This Bible is presented to ......

Lily Calcagnini

...on October 13th, 2006 at
Convent of the Sacred Heart, New York City

GOOD NEWS
BIBLE

WITH DEUTEROCANONICALS / APOCRYPHA

GOOD NEWS TRANSLATION

AMERICAN BIBLE SOCIETY
NEW YORK

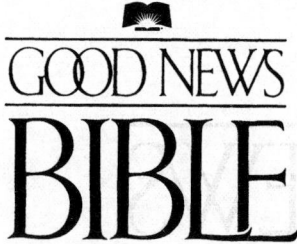

GOOD NEWS BIBLE

GOOD NEWS TRANSLATION

Imprimatur:
✠Most Reverend William H. Keeler, D.D.
President, National Conference of Catholic Bishops

March 10, 1993

Quotation Rights for the Good News Translation

The American Bible Society is glad to grant authors and publishers the right to use up to five hundred (500) verses from the Good News Translation text in church, religious and other publications without the need to seek and receive written permission. However, the extent of quotation must not comprise a complete book nor should it amount to more than 25% of the work. The proper copyright notice must appear on the title or copyright page.

When quotations from the GNT are used in non-saleable media such as church bulletins, orders of service, posters, transparencies or similar media, a complete copyright notice is not required, but the initials (GNT) must appear at the end of each quotation.

Requests for quotations in excess of five hundred (500) verses in any publication must be directed to, and written approval received from, the American Bible Society, 1865 Broadway, New York, NY 10023.

Visit ABS websit! www.americanbible.org

ISBN 1-58516-067-9
ISBN 1-58516-068-7

Printed in Brazil
Eng. Bible GNT 053P/DC Series
104891 – 104892
ABS – 5/06 – 15,000 – 569,000 – BBS 2(9)

NPI 5880

FOREWORD

The *Good News Translation* of the Bible seeks to state clearly and accurately the meaning of the original texts in words and forms that are widely accepted by people who use English as a means of communication. This translation does not follow the traditional vocabulary and style found in the historic English Bible versions. Rather it attempts for our time to set forth the biblical content and message in the standard, everyday, natural form of English.

The aim of this Bible is to give today's reader the best possible understanding of the content of the original texts. The Preface sets forth the basic principles which the translators followed in their work and explains the nature of special aids for readers.

The *Good News Translation* was translated and published by the United Bible Societies for use throughout the world. The Bible Societies trust that the reading and study of this translation will result in a better understanding of the meaning of the Bible. We also earnestly pray that readers will discover the message of saving faith and hope for all people, which the Bible announces anew to each generation.

PREFACE

In September 1966 the American Bible Society published *The New Testament in Today's English Version*, the first publication of a new Bible translation intended for people everywhere for whom English is either their mother tongue or an acquired language. Shortly thereafter the United Bible Societies (UBS) requested the American Bible Society (ABS) to undertake on its behalf a translation of the Old Testament following the same principles. Accordingly the American Bible Society appointed a group of translators to prepare the translation. In 1971 this group added a British consultant recommended by the British and Foreign Bible Society. The translation of the Old Testament, which was completed in 1976, was joined to the fourth edition New Testament, thus completing the first edition of the *Good News Translation*. Though previously known as *Today's English Version* (TEV) and commonly known as the Good News Bible (GNB), the translation is now called the *Good News Translation (GNT)*.

Two ways to present the deuterocanonical books

The translation of the deuterocanonical books and others classed as Apocrypha was completed in 1978, and the first edition of the *Good News Translation* with Deuterocanonicals and Apocrypha was published in 1979, with the Imprimatur of the Most Reverend John F. Whealon, Archbishop of Hartford, Connecticut. This edition was welcomed by Christians from Roman Catholic, Eastern Orthodox, and various Protestant traditions. As an interconfessional edition, the Deuterocanonicals/Apocrypha were grouped in two sections and positioned between the Old and the New Testaments. (The second of these two groupings was given the title "Some Additional Books" and consists of 1 and 2 Esdras and the Prayer of Manasseh.) In 1993, the revised edition of the *Good News Translation (GNT)*, was granted an Imprimatur by the Most Reverend William H. Keeler, D.D., President of the National Conference of Catholic Bishops. Although the interconfessional edition of the Good News Bible has been happily used by Roman Catholics since 1979, some Catholics expressed a desire to have a Good News Bible that includes all of the deuterocanonical books, exclusive of the "Additional Books" listed above, and arranged in the order most commonly used in Roman Catholic Bibles. In response to this plea, the ABS is in the process of preparing a Roman Catholic edition of the Good News Bible. Like the interconfessional edition, the Roman Catholic edition of the Good News Bible bears the Imprimatur of the National Conference of Catholic Bishops.

The text used for this translation

The basic Hebrew (and Aramaic) text for the Old Testament is the Masoretic Text made available through printed editions, published by the UBS, and since 1977 under the title of *Biblia Hebraica Stuttgartensia*. In some instances the words of the printed consonantal text have been divided differently or have been read with a different set of vowels; at times a variant reading in the margin of the Hebrew text (*qere*) has been followed instead of the reading in the text (*kethiv*); and in other instances a variant reading supported by one or more Hebrew manuscripts has been adopted. Where no Hebrew source yields a satisfactory meaning in the context, the translation has either followed one or more of the ancient versions (e.g. Greek, Syriac, Latin) or has adopted a reconstructed text (technically referred to as a conjectural emendation) based on scholarly consensus; such departures from the Hebrew are indicated in footnotes.

The basic text for the deuterocanonical books is the Greek text printed in the Septuagint (3rd edition, 1949), edited by Alfred Rahlfs. For some of these books the more recently published Goettingen edition of the Septuagint has also been consulted.

The basic text for the translation of the New Testament is *The Greek New Testament* published by the UBS (3rd edition, 1975), but in a few instances the translation is based on a variant reading supported by one or more Greek manuscripts.

The translation process

Drafts of the translation in its early stages were sent for comments and suggestions to a Review Panel consisting of prominent theologians and biblical scholars appointed by the American Bible Society Board of Managers in its capacity as trustee for the translation. In addition, drafts were sent to major English-speaking Bible Societies throughout the world. Final approval of the translation on behalf of the United Bible Societies was given by the American Bible Society's Board of Managers upon recommendation of its Translations Committee.

The primary concern of the translators was to provide a faithful translation of the meaning of the Hebrew, Aramaic, and Greek texts. Their first task was to understand correctly the meaning of the original. At times the original meaning cannot be precisely known, not only because the meaning of some words and phrases cannot be determined with a great degree of assurance, but also because the underlying cultural and historical context is sometimes beyond recovery. All aids available were used in this task, including the ancient versions and the modern translations in English and other languages. After ascertaining as accurately as possible the meaning of the original, the translators' next task was to express that meaning in a manner and form easily understood by the readers. Since this translation is intended for all who use English as a means of communication, the translators have tried to avoid words and forms not in current or widespread use; but no artificial limit has been set to the range of the vocabulary employed. Every effort has been made to use language that is natural, clear, simple, and unambiguous. Consequently there has been no attempt to reproduce in English the parts of speech, sentence structure, word order, and grammatical devices of the original languages. Faithfulness in translation also includes a faithful representation of the cultural and historical features of the original. Certain features, however, such as the hours of the day and the measures of weight, capacity, distance, and area, are given their modern equivalents, since the information in those terms conveys more meaning to the reader than the biblical form of those terms.

In cases where a person or place is called by two or more different names in the original, this translation has normally used only the more familiar name in all places; e.g. King Jehoiachin of Judah (Jeremiah 52.31), also called Jeconiah (Jeremiah 24.1) and Coniah (Jeremiah 37.1). Where a proper name is spelled two or more different ways in the original text, this translation has used only one spelling; e.g. Nebuchadnezzar, also spelled Nebuchadrezzar (Jeremiah 29.3 and 29.21), and Priscilla, also spelled Prisca (Acts 18.26 and Romans 16.3).

In view of the differences in vocabulary and form that exist between the American and the British use of the English language, a British edition of the GNT has been published, which incorporates changes that are in keeping with British usage.

Following an ancient tradition, begun by the first translation of the Hebrew Scriptures into Greek (the Septuagint) and followed by the vast majority of English translations, the distinctive Hebrew name for God (usually transliterated *Jehovah* or *Yahweh*) is in this translation represented by "LORD." When *Adonai*, normally translated "Lord," is followed by *Yahweh*, the combination is rendered by the phrase "Sovereign LORD."

The revision of the *Good News Translation*

Since the initial appearance of the full GNT in 1976, some minor editorial changes and corrections of printing errors have been introduced into the text in connection with various printings. The New Testament was already in its fourth edition at the time the full Bible appeared, but for the Old Testament and the Deuterocanonicals/Apocrypha of the Good News Bible there was no revised edition until 1992. The preparation and publication of the second edition of the full Good News Bible in two formats, with and without the Deuterocanonicals and Apocrypha, is the result of a broad international process of careful review and evaluation of the GNT by many scholars and experts over a period of several years.

In December 1986, acting in response to a mounting perception of a need for text revisions, the ABS Board of Managers approved the undertaking of a revision of the GNT. The revision was restricted to two main areas of concern that had been raised and discussed over the years since the first appearance of the translation: (1) passages in which the English style had been unnecessarily exclusive and inattentive to gender concerns, and (2) passages in which the translation had been seen as problematic from either a stylistic or an exegetical viewpoint.

The process followed in preparing this revised edition was one of first inviting and collecting proposals for needed revisions from all English-language Bible Societies and English-speaking UBS translations consultants around the world, as well as numerous scholarly consultants in the United States and representatives of various American churches. The proposals received were then assembled for review and evaluation by the same broad array of experts whose specializations included translation, linguistics, English usage, literary and poetic style, biblical studies, and theology. In a series of four stages, consensus was sought on which proposals were necessary and valid, and at each of these review stages the number of proposals under consideration was reduced until widespread agreement was reached. On the recommendation of the Program Committee of the ABS Board of Trustees, and its Translations Subcommittee, the ABS Board acted to approve the revisions for the Good News Second Edition. These revisions have also been incorporated for use in British usage editions of the *GNT*.

In the decade and a half since the initial publication of the Good News Bible, many Bible readers had become sensitive to the negative effects of exclusive language; that is, to the ways in which the built-in linguistic biases of the ancient languages and the English language toward the masculine gender has led some Bible readers to feel excluded from being addressed by the scriptural Word. This concern has led to the revision of most major English translations during the 1980s, and, increasingly, readers of the *GNT* wrote to request that the Bible Society take this concern into consideration in preparing any revision. In practical terms what this means is that, where references in particular passages are to both men and women, the revision aims at language that is not exclusively masculine-oriented. At the same time, however, great care was taken not to distort the historical reality of the ancient patriarchal culture of Bible times.

Helps for the reader

In order to make the text easier to understand, various kinds of readers' helps are supplied. The text itself has been divided into sections, and headings are provided which indicate the contents of the section. Where there are parallel accounts elsewhere in the Bible as happens frequently in the Gospels, a reference to such a passage appears within parentheses below the heading. There are, in addition, several kinds of notes which appear at the bottom of the page. (1) *Cultural or Historical Notes.* These provide information required to enable the reader to understand the meaning of the text in terms of its original setting (e.g. the explanation of *Rahab* in Psalm 89.10; the explanation of *Day of Atonement* in Acts 27.9). (2) *Textual Notes.* In the Old Testament these indicate primarily those places where the translators were compelled for a variety of reasons to base the translation on some text other than the Hebrew. Where one or more of the ancient versions were followed, the note indicates this by *One ancient translation* (e.g. Genesis 1.26) or *Some ancient translations* (e.g. Genesis 4.8); where a conjectural emendation was adopted, the note reads *Probable text* (e.g. Genesis 10.14). In the New Testament, as well as in the Deuterocanonicals, there are textual notes indicating some of the places where there are significant differences among the ancient manuscripts. These differences may consist of additions to the text (e.g. Matthew 21.43), deletions (e.g. Matthew 24.36), or substitutions (e.g. Mark 1.41). (3) *Alternative Renderings.* In many places the precise meaning of the original text is in dispute, and there are two or more different ways in which the text may be understood. In some of the more important of such instances an alternative rendering is given (e.g. Genesis 2.9; Matthew 6.11). (4) *References to Other Passages.* In addition, many editions of the *GNT* include references, (by book, chapter, and verse) to other places in the Bible where identical or similar matters or ideas are dealt with.

There are several appendices at the end of the volume. A *Word List* identifies many objects or cultural features whose meaning may not be known to all readers. A List of *New Testament Passages Quoted or Paraphrased from the Septuagint* (the ancient Greek translation of the Old Testament) identifies those passages which differ significantly in meaning from the Hebrew Masoretic Text. This list should help readers understand some otherwise puzzling differences in quotations. The *Chronology of the Bible* is a chart that gives the approximate dates of the major events recorded in the Bible. The *Maps* are designed to help the reader to visualize the geographical setting of countries and localities mentioned in the Bible at different points in their history. A *Subject Index* locates by biblical reference some of the more important subjects, persons, places, and events in the Bible.

The line drawings which accompany the text were specially prepared for this translation.

The numbering of chapters and verses in this translation follows the traditional system of major English translations of the Bible. In some instances, however, where the order of thought or events in two or more verses is more clearly represented by a rearrangement of the material, two or more verse numbers are joined (e.g. Exodus 2.15-16; Acts 1.21-22).

A Bible that brings good news

No one knows better than the translators how difficult has been their task. But they have performed it gladly, conscious always of the presence of the Holy Spirit and of the tremendous debt which they owe to the dedication and scholarship of those who have preceded them. The Bible is not simply great literature to be admired and revered; it is Good News for all people everywhere—a message both to be understood and to be applied in daily life. It is with prayer and thankfulness that the translators and staff of the United Bible Societies and the American Bible Society offer this translation to the Lord; it is with humility that we pray God will make it fruitful. And to Christ be the glory forever and ever!

CONTENTS

OLD TESTAMENT

DEUTEROCANONICALS/APOCRYPHA

NEW TESTAMENT

APPENDICES

ALPHABETICAL LISTING
WITH ABBREVIATIONS

OLD TESTAMENT

Amos	Am	1074	Judges	Jg	277
1 Chronicles	1 Ch	469	1 Kings	1 K	392
2 Chronicles	2 Ch	506	2 Kings	2 K	431
Daniel	Dn	1035	Lamentations	Lm	961
Deuteronomy	Dt	201	Leviticus	Lv	119
Ecclesiastes	Ec	784	Malachi	Ml	1126
Esther	Es	583	Micah	Mic	1092
Exodus	Ex	66	Nahum	Nh	1099
Ezekiel	Ez	971	Nehemiah	Ne	562
Ezra	Ezra	548	Numbers	Nu	154
Genesis	Gn	1	Obadiah	Ob	1084
Habakkuk	Hb	1103	Proverbs	Pr	752
Haggai	Hg	1111	Psalms	Ps	639
Hosea	Ho	1056	Ruth	Ru	308
Isaiah	Is	804	1 Samuel	1 S	314
Jeremiah	Jr	884	2 Samuel	2 S	355
Job	Job	593	Song of Songs	Sgs	795
Joel	Jl	1068	Zechariah	Zec	1114
Jonah	Jon	1087	Zephaniah	Zep	1107
Joshua	Js	247			

DEUTEROCANONICALS/APOCRYPHA

Baruch	Ba	1267	2 Maccabees	2 Macc	1328
Bel and the			The Prayer of		
Dragon	Bel	1284	Manasseh	Man	1421
1 Esdras	1 Esd	1361	Sirach	Si	1206
2 Esdras	2 Esd	1383	Song of the Three		
Esther (Greek)	Gk Est	1170	Young Men	S of 3 Y	1277
Judith	Jdt	1150	Susanna	Su	1281
Letter of			Tobit	Tb	1131
Jeremiah	Let Jer	1274	Wisdom of		
1 Maccabees	1 Macc	1287	Solomon	Ws	1185

NEW TESTAMENT

Acts	Ac	1593	Mark	Mk	1472
Colossians	Col	1715	Matthew	Mt	1423
1 Corinthians	1 Co	1661	1 Peter	1 P	1763
2 Corinthians	2 Co	1680	2 Peter	2 P	1769
Ephesians	Eph	1701	Philemon	Phm	1740
Galatians	Ga	1693	Philippians	Phil	1709
Hebrews	He	1742	Revelation	Rev	1784
James	Jas	1758	Romans	Ro	1640
John	Jn	1556	1 Thessalonians	1 Th	1720
1 John	1 Jn	1773	2 Thessalonians	2 Th	1724
2 John	2 Jn	1779	1 Timothy	1 Ti	1727
3 John	3 Jn	1780	2 Timothy	2 Ti	1733
Jude	Jd	1781	Titus	Titus	1737
Luke	Lk	1505			

OTHER ABBREVIATIONS

Circa (around)	*c.*
Old Testament	OT
New Testament	NT
Septuagint	LXX

OLD TESTAMENT

GENESIS

INTRODUCTION

The name *Genesis* means "origin." The book tells about the creation of the universe, the origin of human beings, the beginning of sin and suffering in the world, and about God's way of dealing with people. Genesis can be divided into two main parts:

1) *Chapters 1–11* The creation of the world and the early history of the human race. Here are the accounts of Adam and Eve, Cain and Abel, Noah and the flood, and the Tower of Babylon.

2) *Chapters 12–50* The history of the early ancestors of the Israelites. The first is Abraham, who was notable for his faith and his obedience to God. Then follow the stories of his son Isaac, and grandson Jacob (also called Israel), and of Jacob's twelve sons, the founders of the twelve tribes of Israel. Special attention is given to one of the sons, Joseph, and the events that brought Jacob and his other sons with their families to live in Egypt.

While this book tells stories about people, it is first and foremost an account of what God has done. It begins with the affirmation that God created the universe, and it ends with a promise that God will continue to show his concern for his people. Throughout the book the main character is God, who judges and punishes those who do wrong, leads and helps his people, and shapes their history. This ancient book was written to record the story of a people's faith and to help keep that faith alive.

OUTLINE OF CONTENTS

The Story of Creation

1 In the beginning, when God created the universe,[a] ²the earth was formless and desolate. The raging ocean that covered everything was engulfed in total darkness, and the Spirit of God[b] was moving over the water. ³Then God commanded, "Let there be light"—and light appeared. ⁴God was

---

[a] In the beginning ... the universe; *or* In the beginning God created the universe; *or* When God began to create the universe.   [b] the Spirit of God; *or* the power of God; *or* a wind from God; *or* an awesome wind.

1.3 2 Macc 7.28; 2 Co 4.6

So God made them all, and he was pleased with what he saw. (1.25)

pleased with what he saw. Then he separated the light from the darkness, 5 and he named the light "Day" and the darkness "Night." Evening passed and morning came — that was the first day.

6-7 Then God commanded, "Let there be a dome to divide the water and to keep it in two separate places" — and it was done. So God made a dome, and it separated the water under it from the water above it. 8 He named the dome "Sky." Evening passed and morning came — that was the second day.

9 Then God commanded, "Let the water below the sky come together in one place, so that the land will appear" — and it was done. 10 He named the land "Earth," and the water which had come together he named "Sea." And God was pleased with what he saw. 11 Then he commanded, "Let the earth produce all kinds of plants, those that bear grain and those that bear fruit" — and it was done. 12 So the earth produced all kinds of plants, and God was pleased with what he saw. 13 Evening passed and morning came — that was the third day.

14 Then God commanded, "Let lights appear in the sky to separate day from

night and to show the time when days, years, and religious festivals[c] begin; 15 they will shine in the sky to give light to the earth" — and it was done. 16 So God made the two larger lights, the sun to rule over the day and the moon to rule over the night; he also made the stars. 17 He placed the lights in the sky to shine on the earth, 18 to rule over the day and the night, and to separate light from darkness. And God was pleased with what he saw. 19 Evening passed and morning came — that was the fourth day.

20 Then God commanded, "Let the water be filled with many kinds of living beings, and let the air be filled with birds." 21 So God created the great sea monsters, all kinds of creatures that live in the water, and all kinds of birds. And God was pleased with what he saw. 22 He blessed them all and told the creatures that live in the water to reproduce and to fill the sea, and he told the birds to increase in number. 23 Evening passed and morning came — that was the fifth day.

24 Then God commanded, "Let the earth produce all kinds of animal life: domestic and wild, large and small" — and it was done. 25 So God made them

c *religious festivals; or* seasons.

all, and he was pleased with what he saw.

²⁶Then God said, "And now we will make human beings; they will be like us and resemble us. They will have power over the fish, the birds, and all animals, domestic and wild,ᵈ large and small." ²⁷So God created human beings, making them to be like himself. He created them male and female, ²⁸blessed them, and said, "Have many children, so that your descendants will live all over the earth and bring it under their control. I am putting you in charge of the fish, the birds, and all the wild animals. ²⁹I have provided all kinds of grain and all kinds of fruit for you to eat; ³⁰but for all the wild animals and for all the birds I have provided grass and leafy plants for food"—and it was done. ³¹God looked at everything he had made, and he was very pleased. Evening passed and morning came—that was the sixth day.

2 And so the whole universe was completed. ²By the seventh day God finished what he had been doing and stopped working. ³He blessed the seventh day and set it apart as a special day, because by that day he had completed his creationᵉ and stopped working. ⁴And that is how the universe was created.

The Garden of Eden

When the LORDᶠ God made the universe, ⁵there were no plants on the earth and no seeds had sprouted, because he had not sent any rain, and there was no one to cultivate the land; ⁶but water would come up from beneath the surface and water the ground.

⁷Then the LORD God took some soil from the groundᵍ and formed a manᵍ out of it; he breathed life-giving breath into his nostrils and the man began to live.

⁸Then the LORD God planted a garden in Eden, in the East, and there he put the man he had formed. ⁹He made all kinds of beautiful trees grow there and produce good fruit. In the middle of the garden stood the tree that gives life and the tree that gives knowledge of what is good and what is bad.ʰ

¹⁰A stream flowed in Eden and watered the garden; beyond Eden it divided into four rivers. ¹¹The first river is the Pishon; it flows around the country of Havilah. (¹²Pure gold is found there and also rare perfume and precious stones.) ¹³The second river is the Gihon; it flows around the country of Cush.ⁱ ¹⁴The third river is the Tigris, which flows east of Assyria, and the fourth river is the Euphrates.

¹⁵Then the LORD God placed the man in the Garden of Eden to cultivate it and guard it. ¹⁶He told him, "You may eat the fruit of any tree in the garden, ¹⁷except the tree that gives knowledge of what is good and what is bad.ʲ You must not eat the fruit of that tree; if you do, you will die the same day."

¹⁸Then the LORD God said, "It is not good for the man to live alone. I will

ᵈ One ancient translation animals, domestic and wild; Hebrew domestic animals and all the earth.   ᵉ by that day he had completed his creation; or on that day he completed his creation.   ᶠ THE LORD: Where the Hebrew text has Yahweh, traditionally transliterated as Jehovah, this translation employs LORD with capital letters, following a usage which is widespread in English versions.   ᵍ GROUND ... MAN: The Hebrew words for "man" and "ground" have similar sounds.   ʰ knowledge of what is good and what is bad; or knowledge of everything.   ⁱ Cush (of Mesopotamia); or Ethiopia.   ʲ knowledge of what is good and what is bad; or knowledge of everything.

1.26 Ws 2.23; Si 17.3, 4; 1 Co 11.7   **1.27, 28** Gn 5.1, 2   **1.27** Mt 19.4; Mk 10.6   **2.2, 3** Ex 20.11   **2.2** He 4.4, 10   **2.7** Ws 15.8, 11; 1 Co 15.45   **2.9** Rev 2.7; 22.2, 14 make a suitable companion to help him." ¹⁹ So he took some soil from the ground and formed all the animals and all the birds. Then he brought them to the man to see what he would name them; and that is how they all got their names. ²⁰ So the man named all the birds and all the animals; but not one of them was a suitable companion to help him.

²¹ Then the LORD God made the man fall into a deep sleep, and while he was sleeping, he took out one of the man's ribs and closed up the flesh. ²² He formed a woman out of the rib and brought her to him. ²³ Then the man said,

"At last, here is one of my own
     kind —
Bone taken from my bone, and
     flesh from my flesh.
'Woman' is her name because
     she was taken out
     of man."ᵏ

²⁴ That is why a man leaves his father and mother and is united with his wife, and they become one.

²⁵ The man and the woman were both naked, but they were not embarrassed.

Human Disobedience

3 Now the snake was the most cunning animal that the LORD God had made. The snake asked the woman, "Did God really tell you not to eat fruit from any tree in the garden?"

² "We may eat the fruit of any tree in the garden," the woman answered, ³ "except the tree in the middle of it. God told us not to eat the fruit of that tree or even touch it; if we do, we will die."

⁴ The snake replied, "That's not true; you will not die. ⁵ God said that because he knows that when you eat it, you will be like God ˡ and know what is good and what is bad." ᵐ

⁶ The woman saw how beautiful the tree was and how good its fruit would be to eat, and she thought how wonderful it would be to become wise. So she took some of the fruit and ate it. Then she gave some to her husband, and he

How wonderful it would be to become wise! (3.6)

also ate it. ⁷ As soon as they had eaten it, they were given understanding and realized that they were naked; so they sewed fig leaves together and covered themselves.

⁸ That evening they heard the LORD God walking in the garden, and they hid from him among the trees. ⁹ But the LORD God called out to the man, "Where are you?"

¹⁰ He answered, "I heard you in the garden; I was afraid and hid from you, because I was naked."

¹¹ "Who told you that you were naked?" God asked. "Did you eat the fruit that I told you not to eat?"

¹² The man answered, "The woman you put here with me gave me the fruit, and I ate it."

¹³ The LORD God asked the woman, "Why did you do this?"

ᵏ WOMAN . . . MAN: *The Hebrew words for "woman" and "man" have rather similar sounds.*   ˡ God; *or the gods.*   ᵐ know what is good and what is bad; *or know everything.*

2.24 Mt 19.5; Mk 10.7, 8; 1 Co 6.16; Eph 5.31   **3.1** Ws 2.24; Rev 12.9; 20.2
3.13 2 Co 11.3; 1 Ti 2.14

She replied, "The snake tricked me into eating it."

God Pronounces Judgment

¹⁴Then the LORD God said to the snake, "You will be punished for this; you alone of all the animals must bear this curse: From now on you will crawl on your belly, and you will have to eat dust as long as you live. ¹⁵I will make you and the woman hate each other; her offspring and yours will always be enemies. Her offspring will crush your head, and you will bite her offspring's*ⁿ* heel."

¹⁶And he said to the woman, "I will increase your trouble in pregnancy and your pain in giving birth. In spite of this, you will still have desire for your husband, yet you will be subject to him."

¹⁷And he said to the man, "You listened to your wife and ate the fruit which I told you not to eat. Because of what you have done, the ground will be under a curse. You will have to work hard all your life to make it produce enough food for you. ¹⁸It will produce weeds and thorns, and you will have to eat wild plants. ¹⁹You will have to work hard and sweat to make the soil produce anything, until you go back to the soil from which you were formed. You were made from soil, and you will become soil again."

²⁰Adam*ᵒ* named his wife Eve,*ᵖ* because she was the mother of all human beings. ²¹And the LORD God made clothes out of animal skins for Adam and his wife, and he clothed them.

Adam and Eve Are Sent Out of the Garden

²²Then the LORD God said, "Now these human beings have become like one of us and have knowledge of what is good and what is bad.*�q* They must not be allowed to take fruit from the tree that gives life, eat it, and live forever." ²³So the LORD God sent them out of the Garden of Eden and made them cultivate the soil from which they had been formed. ²⁴Then at the east side of the garden he put living creatures*ʳ* and a flaming sword which turned in all directions. This was to keep anyone from coming near the tree that gives life.

Cain and Abel

4 Then Adam had intercourse with his wife, and she became pregnant. She bore a son and said, "By the LORD's help I have gotten a son." So she named him Cain.*ˢ* ²Later she gave birth to another son, Abel. Abel became a shepherd, but Cain was a farmer. ³After some time Cain brought some of his harvest and gave it as an offering to the LORD. ⁴Then Abel brought the first lamb born to one of his sheep, killed it, and gave the best parts of it as an offering. The LORD was pleased with Abel and his offering, ⁵but he rejected Cain and his offering. Cain became furious, and he scowled in anger. ⁶Then the LORD said to Cain, "Why are you angry? Why that scowl on your face? ⁷If you had done the right thing, you would be smiling;*ᵗ* but because you have done evil, sin is crouching at your door. It wants to rule you, but you must overcome it."

ⁿ her offspring's; *or* their.   *ᵒ* ADAM: *This name in Hebrew means "all human beings."* *ᵖ* EVE: *This name sounds similar to the Hebrew word for "living," which is rendered in this context as "human beings."* *�q* knowledge of what is good and what is bad; *or* knowledge of everything. *ʳ* LIVING CREATURES: *See Word List.* *ˢ* CAIN: *This name sounds like the Hebrew for "gotten."* *ᵗ* you would be smiling; *or* I would have accepted your offering.

3.15 Rev 12.17   **3.17, 18** He 6.8   **3.22** Rev 22.14   **4.4** He 11.4

"Why that scowl on your face?" (4.6)

8 Then Cain said to his brother Abel, "Let's go out in the fields."[u] When they were out in the fields, Cain turned on his brother and killed him.

9 The LORD asked Cain, "Where is your brother Abel?"

He answered, "I don't know. Am I supposed to take care of my brother?"

10 Then the LORD said, "Why have you done this terrible thing? Your brother's blood is crying out to me from the ground, like a voice calling for revenge. **11** You are placed under a curse and can no longer farm the soil. It has soaked up your brother's blood as if it had opened its mouth to receive it when you killed him. **12** If you try to grow crops, the soil will not produce anything; you will be a homeless wanderer on the earth."

13 And Cain said to the LORD, "This punishment is too hard for me to bear. **14** You are driving me off the land and away from your presence. I will be a homeless wanderer on the earth, and anyone who finds me will kill me."

15 But the LORD answered, "No. If anyone kills you, seven lives will be taken in revenge." So the LORD put a mark on Cain to warn anyone who met him not to kill him. **16** And Cain went away from the LORD's presence and lived in a land called "Wandering," which is east of Eden.

The Descendants of Cain

17 Cain and his wife had a son and named him Enoch. Then Cain built a city and named it after his son. **18** Enoch had a son named Irad, who was the father of Mehujael, and Mehujael had a son named Methushael, who was the father of Lamech. **19** Lamech had two wives, Adah and Zillah. **20** Adah gave birth to Jabal, who was the ancestor of those who raise livestock and live in tents. **21** His brother was Jubal, the ancestor of all musicians who play the harp and the flute. **22** Zillah gave birth to Tubal Cain, who made all kinds of tools[v] out of bronze and iron. The sister of Tubal Cain was Naamah.

23 Lamech said to his wives,
"Adah and Zillah, listen to me:
    I have killed a young man
        because he struck me.
24 If seven lives are taken to pay for
        killing Cain,
    Seventy-seven will be taken if
        anyone kills me."

Seth and Enosh

25 Adam and his wife had another son. She said, "God has given me a son to replace Abel, whom Cain killed." So she named him Seth.[w] **26** Seth had a son whom he named Enosh. It was then that people began using the LORD's holy name in worship.

[u] *Some ancient translations* Let's go out in the fields; *Hebrew does not have these words.* [v] who made all kinds of tools; *one ancient translation* ancestor of all metalworkers. [w] SETH: *This name sounds like the Hebrew for "has given."*
4.8 Ws 10.3; Mt 23.35; Lk 11.51; 1 Jn 3.12 **4.10** He 12.24

The Descendants of Adam
(1 Chronicles 1.1-4)

5 This is the list of the descendants of Adam. (When God created human beings, he made them like himself. ²He created them male and female, blessed them, and named them "Human Beings.") ³When Adam was 130 years old, he had a son who was like him, and he named him Seth. ⁴After that, Adam lived another 800 years. He had other children ⁵and died at the age of 930.

⁶When Seth was 105, he had a son, Enosh, ⁷and then lived another 807 years. He had other children ⁸and died at the age of 912.

⁹When Enosh was 90, he had a son, Kenan, ¹⁰and then lived another 815 years. He had other children ¹¹and died at the age of 905.

¹²When Kenan was 70, he had a son, Mahalalel, ¹³and then lived another 840 years. He had other children ¹⁴and died at the age of 910.

¹⁵When Mahalalel was 65, he had a son, Jared, ¹⁶and then lived another 830 years. He had other children ¹⁷and died at the age of 895.

¹⁸When Jared was 162, he had a son, Enoch, ¹⁹and then lived another 800 years. He had other children ²⁰and died at the age of 962.

²¹When Enoch was 65, he had a son, Methuselah. ²²After that, Enoch lived in fellowship with God for 300 years and had other children. ²³He lived to be 365 years old. ²⁴He spent his life in fellowship with God, and then he disappeared, because God took him away.

²⁵When Methuselah was 187, he had a son, Lamech, ²⁶and then lived another 782 years. He had other children ²⁷and died at the age of 969.

²⁸When Lamech was 182, he had a son ²⁹and said, "From the very ground on which the LORD put a curse, this child will bring us relief from all our hard work"; so he named him Noah.ˣ ³⁰Lamech lived another 595 years. He had other children ³¹and died at the age of 777.

³²After Noah was 500 years old, he had three sons, Shem, Ham, and Japheth.

Human Wickedness

6 When people had spread all over the world, and daughters were being born, ²some of the heavenly beingsʸ saw that these young women were beautiful, so they took the ones they liked. ³Then the LORD said, "I will not allow people to live forever; they are mortal. From now on they will live no longer than 120 years." ⁴In those days, and even later, there were giants on the earth who were descendants of human women and the heavenly beings. They were the great heroes and famous men of long ago.

⁵When the LORD saw how wicked everyone on earth was and how evil their thoughts were all the time, ⁶he was sorry that he had ever made them and put them on the earth. He was so filled with regret ⁷that he said, "I will wipe out these people I have created, and also the animals and the birds, because I am sorry that I made any of them." ⁸But the LORD was pleased with Noah.

Noah

⁹⁻¹⁰This is the story of Noah. He had three sons, Shem, Ham, and Japheth. Noah had no faults and was the only good man of his time. He lived in

---

ˣ NOAH: *This name sounds like the Hebrew for "relief."*   ʸ heavenly beings; *or sons of the gods; or sons of God.*

5.1, 2 Gn 1.27, 28   **5.2** Mt 19.4; Mk 10.6   **5.24** Si 44.16; 49.14; He 11.5; Jd 14
6.1-4 Job 1.6; 2.1   **6.4** Nu 13.33; Si 16.7; Ba 3.26   **6.5-8** Mt 24.37; Lk 17.26; 1 P 3.20
6.9 Si 44.17, 18; 2 P 2.5

fellowship with God, [11] but everyone else was evil in God's sight, and violence had spread everywhere. [12] God looked at the world and saw that it was evil, for the people were all living evil lives.

[13] God said to Noah, "I have decided to put an end to all people. I will destroy them completely, because the world is full of their violent deeds. [14] Build a boat for yourself out of good timber; make rooms in it and cover it with tar inside and out. [15] Make it 450 feet long, 75 feet wide, and 45 feet high. [16] Make a roof[z] for the boat and leave a space of 18 inches between the roof[z] and the sides. Build it with three decks and put a door in the side. [17] I am going to send a flood on the earth to destroy every liv-

ing being. Everything on the earth will die, [18] but I will make a covenant with you. Go into the boat with your wife, your sons, and their wives. [19-20] Take into the boat with you a male and a female of every kind of animal and of every kind of bird, in order to keep them alive. [21] Take along all kinds of food for you and for them." [22] Noah did everything that God commanded.

The Flood

7 The LORD said to Noah, "Go into the boat with your whole family; I have found that you are the only one in all the world who does what is right. [2] Take with you seven pairs of each kind of ritually clean animal, but only one pair of each kind of unclean animal. [3] Take also seven pairs of each kind of bird. Do this so that every kind of animal and bird will be kept alive to reproduce again on the earth. [4] Seven days from now I am going to send rain that will fall for forty days and nights, in order to destroy all the living beings that I have made." [5] And Noah did everything that the LORD commanded.

[6] Noah was six hundred years old when the flood came on the earth. [7] He

[z] roof; *or* window.
6.22 He 11.7   **7.7** Mt 24.38, 39; Lk 17.27

Every kind of animal and bird . . . went into the boat. (7.8,9)

and his wife, and his sons and their wives, went into the boat to escape the flood. ⁸A male and a female of every kind of animal and bird, whether ritually clean or unclean, ⁹went into the boat with Noah, as God had commanded. ¹⁰Seven days later the flood came.

¹¹When Noah was six hundred years old, on the seventeenth day of the second month all the outlets of the vast body of water beneath the earth burst open, all the floodgates of the sky were opened, ¹²and rain fell on the earth for forty days and nights. ¹³On that same day Noah and his wife went into the boat with their three sons, Shem, Ham, and Japheth, and their wives. ¹⁴With them went every kind of animal, domestic and wild, large and small, and every kind of bird. ¹⁵A male and a female of each kind of living being went into the boat with Noah, ¹⁶as God had commanded. Then the Lord shut the door behind Noah.

¹⁷The flood continued for forty days, and the water became deep enough for the boat to float. ¹⁸The water became deeper, and the boat drifted on the surface. ¹⁹It became so deep that it covered the highest mountains; ²⁰it went on rising until it was about twenty-five feet above the tops of the mountains. ²¹Every living being on the earth died—every bird, every animal, and every person. ²²Everything on earth that breathed died. ²³The Lord destroyed all living beings on the earth—human beings, animals, and birds. The only ones left were Noah and those who were with him in the boat. ²⁴The water did not start going down for a hundred and fifty days.

The End of the Flood

8 God had not forgotten Noah and all the animals with him in the boat; he caused a wind to blow, and the

Everything on earth that breathed died. (7.22)

water started going down. ²The outlets of the water beneath the earth and the floodgates of the sky were closed. The rain stopped, ³and the water gradually went down for 150 days. ⁴On the seventeenth day of the seventh month the boat came to rest on a mountain in the Ararat range. ⁵The water kept going down, and on the first day of the tenth month the tops of the mountains appeared.

⁶After forty days Noah opened a window ⁷and sent out a raven. It did not come back, but kept flying around until the water was completely gone. ⁸Meanwhile, Noah sent out a dove to see if the water had gone down, ⁹but since the water still covered all the land, the dove did not find a place to light. It flew back to the boat, and Noah reached out and took it in. ¹⁰He waited another seven days and sent out the dove again. ¹¹It returned to him in the evening with a fresh olive leaf in its beak. So Noah knew that the water had gone down.

The water had gone down. (8.11)

¹²Then he waited another seven days and sent out the dove once more; this time it did not come back.

¹³When Noah was 601 years old, on the first day of the first month, the water was gone. Noah removed the covering of the boat, looked around, and saw that the ground was getting dry. ¹⁴By the twenty-seventh day of the second month the earth was completely dry.

¹⁵God said to Noah, ¹⁶"Go out of the boat with your wife, your sons, and their wives. ¹⁷Take all the birds and animals out with you, so that they may reproduce and spread over all the earth." ¹⁸So Noah went out of the boat with his wife, his sons, and their wives. ¹⁹All the animals and birds went out of the boat in groups of their own kind.

Noah Offers a Sacrifice

²⁰Noah built an altar to the LORD; he took one of each kind of ritually clean animal and bird, and burned them whole as a sacrifice on the altar. ²¹The odor of the sacrifice pleased the LORD, and he said to himself, "Never again will I put the earth under a curse because of what people do; I know that from the time they are young their thoughts are evil. Never again will I destroy all living beings, as I have done this time. ²²As long as the world exists, there will be a time for planting and a time for harvest. There will always be cold and heat, summer and winter, day and night."

God's Covenant with Noah

9 God blessed Noah and his sons and said, "Have many children, so that your descendants will live all over the earth. ²All the animals, birds, and fish will live in fear of you. They are all placed under your power. ³Now you can eat them, as well as green plants; I give them all to you for food. ⁴The one thing you must not eat is meat with blood still in it; I forbid this because the life is in the blood. ⁵If anyone takes human life, he will be punished. I will punish with death any animal that takes a human life. ⁶Human beings were made like God, so whoever murders one of them will be killed by someone else.

⁷"You must have many children, so that your descendants will live all over the earth."

⁸God said to Noah and his sons, ⁹"I am now making my covenant with you and with your descendants, ¹⁰and with all living beings — all birds and all animals — everything that came out of the boat with you. ¹¹With these words I make my covenant with you: I promise that never again will all living beings be destroyed by a flood; never again will a flood destroy the earth. ¹²As a sign of this everlasting covenant which I am making with you and with all living beings, ¹³I am putting my bow in the clouds. It will be the sign of my covenant with the world. ¹⁴Whenever I cover the sky with clouds and the rainbow appears, ¹⁵I will remember my promise to you and to all the animals that a flood will never again destroy all living beings. ¹⁶When the rainbow appears in the clouds, I will see it and remember the everlasting covenant between me and all living beings on earth. ¹⁷That is the sign of the promise which I am making to all living beings."

Noah and His Sons

¹⁸The sons of Noah who went out of the boat were Shem, Ham, and Japheth. (Ham was the father of Canaan.) ¹⁹These three sons of Noah were the ancestors of all the people on earth.

9.1 Gn 1.28   **9.4** Lv 7.26, 27; 17.10-14; 19.26; Dt 12.16, 23; 15.23   **9.6** Ex 20.13; Gn 1.26   **9.7** Gn 1.28

The sign of my covenant with the world (9.13)

20 Noah, who was a farmer, was the first man to plant a vineyard. **21** After he drank some of the wine, he became drunk, took off his clothes, and lay naked in his tent. **22** When Ham, the father of Canaan, saw that his father was naked, he went out and told his two brothers. **23** Then Shem and Japheth took a robe and held it behind them on their shoulders. They walked backward into the tent and covered their father, keeping their faces turned away so as not to see him naked. **24** When Noah sobered up and learned what his youngest son had done to him, **25** he said,

"A curse on Canaan!
He will be a slave to his
     brothers.
26 Give praise to the LORD, the
     God of Shem!
Canaan will be the slave of
     Shem.
27 May God cause Japheth[a] to
     increase!

May his descendants live with
     the people of Shem!
Canaan will be the slave of
     Japheth."

28 After the flood Noah lived 350 years **29** and died at the age of 950.

The Descendants of Noah's Sons
(1 Chronicles 1.5-23)

10 These are the descendants of Noah's sons, Shem, Ham, and Japheth. These three had sons after the flood.

2 The sons of Japheth—Gomer, Magog, Madai, Javan, Tubal, Meshech, and Tiras—were the ancestors of the peoples who bear their names. **3** The descendants of Gomer were the people of Ashkenaz, Riphath, and Togarmah. **4** The descendants of Javan were the people of Elishah, Spain, Cyprus, and Rhodes; **5** they were the ancestors of the people who live along the coast and on

---

a JAPHETH: *This name sounds like the Hebrew for "increase."*

the islands. These are the descendants of Japheth, living in their different tribes and countries, each group speaking its own language.

6 The sons of Ham — Cush, Egypt, Libya, and Canaan — were the ancestors of the peoples who bear their names. 7 The descendants of Cush were the people of Seba, Havilah, Sabtah, Raamah, and Sabteca. The descendants of Raamah were the people of Sheba and Dedan. 8 Cush had a son named Nimrod, who became the world's first great conqueror. 9 By the LORD's help he was a great hunter, and that is why people say, "May the LORD make you as great a hunter as Nimrod!" 10 At first his kingdom included Babylon, Erech, and Accad, all three of them in Babylonia. 11 From that land he went to Assyria and built the cities of Nineveh, Rehoboth Ir, Calah, 12 and Resen, which is between Nineveh and the great city of Calah.

13 The descendants of Egypt were the people of Lydia, Anam, Lehab, Naphtuh, 14 Pathrus, Casluh, and of Crete, from whom the Philistines are descended.[b]

15 Canaan's sons — Sidon, the oldest, and Heth — were the ancestors of the peoples who bear their names. 16 Canaan was also the ancestor of the Jebusites, the Amorites, the Girgashites, 17 the Hivites, the Arkites, the Sinites, 18 the Arvadites, the Zemarites, and the Hamathites. The different tribes of the Canaanites spread out, 19 until the Canaanite borders reached from Sidon southward to Gerar near Gaza, and eastward to Sodom, Gomorrah, Admah, and Zeboiim near Lasha. 20 These are the descendants of Ham, living in their different tribes and countries, each group speaking its own language.

21 Shem, the older brother of Japheth, was the ancestor of all the Hebrews. 22 Shem's sons — Elam, Asshur,

Arpachshad, Lud. and Aram — were the ancestors of the peoples who bear their names. 23 The descendants of Aram were the people of Uz, Hul, Gether, and Meshek. 24 Arpachshad was the father of Shelah, who was the father of Eber. 25 Eber had two sons: one was named Peleg,[c] because during his time the people of the world were divided; and the other was named Joktan. 26 The descendants of Joktan were the people of Almodad, Sheleph, Hazarmaveth, Jerah, 27 Hadoram, Uzal, Diklah, 28 Obal, Abimael, Sheba, 29 Ophir, Havilah, and Jobab. All of them were descended from Joktan. 30 The land in which they lived extended from Mesha to Sephar in the eastern hill country. 31 These are the descendants of Shem, living in their different tribes and countries, each group speaking its own language.

32 All these peoples are the descendants of Noah, nation by nation, according to their different lines of descent. After the flood all the nations of the earth were descended from the sons of Noah.

The Tower of Babylon

11 At first, the people of the whole world had only one language and used the same words. 2 As they wandered about in the East, they came to a plain in Babylonia and settled there. 3 They said to one another, "Come on! Let's make bricks and bake them hard." So they had bricks to build with and tar to hold them together. 4 They said, "Now let's build a city with a tower that reaches the sky, so that we can make a name for ourselves and not be scattered all over the earth."

5 Then the LORD came down to see the city and the tower which they had built, 6 and he said, "Now then, these are all one people and they speak one

[b] Probable text and of Crete ... descended; Hebrew from whom the Philistines are descended, and Crete.   [c] PELEG: This name sounds like the Hebrew for "divide."

language; this is just the beginning of what they are going to do. Soon they will be able to do anything they want! [7] Let us go down and mix up their language so that they will not understand each other." [8] So the LORD scattered them all over the earth, and they stopped building the city. [9] The city was called Babylon,[d] because there the LORD mixed up the language of all the people, and from there he scattered them all over the earth.

The Descendants of Shem
(*1 Chronicles 1.24-27*)

[10] These are the descendants of Shem. Two years after the flood, when Shem was 100 years old, he had a son, Arpachshad. [11] After that, he lived another 500 years and had other children.

[12] When Arpachshad was 35 years old, he had a son, Shelah; [13] after that, he lived another 403 years and had other children.

[14] When Shelah was 30 years old, he had a son, Eber; [15] after that, he lived another 403 years and had other children.

[16] When Eber was 34 years old, he had a son, Peleg; [17] after that, he lived another 430 years and had other children.

[18] When Peleg was 30 years old, he had a son, Reu; [19] after that, he lived another 209 years and had other children.

[20] When Reu was 32 years old, he had a son, Serug; [21] after that, he lived another 207 years and had other children.

[22] When Serug was 30 years old, he had a son, Nahor; [23] after that, he lived another 200 years and had other children.

[24] When Nahor was 29 years old, he had a son, Terah; [25] after that, he lived

another 119 years and had other children.

[26] After Terah was 70 years old, he became the father of Abram, Nahor, and Haran.

The Descendants of Terah

[27] These are the descendants of Terah, who was the father of Abram, Nahor, and Haran. Haran was the father of Lot, [28] and Haran died in his hometown of Ur in Babylonia, while his father was still living. [29] Abram married Sarai, and Nahor married Milcah, the daughter of Haran, who was also the father of Iscah. [30] Sarai was not able to have children.

[31] Terah took his son Abram, his grandson Lot, who was the son of Haran, and his daughter-in-law Sarai, Abram's wife, and with them he left the city of Ur in Babylonia to go to the land of Canaan. They went as far as Haran and settled there. [32] Terah died there at the age of 205.

God's Call to Abram

12 The LORD said to Abram, "Leave your country, your relatives, and your father's home, and go to a land that I am going to show you. [2] I will give you many descendants, and they will become a great nation. I will bless you and make your name famous, so that you will be a blessing.
[3] I will bless those who bless you,
But I will curse those who
    curse you.
And through you I will bless all
    the nations."[e]

[4] When Abram was seventy-five years old, he started out from Haran, as the LORD had told him to do; and Lot went with him. [5] Abram took his wife Sarai, his nephew Lot, and all the wealth and all the slaves they had

---

[d] BABYLON: *This name sounds like the Hebrew for "mixed up."*   [e] And through . . . nations; *or* All the nations will ask me to bless them as I have blessed you.
12.1 Ws 10.5; Ac 7.2, 3; He 11.8   **12.3** Ga 3.8

acquired in Haran, and they started out for the land of Canaan.

When they arrived in Canaan, [6]Abram traveled through the land until he came to the sacred tree of Moreh, the holy place at Shechem. (At that time the Canaanites were still living in the land.) [7]The LORD appeared to Abram and said to him, "This is the country that I am going to give to your descendants." Then Abram built an altar there to the LORD, who had appeared to him. [8]After that, he moved on south to the hill country east of the city of Bethel and set up his camp between Bethel on the west and Ai on the east. There also he built an altar and worshiped the LORD. [9]Then he moved on from place to place, going toward the southern part of Canaan.

Abram in Egypt

[10]But there was a famine in Canaan, and it was so bad that Abram went farther south to Egypt, to live there for a while. [11]When he was about to cross the border into Egypt, he said to his wife Sarai, "You are a beautiful woman. [12]When the Egyptians see you, they will assume that you are my wife, and so they will kill me and let you live. [13]Tell them that you are my sister; then because of you they will let me live and treat me well." [14]When he crossed the border into Egypt, the Egyptians did see that his wife was beautiful. [15]Some of the court officials saw her and told the king how beautiful she was; so she was taken to his palace. [16]Because of her the king treated Abram well and gave him flocks of sheep and goats, cattle, donkeys, slaves, and camels.

[17]But because the king had taken Sarai, the LORD sent terrible diseases on him and on the people of his palace. [18]Then the king sent for Abram and asked him, "What have you done to me? Why didn't you tell me that she was your wife? [19]Why did you say that she was your sister, and let me take her as my wife? Here is your wife; take her and get out!" [20]The king gave orders to his men, so they took Abram and put him out of the country, together with his wife and everything he owned.

Abram and Lot Separate

13 Abram went north out of Egypt to the southern part of Canaan with his wife and everything he owned, and Lot went with him. [2]Abram was a very rich man, with sheep, goats, and cattle, as well as silver and gold. [3]Then he left there and moved from place to place, going toward Bethel. He reached the place between Bethel and Ai where he had camped before [4]and had built an altar. There he worshiped the LORD.

[5]Lot also had sheep, goats, and cattle, as well as his own family and servants. [6]And so there was not enough pasture land for the two of them to stay together, because they had too many animals. [7]So quarrels broke out between the men who took care of Abram's animals and those who took care of Lot's animals. (At that time the Canaanites and the Perizzites were still living in the land.)

[8]Then Abram said to Lot, "We are relatives, and your men and my men shouldn't be quarreling. [9]So let's separate. Choose any part of the land you want. You go one way, and I'll go the other."

[10]Lot looked around and saw that the whole Jordan Valley, all the way to Zoar, had plenty of water, like the Garden of the LORD[f] or like the land of Egypt. (This was before the LORD had destroyed the cities of Sodom and Gomorrah.) [11]So Lot chose the whole Jordan Valley for himself and moved away toward the east. That is how the two

---

[f] GARDEN OF THE LORD: *a reference to the Garden of Eden.*
12.7 Ac 7.5; Ga 3.16   **12.13** Gn 20.2; 26.7   **13.10** Gn 2.10

men parted. ¹²Abram stayed in the land of Canaan, and Lot settled among the cities in the valley and camped near Sodom, ¹³whose people were wicked and sinned against the LORD.

Abram Moves to Hebron

¹⁴After Lot had left, the LORD said to Abram, "From where you are, look carefully in all directions. ¹⁵I am going to give you and your descendants all the land that you see, and it will be yours forever. ¹⁶I am going to give you so many descendants that no one will be able to count them all; it would be as easy to count all the specks of dust on earth! ¹⁷Now, go and look over the whole land, because I am going to give it all to you." ¹⁸So Abram moved his camp and settled near the sacred trees of Mamre at Hebron, and there he built an altar to the LORD.

Abram Rescues Lot

14 Four kings, Amraphel of Babylonia, Arioch of Ellasar, Chedorlaomer of Elam, and Tidal of Goiim, ²went to war against five other kings: Bera of Sodom, Birsha of Gomorrah, Shinab of Admah, Shemeber of Zeboiim, and the king of Bela (or Zoar). ³These five kings had formed an alliance and joined forces in Siddim Valley, which is now the Dead Sea. ⁴They had been under the control of Chedorlaomer for twelve years, but in the thirteenth year they rebelled against him. ⁵In the fourteenth year Chedorlaomer and his allies came with their armies and defeated the Rephaim in Ashteroth Karnaim, the Zuzim in Ham, the Emim in the plain of Kiriathaim, ⁶and the Horites in the mountains of Edom, pursuing them as far as Elparan on the edge of the desert. ⁷Then they turned around and came back to Kadesh (then known as Enmishpat). They conquered all the land of the Amalekites

and defeated the Amorites who lived in Hazazon Tamar.

⁸Then the kings of Sodom, Gomorrah, Admah, Zeboiim, and Bela drew up their armies for battle in Siddim Valley and fought ⁹against the kings of Elam, Goiim, Babylonia, and Ellasar, five kings against four. ¹⁰The valley was full of tar pits, and when the kings of Sodom and Gomorrah tried to run away from the battle, they fell into the pits; but the other three kings escaped to the mountains. ¹¹The four kings took everything in Sodom and Gomorrah, including the food, and went away. ¹²Lot, Abram's nephew, was living in Sodom, so they took him and all his possessions.

¹³But a man escaped and reported all this to Abram, the Hebrew, who was living near the sacred trees belonging to Mamre the Amorite. Mamre and his brothers Eshcol and Aner were Abram's allies. ¹⁴When Abram heard that his nephew had been captured, he called together all the fighting men in his camp, 318 in all, and pursued the four kings all the way to Dan. ¹⁵There he divided his men into groups, attacked the enemy by night, and defeated them. He chased them as far as Hobah, north of Damascus, ¹⁶and got back all the loot that had been taken. He also brought back his nephew Lot and his possessions, together with the women and the other prisoners.

Melchizedek Blesses Abram

¹⁷When Abram came back from his victory over Chedorlaomer and the other kings, the king of Sodom went out to meet him in Shaveh Valley (also called King's Valley). ¹⁸And Melchizedek, who was king of Salem and also a priest of the Most High God, brought bread and wine to Abram, ¹⁹blessed him, and said, "May the Most High God, who made heaven and earth, bless

13.15 Ac 7.5   **14.18-20** He 7.1-10

Abram! 20 May the Most High God, who gave you victory over your enemies, be praised!" And Abram gave Melchizedek a tenth of all the loot he had recovered.

21 The king of Sodom said to Abram, "Keep the loot, but give me back all my people."

22 Abram answered, "I solemnly swear before the LORD, the Most High God, Maker of heaven and earth, 23 that I will not keep anything of yours, not even a thread or a sandal strap. Then you can never say, 'I am the one who made Abram rich.' 24 I will take nothing for myself. I will accept only what my men have used. But let my allies, Aner, Eshcol, and Mamre, take their share."

God's Covenant with Abram

15 After this, Abram had a vision and heard the LORD say to him, "Do not be afraid, Abram. I will shield you from danger and give you a great reward."

2 But Abram answered, "Sovereign LORD, what good will your reward do me, since I have no children? My only heir is Eliezer of Damascus.*g* 3 You have given me no children, and one of my slaves will inherit my property."

4 Then he heard the LORD speaking to him again: "This slave Eliezer will not inherit your property; your own son will be your heir." 5 The LORD took him outside and said, "Look at the sky and try to count the stars; you will have as many descendants as that."

6 Abram put his trust in the LORD, and because of this the LORD was pleased with him and accepted him.

7 Then the LORD said to him, "I am the LORD, who led you out of Ur in Babylonia, to give you this land as your own."

8 But Abram asked, "Sovereign LORD, how can I know that it will be mine?"

9 He answered, "Bring me a cow, a goat, and a ram, each of them three years old, and a dove and a pigeon."

10 Abram brought the animals to God, cut them in half, and placed the halves opposite each other in two rows; but he did not cut up the birds. 11 Vultures came down on the bodies, but Abram drove them off.

12 When the sun was going down, Abram fell into a deep sleep, and fear and terror came over him. 13 The LORD said to him, "Your descendants will be strangers in a foreign land; they will be slaves there and will be treated cruelly for four hundred years. 14 But I will punish the nation that enslaves them, and when they leave that foreign land, they will take great wealth with them. 15 You yourself will live to a ripe old age, die in peace, and be buried. 16 It will be four generations before your descendants come back here, because I will not drive out the Amorites until they become so wicked that they must be punished."

17 When the sun had set and it was dark, a smoking fire pot and a flaming torch suddenly appeared and passed between the pieces of the animals. 18 Then and there the LORD made a covenant with Abram. He said, "I promise to give your descendants all this land from the border of Egypt to the Euphrates River, 19 including the lands of the Kenites, the Kenizzites, the Kadmonites, 20 the Hittites, the Perizzites, the Rephaim, 21 the Amorites, the Canaanites, the Girgashites, and the Jebusites."

Hagar and Ishmael

16 Abram's wife Sarai had not borne him any children. But she had an Egyptian slave woman named Hagar, 2 and so she said to

g My ... Damascus; *Hebrew unclear.*

15.5 Ro 4.18; He 11.12   **15.6** 1 Macc 2.52; Ro 4.3; Ga 3.6; Jas 2.23   **15.12** Job 4.13, 14
15.13 Ex 1.1-14; Ac 7.6   **15.14** Ex 12.40, 41; Ac 7.7   **15.18** Ac 7.5

Abram, "The LORD has kept me from having children. Why don't you sleep with my slave? Perhaps she can have a child for me." Abram agreed with what Sarai said. ³So she gave Hagar to him to be his concubine. (This happened after Abram had lived in Canaan for ten years.) ⁴Abram had intercourse with Hagar, and she became pregnant. When she found out that she was pregnant, she became proud and despised Sarai.

⁵Then Sarai said to Abram, "It's your fault that Hagar despises me.ʰ I myself gave her to you, and ever since she found out that she was pregnant, she has despised me. May the LORD judge which of us is right, you or me!"

⁶Abram answered, "Very well, she is your slave and under your control; do whatever you want with her." Then Sarai treated Hagar so cruelly that she ran away.

⁷The angel of the LORD met Hagar at a spring in the desert on the road to Shur ⁸and said, "Hagar, slave of Sarai, where have you come from and where are you going?"

She answered, "I am running away from my mistress."

⁹He said, "Go back to her and be her slave." ¹⁰Then he said, "I will give you so many descendants that no one will be able to count them. ¹¹You are going to have a son, and you will name him Ishmael,ⁱ because the LORD has heard your cry of distress. ¹²But your son will live like a wild donkey; he will be against everyone, and everyone will be against him. He will live apart from all his relatives."

¹³Hagar asked herself, "Have I really seen God and lived to tell about it?"ʲ So she called the LORD, who had spoken to her, "A God Who Sees." ¹⁴That is why people call the well between Kadesh and Bered "The Well of the Living One Who Sees Me."

¹⁵Hagar bore Abram a son, and he named him Ishmael. ¹⁶Abram was eighty-six years old at the time.

Circumcision, the Sign of the Covenant

17 When Abram was ninety-nine years old, the LORD appeared to him and said, "I am the Almighty God. Obey me and always do what is right. ²I will make my covenant with you and give you many descendants." ³Abram bowed down with his face touching the ground, and God said, ⁴"I make this covenant with you: I promise that you will be the ancestor of many nations. ⁵Your name will no longer be Abram, but Abraham,ᵏ because I am making you the ancestor of many nations. ⁶I will give you many descendants, and some of them will be kings. You will have so many descendants that they will become nations.

⁷"I will keep my promise to you and to your descendants in future generations as an everlasting covenant. I will be your God and the God of your descendants. ⁸I will give to you and to your descendants this land in which you are now a foreigner. The whole land of Canaan will belong to your descendants forever, and I will be their God."

⁹God said to Abraham, "You also must agree to keep the covenant with me, both you and your descendants in future generations. ¹⁰You and your descendants must all agree to circumcise every male among you. ¹¹⁻¹²From now on you must circumcise every baby boy when he is eight days old, including slaves born in your homes and

---

ʰ *It's your fault . . . me; or* May you suffer for this wrong done against me.
ⁱ ISHMAEL: *This name in Hebrew means "God hears."*   ʲ *Probable text* lived to tell about it?; *Hebrew unclear.*   ᵏ ABRAHAM: *This name sounds like the Hebrew for "ancestor of many nations."*
16.15 Ga 4.22   **17.5** Ro 4.17   **17.7** Lk 1.55   **17.8** Ac 7.5   **17.10** Ac 7.8; Ro 4.11

slaves bought from foreigners. This will show that there is a covenant between you and me. 13 Each one must be circumcised, and this will be a physical sign to show that my covenant with you is everlasting. 14 Any male who has not been circumcised will no longer be considered one of my people, because he has not kept the covenant with me."

15 God said to Abraham, "You must no longer call your wife Sarai; from now on her name is Sarah.*l* 16 I will bless her, and I will give you a son by her. I will bless her, and she will become the mother of nations, and there will be kings among her descendants."

17 Abraham bowed down with his face touching the ground, but he began to laugh when he thought, "Can a man have a child when he is a hundred years old? Can Sarah have a child at ninety?" 18 He asked God, "Why not let Ishmael be my heir?"

19 But God said, "No. Your wife Sarah will bear you a son and you will name him Isaac.*m* I will keep my covenant with him and with his descendants forever. It is an everlasting covenant. 20 I have heard your request about Ishmael, so I will bless him and give him many children and many descendants. He will be the father of twelve princes, and I will make a great nation of his descendants. 21 But I will keep my covenant with your son Isaac, who will be born to Sarah about this time next year." 22 When God finished speaking to Abraham, he left him.

23 On that same day Abraham obeyed God and circumcised his son Ishmael and all the other males in his household, including the slaves born in his home and those he had bought. 24 Abraham was ninety-nine years old when he was circumcised, 25 and his son Ishmael was thirteen. 26 They were both circumcised on the same day, 27 together with all of Abraham's slaves.

A Son Is Promised to Abraham

18 The LORD appeared to Abraham at the sacred trees of Mamre. As Abraham was sitting at the entrance of his tent during the hottest part of the day, 2 he looked up and saw three men standing there. As soon as he saw them, he ran out to meet them. Bowing down with his face touching the ground, 3 he said, "Sirs, please do not pass by my home without stopping; I am here to serve you. 4 Let me bring some water for you to wash your feet; you can rest here beneath this tree. 5 I will also bring a bit of food; it will give you strength to continue your journey. You have honored me by coming to my home, so let me serve you."

They replied, "Thank you; we accept."

6 Abraham hurried into the tent and said to Sarah, "Quick, take a sack of your best flour, and bake some bread." 7 Then he ran to the herd and picked out a calf that was tender and fat, and gave it to a servant, who hurried to get it ready. 8 He took some cream, some milk, and the meat, and set the food before the men. There under the tree he served them himself, and they ate.

9 Then they asked him, "Where is your wife Sarah?"

"She is there in the tent," he answered.

10 One of them said, "Nine months from now*n* I will come back, and your wife Sarah will have a son."

Sarah was behind him, at the door of the tent, listening. 11 Abraham and Sarah were very old, and Sarah had stopped having her monthly periods. 12 So Sarah laughed to herself and said, "Now that I am old and worn out, can

---

l SARAH: *This name in Hebrew means "princess."*   *m* ISAAC: *This name in Hebrew means "he laughs."*   *n* Nine months from now; *or* This time next year.
18.2 a He 13.2   **18.10** Ro 9.9   **18.12** 1 P 3.6

I still enjoy sex? And besides, my husband is old too."

¹³Then the LORD asked Abraham, "Why did Sarah laugh and say, 'Can I really have a child when I am so old?' ¹⁴Is anything too hard for the LORD? As I said, nine months from now I will return, and Sarah will have a son."

¹⁵Because Sarah was afraid, she denied it. "I didn't laugh," she said.

"Yes, you did," he replied. "You laughed."

Abraham Pleads for Sodom

¹⁶Then the men left and went to a place where they could look down at Sodom, and Abraham went with them to send them on their way. ¹⁷And the LORD said to himself, "I will not hide from Abraham what I am going to do. ¹⁸His descendants will become a great and mighty nation, and through him I will bless all the nations.ᵒ ¹⁹I have chosen him in order that he may command his sons and his descendants to obey me and to do what is right and just. If they do, I will do everything for him that I have promised."

²⁰Then the LORD said to Abraham, "There are terrible accusations against Sodom and Gomorrah, and their sin is very great. ²¹I must go down to find out whether or not the accusations which I have heard are true."

²²Then the two men left and went on toward Sodom, but the LORD remained with Abraham. ²³Abraham approached the LORD and asked, "Are you really going to destroy the innocent with the guilty? ²⁴If there are fifty innocent people in the city, will you destroy the whole city? Won't you spare it in order to save the fifty? ²⁵Surely you won't kill the innocent with the guilty. That's impossible! You can't do that. If you did, the innocent would be punished along with the guilty. That is impossible. The judge of all the earth has to act justly."

²⁶The LORD answered, "If I find fifty innocent people in Sodom, I will spare the whole city for their sake."

²⁷Abraham spoke again: "Please forgive my boldness in continuing to speak to you, Lord. I am only a man and have no right to say anything. ²⁸But perhaps there will be only forty-five innocent people instead of fifty. Will you destroy the whole city because there are five too few?"

The LORD answered, "I will not destroy the city if I find forty-five innocent people."

²⁹Abraham spoke again: "Perhaps there will be only forty."

He replied, "I will not destroy it if there are forty."

³⁰Abraham said, "Please don't be angry, Lord, but I must speak again. What if there are only thirty?"

He said, "I will not do it if I find thirty."

³¹Abraham said, "Please forgive my boldness in continuing to speak to you, Lord. Suppose that only twenty are found?"

He said, "I will not destroy the city if I find twenty."

³²Abraham said, "Please don't be angry, Lord, and I will speak only once more. What if only ten are found?"

He said, "I will not destroy it if there are ten." ³³After he had finished speaking with Abraham, the LORD went away, and Abraham returned home.

The Sinfulness of Sodom

19 When the two angels came to Sodom that evening, Lot was sitting at the city gate. As soon as he saw them, he got up and went to meet them. He bowed down before them ²and said, "Sirs, I am here to serve you.

ᵒ through ... nations; *or* all the nations will ask me to bless them as I have blessed him.
18.14 Lk 1.37

Please come to my house. You can wash your feet and spend the night. In the morning you can get up early and go on your way."

But they answered, "No, we will spend the night here in the city square."

³ He kept on urging them, and finally they went with him to his house. Lot ordered his servants to bake some bread and prepare a fine meal for the guests. When it was ready, they ate it.

⁴ Before the guests went to bed, the men of Sodom surrounded the house. All the men of the city, both young and old, were there. ⁵ They called out to Lot and asked, "Where are the men who came to stay with you tonight? Bring them out to us!" The men of Sodom wanted to have sex with them.

⁶ Lot went outside and closed the door behind him. ⁷ He said to them, "Friends, I beg you, don't do such a wicked thing! ⁸ Look, I have two daughters who are still virgins. Let me bring them out to you, and you can do whatever you want with them. But don't do anything to these men; they are guests in my house, and I must protect them."

⁹ But they said, "Get out of our way, you foreigner! Who are you to tell us what to do? Out of our way, or we will treat you worse than them." They pushed Lot back and moved up to break down the door. ¹⁰ But the two men inside reached out, pulled Lot back into the house, and shut the door. ¹¹ Then they struck all the men outside with blindness, so that they couldn't find the door.

Lot Leaves Sodom

¹² The two men said to Lot, "If you have anyone else here — sons, daughters, sons-in-law, or any other relatives living in the city — get them out of here,

¹³ because we are going to destroy this place. The LORD has heard the terrible accusations against these people and has sent us to destroy Sodom."

¹⁴ Then Lot went to the men that his daughters were going to marry, and said, "Hurry up and get out of here; the LORD is going to destroy this place." But they thought he was joking.

¹⁵ At dawn the angels tried to make Lot hurry. "Quick!" they said. "Take your wife and your two daughters and get out, so that you will not lose your lives when the city is destroyed." ¹⁶ Lot hesitated. The LORD, however, had pity on him; so the men took him, his wife, and his two daughters by the hand and led them out of the city. ¹⁷ Then one of the angels said, "Run for your lives! Don't look back and don't stop in the valley. Run to the hills, so that you won't be killed."

¹⁸ But Lot answered, "No, please don't make us do that, sir. ¹⁹ You have done me a great favor and saved my life. But the hills are too far away; the disaster will overtake me, and I will die before I get there. ²⁰ Do you see that little town? It is near enough. Let me go over there — you can see it is just a small place — and I will be safe."

²¹ He answered, "All right, I agree. I won't destroy that town. ²² Hurry! Run! I can't do anything until you get there."

Because Lot called it small, the town was named Zoar.ᵖ

The Destruction of Sodom and Gomorrah

²³ The sun was rising when Lot reached Zoar. ²⁴ Suddenly the LORD rained burning sulfur on the cities of Sodom and Gomorrah ²⁵ and destroyed them and the whole valley, along with all the people there and everything that

ᵖ ZOAR: *This name sounds like the Hebrew for "small."*
19.5-8 Jg 19.22-24   **19.11** 2 K 6.18   **19.16** 2 P 2.7   **19.24, 25** Mt 10.15; 11.23, 24; Lk 10.12; 17.29; 2 P 2.6; Jdt 7

grew on the land. 26 But Lot's wife looked back and was turned into a pillar of salt.

Lot's wife looked back. (19.26)

27 Early the next morning Abraham hurried to the place where he had stood in the presence of the LORD. 28 He looked down at Sodom and Gomorrah and the whole valley and saw smoke rising from the land, like smoke from a huge furnace. 29 But when God destroyed the cities of the valley where Lot was living, he kept Abraham in mind and allowed Lot to escape to safety.

The Origin of the Moabites and Ammonites

30 Because Lot was afraid to stay in Zoar, he and his two daughters moved up into the hills and lived in a cave. 31 The older daughter said to her sister, "Our father is getting old, and there are no men in the whole world *q* to marry us so that we can have children. 32 Come on, let's get our father drunk, so that we can sleep with him and have children by him." 33 That night they gave him wine to drink, and the older

daughter had intercourse with him. But he was so drunk that he didn't know it.

34 The next day the older daughter said to her sister, "I slept with him last night; now let's get him drunk again tonight, and you sleep with him. Then each of us will have a child by our father." 35 So that night they got him drunk, and the younger daughter had intercourse with him. Again he was so drunk that he didn't know it. 36 In this way both of Lot's daughters became pregnant by their own father. 37 The older daughter had a son, whom she named Moab. *r* He was the ancestor of the present-day Moabites. 38 The younger daughter also had a son, whom she named Benammi. *s* He was the ancestor of the present-day Ammonites.

Abraham and Abimelech

20 Abraham moved from Mamre to the southern part of Canaan and lived between Kadesh and Shur. Later, while he was living in Gerar, 2 he said that his wife Sarah was his sister. So King Abimelech of Gerar had Sarah brought to him. 3 One night God appeared to him in a dream and said, "You are going to die, because you have taken this woman; she is already married."

4 But Abimelech had not come near her, and he said, "Lord, I am innocent! Would you destroy me and my people? 5 Abraham himself said that she was his sister, and she said the same thing. I did this with a clear conscience, and I have done no wrong."

6 God replied in the dream, "Yes, I know that you did it with a clear conscience; so I kept you from sinning against me and did not let you touch

---

q the whole world; *or* this land.   *r* MOAB: *This name sounds like the Hebrew for "from my father."*   *s* BENAMMI: *This name in Hebrew means "son of my relative" and sounds like the Hebrew for "Ammonite."*

19.26 Ws 10.7; Lk 17.32   **20.2** Gn 12.13; 26.7

© United Bible Societies, 1976

ANCIENT WORLD

her. ⁷But now, give the woman back to her husband. He is a prophet, and he will pray for you, so that you will not die. But if you do not give her back, I warn you that you are going to die, you and all your people."

⁸Early the next morning Abimelech called all his officials and told them what had happened, and they were terrified. ⁹Then Abimelech called Abraham and asked, "What have you done to us? What wrong have I done to you to make you bring this disaster on me and my kingdom? No one should ever do what you have done to me. ¹⁰Why did you do it?"

¹¹Abraham answered, "I thought that there would be no one here who has reverence for God and that they would kill me to get my wife. ¹²She really is my sister. She is the daughter of my father, but not of my mother, and I married her. ¹³So when God sent me from my father's house into foreign lands, I said to her, 'You can show how loyal you are to me by telling everyone that I am your brother.' "

¹⁴Then Abimelech gave Sarah back to Abraham, and at the same time he gave him sheep, cattle, and slaves. ¹⁵He said to Abraham, "Here is my whole land; live anywhere you like." ¹⁶He said to Sarah, "I am giving your brother a thousand pieces of silver as proof to all who are with you that you are innocent; everyone will know that you have done no wrong."

¹⁷⁻¹⁸Because of what had happened to Sarah, Abraham's wife, the Lord had made it impossible for any woman in Abimelech's palace to have children. So Abraham prayed for Abimelech, and God healed him. He also healed his wife and his slave women, so that they could have children.

The Birth of Isaac

21 The Lord blessed Sarah, as he had promised, ²and she became pregnant and bore a son to Abraham when he was old. The boy was born at the time God had said he would be born. ³Abraham named him Isaac, ⁴and when Isaac was eight days old, Abraham circumcised him, as God had commanded. ⁵Abraham was a hundred years old when Isaac was born. ⁶Sarah said, "God has brought me joy and laughter.ᵗ Everyone who hears about it will laugh with me." ⁷Then she added, "Who would have said to Abraham that Sarah would nurse children? Yet I have borne him a son in his old age."

⁸The child grew, and on the day that he was weaned, Abraham gave a great feast.

Hagar and Ishmael Are Sent Away

⁹One day Ishmael, whom Hagar the Egyptian had borne to Abraham, was playing withᵘ Sarah's son Isaac.ᵛ ¹⁰Sarah saw them and said to Abraham, "Send this slave and her son away. The son of this woman must not get any part of your wealth, which my son Isaac should inherit." ¹¹This troubled Abraham very much, because Ishmael also was his son. ¹²But God said to Abraham, "Don't be worried about the boy and your slave Hagar. Do whatever Sarah tells you, because it is through Isaac that you will have the descendants I have promised. ¹³I will also give many children to the son of the slave woman, so that they will become a nation. He too is your son."

¹⁴Early the next morning Abraham gave Hagar some food and a leather bag full of water. He put the child on her back and sent her away. She left and

---

ᵗ LAUGHTER: *The name Isaac in Hebrew means "he laughs" (see also 17.17-19).*
ᵘ playing with; *or* making fun of.   ᵛ *Some ancient translations* with Sarah's son Isaac; *Hebrew does not have these words.*
21.2 He 11.11   **21.4** Gn 17.12; Ac 7.8   **21.10** Ga 4.29, 30   **21.12** Ro 9.7; He 11.18

wandered about in the wilderness of Beersheba. [15]When the water was all gone, she left the child under a bush [16]and sat down about a hundred yards away. She said to herself, "I can't bear to see my child die." While she was sitting there, she[w] began to cry.

[17]God heard the boy crying, and from heaven the angel of God spoke to Hagar, "What are you troubled about, Hagar? Don't be afraid. God has heard the boy crying. [18]Get up, go and pick him up, and comfort him. I will make a great nation out of his descendants." [19]Then God opened her eyes, and she saw a well. She went and filled the leather bag with water and gave some to the boy. [20]God was with the boy as he grew up; he lived in the wilderness of Paran and became a skillful hunter. [21]His mother got an Egyptian wife for him.

The Agreement between Abraham and Abimelech

[22]At that time Abimelech went with Phicol, the commander of his army, and said to Abraham, "God is with you in everything you do. [23]So make a vow here in the presence of God that you will not deceive me, my children, or my descendants. I have been loyal to you, so promise that you will also be loyal to me and to this country in which you are living."

[24]Abraham said, "I promise."

[25]Abraham complained to Abimelech about a well which the servants of Abimelech had seized. [26]Abimelech said, "I don't know who did this. You didn't tell me about it, and this is the first I have heard of it." [27]Then Abraham gave some sheep and cattle to Abimelech, and the two of them made an agreement. [28]Abraham separated seven lambs from his flock, [29]and

Abimelech asked him, "Why did you do that?"

[30]Abraham answered, "Accept these seven lambs. By doing this, you admit that I am the one who dug this well." [31]And so the place was called Beersheba,[x] because it was there that the two of them made a vow.

[32]After they had made this agreement at Beersheba, Abimelech and Phicol went back to Philistia. [33]Then Abraham planted a tamarisk tree in Beersheba and worshiped the LORD, the Everlasting God. [34]Abraham lived in Philistia for a long time.

God Commands Abraham to Offer Isaac

22 Some time later God tested Abraham; he called to him, "Abraham!" And Abraham answered, "Yes, here I am!"

[2]"Take your son," God said, "your only son, Isaac, whom you love so much, and go to the land of Moriah. There on a mountain that I will show you, offer him as a sacrifice to me."

[3]Early the next morning Abraham cut some wood for the sacrifice, loaded his donkey, and took Isaac and two servants with him. They started out for the place that God had told him about. [4]On the third day Abraham saw the place in the distance. [5]Then he said to the servants, "Stay here with the donkey. The boy and I will go over there and worship, and then we will come back to you."

[6]Abraham made Isaac carry the wood for the sacrifice, and he himself carried a knife and live coals for starting the fire. As they walked along together, [7]Isaac spoke up, "Father!"

He answered, "Yes, my son?"

Isaac asked, "I see that you have the

---

[w] she; *one ancient translation* the child.   [x] BEERSHEBA: *This name in Hebrew means "Well of the Vow" or "Well of Seven" (see also 26.33).*
21.22 Gn 26.26   **22.1-13** Ws 10.5; Si 44.20; He 11.17-19   **22.2** 2 Ch 3.1

coals and the wood, but where is the lamb for the sacrifice?"

⁸Abraham answered, "God himself will provide one." And the two of them walked on together.

⁹When they came to the place which God had told him about, Abraham built an altar and arranged the wood on it. He tied up his son and placed him on the altar, on top of the wood. ¹⁰Then he picked up the knife to kill him. ¹¹But the angel of the LORD called to him from heaven, "Abraham, Abraham!"

He answered, "Yes, here I am."

¹²"Don't hurt the boy or do anything to him," he said. "Now I know that you honor and obey God, because you have not kept back your only son from him."

"Now I know that you honor and obey God."
(22.12)

¹³Abraham looked around and saw a ram caught in a bush by its horns. He went and got it and offered it as a burnt offering instead of his son. ¹⁴Abraham named that place "The LORD Provides."ʸ And even today people say, "On the LORD's mountain he provides."ᶻ

¹⁵The angel of the LORD called to Abraham from heaven a second time, ¹⁶"I make a vow by my own name — the LORD is speaking — that I will richly bless you. Because you did this and did not keep back your only son from me, ¹⁷I promise that I will give you as many descendants as there are stars in the sky or grains of sand along the seashore. Your descendants will conquer their enemies. ¹⁸All the nations will ask me to bless them as I have blessed your descendants — all because you obeyed my command." ¹⁹Abraham went back to his servants, and they went together to Beersheba, where Abraham settled.

The Descendants of Nahor

²⁰Some time later Abraham learned that Milcah had borne eight children to his brother Nahor: ²¹Uz the first-born, Buz his brother, Kemuel the father of Aram, ²²Chesed, Hazo, Pildash, Jidlaph, and Bethuel, ²³Rebecca's father. Milcah bore these eight sons to Nahor, Abraham's brother. ²⁴Reumah, Nahor's concubine, bore Tebah, Gaham, Tahash, and Maacah.

Sarah Dies and Abraham Buys a Burial Ground

23 Sarah lived to be 127 years old. ²She died in Hebron in the land of Canaan, and Abraham mourned her death.

³He left the place where his wife's body was lying, went to the Hittites, and said, ⁴"I am a foreigner living here among you; sell me some land, so that I can bury my wife."

⁵They answered, ⁶"Listen to us, sir. We look upon you as a mighty leader; bury your wife in the best grave that we have. Any of us would be glad to

---

ʸ Provides; *or* Sees.   ᶻ provides; *or* is seen.

22.9 Jas 2.21   **22.16, 17** He 6.13, 14   **22.17** He 11.12   **22.18** Ac 3.25   **23.4** He 11.9, 13; Ac 7.16

give you a grave, so that you can bury her."

7 Then Abraham bowed before them 8 and said, "If you are willing to let me bury my wife here, please ask Ephron son of Zohar 9 to sell me Machpelah Cave, which is near the edge of his field. Ask him to sell it to me for its full price, here in your presence, so that I can own it as a burial ground."

10 Ephron himself was sitting with the other Hittites at the meeting place at the city gate; he answered in the hearing of everyone there, 11 "Listen, sir; I will give you the whole field and the cave that is in it. Here in the presence of my own people, I will give it to you, so that you can bury your wife."

12 But Abraham bowed before the Hittites 13 and said to Ephron, so that everyone could hear, "May I ask you, please, to listen. I will buy the whole field. Accept my payment, and I will bury my wife there."

14 Ephron answered, 15 "Sir, land worth only four hundred pieces of silver — what is that between us? Bury your wife in it." 16 Abraham agreed and weighed out the amount that Ephron had mentioned in the hearing of the people — four hundred pieces of silver, according to the standard weights used by the merchants.

17 That is how the property which had belonged to Ephron at Machpelah east of Mamre, became Abraham's. It included the field, the cave which was in it, and all the trees in the field up to the edge of the property. 18 It was recognized as Abraham's property by all the Hittites who were there at the meeting.

19 Then Abraham buried his wife Sarah in that cave in the land of Canaan. 20 So the field which had belonged to the Hittites, and the cave in it, became the property of Abraham for a burial ground.

A Wife for Isaac

24 Abraham was now very old, and the LORD had blessed him in everything he did. 2 He said to his oldest servant, who was in charge of all that he had, "Place your hand between my thighs[a] and make a vow. 3 I want you to make a vow in the name of the LORD, the God of heaven and earth, that you will not choose a wife for my son from the people here in Canaan. 4 You must go back to the country where I was born and get a wife for my son Isaac from among my relatives."

5 But the servant asked, "What if the young woman will not leave home to come with me to this land? Shall I send your son back to the land you came from?"

6 Abraham answered, "Make sure that you don't send my son back there! 7 The LORD, the God of heaven, brought me from the home of my father and from the land of my relatives, and he solemnly promised me that he would give this land to my descendants. He will send his angel before you, so that you can get a wife there for my son. 8 If the young woman is not willing to come with you, you will be free from this promise. But you must not under any circumstances take my son back there." 9 So the servant put his hand between the thighs of Abraham, his master, and made a vow to do what Abraham had asked.

10 The servant, who was in charge of Abraham's property, took ten of his master's camels and went to the city where Nahor had lived in northern Mesopotamia. 11 When he arrived, he made the camels kneel down at the well outside the city. It was late afternoon, the time when women came out to get water. 12 He prayed, "LORD, God of my master Abraham, give me success today and keep your promise to my mas-

---

a PLACE ... THIGHS: *This was the way in which a vow was made absolutely unchangeable.*

ter. ¹³Here I am at the well where the young women of the city will be coming to get water. ¹⁴I will say to one of them, 'Please, lower your jar and let me have a drink.' If she says, 'Drink, and I will also bring water for your camels,' may she be the one that you have chosen for your servant Isaac. If this happens, I will know that you have kept your promise to my master."

¹⁵Before he had finished praying, Rebecca arrived with a water jar on her shoulder. She was the daughter of Bethuel, who was the son of Abraham's brother Nahor and his wife Milcah.

Rebecca arrived. (24.15)

¹⁶She was a very beautiful young woman and still a virgin. She went down to the well, filled her jar, and came back. ¹⁷The servant ran to meet her and said, "Please give me a drink of water from your jar."

¹⁸She said, "Drink, sir," and quickly lowered her jar from her shoulder and held it while he drank. ¹⁹When he had finished, she said, "I will also bring water for your camels and let them have all they want." ²⁰She quickly emptied her jar into the animals' drinking trough and ran to the well to get more water, until she had watered all his camels. ²¹The man kept watching her in silence, to see if the LORD had given him success.

²²When she had finished, the man took an expensive gold ring and put it in her nose and put two large gold bracelets on her arms. ²³He said, "Please tell me who your father is. Is there room in his house for my men and me to spend the night?"

²⁴"My father is Bethuel son of Nahor and Milcah," she answered. ²⁵"There is plenty of straw and fodder at our house, and there is a place for you to stay."

²⁶Then the man knelt down and worshiped the LORD. ²⁷He said, "Praise the LORD, the God of my master Abraham, who has faithfully kept his promise to my master. The LORD has led me straight to my master's relatives."

²⁸The young woman ran to her mother's house and told the whole story. ²⁹Now Rebecca had a brother named Laban, and he ran outside to go to the well where Abraham's servant was. ³⁰Laban had seen the nose ring and the bracelets on his sister's arms and had heard her say what the man had told her. He went to Abraham's servant, who was standing by his camels at the well, ³¹and said, "Come home with me. You are a man whom the LORD has blessed. Why are you standing out here? I have a room ready for you in my house, and there is a place for your camels."

³²So the man went into the house, and Laban unloaded the camels and gave them straw and fodder. Then he brought water for Abraham's servant and his men to wash their feet. ³³When food was brought, the man said, "I will not eat until I have said what I have to say."

Laban said, "Go on and speak."

³⁴"I am the servant of Abraham," he began. ³⁵"The LORD has greatly blessed my master and made him a rich man. He has given him flocks of sheep and goats, cattle, silver, gold, male and female slaves, camels, and donkeys. ³⁶Sarah, my master's wife, bore him a son when she was old, and my master has given everything he owns to him.

37 My master made me promise with a vow to obey his command. He said, 'Do not choose a wife for my son from the young women in the land of Canaan. 38 Instead, go to my father's people, to my relatives, and choose a wife for him.' 39 And I asked my master, 'What if she will not come with me?' 40 He answered, 'The LORD, whom I have always obeyed, will send his angel with you and give you success. You will get for my son a wife from my own people, from my father's family. 41 There is only one way for you to be free from your vow: if you go to my relatives and they refuse you, then you will be free.'

42 "When I came to the well today, I prayed, 'LORD, God of my master Abraham, please give me success in what I am doing. 43 Here I am at the well. When a young woman comes out to get water, I will ask her to give me a drink of water from her jar. 44 If she agrees and also offers to bring water for my camels, may she be the one that you have chosen as the wife for my master's son.' 45 Before I had finished my silent prayer, Rebecca came with a water jar on her shoulder and went down to the well to get water. I said to her, 'Please give me a drink.' 46 She quickly lowered her jar from her shoulder and said, 'Drink, and I will also water your camels.' So I drank, and she watered the camels. 47 I asked her, 'Who is your father?' And she answered, 'My father is Bethuel son of Nahor and Milcah.' Then I put the ring in her nose and the bracelets on her arms. 48 I knelt down and worshiped the LORD. I praised the LORD, the God of my master Abraham, who had led me straight to my master's relative, where I found his daughter for my master's son. 49 Now, if you intend to fulfill your responsibility toward my master and treat him fairly, please tell me; if not, say so, and I will decide what to do."

50 Laban and Bethuel answered, "Since this matter comes from the LORD, it is not for us to make a decision. 51 Here is Rebecca; take her and go. Let her become the wife of your master's son, as the LORD himself has said." 52 When the servant of Abraham heard this, he bowed down and worshiped the LORD. 53 Then he brought out clothing and silver and gold jewelry, and gave them to Rebecca. He also gave expensive gifts to her brother and to her mother.

54 Then Abraham's servant and the men with him ate and drank, and spent the night there. When they got up in the morning, he said, "Let me go back to my master."

55 But Rebecca's brother and her mother said, "Let her stay with us a week or ten days, and then she may go."

56 But he said, "Don't make us stay. The LORD has made my journey a success; let me go back to my master."

57 They answered, "Let's call her and find out what she has to say." 58 So they called Rebecca and asked, "Do you want to go with this man?"

"Yes," she answered.

59 So they let Rebecca and her old family servant go with Abraham's servant and his men. 60 And they gave Rebecca their blessing in these words:

"May you, sister, become the
    mother of millions!
May your descendants conquer
    the cities of their enemies!"
61 Then Rebecca and her young women got ready and mounted the camels to go with Abraham's servant, and they all started out.

62 Isaac had come into the wilderness of[b] "The Well of the Living One Who Sees Me" and was staying in the southern part of Canaan. 63 He went out in the early evening to take a walk in the fields and saw camels coming. 64 When Rebecca saw Isaac, she got down from her camel 65 and asked Abraham's serv-

---

[b] Some ancient translations into the wilderness of; Hebrew from coming.

ant, "Who is that man walking toward us in the field?"

"He is my master," the servant answered. So she took her scarf and covered her face.

66 The servant told Isaac everything he had done. 67 Then Isaac brought Rebecca into the tent that his mother Sarah had lived in, and she became his wife. Isaac loved Rebecca, and so he was comforted for the loss of his mother.

Other Descendants of Abraham
(1 Chronicles 1.32, 33)

25 Abraham married another woman, whose name was Keturah. 2 She bore him Zimran, Jokshan, Medan, Midian, Ishbak, and Shuah. 3 Jokshan was the father of Sheba and Dedan, and the descendants of Dedan were the Asshurim, the Letushim, and the Leummim. 4 The sons of Midian were Ephah, Epher, Hanoch, Abida, and Eldaah. All these were Keturah's descendants.

5 Abraham left everything he owned to Isaac; 6 but while he was still alive, he gave presents to the sons his other wives had borne him. Then he sent these sons to the land of the East, away from his son Isaac.

The Death and Burial of Abraham

7-8 Abraham died at the ripe old age of 175. 9 His sons Isaac and Ishmael buried him in Machpelah Cave, in the field east of Mamre that had belonged to Ephron son of Zohar the Hittite. 10 It was the field that Abraham had bought from the Hittites; both Abraham and his wife Sarah were buried there. 11 After the death of Abraham, God blessed his son Isaac, who lived near "The Well of the Living One Who Sees Me."

The Descendants of Ishmael
(1 Chronicles 1.28-31)

12 Ishmael, whom Hagar, the Egyptian slave of Sarah, bore to Abraham, 13 had the following sons, listed in the order of their birth: Nebaioth, Kedar, Adbeel, Mibsam, 14 Mishma, Dumah, Massa, 15 Hadad, Tema, Jetur, Naphish, and Kedemah. 16 They were the ancestors of twelve tribes, and their names were given to their villages and camping places. 17 Ishmael was 137 years old when he died. 18 The descendants of Ishmael lived in the territory between Havilah and Shur, to the east of Egypt on the way to Assyria. They lived apart from the other descendants of Abraham.

The Birth of Esau and Jacob

19 This is the story of Abraham's son Isaac. 20 Isaac was forty years old when he married Rebecca, the daughter of Bethuel (an Aramean from Mesopotamia) and sister of Laban. 21 Because Rebecca had no children, Isaac prayed to the LORD for her. The LORD answered his prayer, and Rebecca became pregnant. 22 She was going to have twins, and before they were born, they struggled against each other in her womb. She said, "Why should something like this happen to me?" So she went to ask the LORD for an answer.

23 The LORD said to her,
"Two nations are within you;
You will give birth to two rival peoples.
One will be stronger than the other;
The older will serve the younger."

24 The time came for her to give birth, and she had twin sons. 25 The first one was reddish, and his skin was like a hairy robe, so he was named Esau.c

---

c ESAU: *This name is taken to refer to Seir, the territory later inhabited by Esau's descendants; Seir sounds like the Hebrew for "hairy."*

25.10 Gn 23.3-16   **25.23** Ro 9.12

26 The second one was born holding on tightly to the heel of Esau, so he was named Jacob.[d] Isaac was sixty years old when they were born.

Esau Sells His Rights as the First-Born Son

27 The boys grew up, and Esau became a skilled hunter, a man who loved the outdoors, but Jacob was a quiet man who stayed at home. 28 Isaac preferred Esau, because he enjoyed eating the animals Esau killed, but Rebecca preferred Jacob.

29 One day while Jacob was cooking some bean soup, Esau came in from hunting. He was hungry 30 and said to Jacob, "I'm starving; give me some of that red stuff." (That is why he was named Edom.[e])

31 Jacob answered, "I will give it to you if you give me your rights as the first-born son."

32 Esau said, "All right! I am about to die; what good will my rights do me?"

33 Jacob answered, "First make a vow that you will give me your rights."

Esau made the vow and gave his rights to Jacob. 34 Then Jacob gave him some bread and some of the soup. He ate and drank and then got up and left. That was all Esau cared about his rights as the first-born son.

Isaac Lives at Gerar

26 There was another famine in the land besides the earlier one during the time of Abraham. Isaac went to Abimelech, king of the Philistines, at Gerar. 2 The LORD had appeared to Isaac and had said, "Do not go to Egypt; stay in this land, where I tell you to stay. 3 Live here, and I will be with you and bless you. I am going to give all this ter-

Then Jacob gave him . . . some of the soup. (25.34)

ritory to you and to your descendants. I will keep the promise I made to your father Abraham. 4 I will give you as many descendants as there are stars in the sky, and I will give them all this territory. All the nations will ask me to bless them as I have blessed your descendants. 5 I will bless you, because Abraham obeyed me and kept all my laws and commands."

6 So Isaac lived at Gerar. 7 When the men there asked about his wife, he said that she was his sister. He would not admit that she was his wife, because he was afraid that the men there would kill him to get Rebecca, who was very beautiful. 8 When Isaac had been there for some time, King Abimelech looked down from his window and saw Isaac and Rebecca making love. 9 Abimelech sent for Isaac and said, "So she is your wife! Why did you say she was your sister?"

He answered, "I thought I would be killed if I said she was my wife."

---

[d] JACOB: *This name sounds like the Hebrew for "heel."*   [e] EDOM: *This name sounds like the Hebrew for "red."*

25.33 He 12.16   **26.3, 4** Gn 22.16-18   **26.7** Gn 12.13; 20.2

[10]"What have you done to us?" Abimelech said. "One of my men might easily have slept with your wife, and you would have been responsible for our guilt." [11]Abimelech warned all the people: "Anyone who mistreats this man or his wife will be put to death."

[12]Isaac sowed crops in that land, and that year he harvested a hundred times as much as he had sown, because the LORD blessed him. [13]He continued to prosper and became a very rich man. [14]Because he had many herds of sheep and cattle and many servants, the Philistines were jealous of him [15]So they filled in all the wells which the servants of his father Abraham had dug while Abraham was alive.

[16]Then Abimelech said to Isaac, "Leave our country. You have become more powerful than we are." [17]So Isaac left and set up his camp in Gerar Valley, where he stayed for some time. [18]He dug once again the wells which had been dug during the time of Abraham and which the Philistines had stopped up after Abraham's death. Isaac gave the wells the same names that his father had given them.

[19]Isaac's servants dug a well in the valley and found water. [20]The shepherds of Gerar quarreled with Isaac's shepherds and said, "This water belongs to us." So Isaac named the well "Quarrel."

[21]Isaac's servants dug another well, and there was a quarrel about that one also, so he named it "Enmity." [22]He moved away from there and dug another well. There was no dispute about this one, so he named it "Freedom." He said, "Now the LORD has given us freedom to live in the land, and we will be prosperous here."

[23]Isaac left and went to Beersheba. [24]That night the LORD appeared to him and said, "I am the God of your father Abraham. Do not be afraid; I am with you. I will bless you and give you many descendants because of my promise to my servant Abraham." [25]Isaac built an altar there and worshiped the LORD. Then he set up his camp there, and his servants dug another well.

The Agreement between Isaac and Abimelech

[26]Abimelech came from Gerar with Ahuzzath his adviser and Phicol the commander of his army to see Isaac. [27]So Isaac asked, "Why have you now come to see me, when you were so unfriendly to me before and made me leave your country?"

[28]They answered, "Now we know that the LORD is with you, and we think that there should be a solemn agreement between us. We want you to promise [29]that you will not harm us, just as we did not harm you. We were kind to you and let you go peacefully. Now it is clear that the LORD has blessed you." [30]Isaac prepared a feast for them, and they ate and drank. [31]Early next morning each man made his promise and sealed it with a vow. Isaac said good-bye to them, and they parted as friends.

[32]On that day Isaac's servants came and told him about the well which they had dug. They said, "We have found water." [33]He named the well "Vow." That is how the city of Beersheba[f] got its name.

Esau's Foreign Wives

[34]When Esau was forty years old, he married two Hittites, Judith the daughter of Beeri, and Basemath the daughter of Elon. [35]They made life miserable for Isaac and Rebecca.

---

[f] BEERSHEBA: *This name in Hebrew means "Well of the Vow" or "Well of Seven" (see also 21.31).*

26.26 Gn 21.22

Isaac Blesses Jacob

27 Isaac was now old and had become blind. He sent for his older son Esau and said to him, "Son!"

"Yes," he answered.

2 Isaac said, "You see that I am old and may die soon. 3 Take your bow and arrows, go out into the country, and kill an animal for me. 4 Cook me some of that tasty food that I like, and bring it to me. After I have eaten it, I will give you my final blessing before I die."

5 While Isaac was talking to Esau, Rebecca was listening. So when Esau went out to hunt, 6 she said to Jacob, "I have just heard your father say to Esau, 7 'Bring me an animal and cook it for me. After I have eaten it, I will give you my blessing in the presence of the LORD before I die.' 8 Now, son," Rebecca continued, "listen to me and do what I say. 9 Go to the flock and pick out two fat young goats, so that I can cook them and make some of that food your father likes so much. 10 You can take it to him to eat, and he will give you his blessing before he dies."

11 But Jacob said to his mother, "You know that Esau is a hairy man, but I have smooth skin. 12 Perhaps my father will touch me and find out that I am deceiving him; in this way, I will bring a curse on myself instead of a blessing."

13 His mother answered, "Let any curse against you fall on me, my son; just do as I say, and go and get the goats for me." 14 So he went to get them and brought them to her, and she cooked the kind of food that his father liked. 15 Then she took Esau's best clothes, which she kept in the house, and put them on Jacob. 16 She put the skins of the goats on his arms and on the hairless part of his neck. 17 She handed him the tasty food, along with the bread she had baked.

18 Then Jacob went to his father and said, "Father!"

"Yes," he answered. "Which of my sons are you?"

19 Jacob answered, "I am your older son Esau; I have done as you told me. Please sit up and eat some of the meat that I have brought you, so that you can give me your blessing."

20 Isaac said, "How did you find it so quickly, son?"

Jacob answered, "The LORD your God helped me find it."

21 Isaac said to Jacob, "Please come closer so that I can touch you. Are you really Esau?" 22 Jacob moved closer to his father, who felt him and said, "Your voice sounds like Jacob's voice, but your arms feel like Esau's arms." 23 He did not recognize Jacob, because his arms were hairy like Esau's. He was about to give him his blessing, 24 but asked again, "Are you really Esau?"

"I am," he answered.

25 Isaac said, "Bring me some of the meat. After I eat it, I will give you my blessing." Jacob brought it to him, and he also brought him some wine to drink. 26 Then his father said to him, "Come closer and kiss me, son." 27 As he came up to kiss him, Isaac smelled his clothes — so he gave him his blessing. He said, "The pleasant smell of my son is like the smell of a field which the

He gave him his blessing. (27.27)

27.27-29 He 11.20

LORD has blessed. [28] May God give you dew from heaven and make your fields fertile! May he give you plenty of grain and wine! [29] May nations be your servants, and may peoples bow down before you. May you rule over all your relatives, and may your mother's descendants bow down before you. May those who curse you be cursed, and may those who bless you be blessed."

Esau Begs for Isaac's Blessing

[30] Isaac finished giving his blessing, and as soon as Jacob left, his brother Esau came in from hunting. [31] He also cooked some tasty food and took it to his father. He said, "Please, father, sit up and eat some of the meat that I have brought you, so that you can give me your blessing."

[32] "Who are you?" Isaac asked.

"Your older son Esau," he answered.

[33] Isaac began to tremble and shake all over, and he asked, "Who was it, then, who killed an animal and brought it to me? I ate it just before you came. I gave him my final blessing, and so it is his forever."

[34] When Esau heard this, he cried out loudly and bitterly and said, "Give me your blessing also, father!"

[35] Isaac answered, "Your brother came and deceived me. He has taken away your blessing."

[36] Esau said, "This is the second time that he has cheated me. No wonder his name is Jacob.[g] He took my rights as the first-born son, and now he has taken away my blessing. Haven't you saved a blessing for me?"

[37] Isaac answered, "I have already made him master over you, and I have made all his relatives his slaves. I have given him grain and wine. Now there is nothing that I can do for you, son!"

[38] Esau continued to plead with his father: "Do you have only one blessing, father? Bless me too, father!" He began to cry.

[39] Then Isaac said to him,
"No dew from heaven for you,
No fertile fields for you.
[40] You will live by your sword,
But be your brother's slave.
Yet when you rebel,[h]
You will break away from his control."

[41] Esau hated Jacob, because his father had given Jacob the blessing. He thought, "The time to mourn my father's death is near; then I will kill Jacob."

[42] But when Rebecca heard about Esau's plan, she sent for Jacob and said, "Listen, your brother Esau is planning to get even with you and kill you. [43] Now, son, do what I say. Go at once to my brother Laban in Haran, [44] and stay with him for a while, until your brother's anger cools down [45] and he forgets what you have done to him. Then I will send someone to bring you back. Why should I lose both of my sons on the same day?"

Isaac Sends Jacob to Laban

[46] Rebecca said to Isaac, "I am sick and tired of Esau's foreign wives. If Jacob also marries one of these Hittites, I might as well die."

28 Isaac called Jacob, greeted him, and told him, "Don't marry a Canaanite. [2] Go instead to Mesopotamia, to the home of your grandfather Bethuel, and marry one of the young women there, one of your uncle Laban's daughters. [3] May Almighty God bless your marriage and give you many children, so that you will become the father of many nations! [4] May he bless you and your descendants as he blessed Abraham, and may you take possession

---

[g] JACOB: *This name sounds like the Hebrew for "cheat."*   [h] rebel; *or* grow restless.

27.29 Gn 12.3   **27.36** Gn 25.29-34   **27.38** He 12.17   **27.39, 40** He 11.20   **27.40** Gn 36.8; 2 K 8.20   **27.42** Ws 10.10   **28.4** Gn 17.4-8 of this land, in which you have lived and which God gave to Abraham!" [5]Isaac sent Jacob away to Mesopotamia, to Laban, who was the son of Bethuel the Aramean and the brother of Rebecca, the mother of Jacob and Esau.

Esau Takes Another Wife

[6]Esau learned that Isaac had blessed Jacob and sent him away to Mesopotamia to find a wife. He also learned that when Isaac blessed him, he commanded him not to marry a Canaanite woman. [7]He found out that Jacob had obeyed his father and mother and had gone to Mesopotamia. [8]Esau then understood that his father Isaac did not approve of Canaanite women. [9]So he went to Ishmael son of Abraham and married his daughter Mahalath, who was the sister of Nebaioth.

Jacob's Dream at Bethel

[10]Jacob left Beersheba and started toward Haran. [11]At sunset he came to a holy place[i] and camped there. He lay down to sleep, resting his head on a stone. [12]He dreamed that he saw a stairway reaching from earth to heaven, with angels going up and coming down on it. [13]And there was the LORD standing beside him.[j] "I am the LORD, the God of Abraham and Isaac," he said. "I will give to you and to your descendants this land on which you are lying. [14]They will be as numerous as the specks of dust on the earth. They will extend their territory in all directions, and through you and your descendants I will bless all the nations.[k] [15]Remember, I will be with you and protect you wherever you go, and I will bring you back to this land. I will not leave you until I have done all that I have promised you."

A stairway reaching from earth to heaven (28.12)

[16]Jacob woke up and said, "The LORD is here! He is in this place, and I didn't know it!" [17]He was afraid and said, "What a terrifying place this is! It must be the house of God; it must be the gate that opens into heaven."

[18]Jacob got up early next morning, took the stone that was under his head, and set it up as a memorial. Then he poured olive oil on it to dedicate it to

---

[i] a holy place; *or* a place.   [j] beside him; *or* on it.   [k] through you ... nations; *or* all the nations will ask me to bless them as I have blessed you and your descendants.
28.10 Ws 10.10   **28.12** Jn 1.51   **28.13** Gn 13.14, 15   **28.14** Gn 12.3; 22.18

God. [19] He named the place Bethel.[l] (The town there was once known as Luz.) [20] Then Jacob made a vow to the LORD: "If you will be with me and protect me on the journey I am making and give me food and clothing, [21] and if I return safely to my father's home, then you will be my God. [22] This memorial stone which I have set up will be the place where you are worshiped, and I will give you a tenth of everything you give me."

Jacob Arrives at Laban's Home

29 Jacob continued on his way and went toward the land of the East. [2] Suddenly he came upon a well out in the fields with three flocks of sheep lying around it. The flocks were watered from this well, which had a large stone over the opening. [3] Whenever all the flocks came together there, the shepherds would roll the stone back and water them. Then they would put the stone back in place.

[4] Jacob asked the shepherds, "My friends, where are you from?"

"From Haran," they answered.

[5] He asked, "Do you know Laban, grandson of Nahor?"

"Yes, we do," they answered.

[6] "Is he well?" he asked.

"He is well," they answered. "Look, here comes his daughter Rachel with his flock."

[7] Jacob said, "Since it is still broad daylight and not yet time to bring the flocks in, why don't you water them and take them back to pasture?"

[8] They answered, "We can't do that until all the flocks are here and the stone has been rolled back; then we will water the flocks."

[9] While Jacob was still talking with them, Rachel arrived with the flock. [10] When Jacob saw Rachel with his uncle Laban's flock, he went to the well, rolled the stone back, and watered the sheep. [11] Then he kissed her and began to cry for joy. [12] He told her, "I am your father's relative, the son of Rebecca."

She ran to tell her father; [13] and when he heard the news about his nephew Jacob, he ran to meet him, hugged him and kissed him, and brought him into the house. When Jacob told Laban everything that had happened, [14] Laban said, "Yes, indeed, you are my own flesh and blood." Jacob stayed there a whole month.

Jacob Serves Laban for Rachel and Leah

[15] Laban said to Jacob, "You shouldn't work for me for nothing just because you are my relative. How much pay do you want?" [16] Laban had two daughters; the older was named Leah, and the younger Rachel. [17] Leah had lovely[m] eyes, but Rachel was shapely and beautiful.

[18] Jacob was in love with Rachel, so he said, "I will work seven years for you, if you will let me marry Rachel."

[19] Laban answered, "I would rather give her to you than to anyone else; stay here with me." [20] Jacob worked seven years so that he could have Rachel, and the time seemed like only a few days to him, because he loved her.

[21] Then Jacob said to Laban, "The time is up; let me marry your daughter." [22] So Laban gave a wedding feast and invited everyone. [23] But that night, instead of Rachel, he took Leah to Jacob, and Jacob had intercourse with her. ([24] Laban gave his slave woman Zilpah to his daughter Leah as her maid.) [25] Not until the next morning did Jacob discover that it was Leah. He went to Laban and said, "Why did you do this to me? I worked to get Rachel. Why have you tricked me?"

[26] Laban answered, "It is not the custom here to give the younger daughter in marriage before the older. [27] Wait until

---

[l] BETHEL: *This name in Hebrew means "house of God."*   [m] lovely; *or* weak.

the week's marriage celebrations are over, and I will give you Rachel, if you will work for me another seven years." [28] Jacob agreed, and when the week of marriage celebrations was over, Laban gave him his daughter Rachel as his wife. ([29] Laban gave his slave woman Bilhah to his daughter Rachel as her maid.) [30] Jacob had intercourse with Rachel also, and he loved her more than Leah. Then he worked for Laban another seven years.

The Children Born to Jacob

[31] When the LORD saw that Leah was loved less than Rachel, he made it possible for her to have children, but Rachel remained childless. [32] Leah became pregnant and gave birth to a son. She said, "The LORD has seen my trouble, and now my husband will love me"; so she named him Reuben.[n] [33] She became pregnant again and gave birth to another son. She said, "The LORD has given me this son also, because he heard that I was not loved"; so she named him Simeon.[o] [34] Once again she became pregnant and gave birth to another son. She said, "Now my husband will be bound more tightly to me, because I have borne him three sons"; so she named him Levi.[p] [35] Then she became pregnant again and gave birth to another son. She said, "This time I will praise the LORD"; so she named him Judah.[q] Then she stopped having children.

30 But Rachel had not borne Jacob any children, and so she became jealous of her sister and said to Jacob, "Give me children, or I will die."

[2] Jacob became angry with Rachel and said, "I can't take the place of God. He is the one who keeps you from having children."

[3] She said, "Here is my slave Bilhah; sleep with her, so that she can have a child for me. In this way I can become a mother through her." [4] So she gave Bilhah to her husband, and he had intercourse with her. [5] Bilhah became pregnant and bore Jacob a son. [6] Rachel said, "God has judged in my favor. He has heard my prayer and has given me a son"; so she named him Dan.[r] [7] Bilhah became pregnant again and bore Jacob a second son. [8] Rachel said, "I have fought a hard fight with my sister, but I have won"; so she named him Naphtali.[s]

[9] When Leah realized that she had stopped having children, she gave her slave Zilpah to Jacob as his wife. [10] Then Zilpah bore Jacob a son. [11] Leah said, "I have been lucky"; so she named him Gad.[t] [12] Zilpah bore Jacob another son, [13] and Leah said, "How happy I am! Now women will call me happy"; so she named him Asher.[u]

[14] During the wheat harvest Reuben went into the fields and found mandrakes,[v] which he brought to his mother Leah. Rachel said to Leah, "Please give me some of your son's mandrakes."

[15] Leah answered, "Isn't it enough that you have taken away my husband? Now you are even trying to take away my son's mandrakes."

Rachel said, "If you will give me your son's mandrakes, you can sleep with Jacob tonight."

[16] When Jacob came in from the

[n] REUBEN: *This name sounds like the Hebrew for "see, a son" and "has seen my trouble."*   [o] SIMEON: *This name sounds like the Hebrew for "hear."*   [p] LEVI: *This name sounds like the Hebrew for "bound."*   [q] JUDAH: *This name sounds like the Hebrew for "praise."*   [r] DAN: *This name sounds like the Hebrew for "judge in favor."*   [s] NAPHTALI: *This name sounds like the Hebrew for "fight."*   [t] GAD: *This name in Hebrew means "luck."*   [u] ASHER: *This name in Hebrew means "happy."*   [v] MANDRAKES: *Plants which were believed to produce fertility and were used as love charms.*

fields in the evening, Leah went out to meet him and said, "You are going to sleep with me tonight, because I have paid for you with my son's mandrakes." So he had intercourse with her that night.

¹⁷God answered Leah's prayer, and she became pregnant and bore Jacob a fifth son. ¹⁸Leah said, "God has given me my reward, because I gave my slave to my husband"; so she named her son Issachar.ʷ ¹⁹Leah became pregnant again and bore Jacob a sixth son. ²⁰She said, "God has given me a fine gift. Now my husband will accept me, because I have borne him six sons"; so she named him Zebulun.ˣ ²¹Later she bore a daughter, whom she named Dinah.

²²Then God remembered Rachel; he answered her prayer and made it possible for her to have children. ²³She became pregnant and gave birth to a son. She said, "God has taken away my disgrace by giving me a son. ²⁴May the LORD give me another son"; so she named him Joseph.ʸ

Jacob's Bargain with Laban

²⁵After the birth of Joseph, Jacob said to Laban, "Let me go, so that I can return home. ²⁶Give me my wives and children that I have earned by working for you, and I will leave. You know how well I have served you."

²⁷Laban said to him, "Let me say this: I have learned by divination that the LORD has blessed me because of you. ²⁸Name your wages, and I will pay them."

²⁹Jacob answered, "You know how I have worked for you and how your flocks have prospered under my care. ³⁰The little you had before I came has grown enormously, and the LORD has

blessed you wherever I went.ᶻ Now it is time for me to look out for my own interests."

³¹"What shall I pay you?" Laban asked.

Jacob answered, "I don't want any wages. I will continue to take care of your flocks if you agree to this suggestion: ³²Let me go through all your flocks today and take every black lambᵃ and every spotted or speckled young goat. That is all the wages I want. ³³In the future you can easily find out if I have been honest. When you come to check up on my wages, if I have any goat that isn't speckled or spotted or any sheep that isn't black, you will know that it has been stolen."

³⁴Laban answered, "Agreed. We will do as you suggest." ³⁵But that day Laban removed the male goats that had stripes or spots and all the females that were speckled and spotted or which had white on them; he also removed all the black sheep. He put his sons in charge of them, ³⁶and then went away from Jacob with this flock as far as he could travel in three days. Jacob took care of the rest of Laban's flocks.

³⁷Jacob got green branches of poplar, almond, and plane trees and stripped off some of the bark so that the branches had white stripes on them. ³⁸He placed these branches in front of the flocks at their drinking troughs. He put them there, because the animals mated when they came to drink. ³⁹So when the goats bred in front of the branches, they produced young that were streaked, speckled, and spotted. ⁴⁰Jacob kept the sheep separate from the goats and made them face in the direction of the streaked and black animals of Laban's flock. In this way he

---

ʷ ISSACHAR: *This name sounds like the Hebrew for "a man is hired" and "there is reward."*   ˣ ZEBULUN: *This name sounds like the Hebrew for "accept" and "gift."* ʸ JOSEPH: *This name sounds like the Hebrew for "may he give another" and "he has taken away."*   ᶻ wherever I went; *or* because of me.   ᵃ *One ancient translation* every black lamb; *Hebrew* every spotted and speckled lamb, and every black lamb.

built up his own flock and kept it apart from Laban's.

⁴¹When the healthy animals were mating, Jacob put the branches in front of them at the drinking troughs, so that they would breed among the branches. ⁴²But he did not put the branches in front of the weak animals. Soon Laban had all the weak animals, and Jacob all the healthy ones. ⁴³In this way Jacob became very wealthy. He had many flocks, slaves, camels, and donkeys.

Jacob Flees from Laban

31 Jacob heard that Laban's sons were saying, "Jacob has taken everything that belonged to our father. He got all his wealth from what our father owned." ²He also saw that Laban was no longer as friendly as he had been earlier. ³Then the LORD said to him, "Go back to the land of your fathers and to your relatives. I will be with you."

⁴So Jacob sent word to Rachel and Leah to meet him in the field where his flocks were. ⁵He said to them, "I have noticed that your father is not as friendly toward me as he used to be; but my father's God has been with me. ⁶You both know that I have worked for your father with all my strength. ⁷Yet he has cheated me and changed my wages ten times. But God did not let him harm me. ⁸Whenever Laban said, 'The speckled goats shall be your wages,' all the flocks produced speckled young. When he said, 'The striped goats shall be your wages,' all the flocks produced striped young. ⁹God has taken flocks away from your father and given them to me.

¹⁰"During the breeding season I had a dream, and I saw that the male goats that were mating were striped, spotted, and speckled. ¹¹The angel of God spoke to me in the dream and said, 'Jacob!' 'Yes,' I answered. ¹²'Look,' he contin-

ued, 'all the male goats that are mating are striped, spotted, and speckled. I am making this happen because I have seen all that Laban is doing to you. ¹³I am the God who appeared to you at Bethel, where you dedicated a stone as a memorial by pouring olive oil on it and where you made a vow to me. Now get ready and go back to the land where you were born.'"

¹⁴Rachel and Leah answered Jacob, "There is nothing left for us to inherit from our father. ¹⁵He treats us like foreigners. He sold us, and now he has spent all the money he was paid for us. ¹⁶All this wealth which God has taken from our father belongs to us and to our children. Do whatever God has told you."

¹⁷⁻¹⁸So Jacob got ready to go back to his father in the land of Canaan. He put his children and his wives on the camels, and drove all his flocks ahead of him, with everything that he had gotten in Mesopotamia. ¹⁹Laban had gone to shear his sheep, and during his absence Rachel stole the household gods that belonged to her father. ²⁰Jacob deceived Laban by not letting him know that he was leaving. ²¹He took everything he owned and left in a hurry. He crossed the Euphrates River and started for the hill country of Gilead.

Laban Pursues Jacob

²²Three days later Laban was told that Jacob had fled. ²³He took his men with him and pursued Jacob for seven days until he caught up with him in the hill country of Gilead. ²⁴In a dream that night God came to Laban and said to him, "Be careful not to threaten Jacob in any way." ²⁵Jacob had set up his camp on a mountain, and Laban set up his camp with his relatives in the hill country of Gilead.

²⁶Laban said to Jacob, "Why did you deceive me and carry off my daughters

31.13 Gn 28.18-22

Jacob drove all his flocks ahead of him. (31.18)

like women captured in war? 27 Why did you deceive me and slip away without telling me? If you had told me, I would have sent you on your way with rejoicing and singing to the music of tambourines and harps. 28 You did not even let me kiss my grandchildren and my daughters good-bye. That was a foolish thing to do! 29 I have the power to do you harm, but last night the God of your father warned me not to threaten you in any way. 30 I know that you left because you were so anxious to get back home, but why did you steal my household gods?"

31 Jacob answered, "I was afraid, because I thought that you might take your daughters away from me. 32 But if you find that anyone here has your gods, he will be put to death. Here, with our men as witnesses, look for anything that belongs to you and take what is yours." Jacob did not know that Rachel had stolen Laban's gods.

33 Laban went and searched Jacob's tent; then he went into Leah's tent, and the tent of the two slave women, but he did not find his gods. Then he went into Rachel's tent. 34 Rachel had taken the household gods and put them in a camel's saddlebag and was sitting on them. Laban searched through the whole tent, but did not find them. 35 Rachel said to her father, "Do not be angry with me, sir, but I am not able to stand up in your presence; I am having my monthly period." Laban searched but did not find his household gods.

36 Then Jacob lost his temper. "What crime have I committed?" he asked angrily. "What law have I broken that gives you the right to hunt me down? 37 Now that you have searched through all my belongings, what household article have you found that belongs to you? Put it out here where your men and mine can see it, and let them decide which one of us is right. 38 I have been with you now for twenty years; your sheep and your goats have not failed to reproduce, and I have not eaten any rams from your flocks. 39 Whenever a sheep was killed by wild animals, I always bore the loss myself. I didn't take it to you to show that it was not my fault. You demanded that I make good anything that was stolen during the day or during the night. 40 Many times I suffered from the heat during the day and from the cold at night. I was not able to sleep. 41 It was like that for the whole twenty years I was with you. For fourteen years I worked to win your two daughters — and six years for your

flocks. And even then, you changed my wages ten times. [42] If the God of my fathers, the God of Abraham and Isaac, had not been with me, you would have already sent me away empty-handed. But God has seen my trouble and the work I have done, and last night he gave his judgment."

The Agreement between Jacob and Laban

[43] Laban answered Jacob, "These young women are my daughters; their children belong to me, and these flocks are mine. In fact, everything you see here belongs to me. But since I can do nothing to keep my daughters and their children, [44] I am ready to make an agreement with you. Let us make a pile of stones to remind us of our agreement."

[45] So Jacob got a stone and set it up as a memorial. [46] He told his men to gather some rocks and pile them up. Then they ate a meal beside the pile of rocks. [47] Laban named it Jegar Sahadutha,[b] while Jacob named it Galeed.[c] [48] Laban said to Jacob, "This pile of rocks will be a reminder for both of us." That is why that place was named Galeed. [49] Laban also said, "May the LORD keep an eye on us while we are separated from each other." So the place was also named Mizpah.[d] [50] Laban went on, "If you mistreat my daughters or if you marry other women, even though I don't know about it, remember that God is watching us. [51] Here are the rocks that I have piled up between us, and here is the memorial stone. [52] Both this pile and this memorial stone are reminders. I will never go beyond this pile to attack you, and you must

never go beyond it or beyond this memorial stone to attack me. [53] The God of Abraham and the God of Nahor[e] will judge between us." Then, in the name of the God whom his father Isaac worshiped, Jacob solemnly vowed to keep this promise. [54] He killed an animal, which he offered as a sacrifice on the mountain, and he invited his men to the meal. After they had eaten, they spent the night on the mountain. [55] Early the next morning Laban kissed his grandchildren and his daughters good-bye, and left to go back home.

Jacob Prepares to Meet Esau

32 As Jacob went on his way, some angels met him. [2] When he saw them, he said, "This is God's camp"; so he named the place Mahanaim.[f]

[3] Jacob sent messengers ahead of him to his brother Esau in the country of Edom. [4] He instructed them to say: "I, Jacob, your obedient servant, report to my master Esau that I have been staying with Laban and that I have delayed my return until now. [5] I own cattle, donkeys, sheep, goats, and slaves. I am sending you word, sir, in the hope of gaining your favor."

[6] When the messengers came back to Jacob, they said, "We went to your brother Esau, and he is already on his way to meet you. He has four hundred men with him." [7] Jacob was frightened and worried. He divided into two groups the people who were with him, and also his sheep, goats, cattle, and camels. [8] He thought, "If Esau comes and attacks the first group, the other may be able to escape."

[9] Then Jacob prayed, "God of my

---

[b] JEGAR SAHADUTHA: *This name in Aramaic means "a pile to remind us."*   [c] GALEED: *This name in Hebrew means "a pile to remind us."*   [d] MIZPAH: *This name sounds like the Hebrew for "place from which to watch."*   [e] ABRAHAM ... NAHOR: *Abraham was Jacob's grandfather and Nahor was Laban's grandfather.*   [f] MAHANAIM: *This name in Hebrew means "two camps."*

grandfather Abraham and God of my father Isaac, hear me! You told me, LORD, to go back to my land and to my relatives, and you would make everything go well for me. ¹⁰I am not worth all the kindness and faithfulness that you have shown me, your servant. I crossed the Jordan with nothing but a walking stick, and now I have come back with these two groups. ¹¹Save me, I pray, from my brother Esau. I am afraid — afraid that he is coming to attack us and destroy us all, even the women and children. ¹²Remember that you promised to make everything go well for me and to give me more descendants than anyone could count, as many as the grains of sand along the seashore."

¹³⁻¹⁵After spending the night there, Jacob chose from his livestock as a present for his brother Esau: 200 female goats and 20 males, 200 female sheep and 20 males, 30 milk camels with their young, 40 cows and 10 bulls, 20 female donkeys and 10 males. ¹⁶He divided them into herds and put one of his servants in charge of each herd. He said to them, "Go ahead of me, and leave a space between each herd and the one behind it." ¹⁷He ordered the first servant, "When my brother Esau meets you and asks, 'Who is your master? Where are you going? Who owns these animals in front of you?' ¹⁸you must answer, 'They belong to your servant Jacob. He sends them as a present to his master Esau. Jacob himself is right behind us.' " ¹⁹He gave the same order to the second, the third, and to all the others who were in charge of the herds: "This is what you must say to Esau when you meet him. ²⁰You must say, 'Yes, your servant Jacob is right behind us.' " Jacob was thinking, "I will win him over with the gifts, and

when I meet him, perhaps he will forgive me." ²¹He sent the gifts on ahead of him and spent that night in camp.

Jacob Wrestles at Peniel

²²That same night Jacob got up, took his two wives, his two concubines, and his eleven children, and crossed the Jabbok River. ²³After he had sent them across, he also sent across all that he owned, ²⁴but he stayed behind, alone.

Then a man came and wrestled with

A man came and wrestled with him. (32.24)

him until just before daybreak. ²⁵When the man saw that he was not winning the struggle, he hit Jacob on the hip, and it was thrown out of joint. ²⁶The man said, "Let me go; daylight is coming."

"I won't, unless you bless me," Jacob answered.

²⁷"What is your name?" the man asked.

"Jacob," he answered.

²⁸The man said, "Your name will no longer be Jacob. You have struggled with God and with men, and you have won; so your name will be Israel."ᵍ

ᵍ ISRAEL: *This name sounds like the Hebrew for "he struggles with God" or "God struggles."*

32.12 Gn 22.17 **32.23** Ws 10.12 **32.24-26** Ho 12.3, 4 **32.28** Gn 35.10

Esau . . . threw his arms around him. (33.4)

²⁹ Jacob said, "Now tell me your name."

But he answered, "Why do you want to know my name?" Then he blessed Jacob.

³⁰ Jacob said, "I have seen God face-to-face, and I am still alive"; so he named the place Peniel.ʰ ³¹ The sun rose as Jacob was leaving Peniel, and he was limping because of his hip. ³² Even today the descendants of Israel do not eat the muscle which is on the hip joint, because it was on this muscle that Jacob was hit.

Jacob Meets Esau

33 Jacob saw Esau coming with his four hundred men, so he divided the children among Leah, Rachel, and the two concubines. ² He put the concubines and their children first, then Leah and her children, and finally Rachel and Joseph at the rear. ³ Jacob went ahead of them and bowed down to the ground seven times as he approached his brother. ⁴ But Esau ran to meet him, threw his arms around him, and kissed him. They were both crying. ⁵ When Esau looked around and saw the women and the children, he asked, "Who are these people with you?"

"These, sir, are the children whom God has been good enough to give me," Jacob answered. ⁶ Then the concubines came up with their children and bowed down; ⁷ then Leah and her children came, and last of all Joseph and Rachel came and bowed down.

⁸ Esau asked, "What about that other group I met? What did that mean?"

Jacob answered, "It was to gain your favor."

⁹ But Esau said, "I have enough, my brother; keep what you have."

¹⁰ Jacob said, "No, please, if I have gained your favor, accept my gift. To see your face is for me like seeing the face of God, now that you have been so friendly to me. ¹¹ Please accept this gift which I have brought for you; God has

---

ʰ **PENIEL**: *This name sounds like the Hebrew for "the face of God."*
32.29 Jg 13.17, 18

been kind to me and given me everything I need." Jacob kept on urging him until he accepted.

¹²Esau said, "Let's get ready and leave. I will go ahead of you."

¹³Jacob answered, "You know that the children are weak, and I must think of the sheep and livestock with their young. If they are driven hard for even one day, the whole herd will die. ¹⁴Please go on ahead of me, and I will follow slowly, going as fast as I can with the livestock and the children until I catch up with you in Edom."

¹⁵Esau said, "Then let me leave some of my men with you."

But Jacob answered, "There is no need for that for I only want to gain your favor."ⁱ ¹⁶So that day Esau started on his way back to Edom. ¹⁷But Jacob went to Sukkoth, where he built a house for himself and shelters for his livestock. That is why the place was named Sukkoth.ʲ

¹⁸On his return from Mesopotamia Jacob arrived safely at the city of Shechem in the land of Canaan and set up his camp in a field near the city. ¹⁹He bought that part of the field from the descendants of Hamor father of Shechem for a hundred pieces of silver. ²⁰He put up an altar there and named it for El, the God of Israel.

The Rape of Dinah

34 One day Dinah, the daughter of Jacob and Leah, went to visit some of the Canaanite women. ²When Shechem son of Hamor the Hivite, who was chief of that region, saw her, he took her and raped her. ³But he found the young woman so attractive that he fell in love with her and tried to win her affection.ᵏ ⁴He told his father, "I want you to get Dinah for me as my wife."

⁵Jacob learned that his daughter had been disgraced, but because his sons were out in the fields with his livestock, he did nothing until they came back. ⁶Shechem's father Hamor went out to talk with Jacob, ⁷just as Jacob's sons were coming in from the fields. When they heard about it, they were shocked and furious that Shechem had done such a thing and had insulted the people of Israel by raping Jacob's daughter. ⁸Hamor said to him, "My son Shechem has fallen in love with your daughter; please let him marry her. ⁹Let us make an agreement that there will be intermarriage between our people and yours. ¹⁰Then you may stay here in our country with us; you may live anywhere you wish, trade freely, and own property."

¹¹Then Shechem said to Dinah's father and brothers, "Do me this favor, and I will give you whatever you want. ¹²Tell me what presents you want, and set the payment for the bride as high as you wish; I will give you whatever you ask, if you will only let me marry her."

¹³Because Shechem had disgraced their sister Dinah, Jacob's sons answered Shechem and his father Hamor in a deceitful way. ¹⁴They said to him, "We cannot let our sister marry a man who is not circumcised; that would be a disgrace for us. ¹⁵We can agree only on the condition that you become like us by circumcising all your males. ¹⁶Then we will agree to intermarriage. We will settle among you and become one people with you. ¹⁷But if you will not accept our terms and be circumcised, we will take her and leave."

¹⁸These terms seemed fair to Hamor and his son Shechem, ¹⁹and the young man lost no time in doing what was suggested, because he was in love with

---

ⁱ for I only want to gain your favor; or if it's all right with you. ʲ SUKKOTH: This name in Hebrew means "shelters." ᵏ tried to win her affection; or comforted her.
33.19 Js 24.32; Jn 4.5

Jacob's daughter. He was the most important member of his family.

20 Hamor and his son Shechem went to the meeting place at the city gate and spoke to the people of the town: 21 "These men are friendly; let them live in the land with us and travel freely. The land is large enough for them also. Let us marry their daughters and give them ours in marriage. 22 But these men will agree to live among us and be one people with us only on the condition that we circumcise all our males, as they are circumcised. 23 Won't all their livestock and everything else they own be ours? So let us agree that they can live among us." 24 All the citizens of the city agreed with what Hamor and Shechem proposed, and all the males were circumcised.

25 Three days later, when the men were still sore from their circumcision, two of Jacob's sons, Simeon and Levi, the brothers of Dinah, took their swords, went into the city without arousing suspicion, and killed all the men, 26 including Hamor and his son Shechem. Then they took Dinah from Shechem's house and left. 27 After the slaughter Jacob's other sons looted the town to take revenge for their sister's disgrace. 28 They took the flocks, the cattle, the donkeys, and everything else in the city and in the fields. 29 They took everything of value, captured all the women and children, and carried off everything in the houses.

30 Jacob said to Simeon and Levi, "You have gotten me into trouble; now the Canaanites, the Perizzites, and everybody else in the land will hate me. I do not have many men; if they all band together against me and attack me, our whole family will be destroyed."

31 But they answered, "We cannot let our sister be treated like a common whore."

God Blesses Jacob at Bethel

35 God said to Jacob, "Go to Bethel at once, and live there. Build an altar there to me, the God who appeared to you when you were running away from your brother Esau."

2 So Jacob said to his family and to all who were with him, "Get rid of the foreign gods that you have; purify yourselves and put on clean clothes. 3 We are going to leave here and go to Bethel, where I will build an altar to the God who helped me in the time of my trouble and who has been with me everywhere I have gone." 4 So they gave Jacob all the foreign gods that they had and also the earrings that they were wearing. He buried them beneath the oak tree near Shechem.

5 When Jacob and his sons started to leave, great fear fell on the people of the nearby towns, and they did not pursue them. 6 Jacob came with all his people to Luz, which is now known as Bethel, in the land of Canaan. 7 He built an altar there and named the place for the God of Bethel, because God had revealed himself to him there when he was running away from his brother. 8 Rebecca's nurse Deborah died and was buried beneath the oak south of Bethel. So it was named "Oak of Weeping."

9 When Jacob returned from Mesopotamia, God appeared to him again and blessed him. 10 God said to him, "Your name is Jacob, but from now on it will be Israel." So God named him Israel. 11 And God said to him, "I am Almighty God. Have many children. Nations will be descended from you, and you will be the ancestor of kings. 12 I will give you the land which I gave to Abraham and to Isaac, and I will also give it to your descendants after you." 13 Then God left him. 14 There, where God had spoken to him, Jacob set up a memorial stone and consecrated it by

---

35.1 Gn 28.11-17   **35.10** Gn 32.28   **35.11, 12** Gn 17.4-8   **35.14, 15** Gn 28.18, 19

pouring wine and olive oil on it. [15] He named the place Bethel.

The Death of Rachel

[16] Jacob and his family left Bethel, and when they were still some distance from Ephrath, the time came for Rachel to have her baby, and she was having difficult labor. [17] When her labor pains were at their worst, the midwife said to her, "Don't be afraid, Rachel; it's another boy." [18] But she was dying, and as she breathed her last, she named her son Benoni,[l] but his father named him Benjamin.[m]

[19] When Rachel died, she was buried beside the road to Ephrath, now known as Bethlehem. [20] Jacob set up a memorial stone there, and it still marks Rachel's grave to this day. [21] Jacob moved on and set up his camp on the other side of the tower of Eder.

The Sons of Jacob
(1 Chronicles 2.1, 2)

[22] While Jacob was living in that land, Reuben had sexual intercourse with Bilhah, one of his father's concubines; Jacob heard about it and was furious.[n]

Jacob had twelve sons. [23] The sons of Leah were Reuben (Jacob's oldest son), Simeon, Levi, Judah, Issachar, and Zebulun. [24] The sons of Rachel were Joseph and Benjamin. [25] The sons of Rachel's slave Bilhah were Dan and Naphtali. [26] The sons of Leah's slave Zilpah were Gad and Asher. These sons were born in Mesopotamia.

The Death of Isaac

[27] Jacob went to his father Isaac at Mamre, near Hebron, where Abraham and Isaac had lived. [28] Isaac lived to be a hundred and eighty years old [29] and died at a ripe old age; and his sons Esau and Jacob buried him.

The Descendants of Esau
(1 Chronicles 1.34-37)

36 These are the descendants of Esau, also called Edom. [2] Esau married Canaanite women: Adah, the daughter of Elon the Hittite; Oholibamah, the daughter of Anah son[o] of Zibeon the Hivite; [3] and Basemath, the daughter of Ishmael and sister of Nebaioth. [4] Adah bore Eliphaz; Basemath bore Reuel; [5] and Oholibamah bore Jeush, Jalam, and Korah. All these sons were born to Esau in the land of Canaan.

[6] Then Esau took his wives, his sons, his daughters, and all the people of his house, along with all his livestock and all the possessions he had gotten in the land of Canaan, and went away from his brother Jacob to another land. [7] He left because the land where he and Jacob were living was not able to support them; they had too much livestock and could no longer stay together. [8] So Esau lived in the hill country of Edom.

[9] These are the descendants of Esau, the ancestor of the Edomites. [10-13] Esau's wife Adah bore him one son, Eliphaz, and Eliphaz had five sons: Teman, Omar, Zepho, Gatam, and Kenaz. And by another wife, Timna, he had one more son, Amalek.

Esau's wife Basemath bore him one son, Reuel, and Reuel had four sons: Nahath, Zerah, Shammah, and Mizzah.

[14] Esau's wife Oholibamah, the daughter of Anah son[o] of Zibeon, bore him three sons: Jeush, Jalam, and Korah.

---

[l] BENONI: *This name in Hebrew means "son of my sorrow."*   [m] BENJAMIN: *This name in Hebrew means "son who will be fortunate."*   [n] *One ancient translation and was furious; Hebrew does not have these words.*   [o] *Some ancient translations son; Hebrew daughter; or granddaughter.*

35.22 Gn 49.4   **35.27** Gn 13.18   **36.2** Gn 26.34   **36.3** Gn 28.9

15These are the tribes descended from Esau. Esau's first son Eliphaz was the ancestor of the following tribes: Teman, Omar, Zepho, Kenaz, 16Korah, Gatam, and Amalek. These were all descendants of Esau's wife Adah.

17Esau's son Reuel was the ancestor of the following tribes: Nahath, Zerah, Shammah, and Mizzah. These were all descendants of Esau's wife Basemath.

18The following tribes were descended from Esau by his wife Oholibamah, the daughter of Anah: Jeush, Jalam, and Korah. 19All these tribes were descended from Esau.

The Descendants of Seir
(1 Chronicles 1.38-42)

20-21The original inhabitants of the land of Edom were divided into tribes which traced their ancestry to the following descendants of Seir, a Horite: Lotan, Shobal, Zibeon, Anah, Dishon, Ezer, and Dishan.

22Lotan was the ancestor of the clans of Hori and Heman. (Lotan had a sister named Timna.)

23Shobal was the ancestor of the clans of Alvan, Manahath, Ebal, Shepho, and Onam.

24Zibeon had two sons, Aiah and Anah. (This is the Anah who found the hot springs in the wilderness when he was taking care of his father's donkeys.) 25-26Anah was the father of Dishon, who was the ancestor of the clans of Hemdan, Eshban, Ithran, and Cheran. Anah also had a daughter named Oholibamah.

27Ezer was the ancestor of the clans of Bilhan, Zaavan, and Akan.

28Dishan was the ancestor of the clans of Uz and Aran.

29-30These are the Horite tribes in the land of Edom: Lotan, Shobal, Zibeon, Anah, Dishon, Ezer, and Dishan.

The Kings of Edom
(1 Chronicles 1.43-54)

31-39Before there were any kings in Israel, the following kings ruled the land of Edom in succession:
> Bela son of Beor from Dinhabah
> Jobab son of Zerah from Bozrah
> Husham from the region of Teman
> Hadad son of Bedad from Avith (he defeated the Midianites in a battle in the country of Moab)
> Samlah from Masrekah
> Shaul from Rehoboth-on-the-River
> Baal Hanan son of Achbor
> Hadad from Pau (his wife was Mehetabel, the daughter of Matred and granddaughter of Mezahab)

40-43Esau was the ancestor of the following Edomite tribes: Timna, Alvah, Jetheth, Oholibamah, Elah, Pinon, Kenaz, Teman, Mibzar, Magdiel, and Iram. The area where each of these tribes lived was known by the name of the tribe.

Joseph and His Brothers

37 Jacob continued to live in the land of Canaan, where his father had lived, 2and this is the story of Jacob's family.

Joseph, a young man of seventeen, took care of the sheep and goats with his brothers, the sons of Bilhah and Zilpah, his father's concubines. He brought bad reports to his father about what his brothers were doing.

3Jacob loved Joseph more than all his other sons, because he had been born to him when he was old. He made a long robe with full sleevesp for him. 4When his brothers saw that their father loved Joseph more than he loved them, they hated their brother so much

---

p robe with full sleeves; *or* decorated robe.

that they would not speak to him in a friendly manner.

⁵One time Joseph had a dream, and when he told his brothers about it, they hated him even more. ⁶He said, "Listen to the dream I had. ⁷We were all in the field tying up sheaves of wheat, when my sheaf got up and stood up straight. Yours formed a circle around mine and bowed down to it."

⁸"Do you think you are going to be a king and rule over us?" his brothers asked. So they hated him even more because of his dreams and because of what he said about them.

⁹Then Joseph had another dream and told his brothers, "I had another dream, in which I saw the sun, the moon, and eleven stars bowing down to me."

¹⁰He also told the dream to his father, and his father scolded him: "What kind of a dream is that? Do you think that your mother, your brothers, and I are going to come and bow down to you?" ¹¹Joseph's brothers were jealous of him, but his father kept thinking about the whole matter.

Joseph Is Sold and Taken to Egypt

¹²One day when Joseph's brothers had gone to Shechem to take care of their father's flock, ¹³Jacob said to Joseph, "I want you to go to Shechem, where your brothers are taking care of the flock."

Joseph answered, "I am ready."

¹⁴His father told him, "Go and see if your brothers are safe and if the flock is all right; then come back and tell me." So his father sent him on his way from Hebron Valley.

Joseph arrived at Shechem ¹⁵and was wandering around in the country when a man saw him and asked him, "What are you looking for?"

¹⁶"I am looking for my brothers, who are taking care of their flock," he answered. "Can you tell me where they are?"

¹⁷The man said, "They have already left. I heard them say that they were going to Dothan." So Joseph went after his brothers and found them at Dothan.

¹⁸They saw him in the distance, and before he reached them, they plotted against him and decided to kill him. ¹⁹They said to one another, "Here comes that dreamer. ²⁰Come on now, let's kill him and throw his body into one of the dry wells. We can say that a wild animal killed him. Then we will see what becomes of his dreams."

²¹Reuben heard them and tried to save Joseph. "Let's not kill him," he said. ²²"Just throw him into this well in the wilderness, but don't hurt him." He said this, planning to save him from them and send him back to his father. ²³When Joseph came up to his brothers, they ripped off his long robe with full sleeves.ᵖ ²⁴Then they took him and threw him into the well, which was dry.

²⁵While they were eating, they suddenly saw a group of Ishmaelites traveling from Gilead to Egypt. Their camels were loaded with spices and resins. ²⁶Judah said to his brothers, "What will we gain by killing our brother and covering up the murder? ²⁷Let's sell him to these Ishmaelites. Then we won't have to hurt him; after all, he is our brother, our own flesh and blood." His brothers agreed, ²⁸and when some Midianite traders came by, the brothers�q pulled Joseph out of the well and sold him for twenty pieces of silver to the Ishmaelites, who took him to Egypt.

²⁹When Reuben came back to the well and found that Joseph was not there, he tore his clothes in sorrow. ³⁰He returned to his brothers and said, "The boy is not there! What am I going to do?"

ᵖ robe with full sleeves; *or* decorated robe.
37.11 Ac 7.9   **37.28** Ws 10.13; Ac 7.9

q the brothers; Hebrew they.

HIGHLIGHTS IN JOSEPH'S LIFE
(Numbers refer to chapter and verse in Genesis)

³¹Then they killed a goat and dipped Joseph's robe in its blood. ³²They took the robe to their father and said, "We found this. Does it belong to your son?" ³³He recognized it and said, "Yes, it is his! Some wild animal has killed him. My son Joseph has been torn to pieces!" ³⁴Jacob tore his clothes in sorrow and put on sackcloth. He mourned for his son a long time. ³⁵All his sons and daughters came to comfort him, but he refused to be comforted and said, "I will go down to the world of the dead still mourning for my son." So he continued to mourn for his son Joseph.

³⁶Meanwhile, in Egypt the Midianites had sold Joseph to Potiphar, one of the king's officers, who was the captain of the palace guard.

Judah and Tamar

38 About that time Judah left his brothers and went to stay with a man named Hirah, who was from the town of Adullam. ²There Judah met a young Canaanite woman whose father was named Shua. He married her, ³and she bore him a son, whom he named Er. ⁴She became pregnant again and bore another son and named him Onan. ⁵Again she had a son and named him Shelah. Judah was at Achzib when the boy was born.

⁶For his first son Er, Judah got a wife whose name was Tamar. ⁷Er's conduct was evil, and it displeased the LORD, so the LORD killed him. ⁸Then Judah said to Er's brother Onan, "Go and sleep with your brother's widow. Fulfill your obligation to her as her husband's brother, so that your brother may have descendants." ⁹But Onan knew that the children would not belong to him, so when he had intercourse with his brother's widow, he let the semen spill on the ground, so that there would be no children for his brother. ¹⁰What he did displeased the LORD, and the LORD killed him also. ¹¹Then Judah said to his daughter-in-law Tamar, "Return to

your father's house and remain a widow until my son Shelah grows up." He said this because he was afraid that Shelah would be killed, as his brothers had been. So Tamar went back home.

¹²After some time Judah's wife died. When he had finished the time of mourning, he and his friend Hirah of Adullam went to Timnah, where his sheep were being sheared. ¹³Someone told Tamar that her father-in-law was going to Timnah to shear his sheep. ¹⁴So she changed from the widow's clothes she had been wearing, covered her face with a veil, and sat down at the entrance to Enaim, a town on the road to Timnah. As she well knew, Judah's youngest son Shelah was now grown up, and yet she had not been given to him in marriage.

¹⁵When Judah saw her, he thought that she was a prostitute, because she had her face covered. ¹⁶He went over to her at the side of the road and said, "All right, how much do you charge?" (He did not know that she was his daughter-in-law.)

She said, "What will you give me?"

¹⁷He answered, "I will send you a young goat from my flock."

She said, "All right, if you will give me something to keep as a pledge until you send the goat."

¹⁸"What shall I give you as a pledge?" he asked.

She answered, "Your seal with its cord and the walking stick you are carrying." He gave them to her. Then they had intercourse, and she became pregnant. ¹⁹Tamar went home, took off her veil, and put her widow's clothes back on.

²⁰Judah sent his friend Hirah to take the goat and get back from the woman the articles he had pledged, but Hirah could not find her. ²¹He asked some men at Enaim, "Where is the prostitute who was here by the road?"

"There has never been a prostitute here," they answered.

²²He returned to Judah and said, "I

couldn't find her. The men of the place said that there had never been a prostitute there."

23 Judah said, "Let her keep the things. We don't want people to laugh at us. I did try to pay her, but you couldn't find her."

24 About three months later someone told Judah, "Your daughter-in-law Tamar has been acting like a whore, and now she is pregnant."

Judah ordered, "Take her out and burn her to death."

25 As she was being taken out, she sent word to her father-in-law: "I am pregnant by the man who owns these things. Look at them and see whose they are — this seal with its cord and this walking stick."

26 Judah recognized them and said, "She is in the right. I have failed in my obligation to her — I should have given her to my son Shelah in marriage." And Judah never had intercourse with her again.

27 When the time came for her to give birth, it was discovered that she was going to have twins. 28 While she was in labor, one of them put out an arm; the midwife caught it, tied a red thread around it, and said, "This one was born first." 29 But he pulled his arm back, and his brother was born first. Then the midwife said, "So this is how you break your way out!" So he was named Perez.*r* 30 Then his brother was born with the red thread on his arm, and he was named Zerah.*s*

Joseph and Potiphar's Wife

39 Now the Ishmaelites had taken Joseph to Egypt and sold him to Potiphar, one of the king's officers, who was the captain of the palace guard. 2 The LORD was with Joseph and made him successful. He lived in the house of his Egyptian master, 3 who saw that the LORD was with Joseph and had made him successful in everything he did. 4 Potiphar was pleased with him and made him his personal servant; so he put him in charge of his house and everything he owned. 5 From then on, because of Joseph the LORD blessed the household of the Egyptian and everything that he had in his house and in his fields. 6 Potiphar turned over everything he had to the care of Joseph and did not concern himself with anything except the food he ate.

Joseph was well-built and good-looking, 7 and after a while his master's wife began to desire Joseph and asked him to go to bed with her. 8 He refused and said to her, "Look, my master does not have to concern himself with anything in the house, because I am here. He has put me in charge of everything he has. 9 I have as much authority in this house as he has, and he has not kept back anything from me except you. How then could I do such an immoral thing and sin against God?" 10 Although she asked Joseph day after day, he would not go to bed with her.

11 But one day when Joseph went into the house to do his work, none of the house servants was there. 12 She caught him by his robe and said, "Come to bed with me." But he escaped and ran outside, leaving his robe in her hand. 13 When she saw that he had left his robe and had run out of the house, 14 she called to her house servants and said, "Look at this! This Hebrew that my husband brought to the house is insulting us. He came into my room and tried to rape me, but I screamed as loud as I could. 15 When he heard me scream, he ran outside, leaving his robe beside me."

16 She kept his robe with her until Joseph's master came home. 17 Then she

---

r PEREZ: *This name in Hebrew means "breaking out."*   *s* ZERAH: *This name sounds like a Hebrew word for the red brightness of dawn.*
39.2 Ac 7.9

told him the same story: "That Hebrew slave that you brought here came into my room and insulted me. 18 But when I screamed, he ran outside, leaving his robe beside me."

19 Joseph's master was furious 20 and had Joseph arrested and put in the prison where the king's prisoners were kept, and there he stayed. 21 But the LORD was with Joseph and blessed him, so that the jailer was pleased with him. 22 He put Joseph in charge of all the other prisoners and made him responsible for everything that was done in the prison. 23 The jailer did not have to look after anything for which Joseph was responsible, because the LORD was with Joseph and made him succeed in everything he did.

Joseph Interprets the Prisoners' Dreams

40 Some time later the king of Egypt's wine steward and his chief baker offended the king. 2 He was angry with these two officials 3 and put them in prison in the house of the captain of the guard, in the same place where Joseph was being kept. 4 They spent a long time in prison, and the captain assigned Joseph as their servant.

5 One night there in prison the wine steward and the chief baker each had a dream, and the dreams had different meanings. 6 When Joseph came to them in the morning, he saw that they were upset. 7 He asked them, "Why do you look so worried today?"

8 They answered, "Each of us had a dream, and there is no one here to explain what the dreams mean."

"It is God who gives the ability to interpret dreams," Joseph said. "Tell me your dreams."

9 So the wine steward said, "In my dream there was a grapevine in front of me 10 with three branches on it. As soon as the leaves came out, the blossoms

appeared, and the grapes ripened. 11 I was holding the king's cup; so I took the grapes and squeezed them into the cup and gave it to him."

12 Joseph said, "This is what it means: the three branches are three days. 13 In three days the king will release you, pardon you, and restore you to your position. You will give him his cup as you did before when you were his wine steward. 14 But please remember me when everything is going well for you, and please be kind enough to mention me to the king and help me get out of this prison. 15 After all, I was kidnapped from the land of the Hebrews, and even here in Egypt I didn't do anything to deserve being put in prison."

16 When the chief baker saw that the interpretation of the wine steward's dream was favorable, he said to Joseph, "I had a dream too; I was carrying three breadbaskets on my head. 17 In the top basket there were all kinds of baked goods for the king, and the birds were eating them."

18 Joseph answered, "This is what it means: the three baskets are three days. 19 In three days the king will release you — and have your head cut off! Then he will hang your body on a pole, and the birds will eat your flesh."

20 On his birthday three days later the king gave a banquet for all his officials; he released his wine steward and his chief baker and brought them before his officials. 21 He restored the wine steward to his former position, 22 but he executed the chief baker. It all happened just as Joseph had said. 23 But the wine steward never gave Joseph another thought — he forgot all about him.

Joseph Interprets the King's Dreams

41 After two years had passed, the king of Egypt dreamed that he was standing by the Nile River, 2 when

39.21 Ac 7.9

seven cows, fat and sleek, came up out of the river and began to feed on the grass. 3 Then seven other cows came up; they were thin and bony. They came and stood by the other cows on the riverbank, 4 and the thin cows ate up the fat cows. Then the king woke up. 5 He fell asleep again and had another dream. Seven heads of grain, full and ripe, were growing on one stalk. 6 Then seven other heads of grain sprouted, thin and scorched by the desert wind, 7 and the thin heads of grain swallowed the full ones. The king woke up and realized that he had been dreaming. 8 In the morning he was worried, so he sent for all the magicians and wise men of Egypt. He told them his dreams, but no one could explain them to him.

9 Then the wine steward said to the king, "I must confess today that I have done wrong. 10 You were angry with the chief baker and me, and you put us in prison in the house of the captain of the guard. 11 One night each of us had a dream, and the dreams had different meanings. 12 A young Hebrew was there with us, a slave of the captain of the guard. We told him our dreams, and he interpreted them for us. 13 Things turned out just as he said: you restored me to my position, but you executed the baker."

14 The king sent for Joseph, and he was immediately brought from the prison. After he had shaved and changed his clothes, he came into the king's presence. 15 The king said to him, "I have had a dream, and no one can explain it. I have been told that you can interpret dreams."

16 Joseph answered, "I cannot, Your Majesty, but God will give a favorable interpretation."

17 The king said, "I dreamed that I was standing on the bank of the Nile, 18 when seven cows, fat and sleek, came up out of the river and began feeding on the grass. 19 Then seven other cows came up which were thin and bony. They were the poorest cows I have ever seen anywhere in Egypt. 20 The thin cows ate up the fat ones, 21 but no one would have known it, because they looked just as bad as before. Then I woke up. 22 I also dreamed that I saw seven heads of grain which were full and ripe, growing on one stalk. 23 Then seven heads of grain sprouted, thin and scorched by the desert wind, 24 and the thin heads of grain swallowed the full ones. I told the dreams to the magicians, but none of them could explain them to me."

25 Joseph said to the king, "The two dreams mean the same thing; God has told you what he is going to do. 26 The seven fat cows are seven years, and the seven full heads of grain are also seven years; they have the same meaning. 27 The seven thin cows which came up later and the seven thin heads of grain scorched by the desert wind are seven years of famine. 28 It is just as I told you — God has shown you what he is going to do. 29 There will be seven years of great plenty in all the land of Egypt. 30 After that, there will be seven years of famine, and all the good years will be forgotten, because the famine will ruin the country. 31 The time of plenty will be entirely forgotten, because the famine which follows will be so terrible. 32 The repetition of your dream means that the matter is fixed by God and that he will make it happen in the near future.

33 "Now you should choose some man with wisdom and insight and put him in charge of the country. 34 You must also appoint other officials and take a fifth of the crops during the seven years of plenty. 35 Order them to collect all the food during the good years that are coming, and give them authority to store up grain in the cities and guard it. 36 The food will be a re-

serve supply for the country during the seven years of famine which are going to come on Egypt. In this way the people will not starve."

Joseph Is Made Governor over Egypt

37 The king and his officials approved this plan, **38** and he said to them, "We will never find a better man than Joseph, a man who has God's spirit in him." **39** The king said to Joseph, "God has shown you all this, so it is obvious that you have greater wisdom and insight than anyone else. **40** I will put you in charge of my country, and all my people will obey your orders. Your authority will be second only to mine. **41** I now appoint you governor over all Egypt." **42** The king removed from his finger the ring engraved with the royal seal and put it on Joseph's finger. He put a fine linen robe on him, and placed a gold chain around his neck. **43** He gave him the second royal chariot to ride in, and his guard of honor went ahead of him and cried out, "Make way! Make way!" And so Joseph was appointed governor over all Egypt. **44** The king said to him, "I am the king — and no one in all Egypt shall so much as lift a hand or a foot without your permission." **45-46** He gave Joseph the Egyptian name Zaphenath Paneah, and he gave him a wife, Asenath, the daughter of Potiphera, a priest in the city of Heliopolis.

Joseph was thirty years old when he began to serve the king of Egypt. He left the king's court and traveled all over the land. **47** During the seven years of plenty the land produced abundant crops, **48** all of which Joseph collected and stored in the cities. In each city he stored the food from the fields around it. **49** There was so much grain that Joseph stopped measuring it — it was like the sand of the sea.

50 Before the years of famine came, Joseph had two sons by Asenath. **51** He said, "God has made me forget all my sufferings and all my father's family"; so he named his first son Manasseh. *t* **52** He also said, "God has given me children in the land of my trouble"; so he named his second son Ephraim. *u*

53 The seven years of plenty that the land of Egypt had enjoyed came to an end, **54** and the seven years of famine began, just as Joseph had said. There was famine in every other country, but there was food throughout Egypt. **55** When the Egyptians began to be hungry, they cried out to the king for food. So he ordered them to go to Joseph and do what he told them. **56** The famine grew worse and spread over the whole country, so Joseph opened all the storehouses and sold grain to the Egyptians. **57** People came to Egypt from all over the world to buy grain from Joseph, because the famine was severe everywhere.

Joseph's Brothers Go to Egypt to Buy Grain

42 When Jacob learned that there was grain in Egypt, he said to his sons, "Why don't you do something? **2** I hear that there is grain in Egypt; go there and buy some to keep us from starving to death." **3** So Joseph's ten half brothers went to buy grain in Egypt, **4** but Jacob did not send Joseph's full brother Benjamin with them, because he was afraid that something might happen to him.

5 The sons of Jacob came with others to buy grain, because there was famine in the land of Canaan. **6** Joseph, as governor of the land of Egypt, was selling grain to people from all over the world.

---

t MANASSEH: *This name sounds like the Hebrew for "cause to forget."*   *u* EPHRAIM: *This name sounds like the Hebrew for "give children."*

41.40 Ac 7.10   **41.42** Dn 5.29   **41.54** Ac 7.11   **41.55** Jn 2.5   **42.2** Ac 7.12

So Joseph's brothers came and bowed down before him with their faces to the ground. [7]When Joseph saw his brothers, he recognized them, but he acted as if he did not know them. He asked them harshly, "Where do you come from?"

"We have come from Canaan to buy food," they answered.

[8]Although Joseph recognized his brothers, they did not recognize him. [9]He remembered the dreams he had dreamed about them and said, "You are spies; you have come to find out where our country is weak."

[10]"No, sir," they answered. "We have come as your slaves, to buy food. [11]We are all brothers. We are not spies, sir, we are honest men."

[12]Joseph said to them, "No! You have come to find out where our country is weak."

[13]They said, "We were twelve brothers in all, sir, sons of the same man in the land of Canaan. One brother is dead, and the youngest is now with our father."

[14]"It is just as I said," Joseph answered. "You are spies. [15]This is how you will be tested: I swear by the name of the king that you will never leave unless your youngest brother comes here. [16]One of you must go and get him. The rest of you will be kept under guard until the truth of what you say can be tested. Otherwise, as sure as the king lives, you are spies." [17]With that, he put them in prison for three days.

[18]On the third day Joseph said to them, "I am a God-fearing man, and I will spare your lives on one condition. [19]To prove that you are honest, one of you will stay in the prison where you have been kept; the rest of you may go and take back to your starving families the grain that you have bought. [20]Then you must bring your youngest brother to me. This will prove that you have

been telling the truth, and I will not put you to death."

They agreed to this [21]and said to one another, "Yes, now we are suffering the consequences of what we did to our brother; we saw the great trouble he was in when he begged for help, but we would not listen. That is why we are in this trouble now."

[22]Reuben said, "I told you not to harm the boy, but you wouldn't listen. And now we are being paid back for his death." [23]Joseph understood what they said, but they did not know it, because they had been speaking to him through an interpreter. [24]Joseph left them and began to cry. When he was able to speak again, he came back, picked out Simeon, and had him tied up in front of them.

Joseph's Brothers Return to Canaan

[25]Joseph gave orders to fill his brothers' packs with grain, to put each man's money back in his sack, and to give them food for the trip. This was done. [26]The brothers loaded their donkeys with the grain they had bought, and then they left. [27]At the place where they spent the night, one of them opened his sack to feed his donkey and found his money at the top of the sack. [28]"My money has been returned to me," he called to his brothers. "Here it is in my sack!" Their hearts sank, and in fear they asked one another, "What has God done to us?"

[29]When they came to their father Jacob in Canaan, they told him all that had happened to them: [30]"The governor of Egypt spoke harshly to us and accused us of spying against his country. [31]'We are not spies,' we answered, 'we are honest men. [32]We were twelve brothers in all, sons of the same father. One brother is dead, and the youngest is still in Canaan with our father.' [33]The man answered, 'This is how I will find

42.9 Gn 37.5-10   **42.22** Gn 37.21, 22

out if you are honest men: One of you will stay with me; the rest will take grain for your starving families and leave. 34 Bring your youngest brother to me. Then I will know that you are not spies, but honest men; I will give your brother back to you, and you can stay here and trade.' "

35 Then when they emptied out their sacks, every one of them found his bag of money; and when they saw the money, they and their father Jacob were afraid. 36 Their father said to them, "Do you want to make me lose all my children? Joseph is gone; Simeon is gone; and now you want to take away Benjamin. I am the one who suffers!"

37 Reuben said to his father, "If I do not bring Benjamin back to you, you can kill my two sons. Put him in my care, and I will bring him back."

38 But Jacob said, "My son cannot go with you; his brother is dead, and he is the only one left. Something might happen to him on the way. I am an old man, and the sorrow you would cause me would kill me."

Joseph's Brothers Return to Egypt with Benjamin

43 The famine in Canaan got worse, 2 and when the family of Jacob had eaten all the grain which had been brought from Egypt, Jacob said to his sons, "Go back and buy a little food for us."

3 Judah said to him, "The man sternly warned us that we would not be admitted to his presence unless we had our brother with us. 4 If you are willing to send our brother with us, we will go and buy food for you. 5 If you are not willing, we will not go, because the man told us we would not be admitted to his presence unless our brother was with us."

6 Jacob said, "Why did you cause me so much trouble by telling the man that you had another brother?"

7 They answered, "The man kept asking about us and our family, 'Is your father still living? Do you have another brother?' We had to answer his questions. How could we know that he would tell us to bring our brother with us?"

8 Judah said to his father, "Send the boy with me, and we will leave at once. Then none of us will starve to death. 9 I will pledge my own life, and you can hold me responsible for him. If I do not bring him back to you safe and sound, I will always bear the blame. 10 If we had not waited so long, we could have been there and back twice by now."

11 Their father said to them, "If that is how it has to be, then take the best products of the land in your packs as a present for the governor: a little resin, a little honey, spices, pistachio nuts, and almonds. 12 Take with you also twice as much money, because you must take back the money that was returned in the top of your sacks. Maybe it was a mistake. 13 Take your brother and return at once. 14 May Almighty God cause the man to have pity on you, so that he will give Benjamin and your other brother back to you. As for me, if I must lose my children, I must lose them."

15 So the brothers took the gifts and twice as much money, and set out for Egypt with Benjamin. There they presented themselves to Joseph. 16 When Joseph saw Benjamin with them, he said to the servant in charge of his house, "Take these men to my house. They are going to eat with me at noon, so kill an animal and prepare it." 17 The servant did as he was commanded and took the brothers to Joseph's house.

18 As they were being brought to the house, they were afraid and thought, "We are being brought here because of the money that was returned in our sacks the first time. They will suddenly attack us, take our donkeys, and make us his slaves." 19 So at the door of the house, they said to the servant in charge, 20 "If you please, sir, we came here once before to buy food. 21 When

we set up camp on the way home, we opened our sacks, and each man found his money in the top of his sack — every bit of it. We have brought it back to you. 22 We have also brought some more money with us to buy more food. We do not know who put our money back in our sacks."

23 The servant said, "Don't worry. Don't be afraid. Your God, the God of your father, must have put the money in your sacks for you. I received your payment." Then he brought Simeon to them.

24 The servant took the brothers into the house. He gave them water so that they could wash their feet, and he fed their donkeys. 25 They got their gifts ready to present to Joseph when he arrived at noon, because they had been told that they were to eat with him. 26 When Joseph got home, they took the gifts into the house to him and bowed down to the ground before him. 27 He asked about their health and then said, "You told me about your old father — how is he? Is he still alive and well?"

28 They answered, "Your humble servant, our father, is still alive and well." And they knelt and bowed down before him.

29 When Joseph saw his brother Benjamin, he said, "So this is your youngest brother, the one you told me about. God bless you, my son." 30 Then Joseph left suddenly, because his heart was full of tender feelings for his brother. He was about to break down, so he went to his room and cried. 31 After he had washed his face, he came out, and controlling himself, he ordered the meal to be served. 32 Joseph was served at one table and his brothers at another. The Egyptians who were eating there were served separately, because they considered it beneath their dignity to eat with Hebrews. 33 The brothers had been seated at the table, facing Joseph, in the order of their age from the oldest to the youngest. When they saw how they had been seated, they looked at one another in amazement. 34 Food was served to them from Joseph's table, and Benjamin was served five times as much as the rest of them. So they ate and drank with Joseph until they were drunk.

The Missing Cup

44 Joseph commanded the servant in charge of his house, "Fill the men's sacks with as much food as they can carry, and put each man's money in the top of his sack. 2 Put my silver cup in the top of the youngest brother's sack, together with the money for his grain." He did as he was told. 3 Early in the morning the brothers were sent on their way with their donkeys. 4 When they had gone only a short distance from the city, Joseph said to the servant in charge of his house, "Hurry after those men. When you catch up with them, ask them, 'Why have you paid back evil for good? 5 Why did you steal my master's silver cup? It is the one he drinks from, the one he uses for divination. You have committed a serious crime!' "

6 When the servant caught up with them, he repeated these words. 7 They answered him, "What do you mean, sir, by talking like this? We swear that we have done no such thing. 8 You know that we brought back to you from the land of Canaan the money we found in the top of our sacks. Why then should we steal silver or gold from your master's house? 9 Sir, if any one of us is found to have it, he will be put to death, and the rest of us will become your slaves."

10 He said, "I agree; but only the one who has taken the cup will become my slave, and the rest of you can go free." 11 So they quickly lowered their sacks to

---

v *One ancient translation* Why did you steal my master's silver cup?; *Hebrew does not have these words.*

the ground, and each man opened his sack. 12 Joseph's servant searched carefully, beginning with the oldest and ending with the youngest, and the cup was found in Benjamin's sack. 13 The brothers tore their clothes in sorrow, loaded their donkeys, and returned to the city.

14 When Judah and his brothers came to Joseph's house, he was still there. They bowed down before him, 15 and Joseph said, "What have you done? Didn't you know that a man in my position could find you out by practicing divination?"

16 "What can we say to you, sir?" Judah answered. "How can we argue? How can we clear ourselves? God has uncovered our guilt. All of us are now your slaves and not just the one with whom the cup was found."

17 Joseph said, "Oh, no! I would never do that! Only the one who had the cup will be my slave. The rest of you may go back safe and sound to your father."

Judah Pleads for Benjamin

18 Judah went up to Joseph and said, "Please, sir, allow me to speak with you freely. Don't be angry with me; you are like the king himself. 19 Sir, you asked us, 'Do you have a father or another brother?' 20 We answered, 'We have a father who is old and a younger brother, born to him in his old age. The boy's brother is dead, and he is the only one of his mother's children still alive; his father loves him very much.' 21 Sir, you told us to bring him here, so that you could see him, 22 and we answered that the boy could not leave his father; if he did, his father would die. 23 Then you said, 'You will not be admitted to my presence again unless your youngest brother comes with you.'

24 "When we went back to our father, we told him what you had said. 25 Then he told us to return and buy a little food.

26 We answered, 'We cannot go; we will not be admitted to the man's presence unless our youngest brother is with us. We can go only if our youngest brother goes also.' 27 Our father said to us, 'You know that my wife Rachel bore me only two sons. 28 One of them has already left me. He must have been torn to pieces by wild animals, because I have not seen him since he left. 29 If you take this one from me now and something happens to him, the sorrow you would cause me would kill me, as old as I am.'

30-31 "And now, sir," Judah continued, "if I go back to my father without the boy, as soon as he sees that the boy is not with me, he will die. His life is wrapped up with the life of the boy, and he is so old that the sorrow we would cause him would kill him. 32 What is more, I pledged my life to my father for the boy. I told him that if I did not bring the boy back to him, I would bear the blame all my life. 33 And now, sir, I will stay here as your slave in place of the boy; let him go back with his brothers. 34 How can I go back to my father if the boy is not with me? I cannot bear to see this disaster come upon my father."

Joseph Tells His Brothers Who He Is

45 Joseph was no longer able to control his feelings in front of his servants, so he ordered them all to leave the room. No one else was with him when Joseph told his brothers who he was. 2 He cried with such loud sobs that the Egyptians heard it, and the news was taken to the king's palace. 3 Joseph said to his brothers, "I am Joseph. Is my father still alive?" But when his brothers heard this, they were so terrified that they could not answer. 4 Then Joseph said to them, "Please come closer." They did, and he said, "I am your brother Joseph, whom you sold into Egypt. 5 Now do not be upset or blame yourselves because you sold me

45.1 Ac 7.13

here. It was really God who sent me ahead of you to save people's lives. [6]This is only the second year of famine in the land; there will be five more years in which there will be neither plowing nor reaping. [7]God sent me ahead of you to rescue you in this amazing way and to make sure that you and your descendants survive. [8]So it was not really you who sent me here, but God. He has made me the king's highest official. I am in charge of his whole country; I am the ruler of all Egypt.

[9]"Now hurry back to my father and tell him that this is what his son Joseph says: 'God has made me ruler of all Egypt; come to me without delay. [10]You can live in the region of Goshen, where you can be near me — you, your children, your grandchildren, your sheep, your goats, your cattle, and everything else that you have. [11]If you are in Goshen, I can take care of you. There will still be five years of famine; and I do not want you, your family, and your livestock to starve.'"

[12]Joseph continued, "Now all of you, and you too, Benjamin, can see that I am really Joseph. [13]Tell my father how powerful I am here in Egypt and tell him about everything that you have seen. Then hurry and bring him here."

[14]He threw his arms around his brother Benjamin and began to cry; Benjamin also cried as he hugged him. [15]Then, still weeping, he embraced each of his brothers and kissed them. After that, his brothers began to talk with him.

[16]When the news reached the palace that Joseph's brothers had come, the king and his officials were pleased. [17]He said to Joseph, "Tell your brothers to load their animals and to return to the land of Canaan. [18]Let them get their father and their families and come back here. I will give them the best land in Egypt, and they will have more than enough to live on. [19]Tell them also to take wagons with them from Egypt for their wives and small children and to bring their father with them. [20]They are not to worry about leaving their possessions behind; the best in the whole land of Egypt will be theirs."

[21]Jacob's sons did as they were told. Joseph gave them wagons, as the king had ordered, and food for the trip. [22]He also gave each of them a change of clothes, but he gave Benjamin three hundred pieces of silver and five changes of clothes. [23]He sent his father ten donkeys loaded with the best Egyptian goods and ten donkeys loaded with grain, bread, and other food for the trip. [24]He sent his brothers off and as they left, he said to them, "Don't quarrel on the way."

[25]They left Egypt and went back home to their father Jacob in Canaan. [26]"Joseph is still alive!" they told him. "He is the ruler of all Egypt!" Jacob was stunned and could not believe them.

[27]But when they told him all that Joseph had said to them, and when he saw the wagons which Joseph had sent to take him to Egypt, he recovered from the shock. [28]"My son Joseph is still alive!" he said. "This is all I could ask for! I must go and see him before I die."

Jacob and His Family Go to Egypt

46 Jacob packed up all he had and went to Beersheba, where he offered sacrifices to the God of his father Isaac. [2]God spoke to him in a vision at night and called, "Jacob, Jacob!"

"Yes, here I am," he answered.

[3]"I am God, the God of your father," he said. "Do not be afraid to go to Egypt; I will make your descendants a great nation there. [4]I will go with you to Egypt, and I will bring your descendants back to this land. Joseph will be with you when you die."

[5]Jacob set out from Beersheba. His sons put him, their small children, and

their wives in the wagons which the king of Egypt had sent. ⁶They took their livestock and the possessions they had acquired in Canaan and went to Egypt. Jacob took all his descendants with him: ⁷his sons, his grandsons, his daughters, and his granddaughters.

⁸The members of Jacob's family who went to Egypt with him were his oldest son Reuben ⁹and Reuben's sons: Hanoch, Pallu, Hezron, and Carmi. ¹⁰Simeon and his sons: Jemuel, Jamin, Ohad, Jachin, Zohar, and Shaul, the son of a Canaanite woman. ¹¹Levi and his sons: Gershon, Kohath, and Merari. ¹²Judah and his sons: Shelah, Perez, and Zerah. (Judah's other sons, Er and Onan, had died in Canaan.) Perez' sons were Hezron and Hamul. ¹³Issachar and his sons: Tola, Puah, Jashub, and Shimron. ¹⁴Zebulun and his sons: Sered, Elon, and Jahleel. ¹⁵These are the sons that Leah had borne to Jacob in Mesopotamia, besides his daughter Dinah. In all, his descendants by Leah numbered thirty-three.

¹⁶Gad and his sons: Zephon, Haggi, Shuni, Ezbon, Eri, Arod, and Areli. ¹⁷Asher and his sons: Imnah, Ishvah, Ishvi, Beriah, and their sister Serah. Beriah's sons were Heber and Malchiel. ¹⁸These sixteen are the descendants of Jacob by Zilpah, the slave woman whom Laban gave to his daughter Leah.

¹⁹Jacob's wife Rachel bore him two sons: Joseph and Benjamin. ²⁰In Egypt Joseph had two sons, Manasseh and Ephraim, by Asenath, the daughter of Potiphera, a priest in Heliopolis. ²¹Benjamin's sons were Bela, Becher, Ashbel, Gera, Naaman, Ehi, Rosh, Muppim, Huppim, and Ard. ²²These fourteen are the descendants of Jacob by Rachel.

²³Dan and his son Hushim. ²⁴Naphtali and his sons: Jahzeel, Guni, Jezer, and Shillem. ²⁵These seven are the descendants of Jacob by Bilhah, the slave woman whom Laban gave to his daughter Rachel.

²⁶The total number of the direct descendants of Jacob who went to Egypt was sixty-six, not including his sons' wives. ²⁷Two sons were born to Joseph in Egypt, bringing to seventy the total number of Jacob's family who went there.

Jacob and His Family in Egypt

²⁸Jacob sent Judah ahead to ask Joseph to meet them in Goshen. When they arrived, ²⁹Joseph got in his chariot and went to Goshen to meet his father. When they met, Joseph threw his arms around his father's neck and cried for a long time. ³⁰Jacob said to Joseph, "I am ready to die, now that I have seen you and know that you are still alive."

³¹Then Joseph said to his brothers and the rest of his father's family, "I must go and tell the king that my brothers and all my father's family, who were living in Canaan, have come to me. ³²I will tell him that you are shepherds and take care of livestock and that you have brought your flocks and herds and everything else that belongs to you. ³³When the king calls for you and asks what your occupation is, ³⁴be sure to tell him that you have taken care of livestock all your lives, just as your ancestors did. In this way he will let you live in the region of Goshen." Joseph said this because Egyptians will have nothing to do with shepherds.

47 So Joseph took five of his brothers and went to the king. He told him, "My father and my brothers have come from Canaan with their flocks, their herds, and all that they own. They are now in the region of Goshen." ²He then presented his brothers to the king. ³The king asked them, "What is your occupation?"

"We are shepherds, sir, just as our ancestors were," they answered. ⁴"We have come to live in this country, because in the land of Canaan the famine is so severe that there is no pasture for our flocks. Please give us permission to live in the region of Goshen." ⁵The king said to Joseph, "Now that your father and your brothers have arrived, ⁶the land of Egypt is theirs. Let them settle in the region of Goshen, the best part of the land. And if there are any capable men among them, put them in charge of my own livestock."

⁷Then Joseph brought his father Jacob and presented him to the king. Jacob gave the king his blessing, ⁸and the king asked him, "How old are you?"

⁹Jacob answered, "My life of wandering has lasted a hundred and thirty years. Those years have been few and difficult, unlike the long years of my ancestors in their wanderings." ¹⁰Jacob gave the king a farewell blessing and left. ¹¹Then Joseph settled his father and his brothers in Egypt, giving them property in the best of the land near the city of Rameses, as the king had commanded. ¹²Joseph provided food for his father, his brothers, and all the rest of his father's family, including the very youngest.

The Famine

¹³The famine was so severe that there was no food anywhere, and the people of Egypt and Canaan became weak with hunger. ¹⁴As they bought grain, Joseph collected all the money and took it to the palace. ¹⁵When all the money in Egypt and Canaan was spent, the Egyptians came to Joseph and said, "Give us food! Don't let us die. Do something! Our money is all gone."

¹⁶Joseph answered, "Bring your livestock; I will give you food in exchange for it if your money is all gone." ¹⁷So they brought their livestock to Joseph, and he gave them food in exchange for their horses, sheep, goats, cattle, and donkeys. That year he supplied them with food in exchange for all their livestock.

¹⁸The following year they came to him and said, "We will not hide the fact from you, sir, that our money is all gone and our livestock belongs to you. There is nothing left to give you except our bodies and our lands. ¹⁹Don't let us die. Do something! Don't let our fields be deserted. Buy us and our land in exchange for food. We will be the king's slaves, and he will own our land. Give us grain to keep us alive and seed so that we can plant our fields."

²⁰Joseph bought all the land in Egypt for the king. Every Egyptian was forced to sell his land, because the famine was so severe; and all the land became the king's property. ²¹Joseph made slaves of the people from one end of Egypt to the other. ²²The only land he did not buy was the land that belonged to the priests. They did not have to sell their lands, because the king gave them an allowance to live on. ²³Joseph said to the people, "You see, I have now bought you and your lands for the king. Here is seed for you to sow in your fields. ²⁴At the time of harvest you must give one-fifth to the king. You can use the rest for seed and for food for yourselves and your families."

²⁵They answered, "You have saved our lives; you have been good to us, sir, and we will be the king's slaves." ²⁶So Joseph made it a law for the land of Egypt that one-fifth of the harvest should belong to the king. This law still remains in force today. Only the lands of the priests did not become the king's property.

Jacob's Last Request

²⁷The Israelites lived in Egypt in the region of Goshen, where they became rich and had many children. ²⁸Jacob lived in Egypt seventeen years, until he was a hundred and forty-seven years

old. ²⁹When the time drew near for him to die, he called for his son Joseph and said to him, "Place your hand between my thighs*w* and make a solemn vow that you will not bury me in Egypt. ³⁰I want to be buried where my fathers are; carry me out of Egypt and bury me where they are buried."

Joseph answered, "I will do as you say."

³¹Jacob said, "Make a vow that you will." Joseph made the vow, and Jacob gave thanks there on his bed.

Jacob Blesses Ephraim and Manasseh

48 Some time later Joseph was told that his father was ill. So he took his two sons, Manasseh and Ephraim, and went to see Jacob. ²When Jacob was told that his son Joseph had come to see him, he gathered his strength and sat up in bed. ³Jacob said to Joseph, "Almighty God appeared to me at Luz in the land of Canaan and blessed me. ⁴He said to me, 'I will give you many children, so that your descendants will become many nations; I will give this land to your descendants as their possession forever.'"

⁵Jacob continued, "Joseph, your two sons, who were born to you in Egypt before I came here, belong to me; Ephraim and Manasseh are just as much my sons as Reuben and Simeon. ⁶If you have any more sons, they will not be considered mine; the inheritance they get will come through Ephraim and Manasseh. ⁷I am doing this because of your mother Rachel. To my great sorrow she died in the land of Canaan, not far from Ephrath, as I was returning from Mesopotamia. I buried her there beside the road to Ephrath." (Ephrath is now known as Bethlehem.)

"May God . . . bless these boys!" (48.15)

⁸When Jacob saw Joseph's sons, he asked, "Who are these boys?"

⁹Joseph answered, "These are my sons, whom God has given me here in Egypt."

Jacob said, "Bring them to me so that I may bless them." ¹⁰Jacob's eyesight was failing because of his age, and he could not see very well. Joseph brought the boys to him, and he hugged them and kissed them. ¹¹Jacob said to Joseph, "I never expected to see you again, and now God has even let me see your children." ¹²Then Joseph took them from Jacob's lap and bowed down before him with his face to the ground.

¹³Joseph put Ephraim at Jacob's left and Manasseh at his right. ¹⁴But Jacob crossed his hands, and put his right hand on the head of Ephraim, even though he was the younger, and his left hand on the head of Manasseh, who was the older. ¹⁵Then he blessed Joseph:*x*

"May God, whom my fathers
    Abraham and Isaac served,
    bless these boys!

---

w PLACE ... THIGHS: *See 24.2.*   *x* JOSEPH: *In blessing Ephraim and Manasseh, Jacob was in fact blessing Joseph.*

47.29, 30 Gn 49.29-32; 50.6   **48.3, 4** Gn 28.13, 14   **48.7** Gn 35.16-19

May God, who has led me to this
very day, bless them!
[16] May the angel, who has rescued
me from all harm, bless
them!
May my name and the name of
my fathers Abraham and
Isaac live on through
these boys!
May they have many children,
many descendants!"

[17] Joseph was upset when he saw
that his father had put his right hand on
Ephraim's head; so he took his father's
hand to move it from Ephraim's head to
the head of Manasseh. [18] He said to his
father, "Not that way, father. This is the
older boy; put your right hand on his
head."

[19] His father refused, saying, "I
know, son, I know. Manasseh's
descendants will also become a great
people. But his younger brother will be
greater than he, and his descendants
will become great nations."

[20] So he blessed them that day, saying, "The Israelites will use your names
when they pronounce blessings. They
will say, 'May God make you like
Ephraim and Manasseh.'" In this way
Jacob put Ephraim before Manasseh.

[21] Then Jacob said to Joseph, "As you
see, I am about to die, but God will be
with you and will take you back to the
land of your ancestors. [22] It is to you and
not to your brothers that I am giving
Shechem, that fertile region which I
took from the Amorites with my sword
and my bow."

The Last Words of Jacob

49 Jacob called for his sons and
said, "Gather around, and I will
tell you what will happen to you in the
future:

[2] "Come together and listen, sons
of Jacob.

Listen to your father Israel.

[3] "Reuben, my first-born, you are
my strength
And the first child of my
manhood,
The proudest and strongest of all
my sons.
[4] You are like a raging flood,
But you will not be the most
important,
For you slept with my concubine
And dishonored your
father's bed.

[5] "Simeon and Levi are brothers.
They use their weapons to
commit violence.
[6] I will not join in their secret
talks,
Nor will I take part in their
meetings,
For they killed people in anger
And they crippled bulls for sport.
[7] A curse be on their anger,
because it is so fierce,
And on their fury, because it is
so cruel.
I will scatter them throughout
the land of Israel.
I will disperse them among its
people.

[8] "Judah, your brothers will
praise you.
You hold your enemies by the
neck.
Your brothers will bow down
before you.
[9] Judah is like a lion,
Killing his victim and returning
to his den,
Stretching out and lying down.
No one dares disturb him.
[10] Judah will hold the royal scepter,
And his descendants will always
rule.

48.20 He 11.21   **49.9** Nu 24.9; Rev 5.5

Nations will bring him tribute[y]
And bow in obedience
    before him.
11 He ties his young donkey to a
    grapevine,
To the very best of the vines.
He washes his clothes in
    blood-red wine.
12 His eyes are bloodshot from
    drinking wine,
His teeth white from drinking
    milk.[z]

13 "Zebulun will live beside the sea.
His shore will be a haven for
    ships.
His territory will reach as far as
    Sidon.

14 "Issachar is no better than a
    donkey
That lies stretched out between
    its saddlebags.
15 But he sees that the resting
    place is good
And that the land is delightful.
So he bends his back to carry
    the load
And is forced to work as a slave.

16 "Dan will be a ruler for his
    people.
They will be like the other tribes
    of Israel.
17 Dan will be a snake at the side
    of the road,
A poisonous snake beside the
    path,
That strikes at the horse's heel,
So that the rider is thrown off
    backward.

18 "I wait for your deliverance,
    LORD.

19 "Gad will be attacked by a band
    of robbers,
But he will turn and pursue
    them.

20 "Asher's land will produce rich
    food.
He will provide food fit for a
    king.

21 "Naphtali is a deer that runs
    free,
Who bears lovely fawns.[a]

22 "Joseph is like a wild donkey by
    a spring,
A wild colt on a hillside.[b]
23 His enemies attack him fiercely
And pursue him with their bows
    and arrows.
24 But his bow remains steady,
And his arms are made strong[c]
By the power of the Mighty God
    of Jacob,
By the Shepherd, the Protector of
    Israel.
25 It is your father's God who
    helps you,
The Almighty God who
    blesses you
With blessings of rain from
    above
And of deep waters from beneath
    the ground,
Blessings of many cattle and
    children,
26 Blessings of grain and flowers,[d]
Blessings of ancient mountains,[e]
Delightful things from
    everlasting hills.

[y] *Probable text* Nations . . . tribute; *Hebrew unclear.*   [z] His eyes . . . milk; *or* His eyes
are darker than wine, his teeth are whiter than milk.   [a] Naphtali . . . fawns; *or*
Naphtali is a spreading tree that puts out lovely branches.   [b] Joseph . . . hillside; *or*
Joseph is like a tree by a spring, a fruitful tree that spreads over a wall.   [c] But . . .
strong; *or* But their bows were broken and splintered, the muscles of their arms torn
apart.   [d] *Probable text* grain and flowers; *Hebrew* your fathers are mightier than.
[e] *One ancient translation* ancient mountains; *Hebrew* my ancestors to.

May these blessings rest on the
head of Joseph,
On the brow of the one set apart
from his brothers.

27"Benjamin is like a vicious wolf.
Morning and evening he kills
and devours."

28 These are the twelve tribes of Israel, and this is what their father said as
he spoke a suitable word of farewell to
each son.

The Death and Burial of Jacob

29 Then Jacob commanded his sons,
"Now that I am going to join my people
in death, bury me with my fathers in
the cave that is in the field of Ephron
the Hittite, 30 at Machpelah east of
Mamre in the land of Canaan. Abraham
bought this cave and field from Ephron
for a burial ground. 31 That is where
they buried Abraham and his wife
Sarah; that is where they buried Isaac
and his wife Rebecca; and that is where
I buried Leah. 32 The field and the cave
in it were bought from the Hittites.
Bury me there." 33 When Jacob had finished giving instructions to his sons, he
lay back down and died.

50 Joseph threw himself on his
father, crying and kissing his
face. 2 Then Joseph gave orders to em-
balm his father's body. 3 It took forty
days, the normal time for embalming.
The Egyptians mourned for him seventy days.

4 When the time of mourning was
over, Joseph said to the king's officials,
"Please take this message to the king:
5 'When my father was about to die, he
made me promise him that I would
bury him in the tomb which he had prepared in the land of Canaan. So please
let me go and bury my father, and then
I will come back.'"

6 The king answered, "Go and bury
your father, as you promised you
would."

7 So Joseph went to bury his father.
All the king's officials, the senior men
of his court, and all the leading men of
Egypt went with Joseph. 8 His family,
his brothers, and the rest of his father's
family all went with him. Only their
small children and their sheep, goats,
and cattle stayed in the region of Goshen. 9 Men in chariots and men on
horseback also went with him; it was a
huge group.

10 When they came to the threshing
place at Atad east of the Jordan, they
mourned loudly for a long time, and Joseph performed mourning ceremonies
for seven days. 11 When the citizens of
Canaan saw those people mourning at
Atad, they said, "What a solemn ceremony of mourning the Egyptians are
holding!" That is why the place was
named Abel Mizraim.f

12 So Jacob's sons did as he had commanded them; 13 they carried his body
to Canaan and buried it in the cave at
Machpelah east of Mamre in the field
which Abraham had bought from
Ephron the Hittite for a burial ground.
14 After Joseph had buried his father, he
returned to Egypt with his brothers and
all who had gone with him for the
funeral.

Joseph Reassures His Brothers

15 After the death of their father, Joseph's brothers said, "What if Joseph
still hates us and plans to pay us back
for all the harm we did to him?" 16 So
they sent a message to Joseph: "Before
our father died, 17 he told us to ask you,

---

f ABEL MIZRAIM: *This name sounds like the Hebrew for "mourning of the Egyptians."*
49.30 Gn 23.3-20   **49.31 a** Gn 25.9, 10; **b** Gn 35.29   **49.33** Ac 7.15   **50.5** Gn 47.29-31
50.13 Ac 7.16

'Please forgive the crime your brothers committed when they wronged you.' Now please forgive us the wrong that we, the servants of your father's God, have done." Joseph cried when he received this message.

18 Then his brothers themselves came and bowed down before him. "Here we are before you as your slaves," they said.

19 But Joseph said to them, "Don't be afraid; I can't put myself in the place of God. **20** You plotted evil against me, but God turned it into good, in order to preserve the lives of many people who are alive today because of what happened. **21** You have nothing to fear. I will take care of you and your children." So he reassured them with kind words that touched their hearts.

50.25 Ex 13.19; Js 24.32; He 11.22

The Death of Joseph

22 Joseph continued to live in Egypt with his father's family; he was a hundred and ten years old when he died. **23** He lived to see Ephraim's children and grandchildren. He also lived to receive the children of Machir son of Manasseh into the family. **24** He said to his brothers, "I am about to die, but God will certainly take care of you and lead you out of this land to the land he solemnly promised to Abraham, Isaac, and Jacob." **25** Then Joseph asked his people to make a vow. "Promise me," he said, "that when God leads you to that land, you will take my body with you." **26** So Joseph died in Egypt at the age of a hundred and ten. They embalmed his body and put it in a coffin.

EXODUS

INTRODUCTION

The name *Exodus* means "departure," and refers to the most important event in Israel's history, which is described in this book—the departure of the people of Israel from Egypt, where they had been slaves. The book has four main parts: 1) the freeing of the Hebrews from slavery; 2) their journey to Mount Sinai; 3) God's covenant with his people at Sinai, which gave them moral, civil, and religious laws to live by; and 4) the building and furnishing of a place of worship for Israel, and laws regarding the priests and the worship of God.

Above all, this book describes what God did, as he liberated his enslaved people and formed them into a nation with hope for the future.

The central human figure in the book is Moses, the man whom God chose to lead his people from Egypt. The most widely known part of the book is the list of the Ten Commandments in chapter 20.

OUTLINE OF CONTENTS

The Israelites Are Treated Cruelly in Egypt

1 The sons of Jacob who went to Egypt with him, each with his family, were ² Reuben, Simeon, Levi, Judah, ³ Issachar, Zebulun, Benjamin, ⁴ Dan, Naphtali, Gad, and Asher. ⁵ The total number of these people directly descended from Jacob was seventy.ᵃ His son Joseph was already in Egypt. ⁶ In the course of time Joseph, his brothers, and all the rest of that generation died, ⁷ but their descendants, the Israelites, had many children and became so numerous and strong that Egypt was filled with them.

⁸ Then, a new king, who knew nothing about Joseph, came to power in Egypt. ⁹ He said to his people, "These Israelites are so numerous and strong that they are a threat to us. ¹⁰ In case of war they might join our enemies in order to fight against us, and might escape fromᵇ the country. We must find some way to keep them from becoming even more numerous." ¹¹ So the Egyptians put slave drivers over them to crush their spirits with hard labor. The Israelites built the cities of Pithom and

---

ᵃ *One ancient translation* seventy-five (*see Ac 7.14*).   ᵇ escape from; *or* take control of.

1.1-4 Gn 46.8-27   **1.7** Ac 7.17   **1.8** Ac 7.18   **1.10** Ac 7.19

Rameses to serve as supply centers for the king. [12] But the more the Egyptians oppressed the Israelites, the more they increased in number and the farther they spread through the land. The Egyptians came to fear the Israelites [13-14] and made their lives miserable by forcing them into cruel slavery. They made them work on their building projects and in their fields, and they had no pity on them.

[15] Then the king of Egypt spoke to Shiphrah and Puah, the two midwives who helped the Hebrew women. [16]"When you help the Hebrew women give birth," he said to them, "kill the baby if it is a boy; but if it is a girl, let it live." [17] But the midwives were God-fearing and so did not obey the king; instead, they let the boys live. [18] So the king sent for the midwives and asked them, "Why are you doing this? Why are you letting the boys live?"

[19] They answered, "The Hebrew women are not like Egyptian women; they give birth easily, and their babies are born before either of us gets there." [20-21] Because the midwives were God-fearing, God was good to them and gave them families of their own. And the Israelites continued to increase and become strong. [22] Finally the king issued a command to all his people: "Take every newborn Hebrew boy and throw him into the Nile, but let all the girls live."

The Birth of Moses

2 During this time a man from the tribe of Levi married a woman of his own tribe, [2] and she bore him a son. When she saw what a fine baby he was, she hid him for three months. [3] But when she could not hide him any longer, she took a basket made of reeds and covered it with tar to make it watertight. She put the baby in it and then placed it in the tall grass at the edge of the river. [4] The baby's sister stood some distance away to see what would happen to him.

[5] The king's daughter came down to the river to bathe, while her servants walked along the bank. Suddenly she noticed the basket in the tall grass and

The king's daughter . . . noticed the basket. (2.5)

sent a slave woman to get it. [6] The princess opened it and saw a baby boy. He was crying, and she felt sorry for him. "This is one of the Hebrew babies," she said.

[7] Then his sister asked her, "Shall I go and call a Hebrew woman to nurse the baby for you?"

[8]"Please do," she answered. So the girl went and brought the baby's own mother. [9] The princess told the woman, "Take this baby and nurse him for me, and I will pay you." So she took the baby and nursed him. [10] Later, when the child was old enough, she took him to the king's daughter, who adopted him as her own son. She said to herself, "I pulled him out of the water, and so I name him Moses."[c]

Moses Escapes to Midian

[11] When Moses had grown up, he went out to visit his people, the

---

[c] MOSES: *This name sounds like the Hebrew for "pull out."*

1.22 Ac 7.19   **2.2** Ac 7.20; He 11.23   **2.10** Ac 7.21   **2.11-14** Ac 7.23-28   **2.11** He 11.24

Hebrews, and he saw how they were forced to do hard labor. He even saw an Egyptian kill a Hebrew, one of Moses' own people. 12 Moses looked all around, and when he saw that no one was watching, he killed the Egyptian and hid his body in the sand. 13 The next day he went back and saw two Hebrew men fighting. He said to the one who was in the wrong, "Why are you beating up a fellow Hebrew?"

14 The man answered, "Who made you our ruler and judge? Are you going to kill me just as you killed that Egyptian?" Then Moses was afraid and said to himself, "People have found out what I have done." 15-16 When the king heard about what had happened, he tried to have Moses killed, but Moses fled and went to live in the land of Midian.

One day, when Moses was sitting by a well, seven daughters of Jethro, the priest of Midian, came to draw water and fill the troughs for their father's sheep and goats. 17 But some shepherds drove Jethro's daughters away. Then Moses went to their rescue and watered their animals for them. 18 When they returned to their father, he asked, "Why have you come back so early today?"

19 "An Egyptian rescued us from the shepherds," they answered, "and he even drew water for us and watered our animals."

20 "Where is he?" he asked his daughters. "Why did you leave the man out there? Go and invite him to eat with us."

21 So Moses decided to live there, and Jethro gave him his daughter Zipporah in marriage, 22 who bore him a son. Moses said to himself, "I am a foreigner in this land, and so I name him Gershom."*d*

23 Years later the king of Egypt died, but the Israelites were still groaning under their slavery and cried out for help. Their cry went up to God, 24 who heard their groaning and remembered his covenant with Abraham, Isaac, and Jacob. 25 He saw the slavery of the Israelites and was concerned for them.*e*

God Calls Moses

3 One day while Moses was taking care of the sheep and goats of his father-in-law Jethro, the priest of Midian, he led the flock across the desert and came to Sinai, the holy mountain. 2 There the angel of the LORD appeared to him as a flame coming from the middle of a bush. Moses saw that the bush was on fire but that it was not burning up. 3 "This is strange," he thought. "Why isn't the bush burning up? I will go closer and see."

4 When the LORD saw that Moses was coming closer, he called to him from the middle of the bush and said, "Moses! Moses!"

He answered, "Yes, here I am."

5 God said, "Do not come any closer. Take off your sandals, because you are standing on holy ground. 6 I am the God of your ancestors, the God of Abraham, Isaac, and Jacob." So Moses covered his face, because he was afraid to look at God.

7 Then the LORD said, "I have seen how cruelly my people are being treated in Egypt; I have heard them cry out to be rescued from their slave drivers. I know all about their sufferings, 8 and so I have come down to rescue them from the Egyptians and to bring them out of Egypt to a spacious land, one which is rich and fertile and in which the Canaanites, the Hittites, the Amorites, the Perizzites, the Hivites, and the Jebusites now live. 9 I have indeed heard the cry of my people, and I see how the Egyptians are oppressing them. 10 Now I am sending you to the king of Egypt

---

d GERSHOM: *This name sounds like the Hebrew for "foreigner."*   *e* was concerned for them; *one ancient translation* revealed himself to them.
2.15 Ac 7.29; He 11.27   **2.24** Gn 15.13, 14   **3.2-10** Ac 7.30-34

so that you can lead my people out of his country."

¹¹But Moses said to God, "I am nobody. How can I go to the king and bring the Israelites out of Egypt?"

¹²God answered, "I will be with you, and when you bring the people out of Egypt, you will worship me on this mountain. That will be the proof that I have sent you."

¹³But Moses replied, "When I go to the Israelites and say to them, 'The God of your ancestors sent me to you,' they will ask me, 'What is his name?' So what can I tell them?"

¹⁴God said, "I am who I am. You must tell them: 'The one who is called

"I am who I am. . . . This is my name forever."
(3.14-15)

I AM*ᶠ* has sent me to you.' ¹⁵Tell the Israelites that I, the LORD, the God of their ancestors, the God of Abraham, Isaac, and Jacob, have sent you to them. This is my name forever; this is what all future generations are to call

me. ¹⁶Go and gather the leaders of Israel together and tell them that I, the LORD, the God of their ancestors, the God of Abraham, Isaac, and Jacob, appeared to you. Tell them that I have come to them and have seen what the Egyptians are doing to them. ¹⁷I have decided that I will bring them out of Egypt, where they are being treated cruelly, and will take them to a rich and fertile land — the land of the Canaanites, the Hittites, the Amorites, the Perizzites, the Hivites, and the Jebusites.

¹⁸"My people will listen to what you say to them. Then you must go with the leaders of Israel to the king of Egypt and say to him, 'The LORD, the God of the Hebrews, has revealed himself to us. Now allow us to travel three days into the desert to offer sacrifices to the LORD, our God.' ¹⁹I know that the king of Egypt will not let you go unless he is forced to do so. ²⁰But I will use my power and will punish Egypt by doing terrifying things there. After that he will let you go.

²¹"I will make the Egyptians respect you so that when my people leave, they will not go empty-handed. ²²Every Israelite woman will go to her Egyptian neighbors and to any Egyptian woman living in her house and will ask for clothing and for gold and silver jewelry. The Israelites will put these things on their sons and daughters and carry away the wealth of the Egyptians."

God Gives Moses Miraculous Power

4 Then Moses answered the LORD, "But suppose the Israelites do not believe me and will not listen to what I say. What shall I do if they say that you did not appear to me?"

ᶠI am who I am ... I AM; or I will be who I will be ... I WILL BE. "I am" sounds like the Hebrew name Yahweh traditionally transliterated as Jehovah. This name is represented in this translation by "the LORD" in capital letters, following a usage which is widespread in English versions.

3.13 Ex 6.2, 3   **3.14** Rev 1.4, 8   **3.21, 22** Ex 12.35, 36   **3.21** Ws 10.17

2 So the LORD asked him, "What are you holding?"

"A walking stick," he answered.

3 The LORD said, "Throw it on the ground." When Moses threw it down, it turned into a snake, and he ran away from it. 4 Then the LORD said to Moses, "Reach down and pick it up by the tail." So Moses reached down and caught it, and it became a walking stick again. 5 The LORD said, "Do this to prove to the Israelites that the LORD, the God of their ancestors, the God of Abraham, Isaac, and Jacob, has appeared to you."

To prove . . . that the LORD has appeared to you (4.5)

6 The LORD spoke to Moses again, "Put your hand inside your robe." Moses obeyed; and when he took his hand out, it was diseased, covered with white spots, like snow. 7 Then the LORD said, "Put your hand inside your robe again." He did so, and when he took it out this time, it was healthy, just like the rest of his body. 8 The LORD said, "If they will not believe you or be convinced by the first miracle, then this one will convince them. 9 If in spite of these two miracles they still will not believe you, and if they refuse to listen to what you say, take some water from the Nile and pour it on the ground. The water will turn into blood."

10 But Moses said, "No, LORD, don't send me. I have never been a good speaker, and I haven't become one since you began to speak to me. I am a poor speaker, slow and hesitant."

11 The LORD said to him, "Who gives man his mouth? Who makes him deaf or dumb? Who gives him sight or makes him blind? It is I, the LORD. 12 Now, go! I will help you to speak, and I will tell you what to say."

13 But Moses answered, "No, Lord, please send someone else."

14 At this the LORD became angry with Moses and said, "What about your brother Aaron, the Levite? I know that he can speak well. In fact, he is now coming to meet you and will be glad to see you. 15 You can speak to him and tell him what to say. I will help both of you to speak, and I will tell you both what to do. 16 He will be your spokesman and speak to the people for you. Then you will be like God, telling him what to say. 17 Take this walking stick with you; for with it you will perform miracles."

Moses Returns to Egypt

18 Then Moses went back to Jethro, his father-in-law, and said to him, "Please let me go back to my relatives in Egypt to see if they are still alive." Jethro agreed and told him good-bye.

19 While Moses was still in Midian, the LORD said to him, "Go back to Egypt, for all those who wanted to kill you are dead." 20 So Moses took his wife and his sons, put them on a donkey, and set out with them for Egypt, carrying the walking stick that God had told him to take.

21 Again the LORD said to Moses, "Now that you are going back to Egypt, be sure to perform before the king all the miracles which I have given you the power to do. But I will make the king stubborn, and he will not let the people go. 22 Then you must tell him that I, the LORD, say, 'Israel is my first-born son. 23 I told you to let my son go, so that he might worship me, but you refused. Now I am going to kill your first-born son.'"

24 At a camping place on the way to Egypt, the LORD met Moses and tried to kill him. 25-26 Then Zipporah, his wife,

took a sharp stone, cut off the foreskin of her son, and touched Moses' feet[g] with it. Because of the rite of circumcision she said to Moses, "You are a husband of blood to me." And so the LORD spared Moses' life.

27 Meanwhile the LORD had said to Aaron, "Go into the desert to meet Moses." So he went to meet him at the holy mountain; and when he met him, he kissed him. 28 Then Moses told Aaron everything that the LORD had said when he told him to return to Egypt; he also told him about the miracles which the LORD had ordered him to perform. 29 So Moses and Aaron went to Egypt and gathered all the Israelite leaders together. 30 Aaron told them everything that the LORD had said to Moses, and then Moses performed all the miracles in front of the people. 31 They believed, and when they heard that the LORD had come to them and had seen how they were being treated cruelly, they bowed down and worshiped.

Moses and Aaron before the King of Egypt

5 Then Moses and Aaron went to the king of Egypt and said, "The LORD, the God of Israel, says, 'Let my people go, so that they can hold a festival in the desert to honor me.'"

2 "Who is the LORD?" the king demanded. "Why should I listen to him and let Israel go? I do not know the LORD; and I will not let Israel go."

3 Moses and Aaron replied, "The God of the Hebrews has revealed himself to us. Allow us to travel three days into the desert to offer sacrifices to the LORD our God. If we don't do so, he will kill us with disease or by war."

4 The king said to Moses and Aaron, "What do you mean by making the people neglect their work? Get those slaves back to work! 5 You people have become

more numerous than the Egyptians. And now you want to stop working!"

6 That same day the king commanded the Egyptian slave drivers and the Israelite foremen: 7 "Stop giving the people straw for making bricks. Make them go and find it for themselves. 8 But still require them to make the same number of bricks as before, not one brick less. They don't have enough work to do, and that is why they keep asking me to let them go and offer sacrifices to their God! 9 Make them work harder and keep them busy, so that they won't have time to listen to a pack of lies."

10 The slave drivers and the Israelite foremen went out and said to the Israelites, "The king has said that he will not supply you with any more straw. 11 He says that you must go and get it for yourselves wherever you can find it, but you must still make the same number of bricks." 12 So the people went all over Egypt looking for straw. 13 The slave drivers kept trying to force them to make the same number of bricks every day as they had made when they were given straw. 14 The Egyptian slave drivers beat the Israelite foremen, whom they had put in charge of the work. They demanded, "Why aren't you people making the same number of bricks that you made before?"

15 Then the foremen went to the king and complained, "Why do you do this to us, Your Majesty? 16 We are given no straw, but we are still ordered to make bricks! And now we are being beaten. It is your people that are at fault."

17 The king answered, "You are lazy and don't want to work, and that is why you ask me to let you go and offer sacrifices to the LORD. 18 Now get back to work! You will not be given any straw, but you must still make the same number of bricks." 19 The foremen realized that they were in trouble when they were told that they had to make the

---

g FEET: *This reference to "feet" is thought by some to be a euphemism for the genitals.*

same number of bricks every day as they had made before.

20 As they were leaving, they met Moses and Aaron, who were waiting for them. 21 They said to Moses and Aaron, "The LORD has seen what you have done and will punish you for making the king and his officers hate us. You have given them an excuse to kill us."

Moses Complains to the LORD

22 Then Moses turned to the LORD again and said, "Lord, why do you mistreat your people? Why did you send me here? 23 Ever since I went to the king to speak for you, he has treated them cruelly. And you have done nothing to help them!"

6 Then the LORD said to Moses, "Now you are going to see what I will do to the king. I will force him to let my people go. In fact, I will force him to drive them out of his land."

God Calls Moses

2 God spoke to Moses and said, "I am the LORD. 3 I appeared to Abraham, to Isaac, and to Jacob as Almighty God, but I did not make myself known to them by my holy name, the LORD.[h] 4 I also made my covenant with them, promising to give them the land of Canaan, the land in which they had lived as foreigners. 5 Now I have heard the groaning of the Israelites, whom the Egyptians have enslaved, and I have remembered my covenant. 6 So tell the Israelites that I say to them, 'I am the LORD; I will rescue you and set you free from your slavery to the Egyptians. I will raise my mighty arm to bring terrible punishment upon them, and I will save you. 7 I will make you my own people, and I will be your God. You will know that I am the LORD your God

when I set you free from slavery in Egypt. 8 I will bring you to the land that I solemnly promised to give to Abraham, Isaac, and Jacob; and I will give it to you as your own possession. I am the LORD.' " 9 Moses told this to the Israelites, but they would not listen to him, because their spirit had been broken by their cruel slavery.

10 Then the LORD said to Moses, 11 "Go and tell the king of Egypt that he must let the Israelites leave his land."

12 But Moses replied, "Even the Israelites will not listen to me, so why should the king? I am such a poor speaker."

13 The LORD commanded Moses and Aaron: "Tell the Israelites and the king of Egypt that I have ordered you to lead the Israelites out of Egypt."

The Family Record of Moses and Aaron

14 Reuben, Jacob's first-born, had four sons: Hanoch, Pallu, Hezron, and Carmi; they were the ancestors of the clans that bear their names. 15 Simeon had six sons: Jemuel, Jamin, Ohad, Jachin, Zohar, and Shaul, the son of a Canaanite woman; they were the ancestors of the clans that bear their names. 16 Levi had three sons: Gershon, Kohath, and Merari; they were the ancestors of the clans that bear their names. Levi lived 137 years. 17 Gershon had two sons: Libni and Shimei, and they had many descendants. 18 Kohath had four sons: Amram, Izhar, Hebron, and Uzziel. Kohath lived 133 years. 19 Merari had two sons: Mahli and Mushi. These are the clans of Levi with their descendants.

20 Amram married his father's sister Jochebed, who bore him Aaron and Moses. Amram lived 137 years. 21 Izhar had three sons: Korah, Nepheg, and

---

[h] THE LORD: See 3.14.

6.2, 3 Gn 17.1; 28.3; 35.11; Ex 3.13-15   **6.16-19** Nu 3.17-20; 26.57, 58; 1 Ch 6.16-19

Zichri. ²²Uzziel also had three sons: Mishael, Elzaphan, and Sithri.

²³Aaron married Elisheba, the daughter of Amminadab and sister of Nahshon; she bore him Nadab, Abihu, Eleazar, and Ithamar. ²⁴Korah had three sons: Assir, Elkanah, and Abiasaph; they were the ancestors of the divisions of the clan of Korah. ²⁵Eleazar, Aaron's son, married one of Putiel's daughters, who bore him Phinehas. These were the heads of the families and the clans of the tribe of Levi.

²⁶Aaron and Moses were the ones to whom the Lord said, "Lead the tribes of Israel out of Egypt." ²⁷They were the men who told the king of Egypt to free the Israelites.

The Lord's Command to Moses and Aaron

²⁸When the Lord spoke to Moses in the land of Egypt, ²⁹he said, "I am the Lord. Tell the king of Egypt everything I tell you."

³⁰But Moses answered, "You know that I am such a poor speaker; why should the king listen to me?"

7 The Lord said, "I am going to make you like God to the king, and your brother Aaron will speak to him as your prophet. ²Tell Aaron everything I command you, and he will tell the king to let the Israelites leave his country. ³⁻⁴But I will make the king stubborn, and he will not listen to you, no matter how many terrifying things I do in Egypt. Then I will bring severe punishment on Egypt and lead the tribes of my people out of the land. ⁵The Egyptians will then know that I am the Lord, when I raise my hand against them and bring the Israelites out of their country." ⁶Moses and Aaron did what the Lord commanded. ⁷At the time when they spoke to the king, Moses was eighty years old, and Aaron was eighty-three.

Aaron's Walking Stick

⁸The Lord said to Moses and Aaron, ⁹"If the king demands that you prove yourselves by performing a miracle, tell Aaron to take his walking stick and throw it down in front of the king, and it will turn into a snake." ¹⁰So Moses and Aaron went to the king and did as the Lord had commanded. Aaron threw his walking stick down in front of the king and his officers, and it turned into a snake. ¹¹Then the king called for his wise men and magicians, and by their magic they did the same thing. ¹²They threw down their walking sticks, and the sticks turned into snakes. But Aaron's stick swallowed theirs. ¹³The king, however, remained stubborn and, just as the Lord had said, the king would not listen to Moses and Aaron.

Disasters Strike Egypt
Blood

¹⁴Then the Lord said to Moses, "The king is very stubborn and refuses to let the people go. ¹⁵So go and meet him in the morning when he goes down to the Nile. Take with you the walking stick that was turned into a snake, and wait for him on the riverbank. ¹⁶Then say to the king, 'The Lord, the God of the Hebrews, sent me to tell you to let his people go, so that they can worship him in the desert. But until now you have not listened. ¹⁷Now, Your Majesty, the Lord says that you will find out who he is by what he is going to do. Look, I am going to strike the surface of the river with this stick, and the water will be turned into blood. ¹⁸The fish will die, and the river will stink so much that the Egyptians will not be able to drink from it.' "

¹⁹The Lord said to Moses, "Tell Aaron to take his stick and hold it out over all the rivers, canals, and pools in

7.3 Ac 7.36   **7.14-24** Ws 11.6-8   **7.17** Rev 16.4

Egypt. The water will become blood, and all over the land there will be blood, even in the wooden tubs and stone jars."

20 Then Moses and Aaron did as the LORD commanded. In the presence of the king and his officers, Aaron raised his stick and struck the surface of the river, and all the water in it was turned into blood. 21 The fish in the river died, and it smelled so bad that the Egyptians could not drink from it. There was blood everywhere in Egypt. 22 Then the king's magicians did the same thing by means of their magic, and the king was as stubborn as ever. Just as the LORD had said, the king refused to listen to Moses and Aaron. 23 Instead, he turned and went back to his palace without paying any attention even to this. 24 All the Egyptians dug along the bank of the river for drinking water, because they were not able to drink water from the river.

25 Seven days passed after the LORD struck the river.

Frogs

8 Then the LORD said to Moses, "Go to the king and tell him that the LORD says, 'Let my people go, so that they can worship me. 2 If you refuse, I will punish your country by covering it with frogs. 3 The Nile will be so full of frogs that they will leave it and go into your palace, your bedroom, your bed, the houses of your officials and your people, and even into your ovens and baking pans. 4 They will jump up on you, your people, and all your officials.' "

5 The LORD said to Moses, "Tell Aaron to hold out his walking stick over the rivers, the canals, and the pools, and make frogs come up and cover the land of Egypt." 6 So Aaron held it out over all the water, and the frogs came out and covered the land. 7 But the magicians used magic, and

They will jump up on you. (8.4)

they also made frogs come up on the land.

8 The king called for Moses and Aaron and said, "Pray to the LORD to take away these frogs, and I will let your people go, so that they can offer sacrifices to the LORD."

9 Moses replied, "I will be glad to pray for you. Just set the time when I am to pray for you, your officers, and your people. Then you will be rid of the frogs, and there will be none left except in the Nile."

10 The king answered, "Pray for me tomorrow."

Moses said, "I will do as you ask, and then you will know that there is no other god like the LORD, our God. 11 You, your officials, and your people will be rid of the frogs, and there will be none left except in the Nile." 12 Then Moses and Aaron left the king, and Moses prayed to the LORD to take away the frogs which he had brought on the king. 13 The LORD did as Moses asked, and the frogs in the houses, the courtyards, and the fields died. 14 The Egyptians piled them up in great heaps, until the land stank with them. 15 When the king saw that the frogs were dead, he became stubborn again and, just as the LORD had said, the king would not listen to Moses and Aaron.

Gnats

16 The LORD said to Moses, "Tell Aaron to strike the ground with his stick, and all over the land of Egypt the dust will change into gnats." **17** So Aaron struck the ground with his stick, and all the dust in Egypt was turned into gnats, which covered the people and the animals. **18** The magicians tried to use their magic to make gnats appear, but they failed. There were gnats everywhere, **19** and the magicians said to the king, "God has done this!" But the king was stubborn and, just as the LORD had said, the king would not listen to Moses and Aaron.

Flies

20 The LORD said to Moses, "Early tomorrow morning go and meet the king as he goes to the river, and tell him that the LORD says, 'Let my people go, so that they can worship me. **21** I warn you that if you refuse, I will punish you by sending flies on you, your officials, and your people. The houses of the Egyptians will be full of flies, and the ground will be covered with them. **22** But I will spare the region of Goshen, where my people live, so that there will be no flies there. I will do this so that you will know that I, the LORD, am at work in this land. **23** I will make a distinction[i] between my people and your people. This miracle will take place tomorrow.' " **24** The LORD sent great swarms of flies into the king's palace and the houses of his officials. The whole land of Egypt was brought to ruin by the flies.

25 Then the king called for Moses and Aaron and said, "Go and offer sacrifices to your God here in this country."

26 "It would not be right to do that," Moses answered, "because the Egyptians would be offended by our sacrificing the animals that we offer to the LORD our God. If we use these animals and offend the Egyptians by sacrificing them where they can see us, they will stone us to death. **27** We must travel three days into the desert to offer sacrifices to the LORD our God, just as he commanded us."

28 The king said, "I will let you go to sacrifice to the LORD, your God, in the desert, if you do not go very far. Pray for me."

29 Moses answered, "As soon as I leave, I will pray to the LORD that tomorrow the flies will leave you, your officials, and your people. But you must not deceive us again and prevent the people from going to sacrifice to the LORD."

30 Moses left the king and prayed to the LORD, **31** and the LORD did as Moses asked. The flies left the king, his officials, and his people; not one fly remained. **32** But even this time the king became stubborn, and again he would not let the people go.

Death of the Animals

9 The LORD said to Moses, "Go to the king and tell him that the LORD, the God of the Hebrews, says, 'Let my people go, so that they may worship me. **2** If you again refuse to let them go, **3** I will punish you by sending a terrible disease on all your animals — your horses, donkeys, camels, cattle, sheep, and goats. **4** I will make a distinction between the animals of the Israelites and those of the Egyptians, and no animal that belongs to the Israelites will die. **5** I, the LORD, have set tomorrow as the time when I will do this.' "

6 The next day the LORD did as he had said, and all the animals of the Egyptians died, but not one of the animals of the Israelites died. **7** The king asked what had happened and was told that none of the animals of the

---

i Some ancient translations a distinction; *Hebrew* redemption.
8.19 Lk 11.20

Israelites had died. But he was stubborn and would not let the people go.

Boils

8 Then the LORD said to Moses and Aaron, "Take a few handfuls of ashes from a furnace; Moses is to throw them into the air in front of the king. 9 They will spread out like fine dust over all the land of Egypt, and everywhere they will produce boils that become open sores on the people and the animals." 10 So they got some ashes and stood before the king; Moses threw them into the air, and they produced boils that became open sores on the people and the animals. 11 The magicians were not able to appear before Moses, because they were covered with boils, like all the other Egyptians. 12 But the LORD made the king stubborn and, just as the LORD had said, the king would not listen to Moses and Aaron.

Hail

13 The LORD then said to Moses, "Early tomorrow morning meet with the king and tell him that the LORD, the God of the Hebrews, says, 'Let my people go, so that they may worship me. 14 This time I will punish not only your officials and your people, but I will punish you as well, so that you may know that there is no one like me in all the world. 15 If I had raised my hand to strike you and your people with disease, you would have been completely destroyed. 16 But to show you my power I have let you live so that my fame might spread over the whole world. 17 Yet you are still arrogant and refuse to let my people go. 18 This time tomorrow I will cause a heavy hailstorm, such as Egypt has never known in all its history. 19 Now give orders for your livestock and everything else you have in the open to be put under shelter. Hail will fall on the people and animals left out-side unprotected, and they will all die.' " 20 Some of the king's officials were afraid because of what the LORD had said, and they brought their slaves and animals indoors for shelter. 21 Others, however, paid no attention to the LORD's warning and left their slaves and animals out in the open.

22 Then the LORD said to Moses, "Raise your hand toward the sky, and hail will fall over the whole land of Egypt — on the people, the animals, and all the plants in the fields." 23 So Moses raised his stick toward the sky, and the LORD sent thunder and hail, and lightning struck the ground. The LORD sent 24 a heavy hailstorm, with lightning flashing back and forth. It was the worst storm that Egypt had ever known in all its history. 25 All over Egypt the hail struck down everything in the open, including all the people and all the animals. It beat down all the plants in the fields and broke all the trees. 26 The region of Goshen, where the Israelites lived, was the only place where there was no hail.

27 The king sent for Moses and Aaron and said, "This time I have sinned; the LORD is in the right, and my people and I are in the wrong. 28 Pray to the LORD! We have had enough of this thunder and hail! I promise to let you go; you don't have to stay here any longer."

29 Moses said to him, "As soon as I go out of the city, I will lift up my hands in prayer to the LORD. The thunder will stop, and there will be no more hail, so that you may know that the earth belongs to the LORD. 30 But I know that you and your officials do not yet fear the LORD God."

31 The flax and the barley were ruined, because the barley was ripe, and the flax was budding. 32 But none of the wheat was ruined, because it ripens later.

33 Moses left the king, went out of the city, and lifted up his hands in prayer to

the LORD. The thunder, the hail, and the rain all stopped. ³⁴When the king saw what had happened, he sinned again. He and his officials remained as stubborn as ever ³⁵and, just as the LORD had foretold through Moses, the king would not let the Israelites go.

Locusts

10 Then the LORD said to Moses, "Go and see the king. I have made him and his officials stubborn, in order that I may perform these miracles among them ²and in order that you may be able to tell your children and grandchildren how I made fools of the Egyptians when I performed the miracles. All of you will know that I am the LORD."

³So Moses and Aaron went to the king and said to him, "The LORD, the God of the Hebrews, says, 'How much longer will you refuse to submit to me? Let my people go, so that they may worship me. ⁴If you keep on refusing, then I will bring locusts into your country tomorrow. ⁵There will be so many that they will completely cover the ground. They will eat everything that the hail did not destroy, even the trees that are left. ⁶They will fill your palaces and the houses of all your officials and all your people. They will be worse than anything your ancestors ever saw.' " Then Moses turned and left.

⁷The king's officials said to him, "How long is this man going to give us trouble? Let the Israelite men go, so that they can worship the LORD their God. Don't you realize that Egypt is ruined?"

⁸So Moses and Aaron were brought back to the king, and he said to them, "You may go and worship the LORD your God. But exactly who will go?"

⁹Moses answered, "We will all go, including our children and our old people. We will take our sons and daughters, our sheep and goats, and our cattle, because we must hold a festival to honor the LORD."

¹⁰The king said, "I swear by the LORD that I will never let you take your women and children! It is clear that you are plotting to revolt. ¹¹No! Only the men may go and worship the LORD if that is what you want." With that, Moses and Aaron were driven out of the king's presence.

¹²Then the LORD said to Moses, "Raise your hand over the land of Egypt to bring the locusts. They will come and eat everything that grows, everything that has survived the hail." ¹³So Moses raised his stick, and the LORD caused a wind from the east to blow on the land all that day and all that night. By morning it had brought the locusts. ¹⁴They came in swarms and settled over the whole country. It was the largest swarm of locusts that had ever been seen or that ever would be seen again. ¹⁵They covered the ground until it was black with them; they ate everything that the hail had left, including all the fruit on the trees. Not a green thing was left on any tree or plant in all the land of Egypt.

¹⁶Then the king hurriedly called Moses and Aaron and said, "I have sinned against the LORD your God and against you. ¹⁷Now forgive my sin this one time and pray to the LORD your God to take away this fatal punishment from me." ¹⁸Moses left the king and prayed to the LORD. ¹⁹And the LORD changed the east wind into a very strong west wind, which picked up the locusts and blew them into the Gulf of Suez.ʲ Not one locust was left in all of Egypt. ²⁰But the LORD made the king stubborn, and he did not let the Israelites go.

ʲ GULF OF SUEZ: *See Red Sea in 13.18.*
10.14, 15 Rev 9.2, 3

Darkness

21 The LORD then said to Moses, "Raise your hand toward the sky, and a darkness thick enough to be felt will cover the land of Egypt." **22** Moses raised his hand toward the sky, and there was total darkness throughout Egypt for three days. **23** The Egyptians could not see each other, and no one left his house during that time. But the Israelites had light where they were living.

24 The king called Moses and said, "You may go and worship the LORD; even your women and children may go with you. But your sheep, goats, and cattle must stay here."

25 Moses answered, "Then you would have to provide us with animals for sacrifices and burnt offerings to offer to the LORD our God. **26** No, we will take our animals with us; not one will be left behind. We ourselves must select the animals with which to worship the LORD our God. And until we get there, we will not know what animals to sacrifice to him."

27 The LORD made the king stubborn, and he would not let them go. **28** He said to Moses, "Get out of my sight! Don't let me ever see you again! On the day I do, you will die!"

29 "You are right," Moses answered. "You will never see me again."

Moses Announces the Death of the First-Born

11 Then the LORD said to Moses, "I will send only one more punishment on the king of Egypt and his people. After that he will let you leave. In fact, he will drive all of you out of here. **2** Now speak to the people of Israel and tell all of them to ask their neighbors for gold and silver jewelry." **3** The LORD made the Egyptians respect the Israelites. Indeed, the officials and all the people considered Moses to be a very great man.

4 Moses then said to the king, "The LORD says, 'At about midnight I will go through Egypt, **5** and every first-born son in Egypt will die, from the king's son, who is heir to the throne, to the son of the slave woman who grinds grain. The first-born of all the cattle will die also. **6** There will be loud crying all over Egypt, such as there has never been before or ever will be again. **7** But not even a dog will bark at the Israelites or their animals. Then you will know that I, the LORD, make a distinction between the Egyptians and the Israelites.' " **8** Moses concluded by saying, "All your officials will come to me and bow down before me, and they will beg me to take all my people and go away. After that, I will leave." Then in great anger Moses left the king.

9 The LORD had said to Moses, "The king will continue to refuse to listen to you, in order that I may do more of my miracles in Egypt." **10** Moses and Aaron performed all these miracles before the king, but the LORD made him stubborn, and he would not let the Israelites leave his country.

The Passover

12 The LORD spoke to Moses and Aaron in Egypt: **2** "This month is to be the first month of the year for you. **3** Give these instructions to the whole community of Israel: On the tenth day of this month each man must choose either a lamb or a young goat for his household. **4** If his family is too small to eat a whole animal, he and his next-door neighbor may share an animal, in proportion to the number of people and the amount that each person can eat.

10.21-23 Ws 17.1-21   **10.22** Ps 105.28; Rev 16.10   **12.1-13** Lv 23.5; Nu 9.1-5; 28.16; Dt 16.1, 2

⁵You may choose either a sheep or a goat, but it must be a one-year-old male without any defects. ⁶Then, on the evening of the fourteenth day of the month, the whole community of Israel will kill the animals. ⁷The people are to take some of the blood and put it on the doorposts and above the doors of the houses in which the animals are to be eaten. ⁸That night the meat is to be roasted, and eaten with bitter herbs and with bread made without yeast. ⁹Do not eat any of it raw or boiled, but eat it roasted whole, including the head, the legs, and the internal organs. ¹⁰You must not leave any of it until morning; if any is left over, it must be burned. ¹¹You are to eat it quickly, for you are to be dressed for travel, with your sandals on your feet and your walking stick in your hand. It is the Passover Festival to honor me, the LORD.

¹²"On that night I will go through the land of Egypt, killing every first-born male, both human and animal, and punishing all the gods of Egypt. I am the LORD. ¹³The blood on the doorposts will be a sign to mark the houses in which you live. When I see the blood, I will pass over you and will not harm you when I punish the Egyptians. ¹⁴You must celebrate this day as a religious festival to remind you of what I, the LORD, have done. Celebrate it for all time to come."

The Festival of Unleavened Bread

¹⁵The LORD said, "For seven days you must not eat any bread made with yeast — eat only unleavened bread. On the first day you are to get rid of all the yeast in your houses, for if anyone during those seven days eats bread made with yeast, he shall no longer be considered one of my people. ¹⁶On the first day and again on the seventh day you are to meet for worship. No work is to be done on those days, but you may prepare food. ¹⁷Keep this festival, because it was on this day that I brought your tribes out of Egypt. For all time to come you must celebrate this day as a festival. ¹⁸From the evening of the fourteenth day of the first month to the evening of the twenty-first day, you must not eat any bread made with yeast. ¹⁹⁻²⁰For seven days no yeast must be found in your houses, for if anyone, native-born or foreign, eats bread made with yeast, he shall no longer be considered one of my people."

The First Passover

²¹Moses called for all the leaders of Israel and said to them, "Each of you is to choose a lamb or a young goat and kill it, so that your families can celebrate Passover. ²²Take a sprig of hyssop, dip it in the bowl containingᵏ the animal's blood, and wipe the blood on the doorposts and the beam above the door of your house. Not one of you is to leave the house until morning. ²³When the LORD goes through Egypt to kill the Egyptians, he will see the blood on the beams and the doorposts and will not let the Angel of Death enter your houses and kill you. ²⁴You and your children must obey these rules forever. ²⁵When you enter the land that the LORD has promised to give you, you must perform this ritual. ²⁶When your children ask you, 'What does this ritual mean?' ²⁷you will answer, 'It is the sacrifice of Passover to honor the LORD, because he passed over the houses of the Israelites in Egypt. He killed the Egyptians, but spared us.'"

The Israelites knelt down and worshiped. ²⁸Then they went and did what the LORD had commanded Moses and Aaron.

ᵏ dip it in the bowl containing; *or* put it on the threshold covered with.
12.14-20 Ex 23.15; 34.18; Lv 23.6-8; Nu 28.17-25; Dt 16.3-8   **12.23** He 11.28

The people filled their baking pans with unleavened dough. (12.34)

The Death of the First-Born

29 At midnight the LORD killed all the first-born sons in Egypt, from the king's son, who was heir to the throne, to the son of the prisoner in the dungeon; all the first-born of the animals were also killed. **30** That night, the king, his officials, and all the other Egyptians were awakened. There was loud crying throughout Egypt, because there was not one home in which there was not a dead son. **31** That same night the king sent for Moses and Aaron and said, "Get out, you and your Israelites! Leave my country; go and worship the LORD, as you asked. **32** Take your sheep, goats, and cattle, and leave. Also pray for a blessing on me."

33 The Egyptians urged the people to hurry and leave the country; they said, "We will all be dead if you don't leave." **34** So the people filled their baking pans with unleavened dough, wrapped them in clothing, and carried them on their shoulders. **35** The Israelites had done as Moses had said, and had asked the Egyptians for gold and silver jewelry and for clothes. **36** The LORD made the Egyptians respect the people and give them what they asked for. In this way the Israelites carried away the wealth of the Egyptians.

The Israelites Leave Egypt

37 The Israelites set out on foot from Rameses for Sukkoth. There were about 600,000 men, not counting women and children. **38** A large number of other people and many sheep, goats, and cattle also went with them. **39** They baked unleavened bread from the dough that they had brought out of Egypt, for they had been driven out of Egypt so suddenly that they did not have time to get their food ready or to prepare leavened dough.

40 The Israelites had lived in Egypt for 430 years. **41** On the day the 430 years ended, all the tribes of the LORD's people left Egypt. **42** It was a night when the LORD kept watch to bring them out of Egypt; this same night is dedicated to the LORD for all time to come as a night when the Israelites must keep watch.

Regulations about Passover

43 The LORD said to Moses and Aaron, "These are the Passover regulations: No foreigner shall eat the Passover meal, **44** but any slave that you have bought may eat it if you circumcise him first. **45** No temporary resident or hired

12.29 Ex 4.22-32   **12.35, 36** Ex 3.21, 22   **12.40** Gn 15.13; Ga 3.17

worker may eat it. ⁴⁶The whole meal must be eaten in the house in which it was prepared; it must not be taken outside. And do not break any of the animal's bones. ⁴⁷The whole community of Israel must celebrate this festival, ⁴⁸but no uncircumcised man may eat it. If a foreigner has settled among you and wants to celebrate Passover to honor the LORD, you must first circumcise all the males of his household. He is then to be treated like a native-born Israelite and may join in the festival. ⁴⁹The same regulations apply to native-born Israelites and to foreigners who settle among you." ⁵⁰All the Israelites obeyed and did what the LORD had commanded Moses and Aaron. ⁵¹On that day the LORD brought the Israelite tribes out of Egypt.

Dedication of the First-Born

13 The LORD said to Moses, ²"Dedicate all the first-born males to me, for every first-born male Israelite and every first-born male animal belongs to me."

The Festival of Unleavened Bread

³Moses said to the people, "Remember this day — the day on which you left Egypt, the place where you were slaves. This is the day the LORD brought you out by his great power. No leavened bread is to be eaten. ⁴You are leaving Egypt on this day in the first month, the month of Abib. ⁵The LORD solemnly promised your ancestors to give you the land of the Canaanites, the Hittites, the Amorites, the Hivites, and the Jebusites. When he brings you into that rich and fertile land, you must celebrate this festival in the first month of every year. ⁶For seven days you must eat unleavened bread and on the seventh day there is to be a festival to honor the LORD. ⁷For seven days you must not eat any bread made with yeast; there must

be no yeast or leavened bread anywhere in your land. ⁸When the festival begins, explain to your sons that you do all this because of what the LORD did for you when you left Egypt. ⁹This observance will be a reminder, like something tied on your hand or on your forehead; it will remind you to continue to recite and study the Law of the LORD, because the LORD brought you out of Egypt by his great power. ¹⁰Celebrate this festival at the appointed time each year.

The First-Born

¹¹"The LORD will bring you into the land of the Canaanites, which he solemnly promised to you and your ancestors. When he gives it to you, ¹²you must offer every first-born male to the LORD. Every first-born male of your animals belongs to the LORD, ¹³but you must buy back from him every first-born male donkey by offering a lamb in its place. If you do not want to buy back the donkey, break its neck. You must buy back every first-born male child of yours. ¹⁴In the future, when your son asks what this observance means, you will answer him, 'By using great power the LORD brought us out of Egypt, the place where we were slaves. ¹⁵When the king of Egypt was stubborn and refused to let us go, the LORD killed every first-born male in the land of Egypt, both human and animal. That is why we sacrifice every first-born male animal to the LORD, but buy back our first-born sons. ¹⁶This observance will be a reminder, like something tied on our hands or on our foreheads; it will remind us that the LORD brought us out of Egypt by his great power.' "

The Pillar of Cloud and the Pillar of Fire

¹⁷When the king of Egypt let the people go, God did not take them by the

12.46 Nu 9.12; Jn 19.36   **13.2** Nu 3.13; Lk 2.23   **13.12** Ex 34.19, 20; Lk 2.23

The LORD went in front of them. (13.21)

road that goes up the coast to Philistia, although it was the shortest way. God thought, "I do not want the people to change their minds and return to Egypt when they see that they are going to have to fight." ¹⁸ Instead, he led them in a roundabout way through the desert toward the Red Sea.*ˡ* The Israelites were armed for battle.

¹⁹ Moses took the body of Joseph with him, as Joseph had made the Israelites solemnly promise to do. Joseph had

said, "When God rescues you, you must carry my body with you from this place."

²⁰ The Israelites left Sukkoth and camped at Etham on the edge of the desert. ²¹ During the day the LORD went in front of them in a pillar of cloud to show them the way, and during the night he went in front of them in a pillar of fire to give them light, so that they could travel night and day. ²² The pillar of cloud was always in front of the people

---

ˡ RED SEA: *(in Hebrew literally "Sea of Reeds") evidently referred to (1) a series of lakes and marshes between the head of the Gulf of Suez and the Mediterranean, the region generally regarded as the site of the events described in Exodus 13, and was also used to designate (2) the Gulf of Suez, and (3) the Gulf of Aqaba.*
13.19 Gn 50.25; Js 24.32 **13.22** Ws 10.17, 18; 18.3

during the day, and the pillar of fire at night.

Crossing the Red Sea

14 Then the LORD said to Moses, 2 "Tell the Israelites to turn back and camp in front of Pi Hahiroth, between Migdol and the Red Sea, near Baal Zephon. 3 The king will think that the Israelites are wandering around in the country and are closed in by the desert. 4 I will make him stubborn, and he will pursue you, and my victory over the king and his army will bring me honor. Then the Egyptians will know that I am the LORD." The Israelites did as they were told.

5 When the king of Egypt was told that the people had escaped, he and his officials changed their minds and said, "What have we done? We have let the Israelites escape, and we have lost them as our slaves!" 6 The king got his war chariot and his army ready. 7 He set out with all his chariots, including the six hundred finest, commanded by their officers. 8 The LORD made the king stubborn, and he pursued the Israelites, who were leaving triumphantly.*m* 9 The Egyptian army, with all the horses, chariots, and drivers, pursued them and caught up with them where they were camped by the Red Sea near Pi Hahiroth and Baal Zephon.

10 When the Israelites saw the king and his army marching against them, they were terrified and cried out to the LORD for help. 11 They said to Moses, "Weren't there any graves in Egypt? Did you have to bring us out here in the desert to die? Look what you have done by bringing us out of Egypt! 12 Didn't we tell you before we left that this would happen? We told you to leave us alone and let us go on being slaves of the Egyptians. It would be better to be slaves there than to die here in the desert."

13 Moses answered, "Don't be afraid! Stand your ground, and you will see what the LORD will do to save you today; you will never see these Egyptians again. 14 The LORD will fight for you, and all you have to do is keep still."

15 The LORD said to Moses, "Why are you crying out for help? Tell the people to move forward. 16 Lift up your walking stick and hold it out over the sea. The water will divide, and the Israelites will be able to walk through the sea on dry ground. 17 I will make the Egyptians so stubborn that they will go in after them, and I will gain honor by my victory over the king, his army, his chariots, and his drivers. 18 When I defeat them, the Egyptians will know that I am the LORD."

19 The angel of God, who had been in front of the army of Israel, moved and went to the rear. The pillar of cloud also moved until it was 20 between the Egyptians and the Israelites. The cloud made it dark for the Egyptians, but gave light to the people of Israel,*n* and so the armies could not come near each other all night.

21 Moses held out his hand over the sea, and the LORD drove the sea back with a strong east wind. It blew all night and turned the sea into dry land. The water was divided, 22 and the Israelites went through the sea on dry ground, with walls of water on both sides. 23 The Egyptians pursued them and went after them into the sea with all their horses, chariots, and drivers. 24 Just before dawn the LORD looked down from the pillar of fire and cloud at the Egyptian army and threw them into a panic. 25 He made the wheels of their chariots get stuck, so that they moved

---

m triumphantly; *or* under the protection of the LORD.   *n* *Probable text* The cloud . . . Israel; *Hebrew unclear.*

14.22 1 Co 10.1, 2; He 11.29

The Egyptians will know that I am the LORD. (14.18)

with great difficulty. The Egyptians said, "The LORD is fighting for the Israelites against us. Let's get out of here!"

²⁶ The LORD said to Moses, "Hold out your hand over the sea, and the water will come back over the Egyptians and their chariots and drivers." ²⁷ So Moses held out his hand over the sea, and at daybreak the water returned to its normal level. The Egyptians tried to escape from the water, but the LORD threw them into the sea. ²⁸ The water returned and covered the chariots, the

drivers, and all the Egyptian army that had followed the Israelites into the sea; not one of them was left. ²⁹ But the Israelites walked through the sea on dry ground, with walls of water on both sides.

³⁰ On that day the LORD saved the people of Israel from the Egyptians, and the Israelites saw them lying dead on the seashore. ³¹ When the Israelites saw the great power with which the LORD had defeated the Egyptians, they stood in awe of the LORD; and they had faith in the LORD and in his servant Moses.

EGYPT AND SINAI

© United Bible Societies, 1976

MEDITERRANEAN SEA

Jerusalem
Hebron
Beersheba
Gaza

CANAAN

Brook of Egypt

Nile Delta

Rameses
Goshen
Pithom
Heliopolis

E G Y P T

Memphis

Nile River

Migdol
Baal Zephon
Bitter Lakes

Wilderness of Shur

SEA OF REEDS (RED SEA)

Marah
Elim
Dophkah

Wilderness of Sin

MT. SINAI (HOREB)

Hazeroth

Sinai Peninsula

Wilderness of Paran

Mt. Shepher

Kadesh Barnea

Wilderness of Zin

Arad
Hormah

▲ MT. NEBO
Dibon
Ar of Moab
Arnon
Dead Sea

LAND OF THE MOABITES

Tophel
Zalmonah

LAND OF THE EDOMITES

Jotbathah

Eziongeber (Elath)

GULF OF AQABA

LAND OF MIDIAN

Miles   100
Kms   100
0

The Song of Moses

15 Then Moses and the Israelites sang this song to the LORD:

"I will sing to the LORD, because
    he has won a glorious
    victory;
  he has thrown the horses and
    their riders into the sea.
2 The LORD is my strong defender;
    he is the one who has
    saved me.
  He is my God, and I will
    praise him,
    my father's God, and I will
    sing about his greatness.
3 The LORD is a warrior;
    the LORD is his name.

4 "He threw Egypt's army and its
    chariots into the sea;
    the best of its officers were
    drowned in the Red Sea.
5 The deep sea covered them;
    they sank to the bottom like a
    stone.

6 "Your right hand, LORD, is
    awesome in power;
    it breaks the enemy in pieces.
7 In majestic triumph you overthrow
    your foes;
    your anger blazes out and
    burns them up like straw.
8 You blew on the sea and the
    water piled up high;
    it stood up straight like a wall;
    the deepest part of the sea
    became solid.
9 The enemy said, 'I will pursue
    them and catch them;
  I will divide their wealth and
    take all I want;
  I will draw my sword and take
    all they have.'
10 But one breath from you, LORD,
    and the Egyptians were
    drowned;

they sank like lead in the
    terrible water.

11 "LORD, who among the gods is
    like you?
  Who is like you, wonderful in
    holiness?
  Who can work miracles and
    mighty acts like yours?
12 You stretched out your right
    hand,
    and the earth swallowed our
    enemies.
13 Faithful to your promise, you led
    the people you had
    rescued;
    by your strength you guided
    them to your sacred land.
14 The nations have heard, and
    they tremble with fear;
    the Philistines are seized with
    terror.
15 The leaders of Edom are
    terrified;
    Moab's mighty men are
    trembling;
    the people of Canaan lose
    their courage.
16 Terror and dread fall upon them.
  They see your strength, O LORD,
    and stand helpless with fear
    until your people have
    marched past—
    the people you set free from
    slavery.
17 You bring them in and plant them
    on your mountain,
    the place that you, LORD, have
    chosen for your home,
    the Temple that you yourself
    have built.
18 You, LORD, will be king forever
    and ever."

The Song of Miriam

19 The Israelites walked through the sea on dry ground. But when the Egyptian chariots with their horses and driv-

15.1 Rev 15.3   **15.2** Ps 118.14; Is 12.2

ers went into the sea, the LORD brought the water back, and it covered them.

²⁰The prophet Miriam, Aaron's sister, took her tambourine, and all the women followed her, playing tambourines and dancing. ²¹Miriam sang for them:

"Sing to the LORD, because he
has won a glorious victory;
he has thrown the horses and
their riders into the sea."

Bitter Water

²²Then Moses led the people of Israel away from the Red Sea into the desert of Shur. For three days they walked through the desert, but found no water. ²³Then they came to a place called Marah, but the water there was so bitter that they could not drink it. That is why it was named Marah.ᵒ ²⁴The people complained to Moses and asked, "What are we going to drink?" ²⁵Moses prayed earnestly to the LORD, and the LORD showed him a piece of wood, which he threw into the water; and the water became fit to drink.

There the LORD gave them laws to live by, and there he also tested them. ²⁶He said, "If you will obey me completely by doing what I consider right and by keeping my commands, I will not punish you with any of the diseases that I brought on the Egyptians. I am the LORD, the one who heals you."

²⁷Next they came to Elim, where there were twelve springs and seventy palm trees; there they camped by the water.

The Manna and the Quails

16 The whole Israelite community set out from Elim, and on the fifteenth day of the second month after they had left Egypt, they came to the desert of Sin, which is between Elim and Sinai. ²There in the desert they all complained to Moses and Aaron ³and said to them, "We wish that the LORD had killed us in Egypt. There we could at least sit down and eat meat and as much other food as we wanted. But you have brought us out into this desert to starve us all to death."

⁴The LORD said to Moses, "Now I am going to cause food to rain down from the sky for all of you. The people must go out every day and gather enough for that day. In this way I can test them to find out if they will follow my instructions. ⁵On the sixth day they are to bring in twice as much as usual and prepare it."

⁶So Moses and Aaron said to all the Israelites, "This evening you will know that it was the LORD who brought you out of Egypt. ⁷In the morning you will see the dazzling light of the LORD's presence. He has heard your complaints against him — yes, against him, because we are only carrying out his instructions." ⁸Then Moses said, "It is the LORD who will give you meat to eat in the evening and as much bread as you want in the morning, because he has heard how much you have complained against him. When you complain against us, you are really complaining against the LORD."

⁹Moses said to Aaron, "Tell the whole community to come and stand before the LORD, because he has heard their complaints." ¹⁰As Aaron spoke to the whole community, they turned toward the desert, and suddenly the dazzling light of the LORD appeared in a cloud. ¹¹The LORD said to Moses, ¹²"I have heard the complaints of the Israelites. Tell them that at twilight they will have meat to eat, and in the morning they will have all the bread they want. Then they will know that I, the LORD, am their God."

¹³In the evening a large flock of quails flew in, enough to cover the

ᵒ MARAH: *This name in Hebrew means "bitter."*
15.25 Si 38.5   **16.4** Ws 16.20-29; Jn 6.31

camp, and in the morning there was dew all around the camp. [14] When the dew evaporated, there was something thin and flaky on the surface of the desert. It was as delicate as frost. [15] When the Israelites saw it, they didn't know what it was and asked each other, "What is it?"

Moses said to them, "This is the food that the LORD has given you to eat.

The food that the LORD has given you to eat (16.15)

[16] The LORD has commanded that each of you is to gather as much of it as he needs, two quarts for each member of his household."

[17] The Israelites did this, some gathering more, others less. [18] When they measured it, those who gathered much did not have too much, and those who gathered less did not have too little. Each had gathered just what he needed. [19] Moses said to them, "No one is to keep any of it for tomorrow." [20] But some of them did not listen to Moses and saved part of it. The next morning it was full of worms and smelled rotten, and Moses was angry with them. [21] Every morning each one gathered as much as he needed; and when the sun grew hot, what was left on the ground melted.

[22] On the sixth day they gathered twice as much food, four quarts for each person. All the leaders of the community came and told Moses about it, [23] and he said to them, "The LORD has commanded that tomorrow is a holy day of rest, dedicated to him. Bake today what you want to bake and boil what you want to boil. Whatever is left should be put aside and kept for tomorrow." [24] As Moses had commanded, they kept what was left until the next day; it did not spoil or get worms in it. [25] Moses said, "Eat this today, because today is the Sabbath, a day of rest dedicated to the LORD, and you will not find any food outside the camp. [26] You must gather food for six days, but on the seventh day, the day of rest, there will be none."

[27] On the seventh day some of the people went out to gather food, but they did not find any. [28] Then the LORD said to Moses, "How much longer will you people refuse to obey my commands? [29] Remember that I, the LORD, have given you a day of rest, and that is why on the sixth day I will always give you enough food for two days. Everyone is to stay where he is on the seventh day and not leave his home." [30] So the people did no work on the seventh day.

[31] The people of Israel called the food manna.[p] It was like a small white seed, and tasted like thin cakes made with honey. [32] Moses said, "The LORD has commanded us to save some manna, to be kept for our descendants, so that they can see the food which he gave us to eat in the desert when he brought us out of Egypt." [33] Moses said to Aaron, "Take a jar, put two quarts of manna in it, and place it in the LORD's presence to be kept for our descendants." [34] As the LORD had commanded Moses, Aaron put it in front of the Covenant

[p] MANNA: *This word sounds like the Hebrew for "what is it?" (see verse 15).*
16.15 1 Co 10.3   **16.18** 2 Co 8.15   **16.23** Ex 20.8-11   **16.31** Nu 11.7, 8   **16.33** He 9.4

They held his arms steady until the sun went down. (17.12)

Box, so that it could be kept. ³⁵ The Israelites ate manna for the next forty years, until they reached the land of Canaan, where they settled. (³⁶ The standard dry measure then in use equaled twenty quarts.)

Water from the Rock
(Numbers 20.1-13)

17 The whole Israelite community left the desert of Sin, moving from one place to another at the command of the LORD. They camped at Rephidim, but there was no water there to drink. ² They complained to Moses and said, "Give us water to drink."

Moses answered, "Why are you complaining? Why are you putting the LORD to the test?"

³ But the people were very thirsty and continued to complain to Moses. They said, "Why did you bring us out of Egypt? To kill us and our children and our livestock with thirst?"

⁴ Moses prayed earnestly to the LORD and said, "What can I do with these people? They are almost ready to stone me."

⁵ The LORD said to Moses, "Take some of the leaders of Israel with you, and go on ahead of the people. Take along the stick with which you struck the Nile. ⁶ I will stand before you on a rock at Mount Sinai. Strike the rock, and water will come out of it for the people to drink." Moses did so in the presence of the leaders of Israel.

⁷ The place was named Massah and Meribah,�q because the Israelites complained and put the LORD to the test when they asked, "Is the LORD with us or not?"

War with the Amalekites

⁸ The Amalekites came and attacked the Israelites at Rephidim. ⁹ Moses said to Joshua, "Pick out some men to go and fight the Amalekites tomorrow. I will stand on top of the hill holding the stick that God told me to carry." ¹⁰ Joshua did as Moses commanded him and went out to fight the Amalekites, while Moses, Aaron, and Hur went up to the top of the hill. ¹¹ As long as Moses held up his arms, the Israelites won, but when he put his arms down, the Amalekites started winning. ¹² When Moses' arms grew tired, Aaron and Hur brought a stone for him to sit on, while they stood beside him and held up his

arms, holding them steady until the sun went down. 13 In this way Joshua totally defeated the Amalekites.

14 Then the LORD said to Moses, "Write an account of this victory, so that it will be remembered. Tell Joshua that I will completely destroy the Amalekites." 15 Moses built an altar and named it "The LORD is my Banner." 16 He said, "Hold high the banner of the LORD! r The LORD will continue to fight against the Amalekites forever!"

Jethro Visits Moses

18 Moses' father-in-law Jethro, the priest of Midian, heard about everything that God had done for Moses and the people of Israel when he led them out of Egypt. 2 So he came to Moses, bringing with him Moses' wife Zipporah, who had been left behind, 3 and Gershom and Eliezer, her two sons. (Moses had said, "I have been a foreigner in a strange land"; so he had named one son Gershom.s 4 He had also said, "The God of my father helped me and saved me from being killed by the king of Egypt"; so he had named the other son Eliezer.t) 5 Jethro came with Moses' wife and her two sons into the desert where Moses was camped at the holy mountain. 6 He had sent word to Moses that they were coming, 7 so Moses went out to meet him, bowed before him, and kissed him. They asked about each other's health and then went into Moses' tent. 8 Moses told Jethro everything that the LORD had done to the king and the people of Egypt in order to rescue the Israelites. He also told him about the hardships the people had faced on the way and how the LORD had saved them. 9 When Jethro heard all this, he was happy 10 and said, "Praise the LORD, who saved

you from the king and the people of Egypt! Praise the LORD, who saved his people from slavery! 11 Now I know that the LORD is greater than all the gods, because he did this when the Egyptians treated the Israelites with such contempt." 12 Then Jethro brought an offering to be burned whole and other sacrifices to be offered to God; and Aaron and all the leaders of Israel went with him to eat the sacred meal as an act of worship.

The Appointment of Judges
(Deuteronomy 1.9-18)

13 The next day Moses was settling disputes among the people, and he was kept busy from morning till night. 14 When Jethro saw everything that Moses had to do, he asked, "What is all this that you are doing for the people? Why are you doing this all alone, with people standing here from morning till night to consult you?"

15 Moses answered, "I must do this because the people come to me to learn God's will. 16 When two people have a dispute, they come to me, and I decide which one of them is right, and I tell them God's commands and laws."

17 Then Jethro said, "You are not doing this right. 18 You will wear yourself out and these people as well. This is too much for you to do alone. 19 Now let me give you some good advice, and God will be with you. It is right for you to represent the people before God and bring their disputes to him. 20 You should teach them God's commands and explain to them how they should live and what they should do. 21 But in addition, you should choose some capable men and appoint them as leaders of the people: leaders of thousands, hundreds, fifties, and tens. They must be

r Probable text Hold . . . LORD; Hebrew unclear.   s GERSHOM: This name sounds like the Hebrew for "foreigner."   t ELIEZER: This name sounds like the Hebrew for "God helps me."

17.14 Dt 25.17-19; 1 S 15.2-9   **18.2, 3** Ex 2.21, 22   **18.3** Ac 7.29

God-fearing men who can be trusted and who cannot be bribed. ²²Let them serve as judges for the people on a permanent basis. They can bring all the difficult cases to you, but they themselves can decide all the smaller disputes. That will make it easier for you, as they share your burden. ²³If you do this, as God commands, you will not wear yourself out, and all these people can go home with their disputes settled."

²⁴Moses took Jethro's advice ²⁵and chose capable men from among all the Israelites. He appointed them as leaders of thousands, hundreds, fifties, and tens. ²⁶They served as judges for the people on a permanent basis, bringing the difficult cases to Moses but deciding the smaller disputes themselves.

²⁷Then Moses said good-bye to Jethro, and Jethro went back home.

The Israelites at Mount Sinai

19 ¹⁻²The people of Israel left Rephidim, and on the first day of the third month after they had left Egypt they came to the desert of Sinai. There they set up camp at the foot of Mount Sinai, ³and Moses went up the mountain to meet with God.

The LORD called to him from the mountain and told him to say to the Israelites, Jacob's descendants: ⁴"You saw what I, the LORD, did to the Egyptians and how I carried you as an eagle carries her young on her wings, and brought you here to me. ⁵Now, if you will obey me and keep my covenant, you will be my own people. The whole earth is mine, but you will be my chosen people, ⁶a people dedicated to me alone, and you will serve me as priests."

⁷So Moses went down and called the leaders of the people together and told them everything that the LORD had commanded him. ⁸Then all the people answered together, "We will do everything that the LORD has said," and Moses reported this to the LORD.

⁹The LORD said to Moses, "I will come to you in a thick cloud, so that the people will hear me speaking with you and will believe you from now on."

Moses told the LORD what the people had answered, ¹⁰and the LORD said to him, "Go to the people and tell them to spend today and tomorrow purifying themselves for worship. They must wash their clothes ¹¹and be ready the day after tomorrow. On that day I will come down on Mount Sinai, where all the people can see me. ¹²Mark a boundary around the mountain that the people must not cross, and tell them not to go up the mountain or even get near it. If any of you set foot on it, you are to be put to death; ¹³you must either be stoned or shot with arrows, without anyone touching you. This applies to both people and animals; they must be put to death. But when the trumpet is blown, then the people are to go up to the mountain."

¹⁴Then Moses came down the mountain and told the people to get ready for worship. So they washed their clothes, ¹⁵and Moses told them, "Be ready by the day after tomorrow and don't have sexual intercourse in the meantime."

¹⁶On the morning of the third day there was thunder and lightning, a thick cloud appeared on the mountain, and a very loud trumpet blast was heard. All the people in the camp trembled with fear. ¹⁷Moses led them out of the camp to meet God, and they stood at the foot of the mountain. ¹⁸All of Mount Sinai was covered with smoke, because the LORD had come down on it in fire. The smoke went up like the smoke of a furnace, and all the people trembled violently. ¹⁹The sound of the trumpet became louder and louder. Moses spoke, and God answered him

19.5, 6 1 P 2.9   **19.5** Dt 4.20; 7.6; 14.2; 26.18; Titus 2.14   **19.6** Rev 1.6; 5.10
19.12, 13 He 12.18-20   **19.16** Rev 4.5   **19.16-18** Dt 4.11, 12

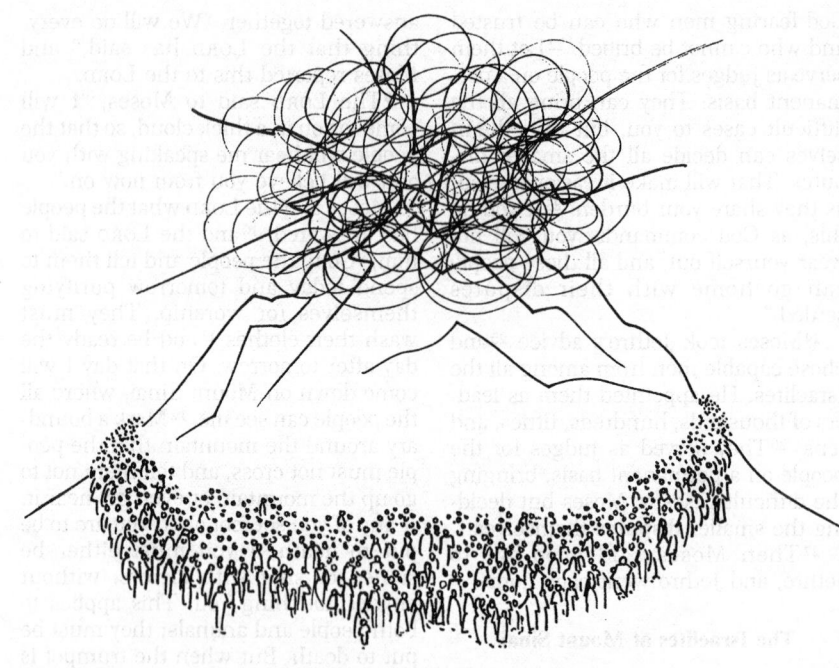

God answered him with thunder. (19.19)

with thunder. [20] The LORD came down on the top of Mount Sinai and called Moses to the top of the mountain. Moses went up [21] and the LORD said to him, "Go down and warn the people not to cross the boundary to come and look at me; if they do, many of them will die. [22] Even the priests who come near me must purify themselves, or I will punish them."

[23] Moses said to the LORD, "The people cannot come up, because you commanded us to consider the mountain sacred and to mark a boundary around it."

[24] The LORD replied, "Go down and bring Aaron back with you. But the priests and the people must not cross the boundary to come up to me, or I will

punish them." [25] Moses then went down to the people and told them what the LORD had said.

The Ten Commandments
(Deuteronomy 5.1-21)

20 God spoke, and these were his words: [2] "I am the LORD your God who brought you out of Egypt, where you were slaves.

[3] "Worship no god but me.

[4] "Do not make for yourselves images of anything in heaven or on earth or in the water under the earth. [5] Do not bow down to any idol or worship it, because I am the LORD your God and I tolerate no rivals. I bring punishment on those who hate me and on their descendants down to the third and fourth genera-

20.4, 5 Ex 34.17; Lv 19.4; 26.1; Dt 4.15-18; 27.15 **20.5, 6** Ex 34.6, 7; Nu 14.18; Dt 7.9, 10 tion. [6]But I show my love to thousands of generations[u] of those who love me and obey my laws.

[7]"Do not use my name for evil purposes, for I, the LORD your God, will punish anyone who misuses my name.

[8]"Observe the Sabbath and keep it holy. [9]You have six days in which to do your work, [10]but the seventh day is a day of rest dedicated to me. On that day no one is to work — neither you, your children, your slaves, your animals, nor the foreigners who live in your country. [11]In six days I, the LORD, made the earth, the sky, the seas, and everything in them, but on the seventh day I rested. That is why I, the LORD, blessed the Sabbath and made it holy.

[12]"Respect your father and your mother, so that you may live a long time in the land that I am giving you.

[13]"Do not commit murder.

[14]"Do not commit adultery.

[15]"Do not steal.

[16]"Do not accuse anyone falsely.

[17]"Do not desire another man's house; do not desire his wife, his slaves, his cattle, his donkeys, or anything else that he owns."

The People's Fear
(Deuteronomy 5.22-33)

[18]When the people heard the thunder and the trumpet blast and saw the lightning and the smoking mountain, they trembled with fear and stood a long way off. [19]They said to Moses, "If you speak to us, we will listen; but we are afraid that if God speaks to us, we will die."

[20]Moses replied, "Don't be afraid; God has only come to test you and make you keep on obeying him, so that you will not sin." [21]But the people continued to stand a long way off, and only Moses went near the dark cloud where God was.

Laws about Altars

[22]The LORD commanded Moses to tell the Israelites: "You have seen how I, the LORD, have spoken to you from heaven. [23]Do not make for yourselves gods of silver or gold to be worshiped in addition to me. [24]Make an altar of earth for me, and on it sacrifice your sheep and your cattle as offerings to be completely burned and as fellowship offerings. In every place that I set aside for you to worship me, I will come to you and bless you. [25]If you make an altar of stone for me, do not build it out of cut stones, because when you use a chisel on stones, you make them unfit for my use. [26]Do not build an altar for me with steps leading up to it; if you do, you will expose yourselves as you go up the steps.

The Treatment of Slaves
(Deuteronomy 15.12-18)

21 "Give the Israelites the following laws: [2]If you buy a Hebrew slave, he shall serve you for six years. In the seventh year he is to be set free without having to pay anything. [3]If he was unmarried when he became your slave, he is not to take a wife with him when he leaves; but if he was married when he became your slave, he may take his wife with him. [4]If his master gave him a wife and she bore him sons

---

[u] thousands of generations; *or* thousands.

20.7 Lv 19.12   **20.8** Ex 16.23-30; 31.12-14   **20.9, 10** Ex 23.12; 31.15; 34.21; 35.2; Lv 23.3   **20.11** Gn 2.1-3; Ex 31.17   **20.12 a** Dt 27.16; Mt 15.4; 19.19; Mk 7.10; 10.19; Lk 18.20; Eph 6.2; **b** Eph 6.3   **20.13** Gn 9.6; Lv 24.17; Mt 5.21; 19.18; Mk 10.19; Lk 18.20; Ro 13.9; Jas 2.11   **20.14** Lv 20.10; Mt 5.27; 19.18; Mk 10.19; Lk 18.20; Ro 13.9; Jas 2.11   **20.15** Lv 19.11; Mt 19.18; Mk 10.19; Lk 18.20; Ro 13.9   **20.16** Ex 23.1; Mt 19.18; Mk 10.19; Lk 18.20   **20.17** Ro 7.7; 13.9   **20.18, 19** He 12.18, 19   **20.25** Dt 27.5-7; Js 8.31   **21.2-6** Lv 25.39-46 or daughters, the woman and her children belong to the master, and the man is to leave by himself. [5] But if the slave declares that he loves his master, his wife, and his children and does not want to be set free, [6] then his master shall take him to the place of worship. There he is to make him stand against the door or the doorpost and put a hole through his ear. Then he will be his slave for life.

[7] "If a man sells his daughter as a slave, she is not to be set free, as male slaves are. [8] If she is sold to someone who intends to make her his wife, but he doesn't like her, then she is to be sold back to her father; her master cannot sell her to foreigners, because he has treated her unfairly. [9] If a man buys a female slave to give to his son, he is to treat her like a daughter. [10] If a man takes a second wife, he must continue to give his first wife the same amount of food and clothing and the same rights that she had before. [11] If he does not fulfill these duties to her, he must set her free and not receive any payment.

Laws about Violent Acts

[12] "Whoever hits someone and kills him is to be put to death. [13] But if it was an accident and he did not mean to kill him, he can escape to a place which I will choose for you, and there he will be safe. [14] But when someone gets angry and deliberately kills someone else, he is to be put to death, even if he has run to my altar for safety.

[15] "Whoever hits his father or his mother is to be put to death.

[16] "Whoever kidnaps someone, either to sell him or to keep him as a slave, is to be put to death.

[17] "Whoever curses his father or his mother is to be put to death.

[18-19] "If there is a fight and someone hits someone else with a stone or with his fist, but does not kill him, he is not to be punished. If the one who was hit has to stay in bed, but later is able to get up and walk outside with the help of a cane, the one who hit him is to pay for his lost time and take care of him until he gets well.

[20] "If a slave owner takes a stick and beats his slave, whether male or female, and the slave dies on the spot, the owner is to be punished. [21] But if the slave does not die for a day or two, the master is not to be punished. The loss of his property is punishment enough.

[22] "If some men are fighting and hurt a pregnant woman so that she loses her child, but she is not injured in any other way, the one who hurt her is to be fined whatever amount the woman's husband demands, subject to the approval of the judges. [23] But if the woman herself is injured, the punishment shall be life for life, [24] eye for eye, tooth for tooth, hand for hand, foot for foot, [25] burn for burn, wound for wound, bruise for bruise.

[26] "If someone hits his male or female slave in the eye and puts it out, he is to free the slave as payment for the eye. [27] If he knocks out a tooth, he is to free the slave as payment for the tooth.

The Responsibility of Owners

[28] "If a bull gores someone to death, it is to be stoned, and its flesh shall not be eaten; but its owner is not to be punished. [29] But if the bull had been in the habit of attacking people and its owner had been warned, but did not keep it penned up — then if it gores someone to death, it is to be stoned, and its owner is to be put to death also. [30] However, if the owner is allowed to pay a fine to save his life, he must pay the full amount required. [31] If the bull kills a boy or a girl, the same rule applies. [32] If

21.12 Lv 24.17   **21.13** Nu 35.10-34; Dt 19.1-13; Js 20.1-9   **21.16** Dt 24.7   **21.17** Lv 20.9;
Mt 15.4; Mk 7.10   **21.24** Lv 24.19, 20; Dt 19.21; Mt 5.38

the bull kills a male or female slave, its owner shall pay the owner of the slave thirty pieces of silver, and the bull shall be stoned to death.

33"If someone takes the cover off a pit or if he digs one and does not cover it, and a bull or a donkey falls into it, 34 he must pay for the animal. He is to pay the money to the owner and may keep the dead animal. 35 If someone's bull kills someone else's bull, the two of them shall sell the live bull and divide the money; they shall also divide up the meat from the dead animal. 36 But if it was known that the bull had been in the habit of attacking and its owner did not keep it penned up, he must make good the loss by giving the other man a live bull, but he may keep the dead animal.

Laws about Repayment

22 "If someone steals a cow or a sheep and kills it or sells it, he must pay five cows for one cow and four sheep for one sheep. 2-4 He must pay for what he stole. If he owns nothing, he shall be sold as a slave to pay for what he has stolen. If the stolen animal, whether a cow, a donkey, or a sheep, is found alive in his possession, he shall pay two for one.

"If a thief is caught breaking into a house at night and is killed, the one who killed him is not guilty of murder. But if it happens during the day, he is guilty of murder.

5"If someone lets his animals graze in a field or a vineyard and they stray away and eat up the crops*v* growing in someone else's field, he must make good the loss with the crops from his own fields or vineyards.

6"If someone starts a fire in his own field and it spreads through the weeds to someone else's field and burns up grain that is growing or that has been cut and stacked, the one who started the fire is to pay for the damage.

They . . . eat up the crops growing in someone else's field. (22.5)

7"If anyone agrees to keep someone else's money or other valuables for him and they are stolen from his house, the thief, if found, shall repay double. 8 But if the thief is not found, the one who was keeping the valuables is to be brought to the place of worship and there he must take an oath that he has not stolen the other one's property.

9"In every case of a dispute about property, whether it involves cattle, donkeys, sheep, clothing, or any other lost object, the two people claiming the property shall be taken to the place of worship. The one whom God declares to be guilty shall pay double to the other one.

10"If anyone agrees to keep someone else's donkey, cow, sheep, or other animal for him, and the animal dies or is injured or is carried off in a raid, and if there was no witness, 11 the man must go to the place of worship and take an oath that he has not stolen the other man's animal. If the animal was not stolen, the owner shall accept the loss, and the other man need not repay him; 12 but if the animal was stolen, the man must repay the owner. 13 If it was killed by wild animals, the man is to bring the remains as evidence; he need not pay for what has been killed by wild animals.

14"If anyone borrows an animal from

---

v If . . . crops; *or* If someone burns off a field or a vineyard, and lets the fire get out of control and burn up the crops.

someone else and it is injured or dies when its owner is not present, he must pay for it. [15] But if that happens when the owner is present, he need not repay. If it is a rented animal, the loss is covered by the rental price.

Moral and Religious Laws

[16] "If a man seduces a virgin who is not engaged, he must pay the bride price for her and marry her. [17] But if her father refuses to let him marry her, he must pay the father a sum of money equal to the bride price for a virgin.

[18] "Put to death any woman who practices magic.

[19] "Put to death any man who has sexual relations with an animal.

[20] "Condemn to death anyone who offers sacrifices to any god except to me, the LORD.

[21] "Do not mistreat or oppress a foreigner; remember that you were foreigners in Egypt. [22] Do not mistreat any widow or orphan. [23] If you do, I, the LORD, will answer them when they cry out to me for help, [24] and I will become angry and kill you in war. Your wives will become widows, and your children will be fatherless.

[25] "If you lend money to any of my people who are poor, do not act like a moneylender and require him to pay interest. [26] If you take someone's cloak as a pledge that he will pay you, you must give it back to him before the sun sets, [27] because it is the only covering he has to keep him warm. What else can he sleep in? When he cries out to me for help, I will answer him because I am merciful.

[28] "Do not speak evil of God, [w] and do not curse a leader of your people.

[29] "Give me the offerings from your grain, your wine, and your olive oil when they are due.

"Give me your first-born sons. [30] Give me the first-born of your cattle and your sheep. Let the first-born male stay with its mother for seven days, and on the eighth day offer it to me.

[31] "You are my people, so you must not eat the meat of any animal that has been killed by wild animals; instead, give it to the dogs.

Justice and Fairness

23 "Do not spread false rumors, and do not help a guilty person by giving false testimony. [2] Do not follow the majority when they do wrong or when they give testimony that perverts justice. [3] Do not show partiality to a poor person at his trial.

[4] "If you happen to see your enemy's cow or donkey running loose, take it back to him. [5] If his donkey has fallen under its load, help him get the donkey to its feet again; don't just walk off.

[6] "Do not deny justice to a poor person when he appears in court. [7] Do not make false accusations, and do not put an innocent person to death, for I will condemn anyone who does such an evil thing. [8] Do not accept a bribe, for a bribe makes people blind to what is right and ruins the cause of those who are innocent.

[9] "Do not mistreat a foreigner; you know how it feels to be a foreigner, because you were foreigners in Egypt.

The Seventh Year and the Seventh Day

[10] "For six years plant your land and gather in what it produces. [11] But in the seventh year let it rest, and do not har-

---

w God; *or* the judges.

22.16, 17 Dt 22.28, 29   **22.18** Dt 18.10, 11   **22.19** Lv 18.23; 20.15, 16; Dt 27.21
22.20 Dt 17.2-7   **22.21, 22** Ex 23.9; Lv 19.33, 34; Dt 24.17, 18; 27.19   **22.25** Lv 25.35-38;
Dt 15.7-11; 23.19, 20   **22.26, 27** Dt 24.10-13   **22.28** Ac 23.5   **22.31** Lv 17.15
23.1 Ex 20.16; Lv 19.11, 12; Dt 5.20   **23.3** Lv 19.15   **23.4, 5** Dt 22.1-4   **23.6-8** Lv 19.15;
Dt 16.19   **23.9** Ex 22.21; Lv 19.33, 34; Dt 24.17, 18; 27.19   **23.10, 11** Lv 25.1-7

vest anything that grows on it. The poor may eat what grows there, and the wild animals can have what is left. Do the same with your vineyards and your olive trees.

12"Work six days a week, but do no work on the seventh day, so that your slaves and the foreigners who work for you and even your animals can rest.

13"Listen to everything that I, the LORD, have said to you. Do not pray to other gods; do not even mention their names.

The Three Great Festivals
(Exodus 34.18-26; Deuteronomy 16.1-17)

14"Celebrate three festivals a year to honor me. 15 In the month of Abib, the month in which you left Egypt, celebrate the Festival of Unleavened Bread in the way that I commanded you. Do not eat any bread made with yeast during the seven days of this festival. Never come to worship me without bringing an offering.

16"Celebrate the Harvest Festival when you begin to harvest your crops.

"Celebrate the Festival of Shelters in the autumn, when you gather the fruit from your vineyards and orchards. 17 Every year at these three festivals all your men must come to worship me, the Lord your God.

18"Do not offer bread made with yeast when you sacrifice an animal to me. The fat of animals sacrificed to me during these festivals is not to be left until the following morning.

19"Each year bring to the house of the LORD your God the first grain that you harvest.

"Do not cook a young sheep or goat in its mother's milk.

Promises and Instructions

20"I will send an angel ahead of you to protect you as you travel and to bring you to the place which I have prepared. 21 Pay attention to him and obey him. Do not rebel against him, for I have sent him, and he will not pardon such rebellion. 22 But if you obey him and do everything I command, I will fight against all your enemies. 23 My angel will go ahead of you and take you into the land of the Amorites, the Hittites, the Perizzites, the Canaanites, the Hivites, and the Jebusites, and I will destroy them. 24 Do not bow down to their gods or worship them, and do not adopt their religious practices. Destroy their gods and break down their sacred stone pillars. 25 If you worship me, the LORD your God, I will bless you with food and water and take away all your sicknesses. 26 In your land no woman will have a miscarriage or be without children. I will give you long lives.

27"I will make the people who oppose you afraid of me; I will bring confusion among the people against whom you fight, and I will make all your enemies turn and run from you. 28 I will throw your enemies into panic;* I will drive out the Hivites, the Canaanites, and the Hittites as you advance. 29 I will not drive them out within a year's time; if I did, the land would become deserted, and the wild animals would be too many for you. 30 Instead, I will drive them out little by little, until there are enough of you to take possession of the land. 31 I will make the borders of your land extend from the Gulf of Aqaba to the Mediterranean Sea and from the desert to the Euphrates River. I will give you power over the inhabitants of the land, and you will drive them out as you advance. 32 Do not make any

---

x I will . . . panic; *or* I will send hornets among your enemies.

23.12 Ex 20.9-11; 31.15; 34.21; 35.2; Lv 23.3; Dt 5.13, 14   **23.15** Ex 12.14-20;
Lv 23.6-8; Nu 28.17-25   **23.16 a** Lv 23.15-21; Nu 28.26-31; **b** Lv 23.39-43
23.19 Dt 26.2; Ex 34.26; Dt 14.21

agreement with them or with their gods. [33] Do not let those people live in your country; if you do, they will make you sin against me. If you worship their gods, it will be a fatal trap for you."

The Covenant Is Sealed

24 The LORD said to Moses, "Come up the mountain to me, you and Aaron, Nadab, Abihu, and seventy of the leaders of Israel; and while you are still some distance away, bow down in worship. [2] You alone, and none of the others, are to come near me. The people are not even to come up the mountain."

[3] Moses went and told the people all the LORD's commands and all the ordinances, and all the people answered together, "We will do everything that the LORD has said." [4] Moses wrote down all the LORD's commands. Early the next morning he built an altar at the foot of the mountain and set up twelve stones, one for each of the twelve tribes of Israel. [5] Then he sent young men, and they burned sacrifices to the LORD and sacrificed some cattle as fellowship offerings. [6] Moses took half of the blood of the animals and put it in bowls; and the other half he threw against the altar. [7] Then he took the book of the covenant, in which the LORD's commands were written, and read it aloud to the people. They said, "We will obey the LORD and do everything that he has commanded."

[8] Then Moses took the blood in the bowls and threw it on the people. He said, "This is the blood that seals the covenant which the LORD made with you when he gave all these commands."

[9] Moses, Aaron, Nadab, Abihu, and seventy of the leaders of Israel went up the mountain [10] and they saw the God of Israel. Beneath his feet was what looked like a pavement of sapphire, as blue as the sky. [11] God did not harm these leading men of Israel; they saw God, and then they ate and drank together.

Moses on Mount Sinai

[12] The LORD said to Moses, "Come up the mountain to me, and while you are here, I will give you two stone tablets which contain all the laws that I have written for the instruction of the people." [13] Moses and his helper Joshua got ready, and Moses began[y] to go up the holy mountain. [14] Moses said to the leaders, "Wait here in the camp for us until we come back. Aaron and Hur are here with you; and so whoever has a dispute to settle can go to them."

[15] Moses went up Mount Sinai, and a cloud covered it. [16-17] The dazzling light of the LORD's presence came down on the mountain. To the Israelites the light looked like a fire burning on top of the mountain. The cloud covered the mountain for six days, and on the seventh day the LORD called to Moses from the cloud. [18] Moses went on up the mountain into the cloud. There he stayed for forty days and nights.

Offerings for the Sacred Tent
(Exodus 35.4-9)

25 The LORD said to Moses, [2] "Tell the Israelites to make an offering to me. Receive whatever offerings anyone wishes to give. [3] These offerings are to be: gold, silver, and bronze; [4] fine linen; blue, purple, and red wool; cloth made of goats' hair; [5] rams' skin dyed red; fine leather; acacia wood; [6] oil for the lamps; spices for the anointing oil and for the sweet-smelling incense; [7] carnelians and other jewels to be set in

---

[y] Moses began; *one ancient translation* they began.

24.8 a Mt 26.28; Mk 14.24; Lk 22.20; 1 Co 11.25; He 10.29; **b** He 9.19, 20   **24.18** Dt 9.9

the ephod[z] of the High Priest and in his breastpiece. [8] The people must make a sacred Tent for me, so that I may live among them. [9] Make it and all its furnishings according to the plan that I will show you.

The Covenant Box
(Exodus 37.1-9)

[10] "Make a Box out of acacia wood, 45 inches long, 27 inches wide, and 27 inches high. [11] Cover it with pure gold inside and out and put a gold border all around it. [12] Make four carrying rings of gold for it and attach them to its four legs, with two rings on each side. [13] Make carrying poles of acacia wood and cover them with gold [14] and put them through the rings on each side of the Box. [15] The poles are to be left in the rings and must not be taken out. [16] Then put in the Box the two stone tablets that I will give you, on which the commandments are written.

[17] "Make a lid of pure gold, 45 inches long and 27 inches wide. [18] Make two winged creatures[a] of hammered gold, [19] one for each end of the lid. Make them so that they form one piece with the lid. [20] The winged creatures are to face each other across the lid, and their outspread wings are to cover it. [21] Put the two stone tablets inside the Box and put the lid on top of it. [22] I will meet you there, and from above the lid between the two winged creatures I will give you all my laws for the people of Israel.

The Table for the Bread Offered to God
(Exodus 37.10-16)

[23] "Make a table out of acacia wood, 36 inches long, 18 inches wide, and 27 inches high. [24] Cover it with pure gold and put a gold border around it. [25] Make a rim 3 inches wide around it and a gold border around the rim. [26] Make four carrying rings of gold for it and put them at the four corners, where the legs are. [27] The rings to hold the poles for carrying the table are to be placed near the rim. [28] Make the poles of acacia wood and cover them with gold. [29] Make plates, cups, jars, and bowls to be used for the wine offerings. All of these are to be made of pure gold. [30] The table is to be placed in front of the Covenant Box, and on the table there is always to be the sacred bread offered to me.

The Lampstand
(Exodus 37.17-24)

[31] "Make a lampstand of pure gold. Make its base and its shaft of hammered gold; its decorative flowers, including buds and petals, are to form one piece with it. [32] Six branches shall extend from its sides, three from each side. [33] Each of the six branches is to have three decorative flowers shaped like almond blossoms with buds and petals. [34] The shaft of the lampstand is to have four decorative flowers shaped like almond blossoms with buds and petals. [35] There is to be one bud below each of the three pairs of branches. [36] The buds, the branches, and the lampstand are to be a single piece of pure hammered gold. [37] Make seven lamps for the lampstand and set them up so that they shine toward the front. [38] Make its tongs and trays of pure gold. [39] Use seventy-five pounds of pure gold to make the lampstand and all this equipment. [40] Take care to make them according to the plan that I showed you on the mountain.

---

[z] EPHOD: *In most contexts the term ephod refers to a type of shoulder garment, in certain respects resembling a vest. It was made of costly and colorful cloth and to it was attached a kind of pouch containing the Urim and Thummim, two objects used in determining God's will.*   [a] WINGED CREATURES: *See Word List.*
25.17 He 9.5   **25.30** Lv 24.5-8   **25.40** Ac 7.44; He 8.5

The Tent of the LORD's Presence [b]
(Exodus 36.8-38)

26 "Make the interior of the sacred Tent, the Tent of my presence, out of ten pieces of fine linen woven with blue, purple, and red wool. Embroider them with figures of winged creatures. 2 Make each piece the same size, 14 yards long and 2 yards wide. 3 Sew five of them together in one set, and do the same with the other five. 4 Make loops of blue cloth on the edge of the outside piece in each set. 5 Put fifty loops on the first piece of the first set and fifty loops matching them on the last piece of the second set. 6 Make fifty gold hooks with which to join the two sets into one piece.

7 "Make a cover for the Tent out of eleven pieces of cloth made of goats' hair. 8 Make them all the same size, 15 yards long and 2 yards wide. 9 Sew five of them together in one set, and the other six in another set. Fold the sixth piece double over the front of the Tent. 10 Put fifty loops on the edge of the last piece of one set, and fifty loops on the edge of the other set. 11 Make fifty bronze hooks and put them in the loops to join the two sets so as to form one cover. 12 Hang the extra half piece over the back of the Tent. 13 The extra half yard on each side of the length is to hang over the sides of the Tent to cover it.

14 "Make two more coverings, one of rams' skin dyed red and the other of fine leather, to serve as the outer cover.

15 "Make upright frames for the Tent out of acacia wood. 16 Each frame is to be 15 feet long and 27 inches wide, 17 with two matching projections, so that the frames can be joined together. All the frames are to have these projections. 18 Make twenty frames for the south side 19 and forty silver bases to go under them, two bases under each frame to hold its two projections. 20 Make twenty frames for the north side of the Tent 21 and forty silver bases, two under each frame. 22 For the back of the Tent on the west, make six frames, 23 and two frames for the corners. 24 These corner frames are to be joined at the bottom and connected all the way to the top. The two frames that form the two corners are to be made in this way. 25 So there will be eight frames with their sixteen silver bases, two under each frame.

26 "Make fifteen crossbars of acacia wood, five for the frames on one side of the Tent, 27 five for the frames on the other side, and five for the frames on the west end, at the back. 28 The middle crossbar, set halfway up the frames, is to extend from one end of the Tent to the other. 29 Cover the frames with gold and fit them with gold rings to hold the crossbars, which are also to be covered with gold. 30 Set up the Tent according to the plan that I showed you on the mountain.

31 "Make a curtain of fine linen woven with blue, purple, and red wool. Embroider it with figures of winged creatures. 32 Hang it on four posts of acacia wood covered with gold, fitted with hooks, and set in four silver bases. 33 Place the curtain under the row of hooks in the roof of the Tent, and put behind the curtain the Covenant Box containing the two stone tablets. The curtain will separate the Holy Place from the Most Holy Place. 34 Put the lid on the Covenant Box. 35 Outside the Most Holy Place put the table against the north side of the Tent and the lampstand against the south side.

36 "For the entrance of the Tent make a curtain of fine linen woven with blue, purple, and red wool and decorated with embroidery. 37 For this curtain make five posts of acacia wood covered

[b] TENT OF THE LORD'S PRESENCE: *See Word List.*
26.33 He 6.19; 9.3-5

with gold and fitted with gold hooks; make five bronze bases for these posts.

The Altar
(Exodus 38.1-7)

27 "Make an altar out of acacia wood. It is to be square, 7½ feet long and 7½ feet wide, and it is to be 4½ feet high. 2 Make projections at the top of the four corners. They are to form one piece with the altar, and the whole is to be covered with bronze. 3 Make pans for the greasy ashes, and make shovels, bowls, hooks, and fire pans. All this equipment is to be made of bronze. 4 Make a bronze grating and put four bronze carrying rings on its corners. 5 Put the grating under the rim of the altar, so that it reaches halfway up the altar. 6 Make carrying poles of acacia wood, cover them with bronze, 7 and put them in the rings on each side of the altar when it is carried. 8 Make the altar out of boards and leave it hollow, according to the plan that I showed you on the mountain.

The Enclosure for the Tent of the LORD's Presence
(Exodus 38.9-20)

9 "For the Tent of my presence make an enclosure out of fine linen curtains. On the south side the curtains are to be 50 yards long, 10 supported by twenty bronze posts in twenty bronze bases, with hooks and rods made of silver. 11 Do the same on the north side of the enclosure. 12 On the west side there are to be curtains 25 yards long, with ten posts and ten bases. 13 On the east side, where the entrance is, the enclosure is also to be 25 yards wide. 14-15 On each side of the entrance there are to be 7½ yards of curtains, with three posts and three bases. 16 For the entrance itself there is to be a curtain 10 yards long made of fine linen woven with blue, purple, and red wool, and decorated with embroidery. It is to be supported by four posts in four bases. 17 All the posts around the enclosure are to be

connected with silver rods, and their hooks are to be made of silver and their bases of bronze. 18 The enclosure is to be 50 yards long, 25 yards wide, and 2½ yards high. The curtains are to be made of fine linen and the bases of bronze. 19 All the equipment that is used in the Tent and all the pegs for the Tent and for the enclosure are to be made of bronze.

Taking Care of the Lamp
(Leviticus 24.1-4)

20 "Command the people of Israel to bring you the best olive oil for the lamp, so that it can be lit each evening. 21 Aaron and his sons are to set up the lamp in the Tent of my presence outside the curtain which is in front of the Covenant Box. There in my presence it is to burn from evening until morning. This command is to be kept forever by the Israelites and their descendants.

Garments for the Priests
(Exodus 39.1-7)

28 "Summon your brother Aaron and his sons, Nadab, Abihu, Eleazar, and Ithamar. Separate them from the people of Israel, so that they may serve me as priests. 2 Make priestly garments for your brother Aaron, to provide him with dignity and beauty. 3 Call all the skilled workers to whom I have given ability, and tell them to make Aaron's clothes, so that he may be dedicated as a priest in my service. 4 Tell them to make a breastpiece, an ephod, a robe, an embroidered shirt, a turban, and a sash. They are to make these priestly garments for your brother Aaron and his sons, so that they can serve me as priests. 5 The skilled workers are to use blue, purple, and red wool, gold thread, and fine linen.

6 "They are to make the ephod of blue, purple, and red wool, gold thread, and fine linen, decorated with embroidery. 7 Two shoulder straps, by which it can be fastened, are to be attached to

the sides. ⁸A finely woven belt made of the same materials is to be attached to the ephod so as to form one piece with it. ⁹Take two carnelian stones and engrave on them the names of the twelve sons of Jacob, ¹⁰in the order of their birth, with six on one stone and six on the other. ¹¹Have a skillful jeweler engrave on the two stones the names of the sons of Jacob, and mount the stones in gold settings. ¹²Put them on the shoulder straps of the ephod to represent the twelve tribes of Israel. In this way Aaron will carry their names on his shoulders, so that I, the LORD, will always remember my people. ¹³Make two gold settings ¹⁴and two chains of pure gold twisted like cords, and attach them to the settings.

The Breastpiece
(Exodus 39.8-21)

¹⁵"Make a breastpiece for the High Priest to use in determining God's will. It is to be made of the same materials as the ephod and with similar embroidery. ¹⁶It is to be square and folded double, 9 inches long and 9 inches wide. ¹⁷Mount four rows of precious stones on it; in the first row mount a ruby, a topaz, and a garnet; ¹⁸in the second row, an emerald, a sapphire, and a diamond; ¹⁹in the third row, a turquoise, an agate, and an amethyst; ²⁰and in the fourth row, a beryl, a carnelian, and a jasper. These are to be mounted in gold settings. ²¹Each of these twelve stones is to have engraved on it the name of one of the sons of Jacob, to represent the tribes of Israel. ²²For the breastpiece make chains of pure gold, twisted like cords. ²³Make two gold rings and attach them to the upper corners of the breastpiece, ²⁴and fasten the two gold cords to the two rings. ²⁵Fasten the other two ends of the cords to the two

settings, and in this way attach them in front to the shoulder straps of the ephod. ²⁶Then make two rings of gold and attach them to the lower corners of the breastpiece on the inside edge next to the ephod. ²⁷Make two more gold rings and attach them to the lower part of the front of the two shoulder straps of the ephod, near the seam and above the finely woven belt. ²⁸Tie the rings of the breastpiece to the rings of the ephod with a blue cord, so that the breastpiece rests above the belt and does not come loose.

²⁹"When Aaron enters the Holy Place, he will wear this breastpiece engraved with the names of the tribes of Israel, so that I, the LORD, will always remember my people. ³⁰Put the Urim and Thummim𝒸 in the breastpiece, so that Aaron will carry them when he comes into my holy presence. At such times he must always wear this breastpiece, so that he can determine my will for the people of Israel.

The Other Priestly Garments
(Exodus 39.22-31)

³¹"The robe that goes under the ephod is to be made entirely of blue wool. ³²It is to have a hole for the head, and this hole is to be reinforced with a woven binding to keep it from tearing. ³³⁻³⁴All around its lower hem put pomegranates of blue, purple, and red wool, alternating with gold bells. ³⁵Aaron is to wear this robe when he serves as priest. When he comes into my presence in the Holy Place or when he leaves it, the sound of the bells will be heard, and he will not be killed.

³⁶"Make an ornament of pure gold and engrave on it 'Dedicated to the LORD.' ³⁷Tie it to the front of the turban with a blue cord. ³⁸Aaron is to wear it on his forehead, so that I, the LORD, will

𝒸 URIM AND THUMMIM: *Two objects used by the priest to determine God's will; it is not known precisely how they were used.*
28.30 Nu 27.21; Dt 33.8; Ezra 2.63; Ne 7.65   **28.33, 34** Si 45.9

accept all the offerings that the Israelites dedicate to me, even if the people commit some error in offering them.

39 "Weave Aaron's shirt of fine linen and make a turban of fine linen and also a sash decorated with embroidery.

40 "Make shirts, sashes, and caps for Aaron's sons, to provide them with dignity and beauty. 41 Put these clothes on your brother Aaron and his sons. Then ordain them and dedicate them by anointing them with olive oil, so that they may serve me as priests. 42 Make linen shorts for them, reaching from the waist to the thighs, so that they will not expose themselves. 43 Aaron and his sons must always wear them when they go into the Tent of my presence or approach the altar to serve as priests in the Holy Place, so that they will not be killed for exposing themselves. This is a permanent rule for Aaron and his descendants.

Instructions for Ordaining Aaron and His Sons as Priests
(Leviticus 8.1-36)

29 "This is what you are to do to Aaron and his sons to dedicate them as priests in my service. Take one young bull and two rams without any defects. 2 Use the best wheat flour, but no yeast, and make some bread with olive oil, some without it, and some in the form of thin cakes brushed with oil. 3 Put them in a basket and offer them to me when you sacrifice the bull and the two rams.

4 "Bring Aaron and his sons to the entrance of the Tent of my presence, and have them take a ritual bath. 5 Then dress Aaron in the priestly garments — the shirt, the robe that goes under the ephod, the ephod, the breastpiece, and the belt. 6 Put the turban on him and tie on it the sacred sign of dedication en-

graved 'Dedicated to the Lord.' 7 Then take the anointing oil, pour it on his head, and anoint him.

8 "Bring his sons and put shirts on them; 9 put sashes around their waists and tie caps on their heads. That is how you are to ordain Aaron and his sons. They and their descendants are to serve me as priests forever.

10 "Bring the bull to the front of the Tent of my presence and tell Aaron and his sons to put their hands on its head. 11 Kill the bull there in my holy presence at the entrance of the Tent. 12 Take some of the bull's blood and with your finger put it on the projections of the altar. Then pour out the rest of the blood at the base of the altar. 13 Next, take all the fat which covers the internal organs, the best part of the liver, and the two kidneys with the fat on them, and burn them on the altar as an offering to me. 14 But burn the bull's flesh, its skin, and its intestines outside the camp. This is an offering to take away the sins of the priests.

15 "Take one of the rams and tell Aaron and his sons to put their hands on its head. 16 Kill it, and take its blood and throw it against all four sides of the altar. 17 Cut the ram in pieces; wash its internal organs and its hind legs, and put them on top of the head and the other pieces. 18 Burn the whole ram on the altar as a food offering. The odor of this offering pleases me.

19 "Take the other ram — the ram used for dedication — and tell Aaron and his sons to put their hands on its head. 20 Kill it, and take some of its blood and put it on the lobes of the right ears of Aaron and his sons, on the thumbs of their right hands and on the big toes of their right feet. Throw the rest of the blood against all four sides of the altar. 21 Take some of the blood that is on the altar and some of the anointing

29.18 Eph 5.2; Phil 4.18

oil, and sprinkle it on Aaron and his clothes and on his sons and their clothes. He, his sons, and their clothes will then be dedicated to me.

22 "Cut away the ram's fat, the fat tail, the fat covering the internal organs, the best part of the liver, the two kidneys with the fat on them, and the right thigh. 23 From the basket of bread which has been offered to me, take one loaf of each kind: one loaf made with olive oil and one made without it and one thin cake. 24 Put all this food in the hands of Aaron and his sons and have them dedicate it to me as a special gift. 25 Then take it from them and burn it on the altar, on top of the burnt offering, as a food offering to me. The odor of this offering pleases me.

26 "Take the breast of this ram and dedicate it to me as a special gift. This part of the animal will be yours.

27 "When a priest is ordained, the breast and the thigh of the ram being used for the ordination are to be dedicated to me as a special gift and set aside for the priests. 28 It is my unchanging decision that when my people make their fellowship offerings, the breast and the thigh of the animal belong to the priests. This is the people's gift to me, the LORD.

29 "Aaron's priestly garments are to be handed on to his sons after his death, for them to wear when they are ordained. 30 The son of Aaron who succeeds him as priest and who goes into the Tent of my presence to serve in the Holy Place is to wear these garments for seven days.

31 "Take the meat of the ram used for the ordination of Aaron and his sons and boil it in a holy place. 32 At the entrance of the Tent of my presence they are to eat it along with the bread left in the basket. 33 They shall eat what was used in the ritual of forgiveness at their ordination. Only priests may eat this food, because it is sacred. 34 If some of the meat or some of the bread is not eaten by morning, it is to be burned; it is not to be eaten, for it is sacred.

35 "Perform the rites of ordination for Aaron and his sons for seven days exactly as I have commanded you. 36 Each day you must offer a bull as a sacrifice, so that sin may be forgiven. This will purify the altar. Then anoint it with olive oil to make it holy. 37 Do this every day for seven days. Then the altar will be completely holy, and anyone or anything that touches it will be harmed by the power of its holiness. d

The Daily Offerings
(Numbers 28.1-8)

38 "Every day for all time to come, sacrifice on the altar two one-year-old lambs. 39 Sacrifice one of the lambs in the morning and the other in the evening. 40 With the first lamb offer two pounds of fine wheat flour mixed with one quart of pure olive oil. Pour out one quart of wine as an offering. 41 Sacrifice the second lamb in the evening, and offer with it the same amounts of flour, olive oil, and wine as in the morning. This is a food offering to me, the LORD, and its odor pleases me. 42 For all time to come, this burnt offering is to be offered in my presence at the entrance of the Tent of my presence. That is where I will meet my people and speak to you. 43 There I will meet the people of Israel, and the dazzling light of my presence will make the place holy. 44 I will make the Tent and the altar holy, and I will set Aaron and his sons apart to serve me as priests. 45 I will live among the people of Israel, and I will be their God. 46 They will know that I am the LORD their God who brought them out of Egypt so that I could live among them. I am the LORD their God.

---

d BE HARMED BY THE POWER OF ITS HOLINESS: *It was believed that ordinary people or things would be harmed by touching something holy.*

The Altar for Burning Incense
(Exodus 37.25-28)

30 "Make an altar out of acacia wood, for burning incense. [2] It is to be square, 18 inches long and 18 inches wide, and it is to be 36 inches high. Its projections at the four corners are to form one piece with it. [3] Cover its top, all four sides, and its projections with pure gold, and put a gold border around it. [4] Make two gold carrying rings for it and attach them below the border on two sides to hold the poles with which it is to be carried. [5] Make these poles of acacia wood and cover them with gold. [6] Put this altar outside the curtain which hangs in front of the Covenant Box. That is the place where I will meet you. [7] Every morning when Aaron comes to take care of the lamps, he is to burn sweet-smelling incense on it. [8] He must do the same when he lights the lamps in the evening. This offering of incense is to continue without interruption for all time to come. [9] Do not offer on this altar any forbidden incense, any animal offering, or any grain offering, and do not pour out any wine offering on it. [10] Once a year Aaron is to perform the ritual for purifying the altar by putting on its four projections the blood of the animal sacrificed for sin. This is to be done every year for all time to come. This altar is to be completely holy, dedicated to me, the LORD."

The Tax for the Tent of the LORD's Presence

[11] The LORD said to Moses, [12] "When you take a census of the people of Israel, each man is to pay me a price for his life, so that no disaster will come on him while the census is being taken. [13] Everyone included in the census must pay the required amount of money, weighed according to the official standard. Everyone must pay this as an offering to me. [14] Everyone being counted in the census, that is, every man twenty years old or older, is to pay me this amount. [15] The rich man is not to pay more, nor the poor man less, when they pay this amount for their lives. [16] Collect this money from the people of Israel and spend it for the upkeep of the Tent of my presence. This tax will be the payment for their lives, and I will remember to protect them."

The Bronze Basin

[17] The LORD said to Moses, [18] "Make a bronze basin with a bronze base. Place it between the Tent and the altar, and put water in it. [19] Aaron and his sons are to use the water to wash their hands and feet [20] before they go into the Tent or approach the altar to offer the food offering. Then they will not be killed. [21] They must wash their hands and feet, so that they will not die. This is a rule which they and their descendants are to observe forever."

The Anointing Oil

[22] The LORD said to Moses, [23] "Take the finest spices — 12 pounds of liquid myrrh, 6 pounds of sweet-smelling cinnamon, 6 pounds of sweet-smelling cane, [24] and 12 pounds of cassia (all weighed according to the official standard). Add one gallon of olive oil, [25] and make a sacred anointing oil, mixed like perfume. [26] Use it to anoint the Tent of my presence, the Covenant Box, [27] the table and all its equipment, the lampstand and its equipment, the altar for burning incense, [28] the altar for burning offerings, together with all its equipment, and the washbasin with its base. [29] Dedicate these things in this way, and they will be completely holy, and anyone or anything that touches them will be harmed by the power of its holiness.[e] [30] Then anoint Aaron and

e HARMED BY THE POWER OF ITS HOLINESS: *See* 29.37.

30.13 Ex 38.25, 26; Mt 17.24   **30.18** Ex 38.8   **30.22-38** Ex 37.29

his sons, and ordain them as priests in my service. [31] Say to the people of Israel, 'This holy anointing oil is to be used in my service for all time to come. [32] It must not be poured on ordinary men, and you must not use the same formula to make any mixture like it. It is holy, and you must treat it as holy. [33] Whoever makes any like it or uses any of it on anyone who is not a priest will no longer be considered one of my people.' "

The Incense

[34] The LORD said to Moses, "Take an equal part of each of the following sweet spices — stacte, onycha, galbanum, and pure frankincense. [35] Use them to make incense, mixed like perfume. Add salt to keep it pure and holy. [36] Beat part of it into a fine powder, take it into the Tent of my presence, and sprinkle it in front of the Covenant Box. Treat this incense as completely holy. [37] Do not use the same formula to make any incense like it for yourselves. Treat it as a holy thing dedicated to me. [38] If anyone makes any like it for use as perfume, he will no longer be considered one of my people."

Craftsmen for the Tent of the LORD's Presence
(Exodus 35.30 − 36.1)

31 The LORD said to Moses, [2] "I have chosen Bezalel, the son of Uri and grandson of Hur, from the tribe of Judah, [3] and I have filled him with my power.*f* I have given him understanding, skill, and ability for every kind of artistic work — [4] for planning skillful designs and working them in gold, silver, and bronze; [5] for cutting jewels to be set; for carving wood; and for every other kind of artistic work. [6] I

have also selected Oholiab son of Ahisamach, from the tribe of Dan, to work with him. I have also given great ability to all the other skilled workers, so that they can make everything I have commanded to be made: [7] the Tent of my presence, the Covenant Box and its lid, all the furnishings of the Tent, [8] the table and its equipment, the lampstand of pure gold and all its equipment, the altar for burning incense, [9] the altar for burnt offerings and all its equipment, the washbasin and its base, [10] the magnificent priestly garments for Aaron and his sons to use when they serve as priests, [11] the anointing oil, and the sweet-smelling incense for the Holy Place. In making all these things, they are to do exactly as I have commanded you."

Sabbath, the Day of Rest

[12] The LORD commanded Moses [13] to tell the people of Israel, "Keep the Sabbath, my day of rest, because it is a sign between you and me for all time to come, to show that I, the LORD, have made you my own people. [14] You must keep the day of rest, because it is sacred. Whoever does not keep it, but works on that day, is to be put to death. [15] You have six days in which to do your work, but the seventh day is a solemn day of rest dedicated to me. Whoever does any work on that day is to be put to death. [16] The people of Israel are to keep this day as a sign of the covenant. [17] It is a permanent sign between the people of Israel and me, because I, the LORD, made heaven and earth in six days, and on the seventh day I stopped working and rested."

[18] When God had finished speaking to Moses on Mount Sinai, he gave him the two stone tablets on which God himself had written the commandments.

f power; *or* spirit.

31.15 Ex 20.8-11; 23.12; 34.21; 35.2; Lv 23.3; Dt 5.12-14   **31.17** Ex 20.11

The Gold Bull-Calf
(Deuteronomy 9.6-29)

32 When the people saw that Moses had not come down from the mountain but was staying there a long time, they gathered around Aaron and said to him, "We do not know what has happened to this man Moses, who led us out of Egypt; so make us a god*g* to lead us."

2 Aaron said to them, "Take off the gold earrings which your wives, your sons, and your daughters are wearing, and bring them to me." 3 So all the people took off their gold earrings and brought them to Aaron. 4 He took the earrings, melted them, poured the gold into a mold, and made a gold bull-calf. The people said, "Israel, this is our god, who led us out of Egypt!"

5 Then Aaron built an altar in front of the gold bull-calf and announced, "Tomorrow there will be a festival to honor the LORD." 6 Early the next morning they brought some animals to burn as sacrifices and others to eat as fellowship offerings. The people sat down to a feast, which turned into an orgy of drinking and sex.

7 The LORD said to Moses, "Hurry and go back down, because your people, whom you led out of Egypt, have sinned and rejected me. 8 They have already left the way that I commanded them to follow; they have made a bull-calf out of melted gold and have worshiped it and offered sacrifices to it. They are saying that this is their god, who led them out of Egypt. 9 I know how stubborn these people are. 10 Now, don't try to stop me. I am angry with them, and I am going to destroy them. Then I will make you and your descendants into a great nation."

11 But Moses pleaded with the LORD his God and said, "LORD, why should you be so angry with your people, whom you rescued from Egypt with great might and power? 12 Why should the Egyptians be able to say that you led your people out of Egypt, planning to kill them in the mountains and destroy them completely? Stop being angry; change your mind and do not bring this disaster on your people. 13 Remember your servants Abraham, Isaac, and Jacob. Remember the solemn promise you made to them to give them as many descendants as there are stars in the sky and to give their descendants all that land you promised would be their possession forever." 14 So the LORD changed his mind and did not bring on his people the disaster he had threatened.

15 Moses went back down the mountain, carrying the two stone tablets with the commandments written on both sides. 16 God himself had made the tablets and had engraved the commandments on them.

17 Joshua heard the people shouting and said to Moses, "I hear the sound of battle in the camp."

18 Moses said, "That doesn't sound like a shout of victory or a cry of defeat; it's the sound of singing."

19 When Moses came close enough to the camp to see the bull-calf and to see the people dancing, he became furious. There at the foot of the mountain, he threw down the tablets he was carrying and broke them. 20 He took the bull-calf which they had made, melted it, ground it into fine powder, and mixed it with water. Then he made the people of Israel drink it. 21 He said to Aaron, "What did these people do to you, that you have made them commit such a terrible sin?"

22 Aaron answered, "Don't be angry with me; you know how determined these people are to do evil. 23 They said

g a god; *or* some gods.

32.1 Ac 7.40 **32.4** 1 K 12.28; Ac 7.41 **32.6** 1 Co 10.7 **32.11-14** Nu 14.13-19
32.13 Gn 22.16, 17; Gn 17.8

to me, 'We don't know what has happened to this man Moses, who brought us out of Egypt; so make us a god to lead us.' ²⁴I asked them to bring me their gold ornaments, and those who had any took them off and gave them to me. I threw the ornaments into the fire and out came this bull-calf!"

²⁵Moses saw that Aaron had let the people get out of control and make fools of themselves in front of their enemies. ²⁶So he stood at the gate of the camp and shouted, "Everyone who is on the LORD's side come over here!" So all the Levites gathered around him, ²⁷and he said to them, "The LORD God of Israel commands every one of you to put on your sword and go through the camp from this gate to the other and kill your brothers, your friends, and your neighbors." ²⁸The Levites obeyed, and killed about three thousand men that day. ²⁹Moses said to the Levites, "Today you have consecrated yourselves[h] as priests in the service of the LORD by killing your sons and brothers, so the LORD has given you his blessing."

³⁰The next day Moses said to the people, "You have committed a terrible sin. But now I will again go up the mountain to the LORD; perhaps I can obtain forgiveness for your sin." ³¹Moses then returned to the LORD and said, "These people have committed a terrible sin. They have made a god out of gold and worshiped it. ³²Please forgive their sin; but if you won't, then remove my name from the book in which you have written the names of your people."

³³The LORD answered, "It is those who have sinned against me whose names I will remove from my book. ³⁴Now go, lead the people to the place I told you about. Remember that my angel will guide you, but the time is coming when I will punish these people for their sin."

³⁵So the LORD sent a disease on the people, because they had caused Aaron to make the gold bull-calf.

The LORD Orders Israel to Leave Mount Sinai

33 The LORD said to Moses, "Leave this place, you and the people you brought out of Egypt, and go to the land that I promised to give to Abraham, Isaac, and Jacob and to their descendants. ²I will send an angel to guide you, and I will drive out the Canaanites, the Amorites, the Hittites, the Perizzites, the Hivites, and the Jebusites. ³You are going to a rich and fertile land. But I will not go with you myself, because you are a stubborn people, and I might destroy you on the way."

⁴When the people heard this, they began to mourn and did not wear jewelry any more. ⁵For the LORD had commanded Moses to tell them, "You are a stubborn people. If I were to go with you even for a moment, I would completely destroy you. Now take off your jewelry, and I will decide what to do with you." ⁶So after they left Mount Sinai, the people of Israel no longer wore jewelry.

The Tent of the LORD's Presence

⁷Whenever the people of Israel set up camp, Moses would take the sacred Tent and put it up some distance outside the camp. It was called the Tent of the LORD's presence, and anyone who wanted to consult the LORD would go out to it. ⁸Whenever Moses went out there, the people would stand at the door of their tents and watch Moses until he entered it. ⁹After Moses had gone in, the pillar of cloud would come down and stay at the door of the Tent, and the

---

[h] *Some ancient translations* Today you have consecrated yourselves; *Hebrew* Consecrate yourselves today; *or* You have been consecrated today.
32.32 Ps 69.28; Rev 3.5   **33.1 a** Gn 12.7; **b** Gn 26.3; **c** Gn 28.13

They would bow down. (33.10)

Lord would speak to Moses from the cloud. [10] As soon as the people saw the pillar of cloud at the door of the Tent, they would bow down. [11] The Lord would speak with Moses face-to-face, just as someone speaks with a friend. Then Moses would return to the camp. But the young man who was his helper, Joshua son of Nun, stayed in the Tent.

The Lord Promises to Be with His People

[12] Moses said to the Lord, "It is true that you have told me to lead these people to that land, but you did not tell me whom you would send with me. You have said that you know me well and are pleased with me. [13] Now if you are, tell me your plans, so that I may serve you and continue to please you. Remember also that you have chosen this nation to be your own."

[14] The Lord said, "I will go with you, and I will give you victory."

[15] Moses replied, "If you do not go with us, don't make us leave this place. [16] How will anyone know that you are pleased with your people and with me if you do not go with us? Your presence with us will distinguish us from any other people on earth."

[17] The Lord said to Moses, "I will do just as you have asked, because I know you very well and I am pleased with you."

[18] Then Moses requested, "Please, let me see the dazzling light of your presence."

[19] The Lord answered, "I will make all my splendor pass before you and in your presence I will pronounce my sacred name. I am the Lord, and I show compassion and pity on those I choose. [20] I will not let you see my face, because no one can see me and stay alive, [21] but here is a place beside me where you can stand on a rock. [22] When the dazzling light of my presence passes by, I will put you in an opening in the rock and cover you with my hand until I have passed by. [23] Then I will take my hand away, and you will see my back but not my face."

The Second Set of Stone Tablets
(*Deuteronomy 10.1-5*)

34 The Lord said to Moses, "Cut two stone tablets like the first ones, and I will write on them the words that were on the first tablets, which you broke. [2] Get ready tomorrow morning, and come up Mount Sinai to meet me there at the top. [3] No one is to come up with you; no one is to be seen on any part of the mountain; and no sheep or cattle are to graze at the foot of the mountain." 4 So Moses cut two more stone tablets, and early the next morning he carried them up Mount Sinai, just as the LORD had commanded.

5 The LORD came down in a cloud, stood with him there, and pronounced his holy name, the LORD.[i] 6 The LORD then passed in front of him and called out, "I, the LORD, am a God who is full of compassion and pity, who is not easily angered and who shows great love and faithfulness. 7 I keep my promise for thousands of generations[j] and forgive evil and sin; but I will not fail to punish children and grandchildren to the third and fourth generation for the sins of their parents."

8 Moses quickly bowed down to the ground and worshiped. 9 He said, "Lord, if you really are pleased with me, I ask you to go with us. These people are stubborn, but forgive our evil and our sin, and accept us as your own people."

The Covenant Is Renewed
(Exodus 23.14-19; Deuteronomy 7.1-5; 16.1-17)

10 The LORD said to Moses, "I now make a covenant with the people of Israel. In their presence I will do great things such as have never been done anywhere on earth among any of the nations. All the people will see what great things I, the LORD, can do, because I am going to do an awesome thing for you. 11 Obey the laws that I am giving you today. I will drive out the Amorites, the Canaanites, the Hittites, the Perizzites, the Hivites, and the Jebusites, as you advance. 12 Do not make any treaties with the people of the country into which you are going, because this could be a fatal trap for you.

13 Instead, tear down their altars, destroy their sacred pillars, and cut down their symbols of the goddess Asherah. 14 "Do not worship any other god, because I, the LORD, tolerate no rivals. 15 Do not make any treaties with the people of the country, because when they worship their pagan gods and sacrifice to them, they will invite you to join them, and you will be tempted to eat the food they offer to their gods. 16 Your sons might marry those foreign women, who would lead them to be unfaithful to me and to worship their pagan gods.

17 "Do not make gods of metal and worship them.

18 "Keep the Festival of Unleavened Bread. As I have commanded you, eat unleavened bread for seven days in that month of Abib, because it was in that month that you left Egypt.

19 "Every first-born son and first-born male domestic animal belongs to me, 20 but you are to buy back every firstborn donkey by offering a lamb in its place. If you do not buy it back, break its neck. Buy back every first-born son.

"No one is to appear before me without an offering.

21 "You have six days in which to do your work, but do not work on the seventh day, not even during plowing time or harvest.

22 "Keep the Harvest Festival when you begin to harvest the first crop of your wheat, and keep the Festival of Shelters in the autumn when you gather your fruit.

23 "Three times a year all of your men must come to worship me, the LORD, the God of Israel. 24 After I have driven out the nations before you and extended your territory, no one will try to

---

[i] THE LORD: See *3.14*, and Word List.   [j] thousands of generations; *or* thousands.

34.6, 7 Ex 20.5, 6; Nu 14.18; Dt 5.9, 10; 7.9, 10   **34.13** Dt 16.21   **34.17** Ex 20.4; Lv 19.4; Dt 5.8; 27.15   **34.18** Ex 12.14-20; Lv 23.6-8; Nu 28.16-25   **34.19** Ex 13.2
34.20 Ex 13.13   **34.21** Ex 20.9, 10; 23.12; 31.15; 35.2; Lv 23.3; Dt 5.13, 14
34.22 a Lv 23.15-21; Nu 28.26-31; **b** Lv 23.39-43

conquer your country during the three festivals.

²⁵"Do not offer bread made with yeast when you sacrifice an animal to me. Do not keep until the following morning any part of the animal killed at the Passover Festival.

²⁶"Each year bring to the house of the LORD the first grain that you harvest.

"Do not cook a young sheep or goat in its mother's milk."

²⁷The LORD said to Moses, "Write these words down, because it is on the basis of these words that I am making a covenant with you and with Israel."

²⁸Moses stayed there with the LORD forty days and nights, eating and drinking nothing. He wrote on the tablets the words of the covenant — the Ten Commandments.

Moses Goes Down from Mount Sinai

²⁹When Moses went down from Mount Sinai carrying the Ten Commandments, his face was shining because he had been speaking with the LORD; but he did not know it. ³⁰Aaron and all the people looked at Moses and saw that his face was shining, and they were afraid to go near him. ³¹But Moses called them, and Aaron and all the leaders of the community went to him, and Moses spoke with them. ³²After that, all the people of Israel gathered around him, and Moses gave them all the laws that the LORD had given him on Mount Sinai. ³³When Moses had finished speaking with them, he covered his face with a veil. ³⁴Whenever Moses went into the Tent of the LORD's presence to speak to the LORD, he would take the veil off. When he came out, he would tell the people of Israel everything that he had been commanded to say, ³⁵and they would see that his face was shining. Then he would put the veil back on until the next time he went to speak with the LORD.

Regulations for the Sabbath

35 Moses called together the whole community of the people of Israel and said to them, "This is what the LORD has commanded you to do: ²You have six days in which to do your work, but the seventh day is to be sacred, a solemn day of rest dedicated to me, the LORD. Anyone who does any work on that day is to be put to death. ³Do not even light a fire in your homes on the Sabbath."

Offerings for the Sacred Tent
(Exodus 25.1-9)

⁴Moses said to all the people of Israel, "This is what the LORD has commanded: ⁵Make an offering to the LORD. Everyone who wishes to do so is to bring an offering of gold, silver, or bronze; ⁶fine linen; blue, purple, and red wool; cloth made of goats' hair; ⁷rams' skin dyed red; fine leather; acacia wood; ⁸oil for the lamps; spices for the anointing oil and for the sweet-smelling incense; ⁹carnelians and other jewels to be set in the High Priest's ephod and in his breastpiece.

Articles for the Tent of the LORD's Presence
(Exodus 39.32-43)

¹⁰"All the skilled workers among you are to come and make everything that the LORD commanded: ¹¹the Tent, its covering and its outer covering, its hooks and its frames, its crossbars, its posts, and its bases; ¹²the Covenant Box, its poles, its lid, and the curtain to screen it off; ¹³the table, its poles, and all its equipment; the bread offered to God; ¹⁴the lampstand for the light and its equipment; the lamps with their oil;

34.25 Ex 12.10   **34.26 a** Dt 26.2; **b** Dt 14.21   **34.29-35** 2 Co 3.7-16   **35.2** Ex 20.8-11;
23.12; 31.15; 34.21; Lv 23.3; Dt 5.12-14

¹⁵the altar for burning incense and its poles; the anointing oil; the sweet-smelling incense; the curtain for the entrance of the Tent; ¹⁶the altar on which to burn offerings, with its bronze grating attached, its poles, and all its equipment; the washbasin and its base; ¹⁷the curtains for the enclosure, its posts and bases; the curtain for the entrance of the enclosure; ¹⁸the Tent pegs and ropes for the Tent and the enclosure; ¹⁹and the magnificent garments the priests are to wear when they serve in the Holy Place — the sacred clothes for Aaron the priest and for his sons."

The People Bring Their Offerings

²⁰All the people of Israel left, ²¹and everyone who wished to do so brought an offering to the LORD for making the Tent of the LORD's presence. They brought everything needed for use in worship and for making the priestly garments. ²²All who wanted to, both men and women, brought decorative pins, earrings, rings, necklaces, and all kinds of gold jewelry and dedicated them to the LORD. ²³Everyone who had fine linen; blue, purple, or red wool; cloth of goats' hair; rams' skin dyed red; or fine leather, brought it. ²⁴All who were able to contribute silver or bronze brought their offering for the LORD, and all who had acacia wood which could be used for any of the work brought it. ²⁵All the skilled women brought fine linen thread and thread of blue, purple, and red wool, which they had made. ²⁶They also made thread of goats' hair. ²⁷The leaders brought carnelians and other jewels to be set in the ephod and the breastpiece ²⁸and spices and oil for the lamps, for the anointing oil, and for the sweet-smelling incense. ²⁹All the people of Israel who wanted to brought their offering to the LORD for the work which he had commanded Moses to do.

Workers to Make the Tent of the LORD's Presence
(Exodus 31.1-11)

³⁰Moses said to the Israelites, "The LORD has chosen Bezalel, the son of Uri and grandson of Hur from the tribe of Judah. ³¹God has filled him with his power[k] and given him skill, ability, and understanding for every kind of artistic work, ³²for planning skillful designs and working them in gold, silver, and bronze; ³³for cutting jewels to be set; for carving wood; and for every other kind of artistic work. ³⁴The LORD has given to him and to Oholiab son of Ahisamach, from the tribe of Dan, the ability to teach their crafts to others. ³⁵He has given them skill in all kinds of work done by engravers, designers, and weavers of fine linen; blue, purple, and red wool; and other cloth. They are able to do all kinds of work and are skillful designers.

36 "Bezalel, Oholiab, and all the other workers to whom the LORD has given skill and understanding, who know how to make everything needed to build the sacred Tent, are to make everything just as the LORD has commanded."

The People Bring Many Gifts

²Moses called Bezalel, Oholiab, and all the other skilled men to whom the LORD had given ability and who were willing to help, and Moses told them to start working. ³They received from him all the offerings which the Israelites had brought for constructing the sacred Tent. But the people of Israel continued to bring Moses their offerings every morning. ⁴Then the skilled men who were doing the work went ⁵and told Moses, "The people are bringing more than is needed for the work which the LORD commanded to be done."

⁶So Moses sent a command throughout the camp that no one was to make

---

k power; *or* spirit.

any further contribution for the sacred Tent; so the people did not bring any more. [7] What had already been brought was more than enough to finish all the work.

Making the Tent of the Lord's Presence
(Exodus 26.1-37)

[8] The most skilled men among those doing the work made the Tent of the Lord's presence. They made it out of ten pieces of fine linen woven with blue, purple, and red wool and embroidered with figures of winged creatures. [9] Each piece was the same size, 14 yards long and 2 yards wide. [10] They sewed five of them together in one set and did the same with the other five. [11] They made loops of blue cloth on the edge of the outside piece in each set. [12] They put fifty loops on the first piece of the first set and fifty loops matching them on the last piece of the second set. [13] They made fifty gold hooks, with which to join the two sets into one piece.

[14] Then they made a cover for the Tent out of eleven pieces of cloth made of goats' hair. [15] They made them all the same size, 15 yards long and 2 yards wide. [16] They sewed five of them together in one set and the other six in another set. [17] They put fifty loops on the edge of the last piece of one set and fifty loops on the edge of the other set. [18] They made fifty bronze hooks to join the two sets, so as to form one cover. [19] They made two more coverings, one of rams' skin dyed red and the other of fine leather, to serve as an outer cover.

[20] They made upright frames of acacia wood for the Tent. [21] Each frame was 15 feet tall and 27 inches wide, [22] with two matching projections, so that the frames could be joined together. All the frames had these projections. [23] They made twenty frames for the south side [24] and forty silver bases to go under them, two bases under each

frame to hold its two projections. [25] They made twenty frames for the north side of the Tent [26] and forty silver bases, two under each frame. [27] For the back of the Tent, on the west, they made six frames [28] and two frames for the corners. [29] These corner frames were joined at the bottom and connected all the way to the top. The two frames that formed the two corners were made in this way. [30] So there were eight frames and sixteen silver bases, two under each frame.

[31] They made fifteen crossbars of acacia wood, five for the frames on one side of the Tent, [32] five for the frames on the other side, and five for the frames on the west end, at the back. [33] The middle crossbar, set halfway up the frames, extended from one end of the Tent to the other. [34] They covered the frames with gold and fitted them with gold rings to hold the crossbars, which were also covered with gold.

[35] They made a curtain of fine linen, woven with blue, purple, and red wool and embroidered it with figures of winged creatures. [36] They made four posts of acacia wood to hold the curtain, covered them with gold, and fitted them with gold hooks. Then they made four silver bases to hold the posts. [37] For the entrance of the Tent they made a curtain of fine linen woven with blue, purple, and red wool and decorated with embroidery. [38] For this curtain they made five posts fitted with hooks, covered their tops and their rods with gold, and made five bronze bases for the posts.

Making the Covenant Box
(Exodus 25.10-22)

37 Bezalel made the Covenant Box out of acacia wood, 45 inches long, 27 inches wide, and 27 inches high. [2] He covered it with pure gold inside and out and put a gold border all around it. [3] He made four carrying rings of gold for it and attached them to its four feet, with two rings on each side. 4 He made carrying poles of acacia wood, covered them with gold, 5 and put them through the rings on each side of the Box. 6 He made a lid of pure gold, 45 inches long and 27 inches wide. 7 He made two winged creatures of hammered gold, 8 one for each end of the lid. He made them so that they formed one piece with the lid. 9 The winged creatures faced each other across the lid, and their outspread wings covered it.

Making the Table for the Bread Offered to God
(Exodus 25.23-30)

10 He made the table out of acacia wood, 36 inches long, 18 inches wide, and 27 inches high. 11 He covered it with pure gold and put a gold border around it. 12 He made a rim 3 inches wide around it and put a gold border around the rim. 13 He made four carrying rings of gold for it and put them at the four corners, where the legs were. 14 The rings to hold the poles for carrying the table were placed near the rim. 15 He made the poles of acacia wood and covered them with gold. 16 He made the dishes of pure gold for the table: the plates, the cups, the jars, and the bowls to be used for the wine offering.

Making the Lampstand
(Exodus 25.31-40)

17 He made the lampstand of pure gold. He made its base and its shaft of hammered gold; its decorative flowers, including buds and petals, formed one piece with it. 18 Six branches extended from its sides, three from each side. 19 Each of the six branches had three decorative flowers shaped like almond blossoms with buds and petals. 20 The shaft of the lampstand had four decorative flowers shaped like almond blossoms with buds and petals. 21 There

was one bud below each of the three pairs of branches. 22 The buds, the branches, and the lampstand were a single piece of pure hammered gold. 23 He made seven lamps for the lampstand, and he made its tongs and trays of pure gold. 24 He used seventy-five pounds of pure gold to make the lampstand and all its equipment.

Making the Altar for Burning Incense
(Exodus 30.1-5)

25 He made an altar out of acacia wood, for burning incense. It was square, 18 inches long and 18 inches wide, and it was 36 inches high. Its projections at the four corners formed one piece with it. 26 He covered its top, all four sides, and its projections with pure gold and put a gold border around it. 27 He made two gold carrying rings for it and attached them below the border on the two sides, to hold the poles with which it was to be carried. 28 He made the poles of acacia wood and covered them with gold.

Making the Anointing Oil and the Incense
(Exodus 30.22-38)

29 He also made the sacred anointing oil and the pure sweet-smelling incense, mixed like perfume.

Making the Altar for Burning Offerings
(Exodus 27.1-8)

38 For burning offerings, he made an altar out of acacia wood. It was square, 7½ feet long and 7½ feet wide, and it was 4½ feet high. 2 He made the projections at the top of the four corners, so that they formed one piece with the altar. He covered it all with bronze. 3 He also made all the equipment for the altar: the pans, the shovels, the bowls, the hooks, and the

37.29 Ex 30.22-38

fire pans. All this equipment was made of bronze. ⁴He made a bronze grating and put it under the rim of the altar, so that it reached halfway up the altar. ⁵He made four carrying rings and put them on the four corners. ⁶He made carrying poles of acacia wood, covered them with bronze, ⁷and put them in the rings on each side of the altar. The altar was made of boards and was hollow.

Making the Bronze Basin
(Exodus 30.18)

⁸He made the bronze basin and its bronze base out of the mirrors belonging to the women who served at the entrance of the Tent of the LORD's presence.

The Enclosure for the Tent of the LORD's Presence
(Exodus 27.9-19)

⁹For the Tent of the LORD's presence he made the enclosure out of fine linen curtains. On the south side the curtains were 50 yards long, ¹⁰supported by twenty bronze posts in twenty bronze bases, with hooks and rods made of silver. ¹¹The enclosure was the same on the north side. ¹²On the west side there were curtains 25 yards long, with ten posts and ten bases and with hooks and rods made of silver. ¹³On the east side, where the entrance was, the enclosure was also 25 yards wide. ¹⁴⁻¹⁵On each side of the entrance there were 7½ yards of curtains, with three posts and three bases. ¹⁶All the curtains around the enclosure were made of fine linen. ¹⁷The bases for the posts were made of bronze, and the hooks, the rods, and the covering of the tops of the posts were made of silver. All the posts around the enclosure were connected with silver rods. ¹⁸The curtain for the entrance of the enclosure was made of fine linen woven with blue, purple, and red wool and decorated with embroi-

dery. It was 10 yards long and 2½ yards high, like the curtains of the enclosure. ¹⁹It was supported by four posts in four bronze bases. Their hooks, the covering of their tops, and their rods were made of silver. ²⁰All the pegs for the Tent and for the surrounding enclosure were made of bronze.

Metals Used in the Tent of the LORD's Presence

²¹Here is a list of the amounts of the metals used in the Tent of the LORD's presence, where the two stone tablets were kept on which the Ten Commandments were written. The list was ordered by Moses and made by the Levites who worked under the direction of Ithamar son of Aaron the priest. ²²Bezalel, the son of Uri and grandson of Hur from the tribe of Judah, made everything that the LORD had commanded. ²³His helper, Oholiab son of Ahisamach, from the tribe of Dan, was an engraver, a designer, and a weaver of fine linen and of blue, purple, and red wool.

²⁴All the gold that had been dedicated to the LORD for the sacred Tent weighed 2,195 pounds, weighed according to the official standard. ²⁵The silver from the census of the community weighed 7,550 pounds, weighed according to the official standard. ²⁶This amount equaled the total paid by all persons enrolled in the census, each one paying the required amount, weighed according to the official standard. There were 603,550 men twenty years old or older enrolled in the census. ²⁷Of the silver, 7,500 pounds were used to make the hundred bases for the sacred Tent and for the curtain, 75 pounds for each base. ²⁸With the remaining 50 pounds of silver Bezalel made the rods, the hooks for the posts, and the covering for their tops. ²⁹The bronze which was dedicated to the

38.8 Ex 30.18   **38.25, 26** Ex 30.11-16   **38.26** Mt 17.24

LORD amounted to 5,310 pounds. [30]With it he made the bases for the entrance of the Tent of the LORD's presence, the bronze altar with its bronze grating, all the equipment for the altar, [31]the bases for the surrounding enclosure and for the entrance of the enclosure, and all the pegs for the Tent and the surrounding enclosure.

Making the Garments for the Priests
(Exodus 28.1-14)

39 With the blue, purple, and red wool they made the magnificent garments which the priests were to wear when they served in the Holy Place. They made the priestly garments for Aaron, as the LORD had commanded Moses.

[2]They made the ephod of fine linen; blue, purple, and red wool; and gold thread. [3]They hammered out sheets of gold and cut them into thin strips to be worked into the fine linen and into the blue, purple, and red wool. [4]They made two shoulder straps for the ephod and attached them to its sides, so that it could be fastened. [5]The finely woven belt, made of the same materials, was attached to the ephod so as to form one piece with it, as the LORD had commanded Moses. [6]They prepared the carnelians and mounted them in gold settings; they were skillfully engraved with the names of the twelve sons of Jacob. [7]They put them on the shoulder straps of the ephod to represent the twelve tribes of Israel, just as the LORD had commanded Moses.

Making the Breastpiece
(Exodus 28.15-30)

[8]They made the breastpiece of the same materials as the ephod and with similar embroidery. [9]It was square and folded double, 9 inches long and 9 inches wide. [10]They mounted four rows of precious stones on it: in the first row they mounted a ruby, a topaz, and a garnet; [11]in the second row, an emerald, a sapphire, and a diamond; [12]in the third row, a turquoise, an agate, and an amethyst; [13]and in the fourth row, a beryl, a carnelian, and a jasper. These were mounted in gold settings. [14]Each of the twelve stones had engraved on it the name of one of the sons of Jacob, in order to represent the twelve tribes of Israel. [15]For the breastpiece they made chains of pure gold, twisted like cords. [16]They made two gold settings and two gold rings and attached the two rings to the upper corners of the breastpiece. [17]They fastened the two gold cords to the two rings [18]and fastened the other two ends of the cords to the two settings and in this way attached them in front to the shoulder straps of the ephod. [19]They made two rings of gold and attached them to the lower corners of the breastpiece, on the inside edge next to the ephod. [20]They made two more gold rings and attached them to the lower part of the front of the two shoulder straps of the ephod, near the seam and above the finely woven belt. [21]Just as the LORD had commanded Moses, they tied the rings of the breastpiece to the rings of the ephod with a blue cord, so that the breastpiece rested above the belt and did not come loose.

Making the Other Priestly Garments
(Exodus 28.31-43)

[22]The robe that goes under the ephod was made entirely of blue wool. [23]The hole for the head was reinforced with a woven binding to keep it from tearing. [24-26]All around its lower hem they put pomegranates of fine linen and of blue, purple, and red wool, alternating with bells of pure gold, just as the LORD had commanded Moses.

[27]They made the shirts for Aaron and his sons, [28]and the turban, the caps, the linen shorts, [29]and the sash of fine linen and of blue, purple, and red wool, decorated with embroidery, as the LORD had commanded Moses. [30]They made the ornament, the sacred sign of

dedication, out of pure gold, and they engraved on it "Dedicated to the LORD." 31 They tied it to the front of the turban with a blue cord, just as the LORD had commanded Moses.

The Completion of the Work
(Exodus 35.10-19)

32 All the work on the Tent of the LORD's presence was finally completed. The Israelites made everything just as the LORD had commanded Moses. 33 They brought to Moses the Tent and all its equipment, its hooks, its frames, its crossbars, its posts, and its bases; 34 the covering of rams' skin dyed red; the covering of fine leather; the curtain; 35 the Covenant Box containing the stone tablets, its poles, and its lid; 36 the table and all its equipment, and the bread offered to God; 37 the lampstand of pure gold, its lamps, all its equipment, and the oil for the lamps; 38 the gold altar; the anointing oil; the sweet-smelling incense; the curtain for the entrance of the Tent; 39 the bronze altar with its bronze grating, its poles, and all its equipment; the washbasin and its base; 40 the curtains for the enclosure and its posts and bases; the curtain for the entrance of the enclosure and its ropes; the Tent pegs; all the equipment to be used in the Tent; 41 and the magnificent garments the priests were to wear in the Holy Place — the sacred clothes for Aaron the priest and for his sons. 42 The Israelites had done all the work just as the LORD had commanded Moses. 43 Moses examined everything and saw that they had made it all just as the LORD had commanded. So Moses blessed them.

Setting Up and Dedicating the Tent of the LORD's Presence

40 The LORD said to Moses, 2 "On the first day of the first month set up the Tent of the LORD's presence. 3 Place in it the Covenant Box containing the Ten Commandments and put

the curtain in front of it. 4 Bring in the table and place the equipment on it. Also bring in the lampstand and set up the lamps on it. 5 Put the gold altar for burning incense in front of the Covenant Box and hang the curtain at the entrance of the Tent. 6 Put in front of the Tent the altar for burning offerings. 7 Put the washbasin between the Tent and the altar and fill it with water. 8 Put up the surrounding enclosure and hang the curtain at its entrance.

9 "Then dedicate the Tent and all its equipment by anointing it with the sacred oil, and it will be holy. 10 Next, dedicate the altar and all its equipment by anointing it, and it will be completely holy. 11 Also dedicate the washbasin and its base in the same way.

12 "Bring Aaron and his sons to the entrance of the Tent, and have them take a ritual bath. 13 Dress Aaron in the priestly garments, anoint him, and in this way consecrate him, so that he can serve me as priest. 14 Bring his sons and put the shirts on them. 15 Then anoint them, just as you anointed their father, so that they can serve me as priests. This anointing will make them priests for all time to come."

16 Moses did everything just as the LORD had commanded. 17 So on the first day of the first month of the second year after they left Egypt, the Tent of the LORD's presence was set up. 18 Moses put down its bases, set up its frames, attached its crossbars, and put up its posts. 19 He spread out the covering over the Tent and put the outer covering over it, just as the LORD had commanded. 20 Then he took the two stone tablets and put them in the Covenant Box. He put the poles in the rings of the Box and put the lid on it. 21 Then he put the Box in the Tent and hung up the curtain. In this way he screened off the Covenant Box, just as the LORD had commanded.

22 He put the table in the Tent, on the north side outside the curtain, 23 and placed on it the bread offered to the

LORD, just as the LORD had commanded. 24 He put the lampstand in the Tent, on the south side, opposite the table, 25 and there in the LORD's presence he lit the lamps, just as the LORD had commanded. 26 He put the gold altar in the Tent, in front of the curtain, 27 and burned the sweet-smelling incense, just as the LORD had commanded. 28 He hung the curtain at the entrance of the Tent, 29 and there in front of the curtain he placed the altar for burning offerings. On it he sacrificed the burnt offering and the grain offering, just as the LORD had commanded. 30 He put the washbasin between the Tent and the altar and filled it with water. 31 Moses, Aaron, and his sons washed their hands and their feet there 32 whenever they went into the Tent or to the altar, just as the LORD had commanded. 33 Moses

40.34 1 K 8.10, 11; Is 6.4; Ez 43.4, 5; Rev 15.8

set up the enclosure around the Tent and the altar and hung the curtain at the entrance of the enclosure. So he finished all the work.

The Cloud over the Tent of the LORD's Presence
(Numbers 9.15-23)

34 Then the cloud covered the Tent and the dazzling light of the LORD's presence filled it. 35 Because of this, Moses could not go into the Tent. 36 The Israelites moved their camp to another place only when the cloud lifted from the Tent. 37 As long as the cloud stayed there, they did not move their camp. 38 During all their wanderings they could see the cloud of the LORD's presence over the Tent during the day and a fire burning above it during the night.

LEVITICUS

INTRODUCTION

Leviticus contains regulations for worship and religious ceremonies in ancient Israel, and for the priests who were responsible for carrying out these instructions.

The main theme of the book is the holiness of God and the ways in which his people were to worship and live so as to maintain their relationship with "the holy God of Israel."

The best known words from the book, found in 19.18, are those which Jesus called the second great commandment: "Love your neighbors as you love yourself."

OUTLINE OF CONTENTS

Sacrifices Burned Whole

1 The LORD called to Moses from the Tent of the LORD's presence and gave him the following rules ²for the Israelites to observe when they offer their sacrifices.

When you offer an animal sacrifice, it may be one of your cattle or one of your sheep or goats. ³If you are offering one of your cattle as a burnt offering, you must bring a bull without any defects. You must present it at the entrance of the Tent of the LORD's presence so that the LORD will accept you. ⁴You shall put your hand on its head, and it will be accepted as a sacrifice to take away your sins. ⁵You shall kill the bull there, and the Aaronite priests shall present the blood to the LORD and then throw it against all four sides of the altar located at the entrance of the Tent. ⁶Then you shall skin the animal and cut it up, ⁷and the priests shall arrange firewood on the altar and light it. ⁸They shall put on the fire the pieces of the animal, including the head and the fat. ⁹You must wash the internal organs and the hind legs, and the officiating priest will burn the whole sacrifice on the altar. The odor of this food offering is pleasing to the LORD.

¹⁰If you are offering one of your sheep or goats, it must be a male without any defects. ¹¹You shall kill it on the north side of the altar, and the priests shall throw its blood on all four sides of the altar. ¹²After you cut it up, the officiating priest shall put on the fire all the parts, including the head and the fat. ¹³You must wash the internal organs and the hind legs, and the priest will present the sacrifice to the LORD and burn all of it on the altar. The odor of this food offering is pleasing to the LORD.

¹⁴If you are offering a bird as a burnt offering, it must be a dove or a pigeon. ¹⁵The priest shall present it at the altar, wring its neck, and burn its head on the altar. Its blood shall be drained out against the side of the altar. ¹⁶He shall

remove the crop and its contents and throw them away on the east side of the altar where the ashes are put. [17] He shall take hold of its wings and tear its body open, without tearing the wings off, and then burn it whole on the altar. The odor of this food offering is pleasing to the LORD.

Grain Offerings

2 When any of you present an offering of grain to the LORD, you must first grind it into flour. You must put olive oil and incense on it [2] and bring it to the Aaronite priests. The officiating priest shall take a handful of the flour and oil and all of the incense and burn it on the altar as a token that it has all been offered to the LORD. The odor of this food offering is pleasing to the LORD. [3] The rest of the grain offering belongs to the priests; it is very holy, since it is taken from the food offered to the LORD.

[4] If the offering is bread baked in an oven, it must be made without yeast. It may be thick loaves made of flour mixed with olive oil or thin cakes brushed with olive oil.

[5] If the offering is bread cooked on a griddle, it is to be made of flour mixed with olive oil but without yeast. [6] Crumble it up and pour the oil on it when you present it as an offering.

[7] If the offering is bread cooked in a pan, it is to be made of flour and olive oil. [8] Bring it as an offering to the LORD and present it to the priest, who will take it to the altar. [9] The priest will take part of it as a token that it has all been offered to the LORD, and he will burn it on the altar. The odor of this food offering is pleasing to the LORD. [10] The rest of the offering belongs to the priests; it is very holy, since it is taken from the food offered to the LORD.

[11] None of the grain offerings which you present to the LORD may be made with yeast; you must never use yeast or honey in food offered to the LORD. [12] An offering of the first grain that you harvest each year shall be brought to the LORD, but it is not to be burned on the altar. [13] Put salt on every grain offering, because salt represents the covenant between you and God. (You must put salt on all your offerings.) [14] When you bring to the LORD an offering of the first grain harvested, offer roasted grain or ground meal. [15] Add olive oil and put incense on it. [16] The priest will burn that part of the meal and oil that is to serve as a token, and also all the incense, as a food offering to the LORD.

Fellowship Offerings

3 When any of you offer one of your cattle as a fellowship offering, it is to be a bull or a cow without any defects. [2] You shall put your hand on the head of the animal and kill it at the entrance of the Tent of the LORD's presence. The Aaronite priests shall throw the blood against all four sides of the altar [3] and present the following parts of the animal as a food offering to the LORD: all the fat on the internal organs, [4] the kidneys and the fat on them, and the best part of the liver. [5] The priests shall burn all this on the altar along with the burnt offerings. The odor of this food offering is pleasing to the LORD.

[6] If a sheep or goat is used as a fellowship offering, it may be male or female, but it must be without any defects. [7] If you offer a sheep, [8] you shall put your hand on its head and kill it in front of the Tent. The priests shall throw its blood against all four sides of the altar [9] and present the following parts of the animal as a food offering to the LORD: the fat, the entire fat tail cut off near the backbone, all the fat covering the internal organs, [10] the kidneys and the fat on them, and the best part of the liver. [11] The officiating priest shall burn all this on the altar as a food offering to the LORD.

[12] If you offer a goat, [13] you shall put

your hand on its head and kill it in front of the Tent. The priests shall throw its blood against all four sides of the altar [14] and present the following parts as a food offering to the LORD: all the fat on the internal organs, [15] the kidneys and the fat on them, and the best part of the liver. [16] The priest shall burn all this on the altar as a food offering pleasing to the LORD. All the fat belongs to the LORD. [17] No Israelite may eat any fat or any blood; this is a rule to be kept forever by all Israelites wherever they live.

Offerings for Unintentional Sins

4 The LORD commanded Moses [2] to tell the people of Israel that anyone who sinned and broke any of the LORD's commands without intending to, would have to observe the following rules.

[3] If it is the High Priest who sins and so brings guilt on the people, he shall present a young bull without any defects and sacrifice it to the LORD for his sin. [4] He shall bring the bull to the entrance of the Tent, put his hand on its head, and kill it there in the LORD's

He shall bring the bull. (4.4)

presence. [5] Then the High Priest shall take some of the bull's blood and carry it into the Tent. [6] He shall dip his finger in the blood and sprinkle it in front of the sacred curtain seven times. [7] Then he shall put some of the blood on the projections at the corners of the incense altar in the Tent. He shall pour out the rest of the blood at the base of the altar used for burning sacrifices, which is at the entrance of the Tent. [8] From this bull he shall take all the fat, the fat on the internal organs, [9] the kidneys and the fat on them, and the best part of the liver. [10] The priest shall take this fat and burn it on the altar used for the burnt offerings, just as he does with the fat from the animal killed for the fellowship offering. [11] But he shall take its skin, all its flesh, its head, its legs, and its internal organs, including the intestines, [12] carry it all outside the camp to the ritually clean place where the ashes are poured out, and there he shall burn it on a wood fire.

[13] If it is the whole community of Israel that sins and becomes guilty of breaking one of the LORD's commands without intending to, [14] then as soon as the sin becomes known, the community shall bring a young bull as a sin offering. They shall bring it to the Tent of the LORD's presence; [15] the leaders of the community shall put their hands on its head, and it shall be killed there. [16] The High Priest shall take some of the bull's blood into the Tent, [17] dip his finger in it, and sprinkle it in front of the curtain seven times. [18] He shall put some of the blood on the projections at the corners of the incense altar inside the Tent and pour out the rest of it at the base of the altar used for burning sacrifices, which is at the entrance of the Tent. [19] Then he shall take all its fat and burn it on the altar. [20] He shall do the same thing with this bull as he does with the bull for the sin offering, and in this way he shall make the sacrifice for the people's sin, and they will be forgiven. [21] Then he shall take the bull outside the camp and burn it, just as he burns the bull offered for his own sin. This is an offering to take away the sin of the community.

22 If it is a ruler who sins and becomes guilty of breaking one of the LORD's commands without intending to, 23 then as soon as the sin is called to his attention, he shall bring as his offering a male goat without any defects. 24 He shall put his hand on its head and kill it on the north side of the altar, where the animals for the burnt offerings are killed. This is an offering to take away sin. 25 The priest shall dip his finger in the blood of the animal, put it on the projections at the corners of the altar, and pour out the rest of it at the base of the altar. 26 Then he shall burn all of its fat on the altar, just as he burns the fat of the animals killed for the fellowship offerings. In this way the priest shall offer the sacrifice for the sin of the ruler, and he will be forgiven.

27 If any of you people sin and become guilty of breaking one of the LORD's commands without intending to, 28 then as soon as the sin is called to your attention, you shall bring as your offering a female goat without any defects. 29 You shall put your hand on its head and kill it on the north side of the altar, where the animals for the burnt offerings are killed. 30 The priest shall dip his finger in the blood of the animal, put it on the projections at the corners of the altar, and pour out the rest of it at the base of the altar. 31 Then he shall remove all its fat, just as the fat is removed from the animals killed for the fellowship offerings, and he shall burn it on the altar as an odor pleasing to the LORD. In this way the priest shall offer the sacrifice for the man's sin, and he will be forgiven.

32 If you bring a sheep as a sin offering, it must be a female without any defects. 33 You shall put your hand on its head and kill it on the north side of the altar, where the animals for the burnt offerings are killed. 34 The priest shall dip his finger in the blood of the animal, put it on the projections at the corners

of the altar, and pour out the rest of it at the base of the altar. 35 Then he shall remove all its fat, just as the fat is removed from the sheep killed for the fellowship offerings, and he shall burn it on the altar along with the food offerings given to the LORD. In this way the priest shall offer the sacrifice for your sin, and you will be forgiven.

Cases Requiring Sin Offerings

5 Sin offerings are required in the following cases.

If you are officially summoned to give evidence in court and do not give information about something you have seen or heard, you must suffer the consequences.

2 If you unintentionally touch anything ritually unclean, such as a dead animal, you are unclean and guilty as soon as you realize what you have done.

3 If you unintentionally touch anything of human origin that is unclean, whatever it may be, you are guilty as soon as you realize what you have done.

4 If you make a careless vow, no matter what it is about, you are guilty as soon as you realize what you have done.

5 When you are guilty, you must confess the sin, 6 and as the penalty for your sin you must bring to the LORD a female sheep or goat as an offering. The priest shall offer the sacrifice for your sin.

7 If you cannot afford a sheep or a goat, you shall bring to the LORD as the payment for your sin two doves or two pigeons, one for a sin offering and the other for a burnt offering. 8 You shall bring them to the priest, who will first offer the bird for the sin offering. He will break its neck without pulling off its head 9 and sprinkle some of its blood against the side of the altar. The rest of the blood will be drained out at the base of the altar. This is an offering to take away sin. 10 Then he shall offer the second bird as a burnt offering, according

4.27-31 Nu 15.27, 28

to the regulations. In this way the priest shall offer the sacrifice for your sin, and you will be forgiven.

¹¹If you cannot afford two doves or two pigeons, you shall bring two pounds of flour as a sin offering. You shall not put any olive oil or any incense on it, because it is a sin offering, not a grain offering. ¹²You shall bring it to the priest, who will take a handful of it as a token that it has all been offered to the LORD, and he will burn it on the altar as a food offering. It is an offering to take away sin. ¹³In this way the priest shall offer the sacrifice for your sin, and you will be forgiven. The rest of the flour belongs to the priest, just as in the case of a grain offering.

Repayment Offerings

¹⁴The LORD gave the following regulations to Moses. ¹⁵If any of you sin unintentionally by failing to hand over the payments that are sacred to the LORD, you shall bring as your repayment offering to the LORD a male sheep or goat without any defects. Its value is to be determined according to the official standard. ¹⁶You must make the payments you have failed to hand over and must pay an additional 20 percent. You shall give it to the priest, and the priest shall offer the animal as a sacrifice for your sin, and you will be forgiven.

¹⁷If any of you sin unintentionally by breaking any of the LORD's commands, you are guilty and must pay the penalty. ¹⁸You must bring to the priest as a repayment offering a male sheep or goat without any defects. Its value is to be determined according to the official standard. The priest shall offer the sacrifice for the sin which you committed unintentionally, and you will be forgiven. ¹⁹It is a repayment offering for the sin you committed against the LORD.

6.1-7 Nu 5.5-8

6 The LORD gave the following regulations to Moses. ²An offering is to be made if any of you sin against the LORD by refusing to return what another Israelite has left as a deposit or by stealing something from him or by cheating him ³or by lying about something that has been lost and swearing that you did not find it. ⁴⁻⁵When you sin in any of these ways, you must repay whatever you got by dishonest means. On the day you are found guilty, you must repay the owner in full, plus an additional 20 percent. ⁶You shall bring to the priest as your repayment offering to the LORD a male sheep or goat without any defects. Its value is to be determined according to the official standard. ⁷The priest shall offer the sacrifice for your sin, and you will be forgiven.

Sacrifices Burned Whole

⁸The LORD commanded Moses ⁹to give Aaron and his sons the following regulations for burnt offerings. A burnt offering is to be left on the altar all night long, and the fire is to be kept burning. ¹⁰Then the priest, wearing his linen robe and linen shorts, shall remove the greasy ashes left on the altar and put them at the side of the altar. ¹¹Then he shall change his clothes and take the ashes outside the camp to a ritually clean place. ¹²The fire on the altar must be kept burning and never allowed to go out. Every morning the priest shall put firewood on it, arrange the burnt offering on it, and burn the fat of the fellowship offering. ¹³The fire must always be kept burning on the altar and never allowed to go out.

Grain Offerings

¹⁴The following are the regulations for grain offerings. An Aaronite priest shall present the grain offering to the LORD in front of the altar. ¹⁵Then he

shall take a handful of the flour and oil, and the incense on it, and burn it on the altar as a token that all of it has been offered to the LORD. The odor of this offering is pleasing to the LORD. 16-17 The priests shall eat the rest of it. It shall be made into bread baked without yeast and eaten in a holy place, the courtyard of the Tent of the LORD's presence. The LORD has given it to the priests as their part of the food offerings. It is very holy, like the sin offerings and the repayment offerings. 18 For all time to come any of the male descendants of Aaron may eat it as their continuing share of the food offered to the LORD. Anyone else who touches a food offering will be harmed by the power of its holiness.

19 The LORD gave Moses the following regulations 20 for the ordination of an Aaronite priest. On the day he is ordained, he shall present as an offering to the LORD two pounds of flour (the same amount as the daily grain offering), half in the morning and half in the evening. 21 It is to be mixed with oil and cooked on a griddle and then crumbled and presented as a grain offering, an odor pleasing to the LORD. 22 For all time to come this offering is to be made by every descendant of Aaron who is serving as High Priest. It shall be completely burned as a sacrifice to the LORD. 23 No part of a grain offering that a priest makes may be eaten; all of it must be burned.

Sin Offerings

24 The LORD commanded Moses 25 to give Aaron and his sons the following regulations for sin offerings. The animal for a sin offering shall be killed on the north side of the altar, where the animals for the burnt offerings are killed. This is a very holy offering. 26 The priest who sacrifices the animal shall eat it in a holy place, the courtyard of the Tent of the LORD's presence. 27 Anyone or anything that touches the flesh of the animal will be harmed by the power of its holiness. If any article of clothing is spattered with the animal's blood, it must be washed in a holy place. 28 Any clay pot in which the meat is boiled must be broken, and if a metal pot is used, it must be scrubbed and rinsed with water. 29 Any male of the priestly families may eat this offering; it is very holy. 30 But if any of the blood is brought into the Tent and used in the ritual to take away sin, the animal must not be eaten; it must be burned.

Repayment Offerings

7 The following are the regulations for repayment offerings, which are very holy. 2 The animal for this offering is to be killed on the north side of the altar, where the animals for the burnt offerings are killed, and its blood is to be thrown against all four sides of the altar. 3 All of its fat shall be removed and offered on the altar: the fat tail, the fat covering the internal organs, 4 the kidneys and the fat on them, and the best part of the liver. 5 The priest shall burn all the fat on the altar as a food offering to the LORD. It is a repayment offering. 6 Any male of the priestly families may eat it, but it must be eaten in a holy place, because it is very holy.

7 There is one regulation that applies to both the sin offering and the repayment offering: the meat belongs to the priest who offers the sacrifice. 8 The skin of an animal offered as a burnt offering belongs to the priest who offers the sacrifice. 9 Every grain offering that has been baked in an oven or prepared in a pan or on a griddle belongs to the priest who has offered it to God. 10 But all uncooked grain offerings, whether mixed with oil or dry, belong to all the Aaronite priests and must be shared equally among them.

Fellowship Offerings

11 The following are the regulations for the fellowship offerings presented to the LORD. 12 If you make this offering as

a thanksgiving offering to God, you shall present, together with the animal to be sacrificed, an offering of bread made without yeast: either thick loaves made of flour mixed with olive oil or thin cakes brushed with olive oil or cakes made of flour mixed with olive oil. 13 In addition, you shall offer loaves of bread baked with yeast. 14 You shall present one part of each kind of bread as a special contribution to the LORD; it belongs to the priest who takes the blood of the animal and throws it against the altar. 15 The flesh of the animal must be eaten on the day it is sacrificed; none of it may be left until the next morning.

16 If you bring a fellowship offering as fulfillment of a vow or as your own freewill offering, not all of it has to be eaten on the day it is offered, but any that is left over may be eaten on the following day. 17 Any meat that still remains on the third day must be burned. 18 If any of it is eaten on the third day, God will not accept your offering. The offering will not be counted to your credit but will be considered unclean, and whoever eats it will suffer the consequences. 19 If the meat comes into contact with anything ritually unclean, it must not be eaten, but must be burned.

Any of you that are ritually clean may eat the meat, 20 but if any of you who are not clean eat it, you shall no longer be considered one of God's people. 21 Also, if you eat the meat of this offering after you have touched anything ritually unclean, whether from a person or an animal, you shall no longer be considered one of God's people.

22 The LORD gave Moses the following regulations 23 for the people of Israel. No fat of cattle, sheep, or goats shall be eaten. 24 The fat of an animal that has died a natural death or has been killed by a wild animal must not

be eaten, but it may be used for any other purpose. 25 Anyone who eats the fat of an animal that may be offered as a food offering to the LORD will no longer be considered one of God's people. 26 No matter where the Israelites live, they must never use the blood of birds or animals for food. 27 Anyone who breaks this law will no longer be considered one of God's people.

28 The LORD gave Moses the following regulations 29 for the people of Israel. When any of you offer a fellowship offering you must bring part of it as a special gift to the LORD, 30 bringing it with your own hands as a food offering. You shall bring the fat of the animal with its breast and present it as a special gift to the LORD. 31 The priest shall burn the fat on the altar, but the breast shall belong to the priests. 32 The right hind leg of the animal shall be given as a special contribution 33 to the priest who offers the blood and the fat of the fellowship offering. 34 The breast of the animal is a special gift, and the right hind leg is a special contribution that the LORD has taken from the people of Israel and given to the priests. This is what the people of Israel must give to the priests for all time to come. 35 This is the part of the food offered to the LORD that was given to Aaron and his sons on the day they were ordained as priests. 36 On that day the LORD commanded the people of Israel to give them this part of the offering. It is a regulation that the people of Israel must obey for all time to come.

37 These, then, are the regulations for the burnt offerings, the grain offerings, the sin offerings, the repayment offerings, the ordination offerings, and the fellowship offerings. 38 There on Mount Sinai in the desert, the LORD gave these commands to Moses on the day he told the people of Israel to make their offerings.

7.26, 27 Gn 9.4; Lv 17.10-14; 19.26; Dt 12.16, 23; 15.23

The Ordination of Aaron and His Sons
(Exodus 29.1-37)

8 The LORD said to Moses, [2]"Take Aaron and his sons to the entrance of the Tent of my presence and bring the priestly garments, the anointing oil, the young bull for the sin offering, the two rams, and the basket of unleavened bread. [3]Then call the whole community together there."

[4]Moses did as the LORD had commanded, and when the community had assembled, [5]he said to them, "What I am now about to do is what the LORD has commanded."

[6]Moses brought Aaron and his sons forward and had them take a ritual bath. [7]He put the shirt and the robe on Aaron and the sash around his waist. He put the ephod[a] on him and fastened it by putting its finely woven belt around his waist. [8]He put the breastpiece on him and put the Urim and Thummim[b] in it. [9]He placed the turban on his head, and on the front of it he put the gold ornament, the sacred sign of dedication, just as the LORD had commanded him.

[10]Then Moses took the anointing oil and put it on the Tent of the LORD's presence and everything that was in it, and in this way he dedicated it all to the LORD. [11]He took some of the oil and sprinkled it seven times on the altar and its equipment and on the basin and its base, in order to dedicate them to the LORD. [12]He ordained Aaron by pouring some of the anointing oil on his head. [13]Next, Moses brought the sons of Aaron forward and put shirts on them, put sashes around their waists, and tied caps on their heads, just as the LORD had commanded.

[14]Then Moses brought the young bull for the sin offering, and Aaron and his sons put their hands on its head. [15]Moses killed it and took some of the blood, and with his finger put it on the projections at the corners of the altar, in order to dedicate it. He then poured out the rest of the blood at the base of the altar. In this way he dedicated it and purified it. [16]Moses took all the fat on the internal organs, the best part of the liver, and the kidneys with the fat on them, and burned it all on the altar. [17]He took the rest of the bull, including its skin, flesh, and intestines, and burned it outside the camp, just as the LORD had commanded.

[18]Next, Moses brought the ram for the burnt offering, and Aaron and his sons put their hands on its head. [19]Moses killed it and threw the blood on all four sides of the altar. [20-21]He cut the ram in pieces, washed the internal organs and the hind legs with water, and burned the head, the fat, and all the rest of the ram on the altar, just as the LORD had commanded. This burnt offering was a food offering, and its odor was pleasing to the LORD.

[22]Then Moses brought the second ram, which was for the ordination of priests, and Aaron and his sons put their hands on its head. [23]Moses killed it and took some of the blood and put it on the lobe of Aaron's right ear, on the thumb of his right hand, and on the big toe of his right foot. [24]Then he brought Aaron's sons forward and put some of the blood on the lobes of their right ears, on the thumbs of their right hands, and on the big toes of their right feet. Moses then threw the rest of the blood on all four sides of the altar. [25]He took the fat, the fat tail, all the fat covering the internal organs, the best part of the liver, the kidneys with the fat on them, and the right hind leg. [26]Then he took one loaf of bread from the basket of unleavened bread dedicated to the LORD, one loaf made with oil, and one thin cake, and he put them on top of the fat and the right hind leg. [27]He put all

---

[a] EPHOD: *See Word List.*   [b] URIM AND THUMMIM: *Two objects used by the priest to determine God's will; it is not known precisely how they were used.*

of this food in the hands of Aaron and his sons, and they presented it as a special gift to the LORD. 28 Then Moses took the food from them and burned it on the altar, on top of the burnt offering, as an ordination offering. This was a food offering, and its odor was pleasing to the LORD. 29 Then Moses took the breast and presented it as a special gift to the LORD. It was Moses' part of the ordination ram. Moses did everything just as the LORD had commanded.

30 Moses took some of the anointing oil and some of the blood that was on the altar and sprinkled them on Aaron and his sons and on their clothes. In this way he consecrated them and their clothes to the LORD.

In this way he consecrated them. (8.30)

31 Moses said to Aaron and his sons, "Take the meat to the entrance of the Tent of the LORD's presence, boil it, and eat it there with the bread that is in the basket of ordination offerings, just as the LORD commanded. 32 Burn up any meat or bread that is left over. 33 You shall not leave the entrance of the Tent for seven days, until your ordination rites are completed. 34 The LORD commanded us to do what we have done today, in order to take away your sin. 35 You must stay at the entrance of the Tent day and night for seven days, doing what the LORD has commanded. If you don't, you will die. This is what the LORD has commanded me." 36 So Aaron and his sons did everything that the LORD had commanded through Moses.

Aaron Offers Sacrifices

9 The day after the ordination rites were completed, Moses called Aaron and his sons and the leaders of Israel. 2 He said to Aaron, "Take a young bull and a ram without any defects and offer them to the LORD, the bull for a sin offering and the ram for a burnt offering. 3 Then tell the people of Israel to take a male goat for a sin offering, a one-year-old calf, and a one-year-old lamb without any defects for a burnt offering, 4 and a bull and a ram for a fellowship offering. They are to sacrifice them to the LORD with the grain offering mixed with oil. They must do this because the LORD will appear to them today."

5 They brought to the front of the Tent everything that Moses had commanded, and the whole community assembled there to worship the LORD. 6 Moses said, "The LORD has commanded you to do all this, so that the dazzling light of his presence can appear to you." 7 Then he said to Aaron, "Go to the altar and offer the sin offering and the burnt offering to take away your sins and the sins of the people. Present this offering to take away the sins of the people, just as the LORD commanded."

8 Aaron went to the altar and killed the young bull which was for his own sin offering. 9 His sons brought him the blood, and he dipped his finger in it, put some of it on the projections at the corners of the altar, and poured out the rest of it at the base of the altar. 10 Then he burned on the altar the fat, the kidneys, and the best part of the liver, just as the

LORD had commanded Moses. [11] But he burned the meat and the skin outside the camp.

[12] He killed the animal which was for his own burnt offering. His sons brought him the blood, and he threw it on all four sides of the altar. [13] They handed him the head and the other pieces of the animal, and he burned them on the altar. [14] Then he washed the internal organs and the hind legs and burned them on the altar on top of the rest of the burnt offering.

[15] After that, he presented the people's offerings. He took the goat that was to be offered for the people's sins, killed it, and offered it, as he had done with his own sin offering. [16] He also brought the animal for the burnt offering and offered it according to the regulations. [17] He presented the grain offering and took a handful of flour and burned it on the altar. (This was in addition to the daily burnt offering.) [18] He killed the bull and the ram as a fellowship offering for the people. His sons brought him the blood, and he threw it on all four sides of the altar. [19] Aaron put the fat parts of the bull and the ram [20] on top of the breasts of the animals and carried it all to the altar. He burned the fat on the altar [21] and presented the breasts and the right hind legs as the special gift to the LORD for the priests, as Moses had commanded.

[22] When Aaron had finished all the sacrifices, he raised his hands over the people and blessed them, and then stepped down. [23] Moses and Aaron went into the Tent of the LORD's presence, and when they came out, they blessed the people, and the dazzling light of the LORD's presence appeared to all the people. [24] Suddenly the LORD sent a fire, and it consumed the burnt offering and the fat parts on the altar. When the people saw it, they all shouted and bowed down with their faces to the ground.

The Sin of Nadab and Abihu

10 Aaron's sons, Nadab and Abihu, each took his fire pan, put live coals in it, added incense, and presented it to the LORD. But this fire was not holy, because the LORD had not commanded them to present it. [2] Suddenly the LORD sent fire, and it burned them to death there in the presence of the LORD. [3] Then Moses said to Aaron, "This is what the LORD was speaking about when he said, 'All who serve me must respect my holiness; I will reveal my glory to my people.' "[c] But Aaron remained silent.

[4] Moses called Mishael and Elzaphan, the sons of Uzziel, Aaron's uncle, and said to them, "Come here and carry your cousins' bodies away from the sacred Tent and put them outside the camp." [5] So they came and took hold of the clothing on the corpses and carried them outside the camp, just as Moses had commanded.

[6] Then Moses said to Aaron and to his sons Eleazar and Ithamar, "Do not leave your hair uncombed or tear your clothes to show that you are in mourning. If you do, you will die, and the LORD will be angry with the whole community. But all other Israelites are allowed to mourn this death caused by the fire which the LORD sent. [7] Do not leave the entrance of the Tent or you will die, because you have been consecrated by the anointing oil of the LORD." So they did as Moses said.

Rules for Priests

[8] The LORD said to Aaron, [9] "You and your sons are not to enter the Tent of my presence after drinking wine or beer; if you do, you will die. This is a

---

[c] I will reveal my glory to my people; *or* my people must honor me.
9.18 Lv 3.1-11   **9.22** Nu 6.22-26

The unclean animals (11)

law to be kept by all your descendants.
¹⁰ You must distinguish between what
belongs to God and what is for general
use, between what is ritually clean and
what is unclean. ¹¹ You must teach the
people of Israel all the laws which I
have given to you through Moses."

¹² Moses said to Aaron and his two remaining sons, Eleazar and Ithamar,
"Take the grain offering that is left over
from the food offered to the LORD, make
unleavened bread with it and eat it beside the altar, because this offering is
very holy. ¹³ Eat it in a holy place; it is
the part that belongs to you and your
sons from the food offered to the LORD.
That is what the LORD commanded me.
¹⁴ But you and your families may eat the
breast and the hind leg that are presented as the special gift and the special contribution to the LORD for the
priests. You may eat them in any ritually clean place. These offerings have
been given to you and your children as
the part that belongs to you from the
fellowship offerings of the people of Israel. ¹⁵ They shall bring the hind leg
and the breast at the time the fat is presented as a food offering to the LORD.
These parts belong to you and your

children forever, just as the LORD commanded."

¹⁶ Moses asked about the goat for the
sin offering and learned that it had already been burned. This made him angry at Eleazar and Ithamar, and he
demanded, ¹⁷ "Why didn't you eat the
sin offering in a sacred place? It is very
holy, and the LORD has given it to you
in order to take away the sin of the community. ¹⁸ Since its blood was not
brought into the sacred Tent, you
should have eaten the sacrifice there,
as I commanded."

¹⁹ Aaron answered, "If I had eaten the
sin offering today, would the LORD have
approved? The people presented their
sin offering to the LORD today, and they
brought their burnt offering, but still
these terrible things have happened to
me." ²⁰ When Moses heard this, he was
satisfied.

Animals That May Be Eaten
(Deuteronomy 14.3-21)

11 The LORD gave Moses and
Aaron the following regula-
tions ² for the people of Israel. You may
eat any land animal ³ that has divided

hoofs and that also chews the cud, 4-6but you must not eat camels, rock badgers, or rabbits. These must be considered unclean; they chew the cud, but do not have divided hoofs. 7Do not eat pigs. They must be considered unclean; they have divided hoofs, but do not chew the cud. 8Do not eat these animals or even touch their dead bodies; they are unclean.

9You may eat any kind of fish that has fins and scales, 10but anything living in the water that does not have fins and scales must not be eaten. 11Such creatures must be considered unclean. You must not eat them or even touch their dead bodies. 12You must not eat anything that lives in the water and does not have fins and scales.

13-19You must not eat any of the following birds: eagles, owls, hawks, falcons; buzzards, vultures, crows; ostriches; seagulls, storks, herons, pelicans, cormorants;*d* hoopoes; or bats.

20All winged insects are unclean, 21except those that hop. 22You may eat locusts, crickets, or grasshoppers. 23But all other small things that have wings and also crawl must be considered unclean.

24-28If you touch the dead bodies of the following animals, you will be unclean until evening: all animals with hoofs, unless their hoofs are divided and they chew the cud, and all four-footed animals with paws. If you carry their dead bodies, you must wash your clothes, but you will still be unclean until evening.

29-30Moles, rats, mice, and lizards must be considered unclean. 31Whoever touches them or their dead bodies will be unclean until evening. 32And if their dead bodies fall on anything, it will be unclean. This applies to any article of wood, cloth, leather, or sacking, no matter what it is used for. It shall be

dipped in water, but it will remain unclean until evening. 33And if their bodies fall into a clay pot, everything that is in it shall be unclean, and you must break the pot. 34Any food which could normally be eaten, but on which water from such a pot has been poured, will be unclean, and anything drinkable in such a pot is unclean. 35Anything on which the dead bodies fall is unclean; a clay stove or oven shall be broken, 36but a spring or a cistern remains clean, although anything else that touches their dead bodies is unclean. 37If one of them falls on seed that is going to be planted, the seed remains clean. 38But if the seed is soaking in water and one of them falls on it, the seed is unclean.

39If any animal that may be eaten dies, anyone who touches it will be unclean until evening. 40And if any of you eat any part of the animal, you must wash your clothes, but you will still be unclean until evening; any of you who carry the dead body must wash your clothes, but you will still be unclean until evening.

41You must not eat any of the small animals that move on the ground, 42whether they crawl, or walk on four legs, or have many legs. 43Do not make yourselves unclean by eating any of these. 44I am the LORD your God, and you must keep yourselves holy, because I am holy. 45I am the LORD who brought you out of Egypt so that I could be your God. You must be holy, because I am holy.

46This, then, is the law about animals and birds, about everything that lives in the water, and everything that moves on the ground. 47You must be careful to distinguish between what is ritually clean and unclean, between animals that may be eaten and those that may not.

d The identification of some of the birds in verses 13-19 is uncertain.
11.44 Lv 19.2; 1 P 1.16

The Purification of Women after Childbirth

12 The LORD gave Moses the following regulations [2] for the people of Israel. For seven days after a woman gives birth to a son, she is ritually unclean, as she is during her monthly period. [3] On the eighth day, the child shall be circumcised. [4] Then it will be thirty-three more days until she is ritually clean from her loss of blood; she must not touch anything that is holy or enter the sacred Tent until the time of her purification is completed.

[5] For fourteen days after a woman gives birth to a daughter, she is ritually unclean, as she is during her monthly period. Then it will be sixty-six more days until she is ritually clean from her loss of blood.

[6] When the time of her purification is completed, whether for a son or daughter, she shall bring to the priest at the entrance of the Tent of the LORD's presence a one-year-old lamb for a burnt offering and a pigeon or a dove for a sin offering. [7] The priest shall present her offering to the LORD and perform the ritual to take away her impurity, and she will be ritually clean. This, then, is what a woman must do after giving birth.

[8] If the woman cannot afford a lamb, she shall bring two doves or two pigeons, one for a burnt offering and the other for a sin offering, and the priest shall perform the ritual to take away her impurity, and she will be ritually clean.

Laws concerning Skin Diseases

13 The LORD gave Moses and Aaron these regulations. [2] If any of you have a sore on your skin or a boil or an inflammation which could develop into a dreaded skin disease, you shall be brought to the Aaronite priest. [3] The priest shall examine the sore, and if the hairs in it have turned white and

the sore appears to be deeper than the surrounding skin, it is a dreaded skin disease, and the priest shall pronounce you unclean. [4] But if the sore is white and does not appear to be deeper than the skin around it and the hairs have not turned white, the priest shall isolate you for seven days. [5] The priest shall examine you again on the seventh day, and if in his opinion the sore looks the same and has not spread, he shall isolate you for another seven days. [6] The priest shall examine you again on the seventh day, and if the sore has faded and has not spread, he shall pronounce you ritually clean; it is only a sore. You shall wash your clothes and be ritually clean. [7] But if the sore spreads after the priest has examined you and pronounced you clean, you must appear before the priest again. [8] The priest will examine you again, and if it has spread, he shall pronounce you unclean; it is a dreaded skin disease.

[9] If any of you have a dreaded skin disease, you shall be brought to the priest, [10] who will examine you. If there is a white sore on your skin which turns the hairs white and is full of pus, [11] it is a chronic skin disease. The priest shall pronounce you unclean; there is no need to isolate you, because you are obviously unclean. [12] If the skin disease spreads and covers you from head to foot, [13] the priest shall examine you again. If he finds that it actually has covered the whole body, he shall pronounce you ritually clean. If your whole skin has turned white, you are ritually clean. [14] But from the moment an open sore appears, you are unclean. [15] The priest shall examine you again, and if he sees an open sore, he shall pronounce you unclean. An open sore means a dreaded skin disease, and you are unclean. [16] But when the sore heals and becomes white again, you shall go to the priest, [17] who will examine you again. If the sore has turned white, you

are ritually clean, and the priest shall pronounce you clean.

18 If any of you have a boil that has healed 19 and if afterward a white swelling or a reddish-white spot appears where the boil was, you shall go to the priest. 20 The priest shall examine you, and if the spot seems to be deeper than the surrounding skin and the hairs in it have turned white, he shall pronounce

The priest shall examine you. (13.20)

you unclean. It is a dreaded skin disease that has started in the boil. 21 But if the priest examines it and finds that the hairs in it have not turned white and that it is not deeper than the surrounding skin, but is light in color, the priest shall isolate you for seven days. 22 If the spot spreads, the priest shall pronounce you unclean; you are diseased. 23 But if it remains unchanged and does not spread, it is only the scar left from the boil, and the priest shall pronounce you ritually clean.

24 In case any of you have been burned, if the raw flesh becomes white or reddish-white, 25 the priest shall examine you. If the hairs in the spot have turned white and it appears deeper than the surrounding skin, it is a dreaded skin disease that has started in

the burn, and the priest shall pronounce you unclean. 26 But if the hairs in it have not turned white and it is not deeper than the surrounding skin, but is light in color, the priest shall isolate you for seven days. 27 The priest shall examine you again on the seventh day, and if it is spreading, it is a dreaded skin disease, and the priest shall pronounce you unclean. 28 But if the spot remains unchanged and does not spread and is light in color, it is not a dreaded skin disease. The priest shall pronounce you ritually clean, because it is only a scar from the burn.

29 When any of you, male or female, have a sore on your head or chin, 30 the priest shall examine it. If it seems to be deeper than the surrounding skin and the hairs in it are yellowish and thin, it is a dreaded skin disease, and he shall pronounce you unclean. 31 If, when the priest examines you, the sore does not appear to be deeper than the surrounding skin, but there are still no healthy hairs in it, he shall isolate you for seven days. 32 The priest shall examine the sore again on the seventh day, and if it has not spread and there are no yellowish hairs in it and it does not seem to be deeper than the surrounding skin, 33 you shall shave the head except the area around the sore. The priest shall then isolate you for another seven days. 34 On the seventh day the priest shall again examine the sore, and if it has not spread and does not seem to be deeper than the surrounding skin, he shall pronounce you ritually clean. You shall wash your clothes, and you will be clean. 35 But if the sore spreads after you have been pronounced clean, 36 the priest shall examine you again. If the sore has spread, he need not look for yellowish hairs; you are obviously unclean. 37 But if in the priest's opinion the sore has not spread and healthy hairs are growing in it, the sore has healed, and the priest shall pronounce you ritually clean.

38 When any of you, male or female,

have white spots on the skin, ³⁹ the priest shall examine you. If the spots are dull white, it is only a blemish that has broken out on the skin; you are ritually clean.

⁴⁰⁻⁴¹ If you lose your hair at the back or the front of your head, this does not make you unclean. ⁴² But if a reddish-white sore appears on the bald spot, it is a dreaded skin disease. ⁴³ The priest shall examine you, and if there is a reddish-white sore, ⁴⁴ the priest shall pronounce you unclean, because of the dreaded skin disease on your head.

⁴⁵ If you have a dreaded skin disease, you must wear torn clothes, leave your hair uncombed, cover the lower part of your face, and call out, "Unclean, unclean!" ⁴⁶ You remain unclean as long as you have the disease, and you must live outside the camp, away from others.

Laws concerning Mildew

⁴⁷ When there is mildew^e on clothing, whether wool or linen, ⁴⁸ or on any piece of linen or wool cloth or on leather or anything made of leather, ⁴⁹ if it is greenish or reddish, it is a spreading mildew and must be shown to the priest. ⁵⁰ The priest shall examine it and put the object away for seven days. ⁵¹ He shall examine it again on the seventh day, and if the mildew has spread, the object is unclean. ⁵² The priest shall burn it, because it is a spreading mildew which must be destroyed by fire.

⁵³ But if, when he examines it, the priest finds that the mildew has not spread on the object, ⁵⁴ he shall order that it be washed and put away for another seven days. ⁵⁵ Then he shall examine it, and if the mildew has not changed color, even though it has not spread, it is still unclean; you must burn the object, whether the rot is on the front or the back. ⁵⁶ But if, when the

priest examines it again, the mildew has faded, he shall tear it out of the clothing or leather. ⁵⁷ Then, if the mildew reappears, it is spreading again, and the owner shall burn the object. ⁵⁸ If he washes the object and the spot disappears, he shall wash it again, and it will be ritually clean.

⁵⁹ This, then, is the law about mildew on clothing, whether it is wool or linen, or on linen or wool cloth or on anything made of leather; this is how the decision is made as to whether it is ritually clean or unclean.

Purification after Having Skin Diseases

14 The LORD gave Moses ² the following regulations about the ritual purification of those of you cured of a dreaded skin disease. On the day you are to be pronounced clean, you shall be brought to the priest, ³ and the priest shall take you outside the camp and examine you. If the disease is healed, ⁴ the priest shall order that two ritually clean birds be brought, along with a piece of cedar wood, a red cord, and a sprig of hyssop. ⁵ Then the priest shall order that one of the birds be killed over a clay bowl containing fresh spring water. ⁶ He shall take the other bird and dip it, together with the cedar wood, the red cord, and the hyssop, in the blood of the bird that was killed. ⁷ He shall sprinkle the blood seven times on the one of you who is to be purified from your skin disease, and then he shall pronounce you clean. He shall let the live bird fly away over the open fields. ⁸ You shall wash your clothes, shave off all your hair, and take a bath; you will then be ritually clean. You may enter the camp, but you must live outside your tent for seven days. ⁹ On the seventh day you shall again shave your head, your beard, your eyebrows, and all the rest of the hair on your body; you shall wash

---

^e MILDEW: *The Hebrew word for "dreaded skin disease" and "mildew" is the same.*
14.2 Mt 8.4; Mk 1.44; Lk 5.14; 17.14

your clothes and take a bath, and then you will be ritually clean.

10 On the eighth day you shall bring two male lambs and one female lamb a year old that are without any defects, five pounds of flour mixed with olive oil, and half a pint of olive oil. 11 The priest shall take you and these offerings to the entrance of the Tent of the LORD's presence. 12 Then the priest shall take one of the male lambs and together with the half pint of oil he shall offer it as a re-payment offering. He shall present them as a special gift to the LORD for the priest. 13 He shall kill the lamb in the holy place where the animals for the sin offerings and the burnt offerings are killed. He must do this because the re-payment offering, like the sin offering, belongs to the priest and is very holy. 14 The priest shall take some of the blood of the lamb and put it on the lobe of the right ear, on the thumb of the right hand, and on the big toe of the right foot of the one of you to be de-clared ritually clean. 15 The priest shall take some of the olive oil and pour it in the palm of his own left hand, 16 dip a finger of his right hand in it, and sprin-kle some of it seven times there in the LORD's presence. 17 He shall take some of the oil that is in the palm of his hand and some of the blood of the lamb and put them on the lobe of the right ear, on the thumb of the right hand, and on the big toe of the right foot of the one of you to be declared ritually clean. 18 He shall put the rest of the oil that is in the palm of his hand on your head. In this way he shall perform the ritual of purification.

19 Then the priest shall offer the sin offering and perform the ritual of purifi-cation. After that, he shall kill the ani-mal for the burnt offering 20 and offer it with the grain offering on the altar. In this way the priest shall perform the rit-ual of purification, and you will be ritu-ally clean.

21 If you are poor and cannot afford any more, you shall bring for your puri-fication only one male lamb as your re-payment offering, a special gift to the LORD for the priest. You shall bring only two pounds of flour mixed with olive oil for a grain offering and half a pint of ol-ive oil. 22 You shall also bring two doves or two pigeons, one for the sin offering and one for the burnt offering. 23 On the eighth day of your purification you shall bring them to the priest at the entrance of the Tent. 24 The priest shall take the lamb and the olive oil and present them as a special gift to the LORD for the priest. 25 He shall kill the lamb and take some of the blood and put it on the lobe of your right ear, on the thumb of your right hand, and on the big toe of your right foot. 26 The priest shall pour some of the oil into the palm of his own left hand 27 and with a finger of his right hand sprinkle some of it seven times there in the LORD's presence. 28 He shall put some of the oil on the same places he put the blood: on the lobe of your right ear, on the thumb of your right hand, and on the big toe of your right foot. 29 The rest of the oil that is in his palm he shall put on your head and in this way perform the ritual of purifi-cation. 30 Then he shall offer one of the doves or pigeons 31 as the sin offering and the other as the burnt offering with the grain offering. In this way the priest shall perform the ritual of purification. 32 This is the law for those who have a dreaded skin disease but who cannot afford the normal offerings required for his purification.

Mildew in Houses

33 The LORD gave Moses and Aaron 34-35 the following regulations about houses affected by spreading mildew. (These were to apply after the people of Israel entered the land of Canaan, which the LORD was going to give them as their possession.) If any of you find that the LORD has sent mildew on your house, then you must go and tell the priest about it. 36 The priest shall order everything to be moved out of the house

before he goes to examine the mildew; otherwise everything in the house will be declared unclean. Then he shall go to the house [37] and examine the mildew. If there are greenish or reddish spots that appear to be eating into the wall, [38] he shall leave the house and lock it up for seven days. [39] On the seventh day he shall return and examine it again. If the mildew has spread, [40] he shall order that the stones on which the mildew is found be removed and thrown into some unclean place out-

The stones shall be removed. (14.40)

side the city. [41] After that he must have all the interior walls scraped and the plaster dumped in an unclean place outside the city. [42] Then other stones are to be used to replace the stones that were removed, and new plaster will be used to cover the walls.

[43] If the mildew breaks out again in the house after the stones have been removed and the house has been scraped and plastered, [44] the priest shall go and look. If it has spread, the house is unclean. [45] It must be torn down, and its stones, its wood, and all its plaster must be carried out of the city to an unclean place. [46] Any who enter the house while it is locked up will be unclean until evening. [47] Any who lie down or eat in the house must wash their clothes.

[48] If, when the priest comes to look,

the mildew has not reappeared after the house has been replastered, he shall pronounce the house ritually clean, because the mildew has been completely removed. [49] To purify the house, he shall take two birds, some cedar wood, a red cord, and a sprig of hyssop. [50] He shall kill one of the birds over a clay bowl containing fresh spring water. [51] Then he shall take the cedar wood, the hyssop, the red cord, and the live bird and shall dip them in the blood of the bird that was killed and in the fresh water. And he shall sprinkle the house seven times. [52] In this way he shall purify the house with the bird's blood, the fresh water, the live bird, the cedar wood, the hyssop, and the red cord. [53] Then he shall let the live bird fly away outside the city over the open fields. In this way he shall perform the ritual of purification for the house, and it will be ritually clean.

[54] These are the laws about dreaded skin diseases; [55-56] sores, boils, or inflammations; and about mildew in clothes or houses. [57] These laws determine when something is unclean and when it is clean.

Unclean Bodily Discharges

15 The LORD gave Moses and Aaron the following regulations [2] for the people of Israel. When any man has a discharge from his penis, the discharge is unclean, [3] whether the penis runs with it or is stopped up by it. [4] Any bed on which he sits or lies is unclean. [5] Anyone who touches his bed [6] or sits on anything the man has sat on must wash his clothes and take a bath, and he remains unclean until evening. [7] Anyone who touches the man with the discharge must wash his clothes and take a bath, and he remains unclean until evening. [8] If the man with the discharge spits on anyone who is ritually clean, that person must wash his clothes and take a bath, and he remains unclean until evening. [9] Any saddle or seat on which the man with the discharge sits is unclean. ¹⁰Anyone who touches anything on which the man sat is unclean until evening. Anyone who carries anything on which the man sat must wash his clothes and take a bath, and he remains unclean until evening. ¹¹If a man who has a discharge touches one of you without first having washed his hands, you must wash your clothes and take a bath, and you remain unclean until evening. ¹²Any clay pot that the man touches must be broken, and any wooden bowl that he touches must be washed.

¹³After the man is cured of his discharge, he must wait seven days and then wash his clothes and take a bath in fresh spring water, and he will be ritually clean. ¹⁴On the eighth day he shall take two doves or two pigeons to the entrance of the Tent of the LORD's presence and give them to the priest. ¹⁵The priest shall offer one of them as a sin offering and the other as a burnt offering. In this way he will perform the ritual of purification for the man.

¹⁶When a man has an emission of semen, he must bathe his whole body, and he remains unclean until evening. ¹⁷Anything made of cloth or leather on which the semen falls must be washed, and it remains unclean until evening. ¹⁸After sexual intercourse both the man and the woman must take a bath, and they remain unclean until evening.

¹⁹When a woman has her monthly period, she remains unclean for seven days. Anyone who touches her is unclean until evening. ²⁰Anything on which she sits or lies during her monthly period is unclean. ²¹⁻²³Any who touch her bed or anything on which she has sat must wash their clothes and take a bath, and they remain unclean until evening. ²⁴If a man has sexual intercourse with her during her period, he is contaminated by her impurity and remains unclean for

seven days, and any bed on which he lies is unclean.

²⁵If a woman has a flow of blood for several days outside her monthly period or if her flow continues beyond her regular period, she remains unclean as long as the flow continues, just as she is during her monthly period. ²⁶Any bed on which she lies and anything on which she sits during this time is unclean. ²⁷Any who touch them are unclean and must wash their clothes and take a bath; they remain unclean until evening. ²⁸After her flow stops, she must wait seven days, and then she will be ritually clean. ²⁹On the eighth day she shall take two doves or two pigeons to the priest at the entrance of the Tent of the LORD's presence. ³⁰The priest shall offer one of them as a sin offering and the other as a burnt offering, and in this way he will perform the ritual of purification for her.

³¹The LORD told Moses to warn the people of Israel about their uncleanness, so that they would not defile the Tent of his presence, which was in the middle of the camp. If they did, they would be killed.

³²These are the regulations about a man who has a discharge or an emission of semen, ³³a woman during her monthly period, or a man who has sexual intercourse with a woman who is ritually unclean.

The Day of Atonement

16 The LORD spoke to Moses after the death of the two sons of Aaron who were killed when they offered unholy fire to the LORD. ²He said, "Tell your brother Aaron that only at the proper time is he to go behind the curtain into the Most Holy Place, because that is where I appear in a cloud above the lid on the Covenant Box. If he disobeys, he will be killed. ³He may enter the Most Holy Place only after he has

16.2 He 6.19 **16.3** He 9.7

brought a young bull for a sin offering and a ram for a burnt offering."

4 Then the LORD gave the following instructions. Before Aaron goes into the Most Holy Place, he must take a bath and put on the priestly garments: the linen robe and shorts, the belt, and the turban.

5 The community of Israel shall give Aaron two male goats for a sin offering and a ram for a burnt offering. 6 He shall offer a bull as a sacrifice to take away his own sins and those of his family. 7 Then he shall take the two goats to the entrance of the Tent of the LORD's presence. 8 There he shall draw lots, using two stones, one marked "for the LORD" and the other "for Azazel."*f*
9 Aaron shall sacrifice the goat chosen by lot for the LORD and offer it as a sin offering. 10 The goat chosen for Azazel shall be presented alive to the LORD and sent off into the desert to Azazel, in order to take away the sins of the people.

11 When Aaron sacrifices the bull as the sin offering for himself and his family, 12 he shall take a fire pan full of burning coals from the altar and two handfuls of fine incense and bring them into the Most Holy Place. 13 There in the LORD's presence he shall put the incense on the fire, and the smoke of the incense will hide the lid of the Covenant Box so that he will not see it and die. 14 He shall take some of the bull's blood and with his finger sprinkle it on the front of the lid and then sprinkle some of it seven times in front of the Covenant Box.

15 After that, he shall kill the goat for the sin offering for the people, bring its blood into the Most Holy Place, and sprinkle it on the lid and then in front of the Covenant Box, as he did with the bull's blood. 16 In this way he will perform the ritual to purify the Most Holy Place from the uncleanness of the people of Israel and from all their sins. He must do this to the Tent, because it stands in the middle of the camp, which is ritually unclean. 17 From the time Aaron enters the Most Holy Place to perform the ritual of purification until he comes out, there must be no one in the Tent. When he has performed the ritual for himself, his family, and the whole community, 18 he must then go out to the altar for burnt offerings and purify it. He must take some of the bull's blood and some of the goat's blood and put it all over the projections at the corners of the altar. 19 With his finger he must sprinkle some of the blood on the altar seven times. In this way he is to purify it from the sins of the people of Israel and make it holy.

The Scapegoat

20 When Aaron has finished performing the ritual to purify the Most Holy Place, the rest of the Tent of the LORD's presence, and the altar, he shall present to the LORD the live goat chosen for Azazel.*g* 21 He shall put both of his hands on the goat's head and confess over it all the evils, sins, and rebellions of the people of Israel, and so transfer them to the goat's head. Then the goat is to be driven off into the desert by someone appointed to do it. 22 The goat will carry all their sins away with him into some uninhabited land.

23 Then Aaron shall go into the Tent, take off the priestly garments that he had put on before entering the Most Holy Place, and leave them there. 24 He must take a bath in a holy place and put on his own clothes. After that, he shall go out and offer the burnt offering to remove his own sins and those of the people. 25 He shall burn on the altar the fat of the animal for the sin offering. 26 The man who drove the goat into the

---

f AZAZEL: *The meaning of this Hebrew word is unknown; it may be the name of a desert demon.* *g* AZAZEL: *See 16.8.*

16.15 He 9.12 **16.21, 22** Tb 8.3 **16.23** Ez 44.19

The goat will carry all their sins away. (16.22)

desert to Azazel must wash his clothes and take a bath before he comes back into camp. 27 The bull and the goat used for the sin offering, whose blood was brought into the Most Holy Place to take away sin, shall be carried outside the camp and burned. Skin, meat, and intestines shall all be burned. 28 The one who burns them must wash his clothes and take a bath before he returns to camp.

Observing the Day of Atonement

29 The following regulations are to be observed for all time to come. On the tenth day of the seventh month the Israelites and the foreigners living among them must fast and must not do any work. 30 On that day the ritual is to be performed to purify them from all their sins, so that they will be ritually clean. 31 That day is to be a very holy day, one on which they fast and do no work at all. These regulations are to be observed for all time to come. 32 The High Priest, properly ordained and consecrated to succeed his father, is to perform the ritual of purification. He shall put on the priestly garments 33 and perform the ritual to purify the Most Holy Place, the rest of the Tent of the LORD's presence, the altar, the priests, and all the people of the community. 34 These regulations are to be observed for all time to come. This ritual must be performed once a year to purify the people of Israel from all their sins.

So Moses[h] did as the LORD had commanded.

The Sacredness of Blood

17 The LORD commanded Moses 2 to give Aaron and his sons and all the people of Israel the following regulations. 3-4 Any Israelites who kill a cow or a sheep or a goat as an offering to the LORD anywhere except at the entrance of the Tent of the LORD's presence have broken the Law. They have shed blood and shall no longer be considered God's people. 5 The meaning of this command is that the people of Israel shall now bring to the LORD the animals which they used to kill in the open country. They shall now bring them to the priest at the entrance of the Tent and kill them as fellowship offerings. 6 The priest shall throw the blood against the sides of the altar at the entrance of the Tent and burn the fat to produce an odor that is pleasing to the LORD. 7 The people of Israel must no longer be unfaithful to the LORD by killing their animals in the fields as sacrifices to the goat demons. The people of Israel must keep this regulation for all time to come.

8 Any Israelites or any foreigners living in the community who offer a burnt offering or any other sacrifice 9 as an offering to the LORD anywhere except at the entrance of the Tent shall no longer be considered God's people.

10 If any Israelites or any foreigners living in the community eat meat with

blood still in it, the LORD will turn against them and no longer consider them his people. [11] The life of every living thing is in the blood, and that is why the LORD has commanded that all blood be poured out on the altar to take away the people's sins. Blood, which is life, takes away sins. [12] That is why the LORD has told the people of Israel that neither they nor any foreigner living among them shall eat any meat with blood still in it.

[13] If any Israelites or any foreigners living in the community catch an animal or a bird which is ritually clean, they must pour its blood out on the ground and cover it with dirt. [14] The life of every living thing is in the blood, and that is why the LORD has told the people of Israel that they shall not eat any meat with blood still in it and that anyone who does so will no longer be considered one of his people.

[15] Any people, Israelites or foreigners, who eat meat from an animal that has died a natural death or has been killed by wild animals must wash their clothes, take a bath, and wait until evening before they are ritually clean. [16] If they do not, they must suffer the consequences.

Forbidden Sexual Practices

18 The LORD told Moses [2] to say to the people of Israel, "I am the LORD your God. [3] Do not follow the practices of the people of Egypt, where you once lived, or of the people in the land of Canaan, where I am now taking you. [4] Obey my laws and do what I command. I am the LORD your God. [5] Follow the practices and the laws that I give you; you will save your life by doing so. I am the LORD."

[6] The LORD gave the following regulations. Do not have sexual intercourse with any of your relatives. [7] Do not disgrace your father by having intercourse with your mother. You must not disgrace your own mother. [8] Do not disgrace your father by having intercourse with any of his other wives. [9] Do not have intercourse with your sister or your stepsister, whether or not she was brought up in the same house with you. [10] Do not have intercourse with your granddaughter; that would be a disgrace to you. [11] Do not have intercourse with a half sister; she, too, is your sister. [12-13] Do not have intercourse with an aunt, whether she is your father's sister or your mother's sister. [14] Do not have intercourse with your uncle's wife; she, too, is your aunt. [15] Do not have intercourse with your daughter-in-law [16] or with your brother's wife. [17] Do not have intercourse with the daughter or granddaughter of a woman with whom you have had intercourse; they may be related to you, and that would be incest. [18] Do not take your wife's sister as one of your wives, as long as your wife is living.

[19] Do not have intercourse with a woman during her monthly period, because she is ritually unclean. [20] Do not have intercourse with another man's wife; that would make you ritually unclean. [21] Do not hand over any of your children to be used in the worship of the god Molech, because that would bring disgrace on the name of God, the LORD. [22] No man is to have sexual relations with another man; God hates that. [23] No man or woman is to have sexual relations with an animal; that perversion makes you ritually unclean.

[24] Do not make yourselves unclean by any of these acts, for that is how the pagans made themselves unclean, those pagans who lived in the land

---

17.11 He 9.22   **18.5** Ne 9.29; Ez 18.9; 20.11-13; Lk 10.28; Ro 10.5; Ga 3.12
18.8 Lv 20.11; Dt 22.30; 27.20   **18.9** Lv 20.17; Dt 27.22   **18.12-14** Lv 20.19, 20
18.15 Lv 20.12   **18.16** Lv 20.21   **18.17** Lv 20.14; Dt 27.23   **18.19** Lv 20.18
18.20 Lv 20.10   **18.21** Lv 20.1-5   **18.22** Lv 20.13   **18.23** Ex 22.19; Lv 20.15, 16; Dt 27.21

before you and whom the LORD is driving out so that you can go in. 25 Their actions made the land unclean, and so the LORD is punishing the land and making it reject the people who lived there. 26-27 They did all these disgusting things and made the land unclean, but you must not do them. All of you, whether Israelites or foreigners living with you, must keep the LORD's laws and commands, 28 and then the land will not reject you, as it rejected the pagans who lived there before you. 29 You know that whoever does any of these disgusting things will no longer be considered one of God's people.

30 And the LORD said, "Obey the commands I give and do not follow the practices of the people who lived in the land before you, and do not make yourselves unclean by doing any of these things. I am the LORD your God."

Laws of Holiness and Justice

19 The LORD told Moses 2 to say to the community of Israel, "Be holy, because I, the LORD your God, am holy. 3 Each of you must respect your mother and your father, and must keep the Sabbath, as I have commanded. I am the LORD your God.

4 "Do not abandon me and worship idols; do not make gods of metal and worship them. I am the LORD your God.

5 "When you kill an animal for a fellowship offering, keep the regulations that I have given you, and I will accept the offering. 6 The meat must be eaten on the day the animal is killed or on the next day. Any meat left on the third day must be burned, 7 because it is ritually unclean, and if anyone eats it, I will not accept the offering. 8 Any who eat it will

be guilty of treating as ordinary what is dedicated to me, and they will no longer be considered my people.

9 "When you harvest your fields, do not cut the grain at the edges of the fields, and do not go back to cut the heads of grain that were left. 10 Do not go back through your vineyard to gather the grapes that were missed or to pick up the grapes that have fallen; leave them here for poor people and foreigners. I am the LORD your God.

11 "Do not steal or cheat or lie. 12 Do not make a promise in my name if you do not intend to keep it; that brings disgrace on my name. I am the LORD your God.

13 "Do not rob or take advantage of anyone. Do not hold back the wages of someone you have hired, not even for one night. 14 Do not curse the deaf or put something in front of the blind so as to make them stumble over it. Obey me; I am the LORD your God.

15 "Be honest and just when you make decisions in legal cases; do not show favoritism to the poor or fear the rich. 16 Do not spread lies about anyone, and when someone is on trial for his life, speak out if your testimony can help him. I am the LORD.

17 "Do not bear a grudge against others, but settle your differences with them, so that you will not commit a sin

"Do not bear a grudge." (19.17)

19.2 Lv 11.44, 45; 1 P 1.16   **19.3 a** Ex 20.12; Dt 5.16; **b** Ex 20.8; Dt 5.12   **19.4 a** Lv 26.1; **b** Ex 20.23; 34.17; Dt 17.25   **19.9, 10** Lv 27.15; Dt 24.19-22   **19.11 a** Ex 20.15; Dt 5.19; **b** Ex 20.16; Dt 5.20   **19.12** Ex 20.7; Dt 5.11; Mt 5.33   **19.13** Dt 24.14, 15   **19.14** Dt 27.18   **19.15** Ex 23.6-8; Dt 16.19   **19.17** Mt 18.15

because of them.[i] 18 Do not take revenge on others or continue to hate them, but love your neighbors as you love yourself. I am the LORD.

19 "Obey my commands. Do not crossbreed domestic animals. Do not plant two kinds of seed in the same field. Do not wear clothes made of two kinds of material.

20 "If a slave woman is the recognized concubine of a man and she has not been paid for and freed, then if another man has sexual relations with her, they will be punished, but not[j] put to death, since she is a slave. 21 The man shall bring a ram to the entrance of the Tent of my presence as his repayment offering, 22 and with it the priest shall perform the ritual of purification to remove the man's sin, and God will forgive him.

23 "When you come into the land of Canaan and plant any kind of fruit tree, consider the fruit ritually unclean for the first three years. During that time you must not eat it. 24 In the fourth year all the fruit shall be dedicated as an offering to show your gratitude to me,[k] the LORD. 25 But in the fifth year you may eat the fruit. If you do all this, your trees will bear more fruit. I am the LORD your God.

26 "Do not eat any meat with blood still in it. Do not practice any kind of magic. 27 Do not cut the hair on the sides of your head or trim your beard 28 or tattoo yourselves or cut gashes in your body to mourn for the dead. I am the LORD.

29 "Do not disgrace your daughters by making them temple prostitutes;[l] if you do, you will turn to other gods and the land will be full of immorality. 30 Keep the Sabbath, and honor the place where I am worshiped. I am the LORD.

31 "Do not go for advice to people who consult the spirits of the dead. If you do, you will be ritually unclean. I am the LORD your God.

32 "Show respect for old people and honor them. Reverently obey me; I am the LORD.

Show respect for old people. (19.32)

33 "Do not mistreat foreigners who are living in your land. 34 Treat them as you would an Israelite, and love them as you love yourselves. Remember that you were once foreigners in the land of Egypt. I am the LORD your God.

35 "Do not cheat anyone by using false measures of length, weight, or quantity. 36 Use honest scales, honest

[i] so . . . them; *or* so that you do not commit this sin against them.   [j] they . . . not; *or* an investigation will be made but they will not be.   [k] to show your gratitude to me; *or* in praise of me.   [l] TEMPLE PROSTITUTES: *These women were found in Canaanite temples, where fertility gods were worshiped. It was believed that intercourse with these prostitutes assured fertile fields and herds.*

19.18 Mt 5.43; 19.19; 22.39; Mk 12.31; Lk 10.27; Ro 13.9; Ga 5.14; Jas 2.8
19.19 Dt 22.9-11   **19.26 a** Gn 9.4; Lv 7.26, 27; 17.10-14; Dt 12.16, 23; 15.23; **b** Dt 18.10
19.27, 28 Lv 21.5; Dt 14.1   **19.29** Dt 23.17   **19.30** Lv 26.2   **19.31** Dt 18.11; 1 S 28.3;
2 K 23.4; Is 8.19   **19.33, 34** Ex 22.21; Dt 24.17, 18; 27.19   **19.35, 36** Dt 25.13-16;
Pr 20.10; Ez 45.10

Love them as you love yourselves. (19.34)

weights, and honest measures. I am the LORD your God, and I brought you out of Egypt. ³⁷Obey all my laws and commands. I am the LORD."

Penalties for Disobedience

20 The LORD told Moses ²to say to the people of Israel, "Any of you or any foreigner living among you who gives any children to be used in the worship of the god Molech shall be stoned to death by the whole community. ³If any of you give one of your children to Molech and make my sacred Tent unclean and disgrace my holy name, I will turn against you and will no longer consider you my people. ⁴But if the community ignores what you have done and does not put you to death, ⁵I myself will turn against you and your whole family and against all who join you in being unfaithful to me and worshiping Molech. I will no longer consider any of you my people.

⁶"If any of you go for advice to people who consult the spirits of the dead, I will turn against you and will no longer consider you one of my people. ⁷Keep yourselves holy, because I am the LORD your God. ⁸Obey my laws, because I am the LORD and I make you holy."

⁹The LORD gave the following regulations. Any of you that curse your father or mother shall be put to death; you are responsible for your own death.

¹⁰If a man commits adultery with the wife of an Israelite, both he and the woman shall be put to death. ¹¹A man who has intercourse with one of his father's wives disgraces his father, and both he and the woman shall be put to death. They are responsible for their own death. ¹²If a man has intercourse with his daughter-in-law, they shall both be put to death. They have committed incest and are responsible for their own death. ¹³If a man has sexual relations with another man, they have done a disgusting thing, and both shall be put to death. They are responsible for their own death. ¹⁴If a man marries a woman and her mother, all three shall be burned to death because of the disgraceful thing they have done; such a thing must not be permitted among you. ¹⁵If a man has sexual relations with an animal, he and the animal shall be put to death. ¹⁶If a woman tries to have sexual relations with an animal, she and the animal shall be put to death. They are responsible for their own death.

¹⁷If a man marries his sister or half sister, they shall be publicly disgraced and driven out of the community. He has had intercourse with his sister and must suffer the consequences. ¹⁸If a man has intercourse with a woman during her monthly period, both of them are to be driven out of the community, because they have broken the regulations about ritual uncleanness.

¹⁹If a man has intercourse with his aunt, both of them must suffer the consequences for incest. ²⁰If a man has intercourse with his uncle's wife, he disgraces his uncle, and he and the

20.9 Ex 21.17; Mt 15.4; Mk 7.10 **20.10** Ex 20.14; Lv 18.20; Dt 5.18 **20.11** Lv 18.8;
Dt 22.30; 27.20 **20.12** Lv 18.15 **20.13** Lv 18.22 **20.14** Lv 18.17; Dt 27.23
20.15, 16 Ex 22.19; Lv 18.23; Dt 27.21 **20.17** Lv 18.9; Dt 27.22 **20.18** Lv 18.19
20.19, 20 Lv 18.12-14

woman will pay the penalty; neither one will have children. 21 If a man takes his brother's wife, they will die childless. He has done a ritually unclean thing and has disgraced his brother.

22 The LORD said, "Keep all my laws and commands, so that you will not be rejected by the land of Canaan, into which I am bringing you. 23 Do not adopt the customs of the people who live there; I am driving out those pagans so that you can enter the land. They have disgusted me with all their evil practices. 24 But I have promised you this rich and fertile land as your possession, and I will give it to you. I am the LORD your God, and I have set you apart from the other nations. 25 So then, you must make a clear distinction between animals and birds that are ritually clean and those that are not. Do not eat unclean animals or birds. I have declared them unclean, and eating them would make you unclean. 26 You shall be holy and belong only to me, because I am the LORD and I am holy. I have set you apart from the other nations so that you would belong to me alone.

27 "Any man or woman who consults the spirits of the dead shall be stoned to death; any of you that do this are responsible for your own death."

The Holiness of the Priests

21 The LORD commanded Moses to tell the Aaronite priests, "No priest is to make himself ritually unclean by taking part in the funeral ceremonies when a relative dies, 2 unless it is his mother, father, son, daughter, brother, 3 or unmarried sister living in his house. 4 He shall not make himself unclean at the death of those related to him by marriage. *m*

5 "No priest shall shave any part of his head or trim his beard or cut gashes on his body to show that he is in mourn-

ing. 6 He must be holy and must not disgrace my name. He offers food offerings to me, and he must be holy. 7 A priest shall not marry a woman who has been a prostitute or a woman who is not a virgin or who is divorced; he is holy. 8 The people must consider the priest holy, because he presents the food offerings to me. I am the LORD; I am holy and I make my people holy. 9 If a priest's daughter becomes a prostitute, she disgraces her father; she shall be burned to death.

10 "The High Priest has had the anointing oil poured on his head and has been consecrated to wear the priestly garments, so he must not leave his hair uncombed or tear his clothes to show that he is in mourning. 11-12 He has been dedicated to me and is not to make himself ritually unclean nor is he to defile my sacred Tent by leaving it and entering a house where there is a dead person, even if it is his own father or mother. 13 He shall marry a virgin, 14 not a widow or a divorced woman or a woman who has been a prostitute. He shall marry only a virgin from his own clan. 15 Otherwise, his children, who ought to be holy, will be ritually unclean. I am the LORD and I have set him apart as the High Priest."

16 The LORD commanded Moses 17 to tell Aaron, "None of your descendants who has any physical defects may present the food offering to me. This applies for all time to come. 18 No man with any physical defects may make the offering: no one who is blind, lame, disfigured, or deformed; 19 no one with a crippled hand or foot; 20 no one who is a hunchback or a dwarf; no one with any eye or skin disease; and no eunuch. 21 No descendant of Aaron the priest who has any physical defects may present the food offering to me. 22 Such a man may eat the food offered to me, both the holy food offering and the very

---

m Verse 4 in Hebrew is unclear.
20.21 Lv 18.16   **21.5** Lv 19.27, 28; Dt 14.1

holy food offering, 23 but because he has a physical defect, he shall not come near the sacred curtain or approach the altar. He must not profane these holy things, because I am the LORD and I make them holy."

24 This, then, is what Moses said to Aaron, the sons of Aaron, and to all the people of Israel.

The Holiness of the Offerings

22 The LORD commanded Moses 2 to tell Aaron and his sons, "You must not bring disgrace on my holy name, so treat with respect the sacred offerings that the people of Israel dedicate to me. I am the LORD. 3 If any of your descendants, while he is ritually unclean, comes near the sacred offerings which the people of Israel have dedicated to me, he can never again serve at the altar. This applies for all time to come. I am the LORD.

4 "None of the descendants of Aaron who has a dreaded skin disease or a discharge may eat any of the sacred offerings until he is ritually clean. Any priest is unclean if he touches anything which is unclean through contact with a corpse or if he has an emission of semen 5 or if he has touched an unclean animal or person. 6 Any priest who becomes unclean remains unclean until evening, and even then he may not eat any of the sacred offerings until he has taken a bath. 7 After the sun sets he is clean, and then he may eat the sacred offerings, which are his food. 8 He shall not eat the meat of any animal that has died a natural death or has been killed by wild animals; it will make him unclean. I am the LORD.

9 "All priests shall observe the regulations that I have given. Otherwise, they will become guilty and die, because they have disobeyed the sacred regulations. I am the LORD and I make them holy.

10 "Only a member of a priestly family may eat any of the sacred offerings; no one else may eat them — not even someone staying with a priest or hired by him. 11 But a priest's slaves, bought with his own money or born in his home, may eat the food the priest receives. 12 A priest's daughter who marries someone who is not a priest may not eat any of the sacred offerings. 13 But a widowed or divorced daughter who has no children and who has returned to live in her father's house as a dependent may eat the food her father receives as a priest. Only a member of a priestly family may eat any of it.

14 "If any people who are not members of a priestly family eat any of the sacred offerings without intending to, they must repay the priest its full value plus an additional 20 percent. 15 The priests shall not profane the sacred offerings 16 by letting any unauthorized people eat them; this would bring guilt and punishment on such people. I am the LORD and I make the offerings holy."

17 The LORD commanded Moses 18 to give Aaron and his sons and all the people of Israel the following regulations. When any Israelite or any foreigner living in Israel presents a burnt offering, whether as fulfillment of a vow or as a freewill offering, the animal must not have any defects. 19 To be accepted, it must be a male without any defects. 20 If you offer any animal that has any defects, the LORD will not accept it. 21 When anyone presents a fellowship offering to the LORD, whether as fulfillment of a vow or as a freewill offering, the animal must be without any defects if it is to be accepted. 22 Do not offer to the LORD any animal that is blind or crippled or mutilated, or that has a running sore or a skin eruption or scabs. Do not offer any such animals on the altar as a food offering. 23 As a freewill offering you may offer an animal that is

22.20 Dt 17.1

stunted or not perfectly formed, but it is not acceptable in fulfillment of a vow. 24 Do not offer to the LORD any animal whose testicles have been crushed, cut, bruised, or torn off. This is not permitted in your land.

25 Do not offer as a food offering any animal obtained from a foreigner. Such animals are considered defective and are not acceptable.

26-27 When a calf or a lamb or a kid is born, it must not be taken from its mother for seven days, but after that it is acceptable as a food offering. 28 Do not sacrifice a cow and its calf or a sheep and its lamb or a goat and its kid on the same day. 29 When you offer a sacrifice of thanksgiving to the LORD, follow the rules so that you will be accepted; 30 eat it the same day and leave none of it until the next morning.

31 The LORD said, "Obey my commands; I am the LORD. 32 Do not bring disgrace on my holy name; all the people of Israel must acknowledge me to be holy. I am the LORD and I make you holy; 33 and I brought you out of Egypt to become your God. I am the LORD."

The Religious Festivals

23 The LORD gave Moses 2 the following regulations for the religious festivals, when the people of Israel are to gather for worship. 3 You have six days in which to do your work, but remember that the seventh day, the Sabbath, is a day of rest. On that day do not work, but gather for worship. The Sabbath belongs to the LORD, no matter where you live. 4 Proclaim the following festivals at the appointed times.

Passover and Unleavened Bread
(Numbers 28.16-25)

5 The Passover, celebrated to honor the LORD, begins at sunset on the four-teenth day of the first month. 6 On the fifteenth day the Festival of Unleavened Bread begins, and for seven days you must not eat any bread made with yeast. 7 On the first of these days you shall gather for worship and do none of your daily work. 8 Offer your food offerings to the LORD for seven days. On the seventh day you shall again gather for worship, but you shall do none of your daily work.

9-10 When you come into the land that the LORD is giving you and you harvest your grain, take the first sheaf to the priest. 11 He shall present it as a special offering to the LORD, so that you may be accepted. The priest shall present it the day after the Sabbath. 12 On the day you present the offering of grain, also sacrifice as a burnt offering a one-year-old male lamb that has no defects. 13 With it you shall present four pounds of flour mixed with olive oil as a food offering. The odor of this offering is pleasing to the LORD. You shall also present with it an offering of one quart of wine. 14 Do not eat any of the new grain, whether raw, roasted, or baked into bread, until you have brought this offering to God. This regulation is to be observed by all your descendants for all time to come.

The Harvest Festival
(Numbers 28.26-31)

15 Count seven full weeks from the day after the Sabbath on which you bring your sheaf of grain to present to the LORD. 16 On the fiftieth day, the day after the seventh Sabbath, present to the LORD another new offering of grain. 17 Each family is to bring two loaves of bread and present them to the LORD as a special gift. Each loaf shall be made of four pounds of flour baked with yeast and shall be presented to the LORD as

23.3 Ex 20.8-10; 23.12; 31.15; 34.21; 35.2; Dt 5.12-14   **23.5** Ex 12.1-13; Dt 16.1, 2
23.6-8 Ex 12.14-20; 23.15; 34.18; Dt 16.3-8   **23.15-21** Ex 23.16; 34.22; Dt 16.9-12

Leave them for poor people. (23.22)

an offering of the first grain to be harvested. 18 And with the bread the community is to present seven one-year-old lambs, one bull, and two rams, none of which may have any defects. They shall be offered as a burnt offering to the Lord, along with a grain offering and a wine offering. The odor of this offering is pleasing to the Lord. 19 Also offer one male goat as a sin offering and two one-year-old male lambs as a fellowship offering. 20 The priest shall present the bread with the two lambs as a special gift to the Lord for the priests. These offerings are holy. 21 On that day do none of your daily work, but gather for worship. Your descendants are to observe this regulation for all time to come, no matter where they live.

22 When you harvest your fields, do not cut the grain at the edges of the fields, and do not go back to cut the heads of grain that were left; leave them for poor people and foreigners. The Lord is your God.

The New Year Festival
(Numbers 29.1-6)

23-24 On the first day of the seventh month observe a special day of rest, and come together for worship when the trumpets sound. 25 Present a food offering to the Lord and do none of your daily work.

The Day of Atonement
(Numbers 29.7-11)

26-27 The tenth day of the seventh month is the day when the annual ritual is to be performed to take away the sins of the people. On that day do not eat anything at all; come together for worship, and present a food offering to the Lord. 28 Do no work on that day, because it is the day for performing the ritual to take away sin. 29 Any who eat anything on that day will no longer be considered God's people. 30 And if any do any work on that day, the Lord himself will put them to death. 31 This regulation applies to all your descendants, no matter where they live. 32 From sunset on the ninth day of the month to sunset on the tenth observe this day as a special day of rest, during which nothing may be eaten.

The Festival of Shelters
(Numbers 29.12-40)

33-34 The Festival of Shelters begins on the fifteenth day of the seventh month and continues for seven days. 35 On the first of these days come together for worship and do none of your daily work. 36 Each day for seven days you shall present a food offering. On the eighth day come together again for worship and present a food offering. It is a day for worship, and you shall do no work.

23.22 Lv 19.9, 10; Dt 24.19-22 **23.26-32** Lv 16.29-34 **23.33-36** Dt 16.13-15

(³⁷These are the religious festivals on which you honor the LORD by gathering together for worship and presenting food offerings, burnt offerings, grain offerings, sacrifices, and wine offerings, as required day by day. ³⁸These festivals are in addition to the regular Sabbaths, and these offerings are in addition to your regular gifts, your offerings as fulfillment of vows, and your freewill offerings that you give to the LORD.)

³⁹When you have harvested your fields, celebrate this festival for seven days, beginning on the fifteenth day of the seventh month. The first day shall be a special day of rest. ⁴⁰On that day take some of the best fruit from your trees, take palm branches and limbs from leafy trees, and begin a religious festival to honor the LORD your God. ⁴¹Celebrate it for seven days. This regulation is to be kept by your descendants for all time to come. ⁴²All the people of Israel shall live in shelters for seven days, ⁴³so that your descendants may know that the LORD made the people of Israel live in simple shelters when he led them out of Egypt. He is the LORD your God.

⁴⁴So in this way Moses gave the people of Israel the regulations for observing the religious festivals to honor the LORD.

Taking Care of the Lamps
(Exodus 27.20, 21)

24 The LORD told Moses ²to give the following orders to the people of Israel: Bring pure olive oil of the finest quality for the lamps in the Tent, so that a light might be kept burning regularly. ³Each evening Aaron shall light them and keep them burning until morning, there in the LORD's presence outside the curtain in front of the Covenant Box, which is in the Most Holy Place. This regulation is to be observed for all time to come. ⁴Aaron shall take care of the lamps on the lampstand of pure gold and must see that they burn regularly in the LORD's presence.

The Bread Offered to God

⁵Take twenty-four pounds of flour and bake twelve loaves of bread. ⁶Put the loaves in two rows, six in each row, on the table covered with pure gold, which is in the LORD's presence. ⁷Put some pure incense on each row, as a token food offering to the LORD to take the place of the bread. ⁸Every Sabbath, for all time to come, the bread must be placed in the presence of the LORD. This is Israel's duty forever. ⁹The bread belongs to Aaron and his descendants, and they shall eat it in a holy place, because this is a very holy part of the food offered to the LORD for the priests.

An Example of Just and Fair Punishment

¹⁰⁻¹¹There was a man whose father was an Egyptian and whose mother was an Israelite named Shelomith, the daughter of Dibri from the tribe of Dan. There in the camp this man quarreled with an Israelite. During the quarrel he cursed the LORD, so they took him to Moses, ¹²put him under guard, and waited for the LORD to tell them what to do with him.

¹³The LORD said to Moses, ¹⁴"Take that man out of the camp. Everyone who heard him curse shall put his hands on the man's head to testify that he is guilty, and then the whole community shall stone him to death. ¹⁵Then tell the people of Israel that anyone who curses God must suffer the consequences ¹⁶and be put to death. Any Israelite or any foreigner living in Israel who curses the LORD shall be stoned to death by the whole community.

¹⁷"Any who commit murder shall be

24.5, 6 Ex 25.30   **24.9** Mt 12.4; Mk 2.26; Lk 6.4   **24.17** Ex 21.12

put to death, [18] and any who kill an animal belonging to someone else must replace it. The principle is a life for a life.

[19] "If any of you injure another person, whatever you have done shall be done to you. [20] If you break a bone, one of your bones shall be broken; if you put out an eye, one of your eyes shall be put out; if you knock out a tooth, one of your teeth shall be knocked out. Whatever injury you cause another person shall be done to you in return. [21] Whoever kills an animal shall replace it, but whoever kills a human being shall be put to death. [22] This law applies to all of you, to Israelites and to foreigners living among you, because I am the LORD your God."

[23] When Moses had said this to the people of Israel, they took the man outside the camp and stoned him to death. In this way the people of Israel did what the LORD had commanded Moses.

The Seventh Year
(Deuteronomy 15.1-11)

25 The LORD spoke to Moses on Mount Sinai and commanded him [2] to give the following regulations to the people of Israel. When you enter the land that the LORD is giving you, you shall honor the LORD by not cultivating the land every seventh year. [3] You shall plant your fields, prune your vineyards, and gather your crops for six years. [4] But the seventh year is to be a year of complete rest for the land, a year dedicated to the LORD. Do not plant your fields or prune your vineyards. [5] Do not even harvest the grain that grows by itself without being planted, and do not gather the grapes from your unpruned vines; it is a year of complete rest for the land. [6] Although the land has not been cultivated during that year, it will provide food for you, your slaves, your hired men, the foreigners living with you, [7] your domestic animals, and the wild animals in your fields. Everything that it produces may be eaten.

The Year of Restoration

[8] Count seven times seven years, a total of forty-nine years. [9] Then, on the tenth day of the seventh month, the Day of Atonement, send someone to blow a trumpet throughout the whole land. [10] In this way you shall set the fiftieth year apart and proclaim freedom to all the inhabitants of the land. During this year all property that has been sold shall be restored to the original owner or the descendants, and any who have been sold as slaves shall return to their families. [11] You shall not plant your fields or harvest the grain that grows by itself or gather the grapes in your unpruned vineyards. [12] The whole year shall be sacred for you; you shall eat only what the fields produce of themselves.

[13] In this year all property that has been sold shall be restored to its original owner. [14] So when you sell land to an Israelite or buy land, do not deal unfairly. [15] The price is to be set according to the number of years the land can produce crops before the next Year of Restoration. [16] If there are many years, the price shall be higher, but if there are only a few years, the price shall be lower, because what is being sold is the number of crops the land can produce. [17] Do not cheat an Israelite, but obey the LORD your God.

The Problem of the Seventh Year

[18] Obey all the LORD's laws and commands, so that you may live in safety in the land. [19] The land will produce its crops, and you will have all you want to eat and will live in safety.

[20] But someone may ask what there will be to eat during the seventh year, when no fields are planted and no crops

24.20 Ex 21.23-25; Dt 19.21; Mt 5.38   **24.22** Nu 15.16   **25.1-7** Ex 23.10, 11

gathered. 21 The LORD will bless the land in the sixth year so that it will produce enough food for two years. 22 When you plant your fields in the eighth year, you will still be eating what you harvested during the sixth year, and you will have enough to eat until the crops you plant that year are harvested.

Restoration of Property

23 Your land must not be sold on a permanent basis, because you do not own it; it belongs to God, and you are like foreigners who are allowed to make use of it.

24 When land is sold, the right of the original owner to buy it back must be recognized. 25 If any of you Israelites become poor and are forced to sell your land, your closest relative is to buy it back. 26 If you have no relative to buy it back, you may later become prosperous and have enough to buy it back yourself. 27 In that case you must pay to the one who bought it a sum that will make up for the years remaining until the next Year of Restoration, when you would in any event recover your land. 28 But if you do not have enough money to buy the land back, it remains under the control of the one who bought it until the next Year of Restoration. In that year it will be returned to its original owner.

29 If you sell a house in a walled city, you have the right to buy it back during the first full year from the date of sale. 30 But if you do not buy it back within the year, you lose the right of repurchase, and the house becomes the permanent property of the purchasers and their descendants; it will not be returned in the Year of Restoration. 31 But houses in unwalled villages are to be treated like fields; the original owner has the right to buy them back, and

they are to be returned in the Year of Restoration. 32 However, Levites have the right to buy back at any time their property in the cities assigned to them. 33 If a house in one of these cities is sold by a Levite and is not bought back, it must be returned in the Year of Restoration,[n] because the houses which the Levites own in their cities are their permanent property among the people of Israel. 34 But the pasture land around the Levite cities shall never be sold; it is their property forever.

Loans to the Poor

35 If any Israelites living near you become poor and cannot support themselves, you must provide for them as you would for a hired worker, so that

You must provide for them. (25.35)

they can continue to live near you. 36 Do not charge Israelites any interest, but obey God and let them live near you. 37 Do not make them pay interest on the money you lend them, and do not make a profit on the food you sell them. 38 This is the command of the LORD your God, who brought you out of Egypt in order to give you the land of Canaan and to be your God.

---

[n] *Probable text* If a house . . . Restoration; *Hebrew unclear.*
25.35 Dt 15.7, 8　**25.37** Ex 22.25; Dt 23.19, 20

Release of Slaves

39 If any Israelites living near you become so poor that they sell themselves to you as a slave, you shall not make them do the work of a slave. **40** They shall stay with you as hired workers and serve you until the next Year of Restoration. **41** At that time they and their children shall leave you and return to their family and to the property of their ancestors. **42** The people of Israel are the LORD's slaves, and he brought them out of Egypt; they must not be sold into slavery. **43** Do not treat them harshly, but obey your God. **44** If you need slaves, you may buy them from the nations around you. **45** You may also buy the children of the foreigners who are living among you. Such children born in your land may become your property, **46** and you may leave them as an inheritance to your children, whom they must serve as long as they live. But you must not treat any Israelites harshly.

47 Suppose a foreigner living with you becomes rich, while some Israelites become poor and sell themselves as slaves to that foreigner or to a member of that foreigner's family. **48** After they are sold, they still have the right to be bought back. A brother **49** or an uncle or a cousin or another close relative may buy them back; or if they themselves earn enough, they may buy their own freedom. **50** They must consult the one who bought them, and they must count the years from the time they sold themselves until the next Year of Restoration and must set the price for their release on the basis of the wages paid hired workers. **51-52** They must refund a part of the purchase price according to the number of years left, **53** as if they had been hired on an annual basis. Their master must not treat them harshly. **54** If they are not set free in any of these ways, they and their children must be set free in the next Year of Restoration. **55** Israelites cannot be permanent slaves, because the people of Israel are the LORD's slaves. He brought them out of Egypt; he is the LORD their God.

Blessings for Obedience
(Deuteronomy 7.12-24; 28.1-14)

26 The LORD said, "Do not make idols or set up statues, stone pillars, or carved stones to worship. I am the LORD your God. **2** Keep the religious festivals and honor the place where I am worshiped. I am the LORD.

3 "If you live according to my laws and obey my commands, **4** I will send you rain at the right time, so that the land will produce crops and the trees will bear fruit. **5** Your crops will be so plentiful that you will still be harvesting grain when it is time to pick grapes, and you will still be picking grapes when it is time to plant grain. You will have all that you want to eat, and you can live in safety in your land.

6 "I will give you peace in your land, and you can sleep without being afraid of anyone. I will get rid of the dangerous animals in the land, and there will be no more war there. **7** You will be victorious over your enemies; **8** five of you will be able to defeat a hundred, and a hundred will be able to defeat ten thousand. **9** I will bless you and give you many children; I will keep my part of the covenant that I made with you. **10** Your harvests will be so plentiful that they will last for a year, and even then you will have to throw away what is left of the old harvest to make room for the new. **11** I will live among you in my sacred Tent, and I will never turn away from you. **12** I will be with you; I will be your God, and you will be my people. **13** I, the LORD your God, brought you out of Egypt so that you would no longer be slaves. I broke the power that held you

25.39-46 Ex 21.2-6; Dt 15.12-18   **26.1 a** Lv 19.4; **b** Ex 20.4; Dt 5.8; 16.21, 22; 27.1
26.3-5 Dt 11.13-15; 28.1-14   **26.12** 2 Co 6.16

down and I let you walk with your head held high."

Punishment for Disobedience
(Deuteronomy 28.15-68)

¹⁴The LORD said, "If you will not obey my commands, you will be punished. ¹⁵If you refuse to obey my laws and commands and break the covenant I have made with you, ¹⁶I will punish you. I will bring disaster on you — incurable diseases and fevers that will make you blind and cause your life to waste away. You will plant your crops, but it will do you no good, because your enemies will conquer you and eat what you have grown. ¹⁷I will turn against you, so that you will be defeated, and those who hate you will rule over you; you will be so terrified that you will run when no one is chasing you.

¹⁸"If even after all of this you still do not obey me, I will increase your punishment seven times. ¹⁹I will break your stubborn pride; there will be no rain, and your land will be dry and as hard as iron. ²⁰All your hard work will do you no good, because your land will not produce crops and the trees will not bear fruit.

²¹"If you still continue to resist me and refuse to obey me, I will again increase your punishment seven times. ²²I will send dangerous animals among you, and they will kill your children, destroy your livestock, and leave so few of you that your roads will be deserted.

²³"If after all of this punishment you still do not listen to me, but continue to defy me, ²⁴then I will turn on you and punish you seven times harder than before. ²⁵I will bring war on you to punish you for breaking our covenant, and if you gather in your cities for safety, I will send incurable diseases among you, and you will be forced to surrender to your enemies. ²⁶I will cut off your food supply, so that ten women will need only one oven to bake all the bread they have. They will ration it out, and when you have eaten it all, you will still be hungry.

²⁷"If after all of this you still continue to defy me and refuse to obey me, ²⁸then in my anger I will turn on you and again make your punishment seven times worse than before. ²⁹Your hunger will be so great that you will eat your own children. ³⁰I will destroy your places of worship on the hills, tear down your incense altars, and throw your dead bodies on your fallen idols. In utter disgust ³¹I will turn your cities into ruins, destroy your places of worship, and refuse to accept your sacrifices. ³²I will destroy your land so completely that the enemies who occupy it will be shocked at the destruction. ³³I will bring war on you and scatter you in foreign lands. Your land will be deserted, and your cities left in ruins. ³⁴⁻³⁵Then the land will enjoy the years of complete rest that you would not give it; it will lie abandoned and get its rest while you are in exile in the land of your enemies.

³⁶"I will make those of you who are in exile so terrified that the sound of a leaf blowing in the wind will make you run. You will run as if you were being pursued in battle, and you will fall when there is no enemy near you. ³⁷You will stumble over one another when no one is chasing you, and you will be unable to fight against any enemy. ³⁸You will die in exile, swallowed up by the land of your enemies. ³⁹The few of you who survive in the land of your enemies will waste away because of your own sin and the sin of your ancestors.

⁴⁰"But your descendants will confess their sins and the sins of their ancestors, who resisted me and rebelled against me, ⁴¹and caused me to turn against them and send them into exile in the land of their enemies. At last,

when your descendants are humbled and they have paid the penalty for their sin and rebellion, [42] I will remember my covenant with Jacob and with Isaac and with Abraham, and I will renew my promise to give my people the land. [43] First, however, the land must be rid of its people, so that it can enjoy its complete rest, and they must pay the full penalty for having rejected my laws and my commands. [44] But even then, when they are still in the land of their enemies, I will not completely abandon them or destroy them. That would put an end to my covenant with them, and I am the LORD their God. [45] I will renew the covenant that I made with their ancestors when I showed all the nations my power by bringing my people out of Egypt, in order that I, the LORD, might be their God."

[46] All these are the laws and commands that the LORD gave to Moses on Mount Sinai for the people of Israel.

Laws concerning Gifts to the LORD

27 The LORD gave Moses [2] the following regulations for the people of Israel. When any of you have been given to the LORD in fulfillment of a special vow, you may be set free by the payment of the following sums of money, [3-7] according to the official standard:

- —adult male, twenty to sixty years old: 50 pieces of silver
- —adult female: 30 pieces of silver
- —young male, five to twenty years old: 20 pieces of silver
- —young female: 10 pieces of silver
- —infant male under five: 5 pieces of silver
- —infant female: 3 pieces of silver
- —male above sixty years of age: 15 pieces of silver
- —female above sixty: 10 pieces of silver

[8] If any of you make a vow and are too poor to pay the standard price, you shall bring the person to the priest, and the priest will set a lower price, according to your ability to pay.

[9] If your vow concerns an animal that is acceptable as an offering to the LORD, then every gift made to the LORD is sacred, [10] and you may not substitute another animal for it. If you do, both animals belong to the LORD. [11] But if your vow concerns a ritually unclean animal, which is not acceptable as an offering to the LORD, you shall take the animal to the priest. [12] The priest shall set a price for it, according to its good or bad qualities, and the price will be final. [13] If you wish to buy it back, you must pay the price plus an additional 20 percent.

[14] When any of you dedicate your house to the LORD, the priest shall set the price according to its good or bad points, and the price will be final. [15] If you wish to buy your house back, you must pay the price plus an additional 20 percent.

[16] If any of you dedicate part of your land to the LORD, the price shall be set according to the amount of seed it takes to sow it, at the rate of ten pieces of silver per bushel of barley. [17] If you dedicate the land immediately after a Year of Restoration, the full price applies. [18] If you dedicate it any time later, the priest shall estimate the cash value according to the number of years left until the next Year of Restoration, and set a reduced price. [19] If you wish to buy your field back, you must pay the price plus an additional 20 percent. [20] If you sell the field to someone else without first buying it back from the LORD, you lose the right to buy it back. [21] At the next Year of Restoration the field will become the LORD's permanent property; it shall belong to the priests.

26.42 a Gn 28.13, 14; **b** Gn 26.3, 4; **c** Gn 17.7, 8

²²If you dedicate to the Lord a field that you have bought, ²³the priest shall estimate its value according to the number of years until the next Year of Restoration, and you must pay the price that very day; the money belongs to the Lord. ²⁴At the Year of Restoration the field shall be returned to the original owner or to the descendants.

²⁵All prices shall be set according to the official standard.

²⁶The first-born of an animal already belongs to the Lord, so no one may dedicate it to him as a freewill offering. A calf, a lamb, or a kid belongs to the Lord, ²⁷but the first-born of an unclean animal may be bought back at the standard price plus an additional 20 percent. If it is not bought back, it may be sold to someone else at the standard price.

²⁸None of you may sell or buy back what you have unconditionally dedicated^o to the Lord, whether it is a hu- man being, an animal, or land. It belongs permanently to the Lord. ²⁹Not even human beings who have been unconditionally dedicated may be bought back; they must be put to death.

³⁰One tenth of all the produce of the land, whether grain or fruit, belongs to the Lord. ³¹If you wish to buy any of it back, you must pay the standard price plus an additional 20 percent. ³²One of every ten domestic animals belongs to the Lord. When the animals are counted, every tenth one belongs to the Lord. ³³You may not arrange the animals so that the poor animals are chosen, and you may not make any substitutions. If you do substitute one animal for another, then both animals will belong to the Lord and may not be bought back.

³⁴These are the commands that the Lord gave Moses on Mount Sinai for the people of Israel.

---

^{o} UNCONDITIONALLY DEDICATED: *Anything dedicated in this way belonged completely to the Lord and could not be used; it had to be destroyed.*
27.28 Nu 18.14   **27.30-33** Nu 18.21; Dt 14.22-29

NUMBERS

INTRODUCTION

The book of *Numbers* tells the story of the Israelites during the nearly forty years from the time they left Mount Sinai until they reached the eastern border of the land that God had promised to give them. The name of the book refers to a prominent feature of the story, that is, the census which Moses took of the Israelites at Mount Sinai before their departure, and again in Moab, east of the Jordan, about a generation later. In the period between the two censuses the Israelites went to Kadesh Barnea on the southern border of Canaan, but failed to enter the promised land from there. After spending many years in that area, they went to the region east of the Jordan River, where part of the people settled and where the rest prepared to cross the river into Canaan.

The book of *Numbers* is an account of a people who were often discouraged and afraid in the face of hardship, and who rebelled against God and against Moses, the man God appointed to lead them. It is the story of God's faithful, persistent care for his people in spite of their weakness and disobedience, and of Moses' steadfast, if sometimes impatient, devotion both to God and to his people.

OUTLINE OF CONTENTS

The First Census of Israel

1 On the first day of the second month in the second year after the people of Israel left Egypt, the LORD spoke to Moses there in the Tent of his presence in the Sinai Desert. He said, ²"You and Aaron are to take a census of the people of Israel by clans and families. List the names of all the men ³twenty years old or older who are fit for military service. ⁴Ask one clan chief from each tribe to help you." ⁵⁻¹⁶These are the men, leaders within their tribes, who were chosen from the community for this work:

Tribe	Clan chief
Reuben	Elizur son of Shedeur
Simeon	Shelumiel son of Zurishaddai
Judah	Nahshon son of Amminadab
Issachar	Nethanel son of Zuar
Zebulun	Eliab son of Helon
Ephraim	Elishama son of Ammihud

Manasseh	Gamaliel son of Pedahzur
Benjamin	Abidan son of Gideoni
Dan	Ahiezer son of Ammishaddai
Asher	Pagiel son of Ochran
Gad	Eliasaph son of Deuel
Naphtali	Ahira son of Enan

[17] With the help of these twelve men Moses and Aaron [18] called together the whole community on the first day of the second month and registered all the people by clans and families. The names of all the men twenty years old or older were recorded and counted, [19] as the LORD had commanded. In the Sinai Desert, Moses registered the people. [20-46] The men twenty years old or older who were fit for military service were registered by name according to clan and family, beginning with the tribe of Reuben, Jacob's oldest son. The totals were as follows:

Tribe	Number
Reuben	46,500
Simeon	59,300
Gad	45,650
Judah	74,600
Issachar	54,400
Zebulun	57,400
Ephraim	40,500
Manasseh	32,200
Benjamin	35,400
Dan	62,700
Asher	41,500
Naphtali	53,400
Total:	603,550

[47] The Levites were not registered with the other tribes, [48] because the LORD had said to Moses, [49] "When you take a census of the men fit for military service, do not include the tribe of Levi. [50] Instead, put the Levites in charge of the Tent of my presence and all its equipment. They shall carry it and its

equipment, serve in it, and set up their camp around it. [51] Whenever you move your camp, the Levites shall take the Tent down and set it up again at each new campsite. Anyone else who comes near the Tent shall be put to death. [52] The rest of the Israelites shall set up camp, company by company, each man with his own group and under his own banner. [53] But the Levites shall camp around the Tent to guard it, so that no one may come near and cause my anger to strike the community of Israel." [54] So the people of Israel did everything that the LORD had commanded Moses.

The Arrangement of the Tribes in Camp

2 The LORD gave Moses and Aaron the following instructions. [2] When the Israelites set up camp, each man will camp under the banner of his division and the flag of his own clan. The camp is to be set up all around the Tent.

[3-9] On the east side, those under the banner of the division of Judah shall camp in their groups, under their leaders, as follows:

Tribe	Leader	Number
Judah	Nahshon son of Amminadab	74,600
Issachar	Nethanel son of Zuar	54,400
Zebulun	Eliab son of Helon	57,400
	Total:	186,400

The division of Judah shall march first.

[10-16] On the south, those under the banner of the division of Reuben shall camp in their groups, under their leaders, as follows:

Tribe	Leader	Number
Reuben	Elizur son of Shedeur	46,500

Simeon	Shelumiel son of	
	Zurishaddai	59,300
Gad	Eliasaph son of	
	Deuel	45,650
	Total:	151,450

The division of Reuben shall march second.

17 Then, between the first two divisions and the last two the Levites are to march carrying the Tent. Each division shall march in the same order as they camp, each in position under its banner.

18-24 On the west, those under the banner of the division of Ephraim shall camp in their groups, under their leaders, as follows:

Tribe	Leader	Number
Ephraim	Elishama son of	
	Ammihud	40,500
Manasseh	Gamaliel son of	
	Pedahzur	32,200
Benjamin	Abidan son of	
	Gideoni	35,400
	Total:	108,100

The division of Ephraim shall march third.

25-31 On the north, those under the banner of the division of Dan shall camp in their groups, under their leaders, as follows:

Tribe	Leader	Number
Dan	Ahiezer son of	
	Ammishaddai	62,700
Asher	Pagiel son of	
	Ochran	41,500
Naphtali	Ahira son of	
	Enan	53,400
	Total:	157,600

The division of Dan shall march last.

32 The total number of the people of Israel enrolled in the divisions, group by group, was 603,550. 33 As the LORD had commanded Moses, the Levites were not registered with the rest of the Israelites.

34 So the people of Israel did everything the LORD had commanded Moses. They camped, each under his own banner, and they marched, each with his own clan.

Aaron's Sons

3 This is the family of Aaron and Moses at the time the LORD spoke to Moses on Mount Sinai. 2 Aaron had four sons: Nadab, the oldest, Abihu, Eleazar, and Ithamar. 3 They were anointed and ordained as priests, 4 but Nadab and Abihu were killed when they offered unholy fire to the LORD in the Sinai Desert. They had no children, so Eleazar and Ithamar served as priests during Aaron's lifetime.

The Levites Are Appointed to Serve the Priests

5 The LORD said to Moses, 6 "Bring forward the tribe of Levi and appoint them as servants of Aaron the priest. 7 They shall do the work required for the Tent of my presence and perform duties for the priests and for the whole community. 8 They shall take charge of all the equipment of the Tent and perform the duties for the rest of the Israelites. 9 The only responsibility the Levites have is to serve Aaron and his sons. 10 You shall appoint Aaron and his sons to carry out the duties of the priesthood; anyone else who tries to do so shall be put to death."

11 The LORD said to Moses, 12-13 "The Levites are now to be mine. When I killed all the first-born of the Egyptians, I consecrated as my own the oldest son of each Israelite family and the first-born of every animal. Now, instead of having the first-born sons of Israel as

3.2 Nu 26.60   3.4 Lv 10.1, 2; Nu 26.61   3.13 Ex 13.2

my own, I have the Levites; they will belong to me. I am the LORD."

The Census of the Levites

¹⁴ In the Sinai Desert the LORD commanded Moses ¹⁵ to register the Levites by clans and families, enrolling every male a month old or older, ¹⁶ and Moses did so. ¹⁷⁻²⁰ Levi had three sons: Gershon, Kohath, and Merari, who were the ancestors of the clans that bear their names. Gershon had two sons: Libni and Shimei; Kohath had four sons: Amram, Izhar, Hebron, and Uzziel; and Merari had two sons: Mahli and Mushi. They were the ancestors of the families that bear their names.

²¹ The clan of Gershon was composed of the families of Libni and Shimei. ²² The total number of males one month old or older that were enrolled was 7,500. ²³ This clan was to camp on the west behind the Tent, ²⁴ with Eliasaph son of Lael as chief of the clan. ²⁵ They were responsible for the Tent, its inner cover, its outer cover, the curtain for the entrance, ²⁶ the curtains for the court which is around the Tent and the altar, and the curtain for the entrance of the court. They were responsible for all the service connected with these items.

²⁷ The clan of Kohath was composed of the families of Amram, Izhar, Hebron, and Uzziel. ²⁸ The total number of males one month old or older that were enrolled was 8,600. ²⁹ This clan was to camp on the south side of the Tent, ³⁰ with Elizaphan son of Uzziel as chief of the clan. ³¹ They were responsible for the Covenant Box, the table, the lampstand, the altars, the utensils the priests use in the Holy Place, and the curtain at the entrance to the Most Holy Place. They were responsible for all the service connected with these items.

³² The chief of the Levites was Eleazar son of Aaron the priest. He was in charge of those who carried out the duties in the Holy Place.

³³ The clan of Merari was composed of the families of Mahli and Mushi. ³⁴ The total number of males one month old or older that were enrolled was 6,200. ³⁵ This clan was to camp on the north side of the Tent, with Zuriel son of Abihail as chief of the clan. ³⁶ They were assigned responsibility for the frames for the Tent, its bars, posts, bases, and all its fittings. They were responsible for all the service connected with these items. ³⁷ They were also responsible for the posts, bases, pegs, and ropes for the outer court.

³⁸ Moses and Aaron and his sons were to camp in front of the Tent on the east. They were responsible for carrying out the services performed in the Holy Place for the people of Israel. Anyone else who tried to do so was to be put to death. ³⁹ The total number of all the Levite males one month old or older that Moses enrolled by clans at the command of the LORD, was 22,000.

The Levites Take the Place of the First-Born Sons

⁴⁰⁻⁴¹ The LORD said to Moses, "All of Israel's first-born sons belong to me. So register by name every first-born male Israelite, one month old or older. But in place of them I claim all the Levites as mine! I am the LORD! I also claim the livestock of the Levites in place of all the first-born of the livestock." ⁴² Moses obeyed, and registered all the first-born males ⁴³ one month old or older; the total was 22,273.

⁴⁴ The LORD said to Moses, ⁴⁵ "Now dedicate the Levites as mine in place of all the first-born Israelite sons, and dedicate the livestock of the Levites in place of the first-born of the Israelites' livestock. ⁴⁶ Since the first-born Israelite sons outnumber the Levites by 273, you must buy back the extra sons. ⁴⁷ For each one pay five pieces of silver, according to the official standard, ⁴⁸ and give this money to Aaron and his sons." ⁴⁹ Moses obeyed and took ⁵⁰ the 1,365

pieces of silver ⁵¹ and gave them to Aaron and his sons.

The Duties of the Levite
Clan of Kohath

4 The LORD told Moses ²to take a census of the Levite clan of Kohath by subclans and families, ³and to register all the men between the ages of thirty and fifty who were qualified to work in the Tent of the LORD's presence. ⁴Their service involves the most holy things.

⁵The LORD gave Moses the following instructions. When it is time to break camp, Aaron and his sons shall enter the Tent, take down the curtain in front of the Covenant Box, and cover the Box with it. ⁶They shall put a fine leather cover over it, spread a cloth of solid blue on top, and then insert the carrying poles.

⁷They shall spread a blue cloth over the table for the bread offered to the LORD and put on it the dishes, the incense bowls, the offering bowls, and the jars for the wine offering. There shall always be bread on the table. ⁸They shall spread a red cloth over all of this, put a fine leather cover over it, and then insert the carrying poles.

⁹They shall take a blue cloth and cover the lampstand, with its lamps, tongs, trays, and all the olive oil containers. ¹⁰They shall wrap it and all its equipment in a fine leather cover and place it on a carrying frame.

¹¹Next they shall spread a blue cloth over the gold altar, put a fine leather cover over it, and then insert the carrying poles. ¹²They shall take all the utensils used in the Holy Place, wrap them in a blue cloth, put a fine leather cover over them, and place them on a carrying frame. ¹³They shall remove the greasy ashes from the altar and spread a purple cloth over it. ¹⁴They shall put

on it all the equipment used in the service at the altar: fire pans, hooks, shovels, and basins. Then they shall put a fine leather cover over it and insert the carrying poles. ¹⁵When it is time to break camp, the clan of Kohath shall come to carry the sacred objects only after Aaron and his sons have finished covering them and all their equipment. The Kohath clan must not touch the sacred objects, or they will die.

These are the responsibilities of the Kohath clan whenever the Tent is moved.

¹⁶Eleazar son of Aaron the priest shall be responsible for the whole Tent and for the oil for the lamps, the incense, the grain offerings, the anointing oil, and everything else in the Tent that has been consecrated to the LORD.

¹⁷The LORD said to Moses and Aaron, ¹⁸"Do not let the clan of Kohath ¹⁹be killed by coming near these most sacred objects. To prevent this from happening, Aaron and his sons shall go in and assign each man his task and tell him what to carry. ²⁰But if the Kohathites enter the Tent and see the priests preparing the sacred objects for moving,^a they will die."

The Duties of the Levite
Clan of Gershon

²¹The LORD told Moses ²²to take a census of the Levite clan of Gershon by subclans and families, ²³and to register all the men between the ages of thirty and fifty who were qualified to work in the Tent of the LORD's presence. ²⁴They shall be responsible for carrying the following objects: ²⁵the Tent, its inner cover, its outer cover, the fine leather cover on top of it, the curtain for the entrance, ²⁶the curtains and ropes for the court that is around the Tent and the altar, the curtains for the en-

^a see . . . moving; or see the sacred objects even for a moment.

Qualified to work in the Tent (4.23)

trance of the court, and all the fittings used in setting up these objects. They shall perform all the tasks required for these things. 27 Moses and Aaron shall see to it that the Gershonites perform all the duties and carry everything that Aaron and his sons assign to them. 28 These are the responsibilities of the Gershon clan in the Tent; they shall carry them out under the direction of Ithamar son of Aaron the priest.

The Duties of the Levite Clan of Merari

29 The LORD told Moses to take a census of the Levite clan of Merari by subclans and families, 30 and to register all the men between the ages of thirty and fifty who were qualified to work in the Tent of the LORD's presence. 31 They shall be responsible for carrying the frames, bars, posts, and bases of the Tent, 32 and the posts, bases, pegs, and ropes of the court around the Tent, with all the fittings used in setting them up. Each man will be responsible for carrying specific items. 33 These are the responsibilities of the Merari clan in their service in the Tent; they shall carry them out under the direction of Ithamar son of Aaron the priest.

The Census of the Levites

34-48 Following the LORD's command, Moses, Aaron, and the leaders of the community took a census of the three Levite clans, Kohath, Gershon, and Merari. They did this by subclans and families and registered all the men between the ages of thirty and fifty who were qualified to work in the Tent of the LORD's presence, as follows:

Clan	Number
Kohath	2,750
Gershon	2,630
Merari	3,200
Total:	8,580

49 Each man was registered as the LORD had commanded Moses; and at the command of the LORD given through Moses, each man was assigned responsibility for his task of serving or carrying.

Unclean People

5 The LORD said to Moses, 2 "Command the people of Israel to expel from the camp everyone with a dreaded skin disease or a bodily discharge and everyone who is unclean by contact with a corpse. 3 Send all these ritually unclean people out, so that they will not defile the camp, where I live among my people." 4 The Israelites obeyed and expelled them all from the camp.

Repayment for Wrongs Done

[5] The LORD gave Moses [6] the following instructions for the people of Israel. When any of you are unfaithful to the LORD and commit a wrong against someone, [7] you must confess your sin and make full repayment, plus an additional 20 percent, to the person you have wronged. [8] But if that person has died and has no near relative to whom payment can be made, it shall be given to the LORD for the priest. This payment is in addition to the ram used to perform the ritual of purification for the guilty person. [9] Also every special contribution which the Israelites offer to the LORD belongs to the priest to whom they present it. [10] Each priest shall keep the offerings presented to him.

Cases of Wives with Suspicious Husbands

[11] The LORD commanded Moses [12-14] to give the Israelites the following instructions. It may happen that a man becomes suspicious that his wife is unfaithful to him and has defiled herself by having intercourse with another man. But the husband may not be certain, for his wife may have kept it secret — there was no witness, and she was not caught in the act. Or it may happen that a husband becomes suspicious of his wife, even though she has not been unfaithful. [15] In either case the man shall take his wife to the priest. He shall also take the required offering of two pounds of barley flour, but he shall not pour any olive oil on it or put any incense on it, because it is an offering from a suspicious husband, made to bring the truth to light. [16] The priest shall bring the woman forward and have her stand in front of the altar. [17] He shall pour some holy water into a clay bowl and take some of the earth that is on the floor of the Tent of the LORD's presence and put it in the water to make it bitter. [18] Then he shall loosen the woman's hair and put the offering of flour in her hands. In his hands the priest shall hold the bowl containing the bitter water that brings a curse. [19] Then the priest shall make the woman agree to this oath spoken by the priest: "If you have not committed adultery, you will not be harmed by the curse that this water brings. [20] But if you have committed adultery, [21] may the LORD make your name a curse among your people. May he cause your genital organs to shrink and your stomach to swell up. [22] May this water enter your stomach and cause it to swell up and your genital organs to shrink."

The woman shall respond, "I agree; may the LORD do so."

[23] Then the priest shall write this curse down and wash the writing off into the bowl of bitter water. [24] Before he makes the woman drink the water, which may then cause her bitter pain, [25] the priest shall take the offering of flour out of the woman's hands, hold it out in dedication to the LORD, and present it on the altar. [26] Then he shall take a handful of it as a token offering and burn it on the altar. Finally, he shall make the woman drink the water. [27] If she has committed adultery, the water will cause bitter pain; her stomach will swell up and her genital organs will shrink. Her name will become a curse among her people. [28] But if she is innocent, she will not be harmed and will be able to bear children.

[29-30] This is the law in cases where a man is jealous and becomes suspicious that his wife has committed adultery. The woman shall be made to stand in front of the altar, and the priest shall perform this ritual. [31] The husband shall be free of guilt, but the woman, if guilty, must suffer the consequences.

Rules for Nazirites

6 The LORD commanded Moses [2]to give the following instructions to the people of Israel. Any of you, male or female, who make a special vow to become a nazirite and dedicate yourself to the LORD [3]shall abstain from wine and beer. You shall not drink any kind of drink made from grapes or eat any grapes or raisins. [4]As long as you are a nazirite, you shall not eat anything that comes from a grapevine, not even the seeds or skins of grapes.

[5]As long as you are under the nazirite vow, you must not cut your hair or shave. You are bound by the vow for the full time that you are dedicated to the LORD, and you shall let your hair grow. [6-7]Your hair is the sign of your dedication to God, and so you must not defile yourself by going near a corpse, not even that of your father, mother, brother, or sister. [8]As long as you are a nazirite, you are consecrated to the LORD.

[9]If your consecrated hair is defiled because you are right beside someone who suddenly dies, you must wait seven days and then shave your head; and so you become ritually clean. [10]On the eighth day you shall bring two doves or two pigeons to the priest at the entrance of the Tent of the LORD's presence. [11]The priest shall offer one as a sin offering and the other as a burnt offering, to perform the ritual of purification for you because of your contact with a corpse. On the same day you shall reconsecrate your hair [12]and rededicate to the LORD your time as a nazirite. The previous period of time doesn't count, because your consecrated hair was defiled. As a repayment offering you shall bring a one-year-old lamb.

[13]When you complete your nazirite vow, you shall perform this ritual. You shall go to the entrance of the Tent [14]and present to the LORD three animals without any defects: a one-year-old male lamb for a burnt offering, a one-year-old ewe lamb for a sin offering, and a ram for a fellowship offering. [15]You shall also offer a basket of bread made without yeast: thick loaves made of flour mixed with olive oil and thin cakes brushed with olive oil, and in addition the required offerings of grain and wine.

[16]The priest shall present all these to the LORD and offer the sin offering and the burnt offering. [17]He shall sacrifice the ram to the LORD as a fellowship offering, and offer it with the basket of bread; he shall also present the offerings of grain and wine. [18]At the entrance of the Tent you nazirites shall shave off your hair and put it on the fire on which the fellowship offering is being burned.

[19]Then, when the shoulder of the ram is boiled, the priest shall take it and put it, together with one thick loaf of bread and one thin cake from the basket, into the hands of the nazirite. [20]Next, the priest shall present them as a special gift to the LORD; they are a sacred offering for the priest, in addition to the breast and the leg of the ram which by law belong to the priest. After that, the nazirite may drink wine.

[21]These are the regulations for you nazirites; but if you promise an offering beyond what your vow requires you to give, you must fulfill exactly the promise you made.

The Priestly Blessing

[22]The LORD commanded Moses [23]to tell Aaron and his sons to use the following words in blessing the people of Israel:

[24]May the LORD bless you and
    take care of you;
[25]May the LORD be kind and
    gracious to you;

6.3 Lk 1.15   **6.13-21** Ac 21.23, 24

26 May the LORD look on you with
favor and give you peace.
27 And the LORD said, "If they pronounce my name as a blessing upon
the people of Israel, I will bless
them."

The Offerings of the Leaders

7 On the day Moses finished setting
up the Tent of the LORD's presence, he anointed and dedicated the
Tent and all its equipment, and the altar and all its equipment. 2 Then the
clan chiefs who were leaders in the
tribes of Israel, the same men who were
in charge of the census, 3 brought their
offerings to the LORD: six wagons and
twelve oxen, a wagon for every two
leaders and an ox for each leader. After
they had presented them, 4 the LORD
said to Moses, 5 "Accept these gifts for
use in the work to be done for the Tent;
give them to the Levites according to
the work they have to do." 6 So Moses
gave the wagons and the oxen to the
Levites. 7 He gave two wagons and
four oxen to the Gershonites, 8 and
four wagons and eight oxen to the
Merarites. All their work was to be
done under the direction of Ithamar
son of Aaron. 9 But Moses gave no
wagons or oxen to the Kohathites,
because the sacred objects they took
care of had to be carried on their
shoulders.

10 The leaders also brought offerings
to celebrate the dedication of the altar.
When they were ready to present their
gifts at the altar, 11 the LORD said to
Moses, "Tell them that each day for a
period of twelve days one of the leaders
is to present his gifts for the dedication
of the altar."

12-83 They presented their offerings in
the following order:

Day	Tribe	Leader
1st	Judah	Nahshon son of Amminadab
2nd	Issachar	Nethanel son of Zuar
3rd	Zebulun	Eliab son of Helon
4th	Reuben	Elizur son of Shedeur
5th	Simeon	Shelumiel son of Zurishaddai
6th	Gad	Eliasaph son of Deuel
7th	Ephraim	Elishama son of Ammihud
8th	Manasseh	Gamaliel son of Pedahzur
9th	Benjamin	Abidan son of Gideoni
10th	Dan	Ahiezer son of Ammishaddai
11th	Asher	Pagiel son of Ochran
12th	Naphtali	Ahira son of Enan

The offerings each one brought were
identical: one silver bowl weighing 50
ounces and one silver basin weighing
30 ounces, by the official standard, both
of them full of flour mixed with oil for
the grain offering; one gold dish weighing 4 ounces, full of incense; one young
bull, one ram, and a one-year-old lamb,
for the burnt offering; one goat for the
sin offering; and two bulls, five rams,
five goats, and five one-year-old lambs,
for the fellowship offering.

84-88 The totals of the offerings
brought by the twelve leaders for the
dedication of the altar were as follows:
—twelve silver bowls and twelve
silver basins weighing a
total of 60 pounds
—twelve gold dishes weighing a
total of 48 ounces, filled
with incense
—twelve bulls, twelve rams, and
twelve one-year-old lambs,
plus the grain offerings
that go with them, for the
burnt offerings
—twelve goats for the sin
offerings

—twenty-four bulls, sixty rams,
        sixty goats, sixty one-
        year-old lambs, for the
        fellowship offerings
89 When Moses went into the Tent to
talk with the LORD, he heard the LORD
speaking to him from above the lid on
the Covenant Box, between the two
winged creatures.b

Placing the Lamps

8 The LORD said to Moses, 2 "Tell
Aaron that when he puts the
seven lamps on the lampstand, he
should place them so that the light
shines toward the front." 3 Aaron
obeyed and placed the lamps facing the
front of the lampstand. 4 From top to
bottom the lampstand was made of
hammered gold, according to the pattern that the LORD had shown Moses.

The Purification and Dedication
of the Levites

5 The LORD said to Moses, 6 "Separate
the Levites from the rest of the people
of Israel and purify them 7 in the following way: sprinkle them with the water
of purification and have them shave
their whole bodies and have them wash
their clothes. Then they will be ritually
clean. 8 Then they are to take a young
bull and the required grain offering of
flour mixed with olive oil; and you are
to take another bull for the sin offering.
9 Then assemble the whole community
of Israel and have the Levites stand in
front of the Tent of my presence. 10 The
people of Israel are to place their hands
on the heads of the Levites, 11 and then
Aaron shall dedicate the Levites to me
as a special gift from the Israelites, so
that they may do my work. 12 The Levites shall then put their hands on the
heads of the two bulls; one is to be offered as a sin offering and the other as

a burnt offering, in order to perform the
ritual of purification for the Levites.
13 "Dedicate the Levites as a special
gift to me, and put Aaron and his sons
in charge of them. 14 Separate the Levites in this way from the rest of the Israelites, so that they will belong to me.
15 After you have purified and dedicated
the Levites, they will be qualified to
work in the Tent. 16 I have claimed
them in the place of all the first-born
sons of the Israelites, and they belong
to me alone. 17 When I killed all the
first-born in Egypt, I consecrated as my
own the oldest son of each Israelite
family and the first-born of every animal. 18 I am now taking the Levites instead of all the first-born of the
Israelites, 19 and I assign the Levites to
Aaron and his sons, as a gift from the
Israelites, to work in the Tent for the
people of Israel and to protect the Israelites from the disaster that would
strike them if they came too near the
Holy Place."
20 So Moses, Aaron, and all the people
of Israel dedicated the Levites, as the
LORD commanded Moses. 21 The Levites purified themselves and washed
their clothes, and Aaron dedicated
them as a special gift to the LORD. He
also performed the ritual of purification
for them. 22 The people did everything
the LORD had commanded Moses concerning the Levites. And so the Levites
were qualified to work in the Tent under Aaron and his sons.
23 The LORD said to Moses, 24 "From
the age of twenty-five each Levite shall
perform his duties in the Tent of my
presence, 25 and at the age of fifty he
shall retire. 26 After that, he may help
his fellow Levites in performing their
duties in the Tent, but he must not perform any service by himself. This is
how you are to regulate the duties of the
Levites."

---

b WINGED CREATURES: *See Word List.*
8.1-4 Ex 25.31-40; 37.17-24   **8.17** Ex 13.2

The Second Passover

9 The LORD spoke to Moses in the Sinai Desert in the first month of the second year after the people of Israel had left Egypt. He said, [2-3]"On the fourteenth day of this month, beginning at sunset, the people of Israel are to observe the Passover according to all the rules and regulations for it." [4]So Moses told the people to observe the Passover, [5]and on the evening of the fourteenth day of the first month they did so in the Sinai Desert. The people did everything just as the LORD had commanded Moses.

[6]But there were some people who were ritually unclean because they had touched a corpse, and they were not able to keep the Passover on that day. They went to Moses and Aaron [7]and said, "We are unclean because we have touched a corpse, but why should we be excluded from presenting the LORD's offering with the rest of the Israelites?"

[8]Moses answered, "Wait until I receive instructions from the LORD."

[9]The LORD told Moses [10]to say to the people of Israel, "When any of you or your descendants are unclean from touching a corpse or are far away on a journey, but still want to keep the Passover, [11]you are permitted to observe it one month later instead, on the evening of the fourteenth day of the second month. Celebrate it with unleavened bread and bitter herbs. [12]Do not leave any of the food until the following morning and do not break any of the animal's bones. Observe the Passover according to all the regulations. [13]But if any of you are ritually clean and not away on a journey and do not observe the Passover, you shall no longer be considered my people, because you did not present the offering to me at the appointed time. You must suffer the consequences of your sin.

[14]"If foreigners living among you want to keep the Passover, they must observe it according to all the rules and regulations. The same law applies to everyone, whether native or foreigner."

The Fiery Cloud
(Exodus 40.34-38)

[15-16]On the day the Tent of the LORD's presence was set up, a cloud came and covered it. At night the cloud looked like fire. [17]Whenever the cloud lifted, the people of Israel broke camp, and they set up camp again in the place where the cloud came down. [18]The people broke camp at the command of the LORD, and at his command they set up camp. As long as the cloud stayed over the Tent, they stayed in the same camp. [19]When the cloud stayed over the Tent for a long time, they obeyed the LORD and did not move on. [20]Sometimes the cloud remained over the Tent for only a few days; in any case, they remained in camp or moved, according to the command of the LORD. [21]Sometimes the cloud remained only from evening until morning, and they moved on as soon as the cloud lifted. Whenever the cloud lifted, they moved on. [22]Whether it was two days, a month, a year, or longer, as long as the cloud remained over the Tent, they did not move on; but when it lifted, they moved. [23]They set up camp and broke camp in obedience to the commands which the LORD gave through Moses.

The Silver Trumpets

10 The LORD said to Moses, [2]"Make two trumpets of hammered silver to use for calling the people together and for breaking camp. [3]When long blasts are sounded on both trumpets, the whole community is to gather around you at the entrance to the Tent of my presence. [4]But when only one trumpet is sounded, then only the leaders of the clans are to gather

9.1-5 Ex 12.1-13   **9.12** Ex 12.46; Jn 19.36

When only one trumpet is sounded (10.4)

around you. ⁵When short blasts are sounded, the tribes camped on the east will move out. ⁶When short blasts are sounded a second time, the tribes on the south will move out. So short blasts are to be sounded to break camp, ⁷but in order to call the community together, long blasts are to be sounded. ⁸The trumpets are to be blown by Aaron's sons, the priests.

"The following rule is to be observed for all time to come. ⁹When you are at war in your land, defending yourselves against an enemy who has attacked you, sound the signal for battle on these trumpets. I, the LORD your God, will help you and save you from your enemies. ¹⁰Also on joyful occasions — at your New Moon Festivals and your other religious festivals — you are to blow the trumpets when you present your burnt offerings and your fellowship offerings. Then I will help you. I am the LORD your God."

The Israelites Break Camp

¹¹On the twentieth day of the second month in the second year after the people left Egypt, the cloud over the Tent of the LORD's presence lifted, ¹²and the Israelites started on their journey out of the Sinai Desert. The cloud came to rest in the wilderness of Paran.

¹³They began to march at the command of the LORD through Moses, ¹⁴and each time they moved, they were in the same order. Those under the banner of the division led by the tribe of Judah started out first, company by company, with Nahshon son of Amminadab in command. ¹⁵Nethanel son of Zuar was in command of the tribe of Issachar, ¹⁶and Eliab son of Helon was in command of the tribe of Zebulun. ¹⁷Then the Tent would be taken down, and the clans of Gershon and Merari, who carried it, would start out.

¹⁸Next, those under the banner of the division led by the tribe of Reuben would start out, company by company, with Elizur son of Shedeur in command. ¹⁹Shelumiel son of Zurishaddai was in command of the tribe of Simeon, ²⁰and Eliasaph son of Deuel was in command of the tribe of Gad.

²¹Then the Levite clan of Kohath would start out, carrying the sacred objects. By the time they arrived at the next camp, the Tent had been set up again.

²²Next, those under the banner of the division led by the tribe of Ephraim would start out, company by company, with Elishama son of Ammihud in command. ²³Gamaliel son of Pedahzur was in command of the tribe of Manasseh, ²⁴and Abidan son of Gideoni was in command of the tribe of Benjamin.

²⁵Finally, those under the banner of the division led by the tribe of Dan, serving as the rear guard of all the divisions, would start out, company by company, with Ahiezer son of Ammishaddai in command. ²⁶Pagiel son of Ochran was in command of the tribe of Asher, ²⁷and Ahira son of Enan was in command of the tribe of Naphtali. ²⁸This, then, was the order of march, company by company, whenever the Israelites broke camp and set out.

²⁹Moses said to his brother-in-law

Hobab son of Jethro the Midianite, "We are about to start out for the place which the LORD said he would give us. He has promised to make Israel prosperous, so come with us, and we will share our prosperity with you."

³⁰Hobab answered, "No, I am going back to my native land."

³¹"Please don't leave us," Moses said. "You know where we can camp in the wilderness, and you can be our guide. ³²If you come with us, we will share with you all the blessings that the LORD gives us."

The People Set Out

³³When the people left Sinai, the holy mountain, they traveled three days. The LORD's Covenant Box always went ahead of them to find a place for

The LORD's Covenant Box always went ahead. (10.33)

them to camp. ³⁴As they moved on from each camp, the cloud of the LORD was over them by day.

³⁵Whenever the Covenant Box started out, Moses would say, "Arise, LORD; scatter your enemies and put to flight those who hate you!" ³⁶And whenever it stopped, he would say, "Return, LORD, to the thousands of families of Israel."ᶜ

The Place Named Taberah

11 The people began to complain to the LORD about their troubles. When the LORD heard them, he became angry and sent fire on the people. It burned among them and destroyed one end of the camp. ²The people cried out to Moses for help; he prayed to the LORD, and the fire died down. ³So the place was named Taberah,ᵈ because there the fire of the LORD burned among them.

Moses Chooses Seventy Leaders

⁴There were foreigners traveling with the Israelites. They had a strong craving for meat, and even the Israelites themselves began to complain: "If only we could have some meat! ⁵In Egypt we used to eat all the fish we wanted, and it cost us nothing. Remember the cucumbers, the watermelons, the leeks, the onions, and the garlic we had? ⁶But now our strength is gone. There is nothing at all to eat — nothing but this manna day after day!"

(⁷Manna was like small seeds, whitish yellow in color. ⁸⁻⁹It fell on the camp at night along with the dew. The next morning the people would go around and gather it, grind it or pound it into flour, and then boil it and make it into flat cakes. It tasted like bread baked with olive oil.)

¹⁰Moses heard all the people complaining as they stood around in groups at the entrances of their tents. He was distressed because the LORD had be-

ᶜ Return ... Israel; *or* Return, LORD, you who are like an army of millions for Israel.
ᵈ TABERAH: *This name sounds like the Hebrew for "burning."*
10.35 Ps 68.1 **11.7, 8** Ex 16.31 **11.9** Ex 16.13-15

come angry with them, [11] and he said to the LORD, "Why have you treated me so badly? Why are you displeased with me? Why have you given me the responsibility for all these people? [12] I didn't create them or bring them to birth! Why should you ask me to act like a nurse and carry them in my arms like babies all the way to the land you promised to their ancestors? [13] Where could I get enough meat for all these people? They keep whining and asking for meat. [14] I can't be responsible for all these people by myself; it's too much

"I can't be responsible for all these people!" (11.14)

for me! [15] If you are going to treat me like this, have pity on me and kill me, so that I won't have to endure your cruelty any longer."

[16] The LORD said to Moses, "Assemble seventy respected men who are recognized as leaders of the people, bring them to me at the Tent of my presence, and tell them to stand there beside you. [17] I will come down and speak with you there, and I will take some of the spirit I have given you and give it to them. Then they can help you bear the responsibility for these people, and you will not have to bear it alone. [18] Now tell the people, 'Purify yourselves for tomorrow; you will have meat to eat. The LORD has heard you whining and saying that you wished you had some meat and that you were better off in Egypt. Now the LORD will give you meat, and you will have to eat it. [19] You will have to eat it not just for one or two days, or five, or ten, or even twenty days, [20] but

for a whole month, until it comes out of your ears, until you are sick of it. This will happen because you have rejected the LORD who is here among you and have complained to him that you should never have left Egypt.'"

[21] Moses said to the LORD, "Here I am leading 600,000 people, and you say that you will give them enough meat for a month? [22] Could enough cattle and sheep be killed to satisfy them? Are all the fish in the sea enough for them?"

[23] "Is there a limit to my power?" the LORD answered. "You will soon see whether what I have said will happen or not!"

[24] So Moses went out and told the people what the LORD had said. He assembled seventy of the leaders and placed them around the Tent. [25] Then the LORD came down in the cloud and spoke to him. He took some of the spirit he had given to Moses and gave it to the seventy leaders. When the spirit came on them, they began to shout like prophets, but not for long.

[26] Two of the seventy leaders, Eldad and Medad, had stayed in the camp and had not gone out to the Tent. There in the camp the spirit came on them, and they too began to shout like prophets. [27] A young man ran out to tell Moses what Eldad and Medad were doing. [28] Then Joshua son of Nun, who had been Moses' helper since he was a young man, spoke up and said to Moses, "Stop them, sir!"

[29] Moses answered, "Are you concerned about my interests? I wish that the LORD would give his spirit to all his people and make all of them shout like prophets!" [30] Then Moses and the seventy leaders of Israel went back to camp.

The LORD Sends Quails

[31] Suddenly the LORD sent a wind that brought quails from the sea, flying three feet above the ground. They settled on the camp and all around it for

Catching quails (11.32)

miles and miles in every direction.*e*
32 So all that day, all night, and all the
next day, the people worked catching
quails; no one gathered less than fifty
bushels. They spread them out to dry
all around the camp. 33 While there was
still plenty of meat for them to eat, the
LORD became angry with the people
and caused an epidemic to break out
among them. 34 That place was named
Kibroth Hattaavah (which means
"Graves of Craving"), because there
they buried the people who had craved
meat.

35 From there the people moved to
Hazeroth, where they made camp.

Miriam Is Punished

12 Moses had married a Cushite*f*
woman, and Miriam and Aaron
criticized him for it. 2 They said, "Has
the LORD spoken only through*g*
Moses? Hasn't he also spoken
through*g* us?" The LORD heard what

they said. (3 Moses was a humble man,
more humble than anyone else on
earth.)

4 Suddenly the LORD said to Moses,
Aaron, and Miriam, "I want the three of
you to come out to the Tent of my presence." They went, 5 and the LORD came
down in a pillar of cloud, stood at the
entrance of the Tent, and called out,
"Aaron! Miriam!" The two of them
stepped forward, 6 and the LORD said,
"Now hear what I have to say! When
there are prophets among you,*h* I reveal myself to them in visions and
speak to them in dreams. 7 It is different
when I speak with my servant Moses;
I have put him in charge of all my
people Israel.*i* 8 So I speak to him
face-to-face, clearly and not in riddles; he has even seen my form! How
dare you speak against my servant
Moses?"

9 The LORD was angry with them;
and so as he departed 10 and the cloud
left the Tent, Miriam's skin was suddenly covered with a dreaded disease
and turned as white as snow. When
Aaron looked at her and saw that she
was covered with the disease, 11 he said
to Moses, "Please, sir, do not make us
suffer this punishment for our foolish

e sea, flying . . . direction; *or* sea. They settled in the camp and all around it for miles
and miles in every direction, until they were piled up three feet deep on the ground.
f Cushite *(compare Hb 3.7); or* Midianite; *or* Ethiopian.   *g* through; *or* to.   *h* Some
ancient translations When . . . you; *Hebrew unclear.*   *i* I have put . . . Israel; *or* he
can be trusted with all my affairs.
12.3 Si 45.4   **12.7** He 3.2

sin. [12]Don't let her become like something born dead with half its flesh eaten away."

[13]So Moses cried out to the LORD, "O God, heal her!"

[14]The LORD answered, "If her father had spit in her face, she would have to bear her disgrace for seven days. So let her be shut out of the camp for a week, and after that she can be brought back in." [15]Miriam was shut out of the camp for seven days, and the people did not move on until she was brought back in. [16]Then they left Hazeroth and set up camp in the wilderness of Paran.

The Spies
(Deuteronomy 1.19-33)

13 The LORD said to Moses, [2]"Choose one of the leaders from each of the twelve tribes and send them as spies to explore the land of Canaan, which I am giving to the Israelites." [3-15]Moses obeyed and from the wilderness of Paran he sent out leaders, as follows:

Tribe	Leader
Reuben	Shammua son of Zaccur
Simeon	Shaphat son of Hori
Judah	Caleb son of Jephunneh
Issachar	Igal son of Joseph
Ephraim	Hoshea son of Nun
Benjamin	Palti son of Raphu
Zebulun	Gaddiel son of Sodi
Manasseh	Gaddi son of Susi
Dan	Ammiel son of Gemalli
Asher	Sethur son of Michael
Naphtali	Nahbi son of Vophsi
Gad	Geuel son of Machi

[16]These are the spies Moses sent to explore the land. He changed the name of Hoshea son of Nun to Joshua.

[17]When Moses sent them out, he said to them, "Go north from here into the southern part of the land of Canaan and then on into the hill country. [18]Find out what kind of country it is, how many people live there, and how strong they are. [19]Find out whether the land is good or bad and whether the people live in open towns or in fortified cities. [20]Find out whether the soil is fertile and whether the land is wooded. And be sure to bring back some of the fruit that grows there." (It was the season when grapes were beginning to ripen.)

[21]So the men went north and explored the land from the wilderness of Zin in the south all the way to Rehob, near Hamath Pass in the north. [22]They went first into the southern part of the land and came to Hebron, where the clans of Ahiman, Sheshai, and Talmai, the descendants of a race of giants called the Anakim, lived. (Hebron was founded seven years before Zoan in Egypt.) [23]They came to Eshcol Valley, and there they cut off a branch which had one bunch of grapes on it so heavy that it took two men to carry it on a pole between them. They also brought back some pomegranates and figs. ([24]That place was named Eshcol[j] Valley

It took two men to carry it. (13.23)

j ESHCOL: *This name in Hebrew means "bunch of grapes."*
12.14 Nu 5.2, 3

because of the bunch of grapes the Israelites cut off there.)

25 After exploring the land for forty days, the spies returned **26** to Moses, Aaron, and the whole community of Israel at Kadesh in the wilderness of Paran. They reported what they had seen and showed them the fruit they had brought. **27** They told Moses, "We explored the land and found it to be rich and fertile; and here is some of its fruit. **28** But the people who live there are powerful, and their cities are very large and well fortified. Even worse, we saw the descendants of the giants there. **29** Amalekites live in the southern part of the land; Hittites, Jebusites, and Amorites live in the hill country; and Canaanites live by the Mediterranean Sea and along the Jordan River."

30 Caleb silenced the people who were complaining against[k] Moses, and said, "We should attack now and take the land; we are strong enough to conquer it."

31 But the men who had gone with Caleb said, "No, we are not strong enough to attack them; the people there are more powerful than we are." **32** So they spread a false report among the Israelites about the land they had explored. They said, "That land doesn't even produce enough to feed the people who live there. Everyone we saw was very tall, **33** and we even saw giants there, the descendants of Anak. We felt as small as grasshoppers, and that is how we must have looked to them."

The People Complain

14 All night long the people cried out in distress. **2** They complained against Moses and Aaron, and said, "It would have been better to die in Egypt or even here in the wilderness! **3** Why is the LORD taking us into that land? We will be killed in battle, and our wives and children will be captured. Wouldn't it be better to go back to Egypt?" **4** So they said to one another, "Let's choose a leader and go back to Egypt!"

5 Then Moses and Aaron bowed to the ground in front of all the people. **6** And Joshua son of Nun and Caleb son of Jephunneh, two of the spies, tore their clothes in sorrow **7** and said to the people, "The land we explored is an excellent land. **8** If the LORD is pleased with us, he will take us there and give us that rich and fertile land. **9** Do not rebel against the LORD and don't be afraid of the people who live there. We will conquer them easily. The LORD is with us and has defeated the gods who protected them; so don't be afraid." **10** The whole community was threatening to stone them to death, but suddenly the people saw the dazzling light of the LORD's presence appear over the Tent.

Moses Prays for the People

11 The LORD said to Moses, "How much longer will these people reject me? How much longer will they refuse to trust in me, even though I have performed so many miracles among them? **12** I will send an epidemic and destroy them, but I will make you the father of a nation that is larger and more powerful than they are!"

13 But Moses said to the LORD, "You brought these people out of Egypt by your power. When the Egyptians hear what you have done to your people, **14** they will tell it to the people who live in this land. These people have already heard that you, LORD, are with us, that you appear in plain sight when your cloud stops over us, and that you go before us in a pillar of cloud by day and a pillar of fire by night. **15** Now if you kill all your people, the nations who have

---

[k] complaining against; *or* gathered around.
13.33 Gn 6.4   **14.9** He 3.16   **14.13-19** Ex 32.11-14

heard of your fame will say [16] that you killed your people in the wilderness because you were not able to bring them into the land you promised to give them. [17] So now, LORD, I pray, show us your power and do what you promised when you said, [18] 'I, the LORD, am not easily angered, and I show great love and faithfulness and forgive sin and rebellion. Yet I will not fail to punish children and grandchildren to the third and fourth generation for the sins of their parents.' [19] And now, LORD, according to the greatness of your unchanging love, forgive, I pray, the sin of these people, just as you have forgiven them ever since they left Egypt."

[20] The LORD answered, "I will forgive them, as you have asked. [21] But I promise that as surely as I live and as surely as my presence fills the earth, [22] none of these people will live to enter that land. They have seen the dazzling light of my presence and the miracles that I performed in Egypt and in the wilderness, but they have tried my patience over and over again and have refused to obey me. [23] They will never enter the land which I promised to their ancestors. None of those who have rejected me will ever enter it. [24] But because my servant Caleb has a different attitude and has remained loyal to me, I will bring him into the land which he explored, and his descendants will possess the land [25] in whose valleys the Amalekites and the Canaanites now live. Turn back tomorrow and go into the wilderness in the direction of the Gulf of Aqaba."

The LORD Punishes the People for Complaining

[26] The LORD said to Moses and Aaron, [27] "How much longer are these wicked people going to complain against me? I have heard enough of these complaints! [28] Now give them this answer: 'I swear that as surely as I live, I will do to you just what you have asked. I, the LORD, have spoken. [29] You will die and your corpses will be scattered across this wilderness. Because you have complained against me, none of you over twenty years of age will enter that land. [30] I promised to let you live there, but not one of you will, except Caleb and Joshua. [31] You said that your children would be captured, but I will bring them into the land that you rejected, and it will be their home. [32] You will die here in this wilderness. [33] Your children will wander in the wilderness for forty years, suffering for your unfaithfulness, until the last one of you dies. [34] You will suffer the consequences of your sin for forty years, one year for each of the forty days you spent exploring the land. You will know what it means to have me against you! [35] I swear that I will do this to you wicked people who have gathered together against me. Here in the wilderness every one of you will die. I, the LORD, have spoken.' "

[36-37] The men Moses had sent to explore the land brought back a false report which caused the people to complain against the LORD. And so the LORD struck them with a disease, and they died. [38] Of the twelve spies only Joshua and Caleb survived.

The First Attempt to Invade the Land
(Deuteronomy 1.41-46)

[39] When Moses told the Israelites what the LORD had said, they mourned bitterly. [40] Early the next morning they started out to invade the hill country, saying, "Now we are ready to go to the place which the LORD told us about. We admit that we have sinned." [41] But Moses said, "Then why are you disobeying the LORD now? You will not

---

14.18 Ex 20.5, 6; 34.6, 7; Dt 5.9, 10; 7.9, 10   **14.21-23** He 3.18   **14.24** Js 14.9-12
14.29 He 3.17   **14.33** Ac 7.36

succeed! ⁴²Don't go. The LORD is not with you, and your enemies will defeat you. ⁴³When you face the Amalekites and the Canaanites, you will die in battle; the LORD will not be with you, because you have refused to follow him."

⁴⁴Yet they still dared to go up into the hill country, even though neither the LORD's Covenant Box nor Moses left the camp. ⁴⁵Then the Amalekites and the Canaanites who lived there attacked and defeated them, and pursued them as far as Hormah.

Laws about Sacrifice

15 The LORD gave Moses ²the following regulations for the people of Israel to observe in the land that he was going to give them. ³A bull, a ram, a sheep, or a goat may be presented to the LORD as a burnt offering or as a sacrifice in fulfillment of a vow or as a freewill offering or as an offering at your regular religious festivals; the odor of these food offerings is pleasing to the LORD. ⁴⁻⁵Whoever presents a sheep or a goat as a burnt offering to the LORD is to bring with each animal 2 pounds of flour mixed with 2 pints of olive oil as a grain offering, together with 2 pints of wine. ⁶When a ram is offered, 4 pounds of flour mixed with 3 pints of olive oil are to be presented as a grain offering, ⁷together with 3 pints of wine. The odor of these sacrifices is pleasing to the LORD. ⁸When a bull is offered to the LORD as a burnt offering or as a sacrifice in fulfillment of a vow or as a fellowship offering, ⁹a grain offering of 6 pounds of flour mixed with 4 pints of olive oil is to be presented, ¹⁰together with 4 pints of wine. The odor of this sacrifice is pleasing to the LORD.

¹¹That is what shall be offered with each bull, ram, sheep, or goat. ¹²When more than one animal is offered, the ac-

companying offering is to be increased proportionately. ¹³All native Israelites are to do this when they present a food offering, an odor pleasing to the LORD. ¹⁴And if at any time foreigners living among you, whether on a temporary or a permanent basis, make a food offering, an odor that pleases the LORD, they are to observe the same regulations. ¹⁵For all time to come, the same[l] rules are binding on you and on the foreigners who live among you. You and they are alike in the LORD's sight; ¹⁶the same laws and regulations apply to you and to them.

¹⁷The LORD gave Moses ¹⁸the following regulations for the people of Israel to observe in the land that he was going to give them. ¹⁹When any food produced there is eaten, some of it is to be set aside as a special contribution to the LORD. ²⁰When you bake bread, the first loaf of the first bread made from the new grain is to be presented as a special contribution to the LORD. This is to be presented in the same way as the special contribution you make from the grain you thresh. ²¹For all time to come, this special gift is to be given to the LORD from the bread you bake.

²²But suppose someone unintentionally fails to keep some of these regulations which the LORD has given Moses. ²³And suppose that in the future the community fails to do everything that the LORD commanded through Moses. ²⁴If the mistake was made because of the ignorance of the community, they are to offer a bull as a burnt offering, an odor that pleases the LORD, with the proper grain offering and wine offering. In addition, they are to offer a male goat as a sin offering. ²⁵The priest shall perform the ritual of purification for the community, and they will be forgiven, because the mistake was unintentional and they brought their sin offering as a food offering to the LORD. ²⁶The whole

---

[l] *Some ancient translations* the same; *Hebrew* the congregation the same.
15.16 Lv 24.22

community of Israel and the foreigners living among them will be forgiven, because everyone was involved in the mistake.

²⁷ If any of you sin unintentionally, you are to offer a one-year-old female goat as a sin offering. ²⁸ At the altar the priest shall perform the ritual of purification to purify you from your sin, and you will be forgiven. ²⁹ The same regulation applies to all who unintentionally commit a sin, whether they are native Israelites or resident foreigners.

³⁰ But any who sin deliberately, whether they are natives or foreigners, are guilty of treating the LORD with contempt, and they shall be put to death, ³¹ because they have rejected what the LORD said and have deliberately broken one of his commands. They are responsible for their own death.

The Man Who Broke the Sabbath

³² Once, while the Israelites were still in the wilderness, a man was found gathering firewood on the Sabbath. ³³ He was taken to Moses, Aaron, and the whole community, ³⁴ and was put under guard, because it was not clear what should be done with him. ³⁵ Then the LORD said to Moses, "The man must be put to death; the whole community is to stone him to death outside the camp." ³⁶ So the whole community took him outside the camp and stoned him to death, as the LORD had commanded.

Rules about Tassels

³⁷ The LORD commanded Moses ³⁸ to say to the people of Israel: "Make tassels on the corners of your garments and put a blue cord on each tassel. You are to do this for all time to come. ³⁹ The tassels will serve as reminders, and each time you see them you will remember all my commands and obey them; then you will not turn away from

me and follow your own wishes and desires. ⁴⁰ The tassels will remind you to keep all my commands, and you will belong completely to me. ⁴¹ I am the LORD your God; I brought you out of Egypt to be your God. I am the LORD."

The Rebellion of Korah, Dathan, and Abiram

16 ¹⁻² Korah son of Izhar, from the Levite clan of Kohath, rebelled against the leadership of Moses. He was joined by three members of the tribe of Reuben — Dathan and Abiram, the sons of Eliab, and On son of Peleth — and by 250 other Israelites, well-known leaders chosen by the community. ³ They assembled before Moses and Aaron and said to them, "You have gone too far! All the members of the community belong to the LORD, and the LORD is with all of us. Why, then, Moses, do you set yourself above the LORD's community?"

⁴ When Moses heard this, he threw himself on the ground and prayed. ⁵ Then he said to Korah and his followers, "Tomorrow morning the LORD will show us who belongs to him; he will let the one who belongs to him, that is, the one he has chosen, approach him at the altar. ⁶⁻⁷ Tomorrow morning you and your followers take fire pans, put live coals and incense on them, and take them to the altar. Then we will see which of us the LORD has chosen. You Levites are the ones who have gone too far!"

⁸ Moses continued to speak to Korah. "Listen, you Levites! ⁹ Do you consider it a small matter that the God of Israel has set you apart from the rest of the community, so that you can approach him, perform your service in the LORD's Tent, and minister to the community and serve them? ¹⁰ He has let you and all the other Levites have this honor — and now you are trying to get the priest-

15.27, 28 Lv 4.27-31   **15.38** Dt 22.12   **16.1-35** Si 45.18-20   **16.1** Jdt 11 hood too! 11 When you complain against Aaron, it is really against the LORD that you and your followers are rebelling."

12 Then Moses sent for Dathan and Abiram, but they said, "We will not come! 13 Isn't it enough that you have brought us out of the fertile land of Egypt to kill us here in the wilderness? Do you also have to lord it over us? 14 You certainly have not brought us into a fertile land or given us fields and vineyards as our possession, and now you are trying to deceive us. We will not come!"

15 Moses became angry and said to the LORD, "Do not accept any offerings these men bring. I have not wronged any of them; I have not even taken one of their donkeys."

16 Moses said to Korah, "Tomorrow you and your 250 followers must come to the Tent of the LORD's presence; Aaron will also be there. 17 Each of you will take his fire pan, put incense on it, and then present it at the altar." 18 So they each took their fire pans, put live coals and incense on them, and stood at the entrance of the Tent with Moses and Aaron. 19 Then Korah gathered the whole community, and they stood facing Moses and Aaron at the entrance of the Tent. Suddenly the dazzling light of the LORD's presence appeared to the whole community, 20 and the LORD said to Moses and Aaron, 21 "Move back from these people, and I will destroy them immediately."

22 But Moses and Aaron bowed down with their faces to the ground and said, "O God, you are the source of all life. When one of us sins, do you become angry with the whole community?"

23 The LORD said to Moses, 24 "Tell the people to move away from the tents of Korah, Dathan, and Abiram."

25 Then Moses, accompanied by the leaders of Israel, went to Dathan and Abiram. 26 He said to the people, "Get away from the tents of these wicked

men and don't touch anything that belongs to them. Otherwise, you will be wiped out with them for all their sins." 27 So they moved away from the tents of Korah, Dathan, and Abiram.

Dathan and Abiram had come out and were standing at the entrance of their tents, with their wives and children. 28 Moses said to the people, "This is how you will know that the LORD has sent me to do all these things and that it is not by my own choice that I have done them. 29 If these men die a natural death without some punishment from God, then the LORD did not send me. 30 But if the LORD does something unheard of, and the earth opens up and swallows them with all they own, so that they go down alive to the world of the dead, you will know that these men have rejected the LORD."

The earth opens up and swallows them. (16.30)

31 As soon as he had finished speaking, the ground under Dathan and Abiram split open 32 and swallowed them and their families, together with all of Korah's followers and their possessions. 33 So they went down alive to the world of the dead, with their possessions. The earth closed over them, and they vanished. 34 All the people of Israel who were there fled when they heard

Between the living and the dead (16.48)

their cry. They shouted, "Run! The earth might swallow us too!"

³⁵ Then the LORD sent a fire that blazed out and burned up the 250 men who had presented the incense.

The Fire Pans

³⁶ Then the LORD said to Moses, ³⁷"Tell Eleazar son of Aaron the priest to remove the bronze fire pans from the remains of those who have been burned, and scatter the coals from the fire pans somewhere else, because the fire pans are holy. ³⁸ They became holy when they were presented at the LORD's altar. So take the fire pans of these who were put to death for their sin, beat them into thin plates, and make a covering for the altar. It will be a warning to the people of Israel." ³⁹ So Eleazar the priest took the fire pans and had them beaten into thin plates to make a covering for the altar. ⁴⁰ This was a warning to the Israelites that no one who was not a descendant of Aaron should come to the altar to burn incense for the LORD. Otherwise he would be destroyed like Korah and his men. All this was done as the LORD had commanded Eleazar through Moses.

Aaron Saves the People

⁴¹ The next day the whole community complained against Moses and Aaron and said, "You have killed some of the LORD's people." ⁴² After they had all gathered to protest to Moses and Aaron, they turned toward the Tent and saw that the cloud was covering it and that the dazzling light of the LORD's presence had appeared. ⁴³ Moses and Aaron went and stood in front of the Tent, ⁴⁴ and the LORD said to Moses, ⁴⁵"Move back from these people, and I will destroy them on the spot!"

The two of them bowed down with their faces to the ground, ⁴⁶ and Moses said to Aaron, "Take your fire pan, put live coals from the altar in it, and put some incense on the coals. Then hurry with it to the people and perform the ritual of purification for them. Hurry! The LORD's anger has already broken out and an epidemic has already begun." ⁴⁷ Aaron obeyed, took his fire pan and ran into the middle of the assembled people. When he saw that the plague had already begun, he put the incense on the coals and performed the ritual of purification for the people. ⁴⁸ This stopped the plague, and he was left standing between the living and the dead. [49] The number of people who died was 14,700, not counting those who died in Korah's rebellion. [50] When the plague had stopped, Aaron returned to Moses at the entrance of the Tent.

Aaron's Walking Stick

17 The LORD said to Moses, [2] "Tell the people of Israel to give you twelve walking sticks, one from the leader of each tribe. Write each man's name on his stick [3] and then write Aaron's name on the stick representing Levi. There will be one stick for each tribal leader. [4] Take them to the Tent of my presence and put them in front of the Covenant Box, where I meet you. [5] Then the stick of the man I have chosen will sprout. In this way I will put a stop to the constant complaining of these Israelites against you."

[6] So Moses spoke to the Israelites, and each of their leaders gave him a stick, one for each tribe, twelve in all, and Aaron's stick was put with them. [7] Moses then put all the sticks in the Tent in front of the LORD's Covenant Box.

[8] The next day, when Moses went into the Tent, he saw that Aaron's stick, representing the tribe of Levi, had sprouted. It had budded, blossomed,

Aaron's stick ... produced ripe almonds. (17.8)

and produced ripe almonds! [9] Moses took all the sticks and showed them to the Israelites. They saw what had hap-

pened, and each leader took his own stick back. [10] The LORD said to Moses, "Put Aaron's stick back in front of the Covenant Box. It is to be kept as a warning to the rebel Israelites that they will die unless their complaining stops." [11] Moses did as the LORD commanded.

[12] The people of Israel said to Moses, "Then that's the end of us! [13] If anyone who even comes near the Tent must die, then we are all as good as dead!"

Duties of Priests and Levites

18 The LORD said to Aaron, "You, your sons, and the Levites must suffer the consequences of any guilt connected with serving in the Tent of my presence; but only you and your sons will suffer the consequences of service in the priesthood. [2] Bring in your relatives, the tribe of Levi, to work with you and help you while you and your sons are serving at the Tent. [3] They are to fulfill their duties to you and their responsibilities for the Tent, but they must not have any contact with sacred objects in the Holy Place or with the altar. If they do, both they and you will be put to death. [4] They are to work with you and fulfill their responsibilities for all the service in the Tent, but no unqualified person may work with you. [5] You and your sons alone must fulfill the responsibilities for the Holy Place and the altar, so that my anger will not again break out against the people of Israel. [6] I am the one who has chosen your relatives the Levites from among the Israelites as a gift to you. They are dedicated to me, so that they can carry out their duties in the Tent. [7] But you and your sons alone shall fulfill all the responsibilities of the priesthood that concern the altar and what is in the Most Holy Place. These things are your responsibility, because I have given you the gift of the priesthood. Any unqualified person who comes near the sacred objects shall be put to death."

The Share of the Priests

8 The LORD said to Aaron, "Remember that I am giving you all the special contributions made to me that are not burned as sacrifices. I am giving them to you and to your descendants as the part assigned to you forever. **9** Of the most sacred offerings not burned on the altar, the following belong to you: the grain offerings, the sin offerings, and the repayment offerings. Everything that is presented to me as a sacred offering belongs to you and your sons. **10** You must eat these things in a holy place, and only males may eat them; consider them holy.

11 "In addition, any other special contributions that the Israelites present to me shall be yours. I am giving them to you, your sons, and your daughters for all time to come. Every member of your family who is ritually clean may eat them.

12 "I am giving you all the best of the first produce which the Israelites give me each year: olive oil, wine, and grain. **13** It all belongs to you. Every member of your family who is ritually clean may eat it.

14 "Everything in Israel that has been unconditionally dedicated to me belongs to you.

15 "Every first-born child or animal that the Israelites present to me belongs to you. But you must accept payment to buy back every first-born child, and must also accept payment for every first-born animal that is ritually unclean. **16** Children shall be bought back at the age of one month for the fixed price of five pieces of silver, according to the official standard. **17** But the first-born of cows, sheep, and goats are not to be bought back; they belong completely to me and are to be sacrificed.

Throw their blood against the altar and burn their fat as a food offering, an odor pleasing to me. **18** The meat from them belongs to you, like the breast and the right hind leg of the special offering.

19 "I am giving to you, to your sons, and to your daughters, for all time to come, all the special contributions which the Israelites present to me. This is an unbreakable covenant that I have made with you and your descendants."

20 The LORD said to Aaron, "You will not receive any property that can be inherited, and no part of the land of Israel will be assigned to you. I, the LORD, am all you need."

The Share of the Levites

21 The LORD said, "I have given to the Levites every tithe that the people of Israel present to me. This is in payment for their service in taking care of the Tent of my presence. **22** The other Israelites must no longer approach the Tent and in this way bring on themselves the penalty of death. **23** From now on only the Levites will take care of the Tent and bear the full responsibility for it. This is a permanent rule that applies also to your descendants. The Levites shall have no permanent property in Israel, **24** because I have given to them as their possession the tithe which the Israelites present to me as a special contribution. That is why I told them that they would have no permanent property in Israel."

The Levites' Tithe

25 The LORD commanded Moses **26** to say to the Levites: "When you receive from the Israelites the tithe that the LORD gives you as your possession, you must present a tenth of it as a special contribution to the LORD. **27** This special contribution will be considered as the equivalent of the offering which the farmer makes of new grain and new

18.14 Lv 27.28   **18.21** Lv 27.30-33; Dt 14.22-29

wine. [28] In this way you also will present the special contribution that belongs to the LORD from all the tithes which you receive from the Israelites. You are to give this special contribution for the LORD to Aaron the priest. [29] Give it from the best that you receive. [30] When you have presented the best part, you may keep the rest, just as the farmer keeps what is left after he makes his offering. [31] You and your families may eat the rest anywhere, because it is your wages for your service in the Tent. [32] You will not become guilty when you eat it, as long as you have presented the best of it to the LORD. But be sure not to profane the sacred gifts of the Israelites by eating any of the gifts before the best part is offered; if you do, you will be put to death."

Ashes of the Red Cow

19 The LORD commanded Moses and Aaron [2] to give the Israelites the following regulations. Bring to Moses and Aaron a red cow which has no defects and which has never been worked, [3] and they will give it to Eleazar the priest. It is to be taken outside the camp and killed in his presence. [m] [4] Then Eleazar is to take some of its blood and with his finger sprinkle it seven times in the direction of the Tent. [5] The whole animal, including skin, meat, blood, and intestines, is to be burned in the presence of the priest. [6] Then he is to take some cedar wood, a sprig of hyssop, and a red cord and throw them into the fire. [7] After that, he is to wash his clothes and pour water over himself, and then he may enter the camp; but he remains ritually unclean until evening. [8] The one who burned the cow must also wash his clothes and pour water over himself, but he also remains unclean until evening. [9] Then

someone who is ritually clean is to collect the ashes of the cow and put them in a ritually clean place outside the camp, where they are to be kept for the Israelite community to use in preparing the water for removing ritual uncleanness. This ritual is performed to remove sin. [10] The one who collected the ashes must wash his clothes, but he remains unclean until evening. This regulation is valid for all time to come, both for the Israelites and for the foreigners living among them.

Contact with a Corpse

[11] Those who touch a corpse are ritually unclean for seven days. [12] They must purify themselves with the water for purification on the third day and on the seventh day, and then they will be clean. But if they do not purify themselves on both the third and the seventh day, they will not be clean. [13] Those who touch a corpse and do not purify themselves remain unclean, because the water for purification has not been thrown over them. They defile the LORD's Tent, and they will no longer be considered God's people.

[14] In the case of a person who dies in a tent, anyone who is in the tent at the time of death or who enters it becomes ritually unclean for seven days. [15] Every jar and pot in the tent that has no lid[n] on it also becomes unclean. [16] If any touch a person who has been killed or has died a natural death outdoors or if any touch a human bone or a grave, they become unclean for seven days.

[17] To remove the uncleanness, some ashes from the red cow which was burned to remove sin shall be taken and put in a pot, and fresh water added. [18] In the first case, someone who is ritually clean is to take a sprig of hyssop, dip it in the water, and sprinkle the tent,

---

[m] It . . . presence; or He is to take it outside to the east of the camp and kill it. [n] no lid; or no lid fastened.
19.9 He 9.13

everything in it, and the people who were there. In the second case, someone who is ritually clean is to sprinkle the water on those who had touched the human bone or the dead body or the grave. ¹⁹On the third day and on the seventh the person who is ritually clean is to sprinkle the water on the unclean persons. On the seventh day he is to purify those, who, after washing their clothes and pouring water over themselves, become ritually clean at sunset.

²⁰Those who have become ritually unclean and do not purify themselves remain unclean, because the water for purification has not been thrown over them. They defile the LORD's Tent and will no longer be considered God's people. ²¹You are to observe this rule for all time to come. The person who sprinkles the water for purification must also wash his clothes; anyone who touches the water remains ritually unclean until evening. ²²Whatever an unclean person touches is unclean, and anyone else who touches it remains unclean until evening.

Events at Kadesh
(Exodus 17.1-7)

20 In the first month the whole community of Israel came to the wilderness of Zin and camped at Kadesh. There Miriam died and was buried.

²There was no water where they camped, so the people gathered around Moses and Aaron ³and complained: "It would have been better if we had died in front of the LORD's Tent along with the other Israelites. ⁴Why have you brought us out into this wilderness? Just so that we can die here with our animals? ⁵Why did you bring us out of Egypt into this miserable place where nothing will grow? There's no grain, no figs, no grapes, no pomegranates. There is not even any water to drink!"

⁶Moses and Aaron moved away from the people and stood at the entrance of the Tent. They bowed down with their faces to the ground, and the dazzling light of the LORD's presence appeared to them.

⁷The LORD said to Moses, ⁸"Take the stick that is in front of the Covenant Box, and then you and Aaron assemble the whole community. There in front of them all speak to that rock over there, and water will gush out of it. In this way you will bring water out of the rock for the people, for them and their animals to drink." ⁹Moses went and got the stick, as the LORD had commanded.

¹⁰He and Aaron assembled the whole community in front of the rock, and Moses said, "Listen, you rebels! Do we have to get water out of this rock for you?" ¹¹Then Moses raised the stick and struck the rock twice with it, and a great stream of water gushed out, and all the people and animals drank.

¹²But the LORD reprimanded Moses and Aaron. He said, "Because you did

A great stream of water gushed out. (20.11)

20.2-13 Ex 17.1-7   **20.11** Ws 11.4

not have enough faith to acknowledge my holy power before the people of Israel, you will not lead them into the land that I promised to give them."

¹³ This happened at Meribah,ᵒ where the people of Israel complained against the LORD and where he showed them that he is holy.

The King of Edom Refuses to Let Israel Pass

¹⁴ Moses sent messengers from Kadesh to the king of Edom. They said, "This message is from your kinsmen, the tribes of Israel. You know the hardships we have suffered, ¹⁵ how our ancestors went to Egypt, where we lived many years. The Egyptians mistreated our ancestors and us, ¹⁶ and we cried to the LORD for help. He heard our cry and sent an angel, who led us out of Egypt. Now we are at Kadesh, a town at the border of your territory. ¹⁷ Please permit us to pass through your land. We and our cattle will not leave the road or go into your fields or vineyards, and we will not drink from your wells. We will stay on the main roadᵖ until we are out of your territory."

¹⁸ But the Edomites answered, "We refuse to let you pass through our country! If you try, we will march out and attack you."

¹⁹ The people of Israel said, "We will stay on the main road, and if we or our animals drink any of your water, we will pay for it — all we want is to pass through."

²⁰ The Edomites repeated, "We refuse!" and they marched out with a powerful army to attack the people of Israel. ²¹ Because the Edomites would not let the Israelites pass through their territory, the Israelites turned and went another way.

The Death of Aaron

²² The whole community of Israel left Kadesh and arrived at Mount Hor, ²³ on the border of Edom. There the LORD said to Moses and Aaron, ²⁴ "Aaron is not going to enter the land which I promised to give to Israel; he is going to die, because the two of you rebelled against my command at Meribah. ²⁵ Take Aaron and his son Eleazar up Mount Hor, ²⁶ and there remove Aaron's priestly robes and put them on Eleazar. Aaron is going to die there." ²⁷ Moses did what the LORD had commanded. They went up Mount Hor in the sight of the whole community, ²⁸ and Moses removed Aaron's priestly robes and put them on Eleazar. There on the top of the mountain Aaron died, and Moses and Eleazar came back down. ²⁹ The whole community learned that Aaron had died, and they all mourned for him for thirty days.

Victory over the Canaanites

21 When the Canaanite king of Arad in the southern part of Canaan heard that the Israelites were coming by way of Atharim, he attacked them and captured some of them. ² Then the Israelites made a vow to the LORD: "If you will let us conquer these people, we will unconditionally dedicate�q them and their cities to you and will destroy them." ³ The LORD heard them and helped them conquer the Canaanites. So the Israelites completely destroyed them and their cities, and named the place Hormah.ʳ

ᵒ MERIBAH: *This name in Hebrew means "complaining."*   ᵖ main road; or King's Highway.   q UNCONDITIONALLY DEDICATE: *Anything dedicated in this way belonged completely to the LORD and could not be used; it had to be destroyed.*   ʳ HORMAH: *This name in Hebrew means "destruction."*
20.28 Ex 29.29; Nu 33.38; Dt 10.6   **21.1** Nu 33.40

The Snake Made of Bronze

⁴The Israelites left Mount Hor by the road that leads to the Gulf of Aqaba, in order to go around the territory of Edom. But on the way the people lost their patience ⁵and spoke against God and Moses. They complained, "Why did you bring us out of Egypt to die in this desert, where there is no food or water? We can't stand any more of this miserable food!" ⁶Then the LORD sent poisonous snakes among the people, and many Israelites were bitten and died. ⁷The people came to Moses and said, "We sinned when we spoke against the LORD and against you. Now pray to the LORD to take these snakes away." So Moses prayed for the people. ⁸Then the LORD told Moses to make a metal snake and put it on a pole, so that anyone who was bitten could look at it and be

Anyone who was bitten could look at it and be healed. (21.8)

healed. ⁹So Moses made a bronze snake and put it on a pole. Anyone who had been bitten would look at the bronze snake and be healed.

From Mount Hor to the Valley of the Moabites

¹⁰The Israelites moved on and camped at Oboth. ¹¹After leaving that place, they camped at the ruins of Aba-

rim in the wilderness east of Moabite territory. ¹²Then they camped in Zered Valley. ¹³From there they moved again and camped on the north side of the Arnon River, in the wilderness which extends into Amorite territory. (The Arnon was the border between the Moabites and the Amorites.) ¹⁴That is why *The Book of the LORD's Battles* speaks of ". . . the town of Waheb in the area of Suphah, and the valleys; the Arnon River, ¹⁵and the slope of the valleys that extend to the town of Ar and toward the border of Moab."

¹⁶From there they went on to a place called Wells, where the LORD said to Moses, "Bring the people together, and I will give them water." ¹⁷At that time the people of Israel sang this song:
"Wells, produce your water;
    And we will greet it with a
        song —
¹⁸The well dug by princes
    And by leaders of the people,
    Dug with a royal scepter
    And with their walking sticks."
They moved from the wilderness to Mattanah, ¹⁹and from there they went on to Nahaliel, and from Nahaliel to Bamoth, ²⁰and from Bamoth to the valley in the territory of the Moabites, below the top of Mount Pisgah, looking out over the desert.

Victory over King Sihon and King Og
(Deuteronomy 2.26 – 3.11)

²¹Then the people of Israel sent messengers to the Amorite king Sihon to say: ²²"Let us pass through your land. We and our cattle will not leave the road and go into your fields or vineyards, and we will not drink water from your wells; we will stay on the main road*s* until we are out of your territory." ²³But Sihon would not permit the people of Israel to pass through his territory. He gathered his army and went out to Jahaz in the

---

s main road; *or* King's Highway.

21.4 Dt 2.1   **21.5, 6** 1 Co 10.9   **21.9** 2 K 18.4; Jn 3.14

wilderness and attacked the Israelites. 24 But the Israelites killed many of the enemy in battle and occupied their land from the Arnon River north to the Jabbok, that is, to the Ammonites, because the Ammonite border was strongly defended.[t] 25 So the people of Israel captured all the Amorite cities, including Heshbon and all the surrounding towns, and settled in them. 26 Heshbon was the capital city of the Amorite king Sihon, who had fought against the former king of Moab and had captured all his land as far as the Arnon River. 27 That is why the poets sing,

"Come to Heshbon, to King
    Sihon's city!
We want to see it rebuilt and
    restored.
28 Once from this city of Heshbon
Sihon's army went forth like a
    fire;
It destroyed the city of Ar in
    Moab
And devoured[u] the hills of the
    upper Arnon.
29 How terrible for you, people of
    Moab!
You worshipers of Chemosh are
    brought to ruin!
Your god let the men become
    refugees,
And the women became captives
    of the Amorite king.
30 But now their descendants are
    destroyed,
All the way from Heshbon to
    Dibon,
From Nashim to Nophah, near
    Medeba."[v]

31 So the people of Israel settled in the territory of the Amorites, 32 and Moses sent men to find the best way to attack the city of Jazer. The Israelites cap-

tured it and its surrounding towns and drove out the Amorites living there.

33 Then the Israelites turned and took the road to Bashan, and King Og of Bashan marched out with his army to attack them at Edrei. 34 The LORD said to Moses, "Do not be afraid of him. I will give you victory over him, all his people, and his land. Do to him what you did to Sihon, the Amorite king who ruled at Heshbon." 35 So the Israelites killed Og, his sons, and all his people, leaving no survivors, and then they occupied his land.

The King of Moab Sends for Balaam

22 The Israelites moved on and set up camp in the plains of Moab east of the Jordan and opposite Jericho.

2 When the king of Moab, Balak son of Zippor, heard what the Israelites had done to the Amorites and how many Israelites there were, 3 he and all his people became terrified. 4 The Moabites said to the leaders of the Midianites, "This horde will soon destroy everything around us, like a bull eating the grass in a pasture." So King Balak 5 sent messengers to summon Balaam son of Beor, who was at Pethor near the Euphrates River in the land of Amaw. They brought him this message from Balak: "I want you to know that a whole nation has come from Egypt; its people are spreading out everywhere and threatening to take over our land. 6 They outnumber us, so please come and put a curse on them for me. Then perhaps we will be able to defeat them and drive them out of the land. I know that when you pronounce a blessing, people are blessed, and when you pronounce a curse, they are placed under a curse."

---

[t] because . . . strongly defended; *some ancient translations* as far as Jazer on the Ammonite border.   [u] *One ancient translation* devoured; *Hebrew* the lords of.
[v] *Verse 30 in Hebrew is unclear.*
21.28, 29 Jr 48.45, 46   **22.5** Nu 31.8; 2 P 2.15, 16; Jdt 11

⁷So the Moabite and Midianite leaders took with them the payment for the curse, went to Balaam, and gave him Balak's message. ⁸Balaam said to them, "Spend the night here, and tomorrow I will report to you whatever the LORD tells me." So the Moabite leaders stayed with Balaam.

⁹God came to Balaam and asked, "Who are these people that are staying with you?"

¹⁰He answered, "King Balak of Moab has sent them to tell me ¹¹that a people who came from Egypt has spread out over the whole land. He wants me to curse them for him, so that he can fight them and drive them out."

¹²God said to Balaam, "Do not go with them, and do not put a curse on the people of Israel, because they have my blessing."

¹³The next morning Balaam went to Balak's messengers and said, "Go back home; the LORD has refused to let me go with you." ¹⁴So they returned to Balak and told him that Balaam had refused to come with them.

¹⁵Then Balak sent a larger number of leaders, who were more important than the first. ¹⁶They went to Balaam and gave him this message from Balak: "Please don't let anything prevent you from coming to me! ¹⁷I will reward you richly and do anything you say. Please come and curse these people for me."

¹⁸But Balaam answered, "Even if Balak gave me all the silver and gold in his palace, I could not disobey the command of the LORD my God in even the smallest matter. ¹⁹But please spend the night, as the others did, so that I may learn whether or not the LORD has something else to tell me."

²⁰That night God came to Balaam and said, "If these men have come to ask you to go with them, get ready and go, but do only what I tell you." ²¹So the next morning Balaam saddled his donkey and went with the Moabite leaders.

Balaam and His Donkey

²²God was angry that Balaam was going, and as Balaam was riding along on his donkey, accompanied by his two servants, the angel of the LORD stood in the road to bar his way. ²³When the donkey saw the angel standing there holding a sword, it left the road and turned into the fields. Balaam beat the donkey and brought it back onto the road. ²⁴Then the angel stood where the road narrowed between two vineyards and had a stone wall on each side. ²⁵When the donkey saw the angel, it moved over against the wall and crushed Balaam's foot against it. Again Balaam beat the donkey. ²⁶Once more the angel moved ahead; he stood in a narrow place where there was no room at all to pass on either side. ²⁷This time, when the donkey saw the angel, it lay down. Balaam lost his temper and began to beat the donkey with his stick. ²⁸Then the LORD gave the donkey the power of speech, and it said to Balaam, "What have I done to you? Why have you beaten me these three times?"

²⁹Balaam answered, "Because you have made a fool of me! If I had a sword, I would kill you."

³⁰The donkey replied, "Am I not the same donkey on which you have ridden all your life? Have I ever treated you like this before?"

"No," he answered.

³¹Then the LORD let Balaam see the angel standing there with his sword; and Balaam threw himself face downward on the ground. ³²The angel demanded, "Why have you beaten your donkey three times like this? I have come to bar your way, because you should not be making this journey.ʷ ³³But your donkey saw me and turned aside three times. If it hadn't, I would have killed you and spared the donkey."

³⁴Balaam replied, "I have sinned. I did not know that you were standing in

ʷ *Probable text* you should . . . journey; *Hebrew unclear.*

HIGHLIGHTS FROM THE STORY OF BALAAM
(Numbers refer to chapter and verse in Numbers)

the road to oppose me; but now if you think it is wrong for me to go on, I will return home."

35 But the angel said, "Go on with these men, but say only what I tell you to say." So Balaam went on with them.

Balak Welcomes Balaam

36 When Balak heard that Balaam was coming, he went to meet him at Ar, a city on the Arnon River at the border of Moab. **37** Balak said to him, "Why didn't you come when I sent for you the first time? Did you think I wasn't able to reward you enough?"

38 Balaam answered, "I came, didn't I? But now, what power do I have? I can say only what God tells me to say." **39** So Balaam went with Balak to the town of Huzoth, **40** where Balak slaughtered cattle and sheep and gave some of the meat to Balaam and the leaders who were with him.

Balaam's First Prophecy

41 The next morning Balak took Balaam up to Bamoth Baal, from where Balaam could see a part of the people of Israel. **23** **1** He said to Balak, "Build seven altars here for me, and bring me seven bulls and seven rams."

2 Balak did as he was told, and he and Balaam offered a bull and a ram on each altar. **3** Then Balaam said to Balak, "Stand here by your burnt offering, while I go to see whether or not the Lord will meet me. I will tell you whatever he reveals to me." So he went alone to the top of a hill, **4** and God met him. Balaam said to him, "I have built the seven altars and offered a bull and a ram on each."

5 The Lord told Balaam what to say and sent him back to Balak to give him his message. **6** So he went back and found Balak still standing by his burnt offering with all the leaders of Moab.

7 Balaam uttered this prophecy:

"Balak king of Moab has
    brought me
From Syria, from the eastern
    mountains.
'Come speak for me,' he said.
'Put a curse on the people of
    Israel.'
8 How can I curse what God has
    not cursed,
Or speak of doom when the
    Lord has not?
9 From the high rocks I can see
    them;
I can watch them from the hills.
They are a nation that lives
    alone;
They know they are blessed
    more than other nations.
10 The descendants of Israel are
    like the dust—
There are too many of them to
    be counted.
Let me end my days like one of
    God's people;
Let me die in peace like the
    righteous."

11 Then Balak said to Balaam, "What have you done to me? I brought you here to curse my enemies, but all you have done is bless them."

12 He answered, "I can say only what the Lord tells me to say."

Balaam's Second Prophecy

13 Then Balak said to Balaam, "Come with me to another place from which you can see only some of the Israelites. Curse them for me from there." **14** He took him to the field of Zophim on the top of Mount Pisgah. There also he built seven altars and offered a bull and a ram on each of them.

15 Balaam said to Balak, "Stand here by your burnt offering, and I will meet God over there."

16 The Lord met Balaam, told him what to say, and sent him back to Balak to give him his message. **17** So he went back and found Balak still standing by his burnt offering, with the leaders of Moab. Balak asked what the LORD had said, [18] and Balaam uttered this prophecy:

"Come, Balak son of Zippor,
And listen to what I have to say.
[19] God is not like people, who lie;
He is not a human who changes
his mind.
Whatever he promises, he does;
He speaks, and it is done.
[20] I have been instructed to bless,
And when God blesses, I cannot
call it back.
[21] I foresee that Israel's future
Will bring her no misfortune or
trouble.
The LORD their God is with
them;
They proclaim that he is their
king.
[22] God has brought them out of
Egypt;
He fights for them like a wild ox.
[23] There is no magic charm, no
witchcraft,
That can be used against the
nation of Israel. [x]
Now people will say about Israel,
'Look what God has done!'
[24] The nation of Israel is like a
mighty lion:
It doesn't rest until it has torn
and devoured,
Until it has drunk the blood of
those it has killed."

[25] Then Balak said to Balaam, "You refuse to curse the people of Israel, but at least don't bless them!"

[26] Balaam answered, "Didn't I tell you that I had to do everything that the LORD told me?"

Balaam's Third Prophecy

[27] Balak said, "Come with me, and I will take you to another place. Perhaps God will be willing to let you curse them for me from there." [28] So he took Balaam to the top of Mount Peor overlooking the desert. [29] Balaam said to him, "Build seven altars for me here and bring me seven bulls and seven rams." [30] Balak did as he was told, and offered a bull and a ram on each altar.

24 By now Balaam knew that the LORD wanted him to bless the people of Israel, so he did not go to look for omens, as he had done before. He turned toward the desert [2] and saw the people of Israel camped tribe by tribe. The spirit of God took control of him, [3] and he uttered this prophecy:

"The message of Balaam son of
Beor,
The words of the man who can
see clearly, [y]
[4] Who can hear what God is
saying.
With staring eyes I see in a
trance
A vision from Almighty God.
[5] The tents of Israel are beautiful,
[6] Like long rows of palms
Or gardens beside a river,
Like aloes planted by the LORD
Or cedars beside the water.
[7] They will have abundant rainfall
And plant their seed in
well-watered fields. [z]
Their king shall be greater than
Agag,
And his rule shall be extended
far and wide.
[8] God brought them out of Egypt;
He fights for them like a wild ox.
They devour their enemies,
Crush their bones, smash their
arrows.

[x] There . . . Israel; *or* No magic charms are used in Israel, no witchcraft is practiced there.   [y] who can see clearly; *or* whose eyes are closed.   [z] *One ancient translation* They . . . fields; *Hebrew unclear.*

⁹The nation is like a mighty lion;
When it is sleeping, no one dares
    wake it.
Whoever blesses Israel will be
    blessed,
And whoever curses Israel will
    be cursed."

¹⁰Balak clenched his fists in anger
and said to Balaam, "I called you to
curse my enemies, but three times now
you have blessed them instead. ¹¹Now
get on home! I promised to reward you,
but the LORD has kept you from getting
the reward."

¹²Balaam answered, "I told the messengers you sent to me that ¹³even if
you gave me all the silver and gold in
your palace, I could not disobey the
command of the LORD by doing anything of myself. I will say only what the
LORD tells me to say."

Balaam's Final Prophecies

¹⁴Balaam said to Balak, "Now I am
going back to my own people, but before I go, I am warning you what the
people of Israel will do to your people in
the future." ¹⁵Then he uttered this
prophecy:

"The message of Balaam son of
    Beor,
The words of the man who can
    see clearly,ᵃ
¹⁶Who can hear what God is
    saying
And receive the knowledge that
    comes from the Most High.
With staring eyes I see in a
    trance
A vision from Almighty God.

¹⁷I look into the future,
And I see the nation of Israel.
A king, like a bright star, will
    arise in that nation.
Like a comet he will come from
    Israel.
He will strike the leaders of
    Moab
And beat down all the people of
    Seth.ᵇ
¹⁸He will conquer his enemies in
    Edom
And make their land his
    property,
While Israel continues victorious.
¹⁹The nation of Israel will trample
    them down
And wipe out the last survivors."

²⁰Then in his vision Balaam saw
the Amalekites and uttered this
prophecy:
"Amalek was the most powerful
    nation of all,
But at the end it will perish
    forever."
²¹In his vision he saw the Kenites,
and uttered this prophecy:
"The place where you live is
    secure,
Safe as a nest set high on a cliff,
²²But you Kenites will be destroyed
When Assyria takes you
    captive."ᶜ
²³Balaam uttered this prophecy:
"Who are these people gathering
    in the north?ᵈ
²⁴Invaders will sail from Cyprus;
They will conquer Assyria and
    Eber,
But they, in turn, will perish
    forever."
²⁵Then Balaam got ready and went
back home, and Balak went on his way.

ᵃ who can see clearly; *or* whose eyes are closed.   ᵇ the people of Seth; *or* who are
proud and violent.   ᶜ *Verse 22 in Hebrew is unclear.*   ᵈ *Probable text* Who . . .
north; *Hebrew unclear.*
24.9 a Gn 49.9; **b** Gn 12.3

The People of Israel at Peor

25 When the Israelites were camped at Acacia Valley, the men began to have sexual intercourse with the Moabite women who were there. [2] These women invited them to sacrificial feasts, where the god of Moab was worshiped. The Israelites ate the food and worshiped the god [3] Baal of Peor. So the LORD was angry with them [4] and said to Moses, "Take all the leaders of Israel and, in obedience to me, execute them in broad daylight,[e] and then I will no longer be angry with the people." [5] Moses said to the officials, "Each of you is to kill every man in your tribe who has become a worshiper of Baal of Peor."

[6] One of the Israelites took a Midianite woman into his tent in the sight of Moses and the whole community, while they were mourning at the entrance of the Tent of the LORD's presence. [7] When Phinehas, the son of Eleazar and grandson of Aaron the priest, saw this, he got up and left the assembly. He took a spear, [8] followed the man and the woman into the tent, and drove the spear through both of them. In this way the epidemic that was destroying Israel was stopped, [9] but it had already killed twenty-four thousand people.

[10] The LORD said to Moses, [11] "Because of what Phinehas has done, I am no longer angry with the people of Israel. He refused to tolerate the worship of any god but me, and that is why I did not destroy them in my anger. [12] So tell him that I am making a covenant with him that is valid for all time to come. [13] He and his descendants are permanently established as priests, because he did not tolerate any rivals to me and brought about forgiveness for the people's sin."

[14] The name of the Israelite who was killed with the Midianite woman was Zimri son of Salu, the head of a family in the tribe of Simeon. [15] The woman's name was Cozbi. Zur, her father, was chief of a group of Midianite clans.

[16] The LORD commanded Moses, [17] "Attack the Midianites and destroy them, [18] because of the evil they did to you when they deceived you at Peor, and because of Cozbi, who was killed at the time of the epidemic at Peor."

The Second Census

26 After the epidemic the LORD said to Moses and Eleazar son of Aaron, [2] "Take a census by families of the whole community of Israel, of all men twenty years old or older who are fit for military service." [3-4] Moses and Eleazar obeyed and called together all the men of that age group. They assembled in the plains of Moab across the Jordan River from Jericho.

These were the Israelites who came out of Egypt:

[5] The tribe of Reuben (Reuben was the oldest son of Jacob): the clans of Hanoch, Pallu, [6] Hezron, and Carmi. [7] These clans numbered 43,730 men. [8] The descendants of Pallu were Eliab [9] and his sons Nemuel, Dathan, and Abiram. (These are the Dathan and Abiram who were chosen by the community. They defied Moses and Aaron and joined the followers of Korah when they rebelled against the LORD. [10] The ground opened and swallowed them, and they died with Korah and his followers when fire destroyed 250 men; they became a warning to the people. [11] But the sons of Korah were not killed.)

[12] The tribe of Simeon: the clans of Nemuel, Jamin, Jachin, [13] Zerah, and Shaul. [14] These clans numbered 22,200 men.

[15] The tribe of Gad: the clans of Ze-

[e] in broad daylight; or publicly.
26.1-51 Nu 1.1-46

phon, Haggi, Shuni, ¹⁶Ozni, Eri, ¹⁷Arod, and Areli. ¹⁸These clans numbered 40,500 men.

¹⁹⁻²¹The tribe of Judah: the clans of Shelah, Perez, Zerah, Hezron, and Hamul. (Two of Judah's sons, Er and Onan, had died in the land of Canaan.) ²²These clans numbered 76,500 men.

²³The tribe of Issachar: the clans of Tola, Puah, ²⁴Jashub, and Shimron. ²⁵These clans numbered 64,300 men.

²⁶The tribe of Zebulun: the clans of Sered, Elon, and Jahleel. ²⁷These clans numbered 60,500 men.

²⁸The tribes of Joseph, who was the father of two sons, Manasseh and Ephraim.

²⁹The tribe of Manasseh. Machir son of Manasseh was the father of Gilead, and the following clans traced their ancestry to Gilead: ³⁰the clans of Iezer, Helek, ³¹Asriel, Shechem, ³²Shemida, and Hepher. ³³Zelophehad son of Hepher had no sons, but only daughters; their names were Mahlah, Noah, Hoglah, Milcah, and Tirzah. ³⁴These clans numbered 52,700 men.

³⁵The tribe of Ephraim: the clans of Shuthelah, Becher, and Tahan. ³⁶The clan of Eran traced its descent from Shuthelah. ³⁷These clans numbered 32,500 men.

These are the clans descended from Joseph.

³⁸The tribe of Benjamin: the clans of Bela, Ashbel, Ahiram, ³⁹Shephupham, and Hupham. ⁴⁰The clans of Ard and Naaman traced their descent from Bela. ⁴¹These clans numbered 45,600 men.

⁴²The tribe of Dan: the clan of Shuham, ⁴³which numbered 64,400 men.

⁴⁴The tribe of Asher: the clans of Imnah, Ishvi, and Beriah. ⁴⁵The clans of Heber and Malchiel traced their descent from Beriah. ⁴⁶Asher had a daughter named Serah. ⁴⁷These clans numbered 53,400 men.

⁴⁸The tribe of Naphtali: the clans of Jahzeel, Guni, ⁴⁹Jezer, and Shillem. ⁵⁰These clans numbered 45,400 men.

⁵¹The total number of the Israelite men was 601,730.

⁵²The LORD said to Moses, ⁵³"Divide the land among the tribes, according to their size. ⁵⁴⁻⁵⁶Divide the land by drawing lots, and give a large share to a large tribe and a small one to a small tribe."

⁵⁷The tribe of Levi consisted of the clans of Gershon, Kohath, and Merari. ⁵⁸Their descendants included the subclans of Libni, Hebron, Mahli, Mushi, and Korah. Kohath was the father of Amram, ⁵⁹who was married to Levi's daughter Jochebed, who was born in Egypt. She bore Amram two sons, Aaron and Moses, and a daughter, Miriam. ⁶⁰Aaron had four sons, Nadab, Abihu, Eleazar, and Ithamar. ⁶¹Nadab and Abihu died when they offered unholy fire to the LORD. ⁶²The male Levites who were one month old or older numbered 23,000. They were listed separately from the rest of the Israelites, because they were not given any property in Israel.

⁶³All these clans were listed by Moses and Eleazar when they took a census of the Israelites in the plains of Moab across the Jordan River from Jericho. ⁶⁴There was not even one man left among those whom Moses and Aaron had listed in the first census in the Sinai Desert. ⁶⁵The LORD had said that all of them would die in the wilderness, and except for Caleb son of Jephunneh and Joshua son of Nun they all did.

The Daughters of Zelophehad

27 Mahlah, Noah, Hoglah, Milcah, and Tirzah were the daughters of Zelophehad son of Hepher, son of Gilead, son of Machir, son of Manasseh, son of Joseph. ²They went and stood before Moses, Eleazar

26.52-56 Nu 34.13; Js 14.1, 2   **26.60** Nu 3.2   **26.61** Lv 10.1, 2; Nu 3.4
26.65 Nu 14.26-35

Take Joshua . . . a capable man. (27.18)

the priest, the leaders, and the whole community at the entrance of the Tent of the LORD's presence and said, 3"Our father died in the wilderness without leaving any sons. He was not among the followers of Korah, who rebelled against the LORD; he died because of his own sin. 4Just because he had no sons, why should our father's name disappear from Israel? Give us property among our father's relatives."

5Moses presented their case to the LORD, 6and the LORD said to him, 7"What the daughters of Zelophehad request is right; give them property among their father's relatives. Let his inheritance pass on to them. 8Tell the people of Israel that whenever a man dies without leaving a son, his daughter is to inherit his property. 9If he has no daughter, his brothers are to inherit it. 10If he has no brothers, his father's brothers are to inherit it. 11If he has no brothers or uncles, then his nearest relative is to inherit it and hold it as his own property. The people of Israel are to observe this as a legal require-

ment, just as I, the LORD, have commanded you."

Joshua Is Chosen as Successor to Moses
(Deuteronomy 31.1-8)

12The LORD said to Moses, "Go up the Abarim Mountains and look out over the land that I am giving to the Israelites. 13After you have seen it, you will die, as your brother Aaron did, 14because both of you rebelled against my command in the wilderness of Zin. When the whole community complained against me at Meribah, you refused to acknowledge my holy power before them." (Meribah is the spring at Kadesh in the wilderness of Zin.)

15Moses prayed, 16"LORD God, source of all life, appoint, I pray, a man who can lead the people 17and can command them in battle, so that your community will not be like sheep without a shepherd."

18The LORD said to Moses, "Take Joshua son of Nun, a capable man, and place your hands on his head. 19Have

27.7 Nu 36.2   27.12-14 Dt 3.23-27; 32.48-52   27.17 1 K 22.17; Ez 34.5; Mt 9.36;
Mk 6.34   27.18 Ex 24.13

him stand in front of Eleazar the priest and the whole community, and there before them all proclaim him as your successor. ²⁰Give him some of your own authority, so that the whole community of Israel will obey him. ²¹He will depend on Eleazar the priest, who will learn my will by using the Urim and Thummim.*f* In this way Eleazar will direct Joshua and the whole community of Israel in all their affairs." ²²Moses did as the LORD had commanded him. He had Joshua stand before Eleazar the priest and the whole community. ²³As the LORD had commanded, Moses put his hands on Joshua's head and proclaimed him as his successor.

The Regular Offerings
(Exodus 29.38-46)

28 The LORD commanded Moses ²to instruct the Israelites to present to God at the appointed times the required food offerings that are pleasing to him.

³These are the food offerings that are to be presented to the LORD: for the daily burnt offering, two one-year-old male lambs without any defects. ⁴Offer the first lamb in the morning, and the second in the evening, ⁵each with a grain offering of 2 pounds of flour, mixed with 2 pints of the best olive oil. ⁶This is the daily offering that is completely burned, which was first offered at Mount Sinai as a food offering, an odor pleasing to the LORD. ⁷As the wine offering with the first lamb, pour out at the altar 2 pints of wine. ⁸In the evening offer the second lamb in the same way as the morning offering, together with its wine offering. It also is a food offering, an odor pleasing to the LORD.

The Sabbath Offering

⁹On the Sabbath day offer two one-year-old male lambs without any defects, 4 pounds of flour mixed with olive oil as a grain offering, and the wine offering. ¹⁰This burnt offering is to be offered every Sabbath in addition to the daily offering with its wine offering.

The Offering on the First Day of the Month

¹¹Present a burnt offering to the LORD at the beginning of each month: two young bulls, one ram, seven one-year-old male lambs, all without any defects. ¹²As a grain offering, offer flour mixed with olive oil: with each bull, 6 pounds of flour; with the ram, 4 pounds; ¹³and with each lamb, 2 pounds. These burnt offerings are food offerings, an odor pleasing to the LORD. ¹⁴The proper wine offering is 4 pints of wine with each bull, 3 pints with the ram, and 2 pints with each lamb. This is the regulation for the burnt offering for the first day of each month throughout the year. ¹⁵And in addition to the daily burnt offering with its wine offering, offer one male goat as a sin offering.

The Offerings at the Festival of Unleavened Bread
(Leviticus 23.5-14)

¹⁶The Passover Festival in honor of the LORD is to be held on the fourteenth day of the first month. ¹⁷On the fifteenth day a religious festival begins which lasts seven days, during which only bread prepared without yeast is to be eaten. ¹⁸On the first day of the festival you are to gather for worship, and no work is to be done. ¹⁹Offer a burnt offering as a food offering to the LORD: two

f URIM AND THUMMIM: *Two objects used by the priest to determine God's will; it is not known precisely how they were used.*
27.21 Ex 28.30; 1 S 14.41; 28.6   **27.23** Dt 31.23   **28.16** Ex 12.1-13; Dt 16.1, 2
28.17-25 Ex 12.14-20; 23.15; 34.18; Dt 16.3-8

young bulls, one ram, and seven one-year-old male lambs, all without any defects. [20] Offer the proper grain offering of flour mixed with olive oil: 6 pounds with each bull, 4 pounds with the ram, [21] and 2 pounds with each lamb. [22] Also offer one male goat as a sin offering, and in this way perform the ritual of purification for the people. [23] Offer these in addition to the regular morning burnt offering. [24] In the same way, for seven days offer to the LORD a food offering, an odor pleasing to him. Offer this in addition to the daily burnt offering and wine offering. [25] Meet for worship on the seventh day and do no work.

The Offerings at the Harvest Festival
(Leviticus 23.15-22)

[26] On the first day of the Harvest Festival, when you present the offering of new grain to the LORD, you are to gather for worship, and no work is to be done. [27] Offer a burnt offering as an odor pleasing to the LORD: two young bulls, one ram, and seven one-year-old male lambs, all without any defects. [28] Offer the proper grain offering of flour mixed with olive oil: 6 pounds with each bull, 4 pounds with the ram, [29] and 2 pounds with each lamb. [30] Also offer one male goat as a sin offering, and in this way perform the ritual of purification for the people. [31] Offer these and the wine offering in addition to the daily burnt offering and grain offering.

The Offerings at the New Year Festival
(Leviticus 23.23-25)

29 On the first day of the seventh month you are to gather for worship, and no work is to be done. On that day trumpets are to be blown. [2] Present a burnt offering to the LORD, an odor pleasing to him: one young bull, one ram, and seven one-year-old male lambs, all without any defects.

[3] Offer the proper grain offering of flour mixed with olive oil: 6 pounds of flour with the bull, 4 pounds with the ram, [4] and 2 pounds with each lamb. [5] Also offer one male goat as a sin offering, and in this way perform the ritual of purification for the people. [6] Offer these in addition to the regular burnt offering for the first day of the month with its grain offering, and the daily burnt offering with its grain offering and wine offering. These food offerings are an odor pleasing to the LORD.

The Offerings at the Day of Atonement
(Leviticus 23.26-32)

[7] Gather for worship on the tenth day of the seventh month; eat no food and do no work. [8] Offer a burnt offering to the LORD, an odor pleasing to him: one young bull, one ram, and seven one-year-old male lambs, all without any defects. [9] Offer the proper grain offering of flour mixed with olive oil: 6 pounds of flour with the bull, 4 pounds with the ram, [10] and 2 pounds with each lamb. [11] Also offer one male goat as a sin offering, in addition to the goat offered in the ritual of purification for the people, and the daily burnt offering with its grain offering and wine offering.

The Offerings at the Festival of Shelters
(Leviticus 23.33-44)

[12] Gather for worship on the fifteenth day of the seventh month. Celebrate this festival in honor of the LORD for seven days and do no work. [13] On this first day offer a food offering to the LORD, an odor pleasing to him: thirteen young bulls, two rams, and fourteen one-year-old male lambs, all without any defects. [14] Offer the proper grain offering of flour mixed with olive oil: 6 pounds of flour with each bull, 4 pounds with each ram, [15] and

28.26-31 Ex 23.16; 34.22; Dt 16.9-12   **29.7-11** Lv 16.29-34   **29.12-38** Lv 23.34; Dt 16.13-15

2 pounds with each lamb, with the required wine offerings. [16] Also offer one male goat as a sin offering. Offer these in addition to the daily burnt offering with its grain offering and wine offering.

[17] On the second day offer twelve young bulls, two rams, and fourteen one-year-old male lambs, all without any defects. [18-19] Offer with them all the other offerings required for the first day.

[20] On the third day offer eleven young bulls, two rams, and fourteen one-year-old male lambs, all without any defects. [21-22] Offer with them all the other offerings required for the first day.

[23] On the fourth day offer ten young bulls, two rams, and fourteen one-year-old male lambs, all without any defects. [24-25] Offer with them all the other offerings required for the first day.

[26] On the fifth day offer nine young bulls, two rams, and fourteen one-year-old male lambs, all without any defects. [27-28] Offer with them all the other offerings required for the first day.

[29] On the sixth day offer eight young bulls, two rams, and fourteen one-year-old male lambs, all without any defects. [30-31] Offer with them all the other offerings required for the first day.

[32] On the seventh day offer seven young bulls, two rams, and fourteen one-year-old male lambs, all without any defects. [33-34] Offer with them all the other offerings required for the first day.

[35] On the eighth day gather for worship and do no work. [36] Offer a burnt offering as a food offering to the LORD, an odor pleasing to him: one young bull, one ram, and seven one-year-old male lambs, all without any defects. [37-38] Offer with them all the other offerings required for the first day.

[39] These are the regulations concerning the burnt offerings, grain offerings, wine offerings, and fellowship offerings that you are to make to the LORD at your appointed festivals. These are in addition to the offerings you give in fulfillment of a vow or as freewill offerings.

[40] So Moses told the people of Israel everything that the LORD had commanded him.

Rules about Vows

30 Moses gave the following instructions to the leaders of the tribes of Israel. [2] When a man makes a vow to give something to the LORD or takes an oath to abstain from something, he must not break his promise, but must do everything that he said he would.

[3] When a young woman still living in her father's house makes a vow to give something to the LORD or promises to abstain from something, [4] she must do everything that she vowed or promised unless her father raises an objection when he hears about it. [5] But if her father forbids her to fulfill the vow when he hears about it, she is not required to keep it. The LORD will forgive her, because her father refused to let her keep it.

[6] If an unmarried woman makes a vow, whether deliberately or carelessly, or promises to abstain from something, and then marries, [7] she must do everything that she vowed or promised unless her husband raises an objection when he hears about it. [8] But if her husband forbids her to fulfill the vow when he hears about it, she is not required to keep it. The LORD will forgive her.

[9] A widow or a divorced woman must keep every vow she makes and every promise to abstain from something.

[10] If a married woman makes a vow or promises to abstain from something, [11] she must do everything that she vowed or promised unless her husband raises an objection when he hears about it. [12] But if her husband forbids her to fulfill the vow when he hears

30.2 Dt 23.21-23; Mt 5.33

about it, she is not required to keep it. The LORD will forgive her, because her husband prevented her from keeping her vow. ¹³ Her husband has the right to affirm or to annul any vow or promise that she has made. ¹⁴ But if, by the day after he hears of the vow, he has raised no objection, she must do everything that she has vowed or promised. He has affirmed the vow by not objecting on the day he heard of it. ¹⁵ But if he later annuls the vow, he must suffer the consequences for the failure to fulfill the vow.

¹⁶ These are the rules that the LORD gave Moses concerning vows made by an unmarried woman living in her father's house or by a married woman.

The Holy War against Midian

31 The LORD said to Moses, ² "Punish the Midianites for what they did to the people of Israel. After you have done that, you will die."

³ So Moses said to the people, "Get ready for war, so that you can attack Midian and punish them for what they did to the LORD. ⁴ From each tribe of Israel send a thousand men to war."

⁵ So a thousand men were chosen from each tribe, a total of twelve thousand men ready for battle. ⁶ Moses sent them to war under the command of Phinehas son of Eleazar the priest, who took charge of the sacred objects and the trumpets for giving signals. ⁷ They attacked Midian, as the LORD had commanded Moses, and killed all the men, ⁸ including the five kings of Midian: Evi, Rekem, Zur, Hur, and Reba. They also killed Balaam son of Beor.

⁹ The people of Israel captured the Midianite women and children, took their cattle and their flocks, plundered all their wealth, ¹⁰ and burned all their cities and camps. ¹¹ They took all the loot that they had captured, including the prisoners and the animals, ¹² and

brought them to Moses and Eleazar and to the community of the people of Israel, who were at the camp on the plains of Moab across the Jordan from Jericho.

The Army Returns

¹³ Moses, Eleazar, and all the other leaders of the community went out of the camp to meet the army. ¹⁴ Moses became angry with the officers, the commanders of battalions and companies, who had returned from the war. ¹⁵ He asked them, "Why have you kept all the women alive? ¹⁶ Remember that it was the women who followed Balaam's instructions and at Peor led the people to be unfaithful to the LORD. That was what brought the epidemic on the LORD's people. ¹⁷ So now kill every boy and kill every woman who has had sexual intercourse, ¹⁸ but keep alive for yourselves all the girls and all the women who are virgins. ¹⁹ Now all of you who have killed anyone or have touched a corpse must stay outside the camp for seven days. On the third day and on the seventh day purify yourselves and the women you have captured. ²⁰ You must also purify every piece of clothing and everything made of leather, goats' hair, or wood."

²¹ Eleazar the priest said to the men who had returned from battle, "These are the regulations that the LORD has given to Moses. ²²⁻²³ Everything that will not burn, such as gold, silver, bronze, iron, tin, or lead, is to be purified by passing it through fire. Everything else is to be purified by the water for purification. ²⁴ On the seventh day you must wash your clothes; then you will be ritually clean and will be permitted to enter the camp."

Division of the Loot

²⁵ The LORD said to Moses, ²⁶ "You and Eleazar, together with the other

leaders of the community, are to count everything that has been captured, including the prisoners and the animals. ²⁷Divide what was taken into two equal parts, one part for the soldiers and the other part for the rest of the community. ²⁸From the part that belongs to the soldiers, withhold as a tax for the LORD one out of every five hundred prisoners and the same proportion of the cattle, donkeys, sheep, and goats. ²⁹Give them to Eleazar the priest as a special contribution to the LORD. ³⁰From the part given to the rest of the people, take one out of every fifty prisoners and the same proportion of the cattle, the donkeys, sheep, and goats. Give them to the Levites who are in charge of the LORD's Tent." ³¹Moses and Eleazar did what the LORD commanded.

³²⁻³⁵The following is a list of what was captured by the soldiers, in addition to what they kept for themselves: 675,000 sheep and goats, 72,000 cattle, 61,000 donkeys, and 32,000 virgins. ³⁶⁻⁴⁰The half share of the soldiers was 337,500 sheep and goats, of which 675 were the tax for the LORD; 36,000 cattle for the soldiers, of which 72 were the tax for the LORD; 30,500 donkeys for the soldiers, of which 61 were the tax for the LORD; and 16,000 virgins for the soldiers, of which 32 were the tax for the LORD. ⁴¹So Moses gave Eleazar the tax as a special contribution to the LORD, as the LORD had commanded.

⁴²⁻⁴⁶The share of the community was the same as that for the soldiers: 337,500 sheep and goats, 36,000 cattle, 30,500 donkeys, and 16,000 virgins. ⁴⁷From this share Moses took one out of every fifty prisoners and animals, and as the LORD had commanded, gave them to the Levites who were in charge of the LORD's Tent.

⁴⁸Then the officers who had commanded the army went to Moses ⁴⁹and reported, "Sir, we have counted the soldiers under our command and not one of them is missing. ⁵⁰So we are bring-

ing the gold ornaments, armlets, bracelets, rings, earrings, and necklaces that each of us has taken. We offer them to the LORD as a payment for our lives, so

The gold ornaments (31.50)

that he will protect us." ⁵¹Moses and Eleazar received the gold, all of which was in the form of ornaments. ⁵²The total contribution of the officers weighed over four hundred pounds. ⁵³Those who were not officers kept the loot they had taken. ⁵⁴So Moses and Eleazar took the gold to the Tent, so that the LORD would protect the people of Israel.

The Tribes East of the Jordan
(Deuteronomy 3.12-22)

32 The tribes of Reuben and Gad had a lot of livestock. When they saw how suitable the land of Jazer and Gilead was for cattle, ²they went to Moses, Eleazar, and the other leaders of the community and said, ³⁻⁴"This region which the LORD has helped the Israelites occupy — the towns of Ataroth, Dibon, Jazer, Nimrah, Heshbon, Elealeh, Sibmah, Nebo, and Beon — is good land for livestock, and we have so much livestock. ⁵Please give us this land as our property, and do not make us cross the Jordan River and settle there."

⁶Moses replied, "Do you want to stay here while the other Israelites go to war? ⁷How dare you try to discourage the people of Israel from crossing the Jordan into the land which the LORD

has given them? [8] That is what your fathers did when I sent them from Kadesh Barnea to explore the land. [9] They went as far as Eshcol Valley and saw the land, but when they returned, they discouraged the people from entering the land which the LORD had given them. [10] The LORD became angry that day and made a promise: [11] 'I swear that because they did not remain loyal to me, none of the men twenty years old or older who came out of Egypt will enter the land that I promised to Abraham, Isaac, and Jacob.' [12] This included everyone, except Caleb son of Jephunneh the Kenizzite and Joshua son of Nun; they remained loyal to the LORD. [13] The LORD became angry with the people and made them wander in the wilderness forty years until that whole generation that had displeased him was dead. [14] And now you have taken your ancestors' place, a new generation of sinful people ready to bring down the fierce anger of the LORD on Israel again. [15] If you people of Reuben and Gad refuse to follow him now, he will once again abandon all these people in the wilderness, and you will be responsible for their destruction."

[16] They approached Moses and said, "First, allow us to build stone enclosures here for our sheep and fortified towns for our dependents. [17] Then we will be ready to go with the other Israelites into battle and lead the attack until we have settled them in the land that will be theirs. In the meantime, our dependents can live here in the fortified towns, safe from the people of this land. [18] We will not return to our homes until all the other Israelites have taken possession of the land assigned to them. [19] We will not take possession of any property among them on the other side of the Jordan, because we have received our share here east of the Jordan."

[20] Moses answered, "If you really mean what you say, then here in the presence of the LORD get ready to go into battle. [21] All your fighting men are to cross the Jordan and under the command of the LORD they are to attack our enemies until the LORD defeats them [22] and takes possession of the land. After that, you may return, because you will have fulfilled your obligation to the LORD and to the other Israelites. Then the LORD will acknowledge that this land east of the Jordan is yours. [23] But if you do not keep your promise, I warn you that you will be sinning against the LORD. Make no mistake about it; you will be punished for your sin. [24] So build your towns and the enclosures for your sheep, but do what you have promised!"

[25] The men of Gad and Reuben said, "Sir, we will do as you command. [26] Our wives and children and our cattle and sheep will remain here in the towns of Gilead. [27] But all of us are ready to go into battle under the LORD's command. We will cross the Jordan and fight, just as you have said."

[28] So Moses gave these commands to Eleazar, Joshua, and the other leaders of Israel: [29] "If the men of Gad and Reuben cross the Jordan ready for battle at the LORD's command and if with their help you are able to conquer the land, then give them the land of Gilead as their property. [30] But if they do not cross the Jordan and go into battle with you, they are to receive their share of the property in the land of Canaan, as you do."

[31] The men of Gad and Reuben answered, "Sir, we will do as the LORD has commanded. [32] Under his command we will cross into the land of Canaan and go into battle, so that we can retain our property here east of the Jordan."

[33] So Moses assigned to the tribes of Gad and Reuben and to half the tribe of Manasseh all the territory of King Sihon of the Amorites and King Og of Bashan, including the towns and the

32.8, 9 Nu 13.17-33   **32.10-13** Nu 14.26-35   **32.28-32** Js 1.12-15

country around them. 34 The tribe of Gad rebuilt the fortified towns of Dibon, Ataroth, Aroer, 35 Atroth Shophan, Jazer, Jogbehah, 36 Beth Nimrah, and Beth Haran. 37 The tribe of Reuben rebuilt Heshbon, Elealeh, Kiriathaim, 38 Nebo, Baal Meon (this name was changed), and Sibmah. They gave new names to the towns they rebuilt.

39 The clan of Machir son of Manasseh invaded the land of Gilead, occupied it, and drove out the Amorites who were there. 40 So Moses gave Gilead to the clan of Machir, and they lived there. 41 Jair, of the tribe of Manasseh, attacked and captured some villages and named them "Villages of Jair." 42 Nobah attacked and captured Kenath and its villages, and he renamed it Nobah, after himself.

The Journey from Egypt to Moab

33 The following account gives the names of the places where the Israelites set up camp after they left Egypt in their tribes under the leadership of Moses and Aaron. 2 At the command of the LORD, Moses wrote down the name of the place each time they set up camp.

3 The people of Israel left Egypt on the fifteenth day of the first month of the year, the day after the first Passover. Under the LORD's protection they left the city of Rameses in full view of the Egyptians, 4 who were burying the first-born sons that the LORD had killed. By doing this, the LORD showed that he was more powerful than the gods of Egypt.

5 The people of Israel left Rameses and set up camp at Sukkoth. 6 Their next camp was at Etham on the edge of the desert. 7 From there they turned back to Pi Hahiroth, east of Baal Zephon, and camped near Migdol. 8 They left Pi Hahiroth and passed through the

Red Sea*g* into the desert of Shur; after a three days' march they camped at Marah. 9 From there they went to Elim, where they camped, because there were twelve springs of water and seventy palm trees there.

10 They left Elim and camped near the Gulf of Suez. 11 Their next camp was in the desert of Sin. 12 Then they camped at Dophkah, 13 and after that at Alush. 14 Next was Rephidim, where there was no water for them to drink.

15-37 From Rephidim to Mount Hor they set up camp at the following places: the Sinai Desert, Kibroth Hattaavah (or "Graves of Craving"), Hazeroth, Rithmah, Rimmon Perez, Libnah, Rissah, Kehelathah, Mount Shepher, Haradah, Makheloth, Tahath, Terah, Mithkah, Hashmonah, Moseroth, Bene Jaakan, Hor Haggidgad, Jotbathah, Abronah, Eziongeber, the wilderness of Zin (that is, Kadesh), and Mount Hor, at the edge of the land of Edom.

38-39 At the command of the LORD, Aaron the priest climbed Mount Hor. At the age of 123 he died there on the first day of the fifth month of the fortieth year after the Israelites had left Egypt.

40 The king of Arad in southern Canaan heard that the Israelites were coming.

41-49 From Mount Hor to the plains of Moab the Israelites set up camp at the following places: Zalmonah, Punon, Oboth, the ruins of Abarim in the territory of Moab, Dibon Gad, Almon Diblathaim, the Abarim Mountains near Mount Nebo, and in the plains of Moab across the Jordan River from Jericho, between Beth Jeshimoth and Acacia Valley.

Instructions before Crossing the Jordan

50 There in the plains of Moab across the Jordan from Jericho the LORD gave

g RED SEA: *See Word List.*

33.38 Nu 20.22-28; Dt 10.6; 32.50   **33.40** Nu 21.1

Moses [51] the following instructions for Israel: "When you cross the Jordan into the land of Canaan, [52] you must drive out all the inhabitants of the land. Destroy all their stone and metal idols and all their places of worship. [53] Occupy the land and settle in it, because I am giving it to you. [54] Divide the land among the various tribes and clans by drawing lots, giving a large piece of property to a large clan and a small one to a small clan. [55] But if you do not drive out the inhabitants of the land, those that are left will be as troublesome as splinters in your eyes and thorns in your sides, and they will fight against you. [56] If you do not drive them out, I will destroy you, as I planned to destroy them."

The Boundaries of the Land

34 The LORD gave Moses [2] the following instructions for the people of Israel: "When you enter Canaan, the land which I am giving you, the borders of your territory will be as follows. [3] The southern border will extend from the wilderness of Zin along the border of Edom. It will begin on the east at the southern end of the Dead Sea. [4] Then it will turn southward toward Akrabbim Pass and continue on through Zin as far south as Kadesh Barnea. Then it will turn northwest to Hazar Addar and on to Azmon, [5] where it will turn toward the valley at the border of Egypt and end at the Mediterranean.

[6] "The western border will be the Mediterranean Sea.

[7] "The northern border will follow a line from the Mediterranean to Mount Hor [8] and from there to Hamath Pass. It will continue to Zedad [9] and to Ziphron, and will end at Hazar Enan.

[10] "The eastern border will follow a line from Hazar Enan to Shepham. [11] It will then go south to Harbel, east of Ain,

and on to the hills on the eastern shore of Lake Galilee, [12] then south along the Jordan River to the Dead Sea.

"These will be the four borders of your land."

[13] So Moses said to the Israelites, "This is the land that you will receive by drawing lots, the land that the LORD has assigned to the nine and one-half tribes. [14] The tribes of Reuben and Gad and the eastern half of Manasseh have received their property, divided according to their families, [15] on the eastern side of the Jordan, opposite Jericho."

The Leaders Responsible for Dividing the Land

[16] The LORD said to Moses, [17] "Eleazar the priest and Joshua son of Nun will divide the land for the people. [18] Take also one leader from each tribe to help them divide it." [19-28] These are the men the LORD chose:

Tribe	Leader
Judah	Caleb son of Jephunneh
Simeon	Shelumiel son of Ammihud
Benjamin	Elidad son of Chislon
Dan	Bukki son of Jogli
Manasseh	Hanniel son of Ephod
Ephraim	Kemuel son of Shiphtan
Zebulun	Elizaphan son of Parnach
Issachar	Paltiel son of Azzan
Asher	Ahihud son of Shelomi
Naphtali	Pedahel son of Ammihud

[29] These are the men that the LORD assigned to divide the property for the people of Israel in the land of Canaan.

33.54 Nu 26.54-56   **34.13** Nu 26.52-56   **34.13-15** Js 14.1-5

The Cities Assigned to the Levites

35 In the plains of Moab across the Jordan from Jericho the LORD said to Moses, ² "Tell the Israelites that from the property they receive they must give the Levites some cities to live in and pasture land around the cities. ³ These cities will belong to the Levites, and they will live there. The pasture land will be for their cattle and all their other animals. ⁴ The pasture land is to extend outward from the city walls five hundred yards in each direction, ⁵ so that there is a square area measuring one thousand yards on each side, with the city in the middle. ⁶ You are to give the Levites six cities of refuge to which any of you can escape if you kill someone accidentally. In addition, give them forty-two other cities ⁷ with their pasture land, making a total of forty-eight. ⁸ The number of Levite cities in each tribe is to be determined according to the size of its territory."

The Cities of Refuge
(Deuteronomy 19.1-13; Joshua 20.1-9)

⁹ The LORD told Moses ¹⁰ to say to the people of Israel: "When you cross the Jordan River and enter the land of Canaan, ¹¹ you are to choose cities of refuge to which any of you can escape if you kill someone accidentally. ¹² There you will be safe from the dead person's relative who seeks revenge. No one accused of manslaughter is to be put to death without a public trial. ¹³ Choose six cities, ¹⁴ three east of the Jordan and three in the land of Canaan. ¹⁵ These will serve as cities of refuge for Israelites and for foreigners who are temporary or permanent residents. Anyone who kills someone accidentally can escape to one of them.

¹⁶⁻¹⁸ "If, however, any of you use a weapon of iron or stone or wood to kill someone, you are guilty of murder and are to be put to death. ¹⁹ The dead person's nearest relative has the responsibility for putting the murderer to death. When he finds you, he is to kill you.

²⁰ "If you hate someone and kill him by pushing him down or by throwing something at him ²¹ or by striking him with your fist, you are guilty of murder and are to be put to death. The dead person's nearest relative has the responsibility for putting the murderer to death. When he finds you, he is to kill you.

²² "But suppose you accidentally kill someone you do not hate, whether by pushing him down or by throwing something at him. ²³ Or suppose that, without looking, you throw a stone that kills someone whom you did not intend to hurt and who was not your enemy. ²⁴ In such cases the community shall judge in your favor and not in favor of the dead person's relative who is seeking revenge. ²⁵ You are guilty only of manslaughter, and the community is to rescue you from the dead person's relative, and they are to return you to the city of refuge to which you had escaped. You must live there until the death of the man who is then High Priest. ²⁶ If you leave the city of refuge to which you have escaped ²⁷ and if the dead person's relative finds you and kills you, this act of revenge is not murder. ²⁸ Any of you guilty of manslaughter must remain in the city of refuge until the death of the High Priest, but after that you may return home. ²⁹ These rules apply to you and your descendants wherever you may live.

³⁰ "Those accused of murder may be found guilty and put to death only on the evidence of two or more witnesses; the evidence of one witness is not sufficient to support an accusation of murder. ³¹ Murderers must be put to death. They cannot escape this penalty by the payment of money. ³² If they have fled to a city of refuge, do not allow them to make a payment in order to return

35.1-8 Js 21.1-42   **35.9-28** Dt 19.2-4; Js 20.1-9   **35.30** Dt 17.6; 19.15

home before the death of the High Priest. [33] If you did this, you would defile the land where you are living. Murder defiles the land, and except by the death of the murderer there is no way to perform the ritual of purification for the land where someone has been murdered. [34] Do not defile the land where you are living, because I am the LORD and I live among the people of Israel."

The Inheritance of Married Women

36 The heads of the families in the clan of Gilead, the son of Machir and grandson of Manasseh son of Joseph, went to Moses and the other leaders. [2] They said, "The LORD commanded you to distribute the land to the people of Israel by drawing lots. He also commanded you to give the property of our relative Zelophehad to his daughters. [3] But remember, if they marry men of another tribe, their property will then belong to that tribe, and the total allotted to us will be reduced. [4] In the Year of Restoration, when all property that has been sold is restored to its original owners, the property of Zelophehad's daughters will be permanently added to

36.2 Nu 27.7

the tribe into which they marry and will be lost to our tribe."

[5] So Moses gave the people of Israel the following command from the LORD. He said, "What the tribe of Manasseh says is right, [6] and so the LORD says that the daughters of Zelophehad are free to marry anyone they wish but only within their own tribe. [7] The property of every Israelite will remain attached to his tribe. [8] Every woman who inherits property in an Israelite tribe must marry a man belonging to that tribe. In this way all Israelites will inherit the property of their ancestors, [9] and the property will not pass from one tribe to another. Each tribe will continue to possess its own property."

[10-11] So Mahlah, Tirzah, Hoglah, Milcah, and Noah, the daughters of Zelophehad, did as the LORD had commanded Moses, and they married their cousins. [12] They married within the clans of the tribe of Manasseh son of Joseph, and their property remained in their father's tribe.

[13] These are the rules and regulations that the LORD gave the Israelites through Moses in the plains of Moab across the Jordan River from Jericho.

DEUTERONOMY

INTRODUCTION

The book of *Deuteronomy* is organized as a series of addresses given by Moses to the people of Israel in the land of Moab, where they had stopped at the end of the long wilderness journey and were about to enter and occupy Canaan.

Some of the most important matters recorded in the book are as follows: 1) Moses recalls the great events of the past forty years. He appeals to the people to remember how God has led them through the wilderness and to be obedient and loyal to God. 2) Moses reviews the Ten Commandments and emphasizes the meaning of the First Commandment, calling the people to devotion to the Lord alone. Then he reviews the various laws that are to govern Israel's life in the promised land. 3) Moses reminds the people of the meaning of God's covenant with them, and calls for them to renew their commitment to its obligations. 4) Joshua is commissioned as the next leader of God's people. After singing a song celebrating God's faithfulness, and pronouncing a blessing on the tribes of Israel, Moses dies in Moab, east of the Jordan River.

The great theme of the book is that God has saved and blessed his chosen people, whom he loves; so his people are to remember this, and love and obey him, so that they may have life and continued blessing.

The key verses of the book are 6.4-6, and contain the words that Jesus called the greatest of all commandments: "Love the LORD your God with all your heart, with all your soul, and with all your strength."

OUTLINE OF CONTENTS

Introduction

1 In this book are the words that Moses spoke to the people of Israel when they were in the wilderness east of the Jordan River. They were in the Jordan Valley near Suph, between the town of Paran on one side and the towns of Tophel, Laban, Hazeroth, and Dizahab on the other. (²It takes eleven days to travel from Mount Sinai to Kadesh Barnea by way of the hill country of Edom.) ³On the first day of the eleventh month of the fortieth year after they had left Egypt, Moses told the people everything the LORD had commanded him to tell them. ⁴This was after the Lord*ᵃ* had defeated King Sihon of the Amorites, who ruled in the town of Heshbon, and King Og of Bashan, who ruled in the towns of Ashtaroth and Edrei. ⁵It was while the people were east of the Jordan in the territory of Moab that Moses began to explain God's laws and teachings.

He said, ⁶"When we were at Mount Sinai, the Lord our God said to us, 'You have stayed long enough at this mountain. ⁷Break camp and move on. Go to the hill country of the Amorites and to all the surrounding regions — to the Jordan Valley, to the hill country and the lowlands, to the southern region, and to the Mediterranean coast. Go to the land of Canaan and on beyond the Lebanon Mountains as far as the great Euphrates River. ⁸All of this is the land which I, the Lord, promised to give to your ancestors, Abraham, Isaac, and Jacob, and to their descendants. Go and occupy it.' "

Moses Appoints Judges
(Exodus 18.13-27)

⁹Moses said to the people, "While we were still at Mount Sinai, I told you, 'The responsibility for leading you is too much for me. I can't do it alone. ¹⁰The Lord your God has made you as numerous as the stars in the sky. ¹¹May the Lord, the God of your ancestors, make you increase a thousand times more and make you prosperous, as he promised! ¹²But how can I alone bear the heavy responsibility for settling your disputes? ¹³Choose some wise, understanding, and experienced men from each tribe, and I will put them in charge of you.' ¹⁴And you agreed that this was a good thing to do. ¹⁵So I took the wise and experienced leaders you chose from your tribes, and I placed them in charge of you. Some were re-

sponsible for a thousand people, some for a hundred, some for fifty, and some for ten. I also appointed other officials throughout the tribes.

¹⁶"At that time I instructed them, 'Listen to the disputes that come up among your people. Judge every dispute fairly, whether it concerns only your own people or involves foreigners who live among you. ¹⁷Show no partiality in your decisions; judge everyone on the same basis, no matter who they are. Do not be afraid of anyone, for the decisions you make come from God. If any case is too difficult for you, bring it to me, and I will decide it.' ¹⁸At the same time I gave you instructions for everything else you were to do.

The Spies Are Sent Out from Kadesh Barnea
(Numbers 13.1-33)

¹⁹"We did what the Lord our God commanded us. We left Mount Sinai and went through that vast and fearful desert on the way to the hill country of the Amorites. When we reached Kadesh Barnea, ²⁰⁻²¹I told you, 'You have now come to the hill country of the Amorites, which the Lord our God, the God of our ancestors, is giving us. Look, there it is. Go and occupy it as he commanded. Do not hesitate or be afraid.'

²²"But you came to me and said, 'Let's send men ahead of us to spy out the land, so that they can tell us the best route to take and what kind of cities are there.'

²³"That seemed like a good thing to do, so I selected twelve men, one from each tribe. ²⁴They went into the hill country as far as Eshcol Valley and explored it. ²⁵They brought us back some fruit they found there, and reported that the land which the Lord our God was giving us was very fertile.

²⁶"But you rebelled against the com-

ᵃ the Lord; *or* Moses.
1.4 Nu 21.21-35 **1.26** Dt 9.23; He 3.16

mand of the LORD your God, and you would not enter the land. 27 You grumbled to one another: 'The LORD hates us. He brought us out of Egypt just to hand us over to these Amorites, so that they could kill us. 28 Why should we go there? We are afraid. The men we sent tell us that the people there are stronger and taller than we are, and that they live in cities with walls that reach the sky. They saw giants there!'

29 "But I told you, 'Don't be afraid of those people. 30 The LORD your God will lead you, and he will fight for you, just as you saw him do in Egypt 31 and in the desert. You saw how he brought you safely all the way to this place, just as a father would carry his son.' 32 But in spite of what I said, you still would not trust the LORD, 33 even though he always went ahead of you to find a place for you to camp. To show you the way, he went in front of you in a pillar of fire by night and in a pillar of cloud by day.

The LORD Punishes Israel
(Numbers 14.20-45)

34 "The LORD heard your complaints and became angry, and so he solemnly declared, 35 'Not one of you from this evil generation will enter the fertile land that I promised to give your ancestors. 36 Only Caleb son of Jephunneh will enter it. He has remained faithful to me, and I will give him and his descendants the land that he has explored.' 37 Because of you the LORD also became angry with me and said, 'Not even you, Moses, will enter the land. 38 But strengthen the determination of your helper, Joshua son of Nun. He will lead Israel to occupy the land.'

39 "Then the LORD said to all of us, 'Your children, who are still too young to know right from wrong, will enter the land — the children you said would be seized by your enemies. I will give the land to them, and they will occupy

it. 40 But as for you people, turn around and go back into the desert on the road to the Gulf of Aqaba.'

41 "You replied, 'Moses, we have sinned against the LORD. But now we will attack, just as the LORD our God commanded us.' Then each one of you got ready to fight, thinking it would be easy to invade the hill country.

42 "But the LORD said to me, 'Warn them not to attack, for I will not be with them, and their enemies will defeat them.' 43 I told you what the LORD had said, but you paid no attention. You rebelled against him, and in your pride you marched into the hill country. 44 Then the Amorites who lived in those hills came out against you like a swarm of bees. They chased you as far as Hormah and defeated you there in the hill country of Edom. 45 So you cried out to the LORD for help, but he would not listen to you or pay any attention to you.

The Years in the Desert

46 "So then, after we had stayed at Kadesh for a long time, 1 we finally turned and went into the desert, on the road to the Gulf of Aqaba, as the LORD had commanded, and we spent a long time wandering about in the hill country of Edom.

2 "Then the LORD told me 3 that we had spent enough time wandering about in those hills and that we should go north. 4 He told me to give you the following instructions: 'You are about to go through the hill country of Edom, the territory of your distant relatives, the descendants of Esau. They will be afraid of you, 5 but you must not start a war with them, because I am not going to give you so much as a square foot of their land. I have given Edom to Esau's descendants. 6 You may buy food and water from them.'

7 "Remember how the LORD your God has blessed you in everything that

---

1.31 Ac 13.18   **1.32** He 3.19   **1.34, 35** He 3.18   **2.1** Nu 21.4   **2.4** Gn 36.8

you have done. He has taken care of you as you wandered through this vast desert. He has been with you these forty years, and you have had everything you needed.

8"So we moved on and left the road that goes from the towns of Elath and Eziongeber to the Dead Sea, and we turned northeast toward Moab. 9The LORD said to me, 'Don't trouble the people of Moab, the descendants of Lot, or start a war against them. I have given them the city of Ar, and I am not going to give you any of their land.'"

(10A mighty race of giants called the Emim used to live in Ar. They were as tall as the Anakim, another race of giants. 11Like the Anakim they were also known as Rephaim; but the Moabites called them Emim. 12The Horites used to live in Edom, but the descendants of Esau chased them out, destroyed their nation, and settled there themselves, just as the Israelites later chased their enemies out of the land that the LORD gave them.)

13"Then we crossed the Zered River as the LORD told us to do. 14This was thirty-eight years after we had left Kadesh Barnea. All the fighting men of that generation had died, as the LORD had said they would. 15The LORD kept on opposing them until he had destroyed them all.

16"After they had all died, 17the LORD said to us, 18'Today you are to pass through the territory of Moab by way of Ar. 19You will then be near the land of the Ammonites, the descendants of Lot. Don't trouble them or start a war against them, because I am not going to give you any of the land that I have given them.'"

(20This territory is also known as the land of the Rephaim, the name of the people who used to live there; the Ammonites called them Zamzummim. 21They were as tall as the Anakim. There were many of them, and they were a mighty race. But the LORD destroyed them, so that the Ammonites took over their land and settled there. 22The LORD had done the same thing for the Edomites, the descendants of Esau, who live in the hill country of Edom. He destroyed the Horites, so that the Edomites took over their land and settled there, where they still live. 23The land along the Mediterranean coast had been settled by people from the island of Crete. They had destroyed the Avvim, the original inhabitants, and had taken over all their land as far south as the city of Gaza.)

24"After we had passed through Moab, the LORD told us, 'Now, start out and cross the Arnon River. I am placing in your power Sihon, the Amorite king of Heshbon, along with his land. Attack him, and begin occupying his land. 25From today on I will make people everywhere afraid of you. Everyone will tremble with fear at the mention of your name.'

Israel Defeats King Sihon
(Numbers 21.21-30)

26"Then I sent messengers from the desert of Kedemoth to King Sihon of Heshbon with the following offer of peace: 27'Let us pass through your country. We will go straight through and not leave the road. 28We will pay for the food we eat and the water we drink. All we want to do is to pass through your country, 29until we cross the Jordan River into the land that the LORD our God is giving us. The descendants of Esau, who live in Edom, and the Moabites, who live in Ar, allowed us to pass through their territory.'

30"But King Sihon would not let us pass through his country. The LORD your God had made him stubborn and rebellious, so that we could defeat him and take his territory, which we still occupy.

2.9 Gn 19.37   2.14 Nu 14.28-35   2.19 Gn 19.38

[31]"Then the LORD said to me, 'Look, I have made King Sihon and his land helpless before you; take his land and occupy it.' [32]Sihon came out with all his men to fight us near the town of Jahaz, [33]but the LORD our God put him in our power, and we killed him, his sons, and all his men. [34]At the same time we captured and destroyed every town, and put everyone to death, men, women, and children. We left no survivors. [35]We took the livestock and plundered the towns. [36]The LORD our God let us capture all the towns from Aroer, on the edge of the Arnon Valley, and the city in the middle of that valley, all the way to Gilead. No town had walls too strong for us. [37]But we did not go near the territory of the Ammonites or to the banks of the Jabbok River or to the towns of the hill country or to any other place where the LORD our God had commanded us not to go.

Israel Conquers King Og
(Numbers 21.31-35)

3 "Next, we moved north toward the region of Bashan, and King Og came out with all his men to fight us near the town of Edrei. [2]But the LORD said to me, 'Don't be afraid of him. I am going to give him, his men, and all his territory to you. Do the same thing to him that you did to Sihon the Amorite king who ruled in Heshbon.'

[3]"So the LORD also placed King Og and his people in our power, and we slaughtered them all. [4]At the same time we captured all his towns — there was not one that we did not take. In all we captured sixty towns — the whole region of Argob, where King Og of Bashan ruled. [5]All these towns were fortified with high walls, gates, and bars to lock the gates, and there were also many villages without walls. [6]We destroyed all the towns and put to death all the men, women, and children, just

as we did in the towns that belonged to King Sihon of Heshbon. [7]We took the livestock and plundered the towns.

[8]"At that time we took from those two Amorite kings the land east of the Jordan River, from the Arnon River to Mount Hermon. ([9]Mount Hermon is called Sirion by the Sidonians, and Senir by the Amorites.) [10]We took all the territory of King Og of Bashan: the cities on the plateau, the regions of Gilead and of Bashan, as far east as the towns of Salecah and Edrei."

([11]King Og was the last of the Rephaim. His coffin,[b] made of stone,[c] was six feet wide and almost fourteen feet long, according to standard measurements. It can still be seen in the Ammonite city of Rabbah.)

The Tribes That Settled East of the Jordan
(Numbers 32.1-42)

[12]"When we took possession of the land, I assigned to the tribes of Reuben and Gad the territory north of the town of Aroer near the Arnon River and part of the hill country of Gilead, along with its towns. [13]To half the tribe of Manasseh I assigned the rest of Gilead and also all of Bashan, where Og had ruled, that is, the entire Argob region."

(Bashan was known as the land of the Rephaim. [14]Jair, from the tribe of Manasseh, took the entire region of Argob, that is, Bashan, as far as the border of Geshur and Maacah. He named the villages after himself, and they are still known as the villages of Jair.)

[15]"I assigned Gilead to the clan of Machir of the tribe of Manasseh. [16]And to the tribes of Reuben and Gad I assigned the territory from Gilead to the Arnon River. The middle of the river was their southern boundary, and their northern boundary was the Jabbok River, part of which formed the Ammonite border. [17]On the west their

---

[b] coffin; *or* bed.   [c] stone; *or* iron.

territory extended to the Jordan River, from Lake Galilee in the north down to the Dead Sea in the south and to the foot of Mount Pisgah on the east.

18 "At the same time, I gave them the following instructions: 'The LORD our God has given you this land east of the Jordan to occupy. Now arm your fighting men and send them across the Jordan ahead of the other tribes of Israel, to help them occupy their land. 19 Only your wives, children, and livestock — I know you have a lot of livestock — will remain behind in the towns that I have assigned to you. 20 Help the other Israelites until they occupy the land that the LORD is giving them west of the Jordan and until the LORD lets them live there in peace, as he has already done here for you. After that, you may return to this land that I have assigned to you.'

21 "Then I instructed Joshua: 'You have seen all that the LORD your God did to those two kings, Sihon and Og; and he will do the same thing to everyone else whose land you invade. 22 Don't be afraid of them, for the LORD your God will fight for you.'

Moses Is Not Permitted to Enter Canaan

23 "At that time I earnestly prayed, 24 'Sovereign LORD, I know that you have shown me only the beginning of the great and wonderful things you are going to do. There is no god in heaven or on earth who can do the mighty things that you have done! 25 Let me cross the Jordan River, LORD, and see the fertile land on the other side, the beautiful hill country and the Lebanon Mountains.'

26 "But because of you people the LORD was angry with me and would not listen. Instead, he said, 'That's enough! Don't mention this again! 27 Go to the peak of Mount Pisgah and look to the north and to the south, to the east and to the west. Look carefully at what you see, because you will never go across the Jordan. 28 Give Joshua his instructions. Strengthen his determination, because he will lead the people across to occupy the land that you see.'

29 "So we remained in the valley opposite the town of Bethpeor."

Moses Urges Israel to Be Obedient

4 Then Moses said to the people, "Obey all the laws that I am teaching you, and you will live and occupy the land which the LORD, the God of your ancestors, is giving you. 2 Do not add anything to what I command you, and do not take anything away. Obey the commands of the LORD your God that I have given you. 3 You yourselves saw what the LORD did at Mount Peor. He destroyed everyone who worshiped Baal there, 4 but those of you who were faithful to the LORD your God are still alive today.

5 "I have taught you all the laws, as the LORD my God told me to do. Obey them in the land that you are about to invade and occupy. 6 Obey them faithfully, and this will show the people of other nations how wise you are. When they hear of all these laws, they will say, 'What wisdom and understanding this great nation has!'

7 "No other nation, no matter how great, has a god who is so near when they need him as the LORD our God is to us. He answers us whenever we call for help. 8 No other nation, no matter how great, has laws so just as those that I have taught you today. 9 Be on your guard! Make certain that you do not forget, as long as you live, what you have seen with your own eyes. Tell your children and your grandchildren 10 about the day you stood in the presence of the LORD your God at Mount Sinai, *d* when

---

d Sinai; *or* Horeb.

3.18-20 Js 1.12-15   **3.23-27** Nu 27.12-14; Dt 32.48-52   **4.2** Rev 22.18, 19   **4.3** Nu 25.1-9 he said to me, 'Assemble the people. I want them to hear what I have to say, so that they will learn to obey me as long as they live and so that they will teach their children to do the same.'

¹¹"Tell your children how you went and stood at the foot of the mountain which was covered with thick clouds of dark smoke and fire blazing up to the sky. ¹²Tell them how the LORD spoke to you from the fire, how you heard him speaking but did not see him in any form at all. ¹³He told you what you must do to keep the covenant he made with you—you must obey the Ten Commandments, which he wrote on two stone tablets. ¹⁴The LORD told me to teach you all the laws that you are to obey in the land that you are about to invade and occupy.

Warning against Idolatry

¹⁵"When the LORD spoke to you from the fire on Mount Sinai, you did not see any form. For your own good, then, make certain ¹⁶that you do not sin by making for yourselves an idol in any form at all—whether man or woman, ¹⁷animal or bird, ¹⁸reptile or fish. ¹⁹Do not be tempted to worship and serve what you see in the sky—the sun, the moon, and the stars. The LORD your God has given these to all other peoples for them to worship. ²⁰But you are the people he rescued from Egypt, that blazing furnace. He brought you out to make you his own people, as you are today. ²¹Because of you the LORD your God was angry with me and solemnly declared that I would not cross the Jordan River to enter the fertile land which he is giving you. ²²I will die in this land and never cross the river, but you are about to go across and occupy that fertile land. ²³Be certain that you do not

forget the covenant that the LORD your God made with you. Obey his command not to make yourselves any kind of idol, ²⁴because the LORD your God is like a flaming fire; he tolerates no rivals.

²⁵"Even when you have been in the land a long time and have children and grandchildren, do not sin by making for yourselves an idol in any form at all. This is evil in the LORD's sight, and it will make him angry. ²⁶I call heaven and earth as witnesses against you today that, if you disobey me, you will soon disappear from the land. You will not live very long in the land across the Jordan that you are about to occupy. You will be completely destroyed. ²⁷The LORD will scatter you among other nations, where only a few of you will survive. ²⁸There you will serve gods made by human hands, gods of wood and stone, gods that cannot see or hear, eat or smell. ²⁹There you will look for the LORD your God, and if you search for him with all your heart, you will find him. ³⁰When you are in trouble and all those things happen to you, then you will finally turn to the LORD and obey him. ³¹He is a merciful God. He will not abandon you or destroy you, and he will not forget the covenant that he himself made with your ancestors.

³²"Search the past, the time before you were born, all the way back to the time when God created human beings on the earth. Search the entire earth. Has anything as great as this ever happened before? Has anyone ever heard of anything like this? ³³Have any people ever lived after hearing a god speak to them from a fire, as you have? ³⁴Has any god ever dared to go and take a people from another nation and make them his own, as the LORD your God did for you in Egypt? Before your very eyes he used his great power and strength; he

4.11, 12 Ex 19.16-18; He 12.18, 19   **4.13** Ex 31.18; 34.28; Dt 9.10   **4.14** Ex 21.1
4.16 Ex 20.4; Lv 26.1; Dt 5.8; 27.15   **4.17, 18a** Ro 1.23   **4.20** Ex 19.5; Dt 7.6; 14.2;
26.18; Titus 2.14; 1 P 2.9   **4.21** Nu 20.12   **4.24** He 12.29   **4.27, 28** Dt 28.36
4.29 Jr 29.13

brought plagues and war, worked miracles and wonders, and caused terrifying things to happen. 35 The LORD has shown you this, to prove to you that he alone is God and that there is no other. 36 He let you hear his voice from heaven so that he could instruct you; and here on earth he let you see his holy fire, and he spoke to you from it. 37 Because he loved your ancestors, he chose you, and by his great power he himself brought you out of Egypt. 38 As you advanced, he drove out nations greater and more powerful than you, so that he might bring you in and give you their land, the land which still belongs to you. 39 So remember today and never forget: the LORD is God in heaven and on earth. There is no other god. 40 Obey all his laws that I have given you today, and all will go well with you and your descendants. You will continue to live in the land that the LORD your God is giving you to be yours forever."

The Cities of Refuge East of the Jordan

41 Then Moses set aside three cities east of the Jordan River 42 to which a man could escape and be safe if he had accidentally killed someone who had not been his enemy. He could escape to one of these cities and not be put to death. 43 For the tribe of Reuben there was the city of Bezer, on the desert plateau; for the tribe of Gad there was Ramoth, in the territory of Gilead; and for the tribe of Manasseh there was Golan, in the territory of Bashan.

Introduction to the Giving of God's Law

44 Moses gave God's laws and teachings to the people of Israel. 45-46 It was after they had come out of Egypt and were in the valley east of the Jordan River, opposite the town of Bethpeor, that he gave them these laws. This was in the territory that had belonged to King Sihon of the Amorites, who had ruled in the town of Heshbon. Moses and the people of Israel defeated him when they came out of Egypt. 47 They occupied his land and the land of King Og of Bashan, the other Amorite king who lived east of the Jordan. 48 This land extended from the town of Aroer, on the edge of the Arnon River, all the way north to Mount Sirion,e that is, Mount Hermon. 49 It also included all the region east of the Jordan River as far south as the Dead Sea and east to the foot of Mount Pisgah.

The Ten Commandments
(Exodus 20.1-17)

5 Moses called together all the people of Israel and said to them, "People of Israel, listen to all the laws that I am giving you today. Learn them and be sure that you obey them. 2 At Mount Sinai the LORD our God made a covenant, 3 not only with our fathers, but with all of us who are living today. 4 There on the mountain the LORD spoke to you face-to-face from the fire. 5 I stood between you and the LORD at that time to tell you what he said, because you were afraid of the fire and would not go up the mountain.

"The LORD said, 6 'I am the LORD your God, who rescued you from Egypt, where you were slaves.

7 " 'Worship no god but me.

8 " 'Do not make for yourselves images of anything in heaven or on earth or in the water under the earth. 9 Do not bow down to any idol or worship it, for I am the LORD your God and I tolerate no rivals. I bring punishment on those who hate me and on their descendants down to the third and fourth genera-

---

e *One ancient translation* Sirion; *Hebrew* Sion.
4.35 Mk 12.32   **4.41-43** Js 20.8, 9   **5.8, 9** Lv 26.1; Dt 4.15-18; 27.15   **5.9, 10** Ex 34.6, 7; Nu 14.18; Dt 7.9, 10

The LORD our God made a covenant. (5.2)

tion. [10] But I show my love to thousands of generations[f] of those who love me and obey my laws.

[11]" 'Do not use my name for evil purposes, for I, the LORD your God, will punish anyone who misuses my name.

[12]" 'Observe the Sabbath and keep it holy, as I, the LORD your God, have commanded you. [13] You have six days in which to do your work, [14] but the seventh day is a day of rest dedicated to me. On that day no one is to work — neither you, your children, your slaves, your animals, nor the foreigners who live in your country. Your slaves must rest just as you do. [15] Remember that you were slaves in Egypt, and that I, the LORD your God, rescued you by my great power and strength. That is why I command you to observe the Sabbath.

[16]" 'Respect your father and your mother, as I, the LORD your God, command you, so that all may go well with

you and so that you may live a long time in the land that I am giving you.

[17]" 'Do not commit murder.

[18]" 'Do not commit adultery.

[19]" 'Do not steal.

[20]" 'Do not accuse anyone falsely.

[21]" 'Do not desire another man's wife; do not desire his house, his land, his slaves, his cattle, his donkeys, or anything else that he owns.'

[22]"These are the commandments the LORD gave to all of you when you were gathered at the mountain. When he spoke with a mighty voice from the fire and from the thick clouds, he gave these commandments and no others. Then he wrote them on two stone tablets and gave them to me.

The People's Fear
(Exodus 20.18-21)

[23]"When the whole mountain was on fire and you heard the voice from the darkness, your leaders and the chiefs of your tribes came to me [24] and said, 'The LORD our God showed us his greatness and his glory when we heard him speak from the fire! Today we have seen that it is possible for people to continue to live, even though God has spoken to them. [25] But why should we risk death again? That terrible fire will destroy us. We are sure to die if we hear the LORD our God speak again. [26] Has any human being ever lived after hearing the living God speak from a fire? [27] Go back, Moses, and listen to everything that the LORD our God says. Then return and tell us what he said to you. We will listen and obey.'

[28]"When the LORD heard this, he

---

[f] thousands of generations; *or* thousands.
5.11 Lv 19.12　**5.12** Ex 16.23-30; 31.12-14　**5.13, 14** Ex 23.12; 31.15; 34.21; 35.2;
Lv 23.3　**5.16 a** Dt 27.16; Si 3.1-16; Mt 15.4; 19.19; Mk 7.10; 10.19;
Lk 18.20; Eph 6.2; **b** Eph 6.3　**5.17** Gn 9.6; Lv 24.17; Mt 5.21; 19.18; Mk 10.19;
Lk 18.20; Ro 13.9; Jas 2.11　**5.18** Lv 20.10; Mt 5.27; 19.18; Mk 10.19; Lk 18.20;
Ro 13.9; Jas 2.11　**5.19** Lv 19.11; Mt 19.18; Mk 10.19; Lk 18.20; Ro 13.9
5.20 Ex 23.1; Mt 19.18; Mk 10.19; Lk 18.20　**5.21** Ro 7.7; 13.9　**5.22-27** He 12.18, 19

said to me, 'I have heard what these people said, and they are right. ²⁹If only they would always feel this way! If only they would always honor me and obey all my commands, so that everything would go well with them and their descendants forever. ³⁰Go and tell them to return to their tents. ³¹But you, Moses, stay here with me, and I will give you all my laws and commands. Teach them to the people, so that they will obey them in the land that I am giving them.'

³²"People of Israel, be sure that you do everything that the LORD your God has commanded you. Do not disobey any of his laws. ³³Obey them all, so that everything will go well with you and so that you will continue to live in the land that you are going to occupy.

The Great Commandment

6 "These are all the laws that the LORD your God commanded me to teach you. Obey them in the land that you are about to enter and occupy. ²As long as you live, you and your descendants are to honor the LORD your God and obey all his laws that I am giving you, so that you may live in that land a long time. ³Listen to them, people of Israel, and obey them! Then all will go well with you, and you will become a mighty nation and live in that rich and fertile land, just as the LORD, the God of our ancestors, has promised.

⁴"Israel, remember this! The LORD — and the LORD alone — is our God.ᵍ ⁵Love the LORD your God with all your heart, with all your soul, and with all your strength. ⁶Never forget these commands that I am giving you today. ⁷Teach them to your children. Repeat them when you are at home and when you are away, when you are rest-

ing and when you are working. ⁸Tie them on your arms and wear them on your foreheads as a reminder. ⁹Write them on the doorposts of your houses and on your gates.

Write them on the doorposts. (6.9)

Warning against Disobedience

¹⁰"Just as the LORD your God promised your ancestors, Abraham, Isaac, and Jacob, he will give you a land with large and prosperous cities which you did not build. ¹¹The houses will be full of good things which you did not put in them, and there will be wells that you did not dig, and vineyards and olive orchards that you did not plant. When the LORD brings you into this land and you have all you want to eat, ¹²make certain that you do not forget the LORD who rescued you from Egypt, where you were slaves. ¹³Honor the LORD your God, worship only him, and make your promises in his name alone. ¹⁴Do not worship other gods, any of the gods of the peoples around you. ¹⁵If you do worship other gods, the LORD's anger will come against you like fire and will destroy you completely, because the LORD your God, who is present with you, tolerates no rivals.

¹⁶"Do not put the LORD your God to the test, as you did at Massah. ¹⁷Be sure that you obey all the laws that he has given you. ¹⁸Do what the LORD says is

ᵍ The LORD . . . is our God; *or* The LORD, our God, is the only God; *or* The LORD our God is one.

6.4 Mk 12.29   **6.5** Mt 22.37; Mk 12.30; Lk 10.27   **6.6-9** Dt 11.18-20   **6.10 a** Gn 12.7; **b** Gn 26.3; **c** Gn 28.13   **6.13** Mt 4.10; Lk 4.8   **6.16 a** Mt 4.7; Lk 4.12; **b** Ex 17.1-7 right and good, and all will go well with you. You will be able to take possession of the fertile land that the LORD promised your ancestors, [19] and you will drive out your enemies, as he promised.

[20]"In times to come your children will ask you, 'Why did the LORD our God command us to obey all these laws?' [21] Then tell them, 'We were slaves of the king of Egypt, and the LORD rescued us by his great power. [22] With our own eyes we saw him work miracles and do terrifying things to the Egyptians and to their king and to all his officials. [23] He freed us from Egypt to bring us here and give us this land, as he had promised our ancestors he would. [24] Then the LORD our God commanded us to obey all these laws and to honor him. If we do, he will always watch over our nation and keep it prosperous. [25] If we faithfully obey everything that God has commanded us, he will be pleased with us.'[h]

The LORD's Own People
(Exodus 34.11-16)

7 "The LORD your God will bring you into the land that you are going to occupy, and he will drive many nations out of it. As you advance, he will drive out seven nations larger and more powerful than you: the Hittites, the Girgashites, the Amorites, the Canaanites, the Perizzites, the Hivites, and the Jebusites. [2] When the LORD your God places these people in your power and you defeat them, you must put them all to death. Do not make an alliance with them or show them any mercy. [3] Do not marry any of them, and do not let your children marry any of them, [4] because then they would lead your children away from the LORD to worship other gods. If that happens, the LORD will be

angry with you and destroy you at once. [5] So then, tear down their altars, break their sacred stone pillars in pieces, cut down their symbols of the goddess Asherah, and burn their idols. [6] Do this because you belong to the LORD your God. From all the peoples on earth he chose you to be his own special people.

[7]"The LORD did not love you and choose you because you outnumbered other peoples; you were the smallest nation on earth. [8] But the LORD loved you and wanted to keep the promise that he made to your ancestors. That is why he saved you by his great might and set you free from slavery to the king of Egypt. [9] Remember that the LORD your God is the only God and that he is faithful. He will keep his covenant and show his constant love to a thousand generations of those who love him and obey his commands, [10] but he will not hesitate to punish those who hate him. [11] Now then, obey what you have been taught; obey all the laws that I have given you today.

The Blessings of Obedience
(Deuteronomy 28.1-14)

[12]"If you listen to these commands and obey them faithfully, then the LORD your God will continue to keep his covenant with you and will show you his constant love, as he promised your ancestors. [13] He will love you and bless you, so that you will increase in number and have many children; he will bless your fields, so that you will have grain, wine, and olive oil; and he will bless you by giving you many cattle and sheep. He will give you all these blessings in the land that he promised your ancestors he would give to you. [14] No people in the world will be as richly blessed as you. None of you nor any of your live-

---

[h] If we faithfully ... with us; *or* The right thing for us to do is to obey faithfully everything that God has commanded us.

7.1 Ac 13.19   **7.5** Dt 12.3   **7.6** Ex 19.5; Dt 4.20; 14.2; 26.18; Titus 2.14; 1 P 2.9
7.9, 10 Ex 20.5, 6; 34.6, 7; Nu 14.18; Dt 5.9, 10   **7.12-16** Dt 11.13-17

stock will be sterile. ¹⁵The LORD will protect you from all sickness, and he will not bring on you any of the dreadful diseases that you experienced in Egypt, but he will bring them on all your enemies. ¹⁶Destroy every nation that the LORD your God places in your power, and do not show them any mercy. Do not worship their gods, for that would be fatal.

¹⁷"Do not tell yourselves that these peoples outnumber you and that you cannot drive them out. ¹⁸Do not be afraid of them; remember what the LORD your God did to the king of Egypt and to all his people. ¹⁹Remember the terrible plagues that you saw with your own eyes, the miracles and wonders, and the great power and strength by which the LORD your God set you free. In the same way that he destroyed the Egyptians, he will destroy all these people that you now fear. ²⁰He will even cause panic*ⁱ* among them and will destroy those who escape and go into hiding. ²¹So do not be afraid of these people. The LORD your God is with you; he is a great God and one to be feared. ²²Little by little he will drive out these nations as you advance. You will not be able to destroy them all at once, for, if you did, the number of wild animals would increase and be a threat to you. ²³The LORD will put your enemies in your power and make them panic until they are destroyed. ²⁴He will put their kings in your power. You will kill them, and they will be forgotten. No one will be able to stop you; you will destroy everyone. ²⁵Burn their idols. Do not desire the silver or gold that is on them, and do not take it for yourselves. If you do, that will be fatal, because the LORD hates idolatry. ²⁶Do not bring any of these idols into your homes, or the same curse will be on you that is on them. You must hate and despise these

idols, because they are under the LORD's curse.

A Good Land to Be Possessed

8 "Obey faithfully all the laws that I have given you today, so that you may live, increase in number, and occupy the land that the LORD promised to your ancestors. ²Remember how the LORD your God led you on this long journey through the desert these past forty years, sending hardships to test you, so that he might know what you intended to do and whether you would obey his commands. ³He made you go hungry, and then he gave you manna to eat, food that you and your ancestors had never eaten before. He did this to teach you that you must not depend on bread alone to sustain you, but on everything that the LORD says. ⁴During these forty years your clothes have not worn out, nor have your feet swollen up. ⁵Remember that the LORD your God corrects and punishes you just as parents discipline their children. ⁶So then, do as the LORD has commanded you: live according to his laws and obey him. ⁷The LORD your God is bringing you into a fertile land — a land that has rivers and springs, and underground streams gushing out into the valleys and hills; ⁸a land that produces wheat and barley, grapes, figs, pomegranates, olives, and honey. ⁹There you will never go hungry or ever be in need. Its rocks have iron in them, and from its hills you can mine copper. ¹⁰You will have all you want to eat, and you will give thanks to the LORD your God for the fertile land that he has given you.

Warnings against Forgetting the LORD

¹¹"Make certain that you do not forget the LORD your God; do not fail to obey any of his laws that I am giving you today. ¹²When you have all you

---

ⁱ cause panic; *or* send hornets, *or* send plagues.
8.3 Mt 4.4; Lk 4.4   **8.5** Ws 11.9, 10   **8.11-16** Ho 13.5, 6

want to eat and have built good houses to live in ¹³and when your cattle and sheep, your silver and gold, and all your other possessions have increased, ¹⁴be sure that you do not become proud and forget the Lord your God who rescued you from Egypt, where you were slaves. ¹⁵He led you through that vast and terrifying desert where there were poisonous snakes and scorpions. In that dry and waterless land he made water flow out of solid rock for you. ¹⁶In the desert he gave you manna to eat, food that your ancestors had never eaten. He sent hardships on you to test you, so that in the end he could bless you with good things. ¹⁷So then, you must never think that you have made yourselves wealthy by your own power and strength. ¹⁸Remember that it is the Lord your God who gives you the power to become rich. He does this because he is still faithful today to the covenant that he made with your ancestors. ¹⁹Never forget the Lord your God or turn to other gods to worship and serve them. If you do, then I warn you today that you will certainly be destroyed. ²⁰If you do not obey the Lord, then you will be destroyed just like those nations that he is going to destroy as you advance.

The People's Disobedience

9 "Listen, people of Israel! Today you are about to cross the Jordan River and occupy the land belonging to nations greater and more powerful than you. Their cities are large, with walls that reach the sky. ²The people themselves are tall and strong; they are giants, and you have heard it said that no one can stand against them. ³But now you will see for yourselves that the Lord your God will go ahead of you like a raging fire. He will defeat them as you advance, so that you will drive them out

and destroy them quickly, as he promised.

⁴"After the Lord your God has driven them out for you, do not say to yourselves that he brought you in to possess this land because you deserved it. No, the Lord is going to drive these people out for you because they are wicked. ⁵It is not because you are good and do what is right that the Lord is letting you take their land. He will drive them out because they are wicked and because he intends to keep the promise that he made to your ancestors, Abraham, Isaac, and Jacob. ⁶You can be sure that the Lord is not giving you this fertile land because you deserve it. No, you are a stubborn people.

⁷"Never forget how you made the Lord your God angry in the desert. From the day that you left Egypt until the day you arrived here, you have rebelled against him. ⁸Even at Mount Sinai you made the Lord angry — angry enough to destroy you. ⁹I went up the mountain to receive the stone tablets on which was written the covenant that the Lord had made with you. I stayed there forty days and nights and did not eat or drink anything. ¹⁰Then the Lord gave me the two stone tablets on which he had written with his own hand what he had said to you from the fire on the day that you were gathered there at the mountain. ¹¹Yes, after those forty days and nights the Lord gave me the two stone tablets on which he had written the covenant.

¹²"Then the Lord said to me, 'Go down the mountain at once, because your people, whom you led out of Egypt, have become corrupt and have done evil. They have already turned away from what I commanded them to do, and they have made an idol for themselves.'

¹³"The Lord also said to me, 'I know how stubborn these people are. ¹⁴Don't try to stop me. I intend to destroy them

I threw the stone tablets down and broke them to pieces. (9.17)

so that no one will remember them any longer. Then I will make you the father of a nation larger and more powerful than they are.'

15 "So I turned and went down the mountain, carrying the two stone tablets on which the covenant was written. Flames of fire were coming from the mountain. 16 I saw that you had already disobeyed the command that the LORD your God had given you, and that you had sinned against him by making yourselves a metal idol in the form of a bull-calf. 17 So there in front of you I threw the stone tablets down and broke them to pieces. 18 Then once again I lay face downward in the LORD's presence for forty days and nights and did not eat or drink anything. I did this because you had sinned against the LORD and had made him angry. 19 I was afraid of the LORD's fierce anger, because he was furious enough to destroy you; but once again the LORD listened to me. 20 The LORD was also angry enough with Aaron to kill him, so I prayed for Aaron at the same time. 21 I took that sinful thing that you had made — that metal bull-calf — and threw it into the

fire. Then I broke it in pieces, ground it to dust, and threw the dust into the stream that flowed down the mountain.

22 "You also made the LORD your God angry when you were at Taberah, Massah, and Kibroth Hattaavah. 23 And when he sent you from Kadesh Barnea with orders to go and take possession of the land that he was giving you, you rebelled against him; you did not trust him or obey him. 24 Ever since I have known you, you have rebelled against the LORD.

25 "So I lay face downward in the LORD's presence those forty days and nights, because I knew that he was determined to destroy you. 26 And I prayed, 'Sovereign LORD, don't destroy your own people, the people you rescued and brought out of Egypt by your great strength and power. 27 Remember your servants, Abraham, Isaac, and Jacob, and do not pay any attention to the stubbornness, wickedness, and sin of this people. 28 Otherwise, the Egyptians will say that you were unable to take your people into the land that you had promised them. They will say that you took your people out into the desert to

9.19 He 12.21   **9.22 a** Nu 11.3; **b** Ex 17.7; **c** Nu 11.34   **9.23 a** Nu 13.17; **b** Dt 1.21; **c** Nu 13.31; Dt 1.26; He 3.16

kill them, because you hated them. [29] After all, these are the people whom you chose to be your own and whom you brought out of Egypt by your great power and might.'

Moses Receives the Commandments Again
(Exodus 34.1-10)

10 "Then the LORD said to me, 'Cut two stone tablets like the first ones and make a wooden Box to put them in. Come up to me on the mountain, [2] and I will write on those tablets what I wrote on the tablets that you broke, and then you are to put them in the Box.'

[3] "So I made a Box of acacia wood and cut two stone tablets like the first ones and took them up the mountain. [4] Then the LORD wrote on those tablets the same words that he had written the first time, the Ten Commandments that he gave you when he spoke from the fire on the day you were gathered at the mountain. The LORD gave me the tablets, [5] and I turned and went down the mountain. Then, just as the LORD had commanded, I put them in the Box that I had made — and they have been there ever since."

([6] The Israelites set out from the wells that belonged to the people of Jaakan, and went to Moserah. There Aaron died and was buried, and his son Eleazar succeeded him as priest. [7] From there they went to Gudgodah and then on to Jotbathah, a well-watered place. [8] At the mountain[j] the LORD appointed the men of the tribe of Levi to be in charge of the Covenant Box, to serve him as priests, and to pronounce blessings in his name. And these are still their duties. [9] That is why the tribe of Levi received no land as the other tribes

did; what they received was the privilege of being the LORD's priests, as the LORD your God promised.)

[10] "I stayed on the mountain forty days and nights, as I did the first time. The LORD listened to me once more and agreed not to destroy you. [11] Then he told me to go and lead you, so that you could take possession of the land that he had promised to give to your ancestors.

What God Demands

[12] "Now, people of Israel, listen to what the LORD your God demands of you: Worship the LORD and do all that he commands. Love him, serve him with all your heart, [13] and obey all his laws. I am giving them to you today for your benefit. [14] To the LORD belong even the highest heavens; the earth is his also, and everything on it. [15] But the LORD's love for your ancestors was so strong that he chose you instead of any other people, and you are still his chosen people. [16] So then, from now on be obedient to the LORD and stop being stubborn. [17] The LORD your God is supreme over all gods and over all powers. He is great and mighty, and he is to be obeyed. He does not show partiality, and he does not accept bribes. [18] He makes sure that orphans and widows are treated fairly; he loves the foreigners who live with our people, and gives them food and clothes. [19] So then, show love for those foreigners, because you were once foreigners in Egypt. [20] Have reverence for the LORD your God and worship only him. Be faithful to him and make your promises in his name alone. [21] Praise him — he is your God, and you have seen with your own eyes the great and astounding things that he has done for you. [22] When your

---

[j] the mountain; *or* that time.

10.6 Nu 20.28; 33.38   **10.8** Nu 3.5-8   **10.10** Ex 34.28   **10.17** 1 Ti 6.15; Rev 17.14; 19.16; Ac 10.34; Ro 2.11; Ga 2.6; Eph 6.9   **10.18** Si 35.12-15   **10.22 a** Gn 46.27; **b** Gn 15.5; 22.17

ancestors went to Egypt, there were only seventy of them. But now the LORD your God has made you as numerous as the stars in the sky.

The LORD's Greatness

11 "Love the LORD your God and always obey all his laws. ²Remember today what you have learned about the LORD through your experiences with him. It was you, not your children, who had these experiences. You saw the LORD's greatness, his power, his might, ³and his miracles. You saw what he did to the king of Egypt and to his entire country. ⁴You saw how the LORD completely wiped out the Egyptian army, along with their horses and chariots, by drowning them in the Red Sea*k* when they were pursuing you. ⁵You know what the LORD did for you in the desert before you arrived here. ⁶You recall what he did to Dathan and Abiram, the sons of Eliab of the tribe of Reuben. In the sight of everyone the earth opened up and swallowed them, along with their families, their tents, and all their servants and animals. ⁷Yes, you are the ones who have seen all these great things that the LORD has done.

The Blessings of the Promised Land

⁸"Obey everything that I have commanded you today. Then you will be able to cross the river and occupy the land that you are about to enter. ⁹And you will live a long time in the rich and fertile land that the LORD promised to give your ancestors and their descendants. ¹⁰The land that you are about to occupy is not like the land of Egypt, where you lived before. There, when you planted grain, you had to work hard to irrigate the fields; ¹¹but the land that you are about to enter is a land of mountains and valleys, a land watered by rain. ¹²The LORD your God takes care of this land and watches over it throughout the year.

¹³"So then, obey the commands that I have given you today; love the LORD your God and serve him with all your heart. ¹⁴If you do, he will send rain on your land when it is needed, in the autumn and in the spring, so that there will be grain, wine, and olive oil for you, ¹⁵and grass for your livestock. You will have all the food you want. ¹⁶Do not let yourselves be led away from the LORD to worship and serve other gods. ¹⁷If you do, the LORD will become angry with you. He will hold back the rain, and your ground will become too dry for crops to grow. Then you will soon die there, even though it is a good land that he is giving you.

¹⁸"Remember these commands and cherish them. Tie them on your arms and wear them on your foreheads as a reminder. ¹⁹Teach them to your children. Talk about them when you are at home and when you are away, when you are resting and when you are working. ²⁰Write them on the doorposts of your houses and on your gates. ²¹Then you and your children will live a long time in the land that the LORD your God promised to give to your ancestors. You will live there as long as there is a sky above the earth.

²²"Obey faithfully everything that I have commanded you: Love the LORD your God, do everything he commands, and be faithful to him. ²³Then he will drive out all those nations as you advance, and you will occupy the land belonging to nations greater and more powerful than you. ²⁴All the ground that you march over will be yours. Your territory will extend from the desert in the south to the Lebanon Mountains in the north, and from the Euphrates

---

k RED SEA: *See Word List.*

11.3 Ex 7.8–12.13   **11.4** Ex 14.28   **11.6** Nu 16.31, 32   **11.13-17** Lv 26.3-5; Dt 7.12-16; 28.1-14   **11.18-20** Dt 6.6-9   **11.24, 25** Js 1.3-5

Teach them to your children. (11.19)

River in the east to the Mediterranean Sea in the west. ²⁵ Wherever you go in that land, the LORD your God will make the people fear you, as he has promised, and no one will be able to stop you.

²⁶ "Today I am giving you the choice between a blessing and a curse — ²⁷ a blessing, if you obey the commands of the LORD your God that I am giving you today; ²⁸ but a curse, if you disobey these commands and turn away to worship other gods that you have never worshiped before. ²⁹ When the LORD brings you into the land that you are going to occupy, you are to proclaim the blessing from Mount Gerizim and the curse from Mount Ebal. (³⁰ These two mountains are west of the Jordan River in the territory of the Canaanites who live in the Jordan Valley. They are toward the west, not far from the sacred trees of Moreh near the town of Gilgal.) ³¹ You are about to cross the Jordan River and occupy the land that the LORD your God is giving you. When you take it and settle there, ³² be sure to obey all the laws that I am giving you today.

The One Place for Worship

12 "Here are the laws that you are to obey as long as you live in the land that the LORD, the God of your ancestors, is giving you. Listen to them! ² In the land that you are taking, destroy all the places where the people worship their gods on high mountains, on hills, and under green trees. ³ Tear down their altars and smash their sacred stone pillars to pieces. Burn their symbols of the goddess Asherah and chop down their idols, so that they will never again be worshiped at those places.

⁴ "Do not worship the LORD your God in the way that these people worship their gods. ⁵ Out of the territory of all

Tear down their altars. (12.3)

your tribes the LORD will choose the one place where the people are to come into his presence and worship him. ⁶ There you are to offer your sacrifices that are to be burned and your other sacrifices, your tithes and your offerings, the gifts that you promise to the LORD, your freewill offerings, and the first-born of your cattle and sheep. ⁷ There, in the presence of the LORD your God, who has blessed you, you and your families will eat and enjoy the good things that you have worked for. ⁸ "When that time comes, you must

11.29 Dt 27.11-14; Js 8.33-35 **12.3** Dt 7.5

not do as you have been doing. Until now you have all been worshiping as you please, [9]because you have not yet entered the land that the LORD your God is giving you, where you can live in peace. [10]When you cross the Jordan River, the LORD will let you occupy the land and live there. He will keep you safe from all your enemies, and you will live in peace. [11]The LORD will choose a single place where he is to be worshiped, and there you must bring to him everything that I have commanded: your sacrifices that are to be burned and your other sacrifices, your tithes and your offerings, and those special gifts that you have promised to the LORD. [12]Be joyful there in his presence, together with your children, your servants, and the Levites who live in your towns; remember that the Levites will have no land of their own. [13]You are not to offer your sacrifices wherever you choose; [14]you must offer them only in the one place that the LORD will choose in the territory of one of your tribes. Only there are you to offer your sacrifices that are to be burned and do all the other things that I have commanded you.

[15]"But you are free to kill and eat your animals wherever you live. You may eat as many as the LORD gives you. All of you, whether ritually clean or unclean, may eat them, just as you would eat the meat of deer or antelope. [16]But you must not eat their blood; you must pour it out on the ground like water. [17]Nothing that you offer to the LORD is to be eaten in the places where you live: neither the tithes of your grain, your wine, or your olive oil, nor the first-born of your cattle and sheep, the gifts that you promise to the LORD, your freewill offerings, or any other offerings. [18]You and your children, together with your servants and the Levites who live in your towns, are to eat these offerings only in the presence of the LORD your

God, in the one place of worship chosen by the LORD your God. And you are to be happy there over everything that you have done. [19]Be sure, also, not to neglect the Levites, as long as you live in your land.

[20]"When the LORD your God enlarges your territory, as he has promised, you may eat meat whenever you want to. [21]If the one place of worship is too far away, then, whenever you wish, you may kill any of the cattle or sheep that the LORD has given you, and you may eat the meat at home, as I have told you. [22]Anyone, ritually clean or unclean, may eat that meat, just as he would eat the meat of deer or antelope. [23]Only do not eat meat with blood still in it, for the life is in the blood, and you must not eat the life with the meat. [24]Do not use the blood for food; instead, pour it out on the ground like water. [25]If you obey this command, the LORD will be pleased, and all will go well for you and your descendants. [26]Take to the one place of worship your offerings and the gifts that you have promised the LORD. [27]Offer there the sacrifices which are to be completely burned on the LORD's altar. Also offer those sacrifices in which you eat the meat and pour the blood out on the altar. [28]Obey faithfully everything that I have commanded you, and all will go well for you and your descendants forever, because you will be doing what is right and what pleases the LORD your God.

Warning against Idolatry

[29]"The LORD your God will destroy the nations as you invade their land, and you will occupy it and settle there. [30]After the LORD destroys those nations, make sure that you don't follow their religious practices, because that would be fatal. Don't try to find out how they worship their gods, so that you can

12.16 Gn 9.4; Lv 7.26, 27; 17.10-14; 19.26; Dt 15.23   **12.23, 24** Lv 17.10-14

worship in the same way. 31 Do not worship the LORD your God in the way they worship their gods, for in the worship of their gods they do all the disgusting things that the LORD hates. They even sacrifice their children in the fires on their altars.

32 "Do everything that I have commanded you; do not add anything to it or take anything from it.

13 "Prophets or interpreters of dreams may promise a miracle or a wonder, 2 in order to lead you to worship and serve gods that you have not worshiped before. Even if what they promise comes true, 3 do not pay any attention to them. The LORD your God is using them to test you, to see if you love the LORD with all your heart. 4 Follow the LORD and honor him; obey him and keep his commands; worship him and be faithful to him. 5 But put to death any interpreters of dreams or prophets that tell you to rebel against the LORD, who rescued you from Egypt, where you were slaves. Such people are evil and are trying to lead you away from the life that the LORD has commanded you to live. They must be put to death, in order to rid yourselves of this evil.

6 "Even your brother or your son or your daughter or the wife you love or your closest friend may secretly encourage you to worship other gods, gods that you and your ancestors have never worshiped. 7 Some of them may encourage you to worship the gods of the people who live near you or the gods of those who live far away. 8 But do not let any of them persuade you; do not even listen to them. Show them no mercy or pity, and do not protect them. 9 Kill them! Be the first to stone them, and then let everyone else stone them too. 10 Stone them to death! They tried to lead you away from the LORD your God, who rescued you from Egypt, where you were slaves. 11 Then all the

people of Israel will hear what happened; they will be afraid, and no one will ever again do such an evil thing.

Do not even listen to them. (13.8)

12 "When you are living in the towns that the LORD your God gives you, you may hear 13 that some worthless people of your nation have misled the people of their town to worship gods that you have never worshiped before. 14 If you hear such a rumor, investigate it thoroughly; and if it is true that this evil thing did happen, 15 then kill all the people in that town and all their livestock too. Destroy that town completely. 16 Bring together all the possessions of the people who live there and pile them up in the town square. Then burn the town and everything in it as an offering to the LORD your God. It must be left in ruins forever and never again be rebuilt. 17 Do not keep for yourselves anything that was condemned to destruction, and then the LORD will turn from his fierce anger and show you mercy. He will be merciful to you and make you a numerous people, as he promised your ancestors, 18 if you obey all his commands that I have given you today, and do what he requires.

12.32 Dt 4.2; Rev 22.18, 19

A Forbidden Mourning Practice

14 "You are the people of the LORD your God. So when you mourn for the dead, don't gash yourselves or shave the front of your head, as other people do. ² You belong to the LORD your God; he has chosen you to be his own people from among all the peoples who live on earth.

Clean and Unclean Animals
(Leviticus 11.1-47)

³ "Do not eat anything that the LORD has declared unclean. ⁴ You may eat these animals: cattle, sheep, goats, ⁵ deer, wild sheep, wild goats, or antelopes — ⁶ any animals that have divided hoofs and that also chew the cud. ⁷ But no animals may be eaten unless they have divided hoofs and also chew the cud. You may not eat camels, rabbits, or rock badgers. They must be considered unclean; they chew the cud but do not have divided hoofs. ⁸ Do not eat pigs. They must be considered unclean; they have divided hoofs but do not chew the cud. Do not eat any of these animals or even touch their dead bodies.

⁹ "You may eat any kind of fish that has fins and scales, ¹⁰ but anything living in the water that does not have fins and scales may not be eaten; it must be considered unclean.

¹¹ "You may eat any clean bird. ¹²⁻¹⁸ But these are the kinds of birds you are not to eat: eagles, owls, hawks, falcons; buzzards, vultures, crows; ostriches; seagulls, storks, herons, pelicans, cormorants;ᶦ hoopoes; and bats.

¹⁹ "All winged insects are unclean; do not eat them. ²⁰ You may eat any clean insect.

²¹ "Do not eat any animal that dies a natural death. You may let the foreign-ers who live among you eat it, or you may sell it to other foreigners. But you belong to the LORD your God; you are his people.

"Do not cook a young sheep or goat in its mother's milk.

The Law of the Tithe

²² "Set aside a tithe — a tenth of all that your fields produce each year. ²³ Then go to the one place where the LORD your God has chosen to be worshiped; and there in his presence eat the tithes of your grain, wine, and olive oil, and the first-born of your cattle and sheep. Do this so that you may learn to honor the LORD your God always. ²⁴ If the place of worship is too far from your home for you to carry there the tithe of the produce that the LORD has blessed you with, then do this: ²⁵ Sell your produce and take the money with you to the one place of worship. ²⁶ Spend it on whatever you want — beef, lamb, wine, beer — and there, in the presence of the LORD your God, you and your families are to eat and enjoy yourselves.

²⁷ "Do not neglect the Levites who live in your towns; they have no property of their own. ²⁸ At the end of every third year bring the tithe of all your crops and store it in your towns. ²⁹ This food is for the Levites, since they own no property, and for the foreigners, orphans, and widows who live in your towns. They are to come and get all they need. Do this, and the LORD your God will bless you in everything you do.

The Seventh Year
(Leviticus 25.1-7)

15 "At the end of every seventh year you are to cancel the debts of those who owe you money. ² This is how it is to be done. Each of you who has lent money to any Israelite is to can-

---

ᶦ *The identification of some of these birds is uncertain.*
14.1 Lv 19.28; 21.5   **14.2** Ex 19.5, 6; Dt 4.20; 7.6; 26.18; Titus 2.14; 1 P 2.9
14.21 Ex 23.19; 34.26   **14.22-29** Lv 27.30-33; Nu 18.21

cel the debt; you must not try to collect the money; the LORD himself has declared the debt canceled. ³ You may collect what a foreigner owes you, but you must not collect what any of your own people owe you.

⁴ "The LORD your God will bless you in the land that he is giving you. Not one of your people will be poor ⁵ if you obey him and carefully observe everything that I command you today. ⁶ The LORD will bless you, as he has promised. You will lend money to many nations, but you will not have to borrow from any; you will have control over many nations, but no nation will have control over you.

⁷ "If in any of the towns in the land that the LORD your God is giving you there are Israelites in need, then do not be selfish and refuse to help them. ⁸ Instead, be generous and lend them as much as they need. ⁹ Do not refuse to lend them something, just because the year when debts are canceled is near. Do not let such an evil thought enter your mind. If you refuse to make the loan, they will cry out to the LORD against you, and you will be held guilty. ¹⁰ Give to them freely and unselfishly, and the LORD will bless you in everything you do. ¹¹ There will always be some Israelites who are poor and in need, and so I command you to be generous to them.

The Treatment of Slaves
(Exodus 21.1-11)

¹² "If any Israelites, male or female, sell themselves[m] to you as slaves, you are to release them after they have served you for six years. When the seventh year comes, you must let them go free. ¹³ When you set them free, do not

send them away empty-handed. ¹⁴ Give to them generously from what the LORD has blessed you with — sheep, grain, and wine. ¹⁵ Remember that you were

Do not send them away empty-handed. (15.13)

slaves in Egypt and the LORD your God set you free; that is why I am now giving you this command.

¹⁶ "But your slave may not want to leave; he may love you and your family and be content to stay. ¹⁷ Then take him to the door of your house and there pierce his ear; he will then be your slave for life. Treat your female slave in the same way. ¹⁸ Do not be resentful when you set slaves free; after all, they have served you for six years at half the cost of hired servants.[n] Do this, and the LORD your God will bless you in all that you do.

The First-Born Cattle and Sheep

¹⁹ "Set aside for the LORD your God all the first-born males of your cattle and sheep; don't use any of these cattle for work and don't shear any of these sheep. ²⁰ Each year you and your family are to eat them in the LORD's presence at the one place of worship. ²¹ But if

---

[m] sell themselves; *or* are sold.   [n] at half . . . servants; *or* and have worked twice as hard as hired servants.

15.7, 8 Lv 25.35   **15.11** Mt 26.11; Mk 14.7; Jn 12.8   **15.12-18** Lv 25.39-46
15.19 Ex 13.12

there is anything wrong with the animals, if they are crippled or blind or have any other serious defect, you must not sacrifice them to the LORD your God. ²²You may eat such animals at home. All of you, whether ritually clean or unclean, may eat them, just as you eat deer or antelope. ²³But do not use their blood for food; instead, you must pour it out on the ground like water.

The Passover
(Exodus 12.1-20)

16 "Honor the LORD your God by celebrating Passover in the month of Abib; it was on a night in that month that he rescued you from Egypt. ²Go to the one place of worship and slaughter there one of your sheep or cattle for the Passover meal to honor the LORD your God. ³When you eat this meal, do not eat bread prepared with yeast. For seven days you are to eat bread prepared without yeast, as you did when you had to leave Egypt in such a hurry. Eat this bread — it will be called the bread of suffering — so that as long as you live you will remember the day you came out of Egypt, that place of suffering. ⁴For seven days no one in your land is to have any yeast in the house; and the meat of the animal killed on the evening of the first day must be eaten that same night.

⁵⁻⁶"Slaughter the Passover animals at the one place of worship — and nowhere else in the land that the LORD your God will give you. Do it at sunset, the time of day when you left Egypt. ⁷Boil the meat and eat it at the one place of worship; and the next morning return home. ⁸For the next six days you are to eat bread prepared without yeast, and on the seventh day assemble to worship the LORD your God, and do no work on that day.

The Harvest Festival
(Exodus 34.22; Leviticus 23.15-21)

⁹"Count seven weeks from the time that you begin to harvest the grain, ¹⁰and then celebrate the Harvest Festival, to honor the LORD your God, by bringing him a freewill offering in proportion to the blessing he has given you. ¹¹Be joyful in the LORD's presence, together with your children, your servants, and the Levites, foreigners, orphans, and widows who live in your towns. Do this at the one place of worship. ¹²Be sure that you obey these commands; do not forget that you were slaves in Egypt.

The Festival of Shelters
(Leviticus 23.33-43)

¹³"After you have threshed all your grain and pressed all your grapes, celebrate the Festival of Shelters for seven days. ¹⁴Enjoy it with your children, your servants, and the Levites, foreigners, orphans, and widows who live in your towns. ¹⁵Honor the LORD your God by celebrating this festival for seven days at the one place of worship. Be joyful, because the LORD has blessed your harvest and your work.

¹⁶"All the men of your nation are to come to worship the LORD three times a year at the one place of worship: at Passover, Harvest Festival, and the Festival of Shelters. Each man is to bring a gift ¹⁷as he is able, in proportion to the blessings that the LORD your God has given him.

The Administration of Justice

¹⁸"Appoint judges and other officials in every town that the LORD your God gives you. These men are to judge the people impartially. ¹⁹They are not to be unjust or show partiality in their judg-

15.23 Gn 9.4; Lv 7.26, 27; 17.10-14; 19.26; Dt 12.16, 23   **16.1-8** Ex 12.1-20; Lv 23.5-8; Nu 28.16-25   **16.9-12** Lv 23.15-21; Nu 28.26-31   **16.13-15** Lv 23.33-36, 39-43; Nu 29.12-38   **16.19** Ex 23.6-8; Lv 19.15

ments; and they are not to accept bribes, for gifts blind the eyes even of wise and honest men, and cause them to give wrong decisions. 20 Always be fair and just, so that you will occupy the land that the LORD your God is giving you and so that you will continue to live there.

21 "When you make an altar for the LORD your God, do not put beside it a wooden symbol of the goddess Asherah. 22 And do not set up any stone pillar for idol worship; the LORD hates them.

17 "Do not sacrifice to the LORD your God cattle or sheep that have any defects; the LORD hates this.

2 "Suppose you hear that in one of your towns some men or women have sinned against the LORD and broken his covenant 3 by worshiping and serving other gods or the sun or the moon or the stars, contrary to the LORD's command. 4 If you hear such a report, then investigate it thoroughly. If it is true that this evil thing has happened in Israel, 5 then take them outside the town and stone them to death. 6 However, they may be put to death only if two or more witnesses testify against them; they are not to be put to death if there is only one witness. 7 The witnesses are to throw the first stones, and then the rest of the people are to stone them; in this way you will get rid of this evil.

8 "It may be that some cases will be too difficult for the local judges to decide, such as certain cases of property rights or of bodily injury or those cases that involve a distinction between murder and manslaughter. When this happens, go to the one place of worship chosen by the LORD your God, 9 and present your case to the levitical priests and to the judge who is in office at that time, and let them decide the case.

10 They will give their decision, and you are to do exactly as they tell you. 11 Accept their verdict and follow their instructions in every detail. 12 Anyone who dares to disobey either the judge or the priest on duty is to be put to death; in this way you will remove this evil from Israel. 13 Then everyone will hear of it and be afraid, and no one else will dare to act in such a way.

Instructions concerning a King

14 "After you have taken possession of the land that the LORD your God is going to give you and have settled there, then you will decide you need a king like all the nations around you. 15 Be sure that the man you choose to be king is the one whom the LORD has chosen. He must be one of your own people; do not make a foreigner your king. 16 The king is not to have a large number of horses for his army, and he is not to send people to Egypt to buy horses,o because the LORD has said that his people are never to return there. 17 The king is not to have many wives, because this would make him turn away from the LORD; and he is not to make himself rich with silver and gold. 18 When he becomes king, he is to have a copy of the book of God's laws and teachings made from the original copy kept by the levitical priests. 19 He is to keep this book near him and read from it all his life, so that he will learn to honor the LORD and to obey faithfully everything that is commanded in it. 20 This will keep him from thinking that he is better than other Israelites and from disobeying the LORD's commands in any way. Then he will reign for many years, and his descendants will rule Israel for many generations.

o to buy horses; or in exchange for horses.

16.21 Ex 34.13   **16.22** Lv 26.1   **17.3** Ex 22.20   **17.6** Nu 35.30; Dt 19.15; Mt 18.16; 2 Co 13.1; 1 Ti 5.19; He 10.28   **17.7** 1 Co 5.13   **17.14** 1 S 8.5   **17.16** 1 K 10.28; 2 Ch 1.16; 9.28   **17.17 a** 1 K 11.1-8; **b** 1 K 10.14-22, 27; 2 Ch 1.15; 9.27

The Share of the Priests

18 "The priestly tribe of Levi is not to receive any share of land in Israel; instead, they are to live on the offerings and other sacrifices given to the LORD. ²They are to own no land, as the other tribes do; their share is the privilege of being the LORD's priests, as the LORD has promised.

³"Whenever cattle or sheep are sacrificed, the priests are to be given the shoulder, the jaw, and the stomach. ⁴They are to receive the first share of the grain, wine, olive oil, and wool. ⁵The LORD chose from all your tribes the tribe of Levi to serve him as priests forever.

⁶"Any Levite who wants to may come from any town in Israel to the one place of worship ⁷and may serve there as a priest of the LORD his God, like the other Levites who are serving there. ⁸He is to receive the same amount of food as the other priests, and he may keep whatever his family sends him.ᵖ

Warning against Pagan Practices

⁹"When you come into the land that the LORD your God is giving you, don't follow the disgusting practices of the nations that are there. ¹⁰Don't sacrifice your children in the fires on your altars; and don't let your people practice divination or look for omens or use spells ¹¹or charms, and don't let them consult the spirits of the dead. ¹²The LORD your God hates people who do these disgusting things, and that is why he is driving those nations out of the land as you advance. ¹³Be completely faithful to the LORD."

The Promise to Send a Prophet

¹⁴Then Moses said, "In the land you are about to occupy, people follow the advice of those who practice divination and look for omens, but the LORD your God does not allow you to do this. ¹⁵Instead, he will send you a prophet like me from among your own people, and you are to obey him.�q

¹⁶"On the day that you were gathered at Mount Sinai, you begged not to hear the LORD speak again or to see his fiery presence any more, because you were afraid you would die. ¹⁷So the LORD said to me, 'They have made a wise request. ¹⁸I will send them a prophet like you from among their own people; I will tell him what to say, and heʳ will tell the people everything I command. ¹⁹He will speak in my name, and Iˢ will punish anyone who refuses to obey him. ²⁰But if any prophet dares to speak a message in my name when I did not command him to do so, he must die for it, and so must any prophet who speaks in the name of other gods.'

²¹"You may wonder how you can tell when a prophet's message does not come from the LORD. ²²If a prophet speaks in the name of the LORD and what he says does not come true, then it is not the LORD's message. That prophet has spoken on his own authority, and you are not to fear him.

The Cities of Refuge
(Numbers 35.9-34; Joshua 20.1-9)

19 "After the LORD your God has destroyed the people whose land he is giving you and after you have taken their cities and houses and settled there, ²⁻³divide the territory into three parts, each with a city that can be easily reached. Then any of you that kill

---

ᵖ *Probable text* and he may keep ... sends him; *Hebrew unclear.*   q a prophet ... him; *or* prophets ... them.   ʳ a prophet ... him ... he; *or* prophets ... them ... they.   ˢ He will speak ... and I; *or* When a prophet speaks in my name, I.
18.2 Nu 18.20   **18.10 a** Lv 19.26; **b** Ex 22.18   **18.11** Lv 19.31   **18.13** Mt 5.48
18.15 Ac 3.22; 7.37   **18.19** Ac 3.23   **19.1-13** Js 20.1-9

It was by accident that you killed someone. (19.6)

will be able to escape to one of them for protection. ⁴If you accidentally kill someone who is not your enemy, you may escape to any of these cities and be safe. ⁵For example, if two of you go into the forest together to cut wood and if, as one of you is chopping down a tree, the ax head comes off the handle and kills the other, you can run to one of those three cities and be safe. ⁶If there were only one city, the distance to it might be too great, and the relative who is responsible for taking revenge for the killing might catch you and angrily kill an innocent person. After all, it was by accident that you killed someone who was not your enemy. ⁷This is why I order you to set aside three cities.

⁸"When the LORD your God enlarges your territory, as he told your ancestors he would, and gives you all the land he has promised, ⁹then you are to select three more cities. (He will give you this land if you do everything that I command you today and if you love the LORD your God and live according to his teachings.) ¹⁰Do this, so that innocent people will not die and so that you will not be guilty of putting them to death in the land that the LORD is giving you.

¹¹"But suppose you deliberately mur-

der your enemy in cold blood and then escape to one of those cities for protection. ¹²In that case, the leaders of your own town are to send for you and hand you over to the relative responsible for taking revenge for the murder, so that you may be put to death. ¹³No mercy will be shown to you. Israel must rid itself of murderers, so that all will go well.

Ancient Property Lines

¹⁴"Do not move your neighbor's property line, established long ago in the land that the LORD your God is giving you.

Concerning Witnesses

¹⁵"One witness is not enough to convict someone of a crime; at least two witnesses are necessary to prove that someone is guilty. ¹⁶If any of you try to harm another by false accusations, ¹⁷both of you are to go to the one place of worship and be judged by the priests and judges who are then in office. ¹⁸The judges will investigate the case thoroughly; and if you have made a false accusation, ¹⁹you are to receive the punishment the accused would

19.14 Dt 27.17   **19.15** Nu 35.30; Dt 17.6; Mt 18.16; Jn 8.17; 2 Co 13.1; 1 Ti 5.19; He 10.28

have received. In this way your nation will get rid of this evil. ²⁰ Then everyone else will hear what happened; they will be afraid, and no one will ever again do such an evil thing. ²¹ In such cases show no mercy; the punishment is to be a life for a life, an eye for an eye, a tooth for a tooth, a hand for a hand, and a foot for a foot.

Concerning War

20 "When you go out to fight against your enemies and you see chariots and horses and an army that outnumbers yours, do not be afraid of them. The Lord your God, who rescued you from Egypt, will be with you. ² Before you start fighting, a priest is to come forward and say to the army, ³ 'Men of Israel, listen! Today you are going into battle. Do not be afraid of your enemies or lose courage or panic. ⁴ The Lord your God is going with you, and he will give you victory.'

⁵ "Then the officers will address the men and say, 'Is there any man here who has just built a house, but has not yet dedicated it? If so, he is to go home. Otherwise, if he is killed in battle, someone else will dedicate his house. ⁶ Is there any man here who has just planted a vineyard, but has not yet had the chance to harvest its grapes? If so, he is to go home. Otherwise, if he is killed in battle, someone else will enjoy the wine. ⁷ Is there anyone here who is engaged to be married? If so, he is to go home. Otherwise, if he is killed in battle, someone else will marry the woman he is engaged to.'

⁸ "The officers will also say to the men, 'Is there any man here who has lost his nerve and is afraid? If so, he is to go home. Otherwise, he will destroy the morale of the others.' ⁹ When the officers have finished speaking to the army, leaders are to be chosen for each unit.

¹⁰ "When you go to attack a city, first give its people a chance to surrender. ¹¹ If they open the gates and surrender, they are all to become your slaves and do forced labor for you. ¹² But if the people of that city will not surrender, but choose to fight, surround it with your army. ¹³ Then, when the Lord your God lets you capture the city, kill every man in it. ¹⁴ You may, however, take for yourselves the women, the children, the livestock, and everything else in the city. You may use everything that belongs to your enemies. The Lord has given it to you. ¹⁵ That is how you are to deal with those cities that are far away from the land you will settle in.

¹⁶ "But when you capture cities in the land that the Lord your God is giving you, kill everyone. ¹⁷ Completely destroy all the people: the Hittites, the Amorites, the Canaanites, the Perizzites, the Hivites, and the Jebusites, as the Lord ordered you to do. ¹⁸ Kill them, so that they will not make you sin against the Lord by teaching you to do all the disgusting things that they do in the worship of their gods.

¹⁹ "When you are trying to capture a city, do not cut down its fruit trees, even though the siege lasts a long time. Eat the fruit, but do not destroy the trees; the trees are not your enemies. ²⁰ You may cut down the other trees and use them in the siege mounds until the city is captured.

Concerning Unsolved Murders

21 "Suppose someone is found murdered in a field in the land that the Lord your God is going to give you, and you do not know who killed him. ² Your leaders and judges are to go out and measure the distance from the place where the body was found to each of the nearby towns. ³ Then the leaders of the town nearest to where the body was found are to select a young cow

19.21 Ex 21.23-25; Lv 24.19, 20; Mt 5.38

that has never been used for work. 4 They are to take it down to a spot near a stream that never runs dry and where the ground has never been plowed or planted, and there they are to break its neck. 5 The levitical priests are to go there also, because they are to decide every legal case involving violence. The LORD your God has chosen them to serve him and to pronounce blessings in his name. 6 Then all the leaders from the town nearest the place where the murdered person was found are to wash their hands over the cow 7 and say, 'We did not murder this one, and we do not know who did it. 8 LORD, forgive your people Israel, whom you rescued from Egypt. Forgive us and do not hold us responsible for the murder of an innocent person.' 9 And so, by doing what the LORD requires, you will not be held responsible for the murder.

Concerning Women Prisoners of War

10 "When the LORD your God gives you victory in battle and you take prisoners, 11 you may see among them a beautiful woman that you like and want to marry. 12 Take her to your home, where she will shave her head,*t* cut her fingernails, 13 and change her clothes. She is to stay in your home and mourn for her parents for a month; after that, you may marry her. 14 Later, if you no longer want her, you are to let her go free. Since you forced her to have intercourse with you, you cannot treat her as a slave and sell her.

Concerning the First Son's Inheritance

15 "Suppose a man has two wives and they both bear him sons, but the first son is not the child of his favorite wife. 16 When the man decides how he is going to divide his property among his children, he is not to show partiality to the son of his favorite wife by giving

him the share that belongs to the first-born son. 17 He is to give a double share of his possessions to his first son, even though he is not the son of his favorite wife. A man must acknowledge his first son and give him the share he is legally entitled to.

Concerning a Disobedient Son

18 "Suppose someone has a son who is stubborn and rebellious, a son who will not obey his parents, even though they punish him. 19 His parents are to take him before the leaders of the town where he lives and make him stand trial. 20 They are to say to them, 'Our son is stubborn and rebellious and refuses to obey us; he wastes money and is a drunkard.' 21 Then the men of the city are to stone him to death, and so you will get rid of this evil. Everyone in Israel will hear what has happened and be afraid.

Various Laws

22 "If someone has been put to death for a crime and the body is hung on a post, 23 it is not to remain there overnight. It must be buried the same day, because a dead body hanging on a post brings God's curse on the land. Bury the body, so that you will not defile the land that the LORD your God is giving you.

22 "If you see an Israelite's cow or sheep running loose, do not ignore it; take it back. 2 But if its owner lives a long way off or if you don't know who owns it, then take it home with you. When its owner comes looking for it, give it to him. 3 Do the same thing if you find a donkey, a piece of clothing, or anything else that an Israelite may have lost.

4 "If an Israelite's donkey or cow has fallen down, don't ignore it; help him get the animal to its feet again.

---

t shave her head; *or* trim her hair.
21.23 Ga 3.13   **22.1-4** Ex 23.4, 5

When its owner comes . . . give it to him. (22.2)

5"Women are not to wear men's clothing, and men are not to wear women's clothing; the LORD your God hates people who do such things.

6"If you happen to find a bird's nest in a tree or on the ground with the mother bird sitting either on the eggs or with her young, you are not to take the mother bird. 7You may take the young birds, but you must let the mother bird go, so that you will live a long and prosperous life.

8"When you build a new house, be sure to put a railing around the edge of the roof. Then you will not be responsible if someone falls off and is killed.

9"Do not plant any crop in the same field with your grapevines; if you do, you are forbidden to use either the grapes or the produce of the other crop.

10"Do not hitch an ox and a donkey together for plowing.

11"Do not wear cloth made by weaving wool and linen together.

12"Sew tassels on the four corners of your clothes.

Laws concerning Sexual Purity

13"Suppose a man marries a young woman and later he decides he doesn't want her. 14So he makes up false charges against her, accusing her of not being a virgin when they got married.

15"If this happens, the young woman's parents are to take the blood-stained wedding sheet that proves she was a virgin, and they are to show it in court to the town leaders. 16Her father will say to them, 'I gave my daughter to this man in marriage, and now he doesn't want her. 17He has made false charges against her, saying that she was not a virgin when he married her. But here is the proof that my daughter was a virgin; look at the bloodstains on the wedding sheet!' 18Then the town leaders are to take the husband and beat him. 19They are also to fine him a hundred pieces of silver and give the money to the young woman's father, because the man has brought disgrace on an Israelite woman. Moreover, she will continue to be his wife, and he can never divorce her as long as he lives.

20"But if the charge is true and there is no proof that she was a virgin, 21then they are to take her out to the entrance of her father's house, where the men of her city are to stone her to death. She has done a shameful thing among our people by having intercourse before she was married, while she was still living in her father's house. In this way you will get rid of this evil.

22"If a man is caught having intercourse with another man's wife, both of them are to be put to death. In this way you will get rid of this evil.

22.9-11 Lv 19.19 **22.12** Nu 15.37-41

²³"Suppose a man is caught in a town having intercourse with a young woman who is engaged to someone else. ²⁴You are to take them outside the town and stone them to death. She is to die because she did not cry out for help, although she was in a town, where she could have been heard. And the man is to die because he had intercourse with someone who was engaged. In this way you will get rid of this evil.

²⁵"Suppose a man out in the countryside rapes a young woman who is engaged to someone else. Then only the man is to be put to death; ²⁶nothing is to be done to the woman, because she has not committed a sin worthy of death. This case is the same as when one man attacks another man and murders him. ²⁷The man raped the engaged woman in the countryside, and although she cried for help, there was no one to help her.

²⁸"Suppose a man is caught raping a young woman who is not engaged. ²⁹He is to pay her father the bride price of fifty pieces of silver, and she is to become his wife, because he forced her to have intercourse with him. He can never divorce her as long as he lives.

³⁰"No man is to disgrace his father by having intercourse with any of his father's wives.

Exclusion from the LORD's People

23 "No man who has been castrated or whose penis has been cut off may be included among the LORD's people.

²"No one born out of wedlock or any descendant of such a person, even in the tenth generation, may be included among the LORD's people.

³"No Ammonite or Moabite — or any of their descendants, even in the tenth generation — may be included among the LORD's people. ⁴They refused to provide you with food and water when you were on your way out of Egypt, and they hired Balaam son of Beor, from the city of Pethor in Mesopotamia, to curse you. ⁵But the LORD your God would not listen to Balaam; instead he turned the curse into a blessing, because he loved you. ⁶As long as you are a nation, never do anything to help these nations or to make them prosperous.

⁷"Do not despise the Edomites; they are your relatives. And do not despise the Egyptians; you once lived in their land. ⁸From the third generation onward their descendants may be included among the LORD's people.

Keeping the Military Camp Clean

⁹"When you are in camp in time of war, you are to avoid anything that would make you ritually unclean. ¹⁰If a man becomes unclean because he has had a wet dream during the night, he is to go outside the camp and stay there. ¹¹Toward evening he is to wash himself, and at sunset he may come back into camp.

¹²"You are to have a place outside the camp where you can go when you need to relieve yourselves. ¹³Carry a stick as part of your equipment, so that when you have a bowel movement you can dig a hole and cover it up. ¹⁴Keep your camp ritually clean, because the LORD your God is with you in your camp to protect you and to give you victory over your enemies. Do not do anything indecent that would cause the LORD to turn his back on you.

Various Laws

¹⁵"If slaves run away from their owners and come to you for protection, do not send them back. ¹⁶They may live in any of your towns that they choose, and you are not to treat them harshly.

22.28, 29 Ex 22.16, 17   **22.30** Lv 18.8; 20.11; Dt 27.20   **23.3-5** Ne 13.1, 2
23.4 Nu 22.1-6   **23.5** Nu 23.7—24.9

You may eat all the grapes you want. (23.24)

But you must not carry any away in a container. (23.24)

17"No Israelite, man or woman, is to become a temple prostitute. **18**Also, no money earned in this way may be brought into the house of the LORD your God in fulfillment of a vow. The LORD hates temple prostitutes.

19"When you lend money or food or anything else to Israelites, do not charge them interest. **20**You may charge interest on what you lend to foreigners, but not on what you lend to Israelites. Obey this rule, and the LORD your God will bless everything you do in the land that you are going to occupy.

21"When you make a vow to the LORD your God, do not put off doing what you promised; the LORD will hold you to your vow, and it is a sin

not to keep it. **22**It is no sin not to make a vow to the LORD, **23**but if you make one voluntarily, be sure that you keep it.

24"When you walk along a path in someone else's vineyard, you may eat all the grapes you want, but you must not carry any away in a container. **25**When you walk along a path in someone else's grainfield, you may eat all the grain you can pull off with your hands, but you must not cut any grain with a sickle.

Divorce and Remarriage

24 "Suppose a man marries a woman and later decides that he doesn't want her, because he finds something about her that he doesn't like.[u] So he writes out divorce papers, gives them to her, and sends her away from his home. **2**Then suppose she marries another man, **3**and he also decides that he doesn't want her, so he also writes out divorce papers, gives them to her, and sends her away from his home. Or suppose her second husband dies. **4**In either case, her first husband is not to marry her again; he is to consider her defiled. If he married her again, it would be offensive to the LORD. You are not to commit such a terrible sin in the land that the LORD your God is giving you.

Various Laws

5"When a man is newly married, he is not to be drafted into military service or any other public duty; he is to be excused from duty for one year, so that he can stay at home and make his wife happy.[v]

6"When you lend someone something, you are not to take as security his

---

[u] something . . . like; *or* that she is guilty of some shameful conduct.   [v] make his wife happy; *or* be happy with his wife.

23.17 Lv 19.29   **23.19, 20** Ex 22.25; Lv 25.36, 37; Dt 15.7-11   **23.21** Nu 30.1-16; Mt 5.33
24.1 Mt 5.31; 19.7; Mk 10.4

millstones used for grinding his grain. This would take away the family's means of preparing food to stay alive.

7"If any of you kidnap Israelites and make them your slaves or sell them into slavery, you are to be put to death. In this way your nation will get rid of this evil.

8"When you are suffering from a dreaded skin disease, be sure to do exactly what the levitical priests tell you; follow the instructions that I have given them. 9 Remember what the LORD your God did to Miriam as you were coming from Egypt.

10"When you lend someone something, do not go into his house to get the garment he is going to give you as security; 11 wait outside and let him bring it to you himself. 12 If he is poor, do not keep it overnight; 13 return it to him each evening, so that he can have it to sleep in. Then he will be grateful, and the LORD your God will be pleased with you.

14"Do not cheat poor and needy hired servants, whether they are Israelites or foreigners living in one of your towns. 15 Each day before sunset pay them for that day's work; they need the money and have counted on getting it. If you do not pay them, they will cry out against you to the LORD, and you will be guilty of sin.

16"Parents are not to be put to death for crimes committed by their children, and children are not to be put to death for crimes committed by their parents; people are to be put to death only for a crime they themselves have committed.

17"Do not deprive foreigners and orphans of their rights; and do not take a widow's garment as security for a loan. 18 Remember that you were slaves in Egypt and that the LORD your God set you free; that is why I have given you this command.

19"When you gather your crops and fail to bring in some of the grain that you have cut, do not go back for it; it is to be left for the foreigners, orphans, and widows, so that the LORD your God will bless you in everything you do. 20 When you have picked your olives once, do not go back and get those that are left; they are for the foreigners, orphans, and widows. 21 When you have gathered your grapes once, do not go back over the vines a second time; the grapes that are left are for the foreigners, orphans, and widows. 22 Never forget that you were slaves in Egypt; that is why I have given you this command.

25 "Suppose two Israelites go to court to settle a dispute, and one is declared innocent and the other guilty. 2 If the guilty one is sentenced to be beaten, the judge is to make him lie face downward and have him whipped. The number of lashes will depend on the crime he has committed. 3 He may be given as many as forty lashes, but no more; more than that would humiliate him publicly.

4"Do not muzzle an ox when you are using it to thresh grain.

Duty to a Dead Brother

5"If two brothers live on the same property and one of them dies, leaving no son, then his widow is not to be married to someone outside the family; it is the duty of the dead man's brother to marry her. 6 The first son that they have will be considered the son of the dead man, so that his family line will continue in Israel. 7 But if the dead man's brother does not want to marry her, she is to go before the town leaders and say, 'My husband's brother will not do his

24.7 Ex 21.16   **24.8** Lv 13.1—14.54   **24.9** Nu 12.10   **24.10-13** Ex 22.26, 27
24.14, 15 Lv 19.13   **24.16** 2 K 14.6; 2 Ch 25.4; Ez 18.20   **24.17, 18** Ex 23.9;
Lv 19.33, 34; Dt 27.19   **24.19-21** Lv 19.9, 10; 23.22   **25.3** 2 Co 11.24   **25.4** 1 Co 9.9;
1 Ti 5.18   **25.5, 6** Mt 22.24; Mk 12.19; Lk 20.28   **25.7-10** Ru 4.7, 8

duty; he refuses to give his brother a descendant among the people of Israel.' 8 Then the town leaders are to summon him and speak to him. If he still refuses to marry her, 9 his brother's widow is to go up to him in the presence of the town leaders, take off one of his sandals, spit in his face, and say, 'This is what happens to the man who refuses to give his brother a descendant.' 10 His family will be known in Israel as 'the family of the man who had his sandal pulled off.'

Other Laws

11 "If two men are having a fight and the wife of one tries to help her husband by grabbing hold of the other man's genitals, 12 show her no mercy; cut off her hand.

13-14 "Do not cheat when you use weights and measures. 15 Use true and honest weights and measures, so that you may live a long time in the land that the LORD your God is giving you. 16 The LORD hates people who cheat.

The Command to Kill the Amalekites

17 "Remember what the Amalekites did to you as you were coming from Egypt. 18 They had no fear of God, and so they attacked you from the rear when you were tired and exhausted, and killed all who were straggling behind. 19 So then, when the LORD your God has given you the land and made you safe from all your enemies who live around you, be sure to kill all the Amalekites, so that no one will remember them any longer. Do not forget!

Harvest Offerings

26 "After you have occupied the land that the LORD your God is giving you and have settled there, 2 each of you must place in a basket the first part of each crop that you harvest and you must take it with you to the one place of worship. 3 Go to the priest in charge at that time and say to him, 'I now acknowledge to the LORD my God that I have entered the land that he promised our ancestors to give us.'

4 "The priest will take the basket from you and place it before the altar of the LORD your God. 5 Then, in the LORD's presence you will recite these words: 'My ancestor was a wandering Aramean, who took his family to Egypt to live. They were few in number when they went there, but they became a large and powerful nation. 6 The Egyptians treated us harshly and forced us to work as slaves. 7 Then we cried out for help to the LORD, the God of our ancestors. He heard us and saw our suffering, hardship, and misery. 8 By his great power and strength he rescued us from Egypt. He worked miracles and wonders, and caused terrifying things to happen. 9 He brought us here and gave us this rich and fertile land. 10 So now I bring to the LORD the first part of the harvest that he has given me.'

"Then set the basket down in the LORD's presence and worship there. 11 Be grateful for the good things that the LORD your God has given you and your family; and let the Levites and the foreigners who live among you join in the celebration.

12 "Every third year give the tithe — a tenth of your crops — to the Levites, the foreigners, the orphans, and the widows, so that in every community they will have all they need to eat. When you have done this, 13 say to the LORD, 'None of the sacred tithe is left in my house; I have given it to the Levites, the foreigners, the orphans, and the widows, as you commanded me to do. I have not disobeyed or forgotten any of your commands concerning the tithe. 14 I have not eaten any of it when I was mourning; I have not taken any of it out

25.13-16 Lv 19.35, 36   **25.17-19** Ex 17.8-14; 1 S 15.2-9   **26.2** Ex 23.19
26.12 Dt 14.28, 29

of my house when I was ritually unclean; and I have not given any of it as an offering for the dead.[w] I have obeyed you, O Lᴏʀᴅ; I have done everything you commanded concerning the tithe. [15] Look down from your holy place in heaven and bless your people Israel; bless also the rich and fertile land that you have given us, as you promised our ancestors.'

The Lᴏʀᴅ's Own People

[16]"Today the Lᴏʀᴅ your God commands you to obey all his laws; so obey them faithfully with all your heart. [17] Today you have acknowledged the Lᴏʀᴅ as your God; you have promised to obey him, to keep all his laws, and to do all that he commands. [18] Today the Lᴏʀᴅ has accepted you as his own people, as he promised you; and he commands you to obey all his laws. [19] He will make you greater than any other nation that he has created, and you will bring praise and honor to his name.[x] You will be his own people, as he promised."

God's Laws Written on Stones

27 Then Moses, together with the leaders of Israel, said to the people, "Obey all the instructions that I am giving you today. [2] On the day you cross the Jordan River and enter the land that the Lᴏʀᴅ your God is giving you, you are to set up some large stones, cover them with plaster, [3] and write on them all these laws and teachings. When you have entered the rich and fertile land that the Lᴏʀᴅ, the God of your ancestors, promised you, [4] and you are on the other side of the Jordan, set up these stones on Mount Ebal, as I am instructing you today, and cover them with plaster. [5] Build an altar there made of stones that have had no iron tools

used on them, [6] because any altar you build for the Lᴏʀᴅ your God must be made of uncut stones. There you are to offer the sacrifices that are to be burned, [7] and there you are to sacrifice and eat your fellowship offerings and be grateful in the presence of the Lᴏʀᴅ your God. [8] On the stones covered with plaster write clearly every word of God's laws."

[9] Then Moses, together with the levitical priests, said to all the people of Israel, "Give me your attention, people of Israel, and listen to me. Today you have become the people of the Lᴏʀᴅ

"People of Israel . . . listen to me." (27.9)

your God; [10] so obey him and keep all his laws that I am giving you today."

The Curses on Disobedience

[11] Then Moses said to the people of Israel, [12]"After you have crossed the Jordan, the following tribes are to stand on Mount Gerizim when the blessings are pronounced on the people: Simeon, Levi, Judah, Issachar, Joseph, and Benjamin. [13] And the following tribes will stand on Mount Ebal when the curses are pronounced: Reuben, Gad, Asher, Zebulun, Dan, and Naphtali. [14] The Levites will speak these words in a loud voice:

[15]" 'God's curse on anyone who

---

[w] for the dead; *or* to the dead.   [x] bring praise . . . name; *or* receive praise and honor.
26.18 Ex 19.5; Dt 4.20; 7.6; 14.2; Titus 2.14; 1 P 2.9   **27.2-8** Js 8.30-32   **27.5, 6** Ex 20.25
27.12 Dt 11.29; Js 8.33-35   **27.15** Ex 20.4; 34.17; Lv 19.4; 26.1; Dt 4.15-18; 5.8

makes an idol of stone, wood, or metal and secretly worships it; the LORD hates idolatry.'

"And all the people will answer, 'Amen!'

16" 'God's curse on anyone who dishonors his father or mother.'

"And all the people will answer, 'Amen!'

17" 'God's curse on anyone who moves a neighbor's property line.'

"And all the people will answer, 'Amen!'

18" 'God's curse on anyone who leads a blind person in the wrong direction.'

"And all the people will answer, 'Amen!'

19" 'God's curse on anyone who deprives foreigners, orphans, and widows of their rights.'

"And all the people will answer, 'Amen!'

20" 'God's curse on anyone who disgraces his father by having intercourse with any of his father's wives.'

"And all the people will answer, 'Amen!'

21" 'God's curse on anyone who has sexual relations with an animal.'

"And all the people will answer, 'Amen!'

22" 'God's curse on anyone who has intercourse with his sister or half sister.'

"And all the people will answer, 'Amen!'

23" 'God's curse on anyone who has intercourse with his mother-in-law.'

"And all the people will answer, 'Amen!'

24" 'God's curse on anyone who secretly commits murder.'

"And all the people will answer, 'Amen!'

25" 'God's curse on anyone who accepts money to murder an innocent person.'

"And all the people will answer, 'Amen!'

26" 'God's curse on anyone who does not obey all of God's laws and teachings.'

"And all the people will answer, 'Amen!'

The Blessings of Obedience
(Leviticus 26.3-13; Deuteronomy 7.12-24)

28 "If you obey the LORD your God and faithfully keep all his commands that I am giving you today, he will make you greater than any other nation on earth. 2Obey the LORD your God and all these blessings will be yours:

3"The LORD will bless your towns and your fields.

4"The LORD will bless you with many children, with abundant crops, and with many cattle and sheep.

5"The LORD will bless your grain crops and the food you prepare from them.

6"The LORD will bless everything you do.

7"The LORD will defeat your enemies when they attack you. They will attack from one direction, but they will run from you in all directions.

8"The LORD your God will bless your work and fill your barns with grain. He will bless you in the land that he is giving you.

9"If you obey the LORD your God and do everything he commands, he will make you his own people, as he has promised. 10Then all the peoples on earth will see that the LORD has chosen you to be his own people, and they will be afraid of you. 11The LORD will give you many children, many cattle, and abundant crops in the land that he promised your ancestors to give you. 12He will send rain in season from his

27.16 Ex 20.12; Dt 5.16   **27.17** Dt 19.14   **27.18** Lv 19.14   **27.19** Ex 22.21; 23.9; Lv 19.33, 34; Dt 24.17, 18   **27.20** Lv 18.8; 20.11; Dt 22.30   **27.21** Ex 22.19; Lv 18.23; 20.15   **27.22** Lv 18.9; 20.17   **27.23** Lv 18.17; 20.14   **27.26** Ga 3.10   **28.1-14** Dt 11.13-17 rich storehouse in the sky and bless all your work, so that you will lend to many nations, but you will not have to borrow from any. ¹³The LORD your God will make you the leader among the nations and not a follower; you will always prosper and never fail if you obey faithfully all his commands that I am giving you today. ¹⁴But you must never disobey them in any way, or worship and serve other gods.

The Consequences of Disobedience
(Leviticus 26.14-46)

¹⁵"But if you disobey the LORD your God and do not faithfully keep all his commands and laws that I am giving you today, all these evil things will happen to you:

But if you disobey the LORD (28.15)

¹⁶"The LORD will curse your towns and your fields.

¹⁷"The LORD will curse your grain crops and the food you prepare from them.

¹⁸"The LORD will curse you by giving you only a few children, poor crops, and few cattle and sheep.

¹⁹"The LORD will curse everything you do.

²⁰"If you do evil and reject the LORD, he will bring on you disaster, confusion, and trouble in everything you do, until you are quickly and completely destroyed. ²¹He will send disease after disease on you until there is not one of you left in the land that you are about to occupy. ²²The LORD will strike you with infectious diseases, with swelling and fever; he will send drought and scorching winds to destroy your crops. These disasters will be with you until you die. ²³No rain will fall, and your ground will become as hard as iron. ²⁴Instead of rain, the LORD will send down duststorms and sandstorms until you are destroyed.

²⁵"The LORD will give your enemies victory over you. You will attack them from one direction, but you will run from them in all directions, and all the people on earth will be terrified when they see what happens to you. ²⁶When you die, birds and wild animals will come and eat your bodies, and there will be no one to scare them off. ²⁷The LORD will send boils on you, as he did on the Egyptians. He will make your bodies break out with sores. You will be covered with scabs, and you will itch, but there will be no cure. ²⁸The LORD will make you lose your mind; he will strike you with blindness and confusion. ²⁹You will grope about in broad daylight like someone blind, and you will not be able to find your way. You will not prosper in anything you do. You will be constantly oppressed and robbed, and there will be no one to help you.

³⁰"You will be engaged to a young woman—but someone else will marry her. You will build a house—but never live in it. You will plant a vineyard—but never eat its grapes. ³¹Your cattle will be butchered before your very eyes, but you will not eat any of the meat. Your donkeys will be dragged away while you look on, and they will not be given back to you. Your sheep will be given to

your enemies, and there will be no one to help you. [32] Your sons and daughters will be given as slaves to foreigners while you look on. Every day you will strain your eyes, looking in vain for your children to return. [33] A foreign nation will take all the crops that you have worked so hard to grow, while you receive nothing but constant oppression and harsh treatment. [34] Your sufferings will make you lose your mind. [35] The LORD will cover your legs with incurable, painful sores; boils will cover you from head to foot.

[36] "The LORD will take you and your king away to a foreign land, where neither you nor your ancestors ever lived before; there you will serve gods made of wood and stone. [37] In the countries to which the LORD will scatter you, the people will be shocked at what has happened to you; they will make fun of you and ridicule you.

[38] "You will plant plenty of seed, but reap only a small harvest, because the locusts will eat your crops. [39] You will plant vineyards and take care of them, but you will not gather their grapes or drink wine from them, because worms will eat the vines. [40] Olive trees will grow everywhere in your land, but you will not have any olive oil, because the olives will drop off. [41] You will have sons and daughters, but you will lose them, because they will be taken away as prisoners of war. [42] All your trees and crops will be devoured by insects.

[43] "Foreigners who live in your land will gain more and more power, while you gradually lose yours. [44] They will have money to lend you, but you will have none to lend them. In the end they will be your rulers.

[45] "All these disasters will come on you, and they will be with you until you are destroyed, because you did not obey the LORD your God and keep all the

laws that he gave you. [46] They will be the evidence of God's judgment on you and your descendants forever. [47] The LORD blessed you in every way, but you would not serve him with glad and joyful hearts. [48] So then, you will serve the enemies that the LORD is going to send against you. You will be hungry, thirsty, and naked — in need of everything. The LORD[y] will oppress you harshly until you are destroyed. [49] The LORD will bring against you a nation from the ends of the earth, a nation whose language you do not know. They will swoop down on you like an eagle. [50] They will be ruthless and show no mercy to anyone, young or old. [51] They will eat your livestock and your crops, and you will starve to death. They will not leave you any grain, wine, olive oil, cattle, or sheep; and you will die. [52] They will attack every town in the land that the LORD your God is giving you, and the high, fortified walls in which you trust will fall.

[53] "When your enemies are besieging your towns, you will become so desperate for food that you will even eat the children that the LORD your God has given you. [54-55] Even the most refined man of noble birth will become so desperate during the siege that he will eat some of his own children because he has no other food. He will not even give any to his brother or to the wife he loves or to any of his children who are left. [56-57] Even the most refined woman of noble birth, so rich that she has never had to walk anywhere, will behave in the same way. When the enemy besieges her town, she will become so desperate for food that she will secretly eat her newborn child and the afterbirth as well. She will not share them with the husband she loves or with any of her children.

[58] "If you do not obey faithfully all of

<hr>

[y] The LORD; or Your enemies.

28.57 2 K 6.28, 29; Lm 4.10

God's teachings that are written in this book and if you do not honor the wonderful and awesome name of the LORD your God, [59] he will send on you and on your descendants incurable diseases and horrible epidemics that can never be stopped. [60] He will bring on you once again all the dreadful diseases you experienced in Egypt, and you will never recover. [61] He will also send all kinds of diseases and epidemics that are not mentioned in this book of God's laws and teachings, and you will be destroyed. [62] Although you become as numerous as the stars in the sky, only a few of you will survive, because you did not obey the LORD your God. [63] Just as the LORD took delight in making you prosper and in making you increase in number, so he will take delight in destroying you and in bringing ruin on you. You will be uprooted from the land that you are about to occupy.

[64] "The LORD will scatter you among all the nations, from one end of the earth to the other, and there you will serve gods made of wood and stone, gods that neither you nor your ancestors have ever worshiped before. [65] You will find no peace anywhere, no place to call your own; the LORD will overwhelm you with anxiety, hopelessness, and despair. [66] Your life will always be in danger. Day and night you will be filled with terror, and you will live in constant fear of death. [67] Your hearts will pound with fear at everything you see. Every morning you will wish for evening; every evening you will wish for morning. [68] The LORD will send you back to Egypt in ships, even though he[z] said that you would never have to go there again. There you will try to sell yourselves to your enemies as slaves, but no one will want to buy you."

The LORD's Covenant with Israel in the Land of Moab

29 These are the terms of the covenant that the LORD commanded Moses to make with the people of Israel in the land of Moab; all this was in addition to the covenant which the LORD had made with them at Mount Sinai.

[2] Moses called together all the people of Israel and said to them, "You saw for yourselves what the LORD did to the king of Egypt, to his officials, and to his entire country. [3] You saw the terrible plagues, the miracles, and the great wonders that the LORD performed. [4] But to this very day he has not let you understand what you have experienced. [5] For forty years the LORD led you through the desert, and your clothes and sandals never wore out. [6] You did not have bread to eat or wine or beer to drink, but the LORD provided for your needs in order to teach you that he is your God. [7] And when we came to this place, King Sihon of Heshbon and King Og of Bashan came out to fight against us. But we defeated them, [8] took their land, and divided it among the tribes of Reuben and Gad, and half the tribe of Manasseh. [9] Obey faithfully all the terms of this covenant, so that you will be successful in everything you do.

[10] "Today you are standing in the presence of the LORD your God, all of you — your leaders and officials, your men, [11] women, and children, and the foreigners who live among you and cut wood and carry water for you. [12] You are here today to enter into this covenant that the LORD your God is making with you and to accept its obligations, [13] so that the LORD may now confirm you as his people and be your God, as he promised you and your ancestors, Abraham, Isaac, and Jacob. [14] You are not the only ones with whom the LORD is making

[z] he; *or* I.
29.7 a Nu 21.21-30; **b** Nu 21.31-35   **29.8** Nu 32.33

this covenant with its obligations. ¹⁵He is making it with all of us who stand here in his presence today and also with our descendants who are not yet born.

¹⁶"You remember what life was like in Egypt and what it was like to travel through the territory of other nations. ¹⁷You saw their disgusting idols made of wood, stone, silver, and gold. ¹⁸Make sure that no man, woman, family, or tribe standing here today turns from the LORD our God to worship the gods of other nations. This would be like a root that grows to be a bitter and poisonous plant. ¹⁹Make sure that there is no one here today who hears these solemn demands and yet convinces himself that all will be well with him, even if he stubbornly goes his own way. That would destroy all of you, good and evil alike. ²⁰The LORD will not forgive such a man. Instead, the LORD's burning anger will flame up against him, and all the disasters written in this book will fall on him until the LORD has destroyed him completely. ²¹The LORD will make an example of him before all the tribes of Israel and will bring disaster on him in accordance with all the curses listed in the covenant that is written in this book of the LORD's teachings.

²²"In future generations your descendants and foreigners from distant lands will see the disasters and sufferings that the LORD has brought on your land. ²³The fields will be a barren waste, covered with sulfur and salt; nothing will be planted, and not even weeds will grow there. Your land will be like the cities of Sodom and Gomorrah, of Admah and Zeboiim, which the LORD destroyed when he was furiously angry. ²⁴Then the whole world will ask, 'Why did the LORD do this to their land? What was the reason for his fierce anger?' ²⁵And the answer will be, 'It is because the LORD's people broke the covenant they had made with him, the

God of their ancestors, when he brought them out of Egypt. ²⁶They served other gods that they had never worshiped before, gods that the LORD had forbidden them to worship. ²⁷And so the LORD became angry with his people and brought on their land all the disasters written in this book. ²⁸The LORD became furiously angry, and in his great anger he uprooted them from their land and threw them into a foreign land, and there they are today.'

²⁹"There are some things that the LORD our God has kept secret; but he has revealed his Law, and we and our descendants are to obey it forever.

Conditions for Restoration and Blessing

30 "I have now given you a choice between a blessing and a curse. When all these things have happened to you, and you are living among the nations where the LORD your God has scattered you, you will remember the choice I gave you. ²If you and your descendants will turn back to the LORD and with all your heart obey his commands that I am giving you today, ³then the LORD your God will have mercy on you. He will bring you back from the nations where he has scattered you, and he will make you prosperous again. ⁴Even if you are scattered to the farthest corners of the earth, the LORD your God will gather you together and bring you back, ⁵so that you may again take possession of the land where your ancestors once lived. And he will make you more prosperous and more numerous than your ancestors ever were. ⁶The LORD your God will give you and your descendants obedient hearts, so that you will love him with all your heart, and you will continue to live in that land. ⁷He will turn all these curses against your enemies, who hated you and oppressed you, ⁸and you will again

29.18 He 12.15   **29.23** Gn 19.24, 25

obey him and keep all his commands that I am giving you today. ⁹The LORD will make you prosperous in all that you do; you will have many children and a lot of livestock, and your fields will produce abundant crops. He will be as glad to make you prosperous as he was to make your ancestors prosperous, ¹⁰but you will have to obey him and keep all his laws that are written in this book of his teachings. You will have to turn to him with all your heart.

¹¹"The command that I am giving you today is not too difficult or beyond your reach. ¹²It is not up in the sky. You do not have to ask, 'Who will go up and bring it down for us, so that we can hear it and obey it?' ¹³Nor is it on the other side of the ocean. You do not have to ask, 'Who will go across the ocean and bring it to us, so that we may hear it and obey it?' ¹⁴No, it is here with you. You know it and can quote it, so now obey it.

¹⁵"Today I am giving you a choice between good and evil, between life and death. ¹⁶If you obey the commands of the LORD your God,ᵃ which I give you today, if you love him, obey him, and keep all his laws, then you will prosper and become a nation of many people. The LORD your God will bless you in the land that you are about to occupy. ¹⁷But if you disobey and refuse to listen, and are led away to worship other gods, ¹⁸you will be destroyed—I warn you here and now. You will not live long in that land across the Jordan that you are about to occupy. ¹⁹I am now giving you the choice between life and death, between God's blessing and God's curse, and I call heaven and earth to witness the choice you make. Choose life. ²⁰Love the LORD your God, obey him and be faithful to him, and then you and your descendants will live long in

Choose life. (30.19)

the land that he promised to give your ancestors, Abraham, Isaac, and Jacob."

Joshua Becomes Moses' Successor

31 Moses continued speaking to the people of Israel, ²and said, "I am now a hundred and twenty years old and am no longer able to be your leader. And besides this, the LORD has told me that I will not cross the Jordan. ³The LORD your God himself will go before you and destroy the nations living there, so that you can occupy their land; and Joshua will be your leader, as the LORD has said. ⁴The LORD will destroy those people, just as he defeated Sihon and Og, kings of the Amorites, and destroyed their country. ⁵The LORD will give you victory over them,

---

ᵃ *One ancient translation* If you obey the commands of the LORD your God; *Hebrew does not have these words.*

30.12-14 Ro 10.6-8 **30.15** Si 15.16, 17 **30.20 a** Gn 12.7; **b** Gn 26.3; **c** Gn 28.13 **31.2** Nu 20.12 **31.4** Nu 21.21-35 and you are to treat them exactly as I have told you. [6] Be determined and confident. Do not be afraid of them. Your God, the LORD himself, will be with you. He will not fail you or abandon you."

[7] Then Moses called Joshua and said to him in the presence of all the people of Israel, "Be determined and confident; you are the one who will lead these people to occupy the land that the LORD promised to their ancestors. [8] The LORD himself will lead you and be with you. He will not fail you or abandon you, so do not lose courage or be afraid."

The Law Is to Be Read Every Seven Years

[9] So Moses wrote down God's Law and gave it to the levitical priests, who were in charge of the LORD's Covenant Box, and to the leaders of Israel. [10] He commanded them, "At the end of every seven years, when the year that debts are canceled comes around, read this aloud at the Festival of Shelters. [11] Read it to the people of Israel when they come to worship the LORD your God at the one place of worship. [12] Call together all the men, women, and children, and the foreigners who live in your towns, so that everyone may hear it and learn to honor the LORD your God and to obey his teachings faithfully. [13] In this way your descendants who have never heard the Law of the LORD your God will hear it. And so they will learn to obey him as long as they live in the land that you are about to occupy across the Jordan."

The LORD's Last Instructions to Moses

[14] Then the LORD said to Moses, "You do not have much longer to live. Call Joshua and bring him to the Tent, so that I may give him his instructions." Moses and Joshua went to the Tent, [15] and the LORD appeared to them there in a pillar of cloud that stood by the door of the Tent.

[16] The LORD said to Moses, "You will soon die, and after your death the people will become unfaithful to me and break the covenant that I made with them. They will abandon me and worship the pagan gods of the land they are about to enter. [17] When that happens, I will become angry with them; I will abandon them, and they will be destroyed. Many terrible disasters will come upon them, and then they will realize that these things are happening to them because I, their God, am no longer with them. [18] And I will refuse to help them then, because they have done evil and worshiped other gods.

[19] "Now, write down this song. Teach it to the people of Israel, so that it will stand as evidence against them. [20] I will take them into this rich and fertile land, as I promised their ancestors. There they will have all the food they want, and they will live comfortably. But they will turn away and worship other gods. They will reject me and break my covenant, [21] and many terrible disasters will come on them. But this song will still be sung, and it will stand as evidence against them. Even now, before I take them into the land that I promised to give them, I know what they are thinking."

[22] That same day Moses wrote down the song and taught it to the people of Israel.

[23] Then the LORD spoke to Joshua son of Nun and told him, "Be confident and determined. You will lead the people of Israel into the land that I promised them, and I will be with you."

[24] Moses wrote God's Law in a book, taking care not to leave out anything. [25] When he finished, he said to the levitical priests, who were in charge of the LORD's Covenant Box, [26] "Take this book of God's Law and place it beside the Covenant Box of the LORD your

31.8 Js 1.5; He 13.5   **31.10 a** Dt 15.12; **b** Dt 16.13-15   **31.23** Nu 27.23; Js 1.6

God, so that it will remain there as a witness against his people. ²⁷I know how stubborn and rebellious they are. They have rebelled against the Lord during my lifetime, and they will rebel even more after I am dead. ²⁸Assemble all your tribal leaders and officials before me, so that I can tell them these things; I will call heaven and earth to be my witnesses against them. ²⁹I know that after my death the people will become wicked and reject what I have taught them. And in time to come they will meet with disaster, because they will have made the Lord angry by doing what he has forbidden."

The Song of Moses

³⁰Then Moses recited the entire song while all the people of Israel listened.

32 "Earth and sky, hear my words,
    listen closely to what I say.
²My teaching will fall like drops of rain
    and form on the earth like dew.
My words will fall like showers on young plants,
    like gentle rain on tender grass.
³I will praise the name of the Lord,
    and his people will tell of his greatness.

⁴"The Lord is your mighty defender,
    perfect and just in all his ways;
Your God is faithful and true;
    he does what is right and fair.
⁵But you are unfaithful, unworthy to be his people,ᵇ
    a sinful and deceitful nation.

⁶Is this the way you should treat the Lord,
    you foolish, senseless people?
He is your father, your Creator,
    he made you into a nation.

⁷"Think of the past, of the time long ago;
    ask your parents to tell you what happened,
    ask the old people to tell of the past.
⁸The Most High assigned nations their lands;
    he determined where peoples should live.
He assigned to each nation a heavenly being,
⁹   but Jacob's descendants he chose for himself.

¹⁰"He found them wandering through the desert,
    a desolate, wind-swept wilderness.
He protected them and cared for them,
    as he would protect himself.
¹¹Like an eagle teaching its young to fly,ᶜ
    catching them safely on its spreading wings,
    the Lord kept Israel from falling.
¹²The Lord alone led his people without the help of a foreign god.

¹³"He let them rule the highlands,
    and they ate what grew in the fields.
They found wild honey among the rocks;
    their olive trees flourished in stony ground.
¹⁴Their cows and goats gave plenty of milk;

ᵇ *Probable text* But you ... people; *Hebrew unclear.*   ᶜ teaching its young to fly; *or* watching over its young.
32.8 Ac 17.26

they had the best sheep,
    goats, and cattle,
the finest wheat, and the
    choicest wine.

15 "The LORD's people grew rich,
    but rebellious;
they were fat and stuffed with
    food.
  They abandoned God their
    Creator
and rejected their mighty
    savior.
16 Their idolatry made the LORD
    jealous;
the evil they did made him
    angry.
17 They sacrificed to gods that are
    not real,
new gods their ancestors had
    never known,
gods that Israel had never
    obeyed.
18 They forgot their God, their
    mighty savior,
the one who had given them
    life.

19 "When the LORD saw this, he
    was angry
and rejected his sons and
    daughters.
20 'I will no longer help them,' he
    said;
'then I will see what happens
    to them,
those stubborn, unfaithful
    people.
21 With their idols they have made
    me angry,
jealous with their so-called
    gods,
gods that are really not gods.
So I will use a so-called nation to
    make them angry;
I will make them jealous with
    a nation of fools.
22 My anger will flame up like fire

and burn everything on earth.
  It will reach to the world below *d*
and consume the roots of the
    mountains.

23 " 'I will bring on them endless
    disasters
and use all my arrows against
    them.
24 They will die from hunger and
    fever;
they will die from terrible
    diseases.
  I will send wild animals to attack
    them,
and poisonous snakes to bite
    them.
25 War will bring death in the
    streets;
terrors will strike in the
    homes.
  Young men and young women
    will die;
neither babies nor old people
    will be spared.
26 I would have destroyed them
    completely,
so that no one would
    remember them.
27 But I could not let their enemies
    boast
that they had defeated my
    people,
when it was I myself who had
    crushed them.'

28 "Israel is a nation without sense;
    they have no wisdom at all.
29 They fail to see why they were
    defeated;
they cannot understand what
    happened.
30 Why were a thousand defeated
    by one,
and ten thousand by
    only two?
  The LORD, their God, had
    abandoned them;

---

d THE WORLD BELOW: *This refers to the world of the dead.*
32.17 1 Co 10.20   **32.21 a** 1 Co 10.22; **b** Ro 10.19

their mighty God had given
them up.

31 Their enemies know that their
own gods are weak,
not mighty like Israel's God.

32 Their enemies, corrupt as Sodom
and Gomorrah,
are like vines that bear bitter
and poisonous grapes,

33 like wine made from the
venom of snakes.

34 "The LORD remembers what their
enemies have done;
he waits for the right time to
punish them.

35 The LORD will take revenge and
punish them;
the time will come when they
will fall;
the day of their doom is near.

36 The LORD will rescue his people
when he sees that their
strength is gone.
He will have mercy on those who
serve him,
when he sees how helpless
they are.

37 Then the LORD will ask his
people,
'Where are those mighty gods
you trusted?

38 You fed them the fat of your
sacrifices
and offered them wine to
drink.
Let them come and help
you now;
let them run to your rescue.

39 " 'I, and I alone, am God;
no other god is real.
I kill and I give life, I wound and
I heal,
and no one can oppose what
I do.

40 As surely as I am the living God,
I raise my hand and I vow

41 that I will sharpen my
flashing sword
and see that justice is done.
I will take revenge on my
enemies
and punish those who
hate me.

42 My arrows will drip with their
blood,
and my sword will kill all who
oppose me.
I will spare no one who fights
against me;
even the wounded and
prisoners will die.'

43 "Nations, you must praise the
LORD's people—
he punishes all who kill them.
He takes revenge on his enemies
and forgives the sins of his
people."

44 Moses and Joshua son of Nun recited this song, so that the people of Israel could hear it.

Moses' Final Instructions

45 When Moses had finished giving
God's teachings to the people, **46** he
said, "Be sure to obey all these commands that I have given you today. Repeat them to your children, so that they
may faithfully obey all of God's teachings. **47** These teachings are not empty
words; they are your very life. Obey
them and you will live long in that land
across the Jordan that you are about to
occupy."

48 That same day the LORD said to
Moses, **49** "Go to the Abarim Mountains
in the land of Moab opposite the city of
Jericho; climb Mount Nebo and look at
the land of Canaan that I am about to
give the people of Israel. **50** You will die
on that mountain as your brother Aaron
died on Mount Hor, **51** because both of

32.35 Ro 12.19; He 10.30   **32.36a** Ps 135.14   **32.43** Ro 15.10; Rev 19.2
32.48-52 Nu 27.12-14; Dt 3.23-27

you were unfaithful to me in the presence of the people of Israel. When you were at the waters of Meribah, near the town of Kadesh in the wilderness of Zin, you dishonored me in the presence of the people. ⁵²You will look at the land from a distance, but you will not enter the land that I am giving the people of Israel."

Moses Blesses the Tribes of Israel

33
These are the blessings that Moses, the man of God, pronounced on the people of Israel before he died.

²The LORD came from Mount Sinai;
he rose like the sun over Edom
and shone on his people from Mount Paran.
Ten thousand angels were with him,
a flaming fire at his right hand.ᵉ
³The LORD loves his peopleᶠ
and protects those who belong to him.
So we bow atᵍ his feet
and obey his commands.
⁴We obey the Law that Moses gave us,
our nation's most treasured possession.
⁵The LORD became king of his people Israel
when their tribes and leaders were gathered together.

⁶Moses said about the tribe of Reuben:

"May Reuben never die out,
Although their people are few."

⁷About the tribe of Judah he said:
"LORD, listen to their cry for help;
Unite them again with the other tribes.
Fight for them, LORD,
And help them against their enemies."ʰ

⁸About the tribe of Levi he said:
"You, LORD, reveal your will by the Urim and Thummimⁱ
Through your faithful servants, the Levites;
You put them to the test at Massah
And proved them true at the waters of Meribah.
⁹They showed greater loyalty to you
Than to parents, brothers, or children.
They obeyed your commands
And were faithful to your covenant.
¹⁰They will teach your people to obey your Law;
They will offer sacrifices on your altar.
¹¹LORD, help their tribe to grow strong;
Be pleased with what they do.
Crush all their enemies;
Let them never rise again."

¹²About the tribe of Benjamin he said:
"This is the tribe the LORD loves and protects;

ᵉ *Probable text* Ten thousand . . . right hand; *Hebrew unclear.*   ᶠ*One ancient translation* his people; *Hebrew* the peoples.   ᵍ*Probable text* bow at; *Hebrew unclear.*   ʰ *Probable text* Fight for . . . enemies; *Hebrew* The tribe of Judah will fight for itself, and the LORD will help it against its enemies.   ⁱ URIM AND THUMMIM: *Two objects used by the priest to determine God's will; it is not known precisely how they were used.*

33.8 a Ex 28.30; **b** Ex 17.7; **c** Ex 17.7; Nu 20.13

He guards them all the day long,
And he dwells in their midst."*j*

13 About the tribe of Joseph he said:
"May the LORD bless their land
    with rain
And with water from under the
    earth.
14 May their land be blessed with
    sun-ripened fruit,
Rich with the best fruits of each
    season.
15 May their ancient hills be covered
    with choice fruit.
16 May their land be filled with all
    that is good,
Blessed by the goodness of the
    LORD,
Who spoke from the burning
    bush.
May these blessings come to the
    tribe of Joseph,
Because he was the leader
    among his brothers.
17 Joseph has the strength of a bull,
The horns of a wild ox.
His horns are Manasseh's
    thousands
And Ephraim's ten thousands.
With them he gores the nations
And pushes them to the ends of
    the earth."

18 About the tribes of Zebulun and Is-
sachar he said:
"May Zebulun be prosperous in
    their trade on the sea,
And may Issachar's wealth
    increase at home.
19 They invite foreigners to their
    mountain
And offer the right sacrifices
    there.
They get their wealth from
    the sea
And from the sand along the
    shore."

20 About the tribe of Gad he said:

"Praise God, who made their
    territory large.
Gad waits like a lion
To tear off an arm or a scalp.
21 They took the best of the land
    for themselves;
A leader's share was assigned
    to them.
They obeyed the LORD's
    commands and laws
When the leaders of Israel were
    gathered together."*k*

22 About the tribe of Dan he said:
"Dan is a young lion;
He leaps out from Bashan."

23 About the tribe of Naphtali he said:
"Naphtali is richly blessed by the
    LORD's good favor;
Their land reaches to the south
    from Lake Galilee."

24 About the tribe of Asher he said:
"Asher is blessed more than the
    other tribes.
May he be the favorite of his
    brothers,
And may his land be rich with
    olive trees.
25 May his towns be protected with
    iron gates,
And may he always live secure."

26 People of Israel, no god is like
    your God,
    riding in splendor across
        the sky,
    riding through the clouds to
        come to your aid.
27 God has always been your
        defense;
    his eternal arms are your
        support.
    He drove out your enemies as
        you advanced,
    and told you to destroy
        them all.

---

j And he . . . midst; or They live under his protection.   *k One ancient translation*
When the leaders . . . together; *Hebrew unclear.*

The LORD showed him the whole land. (34.1)

28 So Jacob's descendants live in
    peace,
   secure in a land full of grain
    and wine,
   where dew from the sky
    waters the ground.
29 Israel, how happy you are!
   There is no one like you,
    a nation saved by the LORD.
   The LORD himself is your shield
    and your sword,
   to defend you and give you
    victory.
   Your enemies will come begging
    for mercy,
   and you will trample them
    down.

The Death of Moses

34 Moses went up from the plains
of Moab to Mount Nebo, to the
top of Mount Pisgah east of Jericho, and
there the LORD showed him the whole
land: the territory of Gilead as far north
as the town of Dan; 2 the entire territory
of Naphtali; the territories of Ephraim
and Manasseh; the territory of Judah as
far west as the Mediterranean Sea; 3 the
southern part of Judah; and the plain
that reaches from Zoar to Jericho, the
city of palm trees. 4 Then the LORD said
to Moses, "This is the land that I promised Abraham, Isaac, and Jacob I would
give to their descendants. I have let you
see it, but I will not let you go there."

5 So Moses, the LORD's servant, died
there in the land of Moab, as the LORD
had said he would. 6 The LORD buried
him in a valley in Moab, opposite the
town of Bethpeor, but to this day no one
knows the exact place of his burial.
7 Moses was a hundred and twenty
years old when he died; he was as
strong as ever, and his eyesight was still
good. 8 The people of Israel mourned for
him for thirty days in the plains of
Moab.

9 Joshua son of Nun was filled with
wisdom, because Moses had appointed
him to be his successor. The people of
Israel obeyed Joshua and kept the commands that the LORD had given them
through Moses.

10 There has never been a prophet in
Israel like Moses; the LORD spoke with
him face-to-face. 11 No other prophet
has ever done miracles and wonders
like those that the LORD sent Moses to
perform against the king of Egypt, his
officials, and the entire country. 12 No
other prophet has been able to do the
great and terrifying things that Moses
did in the sight of all Israel.

34.4 a Gn 12.7; **b** Gn 26.3; **c** Gn 28.13   **34.10** Ex 33.11; Si 45.1-5

The Book of
JOSHUA

INTRODUCTION

The Book of Joshua is the story of the Israelite invasion of Canaan under the leadership of Joshua, the successor of Moses. Notable events recorded in this book include the crossing of the Jordan, the fall of Jericho, the battle at Ai, and the renewal of the covenant between God and his people. One of the best-known passages in the book is, "Decide today whom you will serve. . . . As for my family and me, we will serve the LORD" (24.15).

OUTLINE OF CONTENTS

God Commands Joshua to Conquer Canaan

1 After the death of the LORD's servant Moses, the LORD spoke to Moses' helper, Joshua son of Nun. 2 He said, "My servant Moses is dead. Get ready now, you and all the people of Israel, and cross the Jordan River into the land that I am giving them. 3 As I told Moses, I have given you and all my people the entire land that you will be marching over. 4 Your borders will reach from the desert in the south to the Lebanon Mountains in the north; from the great Euphrates River in the east, through the Hittite country, to the Mediterranean Sea in the west.

5 Joshua, no one will be able to defeat you as long as you live. I will be with you as I was with Moses. I will always be with you; I will never abandon you. 6 Be determined and confident, for you will be the leader of these people as they occupy this land which I promised their ancestors. 7 Just be determined, be confident; and make sure that you obey the whole Law that my servant Moses gave you. Do not neglect any part of it and you will succeed wherever you go. 8 Be sure that the book of the Law is always read in your worship. Study it day and night, and make sure that you obey everything written in it. Then you will be prosperous and successful.

1.3-5 Dt 11.24, 25   **1.5** Dt 31.6, 8; He 13.5   **1.6** Dt 31.6, 7, 23

Explore the land . . . especially the city of Jericho. (2.1)

⁹Remember that I have commanded you to be determined and confident! Do not be afraid or discouraged, for I, the LORD your God, am with you wherever you go."

Joshua Gives Orders to the People

¹⁰Then Joshua ordered the leaders to ¹¹go through the camp and say to the people, "Get some food ready, because in three days you are going to cross the Jordan River to occupy the land that the LORD your God is giving you."

¹²Joshua said to the tribes of Reuben and Gad and to half the tribe of Manasseh, ¹³"Remember how the LORD's servant Moses told you that the LORD your God would give you this land on the east side of the Jordan as your home. ¹⁴Your wives, your children, and your livestock will stay here, but your soldiers, armed for battle, will cross over ahead of the other Israelites in order to help them ¹⁵until they have occupied the land west of the Jordan that the LORD your God has given them. When he has given safety to all the tribes of Israel, then you may come back and settle here in your own land east of the Jordan, which Moses, the LORD's servant, gave to you."

¹⁶They answered Joshua, "We will do everything you have told us and will go anywhere you send us. ¹⁷We will obey you, just as we always obeyed Moses, and may the LORD your God

be with you as he was with Moses! ¹⁸Whoever questions your authority or disobeys any of your orders will be put to death. Be determined and confident!"

Joshua Sends Spies into Jericho

2 Then Joshua sent two spies from the camp at Acacia with orders to go and secretly explore the land of Canaan, especially the city of Jericho. When they came to the city, they went to spend the night in the house of a prostitute named Rahab. ²The king of Jericho heard that some Israelites had come that night to spy out the country, ³so he sent word to Rahab: "The men in your house have come to spy out the whole country! Bring them out!"

⁴⁻⁶"Some men did come to my house," she answered, "but I don't know where they were from. They left at sundown before the city gate was closed. I didn't find out where they were going, but if you start after them quickly, you can catch them." (Now Rahab had taken the two spies up on the roof and hidden them under some stalks of flax that she had put there.) ⁷The king's men left the city, and then the gate was shut. They went looking for the Israelite spies as far as the place where the road crosses the Jordan.

⁸Before the spies settled down for the night, Rahab went up on the roof ⁹and said to them, "I know that the LORD has

1.12-15 Nu 32.28-32; Dt 3.18-20; Js 22.1-6 **2.1** He 11.31; Jas 2.25

given you this land. Everyone in the country is terrified of you. [10]We have heard how the LORD dried up the Red Sea in front of you when you were leaving Egypt. We have also heard how you killed Sihon and Og, the two Amorite kings east of the Jordan. [11]We were afraid as soon as we heard about it; we have all lost our courage because of you. The LORD your God is God in heaven above and here on earth. [12]Now swear by him that you will treat my family as kindly as I have treated you, and give me some sign that I can trust you. [13]Promise me that you will save my father and mother, my brothers and sisters, and all their families! Don't let us be killed!"

[14]The men said to her, "May God take our lives if we don't do as we say![a] If you do not tell anyone what we have been doing, we promise you that when the LORD gives us this land, we will treat you well."

[15]Rahab lived in a house built into the city wall, so she let the men down from the window by a rope. [16]"Go into the hill country," she said, "or the king's men will find you. Hide there for three days until they come back. After that, you can go on your way."

[17]The men said to her, "We will keep the promise that you have made us give. [18]This is what you must do. When we invade your land, tie this red cord to the window you let us down from. Get your father and mother, your brothers, and all your father's family together in your house. [19]If anyone goes out of the house, his death will be his own fault, and we will not be responsible; but if anyone in the house with you is harmed, then we will be responsible. [20]However, if you tell anyone what we have been doing, then we will not have to keep our promise which you have made us give you." [21]She agreed and

sent them away. When they had gone, she tied the red cord to the window.

[22]The spies went into the hills and hid. The king's men looked for them all over the countryside for three days, but they did not find them, so they returned to Jericho. [23]Then the two spies came down from the hills, crossed the river, and went back to Joshua. They told him everything that had happened, [24]and then said, "We are sure that the LORD has given us the whole country. All the people there are terrified of us."

The People of Israel Cross the Jordan

3 The next morning Joshua and all the people of Israel got up early, left the camp at Acacia, and went to the Jordan, where they camped while waiting to cross it. [2]Three days later the leaders went through the camp [3]and told the people, "When you see the priests carrying the Covenant Box of the LORD your God, break camp and follow them. [4]You have never been here before, so they will show you the way to go. But do not get near the Covenant Box; stay about half a mile behind it."

[5]Joshua told the people, "Purify yourselves, because tomorrow the LORD will perform miracles among you." [6]Then he told the priests to take the Covenant Box and go with it ahead of the people. They did as he said.

[7]The LORD said to Joshua, "What I do today will make all the people of Israel begin to honor you as a great man, and they will realize that I am with you as I was with Moses. [8]Tell the priests carrying the Covenant Box that when they reach the river, they must wade in and stand near the bank."

[9]Then Joshua said to the people, "Come here and listen to what the LORD your God has to say. [10]As you advance, he will surely drive out the Canaanites, the Hittites, the Hivites, the Perizzites,

---

[a] May God . . . say; or We will protect you if you protect us.
2.10 a Ex 14.21; **b** Nu 21.21-35

the Girgashites, the Amorites, and the Jebusites. You will know that the living God is among you ¹¹when the Covenant Box of the Lord of all the earth crosses the Jordan ahead of you. ¹²Now choose twelve men, one from each of the tribes of Israel. ¹³When the priests who carry the Covenant Box of the LORD of all the earth put their feet in the water, the Jordan will stop flowing, and the water coming downstream will pile up in one place."

¹⁴⁻¹⁵It was harvest time, and the river was in flood.

When the people left the camp to cross the Jordan, the priests went ahead of them, carrying the Covenant Box. As soon as the priests stepped into the river, ¹⁶the water stopped flowing and piled up, far upstream at Adam, the city beside Zarethan. The flow downstream to the Dead Sea was completely cut off, and the people were able to cross over near Jericho. ¹⁷While the people walked across on dry ground, the priests carrying the LORD's Covenant Box stood on dry ground in the middle of the Jordan until all the people had crossed over.

Memorial Stones Are Set Up

4 When the whole nation had crossed the Jordan, the LORD said to Joshua, ²"Choose twelve men, one from each tribe, ³and command them to take twelve stones out of the middle of the Jordan, from the very place where the priests were standing. Tell them to carry these stones with them and to put them down where you camp tonight."

⁴Then Joshua called the twelve men he had chosen, ⁵and he told them, "Go into the Jordan ahead of the Covenant Box of the LORD your God. Each one of you take a stone on your shoulder, one for each of the tribes of Israel. ⁶These stones will remind the people of what the LORD has done. In the future, when

your children ask what these stones mean to you, ⁷you will tell them that the water of the Jordan stopped flowing when the LORD's Covenant Box crossed the river. These stones will always remind the people of Israel of what happened here."

⁸The men followed Joshua's orders. As the LORD had commanded Joshua, they took twelve stones from the middle of the Jordan, one for each of the tribes of Israel, carried them to the camping place, and put them down there. ⁹Joshua also set up twelve stones in the middle of the Jordan, where the priests carrying the Covenant Box had stood.

Twelve stones in the middle of the Jordan (4.9)

(Those stones are still there.) ¹⁰The priests stood in the middle of the Jordan until everything had been done that the LORD ordered Joshua to tell the people to do. This is what Moses had commanded.

The people hurried across the river. ¹¹When they were all on the other side, the priests with the LORD's Covenant Box went on ahead of the people. ¹²The men of the tribes of Reuben and Gad and of half the tribe of Manasseh, ready for battle, crossed ahead of the rest of the people, as Moses had told them to do. ¹³In the presence of the LORD about forty thousand men ready for war crossed over to the plain near Jericho. ¹⁴What the LORD did that day made the people of Israel consider Joshua a great man. They honored him all his life, just as they had honored Moses.

¹⁵Then the LORD told Joshua ¹⁶to command the priests carrying the Covenant Box to come up out of the Jordan.

The people hurried across the river. (4.10)

¹⁷Joshua did so, ¹⁸and when the priests reached the riverbank, the river began flowing once more and flooded its banks again.

¹⁹The people crossed the Jordan on the tenth day of the first month and camped at Gilgal, east of Jericho. ²⁰There Joshua set up the twelve stones taken from the Jordan. ²¹And he said to the people of Israel, "In the future, when your children ask you what these stones mean, ²²you will tell them about the time when Israel crossed the Jordan on dry ground. ²³Tell them that the LORD your God dried up the water of the Jordan for you until you had crossed, just as he dried up the Red Sea for us. ²⁴Because of this everyone on earth will know how great the LORD's power is, and you will honor the LORD your God forever."

5 All the Amorite kings west of the Jordan and all the Canaanite kings along the Mediterranean Sea heard that the LORD had dried up the Jordan until the people of Israel had crossed it. They became afraid and lost their courage because of the Israelites.

The Circumcision at Gilgal

²Then the LORD told Joshua, "Make some knives out of flint and circumcise the Israelites." ³So Joshua did as the LORD had commanded, and he circumcised the Israelites at a place called Circumcision Hill. ⁴⁻⁶When the people of Israel left Egypt, all the males were already circumcised. However, during the forty years the people spent crossing the desert, none of the baby boys had been circumcised. Also, by the end of that time all the men who were of fighting age when they left Egypt had died because they had disobeyed the LORD. Just as he had sworn, they were not allowed to see the rich and fertile land that he had promised their ancestors. ⁷The sons of these men had never been circumcised, and it was this new generation that Joshua circumcised.

⁸After the circumcision was completed, the whole nation stayed in the camp until the wounds had healed. ⁹The LORD said to Joshua, "Today I have removed from you the disgrace of being slaves in Egypt." That is why the

place was named Gilgal,[b] the name it still has.

10 While the Israelites were camping at Gilgal on the plain near Jericho, they observed Passover on the evening of the fourteenth day of the month. 11 The next day was the first time they ate food grown in Canaan: roasted grain and bread made without yeast. 12 The manna stopped falling then, and the Israelites no longer had any. From that time on they ate food grown in Canaan.

Joshua and the Man with a Sword

13 While Joshua was near Jericho, he suddenly saw a man standing in front of him, holding a sword. Joshua went up to him and asked, "Are you one of our soldiers, or an enemy?"

14 "Neither," the man answered. "I am here as the commander of the LORD's army."

Joshua threw himself on the ground in worship and said, "I am your servant, sir. What do you want me to do?"

15 And the commander of the LORD's army told him, "Take your sandals off; you are standing on holy ground." And Joshua did as he was told.

The Fall of Jericho

6 The gates of Jericho were kept shut and guarded to keep the Israelites out. No one could enter or leave the city. 2 The LORD said to Joshua, "I am putting into your hands Jericho, with its king and all its brave soldiers. 3 You and your soldiers are to march around the city once a day for six days. 4 Seven priests, each carrying a trumpet, are to go in front of the Covenant Box. On the seventh day you and your soldiers are to march around the city seven times while the priests blow the trumpets. 5 Then they are to sound one long note. As soon as you hear it, all the people are to give a loud shout, and the

city walls will collapse. Then the whole army will go straight into the city."

6 Joshua called the priests and told them, "Take the Covenant Box, and seven of you go in front of it, carrying trumpets." 7 Then he ordered the people to start marching around the city, with an advance guard going on ahead of the LORD's Covenant Box.

8-9 So, just as Joshua had ordered, an advance guard started out ahead of the priests who were blowing trumpets; behind these came the priests who were carrying the Covenant Box, followed by a rear guard. All this time the trumpets were sounding. 10 But Joshua had ordered the people not to shout, not to say a word until he gave the order. 11 So he had this group of men take the LORD's Covenant Box around the city one time. Then they came back to camp and spent the night there.

12-13 Joshua got up early the next morning, and for the second time the priests and soldiers marched around the city in the same order as the day before: first, the advance guard; next, the seven priests blowing the seven trumpets; then, the priests carrying the LORD's Covenant Box; and finally, the rear guard. All this time the trumpets were sounding. 14 On this second day they again marched around the city one time and then returned to camp. They did this for six days.

15 On the seventh day they got up at daybreak and marched seven times around the city in the same way — this was the only day that they marched around it seven times. 16 The seventh time around, when the priests were about to sound the trumpets, Joshua ordered the people to shout, and he said, "The LORD has given you the city! 17 The city and everything in it must be totally destroyed as an offering to the LORD. Only the prostitute Rahab and her household will be spared, because

[b] GILGAL: *This name sounds like the Hebrew for "removed."*
5.10 Ex 12.1-13 **5.12** Ex 16.35

They gave a loud shout, and the walls collapsed. (6.20)

she hid our spies. 18 But you are not to take anything that is to be destroyed; if you do, you will bring trouble and destruction on the Israelite camp. 19 Everything made of silver, gold, bronze, or iron is set apart for the LORD. It is to be put in the LORD's treasury."

20 So the priests blew the trumpets. As soon as the people heard it, they gave a loud shout, and the walls collapsed. Then all the army went straight up the hill into the city and captured it. 21 With their swords they killed everyone in the city, men and women, young and old. They also killed the cattle, sheep, and donkeys.

22 Joshua then told the two men who had served as spies, "Go into the prostitute's house, and bring her and her family out, as you promised her." 23 So they went and brought Rahab out, along with her father and mother, her brothers, and the rest of her family. They took them all, family and slaves, to safety near the Israelite camp. 24 Then they set fire to the city and burned it to the ground, along with everything in it, except the things made

of gold, silver, bronze, and iron, which they took and put in the LORD's treasury. 25 But Joshua spared the lives of the prostitute Rahab and all her relatives, because she had hidden the two spies that he had sent to Jericho. (Her descendants have lived in Israel to this day.)

26 At this time Joshua issued a solemn warning: "Anyone who tries to rebuild the city of Jericho will be under the LORD's curse.

Whoever lays the foundation will
　　lose his oldest son;
Whoever builds the gates will
　　lose his youngest."

27 So the LORD was with Joshua, and his fame spread through the whole country.

Achan's Sin

7 The LORD's command to Israel not to take from Jericho anything that was to be destroyed was not obeyed. A man named Achan disobeyed that order, and so the LORD was furious with the Israelites. (Achan was the son of

6.20 He 11.30　**6.25** He 11.31　**6.26** 1 K 16.34

Carmi and grandson of Zabdi, and belonged to the clan of Zerah, a part of the tribe of Judah.)

2 Joshua sent some men from Jericho to Ai, a city east of Bethel, near Bethaven, with orders to go and explore the land. When they had done so, 3 they reported back to Joshua: "There is no need for everyone to attack Ai. Send only about two or three thousand men. Don't send the whole army up there to fight; it is not a large city." 4 So about three thousand Israelites made the attack, but they were forced to retreat. 5 The men of Ai chased them from the city gate as far as some quarries and killed about thirty-six of them on the way down the hill. Then the Israelites lost their courage and were afraid.

6 Joshua and the leaders of Israel tore their clothes in grief, threw themselves to the ground before the LORD's Covenant Box, and lay there till evening, with dust on their heads to show their sorrow. 7 And Joshua said, "Sovereign LORD! Why did you bring us across the Jordan at all? To turn us over to the Amorites? To destroy us? Why didn't we just stay on the other side of the Jordan? 8 What can I say, O Lord, now that Israel has retreated from the enemy? 9 The Canaanites and everyone else in the country will hear about it. They will surround us and kill every one of us! And then what will you do to protect your honor?"

10 The LORD said to Joshua, "Get up! Why are you lying on the ground like this? 11 Israel has sinned! They have broken the agreement with me that I ordered them to keep. They have taken some of the things condemned to destruction. They stole them, lied about it, and put them with their own things. 12 This is why the Israelites cannot stand against their enemies. They retreat from them because they themselves have now been condemned to destruction! I will not stay with you any longer unless you destroy the things you were ordered not to take! 13 Get up!

Purify the people and get them ready to come before me. Tell them to be ready tomorrow, because I, the LORD God of Israel, have this to say: 'Israel, you have in your possession some things that I ordered you to destroy! You cannot stand against your enemies until you get rid of these things!' 14 So tell them that in the morning they will be brought forward, tribe by tribe. The tribe that I pick out will then come forward, clan by clan. The clan that I pick out will come forward, family by family. The family that I pick out will come forward, one by one. 15 The one who is then picked out and found with the condemned goods will be burned, along with his family and everything he owns, for he has brought terrible shame on Israel and has broken my covenant."

16 Early the next morning Joshua brought Israel forward, tribe by tribe, and the tribe of Judah was picked out. 17 He brought the tribe of Judah forward, clan by clan, and the clan of Zerah was picked out. Then he brought the clan of Zerah forward, family by family, and the family of Zabdi was picked out. 18 He then brought Zabdi's family forward, one by one, and Achan, the son of Carmi and grandson of Zabdi, was picked out. 19 Joshua said to him, "My son, tell the truth here before the LORD, the God of Israel, and confess. Tell me now what you have done. Don't try to hide it from me."

20 "It's true," Achan answered. "I have sinned against the LORD, Israel's God, and this is what I did. 21 Among the things we seized I saw a beautiful Babylonian cloak, about five pounds of silver, and a bar of gold weighing over one pound. I wanted them so much that I took them. You will find them buried inside my tent, with the silver at the bottom."

22 So Joshua sent some men, who ran to the tent and found that the condemned things really were buried there, with the silver at the bottom. 23 They brought them out of the tent,

took them to Joshua and all the Israelites, and laid them down in the presence of the LORD. ²⁴ Joshua, along with all the people of Israel, seized Achan, the silver, the cloak, the bar of gold, together with Achan's sons and daughters, his cattle, donkeys, and sheep, his tent, and everything else he owned; and they took them to Trouble Valley. ²⁵ And Joshua said, "Why have you brought such trouble on us? The LORD will now bring trouble on you!" All the people then stoned Achan to death; they also stoned and burned his family and possessions. ²⁶ They put a huge pile of stones over him, which is there to this day. That is why that place is still called Trouble Valley.

Then the LORD was no longer furious.

The Capture and Destruction of Ai

8 The LORD said to Joshua, "Take all the soldiers with you and go on up to Ai. Don't be afraid or discouraged. I will give you victory over the king of Ai; his people, city, and land will be yours. ² You are to do to Ai and its king what you did to Jericho and its king, but this time you may keep its goods and livestock for yourselves. Prepare to attack the city by surprise from the rear."

³ So Joshua got ready to go to Ai with all his soldiers. He picked out thirty thousand of his best troops and sent them out at night ⁴ with these orders: "Hide on the other side of the city, but not too far away from it; be ready to attack. ⁵ My men and I will approach the city. When the men of Ai come out against us, we will turn and run, just as we did the first time. ⁶ They will pursue us until we have led them away from the city. They will think that we are running from them, as we did before. ⁷ Then you will come out of hiding and capture the city. The LORD your God will give it to you. ⁸ After you have taken

the city, set it on fire, just as the LORD has commanded. These are your orders." ⁹ So Joshua sent them out, and they went to their hiding place and waited there, west of Ai, between Ai and Bethel. Joshua spent the night in camp.

¹⁰ Early in the morning Joshua got up and called the soldiers together. Then he and the leaders of Israel led them to Ai. ¹¹ The soldiers with him went toward the main entrance to the city and set up camp on the north side, with a valley between themselves and Ai. ¹² He took about five thousand men and put them in hiding west of the city, between Ai and Bethel. ¹³ The soldiers were arranged for battle with the main camp north of the city and the rest of the men to the west. Joshua spent the night in the valley. ¹⁴ When the king of Ai saw Joshua's men, he acted quickly. He and all his men went out toward the Jordan Valley to fight the Israelites at the same place as before, not knowing that he was about to be attacked from the rear. ¹⁵ Joshua and his men pretended that they were retreating, and ran away toward the barren country. ¹⁶ All the men in the city had been called together to go after them, and as they pursued Joshua, they kept getting farther away from the city. ¹⁷ Every man in Aiᶜ went after the Israelites, and the city was left wide open, with no one to defend it.

¹⁸ Then the LORD said to Joshua, "Point your spear at Ai; I am giving it to you." Joshua did as he was told, ¹⁹ and as soon as he lifted his hand, the men who had been hiding got up quickly, ran into the city and captured it. They immediately set the city on fire. ²⁰ When the men of Ai looked back, they saw the smoke rising to the sky. There was no way for them to escape, because the Israelites who had run toward the barren country now turned around to attack them. ²¹ When Joshua and his

---

ᶜ *One ancient translation* Ai; *Hebrew* Ai and Bethel.

men saw that the others had taken the city and that it was on fire, they turned around and began killing the men of Ai. [22] The Israelites in the city now came down to join the battle. So the men of Ai found themselves completely surrounded by Israelites, and they were all killed. No one got away, and no one lived through it [23] except the king of Ai. He was captured and taken to Joshua.

[24] The Israelites killed every one of the enemy in the barren country where they had chased them. Then they went back to Ai and killed everyone there. [25-26] Joshua kept his spear pointed at Ai and did not put it down until every person there had been killed. The whole population of Ai was killed that day — twelve thousand men and women. [27] The Israelites kept for themselves the livestock and goods captured in the city, as the LORD had told Joshua. [28] Joshua burned Ai and left it in ruins. It is still like that today. [29] He hanged the king of Ai from a tree and left his body there until evening. At sundown Joshua gave orders for the body to be removed, and it was thrown down at the entrance to the city gate. They covered it with a huge pile of stones, which is still there today.

The Law Is Read at Mount Ebal

[30] Then Joshua built on Mount Ebal an altar to the LORD, the God of Israel. [31] He made it according to the instructions that Moses, the LORD's servant, had given the Israelites, as it says in the Law of Moses: "an altar made of stones which have not been cut with iron tools." On it they offered burnt sacrifices to the LORD, and they also presented their fellowship offerings. [32] There, with the Israelites looking on, Joshua made on the stones [d] a copy of

the Law which Moses had written. [33] The Israelites, with their leaders, officers, and judges, as well as the foreigners among them, stood on two sides of the LORD's Covenant Box, facing the levitical priests who carried it. Half of the people stood with their backs to Mount Gerizim and the other half with their backs to Mount Ebal. The LORD's servant Moses had commanded them to do this when the time came for them to receive the blessing. [34] Joshua then read aloud the whole Law, including the blessings and the curses, just as they are written in the book of the Law. [35] Every one of the commandments of Moses was read by Joshua to the whole gathering, which included women and children, as well as the foreigners living among them.

The Gibeonites Deceive Joshua

9 The victories of Israel became known to all the kings west of the Jordan — in the hills, in the foothills, and all along the coastal plain of the Mediterranean Sea as far north as Lebanon; these were the kings of the Hittites, the Amorites, the Canaanites, the Perizzites, the Hivites, and the Jebusites. [2] They all came together and joined forces to fight against Joshua and the Israelites.

[3] But the people of Gibeon, who were Hivites, heard what Joshua had done to Jericho and Ai, [4] and they decided to deceive him. They went and got some food and loaded their donkeys with worn-out sacks and patched-up wineskins. [5] They put on ragged clothes and worn-out sandals that had been mended. The bread they took with them was dry and moldy. [6] Then they went to the camp at Gilgal and said to Joshua and the Israelites, "We have come from a distant land. We want you to make a treaty with us."

[d] the stones; or stones.
8.30-32 Dt 27.2-8 **8.31** Ex 20.25 **8.33-35** Dt 11.29; 27.11-14

[7]But the Israelites said, "Why should we make a treaty with you? Maybe you live nearby."

[8]They said to Joshua, "We are at your service."

Joshua asked them, "Who are you? Where do you come from?"

[9]Then they told him this story: "We have come from a very distant land, sir, because we have heard of the LORD your God. We have heard about everything that he did in Egypt [10]and what he did to the two Amorite kings east of the Jordan: King Sihon of Heshbon and King Og of Bashan, who lived in Ashtaroth. [11]Our leaders and all the people that live in our land told us to get some food ready for a trip and to go and meet you. We were told to put ourselves at your service and ask you to make a treaty with us. [12]Look at our bread. When we left home with it and started out to meet you, it was still warm. But look! Now it is dry and moldy. [13]When we filled these wineskins, they were new, but look! They are torn. Our clothes and sandals are worn out from the long trip."

"But look! They are torn." (9.13)

[14]The Israelites accepted some food from them, but did not consult the LORD about it. [15]Joshua made a treaty of friendship with the people of Gibeon and allowed them to live. The leaders of the community of Israel gave their solemn promise to keep the treaty.

[16]Three days after the treaty had been made, the Israelites learned that these people did indeed live nearby. [17]So the people of Israel started out and three days later arrived at the cities where these people lived: Gibeon, Chephirah, Beeroth, and Kiriath Jearim. [18]But the Israelites could not kill them, because their leaders had made a solemn promise to them in the name of the LORD, Israel's God. All the people complained to the leaders about this, [19]but they answered, "We have made our solemn promise to them in the name of the LORD God of Israel. Now we cannot harm them. [20]We must let them live because of our promise; if we don't, God will punish us. [21]Let them live, but they will have to cut wood and carry water for us." This was what the leaders suggested.

[22]Joshua ordered the people of Gibeon to be brought to him, and he asked them, "Why did you deceive us and tell us that you were from far away, when you live right here? [23]Because you did this, God has condemned you. Your people will always be slaves, cutting wood and carrying water for the sanctuary of my God."

[24]They answered, "We did it, sir, because we learned that it was really true that the LORD your God had commanded his servant Moses to give you the whole land and to kill the people living in it as you advanced. We did it because we were terrified of you; we were in fear of our lives. [25]Now we are in your power; do with us what you think is right." [26]So this is what Joshua did: he protected them and did not allow the people of Israel to kill them. [27]But at the same time he made them slaves, to cut wood and carry water for the people of Israel and for the LORD's altar. To this day they have continued to do this work

9.7 Ex 23.32; 34.12; Dt 7.2   **9.10** Nu 21.21-35

in the place where the LORD has chosen to be worshiped.

The Amorites Are Defeated

10 Adonizedek, the king of Jerusalem,[e] heard that Joshua had captured and totally destroyed Ai and had killed its king, just as he had done to Jericho and its king. He also heard that the people of Gibeon had made peace with the Israelites and were living among them. ²The people of Jerusalem were greatly alarmed at this because Gibeon was as large as any of the cities that had a king; it was larger than Ai, and its men were good fighters. ³So Adonizedek sent the following message to King Hoham of Hebron, King Piram of Jarmuth, King Japhia of Lachish, and to King Debir of Eglon: ⁴"Come and help me attack Gibeon, because its people have made peace with Joshua and the Israelites." ⁵These five Amorite kings, the kings of Jerusalem, Hebron, Jarmuth, Lachish, and Eglon, joined forces, surrounded Gibeon, and attacked it.

⁶The men of Gibeon sent word to Joshua at the camp in Gilgal: "Do not abandon us, sir! Come at once and help us! Save us! All the Amorite kings in the hill country have joined forces and have attacked us!"

⁷So Joshua and his whole army, including the best troops, started out from Gilgal. ⁸The LORD said to Joshua, "Do not be afraid of them. I have already given you the victory. Not one of them will be able to stand against you." ⁹All night Joshua and his army marched from Gilgal to Gibeon, and they made a surprise attack on the Amorites. ¹⁰The LORD made the Amorites panic at the sight of Israel's army. The Israelites slaughtered them at Gibeon and pursued them down the mountain pass at Beth Horon, keeping up the attack as far south as Azekah and Makkedah. ¹¹While the Amorites were running down the pass from the Israelite army, the LORD made large hailstones fall down on them all the way to Azekah. More were killed by the hailstones than by the Israelites.

¹²On the day that the LORD gave the men of Israel victory over the Amorites, Joshua spoke to the LORD. In the presence of the Israelites he said,

"Sun, stand still over Gibeon;
  Moon, stop over Aijalon Valley."
¹³The sun stood still and the moon did not move until the nation had conquered its enemies. This is written in The Book of Jashar. The sun stood still in the middle of the sky and did not go down for a whole day. ¹⁴Never before, and never since, has there been a day like it, when the LORD obeyed a human being. The LORD fought on Israel's side!

¹⁵After this, Joshua and his army went back to the camp at Gilgal.

Joshua Captures the Five Amorite Kings

¹⁶The five Amorite kings, however, had escaped and were hiding in the cave at Makkedah. ¹⁷Someone found them, and Joshua was told where they were hiding. ¹⁸He said, "Roll some big stones in front of the entrance to the cave. Place some guards there, ¹⁹but don't stay there yourselves. Keep on after the enemy and attack them from the rear; don't let them get to their cities! The LORD your God has given you victory over them." ²⁰Joshua and the men of Israel slaughtered them, although some managed to find safety inside their city walls and were not killed. ²¹Then all of Joshua's men came back safe to him at the camp at Makkedah.

No one in the land dared even to speak against the Israelites.

---

e JERUSALEM: *At that time it was a Jebusite city.*
10.13 2 S 1.18; Si 46.4-6

Bring those five kings out to me. (10.22)

22 Then Joshua said, "Open the entrance to the cave and bring those five kings out to me." 23 So the cave was opened, and the kings of Jerusalem, Hebron, Jarmuth, Lachish, and Eglon were brought out 24 and taken to Joshua. Joshua then called all the men of Israel to him and ordered the officers who had gone with him to come and put their feet on the necks of the kings. They did so. 25 Then Joshua said to his officers, "Don't be afraid or discouraged. Be determined and confident because this is what the LORD is going to do to all your enemies." 26 Then Joshua killed the kings and hanged them on five trees, where their bodies stayed until evening. 27 At sundown Joshua gave orders, and their bodies were taken down and thrown into the same cave where they had hidden earlier. Large stones were placed at the entrance to the cave, and they are still there.

Joshua Captures More Amorite Territory

28 Joshua attacked and captured Makkedah and its king that day. He put everyone in the city to death; no one was left alive. He did to the king of Makkedah what he had done to the king of Jericho.

29 After this, Joshua and his army went on from Makkedah to Libnah and attacked it. 30 The LORD also gave the Israelites victory over this city and its king. They spared no one, but killed every person in it. They did to the king what they had done to the king of Jericho.

31 After this, Joshua and his army went on from Libnah to Lachish, surrounded it and attacked it. 32 The LORD gave the Israelites victory over Lachish on the second day of the battle. Just as they had done at Libnah, they spared no one, but killed every person in the city. 33 King Horam of Gezer came to the aid of Lachish, but Joshua defeated him and his army and left none of them alive.

34 Next, Joshua and his army went on from Lachish to Eglon, surrounded it and attacked it. 35 They captured it the same day and put everyone there to death, just as they had done at Lachish.

36 After this, Joshua and his army went from Eglon up into the hills to Hebron, attacked it 37 and captured it. They killed the king and everyone else in the city as well as in the nearby towns. Joshua condemned the city to total destruction, just as he had done to Eglon. No one in it was left alive.

38 Then Joshua and his army turned back to Debir and attacked it. 39 He captured it, with its king and all the nearby towns. They put everyone there to death. Joshua did to Debir and its king what he had done to Hebron and to Libnah and its king.

40 Joshua conquered the whole land. He defeated the kings of the hill country, the eastern slopes, and the western foothills, as well as those of the dry country in the south. He spared no one; everyone was put to death. This was what the LORD God of Israel had commanded. 41 Joshua's campaign took him from Kadesh Barnea in the south to Gaza near the coast, including all the area of Goshen, and as far north as Gibeon. 42 Joshua conquered all these kings and their territory in one campaign because the LORD, Israel's God, was fighting for Israel. 43 After this, Joshua and his army went back to the camp at Gilgal.

Joshua Defeats Jabin and His Allies

11 When the news of Israel's victories reached King Jabin of Hazor, he sent word to King Jobab of Madon, to the kings of Shimron and Achshaph, ²and to the kings in the hill country in the north, in the Jordan Valley south of Lake Galilee, in the foothills, and on the coast near Dor. ³He also sent word to the Canaanites on both sides of the Jordan, to the Amorites, the Hittites, the Perizzites, and the Jebusites in the hill country, as well as to the Hivites who lived at the foot of Mount Hermon in the land of Mizpah. ⁴They came with all their soldiers — an army with as many men as there are grains of sand on the seashore. They also had many horses and chariots. ⁵All of these kings joined forces and came together and set up camp at Merom Brook to fight against Israel.

⁶The Lord said to Joshua, "Do not be afraid of them. By this time tomorrow I will have killed all of them for Israel. You are to cripple their horses and burn their chariots." ⁷So Joshua and all his men attacked them by surprise at Merom Brook. ⁸The Lord gave the Israelites victory over them; the Israelites attacked and pursued them as far north as Misrephoth Maim and Sidon, and as far east as the valley of Mizpah. The fight continued until none of the enemy was left alive. ⁹Joshua did to them what the Lord had commanded: he crippled their horses and burned their chariots.

¹⁰Joshua then turned back, captured Hazor and killed its king. (At that time Hazor was the most powerful of all those kingdoms.) ¹¹They put everyone there to death; no one was left alive, and the city was burned. ¹²Joshua captured all these cities and their kings, putting everyone to death, just as Moses, the Lord's servant, had commanded. ¹³However, the Israelites did not burn any of the cities built on mounds, except Hazor, which

Joshua did burn. ¹⁴The people of Israel took all the valuables and livestock from these cities and kept them for themselves. But they put every person to death; no one was left alive. ¹⁵The Lord had given his commands to his servant Moses, Moses had given them to Joshua, and Joshua obeyed them. He did everything that the Lord had commanded Moses.

The Territory Taken by Joshua

¹⁶Joshua captured all the land — the hill country and foothills, both north and south, all the area of Goshen and the dry country south of it, as well as the Jordan Valley. ¹⁷⁻¹⁸The territory extended from Mount Halak in the south near Edom, as far as Baalgad in the north, in the valley of Lebanon south of Mount Hermon. Joshua was at war with the kings of this territory for a long time, but he captured them all and put them to death. ¹⁹The only city that made peace with the people of Israel was Gibeon, where some of the Hivites lived. All the others were conquered in battle. ²⁰The Lord had made them determined to fight the Israelites, so that they would be condemned to total destruction and all be killed without mercy. This was what the Lord had commanded Moses.

²¹At this time Joshua went and destroyed the race of giants called the Anakim who lived in the hill country — in Hebron, Debir, Anab, and in all the hill country of Judah and Israel. Joshua completely destroyed them and their cities. ²²None of the Anakim were left in the land of Israel; a few, however, were left in Gaza, Gath, and Ashdod.

²³Joshua captured the whole land, as the Lord had commanded Moses. Joshua gave it to the Israelites as their own and divided it into portions, one for each tribe.

So the people rested from war.

11.20 Dt 7.16

The Kings Defeated by Moses

12 The people of Israel had already conquered and occupied the land east of the Jordan, from the Arnon Valley up the Jordan Valley and as far north as Mount Hermon. They defeated two kings. ²One was Sihon, the Amorite king who ruled at Heshbon. His kingdom included half of Gilead: from Aroer (on the edge of the Arnon Valley) and from the city in*f* the middle of that valley, as far as the Jabbok River, the border of Ammon; ³it included the Jordan Valley from Lake Galilee south to Beth Jeshimoth (east of the Dead Sea) and on toward the foot of Mount Pisgah.

⁴They also defeated King Og of Bashan, who was one of the last of the Rephaim; he ruled at Ashtaroth and Edrei. ⁵His kingdom included Mount Hermon, Salecah, and all of Bashan as far as the boundaries of Geshur and Maacah, as well as half of Gilead, as far as the territory of King Sihon of Heshbon.

⁶These two kings were defeated by Moses and the people of Israel. Moses, the LORD's servant, gave their land to the tribes of Reuben and Gad and to half the tribe of Manasseh, to be their possession.

The Kings Defeated by Joshua

⁷Joshua and the people of Israel defeated all the kings in the territory west of the Jordan, from Baalgad in the valley of Lebanon to Mount Halak in the south near Edom. Joshua divided this land among the tribes and gave it to them as a permanent possession. ⁸This portion included the hill country, the western foothills, the Jordan Valley and its foothills, the eastern slopes, and the

dry country in the south. This land had been the home of the Hittites, the Amorites, the Canaanites, the Perizzites, the Hivites, and the Jebusites. ⁹The people of Israel defeated the kings of the following cities: Jericho, Ai (near Bethel), ¹⁰Jerusalem, Hebron, ¹¹Jarmuth, Lachish, ¹²Eglon, Gezer, ¹³Debir, Geder, ¹⁴Hormah, Arad, ¹⁵Libnah, Adullam, ¹⁶Makkedah, Bethel, ¹⁷Tappuah, Hepher, ¹⁸Aphek, Lasharon, ¹⁹Madon, Hazor, ²⁰Shimron Meron, Achshaph, ²¹Taanach, Megiddo, ²²Kedesh, Jokneam (in Carmel), ²³Dor (on the coast), Goiim (in Galilee*g*), ²⁴and Tirzah — thirty-one kings in all.

The Land Still to Be Taken

13 Joshua was now very old. The LORD said to him, "You are very old, but there is still much land to be taken: ²all the territory of Philistia and Geshur, ³as well as all the territory of the Avvim to the south. (The land from the stream Shihor, at the Egyptian border, as far north as the border of Ekron was considered Canaanite; the kings of the Philistines lived at Gaza, Ashdod, Ashkelon, Gath, and Ekron.) ⁴There is still all the Canaanite country, and Mearah (which belonged to the Sidonians), as far as Aphek, at the Amorite border; ⁵the land of the Gebalites; all of Lebanon to the east, from Baalgad, which is south of Mount Hermon, to Hamath Pass. ⁶This includes all the territory of the Sidonians, who live in the hill country between the Lebanon Mountains and Misrephoth Maim. I will drive all these peoples out as the people of Israel advance. You must divide the land among the Israelites, just as I have commanded you to do. ⁷Now then, divide this land among the other nine tribes and half of the tribe of

f Probable text (see 13.16; Dt 2.36) the city in; *Hebrew does not have these words.*
g One ancient translation Galilee; *Hebrew* Gilgal.
12.1-5 Nu 21.21-35; Dt 2.26—3.11　**12.6** Nu 32.33; Dt 3.12　**13.6** Nu 33.54

Manasseh, for them to possess as their own."

The Division of the Territory East of the Jordan

[8] The tribes of Reuben and Gad and the other half of the tribe of Manasseh had already received the land that Moses, the LORD's servant, had given them; it was on the east side of the Jordan River. [9] Their territory extended to Aroer (on the edge of the Arnon Valley) and the city in the middle of that valley and included all of the plateau from Medeba to Dibon. [10] It went as far as the border of Ammon and included all the cities that had been ruled by the Amorite king Sihon, who had ruled at Heshbon. [11] It included Gilead, the regions of Geshur and Maacah, all of Mount Hermon, and all of Bashan as far as Salecah. [12] It included the kingdom of Og, the last of the Rephaim, who had ruled at Ashtaroth and Edrei. Moses had defeated these people and driven them out. [13] However, the Israelites did not drive out the people of Geshur and Maacah; they still live in Israel.

[14] Moses had given no land to the tribe of Levi. As the LORD had told Moses, they were to receive as their possession a share of the sacrifices burned on the altar to the LORD God of Israel.

The Territory Assigned to Reuben

[15] Moses had given a part of the land to the families of the tribe of Reuben as their possession. [16] Their territory extended to Aroer (on the edge of the Arnon Valley) and the city in the middle of that valley and included all the plateau around Medeba. [17] It included Heshbon and all the cities on the plateau: Dibon, Bamoth Baal, Beth Baalmeon, [18] Jahaz, Kedemoth, Mephaath, [19] Kiriathaim, Sibmah, Zereth Shahar on the hill in the valley, [20] Bethpeor, the slopes of Mount Pisgah, and Beth Jeshimoth. [21] It included all the cities of the plateau and the whole kingdom of the Amorite king Sihon, who had ruled at Heshbon. Moses defeated him, as well as the rulers of Midian: Evi, Rekem, Zur, Hur, and Reba. All of them had ruled the land for King Sihon. [22] Among those whom the people of Israel killed was the fortune teller Balaam son of Beor. [23] The Jordan was the western border of the tribe of Reuben. These were the cities and towns given to the families of the tribe of Reuben as their possession.

The Territory Assigned to Gad

[24] Moses had also given a part of the land to the families of the tribe of Gad as their possession. [25] Their territory included Jazer and all the cities of Gilead, half the land of Ammon as far as Aroer, which is east of Rabbah; [26] their land extended from Heshbon to Ramath Mizpeh and Betonim, from Mahanaim to the border of Lodebar. [27] In the Jordan Valley it included Beth Haram, Bethnimrah, Sukkoth, and Zaphon, the rest of the kingdom of King Sihon of Heshbon. Their western border was the Jordan River as far north as Lake Galilee. [28] These were the cities and towns given to the families of the tribe of Gad as their possession.

The Territory Assigned to East Manasseh

[29] Moses had given a part of the land to the families of half the tribe of Manasseh as their possession. [30] Their territory extended to Mahanaim and included all of Bashan — the whole kingdom of Og, the king of Bashan, as well as all sixty of the villages of Jair in Bashan. [31] It included half of Gilead, as well as Ashtaroth and Edrei, the capital cities of Og's kingdom in Bashan. All

13.8 Nu 32.33; Dt 3.12   **13.14** Dt 18.1

DIVISION OF CANAAN

Miles 0 — 40

Kms 0 — 40

Sidon

SIDONIANS

LEBANON MTS.

HITTITES

ARAMEANS

Damascus

MT. HERMON

Tyre

DAN

Dan (Laish)

MEDITERRANEAN

ASHER

NAPHTALI

MANASSEH (EAST)

Hazor

Ashtaroth

SEA

Lake Galilee

MT. CARMEL

ZEBULUN

MT. TABOR

Endor

Shunem

ISSACHAR

Dor Megiddo

Jezreel

MT. GILBOA

Ramoth

MANASSEH (WEST)

Jordan River

Jabesh

Shechem

GAD

Joppa

Shiloh

EPHRAIM

Rabbah

AMMONITES

Bethel

Gilgal

Ai

BENJAMIN

Jericho

Gibeah

Ashdod

Jerusalem

Bethpeor

Libnah

Bethlehem

REUBEN

Ashkelon

PHILISTINES

Gath?

Lachish

Gaza

JUDAH

Hebron

Dead

Gath?

Engedi

Sea

Beersheba

Hormah

MOABITES

SIMEON

The Negev

EDOMITES

© United Bible Societies, 1976

this was given to half the families descended from Machir son of Manasseh.

³²This is how Moses divided the land east of Jericho and the Jordan when he was in the plains of Moab. ³³But Moses did not assign any land to the tribe of Levi. He told them that their possession was to be a share of the offerings to the LORD God of Israel.

The Division of the Territory West of the Jordan

14 What follows is an account of how the land of Canaan west of the Jordan was divided among the people of Israel. Eleazar the priest, Joshua son of Nun, and the leaders of the families of the Israelite tribes divided it among the population. ²As the LORD had commanded Moses, the territories of the nine and one-half tribes west of the Jordan were determined by drawing lots.ʰ ³⁻⁴Moses had already assigned the land east of the Jordan to the other two and one-half tribes. (The descendants of Joseph were divided into two tribes: Manasseh and Ephraim.) However, Moses gave the Levites no portion of the territory. Instead, they received cities to live in, with fields for their cattle and flocks. ⁵The people of Israel divided the land as the LORD had commanded Moses.

Hebron Is Given to Caleb

⁶One day some people from the tribe of Judah came to Joshua at Gilgal. One of them, Caleb son of Jephunneh the Kenizzite, said to him, "You know what the LORD said in Kadesh Barnea about you and me to Moses, the man of God. ⁷I was forty years old when the LORD's servant Moses sent me from Kadesh Barnea to spy out this land. I brought an honest report back to him. ⁸The men

who went with me, however, made our people afraid. But I faithfully obeyed the LORD my God. ⁹Because I did, Moses promised me that my children and I would certainly receive as our possession the land which I walked over. ¹⁰But now, look. It has been forty-five years since the LORD said that to Moses. That was when Israel was going through the desert, and the LORD, as he promised, has kept me alive ever since. Look at me! I am eighty-five years old ¹¹and am just as strong today as I was when Moses sent me out. I am still strong enough for war or for anything else. ¹²Now then, give me the hill country that the LORD promised me on that day when my men and I reported. We told you then that the race of giants called the Anakim were there in large walled cities. Maybe the LORD will be with me, and I will drive them out, just as the LORD said."

¹³Joshua blessed Caleb son of Jephunneh and gave him the city of Hebron as his possession. ¹⁴Hebron still belongs to the descendants of Caleb son of Jephunneh the Kenizzite, because he faithfully obeyed the LORD, the God of Israel. ¹⁵Before this, Hebron was called the city of Arba. (Arba had been the greatest of the Anakim.)

There was now peace in the land.

The Territory Assigned to Judah

15 The families of the tribe of Judah received a part of the land described as follows:

The land reached south to the southernmost point of the wilderness of Zin, at the border of Edom. ²This southern border ran from the south end of the Dead Sea, ³went southward from the Akrabbim Pass and on to Zin. It ran south of Kadesh Barnea, past Hezron

---

ʰ DRAWING LOTS: *This was usually done by using specially marked stones to determine God's will.*

13.33 Nu 18.20; Dt 18.2   **14.2** Nu 26.52-56; 34.13   **14.3, 4** Nu 32.33; 34.14, 15; Dt 3.12-17   **14.6** Nu 14.30   **14.7** Nu 13.1-30   **14.9** Nu 14.24

and up to Addar, turned toward Karka, [4] went on to Azmon, and followed the stream on the border of Egypt to the Mediterranean Sea, where the border ended. That was the southern border of Judah.

[5] The eastern border was the Dead Sea, all the way up to the inlet where the Jordan empties into it.

The northern border began there, [6] extended up to Beth Hoglah, and went north of the ridge overlooking the Jordan Valley. Then it went up to the Stone of Bohan (Bohan was a son of Reuben), [7] from Trouble Valley up to Debir, and then turned north toward Gilgal, which faces Adummim Pass on the south side of the valley. It then went on to the springs of Enshemesh, out to Enrogel, [8] and up through Hinnom Valley on the south side of the hill where the Jebusite city of Jerusalem was located. The border then proceeded up to the top of the hill on the west side of Hinnom Valley, at the northern end of Rephaim Valley. [9] From there it went to the Springs of Nephtoah and out to the cities near Mount Ephron. There it turned toward Baalah (or Kiriath Jearim), [10] where it circled west of Baalah toward the hill country of Edom, went on the north side of Mount Jearim (or Chesalon), down to Beth Shemesh, and on past Timnah. [11] The border then went out to the hill north of Ekron, turned toward Shikkeron, past Mount Baalah, and on to Jamnia. It ended at the Mediterranean Sea, [12] which formed the western border.

Within these borders lived the people of the families of Judah.

Caleb Conquers Hebron and Debir
(*Judges 1.11-15*)

[13] As the LORD commanded Joshua, part of the territory of Judah was given to Caleb son of Jephunneh, from the tribe of Judah. He received Hebron, the city belonging to Arba, father of Anak. [14] Caleb drove the descendants of Anak out of the city — the clans of Sheshai, Ahiman, and Talmai. [15] From there he went to attack the people living in Debir. (This city used to be called Kiriath Sepher.) [16] Caleb said, "I will give my daughter Achsah in marriage to the man who succeeds in capturing Kiriath Sepher." [17] Othniel, the son of Caleb's brother Kenaz, captured the city, so Caleb gave him his daughter Achsah in marriage. [18] On the wedding day Othniel urged her [i] to ask her father for a field. She got down from her donkey, and Caleb asked her what she wanted. [19] She answered, "I want some water holes. The land you have given me is in the dry country." So Caleb gave her the upper and lower springs.

The Cities of Judah

[20] This is the land that the families of the tribe of Judah received as their possession. [21] The cities farthest south that belonged to them, those that were near the border of Edom, were Kabzeel, Eder, Jagur, [22] Kinah, Dimonah, Adadah, [23] Kedesh, Hazor, Ithnan, [24] Ziph, Telem, Bealoth, [25] Hazor Hadattah, Kerioth Hezron (or Hazor), [26] Amam, Shema, Moladah, [27] Hazar Gaddah, Heshmon, Bethpelet, [28] Hazar Shual, Beersheba, Biziothiah, [29] Baalah, Iim, Ezem, [30] Eltolad, Chesil, Hormah, [31] Ziklag, Madmannah, Sansannah, [32] Lebaoth, Shilhim, Ain, and Rimmon: twenty-nine cities in all, along with the towns around them.

[33] The cities in the foothills were Eshtaol, Zorah, Ashnah, [34] Zanoah, Engannim, Tappuah, Enam, [35] Jarmuth, Adullam, Socoh, Azekah, [36] Shaaraim,

---

[i] *Probable text (see Jg 1.14)* Othniel urged her; *Hebrew* she urged Othniel.

15.13, 14 Jg 1.20

Adithaim, Gederah, and Gederothaim: fourteen cities, along with the towns around them.

37 There were also Zenan, Hadashah, Migdalgad, 38 Dilean, Mizpah, Joktheel, 39 Lachish, Bozkath, Eglon, 40 Cabbon, Lahmam, Chitlish, 41 Gederoth, Bethdagon, Naamah, and Makkedah: sixteen cities, along with the towns around them.

42 There were also Libnah, Ether, Ashan, 43 Iphtah, Ashnah, Nezib, 44 Keilah, Achzib, and Mareshah: nine cities, along with the towns around them.

45 There was Ekron with its towns and villages, 46 and all the cities and towns near Ashdod, from Ekron to the Mediterranean Sea.

47 There were Ashdod and Gaza, with their towns and villages, reaching to the stream on the border of Egypt and the coast of the Mediterranean Sea.

48 In the hill country there were Shamir, Jattir, Socoh, 49 Dannah, Kiriath Sepher (or Debir), 50 Anab, Eshtemoa, Anim, 51 Goshen, Holon, and Giloh: eleven cities, along with the towns around them.

52 There were Arab, Dumah, Eshan, 53 Janim, Beth Tappuah, Aphekah, 54 Humtah, Hebron, and Zior: nine cities, along with the towns around them.

55 There were Maon, Carmel, Ziph, Juttah, 56 Jezreel, Jokdeam, Zanoah, 57 Kain, Gibeah, and Timnah: ten cities, along with the towns around them.

58 There were Halhul, Bethzur, Gedor, 59 Maarath, Bethanoth, and Eltekon: six cities, along with the towns around them.

60 There were Kiriath Baal (or Kiriath Jearim) and Rabbah: two cities, along with the towns around them.

61 In the desert there were Beth Arabah, Middin, Secacah, 62 Nibshan, Salt City, and Engedi: six cities, along with the towns around them.

63 But the people of Judah were not able to drive out the Jebusites, who lived in Jerusalem. The Jebusites still live there with the people of Judah.

The Territory Assigned to Ephraim and West Manasseh

16 The southern boundary of the land assigned to the descendants of Joseph started from the Jordan near Jericho, at a point east of the springs of Jericho, and went into the desert. It went from Jericho up into the hill country as far as Bethel. 2 From Bethel it went to Luz, passing on to Ataroth Addar, where the Archites lived. 3 It then went west to the area of the Japhletites, as far as the area of Lower Beth Horon. It went on from there to Gezer and ended at the Mediterranean Sea.

4 The descendants of Joseph, the tribes of Ephraim and West Manasseh, received this land as their possession.

Ephraim

5 This was the territory of the Ephraimite families: their border ran from Ataroth Addar eastward to Upper Beth Horon, 6 and from there to the Mediterranean Sea. Michmethath was on their north. East of there the border bent toward Taanath Shiloh and went past it on the east to Janoah. 7 Then it went down from Janoah to Ataroth and Naarah, reaching Jericho and ending at the Jordan. 8 The border went west from Tappuah to the stream Kanah and ended at the Mediterranean Sea. This was the land given to the families of the tribe of Ephraim as their possession, 9 along with some towns and villages that were within the borders of Manasseh, but given to the Ephraimites. 10 But they did not drive out the Canaanites who lived in Gezer, so the Canaanites have lived among the Ephraimites to this day, but they have been forced to work as slaves.

15.63 Jg 1.21; 2 S 5.6; 1 Ch 11.4   **16.10** Jg 1.29

West Manasseh

17 A part of the land west of the Jordan was assigned to some of the families descended from Joseph's older son Manasseh. Machir, the father of Gilead, was Manasseh's oldest son and a military hero, so Gilead and Bashan, east of the Jordan, were assigned to him. ² Land west of the Jordan was assigned to the rest of the families of Manasseh: Abiezer, Helek, Asriel, Shechem, Hepher, and Shemida. These were male descendants of Manasseh son of Joseph, and they were heads of families. ³ Zelophehad, son of Hepher, son of Gilead, son of Machir, son of Manasseh, did not have any sons, but only daughters. Their names were Mahlah, Noah, Hoglah, Milcah, and Tirzah. ⁴ They went to Eleazar the priest and to Joshua son of Nun and to the leaders, and said, "The LORD commanded Moses to give us, as well as our male relatives, a part of the land to possess." So, as the LORD had commanded, they were given land along with their male relatives. ⁵ This is why Manasseh received ten shares in addition to Gilead and Bashan on the east side of the Jordan, ⁶ since his female descendants as well as his male descendants were assigned land. The land of Gilead was assigned to the rest of the descendants of Manasseh.

⁷ The territory of Manasseh reached from Asher to Michmethath, east of Shechem. The border then went south to include the people of Entappuah. ⁸ The land around Tappuah belonged to Manasseh, but the town of Tappuah, on the border, belonged to the descendants of Ephraim. ⁹ The border then went down to the stream Kanah. The cities south of the stream belonged to Ephraim, even though they were in the territory of Manasseh. The border of Manasseh proceeded along the north side of the stream and ended at the Mediterranean Sea. ¹⁰ Ephraim was to the south, and Manasseh was to the north, with the Mediterranean Sea as their western border. Asher was to the northwest, and Issachar to the northeast. ¹¹ Within the territories of Issachar and Asher, Manasseh possessed Beth Shan and Ibleam, along with their surrounding towns, as well as Dor (the one on the coast),ʲ Endor, Taanach, Megiddo, and their surrounding towns. ¹² The people of Manasseh, however, were not able to drive out the people living in those cities, so the Canaanites continued to live there. ¹³ Even when the Israelites became stronger, they did not drive out all the Canaanites, but they did force them to work for them.

Ephraim and West Manasseh Request More Land

¹⁴ The descendants of Joseph said to Joshua, "Why have you given us only one part of the land to possess as our own? There are very many of us because the LORD has blessed us."

¹⁵ Joshua answered, "If there are so many of you and the hill country of Ephraim is too small for you, then go into the forests and clear ground for yourselves in the land of the Perizzites and the Rephaim."

¹⁶ They replied, "The hill country is not big enough for us, but the Canaanites in the plains have iron chariots, both those who live in Beth Shan and its surrounding towns and those who live in Jezreel Valley."

¹⁷ Joshua said to the tribes of Ephraim and West Manasseh, "There are indeed many of you, and you are very powerful. You shall have more than one share. ¹⁸ The hill country will be yours. Even though it is a forest, you will clear it and take possession of it

---

ʲ *Probable text* Dor (the one on the coast); *Hebrew unclear.*
17.4 Nu 27.1-7 **17.12, 13** Jg 1.27, 28

Go all over the land and map it out. (18.8)

from one end to the other. As for the Canaanites, you will drive them out, even though they do have iron chariots and are a strong people."

The Division of the Rest of the Land

18 After they had conquered the land, the entire community of Israel assembled at Shiloh and set up the Tent of the LORD's presence. ² There were still seven tribes of the people of Israel who had not yet been assigned their share of the land. ³ So Joshua said to the people of Israel, "How long are you going to wait before you go in and take the land that the LORD, the God of your ancestors, has given you? ⁴ Let me have three men from each tribe. I will send them out over the whole country to map out the territory that they would like to have as their possession. Then they are to come back to me. ⁵ The land will be divided among them in seven parts; Judah will stay in its territory in the south, and Joseph in its territory in the north. ⁶ Write down a description of these seven divisions and bring it to me. Then I will draw lots[k] to consult the LORD our God for you. ⁷ The Levites, however, will not

receive a share of the land with the rest of you, because their share is to serve as the LORD's priests. And of course, the tribes of Gad, Reuben, and East Manasseh have already received their land east of the Jordan, which Moses, the LORD's servant, gave to them."

⁸ The men went on their way to map out the land after Joshua had given them these instructions: "Go all over the land and map it out, and come back to me. And then here in Shiloh I will consult the LORD for you by drawing lots." ⁹ So the men went all over the land and set down in writing how they divided it into seven parts, making a list of the towns. Then they went back to Joshua in the camp at Shiloh. ¹⁰ Joshua drew lots to consult the LORD for them, and assigned each of the remaining tribes of Israel a certain part of the land.

The Territory Assigned to Benjamin

¹¹ The territory belonging to the families of the tribe of Benjamin was the first to be assigned. Their land lay between the tribes of Judah and Joseph. ¹² On the north their border began at the Jordan and then went up the slope

[k] DRAW LOTS: See 14.2.

north of Jericho and westward through the hill country as far as the desert of Bethaven. [13] The border then went to the slope on the south side of Luz (also called Bethel), then down to Ataroth Addar, on the mountain south of Lower Beth Horon. [14] The border then went in another direction, turning south from the western side of this mountain and going to Kiriath Baal (or Kiriath Jearim), which belongs to the tribe of Judah. This was the western border. [15] The southern border started on the edge of Kiriath Jearim and went[*l*] to the Springs of Nephtoah. [16] It then went down to the foot of the mountain that overlooks Hinnom Valley, at the north end of Rephaim Valley. It then went south through Hinnom Valley, south of the Jebusite ridge, toward Enrogel. [17] It then turned north to Enshemesh and then on to Geliloth, opposite Adummim Pass. The border then went down to the Stone of Bohan (Bohan was a son of Reuben) [18] and passed north of the ridge overlooking the Jordan Valley. It then went down into the valley, [19] passing north of the ridge of Beth Hoglah, and ended at the northern inlet on the Dead Sea, where the Jordan River empties into it. This was the southern border. [20] The Jordan was the eastern border. These were the borders of the land which the families of the tribe of Benjamin received as their possession.

[21] The cities belonging to the families of the tribe of Benjamin were Jericho, Beth Hoglah, Emek Keziz, [22] Beth Arabah, Zemaraim, Bethel, [23] Avvim, Parah, Ophrah, [24] Chepharammoni, Ophni, and Geba: twelve cities, along with the towns around them. [25] There were also Gibeon, Ramah, Beeroth, [26] Mizpah, Chephirah, Mozah, [27] Rekem, Irpeel, Taralah, [28] Zela, Haeleph, Jebus (or Jerusalem), Gibeah, and Kiriath Jearim: fourteen cities, along with the towns around them. This is the land

which the families of the tribe of Benjamin received as their possession.

The Territory Assigned to Simeon

19 The second assignment made was for the families of the tribe of Simeon. Its territory extended into the land assigned to the tribe of Judah. [2] It included Beersheba, Sheba, Moladah, [3] Hazar Shual, Balah, Ezem, [4] Eltolad, Bethul, Hormah, [5] Ziklag, Beth Marcaboth, Hazar Susah, [6] Beth Lebaoth, and Sharuhen: thirteen cities, along with the towns around them.

[7] There were also Ain, Rimmon, Ether, and Ashan: four cities, along with the towns around them. [8] This included all the towns around these cities as far as Baalath Beer (or Ramah), in the south. This was the land which the families of the tribe of Simeon received as their possession. [9] Since Judah's assignment was larger than was needed, part of its territory was given to the tribe of Simeon.

The Territory Assigned to Zebulun

[10] The third assignment made was for the families of the tribe of Zebulun. The land which they received reached as far as Sarid. [11] From there the border went west to Mareal, touching Dabbesheth and the stream east of Jokneam. [12] On the other side of Sarid it went east to the border of Chisloth Tabor, then to Daberath and up to Japhia. [13] It continued east from there to Gath Hepher and Ethkazin, turning in the direction of Neah on the way to Rimmon. [14] On the north the border turned toward Hannathon, ending at Iphtahel Valley. [15] It included Kattath, Nahalal, Shimron, Idalah, and Bethlehem: twelve cities, along with the towns around them. [16] These cities and their towns were in

---

l Probable text and went; *Hebrew* and went westward.
19.2-8 1 Ch 4.28-33

the land which the families of the tribe of Zebulun received as their possession.

The Territory Assigned to Issachar

17 The fourth assignment made was for the families of the tribe of Issachar. 18 Its area included Jezreel, Chesulloth, Shunem, 19 Hapharaim, Shion, Anaharath, 20 Rabbith, Kishion, Ebez, 21 Remeth, Engannim, Enhaddah, and Bethpazzez. 22 The border also touched Tabor, Shahazumah, and Beth Shemesh, ending at the Jordan. It included sixteen cities along with the towns around them. 23 These cities and their towns were in the land which the families of the tribe of Issachar received as their possession.

The Territory Assigned to Asher

24 The fifth assignment made was for the families of the tribe of Asher. 25 Its area included Helkath, Hali, Beten, Achshaph, 26 Allam Melech, Amad, and Mishal. On the west it touched Carmel and Shihor Libnath. 27 As it turned east, the border went to Bethdagon, touching Zebulun and Iphtahel Valley on the way north to Bethemek and Neiel. It continued north to Cabul, 28 Ebron, Rehob, Hammon, and Kanah, as far as Sidon. 29 The border then turned to Ramah, reaching the fortified city of Tyre; then it turned to Hosah and ended at the Mediterranean Sea. It included Mahalab, Achzib, 30 Ummah, Aphek, and Rehob: twenty-two cities, along with the towns around them. 31 These cities and their towns were in the land which the families of the tribe of Asher received as their possession.

The Territory Assigned to Naphtali

32 The sixth assignment made was for the families of the tribe of Naphtali.

33 Its border went from Heleph to the oak in Zaanannim, on to Adaminekeb and to Jamnia, as far as Lakkum, and ended at the Jordan. 34 There the border turned west to Aznoth Tabor, from there to Hukkok, touching Zebulun on the south, Asher on the west, and the Jordan*m* on the east. 35 The fortified cities were Ziddim, Zer, Hammath, Rakkath, Chinnereth, 36 Adamah, Ramah, Hazor, 37 Kedesh, Edrei, Enhazor, 38 Yiron, Migdalel, Horem, Bethanath, and Beth Shemesh: nineteen cities, along with the towns around them. 39 These cities and their towns were in the land which the families of the tribe of Naphtali received as their possession.

The Territory Assigned to Dan

40 The seventh assignment made was for the families of the tribe of Dan. 41 Its area included Zorah, Eshtaol, Irshemesh, 42 Shaalbim, Aijalon, Ithlah, 43 Elon, Timnah, Ekron, 44 Eltekeh, Gibbethon, Baalath, 45 Jehud, Beneberak, Gathrimmon, 46 Mejarkon, and Rakkon, as well as the territory around Joppa. 47 When the people of Dan lost their land, they went to Laish and attacked it. They captured it, killed its people, and claimed it for themselves. They settled there and changed the name of the city from Laish to Dan, naming it after their ancestor Dan. 48 These cities and their towns were in the land which the families of the tribe of Dan received as their possession.

The Final Assignment of the Land

49 When the people of Israel finished dividing up the land, they gave Joshua son of Nun a part of the land as his own. 50 As the LORD had commanded, they gave him the city he asked for: Timnath Serah, in the hill country of Ephraim. He rebuilt the city and settled there. 51 Eleazar the priest, Joshua son of

---

m One ancient translation the Jordan; *Hebrew* Judah at the Jordan.
19.47 Jg 18.27-29

Nun, and the leaders of the families of the tribes of Israel assigned these parts of the land by drawing lots[n] to consult the LORD at Shiloh, at the entrance of the Tent of the LORD's presence. In this way they finished dividing the land.

The Cities of Refuge

20 Then the LORD told Joshua [2]to say to the people of Israel, "Choose the cities of refuge that I had Moses tell you about. [3]If any of you accidentally kills someone, you can go there and escape the one who is looking for revenge. [4]You can run away to one of these cities, go to the place of judgment at the entrance to the city, and explain to the leaders what happened. Then they will let you into the city and give you a place to live in, so that you can stay there. [5]If the one looking for revenge follows you there, the people of the city must not hand you over to that one. They must protect you because you killed the person accidentally and not out of anger. [6]You may stay in the city until you have received a public trial and until the death of the man who is then the High Priest. Then you may go back home to your own town, from which you had run away."

[7]So, on the west side of the Jordan they set aside Kedesh in Galilee, in the hill country of Naphtali; Shechem, in the hill country of Ephraim; and Hebron, in the hill country of Judah. [8]East of the Jordan, on the desert plateau east of Jericho, they chose Bezer in the territory of Reuben; Ramoth in Gilead, in the territory of Gad; and Golan in Bashan, in the territory of Manasseh. [9]These were the cities of refuge chosen for all the people of Israel and for any foreigner living among them. Any who killed a person accidentally could find protection there from the one looking

for revenge; they could not be killed unless they had first received a public trial.

The Cities of the Levites

21 The leaders of the Levite families went to Eleazar the priest, Joshua son of Nun, and to the heads of the families of all the tribes of Israel. [2]There at Shiloh in the land of Canaan they said to them, "The LORD commanded through Moses that we were to be given cities to live in, as well as pasture land around them for our livestock." [3]So in accordance with the LORD's command the people of Israel gave the Levites certain cities and pasture lands out of their own territories.

[4]The families of the Levite clan of Kohath were the first to be assigned cities. The families who were descended from Aaron the priest were assigned thirteen cities from the territories of Judah, Simeon, and Benjamin. [5]The rest of the clan of Kohath was assigned ten cities from the territories of Ephraim, Dan, and West Manasseh.

[6]The clan of Gershon was assigned thirteen cities from the territories of Issachar, Asher, Naphtali, and East Manasseh.

[7]The families of the clan of Merari were assigned twelve cities from the territories of Reuben, Gad, and Zebulun.

[8]By drawing lots,[n] the people of Israel assigned these cities and their pasture lands to the Levites, as the LORD had commanded through Moses.

[9]These are the names of the cities from the territories of Judah and Simeon which were given [10]to the descendants of Aaron who were of the clan of Kohath, which was descended from Levi. Their assignment was the first to be made. [11]They were given the city of Arba (Arba was Anak's father), now called Hebron, in the hill country of

---

[n] DRAWING LOTS: *See 14.2.*
20.1-9 Nu 35.9-34; Dt 4.41-43; 19.1-13   **21.2** Nu 35.1-8

Judah, along with the pasture land surrounding it. 12 However, the fields of the city, as well as its towns, had already been given to Caleb son of Jephunneh as his possession.

13 In addition to Hebron (one of the cities of refuge), the following cities were assigned to the descendants of Aaron the priest: Libnah, 14 Jattir, Eshtemoa, 15 Holon, Debir, 16 Ain, Juttah, and Beth Shemesh, with their pasture lands: nine cities from the tribes of Judah and Simeon. 17 From the territory of Benjamin they were given four cities: Gibeon, Geba, 18 Anathoth, and Almon, with their pasture lands. 19 Thirteen cities in all, with their pasture lands, were given to the priests, the descendants of Aaron.

20 The other families of the Levite clan of Kohath were assigned some cities from the territory of Ephraim. 21 They were given four cities: Shechem and its pasture lands in the hill country of Ephraim (one of the cities of refuge), Gezer, 22 Kibzaim, and Beth Horon, with their pasture lands. 23 From the territory of Dan they were given four cities: Eltekeh, Gibbethon, 24 Aijalon, and Gathrimmon, with their pasture lands. 25 From the territory of West Manasseh they were given two cities: Taanach and Gathrimmon, with their pasture lands. 26 These families of the clan of Kohath received ten cities in all, with their pasture lands.

27 Another group of Levites, the clan of Gershon, received from the territory of East Manasseh two cities: Golan in Bashan (one of the cities of refuge) and Beeshterah, with their pasture lands. 28 From the territory of Issachar they received four cities: Kishion, Daberath, 29 Jarmuth, and Engannim, with their pasture lands. 30 From the territory of Asher they received four cities: Mishal, Abdon, 31 Helkath, and Rehob, with their pasture lands. 32 From the territory of Naphtali they received three cit-

ies: Kedesh in Galilee, with its pasture lands (one of the cities of refuge), Hammoth Dor, and Kartan, with their pasture lands. 33 The various families of the clan of Gershon received a total of thirteen cities with their pasture lands.

34 The rest of the Levites, the clan of Merari, received from the territory of Zebulun four cities: Jokneam, Kartah, 35 Dimnah, and Nahalal, with their pasture lands. 36 From the territory of Reuben they received four cities: Bezer, Jahaz, 37 Kedemoth, and Mephaath, with their pasture lands. 38 From the tribe of Gad they received four cities: Ramoth in Gilead, with its pasture lands (one of the cities of refuge), Mahanaim, 39 Heshbon, and Jazer, with their pasture lands. 40 So the clan of Merari was assigned a total of twelve cities.

41-42 From the land that the people of Israel possessed, a total of forty-eight cities, with the pasture lands around them, was given to the Levites.

Israel Takes Possession of the Land

43 So the LORD gave to Israel all the land that he had solemnly promised their ancestors he would give them. When they had taken possession of it, they settled down there. 44 The LORD gave them peace throughout the land, just as he had promised their ancestors. Not one of all their enemies had been able to stand against them, because the LORD gave the Israelites the victory over all their enemies. 45 The LORD kept every one of the promises that he had made to the people of Israel.

Joshua Sends the Eastern Tribes Home

22 Then Joshua called together the people of the tribes of Reuben, Gad, and East Manasseh. 2 He said to them, "You have done everything that Moses the LORD's servant ordered you to do, and you have obeyed all my commands. 3 All this time you have

---

22.2 Nu 32.20-32; Js 1.12-15

never once deserted the other Israelites. You have been careful to obey the commands of the LORD your God. ⁴Now, as he promised, the LORD your God has given the other Israelites peace. So go back home to the land which you claimed for your own, the land on the east side of the Jordan, that Moses, the LORD's servant, gave you. ⁵Make sure you obey the law that Moses commanded you: love the LORD your God, do his will, obey his commandments, be faithful to him, and serve him with all your heart and soul." ⁶⁻⁸Joshua sent them home with his blessing and with these words: "You are going back home very rich, with a lot of livestock, silver, gold, bronze, iron, and many clothes. Share with your fellow tribesmen what you took from your enemies." Then they left for home.

Moses had given land east of the Jordan to one half of the tribe of Manasseh, but to the other half Joshua had given land west of the Jordan, along with the other tribes.

⁹So the people of the tribes of Reuben, Gad, and East Manasseh went back home. They left the rest of the people of Israel at Shiloh in the land of Canaan and started out for their own land, the land of Gilead, which they had taken as the LORD had commanded them through Moses.

The Altar by the Jordan

¹⁰When the tribes of Reuben, Gad, and East Manasseh arrived at Geliloth, still on the west side⁰ of the Jordan, they built a large, impressive altar there by the river. ¹¹The rest of the people of Israel were told, "Listen! The people of the tribes of Reuben, Gad, and East Manasseh have built an altar at Geliloth, on our side of the Jordan!" ¹²When the people of Israel heard this, the whole community came together at Shiloh to go to war against the eastern tribes.

¹³Then the people of Israel sent Phinehas, the son of Eleazar the priest, to the people of the tribes of Reuben, Gad, and East Manasseh in the land of Gilead. ¹⁴Ten leading men went with Phinehas, one from each of the western tribes and each one the head of a family among the clans. ¹⁵They came to the land of Gilead, to the people of Reuben, Gad, and East Manasseh, ¹⁶and speaking for the whole community of the LORD, they said to them, "Why have you done this evil thing against the God of Israel? You have rebelled against the LORD by building this altar for yourselves! You are no longer following him! ¹⁷Remember our sin at Peor, when the LORD punished his own people with an epidemic? We are still suffering because of that. Wasn't that sin enough? ¹⁸Are you going to refuse to follow him now? If you rebel against the LORD today, he will be angry with everyone in Israel tomorrow. ¹⁹Now then, if your land is not fit to worship in, come over into the LORD's land, where his Tent is. Claim some land among us. But don't rebel against the LORD or make rebels out of us by building an altar in addition to the altar of the LORD our God. ²⁰Remember how Achan son of Zerah refused to obey the command about the things condemned to destruction; the whole community of Israel was punished for that. Achan was not the only one who died because of his sin."

²¹The people of the tribes of Reuben, Gad, and East Manasseh answered the heads of the families of the western tribes: ²²"The Mighty One is God! He is the LORD! The Mighty One is God! He is the LORD! He knows why we did this, and we want you to know too! If we rebelled and did not keep faith with the

---

⁰ still on the west side; *or* on the east side.

22.16 Dt 12.13, 14   **22.17** Nu 25.1-9   **22.20** Js 7.1-26

LORD, do not let us live any longer! 23 If we disobeyed the LORD and built our own altar to burn sacrifices on or to use for grain offerings or fellowship offerings, let the LORD himself punish us. 24 No! We did it because we were afraid that in the future your descendants would say to ours, 'What do you have to do with the LORD, the God of Israel? 25 He made the Jordan a boundary between us and you people of Reuben and Gad. You have nothing to do with the LORD.' Then your descendants might make our descendants stop worshiping the LORD. 26 So we built an altar, not to burn sacrifices or make offerings, 27 but instead, as a sign for our people and yours, and for the generations after us, that we do indeed worship the LORD before his sacred Tent with our offerings to be burned and with sacrifices and fellowship offerings. This was to keep your descendants from saying that ours have nothing to do with the LORD. 28 It was our idea that, if this should ever happen, our descendants could say, 'Look! Our ancestors made an altar just like the LORD's altar. It was not for burning offerings or for sacrifice, but as a sign for our people and yours.' 29 We would certainly not rebel against the LORD or stop following him now by building an altar to burn offerings on or for grain offerings or sacrifices. We would not build any other altar than the altar of the LORD our God that stands in front of the Tent of his presence."

30 Phinehas the priest and the ten leading men of the community who were with him, the heads of families of the western tribes, heard what the people of the tribes of Reuben, Gad, and East Manasseh had to say, and they were satisfied. 31 Phinehas, the son of Eleazar the priest, said to them, "Now we know that the LORD is with us. You have not rebelled against him, and so you have saved the people of Israel from the LORD's punishment."

32 Then Phinehas and the leaders left the people of Reuben and Gad in the land of Gilead and went back to Canaan, to the people of Israel, and reported to them. 33 The Israelites were satisfied and praised God. They no longer talked about going to war to devastate the land where the people of Reuben and Gad had settled.

34 The people of Reuben and Gad said, "This altar is a witness to all of us that the LORD is God." And so they named it "Witness."

Joshua's Farewell Address

23 Much later the LORD gave Israel security from their enemies around them. By that time Joshua was very old, 2 so he called all Israel, the elders, leaders, judges, and officers of the people, and said, "I am very old now. 3 You have seen everything that the LORD your God has done to all these nations because of you. The LORD your God has been fighting for you. 4 I have assigned as the possession of your tribes the land of the nations that are still left, as well as of all the nations that I have already conquered, from the Jordan River in the east to the Mediterranean Sea in the west. 5 The LORD your God will make them retreat from you, and he will drive them away as you advance. You shall have their land, as the LORD your God has promised you. 6 So be careful to obey and do everything that is written in the book of the Law of Moses. Do not neglect any part of it, 7 and then you will not associate with these peoples left among you or speak the names of their gods or use those names in taking vows or worship those gods or bow down to them. 8 Instead, be faithful to the LORD, as you have been till now. 9 The LORD has driven great and powerful nations out as you advanced, and no one has ever been able to stand against you. 10 Any one of you

23.10 **a** Dt 32.30; **b** Dt 3.22

can make a thousand men run away, because the LORD your God is fighting for you, just as he promised. 11 Be careful, then, to love the LORD your God. 12 If you are disloyal and join with the nations that are still left among you and intermarry with them, 13 you may be sure that the LORD your God will no longer drive these nations out as you advance. Rather, they will be as dangerous for you as a trap or a pit and as painful as a whip on your back or thorns in your eyes. And this will last until none of you are left in this good land which the LORD your God has given you.

14 "Now my time has come to die. Every one of you knows in his heart and soul that the LORD your God has given you all the good things that he promised. Every promise he made has been kept; not one has failed. 15 But just as he kept every promise that he made to you, so he will carry out every threat. 16 If you do not keep the covenant which the LORD your God commanded you to keep and if you serve and worship other gods, then in his anger he will punish you, and soon none of you will be left in this good land that he has given you."

Joshua Speaks to the People at Shechem

24 Joshua gathered all the tribes of Israel together at Shechem. He called the elders, the leaders, the judges, and the officers of Israel, and they came into the presence of God. 2 Joshua said to all the people, "This is what the LORD, the God of Israel, has to say: 'Long ago your ancestors lived on the other side of the Euphrates River and worshiped other gods. One of those ancestors was Terah, the father of Abraham and Nahor. 3 Then I took Abraham, your ancestor, from the land across the Euphrates and led him through the whole land of Canaan. I gave him many descendants. I gave him Isaac, 4 and to Isaac I gave Jacob and Esau. I gave Esau the hill country of Edom as his possession, but your ancestor Jacob and his children went down to Egypt. 5 Later I sent Moses and Aaron, and I brought great trouble on Egypt. But I led you out; 6 I brought your ancestors out of Egypt, and the Egyptians pursued them with chariots and cavalry. But when your ancestors got to the Red Sea 7 they cried out to me for help, and I put darkness between them and the Egyptians. I made the sea come rolling over the Egyptians and drown them. You know what I did to Egypt.

" 'You lived in the desert a long time. 8 Then I brought you to the land of the Amorites, who lived on the east side of the Jordan. They fought you, but I gave you victory over them. You took their land, and I destroyed them as you advanced. 9 Then the king of Moab, Balak son of Zippor, fought against you. He sent word to Balaam son of Beor and asked him to put a curse on you. 10 But I would not listen to Balaam, so he blessed you, and in this way I rescued you from Balak. 11 You crossed the Jordan and came to Jericho. The men of Jericho fought you, as did the Amorites, the Perizzites, the Canaanites, the Hittites, the Girgashites, the Hivites, and the Jebusites. But I gave you victory over them all. 12 As you advanced, I threw them into panic in order to drive out the two Amorite kings. Your swords and bows had nothing to do with it. 13 I gave you a land that you had never worked and cities that you had not built. Now you are living there and eating grapes from vines that you did not

24.2 Gn 11.27   **24.3 a** Gn 12.1-9; **b** Gn 21.1-3   **24.4 a** Gn 25.24-26; **b** Gn 36.8; Dt 2.5; **c** Gn 46.1-7   **24.5** Ex 3.1—12.42   **24.6, 7** Ex 14.1-31   **24.8** Nu 21.21-35 **24.9, 10** Nu 22.1—24.25   **24.11 a** Js 3.14-17; **b** Js 6.1-21   **24.12** Ex 23.28; Dt 7.20 **24.13** Dt 6.10, 11 plant, and olives from trees that you did not plant.'

14 "Now then," Joshua continued, "honor the LORD and serve him sincerely and faithfully. Get rid of the gods which your ancestors used to worship in Mesopotamia and in Egypt, and serve only the LORD. **15** If you are not willing to serve him, decide today whom you will serve, the gods your ancestors worshiped in Mesopotamia or the gods of the Amorites, in whose land you are now living. As for my family and me, we will serve the LORD."

16 The people replied, "We would never leave the LORD to serve other gods! **17** The LORD our God brought our fathers and us out of slavery in Egypt, and we saw the miracles that he performed. He kept us safe wherever we went among all the nations through which we passed. **18** As we advanced into this land, the LORD drove out all the Amorites who lived here. So we also will serve the LORD; he is our God."

19 Joshua said to the people, "But you may not be able to serve the LORD. He is a holy God and will not forgive your sins. He will tolerate no rivals, **20** and if you leave him to serve foreign gods, he will turn against you and punish you. He will destroy you, even though he was good to you before."

21 The people said to Joshua, "No! We will serve the LORD."

22 Joshua told them, "You are your own witnesses to the fact that you have chosen to serve the LORD."

"Yes," they said, "we are witnesses."

23 "Then get rid of those foreign gods that you have," he demanded, "and pledge your loyalty to the LORD, the God of Israel."

24 The people then said to Joshua,

"We will serve the LORD our God. We will obey his commands."

25 So Joshua made a covenant for ᵖ the people that day, and there at Shechem he gave them laws and rules to follow. **26** Joshua wrote these commands in the book of the Law of God. Then he took a large stone and set it up under the oak tree in the LORD's sanctuary. **27** He said to all the people, "This stone will be our witness. It has heard all the words that the LORD has spoken to us. So it will be a witness against you, to keep you from rebelling against your God." **28** Then Joshua sent the people away, and everyone returned to their own part of the land.

Joshua and Eleazar Die

29 After that, the LORD's servant Joshua son of Nun died at the age of a hundred and ten. **30** They buried him on his own land at Timnath Serah in the hill country of Ephraim north of Mount Gaash.

31 As long as Joshua lived, the people of Israel served the LORD, and after his death they continued to do so as long as those leaders were alive who had seen for themselves everything that the LORD had done for Israel.

32 The body of Joseph, which the people of Israel had brought from Egypt, was buried at Shechem, in the piece of land that Jacob had bought from the sons of Hamor, the father of Shechem, for a hundred pieces of silver. This land was inherited by Joseph's descendants.

33 Eleazar son of Aaron died and was buried at Gibeah, the town in the hill country of Ephraim which had been given to his son Phinehas.

ᵖ for; *or* with.

24.30 Js 19.49, 50   **24.32** Gn 33.19; 50.24, 25; Ex 13.19; Jn 4.5; Ac 7.16

The Book of
JUDGES

INTRODUCTION

The Book of Judges is composed of stories from the lawless period of Israel's history between the invasion of Canaan and the establishment of the monarchy. These stories are about the exploits of national heroes called "judges," most of whom were military leaders rather than judges in the legal sense of the word. One of the better known of them is Samson, whose deeds are recorded in chapters 13–16.

The great lesson of the book is that Israel's survival depended on loyalty to God, while disloyalty always led to disaster. But there was more than this: even when the nation was disloyal to God and disaster came, God was always ready to save his people when they repented and turned to him again.

OUTLINE OF CONTENTS

The Tribes of Judah and Simeon Capture Adonibezek

1 After Joshua's death the people of Israel asked the LORD, "Which of our tribes should be the first to go and attack the Canaanites?"

²The LORD answered, "The tribe of Judah will go first. I am giving them control of the land."

³The people of Judah said to the people of Simeon, "Go with us into the territory assigned to us, and we will fight the Canaanites together. Then we will go with you into the territory assigned to you." So the tribes of Simeon ⁴and Judah went into battle together. The LORD gave them victory over the Canaanites and the Perizzites, and they defeated ten thousand men at Bezek. ⁵They found Adonibezek there and fought him. ⁶He ran away, but they chased him, caught him, and cut off his thumbs and big toes. ⁷Adonibezek said, "Seventy kings with their thumbs and big toes cut off have picked up scraps under my table. God has now done to me what I did to them." He was taken to Jerusalem, where he died.

The Tribe of Judah Conquers Jerusalem and Hebron

⁸The people of Judah attacked Jerusalem and captured it. They killed its people and set fire to the city. ⁹After this they went on to fight the Canaanites who lived in the hill country, in the foothills, and in the dry country to the south. ¹⁰They marched against the Canaanites living in the city of Hebron, which used to be called Kiriath Arba. There they defeated the clans of Sheshai, Ahiman, and Talmai.

Othniel Conquers the City of Debir
(Joshua 15.13-19)

¹¹ From there the men of Judah marched against the city of Debir, at that time called Kiriath Sepher. ¹² One of them, called Caleb, said, "I will give my daughter Achsah in marriage to the man who succeeds in capturing Kiriath Sepher." ¹³ Othniel, the son of Caleb's younger brother Kenaz, captured the city, so Caleb gave him his daughter Achsah in marriage. ¹⁴ On the wedding day Othniel urged her *a* to ask her father for a field. She got down from her donkey, and Caleb asked her what she wanted. ¹⁵ She answered, "I want some water holes. The land you have given me is in the dry country." So Caleb gave her the upper and lower springs.

The Victories of the Tribes of Judah and Benjamin

¹⁶ The descendants of Moses' father-in-law, the Kenite, went on with the people of Judah from Jericho, the city of palm trees, into the barren country south of Arad in Judah. There they settled among the Amalekites. *b* ¹⁷ The people of Judah went with the people of Simeon, and together they defeated the Canaanites who lived in the city of Zephath. They put a curse on the city, destroyed it, and named it Hormah. *c* ¹⁸⁻¹⁹ The Lord helped the people of Judah, and they took possession of the hill country. But they did not capture *d* Gaza, Ashkelon, or Ekron, with their surrounding territories. These people living along the coast had iron chariots, and so the people of Judah were not able to drive them out. ²⁰ As Moses had commanded, Hebron was given to Caleb, who drove out of the city the three clans descended from Anak. ²¹ But the people of the tribe of Benjamin did not drive out the Jebusites living in Jerusalem, and the Jebusites have continued to live there with the people of Benjamin ever since.

The Tribes of Ephraim and Manasseh Conquer Bethel

²²⁻²³ The tribes of Ephraim and Manasseh went to attack the city of Bethel, at that time called Luz. The Lord helped them. They sent spies to the city, ²⁴ who saw a man leaving and said to him, "Show us how to get into the city, and we won't hurt you." ²⁵ So he showed them, and the people of Ephraim and Manasseh killed everyone in the city, except this man and his family. ²⁶ He later went to the land of the Hittites, built a city there, and named it Luz, which is still its name.

People Who Were Not Driven Out by the Israelites

²⁷ The tribe of Manasseh did not drive out the people living in the cities of Beth Shan, Taanach, Dor, Ibleam, Megiddo, and the nearby towns; the Canaanites continued to live there. ²⁸ When the Israelites became stronger, they forced the Canaanites to work for them, but still they did not drive them all out.

²⁹ The tribe of Ephraim did not drive out the Canaanites living in the city of Gezer, and so the Canaanites continued to live there with them.

³⁰ The tribe of Zebulun did not drive out the people living in the cities of Kitron and Nahalal, and so the Canaanites continued to live there with them and were forced to work for them.

³¹ The tribe of Asher did not drive out the people living in the cities of Acco,

---

a Some ancient translations Othniel urged her; *Hebrew* she urged Othniel.　　*b Some ancient translations* Amalekites; *Hebrew* people.　　*c* HORMAH: *This name in Hebrew means "destruction."*　　*d One ancient translation* But they did not capture; *Hebrew* And they captured.

1.20 Js 15.13, 14　**1.21** Js 15.63; 2 S 5.6; 1 Ch 11.4　**1.27, 28** Js 17.11-13　**1.29** Js 16.10

Sidon, Ahlab, Achzib, Helbah, Aphek, and Rehob. 32 The people of Asher lived with the local Canaanites, since they had not been driven out.

33 The tribe of Naphtali did not drive out the people living in the cities of Beth Shemesh and Bethanath. The people of Naphtali lived with the local Canaanites, but forced them to work for them.

34 The Amorites forced the people of the tribe of Dan into the hill country and did not let them come down to the plain. 35 The Amorites continued to live at Aijalon, Shaalbim, and Mount Heres, but the tribes of Ephraim and Manasseh kept them under their rule and forced them to work for them.

36 North of Sela, the Edomite*e* border ran through Akrabbim Pass.

The Angel of the LORD at Bochim

2 The angel of the LORD went from Gilgal to Bochim and said to the Israelites, "I took you out of Egypt and brought you to the land that I promised to your ancestors. I said, 'I will never break my covenant with you. 2 You must not make any covenant with the people who live in this land. You must tear down their altars.' But you have not done what I told you. You have done just the opposite! 3 So I tell you now that I will not drive these people out as you advance. They will be your enemies,*f* and you will be trapped by the worship of their gods." 4 When the angel had said this, all the people of Israel began to cry, 5 and that is why the place is called Bochim.*g* There they offered sacrifices to the LORD.

The Death of Joshua

6 Joshua sent the people of Israel on their way, and each man went to take possession of his own share of the land.

7 As long as Joshua lived, the people of Israel served the LORD, and even after his death they continued to do so as long as the leaders were alive who had seen for themselves all the great things that the LORD had done for Israel. 8 The LORD's servant Joshua son of Nun died at the age of a hundred and ten. 9 He was buried in his own part of the land at Timnath Serah in the hill country of Ephraim north of Mount Gaash. 10 That whole generation also died, and the next generation forgot the LORD and what he had done for Israel.

Israel Stops Worshiping the LORD

11 Then the people of Israel sinned against the LORD and began to serve the Baals. 12 They stopped worshiping the LORD, the God of their ancestors, the God who had brought them out of Egypt, and they began to worship other gods, the gods of the peoples around them. They bowed down to them and made the LORD angry. 13 They stopped worshiping the LORD and served the Baals and the Astartes. 14 And so the LORD became furious with Israel and let raiders attack and rob them. He let the enemies all around overpower them, and the Israelites could no longer protect themselves. 15 Every time they would go into battle, the LORD was against them, just as he had said he would be. They were in great distress.

16 Then the LORD gave the Israelites leaders who saved them from the raiders. 17 But the Israelites paid no attention to their leaders. Israel was unfaithful to the LORD and worshiped other gods. Their fathers had obeyed the LORD's commands, but this new generation soon stopped doing so. 18 Whenever the LORD gave Israel a leader, the LORD would help that leader and would save the people from their

Israel . . . worshiped
other gods. (2.17)

enemies as long as that leader lived. The LORD would have mercy on them because they groaned under their suffering and oppression. ¹⁹ But when the leader died, the people would return to the old ways and behave worse than the previous generation. They would serve and worship other gods, and stubbornly continue their own evil ways. ²⁰ Then the LORD would become furious with Israel and say, "This nation has broken the covenant that I commanded their ancestors to keep. Because they have not obeyed me, ²¹ I will no longer drive out any of the nations that were still in the land when Joshua died. ²² I will use them to find out whether or not these Israelites will follow my ways, as their ancestors did." ²³ So the LORD allowed these nations to remain in the land; he did not give Joshua victory over them, nor did he drive them out soon after Joshua's death.

The Nations Remaining in the Land

3 So then, the LORD left some nations in the land to test the Israelites who had not been through the wars in Canaan. ² He did this only in order to teach each generation of Israelites about war, especially those who had

never been in battle before. ³ Those left in the land were the five Philistine cities, all the Canaanites, the Sidonians, and the Hivites who lived in the Lebanon Mountains from Mount Baal Hermon as far as Hamath Pass. ⁴ They were to be a test for Israel, to find out whether or not the Israelites would obey the commands that the LORD had given their ancestors through Moses. ⁵ And so the people of Israel settled down among the Canaanites, the Hittites, the Amorites, the Perizzites, the Hivites, and the Jebusites. ⁶ They intermarried with them and worshiped their gods.

Othniel

⁷ The people of Israel forgot the LORD their God; they sinned against him and worshiped the idols of Baal and Asherah. ⁸ So the LORD became angry with Israel and let King Cushan Rishathaim of Mesopotamia conquer them. They were subject to him for eight years. ⁹ Then the Israelites cried out to the LORD, and he sent someone to free them. This was Othniel, the son of Caleb's younger brother Kenaz. ¹⁰ The spirit of the LORD came upon him, and he became Israel's leader. Othniel went to war, and the LORD gave him the victory over the king of Mesopotamia. ¹¹ There was peace in the land for forty years, and then Othniel died.

Ehud

¹² The people of Israel sinned against the LORD again. Because of this the LORD made King Eglon of Moab stronger than Israel. ¹³ Eglon joined the Ammonites and the Amalekites; they defeated Israel and captured Jericho, the city of palm trees. ¹⁴ The Israelites were subject to Eglon for eighteen years.

¹⁵ Then the Israelites cried out to the LORD, and he sent someone to free them. This was Ehud, a left-handed man, who was the son of Gera, from the

tribe of Benjamin. The people of Israel sent Ehud to King Eglon of Moab with gifts for him. 16 Ehud had made himself a double-edged sword about a foot and a half long. He had it fastened on his right side under his clothes. 17 Then he took the gifts to Eglon, who was a very fat man. 18 When Ehud had given him the gifts, he told the men who had carried them to go back home. 19 But Ehud himself turned back at the carved stones near Gilgal, went back to Eglon, and said, "Your Majesty, I have a secret message for you."

So the king ordered his servants, "Leave us alone!" And they all went out.

20 Then, as the king was sitting there alone in his cool room on the roof, Ehud went over to him and said, "I have a message from God for you." The king stood up. 21 With his left hand Ehud took the sword from his right side and plunged it into the king's belly. 22 The whole sword went in, handle and all, and the fat covered it up. Ehud did not pull it out of the king's belly, and it stuck out behind, between his legs.*h* 23 Then Ehud went outside, closed the doors behind him, locked them, 24 and left. The servants came and saw that the doors were locked, but they only thought that the king was inside, relieving himself. 25 They waited as long as they thought they should, but when he still did not open the door, they took the key and opened it. And there was their master, lying dead on the floor.

26 Ehud got away while they were waiting. He went past the carved stones and escaped to Seirah. 27 When he arrived there in the hill country of Ephraim, he blew a trumpet to call the people of Israel to battle; then he led them down from the hills. 28 He told them, "Follow me! The LORD has given you victory over your enemies, the Moabites." So they followed Ehud down and captured the place where the Mo-

abites were to cross the Jordan; they did not allow anyone to cross. 29 That day they killed about ten thousand of the best Moabite soldiers; none of them escaped. 30 That day the Israelites defeated Moab, and there was peace in the land for eighty years.

Shamgar

31 The next leader was Shamgar son of Anath. He too rescued Israel, and did so by killing six hundred Philistines with an oxgoad.

Deborah and Barak

4 After Ehud died, the people of Israel sinned against the LORD again. 2 So the LORD let them be conquered by Jabin, a Canaanite king who ruled in the city of Hazor. The commander of his army was Sisera, who lived at Harosheth-of-the-Gentiles. 3 Jabin had nine hundred iron chariots, and he ruled the people of Israel with cruelty and violence for twenty years. Then the people of Israel cried out to the LORD for help.

4 Now Deborah, the wife of Lappidoth, was a prophet, and she was serving as a judge for the Israelites at that time. 5 She would sit under a certain palm tree between Ramah and Bethel in the hill country of Ephraim, and the people of Israel would go there for her decisions. 6 One day she sent for Barak son of Abinoam from the city of Kedesh in Naphtali and said to him, "The LORD, the God of Israel, has given you this command: 'Take ten thousand men from the tribes of Naphtali and Zebulun and lead them to Mount Tabor. 7 I will bring Sisera, the commander of Jabin's army, to fight you at the Kishon River. He will have his chariots and soldiers, but I will give you victory over him.'"

8 Then Barak replied, "I will go if you

h Probable text it stuck ... legs; *Hebrew unclear.*

go with me, but if you don't go with me, I won't go either."

⁹She answered, "All right, I will go with you, but you won't get any credit for the victory, because the LORD will hand Sisera over to a woman." So Deborah set off for Kedesh with Barak. ¹⁰Barak called the tribes of Zebulun and Naphtali to Kedesh, and ten thousand men followed him. Deborah went with him.

¹¹In the meantime Heber the Kenite had set up his tent close to Kedesh near the oak tree at Zaanannim. He had moved away from the other Kenites, the descendants of Hobab, the brother-in-law of Moses.

¹²When Sisera learned that Barak had gone up to Mount Tabor, ¹³he called out his nine hundred iron chariots and all his men, and sent them from Harosheth-of-the-Gentiles to the Kishon River.

¹⁴Then Deborah said to Barak, "Go! The LORD is leading you! Today he has given you victory over Sisera." So Barak went down from Mount Tabor with his ten thousand men. ¹⁵When Barak attacked with his army, the LORD threw Sisera into confusion together with all his chariots and men. Sisera got down from his chariot and fled on foot. ¹⁶Barak pursued the chariots and the army to Harosheth-of-the-Gentiles, and Sisera's whole army was killed. Not a man was left.

¹⁷Sisera ran away to the tent of Jael, the wife of Heber the Kenite, because King Jabin of Hazor was at peace with Heber's family. ¹⁸Jael went out to meet Sisera and said to him, "Come in, sir; come into my tent. Don't be afraid." So he went in, and she hid him behind a curtain.ⁱ ¹⁹He said to her, "Please give me a drink of water; I'm thirsty." She opened a leather bag of milk, gave him a drink, and hid him again. ²⁰Then he told her, "Stand at the door of the tent,

and if anyone comes and asks you if anyone is here, say no."

²¹Sisera was so tired that he fell sound asleep. Then Jael took a hammer and a tent peg, quietly went up to him, and killed him by driving the peg right through the side of his head and into the ground. ²²When Barak came looking for Sisera, Jael went out to meet him and said to him, "Come here! I'll show you the man you're looking for." So he went in with her, and there was Sisera on the ground, dead, with the tent peg through his head.

²³That day God gave the Israelites victory over Jabin, the Canaanite king. ²⁴They pressed harder and harder against him until they destroyed him.

The Song of Deborah and Barak

5 On that day Deborah and Barak son of Abinoam sang this song:

²Praise the LORD!
　The Israelites were
　　determined to fight;
　the people gladly volunteered.
³Listen, you kings!
　Pay attention, you rulers!
　I will sing and play music
　to Israel's God, the LORD.
⁴LORD, when you left the
　　mountains of Seir,
　when you came out of the
　　region of Edom,
　the earth shook, and rain fell
　　from the sky.
　Yes, water poured down from
　　the clouds.
⁵The mountains quaked before
　　the LORD of Sinai,
　before the LORD, the God of
　　Israel.

⁶In the days of Shamgar son of
　　Anath,
　in the days of Jael,

ⁱ hid him behind a curtain; *or* covered him with a rug.
5.5 Ex 19.18

caravans no longer went through
the land,
and travelers used the back
roads.
⁷The towns of Israel stood
abandoned, Deborah;
they stood empty until you
came,ʲ
came like a mother for Israel.
⁸Then there was war in the land
when the Israelites chose new
gods.
Of the forty thousand men in
Israel,
did anyone carry shield or
spear?
⁹My heart is with the
commanders of Israel,
with the people who gladly
volunteered.
Praise the LORD!
¹⁰Tell ofᵏ it, you that ride on
white donkeys,
sitting on saddles,
and you that must walk
wherever you go.
¹¹Listen! The noisy crowds around
the wells
are telling of the LORD's
victories,
the victories of Israel's people!

Then the LORD's people marched
down from their cities.ˡ
¹²Lead on, Deborah, lead on!
Lead on! Sing a song!
Lead on!
Forward, Barak son of Abinoam,
lead your captives away!
¹³Then the faithful ones came
down to their leaders;
the LORD's people came to
himᵐ ready to fight.
¹⁴They cameⁿ from Ephraim into
the valley,ᵒ

behind the tribe of Benjamin
and its people.
The commanders came down
from Machir,
the officers down from
Zebulun.
¹⁵The leaders of Issachar came
with Deborah;
yes, Issachar came and
Barak too,
and they followed him into
the valley.
But the tribe of Reuben was
divided;
they could not decide to come.
¹⁶Why did they stay behind with
the sheep?
To listen to shepherds calling
the flocks?
Yes, the tribe of Reuben was
divided;
they could not decide to come.
¹⁷The tribe of Gad stayed east of
the Jordan,
and the tribe of Dan remained
by the ships.
The tribe of Asher stayed by the
seacoast;
they remained along the
shore.
¹⁸But the people of Zebulun and
Naphtali
risked their lives on the
battlefield.

¹⁹At Taanach, by the stream of
Megiddo,
the kings came and fought;
the kings of Canaan fought,
but they took no silver away.
²⁰The stars fought from the sky;
as they moved across the sky,
they fought against Sisera.
²¹A flood in the Kishon swept
them away —
the onrushing Kishon River.

ʲ abandoned, Deborah . . . you came; *or* abandoned; they stood empty until I, Deborah,
came.   ᵏ Tell of; *or* Think about.   ˡ from their cities; *or* to their gates.   ᵐ *One
ancient translation* him; *Hebrew* me.   ⁿ *Probable text* They came; *Hebrew* Their
root.   ᵒ *One ancient translation* into the valley; *Hebrew* in Amalek.

I shall march, march on, with
strength!
22 Then the horses came
galloping on,
stamping the ground with
their hoofs.

23 "Put a curse on Meroz," says the
angel of the LORD,
"a curse, a curse on those
who live there.
They did not come to help the
LORD,
come as soldiers to fight
for him."

24 The most fortunate of women is
Jael,
the wife of Heber the
Kenite —
the most fortunate of women
who live in tents.
25 Sisera asked for water, but she
gave him milk;
she brought him cream in a
beautiful bowl.
26 She took a tent peg in one hand,
a worker's hammer in the
other;
she struck Sisera and crushed
his skull;
she pierced him through the
head.
27 He sank to his knees,
fell down and lay still at her
feet.
At her feet he sank to his knees
and fell;
he fell to the ground, dead.

28 Sisera's mother looked out of the
window;
she gazed[p] from behind the
lattice.
"Why is his chariot so late in
coming?" she asked.
"Why are his horses so slow to
return?"

29 Her wisest friends answered her,
and she told herself over and
over,
30 "They are only finding things to
capture and divide,
a woman or two for every
soldier,
rich cloth for Sisera,
embroidered pieces for the
neck of the queen."[q]

31 So may all your enemies die like
that, O LORD,
but may your friends shine
like the rising sun!

And there was peace in the land for
forty years.

Gideon

6 Once again the people of Israel
sinned against the LORD, so he let
the people of Midian rule them for
seven years. 2 The Midianites were
stronger than Israel, and the people of
Israel hid from them in caves and other
safe places in the hills. 3 Whenever the
Israelites would plant their crops, the
Midianites would come with the Amalekites and the desert tribes and attack
them. 4 They would camp on the land
and destroy the crops as far south as the
area around Gaza. They would take all
the sheep, cattle, and donkeys, and
leave nothing for the Israelites to live
on. 5 They would come with their livestock and tents, as thick as locusts.
They and their camels were too many to
count. They came and devastated the
land, 6 and Israel was helpless against
them.

7 Then the people of Israel cried out
to the LORD for help against the Midianites, 8 and he sent them a prophet who
brought them this message from the
LORD, the God of Israel: "I brought you
out of slavery in Egypt. 9 I rescued you

p Some ancient translations gazed; _Hebrew_ cried out.   _q Probable text_ queen;
Hebrew plunder.

from the Egyptians and from the people who fought you here in this land. I drove them out as you advanced, and I gave you their land. [10] I told you that I am the LORD your God and that you should not worship the gods of the Amorites, whose land you are now living in. But you have not listened to me."

[11] Then the LORD's angel came to the village of Ophrah and sat under the oak tree that belonged to Joash, a man of the clan of Abiezer. His son Gideon was threshing some wheat secretly in a wine press, so that the Midianites would not see him. [12] The LORD's angel appeared to him there and said, 'The LORD is with you, brave and mighty man!"

[13] Gideon said to him, "If I may ask, sir, why has all this happened to us if the LORD is with us? What happened to all the wonderful things that our fathers told us the LORD used to do — how he brought them out of Egypt? The LORD has abandoned us and left us to the mercy of the Midianites."

[14] Then the LORD ordered him, "Go with all your great strength and rescue Israel from the Midianites. I myself am sending you."

[15] Gideon replied, "But Lord, how can I rescue Israel? My clan is the weakest in the tribe of Manasseh, and I am the least important member of my family."

[16] The LORD answered, "You can do it because I will help you. You will crush the Midianites as easily as if they were only one man."

[17] Gideon replied, "If you are pleased with me, give me some proof that you are really the LORD. [18] Please do not leave until I bring you an offering of food."

He said, "I will stay until you come back."

[19] So Gideon went into his house and cooked a young goat and used a bushel of flour to make bread without any yeast. He put the meat in a basket and the broth in a pot, brought them to the LORD's angel under the oak tree, and gave them to him. [20] The angel told him, "Put the meat and the bread on this rock, and pour the broth over them." Gideon did so. [21] Then the LORD's angel reached out and touched the meat and the bread with the end of the stick he was holding. Fire came out of the rock and burned up the meat and the bread. Then the angel disappeared.

[22] Gideon then realized that it was the LORD's angel he had seen, and he said in terror, "Sovereign LORD! I have seen your angel face-to-face!"

[23] But the LORD told him, "Peace. Don't be afraid. You will not die." [24] Gideon built an altar to the LORD there and named it "The LORD is Peace." (It is still standing at Ophrah, which belongs to the clan of Abiezer.)

[25] That night the LORD told Gideon, "Take your father's bull and another bull seven years old,[r] tear down your father's altar to Baal, and cut down the symbol of the goddess Asherah, which is beside it. [26] Build a well-constructed altar to the LORD your God on top of this mound. Then take the second bull[s] and burn it whole as an offering, using for firewood the symbol of Asherah you have cut down." [27] So Gideon took ten of his servants and did what the LORD had told him. He was too afraid of his family and the people in town to do it by day, so he did it at night.

[28] When the people in town got up early the next morning, they found that the altar to Baal and the symbol of Asherah had been cut down, and that the second bull had been burned on the altar that had been built there. [29] They asked each other, "Who did this?" They investigated and found out that Gideon son of Joash had done it. [30] Then they

[r] bull and another bull seven years old; *or* bull, the seven-year-old one.   [s] the second bull; *or* the bull.

said to Joash, "Bring your son out here, so that we can kill him! He tore down the altar to Baal and cut down the symbol of Asherah beside it."

31 But Joash said to all those who confronted him, "Are you arguing for Baal? Are you defending him? Anyone who argues for him will be killed before morning. If Baal is a god, let him defend himself. It is his altar that was torn down." **32** From then on Gideon was known as Jerubbaal,[t] because Joash said, "Let Baal defend himself; it is his altar that was torn down."

33 Then all the Midianites, the Amalekites, and the desert tribes assembled, crossed the Jordan River, and camped in Jezreel Valley. **34** The spirit of the LORD took control of Gideon, and he blew a trumpet to call the men of the clan of Abiezer to follow him. **35** He sent messengers throughout the territory of both parts of Manasseh to call them to follow him. He sent messengers to the tribes of Asher, Zebulun, and Naphtali, and they also came to join him.

36 Then Gideon said to God, "You say that you have decided to use me to rescue Israel. **37** Well, I am putting some wool on the ground where we thresh the wheat. If in the morning there is dew only on the wool but not on the ground, then I will know that you are going to use me to rescue Israel." **38** That is exactly what happened. When Gideon got up early the next morning, he squeezed the wool and wrung enough dew out of it to fill a bowl with water. **39** Then Gideon said to God, "Don't be angry with me; let me speak just once more. Please let me make one more test with the wool. This time let the wool be dry, and the ground be wet." **40** That night God did that very thing. The next morning the wool was dry, but the ground was wet with dew.

Gideon Defeats the Midianites

7 One day Gideon and all his men got up early and camped beside Harod Spring. The Midianite camp was in the valley to the north of them by Moreh Hill.

2 The LORD said to Gideon, "The men you have are too many for me to give them victory over the Midianites. They might think that they had won by themselves, and so give me no credit. **3** Announce to the people, 'Anyone who is afraid should go back home, and we will stay here at Mount Gilead.' " So twenty-two thousand went back, but ten thousand stayed.

4 Then the LORD said to Gideon, "You still have too many men. Take them down to the water, and I will separate them for you there. If I tell you a man should go with you, he will go. If I tell you a man should not go with you, he will not go." **5** Gideon took the men down to the water, and the LORD told him, "Separate everyone who laps up the water with his tongue like a dog from everyone who gets down on his knees to drink." **6** There were three hundred men who scooped up water in their hands and lapped it; all the others got down on their knees to drink. **7** The LORD said to Gideon, "I will rescue you and give you victory over the Midianites with the three hundred men who lapped the water. Tell everyone else to go home." **8** So Gideon sent all the Israelites home, except the three hundred who kept all the supplies and trumpets. The Midianite camp was below them in the valley.

9 That night the LORD commanded Gideon, "Get up and attack the camp; I am giving you victory over it. **10** But if you are afraid to attack, go down to the camp with your servant Purah. **11** You will hear what they are saying, and then you will have the courage to at

---

[t] JERUBBAAL: This name in Hebrew means "Let Baal defend himself."
7.3 Dt 20.8

tack." So Gideon and his servant Purah went down to the edge of the enemy camp. ¹²The Midianites, the Amalekites, and the desert tribesmen were spread out in the valley like a swarm of locusts, and they had as many camels as there are grains of sand on the seashore.

¹³When Gideon arrived, he heard a man telling a friend about a dream. He was saying, "I dreamed that a loaf of barley bread rolled into our camp and hit a tent. The tent collapsed and lay flat on the ground."

¹⁴His friend replied, "It's the sword of the Israelite, Gideon son of Joash! It can't mean anything else! God has given him victory over Midian and our whole army!"

¹⁵When Gideon heard about the man's dream and what it meant, he fell to his knees and worshiped the LORD. Then he went back to the Israelite camp and said, "Get up! The LORD is giving you victory over the Midianite army!" ¹⁶He divided his three hundred men into three groups and gave each man a trumpet and a jar with a torch inside it. ¹⁷He told them, "When I get to the edge of the camp, watch me, and do what I do. ¹⁸When my group and I blow our trumpets, then you blow yours all around the camp and shout, 'For the LORD and for Gideon!'"

¹⁹Gideon and his one hundred men came to the edge of the camp a while before midnight, just after the guard had been changed. Then they blew the trumpets and broke the jars they were holding, ²⁰and the other two groups did the same. They all held the torches in their left hands, the trumpets in their right, and shouted, "A sword for the LORD and for Gideon!" ²¹Every man stood in his place around the camp, and the whole enemy army ran away yelling. ²²While Gideon's men were blowing their trumpets, the LORD made the enemy troops attack each other

with their swords. They ran toward Zarethan as far as Beth Shittah, as far as the town of Abel Meholah near Tabbath.

²³Then men from the tribes of Naphtali, Asher, and both parts of Manasseh were called out, and they pursued the Midianites. ²⁴Gideon sent messengers through all the hill country of Ephraim to say, "Come down and fight the Midianites. Hold the Jordan River and the streams as far as Bethbarah, to keep the Midianites from crossing them." The men of Ephraim were called together, and they held the Jordan River and the streams as far as Bethbarah. ²⁵They captured the two Midianite chiefs, Oreb and Zeeb; they killed Oreb at Oreb Rock, and Zeeb at the Winepress of Zeeb. They continued to pursue the Midianites and brought the heads of Oreb and Zeeb to Gideon, who was now east of the Jordan.

The Final Defeat of the Midianites

8 Then the people of Ephraim said to Gideon, "Why didn't you call us when you went to fight the Midianites? Why did you treat us like this?" They complained bitterly about it.

²But he told them, "What I was able to do is nothing compared with what you have done. Even the little that you people of Ephraim did is worth more than what my whole clan has done. ³After all, through the power of God you killed the two Midianite chiefs, Oreb and Zeeb. What have I done to compare with that?" When he said this, they were no longer so angry.

⁴By this time Gideon and his three hundred men had come to the Jordan River and had crossed it. They were exhausted, but were still pursuing the enemy. ⁵When they arrived at Sukkoth,

8.3-5 Ps 83.11

While Gideon's men were blowing their trumpets, the LORD made the enemy troops attack each other. (7.22)

he said to the men of the town, "Please give my men some loaves of bread. They are exhausted, and I am chasing Zebah and Zalmunna, the Midianite kings."

6 But the leaders of Sukkoth said, "Why should we give your army any food? You haven't captured Zebah and Zalmunna yet."

7 So Gideon said, "All right! When the LORD has handed Zebah and Zalmunna over to me, I will beat you with thorns and briers from the desert!" 8 Gideon went on to Penuel and made the same request of the people there, but the men of Penuel gave the same answer as the men of Sukkoth. 9 So he said to them, "I am going to come back safe and sound, and when I do, I will tear this tower down!"

10 Zebah and Zalmunna were at Karkor with their army. Of the whole army of desert tribesmen, only about 15,000 were left; 120,000 soldiers had been killed. 11 Gideon went on the road along the edge of the desert, east of Nobah and Jogbehah, and attacked the army by surprise. 12 The two Midianite kings, Zebah and Zalmunna, ran away, but he pursued them and captured them, and caused their whole army to panic.

13 When Gideon was returning from the battle by way of Heres Pass, 14 he captured a young man from Sukkoth and questioned him. The young man wrote down for Gideon the names of the seventy-seven leading men of Sukkoth. 15 Then Gideon went to the men of Sukkoth and said, "Remember when you refused to help me? You said that you couldn't give any food to my exhausted army because I hadn't captured Zebah and Zalmunna yet. Well, here they are!" 16 He then took thorns and briers from the desert and used them to punish the leaders of Sukkoth. 17 He also

tore down the tower at Penuel and killed the men of that city.

¹⁸ Then Gideon asked Zebah and Zalmunna, "What about the men you killed at Tabor?"

They answered, "They looked like you — every one of them like the son of a king."

¹⁹ Gideon said, "They were my brothers, my own mother's sons. I solemnly swear that if you had not killed them, I would not kill you." ²⁰ Then he said to Jether, his oldest son, "Go ahead, kill them!" But the boy did not draw his sword. He hesitated, because he was still only a boy.

²¹ Then Zebah and Zalmunna said to Gideon, "Come on, kill us yourself. It takes a man to do a man's job." So Gideon killed them and took the ornaments that were on the necks of their camels.

²² After that, the Israelites said to Gideon, "Be our ruler — you and your descendants after you. You have saved us from the Midianites."

²³ Gideon answered, "I will not be your ruler, nor will my son. The LORD will be your ruler." ²⁴ But he went on to say, "Let me ask one thing of you. Every one of you give me the earrings you took." (The Midianites, like other desert people, wore gold earrings.)

²⁵ The people answered, "We'll be glad to give them to you." They spread out a cloth, and everyone put on it the earrings that he had taken. ²⁶ The gold earrings that Gideon got weighed over forty pounds, and this did not include the ornaments, necklaces, and purple clothes that the kings of Midian wore, nor the collars that were around the necks of their camels. ²⁷ Gideon made an idol from the gold and put it in his hometown, Ophrah. All the Israelites abandoned God and went there to worship the idol. It was a trap for Gideon and his family.

²⁸ So Midian was defeated by the Israelites and was no longer a threat. The land was at peace for forty years, until Gideon died.

The Death of Gideon

²⁹ Gideon went back to his own home and lived there. ³⁰ He had seventy sons, because he had many wives. ³¹ He also had a concubine in Shechem; she bore him a son, and he named him Abimelech. ³² Gideon son of Joash died at a ripe old age and was buried in the tomb of his father Joash, at Ophrah, the town of the clan of Abiezer.

³³ After Gideon's death the people of Israel were unfaithful to God again and worshiped the Baals. They made Baal-of-the-Covenant their god, ³⁴ and no longer served the LORD their God, who had saved them from all their enemies around them. ³⁵ They were not grateful to the family of Gideon for all the good that he had done for Israel.

Abimelech

9 Gideon's son Abimelech went to the town of Shechem, where all his mother's relatives lived, and told them ²to ask the men of Shechem, "Which would you prefer? To have all seventy of Gideon's sons govern you or to have just one man? Remember that Abimelech is your own flesh and blood." ³ His mother's relatives talked to the men of Shechem about this for him, and the men of Shechem decided to follow Abimelech because he was their relative. ⁴ They gave him seventy pieces of silver from the temple of Baal-of-the-Covenant, and with this money he hired a bunch of worthless scoundrels to join him. ⁵ He went to his father's house at Ophrah, and there on top of a single stone he killed his seventy brothers, Gideon's sons. But Jotham, Gideon's youngest son, hid and was not killed. ⁶ Then all the men of Shechem and Bethmillo got together and went to the sacred oak tree at Shechem, where they made Abimelech king.

⁷ When Jotham heard about this, he went and stood on top of Mount Gerizim and shouted out to them, "Listen to me, you men of Shechem, and God may

listen to you! [8]Once upon a time the trees went out to choose a king for themselves. They said to the olive tree, 'Be our king.' [9]The olive tree answered, 'In order to govern you, I would have to stop producing my oil, which is used to honor gods and human beings.' [10]Then the trees said to the fig tree, 'You come and be our king.' [11]But the fig tree answered, 'In order to govern you, I would have to stop producing my good sweet fruit.' [12]So the trees then said to the grapevine, 'You come and be our king.' [13]But the vine answered, 'In order to govern you, I would have to stop producing my wine, that makes gods and human beings happy.' [14]So then all the trees said to the thorn bush, 'You come and be our king.' [15]The thorn bush answered, 'If you really want to make me your king, then come and take shelter in my shade. If you don't, fire will blaze out of my thorny branches and burn up the cedars of Lebanon.'

[16]"Now then," Jotham continued, "were you really honest and sincere when you made Abimelech king? Did you respect Gideon's memory and treat his family properly, as his actions deserved? [17]Remember that my father fought for you. He risked his life to save you from the Midianites. [18]But today you turned against my father's family. You killed his sons — seventy men on a single stone — and just because Abimelech, his son by his servant woman, is your relative, you have made him king of Shechem. [19]Now then, if what you did today to Gideon and his family was sincere and honest, then be happy with Abimelech and let him be happy with you. [20]But if not, may fire blaze out from Abimelech and burn up the men of Shechem and Bethmillo. May fire blaze out from the men of Shechem and Bethmillo and burn Abimelech up." [21]Then because he was afraid of his brother Abimelech, Jotham ran away and went to live at Beer.

[22]Abimelech ruled Israel for three years. [23]Then God made Abimelech and the men of Shechem hostile to each other, and they rebelled against Abimelech. [24]This happened so that Abimelech and the men of Shechem, who encouraged him to murder Gideon's seventy sons, would pay for their crime. [25]The men of Shechem put men in ambush against Abimelech on the mountaintops, and they robbed everyone who passed their way. Abimelech was told about this.

[26]Then Gaal son of Ebed came to Shechem with his brothers, and the men of Shechem put their confidence in him. [27]They all went out into their vineyards and picked the grapes, made wine from them, and held a festival. They went into the temple of their god, where they ate and drank and made fun of Abimelech. [28]Gaal said, "What kind of men are we in Shechem? Why are we serving Abimelech? Who is he, anyway? The son of Gideon! And Zebul takes orders from him, but why should we serve him? Be loyal to your ancestor Hamor, who founded your clan! [29]I wish I were leading this people! I would get rid of Abimelech! I would tell[u] him, 'Reinforce your army, come on out and fight!' "

[30]Zebul, the ruler of the city, became angry when he heard what Gaal had said. [31]He sent messengers to Abimelech at Arumah[v] to say, "Gaal son of Ebed and his brothers have come to Shechem, and they are not going to let you into the city. [32]Now then, you and your men should move by night and hide in the fields. [33]Get up tomorrow morning at sunrise and make a sudden attack on the city. Then when Gaal and his men come out against you, hit them with all you've got!"

---

[u] *One ancient translation* I would tell; *Hebrew* He told. [v] *Probable text* Arumah; *Hebrew unclear.*

³⁴So Abimelech and all his men made their move at night and hid outside Shechem in four groups. ³⁵When Abimelech and his men saw Gaal come out and stand at the city gate, they got up from their hiding places. ³⁶Gaal saw them and said to Zebul, "Look! There are men coming down from the mountaintops!"

"Those are not men," Zebul answered. "They are just shadows on the mountains."

³⁷Gaal said again, "Look! There are men coming down the crest of the mountain and one group is coming along the road from the oak tree of the fortunetellers!"

³⁸Then Zebul said to him, "Where is all your big talk now? You were the one who asked why we should serve this man Abimelech. These are the men you were making fun of. Go on out now and fight them." ³⁹Gaal led the men of Shechem out and fought Abimelech. ⁴⁰Abimelech started after Gaal, and Gaal ran. Many were wounded, even at the city gate. ⁴¹Abimelech lived in Arumah, and Zebul drove Gaal and his brothers out of Shechem, so that they could no longer live there.

⁴²The next day Abimelech found out that the people of Shechem were planning to go out into the fields, ⁴³so he took his men, divided them into three groups, and hid in the fields, waiting. When he saw the people coming out of the city, he came out of hiding to kill them. ⁴⁴While Abimelech and his group hurried forward to guard the city gate, the other two companies attacked the people in the fields and killed them all. ⁴⁵The fighting continued all day long. Abimelech captured the city, killed its people, tore it down, and covered the ground with salt.

⁴⁶When all the leading men in the fort at Shechem heard about this, they sought safety in the stronghold of the temple of Baal-of-the-Covenant. ⁴⁷Abimelech was told that they had gathered there, ⁴⁸so he went up to Mount Zalmon with his men. There he took an ax, cut a limb off a tree, and put it on his shoulder. He told his men to hurry and do the same thing. ⁴⁹So everyone cut off a tree limb; then they followed Abimelech and piled the wood up against the stronghold. They set it on fire, with the people inside, and all the people of the fort died — about a thousand men and women.

⁵⁰Then Abimelech went to Thebez, surrounded that city, and captured it. ⁵¹There was a strong tower there, and every man and woman in the city, including the leaders, ran to it. They locked themselves in and went up to the roof. ⁵²When Abimelech came to attack the tower, he went up to the door to set the tower on fire. ⁵³But a woman threw a millstone down on his head and fractured his skull. ⁵⁴Then he quickly called the young man who was carrying his weapons and told him, "Draw your sword and kill me. I don't want it said that a woman killed me." So the young man ran him through, and he died. ⁵⁵When the Israelites saw that Abimelech was dead, they all went home.

⁵⁶And so it was that God paid Abimelech back for the crime that he committed against his father in killing his seventy brothers. ⁵⁷God also made the men of Shechem suffer for their wickedness, just as Jotham, Gideon's son, said they would when he cursed them.

Tola

10 After Abimelech's death Tola, the son of Puah and grandson of Dodo, came to free Israel. He was from the tribe of Issachar and lived at Shamir in the hill country of Ephraim. ²He was Israel's leader for twenty-three years. Then he died and was buried at Shamir.

Jair

³After Tola came Jair from Gilead. He led Israel for twenty-two years. ⁴He had thirty sons who rode thirty donkeys. They had thirty cities in the land of Gilead, which are still called the villages of Jair. ⁵Jair died and was buried at Kamon.

Jephthah

⁶Once again the Israelites sinned against the Lord by worshiping the Baals and the Astartes, as well as the gods of Syria, of Sidon, of Moab, of Ammon, and of Philistia. They abandoned the Lord and stopped worshiping him. ⁷So the Lord became angry with the Israelites, and let the Philistines and the Ammonites conquer them. ⁸For eighteen years they oppressed and persecuted all the Israelites who lived in Amorite country east of the Jordan River in Gilead. ⁹The Ammonites even crossed the Jordan to fight the tribes of Judah, Benjamin, and Ephraim. Israel was in great distress.

¹⁰Then the Israelites cried out to the Lord and said, "We have sinned against you, for we left you, our God, and worshiped the Baals."

¹¹The Lord gave them this answer: "The Egyptians, the Amorites, the Ammonites, the Philistines, ¹²the Sidonians, the Amalekites, and the Maonites oppressed you in the past, and you cried out to me. Did I not save you from them? ¹³But you still left me and worshiped other gods, so I am not going to rescue you again. ¹⁴Go and cry out to the gods you have chosen. Let them rescue you when you get in trouble."

¹⁵But the people of Israel said to the Lord, "We have sinned. Do whatever you like, but please, save us today." ¹⁶So they got rid of their foreign gods and worshiped the Lord; and he became troubled over Israel's distress.

¹⁷Then the Ammonite army prepared for battle and camped in Gilead. The people of Israel came together and camped at Mizpah in Gilead. ¹⁸There the people and the leaders of the Israelite tribes asked one another, "Who will lead the fight against the Ammonites? Whoever does will be the leader of everyone in Gilead."

11 Jephthah, a brave soldier from Gilead, was the son of a prostitute. His father Gilead ²had other sons by his wife, and when they grew up, they forced Jephthah to leave home. They told him, "You will not inherit anything from our father; you are the son of another woman." ³Jephthah fled from his brothers and lived in the land of Tob. There he attracted a group of worthless men, and they went around with him.

⁴It was some time later that the Ammonites went to war against Israel. ⁵When this happened, the leaders of Gilead went to bring Jephthah back from the land of Tob. ⁶They told him, "Come and lead us, so that we can fight the Ammonites."

⁷But Jephthah answered, "You hated me so much that you forced me to leave my father's house. Why come to me now that you're in trouble?"

⁸They said to Jephthah, "We are turning to you now because we want you to go with us and fight the Ammonites and lead all the people of Gilead."

⁹Jephthah said to them, "If you take me back home to fight the Ammonites and the Lord gives me victory, I will be your ruler."

¹⁰They replied, "We agree. The Lord is our witness." ¹¹So Jephthah went with the leaders of Gilead, and the people made him their ruler and leader. Jephthah stated his terms at Mizpah in the presence of the Lord.

¹²Then Jephthah sent messengers to the king of Ammon to say, "What is your quarrel with us? Why have you invaded our country?"

¹³The king of Ammon answered Jephthah's messengers, "When the Israelites came out of Egypt, they took away my land from the Arnon River to

the Jabbok River and the Jordan River. Now you must give it back peacefully."

¹⁴Jephthah sent messengers back to the king of Ammon ¹⁵with this answer: 'It is not true that Israel took away the land of Moab or the land of Ammon. ¹⁶This is what happened: when the Israelites left Egypt, they went through the desert to the Gulf of Aqaba and came to Kadesh. ¹⁷Then they sent messengers to the king of Edom to ask permission to go through his land. But the king of Edom would not let them. They also asked the king of Moab, but neither would he let them go through his land. So the Israelites stayed at Kadesh. ¹⁸Then they went on through the desert, going around the land of Edom and the land of Moab until they came to the east side of Moab, on the other side of the Arnon River. They camped there, but they did not cross the Arnon because it was the boundary of Moab. ¹⁹Then the Israelites sent messengers to Sihon, the Amorite king of Heshbon, and asked him for permission to go through his country to their own land. ²⁰But Sihon would not let Israel do it. He brought his whole army together, camped at Jahaz, and attacked Israel. ²¹But the LORD, the God of Israel, gave the Israelites victory over Sihon and his army. So the Israelites took possession of all the territory of the Amorites who lived in that country. ²²They occupied all the Amorite territory from the Arnon in the south to the Jabbok in the north and from the desert on the east to the Jordan on the west. ²³So it was the LORD, the God of Israel, who drove out the Amorites for his people, the Israelites. ²⁴Are you going to try to take it back? You can keep whatever your god Chemosh has given you. But we are going to keep everything that the LORD, our God, has taken for us. ²⁵Do you think you are any better than Balak son of Zippor, king of Moab? He never challenged Israel, did he? Did he ever go to war against us? ²⁶For three hundred years Israel has occupied Heshbon and Aroer, and the towns around them, and all the cities on the banks of the Arnon River. Why haven't you taken them back in all this time? ²⁷No, I have not done you any wrong. You are doing wrong by making war on me. The LORD is the judge. He will decide today between the Israelites and the Ammonites." ²⁸But the king of Ammon paid no attention to this message from Jephthah.

²⁹Then the spirit of the LORD came upon Jephthah. He went through Gilead and Manasseh and returned to Mizpah in Gilead and went on to Ammon. ³⁰Jephthah promised the LORD: "If you will give me victory over the Ammonites, ³¹I will burn as an offering the first person that comes out of my house to meet me, when I come back from the victory. I will offer that person to you as a sacrifice."

³²So Jephthah crossed the river to fight the Ammonites, and the LORD gave him victory. ³³He struck at them from Aroer to the area around Minnith, twenty cities in all, and as far as Abel Keramim. There was a great slaughter, and the Ammonites were defeated by Israel.

Jephthah's Daughter

³⁴When Jephthah went back home to Mizpah, there was his daughter coming out to meet him, dancing and playing the tambourine. She was his only child. ³⁵When he saw her, he tore his clothes in sorrow and said, "Oh, my daughter! You are breaking my heart! Why must it be you that causes me pain? I have made a solemn promise to the LORD, and I cannot take it back!"

³⁶She told him, "If you have made a promise to the LORD, do what you said

11.17 Nu 20.14-21   **11.18** Nu 21.4   **11.19-22** Nu 21.21-24   **11.25** Nu 22.1-6
11.35 Nu 30.2

you would do to me, since the LORD has given you revenge on your enemies, the Ammonites." ³⁷But she asked her father, "Do this one thing for me. Leave me alone for two months, so that I can go with my friends to wander in the mountains and grieve that I must die a virgin." ³⁸He told her to go and sent her away for two months. She and her friends went up into the mountains and grieved because she was going to die unmarried and childless. ³⁹After two months she came back to her father. He did what he had promised the LORD, and she died still a virgin.

Dancing and playing the tambourine (11.34)

This was the origin of the custom in Israel ⁴⁰that the Israelite women would go out for four days every year to grieve for the daughter of Jephthah of Gilead.

Jephthah and the Ephraimites

12 The men of Ephraim prepared for battle; they crossed the Jordan River to Zaphon and said to Jephthah, "Why did you cross the border to fight the Ammonites without calling us to go with you? We'll burn the house down over your head!"

²But Jephthah told them, "My people and I had a serious quarrel with the Ammonites. I did call you, but you would not rescue me from them. ³When I saw that you were not going to, I risked my life and crossed the border to fight them, and the LORD gave me victory over them. So why are you coming up to fight me now?" ⁴Then Jephthah brought all the men of Gilead together, fought the men of Ephraim and defeated them. (The Ephraimites had said, "You Gileadites in Ephraim and Manasseh, you are deserters from Ephraim!") ⁵In order to keep the Ephraimites from escaping, the Gileadites captured the places where the Jordan could be crossed. When any Ephraimite who was trying to escape would ask permission to cross, the men of Gilead would ask, "Are you an Ephraimite?" If he said, "No," ⁶they would tell him to say "Shibboleth." But he would say "Sibboleth," because he could not pronounce it correctly. Then they would grab him and kill him there at one of the Jordan River crossings. At that time forty-two thousand of the Ephraimites were killed.

⁷Jephthah led Israel for six years. Then he died and was buried in his hometown[w] in Gilead.

Ibzan, Elon, and Abdon

⁸After Jephthah, Ibzan from Bethlehem led Israel. ⁹He had thirty sons and thirty daughters. He gave his daughters in marriage outside the clan and brought thirty young women from outside the clan for his sons to marry. Ibzan led Israel for seven years, ¹⁰then he died and was buried at Bethlehem.

¹¹After Ibzan, Elon from Zebulun led Israel for ten years. ¹²Then he died and was buried at Aijalon in the territory of Zebulun.

¹³After Elon, Abdon son of Hillel from Pirathon led Israel. ¹⁴He had forty sons and thirty grandsons, who rode on

---

[w] *One ancient translation* his hometown; *Hebrew* the towns.

seventy donkeys. Abdon led Israel for eight years, [15] then he died and was buried at Pirathon in the territory of Ephraim in the hill country of the Amalekites.

The Birth of Samson

13 The Israelites sinned against the LORD again, and he let the Philistines rule them for forty years.

[2] At that time there was a man named Manoah from the town of Zorah. He was a member of the tribe of Dan. His wife had never been able to have children. [3] The LORD's angel appeared to her and said, "You have never been able to have children, but you will soon be pregnant and have a son. [4] Be sure not to drink any wine or beer, or eat any forbidden food; [5] and after your son is born, you must never cut his hair, because from the day of his birth he will be dedicated to God as a nazirite.[x] He will begin the work of rescuing Israel from the Philistines."

[6] Then the woman went and told her husband, "A man of God has come to me, and he looked as frightening as the angel[y] of God. I didn't ask him where he came from, and he didn't tell me his name. [7] But he did tell me that I would become pregnant and have a son. He told me not to drink any wine or beer, or eat any forbidden food, because the boy is to be dedicated to God as a nazirite as long as he lives."

[8] Then Manoah prayed to the LORD, "Please, LORD, let the man of God that you sent come back to us and tell us what we must do with the boy when he is born."

[9] God did what Manoah asked, and his angel came back to the woman while she was sitting in the field. Her husband Manoah was not with her, [10] so she ran at once and told him, "Look! The man who came to me the other day has appeared to me again."

[11] Manoah got up and followed his wife. He went to the man and asked, "Are you the man who talked to my wife?"

"Yes," he answered.

[12] Then Manoah said, "Now then, when your words come true, what must the boy do? What kind of a life must he lead?"

[13] The LORD's angel answered, "Your wife must be sure to do everything that I have told her. [14] She must not eat anything that comes from the grapevine; she must not drink any wine or beer, or eat any forbidden food. She must do everything that I have told her."

[15-16] Not knowing that it was the LORD's angel, Manoah said to him, "Please do not go yet. Let us cook a young goat for you."

But the angel said, "If I do stay, I will not eat your food. But if you want to prepare it, burn it as an offering to the LORD."

[17] Manoah replied, "Tell us your name, so that we can honor you when your words come true."

[18] The angel asked, "Why do you want to know my name? It is a name of wonder."[z]

[19] So Manoah took a young goat and some grain, and offered them on the rock altar to the LORD who works wonders.[a] [20-21] While the flames were going up from the altar, Manoah and his wife saw the LORD's angel go up toward heaven in the flames. Manoah realized then that the man had been the LORD's angel, and he and his wife threw themselves face downward on the ground. They never saw the angel again.

---

[x] NAZIRITE: *A person who showed devotion to God by taking vows not to drink wine or beer or allow any hair to be cut or touch corpses (see Nu 6.1-8).*   [y] the angel; *or an* angel.   [z] name of wonder; *or mysterious name.*   [a] *Some ancient translations* who works wonders; *Hebrew* and working wonders while Manoah and his wife watched.

13.5 Nu 6.1-5

Manoah and his wife saw the Lord's angel.
(13.21)

²²Manoah said to his wife, "We are sure to die, because we have seen God!"

²³But his wife answered, "If the Lord had wanted to kill us, he would not have accepted our offerings; he would not have shown us all this or told us such things at this time."

²⁴The woman gave birth to a son and named him Samson. The child grew and the Lord blessed him. ²⁵And the Lord's power began to strengthen him while he was between Zorah and Eshtaol in the Camp of Dan.

Samson and the Woman from Timnah

14 One day Samson went down to Timnah, where he noticed a certain young Philistine woman. ²He went back home and told his father and mother, "There is a Philistine woman down at Timnah who caught my attention. Get her for me; I want to marry her."

³But his father and mother asked him, "Why do you have to go to those heathen Philistines to get a wife? Can't you find someone in our own clan, among all our people?"

But Samson told his father, "She is the one I want you to get for me. I like her."

⁴His parents did not know that it was the Lord who was leading Samson to do this, for the Lord was looking for a chance to fight the Philistines. At this time the Philistines were ruling Israel.

⁵So Samson went down to Timnah with his father and mother. As they were going through the vineyards there, he heard a young lion roaring. ⁶Suddenly the power of the Lord made Samson strong, and he tore the lion apart with his bare hands, as if it were a young goat. But he did not tell his parents what he had done.

⁷Then he went and talked to the young woman, and he liked her. ⁸A few days later Samson went back to marry her. On the way he left the road to look at the lion he had killed, and he was surprised to find a swarm of bees and some honey inside the dead body. ⁹He scraped the honey out into his hands and ate it as he walked along. Then he went to his father and mother and gave them some. They ate it, but Samson did not tell them that he had taken the honey from the dead body of a lion.

¹⁰His father went to the woman's house, and Samson gave a banquet there. This was a custom among the young men. ¹¹When the Philistines saw him, they sent thirty young men to stay with him. ¹²-¹³Samson said to them, "Let me tell you a riddle. I'll bet each one of you a piece of fine linen and a change of fine clothes that you can't tell me its meaning before the seven days of the wedding feast are over."

"Tell us your riddle," they said. "Let's hear it."

¹⁴He said,

"Out of the eater came
        something to eat;
Out of the strong came
        something sweet."

Three days later they had still not figured out what the riddle meant.

¹⁵On the fourth[b] day they said to Samson's wife, "Trick your husband into telling us what the riddle means. If you don't, we'll set fire to your father's house and burn you with it.[c] You two invited us so that you could rob us, didn't you?"

¹⁶So Samson's wife went to him in tears and said, "You don't love me! You just hate me! You told my friends a riddle and didn't tell me what it means!"

He said, "Look, I haven't even told my father and mother. Why should I tell you?" ¹⁷She cried about it for the whole seven days of the feast. But on the seventh day he told her what the riddle meant, for she nagged him so about it. Then she told the Philistines. ¹⁸So on the seventh day, before Samson went into the bedroom,[d] the men of the city said to him,

"What could be sweeter than
        honey?
What could be stronger than a
        lion?"

Samson replied,

"If you hadn't been plowing with
        my cow,
You wouldn't know the
        answer now."

¹⁹Suddenly the power of the Lord made him strong, and he went down to Ashkelon, where he killed thirty men, stripped them, and gave their fine clothes to the men who had solved the riddle. After that, he went back home, furious about what had happened, ²⁰and his wife was given to the man that had been his best man at the wedding.

15 Some time later Samson went to visit his wife during the wheat harvest and took her a young goat. He told her father, "I want to go to my wife's room."

But he wouldn't let him go in. ²He told Samson, "I really thought that you hated her, so I gave her to your friend. But her younger sister is prettier, anyway. You can have her, instead."

³Samson said, "This time I'm not going to be responsible for what I do to the Philistines!" ⁴So he went and caught three hundred foxes. Two at a time, he tied their tails together and put torches in the knots. ⁵Then he set fire to the torches and turned the foxes loose in the Philistine wheat fields. In this way he burned up not only the wheat that had been harvested but also the wheat that was still in the fields. The olive orchards were also burned. ⁶When the Philistines asked who had done this, they learned that Samson had done it because his father-in-law, a man from Timnah, had given Samson's wife to a friend of Samson's. So the Philistines went and burned the woman to death and burned down her father's house.[e]

⁷Samson told them, "So this is how you act! I swear that I won't stop until I pay you back!" ⁸He attacked them fiercely and killed many of them. Then he went and stayed in the cave in the cliff at Etam.

Samson Defeats the Philistines

⁹The Philistines came and camped in Judah, and attacked the town of Lehi. ¹⁰The men of Judah asked them, "Why are you attacking us?"

They answered, "We came to take Samson prisoner and to treat him as he treated us." ¹¹So these three thousand men of Judah went to the cave in the cliff at Etam and said to Samson, "Don't

---

[b] *Some ancient translations* fourth; *Hebrew* seventh.   [c] set fire . . . you with it; *or* burn you and your family.   [d] *Probable text* bedroom; *Hebrew* sun.   [e] burned the woman . . . house; *or* burned the woman and her family to death.

He tied their tails together and put torches in the knots. (15.4)

you know that the Philistines are our rulers? What have you done to us?"

He answered, "I did to them just what they did to me."

¹²They told him, "We have come here to tie you up, so we can hand you over to them."

Samson said, "Give me your word that you won't kill me yourselves."

¹³"All right," they said, "we are only going to tie you up and hand you over to them. We won't kill you." So they tied him up with two new ropes and brought him back from the cliff.

¹⁴When he got to Lehi, the Philistines came running toward him, shouting at him. Suddenly the power of the LORD made him strong, and he broke the ropes around his arms and hands as if they were burnt thread. ¹⁵Then he found a jawbone of a donkey that had recently died. He reached down and picked it up, and killed a thousand men with it. ¹⁶So Samson sang,

"With the jawbone of a donkey I
  killed a thousand men;

With the jawbone of a donkey I
  piled them up in piles."ᶠ
¹⁷After that, he threw the jawbone

He broke the ropes around his arms. (15.14)

ᶠ PILES: *This word sounds like the Hebrew for "donkey."*

away. The place where this happened was named Ramath Lehi.*g*

18 Then Samson became very thirsty, so he called to the LORD and said, "You gave me this great victory; am I now going to die of thirst and be captured by these heathen Philistines?" 19 Then God opened a hollow place in the ground there at Lehi, and water came out of it. Samson drank it and began to feel much better. So the spring was named Hakkore;*h* it is still there at Lehi.

20 Samson led Israel for twenty years while the Philistines ruled the land.

Samson at Gaza

16 One day Samson went to the Philistine city of Gaza, where he met a prostitute and went to bed with her. 2 The people of Gaza found out that Samson was there, so they surrounded the place and waited for him all night long at the city gate. They were quiet all night, thinking to themselves, "We'll wait until daybreak, and then we'll kill him." 3 But Samson stayed in bed only until midnight. Then he got up and took hold of the city gate and pulled it up — doors, posts, lock, and all. He put them on his shoulders and carried them far off to the top of the hill overlooking Hebron.

Samson and Delilah

4 After this, Samson fell in love with a woman named Delilah, who lived in Sorek Valley. 5 The five Philistine kings went to her and said, "Trick Samson into telling you why he is so strong and how we can overpower him, tie him up, and make him helpless. Each one of us will give you eleven hundred pieces of silver."

6 So Delilah said to Samson, "Please tell me what makes you so strong. If

someone wanted to tie you up and make you helpless, how could he do it?"

7 Samson answered, "If they tie me up with seven new bowstrings that are not dried out, I'll be as weak as anybody else."

8 So the Philistine kings brought Delilah seven new bowstrings that were not dried out, and she tied Samson up. 9 She had some men waiting in another room, so she shouted, "Samson! The Philistines are coming!" But he snapped the bowstrings just as thread breaks when fire touches it. So they still did not know the secret of his strength.

10 Delilah told Samson, "Look, you've been making a fool of me and not telling me the truth. Please tell me how someone could tie you up."

11 He told her, "If they tie me with new ropes that have never been used, I'll be as weak as anybody else."

12 So Delilah got some new ropes and tied him up. Then she shouted, "Samson! The Philistines are coming!" The men were waiting in another room. But he snapped the ropes off his arms like thread.

13 Delilah said to Samson, "You're still making a fool of me and not telling me the truth. Tell me how someone could tie you up."

He told her, "If you weave my seven locks of hair into a loom, and make it tight with a peg, I'll be as weak as anybody else."

14 Delilah then lulled him to sleep, took his seven locks of hair, and wove them into the loom.*i* She made it tight with a peg and shouted, "Samson! The Philistines are coming!" But he woke up and pulled his hair loose from the loom.

15 So she said to him, "How can you say you love me, when you don't mean it? You've made a fool of me three

---

g RAMATH LEHI: *This name in Hebrew means "Jawbone Hill."*   *h* HAKKORE: *This name in Hebrew means "caller."*   *i One ancient translation* and make it tight *(in verse 13) . . .* into the loom *(in verse 14); Hebrew does not have these words.*

times, and you still haven't told me what makes you so strong." ¹⁶ She kept on asking him, day after day. He got so sick and tired of her bothering him about it ¹⁷ that he finally told her the truth. "My hair has never been cut," he said. "I have been dedicated to God as a nazirite ^j from the time I was born. If my hair were cut, I would lose my strength and be as weak as anybody else."

¹⁸ When Delilah realized that he had told her the truth, she sent a message to the Philistine kings and said, "Come back one more time. He has told me the truth." Then they came and brought the money with them. ¹⁹ Delilah lulled Samson to sleep in her lap and then called a man, who cut off ^k Samson's seven locks of hair. Then she began to torment him, for he had lost his strength. ²⁰ Then she shouted, "Samson! The Philistines are coming!" He woke up and thought, "I'll get loose and go free, as always." He did not know that the LORD had left him. ²¹ The Philistines captured him and put his eyes out. They took him to Gaza, chained him with bronze chains, and put him to work grinding at the mill in the prison. ²² But his hair started growing back.

The Death of Samson

²³ The Philistine kings met together to celebrate and offer a great sacrifice to their god Dagon. They sang, "Our god has given us victory over our enemy Samson!" ²⁴⁻²⁵ They were enjoying themselves, and so they said, "Call Samson, and let's make him entertain us!" ^l When they brought Samson out of the prison, they made him entertain them ^m and made him stand between the columns. When the people saw him, they sang praise to their god: "Our

god has given us victory over our enemy, who devastated our land and killed so many of us!" ²⁶ Samson said to the boy who was leading him by the hand, "Let me touch the columns that hold up the building. I want to lean on them." ²⁷ The building was crowded with men and women. All five Philistine kings were there, and there were about three thousand men and women on the roof, watching Samson entertain them. ⁿ

²⁸ Then Samson prayed, "Sovereign LORD, please remember me; please, God, give me my strength just this one time more, so that with this one blow I can get even with the Philistines for putting out my two eyes." ²⁹ So Samson took hold of the two middle columns holding up the building. Putting one hand on each column, he pushed against them ³⁰ and shouted, "Let me die with the Philistines!" He pushed with all his might, and the building fell down on the five kings and everyone else. Samson killed more people at his death than he had killed during his life.

³¹ His brothers and the rest of his

He pushed with all his might. (16.30)

---

^j NAZIRITE: *See 13.5.*   ^k *Probable text* who cut off; *Hebrew* and she cut off.
^l make him entertain us; *or* make fun of him.   ^m made him entertain them; *or* made fun of him.   ⁿ entertain them; *or* and making fun of him.

family came down to get his body. They took him back and buried him between Zorah and Eshtaol in the tomb of his father Manoah. He had been Israel's leader for twenty years.

Micah's Idols

17 There was once a man named Micah, who lived in the hill country of Ephraim. 2 He told his mother, "When someone stole those eleven hundred pieces of silver from you, you put a curse on the robber. I heard you do it. Look, I have the money. I am the one who took it."

His mother said, "May the LORD bless you, my son!" 3 He gave the money back to his mother, and she said, "To keep the curse from falling on my son, I myself am solemnly dedicating the silver to the LORD. It will be used to make a wooden idol covered with silver. So now I will give the pieces of silver back to you." 4 Then he gave them back to his mother. She took two hundred of the pieces of silver and gave them to a metalworker, who made an idol, carving it from wood and covering it with the silver. It was placed in Micah's house.

5 This man Micah had his own place of worship. He made some idols and an ephod,[o] and appointed one of his sons as his priest. 6 There was no king in Israel at that time; everyone did whatever they wanted.

7 At that same time there was a young Levite who had been living in the town of Bethlehem in Judah. 8 He left Bethlehem to find another place to live. While he was traveling, he came to Micah's house in the hill country of Ephraim. 9 Micah asked him, "Where do you come from?"

He answered, "I am a Levite from Bethlehem in Judah. I am looking for a place to live."

10 Micah said, "Stay with me. Be my adviser and priest, and I will give you ten pieces of silver a year, some clothes, and your food."[p] 11 The young Levite agreed to stay with Micah and became like a son to him. 12 Micah appointed him as his priest, and he lived in Micah's home. 13 Micah said, "Now that I have a Levite as my priest, I know that the LORD will make things go well for me."

Micah and the Tribe of Dan

18 There was no king in Israel at that time. In those days the tribe of Dan was looking for territory to claim and settle in because they had not yet received any land of their own among the tribes of Israel. 2 So the people of Dan chose five qualified[q] men out of all the families in the tribe and sent them all from the towns of Zorah and Eshtaol with instructions to explore the land and spy on it. When they arrived in the hill country of Ephraim, they stayed at Micah's house. 3 While they were there, they recognized the accent of the young Levite, so they went up to him and asked, "What are you doing here? Who brought you here?"

4 He answered, "I have an arrangement with Micah, who pays me to serve as his priest."

5 They said to him, "Please ask God if we are going to be successful on our trip."

6 The priest answered, "You have nothing to worry about. The LORD is taking care of you on this trip."

7 So the five men left and went to the town of Laish. They saw how the people there lived in security like the Sidonians. They were a peaceful, quiet people, with no argument with anyone;

---

o EPHOD: *See Word List.*　　　*p Probable text* your food; *Hebrew* your food. So the Levite went.　　　*q* qualified; *or* brave.

17.6 Jg 21.25

they had all they needed.ʳ They lived far away from the Sidonians and had no dealings with any other people. ⁸When the five men returned to Zorah and Eshtaol, the people asked them what they had found out. ⁹"Come on," they replied. "Let's attack Laish. We saw the land, and it's very good. Don't stay here doing nothing; hurry! Go on in and take it over! ¹⁰When you get there, you will find that the people don't suspect a thing. It is a big country; it has everything a person could want, and God has given it to you."

¹¹So six hundred men from the tribe of Dan left Zorah and Eshtaol, ready for battle. ¹²They went up and camped west of Kiriath Jearim in Judah. That is why the place is still called Camp of Dan. ¹³They went on from there and came to Micah's house in the hill country of Ephraim.

¹⁴Then the five men who had gone to spy on the country around Laish said to their companions, "Did you know that here in one of these houses there is a wooden idol covered with silver? There are also other idols and an ephod. What do you think we should do?" ¹⁵So they went into Micah's house, where the young Levite lived, and asked the Levite how he was getting along. ¹⁶Meanwhile the six hundred Danite soldiers, ready for battle, were standing at the gate. ¹⁷The five spies went straight on into the house and took the wooden idol covered with silver, the other idols, and the ephod, while the priest stayed at the gate with the six hundred armed men.

¹⁸When the men went into Micah's house and took the sacred objects, the priest asked them, "What are you doing?"

¹⁹They told him, "Keep quiet. Don't say a word. Come with us and be our priest and adviser. Wouldn't you rather be a priest for a whole Israelite tribe

than for the family of one man?" ²⁰This made the priest very happy, so he took the sacred objects and went along with them.

²¹They turned around and started off, with their children, their livestock, and their belongings going ahead. ²²They had traveled a good distance from the house when Micah called his neighbors out for battle. They caught up with the Danites ²³and shouted at them. The Danites turned around and asked Micah, "What's the matter? Why all this mob?"

²⁴Micah answered, "What do you mean, 'What's the matter?' You take my priest and the gods that I made, and walk off! What have I got left?"

²⁵The Danites told him, "You had better not say anything else unless you want these men to get angry and attack you. You and your whole family would die." ²⁶Then the Danites went on. Micah saw that they were too strong for him, so he turned and went back home.

²⁷⁻²⁸After the Danites had taken the priest and the things that Micah had made, they went and attacked Laish, that town of peaceful, quiet people which was in the same valley as Bethrehob. They killed the inhabitants and burned the town. There was no one to save them, because Laish was a long way from Sidon, and they had no dealings with any other people. The Danites rebuilt the town and settled down there. ²⁹They changed its name from Laish to Dan, after their ancestor Dan, the son of Jacob. ³⁰The Danites set up the idol to be worshiped, and Jonathan, the son of Gershom and grandson of Moses, served as a priest for the Danites, and his descendants served as their priests until the people were taken away into exile. ³¹Micah's idol remained there as long as the Tent where God was worshiped remained at Shiloh.

ʳ *Probable text* They were . . . needed; *Hebrew unclear.*

The Levite and His Concubine

19 In those days before Israel had a king, there was a Levite living far back in the hill country of Ephraim. He took a young woman from Bethlehem in Judah to be his concubine. ²But she became angry with him, went back to her father's house in Bethlehem, and stayed there four months. ³Then the man decided to go after her and try to persuade her to return to him. He took his servant and two donkeys with him. The woman showed the Levite into the house, and when her father saw him, he gave him a hearty greeting. ⁴The father insisted that he stay, and so he stayed for three days. The couple had their meals and spent the nights there. ⁵On the morning of the fourth day they woke up early and got ready to go. But the woman's father said to the Levite, "Have something to eat first. You'll feel better. You can go later."

⁶So the two men sat down and ate and drank together. Then the woman's father told him, "Please spend the night and enjoy yourself."

⁷The Levite got up to go, but the father urged him to stay, so he spent another night there. ⁸Early in the morning of the fifth day he started to leave, but the woman's father said, "Eat something, please. Wait until later in the day." So the two men ate together.

⁹When the man, his concubine, and the servant once more started to leave, the father said, "Look, it's almost evening now; you might as well stay all night. It will be dark soon; stay here and have a good time. Tomorrow you can get up early for the trip and go home."

¹⁰⁻¹¹But the man did not want to spend another night there, so he and his concubine started on their way, with their servant and two donkeys with pack saddles. It was late in the day when they came near Jebus (that is, Jerusalem), so the servant said to his master, "Why don't we stop and spend the night here in this Jebusite city?"

¹²⁻¹³But his master said, "We're not going to stop in a city where the people are not Israelites. We'll pass on by and go a little farther and spend the night at Gibeah or Ramah." ¹⁴So they passed by Jebus and continued on their way. It was sunset when they came to Gibeah in the territory of the tribe of Benjamin. ¹⁵They turned off the road to go and spend the night there. They went into town and sat down in the city square, but no one offered to take them home for the night.

¹⁶While they were there, an old man came by at the end of a day's work on the farm. He was originally from the hill country of Ephraim, but he was now living in Gibeah. (The other people there were from the tribe of Benjamin.) ¹⁷The old man noticed the traveler in the city square and asked him, "Where do you come from? Where are you going?"

¹⁸The Levite answered, "We have been in Bethlehem in Judah, and now we are on our way home*ˢ* deep in the hill country of Ephraim. No one will put us up for the night, ¹⁹even though we have fodder and straw for our donkeys, as well as bread and wine for my concubine and me and for my servant. We have everything we need."

²⁰The old man said, "You are welcome in my home! I'll take care of you; you don't have to spend the night in the square." ²¹So he took them home with him and fed their donkeys. His guests washed their feet and had a meal.

²²They were enjoying themselves when all of a sudden some sexual perverts from the town surrounded the house and started beating on the door. They said to the old man, "Bring out

---

ˢ One ancient translation home; *Hebrew* to the house of the Lᴏʀᴅ.
19.22-24 Gn 19.5-8

that man that came home with you! We want to have sex with him!"

²³ But the old man went outside and said to them, "No, my friends! Please! Don't do such an evil, immoral thing! This man is my guest. ²⁴ Look! Here is his concubine and my own virgin daughter. I'll bring them out now, and you can have them. Do whatever you want to with them. But don't do such an awful thing to this man!" ²⁵ But the men would not listen to him. So the Levite took his concubine and put her outside with them. They raped her and abused her all night long and didn't stop until morning.

²⁶ At dawn the woman came and fell down at the door of the old man's house, where her husband was. She was still there when daylight came. ²⁷ Her husband got up that morning, and when he opened the door to go on his way, he found his concubine lying in front of the house with her hands reaching for the door. ²⁸ He said, "Get up. Let's go." But there was no answer. So he put her body across the donkey and started on his way home. ²⁹ When he arrived, he went in the house and got a knife. He took his concubine's body, cut it into twelve pieces, and sent one piece to each of the twelve tribes of Israel. ³⁰ Everyone who saw it said, "We have never heard of such a thing! Nothing like this has ever happened since the Israelites left Egypt! We have to do something about this! What will it be?"

Israel Prepares for War

20 All the people of Israel from Dan in the north to Beersheba in the south, as well as from the land of Gilead in the east, answered the call. They gathered in one body in the LORD's presence at Mizpah. ² The lead- ers of all the tribes of Israel were present at this gathering of God's peo- ple, and there were 400,000 foot sol- diers. ³ Meanwhile the people of Benjamin heard that all the other Isra- elites had gathered at Mizpah.

The Israelites asked, "Tell us, how was this crime committed?" ⁴ The Le- vite whose concubine had been mur- dered answered, "My concubine and I went to Gibeah in the territory of Benja- min to spend the night. ⁵ The men of Gibeah came to get me and surrounded the house at night. They intended to kill me; instead they raped my concu- bine, and she died. ⁶ I took her body, cut it in pieces, and sent one piece to each of the twelve tribes of Israel. These peo- ple have committed an evil and im- moral act among us. ⁷ All of you here are Israelites. What are we going to do about this?"

⁸ All the people stood up together and said, "None of us, whether he lives in a tent or in a house, will go home. ⁹ This is what we will do: we will draw lots and choose some men to attack Gibeah.^t ¹⁰ One tenth of the men in Israel will provide food for the army, and the oth- ers will go and punish Gibeah^u for this immoral act that they have committed in Israel." ¹¹ So all the men in Israel as- sembled with one purpose — to attack the town.

¹² The Israelite tribes sent messen- gers all through the territory of the tribe of Benjamin to say, "What is this crime that you have committed? ¹³ Now hand over those perverts in Gibeah, so that we can kill them and remove this evil from Israel." But the people of Benja- min paid no attention to the other Isra- elites. ¹⁴ From all the cities of Benjamin they came to Gibeah to fight the other people of Israel. ¹⁵⁻¹⁶ They called out twenty-six thousand soldiers from their

---

^t *One ancient translation* to attack Gibeah; *Hebrew* to Gibeah.   ^u *One ancient translation* Gibeah; *Hebrew* Geba.

19.29 1 S 11.7

cities that day. Besides these, the citizens of Gibeah gathered seven hundred specially chosen men[v] who were left-handed. Every one of them could sling a stone at a strand of hair and never miss. 17 Not counting the tribe of Benjamin, the Israelites gathered 400,000 trained soldiers.

The War against the Benjaminites

18 The Israelites went to the place of worship at Bethel, and there they asked God, "Which tribe should attack the Benjaminites first?"

The LORD answered, "The tribe of Judah."

19 So the Israelites started out the next morning and camped near the city of Gibeah. 20 They went to attack the army of Benjamin, and placed the soldiers in position facing the city. 21 The army of Benjamin came out of the city, and before the day was over they had killed twenty-two thousand Israelite soldiers. 22-23 Then the Israelites went to the place of worship and mourned in the presence of the LORD until evening. They asked him, "Should we go again into battle against our brothers the Benjaminites?"

The LORD answered, "Yes."

So the Israelite army was encouraged, and they placed their soldiers in position again, where they had been the day before. 24 They marched against the army of Benjamin a second time. 25 And for the second time the Benjaminites came out of Gibeah, and this time they killed eighteen thousand trained Israelite soldiers. 26 Then all the people of Israel went up to Bethel and mourned. They sat there in the LORD's presence and did not eat until evening. They offered fellowship sacrifices and burned some sacrifices whole — all in the presence of the LORD. 27-28 God's Covenant Box was there at Bethel in those days, and Phinehas, the son of Eleazar and grandson of Aaron, was in charge of it. The people asked the LORD, "Should we go out to fight our brothers the Benjaminites again, or should we give up?"

The LORD answered, "Fight. Tomorrow I will give you victory over them."

29 So the Israelites put some soldiers in hiding around Gibeah. 30 Then for the third straight day they marched against the army of Benjamin and placed their soldiers in battle position facing Gibeah, as they had done before. 31 The Benjaminites came out to fight and were led away from the city. As they had before, they began killing some Israelites in the open country, on the road to Bethel and on the road to Gibeah. They killed about thirty Israelites. 32 The Benjaminites said, "We've beaten them just as before."

But the Israelites had planned to retreat and lead them away from the city onto the roads. 33 So when the main army of the Israelites pulled back and regrouped at Baaltamar, the men surrounding Gibeah suddenly rushed out of their hiding places in the rocky country around the city.[w] 34 Ten thousand men, specially chosen out of all Israel, attacked Gibeah, and the fighting was hard. The Benjaminites had not realized that they were about to be destroyed. 35 The LORD gave Israel victory over the army of Benjamin. The Israelites killed 25,100 of the enemy that day, 36 and the Benjaminites realized they were defeated.

How the Israelites Won

The main body of the Israelite army had retreated from the Benjaminites because they were relying on the men

---

v *Some ancient translations* men; *Hebrew* men. In all this number there were seven hundred specially chosen men.   w *One ancient translation* the city *(that is, Gibeah)*; *Hebrew* Geba.

that they had put in hiding around Gibeah. ³⁷These men ran quickly toward Gibeah; they spread out in the city and killed everyone there. ³⁸The main Israelite army and the men in hiding had arranged a signal. When they saw a big cloud of smoke going up from the town, ³⁹the Israelites out on the battlefield were to turn around. By this time the Benjaminites had already killed the thirty Israelites. They told themselves, "Yes, we've beaten them just as before." ⁴⁰Then the signal appeared; a cloud of smoke began to go up from the town. The Benjaminites looked behind them and were amazed to see the whole city going up in flames. ⁴¹Then the Israelites turned around, and the Benjaminites were thrown into panic because they realized that they were about to be destroyed. ⁴²They retreated from the Israelites and ran toward the open country, but they could not escape. They were caught between the main army and the men who were now coming out of the city,ˣ and they were destroyed. ⁴³The Israelites had the enemy trapped, and without stopping they pursued them as far as a point east of Gibeah, killing them as they went.ʸ ⁴⁴Eighteen thousand of the best Benjaminite soldiers were killed. ⁴⁵The others turned and ran toward the open country to Rimmon Rock. Five thousand of them were killed on the roads. The Israelites continued to pursue the rest to Gidom, killing two thousand. ⁴⁶In all, twenty-five thousand Benjaminites were killed that day — all of them brave soldiers.

⁴⁷But six hundred men were able to escape to the open country to Rimmon Rock, and they stayed there four months. ⁴⁸The Israelites turned back against the rest of the Benjaminites and killed them all — men, women, and children, and animals as well. They burned every town in the area.

Wives for the Tribe of Benjamin

21 When the Israelites had gathered at Mizpah, they had made a solemn promise to the LORD: "None of us will allow a Benjaminite to marry a daughter of ours." ²So now the people of Israel went to Bethel and sat there in the presence of God until evening. Loudly and bitterly they mourned: ³"LORD God of Israel, why has this happened? Why is the tribe of Benjamin about to disappear from Israel?"

⁴Early the next morning the people got up and built an altar there. They offered fellowship sacrifices and burned some sacrifices whole. ⁵They asked, "Is there any group out of all the tribes of Israel that did not go to the gathering in the LORD's presence at Mizpah?" (They had taken a solemn oath that anyone who had not gone to Mizpah would be put to death.) ⁶The people of Israel felt sorry for their brothers the Benjaminites and said, "Today Israel has lost one of its tribes. ⁷What shall we do to provide wives for the men of Benjamin who are left? We have made a solemn promise to the LORD that we will not give them any of our daughters."

⁸When they asked if there was some group out of the tribes of Israel that had not gone to the gathering at Mizpah, they found out that no one from Jabesh in Gilead had been there; ⁹at the roll call of the army no one from Jabesh had responded. ¹⁰So the assembly sent twelve thousand of their bravest men with the orders, "Go and kill everyone in Jabesh, including women and children. ¹¹Kill all the males, and also every woman who is not a virgin." ¹²They found four hundred young virgins among the people in Jabesh, so they brought them to the camp at Shiloh, which is in the land of Canaan.

¹³Then the whole assembly sent word to the Benjaminites who were at Rimmon Rock and offered to end the

---

ˣ *Probable text* city; *Hebrew* cities.   ʸ *Verse 43 in Hebrew is unclear.*

war. [14] The Benjaminites came back, and the other Israelites gave them the young women from Jabesh whom they had not killed. But there were not enough of them.

[15] The people felt sorry for the Benjaminites because the LORD had broken the unity of the tribes of Israel. [16] So the leaders of the gathering said, "There are no more women in the tribe of Benjamin. What shall we do to provide wives for the men who are left? [17] Israel must not lose one of its twelve tribes. We must find a way for the tribe of Benjamin to survive, [18] but we cannot allow them to marry our daughters, because we have put a curse on anyone who allows a Benjaminite to marry one of our daughters."

[19] Then they thought, "The yearly festival of the LORD at Shiloh is coming soon." (Shiloh is north of Bethel, south of Lebonah, and east of the road between Bethel and Shechem.) [20] They told the Benjaminites, "Go and hide in the vineyards [21] and watch. When the young women of Shiloh come out to dance during the festival, you come out of the vineyards. Each of you take a wife by force from among them and take her back to the territory of Benjamin with you. [22] If their fathers or brothers come to you[z] and protest, you[a] can tell them, 'Please let us keep them, because we did not take them from you in battle to be our wives. And since you did not give them to us, you are not guilty of breaking your promise.'"

[23] The Benjaminites did this; each of them chose a wife from the young women who were dancing at Shiloh and carried her away. Then they went back to their own territory, rebuilt their towns, and lived there. [24] At the same time the rest of the Israelites left, and every man went back to his own tribe and family and to his own property.

[25] There was no king in Israel at that time. Everyone did whatever they pleased.

---

[z] *One ancient translation* you; *Hebrew* us.
21.25 Jg 17.6

[a] *Probable text* you; *Hebrew* we.

The Book of
RUTH

INTRODUCTION

The peaceful story of *Ruth* is set in the violent times of *The Book of Judges*. Ruth, a Moabite woman, is married to an Israelite. When he dies, Ruth shows uncommon loyalty to her Israelite mother-in-law and deep devotion to the God of Israel. In the end she finds a new husband among her former husband's relatives, and through this marriage becomes the great-grandmother of David, Israel's greatest king.

The stories of *Judges* show the disaster that came when God's people turned away from him. *Ruth* shows the blessing that came to a foreigner who turned to Israel's God and so became part of his faithful people.

OUTLINE OF CONTENTS

Elimelech and His Family Move to Moab

1 ¹⁻² Long ago, in the days before Israel had a king, there was a famine in the land. So a man named Elimelech, who belonged to the clan of Ephrath and who lived in Bethlehem in Judah, went with his wife Naomi and their two sons Mahlon and Chilion to live for a while in the country of Moab. While they were living there, ³ Elimelech died, and Naomi was left alone with her two sons, ⁴ who married Moabite women, Orpah and Ruth. About ten years later ⁵ Mahlon and Chilion also died, and Naomi was left all alone, without husband or sons.

Naomi and Ruth Return to Bethlehem

⁶ Some time later Naomi heard that the Lord had blessed his people by giving them good crops; so she got ready to leave Moab with her daughters-in-law. ⁷ They started out together to go back to Judah, but on the way ⁸ she said to them, "Go back home and stay with your mothers. May the Lord be as good to you as you have been to me and to those who have died. ⁹ And may the Lord make it possible for each of you to marry again and have a home."

So Naomi kissed them good-bye. But they started crying ¹⁰ and said to her, "No! We will go with you to your people."

¹¹ "You must go back, my daughters," Naomi answered. "Why do you want to come with me? Do you think I could have sons again for you to marry? ¹² Go back home, for I am too old to get married again. Even if I thought there was still hope, and so got married tonight and had sons, ¹³ would you wait until they had grown up? Would this

keep you from marrying someone else? No, my daughters, you know that's impossible. The LORD has turned against me, and I feel very sorry for you."[a]

[14] Again they started crying. Then Orpah kissed her mother-in-law good-bye and went back home,[b] but Ruth held on to her. [15] So Naomi said to her, "Ruth, your sister-in-law has gone back to her people and to her god.[c] Go back home with her."

[16] But Ruth answered, "Don't ask me to leave you! Let me go with you. Wherever you go, I will go; wherever you live, I will live. Your people will be my people, and your God will be my God. [17] Wherever you die, I will die, and that is where I will be buried. May the LORD's worst punishment come upon me if I let anything but death[d] separate me from you!"

[18] When Naomi saw that Ruth was determined to go with her, she said nothing more.

[19] They went on until they came to Bethlehem. When they arrived, the whole town became excited, and the women there exclaimed, "Is this really Naomi?"

[20] "Don't call me Naomi," she answered; "call me Marah,[e] because Almighty God has made my life bitter. [21] When I left here, I had plenty, but the LORD has brought me back without a thing. Why call me Naomi when the LORD Almighty has condemned me and sent me trouble?"

[22] This, then, was how Naomi came back from Moab with Ruth, her Moabite daughter-in-law. When they arrived in Bethlehem, the barley harvest was just beginning.

Ruth Works in the Field of Boaz

2 Naomi had a relative named Boaz, a rich and influential man who belonged to the family of her husband Elimelech. [2] One day Ruth said to Naomi, "Let me go to the fields to gather the grain that the harvest workers leave. I am sure to find someone who will let me work with him."

Naomi answered, "Go ahead, daughter."

[3] So Ruth went out to the fields and walked behind the workers, picking up the heads of grain which they left. It so happened that she was in a field that belonged to Boaz.

[4] Some time later Boaz himself arrived from Bethlehem and greeted the workers. "The LORD be with you!" he said.

"The LORD bless you!" they answered.

[5] Boaz asked the man in charge, "Who is that young woman?"

[6] The man answered, "She is the foreigner who came back from Moab with Naomi. [7] She asked me to let her follow the workers and gather grain. She has been working since early morning and has just now stopped to rest for a while under the shelter."

[8] Then Boaz said to Ruth, "Let me give you some advice. Don't gather grain anywhere except in this field. Work with the women here; [9] watch them to see where they are reaping and stay with them. I have ordered my men not to molest you. And whenever you are thirsty, go and drink from the water jars that they have filled."

[10] Ruth bowed down with her face touching the ground, and said to Boaz, "Why should you be so concerned

---

[a] sorry for you; or bitter about what has happened to you.   [b] One ancient translation and went back home; Hebrew does not have these words.   [c] god; or gods.
[d] anything but death; or even death.   [e] NAOMI ... MARAH: In Hebrew Naomi means "pleasant" and Marah means "bitter."
2.2 Lv 19.9, 10; Dt 24.19

Ruth went out . . . picking up the heads of grain. (2.3)

about me? Why should you be so kind to a foreigner?"

11 Boaz answered, "I have heard about everything that you have done for your mother-in-law since your husband died. I know how you left your father and mother and your own country and how you came to live among a people you had never known before. 12 May the LORD reward you for what you have done. May you have a full reward from the LORD God of Israel, to whom you have come for protection!"

13 Ruth answered, "You are very kindᶠ to me, sir. You have made me feel better by speaking gently to me, even though I am not the equal of one of your servants."

14 At mealtime Boaz said to Ruth, "Come and have a piece of bread, and dip it in the sauce." So she sat with the workers, and Boaz passed some roasted

grain to her. She ate until she was satisfied, and she still had some food left over. 15-16 After she had left to go and gather grain, Boaz ordered the workers, "Let her gather grain even where the bundles are lying, and don't say anything to stop her. Besides that, pull out some heads of grain from the bundles and leave them for her to pick up."

17 So Ruth gathered grain in the field until evening, and when she had beaten it out, she found she had nearly twenty-five pounds. 18 She took the grain back into town and showed her mother-in-law how much she had gathered. She also gave her the food left over from the meal. 19 Naomi asked her, "Where did you gather all this grain today? Whose field have you been working in? May God bless the man who took an interest in you!"

So Ruth told Naomi that she had

ᶠ You are very kind; *or* Please be kind.

been working in a field belonging to a man named Boaz.

20 "May the LORD bless Boaz!" Naomi exclaimed. "The LORD always keeps his promises to the living and the dead." And she went on, "That man is a close relative of ours, one of those responsible for taking care of us."

21 Then Ruth said, "Best of all, he told me to keep gathering grain with his workers until they finish the harvest."

22 Naomi said to Ruth, "Yes, daughter, it will be better for you to work with the women in Boaz' field. You might be molested if you went to someone else's field." 23 So Ruth worked with them and gathered grain until all the barley and wheat had been harvested. And she continued to live with her mother-in-law.

Ruth Finds a Husband

3 Some time later Naomi said to Ruth, "I must find a husband for you, so that you will have a home of your own. 2 Remember that this man Boaz, whose women you have been working with, is our relative. Now listen. This evening he will be threshing the barley. 3 So wash yourself, put on some perfume, and get dressed in your best clothes. Then go where he is threshing, but don't let him know you are there until he has finished eating and drinking. 4 Be sure to notice where he lies down, and after he falls asleep, go and lift the covers and lie down at his feet. He will tell you what to do."

5 Ruth answered, "I will do everything you say."

6 So Ruth went to the threshing place and did just what her mother-in-law had told her. 7 When Boaz had finished eating and drinking, he was in a good mood. He went to the pile of barley and lay down to sleep. Ruth slipped over quietly, lifted the covers and lay down

at his feet. 8 During the night he woke up suddenly, turned over, and was surprised to find a woman lying at his feet. 9 "Who are you?" he asked.

"It's Ruth, sir," she answered. "Because you are a close relative, you are responsible for taking care of me. So please marry me."

10 "The LORD bless you," he said. "You are showing even greater family loyalty in what you are doing now than in what you did for your mother-in-law. You might have gone looking for a young man, either rich or poor, but you haven't. 11 Now don't worry, Ruth. I will do everything you ask; as everyone in town knows, you are a fine woman. 12 It is true that I am a close relative and am responsible for you, but there is a man who is a closer relative than I am. 13 Stay here the rest of the night, and in the morning we will find out whether or not he will take responsibility for you. If so, well and good; if not, then I swear by the living LORD that I will take the responsibility. Now lie down and stay here till morning."

14 So she lay there at his feet, but she got up before it was light enough for her to be seen, because Boaz did not want anyone to know that she had been there. 15 Boaz said to her, "Take off your cloak and spread it out here." She did, and he poured out almost fifty pounds of barley and helped her lift it to her shoulder. Then she returned to town with it. 16 When she arrived home, her mother-in-law asked her, "How did you get along, daughter?"

Ruth told her everything that Boaz had done for her. 17 She added, "He told me I must not come back to you empty-handed, so he gave me all this barley."

18 Naomi said to her, "Now be patient, Ruth, until you see how this all turns out. Boaz will not rest today until he settles the matter."

2.20 Lv 25.25   **3.12** Ru 2.20

Boaz Marries Ruth

4 Boaz went to the meeting place at the town gate and sat down there. Then Elimelech's nearest relative, the man whom Boaz had mentioned, came by, and Boaz called to him, "Come over here, my friend, and sit down." So he went over and sat down. ²Then Boaz got ten of the leaders of the town and asked them to sit down there too. When they were seated, ³he said to his relative, "Now that Naomi has come back from Moab, she wants to sell the field that belonged to our relative Elimelech, ⁴and I think you ought to know about it. Now then, if you want it, buy it in the presence of these men sitting here. But if you don't want it, say so, because the right to buy it belongs first to you and then to me."

The man said, "I will buy it."

⁵Boaz said, "Very well, if you buy the field from Naomi, then you are also buying Ruth,*ᵍ* the Moabite widow, so that the field will stay in the dead man's family."

⁶The man answered, "In that case I will give up my right to buy the field, because it would mean that my own children would not inherit it. You buy it; I would rather not."

⁷Now in those days, to settle a sale or an exchange of property, it was the custom for the seller to take off his sandal and give it to the buyer. In this way the Israelites showed that the matter was settled.

⁸So when the man said to Boaz, "You buy it," he took off his sandal and gave it to Boaz.*ʰ* ⁹Then Boaz said to the leaders and all the others there, "You are all witnesses today that I have bought from Naomi everything that belonged to Elimelech and to his sons Chilion and Mahlon. ¹⁰In addition, Ruth the Moabite, Mahlon's widow, be-

It was the custom for the seller to take off his sandal. (4.7)

comes my wife. This will keep the property in the dead man's family, and his family line will continue among his people and in his hometown. You are witnesses to this today."

¹¹The leaders and the others said, "Yes, we are witnesses. May the LORD make your wife become like Rachel and Leah, who bore many children to Jacob. May you become rich in the clan of Ephrath and famous in Bethlehem. ¹²May the children that the LORD will give you by this young woman make your family like the family of Perez, the son of Judah and Tamar."

Boaz and His Descendants

¹³So Boaz took Ruth home as his wife. The LORD blessed her, and she became pregnant and had a son. ¹⁴The women said to Naomi, "Praise the LORD! He has given you a grandson today to take care of you. May the boy become famous in Israel! ¹⁵Your

ᵍ Some ancient translations Naomi ... Ruth; *Hebrew* Naomi and from Ruth.   *ʰ One ancient translation* and gave it to Boaz; *Hebrew does not have these words.*
4.7, 8 Dt 25.9   **4.10** Dt 25.5, 6   **4.11** Gn 29.31   **4.12** Gn 38.27-30

daughter-in-law loves you, and has done more for you than seven sons. And now she has given you a grandson, who will bring new life to you and give you security in your old age." ¹⁶Naomi took the child, held him close,*i* and took care of him.

¹⁷The women of the neighborhood named the boy Obed. They told everyone, "A son has been born to Naomi!"

Obed became the father of Jesse, who was the father of David.

18-22 This is the family line from Perez to David: Perez, Hezron, Ram, Amminadab, Nahshon, Salmon, Boaz, Obed, Jesse, David.

---

i held him close; *or* adopted him.

The First Book of
SAMUEL

INTRODUCTION

The book of *First Samuel* records the transition in Israel from the period of the judges to the monarchy. This change in Israel's national life revolved mainly around three men: Samuel, the last of the great judges; Saul, Israel's first king; and David, whose early adventures before coming to power are interwoven with the accounts of Samuel and Saul.

The theme of this book, like that of other historical writings in the Old Testament, is that faithfulness to God brings success, while disobedience brings disaster. This is stated clearly in the Lord's message to the priest Eli in 2.30: "I will honor those who honor me, and I will treat with contempt those who despise me."

The book records mixed feelings about the establishment of the monarchy. The Lord himself was regarded as the real king of Israel, but in response to the people's request the Lord chose a king for them. The important fact was that both the king and the people of Israel lived under the sovereignty and judgment of God (2.7-10). Under God's laws the rights of all people, rich and poor alike, were to be maintained.

OUTLINE OF CONTENTS

Elkanah and His Family at Shiloh

1 There was a man named Elkanah, from the tribe of Ephraim, who lived in the town of Ramah in the hill country of Ephraim. He was the son of Jeroham and grandson of Elihu, and belonged to the family of Tohu, a part of the clan of Zuph. ² Elkanah had two wives, Hannah and Peninnah. Peninnah had children, but Hannah did not. ³ Every year Elkanah went from Ramah to worship and offer sacrifices to the Lord Almighty at Shiloh, where Hophni and Phinehas, the two sons of Eli, were priests of the Lord. ⁴ Each time Elkanah offered his sacrifice, he would give one share of the meat to Peninnah and one share to each of her children. ⁵ And even though he loved Hannah very much he would give her only one share, because *a* the Lord had kept her from having children. ⁶ Peninnah, her rival, would torment and humiliate her, because the Lord had kept

a And even ... because; *or* To Hannah, however, he would give a special share, because he loved her very much, even though.

her childless. ⁷This went on year after year; whenever they went to the house of the LORD, Peninnah would upset Hannah so much that she would cry and refuse to eat anything. ⁸Her husband Elkanah would ask her, "Hannah, why are you crying? Why won't you eat? Why are you always so sad? Don't I mean more to you than ten sons?"

Hannah and Eli

⁹⁻¹⁰One time, after they had finished their meal in the house of the LORD at Shiloh, Hannah got up. She was deeply distressed, and she cried bitterly as she prayed to the LORD. Meanwhile, Eli the priest was sitting in his place by the door. ¹¹Hannah made a solemn promise: "LORD Almighty, look at me, your servant! See my trouble and remember me! Don't forget me! If you give me a son, I promise that I will dedicate him to you for his whole life and that he will never have his hair cut."[b]

¹²Hannah continued to pray to the LORD for a long time, and Eli watched her lips. ¹³She was praying silently; her lips were moving, but she made no sound. So Eli thought that she was drunk, ¹⁴and he said to her, "Stop making a drunken show of yourself! Stop your drinking and sober up!"

¹⁵"No, I'm not drunk, sir," she answered. "I haven't been drinking! I am desperate, and I have been praying, pouring out my troubles to the LORD. ¹⁶Don't think I am a worthless woman. I have been praying like this because I'm so miserable."

¹⁷"Go in peace," Eli said, "and may the God of Israel give you what you have asked him for."

¹⁸"May you always think kindly of me," she replied. Then she went away, ate some food, and was no longer sad.

Samuel's Birth and Dedication

¹⁹The next morning Elkanah and his family got up early, and after worshiping the LORD, they went back home to

"Stop making a drunken show of yourself!" (1.14)

Ramah. Elkanah had intercourse with his wife Hannah, and the LORD answered her prayer. ²⁰So it was that she became pregnant and gave birth to a son. She named him Samuel,[c] and explained, "I asked the LORD for him."

²¹The time came again for Elkanah and his family to go to Shiloh and offer to the LORD the yearly sacrifice and the special sacrifice he had promised. ²²But this time Hannah did not go. She told her husband, "As soon as the child is weaned, I will take him to the house of the LORD, where he will stay all his life."

²³Elkanah answered, "All right, do whatever you think best; stay at home until you have weaned him. And may the LORD make your[d] promise come

---

[b] NEVER HAVE HIS HAIR CUT: *A sign of dedication to the LORD (see Nu 6.5).*
[c] SAMUEL: *This name, which in Hebrew means "name of God," is here related to the Hebrew verb for "ask."*　　[d] *Some ancient translations* your; *Hebrew* his.
1.11 Nu 6.5

true." So Hannah stayed at home and nursed her child.

24 After she had weaned him, she took him to Shiloh, taking along a three-year-old bull,[e] a bushel of flour, and a leather bag full of wine. She took Samuel, young as he was, to the house of the LORD at Shiloh. 25 After they had killed the bull, they took the child to Eli. 26 Hannah said to him, "Excuse me, sir. Do you remember me? I am the woman you saw standing here, praying to the LORD. 27 I asked him for this child, and he gave me what I asked for. 28 So I am dedicating him to the LORD. As long as he lives, he will belong to the LORD."

Then they[f] worshiped the LORD there.

Hannah's Prayer

2 Hannah prayed:

"The LORD has filled my heart
    with joy;
  how happy I am because of
    what he has done!
I laugh at my enemies;
  how joyful I am because God
    has helped me!

2 "No one is holy like the LORD;
  there is none like him,
  no protector like our God.
3 Stop your loud boasting;
  silence your proud words.
For the LORD is a God who
    knows,
  and he judges all that
    people do.
4 The bows of strong soldiers are
    broken,
  but the weak grow strong.
5 The people who once were
    well fed
  now hire themselves out to
    get food,

but the hungry are hungry no
    more.
The childless wife has borne
    seven children,
  but the mother of many is left
    with none.
6 The LORD kills and restores to
    life;
  he sends people to the world
    of the dead
  and brings them back again.
7 He makes some people poor and
    others rich;
  he humbles some and makes
    others great.
8 He lifts the poor from the dust
  and raises the needy from
    their misery.
He makes them companions of
    princes
  and puts them in places of
    honor.
The foundations of the earth
    belong to the LORD;
  on them he has built the
    world.

9 "He protects the lives of his
    faithful people,
  but the wicked disappear in
    darkness;
  a man does not triumph by
    his own strength.
10 The LORD's enemies will be
    destroyed;
  he will thunder against them
    from heaven.
The LORD will judge the whole
    world;
  he will give power to his king,
  he will make his chosen king
    victorious."

11 Then Elkanah went back home to Ramah, but the boy Samuel stayed in Shiloh and served the LORD under the priest Eli.

---

[e] Some ancient translations a three-year-old bull; Hebrew three bulls.   [f] Some ancient translations they; Hebrew he.

2.1-10 Lk 1.46-55   **2.6** Ws 16.13; Tb 13.2

The Sons of Eli

¹²The sons of Eli were scoundrels. They paid no attention to the LORD ¹³or to the regulations concerning what the priests could demand from the people. Instead, when someone was offering a sacrifice, the priest's servant would come with a three-pronged fork. While the meat was still cooking, ¹⁴he would stick the fork into the cooking pot, and whatever the fork brought out belonged to the priest. All the Israelites who came to Shiloh to offer sacrifices were treated like this. ¹⁵In addition, even before the fat was taken off and burned, the priest's servant would come and say to the one offering the sacrifice, "Give me some meat for the priest to roast; he won't accept boiled meat from you, only raw meat."

¹⁶If the person answered, "Let us do what is right and burn the fat first; then take what you want," the priest's servant would say, "No! Give it to me now! If you don't, I will have to take it by force!"

¹⁷This sin of the sons of Eli was extremely serious in the LORD's sight, because they treated the offerings to the LORD with such disrespect.

Samuel at Shiloh

¹⁸In the meantime the boy Samuel continued to serve the LORD, wearing a sacred linen apron. ¹⁹Each year his mother would make a little robe and take it to him when she accompanied her husband to offer the yearly sacrifice. ²⁰Then Eli would bless Elkanah and his wife, and say to Elkanah, "May the LORD give you other children by this woman to take the place of the one you dedicated to him."

After that they would go back home. ²¹The LORD did bless Hannah, and she had three more sons and two daughters. The boy Samuel grew up in the service of the LORD.

Eli and His Sons

²²Eli was now very old. He kept hearing about everything his sons were doing to the Israelites and that they were

Each year his mother would make a little robe. (2.19)

even sleeping with the women who worked at the entrance to the Tent of the LORD's presence. ²³So he said to them, "Why are you doing these things? Everybody tells me about the evil you are doing. ²⁴Stop it, my sons! This is an awful thing the people of the LORD are talking about! ²⁵If anyone sins against someone else, God can defend the one who is wrong; but who can defend someone who sins against the LORD?"

But they would not listen to their father, for the LORD had decided to kill them.

²⁶The boy Samuel continued to grow and to gain favor both with the LORD and with people.

The Prophecy against Eli's Family

²⁷A prophet came to Eli with this message from the LORD: "When your ancestor Aaron and his family were

2.26 Si 46.13; Lk 2.52

slaves of the king of Egypt, I revealed myself to Aaron. 28 From all the tribes of Israel I chose his family to be my priests, to serve at the altar, to burn the incense, and to wear the ephod*g* to consult me. And I gave them the right to keep a share of the sacrifices burned on the altar. 29 Why, then, do you look with greed*h* at the sacrifices and offerings which I require from my people? Why, Eli, do you honor your sons more than me by letting them fatten themselves on the best parts of all the sacrifices my people offer to me? 30 I, the LORD God of Israel, promised in the past that your family and your clan would serve me as priests for all time. But now I say that I won't have it any longer! Instead, I will honor those who honor me, and I will treat with contempt those who despise me. 31 Listen, the time is coming when I will kill all the young men in your family and your clan, so that no man in your family will live to be old. 32 You will be troubled and look with envy*i* on all the blessings I will give to the other people of Israel, but no one in your family will ever again live to old age. 33 Yet I will keep one of your descendants alive, and he will serve me as priest. But he*j* will become blind and lose all hope, and all your other descendants will die a violent death. 34 When your two sons Hophni and Phinehas both die on the same day, this will show you that everything I have said will come true. 35 I will choose a priest who will be faithful to me and do everything I want him to. I will give him descendants, who will always serve in the presence of my chosen king. 36 Any of your descendants who survive will have to go to that priest and ask him for money and food, and beg to be allowed to help the priests, in order to have something to eat."

The LORD Appears to Samuel

3 In those days, when the boy Samuel was serving the LORD under the direction of Eli, there were very few messages from the LORD, and visions from him were quite rare. 2 One night Eli, who was now almost blind, was sleeping in his own room; 3 Samuel was sleeping in the sanctuary, where the sacred Covenant Box was. Before dawn, while the lamp was still burning, 4 the LORD called Samuel. He answered, "Yes, sir!" 5 and ran to Eli and said, "You called me, and here I am."

But Eli answered, "I didn't call you; go back to bed." So Samuel went back to bed.

6-7 The LORD called Samuel again. The boy did not know that it was the LORD, because the LORD had never spoken to him before. So he got up, went to Eli, and said, "You called me, and here I am."

But Eli answered, "My son, I didn't call you; go back to bed."

8 The LORD called Samuel a third time; he got up, went to Eli, and said, "You called me, and here I am."

Then Eli realized that it was the LORD who was calling the boy, 9 so he said to him, "Go back to bed; and if he calls you again, say, 'Speak, LORD, your servant is listening.'" So Samuel went back to bed.

10 The LORD came and stood there, and called as he had before, "Samuel! Samuel!"

Samuel answered, "Speak; your servant is listening."

11 The LORD said to him, "Some day I am going to do something to the people of Israel that is so terrible that everyone who hears about it will be stunned. 12 On that day I will carry out all my threats against Eli's family, from begin-

---

g EPHOD: *See Word List.*   *h One ancient translation* look with greed; *Hebrew unclear.*
i Probable text look with envy; *Hebrew unclear.*   *j One ancient translation* he;
Hebrew you.
2.28 a Ex 28.1-4; **b** Lv 7.35, 36   **2.34** 1 S 4.11

ning to end. [13] I have already told him[k] that I am going to punish his family forever because his sons have spoken evil things against me. Eli knew they were doing this, but he did not stop them. [14] So I solemnly declare to the family of Eli that no sacrifice or offering will ever be able to remove the consequences of this terrible sin."

"Speak; your servant is listening." (3.10)

[15] Samuel stayed in bed until morning; then he got up and opened the doors of the house of the LORD. He was afraid to tell Eli about the vision. [16] Eli called him, "Samuel, my boy!"

"Yes, sir," answered Samuel.

[17] "What did the LORD tell you?" Eli asked. "Don't keep anything from me. God will punish you severely if you don't tell me everything he said." [18] So Samuel told him everything; he did not keep anything back. Eli said, "He is the LORD; he will do whatever seems best to him."

[19] As Samuel grew up, the LORD was with him and made come true everything that Samuel said. [20] So all the people of Israel, from one end of the country to the other, knew that Samuel was indeed a prophet of the LORD. [21] The LORD continued to reveal himself at Shiloh, where he had appeared to Samuel and had spoken to him. And when Samuel spoke, all Israel listened.

The Capture of the Covenant Box

4 At that time the Philistines gathered to go to war against Israel, so[l] the Israelites set out to fight them. The Israelites set up their camp at Ebenezer and the Philistines at Aphek. [2] The Philistines attacked, and after fierce fighting they defeated the Israelites and killed about four thousand men on the battlefield. [3] When the survivors came back to camp, the leaders of Israel said, "Why did the LORD let the Philistines defeat us today? Let's go and bring the LORD's Covenant Box from Shiloh, so that he[m] will go with us and save us from our enemies." [4] So they sent messengers to Shiloh and got the Covenant Box of the LORD Almighty, who is enthroned above the winged creatures.[n] And Eli's two sons, Hophni and Phinehas, came along with the Covenant Box.

[5] When the Covenant Box arrived, the Israelites gave such a loud shout of joy that the earth shook. [6] The Philistines heard the shouting and said, "Listen to all that shouting in the Hebrew camp! What does it mean?" When they found out that the LORD's Covenant Box had arrived in the Hebrew camp, [7] they were afraid, and said, "A god has come into their camp! We're lost! Nothing like this has ever happened to us before! [8] Who can save us from those powerful gods? They are the gods who slaughtered the Egyptians in the desert! [9] Be brave, Philistines! Fight like men, or we will become slaves to the Hebrews, just as they were our slaves. So fight like men!"

[10] The Philistines fought hard and

---

[k] *One ancient translation* I have already told him; *Hebrew* I will tell him.　　[l] *One ancient translation* the Philistines . . . so; *Hebrew does not have these words.*　　[m] he; *or* it.　　[n] WINGED CREATURES: *See Word List.*

4.4 Ex 25.22

defeated the Israelites, who went running to their homes. There was a great slaughter: thirty thousand Israelite soldiers were killed. [11] God's Covenant Box was captured, and Eli's sons, Hophni and Phinehas, were both killed.

The Death of Eli

[12] A man from the tribe of Benjamin ran all the way from the battlefield to Shiloh and arrived there the same day. To show his grief, he had torn his clothes and put dirt on his head. [13] Eli, who was very worried about the Covenant Box, was sitting in his seat beside the road, staring. The man spread the news throughout the town, and everyone cried out in fear. [14] Eli heard the noise and asked, "What is all this noise about?" The man hurried to Eli to tell him the news. ([15] Eli was now ninety-eight years old and almost completely blind.) [16] The man said, "I have escaped from the battle and have run all the way here today."

Eli asked him, "What happened, my son?"

[17] The messenger answered, "Israel ran away from the Philistines; it was a terrible defeat for us! Besides that, your sons Hophni and Phinehas were killed, and God's Covenant Box was captured!"

[18] When the man mentioned the Covenant Box, Eli fell backward from his seat beside the gate. He was so old and fat that the fall broke his neck, and he died. He had been a leader in Israel for forty years.

The Death of the Widow of Phinehas

[19] Eli's daughter-in-law, the wife of Phinehas, was pregnant, and it was almost time for her baby to be born. When she heard that God's Covenant Box had been captured and that her father-in-law and her husband were dead, she suddenly went into labor and gave birth. [20] As she was dying, the women helping her said to her, "Be brave! You have a son!" But she paid no attention and did not answer. [21] She named the boy Ichabod,[o] explaining, "God's glory has left Israel" — referring to the capture of the Covenant Box and the death of her father-in-law and her husband. [22] "God's glory has left Israel," she said, "because God's Covenant Box has been captured."

The Covenant Box among the Philistines

5 After the Philistines captured the Covenant Box, they carried it from Ebenezer to their city of Ashdod, [2] took it into the temple of their god Dagon, and set it up beside his statue. [3] Early the next morning the people of Ashdod saw that the statue of Dagon had fallen face downward on the ground in front of the LORD's Covenant Box. So they lifted it up and put it back in its place. [4] Early the following morning they saw that the statue had again fallen down in front of the Covenant Box. This time its head and both its arms were broken off and were lying in the doorway; only the body was left. ([5] That is why even today the priests of Dagon and all his worshipers in Ashdod step over that place and do not walk on it.)

[6] The LORD punished the people of Ashdod severely and terrified them. He punished them and the people in the surrounding territory by causing them to have tumors.[p] [7] When they saw what was happening, they said, "The God of Israel is punishing us and our god Dagon. We can't let the Covenant Box stay here any longer." [8] So they sent messengers and called together all five of the Philistine kings and asked them,

---

[o] ICHABOD: *This name in Hebrew means "no glory."*   [p] TUMORS: *The association of tumors with an abundance of mice suggests that this was a case of bubonic plague (see 6.5).*

"What shall we do with the Covenant Box of the God of Israel?"

"Take it over to Gath," they answered; so they took it to Gath, another Philistine city. ⁹But after it arrived there, the LORD punished that city too and caused a great panic. He punished them with tumors which developed in all the people of the city, young and old alike. ¹⁰So they sent the Covenant Box to Ekron, another Philistine city; but when it arrived there, the people cried out, "They have brought the Covenant Box of the God of Israel here, in order to kill us all!" ¹¹So again they sent for all the Philistine kings and said, "Send the Covenant Box of Israel back to its own place, so that it won't kill us and our families." There was panic throughout the city because God was punishing them so severely. ¹²Even those who did not die developed tumors and the people cried out to their gods for help.

The Return of the Covenant Box

6 After the LORD's Covenant Box had been in Philistia for seven months, ²the people called the priests and the magicians and asked, "What shall we do with the Covenant Box of the LORD? If we send it back where it belongs, what shall we send with it?"

³They answered, "If you return the Covenant Box of the God of Israel, you must, of course, send with it a gift to him to pay for your sin. The Covenant Box must not go back without a gift. In this way you will be healed, and you will find out why he has kept on punishing you."

⁴"What gift shall we send him?" the people asked.

They answered, "Five gold models of tumors and five gold mice, one of each for each Philistine king. The same plague was sent on all of you and on the five kings. ⁵You must make these models of the tumors and of the mice that are ravaging your country, and you must give honor to the God of Israel.

Perhaps he will stop punishing you, your gods, and your land. ⁶Why should you be stubborn, as the king of Egypt and the Egyptians were? Don't forget how God made fools of them until they let the Israelites leave Egypt. ⁷So prepare a new wagon and two cows that have never been yoked; hitch them to the wagon and drive their calves back to the barn. ⁸Take the LORD's Covenant Box, put it on the wagon, and place in a box beside it the gold models that you are sending to him as a gift to pay for your sins. Start the wagon on its way and let it go by itself. ⁹Then watch it go; if it goes toward the town of Beth Shemesh, this means that it is the God of the Israelites who has sent this terrible disaster on us. But if it doesn't, then we will know that he did not send the plague; it was only a matter of chance."

¹⁰They did what they were told: they took two cows and hitched them to the wagon, and shut the calves in the barn. ¹¹They put the Covenant Box in the wagon, together with the box containing the gold models of the mice and of the tumors. ¹²The cows started off on the road to Beth Shemesh and headed straight toward it, without turning off the road. They were mooing as they went. The five Philistine kings followed them as far as the border of Beth Shemesh.

¹³The people of Beth Shemesh were reaping wheat in the valley, when suddenly they looked up and saw the Covenant Box. They were overjoyed at the sight. ¹⁴The wagon came to a field belonging to a man named Joshua, who lived in Beth Shemesh, and it stopped there near a large rock. The people chopped up the wooden wagon and killed the cows and burned them as a burnt sacrifice to the LORD. ¹⁵The Levites lifted off the Covenant Box of the LORD and the box with the gold models in it, and placed them on the large rock. Then the people of Beth Shemesh offered burnt sacrifices and other sacrifices to the LORD. ¹⁶The five

The wagon came to a field belonging to a man named Joshua. (6.14)

Philistine kings watched them do this and then went back to Ekron that same day.

[17] The Philistines sent the five gold tumors to the LORD as a gift to pay for their sins, one each for the cities of Ashdod, Gaza, Ashkelon, Gath, and Ekron. [18] They also sent gold mice, one for each of the cities ruled by the five Philistine kings, both the fortified towns and the villages without walls. The large rock in the field of Joshua of Beth Shemesh, on which they placed the LORD's Covenant Box, is still there as a witness to what happened.

[19] The LORD killed seventy of the men of Beth Shemesh because they looked inside the Covenant Box. And the people mourned because the LORD had caused such a great slaughter among them.

7.1 2 S 6.2-4; 1 Ch 13.5-7

The Covenant Box at Kiriath Jearim

[20] So the men of Beth Shemesh said, "Who can stand before the LORD, this holy God? Where can we send him to get him away from us?" [21] They sent messengers to the people of Kiriath Jearim to say, "The Philistines have returned the LORD's Covenant Box. Come down and get it."

7 So the people of Kiriath Jearim got the LORD's Covenant Box and took it to the house of a man named Abinadab, who lived on a hill. They consecrated his son Eleazar to be in charge of it.

Samuel Rules Israel

[2] The Covenant Box of the LORD stayed in Kiriath Jearim a long time, some twenty years. During this time all

the Israelites cried to the LORD for help.

³Samuel said to the people of Israel, "If you are going to turn to the LORD with all your hearts, you must get rid of all the foreign gods and the images of the goddess Astarte. Dedicate yourselves completely to the LORD and worship only him, and he will rescue you from the power of the Philistines." ⁴So the Israelites got rid of their idols of Baal and Astarte, and worshiped only the LORD.

⁵Then Samuel called for all the Israelites to meet at Mizpah, telling them, "I will pray to the LORD for you there." ⁶So they all gathered at Mizpah. They drew some water and poured it out as an offering to the LORD and fasted that whole day. They said, "We have sinned against the LORD." (It was at Mizpah where Samuel settled disputes among the Israelites.)

⁷When the Philistines heard that the Israelites had gathered at Mizpah, the five Philistine kings started out with their men to attack them. The Israelites heard about it and were afraid, ⁸and said to Samuel, "Keep praying to the LORD our God to save us from the Philistines." ⁹Samuel killed a young lamb and burned it whole as a sacrifice to the LORD. Then he prayed to the LORD to help Israel, and the LORD answered his prayer. ¹⁰While Samuel was offering the sacrifice, the Philistines moved forward to attack; but just then the LORD thundered from heaven against them. They became completely confused and fled in panic. ¹¹The Israelites marched out from Mizpah and pursued the Philistines almost as far as Bethcar, killing them along the way.

¹²Then Samuel took a stone, set it up between Mizpah and Shen, and said, "The LORD has helped us all the way"— and he named it "Stone of Help." ¹³So the Philistines were defeated, and the LORD prevented them from invading Israel's territory as long as Samuel lived.

¹⁴All the cities which the Philistines had captured between Ekron and Gath were returned to Israel, and so Israel got back all its territory. And there was peace also between the Israelites and the Canaanites.

¹⁵Samuel ruled Israel as long as he lived. ¹⁶Every year he would go around to Bethel, Gilgal, and Mizpah, and in these places he would settle disputes. ¹⁷Then he would go back to his home in Ramah, where also he would serve as judge. In Ramah he built an altar to the LORD.

The People Ask for a King

8 When Samuel grew old, he made his sons judges in Israel. ²The older son was named Joel and the younger one Abijah; they were judges in Beersheba. ³But they did not follow their father's example; they were interested only in making money, so they accepted bribes and did not decide cases honestly.

⁴Then all the leaders of Israel met together, went to Samuel in Ramah, ⁵and said to him, "Look, you are getting old and your sons don't follow your example. So then, appoint a king to rule over us, so that we will have a king, as other countries have." ⁶Samuel was displeased with their request for a king; so he prayed to the LORD, ⁷and the LORD said, "Listen to everything the people say to you. You are not the one they have rejected; I am the one they have rejected as their king. ⁸Ever since I brought them out of Egypt, they have turned away from me and worshiped other gods; and now they are doing to you what they have always done to me. ⁹So then, listen to them, but give them strict warnings and explain how their kings will treat them."

¹⁰Samuel told the people who were asking him for a king everything that the LORD had said to him. ¹¹"This is

how your king will treat you," Samuel explained. "He will make soldiers of your sons; some of them will serve in his war chariots, others in his cavalry, and others will run before his chariots. ¹²He will make some of them officers in charge of a thousand men, and others in charge of fifty men. Your sons will have to plow his fields, harvest his crops, and make his weapons and the equipment for his chariots. ¹³Your daughters will have to make perfumes for him and work as his cooks and his bakers. ¹⁴He will take your best fields, vineyards, and olive groves, and give them to his officials. ¹⁵He will take a tenth of your grain and of your grapes for his court officers and other officials. ¹⁶He will take your servants and your best cattle ᑫ and donkeys, and make them work for him. ¹⁷He will take a tenth of your flocks. And you yourselves will become his slaves. ¹⁸When that time comes, you will complain bitterly because of your king, whom you yourselves chose, but the LORD will not listen to your complaints."

¹⁹The people paid no attention to Samuel, but said, "No! We want a king, ²⁰so that we will be like other nations, with our own king to rule us and to lead us out to war and to fight our battles." ²¹Samuel listened to everything they said and then went and told it to the LORD. ²²The LORD answered, "Do what they want and give them a king." Then Samuel told all the men of Israel to go back home.

Saul Meets Samuel

9 There was a wealthy and influential man named Kish, from the tribe of Benjamin; he was the son of Abiel and grandson of Zeror, and belonged to the family of Becorath, a part of the clan of Aphiah. ²He had a son named Saul, a handsome man in the prime of life. Saul was a foot taller than anyone else in Israel and more handsome as well.

³Some donkeys belonging to Kish had wandered off, so he said to Saul, "Take one of the servants with you and go and look for the donkeys." ⁴They went through the hill country of Ephraim and the region of Shalishah, but did not find them; so they went on through the region of Shaalim, but the donkeys were not there. Then they went through the territory of Benjamin, but still did not find them. ⁵When they came into the region of Zuph, Saul said to his servant, "Let's go back home, or my father might stop thinking about the donkeys and start worrying about us."

⁶The servant answered, "Wait! In this town there is a holy man who is highly respected because everything he says comes true. Let's go to him, and maybe he can tell us where we can find the donkeys."

⁷"If we go to him, what can we give him?" Saul asked. "There is no food left in our packs, and we don't have a thing to give him, do we?"

⁸The servant answered, "I have a small silver coin. I can give him that, and then he will tell us where we can find them."

⁹⁻¹¹Saul replied, "A good idea! Let's go." So they went to the town where the holy man lived. As they were going up the hill to the town, they met some young women who were coming out to draw water. They asked these women, "Is the seer in town?"

(At that time a prophet was called a seer, and so whenever someone wanted to ask God a question, he would say, "Let's go to the seer.")

¹²⁻¹³"Yes, he is," the young women answered. "In fact, he is just ahead of you. If you hurry, you will catch up with him. As soon as you go into town, you will find him. He arrived in town today because the people are going to offer a

---

ᑫ *One ancient translation* cattle; *Hebrew* young men.

sacrifice on the altar on the hill. The people who are invited won't start eating until he gets there, because he has to bless the sacrifice first. If you go now, you will find him before he goes up the hill to eat." ¹⁴So Saul and his servant went on to the town, and as they were going in, they saw Samuel coming out toward them on his way to the place of worship.

¹⁵Now on the previous day the LORD had told Samuel, ¹⁶"Tomorrow about this time I will send you a man from the tribe of Benjamin; anoint him as ruler of my people Israel, and he will rescue them from the Philistines. I have seen the suffering of my people and have heard their cries for help."

¹⁷When Samuel caught sight of Saul, the LORD said to him, "This is the man I told you about. He will rule my people." ¹⁸Then Saul went over to Samuel, who was near the gate, and asked, "Tell me, where does the seer live?"

¹⁹Samuel answered, "I am the seer. Go on ahead of me to the place of worship. Both of you are to eat with me today. Tomorrow morning I will answer all your questions and send you on your way. ²⁰As for the donkeys that were lost three days ago, don't worry about them; they have already been found. But who is it that the people of Israel want so much?ʳ It is you — you and your father's family."

²¹Saul answered, "I belong to the tribe of Benjamin, the smallest tribe in Israel, and my family is the least important one in the tribe. Why, then, do you talk like this to me?"

²²Then Samuel led Saul and his servant into the large room and gave them a place at the head of the table where the guests, about thirty in all, were seated. ²³Samuel said to the cook, "Bring the piece of meat I gave you, which I told you to set aside." ²⁴So the cook brought the choice piece of the leg and placed it before Saul. Samuelˢ

"I am the seer." (9.19)

said, "Look, here is the piece that was kept for you. Eat it. I saved it for you to eat at this time with the people I invited."ᵗ

So Saul ate with Samuel that day. ²⁵When they went down from the place of worship to the town, they fixed up a bed for Saulᵘ on the roof,ᵛ ²⁶and he slept there.ʷ

Samuel Anoints Saul as Ruler

At dawn Samuel called to Saul on the roof, "Get up, and I will send you on your way." Saul got up, and he and Samuel went out to the street together.

ʳ who is it ... much?; *or* who is to have the most desirable thing in Israel?   ˢ *Some ancient translations* Samuel; *Hebrew* He (that is, the cook).   ᵗ *Probable text* I saved it ... invited; *Hebrew unclear.*   ᵘ *One ancient translation* they fixed up a bed for Saul; *Hebrew* he spoke with Saul.   ᵛ ON THE ROOF: *At that time houses had flat roofs, and it was common for people to sleep on them.*   ʷ *Some ancient translations* and he slept there; *Hebrew* and they got up early.

27 When they arrived at the edge of town, Samuel said to Saul, "Tell the servant to go on ahead of us." The servant left, and Samuel continued, "Stay here a minute, and I will tell you what God has said."

10 Then Samuel took a jar of olive oil and poured it on Saul's head, kissed him, and said, "The LORD anoints you as ruler of his people Israel. You will rule his people and protect them from all their enemies. And this is the proof to you that the LORD has chosen you[x] to be the ruler of his people:

"The LORD anoints you as ruler of his people." (10.1)

2 When you leave me today, you will meet two men near Rachel's tomb at Zelzah in the territory of Benjamin. They will tell you that the donkeys you were looking for have been found, so that your father isn't worried any more about them but about you, and he keeps asking, 'What shall I do about my son?' 3 You will go on from there until you come to the sacred tree at Tabor, where you will meet three men on their way to offer a sacrifice to God at Bethel. One of them will be leading three young goats, another one will be carrying three loaves of bread, and the third one will have a leather bag full of wine. 4 They will greet you and offer you two of the loaves, which you are to accept. 5 Then you will go to the Hill of God in Gibeah, where there is a Philistine camp. At the entrance to the town you will meet a group of prophets coming down from the altar on the hill, playing harps, drums, flutes, and lyres. They will be dancing and shouting. 6 Suddenly the spirit of the LORD will take control of you, and you will join in their religious dancing and shouting and will become a different person. 7 When these things happen, do whatever God leads you to do. 8 You will go ahead of me to Gilgal, where I will meet you and offer burnt sacrifices and fellowship sacrifices. Wait there seven days until I come and tell you what to do."

9 When Saul turned to leave Samuel, God gave Saul a new nature. And everything Samuel had told him happened that day. 10 When Saul and his servant arrived at Gibeah, a group of prophets met him. Suddenly the spirit of God took control of him, and he joined in their ecstatic dancing and shouting. 11 People who had known him before saw him doing this and asked one another, "What has happened to the son of Kish? Has Saul become a prophet?" 12 A man who lived there asked, "How about these other prophets — who do you think their fathers are?" This is how the saying originated, "Has even Saul become a prophet?" 13 When Saul finished his ecstatic dancing and shouting, he went to the altar on the hill.

14 Saul's uncle saw him and the serv-

x *Some ancient translations* as ruler of his people ... the LORD has chosen you; *Hebrew does not have these words.*
10.12 1 S 19.23, 24

ant, and he asked them, "Where have you been?"

"Looking for the donkeys," Saul answered. "When we couldn't find them, we went to see Samuel."

¹⁵"And what did he tell you?" Saul's uncle asked.

¹⁶"He told us that the animals had been found," Saul answered — but he did not tell his uncle what Samuel had said about his becoming king.

Saul Is Acclaimed as King

¹⁷Samuel called the people together for a religious gathering at Mizpah ¹⁸and said to them, "The Lord, the God of Israel, says, 'I brought you out of Egypt and rescued you from the Egyptians and all the other peoples who were oppressing you. ¹⁹I am your God, the one who rescues you from all your troubles and difficulties, but today you have rejected me and have asked me to give you a king. Very well, then, gather yourselves before the Lord by tribes and by clans.'"

²⁰Then Samuel had each tribe come forward, and the Lord picked the tribe of Benjamin. ²¹Then Samuel had the families of the tribe of Benjamin come forward, and the family of Matri was picked out. Then the men of the family of Matri came forward,ʸ and Saul son of Kish was picked out. They looked for him, but when they could not find him, ²²they asked the Lord, "Is there still someone else?"

The Lord answered, "Saul is over there, hiding behind the supplies."

²³So they ran and brought Saul out to the people, and they could see that he was a foot taller than anyone else. ²⁴Samuel said to the people, "Here is the man the Lord has chosen! There is no one else among us like him."

All the people shouted, "Long live the king!"

²⁵Samuel explained to the people the rights and duties of a king, and then wrote them in a book, which he deposited in a holy place. Then he sent everyone home. ²⁶Saul also went back home to Gibeah. Some powerful men,ᶻ whose hearts God had touched, went with him. ²⁷But some worthless people said, "How can this fellow do us any good?" They despised Saul and did not bring him any gifts.

Saul Defeats the Ammonites

11 About a month later King Nahash of Ammon led his army against the town of Jabesh in the territory of Gilead and besieged it. The men of Jabesh said to Nahash, "Make a treaty with us, and we will accept you as our ruler."

²Nahash answered, "I will make a treaty with you on one condition: I will put out everyone's right eye and so bring disgrace on all Israel."

³The leaders of Jabesh said, "Give us seven days to send messengers throughout the land of Israel. If no one will help us, then we will surrender to you."

⁴The messengers arrived at Gibeah, where Saul lived, and when they told the news, the people started crying in despair. ⁵Saul was just then coming in from the field with his oxen, and he asked, "What's wrong? Why is everyone crying?" They told him what the messengers from Jabesh had reported. ⁶When Saul heard this, the spirit of God took control of him, and he became furious. ⁷He took two oxen, cut them in pieces, and had messengers carry the pieces throughout the land of Israel with this warning: "Whoever does not

---

ʸ *One ancient translation* Then the men of the family of Matri came forward; *Hebrew does not have these words.*   ᶻ *One ancient translation* Some powerful men; *Hebrew* The army.

follow Saul and Samuel into battle will have this done to his oxen!"

The people of Israel were afraid of what the LORD might do, and all of them, without exception, came out together. ⁸Saul gathered them at Bezek: there were 300,000 from Israel and 30,000 from Judah. ⁹They said to the messengers from Jabesh, "Tell your people that before noon tomorrow they will be rescued." When the people of Jabesh received the message, they were overjoyed ¹⁰and said to Nahash, "Tomorrow we will surrender to you, and you can do with us whatever you wish."

¹¹That night Saul divided his men into three groups, and at dawn the next day they rushed into the enemy camp and attacked the Ammonites. By noon they had slaughtered them. The survivors scattered, each man running off by himself.

¹²Then the people of Israel said to Samuel, "Where are the people who said that Saul should not be our king? Hand them over to us, and we will kill them!"

¹³But Saul said, "No one will be put to death today, for this is the day the LORD rescued Israel." ¹⁴And Samuel said to them, "Let us all go to Gilgal and once more proclaim Saul as our king." ¹⁵So they all went to Gilgal, and there at the holy place they proclaimed Saul king. They offered fellowship sacrifices, and Saul and all the people of Israel celebrated the event.

Samuel Addresses the People

12 Then Samuel said to the people of Israel, "I have done what you asked me to do. I have given you a king to rule you, ²and now you have him to lead you. As for me, I am old and gray,

and my sons are with you. I have been your leader from my youth until now. ³Here I am. If I have done anything wrong, accuse me now in the presence of the LORD and the king he has chosen. Have I taken anybody's cow or anybody's donkey? Have I cheated or oppressed anyone? Have I accepted a bribe from anyone? If I have done any of these things, I will pay back what I have taken."

⁴The people answered, "No, you have not cheated us or oppressed us; you have not taken anything from anyone."

⁵Samuel replied, "The LORD and the king he has chosen are witnesses today that you have found me to be completely innocent."

"Yes, the LORD is our witness," they answered.

⁶Samuel continued, "The LORD is the one who chose Moses and Aaron and who brought your ancestors out of Egypt. ⁷Now stand where you are, and I will accuse you before the LORD by reminding you[a] of all the mighty actions the LORD did to save you and your ancestors. ⁸When Jacob and his family went to Egypt and the Egyptians oppressed them,[b] your ancestors cried to the LORD for help, and he sent Moses and Aaron, who brought them out of Egypt and settled them in this land. ⁹But the people forgot the LORD their God, and so he let the Philistines and the king of Moab and Sisera, commander of the army of the city of Hazor, fight against your ancestors and conquer them. ¹⁰Then they cried to the LORD for help and said, 'We have sinned, because we turned away from you, LORD, and worshiped the idols of Baal and Astarte. Rescue us from our enemies, and we will worship you!'

ᵃ *One ancient translation* by reminding you; *Hebrew does not have these words.*
ᵇ *One ancient translation* and the Egyptians oppressed them; *Hebrew does not have these words.*

12.3 Si 46.19   **12.6** Ex 6.26   **12.8** Ex 2.23   **12.9 a** Jg 4.2; **b** Jg 13.1; **c** Jg 3.12
12.10 Jg 10.10-15

11 And the LORD sent Gideon, Barak,[c] Jephthah, and finally me. Each of us rescued you from your enemies, and you lived in safety. 12 But when you saw that King Nahash of Ammon was about to attack you, you rejected the LORD as your king and said to me, 'We want a king to rule us.'

13 "Now here is the king you chose; you asked for him, and now the LORD has given him to you. 14 All will go well with you if you honor the LORD your God, serve him, listen to him, and obey his commands, and if you and your king follow him. 15 But if you do not listen to the LORD but disobey his commands, he will be against you and your king.[d] 16 So then, stand where you are, and you will see the great thing which the LORD is going to do. 17 It's the dry season, isn't it? But I will pray, and the LORD will send thunder and rain. When this happens, you will realize that you committed a great sin against the LORD when you asked him for a king."

18 So Samuel prayed, and on that same day the LORD sent thunder and rain. Then all the people became afraid of the LORD and of Samuel, 19 and they said to Samuel, "Please, sir, pray to the LORD your God for us, so that we won't die. We now realize that, besides all our other sins, we have sinned by asking for a king."

20 "Don't be afraid," Samuel answered. "Even though you have done such an evil thing, do not turn away from the LORD, but serve him with all your heart. 21 Don't go after[e] false gods; they cannot help you or save you, for they are not real. 22 The LORD has made a solemn promise, and he will not abandon you, for he has decided to make you his own people. 23 As for me, the LORD forbid that I should sin against him by no longer praying for you. Instead, I will teach you what is good and right for you to do. 24 Obey the LORD and serve him faithfully with all your heart. Remember the great things he has done for you. 25 But if you continue to sin, you and your king will be destroyed."

War against the Philistines

13[f] 2 Saul picked three thousand men, keeping two thousand of them with him in Michmash and in the hill country of Bethel and sending one thousand with his son Jonathan to Gibeah, in the territory of the tribe of Benjamin. The rest of the men Saul sent home.

3 Jonathan killed the Philistine commander[g] in Geba, and all the Philistines heard about it. Then Saul sent messengers to call the Hebrews to war by blowing a trumpet throughout the whole country. 4 All the Israelites were told that Saul had killed the Philistine commander and that the Philistines hated them. So the people answered the call to join Saul at Gilgal.

5 The Philistines assembled to fight the Israelites; they had thirty thousand war chariots, six thousand cavalry troops, and as many soldiers as there are grains of sand on the seashore. They went to Michmash, east of Bethaven, and camped there. 6 Then they launched a strong attack against the Israelites, putting them in a desperate situation. Some of the Israelites hid in caves and holes or among the rocks or in pits and wells; 7 others crossed the

---

c Some ancient translations Barak; Hebrew Bedan.   *d One ancient translation your king; Hebrew your ancestors.*   *e Some ancient translations after; Hebrew because after.*   *f One ancient translation does not have verse 1; Hebrew has as verse 1 Saul was . . . years old when he became king, and he was king of Israel for two years. The Hebrew text is defective at two points in this verse.*   *g killed the Philistine commander; or defeated the Philistines camping.*

12.11 a Jg 7.1; **b** Jg 4.6; **c** Jg 11.29; **d** 1 S 3.20   **12.12** 1 S 8.19

Jordan River into the territories of Gad and Gilead.

Saul was still at Gilgal, and the people with him were trembling with fear. [8] He waited seven days for Samuel, as Samuel had instructed him to do, but Samuel still had not come to Gilgal. The people began to desert Saul, [9] so he said to them, "Bring me the burnt sacrifices and the fellowship sacrifices." He offered a burnt sacrifice, [10] and just as he was finishing, Samuel arrived. Saul went out to meet him and welcome him, [11] but Samuel said, "What have you done?"

Saul answered, "The people were deserting me, and you had not come when you said you would; besides that, the Philistines are gathering at Michmash. [12] So I thought, 'The Philistines are going to attack me here in Gilgal, and I have not tried to win the LORD's favor.' So I felt I had to offer a sacrifice."

[13] "That was a foolish thing to do," Samuel answered. "You have not obeyed the command the LORD your God gave you. If you had obeyed, he would have let you and your descendants rule over Israel forever. [14] But now your rule will not continue. Because you have disobeyed him, the LORD will find the kind of man he wants and make him ruler of his people."

[15] Samuel left Gilgal and went on his way. The rest of the people followed Saul as he went to join his soldiers. They went from Gilgal[h] to Gibeah in the territory of Benjamin. Saul inspected his troops, about six hundred men. [16] Saul, his son Jonathan, and their men camped in Geba in the territory of Benjamin; the Philistine camp was at Michmash. [17] The Philistine soldiers went out on raids from their camp in three groups: one group went toward Ophrah in the territory of Shual, [18] another went toward Beth Horon, and the other one went to the border overlooking Zeboim Valley and the wilderness.

[19] There were no blacksmiths in Israel because the Philistines were determined to keep the Hebrews from making swords and spears. ([20] The Israelites had to go to the Philistines to get their plows, hoes, axes, and sickles[i] sharpened; [21] the charge was one small coin for sharpening axes and for fixing goads,[j] and two coins for sharpening plows or hoes.) [22] And so on the day of battle none of the Israelite soldiers except Saul and his son Jonathan had swords or spears.

[23] The Philistines sent a group of soldiers to defend Michmash Pass.

Jonathan's Daring Deed

14 One day Jonathan said to the young man who carried his weapons, "Let's go across to the Philistine camp." But Jonathan did not tell his father Saul, [2] who was camping under a pomegranate tree in Migron, not far from Gibeah; he had about six hundred men with him. [3] (The priest carrying the ephod was Ahijah, the son of Ichabod's brother Ahitub, who was the son of Phinehas and grandson of Eli, the priest of the LORD in Shiloh.) The men did not know that Jonathan had left.

[4] In Michmash Pass, which Jonathan had to go through to get over to the Philistine camp, there were two large jagged rocks, one on each side of the pass: one was called Bozez and the other Seneh. [5] One was on the north side of the pass, facing Michmash, and the other was on the south side, facing Geba.

[6] Jonathan said to the young man, "Let's cross over to the camp of those

---

[h] *Some ancient translations* on his way . . . went from Gilgal; *Hebrew does not have these words.* [i] *One ancient translation* sickles; *Hebrew* plows. [j] *Probable text* the charge . . . fixing goads; *Hebrew unclear.*
13.8 1 S 10.8   **13.14** Ac 13.22

heathen Philistines. Maybe the LORD will help us; if he does, nothing can keep him from giving us the victory, no matter how few of us there are."

⁷The young man answered, "Whatever you want to do,ᵏ I'm with you."

⁸"All right," Jonathan said. "We will go across and let the Philistines see us. ⁹If they tell us to wait for them to come to us, then we will stay where we are. ¹⁰But if they tell us to go to them, then we will, because that will be the sign that the LORD has given us victory over them."

¹¹So they let the Philistines see them, and the Philistines said, "Look! Some Hebrews are coming out of the holes they have been hiding in!" ¹²Then they called out to Jonathan and the young man, "Come on up here! We have something to tellˡ you!"

Jonathan said to the young man, "Follow me. The LORD has given Israel victory over them." ¹³Jonathan climbed up out of the pass on his hands and knees, and the young man followed him. Jonathan attacked the Philistines and knocked them down, and the young man killed them. ¹⁴In that first slaughter Jonathan and the young man killed about twenty men in an area of about half an acre.ᵐ ¹⁵All the Philistines in the countryside were terrified; the raiders and the soldiers in the camp trembled with fear; the earth shook, and there was great panic.

The Defeat of the Philistines

¹⁶Saul's men on watch at Gibeah in the territory of Benjamin saw the Philistines running in confusion. ¹⁷So Saul said to his men, "Count the soldiers and find out who is missing." They did so

and found that Jonathan and the young man who carried his weapons were missing. ¹⁸"Bring the ephodⁿ here," Saul said to Ahijah the priest. (On that day Ahijah was carrying it in front of the people of Israel.)ᵒ ¹⁹As Saul was speaking to the priest, the confusion in the Philistine camp kept getting worse, so Saul said to him, "There's no time to consult the LORD!" ²⁰Then he and his men marched into battle against the Philistines, who were fighting each other in complete confusion. ²¹Some Hebrews, who had been on the Philistine side and had gone with them to the camp, changed sides againᵖ and joined Saul and Jonathan. ²²Others, who had been hiding in the hills of Ephraim, heard that the Philistines were running away, so they also joined in and attacked the Philistines, ²³fighting all the way beyond Bethaven. The LORD saved Israel that day.

Events after the Battle

²⁴The Israelites were weak with hunger that day, because Saul, with a solemn oath, had given the order: "A curse be on anyone who eats any food today before I take revenge on my enemies." So nobody had eaten anything all day. ²⁵They allᑫ came into a wooded area and found honey everywhere. ²⁶The woods were full of honey, but no one ate any of it because they were all afraid of Saul's curse. ²⁷But Jonathan had not heard his father threaten the people with a curse; so he reached out with the stick he was carrying, dipped it in a honeycomb, and ate some honey. At once he felt much better. ²⁸But one of the men told him, "We are all weak from hunger, but your father

---

ᵏ *One ancient translation* you want to do; *Hebrew* you want to do. Turn.   ˡ tell; *or* show.   ᵐ *Probable text* in an area of about half an acre; *Hebrew unclear.*   ⁿ *One ancient translation* ephod *(see 2.28); Hebrew* Covenant Box.   ᵒ *One ancient translation* On that day ... Israel; *Hebrew* Because on that day God's Covenant Box and the people of Israel.   ᵖ *Some ancient translations* changed sides again; *Hebrew* around also.   ᑫ *Probable text* They all; *Hebrew* All the land.

threatened us and said, 'A curse be on anyone who eats any food today.' "

29 Jonathan answered, "What a terrible thing my father has done to our people! See how much better I feel because I ate some honey! 30 How much better it would have been today if our people had eaten the food they took when they defeated the enemy. Just think how many more Philistines they would have killed!"

31 That day the Israelites defeated the Philistines, fighting all the way from Michmash to Aijalon. By this time the Israelites were very weak from hunger, 32 and so they rushed over to what they had captured from the enemy, took sheep and cattle, slaughtered them on the spot, and ate the meat with the blood still in it. 33 Saul was told, "Look, the people are sinning against the LORD by eating meat with the blood in it."

"You are traitors!" Saul cried out. "Roll a big stone over here *r* to me." 34 Then he gave another order: "Go among the people and tell them all to bring their cattle and sheep here. They are to slaughter them and eat them here; they must not sin against the LORD by eating meat with blood in it." So that night they all brought their cattle and slaughtered them there. 35 Saul built an altar to the LORD, the first one that he built.

36 Saul said to his men, "Let's go down and attack the Philistines in the night, plunder them until dawn, and kill them all."

"Do whatever you think best," they answered.

But the priest said, "Let's consult God first."

37 So Saul asked God, "Shall I attack the Philistines? Will you give us vic-

tory?" But God did not answer that day. 38 Then Saul said to the leaders of the people, "Come here and find out what sin was committed today. 39 I promise by the living LORD, who gives Israel victory, that the guilty one will be put to death, even if he is my son Jonathan." But no one said anything. 40 Then Saul said to them, "All of you stand over there, and Jonathan and I will stand over here."

"Do whatever you think best," they answered.

41 Saul said to the LORD, the God of Israel, "LORD, why have you not answered me today? LORD, God of Israel, answer me by the sacred stones. If the guilt is Jonathan's or mine, answer by the Urim; but if it belongs to your people Israel, *s* answer by the Thummim." *t* The answer indicated Jonathan and Saul; and the people were cleared. 42 Then Saul said, "Decide between my son Jonathan and me." And Jonathan was indicated. 43 Then Saul asked Jonathan, "What have you done?"

Jonathan answered, "I ate a little honey with the stick I was holding. Here I am — I am ready to die."

44 Saul said to him, "May God strike me dead if you are not put to death!"

45 But the people said to Saul, "Will Jonathan, who won this great victory for Israel, be put to death? No! We promise by the living LORD that he will not lose even a hair from his head. What he did today was done with God's help." So the people saved Jonathan from being put to death.

46 After that, Saul stopped pursuing the Philistines, and they went back to their own territory.

---

r One ancient translation here; *Hebrew* today.   *s Some ancient translations* answer me by the sacred stones . . . your people Israel; *Hebrew does not have these words.*
t URIM . . . THUMMIM: *Two stones used by the priest to determine God's will; it is not known precisely how they were used.*
14.33 Gn 9.4; Lv 7.26, 27; 17.10-14; 19.26; Dt 12.16, 23; 15.23   **14.41** Nu 27.21; 1 S 28.6

Saul's Reign and Family

47 After Saul became king of Israel, he fought all his enemies everywhere: the people of Moab, of Ammon, and of Edom, the kings of Zobah, and the Philistines. Wherever he fought he was victorious.*u* 48 He fought heroically and defeated even the people of Amalek. He saved the Israelites from all attacks.

49 Saul's sons were Jonathan, Ishvi, and Malchishua. His older daughter was named Merab, and the younger one Michal. 50 His wife was Ahinoam, the daughter of Ahimaaz; his army commander was his cousin Abner, the son of his uncle Ner. 51 Saul's father Kish and Abner's father Ner were sons of Abiel.

52 As long as he lived, Saul had to fight fiercely against the Philistines. So whenever he found a man who was strong or brave, he would enlist him in his army.

War against the Amalekites

15 Samuel said to Saul, "I am the one whom the LORD sent to anoint you king of his people Israel. Now listen to what the LORD Almighty says. 2 He is going to punish the people of Amalek because their ancestors opposed the Israelites when they were coming from Egypt. 3 Go and attack the Amalekites and completely destroy everything they have. Don't leave a thing; kill all the men, women, children, and babies; the cattle, sheep, camels, and donkeys."

4 Saul called his forces together and inspected them at Telem: there were 200,000 soldiers from Israel and 10,000 from Judah. 5 Then he and his men went to the city of Amalek and waited

in ambush in a dry riverbed. 6 He sent a warning to the Kenites, a people whose ancestors had been kind to the Israelites when they came from Egypt: "Go away and leave the Amalekites, so that I won't kill you along with them." So the Kenites left.

7 Saul defeated the Amalekites, fighting all the way from Havilah to Shur, east of Egypt; 8 he captured King Agag of Amalek alive and killed all the people. 9 But Saul and his men spared Agag's life and did not kill the best sheep and cattle, the best calves and lambs,*v* or anything else that was good; they destroyed only what was useless or worthless.*w*

Saul Is Rejected as King

10 The LORD said to Samuel, 11 "I am sorry that I made Saul king; he has turned away from me and disobeyed my commands." Samuel was angry, and all night long he pleaded with the LORD. 12 Early the following morning he went off to find Saul. He heard that Saul had gone to the town of Carmel, where he had built a monument to himself, and then had gone on to Gilgal. 13 Samuel went up to Saul, who greeted him, saying, "The LORD bless you, Samuel! I have obeyed the LORD's command."

14 Samuel asked, "Why, then, do I hear cattle mooing and sheep bleating?"

15 Saul answered, "My men took them from the Amalekites. They kept the best sheep and cattle to offer as a sacrifice to the LORD your God, and the rest we have destroyed completely."*x*

16 "Stop," Samuel ordered, "and I will tell you what the LORD said to me last night."

---

u One ancient translation was victorious; *Hebrew* acted wickedly.   *v One ancient translation* the best calves and lambs; *Hebrew unclear.*   *w Some ancient translations* useless or worthless; *Hebrew unclear.*   *x* DESTROYED COMPLETELY: *These animals had been unconditionally dedicated to the LORD and had to be destroyed (see Lv 27.28).*

15.1 1 S 10.1   **15.2** Ex 17.8-14; Dt 25.17-19

"Tell me," Saul said.

¹⁷ Samuel answered, "Even though you consider yourself of no importance, you are the leader of the tribes of Israel. The LORD anointed you king of Israel, ¹⁸ and he sent you out with orders to destroy those wicked people of Amalek. He told you to fight until you had killed them all. ¹⁹ Why, then, did you not obey him? Why did you rush to grab the loot, and so do what displeases the LORD?"

²⁰ "I did obey the LORD," Saul replied. "I went out as he told me to, brought back King Agag, and killed all the Amalekites. ²¹ But my men did not kill the best sheep and cattle that they captured; instead, they brought them here to Gilgal to offer as a sacrifice to the LORD your God."

²² Samuel said, "Which does the LORD prefer: obedience or offerings and sacrifices? It is better to obey him than to sacrifice the best sheep to him. ²³ Rebellion against him is as bad as witchcraft, and arrogance is as sinful as idolatry. Because you rejected the LORD's command, he has rejected you as king."

²⁴ "Yes, I have sinned," Saul replied. "I disobeyed the LORD's command and your instructions. I was afraid of my men and did what they wanted. ²⁵ But now I beg you, forgive my sin and go back with me, so that I can worship the LORD."

²⁶ "I will not go back with you," Samuel answered. "You rejected the LORD's command, and he has rejected you as king of Israel."

²⁷ Then Samuel turned to leave, but Saul caught hold of his cloak, and it tore. ²⁸ Samuel said to him, "The LORD has torn the kingdom of Israel away from you today and given it to someone who is a better man than you. ²⁹ Israel's majestic God does not lie or change his mind. He is not a human being—he does not change his mind."

³⁰ "I have sinned," Saul replied. "But at least show me respect in front of the

"The LORD has torn the kingdom away from you." (15.28)

leaders of my people and all of Israel. Go back with me so that I can worship the LORD your God." ³¹ So Samuel went back with him, and Saul worshiped the LORD.

³² "Bring King Agag here to me," Samuel ordered. Agag came to him, trembling with fear, thinking to himself, "What a bitter thing it is to die!"ʸ ³³ Samuel said, "As your sword has made many mothers childless, so now your mother will become childless." And he cut Agag to pieces in front of the altar in Gilgal.

³⁴ Then Samuel went to Ramah, and King Saul went home to Gibeah. ³⁵ As long as Samuel lived, he never again saw the king; but he grieved over him. The LORD was sorry that he had made Saul king of Israel.

David Is Anointed King

16 The LORD said to Samuel, "How long will you go on grieving over Saul? I have rejected him as king of Israel. But now get some olive oil and go to Bethlehem, to a man named Jesse, because I have chosen one of his sons to be king."

² "How can I do that?" Samuel asked.

ʸ trembling with fear ... die; *or* confidently, thinking to himself, "Surely the bitter danger of death is past!"

15.27, 28 1 S 28.17; 1 K 11.30, 31

"If Saul hears about it, he will kill me!"

The LORD answered, "Take a calf with you and say that you are there to offer a sacrifice to the LORD. ³Invite Jesse to the sacrifice, and I will tell you what to do. You will anoint as king the man I tell you to."

⁴Samuel did what the LORD told him to do and went to Bethlehem, where the city leaders came trembling to meet him and asked, "Is this a peaceful visit, seer?"

⁵"Yes," he answered. "I have come to offer a sacrifice to the LORD. Purify yourselves and come with me." He also told Jesse and his sons to purify themselves, and he invited them to the sacrifice.

⁶When they arrived, Samuel saw Jesse's son Eliab and said to himself, "This man standing here in the LORD's presence is surely the one he has chosen." ⁷But the LORD said to him, "Pay no attention to how tall and handsome he is. I have rejected him, because I do not judge as people judge. They look at the outward appearance, but I look at the heart."

⁸Then Jesse called his son Abinadab and brought him to Samuel. But Samuel said, "No, the LORD hasn't chosen him either." ⁹Jesse then brought Shammah. "No, the LORD hasn't chosen him either," Samuel said. ¹⁰In this way Jesse brought seven of his sons to Samuel. And Samuel said to him, "No, the LORD hasn't chosen any of these." ¹¹Then he asked him, "Do you have any more sons?"

Jesse answered, "There is still the youngest, but he is out taking care of the sheep."

"Tell him to come here," Samuel said. "We won't offer the sacrifice until he comes." ¹²So Jesse sent for him. He was a handsome, healthy young man, and his eyes sparkled. The LORD said to Samuel, "This is the one — anoint him!" ¹³Samuel took the olive oil and anointed David in front of his brothers. Immediately the spirit of the LORD took control of David and was with him from that day on. Then Samuel returned to Ramah.

David in Saul's Court

¹⁴The LORD's spirit left Saul, and an evil spirit sent by the LORD tormented him. ¹⁵His servants said to him, "We know that an evil spirit sent by God is tormenting you. ¹⁶So give us the order, sir, and we will look for a man who knows how to play the harp. Then when the evil spirit comes on you, the man can play his harp, and you will be all right again."

¹⁷Saul ordered them, "Find me a man who plays well and bring him to me."

¹⁸One of his attendants said, "Jesse of the town of Bethlehem has a son who is a good musician. He is also a brave and handsome man, a good soldier, and an able speaker. The LORD is with him."

¹⁹So Saul sent messengers to Jesse to say, "Send me your son David, the one who takes care of the sheep." ²⁰Jesse sent David to Saul with a young goat, a donkey loaded with bread, and a leather bag full of wine. ²¹David came to Saul and entered his service. Saul liked him very much and chose him as the man to carry his weapons. ²²Then Saul sent a message to Jesse: "I like David. Let him stay here in my service." ²³From then on, whenever the evil spirit sent by God came on Saul, David would get

David would get his harp and play it. (16.23)

"I dare you to pick someone to fight me!" (17.10)

his harp and play it. The evil spirit would leave, and Saul would feel better and be all right again.

Goliath Challenges the Israelites

17 The Philistines gathered for battle in Socoh, a town in Judah; they camped at a place called Ephes Dammim, between Socoh and Azekah. ² Saul and the Israelites assembled and camped in Elah Valley, where they got ready to fight the Philistines. ³ The Philistines lined up on one hill and the Israelites on another, with a valley between them.

⁴ A man named Goliath, from the city of Gath, came out from the Philistine camp to challenge the Israelites. He was over nine feet*ᶻ* tall ⁵ and wore bronze armor that weighed about 125 pounds and a bronze helmet. ⁶ His legs were also protected by bronze armor, and he carried a bronze javelin slung over his shoulder. ⁷ His spear was as thick as the bar on a weaver's loom, and its iron head weighed about fifteen pounds. A soldier walked in front of him carrying his shield. ⁸ Goliath stood and shouted at the Israelites, "What are you doing there, lined up for battle? I am a Philistine, you slaves of Saul! Choose one of your men to fight me. ⁹ If he wins and kills me, we will be your slaves; but if I win and kill him, you will be our slaves. ¹⁰ Here and now I challenge the Israelite army. I dare you to pick someone to fight me!" ¹¹ When Saul and his men heard this, they were terrified.

David in Saul's Camp

¹² David was the son of Jesse, who was an Ephrathite from Bethlehem in Judah. Jesse had eight sons, and at the time Saul was king, he was already a very old man.*ᵃ* ¹³ His three oldest sons had gone with Saul to war. The oldest

---

ᶻ *Hebrew* nine feet; *one ancient Hebrew manuscript and one ancient translation* seven feet.   ᵃ *Some ancient translations* a very old man; *Hebrew unclear.*

was Eliab, the next was Abinadab, and the third was Shammah. ¹⁴David was the youngest son, and while the three oldest brothers stayed with Saul, ¹⁵David would go back to Bethlehem from time to time, to take care of his father's sheep.

¹⁶Goliath challenged the Israelites every morning and evening for forty days.

¹⁷One day Jesse said to David, "Take a half-bushel of this roasted grain and these ten loaves of bread, and hurry with them to your brothers in the camp. ¹⁸And take these ten cheeses to the commanding officer. Find out how your brothers are getting along and bring back something to show that you saw them and that they are well. ¹⁹King Saul, your brothers, and all the other Israelites are in Elah Valley fighting the Philistines."

²⁰David got up early the next morning, left someone else in charge of the sheep, took the food, and went as Jesse had told him to. He arrived at the camp just as the Israelites were going out to their battle line, shouting the war cry. ²¹The Philistine and the Israelite armies took positions for battle, facing each other. ²²David left the food with the officer in charge of the supplies, ran to the battle line, went to his brothers, and asked how they were getting along. ²³As he was talking with them, Goliath came forward and challenged the Israelites as he had done before. And David heard him. ²⁴When the Israelites saw Goliath, they ran away in terror. ²⁵"Look at him!" they said to each other. "Listen to his challenge! King Saul has promised to give a big reward to the man who kills him; the king will also give him his daughter to marry and will not require his father's family to pay taxes."ᵇ

²⁶David asked the men who were near him, "What will the man get who kills this Philistine and frees Israel from this disgrace? After all, who is this heathen Philistine to defy the army of the living God?" ²⁷They told him what would be done for the man who killed Goliath.

²⁸Eliab, David's oldest brother, heard David talking to the men. He became angry with David and said, "What are you doing here? Who is taking care of those sheep of yours out there in the wilderness? You smart aleck, you! You just came to watch the fighting!"

²⁹"Now what have I done?" David asked. "Can't I even ask a question?" ³⁰He turned to another man and asked him the same question, and every time he asked, he got the same answer.

³¹Some men heard what David had said, and they told Saul, who sent for him. ³²David said to Saul, "Your Majesty, no one should be afraid of this Philistine! I will go and fight him."

³³"No," answered Saul. "How could you fight him? You're just a boy, and he has been a soldier all his life!"

³⁴"Your Majesty," David said, "I take care of my father's sheep. Any time a lion or a bear carries off a lamb, ³⁵I go after it, attack it, and rescue the lamb. And if the lion or bear turns on me, I grab it by the throat and beat it to death. ³⁶I have killed lions and bears, and I will do the same to this heathen Philistine, who has defied the army of the living God. ³⁷The LORD has saved me from lions and bears; he will save me from this Philistine."

"All right," Saul answered. "Go, and the LORD be with you." ³⁸He gave his own armor to David for him to wear: a bronze helmet, which he put on David's head, and a coat of armor. ³⁹David strapped Saul's sword over the armor and tried to walk, but he couldn't, because he wasn't used to wearing them. "I can't fight with all this," he said to Saul. "I'm not used to it." So he took it all off. ⁴⁰He took his shepherd's stick and then picked up five smooth stones

---

ᵇ to pay taxes; *or* either to pay taxes or serve him.

David defeated and killed Goliath. (17.50)

from the stream and put them in his bag. With his sling ready, he went out to meet Goliath.

David Defeats Goliath

⁴¹ The Philistine started walking toward David, with his shield bearer walking in front of him. He kept coming closer, ⁴² and when he got a good look at David, he was filled with scorn for him because he was just a nice, good-looking boy. ⁴³ He said to David, "What's that stick for? Do you think I'm a dog?" And he called down curses from his god on David. ⁴⁴ "Come on," he challenged David, "and I will give your body to the birds and animals to eat."

⁴⁵ David answered, "You are coming against me with sword, spear, and javelin, but I come against you in the name of the LORD Almighty, the God of the Israelite armies, which you have defied. ⁴⁶ This very day the LORD will put you in my power; I will defeat you and cut off your head. And I will give the bodies of the Philistine soldiers to the birds and animals to eat. Then the whole world

will know that Israel has a God, ⁴⁷ and everyone here will see that the LORD does not need swords or spears to save his people. He is victorious in battle, and he will put all of you in our power."

⁴⁸ Goliath started walking toward David again, and David ran quickly toward the Philistine battle line to fight him. ⁴⁹ He reached into his bag and took out a stone, which he slung at Goliath. It hit him on the forehead and broke his skull, and Goliath fell face downward on the ground. ⁵⁰ And so, without a sword, David defeated and killed Goliath with a sling and a stone! ⁵¹ He ran to him, stood over him, took Goliath's sword out of its sheath, and cut off his head and killed him.

When the Philistines saw that their hero was dead, they ran away. ⁵² The men of Israel and Judah shouted and ran after them, pursuing them all the way to Gath*c* and to the gates of Ekron. The Philistines fell wounded all along the road that leads to Shaaraim, as far as Gath and Ekron. ⁵³ When the Israelites came back from pursuing the Phi-

c One ancient translation Gath; *Hebrew* a valley.

17.50 2 S 21.19 **17.51** 2 S 21.29

listines, they looted their camp. ⁵⁴David got Goliath's head and took it to Jerusalem, but he kept Goliath's weapons in his own tent.

David Is Presented to Saul

⁵⁵When Saul saw David going out to fight Goliath, he asked Abner, the commander of his army, "Abner, whose son is he?"

"I have no idea, Your Majesty," Abner answered.

⁵⁶"Then go and find out," Saul ordered.

⁵⁷So when David returned to camp after killing Goliath, Abner took him to Saul. David was still carrying Goliath's head. ⁵⁸Saul asked him, "Young man, whose son are you?"

"I am the son of your servant Jesse from Bethlehem," David answered.

18 Saul and David finished their conversation. After that, Saul's son Jonathan was deeply attracted to David and came to love him as much as he loved himself. ²Saul kept David with him from that day on and did not let him go back home. ³Jonathan swore eternal friendship with David because of his deep affection for him. ⁴He took off the robe he was wearing and gave it to David, together with his armor and also his sword, bow, and belt. ⁵David was successful in all the missions on which Saul sent him, and so Saul made him an officer in his army. This pleased all of Saul's officers and men.

Saul Becomes Jealous of David

⁶As David was returning after killing Goliath and as the soldiers were coming back home, women from every town in Israel came out to meet King Saul. They were singing joyful songs, dancing, and playing tambourines and lyres. ⁷In their celebration the women sang, "Saul has killed thousands, but David tens of thousands." ⁸Saul did not like

this, and he became very angry. He said, "For David they claim tens of thousands, but only thousands for me. They will be making him king next!" ⁹And so he was jealous and suspicious of David from that day on.

¹⁰The next day an evil spirit from God suddenly took control of Saul, and he raved in his house like a madman. David was playing the harp, as he did every day, and Saul was holding a spear. ¹¹"I'll pin him to the wall," Saul said to himself, and he threw the spear at him twice; but David dodged each time.

"I'll pin him to the wall." (18.11)

¹²Saul was afraid of David because the LORD was with David but had abandoned him. ¹³So Saul sent him away and put him in command of a thousand men. David led his men in battle ¹⁴and was successful in all he did, because the LORD was with him. ¹⁵Saul noticed David's success and became even more afraid of him. ¹⁶But everyone in Israel and Judah loved David because he was such a successful leader.

David Marries Saul's Daughter

¹⁷Then Saul said to David, "Here is my older daughter Merab. I will give her to you as your wife on condition that you serve me as a brave and loyal soldier, and fight the LORD's battles." (Saul was thinking that in this way the Philistines would kill David, and he would not have to do it himself.)

¹⁸David answered, "Who am I and

18.7 1 S 21.11; 29.5

what is my family that I should become the king's son-in-law?" [19] But when the time came for Merab to be given to David, she was given instead to a man named Adriel from Meholah.

[20] Saul's daughter Michal, however, fell in love with David, and when Saul heard of this, he was pleased. [21] He said to himself, "I'll give Michal to David; I will use her to trap him, and he will be killed by the Philistines." So for the second time Saul said to David, "You will be my son-in-law." [22] He ordered his officials to speak privately with David and tell him, "The king is pleased with you and all his officials like you; now is a good time for you to marry his daughter."

[23] So they told this to David, and he answered, "It's a great honor to become the king's son-in-law, too great for someone poor and insignificant like me."

[24] The officials told Saul what David had said, [25] and Saul ordered them to tell David: "All the king wants from you as payment for the bride are the foreskins of a hundred dead Philistines, as revenge on his enemies." (This was how Saul planned to have David killed by the Philistines.) [26] Saul's officials reported to David what Saul had said, and David was delighted with the thought of becoming the king's son-in-law. Before the day set for the wedding, [27] David and his men went and killed two hundred Philistines. He took their foreskins to the king and counted them all out to him, so that he might become his son-in-law. So Saul had to give his daughter Michal in marriage to David.

[28] Saul realized clearly that the LORD was with David and also that his daughter Michal loved him. [29] So he became even more afraid of David and was his enemy as long as he lived.

[30] The Philistine armies would come and fight, but in every battle David was

more successful than any of Saul's other officers. As a result David became very famous.

David Is Persecuted by Saul

19 Saul told his son Jonathan and all his officials that he planned to kill[d] David. But Jonathan was very fond of David, [2] and so he told him, "My father is trying to kill you. Please be careful tomorrow morning; hide in some secret place and stay there. [3] I will go and stand by my father in the field where you are hiding, and I will speak to him about you. If I find out anything, I will let you know."

[4] Jonathan praised David to Saul and said, "Sir, don't do wrong to your servant David. He has never done you any wrong; on the contrary, everything he has done has been a great help to you. [5] He risked his life when he killed Goliath, and the LORD won a great victory for Israel. When you saw it, you were glad. Why, then, do you now want to do wrong to an innocent man and kill David for no reason at all?"

[6] Saul was convinced by what Jonathan said and made a vow in the LORD's name that he would not kill David. [7] So Jonathan called David and told him everything; then he took him to Saul, and David served the king as he had before.

[8] War with the Philistines broke out again. David attacked them and defeated them so thoroughly that they fled.

[9] One day an evil spirit from the LORD took control of Saul. He was sitting in his house with his spear in his hand, and David was there, playing his harp. [10] Saul tried to pin David to the wall with his spear, but David dodged, and the spear stuck in the wall. David ran away and escaped.

[11] That same night Saul sent some

---

[d] that he planned to kill; *or* to kill.

19.11 Ps 59 Title

men to watch David's house and kill him the next morning. Michal, David's wife, warned him, "If you don't get away tonight, tomorrow you will be dead." ¹²She let him down from a window, and he ran away and escaped. ¹³Then she took the household idol, laid it on the bed, put a pillow made of goats' hair at its head, and put a cover over it. ¹⁴When Saul's men came to get David, Michal told them that he was sick. ¹⁵But Saul sent them back to see David for themselves. He ordered them, "Carry him here in his bed, and I will kill him." ¹⁶They went inside and found the household idol in the bed and the goats' hair pillow at its head. ¹⁷Saul asked Michal, "Why have you tricked me like this and let my enemy escape?"

She answered, "He said he would kill me if I didn't help him escape."

¹⁸David escaped and went to Samuel in Ramah and told him everything that Saul had done to him. Then he and Samuel went to Naioth and stayed there. ¹⁹Saul was told that David was in Naioth in Ramah, ²⁰so he sent some men to arrest him. They saw*e* the group of prophets dancing and shouting, with Samuel as their leader. Then the spirit of God took control of Saul's men, and they also began to dance and shout. ²¹When Saul heard of this, he sent more messengers, and they also began to dance and shout. He sent messengers the third time, and the same thing happened to them. ²²Then he himself started out to Ramah. When he came to the large well in Secu, he asked where Samuel and David were and was told that they were at Naioth. ²³As he was going there, the spirit of God took control of him also, and he danced and shouted all the way to Naioth. ²⁴He took off his clothes and danced and shouted in Samuel's presence, and lay naked all that day and all

that night. (This is how the saying originated, "Has even Saul become a prophet?")

Jonathan Helps David

20 Then David fled from Naioth in Ramah and went to Jonathan. "What have I done?" he asked. "What crime have I committed? What wrong have I done to your father to make him want to kill me?"

²Jonathan answered, "God forbid that you should die! My father tells me everything he does, important or not, and he would not hide this from me. It just isn't so!"

³But David answered,*f* "Your father knows very well how much you like me, and he has decided not to let you know what he plans to do, because you would be deeply hurt. I swear to you by the living LORD that I am only a step away from death!"

⁴Jonathan said, "I'll do anything you want."

⁵"Tomorrow is the New Moon Festival," David replied, "and I am supposed to eat with the king. But if it's all right with you, I will go and hide in the fields until the evening of the day after tomorrow. ⁶If your father notices that I am not at the table, tell him that I begged your permission to hurry home to Bethlehem, since it's the time for the annual sacrifice there for my whole family. ⁷If he says, 'All right,' I will be safe; but if he becomes angry, you will know that he is determined to harm me. ⁸Please do me this favor, and keep the sacred promise you made to me. But if I'm guilty, kill me yourself! Why take me to your father to be killed?"

⁹"Don't even think such a thing!" Jonathan answered. "If I knew for sure that my father was determined to harm you, wouldn't I tell you?"

---

e Some ancient translations They saw; *Hebrew* He saw.   *f One ancient translation* answered; *Hebrew* made a vow again.

19.24 1 S 10.11, 12   **20.5** Nu 28.11

¹⁰David then asked, "Who will let me know if your father answers you angrily?"

¹¹"Let's go out to the fields," Jonathan answered. So they went, ¹²and Jonathan said to David, "May the LORD God of Israel be our witness!ᵍ At this time tomorrow and on the following day I will question my father. If his attitude toward you is good, I will send you word. ¹³If he intends to harm you, may the LORD strike me dead if I don't let you know about it and get you safely away. May the LORD be with you as he was with my father! ¹⁴And if I remain alive, please keep your sacred promise and be loyal to me; but if I die,ʰ ¹⁵show the same kind of loyalty to my family forever. And when the LORD has completely destroyed all your enemies, ¹⁶may our promise to each other still be unbroken. If it is broken, the LORD will punish you."ⁱ

¹⁷Once again Jonathan made David promise to love him, for Jonathan loved David as much as he loved himself. ¹⁸Then Jonathan said to him, "Since tomorrow is the New Moon Festival, your absence will be noticed if you aren't at the meal. ¹⁹The day after tomorrow your absence will be noticedʲ even more; so go to the place where you hid yourself the other time, and hide behind the pile of stones there.ᵏ ²⁰I will then shoot three arrows at it, as though it were a target. ²¹Then I will tell my servant to go and find them. And if I tell him, 'Look, the arrows are on this side of you; get them,' that means that you are safe and can come out. I swear by the living LORD that you will be in no danger. ²²But if I tell him, 'The arrows are on the other side of you,' then leave, because the LORD is sending you away. ²³As for the promise we have made to each other, the LORD will make sure that we will keep it forever."

²⁴So David hid in the fields. At the New Moon Festival, King Saul came to the meal ²⁵and sat in his usual place by the wall. Abner sat next to him, and Jonathan sat across the table from him.ˡ David's place was empty, ²⁶but Saul said nothing that day, because he thought, "Something has happened to him, and he is not ritually pure." ²⁷On the following day, the day after the New Moon Festival, David's place was still empty, and Saul asked Jonathan, "Why didn't David come to the meal either yesterday or today?"

²⁸Jonathan answered, "He begged me to let him go to Bethlehem. ²⁹'Please let me go,' he said, 'because our family is celebrating the sacrificial feast in town, and my brother ordered me to be there. So then, if you are my friend, let me go and see my relatives.' That is why he isn't in his place at your table."

³⁰Saul became furious with Jonathan and said to him, "How rebellious and faithless your mother was! Now I know you are taking sides with David and are disgracing yourself and that mother of yours! ³¹Don't you realize that as long as David is alive, you will never be king of this country? Now go and bring him here — he must die!"

³²"Why should he die?" Jonathan replied. "What has he done?"

³³At that, Saul threw his spear at Jonathan to kill him, and Jonathan realized that his father was really determined to kill David. ³⁴Jonathan got up from the table in a rage and ate nothing

---

ᵍ *One ancient translation* be our witness; *Hebrew does not have these words.*

ʰ *Some ancient translations* if I die; *Hebrew* that I may not die.   ⁱ *Verses 15-16 in Hebrew are unclear.*   ʲ *Some ancient translations* your absence will be noticed; *Hebrew* go down.   ᵏ *Probable text* the pile of stones there; *Hebrew* the Ezel Stone.   ˡ *One ancient translation* sat across the table from him; *Hebrew* stood up.

20.15 2 S 9.1

that day — the second day of the New Moon Festival. He was deeply distressed about David, because Saul had insulted him. 35 The following morning Jonathan went to the fields to meet David, as they had agreed. He took a young boy with him 36 and said to him, "Run and find the arrows I'm going to shoot." The boy ran, and Jonathan shot an arrow beyond him. 37 When the boy reached the place where the arrow had fallen, Jonathan shouted to him, "The arrow is farther on! 38 Don't just stand there! Hurry up!" The boy picked up the arrow and returned to his master, 39 not knowing what it all meant; only Jonathan and David knew. 40 Jonathan gave his weapons to the boy and told him to take them back to town.

41 After the boy had left, David got up from behind the pile of stones,^{m} fell on his knees and bowed with his face to the ground three times. Both he and Jonathan were crying as they kissed each other; David's grief was even greater than Jonathan's.^{n} 42 Then Jonathan said to David, "God be with you. The Lord will make sure that you and I, and your descendants and mine, will forever keep the sacred promise we have made to each other." Then David left, and Jonathan went back to the town.

"God be with you!" (20.42)

David Flees from Saul

21 David went to the priest Ahimelech in Nob. Ahimelech came out trembling to meet him and asked, "Why did you come here all by yourself?"

2 "I am here on the king's business," David answered. "He told me not to let anyone know what he sent me to do. As for my men, I have told them to meet me at a certain place. 3 Now, then, what supplies do you have? Give me five loaves of bread or anything else you have."

4 The priest said, "I don't have any ordinary bread, only sacred bread; you can have it if your men haven't had sexual relations recently."

5 "Of course they haven't," answered David. "My men always keep themselves ritually pure even when we go out on an ordinary mission; how much more this time when we are on a special mission!"

6 So the priest gave David the sacred bread, because the only bread he had was the loaves offered to God, which had been removed from the sacred table and replaced by fresh bread.

(7 Saul's chief herdsman, Doeg, who was from Edom, happened to be there that day, because he had to fulfill a religious obligation.)

8 David said to Ahimelech, "Do you have a spear or a sword you can give me? The king's orders made me leave in such a hurry that I didn't have time to get my sword or any other weapon."

9 Ahimelech answered, "I have the sword of Goliath the Philistine, whom you killed in Elah Valley; it is behind the ephod, wrapped in a cloth. If you want it, take it — it's the only weapon here."

"Give it to me," David said. "There is not a better sword anywhere!"

---

^{m} *Probable text* the pile of stones; *Hebrew* the south. ^{n} *Probable text* David's grief was even greater than Jonathan's; *Hebrew unclear.*

21.1-6 Mt 12.3, 4; Mk 2.25, 26; Lk 6.3   **21.6** Lv 24.5-9   **21.9** 1 S 17.51

10 So David left, fleeing from Saul, and went to King Achish of Gath. 11 The king's officials said to Achish, "Isn't this David, the king of his country? This is the man about whom the women sang, as they danced, 'Saul has killed thousands, but David has killed tens of thousands.'"

12 Their words made a deep impression on David, and he became very much afraid of King Achish. 13 So whenever David was around them, he pretended to be insane and acted like a madman when they tried to restrain him; he would scribble on the city^o gates and let spit drool down his beard. 14 So Achish said to his officials, "Look! The man is crazy! Why did you bring him to me? 15 Don't I have enough madmen already? Why bring another one to bother me with his crazy actions right here in my own house?"

The Slaughter of the Priests

22 David fled from the city of Gath and went to a cave near the town of Adullam. When his brothers and the rest of the family heard that he was there, they joined him. 2 People who were oppressed or in debt or dissatisfied went to him, about four hundred men in all, and he became their leader.

3 David went on from there to Mizpah in Moab and said to the king of Moab, "Please let my father and mother come and stay with you until I find out what God is going to do for me." 4 So David left his parents with the king of Moab, and they stayed there as long as David was hiding out in the cave.

5 Then the prophet Gad came to David and said, "Don't stay here; go at once to the land of Judah." So David left and went to the forest of Hereth.

6 One day Saul was in Gibeah, sitting under a tamarisk tree on a hill, with his spear in his hand, and all his officers were standing around him. He was told that David and his men had been located, 7 and he said to his officers, "Listen, men of Benjamin! Do you think that David will give fields and vineyards to all of you, and make you officers in his army? 8 Is that why you are plotting against me? Not one of you told me that my own son had made an alliance with David. No one is concerned about me or tells me that David, one of my own men, is right now looking for a chance to kill me, and that my son has encouraged him!"

9 Doeg was standing there with Saul's officers, and he said, "I saw David when he went to Ahimelech son of Ahitub in Nob. 10 Ahimelech asked the LORD what David should do, and then he gave David some food and the sword of Goliath the Philistine."

11 So King Saul sent for the priest Ahimelech and all his relatives, who were also priests in Nob, and they came to him. 12 Saul said to Ahimelech, "Listen, Ahimelech!"

"At your service, sir," he answered.

13 Saul asked him, "Why are you and David plotting against me? Why did you give him some food and a sword, and consult God for him? Now he has turned against me and is waiting for a chance to kill me!"

14 Ahimelech answered, "David is the most faithful officer you have! He is your own son-in-law, captain of^p your bodyguard, and highly respected by everyone in the royal court. 15 Yes, I consulted God for him, and it wasn't the first time.^q As for plotting against you, Your Majesty must not accuse me or

---

^o city; *or* palace.   ^p *Some ancient translations* captain of; *Hebrew* he turned to.
^q Yes, I consulted . . . time; *or* Now, have I done something wrong today by consulting God for him? Not at all!

21.11 1 S 18.7; 29.5   **21.12** Ps 56 Title   **21.13** Ps 34 Title   **22.1** Ps 57 Title; Ps 142 Title
22.9, 10 1 S 21.7-9; Ps 52 Title

anyone else in my family. I don't know anything about this matter!"

¹⁶The king said, "Ahimelech, you and all your relatives must die." ¹⁷Then he said to the guards standing near him, "Kill the LORD's priests! They conspired with David and did not tell me that he had run away, even though they knew it all along." But the guards refused to lift a hand to kill the LORD's priests. ¹⁸So Saul said to Doeg, "You kill them!" — and Doeg killed them all. On that day he killed eighty-five priests who were qualified to carry the ephod. ¹⁹Saul also had all the other inhabitants of Nob, the city of priests, put to death: men and women, children and babies, cattle, donkeys, and sheep — they were all killed.

²⁰But Abiathar, one of Ahimelech's sons, escaped, and went and joined David. ²¹He told him how Saul had slaughtered the priests of the LORD. ²²David said to him, "When I saw Doeg there that day, I knew that he would be sure to tell Saul. So I am responsible *ʳ* for the death of all your relatives. ²³Stay with me and don't be afraid. Saul wants to kill both you and me, but you will be safe with me."

David Saves the Town of Keilah

23 David heard that the Philistines were attacking the town of Keilah and were stealing the newly harvested grain. ²So he asked the LORD, "Shall I go and attack the Philistines?"

"Yes," the LORD answered. "Attack them and save Keilah."

³But David's men said to him, "We have enough to be afraid of here in Judah; it will be much worse if we go to Keilah and attack the Philistine forces!"

⁴So David consulted the LORD again, and the LORD said to him, "Go and attack Keilah, because I will give you victory over the Philistines." ⁵So David

and his men went to Keilah and attacked the Philistines; they killed many of them and took their livestock. And so it was that David saved the town.

⁶When Abiathar son of Ahimelech escaped and joined David in Keilah, he took the ephod with him.

⁷Saul was told that David had gone to Keilah, and he said, "God has put him in my power. David has trapped himself by going into a walled town with fortified gates." ⁸So Saul called his troops to war, to march against Keilah and besiege David and his men.

⁹When David heard that Saul was planning to attack him, he said to the priest Abiathar, "Bring the ephod here." ¹⁰Then David said, "LORD, God of Israel, I have heard that Saul is planning to come to Keilah and destroy it on account of me, your servant. ¹¹Will the citizens of Keilah hand me over to Saul? Will Saul really come, as I have heard? LORD, God of Israel, I beg you to answer me!"

The LORD answered, "Saul will come."

¹²"And will the citizens of Keilah hand my men and me over to Saul?" David asked again.

"They will," the LORD answered.

¹³So David and his men — about six hundred in all — left Keilah at once and kept on the move. When Saul heard that David had escaped from Keilah, he gave up his plan.

David in the Hill Country

¹⁴David stayed in hiding in the hill country, in the wilderness near Ziph. Saul was always trying to find him, but God did not turn David over to him. ¹⁵David saw that Saul was out to kill him.

David was at Horesh, in the wilderness near Ziph. ¹⁶Jonathan went to him there and encouraged him with assurances of God's protection, ¹⁷saying to

ʳ Some ancient translations I am responsible; *Hebrew* I have turned.

David . . . cut off a piece of Saul's robe. (24.4)

him, "Don't be afraid. My father Saul won't be able to harm you. He knows very well that you are the one who will be the king of Israel and that I will be next in rank to you." [18] The two of them made a sacred promise of friendship to each other. David stayed at Horesh, and Jonathan went home.

[19] Some people from Ziph went to Saul at Gibeah and said, "David is hiding out in our territory at Horesh on Mount Hachilah, in the southern part of the Judean wilderness. [20] We know, Your Majesty, how much you want to capture him; so come to our territory, and we will make sure that you catch him."

[21] Saul answered, "May the LORD bless you for being so kind to me! [22] Go and make sure once more; find out for certain where he is and who has seen him there. I hear that he is very cunning. [23] Find out exactly the places where he hides, and be sure to bring back a report to me right away. Then I will go with you, and if he is still in the region, I will hunt him down, even if I have to search the whole land of Judah."

[24] So they left and returned to Ziph ahead of Saul. David and his men were in the wilderness of Maon, in a desolate valley in the southern part of the Judean wilderness. [25] Saul and his men set out to look for David, but he heard about it and went to a rocky hill in the wilderness of Maon and stayed there. When Saul heard about this, he went after David. [26] Saul and his men were on one side of the hill, separated from David and his men, who were on the other side. They were hurrying to get away from Saul and his men, who were closing in on them and were about to capture them. [27] Just then a messenger arrived and said to Saul, "Come back at once! The Philistines are invading the country!" [28] So Saul stopped pursuing David and went to fight the Philistines. That is why that place is called Separation Hill. [29] David left and went to the region of Engedi, where he stayed in hiding.

David Spares Saul's Life

24 When Saul came back from fighting the Philistines, he was told that David was in the wilderness near Engedi. [2] Saul took three thousand of the best soldiers in Israel and went looking for David and his men east of

"I could have killed you!" (24.11)

Wild Goat Rocks. ³ He came to a cave close to some sheep pens by the road and went in to relieve himself. It happened to be the very cave in which David and his men were hiding far back in the cave. ⁴ They said to him, "This is your chance! The LORD has told you that he would put your enemy in your power and you could do to him whatever you wanted to." David crept over and cut off a piece of Saul's robe without Saul's knowing it. ⁵ But then David's conscience began to hurt, ⁶ and he said to his men, "May the LORD keep me from doing any harm to my master, whom the LORD chose as king! I must not harm him in the least, because he is the king chosen by the LORD!" ⁷ So David convinced his men that they should not attack Saul.

Saul got up, left the cave, and started away. ⁸ Then David went out after him and called to him, "Your Majesty!" Saul turned around, and David bowed down to the ground in respect ⁹ and said, "Why do you listen to people who say that I am trying to harm you? ¹⁰ You can see for yourself that just now in the cave the LORD put you in my power. Some of my men told me to kill you, but

I felt sorry for you and said that I would not harm you in the least, because you are the one whom the LORD chose to be king. ¹¹ Look, my father, look at the piece of your robe I am holding! I could have killed you, but instead I only cut this off. This should convince you that I have no thought of rebelling against you or of harming you. You are hunting me down to kill me, even though I have not done you any wrong. ¹² May the LORD judge which one of us is wrong! May he punish you for your action against me, for I will not harm you in the least. ¹³ You know the old saying, 'Evil is done only by evil people.' And so I will not harm you. ¹⁴ Look at what the king of Israel is trying to kill! Look at what he is chasing! A dead dog, a flea! ¹⁵ The LORD will judge, and he will decide which one of us is wrong. May he look into the matter, defend me, and save me from you."

¹⁶ When David had finished speaking, Saul said, "Is that really you, David my son?" And he started crying. ¹⁷ Then he said to David, "You are right, and I am wrong. You have been so good to me, while I have done such wrong to you! ¹⁸ Today you have shown how good

24.3 Ps 57 Title; Ps 142 Title **24.6** 1 S 26.11 **24.14** 1 S 26.20

you are to me, because you did not kill me, even though the LORD put me in your power. [19] How often does someone catch an enemy and then let him get away unharmed? The LORD bless you for what you have done to me today! [20] Now I am sure that you will be king of Israel and that the kingdom will continue under your rule. [21] But promise me in the LORD's name that you will spare my descendants, so that my name and my family's name will not be completely forgotten." [22] David promised that he would.

Then Saul went back home, and David and his men went back to their hiding place.

The Death of Samuel

25 Samuel died, and all the Israelites came together and mourned for him. Then they buried him at his home in Ramah.

David and Abigail

After this, David went to the wilderness of Paran. [2-3] There was a man of the clan of Caleb named Nabal, who was from the town of Maon, and who owned land near the town of Carmel. He was a very rich man, the owner of three thousand sheep and one thousand goats. His wife Abigail was beautiful and intelligent, but he was a mean, bad-tempered man.

Nabal was shearing his sheep in Carmel, [4] and David, who was in the wilderness, heard about it, [5] so he sent ten young men with orders to go to Carmel, find Nabal, and give him his greetings. [6] He instructed them to say to Nabal: "David sends you greetings, my friend, with his best wishes for you, your family, and all that is yours. [7] He heard that you were shearing your sheep, and he wants you to know that your shepherds have been with us and we did not harm them. Nothing that belonged to them was stolen all the time they were at Car-

mel. [8] Just ask them, and they will tell you. We have come on a feast day, and David asks you to receive us kindly. Please give what you can to us your servants and to your dear friend David."

[9] David's men delivered this message to Nabal in David's name. Then they waited there, [10] and Nabal finally answered, "David? Who is he? I've never heard of him! The country is full of runaway slaves nowadays! [11] I'm not going to take my bread and water, and the animals I have butchered for my sheepshearers, and give them to people who come from I don't know where!"

[12] David's men went back to him and told him what Nabal had said. [13] "Buckle on your swords!" he ordered, and they all did. David also buckled on his sword and left with about four hundred of his men, leaving two hundred behind with the supplies.

[14] One of Nabal's servants said to Nabal's wife Abigail, "Have you heard? David sent some messengers from the wilderness with greetings for our master, but he insulted them. [15] Yet they were very good to us; they never bothered us, and all the time we were with them in the fields, nothing that belonged to us was stolen. [16] They protected us day and night the whole time we were with them looking after our flocks. [17] Please think this over and decide what to do. This could be disastrous for our master and all his family. He is so mean that he won't listen to anybody!"

[18] Abigail quickly gathered two hundred loaves of bread, two leather bags full of wine, five roasted sheep, two bushels of roasted grain, a hundred bunches of raisins, and two hundred cakes of dried figs, and loaded them on donkeys. [19] Then she said to the servants, "You go on ahead and I will follow you." But she said nothing to her husband.

[20] She was riding her donkey around a bend on a hillside when suddenly she

met David and his men coming toward her. 21 David had been thinking, "Why did I ever protect that fellow's property out here in the wilderness? Not a thing that belonged to him was stolen, and this is how he pays me back for the help I gave him! 22 May God strike me[s] dead if I don't kill every last one of those men before morning!"

23 When Abigail saw David, she quickly dismounted and threw herself

When Abigail saw David . . . (25.23)

on the ground 24 at David's feet, and said to him, "Please, sir, listen to me! Let me take the blame. 25 Please, don't pay any attention to Nabal, that good-for-nothing! He is exactly what his name means — a fool![t] I wasn't there when your servants arrived, sir. 26 It is the LORD who has kept you from taking revenge and killing your enemies. And now I swear to you by the living LORD that your enemies and all who want to harm you will be punished like Nabal. 27 Please, sir, accept this present I have brought you, and give it to your men. 28 Please forgive me, sir, for any wrong I have done. The LORD will make you king, and your descendants also, because you are fighting his battles; and you will not do anything evil[u] as long as you live. 29 If anyone should attack you and try to kill you, the LORD your

God will keep you safe, as someone guards a precious treasure. As for your enemies, however, he will throw them away, as someone hurls stones with a sling. 30 And when the LORD has done all the good things he has promised you and has made you king of Israel, 31 then you will not have to feel regret or remorse, sir, for having killed without cause or for having taken your own revenge. And when the LORD has blessed you, sir, please do not forget me."

32 David said to her, "Praise the LORD, the God of Israel, who sent you today to meet me! 33 Thank God for your good sense and for what you have done today in keeping me from the crime of murder and from taking my own revenge. 34 The LORD has kept me from harming you. But I swear by the living God of Israel that if you had not hurried to meet me, all of Nabal's men would have been dead by morning!" 35 Then David accepted what she had brought him and said to her, "Go back home and don't worry. I will do what you want."

36 Abigail went back to Nabal, who was at home having a feast fit for a king. He was drunk and in a good mood, so she did not tell him anything until the next morning. 37 Then, after he had sobered up, she told him everything. He suffered a stroke and was completely paralyzed. 38 Some ten days later the LORD struck Nabal and he died.

39 When David heard that Nabal had died, he said, "Praise the LORD! He has taken revenge on Nabal for insulting me and has kept me his servant from doing wrong. The LORD has punished Nabal for his evil."

Then David sent a proposal of marriage to Abigail. 40 His servants went to her at Carmel and said to her, "David sent us to take you to him to be his wife."

41 Abigail bowed down to the ground

---

[s] *One ancient translation* me; *Hebrew* my enemies.   [t] A FOOL: *This is the meaning of the Hebrew name Nabal.*   [u] you will not do anything evil; *or* no evil will happen to you.

and said, "I am his servant, ready to wash the feet of his servants." ⁴²She rose quickly and mounted her donkey. Accompanied by her five maids, she went with David's servants and became his wife.

⁴³David had married Ahinoam from Jezreel, and now Abigail also became his wife. ⁴⁴Meanwhile, Saul had given his daughter Michal, who had been David's wife, to Palti son of Laish, who was from the town of Gallim.

David Spares Saul's Life Again

26 Some men from Ziph came to Saul at Gibeah and told him that David was hiding on Mount Hachilah at the edge of the Judean wilderness. ²Saul went at once with three thousand of the best soldiers in Israel to the wilderness of Ziph to look for David, ³and camped by the road on Mount Hachilah. David was still in the wilderness, and when he learned that Saul had come to look for him, ⁴he sent spies and found out that Saul was indeed there. ⁵He went at once and located the exact place where Saul and Abner son of Ner, commander of Saul's army, slept. Saul slept inside the camp, and his men camped around him.

⁶Then David asked Ahimelech the Hittite, and Abishai the brother of Joab (their mother was Zeruiah), "Which of you two will go to Saul's camp with me?"

"I will," Abishai answered.

⁷So that night David and Abishai entered Saul's camp and found Saul sleeping in the center of the camp with his spear stuck in the ground near his head. Abner and the troops were sleeping around him. ⁸Abishai said to David, "God has put your enemy in your power tonight. Now let me plunge his own spear through him and pin him to the ground with just one blow — I won't have to strike twice!"

⁹But David said, "You must not harm him! The LORD will certainly punish whoever harms his chosen king. ¹⁰By the living LORD," David continued, "I know that the LORD himself will kill Saul, either when his time comes to die a natural death or when he dies in battle. ¹¹The LORD forbid that I should try to harm the one whom the LORD has made king! Let's take his spear and his water jar, and go." ¹²So David took the spear and the water jar from right beside Saul's head, and he and Abishai left. No one saw it or knew what had happened or even woke up — they were all sound asleep, because the LORD had sent a heavy sleep on them all.

¹³Then David crossed over to the other side of the valley to the top of the hill, a safe distance away, ¹⁴and shouted to Saul's troops and to Abner, "Abner! Can you hear me?"

"Who is that shouting and waking up the king?" Abner asked.

¹⁵David answered, "Abner, aren't you the greatest man in Israel? So why aren't you protecting your master, the king? Just now someone entered the camp to kill your master. ¹⁶You failed in your duty, Abner! I swear by the living LORD that all of you deserve to die, because you have not protected your master, whom the LORD made king. Look! Where is the king's spear? Where is the water jar that was right by his head?"

¹⁷Saul recognized David's voice and asked, "David, is that you, my son?"

"Yes, Your Majesty," David answered. ¹⁸And he added, "Why, sir, are you still pursuing me, your servant? What have I done? What crime have I committed? ¹⁹Your Majesty, listen to what I have to say. If it is the LORD who has turned you against me, an offering to him will make him change his mind; but if some people have done it, may the LORD's curse fall on them. For they have driven me out from the LORD's land to a country where I can only wor-

25.44 2 S 3.14-16   **26.1** Ps 54 Title   **26.11** 1 S 24.26

ship foreign gods. 20 Don't let me be killed on foreign soil, away from the LORD. Why should the king of Israel come to kill a flea like me? Why should he hunt me down like a wild bird?"

21 Saul answered, "I have done wrong. Come back, David, my son! I will never harm you again, because you have spared my life tonight. I have been a fool! I have done a terrible thing!"

22 David replied, "Here is your spear, Your Majesty. Let one of your men come over and get it. 23 The LORD rewards those who are faithful and righteous. Today he put you in my power, but I did not harm you, whom the LORD made king. 24 Just as I have spared your life today, may the LORD do the same to me and free me from all troubles!"

25 Saul said to David, "God bless you, my son! You will succeed in everything you do!"

So David went on his way, and Saul returned home.

David among the Philistines

27 David said to himself, "One of these days Saul will kill me. The best thing for me to do is to escape to Philistia. Then Saul will give up looking for me in Israel, and I will be safe." 2 So David and his six hundred men went over at once to Achish son of Maoch, king of Gath. 3 David and his men settled there in Gath with their families. David had his two wives with him, Ahinoam from Jezreel, and Abigail, Nabal's widow, from Carmel. 4 When Saul heard that David had fled to Gath, he gave up trying to find him.

5 David said to Achish, "If you are my friend, let me have a small town to live in. There is no need, sir, for me to live with you in the capital city." 6 So Achish gave him the town of Ziklag, and for this reason Ziklag has belonged to the kings of Judah ever since. 7 David lived in Philistia for sixteen months.

8 During that time David and his men would attack the people of Geshur, Girzi, and Amalek, who had been living in the region a very long time. He would raid their land as far as Shur, all the way down to Egypt, 9 killing all the men and women and taking the sheep, cattle, donkeys, camels, and even the clothes. Then he would come back to Achish, 10 who would ask him, "Where did you go on a raid this time?" and David would tell him that he had gone to the southern part of Judah or to the territory of the clan of Jerahmeel or to the territory where the Kenites lived. 11 David would kill everyone, men and women, so that no one could go back to Gath and report what he and his men had really done. This is what David did the whole time he lived in Philistia. 12 But Achish trusted David and said to himself, "He is hated so much by his own people the Israelites that he will have to serve me all his life."

28 Some time later the Philistines gathered their troops to fight Israel, and Achish said to David, "Of course you understand that you and your men are to fight on my side."

2 "Of course," David answered. "I am your servant, and you will see for yourself what I can do."

Achish said, "Good! I will make you my permanent bodyguard."

Saul Consults a Medium

3 Now Samuel had died, and all the Israelites had mourned for him and had buried him in his hometown of Ramah. Saul had forced all the fortunetellers and mediums to leave Israel.

4 The Philistine troops assembled and camped near the town of Shunem; Saul gathered the Israelites and camped at Mount Gilboa. 5 When Saul saw the Philistine army, he was terrified, 6 and so he asked the LORD what to do. But the LORD did not answer him at

28.3 1 S 25.1   **28.3** Lv 20.27; Dt 18.10, 11   **28.6** Nu 27.21

all, either by dreams or by the use of Urim and Thummim or by prophets. [7] Then Saul ordered his officials, "Find me a woman who is a medium, and I will go and consult her."

"There is one in Endor," they answered.

[8] So Saul disguised himself; he put on different clothes, and after dark he went with two of his men to see the woman. "Consult the spirits for me and tell me what is going to happen," he said to her. "Call up the spirit of the man I name."

[9] The woman answered, "Surely you know what King Saul has done, how he forced the fortunetellers and mediums to leave Israel.[v] Why, then, are you trying to trap me and get me killed?"

[10] Then Saul made a sacred vow. "By the living LORD I promise that you will not be punished for doing this," he told her.

[11] "Whom shall I call up for you?" the woman asked.

"Samuel," he answered.

[12] When the woman saw Samuel, she screamed and said to Saul, "Why have you tricked me? You are King Saul!"

[13] "Don't be afraid!" the king said to her. "What do you see?"

"I see a spirit coming up from the earth," she answered.

[14] "What does it look like?" he asked.

"It's an old man coming up," she answered. "He is wearing a cloak."

Then Saul knew that it was Samuel, and he bowed to the ground in respect.

[15] Samuel said to Saul, "Why have you disturbed me? Why did you make me come back?"

Saul answered, "I am in great trouble! The Philistines are at war with me, and God has abandoned me. He doesn't answer me any more, either by prophets or by dreams. And so I have called you, for you to tell me what I must do."

[16] Samuel said, "Why do you call me

when the LORD has abandoned you and become your enemy? [17] The LORD has done to you what he told you through me: he has taken the kingdom away from you and given it to David instead. [18] You disobeyed the LORD's command and did not completely destroy the Amalekites and all they had. That is why the LORD is doing this to you now. [19] He will give you and Israel over to the Philistines. Tomorrow you and your sons will join me, and the LORD will also give the army of Israel over to the Philistines."

[20] At once Saul fell down and lay stretched out on the ground, terrified by what Samuel had said. He was weak, because he had not eaten anything all day and all night. [21] The woman went over to him and saw that he was terrified, so she said to him, "Please, sir, I risked my life by doing what you asked. [22] Now please do what I ask. Let me fix you some food. You must eat so that you will be strong enough to travel."

[23] Saul refused and said he would not eat anything. But his officers also urged him to eat. He finally gave in, got up from the ground, and sat on the bed. [24] The woman quickly killed a calf which she had been fattening. Then she took some flour, prepared it, and baked some bread without yeast. [25] She set the food before Saul and his officers, and they ate it. And they left that same night.

David Is Rejected by the Philistines

29 The Philistines brought all their troops together at Aphek, while the Israelites camped at the spring in Jezreel Valley. [2] The five Philistine kings marched out with their units of a hundred and of a thousand men; David and his men marched in the rear with King Achish. [3] The

[v] he forced . . . Israel; or he put to death the fortunetellers and mediums in Israel.

28.11 Si 46.20   **28.17** 1 S 15.28   **28.18** 1 S 15.3-9

Philistine commanders saw them and asked, "What are these Hebrews doing here?"

Achish answered, "This is David, an official of King Saul of Israel. He has been with me for quite some time now. He has done nothing I can find fault with since the day he came over to me."

⁴But the Philistine commanders were angry with Achish and said to him, "Send that fellow back to the town you gave him. Don't let him go into battle with us; he might turn against us during the fighting. What better way is there for him to win back his master's favor than by the death of our men? ⁵After all, this is David, the one about whom the women sang, as they danced, 'Saul has killed thousands, but David has killed tens of thousands.'"

⁶Achish called David and said to him, "I swear by the living God of Israel that you have been loyal to me; and I would be pleased to have you go with me and fight in this battle. I have not found any fault in you from the day you came over to me. But the other kings don't approve of you. ⁷So go back home in peace, and don't do anything that would displease them."

⁸David answered, "What have I done wrong, sir? If, as you say, you haven't found any fault in me since the day I started serving you, why shouldn't I go with you, my master and king, and fight your enemies?"

⁹"I agree," Achish replied. "I consider you as loyal as an angel of God. But the other kings have said that you can't go with us into battle. ¹⁰So then, David, tomorrow morning all of you who left Saul and came over to me will have to get up early and leave as soon as it's light."

¹¹So David and his men started out early the following morning to go back to Philistia, and the Philistines went on to Jezreel.

The War against the Amalekites

30 Two days later David and his men arrived back at Ziklag. The Amalekites had raided southern Judah and attacked Ziklag. They had burned down the town ²and captured all the women; they had not killed anyone, but had taken everyone with them when they left. ³When David and his men arrived, they found that the town had been burned down and that their wives, sons, and daughters had been carried away. ⁴David and his men started crying and did not stop until they were completely exhausted. ⁵Even David's two wives, Ahinoam and Abigail, had been taken away.

⁶David was now in great trouble, because his men were all very bitter about losing their children, and they were threatening to stone him; but the LORD his God gave him courage. ⁷David said to the priest Abiathar son of Ahimelech, "Bring me the ephod," and Abiathar brought it to him. ⁸David asked the LORD, "Shall I go after those raiders? And will I catch them?"

He answered, "Go after them; you will catch them and rescue the captives."

⁹So David and his six hundred men started out, and when they arrived at Besor Brook, some of them stayed there. ¹⁰David continued on his way with four hundred men; the other two hundred men were too tired to cross the brook and so stayed behind. ¹¹The men with David found a young Egyptian out in the country and brought him to David. They gave him some food and water, ¹²some dried figs, and two bunches of raisins. After he had eaten, his strength returned; he had not had anything to eat or drink for three full days. ¹³David asked him, "Who is your master, and where are you from?"

"I am an Egyptian, the slave of an Amalekite," he answered. "My master

29.5 1 S 18.7; 21.11   **30.5** 1 S 25.42, 43   **30.7** 1 S 22.20-23

left me behind three days ago because I got sick. [14] We had raided the territory of the Cherethites in the southern part of Judah and the territory of the clan of Caleb, and we burned down Ziklag."

[15] "Will you lead me to those raiders?" David asked him.

He answered, "I will if you promise me in God's name that you will not kill me or hand me over to my master." [16] And he led David to them.

The raiders were scattered all over the place, eating, drinking, and celebrating because of the enormous amount of loot they had captured from Philistia and Judah. [17] At dawn the next day David attacked them and fought until evening. Except for four hundred young men who mounted camels and got away, none of them escaped. [18] David rescued everyone and everything the Amalekites had taken, including his two wives; [19] nothing at all was missing. David got back all his men's sons and daughters, and all the loot the Amalekites had taken. [20] He also recovered all the flocks and herds; his men drove all the livestock in front of them[w] and said, "This belongs to David!"

[21] Then David went back to the two hundred men who had been too weak to go with him and had stayed behind at Besor Brook. They came forward to meet David and his men, and David went up to them and greeted them warmly. [22] But some mean and worthless men who had gone with David said, "They didn't go with us, and so we won't give them any of the loot. They can take their wives and children and go away."

[23] But David answered, "My brothers, you can't do this with what the LORD has given us! He kept us safe and gave us victory over the raiders. [24] No one can agree with what you say! All must share alike: whoever stays behind with the supplies gets the same share as the one who goes into battle." [25] David made this a rule, and it has been followed in Israel ever since.

[26] When David returned to Ziklag, he sent part of the loot to his friends, the leaders of Judah, with the message "Here is a present for you from the loot we took from the LORD's enemies." [27] He sent it to the people in Bethel, to the people in Ramah in the southern part of Judah, and to the people in the towns of Jattir, [28] Aroer, Siphmoth, Eshtemoa, [29] and Racal; to the clan of Jerahmeel, to the Kenites, [30] and to the people in the towns of Hormah, Borashan, Athach, [31] and Hebron. He sent it to all the places where he and his men had roamed.

The Death of Saul and His Sons
(1 Chronicles 10.1-12)

31 The Philistines fought a battle against the Israelites on Mount Gilboa. Many Israelites were killed there, and the rest of them, including King Saul and his sons, fled. [2] But the Philistines caught up with them and killed three of Saul's sons, Jonathan, Abinadab, and Malchishua. [3] The fighting was heavy around Saul, and he himself was hit by enemy arrows and badly wounded. [4] He said to the young man carrying his weapons, "Draw your sword and kill me, so that these godless Philistines won't gloat over me and kill me." But the young man was too terrified to do it. So Saul took his own sword and threw himself on it. [5] The young man saw that Saul was dead, so he too threw himself on his own sword and died with Saul. [6] And that is how Saul, his three sons, and the young man died; all of Saul's men died that day. [7] When the Israelites on the other side of Jezreel Valley and east of the Jordan River heard that the Israelite army had fled and that Saul and his sons had

---

[w] *Probable text* his men ... front of them; *Hebrew unclear.*

been killed, they abandoned their towns and fled. Then the Philistines came and occupied the towns.

8 The day after the battle the Philistines went to plunder the corpses, and they found the bodies of Saul and his three sons lying on Mount Gilboa. 9 They cut off Saul's head, stripped off his armor, and sent messengers with them throughout Philistia to tell the good news to their idols and to their people. 10 Then they put his weapons in the temple of the goddess Astarte, and they nailed his body to the wall of the city of Beth Shan.

11 When the people of Jabesh in Gilead heard what the Philistines had done to Saul, 12 the bravest men started out and marched all night to Beth Shan. They took down the bodies of Saul and his sons from the wall, brought them back to Jabesh, and burned them there. 13 Then they took the bones and buried them under the tamarisk tree in town, and fasted for seven days.

The Second Book of
SAMUEL

INTRODUCTION

Second Samuel, the sequel to *First Samuel*, is the history of David's reign as king, first over Judah in the south (chapters 1–4) and then over the whole nation, including Israel in the north (chapters 5–24). It is a vivid account of how David, in order to extend his kingdom and consolidate his position, had to struggle with enemies within the nation as well as with foreign powers. David is shown to be a man of deep faith and devotion to God, and one who was able to win the loyalty of his people. Yet he is also shown as being sometimes ruthless and willing to commit terrible sins to serve his own desires and ambitions. But when he is confronted with his sins by the Lord's prophet Nathan, he confesses them and accepts the punishment that God sends.

The life and achievements of David impressed the people of Israel so much that in later times of national distress, when they longed for another king, it was for one who would be "a son of David," that is, a descendant of David who would be like him.

OUTLINE OF CONTENTS

David Learns of Saul's Death

1 After Saul's death David came back from his victory over the Amalekites and stayed in Ziklag for two days. ² The next day a young man arrived from Saul's camp. To show his grief, he had torn his clothes and put dirt on his head. He went to David and bowed to the ground in respect. ³ David asked him, "Where have you come from?"

"I have escaped from the Israelite camp," he answered.

⁴ "Tell me what happened," David said.

"Our army ran away from the battle," he replied, "and many of our men were killed. Saul and his son Jonathan were also killed."

⁵ "How do you know that Saul and Jonathan are dead?" David asked him.

⁶ He answered, "I happened to be on Mount Gilboa, and I saw that Saul was leaning on his spear and that the chariots and cavalry of the enemy were closing in on him. ⁷ Then he turned around, saw me, and called to me. I answered, 'Yes, sir!' ⁸ He asked who I was, and I told him that I was an Amalekite. ⁹ Then he said, 'Come here and kill me! I have been badly wounded, and I'm about to die.' ¹⁰ So I went up to him and killed him, because I knew that he would die anyway as soon as he fell. Then I took the crown from his head and the bracelet from his arm, and I have brought them to you, sir."

¹¹ David tore his clothes in sorrow, and all his men did the same. ¹² They grieved and mourned and fasted until evening for Saul and Jonathan and for Israel, the people of the LORD, because so many had been killed in battle.

¹³ David asked the young man who had brought him the news, "Where are you from?"

David tore his clothes in sorrow. (1.11)

He answered, "I'm an Amalekite, but I live in your country."

¹⁴ David asked him, "How is it that you dared kill the LORD's chosen king?" ¹⁵ Then David called one of his men and said, "Kill him!" The man struck the Amalekite and mortally wounded him, ¹⁶ and David said to the Amalekite, "You brought this on yourself. You condemned yourself when you confessed that you killed the one whom the LORD chose to be king."

David's Lament for Saul and Jonathan

¹⁷ David sang this lament for Saul and his son Jonathan, ¹⁸ and ordered it[a] to be taught to the people of Judah. (It is recorded in *The Book of Jashar*.)

¹⁹ "On the hills of Israel our leaders are dead!
　The bravest of our soldiers have fallen!
²⁰ Do not announce it in Gath
　or in the streets of Ashkelon.
Do not make the women of
　Philistia glad;

---

[a] *One ancient translation* it; *Hebrew* the bow.
1.6-10 1 S 31.1-6; 1 Ch 10.1-6   **1.18** Js 10.13

do not let the daughters of
pagans rejoice.

21 "May no rain or dew fall on
Gilboa's hills;
may its fields be always
barren!
For the shields of the brave lie
there in disgrace;
the shield of Saul is no longer
polished with oil.
22 Jonathan's bow was deadly,
the sword of Saul was
merciless,
striking down the mighty,
killing the enemy.

23 "Saul and Jonathan, so
wonderful and dear;
together in life, together in
death;
swifter than eagles, stronger
than lions.

24 "Women of Israel, mourn for
Saul!
He clothed you in rich scarlet
dresses
and adorned you with jewels
and gold.

25 "The brave soldiers have fallen,
they were killed in battle.
Jonathan lies dead in the hills.

26 "I grieve for you, my brother
Jonathan;
how dear you were to me!
How wonderful was your love
for me,
better even than the love of
women.

27 "The brave soldiers have fallen,
their weapons abandoned and
useless."

David Is Made King of Judah

2 After this, David asked the LORD,
"Shall I go and take control of one
of the towns of Judah?"

"Yes," the LORD answered.

"Which one?" David asked.

"Hebron," the LORD said. 2 So David
went to Hebron, taking with him his
two wives: Ahinoam, who was from
Jezreel, and Abigail, Nabal's widow,
who was from Carmel. 3 He also took his
men and their families, and they settled
in the towns around Hebron. 4 Then the
men of Judah came to Hebron and
anointed David as king of Judah.

When David heard that the people of
Jabesh in Gilead had buried Saul, 5 he
sent some men there with the message:
"May the LORD bless you for showing
your loyalty to your king by burying
him. 6 And now may the LORD be kind
and faithful to you. I too will treat you
well because of what you have done.
7 Be strong and brave! Saul your king is
dead, and the people of Judah have
anointed me as their king."

Ishbosheth Is Made King of Israel

8 The commander of Saul's army, Abner son of Ner, had fled with Saul's
son Ishbosheth across the Jordan to Mahanaim. 9 There Abner made Ishbosheth
king of the territories of Gilead, Asher,[b]
Jezreel, Ephraim, and Benjamin, and
indeed over all Israel. 10 He was forty
years old when he was made king of Israel, and he ruled for two years.

But the tribe of Judah was loyal to
David, 11 and he ruled in Hebron over
Judah for seven and a half years.

War between Israel and Judah

12 Abner and the officials of Ishbosheth went from Mahanaim to the city
of Gibeon. 13 Joab, whose mother was
Zeruiah, and David's other officials met

---

b One ancient translation Asher; *Hebrew* Assyria.
2.2 1 S 25.42, 43   **2.4** 1 S 31.11-13

them at the pool, where they all sat down, one group on one side of the pool and the other group on the opposite side. ¹⁴Abner said to Joab, "Let's have some of the young men from each side fight an armed contest."

"All right," Joab answered.

¹⁵So twelve men, representing Ish-bosheth and the tribe of Benjamin, fought twelve of David's men. ¹⁶Each man caught his opponent by the head and plunged his sword into his opponent's side, so that all twenty-four of them fell down dead together. And so that place in Gibeon is called "Field of Swords."

¹⁷Then a furious battle broke out, and Abner and the Israelites were defeated by David's men. ¹⁸The three sons of Zeruiah were there: Joab, Abishai, and Asahel. Asahel, who could run as fast as a wild deer, ¹⁹started chasing Abner, running straight for him. ²⁰Abner looked back and said, "Is that you, Asahel?"

"Yes," he answered.

²¹"Stop chasing me!" Abner said. "Run after one of the soldiers and take what he has." But Asahel kept on chasing him. ²²Once more Abner said to him, "Stop chasing me! Why force me to kill you? How could I face your brother Joab?" ²³But Asahel would not quit; so Abner, with a backward thrust*c* of his spear, struck him through the stomach so that the spear came out at his back. Asahel dropped to the ground dead, and everyone who came to the place where he was lying stopped and stood there.

²⁴But Joab and Abishai started out after Abner, and at sunset they came to the hill of Ammah, which is to the east of Giah on the road to the wilderness of Gibeon. ²⁵The men from the tribe of Benjamin gathered around Abner again and took their stand on the top of a hill. ²⁶Abner called out to Joab, "Do

we have to go on fighting forever? Can you see that in the end there will be nothing but bitterness? We are you relatives. How long will it be before you order your men to stop chasing us?"

²⁷"I swear by the living God," Joab answered, "that if you had not spoken my men would have kept on chasing you until tomorrow morning." ²⁸Then Joab blew the trumpet as a signal for his men to stop pursuing the Israelites; and so the fighting stopped.

²⁹Abner and his men marched through the Jordan Valley all that night; they crossed the Jordan River and after marching all the next morning, they arrived back at Mahanaim.

³⁰When Joab gave up the chase, he gathered all his men and found that nineteen of them were missing, in addition to Asahel. ³¹David's men had killed 360 of Abner's men from the tribe of Benjamin. ³²Joab and his men took Asahel's body and buried it in the family tomb at Bethlehem. Then they marched all night and at dawn arrived back at Hebron.

3 The fighting between the forces supporting Saul's family and those supporting David went on for a long time. As David became stronger and stronger, his opponents became weaker and weaker.

David's Sons

²The following six sons, in order of their birth, were born to David at Hebron: Amnon, whose mother was Ahinoam, from Jezreel; ³Chileab, whose mother was Abigail, Nabal's widow from Carmel; Absalom, whose mother was Maacah, the daughter of King Talmai of Geshur; ⁴Adonijah, whose mother was Haggith; Shephatiah whose mother was Abital; ⁵Ithream whose mother was Eglah. All of these sons were born in Hebron.

---

c Probable text with a backward thrust; *Hebrew unclear.*

Abner Joins David

6 As the fighting continued between David's forces and the forces loyal to Saul's family, Abner became more and more powerful among Saul's followers.

7 One day Ishbosheth son of Saul accused Abner of sleeping with Saul's concubine Rizpah, the daughter of Aiah. **8** This made Abner furious. "Do you think that I would betray Saul? Do you really think I'm serving Judah?" he exclaimed. "From the very first I have been loyal to the cause of your father Saul, his brothers, and his friends, and I have kept you from being defeated by David; yet today you find fault with me about a woman! **9-10** The LORD promised David that he would take the kingdom away from Saul and his descendants and would make David king of both Israel and Judah, from one end of the country to the other. Now may God strike me dead if I don't make this come true!" **11** Ishbosheth was so afraid of Abner that he could not say a word.

12 Abner sent messengers to David, who at that time was at Hebron,[d] to say, "Who is going to rule this land? Make an agreement with me, and I will help you win all Israel over to your side."

13 "Good!" David answered. "I will make an agreement with you on one condition: you must bring Saul's daughter Michal to me when you come to see me." **14** And David also sent messengers to Ishbosheth to say, "Give me back my wife Michal. I paid a hundred Philistine foreskins in order to marry her." **15** So Ishbosheth had her taken from her husband Paltiel son of Laish. **16** Paltiel followed her all the way to the town of Bahurim, crying as he went. But when Abner said, "Go back home," he did.

17 Abner went to the leaders of Israel and said to them, "For a long time you have wanted David to be your king. **18** Now here is your chance. Remember that the LORD has said, 'I will use my servant David to rescue my people Israel from the Philistines and from all their other enemies.'" **19** Abner spoke also to the people of the tribe of Benjamin and then went to Hebron to tell David what the people of Benjamin and of Israel had agreed to do.

20 When Abner came to David at Hebron with twenty men, David gave a feast for them. **21** Abner told David, "I will go now and win all Israel over to Your Majesty. They will accept you as king, and then you will get what you have wanted and will rule over the whole land." David gave Abner a guarantee of safety and sent him on his way.

Abner Is Murdered

22 Later on Joab and David's other officials returned from a raid, bringing a large amount of loot with them. Abner, however, was no longer there at Hebron with David, because David had sent him away with a guarantee of safety. **23** When Joab and his men arrived, he was told that Abner had come to King David and had been sent away with a guarantee of safety. **24** So Joab went to the king and said to him, "What have you done? Abner came to you—why did you let him go like that? **25** He came here to deceive you and to find out everything you do and everywhere you go. Surely you know that!"

26 After leaving David, Joab sent messengers to get Abner, and they brought him back from Sirah Well; but David knew nothing about it. **27** When Abner arrived in Hebron, Joab took him aside at the gate, as though he wanted to speak privately with him, and there he stabbed him in the stomach. And so Abner was murdered because he had

---

d One ancient translation at Hebron; *Hebrew* where he (Abner) was.

3.10 1 S 15.28   **3.14** 1 S 18.27

killed Joab's brother Asahel. 28 When David heard the news, he said, "The LORD knows that my subjects and I are completely innocent of the murder of Abner. 29 May the punishment for it fall on Joab and all his family! In every generation may there be some man in his family who has gonorrhea or a dreaded skin disease or is fit only to do a woman's work or is killed in battle or doesn't have enough to eat!" 30 So Joab and his brother Abishai took revenge on Abner for killing their brother Asahel in the battle at Gibeon.

Abner Is Buried

31 Then David ordered Joab and his men to tear their clothes, wear sackcloth, and mourn for Abner. And at the funeral King David himself walked behind the coffin. 32 Abner was buried at Hebron, and the king wept aloud at the grave, and so did all the people. 33 David sang this lament for Abner:

"Why did Abner have to die like a fool?
34 His hands were not tied,
And his feet were not bound;
He died like someone killed by criminals!"

And the people wept for him again.

35 All day long the people tried to get David to eat something, but he made a solemn promise, "May God strike me dead if I eat anything before the day is over!" 36 They took note of this and were pleased. Indeed, everything the king did pleased the people. 37 All of David's people and all the people in Israel understood that the king had no part in the murder of Abner. 38 The king said to his officials, "Don't you realize that this day a great leader in Israel has died? 39 Even though I am the king chosen by God, I feel weak today. These sons of Zeruiah are too violent for me. May the LORD punish these criminals as they deserve!"

Ishbosheth Is Murdered

4 When Saul's son Ishbosheth heard that Abner had been killed in Hebron, he was afraid, and all the people of Israel were alarmed. 2 Ishbosheth had two officers who were leaders of raiding parties, Baanah and Rechab, sons of Rimmon, from Beeroth in the tribe of Benjamin. (Beeroth is counted as part of Benjamin. 3 Its original inhabitants had fled to Gittaim where they have lived ever since.)

4 Another descendant of Saul was Jonathan's son Mephibosheth, who was five years old when Saul and Jonathan were killed. When the news about their death came from the city of Jezreel, his nurse picked him up and fled, but she was in such a hurry that she dropped him, and he became crippled.

5 Rechab and Baanah set out for Ishbosheth's house and arrived there about noon, while he was taking his midday rest. 6 The woman at the door had become drowsy while she was sifting wheat and had fallen asleep, so Rechab and Baanah slipped in.e 7 Once inside, they went to Ishbosheth's bedroom, where he was sound asleep, and killed him. Then they cut off his head, took it with them, and walked all night through the Jordan Valley. 8 They presented the head to King David at Hebron and said to him, "Here is the head of Ishbosheth, the son of your enemy Saul, who tried to kill you. Today the LORD has allowed Your Majesty to take revenge on Saul and his descendants."

9 David answered them, "I take a vow by the living LORD, who has saved me from all dangers! 10 The messenger who came to me at Ziklag and told me of Saul's death thought he was bringing

e Verse 6 follows one ancient translation; Hebrew They went on into the house carrying wheat, and struck him in the belly. Then Rechab and his brother Baanah escaped.

4.4 2 S 9.3   4.10 2 S 1.1-16

good news. I seized him and had him put to death. That was the reward I gave him for his good news! [11] How much worse it will be for evil men who murder an innocent man asleep in his own house! I will now take revenge on you for murdering him and will wipe you off the face of the earth!" [12] David gave the order, and his soldiers killed Rechab and Baanah and cut off their hands and feet, which they hung up near the pool in Hebron. They took Ishbosheth's head and buried it in Abner's tomb there at Hebron.

David Becomes King of Israel and Judah
(1 Chronicles 11.1-9; 14.1-7)

5 Then all the tribes of Israel went to David at Hebron and said to him, "We are your own flesh and blood. [2] In the past, even when Saul was still our king, you led the people of Israel in battle, and the LORD promised you that you would lead his people and be their ruler." [3] So all the leaders of Israel came to King David at Hebron. He made a sacred alliance with them, they anointed him, and he became king of Israel. [4] David was thirty years old when he became king, and he ruled for forty years. [5] He ruled in Hebron over Judah for seven and a half years, and in Jerusalem over all Israel and Judah for thirty-three years.

[6] The time came when King David and his men set out to attack Jerusalem. The Jebusites, who lived there, thought that David would not be able to conquer the city, and so they said to him, "You will never get in here; even the blind and the crippled could keep you out." ([7] But David did capture their fortress of Zion, and it became known as "David's City.")

[8] That day David said to his men, "Does anybody here hate the Jebusites as much as I do? Enough to kill them? Then go up through the water tunnel and attack those poor blind cripples." (That is why it is said, "The blind and the crippled cannot enter the LORD's house.")*f*

[9] After capturing the fortress, David lived in it and named it "David's City." He built the city around it, starting at the place where land was filled in on the east side of the hill. [10] He grew stronger all the time, because the LORD God Almighty was with him.

[11] King Hiram of Tyre sent a trade mission to David; he provided him with cedar logs and with carpenters and stone masons to build a palace. [12] And so David realized that the LORD had established him as king of Israel and was making his kingdom prosperous for the sake of his people.

[13] After moving from Hebron to Jerusalem, David took more concubines and wives, and had more sons and daughters. [14] The following children were born to him in Jerusalem: Shammua, Shobab, Nathan, Solomon, [15] Ibhar, Elishua, Nepheg, Japhia, [16] Elishama, Eliada, and Eliphelet.

Victory over the Philistines
(1 Chronicles 14.8-17)

[17] The Philistines were told that David had been made king of Israel, so their army set out to capture him. When David heard of it, he went down to a fortified place. [18] The Philistines arrived at Rephaim Valley and occupied it. [19] David asked the LORD, "Shall I attack the Philistines? Will you give me the victory?"

"Yes, attack!" the LORD answered. "I will give you the victory!"

[20] So David went to Baal Perazim and there he defeated the Philistines. He said, "The LORD has broken through my enemies like a flood." And so that

f Verse 8 in Hebrew is unclear.
5.4, 5 1 K 2.11; 1 Ch 3.4; 29.27   **5.6** Js 15.63; Jg 1.21

The Israelites were dancing and singing. (6.5)

place is called Baal Perazim.*g* 21 When the Philistines fled, they left their idols behind, and David and his men carried them away.

22 Then the Philistines went back to Rephaim Valley and occupied it again. 23 Once more David consulted the LORD, who answered, "Don't attack them from here, but go around and get ready to attack them from the other side, near the balsam trees. 24 When you hear the sound of marching in the treetops, then attack because I will be marching ahead of you to defeat the Philistine army." 25 David did what the LORD had commanded, and was able to drive the Philistines back from Geba all the way to Gezer.

The Covenant Box Is Brought to Jerusalem
(1 Chronicles 13.1-14; 15.25 — 16.6, 43)

6 Once more David called together the best soldiers in Israel, a total of thirty thousand men, 2 and led them to Baalah*h* in Judah, in order to bring

from there God's Covenant Box, bearing the name of the LORD Almighty, whose throne is above the winged creatures.*i* 3 They took it from Abinadab's home on the hill and placed it on a new cart. Uzzah and Ahio, sons of Abinadab, were guiding the cart, 4 with Ahio walking in front. 5 David and all the Israelites were dancing and singing with all their might*j* to honor the LORD. They were playing harps, lyres, drums, rattles, and cymbals.

6 As they came to the threshing place of Nacon, the oxen stumbled, and Uzzah reached out and took hold of the Covenant Box. 7 At once the LORD God became angry with Uzzah and killed him because of his irreverence.*k* Uzzah died there beside the Covenant Box, 8 and so that place has been called Perez Uzzah*l* ever since. David was furious because the LORD had punished Uzzah in anger.

9 Then David was afraid of the LORD and said, "How can I take the Covenant Box with me now?" 10 So he decided not to take it with him to Jerusalem; in-

---

g BAAL PERAZIM: *This name in Hebrew means "Lord of the Breakthrough."*
h *Probable text (see 1 Ch 13.6) to Baalah; Hebrew from Baaley, or from the leaders.*
i WINGED CREATURES: *See Word List.*   *j* *One ancient translation (and see 1 Ch 13.8) and singing with all their might; Hebrew with all the fir trees.*   *k* *Probable text his irreverence; Hebrew unclear.*   *l* PEREZ UZZAH: *This name in Hebrew means "Punishment of Uzzah."*
6.2 Ex 25.22   **6.3** 1 S 7.1, 2

stead, he turned off the road and took it to the house of Obed Edom, a native of the city of Gath. [11] It stayed there three months, and the LORD blessed Obed Edom and his family.

[12] King David heard that because of the Covenant Box the LORD had blessed Obed Edom's family and all that he had; so he got the Covenant Box from Obed's house to take it to Jerusalem with a great celebration. [13] After the men carrying the Covenant Box had gone six steps, David had them stop while he offered the LORD a sacrifice of a bull and a fattened calf. [14] David, wearing only a linen cloth around his waist, danced with all his might to honor the LORD. [15] And so he and all the Israelites took the Covenant Box up to Jerusalem with shouts of joy and the sound of trumpets.

[16] As the Box was being brought into the city, Michal, Saul's daughter, looked out of the window and saw King David dancing and jumping around in the sacred dance, and she was disgusted with him. [17] They brought the Box and put it in its place in the Tent that David had set up for it. Then he offered sacrifices and fellowship offerings to the LORD. [18] When he had finished offering the sacrifices, he blessed the people in the name of the LORD Almighty [19] and distributed food to them all. He gave each man and woman in Israel a loaf of bread, a piece of roasted meat,[m] and some raisins. Then everyone went home.

[20] Afterward, when David went home to greet his family, Michal came out to meet him. "The king of Israel made a big name for himself today!" she said. "He exposed himself like a fool in the sight of the servant women of his officials!"

[21] David answered, "I was dancing to honor the LORD, who chose me instead of your father and his family to make me the leader of his people Israel. And I will go on dancing to honor the LORD, [22] and will disgrace myself even more. You[n] may think I am nothing, but those women will think highly of me!"

[23] Michal, Saul's daughter, never had any children.

Nathan's Message to David
(1 Chronicles 17.1-15)

7 King David was settled in his palace, and the LORD kept him safe from all his enemies. [2] Then the king said to the prophet Nathan, "Here I am living in a house built of cedar, but God's Covenant Box is kept in a tent!"

[3] Nathan answered, "Do whatever you have in mind, because the LORD is with you." [4] But that night the LORD said to Nathan, [5] "Go and tell my servant David that I say to him, 'You are not the one to build a temple for me to live in. [6] From the time I rescued the people of Israel from Egypt until now, I have never lived in a temple; I have traveled around living in a tent. [7] In all my traveling with the people of Israel I never asked any of the leaders[o] that I appointed why they had not built me a temple made of cedar.'

[8] "So tell my servant David that I, the LORD Almighty, say to him, 'I took you from looking after sheep in the fields and made you the ruler of my people Israel. [9] I have been with you wherever you have gone, and I have defeated all your enemies as you advanced. I will make you as famous as the greatest leaders in the world. [10-11] I have chosen a place for my people Israel and have settled them there, where they will live without being oppressed any more. Ever since they entered this land, they have been attacked by violent people, but this will not happen again. I

---

m a piece of roasted meat; or a cake of dates.   *n One ancient translation You;*
Hebrew I.   *o Probable text (see 1 Ch 17.6) leaders; Hebrew tribes.*
6.11 1 Ch 26.4, 5   **6.19, 20** 1 Ch 16.43

promise to keep you safe from all your enemies and to give you descendants. ¹²When you die and are buried with your ancestors, I will make one of your sons king and will keep his kingdom strong. ¹³He will be the one to build a temple for me, and I will make sure that his dynasty continues forever. ¹⁴I will be his father, and he will be my son. When he does wrong, I will punish him as a father punishes his son. ¹⁵But I will not withdraw my support from him as I did from Saul, whom I removed so that you could be king. ¹⁶You will always have descendants, and I will make your kingdom last forever. Your dynasty will never end.'"

¹⁷Nathan told David everything that God had revealed to him.

David's Prayer of Thanksgiving
(1 Chronicles 17.16-27)

¹⁸Then King David went into the Tent of the Lord's presence, sat down and prayed, "Sovereign Lord, I am not worthy of what you have already done for me, nor is my family. ¹⁹Yet now you are doing even more, Sovereign Lord; you have made promises about my descendants in the years to come. And you let a man see this,ᵖ Sovereign Lord! ²⁰What more can I say to you! You know me, your servant. ²¹It was your will and purpose to do this; you have done all these great things in order to instruct me. ²²How great you are, Sovereign Lord! There is none like you; we have always known that you alone are God. ²³There is no other nation on earth like Israel, whom you rescued from slavery to make them your own people. The great and wonderful things you did for them�q have spread

your fame throughout the world. You drove outʳ other nations and their gods as your people advanced, the people whom you set free from Egypt to be your own. ²⁴You have made Israel your own people forever, and you, Lord, have become their God.

²⁵"And now, Lord God, fulfill for all time the promise you made about me and my descendants, and do what you said you would. ²⁶Your fame will be great, and people will forever say, 'The Lord Almighty is God over Israel.' And you will preserve my dynasty for all time. ²⁷Lord Almighty, God of Israel! I have the courage to pray this prayer to you, because you have revealed all this to me, your servant, and have told me that you will make my descendants kings.

²⁸"And now, Sovereign Lord, you are God; you always keep your promises, and you have made this wonderful promise to me. ²⁹I ask you to bless my descendants so that they will continue to enjoy your favor. You, Sovereign Lord, have promised this, and your blessing will rest on my descendants forever."

David's Military Victories
(1 Chronicles 18.1-17)

8 Some time later King David attacked the Philistines again, defeated them, and ended their control over the land.ˢ

²Then he defeated the Moabites. He made the prisoners lie down on the ground and put two out of every three of them to death. So the Moabites became his subjects and paid taxes to him.

³Then he defeated the king of the

ᵖ *Probable text* you let a man see this; *Hebrew* this is a law for human beings.
�q *Probable text* them; *Hebrew* you *(plural).*   ʳ *One ancient translation (and see*
1 Ch 17.21) You drove out; *Hebrew* for your land.   ˢ *Probable text* over the land;
Hebrew unclear.

7.12 Ps 89.3, 4; 132.11; Jn 7.42; Ac 2.30   **7.14** Ps 89.26, 27; 2 Co 6.18; He 1.5
7.16 Ps 89.36, 37   **7.23** Dt 4.34

Syrian state of Zobah, Hadadezer son of Rehob, as Hadadezer was on his way to restore his control over the territory by the upper Euphrates River. ⁴David captured seventeen hundred of his cavalry and twenty thousand of his foot soldiers. He kept enough horses for a hundred chariots and crippled all the rest.

⁵When the Syrians of Damascus sent an army to help King Hadadezer, David attacked it and killed twenty-two thousand men. ⁶Then he set up military camps in*ᵗ* their territory, and they became his subjects and paid taxes to him. The LORD made David victorious everywhere. ⁷David captured the gold shields carried by Hadadezer's officials and took them to Jerusalem. ⁸He also took a great quantity of bronze from Betah and Berothai, cities ruled by Hadadezer.

⁹King Toi of Hamath heard that David had defeated all of Hadadezer's army. ¹⁰So he sent his son Joram to greet King David and congratulate him for his victory over Hadadezer, against whom Toi had fought many times. Joram took David presents made of gold, silver, and bronze. ¹¹King David dedicated them for use in worship, along with the silver and gold he took from the nations he had conquered — ¹²Edom, Moab, Ammon, Philistia, and Amalek — as well as part of the loot he had taken from Hadadezer.

¹³David became even more famous when he returned from killing eighteen thousand Edomites in Salt Valley. ¹⁴He set up military camps*ᵘ* throughout Edom, and the people there became his subjects. The LORD made David victorious everywhere.

¹⁵David ruled over all of Israel and made sure that his people were always treated fairly and justly. ¹⁶Joab, whose mother was Zeruiah, was the com-

mander of the army; Jehoshaphat son of Ahilud was in charge of the records; ¹⁷Zadok son of Ahitub and Ahimelech son of Abiathar were priests; Seraiah was the court secretary; ¹⁸Benaiah son of Jehoiada was in charge of*ᵛ* David's bodyguards; and David's sons were priests.

David and Mephibosheth

9 One day David asked, "Is there anyone left of Saul's family? If there is, I would like to show him kindness for Jonathan's sake."

²There was a servant of Saul's family named Ziba, and he was told to go to David. "Are you Ziba?" the king asked.

"At your service, sir," he answered.

³The king asked him, "Is there anyone left of Saul's family to whom I can show loyalty and kindness, as I promised God I would?"

Ziba answered, "There is still one of Jonathan's sons. He is crippled."

He is crippled. (9.3)

⁴"Where is he?" the king asked.

"At the home of Machir son of Ammiel in Lodebar," Ziba answered. ⁵So King David sent for him.

ᵗ set up military camps in; or placed military commanders over.   ᵘ set up military camps; or placed military commanders.   ᵛ Some ancient translations was in charge of; Hebrew does not have these words.

8.13 Ps 60 Title   **9.1** 1 S 20.15-17   **9.3** 2 S 4.4

⁶When Mephibosheth, the son of Jonathan and grandson of Saul, arrived, he bowed down before David in respect. David said, "Mephibosheth," and he answered, "At your service, sir."

⁷"Don't be afraid," David replied. "I will be kind to you for the sake of your father Jonathan. I will give you back all the land that belonged to your grandfather Saul, and you will always be welcome at my table."

"Don't be afraid . . . I will be kind to you." (9.7)

⁸Mephibosheth bowed again and said, "I am no better than a dead dog, sir! Why should you be so good to me?"

⁹Then the king called Ziba, Saul's servant, and said, "I am giving Mephibosheth, your master's grandson, everything that belonged to Saul and his family. ¹⁰You, your sons, and your servants will farm the land for your master Saul's family and bring in the harvest, to provide food for them. But Mephibosheth himself will always be a guest at my table." (Ziba had fifteen sons and twenty servants.)

¹¹Ziba answered, "I will do everything Your Majesty commands."

So Mephibosheth ate at the king's*ʷ* table, just like one of the king's sons. ¹²Mephibosheth had a young son

named Mica. All the members of Ziba's family became servants of Mephibosheth. ¹³So Mephibosheth, who was crippled in both feet, lived in Jerusalem, eating all his meals at the king's table.

David Defeats the Ammonites and the Syrians
(1 Chronicles 19.1-19)

10 Some time later King Nahash of Ammon died, and his son Hanun became king. ²King David said, "I must show loyal friendship to Hanun, as his father Nahash did to me." So David sent messengers to express his sympathy.

When they arrived in Ammon, ³the Ammonite leaders said to the king, "Do you think that it is in your father's honor that David has sent these men to express sympathy to you? Of course not! He has sent them here as spies to explore the city, so that he can conquer us!"

⁴Hanun seized David's messengers, shaved off one side of their beards, cut off their clothes at the hips, and sent them away. ⁵They were too ashamed to return home. When David heard about what had happened, he sent word for them to stay in Jericho and not return until their beards had grown again.

⁶The Ammonites realized that they had made David their enemy, so they hired twenty thousand Syrian soldiers from Bethrehob and Zobah, twelve thousand men from Tob, and the king of Maacah with a thousand men. ⁷David heard of it and sent Joab against them with the whole army. ⁸The Ammonites marched out and took up their position at the entrance to Rabbah, their capital city, while the others, both the Syrians and the men from Tob and Maacah, took up their position in the open countryside.

ʷ One ancient translation the king's; *Hebrew* my.

⁹Joab saw that the enemy troops would attack him in front and from the rear, so he chose the best of Israel's soldiers and put them in position facing the Syrians. ¹⁰He placed the rest of his troops under the command of his brother Abishai, who put them in position facing the Ammonites. ¹¹Joab said to him, "If you see that the Syrians are defeating me, come and help me, and if the Ammonites are defeating you, I will go and help you. ¹²Be strong and courageous! Let's fight hard for our people and for the cities of our God. And may the LORD's will be done!"

¹³Joab and his men advanced to attack, and the Syrians fled. ¹⁴When the Ammonites saw the Syrians running away, they fled from Abishai and retreated into the city. Then Joab turned back from fighting the Ammonites and went back to Jerusalem.

¹⁵The Syrians realized that they had been defeated by the Israelites, and so they called all their troops together. ¹⁶King Hadadezer sent for the Syrians who were on the east side of the Euphrates River, and they came to Helam under the command of Shobach, commander of the army of King Hadadezer of Zobah. ¹⁷When David heard of it, he gathered the Israelite troops, crossed the Jordan River, and marched to Helam, where the Syrians took up their position facing him. The fighting began, ¹⁸and the Israelites drove the Syrian army back. David and his men killed seven hundred Syrian chariot drivers and forty thousand cavalry, and they wounded Shobach, the enemy commander, who died on the battlefield. ¹⁹When the kings who were subject to Hadadezer realized that they had been defeated by the Israelites, they made peace with them and became their subjects. And the Syrians were afraid to help the Ammonites any more.

David and Bathsheba

11 The following spring, at the time of the year when kings usually go to war, David sent out Joab with his officers and the Israelite army; they defeated the Ammonites and besieged the city of Rabbah. But David himself stayed in Jerusalem.

²One day, late in the afternoon, David got up from his nap and went to the palace roof. As he walked around up there, he saw a woman taking a bath in her house. She was very beautiful. ³So he sent a messenger to find out who she was, and learned that she was Bathsheba, the daughter of Eliam and the wife of Uriah the Hittite. ⁴David sent messengers to get her; they brought her to him and he made love to her. (She had just finished her monthly ritual of purification.) Then she went back home. ⁵Afterward she discovered that she was pregnant and sent a message to David to tell him.

⁶David then sent a message to Joab: "Send me Uriah the Hittite." So Joab sent him to David. ⁷When Uriah arrived, David asked him if Joab and the troops were well, and how the fighting was going. ⁸Then he said to Uriah, "Go on home and rest a while." Uriah left, and David had a present sent to his home. ⁹But Uriah did not go home; instead he slept at the palace gate with the king's guards. ¹⁰When David heard that Uriah had not gone home, he asked him, "You have just returned after a long absence; why didn't you go home?"

¹¹Uriah answered, "The men of Israel and Judah are away in battle, and the Covenant Box is with them; my commander Joab and his officers are camping out in the open. How could I go home, eat and drink, and sleep with my wife? By all that's sacred, I swear that I could never do such a thing!"

¹²So David said, "Then stay here the

11.1 1 Ch 20.1

UNITED ISRAELITE
KINGDOM

Kadesh

Gebal

SIDONIANS
LEBANON MTS.
BETHREHOB

SYRIA

Damascus

Sidon

MT. HERMON

Tyre

Dan

Abel

MAACAH

Bashan

Hazor

Ashtaroth

Cabul

GESHUR

Edrei

MT. CARMEL

Megiddo

Jezreel

Dor

Ramoth

Taanach

MT. GILBOA

Jabesh

Shechem

Zarethan

Gathrimmon

Jabbok

Joppa

Jazer

Beth

Horon

Rabbah

Gezer

Bethel

Jericho

AMMONITES

Ashdod

Ekron

Heshbon

Jerusalem

Medeba

Ashkelon

Gath?

Dibon

Gaza

Debir

Hebron

Aroer

Gerar

Ziklag?

Dead
Sea

Beersheba

MOABITES

Kir Heres

Tamar

AMALEKITES

Bozrah

Kadesh Barnea

EDOMITES

Sela

The

Negev

MEDITERRANEAN

SEA

Jordan R.

The Desert

Miles
0   60

Kms
0   60

© United Bible Societies, 1976

Eziongeber

GULF OF
AQABA

The rich man had many cattle and sheep. (12.2)
The poor man had only one lamb. (12.3)

rest of the day, and tomorrow I'll send you back." So Uriah stayed in Jerusalem that day and the next. 13 David invited him to supper and got him drunk. But again that night Uriah did not go home; instead he slept on his blanket*x* in the palace guardroom.

14 The next morning David wrote a letter to Joab and sent it by Uriah. 15 He wrote: "Put Uriah in the front line, where the fighting is heaviest, then retreat and let him be killed." 16 So while Joab was besieging the city, he sent Uriah to a place where he knew the enemy was strong. 17 The enemy troops came out of the city and fought Joab's forces; some of David's officers were killed, and so was Uriah.

18 Then Joab sent a report to David telling him about the battle, 19 and he instructed the messenger, "After you have told the king all about the battle, 20 he may get angry and ask you, 'Why did you go so near the city to fight them? Didn't you realize that they would shoot arrows from the walls? 21 Don't you remember how Abimelech son of Gideon was killed? It was at Thebez, where a woman threw a millstone down from the wall and killed him. Why, then, did you go so near the wall?' If the king asks you this, tell him, 'Your officer Uriah was also killed.'"

22 So the messenger went to David and told him what Joab had commanded him to say. 23 He said, "Our enemies were stronger than we were and came out of the city to fight us in the open, but we drove them back to the city gate. 24 Then they shot arrows at us from the wall, and some of Your Majesty's officers were killed; your officer Uriah was also killed."

25 David said to the messenger, "Encourage Joab and tell him not to be upset, since you never can tell who will die in battle. Tell him to launch a stronger attack on the city and capture it."

26 When Bathsheba heard that her husband had been killed, she mourned for him. 27 When the time of mourning was over, David had her brought to the palace; she became his wife and bore him a son. But the LORD was not pleased with what David had done.

Nathan's Message and David's Repentance

12 The LORD sent the prophet Nathan to David. Nathan went to him and said, "There were two men who lived in the same town; one was rich and the other poor. 2 The rich man had many cattle and sheep, 3 while the poor man had only one lamb, which he had bought. He took care of it, and it grew up in his home with his children.

x blanket; *or* cot.

11.21 Jg 9.53   **12.1** Ps 51 Title

He took the poor man's lamb. (12.4)

He would feed it some of his own food, let it drink from his cup, and hold it in his lap. The lamb was like a daughter to him. ⁴One day a visitor arrived at the rich man's home. The rich man didn't want to kill one of his own animals to fix a meal for him; instead, he took the poor man's lamb and prepared a meal for his guest."

⁵David became very angry at the rich man and said, "I swear by the living LORD that the man who did this ought to die! ⁶For having done such a cruel thing, he must pay back four times as much as he took."

⁷"You are that man," Nathan said to David. "And this is what the LORD God of Israel says: 'I made you king of Israel and rescued you from Saul. ⁸I gave you his kingdom and his wives; I made you king over Israel and Judah. If this had not been enough, I would have given you twice as much. ⁹Why, then, have you disobeyed my commands? Why did you do this evil thing? You had Uriah killed in battle; you let the Ammonites kill him, and then you took his wife! ¹⁰Now, in every generation some of your descendants will die a violent death because you have disobeyed me and have taken Uriah's wife. ¹¹I swear to you that I will cause someone from your own family to bring trouble on you. You will see it when I take your wives from you and give them to an-

other man; and he will have intercourse with them in broad daylight. ¹²You sinned in secret, but I will make this happen in broad daylight for all Israel to see.' "

¹³"I have sinned against the LORD," David said.

Nathan replied, "The LORD forgives you; you will not die. ¹⁴But because you have shown such contempt for the LORD in doing this, your child will die." ¹⁵Then Nathan went home.

David's Son Dies

The LORD caused the child that Uriah's wife had borne to David to become very sick. ¹⁶David prayed to God that the child would get well. He refused to eat anything, and every night he went into his room and spent the night lying on the floor. ¹⁷His court officials went to him and tried to make him get up, but he refused and would not eat anything with them. ¹⁸A week later the child died, and David's officials were afraid to tell him the news. They said, "While the child was living, David wouldn't answer us when we spoke to him. How can we tell him that his child is dead? He might do himself some harm!"

¹⁹When David noticed them whispering to each other, he realized that

the child had died. So he asked them, "Is the child dead?"

"Yes, he is," they answered.

20 David got up from the floor, took a bath, combed his hair, and changed his clothes. Then he went and worshiped in the house of the LORD. When he returned to the palace, he asked for food and ate it as soon as it was served. 21 "We don't understand this," his officials said to him. "While the child was alive, you wept for him and would not eat; but as soon as he died, you got up and ate!"

22 "Yes," David answered, "I did fast and weep while he was still alive. I thought that the LORD might be merciful to me and not let the child die. 23 But now that he is dead, why should I fast? Could I bring the child back to life? I will some day go to where he is, but he can never come back to me."

Solomon Is Born

24 Then David comforted his wife Bathsheba. He had intercourse with her, and she bore a son, whom David named Solomon. The LORD loved the boy 25 and commanded the prophet Nathan to name the boy Jedidiah,y because the LORD loved him.

David Captures Rabbah
(1 Chronicles 20.1-3)

26 Meanwhile Joab continued his campaign against Rabbah, the capital city of Ammon, and was about to capture it. 27 He sent messengers to David to report: "I have attacked Rabbah and have captured its water supply. 28 Now gather the rest of your forces, attack the city and take it yourself. I don't want to get the credit for capturing it." 29 So David gathered his forces, went to Rabbah, attacked it, and conquered it. 30 From the head of the idol of the Am-

monite god Molechz David took a gold crown which weighed about seventy-five pounds and had a jewel in it. David took the jewel and put it in his own crown.a He also took a large amount of loot from the city 31 and put its people to work with saws, iron hoes, and iron axes, and forced them to work atb making bricks. He did the same to the people of all the other towns of Ammon. Then he and his men returned to Jerusalem.

Amnon and Tamar

13 David's son Absalom had a beautiful unmarried sister named Tamar. Amnon, another of David's sons, fell in love with her. 2 He was so much in love with her that he became sick, because it seemed impossible for him to have her; as a virgin, she was kept from meeting men. 3 But he had a friend, a very shrewd man named Jonadab, the son of David's brother Shammah. 4 Jonadab said to Amnon, "You are the king's son, yet day after day I see you looking sad. What's the matter?"

"I'm in love with Tamar, the sister of my half brother Absalom," he answered.

5 Jonadab said to him, "Pretend that you are sick and go to bed. When your father comes to see you, say to him, 'Please ask my sister Tamar to come and feed me. I want her to fix the food here where I can see her, and then serve it to me herself.'" 6 So Amnon pretended that he was sick and went to bed.

King David went to see him, and Amnon said to him, "Please let Tamar come and make a few cakes here where I can see her, and then serve them to me herself."

7 So David sent word to Tamar in the

y JEDIDIAH: *This name in Hebrew means "Beloved of the LORD."*   z idol of the Ammonite god Molech; *or* Ammonite king.   a jewel . . . crown; *or* crown and put it on his own head.   b *Probable text (see 1 Ch 20.3)* work at; *Hebrew* pass through.

palace: "Go to Amnon's house and fix him some food." [8] She went there and found him in bed. She took some dough, prepared it, and made some cakes there where he could see her. Then she baked the cakes [9] and emptied them out of the pan for him to eat, but he wouldn't. He said, "Send everyone away" — and they all left. [10] Then he said to her, "Bring the cakes here to my bed and serve them to me yourself." She took the cakes and went over to him. [11] As she offered them to him, he grabbed her and said, "Come to bed with me!"

[12] "No," she said. "Don't force me to do such a degrading thing! That's awful! [13] How could I ever hold up my head in public again? And you — you would be completely disgraced in Israel. Please, speak to the king, and I'm sure that he will give me to you." [14] But he would not listen to her; and since he was stronger than she was, he overpowered her and raped her.

[15] Then Amnon was filled with a deep hatred for her; he hated her now even more than he had loved her before. He said to her, "Get out!"

[16] "No," she answered. "To send me away like this is a greater crime[c] than what you just did!"

But Amnon would not listen to her; [17] he called in his personal servant and said, "Get this woman out of my sight! Throw her out and lock the door!" [18] The servant put her out and locked the door.

Tamar was wearing a long robe with full sleeves,[d] the usual clothing for an unmarried princess in those days.[e] [19] She sprinkled ashes on her head, tore her robe, and with her face buried in her hands went away crying. [20] When her brother Absalom saw her, he asked, "Has Amnon molested you? Please, sis-

ter, don't let it upset you so much. He is your half brother, so don't tell anyone about it." So Tamar lived in Absalom's house, sad and lonely.

[21] When King David heard what had happened, he was furious. [22] And Absalom hated Amnon so much for having raped his sister Tamar that he would no longer even speak to him.

Absalom's Revenge

[23] Two years later Absalom was having his sheep sheared at Baal Hazor, near the town of Ephraim, and he invited all the king's sons to be there. [24] He went to King David and said, "Your Majesty, I am having my sheep sheared. Will you and your officials come and take part in the festivities?"

[25] "No, my son," the king answered. "It would be too much trouble for you if we all went." Absalom insisted, but the king would not give in, and he asked Absalom to leave.

[26] But Absalom said, "Well, then, will you at least let my brother Amnon come?"

"Why should he?" the king asked. [27] But Absalom kept on insisting until David finally let Amnon and all his other sons go with Absalom.

Absalom prepared a banquet fit for a king[f] [28] and instructed his servants: "Notice when Amnon has had too much to drink, and then when I give the order, kill him. Don't be afraid. I will take the responsibility myself. Be brave and don't hesitate!" [29] So the servants followed Absalom's instructions and killed Amnon. All the rest of David's sons mounted their mules and fled.

[30] While they were on their way home, David was told: "Absalom has killed all your sons — not one of them is left!" [31] The king stood up, tore his

---

[c] *Probable text* To send me ... crime; *Hebrew unclear.*   [d] long robe with full sleeves; *or* decorated robe (*see Gn* 37.3).   [e] *Probable text* in those days; *Hebrew* garments.
[f] *Some ancient translations* Absalom prepared a banquet fit for a king; *Hebrew does not have these words.*

clothes in sorrow, and threw himself to the ground. The servants who were there with him tore their clothes also. ³²But Jonadab, the son of David's brother Shammah, said, "Your Majesty, they haven't killed all your sons. Only Amnon is dead. You could tell by looking at Absalom that he had made up his mind to do this from the time that Amnon raped his sister Tamar. ³³So don't believe the news that all your sons are dead; only Amnon was killed."

³⁴In the meantime Absalom had fled.

Just then the soldier on sentry duty saw a large crowd coming down the hill on the road from Horonaim.*g* He went to the king and reported what he had seen.*h* ³⁵Jonadab said to David, "Those are your sons coming, just as I said they would." ³⁶As soon as he finished saying this, David's sons came in; they started crying, and David and his officials also cried bitterly.

³⁷⁻³⁸Absalom fled and went to the king of Geshur, Talmai son of Ammihud, and stayed there three years. David mourned a long time for his son Amnon; ³⁹but when he got over Amnon's death, he was filled with longing for his son Absalom.

Joab Arranges for Absalom's Return

14 Joab knew that King David missed Absalom very much, ²so he sent for a clever woman who lived in Tekoa. When she arrived, he said to her, "Pretend that you are in mourning; put on your mourning clothes, and don't comb your hair. Act like a woman who has been in mourning for a long time. ³Then go to the king and say to him what I tell you to say." Then Joab told her what to say.

⁴The woman went to the king, bowed down to the ground in respect, and said, "Help me, Your Majesty!"

⁵"What do you want?" he asked her.

"I am a poor widow, sir," she answered. "My husband is dead. ⁶Sir, I had two sons, and one day they got into a quarrel out in the fields, where there was no one to separate them, and one of them killed the other. ⁷And now, sir, all my relatives have turned against me and are demanding that I hand my son over to them, so that they can kill him for murdering his brother. If they do this, I will be left without a son. They will destroy my last hope and leave my husband without a son to keep his name alive."

⁸"Go back home," the king answered, "and I will take care of the matter."

⁹"Your Majesty," she said, "whatever you do, my family and I will take the blame; you and the royal family are innocent."

¹⁰The king replied, "If anyone threatens you, bring him to me, and he will never bother you again."

¹¹She said, "Your Majesty, please pray to the LORD your God, so that my relative who is responsible for avenging the death of my son will not commit a greater crime by killing my other son."

"I promise by the living LORD," David replied, "that your son will not be harmed in the least."

¹²"Please, Your Majesty, let me say just one more thing," the woman said.

"All right," he answered.

¹³She said to him, "Why have you done such a wrong to God's people? You have not allowed your own son to return from exile, and so you have condemned yourself by what you have just said. ¹⁴We will all die; we are like water spilled on the ground, which can't be gathered again. Even God does not bring the dead back to life, but the king can at least find a way to bring a man

---

g Probable text from Horonaim; *Hebrew* behind him.   *h One ancient translation* He went . . . had seen; *Hebrew does not have these words.*
13.37 2 S 3.3

back from exile.*i* *15*Now, Your Majesty, the reason I have come to speak to you is that the people threatened me, and so I said to myself that I would speak to you in the hope that you would do what I ask. *16*I thought you would listen to me and save me from the one who is trying to kill my son and me and so remove us from the land God gave his people. *17*I said to myself that your promise, sir, would make me safe, because the king is like God's angel and can distinguish good from evil.*j* May the Lord your God be with you!"

*18*The king answered, "I'm going to ask you a question, and you must tell me the whole truth."

"Ask me anything, Your Majesty," she answered.

19"Did Joab put you up to this?" he asked her.

She answered, "I swear by all that is sacred, Your Majesty, that there is no way to avoid answering your question.*k* It was indeed your officer Joab who told me what to do and what to say. *20*But he did it in order to straighten out this whole matter. Your Majesty is as wise as the angel of God and knows everything that happens."

*21*Later on the king said to Joab, "I have decided to do what you want. Go and get the young man Absalom and bring him back here."

*22*Joab threw himself to the ground in front of David in respect, and said, "God bless you, Your Majesty! Now I know that you are pleased with me, because you have granted my request." *23*Then he got up and went to Geshur and brought Absalom back to Jerusalem. *24*The king, however, gave orders that Absalom should not live in the palace. "I don't want to see him," the king said. So Absalom lived in his own house and did not appear before the king.

Absalom Is Reconciled to David

*25*There was no one in Israel as famous for his good looks as Absalom; he had no defect from head to toe. *26*His hair was very thick, and he had to cut it once a year, when it grew too long and heavy. It would weigh about five pounds according to the royal standard of weights. *27*Absalom had three sons and one daughter named Tamar, a very beautiful woman.

*28*Absalom lived two years in Jerusalem without seeing the king. *29*Then he sent for Joab, to ask him to go to the king for him; but Joab would not come. Again Absalom sent for him, and again Joab refused to come. *30*So Absalom said to his servants, "Look, Joab's field is next to mine, and it has barley growing in it. Go and set fire to it." So they went and set the field on fire.

*31*Joab went to Absalom's house and demanded, "Why did your servants set fire to my field?"

*32*Absalom answered, "Because you wouldn't come when I sent for you. I wanted you to go to the king and ask for me: 'Why did I leave Geshur and come here? It would have been better for me to have stayed there.'" And Absalom went on, "I want you to arrange for me to see the king, and if I'm guilty, then let him put me to death."

*33*So Joab went to King David and told him what Absalom had said. The king sent for Absalom, who went to him and bowed down to the ground in front of him. The king welcomed him with a kiss.

Absalom Plans Rebellion

15 After this, Absalom provided a chariot and horses for himself, and an escort of fifty men. *2*He would get up early and go and stand by the

---

i Probable text Even God . . . from exile; *Hebrew unclear.* *j* can distinguish good from evil; *or* knows everything. *k* there is . . . question; *or* you are absolutely right.
14.17 2 S 19.27

road at the city gate. Whenever someone came there with a dispute that he
wanted the king to settle, Absalom
would call him over and ask him where
he was from. And after the man had
told him what tribe he was from,
3 Absalom would say, "Look, the law
is on your side, but there is no representative of the king to hear
your case." 4 And he would add,
"How I wish I were a judge! Then anyone who had a dispute or a claim
could come to me, and I would give
him justice." 5 When the man would
approach Absalom to bow down before him, Absalom would reach out,
take hold of him, and kiss him. 6 Absalom did this with every Israelite who
came to the king for judgment, and so
he won their loyalty.

7 After four *l* years Absalom said to
King David, "Sir, let me go to Hebron
and keep a promise I made to the LORD.
8 While I was living in Geshur in Syria,
I promised the LORD that if he would
take me back to Jerusalem, I would
worship him in Hebron."*m*

9 "Go in peace," the king said. So
Absalom went to Hebron. 10 But he
sent messengers to all the tribes
of Israel to say, "When you hear the
sound of trumpets, shout, 'Absalom
has become king at Hebron!'" 11 There
were two hundred men who at
Absalom's invitation had gone from
Jerusalem with him; they knew nothing of the plot and went in all good
faith. 12 And while he was offering sacrifices, Absalom also sent to
the town of Gilo for Ahithophel, who
was one of King David's advisers. The
plot against the king gained strength,
and Absalom's followers grew in
number.

David Flees from Jerusalem

13 A messenger reported to David,
"The Israelites are pledging their loyalty to Absalom."

14 So David said to all his officials who
were with him in Jerusalem, "We must
get away at once if we want to escape
from Absalom! Hurry! Or else he will
soon be here and defeat us and kill
everyone in the city!"

15 "Yes, Your Majesty," they answered. "We are ready to do whatever
you say." 16 So the king left, accompanied by all his family and officials, except for ten concubines, whom he left
behind to take care of the palace.

17 As the king and all his men were
leaving the city, they stopped at the last
house. 18 All his officials stood *n* next to
him as the royal bodyguards passed by
in front of him. The six hundred soldiers who had followed him from Gath
also passed by, 19 and the king said to
Ittai, their leader, "Why are you going
with us? Go back and stay with the new
king. You are a foreigner, a refugee
away from your own country. 20 You
have lived here only a short time, so
why should I make you wander around
with me? I don't even know where I'm
going. Go back and take all your people
with you — and may the LORD be kind
and faithful to you."*o*

21 But Ittai answered, "Your Majesty,
I swear to you in the LORD's name that
I will always go with you wherever you
go, even if it means death."

22 "Fine!" David answered. "March
on!" So Ittai went on with all his men
and their dependents. 23 The people
cried loudly as David's followers left.
The king crossed Kidron Brook, followed by his men, and together they
went out toward the wilderness.

---

l Some ancient translations four; *Hebrew* forty.
Hebrew; *Hebrew does not have these words.*
o One ancient translation and may the LORD be kind and faithful to you; *Hebrew*
kindness and faithfulness.

m One ancient translation in
n Probable text stood; *Hebrew* passed.

David went on up the Mount of Olives crying. (15.30)

²⁴Zadok the priest was there, and with him were the Levites, carrying the sacred Covenant Box. They set it down*p* and didn't pick it up again until all the people had left the city. The priest Abiathar was there too.*q* ²⁵Then the king said to Zadok, "Take the Covenant Box back to the city. If the LORD is pleased with me, some day he will let me come back to see it and the place where it stays. ²⁶But if he isn't pleased with me — well, then, let him do to me what he wishes." ²⁷And he went on to say to Zadok, "Look,*r* take your son Ahimaaz and Abiathar's son Jonathan and go back to the city in peace. ²⁸Meanwhile, I will wait at the river crossings in the wilderness until I receive news from you." ²⁹So Zadok and Abiathar took the Covenant Box back into Jerusalem and stayed there.

³⁰David went on up the Mount of Olives crying; he was barefoot and had his head covered as a sign of grief. All who followed him covered their heads and cried also. ³¹When David was told*s* that Ahithophel had joined Absalom's rebellion, he prayed, "Please, LORD, turn Ahithophel's advice into nonsense!"

³²When David reached the top of the hill, where there was a place of worship, his trusted friend Hushai the Archite met him with his clothes torn and with dirt on his head. ³³David said to him, "You will be of no help to me if you come with me, ³⁴but you can help me by returning to the city and telling Absalom that you will now serve him as faithfully as you served his father. And do all you can to oppose any advice that Ahithophel gives. ³⁵The priests Zadok and Abiathar will be there; tell them everything you hear in the king's palace. ³⁶They have their sons Ahimaaz and Jonathan with them, and you can send them to me with all the information you gather."

³⁷So Hushai, David's friend, returned to the city just as Absalom was arriving.

---

p Probable text set it down; *Hebrew* poured it out.   *q Probable text* was there too; *Hebrew* went up.   *r Some ancient translations* Look; *Hebrew* Are you the seer?   *s One ancient translation* was told; *Hebrew* told.

David and Ziba

16 When David had gone a little beyond the top of the hill, he was suddenly met by Ziba, the servant of Mephibosheth, who had with him a couple of donkeys loaded with two hundred loaves of bread, a hundred bunches of raisins, a hundred bunches of fresh fruit, and a leather bag full of wine. ² King David asked him, "What are you going to do with all that?"

Ziba answered, "The donkeys are for Your Majesty's family to ride, the bread and the fruit are for the men to eat, and the wine is for them to drink when they get tired in the wilderness."

³ "Where is Mephibosheth, the grandson of your master Saul?" the king asked him.

"He is staying in Jerusalem," Ziba answered, "because he is convinced that the Israelites will now restore to him the kingdom of his grandfather Saul."

⁴ The king said to Ziba, "Everything that belonged to Mephibosheth is yours."

"I am your servant," Ziba replied. "May I always please Your Majesty!"

David and Shimei

⁵ When King David arrived at Bahurim, one of Saul's relatives, Shimei son of Gera, came out to meet him, cursing him as he came. ⁶ Shimei started throwing stones at David and his officials, even though David was surrounded by his men and his bodyguards. ⁷ Shimei cursed him and said, "Get out! Get out! Murderer! Criminal! ⁸ You took Saul's kingdom, and now the LORD is punishing you for murdering so many of Saul's family. The LORD has given the kingdom to your son Absalom, and you are ruined, you murderer!"

⁹ Abishai, whose mother was Zeru-

iah, said to the king, "Your Majesty, why do you let this dog curse you? Let me go over there and cut off his head!"

¹⁰ "This is none of your business," the king said to Abishai and his brother Joab. "If he curses me because the LORD told him to, who has the right to ask why he does it?" ¹¹ And David said to Abishai and to all his officials, "My own son is trying to kill me; so why should you be surprised at this Benjaminite? The LORD told him to curse; so leave him alone and let him do it. ¹² Perhaps the LORD will notice my misery*ᵗ* and give me some blessings to take the place of his curse." ¹³ So David and his men continued along the road. Shimei kept up with them, walking on the hillside; he was cursing and throwing stones and dirt at them as he went. ¹⁴ The king and all his men were worn out when they reached the Jordan,*ᵘ* and there they rested.

Absalom in Jerusalem

¹⁵ Absalom and all the Israelites with him entered Jerusalem, and Ahithophel was with them. ¹⁶ When Hushai, David's trusted friend, met Absalom, he shouted, "Long live the king! Long live the king!"

¹⁷ "What has happened to your loyalty to your friend David?" Absalom asked him. "Why didn't you go with him?"

¹⁸ Hushai answered, "How could I? I am for the one chosen by the LORD, by these people, and by all the Israelites. I will stay with you. ¹⁹ After all, whom should I serve, if not my master's son? As I served your father, so now I will serve you."

²⁰ Then Absalom turned to Ahithophel and said, "Now that we are here, what do you advise us to do?"

²¹ Ahithophel answered, "Go and

ᵗ Some ancient translations misery; *Hebrew* wickedness.　　*ᵘ One ancient translation* the Jordan; *Hebrew does not have these words.*
16.1 2 S 9.9, 10　**16.3** 2 S 19.25-27

have intercourse with your father's concubines whom he left behind to take care of the palace. Then everyone in Israel will know that your father regards you as his enemy, and your followers will be greatly encouraged."
²² So they set up a tent for Absalom on the palace roof, and in the sight of everyone Absalom went in and had intercourse with his father's concubines.

²³ Any advice that Ahithophel gave in those days was accepted as though it were the very word of God; both David and Absalom followed it.

Hushai Misleads Absalom

17 Not long after that, Ahithophel said to Absalom, "Let me choose twelve thousand men, and tonight I will set out after David. ² I will attack him while he is tired and discouraged. He will be frightened, and all his men will run away. I will kill only the king ³ and then bring back all his men to you, like a bride returning to her husband. You want to kill only one man;ᵛ the rest of the people will be safe." ⁴ This seemed like good advice to Absalom and all the Israelite leaders.

⁵ Absalom said, "Now call Hushai, and let us hear what he has to say." ⁶ When Hushai arrived, Absalom said to him, "This is the advice that Ahithophel has given us; shall we follow it? If not, you tell us what to do."

⁷ Hushai answered, "The advice Ahithophel gave you this time is no good. ⁸ You know that your father David and his men are hard fighters and that they are as fierce as a mother bear robbed of her cubs. Your father is an experienced soldier and does not stay with his men at night. ⁹ Right now he is probably hiding in a cave or some other place. As soon as David attacks your men, whoever hears about it will say

that your men have been defeated. ¹⁰ Then even the bravest men, as fearless as lions, will be afraid because everyone in Israel knows that your father is a great soldier and that his men are hard fighters. ¹¹ My advice is that you bring all the Israelites together from one end of the country to the other, as many as the grains of sand on the seashore, and that you lead them personally in battle. ¹² We will find David wherever he is, and attack him before he knows what's happening. Neither he nor any of his men will survive. ¹³ If he retreats into a city, our people will all bring ropes and just pull the cityʷ into the valley below. Not a single stone will be left there on top of the hill."

¹⁴ Absalom and all the Israelites said, "Hushai's advice is better than Ahithophel's." The LORD had decided that Ahithophel's good advice would not be followed, so that disaster would come on Absalom.

David Is Warned and Escapes

¹⁵ Then Hushai told the priests Zadok and Abiathar what advice he had given to Absalom and the Israelite leaders and what advice Ahithophel had given. ¹⁶ Hushai added, "Quick, now! Send a message to David not to spend the night at the river crossings in the wilderness, but to cross the Jordan at once, so that he and his men won't all be caught and killed."

¹⁷ Abiathar's son Jonathan and Zadok's son Ahimaaz were waiting at the spring of Enrogel, on the outskirts of Jerusalem, because they did not dare be seen entering the city. A servant woman would regularly go and tell them what was happening, and then they would go and tell King David. ¹⁸ But one day a boy happened to see

---

ᵛ *One ancient translation* like a bride . . . only one man; *Hebrew* like the return of the whole, so is the man you seek.　ʷ *Some ancient translations* the city; *Hebrew* him.

16.22 2 S 12.11, 12

them, and he told Absalom; so they hurried off to hide in the house of a certain man in Bahurim. He had a well near his house, and they got down in it. ¹⁹The man's wife took a covering, spread it over the opening of the well and scattered grain over it, so that no one would notice anything. ²⁰Absalom's officials came to the house and asked the woman, "Where are Ahimaaz and Jonathan?"

"They crossed the river," she answered.

The men looked for them but could not find them, and so they returned to Jerusalem. ²¹After they left, Ahimaaz and Jonathan came up out of the well and went and reported to King David. They told him what Ahithophel had planned against him and said, "Hurry up and cross the river." ²²So David and his men started crossing the Jordan, and by daybreak they had all gone across.

²³When Ahithophel saw that his advice had not been followed, he saddled his donkey and went back to his hometown. After putting his affairs in order, he hanged himself. He was buried in the family grave.

²⁴David had reached the town of Mahanaim by the time Absalom and the Israelites had crossed the Jordan. (²⁵Absalom had put Amasa in command of the army in the place of Joab. Amasa was the son of Jether the Ishmaelite;ˣ his mother was Abigail, the daughter of Nahash and the sister of Joab's mother Zeruiah.) ²⁶Absalom and his men camped in the land of Gilead.

²⁷When David arrived at Mahanaim, he was met by Shobi son of Nahash, from the city of Rabbah in Ammon, and by Machir son of Ammiel, from Lodebar, and by Barzillai, from Rogelim in Gilead. ²⁸⁻²⁹They brought bowls, clay pots, and bedding, and also food for David and his men: wheat, barley, meal, roasted grain, beans, peas,ʸ honey, cheese, cream, and some sheep. They knew that David and his men would get hungry, thirsty, and tired in the wilderness.

Absalom Is Defeated and Killed

18 King David brought all his men together, divided them into units of a thousand and of a hundred, and placed officers in command of them. ²Then he sent them out in three groups, with Joab and Joab's brother Abishai and Ittai from Gath, each in command of a group. And the king said to his men, "I will go with you myself."

³"You mustn't go with us," they answered. "It won't make any difference to the enemy if the rest of us turn and run, or even if half of us are killed; but you are worth ten thousand of us. It will be better if you stay here in the city and send us help."

⁴"I will do whatever you think best," the king answered. Then he stood by the side of the gate as his men marched out in units of a thousand and of a hundred. ⁵He gave orders to Joab, Abishai, and Ittai: "For my sake don't harm the young man Absalom." And all the

"Don't harm the young man Absalom." (18.5)

ˣ *One ancient translation (and see 1 Ch 2.17)* Ishmaelite; *Hebrew* Israelite.　　ʸ *Some ancient translations* peas; *Hebrew* peas and roasted grain.

Absalom's head got caught in the branches. (18.9)

troops heard David give this command to his officers.

⁶ David's army went out into the countryside and fought the Israelites in Ephraim Forest. ⁷ The Israelites were defeated by David's men; it was a terrible defeat, with twenty thousand men killed that day. ⁸ The fighting spread over the countryside, and more men died in the forest than were killed in battle.

⁹ Suddenly Absalom met some of David's men. Absalom was riding a mule, and as it went under a large oak tree, Absalom's head got caught in the branches. The mule ran on and Absalom was left hanging in midair. ¹⁰ One of David's men saw him and reported to Joab, "Sir, I saw Absalom hanging in an oak tree!"

¹¹ Joab answered, "If you saw him, why didn't you kill him on the spot? I myself would have given you ten pieces of silver and a belt."

¹² But the man answered, "Even if you gave me a thousand pieces of silver, I wouldn't lift a finger against the king's son. We all heard the king command you and Abishai and Ittai, 'For my sake don't harm the young man Absalom.' ¹³ But if I had disobeyed the king and killed Absalom, the king would have heard about it — he hears about

everything — and you would not have defended me."

¹⁴ "I'm not going to waste any more time with you," Joab said. He took three spears and plunged them into Absalom's chest while he was still alive, hanging in the oak tree. ¹⁵ Then ten of Joab's soldiers closed in on Absalom and finished killing him.

¹⁶ Joab had the trumpet blown to stop the fighting, and his troops came back from pursuing the Israelites. ¹⁷ They took Absalom's body, threw it into a deep pit in the forest, and covered it with a huge pile of stones. All the Israelites fled to their own hometowns.

¹⁸ During his lifetime Absalom had built a monument for himself in King's Valley, because he had no son to keep his name alive. So he named it after himself, and to this day it is known as Absalom's Monument.

David Is Told of Absalom's Death

¹⁹ Then Ahimaaz son of Zadok said to Joab, "Let me run to the king with the good news that the LORD has saved him from his enemies."

²⁰ "No," Joab said, "today you will not take any good news. Some other day you may do so, but not today, for the king's son is dead." ²¹ Then he said to

his Ethiopian[z] slave, "Go and tell the king what you have seen." The slave bowed and ran off.

22 Ahimaaz insisted, "I don't care what happens; please let me take the news also."

"Why do you want to do it, my son?" Joab asked. "You will get no reward for it."

23 "Whatever happens," Ahimaaz said again, "I want to go."

"Then go," Joab said. So Ahimaaz ran off down the road through the Jordan Valley, and soon he passed the slave.

24 David was sitting in the space between the inner and outer gates of the city. The lookout went up to the top of the wall and stood on the roof of the gateway; he looked out and saw a man running alone. 25 He called down and told the king, and the king said, "If he is alone, he is bringing good news." The runner kept coming closer.

26 Then the lookout saw another man running alone, and he called down to the gatekeeper, "Look! There's another man running!"

The king answered, "This one also is bringing good news."

27 The lookout said, "I can see that the first man runs like Ahimaaz."

"He's a good man," the king said, "and he is bringing good news."

28 Ahimaaz called out a greeting to the king, threw himself down to the ground before him, and said, "Praise the Lord your God, who has given you victory over the men who rebelled against Your Majesty!"

29 "Is the young man Absalom all right?" the king asked.

Ahimaaz answered, "Sir, when your officer Joab sent me, I saw a great commotion, but I couldn't tell what it was."

30 "Stand over there," the king told

him; and he went over and stood there.

31 Then the Ethiopian[z] slave arrived and said to the king, "I have good news for Your Majesty! Today the Lord has given you victory over all who rebelled against you!"

32 "Is the young man Absalom all right?" the king asked.

The slave answered, "I wish that what has happened to him would happen to all your enemies, sir, and to all who rebel against you."

33 The king was overcome with grief. He went up to the room over the gateway and wept. As he went, he cried, "O my son! My son Absalom! Absalom, my son! If only I had died in your place, my son! Absalom, my son!"

Joab Reprimands David

19 Joab was told that King David was weeping and mourning for Absalom. 2 And so the joy of victory was turned into sadness for all of David's troops that day, because they heard that the king was mourning for his son. 3 They went back into the city quietly, like soldiers who are ashamed because they are running away from battle. 4 The king covered his face and cried loudly, "O my son! My son Absalom! Absalom, my son!"

5 Joab went to the king's house and said to him, "Today you have humiliated your men — the men who saved your life and the lives of your sons and daughters and of your wives and concubines. 6 You oppose those who love you and support those who hate you! You have made it clear that your officers and men mean nothing to you. I can see that you would be quite happy if Absalom were alive today and all of us were dead. 7 Now go and reassure your men. I swear by the Lord's name that if you

---

z *Hebrew* Cushite: *Cush is the ancient name of the extensive territory south of the First Cataract of the Nile River. This region was called Ethiopia in Graeco-Roman times, and included within its borders most of modern Sudan and some of present-day Ethiopia (Abyssinia).*

"O my son! My son Absalom!" (19.4)

don't, not one of them will be with you by tomorrow morning. That would be the worst disaster you have suffered in all your life." [8] Then the king got up, and went and sat near the city gate. His men heard that he was there, and they all gathered around him.

David Starts Back to Jerusalem

Meanwhile all the Israelites had fled to their own hometowns. [9] All over the country they started quarreling among themselves. "King David saved us from our enemies," they said to one another. "He rescued us from the Philistines, but now he has fled from Absalom and left the country. [10] We anointed Absalom as our king, but he has been killed in battle. So why doesn't somebody try to bring King David back?"

[11] The news of what the Israelites were saying reached King David.[a] So he sent the priests Zadok and Abiathar to ask the leaders of Judah, "Why should you be the last to help bring the king back to his palace? [12] You are my relatives, my own flesh and blood; why should you be the last to bring me back?" [13] David also told them to say to Amasa, "You are my relative. From now on I am putting you in charge of the army in place of Joab. May God strike me dead if I don't!" [14] David's words won the complete loyalty of all the men of Judah, and they sent him word to return with all his officials.

[15] On his way back the king was met at the Jordan River by the men of Judah, who had come to Gilgal to escort him across the river. [16] At the same time the Benjaminite Shimei son of Gera from Bahurim hurried to the Jordan to meet King David. [17] He had with him a thousand men from the tribe of Benjamin. And Ziba, the servant of Saul's family, also came with his fifteen sons and twenty servants, and they arrived at the Jordan before the king. [18] They crossed[b] the river to escort the royal party across and to do whatever the king wanted.

David Shows Kindness to Shimei

As the king was getting ready to cross, Shimei threw himself down in front of him [19] and said, "Your Majesty, please forget the wrong I did that day you left Jerusalem. Don't hold it against me or think about it any more. [20] I know, sir, that I have sinned, and this is why I am the first one from the northern tribes to come and meet Your Majesty today."

[21] Abishai son of Zeruiah spoke up: "Shimei should be put to death because he cursed the one whom the LORD chose as king."

[22] But David said to Abishai and his brother Joab, "Who asked your opinion? Are you going to give me trouble? I am the one who is king of Israel now, and no Israelite will be put to death to-

---

[a] *Some ancient translations* The news . . . David; *Hebrew* The news . . . David, to his palace, *and places this sentence at the end of the verse.*   [b] *Probable text* They crossed; *Hebrew* The crossing crossed.
19.16 2 S 16.5-13

day." ²³And he said to Shimei, "I give you my word that you will not be put to death."

David Shows Kindness to Mephibosheth

²⁴Then Mephibosheth, Saul's grandson, came down to meet the king. He had not washed his feet, trimmed his beard, or washed his clothes from the time the king left Jerusalem until he returned victorious. ²⁵When Mephibosheth arrived from*c* Jerusalem to meet the king, the king said to him, "Mephibosheth, you didn't go with me. Why not?"

²⁶He answered, "As you know, Your Majesty, I am crippled. I told my servant to saddle my donkey so that I could ride along with you, but he betrayed me. ²⁷He lied about me to Your Majesty, but you are like God's angel, so do what seems right to you. ²⁸All of my father's family deserved to be put to death by Your Majesty, but you gave me the right to eat at your table. I have no right to ask for any more favors from Your Majesty."

²⁹The king answered, "You don't have to say anything more. I have decided that you and Ziba will share Saul's property."

³⁰"Let Ziba have it all," Mephibosheth answered. "It's enough for me that Your Majesty has come home safely."

David Shows Kindness to Barzillai

³¹Barzillai, from Gilead, had also come down from Rogelim to escort the king across the Jordan. ³²Barzillai was a very old man, eighty years old. He was very rich and had supplied the king with food while he was staying at Mahanaim. ³³The king said to him, "Come with me to Jerusalem, and I will take care of you."

³⁴But Barzillai answered, "I don't have long to live; why should I go with Your Majesty to Jerusalem? ³⁵I am already eighty years old, and nothing gives me pleasure any more. I can't taste what I eat and drink, and I can't hear the voices of singers. I would only be a burden to Your Majesty. ³⁶I don't deserve such a great reward. So I will go just a little way with you beyond the Jordan. ³⁷Then let me go back home and die near my parents' grave. Here is my son Chimham, who will serve you; take him with you, Your Majesty, and do for him as you think best."

³⁸The king answered, "I will take him with me and do for him whatever you want. And I will do for you anything you ask." ³⁹Then David and all of his men crossed the Jordan. He kissed Barzillai and gave him his blessing, and Barzillai went back home.

Judah and Israel Argue over the King

⁴⁰When the king had crossed, escorted by all the people of Judah and half the people of Israel, he went on to Gilgal, and Chimham went with him. ⁴¹Then all the Israelites went to the king and said to him, "Your Majesty, why did our brothers, the men of Judah, think they had the right to take you away and escort you, your family, and your men across the Jordan?"

⁴²The men of Judah answered, "We did it because the king is one of us. So why should this make you angry? He hasn't paid for our food nor has he given us anything."

⁴³The Israelites replied, "We have ten times as many claims on King David as you have, even if he is one of you. Why do you look down on us? Don't forget that we were the first to talk about bringing the king back!"

But the men of Judah were more

---

c One ancient translation from; *Hebrew* at.
19.24 2 S 9.1-13; 16.1-4   **19.31** 2 S 17.27-29

violent in making their claims than the men of Israel.

Sheba's Rebellion

20 There happened to be in Gilgal a worthless character named Sheba son of Bikri, of the tribe of Benjamin. He blew the trumpet and called out, "Down with David! We won't follow him! Men of Israel, let's go home!" ²So the Israelites deserted David and went with Sheba, but the men of Judah remained loyal and followed David from the Jordan to Jerusalem.

³When David arrived at his palace in Jerusalem, he took the ten concubines he had left to take care of the palace, and put them under guard. He provided for their needs, but did not have intercourse with them. They were kept confined for the rest of their lives, living like widows.

⁴The king said to Amasa, "Call the men of Judah together and be back here with them by the day after tomorrow." ⁵Amasa went to call them, but he did not get back by the time the king had told him to. ⁶So the king said to Abishai, "Sheba will give us more trouble than Absalom. Take my men and go after him, or else he may occupy some fortified towns and escape from us." ⁷So Joab's men, the royal bodyguards, and all the other soldiers left Jerusalem with Abishai to go after Sheba. ⁸When they reached the large rock at Gibeon, Amasa met them. Joab was dressed for battle, with a sword in its sheath fastened to his belt. As he came forward, the sword fell out. ⁹Joab said to Amasa, "How are you, my friend?" and took hold of his beard with his right hand in order to kiss him. ¹⁰Amasa was not on guard against the sword that Joab was holding in his other hand, and Joab stabbed him in the belly, and his insides spilled out on the ground. He died

immediately, and Joab did not have to strike again.

Then Joab and his brother Abishai went on after Sheba. ¹¹One of Joab's men stood by Amasa's body and called out, "Everyone who is for Joab and David follow Joab!" ¹²Amasa's body, covered with blood, was lying in the middle of the road. Joab's man saw that everybody was stopping, so he dragged the body from the road out into the field and threw a blanket over it. ¹³After the body had been removed from the road, everyone followed Joab in pursuit of Sheba.

¹⁴Sheba passed through the territory of all the tribes of Israel and came to the city of Abel Beth Maacah, and all the members of the clan of Bikri*ᵈ* assembled and followed him into the city. ¹⁵Joab's men heard that Sheba was there, and so they went and besieged the city. They built ramps of earth against the outer wall and also began to dig under the wall to make it fall down. ¹⁶There was a wise woman in the city who shouted from the wall, "Listen! Listen! Tell Joab to come here; I want to speak with him." ¹⁷Joab went, and she asked, "Are you Joab?"

"Yes, I am," he answered.

"Listen to me, sir," she said.

"I'm listening," he answered.

¹⁸She said, "Long ago they used to say, 'Go and get your answer in the city of Abel'—and that's just what they did. ¹⁹Ours is a great city, one of the most peaceful and loyal in Israel. Why are you trying to destroy it? Do you want to ruin what belongs to the LORD?"

²⁰"Never!" Joab answered. "I will never ruin or destroy your city! ²¹That is not our plan. A man named Sheba son of Bikri, who is from the hill country of Ephraim, started a rebellion against King David. Hand over this one man, and I will withdraw from the city."

"We will throw his head over the wall to you," she said. ²²Then she went to

---

ᵈ Probable text Bikri; *Hebrew* Beri.
20.1 1 K 12.16; 2 Ch 10.16   **20.3** 2 S 16.22

the people of the city with her plan, and they cut off Sheba's head and threw it over the wall to Joab. He blew the trumpet as a signal for his men to leave the city, and they went back home. And Joab returned to Jerusalem to the king.

David's Officials

23 Joab was in command of the army of Israel; Benaiah son of Jehoiada was in charge of David's bodyguards; 24 Adoniram was in charge of the forced labor; Jehoshaphat son of Ahilud was in charge of the records; 25 Sheva was the court secretary; Zadok and Abiathar were the priests, 26 and Ira from the town of Jair was also one of David's priests.

Saul's Descendants Are Put to Death

21 During David's reign there was a severe famine which lasted for three full years. So David consulted the LORD about it, and the LORD said, "Saul and his family are guilty of murder; he put the people of Gibeon to death." (2 The people of Gibeon were not Israelites; they were a small group of Amorites whom the Israelites had promised to protect, but Saul had tried to destroy them because of his zeal for the people of Israel and Judah.) 3 So David summoned the people of Gibeon and said to them, "What can I do for you? I want to make up for the wrong that was done to you, so that you will bless the LORD's people."

4 They answered, "Our quarrel with Saul and his family can't be settled with silver or gold, nor do we want to kill any Israelite."

"What, then, do you think I should do for you?" David asked.

5 They answered, "Saul wanted to destroy us and leave none of us alive anywhere in Israel. 6 So hand over seven of his male descendants, and we will hang them before the LORD at Gibeah, the hometown of Saul, the LORD's chosen king."

"I will hand them over," the king answered.

7 But because of the sacred promise that he and Jonathan had made to each other, David spared Jonathan's son Mephibosheth, the grandson of Saul. 8 However, he took Armoni and Mephibosheth, the two sons that Rizpah the daughter of Aiah had borne to Saul; he also took the five sons of Saul's daughter Merab, whom she had borne to Adriel son of Barzillai, who was from Meholah. 9 David handed them over to the people of Gibeon, who hanged them on the mountain before the LORD — and all seven of them died together. It was late in the spring, at the beginning of the barley harvest, when they were put to death.

10 Then Saul's concubine Rizpah, the daughter of Aiah, used sackcloth to make a shelter for herself on the rock where the corpses were, and she stayed there from the beginning of harvest until the autumn rains came. During the day she would keep the birds away from the corpses, and at night she would protect them from wild animals.

11 When David heard what Rizpah had done, 12 he went and got the bones of Saul and of his son Jonathan from the people of Jabesh in Gilead. (They had stolen them from the public square in Beth Shan, where the Philistines had hanged the bodies on the day they killed Saul on Mount Gilboa.) 13 David took the bones of Saul and Jonathan and also gathered up the bones of the seven men who had been hanged. 14 Then they buried the bones of Saul and Jonathan in the grave of Saul's father Kish, in Zela in the territory of Benjamin, doing all that the king had commanded. And after that, God answered their prayers for the country.

21.2 Js 9.3-15   **21.7** 1 S 20.15-17; 2 S 9.1-7   **21.8** 1 S 18.19   **21.12** 1 S 31.8-13

Battles against Philistine Giants
(1 Chronicles 20.4-8)

15 There was another war between the Philistines and Israel, and David and his men went and fought the Philistines. During one of the battles David grew tired. 16 A giant named Ishbibenob, who was carrying a bronze spear that weighed about seven and a half pounds and who was wearing a new sword, thought he could kill David. 17 But Abishai son of Zeruiah came to David's help, attacked the giant, and killed him. Then David's men made David promise that he would never again go out with them to battle. "You are the hope of Israel, and we don't want to lose you," they said.

18 After this there was a battle with the Philistines at Gob, during which Sibbecai from Hushah killed a giant named Saph.

19 There was another battle with the Philistines at Gob, and Elhanan son of Jair*e* from Bethlehem killed Goliath from Gath, whose spear had a shaft as thick as the bar on a weaver's loom.

20 Then there was another battle at Gath, where there was a giant who loved to fight. He had six fingers on each hand and six toes on each foot. 21 He defied the Israelites, and Jonathan, the son of David's brother Shammah, killed him.

22 These four were descendants of the giants of Gath, and they were killed by David and his men.

David's Song of Victory
(Psalm 18)

22 When the LORD saved David from Saul and his other enemies, David sang this song to the LORD:

2 The LORD is my protector;
  he is my strong fortress.
3 My God is my protection,

The LORD is my protector! (22.2)

and with him I am safe.
He protects me like a shield;
  he defends me and keeps me
    safe.
He is my savior;
  he protects me and saves me
    from violence.
4 I call to the LORD,
  and he saves me from my
    enemies.
Praise the LORD!

5 The waves of death were all
    around me;
  the waves of destruction rolled
    over me.
6 The danger of death was
    around me,
  and the grave set its trap
    for me.
7 In my trouble I called to the
    LORD;
  I called to my God for help.
In his temple he heard my voice;
  he listened to my cry for help.

8 Then the earth trembled and
    shook;
  the foundations of the sky
    rocked and quivered

---

e Probable text (see 1 Ch 20.5) Jair; *Hebrew* Jaareoregim.
21.17 1 K 11.36; Ps 132.17

because God was angry!

9 Smoke poured out of his nostrils,
   a consuming flame and
   burning coals from
   his mouth.
10 He tore the sky open and came
   down,
   with a dark cloud under his
   feet.
11 He flew swiftly on his winged
   creature;*f*
   he traveled on the wings of
   the wind.
12 He covered himself with
   darkness;
   thick clouds, full of*g* water,
   surrounded him;
13   burning coals flamed up from
   the lightning before him.

14 Then the LORD thundered from
   the sky,
   and the voice of Almighty God
   was heard.
15 He shot his arrows and scattered
   his enemies;
   with flashes of lightning he
   sent them running.
16 The floor of the ocean was laid
   bare,
   and the foundations of the
   earth were uncovered
when the LORD rebuked his
   enemies
   and roared at them in anger.

17 The LORD reached down from
   above and took hold of me;
   he pulled me out of the deep
   waters.
18 He rescued me from my
   powerful enemies
   and from all those who
   hate me —
   they were too strong for me.
19 When I was in trouble, they
   attacked me,
   but the LORD protected me.

20 He helped me out of danger;
   he saved me because he was
   pleased with me.
21 The LORD rewards me because I
   do what is right;
   he blesses me because I am
   innocent.
22 I have obeyed the law of the
   LORD;
   I have not turned away from
   my God.
23 I have observed all his laws;
   I have not disobeyed his
   commands.
24 He knows that I am faultless,
   that I have kept myself from
   doing wrong.
25 And so he rewards me because I
   do what is right,
   because he knows that I am
   innocent.

26 O LORD, you are faithful to those
   who are faithful to you,
   and completely good to those*h*
   who are perfect.
27 You are pure to those who are
   pure,
   but hostile to those who are
   wicked.
28 You save those who are humble,
   but you humble those who are
   proud.

29 You, LORD, are my light;
   you dispel my darkness.
30 You give me strength to attack
   my enemies
   and power to overcome their
   defenses.

31 This God — how perfect are his
   deeds,
   how dependable his words!
He is like a shield
   for all who seek his
   protection.

---

f WINGED CREATURE: *See Word List.*   *g Some ancient translations (and see Ps 18.11)*
full of; *Hebrew unclear.*   *h Probable text (see Ps 18.25)* those; *Hebrew* the strong.

³²The LORD alone is God;
   God alone is our defense.
³³This God is my strong refuge;
   he makesⁱ my pathway safe.
³⁴He makes me sure-footed as a
      deer;
   he keeps me safe on the
      mountains.
³⁵He trains me for battle,
   so that I can use the
      strongest bow.

³⁶O LORD, you protect me and
      save me;
   your help has made me great.
³⁷You have kept me from being
      captured,
   and I have never fallen.
³⁸I pursue my enemies and defeat
      them;
   I do not stop until I destroy
      them.
³⁹I strike them down, and they
      cannot rise;
   they lie defeated before me.
⁴⁰You give me strength for the
      battle
   and victory over my enemies.
⁴¹You make my enemies run
      from me;
   I destroy those who hate me.
⁴²They look for help, but no one
      saves them;
   they call to the LORD, but he
      does not answer.
⁴³I crush them, and they become
      like dust;
   I trample on them like mud in
      the streets.

⁴⁴You saved me from my rebellious
      people
   and maintained my rule over
      the nations;
   people I did not know have
      now become my subjects.
⁴⁵Foreigners bow before me;

⁴⁵when they hear me, they
      obey.
⁴⁶They lose their courage
   and come trembling^j from
      their fortresses.

⁴⁷The LORD lives! Praise my
      defender!
   Proclaim the greatness of the
      strong God who saves me!
⁴⁸He gives me victory over my
      enemies;
   he subdues the nations
      under me
⁴⁹   and saves me from my foes.

   O LORD, you give me victory over
      my enemies
   and protect me from
      violent men.
⁵⁰And so I praise you among the
      nations;
   I sing praises to you.
⁵¹God gives great victories to his
      king;
   he shows constant love to the
      one he has chosen,
   to David and his descendants
      forever.

David's Last Words

23 David son of Jesse was the man
whom God made great, whom
the God of Jacob chose to be king, and
who was the composer of beautiful
songs for Israel. These are David's last
words:

²The spirit of the LORD speaks
      through me;
   his message is on my lips.
³The God of Israel has spoken;
   the protector of Israel said
      to me:
   "The king who rules with justice,

ⁱ *Probable text (see Ps 18.32)* he makes; *Hebrew unclear.*   ^j *Probable text (see* Ps 18.45) come trembling; *Hebrew* come ready to fight.
22.34 Hb 3.19   **22.50** Ro 15.9

who rules in obedience
      to God,
[4] is like the sun shining on a
      cloudless dawn,
   the sun that makes the grass
      sparkle after rain."

[5] And that is how God will bless
      my descendants,
   because he has made an
      eternal covenant with me,
   an agreement that will not be
      broken,
   a promise that will not be
      changed.
That is all I desire;
   that will be my victory,
   and God will surely bring it
      about.
[6] But godless people are like
      thorns that are thrown
      away;
   no one can touch them
      barehanded.
[7] You must use an iron tool or a
      spear;
   they will be burned
      completely.[k]

David's Famous Soldiers
(1 Chronicles 11.10-41)

[8] These are the names of David's famous soldiers: the first was Josheb Bas-
shebeth from Tachemon, who was the
leader of "The Three";[l] he fought with
his spear[m] against eight hundred men
and killed them all in one battle.

[9] The second of the famous three was
Eleazar son of Dodo, of the clan of
Ahoh. One day he and David challenged the Philistines who had gathered for battle. The Israelites fell back,
[10] but he stood his ground and fought
the Philistines until his hand was so

cramped that he could not let go of his
sword. The LORD won a great victory
that day. After it was over, the Israelites
returned to where Eleazar was and
stripped the armor from the dead.

[11] The third of the famous three was
Shammah son of Agee from Harar. The
Philistines had gathered at Lehi, where
there was a field of peas. The Israelites
fled from the Philistines, [12] but Shammah stood his ground in the field, defended it, and killed the Philistines. The
LORD won a great victory that day.

[13] Near the beginning of harvest
time[n] three of "The Thirty" went down
to Adullam Cave, where David was,
while a band of Philistines was camping in Rephaim Valley. [14] At that time
David was on a fortified hill, and a
group of Philistines had occupied Bethlehem. [15] David grew homesick and
said, "How I wish someone would bring
me a drink of water from the well by the
gate at Bethlehem!" [16] The three famous soldiers forced their way through
the Philistine camp, drew some water
from the well, and brought it back to
David. But he would not drink it; instead he poured it out as an offering to
the LORD [17] and said, "LORD, I could
never drink this! It would be like drinking the blood of these men who risked
their lives!" So he refused to drink it.

Those were the brave deeds of the
three famous soldiers.

[18] Joab's brother Abishai (their
mother was Zeruiah) was the leader of
"The Famous Thirty." He fought with
his spear against three hundred men
and killed them, and became famous
among "The Thirty."[o] [19] He was the
most famous of "The Thirty"[p] and became their leader, but he was not as famous as "The Three."

[20] Benaiah son of Jehoiada from

---

[k] *Verses 6-7 in Hebrew are unclear.*   [l] *One ancient translation* "The Three"; *Hebrew*
the third.   [m] *Probable text (see 1 Ch 11.11)* he fought with his spear; *Hebrew*
unclear.   [n] *Probable text* Near the beginning of harvest time; *Hebrew unclear.*
[o] *One ancient translation* "The Thirty"; *Hebrew* "The Three."   [p] *Probable text* "The
Thirty"; *Hebrew* "The Three."

Kabzeel was another famous soldier; he did many brave deeds, including killing two great Moabite warriors. He once went down into a pit on a snowy day and killed a lion. 21 He also killed an Egyptian, a huge man who was armed with a spear. Benaiah attacked him with his club, snatched the spear from the Egyptian's hand, and killed him with it. 22 Those were the brave deeds of Benaiah, who was one of "The Thirty."*p* 23 He was outstanding among them, but was not as famous as "The Three." David put him in charge of his bodyguard.

24-39 Other members of "The Thirty" included:

Asahel, Joab's brother
Elhanan son of Dodo from Bethlehem
Shammah and Elika from Harod
Helez from Pelet
Ira son of Ikkesh from Tekoa
Abiezer from Anathoth
Mebunnai from Hushah
Zalmon from Ahoh
Maharai from Netophah
Heleb son of Baanah from Netophah
Ittai son of Ribai from Gibeah in Benjamin
Benaiah from Pirathon
Hiddai from the valleys near Gaash
Abialbon from Arabah
Azmaveth from Bahurim
Eliahba from Shaalbon
The sons of Jashen
Jonathan
Shammah from Harar
Ahiam son of Sharar from Harar
Eliphelet son of Ahasbai from Maacah
Eliam son of Ahithophel from Gilo
Hezro from Carmel

Paarai from Arab
Igal son of Nathan from Zobah
Bani from Gad
Zelek from Ammon
Naharai from Beeroth, Joab's armorbearer
Ira and Gareb from Jattir
Uriah the Hittite.

There were thirty-seven famous soldiers in all.

David Takes a Census
(1 Chronicles 21.1-27)

24 On another occasion the LORD was angry with Israel, and he made David bring trouble on them. The LORD said to him, "Go and count the people of Israel and Judah." 2 So David gave orders to Joab, the commander of his army: "Go with your officers through all the tribes of Israel from one end of the country to the other, and count the people. I want to know how many there are."

3 But Joab answered the king, "Your Majesty, may the LORD your God make the people of Israel a hundred times more numerous than they are now, and may you live to see him do it. But why does Your Majesty want to do this?" 4 But the king made Joab and his officers obey his order; they left his presence and went out to count the people of Israel.

5 They crossed the Jordan and camped south of Aroer, the city in the middle of the valley, in the territory of Gad.*q* From there they went north to Jazer, 6 and on to Gilead and to Kadesh, in Hittite territory.*r* Then they went to Dan, and from Dan they went*s* west to Sidon. 7 Then they went south to the fortified city of Tyre, on to all the cities of the Hivites and the Canaanites, and

---

p Probable text "The Thirty"; *Hebrew* "The Three."   *q Probable text* Aroer . . . Gad; *Hebrew unclear.*   *r One ancient translation* Kadesh, in Hittite territory; *Hebrew* to the land of Tahtim, Hodshi.   *s Probable text* and from Dan they went; *Hebrew unclear.*

finally to Beersheba, in the southern part of Judah. ⁸So after nine months and twenty days they returned to Jerusalem, having traveled through the whole country. ⁹They reported to the king the total number of men capable of military service: 800,000 in Israel and 500,000 in Judah.

¹⁰But after David had taken the census, his conscience began to hurt, and he said to the LORD, "I have committed a terrible sin in doing this! Please forgive me. I have acted foolishly."

¹¹⁻¹²The LORD said to Gad, David's prophet, "Go and tell David that I am giving him three choices. I will do whichever he chooses." The next morning, after David had gotten up, ¹³Gad went to him, told him what the LORD had said, and asked, "Which is it to be? Three *t* years of famine in your land or three months of running away from your enemies or three days of an epidemic in your land? Now think it over, and tell me what answer to take back to the LORD."

¹⁴David answered, "I am in a desperate situation! But I don't want to be punished by people. Let the LORD himself be the one to punish us, for he is merciful." ¹⁵So the LORD sent an epidemic on Israel, which lasted from that morning until the time that he had chosen. From one end of the country to the other seventy thousand Israelites died. ¹⁶When the LORD's angel was about to destroy Jerusalem, the LORD changed his mind about punishing the people and said to the angel who was killing them, "Stop! That's enough!" The an-

gel was by the threshing place of Araunah, a Jebusite.

¹⁷David saw the angel who was killing the people, and said to the LORD, "I am the guilty one. I am the one who did wrong. What have these poor people done? You should punish me and my family."

¹⁸That same day Gad went to David and said to him, "Go up to Araunah's threshing place and build an altar to the LORD." ¹⁹David obeyed the LORD's command and went as Gad had told him to. ²⁰Araunah looked down and saw the king and his officials coming up to him. He threw himself on the ground in front of David ²¹and asked, "Your Majesty, why are you here?"

David answered, "To buy your threshing place and build an altar for the LORD, in order to stop the epidemic."

²²"Take it, Your Majesty," Araunah said, "and offer to the LORD whatever you wish. Here are these oxen to burn as an offering on the altar; here are their yokes and the threshing boards to use as fuel." ²³Araunah gave it all to the king*u* and said to him, "May the LORD your God accept your offering."

²⁴But the king answered, "No, I will pay you for it. I will not offer to the LORD my God sacrifices that have cost me nothing." And he bought the threshing place and the oxen for fifty pieces of silver. ²⁵Then he built an altar to the LORD and offered burnt offerings and fellowship offerings. The LORD answered his prayer, and the epidemic in Israel was stopped.

---

t Some ancient translations (and see 1 Ch 21.12) Three; Hebrew Seven.   *u Probable text to the king; Hebrew to the king the king.*

The First Book of
KINGS

INTRODUCTION

First Kings continues the history of the Israelite monarchy begun in the books of *Samuel*. It may be divided into three parts: 1) The succession of Solomon as king of Israel and Judah, and the death of his father David. 2) The reign and achievements of Solomon. Especially noteworthy is the building of the Temple in Jerusalem. 3) The division of the nation into the northern and southern kingdoms, and the stories of the kings who ruled them down to the middle of the ninth century B.C.

In the two books of *Kings* each ruler is judged according to his loyalty to God, and national success is seen as depending on this loyalty, while idolatry and disobedience lead to disaster. The kings of the northern kingdom all fail the test, while the record of Judah's kings is mixed.

Prominent in the book of *First Kings* are the prophets of the Lord, those courageous spokesmen for God who warned the people not to worship idols and not to disobey God. Especially notable is Elijah and the story of his contest with the priests of Baal (chapter 18).

OUTLINE OF CONTENTS

King David in His Old Age

1 King David was now a very old man, and although his servants covered him with blankets, he could not keep warm. ² So his officials said to him, "Your Majesty, let us find a young woman to stay with you and take care of you. She will lie close to you and keep you warm." ³ A search was made all over Israel for a beautiful young woman, and in Shunem they found such a woman named Abishag, and brought her to the king. ⁴ She was very beautiful, and waited on the king and took care of him, but he did not have intercourse with her.

Adonijah Claims the Throne

5-6 Now that Absalom was dead, Adonijah, the son of David and Haggith, was the oldest surviving son. He was a very handsome man. David had never reprimanded him about anything, and he was ambitious to be king. He provided for himself chariots, horses, and an escort of fifty men. **7** He talked with Joab (whose mother was Zeruiah) and with Abiathar the priest, and they agreed to support his cause. **8** But Zadok the priest, Benaiah son of Jehoiada, Nathan the prophet, Shimei, Rei, and David's bodyguards were not on Adonijah's side.

9 One day Adonijah offered a sacrifice of sheep, bulls, and fattened calves at Snake Rock, near the spring of Enrogel. He invited the other sons of King David and the king's officials who were from Judah to come to this sacrificial feast, **10** but he did not invite his half brother Solomon or Nathan the prophet or Benaiah or the king's bodyguards.

Solomon Is Made King

11 Then Nathan went to Bathsheba, Solomon's mother, and asked her, "Haven't you heard that Haggith's son Adonijah has made himself king? And King David doesn't know anything about it! **12** If you want to save your life and the life of your son Solomon, I would advise you to **13** go at once to King David and ask him, 'Your Majesty, didn't you solemnly promise me that my son Solomon would succeed you as king? How is it, then, that Adonijah has become king?'" **14** And Nathan added, "Then, while you are still talking with King David, I will come in and confirm your story."

15 So Bathsheba went to see the king in his bedroom. He was very old, and Abishag, the young woman from Shunem, was taking care of him. **16** Bathsheba bowed low before the king, and he asked, "What do you want?"

17 She answered, "Your Majesty, you made me a solemn promise in the name of the LORD your God that my son Solomon would be king after you. **18** But Adonijah has already become king, and you don't know anything about it. **19** He has offered a sacrifice of many bulls, sheep, and fattened calves, and he invited your sons, and Abiathar the priest, and Joab the commander of your army to the feast, but he did not invite your son Solomon. **20** Your Majesty, all the people of Israel are looking to you to tell them who is to succeed you as king. **21** If you don't, as soon as you are dead, my son Solomon and I will be treated as traitors."

22 She was still speaking, when Nathan arrived at the palace. **23** The king was told that the prophet was there, and Nathan went in and bowed low before the king. **24** Then he said, "Your Majesty, have you announced that Adonijah would succeed you as king? **25** This very day he has gone and offered a sacrifice of many bulls, sheep, and fattened calves. He invited all your sons, Joab the commander of your army,[a] and Abiathar the priest, and right now they are feasting with him and shouting, 'Long live King Adonijah!' **26** But he did not invite me, sir, or Zadok the priest or Benaiah or Solomon. **27** Did Your Majesty approve all this and not even tell your officials who is to succeed you as king?"

28 King David said, "Ask Bathsheba to come back in"—and she came and stood before him. **29** Then he said to her, "I promise you by the living LORD, who has rescued me from all my troubles,

---

[a] *One ancient translation* Joab the commander of your army; *Hebrew* your army commanders.

1.5 2 S 3.4   **1.11** 2 S 12.24

30 that today I will keep the promise I made to you in the name of the LORD, the God of Israel, that your son Solomon would succeed me as king."

31 Bathsheba bowed low and said, "May my lord the king live forever!"

32 Then King David sent for Zadok, Nathan, and Benaiah. When they came in, 33 he said to them, "Take my court officials with you; have my son Solomon ride my own mule, and escort him down to Gihon Spring, 34 where Zadok and Nathan are to anoint him as king of Israel. Then blow the trumpet and shout, 'Long live King Solomon!' 35 Follow him back here when he comes to sit on my throne. He will succeed me as king, because he is the one I have chosen to be the ruler of Israel and Judah."

36 "It shall be done," answered Benaiah, "and may the LORD your God confirm it! 37 As the LORD has been with Your Majesty, may he also be with Solomon and make his reign even more prosperous than yours."

38 So Zadok, Nathan, Benaiah, and the royal bodyguards put Solomon on King David's mule and escorted him to Gihon Spring. 39 Zadok took the container of olive oil which he had brought from the Tent of the LORD's presence, and anointed Solomon. They blew the trumpet, and all the people shouted, "Long live King Solomon!" 40 Then they all followed him back, shouting for joy and playing flutes, making enough noise to shake the ground.

41 As Adonijah and all his guests were finishing the feast, they heard the noise. And when Joab heard the trumpet, he asked, "What's the meaning of all that noise in the city?" 42 Before he finished speaking, Jonathan, the son of the priest Abiathar, arrived. "Come on in," Adonijah said. "You're a good man — you must be bringing good news."

43 "I'm afraid not," Jonathan answered. "His Majesty King David has made Solomon king. 44 He sent Zadok, Nathan, Benaiah, and the royal bodyguards to escort him. They had him ride on the king's mule, 45 and Zadok and Nathan anointed him as king at Gihon Spring. Then they went into the city, shouting for joy, and the people are now in an uproar. That's the noise you just heard. 46 Solomon is now the king. 47 What is more, the court officials went in to pay their respects to His Majesty King David and said, 'May your God make Solomon even more famous than you, and may Solomon's reign be even more prosperous than yours.' Then King David bowed in worship on his bed 48 and prayed, 'Let us praise the LORD, the God of Israel, who has today made one of my descendants succeed me as king, and has let me live to see it!' "

49 Then Adonijah's guests were afraid, and they all got up and left, each going his own way. 50 Adonijah, in great fear of Solomon, went to the Tent of the LORD's presence and took hold of the corners of the altar.*b* 51 King Solomon was told that Adonijah was afraid of him and that he was holding on to the corners of the altar and had said, "First, I want King Solomon to swear to me that he will not have me put to death."

52 Solomon replied, "If he is loyal, not even a hair on his head will be touched; but if he is not, he will die." 53 King Solomon then sent for Adonijah and had him brought down from the altar. Adonijah went to the king and bowed low before him, and the king said to him, "You may go home."

David's Last Instructions to Solomon

2 When David was about to die, he called his son Solomon and gave him his last instructions: 2 "My time to die has come. Be confident and deter-

---

b CORNERS OF THE ALTAR: *Small projections at the four corners of the altar that looked like horns. Anyone holding on to them was safe from being killed.*

mined, ³and do what the LORD your God orders you to do. Obey all his laws and commands, as written in the Law of Moses, so that wherever you go you may prosper in everything you do. ⁴If you obey him, the LORD will keep the promise he made when he told me that my descendants would rule Israel as long as they were careful to obey his commands faithfully with all their heart and soul.

⁵"There is something else. You remember what Joab did to me by killing the two commanders of Israel's armies, Abner son of Ner and Amasa son of Jether. You remember how he murdered them in time of peace as revenge for deaths they had caused in time of war. He killed innocent men,ᶜ and now I bear the responsibility for what he did, and I sufferᵈ the consequences. ⁶You know what to do; you must not let him die a natural death.

⁷"But show kindness to the sons of Barzillai from Gilead and take care of them, because they were kind to me when I was fleeing from your brother Absalom.

⁸"There is also Shimei son of Gera, from the town of Bahurim in Benjamin. He cursed me bitterly the day I went to Mahanaim, but when he met me at the Jordan River, I gave him my solemn promise in the name of the LORD that I would not have him killed. ⁹But you must not let him go unpunished. You know what to do, and you must see to it that he is put to death."

The Death of David

¹⁰David died and was buried in David's City. ¹¹He had been king of Israel for forty years, ruling seven years in Hebron and thirty-three years in Jerusalem. ¹²Solomon succeeded his father

David as king, and his royal power was firmly established.

The Death of Adonijah

¹³Then Adonijah, whose mother was Haggith, went to Bathsheba, who was Solomon's mother. "Is this a friendly visit?" she asked.

"It is," he answered, ¹⁴and then he added, "I have something to ask of you."

"What is it?" she asked.

¹⁵He answered, "You know that I should have become king and that everyone in Israel expected it. But it happened differently, and my brother became king because it was the LORD's will. ¹⁶And now I have one request to make; please do not refuse me."

"What is it?" Bathsheba asked.

¹⁷He answered, "Please ask King Solomon—I know he won't refuse you—to let me have Abishag, the young woman from Shunem, as my wife."

¹⁸"Very well," she answered. "I will speak to the king for you."

¹⁹So Bathsheba went to the king to speak to him on behalf of Adonijah. The king stood up to greet his mother and bowed to her. Then he sat on his throne and had another one brought in on which she sat at his right. ²⁰She said, "I have a small favor to ask of you; please do not refuse me."

"What is it, mother?" he asked. "I will not refuse you."

²¹She answered, "Let your brother Adonijah have Abishag as his wife."

²²"Why do you ask me to give Abishag to him?" the king asked. "You might as well ask me to give him the throne too. After all, he is my older brother, and Abiathar the priest and

---

ᶜ *Some ancient translations* innocent men; *Hebrew* men in battle.   ᵈ *Some ancient translations* I bear ... and I suffer; *Hebrew* he bears ... and he suffers.

2.5 a 2 S 3.27; b 2 S 20.10   **2.7** 2 S 17.27-29   **2.8** 2 S 16.5-13; 19.16-23   **2.11** 2 S 5.4, 5; 1 Ch 3.4   **2.12** 1 Ch 29.23   **2.17** 1 K 1.3, 4

Joab are on his side!"*e* 23 Then Solomon made a solemn promise in the LORD's name, "May God strike me dead if I don't make Adonijah pay with his life for asking this! 24 The LORD has firmly established me on the throne of my father David; he has kept his promise and given the kingdom to me and my descendants. I swear by the living LORD that Adonijah will die this very day!"

25 So King Solomon gave orders to Benaiah, who went out and killed Adonijah.

Abiathar's Banishment and Joab's Death

26 Then King Solomon said to Abiathar the priest, "Go to your country home in Anathoth. You deserve to die, but I will not have you put to death now, for you were in charge of the LORD's Covenant Box while you were with my father David, and you shared in all his troubles." 27 Then Solomon dismissed Abiathar from serving as a priest of the LORD, and so made come true what the LORD had said in Shiloh about the priest Eli and his descendants.

28 Joab heard what had happened. (He had supported Adonijah, but not Absalom.) So he fled to the Tent of the LORD's presence and took hold of the corners of the altar.*f* 29 When the news reached King Solomon that Joab had fled to the Tent and was by the altar, Solomon sent a messenger to Joab to ask him why he had fled to the altar. Joab answered that he had fled to the LORD because he was afraid of Solomon. So King Solomon sent Benaiah*g* to kill Joab. 30 He went to the Tent of the LORD's presence and said to Joab, "The king orders you to come out."

"No," Joab answered. "I will die here."

Benaiah went back to the king and told him what Joab had said.

31 "Do what Joab says," Solomon answered. "Kill him and bury him. Then neither I nor any other of David's descendants will any longer be held responsible for what Joab did when he killed innocent men. 32 The LORD will punish Joab for those murders, which he committed*h* without my father David's knowledge. Joab killed two innocent men who were better men than he: Abner, commander of the army of Israel, and Amasa, commander of the army of Judah. 33 The punishment for their murders will fall on Joab and on his descendants forever. But the LORD will always give success to David's descendants who sit on his throne."

34 So Benaiah went to the Tent of the LORD's presence and killed Joab, and he was buried at his home in the open country. 35 The king made Benaiah commander of the army in Joab's place and put Zadok the priest in Abiathar's place.

The Death of Shimei

36 Then the king sent for Shimei and said to him, "Build a house for yourself here in Jerusalem. Live in it and don't leave the city. 37 If you ever leave and go beyond Kidron Brook, you will certainly die — and you yourself will be to blame."

38 "Very well, Your Majesty," Shimei answered. "I will do what you say." So he lived in Jerusalem a long time.

39 Three years later, however, two of Shimei's slaves ran away to the king of Gath, Achish son of Maacah. When Shimei heard that they were in Gath, 40 he saddled his donkey and went to

---

e Some ancient translations and Abiathar the priest . . . on his side; *Hebrew unclear.*
f CORNERS OF THE ALTAR: *See 1.50.*   *g One ancient translation* Solomon sent a messenger . . . sent Benaiah; *Hebrew* Solomon sent Benaiah.   *h* will punish . . . committed; *or* will kill Joab, because he committed those murders.
2.26 a 2 S 15.24; **b** 1 S 22.20-23   **2.27** 1 S 2.27-36

King Achish in Gath, to find his slaves. He found them and brought them back home. ⁴¹When Solomon heard what Shimei had done, ⁴²he sent for him and said, "I made you promise in the LORD's name not to leave Jerusalem. And I warned you that if you ever did, you would certainly die. Did you not agree to it and say that you would obey me? ⁴³Why, then, have you broken your promise and disobeyed my command? ⁴⁴You know very well all the wrong that you did to my father David. The LORD will punish you for it. ⁴⁵But he will bless me, and he will make David's kingdom secure forever."

⁴⁶Then the king gave orders to Benaiah, who went out and killed Shimei. Solomon was now in complete control.

Solomon Prays for Wisdom
(2 Chronicles 1.3-12)

3 Solomon made an alliance with the king of Egypt by marrying his daughter. He brought her to live in David's City until he had finished building his palace, the Temple, and the wall around Jerusalem. ²A temple had not yet been built for the LORD, and so the people were still offering sacrifices at many different altars. ³Solomon loved the LORD and followed the instructions of his father David, but he also slaughtered animals and offered them as sacrifices on various altars.

⁴On one occasion he went to Gibeon to offer sacrifices because that was where the most famous altar was. He had offered hundreds of burnt offerings there in the past. ⁵That night the LORD appeared to him in a dream and asked him, "What would you like me to give you?"

⁶Solomon answered, "You always showed great love for my father David, your servant, and he was good, loyal, and honest in his relation with you. And you have continued to show him your great and constant love by giving him a son who today rules in his place. ⁷O LORD God, you have let me succeed my father as king, even though I am very young and don't know how to rule. ⁸Here I am among the people you have chosen to be your own, a people who are so many that they cannot be counted. ⁹So give me the wisdom I need to rule your people with justice and to know the difference between good and evil. Otherwise, how would I ever be able to rule this great people of yours?"

¹⁰The Lord was pleased that Solomon had asked for this, ¹¹and so he said to him, "Because you have asked for the wisdom to rule justly, instead of long life for yourself or riches or the death of your enemies, ¹²I will do what you have asked. I will give you more wisdom and understanding than anyone has ever had before or will ever have again. ¹³I will also give you what you have not asked for: all your life you will have wealth and honor, more than that of any other king. ¹⁴And if you obey me and keep my laws and commands, as your father David did, I will give you a long life."

¹⁵Solomon woke up and realized that God had spoken to him in the dream. Then he went to Jerusalem and stood in front of the LORD's Covenant Box and offered burnt offerings and fellowship offerings to the LORD. After that he gave a feast for all his officials.

Solomon Judges a Difficult Case

¹⁶One day two prostitutes came and presented themselves before King Solomon. ¹⁷One of them said, "Your Majesty, this woman and I live in the same house, and I gave birth to a baby boy at home while she was there. ¹⁸Two days after my child was born, she also gave birth to a baby boy. Only the two of us were there in the house—no one else

was present. ¹⁹Then one night she accidentally rolled over on her baby and smothered it. ²⁰She got up during the night, took my son from my side while I was asleep, and carried him to her bed; then she put the dead child in my bed. ²¹The next morning, when I woke up and was going to nurse my baby, I saw that it was dead. I looked at it more closely and saw that it was not my child."

²²But the other woman said, "No! The living child is mine, and the dead one is yours!"

The first woman answered back, "No! The dead child is yours, and the living one is mine!"

And so they argued before the king.

²³Then King Solomon said, "Each of you claims that the living child is hers and that the dead child belongs to the other one." ²⁴He sent for a sword, and when it was brought, ²⁵he said, "Cut the living child in two and give each woman half of it."

²⁶The real mother, her heart full of love for her son, said to the king, "Please, Your Majesty, don't kill the child! Give it to her!"

But the other woman said, "Don't give it to either of us; go on and cut it in two."

²⁷Then Solomon said, "Don't kill the child! Give it to the first woman — she is its real mother."

²⁸When the people of Israel heard of Solomon's decision, they were all filled with deep respect for him, because they knew then that God had given him the wisdom to settle disputes fairly.

Solomon's Officials

4 Solomon was king of all Israel, ²and these were his high officials:
The priest: Azariah son of Zadok
³The court secretaries: Elihoreph and Ahijah, sons of Shisha
In charge of the records: Jehoshaphat son of Ahilud

"Don't kill the child!" (3.27)

⁴Commander of the army: Benaiah son of Jehoiada
Priests: Zadok and Abiathar
⁵Chief of the district governors: Azariah son of Nathan
Royal Adviser: the priest Zabud son of Nathan
⁶In charge of the palace servants: Ahishar
In charge of the forced labor: Adoniram son of Abda

⁷Solomon appointed twelve men as district governors in Israel. They were to provide food from their districts for the king and his household, each man being responsible for one month out of the year. ⁸The following are the names of these twelve officers and the districts they were in charge of:

Benhur: the hill country of
Ephraim
9 Bendeker: the cities of Makaz,
Shaalbim, Beth Shemesh,
Elon, and Beth Hanan
10 Benhesed: the cities of Arubboth
and Socoh and all the
territory of Hepher
11 Benabinadab, who was married
to Solomon's daughter
Taphath: the whole region
of Dor
12 Baana son of Ahilud: the cities of
Taanach, Megiddo, and all
the region near Beth Shan,
near the town of Zarethan,
south of the town of
Jezreel, as far as the city of
Abel Meholah and the city
of Jokmeam
13 Bengeber: the city of Ramoth in
Gilead, and the villages in
Gilead belonging to the
clan of Jair, a descendant
of Manasseh, and the
region of Argob in Bashan,
sixty large towns in all,
fortified with walls and
with bronze bars on the
gates
14 Ahinadab son of Iddo: the district
of Mahanaim
15 Ahimaaz, who was married to
Basemath, another of
Solomon's daughters: the
territory of Naphtali
16 Baana son of Hushai: the region
of Asher and the town of
Bealoth
17 Jehoshaphat son of Paruah: the
territory of Issachar
18 Shimei son of Ela: the territory
of Benjamin
19 Geber son of Uri: the region of
Gilead, which had been
ruled by King Sihon of the
Amorites and King Og of
Bashan

Besides these twelve, there was one
governor over the whole land.

Solomon's Prosperous Reign

20 The people of Judah and Israel
were as numerous as the grains of sand
on the seashore; they ate and drank,
and were happy. 21 Solomon's kingdom
included all the nations from the Euphrates River to Philistia and the Egyptian border. They paid him taxes and
were subject to him all his life.

22 The supplies Solomon needed
each day were 150 bushels of fine flour
and 300 bushels of meal; 23 10 stall-fed
cattle, 20 pasture-fed cattle, and 100
sheep, besides deer, gazelles, roebucks,
and poultry.

24 Solomon ruled over all the land
west of the Euphrates River, from Tiphsah on the Euphrates as far west as the
city of Gaza. All the kings west of the
Euphrates were subject to him, and he
was at peace with all the neighboring
countries. 25 As long as he lived, the
people throughout Judah and Israel
lived in safety, each family with its own
grapevines and fig trees.

26 Solomon had forty thousand stalls
for his chariot horses and twelve thousand cavalry horses. 27 His twelve governors, each one in the month assigned
to him, supplied the food King Solomon
needed for himself and for all who ate
in the palace; they always supplied
everything needed. 28 Each governor
also supplied his share of barley and
straw, where it was needed, i for the
chariot horses and the work animals.

29 God gave Solomon unusual wisdom and insight, and knowledge too
great to be measured. 30 Solomon was
wiser than the wise men of the East or
the wise men of Egypt. 31 He was the
wisest of all men: wiser than Ethan the
Ezrahite, and Heman, Calcol, and
Darda, the sons of Mahol, and his fame

i where it was needed; *or* wherever King Solomon was.
4.21 Gn 15.18; 2 Ch 9.26   **4.26** 1 K 10.26; 2 Ch 1.14; 9.25   **4.31** Ps 89 Title

spread throughout all the neighboring countries. [32]He composed three thousand proverbs and more than a thousand songs. [33]He spoke of trees and plants, from the Lebanon cedars to the hyssop that grows on walls; he talked about animals, birds, reptiles, and fish. [34]Kings all over the world heard of his wisdom and sent people to listen to him.

Solomon Prepares to Build the Temple
(2 Chronicles 2.1-18)

5 King Hiram of Tyre had always been a friend of David's, and when he heard that Solomon had succeeded his father David as king, he sent ambassadors to him. [2]Solomon sent back this message to Hiram: [3]"You know that because of the constant wars my father David had to fight against the enemy countries all around him, he could not build a temple for the worship of the LORD his God until the LORD had given him victory over all his enemies. [4]But now the LORD my God has given me peace on all my borders. I have no enemies, and there is no danger of attack. [5]The LORD promised my father David, 'Your son, whom I will make king after you, will build a temple for me.' And I have now decided to build that temple for the worship of the LORD my God. [6]So send your men to Lebanon to cut down cedars for me. My men will work with them, and I will pay your men whatever you decide. As you well know, my men don't know how to cut down trees as well as yours do."

[7]Hiram was extremely pleased when he received Solomon's message, and he said, "Praise the LORD today for giving David such a wise son to succeed him as king of that great nation!" [8]Then Hiram sent Solomon the following message: "I have received your message, and I am ready to do what you ask. I will

provide the cedars and the pine trees. [9]My men will bring the logs down from Lebanon to the sea and will tie them together in rafts to float them down the coast to the place you choose. There my men will untie them, and your men will take charge of them. On your part, I would like you to supply the food for my men."

[10]So Hiram supplied Solomon with all the cedar and pine logs that he wanted, [11]and Solomon provided Hiram with 100,000 bushels of wheat and 110,000 gallons[j] of pure olive oil every year to feed his men.

[12]The LORD kept his promise and gave Solomon wisdom. There was peace between Hiram and Solomon, and they made a treaty with each other.

[13]King Solomon drafted 30,000 men as forced labor from all over Israel [14]and put Adoniram in charge of them. He divided them into three groups of 10,000 men, and each group spent one month in Lebanon and two months back home. [15]Solomon also had 80,000 stone cutters in hill country, with 70,000 men to carry the stones, [16]and he placed 3,300 foremen in charge of them to supervise their work. [17]At King Solomon's command they cut fine large stones for the foundation of the Temple. [18]Solomon's and Hiram's workers and men from the city of Byblos prepared the stones and the timber to build the Temple.

Solomon Builds the Temple

6 Four hundred and eighty years after the people of Israel left Egypt, during the fourth year of Solomon's reign over Israel, in the second month, the month of Ziv, Solomon began work on the Temple. [2]Inside it was 90 feet long, 30 feet wide, and 45 feet high. [3]The entrance room was 15 feet deep

---

[j] Some ancient translations (and see 2 Ch 2.10) 110,000 gallons; Hebrew 1,100 gallons.
4.32 Pr 1.1; 10.1; 25.1; Sgs 1.1   **5.5** 2 S 7.12, 13; 1 Ch 17.11, 12   **5.14** 1 K 12.18

Hiram supplied Solomon with . . . cedar and pine logs. (5.10)

and 30 feet wide, as wide as the sanctuary itself. ⁴The walls of the Temple had openings in them, narrower on the outside than on the inside. ⁵Against the outside walls, on the sides and the back of the Temple, a three-storied annex was built, each story 7½ feet high. ⁶Each room in the lowest story was 7½ feet wide, in the middle story 9 feet wide, and in the top story 10½ feet wide. The Temple wall on each floor was thinner than on the floor below, so that the rooms could rest on the wall without having their beams built into it.

⁷The stones with which the Temple was built had been prepared at the quarry, so that there was no noise made by hammers, axes, or any other iron tools as the Temple was being built.

⁸The entrance to the lowest[k] story of the annex was on the south side of the Temple, with stairs leading up to the second and third stories. ⁹So King Solomon finished building the Temple. He put in a ceiling made of beams and boards of cedar. ¹⁰The three-storied annex, each story[l] 7½ feet high, was built against the outside walls of the Temple, and was joined to them by cedar beams.

¹¹The Lord said to Solomon, ¹²"If you obey all my laws and commands, I will do for you what I promised your father David. ¹³I will live among my people Israel in this Temple that you are building, and I will never abandon them."

---

[k] *Some ancient translations* lowest; *Hebrew* middle.   [l] *Probable text* three-storied annex, each story; *Hebrew* three-storied annex.

JERUSALEM IN OLD TESTAMENT TIMES

Yards 0 — 400
Meters 0 — 400

Wall of Zion (Jebusite)
Solomon's Expansion
Later Monarchic Wall
Post-exilic Wall

Hanael Tower

Altar
Temple

NEW

CITY

Palace

Post-exilic Tombs

Manasseh's Wall?

UPPER

CITY

Central Valley

Solomon's Wall

Nehemiah's Wall

To Mount of Olives

Gate

CITY OF DAVID

OPHEL

Gihon Spring

Hezekiah's Tunnel

Lower Pool

SILOAM

Steps

Old Pool

Royal Garden

H i n n o m

V a l l e y

K i d r o n   V a l l e y

Enrogel Spring

© United Bible Societies, 1976

14 So Solomon finished building the Temple.

The Interior Furnishings of the Temple
(2 Chronicles 3.8-14)

15 The inside walls were covered with cedar panels from the floor to the ceiling, and the floor was made of pine. **16** An inner room, called the Most Holy Place, was built in the rear of the Temple. It was 30 feet long and was partitioned off by cedar boards reaching from the floor to the ceiling.*m* **17** The room in front of the Most Holy Place

was 60 feet long. **18** The cedar panels were decorated with carvings of gourds and flowers; the whole interior was covered with cedar, so that the stones of the walls could not be seen.

19 In the rear of the Temple an inner room was built, where the LORD's Covenant Box was to be placed. **20** This inner room was 30 feet long, 30 feet wide, and 30 feet high, all covered with pure gold. The altar was covered with cedar panels.*n* **21** The inside of the Temple was covered with gold, and gold chains were placed across the entrance of the

m One ancient translation ceiling; *Hebrew* walls.   *n Verse 20 in Hebrew is unclear.*
6.16 Ex 26.33, 34

nner room, which was also covered
with gold. 22 The whole interior of the
Temple was covered with gold, as well
as the altar in the Most Holy Place.

23 Two winged creatures were made
of olive wood and placed in the Most
Holy Place, each one 15 feet tall.
24-26 Both were of the same size and
shape. Each had two wings, each wing
7½ feet long, so that the distance from
one wing tip to the other was 15 feet.
27 They were placed side by side in the
Most Holy Place, so that two of their
outstretched wings touched each other
in the middle of the room, and the other
two wings touched the walls. 28 The two
winged creatures were covered with
gold.

29 The walls of the main room and of
the inner room were all decorated with
carved figures of winged creatures,
palm trees, and flowers. 30 Even the
floor was covered with gold.

31 A double door made of olive wood
was set in place at the entrance of the
Most Holy Place; the top of the doorway
was a pointed arch. 32 The doors were
decorated with carved figures of
winged creatures, palm trees, and flowers. The doors, the winged creatures,
and the palm trees were covered with
gold. 33 For the entrance to the main
room a rectangular doorframe of olive
wood was made. 34 There were two fold-
ing doors made of pine 35 and decorated
with carved figures of winged creatures, palm trees, and flowers, which
were evenly covered with gold.

36 An inner court was built in front of
the Temple, enclosed with walls which
had one layer of cedar beams for every
three layers of stone.

37 The foundation of the Temple was
laid in the second month, the month of
Ziv, in the fourth year of Solomon's
reign. 38 In the eighth month, the
month of Bul, in the eleventh year of
Solomon's reign, the Temple was completely finished exactly as it had been
planned. It had taken Solomon seven
years to build it.

Solomon's Palace

7 Solomon also built a palace for
himself, and it took him thirteen
years. 2-3 The Hall of the Forest of Lebanon*o* was 150 feet long, 75 feet wide,
and 45 feet high. It had three*p* rows of
cedar pillars, 15 in each row, with cedar
beams resting on them. The ceiling was
of cedar, extending over storerooms,
which were supported by the pillars.
4 On each of the two side walls there
were three rows of windows. 5 The doorways and the windows*q* had rectangular frames, and the three rows of
windows in each wall faced the opposite rows.

6 The Hall of Columns was 75 feet
long and 45 feet wide. It had a covered
porch, supported by columns.

7 The Throne Room, also called the
Hall of Judgment, where Solomon decided cases, had cedar panels from the
floor to the rafters.*r*

8 Solomon's own quarters, in another
court behind the Hall of Judgment,
were made like the other buildings. He
also built the same kind of house for his
wife, the daughter of the king of Egypt.

9 All these buildings and the great
court were made of fine stones from the
foundations to the eaves. The stones
were prepared at the quarry and cut to
measure, with their inner and outer
sides trimmed with saws. 10 The foundations were made of large stones prepared at the quarry, some of them
twelve feet long and others fifteen feet

---

o HALL OF THE FOREST OF LEBANON: *A large ceremonial hall in the palace, probably so
called because it was paneled in cedar.*   *p One ancient translation* three; *Hebrew*
four.   *q One ancient translation* windows; *Hebrew* doorposts.   *r Some ancient
translations* rafters; *Hebrew* floor.

6.22 Ex 30.1-3   **6.23-28** Ex 25.18-20   **7.8** 1 K 3.1

long. [11] On top of them were other stones, cut to measure, and cedar beams. [12] The palace court, the inner court of the Temple, and the entrance room of the Temple had walls with one layer of cedar beams for every three layers of cut stones.

Huram's Task

[13] King Solomon sent for a man named Huram, a craftsman living in the city of Tyre, who was skilled in bronze work. [14] His father, who was no longer living, was from Tyre, and had also been a skilled bronze craftsman; his mother was from the tribe of Naphtali. Huram was an intelligent and experienced craftsman. He accepted King Solomon's invitation to be in charge of all the bronze work.

The Two Bronze Columns
(2 Chronicles 3.15-17)

[15] Huram cast two bronze columns, each one 27 feet tall and 18 feet in circumference,[s] and placed them at the entrance of the Temple. [16] He also made two bronze capitals, each one 7½ feet tall, to be placed on top of the columns. [17] The top of each column was decorated with a design of interwoven chains[t] [18] and two rows of bronze pomegranates.

[19] The capitals were shaped like lilies, 6 feet tall, [20] and were placed on a rounded section which was above the chain design. There were 200 pomegranates in two rows around each[u] capital.

[21] Huram placed these two bronze columns in front of the entrance of the Temple: the one on the south side was named Jachin[v] and the one on the north was named Boaz.[w] [22] The lily-shaped bronze capitals were on top of the columns.

And so the work on the columns was completed.

The Bronze Tank
(2 Chronicles 4.2-5)

[23] Huram made a round tank of bronze, 7½ feet deep, 15 feet in diameter, and 45 feet in circumference. [24] All around the outer edge of the rim of the tank[x] were two rows of bronze gourds, which had been cast all in one piece with the rest of the tank. [25] The tank rested on the backs of twelve bronze bulls that faced outward, three facing in each direction. [26] The sides of the tank were 3 inches thick. Its rim was like the rim of a cup, curving outward like the petals of a lily. The tank held about 10,000 gallons.

The Bronze Carts

[27] Huram also made ten bronze carts; each was 6 feet long, 6 feet wide, and 4½ feet high. [28] They were made of square panels which were set in frames, [29] with the figures of lions, bulls, and winged creatures on the panels; and on the frames, above and underneath the lions and bulls, there were spiral figures in relief. [30] Each cart had four bronze wheels with bronze axles. At the four corners were bronze supports for a basin; the supports were decorated with spiral figures in relief. [31] There was a circular frame on top for the basin. It projected upward 18 inches from the top of the cart and 7 inches down into it. It had carvings around it. [32] The wheels were 25 inches high; they were under the panels, and

---

[s] *Some ancient translations* each one ... circumference; *Hebrew* the first column was 27 feet tall and the second column was 18 feet in circumference.   [t] *Verse 17 in Hebrew is unclear.*   [u] *One ancient translation* each; *Hebrew* the second.
[v] JACHIN: *This name sounds like the Hebrew for "he (God) establishes."*   [w] BOAZ: *This name sounds like the Hebrew for "by his (God's) strength."*   [x] *Probable text* All around ... tank; *Hebrew unclear.*

he axles were of one piece with the
carts. 33 The wheels were like chariot
wheels; their axles, rims, spokes, and
hubs were all of bronze. 34 There were
four supports at the bottom corners of
each cart, which were of one piece with
the cart. 35 There was a 9-inch band
around the top of each cart; its supports
and the panels were of one piece with
the cart. 36 The supports and panels
were decorated with figures of winged
creatures, lions, and palm trees, wherever there was space for them, with spiral figures all around. 37 This, then, is
how the carts were made; they were all
alike, having the same size and shape.
38 Huram also made ten basins, one
for each cart. Each basin was 6 feet in
diameter and held 200 gallons. 39 He
placed five of the carts on the south side
of the Temple, and the other five on the
north side; the tank he placed at the
southeast corner.

Summary List of Temple Furnishings
(2 Chronicles 4.11 − 5.1)

40-45 Huram also made pots, shovels,
and bowls. He completed all his work
for King Solomon for the LORD's Tem-
ple. This is what he made:
  The two columns
  The two bowl-shaped capitals on
    top of the columns
  The design of interwoven chains
    on each capital
  The 400 bronze pomegranates,
    in two rows of 100 each
    around the design on each
    capital
  The ten carts
  The ten basins
  The tank
  The twelve bulls supporting the
    tank
  The pots, shovels, and bowls
All this equipment for the Temple,
which Huram made for King Solomon,

was of polished bronze. 46 The king had
it all made in the foundry between Sukkoth and Zarethan, in the Jordan Valley. 47 Solomon did not have these
bronze objects weighed, because there
were too many of them, and so their
weight was never determined.

48 Solomon also had gold furnishings
made for the Temple: the altar, the table for the bread offered to God, 49 the
ten lampstands that stood in front of the
Most Holy Place, five on the south side
and five on the north; the flowers,
lamps, and tongs; 50 the cups, lamp
snuffers, bowls, dishes for incense, and
the pans used for carrying live coals;
and the hinges for the doors of the Most
Holy Place and of the outer doors of the
Temple. All these furnishings were
made of gold.

51 When King Solomon finished all
the work on the Temple, he placed in
the Temple storerooms all the things
that his father David had dedicated to
the LORD — the silver, gold, and other
articles.

**The Covenant Box Is Brought
to the Temple**
(2 Chronicles 5.2 − 6.2)

8 Then King Solomon summoned
all the leaders of the tribes and
clans of Israel to come to him in Jerusalem in order to take the LORD's Covenant Box from Zion, David's City, to the
Temple. 2 They all assembled during
the Festival of Shelters in the seventh
month, in the month of Ethanim.
3 When all the leaders had gathered, the
priests lifted the Covenant Box 4 and
carried it to the Temple. The Levites
and the priests also moved the Tent of
the LORD's presence and all its equipment to the Temple. 5 King Solomon
and all the people of Israel assembled in
front of the Covenant Box and sacrificed a large number of sheep and

7.38 Ex 30.17-21 **7.48 a** Ex 30.1-3; **b** Ex 25.23-30 **7.49** Ex 25.31-40 **7.51** 2 S 8.11;
1 Ch 18.11 **8.1** 2 S 6.12-16; 1 Ch 15.25-29 **8.2** Lv 23.34

cattle — too many to count. ⁶Then the priests carried the Covenant Box into the Temple and put it in the Most Holy Place, beneath the winged creatures. ⁷Their outstretched wings covered the box and the poles it was carried by. ⁸The ends of the poles could be seen by anyone standing directly in front of the Most Holy Place, but from nowhere else. (The poles are still there today.) ⁹There was nothing inside the Covenant Box except the two stone tablets which Moses had placed there at Mount Sinai, when the LORD made a covenant with the people of Israel as they were coming from Egypt.

¹⁰As the priests were leaving the Temple, it was suddenly filled with a cloud ¹¹shining with the dazzling light of the LORD's presence, and they could not go back in to perform their duties. ¹²Then Solomon prayed:

"You, LORD, have placed the sun
    in the sky,^y
  yet you have chosen to live in
    clouds and darkness.
¹³Now I have built a majestic
    temple for you,
  a place for you to live in
    forever."

Solomon's Address to the People
(2 Chronicles 6.3-11)

¹⁴As the people stood there, King Solomon turned to face them, and he asked God's blessing on them. ¹⁵He said, "Praise the LORD God of Israel! He has kept the promise he made to my father David, when he told him, ¹⁶'From the time I brought my people out of Egypt, I have not chosen any city in all the land of Israel in which a temple should be built where I would be worshiped. But I chose you, David, to rule my people.'"

¹⁷And Solomon continued, "My father David planned to build a temple for the worship of the LORD God of Israel, ¹⁸but the LORD said to him, 'You were right in wanting to build a temple for me, ¹⁹but you will never build it. It is your son, your own son, who will build my temple.'

²⁰"And now the LORD has kept his promise. I have succeeded my father as king of Israel, and I have built the Temple for the worship of the LORD God of Israel. ²¹I have also provided a place in the Temple for the Covenant Box containing the stone tablets of the covenant which the LORD made with our ancestors when he brought them out of Egypt."

Solomon's Prayer
(2 Chronicles 6.12-42)

²²Then in the presence of the people Solomon went and stood in front of the altar, where he raised his arms ²³and prayed, "LORD God of Israel, there is no god like you in heaven above or on earth below! You keep your covenant with your people and show them your love when they live in wholehearted obedience to you. ²⁴You have kept the promise you made to my father David; today every word has been fulfilled. ²⁵And now, LORD God of Israel, I pray that you will also keep the other promise you made to my father when you told him that there would always be one of his descendants ruling as king of Israel, provided they obeyed you as carefully as he did. ²⁶So now, O God of Israel, let everything come true that you promised to my father David, your servant.

²⁷"But can you, O God, really live on earth? Not even all of heaven is large enough to hold you, so how can this Temple that I have built be large

^y *One ancient translation* You . . . sky; *Hebrew does not have these words.*
8.9 Dt 10.5   **8.10, 11** Ex 40.34, 35   **8.12** Ps 18.11; 97.2   **8.16** 2 S 7.4-11; 1 Ch 17.3-10
8.17, 18 2 S 7.1-3; 1 Ch 17.1, 2   **8.19** 2 S 7.12, 13; 1 Ch 17.11, 12   **8.25** 1 K 2.4
8.27 2 Ch 2.6

enough? ²⁸ LORD my God, I am your servant. Listen to my prayer, and grant the requests I make to you today. ²⁹ Watch over this Temple day and night, this place where you have chosen to be worshiped. Hear me when I face this Temple and pray. ³⁰ Hear my prayers and the prayers of your people when they face this place and pray. In your home in heaven hear us and forgive us.

³¹ "When a person is accused of wronging another and is brought to your altar in this Temple to take an oath that he is innocent, ³² O LORD, listen in heaven and judge your servants. Punish the guilty one as he deserves, and acquit the one who is innocent.

³³ "When your people Israel are defeated by their enemies because they have sinned against you, and then when they turn to you and come to this Temple, humbly praying to you for forgiveness, ³⁴ listen to them in heaven. Forgive the sins of your people and bring them back to the land which you gave to their ancestors.

³⁵ "When you hold back the rain because your people have sinned against you, and then when they repent and face this Temple, humbly praying to you, ³⁶ listen to them in heaven. Forgive the sins of the king and of the people of Israel, and teach them to do what is right. Then, O LORD, send rain on this land of yours, which you gave to your people as a permanent possession.

³⁷ "When there is famine in the land or an epidemic or the crops are destroyed by scorching winds or swarms of locusts, or when your people are attacked by their enemies, or when there is disease or sickness among them, ³⁸ listen to their prayers. If any of your people Israel, out of heartfelt sorrow, stretch out their hands in prayer toward this Temple, ³⁹ hear their prayer. Listen to them in your home in heaven, forgive them, and help them. You alone know the thoughts of the human heart. Deal with each person as he deserves, ⁴⁰ so that your people may obey you all the time they live in the land which you gave to our ancestors.

⁴¹⁻⁴² "When a foreigner who lives in a distant land hears of your fame and of the great things you have done for your people and comes to worship you and to pray at this Temple, ⁴³ listen to his prayer. In heaven, where you live, hear him and do what he asks you to do, so that all the peoples of the world may know you and obey you, as your people Israel do. Then they will know that this Temple I have built is the place where you are to be worshiped.

⁴⁴ "When you command your people to go into battle against their enemies and they pray to you, wherever they are, facing this city which you have chosen and this Temple which I have built for you, ⁴⁵ listen to their prayers. Hear them in heaven and give them victory.

⁴⁶ "When your people sin against you — and there is no one who does not sin — and in your anger you let their enemies defeat them and take them as prisoners to some other land, even if that land is far away, ⁴⁷ listen to your people's prayers. If there in that land they repent and pray to you, confessing how sinful and wicked they have been, hear their prayers, O LORD. ⁴⁸ If in that land they truly and sincerely repent and pray to you as they face toward this land which you gave to our ancestors, this city which you have chosen, and this Temple which I have built for you, ⁴⁹ then listen to their prayers. In your home in heaven hear them and be merciful to them. ⁵⁰ Forgive all their sins and their rebellion against you, and make their enemies treat them with kindness. ⁵¹ They are your own people, whom you brought out of Egypt, that blazing furnace.

⁵² "Sovereign LORD, may you always

look with favor on your people Israel and their king, and hear their prayer whenever they call to you for help. ⁵³You chose them from all the peoples to be your own people, as you told them through your servant Moses when you brought our ancestors out of Egypt."

The Final Prayer

⁵⁴After Solomon had finished praying to the LORD, he stood up in front of the altar, where he had been kneeling with uplifted hands. ⁵⁵In a loud voice he asked God's blessings on all the people assembled there. He said, ⁵⁶"Praise the LORD who has given his people peace, as he promised he would. He has kept all the generous promises he made through his servant Moses. ⁵⁷May the LORD our God be with us as he was with our ancestors; may he never leave us or abandon us; ⁵⁸may he make us obedient to him, so that we will always live as he wants us to live, keeping all the laws and commands he gave our ancestors. ⁵⁹May the LORD our God remember at all times this prayer and these petitions I have made to him. May he always be merciful to the people of Israel and to their king, according to their daily needs. ⁶⁰And so all the nations of the world will know that the LORD alone is God — there is no other. ⁶¹May you, his people, always be faithful to the LORD our God, obeying all his laws and commands as you do today."

The Dedication of the Temple
(2 Chronicles 7.4-10)

⁶²Then King Solomon and all the people there offered sacrifices to the LORD. ⁶³He sacrificed 22,000 head of cattle and 120,000 sheep as fellowship

offerings. And so the king and all the people dedicated the Temple. ⁶⁴That same day he also consecrated the central part of the courtyard, the area in front of the Temple, and then he offered there the sacrifices burned whole, the grain offerings, and the fat of the animals for the fellowship offerings. He did this because the bronze altar was too small for all these offerings.

⁶⁵There at the Temple, Solomon and all the people of Israel celebrated the Festival of Shelters for seven*ᶻ* days. There was a huge crowd of people from as far away as Hamath Pass in the north and the Egyptian border in the south. ⁶⁶On the eighth day Solomon sent the people home. They all praised him and went home happy because of all the blessings that the LORD had given his servant David and his people Israel.

God Appears to Solomon Again
(2 Chronicles 7.11-22)

9 After King Solomon had finished building the Temple and the palace and everything else he wanted to build, ²the LORD appeared to him again, as he had in Gibeon. ³The LORD said to him, "I have heard your prayer. I consecrate this Temple which you have built as the place where I shall be worshiped forever. I will watch over it and protect it for all time. ⁴If you will serve me in honesty and integrity, as your father David did, and if you obey my laws and do everything I have commanded you, ⁵I will keep the promise I made to your father David when I told him that Israel would always be ruled by his descendants. ⁶But if you or your descendants stop following me, disobey the laws and commands I have given you, and worship other gods, ⁷then I will remove my people Israel from the

---

ᶻ *One ancient translation* seven; *Hebrew* fourteen.
8.56 Dt 12.10; Js 21.44, 45   **9.2** 1 K 3.5; 2 Ch 1.7   **9.5** 1 K 2.4

land that I have given them. I will also abandon this Temple which I have consecrated as the place where I am to be worshiped. People everywhere will ridicule Israel and treat her with contempt. [8] This Temple will become a pile of ruins,[a] and everyone who passes by will be shocked and amazed. 'Why did the LORD do this to this land and this Temple?' they will ask. [9] People will answer, 'It is because they abandoned the LORD their God, who brought their ancestors out of Egypt. They gave their allegiance to other gods and worshiped them. That is why the LORD has brought this disaster on them.'"

Solomon's Agreement with Hiram
(2 Chronicles 8.1, 2)

[10] It took Solomon twenty years to build the Temple and his palace. [11] King Hiram of Tyre had provided him with all the cedar and pine and with all the gold he wanted for this work. After it was finished, King Solomon gave Hiram twenty towns in the region of Galilee. [12] Hiram went to see them, and he did not like them. [13] So he said to Solomon, "So these, my brother, are the towns you have given me!" For this reason the area is still called Cabul.[b] [14] Hiram had sent Solomon almost five tons of gold.

Further Achievements of Solomon
(2 Chronicles 8.3-18)

[15] King Solomon used forced labor to build the Temple and the palace, to fill in land on the east side of the city, and to build the city wall. He also used it to rebuild the cities of Hazor, Megiddo, and Gezer. ([16] The king of Egypt had attacked Gezer and captured it, killing its inhabitants and setting fire to the city.

Then he gave it as a wedding present to his daughter when she married Solomon, [17] and Solomon rebuilt it.) Using his forced labor, Solomon also rebuilt Lower Beth Horon, [18] Baalath, Tamar in the wilderness of Judah, [19] the cities where his supplies were kept, the cities for his horses and chariots, and everything else he wanted to build in Jerusalem, in Lebanon, and elsewhere in his kingdom. [20-21] For his forced labor Solomon used the descendants of the people of Canaan whom the Israelites had not killed when they took possession of their land. These included Amorites, Hittites, Perizzites, Hivites, and Jebusites, whose descendants continue to be slaves down to the present time. [22] Solomon did not make slaves of Israelites; they served as his soldiers, officers, commanders, chariot captains, and cavalry.

[23] There were 550 officials in charge of the forced labor working on Solomon's various building projects.

[24] Solomon filled in the land on the east side of the city, after his wife, the daughter of the king of Egypt, had moved from David's City to the palace Solomon built for her.

[25] Three times a year Solomon offered burnt offerings and fellowship offerings on the altar he had built to the LORD. He also burned incense[c] to the LORD. And so he finished building the Temple.

[26] King Solomon also built a fleet of ships at Eziongeber, which is near Elath on the shore of the Gulf of Aqaba, in the land of Edom. [27] King Hiram sent some experienced sailors from his fleet to serve with Solomon's men. [28] They sailed to the land of Ophir and brought back to Solomon about sixteen tons of gold.

---

[a] *Some ancient translations* a pile of ruins; *Hebrew* high.   [b] CABUL: *This name sounds like "ke-bal," the Hebrew for "worthless."*   [c] *Hebrew has two additional words, the meaning of which is unclear.*

9.8 2 K 25.9; 2 Ch 36.19   **9.25** Ex 23.17; 34.23; Dt 16.16

The queen of Sheba
heard of Solomon's fame. (10.1)

The Visit of the Queen of Sheba
(2 Chronicles 9.1-12)

10 The queen of Sheba heard of Solomon's fame,*d* and she traveled to Jerusalem to test him with difficult questions. ²She brought with her a large group of attendants, as well as camels loaded with spices, jewels, and a large amount of gold. When she and Solomon met, she asked him all the questions that she could think of. ³He answered them all; there was nothing too difficult for him to explain. ⁴The queen of Sheba heard Solomon's wisdom and saw the palace he had built. ⁵She saw the food that was served at his table, the living quarters for his officials, the organization of his palace staff and the uniforms they wore, the servants who waited on him at feasts, and the sacrifices he offered in the Temple. It left her breathless and amazed. ⁶She said to King Solomon, "What I heard in my own country about you*e* and your wisdom is true! ⁷But I couldn't believe it until I had come and seen it all for myself. But I didn't hear even half of it; your wisdom and wealth are much greater than what I was told. ⁸How for-

tunate are your wives!*f* And how fortunate are your servants, who are always in your presence and are privileged to hear your wise sayings! ⁹Praise the LORD your God! He has shown how pleased he is with you by making you king of Israel. Because his love for Israel is eternal, he has made you their king so that you can maintain law and justice."

¹⁰She presented to King Solomon the gifts she had brought: almost five tons of gold and a very large amount of spices and jewels. The amount of spices she gave him was by far the greatest that he ever received at any time.

(¹¹Hiram's fleet, which had brought gold from Ophir, also brought from there a large amount of juniper wood and jewels. ¹²Solomon used the wood to build railings in the Temple and the palace, and also to make harps and lyres for the musicians. It was the finest juniper wood ever imported into Israel; none like it has ever been seen again.)

¹³King Solomon gave the queen of Sheba everything she asked for, besides all the other customary gifts that

---

d Probable text (see 2 Ch 9.1) Solomon's fame; *Hebrew* Solomon's fame concerning the name of the LORD. *e you; or your deeds.* *f Some ancient translations* wives; *Hebrew* men.

10.1-10 Mt 12.42; Lk 11.31

he had generously given her. Then she and her attendants returned to the land of Sheba.

King Solomon's Wealth
(2 Chronicles 9.13-29)

14 Every year King Solomon received over twenty-five tons of gold, 15 in addition to the taxes*g* paid by merchants, the profits from trade, and tribute paid by the Arabian kings and the governors of the Israelite districts.

16 Solomon made two hundred large shields and had each one overlaid with almost fifteen pounds of gold. 17 He also made three hundred smaller shields, overlaying each one of them with nearly four pounds of gold. He had all these shields placed in the Hall of the Forest of Lebanon.*h*

18 He also had a large throne made. Part of it was covered with ivory and the rest of it was covered with the finest gold. 19-20 The throne had six steps leading up to it, with the figure of a lion at each end of every step, a total of twelve lions. At the back of the throne was the figure of a bull's head, and beside each of the two armrests was the figure of a lion. No throne like this had ever existed in any other kingdom.

21 All of Solomon's drinking cups were made of gold, and all the utensils in the Hall of the Forest of Lebanon were of pure gold. No silver was used, since it was not considered valuable in Solomon's day. 22 He had a fleet of ocean-going ships sailing with Hiram's fleet. Every three years his fleet would return, bringing gold, silver, ivory, apes, and monkeys.

23 King Solomon was richer and wiser than any other king, 24 and the whole world wanted to come and listen to the wisdom that God had given him. 25 Everyone who came brought him a gift — articles of silver and gold, robes, weapons, spices, horses, and mules. This continued year after year.

26 Solomon built up a force of fourteen hundred chariots and twelve thousand cavalry horses. Some of them he kept in Jerusalem and the rest he stationed in various other cities. 27 During his reign silver was as common in Jerusalem as stone, and cedar was as plentiful as ordinary sycamore in the foothills of Judah. 28 The king's agents controlled the export of horses from Musri*i* and Cilicia,*j* 29 and the export of chariots from Egypt. They supplied the Hittite and Syrian kings with horses and chariots, selling chariots for 600 pieces of silver each and horses for 150 each.

Solomon Turns Away from God

11 Solomon loved many foreign women. Besides the daughter of the king of Egypt he married Hittite women and women from Moab, Ammon, Edom, and Sidon. 2 He married them even though the LORD had commanded the Israelites not to intermarry with these people, because they would cause the Israelites to give their loyalty to other gods. 3 Solomon married seven hundred princesses and also had three hundred concubines. They made him turn away from God, 4 and by the time he was old they had led him into the worship of foreign gods. He was not faithful to the LORD his God, as his father David had been. 5 He worshiped Astarte, the goddess of Sidon, and Molech, the disgusting god of Ammon.

g Some ancient translations taxes; *Hebrew* men.   *h* HALL OF THE FOREST OF LEBANON: *See 7.2-3.*   *i Probable text* Musri; *Hebrew* Egypt.   *j* MUSRI AND CILICIA: *Two ancient countries in what is now southeast Turkey which were centers of horse breeding in Solomon's time.*

10.26 1 K 4.26   **10.27** Dt 17.17   **10.28** Dt 17.16   **11.1** Dt 17.17   **11.2** Ex 34.16; Dt 7.3, 4

[6] He sinned against the Lord and was not true to him as his father David had been. [7] On the mountain east of Jerusalem he built a place to worship Chemosh, the disgusting god of Moab, and a place to worship Molech, the disgusting god of Ammon. [8] He also built places of worship where all his foreign wives could burn incense and offer sacrifices to their own gods.

[9-10] Even though the Lord, the God of Israel, had appeared to Solomon twice and had commanded him not to worship foreign gods, Solomon did not obey the Lord but turned away from him. So the Lord was angry with Solomon [11] and said to him, "Because you have deliberately broken your covenant with me and disobeyed my commands, I promise that I will take the kingdom away from you and give it to one of your officials. [12] However, for the sake of your father David I will not do this in your lifetime, but during the reign of your son. [13] And I will not take the whole kingdom away from him; instead, I will leave him one tribe for the sake of my servant David and for the sake of Jerusalem, the city I have made my own."

Solomon's Enemies

[14] So the Lord caused Hadad, of the royal family of Edom, to turn against Solomon. [15-16] Long before this, when David had conquered Edom, Joab the commander of his army had gone there to bury the dead. He and his men remained in Edom six months, and during that time they killed every male in Edom [17] except Hadad and some of his father's Edomite servants, who escaped to Egypt. (At that time Hadad was just a child.) [18] They left Midian and went to Paran, where some other men joined

them. Then they traveled to Egypt and went to the king, who gave Hadad some land and a house and provided him with food. [19] Hadad won the friendship of the king, and the king gave his sister-in-law, the sister of Queen Tahpenes, to Hadad in marriage. [20] She bore him a son, Genubath, who was raised by the queen in the palace, where he lived with the king's sons.

[21] When the news reached Hadad in Egypt that David had died and that Joab the commander of the army was dead, Hadad said to the king, "Let me go back to my own country."

[22] "Why?" the king asked. "Have I failed to give you something? Is that why you want to go back home?"

"Just let me go," Hadad answered the king. And he went back to his country.[k]

As king of Edom, Hadad was an evil, bitter enemy of Israel.[l]

[23] God also caused Rezon son of Eliada to turn against Solomon. Rezon had fled from his master, King Hadadezer of Zobah, [24] and had become the leader of a gang of outlaws. (This happened after David had defeated Hadadezer and had slaughtered his Syrian allies.) Rezon and his gang went and lived in Damascus, where his followers made him king of Syria. [25] He was an enemy of Israel during the lifetime of Solomon.

God's Promise to Jeroboam

[26] Another man who turned against King Solomon was one of his officials, Jeroboam son of Nebat, from Zeredah in Ephraim. His mother was a widow named Zeruah. [27] This is the story of the revolt.

Solomon was filling in the land on the east side of Jerusalem and repairing the city walls. [28] Jeroboam was an able young man, and when Solomon noticed

---

[k] *One ancient translation* And he went back to his country; *Hebrew does not have these words.* [l] *One ancient translation* As king ... Israel; *in Hebrew this sentence, with some differences, comes at the end of verse 25.*

how hard he worked, he put him in charge of all the forced labor in the territory of the tribes of Manasseh and Ephraim. ²⁹One day, as Jeroboam was traveling from Jerusalem, the prophet Ahijah from Shiloh met him alone on the road in the open country. ³⁰Ahijah took off the new robe he was wearing, tore it into twelve pieces, ³¹and said to Jeroboam, "Take ten pieces for yourself, because the LORD, the God of Israel, says to you, 'I am going to take the kingdom away from Solomon, and I will

"Take ten pieces for yourself." (11.31)

give you ten tribes. ³²Solomon will keep one tribe for the sake of my servant David and for the sake of Jerusalem, the city I have chosen to be my own from the whole land of Israel. ³³I am going to do this because Solomon has rejected me and has*ᵐ* worshiped foreign gods: Astarte, the goddess of Sidon; Chemosh, the god of Moab; and Molech, the god of Ammon. Solomon has*ⁿ* disobeyed me; he has done wrong and has not kept my laws and commands as his father David did. ³⁴But I will not take the whole kingdom away from Solomon, and I will keep him in power as long as he lives. This I will do for the sake of my servant David, whom I

chose and who obeyed my laws and commands. ³⁵I will take the kingdom away from Solomon's son and will give you ten tribes, ³⁶but I will let Solomon's son keep one tribe, so that I will always have a descendant of my servant David ruling in Jerusalem, the city I have chosen as the place where I am worshiped. ³⁷Jeroboam, I will make you king of Israel, and you will rule over all the territory that you want. ³⁸If you obey me completely, live by my laws, and win my approval by doing what I command, as my servant David did, I will always be with you. I will make you king of Israel and will make sure that your descendants rule after you, just as I have done for David. ³⁹Because of Solomon's sin I will punish the descendants of David, but not for all time.' "

⁴⁰And so Solomon tried to kill Jeroboam, but he escaped to King Shishak of Egypt and stayed there until Solomon's death.

The Death of Solomon
(2 Chronicles 9.29-31)

⁴¹Everything else that Solomon did, his career, and his wisdom, are all recorded in *The History of Solomon*. ⁴²He was king in Jerusalem over all Israel for forty years. ⁴³He died and was buried in David's City, and his son Rehoboam succeeded him as king.

The Northern Tribes Revolt
(2 Chronicles 10.1-19)

12 Rehoboam went to Shechem, where all the people of northern Israel had gathered to make him king. ²When Jeroboam son of Nebat, who had gone to Egypt to escape from King Solomon, heard this news, he returned from*ᵒ* Egypt. ³The people of the northern tribes sent for him, and then they all went together to Rehoboam

---

ᵐ Some ancient translations Solomon has . . . *and has; Hebrew* they have . . . *and have.*
ⁿ Some ancient translations Solomon has; *Hebrew* They have.   *ᵒ Some ancient*
translations (and see 2 Ch 10.2) returned from; *Hebrew* remained in.

and said to him, [4]"Your father Solomon treated us harshly and placed heavy burdens on us. If you make these burdens lighter and make life easier for us, we will be your loyal subjects."

[5]"Come back in three days and I will give you my answer," he replied. So they left.

[6] King Rehoboam consulted the older men who had served as his father Solomon's advisers. "What answer do you advise me to give these people?" he asked.

[7] They replied, "If you want to serve this people well, give a favorable answer to their request, and they will always serve you loyally."

[8] But he ignored the advice of the older men and went instead to the young men who had grown up with him and who were now his advisers. [9]"What do you advise me to do?" he asked. "What shall I say to the people who are asking me to make their burdens lighter?"

[10] They replied, "This is what you should tell them: 'My little finger is thicker than my father's waist!' [11] Tell them, 'My father placed heavy burdens on you; I will make them even heavier. He beat you with whips; I'll flog you with bullwhips!'"

[12] Three days later Jeroboam and all the people returned to King Rehoboam, as he had instructed them. [13] The king ignored the advice of the older men and spoke harshly to the people, [14] as the younger men had advised. He said, "My father placed heavy burdens on you; I will make them even heavier. He beat you with whips; I'll flog you with bullwhips!" [15] It was the will of the LORD to bring about what he had spoken to Jeroboam son of Nebat through the prophet Ahijah from Shiloh. This is why the king did not pay any attention to the people.

[16] When the people saw that the king would not listen to them, they shouted, "Down with David and his family! What have they ever done for us? People of Israel, let's go home! Let Rehoboam look out for himself!"

So the people of Israel rebelled, [17] leaving Rehoboam as king only of the people who lived in the territory of Judah.

[18] Then King Rehoboam sent Adoniram, who was in charge of the forced labor, to go to the Israelites, but they stoned him to death. At this, Rehoboam hurriedly got in his chariot and escaped to Jerusalem. [19] Ever since that time the people of the northern kingdom of Israel have been in rebellion against the dynasty of David.

[20] When the people of Israel heard that Jeroboam had returned from Egypt, they invited him to a meeting of the people and made him king of Israel. Only the tribe of Judah remained loyal to David's descendants.

Shemaiah's Prophecy
(2 Chronicles 11.1-4)

[21] When Rehoboam arrived in Jerusalem, he called together 180,000 of the best soldiers from the tribes of Judah and Benjamin. He intended to go to war and restore his control over the northern tribes of Israel. [22] But God told the prophet Shemaiah [23] to give this message to Rehoboam and to all the people of the tribes of Judah and Benjamin: [24]"Do not attack your own relatives, the people of Israel. Go home, all of you. What has happened is my will." They all obeyed the LORD's command and went back home.

Jeroboam Turns Away from God

[25] King Jeroboam of Israel fortified the town of Shechem in the hill country of Ephraim and lived there for a while. Then he left and fortified the town of Penuel. [26-27] He said to himself, "As things are now, if my people go to Jeru-

salem and offer sacrifices to the LORD in the Temple there, they will transfer their allegiance to King Rehoboam of Judah and will kill me."

28 After thinking it over, he made two bull-calves of gold and said to his people, "You have been going long enough to Jerusalem to worship. People of Israel, here are your gods who brought you out of Egypt!" **29** He placed one of the gold bull-calves in Bethel and the other in Dan. **30** And so the people sinned, going to worship in Bethel and in Dan.ᵖ **31** Jeroboam also built places of worship on hilltops, and he chose priests from families who were not of the tribe of Levi.

Worship at Bethel Is Condemned

32 Jeroboam also instituted a religious festival on the fifteenth day of the eighth month, like the festival in Judah. On the altar in Bethel he offered sacrifices to the gold bull-calves he had made, and he placed there in Bethel the priests serving at the places of worship he had built. **33** And on the fifteenth day of the eighth month, the day that he himself had set, he went to Bethel and offered a sacrifice on the altar in celebration of the festival he had instituted for the people of Israel.

13 At the LORD's command a prophet from Judah went to Bethel and arrived there as Jeroboam stood at the altar to offer the sacrifice. **2** Following the LORD's command, the prophet denounced the altar: "O altar, altar, this is what the LORD says: A child, whose name will be Josiah, will be born to the family of David. He will slaughter on you the priests serving at the pagan altars who offer sacrifices on you, and he will burn human bones on you." **3** And the prophet went on to say,

"This altar will fall apart, and the ashes on it will be scattered. Then you will know that the LORD has spoken through me."

4 When King Jeroboam heard this, he pointed at him and ordered, "Seize that man!" At once the king's arm became paralyzed so that he couldn't pull it back. **5** The altar suddenly fell apart and the ashes spilled to the ground, as the prophet had predicted in the name of the LORD. **6** King Jeroboam said to the prophet, "Please pray for me to the LORD your God, and ask him to heal my arm!"

The prophet prayed to the LORD, and the king's arm was healed. **7** Then the king said to the prophet, "Come home with me and have something to eat. I will reward you for what you have done."

8 The prophet answered, "Even if you gave me half of your wealth, I would not go with you or eat or drink anything with you. **9** The LORD has commanded me not to eat or drink a thing, and not to return home the same way I came." **10** So he did not go back the same way he had come, but by another road.

The Old Prophet of Bethel

11 At that time there was an old prophet living in Bethel. His sons�q came and told him what the prophet from Judah had done in Bethel that day and what he had said to King Jeroboam. **12** "Which way did he go when he left?" the old prophet asked them. They showed himʳ the road **13** and he told them to saddle his donkey for him. They did so, and he rode off **14** down the road after the prophet from Judah and found him sitting under an oak tree. "Are you the prophet from Judah?" he asked.

ᵖ *One ancient translation* in Bethel and in Dan; *Hebrew* in Dan.   q *Some ancient translations* sons; *Hebrew* son.   ʳ *Some ancient translations* showed him; *Hebrew* saw.

12.28 Ex 32.4   **12.32, 33** Lv 23.33, 34   **13.2** 2 K 23.15, 16

"I am," the man answered.

15 "Come home and have a meal with me," he said.

16 But the prophet from Judah answered, "I can't go home with you or accept your hospitality. And I won't eat or drink anything with you here, 17 because the LORD has commanded me not to eat or drink a thing, and not to return home the same way I came."

18 Then the old prophet from Bethel said to him, "I, too, am a prophet just like you, and at the LORD's command an angel told me to take you home with me and offer you my hospitality." But the old prophet was lying.

19 So the prophet from Judah went home with the old prophet and had a meal with him. 20 As they were sitting at the table, the word of the LORD came to the old prophet, 21 and he cried out to the prophet from Judah, "The LORD says that you disobeyed him and did not do what he commanded. 22 Instead, you returned and ate a meal in a place he had ordered you not to eat in. Because of this you will be killed, and your body will not be buried in your family grave."

23 After they had finished eating, the old prophet saddled the donkey for the prophet from Judah, 24 who rode off. On the way a lion met him and killed him. His body lay on the road, and the donkey and the lion stood beside it. 25 Some men passed by and saw the body on the road, with the lion standing near by. They went on into Bethel and reported what they had seen.

26 When the old prophet heard about it, he said, "That is the prophet who disobeyed the LORD's command! And so the LORD sent the lion to attack and kill him, just as the LORD said he would." 27 Then he said to his sons, "Saddle my donkey for me." They did so, 28 and he rode off and found the prophet's body lying on the road, with the donkey and the lion still standing by it. The lion had not eaten the body or attacked the donkey. 29 The old prophet picked up the body, put it on the donkey, and brought

it back to Bethel to mourn over it and bury it. 30 He buried it in his own family grave, and he and his sons mourned over it, saying, "Oh my brother, my brother!" 31 After the burial the prophet said to his sons, "When I die, bury me in this grave and lay my body next to his. 32 The words that he spoke at the LORD's command against the altar in Bethel and against all the places of worship in the towns of Samaria will surely come true."

Jeroboam's Fatal Sin

33 King Jeroboam of Israel still did not turn from his evil ways but continued to choose priests from ordinary families to serve at the altars he had built. He ordained as priest anyone who wanted to be one. 34 This sin on his part brought about the ruin and total destruction of his dynasty.

The Death of Jeroboam's Son

14 At that time King Jeroboam's son Abijah got sick. 2 Jeroboam said to his wife, "Disguise yourself so that no one will recognize you, and go to Shiloh, where the prophet Ahijah lives, the one who said I would be king of Israel. 3 Take him ten loaves of bread, some cakes, and a jar of honey. Ask him what is going to happen to our son, and he will tell you."

4 So she went to Ahijah's home in Shiloh. Old age had made Ahijah blind. 5 The LORD had told him that Jeroboam's wife was coming to ask him about her son, who was sick. And the LORD told Ahijah what to say.

When Jeroboam's wife arrived, she pretended to be someone else. 6 But when Ahijah heard her coming in the door, he said, "Come in. I know you are Jeroboam's wife. Why are you pretending to be someone else? I have bad news for you. 7 Go and tell Jeroboam that this is what the LORD, the God of Israel, says to him: 'I chose you from among the people and made you the uler of my people Israel. [8] I took the kingdom away from David's descendants and gave it to you. But you have not been like my servant David, who was completely loyal to me, obeyed my commands, and did only what I approve of. [9] You have committed far greater sins than those who ruled before you. You have rejected me and have aroused my anger by making idols and metal images to worship. [10] Because of this I will bring disaster on your dynasty and will kill all your male descendants, young and old alike. I will get rid of your family; they will be swept away like dung. [11] Any members of your family who die in the city will be eaten by dogs, and any who die in the open country will be eaten by vultures. I, the LORD, have spoken.' "

[12] And Ahijah went on to say to Jeroboam's wife, "Now go back home. As soon as you enter the town, your son will die. [13] All the people of Israel will mourn for him and bury him. He will be the only member of Jeroboam's family who will be properly buried, because he is the only one with whom the LORD, the God of Israel, is pleased. [14] The LORD is going to place a king over Israel who will put an end to Jeroboam's dynasty.[s] [15] The LORD will punish Israel, and she will shake like a reed shaking in a stream. He will uproot the people of Israel from this good land which he gave to their ancestors, and he will scatter them beyond the Euphrates River, because they have aroused his anger by making idols of the goddess Asherah. [16] The LORD will abandon Israel because Jeroboam sinned and led the people of Israel into sin."

[17] Jeroboam's wife went back to Tirzah. Just as she entered her home, the child died. [18] The people of Israel mourned for him and buried him, as the LORD had said through his servant, the prophet Ahijah.

The Death of Jeroboam

[19] Everything else that King Jeroboam did, the wars he fought and how he ruled, are all recorded in *The History of the Kings of Israel.* [20] Jeroboam ruled as king for twenty-two years. He died and was buried, and his son Nadab succeeded him as king.

King Rehoboam of Judah
(2 Chronicles 11.5 — 12.15)

[21] Solomon's son Rehoboam was forty-one years old when he became king of Judah, and he ruled seventeen years in Jerusalem, the city which the LORD had chosen from all the territory of Israel as the place where he was to be worshiped. Rehoboam's mother was Naamah from Ammon.

[22] The people of Judah sinned against the LORD and did more to arouse his anger against them than all their ancestors had done. [23] They built places of worship for false gods and put up stone pillars and symbols of Asherah to worship on the hills and under shady trees.

They built places of worship for false gods.
(14.23)

[24] Worst of all, there were men and women who served as prostitutes at those pagan places of worship. The people of Judah practiced all the shameful

---

[s] *Hebrew has five additional words, the meaning of which is unclear.*
14.10 1 K 15.29　**14.23** 2 K 17.9, 10　**14.24** Dt 23.17

things done by the people whom the LORD had driven out of the land as the Israelites advanced into the country. 25 In the fifth year of Rehoboam's reign King Shishak of Egypt attacked Jerusalem. 26 He took away all the treasures in the Temple and in the palace, including the gold shields Solomon had made. 27 To replace them, King Rehoboam made bronze shields and entrusted them to the officers responsible for guarding the palace gates. 28 Every time the king went to the Temple, the guards carried the shields and then returned them to the guardroom. 29 Everything else that King Rehoboam did is recorded in *The History of the Kings of Judah.* 30 During all this time Rehoboam and Jeroboam were constantly at war with each other. 31 Rehoboam died and was buried in the royal tombs in David's City and his son Abijah succeeded him as king.

King Abijah of Judah
(2 Chronicles 13.1 — 14.1)

15 In the eighteenth year of the reign of King Jeroboam of Israel, Abijah became king of Judah, 2 and he ruled three years in Jerusalem. His mother was Maacah, the daughter of Absalom. 3 He committed the same sins as his father and was not completely loyal to the LORD his God, as his great-grandfather David had been. 4 But for David's sake the LORD his God gave Abijah a son to rule after him in Jerusalem and to keep Jerusalem secure. 5 The LORD did this because David had done what pleased him and had never disobeyed any of his commands, except in the case of Uriah the Hittite. 6 The war which had begun between Rehoboam and Jeroboam continued throughout Abijah's lifetime. 7 And everything else that Abijah did is recorded in *The History of the Kings of Judah.*

8 Abijah died and was buried in David's City, and his son Asa succeeded him as king.

King Asa of Judah
(2 Chronicles 15.16 — 16.6)

9 In the twentieth year of the reign of King Jeroboam of Israel, Asa became king of Judah, 10 and he ruled forty-one years in Jerusalem. His grandmother was Maacah, the daughter of Absalom. 11 Asa did what pleased the LORD, as his ancestor David had done. 12 He expelled from the country all the male and female prostitutes serving at the pagan places of worship, and he removed all the idols his predecessors had made. 13 He removed his grandmother Maacah from her position as queen mother, because she had made an obscene idol of the fertility goddess Asherah. Asa cut down the idol and burned it in Kidron Valley. 14 Even though Asa did not destroy all the pagan places of worship, he remained faithful to the LORD all his life. 15 He placed in the Temple all the objects his father had dedicated to God, as well as the gold and silver objects that he himself dedicated.

16 King Asa of Judah and King Baasha of Israel were constantly at war with each other as long as they were in power. 17 Baasha invaded Judah and started to fortify Ramah in order to cut off all traffic in and out of Judah. 18 So King Asa took all the silver and gold that was left in the Temple and the palace, and sent it by some of his officials to Damascus, to King Benhadad of Syria, the son of Tabrimmon and grandson of Hezion, with this message: 19 "Let us be allies, as our fathers were. This silver and gold is a present for you. Now break your alliance with King Baa-

---

14.25 2 Ch 12.2-8   **14.26** 1 K 10.16, 17; 2 Ch 9.15, 16   **15.4** 1 K 11.36   **15.5** 2 S 11.1-27
15.6 2 Ch 13.3-21   **15.12** 2 Ch 15.8-15

ha of Israel, so that he will have to pull
his troops out of my territory."

20 King Benhadad agreed to Asa's
proposal and sent his commanding officers and their armies to attack the cit-
es of Israel. They captured Ijon, Dan,
Abel Beth Maacah, the area near Lake
Galilee, and the whole territory of
Naphtali. **21** When King Baasha heard
what had happened, he stopped fortify-
ng Ramah and went to Tirzah.

22 Then King Asa sent out an order
throughout all of Judah requiring
everyone, without exception, to help
carry away from Ramah the stones and
timber that Baasha had been using to
fortify it. With this material Asa fortified
Mizpah and Geba, a city in the territory
of Benjamin.

23 Everything else that King Asa did,
his brave deeds and the towns he fortified, are all recorded in *The History of
the Kings of Judah*. But in his old age he
was crippled by a foot disease. **24** Asa
died and was buried in the royal tombs
in David's City, and his son Jehoshaphat succeeded him as king.

King Nadab of Israel

25 In the second year of the reign of
King Asa of Judah, King Jeroboam's
son Nadab became king of Israel, and
he ruled for two years. **26** Like his father
before him, he sinned against the LORD
and led Israel into sin.

27 Baasha son of Ahijah, of the tribe of
Issachar, plotted against Nadab and
killed him as Nadab and his army were
besieging the city of Gibbethon in Philistia. **28** This happened during the third
year of the reign of King Asa of Judah.
And so Baasha succeeded Nadab as
king of Israel. **29** At once he began killing all the members of Jeroboam's family. In accordance with what the LORD
had said through his servant, the
prophet Ahijah from Shiloh, all of Jeroboam's family were killed; not one sur-

vived. **30** This happened because
Jeroboam aroused the anger of the
LORD, the God of Israel, by the sins that
he committed and that he caused Israel
to commit.

31 Everything else that Nadab did is
recorded in *The History of the Kings of
Israel*. **32** King Asa of Judah and King
Baasha of Israel were constantly at war
with each other as long as they were in
power.

King Baasha of Israel

33 In the third year of the reign of
King Asa of Judah, Baasha son of Ahijah became king of all Israel, and he
ruled in Tirzah for twenty-four years.
34 Like King Jeroboam before him, he
sinned against the LORD and led Israel
into sin.

16 The LORD spoke to the prophet
Jehu son of Hanani and gave
him this message for Baasha: **2** "You
were a nobody, but I made you the
leader of my people Israel. And now you
have sinned like Jeroboam and have led
my people into sin. Their sins have
aroused my anger, **3** and so I will do
away with you and your family, just as
I did with Jeroboam. **4** Any members of
your family who die in the city will be
eaten by dogs, and any who die in the
open country will be eaten by vultures."

5 Everything else that Baasha did and
all his brave deeds are recorded in *The
History of the Kings of Israel*. **6** Baasha
died and was buried in Tirzah, and his
son Elah succeeded him as king.

7 That message from the LORD
against Baasha and his family was
given by the prophet Jehu because of
the sins that Baasha committed against
the LORD. He aroused the LORD's anger
not only because of the evil he did, just
as King Jeroboam had done before him,
but also because he killed all of Jeroboam's family.

King Elah of Israel

[8] In the twenty-sixth year of the reign of King Asa of Judah, Elah son of Baasha became king of Israel, and he ruled in Tirzah for two years. [9] Zimri, one of his officers who was in charge of half of the king's chariots, plotted against him. One day in Tirzah, Elah was getting drunk in the home of Arza, who was in charge of the palace. [10] Zimri entered the house, assassinated Elah, and succeeded him as king. This happened in the twenty-seventh year of the reign of King Asa of Judah.

[11] As soon as Zimri became king he killed off all the members of Baasha's family. Every male relative and friend was put to death. [12] And so, in accordance with what the LORD had said against Baasha through the prophet Jehu, Zimri killed all the family of Baasha. [13] Because of their idolatry and because they led Israel into sin, Baasha and his son Elah had aroused the anger of the LORD, the God of Israel. [14] Everything else that Elah did is recorded in *The History of the Kings of Israel.*

King Zimri of Israel

[15] In the twenty-seventh year of the reign of King Asa of Judah, Zimri ruled in Tirzah over Israel for seven days. The Israelite troops were besieging the city of Gibbethon in Philistia, [16] and when they heard that Zimri had plotted against the king and assassinated him, then and there they all proclaimed their commander Omri king of Israel. [17] Omri and his troops left Gibbethon and went and besieged Tirzah. [18] When Zimri saw that the city had fallen, he went into the palace's inner fortress, set the palace on fire, and died in the flames. [19] This happened because of his sins against the LORD. Like his predecessor Jeroboam, he displeased the LORD by his own sins and by leading Israel into sin. [20] Everything else that Zimri did, including the account of his conspiracy, is recorded in *The History of the Kings of Israel.*

King Omri of Israel

[21] The people of Israel were divided: some of them wanted to make Tibni son of Ginath king, and the others were in favor of Omri. [22] In the end, those in favor of Omri won out; Tibni died and Omri became king. [23] So in the thirty-first year of the reign of King Asa of Judah, Omri became king of Israel, and he ruled for twelve years. The first six years he ruled in Tirzah, [24] and then he bought the hill of Samaria for six thousand pieces of silver from a man named Shemer. Omri fortified the hill, built a town there, and named it Samaria, after Shemer, the former owner of the hill.

[25] Omri sinned against the LORD more than any of his predecessors. [26] Like Jeroboam before him, he aroused the anger of the LORD, the God of Israel, by his sins and by leading the people into sin and idolatry. [27] Everything else that Omri did and all his accomplishments are recorded in *The History of the Kings of Israel.* [28] Omri died and was buried in Samaria, and his son Ahab succeeded him as king.

King Ahab of Israel

[29] In the thirty-eighth year of the reign of King Asa of Judah, Ahab son of Omri became king of Israel, and he ruled in Samaria for twenty-two years. [30] He sinned against the LORD more than any of his predecessors. [31] It was not enough for him to sin like King Jeroboam; he went further and married Jezebel, the daughter of King Ethbaal of Sidon, and worshiped Baal. [32] He built a temple to Baal in Samaria, made an altar for him, and put it in the temple. [33] He also put up an image of the goddess Asherah. He did more to arouse the anger of the LORD, the God of Israel, than all the kings of Israel be-

ore him. 34 During his reign Hiel from Bethel rebuilt Jericho. As the LORD had foretold through Joshua son of Nun, Hiel lost his oldest son Abiram when he laid the foundation of Jericho, and his youngest son Segub when he built the gates.

Elijah and the Drought

17 A prophet named Elijah, from Tishbe in Gilead, said to King Ahab, "In the name of the LORD, the living God of Israel, whom I serve, I tell you that there will be no dew or rain for the next two or three years until I say so."

2 Then the LORD said to Elijah, "Leave this place and go east and hide yourself near Cherith Brook, east of the Jordan. 4 The brook will supply you with water to drink, and I have commanded ravens to bring you food there."

have commanded ravens to bring you food. (17.4)

5 Elijah obeyed the LORD's command, and went and stayed by Cherith Brook. 6 He drank water from the brook, and ravens brought him bread and meat every morning and every evening. After a while the brook dried up because of the lack of rain.

Elijah and the Widow in Zarephath

8 Then the LORD said to Elijah, "Now go to the town of Zarephath, near Sidon, and stay there. I have commanded a widow who lives there to feed

you." 10 So Elijah went to Zarephath, and as he came to the town gate, he saw a widow gathering firewood. "Please bring me a drink of water," he said to her. 11 And as she was going to get it, he called out, "And please bring me some bread, too."

12 She answered, "By the living LORD your God I swear that I don't have any bread. All I have is a handful of flour in a bowl and a bit of olive oil in a jar. I came here to gather some firewood to take back home and prepare what little I have for my son and me. That will be our last meal, and then we will starve to death."

13 "Don't worry," Elijah said to her. "Go on and prepare your meal. But first make a small loaf from what you have and bring it to me, and then prepare the rest for you and your son. 14 For this is what the LORD, the God of Israel, says: 'The bowl will not run out of flour or the jar run out of oil before the day that I, the LORD, send rain.' "

15 The widow went and did as Elijah had told her, and all of them had enough food for many days. 16 As the LORD had promised through Elijah, the bowl did not run out of flour nor did the jar run out of oil.

17 Some time later the widow's son got sick; he got worse and worse, and finally he died. 18 She said to Elijah, "Man of God, why did you do this to me? Did you come here to remind God of my sins and so cause my son's death?"

19 "Give the boy to me," Elijah said. He took the boy from her arms, carried him upstairs to the room where he was staying, and laid him on the bed. 20 Then he prayed aloud, "O LORD my God, why have you done such a terrible thing to this widow? She has been kind enough to take care of me, and now you kill her son!" 21 Then Elijah stretched himself out on the boy three times and prayed, "O LORD my God, restore this child to life!" 22 The LORD answered

Elijah's prayer; the child started breathing again and revived.

²³ Elijah took the boy back downstairs to his mother and said to her, "Look, your son is alive!"

²⁴ She answered, "Now I know that you are a man of God and that the LORD really speaks through you!"

Elijah and the Prophets of Baal

18 After some time, in the third year of the drought, the LORD said to Elijah, "Go and present yourself to King Ahab, and I will send rain." ² So Elijah started out.

The famine in Samaria was at its worst, ³ so Ahab called in Obadiah, who was in charge of the palace. (Obadiah was a devout worshiper of the LORD, ⁴ and when Jezebel was killing the LORD's prophets, Obadiah took a hundred of them, hid them in caves in two groups of fifty, and provided them with food and water.) ⁵ Ahab said to Obadiah, "Let us go and look*ᵗ* at every spring and every stream bed in the land to see if we can find enough grass to keep the horses and mules alive. Maybe we won't have to kill any of our animals." ⁶ They agreed on which part of the land each one would explore, and set off in different directions.

⁷ As Obadiah was on his way, he suddenly met Elijah. He recognized him, bowed low before him, and asked, "Is it really you, sir?"

⁸ "Yes, I'm Elijah," he answered. "Go and tell your master the king that I am here."

⁹ Obadiah answered, "What have I done that you want to put me in danger of being killed by King Ahab? ¹⁰ By the living LORD, your God, I swear that the king has made a search for you in every country in the world. Whenever the ruler of a country reported that you were not in his country, Ahab would require that ruler to swear that you could

not be found. ¹¹ And now you want me to go and tell him that you are here? ¹² What if the spirit of the LORD carries you off to some unknown place as soon as I leave? Then, when I tell Ahab that you are here and he can't find you, he will put me to death. Remember that I have been a devout worshiper of the LORD ever since I was a boy. ¹³ Haven't you heard that when Jezebel was killing the prophets of the LORD I hid a hundred of them in caves, in two groups of fifty, and supplied them with food and water? ¹⁴ So how can you order me to go and tell the king that you are here? He will kill me!"

¹⁵ Elijah answered, "By the living LORD Almighty, whom I serve, I promise that I will present myself to the king today."

¹⁶ So Obadiah went to King Ahab and told him, and Ahab set off to meet Elijah. ¹⁷ When Ahab saw him, he said, "So there you are — the worst troublemaker in Israel!"

¹⁸ "I'm not the troublemaker," Elijah answered. "You are — you and your father. You are disobeying the LORD's commands and worshiping the idols of Baal. ¹⁹ Now order all the people of Israel to meet me at Mount Carmel. Bring along the 450 prophets of Baal and the 400 prophets of the goddess Asherah who are supported by Queen Jezebel."

²⁰ So Ahab summoned all the Israelites and the prophets of Baal to meet at Mount Carmel. ²¹ Elijah went up to the people and said, "How much longer will it take you to make up your minds? If the LORD is God, worship him; but if Baal is God, worship him!" But the people didn't say a word. ²² Then Elijah said, "I am the only prophet of the LORD still left, but there are 450 prophets of Baal. ²³ Bring two bulls; let the prophets of Baal take one, kill it, cut it in pieces, and put it on the wood — but don't light the fire. I will do the same with the other bull. ²⁴ Then let the prophets of

---

ᵗ One ancient translation Let us go and look; *Hebrew* You go and look.

Baal pray to their god, and I will pray to the LORD, and the one who answers by sending fire — he is God."

The people shouted their approval.

25 Then Elijah said to the prophets of Baal, "Since there are so many of you, you take a bull and prepare it first. Pray to your god, but don't set fire to the wood."

26 They took the bull that was brought to them, prepared it, and prayed to Baal until noon. They shouted, "Answer us, Baal!" and kept dancing around the altar they had built. But no answer came.

27 At noon Elijah started making fun of them: "Pray louder! He is a god! Maybe he is day-dreaming or relieving himself, or perhaps he's gone off on a trip! Or maybe he's sleeping, and you've got to wake him up!" 28 So the prophets prayed louder and cut themselves with knives and daggers, according to their ritual, until blood flowed. 29 They kept on ranting and raving until the middle of the afternoon; but no answer came, not a sound was heard.

30 Then Elijah said to the people, "Come closer to me," and they all gathered around him. He set about repairing the altar of the LORD which had been torn down. 31 He took twelve stones, one for each of the twelve tribes named for the sons of Jacob, the man to whom the LORD had given the name Israel. 32 With these stones he rebuilt the altar for the worship of the LORD. He dug a trench around it, large enough to hold about four gallons of water. 33 Then he placed the wood on the altar, cut the bull in pieces, and laid it on the wood. He said, "Fill four jars with water and pour it on the offering and the wood." They did so, 34 and he said, "Do it again" — and they did. "Do it once more," he said — and they did. 35 The water ran down around the altar and filled the trench.

36 At the hour of the afternoon sacrifice the prophet Elijah approached the altar and prayed, "O LORD, the God of Abraham, Isaac, and Jacob, prove now that you are the God of Israel and that I am your servant and have done all this at your command. 37 Answer me, LORD, answer me, so that this people will know that you, the LORD, are God and that you are bringing them back to yourself."[u]

38 The LORD sent fire down, and it burned up the sacrifice, the wood, and the stones, scorched the earth and dried up the water in the trench. 39 When the people saw this, they threw themselves on the ground and exclaimed, "The LORD is God; the LORD alone is God!"

40 Elijah ordered, "Seize the prophets of Baal; don't let any of them get away!" The people seized them all, and Elijah led them down to Kishon Brook and killed them.

The End of the Drought

41 Then Elijah said to King Ahab, "Now, go and eat. I hear the roar of rain approaching." 42 While Ahab went to eat, Elijah climbed to the top of Mount Carmel, where he bowed down to the ground, with his head between his knees. 43 He said to his servant, "Go and look toward the sea."

The servant went and returned, saying, "I didn't see a thing." Seven times in all Elijah told him to go and look. 44 The seventh time he returned and said, "I saw a little cloud no bigger than a man's hand, coming up from the sea."

Elijah ordered his servant, "Go to King Ahab and tell him to get in his

---

you are bringing them back to yourself; *or* you yourself made them turn away from you.

18.31 Gn 32.28; 35.10 **18.42-45** Jas 5.18

The Lord sent fire down. (18.38)

chariot and go back home before the rain stops him."

⁴⁵ In a little while the sky was covered with dark clouds, the wind began to blow, and a heavy rain began to fall. Ahab got in his chariot and started back to Jezreel. ⁴⁶ The power of the LORD came on Elijah; he fastened his clothes tight around his waist and ran ahead of Ahab all the way to Jezreel.

Elijah on Mount Sinai

19 King Ahab told his wife Jezebel everything that Elijah had done and how he had put all the prophets of Baal to death. ² She sent a message to Elijah: "May the gods strike me dead if by this time tomorrow I don't do the same thing to you that you did to the prophets." ³ Elijah was afraid and fled for his life; he took his servant and went to Beersheba in Judah.

Leaving the servant there, ⁴ Elijah walked a whole day into the wilderness. He stopped and sat down in the shade of a tree and wished he would die. "It's too much, LORD," he prayed. "Take away my life; I might as well be dead!"

⁵ He lay down under the tree and fell asleep. Suddenly an angel touched him and said, "Wake up and eat." ⁶ He looked around and saw a loaf of bread and a jar of water near his head. He ate and drank, and lay down again. ⁷ The LORD's angel returned and woke him up a second time, saying, "Get up and eat, or the trip will be too much for you." ⁸ Elijah got up, ate and drank, and the food gave him enough strength to walk forty days to Sinai, the holy mountain. ⁹ There he went into a cave to spend the night.

Suddenly the LORD spoke to him, "Elijah, what are you doing here?"

¹⁰ He answered, "LORD God Almighty, I have always served you – you alone. But the people of Israel have broken their covenant with you, torn down your altars, and killed all your

19.4 Jon 4.3   **19.10, 14** Ro 11.3

prophets. I am the only one left — and they are trying to kill me!"

11 "Go out and stand before me on top of the mountain," the LORD said to him. Then the LORD passed by and sent a furious wind that split the hills and shattered the rocks — but the LORD was not in the wind. The wind stopped blowing, and then there was an earthquake — but the LORD was not in the earthquake. 12 After the earthquake there was a fire — but the LORD was not in the fire. And after the fire there was the soft whisper of a voice.

13 When Elijah heard it, he covered his face with his cloak and went out and stood at the entrance of the cave. A voice said to him, "Elijah, what are you doing here?"

14 He answered, "LORD God Almighty, I have always served you — you alone. But the people of Israel have broken their covenant with you, torn down your altars, and killed all your prophets. I am the only one left — and they are trying to kill me."

15 The LORD said, "Return to the wilderness near Damascus, then enter the city and anoint Hazael as king of Syria; 16 anoint Jehu son of Nimshi as king of Israel, and anoint Elisha son of Shaphat from Abel Meholah to succeed you as prophet. 17 Anyone who escapes being put to death by Hazael will be killed by Jehu, and anyone who escapes Jehu will be killed by Elisha. 18 Yet I will leave seven thousand people alive in Israel — all those who are loyal to me and have not bowed to Baal or kissed his idol."

The Call of Elisha

19 Elijah left and found Elisha plowing with a team of oxen; there were eleven teams ahead of him, and he was plowing with the last one. Elijah took off his cloak and put it on Elisha. 20 Elisha then left his oxen, ran after Elijah, and said, "Let me kiss my father and mother good-bye, and then I will go with you."

Elijah answered, "All right, go back. I'm not stopping you!"*v*

21 Then Elisha went to his team of oxen, killed them, and cooked the meat, using the yoke as fuel for the fire. He gave the meat to the people, and they ate it. Then he went and followed Elijah as his helper.

War with Syria

20 King Benhadad of Syria gathered all his troops, and supported by thirty-two other rulers with their horses and chariots, he marched up, laid siege to Samaria, and launched attacks against it. 2 He sent messengers into the city to King Ahab of Israel to say, "King Benhadad demands that 3 you surrender to him your silver and gold, your women and the strongest of your children."

4 "Tell my lord, King Benhadad, that I agree; he can have me and everything I own," Ahab answered.

5 Later the messengers came back to Ahab with another demand from Benhadad: "I sent you word that you were to hand over to me your silver and gold, your women and your children. 6 Now, however, I will send my officers to search your palace and the homes of your officials, and to take everything they*w* consider valuable. They will be there about this time tomorrow."

7 King Ahab called in all the leaders of the country and said, "You see that this man wants to ruin us. He sent me a message demanding my wives and children, my silver and gold, and I agreed."

v All right . . . you; *or* Go on, but come back, because what I have just done to you is important.   *w Some ancient translations* they; *Hebrew* you.

19.15 2 K 8.7-13   **19.16** 2 K 9.1-6   **19.18** Ro 11.4

⁸The leaders and the people answered, "Don't pay any attention to him; don't give in."

⁹So Ahab replied to Benhadad's messengers, "Tell my lord the king that I agreed to his first demand, but I cannot agree to the second."

The messengers left and then returned with another message ¹⁰from Benhadad: "I will bring enough men to destroy this city of yours and carry off the rubble in their hands. May the gods strike me dead if I don't!"

¹¹King Ahab answered, "Tell King Benhadad that a real soldier does his bragging *after* a battle, not before it."

¹²Benhadad received Ahab's answer as he and his allies, the other rulers, were drinking in their tents. He ordered his men to get ready to attack the city, and so they moved into position.

¹³Meanwhile, a prophet went to King Ahab and said, "The LORD says, 'Don't be afraid of that huge army! I will give you victory over it today, and you will know that I am the LORD.'"

¹⁴"Who will lead the attack?" Ahab asked.

The prophet answered, "The LORD says that the young soldiers under the command of the district governors are to do it."

"Who will command the main force?" the king asked.

"You," the prophet answered.

¹⁵So the king called out the young soldiers who were under the district commanders, 232 in all. Then he called out the Israelite army, a total of seven thousand men.

¹⁶The attack began at noon, as Benhadad and his thirty-two allies were getting drunk in their tents. ¹⁷The young soldiers advanced first. Scouts sent out by Benhadad reported to him that a group of soldiers was coming out of Samaria. ¹⁸He ordered, "Take them alive, no matter whether they are coming to fight or to ask for peace."

¹⁹The young soldiers led the attack, followed by the Israelite army, ²⁰and each one killed the man he fought. The Syrians fled, with the Israelites in hot pursuit, but Benhadad escaped on horseback, accompanied by some of the cavalry. ²¹King Ahab took to the field, captured[x] the horses and chariots, and inflicted a severe defeat on the Syrians.

²²Then the prophet went to King Ahab and said, "Go back and build up your forces and make careful plans, because the king of Syria will attack again next spring."

The Second Syrian Attack

²³King Benhadad's officials said to him, "The gods of Israel are mountain gods, and that is why the Israelites defeated us. But we will certainly defeat them if we fight them in the plains. ²⁴Now, remove the thirty-two rulers from their commands and replace them with field commanders. ²⁵Then call up an army as large as the one that deserted you, with the same number of horses and chariots. We will fight the Israelites in the plains, and this time we will defeat them."

King Benhadad agreed and followed their advice. ²⁶The following spring he called up his men and marched with them to the city of Aphek to attack the Israelites. ²⁷The Israelites were called up and equipped; they marched out and camped in two groups facing the Syrians. The Israelites looked like two small flocks of goats compared to the Syrians, who spread out over the countryside.

²⁸A prophet went to King Ahab and said, "This is what the LORD says: 'Because the Syrians say that I am a god of the hills and not of the plains, I will give you victory over their huge army, and you and your people will know that I am the LORD.'"

---

x One ancient translation captured; *Hebrew* destroyed.

²⁹ For seven days the Syrians and the Israelites stayed in their camps, facing each other. On the seventh day they started fighting, and the Israelites killed a hundred thousand Syrians. ³⁰ The survivors fled into the city of Aphek, where the city walls fell on twenty-seven thousand of them.

Benhadad also escaped into the city and took refuge in the back room of a house. ³¹ His officials went to him and said, "We have heard that the Israelite kings are merciful. Give us permission to go to the king of Israel with sackcloth around our waists and ropes around our necks, and maybe he will spare your life." ³² So they wrapped sackcloth around their waists and ropes around their necks, went to Ahab and said, "Your servant Benhadad pleads with you for his life."

Ahab answered, "Is he still alive? Good! He's like a brother to me!"

They wrapped . . .
ropes around their necks. (20.32)

³³ Benhadad's officials were watching for a good sign, and when Ahab said "brother," they took it up at once, and said, "As you say, Benhadad is your brother!"

"Bring him to me," Ahab ordered. When Benhadad arrived, Ahab invited him to get in the chariot with him.

³⁴ Benhadad said to him, "I will restore to you the towns my father took from your father, and you may set up a commercial center for yourself in Damascus, just as my father did in Samaria."

Ahab replied, "On these terms, then, I will set you free." He made a treaty with him and let him go.

A Prophet Condemns Ahab

³⁵ At the LORD's command a member of a group of prophets ordered a fellow prophet to hit him. But he refused, ³⁶ so he said to him, "Because you have disobeyed the LORD's command, a lion will kill you as soon as you leave me." And as soon as he left, a lion came along and killed him.

³⁷ Then this same prophet went to another man and said, "Hit me!" This man did so; he hit him a hard blow and hurt him. ³⁸ The prophet bandaged his face with a cloth, to disguise himself, and went and stood by the road, waiting for the king of Israel to pass. ³⁹ As the king was passing by, the prophet called out to him and said, "Your Majesty, I was fighting in the battle when a soldier brought a captured enemy to me and said, 'Guard this man; if he escapes, you will pay for it with your life or else pay a fine of three thousand pieces of silver.' ⁴⁰ But I got busy with other things, and the man escaped."

The king answered, "You have pronounced your own sentence, and you will have to pay the penalty."

⁴¹ The prophet tore the cloth from his face, and at once the king recognized him as one of the prophets. ⁴² The prophet then said to the king, "This is the word of the LORD: 'Because you allowed the man to escape whom I had ordered to be killed, you will pay for it with your life, and your army will be destroyed for letting his army escape.'"

⁴³ The king went back home to Samaria, worried and depressed.

Naboth's Vineyard

21 Near King Ahab's palace in Jezreel there was a vineyard owned by a man named Naboth. ²One day Ahab said to Naboth, "Let me have your vineyard; it is close to my palace, and I want to use the land for a vegetable garden. I will give you a better vineyard for it or, if you prefer, I will pay you a fair price."

³"I inherited this vineyard from my ancestors," Naboth replied. "The LORD forbid that I should let you have it!"

⁴Ahab went home, depressed and angry over what Naboth had said to him. He lay down on his bed, facing the wall, and would not eat. ⁵His wife Jezebel went to him and asked, "Why are you so depressed? Why won't you eat?"

⁶He answered, "Because of what Naboth said to me. I offered to buy his vineyard or, if he preferred, to give him another one for it, but he told me that I couldn't have it!"

⁷"Well, are you the king or aren't you?" Jezebel replied. "Get out of bed, cheer up, and eat. I will get you Naboth's vineyard!"

⁸Then she wrote some letters, signed Ahab's name to them, sealed them with his seal, and sent them to the officials and leading citizens of Jezreel. ⁹The letters said: "Proclaim a day of fasting, call the people together, and give Naboth the place of honor. ¹⁰Get a couple of scoundrels to accuse him to his face of cursing God and the king. Then take him out of the city and stone him to death."

¹¹The officials and leading citizens of Jezreel did what Jezebel had commanded. ¹²They proclaimed a day of fasting, called the people together, and gave Naboth the place of honor. ¹³The two scoundrels publicly accused him of cursing God and the king, and so he was taken outside the city and stoned to death. ¹⁴The message was sent to Jezebel: "Naboth has been put to death."

¹⁵As soon as Jezebel received the message, she said to Ahab, "Naboth is dead. Now go and take possession of the vineyard which he refused to sell to you." ¹⁶At once Ahab went to the vineyard to take possession of it.

¹⁷Then the LORD said to Elijah, the prophet from Tishbe, ¹⁸"Go to King Ahab of Samaria. You will find him in Naboth's vineyard, about to take possession of it. ¹⁹Tell him that I, the LORD, say to him, 'After murdering the man, are you taking over his property as well?' Tell him that this is what I say: 'In the very place that the dogs licked up Naboth's blood they will lick up your blood!' "

²⁰When Ahab saw Elijah, he said, "Have you caught up with me, my enemy?"

"Yes, I have," Elijah answered. "You have devoted yourself completely to doing what is wrong in the LORD's sight. ²¹So the LORD says to you, 'I will bring disaster on you. I will do away with you and get rid of every male in your family, young and old alike. ²²Your family will become like the family of King Jeroboam son of Nebat and like the family of King Baasha son of Ahijah, because you have stirred up my anger by leading Israel into sin.' ²³And concerning Jezebel, the LORD says that dogs will eat her body in the city of Jezreel. ²⁴Any of your relatives who die in the city will be eaten by dogs, and any who die in the open country will be eaten by vultures."

(²⁵There was no one else who had devoted himself so completely to doing wrong in the LORD's sight as Ahab — all at the urging of his wife Jezebel. ²⁶He committed the most shameful sins by worshiping idols, as the Amorites had done, whom the LORD had driven out of the land as the people of Israel advanced.)

²⁷When Elijah finished speaking, Ahab tore his clothes, took them off, and put on sackcloth. He refused food, slept in the sackcloth, and went about gloomy and depressed.

²⁸The LORD said to the prophet Elijah, ²⁹"Have you noticed how Ahab has humbled himself before me? Since he has done this, I will not bring disaster on him during his lifetime; it will be during his son's lifetime that I will bring disaster on Ahab's family."

The Prophet Micaiah Warns Ahab
(2 Chronicles 18.2-27)

22 There was peace between Israel and Syria for the next two years, ²but in the third year King Jehoshaphat of Judah went to see King Ahab of Israel.

³Ahab asked his officials, "Why is it that we have not done anything to get back Ramoth in Gilead from the king of Syria? It belongs to us!" ⁴And Ahab asked Jehoshaphat, "Will you go with me to attack Ramoth?"

"I am ready when you are," Jehoshaphat answered, "and so are my soldiers and my cavalry. ⁵But first let's consult the LORD."

⁶So Ahab called in the prophets, about four hundred of them, and asked them, "Should I go and attack Ramoth, or not?"

"Attack it," they answered. "The Lord will give you victory."

⁷But Jehoshaphat asked, "Isn't there another prophet through whom we can consult the LORD?"

⁸Ahab answered, "There is one more, Micaiah son of Imlah. But I hate him because he never prophesies anything good for me; it's always something bad."

"You shouldn't say that!" Jehoshaphat replied.

⁹Then Ahab called in a court official and told him to go and get Micaiah at once.

¹⁰The two kings, dressed in their royal robes, were sitting on their thrones at the threshing place just outside the gate of Samaria, and all the prophets were prophesying in front of them. ¹¹One of them, Zedekiah son of Chenaanah, made iron horns and said to Ahab, "This is what the LORD says: 'With these you will fight the Syrians and totally defeat them.'" ¹²All the other prophets said the same thing. "March against Ramoth and you will win," they said. "The LORD will give you victory."

¹³Meanwhile, the official who had gone to get Micaiah said to him, "All the other prophets have prophesied success for the king, and you had better do the same."

¹⁴But Micaiah answered, "By the living LORD I promise that I will say what he tells me to!"

¹⁵When he appeared before King Ahab, the king asked him, "Micaiah, should King Jehoshaphat and I go and attack Ramoth, or not?"

"Attack!" Micaiah answered. "Of course you'll win. The LORD will give you victory."

¹⁶But Ahab replied, "When you speak to me in the name of the LORD, tell the truth! How many times do I have to tell you that?"

¹⁷Micaiah answered, "I can see the army of Israel scattered over the hills like sheep without a shepherd. And the LORD said, 'These men have no leader; let them go home in peace.'"

¹⁸Ahab said to Jehoshaphat, "Didn't I tell you that he never prophesies anything good for me? It's always something bad!"

¹⁹Micaiah went on: "Now listen to what the LORD says! I saw the LORD sitting on his throne in heaven, with all his angels standing beside him. ²⁰The LORD asked, 'Who will deceive Ahab so

22.17 Nu 27.17; Mt 9.36; Mk 6.34   **22.19** Job 1.6; Is 6.1

that he will go and be killed at Ramoth?' Some of the angels said one thing, and others said something else, 21 until a spirit stepped forward, approached the LORD, and said, 'I will deceive him.' 22 'How?' the LORD asked. The spirit replied, 'I will go and make all of Ahab's prophets tell lies.' The LORD said, 'Go and deceive him. You will succeed.' "

23 And Micaiah concluded: "This is what has happened. The LORD has made these prophets of yours lie to you. But he himself has decreed that you will meet with disaster!"

24 Then the prophet Zedekiah went up to Micaiah, slapped his face, and asked, "Since when did the LORD's spirit leave me and speak to you?"

25 "You will find out when you go into some back room to hide," Micaiah replied.

26 Then King Ahab ordered one of his officers, "Arrest Micaiah and take him to Amon, the governor of the city, and to Prince Joash. 27 Tell them to throw him in prison and to put him on bread and water until I return safely."

28 "If you return safely," Micaiah exclaimed, "then the LORD has not spoken through me!" And he added, "Listen, everyone, to what I have said!"

The Death of Ahab
(2 Chronicles 18.28-34)

29 Then King Ahab of Israel and King Jehoshaphat of Judah went to attack the city of Ramoth in Gilead. 30 Ahab said to Jehoshaphat, "As we go into battle, I will disguise myself, but you wear your royal garments." So the king of Israel went into battle in disguise.

31 The king of Syria had ordered his thirty-two chariot commanders to attack no one else except the king of Israel. 32 So when they saw King Jehoshaphat, they all thought that he was the king of Israel, and they turned to attack him. But when he cried out, 33 they realized that he was not the king of Israel, and they stopped their attack.

34 By chance, however, a Syrian soldier shot an arrow which struck King Ahab between the joints of his armor. "I'm wounded!" he cried out to his chariot driver. "Turn around and pull out of the battle!"

35 While the battle raged on, King Ahab remained propped up in his chariot, facing the Syrians. The blood from his wound ran down and covered the bottom of the chariot, and at evening he died. 36 Near sunset the order went out through the Israelite ranks: "Each of you go back to your own country and city!"

37 So died King Ahab. His body was taken to Samaria and buried. 38 His chariot was cleaned up at the pool of Samaria, where dogs licked up his blood and prostitutes washed themselves, as the LORD had said would happen.

39 Everything else that King Ahab did, including an account of his palace decorated with ivory and of all the cities he built, is recorded in *The History of the Kings of Israel*. 40 At his death his son Ahaziah succeeded him as king.

King Jehoshaphat of Judah
(2 Chronicles 20.31 – 21.1)

41 In the fourth year of the reign of King Ahab of Israel, Jehoshaphat son of Asa became king of Judah 42 at the age of thirty-five, and he ruled in Jerusalem for twenty-five years. His mother was Azubah, the daughter of Shilhi. 43 Like his father Asa before him, he did what was right in the sight of the LORD; but the places of worship were not destroyed, and the people continued to offer sacrifices and burn incense there. 44 Jehoshaphat made peace with the king of Israel.

45 Everything else that Jehoshaphat did, all his bravery and his battles, are recorded in *The History of the Kings of Judah*. 46 He got rid of all the male and female prostitutes serving at the pagan altars who were still left from the days of his father Asa.

47 The land of Edom had no king; it was ruled by a deputy appointed by the king of Judah.

48 King Jehoshaphat had ocean-going ships built to sail to the land of Ophir for gold; but they were wrecked at Eziongeber and never sailed. 49 Then King Ahaziah of Israel offered to let his men sail with Jehoshaphat's men, but Jehoshaphat refused the offer.

50 Jehoshaphat died and was buried in the royal tombs in David's City, and his son Jehoram succeeded him as king.

King Ahaziah of Israel

51 In the seventeenth year of the reign of King Jehoshaphat of Judah, Ahaziah son of Ahab became king of Israel, and he ruled in Samaria for two years. 52 He sinned against the LORD, following the wicked example of his father Ahab, his mother Jezebel, and King Jeroboam, who had led Israel into sin. 53 He worshiped and served Baal, and like his father before him, he aroused the anger of the LORD, the God of Israel.

The Second Book of
KINGS

INTRODUCTION

Second Kings continues the history of the two Israelite kingdoms where *First Kings* leaves off. The book may be divided into two parts: 1) The story of the two kingdoms from the middle of the ninth century B.C. down to the fall of Samaria and the end of the northern kingdom in 722 B.C. 2) The story of the kingdom of Judah from the fall of the kingdom of Israel down to the capture and destruction of Jerusalem by King Nebuchadnezzar of Babylonia in 586 B.C. The book ends with an account of Gedaliah as governor of Judah under the Babylonians and a report of the release of King Jehoiachin of Judah from prison in Babylon.

These national disasters took place because of the unfaithfulness of the kings and people of Israel and Judah. The destruction of Jerusalem and the exile of many of the people of Judah was one of the great turning points of Israelite history.

The prophet who stands out in *Second Kings* is Elijah's successor Elisha.

OUTLINE OF CONTENTS

Elijah and King Ahaziah

1 After the death of King Ahab of Israel the country of Moab rebelled against Israel.

2 King Ahaziah of Israel fell off the balcony on the roof of his palace in Samaria and was seriously injured. So he sent some messengers to consult Baalzebub, the god of the Philistine city of Ekron, in order to find out whether or not he would recover. **3** But an angel of the LORD commanded Elijah, the prophet from Tishbe, to go and meet the messengers of King Ahaziah and ask them, "Why are you going to consult Baalzebub, the god of Ekron? Is it because you think there is no god in Israel? **4** Tell the king that the LORD says, 'You will not recover from your injuries; you will die!' "

Elijah did as the LORD commanded, **5** and the messengers returned to the king. "Why have you come back?" he asked.

6 They answered, "We were met by a man who told us to come back and tell you that the LORD says to you, 'Why are you sending messengers to consult Baalzebub, the god of Ekron? Is it because you think there is no god in Israel? You will not recover from your injuries; you will die!' "

7 "What did the man look like?" the king asked.

8 "He was wearing a cloak made of animal skins, tied with[a] a leather belt," they answered.

"It's Elijah!" the king exclaimed.

9 Then he sent an officer with fifty men to get Elijah. The officer found him sitting on a hill and said to him, "Man of God, the king orders you to come down."

10 "If I am a man of God," Elijah answered, "may fire come down from heaven and kill you and your men!" At once fire came down and killed the officer and his men.

11 The king sent another officer with fifty men, who went up[b] and said to Elijah, "Man of God, the king orders you to come down at once!"

12 "If I am a man of God," Elijah answered, "may fire come down from heaven and kill you and your men!" At once the fire of God came down and killed the officer and his men.

13 Once more the king sent an officer with fifty men. He went up the hill, fell on his knees in front of Elijah, and pleaded, "Man of God, be merciful to me and my men. Spare our lives! **14** The two other officers and their men were killed by fire from heaven; but please be merciful to me!"

15 The angel of the LORD said to Elijah, "Go down with him, and don't be afraid." So Elijah went with the officer to the king **16** and said to him, "This is what the LORD says: 'Because you sent messengers to consult Baalzebub, the god of Ekron — as if there were no god in Israel to consult — you will not get well; you will die!' "

17 Ahaziah died, as the LORD had said through Elijah. Ahaziah had no sons,

---

[a] *was wearing ... with; or was a hairy man and wore.*   [b] *One ancient translation* went up; *Hebrew* answered.
1.8 Mt 3.4; Mk 1.6   **1.10, 12** Lk 9.54

so his brother[c] Joram succeeded him as king in the second year of the reign of Jehoram son of Jehoshaphat, king of Judah.

[18] Everything else that King Ahaziah did is recorded in *The History of the Kings of Israel.*

Elijah Is Taken Up to Heaven

2 The time came for the LORD to take Elijah up to heaven in a whirlwind. Elijah and Elisha set out from Gilgal, [2] and on the way Elijah said to Elisha, "Now stay here; the LORD has ordered me to go to Bethel."

But Elisha answered, "I swear by my loyalty to the living LORD and to you that I will not leave you." So they went on to Bethel.

[3] A group of prophets who lived there went to Elisha and asked him, "Do you know that the LORD is going to take your master away from you today?"

"Yes, I know," Elisha answered. "But let's not talk about it."

[4] Then Elijah said to Elisha, "Now stay here; the LORD has ordered me to go to Jericho."

But Elisha answered, "I swear by my loyalty to the living LORD and to you that I will not leave you." So they went on to Jericho.

[5] A group of prophets who lived there went to Elisha and asked him, "Do you know that the LORD is going to take your master away from you today?"

"Yes, I know," Elisha answered. "But let's not talk about it."

[6] Then Elijah said to Elisha, "Now stay here; the LORD has ordered me to go to the Jordan River."

But Elisha answered, "I swear by my loyalty to the living LORD and to you that I will not leave you." So they went on, [7] and fifty of the prophets followed

them to the Jordan. Elijah and Elisha stopped by the river, and the fifty prophets stood a short distance away. [8] Then Elijah took off his cloak, rolled it up, and struck the water with it; the water divided, and he and Elisha crossed to the other side on dry ground. [9] There, Elijah said to Elisha, "Tell me what you want me to do for you before I am taken away."

"Let me receive the share of your power that will make me your successor,"[d] Elisha answered.

[10] "That is a difficult request to grant," Elijah replied. "But you will receive it if you see me as I am being taken away from you; if you don't see me, you won't receive it."

[11] They kept talking as they walked on; then suddenly a chariot of fire pulled by horses of fire came between them, and Elijah was taken up to heaven by a whirlwind. [12] Elisha saw it and cried out to Elijah, "My father, my father! Mighty defender of Israel! You are gone!" And he never saw Elijah again.

In grief Elisha tore his cloak in two. [13] Then he picked up Elijah's cloak that had fallen from him, and went back and stood on the bank of the Jordan. [14] He struck the water with Elijah's cloak and said, "Where is the LORD, the God of Elijah?" Then he struck the water again, and it divided, and he walked over to the other side. [15] The fifty prophets from Jericho saw him and said, "The power of Elijah is on Elisha!" They went to meet him, bowed down before him, [16] and said, "There are fifty of us here, all strong men. Let us go and look for your master. Maybe the spirit of the LORD has carried him away and left him on some mountain or in some valley."

"No, you must not go," Elisha answered.

[c] *Some ancient translations* his brother; *Hebrew does not have these words.*   [d] THE SHARE ... SUCCESSOR: *Elisha asked for the share that the first-born son inherited by law from his father (see Dt 21.17).*
2.9 Dt 21.17   **2.12** 2 K 13.14; Si 48.9, 12

"My father! . . . You are gone!" (2.12)

¹⁷But they insisted until he gave in and let them go. The fifty of them went and looked high and low for Elijah for three days, but didn't find him. ¹⁸Then they returned to Elisha, who had waited at Jericho, and he said to them, "Didn't I tell you not to go?"

Miracles of Elisha

¹⁹Some men from Jericho went to Elisha and said, "As you know, sir, this is a fine city, but the water is bad and causes miscarriages."

²⁰"Put some salt in a new bowl and bring it to me," he ordered. They brought it to him, ²¹and he went to the spring, threw the salt in the water, and said, "This is what the LORD says: 'I make this water pure, and it will not cause any more deaths or miscarriages.'" ²²And that water has been pure ever since, just as Elisha said it would be.

²³Elisha left Jericho to go to Bethel, and on the way some boys came out of a town and made fun of him. "Get out of here, baldy!" they shouted.

²⁴Elisha turned around, glared at them, and cursed them in the name of the LORD. Then two she-bears came out of the woods and tore forty-two of the boys to pieces.

²⁵Elisha went on to Mount Carmel and later returned to Samaria.

War between Israel and Moab

3 In the eighteenth year of the reign of King Jehoshaphat of Judah, Joram son of Ahab became king of Israel, and he ruled in Samaria for twelve years. ²He sinned against the LORD, but he was not as bad as his father or his mother Jezebel; he pulled down the image his father had made for the worship of Baal. ³Yet, like King Jeroboam son of Nebat before him, he led Israel into sin and would not stop.

⁴King Mesha of Moab raised sheep, and every year he gave as tribute to the king of Israel 100,000 lambs and the wool from 100,000 sheep. ⁵But when

King Ahab of Israel died, Mesha rebelled against Israel. 6 At once King Joram left Samaria and gathered all his troops. 7 He sent word to King Jehoshaphat of Judah: "The king of Moab has rebelled against me; will you join me in war against him?"

"I will," King Jehoshaphat replied. "I am at your disposal, and so are my men and my horses. 8 What route shall we take for the attack?"

"We will go the long way through the wilderness of Edom," Joram answered.

9 So King Joram and the kings of Judah and Edom set out. After marching seven days, they ran out of water, and there was none left for the men or the pack animals. 10 "We're done for!" King Joram exclaimed. "The LORD has put the three of us at the mercy of the king of Moab!"

11 King Jehoshaphat asked, "Is there a prophet here through whom we can consult the LORD?"

An officer of King Joram's forces answered, "Elisha son of Shaphat is here. He was Elijah's assistant."

12 "He is a true prophet," King Jehoshaphat said. So the three kings went to Elisha.

13 "Why should I help you?" Elisha said to the king of Israel. "Go and consult those prophets that your father and mother consulted."

"No!" Joram replied. "It is the LORD who has put us three kings at the mercy of the king of Moab."

14 Elisha answered, "By the living LORD, whom I serve, I swear that I would have nothing to do with you if I didn't respect your ally, King Jehoshaphat of Judah. 15 Now get me a musician."

As the musician played his harp, the power of the LORD came on Elisha, 16 and he said, "This is what the LORD says: 'Dig ditches all over this dry stream bed. 17 Even though you will not see any rain or wind, this stream bed

will be filled with water, and you, your livestock, and your pack animals will have plenty to drink.'" 18 And Elisha

"This is what the LORD says." (3.16)

continued, "But this is an easy thing for the LORD to do; he will also give you victory over the Moabites. 19 You will conquer all their beautiful fortified cities; you will cut down all their fruit trees, stop all their springs, and ruin all their fertile fields by covering them with stones."

20 The next morning, at the time of the regular morning sacrifice, water came flowing from the direction of Edom and covered the ground.

21 When the Moabites heard that the three kings had come to attack them, all the men who could bear arms, from the oldest to the youngest, were called out and stationed at the border. 22 When they got up the following morning, the sun was shining on the water, making it look as red as blood. 23 "It's blood!" they exclaimed. "The three enemy armies must have fought and killed each other! Let's go and loot their camp!"

24 But when they reached the camp, the Israelites attacked them and drove them back. The Israelites kept up the pursuit,^e slaughtering the Moabites 25 and destroying their cities. As they passed by a fertile field, every Israelite would throw a stone on it until finally all the fields were covered; they also stopped up the springs and cut down

---

^e *One ancient translation* kept up the pursuit; *Hebrew unclear.*

the fruit trees. At last only the capital city of Kir Heres _f_ was left, and the slingers surrounded it and attacked it.

26 When the king of Moab realized that he was losing the battle, he took seven hundred swordsmen with him and tried to force his way through the enemy lines and escape to the king of Syria, _g_ but he failed. 27 So he took his oldest son, who was to succeed him as king, and offered him on the city wall as a sacrifice to the god of Moab. The Israelites were terrified _h_ and so they drew back from the city and returned to their own country.

Elisha Helps a Poor Widow

4 The widow of a member of a group of prophets went to Elisha and said, "Sir, my husband has died! As you know, he was a God-fearing man, but now a man he owed money to has come to take away my two sons as slaves in payment for my husband's debt."

2 "What shall I do for you?" he asked. "Tell me, what do you have at home?"

"Nothing at all, except a small jar of olive oil," she answered.

3 "Go to your neighbors and borrow as many empty jars as you can," Elisha told her. 4 "Then you and your sons go into the house, close the door, and start pouring oil into the jars. Set each one aside as soon as it is full."

5 So the woman went into her house with her sons, closed the door, took the small jar of olive oil, and poured oil into the jars as her sons brought them to her. 6 When they had filled all the jars, she asked if there were any more. "That was the last one," one of her sons answered. And the olive oil stopped flowing. 7 She went back to Elisha, the prophet, who said to her, "Sell the olive oil and pay all your debts, and there will

be enough money left over for you and your sons to live on."

So the woman . . . poured oil into the jars. (4.5)

Elisha and the Rich Woman from Shunem

8 One day Elisha went to Shunem, where a rich woman lived. She invited him to a meal, and from then on every time he went to Shunem he would have his meals at her house. 9 She said to her husband, "I am sure that this man who comes here so often is a holy man. 10 Let's build a small room on the roof, put a bed, a table, a chair, and a lamp in it, and he can stay there whenever he visits us."

11 One day Elisha returned to Shunem and went up to his room to rest. 12 He told his servant Gehazi to go and call the woman. When she came, 13 he said to Gehazi, "Ask her what I can do for her in return for all the trouble she has had in providing for our needs. Maybe she would like me to go to the king or the army commander and put in a good word for her."

"I have all I need here among my own people," she answered.

---

f Probable text only the capital city of Kir Heres; _Hebrew unclear._ _g One ancient translation_ Syria; _Hebrew_ Edom. _h_ TERRIFIED, _either because of what Chemosh, the god of the Moabites, might do,_ or _because of what the_ LORD, _the God of the Israelites, might do._

¹⁴Elisha asked Gehazi, "What can I do for her then?"

He answered, "Well, she has no son, and her husband is an old man."

¹⁵"Tell her to come here," Elisha ordered. She came and stood in the doorway, ¹⁶and Elisha said to her, "By this time next year you will be holding a son in your arms."

"Oh!" she exclaimed. "Please, sir, don't lie to me. You are a man of God!"

¹⁷But, as Elisha had said, at about that time the following year she gave birth to a son.

¹⁸Some years later, at harvest time, the boy went out one morning to join his father, who was in the field with the harvest workers. ¹⁹Suddenly he cried out to his father, "My head hurts! My head hurts!"

"Carry the boy to his mother," the father said to a servant. ²⁰The servant carried the boy back to his mother, who held him in her lap until noon, at which time he died. ²¹She carried him up to Elisha's room, put him on the bed and left, closing the door behind her. ²²Then she called her husband and said to him, "Send a servant here with a donkey. I need to go to the prophet Elisha. I'll be back as soon as I can."

²³"Why do you have to go today?" her husband asked. "It's neither a Sabbath nor a New Moon Festival."ⁱ

"Never mind," she answered. ²⁴Then she had the donkey saddled, and ordered the servant, "Make the donkey go as fast as it can, and don't slow down unless I tell you to." ²⁵So she set out and went to Mount Carmel, where Elisha was.

Elisha saw her coming while she was still some distance away, and he said to his servant Gehazi, "Look, there comes the woman from Shunem! ²⁶Hurry to her and find out if every-

thing is all right with her, her husband, and her son."

She told Gehazi that everything was all right, ²⁷but when she came to Elisha, she bowed down before him and took hold of his feet. Gehazi was about to push her away, but Elisha said, "Leave her alone. Can't you see she's deeply distressed? And the LORD has not told me a thing about it."

²⁸The woman said to him, "Sir, did I ask you for a son? Didn't I tell you not to get my hopes up?"

²⁹Elisha turned to Gehazi and said, "Hurry! Take my walking stick and go. Don't stop to greet anyone you meet, and if anyone greets you, don't take time to answer. Go straight to the house and hold my stick over the boy."

³⁰The woman said to Elisha, "I swear by my loyalty to the living LORD and to you that I will not leave you!" So the two of them started back together. ³¹Gehazi went on ahead and held Elisha's stick over the child, but there was no sound or any other sign of life. So he went back to meet Elisha and said, "The boy didn't wake up."

³²When Elisha arrived, he went alone into the room and saw the boy lying dead on the bed. ³³He closed the door and prayed to the LORD. ³⁴Then he lay down on the boy, placing his mouth, eyes, and hands on the boy's mouth, eyes, and hands. As he lay stretched out over the boy, the boy's body started to get warm. ³⁵Elisha got up, walked around the room, and then went back and again stretched himself over the boy. The boy sneezed seven times and then opened his eyes. ³⁶Elisha called Gehazi and told him to call the boy's mother. When she came in, he said to her, "Here's your son." ³⁷She fell at Elisha's feet, with her face touching the ground; then she took her son and left.

ⁱ SABBATH . . . NEW MOON FESTIVAL: *Such holy days were thought to be the best time to consult a prophet.*

4.16 Gn 18.4   **4.34, 35** 1 K 17.21

Two More Miracles

38 Once, when there was a famine throughout the land, Elisha returned to Gilgal. While he was teaching a group of prophets, he told his servant to put a big pot on the fire and make some stew for them. **39** One of them went out in the fields to get some herbs. He found a wild vine and picked as many gourds as he could carry. He brought them back and sliced them up into the stew, not knowing what they were. **40** The stew was poured out for the men to eat, but as soon as they tasted it they exclaimed to Elisha, "It's poisoned!"—and wouldn't eat it. **41** Elisha asked for some meal, threw it into the pot, and said, "Pour out some more stew for them." And then there was nothing wrong with it.

42 Another time, a man came from Baal Shalishah, bringing Elisha twenty loaves of bread made from the first barley harvested that year, and some freshly-cut heads of grain. Elisha told his servant to feed the group of prophets with this, **43** but he answered, "Do you think this is enough for a hundred men?"

Elisha replied, "Give it to them to eat, because the LORD says that they will eat and still have some left over." **44** So the servant set the food before them, and as the LORD had said, they all ate, and there was still some left over.

Naaman Is Cured

5 Naaman, the commander of the Syrian army, was highly respected and esteemed by the king of Syria, because through Naaman the LORD had given victory to the Syrian forces. He was a great soldier, but he suffered from a dreaded skin disease. **2** In one of their raids against Israel, the Syrians had carried off a little Israelite girl, who became a servant of Naaman's wife. **3** One day she said to her mistress, "I wish that my master could go to the prophet who lives in Samaria! He would cure him of his disease." **4** When Naaman heard of this, he went to the king and told him what the girl had said. **5** The king said, "Go to the king of Israel and take this letter to him."

So Naaman set out, taking thirty thousand pieces of silver, six thousand pieces of gold, and ten changes of fine clothes. **6** The letter that he took read: "This letter will introduce my officer Naaman. I want you to cure him of his disease."

7 When the king of Israel read the letter, he tore his clothes in dismay and exclaimed, "How can the king of Syria expect me to cure this man? Does he think that I am God,[j] with the power of life and death? It's plain that he is trying to start a quarrel with me!"

8 When the prophet Elisha heard what had happened, he sent word to the king: "Why are you so upset? Send the man to me, and I'll show him that there is a prophet in Israel!"

9 So Naaman went with his horses and chariot and stopped at the entrance to Elisha's house. **10** Elisha sent a servant out to tell him to go and wash himself seven times in the Jordan River, and he would be completely cured of his disease. **11** But Naaman left in a rage, saying, "I thought that he would at least come out to me, pray to the LORD his God, wave his hand over the diseased spot,[k] and cure me! **12** Besides, aren't the rivers Abana and Pharpar, back in Damascus, better than any river in Israel? I could have washed in them and been cured!"

13 His servants went up to him and said, "Sir, if the prophet had told you to do something difficult, you would have done it. Now why can't you just wash yourself, as he said, and be cured?" **14** So Naaman went down to the Jordan,

---

j God; *or* a god.   *k* the diseased spot; *or* this place.
5.1-14 Lk 4.27

"If the prophet had told you to do something difficult, you would have done it." (5.13)

dipped himself in it seven times, as Elisha had instructed, and he was completely cured. His flesh became firm and healthy like that of a child. ¹⁵ He returned to Elisha with all his men and said, "Now I know that there is no god but the God of Israel; so please, sir, accept a gift from me."

¹⁶ Elisha answered, "By the living LORD, whom I serve, I swear that I will not accept a gift."

Naaman insisted that he accept it, but he would not. ¹⁷ So Naaman said, "If you won't accept my gift, then let me have two mule-loads of earth to take home with me,[*l*] because from now on I will not offer sacrifices or burnt offerings to any god except the LORD. ¹⁸ So I hope that the LORD will forgive me when I accompany my king to the temple of Rimmon, the god of Syria, and worship him. Surely the LORD will forgive me!"

¹⁹ "Go in peace," Elisha said. And Naaman left.

He had gone only a short distance, ²⁰ when Elisha's servant Gehazi said to himself, "My master has let Naaman get away without paying a thing! He should have accepted what that Syrian offered him. By the living LORD I will run after him and get something from him." ²¹ So he set off after Naaman.

When Naaman saw a man running after him, he got down from his chariot to meet him, and asked, "Is something wrong?"

²² "No," Gehazi answered. "But my master sent me to tell you that just now two members of the group of prophets in the hill country of Ephraim arrived, and he would like you to give them three thousand pieces of silver and two changes of fine clothes."

²³ "Please take six thousand pieces of silver," Naaman replied. He insisted on it, tied up the silver in two bags, gave them and two changes of fine clothes to two of his servants, and sent them on ahead of Gehazi. ²⁴ When they reached the hill where Elisha lived, Gehazi took the two bags and carried them into the house. Then he sent Naaman's servants back. ²⁵ He went back into the house, and Elisha asked him, "Where have you been?"

"Oh, nowhere, sir," he answered.

²⁶ But Elisha said, "Wasn't I there in spirit when the man got out of his chariot to meet you? This is no time to accept money and clothes, olive groves and vineyards, sheep and cattle, or servants! ²⁷ And now Naaman's disease will come upon you, and you and your descendants will have it forever!"

When Gehazi left, he had the disease—his skin was as white as snow.

The Recovery of the Ax Head

6 One day the group of prophets that Elisha was in charge of complained to him, "The place where we live is too small! ² Give us permission to go to the Jordan and cut down some trees, so that we can build a place to live."

"All right," Elisha answered.

³ One of them urged him to go with them; he agreed, ⁴ and they set out

---

[*l*] EARTH TO TAKE HOME WITH ME: *It was then believed that a god could be worshiped only on his own land.*

together. When they arrived at the Jordan, they began to work. 5As one of them was cutting down a tree, suddenly his iron ax head fell in the water. "What shall I do, sir?" he exclaimed to Elisha. "It was a borrowed ax!"

6"Where did it fall?" Elisha asked.

The man showed him the place, and Elisha cut off a stick, threw it in the water, and made the ax head float. 7"Take it out," he ordered, and the man reached down and picked it up.

The Syrian Army Is Defeated

8The king of Syria was at war with Israel. He consulted his officers and chose a place to set up his camp. 9But Elisha sent word to the king of Israel, warning him not to go near that place, because the Syrians were waiting in ambush there. 10So the king of Israel warned the people who lived in that place, and they were on guard. This happened several times.

11The Syrian king became greatly upset over this; he called in his officers and asked them, "Which one of you is on the side of the king of Israel?"

12One of them answered, "No one is, Your Majesty. The prophet Elisha tells the king of Israel what you say even in the privacy of your own room."

13"Find out where he is," the king ordered, "and I will capture him."

When he was told that Elisha was in Dothan, 14he sent a large force there with horses and chariots. They reached the town at night and surrounded it. 15Early the next morning Elisha's servant got up, went out of the house, and saw the Syrian troops with their horses and chariots surrounding the town. He went back to Elisha and exclaimed, "We are doomed, sir! What shall we do?"

16"Don't be afraid," Elisha answered. "We have more on our side than they have on theirs." 17Then he prayed,

"O LORD, open his eyes and let him see!" The LORD answered his prayer, and Elisha's servant looked up and saw the hillside covered with horses and chariots of fire all around Elisha.

18When the Syrians attacked, Elisha prayed, "O LORD, strike these men blind!" The LORD answered his prayer and struck them blind. 19Then Elisha went to them and said, "You are on the wrong road; this is not the town you are looking for. Follow me, and I will lead you to the man you are after." And he led them to Samaria.

20As soon as they had entered the city, Elisha prayed, "Open their eyes, LORD, and let them see." The LORD answered his prayer; he restored their sight, and they saw that they were inside Samaria.

21When the king of Israel saw the Syrians, he asked Elisha, "Shall I kill them, sir? Shall I kill them?"

22"No," he answered. "Not even soldiers you had captured in combat would you put to death. Give them something to eat and drink, and let them return to their king." 23So the king of Israel provided a great feast for them; and after they had eaten and drunk, he sent them back to the king of Syria. From then on the Syrians stopped raiding the land of Israel.

The Siege of Samaria

24Some time later King Benhadad of Syria led his entire army against Israel and laid siege to the city of Samaria. 25As a result of the siege the food shortage in the city was so severe that a donkey's head cost eighty pieces of silver, and half a pound of dove's dung[m] cost five pieces of silver.

26The king of Israel was walking by on the city wall when a woman cried out, "Help me, Your Majesty!"

27He replied, "If the LORD won't help you, what help can I provide? Do I have

---

m DOVE'S DUNG: *This may be a popular term for a vegetable such as wild onions.*

any wheat or wine? 28 What's your trouble?"

She answered, "The other day this woman here suggested that we eat my child, and then eat her child the next day. 29 So we cooked my son and ate him. The next day I told her that we would eat her son, but she had hidden him!"

30 Hearing this, the king tore his clothes in dismay, and the people who were close to the wall could see that he was wearing sackcloth under his clothes. 31 He exclaimed, "May God strike me dead if Elisha is not beheaded before the day is over!" 32 And he sent a messenger to get Elisha.

Meanwhile Elisha was at home with some elders who were visiting him. Before the king's messenger arrived, Elisha said to the elders, "That murderer is sending someone to kill me! Now, when he gets here, shut the door and don't let him come in. The king himself will be right behind him." 33 He had hardly finished saying this, when the king[n] arrived and said, "It's the LORD who has brought this trouble on us! Why should I wait any longer for him to do something?"

7 Elisha answered, "Listen to what the LORD says! By this time tomorrow you will be able to buy in Samaria ten pounds of the best wheat or twenty pounds of barley for one piece of silver."

2 The personal attendant of the king said to Elisha, "That can't happen — not even if the LORD himself were to send grain[o] at once!"

"You will see it happen, but you won't get to eat any of the food," Elisha replied.

The Syrian Army Leaves

3 Four men who were suffering from a dreaded skin disease were outside the gates of Samaria, and they said to each other, "Why should we wait here until we die? 4 It's no use going into the city, because we would starve to death in there; but if we stay here, we'll die also. So let's go to the Syrian camp; the worst they can do is kill us, but maybe they will spare our lives." 5 So, as it began to get dark, they went to the Syrian camp, but when they reached it, no one was there. 6 The Lord had made the Syrians hear what sounded like the advance of a large army with horses and chariots, and the Syrians thought that the king of Israel had hired Hittite and Egyptian kings and their armies to attack them. 7 So that evening the Syrians had fled for their lives, abandoning their tents, horses, and donkeys, and leaving the camp just as it was.

8 When the four men reached the edge of the camp, they went into a tent, ate and drank what was there, grabbed the silver, gold, and clothing they found, and went off and hid them; then they returned, entered another tent, and did the same thing. 9 But then they said to each other, "We shouldn't be doing this! We have good news, and we shouldn't keep it to ourselves. If we wait until morning to tell it, we are sure to be punished. Let's go right now and tell the king's officers!" 10 So they left the Syrian camp, went back to Samaria, and called out to the guards at the gates: "We went to the Syrian camp and didn't see or hear anybody; the horses and donkeys have not been untied, and the tents are just as the Syrians left them."

11 The guards announced the news, and it was reported in the palace. 12 It was still night, but the king got out of bed and said to his officials, "I'll tell you what the Syrians are planning! They know about the famine here, so they have left their camp to go and hide in the countryside. They think that we will leave the city to find food, and then

---

[n] Probable text king; Hebrew messenger.   [o] grain; or rain.
6.29 Dt 28.57; Lm 4.10

they will take us alive and capture the city."

13 One of his officials said, "The people here in the city are doomed anyway, like those that have already died. So let's send some men with five of the horses that are left, so that we can find out what has happened."[p] 14 They chose some men, and the king sent them in two chariots with instructions to go and find out what had happened to the Syrian army. 15 The men went as far as the Jordan, and all along the road they saw the clothes and equipment that the Syrians had abandoned as they fled. Then they returned and reported to the king. 16 The people of Samaria rushed out and looted the Syrian camp. And as the LORD had said, ten pounds of the best wheat or twenty pounds of barley were sold for one piece of silver.

17 It so happened that the king of Israel had put the city gate under the command of the officer who was his personal attendant. The officer was trampled to death there by the people and died, as Elisha had predicted when the king went to see him. 18 Elisha had told the king that by that time the following day ten pounds of the best wheat or twenty pounds of barley would be sold in Samaria for one piece of silver, 19 to which the officer had answered, "That can't happen — not even if the LORD himself were to send grain[q] at once!" And Elisha had replied, "You will see it happen, but you won't get to eat any of the food." 20 And that is just what happened to him — he died, trampled to death by the people at the city gate.

The Woman from Shunem Returns

8 Now Elisha had told the woman who lived in Shunem, whose son he had brought back to life, that the LORD was sending a famine on the land, which would last for seven years, and that she should leave with her family and go and live somewhere else. 2 She had followed his instructions and had gone with her family to live in Philistia for the seven years.

3 At the end of the seven years she returned to Israel and went to the king to ask that her house and her land be restored to her. 4 She found the king talking with Gehazi, Elisha's servant; the king wanted to know about Elisha's miracles. 5 While Gehazi was telling the king how Elisha had brought a dead person back to life, the woman made her appeal to the king. Gehazi said to him, "Your Majesty, here is the woman and here is her son whom Elisha brought back to life!" 6 In answer to the king's question, she confirmed Gehazi's story, and so the king called an official and told him to give back to her everything that was hers, including the value of all the crops that her fields had produced during the seven years she had been away.

Elisha and King Benhadad of Syria

7 Elisha went to Damascus at a time when King Benhadad of Syria was sick. When the king was told that Elisha was there, 8 he said to Hazael, one of his officials, "Take a gift to the prophet and ask him to consult the LORD to find out whether or not I am going to get well." 9 So Hazael loaded forty camels with all kinds of the finest products of Damascus and went to Elisha. When Hazael met him, he said, "Your servant King Benhadad has sent me to ask you whether or not he will recover from his sickness."

10 Elisha answered, "The LORD has revealed to me that he will die; but go to him and tell him that he will recover." 11 Then Elisha stared at him with a horrified look on his face until

---

[p] *Verse 13 in Hebrew is unclear.*   [q] grain; *or* rain.
8.1 2 K 4.8-37

Hazael became ill at ease. Suddenly Elisha burst into tears. ¹²"Why are you crying, sir?" Hazael asked.

"Because I know the horrible things you will do against the people of Israel," Elisha answered. "You will set their fortresses on fire, slaughter their finest young men, batter their children to death, and rip open their pregnant women."

¹³"How could I ever be that powerful?" Hazael asked. "I'm a nobody!"

"The LORD has shown me that you will be king of Syria," Elisha replied.

¹⁴Hazael went back to Benhadad, who asked him, "What did Elisha say?"

"He told me that you would certainly get well," Hazael answered. ¹⁵But on the following day Hazael took a blanket, soaked it in water, and smothered the king.

And Hazael succeeded Benhadad as king of Syria.

King Jehoram of Judah
(2 Chronicles 21.1-20)

¹⁶In the fifth year of the reign of Joram son of Ahab as king of Israel,ʳ Jehoram son of Jehoshaphat became king of Judah ¹⁷at the age of thirty-two, and he ruled in Jerusalem for eight years. ¹⁸His wife was Ahab's daughter, and like the family of Ahab he followed the evil ways of the kings of Israel. He sinned against the LORD, ¹⁹but the LORD was not willing to destroy Judah, because he had promised his servant David that his descendants would always continue to rule.

²⁰During Jehoram's reign Edom revolted against Judah and became an independent kingdom. ²¹So Jehoram set out with all his chariots to Zair, where the Edomite army surrounded them. During the night he and his chariot commanders managed to break out and escape, and his soldiers scattered to their homes. ²²Edom has been independent ofˢ Judah ever since. During this same period the city of Libnah also revolted.

²³Everything else that Jehoram did is recorded in *The History of the Kings of Judah*. ²⁴Jehoram died and was buried in the royal tombs in David's City, and his son Ahaziah succeeded him as king.

King Ahaziah of Judah
(2 Chronicles 22.1-6)

²⁵In the twelfth year of the reign of Joram son of Ahab as king of Israel, Ahaziah son of Jehoram became king of Judah ²⁶at the age of twenty-two, and he ruled in Jerusalem for one year. His mother was Athaliah, the daughter of King Ahab and granddaughter of King Omri of Israel. ²⁷Since Ahaziah was related to King Ahab by marriage, he sinned against the LORD, just as Ahab's family did.

²⁸King Ahaziah joined King Joram of Israel in a war against King Hazael of Syria. The armies clashed at Ramoth in Gilead, and Joram was wounded in battle. ²⁹He returned to the city of Jezreel to recover from his wounds, and Ahaziah went there to visit him.

Jehu Is Anointed King of Israel

9 Meanwhile the prophet Elisha called one of the young prophets and said to him, "Get ready and go to Ramoth in Gilead. Take this jar of olive oil with you, ²and when you get there look for Jehu, the son of Jehoshaphat and grandson of Nimshi. Take him to a private room away from his companions, ³pour this olive oil on his head, and say, 'The LORD proclaims that he anoints you king of Israel.' Then leave there as fast as you can."

⁴So the young prophet went to

ʳ *Some ancient translations* Israel; *Hebrew* Israel, Jehoshaphat being king of Judah.
ˢ independent of; *or* in revolt against.

8.13 1 K 19.15   **8.19** 1 K 11.36   **8.20** Gn 27.40

Ramoth, ⁵where he found the army officers in a conference. He said, "Sir, I have a message for you."

Jehu asked, "Which one of us are you speaking to?"

"To you, sir," he replied. ⁶Then the two of them went indoors, and the young prophet poured the olive oil on Jehu's head and said to him, "The Lord, the God of Israel, proclaims: 'I anoint you king of my people Israel. ⁷You are to kill your master the king, that son of Ahab, so that I may punish Jezebel for murdering my prophets and my other servants. ⁸All of Ahab's family and descendants are to die; I will get rid of every male in his family, young and old alike. ⁹I will treat his family as I did the families of King Jeroboam of Israel and of King Baasha of Israel. ¹⁰Jezebel will not be buried; her body will be eaten by dogs in the territory of Jezreel.'" After saying this, the young prophet left the room and fled.

¹¹Jehu went back to his fellow officers, who asked him, "Is everything all right? What did that crazy fellow want with you?"

"You know what he wanted," Jehu answered.

¹²"No we don't!" they replied. "Tell us what he said!"

"He told me that the Lord proclaims: 'I anoint you king of Israel.'"

¹³At once Jehu's fellow officers spread their cloaks at the top of the steps for Jehu to stand on, blew trumpets, and shouted, "Jehu is king!"

King Joram of Israel Is Killed

¹⁴⁻¹⁵Then Jehu plotted against King Joram, who was in Jezreel, where he had gone to recover from the wounds which he had received in the battle at Ramoth against King Hazael of Syria. So Jehu said to his fellow officers, "If you are with me, make sure that no one slips out of Ramoth to go and warn the people in Jezreel." ¹⁶Then he got into his chariot and set off for Jezreel. Joram had still not recovered, and King Ahaziah of Judah was there, visiting him.

¹⁷A guard on duty in the watchtower at Jezreel saw Jehu and his men approaching. "I see some men riding up!" he called out.

Joram replied, "Send a rider to find out if they are friends or enemies."

¹⁸The messenger rode out to Jehu and said to him, "The king wants to know if you come as a friend."

"That's none of your business!" Jehu answered. "Fall in behind me."

The guard on the watchtower reported that the messenger had reached the group but was not returning. ¹⁹Another messenger was sent out, who asked Jehu the same question. Again Jehu answered, "That's none of your business! Fall in behind me."

²⁰Once more the guard reported that the messenger had reached the group but was not returning. And he added, "The leader of the group is driving his chariot like a madman, just like Jehu!"

²¹"Get my chariot ready," King Joram ordered. It was done, and he and King Ahaziah rode out, each in his own chariot, to meet Jehu. They met him at the field which had belonged to Naboth. ²²"Are you coming in peace?" Joram asked him.

"How can there be peace," Jehu answered, "when we still have all the witchcraft and idolatry that your mother Jezebel started?"

²³"It's treason, Ahaziah!" Joram cried out, as he turned his chariot around and fled. ²⁴Jehu drew his bow, and with all his strength shot an arrow that struck Joram in the back and pierced his heart. Joram fell dead in his chariot, ²⁵and Jehu said to his aide Bidkar, "Get his body and throw it in the field that belonged to Naboth. Remember that when you and I were riding together behind King Joram's father

Ahab, the LORD spoke these words against Ahab: 26'I saw the murder of Naboth and his sons yesterday. And I promise that I will punish you here in this same field.' So take Joram's body," Jehu ordered his aide, "and throw it in the field that belonged to Naboth, so as to fulfill the LORD's promise."

King Ahaziah of Judah Is Killed

27 King Ahaziah saw what happened, so he fled in his chariot toward the town of Beth Haggan, pursued by Jehu. "Kill him too!" Jehu ordered his men, and they wounded him*t* as he drove his chariot on the road up to Gur, near the town of Ibleam. But he managed to keep on going until he reached the city of Megiddo, where he died. 28 His officials took his body back to Jerusalem in a chariot and buried him in the royal tombs in David's City.

29 Ahaziah had become king of Judah in the eleventh year that Joram son of Ahab was king of Israel.

Queen Jezebel Is Killed

30 Jehu arrived in Jezreel. Jezebel, having heard what had happened, put on eye shadow, arranged her hair, and stood looking down at the street from a window in the palace. 31 As Jehu came through the gate, she called out, "You Zimri!*u* You assassin! Why are you here?"

32 Jehu looked up and shouted, "Who is on my side?" Two or three palace officials looked down at him from a window, 33 and Jehu said to them, "Throw her down!" They threw her down, and her blood spattered on the wall and on the horses. Jehu drove his horses and chariot over her body, 34 entered the

palace, and had a meal. Only then did he say, "Take that cursed woman and bury her; after all, she is a king's daughter." 35 But the men who went out to bury her found nothing except her skull and the bones of her hands and feet. 36 When they reported this to Jehu, he said, "This is what the LORD said would happen, when he spoke through his servant Elijah: 'Dogs will eat Jezebel's body in the territory of Jezreel. 37 Her remains will be scattered there like dung, so that no one will be able to identify them.'"

The Descendants of Ahab Are Killed

10 There were seventy descendants of King Ahab living in the city of Samaria. Jehu wrote a letter and sent copies to the rulers of the city,*v* to the leading citizens, and to the guardians of Ahab's descendants. The letter read: 2 "You are in charge of the king's descendants, and you have at your disposal chariots, horses, weapons, and fortified cities. So then, as soon as you receive this letter, 3 you are to choose the best qualified of the king's descendants, make him king, and fight to defend him."

4 The rulers of Samaria were terrified. "How can we oppose Jehu," they said, "when neither King Joram nor King Ahaziah could?" 5 So the officer in charge of the palace and the official in charge of the city, together with the leading citizens and the guardians, sent this message to Jehu: "We are your servants, and we are ready to do anything you say. But we will not make anyone king; do whatever you think best."

6 Jehu wrote them another letter: "If you are with me and are ready to follow

---

t Some ancient translations and they wounded him; *Hebrew does not have these words.*
u ZIMRI: *An Israelite army officer who assassinated the king of Israel (see 1 K 16.8-12).*
v Some ancient translations the city; *Hebrew* Jezreel.
9.26 1 K 21.19   **9.36** 1 K 21.23

my orders, bring the heads of King Ahab's descendants to me at Jezreel by this time tomorrow."

The seventy descendants of King Ahab were under the care of the leading citizens of Samaria, who were bringing them up. 7When Jehu's letter was received, the leaders of Samaria killed all seventy of Ahab's descendants, put their heads in baskets, and sent them to Jehu at Jezreel.

8When Jehu was told that the heads of Ahab's descendants had been brought, he ordered them to be piled up in two heaps at the city gate and to be left there until the following morning. 9In the morning he went out to the gate and said to the people who were there, "I was the one who plotted against King Joram and killed him; you are not responsible for that. But who killed all these? 10This proves that everything that the LORD said about the descendants of Ahab will come true. The LORD has done what he promised through his prophet Elijah." 11Then Jehu put to death all the other relatives of Ahab living in Jezreel, and all his officers, close friends, and priests; not one of them was left alive.

The Relatives of King Ahaziah Are Killed

12Jehu left Jezreel to go to Samaria. On the way, at a place called "Shepherds' Camp," 13he met some relatives of the late King Ahaziah of Judah and asked them, "Who are you?"

"Ahaziah's relatives," they answered. "We are going to Jezreel to pay our respects to the children of Queen Jezebel and to the rest of the royal family." 14Jehu ordered his men, "Take them alive!" They seized them, and he put them to death near a pit there. There were forty-two people in all, and not one of them was left alive.

All Remaining Relatives of Ahab Are Killed

15Jehu started out again, and on his way he was met by Jonadab son of Rechab. Jehu greeted him and said, "You and I think alike. Will you support me?"

"I will," Jonadab answered.

"Give me your hand, then," Jehu replied. They clasped hands, and Jehu helped him up into the chariot, 16saying, "Come with me and see for yourself how devoted I am to the LORD." And they rode on together to Samaria. 17When they arrived there, Jehu killed all of Ahab's relatives, not sparing even one. This is what the LORD had told Elijah would happen.

The Worshipers of Baal Are Killed

18Jehu called the people of Samaria together and said, "King Ahab served the god Baal a little, but I will serve him much more. 19Call together all the prophets of Baal, all his worshipers, and all his priests. No one is excused; I am going to offer a great sacrifice to Baal, and whoever is not present will be put to death." (This was a trick on the part of Jehu by which he meant to kill all the worshipers of Baal.) 20Then Jehu ordered, "Proclaim a day of worship in honor of Baal!" The proclamation was made, 21and Jehu sent word throughout all the land of Israel. All who worshiped Baal came; not one of them failed to come. They all went into the temple of Baal, filling it from one end to the other. 22Then Jehu ordered the priest in charge of the sacred robes to bring the robes out and give them to the worshipers. 23After that, Jehu himself went into the temple with Jonadab son of Rechab and said to the people there, "Make sure that only worshipers of Baal are present and that no worshiper of the LORD has come in." 24Then he and Jon-

10.11 Ho 1.4

adab went in to offer sacrifices and burnt offerings to Baal. He had stationed eighty men outside the temple and had instructed them: "You are to kill all these people; anyone who lets one of them escape will pay for it with his life!"

25 As soon as Jehu had presented the offerings, he said to the guards and officers, "Go in and kill them all; don't let anyone escape!" They went in with drawn swords, killed them all, and dragged the bodies outside. Then they went on into the inner sanctuary of the temple, 26 brought out the sacred pillar that was there, and burned it. 27 So they destroyed the sacred pillar and the temple, and turned the temple into a latrine — which it still is today.

28 That was how Jehu wiped out the worship of Baal in Israel. 29 But he imitated the sin of King Jeroboam, who led Israel into the sin of worshiping the gold bull-calves he set up in Bethel and in Dan. 30 The LORD said to Jehu, "You have done to Ahab's descendants everything I wanted you to do. So I promise you that your descendants, down to the fourth generation, will be kings of Israel." 31 But Jehu did not obey with all his heart the Law of the LORD, the God of Israel; instead, he followed the example of Jeroboam, who led Israel into sin.

The Death of Jehu

32 At that time the LORD began to reduce the size of Israel's territory. King Hazael of Syria conquered all the Israelite territory 33 east of the Jordan, as far south as the town of Aroer on the Arnon River — this included the territories of Gilead and Bashan, where the tribes of Gad, Reuben, and East Manasseh lived.

34 Everything else that Jehu did, including his brave deeds, is recorded in *The History of the Kings of Israel.* 35 He died and was buried in Samaria, and his son Jehoahaz succeeded him as king. 36 Jehu had ruled in Samaria as king of Israel for twenty-eight years.

Queen Athaliah of Judah
(2 Chronicles 22.10 − 23.15)

11 As soon as King Ahaziah's mother Athaliah learned of her son's murder, she gave orders for all the members of the royal family to be killed. 2 Only Ahaziah's son Joash escaped. He was about to be killed with the others, but was rescued by his aunt Jehosheba, who was King Jehoram's daughter and Ahaziah's half sister. She took him and his nurse into a bedroom in the Temple and hid him from Athaliah, so that he was not killed. 3 For six years Jehosheba took care of the boy and kept him hidden in the Temple, while Athaliah ruled as queen.

4 But in the seventh year Jehoiada the priest sent for the officers in charge of the royal bodyguard and of the palace guards, and told them to come to the Temple, where he made them agree under oath to what he planned to do. He showed them King Ahaziah's son Joash 5 and gave them the following orders: "When you come on duty on the Sabbath, one third of you are to guard the palace; 6 another third are to stand guard at the Sur Gate, and the other third are to stand guard at the gate behind the other guards. w 7 The two groups that go off duty on the Sabbath are to stand guard at the Temple to protect the king. 8 You are to guard King Joash with drawn swords and stay with him wherever he goes. Anyone who comes near you is to be killed."

9 The officers obeyed Jehoiada's instructions and brought their men to him — those going off duty on the

---

w *Hebrew has an additional word, the meaning of which is unclear.*
10.29 1 K 12.28-30

Sabbath and those going on duty. [10] He gave the officers the spears[x] and shields that had belonged to King David and had been kept in the Temple, [11] and he stationed the men with drawn swords all around the front of the Temple, to protect the king. [12] Then Jehoiada led Joash out, placed the crown on his head, and gave him a copy of the laws governing kingship. Then Joash was anointed and proclaimed king. The people clapped their hands and shouted, "Long live the king!"

[13] Queen Athaliah heard the noise being made by the guards and the people, so she hurried to the Temple, where the crowd had gathered. [14] There she saw the new king standing by the column at the entrance of the Temple, as was the custom. He was surrounded by the officers and the trumpeters, and the people were all shouting joyfully and blowing trumpets. Athaliah tore her clothes in distress and shouted, "Treason! Treason!"

Athaliah tore her clothes in distress. (11.14)

[15] Jehoiada did not want Athaliah killed in the Temple area, so he ordered the army officers: "Take her out between the rows of guards, and kill anyone who tries to rescue her." [16] They seized her, took her to the palace, and there at the Horse Gate they killed her.

Jehoiada's Reforms
(2 Chronicles 23.16-21)

[17] The priest Jehoiada had King Joash and the people make a covenant with the Lord that they would be the Lord's people; he also made a covenant between the king and the people. [18] Then the people went to the temple of Baal and tore it down; they smashed the altars and the idols, and killed Mattan, the priest of Baal, in front of the altars.

Jehoiada put guards on duty at the Temple, [19] and then he, the officers, the royal bodyguard, and the palace guards escorted the king from the Temple to the palace, followed by all the people. Joash entered by the Guard Gate and took his place on the throne. [20] All the people were filled with happiness, and the city was quiet, now that Athaliah had been killed in the palace.

[21] Joash became king of Judah at the age of seven.

King Joash of Judah
(2 Chronicles 24.1-16)

12 In the seventh year of the reign of King Jehu of Israel, Joash became king of Judah, and he ruled in Jerusalem for forty years. His mother was Zibiah from the city of Beersheba. [2] Throughout his life he did what pleased the Lord, because Jehoiada the priest instructed him. [3] However, the pagan places of worship were not destroyed, and the people continued to offer sacrifices and burn incense there.

[4] Joash called the priests and ordered them to save up the money paid in connection with the sacrifices in the Temple, both the dues paid for the regular sacrifices and the money given as freewill gifts. [5] Each priest was to be responsible for the money brought by those he served, and the money was to

---

[x] *Some ancient translations (and see 2 Ch 23.9)* spears; *Hebrew* spear.
11.14 2 K 23.3   **12.4** Ex 30.11-16

be used to repair the Temple, as needed.

6 But by the twenty-third year of Joash's reign the priests still had not made any repairs in the Temple. 7 So he called in Jehoiada and the other priests and asked them, "Why aren't you repairing the Temple? From now on you are not to keep the money you receive; you must hand it over, so that the repairs can be made." 8 The priests agreed to this and also agreed not to make the repairs in the Temple.

9 Then Jehoiada took a box, made a hole in the lid, and placed the box by the altar, on the right side as one enters the Temple. The priests on duty at the entrance put in the box all the money given by the worshipers. 10 Whenever there was a large amount of money in the box, the royal secretary and the High Priest would come, melt down the silver, and weigh it.y 11 After recording the exact amount, they would hand the silver over to the men in charge of the work in the Temple, and these would pay the carpenters, the builders, 12 the masons, and the stone cutters, buy the timber and the stones used in the repairs, and pay all other necessary expenses. 13 None of the money, however, was used to pay for making silver cups, bowls, trumpets, or tools for tending the lamps, or any other article of silver or of gold. 14 It was all used to pay the workers and to buy the materials used in the repairs. 15 The men in charge of the work were thoroughly honest, so there was no need to require them to account for the funds. 16 The money given for the repayment offerings and for the offerings for sin was not deposited in the box; it belonged to the priests.

17 At that time King Hazael of Syria attacked the city of Gath and conquered it; then he decided to attack Jerusalem.

18 King Joash of Judah took all the offerings that his predecessors Jehoshaphat, Jehoram, and Ahaziah had dedicated to the LORD, added to them his own offerings and all the gold in the treasuries of the Temple and the palace, and sent them all as a gift to King Hazael, who then led his army away from Jerusalem.

19 Everything else that King Joash did is recorded in *The History of the Kings of Judah.*

20-21 King Joash's officials plotted against him, and two of them, Jozacar son of Shimeath and Jehozabad son of Shomer, killed him at the house built on the land that was filled in on the east side of Jerusalem, on the road that goes down to Silla. Joash was buried in the royal tombs in David's City, and his son Amaziah succeeded him as king.

King Jehoahaz of Israel

13 In the twenty-third year of the reign of Joash son of Ahaziah as king of Judah, Jehoahaz son of Jehu became king of Israel, and he ruled in Samaria for seventeen years. 2 Like King Jeroboam before him, he sinned against the LORD and led Israel into sin; he never gave up his evil ways. 3 So the LORD was angry with Israel, and he allowed King Hazael of Syria and his son Benhadad to defeat Israel time after time. 4 Then Jehoahaz prayed to the LORD, and the LORD, seeing how harshly the king of Syria was oppressing the Israelites, answered his prayer. 5 The LORD sent Israel a leader, who freed them from the Syrians, and so the Israelites lived in peace, as before. 6 But they still did not give up the sins into which King Jeroboam had led Israel, but kept onz committing them; and

---

y melt down the silver, and weigh it; *or* count the money, and tie it up in bags.
z *Some ancient translations* kept on; *Hebrew* he kept on.
12.15 2 K 22.7   **12.16** Lv 7.7

the image of the goddess Asherah remained in Samaria.

7 Jehoahaz had no armed forces left except fifty cavalry troops, ten chariots, and ten thousand foot soldiers, because the king of Syria had destroyed the rest, trampling them down like dust.

8 Everything else that Jehoahaz did and all his brave deeds are recorded in *The History of the Kings of Israel.* 9 He died and was buried in Samaria, and his son Jehoash succeeded him as king.

King Jehoash of Israel

10 In the thirty-seventh year of the reign of King Joash of Judah, Jehoash son of Jehoahaz became king of Israel, and he ruled in Samaria for sixteen years. 11 He too sinned against the LORD and followed the evil example of King Jeroboam, who had led Israel into sin. 12 Everything else that Jehoash did, including his bravery in the war against King Amaziah of Judah, is recorded in *The History of the Kings of Israel.* 13 Jehoash died and was buried in the royal tombs in Samaria, and his son Jeroboam II succeeded him as king.

The Death of Elisha

14 The prophet Elisha was sick with a fatal disease, and as he lay dying, King Jehoash of Israel went to visit him. "My father, my father!" he exclaimed as he wept. "You have been the mighty defender of Israel!"

15 "Get a bow and some arrows," Elisha ordered him. Jehoash got them, 16 and Elisha told him to get ready to shoot. The king did so, and Elisha placed his hands on the king's hands. 17 Then, following the prophet's instructions, the king opened the window that faced toward Syria. "Shoot the arrow!" Elisha ordered. As soon as the king shot the arrow, the prophet exclaimed, "You are the LORD's arrow,

with which he will win victory over Syria. You will fight the Syrians in Aphek until you defeat them."

18 Then Elisha told the king to take the other arrows and strike the ground with them. The king struck the ground three times, and then stopped. 19 This made Elisha angry, and he said to the king, "You should have struck five or six times, and then you would have won complete victory over the Syrians; but now you will defeat them only three times."

20 Elisha died and was buried.

Every year bands of Moabites used to invade the land of Israel. 21 One time during a funeral, one of those bands was seen, and the people threw the corpse into Elisha's tomb and ran off.*a* As soon as the body came into contact with Elisha's bones, the man came back to life and stood up.

War between Israel and Syria

22 King Hazael of Syria oppressed the Israelites during all of Jehoahaz' reign, 23 but the LORD was kind and merciful to them. He would not let them be destroyed, but helped them because of his covenant with Abraham, Isaac, and Jacob. He has never forgotten his people.

24 At the death of King Hazael of Syria his son Benhadad became king. 25 Then King Jehoash of Israel defeated Benhadad three times and recaptured the cities that had been taken by Benhadad during the reign of Jehoahaz, the father of Jehoash.

King Amaziah of Judah
(2 Chronicles 25.1-24)

14 In the second year of the reign of Jehoash son of Jehoahaz as king of Israel, Amaziah son of Joash became king of Judah 2 at the age of twenty-five, and he ruled in Jerusalem for twenty-nine years. His mother was

---

a One ancient translation and ran off; *Hebrew* and he ran off.
13.14 2 K 2.12

Jehoaddin from Jerusalem. ³He did what was pleasing to the LORD, but he was not like his ancestor King David; instead, he did what his father Joash had done. ⁴He did not tear down the pagan places of worship, and the people continued to offer sacrifices and burn incense there.

⁵As soon as Amaziah was firmly in power, he executed the officials who had killed his father, the king. ⁶However, he did not kill their children but followed what the LORD had commanded in the Law of Moses: "Parents are not to be put to death for crimes committed by their children, and children are not to be put to death for crimes committed by their parents; people are to be put to death only for a crime they themselves have committed."

⁷Amaziah killed ten thousand Edomite soldiers in Salt Valley; he captured the city of Sela in battle and called it Joktheel, the name it still has.

⁸Then Amaziah sent messengers to King Jehoash of Israel, challenging him to fight.ᵇ ⁹But King Jehoash sent back the following reply: "Once a thorn bush on the Lebanon Mountains sent a message to a cedar: 'Give your daughter in marriage to my son.' A wild animal passed by and trampled the bush down. ¹⁰Now Amaziah, you have defeated the Edomites, and you are filled with pride. Be satisfied with your fame and stay at home. Why stir up trouble that will only bring disaster on you and your people?"

¹¹But Amaziah refused to listen, so King Jehoash marched out with his men and fought against him at Beth Shemesh in Judah. ¹²Amaziah's army was defeated, and all his soldiers fled to their homes. ¹³Jehoash took Amaziah prisoner, advanced on Jerusalem, and tore down the city wall from Ephraim Gate to the Corner Gate, a distance of two hundred yards. ¹⁴He took all the silver and gold he could find, all the Temple equipment and all the palace treasures, and carried them back to Samaria. He also took hostages with him.

¹⁵Everything else that Jehoash did, including his bravery in the war against King Amaziah of Judah, is recorded in *The History of the Kings of Israel.* ¹⁶Jehoash died and was buried in the royal tombs in Samaria, and his son Jeroboam II succeeded him as king.

The Death of King Amaziah of Judah
(2 Chronicles 25.25-28)

¹⁷King Amaziah of Judah lived fifteen years after the death of King Jehoash of Israel. ¹⁸Everything else that Amaziah did is recorded in *The History of the Kings of Judah.*

¹⁹There was a plot in Jerusalem to assassinate Amaziah, so he fled to the city of Lachish, but his enemies followed him there and killed him. ²⁰His body was carried back to Jerusalem on a horse and was buried in the royal tombs in David's City. ²¹The people of Judah then crowned his sixteen-year-old son Uzziah as king. ²²Uzziah reconquered and rebuilt Elath after his father's death.

King Jeroboam II of Israel

²³In the fifteenth year of the reign of Amaziah son of Joash as king of Judah, Jeroboam son of Jehoash became king of Israel, and he ruled in Samaria for forty-one years. ²⁴He sinned against the LORD, following the wicked example of his predecessor King Jeroboam son of Nebat, who led Israel into sin. ²⁵He reconquered all the territory that had belonged to Israel, from Hamath Pass in the north to the Dead Sea in the south. This was what the LORD, the God of Israel, had promised through his servant the prophet Jonah son of Amittai from Gath Hepher.

ᵇ challenging him to fight; *or* inviting him to a conference.
14.6 Dt 24.16   **14.25** Jon 1.1

²⁶The LORD saw the terrible*c* suffering of the Israelites; there was no one at all to help them. ²⁷But it was not the LORD's purpose to destroy Israel completely and forever, so he rescued them through King Jeroboam II.

²⁸Everything else that Jeroboam II did, his brave battles, and how he restored Damascus and Hamath to Israel,*d* are all recorded in *The History of the Kings of Israel.* ²⁹Jeroboam died and was buried in the royal tombs, and his son Zechariah succeeded him as king.

King Uzziah of Judah
(2 Chronicles 26.1-23)

15 In the twenty-seventh year of the reign of King Jeroboam II of Israel, Uzziah son of Amaziah became king of Judah ²at the age of sixteen, and he ruled in Jerusalem for fifty-two years. His mother was Jecoliah from Jerusalem. ³Following the example of his father, he did what was pleasing to the LORD. ⁴But the pagan places of worship were not destroyed, and the people continued to offer sacrifices and burn incense there. ⁵The LORD struck Uzziah with a dreaded skin disease that stayed with him the rest of his life. He lived in a separate house, relieved of all duties, while his son Jotham governed the country.

⁶Everything else that Uzziah did is recorded in *The History of the Kings of Judah.* ⁷Uzziah died and was buried in the royal burial ground in David's City, and his son Jotham succeeded him as king.

King Zechariah of Israel

⁸In the thirty-eighth year of the reign of King Uzziah of Judah, Zechariah son of Jeroboam II became king of Israel, and he ruled in Samaria for six months. ⁹He, like his predecessors, sinned against the LORD. He followed the wicked example of King Jeroboam son of Nebat, who led Israel into sin. ¹⁰Shallum son of Jabesh conspired against King Zechariah, assassinated him at Ibleam,*e* and succeeded him as king.

¹¹Everything else that Zechariah did is recorded in *The History of the Kings of Israel.*

¹²So the promise was fulfilled which the LORD had made to King Jehu: "Your descendants down to the fourth generation*f* will be kings of Israel."

King Shallum of Israel

¹³In the thirty-ninth year of the reign of King Uzziah of Judah, Shallum son of Jabesh became king of Israel, and he ruled in Samaria for one month.

¹⁴Menahem son of Gadi went from Tirzah to Samaria, assassinated Shallum, and succeeded him as king. ¹⁵Everything else that Shallum did, including an account of his conspiracy, is recorded in *The History of the Kings of Israel.* ¹⁶As Menahem was on his way from Tirzah, he completely destroyed the city of Tappuah,*g* its inhabitants, and the surrounding territory, because the city did not surrender to him. He even ripped open the bellies of all the pregnant women.

King Menahem of Israel

¹⁷In the thirty-ninth year of the reign of King Uzziah of Judah, Menahem son of Gadi became king of Israel, and he ruled in Samaria for ten years. ¹⁸He sinned against the LORD, for until the day of his death he followed the wicked

---

c Some ancient translations terrible; *Hebrew* rebellious.   *d One ancient translation* to Israel; *Hebrew* for Judah in Israel.   *e One ancient translation* at Ibleam; *Hebrew* before people.   *f* FOURTH GENERATION: *Zechariah was Jehu's great-great-grandson.*   *g One ancient translation* Tappuah; *Hebrew* Tiphsah.

15.7 Is 6.1   **15.12** 2 K 10.30

example of King Jeroboam son of Nebat, who led Israel into sin. ¹⁹Tiglath Pileser, the emperor of Assyria, invaded Israel, and Menahem gave him thirty-eight tons of silver to gain his support in strengthening Menahem's power over the country. ²⁰Menahem got the money from the rich men of Israel by forcing each one to contribute fifty pieces of silver. So Tiglath Pileser went back to his own country.

²¹Everything else that Menahem did is recorded in *The History of the Kings of Israel.* ²²He died and was buried, and his son Pekahiah succeeded him as king.

King Pekahiah of Israel

²³In the fiftieth year of the reign of King Uzziah of Judah, Pekahiah son of Menahem became king of Israel, and he ruled in Samaria for two years. ²⁴He sinned against the LORD, following the wicked example of King Jeroboam son of Nebat, who led Israel into sin. ²⁵An officer of Pekahiah's forces, Pekah son of Remaliah, plotted with fifty men from Gilead, assassinated Pekahiah in the palace's inner fortress *ʰ* in Samaria, and succeeded him as king.

²⁶Everything else that Pekahiah did is recorded in *The History of the Kings of Israel.*

King Pekah of Israel

²⁷In the fifty-second year of the reign of King Uzziah of Judah, Pekah son of Remaliah became king of Israel, and he ruled in Samaria for twenty years. ²⁸He sinned against the LORD, following the wicked example of King Jeroboam son of Nebat, who led Israel into sin.

²⁹It was while Pekah was king that Tiglath Pileser, the emperor of Assyria, captured the cities of Ijon, Abel Beth Maacah, Janoah, Kedesh, and Hazor, and the territories of Gilead, Galilee,

and Naphtali, and took the people to Assyria as prisoners.

³⁰In the twentieth year of the reign of Jotham son of Uzziah as king of Judah, Hoshea son of Elah plotted against King Pekah, assassinated him, and succeeded him as king. ³¹Everything else that Pekah did is recorded in *The History of the Kings of Israel.*

King Jotham of Judah
(2 Chronicles 27.1-9)

³²In the second year of the reign of Pekah son of Remaliah as king of Israel, Jotham son of Uzziah became king of Judah ³³at the age of twenty-five, and he ruled in Jerusalem for sixteen years. His mother was Jerusha, the daughter of Zadok. ³⁴Following the example of his father Uzziah, Jotham did what was pleasing to the LORD. ³⁵But the pagan places of worship were not destroyed, and the people continued to offer sacrifices and burn incense there. It was Jotham who built the North Gate of the Temple.

³⁶Everything else that Jotham did is recorded in *The History of the Kings of Judah.* ³⁷It was while he was king that the LORD first sent King Rezin of Syria and King Pekah of Israel to attack Judah. ³⁸Jotham died and was buried in the royal tombs in David's City, and his son Ahaz succeeded him as king.

King Ahaz of Judah
(2 Chronicles 28.1-27)

16 In the seventeenth year of the reign of Pekah son of Remaliah as king of Israel, Ahaz son of Jotham became king of Judah ²at the age of twenty, and he ruled in Jerusalem for sixteen years. He did not follow the good example of his ancestor King David; instead, he did what was not pleasing to the LORD his God ³and followed the example of the kings of Israel. He

---

ʰ Hebrew has two additional words, the meaning of which is unclear.
16.3 Dt 12.31

even sacrificed his own son as a burnt offering to idols, imitating the disgusting practice of the people whom the LORD had driven out of the land as the Israelites advanced. ⁴At the pagan places of worship, on the hills, and under every shady tree, Ahaz offered sacrifices and burned incense.

⁵King Rezin of Syria and King Pekah of Israel attacked Jerusalem and besieged it, but could not defeat Ahaz. (⁶At the same time the king of Edom*i* regained control of the city of Elath and drove out the Judeans who lived there. The Edomites settled in Elath and still live there.) ⁷Ahaz sent men to Tiglath Pileser, the emperor of Assyria, with this message: "I am your devoted servant. Come and rescue me from the kings of Syria and of Israel, who are attacking me." ⁸Ahaz took the silver and gold from the Temple and the palace treasury, and sent it as a present to the emperor. ⁹Tiglath Pileser, in answer to Ahaz' plea, marched out with his army against Damascus, captured it, killed King Rezin, and took the people to Kir as prisoners.

¹⁰When King Ahaz went to Damascus to meet Emperor Tiglath Pileser, he saw the altar there and sent back to Uriah the priest an exact model of it, down to the smallest details. ¹¹So Uriah built an altar just like it and finished it before Ahaz returned. ¹²On his return from Damascus, Ahaz saw that the altar was finished, ¹³so he burned animal sacrifices and grain offerings on it and poured a wine offering and the blood of a fellowship offering on it. ¹⁴The bronze altar dedicated to the LORD was between the new altar and the Temple, so Ahaz moved it to the north side of his new altar. ¹⁵Then he ordered Uriah: "Use this large altar of mine for the morning burnt offerings and the evening grain offerings, for the burnt offerings and grain offerings of the king and the people, and for the people's wine offerings. Pour on it the blood of all the animals that are sacrificed. But keep the bronze altar for me to use for divination." ¹⁶Uriah did as the king commanded.

¹⁷King Ahaz took apart the bronze carts used in the Temple and removed the basins that were on them. He also took the bronze tank from the backs of the twelve bronze bulls and placed it on a stone foundation. ¹⁸And in order to please the Assyrian emperor, Ahaz also removed from the Temple the platform for the royal throne and closed up the king's private entrance to the Temple.*j*

¹⁹Everything else that King Ahaz did is recorded in *The History of the Kings of Judah.* ²⁰Ahaz died and was buried in the royal tombs in David's City, and his son Hezekiah succeeded him as king.

King Hoshea of Israel

17 In the twelfth year of the reign of King Ahaz of Judah, Hoshea son of Elah became king of Israel, and he ruled in Samaria for nine years. ²He sinned against the LORD, but not as much as the kings who had ruled Israel before him. ³Emperor Shalmaneser of Assyria made war against him; Hoshea surrendered to Shalmaneser and paid him tribute every year. ⁴But one year Hoshea sent messengers to So, king of Egypt,*k* asking for his help, and stopped paying the annual tribute to Assyria. When Shalmaneser learned of this, he had Hoshea arrested and put in prison.

The Fall of Samaria

⁵Then Shalmaneser invaded Israel and besieged Samaria. In the third year of the siege, ⁶which was the ninth year of the reign of Hoshea, the Assyrian

---

i Probable text the king of Edom; *Hebrew* King Rezin of Syria.   *is unclear.*   *k So,* king of Egypt; *or* the king of Egypt at Sais.   *j Verse 18 in Hebrew*

16.5 Is 7.1 **16.14** Ex 27.1, 2; 2 Ch 4.1 **16.17** 1 K 7.23-39; 2 Ch 4.2-6 **16.20** Is 14.28

emperor *l* captured Samaria, took the Israelites to Assyria as prisoners, and settled some of them in the city of Halah, some near the Habor River in the district of Gozan and some in the cities of Media.

⁷Samaria fell because the Israelites sinned against the LORD their God, who had rescued them from the king of Egypt and had led them out of Egypt.

They worshiped other gods. (17.7)

They worshiped other gods, ⁸followed the customs of the people whom the LORD had driven out as his people advanced, and adopted customs introduced by the kings of Israel.*m* ⁹The Israelites did*n* things that the LORD their God disapproved of. They built pagan places of worship in all their towns, from the smallest village to the largest city. ¹⁰On all the hills and under every shady tree they put up stone pillars and images of the goddess Asherah, ¹¹and they burned incense on all the pagan altars, following the practice of the people whom the LORD had driven out of the land. They aroused the LORD's anger with all their wicked deeds ¹²and disobeyed the LORD's command not to worship idols.

¹³The LORD had sent his messengers and prophets to warn Israel and Judah: 'Abandon your evil ways and obey my commands, which are contained in the Law I gave to your ancestors and which

I handed on to you through my servants the prophets." ¹⁴But they would not obey; they were stubborn like their ancestors, who had not trusted in the LORD their God. ¹⁵They refused to obey his instructions, they did not keep the covenant he had made with their ancestors, and they disregarded his warnings. They worshiped worthless idols and became worthless themselves, and they followed the customs of the surrounding nations, disobeying the LORD's command not to imitate them. ¹⁶They broke all the laws of the LORD their God and made two metal bullcalves to worship; they also made an image of the goddess Asherah, worshiped the stars, and served the god Baal. ¹⁷They sacrificed their sons and daughters as burnt offerings to pagan gods; they consulted mediums and fortunetellers, and they devoted themselves completely to doing what is wrong in the LORD's sight, and so aroused his anger. ¹⁸The LORD was angry with the Israelites and banished them from his sight, leaving only the kingdom of Judah.

¹⁹But even the people of Judah did not obey the laws of the LORD their God; they imitated the customs adopted by the people of Israel. ²⁰The LORD rejected all the Israelites, punishing them and handing them over to cruel enemies until at last he had banished them from his sight.

²¹After the LORD had separated Israel from Judah, the Israelites made Jeroboam son of Nebat their king. Jeroboam caused them to abandon the LORD and led them into terrible sins. ²²They followed Jeroboam and continued to practice all the sins he had committed, ²³until at last the LORD banished them from his sight, as he had warned through his servants the prophets that he would do. So the

ASSYRIAN EMPEROR: *Probably Sargon II, the successor of Shalmaneser.*   *m Probable text and adopted ... Israel; Hebrew unclear.*   *n did; or said.*

17.10 1 K 14.23   **17.16** 1 K 12.28   **17.17** Dt 18.10

people of Israel were taken into exile to Assyria, where they still live.

The Assyrians Settle in Israel

24 The emperor of Assyria took people from the cities of Babylon, Cuth, Ivvah, Hamath, and Sepharvaim, and settled them in the cities of Samaria*o* in place of the exiled Israelites. They took possession of these cities and lived there. 25 When they first settled there, they did not worship the LORD, and so he sent lions, which killed some of them. 26 The emperor of Assyria was told that the people he had settled in the cities of Samaria did not know the law of the god of that land, and so the god had sent lions, which were killing them. 27 So the emperor commanded: "Send back one of the priests we brought as prisoners; have him*p* go back and live there, in order to teach the people the law of the god of that land." 28 So an Israelite priest who had been deported from Samaria went and lived in Bethel, where he taught the people how to worship the LORD.

29 But the people who settled in Samaria continued to make their own idols, and they placed them in the shrines that the Israelites had built. Each different group made idols in the cities they were living in: 30 the people of Babylon made idols of the god Succoth Benoth; the people of Cuth, idols of Nergal; the people of Hamath, idols of Ashima; 31 the people of Ivvah, idols of Nibhaz and Tartak; and the people of Sepharvaim sacrificed their children as burnt offerings to their gods Adrammelech and Anammelech. 32 These people also worshiped the LORD and chose from among their own number all sorts of people to serve as priests at the pagan places of worship and to offer sacrifices for them there. 33 So they worshiped the

LORD, but they also worshiped their own gods according to the customs of the countries from which they had come.

34 They still carry on their old customs to this day. They do not worship the LORD nor do they obey the laws and commands which he gave to the descendants of Jacob, whom he named Israel. 35 The LORD had made a covenant with them and had ordered them: "Do not worship other gods; do not bow down to them or serve them or offer sacrifices to them. 36 You shall obey me, the LORD, who brought you out of Egypt with great power and strength; you are to bow down to me and offer sacrifices to me. 37 You shall always obey the laws and commands that I wrote for you. You shall not obey other gods, 38 and you shall not forget the covenant I made with you. 39 You shall obey me, the LORD your God, and I will rescue you from your enemies." 40 But those people would not listen, and they continued to follow their old customs.

41 So those people worshiped the LORD, but they also worshiped their idols; and to this day their descendants continue to do the same.

King Hezekiah of Judah
(2 Chronicles 29.1, 2; 31.1)

18 In the third year of the reign of Hoshea son of Elah as king of Israel, Hezekiah son of Ahaz became king of Judah 2 at the age of twenty-five, and he ruled in Jerusalem for twenty-nine years. His mother was Abijah, the daughter of Zechariah. 3 Following the example of his ancestor King David, he did what was pleasing to the LORD. 4 He destroyed the pagan places of worship, broke the stone pillars, and cut down the images of the goddess Asherah. He also broke in pieces the bronze snake

---

o SAMARIA: *The name of the capital city was applied to the territory of the former kingdom of Israel.*   *p* *Some ancient translations* him; *Hebrew* them.
17.34 Gn 32.28; 35.10   **17.35** Ex 20.5; Dt 5.9   **17.36** Dt 6.13   **18.4** Nu 21.9

that Moses had made, which was called Nehushtan. Up to that time the people of Israel had burned incense in its honor. ⁵Hezekiah trusted in the LORD, the God of Israel; Judah never had another king like him, either before or after his time. ⁶He was faithful to the LORD and never disobeyed him, but carefully kept all the commands that the LORD had given Moses. ⁷So the LORD was with him, and he was successful in everything he did. He rebelled against the emperor of Assyria and refused to submit to him. ⁸He defeated the Philistines and raided their settlements, from the smallest village to the largest city, including Gaza and its surrounding territory.

⁹In the fourth year of Hezekiah's reign — which was the seventh year of King Hoshea's reign over Israel — Emperor Shalmaneser of Assyria invaded Israel and besieged Samaria. ¹⁰In the third year of the siege Samaria fell; this was the sixth year of Hezekiah's reign and the ninth year of Hoshea's reign. ¹¹The Assyrian emperor*q* took the Israelites to Assyria as prisoners and settled some of them in the city of Halah, some near the Habor River in the district of Gozan, and some in the cities of Media.

¹²Samaria fell because the Israelites did not obey the LORD their God, but broke the covenant he had made with them and disobeyed all the laws given by Moses, the servant of the LORD. They would not listen and they would not obey.

The Assyrians Threaten Jerusalem
(2 Chronicles 32.1-19; Isaiah 36.1-22)

¹³In the fourteenth year of the reign of King Hezekiah, Sennacherib, the emperor of Assyria, attacked the fortified cities of Judah and conquered them. ¹⁴Hezekiah sent a message to

Sennacherib . . . attacked the fortified cities. (18.13)

Sennacherib, who was in Lachish: "I have done wrong; please stop your attack, and I will pay whatever you demand." The emperor's answer was that Hezekiah should send him ten tons of silver and one ton of gold. ¹⁵Hezekiah sent him all the silver in the Temple and in the palace treasury; ¹⁶he also stripped the gold from the temple doors and the gold with which he himself had covered the doorposts, and he sent it all to Sennacherib. ¹⁷The Assyrian emperor sent a large army from Lachish to attack Hezekiah at Jerusalem; it was commanded by his three highest officials. When they arrived at Jerusalem, they occupied the road where the cloth makers work by the ditch that brings water from the upper pool. ¹⁸Then they sent for King Hezekiah, and three of his officials went out to meet them: Eliakim son of Hilkiah, who was in charge of the palace; Shebna, the court secretary; and Joah son of Asaph, who was in charge of the records. ¹⁹One of the Assyrian officials told them that the emperor wanted to know what made King Hezekiah so confident. ²⁰He demanded, "Do you think that words can take the place of military skill and might? Who do you think will help you rebel against Assyria? ²¹You are

q ASSYRIAN EMPEROR: *See 17.6.*

expecting Egypt to help you, but that would be like using a reed as a walking stick — it would break and jab your hand. That is what the king of Egypt is like when anyone relies on him."

22 The Assyrian official went on, "Or will you tell me that you are relying on the LORD your God? It was the LORD's shrines and altars that Hezekiah destroyed, when he told the people of Judah and Jerusalem to worship only at the altar in Jerusalem. 23 I will make a bargain with you in the name of the emperor. I will give you two thousand horses if you can find that many men to ride them! 24 You are no match for even the lowest ranking Assyrian official, and yet you expect the Egyptians to send you chariots and cavalry! 25 Do you think I have attacked your country and destroyed it without the LORD's help? The LORD himself told me to attack it and destroy it."

26 Then Eliakim, Shebna, and Joah told the official, "Speak Aramaic to us, sir. We understand it. Don't speak Hebrew; all the people on the wall are listening."

27 He replied, "Do you think you and the king are the only ones the emperor sent me to say all these things to? No, I am also talking to the people who are sitting on the wall, who will have to eat their excrement and drink their urine, just as you will."

28 Then the official stood up and shouted in Hebrew, "Listen to what the emperor of Assyria is telling you! 29 He warns you not to let Hezekiah deceive you. Hezekiah can't save you. 30 And don't let him persuade you to rely on the LORD. Don't think that the LORD will save you and that he will stop our Assyrian army from capturing your city. 31 Don't listen to Hezekiah. The emperor of Assyria commands you to come out of the city and surrender. You will all be allowed to eat grapes from your own vines and figs from your own trees, and to drink water from your own wells — 32 until the emperor resettles

you in a country much like your own, where there are vineyards to give wine and there is grain for making bread; it is a land of olives, olive oil, and honey. If you do what he commands, you will not die, but live. Don't let Hezekiah fool you into thinking that the LORD will rescue you. 33 Did the gods of any other nations save their countries from the emperor of Assyria? 34 Where are they now, the gods of Hamath and Arpad? Where are the gods of Sepharvaim, Hena, and Ivvah? Did anyone save Samaria? 35 When did any of the gods of all these countries ever save their country from our emperor? Then what makes you think the LORD can save Jerusalem?"

36 The people kept quiet, just as King Hezekiah had told them to; they did not say a word. 37 Then Eliakim, Shebna, and Joah tore their clothes in grief, and went and reported to the king what the Assyrian official had said.

The King Asks Isaiah's Advice
(Isaiah 37.1-7)

19 As soon as King Hezekiah heard their report, he tore his clothes in grief, put on sackcloth, and went to the Temple of the LORD. 2 He sent Eliakim, the official in charge of the palace, Shebna, the court secretary, and the senior priests to the prophet Isaiah son of Amoz. They also were wearing sackcloth. 3 This is the message which he told them to give Isaiah: "Today is a day of suffering; we are being punished and are in disgrace. We are like a woman who is ready to give birth, but is too weak to do it. 4 The Assyrian emperor has sent his chief official to insult the living God. May the LORD your God hear these insults and punish those who spoke them. So pray to God for those of our people who survive."

5 When Isaiah received King Hezekiah's message, 6 he sent back this an-

swer: "The LORD tells you not to let the Assyrians frighten you with their claims that he cannot save you. ⁷The LORD will cause the emperor to hear a rumor that will make him go back to his own country, and the LORD will have him killed there."

The Assyrians Send Another Threat
(Isaiah 37.8-20)

⁸The Assyrian official learned that the emperor had left Lachish and was fighting against the nearby city of Libnah; so he went there to consult him. ⁹Word reached the Assyrians that the Egyptian army, led by King Tirhakah of Ethiopia,ʳ was coming to attack them. When the emperor heard this, he sent a letter to King Hezekiah of Judah ¹⁰to tell him, "The god you are trusting in has told you that you will not fall into my hands, but don't let that deceive you. ¹¹You have heard what an Assyrian emperor does to any country he decides to destroy. Do you think that you can escape? ¹²My ancestors destroyed the cities of Gozan, Haran, and Rezeph, and killed the people of Betheden who lived in Telassar, and none of their gods could save them. ¹³Where are the kings of the cities of Hamath, Arpad, Sepharvaim, Hena, and Ivvah?"

¹⁴King Hezekiah took the letter from the messengers and read it. Then he went to the Temple, placed the letter there in the presence of the LORD, ¹⁵and prayed, "O LORD, the God of Israel, seated on your throne above the winged creatures, you alone are God, ruling all the kingdoms of the world. You created the earth and the sky. ¹⁶Now, LORD, look at what is happen-ing to us. Listen to all the things that Sennacherib is saying to insult you, the living God. ¹⁷We all know, LORD, that the emperors of Assyria have destroyed many nations, made their lands desolate, ¹⁸and burned up their gods — which were no gods at all, only images of wood and stone made by human hands. ¹⁹Now, LORD our God, rescue us from the Assyrians, so that all the nations of the world will know that only you, O LORD, are God."

Isaiah's Message to the King
(Isaiah 37.21-38)

²⁰Then Isaiah sent a message telling King Hezekiah that in answer to the king's prayer ²¹the LORD had said, "The city of Jerusalem laughs at you, Sennacherib, and makes fun of you. ²²Whom do you think you have been insulting and ridiculing? You have been disrespectful to me, the holy God of Israel. ²³You sent your messengers to boast to me that with all your chariots you had conquered the highest mountains of Lebanon. You boasted that there you cut down the tallest cedars and the finest cypress trees and that you reached the deepest parts of the forests. ²⁴You boasted that you dug wells and drank water in foreign lands and that the feet of your soldiers tramped the Nile River dry.

²⁵"Have you never heard that I planned all this long ago? And now I have carried it out. I gave you the power to turn fortified cities into piles of rubble. ²⁶The people who lived there were powerless; they were frightened and stunned. They were like grass in a field or weeds growing on a roof when the hot east wind blasts them.ˢ

ʳ *Hebrew* Cush: *Cush is the ancient name of the extensive territory south of the First Cataract of the Nile River. This region was called Ethiopia in Graeco-Roman times, and included within its borders most of modern Sudan and some of present-day Ethiopia (Abyssinia).* ˢ *Probable text* when the hot east wind blasts them; *Hebrew* blasted before they are grown.
19.15 Ex 25.22

27"But I know everything about you, what you do and where you go. I know how you rage against me. **28**I have received the report of that rage and that pride of yours, and now I will put a hook through your nose and a bit in your mouth, and take you back by the same road you came."

29Then Isaiah said to King Hezekiah, "Here is a sign of what will happen. This year and next you will have only wild grain to eat, but the following year you will be able to plant your grain and harvest it, and plant vines and eat grapes. **30**Those in Judah who survive will flourish like plants that send roots deep into the ground and produce fruit. **31**There will be people in Jerusalem and on Mount Zion who will survive, because the Lord is determined to make this happen.

32"And this is what the Lord has said about the Assyrian emperor: 'He will not enter this city or shoot a single arrow against it. No soldiers with shields will come near the city, and no siege mounds will be built around it. **33**He will go back by the same road he came, without entering this city. I, the Lord, have spoken. **34**I will defend this city and protect it, for the sake of my own honor and because of the promise I made to my servant David.'"

35That night an angel of the Lord went to the Assyrian camp and killed 185,000 soldiers. At dawn the next day there they lay, all dead! **36**Then the Assyrian emperor Sennacherib withdrew and returned to Nineveh. **37**One day, when he was worshiping in the temple of his god Nisroch, two of his sons, Adrammelech and Sharezer, killed him with their swords and then escaped to the land of Ararat. Another of his sons, Esarhaddon, succeeded him as emperor.

King Hezekiah's Illness and Recovery
(Isaiah 38.1-8, 21, 22; 2 Chronicles 32.24-26)

20 About this time King Hezekiah became sick and almost died. The prophet Isaiah son of Amoz went to see him and said to him, "The Lord tells you that you are to put everything in order, because you will not recover. Get ready to die."

2Hezekiah turned his face to the wall and prayed: **3**"Remember, Lord, that I have served you faithfully and loyally and that I have always tried to do what you wanted me to." And he began to cry bitterly.

4Isaiah left the king, but before he had passed through the central courtyard of the palace the Lord told him **5**to go back to Hezekiah, ruler of the Lord's people, and say to him, "I, the Lord, the God of your ancestor David, have heard your prayer and seen your tears. I will heal you, and in three days you will go to the Temple. **6**I will let you live fifteen years longer. I will rescue you and this city Jerusalem from the emperor of Assyria. I will defend this city, for the sake of my own honor and because of the promise I made to my servant David."

7Then Isaiah told the king's attendants to put on his boil a paste made of figs, and he would get well.*t* **8**King Hezekiah asked, "What is the sign to prove that the Lord will heal me and that three days later I will be able to go to the Temple?"

9Isaiah replied, "The Lord will give you a sign to prove that he will keep his promise. Now, would you prefer to have the shadow on the stairway go forward ten steps or go back ten steps?"*u*

---

*t One ancient translation (and see Is 38.21) figs, and he would get well; *Hebrew* figs. They did so, and he got well.   u stairway . . . steps . . . steps . . . ; *or* sundial . . . degrees . . . degrees.

¹⁰Hezekiah answered, "It's easy to have the shadow go forward ten steps!ᵛ Have it go back ten steps."ᵛ

¹¹Isaiah prayed to the LORD, and the LORD made the shadow go back ten stepsᵛ on the stairwayʷ set up by King Ahaz.

Messengers from Babylonia
(Isaiah 39.1-8)

¹²About that same time the king of Babylonia, Merodach Baladan, the son of Baladan, heard that King Hezekiah had been sick, so he sent him a letter and a present. ¹³Hezekiah welcomed the messengers and showed them his wealth — his silver and gold, his spices and perfumes, and all his military equipment. There was nothing in his storerooms or anywhere in his kingdom that he did not show them. ¹⁴Then the prophet Isaiah went to King Hezekiah and asked, "Where did these men come from and what did they say to you?"

Hezekiah answered, "They came from a very distant country, from Babylonia."

¹⁵"What did they see in the palace?"

"They saw everything. There is nothing in the storerooms that I didn't show them."

¹⁶Isaiah then told the king, "The LORD Almighty says that ¹⁷a time is coming when everything in your palace, everything that your ancestors have stored up to this day, will be carried off to Babylonia. Nothing will be left. ¹⁸Some of your own direct descendants will be taken away and made eunuchs to serve in the palace of the king of Babylonia."

¹⁹King Hezekiah understood this to mean that there would be peace and security during his lifetime, so he replied, "The message you have given me from the LORD is good."

The End of Hezekiah's Reign
(2 Chronicles 32.32, 33)

²⁰Everything else that King Hezekiah did, his brave deeds, and an account of how he built a reservoir and dug a tunnel to bring water into the city, are all recorded in *The History of the Kings of Judah.* ²¹Hezekiah died, and his son Manasseh succeeded him as king.

King Manasseh of Judah
(2 Chronicles 33.1-20)

21 Manasseh was twelve years old when he became king of Judah, and he ruled in Jerusalem for fifty-five years. His mother was Hephzibah. ²Following the disgusting practices of the nations whom the LORD had driven out of the land as his people advanced, Manasseh sinned against the LORD. ³He rebuilt the pagan places of worship that his father Hezekiah had destroyed; he built altars for the worship of Baal and made an image of the goddess Asherah, as King Ahab of Israel had done. Manasseh also worshiped the stars. ⁴He built pagan altars in the Temple, the place that the LORD had said was where he should be worshiped. ⁵In the two courtyards of the Temple he built altars for the worship of the stars. ⁶He sacrificed his son as a burnt offering. He practiced divination and magic and consultedˣ fortune-tellers and mediums. He sinned greatly against the LORD and stirred up his anger. ⁷He placed the symbol of the goddess Asherah in the Temple, the place about which the LORD had said to David and his son Solomon: "Here in

---

ᵛ steps; *or* degrees.   ʷ stairway; *or* sundial. *Archaeological evidence suggests that the stairway referred to in this passage was one specially constructed to tell time.*
ˣ consulted; *or* brought back.

20.17 2 K 24.13; 2 Ch 36.10   **20.18** 2 K 24.14, 15; Dn 1.1-7   **21.2** Jr 15.4   **21.4** 2 S 7.13
21.7, 8 1 K 9.3-5; 2 Ch 7.12-18

Jerusalem, in this Temple, is the place that I have chosen out of all the territory of the twelve tribes of Israel as the place where I am to be worshiped. ⁸And if the people of Israel will obey all my commands and keep the whole Law that my servant Moses gave them, then I will not allow them to be driven out of the land that I gave to their ancestors." ⁹But the people of Judah did not obey the LORD, and Manasseh led them to commit even greater sins than those committed by the nations whom the LORD had driven out of the land as his people advanced.

¹⁰Through his servants the prophets the LORD said, ¹¹"King Manasseh has done these disgusting things, things far worse than what the Canaanites did; and with his idols he has led the people of Judah into sin. ¹²So I, the LORD God of Israel, will bring such a disaster on Jerusalem and Judah that everyone who hears about it will be stunned. ¹³I will punish Jerusalem as I did Samaria, as I did King Ahab of Israel and his descendants. I will wipe Jerusalem clean of its people, as clean as a plate that has been wiped and turned upside down. ¹⁴I will abandon the people who survive, and will hand them over to their enemies, who will conquer them and plunder their land. ¹⁵I will do this to my people because they have sinned against me and have stirred up my anger from the time their ancestors came out of Egypt to this day."

¹⁶Manasseh killed so many innocent people that the streets of Jerusalem were flowing with blood; he did this in addition to leading the people of Judah into idolatry, causing them to sin against the LORD.

¹⁷Everything else that Manasseh did, including the sins he committed, is recorded in *The History of the Kings of Judah*. ¹⁸Manasseh died and was buried in the palace garden, the garden of Uzza, and his son Amon succeeded him as king.

King Amon of Judah
(2 Chronicles 33.21-25)

¹⁹Amon was twenty-two years old when he became king of Judah, and he ruled in Jerusalem for two years. His mother was Meshullemeth, the daughter of Haruz from the town of Jotbah. ²⁰Like his father Manasseh, he sinned against the LORD; ²¹he imitated his father's actions, and he worshiped the idols that his father had worshiped. ²²He rejected the LORD, the God of his ancestors, and disobeyed the LORD's commands.

²³Amon's officials plotted against him and assassinated him in the palace. ²⁴The people of Judah killed Amon's assassins and made his son Josiah king.

²⁵Everything else that Amon did is recorded in *The History of the Kings of Judah*. ²⁶Amon was buried in the tomb in the garden of Uzza, and his son Josiah succeeded him as king.

King Josiah of Judah
(2 Chronicles 34.1, 2)

22 Josiah was eight years old when he became king of Judah, and he ruled in Jerusalem for thirty-one years. His mother was Jedidah, the daughter of Adaiah from the town of Bozkath. ²Josiah did what was pleasing to the LORD; he followed the example of his ancestor King David, strictly obeying all the laws of God.

The Book of the Law Is Discovered
(2 Chronicles 34.8-28)

³In the eighteenth year of his reign, King Josiah sent the court secretary Shaphan, the son of Azaliah and grandson of Meshullam, to the Temple with the order: ⁴"Go to the High Priest Hilkiah and get a report on the amount of

22.1 Jr 3.6

money that the priests on duty at the entrance to the Temple have collected from the people. ⁵Tell him to give the money to the men who are in charge of the repairs in the Temple. They are to pay ⁶the carpenters, the builders, and the masons, and buy the timber and the stones used in the repairs. ⁷The men in charge of the work are thoroughly honest, so there is no need to require them to account for the funds."

⁸Shaphan delivered the king's order to Hilkiah, and Hilkiah told him that he had found the book of the Law in the Temple. Hilkiah gave him the book, and Shaphan read it. ⁹Then he went back to the king and reported: "Your servants have taken the money that was in the Temple and have handed it over to the men in charge of the repairs." ¹⁰And then he said, "I have here a book that Hilkiah gave me." And he read it aloud to the king.

¹¹When the king heard the book being read, he tore his clothes in dismay, ¹²and gave the following order to Hilkiah the priest, to Ahikam son of Shaphan, to Achbor son of Micaiah, to Shaphan, the court secretary, and to Asaiah, the king's attendant: ¹³"Go and consult the LORD for me and for all the people of Judah about the teachings of this book. The LORD is angry with us because our ancestors have not done what this book says must be done."

¹⁴Hilkiah, Ahikam, Achbor, Shaphan, and Asaiah went to consult a woman named Huldah, a prophet who lived in the newer part of Jerusalem. (Her husband Shallum, the son of Tikvah and grandson of Harhas, was in charge of the Temple robes.) They described to her what had happened, ⁵and she told them to go back to the king and give him ¹⁶the following message from the LORD: "I am going to punish Jerusalem and all its people, as written in the book that the king has read. ¹⁷They have rejected me and

have offered sacrifices to other gods, and so have stirred up my anger by all they have done. My anger is aroused against Jerusalem, and it will not die down. ¹⁸As for the king himself, this is what I, the LORD God of Israel, say: You listened to what is written in the book, ¹⁹and you repented and humbled yourself before me, tearing your clothes and weeping, when you heard how I threatened to punish Jerusalem and its people. I will make it a terrifying sight, a place whose name people will use as a curse. But I have heard your prayer, ²⁰and the punishment which I am going to bring on Jerusalem will not come until after your death. I will let you die in peace."

The men returned to King Josiah with this message.

Josiah Does Away with Pagan Worship
(2 Chronicles 34.3-7, 29-33)

23 King Josiah summoned all the leaders of Judah and Jerusalem, ²and together they went to the Temple, accompanied by the priests and the prophets and all the rest of the people, rich and poor alike. Before them all the king read aloud the whole book of the covenant which had been found in the Temple. ³He stood by the royal column and made a covenant with the LORD to obey him, to keep his laws and commands with all his heart and soul, and to put into practice the demands attached to the covenant, as written in the book. And all the people promised to keep the covenant.

⁴Then Josiah ordered the High Priest Hilkiah, his assistant priests, and the guards on duty at the entrance to the Temple to bring out of the Temple all the objects used in the worship of Baal, of the goddess Asherah, and of the stars. The king burned all these objects outside the city near Kidron Valley and then had the ashes taken to Bethel. ⁵He

removed from office the priests that the kings of Judah had ordained to offer sacrifices[y] on the pagan altars in the cities of Judah and in places near Jerusalem — all the priests who offered sacrifices to Baal, to the sun, the moon, the planets, and the stars. [6] He removed from the Temple the symbol of the goddess Asherah, took it out of the city to Kidron Valley, burned it, pounded its ashes to dust, and scattered it over the public burying ground. [7] He destroyed

The king burned all these objects outside the city. (23.4)

the living quarters in the Temple occupied by the temple prostitutes.[z] (It was there that women wove robes used in the worship of Asherah.) [8] He brought to Jerusalem the priests who were in the cities of Judah, and throughout the whole country he desecrated the altars where they had offered sacrifices. He also tore down the altars dedicated to the goat demons near the gate built by

Joshua, the city governor, which was to the left of the main gate as one enters the city. [9] Those priests were not allowed to serve in the Temple, but they could eat the unleavened bread provided for their fellow priests.

[10] King Josiah also desecrated Topheth, the pagan place of worship in Hinnom Valley, so that no one could sacrifice his son or daughter as a burnt offering to the god Molech. [11] He also removed the horses that the kings of Judah had dedicated to the worship of the sun, and he burned the chariots used in this worship. (These were kept in the temple courtyard, near the gate and not far from the living quarters of Nathan Melech, a high official.) [12] The altars which the kings of Judah had built on the palace roof above King Ahaz' quarters, King Josiah tore down, along with the altars put up by King Manasseh in the two courtyards of the Temple; he smashed the altars to bits[a] and threw them into Kidron Valley. [13] Josiah desecrated the altars that King Solomon had built east of Jerusalem, south of the Mount of Olives,[b] for the worship of disgusting idols — Astarte the goddess of Sidon, Chemosh the god of Moab, and Molech the god of Ammon. [14] King Josiah broke the stone pillars to pieces, cut down the symbols of the goddess Asherah, and the ground where they had stood he covered with human bones.

[15] Josiah also tore down the place of worship in Bethel, which had been built by King Jeroboam son of Nebat who led Israel into sin. Josiah pulled down the altar, broke its stones into pieces,[c] and pounded them to dust; he

[y] *Some ancient translations* to offer sacrifices; *Hebrew* and he offered sacrifices.
[z] TEMPLE PROSTITUTES: *Men and women who practiced prostitution in the worship of fertility gods.*   [a] *Probable text* smashed . . . to bits; *Hebrew unclear.*   [b] MOUNT OF OLIVES: *Hebrew here refers to it as "Mount of Destruction" or "Mount of Sin."*
[c] *One ancient translation* broke its stones into pieces; *Hebrew* burned the altar.
23.10 a Jr 7.31; 19.1-6; 32.35; **b** Lv 18.21   **23.12** 2 K 21.5; 2 Ch 33.5   **23.13** 1 K 11.7
23.15 1 K 12.33

also burned the image of Asherah.
¹⁶Then Josiah looked around and saw
some tombs there on the hill; he had
the bones taken out of them and
burned on the altar. In this way he desecrated the altar, doing what the
prophet had predicted long before during the festival as King Jeroboam was
standing by the altar. King Josiah
looked around and saw the tomb of
the prophet*d* who had made this
prediction. ¹⁷"Whose tomb is that?"
he asked.

The people of Bethel answered, "It is
the tomb of the prophet who came from
Judah and predicted these things that
you have done to this altar."

¹⁸"Leave it as it is," Josiah ordered.
"His bones are not to be moved."

So his bones were not moved, neither were those of the prophet who had
come from Samaria.

¹⁹In every city of Israel King Josiah
tore down all the pagan places of worship which had been built by the kings
of Israel, who thereby aroused the
LORD's anger. He did to all those altars
what he had done in Bethel. ²⁰He killed
all the pagan priests on the altars where
they served, and he burned human
bones on every altar. Then he returned
to Jerusalem.

Josiah Celebrates the Passover
(2 Chronicles 35.1-19)

²¹King Josiah ordered the people to
celebrate the Passover in honor of the
LORD their God, as written in the book
of the covenant. ²²No Passover like this
one had ever been celebrated by any of
the kings of Israel or of Judah, since the
time when judges ruled the nation.
²³Now at last, in the eighteenth year of
the reign of Josiah, the Passover was
celebrated in Jerusalem.

Other Changes Made by Josiah

²⁴In order to enforce the laws written
in the book that the High Priest Hilkiah
had found in the Temple, King Josiah
removed from Jerusalem and the rest of
Judah all the mediums and fortunetellers, and all the household gods, idols,
and all other pagan objects of worship.
²⁵There had never been a king like him
before, who served the LORD with all
his heart, mind, and strength, obeying
all the Law of Moses; nor has there
been a king like him since.

²⁶But the LORD's fierce anger had
been aroused against Judah by what
King Manasseh had done, and even
now it did not die down. ²⁷The LORD
said, "I will do to Judah what I have
done to Israel: I will banish the people
of Judah from my sight, and I will reject
Jerusalem, the city I chose, and the
Temple, the place I said was where I
should be worshiped."

The End of Josiah's Reign
(2 Chronicles 35.20 − 36.1)

²⁸Everything else that King Josiah
did is recorded in *The History of the
Kings of Judah*. ²⁹While Josiah was
king, King Neco of Egypt led an army
to the Euphrates River to help the emperor of Assyria. King Josiah tried to
stop the Egyptian army at Megiddo and
was killed in battle. ³⁰His officials
placed his body in a chariot and took it
back to Jerusalem, where he was buried in the royal tombs.

The people of Judah chose Josiah's
son Joahaz and anointed him king.

King Joahaz of Judah
(2 Chronicles 36.2-4)

³¹Joahaz was twenty-three years old
when he became king of Judah, and he
ruled in Jerusalem for three months.

---

d One ancient translation during the festival . . . the prophet; *Hebrew does not have
these words.*

23.16 1 K 13.2　　**23.17** 1 K 13.30-32

His mother was Hamutal, the daughter of Jeremiah from the city of Libnah. ³²Following the example of his ancestors, he sinned against the LORD. ³³His reign ended when King Neco of Egypt took him prisoner in Riblah, in the land of Hamath, and made Judah pay 7,500 pounds of silver and 75 pounds of gold as tribute. ³⁴King Neco made Josiah's son Eliakim king of Judah as successor to Josiah, and changed his name to Jehoiakim. Joahaz was taken to Egypt by King Neco, and there he died.

King Jehoiakim of Judah
(2 Chronicles 36.5-8)

³⁵King Jehoiakim collected a tax from the people in proportion to their wealth, in order to raise the amount needed to pay the tribute demanded by the king of Egypt.

³⁶Jehoiakim was twenty-five years old when he became king of Judah, and he ruled in Jerusalem for eleven years. His mother was Zebidah, the daughter of Pedaiah from the town of Rumah. ³⁷Following the example of his ancestors, Jehoiakim sinned against the LORD.

24 While Jehoiakim was king, King Nebuchadnezzar of Babylonia invaded Judah, and for three years Jehoiakim was forced to submit to his rule; then he rebelled. ²The LORD sent armed bands of Babylonians, Syrians, Moabites, and Ammonites against Jehoiakim to destroy Judah, as the LORD had said through his servants the prophets that he would do. ³This happened at the LORD's command, in order to banish the people of Judah from his sight because of all the sins that King Manasseh had committed, ⁴and especially because of all the innocent people he had killed. The LORD could not forgive Manasseh for that.

⁵Everything that Jehoiakim did is recorded in *The History of the Kings of Judah*. ⁶Jehoiakim died, and his son Jehoiachin succeeded him as king.

⁷The king of Egypt and his army never marched out of Egypt again, because the king of Babylonia now controlled all the territory that had belonged to Egypt, from the Euphrates River to the northern border of Egypt.

King Jehoiachin of Judah
(2 Chronicles 36.9, 10)

⁸Jehoiachin was eighteen years old when he became king of Judah, and he ruled in Jerusalem for three months. His mother was Nehushta, the daughter of Elnathan from Jerusalem. ⁹Following the example of his father, Jehoiachin sinned against the LORD.

¹⁰It was during his reign that the Babylonian army, commanded by King Nebuchadnezzar's officers, marched against Jerusalem and besieged it. ¹¹During the siege Nebuchadnezzar himself came to Jerusalem, ¹²and King Jehoiachin, along with his mother, his sons, his officers, and the palace officials, surrendered to the Babylonians. In the eighth year of Nebuchadnezzar's reign he took Jehoiachin prisoner ¹³and carried off to Babylon all the treasures in the Temple and the palace. As the LORD had foretold, Nebuchadnezzar broke up all the gold utensils which King Solomon had made for use in the Temple. ¹⁴Nebuchadnezzar carried away as prisoners the people of Jerusalem, all the royal princes, and all the leading men, ten thousand in all. He also deported all the skilled workers, including the blacksmiths, leaving only the poorest of the people behind in Judah.

¹⁵Nebuchadnezzar took Jehoiachin to Babylon as a prisoner, together with Jehoiachin's mother, his wives, his officials, and the leading men of Judah.

23.34 Jr 22.11, 12   **23.36** Jr 22.18, 19; 26.1-6; 35.1-19   **24.1** Jr 25.1-38; Dn 1.1, 2
24.12 Jr 22.24-30; 24.1-10; 29.1, 2   **24.15** Ez 17.12

⁶Nebuchadnezzar deported all the important men to Babylonia, seven thousand in all, and one thousand skilled workers, including the blacksmiths, all of them able-bodied men fit for military duty.

¹⁷Nebuchadnezzar made Jehoiachin's uncle Mattaniah king of Judah and changed his name to Zedekiah.

King Zedekiah of Judah
(2 Chronicles 36.11, 12; Jeremiah 52.1-3a)

¹⁸Zedekiah was twenty-one years old when he became king of Judah, and he ruled in Jerusalem for eleven years. His mother was Hamutal, the daughter of Jeremiah from the city of Libnah. ¹⁹King Zedekiah sinned against the LORD, just as King Jehoiakim had done. ²⁰The LORD became so angry with the people of Jerusalem and Judah that he banished them from his sight.

The Fall of Jerusalem
(2 Chronicles 36.13-21; Jeremiah 52.3b-11)

25 Zedekiah rebelled against King Nebuchadnezzar of Babylonia, and so Nebuchadnezzar came with all his army and attacked Jerusalem on the tenth day of the tenth month of the ninth year of Zedekiah's reign. They set up camp outside the city, built siege walls around it, ²and kept it under siege until Zedekiah's eleventh year. ³On the ninth day of the fourth month*ᵉ* of that same year, when the famine was so bad that the people had nothing left to eat, ⁴the city walls were broken through. Although the Babylonians were surrounding the city, all the soldiers escaped during the night. They left by way of the royal garden, went through the gateway connecting the two walls, and fled in the direction of the Jordan Valley. ⁵But the Babylonian army pursued King Zedekiah, captured him in the plains near Jericho, and all his soldiers deserted him. ⁶Zedekiah was taken to King Nebuchadnezzar, who was in the city of Riblah, and there Nebuchadnezzar passed sentence on him. ⁷While Zedekiah was looking on, his sons were put to death; then Nebuchadnezzar had Zedekiah's eyes put out, placed him in chains, and took him to Babylon.

The Destruction of the Temple
(Jeremiah 52.12-33)

⁸On the seventh day of the fifth month of the nineteenth year of King Nebuchadnezzar of Babylonia, Nebuzaradan, adviser to the king and commander of his army, entered Jerusalem. ⁹He burned down the Temple, the palace, and the houses of all the important people in Jerusalem, ¹⁰and his soldiers tore down the city walls. ¹¹Then Nebuzaradan took away to Babylonia the people who were left in the city, the remaining skilled workers,*ᶠ* and those who had deserted to the Babylonians. ¹²But he left in Judah some of the poorest people, who owned no property, and put them to work in the vineyards and fields.

¹³The Babylonians broke in pieces the bronze columns and the carts that were in the Temple, together with the large bronze tank, and they took all the bronze to Babylon. ¹⁴They also took away the shovels and the ash containers used in cleaning the altar, the tools used in tending the lamps, the bowls used for catching the blood from the

---

ᵉ *Probable text (see Jr 52.6)* the fourth month; *Hebrew* the month.   ᶠ *Probable text (see Jr 52.15)* skilled workers; *Hebrew* crowd.

24.17 Jr 37.1; Ez 17.13   **24.18** Jr 27.1-22; 28.1-17   **24.20** Ez 17.15   **25.1** Jr 21.1-10; 34.1-5; Ez 24.2   **25.4** Ez 33.21   **25.7** Ez 12.13   **25.9** 1 K 9.8   **25.13 a** 1 K 7.15-26; 2 Ch 3.15-17; **b** 1 K 7.23-26; 2 Ch 4.2-5   **25.14** 1 K 7.45; 2 Ch 4.16

sacrifices, the bowls used for burning incense, and all the other bronze articles used in the Temple service. [15] They took away everything that was made of gold or silver, including the small bowls and the pans used for carrying live coals. [16] The bronze objects that King Solomon had made for the Temple — the two columns, the carts, and the large tank — were too heavy to weigh. [17] The two columns were identical: each one was 27 feet high, with a bronze capital on top, 4½ feet high. All around each capital was a bronze grillwork decorated with pomegranates made of bronze.

The People of Judah Are Taken to Babylonia
(Jeremiah 52.24-27)

[18] In addition, Nebuzaradan, the commanding officer, took away as prisoners Seraiah the High Priest, Zephaniah the priest next in rank, and the three other important Temple officials. [19] From the city he took the officer who had been in command of the troops, five of the king's personal advisers who were still in the city, the commander's assistant, who was in charge of military records, and sixty other important men. [20] Nebuzaradan took them to the king of Babylonia, who was in the city of Riblah [21] in the territory of Hamath. There the king had them beaten and put to death.

So the people of Judah were carried away from their land into exile.

Gedaliah, Governor of Judah
(Jeremiah 40.7-9; 41.1-3)

[22] King Nebuchadnezzar of Babylonia made Gedaliah, the son of Ahikam and grandson of Shaphan, governor of Judah, and placed him in charge of all those who had not been taken away to Babylonia. [23] When the Judean officers and soldiers who had not surrendered heard about this, they joined Gedaliah at Mizpah. These officers were Ishmael son of Nethaniah, Johanan son of Kareah, Seraiah son of Tanhumeth from the town of Netophah, and Jezaniah from Maacah. [24] Gedaliah said to them, "I give you my word that there is no need for you to be afraid of the Babylonian officials. Settle in this land, serve the king of Babylonia, and all will go well with you."

[25] But in the seventh month of that year, Ishmael, the son of Nethaniah and grandson of Elishama, a member of the royal family, went to Mizpah with ten men, attacked Gedaliah, and killed him. He also killed the Israelites and Babylonians who were there with him. [26] Then all the Israelites, rich and poor alike, together with the army officers, left and went to Egypt, because they were afraid of the Babylonians.

Jehoiachin Is Released from Prison
(Jeremiah 52.31-34)

[27] In the year that Evilmerodach became king of Babylonia, he showed kindness to King Jehoiachin of Judah by releasing him from prison. This happened on the twenty-seventh day of the twelfth month of the thirty-seventh year after Jehoiachin had been taken away as prisoner. [28] Evilmerodach treated him kindly and gave him a position of greater honor than he gave the other kings who were exiles with him in Babylonia. [29] So Jehoiachin was permitted to change from his prison clothes and to dine at the king's table for the rest of his life. [30] Each day, for as long as he lived, he was given a regular allowance for his needs.

25.22-24 Jr 40.7-9   25.25 Jr 41.1-3   25.26 Jr 43.5-7

The First Book of
CHRONICLES

INTRODUCTION

First and *Second Chronicles* are largely a retelling of events recorded in the books of *Samuel* and *Kings,* but from a different point of view. Two main purposes govern the account of the history of the Israelite monarchy in the books of *Chronicles:*

1) To show that in spite of the disasters that had fallen upon the kingdoms of Israel and Judah, God was still keeping his promises to the nation and was working out his plan for his people through those who were living in Judah. As a basis for this assurance, the writer looked to the great achievements of David and Solomon, to the reforms of Jehoshaphat, Hezekiah, and Josiah, and to the people who remained faithful to God.

2) To describe the origin of the worship of God in the Temple at Jerusalem and especially the organization of the priests and Levites, by which the worship was carried out. David is presented as the real founder of the Temple and its ritual, even though it is Solomon who builds the Temple.

OUTLINE OF CONTENTS

From Adam to Abraham
(Genesis 5.1-32; 10.1-32; 11.10-26)

1 Adam was the father of Seth, Seth was the father of Enosh, Enosh the father of Kenan, ² Kenan the father of Mahalalel, Mahalalel the father of Jared. ³ Jared was the father of Enoch, who was the father of Methuselah; Methuselah was the father of Lamech, ⁴ who was the father of Noah. Noah had three sons: Shem, Ham, and Japheth.

⁵ The sons of Japheth — Gomer, Magog, Madai, Javan, Tubal, Meshech, and Tiras — were the ancestors of the peoples who bear their names. ⁶ The descendants of Gomer were the people of Ashkenaz, Riphath, and Togarmah. ⁷ The descendants of Javan were the people of Elishah, Spain, Cyprus, and Rhodes.

⁸ The sons of Ham — Cush, Egypt, Libya, and Canaan — were the ancestors of the peoples who bear their names. ⁹ The descendants of Cush were the people of Seba, Havilah, Sabtah, Raamah, and Sabteca. The descendants of Raamah were the people of Sheba and Dedan. (¹⁰ Cush had a son named Nimrod, who became the world's first great conqueror.) ¹¹ The descendants of Egypt were the people of Lydia, Anam, Lehab, Naphtuh,

12 Pathrus, Casluh, and of Crete (from whom the Philistines were descended). 13 Canaan's sons — Sidon, the oldest, and Heth — were the ancestors of the peoples who bear their names. 14 Canaan was also the ancestor of the Jebusites, the Amorites, Girgashites, 15 Hivites, Arkites, Sinites, 16 Arvadites, Zemarites, and Hamathites.

17 Shem's sons — Elam, Asshur, Arpachshad, Lud, Aram, Uz, Hul, Gether, and Meshek — were the ancestors of the peoples who bear their names. 18 Arpachshad was the father of Shelah, who was the father of Eber. 19 Eber had two sons; one was named Peleg,*a* because during his time the people of the world were divided, and the other was named Joktan. 20 The descendants of Joktan were the people of Almodad, Sheleph, Hazarmaveth, Jerah, 21 Hadoram, Uzal, Diklah, 22 Ebal, Abimael, Sheba, 23 Ophir, Havilah, and Jobab.

24 The family line from Shem to Abram is as follows: Shem, Arpachshad, Shelah, 25 Eber, Peleg, Reu, 26 Serug, Nahor, Terah, 27 and Abram (also known as Abraham).

The Descendants of Ishmael
(Genesis 25.12-16)

28 Abraham had two sons, Isaac and Ishmael. 29 The sons of Ishmael became the heads of twelve tribes: Nebaioth (from the name of Ishmael's oldest son), Kedar, Adbeel, Mibsam, 30 Mishma, Dumah, Massa, Hadad, Tema, 31 Jetur, Naphish, and Kedemah.

32 Abraham had a concubine named Keturah, who bore him six sons: Zimran, Jokshan, Medan, Midian, Ishbak, and Shuah. Jokshan had two sons: Sheba and Dedan. 33 Midian had five sons: Ephah, Epher, Hanoch, Abida, and Eldaah.

The Descendants of Esau
(Genesis 36.1-19)

34 Abraham's son Isaac had two sons, Esau and Jacob. 35 Esau's sons were Eliphaz, Reuel, Jeush, Jalam, and Korah. 36 Eliphaz became the ancestor of the following tribes: Teman, Omar, Zephi, Gatam, Kenaz, Timna, and Amalek. 37 And Reuel became the ancestor of the tribes of Nahath, Zerah, Shammah, and Mizzah.

The Original Inhabitants of Edom
(Genesis 36.20-30)

38-42 The original inhabitants of Edom were descended from the following sons of Seir:

Lotan, who was the ancestor of the clans of Hori and Homam. (Lotan had a sister named Timna.)

Shobal, who was the ancestor of the clans of Alvan, Manahath, Ebal, Shephi, and Onam.

Zibeon, who had two sons, Aiah and Anah. Anah was the father of Dishon, and Dishon was the ancestor of the clans of Hamran, Eshban, Ithran, and Cheran.

Ezer, who was the ancestor of the clans of Bilhan, Zaavan, and Jaakan.

Dishan, who was the ancestor of the clans of Uz and Aran.

The Kings of Edom
(Genesis 36.31-43)

43-50 The following kings ruled the land of Edom one after the other, in the time before there were any kings in Israel:

Bela son of Beor from
    Dinhabah
Jobab son of Zerah from
    Bozrah
Husham from the region of
    Teman

---

a PELEG: *This name sounds like the Hebrew for "divide."*

Hadad son of Bedad from Avith (he defeated the Midianites in a battle in the country of Moab)

Samlah from Masrekah

Shaul from Rehoboth-on-the-River

Baal Hanan son of Achbor

Hadad from Pau (his wife was Mehetabel, the daughter of Matred and granddaughter of Mezahab)

⁵¹ The people of Edom were divided into the following tribes: Timna, Alvah, Jetheth, ⁵² Oholibamah, Elah, Pinon, ⁵³ Kenaz, Teman, Mibzar, ⁵⁴ Magdiel, and Iram.

The Descendants of Judah

2 Jacob had twelve sons: Reuben, Simeon, Levi, Judah, Issachar, Zebulun, ² Dan, Joseph, Benjamin, Naphtali, Gad, and Asher.

³ Judah had five sons in all. By his wife Bathshua, a Canaanite, he had three sons: Er, Onan, and Shelah. His oldest son, Er, was so evil that the LORD killed him. ⁴ By his daughter-in-law Tamar, Judah had two more sons, Perez and Zerah.

⁵ Perez had two sons, Hezron and Hamul. ⁶ His brother Zerah had five sons: Zimri, Ethan, Heman, Calcol, and Darda. ⁷ Achan[b] son of Carmi, one of Zerah's descendants, brought disaster on the people of Israel by keeping loot that had been devoted to God.

⁸ Ethan had one son, Azariah.

The Family Tree of King David

⁹ Hezron had three sons: Jerahmeel, Ram, and Caleb.

¹⁰ The family line from Ram to Jesse is as follows: Ram, Amminadab, Nahshon (a prominent man of the tribe of Judah), ¹¹ Salmon, Boaz, ¹² Obed, and Jesse.

¹³ Jesse had seven sons. In order of age they were: Eliab, Abinadab, Shammah, ¹⁴ Nethanel, Raddai, ¹⁵ Ozem, and David. ¹⁶ He also had two daughters, Zeruiah and Abigail.

Jesse's daughter Zeruiah had three sons: Abishai, Joab, and Asahel. ¹⁷ His other daughter Abigail married Jether, a descendant of Ishmael, and they had a son named Amasa.

The Descendants of Hezron

¹⁸ Hezron's son Caleb married Azubah and had a daughter named Jerioth. She had[c] three sons: Jesher, Shobab, and Ardon. ¹⁹ After the death of Azubah, Caleb married Ephrath, and they had a son named Hur. ²⁰ Hur's son was Uri, and his grandson was Bezalel.

²¹ When Hezron was sixty years old, he married Machir's daughter, the sister of Gilead. They had a son named Segub, ²² and Segub had a son named Jair. Jair ruled[d] twenty-three cities in the territory of Gilead. ²³ But the kingdoms of Geshur and Aram conquered sixty towns there, including the villages of Jair and Kenath, and the towns nearby. All the people who lived there were descendants of Machir, the father of Gilead. ²⁴ After Hezron died, his son Caleb married Ephrath, his father's widow.[e] They had a son named Ashhur, who founded the town of Tekoa.

The Descendants of Jerahmeel

²⁵ Jerahmeel, the oldest son of Hezron, had five sons: Ram, the oldest, Bunah, Oren, Ozem, and Ahijah. ²⁶-²⁷ Ram

---

[b] ACHAN: *This is his name in Js 7.1. The Hebrew text here calls him "Achar," which means "disaster."* [c] *Some ancient translations had a daughter. . . . She had; Hebrew unclear.* [d] ruled; *or* owned. [e] *Some ancient translations his son . . . widow; Hebrew unclear.*

2.7 Js 7.1

had three sons: Maaz, Jamin, and Eker. Jerahmeel had another wife, a woman named Atarah, and they had a son, Onam. 28 Onam had two sons, Shammai and Jada, and Shammai also had two sons, Nadab and Abishur.

29 Abishur married a woman named Abihail, and they had two sons, Ahban and Molid. 30 Abishur's brother Nadab had two sons. Seled and Appaim, but Seled died without having any sons. 31 Appaim was the father of Ishi, Ishi was the father of Sheshan, and Sheshan the father of Ahlai.

32 Jada, the brother of Shammai, had two sons, Jether and Jonathan, but Jether died without having any sons. 33 Jonathan had two sons, Peleth and Zaza. All these were descendants of Jerahmeel.

34 Sheshan had no sons, only daughters. He had an Egyptian servant named Jarha, 35 to whom he gave one of his daughters in marriage. They had a son named Attai. 36 The family line from Attai to Elishama is as follows: Attai, Nathan, Zabad, 37 Ephlal, Obed, 38 Jehu, Azariah, 39 Helez, Eleasah, 40 Sismai, Shallum, 41 Jekamiah, and Elishama.

Other Descendants of Caleb

42 The oldest son of Caleb, Jerahmeel's brother, was named Mesha. Mesha was the father of Ziph, who was the father of Mareshah, who was the father of Hebron.f 43 Hebron had four sons: Korah, Tappuah, Rekem, and Shema. 44 Shema was the father of Raham and the grandfather of Jorkeam. Rekem, Shema's brother, was the father of Shammai, 45 who was the father of Maon, who was the father of Bethzur.

46 Caleb had a concubine named Ephah, and by her he had three more sons: Haran, Moza, and Gazez. Haran also had a son named Gazez.

(47 A man named Jahdai had six sons: Regem, Jotham, Geshan, Pelet, Ephah, and Shaaph.)

48 Caleb had another concubine, Maacah, who bore him two sons, Sheber and Tirhanah. 49 Later she had two more sons: Shaaph, who founded the town of Madmannah; and Shevah, who founded the towns of Machbenah and Gibea.

In addition, Caleb had a daughter named Achsah.

50 The following are also descendants of Caleb.

Hur was the oldest son of Caleb and his wife Ephrath. Hur's son Shobal founded Kiriath Jearim, 51 his second son Salma founded Bethlehem, and his third son Hareph founded Bethgader.

52 Shobal, the founder of Kiriath Jearim, was the ancestor of the people of Haroeh, of half the inhabitants of Menuhoth, 53 and of the following clans that lived in Kiriath Jearim: the Ithrites, Puthites, Shumathites, and Mishraites. (The people of the cities of Zorah and Eshtaol were members of these clans.)

54 Salma, the founder of Bethlehem, was the ancestor of the people of Netophath, of Atroth Beth Joab, and of the Zorites, who were one of the two clans in Manahath.

(55 The following clans of experts in writing and copying documents lived in the town of Jabez: the Tirathites, Shimeathites, and Sucathites. They were Kenites who had intermarried with the Rechabites.)

King David's Children

3 1-3 The following, in order of age, are David's sons who were born while he was in Hebron:

Amnon, whose mother was
Ahinoam from Jezreel
Daniel, whose mother was
Abigail from Carmel

f Probable text father of Mareshah . . . Hebron; Hebrew unclear.

Absalom, whose mother was
   Maacah, daughter of King
   Talmai of Geshur
Adonijah, whose mother was
   Haggith
Shephatiah, whose mother
   was Abital
Ithream, whose mother was
   Eglah

⁴All six were born in Hebron during the seven and a half years that David ruled there.

In Jerusalem he ruled as king for thirty-three years, ⁵and many sons were born to him there.

His wife Bathsheba, daughter of Ammiel, bore him four sons: Shimea, Shobab, Nathan, and Solomon.

⁶He had nine other sons: Ibhar, Elishua, Elpelet, ⁷Nogah, Nepheg, Japhia, ⁸Elishama, Eliada, and Eliphelet. ⁹In addition to all these sons, David had sons by his concubines. He also had a daughter, Tamar.

The Descendants of King Solomon

¹⁰This is the line of King Solomon's descendants from father to son: Solomon, Rehoboam, Abijah, Asa, Jehoshaphat, ¹¹Jehoram, Ahaziah, Joash, ¹²Amaziah, Uzziah, Jotham, ¹³Ahaz, Hezekiah, Manasseh, ¹⁴Amon, and Josiah. ¹⁵Josiah had four sons: Johanan, Jehoiakim, Zedekiah, and Joahaz. ¹⁶Jehoiakim had two sons: Jehoiachin and Zedekiah.

The Descendants of King Jehoiachin

¹⁷These are the descendants of King Jehoiachin, who was taken prisoner by the Babylonians. Jehoiachin had seven sons: Shealtiel, ¹⁸Malchiram, Pedaiah, Shenazzar, Jekamiah, Hoshama, and Nedabiah. ¹⁹Pedaiah had two sons, Zerubbabel and Shimei. Zerubbabel was

the father of two sons, Meshullam and Hananiah, and one daughter, Shelomith. ²⁰He had five other sons: Hashubah, Ohel, Berechiah, Hasadiah, and Jushab Hesed.

²¹Hananiah had two sons, Pelatiah and Jeshaiah. Jeshaiah was the father of Rephaiah, who was the father of Arnan, the father of Obadiah, the father of Shecaniah.ᵍ ²²Shecaniah had one son, Shemaiah, and five grandsons: Hattush, Igal, Bariah, Neariah, and Shaphat. ²³Neariah had three sons: Elioenai, Hizkiah, and Azrikam. ²⁴Elioenai had seven sons: Hodaviah, Eliashib, Pelaiah, Akkub, Johanan, Delaiah, and Anani.

The Descendants of Judah

4 These are some of the descendants of Judah: Perez, Hezron, Carmi, Hur, and Shobal. ²Shobal was the father of Reaiah, who was the father of Jahath, the father of Ahumai and Lahad, the ancestors of the people who lived in Zorah.

³⁻⁴Hur was the oldest son of his father Caleb's wife Ephrath, and his descendants founded the city of Bethlehem. Hur had three sons: Etam, Penuel, and Ezer. Etam had three sons:ʰ Jezreel, Ishma, and Idbash, and one daughter, Hazzelelponi. Penuel founded the city of Gedor, and Ezer founded Hushah.

⁵Ashhur, who founded the town of Tekoa, had two wives, Helah and Naarah. ⁶He and Naarah had four sons: Ahuzzam, Hepher, Temeni, and Haahashtari. ⁷Ashhur and Helah had three sons: Zereth, Izhar, and Ethnan.

⁸Koz was the father of Anub and Zobebah, and the ancestor of the clans descended from Aharhel son of Harum.

⁹There was a man named Jabez, who was the most respected member of his family. His mother had given him the

---

ᵍ *Verse 21 in Hebrew is unclear.*   ʰ *Some ancient translations* sons; *Hebrew* fathers.
3.4 2 S 5.4, 5; 1 K 2.11; 1 Ch 29.27   **3.5** 2 S 11.3

name Jabez,[i] because his birth had been very painful. [10]But Jabez prayed to the God of Israel, "Bless me, God, and give me much land. Be with me and keep me from anything evil that might cause me pain." And God gave him what he prayed for.

Other Family Lists

[11]Caleb, the brother of Shuhah, had a son, Mehir. Mehir was the father of Eshton, [12]who had three sons: Bethrapha, Paseah, and Tehinnah. Tehinnah was the founder of the city of Nahash. The descendants of these men lived in Recah.

[13]Kenaz had two sons, Othniel and Seraiah. Othniel also had two sons, Hathath and Meonothai.[j] [14]Meonothai was the father of Ophrah.

Seraiah was the father of Joab, the founder of Handcraft Valley, where all the people were skilled workers.

[15]Caleb son of Jephunneh had three sons: Iru, Elah, and Naam. And Elah was the father of Kenaz.

[16]Jehallelel had four sons: Ziph, Ziphah, Tiria, and Asarel.

[17-18]Ezrah had four sons: Jether, Mered, Epher, and Jalon. Mered married Bithiah, a daughter of the king of Egypt, and they had a daughter, Miriam, and two sons, Shammai and Ishbah. Ishbah founded the town of Eshtemoa. Mered also married a woman from the tribe of Judah, and they had three sons: Jered, who founded the town of Gedor; Heber, founder of the town of Soco; and Jekuthiel, founder of the town of Zanoah.

[19]Hodiah married the sister of Naham. Their descendants founded the clan of Garm, which lived in the town of Keilah, and the clan of Maacath, which lived in the town of Eshtemoa.[k]

Potters in the service of the king (4.23)

[20]Shimon had four sons: Amnon, Rinnah, Benhanan, and Tilon.

Ishi had two sons: Zoheth and Benzoheth.

The Descendants of Shelah

[21]Shelah was one of Judah's sons. His descendants included Er, who founded the town of Lecah; Laadah, founder of the town of Mareshah; the clan of linen weavers, who lived in the town of Beth Ashbea; [22]Jokim and the people who lived in the town of Cozeba; and Joash and Saraph, who married Moabite women and then settled in Bethlehem.[l] (These traditions are very old.) [23]They were potters in the service of the king and lived in the towns of Netaim and Gederah.

The Descendants of Simeon

[24]Simeon had five sons: Nemuel, Jamin, Jarib, Zerah, and Shaul. [25]Shaul's son was Shallum, his grandson was Mibsam, and his great-grandson was Mishma. [26]Then from Mishma the line descended through Hammuel, Zaccur, and Shimei. [27]Shimei had sixteen sons and six daughters, but his relatives had fewer children, and the tribe of Simeon did not grow as much as the tribe of Judah did.

[28]Down to the time of King David the descendants of Simeon lived in the fol-

---

[i] JABEZ: *This name sounds like the Hebrew for "pain."* Meonothai; *Hebrew does not have this name.*   [j] *Some ancient translations*   [k] *Verse 19 in Hebrew is unclear.*
[l] *Probable text* settled in Bethlehem; *Hebrew unclear.*
4.28-33 Js 19.2-8

lowing towns: Beersheba, Moladah, Hazarshual, 29 Bilhah, Ezem, Tolad, 30 Bethuel, Hormah, Ziklag, 31 Beth Marcaboth, Hazarsusim, Bethbiri, and Shaaraim. 32 They also lived in five other places: Etam, Ain, Rimmon, Tochen, and Ashan, 33 and the surrounding villages, as far southwest as the town of Baalath. These are the records which they kept of their families and of the places where they lived.

34-38 The following men were the heads of their clans:

> Meshobab, Jamlech, Joshah son of Amaziah, Joel,
> Jehu (the son of Joshibiah, the son of Seraiah, the son of Asiel),
> Elioenai, Jaakobah, Jeshohaiah, Asaiah, Adiel, Jesimiel, Benaiah,
> Ziza (the son of Shiphi, the son of Allon, a descendant of Jedaiah, Shimri, and Shemaiah).

Because their families continued to grow, 39 they spread out westward almost to Gerar[m] and pastured their sheep on the eastern side of the valley

They . . . pastured their sheep. (4.39)

in which that city is located. 40 They found plenty of fertile pasture lands there in a stretch of open country that was quiet and peaceful. The people who had lived there before were Hamites.

41 In the time of King Hezekiah of Judah, the men named above went to Gerar and destroyed the tents and huts of the people who lived there.[n] They drove the people out and settled there permanently because there was plenty of pasture for their sheep. 42 Five hundred other members of the tribe of Simeon went east to Edom. They were led by the sons of Ishi: Pelatiah, Neariah, Rephaiah, and Uzziel. 43 There they killed the surviving Amalekites, and they have lived there ever since.

The Descendants of Reuben

5 These are the descendants of Reuben, the oldest of Jacob's sons. (Because he had sex with one of his father's concubines, he lost the rights belonging to the first-born son, and those rights were given to Joseph. 2 It was the tribe of Judah, however, that became the strongest and provided a ruler for all the tribes.) 3 Reuben, the oldest of Jacob's sons, had four sons: Hanoch, Pallu, Hezron, and Carmi.

4-6 These are the descendants of Joel from generation to generation: Shemaiah, Gog, Shimei, Micah, Reaiah, Baal, and Beerah. The Assyrian emperor, Tiglath Pileser, captured Beerah, a leader of the tribe, and deported him.

7 The family records list the following clan leaders in the tribe of Reuben: Jeiel, Zechariah, 8 and Bela, the son of Azaz and grandson of Shema, of the clan of Joel. This clan lived in Aroer and in the territory from there north to Nebo and Baal Meon. 9 They had large herds in the land of Gilead, and so they occupied the land as far east as the desert that stretches all the way to the Euphrates River.

---

[m] Some ancient translations Gerar; Hebrew Gedor.   [n] the tents and huts . . . there; or the tents of the people who lived there, and the Meunites also.

5.1 Gn 35.22; 49.3, 4   5.2 Gn 49.8-10   5.6 2 K 15.29

[10] In the time of King Saul the tribe of Reuben attacked the Hagrites, killed them in battle, and occupied their land in the eastern part of Gilead.

The Descendants of Gad

[11] The tribe of Gad lived to the north of Reuben in the land of Bashan as far east as Salecah. [12] Joel was the founder of the leading clan, and Shapham of the second most important clan. Janai and Shaphat were founders of other clans in Bashan. [13] The other members of the tribe belonged to the following seven clans: Michael, Meshullam, Sheba, Jorai, Jacan, Zia, and Eber. [14] They were descendants of Abihail son of Huri, whose ancestors were traced back as follows: Abihail, Huri, Jaroah, Gilead, Michael, Jeshishai, Jahdo, Buz. [15] Ahi, the son of Abdiel and grandson of Guni, was head of these clans. [16] They lived in the territory of Bashan and Gilead, in the towns there and all over the pasture lands of Sharon. ([17] These records were compiled in the days of King Jotham of Judah and King Jeroboam II of Israel.)

The Armies of the Eastern Tribes

[18] In the tribes of Reuben, Gad, and East Manasseh there were 44,760 soldiers, well-trained in the use of shields, swords, and bows. [19] They went to war against the Hagrite tribes of Jetur, Naphish, and Nodab. [20] They put their trust in God and prayed to him for help, and God answered their prayers and made them victorious over the Hagrites and their allies. [21] They captured from the enemy 50,000 camels, 250,000 sheep, and 2,000 donkeys, and took 100,000 prisoners of war. [22] They killed many of the enemy, because the war was God's will. And they went on living in that territory until the exile.[o]

The People of East Manasseh

[23] The people of East Manasseh settled in the territory of Bashan as far north as Baal Hermon, Senir, and Mount Hermon, and their population increased greatly. [24] The following were the heads of their clans: Epher, Ishi, Eliel, Azriel, Jeremiah, Hodaviah, and Jahdiel. They were all outstanding soldiers, well-known leaders of their clans.

The Eastern Tribes Are Deported

[25] But the people were unfaithful to the God of their ancestors and deserted him to worship the gods of the nations whom God had driven out of the land. [26] So God caused Emperor Pul of Assyria (also known as Tiglath Pileser) to invade their country. He deported the tribes of Reuben, Gad, and East Manasseh and settled them permanently in Halah, Habor, and Hara, and by the Gozan River.

The Family Line of the High Priests

6 Levi had three sons: Gershon, Kohath, and Merari. [2] Kohath had four sons: Amram, Izhar, Hebron, and Uzziel.

[3] Amram had two sons, Aaron and Moses, and one daughter, Miriam.

Aaron had four sons: Nadab, Abihu, Eleazar, and Ithamar.

[4] The descendants of Eleazar from generation to generation are as follows: Phinehas, Abishua, [5] Bukki, Uzzi, [6] Zerahiah, Meraioth, [7] Amariah, Ahitub, [8] Zadok, Ahimaaz, [9] Azariah, Johanan, [10] Azariah (the one who served in the Temple which King Solomon built in Jerusalem), [11] Amariah, Ahitub, [12] Zadok, Shallum, [13] Hilkiah, Azariah, [14] Seraiah, Jehozadak. [15] King Nebuchadnezzar deported Jehozadak along with the other people of Judah

---

o THE EXILE: *About 733 B.C. the Assyrians conquered northern Israel and the Israelite territory east of the Jordan River and deported the people (see 2 K 15.29).*
5.26 a 2 K 15.19; **b** 2 K 15.29; **c** 2 K 17.6

and Jerusalem whom the LORD sent into exile.

Other Descendants of Levi

16 Levi had three sons: Gershon, Kohath, and Merari. 17 Each of them also had sons. Gershon was the father of Libni and Shimei; 18 Kohath was the father of Amram, Izhar, Hebron, and Uzziel; 19 and Merari was the father of Mahli and Mushi.

20 These are the descendants of Gershon from generation to generation: Libni, Jahath, Zimmah, 21 Joah, Iddo, Zerah, Jeatherai.

22 These are the descendants of Kohath from generation to generation: Amminadab, Korah, Assir, 23 Elkanah, Ebiasaph, Assir, 24 Tahath, Uriel, Uzziah, Shaul.

25 Elkanah had two sons, Amasai and Ahimoth. 26 These are Ahimoth's descendants from generation to generation: Elkanah, Zophai, Nahath, 27 Eliab, Jeroham, Elkanah.

28 Samuel had two sons: Joel,[p] the older, and Abijah, the younger.

29 These are the descendants of Merari from generation to generation: Mahli, Libni, Shimei, Uzzah, 30 Shimea, Haggiah, Asaiah.

The Temple Musicians

31 These are the men whom King David put in charge of the music at the place of worship in Jerusalem after the Covenant Box was moved there. 32 They took regular turns of duty at the Tent of the LORD's presence during the time before King Solomon built the Temple. 33 The family lines of those who held this office are as follows:

The clan of Kohath: Heman, the leader of the first choir, was the son of Joel. His family line went back to Jacob as follows: Heman, Joel, Samuel, 34 Elkanah, Jeroham, Eliel, Toah, 35 Zuph, Elkanah, Mahath, Amasai, 36 Elkanah, Joel, Azariah, Zephaniah, 37 Tahath, Assir, Ebiasaph, Korah, 38 Izhar, Kohath, Levi, Jacob.

39 Asaph was leader of the second choir. His family line went back to Levi as follows: Asaph, Berechiah, Shimea, 40 Michael, Baaseiah, Malchijah, 41 Ethni, Zerah, Adaiah, 42 Ethan, Zimmah, Shimei, 43 Jahath, Gershon, Levi.

44 Ethan of the clan of Merari was the leader of the third choir. His family line went back to Levi as follows: Ethan, Kishi, Abdi, Malluch, 45 Hashabiah, Amaziah, Hilkiah, 46 Amzi, Bani, Shemer, 47 Mahli, Mushi, Merari, Levi.

48 The other Levites were assigned all the other duties at the place of worship.

The Descendants of Aaron

49 Aaron and his descendants presented the offerings of incense and offered the sacrifices that were burnt on the altar. They were responsible for all the worship in the Most Holy Place and for the sacrifices by which God forgives Israel's sins. They did all this in accordance with the instructions given by Moses, God's servant. 50 This is the line of Aaron's descendants: Eleazar, Phinehas, Abishua, 51 Bukki, Uzzi, Zerahiah, 52 Meraioth, Amariah, Ahitub, 53 Zadok, Ahimaaz.

Where the Levites Lived

54 This is the territory assigned to the descendants of Aaron of the clan of Kohath. They received the first share of the land assigned to the Levites. 55 This included Hebron in the territory of Judah and the pasture lands around it. 56 The fields and villages, however, that belonged to the city were assigned to Caleb son of Jephunneh. 57-59 The following towns were assigned to Aaron's descendants: Hebron, a city of

---

p Some ancient translations (see also 1 S 8.2) Joel; *Hebrew does not have this name.*
6.16-19 Ex 6.16-19

refuge,q Jattir, and the towns of Libnah, Eshtemoa, Hilen, Debir, Ashan, and Beth Shemesh, with their pasture lands. 60 In the territory of Benjamin they were assigned the following towns with their pasture lands: Geba, Alemeth, and Anathoth. This made a total of thirteen towns for all their families to live in. 61 Ten towns in the territory of West Manasseh were assigned by lot to the rest of the clan of Kohath, family by family.

62 To the clan of Gershon, family by family, were assigned thirteen towns in the territories of Issachar, Asher, Naphtali, and East Manasseh in Bashan. 63 In the same way, twelve towns in the territories of Reuben, Gad, and Zebulun were assigned to the clan of Merari, family by family. 64 In this way the people of Israel assigned towns for the Levites to live in, together with the pasture lands around the towns. (65 The towns in the territories of Judah, Simeon, and Benjamin, mentioned above, were also assigned by drawing lots.)

66 Some of the families of the clan of Kohath were assigned towns and pasture lands in the territory of Ephraim: 67 Shechem, the city of refuge in the hills of Ephraim, Gezer, 68 Jokmeam, Beth Horon, 69 Aijalon, and Gath Rimmon. 70 In the territory of West Manasseh they were assigned the towns of Aner and Bileam with the surrounding pasture lands.

71 The families of the clan of Gershon were assigned the following towns, with the surrounding pasture lands:

In the territory of East Manasseh: Golan in Bashan, and Ashtaroth.

72 In the territory of Issachar: Kedesh, Daberath, 73 Ramoth, and Anem.

74 In the territory of Asher: Mashal, Abdon, 75 Hukok, and Rehob.

76 In the territory of Naphtali: Kedesh in Galilee, Hammon, and Kiriathaim.

77 The remaining families of the clan of Merari were assigned the following towns with the surrounding pasture lands:

In the territory of Zebulun: Rimmono and Tabor.

78 In the territory of Reuben, east of the Jordan River beyond Jericho: Bezer on the plateau, Jahzah, 79 Kedemoth, and Mephaath.

80 In the territory of Gad: Ramoth in Gilead, Mahanaim, 81 Heshbon, and Jazer.

The Descendants of Issachar

7 Issachar had four sons: Tola, Puah, Jashub, and Shimron.

2 Tola had six sons: Uzzi, Rephaiah, Jeriel, Jahmai, Ibsam, and Shemuel. They were heads of families of the clan of Tola and were famous soldiers. At the time of King David their descendants numbered 22,600.

3 Uzzi had one son, Izrahiah. Izrahiah and his four sons, Michael, Obadiah, Joel, and Isshiah, were all heads of families. 4 They had so many wives and children that their descendants were able to provide 36,000 men for military duty.

5 The official records of all the families of the tribe of Issachar listed 87,000 men eligible for military duty.

The Descendants of Benjamin and Dan

6 Benjamin had three sons: Bela, Becher, and Jediael.

7 Bela had five sons: Ezbon, Uzzi, Uzziel, Jerimoth, and Iri. They were heads of families in the clan and were all famous soldiers. Their descendants included 22,034 men eligible for military duty.

8 Becher had nine sons: Zemirah, Joash, Eliezer, Elioenai, Omri, Jeremoth, Abijah, Anathoth, and Alemeth. 9 The official record of their descendants by

---

q CITY OF REFUGE: *If anyone accidentally killed someone, he could escape to one of these cities and be safe from revenge (see Js 20.1-9).*

families listed 20,200 men eligible for military duty.

[10] Jediael had one son, Bilhan, and Bilhan had seven sons: Jeush, Benjamin, Ehud, Chenaanah, Zethan, Tarshish, and Ahishahar. [11] They were heads of families in the clan and were all famous soldiers. Their descendants included 17,200 men eligible for military duty. [12] Shuppim and Huppim also belonged to this tribe.

Dan had one son, Hushim.[r]

The Descendants of Naphtali

[13] Naphtali had four sons: Jahziel, Guni, Jezer, and Shallum. (They were descendants of Bilhah.[s])

The Descendants of Manasseh

[14] By his Aramean concubine, Manasseh had two sons, Asriel and Machir. Machir was the father of Gilead. [15] Machir found a wife for Huppim and one for Shuppim. His sister's name was Maacah. Machir's second son was Zelophehad, and he had only daughters.

[16] Maacah, Machir's wife, gave birth to two sons, whom they named Peresh and Sheresh. Peresh had two sons, Ulam and Rakem, [17] and Ulam had a son named Bedan. These are all descendants of Gilead, the son of Machir and grandson of Manasseh.

[18] Gilead's sister Hammolecheth had three sons: Ishod, Abiezer, and Mahlah. ([19] Shemida had four sons: Ahian, Shechem, Likhi, and Aniam.)

The Descendants of Ephraim

[20] These are the descendants of Ephraim from generation to generation: Shuthelah, Bered, Tahath, Eleadah, Tahath, [21] Zabad, Shuthelah. Ephraim had two other sons besides Shuthelah: Ezer and Elead, who were killed when they tried to steal the livestock belonging to the native inhabitants of Gath. [22] Their father Ephraim mourned for them for many days, and his relatives came to comfort him. [23] Then he had intercourse with his wife again, and she became pregnant and had a son. They named him Beriah,[t] because of the trouble that had come to their family.

[24] Ephraim had a daughter named Sheerah. She built the towns of Upper and Lower Beth Horon, and Uzzen Sheerah.

[25] Ephraim also had a son named Rephah, whose descendants were as follows: Resheph, Telah, Tahan, [26] Ladan, Ammihud, Elishama, [27] Nun, Joshua.

[28] The territory which they took and settled included Bethel and the towns around it, as far east as Naaran and as far west as Gezer and the towns around it. It also included the cities of Shechem and Ayyah, and the towns around them.

[29] The descendants of Manasseh controlled the cities of Beth Shan, Taanach, Megiddo, and Dor, and the towns around them.

All these are the places where the descendants of Joseph son of Jacob lived.

The Descendants of Asher

[30] These are the descendants of Asher. He had four sons: Imnah, Ishvah, Ishvi, and Beriah; and one daughter, Serah.

[31] Beriah had two sons, Heber and Malchiel. (Malchiel founded the city of Birzaith.)

[32] Heber had three sons: Japhlet, Shomer, and Hotham; and one daughter, Shua.

---

[r] *Probable text* Shuppim . . . Hushim *(see Gn 46.23; Nu 26.39, 42); Hebrew* And Shuppim and Huppim, sons of Ir; Hushim son of Aher.   [s] BILHAH: *A concubine of Jacob and the mother of his two sons Dan and Naphtali.*   [t] BERIAH: *This name sounds like the Hebrew for "in trouble."*

33 Japhlet also had three sons: Pasach, Bimhal, and Ashvath.

34 His brother Shomer had three sons: Rohgah, Jehubbah, and Aram.

35 His brother Hotham[u] had four sons: Zophah, Imna, Shelesh, and Amal.

36 The descendants of Zophah were Suah, Harnepher, Shual, Beri, Imrah, 37 Bezer, Hod, Shamma, Shilshah, Ithran, and Beera.

38 The descendants of Jether were Jephunneh, Pispa, and Ara, 39 and the descendants of Ulla were Arah, Hanniel, and Rizia.

40 All of these were descendants of Asher. They were heads of families, famous fighting men, outstanding leaders. Asher's descendants included 26,000 men eligible for military duty.

The Descendants of Benjamin

8 Benjamin had five sons. In order of age they were Bela, Ashbel, Aharah, 2 Nohah, and Rapha.

3 The descendants of Bela were Addar, Gera, Abihud, 4 Abishua, Naaman, Ahoah, 5 Gera, Shephuphan, and Huram.

6-7 The descendants of Ehud were Naaman, Ahijah, and Gera. They were heads of families that lived in Geba, but which were forced out and went to live in Manahath. Gera, the father of Uzza and Ahihud, led them in this move.

8-9 Shaharaim divorced two wives, Hushim and Baara. Later, when he lived in the country of Moab, he married Hodesh and had seven sons: Jobab, Zibia, Mesha, Malcam, 10 Jeuz, Sachia, and Mirmah. His sons all became heads of families.

11 He also had two sons by Hushim: Abitub and Elpaal.

12 Elpaal had three sons: Eber, Misham, and Shemed. It was Shemed who built the cities of Ono and Lod and the surrounding villages.

The Benjaminites in Gath and Aijalon

13 Beriah and Shema were heads of families that settled in the city of Aijalon and drove out the people who lived in the city of Gath. 14 Beriah's descendants included Ahio, Shashak, Jeremoth, 15 Zebadiah, Arad, Eder, 16 Michael, Ishpah, and Joha.

The Benjaminites in Jerusalem

17 Elpaal's descendants included Zebadiah, Meshullam, Hizki, Heber, 18 Ishmerai, Izliah, and Jobab.

19 Shimei's descendants included Jakim, Zichri, Zabdi, 20 Elienai, Zillethai, Eliel, 21 Adaiah, Beraiah, and Shimrath.

22 Shashak's descendants included Ishpan, Eber, Eliel, 23 Abdon, Zichri, Hanan, 24 Hananiah, Elam, Anthothijah, 25 Iphdeiah, and Penuel.

26 Jeroham's descendants included Shamsherai, Shehariah, Athaliah, 27 Jaareshiah, Elijah, and Zichri.

28 These were the ancestral heads of families and their principal descendants who lived in Jerusalem.

The Benjaminites in Gibeon and Jerusalem

29 Jeiel[v] founded the city of Gibeon and settled there. His wife was named Maacah, 30 and his oldest son, Abdon. His other sons were Zur, Kish, Baal, Ner,[w] Nadab, 31 Gedor, Ahio, Zechariah, 32 and Mikloth, the father of Shimeah. Their descendants lived in Jerusalem near other families of their clan.

The Family of King Saul

33 Ner was the father of Kish, and Kish was the father of King Saul. Saul

---

u *Probable text (see verse 32)* Hotham; *Hebrew* Helem.   v *Probable text (and see*
9.35) Jeiel; *Hebrew does not have this name.*   w *One ancient translation (and see*
9.36) Ner; *Hebrew does not have this name.*

had four sons: Jonathan, Malchishua, Abinadab, and Eshbaal.[x] [34] Jonathan was the father of Meribbaal,[y] who was the father of Micah.

[35] Micah had four sons: Pithon, Melech, Tarea, and Ahaz. [36] Ahaz was the father of Jehoaddah, who was the father of three sons: Alemeth, Azmaveth, and Zimri. Zimri was the father of Moza, [37] Moza the father of Binea, Binea of Raphah, Raphah of Eleasah, and Eleasah of Azel.

[38] Azel had six sons: Azrikam, Bocheru, Ishmael, Sheariah, Obadiah, and Hanan. [39] Azel's brother Eshek had three sons: Ulam, Jeush, and Eliphelet.

[40] Ulam's sons were outstanding soldiers and archers. He had a hundred and fifty sons and grandsons in all. All those named above were members of the tribe of Benjamin.

The People Who Returned from Captivity

9 All the people of Israel were listed according to their families, and this information was recorded in *The Book of the Kings of Israel*.

The people of Judah had been deported to Babylon as punishment for their sins. [2] The first to return to their property in the cities included Israelite citizens, priests, Levites, and Temple workers. [3] People from the tribes of Judah, Benjamin, Ephraim, and Manasseh went to live in Jerusalem.

[4-6] There were 690 families of the tribe of Judah who lived in Jerusalem.

The descendants of Judah's son Perez had as their leader Uthai, the son of Ammihud and grandson of Omri. His other ancestors included Imri and Bani.

The descendants of Judah's son Shelah had as their leader Asaiah, who was the head of his family.

The descendants of Judah's son Zerah had Jeuel as their leader.

[7-8] The following members of the tribe of Benjamin lived in Jerusalem:

Sallu son of Meshullam, who was the son of Hodaviah, the son of Hassenuah

Ibneiah son of Jeroham

Elah, the son of Uzzi and grandson of Michri

Meshullam son of Shephatiah, who was the son of Reuel, the son of Ibnijah

[9] There were 956 families of this tribe living there. All the men named above were heads of families.

The Priests Who Lived in Jerusalem

[10-12] The following priests lived in Jerusalem:

Jedaiah, Jehoiarib, and Jachin

Azariah son of Hilkiah (the chief official in the Temple), whose ancestors included Meshullam, Zadok, Meraioth, and Ahitub

Adaiah son of Jeroham, whose ancestors included Pashhur and Malchijah

Maasai son of Adiel, whose ancestors included Jahzerah, Meshullam, Meshillemith, and Immer

[13] The priests who were heads of families totaled 1,760. They were experts in all the work carried on in the Temple.

The Levites Who Lived in Jerusalem

[14-16] The following Levites lived in Jerusalem:

Shemaiah son of Hasshub, whose ancestors included Azrikam and Hashabiah, of the clan of Merari

---

[x] ESHBAAL: *Called Ishbosheth in 2 S 2.8 and elsewhere in 2 Samuel.*   [y] MERIBBAAL: *Called Mephibosheth in 2 S 4.4 and elsewhere in 2 Samuel.*
9.2, 3 Ezra 2.27; Ne 7.73

Bakbakkar, Heresh, and Galal

Mattaniah son of Mica, whose ancestors included Zichri and Asaph

Obadiah son of Shemaiah, whose ancestors included Galal and Jeduthun

Berechiah, the son of Asa and grandson of Elkanah, who lived in the territory that belonged to the town of Netophah

The Temple Guards Who Lived in Jerusalem

[17] The following Temple guards lived in Jerusalem: Shallum, Akkub, Talmon, and Ahiman. Shallum was their leader. [18] Down to that time members of their clans had been stationed at the eastern entrance to the King's Gate.[z] Formerly they had stood guard at the gates to the camps of the Levites. [19] Shallum, the son of Kore and grandson of Ebiasaph, together with his fellow members of the clan of Korah, was responsible for guarding the entrance to the Tent of the LORD's presence, just as their ancestors had been when they were in charge of the LORD's camp. [20] Phinehas son of Eleazar — may the LORD be with him! — had supervised them at one time. [21] Zechariah son of Meshelemiah was also a guard at the entrance to the Tent of the LORD's presence.

[22] In all, 212 men were chosen as guards for the entrances and gates. They were registered according to the villages where they lived. It was King David and the prophet Samuel who had put their ancestors in these responsible positions. [23] They and their descendants continued to guard the gates to the Temple. [24] There was a gate facing in each direction, north, south, east, and west, and each had a chief guard. [25] These guards were assisted by their relatives, who lived in the villages and who had to take turns at guard duty for seven days at a time. [26] The four chief guards were Levites and had the final responsibility. They were also responsible for the rooms in the Temple and for the supplies kept there. [27] They lived near the Temple, because it was their duty to guard it and to open the gates every morning.

The Other Levites

[28] Other Levites were responsible for the utensils used in worship. They checked them out and checked them back in every time they were used. [29] Others were in charge of the other sacred equipment, and of the flour, wine, olive oil, incense, and spices. [30] But the responsibility for mixing the spices belonged to the priests. [31] A Levite named Mattithiah, oldest son of Shallum, of the clan of Korah, was responsible for preparing the baked offerings.[a] [32] Members of the clan of Kohath were responsible for preparing the sacred bread[b] for the Temple every Sabbath. [33] Some Levite families were responsible for the Temple music. The heads of these families lived in some of the Temple buildings and were free from other duties, because they were on call day and night. [34] The men named above were heads of Levite families, according to their ancestral lines. They were the leaders who lived in Jerusalem.

[z] KING'S GATE: *The east gate of the Temple, through which the king usually entered.*
[a] BAKED OFFERINGS: *Thin cakes of flour and olive oil which were baked and then presented as offerings to God (see Lv 2.4-6).*   [b] SACRED BREAD: *Twelve loaves of bread which were placed on a table in the Temple each Sabbath as an offering to God (see Lv 24.5-9).*

The Ancestors and Descendants of King Saul
(1 Chronicles 8.29-38)

³⁵ Jeiel founded the city of Gibeon and settled there. His wife was named Maacah. ³⁶ His oldest son was Abdon, and his other sons were Zur, Kish, Baal, Ner, Nadab, ³⁷ Gedor, Ahio, Zechariah, and Mikloth, ³⁸ the father of Shimeah. Their descendants lived in Jerusalem near other families of their clan.

³⁹ Ner was the father of Kish, and Kish was the father of Saul. Saul had four sons: Jonathan, Malchishua, Abinadab, and Eshbaal.ᶜ ⁴⁰ Jonathan was the father of Meribbaal,ᵈ who was the father of Micah. ⁴¹ Micah had four sons: Pithon, Melech, Tarea, and Ahaz.ᵉ ⁴² Ahaz was the father of Jarah, who was the father of three sons: Alemeth, Azmaveth, and Zimri. Zimri was the father of Moza, ⁴³ Moza the father of Binea, Binea of Rephaiah, Rephaiah of Eleasah, and Eleasah of Azel.

⁴⁴ Azel had six sons: Azrikam, Bocheru, Ishmael, Sheariah, Obadiah, and Hanan.

The Death of King Saul
(1 Samuel 31.1-13)

10 The Philistines fought a battle against the Israelites on Mount Gilboa. Many Israelites were killed there, and the rest of them, including King Saul and his sons, fled. ² But the Philistines caught up with them and killed three of Saul's sons, Jonathan, Abinadab, and Malchishua. ³ The fighting was heavy around Saul, and he was hit by enemy arrows and badly wounded. ⁴ He said to the young man carrying his weapons, "Draw your sword and kill me, to keep these godless Philistines from gloating over me." But the young man was too terrified to do it.

So Saul took his own sword and threw himself on it. ⁵ The young man saw that Saul was dead, so he too threw himself on his sword and died. ⁶ So Saul and his three sons all died together, and none of his descendants ever ruled. ⁷ When the Israelites who lived in Jezreel Valley heard that the army had fled and that Saul and his sons had died, they abandoned their towns and ran off. Then the Philistines came and occupied them.

⁸ The day after the battle the Philistines went to plunder the corpses, and they found the bodies of Saul and his sons lying on Mount Gilboa. ⁹ They cut off Saul's head, stripped off his armor, and sent messengers with them throughout Philistia to tell the good news to their idols and to their people. ¹⁰ They put his weapons in one of their temples and hung his head in the temple of their god Dagon. ¹¹ When the people of Jabesh in Gilead heard what the Philistines had done to Saul, ¹² the bravest men went and got the bodies of Saul and his sons and took them to Jabesh. They buried them there under an oak and fasted for seven days.

¹³ Saul died because he was unfaithful to the LORD. He disobeyed the LORD's commands; he tried to find guidance by consulting the spirits of the dead ¹⁴ instead of consulting the LORD. So the LORD killed him and gave control of the kingdom to David son of Jesse.

David Becomes King of Israel and Judah
(2 Samuel 5.1-10)

11 All the people of Israel went to David at Hebron and said to him, "We are your own flesh and blood. ² In the past, even when Saul was still our king, you led the people of Israel in

---

ᶜ ESHBAAL: *Called Ishbosheth in 2 S 2.8 and elsewhere in 2 Samuel.*   ᵈ MERIBBAAL: *Called Mephibosheth in 2 S 4.4 and elsewhere in 2 Samuel.*   ᵉ *Some ancient translations* Ahaz *(see 1 Ch 8.35); Hebrew does not have this name.*
10.13 a 1 S 13.8-14; 15.1-24; **b** Lv 19.31; 20.6; 1 S 28.7, 8

The three famous soldiers (11.18)

battle, and the LORD your God promised you that you would lead his people and be their ruler." ³ So all the leaders of Israel came to King David at Hebron. He made a sacred alliance with them, they anointed him, and he became king of Israel, just as the LORD had promised through Samuel.

⁴ King David and all the Israelites went and attacked the city of Jerusalem. It was then known as Jebus, and the Jebusites, the original inhabitants of the land, were still living there. ⁵ The Jebusites told David he would never get inside the city, but David captured their fortress of Zion, and it became known as "David's City." ⁶ David said, "The first man to kill a Jebusite will be commander of the army!" Joab, whose mother was Zeruiah, led the attack and became commander. ⁷ Because David went to live in the fortress, it came to be called "David's City." ⁸ He rebuilt the city, starting at the place where land was filled in on the east side of the hill, and Joab restored the rest of the city. ⁹ David grew stronger and stronger, because the LORD Almighty was with him.

David's Famous Soldiers
(2 Samuel 23.8-39)

¹⁰ This is the list of David's famous soldiers. Together with the rest of the people of Israel, they helped him become king, as the LORD had promised, and they kept his kingdom strong.

¹¹ First was Jashobeam of the clan of Hachmon, the leader of "The Three."ᶠ He fought with his spear against three hundred men and killed them all in one battle. ¹² Next among the famous "Three" was Eleazar son of Dodo, of the clan of Ahoh. ¹³ He fought on David's side against the Philistines at the battle of Pas Dammim. He was in a barley field when the Israelites started to run away, ¹⁴ so he and his men took a stand in the middle of the field and fought the Philistines. The LORD gave him a great victory.

¹⁵ One day three of the thirty leading soldiers went to a rock where David was staying near Adullam Cave, while a band of Philistines was camping in Rephaim Valley. ¹⁶ At that time David was on a fortified hill, and a group of Philistines had occupied Bethlehem. ¹⁷ David got homesick and said, "How I wish someone would bring me a drink of water from the well by the gate in Bethlehem!" ¹⁸ The three famous soldiers forced their way through the Philistine camp, drew some water from the well, and brought it back to David. But he would not drink it; instead he poured it out as an offering to the LORD ¹⁹ and said, "I could never drink this! It

ᶠ *One ancient translation (see also 2 S 23.8)* "The Three"; *Hebrew* "The Thirty."
11.4 Js 15.63; Jg 1.21

would be like drinking the blood of these men who risked their lives!" So he refused to drink it. These were the brave deeds of the three famous soldiers.

20 Joab's brother Abishai was the leader of "The Famous Thirty."*g* He fought with his spear against three hundred men and killed them, and became famous among "The Thirty."*h* **21** He was the most famous of "The Thirty"*i* and became their leader, but he was not as famous as "The Three."

22 Benaiah son of Jehoiada from Kabzeel was a famous soldier; he did many brave deeds, including killing two great Moabite warriors. He once went down into a pit on a snowy day and killed a lion. **23** He also killed an Egyptian, a huge man seven and a half feet tall, who was armed with a gigantic spear. Benaiah attacked him with a club, snatched the spear from the Egyptian's hand, and killed him with it. **24** Those were the brave deeds of Benaiah, who was one of "The Thirty."*j* **25** He was outstanding among "The Thirty," but not as famous as "The Three." David put him in charge of his bodyguard.

26-47 These are the other outstanding soldiers:

Asahel, Joab's brother
Elhanan son of Dodo from Bethlehem
Shammoth from Harod
Helez from Pelet
Ira son of Ikkesh from Tekoa
Abiezer from Anathoth
Sibbecai from Hushah
Ilai from Ahoh
Maharai from Netophah
Heled son of Baanah from Netophah

Ithai son of Ribai from Gibeah in Benjamin
Benaiah from Pirathon
Hurai from the valleys near Gaash
Abiel from Arbah
Azmaveth from Bahurum
Eliahba from Shaalbon
Hashem*k* from Gizon
Jonathan son of Shagee from Harar
Ahiam son of Sachar from Harar
Eliphal son of Ur
Hepher from Mecherah
Ahijah from Pelon
Hezro from Carmel
Naarai son of Ezbai
Joel brother of Nathan
Mibhar son of Hagri
Zelek from Ammon
Naharai, Joab's armorbearer, from Beeroth
Ira and Gareb from Jattir
Uriah the Hittite
Zabad son of Ahlai
Adina son of Shiza (a leading member of the tribe of Reuben, with his own group of thirty soldiers)
Hanan son of Maacah
Joshaphat from Mithan
Uzzia from Ashterah
Shamma and Jeiel, sons of Hotham, from Aroer
Jediael and Joha, sons of Shimri, from Tiz
Eliel from Mahavah
Jeribai and Joshaviah, sons of Elnaam
Ithmah from Moab
Eliel, Obed, and Jaasiel from Zobah*l*

---

g One ancient translation Thirty; *Hebrew* Three. *h One ancient translation (see also 2 S 23.18)* "The Thirty"; *Hebrew* "The Three." *i Probable text (see 2 S 23.19)* most famous of "The Thirty"; *Hebrew unclear.* *j Probable text* "The Thirty"; *Hebrew* "The Three." *k Probable text* Hashem; *Hebrew* the sons of Hashem. *l Probable text* from Zobah; *Hebrew unclear.*

David's Early Followers from the Tribe of Benjamin

12 David was living in Ziklag, where he had gone to escape from King Saul. There he was joined by many experienced, reliable soldiers, [2] members of the tribe of Benjamin, to which Saul belonged. They could shoot arrows and sling stones either right-handed or left-handed. [3-7] They were under the command of Ahiezer and Joash, sons of Shemaah, from Gibeah.

These were the soldiers:

Jeziel and Pelet, sons of
    Azmaveth
Beracah and Jehu from
    Anathoth
Ishmaiah from Gibeon, a
    famous soldier and one of
    the leaders of "The Thirty"
Jeremiah, Jahaziel, Johannan,
    and Jozabad, from Gederah
Eluzai, Jerimoth, Bealiah,
    Shemariah, and
    Shephatiah, from Hariph
Elkanah, Isshiah, Azarel,
    Joezer, and Jashobeam, of
    the clan of Korah
Joelah and Zebadiah, sons of
    Jeroham, from Gedor

David's Followers from the Tribe of Gad

[8] These are the names of the famous, experienced soldiers from the tribe of Gad who joined David's troops when he was at the desert fort. They were experts with shields and spears, as fierce looking as lions and as quick as mountain deer. [9-13] They were ranked in the following order: Ezer, Obadiah, Eliab, Mishmannah, Jeremiah, Attai, Eliel, Johanan, Elzabad, Jeremiah, and Machbannai.

[14] Some of these men from the tribe of Gad were senior officers in command of a thousand men, and others were junior officers in command of a hundred. [15] In the first month of one year, the time when the Jordan River overflowed its banks, they crossed the river, scattering the people who lived in the valleys both east and west of the river.

Followers from Benjamin and Judah

[16] Once a group of men from the tribes of Benjamin and Judah went out to the fort where David was. [17] David went to meet them and said, "If you are coming as friends to help me, you are welcome here. Join us! But if you intend to betray me to my enemies, even though I have not tried to hurt you, the God of our ancestors will know it and punish you."

[18] God's spirit took control of one of them, Amasai, who later became the commander of "The Thirty," and he called out,

"David son of Jesse, we are
    yours!
Success to you and those who
    help you!
God is on your side."

David welcomed them and made them officers in his army.

Followers from Manasseh

[19] Some soldiers from the tribe of Manasseh went over to David's side when he was marching out with the Philistines to fight King Saul. Actually he did not help the Philistines, for their kings were afraid that he would betray them to his former master Saul, so they sent him back to Ziklag. [20] These are the soldiers from Manasseh who went over to David's side when he was returning: Adnah, Jozabad, Jediael, Michael, Jozabad, Elihu, and Zillethai. In Manasseh they had all commanded units of a thousand men. [21] They served David as officers over his troops, [m] because they were all outstanding soldiers. Later

[m] They served David . . . troops; or They helped David fight against the bands of raiders.

they were officers in the Israelite army. ²Almost every day new men joined David's forces, so that his army was soon enormous.

List of David's Forces

²³⁻³⁷When David was at Hebron, many trained soldiers joined his army to help make him king in place of Saul, as the LORD had promised. Their numbers were as follows:

Judah: 6,800 well-equipped men, armed with shields and spears;

Simeon: 7,100 well-trained men;

Levi: 4,600 men;

Followers of Jehoiada, descendant of Aaron: 3,700 men;

Relatives of Zadok, an able young fighter: 22 leading men;

Benjamin (Saul's own tribe): 3,000 men (most of the people of Benjamin had remained loyal to Saul);

Ephraim: 20,800 men famous in their own clans;

West Manasseh: 18,000 men chosen to go and make David king;

Issachar: 200 leaders, together with the men under their command (these leaders knew what Israel should do and the best time to do it);

Zebulun: 50,000 loyal and reliable men ready to fight, trained to use all kinds of weapons;

Naphtali: 1,000 leaders, together with 37,000 men armed with shields and spears;

Dan: 28,600 trained men;

Asher: 40,000 men ready for battle;

Tribes east of the Jordan — Reuben, Gad, and East Manasseh: 120,000 men trained to use all kinds of weapons.

³⁸All these soldiers, ready for battle, went to Hebron, determined to make David king over all Israel. All the rest of the people of Israel were united in the same purpose. ³⁹They spent three days there with David, feasting on the food and drink which their relatives had prepared for them. ⁴⁰From as far away as the northern tribes of Issachar, Zebulun, and Naphtali, people came bringing donkeys, camels, mules, and oxen loaded with food — flour, figs, raisins, wine, and olive oil. They also brought cattle and sheep to kill and eat. All this was an expression of the joy that was felt throughout the whole country.

The Covenant Box Is Moved from Kiriath Jearim
(2 Samuel 6.1-11)

13 King David consulted with all the officers in command of units of a thousand men and units of a hundred men. ²Then he announced to all the people of Israel, "If you give your approval and if it is the will of the LORD our God, let us send messengers to the rest of our people and to the priests and Levites in their towns, and tell them to assemble here with us. ³Then we will go and get God's Covenant Box, which was ignored while Saul was king." ⁴The people were pleased with the suggestion and agreed to it.

⁵So David assembled the people of Israel from all over the country, from the Egyptian border in the south to Hamath Pass in the north, in order to bring the Covenant Box from Kiriath Jearim to Jerusalem. ⁶David and the people went to the city of Baalah, that is, to Kiriath Jearim, in the territory of Judah, to get the Covenant Box of God, which bears the name of the LORD enthroned above the winged creatures. ⁷At Abinadab's house they brought out the Covenant Box and put it on a new cart. Uzzah and Ahio guided the cart, ⁸while David and all the people danced with all their might to honor God. They sang and played musical instruments — harps, drums, cymbals, and trumpets. ⁹As they came to the threshing place

of Chidon, the oxen stumbled, and Uzzah reached out and took hold of the Covenant Box. [10]At once the LORD became angry with Uzzah and killed him for touching the Box. He died there in God's presence, [11]and so that place has been called Perez Uzzah[n] ever since. David was furious because the LORD had punished Uzzah in anger.

[12]Then David was afraid of God and said, "How can I take the Covenant Box with me now?" [13]So David did not take it with him to Jerusalem. Instead, he left it at the house of a man named Obed Edom, a native of the city of Gath. [14]It stayed there three months, and the LORD blessed Obed Edom's family and everything that belonged to him.

David's Activities in Jerusalem
(2 Samuel 5.11-16)

14 King Hiram of Tyre sent a trade mission to David; he provided him with cedar logs and with stonemasons and carpenters to build a palace. [2]And so David realized that the LORD had established him as king of Israel and was making his kingdom prosperous for the sake of his people.

[3]There in Jerusalem, David married more wives and had more sons and daughters. [4]The following children were born to him in Jerusalem: Shammua, Shobab, Nathan, Solomon, [5]Ibhar, Elishua, Elpelet, [6]Nogah, Nepheg, Japhia, [7]Elishama, Beeliada,[o] and Eliphelet.

Victory over the Philistines
(2 Samuel 5.17-25)

[8]When the Philistines heard that David had now been made king over the whole country of Israel, their army went out to capture him. So David marched out to meet them. [9]The Philistines arrived at Rephaim Valley and began plundering. [10]David asked God, "Shall I attack the Philistines? Will you give me the victory?"

The LORD answered, "Yes, attack! I will give you the victory!"

[11]So David attacked them at Baal Perazim and defeated them. He said, "God has used me to break through the enemy army like a flood." So that place is called Baal Perazim.[p] [12]When the Philistines fled, they left their idols behind, and David gave orders for them to be burned.

[13]Soon the Philistines returned to the valley and started plundering it again. [14]Once more David consulted God, who answered, "Don't attack them from here, but go around and get ready to attack them from the other side, near the balsam trees. [15]When you hear the sound of marching in the treetops, then attack, because I will be marching ahead of you to defeat the Philistine army." [16]David did what God had commanded, and so he drove the Philistines back from Gibeon all the way to Gezer. [17]David's fame spread everywhere, and the LORD made every nation afraid of him.

Getting Ready to Move the Covenant Box

15 For his own use, David built houses in David's City.[q] He also prepared a place for God's Covenant Box and put up a tent for it. [2]Then he said, "Only Levites should carry the Covenant Box, because they are the ones the LORD chose to carry it and to serve him forever." [3]So David summoned all the people of Israel to Jerusalem in order to bring the Covenant Box

[n] PEREZ UZZAH: *This name in Hebrew means "Punishment of Uzzah."*   [o] BEELIADA: *Called Eliada in 3.8.*   [p] BAAL PERAZIM: *This name in Hebrew means "Lord of the Breakthrough."*   [q] DAVID'S CITY: *That part of Jerusalem which David had captured from the original inhabitants, the Jebusites (see 2 S 5.6-10).*
13.12 2 Macc 7.19   **13.14** 1 Ch 26.4, 5   **15.2** Dt 10.8

to the place he had prepared for it. 4 Next he sent for the descendants of Aaron and for the Levites. 5 From the Levite clan of Kohath came Uriel, in charge of 120 members of his clan; 6 from the clan of Merari came Asaiah, in charge of 220; 7 from the clan of Gershon, Joel, in charge of 130; 8 from the clan of Elizaphan, Shemaiah, in charge of 200; 9 from the clan of Hebron, Eliel, in charge of 80; 10 and from the clan of Uzziel, Amminadab, in charge of 112.

11 David called in the priests Zadok and Abiathar and the six Levites, Uriel, Asaiah, Joel, Shemaiah, Eliel, and Amminadab. 12 He said to the Levites, "You are the leaders of the Levite clans. Purify yourselves and your fellow Levites, so that you can bring the Covenant Box of the Lord God of Israel to the place I have prepared for it. 13 Because you were not there to carry it the first time, the Lord our God punished us for not worshiping him as we should have done."

14 Then the priests and the Levites purified themselves in order to move the Covenant Box of the Lord God of Israel. 15 The Levites carried it on poles on their shoulders, as the Lord had commanded through Moses.

16 David commanded the leaders of the Levites to assign various Levites to sing and to play joyful music on harps and cymbals. 17-21 From the clans of singers they chose the following men to play the brass cymbals: Heman son of Joel, his relative Asaph son of Berechiah, and Ethan son of Kushaiah, of the clan of Merari. To assist them they chose the following Levites to play the high-pitched harps: Zechariah, Jaaziel, Shemiramoth, Jehiel, Unni, Eliab, Maaseiah, and Benaiah.

To play the low-pitched harps they chose the following Levites: Mattithiah, Eliphelehu, Mikneiah, Azaziah, and the Temple guards, Obed Edom and Jeiel.

22 Because of his skill in music Chenaniah was chosen to be in charge of the levitical musicians. 23-24 Berechiah and Elkanah, along with Obed Edom and Jehiah, were chosen as guards for the Covenant Box. The priests Shebaniah, Joshaphat, Nethanel, Amasai, Zechariah, Benaiah, and Eliezer were chosen to blow trumpets in front of the Covenant Box.

Moving the Covenant Box to Jerusalem
(2 Samuel 6.12-22)

25 So King David, the leaders of Israel, and the military commanders went to the house of Obed Edom to get the Covenant Box, and they had a great celebration. 26 They sacrificed seven bulls and seven sheep, to make sure that God would help the Levites who were carrying the Covenant Box. 27 David was wearing a robe made of the finest linen, and so were the musicians, Chenaniah their leader, and the Levites who carried the Box. David also wore a linen ephod. 28 So all the Israelites accompanied the Covenant Box up to Jerusalem with shouts of joy, the sound of trumpets, horns, and cymbals, and the music of harps.

29 As the Box was being brought into the city, Michal, Saul's daughter, looked out of the window and saw King David dancing and leaping for joy, and she was disgusted with him.

16 They took the Covenant Box to the tent which David had prepared for it and put it inside. Then they offered sacrifices and fellowship offerings to God. 2 After David had finished offering the sacrifices, he blessed the people in the name of the Lord 3 and distributed food to them all. He gave each man and woman in Israel a loaf of

bread, a piece of roasted meat,[r] and some raisins.

[4] David appointed some of the Levites to lead the worship of the LORD, the God of Israel, in front of the Covenant Box, by singing and praising him. [5] Asaph was appointed leader, with Zechariah as his assistant. Jeiel, Shemiramoth, Jehiel, Mattithiah, Eliab, Benaiah, Obed Edom, and Jeiel were to play harps. Asaph was to sound the cymbals, [6] and two priests, Benaiah and Jahaziel, were to blow trumpets regularly in front of the Covenant Box. [7] It was then that David first gave Asaph and the other Levites the responsibility for singing praises to the LORD.

A Song of Praise
(Psalms 105.1-15; 96.1-13; 106.1, 47, 48)

[8] Give thanks to the LORD,
    proclaim his greatness;
    tell the nations what he has
        done.
[9] Sing praise to the LORD;
    tell the wonderful things he
        has done.
[10] Be glad that we belong to him;
    let all who worship him
        rejoice!
[11] Go to the LORD for help,
    and worship him continually.

[r] *a piece of roasted meat; or a cake of dates.*

[12-13] You descendants of Jacob, God's
        servant,
    descendants of Israel, whom
        God chose,
    remember the miracles that
        God performed
    and the judgments that he
        gave.
[14] The LORD is our God;
    his commands are for all the
        world.
[15] Never forget God's covenant,
    which he made to last forever,
[16] the covenant he made with
        Abraham,
    the promise he made to Isaac.
[17] The LORD made a covenant with
        Jacob,
    one that will last forever.
[18] "I will give you the land of
        Canaan," he said.
    "It will be your own
        possession."

16.16 a Gn 12.7; **b** Gn 26.3   **16.17, 18** Gn 28.13

With shouts of joy (15.28)

¹⁹God's people were few in
　　number,
　　strangers in the land of
　　Canaan.
²⁰They wandered from country to
　　country,
　　from one kingdom to another.
²¹But God let no one oppress
　　them;
　　to protect them, he warned
　　the kings:
²²"Don't harm my chosen servants;
　　do not touch my prophets."

²³Sing to the LORD, all the world!
　　Proclaim every day the good
　　news that he has saved us.
²⁴Proclaim his glory to the nations,
　　his mighty deeds to all
　　peoples.

²⁵The LORD is great and is to be
　　highly praised;
　　he is to be honored more than
　　all the gods.
²⁶The gods of all other nations are
　　only idols,
　　but the LORD created the
　　heavens.
²⁷Glory and majesty surround him,
　　power and joy fill his Temple.

²⁸Praise the LORD, all people on
　　earth,
　　praise his glory and might.
²⁹Praise the LORD's glorious name;
　　bring an offering and come
　　into his Temple.
　　Bow down before the Holy One
　　when he appears;ˢ
³⁰　　tremble before him, all the
　　earth!
　　The earth is set firmly in place
　　and cannot be moved.

³¹Be glad, earth and sky!
　　Tell the nations that the LORD
　　is king.
³²Roar, sea, and every creature
　　in you;
　　be glad, fields, and everything
　　in you!
³³The trees in the woods will shout
　　for joy
　　when the LORD comes to rule
　　the earth.

³⁴Give thanks to the LORD,
　　because he is good;
　　his love is eternal.
³⁵Say to him, "Save us, O God our
　　Savior;
　　gather us together; rescue us
　　from the nations,
　　so that we may be thankful
　　and praise your holy name."
³⁶Praise the LORD, the God of
　　Israel!
　　Praise him now and forever!

Then all the people said, "Amen,"
and praised the LORD.

Worship at Jerusalem and Gibeon

³⁷King David put Asaph and the
other Levites in permanent charge of
the worship that was held at the place
where the Covenant Box was kept.
They were to perform their duties there
day by day. ³⁸Obed Edom son of Jeduthun and sixty-eight men of his clan
were to assist them. Hosah and Obed
Edom were in charge of guarding the
gates.
³⁹Zadok the priest and his fellow
priests, however, were in charge of the
worship of the LORD at the place of worship in Gibeon. ⁴⁰Every morning and
evening they were to burn sacrifices

ˢ when he appears; *or* in garments of worship.

16.21, 22 Gn 20.3-7　　**16.34** 2 Ch 5.13; 7.3; Ezra 3.11; Ps 100.5; 106.1; 107.1; 118.1;
136.1; Jr 33.11

whole on the altar in accordance with what was written in the Law which the LORD gave to Israel. [41] There with them were Heman and Jeduthun and the others who were specifically chosen to sing praises to the LORD for his eternal love. [42] Heman and Jeduthun also had charge of the trumpets and cymbals and the other instruments which were played when the songs of praise were sung. The members of Jeduthun's clan were in charge of guarding the gates.

[43] Then everyone went home, and David went home to spend some time with his family.

Nathan's Message to David
(2 Samuel 7.1-17)

17 King David was now living in his palace. One day he sent for the prophet Nathan and said to him, "Here I am living in a house built of cedar, but the LORD's Covenant Box is kept in a tent!"

[2] Nathan answered, "Do whatever you have in mind, because God is with you."

[3] But that night God said to Nathan, [4] "Go and tell my servant David that I say to him, 'You are not the one to build a temple for me to live in. [5] From the time I rescued the people of Israel from Egypt until now I have never lived in a temple; I have always lived in tents and moved from place to place. [6] In all my traveling with the people of Israel I never asked any of the leaders that I appointed why they had not built me a temple made of cedar.'

[7] "So tell my servant David that I, the LORD Almighty, say to him, 'I took you from looking after sheep in the fields and made you the ruler of my people Israel. [8] I have been with you wherever you have gone, and I have defeated all your enemies as you advanced. I will

make you as famous as the greatest leaders in the world. [9-10] I have chosen a place for my people Israel and have settled them there, where they will live without being oppressed any more. Ever since they entered this land they have been attacked by violent people, but this will not happen again. I promise to defeat all your enemies and to give you descendants. [11] When you die and are buried with your ancestors, I will make one of your sons king and will keep his kingdom strong. [12] He will be the one to build a temple for me, and I will make sure that his dynasty continues forever. [13] I will be his father, and he will be my son. I will not withdraw my support from him as I did from Saul, whom I removed so that you could be king. [14] I will put him in charge of my people and my kingdom forever. His dynasty will never end.' "

[15] Nathan told David everything that God had revealed to him.

David's Prayer of Thanksgiving
(2 Samuel 7.18-29)

[16] Then King David went into the Tent of the LORD's presence, sat down, and prayed, "I am not worthy of what you have already done for me, LORD God, nor is my family. [17] Yet now you are doing even more; you have made promises about my descendants in the years to come, and you, LORD God, are already treating me like someone great.[t] [18] What more can I say to you! You know me well, and yet you honor me, your servant. [19] It was your will and purpose to do this for me and to show me my future greatness. [20] LORD, there is none like you; we have always known that you alone are God. [21] There is no other nation on earth like Israel, whom you rescued from slavery to make them your own people. The great and won-

---

[t] *Probable text* and you, LORD God . . . great; *Hebrew unclear.*
16.43 2 S 6.19, 20   **17.13** 2 Co 6.18; He 1.5

derful things you did for them spread your fame throughout the world. You rescued your people from Egypt and drove out other nations as your people advanced. 22 You have made Israel your own people forever, and you, LORD, have become their God.

23 "And now, O LORD, fulfill for all time the promise you made about me and my descendants, and do what you said you would. 24 Your fame will be great, and people will forever say, 'The LORD Almighty is God over Israel.' And you will preserve my dynasty for all time. 25 I have the courage to pray this prayer to you, my God, because you have revealed all this to me, your servant, and have told me that you will make my descendants kings. 26 You, LORD, are God, and you have made this wonderful promise to me. 27 I ask you to bless my descendants so that they will continue to enjoy your favor. You, LORD, have blessed them, and your blessing will rest on them forever."

David's Military Victories
(2 Samuel 8.1-18)

18 Some time later King David attacked the Philistines again and defeated them. He took out of their control the city of Gath and its surrounding villages. 2 He also defeated the Moabites, who became his subjects and paid taxes to him.

3 Next, David attacked King Hadadezer of the Syrian state of Zobah, near the territory of Hamath, because Hadadezer was trying to gain control of the territory by the upper Euphrates River. 4 David captured a thousand of his chariots, seven thousand cavalry troops, and twenty thousand foot soldiers. He kept enough horses for a hundred chariots and crippled all the rest.

5 When the Syrians of Damascus sent an army to help King Hadadezer, David attacked it and killed twenty-two thousand men. 6 Then he set up military camps in their territory, and they became his subjects and paid taxes to him. The LORD made David victorious everywhere. 7 David captured the gold shields carried by Hadadezer's officials and took them to Jerusalem. 8 He also took a great quantity of bronze from Tibhath and Kun, cities ruled by Hadadezer. (Solomon later used this bronze to make the tank, the columns, and the bronze utensils for the Temple.)

9 King Toi of Hamath heard that David had defeated Hadadezer's entire army. 10 So he sent his son Joram to greet King David and congratulate him for his victory over Hadadezer, against whom Toi had fought many times. Joram brought David presents made of gold, silver, and bronze. 11 King David dedicated them for use in worship, along with the silver and gold he took from the nations he conquered — Edom, Moab, Ammon, Philistia, and Amalek.

12 Abishai, whose mother was Zeruiah, defeated the Edomites in Salt Valley and killed eighteen thousand of them. 13 He set up military camps throughout Edom, and the people there became King David's subjects. The LORD made David victorious everywhere.

14 David ruled over all Israel and made sure that his people were always treated fairly and justly. 15 Abishai's brother Joab was commander of the army; Jehoshaphat son of Ahilud was in charge of the records; 16 Zadok son of Ahitub and Ahimelech son of Abiathar were priests; Seraiah^u was court secretary; 17 Benaiah son of Jehoiada was in charge of David's bodyguards; and King David's sons held high positions in his service.

---

^u *Probable text (see* 2 S 8.17) Seraiah; *Hebrew* Shavsha.
18.8 1 K 7.40-47; 2 Ch 4.11-18   **18.12** Ps 60 Title

David Defeats the Ammonites and the Syrians
(2 Samuel 10.1-19)

19 Some time later King Nahash of Ammon died, and his son Hanun became king. ² King David said, "I must show loyal friendship to Hanun, as his father Nahash did to me." So David sent messengers to express his sympathy.

When they arrived in Ammon and called on King Hanun, ³ the Ammonite leaders said to the king, "Do you think that it is in your father's honor that David has sent these men to express sympathy to you? Of course not! He has sent them here as spies to explore the land, so that he can conquer it!"

⁴ Hanun seized David's messengers, shaved off their beards, cut off their clothes at the hips, and sent them away. ⁵ They were too ashamed to return home. When David heard what had happened, he sent word for them to stay in Jericho and not return until their beards had grown again.

⁶ King Hanun and the Ammonites realized that they had made David their enemy, so they paid nearly forty tons of silver to hire chariots and charioteers from Upper Mesopotamia and from the Syrian states of Maacah and Zobah. ⁷ The thirty-two thousand chariots they hired and the army of the king of Maacah came and camped near Medeba. The Ammonites too came out from all their cities and got ready to fight.

⁸ When David heard what was happening, he sent out Joab and the whole army. ⁹ The Ammonites marched out and took up their position at the entrance to Rabbah, their capital city, and the kings who had come to help took up their position in the open countryside.

¹⁰ Joab saw that the enemy troops would attack him in front and from the rear, so he chose the best of Israel's soldiers and put them in position facing the Syrians. ¹¹ He placed the rest of his troops under the command of his brother Abishai, who put them in position facing the Ammonites. ¹² Joab said to him, "If you see that the Syrians are defeating me, come and help me, and if the Ammonites are defeating you, I will go and help you. ¹³ Be strong and courageous! Let's fight hard for our people and for the cities of our God. And may the LORD's will be done."

¹⁴ Joab and his men advanced to attack, and the Syrians fled. ¹⁵ When the Ammonites saw the Syrians running away, they fled from Abishai and retreated into the city. Then Joab went back to Jerusalem.

¹⁶ The Syrians realized that they had been defeated by the Israelites, so they brought troops from the Syrian states on the east side of the Euphrates River and placed them under the command of Shobach, commander of the army of King Hadadezer of Zobah. ¹⁷ When David heard of it, he gathered the Israelite troops, crossed the Jordan River, and put them in position facing the Syrians. The fighting began, ¹⁸ and the Israelites drove the Syrian army back. David and his men killed seven thousand Syrian chariot drivers and forty thousand foot soldiers. They also killed the Syrian commander, Shobach. ¹⁹ When the kings who were subject to Hadadezer realized that they had been defeated by Israel, they made peace with David and became his subjects. ²⁰ The Syrians were never again willing to help the Ammonites.

David Captures Rabbah
(2 Samuel 12.26-31)

20 The following spring, at the time of the year when kings usually go to war, Joab led out the army and invaded the land of Ammon; King David, however, stayed in Jerusalem. They besieged the city of Rabbah, attacked it, and destroyed it. ²The Ammonite idol Molech*ᵛ* had a gold crown which weighed about seventy-five pounds. In it there was a jewel, which David took and put in his own crown. He also took a large amount of loot from the city. ³He took the people of the city and put them to work with saws, iron hoes, and axes. He did the same to the people of all the other towns of Ammon. Then he and his men returned to Jerusalem.

Battles against Philistine Giants
(2 Samuel 21.15-22)

⁴Later on, war broke out again with the Philistines at Gezer. This was when Sibbecai from Hushah killed a giant named Sippai, and the Philistines were defeated.

⁵There was another battle with the Philistines, and Elhanan son of Jair killed Lahmi, the brother of Goliath from Gath, whose spear had a shaft as thick as the bar on a weaver's loom.

⁶Another battle took place at Gath, where there was a giant with six fingers on each hand and six toes on each foot. He was a descendant of the ancient giants. ⁷He defied the Israelites, and Jonathan, the son of David's brother Shammah, killed him.

⁸These three, who were killed by David and his men, were descendants of the giants at Gath.

David Takes a Census
(2 Samuel 24.1-25)

21 Satan wanted to bring trouble on the people of Israel, so he made David decide to take a census. ²David gave orders to Joab and the other officers, "Go through Israel, from one end of the country to the other, and count the people. I want to know how many there are."

³Joab answered, "May the LORD

make the people of Israel a hundred times more numerous than they are now! Your Majesty, they are all your servants. Why do you want to do this and make the whole nation guilty?" ⁴But the king made Joab obey the order. Joab went out, traveled through the whole country of Israel, and then returned to Jerusalem. ⁵He reported to King David the total number of men capable of military service: 1,100,000 in Israel and 470,000 in Judah. ⁶Because Joab disapproved of the king's command, he did not take any census of the tribes of Levi and Benjamin.

⁷God was displeased with what had been done, so he punished Israel. ⁸David said to God, "I have committed a terrible sin in doing this! Please forgive me. I have acted foolishly."

⁹Then the LORD said to Gad, David's prophet, ¹⁰"Go and tell David that I am giving him three choices. I will do whichever he chooses."

¹¹Gad went to David, told him what the LORD had said, and asked, "Which is it to be? ¹²Three years of famine? Or three months of running away from the armies of your enemies? Or three days during which the LORD attacks you with his sword and sends an epidemic on your land, using his angel to bring death throughout Israel? What answer shall I give the LORD?"

¹³David replied to Gad, "I am in a desperate situation! But I don't want to be punished by people. Let the LORD himself be the one to punish me, because he is merciful."

¹⁴So the LORD sent an epidemic on the people of Israel, and seventy thousand of them died. ¹⁵Then he sent an angel to destroy Jerusalem, but he changed his mind and said to the angel, "Stop! That's enough!" The angel was standing by the threshing place of Araunah, a Jebusite.

¹⁶David saw the angel standing in

ᵛ Ammonite idol Molech; *or* Ammonite king.
20.5 1 S 17.4-7

midair, holding his sword in his hand, ready to destroy Jerusalem. Then David and the leaders of the people — all of whom were wearing sackcloth — bowed low, with their faces touching the ground. 17 David prayed, "O God, I am the one who did wrong. I am the one who ordered the census. What have these poor people done? LORD, my God, punish me and my family, and spare your people."

18 The angel of the LORD told Gad to command David to go and build an altar to the LORD at Araunah's threshing place. 19 David obeyed the LORD's command and went, as Gad had told him to. 20 There at the threshing place Araunah and his four sons were threshing wheat, and when they saw the angel, the sons ran and hid. 21 As soon as Araunah saw King David approaching, he left the threshing place and bowed low, with his face touching the ground. 22 David said to him, "Sell me your threshing place, so that I can build an altar to the LORD, to stop the epidemic. I'll give you the full price."

23 "Take it, Your Majesty," Araunah said, "and do whatever you wish. Here are these oxen to burn as an offering on the altar, and here are the threshing boards to use as fuel, and wheat to give as an offering. I give it all to you."

24 But the king answered, "No, I will pay you the full price. I will not give as an offering to the LORD something that belongs to you, something that costs me nothing." 25 And he paid Araunah six hundred gold coins for the threshing place. 26 He built an altar to the LORD there and offered burnt offerings and fellowship offerings. He prayed, and the LORD answered him by sending fire from heaven to burn the sacrifices on the altar.

27 The LORD told the angel to put his sword away, and the angel obeyed. 28 David saw by this that the LORD had answered his prayer, so he offered sacrifices on the altar at Araunah's threshing place. 29 The Tent of the LORD's presence which Moses had made in the wilderness, and the altar on which sacrifices were burned were still at the place of worship at Gibeon at this time; 30 but David was not able to go there to worship God, because he was afraid of the sword of the LORD's angel.

22 So David said, "This is where the Temple of the LORD God will be. Here is the altar where the people of Israel are to offer burnt offerings."

Preparations for Building the Temple

2 King David gave orders for all the foreigners living in the land of Israel to assemble, and he put them to work. Some of them prepared stone blocks for building the Temple. 3 He supplied a large amount of iron for making nails and clamps for the wooden gates, and so much bronze that no one could weigh it. 4 He had the people of Tyre and Sidon bring him a large number of cedar logs. 5 David thought, "The Temple that my son Solomon is to build must be splendid and world-famous. But he is young and inexperienced, so I must make preparations for it." So David got large amounts of the materials ready before he died.

6 He sent for his son Solomon and commanded him to build a temple for the LORD, the God of Israel. 7 David said to him, "Son, I wanted to build a temple to honor the LORD my God. 8 But the LORD told me that I had killed too many people and fought too many wars. And so, because of all the bloodshed I have caused, he would not let me build a temple for him. 9 He did, however, make me a promise. He said, 'You will have a son who will rule in peace, because I will give him peace from all his

enemies. His name will be Solomon,[w] because during his reign I will give Israel peace and security. 10 He will build a temple for me. He will be my son, and I will be his father. His dynasty will rule Israel forever.'"

11 David continued, "Now, son, may the LORD your God be with you, and may he keep his promise to make you successful in building a temple for him. 12 And may the LORD your God give you insight and wisdom so that you may govern Israel according to his Law. 13 If you obey all the laws which the LORD gave to Moses for Israel, you will be successful. Be determined and confident, and don't let anything make you afraid. 14 As for the Temple, by my efforts I have accumulated almost four thousand tons of gold and nearly forty thousand tons of silver to be used in building it. Besides that, there is an unlimited supply of bronze and iron. I also have wood and stone ready, but you must get more. 15 You have many workers. There are stonecutters to work in the quarries, and there are masons and carpenters, as well as a large number of skilled workers of every sort who can work 16 with gold, silver, bronze, and iron. Now begin the work, and may the LORD be with you."

17 David commanded all the leaders of Israel to help Solomon. 18 He said, "The LORD your God has been with you and given you peace on all sides. He let me conquer all the people who used to live in this land, and they are now subject to you and to the LORD. 19 Now serve the LORD your God with all your heart and soul. Start building the Temple, so that you can place in it the Covenant Box of the LORD and all the other sacred objects used in worshiping him."

23

When David was very old, he made his son Solomon king of Israel.

The Work of the Levites

2 King David brought together all the Israelite leaders and all the priests and

"Now begin the work." (22.16)

Levites. 3 He took a census of all the male Levites aged thirty or older. The total was thirty-eight thousand. 4 The king assigned twenty-four thousand to administer the work of the Temple, six thousand to keep records and decide disputes, 5 four thousand to do guard duty, and four thousand to praise the LORD, using the musical instruments provided by the king for this purpose.

6 David divided the Levites into three groups, according to their clans: Gershon, Kohath, and Merari.

7 Gershon had two sons: Ladan and Shimei. 8 Ladan had three sons: Jehiel, Zetham, and Joel, 9 who were the heads of the clans descended from Ladan. (Shimei had three sons: Shelomoth, Haziel, and Haran.)[x] 10-11 Shimei had four sons: Jahath, Zina, Jeush, and Beriah, in order of age. Jeush and Beriah did not have many descendants, so they were counted as one clan.

---

[w] SOLOMON: *This name is formed from the Hebrew word "shalom," which means "peace and security."*   [x] SHIMEI ... HARAN: *The relation of this list to the list of Shimei's sons in verse 10 is not clear.*

22.13 Js 1.6-9   **23.1** 1 K 1.1-40

¹²Kohath had four sons: Amram, Izhar, Hebron, and Uzziel. ¹³His oldest son, Amram, was the father of Aaron and Moses. (Aaron and his descendants were set apart to be in charge of the sacred objects forever, to burn incense in the worship of the Lord, to serve him, and to bless the people in his name. ¹⁴But the sons of Moses, the man of God, were included among the Levites.) ¹⁵Moses had two sons, Gershom and Eliezer. ¹⁶The leader among Gershom's sons was Shebuel. ¹⁷Eliezer had only one son, Rehabiah, but Rehabiah had many descendants.

¹⁸Kohath's second son, Izhar, had a son, Shelomith, the head of the clan. ¹⁹Kohath's third son, Hebron, had four sons: Jeriah, Amariah, Jahaziel, and Jekameam. ²⁰Kohath's fourth son, Uzziel, had two sons, Micah and Isshiah.

²¹Merari had two sons, Mahli and Mushi. Mahli also had two sons, Eleazar and Kish, ²²but Eleazar died without having any sons, only daughters. His daughters married their cousins, the sons of Kish. ²³Merari's second son, Mushi, had three sons: Mahli, Eder, and Jeremoth.

²⁴These were the descendants of Levi, by clans and families, every one of them registered by name. Each of his descendants, twenty years of age or older, had a share in the work of the Lord's Temple. ²⁵David said, "The Lord God of Israel has given peace to his people, and he himself will live in Jerusalem forever. ²⁶So there is no longer any need for the Levites to carry the Tent of the Lord's presence and all the equipment used in worship." ²⁷On the basis of David's final instructions all Levites were registered for service when they reached the age of twenty, ²⁸and were assigned the following duties: to help the priests descended from Aaron with the Temple worship, to take care of its courtyards and its rooms, and to keep undefiled everything that is sacred; ²⁹to be responsible for the bread offered to God, the flour used in offerings, the wafers made without yeast, the baked offerings, and the flour mixed with olive oil; to weigh and measure the Temple offerings; ³⁰and to praise and glorify the Lord every morning and every evening ³¹and whenever offerings to the Lord are burned on the Sabbath, the New Moon Festival, and other festivals. Rules were made specifying the number of Levites assigned to do this work each time. The Levites were assigned the duty of worshiping the Lord for all time. ³²They were given the responsibility of taking care of the Tent of the Lord's presence and the Temple, and of assisting their relatives, the priests descended from Aaron, in the Temple worship.

The Work Assigned to the Priests

24 These are the groups to which the descendants of Aaron belong. Aaron had four sons: Nadab, Abihu, Eleazar, and Ithamar. ²Nadab and Abihu died before their father did, and left no descendants, so their brothers Eleazar and Ithamar became priests. ³King David organized the descendants of Aaron into groups according to their duties. He was assisted in this by Zadok, a descendant of Eleazar, and by Ahimelech, a descendant of Ithamar. ⁴The descendants of Eleazar were organized into sixteen groups, while the descendants of Ithamar were organized into eight; this was done because there were more male heads of families among the descendants of Eleazar. ⁵Since there were Temple officials and spiritual leaders among the descendants of both Eleazar and Ithamar, assignments were made by drawing lots. ⁶The descendants of Eleazar and of Ithamar took turns drawing lots. Then they were registered by Shema-

23.13 Ex 28.1   **23.26** Dt 10.8   **23.28-32** Nu 3.5-9   **24.2** Lv 10.1, 2 iah son of Nethanel, a Levite secretary. The king, his officials, the priest Zadok, Ahimelech son of Abiathar, and the heads of the priestly families and of the Levite families, were all witnesses.

7-18 This is the order in which the twenty-four family groups were given their assignments: 1) Jehoiarib; 2) Jedaiah; 3) Harim; 4) Seorim; 5) Malchijah; 6) Mijamin; 7) Hakkoz; 8) Abijah; 9) Jeshua; 10) Shecaniah; 11) Eliashib; 12) Jakim; 13) Huppah; 14) Jeshebeab; 15) Bilgah; 16) Immer; 17) Hezir; 18) Happizzez; 19) Pethahiah; 20) Jehezkel; 21) Jachin; 22) Gamul; 23) Delaiah; 24) Maaziah.

19These men were registered according to their assignments for going to the Temple and performing the duties established by their ancestor Aaron in obedience to the commands of the LORD God of Israel.

The List of the Levites

20These are other heads of families descended from Levi:

Jehdeiah, a descendant of Amram through Shebuel;

21Isshiah, a descendant of Rehabiah;

22Jahath, a descendant of Izhar through Shelomith;

23Jeriah, Amariah, Jehaziel, and Jekameam, sons of Hebron, in order of age;

24Shamir, a descendant of Uzziel through Micah;

25Zechariah, a descendant of Uzziel through Isshiah, Micah's brother;

26Mahli, Mushi, and Jaaziah, descendants of Merari. **27**Jaaziah had three sons: Shoham, Zaccur, and Ibri. **28-29**Mahli had two sons, Eleazar and Kish. Eleazar had no sons, but Kish had one son, Jerahmeel. **30**Mushi had three sons: Mahli, Eder, and Jeremoth.

These are the families of the Levites.

31The head of each family and one of his younger brothers drew lots for their assignments, just as their relatives, the priests descended from Aaron, had done. King David, Zadok, Ahimelech, and the heads of families of the priests and of the Levites were witnesses.

The Temple Musicians

25 King David and the leaders of the Levites chose the following Levite clans to lead the worship services: Asaph, Heman, and Jeduthun. They were to proclaim God's messages, accompanied by the music of harps and cymbals. This is the list of persons chosen to lead the worship, with the type of service that each group performed:

2The four sons of Asaph: Zaccur, Joseph, Nethaniah, and Asharelah. They were under the direction of Asaph, who proclaimed God's messages whenever the king commanded.

3The six sons of Jeduthun: Gedaliah, Zeri, Jeshaiah, Shimei, Hashabiah, and Mattithiah. Under the direction of their father they proclaimed God's message, accompanied by the music of harps, and sang praise and thanks to the LORD.

4The fourteen sons of Heman: Bukkiah, Mattaniah, Uzziel, Shebuel, Jerimoth, Hananiah, Hanani, Eliathah, Giddalti, Romamti Ezer, Joshbekashah, Mallothi, Hothir, and Mahazioth. **5**God gave to Heman, the king's prophet, these fourteen sons and also three daughters, as he had promised, in order to give power to Heman. **6**All of his sons played cymbals and harps under their father's direction, to accompany the Temple worship. And Asaph, Jeduthun, and Heman were under orders from the king.

7All these twenty-four men were experts; and their fellow Levites were trained musicians. There were 288 men in all.

8To determine the assignment of duties they all drew lots, whether they were young or old, experts or beginners.

9-31 These 288 men were divided according to families into twenty-four groups of twelve, with a leader in charge of each group. This is the order in which they were on duty: 1) Joseph of the family of Asaph; 2) Gedaliah; 3) Zaccur; 4) Zeri; 5) Nethaniah; 6) Bukkiah; 7) Asharelah; 8) Jeshaiah; 9) Mattaniah; 10) Shimei; 11) Uzziel; 12) Hashabiah; 13) Shebuel; 14) Mattithiah; 15) Jerimoth; 16) Hananiah; 17) Joshbekashah; 18) Hanani; 19) Mallothi; 20) Eliathah; 21) Hothir; 22) Giddalti; 23) Mahazioth; 24) Romamti Ezer.

The Temple Guards

26 These are the assignments of work for the Levites who served as Temple guards. From the clan of Korah there was Meshelemiah son of Kore, of the family of Asaph. ²He had seven sons, listed in order of age: Zechariah, Jediael, Zebadiah, Jathniel, ³Elam, Jehohanan, and Eliehoenai.

⁴There was also Obed Edom, whom God blessed by giving him eight sons, listed in order of age: Shemaiah, Jehozabad, Joah, Sachar, Nethanel, ⁵Ammiel, Issachar, and Peullethai.

⁶⁷Obed Edom's oldest son, Shemaiah, had six sons: Othni, Rephael, Obed, Elzabad, Elihu, and Semachiah. They were important men in their clan because of their great ability; the last two were especially talented.

⁸Obed Edom's family furnished a total of sixty-two highly qualified men for this work.

⁹Meshelemiah's family furnished eighteen qualified men.

¹⁰From the clan of Merari there was Hosah, who had four sons: Shimri (his father made him the leader, even though he was not the oldest son), ¹¹Hilkiah, Tebaliah, and Zechariah. In all there were thirteen members of Hosah's family who were Temple guards.

¹²The Temple guards were divided into groups, according to families, and they were assigned duties in the Temple, just as the other Levites were. ¹³Each family, regardless of size, drew lots to see which gate it would be responsible for. ¹⁴Shelemiah drew the east gate, and his son Zechariah, a man who always gave good advice, drew the north gate. ¹⁵Obed Edom was allotted the south gate, and his sons were allotted to guard the storerooms. ¹⁶Shuppim and Hosah were allotted the west gate and the Shallecheth Gate on the upper road. Guard duty was divided into assigned periods, one after another. ¹⁷On the east, six guards were on duty each day, on the north, four, and on the south, four. Four guards were stationed at the storerooms daily, two at each storeroom. ¹⁸Near the western pavilion there were four guards by the road and two at the pavilion itself. ¹⁹This is the assignment of guard duty to the clan of Korah and the clan of Merari.

Other Temple Duties

²⁰Others of their fellow Levites^y were in charge of the Temple treasury and the storerooms for gifts dedicated to God. ²¹Ladan, one of the sons of Gershon, was the ancestor of several family groups, including the family of his son Jehiel. ²²Ladan's two other sons, Zetham and Joel, had charge of the Temple treasury and storerooms.

²³Duties were also assigned to the descendants of Amram, Izhar, Hebron, and Uzziel.

²⁴Shebuel, of the clan of Moses' son Gershom, was the chief official responsible for the Temple treasury. ²⁵Through Gershom's brother Eliezer he was related to Shelomith. Eliezer was the father of Rehabiah, who was the father of Jeshaiah, the father of Joram, the father of Zichri, the father of Shelomith. ²⁶Shelomith and the mem-

---

^y *One ancient translation* fellow Levites; *Hebrew* Levites, Ahijah.
26.4, 5 2 S 6.11; 1 Ch 13.14

ers of his family were in charge of all the gifts dedicated to God by King David, the heads of families, leaders of clan groups, and army officers. 27 They took some of the loot they captured in battle and dedicated it for use in the Temple. 28 Shelomith and his family were in charge of everything that had been dedicated for use in the Temple, including the gifts brought by the prophet Samuel, by King Saul, by Abner son of Ner, and by Joab son of Zeruiah.

Duties of Other Levites

29 Among the descendants of Izhar, Chenaniah and his sons were assigned administrative duties: keeping records and settling disputes for the people of Israel.

30 Among the descendants of Hebron, Hashabiah and seventeen hundred of his relatives, all outstanding men, were put in charge of the administration of all religious and civil matters in Israel west of the Jordan River. 31 Jeriah was the leader of the descendants of Hebron. In the fortieth year that David was king, an investigation was made of the family line of Hebron's descendants, and outstanding soldiers belonging to this family were found living at Jazer in the territory of Gilead. 32 King David chose twenty-seven hundred outstanding heads of families from Jeriah's relatives and put them in charge of administering all religious and civil matters in Israel east of the Jordan River—the territories of Reuben, Gad, and East Manasseh.

Military and Civil Organization

27 This is the list of the Israelite heads of families and clan leaders and their officials who administered the work of the kingdom. Each month

of the year a different group of twenty-four thousand men was on duty under the commander for that month.

2-15 The following were the commanders for each month:

First month: Jashobeam son of Zabdiel (he was a member of the clan of Perez, a part of the tribe of Judah)

Second month: Dodai, a descendant of Ahohi (Mikloth was his second in command)ᶻ

Third month: Benaiah son of Jehoiada the priest; he was the leader of "The Thirty" (his son Ammizabad succeeded him as commander of this group)

Fourth month: Asahel, brother of Joab (his son Zebadiah succeeded him)

Fifth month: Shamhuth, a descendant of Izhar

Sixth month: Ira son of Ikkesh from Tekoa

Seventh month: Helez, an Ephraimite from Pelon

Eighth month: Sibbecai from Hushah (he was a member of the clan of Zerah, a part of the tribe of Judah)

Ninth month: Abiezer from Anathoth in the territory of the tribe of Benjamin

Tenth month: Maharai from Netophah (he was a member of the clan of Zerah)

Eleventh month: Benaiah from Pirathon in the territory of the tribe of Ephraim

Twelfth month: Heldai from Netophah (he was a descendant of Othniel)

ᶻ *Probable text* Mikloth ... command; *Hebrew unclear.*

Administration of the Tribes of Israel

16-22 This is the list of the administrators of the tribes of Israel:

Tribe	Administrator
Reuben	Eliezer son of Zichri
Simeon	Shephatiah son of Maacah
Levi	Hashabiah son of Kemuel
Aaron	Zadok
Judah	Elihu, one of King David's brothers
Issachar	Omri son of Michael
Zebulun	Ishmaiah son of Obadiah
Naphtali	Jeremoth son of Azriel
Ephraim	Hoshea son of Azaziah
West Manasseh	Joel son of Pedaiah
East Manasseh	Iddo son of Zechariah
Benjamin	Jaasiel son of Abner
Dan	Azarel son of Jeroham

23 King David did not take a census of the people who were under the age of twenty, because of the LORD's promise to make the people of Israel as numerous as the stars in the sky. 24 Joab, whose mother was Zeruiah, began to take a census, but he did not complete it. God punished Israel because of this census, so the final figures were never recorded in King David's official records.

Administrators of the Royal Property

25-31 This is the list of those who administered the royal property:

Royal storerooms: Azmaveth son of Adiel

Local storerooms: Jonathan son of Uzziah

Farm labor: Ezri son of Chelub

Vineyards: Shimei from Ramah

Wine cellars: Zabdi from Shepham

Olive and sycamore trees (in the western foothills): Baal Hanan from Geder

Olive oil storage: Joash

Cattle in the Plain of Sharon: Shitrai from Sharon

Cattle in the valleys: Shaphat son of Adlai

Camels: Obil, an Ishmaelite

Donkeys: Jehdeiah from Meronoth

Sheep and goats: Jaziz, a Hagrite

David's Personal Advisers

32 Jonathan, King David's uncle, was a skillful adviser and a scholar. He and Jehiel son of Hachmoni were in charge of the education of the king's sons. 33 Ahithophel was adviser to the king, and Hushai the Archite was the king's friend and counselor. 34 After Ahithophel died, Abiathar and Jehoiada son of Benaiah became advisers. Joab was commander of the royal army.

David's Instructions for the Temple

28 King David commanded all the officials of Israel to assemble in Jerusalem. So all the officials of the tribes, the officials who administered the work of the kingdom, the leaders of the clans, the supervisors of the property and livestock that belonged to the king and his sons — indeed all the palace officials, leading soldiers, and important men — gathered in Jerusalem. 2 David stood before them and addressed them: "My friends, listen to me. I wanted to build a permanent home for the Covenant Box, the footstool of the

27.23 Gn 15.5; 22.17; 26.4   **27.24** 2 S 24.15; 1 Ch 21.1-14   **28.2-7** 2 S 7.1-16; 1 Ch 17.1-14

LORD our God. I have made preparations for building a temple to honor him, [3] but he has forbidden me to do it, because I am a soldier and have shed too much blood. [4] The LORD, the God of Israel, chose me and my descendants to rule Israel forever. He chose the tribe of Judah to provide leadership, and out of Judah he chose my father's family. From all that family it was his pleasure to take me and make me king over all Israel. [5] He gave me many sons, and out of them all he chose Solomon to rule over Israel, the LORD's kingdom.

[6] "The LORD said to me, 'Your son Solomon is the one who will build my Temple. I have chosen him to be my son, and I will be his father. [7] I will make his kingdom last forever if he continues to obey carefully all my laws and commands as he does now.'

[8] "So now, my people, in the presence of our God and of this assembly of all Israel, the LORD's people, I charge you to obey carefully everything that the LORD our God has commanded us, so that you may continue to possess this good land and so that you may hand it on to succeeding generations forever."

[9] And to Solomon he said, "My son, I charge you to acknowledge your father's God and to serve him with an undivided heart and a willing mind. He knows all our thoughts and desires. If you go to him, he will accept you; but if you turn away from him, he will abandon you forever. [10] You must realize that the LORD has chosen you to build his holy Temple. Now do it — and do it with determination."

[11] David gave Solomon the plans for all the Temple buildings, for the storerooms and all the other rooms, and for the Most Holy Place, where sins are forgiven. [12] He also gave him the plans for all he had in mind for the courtyards and the rooms around them, and for the storerooms for the Temple equipment

and the gifts dedicated to the LORD. [13] David also gave him the plans for organizing the priests and Levites to perform their duties, to do the work of the Temple, and to take care of all the Temple utensils. [14] He gave instructions as to how much silver and gold was to be used for making the utensils, [15] for each lamp and lampstand, [16] for the silver tables, and for each gold table on which were placed the loaves of bread offered to God. [17] He also gave instructions as to how much pure gold was to be used in making forks, bowls, and jars, how much silver and gold in making dishes, [18] and how much pure gold in making the altar on which incense was burned and in making the chariot for the winged creatures that spread their wings over the LORD's Covenant Box. [19] King David said, "All this is contained in the plan written according to the instructions which the LORD himself gave me to carry out."

[20] King David said to his son Solomon, "Be confident and determined. Start the work and don't let anything stop you. The LORD God, whom I serve, will be with you. He will not abandon you, but he will stay with you until you finish the work to be done on his Temple. [21] The priests and the Levites have been assigned duties to perform in the Temple. Workers with every kind of skill are eager to help you, and all the people and their leaders are at your command."

Gifts for Building the Temple

29 King David announced to the whole assembly: "My son Solomon is the one whom God has chosen, but he is still young and lacks experience. The work to be done is tremendous, because this is not a palace for people but a temple for the LORD God. [2] I have made every effort to prepare materials for the Temple — gold, silver,

29.1, 2 1 Ch 22.5

"My son Solomon is the one." (29.1)

bronze, iron, timber, precious stones and gems, stones for mosaics, and quantities of marble. ³Over and above all this that I have provided, I have given silver and gold from my personal property because of my love for God's Temple. ⁴I have given 115 tons of the finest gold and 265 tons of pure silver for decorating the walls of the Temple ⁵and for all the objects which the skilled workers are to make. Now who else is willing to give a generous offering to the Lord?"

⁶Then the heads of the clans, the officials of the tribes, the commanders of the army, and the administrators of the royal property volunteered to give ⁷the following for the work on the Temple: 190 tons of gold, 380 tons of silver, 675 tons of bronze, and 3,750 tons of iron. ⁸Those who had precious stones gave them to the Temple treasury, which was administered by Jehiel of the Levite clan of Gershon. ⁹The people had given willingly to the Lord, and they were happy that so much had been

given. King David also was extremely happy.

David Praises God

¹⁰There in front of the whole assembly King David praised the Lord. He said, "Lord God of our ancestor Jacob, may you be praised forever and ever! ¹¹You are great and powerful, glorious, splendid, and majestic. Everything in heaven and earth is yours, and you are king, supreme ruler over all. ¹²All riches and wealth come from you; you rule everything by your strength and power; and you are able to make anyone great and strong. ¹³Now, our God, we give you thanks, and we praise your glorious name.

¹⁴"Yet my people and I cannot really give you anything, because everything is a gift from you, and we have only given back what is yours already. ¹⁵You know, O Lord, that we pass through life like exiles and strangers, as our ancestors did. Our days are like a passing shadow, and we cannot escape death.

¹⁶O LORD, our God, we have brought together all this wealth to build a temple to honor your holy name, but it all came from you and all belongs to you. ¹⁷I know that you test everyone's heart and are pleased with people of integrity. In honesty and sincerity I have willingly given all this to you, and I have seen how your people who are gathered here have been happy to bring offerings to you. ¹⁸LORD God of our ancestors Abraham, Isaac, and Jacob, keep such devotion forever strong in your people's hearts and keep them always faithful to you. ¹⁹Give my son Solomon a whole-hearted desire to obey everything that you command and to build the Temple for which I have made these preparations."

²⁰Then David commanded the people, "Praise the LORD your God!" And the whole assembly praised the LORD, the God of their ancestors, and they bowed low and gave honor to the LORD and also to the king.

²¹The following day they killed animals as sacrifices, dedicating them to the LORD, and then gave them to the people to eat. In addition, they sacrificed a thousand bulls, a thousand rams, and a thousand lambs, which they burned whole on the altar. They also brought the offerings of wine. ²²So that day they were very happy as they ate and drank in the presence of the LORD.

For a second time they proclaimed Solomon king. In the name of the LORD they anointed him as their ruler and Zadok as priest. ²³So Solomon succeeded his father David on the throne which the LORD had established. He was a successful king, and the whole nation of Israel obeyed him. ²⁴All the officials and soldiers, and even all of David's other sons, promised to be loyal to Solomon as king. ²⁵The LORD made the whole nation stand in awe of Solomon, and he made him more glorious than any other king that had ruled Israel.

Summary of David's Reign

²⁶David son of Jesse ruled over all Israel ²⁷for forty years. He ruled in Hebron for seven years and in Jerusalem for thirty-three. ²⁸He died at a ripe old age, wealthy and respected, and his son Solomon succeeded him as king. ²⁹The history of King David from beginning to end is recorded in the records of the three prophets, Samuel, Nathan, and Gad. ³⁰The records tell how he ruled, how powerful he was, and all the things that happened to him, to Israel, and to the surrounding kingdoms.

29.23 1 K 2.12   **29.27** 2 S 5.4, 5; 1 Ch 3.4

The Second Book of
CHRONICLES

INTRODUCTION

Second Chronicles begins where *First Chronicles* ends. It describes the rule of King Solomon, records the revolt of the northern tribes led by Jeroboam against Rehoboam, King Solomon's son and successor, and continues an account of the history of the kingdom of Judah until the fall of Jerusalem in 586 B.C.

OUTLINE OF CONTENTS

King Solomon Prays for Wisdom
(1 Kings 3.1-15)

1 Solomon, the son of King David, took firm control of the kingdom of Israel, and the LORD his God blessed him and made him very powerful.

² King Solomon gave an order to all the officers in charge of units of a thousand men and of a hundred men, all the government officials, all the heads of families, and all the rest of the people, ³ commanding them to go with him to the place of worship at Gibeon. They went there because that was where the Tent of the LORD's presence was located, which Moses, the LORD's servant, had made in the wilderness. (⁴ The Covenant Box, however, was in Jerusalem, kept in a tent which King David had set up when he brought the Box from Kiriath Jearim.) ⁵ The bronze altar which had been made by Bezalel, the

son of Uri and grandson of Hur, was also in Gibeon in front of the Tent of the LORD's presence. King Solomon and all the people worshiped the LORD there. ⁶ In front of the Tent the king worshiped the LORD by offering sacrifices on the bronze altar; he had a thousand animals killed and burned whole on it.

⁷ That night God appeared to Solomon and asked, "What would you like me to give you?"

⁸ Solomon answered, "You always showed great love for my father David, and now you have let me succeed him as king. ⁹ O LORD God, fulfill the promise you made to my father. You have made me king over a people who are so many that they cannot be counted, ¹⁰ so give me the wisdom and knowledge I need to rule over them. Otherwise, how would I ever be able to rule this great people of yours?"

1.4 2 S 6.1-17; 1 Ch 13.5-14; 15.25—16.1   **1.5** Ex 38.1-7   **1.9** Gn 13.16; 28.14

¹¹God replied to Solomon, "You have made the right choice. Instead of asking for wealth or treasure or fame or the death of your enemies or even for long life for yourself, you have asked for wisdom and knowledge so that you can rule my people, over whom I have made you king. ¹²I will give you wisdom and knowledge. And in addition, I will give you more wealth, treasure, and fame than any king has ever had before or will ever have again."

King Solomon's Power and Wealth
(1 Kings 10.26-29)

¹³So Solomon left*ᵃ* the place of worship at Gibeon, where the Tent of the LORD's presence was, and returned to Jerusalem. There he ruled over Israel. ¹⁴He built up a force of fourteen hundred chariots and twelve thousand cavalry horses. Some of them he kept in Jerusalem, and the rest he stationed in various other cities. ¹⁵During his reign silver and gold became as common in Jerusalem as stone, and cedar was as plentiful as ordinary sycamore in the foothills of Judah. ¹⁶The king's agents controlled the export of horses from Musri*ᵇ* and Cilicia,*ᶜ* ¹⁷and the export of chariots from Egypt. They supplied the Hittite and Syrian kings with horses and chariots, selling chariots for 600 pieces of silver each and horses for 150 each.*ᵈ*

Preparations for Building the Temple
(1 Kings 5.1-18)

2 King Solomon decided to build a temple where the LORD would be worshiped, and also to build a palace for himself. ²He put 70,000 men to work transporting materials, and 80,000 to work cutting stone in the hill country.

There were 3,600 others responsible for supervising the work.

³Solomon sent a message to King Hiram of Tyre: "Do business with me as you did with my father, King David, when you sold him cedar logs for building his palace. ⁴I am building a temple to honor the LORD my God. It will be a holy place where my people and I will worship him by burning incense of fragrant spices, where we will present offerings of sacred bread to him continuously, and where we will offer burnt offerings every morning and evening, as well as on Sabbaths, New Moon Festivals, and other holy days honoring the LORD our God. He has commanded Israel to do this forever. ⁵I intend to build a great temple, because our God is greater than any other god. ⁶Yet no one can really build a temple for God, because even all the vastness of heaven cannot contain him. How then can I build a temple that would be anything more than a place to burn incense to God? ⁷Now send me a man with skill in engraving, in working gold, silver, bronze, and iron, and in making blue, purple, and red cloth. He will work with the craftsmen of Judah and Jerusalem whom my father David selected. ⁸I know how skillful your lumbermen are, so send me cedar, cypress, and juniper logs from Lebanon. I am ready to send my men to assist yours ⁹in preparing large quantities of timber, because this temple I intend to build will be large and magnificent. ¹⁰As provisions for your lumbermen, I will send you 100,000 bushels of wheat, 100,000 bushels of barley, 110,000 gallons of wine, and 110,000 gallons of olive oil."

¹¹King Hiram sent Solomon a letter in reply. He wrote, "Because the LORD loves his people, he has made you their

---

ᵃ Some ancient translations left; *Hebrew* came to.   *ᵇ Probable text* Musri; *Hebrew* Egypt.   *ᶜ* MUSRI AND CILICIA: *Two ancient countries in what is now southeast Turkey which were centers of horse breeding in Solomon's time.*   *ᵈ Verses 16-17 in Hebrew are unclear.*

1.14 1 K 4.26   **1.16** Dt 17.16   **2.6** 1 K 8.27; 2 Ch 6.18

king. ¹²Praise the LORD God of Israel, Creator of heaven and earth! He has given King David a wise son, full of understanding and skill, who now plans to build a temple for the LORD and a palace for himself. ¹³I am sending you a wise and skillful master metalworker named Huram. ¹⁴His mother was a member of the tribe of Dan and his father was a native of Tyre. He knows how to make things out of gold, silver, bronze, iron, stone, and wood. He can work with blue, purple, and red cloth, and with linen. He can do all sorts of engraving and can follow any design suggested to him. Let him work with your skilled workers and with those who worked for your father, King David. ¹⁵So now send us the wheat, barley, wine, and olive oil that you promised. ¹⁶In the mountains of Lebanon we will cut down all the cedars you need, tie them together in rafts, and float them by sea as far as Joppa. From there you can take them to Jerusalem."

Construction of the Temple Begins
(1 Kings 6.1-38)

¹⁷King Solomon took a census of all the foreigners living in the land of Israel, similar to the census his father David had taken. There were 153,600 resident foreigners. ¹⁸He assigned 70,000 of them to transport materials and 80,000 to cut stones in the mountains, and appointed 3,600 supervisors to make sure the work was done.

3 King David, Solomon's father, had already prepared a place for the Temple. It was in Jerusalem, on Mount Moriah, where the LORD appeared to David, at the place which Araunah the Jebusite had used as a threshing place. King Solomon began the construction ²in the second month of the fourth year that he was king. ³The Temple which King Solomon built was 90 feet long

and 30 feet wide. ⁴The entrance room was the full width of the Temple, 30 feet, and was 180 feet high. The inside of the room was overlaid with pure gold. ⁵The main room was paneled with cedar and overlaid with fine gold, in which were worked designs of palm trees and chain patterns. ⁶The king decorated the Temple with beautiful precious stones and with gold imported from the land of Parvaim. ⁷He used the gold to overlay the Temple walls, the rafters, the entryways, and the doors. On the walls the workers carved designs of winged creatures.ᵉ ⁸The inner room, called the Most Holy Place, was 30 feet long and 30 feet wide, which was the full width of the Temple. Twenty-five tons of gold were used to cover the walls of the Most Holy Place; ⁹twenty ounces of gold were used for making nails, and the walls of the upper rooms were also covered with gold.

¹⁰The king also had his workers make two winged creatures out of metal, cover them with gold, and place them in the Most Holy Place, ¹¹⁻¹³where they stood side by side facing the entrance. Each had two wings, each wing 7½ feet long, which were spread out so that they touched each other in the center of the room and reached to the wall on either side of the room, stretching across the full width of 30 feet. ¹⁴A curtain for the Most Holy Place was made of linen and of other material, which was dyed blue, purple, and red, with designs of the winged creatures worked into it.

The Two Bronze Columns
(1 Kings 7.15-22)

¹⁵The king had two columns made, each one 52 feet tall, and placed them in front of the Temple. Each one had a capital 7½ feet tall. ¹⁶The tops of the columns were decorated with a design

---

ᵉ WINGED CREATURES: *See Word List.*

3.1 Gn 22.22   **3.8** Ex 26.33, 34   **3.10-13** Ex 25.18-20   **3.14** Ex 26.31

f interwoven chains and one hundred ronze pomegranates.*f* ¹⁷ The columns were set at the sides of the Temple entrance: the one on the south side was named Jachin*g* and the one on the north side was named Boaz.*h*

Equipment for the Temple
(1 Kings 7.23-51)

4 King Solomon had a bronze altar made, which was 30 feet square and 15 feet high. ²He also made a round tank of bronze, 7½ feet deep, 15 feet in diameter, and 45 feet in circumference. ³All around the outer edge of the rim of the tank*i* were two rows of decorations, one above the other. The decorations were in the shape of bulls, which had been cast all in one piece with the rest of the tank. ⁴The tank rested on the backs of twelve bronze bulls that faced outward, three facing in each direction. ⁵The sides of the tank were 3 inches thick. Its rim was like the rim of a cup, curving outward like the petals of a flower. The tank held about 15,000 gallons. ⁶They also made ten basins, five to be placed on the south side of the Temple and five on the north side. They were to be used to rinse the parts of the animals that were burned as sacrifices. The water in the large tank was for the priests to use for washing.

⁷⁻⁸They made ten gold lampstands according to the usual pattern, and ten tables, and placed them in the main room of the Temple, five lampstands and five tables on each side. They also made a hundred gold bowls.

⁹They made an inner courtyard for the priests, and also an outer courtyard. The doors in the gates between the courtyards were covered with bronze. ¹⁰The tank was placed near the southeast corner of the Temple.

¹¹⁻¹⁶Huram also made pots, shovels, and bowls. He completed all the objects that he had promised King Solomon he would make for the Temple:

The two columns
The two bowl-shaped capitals on top of the columns
The design of interwoven chains on each capital
The 400 bronze pomegranates arranged in two rows around the design of each capital
The ten*j* carts
The ten basins
The tank
The twelve bulls supporting the tank
The pots, shovels, and forks

Huram the master metalworker made all these objects*k* out of polished bronze, as King Solomon had commanded, for use in the Temple of the LORD.

¹⁷The king had them all made in the foundry between Sukkoth and Zeredah*l* in the Jordan Valley. ¹⁸So many objects were made that no one determined the total weight of the bronze used.

¹⁹King Solomon also had gold furnishings made for the Temple: the altar and the tables for the bread offered to God; ²⁰the lampstands and the lamps of fine gold that were to burn in front of the Most Holy Place, according to plan; ²¹the flower decorations, the lamps, and the tongs; ²²the lamp snuffers, the bowls, the dishes for incense, and the pans used for carrying live coals. All these objects were made of pure gold.

---

f Verse 16 in Hebrew is unclear.   *g* JACHIN: *This name sounds like the Hebrew for "he (God) establishes."*   *h* BOAZ: *This name sounds like the Hebrew for "by his (God's) strength."*   *i Probable text* All around . . . tank; *Hebrew unclear.*
j Probable text (see 1 K 7.40-45) ten; *Hebrew* he made.   *k One ancient translation* all these objects; *Hebrew* all their objects.   *l* ZEREDAH *(see Zarethan, 1 K 7.46).*
4.1 Ex 27.1, 2   **4.6** Ex 30.17-21   **4.7** Ex 25.31-40   **4.8** Ex 25.23-30

The outer doors of the Temple and the doors to the Most Holy Place were overlaid with gold.

5 When King Solomon finished all the work on the Temple, he placed in the Temple storerooms all the things that his father David had dedicated to the LORD — the silver, gold, and other articles.

The Covenant Box Is Brought to the Temple
(1 Kings 8.1-9)

2 Then King Solomon summoned all the leaders of the tribes and clans of Israel to assemble in Jerusalem, in order to take the LORD's Covenant Box from Zion, David's City,*m* to the Temple. 3 They all assembled at the time of the Festival of Shelters. 4 When all the leaders had gathered, then the Levites lifted the Covenant Box 5 and carried it to the Temple. The priests and the Levites also moved the Tent of the LORD's presence and all its equipment to the Temple. 6 King Solomon and all the people of Israel assembled in front of the Covenant Box and sacrificed a large number of sheep and cattle — too many to count. 7 Then the priests carried the Covenant Box of the LORD into the Temple and put it in the Most Holy Place, beneath the winged creatures. 8 Their outstretched wings covered the Box and the poles it was carried by. 9 The ends of the poles could be seen by anyone standing directly in front of the Most Holy Place, but from nowhere else. (The poles are still there today.) 10 There was nothing inside the Covenant Box except the two stone tablets which Moses had placed there at Mount Sinai, when the LORD made a covenant with the people of Israel as they were coming from Egypt.

The Glory of the LORD

11-14 All the priests present, regardless of the group to which they belonged, had consecrated themselves. And all the Levite musicians — Asaph, Heman, and Jeduthun, and the members of their clans — were wearing linen clothing. The Levites stood near the east side of the altar with cymbals and harps, and with them were 120 priests playing trumpets. The singers were accompanied in perfect harmony by trumpets, cymbals, and other instruments, as they praised the LORD singing:
> "Praise the LORD, because he is good,
> And his love is eternal."

As the priests were leaving the Temple, it was suddenly filled with a cloud shining with the dazzling light of the LORD's presence, and they could not continue the service of worship.

Solomon's Address to the People
(1 Kings 8.12-21)

6 Then King Solomon prayed, "LORD, you have chosen to live in clouds and darkness.
2 Now I have built a majestic temple for you, a place for you to live in forever."

3 All the people of Israel were standing there. The king turned to face them and asked God's blessing on them. 4 He said, "Praise the LORD God of Israel! He has kept the promise he made to my father David when he said to him, 5 'From the time I brought my people out of Egypt until now, I did not choose any city in the land of Israel as the place to build a temple where I would be worshiped, and I did not choose anyone to

---

m DAVID'S CITY: *See Word List.*

5.1 2 S 8.11; 1 Ch 18.11   **5.2** 2 S 6.12-15; 1 Ch 15.25-28   **5.10** Dt 10.5   **5.13** 1 Ch 16.34;
2 Ch 7.3; Ezra 3.11; Ps 100.5; 106.1; 107.1; 118.1; 136.1; Jr 33.11
5.13, 14 Ex 40.34, 35   **6.4-9** 2 S 7.1-13; 1 Ch 17.1-12

lead my people Israel. ⁶But now I have chosen Jerusalem as the place where I will be worshiped, and you, David, to rule my people.'"

⁷And Solomon continued, "My father David planned to build a temple for the worship of the LORD God of Israel, ⁸but the LORD said to him, 'You were right in wanting to build a temple for me, ⁹but you will never build it. It is your son, your own son, who will build my temple.'

¹⁰"Now the LORD has kept his promise: I have succeeded my father as king of Israel, and I have built a temple for the worship of the LORD God of Israel. ¹¹I have placed in the Temple the Covenant Box, which contains the stone tablets of the covenant which the LORD made with the people of Israel."

Solomon's Prayer
(1 Kings 8.22-53)

¹²Then in the presence of the people Solomon went and stood in front of the altar and raised his arms in prayer.

Solomon . . . raised his arms in prayer. (6.12)

(¹³Solomon had made a bronze platform and put it in the middle of the courtyard. It was eight feet square and five feet high. He mounted this platform, knelt down where everyone could see him, and raised his hands toward heaven.) ¹⁴He prayed, "LORD God of Israel, in all heaven and earth there is no god like you. You keep your covenant with your people and show them your

love when they live in wholehearted obedience to you. ¹⁵You have kept the promise you made to my father David; today every word has been fulfilled. ¹⁶Now, LORD God of Israel, keep the other promise you made to my father when you told him that there would always be one of his descendants ruling as king of Israel, provided that they carefully obeyed your Law just as he did. ¹⁷So now, LORD God of Israel, let everything come true that you promised to your servant David.

¹⁸"But can you, O God, really live on earth among men and women? Not even all of heaven is large enough to hold you, so how can this Temple that I have built be large enough? ¹⁹LORD my God, I am your servant. Listen to my prayer and grant the requests I make to you. ²⁰Watch over this Temple day and night. You have promised that this is where you will be worshiped, so hear me when I face this Temple and pray. ²¹Hear my prayers and the prayers of your people Israel when they face this place and pray. In your home in heaven hear us and forgive us.

²²"When people are accused of wronging others and are brought to your altar in this Temple to take an oath that they are innocent, ²³O LORD, listen in heaven and judge your servants. Punish the guilty ones as they deserve and acquit the innocent.

²⁴"When your people Israel are defeated by their enemies because they have sinned against you and then when they turn to you and come to this Temple, humbly praying to you for forgiveness, ²⁵listen to them in heaven. Forgive the sins of your people and bring them back to the land which you gave to them and to their ancestors.

²⁶"When you hold back the rain because your people have sinned against you and then when they repent and face this Temple, humbly praying to you, ²⁷O LORD, listen to them in

heaven and forgive the sins of your servants, the people of Israel, and teach them to do what is right. Then, O LORD, send rain on this land of yours, which you gave to your people as a permanent possession.

28"When there is famine in the land or an epidemic or the crops are destroyed by scorching winds or swarms of locusts, or when your people are attacked by their enemies, or when there is disease or sickness among them, 29listen to their prayers. If any of your people Israel, out of heartfelt sorrow, stretch out their hands in prayer toward this Temple, 30hear their prayer. Listen to them in your home in heaven and forgive them. You alone know the thoughts of the human heart. Deal with each of us as we deserve, 31so that your people may honor you and obey you all the time they live in the land which you gave to our ancestors.

32"When foreigners who live in a distant land hear how great and powerful you are and how you are always ready to act, and then they come to pray at this Temple, 33listen to their prayers. In heaven, where you live, hear them and do what they ask you to do, so that all the peoples of the world may know you and obey you, as your people Israel do. Then they will know that this Temple I have built is where you are to be worshiped.

34"When you command your people to go into battle against their enemies and they pray to you, wherever they are, facing this city which you have chosen and this Temple which I have built for you, 35listen to their prayers. Hear them in heaven and give them victory.

36"When your people sin against you — and there is no one who does not sin — and in your anger you let their enemies defeat them and take them as prisoners to some other land, even if that land is far away, 37listen to your people's prayers. If there in that land they repent and pray to you, confessing how sinful and wicked they have been, hear their prayers, O LORD. 38If in that land they truly and sincerely repent and pray to you as they face toward this land which you gave to our ancestors, this city which you have chosen, and this Temple which I have built for you, 39then listen to their prayers. In your home in heaven hear them and be merciful to them and forgive all the sins of your people.

40"Now, O my God, look on us and listen to the prayers offered in this place. 41Rise up now, LORD God, and with the Covenant Box, the symbol of your power, enter the Temple and stay here forever. Bless your priests in all they do, and may all your people be happy because of your goodness to them. 42LORD God, do not reject the king you have chosen. Remember the love you had for your servant David."[n]

The Dedication of the Temple
(1 Kings 8.62-66)

7 When King Solomon finished his prayer, fire came down from heaven and burned up the sacrifices that had been offered, and the dazzling light of the LORD's presence filled the Temple. 2Because the Temple was full of the dazzling light, the priests could not enter it. 3When the people of Israel saw the fire fall from heaven and the light fill the Temple, they fell face downward on the pavement, worshiping God and praising him for his goodness and his eternal love. 4Then Solomon and all the people offered sacrifices to the LORD. 5He sacrificed 22,000 head of cattle and 120,000 sheep as fellowship offerings. And so

[n] the love you . . . David; or your servant David's loyal service.
6.41-42 Ps 132.8-10   **7.1** Lv 9.23-24   **7.3** 1 Ch 16.34; 2 Ch 5.13; Ezra 3.11; Ps 100.5; 106.1; 107.1; 118.1; 136.1; Jr 33.11

he and all the people dedicated the Temple. ⁶The priests stood in the places that were assigned to them, and facing them stood the Levites, praising the Lᴏʀᴅ with the musical instruments that King David had provided and singing the hymn, "His Love Is Eternal!" as they had been commissioned by David. The priests blew trumpets while all the people stood.

⁷Solomon consecrated the central part of the courtyard, the area in front of the Temple, and then offered there the sacrifices burned whole, the grain offerings, and the fat from the fellowship offerings. He did this because the bronze altar which he had made was too small for all these offerings.

⁸Solomon and all the people of Israel celebrated the Festival of Shelters for seven days. There was a huge crowd of people from as far away as Hamath Pass in the north and the Egyptian border in the south. ⁹They had spent seven days for the dedication of the altar and then seven more days for the festival. On the last day they had a closing celebration, ¹⁰and on the following day, the twenty-third day of the seventh month, Solomon sent the people home. They were happy about all the blessings that the Lᴏʀᴅ had given to his people Israel, to David, and to Solomon.

God Appears to Solomon Again
(1 Kings 9.1-9)

¹¹After King Solomon had finished the Temple and the palace, successfully completing all his plans for them, ¹²the Lᴏʀᴅ appeared to him at night. He said to him, "I have heard your prayer, and I accept this Temple as the place where sacrifices are to be offered to me. ¹³Whenever I hold back the rain or send locusts to eat up the crops or send an epidemic on my people, ¹⁴if they pray to me and repent and turn away from the evil they have been do-

ing, then I will hear them in heaven, forgive their sins, and make their land prosperous again. ¹⁵I will watch over this Temple and be ready to hear all the prayers that are offered here, ¹⁶because I have chosen it and consecrated it as the place where I will be worshiped forever. I will watch over it and protect it for all time. ¹⁷If you serve me faithfully as your father David did, obeying my laws and doing everything I have commanded you, ¹⁸I will keep the promise I made to your father David when I told him that Israel would always be ruled by his descendants. ¹⁹But if you and your people ever disobey the laws and commands I have given you and worship other gods, ²⁰then I will remove you from the land that I gave you, and I will abandon this Temple that I have consecrated as the place where I am to be worshiped. People everywhere will ridicule it and treat it with contempt.

²¹"The Temple is now greatly honored, but then everyone who passes by it will be amazed and will ask, 'Why did the Lᴏʀᴅ do this to this land and this Temple?' ²²People will answer, 'It is because they abandoned the Lᴏʀᴅ their God, who brought their ancestors out of Egypt. They gave their allegiance to other gods and worshiped them. That is why the Lᴏʀᴅ has brought this disaster on them.'"

Solomon's Achievements
(1 Kings 9.10-28)

8 It took Solomon twenty years to build the Temple and his palace. ²He also rebuilt the cities that King Hiram had given him, and sent Israelites to settle in them. ³He captured the territory of Hamath and Zobah ⁴and fortified the city of Palmyra in the desert. He rebuilt all the cities in Hamath that were centers for storing supplies. ⁵Solomon also rebuilt the following cities: Upper Beth Horon and Lower Beth

Horon (fortified cities with gates that could be barred), [6] the city of Baalath, all the cities where he stored supplies, and the cities where his horses and chariots were stationed. He carried out all his plans for building in Jerusalem, in Lebanon, and throughout the territory that he ruled over. [7-8] Solomon employed at forced labor all the descendants of the people of Canaan whom the Israelites had not killed when they took possession of the land. These included Hittites, Amorites, Perizzites, Hivites, and Jebusites, whose descendants continue to be slaves down to the present time. [9] Israelites were not used at forced labor, but served as soldiers, officers, chariot commanders, and cavalry troops. [10] There were 250 officials in charge of the forced labor working on the various building projects.

[11] Solomon moved his wife, the daughter of the king of Egypt, from David's City to a house he built for her. He said, "She must not live in the palace of King David of Israel, because any place where the Covenant Box has been is holy."

[12] Solomon offered sacrifices to the LORD on the altar which he had built in front of the Temple. [13] He offered burnt offerings according to the requirements of the Law of Moses for each holy day: Sabbaths, New Moon Festivals, and the three annual festivals — the Festival of Unleavened Bread, the Harvest Festival, and the Festival of Shelters. [14] Following the rules laid down by his father David, he organized the daily work of the priests and of the Levites who assisted the priests in singing hymns and in doing their work. He also organized the Temple guards in sections for performing their daily duties at each gate, in accordance with the commands of David, the man of God. [15] The instructions which David had given the priests and the Levites concerning the storehouses and other matters were carried out in detail.

[16] By this time all of Solomon's projects had been completed. From the laying of the foundation of the LORD's Temple to its completion, all the work had been successful.

[17] Then Solomon went to Eziongeber and Elath, ports on the shore of the Gulf of Aqaba, in the land of Edom. [18] King Hiram sent him ships under the command of his own officers and with experienced sailors. They sailed with Solomon's officers to the land of Ophir and brought back to Solomon about sixteen tons of gold.

The Visit of the Queen of Sheba
(1 Kings 10.1-13)

9 The queen of Sheba heard of King Solomon's fame, and she traveled to Jerusalem to test him with difficult questions. She brought with her a large group of attendants, as well as camels loaded with spices, jewels, and a large amount of gold. When she and Solomon met, she asked him all the questions that she could think of. [2] He answered them all; there was nothing too difficult for him to explain. [3] The queen of Sheba heard Solomon's wisdom and saw the palace he had built. [4] She saw the food that was served at his table, the living quarters for his officials, the organization of his palace staff and the uniforms they wore, the clothing of the servants who waited on him at feasts, and the sacrifices he offered[o] in the Temple. It left her breathless and amazed.

[5] She said to the king, "What I heard in my own country about you[p] and

---

[o] *Probable text (see 1 K 10.5)* sacrifices he offered; *Hebrew* his upper rooms.   [p] you; *or your deeds.*

8.13 a Nu 28.9, 10; **b** Nu 28.11-15; **c** Ex 23.14-17; 34.22, 23; Nu 28.16—29.39; Dt 16.16
9.1-9 Mt 12.42; Lk 11.31

your wisdom is true! 6I did not believe what they told me until I came and saw for myself. I had not heard of even half your wisdom. You are even wiser than people say. 7How fortunate are those who serve you, who are always in your presence and are privileged to hear your wise sayings! 8Praise the LORD your God! He has shown how pleased he is with you by making you king, to rule in his name. Because he loves his people Israel and wants to preserve them forever, he has made you their king so that you can maintain law and justice."

9She presented to King Solomon the gifts she had brought: almost five tons of gold and a very large amount of spices and jewels. There have never been any other spices as fine as those that the queen of Sheba gave to King Solomon.

(10The sailors of King Hiram and of King Solomon who brought gold from Ophir also brought juniper wood and jewels. 11Solomon used the wood to make stairs for the Temple and for his palace, and to make harps and lyres for the musicians. Nothing like that had ever been seen before in the land of Judah.)

12King Solomon gave the queen of Sheba everything she asked for. This was in addition to what he gave her in exchange for the gifts*q* she brought to him. Then she and her attendants returned to the land of Sheba.

King Solomon's Wealth
(1 Kings 10.14-25)

13Every year King Solomon received over twenty-five tons of gold, 14in addition to the taxes paid by the traders and merchants. The kings of Arabia and the governors of the Israelite districts also brought him silver and gold. 15Solomon made two hundred large shields, each of which was covered with about fifteen pounds of beaten gold, 16and three hundred smaller shields, each covered with about eight pounds of beaten gold. He had them all placed in the Hall of the Forest of Lebanon.*r*

17The king also had a large throne made. Part of it was covered with ivory and the rest of it was covered with pure gold. 18Six steps led up to the throne, and there was a footstool attached to it, covered with gold. There were arms on each side of the throne, and the figure of a lion stood at each side. 19Twelve figures of lions were on the steps, one at either end of each step. No throne like this had ever existed in any other kingdom.

20All of King Solomon's drinking cups were made of gold, and all the utensils in the Hall of the Forest of Lebanon were of pure gold. Silver was not considered valuable in Solomon's day. 21He had a fleet of ocean-going ships sailing with King Hiram's fleet. Every three years his fleet would return, bringing gold, silver, ivory, apes, and monkeys.

22King Solomon was richer and wiser than any other king in the world. 23They all consulted him, to hear the wisdom that God had given him. 24Each of them brought Solomon gifts — articles of silver and gold, robes, weapons, spices, horses, and mules. This continued year after year.

25King Solomon also had four thousand stalls for his chariots and horses, and had twelve thousand cavalry horses. Some of them he kept in Jerusalem and the rest he stationed in various other cities. 26He was supreme ruler of all the kings in the territory from the Euphrates River to Philistia and the

q Probable text he gave her in exchange for the gifts; *Hebrew unclear.*   *r* HALL OF THE FOREST OF LEBANON: *A large ceremonial hall in the palace, probably so called because it was paneled in cedar.*

9.25 1 K 4.26   **9.26** Gn 15.18; 1 K 4.21

Egyptian border. [27] During his reign silver was as common in Jerusalem as stone, and cedar was as plentiful as ordinary sycamore in the foothills of Judah. [28] Solomon imported horses from Musri[s] and from every other country.

Summary of Solomon's Reign
(1 Kings 11.41-43)

[29] The rest of the history of Solomon from beginning to end is recorded in *The History of Nathan the Prophet*, in *The Prophecy of Ahijah of Shiloh*, and in *The Visions of Iddo the Prophet*, which also deal with the reign of King Jeroboam of Israel. [30] Solomon ruled in Jerusalem over all Israel for forty years. [31] He died and was buried in David's City, and his son Rehoboam succeeded him as king.

The Northern Tribes Revolt
(1 Kings 12.1-20)

10 Rehoboam went to Shechem, where all the people of northern Israel had gathered to make him king. [2] When Jeroboam son of Nebat, who had gone to Egypt to escape from King Solomon, heard this news, he returned home. [3] The people of the northern tribes sent for him, and they all went together to Rehoboam and said to him, [4] "Your father placed heavy burdens on us. If you make these burdens lighter and make life easier for us, we will be your loyal subjects."

[5] Rehoboam replied, "Give me three days to consider the matter. Then come back." So the people left.

[6] King Rehoboam consulted the older men who had served as his father Solomon's advisers. "What answer do you advise me to give these people?" he asked.

[7] They replied, "If you are kind to these people and try to please them by giving a considerate answer, they will always serve you loyally."

[8] But he ignored the advice of the older men and went instead to the young men who had grown up with him and who were now his advisers. [9] "What do you advise me to do?" he asked. "What shall I say to the people who are asking me to make their burdens lighter?"

[10] They replied, "This is what you should tell them: 'My little finger is thicker than my father's waist.' [11] Tell them, 'My father placed heavy burdens on you; I will make them even heavier. He beat you with whips; I'll flog you with bullwhips!'"

[12] Three days later Jeroboam and all the people returned to King Rehoboam, as he had instructed them. [13] The king ignored the advice of the older men and spoke harshly to the people, [14] as the younger men had advised. He said, "My father placed heavy burdens on you; I will make them even heavier. He beat you with whips; I'll flog you with bullwhips!" [15] It was the will of the LORD God to bring about what he had spoken to Jeroboam son of Nebat through the prophet Ahijah from Shiloh. This is why the king did not pay any attention to the people.

[16] When the people saw that the king would not listen to them, they shouted, "Down with David and his family! What have they ever done for us? People of Israel, let's go home! Let Rehoboam look out for himself!"

So the people of Israel rebelled, [17] leaving Rehoboam as king only of the people who lived in the territory of Judah.

[18] Then King Rehoboam sent Adoniram, who was in charge of the forced labor, to go to the Israelites, but they stoned him to death. At this, Rehoboam hurriedly got in his chariot and escaped to Jerusalem. [19] Ever since that time the

---

[s] *Probable text (see 1.16)* Musri; *Hebrew* Egypt.
9.28 Dt 17.16   **10.16** 2 S 20.1

people of the northern kingdom of Israel have been in rebellion against the dynasty of David.

Shemaiah's Prophecy
(1 Kings 12.21-24)

11 When King Rehoboam arrived in Jerusalem, he called together 180,000 of the best soldiers from the tribes of Benjamin and Judah. He intended to go to war and restore his control over the northern tribes of Israel. ²But the LORD told the prophet Shemaiah ³to give this message to King Rehoboam and to all the people of the tribes of Judah and Benjamin: ⁴"Do not attack your own relatives. Go home, all of you. What has happened is my will." They obeyed the LORD's command and did not go to fight Jeroboam.

Rehoboam Fortifies the Cities

⁵Rehoboam remained in Jerusalem and had fortifications built for the following cities of Judah and Benjamin: ⁶Bethlehem, Etam, Tekoa, ⁷Bethzur, Soco, Adullam, ⁸Gath, Mareshah, Ziph, ⁹Adoraim, Lachish, Azekah, ¹⁰Zorah, Aijalon, and Hebron. ¹¹He had them strongly fortified and appointed a commander for each of them, and in each one he placed supplies of food, olive oil, and wine, ¹²and also shields and spears. In this way he kept Judah and Benjamin under his control.

Priests and Levites Come to Judah

¹³From all the territory of Israel priests and Levites came south to Judah. ¹⁴The Levites abandoned their pastures and other land and moved to Judah and Jerusalem, because King Jeroboam of Israel and his successors would not let them serve as priests of the LORD. ¹⁵Jeroboam appointed priests of his own to serve at the pagan places of worship and to worship demons and the idols he made in the form of bull-calves. ¹⁶From all the tribes of Israel people who sincerely wanted to worship the LORD, the God of Israel, followed the Levites to Jerusalem, so that they could offer sacrifices to the LORD, the God of their ancestors. ¹⁷This strengthened the kingdom of Judah, and for three years they supported Rehoboam son of Solomon and lived as they had under the rule of King David and King Solomon.

Rehoboam's Family

¹⁸Rehoboam married Mahalath, whose father was Jerimoth son of David and whose mother was Abihail, the daughter of Eliab and granddaughter of Jesse. ¹⁹They had three sons, Jeush, Shemariah, and Zaham. ²⁰Later he married Maacah, the daughter of Absalom, and they had four sons: Abijah, Attai, Ziza, and Shelomith. ²¹In all, Rehoboam had eighteen wives and sixty concubines, and he fathered twenty-eight sons and sixty daughters. Of all his wives and concubines he loved Maacah best, ²²and he favored her son Abijah over all his other children, choosing him as the one to succeed him as king. ²³Rehoboam wisely assigned responsibilities to his sons and stationed them throughout Judah and Benjamin in the fortified cities. He provided generously for them and also secured many wives for them.

An Egyptian Invasion of Judah
(1 Kings 14.25-28)

12 As soon as Rehoboam had established his authority as king, he and all his people abandoned the Law of the LORD. ²In the fifth year of Rehoboam's reign their disloyalty to the LORD was punished. King Shishak of Egypt attacked Jerusalem ³with an army of twelve hundred chariots, sixty thousand cavalry, and more soldiers

11.15 1 K 12.31

than could be counted, including Libyan, Sukkite, and Ethiopian[t] troops. [4]He captured the fortified cities of Judah and advanced as far as Jerusalem.

[5]Shemaiah the prophet went to King Rehoboam and the Judean leaders who had gathered in Jerusalem to escape Shishak. He said to them, "This is the LORD's message to you: 'You have abandoned me, so now I have abandoned you to Shishak.' "

[6]The king and the leaders admitted that they had sinned, and they said, "What the LORD is doing is just."

[7]When the LORD saw this, he spoke again to Shemaiah and said to him, "Because they admit their sin, I will not destroy them. But when Shishak attacks, they will barely survive. Jerusalem will not feel the full force of my anger, [8]but Shishak will conquer them, and they will learn the difference between serving me and serving earthly rulers."

[9]King Shishak came to Jerusalem and took the treasures from the Temple and from the palace. He took everything, including the gold shields that King Solomon had made. [10]To replace them, Rehoboam made bronze shields and entrusted them to the officers responsible for guarding the palace gates. [11]Every time the king went to the Temple, the guards carried the shields and then returned them to the guardroom. [12]Because he submitted to the LORD, the LORD's anger did not completely destroy him, and things went well for Judah.

Summary of Rehoboam's Reign

[13]Rehoboam ruled in Jerusalem and increased his power as king. He was forty-one years old when he became king, and he ruled for seventeen years in Jerusalem, the city which the LORD had chosen from all the territory of Israel as the place where he was to be worshiped. Rehoboam's mother was Naamah, from the land of Ammon. [14]He did what was evil, because he did not try to find the LORD's will.

[15]Rehoboam's acts from beginning to end and his family records are found in *The History of Shemaiah the Prophet* and *The History of Iddo the Prophet.* Rehoboam and Jeroboam were constantly at war with each other. [16]Rehoboam died and was buried in the royal tombs in David's City and his son Abijah succeeded him as king.

Abijah's War with Jeroboam
(1 Kings 15.1-8)

13 In the eighteenth year of the reign of King Jeroboam of Israel, Abijah became king of Judah, [2]and he ruled three years in Jerusalem. His mother was Micaiah daughter of Uriel, from the city of Gibeah.

War broke out between Abijah and Jeroboam. [3]Abijah raised an army of 400,000 soldiers, and Jeroboam opposed him with an army of 800,000.

[4]The armies met in the hill country of Ephraim. King Abijah went up Mount Zemaraim and called out to Jeroboam and the Israelites: "Listen to me!" he said. [5]"Don't you know that the LORD, the God of Israel, made an unbreakable covenant with David, giving him and his descendants kingship over Israel forever? [6]Jeroboam son of Nebat rebelled against Solomon, his king. [7]Later he gathered together a group of worthless scoundrels, and they forced their will on Rehoboam son of Solomon, who was too young and inexperienced to resist them. [8]Now you propose to

---

[t] *Hebrew* Cushite(s): *Cush is the ancient name of the extensive territory south of the First Cataract of the Nile River. This region was called Ethiopia in Graeco-Roman times, and included within its borders most of modern Sudan and some of present-day Ethiopia (Abyssinia).*

12.9 1 K 10.16, 17; 2 Ch 9.15, 16

ight against the royal authority that the LORD gave to David's descendants. You have a huge army and have with you the gold bull-calves that Jeroboam made to be your gods. ⁹You drove out the LORD's priests, the descendants of Aaron, and you drove out the Levites. In their place you appointed priests in the same way that other nations do. Anybody who comes along with a bull or seven sheep can get himself consecrated as a priest of those so-called gods of yours.

¹⁰"But we still serve the LORD our God and have not abandoned him. Priests descended from Aaron perform their duties, and Levites assist them. ¹¹Every morning and every evening they offer him incense and animal sacrifices burned whole. They present the offerings of bread on a table that is ritually clean, and every evening they light the lamps on the gold lampstand. We do what the LORD has commanded, but you have abandoned him. ¹²God himself is our leader and his priests are here with trumpets, ready to blow them and call us to battle against you. People of Israel, don't fight against the LORD, the God of your ancestors! You can't win!"

¹³Meanwhile Jeroboam had sent some of his troops to ambush the Judean army from the rear, while the rest faced them from the front. ¹⁴The Judeans looked around and saw that they were surrounded. They cried to the LORD for help, and the priests blew the trumpets. ¹⁵The Judeans gave a loud shout, and led by Abijah, they attacked; God defeated Jeroboam and the Israelite army. ¹⁶The Israelites fled from the Judeans, and God let the Judeans overpower them. ¹⁷Abijah and his army dealt the Israelites a crushing defeat — half a million of Israel's best soldiers were killed. ¹⁸And so the people of Judah were victorious over Israel, because they relied on the LORD, the God of their ancestors.

¹⁹Abijah pursued Jeroboam's army and occupied some of his cities: Bethel, Jeshanah, and Ephron, and the villages near each of these cities. ²⁰Jeroboam never regained his power during Abijah's reign. Finally the LORD struck him down, and he died.

²¹Abijah, however, grew more powerful. He had fourteen wives and fathered twenty-two sons and sixteen daughters. ²²The rest of the history of Abijah, what he said and what he did, is written in *The History of Iddo the Prophet.*

King Asa Defeats the Ethiopians

14 King Abijah died and was buried in the royal tombs in David's City. His son Asa succeeded him as king, and under Asa the land enjoyed peace for ten years. ²Asa pleased the LORD, his God, by doing what was right and good. ³He removed the foreign altars and the pagan places of worship, broke down the sacred stone columns, and cut down the symbols of the goddess Asherah. ⁴He commanded the people of Judah to do the will of the LORD, the God of their ancestors, and to obey his teachings and commands. ⁵Because he abolished the pagan places of worship and the incense altars from all the cities of Judah, the kingdom was at peace under his rule. ⁶He built fortifications for the cities of Judah during this time, and for several years there was no war, because the LORD gave him peace. ⁷He told the people of Judah, "Let us fortify the cities by building walls and towers, and gates that can be shut and barred. We have control of the land because we have done the will of the LORD our God. He has protected us and given us security on every side." And so they built and prospered. ⁸King Asa had an army of 300,000 men from Judah, armed with shields and spears, and 280,000 men from Benjamin, armed with shields and bows. All of them were brave, well-trained men.

⁹An Ethiopian^t named Zerah invaded Judah with an army of a million men and three hundred chariots and advanced as far as Mareshah. ¹⁰Asa went out to fight him, and both sides took up their positions at Zephathah Valley near Mareshah. ¹¹Asa prayed to the LORD his God, "O LORD, you can help a weak army as easily as a powerful one. Help us now, O LORD our God, because' we are relying on you, and in your name we have come out to fight against this huge army. LORD, you are our God; no one can hope to defeat you."

¹²The LORD defeated the Ethiopian^t army when Asa and the Judean army attacked them. They fled, ¹³and Asa and his troops pursued them as far as Gerar. So many of the Ethiopians^t were killed that the army was unable to rally and fight.^u They were overpowered by the LORD and his army, and the army took large amounts of loot. ¹⁴Then they were able to destroy the cities in the area around Gerar, because the people there were terrified of the LORD. The army plundered all those cities and captured large amounts of loot. ¹⁵They also attacked the camps of some shepherds, capturing large numbers of sheep and camels. Then they returned to Jerusalem.

Asa's Reforms

15 The spirit of God came upon Azariah son of Oded, ²and he went to meet King Asa. He called out, "Listen to me, King Asa, and all you people of Judah and Benjamin! The LORD is with you as long as you are with him. If you look for him, he will let you find him, but if you turn away, he will abandon you. ³For a long time Israe lived without the true God, withou priests to teach them, and without a law. ⁴But when trouble came, the turned to the LORD, the God of Israel They searched for him and found him ⁵In those days no one could come an go in safety, because there was trouble and disorder in every land. ⁶One natior oppressed another nation, and one city oppressed another city, because Goc was bringing trouble and distress or them. ⁷But you must be strong and no be discouraged. The work that you dc will be rewarded."

⁸When Asa heard the prophecy tha Azariah son of^v Oded had spoken, he was encouraged. He did away with al the idols in the land of Judah and Ben jamin and all the idols in the cities he had captured in the hill country o: Ephraim. He also repaired the altar o: the LORD that stood in the Temple courtyard.

⁹Many people had come over to Asa's side from Ephraim, Manasseh, anc Simeon, and were living in his king dom, because they had seen that the LORD was with him. Asa summoned al of them and the people of Judah anc Benjamin. ¹⁰They assembled in Jerusa lem in the third month of the fifteentl year that Asa was king. ¹¹On that day they offered sacrifices to the LORD from the loot they had brought back: sever hundred head of cattle and seven thou sand sheep. ¹²They made a covenant ir which they agreed to worship the LORD the God of their ancestors, with all thei heart and soul. ¹³Anyone, young or old male or female, who did not worshir him was to be put to death. ¹⁴In a louc voice they took an oath in the LORD': name that they would keep the cove

---

^t Hebrew Cushite(s): *Cush is the ancient name of the extensive territory south of the First Cataract of the Nile River. This region was called Ethiopia in Graeco-Roman times, and included within its borders most of modern Sudan and some of present-day Ethiopia (Abyssinia).*   ^u So many of the Ethiopians . . . fight; *or* The Ethiopians were completely defeated; not one of them was left alive.   ^v *Some ancient translations* Azariah son of; *Hebrew does not have these words.*

nant, and then they shouted and blew trumpets. 15 All the people of Judah were happy because they had made this covenant with all their heart. They took delight in worshiping the LORD, and he accepted them and gave them peace on every side.

16 King Asa removed his grandmother Maacah from her position as queen mother, because she had made an obscene idol of the fertility goddess Asherah. Asa cut down the idol, chopped it up, and burned the pieces in Kidron Valley. 17 Even though Asa did not destroy all the pagan places of worship in the land, he remained faithful to the LORD all his life. 18 He placed in the Temple all the objects his father Abijah had dedicated to God, as well as the gold and silver objects that he himself dedicated. 19 There was no more war until the thirty-fifth year of his reign.

Troubles with Israel
(1 Kings 15.17-22)

16 In the thirty-sixth year of the reign of King Asa of Judah, King Baasha of Israel invaded Judah and started to fortify Ramah in order to cut off all traffic in and out of Judah. 2 So Asa took silver and gold from the treasuries of the Temple and the palace and sent it to Damascus, to King Benhadad of Syria, with this message: 3 "Let us be allies, as our fathers were. This silver and gold is a present for you. Now break your alliance with King Baasha of Israel so that he will have to pull his troops out of my territory."

4 Benhadad agreed to Asa's proposal and sent his commanding officers and their armies to attack the cities of Israel. They captured Ijon, Dan, Abel Beth Maacah, and all the cities of Naphtali where supplies were stored.

5 When King Baasha heard what was happening, he stopped fortifying Ramah and abandoned the work. 6 Then King Asa gathered men from throughout Judah and had them carry off the stones and timbers that Baasha had been using at Ramah, and they used them to fortify the cities of Geba and Mizpah.

The Prophet Hanani

7 At that time the prophet Hanani went to King Asa and said, "Because you relied on the king of Syria instead of relying on the LORD your God, the army of the king of Israel[w] has escaped from you. 8 Didn't the Ethiopians[x] and the Libyans have large armies with many chariots and cavalry troops? But because you relied on the LORD, he gave you victory over them. 9 The LORD keeps close watch over the whole world, to give strength to those whose hearts are loyal to him. You have acted foolishly, and so from now on you will always be at war." 10 This made Asa so angry with the prophet that he had him put in chains. It was at this same time that Asa began treating some of the people cruelly.

The End of Asa's Reign
(1 Kings 15.23, 24)

11 All the events of Asa's reign from beginning to end are recorded in *The History of the Kings of Judah and Israel.* 12 In the thirty-ninth year that Asa was king, he was crippled by a severe foot disease; but even then he did not turn to the LORD for help, but to doctors. 13 Two years later he died 14 and was buried in the rock tomb which he had carved out for himself in David's City. They used spices and perfumed oils to prepare his body for burial, and

---

w One ancient translation Israel; *Hebrew* Syria.   *x Hebrew* Cushites: *Cush is the ancient name of the extensive territory south of the First Cataract of the Nile River. This region was called Ethiopia in Graeco-Roman times, and included within its borders most of modern Sudan and some of present-day Ethiopia (Abyssinia).*

they built a huge bonfire to mourn his death.

Jehoshaphat Becomes King

17 Jehoshaphat succeeded his father Asa as king and strengthened his position against Israel. ² He stationed troops in the fortified cities of Judah, in the Judean countryside, and in the cities which Asa had captured in the territory of Ephraim. ³ The LORD blessed Jehoshaphat because he followed the example of his father's early life and did not worship Baal. ⁴ He served his father's God, obeyed God's commands, and did not act the way the kings of Israel did. ⁵ The LORD gave Jehoshaphat firm control over the kingdom of Judah, and all the people brought him gifts, so that he became wealthy and highly honored. ⁶ He took pride in serving the LORD and destroyed all the pagan places of worship and the symbols of the goddess Asherah in Judah.

⁷ In the third year of his reign he sent out the following officials to teach in the cities of Judah: Benhail, Obadiah, Zechariah, Nethanel, and Micaiah. ⁸ They were accompanied by nine Levites and two priests. The Levites were Shemaiah, Nethaniah, Zebadiah, Asahel, Shemiramoth, Jehonathan, Adonijah, Tobijah, and Tobadonijah; and the priests were Elishama and Jehoram. ⁹ They took the book of the Law of the LORD and went through all the towns of Judah, teaching it to the people.

Jehoshaphat's Greatness

¹⁰ The LORD made all the surrounding kingdoms afraid to go to war against King Jehoshaphat. ¹¹ Some of the Philistines brought Jehoshaphat a large amount of silver and other gifts, and some Arabs brought him 7,700 sheep and 7,700 goats. ¹² So Jehoshaphat continued to grow more and more powerful. Throughout Judah he built

fortifications and cities, ¹³ where supplies were stored in huge amounts.

In Jerusalem he stationed outstanding officers, ¹⁴ according to their clans. Adnah was the commander of the troops from the clans of Judah, and he had 300,000 soldiers under him. ¹⁵ Second in rank was Jehohanan, with 280,000 soldiers, ¹⁶ and third was Amasiah son of Zichri, with 200,000. (Amasiah had volunteered to serve the LORD.) ¹⁷ The commander of the troops from the clans of Benjamin was Eliada, an outstanding soldier, in command of 200,000 men armed with shields and bows. ¹⁸ His second in command was Jehozabad with 180,000 men, well-equipped for battle. ¹⁹ These soldiers served the king in Jerusalem, and in addition he stationed others in the other fortified cities of Judah.

The Prophet Micaiah Warns Ahab
(1 Kings 22.1-28)

18 When King Jehoshaphat of Judah became rich and famous, he arranged a marriage between a member of his family and the family of King Ahab of Israel. ² A number of years later Jehoshaphat went to the city of Samaria to visit Ahab. To honor Jehoshaphat and those with him, Ahab had a large number of sheep and cattle slaughtered for a feast. He tried to persuade Jehoshaphat to join him in attacking the city of Ramoth in Gilead. ³ He asked, "Will you go with me to attack Ramoth?"

Jehoshaphat replied, "I am ready when you are, and so is my army. We will join you." ⁴ Then he added, "But first let's consult the LORD."

⁵ So Ahab called in the prophets, about four hundred of them, and asked them, "Should I go and attack Ramoth, or not?"

"Attack it," they answered. "God will give you victory."

⁶ But Jehoshaphat asked, "Isn't there

another prophet through whom we can consult the LORD?"

⁷Ahab answered, "There is one more, Micaiah son of Imlah. But I hate him because he never prophesies anything good for me; it's always something bad."

"You shouldn't say that!" Jehoshaphat replied.

⁸So King Ahab called in a court official and told him to go and get Micaiah at once.

⁹The two kings, dressed in their royal robes, were sitting on their thrones at the threshing place just outside the gate of Samaria, and all the prophets were prophesying in front of

All the prophets were prophesying in front of them. (18.9)

them. ¹⁰One of them, Zedekiah son of Chenaanah, made iron horns and said to Ahab, "This is what the LORD says, 'With these you will fight the Syrians and totally defeat them.'" ¹¹All the other prophets said the same thing. "March against Ramoth and you will win," they said. "The LORD will give you victory."

¹²Meanwhile, the official who had gone to get Micaiah said to him, "All the other prophets have prophesied success for the king, and you had better do the same."

¹³But Micaiah answered, "By the liv-

ing LORD I will say what my God tells me to!"

¹⁴When he appeared before King Ahab, the king asked him, "Micaiah, should King Jehoshaphat and I go and attack Ramoth, or not?"

"Attack!" Micaiah answered. "Of course you'll win. The LORD will give you victory."

¹⁵But Ahab replied, "When you speak to me in the name of the LORD, tell me the truth! How many times do I have to tell you that?"

¹⁶Micaiah answered, "I can see the army of Israel scattered over the hills like sheep without a shepherd. And the LORD said, 'These men have no leader; let them go home in peace.'"

¹⁷Ahab said to Jehoshaphat, "I told you that he never prophesies anything good for me; it's always something bad!"

¹⁸Micaiah went on: "Now listen to what the LORD says! I saw the LORD sitting on his throne in heaven, with all his angels standing beside him. ¹⁹The LORD asked, 'Who will deceive Ahab so that he will go and get killed at Ramoth?' Some of the angels said one thing, and others said something else, ²⁰until a spirit stepped forward, approached the LORD, and said, 'I will deceive him.' 'How?' the LORD asked. ²¹The spirit replied, 'I will go and make all of Ahab's prophets tell lies.' The LORD said, 'Go and deceive him. You will succeed.'"

²²And Micaiah concluded: "This is what has happened. The LORD has made these prophets of yours lie to you. But he himself has decreed that you will meet with disaster!"

²³Then the prophet Zedekiah went up to Micaiah, slapped his face, and asked, "Since when did the LORD's spirit leave me and speak to you?"

²⁴"You will find out when you go into some back room to hide," Micaiah replied.

18.16 Nu 27.17; Ez 34.5; Mt 9.36; Mk 6.34

²⁵Then King Ahab ordered one of his officers, "Arrest Micaiah and take him to Amon, the governor of the city, and to Prince Joash. ²⁶Tell them to throw him in prison and to put him on bread and water until I return safely."

²⁷"If you return safely," Micaiah exclaimed, "then the LORD has not spoken through me!" And he added, "Listen, everyone, to what I have said!"

The Death of Ahab
(1 Kings 22.29-35)

²⁸Then King Ahab of Israel and King Jehoshaphat of Judah went to attack the city of Ramoth in Gilead. ²⁹Ahab said to Jehoshaphat, "As we go into battle, I will disguise myself, but you wear your royal garments." So the king of Israel went into battle in disguise.

³⁰The king of Syria had ordered his chariot commanders to attack no one else except the king of Israel. ³¹So when they saw King Jehoshaphat, they all thought that he was the king of Israel, and they turned to attack him. But Jehoshaphat gave a shout, and the LORD God rescued him and turned the attack away from him. ³²The chariot commanders saw that he was not the king of Israel, so they stopped pursuing him. ³³By chance, however, a Syrian soldier shot an arrow which struck King Ahab between the joints of his armor. "I'm wounded!" he cried out to his chariot driver. "Turn around and pull out of the battle!" ³⁴While the battle raged on, King Ahab remained propped up in his chariot, facing the Syrians. At sunset he died.

A Prophet Reprimands Jehoshaphat

19 King Jehoshaphat of Judah returned safely to his palace in Jerusalem. ²A prophet, Jehu son of Hanani, went to meet the king and said to him, "Do you think it is right to help those who are wicked and to take the side of those who hate the LORD? What you have done has brought the LORD's anger on you. ³But even so, there is some good in you. You have removed all the symbols of the goddess Asherah which people worshiped, and you have tried to follow God's will."

Jehoshaphat's Reforms

⁴Even though King Jehoshaphat lived in Jerusalem, he traveled regularly among the people, from Beersheba in the south to the edge of the hill country of Ephraim in the north, in order to call the people back to the LORD, the God of their ancestors. ⁵He appointed judges in each of the fortified cities of Judah ⁶and instructed them: "Be careful in pronouncing judgment; you are not acting on human authority, but on the authority of the LORD, and he is with you when you pass sentence. ⁷Honor the LORD and act carefully, because the LORD our God does not tolerate fraud or partiality or the taking of bribes."

⁸In Jerusalem Jehoshaphat appointed Levites, priests, and some of the leading citizens as judges in cases involving a violation of the Law of the LORD or legal disputes between inhabitants of the city.ʸ ⁹He gave them the following instructions: "You must perform your duties in reverence for the LORD, faithfully obeying him in everything you do. ¹⁰Whenever your fellow citizens from any of the cities bring before you a case of homicide or any other violation of a law or commandment, you must instruct them carefully how to conduct themselves during the trial, so that they do not become guilty of sinning against the LORD. Unless you do, you and your fellow citizens will feel the force of the LORD's anger. But if you do your duty, you will not be guilty. ¹¹Amariah the High Priest will have final authority in all religious cases, and

---

ʸ *Some ancient translations* between . . . city; *Hebrew unclear.*

Zebadiah son of Ishmael, governor of Judah, will have final authority in all civil cases. The Levites have the responsibility of seeing that the decisions of the courts are carried out. Be courageous and carry out these instructions, and may the LORD be on the side of the right!"

War against Edom

20 Some time later the armies of Moab and Ammon, together with their allies, the Meunites,ᶻ invaded Judah. ²Some messengers came and announced to King Jehoshaphat: "A large army from Edom has come from the other side of the Dead Sea to attack you. They have already captured Hazazon Tamar." (This is another name for Engedi.) ³Jehoshaphat was frightened and prayed to the LORD for guidance. Then he gave orders for a fast to be observed throughout the country. ⁴From every city of Judah people hurried to Jerusalem to ask the LORD for guidance, ⁵and they and the people of Jerusalem gathered in the new courtyard of the Temple. King Jehoshaphat went and stood before them ⁶and prayed aloud, "O LORD God of our ancestors, you rule in heaven over all the nations of the world. You are powerful and mighty, and no one can oppose you. ⁷You are our God. When your people Israel moved into this land, you drove out the people who were living here and gave the land to the descendants of Abraham, your friend, to be theirs forever. ⁸They have lived here and have built a temple to honor you, knowing ⁹that if any disaster struck them to punish them — a war,ᵃ an epidemic, or a famine — then they could come and stand in front of this Temple

where you are worshiped. They could pray to you in their trouble, and you would hear them and rescue them.

¹⁰"Now the people of Ammon, Moab, and Edom have attacked us. When our ancestors came out of Egypt, you did not allow them to enter those lands, so our ancestors went around them and did not destroy them. ¹¹This is how they repay us — they come to drive us out of the land that you gave us. ¹²You are our God! Punish them, for we are helpless in the face of this large army that is attacking us. We do not know what to do, but we look to you for help."

¹³All the men of Judah, with their wives and children, were standing there at the Temple. ¹⁴The spirit of the LORD came upon a Levite who was present in the crowd. His name was Jahaziel son of Zechariah; he was a member of the clan of Asaph and was descended from Asaph through Mattaniah, Jeiel, and Benaiah. ¹⁵Jahaziel said, "Your Majesty and all you people of Judah and Jerusalem, the LORD says that you must not be discouraged or be afraid to face this large army. The battle depends on God, not on you. ¹⁶Attack them tomorrow as they come up the pass at Ziz. You will meet them at the end of the valley that leads to the wild country near Jeruel. ¹⁷You will not have to fight this battle. Just take up your positions and wait; you will see the LORD give you victory. People of Judah and Jerusalem, do not hesitate or be afraid. Go out to battle, and the LORD will be with you!"

¹⁸Then King Jehoshaphat bowed low, with his face touching the ground, and all the people bowed with him and worshiped the LORD. ¹⁹The members of the Levite clans of Kohath and Korah stood up and with a loud shout praised the LORD, the God of Israel.

ᶻ *One ancient translation* Meunites; *Hebrew* Ammonites.   ᵃ struck ... war; *or* struck them—a devastating war.

20.7 Is 41.8; Jas 2.23   **20.10** Dt 2.4-19   **20.15-17** Dt 20.1-4   **20.17** Ex 14.13, 14

*The Judean army saw that the enemy were all lying
on the ground dead. (20.24)*

²⁰ Early the next morning the people went out to the wild country near Tekoa. As they were starting out, Jehoshaphat addressed them with these words: "People of Judah and Jerusalem! Put your trust in the LORD your God, and you will stand your ground. Believe what his prophets tell you, and you will succeed." ²¹ After consulting with the people, the king ordered some musicians to put on the robes they wore on sacred occasions and to march ahead of the army, singing: "Praise the LORD! His love is eternal!"

²² When they began to sing, the LORD threw the invading armies into a panic. ²³ The Ammonites and the Moabites attacked the Edomite army and completely destroyed it, and then they turned on each other in savage fighting. ²⁴ When the Judean army reached a tower that was in the desert, they looked toward the enemy and saw that they were all lying on the ground dead. Not one had escaped.

²⁵ Jehoshaphat and his troops moved in to take the loot, and they found many cattle,ᵇ supplies, clothing, and other valuable objects. They spent three days gathering the loot, but there was so much that they could not take everything. ²⁶ On the fourth day they assembled in Beracah Valley and praised the LORD for all he had done. That is why the valley is called "Beracah."ᶜ ²⁷ Jehoshaphat led his troops back to Jerusalem in triumph, because the LORD had defeated their enemies. ²⁸ When they reached the city, they marched to the Temple to the music of harps and trumpets. ²⁹ Every nation that heard how the LORD had defeated Israel's enemies was terrified, ³⁰ so Jehoshaphat ruled in peace, and God gave him security on every side.

The End of Jehoshaphat's Reign
(1 Kings 22.41-50)

³¹ Jehoshaphat had become king of Judah at the age of thirty-five and had ruled in Jerusalem for twenty-five years. His mother was Azubah, the daughter of Shilhi. ³² Like his father Asa before him, he did what was right in the sight of the LORD; ³³ but the pagan places of worship were not destroyed. The people still did not turn wholeheartedly to the worship of the God of their ancestors.

³⁴ Everything else that Jehoshaphat did, from the beginning of his reign to its end, is recorded in *The History of Jehu Son of Hanani,* which is a part of *The History of the Kings of Israel.*

³⁵ At one time King Jehoshaphat of Judah made an alliance with King Ahaziah of Israel, who did many wicked things. ³⁶ At the port of Eziongeber they built ocean-going ships. ³⁷ But Eliezer son of Dodavahu, from the town of Mareshah, warned Jehoshaphat, "Because you have made an alliance with Ahaziah, the LORD will destroy what you have built." And the ships were wrecked and never sailed.

ᵇ *One ancient translation* cattle; *Hebrew* among them.   ᶜ ʙᴇʀᴀᴄᴀʜ: *This name in Hebrew means "praise."*

21

Jehoshaphat died and was buried in the royal tombs in David's City and his son Jehoram succeeded him as king.

King Jehoram of Judah
(2 Kings 8.17-24)

[2] Jehoram son of King Jehoshaphat of Judah had six brothers: Azariah, Jehiel, Zechariah, Azariahu, Michael, and Shephatiah. [3] Their father gave them large amounts of gold, silver, and other valuable possessions, and placed each one in charge of one of the fortified cities of Judah. But because Jehoram was the oldest, Jehoshaphat made him his successor. [4] When Jehoram was in firm control of the kingdom, he had all his brothers killed, and also some Israelite officials.

[5] Jehoram became king at the age of thirty-two, and he ruled in Jerusalem for eight years. [6] He followed the wicked example of King Ahab and the other kings of Israel, because he had married one of Ahab's daughters. He sinned against the LORD, [7] but the LORD was not willing to destroy the dynasty of David, because he had made a covenant with David and promised that his descendants would always continue to rule.

[8] During Jehoram's reign Edom revolted against Judah and became an independent kingdom. [9] So Jehoram and his officers set out with chariots and invaded Edom. There the Edomite army surrounded them, but during the night they managed to break out and escape. [10] Edom has been independent of[d] Judah ever since. During this same period the city of Libnah also revolted, because Jehoram had abandoned the LORD, the God of his ancestors. [11] He even built pagan places of worship in the Judean highlands and led the people of Judah and Jerusalem to sin against the LORD.

[12] The prophet Elijah sent Jehoram a letter, which read as follows: "The LORD, the God of your ancestor David, condemns you, because you did not follow the example of your father, King Jehoshaphat, or that of your grandfather, King Asa. [13] Instead, you have followed the example of the kings of Israel and have led the people of Judah and Jerusalem into being unfaithful to God, just as Ahab and his successors led Israel into unfaithfulness. You even murdered your brothers, who were better men than you are. [14] As a result, the LORD will severely punish your people, your children, and your wives, and will destroy your possessions. [15] You yourself will suffer a painful intestinal disease that will grow worse day by day."

[16] Some Philistines and Arabs lived near where some Ethiopians[e] had settled along the coast. The LORD caused them to go to war against Jehoram. [17] They invaded Judah, looted the royal palace, and carried off as prisoners all the king's wives and sons except Ahaziah, his youngest son.

[18] Then after all this, the LORD brought on the king a painful disease of the intestines. [19] For almost two years it grew steadily worse until finally the king died in agony. His subjects did not light a bonfire in mourning for him as had been done for his ancestors.

[20] Jehoram had become king at the age of thirty-two and had ruled in Jerusalem for eight years. Nobody was sorry when he died. They buried him in David's City, but not in the royal tombs.

---

[d] independent of; or in revolt against.   [e] Hebrew Cushites: Cush is the ancient name of the extensive territory south of the First Cataract of the Nile River. This region was called Ethiopia in Graeco-Roman times, and included within its borders most of modern Sudan and some of present-day Ethiopia (Abyssinia).

21.7 1 K 11.36   **21.8** Gn 27.40

King Ahaziah of Judah
(2 Kings 8.25-29; 9.21-28)

22 Some Arabs had led a raid and killed all of King Jehoram's sons except Ahaziah, the youngest. So now the people of Jerusalem made Ahaziah king as his father's successor. ²⁻³ Ahaziah became king at the age of twenty-two,ᶠ and he ruled in Jerusalem for one year. Ahaziah also followed the example of King Ahab's family, since his mother Athaliah — the daughter of King Ahab and granddaughter of King Omri of Israel — gave him advice that led him into evil. ⁴ He sinned against the LORD, because after his father's death other members of King Ahab's family became his advisers, and they led to his downfall. ⁵ Following their advice, he joined King Joram of Israel in a war against King Hazael of Syria. The armies clashed at Ramoth in Gilead, and Joram was wounded in battle. ⁶ He returned to the city of Jezreel to recover from his wounds, and Ahaziah went there to visit him.

⁷ God used this visit to Joram to bring about Ahaziah's downfall. While Ahaziah was there, he and Joram were confronted by a man named Jehu son of Nimshi, whom the LORD had chosen to destroy the dynasty of Ahab. ⁸ As Jehu was carrying out God's sentence on the dynasty, he came across a group made up of Judean leaders and of Ahaziah's nephews that had accompanied Ahaziah on his visit. Jehu killed them all. ⁹ A search was made for Ahaziah, and he was found hiding in Samaria. They took him to Jehu and put him to death. But they did bury his body out of respect for his grandfather King Jehoshaphat, who had done all he could to serve the LORD.

No member of Ahaziah's family was left who could rule the kingdom.

Queen Athaliah of Judah
(2 Kings 11.1-3)

¹⁰ As soon as King Ahaziah's mother Athaliah learned of her son's murder, she gave orders for all the members of the royal family of Judah to be killed. ¹¹ Ahaziah had a half sister, Jehosheba, who was married to a priest named Jehoiada. She secretly rescued one of Ahaziah's sons, Joash, took him away from the other princes who were about to be murdered and hid him and a nurse in a bedroom at the Temple. By keeping him hidden, she saved him from death at the hands of Athaliah. ¹² For six years he remained there in hiding, while Athaliah ruled as queen.

The Revolt against Athaliah
(2 Kings 11.4-16)

23 After waiting six years Jehoiada the priest decided that it was time to take action. He made a pact with five army officers: Azariah son of Jeroham, Ishmael son of Jehohanan, Azariah son of Obed, Maaseiah son of Adaiah, and Elishaphat son of Zichri. ² They traveled to all the cities of Judah and brought back with them to Jerusalem the Levites and all the heads of the clans.

³ They all gathered in the Temple, and there they made a covenant with Joash, the king's son. Jehoiada said to them, "Here is the son of the late king. He is now to be king, as the LORD promised that King David's descendants would be. ⁴ This is what we will do. When the priests and Levites come on duty on the Sabbath, one third of them will guard the Temple gates, ⁵ another third will guard the royal palace, and the rest will be stationed at the Foundation Gate. All the people will assemble in the Temple courtyard. ⁶ No one is to enter the Temple buildings except the

---

ᶠ *Some ancient translations (and see 2 K 8.26)* twenty-two; *Hebrew* forty-two.
23.3 2 S 7.12

priests and the Levites who are on duty. They may enter, because they are consecrated, but the rest of the people must obey the LORD's instructions and stay outside. ⁷The Levites are to stand guard around the king, with their swords drawn, and are to stay with the king wherever he goes. Anyone who tries to enter the Temple is to be killed."

⁸The Levites and the people of Judah carried out Jehoiada's instructions. The men were not dismissed when they went off duty on the Sabbath, so the commanders had available both those coming on duty and those going off. ⁹Jehoiada gave the officers the spears and shields that had belonged to King David and had been kept in the Temple. ¹⁰He stationed the men with drawn swords all around the front of the Temple, to protect the king. ¹¹Then Jehoiada led Joash out, placed the crown on his head, and gave him a copy of the laws governing kingship. And so he was made king. Jehoiada the priest and his sons anointed Joash, and everyone shouted, "Long live the king!"

¹²Athaliah heard the people cheering for the king, so she hurried to the Temple, where the crowd had gathered. ¹³There she saw the new king at the Temple entrance, standing by the column reserved for kings and surrounded by the army officers and the trumpeters. All the people were shouting joyfully and blowing trumpets, and the Temple musicians with their instruments were leading the celebration. She tore her clothes in distress and shouted, "Treason! Treason!"

¹⁴Jehoiada did not want Athaliah killed in the Temple area, so he called out the army officers and said, "Take her out between the rows of guards, and kill anyone who tries to rescue her."

¹⁵They seized her, took her to the palace, and there at the Horse Gate they killed her.

Jehoiada's Reforms
(2 Kings 11.17-20)

¹⁶The priest Jehoiada had King Joash and the people join him in making a covenant that they would be the LORD's people. ¹⁷Then they all went to the temple of Baal and tore it down. They smashed the altars and idols there and killed Mattan, the priest of Baal, in front of the altars. ¹⁸Jehoiada put the priests and Levites in charge of the work of the Temple. They were to carry out the duties assigned to them by King David and to burn the sacrifices offered to the LORD in accordance with the Law of Moses. They were also in charge of the music and the celebrations. ¹⁹Jehoiada also put guards on duty at the Temple gates to keep out anyone who was ritually unclean.

²⁰The army officers, the leading citizens, the officials, and all the rest of the people joined Jehoiada in a procession that brought the king from the Temple to the palace. They entered by the main gate, and the king took his place on the throne. ²¹All the people were filled with happiness, and the city was quiet, now that Athaliah had been killed.

King Joash of Judah
(2 Kings 12.1-16)

24 Joash became king of Judah at the age of seven, and he ruled in Jerusalem for forty years. His mother was Zibiah from the city of Beersheba. ²He did what was pleasing to the LORD as long as Jehoiada the priest was alive. ³Jehoiada chose two wives for King Joash, and they bore him sons and daughters.

⁴After he had been king for a while, Joash decided to have the Temple repaired. ⁵He ordered the priests and the Levites to go to the cities of Judah and collect from all the people enough money to make the annual repairs on the Temple. He told them to act promptly, but the Levites delayed,

⁶so he called in Jehoiada, their leader, and demanded, "Why haven't you seen to it that the Levites collect from Judah and Jerusalem the tax which Moses, the servant of the LORD, required the people*g* to pay for support of the Tent of the LORD's presence?"

(⁷The followers of Athaliah, that corrupt woman,*h* had damaged the Temple and had used many of the sacred objects in the worship of Baal.)

⁸The king ordered the Levites to make a box for contributions and to place it at the Temple gate. ⁹They sent word throughout Jerusalem and Judah for everyone to bring to the LORD the tax which Moses, God's servant, had first collected in the wilderness. ¹⁰This pleased the people and their leaders, and they brought their tax money and

They brought their tax money. (24.10)

filled the box with it. ¹¹Every day the Levites would take the box to the royal official who was in charge of it. Whenever it was full, the royal secretary and the High Priest's representative would take the money out and return the box to its place. And so they collected a large sum of money. ¹²The king and Jehoiada would give the money to those who were in charge of repairing the Temple, and they hired

stonemasons, carpenters, and metalworkers to make the repairs. ¹³All of them worked hard, and they restored the Temple to its original condition, as solid as ever. ¹⁴When the repairs were finished, the remaining gold and silver was given to the king and Jehoiada, who used it to have bowls and other utensils made for the Temple.

Jehoiada's Policies Are Reversed

As long as Jehoiada was alive, sacrifices were offered regularly at the Temple. ¹⁵After reaching the very old age of a hundred and thirty, he died. ¹⁶They buried him in the royal tombs in David's City in recognition of the service he had done for the people of Israel, for God, and for the Temple.

¹⁷But once Jehoiada was dead, the leaders of Judah persuaded King Joash to listen to them instead. ¹⁸And so the people stopped worshiping in the Temple of the LORD, the God of their ancestors, and began to worship idols and the images of the goddess Asherah. Their guilt for these sins brought the LORD's anger on Judah and Jerusalem. ¹⁹The LORD sent prophets to warn them to return to him, but the people refused to listen. ²⁰Then the spirit of God took control of Zechariah son of Jehoiada the priest. He stood where the people could see him and called out, "The LORD God asks why you have disobeyed his commands and are bringing disaster on yourselves! You abandoned him, so he has abandoned you!" ²¹King Joash joined in a conspiracy against Zechariah, and on the king's orders the people stoned Zechariah in the Temple courtyard. ²²The king forgot about the loyal service that Zechariah's father Jehoiada had given him, and he had Zechariah killed. As Zechariah was dy-

g Probable text required the people; *Hebrew unclear.*   *h* that corrupt woman; *or* whom she corrupted.

24.6 Ex 30.11-16   **24.20, 21** Mt 23.35; Lk 11.51

ng, he called out, "May the LORD see what you are doing and punish you!"

The End of Joash's Reign

23 When autumn came that year, the Syrian army attacked Judah and Jerusalem, killed all the leaders, and took large amounts of loot back to Damascus. 24 The Syrian army was small, but the LORD let them defeat a much larger Judean army because the people had abandoned him, the LORD God of their ancestors. In this way King Joash was punished. 25 He was severely wounded, and when the enemy withdrew, two of his officials plotted against him and killed him in his bed to avenge the murder of the son[i] of Jehoiada the priest. He was buried in David's City, but not in the royal tombs. (26 Those who plotted against him were Zabad, the son of an Ammonite woman named Shimeath, and Jehozabad, the son of a Moabite woman named Shimrith.) 27 The *Commentary on the Book of Kings* contains the stories of the sons of Joash, the prophecies spoken against him, and the record of how he rebuilt the Temple. His son Amaziah succeeded him as king.

King Amaziah of Judah
(2 *Kings* 14.2-6)

25 Amaziah became king at the age of twenty-five, and he ruled in Jerusalem for twenty-nine years. His mother was Jehoaddin from Jerusalem. 2 He did what was pleasing to the LORD, but did it reluctantly. 3 As soon as he was firmly in power, he executed the officials who had murdered his father. 4 He did not, however, execute their children, but followed what the LORD had commanded in the Law of Moses: "Parents are not to be put to death for crimes committed by their

children, and children are not to be put to death for crimes committed by their parents; people are to be put to death only for crimes they themselves have committed."

War against Edom
(2 *Kings* 14.7)

5 King Amaziah organized all the men of the tribes of Judah and Benjamin into army units, according to the clans they belonged to, and placed officers in command of units of a thousand and units of a hundred. This included all men twenty years of age or older, 300,000 in all. They were picked troops, ready for battle, skilled in using spears and shields. 6 In addition, he hired 100,000 soldiers from Israel at a cost of about four tons of silver. 7 But a prophet went to the king and said to him, "Don't take these Israelite soldiers with you. The LORD is not with these people from the Northern Kingdom. 8 You may think that they will make you stronger[j] in battle, but it is God who has the power to give victory or defeat, and he will let your enemies defeat you."

9 Amaziah asked the prophet, "But what about all that silver I have already paid for them?"

The prophet replied, "The LORD can give you back more than that!" 10 So Amaziah sent the hired troops away and told them to go home. At this they went home, bitterly angry with the people of Judah.

11 Amaziah summoned up his courage and led his army to Salt Valley. There they fought and killed ten thousand Edomite soldiers 12 and captured another ten thousand. They took the prisoners to the top of the cliff at the city of Sela and threw them off, so that they were killed on the rocks below.

---

[i] *Some ancient translations* son; *Hebrew* sons.
. . stronger; *Hebrew unclear.*

[j] *Some ancient translations* You may

25.4 Dt 24.16

13 Meanwhile the Israelite soldiers that Amaziah had not allowed to go into battle with him attacked the Judean cities between Samaria and Beth Horon, killed three thousand men, and captured quantities of loot.

14 When Amaziah returned from defeating the Edomites, he brought their idols back with him, set them up, worshiped them, and burned incense to them. 15 This made the LORD angry, so he sent a prophet to Amaziah. The prophet demanded, "Why have you worshiped foreign gods that could not even save their own people from your power?"

16 "Since when," Amaziah interrupted, "have we made you adviser to the king? Stop talking, or I'll have you killed!"

The prophet stopped, but not before saying, "Now I know that God has decided to destroy you because you have done all this and have ignored my advice."

War against Israel
(2 Kings 14.8-20)

17 King Amaziah of Judah and his advisers plotted against Israel. He then sent a message to King Jehoash of Israel, who was the son of Jehoahaz and grandson of Jehu, challenging him to fight.[k] 18 Jehoash sent this answer to Amaziah: "Once a thorn bush in the Lebanon Mountains sent a message to a cedar: 'Give your daughter in marriage to my son.' A wild animal passed by and trampled the bush down. 19 Now Amaziah, you boast that you have defeated the Edomites, but I advise you to stay at home. Why stir up trouble that will only bring disaster on you and your people?"

20 But Amaziah refused to listen. It was God's will for Amaziah to be defeated, because he had worshiped the Edomite idols. 21 So King Jehoash of Is-

rael went into battle against King Amaziah of Judah. They met at Beth Shemesh in Judah, 22 the Judean army was defeated, and the soldiers fled to their homes. 23 Jehoash captured Amaziah and took him to Jerusalem. There he tore down the city wall from Ephraim Gate to the Corner Gate, a distance of two hundred yards. 24 He took back to Samaria as loot all the gold and silver in the Temple, the Temple equipment guarded by the descendants of Obed Edom, and the palace treasures. He also took hostages with him.

25 King Amaziah of Judah outlived King Jehoash of Israel by fifteen years. 26 All the other things that Amaziah did from the beginning to the end of his reign are recorded in *The History of the Kings of Judah and Israel.* 27 Ever since the time when he rebelled against the LORD, there had been a plot against him in Jerusalem. Finally he fled to the city of Lachish, but his enemies followed him there and killed him. 28 His body was carried to Jerusalem on a horse, and he was buried in the royal tombs in David's City.

King Uzziah of Judah
(2 Kings 14.21, 22; 15.1-7)

26 All the people of Judah chose Amaziah's sixteen-year-old son Uzziah to succeed his father as king. (2 It was after the death of Amaziah that Uzziah recaptured Elath and rebuilt the city.)

3 Uzziah became king at the age of sixteen, and he ruled in Jerusalem for fifty-two years. His mother was Jecoliah from Jerusalem. 4 Following the example of his father, he did what was pleasing to the LORD. 5 As long as Zechariah, his religious adviser, was living, he served the LORD faithfully, and God blessed him.

6 Uzziah went to war against the Philistines. He tore down the walls of the

---

[k] challenging him to fight; *or* inviting him to a conference.

ities of Gath, Jamnia, and Ashdod, and uilt fortified cities near Ashdod and in ne rest of Philistia. [7]God helped him efeat the Philistines, the Arabs living t Gurbaal, and the Meunites. [8]The mmonites paid tribute to Uzziah, and e became so powerful that his fame pread even to Egypt.

[9]Uzziah strengthened the fortifications of Jerusalem by building towers at ne Corner Gate, at the Valley Gate, and /here the wall turned. [10]He also built ortified towers in the open country and ug many cisterns, because he had arge herds of livestock in the western oothills and plains. Because he loved arming, he encouraged the people to lant vineyards in the hill country and o farm the fertile land.

[11]He had a large army ready for battle. Its records were kept by his secrearies Jeiel and Maaseiah under the upervision of Hananiah, a member of ne king's staff. [12]The army was commanded by 2,600 officers. [13]Under hem were 307,500 soldiers able to ight effectively for the king against his nemies. [14]Uzziah supplied the army /ith shields, spears, helmets, coats of rmor, bows and arrows, and stones for linging. [15]In Jerusalem his inventors nade equipment for shooting arrows nd for throwing large stones from the owers and corners of the city wall. His ame spread everywhere, and he became very powerful because of the help e received from God.

Uzziah Is Punished for His Pride

[16]But when King Uzziah became trong, he grew arrogant, and that led o his downfall. He defied the LORD his God by going into the Temple to burn ncense on the altar of incense. [17]Azaiah the priest, accompanied by eighty trong and courageous priests, followed he king [18]to resist him. They said, "Uz-

ziah! You have no right to burn incense to the LORD. Only the priests who are descended from Aaron have been consecrated to do this. Leave this holy place. You have offended the LORD God, and you no longer have his blessing."

[19]Uzziah was standing there in the Temple beside the incense altar and was holding an incense burner. He became angry with the priests, and immediately a dreaded skin disease broke out on his forehead. [20]Azariah and the other priests stared at the king's forehead in horror and then forced him to leave the Temple. He hurried to get out, because the LORD had punished him.

[21]For the rest of his life King Uzziah was ritually unclean because of his disease. Unable to enter the Temple again, he lived in his own house, relieved of all duties, while his son Jotham governed the country.

[22]The prophet Isaiah son of Amoz recorded all the other things that King Uzziah did during his reign. [23]Uzziah died and was buried in the royal burial ground, but because of his disease he was not buried in the royal tombs. His son Jotham succeeded him as king.

King Jotham of Judah
(2 Kings 15.32-38)

27 Jotham became king at the age of twenty-five, and he ruled in Jerusalem for sixteen years. His mother was Jerushah, the daughter of Zadok. [2]He did what was pleasing to the LORD, just as his father had done; but unlike his father he did not sin by burning incense[l] in the Temple. The people, however, went on sinning.

[3]It was Jotham who built the North Gate of the Temple and did extensive work on the city wall in the area of Jerusalem called Ophel. [4]In the mountains of Judah he built cities, and in the

he did not sin by burning incense; *or* he did not take part in the worship.
6.18 Ex 30.7, 8; Nu 3.10   **26.23** Is 6.1

forests he built forts and towers. ⁵He fought against the king of Ammon and his army and defeated them. Then he forced the Ammonites to pay him the following tribute each year for three years: four tons of silver, fifty thousand bushels of wheat, and fifty thousand bushels of barley. ⁶Jotham grew powerful because he faithfully obeyed the LORD his God. ⁷The other events of Jotham's reign, his wars, and his policies, are all recorded in *The History of the Kings of Israel and Judah.* ⁸Jotham was twenty-five years old when he became king, and he ruled in Jerusalem for sixteen years. ⁹He died and was buried in David's City and his son Ahaz succeeded him as king.

King Ahaz of Judah
(2 Kings 16.1-4)

28 Ahaz became king at the age of twenty, and he ruled in Jerusalem for sixteen years. He did not follow the good example of his ancestor King David; instead, he did what was not pleasing to the LORD ²and followed the example of the kings of Israel. He had metal images of Baal made, ³burned incense in Hinnom Valley, and even sacrificed his own sons as burnt offerings to idols, imitating the disgusting practice of the people whom the LORD had driven out of the land as the Israelites advanced. ⁴At the pagan places of worship, on the hills, and under every shady tree Ahaz offered sacrifices and burned incense.

War with Syria and Israel
(2 Kings 16.5)

⁵⁻⁶Because King Ahaz sinned, the LORD his God let the king of Syria defeat him and take a large number of Judeans back to Damascus as prisoners. The LORD also let the king of Israel, Pekah son of Remaliah, defeat Ahaz and kill 120,000 of the bravest Judean sol-

diers in one day. The LORD, the God o their ancestors, permitted this to hap pen, because the people of Judah ha abandoned him. ⁷An Israelite soldie named Zichri killed King Ahaz' son Ma aseiah, the palace administrator Azri kam, and Elkanah, who was second i command to the king. ⁸Even thoug the Judeans were their own relatives the Israelite army captured 200,00 women and children as prisoners an took them back to Samaria, along wit large amounts of loot.

The Prophet Oded

⁹A man named Oded, a prophet o the LORD, lived in the city of Samaria He met the returning Israelite arm with its Judean prisoners as it wa about to enter the city, and he saic "The LORD God of your ancestors wa angry with Judah and let you defea them, but now he has heard of the vi cious way you slaughtered them. ¹⁰An now you intend to make the men an women of Jerusalem and Judah you slaves. Don't you know that you als have committed sins against the LOR your God? ¹¹Listen to me! These pris oners are your brothers and sisters. Le them go, or the LORD will punish you i his anger."

¹²Four of the leading men of th Northern Kingdom, Azariah son of Je hohanan, Berechiah son of Meshille moth, Jehizkiah son of Shallum, an Amasa son of Hadlai also opposed th actions of the army. ¹³They said, "Don bring those prisoners here! We have al ready sinned against the LORD an made him angry enough to punish us Now you want to do something that wi increase our guilt." ¹⁴So then the arm handed the prisoners and the loot ove to the people and their leaders, ¹⁵an the four men were appointed to provid the prisoners with clothing from th captured loot. They gave them clothe

28.5, 6 2 K 16.5; Is 7.1

nd sandals to wear, gave them enough ɔ eat and drink, and put olive oil on heir wounds. Those who were too veak to walk were put on donkeys, and ll the prisoners were taken back to Ju-ean territory at Jericho, the city of ‹alm trees. Then the Israelites re-ırned home to Samaria.

Ahaz Asks Assyria for Help
(2 Kings 16.7-9)

16-17 The Edomites began to raid Ju-ah again and captured many prison-rs, so King Ahaz asked Tiglath Pileser, he emperor of Assyria, to send help.

hose who were too weak to walk . . . (28.15)

ᵃ At this same time the Philistines were aiding the towns in the western foot-ills and in southern Judah. They cap-ured the cities of Beth Shemesh, ijalon, and Gederoth, and the cities of ɔoco, Timnah, and Gimzo with their illages, and settled there permanently. ᵑ Because King Ahaz of Judah had vio-ated the rights of his people and had defied the LORD, the LORD brought troubles on Judah. **20** The Assyrian em-peror, instead of helping Ahaz, opposed him and caused him trouble. **21** So Ahaz took the gold from the Temple, the pal-ace, and the homes of the leaders of the people, and gave it to the emperor, but even this did not help.

The Sins of Ahaz

22 When his troubles were at their worst, that man Ahaz sinned against the LORD more than ever. **23** He offered sacrifices to the gods of the Syrians, who had defeated him. He said, "The Syrian gods helped the kings of Syria, so if I sacrifice to them, they may help me too." This brought disaster on him and on his nation. **24** In addition, he took all the Temple equipment and broke it in pieces. He closed the Temple and set up altars in every part of Jerusalem. **25** In every city and town in Judah he built pagan places of worship, where in-cense was to be burned to foreign gods. In this way he brought on himself the anger of the LORD, the God of his ancestors.

26 All the other events of his reign, from beginning to end, are recorded in *The History of the Kings of Judah and Israel.* **27** King Ahaz died and was bur-ied in Jerusalem, but not in the royal tombs. His son Hezekiah succeeded him as king.

King Hezekiah of Judah
(2 Kings 18.1-3)

29 Hezekiah became king of Ju-dah at the age of twenty-five, and he ruled in Jerusalem for twenty-nine years. His mother was Abijah, the daughter of Zechariah. **2** Following the example of his ancestor King David, he did what was pleasing to the LORD.

8.27 Is 14.28

The Purification of the Temple

³In the first month of the year after Hezekiah became king, he reopened the gates of the Temple and had them repaired. ⁴He assembled a group of priests and Levites in the east courtyard of the Temple ⁵and spoke to them there. He said, "You Levites are to consecrate yourselves and purify the Temple of the LORD, the God of your ancestors. Remove from the Temple everything that defiles it. ⁶Our ancestors were unfaithful to the LORD our God and did what was displeasing to him. They abandoned him and turned their backs on the place where he dwells. ⁷They closed the doors of the Temple, let the lamps go out, and failed to burn incense or offer burnt offerings in the Temple of the God of Israel. ⁸Because of this the LORD has been angry with Judah and Jerusalem, and what he has done to them has shocked and frightened everyone. You know this very well. ⁹Our fathers were killed in battle, and our wives and children have been taken away as prisoners.

¹⁰"I have now decided to make a covenant with the LORD, the God of Israel, so that he will no longer be angry with us. ¹¹My sons, do not lose any time. You are the ones that the LORD has chosen to burn incense to him and to lead the people in worshiping him."

¹²⁻¹⁴The following Levites were there:

From the clan of Kohath,
   Mahath son of Amasai and
   Joel son of Azariah
From the clan of Merari, Kish
   son of Abdi and Azariah
   son of Jehallelel
From the clan of Gershon, Joah
   son of Zimmah and Eden
   son of Joah
From the clan of Elizaphan,
   Shimri and Jeuel

From the clan of Asaph,
   Zechariah and Mattaniah
From the clan of Heman, Jehuel
   and Shimei
From the clan of Jeduthun,
   Shemaiah and Uzziel

¹⁵These men assembled their fellow Levites, and they all made themselves ritually clean. Then, as the king had commanded them to do, they began to make the Temple ritually clean, according to the Law of the LORD.ᵐ ¹⁶The priests went inside the Temple to purify it, and they carried out into the Temple courtyard everything that was ritually unclean. From there the Levites took it all outside the city to Kidron Valley.

¹⁷The work was begun on the first day of the first month, and by the eighth day they had finished it all, including the entrance room to the Temple. Then they worked for the next eight days, until the sixteenth of the month, preparing the Temple for worship.

The Temple Is Rededicated

¹⁸The Levites made the following report to King Hezekiah: "We have completed the ritual purification of the whole Temple, including the altar for burnt offerings, the table for the sacred bread, and all their equipment. ¹⁹We have also brought back all the equipment which King Ahaz took away during those years he was unfaithful to God, and we have rededicated it. It is all in front of the LORD's altar."

²⁰Without delay King Hezekiah assembled the leading men of the city and together they went to the Temple. ²¹As an offering to take away the sins of the royal family and of the people of Judah and to purify the Temple, they took seven bulls, seven sheep, seven lambs and seven goats. The king told the priests, who were descendants of

---

ᵐ Then, as the king . . . LORD; *or* Then they began to make the Temple ritually clean, as the king, who was acting at the LORD's command, had ordered them to do.

Aaron, to offer the animals as sacrifices on the altar. 22 The priests killed the bulls first, then the sheep, and then the lambs, and sprinkled the blood of each sacrifice on the altar. 23 Finally they took the goats to the king and to the other worshipers, who laid their hands on them. 24 Then the priests killed the goats and poured their blood on the altar as a sacrifice to take away the sin of all the people, for the king had commanded that burnt offerings and sin offerings be made for all Israel.

25 The king followed the instructions that the LORD had given to King David through Gad, the king's prophet, and through the prophet Nathan; he stationed Levites in the Temple, with harps and cymbals, 26 instruments like those that King David had used. The priests also stood there with trumpets. 27 Hezekiah gave the order for the burnt offering to be presented; and as the offering began, the people sang praise to the LORD, and the musicians began to play the trumpets and all the other instruments. 28 Everyone who was there joined in worship, and the singing and the rest of the music continued until all the sacrifices had been burned. 29 Then King Hezekiah and all the people knelt down and worshiped God. 30 The king and the leaders of the nation told the Levites to sing to the LORD the songs of praise that were written by David and by Asaph the prophet. So everyone sang with great joy as they knelt and worshiped God.

31 Hezekiah said to the people, "Now that you are ritually clean, bring sacrifices as offerings of thanksgiving to the LORD." They obeyed, and some of them also voluntarily brought animals to be sacrificed as burnt offerings. 32 They brought 70 bulls, 100 sheep, and 200 lambs as burnt offerings for the LORD; 33 they also brought 600 bulls and 3,000 sheep as sacrifices for the people to eat. 34 Since there were not enough priests

to kill all these animals, the Levites helped them until the work was finished. By then more priests had made themselves ritually clean. (The Levites were more faithful in keeping ritually clean than the priests were.) 35 In addition to offering the sacrifices that were burned whole, the priests were responsible for burning the fat that was offered from the sacrifices which the people ate, and for pouring out the wine that was presented with the burnt offerings.

And so worship in the Temple was begun again. 36 King Hezekiah and the people were happy, because God had helped them to do all this so quickly.

Preparations for Passover

30 1-3 The people had not been able to celebrate the Passover Festival at the proper time in the first month, because not enough priests were ritually clean and not many people had assembled in Jerusalem. So King Hezekiah, his officials, and the people of Jerusalem agreed to celebrate it in the second month, and the king sent word to all the people of Israel and Judah. He took special care to send letters to the tribes of Ephraim and Manasseh, inviting them to come to the Temple in Jerusalem to celebrate the Passover in honor of the LORD, the God of Israel. 4 The king and the people were pleased with their plan, 5 so they invited all the Israelites, from Dan in the north to Beersheba in the south, to come together in Jerusalem and celebrate the Passover according to the Law, in larger numbers than ever before. 6 Messengers went out at the command of the king and his officials through all Judah and Israel with the following invitation:

"People of Israel, you have survived the Assyrian conquest of the land. Now return to the LORD, the God of Abraham, Isaac, and Jacob, and he will

---

30.2, 3 Nu 9.9-11

return to you. [7] Do not be like your ancestors and your Israelite relatives who were unfaithful to the LORD their God. As you can see, he punished them severely. [8] Do not be stubborn as they were, but obey the LORD. Come to the Temple in Jerusalem, which the LORD your God has made holy forever, and worship him so that he will no longer be angry with you. [9] If you return to the LORD, then those who have taken your relatives away as prisoners will take pity on them and let them come back home. The LORD your God is kind and merciful, and if you return to him, he will accept you."

[10] The messengers went to every city in the territory of the tribes of Ephraim and Manasseh, and as far north as the tribe of Zebulun, but people laughed at them and made fun of them. [11] Still, there were some from the tribes of Asher, Manasseh, and Zebulun who were willing to come to Jerusalem. [12] God was also at work in Judah and united the people in their determination to obey his will by following the commands of the king and his officials.

Passover Is Celebrated

[13] A great number of people gathered in Jerusalem in the second month to celebrate the Festival of Unleavened Bread. [14] They took all the altars that had been used in Jerusalem for offering sacrifices and burning incense and threw them into Kidron Valley. [15] And on the fourteenth day of the month they killed the lambs for the Passover sacrifice. The priests and Levites who were not ritually clean became so ashamed that they dedicated themselves to the LORD, and now they could sacrifice burnt offerings in the Temple. [16] They took their places in the Temple according to the instructions in the Law of Moses, the man of God. The Levites gave the blood of the sacrifices to the priests, who sprinkled it on the altar. [17] Because many of the people were not ritually clean, they could not kill the Passover lambs, so the Levites did it for them and dedicated the lambs to the LORD. [18] In addition, many of those who had come from the tribes of Ephraim, Manasseh, Issachar, and Zebulun had not performed the ritual of purification, and so they were observing Passover improperly. King Hezekiah offered this prayer for them: [19] "O LORD, the God of our ancestors, in your goodness forgive those who are worshiping you with all their heart, even though they are not ritually clean." [20] The LORD answered Hezekiah's prayer; he forgave the people and did not harm them. [21] For seven days the people who had gathered in Jerusalem celebrated the Festival of Unleavened Bread with great joy, and day after day the Levites and the priests praised the LORD with all their strength.[n] [22] Hezekiah praised the Levites for their skill in conducting the worship of the LORD.

A Second Celebration

After the seven days during which they offered sacrifices in praise of the LORD, the God of their ancestors, [23] they all decided to celebrate for another seven days. So they celebrated with joy. [24] King Hezekiah contributed 1,000 bulls and 7,000 sheep for the people to kill and eat, and the officials gave them another 1,000 bulls and 10,000 sheep. A large number of priests went through the ritual of purification. [25] So everyone was happy — the people of Judah, the priests, the Levites, the people who had come from the north, and the foreigners who had settled permanently in Israel and Judah. [26] The city of Jerusalem was filled with joy, because nothing like this had happened since the days of King Solomon, the son of David. [27] The priests and the Levites asked the

---

[n] *Probable text* with all their strength; *Hebrew* with mighty instruments.

LORD's blessing on the people. In his home in heaven God heard their prayers and accepted them.

Hezekiah Reforms Religious Life

31 After the festival ended, all the people of Israel went to every city in Judah and broke the stone pillars, cut down the symbols of the godless Asherah, and destroyed the altars and the pagan places of worship. They did the same thing throughout the rest of Judah, and the territories of Benjamin, Ephraim, and Manasseh; then they all returned home.

2 King Hezekiah reestablished the organization of the priests and Levites, under which they each had specific duties. These included offering the burnt offerings and the fellowship offerings, taking part in the Temple worship, and giving praise and thanks in the various parts of the Temple. 3 From his own flocks and herds he provided animals for the burnt offerings each morning and evening, and for those offered on the Sabbath, at the New Moon Festival, and at the other festivals which are required by the Law of the LORD.

4 In addition, the king told the people of Jerusalem to bring the offerings to which the priests and the Levites were entitled, so that they could give all their time to the requirements of the Law of the LORD. 5 As soon as the order was given, the people of Israel brought gifts of their finest grain, wine, olive oil, honey, and other farm produce, and they also brought the tithes⁰ of everything they had. 6 All the people who lived in the cities of Judah brought tithes of their cattle and sheep, and they also brought large quantities of gifts which they dedicated to the LORD their God. 7 The gifts started arriving in the third month and continued to pile up for the next four months. 8 When King Hezekiah and his officials saw how much had been given, they praised the LORD and praised his people Israel. 9 The king spoke to the priests and the Levites about these gifts, 10 and Azariah the High Priest, a descendant of Zadok, said to him, "Since the people started bringing their gifts to the Temple, there has been enough to eat and a large surplus besides. We have all this because the LORD has blessed his people."

11 On the king's orders they prepared storerooms in the Temple area 12 and put all the gifts and tithes in them for safekeeping. They placed a Levite named Conaniah in charge and made his brother Shimei his assistant. 13 Ten Levites were assigned to work under them: Jehiel, Azaziah, Nahath, Asahel, Jerimoth, Jozabad, Eliel, Ismachiah, Mahath, and Benaiah. All this was done under the authority of King Hezekiah and Azariah the High Priest. 14 Kore son of Imnah, a Levite who was chief guard at the East Gate of the Temple, was in charge of receiving the gifts offered to the LORD and of distributing them. 15 In the other cities where priests lived, he was faithfully assisted in this by other Levites: Eden, Miniamin, Jeshua, Shemaiah, Amariah, and Shecaniah. They distributed the food equally to their fellow Levites according to what their duties were, 16 and not by clans. They gave a share to all males thirtyᵖ years of age or older who had daily responsibilities in the Temple in accordance with their positions. 17 The priests were assigned their duties by clans, and the Levites twenty years of age or older were assigned theirs by work groups. 18 They were all registered together with their wives, children, and other dependents, because they were required to be ready to perform their sacred duties at any time. 19 Among the priests who lived in

---

ᵒ GIFTS . . . TITHES: *The gifts were for the priests, and the tithes for the Levites (see Nu 18).*   ᵖ *Probable text* thirty; *Hebrew* three.

31.3 Nu 28.1−29.39   **31.4, 5** Nu 18.12, 13, 21

Receiving the gifts offered to the LORD and distributing them (31.14)

the cities assigned to Aaron's descendants or in the pasture lands belonging to these cities, there were responsible men who distributed the food to all the males in the priestly families and to everyone who was on the rolls of the Levite clans.

²⁰ Throughout all Judah, King Hezekiah did what was right and what was pleasing to the LORD his God. ²¹ He was successful, because everything he did for the Temple or in observance of the Law, he did in a spirit of complete loyalty and devotion to his God.

The Assyrians Threaten Jerusalem
(*2 Kings 18.13-37; 19.14-19, 35-37; Isaiah 36.1-22; 37.8-38*)

32 After these events, in which King Hezekiah served the LORD faithfully, Sennacherib, the emperor of Assyria, invaded Judah. He besieged the fortified cities and gave orders for his army to break their way through the walls. ² When Hezekiah saw that Sennacherib intended to attack Jerusalem also, ³⁻⁴ he and his officials decided to cut off the supply of water outside the city in order to keep the Assyrians from having any water when they got near Jerusalem. The officials led a large number of people out and stopped up all the springs, so that

no more water flowed out of them. ⁵ The king strengthened the city's defenses by repairing the wall, building towers on it,�q and building an outer wall. In addition, he repaired the defenses built on the land that was filled in on the east side of the old part of Jerusalem. He also had a large number of spears and shields made. ⁶ He placed all the men in the city under the command of army officers and had them assemble in the open square at the city gate. He said to them, ⁷ "Be determined and confident and don't be afraid of the Assyrian emperor or of the army he is leading. We have more power on our side than he has on his. ⁸ He has human power, but we have the LORD our God to help us and to fight our battles." The people were encouraged by these words of their king.

⁹ Some time later, while Sennacherib and his army were still at Lachish, he sent the following message to Hezekiah and the people of Judah who were with him in Jerusalem: ¹⁰ "I, Sennacherib, Emperor of Assyria, ask what gives you people the confidence to remain in Jerusalem under siege. ¹¹ Hezekiah tells you that the LORD your God will save you from our power, but Hezekiah is deceiving you and will let you die of hunger and thirst. ¹² He is the one who

---

q *Some ancient translations* building towers on it; *Hebrew* building on the towers.

destroyed the LORD's shrines and altars and then told the people of Judah and Jerusalem to worship and burn incense at one altar only. 13 Don't you know what my ancestors and I have done to the people of other nations? Did the gods of any other nation save their people from the emperor of Assyria? 14 When did any of the gods of all those countries ever save their country from us? Then what makes you think that our god can save you? 15 Now don't let Hezekiah deceive you or mislead you like that. Don't believe him! No god of any nation has ever been able to save his people from any Assyrian emperor. So certainly this god of yours can't save you!"

16 The Assyrian officials said even worse things about the LORD God and Hezekiah, the LORD's servant. 17 The letter that the emperor wrote defied the LORD, the God of Israel. It said, "The gods of the nations have not saved their people from my power, and neither will Hezekiah's god save his people from me." 18 The officials shouted this in Hebrew in order to frighten and discourage the people of Jerusalem who were on the city wall, so that it would be easier to capture the city. 19 They talked about the God of Jerusalem in the same way that they talked about the gods of the other peoples, idols made by human hands.

20 Then King Hezekiah and the prophet Isaiah son of Amoz prayed to God and cried out to him for help. 21 The LORD sent an angel that killed the soldiers and officers of the Assyrian army. So the emperor went back to Assyria disgraced. One day when he was in the temple of his god, some of his sons killed him with their swords.

22 In this way the LORD rescued King Hezekiah and the people of Jerusalem from the power of Sennacherib, the emperor of Assyria, and also from their other enemies. He let the people live in peace[r] with all the neighboring countries. 23 Many people came to Jerusalem, bringing offerings to the LORD and gifts to Hezekiah, so that from then on all the nations held Hezekiah in honor.

Hezekiah's Illness and Pride
(2 Kings 20.1-3, 12-19; Isaiah 38.1-3; 39.1-8)

24 About this time King Hezekiah became sick and almost died. He prayed, and the LORD gave him a sign that he would recover. 25 But Hezekiah was too proud to show gratitude for what the LORD had done for him, and Judah and Jerusalem suffered for it. 26 Finally, however, Hezekiah and the people of Jerusalem humbled themselves, and so the LORD did not punish the people until after Hezekiah's death.

Hezekiah's Wealth and Splendor

27 King Hezekiah became very wealthy, and everyone held him in honor. He had storerooms built for his gold, silver, precious stones, spices, shields, and other valuable objects. 28 In addition, he had storehouses built for his grain, wine, and olive oil; barns for his cattle; and pens for his sheep. 29 Besides all this, God gave him sheep and cattle and so much other wealth that he built many cities. 30 It was King Hezekiah who blocked the outlet for Gihon Spring and channeled the water to flow through a tunnel to a point inside the walls of Jerusalem. Hezekiah succeeded in everything he did, 31 and even when the Babylonian ambassadors came to inquire about the unusual event that had happened in the land, God let Hezekiah go his own way only in order to test his character.

Some ancient translations He let the people live in peace; *Hebrew* He led the people.

The End of Hezekiah's Reign
(2 Kings 20.20, 21)

³²Everything else that King Hezekiah did and his devotion to the LORD are recorded in *The Vision of the Prophet Isaiah Son of Amoz* and in *The History of the Kings of Judah and Israel.* ³³Hezekiah died and was buried in the upper section of the royal tombs. All the people of Judah and Jerusalem paid him great honor at his death. His son Manasseh succeeded him as king.

King Manasseh of Judah
(2 Kings 21.1-9)

33 Manasseh was twelve years old when he became king of Judah, and he ruled in Jerusalem for fifty-five years. ²Following the disgusting practices of the nations whom the LORD had driven out of the land as his people advanced, Manasseh sinned against the LORD. ³He rebuilt the pagan places of worship that his father Hezekiah had destroyed. He built altars for the worship of Baal, made images of the goddess Asherah, and worshiped the stars. ⁴He built pagan altars in the Temple, the place that the LORD had said was where he should be worshiped forever. ⁵In the two courtyards of the Temple he built altars for the worship of the stars. ⁶He sacrificed his sons in Hinnom Valley as burnt offerings. He practiced divination and magic and consulted fortunetellers and mediums. He sinned greatly against the LORD and stirred up his anger. ⁷He placed an image in the Temple, the place about which God had said to David and his son Solomon: "Here in Jerusalem, in this Temple, is the place that I have chosen out of all the territory of the twelve tribes of Israel as the place where I am to be worshiped. ⁸And if the people of Israel will obey all my commands and keep the whole Law that my servant Moses gave them, then I will not allow them to be driven out of the land that I gave to their ancestors." ⁹Manasseh led the people of Judah to commit even greater sins than those committed by the nations whom the LORD had driven out of the land as his people advanced.

Manasseh Repents

¹⁰Although the LORD warned Manasseh and his people, they refused to listen. ¹¹So the LORD let the commanders of the Assyrian army invade Judah. They captured Manasseh, stuck hooks in him, put him in chains, and took him to Babylon. ¹²In his suffering he became humble, turned to the LORD his God, and begged him for help. ¹³God accepted Manasseh's prayer and answered it by letting him go back to Jerusalem and rule again. This convinced Manasseh that the LORD was God.

¹⁴After this, Manasseh increased the height of the outer wall on the east side of David's City, from a point in the valley near Gihon Spring north to the Fish Gate and the area of the city called Ophel. He also stationed an army officer in command of a unit of troops in each of the fortified cities of Judah. ¹⁵He removed from the Temple the foreign gods and the image that he had placed there, and the pagan altars that were on the hill where the Temple stood and in other places in Jerusalem; he took all these things outside the city and threw them away. ¹⁶He also repaired the altar where the LORD was worshiped, and he sacrificed fellowship offerings and thanksgiving offerings on it. He commanded all the people of Judah to worship the LORD, the God of Israel. ¹⁷Although the people continued to offer sacrifices at other places of worship, they offered them only to the LORD.

33.2 Jr 15.4   33.4 2 Ch 6.6   33.7, 8 1 K 9.3-5; 2 Ch 7.12-18

The End of Manasseh's Reign
(2 Kings 21.17, 18)

18 Everything else that Manasseh id, the prayer he made to his God, and he messages of the prophets who poke to him in the name of the LORD, he God of Israel, are all recorded in *The History of the Kings of Israel.* 19 The ing's prayer and God's answer to it, nd an account of the sins he committed before he repented — the evil he did, he pagan places of worship and the ymbols of the goddess Asherah that he nade and the idols that he worshiped — re all recorded in *The History of the Prophets.* 20 Manasseh died and was uried at the palace, and his son Amon ucceeded him as king.

King Amon of Judah
(2 Kings 21.19-26)

21 Amon was twenty-two years old when he became king of Judah, and he uled in Jerusalem for two years. 22 Like is father Manasseh, he sinned against he LORD, and he worshiped the idols hat his father had worshiped. 23 But nlike his father, he did not become umble and turn to the LORD; he was ven more sinful than his father had een.

24 Amon's officials plotted against im and assassinated him in the palace. 25 The people of Judah killed Amon's ssassins and made his son Josiah ing.

King Josiah of Judah
(2 Kings 22.1, 2)

34 Josiah was eight years old when he became king of Judah, and he ruled in Jerusalem for hirty-one years. 2 He did what was leasing to the LORD; he followed the xample of his ancestor King David, trictly obeying all the laws of God.

Josiah Attacks Pagan Worship

3 In the eighth year that Josiah was king, while he was still very young, he began to worship the God of his ancestor King David. Four years later he began to destroy the pagan places of worship, the symbols of the goddess Asherah, and all the other idols. 4 Under his direction the altars where Baal was worshiped were smashed, and the incense altars near them were torn down. They ground to dust the images of Asherah and all the other idols and then scattered the dust on the graves of the people who had sacrificed to them. 5 He burned the bones of the pagan priests on the altars where they had worshiped. By doing all this, he made Judah and Jerusalem ritually clean again. 6 He did the same thing in the cities and the devastated areas of Manasseh, Ephraim, and Simeon, and as far north as Naphtali. 7 Throughout the territory of the Northern Kingdom he smashed the altars and the symbols of Asherah, ground the idols to dust, and broke into bits all the incense altars. Then he returned to Jerusalem.

The Book of the Law Is Discovered
(2 Kings 22.3-20)

8 In the eighteenth year of his reign, after he had purified the land and the Temple by ending pagan worship, King Josiah sent three men to repair the Temple of the LORD God: Shaphan son of Azaliah, Maaseiah, the governor of Jerusalem, and Joah son of Joahaz, a high official. 9 The money that the Levite guards had collected in the Temple was turned over to Hilkiah the High Priest. (It had been collected from the people of Ephraim and Manasseh and the rest of the Northern Kingdom, and from the people of Judah, Benjamin, and Jerusalem.) 10 This money was then handed over to the three men in

4.1 Jr 3.6   **34.4** 2 K 21.3; 2 Ch 33.3   **34.5** 1 K 13.2

charge of the Temple repairs, and they gave it to [11] the carpenters and the builders to buy the stones and the timber used to repair the buildings that the kings of Judah had allowed to decay. [12] The men who did the work were thoroughly honest. They were supervised by four Levites: Jahath and Obadiah of the clan of Merari, and Zechariah and Meshullam of the clan of Kohath. (The Levites were all skillful musicians.) [13] Other Levites were in charge of transporting materials and supervising the workers on various jobs, and others kept records or served as guards.

[14] While the money was being taken out of the storeroom, Hilkiah found the book of the Law of the LORD, the Law that God had given to Moses. [15] He said to Shaphan, "I have found the book of the Law here in the Temple." He gave Shaphan the book, [16] and Shaphan took it to the king. He reported, "We have done everything that you commanded. [17] We have taken the money that was kept in the Temple and handed it over to the workers and their supervisors." [18] Then he added, "I have here a book that Hilkiah gave me." And he read it aloud to the king.

[19] When the king heard the book being read, he tore his clothes in dismay [20] and gave the following order to Hilkiah, to Ahikam son of Shaphan, to Abdon[s] son of Micaiah, to Shaphan, the court secretary, and to Asaiah, the king's attendant: [21] "Go and consult the LORD for me and for the people who still remain in Israel and Judah. Find out about the teachings of this book. The LORD is angry with us because our ancestors have not obeyed the word of the LORD and have not done what this book says must be done."

[22] At the king's command, Hilkiah and the others went to consult a woman named Huldah, a prophet who lived in the newer part of Jerusalem. (Her husband Shallum, the son of Tikvah and grandson of Harhas, was in charge of the Temple robes.) They described to her what had happened, [23] and she told them to go back to the king and give him [24] the following message from the LORD: "I am going to punish Jerusalem and all its people with the curses written in the book that was read to the king. [25] They have rejected me and have offered sacrifices to other gods and so have stirred up my anger by all they have done. My anger is aroused against Jerusalem, and it will not die down. [26] As for the king himself, this is what I, the LORD God of Israel, say: You listened to what is written in the book [27] and you repented and humbled yourself before me, tearing your clothes and weeping, when you heard how I threatened to punish Jerusalem and its people. I have heard your prayer, [28] and the punishment which I am going to bring on Jerusalem will not come until after your death. I will let you die in peace."

The men returned to King Josiah with this message.

Josiah Makes a Covenant to Obey the LORD
(2 Kings 23.1-20)

[29] King Josiah summoned all the leaders of Judah and Jerusalem, [30] and together they went to the Temple, accompanied by the priests and the Levites and all the rest of the people, rich and poor alike. Before them all the king read aloud the whole book of the covenant, which had been found in the Temple. [31] He stood by the royal column[t] and made a covenant with the LORD to obey him, to keep his laws and commands with all his heart and soul, and to put into practice the demands attached to the covenant, as written in

---

[s] ABDON: *Achbor in 2 K 22.12.*   [t] *Probable text (see 2 K 23.3) by the royal column;* Hebrew *in his place.*

the book. [32] He made the people of Benjamin and everyone else present in Jerusalem promise to keep the covenant. And so the people of Jerusalem obeyed the requirements of the covenant they had made with the God of their ancestors. [33] King Josiah destroyed all the disgusting idols that were in the territory belonging to the people of Israel, and as long as he lived, he required the people to serve the LORD, the God of their ancestors.

Josiah Celebrates the Passover
(2 Kings 23.21-23)

35 King Josiah celebrated the Passover at Jerusalem in honor of the LORD; on the fourteenth day of the first month they killed the animals for the festival. [2] He assigned to the priests the duties they were to perform in the Temple and encouraged them to do them well. [3] He also gave these instructions to the Levites, the teachers of Israel, who were dedicated to the LORD: "Put the sacred Covenant Box in the Temple that King Solomon, the son of David, built. You are no longer to carry it from place to place, but you are to serve the LORD your God and his people Israel. [4] Take your places in the Temple by clans, according to the responsibilities assigned to you by King David and his son King Solomon, [5] and arrange yourselves so that some of you will be available to help each family of the people of Israel. [6] You are to kill the Passover lambs and goats. Now make yourselves ritually clean and prepare the sacrifices in order that your fellow Israelites may follow the instructions which the LORD gave through Moses."

[7] For the use of the people at the Passover, King Josiah contributed from his own herds and flocks 30,000 sheep, lambs, and young goats, and 3,000 bulls. [8] His officials also made contributions for the people, the priests, and the Levites to use. And the officials in charge of the Temple — Hilkiah, the High Priest, Zechariah, and Jehiel — gave the priests 2,600 lambs and young goats and 300 bulls for sacrifices during the festival. [9] The leaders of the Levites — Conaniah, Shemaiah and his brother Nethanel, Hashabiah, Jeiel, and Jozabad — contributed 5,000 lambs and young goats and 500 bulls for the Levites to offer as sacrifices.

[10] When everything was arranged for the Passover, the priests and the Levites took their posts, as commanded by the king. [11] After the lambs and goats had been killed, the Levites skinned them, and the priests sprinkled the blood on the altar. [12] Then they divided among the people, by family groups, the animals for burnt offerings, so that they could offer them according to the instructions in the Law of Moses. [13] The Levites roasted the Passover sacrifices over the fire, according to the regulations, and boiled the sacred offerings in pots, kettles, and pans, and quickly distributed the meat to the people. [14] After this was done, the Levites provided meat for themselves and for the priests descended from Aaron, for the priests were kept busy until night, burning the animals that were burned whole and the fat of the sacrifices. [15] The following musicians of the Levite clan of Asaph were in the places assigned to them by King David's instructions: Asaph, Heman, and Jeduthun, the king's prophet. The guards at the Temple gates did not need to leave their posts, because the other Levites prepared the Passover for them. [16] So, as King Josiah had commanded, everything was done that day for the worship of the LORD, the keeping of the Passover Festival, and the offering of burnt offerings on the altar. [17] For seven days all the people of Israel

35.4 2 Ch 8.14   35.13 Ex 12.8, 9   35.15 1 Ch 25.1   35.17 Ex 12.1-20 who were present celebrated the Passover and the Festival of Unleavened Bread. [18] Since the days of the prophet Samuel, the Passover had never been celebrated like this. None of the former kings had ever celebrated a Passover like this one celebrated by King Josiah, the priests, the Levites, and the people of Judah, Israel, and Jerusalem [19] in the eighteenth year of Josiah's reign.

The End of Josiah's Reign
(2 Kings 23.28-30)

[20] After King Josiah had done all this for the Temple, King Neco of Egypt led an army to fight at Carchemish on the Euphrates River. Josiah tried to stop him, [21] but Neco sent Josiah this message: "This war I am fighting does not concern you, King of Judah. I have not come to fight you, but to fight my enemies, and God has told me to hurry. God is on my side, so don't oppose me, or he will destroy you." [22] But Josiah was determined to fight. He refused to listen to what God was saying through King Neco, so he disguised himself and went into battle on the plain of Megiddo.

[23] During the battle King Josiah was struck by Egyptian arrows. He ordered his servants, "Take me away; I'm badly hurt!" [24] They lifted him out of his chariot, placed him in a second chariot which he had there, and took him to Jerusalem. There he died and was buried in the royal tombs. All the people of Judah and Jerusalem mourned his death.

[25] The prophet Jeremiah composed a lament for King Josiah. It has become a custom in Israel for the singers, both men and women, to use this song when they mourn for him. The song is found in the collection of laments.

[26] Everything that Josiah did — his devotion to the LORD, his obedience to the Law, [27] and his history from beginning to end — is all recorded in *The History of the Kings of Israel and Judah.*

King Joahaz of Judah
(2 Kings 23.30-35)

36 The people of Judah chose Josiah's son Joahaz and anointed him king in Jerusalem. [2] Joahaz was twenty-three years old when he became king of Judah, and he ruled in Jerusalem for three months. [3] King Neco of Egypt took him prisoner and made Judah pay 7,500 pounds of silver and 75 pounds of gold as tribute. [4] Neco made Joahaz' brother Eliakim king of Judah and changed his name to Jehoiakim. Joahaz was taken to Egypt by Neco.

King Jehoiakim of Judah
(2 Kings 23.36 − 24.7)

[5] Jehoiakim was twenty-five years old when he became king of Judah, and he ruled in Jerusalem for eleven years. He sinned against the LORD his God. [6] King Nebuchadnezzar of Babylonia invaded Judah, captured Jehoiakim, and took him to Babylonia in chains. [7] Nebuchadnezzar carried off some of the treasures of the Temple and put them in his palace in Babylon. [8] Everything that Jehoiakim did, including his disgusting practices and the evil he committed, is recorded in *The History of the Kings of Israel and Judah.* His son Jehoiachin succeeded him as king.

King Jehoiachin of Judah
(2 Kings 24.8-17)

[9] Jehoiachin was eighteen[u] years old when he became king of Judah, and he ruled in Jerusalem for three months and ten days. He too sinned against the LORD. [10] When spring came, King Nebuchadnezzar took Jehoiachin to Baby-

[u] *Some ancient translations (and see 2 K 24.8)* eighteen; *Hebrew* eight.
36.4 Jr 22.11, 12   **36.5** Jr 22.18, 19; 26.1-6; 35.1-19   **36.6** Jr 25.1-38; 36.1-32; 45.1-5; Dn 1.1, 2   **36.10 a** Jr 22.24-30; 24.1-10; 29.1, 2; Ez 17.12; **b** Jr 37.1; Ez 17.13

lonia as a prisoner and carried off the treasures of the Temple. Then Nebuchadnezzar made Jehoiachin's uncle[v] Zedekiah king of Judah and Jerusalem.

King Zedekiah of Judah
(2 Kings 24.18-20; Jeremiah 52.1-3a)

11 Zedekiah was twenty-one years old when he became king of Judah, and he ruled in Jerusalem for eleven years. 12 He sinned against the LORD and did not listen humbly to the prophet Jeremiah, who spoke the word of the LORD.

The Fall of Jerusalem
(2 Kings 25.1-21; Jeremiah 52.3b-11)

13 Zedekiah rebelled against King Nebuchadnezzar, who had forced him to swear in God's name that he would be loyal. He stubbornly refused to repent and return to the LORD, the God of Israel. 14 In addition, the leaders of Judah, the priests, and the people followed the sinful example of the nations around them in worshiping idols, and so they defiled the Temple, which the LORD himself had made holy. 15 The LORD, the God of their ancestors, had continued to send prophets to warn his people, because he wanted to spare them and the Temple. 16 But they made fun of God's messengers, ignoring his words and laughing at his prophets, until at last the LORD's anger against his people was so great that there was no escape.

17 So the LORD brought the king of Babylonia to attack them. The king killed the young men of Judah even in the Temple. He had no mercy on anyone, young or old, man or woman, sick or healthy. God handed them all over to him. 18 The king of Babylonia looted the Temple, the Temple treasury, and the wealth of the king and his officials, and took everything back to Babylon. 19 He burned down the Temple and the city, with all its palaces and its wealth, and broke down the city wall. 20 He took all the survivors to Babylonia, where they served him and his descendants as slaves until the rise of the Persian Empire. 21 And so what the LORD had foretold through the prophet Jeremiah was fulfilled: "The land will lie desolate for seventy years, to make up for the Sabbath rest[w] that has not been observed."

Cyrus Commands the Jews to Return
(Ezra 1.1-4)

22 In the first year that Cyrus of Persia was emperor,[x] the LORD made what he had said through the prophet Jeremiah come true. He prompted Cyrus to issue the following command and send it out in writing to be read aloud everywhere in his empire:

23 "This is the command of Cyrus, Emperor of Persia. The LORD, the God of Heaven, has made me ruler over the whole world and has given me the responsibility of building a temple for him in Jerusalem in Judah. Now, all of you who are God's people, go there, and may the LORD your God be with you."

---

v Some ancient translations (and see 2 K 24.17) uncle; Hebrew brother.   w SABBATH REST: A reference to the requirement of the Law that every seventh year the land was not to be farmed (see Lv 25.1-7).   x EMPEROR: King Cyrus of Persia occupied the city of Babylon in 539 B.C. and began to reign as the emperor of Babylonia.

36.11 Jr 27.1-22; 28.1-17   **36.13** Ez 17.15   **36.17** Jr 21.1-10; 34.1-5   **36.19** 1 K 9.8   **36.21** Jr 25.11; 29.10   **36.23** Is 44.28

The Book of
EZRA

INTRODUCTION

The Book of Ezra, as a sequel to *Chronicles,* describes the return of some of the Jewish exiles from Babylon and the restoration of life and worship in Jerusalem. These events are presented in the following stages: 1) The first group of Jewish exiles returns from Babylonia at the order of Cyrus, the Persian emperor. 2) The Temple is rebuilt and dedicated, and the worship of God restored in Jerusalem. 3) Years later another group of Jews returns to Jerusalem under the leadership of Ezra, an expert in the Law of God, who helps the people reorganize their religious and social life in order to safeguard the spiritual heritage of Israel.

OUTLINE OF CONTENTS

Cyrus Commands the Jews to Return

1 In the first year that Cyrus of Persia was emperor,[a] the LORD made what he had said through the prophet Jeremiah come true. He prompted Cyrus to issue the following command and send it out in writing to be read aloud everywhere in his empire:

2 "This is the command of Cyrus, Emperor of Persia. The LORD, the God of Heaven, has made me ruler over the whole world and has given me the responsibility of building a temple for him in Jerusalem in Judah. 3 May God be with all of you who are his people. You are to go to Jerusalem and rebuild the Temple of the LORD, the God of Israel, the God who is worshiped in Jerusalem. 4 If any of his people in exile need help to return, their neighbors are to give them this help. They are to provide them with silver and gold, supplies and pack animals, as well as offerings to present in the Temple of God in Jerusalem."

5 Then the heads of the clans of the tribes of Judah and Benjamin, the priests and Levites, and everyone else whose heart God had moved got ready to go and rebuild the LORD's Temple in Jerusalem. 6 All their neighbors helped them by giving them many things: silver utensils, gold, supplies, pack animals, other valuables, and offerings for the Temple.

7 Emperor Cyrus gave them back the bowls and cups that King Nebuchadnezzar had taken from the Temple in

---

[a] EMPEROR: *King Cyrus of Persia occupied the city of Babylon in 539 B.C. and began to reign as the emperor of Babylonia.*
1.1 Jr 25.11; 29.10   1.2 Is 44.28

Jerusalem and had put in the temple of his gods. [8] He handed them over to Mithredath, chief of the royal treasury, who made an inventory of them for Sheshbazzar, the governor of Judah, [9-10] as follows:

gold bowls for offerings   30
silver bowls for offerings 1,000
other bowls   29
small gold bowls   30
small silver bowls   410
other utensils   1,000

[11] In all there were 5,400 gold and silver bowls and other articles which Sheshbazzar took with him when he and the other exiles went from Babylon to Jerusalem.

The List of Those Who Returned from Exile
(Nehemiah 7.4-73)

2 Many of the exiles left the province of Babylon and returned to Jerusalem and Judah, all to their own hometowns. Their families had been living in exile in Babylonia ever since King Nebuchadnezzar had taken them there as prisoners. [2] Their leaders were Zerubbabel, Joshua, Nehemiah, Seraiah, Reelaiah, Mordecai, Bilshan, Mispar, Bigvai, Rehum, and Baanah.

This is the list of the clans of Israel, with the number of those from each clan who returned from exile:

[3-20] Parosh - 2,172
Shephatiah - 372
Arah - 775
Pahath Moab (descendants of Jeshua and Joab) - 2,812

Elam - 1,254
Zattu - 945
Zaccai - 760
Bani - 642
Bebai - 623
Azgad - 1,222
Adonikam - 666
Bigvai - 2,056
Adin - 454
Ater (also called Hezekiah) - 98
Bezai - 323
Jorah - 112
Hashum - 223
Gibbar - 95

[21-35] People whose ancestors had lived in the following towns also returned:

Bethlehem - 123
Netophah - 56
Anathoth - 128
Azmaveth - 42
Kiriath Jearim, Chephirah, and Beeroth - 743
Ramah and Geba - 621
Michmash - 122
Bethel and Ai - 223
Nebo - 52
Magbish - 156
The other Elam - 1,254
Harim - 320
Lod, Hadid, and Ono - 725
Jericho - 345
Senaah - 3,630

[36-39] This is the list of the priestly clans that returned from exile:

Many of the exiles left. (2.1)

Jedaiah (descendants of
    Jeshua) - 973
Immer - 1,052
Pashhur - 1,247
Harim - 1,017

40-42 Clans of Levites who returned from exile:

Jeshua and Kadmiel
    (descendants of
    Hodaviah) - 74
Temple musicians (descendants
    of Asaph) - 128
Temple guards (descendants of
    Shallum, Ater, Talmon,
    Akkub, Hatita, and
    Shobai) - 139

43-54 Clans of Temple workers who returned from exile:

Ziha, Hasupha, Tabbaoth,
    Keros, Siaha, Padon,
    Lebanah, Hagabah, Akkub,
    Hagab, Shamlai, Hanan,
    Giddel, Gahar, Reaiah,
    Rezin, Nekoda, Gazzam,
    Uzza, Paseah, Besai,
    Asnah, Meunim, Nephisim,
    Bakbuk, Hakupha, Harhur,
    Bazluth, Mehida, Harsha,
    Barkos, Sisera, Temah,
    Neziah, and Hatipha

55-57 Clans of Solomon's servants who returned from exile:

Sotai, Hassophereth, Peruda,
    Jaalah, Darkon, Giddel,
    Shephatiah, Hattil, Pochereth
    Hazzebaim, and Ami

58 The total number of descendants of the Temple workers and of Solomon's servants who returned from exile was 392.

59-60 There were 652 belonging to the clans of Delaiah, Tobiah, and Nekoda who returned from the towns of Tel Melah, Tel Harsha, Cherub, Addan, and Immer; but they could not prove

that they were descendants of Israelites.

61-62 The following priestly clans could find no record to prove their ancestry: Habaiah, Hakkoz, and Barzillai. (The ancestor of the priestly clan of Barzillai had married a woman from the clan of Barzillai of Gilead and had taken the name of his father-in-law's clan.) Since they were unable to prove who their ancestors were, they were not accepted as priests. 63 The Jewish governor told them that they could not eat the food offered to God until there was a priest who could use the Urim and Thummim.*b*

64-67 Total number of exiles who
    returned - 42,360
Their male and female
    servants - 7,337
Male and female musicians - 200
Horses - 736
Mules - 245
Camels - 435
Donkeys - 6,720

68 When the exiles arrived at the LORD's Temple in Jerusalem, some of the leaders of the clans gave freewill offerings to help rebuild the Temple on its old site. 69 They gave as much as they could for this work, and the total came to 1,030 pounds of gold, 5,740 pounds of silver, and 100 robes for priests.

70 The priests, the Levites, and some of the people settled in or near Jerusalem;*c* the musicians, the Temple guards, and the Temple workers settled in nearby towns; and the rest of the Israelites settled in the towns where their ancestors had lived.

Worship Begins Again

3 By the seventh month the people of Israel were all settled in their towns. Then they all assembled in Jeru-

b URIM AND THUMMIM: *Two objects used by the priest to determine God's will; it is not known precisely how they were used.*   *c One ancient translation* in or near Jerusalem; *Hebrew does not have these words.*
2.63 Nu 27.21   **2.70** 1 Ch 9.2; Ne 11.3

salem, [2] and Joshua son of Jehozadak, his fellow priests, and Zerubbabel son of Shealtiel, together with his relatives, rebuilt the altar of the God of Israel, so that they could burn sacrifices on it according to the instructions written in the Law of Moses, the man of God. [3] Even though[d] the returning exiles were afraid of the people who were living in the land, they rebuilt the altar where it had stood before. Then they began once again to burn on it the regular morning and evening sacrifices. [4] They celebrated the Festival of Shelters according to the regulations; each day they offered the sacrifices required for that day; [5] and in addition they offered the regular sacrifices to be burned whole and those to be offered at the New Moon Festival and at all the other regular assemblies at which the LORD is worshiped, as well as all the offerings that were given to the LORD voluntarily. [6] Although the people had not yet started to rebuild the Temple, they began on the first day of the seventh month to burn sacrifices to the LORD.

The Rebuilding of the Temple Begins

[7] The people gave money to pay the stonemasons and the carpenters and gave food, drink, and olive oil to be sent to the cities of Tyre and Sidon in exchange for cedar trees from Lebanon, which were to be brought by sea to Joppa. All this was done with the permission of Emperor Cyrus of Persia. [8] So in the second month of the year after they came back to the site of the Temple in Jerusalem, they began work. Zerubbabel, Joshua, and the rest of their people, the priests, and the Levites, in fact all the exiles who had come back to Jerusalem, joined in the work. All the Levites twenty years of age or older were put in charge of the work of rebuilding the Temple. [9] The Levite Jeshua and his sons and relatives, and Kadmiel and his sons (the clan of Hodaviah[e]) joined together in taking charge of the rebuilding of the Temple. (They were helped by the Levites of the clan of Henadad.)

[10] When the builders started to lay the foundation of the Temple, the priests in their robes took their places with trumpets in their hands, and the Levites of the clan of Asaph stood there with cymbals. They praised the LORD according to the instructions handed down from the time of King David. [11] They sang the LORD's praises, repeating the refrain:

"The LORD is good, and his love
   for Israel is eternal."

Everyone shouted with all their might, praising the LORD, because the work on the foundation of the Temple had been started. [12] Many of the older priests, Levites, and heads of clans had seen the first Temple, and as they watched the foundation of this Temple being laid, they cried and wailed. But the others who were there shouted for joy. [13] No one could distinguish between the joyful shouts and the crying, because the noise they made was so loud that it could be heard for miles.

Opposition to the Rebuilding
of the Temple

4 The enemies of the people of Judah and Benjamin heard that those who had returned from exile were rebuilding the Temple of the LORD, the God of Israel. [2] So they went to see Zerubbabel and the heads of the clans and said, "Let us join you in building the

---

Even though; *or* Because.   *e Probable text (see 2.40)* Hodaviah; *Hebrew* Judah.
3.2 Ex 27.1   **3.3** Nu 28.1-8   **3.4** Nu 29.12-38   **3.5** Nu 28.11—29.39   **3.10** 1 Ch 25.1
3.11 1 Ch 16.34; 2 Ch 5.13; 7.3; Ps 100.5; 106.1; 107.1; 118.1; 136.1; Jr 33.11
3.12 Tb 14.5   **4.2** 2 K 17.24-41

The foundation of the Temple had been started. (3.11)

Temple. We worship the same God you worship, and we have been offering sacrifices to him ever since Emperor Esarhaddon of Assyria sent us here to live."

³Zerubbabel, Joshua, and the heads of the clans told them, "We don't need your help to build a temple for the LORD our God. We will build it ourselves, just as Emperor Cyrus of Persia commanded us."

⁴Then the people who had been living in the land tried to discourage and frighten the Jews and keep them from building. ⁵They also bribed Persian government officials to work against them. They kept on doing this throughout the reign of Emperor Cyrus and into the reign of Emperor Darius.*f*

Opposition to the Rebuilding of Jerusalem

⁶At the beginning of the reign of Emperor Xerxes, the enemies of the people living in Judah and Jerusalem brought written charges against them.

⁷Again in the reign of Emperor Artaxerxes of Persia, Bishlam, Mithredath, Tabeel, and their associates wrote a letter to the emperor. The letter was written in Aramaic*g* and was to be translated when read.*h*

⁸Also Rehum, the governor, and Shimshai, the secretary of the province wrote the following letter to Emperor Artaxerxes about Jerusalem:

⁹"From Rehum, the governor from Shimshai, secretary of the province, from their associates, the judges, and from all the other officials, who are originally from Erech, Babylon, and Susa in the land of Elam, ¹⁰together with the other peoples whom the great and powerful Ashurbanipal moved from their homes and settled in the city

---

f EMPEROR DARIUS: *The account of these events is continued at verse 24. The material in verses 6-23 describes events which took place almost a century later.* *g* ARAMAIC: *From 4.8 to 6.18 this book is not in Hebrew, but Aramaic, the official language of the Persian Empire.* *h* The letter . . . read; *or* It was in Aramaic and was written in the Aramaic script.
4.6 Es 1.1

of Samaria and elsewhere in West-of-Euphrates Province."[i]

11 This is the text of the letter:

"To Emperor Artaxerxes from his servants who live in West-of-Euphrates.

12 "We want Your Majesty to know that the Jews who came here from your other territories have settled in Jerusalem and are rebuilding that evil and rebellious city. They have begun to rebuild the walls and will soon finish them. 13 Your Majesty, if this city is rebuilt and its walls are completed, the people will stop paying taxes, and your royal revenues will decrease. 14 Now, because we are under obligation to Your Majesty, we do not want to see this happen, and so we suggest 15 that you order a search to be made in the records your ancestors kept. If you do, you will discover that this city has always been rebellious and that from ancient times it has given trouble to kings and to rulers of provinces. Its people have always been hard to govern. This is why the city was destroyed. 16 We therefore are convinced that if this city is rebuilt and its walls are completed, Your Majesty will no longer be able to control West-of-Euphrates Province."

17 The emperor sent this answer:

"To Rehum, the governor, to Shimshai, secretary of the province, and to their associates who live in Samaria and in the rest of West-of-Euphrates, greetings.

18 "The letter which you sent has been translated and read to me. 19 I gave orders for an investigation to be made, and it has indeed been found that from ancient times Jerusalem has revolted against royal authority and that it has been full of rebels and troublemakers. 20 Powerful kings have reigned there and have ruled over the entire province of West-of-Euphrates, collecting taxes and revenue. 21 Therefore you are to issue orders that those men are to stop rebuilding the city until I give further commands. 22 Do this at once, so that no more harm may be done to my interests."

23 As soon as this letter from Emperor Artaxerxes was read to Rehum, Shimshai, and their associates, they hurried to Jerusalem and forced the Jews to stop rebuilding the city.

Work on the Temple Begins Again

24 Work on the Temple had been stopped and had remained at a standstill until the second year of the reign of Emperor Darius of Persia. 1 At that time two prophets, Haggai and Zechariah son of Iddo, began to speak in the name of the God of Israel to the Jews who lived in Judah and Jerusalem. 2 When Zerubbabel son of Shealtiel and Joshua son of Jehozadak heard their messages, they began to rebuild the Temple in Jerusalem, and the two prophets helped them.

3 Almost at once Governor Tattenai of West-of-Euphrates, Shethar Bozenai, and their fellow officials came to Jerusalem and demanded: "Who gave you orders to build this Temple and equip it?" 4 They[j] also asked for the names of all the men who were helping build the Temple. 5 But God was watching over the Jewish leaders, and the Persian officials decided to take no action until they could write to Emperor Darius and receive a reply. 6 This is the report that they sent to the emperor:

---

[i] WEST-OF-EUPHRATES PROVINCE: *Under Persian rule the land of Judah was part of this large Persian province west of the Euphrates River.*   [j] *Some ancient translations* They; *Aramaic* We.

4.24 Hg 1.1; Zec 1.1   **5.1** Hg 1.1; Zec 1.1   **5.2** Hg 1.12; Zec 4.6-9

7"To Emperor Darius, may you rule in peace.

8"Your Majesty should know that we went to the province of Judah and found that the Temple of the great God is being rebuilt with large stone blocks and with wooden beams set in the wall. The work is being done with great care and is moving ahead steadily.

9"We then asked the leaders of the people to tell us who had given them authority to rebuild the Temple and to equip it. 10We also asked them their names so that we could inform you who the leaders of this work are.

11"They answered, 'We are servants of the God of heaven and earth, and we are rebuilding the Temple which was originally built and equipped many years ago by a powerful king of Israel. 12But because our ancestors made the God of Heaven angry, he let them be conquered by King Nebuchadnezzar of Babylonia, a king of the Chaldean dynasty. The Temple was destroyed, and the people were taken into exile in Babylonia. 13Then in the first year of the reign of King Cyrus as emperor of Babylonia, Cyrus issued orders for the Temple to be rebuilt. 14He restored the gold and silver Temple utensils which Nebuchadnezzar had taken from the Temple in Jerusalem and had placed in the temple in Babylon. Emperor Cyrus turned these utensils over to a man named Sheshbazzar, whom he appointed governor of Judah. 15The emperor told him to take them and return them to the Temple in Jerusalem, and to rebuild the Temple where it had stood before. 16So Sheshbazzar came and laid its foundation; construction has continued from then until the present, but it is still not finished.'

17"Now, if it please Your Majesty, have a search made in the royal records in Babylon to find whether or not Emperor Cyrus gave orders for this Temple in Jerusalem to be rebuilt, and then inform us what your will is in this matter."

Emperor Cyrus' Order Is Rediscovered

6 So Emperor Darius issued orders for a search to be made in the royal records that were kept in Babylon. 2But it was in the city of Ecbatana in the province of Media that a scroll was found, containing the following record:

3"In the first year of his reign Emperor Cyrus commanded that the Temple in Jerusalem be rebuilt as a place where sacrifices are made and offerings are burned. The Temple is to be ninety feet high and ninety feet wide. 4The walls are to be built with one layer of wood on top of each three layers of stone. All expenses are to be paid by the royal treasury. 5Also the gold and silver utensils which King Nebuchadnezzar brought to Babylon from the Temple in Jerusalem are to be returned to their proper place in the Jerusalem Temple."

Emperor Darius Orders the Work to Continue

6Then Emperor Darius sent the following reply:

"To Tattenai, governor of West-of-Euphrates, Shethar Bozenai, and your fellow officials in West-of-Euphrates.

"Stay away from the Temple 7and do not interfere with its construction. Let the governor of Judah and the Jewish leaders rebuild the Temple of God where it stood before. 8I hereby command you to help them rebuild it. Their expenses are to be paid promptly out of the royal funds received from taxes in West-of-Euphrates, so that the work is not interrupted. [9] Day by day, without fail, you are to give the priests in Jerusalem whatever they tell you they need: young bulls, sheep, or lambs to be burned as offerings to the God of Heaven, or wheat, salt, wine, or olive oil. [10] This is to be done so that they can offer sacrifices that are acceptable to the God of Heaven and pray for his blessing on me and my sons. [11] I further command that if any disobey this order, a wooden beam is to be torn out of their houses, sharpened on one end, and then driven through their bodies. And their houses are to be made a rubbish heap. [12] May the God who chose Jerusalem as the place where he is to be worshiped overthrow any king or nation that defies this command and tries to destroy the Temple there. I, Darius, have commanded. My command is to be fully obeyed."

The Temple Is Dedicated

[13] Then Governor Tattenai, Shethar Bozenai, and their fellow officials did exactly as the emperor had commanded. [14] The Jewish leaders made good progress with the building of the Temple, encouraged by the prophets Haggai and Zechariah. They completed the Temple as they had been commanded by the God of Israel and by Cyrus, Darius, and Artaxerxes, emperors of Persia. [15] They finished the Temple on the third day of the month Adar in the sixth year of the reign of Emperor Darius. [16] Then the people of Israel — the priests, the Levites, and all the others who had returned from exile — joyfully dedicated the Temple.

[17] For the dedication they offered 100 bulls, 200 sheep, and 400 lambs as sacrifices, and 12 goats as offerings for sin, one for each tribe of Israel. [18] They also organized the priests and the Levites for the Temple services in Jerusalem, according to the instructions contained in the book of Moses.

The Passover

[19] The people who had returned from exile celebrated Passover on the fourteenth day of the first month of the following year. [20] All the priests and the Levites had purified themselves and were ritually clean. The Levites killed the animals for the Passover sacrifices for all the people who had returned, for the priests, and for themselves. [21] The sacrifices were eaten by all the Israelites who had returned from exile and by all those who had given up the pagan ways of the other people who were living in the land and who had come to worship the LORD God of Israel. [22] For seven days they joyfully celebrated the Festival of Unleavened Bread. They were full of joy because the LORD had made the emperor of Assyria[k] favorable to them, so that he supported them in their work of rebuilding the Temple of the God of Israel.

Ezra Arrives in Jerusalem

7 Many years later, when Artaxerxes was emperor of Persia, there was a man named Ezra. He traced his ancestors back to Aaron, the High Priest, as follows: Ezra was the son of Seraiah, son of Azariah, son of Hilkiah, [2] son of Shallum, son of Zadok, son of Ahitub, [3] son of Amariah, son of Azariah, son of Meraioth, [4] son of Zerahiah, son of Uzzi, son of Bukki, [5] son of Abishua, son of Phinehas, son of Eleazar, son of Aaron.

---

[k] EMPEROR OF ASSYRIA: *Apparently a reference to the Persian emperor who then also ruled the territory once occupied by Assyria, Israel's ancient enemy.*
6.14 a Hg 1.1; **b** Zec 1.1 **6.19** Ex 12.1-20

6-7 Ezra was a scholar with a thorough knowledge of the Law which the LORD, the God of Israel, had given to Moses. Because Ezra had the blessing of the LORD his God, the emperor gave him everything he asked for. In the seventh year of the reign of Artaxerxes, Ezra set out from Babylonia for Jerusalem with a group of Israelites which included priests, Levites, Temple musicians, Temple guards, and workers. 8-9 They left Babylonia on the first day of the first month, and with God's help they arrived in Jerusalem on the first day of the fifth month. 10 Ezra had devoted his life to studying the Law of the LORD, to practicing it, and to teaching all its laws and regulations to the people of Israel.

The Document Which Emperor Artaxerxes Gave to Ezra

11 Emperor Artaxerxes gave the following document to Ezra, the priest and scholar, who had a thorough knowledge of the laws and commands which the LORD had given to Israel:

12 "From Emperor Artaxerxes[l] to the priest Ezra, scholar in the Law of the God of Heaven.[m]

13 "I command that throughout my empire all the Israelite people, priests, and Levites that so desire be permitted to go with you to Jerusalem. 14 I, together with my seven counselors, send you to investigate the conditions in Jerusalem and Judah in order to see how well the Law of your God, which has been entrusted to you, is being obeyed. 15 You are to take with you the gold and silver offerings which I and my counselors desire to give to the God of Israel, whose Temple is in Jerusalem. 16 You are also to take all the silver and gold which you collect throughout the province of Babylon and the offerings which the Israelite people and their priests give for the Temple of their God in Jerusalem.

17 "You are to spend this money carefully and buy bulls, rams, lambs, grain, and wine and offer them on the altar of the Temple in Jerusalem. 18 You may use the silver and gold that is left over for whatever you and your people desire, in accordance with the will of your God. 19 You are to present to God in Jerusalem all the utensils that have been given to you for use in the Temple services. 20 And anything else which you need for the Temple, you may get from the royal treasury.

21 "I command all the treasury officials in West-of-Euphrates Province to provide promptly for Ezra, the priest and scholar in the Law of the God of Heaven, everything he asks you for, 22 up to a limit of 7,500 pounds of silver, 500 bushels of wheat, 550 gallons of wine, 550 gallons of olive oil, and as much salt as needed. 23 You must be careful to provide everything which the God of Heaven requires for his Temple, and so make sure that he is never angry with me or with those who reign after me. 24 You are forbidden to collect any taxes from the priests, Levites, musicians, guards, workers, or anyone else connected with this Temple.

25 "You, Ezra, using the wisdom which your God has given you, are to appoint administrators and judges to govern all the people in West-of-Euphrates who live by the Law of your God. You must teach that Law to anyone who does not know it. 26 If any disobey the laws of your God or the laws of the empire, they are to be punished promptly:

---

l Verses 12-26 are in Aramaic (see also 4.7).
meaning of which is unclear.

m Aramaic has an additional word, the

by death or by exile or by confiscation of their property or by imprisonment."

Ezra Praises God

27 Ezra said, "Praise the LORD, the God of our ancestors! He has made the emperor willing to honor in this way the Temple of the LORD in Jerusalem. 28 By God's grace I have won the favor of the emperor, of his counselors, and of all his powerful officials; the LORD my God has given me courage, and I have been able to persuade many of the heads of the clans of Israel to return with me."

I have been able to persuade many ... to return with me. (7.28)

The People Who Returned from Exile

8 This is the list of the heads of the clans who had been in exile in Babylonia and who returned with Ezra to Jerusalem when Artaxerxes was emperor:

2-14 Gershom, of the clan of Phinehas

Daniel, of the clan of Ithamar

Hattush son of Shecaniah, of the clan of David

Zechariah, of the clan of Parosh, with 150 men of his clan (there were records of their family lines)

Eliehoenai son of Zerahiah, of the clan of Pahath Moab, with 200 men

Shecaniah son of Jahaziel, of the clan of Zattu,ⁿ with 300 men

Ebed son of Jonathan, of the clan of Adin, with 50 men

Jeshaiah son of Athaliah, of the clan of Elam, with 70 men

Zebadiah son of Michael, of the clan of Shephatiah, with 80 men

Obadiah son of Jehiel, of the clan of Joab, with 218 men

Shelomith son of Josiphiah, of the clan of Bani,ᵒ with 160 men

Zechariah son of Bebai, of the clan of Bebai, with 28 men

Johanan son of Hakkatan, of the clan of Azgad, with 110 men

Eliphelet, Jeuel, and Shemaiah, of the clan of Adonikam, with 60 men (they returned at a later date)

Uthai and Zaccur, of the clan of Bigvai, with 70 men

Ezra Finds Levites for the Temple

15 I assembled the entire group by the canal that runs to the town of Ahava, and we camped there three days. I found that there were priests in the group, but no Levites. 16 I sent for nine of the leaders: Eliezer, Ariel, Shemaiah, Elnathan, Jarib, Elnathan, Nathan, Zechariah, and Meshullam, and for two teachers, Joiarib and Elnathan. 17 I sent them to Iddo, head of the community at Casiphia, to ask him and his associates, the Temple workers, to send us people to serve God in the Temple. 18 Through God's grace they sent us Sherebiah, an able man, a Levite from the clan of Mahli; and eighteen of his sons and brothers came with him. 19 They also sent Hashabiah and Jeshaiah of the clan of Merari, with twenty of their relatives. 20 In addition there were 220 Temple workers whose ancestors had

---

ⁿ *One ancient translation (see also 2.8)* Zattu; *Hebrew does not have this name.*

ᵒ *One ancient translation (see also 2.10)* Bani; *Hebrew does not have this name.*

been designated by King David and his officials to assist the Levites. They were all listed by name.

Ezra Leads the People in Fasting and Prayer

21 There by the Ahava Canal I gave orders for us all to fast and humble ourselves before our God and to ask him to lead us on our journey and protect us and our children and all our possessions. 22 I would have been ashamed to ask the emperor for a troop of cavalry to guard us from any enemies during our journey, because I had told him that our God blesses everyone who trusts him, but that he is displeased with and punishes anyone who turns away from him. 23 So we fasted and prayed for God to protect us, and he answered our prayers.

The Gifts for the Temple

24 From among the leading priests I chose Sherebiah, Hashabiah, and ten others. 25 Then I weighed out the silver, the gold, and the utensils which the emperor, his advisers and officials, and the people of Israel had given to be used in the Temple, and I gave it to the priests. 26-27 This is what I gave them:

    silver - 25 tons

    100 silver utensils - 150 pounds

    gold - 7,500 pounds

    20 gold bowls - 270 ounces

    2 fine bronze bowls, equal in
      value to gold bowls

28 I said to them, "You are sacred to the LORD, the God of your ancestors, and so are all the silver and gold utensils brought to him as freewill offerings. 29 Guard them carefully until you reach the Temple. There in the priests' rooms weigh them and turn them over to the leaders of the priests and of the Levites, and to the leaders of the people of Israel in Jerusalem." 30 So the priests and the Levites took charge of the silver, the gold, and the utensils, to take them to the Temple in Jerusalem.

The Return to Jerusalem

31 It was on the twelfth day of the first month that we left the Ahava Canal to go to Jerusalem. Our God was with us and protected us from enemy attacks and from ambush as we traveled. 32 When we reached Jerusalem, we rested three days. 33 Then on the fourth day we went to the Temple, weighed the silver, the gold, and the utensils, and turned them over to Meremoth the priest, son of Uriah. With him were Eleazar son of Phinehas and two Levites, Jozabad son of Jeshua and Noadiah son of Binnui. 34 Everything was counted and weighed, and a complete record was made at the same time.

35 All those who had returned from exile then brought offerings to be burned as sacrifices to the God of Israel. They offered 12 bulls for all Israel, 96 rams, and 77 lambs; they also offered 12 goats to purify themselves from sin. All these animals were burned as sacrifices to the LORD. 36 They also took the document the emperor had given them and gave it to the governors and officials of West-of-Euphrates Province, who then gave their support to the people and the Temple worship.

Ezra Learns of Intermarriages with Non-Jews

9 After all this had been done, some of the leaders of the people of Israel came and told me that the people, the priests, and the Levites had not kept themselves separate from the people in the neighboring countries of Ammon, Moab, and Egypt or from the Canaanites, Hittites, Perizzites, Jebusites, and Amorites. They were doing the same disgusting things which these people did. 2 Jewish men were marrying foreign women, and so God's holy people had become contaminated. The leaders and officials were the chief offenders. 3 When I heard this, I tore my clothes in despair, tore my hair and my beard, and sat down crushed with grief.

⁴I sat there grieving until the time for the evening sacrifice to be offered, and people began to gather around me — all those who were frightened because of what the God of Israel had said about the sins of those who had returned from exile.

⁵When the time came for the evening sacrifice, I got up from where I had been grieving, and still wearing my torn clothes, I knelt in prayer and stretched out my hands to the LORD my God. ⁶I said, "O God, I am too ashamed to raise my head in your presence. Our sins pile up higher than our heads; they reach as high as the heavens. ⁷From the days of our ancestors until now, we, your people, have sinned greatly. Because of our sins we, our kings, and our priests have fallen into the hands of foreign kings, and we have been slaughtered, robbed, and carried away as prisoners. We have been totally disgraced, as we still are today. ⁸Now for a short time, O LORD our God, you have been gracious to us and have let some of us escape from slavery and live in safety in this holy place. You have let us escape from slavery and have given us new life. ⁹We were slaves, but you did not leave us in slavery. You made the emperors of Persia favor us and permit us to go on living and to rebuild your Temple, which was in ruins, and to find safety here in Judah and Jerusalem.

¹⁰"But now, O God, what can we say after all that has happened? We have again disobeyed the commands ¹¹that you gave us through your servants, the prophets. They told us that the land we were going to occupy was an impure land because the people who lived in it filled it from one end to the other with disgusting, filthy actions. ¹²They told us that we were never to intermarry with those people and never to help them prosper or succeed if we wanted to enjoy the land and pass it on to our descendants forever. ¹³Even after everything that has happened to us in punishment for our sins and wrongs, we know that you, our God, have punished us less than we deserve and have allowed us to survive. ¹⁴Then how can we ignore your commandments again and intermarry with these wicked people? If we do, you will be so angry that you will destroy us completely and let no one survive. ¹⁵LORD God of Israel, you are just, but you have let us survive. We confess our guilt to you; we have no right to come into your presence."

The Plan for Ending Mixed Marriages

10 While Ezra was bowing in prayer in front of the Temple, weeping and confessing these sins, a large group of Israelites — men, women, and children — gathered around him, weeping bitterly. ²Then Shecaniah son of Jehiel, of the clan of Elam, said to Ezra, "We have broken faith with God by marrying foreign women, but even so there is still hope for Israel. ³Now we must make a solemn promise to our God that we will send these women and their children away. We will do what you and the others who honor God's commands advise us to do. We will do what God's Law demands. ⁴It is your responsibility to act. We are behind you, so go ahead and get it done."

⁵So Ezra began by making the leaders of the priests, of the Levites, and of the rest of the people take an oath that they would do what Shecaniah had proposed. ⁶Then he went from in front of the Temple into the living quarters of Jehohanan son of Eliashib, and spent the night*ᵖ* there grieving over the unfaithfulness of the exiles. He did not eat or drink anything.

ᵖ One ancient translation spent the night; *Hebrew* went.
9.12 Ex 34.11-16; Dt 7.1-5

"The crowd is too big, and it's raining hard." (10.13)

⁷ A message was sent throughout Jerusalem and Judah that all those who had returned from exile were to meet in Jerusalem ⁸ by order of the leaders of the people. If any failed to come within three days, all their property would be confiscated, and they would lose their right to be members of the community. ⁹ Within the three days, on the twentieth day of the ninth month, all the men living in the territory of Judah and Benjamin came to Jerusalem and assembled in the Temple square. It was raining hard, and because of the weather and the importance of the meeting everyone was trembling.

¹⁰ Ezra the priest stood up and spoke to them. He said, "You have been faithless and have brought guilt on Israel by marrying foreign women. ¹¹ Now then, confess your sins to the LORD, the God of your ancestors, and do what pleases him. Separate yourselves from the foreigners living in our land and get rid of your foreign wives."

¹² The people shouted in answer, "We will do whatever you say." ¹³ But they added, "The crowd is too big, and it's raining hard. We can't stand here in the open like this. This isn't something that can be done in one or two days, because so many of us are involved in this sin. ¹⁴ Let our officials stay in Jerusalem and take charge of the matter. Then let anyone who has a foreign wife come at a set time, together with the leaders and the judges of his city. In this way God's anger over this situation will be turned away." ¹⁵ No one was opposed to the plan except Jonathan son of Asahel and Jahzeiah son of Tikvah, who had the support of Meshullam and of Shabbethai, a Levite.

¹⁶ The returned exiles accepted the plan, so Ezra the priest appointed^q men from among the heads of the clans and recorded their names. On the first day of the tenth month they began their investigation, ¹⁷ and within the next three months they investigated all the cases of men with foreign wives.

^q *Some ancient translations* appointed; *Hebrew unclear.*

The Men Who Had Foreign Wives

18 This is the list of the men who had foreign wives:

Priests, listed by clans:

Clan of Joshua and his brothers, sons of Jehozadak: Maaseiah, Eliezer, Jarib, and Gedaliah. **19** They promised to divorce their wives, and they offered a ram as a sacrifice for their sins.

20 Clan of Immer: Hanani and Zebadiah

21 Clan of Harim: Maaseiah, Elijah, Shemaiah, Jehiel, and Uzziah

22 Clan of Pashhur: Elioenai, Maaseiah, Ishmael, Nethanel, Jozabad, and Elasah

23 *Levites:*

Jozabad, Shimei, Kelaiah (also called Kelita), Pethahiah, Judah, and Eliezer

24 *Musicians:*

Eliashib

Temple guards:

Shallum, Telem, and Uri

25 *Others:*

Clan of Parosh: Ramiah, Izziah, Malchijah, Mijamin, Eleazar, Malchijah, and Benaiah

---

r Verse 44 in Hebrew is unclear.

26 Clan of Elam: Mattaniah, Zechariah, Jehiel, Abdi, Jeremoth, and Elijah

27 Clan of Zattu: Elioenai, Eliashib, Mattaniah, Jeremoth, Zabad, and Aziza

28 Clan of Bebai: Jehohanan, Hananiah, Zabbai, and Athlai

29 Clan of Bani: Meshullam, Malluch, Adaiah, Jashub, Sheal, and Jeremoth

30 Clan of Pahath Moab: Adna, Chelal, Benaiah, Maaseiah, Mattaniah, Bezalel, Binnui, and Manasseh

31-32 Clan of Harim: Eliezer, Isshijah, Malchijah, Shemaiah, Shimeon, Benjamin, Malluch, and Shemariah

33 Clan of Hashum: Mattenai, Mattattah, Zabad, Eliphelet, Jeremai, Manasseh, and Shimei

34-37 Clan of Bani: Maadai, Amram, Uel, Benaiah, Bedeiah, Cheluhi, Vaniah, Meremoth, Eliashib, Mattaniah, Mattenai, and Jaasu

38-42 Clan of Binnui: Shimei, Shelemiah, Nathan, Adaiah, Machnadebai, Shashai, Sharai, Azarel, Shelemiah, Shemariah, Shallum, Amariah, and Joseph

43 Clan of Nebo: Jeiel, Mattithiah, Zabad, Zebina, Jaddai, Joel, and Benaiah

44 All these men had foreign wives. They divorced them and sent them and their children away. *r*

The Book of
NEHEMIAH

INTRODUCTION

The Book of Nehemiah may be divided into four parts: 1) The return of Nehemiah to Jerusalem, where he has been sent by the Persian emperor to govern Judah. 2) The rebuilding of the walls of Jerusalem. 3) The solemn reading of the Law of God by Ezra and the people's confession of sin. 4) Further activities of Nehemiah as governor of Judah.

A notable feature of the book is the record of Nehemiah's deep dependence on God and his frequent prayers to him.

OUTLINE OF CONTENTS

---

1 This is the account of what Nehemiah son of Hacaliah accomplished.

Nehemiah's Concern for Jerusalem

In the month of Kislev in the twentieth year that Artaxerxes was emperor of Persia, I, Nehemiah, was in Susa, the capital city. ²Hanani, one of my brothers, arrived from Judah with another group, and I asked them about Jerusalem and about the other Jews who had returned from exile in*ᵃ* Babylonia. ³They told me that those who had survived and were back in the homeland*ᵇ* were in great difficulty and that the foreigners who lived nearby looked down on them. They also told me that the walls of Jerusalem were still broken down and that the gates had not been

restored since the time they were burned. ⁴When I heard all this, I sat down and wept.

For several days I mourned and did not eat. I prayed to God, ⁵"LORD God of Heaven! You are great, and we stand in fear of you. You faithfully keep your covenant with those who love you and do what you command. ⁶Look at me, LORD, and hear my prayer, as I pray day and night for your servants, the people of Israel. I confess that we, the people of Israel, have sinned. My ancestors and I have sinned. ⁷We have acted wickedly against you and have not done what you commanded. We have not kept the laws which you gave us through Moses, your servant. ⁸Remember now what you told Moses: 'If you people of Israel are unfaithful to me, I

ᵃ had returned from exile in; *or* had not been exiled to.   *ᵇ* had survived and . . . homeland; *or* had remained in the homeland and had not gone into exile.
1.8 Lv 26.33

will scatter you among the other nations. 9 But then if you turn back to me and do what I have commanded you, I will bring you back to the place where I have chosen to be worshiped, even though you are scattered to the ends of the earth.'

10 "Lord, these are your servants, your own people. You rescued them by your great power and strength. 11 Listen now to my prayer and to the prayers of all your other servants who want to honor you. Give me success today and make the emperor merciful to me."

In those days I was the emperor's wine steward.

Nehemiah Goes to Jerusalem

2 One day four months later, when Emperor Artaxerxes was dining, I took the wine to him. He had never seen me look sad before, 2 so he asked, "Why are you looking so sad? You aren't sick, so it must be that you're unhappy."

"Why are you looking so sad?" (2.2)

I was startled 3 and answered, "May Your Majesty live forever! How can I keep from looking sad when the city where my ancestors are buried is in ruins and its gates have been destroyed by fire?"

4 The emperor asked, "What is it that you want?"

I prayed to the God of Heaven, 5 and then I said to the emperor, "If Your Majesty is pleased with me and is willing to grant my request, let me go to the land of Judah, to the city where my ancestors are buried, so that I can rebuild the city."

6 The emperor, with the empress sitting at his side, approved my request. He asked me how long I would be gone and when I would return, and I told him.

7 Then I asked him to grant me the favor of giving me letters to the governors of West-of-Euphrates Province,c instructing them to let me travel to Judah. 8 I asked also for a letter to Asaph, keeper of the royal forests, instructing him to supply me with timber for the gates of the fort that guards the Temple, for the city walls, and for the house I was to live in. The emperor gave me all I asked for, because God was with me.

9 The emperor sent some army officers and a troop of cavalry with me, and I made the journey to West-of-Euphrates. There I gave the emperor's letters to the governors. 10 But Sanballat, from the town of Beth Horon, and Tobiah, an official in the province of Ammon, heard that someone had come to work for the good of the people of Israel, and they were highly indignant.

11 I went on to Jerusalem, and for three days 12 I did not tell anyone what God had inspired me to do for Jerusalem. Then in the middle of the night I got up and went out, taking a few of my companions with me. The only animal we took was the donkey that I rode on. 13 It was still night as I left the city through the Valley Gate on the west and went south past Dragon's Fountain to the Rubbish Gate. As I went, I inspected the broken walls of the city and

---

c WEST-OF-EUPHRATES PROVINCE: *Under Persian rule the land of Israel was part of this large Persian province west of the Euphrates River.*

1.9 Dt 30.1-5   **2.3** 2 K 25.8-10; 2 Ch 36.19; Jr 52.12-14

This is how the city wall was rebuilt. (3.1)

the gates that had been destroyed by fire. ¹⁴Then on the east side of the city I went north to the Fountain Gate and the King's Pool. The donkey I was riding could not find any path through the rubble, ¹⁵so I went down into Kidron Valley and rode along, looking at the wall. Then I returned the way I had come and went back into the city through the Valley Gate.

¹⁶None of the local officials knew where I had gone or what I had been doing. So far I had not said anything to any of the other Jews — the priests, the leaders, the officials, or anyone else who would be taking part in the work. ¹⁷But now I said to them, "See what trouble we are in because Jerusalem is in ruins and its gates are destroyed! Let's rebuild the city walls and put an end to our disgrace." ¹⁸And I told them how God had been with me and helped me, and what the emperor had said to me.

They responded, "Let's start rebuilding!" And they got ready to start the work.

¹⁹When Sanballat, Tobiah, and an Arab named Geshem heard what we were planning to do, they laughed at us and said, "What do you think you're doing? Are you going to rebel against the emperor?"

²⁰I answered, "The God of Heaven will give us success. We are his servants, and we are going to start building. But you have no right to any property in Jerusalem, and you have no share in its traditions."

Rebuilding the Wall of Jerusalem

3 This is how the city wall was rebuilt.*ᵈ* The High Priest Eliashib and his fellow priests rebuilt the Sheep Gate, dedicated it, and put the gates in place. They dedicated the wall as far as the Tower of the Hundred and the Tower of Hananel.

²The men of Jericho built the next section.

Zaccur son of Imri built the next section.

³The clan of Hassenaah built the Fish Gate. They put the beams and the gates in place, and put in the bolts and bars for locking the gate.

⁴Meremoth, the son of Uriah and grandson of Hakkoz, built the next section.

Meshullam, the son of Berechiah and grandson of Meshezabel, built the next section.

ᵈ CITY WALL WAS REBUILT: *According to the following report, the rebuilding of the wall started at the middle of the north side and proceeded counterclockwise around the city. Many of the places mentioned cannot be identified.*

Zadok son of Baana built the next section.

5 The men of Tekoa built the next section, but the leading men of the own refused to do the manual labor assigned them by the supervisors.

6 Joiada son of Paseah and Meshullam son of Besodeiah rebuilt Jeshanah Gate.ᵉ They put the beams and the gates in place, and put in the bolts and bars for locking the gate.

7 Melatiah from Gibeon, Jadon from Meronoth, and the men of Gibeon and Mizpah built the next section, as far as he residence of the governor of West-of-Euphrates.

8 Uzziel son of Harhaiah, a goldsmith, built the next section.

Hananiah, a maker of perfumes, built the next section, as far as Broad Wall.

9 Rephaiah son of Hur, ruler of half of the Jerusalem District, built the next section.

10 Jedaiah son of Harumaph built the next section, which was near his own house.

Hattush son of Hashabneiah built the next section.

11 Malchijah son of Harim and Hasshub son of Pahath Moab built both the next section and the Tower of the Ovens.

12 Shallum son of Hallohesh, ruler of the other half of the Jerusalem District, built the next section. (His daughters helped with the work.)

13 Hanun and the inhabitants of the city of Zanoah rebuilt the Valley Gate. They put the gates in place, put in the bolts and the bars for locking the gate, and repaired the wall for fifteen hundred feet, as far as the Rubbish Gate.

14 Malchijah son of Rechab, ruler of the Beth Haccherem District, rebuilt the Rubbish Gate. He put the gates in place, and put in the bolts and the bars for locking the gate.

15 Shallum son of Colhozeh, ruler of the Mizpah District, rebuilt the Fountain Gate. He covered the gateway, put the gates in place, and put in the bolts and the bars. At the Pool of Shelah he built the wall next to the royal garden, as far as the stairs leading down from David's City.

16 Nehemiah son of Azbuk, ruler of half of the Bethzur District, built the next section, as far as David's tomb, the pool, and the barracks.

Levites Who Worked on the Wall

17 The following Levites rebuilt the next several sections of the wall:

Rehum son of Bani built the next section;

Hashabiah, ruler of half of the Keilah District, built the next section on behalf of his district;

18 Bavvai son of Henadad, ruler of the other half of the Keilah District, built the next section;

19 Ezer son of Jeshua, ruler of Mizpah, built the next section in front of the armory, as far as the place where the wall turns;

20 Baruch son of Zabbai built the next section, as far as the entrance to the house of the High Priest Eliashib;

21 Meremoth, the son of Uriah and grandson of Hakkoz, built the next section, up to the far end of Eliashib's house.

Priests Who Worked on the Wall

22 The following priests rebuilt the next several sections of the wall:

Priests from the area around Jerusalem built the next section;

23 Benjamin and Hasshub built the next section, which was in front of their houses;

Azariah, the son of Maaseiah and grandson of Ananiah, built the next section, which was in front of his house;

24 Binnui son of Henadad built the

ᵉ Jeshanah Gate; *or* the Old Gate.

next section, from Azariah's house to the corner of the wall;

25-26 Palal son of Uzai built the next section, beginning at the corner of the wall and the tower of the upper palace near the court of the guard;

Pedaiah son of Parosh built the next section, to a point on the east near the Water Gate and the tower guarding the Temple. (This was near that part of the city called Ophel, where the Temple workers lived.)

Other Builders

27 The men of Tekoa built the next section, their second one, from a point opposite the large tower guarding the Temple as far as the wall near Ophel.

28 A group of priests built the next section, going north from the Horse Gate, each one building in front of his own house.

29 Zadok son of Immer built the next section, which was in front of his house.

Shemaiah son of Shecaniah, keeper of the East Gate, built the next section.

30 Hananiah son of Shelemiah and Hanun, the sixth son of Zalaph, built the next section, their second one.

Meshullam son of Berechiah built the next section, which was in front of his house.

31 Malchijah, a goldsmith, built the next section, as far as the building used by the Temple workers and the merchants, which was by the Miphkad/ Gate to the Temple, near the room on top of the northeast corner of the wall.

32 The goldsmiths and the merchants built the last section, from the room at the corner as far as the Sheep Gate.

Nehemiah Overcomes Opposition to His Work

4 When Sanballat heard that we Jews had begun rebuilding the wall, he became furious and began to ridicule us. 2 In front of his companions and the Samaritan troops he said, "What do these miserable Jews think they're doing? Do they intend to rebuild the city? Do they think that by offering sacrifices they can finish the work in one day? Can they make building stones out of heaps of burnt rubble?"

3 Tobiah was standing there beside him, and he added, "What kind of wall could they ever build? Even a fox could knock it down!"

4 I prayed, "Hear how they make fun of us, O God! Let their ridicule fall on their own heads. Let them be robbed of everything they have, and let them be taken as prisoners to a foreign land. 5 Don't forgive the evil they do and don't forget their sins, for they have insulted us who are building."

6 So we went on rebuilding the wall and soon it was half its full height because the people were eager to work.

7 Sanballat, Tobiah, and the people of Arabia, Ammon, and Ashdod heard that we were making progress in rebuilding the wall of Jerusalem and that the gaps in the wall were being closed, and they became very angry. 8 So they all plotted together to come and attack Jerusalem and create confusion, 9 but we prayed to our God and kept men on guard against them day and night.

10 The people of Judah had a song they sang:

"We grow weak carrying
      burdens;
There's so much rubble to take
      away.
How can we build the wall
      today?"

11 Our enemies thought we would not see them or know what was happening until they were already upon us, killing us and putting an end to our work. 12 But time after time Jews who were living among our enemies came to

/ Miphkad; or Mustering, or Watch.

They worked with one hand and kept a weapon in the other. (4.17)

warn us of the plans our enemies were making against us.*g* 13 So I armed the people with swords, spears, and bows, and stationed them by clans behind the wall, wherever it was still unfinished.

14 I saw that the people were worried, so I said to them and to their leaders and officials, "Don't be afraid of our enemies. Remember how great and terrifying the Lord is, and fight for your relatives, your children, your wives, and your homes." 15 Our enemies heard that we had found out what they were plotting, and they realized that God had defeated their plans. Then all of us went back to rebuilding the wall.

16 From then on half of my men worked and half stood guard, wearing coats of armor and armed with spears, shields, and bows. And our leaders gave their full support to the people 17 who were rebuilding the wall. Even those who carried building materials worked with one hand and kept a weapon in the other, 18 and everyone who was building kept a sword strapped to their waist. The man who was to sound the alarm on the bugle stayed with me. 19 I told the people and their officials and leaders, "The work is spread out over such a distance that we are widely separated from one another on the wall. 20 If you hear the bugle, gather around me. Our God will fight for us." 21 So every day, from dawn until the stars came out at night, half of us worked on the wall, while the other half stood guard with spears.

22 During this time I told the men in charge that they and all their helpers had to stay in Jerusalem at night, so that we could guard the city at night as well as work in the daytime. 23 I didn't take off my clothes even at night, neither did any of my companions nor my servants nor my bodyguards. And we all kept our weapons at hand.*h*

g Probable text the plans our enemies were making against us; *Hebrew unclear.*
h Probable text weapons at hand; *Hebrew unclear.*

Oppression of the Poor

5 Some time later many of the people, both men and women, began to complain against the other Jews. [2] Some said, "We have large families, we need grain to keep us alive."

[3] Others said, "We have had to mortgage our fields and vineyards and houses to get enough grain to keep us from starving."

[4] Still others said, "We had to borrow money to pay the royal tax on our fields and vineyards. [5] We are of the same race as the other Jews. Aren't our children just as good as theirs? But we have to make slaves of our children. Some of our daughters have already been sold as slaves. We are helpless because our fields and vineyards have been taken away from us."

[6] When I heard their complaints, I grew angry [7] and decided to act. I denounced the leaders and officials of the people and told them, "You are oppressing your own relatives!"

I called a public assembly to deal with the problem [8] and said, "As far as we have been able, we have been buying back our Jewish relatives who had to sell themselves to foreigners. Now you are forcing your own relatives to sell themselves to you, their own people!" The leaders were silent and could find nothing to say.

[9] Then I said, "What you are doing is wrong! You ought to obey God and do what's right. Then you would not give our enemies, the Gentiles, any reason to ridicule us. [10] I have let the people borrow money and grain from me, and so have my companions and those who work for me. Now let's give up all our claims to repayment. [11] Cancel all the debts[i] they owe you — money or grain

or wine or olive oil. And give them back their fields, vineyards, olive groves, and houses right now!"

[12] The leaders replied, "We'll do as you say. We'll give the property back and not try to collect the debts."

I called in the priests and made the leaders swear in front of them to keep the promise they had just made. [13] Then I took off the sash[j] I was wearing around my waist and shook it out. "This is how God will shake any of you who don't keep your promise," I said. "God will take away your houses and everything you own, and will leave you with nothing."

Everyone who was present said "Amen!" and praised the LORD. And the leaders kept their promise.

Nehemiah's Unselfishness

[14] During all the twelve years that I was governor of the land of Judah, from the twentieth year that Artaxerxes was emperor until his thirty-second year, neither my relatives nor I ate the food I was entitled to have as governor. [15] Every governor who had been in office before me had been a burden to the people and had demanded forty silver coins a day[k] for food and wine. Even their servants had oppressed the people. But I acted differently, because I honored God. [16] I put all my energy into rebuilding the wall and did not acquire any property. Everyone who worked for me joined in the rebuilding. [17] I regularly fed at my table a hundred and fifty of the Jewish people and their leaders, besides all the people who came to me from the surrounding nations. [18] Every day I served one beef, six of the best sheep, and many chickens, and every ten days I provided a fresh supply of

---

[i] *One ancient translation* debts; *Hebrew unclear.*   [j] SASH: *Clothing in those days had no pockets, so small items were tucked into the sash that was worn like a belt around the waist. Shaking it out was a symbol of losing everything.*   [k] *One ancient translation* a day; *Hebrew unclear.*

5.7 Ex 22.25; Lv 25. 35-37; Dt 23.19, 20

wine. But I knew what heavy burdens the people had to bear, and so I did not claim the allowance that the governor is entitled to.

¹⁹ I pray you, O God, remember to my credit everything that I have done for this people.

Plots against Nehemiah

6 Sanballat, Tobiah, Geshem, and the rest of our enemies heard that we had finished building the wall and that there were no gaps left in it, although we still had not set up the gates in the gateways. ² So Sanballat and Geshem sent me a message, suggesting that I meet with them in one of the villages in the Plain of Ono. This was a trick of theirs to try to harm me. ³ I sent messengers to say to them, "I am doing important work and can't go down there. I am not going to let the work stop just to go and see you."

⁴ They sent me the same message four times, and each time I sent them the same reply.

⁵ Then Sanballat sent one of his servants to me with a fifth message, this one in the form of an unsealed letter.[l] ⁶ It read:

"Geshem tells me that a rumor is going around among the neighboring peoples that you and the Jewish people intend to revolt and that this is why you are rebuilding the wall. He also says you plan to make yourself king ⁷ and that you have arranged for some prophets to proclaim in Jerusalem that you are the king of Judah. His Majesty is certain to hear about this, so I suggest that you and I meet to talk the situation over."

⁸ I sent a reply to him: "Nothing of what you are saying is true. You have made it all up yourself."

⁹ They were trying to frighten us into stopping work. I prayed, "But now, God, make me strong!"

¹⁰ About this time I went to visit Shemaiah, the son of Delaiah and grandson of Mehetabel, who was unable to leave his house. He said to me, "You and I must go and hide together in the Holy Place of the Temple and lock the doors, because they are coming to kill you. Any night now they will come to kill you."

¹¹ I answered, "I'm not the kind of person that runs and hides. Do you think I would try to save my life by hiding in the Temple? I won't do it."

¹² When I thought it over, I realized that God had not spoken to Shemaiah, but that Tobiah and Sanballat had bribed him to give me this warning. ¹³ They hired him to frighten me into sinning, so that they could ruin my reputation and humiliate me.

¹⁴ I prayed, "God, remember what Tobiah and Sanballat have done and punish them. Remember that woman Noadiah and all the other prophets who tried to frighten me."

The Conclusion of the Work

¹⁵ After fifty-two days of work the entire wall was finished on the twenty-fifth day of the month of Elul. ¹⁶ When our enemies in the surrounding nations heard this, they realized that they had lost face, since everyone knew that the work had been done with God's help.

¹⁷ During all this time the Jewish leaders had been in correspondence with Tobiah. ¹⁸ Many people in Judah were on his side because of his Jewish father-in-law, Shecaniah son of Arah. In addition, his son Jehohanan had married the daughter of Meshullam son of Berechiah. ¹⁹ People would talk in front of me about all the good deeds Tobiah had done and would tell him

---

[l] UNSEALED LETTER: *Leaving a letter unsealed was a deliberate way of making certain that its contents would become widely known.*

everything I said. And he kept sending me letters to try to frighten me.

7 And now the wall had been rebuilt, the gates had all been put in place, and the Temple guards, the members of the sacred choir, and the other Levites had been assigned their work. ²I put two men in charge of governing the city of Jerusalem: my brother Hanani and Hananiah, commanding officer of the fortress. Hananiah was a reliable and God-fearing man without equal. ³I told them not to have the gates of Jerusalem opened in the morning until well after sunrise and to have them closed and barred before the guards went off duty at sunset. I also told them to appoint guards from among the people who lived in Jerusalem and to assign some of them to specific posts and others to patrol the area around their own houses.

The List of Those Who Returned from Exile
(Ezra 2.1-70)

⁴Jerusalem was a large city, but not many people were living in it, and not many houses had been built yet. ⁵God inspired me to assemble the people and their leaders and officials and to check their family records. I located the records of those who had first returned from captivity, and this is the information I found:

⁶Many of the exiles left the province of Babylon and returned to Jerusalem and Judah, each to his own hometown. Their families had been living in exile in Babylonia ever since King Nebuchadnezzar had taken them there as prisoners. ⁷Their leaders were Zerubbabel, Joshua, Nehemiah, Azariah, Raamiah, Nahamani, Mordecai, Bilshan, Mispereth, Bigvai, Nehum, and Baanah.

⁸⁻²⁵This is the list of the clans of Israel, with the number of those from each clan who returned from exile:

Parosh - 2,172
Shephatiah - 372
Arah - 652
Pahath Moab (descendants of Jeshua and Joab) - 2,818
Elam - 1,254
Zattu - 845
Zaccai - 760
Binnui - 648
Bebai - 628
Azgad - 2,322
Adonikam - 667
Bigvai - 2,067
Adin - 655
Ater (also called Hezekiah) - 98
Hashum - 328
Bezai - 324
Hariph - 112
Gibeon - 95

²⁶⁻³⁸People whose ancestors had lived in the following towns also returned:

Bethlehem and Netophah - 188
Anathoth - 128
Beth Azmaveth - 42
Kiriath Jearim, Chephirah, and Beeroth - 743
Ramah and Geba - 621
Michmash - 122
Bethel and Ai - 123
The other Nebo - 52
The other Elam - 1,254
Harim - 320
Jericho - 345
Lod, Hadid, and Ono - 721
Senaah - 3,930

³⁹⁻⁴²This is the list of the priestly clans that returned from exile:

Jedaiah (descendants of Jeshua) - 973
Immer - 1,052
Pashhur - 1,247
Harim - 1,017

⁴³⁻⁴⁵Clans of Levites who returned from exile:

Jeshua and Kadmiel (descendants of Hodaviah) - 74
Temple musicians (descendants of Asaph) - 148

Temple guards (descendants of
  Shallum, Ater, Talmon,
  Akkub, Hatita, and
  Shobai) - 138

46-56 Clans of Temple workers who returned from exile:
  Ziha, Hasupha, Tabbaoth,
  Keros, Sia, Padon,
  Lebana, Hagaba, Shalmai,
  Hanan, Giddel, Gahar,
  Reaiah, Rezin, Nekoda,
  Gazzam, Uzza, Paseah,
  Besai, Meunim, Nephushesim,
  Bakbuk, Hakupha, Harhur,
  Bazlith, Mehida, Harsha,
  Barkos, Sisera, Temah,
  Neziah, and Hatipha.

57-59 Clans of Solomon's servants who returned from exile:
  Sotai, Sophereth, Perida,
  Jaalah, Darkon, Giddel,
  Shephatiah, Hattil, Pochereth
    Hazzebaim, and Amon.

60 The total number of descendants of the Temple workers and of Solomon's servants who returned from exile was 392.

61-62 There were 642 belonging to the clans of Delaiah, Tobiah, and Nekoda who returned from the towns of Tel Melah, Tel Harsha, Cherub, Addon, and Immer; but they could not prove that they were descendants of Israelites.

63-64 The following priestly clans could find no record to prove their ancestry: Hobaiah, Hakkoz, and Barzillai. (The ancestor of the priestly clan of Barzillai had married a woman from the clan of Barzillai of Gilead and taken the name of his father-in-law's clan.) Since they were unable to prove who their ancestors were, they were not accepted as priests. 65 The Jewish governor told them that they could not eat the food offered to God until there was a priest who could use the Urim and Thummim.[m]

66-69 Total number of exiles who returned - 42,360.

  Their male and female
    servants - 7,337
  Male and female musicians - 245
  Horses - 736
  Mules - 245
  Camels - 435
  Donkeys - 6,720

70-72 Many of the people contributed to help pay the cost of restoring the Temple:

The governor	270	ounces of gold
	50	ceremonial bowls
	530	robes for priests
Heads of clans	337	pounds of gold
	3,215	pounds of silver
The rest of the people	337	pounds of gold
	2,923	pounds of silver
	67	robes for priests

73 The priests, the Levites, the Temple guards, the musicians, many of the ordinary people, the Temple workers — all the people of Israel — settled in the towns and cities of Judah.

Ezra Reads the Law to the People

8 By the seventh month the people of Israel were all settled in their towns. On the first day of that month they all assembled in Jerusalem, in the square just inside the Water Gate. They asked Ezra, the priest and scholar of the Law which the LORD had given Israel through Moses, to get the book of the Law. 2 So Ezra brought it to the place where the people had gathered — men, women, and the children who

---

m URIM AND THUMMIM: *Two objects used by the priest to determine God's will; it is not known precisely how they were used.*

7.65 Ex 28.30; Dt 33.8   **7.73** 1 Ch 9.2; Ne 11.3

were old enough to understand. [3] There in the square by the gate he read the Law to them from dawn until noon, and they all listened attentively.

[4] Ezra was standing on a wooden platform that had been built for the occasion. The following men stood at his right: Mattithiah, Shema, Anaiah, Uriah, Hilkiah, and Maaseiah; and the following stood at his left: Pedaiah, Mishael, Malchijah, Hashum, Hashbaddanah, Zechariah, and Meshullam. [5] As Ezra stood there on the platform high above the people, they all kept their eyes fixed on him. As soon as he opened the book, they all stood up. [6] Ezra said, "Praise the Lord, the great God!"

All the people raised their arms in the air and answered, "Amen! Amen!" They knelt in worship, with their faces to the ground.

[7] Then they rose and stood in their places, and the following Levites explained the Law to them: Jeshua, Bani, Sherebiah, Jamin, Akkub, Shabbethai, Hodiah, Maaseiah, Kelita, Azariah, Jozabad, Hanan, and Pelaiah. [8] They gave an oral translation[n] of God's Law and explained[o] it so that the people could understand it.

[9] When the people heard what the Law required, they were so moved that they began to cry. So Nehemiah, who was the governor, Ezra, the priest and scholar of the Law, and the Levites who were explaining the Law told all the people, "This day is holy to the Lord your God, so you are not to mourn or cry. [10] Now go home and have a feast. Share your food and wine with those who don't have enough. Today is holy to our Lord, so don't be sad. The joy that the Lord gives you will make you strong."

[11] The Levites went around calming the people and telling them not to be sad on such a holy day. [12] So all the people went home and ate and drank joyfully and shared what they had with others, because they understood what had been read to them.

The Festival of Shelters

[13] The next day the heads of the clans, together with the priests and the Levites, went to Ezra to study the teachings of the Law. [14] They discovered that the Law, which the Lord gave through Moses, ordered the people of Israel to live in temporary shelters during the Festival of Shelters. [15] So they gave the following instructions and sent them[p] all through Jerusalem and the other cities and towns: "Go out to the hills and get branches from pines, olives, myrtles, palms, and other trees to make shelters according to the instructions written in the Law."

[16] So the people got branches and built shelters on the flat roofs of their houses, in their yards, in the Temple courtyard, and in the public squares by the Water Gate and by the Ephraim Gate. [17] All the people who had come back from captivity built shelters and lived in them. This was the first time it had been done since the days of Joshua son of Nun, and everybody was excited and happy. [18] From the first day of the festival to the last they read a part of God's Law every day. They celebrated for seven days, and on the eighth day there was a closing ceremony, as required in the Law.

---

[n] TRANSLATION: *The Law was written in Hebrew, but in Babylonia the Jews had adopted Aramaic as the language for daily life. Because of this a translation was necessary.*   [o] *They gave ... explained;* or *They read God's Law and then translated it, explaining.*   [p] *Probable text* So they ... sent them; *Hebrew* It also ordered that the following instructions be sent.

8.14, 15 Lv 23.33-36, 39-43; Dt 16.13-15

The People Confess Their Sins

9 **1-2** On the twenty-fourth day of the same month the people of Israel gathered to fast in order to show sorrow for their sins. They had already separated themselves from all foreigners. They wore sackcloth and put dust on their heads as signs of grief. Then they stood and began to confess the sins that they and their ancestors had committed. **3** For about three hours the Law of the LORD their God was read to them, and for the next three hours they confessed their sins and worshiped the LORD their God.

4 There was a platform for the Levites, and on it stood Jeshua, Bani, Kadmiel, Shebaniah, Bunni, Sherebiah, Bani, and Chenani. They prayed aloud to the LORD their God.

5 The following Levites gave a call to worship: Jeshua, Kadmiel, Bani, Hashabneiah, Sherebiah, Hodiah, Shebaniah, and Pethahiah. They said:

"Stand up and praise the LORD
    your God;
  praise him forever and ever!
Let everyone praise his glorious
    name,
  although no human praise is
    great enough."

The Prayer of Confession

6 And then the people of Israel prayed this prayer:

"You, LORD, you alone are LORD;
  you made the heavens and
    the stars of the sky.
You made land and sea and
    everything in them;
  you gave life to all.
The heavenly powers bow down
    and worship you.
7 You, LORD God, chose Abram
  and led him out of Ur in
    Babylonia;

you changed his name to
    Abraham.
8 You found that he was faithful
    to you,
  and you made a covenant
    with him.
You promised to give him the
    land of the Canaanites,
  the land of the Hittites and
    the Amorites,
  the land of the Perizzites, the
    Jebusites, the Girgashites,
  to be a land where his
    descendants would live.
You kept your promise, because
    you are faithful.

9 "You saw how our ancestors
    suffered in Egypt;
  you heard their call for help at
    the Red Sea.
10 You worked amazing miracles
    against the king,
  against his officials and the
    people of his land,
  because you knew how they
    oppressed your people.
You won then the fame you still
    have today.
11 Through the sea you made a
    path for your people
  and led them through on dry
    ground.
Those who pursued them
    drowned in deep water,
  as a stone sinks in the
    raging sea.
12 With a cloud you led them in
    daytime,
  and at night you lighted their
    way with fire.
13 At Mount Sinai you came down
    from heaven;
  you spoke to your people
  and gave them good laws and
    sound teachings.

9.7 a Gn 11.31; 12.1; **b** Gn 17.5 **9.8** Gn 15.18-21 **9.9** a Ex 3.7; **b** Ex 14.10-12 **9.10** Ex 7.8—12.32 **9.11** a Ex 14.21-29; **b** Ex 15.4, 5 **9.12** Ex 13.21, 22 **9.13, 14** Ex 19.18—23.33

¹⁴You taught them to keep your
　　Sabbaths holy,
　　and through your servant
　　　Moses you gave them
　　　your laws.

¹⁵"When they were hungry, you
　　gave them bread from
　　heaven,
　　and water from a rock when
　　　they were thirsty.
You told them to take control of
　　the land
　　which you had promised to
　　　give them.
¹⁶But our ancestors grew proud
　　and stubborn
　　and refused to obey your
　　　commands.
¹⁷They refused to obey; they forgot
　　all you did;
　　they forgot the miracles you
　　　had performed.
In their pride they chose a leader
　　to take them back to slavery
　　　in Egypt.
But you are a God who forgives;
　　you are gracious and loving,
　　　slow to be angry.
Your mercy is great; you did not
　　forsake them.
¹⁸They made an idol in the shape
　　of a bull-calf
　　and said it was the god who
　　　led them from Egypt!
How much they insulted you,
　　LORD!
¹⁹But you did not abandon them
　　there in the desert,
　　for your mercy is great.
You did not take away the cloud
　　or the fire
　　that showed them the path by
　　　day and night.
²⁰In your goodness you told them
　　what they should do;

you fed them manna and gave
　　them water to drink.
²¹Through forty years in the desert
　　you provided all that they
　　needed;
　　their clothing never wore out,
　　and their feet were not
　　　swollen with pain.

²²"You let them conquer nations
　　and kingdoms,
　　lands that bordered their own.
They conquered the land of
　　Heshbon, where
　　Sihon ruled,
　　and the land of Bashan,
　　　where Og was king.
²³You gave them as many children
　　as there are stars in
　　the sky,
　　and let them conquer and live
　　　in the land
　　that you had promised their
　　　ancestors to give them.
²⁴They conquered the land of
　　Canaan;
　　you overcame the people
　　　living there.
You gave your people the power
　　to do as they pleased
　　with the people and kings of
　　　Canaan.
²⁵Your people captured fortified
　　cities,
　　fertile land, houses full of
　　　wealth,
　　cisterns already dug,
　　olive trees, fruit trees, and
　　　vineyards.
They ate all they wanted and
　　grew fat;
　　they enjoyed all the good
　　　things you gave them.

²⁶"But your people rebelled and
　　disobeyed you;

9.15 a Ex 16.4-15; b Ex 17.1-7; c Dt 1.21　9.16, 17 Nu 14.1-4; Dt 1.26-33　9.17 Ex 34.6;
Nu 14.18　9.18 Ex 32.1-4　9.19-21 Dt 8.2-4　9.22 Nu 21.21-35　9.23 a Gn 15.5; 22.17;
b Js 3.14-17　9.24 Js 11.23　9.25 Dt 6.10, 11　9.26-28 Jg 2.11-16　9.26 Ws 2.10-20

they turned their backs on
    your Law.
They killed the prophets who
    warned them,
    who told them to turn back
      to you.
They insulted you time after
    time,
27 so you let their enemies
    conquer and rule them.
In their trouble they called to
    you for help,
and you answered them from
    heaven.
In your great mercy you sent
    them leaders
who rescued them from their
    foes.
28 When peace returned, they
    sinned again,
and again you let their
    enemies conquer them.
Yet when they repented and
    asked you to save them,
in heaven you heard, and time
    after time
you rescued them in your
    great mercy.
29 You warned them to obey your
    teachings,
    but in pride they rejected your
      laws,
    although keeping your Law is
      the way to life.
Hard-headed and stubborn, they
    refused to obey.
30 Year after year you patiently
    warned them.
You inspired your prophets to
    speak,
    but your people were deaf,
so you let them be conquered
    by other nations.
31 And yet, because your mercy is
    great,
    you did not forsake or destroy
      them.
You are a gracious and
    merciful God!

32 "O God, our God, how great
    you are!
How terrifying, how powerful!
You faithfully keep your
    covenant promises.
From the time when Assyrian
    kings oppressed us,
    even till now, how much we
      have suffered!
Our kings, our leaders, our
    priests and prophets,
    our ancestors, and all our
      people have suffered.
Remember how much we have
    suffered!
33 You have done right to
    punish us;
    you have been faithful, even
      though we have sinned.
34 Our ancestors, our kings,
    leaders, and priests
    have not kept your Law.
They did not listen to your
    commands and warnings.
35 With your blessing, kings ruled
    your people
    when they lived in the broad,
      fertile land you gave them;
    but they failed to turn from
      sin and serve you.
36 And now we are slaves in the
    land that you gave us,
    this fertile land which gives
      us food.
37 What the land produces goes to
    the kings
    that you put over us because
      we sinned.
They do as they please with us
    and our livestock,
    and we are in deep distress!"

The People Sign an Agreement

38 Because of all that has happened,
we, the people of Israel, hereby make a
solemn written agreement, and our
leaders, our Levites, and our priests put
their seals to it.

9.29 Lv 18.5   **9.30** 2 K 17.13-18; 2 Ch 36.15, 16   **9.32** 2 K 15.19, 29; 17.3-6; Ezra 4.2, 10

10

The first to sign was the governor, Nehemiah son of Hacaliah, and then Zedekiah signed. The following also signed:

²⁻⁸ *Priests:*
Seraiah, Azariah, Jeremiah,
Pashhur, Amariah, Malchijah,
Hattush, Shebaniah, Malluch,
Harim, Meremoth, Obadiah,
Daniel, Ginnethon, Baruch,
Meshullam, Abijah, Mijamin,
Maaziah, Bilgai, and Shemaiah.

⁹⁻¹³ *Levites:*
Jeshua son of Azaniah,
Binnui of the clan of Henadad,
Kadmiel, Shebaniah, Hodiah,
Kelita, Pelaiah, Hanan,
Mica, Rehob, Hashabiah,
Zaccur, Sherebiah, Shebaniah,
Hodiah, Bani, and Beninu.

¹⁴⁻²⁷ *Leaders of the people:*
Parosh, Pahath Moab,
Elam, Zattu, Bani,
Bunni, Azgad, Bebai,
Adonijah, Bigvai, Adin,
Ater, Hezekiah, Azzur,
Hodiah, Hashum, Bezai,
Hariph, Anathoth, Nebai,
Magpiash, Meshullam, Hezir,
Meshezabel, Zadok, Jaddua,
Pelatiah, Hanan, Anaiah,
Hoshea, Hananiah, Hasshub,
Hallohesh, Pilha, Shobek,
Rehum, Hashabnah, Maaseiah,
Ahiah, Hanan, Anan,
Malluch, Harim, and Baanah.

The Agreement

²⁸ We, the people of Israel, the priests, the Levites, the Temple guards, the Temple musicians, the Temple workers, and all others who in obedience to God's Law have separated themselves from the foreigners living in our land, we, together with our wives and all our children old enough to understand, ²⁹ do hereby join with our leaders in an oath, under penalty of a curse if we break it, that we will live according to God's Law, which God gave through his servant Moses; that we will obey all that the LORD, our Lord, commands us; and that we will keep all his laws and requirements.

³⁰ We will not intermarry with the foreigners living in our land.

³¹ If foreigners bring grain or anything else to sell to us on the Sabbath or on any other holy day, we will not buy from them.

Every seventh year we will not farm the land, and we will cancel all debts.

³² Every year we will each contribute one-eighth of an ounce of silver to help pay the expenses of the Temple.

³³ We will provide for the Temple worship the following: the sacred bread, the daily grain offering, the animals to be burned each day as sacrifices, the sacred offerings for Sabbaths, New Moon Festivals, and other festivals, the other sacred offerings, the offerings to take away the sins of Israel, and anything else needed for the Temple.

³⁴ We, the people, priests, and Levites, will draw lots each year to determine which clans are to provide wood to burn the sacrifices offered to the LORD our God, according to the requirements of the Law.

³⁵ We will take to the Temple each year an offering of the first grain we harvest and of the first fruit that ripens on our trees.

³⁶ The first son born to each of us we will take to the priests in the Temple and there, as required by the Law, dedicate him to God. We will also dedicate the first calf born to each of our cows, and the first lamb or kid born to each of our sheep or goats.

10.30 Ex 34.16; Dt 7.3   **10.31 a** Ex 23.10, 11; Lv 25.1-7; **b** Dt 15.1, 2   **10.32** Ex 30.11-16
10.35 Ex 23.19; 34.26; Dt 26.2   **10.36** Ex 13.2

[37]We will take to the priests in the Temple the dough made from the first grain harvested each year and our other offerings of wine, olive oil, and all kinds of fruit.

We will take to the Levites, who collect tithes in our farming villages, the tithes from the crops that grow on our land. [38]Priests who are descended from Aaron are to be with the Levites when tithes are collected, and for use in the Temple the Levites are to take to the Temple storerooms one-tenth of all the tithes they collect. [39]The people of Israel and the Levites are to take the contributions of grain, wine, and olive oil to the storerooms where the utensils for the Temple are kept and where the priests who are on duty, the Temple guards, and the members of the Temple choir have their quarters.

We will not neglect the house of our God.

The People Who Lived in Jerusalem

11 The leaders settled in Jerusalem, and the rest of the people drew lots to choose one family out of every ten to go and live in the holy city of Jerusalem, while the rest were to live in the other cities and towns. [2]The people praised anyone else who volunteered to live in Jerusalem. [3]In the other towns and cities the people of Israel, the priests, the Levites, the Temple workers, and the descendants of Solomon's servants lived on their own property in their own towns.

The following is the list of the leading citizens of the province of Judah who lived in Jerusalem:

[4]*Members of the tribe of Judah:*

Athaiah, the son of Uzziah and grandson of Zechariah. His other ancestors included Amariah, Shephatiah,

and Mahalalel, descendants of Judah's son Perez.

[5]Maaseiah, the son of Baruch and grandson of Colhozeh. His other ancestors included Hazaiah, Adaiah, Joiarib, and Zechariah, descendants of Judah's son Shelah.

[6]Of the descendants of Perez, 468 outstanding soldiers lived in Jerusalem.

[7]*Members of the tribe of Benjamin:*

Sallu, the son of Meshullam and grandson of Joed. His other ancestors included Pedaiah, Kolaiah, Maaseiah, Ithiel, and Jeshaiah.

[8]Gabbai and Sallai, close relatives[q] of Sallu.

In all, 928 Benjaminites lived in Jerusalem. [9]Joel son of Zichri was their leader, and Judah son of Hassenuah was the second ranking official in the city.

[10]*Priests:*

Jedaiah son of Joiarib, and Jachin. [11]Seraiah, the son of Hilkiah and grandson of Meshullam. His ancestors included Zadok, Meraioth, and Ahitub, who was the High Priest. [12]In all, 822 members of this clan served in the Temple.

Adaiah, the son of Jeroham and grandson of Pelaliah. His ancestors included Amzi, Zechariah, Pashhur, and Malchijah. [13]In all, 242 members of this clan were heads of families.

Amashsai, the son of Azarel and grandson of Ahzai. His ancestors included Meshillemoth and Immer. [14]There were 128 members of this clan who were outstanding soldiers. Their leader was Zabdiel, a member of a leading family.[r]

[15]*Levites:*

Shemaiah, the son of Hasshub and

---

[q] *One ancient translation* close relatives; *Hebrew* after him.   [r] a member of a leading family; *or* son of Haggedolim.

10.37 Nu 18.21   **10.38** Nu 18.26   **11.3, 4** Ne 7.73

grandson of Azrikam. His ancestors included Hashabiah and Bunni.

16 Shabbethai and Jozabad, prominent Levites in charge of the work outside the Temple.

17 Mattaniah, the son of Mica and grandson of Zabdi, a descendant of Asaph. He led the Temple choir in singing the prayer of thanksgiving.

Bakbukiah, who was Mattaniah's assistant.

Abda, the son of Shammua and grandson of Galal, a descendant of Jeduthun.

18 In all, 284 Levites lived in the holy city of Jerusalem.

19 *Temple guards:*

Akkub, Talmon, and their relatives, 172 in all.

20 The rest of the people of Israel and the remaining priests and Levites lived on their own property in the other cities and towns of Judah. 21 The Temple workers lived in the part of Jerusalem called Ophel and worked under the supervision of Ziha and Gishpa.

22 The supervisor of the Levites who lived in Jerusalem was Uzzi, the son of Bani and grandson of Hashabiah. His ancestors included Mattaniah and Mica, and he belonged to the clan of Asaph, the clan that was responsible for the music in the Temple services. 23 There were royal regulations stating how the clans should take turns in leading the Temple music each day.

24 Pethahiah son of Meshezabel, of the clan of Zerah and the tribe of Judah, represented the people of Israel at the Persian court.

The People in Other Towns and Cities

25 Many of the people lived in towns near their farms. Those who were of the tribe of Judah lived in Kiriath Arba, Dibon, and Jekabzeel, and in the villages near these cities. 26 They also lived in the cities of Jeshua, Moladah, Bethpelet, 27 and Hazarshual, and in Beer-

sheba and the villages around it. 28 They lived in the city of Ziklag, in Meconah and its villages, 29 in Enrimmon, in Zorah, in Jarmuth, 30 in Zanoah, in Adullam, and in the villages near these towns. They lived in Lachish and on the farms nearby, and in Azekah and its villages. That is to say, the people of Judah lived in the territory between Beersheba in the south and Hinnom Valley in the north.

31 The people of the tribe of Benjamin lived in Geba, Michmash, Ai, Bethel and the nearby villages, 32 Anathoth, Nob, Ananiah, 33 Hazor, Ramah, Gittaim, 34 Hadid, Zeboim, Neballat, 35 Lod, and Ono, and in Craftsmen's Valley. 36 Some groups of Levites that had lived in the territory of Judah were assigned to live with the people of Benjamin.

List of Priests and Levites

12 The following is a list of the priests and Levites who returned from exile with Zerubbabel son of Shealtiel and with the High Priest Joshua:

2-7 *Priests:*

Seraiah, Jeremiah, Ezra, Amariah, Malluch, Hattush, Shecaniah, Rehum, Meremoth, Iddo, Ginnethoi, Abijah, Mijamin, Maadiah, Bilgah, Shemaiah, Joiarib, Jedaiah, Sallu, Amok, Hilkiah, and Jedaiah.

These men were leaders among all their fellow priests in the days of Joshua.

8 *Levites:*

The following were in charge of the singing of hymns of thanksgiving: Jeshua, Binnui, Kadmiel, Sherebiah, Judah, and Mattaniah.

9 The following formed the choir that sang the responses: Bakbukiah, Unno, and their fellow Levites.

Descendants of the High Priest Joshua

¹⁰Joshua was the father of Joiakim; Joiakim was the father of Eliashib; Eliashib was the father of Joiada; ¹¹Joiada was the father of Jonathan; and Jonathan was the father of Jaddua.

Heads of the Priestly Clans

¹²⁻²¹When Joiakim was High Priest, the following priests were the heads of the priestly clans:

Priest	Clan
Meraiah	Seraiah
Hananiah	Jeremiah
Meshullam	Ezra
Jehohanan	Amariah
Jonathan	Malluchi
Joseph	Shebaniah
Adna	Harim
Helkai	Meraioth
Zechariah	Iddo
Meshullam	Ginnethon
Zichri	Abijah
. . .ˢ	Miniamin
Piltai	Moadiah
Shammua	Bilgah
Jehonathan	Shemaiah
Mattenai	Joiarib
Uzzi	Jedaiah
Kallai	Sallai
Eber	Amok
Hashabiah	Hilkiah
Nethanel	Jedaiah

Record of the Priestly and Levite Families

²²A record was kept of the heads of the Levite families and of the priestly families during the lifetimes of the following High Priests: Eliashib, Joiada, Jonathan, and Jaddua. This record was finished when Darius was emperor of Persia.

²³The heads of the Levite families, however, were recorded in the official records only until the time of Jonathan, the grandson of Eliashib.

Assignment of Duties in the Temple

²⁴Under the direction of Hashabiah, Sherebiah, Jeshua, Binnui,ᵗ and Kadmiel, the Levites were organized into groups. Two groups at a time praised God responsively and gave thanks to him, in accordance with the instructions given by King David, the man of God.

²⁵The following Temple guards were in charge of guarding the storerooms by the gates to the Temple: Mattaniah, Bakbukiah, Obadiah, Meshullam, Talmon, and Akkub.

²⁶These people lived during the time of Joiakim, the son of Joshua and grandson of Jehozadak, and the time of Nehemiah the governor, and the time of Ezra, the priest who was a scholar of the Law.

Nehemiah Dedicates the City Wall

²⁷When the city wall of Jerusalem was dedicated, the Levites were brought in from wherever they were living, so that they could join in celebrating the dedication with songs of thanksgiving and with the music of cymbals and harps. ²⁸The Levite families of singers gathered from the area where they had settled around Jerusalem and from the towns around Netophah, ²⁹and from Bethgilgal, Geba, and Azmaveth. ³⁰The priests and the Levites performed ritual purification for themselves, the people, the gates, and the city wall.

³¹I assembled the leaders of Judah on top of the wall and put them in charge of two large groups to march around the city, giving thanks to God.

The first group went to the right on top of the wall toward the Rubbish

---

ˢ In Hebrew a name is missing from the list. Binnui; *Hebrew* son of.

ᵗ Probable text (see 10.9 and 12.8)

Gate.[u] [32]Hoshaiah marched behind the singers, followed by half the leaders of Judah. [33-35]The following priests, blowing trumpets, marched next: Azariah, Ezra, Meshullam, Judah, Benjamin, Shemaiah, and Jeremiah. Next came Zechariah, the son of Jonathan and grandson of Shemaiah. (His ancestors also included Mattaniah, Micaiah, and Zaccur, of the clan of Asaph.) [36]He was followed by other members of his clan — Shemaiah, Azarel, Milalai, Gilalai, Maai, Nethanel, Judah, and Hanani — all of whom carried musical instruments of the kind played by King David, the man of God. Ezra the scholar led this group in the procession. [37]At the Fountain Gate they went up the steps that led to David's City, past David's palace, and back to the wall at the Water Gate, on the east side of the city.

[38]The other group of those who gave thanks went to the left along the top of the wall, and I followed with half of the people. We marched past the Tower of

The other group . . . went to the left. (12.38)

the Ovens to the Broad Wall, [39]and from there we went past Ephraim Gate, Jeshanah Gate,[v] the Fish Gate, the Tower of Hananel, and the Tower of the Hundred, to the Sheep Gate. We ended our march near the gate to the Temple.

[40]So both the groups that were giving thanks to God reached the Temple area.

In addition to the leaders who were with me, [41]my group included the following priests, blowing trumpets: Eliakim, Maaseiah, Miniamin, Micaiah, Elioenai, Zechariah, and Hananiah; [42]and they were followed by Maaseiah Shemaiah, Eleazar, Uzzi, Jehohanan, Malchijah, Elam, and Ezer. The singers, led by Jezrahiah, sang at the top of their voices.

[43]That day many sacrifices were offered, and the people were full of joy because God had made them very happy. The women and the children joined in the celebration, and the noise they all made could be heard for miles.

Providing for Worship in the Temple

[44]At that time men were put in charge of the storerooms where contributions for the Temple were kept, including the tithes and the first grain and fruit that ripened each year. These men were responsible for collecting from the farms near the various cities the contributions for the priests and the Levites which the Law required. All the people of Judah were pleased with the priests and the Levites, [45]because they performed the ceremonies of purification and the other rituals that God had commanded. The Temple musicians and the Temple guards also performed their duties in accordance with the regulations made by King David and his son Solomon. [46]From the time of King David and the musician Asaph long ago, the musicians have led songs of praise and thanksgiving to God. [47]In the time of Zerubbabel and also in the time of Nehemiah, all the people of Israel gave daily gifts for the support of the Temple musicians and the Temple guards. The people gave a sacred offer-

[u] RUBBISH GATE: *The two groups started somewhere on the southwestern part of the city wall and went in opposite directions until they met in front of the Temple in the northeastern part of the city.*   [v] Ephraim Gate, Jeshanah Gate; *or* Ephraim Gate (also called the Old Gate).
12.45 a 1Ch 25.1-8; **b** 1Ch 26.12

ng to the Levites, and the Levites gave he required portion to the priests.

Separation from Foreigners

13 When the Law of Moses was being read aloud to the people, hey came to the passage that said that no Ammonite or Moabite was ever to be permitted to join God's people. [2] This was because the people of Ammon and Moab did not give food and water to the sraelites on their way out of Egypt. Instead, they paid money to Balaam to curse Israel, but our God turned the curse into a blessing. [3] When the people of Israel heard this law read, they excluded all foreigners from the community.

Nehemiah's Reforms

[4] The priest Eliashib, who was in charge of the Temple storerooms, had for a long time been on good terms with Tobiah. [5] He allowed Tobiah to use a large room that was intended only for storing offerings of grain and incense, the equipment used in the Temple, the offerings for the priests, and the tithes of grain, wine, and olive oil given to the Levites, to the Temple musicians, and to the Temple guards. [6] While this was going on, I was not in Jerusalem, because in the thirty-second year that Artaxerxes[w] was king of Babylon I had gone back to report to him. After some time I received his permission [7] and returned to Jerusalem. There I was shocked to find that Eliashib had allowed Tobiah to use a room in the Temple. [8] I was furious and threw out all of Tobiah's belongings. [9] I gave orders for the rooms to be ritually purified and for the Temple equipment, grain offerings, and incense to be put back.

[10] I also learned that the Temple musicians and other Levites had left Jerusalem and gone back to their farms, because the people had not been giving them enough to live on. [11] I reprimanded the officials for letting the Temple be neglected. And I brought the Levites and musicians back to the Temple and put them to work again. [12] Then all the people of Israel again started bringing to the Temple storerooms their tithes of grain, wine, and olive oil. [13] I put the following men in charge of the storerooms: Shelemiah, a priest; Zadok, a scholar of the Law; and Pedaiah, a Levite. Hanan, the son of Zaccur and grandson of Mattaniah, was to be their assistant. I knew I could trust these men to be honest in distributing the supplies to the other workers.

[14] Remember, my God, all these things that I have done for your Temple and its worship.

[15] At that time I saw people in Judah pressing juice from grapes on the Sabbath. Others were loading grain, wine, grapes, figs, and other things on their donkeys and taking them into Jerusalem; I warned them not to sell anything on the Sabbath. [16] Some people from the city of Tyre were living in Jerusalem, and they brought fish and all kinds of goods into the city to sell to our people on the Sabbath. [17] I reprimanded the Jewish leaders and told them, "Look at the evil you're doing! You're making the Sabbath unholy. [18] This is exactly why God punished your ancestors when he brought destruction on this city. And yet you insist on bringing more of God's anger down on Israel by profaning the Sabbath."

[19] So I gave orders for the city gates to be shut at the beginning of every Sabbath, as soon as evening[x] began to fall, and not to be opened again until

---

[w] ARTAXERXES: *As emperor of Persia, Artaxerxes also had the title "King of Babylon."*
[x] EVENING: *The Jewish day begins at sunset.*
13.1, 2 Dt 23.3-5   **13.2** Nu 22.1-6   **13.10** Dt 12.19   **13.12** Ml 3.10   **13.15** Ex 20.8-10; Dt 5.12-14; Jr 17.21, 22

You're making the Sabbath unholy. (13.17)

the Sabbath was over. I stationed some of my men at the gates to make sure that nothing was brought into the city on the Sabbath. [20] Once or twice merchants who sold all kinds of goods spent Friday night outside the city walls. [21] I warned them, "It's no use waiting out there for morning to come. If you try this again, I'll use force on you." From then on they did not come back on the Sabbath. [22] I ordered the Levites to purify themselves and to go and guard the gates to make sure that the Sabbath was kept holy.

Remember me, O God, for this also, and spare me because of your great love.

[23] At that time I also discovered that many of the Jewish men had married women from Ashdod, Ammon, and Moab. [24] Half of their children spoke the language of Ashdod or some other language and didn't know how to speak our language. [25] I reprimanded the men, called down curses on them, beat them, and pulled out their hair. Then I made them take an oath in God's name that never again would they or their children intermarry with foreigners. [26] I

told them, "It was foreign women that made King Solomon sin. Here was a man who was greater than any of the kings of other nations. God loved him and made him king over all of Israel, and yet he fell into this sin. [27] Are we then to follow your example and disobey our God by marrying foreign women?"

[28] Joiada was the son of Eliashib the High Priest, but one of Joiada's sons married the daughter of Sanballat, from the town of Beth Horon, so I made Joiada leave Jerusalem.

[29] Remember, God, how those people defiled both the office of priest and the covenant you made with the priests and the Levites.

[30] I purified the people from everything foreign; I prepared regulations for the priests and the Levites so that all of them would know their duties; [31] I arranged for the wood used for burning the offerings to be brought at the proper times, and for the people to bring their offerings of the first grain and the first fruits that ripened.

Remember all this, O God, and give me credit for it.

13.23-25 Ex 34.11-16; Dt 7.1-5 **13.26 a** 2 S 12.24, 25; **b** 1 K 11.1-8 **13.28** Ne 4.1

The Book of
ESTHER

INTRODUCTION

The events of *The Book of Esther,* which take place at the winter residence of the Persian emperor, center around a Jewish heroine named Esther, who by her great courage and devotion to her people saved them from being exterminated by their enemies. The book explains the background and meaning of the Jewish festival of Purim.

OUTLINE OF CONTENTS

Queen Vashti Defies King Xerxes

1 ¹⁻²From his royal throne in Persia's capital city of Susa, King Xerxes ruled 127 provinces, all the way from India to Ethiopia.*ᵃ*

³In the third year of his reign he gave a banquet for all his officials and administrators. The armies of Persia and Media were present, as well as the governors and noblemen of the provinces. ⁴For six whole months he made a show of the riches of the imperial court with all its splendor and majesty.

⁵After that, the king gave a banquet for all the people in the capital city of Susa, rich and poor alike. It lasted a whole week and was held in the gardens of the royal palace. ⁶The courtyard there was decorated with blue and white cotton curtains, tied by cords of fine purple linen to silver rings on marble columns. Couches made of gold and silver had been placed in the courtyard, which was paved with white marble, red feldspar, shining mother-of-pearl, and blue turquoise. ⁷Drinks were served in gold cups, no two of them alike, and the king was generous with the royal wine. ⁸There were no limits on the drinks; the king had given orders to the palace servants that everyone could have as much as they wanted.*ᵇ*

⁹Meanwhile, inside the royal palace Queen Vashti was giving a banquet for the women.

ᵃ Hebrew Cush: *Cush is the ancient name of the extensive territory south of the First Cataract of the Nile River. This region was called Ethiopia in Graeco-Roman times, and included within its borders most of modern Sudan and some of present-day Ethiopia (Abyssinia).* *ᵇ* There were no limits ... wanted; *or* But no one was forced to drink; the king had given orders to the palace servants that everyone could have as much or as little as they wanted.
1.1 Ezra 4.6

¹⁰On the seventh day of his banquet the king was drinking and feeling happy, so he called in the seven eunuchs who were his personal servants, Mehuman, Biztha, Harbona, Bigtha, Abagtha, Zethar, and Carkas. ¹¹He ordered them to bring in Queen Vashti, wearing her royal crown. The queen was a beautiful woman, and the king wanted to show off her beauty to the officials and all his guests. ¹²But when the servants told Queen Vashti of the king's command, she refused to come. This made the king furious.

¹³Now it was the king's custom to ask for expert opinion on questions of law and order, so he called for his advisers, who would know what should be done. ¹⁴Those he most often turned to for advice were Carshena, Shethar, Admatha, Tarshish, Meres, Marsena, and Memucan — seven officials of Persia and Media who held the highest offices in the kingdom. ¹⁵He said to these men, "I, King Xerxes, sent my servants to Queen Vashti with a command, and she refused to obey it! What does the law say that we should do with her?"

¹⁶Then Memucan declared to the king and his officials: "Queen Vashti has insulted not only the king but also his officials — in fact, every man in the empire! ¹⁷Every woman in the empire will start looking down on her husband as soon as she hears what the queen has done. They'll say, 'King Xerxes commanded Queen Vashti to come to him, and she refused.' ¹⁸When the wives of the royal officials of Persia and Media hear about the queen's behavior, they will be telling their husbands about it before the day is out. Wives everywhere will have no respect for their husbands, and husbands will be angry with their wives. ¹⁹If it please Your Majesty, issue a royal proclamation that Vashti may never again appear before the king. Have it written into the laws of Persia and Media, so that it can never be changed. Then give her place as queen to some better woman. ²⁰When your proclamation is made known all over this huge empire, every woman will treat her husband with proper respect, whether he's rich or poor."

²¹The king and his officials liked this idea, and the king did what Memucan suggested. ²²To each of the royal provinces he sent a message in the language and the system of writing of that province, saying[c] that every husband should be the master of his home and speak with final authority.

Esther Becomes Queen

2 Later, even after the king's anger had cooled down, he kept thinking about what Vashti had done and about his proclamation against her. ²So some of the king's advisers who were close to him suggested, "Why don't you make a search to find some beautiful young virgins? ³You can appoint officials in every province of the empire and have them bring all these beautiful young women to your harem here in Susa, the capital city. Put them in the care of Hegai, the eunuch who is in charge of your women, and let them be given a beauty treatment. ⁴Then take the young woman you like best and make her queen in Vashti's place."

The king thought this was good advice, so he followed it.

⁵There in Susa lived a Jew named Mordecai son of Jair; he was from the tribe of Benjamin and was a descendant of Kish and Shimei. ⁶When King Nebuchadnezzar of Babylon took King Jehoiachin of Judah into exile from Jerusalem, along with a group of captives, Mordecai was among them. ⁷He had a cousin, Esther, whose Hebrew name was Hadassah; she was a beautiful

c saying; *or* in order.
2.6 2 K 24.10-16; 2 Ch 36.10

young woman, and had a good figure. At the death of her parents, Mordecai had adopted her and brought her up as his own daughter.

⁸When the king had issued his new proclamation and many young women were being brought to Susa, Esther was among them. She too was put in the royal palace in the care of Hegai, who had charge of the harem. ⁹Hegai liked Esther, and she won his favor. He lost no time in beginning her beauty treatment of massage and special diet. He gave her the best place in the harem and assigned seven young women specially chosen from the royal palace to serve her.

¹⁰Now, on the advice of Mordecai, Esther had kept it secret that she was Jewish. ¹¹Every day Mordecai would walk back and forth in front of the courtyard of the harem, in order to find out how she was getting along and what was going to happen to her.

¹²The regular beauty treatment for the women lasted a year — massages with oil of myrrh for six months and with oil of balsam for six more. After that, each woman would be taken in turn to King Xerxes. ¹³When she went from the harem to the palace, she could wear whatever she wanted. ¹⁴She would go there in the evening, and the next morning she would be taken to another harem and put in the care of Shaashgaz, the eunuch in charge of the king's concubines. She would not go to the king again unless he liked her enough to ask for her by name.

¹⁵The time came for Esther to go to the king. Esther — the daughter of Abihail and the cousin of Mordecai, who had adopted her as his daughter; Esther — admired by everyone who saw her. When her turn came, she wore just what Hegai, the eunuch in charge of the harem, advised her to wear. ¹⁶So in Xerxes' seventh year as king, in the tenth month, the month of Tebeth, Es-

ther was brought to King Xerxes in the royal palace. ¹⁷The king liked her more than any of the other women, and more

Esther was brought to King Xerxes. (2.16)

than any of the others she won his favor and affection. He placed the royal crown on her head and made her queen in place of Vashti. ¹⁸Then the king gave a great banquet in Esther's honor and invited all his officials and administrators. He proclaimed a holiday[d] for the whole empire and distributed gifts worthy of a king.

Mordecai Saves the King's Life

¹⁹Meanwhile Mordecai had been appointed by the king to an administrative position. ²⁰As for Esther, she had still not let it be known that she was Jewish. Mordecai had told her not to tell anyone, and she obeyed him in this, just as she had obeyed him when she was a little girl under his care.

²¹During the time that Mordecai held office in the palace, Bigthana and Teresh, two of the palace eunuchs who guarded the entrance to the king's rooms, became hostile to King Xerxes and plotted to assassinate him. ²²Mordecai learned about it and told Queen

---

[d] holiday; *or* remission of taxes.

Esther, who then told the king what Mordecai had found out. 23 There was an investigation, and it was discovered that the report was true, so both men were hanged on the gallows. The king ordered an account of this to be written down in the official records of the empire.

Haman Plots to Destroy the Jews

3 Some time later King Xerxes promoted a man named Haman to the position of prime minister. Haman was the son of Hammedatha, a descendant of Agag.*e* 2 The king ordered all the officials in his service to show their respect for Haman by kneeling and bowing to him. They all did so, except for Mordecai, who refused to do it. 3 The other officials in the royal service asked him why he was disobeying the king's command; 4 day after day they urged him to give in, but he would not listen to them. "I am a Jew," he explained, "and I cannot bow to Haman." So they told Haman about this, wondering if he would tolerate Mordecai's conduct. 5 Haman was furious when he realized that Mordecai was not going to kneel and bow to him, 6 and when he learned that Mordecai was a Jew, he decided to do more than punish Mordecai alone. He made plans to kill every Jew in the whole Persian Empire.

7 In the twelfth year of King Xerxes' rule, in the first month, the month of Nisan, Haman ordered the lots to be cast ("purim," they were called) to find out the right day and month to carry out his plot. The thirteenth day of the twelfth month, the month of Adar, was decided on.

8 So Haman told the king, "There is a certain race of people scattered all over your empire and found in every province. They observe customs that are not like those of any other people. More-over, they do not obey the laws of the empire, so it is not in your best interests to tolerate them. 9 If it please Your Majesty, issue a decree that they are to be put to death. If you do, I guarantee that I will be able to put 375 tons of silver into the royal treasury for the administration of the empire."

10 The king took off his ring, which was used to stamp proclamations and make them official, and gave it to the enemy of the Jewish people, Haman son of Hammedatha, the descendant of Agag. 11 The king told him, "The people and their money are yours; do as you like with them."

12 So on the thirteenth day of the first month Haman called the king's secretaries and dictated a proclamation to be translated into every language and system of writing used in the empire and to be sent to all the rulers, governors, and officials. It was issued in the name of King Xerxes and stamped with his ring. 13 Runners took this proclamation to every province of the empire. It contained the instructions that on a single day, the thirteenth day of Adar, all Jews — young and old, women and children — were to be killed. They were to be slaughtered without mercy and their belongings were to be taken. 14 The contents of the proclamation were to be made public in every province, so that everyone would be prepared when that day came.

15 At the king's command the decree was made public in the capital city of Susa, and runners carried the news to the provinces. The king and Haman sat down and had a drink while the city of Susa was being thrown into confusion.

Mordecai Asks for Esther's Help

4 When Mordecai learned of all that had been done, he tore his clothes in anguish. Then he dressed in sack-

e AGAG: *An Amalekite king; his people were traditional enemies of the people of Israel.*
3.8 Ws 2.14, 15

cloth, covered his head with ashes, and walked through the city, wailing loudly and bitterly, ²until he came to the entrance of the palace. He did not go in because no one wearing sackcloth was allowed inside. ³Throughout all the provinces, wherever the king's proclamation was made known, there was loud mourning among the Jews. They fasted, wept, wailed, and most of them put on sackcloth and lay in ashes.

There was loud mourning among the Jews. (4.3)

⁴When Esther's servant women and eunuchs told her what Mordecai was doing, she was deeply disturbed. She sent Mordecai some clothes to put on instead of the sackcloth, but he would not accept them. ⁵Then she called Hathach, one of the palace eunuchs appointed as her servant by the king, and told him to go to Mordecai and find out what was happening and why. ⁶Hathach went to Mordecai in the city square at the entrance of the palace. ⁷Mordecai told him everything that had happened to him and just how much money Haman had promised to put into the royal treasury if all the Jews were killed. ⁸He gave Hathach a copy of the proclamation that had been issued in Susa, ordering the destruction of the Jews. Mordecai asked him to take it to Esther, explain the situation to her, and have her go and plead with the king and beg him to have mercy on her people. ⁹Hathach did this, ¹⁰and Esther gave him this message to take back to Mordecai: ¹¹"If anyone, man or woman, goes to the inner courtyard and sees the king without being summoned, that person must die. That is the law; everyone, from the king's advisers to the people in the provinces, knows that. There is only one way to get around this law: if the king holds out his gold scepter to someone, then that person's life is spared. But it has been a month since the king sent for me."

¹²When Mordecai received Esther's message, ¹³he sent her this warning: "Don't imagine that you are safer than any other Jew just because you are in the royal palace. ¹⁴If you keep quiet at a time like this, help will come from heaven to the Jews, and they will be saved, but you will die and your father's family will come to an end. Yet who knows — maybe it was for a time like this that you were made queen!"

¹⁵Esther sent Mordecai this reply: ¹⁶"Go and get all the Jews in Susa together; hold a fast and pray for me. Don't eat or drink anything for three days and nights. My servant women and I will be doing the same. After that, I will go to the king, even though it is against the law. If I must die for doing it, I will die."

¹⁷Mordecai then left and did everything that Esther had told him to do.

Esther Invites the King and Haman to a Banquet

5 On the third day of her fast Esther put on her royal robes and went and stood in the inner courtyard of the palace, facing the throne room. The king was inside, seated on the royal throne, facing the entrance. ²When the king saw Queen Esther standing outside, she won his favor, and he held out to her the gold scepter. She then came up and touched the tip of it. ³"What is it, Queen Esther?" the king asked. "Tell me what you want, and you shall have it — even if it is half my empire."

⁴Esther replied, "If it please Your Majesty, I would like you and Haman to be my guests tonight at a banquet I am preparing for you."

5 The king then ordered Haman to come quickly, so that they could be Esther's guests. So the king and Haman went to Esther's banquet. 6 Over the wine the king asked her, "Tell me what you want, and you shall have it. I will grant your request, even if you ask for half my empire."

7 Esther replied, 8 "If Your Majesty is kind enough to grant my request, I would like you and Haman to be my guests tomorrow at another banquet that I will prepare for you. At that time I will tell you what I want."

Haman Plots to Kill Mordecai

9 When Haman left the banquet he was happy and in a good mood. But then he saw Mordecai at the entrance of the palace, and when Mordecai did not rise or show any sign of respect as he passed, Haman was furious with him. 10 But he controlled himself and went on home. Then he invited his friends to his house and asked his wife Zeresh to join them. 11 He boasted to them about how rich he was, how many sons he had, how the king had promoted him to high office, and how much more important he was than any of the king's other officials. 12 "What is more," Haman went on, "Queen Esther gave a banquet for no one but the king and me, and we are invited back tomorrow. 13 But none of this means a thing to me as long as I see that Jew Mordecai sitting at the entrance of the palace."

14 So his wife and all his friends suggested, "Why don't you have a gallows built, seventy-five feet tall? Tomorrow morning you can ask the king to have Mordecai hanged on it, and then you can go to the banquet happy."

Haman thought this was a good idea, so he had the gallows built.

f ORNAMENT: *Probably a type of crown.*
6.2 Es 2.21, 22

The King Honors Mordecai

6 That same night the king could not get to sleep, so he had the official records of the empire brought and read to him. 2 The part they read included the account of how Mordecai had uncovered a plot to assassinate the king—the plot made by Bigthana and Teresh, the two palace eunuchs who had guarded the king's rooms. 3 The king asked, "How have we honored and rewarded Mordecai for this?"

His servants answered, "Nothing has been done for him."

4 "Are any of my officials in the palace?" the king asked.

Now Haman had just entered the courtyard; he had come to ask the king to have Mordecai hanged on the gallows that was now ready. 5 So the servants answered, "Haman is here, waiting to see you."

"Show him in," said the king.

6 So Haman came in, and the king said to him, "There is someone I wish very much to honor. What should I do for this man?"

Haman thought to himself, "Now who could the king want to honor so much? Me, of course."

7-8 So he answered the king, "Have royal robes brought for this man—robes that you yourself wear. Have a royal ornament*f* put on your own horse. 9 Then have one of your highest noblemen dress the man in these robes and lead him, mounted on the horse, through the city square. Have the nobleman announce as they go: 'See how the king rewards someone he wishes to honor!' "

10 Then the king said to Haman, "Hurry and get the robes and the horse, and provide these honors for Mordecai the Jew. Do everything for him that you have suggested. You will find him sitting at the entrance of the palace."

"See how the king rewards a man he wishes to honor!" (6.11)

11 So Haman got the robes and the horse, and he put the robes on Mordecai. Mordecai got on the horse, and Haman led him through the city square, announcing to the people as they went: "See how the king rewards a man he wishes to honor!"

12 Mordecai then went back to the palace entrance while Haman hurried home, covering his face in embarrassment. 13 He told his wife and all his friends everything that had happened to him. Then she and those wise friends of his told him, "You are beginning to lose power to Mordecai. He is a Jew, and you cannot overcome him. He will certainly defeat you."

Haman Is Put to Death

14 While they were still talking, the palace eunuchs arrived in a hurry to take Haman to Esther's banquet.

7 1 And so the king and Haman went to eat with Esther 2 for a second time. Over the wine the king asked her again, "Now, Queen Esther, what do you want? Tell me and you shall

have it. I'll even give you half the empire."

3 Queen Esther answered, "If it please Your Majesty to grant my humble request, my wish is that I may live and that my people may live. 4 My people and I have been sold for slaughter. If it were nothing more serious than being sold into slavery, I would have kept quiet and not bothered you about it;*g* but we are about to be destroyed — exterminated!"

5 Then King Xerxes asked Queen Esther, "Who dares to do such a thing? Where is this man?"

6 Esther answered, "Our enemy, our persecutor, is this evil man Haman!"

Haman faced the king and queen with terror. 7 The king got up in a fury, left the room, and went outside to the palace gardens. Haman could see that the king was determined to punish him for this, so he stayed behind to beg Queen Esther for his life. 8 He had just thrown himself down on Esther's couch to beg for mercy, when the king came back into the room from the gardens. Seeing this, the king cried out, "Is

g Probable text and not . . . it; *Hebrew unclear.*

this man going to rape the queen right here in front of me, in my own palace?"

The king had no sooner said this than the eunuchs covered Haman's head. ⁹Then one of them, who was named Harbonah, said, "Haman even went so far as to build a gallows at his house so that he could hang Mordecai, who saved Your Majesty's life. And it's seventy-five feet tall!"

"Hang Haman on it!" the king commanded.

¹⁰So Haman was hanged on the gallows that he had built for Mordecai. Then the king's anger cooled down.

The Jews Are Told to Fight Back

8 That same day King Xerxes gave Queen Esther all the property of Haman, the enemy of the Jews. Esther told the king that Mordecai was related to her, and from then on Mordecai was allowed to enter the king's presence. ²The king took off his ring with his seal on it (which he had taken back from Haman) and gave it to Mordecai. Esther put Mordecai in charge of Haman's property.

³Then Esther spoke to the king again, throwing herself at his feet and crying. She begged him to do something to stop the evil plot that Haman, the descendant of Agag,[h] had made against the Jews. ⁴The king held out the gold scepter to her, so she stood up and said, ⁵"If it please Your Majesty, and if you care about me and if it seems right to you, please issue a proclamation to keep Haman's orders from being carried out — those orders that the son of Hammedatha the descendant of Agag gave for the destruction of all the Jews in the empire. ⁶How can I endure it if this disaster comes on my people, and my own relatives are killed?"

⁷King Xerxes then said to Queen Esther and Mordecai, the Jew, "Look, I have hanged Haman for his plot against the Jews, and I have given Esther his property. ⁸But a proclamation issued in the king's name and stamped with the royal seal cannot be revoked. You may, however, write to the Jews whatever you like; and you may write it in my name and stamp it with the royal seal."

⁹This happened on the twenty-third day of the third month, the month of Sivan. Mordecai called the king's secretaries and dictated letters to the Jews and to the governors, administrators, and officials of all the 127 provinces from India to Ethiopia.[i] The letters were written to each province in its own language and system of writing and to the Jews in their language and system of writing. ¹⁰Mordecai had the letters written in the name of King Xerxes, and he stamped them with the royal seal. They were delivered by riders mounted on fast horses from the royal stables.

¹¹These letters explained that the king would allow the Jews in every city to organize for self-defense. If armed men of any nationality in any province attacked the Jewish men, their children, or their women, the Jews could fight back and destroy the attackers; they could slaughter them to the last man and take their possessions. ¹²This decree was to take effect throughout the Persian Empire on the day set for the slaughter of the Jews, the thirteenth of Adar, the twelfth month. ¹³It was to be proclaimed as law and made known to everyone in every province, so that the Jews would be ready to take revenge on their enemies when that day came. ¹⁴At the king's command the riders mounted royal horses and rode off at

---

[h] AGAG: See 3.1.   [i] *Hebrew* Cush: *Cush is the ancient name of the extensive territory south of the First Cataract of the Nile River. This region was called Ethiopia in Graeco-Roman times, and included within its borders most of modern Sudan and some of present-day Ethiopia (Abyssinia).*

op speed. The decree was also made
public in Susa, the capital city.

¹⁵ Mordecai left the palace, wearing
royal robes of blue and white, a cloak of
fine purple linen, and a magnificent
gold crown. Then the streets of Susa
rang with cheers and joyful shouts.
¹⁶ For the Jews there was joy and relief,
happiness and a sense of victory. ¹⁷ In
every city and province, wherever the
king's proclamation was read, the Jews
held a joyful holiday with feasting and
happiness. In fact, many other people
became Jews, because they were afraid
of them now.

The Jews Destroy Their Enemies

9 The thirteenth day of Adar came,
the day on which the royal proclamation was to take effect, the day when
the enemies of the Jews were hoping to
get them in their power. But instead,
the Jews triumphed over them. ² In the
Jewish quarter of every city*ʲ* in the empire the Jews organized to attack anyone who tried to harm them. People
everywhere were afraid of them, and no
one could stand against them. ³ In fact,
all the provincial officials — governors, administrators, and royal
representatives — helped the Jews because they were all afraid of Mordecai.
⁴ It was well-known throughout the empire that Mordecai was now a powerful
man in the palace and was growing
more powerful. ⁵ So the Jews could do
what they wanted with their enemies.
They attacked them with swords and
slaughtered them.

⁶ In Susa, the capital city itself, the
Jews killed five hundred people.
⁷⁻¹⁰ Among them were the ten sons of
Haman son of Hammedatha, the enemy of the Jews: Parshandatha, Dal-
phon, Aspatha, Poratha, Adalia,
Aridatha, Parmashta, Arisai, Aridai,
and Vaizatha. However, there was no
looting.

¹¹ That same day the number of people killed in Susa was reported to the
king. ¹² He then said to Queen Esther,
"In Susa alone the Jews have killed five
hundred people, including Haman's
ten sons. What must they have done
out in the provinces! What do you want
now? You shall have it. Tell me what
else you want, and you shall have it."

¹³ Esther answered, "If it please Your
Majesty, let the Jews in Susa do again
tomorrow what they were allowed to do
today. And have the bodies of Haman's
ten sons hung from the gallows." ¹⁴ The
king ordered this to be done, and the
proclamation was issued in Susa. The
bodies of Haman's ten sons were publicly displayed. ¹⁵ On the fourteenth day
of Adar the Jews of Susa got together
again and killed three hundred more
people in the city. But again, they did
no looting.

¹⁶ The Jews in the provinces also organized and defended themselves.
They rid themselves of their enemies by
killing seventy-five thousand people
who hated them. But they did no looting. ¹⁷ This was on the thirteenth day of
Adar. On the next day, the fourteenth,
there was no more killing, and they
made it a joyful day of feasting. ¹⁸ The
Jews of Susa, however, made the fifteenth a holiday, since they had slaughtered their enemies on the thirteenth
and fourteenth and then stopped on the
fifteenth. ¹⁹ This is why Jews who live
in small towns observe the fourteenth
day of the month of Adar as a joyous
holiday, a time for feasting and giving
gifts of food to one another.

The Festival of Purim

²⁰ Mordecai had these events written
down and sent letters to all the Jews,
near and far, throughout the Persian
Empire, ²¹ telling them to observe the
fourteenth and fifteenth days of Adar as
holidays every year. ²² These were the

ʲ In the Jewish quarter of every city; *or* In every Jewish city.

days on which the Jews had rid themselves of their enemies; this was a
month that had been turned from a
time of grief and despair into a time of
joy and happiness. They were told to
observe these days with feasts and parties, giving gifts of food to one another
and to the poor. 23 So the Jews followed
Mordecai's instructions, and the celebration became an annual custom.

24 Haman son of Hammedatha — the
descendant of Agag and the enemy of
the Jewish people — had cast lots ("purim," they were called) to determine the
day for destroying the Jews; he had
planned to wipe them out. 25 But Esther
went to the king, and the king issued
written orders with the result that Haman suffered the fate he had planned
for the Jews — he and his sons were
hanged from the gallows. 26 That is why
the holidays are called Purim. Because
of Mordecai's letter and because of all
that had happened to them, 27 the Jews
made it a rule for themselves, their
descendants, and anyone who might
become a Jew, that at the proper time
each year these two days would be regularly observed according to Mordecai's
instructions. 28 It was resolved that
every Jewish family of every future generation in every province and every city
should remember and observe the days
of Purim for all time to come.

29 Then Queen Esther, the daughter

9.24 Es 3.7

of Abihail, along with Mordecai, also
wrote a letter, putting her full authority
behind the letter about Purim, which
Mordecai had written earlier. 30 The letter was addressed to all the Jews, and
copies were sent to all the 127 provinces of the Persian Empire. It wished
the Jews peace and security 31 and directed them and their descendants to
observe the days of Purim at the proper
time, just as they had adopted rules for
the observance of fasts and times of
mourning. This was commanded by
both Mordecai and Queen Esther.
32 Esther's command, confirming the
rules for Purim, was written down on a
scroll.

The Greatness of Xerxes and Mordecai

10 King Xerxes imposed forced labor on the people of the coastal
regions of his empire as well as on those
of the interior. 2 All the great and wonderful things he did, as well as the
whole story of how he promoted Mordecai to high office, are recorded in the
official records of the kings of Persia
and Media. 3 Mordecai the Jew was second in rank only to King Xerxes himself. He was honored and well-liked by
his fellow Jews. He worked for the good
of his people and for the security of all
their descendants.

The Book of
JOB

INTRODUCTION

The Book of Job is the story of a good man who suffers total disaster — he loses all his children and property and is afflicted with a repulsive disease. Then in three series of poetic dialogues the author shows how Job's friends and Job himself react to these calamities. In the end, God himself, whose dealings with the human race have been a prominent part of the discussion, appears to Job.

The friends of Job explain his suffering in traditional religious terms. Since God, so they assume, always rewards good and punishes evil, the sufferings of Job can only mean that he has sinned. But for Job this is too simple; he does not deserve such cruel punishment, because he has been an unusually good and righteous man. He cannot understand how God can let so much evil happen to one like himself, and he boldly challenges God. Job does not lose his faith, but he does long to be justified before God and to regain his honor as a good man.

God does not give an answer to Job's questions, but he does respond to Job's faith by overwhelming him with a poetic picture of his divine power and wisdom. Job then humbly acknowledges God as wise and great, and repents of the wild and angry words he had used.

The prose conclusion records how Job is restored to his former condition, with even greater prosperity than before. God reprimands Job's friends for failing to understand the meaning of Job's suffering. Only Job had really sensed that God is greater than traditional religion had depicted him.

OUTLINE OF CONTENTS

Satan Tests Job

1 There was a man named Job, living in the land of Uz,[a] who worshiped God and was faithful to him. He was a good man, careful not to do anything evil. [2] He had seven sons and three daughters, [3] and owned seven thousand sheep, three thousand camels, one thousand head of cattle, and five hundred donkeys. He also had a large number of servants and was the richest man in the East.

[4] Job's sons used to take turns giving a feast, to which all the others would come, and they always invited their three sisters to join them. [5] The morning after each feast, Job would get up early and offer sacrifices for each of his children in order to purify them. He always did this because he thought that one of them might have sinned by insulting God unintentionally.

[6] When the day came for the heavenly beings[b] to appear before the LORD, Satan[c] was there among them. [7] The LORD asked him, "What have you been doing?"

Satan answered, "I have been walking here and there, roaming around the earth."

[8] "Did you notice my servant Job?" the LORD asked. "There is no one on earth as faithful and good as he is. He worships me and is careful not to do anything evil."

[9] Satan replied, "Would Job worship you if he got nothing out of it? [10] You have always protected him and his family and everything he owns. You bless everything he does, and you have given him enough cattle to fill the whole country. [11] But now suppose you take away everything he has — he will curse you to your face!"

[12] "All right," the LORD said to Satan, "everything he has is in your power, but you must not hurt Job himself." So Satan left.

Job's Children and Wealth Are Destroyed

[13] One day when Job's children were having a feast at the home of their oldest brother, [14] a messenger came running to Job. "We were plowing the fields with the oxen," he said, "and the donkeys were in a nearby pasture. [15] Suddenly the Sabeans[d] attacked and stole them all. They killed every one of your servants except me. I am the only one who escaped to tell you."

[16] Before he had finished speaking, another servant came and said, "Lightning struck the sheep and the shepherds and killed them all. I am the only one who escaped to tell you."

[17] Before he had finished speaking, another servant came and said, "Three bands of Chaldean[e] raiders attacked us, took away the camels, and killed all your servants except me. I am the only one who escaped to tell you."

[18] Before he had finished speaking, another servant came and said, "Your children were having a feast at the home of your oldest son, [19] when a storm swept in from the desert. It blew the house down and killed them all. I am the only one who escaped to tell you."

[20] Then Job got up and tore his clothes in grief. He shaved his head and threw himself face downward on the ground. [21] He said, "I was born with nothing, and I will die with nothing.

---

[a] UZ: *An area whose exact location is unknown.*   [b] HEAVENLY BEINGS: *Supernatural beings who serve God in heaven.*   [c] SATAN: *A supernatural being whose name indicates he was regarded as the opponent of human beings.*   [d] SABEANS: *A tribe of wandering raiders from the south.*   [e] CHALDEANS: *A tribe of wandering raiders from the north.*

1.6 Gn 6.2   **1.9-11** Rev 12.10   **1.21** Si 40.1; 11.14

"The LORD gave, and now he has taken away."
(1.21)

The LORD gave, and now he has taken away. May his name be praised!"

²² In spite of everything that had happened, Job did not sin by blaming God.

Satan Tests Job Again

2 When the day came for the heavenly beings to appear before the LORD again, Satan was there among them. ² The LORD asked him, "Where have you been?"

Satan answered, "I have been walking here and there, roaming around the earth."

³ "Did you notice my servant Job?" the LORD asked. "There is no one on earth as faithful and good as he is. He worships me and is careful not to do anything evil. You persuaded me to let you attack him for no reason at all, but Job is still as faithful as ever."

⁴ Satan replied, "A person will give up everything in order to stay alive. ⁵ But now suppose you hurt his body — he will curse you to your face!"

⁶ So the LORD said to Satan, "All right, he is in your power, but you are not to kill him."

⁷ Then Satan left the LORD's presence and made sores break out all over Job's body. ⁸ Job went and sat by the garbage dump and took a piece of broken pottery to scrape his sores. ⁹ His wife said to him, "You are still as faithful as ever, aren't you? Why don't you curse God and die?"

¹⁰ Job answered, "You are talking nonsense! When God sends us something good, we welcome it. How can we complain when he sends us trouble?" Even in all this suffering Job said nothing against God.

Job's Friends Come

¹¹ Three of Job's friends were Eliphaz, from the city of Teman, Bildad, from the land of Shuah, and Zophar, from the land of Naamah. When they heard how much Job had been suffering, they decided to go and comfort him. ¹² While they were still a long way off they saw Job, but did not recognize him. When they did, they began to weep and wail, tearing their clothes in grief and throwing dust into the air and on their heads. ¹³ Then they sat there on the ground with him for seven days and nights without saying a word, because they saw how much he was suffering.

Job's Complaint to God

3 Finally Job broke the silence and cursed the day on which he had been born.

Job

²⁻³ O God, put a curse on the day I
    was born;
   put a curse on the night when
    I was conceived!
⁴ Turn that day into darkness,
    God.
  Never again remember
    that day;

"Why don't you curse God and die?" (2.9)

never again let light shine on it.
5 Make it a day of gloom and thick
     darkness;
     cover it with clouds, and blot
   out the sun.
6 Blot that night out of the year,
     and never let it be counted
   again;
7   make it a barren, joyless
   night.
8 Tell the sorcerers to curse
   that day,
     those who know how to
   control Leviathan.ƒ
9 Keep the morning star from
   shining;
     give that night no hope of
   dawn.
10 Curse that night for letting me
   be born,
     for exposing me to trouble
   and grief.

11 I wish I had died in my mother's
   womb
     or died the moment I was
   born.

12 Why did my mother hold me on
   her knees?
     Why did she feed me at her
   breast?
13 If I had died then, I would be at
   rest now,
14   sleeping like the kings and
   rulers
     who rebuilt ancient palaces.
15 Then I would be sleeping like
   princes
     who filled their houses with
   gold and silver,
16   or sleeping like a stillborn
   child.
17 In the grave wicked people stop
   their evil,
     and tired workers find rest at
   last.
18 Even prisoners enjoy peace,
     free from shouts and harsh
   commands.
19 Everyone is there, the famous
   and the unknown,
     and slaves at last are free.

20 Why let people go on living in
   misery?
     Why give light to those in
   grief?
21 They wait for death, but it never
   comes;
     they prefer a grave to any
   treasure.
22 They are not happy till they are
   dead and buried;
23   God keeps their future hidden
     and hems them in on every
   side.
24 Instead of eating, I mourn,
     and I can never stop
   groaning.
25 Everything I fear and dread
   comes true.
26 I have no peace, no rest,
     and my troubles never end.

ƒ LEVIATHAN: *Some take this to be the crocodile, others a legendary monster. Magicians
were thought to be able to make him cause eclipses of the sun.*
3.3 Si 23.14 **3.21** Rev 9.6

The First Dialogue
(4.1 — 14.22)

4

Eliphaz

1-2 Job, will you be annoyed if I
   speak?
   I can't keep quiet any longer.
3 You have taught many people
   and given strength to feeble
   hands.
4 When someone stumbled, weak
   and tired,
   your words encouraged him to
   stand.
5 Now it's your turn to be in
   trouble,
   and you are too stunned to
   face it.
6 You worshiped God, and your life
   was blameless;
   and so you should have
   confidence and hope.
7 Think back now. Name a single
   case
   where someone righteous met
   with disaster.
8 I have seen people plow fields of
   evil
   and plant wickedness like
   seed;
   now they harvest wickedness
   and evil.
9 Like a storm, God destroys them
   in his anger.
10 The wicked roar and growl like
   lions,
   but God silences them and
   breaks their teeth.
11 Like lions with nothing to kill
   and eat,
   they die, and all their children
   are scattered.

12 Once a message came quietly,

so quietly I could hardly
   hear it.
13 Like a nightmare it disturbed my
   sleep.
14   I trembled and shuddered;
   my whole body shook with
   fear.
15 A light breeze touched my face,
   and my skin crawled with
   fright.
16 I could see something standing
   there;
   I stared, but couldn't tell what
   it was.
   Then I heard a voice out of the
   silence:
17 "Can anyone be righteous in the
   sight of[g] God
   or be pure before[h] his
   Creator?
18 God does not trust his heavenly
   servants;
   he finds fault even with his
   angels.
19 Do you think he will trust a
   creature of clay,
   a thing of dust that can be
   crushed like a moth?
20 We may be alive in the morning,
   but die unnoticed before
   evening comes.
21 All that we have is taken away;
   we die, still lacking wisdom."

5

Call out, Job. See if anyone
   answers.
   Is there any angel to whom
   you can turn?
2 To worry yourself to death with
   resentment
   would be a foolish, senseless
   thing to do.
3 I have seen fools who looked
   secure,
   but I called down a sudden
   curse on their homes.

---

righteous in the sight of; *or* more righteous than.   [h] be pure before; *or* be more
pure than.

.13 Job 33.15

4 Their children can never find
safety;
no one stands up to defend
them in court.
5 Hungry people will eat the fool's
crops —
even the grain growing
among thorns[i] —
and thirsty people will envy
his wealth.
6 Evil does not grow in the soil,
nor does trouble grow out of
the ground.
7 No indeed! We bring trouble on
ourselves,
as surely as sparks fly up from
a fire.[j]

8 If I were you, I would turn
to God
and present my case to him.
9 We cannot understand the great
things he does,
and to his miracles there is
no end.
10 He sends rain on the land
and he waters the fields.
11 Yes, it is God who raises the
humble
and gives joy to all who
mourn.
12-13 He upsets the plans of cunning
people,
and traps the wise in their
own schemes,
so that nothing they do
succeeds;
14   even at noon they grope in
darkness.
15 But God saves the poor[k] from
death;
he saves the needy from
oppression.
16 He gives hope to the poor and
silences the wicked.

17 Happy is the person whom God
corrects!
Do not resent it when he
rebukes you.
18 God bandages the wounds he
makes;
his hand hurts you, and his
hand heals.
19 Time after time he will save you
from harm;
20   when famine comes, he will
keep you alive,
and in war protect you from
death.
21 God will rescue you from
slander;
he will save you when
destruction comes.
22 You will laugh at violence and
hunger
and not be afraid of wild
animals.
23 The fields you plow will be free
of rocks;
wild animals will never
attack you.
24 Then you will live at peace in
your tent;
when you look at your sheep,
you will find them safe.
25 You will have as many children
as there are blades of grass in
a pasture.
26 Like wheat that ripens till
harvest time,
you will live to a ripe old age.
27 Job, we have learned this by long
study.
It is true, so now accept it.

6
Job

1-2 If my troubles and griefs were
weighed on scales,
3   they would weigh more than
the sands of the sea,

---

i Probable text even . . . thorns; *Hebrew unclear.*   *j* sparks fly up from a fire; *or* birds
fly up to the sky.   *k Probable text* poor; *Hebrew unclear.*
5.9 Si 43.32   **5.13** 1 Co 3.19   **5.17** Pr 3.11, 12; He 12.5, 6   **5.18** Ho 6.1

so my wild words should not
surprise you.
⁴Almighty God has shot me with
arrows,
and their poison spreads
through my body.
God has lined up his terrors
against me.

⁵A donkey is content when eating
grass,
and a cow is quiet when
eating hay.
⁶But who can eat flat, unsalted
food?
What taste is there in the
white of an egg?
⁷I have no appetite for food like
that,
and everything I eat makes
me sick.ˡ

⁸Why won't God give me what
I ask?
Why won't he answer my
prayer?
⁹If only he would go ahead and
kill me!
¹⁰If I knew he would, I would leap
for joy,
no matter how great my pain.
I know that God is holy;
I have never opposed what he
commands.
¹¹What strength do I have to keep
on living?
Why go on living when I have
no hope?
¹²Am I made of stone? Is my body
bronze?
¹³I have no strength left to save
myself;
there is nowhere I can turn
for help.

¹⁴In troubleᵐ like this I need loyal
friends —
whether I've forsaken God
or not.
¹⁵But you, my friends, you deceive
me like streams
that go dry when no rain
comes.
¹⁶The streams are choked with
snow and ice,
¹⁷ but in the heat they
disappear,
and the stream beds lie bare
and dry.
¹⁸Caravans get lost looking for
water;
they wander and die in the
desert.
¹⁹Caravans from Sheba and Tema
search,
²⁰ but their hope dies beside dry
streams.
²¹You are likeⁿ those streams
to me,ᵒ
you see my fate and draw
back in fear.
²²Have I asked you to give me a
gift
or to bribe someone on my
behalf
²³ or to save me from some
enemy or tyrant?

²⁴All right, teach me; tell me my
faults.
I will be quiet and listen
to you.
²⁵Honest words are convincing,
but you are talking nonsense.
²⁶You think I am talking nothing
but wind;
then why do you answer my
words of despair?
²⁷You would even roll dice for
orphan slaves

ˡProbable text sick; *Hebrew unclear.*   ᵐ Probable text trouble; *Hebrew unclear.*
ⁿProbable text like; *Hebrew because.*   ᵒ *Some ancient translations* and one; *Hebrew
manuscript* to me; *most Hebrew manuscripts have two different expressions:* nothing
the text and to him *in the margin.*

"You think I am talking nothing but wind." (6.26)

and make yourselves rich off
    your closest friends!
²⁸ Look me in the face. I won't lie.
²⁹ You have gone far enough. Stop
    being unjust.
    Don't condemn me. I'm in the
      right.
³⁰ But you think I am lying—
    you think I can't tell right
      from wrong.

7   Human life is like forced army
      service,
    like a life of hard manual
      labor,
²   like a slave longing for cool
      shade;
    like a worker waiting to be
      paid.
³ Month after month I have
    nothing to live for;
    night after night brings me
      grief.
⁴ When I lie down to sleep, the
    hours drag;
    I toss all night and long for
      dawn.

⁵ My body is full of worms;
    it is covered with scabs;
    pus runs out of my sores.
⁶ My days pass by without hope,
    pass faster than a weaver's
      shuttle.ᵖ

⁷ Remember, O God, my life is
    only a breath;
    my happiness has already
      ended.
⁸ You see me now, but never
      again.
    If you look for me, I'll be
      gone.
⁹⁻¹⁰ Like a cloud that fades and is
      gone,
    we humans die and never
      return;
    we are forgotten by all who
      knew us.
¹¹ No! I can't be quiet!
    I am angry and bitter.
    I have to speak.

¹² Why do you keep me under
      guard?
    Do you think I am a sea
      monster?�q
¹³ I lie down and try to rest;
    I look for relief from my pain.
¹⁴ But you—you terrify me with
      dreams;
    you send me visions and
      nightmares
¹⁵   until I would rather be
      strangled
    than live in this miserable
      body.
¹⁶ I give up; I am tired of living.
    Leave me alone. My life makes
      no sense.

¹⁷ Why are people so important
    to you?

ᵖ **WEAVER'S SHUTTLE:** *A small device in the loom which carries threads back and forth
rapidly in weaving cloth.*   �q **SEA MONSTER:** *A reference to ancient stories in which
sea monsters had to be guarded so that they would not escape and do damage.*
7.9, 10 Ws 2.1-4   **7.17** Ps 8.4; 144.3

"I give up; I am tired of living." (7.16)

Why pay attention to what
  they do?
¹⁸You inspect them every morning
  and test them every minute.
¹⁹Won't you look away long
  enough
  for me to swallow my spit?
²⁰Are you harmed by my sin, you
  jailer?
  Why use me for your target
  practice?
  Am I so great a burden
  to you?
²¹Can't you ever forgive my sin?
  Can't you pardon the wrong
  I do?
  Soon I will be in my grave,
  and I'll be gone when you
  look for me.

8

Bildad
¹⁻²Are you finally through with your
  windy speech?
  ³God never twists justice;
  he never fails to do what is
  right.

⁴Your children must have sinned
  against God,
  and so he punished them as
  they deserved.
⁵But turn now and plead with
  Almighty God;
⁶ if you are so honest and pure,
  then God will come and
  help you
  and restore your household as
  your reward.
⁷All the wealth you lost will be
  nothing
  compared with what God will
  give you then.

⁸Look for a moment at ancient
  wisdom;
  consider the truths our
  ancestors learned.
⁹Our life is short, we know
  nothing at all;
  we pass like shadows across
  the earth.
¹⁰But let the ancient wise people
  teach you;
  listen to what they had to say:

¹¹"Reeds can't grow where there is
  no water;
  they are never found outside a
  swamp.
¹²If the water dries up, they are
  the first to wither,
  while still too small to be cut
  and used.
¹³Godless people are like those
  reeds;
  their hope is gone, once God
  is forgotten.
¹⁴They trust a thread — a
  spider's web.
¹⁵ If they lean on a web, will it
  hold them up?
  If they grab for a thread, will
  it help them stand?"

¹⁶Evil people sprout like weeds in
  the sun,

8.8 Si 8.9

like weeds that spread all
through the garden.
17 Their roots wrap around the
stones
and hold fast to[r] every rock.
18 But then pull them up —
no one will ever know they
were there.
19 Yes, that's all the joy evil people
have;
others now come and take
their places.

20 But God will never abandon the
faithful
or ever give help to evil
people.
21 He will let you laugh and shout
again,
22   but he will bring disgrace on
those who hate you,
and the homes of the wicked
will vanish.

9

Job

1-2 Yes, I've heard all that before.
But how can a human being
win a case against God?
3 How can anyone argue
with him?
He can ask a thousand
questions
that no one could ever
answer.[s]
4 God is so wise and powerful;
no one can stand up
against him.
5 Without warning he moves
mountains
and in anger he destroys
them.

6 God sends earthquakes and
shakes the ground;
he rocks the pillars that
support the earth.
7 He can keep the sun from rising,
and the stars from shining at
night.
8 No one helped God spread out
the heavens
or trample the sea monster's
back.[t]
9 God hung the stars in the
sky — the Dipper,
Orion, the Pleiades, and the
stars of the south.
10 We cannot understand the great
things he does,
and to his miracles there is
no end.

11 God passes by, but I cannot
see him.
12 He takes what he wants, and no
one can stop him;
no one dares ask him, "What
are you doing?"
13 God's anger is constant. He
crushed his enemies
who helped Rahab,[u] the sea
monster, oppose him.
14 So how can I find words to
answer God?
15 Though I am innocent, all I
can do
is beg for mercy from God my
judge.
16 Yet even then, if he lets me
speak,
I can't believe he would listen
to me.
17 He sends storms to batter and
bruise me
without any reason at all.

---

[r] *Probable text* hold fast to; *Hebrew* see.   [s] He can ask . . . answer; *or* Someone could
ask him a thousand questions, and he would not answer.   [t] TRAMPLE THE SEA
MONSTER'S BACK: *A reference to ancient stories in which a sea monster was killed and
then trampled (see also 26.13).*   [u] RAHAB: *A legendary sea monster which
represented the forces of chaos and evil.*
9.2 Job 4.17   **9.7, 8** Ba 3.34, 35   **9.9** Job 38.31; Am 5.8

¹⁸He won't let me catch my
breath;
he has filled my life with
bitterness.
¹⁹Should I try force? Try force
on God?
Should I take him to court?
Could anyone make
him go?ᵛ
²⁰I am innocent and faithful, but
my words sound guilty,
and everything I say seems to
condemn me.
²¹⁻²²I am innocent, but I no longer
care.
I am sick of living. Nothing
matters;
innocent or guilty, God will
destroy us.
²³When an innocent person
suddenly dies,
God laughs.
²⁴God gave the world to the
wicked.
He made all the judges blind.
And if God didn't do it, who did?
²⁵My days race by, not one of
them good.
²⁶My life passes like the swiftest
boat,
as fast as an eagle swooping
down on a rabbit.
²⁷⁻²⁸If I smile and try to forget my
pain,
all my suffering comes back
to haunt me;
I know that God does hold me
guilty.
²⁹Since I am held guilty, why
should I bother?
³⁰ No soap can wash away my
sins.
³¹God throws me into a pit with
filth,
and even my clothes are
ashamed of me.

³²If God were human, I could
answer him;
we could go to court to decide
our quarrel.
³³But there is no one to step
between us —
no one to judge both God
and me.
³⁴Stop punishing me, God!
Keep your terrors away!
³⁵I am not afraid. I am going to
talk
because I know my own
heart.

10 I am tired of living.
Listen to my bitter
complaint.
²Don't condemn me, God.
Tell me! What is the charge
against me?
³Is it right for you to be so cruel?
To despise what you yourself
have made?
And then to smile on the
schemes of wicked people?
⁴Do you see things as we do?
⁵ Is your life as short as ours?
⁶Then why do you track down all
my sins
and hunt down every fault I
have?
⁷You know that I am not guilty,
that no one can save me
from you.

⁸Your hands formed and
shaped me,
and nowʷ those same hands
destroy me.
⁹Remember that you made me
from clay;ˣ
are you going to crush me
back to dust?
¹⁰You gave my father strength to
beget me;

Probable text make him go; *Hebrew* make me go.   ʷ *Some ancient translations* and now; *Hebrew* together.   ˣ *One ancient translation* from clay; *Hebrew* like clay.
10.7 Ws 16.15   **10.10** Ws 7.1, 2

you made me grow in my
mother's womb.
¹¹ You formed my body with bones
and sinews
and covered the bones with
muscles and skin.
¹² You have given me life and
constant love,
and your care has kept me
alive.
¹³ But now I know that all that
time
you were secretly planning to
harm me.
¹⁴ You were watching to see if I
would sin,
so that you could refuse to
forgive me.
¹⁵ As soon as I sin, I'm in trouble
with you,
but when I do right, I get no
credit.
I am miserable and covered with
shame.^y
¹⁶ If I have any success at all,
you hunt me down like a lion;
to hurt me you even work
miracles.
¹⁷ You always have some witness
against me;
your anger toward me grows
and grows;
you always plan some new
attack.

¹⁸ Why, God, did you let me be
born?
I should have died before
anyone saw me.
¹⁹ To go from the womb straight to
the grave
would have been as good as
never existing.
²⁰ Isn't my life almost over? Leave
me alone!
Let me enjoy the time I have
left.
²¹ I am going soon and will never
come back—

going to a land that is dark
and gloomy,
²² a land of darkness, shadows,
and confusion,
where the light itself is
darkness.

11

Zophar

¹⁻² Will no one answer all this
nonsense?
Does talking so much put you
in the right?
³ Job, do you think we can't
answer you?
That your mocking words will
leave us speechless?
⁴ You claim that what you say is
true;
you claim you are pure in the
sight of God.
⁵ How I wish God would
answer you!
⁶ He would tell you there are
many sides to wisdom;
there are things too deep for
human knowledge.
God is punishing you less than
you deserve.

⁷ Can you discover the limits and
bounds
of the greatness and power
of God?
⁸ The sky is no limit for God,
but it lies beyond your reach.
God knows the world of the
dead,
but you do not know it.
⁹ God's greatness is broader than
the earth,
wider than the sea.
¹⁰ If God arrests you and brings you
to trial,
who is there to stop him?
¹¹ God knows which people are
worthless;
he sees all their evil deeds.

^y *Probable text* covered with shame; *Hebrew* see my shame.

12 Stupid people will start being
    wise
    when wild donkeys are born
    tame.

13 Put your heart right, Job. Reach
    out to God.

14 Put away evil and wrong from
    your home.

15 Then face the world again, firm
    and courageous.

16 Then all your troubles will fade
    from your memory,
    like floods that are past and
    remembered no more.

17 Your life will be brighter than
    sunshine at noon,
    and life's darkest hours will
    shine like the dawn.

18 You will live secure and full of
    hope;
    God will protect you and give
    you rest.

19 You won't be afraid of your
    enemies;
    many people will ask you for
    help.

20 But the wicked will look around
    in despair
    and find that there is no way
    to escape.
    Their one hope is that death will
    come.

12

Job

1-2 Yes, you are the voice of the
    people.
    When you die, wisdom will
    die with you.

3 But I have as much sense as you
    have;
    I am in no way inferior
    to you;
    everyone knows all that you
    have said.

4 Even my friends laugh at
    me now;
    they laugh, although I am
    righteous and blameless;

but there was a time when
    God answered my prayers.

5 You have no troubles, and yet
    you make fun of me;
    you hit someone who is about
    to fall.

6 But thieves and godless people
    live in peace,
    though their only god is their
    own strength.

7 Even birds and animals have
    much they could
    teach you;

8   ask the creatures of earth and
    sea for their wisdom.

9 All of them know that the LORD's
    hand made them.

10 It is God who directs the lives of
    his creatures;
    everyone's life is in his power.

11 But just as your tongue enjoys
    tasting food,
    your ears enjoy hearing
    words.

12-13 Old people have wisdom,
    but God has wisdom and
    power.
    Old people have insight;
    God has insight and power
    to act.

14 When God tears down, who can
    rebuild,
    and who can free those God
    imprisons?

15 Drought comes when God
    withholds rain;
    floods come when he turns
    water loose.

16 God is strong and always
    victorious;
    both deceived and deceiver
    are in his power.

17 He takes away the wisdom of
    rulers
    and makes leaders act like
    fools.

18 He dethrones kings and makes
    them prisoners;

19   he humbles priests and men
of power.

20 He silences those who are
trusted,

and takes the wisdom of old
people away.

21 He disgraces those in power
and puts an end to the
strength of rulers.

22 He sends light to places dark as
death.

23 He makes nations strong and
great,

but then he defeats and
destroys them.

24 He makes their leaders foolish
and lets them wander
confused and lost;

25   they grope in the dark and
stagger like drunkards.

13

1-2 Everything you say, I have
heard before.

I understand it all; I know as
much as you do.

I'm not your inferior.

3 But my dispute is with God,
not you;

I want to argue my case
with him.

4 You cover up your ignorance
with lies;

you are like doctors who can't
heal anyone.

5 Say nothing, and someone may
think you are wise!

6 Listen while I state my case.

7   Why are you lying?

Do you think your lies will
benefit God?

8 Are you trying to defend him?

Are you going to argue his
case in court?

9 If God looks at you closely, will
he find anything good?

Do you think you can fool God
the way you fool others?

10 Even though your prejudice is
hidden,

he will reprimand you,

11   and his power will fill you
with terror.

12 Your proverbs are as useless as
ashes;

your arguments are as weak
as clay.

13 Be quiet and give me a chance
to speak,

and let the results be what
they will.

"Be quiet and give me a chance to speak."
(13.13)

14 I am[z] ready to risk my life.

15 I've lost all hope, so what if God
kills me?

I am going to state my case
to him.

16 It may even be that my boldness
will save me,

since no wicked person would
dare to face God.

17 Now listen to my words of
explanation.

18 I am ready to state my case,
because I know I am in the
right.

[z] *One ancient translation* I am; *Hebrew* Why am I.

¹⁹ Are you coming to accuse
me, God?
If you do, I am ready to be
silent and die.
²⁰ Let me ask for two things; agree
to them,
and I will not try to hide
from you:
²¹   stop punishing me, and don't
crush me with terror.

²² Speak first, O God, and I will
answer.
Or let me speak, and you
answer me.
²³ What are my sins? What wrongs
have I done?
What crimes am I charged
with?
²⁴ Why do you avoid me?
Why do you treat me like an
enemy?
²⁵ Are you trying to frighten me?
I'm nothing but a leaf;
you are attacking a piece of
dry straw.

²⁶ You bring bitter charges
against me,
even for what I did when I
was young.
²⁷ You bind chains on my feet;
you watch every step I take,
and even examine my
footprints.
²⁸ As a result, I crumble like rotten
wood,
like a moth-eaten coat.

14 We are all born weak and
helpless.
All lead the same short,
troubled life.
² We grow and wither as quickly
as flowers;
we disappear like shadows.

³ Will you even look at me, God,
or put me on trial and
judge me?
⁴ Nothing clean can ever come
from anything as unclean as
human beings.
⁵ The length of our lives is decided
beforehand —
the number of months we
will live.
You have settled it, and it can't
be changed.
⁶ Look away from us and leave us
alone;ᵃ
let us enjoy our hard life — if
we can.ᵇ

⁷ There is hope for a tree that has
been cut down;
it can come back to life and
sprout.

*There is hope for a tree that has been cut
down. (14.7)*

⁸ Even though its roots grow old,
and its stump dies in the
ground,

One Hebrew manuscript and leave us alone; *most Hebrew manuscripts* so that we
may rest.   ᵇ let us . . . can; *or* until we finish our day of hard work.
3.27 Job 33.11   **14.1, 2** Ws 2.1; Si 40.1-11; 41.1-4

9   with water it will sprout like a
      young plant.
10 But we die, and that is the end
      of us;
    we die, and where are we
      then?

11 Like rivers that stop running,
      and lakes that go dry,
12   people die, never to rise.
    They will never wake up while
      the sky endures;
      they will never stir from their
      sleep.

13 I wish you would hide me in the
      world of the dead;
    let me be hidden until your
      anger is over,
    and then set a time to
      remember me.
14 If a man dies, can he come back
      to life?
    But I will wait for better times,
      wait till this time of trouble is
      ended.
15 Then you will call, and I will
      answer,
    and you will be pleased with
      me, your creature.
16 Then you will watch every step
      I take,
    but you will not keep track of
      my sins.
17 You will forgive them and put
      them away;
    you will wipe out all the
      wrongs I have done.

18 There comes a time when
      mountains fall
    and solid cliffs are moved
      away.
19 Water will wear down rocks,
    and heavy rain will wash
      away the soil;
    so you destroy our hope for
      life.
20 You overpower us and send us
      away forever;
    our faces are twisted in death.

21 Our children win honor, but we
      never know it,
    nor are we told when they are
      disgraced.
22 We feel only the pain of our own
      bodies
    and the grief of our own
      minds.

The Second Dialogue
(15.1 – 21.34)

15

Eliphaz
1-2 Empty words, Job! Empty words!
3 No one who is wise would talk
      the way you do
    or defend himself with such
      meaningless words.
4 If you had your way, no one
      would fear God;
    no one would pray to him.
5 Your wickedness is evident by
      what you say;
    you are trying to hide behind
      clever words.
6 There is no need for me to
      condemn you;
    you are condemned by every
      word you speak.

7 Do you think you were the first
      person born?
    Were you there when God
      made the mountains?
8 Did you overhear the plans God
      made?
    Does human wisdom belong
      to you alone?
9 There is nothing you know that
      we don't know.
10 We learned our wisdom from
      gray-haired people —
    those born before your father

11 God offers you comfort; why still
      reject it?
    We have spoken for him with
      calm, even words.

¹²But you are excited and glare at
us in anger.
¹³You are angry with God and
denounce him.

¹⁴Can any human being be really
pure?
Can anyone be right
with God?
¹⁵Why, God does not trust even his
angels;
even they are not pure in his
sight.
¹⁶And we drink evil as if it were
water;
yes, we are corrupt; we are
worthless.

¹⁷Now listen, Job, to what I know.
¹⁸Those who are wise have taught
me truths
which they learned from their
ancestors,
and they kept no secrets
hidden.
¹⁹Their land was free from
foreigners;
there was no one to lead them
away from God.

²⁰The wicked who oppress others
will be in torment as long as
they live.
²¹Voices of terror will scream in
their ears,
and robbers attack when they
think they are safe.
²²They have no hope of escaping
from darkness,
for somewhere a sword is
waiting to kill them,
²³   and vultures*c* are waiting*d* to
eat their corpses.
They know their future is dark;

²⁴   disaster, like a powerful king,
is waiting to attack them.

²⁵That is the fate of those
who shake their fists at God
and defy the Almighty.
²⁶⁻²⁷They are proud and rebellious;
they stubbornly hold up their
shields
and rush to fight against God.

²⁸They are the ones who captured
cities
and seized houses whose
owners had fled,
but war will destroy those
cities and houses.
²⁹They will not remain rich for
long;
nothing they own will last.
Even their shadows*e* will
vanish,
³⁰   and they will not escape from
darkness.
They will be like trees
whose branches are burned
by fire,
whose blossoms*f* are blown
away by the wind.
³¹If they are foolish enough to
trust in evil,
then evil will be their reward.
³²Before their time is up they will
wither,*g*
wither like a branch and
never be green again.
³³They will be like vines that lose
their unripe grapes;
like olive trees that drop their
blossoms.
³⁴There will be no descendants for
godless people,
and fire will destroy the homes
built by bribery.
³⁵These are the ones who plan
trouble and do evil;

c One ancient translation vultures; *Hebrew* where is he?   *d One ancient translation*
are waiting; *Hebrew* he wanders.   *e One ancient translation* shadows; *Hebrew*
unclear.   *f One ancient translation* blossoms; *Hebrew* mouth.   *g Some ancient*
translations wither; *Hebrew* be filled.

15.14-16 Job 25.4-6

their hearts are always full of
deceit.

16

Job

1-2 I have heard words like that
before;
the comfort you give is only
torment.

"The comfort you give is only torment." (16.1)

3 Are you going to keep on talking
forever?
Do you always have to have
the last word?
4 If you were in my place and I in
yours,
I could say everything you are
saying.
I could shake my head wisely
and drown you with a flood of
words.
5 I could strengthen you with
advice
and keep talking to
comfort you.

6 But nothing I say helps,
and being silent does not calm
my pain.
7 You have worn me out, God;

you have let my family be
killed.
8 You have seized me; you are
my enemy.
I am skin and bones,
and people take that as proof
of my guilt.[h]

9 In anger God tears me limb from
limb;
he glares at me with hate.
10 People sneer at me;
they crowd around me and
slap my face.
11 God has handed me over to evil
people.
12 I was living in peace,
but God took me by the throat
and battered me and
crushed me.
God uses me for target practice
13 and shoots arrows at me from
every side —
arrows that pierce and
wound me;
and even then he shows no
pity.
14 He wounds me again and again;
he attacks like a soldier gone
mad with hate.

15 I mourn and wear clothes made
of sackcloth,
and I sit here in the dust
defeated.
16 I have cried until my face is red,
and my eyes are swollen and
circled with shadows,
17 but I am not guilty of any
violence,
and my prayer to God is
sincere.

18 O Earth, don't hide the wrongs
done to me!
Don't let my call for justice be
silenced!

h Verses 7-8 in Hebrew are unclear.

¹⁹There is someone in heaven
    to stand up for me and take
    my side.
²⁰My friends scorn me;
    my eyes pour out tears to God.
²¹I want someone to plead with
    God for me,
    as one pleads for a friend.
²²My years are passing now,
    and I walk the road of no
    return.

17 ¹The end of my life is near. I
    can hardly breathe;
    there is nothing left for me
    but the grave.
²I watch how bitterly everyone
    mocks me.
³I am being honest, God. Accept
    my word.
    There is no one else to
    support what I say.
⁴You have closed their minds to
    reason;
    don't let them triumph over
    me now.
⁵In the old proverb someone
    betrays his friends for
    money,
    and his children suffer for it. ⁱ
⁶And now people use this proverb
    against me;
    they come and spit in my
    face.
⁷My grief has almost made me
    blind;
    my arms and legs are as thin
    as shadows.
⁸Those who claim to be honest
    are shocked,
    and they all condemn me as
    godless.
⁹Those who claim to be
    respectable
    are more and more convinced
    they are right.
¹⁰But if all of them came and stood
    before me,

I would not find even one of
    them wise.
¹¹My days have passed; my plans
    have failed;
    my hope is gone.
¹²But my friends say night is
    daylight;
    they say that light is near,
    but I know I remain in
    darkness.
¹³My only hope is the world of the
    dead,
    where I will lie down to sleep
    in the dark.
¹⁴I will call the grave my father,
    and the worms that eat me
    I will call my mother and my
    sisters.
¹⁵Where is there any hope for me?
    Who sees any?
¹⁶Hope will not go with me ʲ
    when I go down to the world
    of the dead.

18
Bildad
¹⁻²Job, can't people like you ever be
    quiet?
    If you stopped to listen, we
    could talk to you.
³What makes you think we are as
    stupid as cattle?
⁴You are only hurting yourself
    with your anger.
    Will the earth be deserted
    because you are angry?
    Will God move mountains to
    satisfy you?

⁵The light of the wicked will still
    be put out;
    its flame will never burn
    again.
⁶The lamp in their tents will be
    darkened.

someone . . . suffer for it; *or* someone entertains his friends while his children go
ungry.   *ʲ One ancient translation* with me; *Hebrew unclear.*
16.19 Job 19.25   **18.5, 6** Job 21.17

7 Their steps were firm, but now
  they stumble;
    they fall — victims of their own
    advice.

8 They walk into a net, and their
  feet are caught;

9   a trap catches their heels and
    holds them.

10 On the ground a snare is hidden;
   a trap has been set in their
   path.

11 All around them terror is
   waiting;
     it follows them at every step.

12 They used to be rich, but now
   they go hungry;
     disaster stands and waits at
     their side.

13 A deadly disease spreads over
   their bodies
     and causes their arms and
     legs to rot.

14 They are torn from the tents
   where they lived secure,
     and are dragged off to face
     King Death.

15 Now anyone may live in their
   tents — k
     after sulfur is sprinkled to
     disinfect them!l

16 Their roots and branches are
   withered and dry.

17 Their fame is ended at home and
   abroad;
     no one remembers them any
     more.

18 They will be driven out of the
   land of the living,
     driven from light into
     darkness.

19 They have no descendants, no
   survivors.

20 From east to west, all who hear
   of their fate
     shudder and tremble with
     fear.

21 That is the fate of evil people,
   the fate of those who care
   nothing for God.

19
Job

1-2 Why do you keep tormenting me
   with words?

3 Time after time you insult me
  and show no shame for the
  way you abuse me.

4 Even if I have done wrong,
  how does that hurt you?

5 You think you are better than
  I am,
    and regard my troubles as
    proof of my guilt.

6 Can't you see it is God who has
  done this?
    He has set a trap to catch me.

7 I protest his violence,
  but no one is listening;
    no one hears my cry for
    justice.

8 God has blocked the way, and I
  can't get through;
    he has hidden my path in
    darkness.

9 He has taken away all my wealth
  and destroyed my reputation.

10 He batters me from every side.
   He uproots my hope
     and leaves me to wither
     and die.

11 God is angry and rages
   against me;
     he treats me like his worst
     enemy.

12 He sends his army to attack me;
   they dig trenches and lay
   siege to my tent.

13 God has made my own family
   forsake me;
     I am a stranger to those who
     knew me;

---

k *Now anyone may live in their tents; Hebrew unclear.*   l TO DISINFECT THEM: *Sulfur
was used in the ancient world as a disinfectant and to clean rooms that had contained
corpses.*

14   my relatives and friends
     gone.
15 Those who were guests in my
     house have forgotten me;
   my servant women treat me
     like a stranger and a
     foreigner.
16 When I call a servant, he doesn't
     answer—
   even when I beg him to
     help me.
17 My wife can't stand the smell of
     my breath,
   and my own brothers won't
     come near me.
18 Children despise me and laugh
     when they see me.
19 My closest friends look at me
     with disgust;
   those I loved most have
     turned against me.
20 My skin hangs loose on my
     bones;
   I have barely escaped with my
     life.*m*
21 You are my friends! Take pity
     on me!
   The hand of God has struck
     me down.
22 Why must you persecute me the
     way God does?
   Haven't you tormented me
     enough?

23 How I wish that someone would
     remember my words
   and record them in a book!
24 Or with a chisel carve my words
     in stone
   and write them so that they
     would last forever.*n*
25 But I know there is someone in
     heaven
   who will come at last to my
     defense.

26 Even after my skin is eaten by
     disease,
   while still in this body*o* I will
     see God.*p*
27 I will see him with my own eyes,
   and he will not be a stranger.

   My courage failed because you
     said,
28   "How can we torment him?"
   You looked for some excuse to
     attack me.
29 But now, be afraid of the
     sword—
   the sword that brings God's
     wrath on sin,
   so that you will know there is
     one who judges.*q*

20

Zophar
1-2 Job, you upset me. Now I'm
     impatient to answer.
3   What you have said is an
       insult,
   but I know how to reply
     to you.

4 Surely you know that from
     ancient times,
   when we humans were first
     placed on earth,
5   no wicked people have been
       happy for long.
6 They may grow great, towering
     to the sky,
   so great that their heads reach
     the clouds,
7   but they will be blown away
       like dust.
   Those who used to know them
     will wonder where they have
     gone.
8 They will vanish like a dream,
   like a vision at night,

---

m Verse 20 in Hebrew is unclear.   *n* last forever; *or* be on record.   *o* while still in his body; *or* although not in this body.   *p Verse 26 in Hebrew is unclear.*   *q* one who judges; *or* a judgment.

9.19 Si 6.8   **20.8** Ws 5.14

and never be seen again.
9 The wicked will disappear from
the place where they
used to live;
10 and their children will make
good what they stole
from the poor.
11 Their bodies used to be young
and vigorous,
but soon they will turn to
dust.

12-13 Evil tastes so good to them
that they keep some in their
mouths to enjoy its flavor.
14 But in their stomachs the food
turns bitter,
as bitter as any poison
could be.
15 The wicked vomit up the wealth
they stole;
God takes it back, even out of
their stomachs.
16 What the evil people swallow is
like poison;
it kills them like the bite of a
deadly snake.
17 They will not live to see rivers of
olive oil*r*
or streams that flow with milk
and honey.
18 They will have to give up all they
have worked for;
they will have no chance to
enjoy their wealth,
19 because they oppressed and
neglected the poor
and seized houses someone
else had built.
20 Their greed is never satisfied.
21 When they eat, there is nothing
left over,
but now their prosperity
comes to an end.
22 At the height of their success
all the weight of misery will
crush them.
23 Let them eat all they want!

God will punish them in fury
and anger.
24 When they try to escape from an
iron sword,
a bronze bow will shoot them
down.
25 Arrows stick through their
bodies;
the shiny points drip with
their blood,
and terror grips their hearts.
26 Everything they have saved is
destroyed;
a fire not lit by human hands
burns them and all their
family.
27 Heaven reveals their sin,
and the earth gives testimony
against them.
28 All their wealth will be destroyed
in the flood of God's anger.

29 This is the fate of wicked people,
the fate that God assigns to
them.

21
Job

1-2 Listen to what I am saying;
that is all the comfort I ask
from you.
3 Give me a chance to speak and
then,
when I am through, sneer if
you like.

4 My quarrel is not with mortals;
I have good reason to be
impatient.
5 Look at me. Isn't that enough
to make you stare in shocked
silence?
6 When I think of what has
happened to me,
I am stunned, and I tremble
and shake.

r Probable text They will . . . oil; *Hebrew unclear.*
20.24 Ws 5.17-23

7 Why does God let evil people
live,
    let them grow old and
prosper?
8 They have children and
grandchildren,
    and live to watch them all
grow up.
9 God does not bring disaster on
their homes;
    they never have to live in
terror.
10 Yes, all their cattle breed
    and give birth without trouble.
11 Their children run and play like
lambs
12   and dance to the music of
harps and flutes.
13 They live out their lives in peace
    and quietly die without
suffering.

14 The wicked tell God to leave
them alone;
    they don't want to know his
will for their lives.
15 They think there is no need to
serve God
    nor any advantage in praying
to him.
16 They claim they succeed by their
own strength,
    but their way of thinking I
can't accept.

17 Was a wicked person's light ever
put out?
    Did one of them ever meet
with disaster?
    Did God ever punish the wicked
in anger
18   and blow them away like
straw in the wind,
    or like dust carried away in a
storm?

19 You claim God punishes a child
for the sins of his father.
    No! Let God punish the sinners
themselves;

let him show that he does it
because of *their* sins.
20 Let sinners bear their own
punishment;
    let them feel the wrath of
Almighty God.
21 When our lives are over,
    do we really care whether our
children are happy?
22 Can anyone teach God,
    who judges even those in
high places?

23-24 Some people stay healthy till the
day they die;
    they die happy and at ease,
their bodies well-nourished.
25 Others have no happiness at all;
    they live and die with bitter
hearts.
26 But all alike die and are buried;
    they all are covered with
worms.

27 I know what spiteful thoughts
you have.
28 You ask, "Where are the homes
of great people now,
    those who practiced evil?"

29 Haven't you talked with people
who travel?
    Don't you know the reports
they bring back?
30 On the day God is angry and
punishes,
    it is the wicked who are
always spared.
31 There is no one to accuse the
wicked
    or pay them back for all they
have done.
32 When they are carried to the
graveyard,
    to their well-guarded tombs,
33   thousands join the funeral
procession,
    and even the earth lies gently
on their bodies.

34 And you! You try to comfort me
with nonsense!
Every answer you give is a lie!

The Third Dialogue
(22.1 – 27.23)

22

Eliphaz

1-2 Is there anyone, even the wisest,
who could ever be of use
to God?
3 Does your doing right
benefit God,
or does your being good help
him at all?
4 It is not because you stand in
awe of God
that he reprimands you and
brings you to trial.
5 No, it's because you have sinned
so much;
it's because of all the evil
you do.
6 To make a brother repay you the
money he owed,
you took away his clothes and
left him nothing to wear.
7 You refused water to those who
were tired,
and refused to feed those who
were hungry.
8 You used your power and your
position
to take over the whole land.
9 You not only refused to help
widows,
but you also robbed and
mistreated orphans.
10 So now there are pitfalls all
around you,
and suddenly you are full of
fear.
11 It has grown so dark that you
cannot see,
and a flood overwhelms you.

12 Doesn't God live in the highest
heavens
and look down on the stars,
even though they are high?
13 And yet you ask, "What does God
know?
He is hidden by clouds—how
can he judge us?"
14 You think the thick clouds keep
him from seeing,
as he walks on the dome of
the sky.
15 Are you determined to walk in
the paths
that evil people have always
followed?
16 Even before their time had come
they were washed away by a
flood.
17 These are the ones who
rejected God
and believed that he could do
nothing to them.
18 And yet it was God who made
them prosperous—
I can't understand the
thoughts of the wicked.
19 Good people are glad and the
innocent laugh
when they see the wicked
punished.
20 All that the wicked own is
destroyed,
and fire burns up anything
that is left.

21 Now, Job, make peace with God
and stop treating him like an
enemy;
if you do, then he will
bless you.
22 Accept the teaching he gives;
keep his words in your heart.
23 Yes, you must humbly[s] return
to God
and put an end to all the evil
that is done in your house.

s *One ancient translation* humbly; *Hebrew* be built up.
22.2, 3 Job 35.6-8

24 Throw away your gold;
    dump your finest gold in the
      dry stream bed.
25 Let Almighty God be your gold,
    and let him be silver, piled
      high for you.
26 Then you will always trust
      in God
    and find that he is the source
      of your joy.
27 When you pray, he will
      answer you,
    and you will keep the vows
      you made.
28 You will succeed in all you do,
    and light will shine on your
      path.
29 God brings down the proud[t]
    and saves the humble.
30 He will rescue you if you are
      innocent,[u]
    if what you do is right.[v]

23

Job

1-2 I still rebel and complain
      against God;
    I cannot keep from groaning.
3 How I wish I knew where to
      find him,
    and knew how to go where
      he is.
4 I would state my case before him
    and present all the arguments
      in my favor.
5 I want to know what he
      would say
    and how he would
      answer me.
6 Would God use all his strength
      against me?
    No, he would listen as I
      spoke.
7 I am honest; I could reason
      with God;

he would declare me
    innocent[w] once and for all.

8 I have searched in the East, but
      God is not there;
    I have not found him when I
      searched in the West.
9 God has been at work in the
      North and the South,
    but still I have not seen him.
10 Yet God knows every step I take;
    if he tests me, he will find me
      pure.
11 I follow faithfully the road he
      chooses,
    and never wander to either
      side.
12 I always do what God
      commands;
    I follow his will, not my own
      desires.
13 He never changes. No one can
      oppose him
    or stop him from doing what
      he wants to do.
14 He will fulfill what he has
      planned for me;
    that plan is just one of the
      many he has;
15   I tremble with fear
      before him.
16-17 Almighty God has destroyed my
      courage.
    It is God, not the dark, that
      makes me afraid—
    even though the darkness has
      made me blind.

24

Why doesn't God set a time
      for judging,
    a day of justice for those who
      serve him?
2 People move property lines to get
      more land;

---

[t] *Probable text* proud; *Hebrew unclear.*   [u] *Some ancient translations* innocent;
Hebrew not innocent.   [v] *Verse 30 in Hebrew is unclear.*   [w] he would declare me
innocent; *or* then my rights would be safe.

"I tremble with fear before him." (23.15)

they steal sheep and put them
    with their own flocks.
³They take donkeys that belong to
    orphans,
    and keep a widow's ox till she
    pays her debts.
⁴They prevent the poor from
    getting their rights
    and force the needy to run
    and hide.

⁵So the poor, like wild donkeys,
    search for food in the dry
    wilderness;
    nowhere else can they find
    food for their children.
⁶They have to harvest fields they
    don't own,ˣ
    and gather grapes in
    vineyards of the wicked.
⁷At night they sleep with nothing
    to cover them,
    nothing to keep them from
    the cold.
⁸They are drenched by the rain
    that falls on the mountains,
    and they huddle beside the
    rocks for shelter.

⁹Evil people make slaves of
    fatherless infants
    and take the children of the
    poor in payment for debts.
¹⁰But the poor must go out with no
    clothes to protect them;
    they must go hungry while
    harvesting wheat.
¹¹They press olives for oil, and
    grapes for wine,
    but they themselves are
    thirsty.
¹²In the cities the wounded and
    dying cry out,
    but God ignores their prayers.

¹³There are those who reject the
    light;
    they don't understand it or go
    where it leads.
¹⁴At dawn the murderer gets up
    and goes out to kill the poor,
    and at night he steals.
¹⁵The adulterer waits for twilight
    to come;
    he covers his face so that no
    one can see him.
¹⁶At night thieves break into
    houses,
    but by day they hide and
    avoid the light.
¹⁷They fear the light of day,
    but darkness holds no terror
    for them.

[Zophar]ʸ
¹⁸The wicked are swept away by
    floods,
    and the land they own is
    under God's curse;
    they no longer go to work in
    their vineyards.
¹⁹As snow vanishes in heat and
    drought,
    so sinners vanish from the
    land of the living.

ˣ FIELDS THEY DON'T OWN: *Having been cheated out of their own land, the poor are forced to work for others for very small pay.* ʸ Zophar *is not named in the text, but this speech is usually assigned to him.*

20 Not even their mothers
remember them now;
they are eaten by worms and
destroyed like fallen trees.
21 That happens because they
mistreated widows
and showed no kindness to
childless women.
22 God, in his strength, destroys the
mighty;
God acts — and the
wicked die.
23 God may let them live secure,
but keeps an eye on them all
the time.
24 For a while the wicked prosper,
but then they wither like
weeds,
like stalks of grain that have
been cut down.
25 Can anyone deny that this is so?
Can anyone prove that my words
are not true?

25

Bildad

1-2 God is powerful; all must stand
in awe of him;
he keeps his heavenly
kingdom in peace.
3 Can anyone count the angels
who serve him?
Is there any place where God's
light does not shine?
4 Can anyone be righteous or pure
in God's sight?
5 In his eyes even the moon is not
bright,
or the stars pure.
6 Then what about a human
being, that worm,
that insect?
What is a human life worth in
God's eyes?

26

Job

1-2 What a big help you are to me —
poor, weak man that I am!
3 You give such good advice
and share your knowledge
with a fool like me!
4 Who do you think will hear all
your words?
Who inspired you to speak
like this?

*[Bildad]*z

5 The spirits of the dead tremble
in the waters under the earth.
6 The world of the dead lies open
to God;
no covering shields it from his
sight.
7 God stretched out the
northern sky
and hung the earth in empty
space.
8 It is God who fills the clouds
with water
and keeps them from bursting
with the weight.
9 He hides the full moon behind a
cloud.
10 He divided light from darkness
by a circle drawn on the face
of the sea.
11 When he threatens the pillars
that hold up the sky,
they shake and tremble with
fear.
12 It is his strength that conquered
the sea;a
by his skill he destroyed the
monster Rahab.b
13 It is his breath that made the sky
clear,
and his hand that killed the
escaping monster.c
14 But these are only hints of his
power,

z Bildad *is not named in the text, but this speech is usually assigned to him.*
a CONQUERED THE SEA: *A reference to an ancient story in which the sea fought against*
God.   b RAHAB: *See 9.13.*   c ESCAPING MONSTER: *See 9.8.*

only the whispers that we
have heard.
Who can know how truly great
God is?

27
Job

1-2 I swear by the living
Almighty God,
who refuses me justice and
makes my life bitter —
3 as long as God gives me
breath,
4 my lips will never say
anything evil,
my tongue will never tell a lie.
5 I will never say that you men are
right;
I will insist on my innocence
to my dying day.
6 I will never give up my claim to
be right;
my conscience is clear.

7 May all who oppose me and fight
against me
be punished like the wicked
and the unrighteous.
8 What hope is there for the
godless
in the hour when God
demands their life?
9 When trouble comes, will God
hear their cries?
10 They should have desired the joy
he gives;
they should have constantly
prayed to him.

11 Let me teach you how great is
God's power,
and explain what Almighty
God has planned.
12 But no, after all, you have seen
for yourselves;

so why do you talk such
nonsense?

[Zophar]d

13 This is how Almighty God
punishes wicked, violent
people.
14 They may have many sons,
but all will be killed in war;
their children never have
enough to eat.
15 Those who survive will die from
disease,
and even their widows will
not mourn their death.
16 The wicked may have too much
silver to count
and more clothes than anyone
needs,
17 but some good person will wear
the clothes,
and someone honest will get
the silver.
18 The wicked build houses like a
spider's web[e]
or like the hut of a slave
guarding the fields.
19 One last time[f] they will lie
down rich,
and when they wake up, they
will find their wealth gone.
20 Terror will strike like a sudden
flood;
a wind in the night will blow
them away;
21 the east wind will sweep them
from their homes;
22 it will blow down on them
without pity
while they try their best to
escape.
23 The wind howls at them as
they run,
frightening them with
destructive power.

---

d *Zophar* is not named in the text, but this speech is usually assigned to him.
e *Some ancient translations* spider's web; *Hebrew* moth *or* bird's nest.   f *Some
ancient translations* One last time; *Hebrew* They will not be gathered.

In Praise of Wisdom [g]

28 There are mines where silver
is dug;
There are places where gold is
refined.
2 We dig iron out of the ground
And melt copper out of the
stones.
3 Miners explore the deepest
darkness.
They search the depths of the
earth
And dig for rocks in the
darkness.
4 Far from where anyone lives
Or human feet ever travel,
They dig the shafts of mines.
There they work in loneliness,
Clinging to ropes in the pits.
5 Food grows out of the earth,
But underneath the same earth
All is torn up and crushed.
6 The stones of the earth contain
sapphires,
And its dust contains gold.
7 No hawk sees the roads to the
mines,
And no vulture ever flies over
them.
8 No lion or other fierce beast
Ever travels those lonely roads.

9 Miners dig the hardest rocks,
Dig mountains away at their
base.
10 As they tunnel through the
rocks,
They discover precious stones.
11 They dig to the sources of [h]
rivers
And bring to light what is
hidden.
12 But where can wisdom be
found?
Where can we learn to
understand?

13 Wisdom is not to be found
among mortals;
No one knows its true value.
14 The depths of the oceans and
seas
Say that wisdom is not found
there.
15 It cannot be bought with silver
or gold.
16 The finest gold and jewels
Cannot equal its value.
17 It is worth more than gold,
Than a gold vase or finest glass.
18 The value of wisdom is more
Than coral or crystal or rubies.
19 The finest topaz and the purest
gold
Cannot compare with the value
of wisdom.

20 Where, then, is the source of
wisdom?
Where can we learn to
understand?
21 No living creature can see it,
Not even a bird in flight.
22 Even death and destruction
Admit they have heard only
rumors.

23 God alone knows the way,
Knows the place where wisdom
is found,
24 Because he sees the ends of the
earth,
Sees everything under the sky.
25 When God gave the wind its
power
And determined the size of
the sea;
26 When God decided where the
rain would fall,
And the path that the
thunderclouds travel;
27 It was then he saw wisdom and
tested its worth—
He gave it his approval.

g The Hebrew text does not indicate who is speaking in this chapter. *h Some
ancient translations* dig to the sources of; *Hebrew* bind from trickling.
28.12 Si 1.6; Ba 3.15   **28.13** Ba 3.29-31   **28.23** Ba 3.35-37   **28.27** Si 1.9, 19

²⁸God said to us humans,
"To be wise, you must have
reverence for the Lord.
To understand, you must turn
from evil."

Job's Final Statement of His Case

29 Job began speaking again.

Job

²If only my life could once again
be as it was when God
watched over me.
³God was always with me then
and gave me light as I walked
through the darkness.
⁴Those were the days when I was
prosperous,
and the friendship of God
protected my home.
⁵Almighty God was with me then,
and I was surrounded by all
my children.
⁶My cows and goats gave plenty
of milk,
and my olive trees grew in the
rockiest soil.
⁷Whenever the city elders met
and I took my place among
them,
⁸   young men stepped aside as
soon as they saw me,
and old men stood up to show
me respect.
⁹The leaders of the people would
stop talking;
¹⁰   even the most important men
kept silent.

¹¹Everyone who saw me or heard
of me
had good things to say about
what I had done.
¹²When the poor cried out, I
helped them;
I gave help to orphans who
had nowhere to turn.

¹³People who were in deepest
misery praised me,
and I helped widows find
security.
¹⁴I have always acted justly and
fairly.
¹⁵I was eyes for the blind,
and feet for the lame.
¹⁶I was like a father to the poor
and took the side of strangers
in trouble.
¹⁷I destroyed the power of
cruel men
and rescued their victims.

¹⁸I always expected to live a long
life
and to die at home in comfort.
¹⁹I was like a tree whose roots
always have water
and whose branches are wet
with dew.
²⁰Everyone was always
praising me,
and my strength never
failed me.
²¹When I gave advice, people were
silent
and listened carefully to what
I said;
²²   they had nothing to add when
I had finished.
My words sank in like drops of
rain;
²³   everyone welcomed them
just as farmers welcome rain
in spring.
²⁴I smiled on them when they had
lost confidence;
my cheerful face encouraged
them.
²⁵I took charge and made the
decisions;
I led them as a king leads his
troops,
and gave them comfort in
their despair.

28.28 Ps 111.10; Pr 1.7; 9.10

30 But men younger than I am
make fun of me now!
Their fathers have always been
so worthless
that I wouldn't let them help
my dogs guard sheep.
2 They were a bunch of
worn-out men,
too weak to do any work
for me.
3 They were so poor and hungry
that they would gnaw dry
roots —
at night, in wild, desolate
places.
4 They pulled up the plants of the
desert and ate them,
even the tasteless roots of the
broom tree!
5 Everyone drove them away with
shouts,
as if they were shouting at
thieves.
6 They had to live in caves,
in holes dug in the sides of
cliffs.
7 Out in the wilds they howled like
animals
and huddled together under
the bushes.
8 A worthless bunch of nameless
nobodies!
They were driven out of the
land.

9 Now they come and laugh at me;
I am nothing but a joke to
them.
10 They treat me with disgust;
they think they are too good
for me,
and even come and spit in my
face.
11 Because God has made me weak
and helpless,
they turn against me with all
their fury.
12 This mob attacks me head-on;

they send me running; they
prepare their final assault.
13 They cut off my escape and try
to destroy me;
and there is no one to stop[i]
them.
14 They pour through the holes in
my defenses
and come crashing down on
top of me;
15 I am overcome with terror;
my dignity is gone like a puff
of wind,
and my prosperity like a
cloud.

16 Now I am about to die;
there is no relief for my
suffering.
17 At night my bones all ache;
the pain that gnaws me never
stops.
18 God seizes me by my collar
and twists my clothes out of
shape.
19 He throws me down in the mud;
I am no better than dirt.

"He throws me down in the mud." (30.19)

20 I call to you, O God, but you
never answer;
and when I pray, you pay no
attention.

---

i Probable text stop; *Hebrew* help.

²¹ You are treating me cruelly;
   you persecute me with all
      your power.
²² You let the wind blow me away;
   you toss me about in a raging
      storm.
²³ I know you are taking me off to
      my death,
   to the fate in store for
      everyone.
²⁴ Why do you attack a ruined man,
   one who can do nothing but
      beg for pity?ʲ
²⁵ Didn't I weep with people in
      trouble
   and feel sorry for those in
      need?
²⁶ I hoped for happiness and light,
   but trouble and darkness
      came instead.
²⁷ I am torn apart by worry and
      pain;
   I have had day after day of
      suffering.
²⁸ I go about in gloom, without any
      sunshine;
   I stand up in public and plead
      for help.
²⁹ My voice is as sad and lonely
   as the cries of a jackal or an
      ostrich.
³⁰ My skin has turned dark; I am
      burning with fever.
³¹ Where once I heard joyful
      music,
   now I hear only mourning
      and weeping.

31 I have made a solemn
         promise
   never to look with lust at a
      woman.

² What does Almighty God do
      to us?
   How does he repay human
      deeds?

³ He sends disaster and ruin
   to those who do wrong.
⁴ God knows everything I do;
   he sees every step I take.
⁵ I swear I have never acted
      wickedly
   and never tried to deceive
      others.
⁶ Let God weigh me on honest
      scales,
   and he will see how innocent
      I am.
⁷ If I have turned from the right
      path
   or let myself be attracted to
      evil,
   if my hands are stained
      with sin,
⁸ then let my crops be
      destroyed,
   or let others eat the food I
      grow.
⁹ If I have been attracted to my
      neighbor's wife,
   and waited, hidden, outside
      her door,
¹⁰ then let my wife cook another
      man's food
   and sleep in another
      man's bed.
¹¹ Such wickedness should be
      punished by death.
¹² It would be like a destructive,
      hellish fire,
   consuming everything I have.
¹³ When any of my servants
      complained against me,
   I would listen and treat them
      fairly.
¹⁴ If I did not, how could I then
      face God?
   What could I say when God
      came to judge me?
¹⁵ The same God who created me
   created my servants also.

ʲ *Verse 24 in Hebrew is unclear.*

¹⁶I have never refused to help the
poor;
never have I let widows live
in despair
¹⁷   or let orphans go hungry
while I ate.
¹⁸All my life I have taken care of
them.ᵏ

¹⁹When I found someone in need,
too poor to buy clothes,
²⁰   I would give him clothing
made of wool
that had come from my own
flock of sheep.
Then he would praise me with
all his heart.

²¹If I have ever cheated an orphan,
knowing I could win in court,
²²   then may my arms be broken;
may they be torn from my
shoulders.
²³Because I fear God's
punishment,
I could never do such a thing.

²⁴I have never trusted in riches
²⁵   or taken pride in my wealth.
²⁶I have never worshiped the sun
in its brightness
or the moon in all its beauty.
²⁷I have not been led astray to
honor them
by kissing my hand in
reverence to them.
²⁸Such a sin should be punished
by death;
it denies Almighty God.

²⁹I have never been glad when my
enemies suffered,
or pleased when they met
with disaster;
³⁰   I never sinned by praying for
their death.
³¹All those who work for me know

that I have always welcomed
strangers.
³²I invited travelers into my home
and never let them sleep in
the streets.

³³Others try to hide their sins,
but I have never concealed
mine.
³⁴I have never feared what people
would say;
I have never kept quiet or
stayed indoors
because I feared their scorn.

³⁵Will no one listen to what I am
saying?
I swear that every word is true.
Let Almighty God answer me.

If the charges my opponent
brings against me
were written down so that I
could see them,
³⁶I would wear them proudly on
my shoulder
and place them on my head
like a crown.
³⁷I would tell God everything I
have done,
and hold my head high in his
presence.

³⁸If I have stolen the land I farm
and taken it from its rightful
owners —
³⁹   if I have eaten the food that
grew there
but let the farmers that grew
it starve —
⁴⁰   then instead of wheat and
barley,
may weeds and thistles grow.

The words of Job are ended.

ᵏ All my life . . . them; *Hebrew unclear.*
31.16-18 Tb 4.7-11, 16   **31.24** Si 31.5-10

The Speeches of Elihu
(32.1 – 37.24)

32 Because Job was convinced of his own innocence, the three men gave up trying to answer him. ²But a bystander named Elihu could not control his anger any longer, because Job was justifying himself and blaming God. (Elihu was the son of Barakel, a descendant of Buz, and belonged to the clan of Ram.) ³He was also angry with Job's three friends. They could not find any way to answer Job, and this made it appear that God was in the wrong. ⁴Because Elihu was the youngest one there, he had waited until everyone finished speaking. ⁵When he saw that the three men could not answer Job, he was angry ⁶and began to speak.

Elihu

I am young, and you are old,
    so I was afraid to tell you
        what I think.
⁷I told myself that you ought to
        speak,
    that you older men should
        share your wisdom.
⁸But it is the spirit of
    Almighty God
    that comes to us and gives us
        wisdom.
⁹It is not growing old that makes
        us wise
    or helps us to know what is
        right.
¹⁰So now I want you to listen
        to me;
    let me tell you what I think.

¹¹I listened patiently while you
        were speaking
    and waited while you
        searched for wise phrases.
¹²I paid close attention and heard
        you fail;
    you have not disproved what
        Job has said.

¹³How can you claim you have
        discovered wisdom?
    God must answer Job, for you
        have failed.
¹⁴Job was speaking to you, not
        to me,
    but I would never answer the
        way you did.

¹⁵Words have failed them, Job;
    they have no answer for you.
¹⁶Shall I go on waiting when they
        are silent?
    They stand there with nothing
        more to say.
¹⁷No, I will give my own
        answer now
    and tell you what I think.
¹⁸I can hardly wait to speak.
    I can't hold back the words.
¹⁹If I don't get a chance to speak,
    I will burst like a wineskin
        full of new wine.
²⁰I can't stand it; I have to speak.
²¹I will not take sides in this
        debate;
    I am not going to flatter
        anyone.
²²I don't know how to flatter,
    and God would quickly punish
        me if I did.

33 And now, Job, listen carefully to all that I have
        to say.
²I am ready to say what's on my
        mind.
³All my words are sincere,
    and I am speaking the truth.
⁴God's spirit made me and gave
        me life.

⁵Answer me if you can. Prepare
        your arguments.
⁶You and I are the same in God's
        sight,
    both of us were formed from
        clay.
⁷So you have no reason to
        fear me;
    I will not overpower you.

8 Now this is what I heard
   you say:
9 "I am not guilty; I have done
   nothing wrong.
   I am innocent and free
   from sin.
10 But God finds excuses for
   attacking me
   and treats me like an enemy.
11 He binds chains on my feet;
   he watches every move I
   make."

12 But I tell you, Job, you are
   wrong.
   God is greater than any
   human being.
13 Why do you accuse God
   of never answering our
   complaints?
14 Although God speaks again and
   again,
   no one pays attention to what
   he says.
15 At night when people are asleep,
   God speaks in dreams and
   visions.
16 He makes them listen to what he
   says,
   and they are frightened at his
   warnings.
17 God speaks to make them stop
   their sinning
   and to save them from
   becoming proud.
18 He will not let them be
   destroyed;
   he saves them from death
   itself.
19 God corrects us by sending
   sickness
   and filling our bodies with
   pain.
20 Those who are sick lose their
   appetites,
   and even the finest food looks
   revolting.
21 Their bodies waste away to
   nothing;

you can see all their bones;
22   they are about to go to the
       world of the dead.

23 Perhaps an angel may come to
   their aid —
   one of God's thousands of
   angels,
   who remind us of our duty.
24 In mercy the angel will say,
   "Release them!
   They are not to go down to
   the world of the dead.
   Here is the ransom to set
   them free."
25 Their bodies will grow young and
   strong again;
26   when they pray, God will
       answer;
   they will worship God
   with joy;
   God will set things right for
   them again.
27 Each one will say in public, "I
   have sinned.
   I have not done right, but God
   spared me.
28 He kept me from going to the
   world of the dead,
   and I am still alive."

29 God does all this again and
   again;
30   each one saves a person's life,
       and gives him the joy of
       living.

31 Now, Job, listen to what I am
   saying;
   be quiet and let me speak.
32 But if you have something to say,
   let me hear it;
   I would gladly admit you are
   in the right.
33 But if not, be quiet and listen
   to me,
   and I will teach you how to be
   wise.

33.11 Job 13.27   **33.15** Job 4.13

34

¹⁻²You men are so wise, so
clever;
listen now to what I am
saying.
³You know good food when you
taste it,
but not wise words when you
hear them.
⁴It is up to us to decide the case.
⁵Job claims that he is innocent,
that God refuses to give him
justice.
⁶He asks, "How could I lie and
say I am wrong?
I am fatally wounded, but I
am sinless."

⁷Have you ever seen anyone like
this man Job?
He never shows respect
for God.
⁸He likes the company of evil
people
and goes around with sinners.
⁹He says that it never does any
good
to try to follow God's will.

¹⁰Listen to me, you men who
understand!
Will Almighty God do what is
wrong?
¹¹He rewards people for what
they do
and treats them as they
deserve.
¹²Almighty God does not do evil;
he is never unjust to anyone.
¹³Did God get his power from
someone else?
Did someone put him in
charge of the world?
¹⁴If God took back the breath of
life,
¹⁵ then everyone living
would die
and turn into dust again.

¹⁶Now listen to me, if you are
wise.
¹⁷Are you condemning the
righteous God?
Do you think that *he* hates
justice?
¹⁸God condemns kings and rulers
when they are worthless or
wicked.
¹⁹He does not take the side of
rulers
nor favor the rich over the
poor,
for he created everyone.
²⁰We may suddenly die at night.
God strikes us down and we
perish;
he kills the mighty with no
effort at all.
²¹He watches every step we take.
²²There is no darkness dark
enough
to hide a sinner from God.
²³God does not need to set a time*l*
for us to go and be judged
by him.
²⁴He does not need an
investigation
to remove leaders and replace
them with others.
²⁵Because he knows what they do;
he overthrows them and
crushes them by night.
²⁶He punishes sinners where all
can see it,
²⁷ because they have stopped
following him
and ignored all his
commands.
²⁸They forced the poor to cry out
to God,
and he heard their calls for
help.

²⁹If God decided to do nothing
at all,
no one could criticize him.

---

l Probable text a time; *Hebrew* yet.
34.11 Ps 62.12

If he hid his face, we would be
    helpless.
30 There would be nothing that
    nations could do
    to keep godless oppressors
    from ruling them.

31 Job, have you confessed your
    sins to God
    and promised not to sin
    again?
32 Have you asked God to show you
    your faults,
    and have you agreed to stop
    doing evil?
33 Since you object to what God
    does,
    can you expect him to do
    what you want?
    The decision is yours, not mine;
    tell us now what you think.

34 Any sensible person will surely
    agree;
    and the wise who hear me
    will say
35   that Job is speaking from
    ignorance
    and that nothing he says
    makes sense.
36 Think through everything that
    Job says;
    you will see that he talks like
    an evil man.
37 To his sins he adds rebellion;
    in front of us all he
    mocks God.

35 1-2 It is not right, Job, for you
    to say
    that you are innocent in God's
    sight,
3 or to ask God, "How does my sin
    affect you?
    What have I gained by not
    sinning?"
4 I am going to answer you and
    your friends too.

5 Look at the sky! See how high
    the clouds are!
6 If you sin, that does no harm
    to God.
    If you do wrong many times,
    does that affect him?
7 Do you help God by being so
    righteous?
    There is nothing God needs
    from you.
8 Others suffer from your sins,
    and the good you do helps
    them.

9 When people are oppressed, they
    groan;
    they cry for someone to save
    them.
10 But they don't turn to God, their
    Creator,
    who gives them hope in their
    darkest hours.
11 They don't turn to God, who
    makes us wise,
    wiser than any animal or bird.
12 They cry for help, but God
    doesn't answer,
    for they are proud and evil.
13 It is useless for them to cry out;
    Almighty God does not see or
    hear them.

14 Job, you say you can't see God;
    but wait patiently — your case
    is before him.
15 You think that God does not
    punish,
    that he pays little attention
    to sin.
16 It is useless for you to go on
    talking;
    it is clear you don't know
    what you are saying.

36 1-2 Be patient and listen a
    little longer
    to what I am saying on God's
    behalf.
3 My knowledge is wide; I will use
    what I know

to show that God, my Creator,
is just.
⁴ Nothing I say to you is false;
you see before you a truly
wise man.

⁵ How strong God is! He despises
no one;
there is nothing he doesn't
understand.
⁶ He does not let sinners live on,
and he always treats the poor
with justice.
⁷ He protects those who are
righteous;
he allows them to rule like
kings
and lets them be honored
forever.
⁸ But if people are bound in
chains,
suffering for what they have
done,
⁹ God shows them their sins
and their pride.
¹⁰ He makes them listen to his
warning
to turn away from evil.
¹¹ If they obey God and serve him,
they live out their lives in
peace and prosperity.
¹² But if not, they will die in
ignorance
and cross the stream into the
world of the dead.

¹³ Those who are godless keep on
being angry,
and even when punished,
they don't pray for help.
¹⁴ They die while they are still
young,
worn out by a life of disgrace.
¹⁵ But God teaches people through
suffering
and uses distress to open their
eyes.
¹⁶ God brought you out of trouble,

and let you enjoy security;
your table was piled high with
food.
¹⁷ But now you are being punished
as you deserve.
¹⁸ Be careful not to let bribes
deceive you,
or riches lead you astray.
¹⁹ It will do you no good to cry out
for help;
all your strength can't help
you now.
²⁰ Don't wish for night to come,
the time when nations will
perish.
²¹ Be careful not to turn to evil;
your suffering was sent to
keep you from it.

²² Remember how great is God's
power;
he is the greatest teacher
of all.
²³ No one can tell God what to do
or accuse him of doing evil.
²⁴ He has always been praised for
what he does;
you also must praise him.
²⁵ Everyone has seen what he has
done;
but we can only watch from a
distance.ᵐ
²⁶ We cannot fully know his
greatness
or count the number of his
years.

²⁷ It is God who takes water from
the earth
and turns it into drops of rain.
²⁸ He lets the rain pour from the
clouds
in showers for all human
beings.
²⁹ No one knows how the clouds
move
or how the thunder roars
through the sky, where God
dwells.

ᵐ but we can only watch from a distance; *or* no one understands it all.

Everyone has seen what he has done. (36.25)

³⁰He sends lightning through all
the sky,
but the depths of the sea
remain dark.
³¹This is how he feeds[n] the people
and provides an abundance
of food.
³²He seizes the lightning with his
hands
and commands it to hit the
mark.
³³Thunder announces the
approaching storm,
and the cattle know it is
coming.

37 ¹The storm makes my heart
beat wildly.
²Listen, all of you, to the voice
of God,
to the thunder that comes
from his mouth.
³He sends the lightning across
the sky,

from one end of the earth to
the other.
⁴Then the roar of his voice is
heard,
the majestic sound of
thunder,
and all the while the lightning
flashes.
⁵At God's command amazing
things happen,
wonderful things that we
can't understand.
⁶He commands snow to fall on
the earth,
and sends torrents of
drenching rain.
⁷He brings our work to a stop;
he shows us what he
can do.[o]
⁸The wild animals go to their
dens.
⁹The storm winds come from the
south,

---

[n] *Probable text* feeds; *Hebrew* judges.
Hebrew this to those whom he has made.

[o] *One ancient translation* us what he can do;

and the biting cold from the
north.

¹⁰ The breath of God freezes the
waters,
and turns them to solid ice.

¹¹ Lightning flashes from the
clouds,ᵖ

¹² as they move at God's will.
They do all that God commands,
everywhere throughout the
world.

¹³ God sends rain to water the
earth;
he may send it to punish us,
or to show us his favor.

¹⁴ Pause a moment, Job, and listen;
consider the wonderful things
God does.

¹⁵ Do you know how God gives the
command
and makes lightning flash
from the clouds?

¹⁶ Do you know how clouds float in
the sky,
the work of God's amazing
skill?

¹⁷ No, you can only suffer in the
heat
when the south wind
oppresses the land.

¹⁸ Can you help God stretch out
the sky
and make it as hard as
polished metal?

¹⁹ Teach us what to say to God;
our minds are blank; we have
nothing to say.

²⁰ I won't ask to speak with God;
why should I give him a
chance to destroy me?

²¹ And now the light in the sky is
dazzling,
too bright for us to look at it;
and the sky has been swept
clean by the wind.

²² A golden glow is seen in the
north,
and the glory of God fills us
with awe.

²³ God's power is so great that we
cannot come near him;
he is righteous and just in his
dealings with us.

²⁴ No wonder, then, that everyone
is awed by him,
and that he ignores those who
claim to be wise.

The LORD Answers Job

38 Then out of the storm the LORD
spoke to Job.

The LORD

² Who are you to question my
wisdom
with your ignorant, empty
words?

³ Now stand up straight
and answer the questions I
ask you.

⁴ Were you there when I made the
world?
If you know so much, tell me
about it.

⁵ Who decided how large it
would be?
Who stretched the measuring
line over it?
Do you know all the answers?

⁶ What holds up the pillars that
support the earth?
Who laid the cornerstone of
the world?

⁷ In the dawn of that day the stars
sang together,
and the heavenly beings�q
shouted for joy.

⁸ Who closed the gates to hold
back the seaʳ

ᵖ *Verse 11 in Hebrew is unclear.*   q HEAVENLY BEINGS: *See 1.6.*   ʳ TO HOLD BACK
THE SEA: *See 26.12.*
38.7 Ba 3.34   **38.8-11** Jr 5.22

when it burst from the womb
of the earth?
⁹ It was I who covered the sea
with clouds
and wrapped it in darkness.
¹⁰ I marked a boundary for the sea
and kept it behind bolted
gates.
¹¹ I told it, "So far and no farther!
Here your powerful waves
must stop."
¹² Job, have you ever in all your life
commanded a day to dawn?
¹³ Have you ordered the dawn to
seize the earth
and shake the wicked from
their hiding places?
¹⁴ Daylight makes the hills and
valleys stand out
like the folds of a garment,
clear as the imprint of a seal
on clay.
¹⁵ The light of day is too bright for
the wicked
and restrains them from doing
violence.

¹⁶ Have you been to the springs in
the depths of the sea?
Have you walked on the floor
of the ocean?
¹⁷ Has anyone ever shown you the
gates
that guard the dark world of
the dead?
¹⁸ Have you any idea how big the
world is?
Answer me if you know.

¹⁹ Do you know where the light
comes from
or what the source of
darkness is?
²⁰ Can you show them how far
to go,
or send them back again?
²¹ I am sure you can, because
you're so old

and were there when the
world was made!

²² Have you ever visited the
storerooms,
where I keep the snow and
the hail?
²³ I keep them ready for times of
trouble,
for days of battle and war.
²⁴ Have you been to the place
where the sun comes up,
or the place from which the
east wind blows?

²⁵ Who dug a channel for the
pouring rain
and cleared the way for the
thunderstorm?
²⁶ Who makes rain fall where no
one lives?
²⁷ Who waters the dry and thirsty
land,
so that grass springs up?
²⁸ Does either the rain or the dew
have a father?
²⁹ Who is the mother of the ice and
the frost,
30 which turn the waters to
stone
and freeze the face of the sea?

³¹ Can you tie the Pleiades together
or loosen the bonds that hold
Orion?
³² Can you guide the stars season
by season
and direct the Big and the
Little Dipper?
³³ Do you know the laws that
govern the skies,
and can you make them apply
to the earth?

³⁴ Can you shout orders to the
clouds
and make them drench you
with rain?

38.31 Job 9.9; Am 5.8

35 And if you command the
　　lightning to flash,
　　will it come to you and say,
　　"At your service"?
36 Who tells the ibis[s] when the
　　Nile will flood,
　　or who tells the rooster that
　　rain will fall?[t]
37 Who is wise enough to count the
　　clouds
　　and tilt them over to pour out
　　the rain,
38　　rain that hardens the dust
　　into lumps?

39 Do you find food for lions to eat,
　　and satisfy hungry young
　　lions
40　　when they hide in their caves,
　　or lie in wait in their dens?
41 Who is it that feeds the ravens
　　when they wander about
　　hungry,
　　when their young cry to me
　　for food?

39 1 Do you know when
　　　　mountain goats are
　　　　born?
　　Have you watched wild deer
　　give birth?
2 Do you know how long they
　　carry their young?
　　Do you know the time for
　　their birth?
3 Do you know when they will
　　crouch down
　　and bring their young into the
　　world?
4 In the wilds their young grow
　　strong;
　　they go away and don't come
　　back.

5 Who gave the wild donkeys their
　　freedom?
　　Who turned them loose and
　　let them roam?

6 I gave them the desert to be
　　their home,
　　and let them live on the salt
　　plains.
7 They keep far away from the
　　noisy cities,
　　and no one can tame them
　　and make them work.
8 The mountains are the pastures
　　where they feed,
　　where they search for
　　anything green to eat.

9 Will a wild ox work for you?
　　Is he willing to spend the
　　night in your stable?
10 Can you hold one with a rope
　　and make him plow?
　　Or make him pull a harrow in
　　your fields?
11 Can you rely on his great
　　strength
　　and expect him to do your
　　heavy work?
12 Do you expect him to bring in
　　your harvest
　　and gather the grain from
　　your threshing place?

13 How fast the wings of an ostrich
　　beat!
　　But no ostrich can fly like a
　　stork.[u]
14 The ostrich leaves her eggs on
　　the ground
　　for the heat in the soil to
　　warm them.
15 She is unaware that a foot may
　　crush them
　　or a wild animal break them.
16 She acts as if the eggs were not
　　hers,
　　and is unconcerned that her
　　efforts were wasted.
17 It was I who made her foolish
　　and did not give her wisdom.
18 But when she begins to run,[v]

[s] IBIS: *A bird in ancient Egypt that was believed to announce the flooding of the Nile
River.*　　[t] *Verse 36 in Hebrew is unclear.*　　[u] *Verse 13 in Hebrew is unclear.*
[v] *Probable text* run; *Hebrew unclear.*

The ostrich . . . the horses . . . an eagle . . . the monster . . . (39.14, 24, 27; 40.15)

she can laugh at any horse
and rider.

¹⁹Was it you, Job, who made
horses so strong
and gave them their flowing
manes?
²⁰Did you make them leap like
locusts
and frighten people with their
snorting?
²¹They eagerly paw the ground in
the valley;
they rush into battle with all
their strength.
²²They do not know the meaning
of fear,
and no sword can turn them
back.
²³The weapons which their riders
carry
rattle and flash in the sun.
²⁴Trembling with excitement, the
horses race ahead;
when the trumpet blows, they
can't stand still.
²⁵At each blast of the trumpet they
snort;
they can smell a battle before
they get near,
and they hear the officers
shouting commands.

²⁶Does a hawk learn from you how
to fly
when it spreads its wings
toward the south?

²⁷Does an eagle wait for your
command
to build its nest high in the
mountains?
²⁸It makes its home on the highest
rocks
and makes the sharp peaks its
fortress.
²⁹From there it watches near
and far
for something to kill and eat.
³⁰Around dead bodies the eagles
gather,
and the young eagles drink
the blood.

40 ¹⁻²Job, you challenged
Almighty God;
will you give up now, or will
you answer?

Job

³⁻⁴I spoke foolishly, LORD. What
can I answer?
I will not try to say anything
else.
⁵I have already said more than I
should.

⁶Then out of the storm the LORD
spoke to Job once again.

The LORD

⁷Now stand up straight
and answer my questions.
⁸Are you trying to prove that I am
unjust —

39.30 Mt 24.28; Lk 17.37

to put me in the wrong and
yourself in the right?
9 Are you as strong as I am?
Can your voice thunder as
loud as mine?
10 If so, stand up in your honor
and pride;
clothe yourself with majesty
and glory.
11 Look at those who are proud;
pour out your anger and
humble them.
12 Yes, look at them and bring
them down;
crush the wicked where they
stand.
13 Bury them all in the ground;
bind them in the world of the
dead.
14 Then I will be the first to
praise you
and admit that you won the
victory yourself.

15 Look at the monster Behemoth; w
I created him and I
created you.
He eats grass like a cow,
16   but what strength there is in
his body,
and what power there is in his
muscles!
17 His tail stands up like a cedar,
and the muscles in his legs
are strong.
18 His bones are as strong as
bronze,
and his legs are like iron bars.

19 The most amazing of all my
creatures!
Only his Creator can
defeat him.
20 Grass to feed him grows
on the hills where wild beasts
play. x

21 He lies down under the thorn
bushes,
and hides among the reeds in
the swamp.
22 The thorn bushes and the
willows by the stream
give him shelter in their
shade.
23 He is not afraid of a rushing
river;
he is calm when the Jordan
dashes in his face.
24 Who can blind his eyes and
capture him?
Or who can catch his snout in
a trap?

41 Can you catch Leviathan y
with a fishhook
or tie his tongue down with
a rope?
2 Can you put a rope through his
snout
or put a hook through his
jaws?
3 Will he beg you to let him go?
Will he plead with you for
mercy?
4 Will he make an agreement
with you
and promise to serve you
forever?
5 Will you tie him like a pet bird,
like something to amuse your
servant women?
6 Will fishermen bargain
over him?
Will merchants cut him up
to sell?
7 Can you fill his hide with fishing
spears
or pierce his head with a
harpoon?
8 Touch him once and you'll never
try it again;
you'll never forget the fight!

---

w BEHEMOTH: *Some identify this with the hippopotamus, others with a legendary
creature.*   x *Verse 20 in Hebrew is unclear.*   y LEVIATHAN: *See 3.8.*
41.1 Ps 74.14; 104.26; Is 27.1

9 Anyone who sees Leviathan
　　loses courage and falls to the
　　ground.
10 When he is aroused, he is fierce;
　　no one would dare to stand
　　before him.
11 Who can attack him and still be
　　safe?
　　No one in all the world can
　　do it. z

12 Let me tell you about Leviathan's
　　legs
　　and describe how great and
　　strong he is.
13 No one can tear off his outer
　　coat
　　or pierce the armor a he
　　wears.
14 Who can make him open his
　　jaws,
　　ringed with those terrifying
　　teeth?
15 His back b is made of rows of
　　shields,
　　fastened together and hard as
　　stone.
16 Each one is joined so tight to the
　　next,
　　not even a breath can come
　　between.
17 They all are fastened so firmly
　　together
　　that nothing can ever pull
　　them apart.
18 Light flashes when he sneezes,
　　and his eyes glow like the
　　rising sun.
19 Flames blaze from his mouth,
　　and streams of sparks fly out.
20 Smoke comes pouring out of his
　　nose,
　　like smoke from weeds
　　burning under a pot.
21 His breath starts fires burning;
　　flames leap out of his mouth.
22 His neck is so powerful

that all who meet him are
　　terrified.
23 There is not a weak spot in his
　　skin;
　　it is as hard and unyielding as
　　iron.
24 His stony heart is without fear,
　　as unyielding and hard as a
　　millstone.
25 When he rises up, even the
　　strongest c are frightened;
　　they are helpless with fear.
26 There is no sword that can
　　wound him;
　　no spear or arrow or lance
　　that can harm him.
27 For him iron is as flimsy as
　　straw,
　　and bronze as soft as rotten
　　wood.
28 There is no arrow that can make
　　him run;
　　rocks thrown at him are like
　　bits of straw.
29 To him a club is a piece of straw,
　　and he laughs when men
　　throw spears.
30 The scales on his belly are like
　　jagged pieces of pottery;
　　they tear up the muddy
　　ground like a threshing
　　sledge. d
31 He churns up the sea like boiling
　　water
　　and makes it bubble like a pot
　　of oil.
32 He leaves a shining path
　　behind him
　　and turns the sea to white
　　foam.
33 There is nothing on earth to
　　compare with him;
　　he is a creature that has no
　　fear.
34 He looks down on even the
　　proudest animals;
　　he is king of all wild beasts.

z *Verse 11 in Hebrew is unclear.*　　a *One ancient translation* armor; *Hebrew* bridle.
b *Some ancient translations* back; *Hebrew* pride.　　c strongest; *or* gods.
d THRESHING SLEDGES: *These had sharp pieces of iron or stone fastened beneath them.*

42

Then Job answered the LORD.

Job

2 I know, LORD, that you are
   all-powerful;
   that you can do everything
   you want.
3 You ask how I dare question
   your wisdom
   when I am so very ignorant.
   I talked about things I did not
   understand,
   about marvels too great for me
   to know.
4 You told me to listen while you
   spoke
   and to try to answer your
   questions.
5 In the past I knew only what
   others had told me,
   but now I have seen you with
   my own eyes.
6 So I am ashamed of all I have
   said
   and repent in dust and ashes.

Conclusion

7 After the LORD had finished speaking to Job, he said to Eliphaz, "I am angry with you and your two friends, because you did not speak the truth about me, the way my servant Job did. 8 Now take seven bulls and seven rams to Job and offer them as a sacrifice for yourselves. Job will pray for you, and I will answer his prayer and not disgrace you the way you deserve. You did not speak the truth about me as he did."

9 Eliphaz, Bildad, and Zophar did what the LORD had told them to do, and the LORD answered Job's prayer.

10 Then, after Job had prayed for his three friends, the LORD made him prosperous again and gave him twice as much as he had had before. 11 All Job's brothers and sisters and former friends came to visit him and feasted with him

The LORD made him prosperous again. (42.10)

in his house. They expressed their sympathy and comforted him for all the troubles the LORD had brought on him. Each of them gave him some money and a gold ring.

12 The LORD blessed the last part of Job's life even more than he had blessed the first. Job owned fourteen thousand sheep, six thousand camels, two thousand head of cattle, and one thousand donkeys. 13 He was the father of seven sons and three daughters. 14 He called the oldest daughter Jemimah, the second Keziah, and the youngest Keren Happuch.[e] 15 There were no other women in the whole world as beautiful as Job's daughters. Their father gave them a share of the inheritance along with their brothers.

16 Job lived a hundred and forty years after this, long enough to see his grandchildren and great-grandchildren. 17 And then he died at a very great age.

---

e In Hebrew the names of Job's daughters suggest beauty both by their sound and by their meaning. JEMIMAH *means "dove";* KEZIAH *means "cassia," a variety of cinnamon used as a perfume; and* KEREN HAPPUCH *means a small box used for eye make-up.*

42.3 Job 38.2   **42.4** Job 38.3   **42.10** Job 1.1-3

PSALMS

INTRODUCTION

The book of *Psalms* is the hymnbook and prayer book of the Bible. Composed by different authors over a long period of time, these hymns and prayers were collected and used by the people of Israel in their worship, and eventually this collection was included in their Scriptures.

These religious poems are of many kinds: there are hymns of praise and worship of God; prayers for help, protection, and salvation; pleas for forgiveness; songs of thanksgiving for God's blessings; and petitions for the punishment of enemies. These prayers are both personal and national; some portray the most intimate feelings of one person, while others represent the needs and feelings of all the people of God.

The psalms were used by Jesus, quoted by the writers of the New Testament, and became the treasured book of worship of the Christian Church from its beginning.

OUTLINE OF CONTENTS

The 150 psalms are grouped into five collections, or books, as follows:

BOOK ONE
(Psalms 1–41)

True Happiness

1 Happy are those
who reject the advice of evil
people,
who do not follow the example
of sinners
or join those who have no use
for God.
[2] Instead, they find joy in obeying
the Law of the LORD,
and they study it day and night.
[3] They are like trees that grow beside
a stream,
that bear fruit at the right time,
and whose leaves do not
dry up.
They succeed in everything
they do.

[4] But evil people are not like this
at all;
they are like straw that the wind
blows away.
[5] Sinners will be condemned by God
and kept apart from God's own
people.
[6] The righteous are guided and
protected by the LORD,
but the evil are on the way to
their doom.

God's Chosen King

2 Why do the nations plan
rebellion?
Why do people make their
useless plots?
[2] Their kings revolt,
their rulers plot together against
the LORD
and against the king he chose.
[3] "Let us free ourselves from their
rule," they say;
"let us throw off their control."

[4] From his throne in heaven the
Lord laughs
and mocks their feeble plans.
[5] Then he warns them in anger
and terrifies them with his fury.
[6] "On Zion,[a] my sacred hill," he
says,
"I have installed my king."

[7] "I will announce," says the king,
"what the LORD has declared.
He said to me: 'You are my son;
today I have become your father.
[8] Ask, and I will give you all the
nations;
the whole earth will be yours.
[9] You will break them with an
iron rod;
you will shatter them in pieces
like a clay pot.'"

[10] Now listen to this warning, you
kings;
learn this lesson, you rulers of
the world:

[11] Serve the LORD with fear;
tremble [12] and bow down
to him;[b]
or else his anger will be quickly
aroused,
and you will suddenly die.
Happy are all who go to him for
protection.

Morning Prayer for Help[c]

3 I have so many enemies, LORD,
so many who turn against
me!
[2] They talk about me and say,
"God will not help him."

[3] But you, O LORD, are always my
shield from danger;
you give me victory
and restore my courage.
[4] I call to the LORD for help,
and from his sacred hill[d] he
answers me.

[5] I lie down and sleep,
and all night long the LORD
protects me.
[6] I am not afraid of the thousands
of enemies
who surround me on every
side.

[7] Come, LORD! Save me, my God!
You punish all my enemies
and leave them powerless to
harm me.
[8] Victory comes from the LORD —
may he bless his people.

---

[a] ZION: *The term "Zion" (originally a designation for "David's City," the Jebusite
stronghold captured by King David's forces) was later extended in meaning to refer to
the hill on which the Temple stood.* [b] *Probable text* tremble . . . him; *some other
possible texts* with trembling kiss his feet *and* with trembling kiss the Son *and* tremble
and kiss the mighty one; *Hebrew unclear.* [c] HEBREW TITLE: *A psalm by David, after
he ran away from his son Absalom.* [d] SACRED HILL: *See 2.6.*
2.1, 2 Ac 4.25, 26 **2.7** Ac 13.33; He 1.5; 5.5 **2.9** Rev 2.26, 27; 12.5; 19.15
3 Title 2 S 15.13—17.22

Evening Prayer for Help[e]

4 Answer me when I pray,
O God, my defender!
When I was in trouble, you
helped me.
Be kind to me now and hear
my prayer.

2 How long will you people insult
me?
How long will you love what is
worthless
and go after what is false?

3 Remember that the LORD has
chosen the righteous
for his own,
and he hears me when I call
to him.

4 Tremble with fear and stop
sinning;
think deeply about this,
when you lie in silence on your
beds.

5 Offer the right sacrifices to the
LORD,
and put your trust in him.

6 There are many who pray:
"Give us more blessings,
O LORD.
Look on us with kindness!"

7 But the joy that you have given me
is more than they will ever have
with all their grain and wine.

8 When I lie down, I go to sleep in
peace;
you alone, O LORD, keep me
perfectly safe.

A Prayer for Protection[e]

5 Listen to my words, O LORD,
and hear my sighs.
2 Listen to my cry for help,
my God and king!

I pray to you, O LORD;
3   you hear my voice in the
morning;
at sunrise I offer my prayer[f]
and wait for your answer.

4 You are not a God who is pleased
with wrongdoing;
you allow no evil in your
presence.
5 You cannot stand the sight of the
proud;
you hate all wicked people.
6 You destroy all liars
and despise violent, deceitful
people.

7 But because of your great love
I can come into your house;
I can worship in your holy Temple
and bow down to you in
reverence.
8 LORD, I have so many enemies!
Lead me to do your will;
make your way plain for me to
follow.

9 What my enemies say can never
be trusted;
they only want to destroy.
Their words are flattering and
smooth,
but full of deadly deceit.
10 Condemn and punish them, O God;
may their own plots cause their
ruin.
Drive them out of your presence
because of their many sins
and their rebellion against you.

11 But all who find safety in you will
rejoice;
they can always sing for joy.
Protect those who love you;
because of you they are truly
happy.
12 You bless those who obey you,
LORD;

e HEBREW TITLE: *A psalm by David.*   f prayer; *or* sacrifice.
4.4 Eph 4.26   **5.9** Ro 3.13

your love protects them like a
shield.

A Prayer for Help in Time
of Trouble [g]

6 LORD, don't be angry and
rebuke me!
Don't punish me in your anger!
[2] I am worn out, O LORD; have pity
on me!
Give me strength; I am
completely exhausted
[3] and my whole being is deeply
troubled.
How long, O LORD, will you wait to
help me?

[4] Come and save me, LORD;
in your mercy rescue me from
death.
[5] In the world of the dead you are
not remembered;
no one can praise you there.

[6] I am worn out with grief;
every night my bed is damp
from my weeping;
my pillow is soaked with tears.
[7] I can hardly see;
my eyes are so swollen
from the weeping caused by my
enemies.

[8] Keep away from me, you evil
people!
The LORD hears my weeping;
[9]   he listens to my cry for help
and will answer my prayer.
[10] My enemies will know the bitter
shame of defeat;
in sudden confusion they will be
driven away.

A Prayer for Justice [h]

7 O LORD, my God, I come to you
for protection;
rescue me and save me from all
who pursue me,
[2] or else like a lion they will carry
me off
where no one can save me,
and there they will tear me to
pieces.

[3-4] O LORD, my God, if I have
wronged anyone,
if I have betrayed a friend
or without cause done violence
to my enemy [i] —
if I have done any of these
things —
[5] then let my enemies pursue me
and catch me,
let them cut me down and
kill me
and leave me lifeless on the
ground!

[6] Rise in your anger, O LORD!
Stand up against the fury of my
enemies;
rouse yourself and help me!
Justice is what you demand,
[7]   so bring together all the peoples
around you,
and rule over them from
above. [j]
[8] You are the judge of all people.
Judge in my favor, O LORD;
you know that I am innocent.
[9] You are a righteous God
and judge our thoughts and
desires.
Stop the wickedness of evildoers
and reward those who are good.

[10] God is my protector;
he saves those who obey him.

---

[g] HEBREW TITLE: *A psalm by David.*   [h] HEBREW TITLE: *A song which David sang to
the LORD because of Cush the Benjaminite.*   [i] without cause done violence to my
enemy; *or* shown mercy to someone who wronged me unjustly.   [j] *Probable text* rule
over them from above; *Hebrew* return above over them.
6.1 Ps 38.1   **6.8** Mt 7.23; Lk 13.27   **7.9** Rev 2.23

¹¹God is a righteous judge
and always condemns the
wicked.
¹²If they do not change their ways,
God will sharpen his sword.
He bends his bow and makes it
ready;
¹³   he takes up his deadly weapons
and aims his burning arrows.

¹⁴See how wicked people think up
evil;
they plan trouble and practice
deception.
¹⁵But in the traps they set for others,
they themselves get caught.
¹⁶So they are punished by their own
evil
and are hurt by their own
violence.

¹⁷I thank the LORD for his justice;
I sing praises to the LORD, the
Most High.

God's Glory and Human Dignity ^k

8 O LORD, our Lord,
    your greatness is seen in all
the world!
Your praise reaches up to the
heavens;
²   it is sung by children and
babies.
You are safe and secure from all
your enemies;
you stop anyone who opposes
you.

³When I look at the sky, which you
have made,
at the moon and the stars,
which you set in their
places —

⁴what are human beings, that you
think of them;
mere mortals, that you care for
them?

⁵Yet you made them inferior only to
yourself; ^l
you crowned them with glory
and honor.
⁶You appointed them rulers over
everything you made;
you placed them over all
creation:
⁷   sheep and cattle, and the wild
animals too;
⁸   the birds and the fish
and the creatures in the seas.

⁹O LORD, our Lord,
your greatness is seen in all the
world!

Thanksgiving to God for His Justice ^m

9 I will praise you, LORD, with all
    my heart;
I will tell of all the wonderful
things you have done.
²I will sing with joy because of you.
I will sing praise to you,
Almighty God.

³My enemies turn back when you
appear;
they fall down and die.
⁴You are fair and honest in your
judgments,
and you have judged in my
favor.

⁵You have condemned the heathen
and destroyed the wicked;
they will be remembered no
more.

---

^k HEBREW TITLE: *A psalm by David.*   ^l yourself; *or* the gods, *or* the angels.
^m HEBREW TITLE: *A psalm by David.*
8.2 Mt 21.16   **8.4** Job 7.17, 18; Ps 144.3; He 2.6-8   **8.5** Ws 2.23; Si 17.1-4   **8.6** 1 Co 15.27;
Eph 1.22; He 2.8

I will praise you, LORD. (9.1)

⁶Our enemies are finished forever;
  you have destroyed their cities,
  and they are completely
    forgotten.

⁷But the LORD is king forever;
  he has set up his throne for
    judgment.
⁸He rules the world with
    righteousness;
  he judges the nations with
    justice.

⁹The LORD is a refuge for the
    oppressed,
  a place of safety in times of
    trouble.
¹⁰Those who know you, LORD, will
    trust you;
  you do not abandon anyone who
    comes to you.

¹¹Sing praise to the LORD, who rules
    in Zion!
  Tell every nation what he has
    done!
¹²God remembers those who suffer;
  he does not forget their cry,

and he punishes those who
  wrong them.

¹³Be merciful to me, O LORD!
  See the sufferings my enemies
    cause me!
Rescue me from death, O LORD,
¹⁴ that I may stand before the
    people of Jerusalem
  and tell them all the things for
    which I praise you.
I will rejoice because you
    saved me.

¹⁵The heathen have dug a pit and
    fallen in;
  they have been caught in their
    own trap.
¹⁶The LORD has revealed himself by
    his righteous judgments,
  and the wicked are trapped by
    their own deeds.

¹⁷Death is the destiny of all the
    wicked,
  of all those who reject God.
¹⁸The needy will not always be
    neglected;

9.13 Ws 16.13

the hope of the poor will not be
  crushed forever.

¹⁹ Come, Lord! Do not let anyone
  defy you!
  Bring the heathen before you
  and pronounce judgment on
  them.
²⁰ Make them afraid, O Lord;
  make them know that they are
  only mortal beings.

A Prayer for Justice

10 Why are you so far away,
  O Lord?
Why do you hide yourself when
  we are in trouble?
² The wicked are proud and
  persecute the poor;
  catch them in the traps they
  have made.

³ The wicked are proud of their evil
  desires;
  the greedy curse and reject the
  Lord.
⁴ The wicked do not care about the
  Lord;
  in their pride they think that
  God doesn't matter.

⁵ The wicked succeed in everything.
  They cannot understand God's
  judgments;
  they sneer at their enemies.
⁶ They say to themselves, "We will
  never fail;
  we will never be in trouble."
⁷ Their speech is filled with curses,
  lies, and threats;
  they are quick to speak hateful,
  evil words.

⁸ They hide themselves in the
  villages,
  waiting to murder innocent
  people.

They spy on their helpless victims;
⁹   they wait in their hiding place
  like lions.
They lie in wait for the poor;
  they catch them in their traps
  and drag them away.

¹⁰ The helpless victims lie crushed;
  brute strength has defeated
  them.
¹¹ The wicked say to themselves, "God
  doesn't care!
  He has closed his eyes and will
  never see me!"

¹² O Lord, punish those wicked
  people!
  Remember those who are
  suffering!
¹³ How can the wicked despise God
  and say to themselves, "He will
  not punish me"?

¹⁴ But you do see; you take notice of
  trouble and suffering
  and are always ready to help.
The helpless commit themselves
  to you;
  you have always helped the
  needy.

¹⁵ Break the power of wicked and evil
  people;
  punish them for the wrong they
  have done
  until they do it no more.

¹⁶ The Lord is king forever and ever.
  Those who worship other gods
  will vanish from his land.

¹⁷ You will listen, O Lord, to the
  prayers of the lowly;
  you will give them courage.
¹⁸ You will hear the cries of the
  oppressed and the orphans;
  you will judge in their favor,

10.7 Ro 3.14

so that mortal men may cause
terror no more.

Confidence in the LORD [n]

11 I trust in the LORD for safety.
How foolish of you to say
to me,
"Fly away like a bird to the
mountains,[o]

2   because the wicked have drawn
their bows and aimed their
arrows
to shoot from the shadows at
good people.

3 There is nothing a good person
can do
when everything falls apart."

4 The LORD is in his holy temple;
he has his throne in heaven.
He watches people everywhere
and knows what they are doing.

5 He examines the good and the
wicked alike;
the lawless he hates with all
his heart.

6 He sends down flaming coals [p] and
burning sulfur on the wicked;
he punishes them with
scorching winds.

7 The LORD is righteous and loves
good deeds;
those who do them will live in
his presence.

A Prayer for Help [q]

12 Help us, LORD!
There is not a good person
left;
honest people can no longer be
found.

2 All of them lie to one another;
they deceive each other with
flattery.

3 Silence those flattering tongues,
O LORD!
Close those boastful mouths
that say,

4 "With our words we get what we
want.
We will say what we wish,
and no one can stop us."

Those who do them will live in his presence.
(11.7)

5 "But now I will come," says the
LORD,
"because the needy are
oppressed
and the persecuted groan in
pain.
I will give them the security they
long for."

6 The promises of the LORD can be
trusted;
they are as genuine as silver
refined seven times in the
furnace.

7-8 The wicked are everywhere,
and everyone praises what is
evil.
Keep us always safe, O LORD,
and preserve us from such
people.

---

[n] HEBREW TITLE: *By David.*   [o] *Some ancient translations* like a bird to the
mountains; *Hebrew* bird, to your *(plural)* mountain.   [p] *One ancient translation*
coals; *Hebrew* traps.   [q] HEBREW TITLE: *A psalm by David.*

A Prayer for Help [q]

13 How much longer will you
forget me, LORD?
Forever?
How much longer will you hide
yourself from me?
2 How long must I endure trouble?
How long will sorrow fill my
heart day and night?
How long will my enemies
triumph over me?

3 Look at me, O LORD my God, and
answer me.
Restore my strength; don't let
me die.
4 Don't let my enemies say, "We
have defeated him."
Don't let them gloat over my
downfall.

5 I rely on your constant love;
I will be glad, because you will
rescue me.
6 I will sing to you, O LORD,
because you have been good
to me.

Human Wickedness [r]
(Psalm 53)

14 Fools say to themselves,
"There is no God!"
They are all corrupt,
and they have done terrible
things;
there is no one who does what
is right.

2 The LORD looks down from heaven
at us humans
to see if there are any who are
wise,
any who worship him.
3 But they have all gone wrong;
they are all equally bad.

Not one of them does what is right,
not a single one.

4 "Don't they know?" asks the LORD.
"Are all these evildoers ignorant?
They live by robbing my people,
and they never pray to me."

5 But then they will be terrified,
for God is with those who obey
him.
6 Evildoers frustrate the plans of the
humble,
but the LORD is their protection.

7 How I pray that victory
will come to Israel from Zion.
How happy the people of Israel
will be
when the LORD makes them
prosperous again!

What God Requires [s]

15 LORD, who may enter your
Temple?
Who may worship on Zion, your
sacred hill? [t]

2 Those who obey God in everything
and always do what is right,
whose words are true and sincere,
3 and who do not slander others.
They do no wrong to their friends
nor spread rumors about their
neighbors.
4 They despise those whom God
rejects,
but honor those who obey the
LORD.
They always do what they promise,
no matter how much it may
cost.
5 They make loans without charging
interest
and cannot be bribed to testify
against the innocent.

[q] HEBREW TITLE: *A psalm by David.*   [r] HEBREW TITLE: *By David.*   [s] HEBREW
TITLE: *A psalm by David.*   [t] SACRED HILL: *See 2.6.*
14.1-3 Ro 3.10-12

Whoever does these things will
    always be secure.

A Prayer of Confidence [u]

16 Protect me, O God; I trust in
        you for safety.
[2] I say to the LORD, "You are my
        Lord;
    all the good things I have come
        from you."

[3] How excellent are the LORD's
        faithful people!
    My greatest pleasure is to be
        with them.

[4] Those who rush to other gods
        bring many troubles on
        themselves. [v]
    I will not take part in their
        sacrifices;
    I will not worship their gods.

[5] You, LORD, are all I have,
        and you give me all I need;
    my future is in your hands.
[6] How wonderful are your gifts
        to me;
    how good they are!

[7] I praise the LORD, because he
        guides me,
    and in the night my conscience
        warns me.
[8] I am always aware of the LORD's
        presence;
    he is near, and nothing can
        shake me.

[9] And so I am thankful and glad,
        and I feel completely secure,
[10] because you protect me from the
        power of death.
    I have served you faithfully,
        and you will not abandon me to
        the world of the dead.

[11] You will show me the path that
        leads to life;
    your presence fills me with joy
        and brings me pleasure forever.

The Prayer of an Innocent Person [w]

17 Listen, O LORD, to my plea
        for justice;
    pay attention to my cry for help!
    Listen to my honest prayer.
[2] You will judge in my favor,
        because you know what is right.

[3] You know my heart.
    You have come to me at night;
    you have examined me
        completely
    and found no evil desire in me.
    I speak no evil, [4] as others do;
    I have obeyed your command
    and have not followed paths of
        violence.
[5] I have always walked in your way
    and have never strayed from it.

[6] I pray to you, O God, because you
        answer me;
    so turn to me and listen to my
        words.
[7] Reveal your wonderful love and
        save me;
    at your side I am safe from my
        enemies.

[8] Protect me as you would your very
        eyes;
    hide me in the shadow of your
        wings
[9]   from the attacks of the wicked.

    Deadly enemies surround me;
[10]   they have no pity and speak
        proudly.
[11] They are around me now, wherever
        I turn,

---

[u] HEBREW TITLE: *A psalm by David.*   [v] *Probable text* Those . . . themselves; *Hebrew
unclear.*   [w] HEBREW TITLE: *A prayer by David.*
16.10 Ac 13.35   **16.8-11** Ac 2.25-28

watching for a chance to pull
me down.

12 They are like lions, waiting for me,
wanting to tear me to pieces.

13 Come, LORD! Oppose my enemies
and defeat them!
Save me from the wicked by your
sword;
14   save me from those who in this
life have all they want.
Punish them with the sufferings
you have stored up for them;
may there be enough for their
children
and some left over for their
children's children!

15 But I will see you, because I have
done no wrong;
and when I awake, your
presence will fill me with joy.

David's Song of Victory [x]
(2 Samuel 22.1-51)

18 How I love you, LORD!
You are my defender.

2 The LORD is my protector;
he is my strong fortress.
My God is my protection,
and with him I am safe.
He protects me like a shield;
he defends me and keeps me
safe.
3 I call to the LORD,
and he saves me from my
enemies.
Praise the LORD!

4 The danger of death was all
around me;
the waves of destruction rolled
over me.

5 The danger of death was around
me,
and the grave set its trap for me.
6 In my trouble I called to the LORD;
I called to my God for help.
In his temple he heard my voice;
he listened to my cry for help.

7 Then the earth trembled and
shook;
the foundations of the
mountains rocked and
quivered,
because God was angry.
8 Smoke poured out of his nostrils,
a consuming flame and burning
coals from his mouth.
9 He tore the sky open and came
down
with a dark cloud under his feet.
10 He flew swiftly on his winged
creature; [y]
he traveled on the wings of the
wind.
11 He covered himself with darkness;
thick clouds, full of water,
surrounded him.
12 Hailstones and flashes of fire
came from the lightning before
him
and broke through the dark
clouds.

13 Then the LORD thundered from
the sky;
and the voice of the Most High
was heard. [z]
14 He shot his arrows and scattered
his enemies;
with flashes of lightning he sent
them running.
15 The floor of the ocean was laid
bare,
and the foundations of the earth
were uncovered,

---

[x] HEBREW TITLE: *The words that David, the* LORD's *servant, sang to the* LORD *on the day
the* LORD *saved him from Saul and all his other enemies.*   [y] WINGED CREATURE: *See
Word List.*   [z] *One ancient translation (and see 2 S 22.14) was heard; Hebrew was
heard hailstones and flashes of fire.*

when you rebuked your enemies,
LORD,
and roared at them in anger.

16 The LORD reached down from
above and took hold of me;
he pulled me out of the deep
waters.
17 He rescued me from my powerful
enemies
and from all those who hate
me —
they were too strong for me.
18 When I was in trouble, they
attacked me,
but the LORD protected me.
19 He helped me out of danger;
he saved me because he was
pleased with me.

20 The LORD rewards me because I do
what is right;
he blesses me because I am
innocent.
21 I have obeyed the law of the LORD;
I have not turned away from
my God.
22 I have observed all his laws;
I have not disobeyed his
commands.
23 He knows that I am faultless,
that I have kept myself from
doing wrong.
24 And so he rewards me because I do
what is right,
because he knows that I am
innocent.

25 O LORD, you are faithful to those
who are faithful to you;
completely good to those who
are perfect.
26 You are pure to those who are
pure,
but hostile to those who are
wicked.

27 You save those who are humble,
but you humble those who are
proud.

28 O LORD, you give me light;
you dispel my darkness.
29 You give me strength to attack my
enemies
and power to overcome their
defenses.

30 This God — how perfect are his
deeds!
How dependable his words!
He is like a shield
for all who seek his protection.
31 The LORD alone is God;
God alone is our defense.
32 He is the God who makes me
strong,
who makes my pathway safe.
33 He makes me sure-footed as a deer;
he keeps me safe on the
mountains.
34 He trains me for battle,
so that I can use the strongest
bow.

35 O LORD, you protect me and save
me;
your care has made me great,
and your power has kept me
safe.
36 You have kept me from being
captured,
and I have never fallen.
37 I pursue my enemies and catch
them;
I do not stop until I destroy
them.
38 I strike them down, and they
cannot rise;
they lie defeated before me.
39 You give me strength for the battle
and victory over my enemies.
40 You make my enemies run from
me;
I destroy those who hate me.

18.33 Hb 3.19

⁴¹They cry for help, but no one saves
them;
   they call to the LORD, but he
does not answer.
⁴²I crush them, so that they become
like dust
   which the wind blows away.
  I trample on them like mud in the
streets.

⁴³You saved me from a rebellious
people
   and made me ruler over the
nations;
   people I did not know have now
become my subjects.
⁴⁴Foreigners bow before me;
   when they hear me, they obey.
⁴⁵They lose their courage
   and come trembling from their
fortresses.

⁴⁶The LORD lives! Praise my
defender!
   Proclaim the greatness of the
God who saves me.
⁴⁷He gives me victory over my
enemies;
   he subdues the nations under
me
⁴⁸   and saves me from my foes.

O LORD, you give me victory over
my enemies
   and protect me from violent
people.
⁴⁹And so I praise you among the
nations;
   I sing praises to you.

⁵⁰God gives great victories to his
king;
   he shows constant love to the
one he has chosen,
   to David and his descendants
forever.

God's Glory in Creation [a]

19 How clearly the sky reveals
   God's glory!
  How plainly it shows what he
has done!
²Each day announces it to the
following day;
   each night repeats it to the next.
³No speech or words are used,
   no sound is heard;
⁴yet their message[b] goes out to all
the world
   and is heard to the ends of the
earth.
God made a home in the sky for
the sun;
⁵   it comes out in the morning like
a happy bridegroom,
   like an athlete eager to run a
race.
⁶It starts at one end of the sky
   and goes across to the other.
  Nothing can hide from its heat.

The Law of the LORD

⁷The law of the LORD is perfect;
   it gives new strength.
  The commands of the LORD are
trustworthy,
   giving wisdom to those who
lack it.
⁸The laws of the LORD are right,
   and those who obey them are
happy.
  The commands of the LORD are
just
   and give understanding to the
mind.
⁹Reverence for the LORD is good;
   it will continue forever.
  The judgments of the LORD are
just;
   they are always fair.
¹⁰They are more desirable than the
finest gold;

---

[a] HEBREW TITLE: *A psalm by David.*
[b] *Some ancient translations* message; *Hebrew*
line.
18.49 Ro 15.9   **19.4** Ro 10.18

they are sweeter than the purest
  honey.
11 They give knowledge to me, your
  servant;
  I am rewarded for obeying them.

12 None of us can see our own errors;
  deliver me, LORD, from hidden
  faults!
13 Keep me safe, also, from willful
  sins;
  don't let them rule over me.
  Then I shall be perfect
  and free from the evil of sin.

14 May my words and my thoughts be
  acceptable to you,
  O LORD, my refuge and my
  redeemer!

A Prayer for Victory *c*

20 May the LORD answer you
  when you are in
  trouble!
  May the God of Jacob protect
  you!
2 May he send you help from his
  Temple
  and give you aid from Mount
  Zion.
3 May he accept all your offerings
  and be pleased with all your
  sacrifices.
4 May he give you what you desire
  and make all your plans
  succeed.
5 Then we will shout for joy over
  your victory
  and celebrate your triumph by
  praising our God.
  May the LORD answer all your
  requests.

6 Now I know that the LORD gives
  victory to his chosen king;
  he answers him from his holy
  heaven

and by his power gives him
  great victories.
7 Some trust in their war chariots
  and others in their horses,
  but we trust in the power of the
  LORD our God.
8 Such people will stumble and fall,
  but we will rise and stand firm.

9 Give victory to the king, O LORD;
  answer *d* us when we call.

Praise for Victory *e*

21 The king is glad, O LORD,
  because you gave
  him strength;
  he rejoices because you made
  him victorious.
2 You have given him his heart's
  desire;
  you have answered his request.

3 You came to him with great
  blessings
  and set a crown of gold on his
  head.
4 He asked for life, and you gave it,
  a long and lasting life.

5 His glory is great because of your
  help;
  you have given him fame and
  majesty.
6 Your blessings are with him
  forever,
  and your presence fills him
  with joy.

7 The king trusts in the LORD
  Almighty;
  and because of the LORD's
  constant love
  he will always be secure.
8 The king will capture all his
  enemies;
  he will capture everyone who
  hates him.

---

c HEBREW TITLE: *A psalm by David.*   *d Some ancient translations* answer; *Hebrew*
he will answer.   *e* HEBREW TITLE: *A psalm by David.*

9 He will destroy them like a blazing
   fire
     when he appears.

The LORD will devour them in his
   anger,
     and fire will consume them.
10 None of their descendants will
   survive;
     the king will kill them all.

11 They make their plans, and plot
   against him,
     but they will not succeed.
12 He will shoot his arrows at them
     and make them turn and run.

13 We praise you, LORD, for your great
   strength!
     We will sing and praise your
     power.

A Cry of Anguish and a Song
of Praise [e]

22 My God, my God, why have
     you abandoned me?
I have cried desperately for help,
     but still it does not come.
2 During the day I call to you, my
   God,
     but you do not answer;
I call at night,
     but get no rest.
3 But you are enthroned as the
   Holy One,
     the one whom Israel praises.
4 Our ancestors put their trust in
   you;
     they trusted you, and you saved
     them.
5 They called to you and escaped
   from danger;
     they trusted you and were not
     disappointed.

6 But I am no longer a human being;
   I am a worm,
     despised and scorned by
     everyone!
7 All who see me make fun of me;
     they stick out their tongues and
     shake their heads.
8 "You relied on the LORD," they say.
   "Why doesn't he save you?
If the LORD likes you,
     why doesn't he help you?"

9 It was you who brought me safely
   through birth,
     and when I was a baby, you
     kept me safe.
10 I have relied on you since the day I
   was born,
     and you have always been my
     God.
11 Do not stay away from me!
   Trouble is near,
     and there is no one to help.

12 Many enemies surround me like
   bulls;
     they are all around me,
     like fierce bulls from the land of
     Bashan.
13 They open their mouths like lions,
     roaring and tearing at me.

14 My strength is gone,
     gone like water spilled on the
     ground.
All my bones are out of joint;
     my heart is like melted wax.
15 My throat [f] is as dry as dust,
     and my tongue sticks to the roof
     of my mouth.
You have left me for dead in the
   dust.

16 An evil gang is around me;
     like a pack of dogs they close in
     on me;
     they tear at [g] my hands and feet.

_e_ HEBREW TITLE: *A psalm by David.*   _f_ *Probable text* throat; *Hebrew* strength.
_g_ *Some ancient translations* they tear at; *others* they tie; *Hebrew* like a lion.
22.1 Mt 27.46; Mk 15.34   **22.7** Mt 27.39; Mk 15.29; Lk 23.35   **22.8** Mt 27.43

17 All my bones can be seen.
    My enemies look at me and
      stare.
18 They gamble for my clothes
    and divide them among
      themselves.

19 O LORD, don't stay away from me!
    Come quickly to my rescue!
20 Save me from the sword;
    save my life from these dogs.
21 Rescue me from these lions;
    I am helpless *h* before these wild
      bulls.

22 I will tell my people what you have
      done;
    I will praise you in their
      assembly:
23 "Praise him, you servants of the
      LORD!
    Honor him, you descendants of
      Jacob!
    Worship him, you people of
      Israel!
24 He does not neglect the poor or
      ignore their suffering;
    he does not turn away from
      them,
    but answers when they call for
      help."

25 In the full assembly I will praise
    you for what you have done;
    in the presence of those who
      worship you
    I will offer the sacrifices I
      promised.
26 The poor will eat as much as they
      want;
    those who come to the LORD will
      praise him.
    May they prosper forever!

27 All nations will remember the
      LORD.

From every part of the world
    they will turn to him;
    all races will worship him.
28 The LORD is king,
    and he rules the nations.

29 All proud people will bow down to
      him; *i*
    all mortals will bow down before
      him.
30 Future generations will serve him;
    they will speak of the Lord to
      the coming generation.
31 People not yet born will be told:
    "The Lord saved his people."

The LORD Our Shepherd *j*

23 The LORD is my shepherd;
    I have everything I need.
2 He lets me rest in fields of green
      grass
    and leads me to quiet pools of
      fresh water.
3 He gives me new strength.
    He guides me in the right paths,
    as he has promised.
4 Even if I go through the deepest
      darkness,
    I will not be afraid, LORD,
    for you are with me.
    Your shepherd's rod and staff
      protect me.

5 You prepare a banquet for me,
    where all my enemies can see
      me;
    you welcome me as an honored
      guest
    and fill my cup to the brim.
6 I know that your goodness and love
    will be with me all my life;
    and your house will be my home
    as long as I live.

---

h Some ancient translations I am helpless; *Hebrew* you answered me.   *i Probable text* will bow down to him; *Hebrew* will eat and bow down.   *j* HEBREW TITLE: *A psalm by David.*

22.18 Mt 27.35; Mk 15.24; Lk 23.34; Jn 19.24   **22.22** He 2.12   **23.2** Rev 7.17

The Great King[j]

24 The world and all that is in it
belong to the LORD;
the earth and all who live on it
are his.

*Even if I go through the deepest darkness . . .
(23.4)*

2 He built it on the deep waters
beneath the earth
and laid its foundations in the
ocean depths.

3 Who has the right to go up the
LORD's hill?[k]
Who may enter his holy
Temple?
4 Those who are pure in act and in
thought,
who do not worship idols
or make false promises.
5 The LORD will bless them and save
them;
God will declare them innocent.
6 Such are the people who come to
God,
who come into the presence of
the God of Jacob.

7 Fling wide the gates,
open the ancient doors,
and the great king will come in.

8 Who is this great king?
He is the LORD, strong and mighty,
the LORD, victorious in battle.

9 Fling wide the gates,
open the ancient doors,
and the great king will come in.
10 Who is this great king?
The triumphant LORD — he is the
great king!

A Prayer for Guidance and Protection[l]

25 To you, O LORD, I offer my
prayer;
2   in you, my God, I trust.
Save me from the shame of defeat;
don't let my enemies gloat over
me!
3 Defeat does not come to those who
trust in you,
but to those who are quick to
rebel against you.

4 Teach me your ways, O LORD;
make them known to me.
5 Teach me to live according to your
truth,
for you are my God, who saves
me.
I always trust in you.

6 Remember, O LORD, your kindness
and constant love
which you have shown from
long ago.
7 Forgive the sins and errors of my
youth.
In your constant love and goodness,
remember me, LORD!

8 Because the LORD is righteous and
good,

---

j HEBREW TITLE: *A psalm by David.*   k THE LORD'S HILL: *The hill in Jerusalem on
which the Temple was built.*   l HEBREW TITLE: *By David.*
24.1 1 Co 10.26   **24.4** Mt 5.8

he teaches sinners the path they
should follow.

9 He leads the humble in the right
way

and teaches them his will.

10 With faithfulness and love he leads
all who keep his covenant and
obey his commands.

11 Keep your promise, LORD, and
forgive my sins,

for they are many.

12 Those who have reverence for the
LORD

will learn from him the path
they should follow.

13 They will always be prosperous,
and their children will possess
the land.

14 The LORD is the friend of those
who obey him

and he affirms his covenant with
them.

15 I look to the LORD for help at all
times,

and he rescues me from danger.

16 Turn to me, LORD, and be merciful
to me,

because I am lonely and weak.

17 Relieve me of my worries
and save me from all my
troubles.

18 Consider my distress and suffering
and forgive all my sins.

19 See how many enemies I have;
see how much they hate me.

20 Protect me and save me;
keep me from defeat.

I come to you for safety.

21 May my goodness and honesty
preserve me,

because I trust in you.

22 From all their troubles, O God,
save your people Israel!

The Prayer of a Good Person[l]

26 Declare me innocent,
O LORD,

because I do what is right
and trust you completely.

2 Examine me and test me, LORD;
judge my desires and thoughts.

3 Your constant love is my guide;
your faithfulness always
leads me.[m]

4 I do not keep company with
worthless people;

I have nothing to do with
hypocrites.

5 I hate the company of the evil
and avoid the wicked.

6 LORD, I wash my hands to show
that I am innocent

and march in worship around
your altar.

7 I sing a hymn of thanksgiving
and tell of all your wonderful
deeds.

8 I love the house where you live,
O LORD,

the place where your glory
dwells.

9 Do not destroy me with the
sinners;

spare me from the fate of
murderers —

10   those who do evil all the time
and are always ready to take
bribes.

11 As for me, I do what is right;
be merciful to me and save me!

12 I am safe from all dangers;
in the assembly of his people I
praise the LORD.

---

[l] HEBREW TITLE: *By David*.   [m] your faithfulness always leads me; *or* I live in loyalty
to you.

A Prayer of Praise [n]

27 The LORD is my light and my
salvation;
I will fear no one.
The LORD protects me from all
danger;
I will never be afraid.

2 When evil people attack me and try
to kill me,
they stumble and fall.
3 Even if a whole army surrounds
me,
I will not be afraid;
even if enemies attack me,
I will still trust God. [o]

4 I have asked the LORD for one
thing;
one thing only do I want:
to live in the LORD's house all my
life,
to marvel there at his goodness,
and to ask for his guidance.
5 In times of trouble he will shelter
me;
he will keep me safe in his
Temple
and make me secure on a high
rock.
6 So I will triumph over my enemies
around me.
With shouts of joy I will offer
sacrifices in his Temple;
I will sing, I will praise the
LORD.

7 Hear me, LORD, when I call to you!
Be merciful and answer me!
8 When you said, "Come
worship me,"
I answered, "I will come, LORD."
9 Don't hide yourself from me!

Don't be angry with me;
don't turn your servant away.

You have been my help;
don't leave me, don't abandon
me,
O God, my savior.
10 My father and mother may
abandon me,
but the LORD will take care
of me.

11 Teach me, LORD, what you want
me to do,
and lead me along a safe path,
because I have many enemies.
12 Don't abandon me to my enemies,
who attack me with lies and
threats.

13 I know that I will live to see
the LORD's goodness in this
present life.
14 Trust in the LORD.
Have faith, do not despair.
Trust in the LORD.

A Prayer for Help [p]

28 O LORD, my defender, I call
to you.
Listen to my cry!
If you do not answer me,
I will be among those who go
down to the world
of the dead.
2 Hear me when I cry to you for
help,
when I lift my hands toward
your holy Temple.
3 Do not condemn me with the
wicked,
with those who do evil —
those whose words are friendly,
but who have hatred in their
hearts.

4 Punish them for what they have
done,
for the evil they have committed.

---

[n] HEBREW TITLE: *By David.*   [o] still trust God; *or* not lose courage.   [p] HEBREW
TITLE: *By David.*
28.4 Rev 22.12

Punish them for all their deeds;
  give them what they deserve!
[5] They take no notice of what the
    LORD has done
    or of what he has made;
so he will punish them
  and destroy them forever.

[6] Give praise to the LORD;
  he has heard my cry for help.
[7] The LORD protects and defends me;
  I trust in him.
He gives me help and makes me
    glad;
  I praise him with joyful songs.

[8] The LORD protects his people;
  he defends and saves his chosen
    king.
[9] Save your people, LORD,
  and bless those who are yours.
Be their shepherd,
  and take care of them forever.

The Voice of the LORD in the Storm [q]

29 Praise the LORD, you
          heavenly beings;
  praise his glory and power.
[2] Praise the LORD's glorious name;
  bow down before the Holy One
    when he appears. [r]

[3] The voice of the LORD is heard on
    the seas;
  the glorious God thunders,
  and his voice echoes over the
    ocean.
[4] The voice of the LORD is heard
  in all its might and majesty.

[5] The voice of the LORD breaks the
    cedars,
  even the cedars of Lebanon.

[6] He makes the mountains of
    Lebanon jump like calves
  and makes Mount Hermon leap
    like a young bull.

[7] The voice of the LORD makes the
    lightning flash.
[8] His voice makes the desert shake;
  he shakes the desert of Kadesh.
[9] The LORD's voice shakes the oaks [s]
  and strips the leaves from the
    trees
while everyone in his Temple
  shouts, "Glory to God!"

[10] The LORD rules over the deep
    waters;
  he rules as king forever.
[11] The LORD gives strength to his
    people
  and blesses them with peace.

A Prayer of Thanksgiving [t]

30 I praise you, LORD, because
          you have saved me
  and kept my enemies from
    gloating over me.
[2] I cried to you for help, O LORD
    my God,
  and you healed me;
[3]   you kept me from the grave.
I was on my way to the depths
    below, [u]
  but you restored my life.

[4] Sing praise to the LORD,
  all his faithful people!
Remember what the Holy One
    has done,
  and give him thanks!
[5] His anger lasts only a moment,
  his goodness for a lifetime.
Tears may flow in the night,
  but joy comes in the morning.

---

[q] HEBREW TITLE: *A psalm by David.*   [r] *when he appears; or in garments of worship;*
or in his beautiful Temple.   [s] *Probable text* shakes the oaks; *Hebrew* makes the deer
give birth.   [t] HEBREW TITLE: *A song for the dedication of the Temple; a psalm by
David.*   [u] THE DEPTHS BELOW: *The world of the dead (see 6.5).*
29.1, 2 Ps 96.7-9

⁶I felt secure and said to myself,
  "I will never be defeated."
⁷You were good to me, LORD;
  you protected me like a
    mountain fortress.
But then you hid yourself from me,
  and I was afraid.

⁸I called to you, LORD;
  I begged for your help:
⁹"What will you gain from my
    death?
  What profit from my going to
    the grave?
Are dead people able to praise you?
  Can they proclaim your
    unfailing goodness?
¹⁰Hear me, LORD, and be merciful!
  Help me, LORD!"

¹You have changed my sadness into
    a joyful dance;
  you have taken away my sorrow
    and surrounded me with joy.
²So I will not be silent;
  I will sing praise to you.
LORD, you are my God;
  I will give you thanks forever.

A Prayer of Trust in God ᵛ

31 I come to you, LORD, for
         protection;
  never let me be defeated.
You are a righteous God;
  save me, I pray!
²Hear me! Save me now!
Be my refuge to protect me;
  my defense to save me.

³You are my refuge and defense;
  guide me and lead me as you
    have promised.
⁴Keep me safe from the trap that
    has been set for me;
  shelter me from danger.

⁵I place myself in your care.
  You will save me, LORD;
  you are a faithful God.

⁶You hate those who worship false
    gods,
  but I trust in you.
⁷I will be glad and rejoice
  because of your constant love.
You see my suffering;
  you know my trouble.
⁸You have not let my enemies
    capture me;
  you have given me freedom to
    go where I wish.

⁹Be merciful to me, LORD,
  for I am in trouble;
my eyes are tired from so much
    crying;
  I am completely worn out.
¹⁰I am exhausted by sorrow,
  and weeping has shortened my
    life.
I am weak from all my troubles; ʷ
  even my bones are wasting
    away.

¹¹All my enemies, and especially my
    neighbors,
  treat me with contempt.
Those who know me are afraid
    of me;
  when they see me in the street,
    they run away.
¹²Everyone has forgotten me, as
    though I were dead;
  I am like something thrown
    away.
¹³I hear many enemies whispering;
  terror is all around me.
They are making plans against me,
  plotting to kill me.

¹⁴But my trust is in you, O LORD;
  you are my God.

HEBREW TITLE: *A psalm by David.*   ʷ *Some ancient translations* troubles; *Hebrew*
niquity.

1.5 Lk 23.46

15 I am always in your care;
   save me from my enemies,
   from those who persecute me.
16 Look on your servant with
   kindness;
   save me in your constant love.
17 I call to you, LORD;
   don't let me be disgraced.
   May the wicked be disgraced;
   may they go silently down to the
   world of the dead.
18 Silence those liars —
   all the proud and arrogant
   who speak with contempt about
   the righteous.

19 How wonderful are the good things
   you keep for those who honor
   you!
   Everyone knows how good you are,
   how securely you protect those
   who trust you.
20 You hide them in the safety of your
   presence
   from the plots of others;
   in a safe shelter you hide them
   from the insults of their
   enemies.

21 Praise the LORD!
   How wonderfully he showed his
   love for me
   when I was surrounded and
   attacked!
22 I was afraid and thought
   that he had driven me out of his
   presence.
   But he heard my cry,
   when I called to him for help.

23 Love the LORD, all his faithful
   people.
   The LORD protects the faithful,
   but punishes the proud as they
   deserve.

24 Be strong, be courageous,
   all you that hope in the LORD.

Confession and Forgiveness x

32 Happy are those whose sins
      are forgiven,
whose wrongs are pardoned.
2 Happy is the one whom the LORD
   does not accuse of doing
   wrong
   and who is free from all deceit.

3 When I did not confess my sins,
   I was worn out from crying all
   day long.
4 Day and night you punished me,
   LORD;
   my strength was completely
   drained,
   as moisture is dried up by the
   summer heat.

5 Then I confessed my sins to you;
   I did not conceal my
   wrongdoings.
   I decided to confess them to you,
   and you forgave all my sins.

6 So all your loyal people should pray
   to you in times of need; y
   when a great flood of trouble
   comes rushing in,
   it will not reach them.
7 You are my hiding place;
   you will save me from trouble.
   I sing aloud of your salvation,
   because you protect me.

8 The LORD says, "I will teach you
   the way you should go;
   I will instruct you and advise
   you.
9 Don't be stupid like a horse or a
   mule,

---

x HEBREW TITLE: *A poem by David.*   y *Some ancient translations* need; *Hebrew*
finding only.
32.1, 2 Ro 4.7, 8

which must be controlled with a
  bit and bridle
to make it submit."

10 The wicked will have to suffer,
  but those who trust in the LORD
  are protected by his constant
  love.
11 You that are righteous, be glad and
  rejoice
because of what the LORD has
  done.
You that obey him, shout for joy!

A Song of Praise

33 All you that are righteous,
  shout for joy for what the
  LORD has done;
  praise him, all you that obey
  him.
2 Give thanks to the LORD with
  harps,
  sing to him with stringed
  instruments.
3 Sing a new song to him,
  play the harp with skill, and
  shout for joy!

4 The words of the LORD are true,
  and all his works are
  dependable.
5 The LORD loves what is righteous
  and just;
  his constant love fills the earth.

6 The LORD created the heavens by
  his command,
  the sun, moon, and stars by his
  spoken word.
7 He gathered all the seas into one
  place;
  he shut up the ocean depths in
  storerooms.

8 Worship the LORD, all the earth!

Honor him, all peoples of the
  world!
9 When he spoke, the world was
  created;
  at his command everything
  appeared.

10 The LORD frustrates the purposes
  of the nations;
  he keeps them from carrying out
  their plans.
11 But his plans endure forever;
  his purposes last eternally.
12 Happy is the nation whose God is
  the LORD;
  happy are the people he has
  chosen for his own!

13 The LORD looks down from heaven
  and sees all of us humans.
14 From where he rules, he looks
  down
  on all who live on earth.
15 He forms all their thoughts
  and knows everything they do.

16 A king does not win because of his
  powerful army;
  a soldier does not triumph
  because of his strength.
17 War horses are useless for victory;
  their great strength cannot save.

18 The LORD watches over those who
  obey him,
  those who trust in his constant
  love.
19 He saves them from death;
  he keeps them alive in times of
  famine.

20 We put our hope in the LORD;
  he is our protector and our help.
21 We are glad because of him;
  we trust in his holy name.

22 May your constant love be with us,
  LORD,
  as we put our hope in you.

3.16 Jdt 9.7; 1 Macc 3.19

In Praise of God's Goodness [z]

34 I will always thank the LORD;
 I will never stop praising
  him.
[2] I will praise him for what he has
  done;
 may all who are oppressed listen
  and be glad!
[3] Proclaim with me the LORD's
  greatness;
 let us praise his name together!

[4] I prayed to the LORD, and he
  answered me;
 he freed me from all my fears.
[5] The oppressed look to him and are
  glad;
 they will never be disappointed.
[6] The helpless call to him, and he
  answers;
 he saves them from all their
  troubles.
[7] His angel guards those who honor
  the LORD
 and rescues them from danger.

[8] Find out for yourself how good the
  LORD is.
 Happy are those who find safety
  with him.
[9] Honor the LORD, all his people;
 those who obey him have all
  they need.
[10] Even lions go hungry for lack of
  food,
 but those who obey the LORD
  lack nothing good.

[11] Come, my young friends, and listen
  to me,
 and I will teach you to honor
  the LORD.
[12] Would you like to enjoy life?
 Do you want long life and
  happiness?
[13] Then keep from speaking evil

and from telling lies.
[14] Turn away from evil and do good;
 strive for peace with all your
  heart.

[15] The LORD watches over the
  righteous
 and listens to their cries;
[16] but he opposes those who do evil,
 so that when they die, they are
  soon forgotten.
[17] The righteous call to the LORD, and
  he listens;
 he rescues them from all their
  troubles.
[18] The LORD is near to those who are
  discouraged;
 he saves those who have lost all
  hope.

[19] Good people suffer many troubles,
 but the LORD saves them from
  them all;
[20] the LORD preserves them
  completely;
 not one of their bones is broken.
[21] Evil will kill the wicked;
 those who hate the righteous
  will be punished.

[22] The LORD will save his people;
 those who go to him for
  protection will be spared.

A Prayer for Help [a]

35 Oppose those who oppose
 me, LORD,
 and fight those who fight
  against me!
[2] Take your shield and armor
 and come to my rescue.
[3] Lift up your spear and war ax
 against those who pursue me.
 Promise that you will save me.
[4] May those who try to kill me

---

[z] HEBREW TITLE: *By David, who left the presence of Abimelech after pretending to be crazy and being sent away by him.*   [a] HEBREW TITLE: *By David.*

34 Title 1 S 21.13-15   **34.8** 1 P 2.3   **34.12-16** 1 P 3.10-12   **34.20** Jn 19.36

be defeated and disgraced!
May those who plot against me
  be turned back and confused!
⁵ May they be like straw blown by
    the wind
  as the angel of the LORD
    pursues them!
⁶ May their path be dark and slippery
  while the angel of the LORD
    strikes them down!

⁷ Without any reason they laid a trap
    for me
  and dug a deep hole to catch
    me.
⁸ But destruction will catch them
    before they know it;
  they will be caught in their own
    trap
  and fall to their destruction!

⁹ Then I will be glad because of the
    LORD;
  I will be happy because he
    saved me.
¹⁰ With all my heart I will say to the
    LORD,
  "There is no one like you.
  You protect the weak from the
    strong,
  the poor from the oppressor."

¹¹ Evil people testify against me
  and accuse me of crimes I know
    nothing about.
¹² They pay me back evil for good,
  and I sink in despair.
¹³ But when they were sick, I dressed
    in mourning;
  I deprived myself of food;
I prayed with my head bowed low,
  as I would pray for a friend or a
    brother.
I went around bent over in
    mourning,
  as one who mourns for his
    mother.

¹⁵ But when I was in trouble, they
    were all glad
  and gathered around to make
    fun of me;
strangers beat me
  and kept striking me.
¹⁶ Like those who would mock a
    cripple, ᵇ
  they glared at me with hate.

¹⁷ How much longer, Lord, will you
    just look on?
  Rescue me from their attacks;
  save my life from these lions!
¹⁸ Then I will thank you in the
    assembly of your people;
  I will praise you before them all.

¹⁹ Don't let my enemies, those liars,
    gloat over my defeat.
Don't let those who hate me for no
    reason
  smirk with delight over my
    sorrow.

²⁰ They do not speak in a friendly
    way;
  instead they invent all kinds of
    lies about peace-loving
    people.
²¹ They accuse me, shouting,
  "We saw what you did!"
²² But you, O LORD, have seen this.
  So don't be silent, Lord;
  don't keep yourself far away!
²³ Rouse yourself, O Lord, and defend
    me;
  rise up, my God, and plead my
    cause.
²⁴ You are righteous, O LORD, so
    declare me innocent;
  don't let my enemies gloat
    over me.
²⁵ Don't let them say to themselves,
  "We are rid of him!
  That's just what we wanted!"

Probable text Like those ... cripple; *Hebrew unclear.*
5.19 Ps 69.4; Jn 15.25

26 May those who gloat over my
   suffering
   be completely defeated and
   confused;
   may those who claim to be better
   than I am
   be covered with shame and
   disgrace.

27 May those who want to see me
   acquitted
   shout for joy and say again and
   again,
   "How great is the LORD!
   He is pleased with the success
   of his servant."
28 Then I will proclaim your
   righteousness,
   and I will praise you all day
   long.

Human Wickedness [c]

36 Sin speaks to the wicked
         deep in their hearts;
   they reject God and do not have
   reverence for him.
2 Because they think so highly of
   themselves,
   they think that God will not
   discover their sin and
   condemn it.
3 Their speech is wicked and full of
   lies;
   they no longer do what is wise
   and good.
4 They make evil plans as they lie
   in bed;
   nothing they do is good,
   and they never reject anything
   evil.

The Goodness of God

5 LORD, your constant love reaches
   the heavens;
   your faithfulness extends to the
   skies.

6 Your righteousness is towering like
   the mountains;
   your justice is like the depths of
   the sea.
   People and animals are in your
   care.

7 How precious, O God, is your
   constant love!
   We find[d] protection under the
   shadow of your wings.
8 We feast on the abundant food you
   provide;
   you let us drink from the river of
   your goodness.
9 You are the source of all life,
   and because of your light we see
   the light.

10 Continue to love those who know
   you
   and to do good to those who are
   righteous.
11 Do not let proud people attack me
   or the wicked make me run
   away.

12 See where evil people have fallen.
   There they lie, unable to rise.

The Destiny of the Wicked and
of the Good [e]

37 Don't be worried on account
         of the wicked;
   don't be jealous of those who do
   wrong.
2 They will soon disappear like grass
   that dries up;
   they will die like plants that
   wither.

3 Trust in the LORD and do good;
   live in the land and be safe.
4 Seek your happiness in the LORD,
   and he will give you your heart's
   desire.

[c] HEBREW TITLE: *By David, the LORD's servant.*   [d] precious, O God, is . . . find; *or*
precious is your constant love! Gods and people find.   [e] HEBREW TITLE: *By David.*
36.1 Ro 3.18

⁵Give yourself to the LORD;
 trust in him, and he will help
  you;
⁶he will make your righteousness
  shine like the noonday sun.

⁷Be patient and wait for the LORD
  to act;
 don't be worried about those
  who prosper
 or those who succeed in their
  evil plans.

⁸Don't give in to worry or anger;
 it only leads to trouble.
⁹Those who trust in the LORD will
  possess the land,
 but the wicked will be driven
  out.

¹⁰Soon the wicked will disappear;
 you may look for them, but you
  won't find them;
¹¹but the humble will possess the
  land
 and enjoy prosperity and peace.

¹²The wicked plot against good
  people
 and glare at them with hate.
¹³But the Lord laughs at wicked
  people,
 because he knows they will soon
  be destroyed.

¹⁴The wicked draw their swords and
  bend their bows
 to kill the poor and needy,
 to slaughter those who do what
  is right;
¹⁵but they will be killed by their own
  swords,
 and their bows will be smashed.

¹⁶The little that a good person owns
 is worth more than the wealth of
  all the wicked,
¹⁷because the LORD will take away
  the strength of the wicked,

but protect those who are good.

¹⁸The LORD takes care of those who
  obey him,
 and the land will be theirs
  forever.
¹⁹They will not suffer when times are
  bad;
 they will have enough in time of
  famine.
²⁰But the wicked will die;
 the enemies of the LORD will
  vanish like wild flowers;
 they will disappear like smoke.

²¹The wicked borrow and never pay
  back,
 but good people are generous
  with their gifts.
²²Those who are blessed by the LORD
  will possess the land,
 but those who are cursed by him
  will be driven out.

²³The LORD guides us in the way we
  should go
 and protects those who please
  him.
²⁴If they fall, they will not stay down,
 because the LORD will help
  them up.

²⁵I am old now; I have lived a long
  time,
 but I have never seen good
  people abandoned by
  the LORD
 or their children begging for
  food.
²⁶At all times they give freely and
  lend to others,
 and their children are a blessing.

²⁷Turn away from evil and do good,
 and your descendants will
  always live in the land;
²⁸for the LORD loves what is right
 and does not abandon his
  faithful people.

He protects them forever,
but the descendants of the
wicked will be driven out.
29 The righteous will possess the land
and live in it forever.

30 The words of good people are wise,
and they are always fair.
31 They keep the law of their God in
their hearts
and never depart from it.

32 Wicked people watch good people
and try to kill them;
33 but the LORD will not abandon
them to their enemy's power
or let them be condemned when
they are on trial.

34 Put your hope in the LORD and
obey his commands;
he will honor you by giving you
the land,
and you will see the wicked
driven out.

35 I once knew someone wicked who
was a tyrant;
he towered over everyone like a
cedar of Lebanon; *f*
36 but later I *g* passed by, and he
wasn't there;
I looked for him, but couldn't
find him.

37 Notice good people, observe the
righteous;
peaceful people have
descendants,
38 but sinners are completely
destroyed,
and their descendants are
wiped out.

39 The LORD saves the righteous
and protects them in times of
trouble.
40 He helps them and rescues them;

he saves them from the wicked,
because they go to him for
protection.

The Prayer of a Sufferer *h*

38
O LORD, don't punish me in
your anger!
2 You have wounded me with your
arrows;
you have struck me down.

3 Because of your anger, I am in
great pain;
my whole body is diseased
because of my sins.
4 I am drowning in the flood of my
sins;
they are a burden too heavy to
bear.

5 Because I have been foolish,
my sores stink and rot.
6 I am bent over, I am crushed;
I mourn all day long.
7 I am burning with fever
and I am near death.
8 I am worn out and utterly crushed;
my heart is troubled, and I
groan with pain.

9 O Lord, you know what I long for;
you hear all my groans.
10 My heart is pounding, my strength
is gone,
and my eyes have lost their
brightness.
11 My friends and neighbors will not
come near me,
because of my sores;
even my family keeps away
from me.
12 Those who want to kill me lay traps
for me,
and those who want to hurt me
threaten to ruin me;
they never stop plotting against
me.

---

f One ancient translation like a cedar of Lebanon; *Hebrew unclear.*   *g Some ancient
translations* I; *Hebrew* he.   *h* HEBREW TITLE: *A psalm by David; a lament.*

¹³I am like the deaf and cannot hear,
  like the dumb and cannot speak.
¹⁴I am like those who do not answer,
  because they cannot hear.

¹⁵But I trust in you, O LORD;
  and you, O Lord my God, will
    answer me.
¹⁶Don't let my enemies gloat over my
    distress;
  don't let them boast about my
    downfall!
¹⁷I am about to fall
  and am in constant pain.
¹⁸I confess my sins;
  they fill me with anxiety.
¹⁹My enemies are healthy and
    strong;
  there are many who hate me for
    no reason.
²⁰Those who pay back evil for good
  are against me because I try to
    do right.

²¹Do not abandon me, O LORD;
  do not stay away, my God!
²²Help me now, O Lord my savior!

The Confession of a Sufferer [i]

39 I said, "I will be careful about
        what I do
and will not let my tongue make
    me sin;
I will not say anything
    while evil people are near."
²I kept quiet, not saying a word,
    not even about anything good!
But my suffering only grew worse,
³   and I was overcome with
        anxiety.
The more I thought, the more
    troubled I became;
  I could not keep from asking:
⁴"LORD, how long will I live?
  When will I die?
  Tell me how soon my life
    will end."

HEBREW TITLE: *A psalm by David.*

⁵How short you have made my life!
  In your sight my lifetime seems
    nothing.
Indeed every living being is no
    more than a puff of wind,
⁶   no more than a shadow.
All we do is for nothing;
  we gather wealth, but don't
    know who will get it.

⁷What, then, can I hope for, Lord?
  I put my hope in you.
⁸Save me from all my sins,
  and don't let fools make fun
    of me.
⁹I will keep quiet, I will not say a
    word,
  for you are the one who made
    me suffer like this.
¹⁰Don't punish me any more!
  I am about to die from your
    blows.
¹¹You punish our sins by your
    rebukes,
  and like a moth you destroy
    what we love.
Indeed we are no more than a puff
    of wind!

¹²Hear my prayer, LORD,
  and listen to my cry;
  come to my aid when I weep.
Like all my ancestors
  I am only your guest for a little
    while.
¹³Leave me alone so that I may have
    some happiness
  before I go away and am no
    more.

A Song of Praise [i]

40 I waited patiently for the
        LORD's help;
  then he listened to me and
    heard my cry.
²He pulled me out of a dangerous
    pit,
  out of the deadly quicksand.

He set me safely on a rock
and made me secure.
³He taught me to sing a new song,
a song of praise to our God.
Many who see this will take
warning
and will put their trust in the
LORD.

⁴Happy are those who trust the
LORD,
who do not turn to idols
or join those who worship false
gods.
⁵You have done many things for us,
O LORD our God;
there is no one like you!
You have made many wonderful
plans for us.
I could never speak of them all —
their number is so great!

⁶You do not want sacrifices and
offerings;
you do not ask for animals
burned whole on the altar
or for sacrifices to take away
sins.
Instead, you have given me ears to
hear you,
⁷   and so I answered, "Here I am;
your instructions for me are in
the book of the Law.ʲ
⁸How I love to do your will, my God!
I keep your teaching in my
heart."

⁹In the assembly of all your people,
LORD,
I told the good news that you
save us.
You know that I will never stop
telling it.
¹⁰I have not kept the news of
salvation to myself;
I have always spoken of your
faithfulness and help.

I told the good news. (40.9)

In the assembly of all your people I
have not been silent
about your loyalty and constant
love.

¹¹LORD, I know you will never stop
being merciful to me.
Your love and loyalty will always
keep me safe.

A Prayer for Help
(Psalm 70)

¹²I am surrounded by many
troubles —
too many to count!
My sins have caught up with me,
and I can no longer see;
they are more than the hairs of my
head,
and I have lost my courage.
¹³Save me, LORD! Help me now!
¹⁴May those who try to kill me
be completely defeated and
confused.
May those who are happy because
of my troubles
be turned back and disgraced.
¹⁵May those who make fun of me
be dismayed by their defeat.

¹⁶May all who come to you
be glad and joyful.
May all who are thankful for your
salvation

ʲ your instructions ... Law; *or* my devotion to you is recorded in your book.
40.6-8 He 10.5-7

always say, "How great is the
LORD!"

⁷I am weak and poor, O Lord,
but you have not forgotten me.
You are my savior and my God —
hurry to my aid!

A Prayer in Sickness ᵏ

41 Happy are those who are
concerned for the poor;
the LORD will help them when
they are in trouble.
²The LORD will protect them and
preserve their lives;
he will make them happy in the
land;
he will not abandon them to the
power of their enemies.
³The LORD will help them when
they are sick
and will restore them to health.

⁴I said, "I have sinned against you,
LORD;
be merciful to me and heal me."
⁵My enemies say cruel things
about me.
They want me to die and be
forgotten.
⁶Those who come to see me are not
sincere;
they gather bad news about me
and then go out and tell it
everywhere.
⁷All who hate me whisper to each
other about me,
they imagine the worst about ˡ
me.
⁸They say, "He is fatally ill;
he will never leave his bed
again."
⁹Even my best friend, the one I
trusted most,
the one who shared my food,
has turned against me.

¹⁰Be merciful to me, LORD, and
restore my health,
and I will pay my enemies back.
¹¹They will not triumph over me,
and I will know that you are
pleased with me.
¹²You will help me, because I do
what is right;
you will keep me in your
presence forever.

¹³Praise the LORD, the God of Israel!
Praise him now and forever!

Amen! Amen!

BOOK TWO
(Psalms 42–72)

The Prayer of Someone in Exile ᵐ

42 As a deer longs for a stream
of cool water,
so I long for you, O God.
²I thirst for you, the living God.
When can I go and worship in
your presence?
³Day and night I cry,
and tears are my only food;
all the time my enemies ask me,
"Where is your God?"

⁴My heart breaks when I remember
the past,
when I went with the crowds to
the house of God
and led them as they walked
along,
a happy crowd, singing and
shouting praise to God.
⁵Why am I so sad?
Why am I so troubled?
I will put my hope in God,
and once again I will praise him,
my savior and my God.

⁶⁻⁷Here in exile my heart is breaking,

ᵏ HEBREW TITLE: *A psalm by David.*   ˡ imagine the worst about; *or* make evil plans
harm.   ᵐ HEBREW TITLE: *A poem by the clan of Korah.*
41.9 Mt 26.23; Mk 14.18; Lk 22.21; Jn 13.18   **41.13** Ps 106.48

and so I turn my thoughts to
  him.
He has sent waves of sorrow over
  my soul;
chaos roars at me like a flood,
like waterfalls thundering down
  to the Jordan
from Mount Hermon and Mount
  Mizar.
8 May the LORD show his constant
  love during the day,
so that I may have a song at
  night,
a prayer to the God of my life.

9 To God, my defender, I say,
  "Why have you forgotten me?
Why must I go on suffering
  from the cruelty of my
  enemies?"
10 I am crushed by their insults,
  as they keep on asking me,
  "Where is your God?"

11 Why am I so sad?
  Why am I so troubled?
I will put my hope in God,
  and once again I will praise him,
  my savior and my God.

The Prayer of Someone in Exile
(Continuation of Psalm 42)

43 O God, declare me innocent,
  and defend my cause
  against the ungodly;
deliver me from lying and evil
  people!
2 You are my protector;
  why have you abandoned me?
Why must I go on suffering
  from the cruelty of my enemies?

3 Send your light and your truth;
  may they lead me
  and bring me back to Zion, your
    sacred hill,[n]

and to your Temple, where you
  live.
4 Then I will go to your altar, O God;
  you are the source of my
  happiness.
I will play my harp and sing praise
  to you,
  O God, my God.

5 Why am I so sad?
  Why am I so troubled?
I will put my hope in God,
  and once again I will praise him
  my savior and my God.

A Prayer for Protection[o]

44 With our own ears we have
  heard it, O God—
our ancestors have told us
  about it,
about the great things you did in
  their time,
  in the days of long ago:
2 how you yourself drove out the
  heathen
and established your people in
  their land;
how you punished the other
  nations
and caused your own to prosper
3 Your people did not conquer the
  land with their swords;
they did not win it by their own
  power;
it was by your power and your
  strength,
by the assurance of your
  presence,
which showed that you loved
  them.

4 You are my king and my God;
  you give[p] victory to your people,
5   and by your power we defeat ou
  enemies.
6 I do not trust in my bow
  or in my sword to save me;

---

[n] SACRED HILL: *See 2.6.*   [o] HEBREW TITLE: *A poem by the clan of Korah.*   [p] *Some
ancient translations* and my God; you give; *Hebrew* O God; give.

7but you have saved us from our
    enemies
  and defeated those who hate us.
8We will always praise you
  and give thanks to you forever.

9But now you have rejected us and
    let us be defeated;
  you no longer march out with
    our armies.
10You made us run from our
    enemies,
  and they took for themselves
    what was ours.
11You allowed us to be slaughtered
    like sheep;
  you scattered us in foreign
    countries.
12You sold your own people for a
    small price
  as though they had little value.q

13Our neighbors see what you did
    to us,
  and they mock us and laugh
    at us.
14You have made us a joke among
    the nations;
  they shake their heads at us
    in scorn.
15I am always in disgrace;
  I am covered with shame
16 from hearing the sneers and
    insults
  of my enemies and those who
    hate me.

17All this has happened to us,
  even though we have not
    forgotten you
  or broken the covenant you
    made with us.
18We have not been disloyal to you;
  we have not disobeyed your
    commands.
19Yet you left us helpless among wild
    animals;

  you abandoned us in deepest
    darkness.

20If we had stopped worshiping our
    God
  and prayed to a foreign god,
21you would surely have discovered
    it,
  because you know our secret
    thoughts.
22But it is on your account that we
    are being killed all the time,
  that we are treated like sheep to
    be slaughtered.

23Wake up, Lord! Why are you
    asleep?
  Rouse yourself! Don't reject us
    forever!
24Why are you hiding from us?
  Don't forget our suffering and
    trouble!

25We fall crushed to the ground;
  we lie defeated in the dust.
26Come to our aid!
  Because of your constant love
    save us!

A Royal Wedding Song r

45 Beautiful words fill my mind,
    as I compose this song for
    the king.
Like the pen of a good writer
  my tongue is ready with a poem.

2You are the most handsome of
    men;
  you are an eloquent speaker.
  God has always blessed you.
3Buckle on your sword, mighty king;
  you are glorious and majestic.

4Ride on in majesty to victory

as . . . value; or and made no profit from the sale.   r HEBREW TITLE: A poem by the
clan of Korah; a love song.
4.22 Ro 8.36

for the defense of truth and
justice!*s*

Your strength will win you great
victories!

5 Your arrows are sharp,
they pierce the hearts of your
enemies;
nations fall down at your feet.

6 The kingdom that God has given
you*t*
will last forever and ever.
You rule over your people with
justice;
7   you love what is right and hate
what is evil.
That is why God, your God, has
chosen you
and has poured out more
happiness on you
than on any other king.

8 The perfume of myrrh and aloes is
on your clothes;
musicians entertain you in
palaces decorated with ivory.

9 Among the women of your court
are daughters of kings,
and at the right of your throne
stands the queen,
wearing ornaments of finest
gold.

10 Bride of the king, listen to what I
say —
forget your people and your
relatives.

11 Your beauty will make the king
desire you;
he is your master, so you must
obey him.

12 The people of Tyre will bring you
gifts;
rich people will try to win your
favor.

13 The princess is in the palace — how
beautiful she is!
Her gown is made of gold
thread.

14 In her colorful gown she is led to
the king,
followed by her bridesmaids,
and they also are brought to
him.

15 With joy and gladness they come
and enter the king's palace.

16 You, my king, will have many sons
to succeed your ancestors as
kings,
and you will make them rulers
over the whole earth.

17 My song will keep your fame alive
forever,
and everyone will praise you for
all time to come.

God Is with Us*u*

46 God is our shelter and
strength,
always ready to help in times of
trouble.
2 So we will not be afraid, even if the
earth is shaken
and mountains fall into the
ocean depths;
3 even if the seas roar and rage,
and the hills are shaken by the
violence.

4 There is a river that brings joy to
the city of God,
to the sacred house of the Most
High.
5 God is in that city, and it will never
be destroyed;
at early dawn he will come to
its aid.
6 Nations are terrified, kingdoms are
shaken;

---

s Probable text and justice; *Hebrew* and meekness of justice.   *t The kingdom that
God has given you; or* Your kingdom, O God; *or* Your divine kingdom.   *u* HEBREW
TITLE: *A song by the clan of Korah.*
45.6, 7 He 1.8, 9

We will not be afraid. (46.2)

God thunders, and the earth
    dissolves.
[7] The LORD Almighty is with us;
    the God of Jacob is our refuge.

[8] Come and see what the LORD
    has done.
    See what amazing things he has
        done on earth.
[9] He stops wars all over the world;
    he breaks bows, destroys spears,
    and sets shields on fire.
[10] "Stop fighting," he says, "and know
    that I am God,
    supreme among the nations,
    supreme over the world."

[11] The LORD Almighty is with us;
    the God of Jacob is our refuge.

The Supreme Ruler [v]

47 Clap your hands for joy, all
    peoples!
    Praise God with loud songs!

[2] The LORD, the Most High, is to
    be feared;
    he is a great king, ruling over all
        the world.
[3] He gave us victory over the
        peoples;
    he made us rule over the
        nations.
[4] He chose for us the land where
    we live,
    the proud possession of his
        people, whom he loves.

[5] God goes up to his throne.
    There are shouts of joy and the
        blast of trumpets,
    as the LORD goes up.
[6] Sing praise to God;
    sing praise to our king!
[7] God is king over all the world;
    praise him with songs!

[8] God sits on his sacred throne;
    he rules over the nations.
[9] The rulers of the nations assemble

HEBREW TITLE: *A psalm by the clan of Korah.*

with the people[w] of the God of
Abraham.
More powerful than all armies
is he;
he rules supreme.

Zion, the City of God[x]

48 The LORD is great and is to
be highly praised
in the city of our God, on his
sacred hill.[y]
2 Zion, the mountain of God, is high
and beautiful;
the city of the great king brings
joy to all the world.
3 God has shown that there is safety
with him
inside the fortresses of the city.

4 The kings gathered together
and came to attack Mount Zion.
5 But when they saw it, they were
amazed;
they were afraid and ran away.
6 There they were seized with fear
and anguish,
like a woman about to bear a
child,
7 like ships tossing in a furious
storm.

8 We have heard what God has done,
and now we have seen it
in the city of our God, the LORD
Almighty;
he will keep the city safe forever.

9 Inside your Temple, O God,
we think of your constant love.
10 You are praised by people
everywhere,
and your fame extends over all
the earth.
You rule with justice;
11 let the people of Zion be glad!

You give right judgments;
let there be joy in the cities of
Judah!

12 People of God, walk around Zion
and count the towers;
13 take notice of the walls and
examine the fortresses,
so that you may tell the next
generation:
14 "This God is our God forever and
ever;
he will lead us for all time to
come."

The Foolishness of Trusting in Riches[z]

49 Hear this, everyone!
Listen, all people everywhere
2 great and small alike,
rich and poor together.
3 My thoughts will be clear;
I will speak words of wisdom.
4 I will turn my attention to proverbs
and explain their meaning as I
play the harp.

5 I am not afraid in times of danger
when I am surrounded by
enemies,
6 by evil people who trust in their
riches
and boast of their great wealth.
7 We can never redeem ourselves;
we cannot pay God the price for
our lives,
8 because the payment for a
human life is too great.
What we could pay would never
be enough
9 to keep us from the grave,
to let us live forever.

10 Anyone can see that even the
wise die,

---

w Probable text with the people; *Hebrew* the people.   *x* HEBREW TITLE: *A psalm by
the clan of Korah; a song.*   *y* SACRED HILL: *See 2.6.*   *z* HEBREW TITLE: *A psalm by
the clan of Korah.*
48.2 Mt 5.35   **49.10** Si 11.19

as well as the foolish and stupid.
They all leave their riches to
their descendants.
[1] Their graves [a] are their homes
forever;
there they stay for all time,
though they once had lands of
their own.
[2] Our greatness cannot keep us from
death;
we will still die like the animals.

[3] See what happens to those who
trust in themselves,
the fate of those [b] who are
satisfied with their wealth —
[4] they are doomed to die like sheep,
and Death will be their
shepherd.
The righteous will triumph over
them,
as their bodies quickly decay
in the world of the dead far from
their homes. [c]
[5] But God will rescue me;
he will save me from the power
of death.

[6] Don't be upset when someone
becomes rich,
when his wealth grows even
greater;
[7] he cannot take it with him when
he dies;
his wealth will not go with him
to the grave.
[8] Even if someone is satisfied with
this life
and is praised because he is
successful,
[9] he will join all his ancestors in
death,
where the darkness lasts forever.
[10] Our greatness cannot keep us from
death;
we will still die like the animals.

True Worship [d]

50 The Almighty God, the LORD,
speaks;
he calls to the whole earth from
east to west.

He cannot take it with him when he dies. (49.17)

[2] God shines from Zion,
the city perfect in its beauty.

[3] Our God is coming, but not in
silence;
a raging fire is in front of him,
a furious storm around him.
[4] He calls heaven and earth as
witnesses
to see him judge his people.
[5] He says, "Gather my faithful people
to me,
those who made a covenant with
me by offering a sacrifice."
[6] The heavens proclaim that God is
righteous,
that he himself is judge.

[7] "Listen, my people, and I will
speak;
I will testify against you, Israel.
I am God, your God.
[8] I do not reprimand you because of
your sacrifices
and the burnt offerings you
always bring me.
[9] And yet I do not need bulls from
your farms

Some ancient translations graves; *Hebrew* inner thoughts.   [b] *One ancient translation* the fate of those; *Hebrew* after them.   [c] in . . . homes.; *Hebrew unclear.*
HEBREW TITLE: *A psalm by Asaph.*

or goats from your flocks;
¹⁰ all the animals in the forest are
mine
and the cattle on thousands of
hills.

All the animals in the forest are mine. (50.10)

¹¹ All the wild birds are mine
and all living things in the
fields.

¹²"If I were hungry, I would not ask
you for food,
for the world and everything in
it is mine.
¹³ Do I eat the flesh of bulls
or drink the blood of goats?
¹⁴ Let the giving of thanks be your
sacrifice to God,ᵉ
and give the Almighty all that
you promised.
¹⁵ Call to me when trouble comes;
I will save you,
and you will praise me."

¹⁶ But God says to the wicked,
"Why should you recite my
commandments?

Why should you talk about my
covenant?
¹⁷ You refuse to let me correct you;
you reject my commands.
¹⁸ You become the friend of every
thief you see,
and you associate with
adulterers.

¹⁹"You are always ready to speak evil,
you never hesitate to tell lies.
²⁰ You are ready to accuse your own
relatives
and to find fault with them.
²¹ You have done all this, and I have
said nothing,
so you thought that I am like
you.
But now I reprimand you
and make the matter plain to
you.

²²"Listen to this, you that ignore me,
or I will destroy you,
and there will be no one to
save you.
²³ Giving thanks is the sacrifice that
honors me,
and I will surely save all who
obey me."

A Prayer for Forgivenessᶠ

51 Be merciful to me, O God,
because of your constant
love.
Because of your great mercy
wipe away my sins!
² Wash away all my evil
and make me clean from my
sin!

³ I recognize my faults;
I am always conscious of my
sins.

ᵉ *Let the giving ... to God; or* Offer your thanksgiving sacrifice to God.   ᶠ HEBREW
TITLE: *A psalm by David, after the prophet Nathan had spoken to him about his
adultery with Bathsheba.*
51 Title 2 S 12.1-15

4 I have sinned against you — only
    against you —
  and done what you consider evil.
So you are right in judging me;
    you are justified in condemning
    me.
5 I have been evil from the day I was
    born;
  from the time I was conceived, I
    have been sinful.

6 Sincerity and truth are what you
    require;
  fill my mind with your wisdom.
7 Remove my sin, and I will be
    clean;
  wash me, and I will be whiter
    than snow.
8 Let me hear the sounds of joy and
    gladness;
  and though you have crushed
    me and broken me,
  I will be happy once again.
9 Close your eyes to my sins
  and wipe out all my evil.

10 Create a pure heart in me, O God,
  and put a new and loyal spirit
    in me.
11 Do not banish me from your
    presence;
  do not take your holy spirit away
    from me.
12 Give me again the joy that comes
    from your salvation,
  and make me willing to obey
    you.
13 Then I will teach sinners your
    commands,
  and they will turn back to you.

14 Spare my life, O God, and save
    me,[g]
  and I will gladly proclaim your
    righteousness.

15 Help me to speak, Lord,
  and I will praise you.

16 You do not want sacrifices,
  or I would offer them;
  you are not pleased with burnt
    offerings.
17 My sacrifice is a humble spirit,
    O God;
  you will not reject a humble and
    repentant heart.

18 O God, be kind to Zion and help
    her;
  rebuild the walls of Jerusalem.
19 Then you will be pleased with
    proper sacrifices
  and with our burnt offerings;
  and bulls will be sacrificed on
    your altar.

God's Judgment and Grace [h]

52 Why do you boast, great one,
      of your evil?
  God's faithfulness is eternal.
2 You make plans to ruin others;
  your tongue is like a sharp razor.
  You are always inventing lies.
3 You love evil more than good
  and falsehood more than truth.
4 You love to hurt people with your
    words, you liar!

5 So God will ruin you forever;
  he will take hold of you and
    snatch you from your home;
  he will remove you from the
    world of the living.
6 Righteous people will see this and
    be afraid;
  then they will laugh at you
    and say,
7 "Look, here is someone who did not
    depend on God for safety,
  but trusted instead in great
    wealth

Spare my life . . . me; or O God my savior, keep me from the crime of murder.
HEBREW TITLE: A poem by David, after Doeg the Edomite went to Saul and told him
that David had gone to the house of Ahimelech.
14.4 Ro 3.4   **52 Title** 1 S 22.9, 10

and looked for security in being wicked."

8 But I am like an olive tree growing in the house of God;
I trust in his constant love forever and ever.
9 I will always thank you, God, for what you have done;
in the presence of your people I will proclaim that you are good.

Human Wickedness [i]
(Psalm 14)

53 Fools say to themselves,
"There is no God."
They are all corrupt,
and they have done terrible things;
there is no one who does what is right.

2 God looks down from heaven at people
to see if there are any who are wise,
any who worship him.
3 But they have all turned away;
they are all equally bad.
Not one of them does what is right,
not a single one.

4 "Don't they know?" God asks.
"Are these evildoers ignorant?
They live by robbing my people,
and they never pray to me."

5 But then they will become terrified,
as they have never been before,
for God will scatter the bones of the enemies of his people.
God has rejected them,
and so Israel will totally defeat them.

6 How I pray that victory
will come to Israel from Zion.
How happy the people of Israel will be
when God makes them prosperous again!

A Prayer for Protection from Enemies [j]

54 Save me by your power,
O God;
set me free by your might!
2 Hear my prayer, O God;
listen to my words!
3 Proud people are coming to attack me;
cruel people are trying to kill me —
those who do not care about God.

4 But God is my helper.
The Lord is my defender.
5 May God use their own evil to punish my enemies.
He will destroy them because he is faithful.

6 I will gladly offer you a sacrifice,
O LORD;
I will give you thanks
because you are good.
7 You have rescued me from all my troubles,
and I have seen my enemies defeated.

The Prayer of Someone Betrayed by a Friend [k]

55 Hear my prayer, O God;
don't turn away from my plea!
2 Listen to me and answer me;
I am worn out by my worries.

---

[i] HEBREW TITLE: *A poem by David.*   [j] HEBREW TITLE: *A poem by David, after the men from Ziph went to Saul and told him that David was hiding in their territory.* [k] HEBREW TITLE: *A poem by David.*

53.1-3 Ro 3.10-12   **54 Title** 1 S 23.19; 26.1

I am terrified by the threats of my
enemies,
crushed by the oppression of the
wicked.
They bring trouble on me;
they are angry with me and
hate me.

I am terrified,
and the terrors of death crush
me.
I am gripped by fear and trembling;
I am overcome with horror.
I wish I had wings like a dove.
I would fly away and find rest.
I would fly far away
and make my home in the
desert.
I would hurry and find myself a
shelter
from the raging wind and the
storm.
Confuse the speech of my enemies,
O Lord!

I see violence and riots in the city,
surrounding it day and night,
filling it with crime and trouble.
There is destruction everywhere;
the streets are full of oppression
and fraud.

If it were an enemy making fun
of me,
I could endure it;
if it were an opponent boasting
over me,
I could hide myself from him.
But it is you, my companion,
my colleague and close friend.
We had intimate talks with each
other
and worshiped together in the
Temple.
May my enemies die before their
time;
may they go down alive into the
world of the dead!

Evil is in their homes and in their
hearts.

16 But I call to the LORD God for help,
and he will save me.
17 Morning, noon, and night
my complaints and groans go up
to him,
and he will hear my voice.
18 He will bring me safely back
from the battles that I fight
against so many enemies.
19 God, who has ruled from eternity,
will hear me and defeat them;
for they refuse to change,
and they do not fear him.

20 My former companion attacked his
friends;
he broke his promises.
21 His words were smoother than
cream,
but there was hatred in his
heart;
his words were as soothing as oil,
but they cut like sharp swords.

22 Leave your troubles with the LORD,
and he will defend you;
he never lets honest people be
defeated.

23 But you, O God, will bring those
murderers and liars
to their graves
before half their life is over.
As for me, I will trust in you.

A Prayer of Trust in God [l]

56 Be merciful to me, O God,
because I am under
attack;
my enemies persecute me all the
time.
2 All day long my opponents attack
me.

HEBREW TITLE: *A psalm by David, after the Philistines captured him in Gath.*
Title 1 S 21.13-15

There are so many who fight
against me.
3 When I am afraid, O LORD
Almighty,
I put my trust in you.
4 I trust in God and am not afraid;
I praise him for what he has
promised.
What can a mere human being
do to me?

5 My enemies make trouble for me
all day long;
they are always thinking up
some way to hurt me!
6 They gather in hiding places
and watch everything I do,
hoping to kill me.
7 Punish[m] them, O God, for their
evil;
defeat those people in your
anger!

8 You know how troubled I am;
you have kept a record of my
tears.
Aren't they listed in your book?
9 The day I call to you,
my enemies will be turned back.
I know this: God[n] is on my side —
10   the LORD, whose promises I
praise.
11 In him I trust, and I will not be
afraid.
What can a mere human being
do to me?

12 O God, I will offer you what I have
promised;
I will give you my offering of
thanksgiving,
13 because you have rescued me from
death
and kept me from defeat.
And so I walk in the presence
of God,

in the light that shines on the
living.

A Prayer for Help[o]

57 Be merciful to me, O God, be
merciful,
because I come to you for safety.
In the shadow of your wings I find
protection
until the raging storms are over.

2 I call to God, the Most High,
to God, who supplies my every
need.
3 He will answer from heaven and
save me;
he will defeat my oppressors.
God will show me his constant
love and faithfulness.

4 I am surrounded by enemies,
who are like lions hungry for
human flesh.
Their teeth are like spears and
arrows;
their tongues are like sharp
swords.

5 Show your greatness in the sky,
O God,
and your glory over all the earth.

6 My enemies have spread a net to
catch me;
I am overcome with distress.
They dug a pit in my path,
but fell into it themselves.

7 I have complete confidence, O God;
I will sing and praise you!
8 Wake up, my soul!
Wake up, my harp and lyre!
I will wake up the sun.
9 I will thank you, O Lord, among
the nations.

---

[m] *Probable text* Punish; *Hebrew* Save.   [n] I know this: God; *or* Because I know that
God.   [o] HEBREW TITLE: *A psalm by David, after he fled from Saul in the cave.*
57 Title 1 S 22.1; 24.3

I will praise you among the
   peoples.
¹⁰Your constant love reaches the
   heavens;
   your faithfulness touches the
    skies.
¹¹Show your greatness in the sky,
   O God,
   and your glory over all the earth.

A Prayer for God to Punish the Wicked *p*

58 Do you rulers *q* ever give a
      just decision?
   Do you judge everyone fairly?
²No! You think only of the evil you
   can do,
   and commit crimes of violence
    in the land.

³Evildoers go wrong all their lives;
   they tell lies from the day they
    are born.
⁴They are full of poison like snakes;
   they stop up their ears like a
    deaf cobra,
⁵which does not hear the voice of
   the snake charmer,
   or the chant of the clever
    magician.

⁶Break the teeth of these fierce
   lions, O God.
⁷May they disappear like water
   draining away;
   may they be crushed like weeds
    on a path. *r*
⁸May they be like snails that
   dissolve into slime;
   may they be like a baby born
    dead that never sees
    the light.
⁹Before they know it, they are cut
   down like weeds;

in his fierce anger God will blow
   them away
   while they are still living. *s*

¹⁰The righteous will be glad when
   they see sinners punished;
   they will wade through the blood
    of the wicked.
¹¹People will say, "The righteous are
   indeed rewarded;
   there is indeed a God who
    judges the world."

A Prayer for Safety *t*

59 Save me from my enemies,
      my God;
   protect me from those who
    attack me!
²Save me from those evil people;
   rescue me from those
    murderers!

³Look! They are waiting to kill me;
   cruel people are gathering
    against me.
  It is not because of any sin or
    wrong I have done,
⁴   nor because of any fault of mine,
    O LORD,
   that they hurry to their places.

⁵Rise, LORD God Almighty, and
   come to my aid;
   see for yourself, God of Israel!
  Wake up and punish the heathen;
   show no mercy to evil traitors!

⁶They come back in the evening,
   snarling like dogs as they go
    about the city.
⁷Listen to their insults and threats.
   Their tongues are like swords in
    their mouths,

---

p HEBREW TITLE: *A psalm by David.*   *q* rulers; *or* gods.   *r Probable text may . . .*
ath; Hebrew unclear.   *s Verse 9 in Hebrew is unclear.*   *t* HEBREW TITLE: *A*
psalm by David, after Saul sent men to watch his house in order to kill him.
59 Title 1 S 19.11

yet they think that no one hears
them.

[8] But you laugh at them, LORD;
you mock all the heathen.
[9] I have confidence in your strength;
you are my refuge, O God.
[10] My God loves me and will come
to me;
he will let me see my enemies
defeated.

[11] Do not kill them, O God, or my
people may forget.
Scatter them by your strength
and defeat them,
O Lord, our protector.
[12] Sin is on their lips; all their words
are sinful;
may they be caught in their
pride!
Because they curse and lie,
[13]   destroy them in your anger;
destroy them completely.
Then everyone will know that God
rules in Israel,
that his rule extends over all the
earth.

[14] My enemies come back in the
evening,
snarling like dogs as they go
about the city,
[15]   like dogs roaming about for food
and growling if they do not find
enough.

[16] But I will sing about your strength;
every morning I will sing aloud
of your constant love.
You have been a refuge for me,
a shelter in my time of trouble.
[17] I will praise you, my defender.
My refuge is God,
the God who loves me.

A Prayer for Deliverance [u]

60 You have rejected us, God,
and defeated us;
you have been angry with
us — but now turn
back to us. [v]
[2] You have made the land tremble,
and you have cut it open;
now heal its wounds, because it
is falling apart.
[3] You have made your people suffer
greatly;
we stagger around as though we
were drunk.
[4] You have warned those who have
reverence for you,
so that they might escape
destruction.
[5] Save us by your might; answer our
prayer,
so that the people you love may
be rescued.

[6] From his sanctuary [w] God has said,
"In triumph I will divide
Shechem
and distribute Sukkoth Valley to
my people.
[7] Gilead is mine, and Manasseh too;
Ephraim is my helmet
and Judah my royal scepter.
[8] But I will use Moab as my
washbowl,
and I will throw my sandals
on Edom,
as a sign that I own it.
Did the Philistines think they
would shout in triumph
over me?"

[9] Who, O God, will take me into the
fortified city?
Who will lead me to Edom?
[10] Have you really rejected us?

[u] HEBREW TITLE: *A psalm by David, for teaching, when he fought against the Arameans
from Naharaim and from Zobah, and Joab turned back and killed 12,000 Edomites in
Salt Valley.*   [v] angry with us . . . us; *or* angry with us and turned your back on us.
[w] From his sanctuary; *or* In his holiness.
60 Title 2 S 8.13; 1 Ch 18.12

Aren't you going to march out
    with our armies?
[1] Help us against the enemy;
    human help is worthless.
[2] With God on our side we will win;
    he will defeat our enemies.

A Prayer for Protection [x]

61 Hear my cry, O God;
        listen to my prayer!
[2] In despair and far from home
    I call to you!

Take me to a safe refuge,
[3]   for you are my protector,
    my strong defense against my
        enemies.

[4] Let me live in your sanctuary all
        my life;
    let me find safety under your
        wings.
[5] You have heard my promises,
        O God,
    and you have given me what
        belongs to those who
        honor you.

[6] Add many years to the king's life;
    let him live on and on!
[7] May he rule forever in your
        presence, O God;
    protect him with your constant
        love and faithfulness.

[8] So I will always sing praises to you,
    as I offer you daily what I have
        promised.

Confidence in God's Protection [y]

62 I wait patiently for God to
        save me;
    I depend on him alone.
[2] He alone protects and saves me;

he is my defender,
    and I shall never be defeated.

[3] How much longer will all of you
        attack someone
    who is no stronger than a
        broken-down fence?
[4] You only want to bring him down
        from his place of honor;
    you take pleasure in lies.
    You speak words of blessing,
        but in your heart you curse him.

[5] I depend on God alone;
    I put my hope in him.
[6] He alone protects and saves me;
    he is my defender,
    and I shall never be defeated.
[7] My salvation and honor depend
        on God;
    he is my strong protector;
    he is my shelter.

[8] Trust in God at all times, my
        people.
    Tell him all your troubles,
    for he is our refuge.

[9] Human beings are all like a puff of
        breath;
    great and small alike are
        worthless.
    Put them on the scales, and they
        weigh nothing;
    they are lighter than a mere
        breath.
[10] Don't put your trust in violence;
    don't hope to gain anything by
        robbery;
    even if your riches increase,
        don't depend on them.

[11] More than once I have heard
        God say
    that power belongs to him
[12]   and that his love is constant.

HEBREW TITLE: *By David.*   [y] HEBREW TITLE: *A psalm by David.*
2.12 Job 34.11; Jr 17.10; Mt 16.27; Ro 2.6; Rev 2.23

You yourself, O Lord, reward
   everyone according to
   their deeds.

Longing for God [z]

63 O God, you are my God,
   and I long for you.
My whole being desires you;
   like a dry, worn-out, and
      waterless land,
   my soul is thirsty for you.
2 Let me see you in the sanctuary;
   let me see how mighty and
      glorious you are.
3 Your constant love is better than
      life itself,
   and so I will praise you.
4 I will give you thanks as long as
      I live;
   I will raise my hands to you in
      prayer.
5 My soul will feast and be satisfied,
   and I will sing glad songs of
      praise to you.

6 As I lie in bed, I remember you;
   all night long I think of you,
7   because you have always been
      my help.
In the shadow of your wings I sing
      for joy.
8 I cling to you,
   and your hand keeps me safe.

9 Those who are trying to kill me
   will go down into the world of
      the dead.
10 They will be killed in battle,
   and their bodies eaten by
      wolves.
11 Because God gives him victory,
   the king will rejoice.
Those who make promises in God's
   name will praise him,

but the mouths of liars will be
   shut.

A Prayer for Protection [a]

64 I am in trouble, God — listen
   to my prayer!
I am afraid of my
   enemies — save my life!
2 Protect me from the plots of the
      wicked,
   from mobs of evil people.
3 They sharpen their tongues like
      swords
   and aim cruel words like arrows.
4 They are quick to spread their
      shameless lies;
   they destroy good people with
      cowardly slander.
5 They encourage each other in their
      evil plots;
   they talk about where they will
      place their traps.
   "No one can see them," they
      say.
6 They make evil plans and say,
   "We have planned a perfect
      crime."
The human heart and mind are a
   mystery.

7 But God shoots his arrows at them,
   and suddenly they are wounded.
8 He will destroy them because of
      those words; [b]
   all who see them will shake
      their heads.
9 They will all be afraid;
   they will think about what God
      has done
   and tell about his deeds.
10 All righteous people will rejoice
   because of what the LORD has
      done.
They will find safety in him;
   all good people will praise him.

[z] HEBREW TITLE: *A psalm by David, when he was in the desert of Judea.*   [a] HEBREW
TITLE: *A psalm by David.*   [b] *Probable text* He will destroy them because of those
words; *Hebrew* They will destroy him, those words are against them.
63 Title 1 S 23.14

Praise and Thanksgiving [c]

65 O God, it is right for us to
praise you in Zion
and keep our promises to you,
2 because you answer prayers.
People everywhere will come to you
3 on account of their sins.
Our faults defeat us,[d]
but you forgive them.
4 Happy are those whom you choose,
whom you bring to live in your
sanctuary.
We shall be satisfied with the good
things of your house,
the blessings of your sacred
Temple.

5 You answer us by giving us victory,
and you do wonderful things to
save us.
People all over the world
and across the distant seas trust
in you.
6 You set the mountains in place by
your strength,
showing your mighty power.
7 You calm the roar of the seas
and the noise of the waves;
you calm the uproar of the
peoples.
8 The whole world stands in awe
of the great things that you have
done.
Your deeds bring shouts of joy
from one end of the earth to the
other.

9 You show your care for the land by
sending rain;
you make it rich and fertile.
You fill the streams with water;
you provide the earth with crops.
This is how you do it:
10 you send abundant rain on the
plowed fields
and soak them with water;

you soften the soil with showers
and cause the young plants to
grow.
11 What a rich harvest your goodness
provides!
Wherever you go there is plenty.
12 The pastures are filled with flocks;
the hillsides are full of joy.
13 The fields are covered with sheep;
the valleys are full of wheat.
Everything shouts and sings
for joy.

A Song of Praise and Thanksgiving [e]

66 Praise God with shouts of joy,
all people!
2 Sing to the glory of his name;
offer him glorious praise!

Sing to the glory of his name! (66.2)

3 Say to God, "How wonderful are
the things you do!
Your power is so great
that your enemies bow down in
fear before you.
4 Everyone on earth worships you;
they sing praises to you,
they sing praises to your name."

5 Come and see what God has done,
his wonderful acts among
people.
6 He changed the sea into dry land;
our ancestors crossed the river
on foot.
There we rejoiced because of what
he did.
7 He rules forever by his might

HEBREW TITLE: *A psalm by David; a song.*   [d] *One ancient translation* us; *Hebrew*
ne.   [e] HEBREW TITLE: *A song.*
66.6 a Ex 14.21; **b** Js 3.14-17

and keeps his eyes on the
nations.
Let no rebels rise against him.
⁸ Praise our God, all nations;
let your praise be heard.
⁹ He has kept us alive
and has not allowed us to fall.

¹⁰ You have put us to the test, God;
as silver is purified by fire,
so you have tested us.
¹¹ You let us fall into a trap
and placed heavy burdens on
our backs.
¹² You let our enemies trample us;
we went through fire and flood,
but now you have brought us to
a place of safety. ʲ

¹³ I will bring burnt offerings to your
house;
I will offer you what I promised.
¹⁴ I will give you what I said I would
when I was in trouble.
¹⁵ I will offer sheep to be burned on
the altar;
I will sacrifice bulls and goats,
and the smoke will go up to
the sky.

¹⁶ Come and listen, all who honor
God,
and I will tell you what he has
done for me.
¹⁷ I cried to him for help;
I praised him with songs.
¹⁸ If I had ignored my sins,
the Lord would not have listened
to me.
¹⁹ But God has indeed heard me;
he has listened to my prayer.

²⁰ I praise God,
because he did not reject my
prayer
or keep back his constant love
from me.

A Song of Thanksgiving ᵍ

67 God, be merciful to us and
bless us;
look on us with kindness,
² so that the whole world may know
your will;
so that all nations may know
your salvation.

³ May the peoples praise you, O God;
may all the peoples praise you!

⁴ May the nations be glad and sing
for joy,
because you judge the peoples
with justice
and guide every nation on earth.

⁵ May the peoples praise you, O God;
may all the peoples praise you!

⁶ The land has produced its harvest;
God, our God, has blessed us.
⁷ God has blessed us;
may all people everywhere honor
him.

A National Song of Triumph ʰ

68 God rises up and scatters his
enemies.
Those who hate him run away
in defeat.
² As smoke is blown away, so he
drives them off;
as wax melts in front of the fire,
so do the wicked perish in God's
presence.
³ But the righteous are glad and
rejoice in his presence;
they are happy and shout
for joy.

⁴ Sing to God, sing praises to his
name;
prepare a way for him who rides
on the clouds. ⁱ

ʲ *Some ancient translations* safety; *Hebrew* overflowing.
a song.   ʰ HEBREW TITLE: *A psalm by David; a song.*
the desert.

ᵍ HEBREW TITLE: *A psalm;*
ⁱ on the clouds; *or across*

His name is the LORD—be glad
in his presence!

5 God, who lives in his sacred
Temple,
cares for orphans and protects
widows.
6 He gives the lonely a home to
live in
and leads prisoners out into
happy freedom,
but rebels will have to live in a
desolate land.

7 O God, when you led your people,
when you marched across the
desert,
8 the earth shook, and the sky
poured down rain,
because of the coming of the
God of Sinai,*j*
the coming of the God of Israel.
9 You caused abundant rain to fall
and restored your worn-out land;
10 your people made their home there;
in your goodness you provided
for the poor.

11 The Lord gave the command,
and many women carried the
news:
12 "Kings and their armies are
running away!"
The women at home divided
what was captured:
13 figures of doves covered with
silver,
whose wings glittered with fine
gold.
(Why did some of you stay among
the sheep pens on the
day of battle?)
14 When Almighty God scattered the
kings on Mount Zalmon,
he caused snow to fall there.

15 What a mighty mountain is
Bashan,
a mountain of many peaks!
16 Why from your mighty peaks do
you look with scorn
on the mountain*k* on which God
chose to live?
The LORD will live there forever!

17 With his many thousands of mighty
chariots
the Lord comes from Sinai*l*
into the holy place.
18 He goes up to the heights,
taking many captives with him;
he receives gifts from rebellious
people.
The LORD God will live there.

19 Praise the Lord,
who carries our burdens day
after day;
he is the God who saves us.

Praise the LORD, who carries our burdens day after day. (68.19)

20 Our God is a God who saves;
he is the LORD, our Lord,
who rescues us from death.

GOD OF SINAI: *As the people of Israel went from Egypt to Canaan, God revealed himself to them at Mount Sinai (see Ex 19.16-25).* *k* MOUNTAIN: *See 2.6.* *Probable text comes from Sinai; Hebrew in them, Sinai.*
8.8 Ex 19.18   **68.18** Eph 4.8

21 God will surely break the heads of
his enemies,
of those who persist in their
sinful ways.
22 The Lord has said, "I will bring
your enemies back from
Bashan;
I will bring them back from the
depths of the ocean,
23 so that you may wade in their
blood,
and your dogs may lap up as
much as they want."

24 O God, your march of triumph is
seen by all,
the procession of God, my king,
into his sanctuary.
25 The singers are in front, the
musicians are behind,
in between are the young
women beating the
tambourines.
26 "Praise God in the meeting of his
people;
praise the LORD, all you
descendants of Jacob!"
27 First comes Benjamin, the smallest
tribe,
then the leaders of Judah with
their group,
followed by the leaders of
Zebulun and Naphtali.

28 Show your power, O God,
the power you have used on our
behalf
29   from your Temple in Jerusalem,
where kings bring gifts to you.
30 Rebuke Egypt, that wild animal in
the reeds;
rebuke the nations, that herd of
bulls with their calves,
until they all bow down and
offer you their silver.
Scatter those people who love to
make war!_m_
31 Ambassadors _n_ will come from
Egypt;
the Ethiopians_o_ will raise their
hands in prayer to God.

32 Sing to God, kingdoms of the
world,
sing praise to the Lord,
33   to him who rides in the sky,
the ancient sky.
Listen to him shout with a
mighty roar.
34 Proclaim God's power;
his majesty is over Israel,
his might is in the skies.
35 How awesome is God as he comes
from his sanctuary—
the God of Israel!
He gives strength and power to his
people.

Praise God!

A Cry for Help _p_

69 Save me, O God!
The water is up to my
neck;
2 I am sinking in deep mud,
and there is no solid ground;
I am out in deep water,
and the waves are about to
drown me.
3 I am worn out from calling for
help,
and my throat is aching.
I have strained my eyes,
looking for your help.

4 Those who hate me for no reason

---

m Verse 30 in Hebrew is unclear.   _n Some ancient translations_ Ambassadors; _Hebrew
unclear._   _o Hebrew_ Cushites: _Cush is the ancient name of the extensive territory
south of the First Cataract of the Nile River. This region was called Ethiopia in
Graeco-Roman time, and included within its borders most of modern Sudan and some
of present-day Ethiopia (Abyssinia)._   _p_ HEBREW TITLE: _By David._
69.4 Ps 35.19; Jn 15.25

are more numerous than the
    hairs of my head.
My enemies tell lies against me;
    they are strong and want to
    kill me.
They made me give back things I
    did not steal.
5 My sins, O God, are not hidden
    from you;
    you know how foolish I have
    been.
6 Don't let me bring shame on those
    who trust in you,
    Sovereign LORD Almighty!
Don't let me bring disgrace to those
    who worship you,
    O God of Israel!
7 It is for your sake that I have been
    insulted
    and that I am covered with
    shame.
8 I am like a stranger to my relatives,
    like a foreigner to my family.

9 My devotion to your Temple burns
    in me like a fire;
    the insults which are hurled at
    you fall on me.
0 I humble myself *q* by fasting,
    and people insult me;
1 I dress myself in clothes of
    mourning,
    and they laugh at me.
2 They talk about me in the streets,
    and drunkards make up songs
    about me.

3 But as for me, I will pray to you,
    LORD;
    answer me, God, at a time you
    choose.
Answer me because of your great
    love,
    because you keep your promise
    to save.
4 Save me from sinking in the mud;
    keep me safe from my enemies,

    safe from the deep water.
15 Don't let the flood come over me;
    don't let me drown in the depths
    or sink into the grave.

16 Answer me, LORD, in the goodness
    of your constant love;
    in your great compassion turn
    to me!
17 Don't hide yourself from your
    servant;
    I am in great trouble — answer
    me now!
18 Come to me and save me;
    rescue me from my enemies.

19 You know how I am insulted,
    how I am disgraced and
    dishonored;
    you see all my enemies.
20 Insults have broken my heart,
    and I am in despair.
I had hoped for sympathy, but
    there was none;
    for comfort, but I found none.
21 When I was hungry, they gave me
    poison;
    when I was thirsty, they offered
    me vinegar.

22 May their banquets cause their
    ruin;
    may their sacred feasts cause
    their downfall.
23 Strike them with blindness!
    Make their backs always weak!
24 Pour out your anger on them;
    let your indignation overtake
    them.
25 May their camps be left deserted;
    may no one be left alive in their
    tents.
26 They persecute those whom you
    have punished;
    they talk about the sufferings of
    those you have wounded.
27 Keep a record of all their sins;

Some ancient translations humble myself; *Hebrew* cry.
9.9 a Jn 2.17; **b** Ro 15.3   **69.21** Mt 27.48; Mk 15.36; Lk 23.26; Jn 19.28, 29
9.22, 23 Ro 11.9, 10   **69.25** Ac 1.20

don't let them have any part in
your salvation.
28 May their names be erased from
the book of the living;
may they not be included in the
list of your people.

29 But I am in pain and despair;
lift me up, O God, and save me!

30 I will praise God with a song;
I will proclaim his greatness by
giving him thanks.
31 This will please the LORD more
than offering him cattle,
more than sacrificing a
full-grown bull.
32 When the oppressed see this, they
will be glad;
those who worship God will be
encouraged.
33 The LORD listens to those in need
and does not forget his people in
prison.

34 Praise God, O heaven and earth,
seas and all creatures in them.
35 He will save Jerusalem
and rebuild the towns of Judah.
His people will live there and
possess the land;
36   the descendants of his servants
will inherit it,
and those who love him will live
there.

A Prayer for Help *r*
(Psalm 40.13-17)

70 Save me, O God!
LORD, help me now!
2 May those who try to kill me
be defeated and confused.
May those who are happy because
of my troubles
be turned back and disgraced.

3 May those who make fun of me
be dismayed by their defeat.

4 May all who come to you
be glad and joyful.
May all who are thankful for your
salvation
always say, "How great is God!"

5 I am weak and poor;
come to me quickly, O God.
You are my savior and my LORD —
hurry to my aid!

The Prayer of an Elderly Person

71 LORD, I have come to you for
protection;
never let me be defeated!
2 Because you are righteous, help me
and rescue me.
Listen to me and save me!
3 Be my secure shelter
and a strong fortress *s* to
protect me;
you are my refuge and defense.

4 My God, rescue me from wicked
people,
from the power of cruel and evil
people.
5 Sovereign LORD, I put my hope
in you;
I have trusted in you since I was
young.
6 I have relied on you all my life;
you have protected *t* me since
the day I was born.
I will always praise you.

7 My life has been an example to
many,
because you have been my
strong defender.
8 All day long I praise you
and proclaim your glory.

---

r HEBREW TITLE: *A psalm by David; a lament.*
fortress; *Hebrew* to go always you commanded.
protected; *Hebrew unclear.*
69.28 Ex 32.32; Rev 3.5; 13.8; 17.8

s One ancient translation a strong
t Some ancient translations

9 Do not reject me now that I
    am old;
    do not abandon me now that I
      am feeble.
10 My enemies want to kill me;
    they talk and plot against me.
11 They say, "God has abandoned
    him;
    let's go after him and catch him;
    there is no one to rescue him."

12 Don't stay so far away, O God;
    my God, hurry to my aid!
13 May those who attack me
    be defeated and destroyed.
May those who try to hurt me
    be shamed and disgraced.
14 I will always put my hope in you;
    I will praise you more and more.
15 I will tell of your goodness;
    all day long I will speak of your
      salvation,
    though it is more than I can
      understand.
16 I will go in the strength of the
    Lord God;
    I will proclaim your goodness,
      yours alone.

17 You have taught me ever since I
    was young,
    and I still tell of your wonderful
      acts.
18 Now that I am old and my hair is
    gray,
    do not abandon me, O God!
Be with me while I proclaim your
    power and might
    to all generations to come.

19 Your righteousness, God, reaches
    the skies.
    You have done great things;
    there is no one like you.
20 You have sent troubles and
    suffering on me,
    but you will restore my strength;
    you will keep me from the grave.

21 You will make me greater than
    ever;
    you will comfort me again.
22 I will indeed praise you with the
    harp;

Now that I am old . . . (71.18)

    I will praise your faithfulness,
      my God.
On my harp I will play hymns
    to you,
    the Holy One of Israel.
23 I will shout for joy as I play
    for you;
    with my whole being I will sing
    because you have saved me.
24 I will speak of your righteousness
    all day long,
    because those who tried to
      harm me
    have been defeated and
      disgraced.

A Prayer for the King [u]

72 Teach the king to judge with
    your righteousness,
    O God;
    share with him your own
      justice,
2 so that he will rule over your
    people with justice

[u] HEBREW TITLE: *By Solomon.*

and govern the oppressed with
   righteousness.
³ May the land enjoy prosperity;
   may it experience righteousness.
⁴ May the king judge the poor fairly;
   may he help the needy
   and defeat their oppressors.
⁵ May your people worship you as
      long as the sun shines,
   as long as the moon gives light,
      for ages to come.

⁶ May the king be like rain on the
      fields,
   like showers falling on the land.
⁷ May righteousness flourish in his
      lifetime,
   and may prosperity last as long
      as the moon gives light.

⁸ His kingdom will reach from sea
      to sea,
   from the Euphrates to the ends
      of the earth.
⁹ The peoples of the desert will bow
      down before him;
   his enemies will throw
      themselves to the ground.
¹⁰ The kings of Spain and of the
      islands will offer him gifts;
   the kings of Sheba and Seba*v*
      will bring him offerings.
¹¹ All kings will bow down before
      him;
   all nations will serve him.

¹² He rescues the poor who call to
      him,
   and those who are needy and
      neglected.
¹³ He has pity on the weak and poor;
   he saves the lives of those in
      need.
¹⁴ He rescues them from oppression
      and violence;
   their lives are precious to him.

¹⁵ Long live the king!
   May he be given gold from
      Sheba;*w*
   may prayers be said for him at
      all times;
   may God's blessings be on him
      always!
¹⁶ May there be plenty of grain in the
      land;
   may the hills be covered with
      crops,
   as fruitful as those of Lebanon.
   May the cities be filled with people,
      like fields full of grass.
¹⁷ May the king's name never be
      forgotten;
   may his fame last as long as
      the sun.
   May all nations ask God to bless
      them
   as he has blessed the king.*x*

¹⁸ Praise the LORD, the God of Israel!
   He alone does these wonderful
      things.
¹⁹ Praise his glorious name forever!
   May his glory fill the whole world.

Amen! Amen!

²⁰ This is the end of the prayers of
      David son of Jesse.

BOOK THREE
(Psalms 73–89)

The Justice of God *y*

73 God is indeed good to Israel,
      to those who have pure
      hearts.
² But I had nearly lost confidence;
   my faith was almost gone
³ because I was jealous of the proud
   when I saw that things go well
      for the wicked.

v SHEBA AND SEBA: *Sheba was toward the south in Arabia and Seba was on the opposite side of the Red Sea.*   *w* SHEBA: *See 72.10.*   *x* as he has blessed the king; *or* and may they wish happiness for the king.   *y* HEBREW TITLE: *By Asaph.*
72.8 Zec 9.10; Si 44.21

⁴They do not suffer pain;
     they are strong and healthy.
⁵They do not suffer as other
          people do;
     they do not have the troubles
          that others have.
⁶And so they wear pride like a
          necklace
     and violence like a robe;
⁷their hearts pour out evil,ᶻ
     and their minds are busy with
          wicked schemes.
⁸They laugh at other people and
          speak of evil things;
     they are proud and make plans
          to oppress others.
⁹They speak evil of God in heaven
     and give arrogant orders to
          everyone on earth,
¹⁰so that even God's people turn to
          them
     and eagerly believe whatever
          they say.ᵃ
¹¹They say, "God will not know;
     the Most High will not find out."
¹²That is what the wicked are like.
     They have plenty and are always
          getting more.

¹³Is it for nothing, then, that I have
          kept myself pure
     and have not committed sin?
¹⁴O God, you have made me suffer
          all day long;
     every morning you have
          punished me.

¹⁵If I had said such things,
     I would not be acting as one of
          your people.
¹⁶I tried to think this problem
          through,
     but it was too difficult for me
¹⁷   until I went into your Temple.
     Then I understood what will
          happen to the wicked.

¹⁸You will put them in slippery
          places
     and make them fall to
          destruction!
¹⁹They are instantly destroyed;
     they go down to a horrible end.
²⁰They are like a dream that goes
          away in the morning;
     when you rouse yourself,
          O Lord, they disappear.

²¹When my thoughts were bitter
     and my feelings were hurt,
²²I was as stupid as an animal;
     I did not understand you.
²³Yet I always stay close to you,
     and you hold me by the hand.
²⁴You guide me with your instruction
     and at the end you will receive
          me with honor.
²⁵What else do I have in heaven
          but you?
     Since I have you, what else
          could I want on earth?
²⁶My mind and my body may grow
          weak,
     but God is my strength;
     he is all I ever need.

²⁷Those who abandon you will
          certainly perish;
     you will destroy those who are
          unfaithful to you.
²⁸But as for me, how wonderful to
          be near God,
     to find protection with the
          Sovereign LORD
     and to proclaim all that he has
          done!

A Prayer for National Deliverance ᵇ

74 Why have you abandoned us
          like this, O God?
     Will you be angry with your own
          people forever?

ᶻ *Some ancient translations* their hearts pour out evil; *Hebrew unclear.*   ᵃ *Verse 10
n Hebrew is unclear.*   ᵇ HEBREW TITLE: *A poem by Asaph.*

2 Remember your people, whom you
      chose for yourself long ago,
  whom you brought out of slavery
      to be your own tribe.
  Remember Mount Zion, where
      once you lived.
3 Walk over these total ruins;
  our enemies have destroyed
      everything in the Temple.

4 Your enemies have shouted in
      triumph in your Temple;
  they have placed their flags
      there as signs of victory.
5 They looked like woodsmen
      cutting down trees with their
      axes.c
6 They smashed all the wooden
      panels
  with their axes and sledge
      hammers.
7 They wrecked your Temple and set
      it on fire;
  they desecrated the place where
      you are worshiped.
8 They wanted to crush us
      completely;
  they burned down every holy
      place in the land.

9 All our sacred symbols are gone;
  there are no prophets left,
  and no one knows how long this
      will last.
10 How long, O God, will our enemies
      laugh at you?
  Will they insult your name
      forever?
11 Why have you refused to help us?
  Why do you keep your hands
      behind you?d

12 But you have been our king from
      the beginning, O God;
  you have saved us many times.
13 With your mighty strength you
      divided the sea
  and smashed the heads of the
      sea monsters;
14 you crushed the heads of the
      monster Leviathan e
  and fed his body to desert
      animals.f
15 You made springs and fountains
      flow;
  you dried up large rivers.
16 You created the day and the night;
  you set the sun and the moon in
      their places;
17 you set the limits of the earth;
  you made summer and winter.

18 But remember, O LORD, that your
      enemies laugh at you,
  that they are godless and despise
      you.
19 Don't abandon your helpless people
      to their cruel enemies;
  don't forget your persecuted
      people!

20 Remember the covenant you made
      with us.
  There is violence in every dark
      corner of the land.
21 Don't let the oppressed be put to
      shame;
  let those poor and needy people
      praise you.

22 Rouse yourself, God, and defend
      your cause!
  Remember that godless people
      laugh at you all day long.
23 Don't forget the angry shouts of
      your enemies,

c Verse 5 in Hebrew is unclear.   d Probable text Why do you keep your hands behind
you; Hebrew unclear.   e LEVIATHAN: A legendary monster which was a symbol of the
forces of chaos and evil.   f animals; or people.
74.13 Ex 14.21   74.14 Job 41.1; Ps 104.26; Is 27.1

the continuous noise made by
your foes.

God the Judge [g]

75 We give thanks to you,
O God, we give thanks
to you!
We proclaim how great you are
and tell of [h] the wonderful
things you have done.

2 "I have set a time for judgment,"
says God,
"and I will judge with fairness.
3 Though every living creature
tremble
and the earth itself be shaken,
I will keep its foundations firm.
4 I tell the wicked not to be arrogant;
5   I tell them to stop their
boasting."

6 Judgment does not come from the
east or from the west,
from the north or from the
south; [i]
7 it is God who is the judge,
condemning some and
acquitting others.
8 The LORD holds a cup in his hand,
filled with the strong wine of
his anger.
He pours it out, and all the wicked
drink it;
they drink it down to the last
drop.

9 But I will never stop speaking of
the God of Jacob
or singing praises to him.
10 He will break the power of the
wicked,
but the power of the righteous
will be increased.

God the Victor [j]

76 God is known in Judah;
his name is honored in
Israel.
2 He has his home in Jerusalem;
he lives on Mount Zion.
3 There he broke the arrows of the
enemy,
their shields and swords, yes, all
their weapons.

4 How glorious you are, O God!
How majestic, as you return
from the mountains
where you defeated your foes.
5 Their brave soldiers have been
stripped of all they had
and now are sleeping the sleep
of death;
all their strength and skill was
useless.
6 When you threatened them, O God
of Jacob,
the horses and their riders fell
dead.

7 But you, LORD, are feared by all.
No one can stand in your
presence
when you are angry.
8 You made your judgment known
from heaven;
the world was afraid and kept
silent,
9 when you rose up to pronounce
judgment,
to save all the oppressed on
earth.

10 Human anger only results in more
praise for you;
those who survive the wars will
keep your festivals. [k]

---

[g] HEBREW TITLE: *A psalm by Asaph; a song.*   [h] *Some ancient translations* We
proclaim how great you are and tell of; *Hebrew* Your name is near and they tell of.
[i] *Probable text* from the north or from the south; *Hebrew* from the wilderness of the
mountains.   [j] HEBREW TITLE: *A psalm by Asaph; a song.*   [k] *One ancient
translation* will keep your festivals; *verse 10 in Hebrew is unclear.*

11 Give the LORD your God what you
     promised him;
   bring gifts to him, all you nearby
     nations.
   God makes everyone fear him;
12   he humbles proud princes
     and terrifies great kings.

Comfort in Time of Distress [l]

77 I cry aloud to God;
       I cry aloud, and he hears
       me.
2 In times of trouble I pray to the
     Lord;
   all night long I lift my hands in
     prayer,
   but I cannot find comfort.
3 When I think of God, I sigh;
   when I meditate, I feel
     discouraged.

4 He keeps me awake all night;
   I am so worried that I cannot
     speak.
5 I think of days gone by
   and remember years of
     long ago.
6 I spend the night in deep
     thought; [m]
   I meditate, and this is what I
     ask myself:
7 "Will the Lord always reject us?
   Will he never again be pleased
     with us?
8 Has he stopped loving us?
   Does his promise no longer
     stand?
9 Has God forgotten to be merciful?
   Has anger taken the place of his
     compassion?"
10 Then I said, "What hurts me most
     is this —

that God is no longer
  powerful." [n]

11 I will remember your great deeds,
     LORD;
   I will recall the wonders you did
     in the past.
12 I will think about all that you have
     done;
   I will meditate on all your
     mighty acts.

13 Everything you do, O God,
     is holy.
   No god is as great as you.
14 You are the God who works
     miracles;
   you showed your might among
     the nations.
15 By your power you saved your
     people,
   the descendants of Jacob and of
     Joseph.

16 When the waters saw you, O God,
     they were afraid,
   and the depths of the sea
     trembled.
17 The clouds poured down rain;
   thunder crashed from the sky,
   and lightning flashed in all
     directions.
18 The crash of your thunder rolled
     out,
   and flashes of lightning lit up
     the world;
   the earth trembled and shook.
19 You walked through the waves;
   you crossed the deep sea,
   but your footprints could not
     be seen.
20 You led your people like a
     shepherd,
   with Moses and Aaron in
     charge.

---

[l] HEBREW TITLE: *A psalm by Asaph.*   [m] *Some ancient translations* deep thought;
Hebrew song.   [n] *Verse 10 in Hebrew is unclear.*

God and His People [o]

78 Listen, my people, to my teaching,
and pay attention to what I say.
2 I am going to use wise sayings
and explain mysteries from the past,
3 things we have heard and known,
things that our ancestors told us.
4 We will not keep them from our children;
we will tell the next generation
about the LORD's power and his great deeds
and the wonderful things he has done.

5 He gave laws to the people of Israel
and commandments to the descendants of Jacob.
He instructed our ancestors
to teach his laws to their children,
6 so that the next generation might learn them
and in turn should tell their children.
7 In this way they also will put their trust in God
and not forget what he has done,
but always obey his commandments.
8 They will not be like their ancestors,
a rebellious and disobedient people,
whose trust in God was never firm
and who did not remain faithful to him.

9 The Ephraimites, armed with bows and arrows,
ran away on the day of battle.

10 They did not keep their covenant with God;
they refused to obey his law.
11 They forgot what he had done,
the miracles they had seen him perform.
12 While their ancestors watched, God performed miracles
in the plain of Zoan in the land of Egypt.
13 He divided the sea and took them through it;
he made the waters stand like walls.
14 By day he led them with a cloud
and all night long with the light of a fire.
15 He split rocks open in the desert
and gave them water from the depths.
16 He caused a stream to come out of the rock
and made water flow like a river.

17 But they continued to sin against God,
and in the desert they rebelled against the Most High.
18 They deliberately put God to the test
by demanding the food they wanted.
19 They spoke against God and said,
"Can God supply food in the desert?
20 It is true that he struck the rock,
and water flowed out in a torrent;
but can he also provide us with bread
and give his people meat?"

21 And so the LORD was angry when he heard them;
he attacked his people with fire,

---

o HEBREW TITLE: *A poem by Asaph.*

78.2 Mt 13.35   **78.12** Ex 7.8—12.32   **78.13** Ex 14.21, 22   **78.14** Ex 13.21, 22
78.12-16 Ws 16.1—19.22   **78.15, 16** Ex 17.1-7; Nu 20.2-13   **78.18-31** Ex 16.2-15;
Nu 11.4-23, 31-35

and his anger against them grew,

²²because they had no faith in him
and did not believe that he
would save them.

²³But he spoke to the sky above
and commanded its doors to
open;

²⁴he gave them grain from heaven,
by sending down manna for
them to eat.

²⁵So they ate the food of angels,
and God gave them all they
wanted.

²⁶He also caused the east wind to
blow,
and by his power he stirred up
the south wind;

²⁷and to his people he sent down
birds,
as many as the grains of sand
on the shore;

²⁸they fell in the middle of the camp
all around the tents.

²⁹So the people ate and were
satisfied;
God gave them what they
wanted.

³⁰But they had not yet satisfied their
craving
and were still eating,

³¹when God became angry with them
and killed their strongest men,
the best young men of Israel.

³²In spite of all this the people kept
sinning;
in spite of his miracles they did
not trust him.

³³So he ended their days like a
breath
and their lives with sudden
disaster.

³⁴Whenever he killed some of them,
the rest would turn to him;
they would repent and pray
earnestly to him.

³⁵They remembered that God was
their protector,
that the Almighty came to their
aid.

³⁶But their words were all lies;
nothing they said was sincere.

³⁷They were not loyal to him;
they were not faithful to their
covenant with him.

³⁸But God was merciful to his people.
He forgave their sin
and did not destroy them.
Many times he held back his anger
and restrained his fury.

³⁹He remembered that they were
only mortal beings,
like a wind that blows by and is
gone.

⁴⁰How often they rebelled against
him in the desert;
how many times they made
him sad!

⁴¹Again and again they put God to
the test
and brought pain to the
Holy God of Israel.

⁴²They forgot his great power
and the day when he saved
them from their enemies

⁴³   and performed his mighty acts
and miracles
in the plain of Zoan in the land
of Egypt.

⁴⁴He turned the rivers into blood,
and the Egyptians had no water
to drink.

⁴⁵He sent flies among them, that
tormented them,
and frogs that ruined their land.

⁴⁶He sent locusts to eat their crops
and to destroy their fields.

⁴⁷He killed their grapevines with hail
and their fig trees with frost.

⁴⁸He killed their cattle with hail
and their flocks with lightning.ᵖ

ᵖ hail ... lightning; *or* terrible disease ... deadly plague.
78.24 Ws 16.20-29; Jn 6.31   **78.37** Ac 8.21   **78.44** Ex 7.17-21   **78.45 a** Ex 8.20-24;
b Ex 8.1-6   **78.46** Ex 10.12-15   **78.47, 48** Ex 9.22-25

⁴⁹He caused them great distress
    by pouring out his anger and
        fierce rage,
    which came as messengers of
        death.
⁵⁰He did not restrain his anger
    or spare their lives,
    but killed them with a plague.
⁵¹He killed the first-born sons
    of all the families of Egypt.

⁵²Then he led his people out like a
        shepherd
    and guided them through the
        desert.
⁵³He led them safely, and they were
        not afraid;
    but the sea came rolling over
        their enemies.
⁵⁴He brought them to his holy land,
    to the mountains which he
        himself conquered.
⁵⁵He drove out the inhabitants as his
        people advanced;
    he divided their land among the
        tribes of Israel
    and gave their homes to his
        people.

⁵⁶But they rebelled against
        Almighty God
    and put him to the test.
    They did not obey his
        commandments,
⁵⁷   but were rebellious and disloyal
        like their ancestors,
    unreliable as a crooked arrow.
⁵⁸They angered him with their
        heathen places of worship,
    and with their idols they made
        him furious.
⁵⁹God was angry when he saw it,
    so he rejected his people
        completely.
⁶⁰He abandoned his tent in Shiloh,�q

the home where he had lived
    among us.
⁶¹He allowed our enemies to capture
    the Covenant Box,
    the symbol of his power and
        glory.
⁶²He was angry with his own people
    and let them be killed by their
        enemies.
⁶³Young men were killed in war,
    and young women had no one to
        marry.
⁶⁴Priests died by violence,
    and their widows were not
        allowed to mourn.

⁶⁵At last the Lord woke up as though
        from sleep;
    he was like a strong man excited
        by wine.
⁶⁶He drove his enemies back
    in lasting and shameful defeat.
⁶⁷But he rejected the descendants of
        Joseph;
    he did not select the tribe of
        Ephraim.
⁶⁸Instead he chose the tribe of Judah
    and Mount Zion, which he
        dearly loves.
⁶⁹There he built his Temple
    like his home in heaven;
    he made it firm like the earth itself,
        secure for all time.

⁷⁰He chose his servant David;
    he took him from the pastures,
⁷¹   where he looked after his flocks,
    and he made him king of Israel,
    the shepherd of the people
        of God.
⁷²David took care of them with
        unselfish devotion
    and led them with skill.

�q SHILOH: *The central place of worship for the people of Israel before the time of King David.*

78.51 Ex 12.29   **78.52** Ex 13.17-22   **78.53** Ex 14.26-28   **78.54** Ex 15.17; Js 3.14-17
78.55 Js 11.16-23   **78.56** Jg 2.11-15   **78.60** Js 18.1; Jr 7.12-14; 26.6   **78.61** 1 S 4.4-22
78.70, 71 1 S 16.11, 12; 2 S 7.8; 1 Ch 17.7

A Prayer for the Nation's Deliverance [r]

79 O God, the heathen have invaded your land.
They have desecrated your holy Temple
and left Jerusalem in ruins.
2 They left the bodies of your people for the vultures,
the bodies of your servants for wild animals to eat.
3 They shed your people's blood like water;
blood flowed like water all through Jerusalem,
and no one was left to bury the dead.
4 The surrounding nations insult us;
they laugh at us and mock us.

5 LORD, will you be angry with us forever?
Will your anger continue to burn like fire?
6 Turn your anger on the nations that do not worship you,
on the people who do not pray to you.
7 For they have killed your people;
they have ruined your country.

8 Do not punish us for the sins of our ancestors.
Have mercy on us now;
we have lost all hope.
9 Help us, O God, and save us;
rescue us and forgive our sins for the sake of your own honor.
10 Why should the nations ask us, "Where is your God?"
Let us see you punish the nations for shedding the blood of your servants.

11 Listen to the groans of the prisoners,
and by your great power free those who are condemned to die.
12 Lord, pay the other nations back seven times
for all the insults they have hurled at you.
13 Then we, your people, the sheep of your flock,
will thank you forever
and praise you for all time to come.

A Prayer for the Nation's Restoration [s]

80 Listen to us, O Shepherd of Israel;
hear us, leader of your flock.
Seated on your throne above the winged creatures,
2 reveal yourself to the tribes of Ephraim, Benjamin, and Manasseh.
Show us your strength;
come and save us!

3 Bring us back, O God!
Show us your mercy, and we will be saved!

4 How much longer, LORD God Almighty,
will you be angry with your people's prayers?
5 You have given us sorrow to eat,
a large cup of tears to drink.
6 You let the surrounding nations fight over our land;
our enemies insult us.

7 Bring us back, Almighty God!
Show us your mercy, and we will be saved!

[r] HEBREW TITLE: *A psalm by Asaph.*   [s] HEBREW TITLE: *A psalm by Asaph; a testimony.*
79.1 2 K 25.8-10; 2 Ch 36.17-19; Jr 52.12-14   **80.1** Ex 25.22

8 You brought a grapevine out of
    Egypt;
      you drove out other nations and
        planted it in their land.
9 You cleared a place for it to grow;
      its roots went deep, and it
        spread out over the
        whole land.
10 It covered the hills with its shade;
      its branches overshadowed the
        giant cedars.
11 It extended its branches to the
      Mediterranean Sea
      and as far as the Euphrates
        River.
12 Why did you break down the
      fences around it?
    Now anyone passing by can
      steal its grapes;
13   wild hogs trample it down,
      and wild animals feed on it.

14 Turn to us, Almighty God!
    Look down from heaven at us;
    come and save your people!
15 Come and save this grapevine that
    you planted,
      this young vine you made grow
      so strong!

16 Our enemies have set it on fire and
    cut it down;
      look at them in anger and
      destroy them!
17 Preserve and protect the people you
    have chosen,
      the nation you made so strong.
18 We will never turn away from
    you again;
      keep us alive, and we will
      praise you.

19 Bring us back, LORD God Almighty.
    Show us your mercy, and we
      will be saved.

A Song for a Festival [t]

81 Shout for joy to God our
      defender;
    sing praise to the God of Jacob!
2 Start the music and beat the
    tambourines;
      play pleasant music on the harps
      and the lyres.
3 Blow the trumpet for the festival,
    when the moon is new and
      when the moon is full.
4 This is the law in Israel,
    an order from the God of Jacob.
5 He gave it to the people of Israel
    when he attacked the land of
      Egypt.

    I hear an unknown voice saying,
6 "I took the burdens off your backs;
    I let you put down your loads of
      bricks.
7 When you were in trouble, you
    called to me, and I saved you.
    From my hiding place in the
      storm, I answered you.
    I put you to the test at the
      springs of Meribah.
8 Listen, my people, to my warning;
    Israel, how I wish you would
      listen to me!
9 You must never worship
    another god.
10 I am the LORD your God,
    who brought you out
      of Egypt.
    Open your mouth, and
      I will feed you.

11 "But my people would not listen
    to me;
      Israel would not obey me.
12 So I let them go their stubborn
    ways
      and do whatever they wanted.

[t] HEBREW TITLE: *By Asaph.*
81.3 Nu 10.10   **81.7** Ex 17.7; Nu 20.13   **81.9** Ex 20.2, 3; Dt 5.6, 7

13 How I wish my people would listen
to me;
how I wish they would obey me!
14 I would quickly defeat their
enemies
and conquer all their foes.
15 Those who hate me would bow in
fear before me;
their punishment would last
forever.
16 But I would feed you with the
finest wheat
and satisfy you with wild
honey."

God the Supreme Ruler [u]

82 God presides in the heavenly
council;
in the assembly of the gods he
gives his decision:
2 "You must stop judging unjustly;
you must no longer be partial to
the wicked!
3 Defend the rights of the poor and
the orphans;
be fair to the needy and the
helpless.
4 Rescue them from the power of evil
people.

5 "How ignorant you are! How
stupid!
You are completely corrupt,
and justice has disappeared from
the world.
6 'You are gods,' I said;
'all of you are children of the
Most High.'
7 But you will die like mortals;
your life will end like that of any
prince."

8 Come, O God, and rule the world;
all the nations are yours.

A Prayer for the Defeat of Israel's Enemies [v]

83 O God, do not keep silent;
do not be still, do not be
quiet!
2 Look! Your enemies are in revolt,
and those who hate you are
rebelling.
3 They are making secret plans
against your people;
they are plotting against those
you protect.
4 "Come," they say, "let us destroy
their nation,
so that Israel will be forgotten
forever."

5 They agree on their plan
and form an alliance against
you:
6 the people of Edom and the
Ishmaelites;
the people of Moab and the
Hagrites;
7 the people of Gebal, Ammon, and
Amalek,
and of Philistia and Tyre.
8 Assyria has also joined them
as a strong ally of the
Ammonites and Moabites,
the descendants of Lot.

9 Do to them what you did to the
Midianites,
and to Sisera and Jabin at the
Kishon River.
10 You defeated them at Endor,
and their bodies rotted on the
ground.
11 Do to their leaders what you did to
Oreb and Zeeb;
defeat all their rulers as you did
Zebah and Zalmunna,
12 who said, "We will take for our own
the land that belongs to God."

[u] HEBREW TITLE: *A psalm by Asaph.*   [v] HEBREW TITLE: *A psalm by Asaph; a song.*
82.6 Jn 10.34   **83.9 a** Jg 7.1-23; **b** Jg 4.6-22   **83.11 a** Jg 7.25; **b** Jg 8.12

¹³Scatter them like dust, O God,
   like straw blown away by the
      wind.
¹⁴As fire burns the forest,
   as flames set the hills on fire,
¹⁵chase them away with your storm
   and terrify them with your fierce
      winds.
¹⁶Cover their faces with shame,
   O LORD,
      and make them acknowledge
         your power.
¹⁷May they be defeated and terrified
   forever;
      may they die in complete
         disgrace.
¹⁸May they know that you alone are
   the LORD,
      supreme ruler over all the earth.

Longing for God's House ʷ

84 How I love your Temple,
      LORD Almighty!
²   How I want to be there!
    I long to be in the LORD's
       Temple.
    With my whole being I sing for joy
       to the living God.
³Even the sparrows have built a
    nest,
       and the swallows have their own
          home;
    they keep their young near your
       altars,
    LORD Almighty, my king and
       my God.
⁴How happy are those who live in
    your Temple,
       always singing praise to you.

⁵How happy are those whose
       strength comes from you,
    who are eager to make the
       pilgrimage to Mount Zion.
⁶As they pass through the dry valley
    of Baca,

it becomes a place of springs;
   the autumn rain fills it with
      pools.

Even the sparrows have built a nest. (84.3)

⁷They grow stronger as they go;
   they will see the God of gods on
      Zion.

⁸Hear my prayer, LORD God
      Almighty.
   Listen, O God of Jacob!
⁹Bless our king, O God,
   the king you have chosen.

¹⁰One day spent in your Temple
   is better than a thousand
      anywhere else;
   I would rather stand at the gate of
      the house of my God
   than live in the homes of the
      wicked.
¹¹The LORD is our protector and
      glorious king,
   blessing us with kindness and
      honor.
He does not refuse any good
      thing
   to those who do what is right.
¹²LORD Almighty, how happy are
   those who trust in you!

ʷ HEBREW TITLE: *A psalm by the clan of Korah.*

A Prayer for the Nation's Welfare [w]

85 LORD, you have been
merciful to your land;
you have made Israel prosperous
again.
2 You have forgiven your people's
sins
and pardoned all their wrongs.
3 You stopped being angry with them
and held back your furious rage.

4 Bring us back, O God our savior,
and stop being displeased
with us!
5 Will you be angry with us forever?
Will your anger never cease?
6 Make us strong again,
and we, your people, will
praise you.
7 Show us your constant love, O LORD,
and give us your saving help.

8 I am listening to what the LORD
God is saying;
he promises peace to us, his
own people,
if we do not go back to our
foolish ways.
9 Surely he is ready to save those
who honor him,
and his saving presence will
remain in our land.

10 Love and faithfulness will meet;
righteousness and peace will
embrace.
11 Human loyalty will reach up from
the earth,
and God's righteousness will
look down from heaven.
12 The LORD will make us prosperous,
and our land will produce rich
harvests.
13 Righteousness will go before the
LORD
and prepare the path for him.

A Prayer for Help [x]

86 Listen to me, LORD, and
answer me,
for I am helpless and weak.
2 Save me from death, because I am
loyal to you;
save me, for I am your servant
and I trust in you.

3 You are my God, so be merciful
to me;
I pray to you all day long.
4 Make your servant glad, O Lord,
because my prayers go up
to you.
5 You are good to us and forgiving,
full of constant love for all who
pray to you.

6 Listen, LORD, to my prayer;
hear my cries for help.
7 I call to you in times of trouble,
because you answer my prayers.

8 There is no god like you, O Lord,
not one has done what you have
done.
9 All the nations that you have
created
will come and bow down to you;
they will praise your greatness.
10 You are mighty and do wonderful
things;
you alone are God.

11 Teach me, LORD, what you want
me to do,
and I will obey you faithfully;
teach me to serve you with
complete devotion.
12 I will praise you with all my heart,
O Lord my God;
I will proclaim your greatness
forever.

[w] HEBREW TITLE: *A psalm by the clan of Korah.*
David.
86.9 Rev 15.4

[x] HEBREW TITLE: *A prayer by*

13 How great is your constant love
     for me!
  You have saved me from the
     grave itself.
14 Proud people are coming against
     me, O God;
  a cruel gang is trying to kill
     me —
  people who pay no attention
     to you.
15 But you, O Lord, are a merciful
     and loving God,
  always patient, always kind and
     faithful.
16 Turn to me and have mercy on me;
  strengthen me and save me,
  because I serve you just as my
     mother did.
17 Show me proof of your goodness,
     LORD;
  those who hate me will be
     ashamed
  when they see that you have
     given me comfort and help.

In Praise of Jerusalem *y*

87 The LORD built his city on
     the sacred hill; *z*
2   more than any other place in
     Israel
  he loves the city of Jerusalem.
3 Listen, city of God,
  to the wonderful things he says
     about you:

4 "I will include Egypt and Babylonia
  when I list the nations that
     obey me;
  the people of Philistia, Tyre, and
     Ethiopia *a*
  I will number among the
     inhabitants of Jerusalem."

5 Of Zion it will be said
  that all nations belong there
  and that the Almighty will make
     her strong.
6 The LORD will write a list of the
     peoples
  and include them all as citizens
     of Jerusalem.
7 They dance and sing,
  "In Zion is the source of all our
     blessings."

A Cry for Help *b*

88 LORD God, my savior, I cry
     out all day,
  and at night I come before you.
2 Hear my prayer;
  listen to my cry for help!

3 So many troubles have fallen on me
  that I am close to death.
4 I am like all others who are about
     to die;
  all my strength is gone. *c*
5 I am abandoned among the dead;
  I am like the slain lying in their
     graves,
  those you have forgotten
     completely,
  who are beyond your help.
6 You have thrown me into the
     depths of the tomb,
  into the darkest and deepest pit.
7 Your anger lies heavy on me,
  and I am crushed beneath its
     waves.

8 You have caused my friends to
     abandon me;
  you have made me repulsive to
     them.
  I am closed in and cannot escape;

---

y HEBREW TITLE: *A psalm by the clan of Korah; a song.*   *z* SACRED HILL: *See 2.6.*
a Hebrew Cush: *Cush is the ancient name of the extensive territory south of the First
Cataract of the Nile River. This region was called Ethiopia in Graeco-Roman time, and
included within its borders most of modern Sudan and some of present-day Ethiopia
(Abyssinia).*   *b* HEBREW TITLE: *A psalm by the clan of Korah; a song. A poem by
Heman the Ezrahite.*   *c* all my strength is gone; *or* there is no help for me.

9   my eyes are weak from
          suffering.
    LORD, every day I call to you
          and lift my hands to you in
          prayer.

10 Do you perform miracles for the
          dead?
    Do they rise up and praise you?
11 Is your constant love spoken of in
          the grave
      or your faithfulness in the place
          of destruction?
12 Are your miracles seen in that
          place of darkness
      or your goodness in the land of
          the forgotten?

13 LORD, I call to you for help;
      every morning I pray to you.
14 Why do you reject me, LORD?
      Why do you turn away from me?
15 Ever since I was young, I have
          suffered and been near death;
    I am worn out[d] from the
          burden of your punishments.
16 Your furious anger crushes me;
      your terrible attacks destroy me.
17 All day long they surround me like
          a flood;
      they close in on me from every
          side.
18 You have made even my closest
          friends abandon me,
    and darkness is my only
          companion.

A Hymn in Time of National
Trouble[e]

89 O LORD, I will always sing of
          your constant love;
    I will proclaim your faithfulness
          forever.
2 I know that your love will last for
          all time,

that your faithfulness is as
          permanent as the sky.
3 You said, "I have made a covenant
          with the man I chose;
    I have promised my servant
          David,
4 'A descendant of yours will always
          be king;
    I will preserve your dynasty
          forever.' "

5 The heavens sing of the wonderful
          things you do;
    the holy ones sing of your
          faithfulness, LORD.
6 No one in heaven is like you,
          LORD;
    none of the heavenly beings is
          your equal.
7 You are feared in the council of the
          holy ones;
    they all stand in awe of you.

8 LORD God Almighty, none is as
          mighty as you;
    in all things you are faithful,
          O LORD.
9 You rule over the powerful sea;
      you calm its angry waves.
10 You crushed the monster Rahab[f]
          and killed it;
    with your mighty strength you
          defeated your enemies.
11 Heaven is yours, the earth also;
      you made the world and
          everything in it.
12 You created the north and the
          south;
    Mount Tabor and Mount
          Hermon sing to you for joy.
13 How powerful you are!
      How great is your strength!
14 Your kingdom is founded on
          righteousness and justice;
    love and faithfulness are shown
          in all you do.

---

[d] *Probable text* I am worn out; *Hebrew unclear.*   [e] HEBREW TITLE: *A poem by Ethan*
the Ezrahite.   [f] RAHAB: *A legendary sea monster which represented the forces of*
chaos and evil.
89 Title 1 K 4.31   **89.4** 2 S 7.12-16; 1 Ch 17.11-14; Ps 132.11; Ac 2.30

15 How happy are the people who
    worship you with songs,
  who live in the light of your
    kindness!
16 Because of you they rejoice all day
    long,
  and they praise you for your
    goodness.
17 You give us great victories;
  in your love you make us
    triumphant.
18 You, O LORD, chose our protector;
  you, the Holy God of Israel, gave
    us our king.

God's Promise to David

19 In a vision long ago you said to
    your faithful servants,
  "I have given help to a famous
    soldier;
  I have given the throne to one I
    chose from the people.
20 I have made my servant David king
  by anointing him with holy oil.
21 My strength will always be with
    him,
  my power will make him strong.
22 His enemies will never succeed
    against him;
  the wicked will not defeat him.
23 I will crush his foes
  and kill everyone who hates
    him.
24 I will love him and be loyal to him;
  I will make him always
    victorious.
25 I will extend his kingdom
  from the Mediterranean to the
    Euphrates River.
26 He will say to me,
  'You are my father and my God;
  you are my protector and savior.'
27 I will make him my first-born son,
  the greatest of all kings.
28 I will always keep my promise to
    him,
  and my covenant with him will
    last forever.

29 His dynasty will be as permanent
    as the sky;
  a descendant of his will always
    be king.

30 "But if his descendants disobey
    my law
  and do not live according to my
    commands,
31 if they disregard my instructions
  and do not keep my
    commandments,
32 then I will punish them for their
    sins;
  I will make them suffer for their
    wrongs.
33 But I will not stop loving David
  or fail to keep my promise
    to him.
34 I will not break my covenant with
    him
  or take back even one promise I
    made him.

35 "Once and for all I have promised
    by my holy name:
  I will never lie to David.
36 He will always have descendants,
  and I will watch over his
    kingdom as long as the sun
    shines.
37 It will be as permanent as the
    moon,
  that faithful witness in the sky."

Lament over the Defeat of the King

38 But you are angry with your chosen
    king;
  you have deserted and rejected
    him.
39 You have broken your covenant
    with your servant
  and thrown his crown in the
    dirt.
40 You have torn down the walls of
    his city
  and left his forts in ruins.

89.20 a 1 S 13.14; Ac 13.22; b 1 S 16.12   89.27 Rev 1.5

41 All who pass by steal his
     belongings;
   all his neighbors laugh at him.
42 You have given the victory to his
     enemies;
   you have made them all happy.
43 You have made his weapons
     useless
   and let him be defeated in
     battle.
44 You have taken away his royal
     scepter *g*
   and knocked his throne to the
     ground.
45 You have made him old before his
     time
   and covered him with disgrace.

A Prayer for Deliverance

46 LORD, will you hide yourself
     forever?
   How long will your anger burn
     like fire?
47 Remember how short my life is;
   remember that you created all of
     us mortal!
48 Who can live and never die?
   How can we humans keep
     ourselves from the grave?

49 Lord, where are the former proofs
     of your love?
   Where are the promises you
     made to David?
50 Don't forget how I, your servant,
     am insulted,
   how I endure all the curses *h* of
     the heathen.
51 Your enemies insult your chosen
     king, O LORD!
   They insult him wherever he
     goes.

52 Praise the LORD forever!

         Amen! Amen!

BOOK FOUR
(*Psalms 90–106*)

Of God and Human Beings *i*

90 O Lord, you have always
         been our home.
2 Before you created the hills
   or brought the world into being,
   you were eternally God,
   and will be God forever.

3 You tell us to return to what we
     were;
   you change us back to dust.
4 A thousand years to you are like
     one day;
   they are like yesterday, already
     gone,
   like a short hour in the night.
5 You carry us away like a flood;
   we last no longer than a dream.
   We are like weeds that sprout in
     the morning,
6   that grow and burst into bloom,
     then dry up and die in the
       evening.

7 We are destroyed by your anger;
   we are terrified by your fury.
8 You place our sins before you,
   our secret sins where you can
     see them.

9 Our life is cut short by your anger;
   it fades away like a whisper.
10 Seventy years is all we have —
   eighty years, if we are strong;
   yet all they bring us is trouble and
     sorrow;
   life is soon over, and we are
     gone.

11 Who has felt the full power of your
     anger?
   Who knows what fear your fury
     can bring?

g Probable text royal scepter; *Hebrew* purity.
h Probable text curses; *Hebrew* crowds.
i HEBREW TITLE: *A prayer by Moses, the man of God.*
90.4 2 P 3.8   **90.10** Si 18.8, 9

2 Teach us how short our life is,
so that we may become wise.

3 How much longer will your anger
last?
Have pity, O LORD, on your
servants!

4 Fill us each morning with your
constant love,
so that we may sing and be glad
all our life.

5 Give us now as much happiness as
the sadness you gave us
during all our years of misery.

6 Let us, your servants, see your
mighty deeds;
let our descendants see your
glorious might.

7 Lord our God, may your blessings
be with us.
Give us success in all we do!

God Our Protector

91 Whoever goes to the LORD for
safety,
whoever remains under the
protection of the Almighty,

2 can say to him,
"You are my defender and
protector.
You are my God; in you I trust."

3 He will keep you safe from all
hidden dangers
and from all deadly diseases.

4 He will cover you with his wings;
you will be safe in his care;
his faithfulness will protect and
defend you.

5 You need not fear any dangers at
night
or sudden attacks during the day

6   or the plagues that strike in the
dark
or the evils that kill in daylight.

7 A thousand may fall dead beside
you,

ten thousand all around you,
but you will not be harmed.

8 You will look and see
how the wicked are punished.

9 You have made the LORD your^j
defender,
the Most High your protector,

10 and so no disaster will strike you,
no violence will come near your
home.

11 God will put his angels in charge
of you
to protect you wherever you go.

12 They will hold you up with their
hands
to keep you from hurting your
feet on the stones.

13 You will trample down lions and
snakes,
fierce lions and poisonous
snakes.

14 God says, "I will save those who
love me
and will protect those who
acknowledge me as LORD.

15 When they call to me, I will answer
them;
when they are in trouble, I will
be with them.
I will rescue them and honor
them.

16 I will reward them with long life;
I will save them."

A Song of Praise^k

92 How good it is to give thanks
to you, O LORD,
to sing in your honor, O Most
High God,

2 to proclaim your constant love
every morning
and your faithfulness every
night,

Probable text your; *Hebrew* my.   ^k HEBREW TITLE: *A psalm; a song for the Sabbath.*
91.11 Mt 4.6; Lk 4.10   **91.12** Mt 4.6; Lk 4.11   **91.13** Lk 10.19

³with the music of stringed
    instruments
  and with melody on the harp.
⁴Your mighty deeds, O LORD, make
    me glad;
  because of what you have done,
    I sing for joy.

⁵How great are your actions, LORD!
  How deep are your thoughts!
⁶This is something a fool cannot
    know;
  someone who is stupid cannot
    understand:
⁷the wicked may grow like weeds,
  those who do wrong may
    prosper;
  yet they will be totally destroyed,
⁸   because you, LORD, are supreme
    forever.

⁹We know that your enemies will
    die,
  and all the wicked will be
    defeated.
¹⁰You have made me as strong as a
    wild ox;
  you have blessed me with
    happiness.
¹¹I have seen the defeat of my
    enemies
  and heard the cries of the
    wicked.

¹²The righteous will flourish like
    palm trees;
  they will grow like the cedars of
    Lebanon.
¹³They are like trees planted in the
    house of the LORD,
  that flourish in the Temple of
    our God,
¹⁴   that still bear fruit in old age
  and are always green and
    strong.
¹⁵This shows that the LORD is just,
  that there is no wrong in my
    protector.

92.6 Ws 13.1

God the King

93 The LORD is king.
    He is clothed with majesty
      and strength.
The earth is set firmly in place
  and cannot be moved.
²Your throne, O LORD, has been
    firm from the beginning,
  and you existed before time
    began.

³The ocean depths raise their voice,
    O LORD;
  they raise their voice and roar.
⁴The LORD rules supreme in heaven,
  greater than the roar of the
    ocean,
  more powerful than the waves of
    the sea.

⁵Your laws are eternal, LORD,
  and your Temple is holy indeed,
    forever and ever.

God the Judge of All

94 LORD, you are a God who
      punishes;
  reveal your anger!
²You are the judge of us all;
  rise and give the proud what
    they deserve!
³How much longer will the wicked
    be glad?
  How much longer, LORD?
⁴How much longer will criminals be
    proud
  and boast about their crimes?

⁵They crush your people, LORD;
  they oppress those who belong
    to you.
⁶They kill widows and orphans,
  and murder the strangers who
    live in our land.
⁷They say, "The LORD does not
    see us;
  the God of Israel does not
    notice."

⁸My people, how can you be such
   stupid fools?
   When will you ever learn?
⁹God made our ears — can't he hear?
   He made our eyes — can't he
      see?
¹⁰He scolds the nations — won't he
   punish them?ˡ
   He is the teacher of us
      all — hasn't he any
      knowledge?
¹¹The LORD knows what we think;
   he knows how senseless our
      reasoning is.

¹²LORD, how happy are those you
   instruct,
   the ones to whom you teach
      your law!
¹³You give them rest from days of
   trouble
   until a pit is dug to trap the
      wicked.
¹⁴The LORD will not abandon his
   people;
   he will not desert those who
      belong to him.
¹⁵Justice will again be found in the
   courts,
   and all righteous people will
      support it.

¹⁶Who stood up for me against the
   wicked?
   Who took my side against the
      evildoers?
¹⁷If the LORD had not helped me,
   I would have gone quickly to the
      land of silence.ᵐ
¹⁸I said, "I am falling";
   but your constant love, O LORD,
      held me up.
¹⁹Whenever I am anxious and
   worried,
   you comfort me and make me
      glad.

²⁰You have nothing to do with
   corrupt judges,
   who make injustice legal,
²¹ who plot against good people
   and sentence the innocent to
      death.
²²But the LORD defends me;
   my God protects me.
²³He will punish them for their
   wickedness
   and destroy them for their sins;
   the LORD our God will destroy
      them.

A Song of Praise

95 Come, let us praise the LORD!
   Let us sing for joy to God,
      who protects us!
²Let us come before him with
   thanksgiving
   and sing joyful songs of praise.
³For the LORD is a mighty God,
   a mighty king over all the gods.
⁴He rules over the whole earth,
   from the deepest caves to the
      highest hills.
⁵He rules over the sea, which he
   made;
   the land also, which he himself
      formed.

⁶Come, let us bow down and
   worship him;
   let us kneel before the LORD,
      our Maker!
⁷He is our God;
   we are the people he cares for,
   the flock for which he provides.

Listen today to what he says:
⁸"Don't be stubborn, as your
   ancestors were at Meribah,
   as they were that day in the
      desert at Massah.

---

them?; *or our wicked leaders?*
see 6.5).

ᵐ LAND OF SILENCE: *The world of the dead*

94.11 1 Co 3.20   **95.7-11** He 3.7-11   **95.7, 8** He 3.15; 4.7   **95.8, 9** Ex 17.1-7; Nu 20.2-13

⁹There they put me to the test and
  tried me,
  although they had seen what I
  did for them.
¹⁰For forty years I was disgusted with
  those people.
  I said, 'How disloyal they are!
  They refuse to obey my
  commands.'
¹¹I was angry and made a solemn
  promise:
  'You will never enter the land
  where I would have given you
  rest.' "

God the Supreme King
(1 Chronicles 16.23-33)

96 Sing a new song to the LORD!
     Sing to the LORD, all the
     world!
²Sing to the LORD, and praise him!
  Proclaim every day the good
  news that he has saved us.
³Proclaim his glory to the nations,
  his mighty deeds to all peoples.

⁴The LORD is great and is to be
  highly praised;
  he is to be honored more than
  all the gods.
⁵The gods of all other nations are
  only idols,
  but the LORD created the
  heavens.
⁶Glory and majesty surround him;
  power and beauty fill his
  Temple.

⁷Praise the LORD, all people on
  earth;
  praise his glory and might.
⁸Praise the LORD's glorious name;
  bring an offering and come into
  his Temple.

⁹Bow down before the Holy One
  when he appears; ⁿ
  tremble before him, all the
  earth!

¹⁰Say to all the nations, "The LORD is
  king!
  The earth is set firmly in place
  and cannot be moved;
  he will judge the peoples with
  justice."
¹¹Be glad, earth and sky!
  Roar, sea, and every creature
  in you;
¹²   be glad, fields, and everything
  in you!
  The trees in the woods will shout
  for joy
¹³   when the LORD comes to rule
  the earth.

*The trees in the woods will shout for joy.
(96.12)*

ⁿ when he appears; *or* in garments of worship.
95.11 a Nu 14.20-23; Dt 1.34-36; He 4.3, 5; **b** Dt 12.9, 10   **96.7-9** Ps 29.1, 2

He will rule the peoples of the
world
with justice and fairness.

God the Supreme Ruler

97 The LORD is king! Earth, be
glad!
Rejoice, you islands of the seas!
² Clouds and darkness surround him;
he rules with righteousness and
justice.
³ Fire goes in front of him
and burns up his enemies
around him.
⁴ His lightning lights up the world;
the earth sees it and trembles.
⁵ The hills melt like wax before the
LORD,
before the Lord of all the earth.
⁶ The heavens proclaim his
righteousness,
and all the nations see his glory.

⁷ Everyone who worships idols is put
to shame;
all the gods bow down⁰ before
the LORD.
⁸ The people of Zion are glad,
and the cities of Judah rejoice
because of your judgments,
O LORD.
⁹ LORD Almighty, you are ruler of all
the earth;
you are much greater than all
the gods.

¹⁰ The LORD loves those who hate
evil; ᵖ
he protects the lives of his
people;
he rescues them from the power
of the wicked.
¹¹ Light shines on the righteous,
and gladness on the good.
¹² All you that are righteous be glad

because of what the LORD has
done!
Remember what the holy God has
done,
and give thanks to him.

God the Ruler of the World �q

98 Sing a new song to the LORD;
he has done wonderful
things!
By his own power and holy
strength
he has won the victory.
² The LORD announced his victory;
he made his saving power
known to the nations.
³ He kept his promise to the people
of Israel
with loyalty and constant love
for them.
All people everywhere have seen
the victory of our God.

⁴ Sing for joy to the LORD, all the
earth;
praise him with songs and
shouts of joy!
⁵ Sing praises to the LORD!
Play music on the harps!
⁶ Blow trumpets and horns,
and shout for joy to the LORD,
our king.

⁷ Roar, sea, and every creature
in you;
sing, earth, and all who live
on you!
⁸ Clap your hands, you rivers;
you hills, sing together with joy
before the LORD,
⁹ because he comes to rule the
earth.
He will rule the peoples of the
world
with justice and fairness.

ᵒ all the gods bow down; *or* bow down, all gods.   ᵖ *Probable text* The LORD loves
those who hate evil; *Hebrew* Hate evil, you who love the LORD.   �q HEBREW TITLE: A
psalm.

God the Supreme King

99 The LORD is king,
    and the people tremble.
He sits on his throne above the
    winged creatures,
    and the earth shakes.
2 The LORD is mighty in Zion;
    he is supreme over all the
    nations.
3 Everyone will praise his great and
    majestic name.
    Holy is he!

4 Mighty king,*r* you love what is
    right;
    you have established justice in
    Israel;
    you have brought righteousness
    and fairness.
5 Praise the LORD our God;
    worship before his throne!
    Holy is he!

6 Moses and Aaron were his priests,
    and Samuel was one who prayed
    to him;
    they called to the LORD, and he
    answered them.
7 He spoke to them from the pillar of
    cloud;
    they obeyed the laws and
    commands that he gave
    them.

8 O LORD, our God, you answered
    your people;
    you showed them that you are a
    God who forgives,
    even though you punished them
    for their sins.
9 Praise the LORD our God,
    and worship at his sacred hill!*s*
The LORD our God is holy.

A Hymn of Praise*t*

100 Sing to the LORD, all the
    world!
2 Worship the LORD with joy;
    come before him with happy
    songs!

3 Acknowledge that the LORD is God.
    He made us, and we belong to
    him;
    we are his people, we are his
    flock.

4 Enter the Temple gates with
    thanksgiving;
    go into its courts with praise.
    Give thanks to him and praise
    him.

5 The LORD is good;
    his love is eternal
    and his faithfulness lasts forever

A King's Promise*u*

101 My song is about loyalty
    and justice,
    and I sing it to you, O LORD.
2 My conduct will be faultless.
    When will you come to me?

    I will live a pure life in my house
3   and will never tolerate evil.
    I hate the actions of those who
    turn away from God;
    I will have nothing to do with
    them.
4 I will not be dishonest*v*
    and will have no dealings with
    evil.*w*
5 I will get rid of anyone
    who whispers evil things about
    someone else;
    I will not tolerate anyone
    who is proud and arrogant.

---

r Probable text Mighty king; *Hebrew* The might of the king.   *s* SACRED HILL: *See 2.6.*
t HEBREW TITLE: *A psalm of thanksgiving.*   *u* HEBREW TITLE: *A psalm by David.*
v not be dishonest; *or* stay away from dishonest people.   *w* evil; *or* evil people.
99.1 Ex 25.22   **99.7** Ex 33.9   **100.5** 1 Ch 16.34; 2 Ch 5.13; 7.3; Ezra 3.11; Ps 106.1;
107.1; 118.1; 136.1; Jr 33.11

⁶I will approve of those who are
   faithful to God
   and will let them live in my
      palace.
   Those who are completely honest
      will be allowed to serve me.

⁷No liar will live in my palace;
   no hypocrite will remain in my
      presence.
⁸Day after day I will destroy
   the wicked in our land;
   I will expel all who are evil
      from the city of the LORD.

The Prayer of a Troubled Youth ˣ

102 Listen to my prayer,
            O LORD,
   and hear my cry for help!
²When I am in trouble,
   don't turn away from me!
   Listen to me,
      and answer me quickly when
         I call!

³My life is disappearing like smoke;
   my body is burning like fire.
⁴I am beaten down like dry grass;
   I have lost my desire for food.
⁵I groan aloud;
   I am nothing but skin and
      bones.
⁶I am like a wild bird in the desert,
   like an owl in abandoned ruins.
⁷I lie awake;
   I am like a lonely bird on a
      housetop.
⁸All day long my enemies insult me;
   those who mock me use my
      name in cursing.
⁹⁻¹⁰Because of your anger and fury,
   ashes are my food,
   and my tears are mixed with my
      drink.
   You picked me up and threw me
      away.

¹¹My life is like the evening shadows;
   I am like dry grass.
¹²But you, O LORD, are king forever;
   all generations will remember
      you.
¹³You will rise and take pity on Zion;
   the time has come to have
      mercy on her;
   this is the right time.
¹⁴Your servants love her,
   even though she is destroyed;
   they have pity on her,
   even though she is in ruins.

¹⁵The nations will fear the LORD;
   all the kings of the earth will
      fear his power.
¹⁶When the LORD rebuilds Zion,
   he will reveal his greatness.
¹⁷He will hear his forsaken people
   and listen to their prayer.

¹⁸Write down for the coming
      generation what the LORD
      has done,
   so that people not yet born will
      praise him.
¹⁹The LORD looked down from his
      holy place on high,
   he looked down from heaven to
      earth.
²⁰He heard the groans of prisoners
   and set free those who were
      condemned to die.
²¹And so his name will be proclaimed
      in Zion,
   and he will be praised in
      Jerusalem
²²   when nations and kingdoms
      come together
   and worship the LORD.

²³The LORD has made me weak while
   I am still young;
   he has shortened my life.
²⁴O God, do not take me away now
   before I grow old.

ˣ HEBREW TITLE: *A prayer by a weary sufferer who pours out his complaints to the*
LORD.

O LORD, you live forever;
25 long ago you created the earth,
    and with your own hands you
    made the heavens.
26 They will disappear, but you will
    remain;
    they will all wear out like
    clothes.
    You will discard them like clothes,
    and they will vanish.
27 But you are always the same,
    and your life never ends.
28 Our children will live in safety,
    and under your protection
    their descendants will be secure.

The Love of God [y]

103 Praise the LORD, my soul!
        All my being, praise his
        holy name!
2 Praise the LORD, my soul,
    and do not forget how kind
    he is.
3 He forgives all my sins
    and heals all my diseases.
4 He keeps me from the grave
    and blesses me with love and
    mercy.
5 He fills my life [z] with good things,
    so that I stay young and strong
    like an eagle.

6 The LORD judges in favor of the
    oppressed
    and gives them their rights.
7 He revealed his plans to Moses
    and let the people of Israel see
    his mighty deeds.
8 The LORD is merciful and loving,
    slow to become angry and full of
    constant love.
9 He does not keep on rebuking;
    he is not angry forever.
10 He does not punish us as we
    deserve
    or repay us according to our sins
    and wrongs.

11 As high as the sky is above the
    earth,
    so great is his love for those who
    honor him.
12 As far as the east is from the west,
    so far does he remove our sins
    from us.
13 As a father is kind to his children,
    so the LORD is kind to those who
    honor him.
14 He knows what we are made of;
    he remembers that we are dust.

15 As for us, our life is like grass.
    We grow and flourish like a wild
    flower;
16 then the wind blows on it, and it
    is gone—
    no one sees it again.

*Then the wind blows on it,
and it is gone. (103.16)*

17 But for those who honor the LORD,
    his love lasts forever,
    and his goodness endures for all
    generations
18 of those who are true to his
    covenant
    and who faithfully obey his
    commands.

19 The LORD placed his throne in
    heaven;
    he is king over all.
20 Praise the LORD, you strong and
    mighty angels,

who obey his commands,
who listen to what he says.
21 Praise the LORD, all you heavenly
powers,
you servants of his, who do his
will!
22 Praise the LORD, all his creatures
in all the places he rules.
Praise the LORD, my soul!

In Praise of the Creator

104 Praise the LORD, my soul!
O LORD, my God, how
great you are!
You are clothed with majesty and
glory;
2   you cover yourself with light.
You have spread out the heavens
like a tent
3   and built your home on the
waters above.[a]
You use the clouds as your chariot
and ride on the wings of the
wind.
4 You use the winds as your
messengers
and flashes of lightning as your
servants.

5 You have set the earth firmly on its
foundations,
and it will never be moved.
6 You placed the ocean over it like a
robe,
and the water covered the
mountains.
7 When you rebuked the waters, they
fled;
they rushed away when they
heard your shout of
command.
8 They flowed over the mountains
and into the valleys,
to the place you had made for
them.
9 You set a boundary they can never
pass,

to keep them from covering the
earth again.

10 You make springs flow in the
valleys,
and rivers run between the hills.
11 They provide water for the wild
animals;
there the wild donkeys quench
their thirst.
12 In the trees near by,
the birds make their nests and
sing.
13 From the sky you send rain on the
hills,
and the earth is filled with your
blessings.
14 You make grass grow for the cattle
and plants for us to use,
so that we can grow our crops
15   and produce wine to make us
happy,
olive oil to make us cheerful,
and bread to give us strength.

16 The cedars of Lebanon get plenty
of rain —
the LORD's own trees, which he
planted.
17 There the birds build their nests;
the storks nest in the fir trees.
18 The wild goats live in the high
mountains,
and the rock badgers hide in the
cliffs.

19 You created the moon to mark the
months;
the sun knows the time to set.
20 You made the night, and in the
darkness
all the wild animals come out.
21 The young lions roar while they
hunt,
looking for the food that God
provides.
22 When the sun rises, they go back

---

[a] THE WATERS ABOVE: *A reference to the waters above the celestial dome (Gn 1.6, 7).*
104.4 He 1.7

and lie down in their dens.
23 Then people go out to do their
 work
and keep working until evening.

24 LORD, you have made so many
 things!
How wisely you made them all!
The earth is filled with your
 creatures.
25 There is the ocean, large and wide,
where countless creatures live,
 large and small alike.
26 The ships sail on it, and in it plays
 Leviathan,
that sea monster which you
 made.*b*

27 All of them depend on you
to give them food when they
 need it.
28 You give it to them, and they eat it;
you provide food, and they are
 satisfied.
29 When you turn away, they are
 afraid;
when you take away your
 breath, they die
and go back to the dust from
 which they came.
30 But when you give them breath,*c*
 they are created;
you give new life to the earth.

31 May the glory of the LORD last
 forever!
May the LORD be happy with
 what he has made!
32 He looks at the earth, and it
 trembles;
he touches the mountains, and
 they pour out smoke.

33 I will sing to the LORD all my life;
as long as I live I will sing
 praises to my God.
34 May he be pleased with my song,

for my gladness comes from
 him.
35 May sinners be destroyed from the
 earth;
may the wicked be no more.

Praise the LORD, my soul!
Praise the LORD!

God and His People
(1 Chronicles 16.8-22)

105 Give thanks to the LORD,
 proclaim his
 greatness;
tell the nations what he has
 done.
2 Sing praise to the LORD;
tell the wonderful things he has
 done.
3 Be glad that we belong to him;
let all who worship him rejoice.
4 Go to the LORD for help;
and worship him continually.
5-6 You descendants of Abraham, his
 servant;
you descendants of Jacob, the
 man he chose:
remember the miracles that God
 performed
and the judgments that he gave.

7 The LORD is our God;
his commands are for all the
 world.
8 He will keep his covenant forever,
his promises for a thousand
 generations.
9 He will keep the agreement he
 made with Abraham
and his promise to Isaac.
10 The LORD made a covenant with
 Jacob,
one that will last forever.
11 "I will give you the land of
 Canaan," he said.
"It will be your own possession."

b in it plays . . . made; *or* Leviathan is there, that sea monster you made to amuse you.
c give them breath; *or* send out your spirit.
104.26 Job 41.1; Ps 74.14; Is 27.1   **105.9 a** Gn 12.7; 17.8; **b** Gn 26.3   **105.10, 11** Gn 28.13

¹²God's people were few in number,
strangers in the land of Canaan.
¹³They wandered from country to
country,
from one kingdom to another.
¹⁴But God let no one oppress them;
to protect them, he warned the
kings:
¹⁵"Don't harm my chosen servants;
do not touch my prophets."

¹⁶The LORD sent famine to their
country
and took away all their food.
¹⁷But he sent a man ahead of them,
Joseph, who had been sold as a
slave.
¹⁸His feet were kept in chains,
and an iron collar was around
his neck,
¹⁹ until what he had predicted
came true.
The word of the LORD proved him
right.
²⁰Then the king of Egypt had him
released;
the ruler of nations set him free.
²¹He put him in charge of his
government
and made him ruler over all the
land,
²² with power over the king's
officials
and authority to instruct his
advisers.

²³Then Jacob went to Egypt
and settled in that country.
²⁴The LORD gave many children to
his people
and made them stronger than
their enemies.
²⁵He made the Egyptians hate his
people

and treat his servants with
deceit.

²⁶Then he sent his servant Moses,
and Aaron, whom he had
chosen.
²⁷They did God's mighty acts
and performed miracles in
Egypt.
²⁸God sent darkness on the country,
but the Egyptians did not obey ᵈ
his command.
²⁹He turned their rivers into blood
and killed all their fish.
³⁰Their country was overrun with
frogs;
even the palace was filled with
them.
³¹God commanded, and flies and
gnats
swarmed throughout the whole
country.
³²He sent hail and lightning on their
land
instead of rain;
³³he destroyed their grapevines and
fig trees
and broke down all the trees.
³⁴He commanded, and the locusts
came,
countless millions of them;
³⁵they ate all the plants in the land;
they ate all the crops.
³⁶He killed the first-born sons
of all the families of Egypt.

³⁷Then he led the Israelites out;
they carried silver and gold,
and all of them were healthy
and strong.
³⁸The Egyptians were afraid of them

ᵈ *Some ancient translations* did not obey; *Hebrew* obeyed.
105.14, 15 Gn 20.3-7   **105.16** Gn 41.53-57   **105.17** Gn 37.28; 45.5
105.18, 19 Gn 39.20—40.23   **105.20** Gn 41.14   **105.21** Gn 41.39-41   **105.23 a** Gn 46.6;
b Gn 47.11   **105.24, 25** Ex 1.7-14   **105.26** Ex 3.1—4.17   **105.28** Ex 10.21-23
105.29 Ex 7.17-21   **105.30** Ex 8.1-6   **105.31 a** Ex 8.20-24; **b** Ex 8.16, 17
105.32, 33 Ex 9.22-25   **105.34, 35** Ex 10.12-15   **105.36** Ex 12.29   **105.37, 38** Ex 12.33-36

and were glad when they left.
39 God put a cloud over his people
and a fire at night to give them
light.
40 They e asked, and he sent quails;
he gave them food from heaven
to satisfy them.
41 He opened a rock, and water
gushed out,
flowing through the desert like a
river.
42 He remembered his sacred promise
to Abraham his servant.

43 So he led his chosen people out,
and they sang and shouted
for joy.
44 He gave them the lands of other
peoples
and let them take over their
fields,
45 so that his people would obey his
laws
and keep all his commands.

Praise the LORD!

The LORD's Goodness to His People

106

Praise the LORD!

Give thanks to the LORD, because
he is good;
his love is eternal.
2 Who can tell all the great things he
has done?
Who can praise him enough?
3 Happy are those who obey his
commands,
who always do what is right.

4 Remember me, LORD, when you
help your people;

include me when you save
them.
5 Let me see the prosperity of your
people
and share in the happiness of
your nation,
in the glad pride of those who
belong to you.

6 We have sinned as our ancestors
did;
we have been wicked and evil.
7 Our ancestors in Egypt did not
understand God's wonderful
acts;
they forgot the many times he
showed them his love,
and they rebelled against the
Almighty f at the Red Sea.
8 But he saved them, as he had
promised,
in order to show his great power.
9 He gave a command to the Red
Sea,
and it dried up;
he led his people across on dry
land.
10 He saved them from those who
hated them;
he rescued them from their
enemies.
11 But the water drowned their
enemies;
not one of them was left.
12 Then his people believed his
promises
and sang praises to him.

13 But they quickly forgot what he
had done
and acted without waiting for
his advice.

e *Some ancient translations* They; *Hebrew* He.   f *Probable text* the Almighty;
Hebrew the sea.

105.39 Ex 13.21, 22   **105.40** Ex 16.2-15   **105.41** Ex 17.1-7; Nu 20.2-13
105.44 Js 11.16-23   **106.1** 1 Ch 16.34; 2 Ch 5.13; 7.3; Ezra 3.11; Ps 100.5;
107.1; 118.1; 136.1; Jr 33.11   **106.7** Ex 14.10-12   **106.9-12** Ex 14.21-31
106.12 Ex 15.1-21

14 They were filled with craving in the desert
   and put God to the test;
15 so he gave them what they asked for,
   but also sent a terrible disease among them.

16 There in the desert they were jealous of Moses
   and of Aaron, the LORD's holy servant.
17 Then the earth opened up and swallowed Dathan
   and buried Abiram and his family;
18 fire came down on their followers
   and burned up those wicked people.

19 They made a gold bull-calf at Sinai
   and worshiped that idol;
20 they exchanged the glory of God
   for the image of an animal that eats grass.
21 They forgot the God who had saved them
   by his mighty acts in Egypt.
22 What wonderful things he did there!
   What amazing things at the Red Sea!
23 When God said that he would destroy his people,
   his chosen servant, Moses, stood up against God
   and kept his anger from destroying them.

24 Then they rejected the pleasant land,
   because they did not believe God's promise.
25 They stayed in their tents and grumbled
   and would not listen to the LORD.
26 So he gave them a solemn warning
   that he would make them die in the desert
27 and scatter their descendants among the heathen,
   letting them die in foreign countries.

28 Then at Peor, God's people joined in the worship of Baal
   and ate sacrifices offered to dead gods.
29 They stirred up the LORD's anger by their actions,
   and a terrible disease broke out among them.
30 But Phinehas stood up and punished the guilty,
   and the plague was stopped.
31 This has been remembered in his favor ever since
   and will be for all time to come.

32 At the springs of Meribah the people made the LORD angry,
   and Moses was in trouble on their account.
33 They made him so bitter
   that he spoke without stopping to think.

34 They did not kill the heathen,
   as the LORD had commanded them to do,
35 but they intermarried with them
   and adopted their pagan ways.
36 God's people worshiped idols,
   and this caused their destruction.
37 They offered their own sons and daughters
   as sacrifices to the idols of Canaan.

106.14, 15 Nu 11.4-34   **106.16-18** Nu 16.1-35   **106.19-23** Ex 32.1-14
106.24-26 Nu 14.1-35   **106.27** Lv 26.33   **106.28-31** Nu 25.1-13
106.32, 33 Nu 20.2-13   **106.34-36** Jg 2.1-3; 3.5, 6   **106.37** 2 K 17.17

³⁸They killed those innocent
children,
and the land was defiled by
those murders.
³⁹They made themselves impure by
their actions
and were unfaithful to God.

⁴⁰So the LORD was angry with his
people;
he was disgusted with them.
⁴¹He abandoned them to the power
of the heathen,
and their enemies ruled over
them.
⁴²They were oppressed by their
enemies
and were in complete subjection
to them.
⁴³Many times the LORD rescued his
people,
but they chose to rebel against
him
and sank deeper into sin.
⁴⁴Yet the LORD heard them when
they cried out,
and he took notice of their
distress.
⁴⁵For their sake he remembered his
covenant,
and because of his great love he
relented.
⁴⁶He made all their oppressors
feel sorry for them.

⁴⁷Save us, O LORD our God,
and bring us back from among
the nations,
so that we may be thankful
and praise your holy name.

⁴⁸Praise the LORD, the God of Israel;
praise him now and forever!
Let everyone say, "Amen!"

Praise the LORD!

BOOK FIVE
(Psalms 107–150)

In Praise of God's Goodness

107 "Give thanks to the LORD,
because he is good;
his love is eternal!"
²Repeat these words in praise to the
LORD,
all you whom he has saved.
He has rescued you from your
enemies
³   and has brought you back from
foreign countries,
from east and west, from north
and south.⁹

⁴Some wandered in the trackless
desert
and could not find their way to a
city to live in.
⁵They were hungry and thirsty
and had given up all hope.
⁶Then in their trouble they called to
the LORD,
and he saved them from their
distress.
⁷He led them by a straight road
to a city where they could live.
⁸They must thank the LORD for his
constant love,
for the wonderful things he did
for them.
⁹He satisfies those who are thirsty
and fills the hungry with good
things.

¹⁰Some were living in gloom and
darkness,
prisoners suffering in chains,
¹¹because they had rebelled against
the commands of
Almighty God
and had rejected his
instructions.

---

⁹ *Probable text* south; *Hebrew* the Mediterranean Sea (*meaning* "*west*").
106.38 Nu 35.33   **106.40-46** Jg 2.14-18   **106.47, 48** 1 Ch 16.35, 36   **107.1** 1 Ch 16.34;
2 Ch 5.13; 7.3; Ezra 3.11; Ps 100.5; 106.1; 118.1; 136.1; Jr 33.11

He brought them safe to the port. (107.30)

² They were worn out from hard
work;
they would fall down, and no
one would help.
³ Then in their trouble they called to
the LORD,
and he saved them from their
distress.
⁴ He brought them out of their gloom
and darkness
and broke their chains in pieces.
⁵ They must thank the LORD for his
constant love,
for the wonderful things he did
for them.
⁶ He breaks down doors of bronze
and smashes iron bars.

⁷ Some were fools, suffering because
of their sins
and because of their evil;
⁸ they couldn't stand the sight of
food
and were close to death.
⁹ Then in their trouble they called to
the LORD,
and he saved them from their
distress.
¹⁰ He healed them with his command
and saved them from the grave.
¹¹ They must thank the LORD for his
constant love,
for the wonderful things he did
for them.

²² They must thank him with
sacrifices,
and with songs of joy must tell
all that he has done.

²³ Some sailed over the ocean in
ships,
earning their living on the seas.
²⁴ They saw what the LORD can do,
his wonderful acts on the seas.
²⁵ He commanded, and a mighty wind
began to blow
and stirred up the waves.
²⁶ The ships were lifted high in
the air
and plunged down into the
depths.
In such danger the sailors lost their
courage;
²⁷ they stumbled and staggered
like drunks —
all their skill was useless.
²⁸ Then in their trouble they called to
the LORD,
and he saved them from their
distress.
²⁹ He calmed the raging storm,
and the waves became quiet.
³⁰ They were glad because of the
calm,
and he brought them safe to the
port they wanted.
³¹ They must thank the LORD for his
constant love,

for the wonderful things he did
for them.
32 They must proclaim his greatness
in the assembly of the people
and praise him before the
council of the leaders.

33 The LORD made rivers dry up
completely
and stopped springs from
flowing.
34 He made rich soil become a salty
wasteland
because of the wickedness of
those who lived there.
35 He changed deserts into pools of
water
and dry land into flowing
springs.
36 He let hungry people settle there,
and they built a city to live in.
37 They sowed the fields and planted
grapevines
and reaped an abundant harvest.
38 He blessed his people, and they
had many children;
he kept their herds of cattle
from decreasing.

39 When God's people were defeated
and humiliated
by cruel oppression and
suffering,
40 he showed contempt for their
oppressors
and made them wander in
trackless deserts.
41 But he rescued the needy from
their misery
and made their families increase
like flocks.
42 The righteous see this and are glad,
but all the wicked are put to
silence.

43 May those who are wise think
about these things;

h HEBREW TITLE: *A psalm by David; a song.*
holiness.
107.34 Si 39.23

may they consider the LORD's
constant love.

A Prayer for Help against Enemies *h*
(Psalm 57.7-11; 60.5-12)

108
I have complete
confidence, O God!
I will sing and praise you!
Wake up, my soul!
2　Wake up, my harp and lyre!
I will wake up the sun.
3 I will thank you, O LORD, among
the nations.
I will praise you among the
peoples.
4 Your constant love reaches above
the heavens;
your faithfulness touches the
skies.

5 Show your greatness in the sky,
O God,
and your glory over all the earth
6 Save us by your might; answer my
prayer,
so that the people you love may
be rescued.

7 From his sanctuary *i* God has said,
"In triumph I will divide
Shechem
and distribute Sukkoth Valley to
my people.
8 Gilead is mine, and Manasseh too;
Ephraim is my helmet
and Judah my royal scepter.
9 But I will use Moab as my
washbowl,
and I will throw my sandals on
Edom,
as a sign that I own it.
I will shout in triumph over the
Philistines."

10 Who, O God, will take me into the
fortified city?

i From his sanctuary; *or* In his

Who will lead me to Edom?
11 Have you really rejected us?
　　Aren't you going to march out
　　　with our armies?
12 Help us against the enemy;
　　human help is worthless.
13 With God on our side we will win;
　　he will defeat our enemies.

The Complaint of Someone in Trouble *j*

109 I praise you, God; don't remain silent!
2 Wicked people and liars have
　　attacked me.
　They tell lies about me,
3　　and they say evil things about
　　me,
　　attacking me for no reason.
4 They oppose me, even though I
　　love them
　　and have prayed for them. *k*
5 They pay me back evil for good
　　and hatred for love.

6 Choose some corrupt judge to try
　　my enemy,
　　and let one of his own enemies
　　accuse him.
7 May he be tried and found guilty;
　　may even his prayer be
　　considered a crime!
8 May his life soon be ended;
　　may someone else take his job!
9 May his children become orphans,
　　and his wife a widow!
10 May his children be homeless
　　beggars;
　　may they be driven from *l* the
　　ruins they live in!
11 May his creditors take away all his
　　property,
　　and may strangers get
　　everything he worked for.
12 May no one ever be kind to him

or care for the orphans he leaves
　　behind.
13 May all his descendants die,
　　and may his name be forgotten
　　in the next generation.
14 May the LORD remember the evil of
　　his ancestors
　　and never forgive his mother's
　　sins.
15 May the LORD always remember
　　their sins,
　　but may they themselves be
　　completely forgotten!

16 That man never thought of being
　　kind;
　　he persecuted and killed
　　the poor, the needy, and the
　　helpless.
17 He loved to curse — may he be
　　cursed!
　　He hated to give blessings — may
　　no one bless him!
18 He cursed as naturally as he
　　dressed himself;
　　may his own curses soak into
　　his body like water
　　and into his bones like oil!
19 May they cover him like clothes
　　and always be around him like a
　　belt!

20 LORD, punish my enemies in that
　　way —
　　those who say such evil things
　　against me!
21 But my Sovereign LORD, help me
　　as you have promised,
　　and rescue me because of the
　　goodness of your love.
22 I am poor and needy;
　　I am hurt to the depths of my
　　heart.
23 Like an evening shadow I am about
　　to vanish;
　　I am blown away like an insect.

HEBREW TITLE: *A psalm by David.*　*k Probable text* have prayed for them; *Hebrew unclear.*　*l One ancient translation* be driven from; *Hebrew* seek.
109.8 Ac 1.20

²⁴My knees are weak from lack of
food;
I am nothing but skin and
bones.
²⁵When people see me, they laugh
at me;
they shake their heads in scorn.

²⁶Help me, O LORD my God;
because of your constant love,
save me!
²⁷Make my enemies know
that you are the one who saves
me.
²⁸They may curse me, but you will
bless me.
May my persecutors be
defeated,^m
and may I, your servant, be glad.
²⁹May my enemies be covered with
disgrace;
may they wear their shame like
a robe.

³⁰I will give loud thanks to the LORD;
I will praise him in the assembly
of the people,
³¹because he defends the poor
and saves them from those who
condemn them to death.

The LORD and His Chosen King ⁿ

110
The LORD said to my lord,
"Sit here at my right
side
until I put your enemies under
your feet."
²From Zion the LORD will extend
your royal power.
"Rule over your enemies," he
says.
³On the day you fight your enemies,
your people will volunteer.

Like the dew of early morning
your young men will come to
you on the sacred hills.^o

⁴The LORD made a solemn promise
and will not take it back:
"You will be a priest forever
in the priestly order of
Melchizedek."^p

⁵The Lord is at your right side;
when he becomes angry, he will
defeat kings.
⁶He will pass judgment on the
nations
and fill the battlefield with
corpses;
he will defeat kings all over the
earth.
⁷The king will drink from the
stream by the road,
and strengthened, he will stand
victorious.

In Praise of the LORD

111
Praise the LORD!
With all my heart I will thank the
LORD
in the assembly of his people.
²How wonderful are the things the
LORD does!
All who are delighted with them
want to understand them.
³All he does is full of honor and
majesty;
his righteousness is eternal.

⁴The LORD does not let us forget his
wonderful actions;
he is kind and merciful.
⁵He provides food for those who
honor him;

---

^m *One ancient translation* May my persecutors be defeated; *Hebrew* They persecuted
me and were defeated.   ⁿ HEBREW TITLE: *A psalm by David.*   ^o *Verse 3 in*
Hebrew is unclear.   ^p in the priestly order of Melchizedek; *or* like Melchizedek; *or*
in the line of succession to Melchizedek.
109.25 Mt 27.39; Mk 15.29   **110.1** Mt 22.44; Mk 12.36; Lk 20.42, 43; Ac 2.34, 35;
1 Co 15.25; Eph 1.20-22; Col 3.1; He 1.13; 8.1; 10.12, 13   **110.4** He 5.6; 6.20; 7.17, 21

he never forgets his covenant.
⁶ He has shown his power to his
people
by giving them the lands of
foreigners.

⁷ In all he does he is faithful and
just;
all his commands are
dependable.
⁸ They last for all time;
they were given in truth and
righteousness.
⁹ He set his people free
and made an eternal covenant
with them.
Holy and mighty is he!
¹⁰ The way to become wise is to
honor the Lord; ⁹
he gives sound judgment to all
who obey his commands.
He is to be praised forever.

The Happiness of a Good Person

112   Praise the Lord!

Happy is the person who honors
the Lord,
who takes pleasure in obeying
his commands.
² The good man's children will be
powerful in the land;
his descendants will be blessed.
³ His family will be wealthy and rich,
and he will be prosperous
forever.

⁴ Light shines in the darkness for
good people,
for those who are merciful, kind,
and just.
⁵ Happy is the person who is
generous with his loans,
who runs his business honestly.
⁶ A good person will never fail;
he will always be remembered.

⁷ He is not afraid of receiving bad
news;
his faith is strong, and he trusts
in the Lord.
⁸ He is not worried or afraid;
he is certain to see his enemies
defeated.
⁹ He gives generously to the needy,
and his kindness never fails;
he will be powerful and
respected.
¹⁰ The wicked see this and are angry;
they glare in hate and disappear;
their hopes are gone forever.

In Praise of the Lord's Goodness

113   Praise the Lord!

You servants of the Lord,
praise his name!
² May his name be praised,
now and forever.
³ From the east to the west
praise the name of the Lord!
⁴ The Lord rules over all nations;
his glory is above the heavens.

⁵ There is no one like the Lord
our God.
He lives in the heights above,
⁶   but he bends down
to see the heavens and the
earth.
⁷ He raises the poor from the dust;
he lifts the needy from their
misery
⁸ and makes them companions of
princes,
the princes of his people.
⁹ He honors the childless wife in her
home;
he makes her happy by giving
her children.

Praise the Lord!

The way . . . the Lord; *or* The most important part of wisdom is honoring the Lord.
11.10 Job 28.28; Pr 1.7; 9.10   **112.9** 2 Co 9.9

A Passover Song

114 When the people of Israel
left Egypt,
when Jacob's descendants left
that foreign land,
2 Judah became the Lord's holy
people,
Israel became his own
possession.

3 The Red Sea looked and ran away;
the Jordan River stopped
flowing.
4 The mountains skipped like goats;
the hills jumped around like
lambs.

5 What happened, Sea, to make you
run away?
And you, O Jordan, why did you
stop flowing?
6 You mountains, why did you skip
like goats?
You hills, why did you jump
around like lambs?

7 Tremble, earth, at the Lord's
coming,
at the presence of the God of
Jacob,
8 who changes rocks into pools of
water
and solid cliffs into flowing
springs.

The One True God

115 To you alone, O LORD, to
you alone,
and not to us, must glory be
given
because of your constant love
and faithfulness.

2 Why should the nations ask us,
"Where is your God?"
3 Our God is in heaven;

he does whatever he wishes.
4 Their gods are made of silver and
gold,
formed by human hands.
5 They have mouths, but cannot
speak,
and eyes, but cannot see.
6 They have ears, but cannot hear,
and noses, but cannot smell.
7 They have hands, but cannot feel,
and feet, but cannot walk;
they cannot make a sound.
8 May all who made them and who
trust in them
become *r* like the idols they
have made.

9 Trust in the LORD, you people of
Israel.
He helps you and protects you.
10 Trust in the LORD, you priests
of God.
He helps you and protects you.
11 Trust in the LORD, all you that
worship him.
He helps you and protects you.

12 The LORD remembers us and will
bless us;
he will bless the people of Israel
and all the priests of God.
13 He will bless everyone who honors
him,
the great and the small alike.

14 May the LORD give you children —
you and your descendants!
15 May you be blessed by the LORD,
who made heaven and earth!

16 Heaven belongs to the LORD alone,
but he gave the earth to us
humans.
17 The LORD is not praised by the
dead,

r May all ... become; *or* All who made them and who trust in them will become.
114.1 Ex 12.51   **114.3 a** Ex 14.21; **b** Js 3.16   **114.8** Ex 17.1-7; Nu 20.2-13
115.4-8 Ps 135.15-18; Let Jer 4-73; Rev 9.20   **115.13** Rev 11.18; 19.5

by any who go down to the land
　of silence.[s]
[8] But we, the living, will give thanks
　to him
　now and forever.

Praise the LORD!

Someone Saved from Death Praises God

116 I love the LORD, because
　　　he hears me;
he listens to my prayers.
[2] He listens to me
　every time I call to him.
[3] The danger of death was all around
　me;
　the horrors of the grave closed
　in on me;
　I was filled with fear and
　anxiety.
[4] Then I called to the LORD,
　"I beg you, LORD, save me!"

[5] The LORD is merciful and good;
　our God is compassionate.
[6] The LORD protects the helpless;
　when I was in danger, he
　saved me.
[7] Be confident, my heart,
　because the LORD has been good
　to me.

[8] The LORD saved me from death;
　he stopped my tears
　and kept me from defeat.
[9] And so I walk in the presence of
　the LORD
　in the world of the living.
[10] I kept on believing, even when
　I said,
　"I am completely crushed,"
[11] even when I was afraid and said,
　"No one can be trusted."

[12] What can I offer the LORD

for all his goodness to me?
[13] I will bring a wine offering to the
　LORD,
　to thank him for saving me.
[14] In the assembly of all his people
　I will give him what I have
　promised.

[15] How painful it is to the LORD
　when one of his people dies!
[16] I am your servant, LORD;
　I serve you just as my mother
　did.
You have saved me from death.
[17] I will give you a sacrifice of
　thanksgiving
　and offer my prayer to you.
[18-19] In the assembly of all your
　people,
　in the sanctuary of your Temple
　in Jerusalem,
　I will give you what I have
　promised.

Praise the LORD!

In Praise of the LORD

117 Praise the LORD, all
　　　nations!
Praise him, all peoples!
[2] His love for us is strong,
　and his faithfulness is eternal.

Praise the LORD!

A Prayer of Thanks for Victory

118 Give thanks to the LORD,
　　　because he is good,
and his love is eternal.
[2] Let the people of Israel say,
　"His love is eternal."
[3] Let the priests of God say,
　"His love is eternal."
[4] Let all who worship him say,
　"His love is eternal."

[s] LAND OF SILENCE: *The world of the dead (see 6.5).*
116.10 2 Co 4.13　**117.1** Ro 15.11　**118.1** 1 Ch 16.34; 2 Ch 5.13; 7.3; Ezra 3.11; Ps 100.5;
106.1; 107.1; 136.1; Jr 33.11

⁵In my distress I called to the LORD;
  he answered me and set me
    free.
⁶The LORD is with me, I will not be
    afraid;
  what can anyone do to me?

Praise the LORD, all nations! (117.1)

⁷It is the LORD who helps me,
  and I will see my enemies
    defeated.
⁸It is better to trust in the LORD
  than to depend on people.
⁹It is better to trust in the LORD
  than to depend on human
    leaders.

¹⁰Many enemies were around me;
  but I destroyed them by the
    power of the LORD!
¹¹They were around me on every
    side;
  but I destroyed them by the
    power of the LORD!
¹²They swarmed around me like
    bees,
  but they burned out as quickly
    as a brush fire;
  by the power of the LORD I
    destroyed them.

¹³I was fiercely attacked and was
    being defeated,
  but the LORD helped me.
¹⁴The LORD makes me powerful and
    strong;
  he has saved me.

¹⁵Listen to the glad shouts of victory
    in the tents of God's people:
  "The LORD's mighty power has
    done it!
¹⁶ His power has brought us
    victory —
  his mighty power in battle!"

¹⁷I will not die; instead, I will live
  and proclaim what the LORD has
    done.
¹⁸He has punished me severely,
  but he has not let me die.

¹⁹Open to me the gates of the
    Temple;
  I will go in and give thanks to
    the LORD!

²⁰This is the gate of the LORD;
  only the righteous can come in.

²¹I praise you, LORD, because you
    heard me,
  because you have given me
    victory.

²²The stone which the builders
    rejected as worthless
  turned out to be the most
    important of all.
²³This was done by the LORD;
  what a wonderful sight it is!
²⁴This is the day of the LORD's
    victory;
  let us be happy, let us celebrate!
²⁵Save us, LORD, save us!
  Give us success, O LORD!

118.6 He 13.6 **118.14** Ex 15.2; Is 12.2 **118.22** Lk 20.17; Ac 4.11; 1 P 2.7
118.22, 23 Mt 21.42; Mk 12.10, 11 **118.25** Mt 21.9; Mk 11.9; Jn 12.13

6 May God bless the one who comes
     in the name of the LORD!
   From the Temple of the LORD
     we bless you.
7 The LORD is God; he has been good
     to us.
   With branches in your hands, start
     the festival
   and march around the altar.

8 You are my God, and I give you
     thanks;
   I will proclaim your greatness.

9 Give thanks to the LORD, because
     he is good,
   and his love is eternal.

The Law of the LORD

119 Happy are those whose
           lives are faultless,
   who live according to the law of
     the LORD.
2 Happy are those who follow his
     commands,
   who obey him with all their
     heart.
3 They never do wrong;
   they walk in the LORD's ways.
4 LORD, you have given us your laws
   and told us to obey them
     faithfully.
5 How I hope that I shall be faithful
   in keeping your instructions!
6 If I pay attention to all your
     commands,
   then I will not be put to shame.
7 As I learn your righteous
     judgments,
   I will praise you with a pure
     heart.
8 I will obey your laws;
   never abandon me!

Obedience to the Law of the LORD

9 How can young people keep their
     lives pure?

By obeying your commands.
10 With all my heart I try to serve
     you;
   keep me from disobeying your
     commandments.
11 I keep your law in my heart,
   so that I will not sin against you.
12 I praise you, O LORD;
   teach me your ways.
13 I will repeat aloud
   all the laws you have given.
14 I delight in following your
     commands
   more than in having great
     wealth.
15 I study your instructions;
   I examine your teachings.
16 I take pleasure in your laws;
   your commands I will
     not forget.

Happiness in the Law of the LORD

17 Be good to me, your servant,
   so that I may live and obey your
     teachings.
18 Open my eyes, so that I may see
   the wonderful truths in your
     law.
19 I am here on earth for just a little
     while;
   do not hide your commands
     from me.
20 My heart aches with longing;
   I want to know your judgments
     at all times.
21 You reprimand the proud;
   cursed are those who disobey
     your commands.
22 Free me from their insults and
     scorn,
   because I have kept your laws.
23 The rulers meet and plot against
     me,
   but I will study your teachings.
24 Your instructions give me pleasure;
   they are my advisers.

118.26 Mt 21.9; 23.39; Mk 11.9; Lk 13.35; 19.38; Jn 12.13

Determination to Obey the Law
of the LORD

25 I lie defeated in the dust;
   revive me, as you have
      promised.
26 I confessed all I have done, and
      you answered me;
   teach me your ways.
27 Help me to understand your laws,
   and I will meditate on your
      wonderful teachings.[t]
28 I am overcome by sorrow;
   strengthen me, as you have
      promised.
29 Keep me from going the wrong
      way,
   and in your goodness teach me
      your law.
30 I have chosen to be obedient;
   I have paid attention to your
      judgments.
31 I have followed your instructions,
      LORD;
   don't let me be put to shame.
32 I will eagerly obey your commands,
   because you will give me more
      understanding.

A Prayer for Understanding

33 Teach me, LORD, the meaning of
      your laws,
   and I will obey them at all
      times.
34 Explain your law to me, and I will
      obey it;
   I will keep it with all my heart.
35 Keep me obedient to your
      commandments,
   because in them I find
      happiness.
36 Give me the desire to obey your
      laws
   rather than to get rich.
37 Keep me from paying attention to
      what is worthless;
   be good to me, as you have
      promised.

38 Keep your promise to me, your
      servant —
   the promise you make to those
      who obey you.
39 Save me from the insults I fear;
   how wonderful are your
      judgments!
40 I want to obey your commands;
   give me new life, for you are
      righteous.

Trusting the Law of the LORD

41 Show me how much you love me,
      LORD,
   and save me according to your
      promise.
42 Then I can answer those who
      insult me
   because I trust in your word.
43 Enable me to speak the truth at all
      times,
   because my hope is in your
      judgments.
44 I will always obey your law,
   forever and ever.
45 I will live in perfect freedom,
   because I try to obey your
      teachings.
46 I will announce your commands
      to kings
   and I will not be ashamed.
47 I find pleasure in obeying your
      commands,
   because I love them.
48 I respect and love your
      commandments;
   I will meditate on your
      instructions.

Confidence in the Law of the LORD

49 Remember your promise to me,
      your servant;
   it has given me hope.
50 Even in my suffering I was
      comforted
   because your promise gave
      me life.

---

t teachings; or deeds.

⁶¹The proud are always scornful
of me,
but I have not departed from
your law.
⁶²I remember your judgments of
long ago,
and they bring me comfort,
O LORD.
⁶³When I see the wicked breaking
your law,
I am filled with anger.
⁶⁴During my brief earthly life
I compose songs about your
commands.
⁶⁵In the night I remember you,
LORD,
and I think about your law.
⁶⁶I find my happiness
in obeying your commands.

Devotion to the Law of the LORD

⁵⁷You are all I want, O LORD;
I promise to obey your laws.
⁵⁸I ask you with all my heart
to have mercy on me, as you
have promised!
⁵⁹I have considered my conduct,
and I promise to follow your
instructions.
⁶⁰Without delay I hurry
to obey your commands.
⁶¹The wicked have laid a trap for me,
but I do not forget your law.
⁶²In the middle of the night I
wake up
to praise you for your righteous
judgments.
⁶³I am a friend of all who serve you,
of all who obey your laws.
⁶⁴LORD, the earth is full of your
constant love;
teach me your commandments.

The Value of the Law of the LORD

⁶⁵You have kept your promise, LORD,
and you are good to me, your
servant.
⁶⁶Give me wisdom and knowledge,

because I trust in your
commands.
⁶⁷Before you punished me, I used to
go wrong,
but now I obey your word.
⁶⁸How good you are — how kind!
Teach me your commands.
⁶⁹The proud have told lies about me,
but with all my heart I obey
your instructions.
⁷⁰They have no understanding,
but I find pleasure in your law.
⁷¹My punishment was good for me,
because it made me learn your
commands.
⁷²The law that you gave means more
to me
than all the money in the world.

The Justice of the Law of the LORD

⁷³You created me, and you keep me
safe;
give me understanding, so that I
may learn your laws.
⁷⁴Those who honor you will be glad
when they see me,
because I trust in your promise.
⁷⁵I know that your judgments are
righteous, LORD,
and that you punished me
because you are faithful.
⁷⁶Let your constant love comfort me,
as you have promised me, your
servant.
⁷⁷Have mercy on me, and I will live
because I take pleasure in
your law.
⁷⁸May the proud be ashamed for
falsely accusing me;
as for me, I will meditate on
your instructions.
⁷⁹May those who honor you come
to me —
all those who know your
commands.
⁸⁰May I perfectly obey your
commandments
and be spared the shame of
defeat.

A Prayer for Deliverance

81 I am worn out, LORD, waiting for
you to save me;
I place my trust in your word.
82 My eyes are tired from watching for
what you promised,
while I ask, "When will you
help me?"
83 I am as useless as a discarded
wineskin;
yet I have not forgotten your
commands.
84 How much longer must I wait?
When will you punish those who
persecute me?
85 The proud, who do not obey your
law,
have dug pits to trap me.
86 Your commandments are all
trustworthy;
people persecute me with
lies — help me!
87 They have almost succeeded in
killing me,
but I have not neglected your
commands.
88 Because of your constant love be
good to me,
so that I may obey your laws.

Faith in the Law of the LORD

89 Your word, O LORD, will last
forever;
it is eternal in heaven.
90 Your faithfulness endures through
all the ages;
you have set the earth in place,
and it remains.
91 All things remain to this day
because of your command,
because they are all your
servants.
92 If your law had not been the source
of my joy,
I would have died from my
sufferings.
93 I will never neglect your
instructions,
because by them you have kept
me alive.

94 I am yours — save me!
I have tried to obey your
commands.
95 The wicked are waiting to kill me,
but I will meditate on your laws.
96 I have learned that everything has
limits;
but your commandment is
perfect.

Love for the Law of the LORD

97 How I love your law!
I think about it all day long.
98 Your commandment is with me all
the time
and makes me wiser than my
enemies.
99 I understand more than all my
teachers,
because I meditate on your
instructions.
100 I have greater wisdom than those
who are old,
because I obey your commands.
101 I have avoided all evil conduct,
because I want to obey your
word.
102 I have not neglected your
instructions,
because you yourself are my
teacher.
103 How sweet is the taste of your
instructions —
sweeter even than honey!
104 I gain wisdom from your laws,
and so I hate all bad conduct.

Light from the Law of the LORD

105 Your word is a lamp to guide me
and a light for my path.
106 I will keep my solemn promise
to obey your just instructions.
107 My sufferings, LORD, are terrible
indeed;
keep me alive, as you have
promised.
108 Accept my prayer of thanks,
O LORD,
and teach me your commands.
109 I am always ready to risk my life;

I[u] have not forgotten your law.
110 The wicked lay a trap for me,
 but I have not disobeyed your
  commands.
111 Your commandments are my
  eternal possession;
 they are the joy of my heart.
112 I have decided to obey your laws
 until the day I die.

Safety in the Law of the LORD

113 I hate those who are not
  completely loyal to you,
 but I love your law.
114 You are my defender and
  protector;
 I put my hope in your promise.
115 Go away from me, you sinful
  people.
 I will obey the commands of
  my God.
116 Give me strength, as you
  promised, and I shall live;
 don't let me be disappointed in
  my hope!
117 Hold me, and I will be safe,
 and I will always pay attention
  to your commands.
118 You reject everyone who disobeys
  your laws;
 their deceitful schemes are
  useless.
119 You treat all the wicked like
  rubbish,
 and so I love your instructions.
120 Because of you I am afraid;
 I am filled with fear because of
  your judgments.

Obedience to the Law of the LORD

121 I have done what is right and
  good;
 don't abandon me to my
  enemies!
122 Promise that you will help your
  servant;

don't let the arrogant oppress
  me!
123 My eyes are tired from watching
  for your saving help,
 for the deliverance you
  promised.
124 Treat me according to your
  constant love,
 and teach me your commands.
125 I am your servant; give me
  understanding,
 so that I may know your
  teachings.
126 LORD, it is time for you to act,
 because people are disobeying
  your law.
127 I love your commands more than
  gold,
 more than the finest gold.
128 And so I follow all your
  instructions;[v]
 I hate all wrong ways.

Desire to Obey the Law of the LORD

129 Your teachings are wonderful;
 I obey them with all my heart.
130 The explanation of your teachings
  gives light
 and brings wisdom to the
  ignorant.
131 In my desire for your commands
 I pant with open mouth.
132 Turn to me and have mercy on me
 as you do on all those who
  love you.
133 As you have promised, keep me
  from falling;
 don't let me be overcome by evil.
134 Save me from those who oppress
  me,
 so that I may obey your
  commands.
135 Bless me with your presence
 and teach me your laws.
136 My tears pour down like a river,
 because people do not obey your
  law.

[u] I am always ready to risk my life; I; *or* My life is in constant danger, but I.   [v] *Some ancient translations* all your instructions; *Hebrew unclear.*

The Justice of the Law of the LORD

137 You are righteous, LORD,
  and your laws are just.
138 The rules that you have given
  are completely fair and right.
139 My anger burns in me like a fire,
  because my enemies disregard
    your commands.
140 How certain your promise is!
  How I love it!
141 I am unimportant and despised,
  but I do not neglect your
    teachings.
142 Your righteousness will last
    forever,
  and your law is always true.
143 I am filled with trouble and
    anxiety,
  but your commandments bring
    me joy.
144 Your instructions are always just;
  give me understanding, and I
    shall live.

A Prayer for Deliverance

145 With all my heart I call to you;
  answer me, LORD, and I will
    obey your commands!
146 I call to you;
  save me, and I will keep your
    laws.
147 Before sunrise I call to you for
    help;
  I place my hope in your promise.
148 All night long I lie awake,
  to meditate on your instructions.
149 Because your love is constant, hear
    me, O LORD;
  show your mercy, and preserve
    my life!
150 My cruel persecutors are coming
    closer,
  people who never keep your law.
151 But you are near to me, LORD,
  and all your commands are
    permanent.
152 Long ago I learned about your
    instructions;
  you made them to last forever.

A Plea for Help

153 Look at my suffering, and save
    me,
  because I have not neglected
    your law.
154 Defend my cause, and set me free;
  save me, as you have promised.
155 The wicked will not be saved,
  for they do not obey your laws.
156 But your compassion, LORD, is great
  show your mercy and save me!
157 I have many enemies and
    oppressors,
  but I do not fail to obey your
    laws.
158 When I look at those traitors, I am
    filled with disgust,
  because they do not keep your
    commands.
159 See how I love your instructions,
    LORD.
  Your love never changes, so
    save me!
160 The heart of your law is truth,
  and all your righteous
    judgments are eternal.

Dedication to the Law of the LORD

161 Powerful people attack me
    unjustly,
  but I respect your law.
162 How happy I am because of your
    promises —
  as happy as someone who finds
    rich treasure.
163 I hate and detest all lies,
  but I love your law.
164 Seven times each day I thank you
  for your righteous judgments.
165 Those who love your law have
    perfect security,
  and there is nothing that can
    make them fall.
166 I wait for you to save me, LORD,
  and I do what you command.
167 I obey your teachings;
  I love them with all my heart.
168 I obey your commands and your
    instructions;
  you see everything I do.

A Prayer for Help

⁶⁹ Let my cry for help reach you,
LORD!
Give me understanding, as you
have promised.
⁷⁰ Listen to my prayer,
and save me according to your
promise!
⁷¹ I will always praise you,
because you teach me your laws.
⁷² I will sing about your law,
because your commands are
just.
⁷³ Always be ready to help me,
because I follow your
commands.
⁷⁴ How I long for your saving help,
O LORD!
I find happiness in your law.
⁷⁵ Give me life, so that I may
praise you;
may your instructions help me.
⁷⁶ I wander about like a lost sheep;
so come and look for me, your
servant,
because I have not neglected
your laws.

A Prayer for Help

120

When I was in trouble, I
called to the LORD,
and he answered me.
² Save me, LORD,
from liars and deceivers.

³ You liars, what will God do to you?
How will he punish you?
⁴ With a soldier's sharp arrows,
with red-hot coals!

⁵ Living among you is as bad as
living in Meshech
or among the people of Kedar.ʷ
⁶ I have lived too long
with people who hate peace!
⁷ When I speak of peace,
they are for war.

The LORD Our Protector

121

I look to the mountains;
where will my help
come from?
² My help will come from the LORD,
who made heaven and earth.

³ He will not let you fall;
your protector is always awake.

⁴ The protector of Israel
never dozes or sleeps.
⁵ The LORD will guard you;
he is by your side to protect you.
⁶ The sun will not hurt you during
the day,
nor the moon during the night.

⁷ The LORD will protect you from all
danger;
he will keep you safe.
⁸ He will protect you as you come
and go
now and forever.

In Praise of Jerusalem ˣ

122

I was glad when they said
to me,
"Let us go to the LORD's house."
² And now we are here,
standing inside the gates of
Jerusalem!

³ Jerusalem is a city restored
in beautiful order and harmony.
⁴ This is where the tribes come,
the tribes of Israel,
to give thanks to the LORD
according to his command.
⁵ Here the kings of Israel
sat to judge their people.

⁶ Pray for the peace of Jerusalem:
"May those who love you
prosper.

ʷ MESHECH ... KEDAR: *Two distant regions, whose people were regarded as savages.*
HEBREW TITLE: *By David.*

Let us go to the LORD's house. (122.1)

7 May there be peace inside your
    walls
  and safety in your palaces."
8 For the sake of my relatives and
    friends
  I say to Jerusalem, "Peace be
    with you!"
9 For the sake of the house of the
    LORD our God
  I pray for your prosperity.

A Prayer for Mercy

123 LORD, I look up to you,
       up to heaven, where
       you rule.
2 As a servant depends on his
    master,
  as a maid depends on her
    mistress,
so we will keep looking to you,
  O LORD our God,
  until you have mercy on us.

3 Be merciful to us, LORD, be
    merciful;
  we have been treated with so
    much contempt.
4 We have been mocked too long by
    the rich
  and scorned by proud
    oppressors.

ⁿ HEBREW TITLE: *By David.*

God the Protector of His People ˣ

124 What if the LORD had not
       been on our side?
Answer, O Israel!

2 "If the LORD had not been on
    our side
  when our enemies attacked us,
3 then they would have swallowed us
    alive
  in their furious anger against us;
4 then the flood would have carried
    us away,
  the water would have covered
    us,
5   the raging torrent would have
    drowned us."

6 Let us thank the LORD,
  who has not let our enemies
    destroy us.
7 We have escaped like a bird from a
    hunter's trap;
  the trap is broken, and we are
    free!
8 Our help comes from the LORD,
  who made heaven and earth.

The Security of God's People

125 Those who trust in the
       LORD are like
       Mount Zion,
  which can never be shaken,
    never be moved.
2 As the mountains surround
    Jerusalem,
  so the LORD surrounds his
    people,
  now and forever.

3 The wicked will not always rule
    over the land of the
    righteous;
  if they did, the righteous
    themselves might do evil.

⁴ LORD, do good to those who are
good,
to those who obey your
commands.
⁵ But when you punish the wicked,
punish also those who abandon
your ways.

Peace be with Israel!

A Prayer for Deliverance

126 When the LORD brought
us back to
Jerusalem,^y
it was like a dream!
² How we laughed, how we sang
for joy!
Then the other nations said
about us,
"The LORD did great things for
them."
³ Indeed he did great things for us;
how happy we were!

⁴ LORD, make us prosperous again,^z
just as the rain brings water
back to dry riverbeds.
⁵ Let those who wept as they planted
their crops,
gather the harvest with joy!

⁶ Those who wept as they went out
carrying the seed
will come back singing for joy,
as they bring in the harvest.

In Praise of God's Goodness ^a

127 If the LORD does not build
the house,
the work of the builders is
useless;
if the LORD does not protect the
city,
it does no good for the sentries
to stand guard.
² It is useless to work so hard for a
living,

Gather the harvest with joy. (126.5)

getting up early and going to
bed late.
For the LORD provides for those he
loves,
while they are asleep.

³ Children are a gift from the LORD;
they are a real blessing.
⁴ The sons a man has when he is
young
are like arrows in a soldier's
hand.
⁵ Happy is the man who has many
such arrows.
He will never be defeated
when he meets his enemies in
the place of judgment.

The Reward of Obedience to the LORD

128 Happy are those who obey
the LORD,
who live by his commands.

² Your work will provide for your
needs;
you will be happy and
prosperous.
³ Your wife will be like a fruitful vine
in your home,

^y brought us back to Jerusalem; *or* made Jerusalem prosperous again.   ^z make us
prosperous again; *or* take us back to our land.   ^a HEBREW TITLE: *By Solomon.*

and your children will be like
  young olive trees around
  your table.
⁴A man who obeys the Lord
  will surely be blessed like this.

⁵May the Lord bless you from Zion!
  May you see Jerusalem prosper
  all the days of your life!
⁶May you live to see your
  grandchildren!

Peace be with Israel!

A Prayer against Israel's Enemies

129 Israel, tell us how your
        enemies have
        persecuted you
ever since you were young.

²"Ever since I was young,
  my enemies have persecuted me
  cruelly,
  but they have not overcome me.
³They cut deep wounds in my back
  and made it like a plowed field.
⁴But the Lord, the righteous one,
  has freed me from slavery."

⁵May everyone who hates Zion
  be defeated and driven back.
⁶May they all be like grass growing
  on the housetops,
  which dries up before it can
  grow;
⁷ no one gathers it up
  or carries it away in bundles.
⁸No one who passes by will say,
  "May the Lord bless you!
  We bless you in the name of the
  Lord."

A Prayer for Help

130 From the depths of my
        despair I call to
        you, Lord.
²Hear my cry, O Lord;

listen to my call for help!
³If you kept a record of our sins,
  who could escape being
  condemned?
⁴But you forgive us,
  so that we should stand in awe
  of you.

⁵I wait eagerly for the Lord's help,
  and in his word I trust.
⁶I wait for the Lord
  more eagerly than sentries wait
  for the dawn—
  than sentries wait for the dawn.

*. . . more eagerly than sentries wait for the
dawn. (130.6)*

⁷Israel, trust in the Lord,
  because his love is constant
  and he is always willing to save.
⁸He will save his people Israel
  from all their sins.

A Prayer of Humble Trust ᵇ

131 Lord, I have given up my
        pride
and turned away from my
  arrogance.
I am not concerned with great
  matters
  or with subjects too difficult
  for me.
²Instead, I am content and at peace.

ᵇ HEBREW TITLE: *By David.*
130.8 Mt 1.21; Titus 2.14

As a child lies quietly in its
   mother's arms,
   so my heart is quiet within me.
³Israel, trust in the LORD
   now and forever!

In Praise of the Temple

132 LORD, do not forget David
   and all the hardships
he endured.
²Remember, LORD, what he
   promised,
   the vow he made to you, the
   Mighty God of Jacob:
³"I will not go home or go to bed;
⁴ I will not rest or sleep,
⁵ until I provide a place for the
   LORD,
   a home for the Mighty God of
   Jacob."

⁶In Bethlehem we heard about the
   Covenant Box,
   and we found it in the fields of
   Jearim.
⁷We said, "Let us go to the LORD's
   house;
   let us worship before his
   throne."

⁸Come to the Temple, LORD, with
   the Covenant Box,
   the symbol of your power,
   and stay here forever.
⁹May your priests do always what is
   right;
   may your people shout for joy!

¹⁰You made a promise to your
   servant David;
   do not reject your chosen king,
   LORD.
¹¹You made a solemn promise to
   David —

a promise you will not take
   back:
   "I will make one of your sons king,
   and he will rule after you.
¹²If your sons are true to my
   covenant
   and to the commands I give
   them,
   their sons, also, will succeed you
   for all time as kings."

¹³The LORD has chosen Zion;
   he wants to make it his home:
¹⁴"This is where I will live forever;
   this is where I want to rule.
¹⁵I will richly provide Zion with all
   she needs;
   I will satisfy her poor with food.
¹⁶I will bless her priests in all
   they do,
   and her people will sing and
   shout for joy.
¹⁷Here I will make one of David's
   descendants a great king;
   here I will preserve the rule of
   my chosen king.
¹⁸I will cover his enemies with
   shame,
   but his kingdom will prosper
   and flourish."

In Praise of Living in Peace ᵇ

133 How wonderful it is, how
   pleasant,
   for God's people to live together
   in harmony!
²It is like the precious anointing oil
   running down from Aaron's
   head and beard,
   down to the collar of his robes.
³It is like the dew on Mount
   Hermon,
   falling on the hills of Zion.

HEBREW TITLE: *By David.*

132.6-10 2 Ch 6.41, 42   **132.11** 2 S 7.12-16; 1 Ch 17.11-14; Ps 89.3, 4; Ac 2.30
132.17 1 K 11.36

That is where the LORD has
  promised his blessing —
life that never ends.

A Call to Praise God

134 Come, praise the LORD,
    all his servants,
all who serve in his Temple at
  night.
2 Raise your hands in prayer in the
  Temple,
  and praise the LORD!

3 May the LORD, who made heaven
  and earth,
  bless you from Zion!

A Hymn of Praise

135 Praise the LORD!

Praise his name, you servants of
  the LORD,
2   who stand in the LORD's house,
  in the Temple of our God.
3 Praise the LORD, because he is
  good;
  sing praises to his name,
  because he is kind.[c]
4 He chose Jacob for himself,
  the people of Israel for his own.

5 I know that our LORD is great,
  greater than all the gods.
6 He does whatever he wishes
  in heaven and on earth,
  in the seas and in the depths
  below.
7 He brings storm clouds from the
  ends of the earth;
  he makes lightning for the
  storms,
  and he brings out the wind from
  his storeroom.

8 In Egypt he killed all the first-born
  of people and animals alike.
9 There he performed miracles and
  wonders
  to punish the king and all his
  officials.
10 He destroyed many nations
  and killed powerful kings:
11 Sihon, king of the Amorites,
  Og, king of Bashan,
  and all the kings in Canaan.
12 He gave their lands to his people;
  he gave them to Israel.

13 LORD, you will always be
  proclaimed as God;
  all generations will remember
  you.
14 The LORD will defend his people;
  he will take pity on his servants.

15 The gods of the nations are made
  of silver and gold;
  they are formed by human
  hands.
16 They have mouths, but cannot
  speak,
  and eyes, but cannot see.
17 They have ears, but cannot hear;
  they are not even able to
  breathe.
18 May all who made them and who
  trust in them
  become[d] like the idols they
  have made!

19 Praise the LORD, people of Israel;
  praise him, you priests of God!
20 Praise the LORD, you Levites;
  praise him, all you that worship
  him!
21 Praise the LORD in Zion,
  in Jerusalem, his home.

Praise the LORD!

---

[c] he is kind; *or* it is pleasant to do so.
135.15-18 Ps 115.4-8; Rev 9.20

[d] May all ... become; *or* All who made them
and who trust in them will become.

A Hymn of Thanksgiving

136 Give thanks to the LORD,
because he is good;
his love is eternal.

2 Give thanks to the greatest of all
gods;
his love is eternal.

3 Give thanks to the mightiest of all
lords;
his love is eternal.

4 He alone performs great miracles;
his love is eternal.

5 By his wisdom he made the
heavens;
his love is eternal;

6 he built the earth on the deep
waters;
his love is eternal.

7 He made the sun and the moon;
his love is eternal;

8 the sun to rule over the day;
his love is eternal;

9 the moon and the stars to rule over
the night;
his love is eternal.

10 He killed the first-born sons of the
Egyptians;
his love is eternal.

11 He led the people of Israel out
of Egypt;
his love is eternal;

12 with his strong hand, his
powerful arm;
his love is eternal.

13 He divided the Red Sea;
his love is eternal;

14 he led his people through it;
his love is eternal;

15 but he drowned the king of Egypt
and his army;
his love is eternal.

16 He led his people through the
desert;

his love is eternal.

17 He killed powerful kings;
his love is eternal;

18 he killed famous kings;
his love is eternal;

19 Sihon, king of the Amorites;
his love is eternal;

20 and Og, king of Bashan;
his love is eternal.

21 He gave their lands to his people;
his love is eternal;

22 he gave them to Israel, his servant;
his love is eternal.

23 He did not forget us when we were
defeated;
his love is eternal;

24 he freed us from our enemies;
his love is eternal.

25 He gives food to every living
creature;
his love is eternal.

26 Give thanks to the God of heaven;
his love is eternal.

A Lament of Israelites in Exile

137 By the rivers of Babylon
we sat down;
there we wept when we
remembered Zion.

2 On the willows near by
we hung up our harps.

3 Those who captured us told us
to sing;
they told us to entertain them:
"Sing us a song about Zion."

4 How can we sing a song to the
LORD
in a foreign land?

5 May I never be able to play the
harp again
if I forget you, Jerusalem!

6 May I never be able to sing again
if I do not remember you,

36.1 1 Ch 16.34; 2 Ch 5.13; 7.3; Ezra 3.11; Ps 100.5; 106.1; 107.1; 118.1; Jr 33.11
36.5 Gn 1.1   **136.6** Gn 1.2   **136.7-9** Gn 1.16   **136.10** Ex 12.29   **136.11** Ex 12.51
36.13-15 Ex 14.21-29   **136.19** Nu 21.21-30   **136.20** Nu 21.31-35

if I do not think of you as my
greatest joy!

7 Remember, LORD, what the
Edomites did
the day Jerusalem was captured.
Remember how they kept saying,
"Tear it down to the ground!"

8 Babylon, you will be destroyed.
Happy are those who pay you back
for what you have done to us —
9   who take your babies
and smash them against a rock.

A Prayer of Thanksgiving [e]

138 I thank you, LORD, with
all my heart;
I sing praise to you before the
gods.
2 I face your holy Temple,
bow down, and praise your
name
because of your constant love and
faithfulness,
because you have shown that
your name and your
commands are supreme. [f]
3 You answered me when I called
to you;
with your strength you
strengthened me.

4 All the kings in the world will
praise you, LORD,
because they have heard your
promises.
5 They will sing about what you have
done
and about your great glory.
6 Even though you are so high
above,
you care for the lowly,
and the proud cannot hide from
you.

7 When I am surrounded by troubles,
you keep me safe.
You oppose my angry enemies
and save me by your power.
8 You will do everything you have
promised;
LORD, your love is eternal.
Complete the work that you
have begun.

God's Complete Knowledge and Care [g]

139 LORD, you have examined
me and you
know me.
2 You know everything I do;
from far away you understand
all my thoughts.
3 You see me, whether I am working
or resting;
you know all my actions.
4 Even before I speak,
you already know what I
will say.
5 You are all around me on every
side;
you protect me with your power.
6 Your knowledge of me is too deep;
it is beyond my understanding.

7 Where could I go to escape from
you?
Where could I get away from
your presence?
8 If I went up to heaven, you would
be there;
if I lay down in the world of the
dead, you would be there.
9 If I flew away beyond the east
or lived in the farthest place in
the west,
10 you would be there to lead me,
you would be there to help me.
11 I could ask the darkness to hide me

---

e HEBREW TITLE: *By David.*   *f Probable text* your name and your commands are
supreme; *Hebrew* your command is greater than all your name.   *g* HEBREW TITLE: *A*
psalm by David.
137.8 Rev 18.6

or the light around me to turn
    into night,
12 but even darkness is not dark
    for you,
    and the night is as bright as
        the day.
    Darkness and light are the same
        to you.

13 You created every part of me;
    you put me together in my
        mother's womb.
14 I praise you because you are to be
        feared;
    all you do is strange and
        wonderful.
    I know it with all my heart.
15 When my bones were being
        formed,
    carefully put together in my
        mother's womb,
  when I was growing there in
        secret,
    you knew that I was there —
16   you saw me before I was born.
  The days allotted to me
    had all been recorded in your
        book,
    before any of them ever began.
17 O God, how difficult I find your
        thoughts; *h*
    how many of them there are!
18 If I counted them, they would be
        more than the grains of sand.
    When I awake, I am still
        with you.

19 O God, how I wish you would kill
        the wicked!
    How I wish violent people would
        leave me alone!
20 They say wicked things about you;
    they speak evil things against
        your name. *i*
21 O LORD, how I hate those who
        hate you!

How I despise those who rebel
    against you!
22 I hate them with a total hatred;
    I regard them as my enemies.

23 Examine me, O God, and know my
        mind;
    test me, and discover my
        thoughts.
24 Find out if there is any evil in me
    and guide me in the everlasting
        way. *j*

A Prayer for Protection *k*

140 Save me, LORD, from
        evildoers;
    keep me safe from violent
        people.
2 They are always plotting evil,
    always stirring up quarrels.
3 Their tongues are like deadly
        snakes;
    their words are like a cobra's
        poison.

4 Protect me, LORD, from the power
        of the wicked;
    keep me safe from violent people
        who plot my downfall.
5 The proud have set a trap for me;
    they have laid their snares,
    and along the path they have set
        traps to catch me.

6 I say to the LORD, "You are my
        God."
    Hear my cry for help, LORD!
7 My Sovereign LORD, my strong
        defender,
    you have protected me in battle.
8 LORD, don't give the wicked what
        they want;
    don't let their plots succeed.

h how difficult I find your thoughts; *or* how precious are your thoughts to me.
i *Probable text* they speak . . . name; *Hebrew unclear.*   *j* the everlasting way; *or* the
ways of my ancestors.   *k* HEBREW TITLE: *A psalm by David.*
139.17 Si 18.5-7   **140.3** Ro 3.13

9 Don't let my enemies be
    victorious; [l]
  make their threats against me
    fall back on them.
10 May red-hot coals fall on them;
  may they be thrown into a pit
    and never get out.
11 May those who accuse others
    falsely not succeed;
  may evil overtake violent people
    and destroy them.

12 Lord, I know that you defend the
    cause of the poor
  and the rights of the needy.
13 The righteous will praise you
    indeed;
  they will live in your presence.

An Evening Prayer [m]

141 I call to you, Lord; help
    me now!
  Listen to me when I call to you.
2 Receive my prayer as incense,
  my uplifted hands as an evening
    sacrifice.

3 Lord, place a guard at my mouth,
  a sentry at the door of my lips.
4 Keep me from wanting to do wrong
  and from joining evil people in
    their wickedness.
  May I never take part in their
    feasts.

5 Good people may punish me and
    rebuke me in kindness,
  but I will never accept honor
    from evil people,
  because I am always praying
    against their evil deeds.
6 When their rulers are thrown down
    from rocky cliffs,
  the people will admit that my
    words were true.

7 Like wood that is split and chopped
    into bits,
  so their bones are scattered at
    the edge of the grave. [n]

8 But I keep trusting in you, my
    Sovereign Lord.
  I seek your protection;
    don't let me die!
9 Protect me from the traps they
    have set for me,
  from the snares of those
    evildoers.
10 May the wicked fall into their own
    traps
  while I go by unharmed.

A Prayer for Help [o]

142 I call to the Lord for help;
    I plead with him.
2 I bring him all my complaints;
  I tell him all my troubles.
3 When I am ready to give up,
  he knows what I should do.
  In the path where I walk,
    my enemies have hidden a trap
    for me.
4 When I look beside me,
  I see that there is no one to
    help me,
  no one to protect me.
  No one cares for me.

5 Lord, I cry to you for help;
  you, Lord, are my protector;
  you are all I want in this life.
6 Listen to my cry for help,
  for I am sunk in despair.
  Save me from my enemies;
    they are too strong for me.
7 Set me free from my distress; [p]
  then in the assembly of your
    people I will praise you
  because of your goodness to me.

[l] *Probable text* Don't let my enemies be victorious; *Hebrew unclear.*   [m] HEBREW
TITLE: *A psalm by David.*   [n] *Verses 5-7 in Hebrew are unclear.*   [o] HEBREW TITLE:
A poem by David, when he was in the cave; a prayer.   [p] distress; *or* prison.
141.2 Rev 5.8   **142 Title** 1 S 22.1; 24.3

A Prayer for Help [q]

143
Lord, hear my prayer!
   In your righteousness
      listen to my plea;
  answer me in your faithfulness!
2 Don't put me, your servant, on
    trial;
  no one is innocent in your sight.

3 My enemies have hunted me down
   and completely defeated me.
  They have put me in a dark prison,
   and I am like those who died
      long ago.
4 So I am ready to give up;
  I am in deep despair.

5 I remember the days gone by;
   I think about all that you have
      done,
  I bring to mind all your deeds.
6 I lift up my hands to you in prayer;
   like dry ground my soul is
      thirsty for you.

7 Answer me now, Lord!
   I have lost all hope.
  Don't hide yourself from me,
   or I will be among those who go
      down to the world of
      the dead.
8 Remind me each morning of your
    constant love,
   for I put my trust in you.
  My prayers go up to you;
   show me the way I should go.

9 I go to you for protection, Lord;
   rescue me from my enemies.
10 You are my God;
   teach me to do your will.
  Be good to me, and guide me on a
    safe path.

11 Rescue me, Lord, as you have
    promised;

in your goodness save me from
   my troubles!
12 Because of your love for me, kill
    my enemies
  and destroy all my oppressors,
  for I am your servant.

A King Thanks God for Victory [r]

144
Praise the Lord, my
      protector!
He trains me for battle
  and prepares me for war.
2 He is my protector and defender,
   my shelter and savior,
   in whom I trust for safety.
He subdues the nations under me.

3 Lord, what are mortals, that you
    notice them;
   mere mortals, that you pay
      attention to us?
4 We are like a puff of wind;
   our days are like a passing
      shadow.

5 O Lord, tear the sky open and
    come down;
   touch the mountains, and they
      will pour out smoke.
6 Send flashes of lightning and
    scatter your enemies;
   shoot your arrows and send
      them running.
7 Reach down from above,
   pull me out of the deep water,
    and rescue me;
  save me from the power of
      foreigners,
8   who never tell the truth
   and lie even under oath.

9 I will sing you a new song, O God;
   I will play the harp and sing
      to you.
10 You give victory to kings
   and rescue your servant David.
11 Save me from my cruel enemies;

---

[q] HEBREW TITLE: *A psalm by David.*   [r] HEBREW TITLE: *By David.*
143.2 Ro 3.20; Ga 2.16   **144.3** Job 7.17, 18; Ps 8.4

rescue me from the power of
foreigners,
who never tell the truth
and lie even under oath.

12 May our sons in their youth
be like plants that grow up
strong.
May our daughters be like stately
columns
which adorn the corners of a
palace.
13 May our barns be filled
with crops of every kind.
May the sheep in our fields
bear young by the tens of
thousands.
14 May our cattle reproduce plentifully
without miscarriage or loss.
May there be no cries of distress in
our streets.

15 Happy is the nation of whom this
is true;
happy are the people whose God
is the LORD!

A Hymn of Praise [s]

145 I will proclaim your
greatness, my God
and king;
I will thank you forever and
ever.
2 Every day I will thank you;
I will praise you forever and
ever.
3 The LORD is great and is to be
highly praised;
his greatness is beyond
understanding.

4 What you have done will be praised
from one generation to
the next;
they will proclaim your mighty
acts.
5 They will speak of your glory and
majesty,

and I will meditate on your
wonderful deeds.
6 People will speak of your mighty
deeds,
and I will proclaim your
greatness.
7 They will tell about all your
goodness
and sing about your kindness.
8 The LORD is loving and merciful,
slow to become angry and full of
constant love.
9 He is good to everyone
and has compassion on all he
made.

10 All your creatures, LORD, will
praise you,
and all your people will give you
thanks.
11 They will speak of the glory of your
royal power
and tell of your might,
12 so that everyone will know your
mighty deeds
and the glorious majesty of your
kingdom.
13 Your rule is eternal,
and you are king forever.

The LORD is faithful to his
promises;
he is merciful in all his acts.
14 He helps those who are in trouble;
he lifts those who have fallen.

15 All living things look hopefully
to you,
and you give them food when
they need it.
16 You give them enough
and satisfy the needs of all.

17 The LORD is righteous in all he
does,
merciful in all his acts.
18 He is near to those who call to him,
who call to him with sincerity.

---

[s] HEBREW TITLE: *A song of praise by David.*

¹⁹ He supplies the needs of those who
   honor him;
   he hears their cries and saves
   them.
²⁰ He protects everyone who loves
   him,
   but he will destroy the wicked.

²¹ I will always praise the LORD;
   let all his creatures praise his
   holy name forever.

In Praise of God the Savior

146 Praise the LORD!
         Praise the LORD, my
         soul!
² I will praise him as long as I live;
   I will sing to my God all my life.

³ Don't put your trust in human
   leaders;
   no human being can save you.
⁴ When they die, they return to the
   dust;
   on that day all their plans come
   to an end.

⁵ Happy are those who have the God
   of Jacob to help them
   and who depend on the LORD
   their God,
⁶   the Creator of heaven, earth,
   and sea,
   and all that is in them.
   He always keeps his promises;
⁷   he judges in favor of the
   oppressed
   and gives food to the hungry.

   The LORD sets prisoners free
⁸   and gives sight to the blind.
   He lifts those who have fallen;
   he loves his righteous people.
⁹ He protects the strangers who live
   in our land;
   he helps widows and orphans,
   but takes the wicked to their
   ruin.

¹⁰ The LORD is king forever.
   Your God, O Zion, will reign for
   all time.

Praise the LORD!

In Praise of God the Almighty

147 Praise the LORD!

It is good to sing praise to our God;
   it is pleasant and right to
   praise him.
² The LORD is restoring Jerusalem;
   he is bringing back the exiles.
³ He heals the broken-hearted
   and bandages their wounds.

⁴ He has decided the number of the
   stars
   and calls each one by name.
⁵ Great and mighty is our Lord;
   his wisdom cannot be measured.
⁶ He raises the humble,
   but crushes the wicked to the
   ground.

⁷ Sing hymns of praise to the LORD;
   play music on the harp to
   our God.
⁸ He spreads clouds over the sky;
   he provides rain for the earth
   and makes grass grow on the
   hills.
⁹ He gives animals their food
   and feeds the young ravens
   when they call.

¹⁰ His pleasure is not in strong
   horses,
   nor his delight in brave soldiers;
¹¹ but he takes pleasure in those who
   honor him,
   in those who trust in his
   constant love.

¹² Praise the LORD, O Jerusalem!
   Praise your God, O Zion!

146.6 Ac 4.24; 14.15

¹³ He keeps your gates strong;
    he blesses your people.
¹⁴ He keeps your borders safe
    and satisfies you with the finest
      wheat.

¹⁵ He gives a command to the earth,
    and what he says is quickly
      done.
¹⁶ He spreads snow like a blanket
    and scatters frost like dust.
¹⁷ He sends hail like gravel;
    no one can endure the cold he
      sends!
¹⁸ Then he gives a command, and the
      ice melts;
    he sends the wind, and the
      water flows.

¹⁹ He gives his message to his people,
    his instructions and laws to
      Israel.
²⁰ He has not done this for other
      nations;
    they do not know his laws.

Praise the LORD!

A Call for the Universe to Praise God

148
Praise the LORD!

Praise the LORD from heaven,
    you that live in the heights
      above.
² Praise him, all his angels,
    all his heavenly armies.

³ Praise him, sun and moon;
    praise him, shining stars.
⁴ Praise him, highest heavens,
    and the waters above the sky.ᵗ

⁵ Let them all praise the name of the
      LORD!
He commanded, and they were
      created;

⁶ by his command they were fixed
    in their places forever,
    and they cannot disobey.ᵘ

⁷ Praise the LORD from the earth,
    sea monsters and all ocean
      depths;
⁸ lightning and hail, snow and
      clouds,
    strong winds that obey his
      command.

⁹ Praise him, hills and mountains,
    fruit trees and forests;
¹⁰ all animals, tame and wild,
    reptiles and birds.

¹¹ Praise him, kings and all peoples,
    princes and all other rulers;
¹² young women and young men,
    old people and children too.

¹³ Let them all praise the name of the
      LORD!
His name is greater than all others;
    his glory is above earth and
      heaven.
¹⁴ He made his nation strong,
    so that all his people praise
      him —
    the people of Israel, so dear
      to him.

Praise the LORD!

A Hymn of Praise

149
Praise the LORD!

Sing a new song to the LORD;
    praise him in the assembly of
      his faithful people!
² Be glad, Israel, because of your
      Creator;
    rejoice, people of Zion, because
      of your king!
³ Praise his name with dancing;

ᵗ WATERS ABOVE THE SKY: *See Gn 1.6, 7.*   ᵘ by his command . . . disobey; *or* he has
fixed them in their places for all time, by a command that lasts forever.

"Praise the LORD!" (150.1)

play drums and harps in praise
    of him.

4 The LORD takes pleasure in his
    people;
  he honors the humble with
    victory.
5 Let God's people rejoice in their
    triumph
  and sing joyfully all night long.
6 Let them shout aloud as they
    praise God,
  with their sharp swords in their
    hands
7   to defeat the nations
  and to punish the peoples;
8   to bind their kings in chains,
  their leaders in chains of iron;
9   to punish the nations as God has
    commanded.
This is the victory of God's people.

Praise the LORD!

149.6 2 Macc 15.27

Praise the LORD!

150   Praise the LORD!
Praise God in his Temple!
  Praise his strength in heaven!
2 Praise him for the mighty things he
    has done.
  Praise his supreme greatness.

3 Praise him with trumpets.
  Praise him with harps and
    lyres.
4 Praise him with drums and
    dancing.
  Praise him with harps and
    flutes.
5 Praise him with cymbals.
  Praise him with loud cymbals.
6 Praise the LORD, all living
    creatures!

Praise the LORD!

PROVERBS

INTRODUCTION

The book of *Proverbs* is a collection of moral and religious teachings in the form of sayings and proverbs. Much of it has to do with practical, everyday concerns. It begins with the reminder that "To have knowledge, you must first have reverence for the LORD," and then goes on to deal with matters not only of religious morality, but also of common sense and good manners. Its many short sayings reveal the insights of ancient Israelite teachers about what a wise person will do in certain situations. Some of these concern family relations, others, business dealings. Some deal with matters of etiquette in social relationships, and others with the need of self-control. Much is said about such qualities as humility, patience, respect for the poor, and loyalty to friends.

OUTLINE OF CONTENTS

The Value of Proverbs

1 The proverbs of Solomon, son of David and king of Israel.

² Here are proverbs that will help you recognize wisdom and good advice, and understand sayings with deep meaning. ³ They can teach you how to live intelligently and how to be honest, just, and fair. ⁴ They can make an inexperienced person clever and teach young people how to be resourceful. ⁵ These proverbs can even add to the knowledge of the wise and give guidance to the educated, ⁶ so that they can understand the hidden meanings of proverbs and the problems that the wise raise.

Advice to the Young

⁷ To have knowledge, you must first have reverence for the LORD.*ᵃ* Stupid people have no respect for wisdom and refuse to learn.

⁸ My child, pay attention to what your father and mother tell you. ⁹ Their teaching will improve your character as a handsome turban or a necklace improves your appearance.

¹⁰ My child, when sinners tempt you, don't give in. ¹¹ Suppose they say, "Come on; let's find someone to kill! Let's attack some innocent people for the fun of it! ¹² They may be alive and well when we find them, but they'll be dead when we're through with them! ¹³ We'll find all kinds of riches and fill our houses with loot! ¹⁴ Come and join us, and we'll all share what we steal."

¹⁵ My child, don't go with people like that. Stay away from them. ¹⁶ They

---

ᵃ To ... LORD; *or* The most important part of knowledge is having reverence for the LORD.

1.1 1 K 4.32   **1.7** Job 28.28; Ps 111.10; Pr 9.10; Si 1.14

1.9   1.11–15   1.28   1.33   2.2

can't wait to do something bad. They're always ready to kill. ¹⁷It does no good to spread a net when the bird you want to catch is watching, ¹⁸but people like that are setting a trap for themselves, a trap in which they will die. ¹⁹Robbery always claims the life of the robber — this is what happens to^b anyone who lives by violence.

Wisdom Calls

²⁰Listen! Wisdom is calling out in the streets and marketplaces, ²¹calling loudly at the city gates and wherever people come together:

²²"Foolish people! How long do you want to be foolish? How long will you enjoy making fun of knowledge? Will you never learn? ²³Listen when I reprimand you; I will give you good advice and share my knowledge with you. ²⁴I have been calling you, inviting you to come, but you would not listen. You paid no attention to me. ²⁵You have ignored all my advice and have not been willing to let me correct you. ²⁶So when you get into trouble, I will laugh at you. I will make fun of you when terror strikes — ²⁷when it comes on you like a storm, bringing fierce winds of trouble, and you are in pain and misery. ²⁸Then you will call for wisdom, but I will not answer. You may look for me everywhere, but you will not find me. ²⁹You have never had any use for knowledge and have always refused to obey the LORD. ³⁰You have never wanted my advice or paid any attention when I corrected you. ³¹So then, you

will get what you deserve, and your own actions will make you sick. ³²Inexperienced people die because they reject wisdom. Stupid people are destroyed by their own lack of concern. ³³But whoever listens to me will have security. He will be safe, with no reason to be afraid."

The Rewards of Wisdom

2 My child, learn what I teach you and never forget what I tell you to do. ²Listen to what is wise and try to understand it. ³Yes, beg for knowledge; plead for insight. ⁴Look for it as hard as you would for silver or some hidden treasure. ⁵If you do, you will know what it means to fear the LORD and you will succeed in learning about God. ⁶It is the LORD who gives wisdom; from him come knowledge and understanding. ⁷He provides help and protection for those who are righteous and honest. ⁸He protects those who treat others fairly, and guards those who are devoted to him.

⁹If you listen to me, you will know what is right, just, and fair. You will know what you should do. ¹⁰You will become wise, and your knowledge will give you pleasure. ¹¹Your insight and understanding will protect you ¹²and prevent you from doing the wrong thing. They will keep you away from people who stir up trouble by what they say — ¹³those who have abandoned a righteous life to live in the darkness of sin, ¹⁴those who find pleasure in doing wrong and who enjoy senseless evil,

^b *One ancient translation* what happens to; *Hebrew* the path of.
1.20, 21 Pr 8.1-3   **2.6** Ws 9.10; Si 1.1

2.16   3.12   3.20   3.23   3.29

¹⁵unreliable people who cannot be trusted.

¹⁶You will be able to resist any immoral woman who tries to seduce you with her smooth talk, ¹⁷who is faithless to her own husband and forgets her sacred vows. ¹⁸If you go to her house, you are traveling the road to death. To go there is to approach the world of the dead. ¹⁹No one who visits her ever comes back. He never returns to the road to life. ²⁰So you must follow the example of good people and live a righteous life. ²¹Righteous people — people of integrity — will live in this land of ours. ²²But God will snatch the wicked from the land and pull sinners out of it like plants from the ground.

Advice to the Young

3 My child, don't forget what I teach you. Always remember what I tell you to do. ²My teaching will give you a long and prosperous life. ³Never let go of loyalty and faithfulness. Tie them around your neck; write them on your heart. ⁴If you do this, both God and people will be pleased with you.

⁵Trust in the LORD with all your heart. Never rely on what you think you know. ⁶Remember the LORD in everything you do, and he will show you the right way. ⁷Never let yourself think that you are wiser than you are; simply obey the LORD and refuse to do wrong. ⁸If you do, it will be like good medicine, healing your wounds and easing your pains. ⁹Honor the LORD by making him an offering from the best of all that your land produces. ¹⁰If you do, your barns will be filled with grain, and you will have too much wine to store it all.

¹¹My child, when the LORD corrects you, pay close attention and take it as a warning. ¹²The LORD corrects those he loves, as parents correct a child of whom they are proud. ¹³Happy is anyone who becomes wise — who comes to have understanding. ¹⁴There is more profit in it than there is in silver; it is worth more to you than gold. ¹⁵Wisdom is more valuable than jewels; nothing you could want can compare with it. ¹⁶Wisdom offers you long life, as well as wealth and honor. ¹⁷Wisdom can make your life pleasant and lead you safely through it. ¹⁸Those who become wise are happy; wisdom will give them life.

¹⁹The LORD created the earth by
his wisdom;
by his knowledge he set the
sky in place.
²⁰His wisdom caused the rivers to
flow
and the clouds to give rain to
the earth.

²¹My child, hold on to your wisdom and insight. Never let them get away from you. ²²They will provide you with life — a pleasant and happy life. ²³You can go safely on your way and never even stumble. ²⁴You will not be afraid when you go to bed, and you will sleep soundly through the night. ²⁵You will not have to worry about sudden disasters, such as come on the wicked like a storm. ²⁶The LORD will keep you safe. He will not let you fall into a trap.

²⁷Whenever you possibly can, do

3.4 Lk 2.52 **3.7** Ro 12.16 **3.11** Job 5.17 **3.11, 12** He 12.5, 6 **3.12** Rev 3.19
3.27, 28 Si 4.3

4.15   4.25   5.3   5.8   5.13

good to those who need it. 28 Never tell
your neighbors to wait until tomorrow if
you can help them now. 29 Don't plan
anything that will hurt your neighbors;
they live beside you, trusting you.
30 Don't argue with others for no reason
when they have never done you any
harm. 31 Don't be jealous of violent people or decide to act as they do, 32 because the LORD hates people who do
evil, but he takes righteous people into
his confidence. 33 The LORD puts a
curse on the homes of the wicked, but
blesses the homes of the righteous.
34 He has no use for conceited people,
but shows favor to those who are humble. 35 Wise people will gain an honorable reputation, but stupid people will
only add to their own disgrace.

The Benefits of Wisdom

4 My children, listen to what your
father teaches you. Pay attention,
and you will have understanding.
2 What I am teaching you is good, so remember it all. 3 When I was only a little
boy, my parents' only son, 4 my father
would teach me. He would say, "Remember what I say and never forget it.
Do as I tell you, and you will live. 5 Get
wisdom and insight! Do not forget or ignore what I say. 6 Do not abandon wisdom, and she will protect you; love her,
and she will keep you safe. 7 Getting
wisdom is the most important thing you
can do. Whatever else you get, get insight. 8 Love wisdom, and she will make
you great. Embrace her,c and she will
bring you honor. 9 She will be your
crowning glory."

10 Listen to me, my child. Take seriously what I am telling you, and you
will live a long life. 11 I have taught you
wisdom and the right way to live.
12 Nothing will stand in your way if you
walk wisely, and you will not stumble
when you run. 13 Always remember
what you have learned. Your education
is your life — guard it well. 14 Do not go
where evil people go. Do not follow the
example of the wicked. 15 Don't do it!
Keep away from evil! Refuse it and go
on your way. 16 Wicked people cannot
sleep unless they have done something
wrong. They lie awake unless they
have hurt someone. 17 Wickedness
and violence are like food and drink
to them.

18 The road the righteous travel is like
the sunrise, getting brighter and
brighter until daylight has come. 19 The
road of the wicked, however, is dark as
night. They fall, but cannot see what
they have stumbled over.

20 My child, pay attention to what I
say. Listen to my words. 21 Never let
them get away from you. Remember
them and keep them in your heart.
22 They will give life and health to anyone who understands them. 23 Be careful how you think; your life is shaped
by your thoughts. 24 Never say anything that isn't true. Have nothing to
do with lies and misleading words.
25 Look straight ahead with honest confidence; don't hang your head in
shame. 26 Plan carefully what you do,
and whatever you do will turn out
right. 27 Avoid evil and walk straight
ahead. Don't go one step off the
right way.

c Embrace her; or Prize her highly.
3.34 Jas 4.6; 1 P 5.5   **4.26** He 12.13

5.15   6.5   6.6   6.13   6.23

Warning against Adultery

5 My child, pay attention and listen to my wisdom and insight. ²Then you will know how to behave properly, and your words will show that you have knowledge. ³The lips of another man's wife may be as sweet as honey and her kisses as smooth as olive oil, ⁴but when it is all over, she leaves you nothing but bitterness and pain. ⁵She will take you down to the world of the dead; the road she walks is the road to death. ⁶She does not stay on the road to life; but wanders off, and does not realize what is happening.

⁷Now listen to me, sons, and never forget what I am saying. ⁸Keep away from such a woman! Don't even go near her door! ⁹If you do, others will gain the respect that you once had, and you will die young at the hands of merciless people. ¹⁰Yes, strangers will take all your wealth, and what you have worked for will belong to someone else. ¹¹You will lie groaning on your deathbed, your flesh and muscles being eaten away, ¹²and you will say, "Why would I never learn? Why would I never let anyone correct me? ¹³I wouldn't listen to my teachers. I paid no attention to them. ¹⁴And suddenly I found myself*d* publicly disgraced."

¹⁵Be faithful to your own wife and give your love to her alone. ¹⁶Children that you have by other women will do you no good. ¹⁷Your children should grow up to help you, not strangers. ¹⁸So be happy with your wife and find your joy with the woman you married — ¹⁹pretty and graceful as a deer. Let her charms keep you happy; let her surround you with her love. ²⁰Son, why should you give your love to another woman? Why should you prefer the charms of another man's wife? ²¹The LORD sees everything you do. Wherever you go, he is watching. ²²The sins of the wicked are a trap. They get caught in the net of their own sin. ²³They die because they have no self-control. Their utter stupidity will send them to their graves.

More Warnings

6 My child, have you promised to be responsible for someone else's debts? ²Have you been caught by your own words, trapped by your own promises? ³Well then, my child, you are in that person's power, but this is how to get out of it: hurry to him, and beg him to release you. ⁴Don't let yourself go to sleep or even stop to rest. ⁵Get out of the trap like a bird or a deer escaping from a hunter.

⁶Lazy people should learn a lesson from the way ants live. ⁷They have no leader, chief, or ruler, ⁸but they store up their food during the summer, getting ready for winter. ⁹How long is the lazy man going to lie around? When is he ever going to get up? ¹⁰"I'll just take a short nap," he says; "I'll fold my hands and rest a while." ¹¹But while he sleeps, poverty will attack him like an armed robber.

¹²Worthless, wicked people go around telling lies. ¹³They wink and make gestures to deceive you, ¹⁴all the while planning evil in their perverted

---

d And suddenly . . . myself; *or* I was about to be.

6.1-5 Si 29.14-20   **6.10, 11** Pr 24.33, 34   **6.13, 14** Si 27.22

7.6   7.10   7.13   7.22   8.13

minds, stirring up trouble everywhere. ¹⁵ Because of this, disaster will strike them without warning, and they will be fatally wounded.

¹⁶⁻¹⁹ There are seven things that the LORD hates and cannot tolerate:
A proud look,
> a lying tongue,
> hands that kill innocent people,
> a mind that thinks up wicked plans,
> feet that hurry off to do evil,
> a witness who tells one lie after another,
> and someone who stirs up trouble among friends.

Warning against Adultery

²⁰ Son, do what your father tells you and never forget what your mother taught you. ²¹ Keep their words with you always, locked in your heart. ²² Their teaching will lead you when you travel, protect you at night, and advise you during the day. ²³ Their instructions are a shining light; their correction can teach you how to live. ²⁴ It can keep you away from bad women, from the seductive words of other men's wives. ²⁵ Don't be tempted by their beauty; don't be trapped by their flirting eyes. ²⁶ A man can hire a prostitute for the price of a loaf of bread, but adultery will cost him all he has.

²⁷ Can you carry fire against your chest without burning your clothes? ²⁸ Can you walk on hot coals without burning your feet? ²⁹ It is just as dangerous to sleep with another man's wife. Whoever does it will suffer. ³⁰ People don't despise a thief if he steals

food when he is hungry;ᵉ ³¹ yet if he is caught, he must pay back seven times more — he must give up everything he has. ³² But a man who commits adultery doesn't have any sense. He is just destroying himself. ³³ He will be dishonored and beaten up; he will be permanently disgraced. ³⁴ A husband is never angrier than when he is jealous; his revenge knows no limits. ³⁵ He will not accept any payment; no amount of gifts will satisfy his anger.

7 My child, remember what I say and never forget what I tell you to do. ² Do what I say, and you will live. Be as careful to follow my teaching as you are to protect your eyes. ³ Keep my teaching with you all the time; write it on your heart. ⁴ Treat wisdom as your sister, and insight as your closest friend. ⁵ They will keep you away from other men's wives, from women with seductive words.

The Immoral Woman

⁶ Once I was looking out the window of my house, ⁷ and I saw many inexperienced young men, but noticed one foolish fellow in particular. ⁸ He was walking along the street near the corner where a certain woman lived. He was passing near her house ⁹ in the evening after it was dark. ¹⁰ And then she met him; she was dressed like a prostitute and was making plans. ¹¹ She was a bold and shameless woman who always walked the streets ¹² or stood waiting at a corner, sometimes in the streets, sometimes in the marketplace. ¹³ She threw her arms around the young man, kissed him, looked him

---

ᵉ People don't despise . . . hungry; *or* Don't people despise . . . hungry?

straight in the eye, and said, ¹⁴"I made
my offerings today and have the meat
from the sacrifices. ¹⁵So I came out
looking for you. I wanted to find you,
and here you are! ¹⁶I've covered my bed
with sheets of colored linen from Egypt.
¹⁷I've perfumed it with myrrh, aloes,
and cinnamon. ¹⁸Come on! Let's make
love all night long. We'll be happy in
each other's arms. ¹⁹My husband isn't
at home. He's on a long trip. ²⁰He took
plenty of money with him and won't be
back for two weeks." ²¹So she tempted
him with her charms, and he gave in to
her smooth talk. ²²Suddenly he was going with her like an ox on the way to be
slaughtered, like a deer prancing into a
trapᶠ ²³where an arrow would pierce
its heart. He was like a bird going into
a net — he did not know that his life was
in danger.

²⁴Now then, sons, listen to me. Pay
attention to what I say. ²⁵Do not let
such a woman win your heart; don't go
wandering after her. ²⁶She has been
the ruin of many men and caused the
death of too many to count. ²⁷If you go
to her house, you are on the way to the
world of the dead. It is a shortcut to
death.

In Praise of Wisdom

8 Listen! Wisdom is calling out.
Reason is making herself
heard.
²On the hilltops near the road
and at the crossroads she
stands.
³At the entrance to the city,
beside the gates, she calls:
⁴"I appeal to all of you;
I call to everyone on earth.
⁵Are you immature? Learn to be
mature.
Are you foolish? Learn to have
sense.
⁶Listen to my excellent words;

all I tell you is right.
⁷What I say is the truth;
lies are hateful to me.
⁸Everything I say is true;
nothing is false or misleading.
⁹To those with insight, it is
all clear;
to the well-informed, it is
all plain.
¹⁰Choose my instruction instead
of silver;
choose knowledge rather than
the finest gold.

¹¹"I am Wisdom, I am better than
jewels;
nothing you want can
compare with me.
¹²I am Wisdom, and I have
insight;
I have knowledge and sound
judgment.
¹³To honor the LORD is to hate
evil;
I hate pride and arrogance,
evil ways and false words.
¹⁴I make plans and carry them out.
I have understanding, and I
am strong.
¹⁵I help kings to govern
and rulers to make good laws.
¹⁶Every ruler on earth governs
with my help,
officials and nobles alike.
¹⁷I love those who love me;
whoever looks for me can
find me.
¹⁸I have riches and honor to give,
prosperity and success.
¹⁹What you get from me is better
than the finest gold,
better than the purest silver.
²⁰I walk the way of righteousness;
I follow the paths of justice,
²¹giving wealth to those who
love me,
filling their houses with
treasures.

ᶠ *Probable text* like a deer prancing into a trap; *Hebrew unclear.*
8.1-3 Pr 1.20, 21   **8.11-21** Si 24.1-22

8.34   9.9   9.13-14   10.5   10.26

22"The LORD created me first of all,
    the first of his works,
      long ago.
23 I was made in the very
    beginning,
    at the first, before the world
      began.
24 I was born before the oceans,
    when there were no springs of
      water.
25 I was born before the mountains,
    before the hills were set in
      place,
26 before God made the earth and
    its fields
    or even the first handful of
      soil.
27 I was there when he set the sky
    in place,
    when he stretched the
      horizon across the ocean,
28 when he placed the clouds in
    the sky,
    when he opened the springs
      of the ocean
29 and ordered the waters of the sea
    to rise no further than he
      said.
    I was there when he laid the
      earth's foundations.
30 I was beside him like an
    architect,*g*
    I was his daily source of joy,
    always happy in his
      presence —
31 happy with the world
    and pleased with the human
      race.

32"Now, young people, listen
    to me.

Do as I say, and you will be
    happy.
33 Listen to what you are taught.
    Be wise; do not neglect it.
34 Those who listen to me will be
    happy —
    those who stay at my door
      every day,
    waiting at the entrance to my
      home.
35 Those who find me find life,
    and the LORD will be pleased
      with them.
36 Those who do not find me hurt
    themselves;
    anyone who hates me loves
      death."

Wisdom and Stupidity

9 Wisdom has built her house and made seven columns for it. 2 She has had an animal killed for a feast, mixed spices in the wine, and set the table. 3 She has sent her servant women to call out from the highest place in town: 4"Come in, ignorant people!" And to the foolish she says, 5"Come, eat my food and drink the wine that I have mixed. 6 Leave the company of ignorant people, and live. Follow the way of knowledge."

7 If you correct conceited people, you will only be insulted. If you reprimand evil people, you will only get hurt. 8 Never correct conceited people; they will hate you for it. But if you correct the wise, they will respect you. 9 Anything you say to the wise will make them wiser. Whatever you tell the righteous will add to their knowledge.

g an architect; *or* a little child.

8.22 Si 1.4, 9; Rev 3.14   **8.27-31** Ws 9.9; Si 24.3-6   **8.32** Si 14.20-27

¹⁰To be wise you must first have reverence for the Lord. If you know the Holy One, you have understanding. ¹¹Wisdom will add years to your life. ¹²You are the one who will profit if you have wisdom, and if you reject it, you are the one who will suffer.

¹³Stupidity is like a loud, ignorant, shameless woman.[h] ¹⁴She sits at the door of her house or on a seat in the highest part of town, ¹⁵and calls out to people passing by, who are minding their own business: ¹⁶"Come in, ignorant people!" To the foolish she says, ¹⁷"Stolen water is sweeter. Stolen bread tastes better." ¹⁸Her victims do not know that the people die who go to her house, that those who have already entered are now deep in the world of the dead.

Solomon's Proverbs

10 These are Solomon's proverbs:
Wise children make their fathers proud of them; foolish ones bring their mothers grief.

²Wealth you get by dishonesty will do you no good, but honesty can save your life.

³The Lord will not let good people go hungry, but he will keep the wicked from getting what they want.

⁴Being lazy will make you poor, but hard work will make you rich.

⁵A sensible person gathers the crops when they are ready; it is a disgrace to sleep through the time of harvest.

⁶Good people will receive blessings. The words of the wicked hide a violent nature.

⁷Good people will be remembered as a blessing, but the wicked will soon be forgotten.

⁸Sensible people accept good advice. People who talk foolishly will come to ruin.

⁹Honest people are safe and secure, but the dishonest will be caught.

¹⁰Someone who holds back the truth causes trouble, but one who openly criticizes works for peace.[i]

¹¹A good person's words are a fountain of life, but a wicked person's words hide a violent nature.

¹²Hate stirs up trouble, but love forgives all offenses.

¹³Intelligent people talk sense, but stupid people need to be punished.

¹⁴The wise get all the knowledge they can, but when fools speak, trouble is not far off.

¹⁵Wealth protects the rich; poverty destroys the poor.

¹⁶The reward for doing good is life, but sin leads only to more sin.

¹⁷People who listen when they are corrected will live, but those who will not admit that they are wrong are in danger.

¹⁸Anyone who hides hatred is a liar. Anyone who spreads gossip is a fool.

¹⁹The more you talk, the more likely you are to sin. If you are wise, you will keep quiet.

²⁰A good person's words are like pure silver; a wicked person's ideas are worthless.

²¹A good person's words will benefit many people, but you can kill yourself with stupidity.

²²It is the Lord's blessing that makes you wealthy. Hard work can make you no richer.[j]

²³It is foolish to enjoy doing wrong. Intelligent people take pleasure in wisdom.

²⁴The righteous get what they want, but the wicked will get what they fear most.

²⁵Storms come, and the wicked are

---

[h] *Verse 13 in Hebrew is unclear.*   [i] *One ancient translation* but one ... peace; *Hebrew repeats verse 8b.*   [j] Hard work ... richer; *or* And the Lord does not add sorrow to your wealth.

9.10 Job 28.28; Ps 111.10; Pr 1.7   **10.12** Jas 5.20; 1 P 4.8

11.1   11.12   11.22   11.25   11.28

blown away, but honest people are always safe.

²⁶ Never get a lazy person to do something for you; he will be as irritating as vinegar on your teeth or smoke in your eyes.

²⁷ Obey the Lᴏʀᴅ, and you will live longer. The wicked die before their time.

²⁸ The hopes of good people lead to joy, but wicked people can look forward to nothing.

²⁹ The Lᴏʀᴅ protects honest people, but destroys those who do wrong.

³⁰ Righteous people will always have security, but the wicked will not survive in the land.

³¹ Righteous people speak wisdom, but the tongue that speaks evil will be stopped.

³² Righteous people know the kind thing to say, but the wicked are always saying things that hurt.

11 The Lᴏʀᴅ hates people who use dishonest scales. He is happy with honest weights.

² People who are proud will soon be disgraced. It is wiser to be modest.

³ If you are good, you are guided by honesty. People who can't be trusted are destroyed by their own dishonesty.

⁴ Riches will do you no good on the day you face death, but honesty can save your life.

⁵ Honesty makes a good person's life easier, but the wicked will cause their own downfall.

⁶ Righteousness rescues those who are honest, but those who can't be trusted are trapped by their own greed.

⁷ When the wicked die, their hope dies with them. Confidence placed in riches comes to nothing.

⁸ The righteous are protected from trouble; it comes to the wicked instead.

⁹ You can be ruined by the talk of godless people, but the wisdom of the righteous can save you.

¹⁰ A city is happy when honest people have good fortune, and there are joyful shouts when the wicked die.

¹¹ A city becomes great when the righteous give it their blessing; but a city is brought to ruin by the words of the wicked.

¹² It is foolish to speak scornfully of others. If you are smart, you will keep quiet.

¹³ No one who gossips can be trusted with a secret, but you can put confidence in someone who is trustworthy.

¹⁴ A nation will fall if it has no guidance. Many advisers mean security.

¹⁵ If you promise to pay a stranger's debt, you will regret it. You are better off if you don't get involved.

¹⁶ A gracious woman is respected, but a woman without virtue is a disgrace.

Lazy people will never have money,ᵏ but aggressive people will get rich.

¹⁷ You do yourself a favor when you are kind. If you are cruel, you only hurt yourself.

¹⁸ Wicked people do not really gain anything, but if you do what is right, you are certain to be rewarded.

¹⁹ Anyone who is determined to do right will live, but anyone who insists on doing wrong will die.

ᵏ *One ancient translation* but a woman . . . money; *Hebrew does not have these words.*
11.14 Ws 6.24

12.10   12.18   12.27   13.1   13.59

²⁰The LORD hates evil-minded people, but loves those who do right.

²¹You can be sure that evil people will be punished, but the righteous will escape.

²²Beauty in a woman without good judgment is like a gold ring in a pig's snout.

²³What good people want always results in good; when the wicked get what they want, everyone is angry.ˡ

²⁴Some people spend their money freely and still grow richer. Others are cautious, and yet grow poorer.

²⁵Be generous, and you will be prosperous. Help others, and you will be helped.

²⁶People curse someone who hoards grain, waiting for a higher price, but they praise the one who puts it up for sale.

²⁷If your goals are good, you will be respected, but if you are looking for trouble, that is what you will get.

²⁸Those who depend on their wealth will fall like the leaves of autumn, but the righteous will prosper like the leaves of summer.

²⁹Those who bring trouble on their families will have nothing at the end.

Foolish people will always be servants to the wise.

³⁰Righteousnessᵐ gives life, but violenceⁿ takes it away.

³¹Those who are good are rewarded here on earth, so you can be sure that wicked and sinful people will be punished.

12 Any who love knowledge want to be told when they are wrong. It is stupid to hate being corrected.

²The LORD is pleased with good people, but condemns those who plan evil.

³Wickedness does not give security, but righteous people stand firm.

⁴A good wife is her husband's pride and joy; but a wife who brings shame on her husband is like a cancer in his bones.

⁵Honest people will treat you fairly; the wicked only want to deceive you.

⁶The words of the wicked are murderous, but the words of the righteous rescue those who are threatened.

⁷The wicked meet their downfall and leave no descendants, but the families of the righteous live on.

⁸If you are intelligent, you will be praised; if you are stupid, people will look down on you.

⁹It is better to be an ordinary person working for a living than to play the part of someone great but go hungry.

¹⁰Good people take care of their animals, but wicked people are cruel to theirs.

¹¹A hard-working farmer has plenty to eat, but it is stupid to waste time on useless projects.

¹²All that wicked people want is to find evil things to do, but the righteous stand firm.ᵒ

¹³The wicked are trapped by their own words, but honest people get themselves out of trouble.

¹⁴Your reward depends on what you

ˡ everyone is angry; *or* God punishes them. Righteousness; *Hebrew* A righteous person. wise person.   ᵒ *Verse 12 in Hebrew is unclear.*

ᵐ *One ancient translation*
ⁿ *Probable text* violence; *Hebrew* a

11.31 1 P 4.18   **12.1** Si 21.6

say and what you do; you will get what you deserve.

¹⁵ Stupid people always think they are right. Wise people listen to advice.

¹⁶ When a fool is annoyed, he quickly lets it be known. Smart people will ignore an insult.

¹⁷ When you tell the truth, justice is done, but lies lead to injustice.

¹⁸ Thoughtless words can wound as deeply as any sword, but wisely spoken words can heal.

¹⁹ A lie has a short life, but truth lives on forever.

²⁰ Those who plan evil are in for a rude surprise, but those who work for good will find happiness.

²¹ Nothing bad happens to righteous people, but the wicked have nothing but trouble.

²² The LORD hates liars, but is pleased with those who keep their word.

²³ Smart people keep quiet about what they know, but stupid people advertise their ignorance.

²⁴ Hard work will give you power; being lazy will make you a slave.

²⁵ Worry can rob you of happiness, but kind words will cheer you up.

²⁶ The righteous person is a guide to his friend, but the path of the wicked leads them astray.

²⁷ If you are lazy, you will never get what you are after, but if you work hard, you will get a fortune.ᵖ

²⁸ Righteousness is the road to life; wickedness�q is the road to death.

13 Wise children pay attention when their parents correct them, but arrogant people never admit they are wrong.

² Good people will be rewarded for what they say, but those who are deceitful are hungry for violence.

³ Be careful what you say and protect your life. A careless talker destroys himself.

⁴ No matter how much a lazy person may want something, he will never get it. A hard worker will get everything he wants.

⁵ Honest people hate lies, but the words of wicked people are shameful and disgraceful.

⁶ Righteousness protects the innocent; wickedness is the downfall of sinners.

⁷ Some people pretend to be rich, but have nothing. Others pretend to be poor, but own a fortune.

⁸ The rich have to use their money to save their lives, but no one threatens the poor.

⁹ The righteous are like a light shining brightly; the wicked are like a lamp flickering out.

¹⁰ Arrogance causes nothing but trouble. It is wiser to ask for advice.

¹¹ The more easily you get your wealth, the sooner you will lose it. The harder it is to earn, the more you will have.

¹² When hope is crushed, the heart is crushed, but a wish come true fills you with joy.

¹³ If you refuse good advice, you are asking for trouble; follow it and you are safe.

¹⁴ The teachings of the wise are a fountain of life; they will help you escape when your life is in danger.

¹⁵ Intelligence wins respect, but those who can't be trusted are on the road to ruin.ʳ

¹⁶ Sensible people always think before they act, but stupid people advertise their ignorance.

¹⁷ Unreliable messengers cause trouble, but those who can be trusted bring peace.

¹⁸ Someone who will not learn will be poor and disgraced. Anyone who listens to correction is respected.

¹⁹ How good it is to get what you

ᵖ *Verse 27 in Hebrew is unclear.*   q *One ancient translation* wickedness; *Hebrew* path.   ʳ *One ancient translation* road to ruin; *Hebrew* permanent road.

13.3 Si 28.25, 26

13.24   14.1   14.4   14.20   14.31

want! Stupid people refuse to turn away from evil.

²⁰Keep company with the wise and you will become wise. If you make friends with stupid people, you will be ruined.

²¹Trouble follows sinners everywhere, but righteous people will be rewarded with good things.

²²Good people will have wealth to leave to their grandchildren, but the wealth of sinners will go to the righteous.

²³Unused fields could yield plenty of food for the poor, but unjust people keep them from being farmed.ˢ

²⁴If you don't punish your children, you don't love them. If you do love them, you will correct them.

²⁵The righteous have enough to eat, but the wicked are always hungry.

14 Homes are made by the wisdom of women, but are destroyed by foolishness.

²Be honest and you show that you have reverence for the LORD; be dishonest and you show that you do not.

³Proud fools talk too much; the words of the wise protect them.

⁴Without any oxen to pull the plow your barn will be empty, but with them it will be full of grain.ᵗ

⁵A reliable witness always tells the truth, but an unreliable one tells nothing but lies.

⁶Conceited people can never become wise, but intelligent people learn easily.

⁷Stay away from foolish people; they have nothing to teach you.

⁸Why is a clever person wise? Because he knows what to do. Why is a stupid person foolish? Because he only thinks he knows.

⁹Foolish people don't care if they sin, but good people want to be forgiven.ᵘ

¹⁰Your joy is your own; your bitterness is your own. No one can share them with you.

¹¹A good person's house will still be standing after an evildoer's house has been destroyed.

¹²What you think is the right road may lead to death.

¹³Laughter may hide sadness. When happiness is gone, sorrow is always there.

¹⁴Bad people will get what they deserve. Good people will be rewarded for their deeds.ᵛ

¹⁵A fool will believe anything; smart people watch their step.

¹⁶Sensible people are careful to stay out of trouble, but stupid people are careless and act too quickly.

¹⁷People with a hot temper do foolish things; wiser people remain calm.ʷ

¹⁸Ignorant people get what their foolishness deserves, but the clever are rewarded with knowledge.

¹⁹Evil people will have to bow down to the righteous and humbly beg their favor.

²⁰No one likes the poor, not even their neighbors, but the rich have many friends.

ˢ *Verse 23 in Hebrew is unclear.*   ᵗ your barn will be . . . grain; *or* you may grow a little grain, but with them you can grow much more.   ᵘ *Verse 9 in Hebrew is unclear.*   ᵛ *Probable text* for their deeds; *Hebrew* from upon them.   ʷ *One ancient translation* remain calm; *Hebrew* are hated.

13.20 Si 6.33, 34   **14.12** Pr 16.25

15.1   15.13   15.17(1)   15.17(2)   15.19

21 If you want to be happy, be kind to the poor; it is a sin to despise anyone.

22 You will earn the trust and respect of others if you work for good; if you work for evil, you are making a mistake.

23 Work and you will earn a living; if you sit around talking you will be poor.

24 Wise people are rewarded with wealth, but fools are known by[x] their foolishness.

25 A witness saves lives when he tells the truth; when he tells lies, he betrays people.

26 Reverence for the LORD gives confidence and security to a man and his family.

27 Do you want to avoid death? Reverence for the LORD is a fountain of life.

28 A king's greatness depends on how many people he rules; without them he is nothing.

29 If you stay calm, you are wise, but if you have a hot temper, you only show how stupid you are.

30 Peace of mind makes the body healthy, but jealousy is like a cancer.

31 If you oppress poor people, you insult the God who made them; but kindness shown to the poor is an act of worship.

32 Wicked people bring about their own downfall by their evil deeds, but good people are protected by their integrity.[y]

33 Wisdom is in every thought of intelligent people; fools know nothing[z] about wisdom.

34 Righteousness makes a nation great; sin is a disgrace to any nation.

35 Kings are pleased with competent officials, but they punish those who fail them.

15 A gentle answer quiets anger, but a harsh one stirs it up.

2 When wise people speak, they make knowledge attractive, but stupid people spout nonsense.

3 The LORD sees what happens everywhere; he is watching us, whether we do good or evil.

4 Kind words bring life, but cruel words crush your spirit.

5 It is foolish to ignore what your parents taught you; it is wise to accept their correction.

6 Righteous people keep their wealth, but the wicked lose theirs when hard times come.

7 Knowledge is spread by people who are wise, not by fools.

8 The LORD is pleased when good people pray, but hates the sacrifices that the wicked bring him.

9 The LORD hates the ways of evil people, but loves those who do what is right.

10 If you do what is wrong, you will be severely punished; you will die if you do not let yourself be corrected.

11 Not even the world of the dead can keep the LORD from knowing what is there; how then can we hide our thoughts from God?

12 Conceited people do not like to be corrected; they never ask for advice from those who are wiser.

13 When people are happy, they smile, but when they are sad, they look depressed.

14 Intelligent people want to learn,

---

x Probable text are known by; *Hebrew unclear.*   *y Some ancient translations* integrity; *Hebrew death.*   *z One ancient translation* nothing; *Hebrew does not have this word.*

15.24   15.30   16.11   16.22   16.27

but stupid people are satisfied with ignorance.

¹⁵ The life of the poor is a constant struggle, but happy people always enjoy life.

¹⁶ Better to be poor and fear the LORD than to be rich and in trouble.

¹⁷ Better to eat vegetables with people you love than to eat the finest meat where there is hate.

¹⁸ Hot tempers cause arguments, but patience brings peace.

¹⁹ If you are lazy, you will meet difficulty everywhere, but if you are honest, you will have no trouble.

²⁰ Wise children make their fathers happy. Only fools despise their mothers.

²¹ Stupid people are happy with their foolishness, but the wise will do what is right.

²² Get all the advice you can, and you will succeed; without it you will fail.

²³ What a joy it is to find just the right word for the right occasion!

²⁴ Wise people walk the road that leads upward to life, not the road that leads downward to death.

²⁵ The LORD will destroy the homes of arrogant men, but he will protect a widow's property.

²⁶ The LORD hates evil thoughts, but he is pleased with friendly words.

²⁷ Try to make a profit dishonestly, and you get your family in trouble. Don't take bribes and you will live longer.

²⁸ Good people think before they answer. Evil people have a quick reply, but it causes trouble.

²⁹ When good people pray, the LORD listens, but he ignores those who are evil.

³⁰ Smiling faces make you happy, and good news makes you feel better.

³¹ If you pay attention when you are corrected, you are wise.

³² If you refuse to learn, you are hurting yourself. If you accept correction, you will become wiser.

³³ Reverence for the LORD is an education in itself. You must be humble before you can ever receive honors.

16 We may make our plans, but God has the last word.ᵃ

² You may think everything you do is right, but the LORD judges your motives.

³ Ask the LORD to bless your plans, and you will be successful in carrying them out.

⁴ Everything the LORD has made has its destiny; and the destiny of the wicked is destruction.

⁵ The LORD hates everyone who is arrogant; he will never let them escape punishment.

⁶ Be loyal and faithful, and God will forgive your sin. Obey the LORD and nothing evil will happen to you.

⁷ When you please the LORD, you can makeᵇ your enemies into friends.

⁸ It is better to have a little, honestly earned, than to have a large income, dishonestly gained.

⁹ You may make your plans, but God directs your actions.

¹⁰ The king speaks with divine authority; his decisions are always right.

¹¹ The LORD wants weights and measures to be honest and every sale to be fair.

ᵃ God . . . word; *or* God inspires our words.
16.6 Tb 12.9   **16.8** Tb 12.8

ᵇ you can make; *or* he will make.

16.30   16.31   17.6   17.14   17.17

¹²Kings cannot tolerate evil,ᶜ because justice is what makes a government strong.

¹³A king wants to hear the truth and will favor those who speak it.

¹⁴A wise person will try to keep the king happy; if the king becomes angry, someone may die.

¹⁵The king's favor is like the clouds that bring rain in the springtime—life is there.

¹⁶It is better—much better—to have wisdom and knowledge than gold and silver.

¹⁷Those who are good travel a road that avoids evil; so watch where you are going—it may save your life.

¹⁸Pride leads to destruction, and arrogance to downfall.

¹⁹It is better to be humble and stay poor than to be one of the arrogant and get a share of their loot.

²⁰Pay attention to what you are taught, and you will be successful; trust in the LORD and you will be happy.

²¹A wise, mature person is known for his understanding. The more pleasant his words, the more persuasive he is.

²²Wisdom is a fountain of life to the wise, but trying to educate stupid people is a waste of time.

²³Intelligent people think before they speak; what they say is then more persuasive.

²⁴Kind words are like honey—sweet to the taste and good for your health.

²⁵What you think is the right road may lead to death.

²⁶A laborer's appetite makes him work harder, because he wants to satisfy his hunger.

²⁷Evil people look for ways to harm others; even their words burn with evil.

²⁸Gossip is spread by wicked people; they stir up trouble and break up friendships.

²⁹Violent people deceive their friends and lead them to disaster.

³⁰Watch out for people who grin and wink at you; they have thought of something evil.

³¹Long life is the reward of the righteous; gray hair is a glorious crown.

³²It is better to be patient than powerful. It is better to win control over yourself than over whole cities.

³³People cast lots to learn God's will, but God himself determines the answer.

17 Better to eat a dry crust of bread with peace of mind than have a banquet in a house full of trouble.

²A shrewd servant will gain authority over a master's worthless son and receive a part of the inheritance.

³Gold and silver are tested by fire, and a person's heart is tested by the LORD.

⁴Evil people listen to evil ideas, and liars listen to lies.

⁵If you make fun of poor people, you insult the God who made them. You will be punished if you take pleasure in someone's misfortune.

⁶Grandparents are proud of their grandchildren, just as children are proud of their parents.

⁷Respected people do not tell lies, and fools have nothing worthwhile to say.

⁸Some people think a bribe works

ᶜ Kings . . . evil; *or* It is intolerable for kings to do evil.
16.25 Pr 14.12   **16.28** Si 28.13-26

17.20   18.4   18.6   18.8   18.10

like magic; they believe it can do anything.

⁹ If you want people to like you, forgive them when they wrong you. Remembering wrongs can break up a friendship.

¹⁰ An intelligent person learns more from one rebuke than a fool learns from being beaten a hundred times.

¹¹ Death will come like a cruel messenger to wicked people who are always stirring up trouble.

¹² It is better to meet a mother bear robbed of her cubs than to meet some fool busy with a stupid project.

¹³ If you repay good with evil, you will never get evil out of your house.

¹⁴ The start of an argument is like the first break in a dam; stop it before it goes any further.

¹⁵ Condemning the innocent or letting the wicked go — both are hateful to the Lord.

¹⁶ It does a fool no good to spend money on an education, because he has no common sense.

¹⁷ Friends always show their love. What are relatives for if not to share trouble?

¹⁸ Only someone with no sense would promise to be responsible for someone else's debts.

¹⁹ To like sin is to like making trouble. If you brag all the time,ᵈ you are asking for trouble.

²⁰ Anyone who thinks and speaks evil can expect to find nothing good — only disaster.

²¹ There is nothing but sadness and sorrow for parents whose children do foolish things.

²² Being cheerful keeps you healthy. It is slow death to be gloomy all the time.

²³ Corrupt judges accept secret bribes, and then justice is not done.

²⁴ An intelligent person aims at wise action, but a fool starts off in many directions.

²⁵ Foolish children bring grief to their fathers and bitter regrets to their mothers.

²⁶ It is not right to make an innocent person pay a fine; justice is perverted when good people are punished.

²⁷ Those who are sure of themselves do not talk all the time. People who stay calm have real insight. ²⁸ After all, even fools may be thought wise and intelligent if they stay quiet and keep their mouths shut.

18 People who do not get along with others are interested only in themselves; they will disagree with what everyone else knows is right.

² A fool does not care whether he understands a thing or not; all he wants to do is show how smart he is.

³ Sin and shame go together. Lose your honor, and you will get scorn in its place.

⁴ A person's words can be a source of wisdom, deep as the ocean, fresh as a flowing stream.

⁵ It is not right to favor the guilty and keep the innocent from receiving justice.

⁶ When some fool starts an argument, he is asking for a beating.

⁷ When a fool speaks, he is ruining himself; he gets caught in the trap of his own words.

ᵈ brag . . . time; *or* make a show of your wealth.
17.17 Si 6.7-10   **17.28** Si 20.5

18.14   18.22   18.23   19.3   19.6

⁸Gossip is so tasty — how we love to swallow it!

⁹A lazy person is as bad as someone who is destructive.

¹⁰The LORD is like a strong tower, where the righteous can go and be safe.

¹¹Rich people, however, imagine that their wealth protects them like high, strong walls around a city.

¹²No one is respected unless he is humble; arrogant people are on the way to ruin.

¹³Listen before you answer. If you don't, you are being stupid and insulting.

¹⁴Your will to live can sustain you when you are sick, but if you lose it, your last hope is gone.

¹⁵Intelligent people are always eager and ready to learn.

¹⁶Do you want to meet an important person? Take a gift and it will be easy.

¹⁷The first person to speak in court always seems right until his opponent begins to question him.

¹⁸If two powerful people are opposing each other in court, casting lots can settle the issue.

¹⁹Help your relatives and they will protect you like a strong city wall,ᵉ but if you quarrel with them, they will close their doors to you.

²⁰You will have to live with the consequences of everything you say.

²¹What you say can preserve life or destroy it; so you must accept the consequences of your words.

²²Find a wife and you find a good thing; it shows that the LORD is good to you.

²³When the poor speak, they have to be polite, but when the rich answer, they are rude.

²⁴Some friendships doᶠ not last, but some friends are more loyal than brothers.

19 It is better to be poor but honest than to be a lying fool.

²Enthusiasm without knowledge is not good; impatience will get you into trouble.

³Some people ruin themselves by their own stupid actions and then blame the LORD.

⁴Rich people are always finding new friends, but the poor cannot keep the few they have.

⁵If you tell lies in court, you will be punished — there will be no escape.

⁶Everyone tries to gain the favor of important people; everyone claims the friendship of those who give out favors.

⁷Even the relatives of a poor person have no use for him; no wonder he has no friends. No matter how hard he tries, he cannot win any.ᵍ

⁸Do yourself a favor and learn all you can; then remember what you learn and you will prosper.

⁹No one who tells lies in court can escape punishment; he is doomed.

¹⁰Fools should not live in luxury, and slaves should not rule over noblemen.

¹¹If you are sensible, you will control your temper. When someone wrongs you, it is a great virtue to ignore it.

¹²The king's anger is like the roar of

ᵉ *Some ancient translations* Help ... wall; *Hebrew unclear.*   ᶠ *Some ancient translations* Some friendships do; *Hebrew* Someone with friends does.   ᵍ *Probable text* No matter ... any; *Hebrew unclear.*

18.13 Si 11.8   **18.22** Si 26.1-4

20.1   20.12   20.20   20.29   21.8

a lion, but his favor is like welcome rain.

¹³Stupid children can bring their parents to ruin. A nagging wife is like water going drip-drip-drip.

¹⁴A man can inherit a house and money from his parents, but only the LORD can give him a sensible wife.

¹⁵Go ahead and be lazy; sleep on, but you will go hungry.

¹⁶Keep God's laws and you will live longer; if you ignore them, you will die.

¹⁷When you give to the poor, it is like lending to the LORD, and the LORD will pay you back.

¹⁸Discipline your children while they are young enough to learn. If you don't, you are helping them destroy themselves.ʰ

¹⁹If someone has a hot temper, let him take the consequences. If you get him out of trouble once, you will have to do it again.ⁱ

²⁰If you listen to advice and are willing to learn, one day you will be wise.

²¹People may plan all kinds of things, but the LORD's will is going to be done.

²²It is a disgrace to be greedy;ʲ poor people are better off than liars.

²³Obey the LORD and you will live a long life, content and safe from harm.

²⁴Some people are too lazy to put food in their own mouths.

²⁵Arrogance should be punished, so that people who don't know any better can learn a lesson. If you are wise, you will learn when you are corrected.

²⁶Only a shameful, disgraceful person would mistreat his father or turn his mother away from his home.

²⁷My child, when you stop learning, you will soon neglect what you already know.

²⁸There is no justice where a witness is determined to hurt someone. Wicked people love the taste of evil.

²⁹A conceited fool is sure to get a beating.

20 Drinking too much makes you loud and foolish. It's stupid to get drunk.

²Fear an angry king as you would a growling lion; making him angry is suicide.

³Any fool can start arguments; the honorable thing is to stay out of them.

⁴A farmer too lazy to plow his fields at the right time will have nothing to harvest.

⁵A person's thoughts are like water in a deep well, but someone with insight can draw them out.

⁶Everyone talks about how loyal and faithful he is, but just try to find someone who really is!

⁷Children are fortunate if they have a father who is honest and does what is right.

⁸The king sits in judgment and knows evil when he sees it.

⁹Can anyone really say that his conscience is clear, that he has gotten rid of his sin?

¹⁰The LORD hates people who use dishonest weights and measures.

¹¹Even children show what they are by what they do; you can tell if they are honest and good.

¹²The LORD has given us eyes to see with and ears to listen with.

¹³If you spend your time sleeping,

ʰ If you ... themselves; or But don't punish them so hard that you kill them.

ⁱ get him out ... again; or try to get him out of trouble, you only make things worse.

ʲ It ... greedy; or Loyalty is what is desired in a person.

21.9   21.13   21.14   21.23   21.25

you will be poor. Keep busy and you will have plenty to eat.

¹⁴The customer always complains that the price is too high, but then he goes off and brags about the bargain he got.

¹⁵If you know what you are talking about, you have something more valuable than gold or jewels.

¹⁶Anyone stupid enough to promise to be responsible for a stranger's debts ought to have their own property held to guarantee payment.

¹⁷What you get by dishonesty may enjoy like the finest food, but sooner or later it will be like a mouthful of sand.

¹⁸Get good advice and you will succeed; don't go charging into battle without a plan.

¹⁹A gossip can never keep a secret. Stay away from people who talk too much.

²⁰If you curse your parents, your life will end like a lamp that goes out in the dark.

²¹The more easily you get your wealth, the less good it will do you.

²²Don't take it on yourself to repay a wrong. Trust the LORD and he will make it right.

²³The LORD hates people who use dishonest scales and weights.

²⁴The LORD has determined our path; how then can anyone understand the direction his own life is taking?

²⁵Think carefully before you promise an offering to God. You might regret it later.

²⁶A wise king will find out who is doing wrong, and will punish him without pity.

²⁷The LORD gave us mind and conscience; we cannot hide from ourselves.

²⁸A king will remain in power as long as his rule is honest, just, and fair.

²⁹We admire the strength of youth and respect the gray hair of age.

³⁰Sometimes it takes a painful experience to make us change our ways.

21 The LORD controls the mind of a king as easily as he directs the course of a stream.

²You may think that everything you do is right, but remember that the LORD judges your motives.

³Do what is right and fair; that pleases the LORD more than bringing him sacrifices.

⁴Wicked people are controlled by their conceit and arrogance, and this is sinful.

⁵Plan carefully and you will have plenty; if you act too quickly, you will never have enough.

⁶The riches you get by dishonesty soon disappear, but not before they lead you into the jaws of death.

⁷The wicked are doomed by their own violence; they refuse to do what is right.

⁸Guilty people walk a crooked path; the innocent do what is right.

⁹Better to live on the roof than share the house with a nagging wife.

¹⁰Wicked people are always hungry for evil; they have no mercy on anyone.

¹¹When someone who is conceited gets his punishment, even an unthinking person learns a lesson. One who is wise will learn from what he is taught.

¹²God, the righteous one, knows what goes on in the homes of the

21.31   22.5   22.9   22.17   23.1

wicked, and he will bring the wicked down to ruin.

¹³ If you refuse to listen to the cry of the poor, your own cry for help will not be heard.

¹⁴ If someone is angry with you, a gift given secretly will calm him down.

¹⁵ When justice is done, good people are happy, but evil people are brought to despair.

¹⁶ Death is waiting for anyone who wanders away from good sense.

¹⁷ Indulging in luxuries, wine, and rich food will never make you wealthy.

¹⁸ The wicked bring on themselves the suffering they try to cause good people.

¹⁹ Better to live out in the desert than with a nagging, complaining wife.

²⁰ Wise people live in wealth and luxury, but stupid people spend their money as fast as they get it.

²¹ Be kind and honest and you will live a long life; others will respect you and treat you fairly.

²² A shrewd general can take a city defended by strong men, and destroy the walls they relied on.

²³ If you want to stay out of trouble, be careful what you say.

²⁴ Show me a conceited person and I will show you someone who is arrogant, proud, and inconsiderate.

²⁵ Lazy people who refuse to work are only killing themselves; ²⁶ all they do is think about what they would like to have. The righteous, however, can give, and give generously.

²⁷ The LORD hates it when wicked people offer him sacrifices, especially if they do it from evil motives.

²⁸ The testimony of a liar is not be-

lieved, but the word of someone who thinks matters through is accepted.

²⁹ Righteous people are sure of themselves; the wicked have to pretend as best they can.

³⁰ Human wisdom, brilliance, insight — they are of no help if the LORD is against you.

³¹ You can get horses ready for battle, but it is the LORD who gives victory.

22 If you have to choose between a good reputation and great wealth, choose a good reputation.

² The rich and the poor have this in common: the LORD made them both.

³ Sensible people will see trouble coming and avoid it, but an unthinking person will walk right into it and regret it later.

⁴ Obey the LORD, be humble, and you will get riches, honor, and a long life.

⁵ If you love your life, stay away from the traps that catch the wicked along the way.

⁶ Teach children how they should live, and they will remember it all their life.

⁷ Poor people are slaves of the rich. Borrow money and you are the lender's slave.

⁸ If you plant the seeds of injustice, disaster will spring up, and your oppression of others will end.

⁹ Be generous and share your food with the poor. You will be blessed for it.

¹⁰ Get rid of a conceited person, and then there will be no more arguments, quarreling, or name-calling.

¹¹ If you love purity of heart and graciousness of speech, the king will be your friend.

¹² The LORD sees to it that truth is

21.27 Si 7.9   **22.6** Si 6.18

kept safe by disproving the words of liars.

¹³Lazy people stay at home; they say a lion might get them if they go outside.

¹⁴Adultery is a trap — it catches those with whom the LORD is angry.

¹⁵Children just naturally do silly, careless things, but a good spanking will teach them how to behave.

¹⁶If you make gifts to rich people or oppress the poor to get rich, you will become poor yourself.

The Thirty Wise Sayings

¹⁷Listen, and I will teach you what the wise have said. Study their teachings, ¹⁸and you will be glad if you remember them and can quote them. ¹⁹I want you to put your trust in the LORD; that is why I am going to tell them to you now. ²⁰I have written down thirty sayings for you. They contain knowledge and good advice, ²¹and will teach you what the truth really is. Then when you are sent to find it out, you will bring back the right answer.

-1-

²²Don't take advantage of the poor just because you can; don't take advantage of those who stand helpless in court. ²³The LORD will argue their case for them and threaten the life of anyone who threatens theirs.

-2-

²⁴Don't make friends with people who have hot, violent tempers. ²⁵You might learn their habits and not be able to change.

-3-

²⁶Don't promise to be responsible for someone else's debts. ²⁷If you should be unable to pay, they will take away even your bed.

-4-

²⁸Never move an old property line that your ancestors established.

-5-

²⁹Show me someone who does a good job, and I will show you someone who is better than most and worthy of the company of kings.

-6-

23 When you sit down to eat with someone important, keep in mind who he is.ᵏ ²If you have a big appetite, restrain yourself. ³Don't be greedy for the fine food he serves; he may be trying to trick you.

-7-

⁴Be wise enough not to wear yourself out trying to get rich. ⁵Your money can be gone in a flash, as if it had grown wings and flown away like an eagle.

-8-

⁶Don't eat at the table of a stingy person or be greedy for the fine food he serves. ⁷"Come on and have some more," he says, but he doesn't mean it. What he thinks is what he really is. ⁸You will vomit up what you have eaten, and all your flattery will be wasted.

-9-

⁹Don't try to talk sense to a fool; he can't appreciate it.

-10-

¹⁰Never move an old property line or take over land owned by orphans. ¹¹The LORD is their powerful defender, and he will argue their case against you.

ᵏ keep . . . is; *or* notice carefully what is before you.

23.6   23.21   23.22   23.31   23.32

-11-

¹²Pay attention to your teacher and learn all you can.

-12-

¹³Don't hesitate to discipline children. A good spanking won't kill them. ¹⁴As a matter of fact, it may save their lives.

-13-

¹⁵My child, if you become wise, I will be very happy. ¹⁶I will be proud when I hear you speaking words of wisdom.

-14-

¹⁷Don't be envious of sinful people; let reverence for the LORD be the concern of your life. ¹⁸If it is, you have a bright future.

-15-

¹⁹Listen, my child, be wise and give serious thought to the way you live. ²⁰Don't associate with people who drink too much wine or stuff themselves with food. ²¹Drunkards and gluttons will be reduced to poverty. If all you do is eat and sleep, you will soon be wearing rags.

-16-

²²Listen to your father; without him you would not exist. When your mother is old, show her your appreciation. ²³Truth, wisdom, learning, and good sense — these are worth paying for, but too valuable for you to sell. ²⁴A righteous person's parents have good reason to be happy. You can take pride in a wise child. ²⁵Let your father and mother be proud of you; give your mother that happiness.

-17-

²⁶Pay close attention, son, and let my life be your example. ²⁷Prostitutes and immoral women are a deadly trap. ²⁸They wait for you like robbers and cause many men to be unfaithful.

-18-

²⁹⁻³⁰Show me people who drink too much, who have to try out fancy drinks, and I will show you people who are miserable and sorry for themselves, always causing trouble and always complaining. Their eyes are bloodshot, and they have bruises that could have been avoided. ³¹Don't let wine tempt you, even though it is rich red, and it sparkles in the cup, and it goes down smoothly. ³²The next morning you will feel as if you had been bitten by a poisonous snake. ³³Weird sights will appear before your eyes, and you will not be able to think or speak clearly. ³⁴You will feel as if you were out on the ocean, seasick, swinging high up in the rigging of a tossing ship. ³⁵"I must have been hit," you will say; "I must have been beaten up, but I don't remember it. Why can't I wake up? I need another drink."

-19-

24 Don't be envious of evil people, and don't try to make friends with them. ²Causing trouble is all they ever think about; every time they open their mouth someone is going to be hurt.

-20-

³Homes are built on the foundation

of wisdom and understanding.*l*
Where there is knowledge, the rooms
are furnished with valuable, beautiful
things.

-21-

5 Being wise is better than being
strong;*m* yes, knowledge is more important than strength. 6 After all, you
must make careful plans before you
fight a battle, and the more good advice
you get, the more likely you are to win.

-22-

7 Wise sayings are too deep for stupid
people to understand. They have nothing to say when important matters are
being discussed.

-23-

8 If you are always planning evil, you
will earn a reputation as a troublemaker. 9 Any scheme a fool thinks up is
sinful. People hate a person who has
nothing but scorn for others.

-24-

10 If you are weak in a crisis, you are
weak indeed.

-25-

11 Don't hesitate to rescue someone
who is about to be executed unjustly.
12 You may say that it is none of your
business, but God knows and judges
your motives. He keeps watch on you;
he knows. And he will reward you according to what you do.

-26-

13 My child, eat honey; it is good. And
just as honey from the comb is sweet on
your tongue, 14 you may be sure that
wisdom is good for the soul. Get wisdom and you have a bright future.

-27-

15 Don't be like the wicked who
scheme to rob honest people or to take
away their homes. 16 No matter how often honest people fall, they always get
up again; but disaster destroys the
wicked.

-28-

17 Don't be glad when your enemies
meet disaster, and don't rejoice when
they stumble. 18 The LORD will know if
you are gloating, and he will not like it;
and then maybe he won't punish them.

-29-

19 Don't let evil people worry you;
don't be envious of them. 20 A wicked
person has no future — nothing to look
forward to.

-30-

21 Have reverence for the LORD, my
child, and honor the king. Have nothing to do with people who rebel against
them; 22 such people could be ruined in
a moment. Do you realize the disaster
that God or the king can cause?

More Wise Sayings

23 The wise have also said these
things:
It is wrong for judges to be prejudiced. 24 If they pronounce a guilty person innocent, they will be cursed and
hated by everyone. 25 Judges who
punish the guilty, however, will be prosperous and enjoy a good reputation.

26 An honest answer is a sign of true
friendship.

27 Don't build your house and establish a home until your fields are ready,
and you are sure that you can earn a
living.

28 Don't give evidence against others
without good reason, or say misleading
things about them. 29 Don't say, "I'll do
to them just what they did to me! I'll get
even with them!"

---

l Homes . . . understanding; *or* It takes care to lay the foundations of a house, and skill
to build it.   *m* *Some ancient translations* Being wise is better than being strong;
Hebrew A person is wise in strength.

23.34   24.11   25.9   25.13   25.14

30 I walked through the fields and vineyards of a lazy, stupid person. 31 They were full of thorn bushes and overgrown with weeds. The stone wall around them had fallen down. 32 I looked at this, thought about it, and learned a lesson from it: 33 Go ahead and take your nap; go ahead and sleep. Fold your hands and rest awhile, 34 but while you are asleep, poverty will attack you like an armed robber.

More of Solomon's Proverbs

25 Here are more of Solomon's proverbs, copied by scribes at the court of King Hezekiah of Judah.

2 We honor God for what he conceals; we honor kings for what they explain.

3 You never know what a king is thinking; his thoughts are beyond us, like the heights of the sky or the depths of the ocean.

4 Take the impurities out of silver and the artist can produce a thing of beauty. 5 Keep evil advisers away from the king and his government will be known for its justice.

6 When you stand before the king, don't try to impress him and pretend to be important. 7 It is better to be asked to take a higher position than to be told to give your place to someone more important.

8 Don't be too quick to go to court about something you have seen. If another witness later proves you wrong, what will you do then?

9 If you and your neighbor have a difference of opinion, settle it between yourselves and do not reveal any secrets. 10 Otherwise everyone will learn that you can't keep a secret, and you will never live down the shame.

11 An idea well-expressed is like a design of gold, set in silver.

12 A warning given by an experienced person to someone willing to listen is more valuable than gold rings or jewelry made of the finest gold.

13 A reliable messenger is refreshing to the one who sends him, like cold water in the heat of harvest time.

14 People who promise things that they never give are like clouds and wind that bring no rain.

15 Patient persuasion can break down the strongest resistance and can even convince rulers.

16 Never eat more honey than you need; too much may make you vomit. 17 Don't visit your neighbors too often; they may get tired of you and come to hate you.

18 A false accusation is as deadly as a sword, a club, or a sharp arrow.

19 Depending on an unreliable person in a crisis is like trying to chew with a loose tooth or walk with a crippled foot.

20 Singing to a person who is depressed is like taking off a person's clothes on a cold day or like rubbing salt in a wound.

21 If your enemies are hungry, feed them; if they are thirsty, give them a drink. 22 You will make them burn with shame, and the LORD will reward you.

23 Gossip brings anger just as surely as the north wind brings rain.

24 Better to live on the roof than share the house with a nagging wife.

25 Finally hearing good news from a distant land is like a drink of cold water when you are dry and thirsty.

24.33, 34 Pr 6.10, 11   **25.6, 7** Lk 14.8-10   **25.21, 22** Ro 12.20

5.18   25.25   26.3   26.11   26.17

26 A good person who gives in to someone who is evil reminds you of a polluted spring or a poisoned well.

27 Too much honey is bad for you, and so is trying to win too much praise.[n]

28 If you cannot control your anger, you are as helpless as a city without walls, open to attack.

26

Praise for a fool is out of place, like snow in summer or rain at harvest time.

2 Curses cannot hurt you unless you deserve them. They are like birds that fly by and never light.

3 You have to whip a horse, you have to bridle a donkey, and you have to beat a fool.

4 If you answer a silly question, you are just as silly as the person who asked it.

5 Give a silly answer to a silly question, and the one who asked it will realize that he's not as smart as he thinks.

6 If you let a fool deliver a message, you might as well cut off your own feet; you are asking for trouble.

7 A fool can use a proverb about as well as crippled people can use their legs.

8 Praising someone who is stupid makes as much sense as tying a stone in a sling.

9 A fool quoting a wise saying reminds you of a drunk trying to pick a thorn out of his hand.

10 An employer who hires any fool that comes along is only hurting everybody concerned.[o]

11 A fool doing some stupid thing a second time is like a dog going back to its vomit.

12 The most stupid fool is better off than those who think they are wise when they are not.

13 Why don't lazy people ever get out of the house? What are they afraid of? Lions?

14 Lazy people turn over in bed. They get no farther than a door swinging on its hinges.

15 Some people are too lazy to put food in their own mouths.

16 A lazy person will think he is smarter than seven men who can give good reasons for their opinions.

17 Getting involved in an argument that is none of your business is like going down the street and grabbing a dog by the ears.

18-19 Someone who tricks someone else and then claims that he was only joking is like a crazy person playing with a deadly weapon.

20 Without wood, a fire goes out; without gossip, quarreling stops.

21 Charcoal keeps the embers glowing, wood keeps the fire burning, and troublemakers keep arguments alive.

22 Gossip is so tasty! How we love to swallow it!

23 Insincere[p] talk that hides what you are really thinking is like a fine glaze[q] on a cheap clay pot.

24 A hypocrite hides hate behind flattering words. **25** They may sound fine, but don't believe him, because his heart is filled to the brim with hate. **26** He may

---

[n] *Probable text* and so . . . praise; *Hebrew unclear.*

[o] *Verse 10 in Hebrew is unclear.*

[p] *One ancient translation* Insincere; *Hebrew* Burning.

[q] *Probable text* fine glaze; *Hebrew* unrefined silver.

26.11 2 P 2.22

26.20   26.27   27.9   27.18   27.23

disguise his hatred, but everyone will see the evil things he does.

²⁷ People who set traps for others get caught themselves. People who start landslides get crushed.

²⁸ You have to hate someone to want to hurt him with lies. Insincere talk brings nothing but ruin.

27 Never boast about tomorrow. You don't know what will happen between now and then.

² Let other people praise you — even strangers; never do it yourself.

³ The weight of stone and sand is nothing compared to the trouble that stupidity can cause.

⁴ Anger is cruel and destructive, but it is nothing compared to jealousy.

⁵ Better to correct someone openly than to let him think you don't care for him at all.

⁶ Friends mean well, even when they hurt you. But when an enemy puts his arm around your shoulder — watch out!

⁷ When you are full, you will refuse honey, but when you are hungry, even bitter food tastes sweet.

⁸ Anyone away from home is like a bird away from its nest.

⁹ Perfume and fragrant oils make you feel happier, but trouble shatters your peace of mind.ʳ

¹⁰ Do not forget your friends or your father's friends. If you are in trouble, don't ask a relative for help; a nearby neighbor can help you more than relatives who are far away.

¹¹ Be wise, my child, and I will be happy; I will have an answer for anyone who criticizes me.

¹² Sensible people will see trouble coming and avoid it, but an unthinking person will walk right into it and regret it later.

¹³ Any people stupid enough to promise to be responsible for a stranger'sˢ debtsˢ deserve to have their own property held to guarantee payment.

¹⁴ You might as well curse your friends as wake them up early in the morning with a loud greeting.

¹⁵ A nagging wife is like water going drip-drip-drip on a rainy day. ¹⁶ How can you keep her quiet? Have you ever tried to stop the wind or ever tried to hold a handful of oil?ᵗ

¹⁷ People learn from one another, just as iron sharpens iron.

¹⁸ Take care of a fig tree and you will have figs to eat. Servants who take care of their master will be honored.

¹⁹ It is your own face that you see reflected in the water and it is your own self that you see in your heart.

²⁰ Human desires are like the world of the dead — there is always room for more.

²¹ Fire tests gold and silver; a person's reputation can also be tested.

²² Even if you beat fools half to death, you still can't beat their foolishness out of them.

²³ Look after your sheep and cattle as carefully as you can, ²⁴ because wealth is not permanent. Not even nations last forever. ²⁵ You cut the hay and then cut the grass on the hillsides while the next

---

ʳ One ancient translation but trouble ... mind; Hebrew unclear.   ˢ One ancient translation stranger's debts; Hebrew stranger's debts or those of an immoral woman.   ᵗ Probable text or ever ... oil; Hebrew unclear.

26.27 Si 27.25-27   **27.1** Jas 4.13-16

28.1   28.15   28.27   29.1   29.17

crop of hay is growing. ²⁶You can make clothes from the wool of your sheep and buy land with the money you get from selling some of your goats. ²⁷The rest of the goats will provide milk for you and your family, and for your servant women as well.

28 The wicked run when no one is chasing them, but an honest person is as brave as a lion.

²When a nation sins, it will have one ruler after another. But a nation will be strong and endure when it has intelligent, sensible leaders.

³Someone in authority who oppresses poor people is like a driving rain that destroys the crops.

⁴If you have no regard for the law, you are on the side of the wicked; but if you obey it, you are against them.

⁵Evil people do not know what justice is, but those who worship the LORD understand it well.

⁶Better to be poor and honest than rich and dishonest.

⁷Young people who obey the law are intelligent. Those who make friends with good-for-nothings are a disgrace to their parents.

⁸If you get rich by charging interest and taking advantage of people, your wealth will go to someone who is kind to the poor.

⁹If you do not obey the law, God will find your prayers too hateful to hear.

¹⁰If you trick an honest person into doing evil, you will fall into your own trap.

The innocent will be well rewarded.

¹¹Rich people always think they are wise, but a poor person who has insight into character knows better.

¹²When good people come to power, everybody celebrates, but when bad people rule, people stay in hiding.

¹³You will never succeed in life if you try to hide your sins. Confess them and give them up; then God will show mercy to you.

¹⁴Always obey the LORD and you will be happy. If you are stubborn, you will be ruined.

¹⁵Poor people are helpless against a wicked ruler; he is as dangerous as a growling lion or a prowling bear.

¹⁶A ruler without good sense will be a cruel tyrant. One who hates dishonesty will rule a long time.

¹⁷Someone guilty of murder is digging his own grave as fast as he can. Don't try to stop him.

¹⁸Be honest and you will be safe. If you are dishonest, you will suddenly fall.

¹⁹A hard-working farmer has plenty to eat. People who waste time will always be poor.

²⁰Honest people will lead a full, happy life. But if you are in a hurry to get rich, you are going to be punished.

²¹Prejudice is wrong. But some judges will do wrong to get even the smallest bribe.

²²Selfish people are in such a hurry to get rich that they do not know when poverty is about to strike.

²³Correct someone, and afterward he will appreciate it more than flattery.

²⁴Anyone who thinks it isn't wrong to steal from his parents is no better than a common thief.

²⁵Selfishness only causes trouble. You are much better off to trust the LORD.

²⁶It is foolish to follow your own

opinions. Be safe, and follow the teachings of wiser people.

27 Give to the poor and you will never be in need. If you close your eyes to the poor, many people will curse you.

28 People stay in hiding when the wicked come to power. But when they fall from power, the righteous will rule again.

29 If you get more stubborn every time you are corrected, one day you will be crushed and never recover.

2 Show me a righteous ruler and I will show you a happy people. Show me a wicked ruler and I will show you a miserable people.

3 If you appreciate wisdom, your parents will be proud of you.

It is a foolish waste to spend money on prostitutes.

4 When the king is concerned with justice, the nation will be strong, but when he is only concerned with money, he will ruin his country.

5 If you flatter your friends, you set a trap for yourself. *u*

6 Evil people are trapped in their own sins, while honest people are happy and free.

7 A good person knows the rights of the poor, but wicked people cannot understand such things.

8 People with no regard for others can throw whole cities into turmoil. Those who are wise keep things calm.

9 When an intelligent person brings a lawsuit against a fool, the fool only laughs and becomes loud and abusive.

10 Bloodthirsty people hate anyone who's honest, but righteous people will protect*v* the life of such a person.

11 Stupid people express their anger openly, but sensible people are patient and hold it back.

12 If a ruler pays attention to false information, all his officials will be liars.

13 A poor person and his oppressor have this in common — the LORD gave eyes to both of them.

14 If a king defends the rights of the poor, he will rule for a long time.

15 Correction and discipline are good for children. If they have their own way, they will make their mothers ashamed of them.

16 When evil people are in power, crime increases. But the righteous will live to see the downfall of such people.

17 Discipline your children and you can always be proud of them. They will never give you reason to be ashamed.

18 A nation without God's guidance is a nation without order. Happy are those who keep God's law!

19 You cannot correct servants just by talking to them. They may understand you, but they will pay no attention.

20 There is more hope for a stupid fool than for someone who speaks without thinking.

21 If you give your servants everything they want from childhood on, some day they will take over everything you own. *w*

22 People with quick tempers cause a lot of quarreling and trouble.

23 Arrogance will bring your downfall, but if you are humble, you will be respected.

24 A thief's partner is his own worst enemy. He will be punished if he tells the truth in court, and God will curse him if he doesn't.

25 It is dangerous to be concerned with what others think of you, but if you trust the LORD, you are safe.

26 Everybody wants the good will of the ruler, but only from the LORD can you get justice.

27 The righteous hate the wicked, and the wicked hate the righteous.

---

u yourself; *or* them. *v Probable text* protect; *Hebrew* seek. *w* they . . . own; *or* you will not be able to control them.
29.19 Si 33.25-30

The Words of Agur

30 These are the solemn words of Agur son of Jakeh:

"God is not with me, God is
   not with me,
   and I am helpless.[x]
2 I am more like an animal than a
      human being;
   I do not have the sense we
      humans should have.
3 I have never learned any
      wisdom,
   and I know nothing at all
      about God.
4 Have any ever mastered
      heavenly knowledge?
   Have any ever caught the
      wind in their hands?
   Or wrapped up water in a
      piece of cloth?
   Or fixed the boundaries of the
      earth?
   Who are they, if you know? Who
      are their children?
5 "God keeps every promise he
makes. He is like a shield for all who
seek his protection. 6 If you claim that
he said something that he never said,
he will reprimand you and show that
you are a liar."

More Proverbs

7 I ask you, God, to let me have two
things before I die: 8 keep me from lying, and let me be neither rich nor poor.
So give me only as much food as I need.
9 If I have more, I might say that I do not
need you. But if I am poor, I might steal
and bring disgrace on my God.

10 Never criticize servants to their
master. You will be cursed and suffer
for it.

11 There are people who curse their
fathers and do not show their appreciation for their mothers.

12 There are people who think they

are pure when they are as filthy as they
can be.

13 There are people who think they
are so good — oh, how good they think
they are!

14 There are people who take cruel
advantage of the poor and needy; that is
the way they make their living.

15 A leech has two daughters, and
both are named "Give me!"

There are four things that are never
satisfied:
16 the world of the dead,
   a woman without children,
   dry ground that needs rain,
   and a fire burning out of control.

17 If you make fun of your father or
despise your mother in her old age,[y]
you ought to be eaten by vultures or
have your eyes picked out by wild
ravens.

18 There are four things that are too
mysterious for me to understand:
19 an eagle flying in the sky,
   a snake moving on a rock,
   a ship finding its way over
      the sea,
   and a man and a woman falling
      in love.

20 This is how an unfaithful wife acts:
she commits adultery, takes a bath, and
says, "But I haven't done anything
wrong!"

21 There are four things that the earth
itself cannot tolerate:
22 a slave who becomes a king,
   a fool who has all he wants
      to eat,
23 a hateful woman who gets
      married,
   and a servant woman who takes
      the place of her mistress.

24 There are four animals in the world
that are small, but very, very clever:
25 Ants: they are weak, but they
      store up their food in the
      summer.

---

x Probable text "God ... helpless; Hebrew unclear.   y One ancient translation
mother in her old age; Hebrew mother's obedience.
30.19 Ws 5.10-12

30.13   30.19   30.32   31.8   31.28

²⁶ Rock badgers: they are not strong either, but they make their homes among the rocks.

²⁷ Locusts: they have no king, but they move in formation.

²⁸ Lizards: you can hold one in your hand, but you can find them in palaces.

²⁹ There are four things that are impressive to watch as they walk:

³⁰ lions, strongest of all animals and afraid of none;

³¹ goats, strutting roosters, and kings in front of their people.ᶻ

³² If you have been foolish enough to be arrogant and plan evil, stop and think! ³³ If you churn milk, you get butter. If you hit someone's nose, it bleeds. If you stir up anger, you get into trouble.

Advice to a King

31 These are the solemn words which King Lemuel's mother said to him:

² "You are my own dear son, the answer to my prayers. What shall I tell you? ³ Don't spend all your energy on sex and all your money on women; they have destroyed kings. ⁴ Listen, Lemuel. Kings should not drink wine or have a craving for alcohol. ⁵ When they drink, they forget the laws and ignore the rights of people in need. ⁶ Alcohol is for people who are dying, for those who are in misery. ⁷ Let them drink and forget their poverty and unhappiness.

⁸ "Speak up for people who cannot speak for themselves. Protect the rights

of all who are helpless. ⁹ Speak for them and be a righteous judge. Protect the rights of the poor and needy."

The Capable Wife

¹⁰ How hard it is to find a capable wife! She is worth far more than jewels!

¹¹ Her husband puts his confidence in her, and he will never be poor.

¹² As long as she lives, she does him good and never harm.

¹³ She keeps herself busy making wool and linen cloth.

¹⁴ She brings home food from out-of-the-way places, as merchant ships do.

¹⁵ She gets up before daylight to prepare food for her family and to tell her servant women what to do.

¹⁶ She looks at land and buys it, and with money she has earned she plants a vineyard.

¹⁷ She is a hard worker, strong and industrious.

¹⁸ She knows the value of everything she makes, and works late into the night.

¹⁹ She spins her own thread and weaves her own cloth.

²⁰ She is generous to the poor and needy.

²¹ She doesn't worry when it snows, because her family has warm clothing.

²² She makes bedspreads and wears clothes of fine purple linen.

²³ Her husband is well known, one of the leading citizens.

²⁴ She makes clothes and belts, and sells them to merchants.

²⁵ She is strong and respected and not afraid of the future.

ᶻ *Verse 31 in Hebrew is unclear.*

²⁶ She speaks with a gentle wisdom.
²⁷ She is always busy and looks after her family's needs.
²⁸ Her children show their appreciation, and her husband praises her.
²⁹ He says, "Many women are good wives, but you are the best of them all."
³⁰ Charm is deceptive and beauty disappears, but a woman who honors the LORD should be praised.
³¹ Give her credit for all she does. She deserves the respect of everyone.

ECCLESIASTES

INTRODUCTION

The book of *Ecclesiastes* contains the thoughts of "the Philosopher," a man who reflected deeply on how short and contradictory human life is, with its mysterious injustices and frustrations, and concluded that "life is useless." He could not understand the ways of God, who controls human destiny. Yet, in spite of this, he advised people to work hard, and to enjoy the gifts of God as much and as long as they could.

Many of the Philosopher's thoughts appear negative and even depressing. But the fact that this book is in the Bible shows that biblical faith is broad enough to take into account such pessimism and doubt. Many have taken comfort in seeing themselves in the mirror of *Ecclesiastes,* and have discovered that the same Bible which reflects these thoughts also offers the hope in God that gives life its greater meaning.

Life Is Useless

1 These are the words of the Philosopher, David's son, who was king in Jerusalem.

² It is useless, useless, said the Philosopher. Life is useless, all useless. ³ You spend your life working, laboring, and what do you have to show for it? ⁴ Generations come and generations go, but the world stays just the same. ⁵ The sun still rises, and it still goes down, going wearily back to where it must start all over again. ⁶ The wind blows south, the wind blows north — round and round and back again. ⁷ Every river flows into the sea, but the sea is not yet full. The water returns to where the rivers began, and starts all over again. ⁸ Everything leads to weariness — a weariness too great for words. Our eyes

"I tell you, it is all useless." (1.14)

can never see enough to be satisfied; our ears can never hear enough. ⁹ What has happened before will happen again. What has been done before will be done again. There is nothing new in the whole world. [10]"Look," they say, "here is something new!" But no, it has all happened before, long before we were born. [11]No one remembers what has happened in the past, and no one in days to come will remember what happens between now and then.

The Philosopher's Experience

[12]I, the Philosopher, have been king over Israel in Jerusalem. [13]I determined that I would examine and study all the things that are done in this world.

God has laid a miserable fate upon us. [14]I have seen everything done in this world, and I tell you, it is all useless. It is like chasing the wind. [15]You can't straighten out what is crooked; you can't count things that aren't there.

[16]I told myself, "I have become a great man, far wiser than anyone who ruled Jerusalem before me. I know what wisdom and knowledge really are." [17]I was determined to learn the difference between knowledge and foolishness, wisdom and madness. But I found out that I might as well be chasing the wind. [18]The wiser you are, the more worries you have; the more you know, the more it hurts.

2 I decided to enjoy myself and find out what happiness is. But I found that this is useless, too. [2]I discovered that laughter is foolish, that pleasure does you no good. [3]Driven on by my desire for wisdom, I decided to cheer myself up with wine and have a good time. I thought that this might be the best way people can spend their short lives on earth.

[4]I accomplished great things. I built myself houses and planted vineyards. [5]I planted gardens and orchards, with all kinds of fruit trees in them; [6]I dug ponds to irrigate them. [7]I bought many slaves, and there were slaves born in my household. I owned more livestock than anyone else who had ever lived in Jerusalem. [8]I also piled up silver and gold from the royal treasuries of the lands I ruled. Men and women sang to entertain me, and I had all the women a man could want.

[9]Yes, I was great, greater than anyone else who had ever lived in Jerusalem, and my wisdom never failed me. [10]Anything I wanted, I got. I did not deny myself any pleasure. I was proud of everything I had worked for, and all

Anything I wanted, I got. (2.10)

this was my reward. [11]Then I thought about all that I had done and how hard I had worked doing it, and I realized that it didn't mean a thing. It was like chasing the wind — of no use at all. [12]After all, a king can only do what previous kings have done.

So I started thinking about what it meant to be wise or reckless or foolish. [13]Oh, I know, "Wisdom is better than foolishness, just as light is better than darkness. [14]The wise can see where they are going, and fools cannot." But I also know that the same fate is waiting for us all. [15]I thought to myself, "What happens to fools is going to happen to me, too. So what have I gained from being so wise?" "Nothing," I answered, "not a thing." [16] No one remembers the wise, and no one remembers fools. In days to come, we will all be forgotten. We must all die — wise and foolish alike. [17] So life came to mean nothing to me, because everything in it had brought me nothing but trouble. It had all been useless; I had been chasing the wind.

[18] Nothing that I had worked for and earned meant a thing to me, because I knew that I would have to leave it to my successor, [19] and he might be wise, or he might be foolish — who knows? Yet he will own everything I have worked for, everything my wisdom has earned for me in this world. It is all useless. [20] So I came to regret that I had worked so hard. [21] You work for something with all your wisdom, knowledge, and skill, and then you have to leave it all to someone who hasn't had to work for it. It is useless, and it isn't right! [22] You work and worry your way through life, and what do you have to show for it? [23] As long as you live, everything you do brings nothing but worry and heartache. Even at night your mind can't rest. It is all useless.

[24] The best thing we can do is eat and drink and enjoy what we have earned. And yet, I realized that even this comes from God. [25] How else could you have anything to eat or enjoy yourself at all? [26] God gives wisdom, knowledge, and happiness to those who please him, but he makes sinners work, earning and saving, so that what they get can be given to those who please him. It is all useless. It is like chasing the wind.

A Time for Everything

3 Everything that happens in this world happens at the time God chooses.

[2] He sets the time for birth and the time for death,

It is like chasing the wind. (2.26)

the time for planting and the time for pulling up,
[3] the time for killing and the time for healing,
the time for tearing down and the time for building.
[4] He sets the time for sorrow and the time for joy,
the time for mourning and the time for dancing,
[5] the time for making love and the time for not making love,
the time for kissing and the time for not kissing,
[6] He sets the time for finding and the time for losing,
the time for saving and the time for throwing away,
[7] the time for tearing and the time for mending,
the time for silence and the time for talk.
[8] He sets the time for love and the time for hate,
the time for war and the time for peace.
[9] What do we gain from all our work? [10] I know the heavy burdens that God has laid on us. [11] He has set the right time for everything. He has given us a desire to know the future, but never gives us the satisfaction of fully under-

2.23 Job 5.7; 14.1   **2.24** Ec 3.13; 5.18; 9.7; Is 56.12; Lk 12.19; 1 Co 15.32
2.26 Job 32.8; Pr 2.6

standing what he does. 12 So I realized that all we can do is be happy and do the best we can while we are still alive. 13 All of us should eat and drink and enjoy what we have worked for. It is God's gift.

14 I know that everything God does will last forever. You can't add anything to it or take anything away from it. And one thing God does is to make us stand in awe of him. 15 Whatever happens or can happen has already happened before. God makes the same thing happen again and again.

Injustice in the World

16 In addition, I have also noticed that in this world you find wickedness where justice and right ought to be. 17 I told myself, "God is going to judge the righteous and the evil alike, because every thing, every action, will happen at its own set time."*a* 18 I decided that God is testing us, to show us that we are no better than animals. 19 After all, the same fate awaits human beings and animals alike. One dies just like the other. They are the same kind of creature. A human being is no better off than an animal, because life has no meaning for either. 20 They are both going to the same place — the dust. They both came from it; they will both go back to it. 21 How can anyone be sure that the human spirit goes upward while an animal's spirit goes down into the ground? 22 So I realized then that the best thing we can do is enjoy what we have worked for. There is nothing else we can do.*b* There is no way for us to know what will happen after we die.

4 Then I looked again at all the injustice that goes on in this world. The oppressed were crying, and no one would help them. No one would help them, because their oppressors had power on their side. 2 I envy those who

are dead and gone; they are better off than those who are still alive. 3 But better off than either are those who have never been born, who have never seen the injustice that goes on in this world.

4 I have also learned why people work so hard to succeed: it is because they envy the things their neighbors have. But it is useless. It is like chasing the wind. 5 They say that we would be fools to fold our hands and let ourselves starve to death. 6 Maybe so, but it is better to have only a little, with peace of mind, than be busy all the time with both hands, trying to catch the wind.

7 I have noticed something else in life that is useless. 8 Here is someone who lives alone. He has no son, no brother, yet he is always working, never satisfied with the wealth he has. For whom is he working so hard and denying himself any pleasure? This is useless, too — and a miserable way to live.

9 Two are better off than one, because together they can work more effectively. 10 If one of them falls down, the other can help him up. But if someone is alone and falls, it's just too bad, because there is no one to help him. 11 If it is cold, two can sleep together and stay warm, but how can you keep warm by yourself? 12 Two people can resist an attack that would defeat one person alone. A rope made of three cords is hard to break.

13-14 Someone may rise from poverty to become king of his country, or go from prison to the throne, but if in his old age he is too foolish to take advice, he is not as well off as a young man who is poor but intelligent. 15 I thought about all the people who live in this world, and I realized that somewhere among them there is a young man who will take the king's place. 16 There may be no limit to the number of people a king rules; when he is gone, no one will

---

a Probable text its own set time; *Hebrew* its own set time there.   *b what we have . . .* do; *or our work, because we are going to have to do it anyway.*

be grateful for what he has done. It is useless. It is like chasing the wind.

Don't Make Rash Promises

5 Be careful about going to the Temple. It is better to go there to learn than to offer sacrifices like foolish people who don't know right from wrong. ²Think before you speak, and don't make any rash promises to God. He is in heaven and you are on earth, so don't say any more than you have to. ³The more you worry, the more likely you are to have bad dreams, and the more you talk, the more likely you are to say something foolish. ⁴So when you make a promise to God, keep it as quickly as possible. He has no use for a fool. Do what you promise to do. ⁵Better not to promise at all than to make a promise and not keep it. ⁶Don't let your own words lead you into sin, so that you have to tell God's priest that you didn't mean it. Why make God angry with you? Why let him destroy what you have worked for? ⁷No matter how much you dream, how much useless work you do, or how much you talk, you must still stand in awe of God.

Life Is Useless

⁸Don't be surprised when you see that the government oppresses the poor and denies them justice and their rights. Every official is protected by someone higher, and both are protected by still higher officials. ⁹Even a king depends on the harvest.ᶜ

¹⁰If you love money, you will never be satisfied; if you long to be rich, you will never get all you want. It is useless. ¹¹The richer you are, the more mouths you have to feed. All you gain is the knowledge that you are rich. ¹²Workers may or may not have enough to eat, but

Workers . . . at least they can get a good night's sleep. (5.12)

at least they can get a good night's sleep. The rich, however, have so much that they stay awake worrying.

¹³Here is a terrible thing that I have seen in this world: people save up their money for a time when they may need it,ᵈ ¹⁴and then lose it all in some bad deal and end up with nothing left to pass on to their children. ¹⁵We leave this world just as we entered it — with nothing. In spite of all our work there is nothing we can take with us. ¹⁶It isn't right! We go just as we came. We labor,

The rich . . . stay awake worrying. (5.12)

trying to catch the wind, and what do we get? ¹⁷We get to live our lives in darkness and grief,ᵉ worried, angry, and sick.

¹⁸Here is what I have found out: the best thing we can do is eat and drink and enjoy what we have worked for during the short life that God has given

---

ᶜ *Verse 9 in Hebrew is unclear.*   ᵈ *for . . . it; or to their own hurt.*   ᵉ *Some ancient translations* in darkness and grief; *Hebrew* eating in darkness.

5.4 Ps 66.13, 14   **5.15** Job 1.21; Ps 49.17; 1 Ti 6.7

. . . to have stupid people
sing your praises. (7.5)

. . . take a bribe. (7.7)

us; this is our fate. ¹⁹If God gives us wealth and property and lets us enjoy them, we should be grateful and enjoy what we have worked for. It is a gift from God. ²⁰Since God has allowed us to be happy, we will not worry too much about how short life is.

6 I have noticed that in this world a serious injustice is done. ²God will give us wealth, honor, and property, yes, everything we want, but then will not let us enjoy it. Some stranger will enjoy it instead. It is useless, and it just isn't right. ³We may have a hundred children and live a long time, but no matter how long we live, if we do not get our share of happiness and do not receive a decent burial, then I say that a baby born dead is better off. ⁴It does that baby no good to be born; it disappears into darkness, where it is forgotten. ⁵It never sees the light of day or knows what life is like, but at least it has found rest — ⁶more so than the man who never enjoys life, though he may live two thousand years. After all, both of them are going to the same place.

⁷We do all our work just to get something to eat, but we never have enough. ⁸How are the wise better off than fools? What good does it do the poor to know how to face life? ⁹It is useless; it is like chasing the wind. It is better to be satisfied with what you have than to be always wanting something else.

¹⁰Everything that happens was already determined long ago, and we all know that you*f* cannot argue with someone who is stronger than you. ¹¹The longer you argue, the more useless it is, and you are no better off. ¹²How can anyone know what is best for us in this short, useless life of ours — a life that passes like a shadow? How can we know what will happen in the world after we die?

Thoughts about Life

7 A good reputation is better than expensive perfume; and the day you die is better than the day you are born.

²It is better to go to a home where there is mourning than to one where there is a party, because the living should always remind themselves that death is waiting for us all.

³Sorrow is better than laughter; it may sadden your face, but it sharpens your understanding.

⁴Someone who is always thinking about happiness is a fool. A wise person thinks about death.

⁵It is better to have wise people

f and we . . . you; *or* and our nature is already known; you.
7.1 Pr 22.1

reprimand you than to have stupid people sing your praises.

⁶When a fool laughs, it is like thorns crackling in a fire. It doesn't mean a thing.

⁷You may be wise, but if you cheat someone, you are acting like a fool. If you take a bribe, you ruin your character.

⁸The end of something is better than its beginning.

Patience is better than pride.

⁹Keep your temper under control; it is foolish to harbor a grudge.

¹⁰Never ask, "Oh, why were things so much better in the old days?" It's not an intelligent question.

¹¹Everyone who lives ought to be wise; it is as good as receiving an inheritance ¹²and will give you as much security as money can. Wisdom keeps you safe — this is the advantage of knowledge.

¹³Think about what God has done. How can anyone straighten out what God has made crooked? ¹⁴When things are going well for you, be glad, and when trouble comes, just remember: God sends both happiness and trouble; you never know what is going to happen next.ᵍ

¹⁵My life has been useless, but in it I have seen everything. Some good people may die while others live on, even though they are evil. ¹⁶So don't be too good or too wise — why kill yourself? ¹⁷But don't be too wicked or too foolish, either — why die before you have to? ¹⁸Avoid both extremes. If you have reverence for God, you will be successful anyway.

¹⁹Wisdom does more for a person than ten rulers can do for a city.

²⁰There is no one on earth who does what is right all the time and never makes a mistake.

None of us knows. (8.7)

²¹Don't pay attention to everything people say — you may hear your servant insulting you, ²²and you know yourself that you have insulted other people many times.

²³I used my wisdom to test all of this. I was determined to be wise, but it was beyond me. ²⁴How can anyone discover what life means? It is too deep for us, too hard to understand. ²⁵But I devoted myself to knowledge and study; I was determined to find wisdom and the answers to my questions, and to learn how wicked and foolish stupidity is.

²⁶I found something more bitter than death — the woman who is like a trap. The love she offers you will catch you like a net, and her arms around you will hold you like a chain. A man who pleases God can get away, but she will catch the sinner. ²⁷Yes, said the Philosopher, I found this out little by little while I was looking for answers. ²⁸I have looked for other answers but have found none. I found one man in a thousand that I could respect, but not one woman. ²⁹This is all that I have learned: God made us plain and simple, but we have made ourselves very complicated.

ᵍ you . . . next; *or* you cannot find fault with him.
7.9 Jas 1.19

8 Only the wise know what things really mean. Wisdom makes them smile and makes their frowns disappear.

Obey the King

² Do what the king says,[h] and don't make any rash promises to God. ³ The king can do anything he likes, so depart from his presence; don't stay in such a dangerous place. ⁴ The king acts with authority, and no one can challenge what he does. ⁵ As long as you obey his commands, you are safe, and a wise person knows how and when to do it. ⁶ There is a right time and a right way to do everything, but we know so little! ⁷ None of us knows what is going to happen, and there is no one to tell us. ⁸ No one can keep from dying or put off the day of death. That is a battle we cannot escape; we cannot cheat our way out.

The Wicked and the Righteous

⁹ I saw all this when I thought about the things that are done in this world, a world where some people have power and others have to suffer under them. ¹⁰ Yes, I have seen the wicked buried and in their graves, but on the way back from the cemetery people praise them in the very city where they did their evil.[i] It is useless. ¹¹ Why do people commit crimes so readily? Because crime is not punished quickly enough. ¹² A sinner may commit a hundred crimes and still live. Oh yes, I know what they say: "If you obey God, everything will be all right, ¹³ but it will not go well for the wicked. Their life is like a shadow and they will die young, because they do not obey God." ¹⁴ But this is nonsense. Look at what happens in the world: sometimes the righteous get the punishment of the wicked, and the wicked get the reward of the righteous. I say it is useless.

¹⁵ So I am convinced that we should enjoy ourselves, because the only pleasure we have in this life is eating and drinking and enjoying ourselves. We can at least do this as we labor during the life that God has given us in this world.

¹⁶ Whenever I tried to become wise and learn what goes on in the world, I realized that you could stay awake night and day ¹⁷ and never be able to understand what God is doing. However hard you try, you will never find out. The wise may claim to know, but they don't.

The wise may claim to know . . . (8.17)

9 I thought long and hard about all this and saw that God controls the actions of wise and righteous people, even their love and their hate. No one knows anything about what lies ahead. ² It makes no difference.[j] The same fate comes to the righteous and the wicked, to the good and the bad,[k] to those who are religious and those who are not, to those who offer sacrifices and those who do not. A good person is no better off than a sinner; one who takes an oath is no better off than one who does not. ³ One fate comes to all alike, and this is as wrong as anything

---

[h] *Some ancient translations* Do what the king says; *Hebrew unclear.*

[i] *Verse 10 in Hebrew is unclear.*   [j] hate. No one . . . difference; *or* hate, but no one knows whether it is out of love or hate. ²It makes no difference what lies ahead of us.

[k] *Some ancient translations* and the bad; *Hebrew does not have these words.*

that happens in this world. As long as people live, their minds are full of evil and madness, and suddenly they die. ⁴But anyone who is alive in the world of the living has some hope; a live dog is better off than a dead lion. ⁵Yes, the living know they are going to die, but the dead know nothing. They have no further reward; they are completely forgotten. ⁶Their loves, their hates, their passions, all died with them. They will never again take part in anything that happens in this world.

⁷Go ahead — eat your food and be happy; drink your wine and be cheerful. It's all right with God. ⁸Always look happy and cheerful. ⁹Enjoy life with the one you love, as long as you live the useless life that God has given you in this world. Enjoy every useless day of it, because that is all you will get for all your trouble. ¹⁰Work hard at whatever you do, because there will be no action, no thought, no knowledge, no wisdom in the world of the dead — and that is where you are going.

¹¹I realized another thing, that in this world fast runners do not always win the races, and the brave do not always win the battles. The wise do not always earn a living, intelligent people do not always get rich, and capable people do not always rise to high positions. Bad luck happens to everyone. ¹²You never know when your time is coming. Like birds suddenly caught in a trap, like fish caught in a net, we are trapped at some evil moment when we least expect it.

Thoughts on Wisdom and Foolishness

¹³There is something else I saw, a good example of how wisdom is regarded in this world. ¹⁴There was a little town without many people in it. A powerful king attacked it. He surrounded it and prepared to break through the walls. ¹⁵Someone lived there who was poor, but so clever that he could have saved the town. But no one thought about him.^l ¹⁶I have always said that wisdom is better than strength, but no one thinks of the poor as wise or pays any attention to what they say. ¹⁷It is better to listen to the quiet words of someone wise than to the shouts of a ruler at a council of fools. ¹⁸Wisdom does more good than weapons, but one sinner can undo a lot of good.

10 Dead flies can make a whole bottle of perfume stink, and a little stupidity can cancel out the greatest wisdom.

²It is natural for the wise to do the right thing and for fools to do the wrong thing. ³Their stupidity will be evident even to strangers they meet along the way; they let everyone know that they are fools.

⁴If your ruler becomes angry with you, do not hand in your resignation; serious wrongs may be pardoned if you keep calm.^m

⁵Here is an injustice I have seen in the world — an injustice caused by rulers. ⁶Stupid people are given positions of authority while the rich are ignored. ⁷I have seen slaves on horseback while noblemen go on foot like slaves.

It is better to listen to the quiet words of someone wise . . . (9.17)

^l he could have . . . him; *or* he saved the town. But later on no one remembered him.
^m keep calm; *or* submit to him.

⁸If you dig a pit, you fall in it; if you break through a wall, a snake bites you. ⁹If you work in a stone quarry, you get hurt by stones. If you split wood, you get hurt doing it. ¹⁰If your ax is dull and you don't sharpen it, you have to work harder to use it. It is smarter to plan ahead. ¹¹Knowing how to charm a

I have seen slaves on horseback. (10.7)

snake is of no use if you let the snake bite first. ¹²What the wise say brings them honor, but fools are destroyed by their own words. ¹³They start out with silly talk and end up with pure madness. ¹⁴A fool talks on and on.

No one knows what is going to happen next, and no one can tell us what will happen after we die.

¹⁵Only someone too stupid to find his way home would wear himself out with work.

¹⁶A country is in trouble when its king is a youth and its leaders feast all night long. ¹⁷But a country is fortunate to have a king who makes his own decisions and leaders who eat at the proper time, who control themselves and don't get drunk.

¹⁸When you are too lazy to repair your roof, it will leak, and the house will fall in.

¹⁹Feasting makes you happy and wine cheers you up, but you can't have either without money.

²⁰Don't criticize the king, even silently, and don't criticize the rich, even in the privacy of your bedroom. A bird might carry the message and tell them what you said.

What a Wise Person Does

11 Invest your money in foreign trade, and one of these days you will make a profit. ²Put your investments in several places — many places even — because you never know what kind of bad luck you are going to have in this world.

³No matter which direction a tree falls, it will lie where it fell. When the clouds are full, it rains. ⁴If you wait until the wind and the weather are just right, you will never plant anything and never harvest anything. ⁵God made everything, and you can no more understand what he does than you understand how new life begins in the

When you are too lazy to repair your roof . . . (10.18)

womb of a pregnant woman. ⁶Do your planting in the morning and in the evening, too. You never know whether it will all grow well or whether one planting will do better than the other.

⁷It is good to be able to enjoy the pleasant light of day. ⁸Be grateful for every year you live. No matter how long you live, remember that you will be

10.8 Ps 7.15; Pr 26.27; Si 27.26, 27

dead much longer. There is nothing at all to look forward to.

Advice to Young People

9 Young people, enjoy your youth. Be happy while you are still young. Do what you want to do, and follow your heart's desire. But remember that God is going to judge you for whatever you do.

10 Don't let anything worry you or cause you pain. You aren't going to be young very long.

12 So remember your Creator[n] while you are still young, before those dismal days and years come when you will say, "I don't enjoy life." 2 That is when the light of the sun, the moon, and the stars will grow dim for you, and the rain clouds will never pass away. 3 Then your arms, that have protected you, will tremble, and your legs, now strong, will grow weak. Your teeth will be too few to chew your food, and your eyes too dim to see clearly. 4 Your ears will be deaf to the noise of the street. You will barely be able to hear the mill as it grinds or music as it plays, but even the song of a bird will wake you from sleep. 5 You will be afraid of high places, and walking will be dangerous. Your hair will turn white; you will hardly be able to drag yourself along, and all desire will be gone.

We are going to our final resting place, and then there will be mourning in the streets. 6 The silver chain will snap, and the golden lamp will fall and break; the rope at the well will break, and the water jar will be shattered. 7 Our bodies will return to the dust of the earth, and the breath of life will go back to God, who gave it to us.

8 Useless, useless, said the Philosopher. It is all useless.

The Summing Up

9 But because the Philosopher was wise, he kept on teaching the people what he knew. He studied proverbs and honestly tested their truth. 10 The Philosopher tried to find comforting words, but the words he wrote were honest. 11 The sayings of the wise are like the sharp sticks that shepherds use to guide sheep, and collected proverbs are as lasting as firmly driven nails. They have been given by God, the one Shepherd of us all.

12 My child, there is something else to watch out for. There is no end to the writing of books, and too much study will wear you out.

13 After all this, there is only one thing to say: Have reverence for God, and obey his commands, because this is all that we were created for. 14 God is going to judge everything we do, whether good or bad, even things done in secret.

---

[n] *The Hebrew expression for* your Creator *sounds like the Hebrew for* your grave.

SONG OF SONGS

INTRODUCTION

The *Song of Songs* is a series of love poems, for the most part in the form of songs addressed by a man to a woman, and by the woman to the man. In some translations, the book is called *The Song of Solomon,* because it is attributed to Solomon in the Hebrew title.

These songs have often been interpreted by Jews as a picture of the relationship between God and his people, and by Christians as a picture of the relationship between Christ and the Church.

OUTLINE OF CONTENTS

1 The most beautiful of songs, by Solomon.*a*

The First Song

The Woman

² Your lips cover me with kisses;
  your love is better than wine.
³ There is a fragrance about you;
  the sound of your name
    recalls it.
  No woman could keep from
    loving you.
⁴ Take me with you, and we'll run
    away;
  be my king and take me to
    your room.
  We will be happy together,
    drink deep, and lose ourselves
      in love.
  No wonder all women
    love you!

⁵ Women of Jerusalem, I am dark
    but*b* beautiful,
  dark as the desert tents of
    Kedar,
  but beautiful as the draperies
    in Solomon's palace.
⁶ Don't look down on me because
    of my color,
  because the sun has
    tanned me.
  My brothers were angry with me
    and made me work in the
      vineyard.
  I had no time to care for
    myself.
⁷ Tell me, my love,
  Where will you lead your flock
    to graze?
  Where will they rest from the
    noonday sun?
  Why should I need to look
    for you

---

a by Solomon; *or* dedicated to Solomon, *or* about Solomon.   *b* but; *or* and.
1.1 1 K 4.32

among the flocks of the other
shepherds?[c]

The Man

8 Don't you know the place,
    loveliest of women?
Go and follow the flock;
    find pasture for your goats
    near the tents of the
      shepherds.

Loveliest of women (1.8)

9 You, my love, excite men
    as a mare excites the stallions
      of Pharaoh's chariots.
10 Your hair is beautiful upon your
      cheeks
    and falls along your neck like
      jewels.
11 But we will make for you a chain
      of gold
    with ornaments of silver.

The Woman

12 My king was lying on his couch,
    and my perfume filled the air
      with fragrance.
13 My lover has the scent of myrrh
    as he lies upon my breasts.
14 My lover is like the wild flowers
    that bloom in the vineyards at
      Engedi.

The Man

15 How beautiful you are, my love;
    how your eyes shine with
      love!

The Woman

16 How handsome you are, my
      dearest;
    how you delight me!
The green grass will be our bed;
17   the cedars will be the beams
      of our house,
    and the cypress trees the
      ceiling.

2 I am only a wild flower in
      Sharon,
    a lily in a mountain valley.

The Man

2 Like a lily among thorns
    is my darling among women.

"How beautiful you are!" (1.15)

The Woman

3 Like an apple tree among the
      trees of the forest,
    so is my dearest compared to
      other men.
I love to sit in its shadow,
    and its fruit is sweet to my
      taste.
4 He brought me to his banquet
      hall

[c] *Probable text* Why should I . . . shepherds; *Hebrew unclear.*

and raised the banner of love
over me.
⁵ Restore my strength with raisins
and refresh me with apples!
I am weak from passion.
⁶ His left hand is under my head,
and his right hand
caresses me.
⁷ Promise me, women of
Jerusalem;
swear by the swift deer and
the gazelles
that you will not interrupt our
love.

The Second Song

The Woman
⁸ I hear my lover's voice.
He comes running over the
mountains,
racing across the hills to me.
⁹ My lover is like a gazelle,
like a young stag.
There he stands beside the wall.
He looks in through the window
and glances through the
lattice.
¹⁰ My lover speaks to me.

The Man
Come then, my love;
my darling, come with me.
¹¹ The winter is over; the rains
have stopped;
¹² in the countryside the flowers
are in bloom.
This is the time for singing;
the song of doves is heard in
the fields.
¹³ Figs are beginning to ripen;
the air is fragrant with
blossoming vines.
Come then, my love;
my darling, come with me.
¹⁴ You are like a dove that hides
in the crevice of a rock.
Let me see your lovely face

and hear your enchanting
voice.

¹⁵ Catch the foxes, the little foxes,
before they ruin our vineyard
in bloom.

The Woman
¹⁶ My lover is mine, and I am his.
He feeds his flock among the
lilies
¹⁷   until the morning breezes
blow
and the darkness disappears.
Return, my darling, like a
gazelle,
like a stag on the mountains
of Bether.ᵈ

3 Asleep on my bed, night after
night
I dreamed of the one I love;
I was looking for him, but
couldn't find him.
² I went wandering through
the city,
through its streets and alleys.
I looked for the one I love.
I looked, but couldn't
find him.
³ The sentries patrolling the city
saw me.
I asked them, "Have you
found my lover?"
⁴ As soon as I left them, I
found him.
I held him and wouldn't let
him go
until I took him to my
mother's house,
to the room where I was born.

⁵ Promise me, women of
Jerusalem;
swear by the swift deer and
the gazelles
that you will not interrupt
our love.

ᵈ mountains of Bether; *or* rugged mountains.

The Third Song

The Woman

6 What is this coming from the
  desert like a column
  of smoke,
    fragrant with incense and
    myrrh,
    the incense sold by the
    traders?
7 Solomon is coming, carried on
  his throne;
    sixty soldiers form the
    bodyguard,
    the finest soldiers in Israel.
8 All of them are skillful with the
  sword;
    they are battle-hardened
    veterans.
  Each of them is armed with a
  sword,
    on guard against a night
    attack.
9 King Solomon is carried on a
  throne
  made of the finest wood.
10 Its posts are covered with silver;
  over it is cloth embroidered
    with gold.
  Its cushions are covered with
    purple cloth,
    lovingly woven by the women
    of Jerusalem.
11 Women of Zion, come and see
  King Solomon.
  He is wearing the crown that his
    mother placed on his head
    on his wedding day,
    on the day of his gladness
    and joy.

The Man

4 How beautiful you are, my love!
  How your eyes shine with love
    behind your veil.
  Your hair dances like a flock of
    goats
    bounding down the hills of
    Gilead.

2 Your teeth are as white as sheep
  that have just been shorn and
  washed.
  Not one of them is missing;
    they are all perfectly matched.
3 Your lips are like a scarlet
  ribbon;
    how lovely they are when you
    speak.
  Your cheeks glow behind your
  veil.
4 Your neck is like the tower of
  David,
    round and smooth,*e*
    with a necklace like a
    thousand shields hung
    around it.
5 Your breasts are like gazelles,
    twin deer feeding among
    lilies.
6 I will stay on the hill of myrrh,
    the hill of incense,
    until the morning breezes
    blow
    and the darkness disappears.
7 How beautiful you are, my love;
    how perfect you are!

8 Come with me from the Lebanon
    Mountains, my bride;
    come with me from Lebanon.
  Come down from the top of
    Mount Amana,
    from Mount Senir and Mount
    Hermon,
    where the lions and leopards
    live.
9 The look in your eyes, my
    sweetheart and bride,
    and the necklace you are
    wearing
    have stolen my heart.
10 Your love delights me,
    my sweetheart and bride.
  Your love is better than wine;
    your perfume more fragrant
    than any spice.

---

e round and smooth; *Hebrew unclear.*

11 The taste of honey is on your
   lips, my darling;
  your tongue is milk and honey
   for me.
Your clothing has all the
   fragrance of Lebanon.

12 My sweetheart, my bride, is a
   secret garden,
  a walled garden, a private
   spring;
13 there the plants flourish.
They grow like an orchard of
   pomegranate trees
  and bear the finest fruits.
There is no lack of henna and
   nard,
14 of saffron, calamus, and
   cinnamon,
  or incense of every kind.
Myrrh and aloes grow there
  with all the most fragrant
   perfumes.
15 Fountains water the garden,
  streams of flowing water,
  brooks gushing down from
   the Lebanon Mountains.

The Woman
16 Wake up, North Wind.
South Wind, blow on my garden;
  fill the air with fragrance.
Let my lover come to his garden
  and eat the best of its fruits.

The Man

5 I have entered my garden,
  my sweetheart, my bride.
I am gathering my spices and
  myrrh;
  I am eating my honey and
   honeycomb;
  I am drinking my wine and
   milk.

The Women
Eat, lovers, and drink
  until you are drunk with love!

The Fourth Song

The Woman
2 While I slept, my heart was
  awake.
I dreamed my lover knocked at
  the door.

The Man
Let me come in, my darling,
  my sweetheart, my dove.
My head is wet with dew,
  and my hair is damp from the
   mist.

The Woman
3 I have already undressed;
  why should I get dressed
   again?
I have washed my feet;
  why should I get them dirty
   again?

4 My lover put his hand to the
  door,
  and I was thrilled that he was
   near.
5 I was ready to let him
   come in.
My hands were covered with
  myrrh,
  my fingers with liquid myrrh,
  as I grasped the handle of the
   door.
6 I opened the door for my lover,
  but he had already gone.
How I wanted to hear his voice!
I looked for him, but couldn't
   find him;
  I called to him, but heard no
   answer.

7 The sentries patrolling the city
  found me;
  they struck me and
   bruised me;
  the guards at the city wall
   tore off my cape.
8 Promise me, women of
  Jerusalem,

that if you find my lover,
  you will tell him I am weak
    from passion.

The Women

9 Most beautiful of women,
  is your lover different from
    everyone else?
  What is there so wonderful
    about him
  that we should give you our
    promise?

The Woman

10 My lover is handsome and
    strong;
  he is one in ten thousand.
11 His face is bronzed and smooth;
  his hair is wavy,
    black as a raven.
12 His eyes are as beautiful as
    doves by a flowing brook,
  doves washed in milk and
    standing by the stream.ᶠ
13 His cheeks are as lovely as a
    garden
  that is full of herbs and
    spices.
  His lips are like lilies,
    wet with liquid myrrh.
14 His hands are well-formed,
  and he wears rings set with
    gems.
  His body is like smooth ivory,ᵍ
    with sapphires set in it.
15 His thighs are columns of
    alabaster
  set in sockets of gold.
  He is majestic, like the Lebanon
    Mountains
  with their towering cedars.
16 His mouth is sweet to kiss;
  everything about him
    enchants me.
  This is what my lover is like,
    women of Jerusalem.

The Women

6 Most beautiful of women,
    where has your lover gone?
  Tell us which way your lover
    went,
  so that we can help you
    find him.

The Woman

2 My lover has gone to his garden,
  where the balsam trees grow.
  He is feeding his flock in the
    garden
  and gathering lilies.
3 My lover is mine, and I am his;
  he feeds his flock among the
    lilies.

The Fifth Song

The Man

4 My love, you are as beautiful as
    Jerusalem,
  as lovely as the city of Tirzah,
  as breathtaking as these great
    cities.ʰ
5 Turn your eyes away from me;
  they are holding me captive.
  Your hair dances like a flock of
    goats
  bounding down the hills of
    Gilead.
6 Your teeth are as white as a
    flock of sheep
  that have just been washed.
  Not one of them is missing;
  they are all perfectly matched.
7 Your cheeks glow behind your
    veil.
8 Let the king have sixty queens,
    eighty concubines,
  young women without
    number!
9 But I love only one,
  and she is as lovely as a dove.
  She is her mother's only
    daughter,
  her mother's favorite child.

ᶠ and standing by the stream; *Hebrew unclear.*
ʰ as breathtaking as . . . cities; *Hebrew unclear.*

ᵍ like smooth ivory; *Hebrew unclear.*

All women look at her and
    praise her;
    queens and concubines sing
      her praises.

10 Who is this whose glance is like
    the dawn?
She is beautiful and bright,
    as dazzling as the sun or the
    moon. *i*
11 I have come down among the
    almond trees
    to see the young plants in the
      valley,
    to see the new leaves on the
      vines
    and the blossoms on the
      pomegranate trees.
12 I am trembling; you have made
    me as eager for love
    as a chariot driver is for
      battle. *j*

The Women
13 Dance, dance, *k* girl of Shulam.
    Let us watch you as you dance.

The Woman
    Why do you want to watch me
    as I dance between the rows
      of onlookers?

The Man

7 What a magnificent young
    woman you are!
    How beautiful are your feet in
      sandals.
The curve of your thighs
    is like the work of an artist.
2 A bowl is there,
    that never runs out of spiced
      wine.
A sheaf of wheat is there,
    surrounded by lilies.
3 Your breasts are like twin deer,
    like two gazelles.
4 Your neck is like a tower of
    ivory.

Let us watch you as you dance. (6.13)

Your eyes are like the pools in
    the city of Heshbon,
    near the gate of that great
      city.
Your nose is as lovely as the
    tower of Lebanon
    that stands guard at
      Damascus.
5 Your head is held high like
    Mount Carmel.
Your braided hair shines like the
    finest satin;
    its beauty *l* could hold a king
      captive.

6 How pretty you are, how
    beautiful;
    how complete the delights of
      your love.
7 You are as graceful as a palm
    tree,
    and your breasts are clusters
      of dates.
8 I will climb the palm tree
    and pick its fruit.
To me your breasts are like
    bunches of grapes,

---

as dazzling as . . . moon; *Hebrew unclear.*
Dance, dance; *or* Come back, come back.

j Verse 12 in Hebrew is unclear.
l beauty; *Hebrew unclear.*

your breath like the fragrance
of apples,
9   and your mouth like the finest
wine.

The Woman
Then let the wine flow straight
to my lover,
flowing over his lips and
teeth.*m*
10 I belong to my lover, and he
desires me.
11 Come, darling, let's go out to the
countryside
and spend the night in the
villages.*n*
12 We will get up early and look at
the vines
to see whether they've started
to grow,
whether the blossoms are
opening
and the pomegranate trees are
in bloom.
There I will give you my love.
13 You can smell the scent of
mandrakes,
and all the pleasant fruits are
near our door.
Darling, I have kept for you
the old delights and the new.

8 I wish that you were my
brother,
that my mother had nursed
you at her breast.
Then, if I met you in the street,
I could kiss you and no one
would mind.
2 I would take you to my mother's
house,
where you could teach me
love.
I would give you spiced wine,
my pomegranate wine to
drink.

3 Your left hand is under my head,

and your right hand
caresses me.

4 Promise me, women of
Jerusalem,
that you will not interrupt our
love.

The Sixth Song

The Women
5 Who is this coming from the
desert,
arm in arm with her lover?

The Woman
Under the apple tree I woke you,
in the place where you were
born.
6 Close your heart to every love
but mine;
hold no one in your arms
but me.
Love is as powerful as death;
passion is as strong as death
itself.
It bursts into flame
and burns like a raging fire.
7 Water cannot put it out;
no flood can drown it.
But if any tried to buy love with
their wealth,
contempt is all they
would get.

The Woman's Brothers
8 We have a young sister,
and her breasts are still small.
What will we do for her
when a young man comes
courting?
9 If she is a wall,
we will build her a silver
tower.
But if she is a gate,
we will protect her with
panels of cedar.

---

m Some ancient translations lips and teeth; *Hebrew* lips of those who sleep.
n villages; *or* fields.

The Woman
10 I am a wall,
  and my breasts are its towers.
  My lover knows that with him
   I find contentment and peace.

The Man
11 Solomon has a vineyard
   in a place called Baal Hamon.
  There are farmers who rent it
   from him;
  each one pays a thousand
   silver coins.
12 Solomon is welcome to his
   thousand coins,

and the farmers to two
 hundred as their share;
I have a vineyard of my own!

13 Let me hear your voice from the
  garden, my love;
 my companions are waiting to
  hear you speak.

The Woman
14 Come to me, my lover, like a
  gazelle,
 like a young stag on the
  mountains where spices
  grow.

The Book of
ISAIAH

INTRODUCTION

The Book of Isaiah is named for a great prophet who lived in Jerusalem in the latter half of the eighth century B.C. This book may be divided into three principal parts:

1) *Chapters 1–39* come from a time when Judah, the southern kingdom, was threatened by a powerful neighbor, Assyria. Isaiah saw that the real threat to the life of Judah was not simply the might of Assyria, but the nation's own sin and disobedience toward God, and their lack of trust in him. In vivid words and actions the prophet called the people and their leaders to a life of righteousness and justice, and warned that failure to listen to God would bring doom and destruction. Isaiah also foretold a time of world-wide peace and the coming of a descendant of David who would be the ideal king.

2) *Chapters 40–55* speak to a time when many of the people of Judah were in exile in Babylon, crushed and without hope. The prophet proclaimed that God would set his people free and take them home to Jerusalem to begin a new life. A notable theme of these chapters is that God is the Lord of history, and his plan for his people includes their mission to all nations, who will be blessed through Israel. The passages about "the Servant of the Lord" are among the best known of the Old Testament.

3) *Chapters 56–66* for the most part speak to a time when people were back in Jerusalem and needed reassurance that God was going to fulfill his promises to the nation. Concern is expressed for righteousness and justice, and also for Sabbath observance, sacrifice, and prayer. A notable passage is 61.1-2, words used by Jesus at the beginning of his ministry to express his calling.

OUTLINE OF CONTENTS

1 This book contains the messages about Judah and Jerusalem which God revealed to Isaiah son of Amoz during the time when Uzziah, Jotham, Ahaz, and Hezekiah were kings of Judah.

God Reprimands His People

²The LORD said, "Earth and sky, listen to what I am saying! The children I brought up have rebelled against me. ³Cattle know who owns them, and donkeys know where their master feeds them. But that is more than my people Israel know. They don't understand at all."

⁴You are doomed, you sinful nation, you corrupt and evil people! Your sins drag you down! You have rejected the LORD, the holy God of Israel, and have turned your backs on him. ⁵Why do you keep on rebelling? Do you want to be punished even more? Israel, your head is already covered with wounds, and your heart and mind are sick. ⁶From head to foot there is not a healthy spot on your body. You are covered with bruises and sores and open wounds. Your wounds have not been cleaned or bandaged. No medicine has been put on them.

⁷Your country has been devastated, and your cities have been burned to the ground. While you look on, foreigners take over your land and bring everything to ruin. ⁸Jerusalem alone is left, a city under siege — as defenseless as a guard's hut in a vineyard or a shed in a cucumber field. ⁹If the LORD Almighty had not let some of the people survive, Jerusalem would have been totally destroyed, just as Sodom and Gomorrah were.

¹⁰Jerusalem, your rulers and your people are like those of Sodom and Gomorrah. Listen to what the LORD is saying to you. Pay attention to what our God is teaching you. ¹¹He says, "Do you think I want all these sacrifices you keep offering to me? I have had more than enough of the sheep you burn as sacrifices and of the fat of your fine animals. I am tired of the blood of bulls and

Israel, your head is already covered with wounds. (1.5)

sheep and goats. ¹²Who asked you to bring me all this when you come to worship me? Who asked you to do all this tramping around in my Temple? ¹³It's useless to bring your offerings. I am disgusted with the smell of the incense you burn. I cannot stand your New Moon Festivals, your Sabbaths, and your religious gatherings; they are all corrupted by your sins. ¹⁴I hate your New Moon Festivals and holy days; they are a burden that I am tired of bearing.

¹⁵"When you lift your hands in prayer, I will not look at you. No matter how much you pray, I will not listen, for your hands are covered with blood. ¹⁶Wash yourselves clean. Stop all this evil that I see you doing. Yes, stop doing evil ¹⁷and learn to do right. See that

1.1 a 2 K 15.1-7; 2 Ch 26.1-23; **b** 2 K 15.32-38; 2 Ch 27.1-9; **c** 2 K 16.1-20; 2 Ch 28.1-27; **d** 2 K 18.1—20.21; 2 Ch 29.1—32.33 **1.9** Gn 19.24; Ro 9.29 **1.11-14** Am 5.21, 22

justice is done—help those who are oppressed, give orphans their rights, and defend widows."

¹⁸The LORD says, "Now, let's settle the matter. You are stained red with

When you lift your hands in prayer . . . (1.15)

sin, but I will wash you as clean as snow.ᵃ Although your stains are deep red, you will be as white as wool.ᵇ ¹⁹If you will only obey me, you will eat the good things the land produces. ²⁰But if you defy me, you are doomed to die. I, the LORD, have spoken."

The Sinful City

²¹The city that once was faithful is behaving like a whore! At one time it was filled with righteous people, but now only murderers remain. ²²Jerusalem, you were once like silver, but now you are worthless; you were like good wine, but now you are only water. ²³Your leaders are rebels and friends of thieves; they are always accepting gifts and bribes. They never defend orphans in court or listen when widows present their case.

²⁴So now, listen to what the LORD Almighty, Israel's powerful God, is saying: "I will take revenge on you, my enemies, and you will cause me no more trouble. ²⁵I will take action against you.

I will purify you the way metal is refined, and will remove all your impurity. ²⁶I will give you rulers and advisers like those you had long ago. Then Jerusalem will be called the righteous, faithful city."

²⁷Because the LORD is righteous, he will save Jerusalem and everyone there who repents. ²⁸But he will crush everyone who sins and rebels against him; he will kill everyone who forsakes him.

²⁹You will be sorry that you ever worshiped trees and planted sacred gardens.ᶜ ³⁰You will wither like a dying oak, like a garden that no one waters. ³¹Just as straw is set on fire by a spark, so powerful people will be destroyed by their own evil deeds, and no one will be able to stop the destruction.

Everlasting Peace
(Micah 4.1-3)

2 Here is the message which God gave to Isaiah son of Amoz about Judah and Jerusalem:

²In days to come
　the mountain where the
　　Temple stands
　will be the highest one of all,
　　towering above all the hills.
Many nations will come
　　streaming to it,
³　and their people will say,
"Let us go up the hill of the
　　LORD,ᵈ
　to the Temple of Israel's God.
He will teach us what he wants
　　us to do;
　we will walk in the paths he
　　has chosen.
For the LORD's teaching comes
　　from Jerusalem;
　from Zion he speaks to his
　　people."

ᵃ sin, but . . . snow; *or* sin; do you think I will wash you as clean as snow?
ᵇ Although your . . . wool; *or* Your stains are deep red; do you think you will be as white as wool?　ᶜ SACRED GARDENS: *People believed that dedicating a garden to a fertility god would cause him to bless their crops.*　ᵈ HILL OF THE LORD: *Mount Zion, the hill in Jerusalem which formed part of the area on which the Temple was built.*

To escape from the Lord's anger (2.19,21)

⁴He will settle disputes among
   great nations.
They will hammer their swords
      into plows
   and their spears into pruning
      knives.
Nations will never again go
      to war,
   never prepare for battle again.
⁵Now, descendants of Jacob, let us
walk in the light which the Lord
gives us!

Arrogance Will Be Destroyed

⁶O God, you have forsaken your people, the descendants of Jacob! The land
is full of magic practices from the East
and from Philistia.ᵉ The people follow
foreign customs. ⁷Their land is full of
silver and gold, and there is no end to
their treasures. Their land is full of
horses, and there is no end to their
chariots. ⁸Their land is full of idols, and
they worship objects that they have
made with their own hands.

⁹Everyone will be humiliated and
disgraced. Do not forgive them, Lord!

¹⁰They will hide in caves in the rocky
hills or dig holes in the ground to try to
escape from the Lord's anger and to
hide from his power and glory! ¹¹A day
is coming when human pride will be
ended and human arrogance destroyed. Then the Lord alone will be
exalted. ¹²On that day the Lord
Almighty will humble everyone who is
powerful, everyone who is proud and
conceited. ¹³He will destroy the tall cedars of Lebanon and all the oaks in the
land of Bashan. ¹⁴He will level the high
mountains and hills, ¹⁵every high
tower, and the walls of every fortress.
¹⁶He will sink even the largest and
most beautiful ships. ¹⁷⁻¹⁸Human pride
will be ended, and human arrogance
will be destroyed. Idols will completely
disappear, and the Lord alone will be
exalted on that day.

¹⁹People will hide in caves in the
rocky hills or dig holes in the ground to
try to escape from the Lord's anger and
to hide from his power and glory, when
he comes to shake the earth. ²⁰When
that day comes, they will throw away
the gold and silver idols they have
made, and abandon them to the moles
and the bats. ²¹When the Lord comes
to shake the earth, people will hide in
holes and caves in the rocky hills to try
to escape from his anger and to hide
from his power and glory.

²²Put no more confidence in mortals.
What are they worth?

ᵉ *Probable text* The land . . . Philistia; *Hebrew unclear.*
2.4 Jl 3.10; Mic 4.3   **2.10** Rev 6.15; 2 Th 1.9

Chaos in Jerusalem

3 Now the Lord, the Almighty LORD, is about to take away from Jerusalem and Judah everything and everyone that the people depend on. He is going to take away their food and their water, ²their heroes and their soldiers, their judges and their prophets, their fortunetellers and their statesmen, ³their military and civilian leaders, their politicians and everyone who uses magic to control events. ⁴The LORD will let the people be governed by immature boys. ⁵Everyone will take advantage of everyone else. Young people will not respect their elders, and worthless people will not respect their superiors.

⁶A time will come when the members of a clan will choose one of their number and say to him, "You at least have something to wear, so be our leader in this time of trouble."

⁷But he will answer, "Not me! I can't help you. I don't have any food or clothes either. Don't make me your leader!"

⁸Yes, Jerusalem is doomed! Judah is collapsing! Everything they say and do is against the LORD; they openly insult God himself. ⁹Their prejudices will be held against them. They sin as openly as the people of Sodom did. They are doomed, and they have brought it on themselves.

¹⁰The righteous will be happy,ᶠ and things will go well for them. They will get to enjoy what they have worked for. ¹¹But evil people are doomed; what they have done to others will now be done to them.

¹²Moneylenders oppress my people, and their creditors cheat them.

My people, your leaders are misleading you, so that you do not know which way to turn.

The LORD Judges His People

¹³The LORD is ready to state his case; he is ready to judge his people.ᵍ ¹⁴The LORD is bringing the elders and leaders of his people to judgment. He makes this accusation: "You have plundered vineyards, and your houses are full of what you have taken from the poor. ¹⁵You have no right to crush my people and take advantage of the poor. I, the Sovereign LORD Almighty, have spoken."

A Warning to the Women of Jerusalem

¹⁶The LORD said, "Look how proud the women of Jerusalem are! They walk along with their noses in the air. They

With their noses in the air. (3.16)
Dressed in rags (3.24)

are always flirting. They take dainty little steps, and the bracelets on their ankles jingle. ¹⁷But I will punish them — I will shave their heads and leave them bald."

¹⁸A day is coming when the Lord will

ᶠ *Probable text* The righteous will be happy; *Hebrew* Say to the righteous.   ᵍ *Some ancient translations* his people; *Hebrew* the peoples.

take away from the women of Jerusalem everything they are so proud of — the ornaments they wear on their ankles, on their heads, on their necks, ¹⁹ and on their wrists. He will take away their veils ²⁰ and their hats; the magic charms they wear on their arms and at their waists; ²¹ the rings they wear on their fingers and in their noses; ²² all their fine robes, gowns, cloaks, and purses; ²³ their revealing garments, their linen handkerchiefs, and the scarves and long veils they wear on their heads.

²⁴ Instead of using perfumes, they will stink; instead of fine belts, they will wear coarse ropes; instead of having beautiful hair, they will be bald; instead of fine clothes, they will be dressed in rags; their beauty will be turned to shame!

²⁵ The men of the city, yes, even the strongest men, will be killed in war. ²⁶ The city gates will mourn and cry, and the city itself will be like a woman sitting on the ground, stripped naked.

4 When that time comes, seven women will grab hold of one man and say, "We can feed and clothe ourselves, but please let us say you are our husband, so that we won't have to endure the shame of being unmarried."

Jerusalem Will Be Restored

² The time is coming when the LORD will make every plant and tree in the land grow large and beautiful. All the people of Israel who survive will take delight and pride in the crops that the land produces. ³ Everyone who is left in Jerusalem, whom God has chosen for survival, will be called holy. ⁴ By his power the Lord will judge and purify the nation and wash away the guilt of Jerusalem and the blood that has been shed there. ⁵ Then over Mount Zion and over all who are gathered there, the LORD will send a cloud in the daytime and smoke and a bright flame at night. God's glory will cover and protect the whole city. ⁶ His glory will shade the city from the heat of the day and make it a place of safety, sheltered from the rain and storm.

The Song of the Vineyard

5 Listen while I sing you this song,
a song of my friend and his vineyard:
My friend had a vineyard
on a very fertile hill.
² He dug the soil and cleared it of stones;
he planted the finest vines.
He built a tower to guard them,
dug a pit for treading the grapes.
He waited for the grapes to ripen,
but every grape was sour.
³ So now my friend says, "You people who live in Jerusalem and Judah, judge between my vineyard and me. ⁴ Is there anything I failed to do for it? Then why did it produce sour grapes and not the good grapes I expected?

⁵ "Here is what I am going to do to my vineyard: I will take away the hedge around it, break down the wall that protects it, and let wild animals eat it and trample it down. ⁶ I will let it be overgrown with weeds. I will not trim the vines or hoe the ground; instead, I will let briers and thorns cover it. I will even forbid the clouds to let rain fall on it."

⁷ Israel is the vineyard of the LORD Almighty;
the people of Judah are the vines he planted.
He expected them to do what was good,

4.5 Ex 13.21; 24.16   **5.1, 2** Mt 21.33; Mk 12.1; Lk 20.9

but instead they committed
murder.
He expected them to do what
was right,
but their victims cried out for
justice.

The Evil That People Do

8 You are doomed! You buy more
houses and fields to add to those you already have. Soon there will be no place
for anyone else to live, and you alone
will live in the land. **9** I have heard the
LORD Almighty say, "All these big, fine
houses will be empty ruins. **10** The
grapevines growing on five acres of
land will yield only five gallons of wine.
Ten bushels of seed will produce only
one bushel of grain."

11 You are doomed! You get up early
in the morning to start drinking, and
you spend long evenings getting drunk.
12 At your feasts you have harps and
tambourines and flutes — and wine.
But you don't understand what the
LORD is doing, **13** and so you will be carried away as prisoners. Your leaders
will starve to death, and the common
people will die of thirst. **14** The world
of the dead is hungry for them, and
it opens its mouth wide. It gulps
down the nobles of Jerusalem along
with the noisy crowd of common
people.

15 Everyone will be disgraced, and all
who are proud will be humbled. **16** But
the LORD Almighty shows his greatness
by doing what is right, and he reveals
his holiness by judging his people.
17 In the ruins of the cities lambs will
eat grass and young goats will find
pasture.[h]

18 You are doomed! You are unable to
break free from your sins. **19** You say,
"Let the LORD hurry up and do what he

*A very fertile hill . . . he dug the soil . . . cleared
it of stones . . . he planted the finest vines . . .
he built a tower . . . dug a pit . . . he waited for
the grapes to ripen, but every grape was sour.
(5.1-2)*

[h] *Verse 17 in Hebrew is unclear.*
5.11 Ws 2.7-9

In the ruins of the cities. (5.17)

says he will, so that we can see it. Let Israel's holy God carry out his plans; let's see what he has in mind."

²⁰ You are doomed! You call evil good and call good evil. You turn darkness into light and light into darkness. You make what is bitter sweet, and what is sweet you make bitter.

²¹ You are doomed! You think you are wise, so very clever.

²² You are doomed! Heroes of the wine bottle! Brave and fearless when it comes to mixing drinks! ²³ But for just a bribe you let the guilty go free, and you keep the innocent from getting justice. ²⁴ So now, just as straw and dry grass shrivel and burn in the fire, your roots will rot and your blossoms will dry up and blow away, because you have rejected what the LORD Almighty, Israel's holy God, has taught us. ²⁵ The LORD is angry with his people and has stretched out his hand to punish them. The mountains will shake, and the bodies of those who die will be left in the streets like rubbish. Yet even then the LORD's anger will not be ended, but his hand will still be stretched out to punish.

²⁶ The LORD gives a signal to call for a distant nation.ⁱ He whistles for them to come from the ends of the earth. And here they come, swiftly, quickly! ²⁷ None of them grow tired; none of them stumble. They never doze or sleep. Not a belt is loose; not a sandal strap is broken. ²⁸ Their arrows are sharp, and their bows are ready to shoot. Their horses' hoofs are as hard as flint, and their chariot wheels turn like a whirlwind. ²⁹ The soldiers roar like lions that have killed an animal and are carrying it off where no one can take it away from them.

³⁰ When that day comes, they will roar over Israel as loudly as the sea. Look at this country! Darkness and distress! The light is swallowed by darkness.

Heroes of the wine bottle! (5.22)

ⁱ *Probable text* a distant nation; *Hebrew* distant nations.

God Calls Isaiah to Be a Prophet

6 In the year that King Uzziah died, I saw the Lord. He was sitting on his throne, high and exalted, and his robe filled the whole Temple. ²Around him flaming creatures were standing, each of which had six wings. Each creature covered its face with two wings, and its body with two, and used the other two for flying. ³They were calling out to each other:

"Holy, holy, holy!
The LORD Almighty is holy!
His glory fills the world."

⁴The sound of their voices made the foundation of the Temple shake, and the Temple itself became filled with smoke.

⁵I said, "There is no hope for me! I am doomed because every word that passes my lips is sinful, and I live among a people whose every word is sinful. And yet, with my own eyes I have seen the King, the LORD Almighty."

⁶Then one of the creatures flew down to me, carrying a burning coal that he had taken from the altar with a pair of tongs. ⁷He touched my lips with the burning coal and said, "This has touched your lips, and now your guilt is gone, and your sins are forgiven."

⁸Then I heard the Lord say, "Whom shall I send? Who will be our messenger?"

I answered, "I will go! Send me!"

⁹So he told me to go and give the people this message: "No matter how much you listen, you will not understand. No matter how much you look, you will not know what is happening." ¹⁰Then he said to me, "Make the minds of these people dull, their ears deaf, and their eyes blind, so that they cannot see or hear or understand. If they did, they might turn to me and be healed."

¹¹I asked, "How long will it be like this, Lord?"

He answered, "Until the cities are ruined and empty — until the houses are uninhabited — until the land itself is a desolate wasteland. ¹²I will send the people far away and make the whole land desolate. ¹³Even if one person out of ten remains in the land, he too will be destroyed; he will be like the stump of an oak tree that has been cut down."

(The stump represents a new beginning for God's people.)

A Message for King Ahaz

7 When King Ahaz, the son of Jotham and grandson of Uzziah, ruled Judah, war broke out. Rezin, king of Syria, and Pekah son of Remaliah, king of Israel, attacked Jerusalem, but were unable to capture it.

²When word reached the king of Judah that the armies of Syria were already in the territory of Israel, he and all his people were so terrified that they trembled like trees shaking in the wind.

³The LORD said to Isaiah, "Take your son Shear Jashub,ʲ and go to meet King Ahaz. You will find him on the road where the cloth makers work, at the end of the ditch that brings water from the upper pool. ⁴Tell him to keep alert, to stay calm, and not to be frightened or disturbed. The anger of King Rezin and his Syrians and of King Pekah is no more dangerous than the smoke from two smoldering sticks of wood. ⁵Syria, together with Israel and its king, has made a plot. ⁶They intend to invade Judah, terrify the people into joining their side, and then put Tabeel's son on the throne.

⁷"But I, the LORD, declare that this will never happen. ⁸Why? Because Syria is no stronger than Damascus, its capital city, and Damascus is no

---

ʲ SHEAR JASHUB: *This name in Hebrew means "A few will come back" (see 10.20-22).*
6.1 2 K 15.7; 2 Ch 26.23   **6.3** Rev 4.8   **6.4** Rev 15.8   **6.9, 10** Mt 13.14, 15; Mk 4.12; Lk 8.10; Jn 12.40; Ac 28.26, 27   **7.1** 2 K 16.5; 2 Ch 28.5, 6

stronger than King Rezin. As for Israel, within sixty-five years it will be too shattered to survive as a nation. ⁹Israel is no stronger than Samaria, its capital city, and Samaria is no stronger than King Pekah.

"If your faith is not enduring, you will not endure."

The Sign of Immanuel

¹⁰The LORD sent another message to Ahaz: ¹¹"Ask the LORD your God to give you a sign. It can be from deep in the world of the dead or from high up in heaven."

¹²Ahaz answered, "I will not ask for a sign. I refuse to put the LORD to the test."

¹³To that Isaiah replied, "Listen, now, descendants of King David. It's bad enough for you to wear out the patience of people — do you have to wear out God's patience too? ¹⁴Well then, the Lord himself will give you a sign: a young woman*k* who is pregnant will have a son and will name him 'Immanuel.'*l* ¹⁵By the time he is old enough to make his own decisions, people will be drinking milk and eating honey.*m* ¹⁶Even before that time comes, the lands of those two kings who terrify you will be deserted.

¹⁷"The LORD is going to bring on you, on your people, and on the whole royal family, days of trouble worse than any that have come since the kingdom of Israel separated from Judah — he is going to bring the king of Assyria.

¹⁸"When that time comes, the LORD will whistle as a signal for the Egyptians to come like flies from the farthest branches of the Nile, and for the Assyrians to come from their land like bees. ¹⁹They will swarm in the rugged valleys and in the caves in the rocks, and they will cover every thorn bush and every pasture.

²⁰"When that time comes, the Lord will hire a barber from across the Euphrates — the emperor of Assyria! — and he will shave off your beards and the hair on your heads and your bodies.

²¹"When that time comes, even if a farmer has been able to save only one young cow and two goats, ²²they will give so much milk that he will have all he needs. Yes, the few survivors left in the land will have milk and honey to eat.

²³"When that time comes, the fine vineyards, each with a thousand vines and each worth a thousand pieces of silver, will be overgrown with thorn bushes and briers. ²⁴People will go hunting there with bows and arrows. Yes, the whole country will be full of briers and thorn bushes. ²⁵All the hills where crops were once planted will be so overgrown with thorns that no one will go there. It will be a place where cattle and sheep graze."

Isaiah's Son as a Sign to the People

8 The LORD said to me, "Take a large piece of writing material and write on it in large letters:*n* 'Quick Loot, Fast Plunder.' ²Get two reliable men, the priest Uriah and Zechariah son of Jeberechiah, to serve as witnesses."

³Some time later my wife became pregnant. When our son was born, the LORD said to me, "Name him 'Quick-Loot-Fast-Plunder.' ⁴Before the boy is

---

k YOUNG WOMAN: *The Hebrew word here translated "young woman" is not the specific term for "virgin," but refers to any young woman of marriageable age. The use of "virgin" in Mt 1.23 reflects a Greek translation of the Old Testament, made some 500 years after Isaiah.*   *l* IMMANUEL: *This name in Hebrew means "God is with us."*

m MILK AND HONEY: *These foods were associated with the earlier days of Israel's history.*   *n* large letters; *or* letters that everyone can read.

7.14 Mt 1.23

old enough to say 'Mamma' and 'Daddy,' all the wealth of Damascus and all the loot of Samaria will be carried off by the king of Assyria."

The Emperor of Assyria Is Coming

5 The LORD spoke to me again. 6 He said, "Because these people have rejected the quiet waters of Shiloah Brook[o] and tremble[p] before King Rezin and King Pekah, 7 I, the Lord, will bring the emperor of Assyria and all his forces to attack Judah. They will advance like the flood waters of the Euphrates River, overflowing all its banks. 8 They will sweep through Judah in a flood, rising shoulder high and covering everything."

God is with us! His outspread wings protect the land.[q]

9 Gather together in fear, you nations! Listen, you distant parts of the earth. Get ready to fight, but be afraid! Yes, get ready, but be afraid! 10 Make your plans! But they will never succeed. Talk all you want to! But it is all useless, because God is with us.

The LORD Warns the Prophet

11 With his great power the LORD warned me not to follow the road which the people were following. He said, 12 "Do not join in the schemes of the people and do not be afraid of the things that they fear. 13 Remember that I, the LORD Almighty, am holy; I am the one you must fear. 14 Because of my awesome holiness I am like a stone that people stumble over; I am like a trap that will catch the people of the kingdoms of Judah and Israel and the people of Jerusalem. 15 Many will stumble; they will fall and be crushed. They will be caught in a trap."

Warning against Consulting the Dead

16 You, my disciples, are to guard and preserve the messages that God has given me. 17 The LORD has hidden himself from his people, but I trust him and place my hope in him.

18 Here I am with the children the LORD has given me. The LORD Almighty, whose throne is on Mount Zion, has sent us as living messages to the people of Israel.

19 But people will tell you to ask for messages from fortunetellers and mediums, who chirp and mutter. They will say, "After all, people should ask for messages from the spirits and consult the dead on behalf of the living."

20 You are to answer them, "Listen to what the LORD is teaching you! Don't listen to mediums — what they tell you cannot keep trouble away."[r]

A Time of Trouble

21 The people will wander through the land, discouraged and hungry. In their hunger and their anger they will curse their king and their God. They may look up to the sky 22 or stare at the ground, but they will see nothing but trouble and darkness, terrifying darkness into which they are being driven.

9 1 There will be no way for them to escape from this time of trouble.

The Future King

The land of the tribes of Zebulun and Naphtali was once disgraced, but the future will bring honor to this region, from the Mediterranean eastward to the land on the other side of the Jordan, and even to Galilee itself, where the foreigners live.

---

[o] SHILOAH BROOK: *A stream which flowed from the large spring on the eastern side of Jerusalem.*   [p] *Probable text* tremble; *Hebrew* rejoice.   [q] everything." God . . . land; *or* everything. They will spread out over the land. God be with us!"   [r] *Verse 20 in Hebrew is unclear.*

8.12, 13 1 P 3.14, 15   **8.14, 15** 1 P 2.8   **8.17** He 2.13   **8.18** He 2.13   **9.1** Mt 4.15

Now light is shining on them. (9.2)

2 The people who walked in
        darkness
    have seen a great light.
  They lived in a land of shadows,
    but now light is shining on
        them.
3 You have given them great joy,[s]
        Lord;
    you have made them happy.
  They rejoice in what you have
        done,
    as people rejoice when they
        harvest grain
    or when they divide captured
        wealth.
4 For you have broken the yoke
        that burdened them
    and the rod that beat their
        shoulders.
  You have defeated the nation
    that oppressed and exploited
        your people,
    just as you defeated the army
        of Midian long ago.
5 The boots of the invading army
    and all their bloodstained
        clothing
    will be destroyed by fire.
6 A child is born to us!
    A son is given to us!
  And he will be our ruler.
  He will be called, "Wonderful[t]
        Counselor,"

"Mighty God," "Eternal
        Father,"
    "Prince of Peace."
7 His royal power will continue
        to grow;
    his kingdom will always be
        at peace.
  He will rule as King David's
        successor,
    basing his power on right and
        justice,
    from now until the end of
        time.
  The LORD Almighty is
    determined to do all this.

The LORD Will Punish Israel

8 The Lord has pronounced judgment on the kingdom of Israel, on the
descendants of Jacob. 9 All the people of
Israel, everyone who lives in the city of
Samaria, will know that he has done
this. Now they are proud and arrogant.
They say, 10 "The brick buildings have
fallen down, but we will replace them
with stone buildings. The beams of sycamore wood have been cut down, but

[s] *Probable text* You have given them great joy; *Hebrew* You have increased the nation.
[t] Wonderful; *or* Wise.
9.2 Mt 4.16; Lk 1.79   **9.7** Lk 1.32, 33

we will replace them with the finest cedar."

¹¹The LORD has stirred up their enemies[u] to attack them. ¹²Syria on the east and Philistia on the west have opened their mouths to devour Israel. Yet even so the LORD's anger is not ended; his hand is still stretched out to punish.

¹³The people of Israel have not repented; even though the LORD Almighty has punished them, they have not returned to him. ¹⁴In a single day the LORD will punish Israel's leaders and its people; he will cut them off, head and tail. ¹⁵The old and honorable men are the head — and the tail is the prophets whose teachings are lies! ¹⁶Those who lead these people have misled them and totally confused them. ¹⁷And so the Lord will not let any of the young men escape, and he will not show pity on any of the widows and orphans, because all the people are godless and wicked and everything they say is evil. Yet even so the LORD's anger will not be ended, but his hand will still be stretched out to punish.

¹⁸The wickedness of the people burns like a fire that destroys thorn bushes and thistles. It burns like a forest fire that sends up columns of

Like a forest fire (9.18)

smoke. ¹⁹Because the LORD Almighty is angry, his punishment burns like a fire throughout the land and destroys the people, and it is each of us for ourselves. ²⁰Everywhere in the country people snatch and eat any bit of food they can find, but their hunger is never satisfied.

They even eat their own children! ²¹The people of Manasseh and the people of Ephraim attack each other, and together they attack Judah. Yet even so the LORD's anger is not ended; his hand is still stretched out to punish.

10 You are doomed! You make unjust laws that oppress my people. ²That is how you keep the poor from having their rights and from getting justice. That is how you take the property that belongs to widows and orphans. ³What will you do when God punishes you? What will you do when he brings disaster on you from a distant country? Where will you run to find help? Where will you hide your wealth? ⁴You will be killed in battle or dragged off as prisoners. Yet even so the LORD's anger will not be ended; his hand will still be stretched out to punish.

The Emperor of Assyria as the Instrument of God

⁵The LORD said, "Assyria! I use Assyria like a club to punish those with whom I am angry. ⁶I sent Assyria to attack a godless nation, people who have made me angry. I sent them to loot and steal and trample the people like dirt in the streets."

⁷But the Assyrian emperor has his own violent plans in mind. He is determined to destroy many nations. ⁸He boasts, "Every one of my commanders is a king! ⁹I conquered the cities of Calno and Carchemish, the cities of Hamath and Arpad. I conquered Samaria and Damascus. ¹⁰I reached out to punish those kingdoms that worship idols, idols more numerous than those of Jerusalem and Samaria. ¹¹I have destroyed Samaria and all its idols, and I will do the same to Jerusalem and the images that are worshiped there."

¹²But the Lord says, "When I finish what I am doing on Mount Zion and in

---

[u] *Probable text* their enemies; *Hebrew* the enemies of Rezin.
10.5-34 Is 14.24-27; Nh 1.1 — 3.19; Zep 2.13-15

Jerusalem, I will punish the emperor of Assyria for all his boasting and all his pride."

¹³The emperor of Assyria boasts, "I have done it all myself. I am strong and wise and clever. I wiped out the boundaries between nations and took the supplies they had stored. Like a bull I have trampled the people who live there. ¹⁴The nations of the world were like a bird's nest, and I gathered their wealth as easily as gathering eggs. Not a wing fluttered to scare me off; no beak opened to scream at me!"

¹⁵But the LORD says, "Can an ax claim to be greater than the one who uses it? Is a saw more important than the one who saws with it? A club doesn't lift up a person; a person lifts up a club."

¹⁶The LORD Almighty is going to send disease to punish those who are now well-fed. In their bodies there will be a fire that burns and burns. ¹⁷God, the light of Israel, will become a fire. Israel's holy God will become a flame, which in a single day will burn up everything, even the thorns and thistles. ¹⁸The rich forests and farmlands will be totally destroyed, in the same way that a fatal sickness destroys someone. ¹⁹There will be so few trees left that even a child will be able to count them.

A Few Will Come Back

²⁰A time is coming when the people of Israel who have survived will not rely any more on the nation that almost destroyed them. They will truly put their trust in the LORD, Israel's holy God. ²¹A few of the people of Israel will come back to their mighty God. ²²Even though now there are as many people of Israel as there are grains of sand by the sea, only a few will come back. Destruction is in store for the people, and it is fully deserved. ²³Yes, throughout the whole country the Sovereign LORD Almighty will bring destruction, as he said he would.

The LORD Will Punish Assyria

²⁴The Sovereign LORD Almighty says to his people who live in Zion, "Do not be afraid of the Assyrians, even though they oppress you as the Egyptians used to do. ²⁵In only a little while I will finish punishing you, and then I will destroy them. ²⁶I, the LORD Almighty, will beat them with my whip as I did the people of Midian at Oreb Rock. I will punish Assyria as I punished Egypt. ²⁷When that time comes, I will free you from the power of Assyria, and their yoke will no longer be a burden on your shoulders."ᵛ

The Invader Attacks

²⁸The enemy army has captured the city of Ai!ʷ They have passed through Migron! They left their supplies at Michmash! ²⁹They have crossed the pass and are spending the night at Geba! The people in the town of Ramah are terrified, and the people in King Saul's hometown of Gibeah have run away. ³⁰Shout, people of Gallim! Listen, people of Laishah! Answer, people of Anathoth! ³¹The people of Madmenah and Gebim are running for their lives. ³²Today the enemy are in the town of Nob, and there they are shaking their fists at Mount Zion, at the city of Jerusalem.

³³The LORD Almighty will bring them crashing down like branches cut off a tree. The proudest and highest of them will be cut down and humiliated. ³⁴The LORD will cut them down as trees

---

ᵛ *Hebrew has three additional words, the meaning of which is unclear.*   ʷ AI: *This and the other places mentioned in verses 28-32 were located near Jerusalem, along the way by which an invader would come to attack from the north.*
10.22, 23 Ro 9.27

in the heart of the forest are cut down with an ax, as even the finest trees of Lebanon fall!

The Peaceful Kingdom

11 The royal line of David is like a tree that has been cut down; but just as new branches sprout from a stump, so a new king will arise from among David's descendants.

2 The spirit of the LORD will give
　　him wisdom
　　and the knowledge and skill
　　　to rule his people.
He will know the LORD's will and
　　honor him,
3 　　and find pleasure in
　　obeying him.
He will not judge by appearance
　　or hearsay;
4 　he will judge the poor fairly
　　and defend the rights of the
　　helpless.
At his command the people will
　　be punished,
　　and evil persons will die.
5 He will rule his people with
　　justice and integrity.

6 Wolves and sheep will live
　　together in peace,
　　and leopards will lie down
　　with young goats.
Calves and lion cubs will feed[x]
　　together,
　　and little children will take
　　care of them.
7 Cows and bears will eat together,
　　and their calves and cubs will
　　lie down in peace.
Lions will eat straw as cattle do.

8 Even a baby will not be harmed
　　if it plays near a poisonous
　　snake.
9 On Zion, God's sacred hill,
　　there will be nothing harmful
　　or evil.

And little children will take care of them. (11.6)

The land will be as full of
　　knowledge of the LORD
　　as the seas are full of water.

The Exiled People Will Return

10 A day is coming when the new king from the royal line of David will be a symbol to the nations. They will gather in his royal city and give him honor. 11 When that day comes, the Lord will once again use his power and bring back home those of his people who are left in Assyria and Egypt, in the lands of Pathros, Ethiopia,[y] Elam, Babylonia, and Hamath, and in the coastlands and on the islands of the sea. 12 The Lord will raise a signal flag to show the nations that he is gathering together again the scattered people of Israel and Judah and bringing them back from the four corners of the earth. 13 The kingdom of Israel will not be jealous of Judah any more, and Judah will

---

[x] *Some ancient translations* will feed; *Hebrew* and well-fed cattle.　　[y] *Hebrew* Cush: *Cush is the ancient name of the extensive territory south of the First Cataract of the Nile River. This region was called Ethiopia in Graeco-Roman times, and included within its borders most of modern Sudan and some of present-day Ethiopia (Abyssinia).*

11.1 Rev 5.5; 22.16　　**11.4** 2 Th 2.8　　**11.5** Eph 6.14　　**11.6-9** Is 65.25　　**11.9** Hb 2.14
11.10 Ro 15.12

not be the enemy of Israel. ¹⁴Together they will attack the Philistines on the west and plunder the people who live to the east. They will conquer the people of Edom and Moab, and the people of Ammon will obey them. ¹⁵The LORD will dry up the Gulf of Suez, and he will bring a hot wind to dry up the Euphrates, leaving only seven tiny streams, so that anyone can walk across. ¹⁶There will be a highway out of Assyria for those of his people Israel who have survived there, just as there was for their ancestors when they left Egypt.

Hymn of Thanksgiving

12 A day is coming when people will sing,

"I praise you, LORD! You were
    angry with me,
but now you comfort me and
    are angry no longer.
²God is my savior;
    I will trust him and not be
    afraid.
The LORD gives me power and
    strength;
    he is my savior.
³As fresh water brings joy to the
    thirsty,
    so God's people rejoice when
    he saves them."

⁴A day is coming when people will sing,

"Give thanks to the LORD! Call
    for him to help you!
Tell all the nations what he
    has done!
Tell them how great he is!
⁵Sing to the LORD because of the
    great things he has done.
Let the whole world hear the
    news.
⁶Let everyone who lives in Zion
    shout and sing!
Israel's holy God is great,

and he lives among his
    people."

God Will Punish Babylon

13 This is a message about Babylon, which Isaiah son of Amoz received from God.

²On the top of a barren hill raise the battle flag! Shout to the soldiers and raise your arm as the signal for them to attack the gates of the proud city. ³The LORD has called out his proud and confident soldiers to fight a holy war and punish those he is angry with.

⁴Listen to the noise on the mountains — the sound of a great crowd of people, the sound of nations and kingdoms gathering. The LORD of Armies is preparing his troops for battle. ⁵They are coming from far-off countries at the ends of the earth. In his anger the LORD is coming to devastate the whole country.

⁶Howl in pain! The day of the LORD is near, the day when the Almighty brings destruction. ⁷Everyone's hands will hang limp, and everyone's courage will fail. ⁸They will all be terrified and overcome with pain, like the pain of a woman in labor. They will look at each other in fear, and their faces will burn with shame. ⁹The day of the LORD is coming — that cruel day of his fierce anger and fury. The earth will be made a wilderness, and every sinner will be destroyed. ¹⁰Every star and every constellation will stop shining, the sun will be dark when it rises, and the moon will give no light.

¹¹The LORD says, "I will bring disaster on the earth and punish all wicked people for their sins. I will humble everyone who is proud and punish everyone who is arrogant and cruel. ¹²Those who survive will be scarcer than gold. ¹³I will make the heavens tremble, and the earth will be shaken

---

11.15 Rev 16.12   **12.2** Ex 15.2; Ps 118.14   **13.1—14.23** Is 47.1-15; Jr 50.1—51.64
13.6 Jl 1.15   **13.10** Ez 32.7; Mt 24.29; Mk 13.24, 25; Lk 21.25; Rev 6.12, 13; 8.12

out of its place on that day when I, the LORD Almighty, show my anger.

14 "The foreigners living in Babylon will run away to their homelands, scattering like deer escaping from hunters, like sheep without a shepherd. 15 Anyone who is caught will be stabbed to death. 16 While they look on helplessly, their babies will be battered to death, their houses will be looted, and their wives will be raped."

17 The LORD says, "I am stirring up the Medes[z] to attack Babylon. They care nothing for silver and are not tempted by gold. 18 With their bows and arrows they will kill the young men. They will show no mercy to babies and take no pity on children. 19 Babylonia is the most beautiful kingdom of all; it is the pride of its people. But I, the LORD, will overthrow Babylon as I did Sodom and Gomorrah! 20 No one will ever live there again. No wandering Arab will ever pitch a tent there, and no shepherd will ever pasture a flock there. 21 It will be a place where desert animals live and where owls build their nests. Ostriches will live there, and wild goats will prance through the ruins. 22 The towers and palaces will echo with the cries of hyenas and jackals. Babylon's time has come! Her days are almost over."

The Return from Exile

14 The LORD will once again be merciful to his people Israel and choose them as his own. He will let them live in their own land again, and foreigners will come and live there with them. 2 Many nations will help the people of Israel return to the land which the LORD gave them, and there the nations will serve Israel as slaves. Those who once captured Israel will now be

captured by Israel, and the people of Israel will rule over those who once oppressed them.

The King of Babylon in the World of the Dead

3 The LORD will give the people of Israel relief from their pain and suffering and from the hard work they were forced to do. 4 When he does this, they are to mock the king of Babylon and say:

"The cruel king has fallen! He will never oppress anyone again! 5 The LORD has ended the power of the evil rulers 6 who angrily oppressed the peoples and never stopped persecuting the nations they had conquered. 7 Now at last the whole world enjoys rest and peace, and everyone sings for joy. 8 The cypress trees and the cedars of Lebanon rejoice over the fallen king, because there is no one to cut them down, now that he is gone!

9 "The world of the dead is getting ready to welcome the king of Babylon. The ghosts of those who were powerful on earth are stirring about. The ghosts of kings are rising from their thrones. 10 They all call out to him, 'Now you are as weak as we are! You are one of us! 11 You used to be honored with the music of harps, but now here you are in the world of the dead. You lie on a bed of maggots and are covered with a blanket of worms.' "

12 King of Babylon, bright morning star, you have fallen from heaven! In the past you conquered nations, but now you have been thrown to the ground. 13 You were determined to climb up to heaven and to place your throne above the highest stars. You thought you would sit like a king on that mountain in the north where the

---

[z] MEDES: *People of a nation northeast of Babylonia, which became part of the Persian Empire.*

13.19 Gn 19.24   **13.21** Is 34.14; Zep 2.14; Rev 18.2   **14.12** Rev 8.10; 9.1
14.13-15 Mt 11.23; Lk 10.15

gods assemble. [14] You said you would climb to the tops of the clouds and be like the Almighty. [15] But instead, you have been brought down to the deepest part of the world of the dead.

[16] The dead will stare and gape at you. They will ask, "Is this the man who shook the earth and made kingdoms tremble? [17] Is this the man who destroyed cities and turned the world into a desert? Is this the man who never freed his prisoners or let them go home?"

[18] All the kings of the earth lie in their magnificent tombs, [19] but you have no tomb, and your corpse is thrown out to rot. It is covered by the bodies of soldiers killed in battle, thrown with them into a rocky pit, and trampled down. [20] Because you ruined your country and killed your own people, you will not be buried like other kings. None of your evil family will survive. [21] Let the slaughter begin! The sons of this king will die because of their ancestors' sins. None of them will ever rule the earth or cover it with cities.

God Will Destroy Babylon

[22] The LORD Almighty says, "I will attack Babylon and bring it to ruin. I will leave nothing — no children, no survivors at all. I, the LORD, have spoken. [23] I will turn Babylon into a marsh, and owls will live there. I will sweep Babylon with a broom that will sweep everything away. I, the LORD Almighty, have spoken."

God Will Destroy the Assyrians

[24] The LORD Almighty has sworn an oath: "What I have planned will happen. What I have determined to do will be done. [25] I will destroy the Assyrians in my land of Israel and trample them on my mountains. I will free my people from the Assyrian yoke and from the burdens they have had to bear. [26] This is my plan for the world, and my arm is stretched out to punish the nations." [27] The LORD Almighty is determined to do this; he has stretched out his arm to punish, and no one can stop him.

God Will Destroy the Philistines

[28] This is a message that was proclaimed in the year that King Ahaz died.

[29] People of Philistia, the rod that beat you is broken, but you have no reason to be glad. When one snake dies, a worse one comes in its place. A snake's egg hatches a flying dragon. [30] The LORD will be a shepherd to the poor of his people and will let them live in safety. But he will send a terrible famine on you Philistines, and it will not leave any of you alive.

[31] Howl and cry for help, all you Philistine cities! Be terrified, all of you! A cloud of dust is coming from the north — it is an army with no cowards in its ranks.

[32] How shall we answer the messengers that come to us from Philistia? We will tell them that the LORD has established Zion and that his suffering people will find safety there.

God Will Destroy Moab

15 This is a message about Moab. The cities of Ar and Kir are destroyed in a single night, and silence covers the land of Moab. [2] The people of Dibon[a] climb the hill to weep at the shrine. The people of Moab wail in grief over the cities of Nebo and Medeba; they have shaved their heads and their

---

[a] *Probable text* people of Dibon; *Hebrew* people and Dibon.
14.24-27 Is 10.5-34; Nh 1.1−3.19; Zep 2.13-15   **14.28** 2 K 16.20; 2 Ch 28.27
14.29-31 Jr 47.1-7; Ez 25.15-17; Jl 3.4-8; Am 1.6-8; Zep 2.4-7; Zec 9.5-7
15.1−16.14 Is 25.10-12; Jr 48.1-47; Ez 25.8-11; Am 2.1-3; Zep 2.8-11

beards in grief. ³The people in the streets are dressed in sackcloth; in the city squares and on the rooftops people

The people of Moab wail in grief. (15.2)

mourn and cry. ⁴The people of Heshbon and Elealeh cry out, and their cry can be heard as far away as Jahaz. Even the soldiers tremble; their courage is gone. ⁵My heart cries out for Moab! The people have fled to the town of Zoar, and to Eglath Shelishiyah. Some climb the road to Luhith, weeping as they go; some escape to Horonaim, grieving loudly. ⁶Nimrim Brook is dry, the grass beside it has withered, and nothing green is left. ⁷The people go across the Valley of Willows, trying to escape with all their possessions.

Trying to escape with all their possessions (15.7)

⁸Everywhere at Moab's borders the sound of crying is heard. It is heard at the towns of Eglaim and Beerelim. ⁹At the town of Dibon the river is red with blood, and God has something even worse in store for the people there. Yes,

there will be a bloody slaughter of everyone left in Moab.

Moab's Hopeless Situation

16 From the city of Sela in the desert the people of Moab send a lamb as a present to the one who rules in Jerusalem. ²They wait on the banks of the Arnon River and move aimlessly back and forth, like birds driven from their nest.

³They say to the people of Judah, "Tell us what to do. Protect us like a tree that casts a cool shadow in the heat of noon, and let us rest in your shade. We are refugees; hide us where no one can find us. ⁴Let us stay in your land. Protect us from those who want to destroy us."

(Oppression and destruction will end, and those who are devastating the country will be gone. ⁵Then one of David's descendants will be king, and he will rule the people with faithfulness and love. He will be quick to do what is right, and he will see that justice is done.)

⁶The people of Judah say, "We have heard how proud the people of Moab are. We know that they are arrogant and conceited, but their boasts are empty."

⁷The people of Moab will weep because of the troubles they suffer. They will all weep when they remember the fine food they used to eat in the city of Kir Heres. They will be driven to despair. ⁸The farms near Heshbon and the vineyards of Sibmah are destroyed — those vineyards whose wine used to make the rulers of the nations drunk. At one time the vines spread as far as the city of Jazer, and eastward into the desert, and westward to the other side of the Dead Sea. ⁹Now I weep for Sibmah's vines as I weep for Jazer. My tears fall for Heshbon and Elealeh, because there is no harvest to make the people glad. ¹⁰No one is

happy now in the fertile fields. No one shouts or sings in the vineyards. No one tramples grapes to make wine; the shouts of joy are ended.[b] ¹¹I groan with sadness for Moab, with grief for Kir Heres. ¹²The people of Moab wear themselves out going to their mountain shrines and to their temples to pray, but it will do them no good.

¹³That is the message the LORD gave earlier about Moab. ¹⁴And now the LORD says, "In exactly three years Moab's great wealth will disappear. Of its many people, only a few will survive, and they will be weak."

God Will Punish Syria and Israel

17 The LORD said, "Damascus will not be a city any longer; it will be only a pile of ruins. ²The cities of Syria will be deserted forever.[c] They will be a pasture for sheep and cattle, and no one will drive them away. ³Israel will be defenseless, and Damascus will lose its independence. Those Syrians who survive will be in disgrace like the people of Israel. I, the LORD Almighty, have spoken."

⁴The LORD said, "A day is coming when Israel's greatness will come to an end, and its wealth will be replaced by poverty. ⁵Israel will be like a field where the grain has been cut and harvested, as desolate as a field in Rephaim Valley when it has been picked bare. ⁶Only a few people will survive, and Israel will be like an olive tree from which all the olives have been picked except two or three at the very top, or a few that are left on the lower branches. I, the LORD God of Israel, have spoken."

⁷When that day comes, people will turn for help to their Creator, the holy God of Israel. ⁸They will no longer rely on the altars they made with their own hands, or trust in their own handiwork — symbols of the goddess Asherah and altars for burning incense.

Israel will be like an olive tree. (17.6)

⁹When that day comes, well-defended cities will be deserted and left in ruins like the cities that the Hivites and the Amorites[d] abandoned as they fled from the people of Israel.

¹⁰Israel, you have forgotten the God who rescues you and protects you like a mighty rock. Instead, you plant sacred gardens[e] in order to worship a foreign god. ¹¹But even if they sprouted and blossomed the very morning you planted them, there would still be no harvest. There would be only trouble and incurable pain.

Enemy Nations Are Defeated

¹²Powerful nations are in commotion with a sound like the roar of the sea, like the crashing of huge waves. ¹³The nations advance like rushing waves, but God reprimands them and they retreat, driven away like dust on a mountainside, like straw in a whirlwind. ¹⁴At evening they cause terror, but by morning they are gone. That is the fate of everyone who plunders our land.

---

[b] *One ancient translation* the shouts of joy are ended; *Hebrew* I have ended the shouts of joy.   [c] *One ancient translation* The cities . . . forever; *Hebrew* The cities of Aroer are deserted.   [d] *One ancient translation* the Hivites and the Amorites; *Hebrew* woodland and hill country.   [e] SACRED GARDENS: *See 1.29.*

17.1-3 Jr 49.23-27; Am 1.3-5; Zec 9.1

God Will Punish Ethiopia

18 Beyond the rivers of Ethiopia*f* there is a land where the sound of wings is heard. ²From that land ambassadors come down the Nile in boats made of reeds. Go back home, swift messengers! Take a message back to your land divided by rivers, to your strong and powerful nation, to your tall and smooth-skinned people, who are feared all over the world.

³Listen, everyone who lives on earth! Look for a signal flag to be raised on the mountaintops! Listen for the blowing of the bugle! ⁴The LORD said to me, "I will look down from heaven as quietly as the dew forms in the warm nights of harvest time, as serenely as the sun shines in the heat of the day. ⁵Before the grapes are gathered, when the blossoms have all fallen and the grapes are ripening, the enemy will destroy the Ethiopians*f* as easily as a knife cuts branches from a vine. ⁶The corpses of their soldiers will be left exposed to the birds and the wild animals. In summer the birds will feed on them, and in winter, the animals."

⁷A time is coming when the LORD Almighty will receive offerings from this land divided by rivers, this strong and powerful nation, this tall and smooth-skinned people, who are feared all over the world. They will come to Mount Zion, where the LORD Almighty is worshiped.

God Will Punish Egypt

19 This is a message about Egypt. The LORD is coming to Egypt, riding swiftly on a cloud. The Egyptian idols tremble before him, and the people of Egypt lose their courage. ²The LORD says, "I will stir up civil war in Egypt and turn brother against brother and neighbor against neighbor. Rival cities will fight each other, and rival kings will struggle for power. ³I am going to frustrate the plans of the Egyptians and destroy their morale. They will ask their idols to help them, and they will go and consult mediums and ask the spirits of the dead for advice. ⁴I will hand the Egyptians over to a tyrant, to a cruel king who will rule them. I, the LORD Almighty, have spoken."

⁵The water will be low in the Nile, and the river will gradually dry up. ⁶The channels of the river will stink as they slowly go dry. Reeds and rushes will wither, ⁷and all the crops planted along the banks of the Nile will dry up and be blown away. ⁸Everyone who earns a living by fishing in the Nile will groan and cry; their hooks and their

Their hooks and their nets will be useless. (19.8)

nets will be useless. ⁹Those who make linen cloth will be in despair; ¹⁰weavers and skilled workers will be broken and depressed.

¹¹The leaders of the city of Zoan are fools! Egypt's wisest people give stupid advice! How do they dare to tell the king that they are successors to the ancient scholars and kings? ¹²King of Egypt, where are those clever advisers

---

f Hebrew Cush(ites): *Cush is the ancient name of the extensive territory south of the First Cataract of the Nile River. This region was called Ethiopia in Graeco-Roman times, and included within its borders most of modern Sudan and some of present-day Ethiopia (Abyssinia).*

18.1-7 Zep 2.12   **19.1-25** Jr 46.2-26; Ez 29.1−32.32

of yours? Perhaps they can tell you what plans the LORD Almighty has for Egypt. 13 The leaders of Zoan and Memphis are fools. They were supposed to lead the nation, but they have misled it. 14 The LORD has made them give confusing advice. As a result, Egypt does everything wrong and staggers like a drunk slipping on his own vomit. 15 No one in Egypt, rich or poor, important or unknown, can offer help.

Egypt Will Worship the LORD

16 A time is coming when the people of Egypt will be as timid as women. They will tremble in terror when they see that the LORD Almighty has stretched out his hand to punish them. 17 The people of Egypt will be terrified of Judah every time they are reminded of the fate that the LORD Almighty has prepared for them.

18 When that time comes, the Hebrew language will be spoken in five Egyptian cities. The people there will take their oaths in the name of the LORD Almighty. One of the cities will be called, "City of the Sun."

19 When that time comes, there will be an altar to the LORD in the land of Egypt and a stone pillar dedicated to him at the Egyptian border. 20 They will be symbols of the LORD Almighty's presence in Egypt. When the people there are oppressed and call out to the LORD for help, he will send someone to rescue them. 21 The LORD will reveal himself to the Egyptian people, and then they will acknowledge and worship him, and bring him sacrifices and offerings. They will make solemn promises to him and do what they promise. 22 The LORD will punish the Egyptians, but then he will heal them.

They will turn to him, and he will hear their prayers and heal them.

23 When that time comes, there will be a highway between Egypt and Assyria. The people of these two countries will travel back and forth between them, and the two nations will worship together. 24 When that time comes, Israel will rank with Egypt and Assyria, and these three nations will be a blessing to all the world. 25 The LORD Almighty will bless them and say, "I will bless you, Egypt, my people; you, Assyria, whom I created; and you, Israel, my chosen people."

The Sign of the Naked Prophet

20 Under the orders of Emperor Sargon of Assyria, the commander-in-chief of the Assyrian army attacked the Philistine city of Ashdod. 2 Three years earlier the LORD had told Isaiah son of Amoz to take off his sandals and the sackcloth he was wearing. He obeyed and went around naked and barefoot. 3 When Ashdod was captured, the LORD said, "My servant Isaiah has been going around naked and barefoot for three years. This is a sign of what will happen to Egypt and Ethiopia.ƒ 4 The emperor of Assyria will lead away naked the prisoners he captures from those two countries. Young and old, they will walk barefoot and naked, with their buttocks exposed, bringing shame on Egypt. 5 Those who have put their trust in Ethiopiaƒ and have boasted about Egypt will be disillusioned, their hopes shattered. 6 When that time comes, the people who live along the coast of Philistia will say, 'Look at what has happened to the people we relied on to protect us from the emperor of Assyria! How will we ever survive?' "

ƒ *Hebrew* Cush(ites): *Cush is the ancient name of the extensive territory south of the First Cataract of the Nile River. This region was called Ethiopia in Graeco-Roman times, and included within its borders most of modern Sudan and some of present-day Ethiopia (Abyssinia).*

A Vision of the Fall of Babylon

21 This is a message about Babylonia.

Like a whirlwind sweeping across the desert, disaster will come from a terrifying land. ²I have seen a vision of cruel events, a vision of betrayal and destruction.

Army of Elam, attack! Army of Media, lay siege to the cities! God will put an end to the suffering which Babylon has caused.

³What I saw and heard in the vision has filled me with terror and pain, pain like that of a woman in labor. ⁴My head is spinning, and I am trembling with fear. I had been longing for evening to come, but it has brought me nothing but terror.

⁵In the vision a banquet is ready; rugs are spread for the guests to sit on. They are eating and drinking. Suddenly the command rings out: "Officers! Prepare your shields!"

⁶Then the Lord said to me, "Go and post a sentry, and tell him to report what he sees. ⁷If he sees riders coming on horseback, two by two, and riders on donkeys and camels, he is to observe them carefully."

⁸The sentry calls out, "Sir, I have been standing guard at my post day and night."

⁹Suddenly, here they come! Riders on horseback, two by two. The sentry gives the news, "Babylon has fallen! All the idols they worshiped lie shattered on the ground."

¹⁰My people Israel, you have been threshed like wheat, but now I have announced to you the good news that I have heard from the LORD Almighty, the God of Israel.

A Message about Edom

¹¹This is a message about Edom.

Someone calls to me from Edom, "Sentry, how soon will the night be over? Tell me how soon it will end."

¹²I answer, "Morning is coming, but night will come again. If you want to ask again, come back and ask."

A Message about Arabia

¹³This is a message about Arabia.

People of Dedan, you whose caravans camp in the barren country of Arabia, ¹⁴give water to the thirsty people who come to you. You people of the land of Tema, give food to the refugees. ¹⁵People are fleeing to escape from swords that are ready to kill them, from bows that are ready to shoot, from all the dangers of war.

¹⁶Then the Lord said to me, "In exactly one year the greatness of the tribes of Kedar will be at an end. ¹⁷The archers are the bravest warriors of Kedar, but few of them will be left. I, the LORD God of Israel, have spoken."

A Message about Jerusalem

22 This is a message about the Valley of Vision.

What is happening? Why are all the people of the city celebrating on the roofs of the houses? ²The whole city is in an uproar, filled with noise and excitement.

Your people who died in this war did not die fighting. ³All your leaders ran away and were captured before they shot a single arrow. ⁴Now leave me alone to weep bitterly over all those of my people who have died. Don't try to comfort me. ⁵This is a time of panic, defeat, and confusion in the Valley of Vision, and the Sovereign LORD Almighty has sent it on us. The walls of our city have been battered down, and cries for help have echoed among the hills.

⁶The soldiers from the land of Elam came riding on horseback, armed with

21.9 Rev 14.8; 18.2

bows and arrows. Soldiers from the land of Kir had their shields ready. 7 The fertile valleys of Judah were filled with chariots; soldiers on horseback stood in front of Jerusalem's gates. 8 All of Judah's defenses crumbled.

When that happened, you brought weapons out of the arsenal. 9-10 You found the places where the walls of Jerusalem needed repair. You inspected all the houses in Jerusalem and tore some of them down to get stones to repair the city walls. In order to store water, 11 you built a reservoir inside the city to hold the water flowing down from the old pool. But you paid no attention to God, who planned all this long ago and who caused it to happen.

12 The Sovereign LORD Almighty was calling you then to weep and mourn, to shave your heads and wear sackcloth. 13 Instead, you laughed and celebrated. You killed sheep and cattle to eat, and you drank wine. You said, "We might as well eat and drink! Tomorrow we'll be dead."

14 The Sovereign LORD Almighty himself spoke to me and said, "This evil will never be forgiven them as long as they live. I, the Sovereign LORD Almighty, have spoken."

A Warning to Shebna

15 The Sovereign LORD Almighty told me to go to Shebna, the manager of the royal household, and say to him, 16 "Who do you think you are? What right do you have to carve a tomb for yourself out of the rocky hillside? 17 You may be important, but the LORD will pick you up and throw you away. 18 He will pick you up like a ball and throw you into a much larger country. You will die there beside the chariots you were so proud of. You are a disgrace to your master's household. 19 The LORD will remove you from office and bring you down from your high position."

20 The LORD said to Shebna, "When that happens, I will send for my servant Eliakim son of Hilkiah. 21 I will put your official robe and belt on him and give him all the authority you have had. He will be like a father to the people of Jerusalem and Judah. 22 I will give him complete authority under the king, the descendant of David. He will have the keys of office; what he opens, no one will shut, and what he shuts, no one will open. 23 I will fasten him firmly in place like a peg, and he will be a source of honor to his whole family.

24 "But all his relatives and dependents will become a burden to him. They will hang on him like pots and bowls hanging from a peg! 25 When that happens, the peg that was firmly fastened will pull loose and fall. And that will be the end of everything that was hanging on it." The LORD has spoken.

A Message about Phoenicia

23 This is a message about Tyre.
Howl with grief, you sailors out on the ocean! Your home port of Tyre has been destroyed; its houses and its harbor are in ruins. As your ships return from Cyprus, you learn the news. 2 Wail, you merchants of Sidon! You sent agents 3 across the sea to buy and sell the grain that grew in Egypt and to do business with all the nations.

4 City of Sidon, you are disgraced! The sea and the great ocean depths disown you and say, "I never had any children. I never raised sons or daughters."

5 Even the Egyptians will be shocked and dismayed when they learn that Tyre has been destroyed.

6 Howl with grief, you people of Phoenicia! Try to escape to Spain! 7 Can this

22.13 1 Co 15.32 **22.22** Rev 3.7 **23.1-18** Ez 26.1—28.19; Jl 3.4-8; Am 1.9, 10; Zec 9.1-4; Mt 11.21, 22; Lk 10.13, 14

be the joyful city of Tyre, founded so long ago? Is this the city that sent settlers across the sea to establish colonies? 8 Who was it that planned to bring all this on Tyre, that imperial city, whose merchant princes were the most honored men on earth? 9 The LORD Almighty planned it. He planned it in order to put an end to their pride in what they had done and to humiliate their honored ones.

10 Go and farm the land, you people in the colonies in Spain! There is no one to protect you any more.*g* 11 The LORD has stretched out his hand over the sea and overthrown kingdoms. He has commanded that the Phoenician centers of commerce be destroyed. 12 City of Sidon, your happiness has ended, and your people are oppressed. Even if they escape to Cyprus, they will still not be safe.

(13 It was the Babylonians, not the Assyrians, who let the wild animals overrun Tyre. It was the Babylonians who put up siege towers, tore down the fortifications of Tyre, and left the city in ruins.*h*)

14 Howl with grief, you sailors out on the ocean! The city you relied on has been destroyed.

15 A time is coming when Tyre will be forgotten for seventy years, the lifetime of a king. When those years are over, Tyre will be like the prostitute in the song:

16 Take your harp, go round the
    town,
   you poor forgotten whore!
Play and sing your songs again
   to bring men back once more.

17 When the seventy years are over, the LORD will let Tyre go back to her old trade, and she will hire herself out to all the kingdoms of the world. 18 The money she earns by commerce will be dedicated to the LORD. She will not store it away, but those who worship the LORD will use her money to buy the food and the clothing they need.

The LORD Will Punish the Earth

24 The LORD is going to devastate the earth and leave it desolate. He will twist the earth's surface and scatter its people. 2 Everyone will meet the same fate — the priests and the people, slaves and masters, buyers and sellers, lenders and borrowers, rich and poor. 3 The earth will lie shattered and ruined. The LORD has spoken and it will be done.

4 The earth dries up and withers; the whole world grows weak; both earth and sky decay. 5 The people have defiled the earth by breaking God's laws and by violating the covenant he made to last forever. 6 So God has pronounced a curse on the earth. Its people are paying for what they have done. Fewer and fewer remain alive. 7 The grapevines wither, and wine is becoming scarce. Everyone who was once happy is now sad, 8 and the joyful music of their harps and drums has ceased. 9 There is no more happy singing over wine; no one enjoys its taste any more. 10 In the city everything is in chaos, and people lock themselves in their houses for safety. 11 People shout in the streets because there is no more wine. Happiness is gone forever; it has been banished from the land. 12 The city is in ruins, and its gates have been broken down. 13 This is what will happen in every nation all over the world. It will be like the end of harvest, when the olives have been beaten off every tree and the last grapes picked from the vines.

14 Those who survive will sing for joy. Those in the West will tell how great the LORD is, 15 and those in the East will praise him. The people who live along the sea will praise the LORD, the God of Israel. 16 From the most distant parts of

---

g Verse 10 in Hebrew is unclear.   *h Verse 13 in Hebrew is unclear.*

the world we will hear songs in praise of Israel, the righteous nation.

But there is no hope for me! I am wasting away! Traitors continue to betray, and their treachery grows worse and worse. 17 Listen to me, everyone! There are terrors, pits, and traps waiting for you. 18 Anyone who tries to escape from the terror will fall in a pit, and anyone who escapes from the pit will be caught in a trap. Torrents of rain will pour from the sky, and earth's foundations will shake. 19 The earth will crack and shatter and split open. 20 The earth itself will stagger like a drunk, sway like a hut in a storm. The world is weighed down by its sins; it will collapse and never rise again.

21 A time is coming when the LORD will punish the powers above and the rulers of the earth. 22 God will crowd kings together like prisoners in a pit. He will shut them in prison until the

Kings together like prisoners in a pit (24.22)

time of their punishment comes. 23 The moon will grow dark, and the sun will no longer shine, for the LORD Almighty will be king. He will rule in Jerusalem on Mount Zion, and the leaders of the people will see his glory.

A Hymn of Praise

25 LORD, you are my God;
     I will honor you and praise your name.
You have done amazing things;
     you have faithfully carried out the plans you made long ago.
2 You have turned cities into ruins
     and destroyed their fortifications.
The palaces which our enemies built
     are gone forever.
3 The people of powerful nations will praise you;
     you will be feared in the cities of cruel nations.
4 The poor and the helpless have fled to you
     and have been safe in times of trouble.
You give them shelter from storms
     and shade from the burning heat.
Cruel enemies attack like a winter storm,[i]
5   like drought in a dry land.
But you, LORD, have silenced our enemies;
     you silence the shouts of cruel people,
     as a cloud cools a hot day.

God Prepares a Banquet

6 Here on Mount Zion the LORD Almighty will prepare a banquet for all the nations of the world — a banquet of the richest food and the finest wine. 7 Here he will suddenly remove the cloud of sorrow that has been hanging over all the nations. 8 The Sovereign LORD will destroy death forever! He will wipe away the tears from everyone's eyes and take away the disgrace his people have suffered throughout the world. The LORD himself has spoken.

---

[i] *Probable text* winter storm; *Hebrew* storm against a wall.
25.8 a 1 Co 15.54; **b** Rev 7.17; 21.4

⁹When it happens, everyone will say, "He is our God! We have put our trust in him, and he has rescued us. He is the LORD! We have put our trust in him, and now we are happy and joyful because he has saved us."

God Will Punish Moab

¹⁰The LORD will protect Mount Zion, but the people of Moab will be trampled down the way straw is trampled in manure. ¹¹They will reach out their hands as if they were trying to swim, but God will humiliate them, and their hands will sink helplessly. ¹²He will destroy the fortresses of Moab with their high walls and bring them tumbling down into the dust.

God Will Give His People Victory

26 A day is coming when the people will sing this song in the land of Judah:
Our city is strong!
God himself defends its walls!
²Open the city gates
and let the faithful nation
enter,
the nation whose people do
what is right.
³You, LORD, give perfect peace
to those who keep their
purpose firm
and put their trust in you.
⁴Trust in the LORD forever;
he will always protect us.
⁵He has humbled those who were
proud;
he destroyed the strong city
they lived in,
and sent its walls crashing
into the dust.
⁶Those who were oppressed walk
over it now
and trample it under their
feet.

⁷LORD, you make the path smooth
for good people;
the road they travel is level.
⁸We follow your will and put our
hope in you;
you are all that we desire.
⁹At night I long for you with all
my heart;
when you judge the earth and
its people,
they will all learn what
justice is.
¹⁰Even though you are kind to the
wicked,
they never learn to do what
is right.
Even here in a land of righteous
people
they still do wrong;
they refuse to recognize your
greatness.
¹¹Your enemies do not know that
you will punish them.
LORD, put them to shame and let
them suffer;
let them suffer the
punishment you have
prepared.
Show them how much you love
your people.

¹²You will give us prosperity,
LORD;
everything that we achieve
is the result of what you do.ʲ
¹³LORD our God, we have been
ruled by others,
but you alone are our LORD.
¹⁴Now they are dead and will not
live again;
their ghosts will not rise,
for you have punished them
and destroyed them.
No one remembers them any
more.
¹⁵LORD, you have made our nation
grow,

ʲ everything that ... do; or you treat us according to what we do.
25.10-12 Is 15.1—16.14; Jr 48.1-47; Ez 25.8-11; Am 2.1-3; Zep 2.8-11   **26.11** He 10.27

enlarging its territory on
　　every side;
and this has brought you
　　honor.
16 You punished your people, LORD,
　　and in anguish they prayed
　　　to you.*k*
17 You, LORD, have made us
　　cry out,
　　as a woman in labor cries
　　　out in pain.
18 We were in pain and agony,
　　but we gave birth to nothing.
　　We have won no victory for our
　　　land;
　　we have accomplished
　　　nothing.*l*

19 Those of our people who have
　　died will live again!
　　Their bodies will come back
　　　to life.
　　All those sleeping in their graves
　　　will wake up and sing for joy.
　　As the sparkling dew refreshes
　　　the earth,
　　so the LORD will revive those
　　　who have long been dead.

Judgment and Restoration

20 Go into your houses, my people,
and shut the door behind you. Hide
yourselves for a little while until God's
anger is over. 21 The LORD is coming
from his heavenly dwelling place to
punish the people of the earth for their
sins. The murders that were secretly
committed on the earth will be revealed, and the ground will no longer
hide those who have been killed.

27 On that day the LORD will use
his powerful and deadly sword
to punish Leviathan, that wriggling,
twisting dragon, and to kill the monster *m* that lives in the sea.

2 On that day the LORD will say of his
pleasant vineyard, 3 "I watch over it and
water it continually. I guard it night
and day so that no one will harm it. 4 I
am no longer angry with the vineyard.
If there were thorns and briers to fight
against, I would burn them up completely. 5 But if the enemies of my people want my protection, let them make
peace with me. Yes, let them make
peace with me."

6 In the days to come the people of Israel, the descendants of Jacob, will take
root like a tree, and they will blossom
and bud. The earth will be covered with
the fruit they produce.

7 Israel has not been punished by the
LORD as severely as its enemies nor lost
as many people. 8 The LORD punished
his people by sending them into exile.
He took them away with a cruel wind
from the east. *n* 9 But Israel's sins will
be forgiven only when the stones of pagan altars are ground up like chalk, and
no more incense altars or symbols of
the goddess Asherah are left.

10 The fortified city lies in ruins. It is
deserted like an empty wilderness. It
has become a pasture for cattle, where
they can rest and graze. 11 The
branches of the trees are withered and
broken, and women gather them for
firewood. Because the people have
understood nothing, God their Creator
will not pity them or show them any
mercy.

12 On that day, from the Euphrates to
the Egyptian border, the LORD will
gather his people one by one, as threshing separates the wheat from the chaff.
13 When that day comes, a trumpet
will be blown to call back from Assyria
and Egypt all the Israelites who are in
exile there. They will come and worship
the LORD in Jerusalem, on his sacred
hill.*o*

---

k Verse 16 in Hebrew is unclear.　　　*l We have won . . . nothing; Hebrew unclear.*
m LEVIATHAN . . . MONSTER: *Legendary monsters which were symbols of the nations
oppressing Israel.*　　　*n Verse 8 in Hebrew is unclear.*　　　*o* SACRED HILL: *See 2.3.*
27.1 Job 41.1; Ps 74.14; 104.26

The fortified city lies in ruins. (27.10)

A Warning to the Northern Kingdom

28 The kingdom of Israel is doomed! Its glory is fading like the crowns of flowers on the heads of its drunken leaders. Their proud heads are well perfumed, but there they lie, dead drunk. ²The Lord has someone strong and powerful ready to attack them, someone who will come like a hailstorm, like a torrent of rain, like a rushing, overpowering flood, and will overwhelm the land. ³The pride of those drunken leaders will be trampled underfoot. ⁴The fading glory of those proud leaders will disappear like the first figs of the season, picked and eaten as soon as they are ripe.

⁵A day is coming when the LORD Almighty will be like a glorious crown of flowers for his people who survive. ⁶He will give a sense of justice to those who serve as judges, and courage to those who defend the city gates from attack.

Isaiah and the Drunken Prophets of Judah

⁷Even the prophets and the priests are so drunk that they stagger. They have drunk so much wine and liquor that they stumble in confusion. The prophets are too drunk to understand the visions that God sends, and the priests are too drunk to decide the cases that are brought to them. ⁸The tables where they sit are all covered with vomit, and not a clean spot is left.

⁹They complain about me. They say, "Who does that man think he's teaching? Who needs his message? It's only good for babies that have just stopped nursing! ¹⁰He is trying to teach us letter by letter, line by line, lesson by lesson."

¹¹If you won't listen to me, then God will use foreigners speaking some strange-sounding language to teach you a lesson. ¹²He offered rest and comfort to all of you, but you refused to listen to him. ¹³That is why the LORD is going to teach you letter by letter, line

So drunk that they stagger (28.7)

y line, lesson by lesson. Then you will stumble with every step you take. You will be wounded, trapped, and taken prisoner.

A Cornerstone for Zion

14 Now you arrogant leaders who rule here in Jerusalem over this people, listen to what the LORD is saying. 15 You boast that you have made a treaty with death and reached an agreement with the world of the dead. You are certain that disaster will spare you when it comes, because you depend on lies and deceit to keep you safe. 16 This, now, is what the Sovereign LORD says: "I am placing in Zion a foundation that is firm and strong. In it I am putting a solid cornerstone on which are written the words, 'Faith that is firm is also patient.' 17 Justice will be the measuring line for the foundation, and honesty will be its plumb line."

Hailstorms will sweep away all the lies you depend on, and floods will destroy your security. 18 The treaty you have made with death will be abolished, and your agreement with the world of the dead will be canceled. When disaster sweeps down, you will be overcome. 19 It will strike you again and again, morning after morning. You will have to bear it day and night. Each new message from God will bring new terror! 20 You will be like the person in the proverb, who tries to sleep in a bed too short to stretch out on, with a blanket too narrow to wrap himself in. 21 The LORD will fight as he did at Mount Perazim and in the valley of Gibeon, in order to do what he intends to do — strange as his actions may seem. He will complete his work, his mysterious work.

22 Don't laugh at the warning I am giving you! If you do, it will be even harder for you to escape. I have heard the LORD Almighty's decision to destroy the whole country.

God's Wisdom

23 Listen to what I am saying; pay attention to what I am telling you. 24 Farmers don't constantly plow their fields and keep getting them ready for planting. 25 Once they have prepared the soil, they plant the seeds of herbs such as dill and cumin. They plant rows of wheat and barley,p and at the edges of their fields they plant other grain. 26 They know how to do their work, because God has taught them. 27 They never use a heavy club to beat out dill seeds or cumin seeds; instead they use light sticks of the proper size. 28 They do not ruin the wheat by threshing it endlessly, and they know how to thresh it by driving a cart over it without bruising the grains. 29 All this wisdom comes from the LORD Almighty. The plans God makes are wise, and they always succeed.

The Fate of Jerusalem

29 God's altar, Jerusalem itself, is doomed! The city where David camped is doomed! Let another year or two come and go, with its feasts and festivals, 2 and then God will bring disaster on the city that is called "God's altar." There will be weeping and wailing, and the whole city will be like an altar covered with blood. 3 God will attack the city, surround it, and besiege it. 4 Jerusalem will be like a ghost struggling to speak from under the ground, a muffled voice coming from the dust.

5 Jerusalem, all the foreigners who attack you will be blown away like dust, and their terrifying armies will fly away like straw. Suddenly and unexpectedly 6 the LORD Almighty will rescue you with violent thunderstorms and

---

p *Hebrew has an additional word, the meaning of which is unclear.*
28.15 Ws 1.16; Si 14.12   **28.16** Ps 118.22, 23; Ro 9.33; 10.11; 1 P 2.6   **28.21 a** 2 S 5.20; 1 Ch 14.11; **b** Js 10.10-12

earthquakes. He will send windstorms and raging fire; [7] then all the armies of the nations attacking the city of God's altar, all their weapons and equipment — everything — will vanish like a dream, like something imagined in the night. [8] All the nations that assemble to attack Jerusalem will be like a starving person who dreams he is eating and wakes up hungry, or like someone dying of thirst who dreams he is drinking and wakes with a dry throat.

Disregarded Warnings

[9] Go ahead and be stupid! Go ahead and be blind! Get drunk without any wine! Stagger without drinking a drop! [10] The LORD has made you drowsy, ready to fall into a deep sleep. The prophets should be the eyes of the people, but God has blindfolded them. [11] The meaning of every prophetic vision will be hidden from you; it will be like a sealed scroll. If you take it to someone who knows how to read and ask him to read it to you, he will say he can't because it is sealed. [12] If you give it to someone who can't read and ask him to read it to you, he will answer that he doesn't know how.

[13] The Lord said, "These people claim to worship me, but their words are meaningless, and their hearts are somewhere else. Their religion is nothing but human rules and traditions, which they have simply memorized. [14] So I will startle them with one unexpected blow after another. Those who are wise will turn out to be fools, and all their cleverness will be useless."

Hope for the Future

[15] Those who try to hide their plans from the LORD are doomed! They carry out their schemes in secret and think no one will see them or know what they are doing. [16] They turn everything up-side down. Which is more important, the potter or the clay? Can something you have made say, "You didn't make me"? Or can it say, "You don't know what you are doing"?

[17] As the saying goes, before long the dense forest will become farmland, and the farmland will go back to forest.

[18] When that day comes, the deaf will be able to hear a book being read aloud, and the blind, who have been living in darkness, will open their eyes and see. [19] Poor and humble people will once again find the happiness which the LORD, the holy God of Israel, gives. [20] It will be the end of those who oppress others and show contempt for God. Every sinner will be destroyed. [21] God will destroy those who slander others, those who prevent the punishment of criminals, and those who tell lies to keep honest people from getting justice.

[22] So now the LORD, the God of Israel, who rescued Abraham from trouble, says, "My people, you will not be disgraced any longer, and your faces will no longer be pale with shame. [23] When you see the children that I will give you, then you will acknowledge that I am the holy God of Israel. You will honor me and stand in awe of me. [24] Foolish people will learn to understand, and those who are always grumbling will be glad to be taught."

A Useless Treaty with Egypt

30 The LORD has spoken: "Those who rule Judah are doomed because they rebel against me. They follow plans that I did not make, and sign treaties against my will, piling one sin on another. [2] They go to Egypt for help without asking for my advice. They want Egypt to protect them, so they put their trust in Egypt's king. [3] But the king will be powerless to help them,

29.10 Ro 11.8   **29.13** Mt 15.8, 9; Mk 7.6, 7   **29.14** 1 Co 1.19   **29.16** Is 45.9; Si 33.13; Ro 9.20

and Egypt's protection will end in disaster. 4 Although their ambassadors have already arrived at the Egyptian cities of Zoan and Hanes, 5 the people of Judah will regret that they ever trusted that unreliable nation, a nation that fails them when they expect help."

6 This is God's message about the animals of the southern desert: "The ambassadors travel through dangerous country, where lions live and where there are poisonous snakes and flying dragons. They load their donkeys and camels with expensive gifts for a nation that cannot give them any help. 7 The help that Egypt gives is useless. So I have nicknamed Egypt, 'The Harmless Dragon.'"

The Disobedient People

8 God told me to write down in a book what the people are like, so that there would be a permanent record of how evil they are. 9 They are always rebelling against God, always lying, always refusing to listen to the LORD's teachings. 10 They tell the prophets to keep quiet. They say, "Don't talk to us about what's right. Tell us what we want to hear. Let us keep our illusions. 11 Get out of our way and stop blocking our path. We don't want to hear about your holy God of Israel."

12 But this is what the holy God of Israel says: "You ignore what I tell you and rely on violence and deceit. 13 You are guilty. You are like a high wall with a crack running down it; suddenly you will collapse. 14 You will be shattered like a clay pot, so badly broken that there is no piece big enough to pick up hot coals with or to dip water from a cistern."

15 The Sovereign LORD, the Holy One of Israel, says to the people, "Come back and quietly trust in me. Then you will be strong and secure." But you refuse to do it. 16 Instead, you plan to escape from your enemies by riding fast horses. And you are right — escape is

what you will have to do! You think your horses are fast enough, but those who pursue you will be faster! 17 A thousand of you will run away when you see one enemy soldier, and five soldiers will be enough to make you all run away. Nothing will be left of your army except a lonely flagpole on the top of a hill. 18 And yet the LORD is waiting to be merciful to you. He is ready to take pity on you because he always does what is right. Happy are those who put their trust in the LORD.

God Will Bless His People

19 You people who live in Jerusalem will not weep any more. The LORD is compassionate, and when you cry to him for help, he will answer you. 20 The Lord will make you go through hard times, but he himself will be there to teach you, and you will not have to search for him any more. 21 If you wander off the road to the right or the left, you will hear his voice behind you saying, "Here is the road. Follow it." 22 You will take your idols plated with silver and your idols covered with gold, and will throw them away like filth, shouting, "Out of my sight!" 23 Whenever you plant your crops, the Lord will send rain to make them grow and will give you a rich harvest, and your livestock will have plenty of pasture. 24 The oxen and donkeys that plow your fields will eat

The finest and best fodder (30.24)

the finest and best fodder. 25 On the day when the forts of your enemies are captured and their people are killed, streams of water will flow from every mountain and every hill. 26 The moon will be as bright as the sun, and the sun will be seven times brighter than usual, like the light of seven days in one. This will all happen when the LORD bandages and heals the wounds he has given his people.

God Will Punish Assyria

27 The LORD's power and glory can be seen in the distance. Fire and smoke show his anger. He speaks, and his words burn like fire. 28 He sends the wind in front of him like a flood that carries everything away. It sweeps nations to destruction and puts an end to their evil plans. 29 But you, God's people, will be happy and sing as you do on the night of a sacred festival. You will be as happy as those who walk to the music of flutes on their way to the Temple of the LORD, the defender of Israel. 30 The LORD will let everyone hear his majestic voice and feel the force of his anger. There will be flames, cloudbursts, hailstones, and torrents of rain. 31 The Assyrians will be terrified when they hear the LORD's voice and feel the force of his punishment. 32 As the LORD strikes them again and again, his people will keep time with the music of drums and harps. God himself will fight against the Assyrians. 33 Long ago a place was prepared where a huge fire will burn the emperor of Assyria. It is deep and wide, and piled high with wood. The LORD will breathe out a stream of flame to set it on fire.

God Will Protect Jerusalem

31 Those who go to Egypt for help are doomed! They are relying on Egypt's vast military strength — horses, chariots, and soldiers. But they do not rely on the LORD, the holy God of Israel, or ask him for help. 2 He knows what he is doing! He sends disaster. He carries out his threats to punish evil people and those who protect them. 3 The Egyptians are not gods — they are only human. Their horses are not supernatural. When the LORD acts, the strong nation will crumble, and the weak nation it helped will fall. Both of them will be destroyed.

4 The LORD said to me, "No matter how shepherds yell and shout, they can't scare away a lion from an animal that it has killed; in the same way, there is nothing that can keep me, the LORD Almighty, from protecting Mount Zion. 5 Just as a bird hovers over its nest to protect its young, so I, the LORD Almighty, will protect Jerusalem and defend it."

As a bird hovers over its nest (31.5)

6 God said, "People of Israel, you have sinned against me and opposed me. But now, come back to me! 7 A time is coming when all of you will throw away the sinful idols you made out of silver and gold. 8 Assyria will be destroyed in war, but not by human power. The Assyrians will run from battle, and their young men will be made slaves. 9 Their emperor will run away in terror, and the officers will be so frightened that they

vill abandon their battle flags." The
₋ORD has spoken — the LORD who is
worshiped in Jerusalem and whose fire
ɔurns there for sacrifices.

A King with Integrity

32 Some day there will be a king
who rules with integrity, and
national leaders who govern with justice. ² Each of them will be like a shelter
from the wind and a place to hide from
storms. They will be like streams flowing in a desert, like the shadow of a giant rock in a barren land. ³ Their eyes
and ears will be open to the needs of the
people. ⁴ They will not be impatient any
longer, but they will act with understanding and will say what they mean.
⁵ No one will think that a fool is honorable or say that a scoundrel is honest.
⁶ A fool speaks foolishly and thinks up
evil things to do. What he does and
what he says are an insult to the LORD,
and he never feeds the hungry or gives
thirsty people anything to drink. ⁷ A stupid person is evil and does evil things;
he plots to ruin the poor with lies and to
keep them from getting their rights.
⁸ But an honorable person acts honestly
and stands firm for what is right.

Judgment and Restoration

⁹ You women who live an easy life,
free from worries, listen to what I am
saying. ¹⁰ You may be satisfied now, but
this time next year you will be in despair because there will be no grapes
for you to gather. ¹¹ You have been living an easy life, free from worries; but
now, tremble with fear! Strip off your
clothes and tie rags around your waist.
¹² Beat your breasts in grief because the
fertile fields and the vineyards have
been destroyed, ¹³ and thorn bushes
and briers are growing on my people's
land. Weep for all the houses where
people were happy and for the city that
was full of life. ¹⁴ Even the palace will be
abandoned and the capital city totally
deserted. Homes and the forts that

guarded them will be in ruins forever.
Wild donkeys will roam there, and
sheep will find pasture there.
¹⁵ But once more God will send us his
spirit. The wasteland will become fertile, and fields will produce rich crops.
¹⁶ Everywhere in the land righteousness and justice will be done. ¹⁷ Because everyone will do what is right,
there will be peace and security forever.
¹⁸ God's people will be free from worries, and their homes peaceful and safe.
(¹⁹ But hail will fall on the forests, and
the city will be torn down.) ²⁰ How
happy everyone will be with plenty of
water for the crops and safe pasture
everywhere for the donkeys and cattle.

A Prayer for Help

33 Our enemies are doomed!
They have robbed and be-
trayed, although no one has robbed
them or betrayed them. But their time
to rob and betray will end, and they
themselves will become victims of robbery and treachery.
² LORD, have mercy on us. We have
put our hope in you. Protect us day by
day and save us in times of trouble.
³ When you fight for us, nations run
away from the noise of battle. ⁴ Their
belongings are pounced upon and
taken as loot.
⁵ How great the LORD is! He rules
over everything. He will fill Jerusalem
with justice and integrity ⁶ and give sta-
bility to the nation. He always protects
his people and gives them wisdom and
knowledge. Their greatest treasure is
their reverence for the LORD.
⁷ The brave are calling for help. The
ambassadors who tried to bring about
peace are crying bitterly. ⁸ The high-
ways are so dangerous that no one travels on them. Treaties are broken and
agreements are violated. No one is respected any more. ⁹ The land lies idle
and deserted. The forests of Lebanon
have withered, the fertile valley of
Sharon is like a desert, and in Bashan

and on Mount Carmel the leaves are falling from the trees.

The LORD Warns His Enemies

¹⁰The LORD says to the nations, "Now I will act. I will show how powerful I am. ¹¹You make worthless plans and everything you do is useless. My spirit is like a fire that will destroy you.�q ¹²You will crumble like rocks burned to make lime, like thorns burned to ashes. ¹³Let everyone near and far hear what I have done and acknowledge my power."

¹⁴The sinful people of Zion are trembling with fright. They say, "God's judgment is like a fire that burns forever. Can any of us survive a fire like that?" ¹⁵You can survive if you say and do what is right. Don't use your power to cheat the poor and don't accept bribes. Don't join with those who plan to commit murder or to do other evil things. ¹⁶Then you will be safe; you will be as secure as if in a strong fortress. You will have food to eat and water to drink.

The Glorious Future

¹⁷Once again you will see a king ruling in splendor over a land that stretches in all directions. ¹⁸Your old fears of foreign tax collectors and spies will be only a memory. ¹⁹You will no longer see any arrogant foreigners who speak a language that you can't understand. ²⁰Look at Zion, the city where we celebrate our religious festivals. Look at Jerusalem! What a safe place it will be to live in! It will be like a tent that is never moved, whose pegs are never pulled up and whose ropes never break. ²¹The LORD will show us his

glory. We will live beside broad rivers and streams, but hostile ships will not sail on them.ʳ ²²⁻²³All the rigging on those ships is useless; the sails cannot be spread! We will seize all the wealth of enemy armies, and there will be so much that even the lame can get a share. The LORD himself will be our king; he will rule over us and protect us. ²⁴No one who lives in our land will ever again complain of being sick, and all sins will be forgiven.

God Will Punish His Enemies

34 Come, people of all nations! Gather around and listen. Let the whole earth and everyone living on it come here and listen. ²The LORD is angry with all the nations and all their armies. He has condemned them to destruction. ³Their corpses will not be buried, but will lie there rotting and stinking; and the mountains will be red with blood. ⁴The sun, moon, and stars will crumble to dust. The sky will disappear like a scroll being rolled up, and the stars will fall like leaves dropping from a vine or a fig tree.

⁵The LORD has prepared his sword in heaven, and now it will strike Edom, those people whom he has condemned to destruction. ⁶His sword will be covered with their blood and fat, like the blood and fat of lambs and goats that are sacrificed. The LORD will offer this sacrifice in the city of Bozrah; he will make this a great slaughter in the land of Edom. ⁷The people will fall like wild oxen and young bulls, and the earth will be red with blood and covered with fat. ⁸This is the time when the LORD will rescue Zion and take vengeance on her enemies.

�q One ancient translation My spirit . . . you; Hebrew You are destroying yourselves.
ʳ Verse 21 in Hebrew is unclear.
34.4 Mt 24.29; Mk 13.25; Lk 21.26; Rev 6.13, 14 **34.5-17** Is 63.1-6; Jr 49.7-22; Ez 25.12-14; 35.1-15; Am 1.11, 12; Ob 1-14; Ml 1.2-5

⁹The rivers of Edom will turn into ar, and the soil will turn into sulfur. The whole country will burn like tar. ¹⁰It will burn day and night, and smoke will rise from it forever. The land will lie waste age after age, and no one will ever travel through it again. ¹¹Owls and ravens will take over the land. The LORD will make it a barren waste again,

Owls and ravens will take over the land. (34.11)

as it was before the creation. ¹²There will be no king to rule the country, and the leaders will all be gone.ˢ ¹³Thorns and thistles will grow up in all the palaces and walled towns, and jackals and owls will live in them. ¹⁴Wild animals will roam there, and demons will call to each other. The night monsterᵗ will come there looking for a place to rest. ¹⁵Owls will build their nests, lay eggs, hatch their young, and care for them there. Vultures will gather there, one after another.

¹⁶Search in the LORD's book of living creatures and read what it says. Not one of these creatures will be missing, and not one will be without its mate. The LORD has commanded it to be so; he himself will bring them together. ¹⁷It is the LORD who will divide the land among them and give each of them a share. They will live in the land age after age, and it will belong to them forever.

The Road of Holiness

35 The desert will rejoice,
 and flowers will bloom in
 the wastelands.
²The desert will sing and shout
 for joy;
 it will be as beautiful as the
 Lebanon Mountains
 and as fertile as the fields of
 Carmel and Sharon.
Everyone will see the LORD's
 splendor,
 see his greatness and power.

³Give strength to hands that are
 tired
 and to knees that tremble
 with weakness.
⁴Tell everyone who is
 discouraged,
 "Be strong and don't be afraid!
 God is coming to your rescue,
 coming to punish your
 enemies."

⁵The blind will be able to see,
 and the deaf will hear.
⁶The lame will leap and dance,
 and those who cannot speak
 will shout for joy.
Streams of water will flow
 through the desert;
⁷ the burning sand will become
 a lake,
 and dry land will be filled
 with springs.
Where jackals used to live,
 marsh grass and reeds will
 grow.

⁸There will be a highway there,
 called "The Road of Holiness."
No sinner will ever travel that
 road;

ˢ *Verse 12 in Hebrew begins with a word, the meaning of which is unclear.*   ᵗ NIGHT
MONSTER: *A female demon, believed to live in desolate places.*
34.10 Rev 14.11; 19.3   **35.3** He 12.12   **35.5, 6** Mt 11.5; Lk 7.22

no fools will mislead those
    who follow it.[u]
9 No lions will be there;
    no fierce animals will pass
        that way.
Those whom the LORD has
        rescued
    will travel home by that road.
10 They will reach Jerusalem with
        gladness,
    singing and shouting for joy.
They will be happy forever,
    forever free from sorrow and
        grief.

The Assyrians Threaten Jerusalem
(2 *Kings* 18.13-27; 2 *Chronicles* 32.1-19)

36 In the fourteenth year that Hezekiah was king of Judah, Sennacherib, the emperor of Assyria, attacked the fortified cities of Judah and captured them. 2 Then he ordered his chief official to go from Lachish to Jerusalem with a large military force to demand that King Hezekiah surrender. The official occupied the road where the cloth makers work, by the ditch that brings water from the upper pool. 3 Three Judeans came out to meet him: the official in charge of the palace, Eliakim son of Hilkiah; the court secretary, Shebna; and the official in charge of the records, Joah son of Asaph. 4 The Assyrian official told them that the emperor wanted to know what made King Hezekiah so confident. 5 He demanded, "Do you think that words can take the place of military skill and might? Who do you think will help you rebel against Assyria? 6 You are expecting Egypt to help you, but that would be like using a reed as a walking stick — it would break and would jab your hand. That is what the king of Egypt is like when anyone relies on him."

7 The Assyrian official went on, "Or will you tell me that you are relying on the LORD your God? It was the LORD's shrines and altars that Hezekiah destroyed when he told the people of Judah and Jerusalem to worship at one altar only. 8 I will make a bargain with you in the name of the emperor. I will give you two thousand horses if you can find that many riders. 9 You are no match for even the lowest ranking Assyrian official, and yet you expect the Egyptians to send you chariots and horsemen. 10 Do you think I have attacked your country and destroyed it without the LORD's help? The LORD himself told me to attack it and destroy it."

11 Then Eliakim, Shebna, and Joah told the official, "Speak Aramaic to us. We understand it. Don't speak Hebrew; all the people on the wall are listening."

12 He replied, "Do you think you and the king are the only ones the emperor sent me to say all these things to? No, I am also talking to the people who are sitting on the wall, who will have to eat their excrement and drink their urine, just as you will."

13 Then the official stood up and shouted in Hebrew, "Listen to what the emperor of Assyria is telling you. 14 He warns you not to let Hezekiah deceive you. Hezekiah can't save you. 15 And don't let him persuade you to rely on the LORD. Don't think that the LORD will save you and that he will stop our Assyrian army from capturing your city. 16 Don't listen to Hezekiah! The emperor of Assyria commands you to come out of the city and surrender. You will all be allowed to eat grapes from your own vines and figs from your own trees, and to drink water from your own wells — 17 until the emperor resettles you in a country much like your own, where there are vineyards to give wine and there is grain for making bread. 18 Don't let Hezekiah fool you into thinking that the LORD will rescue you.

[u] *Probable text* no fools . . . follow it; *Hebrew unclear.*
36.6 Ez 29.6, 7

The people kept quiet. (36.21)

Did the gods of any other nations save their countries from the emperor of Assyria? ¹⁹ Where are they now, the gods of Hamath and Arpad? Where are the gods of Sepharvaim? Did anyone save Samaria? ²⁰ When did any of the gods of all these countries ever save their country from our emperor? Then what makes you think the Lord can save Jerusalem?"

²¹ The people kept quiet, just as King Hezekiah had told them to; they did not say a word. ²² Then Eliakim, Shebna, and Joah tore their clothes in grief and went and reported to the king what the Assyrian official had said.

The King Asks Isaiah's Advice
(2 Kings 19.1-7)

37 As soon as King Hezekiah heard their report, he tore his clothes in grief, put on sackcloth, and went to the Temple of the Lord. ² He sent Eliakim, the official in charge of the palace, Shebna, the court secretary, and the senior priests to the prophet Isaiah son of Amoz. They also were wearing sackcloth. ³ This is the message which he told them to give to Isaiah: "Today is a day of suffering; we are being punished and are in disgrace. We are like a woman who is ready to give birth, but is too weak to do it. ⁴ The As-

syrian emperor has sent his chief official to insult the living God. May the Lord your God hear these insults and punish those who spoke them. So pray to God for those of our people who survive."

⁵ When Isaiah received King Hezekiah's message, ⁶ he sent back this answer: "The Lord tells you not to let the Assyrians frighten you by their claims that he cannot save you. ⁷ The Lord will cause the emperor to hear a rumor that will make him go back to his own country, and the Lord will have him killed there."

The Assyrians Send Another Threat
(2 Kings 19.8-19)

⁸ The Assyrian official learned that the emperor had left Lachish and was fighting against the nearby city of Libnah; so he went there to consult him. ⁹ Word reached the Assyrians that the Egyptian army, led by King Tirhakah of Ethiopia,ᵛ was coming to attack them. When the emperor heard this, he sent a letter to King Hezekiah ¹⁰ of Judah to tell him: "The god you are trusting in has told you that you will not fall into my hands, but don't let that deceive you. ¹¹ You have heard what an Assyrian emperor does to any country he decides to destroy. Do you think that

---

ᵛ *Hebrew* Cush: *Cush is the ancient name of the extensive territory south of the First Cataract of the Nile River. This region was called Ethiopia in Graeco-Roman times, and included within its borders most of modern Sudan and some of present-day Ethiopia (Abyssinia).*

you can escape? ¹²My ancestors destroyed the cities of Gozan, Haran, and Rezeph, and killed the people of Betheden who lived in Telassar, and none of their gods could save them. ¹³Where are the kings of the cities of Hamath, Arpad, Sepharvaim, Hena, and Ivvah?"

¹⁴King Hezekiah took the letter from the messengers and read it. Then he went to the Temple, placed the letter there in the presence of the LORD, ¹⁵and prayed, ¹⁶"Almighty LORD, God of Israel, seated above the winged creatures, you alone are God, ruling all the kingdoms of the world. You created the earth and the sky. ¹⁷Now, LORD, hear us and look at what is happening to us. Listen to all the things that Sennacherib is saying to insult you, the living God. ¹⁸We all know, LORD, that the emperors of Assyria have destroyed many nations, made their lands desolate, ¹⁹and burned up their gods — which were no gods at all, only images of wood and stone made by human hands. ²⁰Now, LORD our God, rescue us from the Assyrians, so that all the nations of the world will know that you alone are God."

Isaiah's Message to the King
(*2 Kings 19.20-37*)

²¹Then Isaiah sent a message telling King Hezekiah that in answer to the king's prayer ²²the LORD had said, "The city of Jerusalem laughs at you, Sennacherib, and makes fun of you. ²³Whom do you think you have been insulting and ridiculing? You have been disrespectful to me, the holy God of Israel. ²⁴You sent your servants to boast to me that with all your chariots you had conquered the highest mountains of Lebanon. You boasted that there you cut down the tallest cedars and the finest cypress trees, and that you reached the deepest parts of the forests. ²⁵You boasted that you dug wells and drank water in foreign lands, and that the feet of your soldiers tramped the Nile River dry.

²⁶"Have you never heard that I planned all this long ago? And now I have carried it out. I gave you the power to turn fortified cities into piles of rubble. ²⁷The people who lived there were powerless; they were frightened and stunned. They were like grass in a field or weeds growing on a roof when the hot east wind blasts them.ʷ

²⁸"But I know everything about you, what you do and where you go. I know how you rage against me. ²⁹I have received the report of that rage and that pride of yours, and now I will put a hook through your nose and a bit in your mouth and will take you back by the same road you came."

³⁰Then Isaiah said to King Hezekiah, "Here is a sign of what will happen. This year and next you will have only wild grain to eat, but the following year you will be able to plant grain and harvest it, and plant vines and eat grapes. ³¹Those in Judah who survive will flourish like plants that send roots deep into the ground and produce fruit. ³²There will be people in Jerusalem and on Mount Zion who will survive, because the LORD Almighty is determined to make this happen.

³³"And this is what the LORD has said about the Assyrian emperor: 'He will not enter this city or shoot a single arrow against it. No soldiers with shields will come near the city, and no siege mounds will be built around it. ³⁴He will go back by the same road he came, without entering this city. I, the LORD, have spoken. ³⁵I will defend this city and protect it, for the sake of my own honor and because of the promise I made to my servant David.'"

ʷ *Probable text* when the hot east wind blasts them; *Hebrew* blasted before they are grown.
37.16 Ex 25.22

An angel of the LORD went to the Assyrian camp. (37.36)

36 An angel of the LORD went to the Assyrian camp and killed 185,000 soldiers. At dawn the next day there they lay, all dead! **37** Then the Assyrian emperor Sennacherib withdrew and returned to Nineveh. **38** One day when he was worshiping in the temple of his god Nisroch, two of his sons, Adrammelech and Sharezer, killed him with their swords and then escaped to the land of Ararat. Another of his sons, Esarhaddon, succeeded him as emperor.

King Hezekiah's Illness and Recovery
(2 Kings 20.1-11; 2 Chronicles 32.24-26)

38 About this time King Hezekiah became sick and almost died. The prophet Isaiah son of Amoz went to see him and said to him, "The LORD tells you that you are to put everything in order because you will not recover. Get ready to die."

2 Hezekiah turned his face to the wall and prayed: **3** "Remember, LORD, that I have served you faithfully and loyally, and that I have always tried to do what you wanted me to." And he began to cry bitterly.

4 Then the LORD commanded Isaiah **5** to go back to Hezekiah and say to him, "I, the LORD, the God of your ancestor David, have heard your prayer and seen your tears; I will let you live fifteen years longer. **6** I will rescue you and this city of Jerusalem from the emperor of Assyria, and I will continue to protect the city."

21 Isaiah told the king to put a paste made of figs on his boil, and he would get well. **22** Then King Hezekiah asked, "What is the sign to prove that I will be able to go to the Temple?"ˣ

7 Isaiah replied, "The LORD will give you a sign to prove that he will keep his promise. **8** On the stairway built by King Ahaz, the LORD will make the shadow go back ten steps." And the shadow moved back ten steps.ʸ

9 After Hezekiah recovered from his illness, he wrote this song of praise:

10 I thought that in the prime of
   life
  I was going to the world of the
    dead,
  Never to live out my life.
11 I thought that in this world of
   the living
  I would never again see the
    LORD
  Or any living person.
12 My life was cut off and ended,
  Like a tent that is taken down,
  Like cloth that is cut from a
    loom.
  I thought that God was ending
    my life.ᶻ

ˣ *Verses 21-22 are moved here from the end of the chapter (see 2 K 20.6-9).*
ʸ stairway ... ten steps ... steps; *or* sundial ... ten degrees ... degrees (*see* 2 K 20.9-11).   ᶻ I thought ... my life; *Hebrew unclear.*

13 All night I cried out with pain,
　As if a lion were breaking my
　　bones.
　I thought that God was ending
　　my life.*a*
14 My voice was thin and weak,
　And I moaned like a dove.
　My eyes grew tired from looking
　　to heaven.
　LORD, rescue me from all this
　　trouble.
15 What can I say? The LORD has
　　done this.
　My heart is bitter, and I cannot
　　sleep.*b*

16 Lord, I will live for you, for you
　　alone;
　Heal me and let me live.*c*
17 My bitterness will turn into
　　peace.
　You save*d* my life from all
　　danger;
　You forgive all my sins.
18 No one in the world of the dead
　　can praise you;
　The dead cannot trust in your
　　faithfulness.
19 It is the living who praise you,
　As I praise you now.
　Parents tell their children how
　　faithful you are.
20 LORD, you have healed me.
　We will play harps and sing your
　　praise,
　Sing praise in your Temple as
　　long as we live.*e*

Messengers from Babylonia
(2 Kings 20.12-19)

39 About that same time the king
of Babylonia, Merodach Baladan, son of Baladan, heard that King
Hezekiah had been sick, so he sent him
a letter and a present. 2 Hezekiah welcomed the messengers and showed
them his wealth — his silver and gold,
his spices and perfumes, and all his
military equipment. There was nothing
in his storerooms or anywhere in his
kingdom that he did not show them.
3 Then the prophet Isaiah went to King
Hezekiah and asked, "Where did these
messengers come from and what did
they say to you?"

Hezekiah answered, "They came
from a very distant country, from
Babylonia."

4 "What did they see in the palace?"

"They saw everything. There is nothing in the storerooms that I didn't
show them."

5 Isaiah then told the king, "The
LORD Almighty says that 6 a time is
coming when everything in your palace, everything that your ancestors
have stored up to this day, will be carried off to Babylonia. Nothing will be
left. 7 Some of your own direct descendants will be taken away and made eunuchs to serve in the palace of the king
of Babylonia."

8 King Hezekiah understood this to
mean that there would be peace and security during his lifetime, so he replied,
"The message you have given me from
the LORD is good."

Words of Hope

40 "Comfort my people," says
our God. "Comfort
them!
2 Encourage the people of
　Jerusalem.
Tell them they have suffered
　long enough
and their sins are now
　forgiven.*f*

---

a Verse 13 in Hebrew is unclear.　　*b* One ancient translation suggests I cannot sleep;
Hebrew unclear.　　*c* Verses 15 and 16 in Hebrew are unclear.　　*d* Some ancient
translations save; Hebrew love.　　*e* Verses 21-22 are placed after verse 6.　　*f* and
their sins are now forgiven; or they have paid for what they did.
38.18 Si 17.27; Ba 2.17　　**39.7** Dn 1.1-7; 2 K 24.10-16; 2 Ch 36.10

I have punished them in full for
all their sins."

³A voice cries out,
"Prepare in the wilderness a road
for the LORD!
Clear the way in the desert for
our God!
⁴Fill every valley;
level every mountain.
The hills will become a plain,
and the rough country will be
made smooth.
⁵Then the glory of the LORD will
be revealed,
and all people will see it.
The LORD himself has promised
this."

⁶A voice cries out, "Proclaim a
message!"
"What message shall I
proclaim?" I ask.
"Proclaim that all human beings
are like grass;
they last no longer than wild
flowers.
⁷Grass withers and flowers fade
when the LORD sends the
wind blowing over them.
People are no more enduring
than grass.
⁸Yes, grass withers and flowers
fade,
but the word of our God
endures forever."

⁹Jerusalem, go up on a high
mountain
and proclaim the good news!
Call out with a loud voice, Zion;
announce the good news!ᵍ
Speak out and do not be afraid.

Tell the towns of Judah
that their God is coming!

¹⁰The Sovereign LORD is coming to
rule with power,
bringing with him the people
he has rescued.ʰ
¹¹He will take care of his flock like
a shepherd;
he will gather the lambs
together
and carry them in his arms;
he will gently lead their
mothers.

Israel's Incomparable God

¹²Can anyone measure the ocean
by handfuls
or measure the sky with his
hands?
Can anyone hold the soil of the
earth in a cup
or weigh the mountains and
hills on scales?
¹³Can anyone tell the LORD what
to do?
Who can teach him or give
him advice?
¹⁴With whom does God consult
in order to know and
understand
and to learn how things
should be done?

¹⁵To the LORD the nations are
nothing,
no more than a drop of water;
the distant islands are as light
as dust.
¹⁶All the animals in the forests of
Lebanon
are not enough for a sacrifice
to our God,

ᵍ Jerusalem, go up ... news!; *or* Go up on a high mountain and proclaim the good
news to Jerusalem! Call out with a loud voice and announce the good news to Zion!
ʰ the people he has rescued; *or* the rewards he has for his people.
40.3 Si 48.10; Ba 5.7; Mt 3.3; Mk 1.3; Jn 1.23   **40.3-5** Lk 3.4-6   **40.6-8** Jas 1.10, 11;
1 P 1.24, 25   **40.10** Is 62.11; Rev 22.12   **40.11** Ez 34.15; Jn 10.11   **40.13** Ro 11.34;
1 Co 2.16   **40.15** Ws 11.22; Si 10.16, 17

and its trees are too few to
kindle the fire.
¹⁷ The nations are nothing at all
to him.

¹⁸ To whom can God be compared?
How can you describe what
he is like?
¹⁹ He is not like an idol that
workers make,
that metalworkers cover with
gold
and set in a base of silver.
²⁰ Anyone who cannot afford silver
or gold ⁱ
chooses wood that will not rot.
He finds a skillful worker
to make an image that won't
fall down.

²¹ Do you not know?
Were you not told long ago?
Have you not heard how the
world began?
²² It was made by the one who sits
on his throne
above the earth and beyond
the sky;
the people below look as tiny
as ants.
He stretched out the sky like a
curtain,
like a tent in which to live.

²³ He brings down powerful rulers
and reduces them to nothing.
²⁴ They are like young plants,
just set out and barely rooted.
When the LORD sends a wind,
they dry up and blow away
like straw.

²⁵ To whom can the holy God be
compared?
Is there anyone else like him?
²⁶ Look up at the sky!
Who created the stars you see?

The one who leads them out
like an army,
he knows how many there are
and calls each one by name!
His power is so great —
not one of them is ever
missing!

²⁷ Israel, why then do you complain
that the LORD doesn't know
your troubles
or care if you suffer injustice?
²⁸ Don't you know? Haven't you
heard?
The LORD is the everlasting God;
he created all the world.
He never grows tired or weary.
No one understands his
thoughts.
²⁹ He strengthens those who are
weak and tired.
³⁰ Even those who are young grow
weak;
young people can fall
exhausted.
³¹ But those who trust in the LORD
for help
will find their strength
renewed.
They will rise on wings like
eagles;
they will run and not get
weary;
they will walk and not grow
weak.

God's Assurance to Israel

41 God says,
"Be silent and listen to
me, you distant lands!
Get ready to present your case
in court;
you will have your chance to
speak.
Let us come together to decide
who is right.

ⁱ *Verses 19-20a in Hebrew are unclear.*
40.18, 19 Ac 17.29   **40.20** Ws 13.11-19; Let Jer 8-40   **40.26** Ba 3.34, 35

2"Who was it that brought the
      conqueror from the east[j]
   and makes him triumphant
      wherever he goes?
   Who gives him victory over kings
      and nations?
   His sword strikes them down
      as if they were dust.
   His arrows scatter them like
      straw before the wind.
3He follows in pursuit and
      marches safely on,
   so fast that he hardly touches
      the ground!
4Who was it that made this
      happen?
   Who has determined the
      course of history?
   I, the LORD, was there at the
      beginning,
   and I, the LORD, will be there
      at the end.

5"The people of distant lands have
      seen what I have done;
   they are frightened and
      tremble with fear.
   So they all assemble and
      come.
6The skilled workers help and
      encourage each other.
7The carpenter says to the
      goldsmith, 'Well done!'
   The one who beats the idol
      smooth
   encourages the one who nails
      it together.
   They say, 'The soldering is
      good' —
   and they fasten the idol in
      place with nails.

8"But you, Israel my servant,
      you are the people that I have
         chosen,
   the descendants of Abraham,
      my friend.

9I brought you from the ends of
      the earth;
   I called you from its farthest
      corners
   and said to you, 'You are my
      servant.'
   I did not reject you, but
      chose you.
10Do not be afraid — I am with you!
   I am your God — let nothing
      terrify you!
   I will make you strong and
      help you;
   I will protect you and
      save you.

11"Those who are angry with you
      will know the shame of
         defeat.
   Those who fight against you
      will die
12   and will disappear from the
         earth.
13I am the LORD your God;
   I strengthen you and tell you,
   'Do not be afraid; I will
      help you.' "

14The LORD says,
   "Small and weak as you are,
      Israel,
   don't be afraid; I will
      help you.
   I, the holy God of Israel, am the
      one who saves you.
15I will make you like a threshing
      board,
   with spikes that are new and
      sharp.
   You will thresh mountains and
      destroy them;
   hills will crumble into dust.
16You will toss them in the air;
   the wind will carry them off,
   and they will be scattered by
      the storm.

---

[j] THE CONQUEROR FROM THE EAST: *Cyrus, the emperor of Persia (see 45.1).*
41.8 2 Ch 20.7; Jas 2.23

I will turn the desert into pools of water. (41.18)

Then you will be happy because
    I am your God;
    you will praise me, the holy
      God of Israel.

¹⁷"When my people in their need
    look for water,
    when their throats are dry
      with thirst,
then I, the LORD, will answer
    their prayer;
    I, the God of Israel, will never
      abandon them.
¹⁸I will make rivers flow among
    barren hills
    and springs of water run in
      the valleys.
I will turn the desert into pools
    of water
    and the dry land into flowing
      springs.
¹⁹I will make cedars grow in the
    desert,
    and acacias and myrtles and
      olive trees.
Forests will grow in barren land,
    forests of pine and juniper
      and cypress.
²⁰People will see this and know
    that I, the LORD, have done it.
They will come to understand
    that Israel's holy God has
      made it happen."

^k A MAN WHO LIVES IN THE EAST: *See 41.2.*

The LORD's Challenge to False Gods

²¹The LORD, the king of Israel, has
this to say:
    "You gods of the nations, present
      your case.
    Bring the best arguments you
      have!
²²Come here and predict what will
    happen,
    so that we will know it when
      it takes place.
Explain to the court the events
    of the past,
    and tell us what they mean.
²³Tell us what the future holds —
    then we will know that you
      are gods!
Do something good or bring
    some disaster;
    fill us with fear and awe!
²⁴You and all you do are nothing;
    those who worship you are
      disgusting!

²⁵"I have chosen a man who lives
    in the east;^k
    I will bring him to attack from
      the north.
He tramples on rulers as if they
    were mud,
    like a potter trampling clay.
²⁶Which of you predicted that this
    would happen,

so that we could say that you
were right?
None of you said a word about it;
no one heard you say a thing!
27 I, the LORD, was the first to tell
Zion the news;
I sent a messenger to
Jerusalem to say,
'Your people are coming!
They are coming home!'[l]
28 When I looked among the gods,
none of them had a thing
to say;
not one could answer the
questions I asked.
29 All these gods are useless;
they can do nothing at all —
these idols are weak and
powerless."

The LORD's Servant

42 The LORD says,
"Here is my servant,
whom I strengthen —
the one I have chosen, with
whom I am pleased.
I have filled him with my Spirit,
and he will bring justice to
every nation.
2 He will not shout or raise his
voice
or make loud speeches in the
streets.
3 He will not break off a bent reed
nor put out a flickering lamp.
He will bring lasting justice
to all.
4 He will not lose hope or courage;
he will establish justice on the
earth.
Distant lands eagerly wait for
his teaching."

5 God created the heavens and
stretched them out;

he fashioned the earth and all
that lives there;
he gave life and breath to all
its people.
And now the LORD God says to
his servant,
6 "I, the LORD, have called you and
given you power
to see that justice is done on
earth.
Through you I will make a
covenant with all peoples;
through you I will bring light
to the nations.
7 You will open the eyes of the
blind
and set free those who sit in
dark prisons.

8 "I alone am the LORD your God.
No other god may share my
glory;
I will not let idols share my
praise.
9 The things I predicted have now
come true.
Now I will tell you of new things
even before they begin to
happen."

A Song of Praise

10 Sing a new song to the LORD;
sing his praise, all the world!
Praise him, you that sail the sea;
praise him, all creatures of
the sea!
Sing, distant lands and all who
live there!
11 Let the desert and its towns
praise God;
let the people of Kedar
praise him!
Let those who live in the city of
Sela
shout for joy from the tops of
the mountains!

Verse 27 in Hebrew is unclear.

42.1 Mt 3.17; 17.5; Mk 1.11; Lk 3.22; 9.35   **42.1-4** Mt 12.18-21   **42.5** Ac 17.24, 25
42.6 Is 49.6; Lk 2.32; Ac 13.47; 26.23

¹²Let those who live in distant
lands
give praise and glory to the
LORD!
¹³The LORD goes out to fight like a
warrior;
he is ready and eager for
battle.
He gives a war cry, a battle
shout;
he shows his power against
his enemies.

God Promises to Help His People

¹⁴God says,
"For a long time I kept silent;
I did not answer my people.
But now the time to act has
come;
I cry out like a woman in
labor.
¹⁵I will destroy the hills and
mountains
and dry up the grass and
trees.
I will turn the river valleys into
deserts ᵐ
and dry up the pools of water.

¹⁶"I will lead my blind people
by roads they have never
traveled.
I will turn their darkness into
light
and make rough country
smooth before them.
These are my promises,
and I will keep them without
fail.
¹⁷All who trust in idols,
who call images their gods,
will be humiliated and
disgraced."

Israel's Failure to Learn

¹⁸The LORD says,
"Listen, you deaf people!

Look closely, you that are
blind!
¹⁹Is anyone more blind than my
servant,
more deaf than the messenger
I send?
²⁰Israel, you have seen so much,
but what has it meant to you?
You have ears to hear with,
but what have you really
heard?"

²¹The LORD is a God who is eager
to save,
so he exalted his laws and
teachings,
and he wanted his people to
honor them.
²²But now his people have been
plundered;

When you pass through deep waters . . . (43.2)

they are locked up in
dungeons
and hidden away in prisons.
They were robbed and
plundered,
with no one to come to their
rescue.

²³Will any of you listen to this?
From now on will you listen
with care?
²⁴Who gave Israel up to the
looters?
It was the LORD himself,
against whom we sinned!

ᵐ *Probable text* deserts; *Hebrew* coastlands.

We would not live as he wanted
 us to live
 or obey the teachings he
  gave us.
25 So he made us feel the force of
 his anger
 and suffer the violence of war.
Like fire his anger burned
 throughout Israel,
 but we never knew what was
  happening;
 we learned nothing at all
  from it.

God Promises to Rescue His People

43 Israel, the LORD who created
you says,
"Do not be afraid — I will
 save you.
I have called you by name —
 you are mine.
2 When you pass through deep
 waters, I will be with you;
your troubles will not
 overwhelm you.
When you pass through fire, you
 will not be burned;
 the hard trials that come will
 not hurt you.
3 For I am the LORD your God,
 the holy God of Israel, who
 saves you.
I will give up Egypt to set you
 free;
I will give up Ethiopia[n] and
 Seba.
4 I will give up whole nations to
 save your life,
 because you are precious
 to me
 and because I love you and
 give you honor.
5 Do not be afraid — I am with you!

"From the distant east and the
 farthest west
I will bring your people home.

I will bring your people home. (43.5)

6 I will tell the north to let
 them go
 and the south not to hold
 them back.
Let my people return from
 distant lands,
 from every part of the world.
7 They are my own people,
 and I created them to bring
 me glory."

Israel Is the LORD's Witness

8 God says,
"Summon my people to court.
 They have eyes, but they are
 blind;
 they have ears, but they are
 deaf!
9 Summon the nations to come to
 the trial.
 Which of their gods can
 predict the future?

---

[n] *Hebrew* Cush: *Cush is the ancient name of the extensive territory south of the First Cataract of the Nile River. This region was called Ethiopia in Graeco-Roman times, and included within its borders most of modern Sudan and some of present-day Ethiopia (Abyssinia).*

The Lord made a road through the sea. (43.16)

Which of them foretold what
is happening now?
Let these gods bring in their
witnesses
to prove that they are right,
to testify to the truth of their
words.

10"People of Israel, you are my
witnesses;
I chose you to be my servant,
so that you would know me and
believe in me
and understand that I am the
only God.
Besides me there is no other god;
there never was and never
will be.

11"I alone am the Lord,
the only one who can
save you.
12I predicted what would happen,
and then I came to your aid.
No foreign god has ever done
this;
you are my witnesses.
13I am God and always will be.

No one can escape from my
power;
no one can change what
I do."

Escape from Babylon

14Israel's holy God, the Lord who
saves you, says,
"To save you, I will send an
army against Babylon;
I will break down the city
gates,
and the shouts of her people
will turn into crying.
15I am the Lord, your holy God.
I created you, Israel, and I am
your king."

16Long ago the Lord made a road
through the sea,
a path through the swirling
waters.
17He led a mighty army to
destruction,
an army of chariots and
horses.
Down they fell, never to rise,
snuffed out like the flame of
a lamp!

18 But the LORD says,
"Do not cling to events of the
past
or dwell on what happened
long ago.
19 Watch for the new thing I am
going to do.
It is happening already — you
can see it now!
I will make a road through the
wilderness
and give you streams of water
there.
20 Even the wild animals will
honor me;
jackals and ostriches will
praise me
when I make rivers flow in the
desert
to give water to my chosen
people.
21 They are the people I made for
myself,
and they will sing my
praises!"

Israel's Sin

22 The LORD says,
"But you were tired of me, Israel;
you did not worship me.
23 You did not bring me your burnt
offerings of sheep;
you did not honor me with
your sacrifices.
I did not burden you by
demanding offerings
or wear you out by asking for
incense.
24 You didn't buy incense for me
or satisfy me with the fat of
your animals.
Instead you burdened me with
your sins;
you wore me out with the
wrongs you have
committed.

25 And yet, I am the God who
forgives your sins,
and I do this because of who
I am.
I will not hold your sins
against you.

26 "Let us go to court; bring your
accusation!
Present your case to prove you
are in the right!
27 Your earliest ancestor*o* sinned;
your leaders sinned
against me,
28   and your rulers profaned*p* my
sanctuary.
So I brought destruction on
Israel;
I let my own people be
insulted."

The LORD Is the Only God

44 The LORD says,
"Listen now, Israel, my
servant,
my chosen people, the
descendants of Jacob.
2 I am the LORD who created you;
from the time you were born,
I have helped you.
Do not be afraid; you are my
servant,
my chosen people whom I
love.

3 "I will give water to the thirsty
land
and make streams flow on the
dry ground.
I will pour out my spirit on your
children
and my blessing on your
descendants.
4 They will thrive like well-watered
grass,
like willows by streams of
running water.

YOUR EARLIEST ANCESTOR: *A reference to Jacob or to Abraham, or possibly to Adam.*
One ancient translation your rulers profaned; *Hebrew* I profaned the rulers of.

5"One by one, people will say, 'I
  am the LORD's.'
They will come to join the
  people of Israel.
They each will mark the name of
  the LORD on their arms
and call themselves one of
  God's people."

6The LORD, who rules and
  protects Israel,
  the LORD Almighty, has this
  to say:
"I am the first, the last, the
  only God;
  there is no other god but me.
7Could anyone else have done
  what I did?
Who could have predicted all
  that would happen
from the very beginning to
  the end of time?q
8Do not be afraid, my people!
You know that from ancient
  times until now
I have predicted all that would
  happen,
and you are my witnesses.
Is there any other god?
Is there some powerful god I
  never heard of?"

Idolatry Is Ridiculed

9All those who make idols are worthless, and the gods they prize so highly
are useless. Those who worship these
gods are blind and ignorant — and they
will be disgraced. 10It does no good to
make a metal image to worship as a
god! 11Everyone who worships it will be
humiliated. The people who make idols
are human beings and nothing more.
Let them come and stand trial — they
will be terrified and will suffer disgrace.
12The metalworker takes a piece of
metal and works with it over a fire. His

Bowing down to a block of wood (44.19)

strong arm swings a hammer to pound
the metal into shape. As he works, he
gets hungry, thirsty, and tired.
13The carpenter measures the wood.
He outlines a figure with chalk, carves
it out with his tools, and makes it in the
form of a man, a handsome human figure, to be placed in his house. 14He
might cut down cedars to use, or
choose oak or cypress wood from the
forest. Or he might plant a laurel tree
and wait for the rain to make it grow.
15A person uses part of a tree for fuel
and part of it for making an idol. With
one part he builds a fire to warm himself and bake bread; with the other part
he makes a god and worships it. 16With
some of the wood he makes a fire; he
roasts meat, eats it, and is satisfied. He
warms himself and says, "How nice and
warm! What a beautiful fire!" 17The
rest of the wood he makes into an idol
and then he bows down and worships
it. He prays to it and says, "You are my
god — save me!"
18Such people are too stupid to know
what they are doing. They close their
eyes and their minds to the truth. 19The
maker of idols hasn't the wit or the
sense to say, "Some of the wood I
burned up. I baked some bread on the
coals, and I roasted meat and ate it. And
the rest of the wood I made into an idol

Here I am bowing down to a block of wood!"

²⁰ It makes as much sense^r as eating ashes. His foolish ideas have so misled him that he is beyond help. He won't admit to himself that the idol he holds in his hand is not a god at all.

The LORD, the Creator and Savior

²¹ The LORD says,
"Israel, remember this;
    remember that you are my
      servant.
I created you to be my servant,
    and I will never forget you.
²² I have swept your sins away like
    a cloud.
    Come back to me; I am the
      one who saves you."

²³ Shout for joy, you heavens!
    Shout, deep places of the
      earth!
Shout for joy, mountains, and
      every tree of the forest!
The LORD has shown his
    greatness
    by saving his people Israel.

The idol he holds in his hand is not a god at all.
(44.20)

²⁴ "I am the LORD, your savior;
    I am the one who created you.
I am the LORD, the Creator of all
    things.
    I alone stretched out the
      heavens;
    when I made the earth, no
      one helped me.
²⁵ I make fools of fortunetellers
    and frustrate the predictions
      of astrologers.
The words of the wise I refute
    and show that their wisdom is
      foolishness.
²⁶ But when my servant makes a
    prediction,
    when I send a messenger to
      reveal my plans,
    I make those plans and
      predictions come true.
I tell Jerusalem that people will
    live there again,
    and the cities of Judah that
      they will be rebuilt.
    Those cities will rise from the
      ruins.
²⁷ With a word of command I dry
    up the ocean.
²⁸ I say to Cyrus, 'You are the one
    who will rule for me;
    you will do what I want you
      to do:
    you will order that Jerusalem
      be rebuilt
    and that the foundations of
      the Temple be laid.' "

The LORD Appoints Cyrus

45 The LORD has chosen Cyrus
    to be king.
He has appointed him to conquer
    nations;
    he sends him to strip kings of
      their power;
    the LORD will open the gates
      of cities for him.

It makes as much sense; *or* It will do him as much good.
44.25 1 Co 1.20   **44.28** 2 Ch 36.23; Ezra 1.2

To Cyrus the LORD says,
² "I myself will prepare your way,
    leveling mountains and hills.
  I will break down bronze gates
    and smash their iron bars.
³ I will give you treasures from
    dark, secret places;
  then you will know that I am
    the LORD
  and that the God of Israel has
    called you by name.
⁴ I appoint you to help my servant
    Israel,
  the people that I have chosen.
  I have given you great honor,
    although you do not know me.

⁵ "I am the LORD; there is no
    other god.
  I will give you the strength
    you need,
  although you do not know me.
⁶ I do this so that everyone
  from one end of the world to
    the other
  may know that I am the LORD
  and that there is no other god.
⁷ I create both light and darkness;
  I bring both blessing and
    disaster.
  I, the LORD, do all these
    things.
⁸ I will send victory from the sky
    like rain;
  the earth will open to
    receive it
  and will blossom with freedom
    and justice.
  I, the LORD, will make this
    happen."

The LORD of Creation and History

⁹ Does a clay pot dare argue with
    its maker,
  a pot that is like all the
    others?
  Does the clay ask the potter what
    he is doing?
  Does the pot complain that its
    maker has no skill?
¹⁰ Do we dare say to our parents,
    "Why did you make me like
    this?"
¹¹ The LORD, the holy God of Israel,
    the one who shapes the
    future, says:
  "You have no right to question
    me about my children
  or to tell me what I ought
    to do!
¹² I am the one who made the
    earth
  and created human beings to
    live there.
  By my power I stretched out the
    heavens;
  I control the sun, the moon,
    and the stars.
¹³ I myself have stirred Cyrus to
    action
  to fulfill my purpose and put
    things right.
  I will straighten out every road
    that he travels.
  He will rebuild my city,
    Jerusalem,
  and set my captive people
    free.
  No one has hired him or bribed
    him to do this."
  The LORD Almighty has spoken.

¹⁴ The LORD says to Israel,
  "The wealth of Egypt and
    Ethiopiaˢ will be yours,
  and the tall men of Seba will
    be your slaves;
  they will follow you in chains.

ˢ *Hebrew* Cush: *Cush is the ancient name of the extensive territory south of the First Cataract of the Nile River. This region was called Ethiopia in Graeco-Roman times, and included within its borders most of modern Sudan and some of present-day Ethiopia (Abyssinia).*
45.9 Is 29.16; Ro 9.20

They will bow down to you and
confess,
  'God is with you—he alone
    is God.

15 The God of Israel, who saves his
people,
  is a God who conceals
    himself.

16 Those who make idols will all be
ashamed;
  all of them will be disgraced.

17 But Israel is saved by the LORD,
  and her victory lasts forever;
  her people will never be
    disgraced.'"

18 The LORD created the heavens—
  he is the one who is God!
He formed and made the earth—
  he made it firm and lasting.
He did not make it a desolate
waste,
  but a place for people to live.
It is he who says, "I am the
LORD,
  and there is no other god.

19 I have not spoken in secret
  or kept my purpose hidden.
I did not require the people of
Israel
  to look for me in a desolate
    waste.
I am the LORD, and I speak the
truth;
  I make known what is right."

The LORD of the World and the Idols of Babylon

20 The LORD says,
"Come together, people of the
nations,
  all who survive the fall of the
    empire;
  present yourselves for the
    trial!
The people who parade with
  their idols of wood

and pray to gods that cannot
save them—
  those people know nothing
    at all!

21 Come and present your case in
court;
  let the defendants consult one
    another.
Who predicted long ago what
  would happen?
Was it not I, the LORD, the God
  who saves his people?
There is no other god.

22 "Turn to me now and be saved,
  people all over the world!
I am the only God there is.

23 My promise is true,
  and it will not be changed.
I solemnly promise by all that
  I am:
  Everyone will come and kneel
    before me
  and vow to be loyal to me.

24 "They will say that only
  through me
  are victory and strength to be
    found;
  but all who hate me will
    suffer disgrace.

25 I, the LORD, will rescue all the
  descendants of Jacob,
  and they will give me praise.

46

"This is the end for Babylon's
  gods!
Bel and Nebo once were
  worshiped,
but now they are loaded on
  donkeys,
  a burden for the backs of tired
    animals.

2   The idols cannot save
    themselves;
  they are captured and carried
    away.
This is the end for Babylon's
  gods!

45.23 Ro 14.11; Phil 2.10, 11

The idols cannot save themselves. (46.2)

³"Listen to me, descendants of
        Jacob,
    all who are left of my people.
I have cared for you from the
        time you were born.
⁴I am your God and will take care
        of you
    until you are old and your hair
        is gray.
I made you and will care for you;
    I will give you help and
        rescue you.

⁵"To whom will you compare
        me?" says the LORD.
    "Is there anyone else like me?
⁶People open their purses and
        pour out gold;
    they weigh out silver on the
        scales.
They hire a goldsmith to make
        a god;
    then they bow down and
        worship it.
⁷They lift it to their shoulders and
        carry it;
    they put it in place, and there
        it stands,
    unable to move from where
        it is.
If any pray to it, it cannot
        answer
    or save them from disaster.

⁸"Remember this, you sinners;
    consider what I have done.

⁹Remember what happened
        long ago;
    acknowledge that I alone
        am God
    and that there is no one else
        like me.
¹⁰From the beginning I predicted
        the outcome;
    long ago I foretold what would
        happen.
I said that my plans would never
        fail,
    that I would do everything I
        intended to do.
¹¹I am calling a man to come from
        the east;ᵗ
    he will swoop down like a
        hawk
    and accomplish what I have
        planned.
I have spoken, and it will be
        done.

¹²"Listen to me, you stubborn
        people
    who think that victory is far
        away.
¹³I am bringing the day of victory
        near—
    it is not far away at all.
My triumph will not be delayed.
    I will save Jerusalem
    and bring honor to Israel
        there."

Judgment on Babylon

47 The LORD says,
    "Babylon, come down from
        your throne,
    and sit in the dust on the
        ground.
You were once like a virgin, a
        city unconquered,
    but you are soft and delicate
        no longer!
You are now a slave!

ᵗ A MAN TO COME FROM THE EAST: *See* 41.2.
47.1-15 Is 13.1—14.23; Jr 50.1—51.64

2 Turn the millstone! Grind the
    flour!
Off with your veil! Strip off your
    fine clothes!
Lift up your skirts to cross the
    streams!ᵘ
3 People will see you naked;
    they will see you humbled
    and shamed.
I will take vengeance, and no
    one will stop me."

4 The holy God of Israel sets us
    free —
    his name is the LORD
    Almighty.

5 The LORD says to Babylon,
"Sit in silence and darkness;
    no more will they call you the
    queen of nations!
6 I was angry with my people;
    I treated them as no longer
    mine:
I put them in your power,
    and you showed them no
    mercy;
    even the aged you treated
    harshly.
7 You thought you would always
    be a queen,
    and did not take these things
    to heart
    or think how it all would end.

8 "Listen to this, you lover of
    pleasure,
    you that think you are safe
    and secure.
You claim you are as great
    as God —
    that there is no one else
    like you.
You thought that you would
    never be a widow
    or suffer the loss of your
    children.

9 But in a moment, in a
    single day,
    both of these things will
    happen.
In spite of all the magic you use,
    you will lose your husband
    and children.

10 "You felt sure of yourself in
    your evil;
    you thought that no one could
    see you.
Your wisdom and knowledge led
    you astray,
    and you said to yourself, 'I
    am God —
    there is no one else like me.'
11 Disaster will come upon you,
    and none of your magic can
    stop it.
Ruin will come on you
    suddenly —
    ruin you never dreamed of!
12 Keep all your magic spells and
    charms;
    you have used them since you
    were young.
Perhaps they will be of some
    help to you;
    perhaps you can frighten your
    enemies.
13 You are powerless in spite of the
    advice you get.
Let your astrologers come
    forward and save you —
    those people who study the
    stars,
    who map out the zones of the
    heavens
    and tell you from month to
    month
    whatᵛ is going to happen
    to you.

14 "They will be like bits of straw,
    and a fire will burn them up!

ᵘ CROSS THE STREAMS: *This probably refers to going into exile.*   ᵛ *Some ancient*
translations what; *Hebrew* from what.
47.8, 9 Rev 18.7, 8

Those people who study the stars (47.13)

They will not even be able to
    save themselves —
    the flames will be too hot for
    them,
    not a cozy fire to warm
    themselves by.
¹⁵ That is all the good they will
    do you —
    those astrologers you've
    consulted all your life.
They all will leave you and go
    their own way,
    and none will be left to
    save you."

God Is Lord of the Future

48 Listen to this, people of
    Israel,
    you that are descended from
    Judah:
You swear by the name of the
    Lord
    and claim to worship the God
    of Israel —
    but you don't mean a word
    you say.
² And yet you are proud to say
    that you are citizens of the
    holy city

and that you depend on
    Israel's God,
    whose name is the Lord
    Almighty.

³ The Lord says to Israel,
    "Long ago I predicted what
    would take place;
    then suddenly I made it
    happen.
⁴ I knew that you would prove to
    be stubborn,
    as rigid as iron and unyielding
    as bronze.
⁵ And so I predicted your future
    long ago,
    announcing events before
    they took place,
    to keep you from claiming
    that your idols and images
    made them happen.

⁶ "All I foretold has now taken
    place;
    you have to admit my
    predictions were right.
Now I will tell you of new things
    to come,
    events that I did not reveal
    before.
⁷ Only now am I making them
    happen;
    nothing like this took place in
    the past.
If it had, you would claim that
    you knew all about it.
⁸ I knew that you couldn't be
    trusted,
    that you have always been
    known as a rebel.
That is why you never heard of
    this at all,
    why no word of it ever came
    to your ears.

⁹ "In order that people will praise
    my name,
    I am holding my anger in
    check;
    I am keeping it back and will
    not destroy you.

¹⁰I have tested you in the fire of
    suffering,
    as silver is refined in a
        furnace.
But I have found that you are
    worthless.
¹¹What I do is done for my own
    sake —
    I will not let my name be
        dishonored
    or let anyone else share the
        glory
    that should be mine and mine
        alone."

Cyrus, the LORD's Chosen Leader

¹²The LORD says,
    "Listen to me, Israel, the people
        I have called!
    I am God, the first, the last, the
        only God!
¹³My hands made the earth's
        foundations
    and spread the heavens out.
    When I summon earth and sky,
        they come at once and
        present themselves.

¹⁴"Assemble and listen, all of you!
    None of the gods could predict
        that the man I have chosen
        would attack Babylon;
    he will do what I want him
        to do.
¹⁵I am the one who spoke and
        called him;
    I led him out and gave him
        success.

¹⁶"Now come close to me and hear
        what I say.
    From the beginning I have
        spoken openly
    and have always made my
        words come true."
Now the Sovereign LORD has given me
his power and sent me.)

The LORD's Plan for His People

¹⁷The holy God of Israel,
    the LORD who saves you, says:
"I am the LORD your God,
    the one who wants to teach
        you for your own good
    and direct you in the way you
        should go.

¹⁸"If only you had listened to my
        commands!
    Then blessings would have
        flowed for you
    like a stream that never
        goes dry.
    Victory would have come to you
        like the waves that roll on the
        shore.
¹⁹Your descendants would be as
        numerous as grains
        of sand,
    and I would have made sure
        they were never destroyed."

²⁰Go out from Babylon, go free!
    Shout the news gladly; make it
        known everywhere:
    "The LORD has saved his
        servant Israel!"
²¹When the LORD led his people
        through a hot, dry desert,
    they did not suffer from thirst.
    He made water come from a rock
        for them;
    he split the rock open, and
        water flowed out.

²²"There is no safety for sinners,"
    says the LORD.

Israel, A Light to the Nations

49 Listen to me, distant nations,
    you people who live far
        away!
Before I was born, the LORD
        chose me
    and appointed me to be his
        servant.

48.12 Is 44.6; Rev 1.17; 22.13   **48.20** Rev 18.4   **48.22** Is 57.21   **49.1** Jr 1.5

²He made my words as sharp as
a sword.
With his own hand he
protected me. ^w
He made me like an arrow,
sharp and ready for use.
³He said to me, "Israel, you are
my servant;
because of you, people will
praise me."

⁴I said, "I have worked, but how
hopeless it is!
I have used up my strength,
but have accomplished
nothing."
Yet I can trust the LORD to
defend my cause;
he will reward me for what
I do.

⁵Before I was born, the LORD
appointed me;
he made me his servant to
bring back his people,
to bring back the scattered
people of Israel.
The LORD gives me honor;
he is the source of my
strength.

⁶The LORD said to me,
"I have a greater task for you,
my servant.
Not only will you restore to
greatness
the people of Israel who have
survived,
but I will also make you a light
to the nations —
so that all the world may be
saved."

⁷Israel's holy God and savior says
to the one who is deeply
despised,
who is hated by the nations

and is the servant of rulers:
"Kings will see you released
and will rise to show their
respect;
princes also will see it,
and they will bow low to
honor you."

This will happen because the
LORD has chosen his
servant;
the holy God of Israel keeps his
promises.

The Restoration of Jerusalem

⁸The LORD says to his people,
"When the time comes to save
you, I will show you favor
and answer your cries for
help.
I will guard and protect you
and through you make a
covenant with all peoples.
I will let you settle once again
in your land that is now laid
waste.
⁹I will say to the prisoners, 'Go
free!'
and to those who are in
darkness,
'Come out to the light!'
They will be like sheep that
graze on the hills;
¹⁰   they will never be hungry or
thirsty.
Sun and desert heat will not hurt
them,
for they will be led by one
who loves them.
He will lead them to springs
of water.

¹¹"I will make a highway across
the mountains
and prepare a road for my
people to travel.

^w With his own hand . . . me; *or* He kept me hidden in his hand.
49.2 He 4.12; Rev 1.16   **49.6 a** Is 42.6; Lk 2.32; Ac 26.23; **b** Ac 13.47   **49.8** 2 Co 6.2
49.10 Rev 7.16, 17

¹²My people will come from far
    away,
    from the north and the west,
    and from Aswan˟ in the
        south."

¹³Sing, heavens! Shout for joy,
        earth!
    Let the mountains burst into
        song!
The LORD will comfort his
        people;
    he will have pity on his
        suffering people.

¹⁴But the people of Jerusalem said,
    "The LORD has abandoned us!
    He has forgotten us."
¹⁵So the LORD answers,
    "Can a woman forget her own
        baby
    and not love the child she
        bore?
    Even if a mother should forget
        her child,
    I will never forget you.
¹⁶Jerusalem, I can never
        forget you!
    I have written your name on
        the palms of my hands.

¹⁷"Those who will rebuild you are
        coming soon,
    and those who destroyed you
        will leave.
¹⁸Look around and see what is
        happening!
    Your people are assembling—
        they are coming
        home!
As surely as I am the living God,
    you will be proud of your
        people,
    as proud as a bride is of her
        jewels.

¹⁹"Your country was ruined and
        desolate—

but now it will be too small
    for those who are coming to
        live there.
And those who left you in ruins
    will be far removed from you.
²⁰Your people who were born in
        exile
    will one day say to you,
    'This land is too small—
    we need more room to live in!'
²¹Then you will say to yourself,
    'Who bore all these children
        for me?
    I lost my children and could
        have no more.
    I was exiled and driven away—
    who brought these
        children up?
    I was left all alone—
    where did these children
        come from?' "

²²The Sovereign LORD says to his
people:
    "I will signal to the nations,
    and they will bring your
        children home.
²³Kings will be like fathers to you;
    queens will be like mothers.
    They will bow low before you
        and honor you;
    they will humbly show their
        respect for you.
    Then you will know that I am
        the LORD;
    no one who waits for my help
        will be disappointed."

²⁴Can you take away a soldier's
        loot?
    Can you rescue the prisoners
        of a tyrant?

²⁵The LORD replies,
    "That is just what is going to
        happen.
    The soldier's prisoners will be
        taken away,

˟ ASWAN: *A city in southern Egypt, where a large Jewish community had settled.*
49.22 Ba 5.6

and the tyrant's loot will be
  seized.
I will fight against whoever
  fights you,
and I will rescue your
  children.
26 I will make your oppressors kill
  each other;
  they will be drunk with
    murder and rage.
Then all people will know that I
  am the LORD,
  the one who saves you and
    sets you free.
They will know that I am Israel's
  powerful God."

50

The LORD says,
  "Do you think I sent my
    people away
  like a man who divorces his
    wife?
Where, then, are the papers of
  divorce?
Do you think I sold you into
  captivity
  like a man who sells his
    children as slaves?
No, you went away captive
  because of your sins;
  you were sent away because
    of your crimes.

2 "Why did my people fail to
  respond
  when I went to them to save
    them?
Why did they not answer when I
  called?
Am I too weak to save them?
I can dry up the sea with a
  command
  and turn rivers into a desert,
  so that the fish in them die
    for lack of water.
3 I can make the sky turn dark,
  as if it were in mourning for
    the dead."

The Obedience of the LORD's Servant

4 The Sovereign LORD has taught
  me what to say,
  so that I can strengthen the
    weary.
Every morning he makes me
  eager
  to hear what he is going to
    teach me.
5 The LORD has given me
  understanding,
  and I have not rebelled
  or turned away from him.
6 I bared my back to those who
  beat me.
  I did not stop them when they
    insulted me,
  when they pulled out the
    hairs of my beard
  and spit in my face.

7 But their insults cannot hurt me
  because the Sovereign LORD
    gives me help.
I brace myself to endure them.
I know that I will not be
  disgraced,
8   for God is near,
  and he will prove me
    innocent.
Does anyone dare bring charges
  against me?
  Let us go to court together!
  Let him bring his accusation!
9 The Sovereign LORD himself
  defends me —
  who, then, can prove me
    guilty?
All my accusers will disappear;
  they will vanish like
    moth-eaten cloth.

10 All of you that honor the LORD
  and obey the words of his
    servant,

50.1 Ba 4.6   50.6 Mt 26.67; Mk 14.65   50.8, 9 Ro 8.33, 34

the path you walk may be dark
indeed,
but trust in the LORD, rely on
your God.
[11] All of you that plot to destroy
others
will be destroyed by your own
plots.
The LORD himself will make this
happen;
you will suffer a miserable
fate.

Words of Comfort to Jerusalem

51 The LORD says,
"Listen to me, you that
want to be saved,
you that come to me for help.
Think of the rock from which
you came,
the quarry from which you
were cut.
[2] Think of your ancestor,
Abraham,
and of Sarah, from whom you
are descended.
When I called Abraham, he was
childless,
but I blessed him and gave
him children;
I made his descendants
numerous.

[3] "I will show compassion to
Jerusalem,
to all who live in her ruins.
Though her land is a desert, I
will make it a garden,
like the garden I planted in
Eden.
Joy and gladness will be there,
and songs of praise and
thanks to me.

[4] "Listen to me, my people,
listen to what I say:

I give my teaching to the
nations;
my laws will bring them light.
[5] I will come quickly and save
them;
the time of my victory is near.
I myself will rule over the
nations.
Distant lands wait for me to
come;
they wait with hope for me to
save them.
[6] Look up at the heavens; look at
the earth!
The heavens will disappear
like smoke;
the earth will wear out like
old clothing,
and all its people will die like
flies.
But the deliverance I bring will
last forever;
my victory will be final.

[7] "Listen to me, you that know
what is right,
who have my teaching fixed
in your hearts.
Do not be afraid when people
taunt and insult you;
[8]   they will vanish like
moth-eaten clothing!
But the deliverance I bring will
last forever;
my victory will endure for all
time."

[9] Wake up, LORD, and help us!
Use your power and save us;
use it as you did in ancient
times.
It was you that cut the sea
monster Rahab[y] to pieces.
[10] It was you also who dried up
the sea

RAHAB: *A legendary sea monster, which represented the forces of chaos and evil, was*
ometimes a symbol of Egypt.

and made a path through the
water,
so that those you were saving
could cross.
¹¹ Those whom you have rescued
will reach Jerusalem with
gladness,
singing and shouting for joy.
They will be happy forever,
forever free from sorrow and
grief.

¹² The LORD says,
"I am the one who
strengthens you.
Why should you fear mortals,
who are no more enduring
than grass?
¹³ Have you forgotten the LORD
who made you,
who stretched out the
heavens
and laid the earth's
foundations?
Why should you live in constant
fear
of the fury of those who
oppress you,
of those who are ready to
destroy you?
Their fury can no longer
touch you.
¹⁴ Those who are prisoners will
soon be set free;
they will live a long life
and have all the food they
need.

¹⁵ "I am the LORD your God;
I stir up the sea
and make its waves roar.
My name is the LORD Almighty!
¹⁶ I stretched out ᶻ the heavens
and laid the earth's
foundations;
I say to Jerusalem, 'You are my
people!
I have given you my teaching,
and I protect you with my
hand.'"

The End of Jerusalem's Suffering

¹⁷ Jerusalem, wake up!
Rouse yourself and get up!
You have drunk the cup of
punishment
that the LORD in his anger
gave you to drink;
you drank it down, and it
made you stagger.
¹⁸ There is no one to lead you,
no one among your people
to take you by the hand.

¹⁹ A double disaster has fallen
on you:
your land has been devastated
by war,
and your people have starved.
There is no one to show you
sympathy.
²⁰ At the corner of every street
your people collapse from
weakness;
they are like deer caught in a
hunter's net.
They have felt the force of
God's anger.

²¹ You suffering people of
Jerusalem,
you that stagger as though
you were drunk,
²² the LORD your God defends you
and says,
"I am taking away the cup
that I gave you in my anger.
You will no longer have to drink
the wine that makes you
stagger.
²³ I will give it to those who
oppressed you,
to those who made you lie
down in the streets
and trampled on you as if you
were dirt."

ᶻ *One ancient translation* stretched out; *Hebrew* planted.
51.17 Rev 14.10; 16.19

God Will Rescue Jerusalem

52 Jerusalem, be strong and
            great again!
Holy city of God, clothe
      yourself with splendor!
The heathen will never enter
      your gates again.
[2] Shake yourself free, Jerusalem!
      Rise from the dust and sit on
            your throne!
Undo the chains that bind you,
      captive people of Zion!

[3] The Sovereign LORD says to his people, "When you became slaves, no money was paid for you; in the same way nothing will be paid to set you free. [4] When you went to live in Egypt as foreigners, you did so of your own free will; Assyria, however, took you away by force and paid nothing for you. [5] And now in Babylonia the same thing has happened: you are captives, and nothing was paid for you. Those who rule over you boast and brag and constantly show contempt for me. [6] In time to come you will acknowledge that I am God and that I have spoken to you."

[7] How wonderful it is to see
      a messenger coming across
            the mountains,
      bringing good news, the news
            of peace!
He announces victory and says
      to Zion,
      "Your God is king!"
[8] Those who guard the city are
      shouting,
      shouting together for joy.
They can see with their own
      eyes
      the return of the LORD to
            Zion.

[9] Break into shouts of joy,
      you ruins of Jerusalem!
The LORD will rescue his city
      and comfort his people.

A messenger coming across the mountains (52.7)

[10] The LORD will use his holy
      power;
      he will save his people,
      and all the world will see it.
[11] Be sure to leave Babylonia,
      all you that carry the Temple
            equipment.
Touch no forbidden thing;[a]
      keep yourselves holy and
            leave.
[12] This time you will not have to
      leave in a hurry;
      you will not be trying to
            escape.
The LORD your God will lead you
      and protect you on every side.

The Suffering Servant

[13] The LORD says,
"My servant will succeed in his
      task;
      he will be highly honored.[b]
[14] Many people were shocked when
      they saw him;
      he was so disfigured that he
            hardly looked human.
[15] But now many nations will
      marvel at him,

FORBIDDEN THING: *Any object that was considered ritually unclean.*   [b] he will be highly honored; *or* he will be restored to greatness and honor.

2.1 Rev 21.2, 27   **52.5** Ro 2.24   **52.7** Nh 1.15; Ro 10.15; Eph 6.15   **52.11** 2 Co 6.17
2.15 Ro 15.21

and kings will be speechless
    with amazement.
They will see and understand
    something they had never
        known."

53 The people reply,
    "Who would have believed
        what we now report?
Who could have seen the
    LORD's hand in this?
² It was the will of the LORD that
    his servant
    grow like a plant taking root
        in dry ground.
He had no dignity or beauty
    to make us take notice of him.
There was nothing attractive
    about him,
    nothing that would draw us
        to him.
³ We despised him and
    rejected him;
    he endured suffering and
        pain.
No one would even look
    at him —
    we ignored him as if he were
        nothing.

⁴ "But he endured the suffering
    that should have
        been ours,
    the pain that we should have
        borne.
All the while we thought that his
    suffering
    was punishment sent by God.
⁵ But because of our sins he was
    wounded,
    beaten because of the evil
        we did.
We are healed by the
    punishment he suffered,
    made whole by the blows he
        received.

⁶ All of us were like sheep that
    were lost,
    each of us going his own way.
But the LORD made the
    punishment fall on him,
    the punishment all of us
        deserved.

⁷ "He was treated harshly, but
    endured it humbly;
    he never said a word.
Like a lamb about to be
    slaughtered,
    like a sheep about to be sheared,
    he never said a word.

He never said a word. (53.7)

⁸ He was arrested and sentenced
    and led off to die,
    and no one cared about his
        fate.
He was put to death for the sins
    of our people.
⁹ He was placed in a grave with
    those who are evil,
    he was buried with the rich,
even though he had never
    committed a crime
    or ever told a lie."

¹⁰ The LORD says,
    "It was my will that he should
        suffer;

53.1 Ro 10.16; Jn 12.38 **53.4** Mt 8.17 **53.5** 1 P 2.24 **53.6** 1 P 2.25 **53.7** Rev 5.6
53.7, 8 Ac 8.32, 33 **53.9** 1 P 2.22

his death was a sacrifice to
    bring forgiveness.
And so he will see his
    descendants;
  he will live a long life,
  and through him my purpose
    will succeed.
11 After a life of suffering, he will
    again have joy;
  he will know that he did not
    suffer in vain.
My devoted servant, with whom
    I am pleased,
  will bear the punishment of
    many
  and for his sake I will forgive
    them.
12 And so I will give him a place of
    honor,
  a place among the great and
    powerful.
He willingly gave his life
  and shared the fate of
    evil men.
He took the place of many
    sinners
  and prayed that they might be
    forgiven."c

The LORD's Love for Israel

54 Jerusalem, you have been
        like a childless woman,
  but now you can sing and
    shout for joy.
Now you will have more children
  than a woman whose husband
    never left her.
2 Make the tent you live in larger;
  lengthen its ropes and
    strengthen the pegs!
3 You will extend your boundaries
    on all sides;
  your people will get back the
    land
  that the other nations now
    occupy.

Cities now deserted will be
  filled with people.

4 Do not be afraid — you will not be
    disgraced again;
  you will not be humiliated.
You will forget your unfaithfulness
    as a young wife,
  and your desperate loneliness
    as a widow.
5 Your Creator will be like a
    husband to you —
  the LORD Almighty is his
    name.
The holy God of Israel will
    save you —
  he is the ruler of all the
    world.

6 Israel, you are like a young wife,
  deserted by her husband and
    deeply distressed.
But the LORD calls you back to
  him and says:
7 "For one brief moment I left you;
  with deep love I will take you
    back.
8 I turned away angry for only a
    moment,
  but I will show you my love
    forever."
So says the LORD who saves you.

9 "In the time of Noah I promised
  never again to flood the earth.
Now I promise not to be angry
  with you again;
  I will not reprimand or
    punish you.
10 The mountains and hills may
    crumble,
  but my love for you will
    never end;
  I will keep forever my promise
    of peace."
So says the LORD who loves you.

prayed that they might be forgiven; or suffered the punishment they deserved.
53.12 Mk 15.28; Lk 22.37   **54.1** Ga 4.27   **54.9** Gn 9.8-17   **54.10** Jdt 16.15

The Future Jerusalem

[11] The LORD says,
"O Jerusalem, you suffering,
    helpless city,
  with no one to comfort you,
I will rebuild your foundations
    with precious stones.
[12] I will build your towers with
    rubies,
  your gates with stones that
    glow like fire,
  and the wall around you with
    jewels.

[13] "I myself will teach your people
    and give them prosperity and
    peace.
[14] Justice and right will make you
    strong.
  You will be safe from
    oppression and terror.
[15] Whoever attacks you,
    does it without my consent;
  whoever fights against you will
    fall.

[16] "I create the blacksmith,
    who builds a fire and forges
    weapons.
  I also create the soldier,
    who uses the weapons to kill.
[17] But no weapon will be able to
    hurt you;
  you will have an answer for
    all who accuse you.
  I will defend my servants
    and give them victory."

The LORD has spoken.

God's Offer of Mercy

55 The LORD says,
"Come, everyone who is
    thirsty —
  here is water!
Come, you that have no
    money —

buy grain and eat!
Come! Buy wine and milk —
  it will cost you nothing!
[2] Why spend money on what does
    not satisfy?
  Why spend your wages and
    still be hungry?
Listen to me and do what I say,
  and you will enjoy the best
    food of all.

[3] "Listen now, my people, and
    come to me;
  come to me, and you will have
    life!
I will make a lasting covenant
    with you
  and give you the blessings I
    promised to David.
[4] I made him a leader and
    commander of nations,
  and through him I showed
    them my power.
[5] Now you will summon foreign
    nations;
  at one time they did not
    know you,
  but now they will come
    running to join you!
I, the LORD your God, the holy
    God of Israel,
  will make all this happen;
  I will give you honor and
    glory."

[6] Turn to the LORD and pray
    to him,
  now that he is near.
[7] Let the wicked leave their way
    of life
  and change their way of
    thinking.
Let them turn to the LORD,
    our God;
  he is merciful and quick to
    forgive.
[8] "My thoughts," says the LORD,
  "are not like yours,

54.11, 12 Rev 21.18-21   **54.11** Tb 13.16, 17   **54.13** Jn 6.45   **55.1** Rev 21.6; 22.17
55.2 Si 24.19-22   **55.3** Ac 13.34

and my ways are different
from yours.
9 As high as the heavens are above
the earth,
so high are my ways and
thoughts above yours.

10 "My word is like the snow and
the rain
that come down from the sky
to water the earth.
They make the crops grow
and provide seed for planting
and food to eat.
11 So also will be the word that I
speak —
it will not fail to do what I
plan for it;
it will do everything I send it
to do.

12 "You will leave Babylon with joy;
you will be led out of the city
in peace.
The mountains and hills will
burst into singing,
and the trees will shout
for joy.
13 Cypress trees will grow where
now there are briers;
myrtle trees will come up in
place of thorns.
This will be a sign that will last
forever,
a reminder of what I, the
LORD, have done."

God's People Will Include All Nations

56 The LORD says to his people,
"Do what is just and right, for
soon I will save you. 2 I will bless those
who always observe the Sabbath and do
not misuse it. I will bless those who do
nothing evil."

3 A foreigner who has joined the
LORD's people should not say, "The
LORD will not let me worship with his
people."

A man who has been castrated
should never think that because he
cannot have children, he can never be
part of God's people. 4 The LORD says to
such a man, "If you honor me by observing the Sabbath and if you do what
pleases me and faithfully keep my covenant, 5 then your name will be remembered in my Temple and among my
people longer than if you had sons and
daughters. You will never be forgotten."

6 And the LORD says to those foreigners who become part of his people, who
love him and serve him, who observe
the Sabbath and faithfully keep his covenant: 7 "I will bring you to Zion, my sacred hill,*d* give you joy in my house of
prayer, and accept the sacrifices you offer on my altar. My Temple will be
called a house of prayer for the people
of all nations."

8 The Sovereign LORD, who has
brought his people Israel home from
exile, has promised that he will bring
still other people to join them.

Israel's Leaders Are Condemned

9 The LORD has told the foreign nations to come like wild animals and devour his people. 10 He says, "All the
leaders, who are supposed to warn my
people, are blind! They know nothing.
They are like watch dogs that don't
bark — they only lie around and dream.
How they love to sleep! 11 They are like
greedy dogs that never get enough.
These leaders have no understanding.
They each do as they please and seek
their own advantage. 12 'Let's get some
wine,' these drunkards say, 'and drink
all we can hold! Tomorrow will be even
better than today!' "

SACRED HILL: *See 2.3.*
5.10 2 Co 9.10   **56.4, 5** Ws 3.14, 15   **56.7** Mt 21.13; Mk 11.17; Lk 19.46

How they love to sleep! (56.10)

Israel's Idolatry Is Condemned

57 Good people die, and no one understands or even cares. But when they die, no calamity can hurt them. 2 Those who live good lives find peace and rest in death.

3 Come here to be judged, you sinners! You are no better than sorcerers, adulterers, and prostitutes. 4 Who are you making fun of? Who are you liars jeering at? 5 You worship the fertility gods by having sex under those sacred trees of yours. You offer your children as sacrifices in the rocky caves near stream beds. 6 You take smooth stones from there and worship them as gods. You pour out wine as offerings to them and bring them grain offerings. Do you think I am pleased with all this? 7 You go to the high mountains to offer sacrifices and have sex. 8 You set up your obscene idols just inside your front doors. You forsake me; you take off your clothes and climb in your large beds with your lovers, whom you pay to sleep with you. And there you satisfy your lust. 9 You put on your perfumes and ointments and go to worship the god Molech. To find gods to worship, you send messengers far and wide, even to the world of the dead. 10 You wear yourselves out looking for other gods, but you never give up. You think your ob-

scene idols give you strength, and so you never grow weak.

11 The LORD says, "Who are these gods that make you afraid, so that you tell me lies and forget me completely? Have you stopped honoring me because I have kept silent for so long? 12 You think that what you do is right, but I will expose your conduct, and your idols will not be able to help you. 13 When you cry for help, let those idols of yours save you! A puff of wind will carry them off! But those who trust in me will live in the land and will worship me in my Temple."

God's Promise of Help and Healing

14 The LORD says, "Let my people return to me. Remove every obstacle from their path! Build the road and make it ready!

15 "I am the high and holy God, who lives forever. I live in a high and holy place, but I also live with people who are humble and repentant, so that I can restore their confidence and hope. 16 gave my people life, and I will not continue to accuse them or be angry with them forever.*e* 17 I was angry with them because of their sin and greed, and so I punished them and abandoned them. But they were stubborn and kept on going their own way.

---

e I gave my people . . . forever; *or* I will not continue to accuse them or be angry with them forever, for then they would die—the very people to whom I gave life.

18"I have seen how they acted, but I will heal them. I will lead them and help them, and I will comfort those who mourn. 19I offer peace to all, both near and far! I will heal my people. 20But evil people are like the restless sea, whose waves never stop rolling in, bringing filth and muck. 21There is no safety for sinners," says the LORD.

True Fasting

58 The LORD says, "Shout as loud as you can! Tell my people Israel about their sins! 2They worship me every day, claiming that they are eager to know my ways and obey my laws. They say they want me to give them just laws and that they take pleasure in worshiping me."

3The people ask, "Why should we fast if the LORD never notices? Why should we go without food if he pays no attention?"

The LORD says to them, "The truth is that at the same time you fast, you pursue your own interests and oppress your workers. 4Your fasting makes you violent, and you quarrel and fight. Do you think this kind of fasting will make me listen to your prayers? 5When you fast, you make yourselves suffer; you bow your heads low like a blade of grass and spread out sackcloth and ashes to lie on. Is that what you call fasting? Do you think I will be pleased with that?

6"The kind of fasting I want is this: Remove the chains of oppression and the yoke of injustice, and let the oppressed go free. 7Share your food with the hungry and open your homes to the homeless poor. Give clothes to those who have nothing to wear, and do not refuse to help your own relatives.

8"Then my favor will shine on you like the morning sun, and your wounds will be quickly healed. I will always be with you to save you; my presence will protect you on every side. 9When you pray, I will answer you. When you call to me, I will respond.

"If you put an end to oppression, to every gesture of contempt, and to every evil word; 10if you give food to the hungry and satisfy those who are in need, then the darkness around you will turn to the brightness of noon. 11And I will always guide you and satisfy you with good things. I will keep you strong and well. You will be like a garden that has plenty of water, like a spring of water that never goes dry. 12Your people will rebuild what has long been in ruins, building again on the old foundations. You will be known as the people who rebuilt the walls, who restored the ruined houses."

The Reward for Keeping the Sabbath

13The LORD says, "If you treat the Sabbath as sacred and do not pursue your own interests on that day; if you value my holy day and honor it by not traveling, working, or talking idly on that day, 14then you will find the joy that comes from serving me. I will make you honored all over the world, and you will enjoy the land I gave to

57.19 Eph 2.17   **57.21** Is 48.22   **58.7** Mt 25.34

The kind of fasting I want is this. (58.6-7)

your ancestor, Jacob. I, the LORD, have spoken."

The Prophet Condemns the People's Sins

59 Don't think that the LORD is too weak to save you or too deaf to hear your call for help! ² It is because of your sins that he doesn't hear you. It is your sins that separate you from God when you try to worship him. ³ You are guilty of lying, violence, and murder.

⁴ You go to court, but you do not have justice on your side. You depend on lies to win your case. You carry out your plans to hurt others. ⁵⁻⁶ The evil plots you make are as deadly as the eggs of a poisonous snake. Crush an egg, out comes a snake! But your plots will do you no good — they are as useless as clothing made of cobwebs! ⁷ You are always planning something evil, and you can hardly wait to do it. You never hesitate to murder innocent people. You leave ruin and destruction wherever you go, ⁸ and no one is safe when you are around. Everything you do is unjust. You follow a crooked path, and no one who walks that path will ever be safe.

The People Confess Their Sin

⁹ The people say, "Now we know why God does not save us from those who oppress us. We hope for light to walk by, but there is only darkness, ¹⁰ and we grope about like blind people. We stumble at noon, as if it were night, as if we were in the dark world of the dead. ¹¹ We are frightened and distressed. We long for God to save us from oppression and wrong, but nothing happens.

¹² "LORD, our crimes against you are many. Our sins accuse us. We are well aware of them all. ¹³ We have rebelled against you, rejected you, and refused to follow you. We have oppressed others

and turned away from you. Our thoughts are false; our words are lies. ¹⁴ Justice is driven away, and right cannot come near. Truth stumbles in the public square, and honesty finds no place there. ¹⁵ There is so little honesty that those who stop doing evil find themselves the victims of crime."

The LORD Prepares to Rescue His People

The LORD has seen this, and he is displeased that there is no justice. ¹⁶ He is astonished to see that there is no one to help the oppressed. So he will use his own power to rescue them and to win the victory. ¹⁷ He will wear justice like a coat of armor and saving power like a helmet. He will clothe himself with the strong desire to set things right and to punish and avenge the wrongs that

Like a strong wind (59.19)

59.7, 8 Ro 3.15-17   **59.16** Is 63.5   **59.17** Ws 5.17-23; Eph 6.14, 17; 1 Th 5.8

Great caravans of camels will come. (60.6)

people suffer. ¹⁸ He will punish his enemies according to what they have done, even those who live in distant lands. ¹⁹ From east to west everyone will fear him and his great power. He will come like a rushing river, like a strong wind.

²⁰ The LORD says to his people, "I will come to Jerusalem to defend you and to save all of you that turn from your sins. ²¹ And I make a covenant with you: I have given you my power and my teachings to be yours forever, and from now on you are to obey me and teach your children and your descendants to obey me for all time to come."

The Future Glory of Jerusalem

60 Arise, Jerusalem, and shine like the sun;
The glory of the LORD is shining on you!
² Other nations will be covered by darkness,
But on you the light of the LORD will shine;
The brightness of his presence will be with you.
³ Nations will be drawn to your light,
And kings to the dawning of your new day.

⁴ Look around you and see what is happening:
Your people are gathering to come home!
Your sons will come from far away;
Your daughters will be carried like children.
⁵ You will see this and be filled with joy;
You will tremble with excitement.
The wealth of the nations will be brought to you;
From across the sea their riches will come.

⁶ Great caravans of camels will come, from Midian and Ephah.
They will come from Sheba, bringing gold and incense.
People will tell the good news of what the LORD has done!
⁷ All the sheep of Kedar and Nebaioth
Will be brought to you as sacrifices
And offered on the altar to please the LORD.
The LORD will make his Temple more glorious than ever.

⁸ What are these ships that skim along like clouds,
Like doves returning home?
⁹ They are ships coming from distant lands,
Bringing God's people home.

What are these ships? (60.8)

They bring with them silver and
gold
To honor the name of the LORD,
The holy God of Israel,
Who has made all nations honor
his people.

¹⁰The LORD says to Jerusalem,
"Foreigners will rebuild your
walls,
And their kings will serve you.
In my anger I punished you,
But now I will show you my
favor and mercy.
¹¹Day and night your gates will be
open,
So that the kings of the nations
May bring you their wealth.
¹²But nations that do not serve you
Will be completely destroyed.

¹³"The wood of the pine, the
juniper, and the cypress,
The finest wood from the forests
of Lebanon,
Will be brought to rebuild you,
Jerusalem,
To make my Temple beautiful,
To make my city glorious.
¹⁴The descendants of those who
oppressed you will come
And bow low to show their
respect.
All who once despised you will
worship at your feet.

They will call you 'The City of
the LORD,'
'Zion, the City of Israel's
Holy God.'

¹⁵"You will no longer be forsaken
and hated,
A city deserted and desolate.
I will make you great and
beautiful,
A place of joy forever and ever.
¹⁶Nations and kings will care
for you
As a mother nurses her child.
You will know that I, the LORD,
have saved you,
That the mighty God of Israel
sets you free.

¹⁷"I will bring you gold instead of
bronze,
Silver and bronze instead of iron
and wood,
And iron instead of stone.
Your rulers will no longer
oppress you;
I will make them rule with
justice and peace.
¹⁸The sounds of violence will be
heard no more;

*The finest wood from the forests of Lebanon
(60.13)*

Destruction will not shatter your
country again.
I will protect and defend you like
a wall;
You will praise me because I
have saved you.

¹⁹"No longer will the sun be your
  light by day
Or the moon be your light by
  night;
I, the LORD, will be your eternal
  light;
The light of my glory will shine
  on you.
²⁰ Your days of grief will come to
  an end.
I, the LORD, will be your eternal
  light,
More lasting than the sun and
  moon.
²¹ Your people will all do what is
  right,
And will possess the land forever.
I planted them, I made them,
To reveal my greatness to all.
²² Even your smallest and humblest
  family
Will become as great as a
  powerful nation.
When the right time comes,
I will make this happen quickly.
I am the LORD!"

The Good News of Deliverance

61 The Sovereign LORD has
  filled me with his
  Spirit.
He has chosen me and sent me
To bring good news to the poor,
To heal the broken-hearted,
To announce release to captives
And freedom to those in prison.
² He has sent me to proclaim
That the time has come
When the LORD will save his
  people
And defeat their enemies.
He has sent me to comfort all
  who mourn,
³ To give to those who mourn in
  Zion
Joy and gladness instead of grief,
A song of praise instead of
  sorrow.

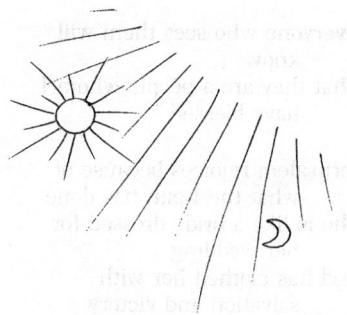

I . . . will be your eternal light. (60.19)

They will be like trees
That the LORD himself has
  planted.
They will all do what is right,
And God will be praised for what
  he has done.
⁴ They will rebuild cities that have
  long been in ruins.

⁵ My people, foreigners will
  serve you.
They will take care of your flocks
And farm your land and tend
  your vineyards.
⁶ And you will be known as the
  priests of the LORD,
The servants of our God.
You will enjoy the wealth of the
  nations
And be proud that it is yours.
⁷ Your shame and disgrace are
  ended.
You will live in your own land,
And your wealth will be doubled;
Your joy will last forever.

⁸ The LORD says,
"I love justice and I hate
  oppression and crime.
I will faithfully reward my people
And make an eternal covenant
  with them.
⁹ They will be famous among the
  nations;

Everyone who sees them will
        know
That they are a people whom I
        have blessed."

10 Jerusalem rejoices because of
        what the LORD has done.
She is like a bride dressed for
        her wedding.
God has clothed her with
        salvation and victory.
11 As surely as seeds sprout and
        grow,
The Sovereign LORD will save his
        people,
And all the nations will
        praise him.

62 I will speak out to encourage
        Jerusalem;
I will not be silent until she is
        saved,
And her victory shines like a
        torch in the night.
2 Jerusalem, the nations will see
        you victorious!
All their kings will see your
        glory.
You will be called by a new
        name,
A name given by the LORD
        himself.
3 You will be like a beautiful
        crown for the LORD.
4 No longer will you be called
        "Forsaken,"
Or your land be called "The
        Deserted Wife."
Your new name will be "God Is
        Pleased with Her."
Your land will be called "Happily
        Married,"
Because the LORD is pleased
        with you
And will be like a husband to
        your land.
5 Like a young man taking a virgin
        as his bride,

He who formed you will
        marry you.
As a groom is delighted with his
        bride,
So your God will delight in you.

6 On your walls, Jerusalem, I have
        placed sentries;
They must never be silent day or
        night.
They must remind the LORD of
        his promises
And never let him forget them.
7 They must give him no rest until
        he restores Jerusalem
And makes it a city the whole
        world praises.

8 The LORD has made a solemn
        promise,
And by his power he will carry
        it out:
"Your grain will no longer be
        food for your enemies,
And foreigners will no longer
        drink your wine.
9 But you that planted and
        harvested the grain
Will eat the bread and praise the
        LORD.
You that tended and gathered
        the grapes
Will drink the wine in the courts
        of my Temple."

10 People of Jerusalem, go out of
        the city
And build a road for your
        returning people!
Prepare a highway; clear it of
        stones!
Put up a signal so that the
        nations can know
11 That the LORD is announcing to
        all the earth:
"Tell the people of Jerusalem
That the LORD is coming to
        save you,

tions and shattered them. I poured out their lifeblood on the ground."

The LORD's Goodness to Israel

⁷I will tell of the LORD's unfailing
    love;
I praise him for all he has
    done for us.
He has richly blessed the people
    of Israel
because of his mercy and
    constant love.

⁸The LORD said, "They are my people; they will not deceive me." And so he saved them ⁹from all their suffering. It was not an angel, but the LORD himself who saved them. In his love and compassion he rescued them. He had always taken care of them in the past, ¹⁰but they rebelled against him and made his holy spirit sad. So the LORD became their enemy and fought against them.

¹¹But then they^g remembered the past, the days of Moses, the servant of the LORD, and they asked, "Where now is the LORD, who saved the leaders of his people from the sea? Where is the LORD, who gave his spirit to Moses? ¹²⁻¹³Where is the LORD, who by his power did great things through Moses, dividing the waters of the sea and leading his people through the deep water, to win everlasting fame for himself?"

Led by the LORD, they were as surefooted as wild horses, and never stumbled. ¹⁴As cattle are led into a fertile valley, so the LORD gave his people rest. He led his people and brought honor to his name.

A Prayer for Mercy and Help

¹⁵LORD, look upon us from heaven, where you live in your holiness and glory. Where is your great concern for

Build a road for your returning people! (62.10)

Bringing with him the people he
    has rescued."
¹²You will be called "God's Holy
    People,"
"The People the LORD Has
    Saved."
Jerusalem will be called "The
    City That God Loves,"
"The City That God Did Not
    Forsake."

The LORD's Victory over the Nations

63 "Who is this coming from the city of Bozrah in Edom? Who is this so splendidly dressed in red, marching along^f in power and strength?"

It is the LORD, powerful to save, coming to announce his victory.

²"Why is his clothing so red, like that of someone who tramples grapes to make wine?"

³The LORD answers, "I have trampled the nations like grapes, and no one came to help me. I trampled them in my anger, and their blood has stained all my clothing. ⁴I decided that the time to save my people had come; it was time to punish their enemies. ⁵I was amazed when I looked and saw that there was no one to help me. But my anger made me strong, and I won the victory myself. ⁶In my anger I trampled whole na-

^f *Some ancient translations* marching along; *Hebrew* bowed down.   ^g *Probable text* they; *Hebrew* he.

63.1-6 Is 34.5-17; Jr 49.7-22; Ez 25.12-14; 35.1-15; Am 1.11, 12; Ob 1-14; Ml 1.2-5
63.3 a Rev 14.20; 19.15; **b** Rev 19.13   **63.5** Is 59.16   **63.12** Ex 14.21

us? Where is your power? Where are your love and compassion? Do not ignore us. ¹⁶You are our father. Our ancestors Abraham and Jacob do not acknowledge us, but you, LORD, are our father, the one who has always rescued us. ¹⁷Why do you let us stray from your ways? Why do you make us so stubborn that we turn away from you? Come back, for the sake of those who serve you, for the sake of the people who have always been yours.

¹⁸We, your holy people, were driven out by our enemies for a little while; they trampled down your sanctuary.ʰ ¹⁹You treat us as though you had never been our ruler, as though we had never been your people.

64 Why don't you tear the sky open and come down? The mountains would see you and shake with fear. ²They would tremble like water boiling over a hot fire. Come and reveal your power to your enemies, and make the nations tremble at your presence! ³There was a time when you came and did terrifying things that we did not expect; the mountains saw you and shook with fear. ⁴No one has ever seen or heard of a God like you, who does such deeds for those who put their hope in him. ⁵You welcome those who find joy in doing what is right, those who remember how you want them to live. You were angry with us, but we went on sinning; in spite of your great anger we have continued to do wrong since ancient times.ⁱ ⁶All of us have been sinful; even our best actions are filthy through and through. Because of our sins we are like leaves that wither and are blown away by the wind. ⁷No one turns to you in prayer; no one goes to you for help. You have hidden yourself from us and have abandonedʲ us because of our sins.

⁸But you are our father, LORD. We are like clay, and you are like the potter. You created us, ⁹so do not be too angry with us or hold our sins against us forever. We are your people; be merciful to us. ¹⁰Your sacred cities are like a desert; Jerusalem is a deserted ruin, ¹¹and our Temple, the sacred and beautiful place where our ancestors praised you, has been destroyed by fire. All the places we loved are in ruins. ¹²LORD, are you unmoved by all this? Are you going to do nothing and make us suffer more than we can endure?

God's Punishment of the Rebellious

65 The LORD said, "I was ready to answer my people's prayers, but they did not pray. I was ready for them to find me, but they did not even try. The nation did not pray to me, even though I was always ready to answer, 'Here I am; I will help you.' ²I have always been ready to welcome my people, who stubbornly do what is wrong and go their own way. ³They shamelessly keep on making me angry. They offer pagan sacrifices at sacred gardensᵏ and burn incense on pagan altars. ⁴At night they go to caves and tombs to consult the spirits of the dead. They eat pork and drink broth made from meat offered in pagan sacrifices. ⁵And then they say to others, 'Keep away from us; we are too holy for you to touch!' I cannot stand people like that—my anger against them is like a fire that never goes out.

⁶"I have already decided on their punishment, and their sentence is written down. I will not overlook what they have done, but will repay them ⁷for their sins and the sins of their ancestors. They have burned incense at pagan hill shrines and spoken evil of me.

ʰ *Verse 18 in Hebrew is unclear.*   ⁱ *Probable text* in spite of . . . ancient times; *Hebrew unclear.*   ʲ *Some ancient translations* abandoned; *Hebrew* melted.
ᵏ SACRED GARDENS: *See* 1.29.
64.4 1 Co 2.9   **65.1** Ro 10.20   **65.2** Ro 10.21

So I will punish them as their past deeds deserve."

[8] The LORD says, "No one destroys good grapes; instead, they make wine with them. Neither will I destroy all my people — I will save those who serve me. [9] I will bless the Israelites who belong to the tribe of Judah, and their descendants will possess my land of mountains. My chosen people, who serve me, will live there. [10] They will worship me and will lead their sheep and cattle to pasture in the Plain of Sharon in the west and in Trouble Valley in the east.

[11] "But it will be different for you that forsake me, who ignore Zion, my sacred hill,[l] and worship Gad and Meni, the gods of luck and fate. [12] It will be your fate to die a violent death, because you did not answer when I called you or listen when I spoke. You chose to disobey me and do evil. [13] And so I tell you that those who worship and obey me will have plenty to eat and drink, but you will be hungry and thirsty. They will be happy, but you will be disgraced. [14] They will sing for joy, but you will cry with a broken heart. [15] My chosen people will use your name as a curse. I, the Sovereign LORD, will put you to death. But I will give a new name to those who obey me. [16] Anyone in the land who asks for a blessing will ask to be blessed by the faithful God. Whoever takes an oath will swear by the name of the faithful God. The troubles of the past will be gone and forgotten."

The New Creation

[17] The LORD says, "I am making a new earth and new heavens. The events of the past will be completely forgotten. [18] Be glad and rejoice forever in what I create. The new Jerusalem I make will be full of joy, and her people will be happy. [19] I myself will be filled with joy because of Jerusalem and her people. There will be no weeping there, no calling for help. [20] Babies will no longer die in infancy, and all people will live out their life span. Those who live to be a hundred will be considered young. To die before that would be a sign that I had punished them. [21-22] People will build houses and get to live in them — they will not be used by someone else. They will plant vineyards and enjoy the wine — it will not be drunk by others. Like trees, my people will live long lives. They will fully enjoy the things that they have worked for. [23] The work they do will be successful, and their children will not meet with disaster. I will bless them and their descendants for all time to come. [24] Even before they finish praying to me, I will answer their prayers. [25] Wolves and lambs will eat together; lions will eat straw, as cattle do, and snakes will no longer be dangerous. On Zion, my sacred hill,[l] there will be nothing harmful or evil."

The LORD Judges the Nations

66 The LORD says, "Heaven is my throne, and the earth is my footstool. What kind of house, then, could you build for me, what kind of place for me to live in? [2] I myself created the whole universe! I am pleased with those who are humble and repentant, who fear me and obey me.

[3] "The people do as they please. It's all the same to them whether they kill a bull as a sacrifice or sacrifice a human being; whether they sacrifice a lamb or break a dog's neck; whether they

---

[l] SACRED HILL: *See* 2.3.

65.10 Js 7.24-26   **65.17** Is 66.22; 2 P 3.13; Rev 21.1   **65.19** Rev 21.4   **65.25** Is 11.6-9
66.1 a Mt 5.34; 23.22; **b** Mt 5.35   **66.1, 2a** Ac 7.49, 50

present a grain offering or offer pigs' blood; whether they offer incense or pray to an idol. They take pleasure in disgusting ways of worship. ⁴So I will bring disaster upon them — the very things they are afraid of — because no one answered when I called or listened when I spoke. They chose to disobey me and do evil."

⁵Listen to what the LORD says, you that fear him and obey him: "Because you are faithful to me, some of your own people hate you and will have nothing to do with you. They mock you and say, 'Let the LORD show his greatness and save you, so that we may see you rejoice.' But they themselves will be disgraced! ⁶Listen! That loud noise in the city, that sound in the Temple, is the sound of the LORD punishing his enemies!

⁷"My holy city is like a woman who suddenly gives birth to a child without ever going into labor. ⁸Has anyone ever seen or heard of such a thing? Has a nation ever been born in a day? Zion will not have to suffer long, before the nation is born. ⁹Do not think that I will bring my people to the point of birth and not let them be born." The LORD has spoken.

¹⁰Rejoice with Jerusalem; be glad
    for her,
    all you that love this city!
Rejoice with her now,
    all you that have mourned
        for her!
¹¹You will enjoy her prosperity,
    like a child at its mother's
        breast.

¹²The LORD says, "I will bring you lasting prosperity; the wealth of the nations will flow to you like a river that never goes dry. You will be like a child that is nursed by its mother, carried in her arms, and treated with love. ¹³I will comfort you in Jerusalem, as a mother comforts her child. ¹⁴When you see this happen, you will be glad; it will make you strong and healthy. Then you will know that I, the LORD, help those who obey me, and I show my anger against my enemies."

¹⁵The LORD will come with fire. He will ride on the wings of a storm to punish those he is angry with. ¹⁶By fire and sword he will punish all the people of the world whom he finds guilty — and many will be put to death.

¹⁷The LORD says, "The end is near for those who purify themselves for pagan worship, who go in procession to sacred gardens, *m* and who eat pork and mice and other disgusting foods. ¹⁸I know*n* their thoughts and their deeds. I am coming*o* to gather the people of all the nations. When they come together, they will see what my power can do ¹⁹and will know that I am the one who punishes them.

"But I will spare some of them and send them to the nations and the distant lands that have not heard of my fame or seen my greatness and power: to Spain, Libya,*p* and Lydia, with its skilled archers, and to Tubal and Greece. Among these nations they will proclaim my greatness. ²⁰They will bring back all your people from the nations as a gift to me. They will bring them to my sacred hill*q* in Jerusalem on horses, mules, and camels, and in chariots and wagons, just as Israelites bring grain offerings to the Temple in ritually clean containers. ²¹I will make some of them priests and Levites.

²²"Just as the new earth and the new heavens will endure by my power, so your descendants and your name will endure. ²³On every New Moon Festival and every Sabbath people of every na-

---

m SACRED GARDENS: See 1.29.   *n* *Some ancient translations* I know; *Hebrew* I.
o *Some ancient translations* I am coming; *Hebrew* He is coming.   *p* *One ancient translation* Libya; *Hebrew* Pul.   *q* SACRED HILL: See 2.3.
66.7 Rev 12.5   **66.22** Is 65.17; 2 P 3.13; Rev 21.1

tion will come to worship me here in Jerusalem," says the LORD. 24"As they leave, they will see the dead bodies of those who have rebelled against me. The worms that eat them will never die, and the fire that burns them will never be put out. The sight of them will be disgusting to all people."

66.24 Jdt 16.17; Mk 9.48

The Book of
JEREMIAH

INTRODUCTION

The prophet Jeremiah lived during the latter part of the seventh century and the first part of the sixth century B.C. During his long ministry he warned God's people of the catastrophe that was to fall upon the nation because of their idolatry and sin. He lived to see this prediction come true with the fall of Jerusalem to the Babylonian king, Nebuchadnezzar, the destruction of the city and the Temple, and the exile to Babylonia of Judah's king and many of the people. He also foretold the eventual return of the people from exile and the restoration of the nation.

The Book of Jeremiah may be divided into the following parts: 1) The call of Jeremiah. 2) Messages from God to the nation of Judah and its rulers during the reigns of Josiah, Jehoiakim, Jehoiachin, and Zedekiah. 3) Material from the memoirs of Baruch, Jeremiah's secretary, including various prophecies and important events from the life of Jeremiah. 4) Messages from the Lord about various foreign nations. 5) A historical appendix, giving an account of the fall of Jerusalem, and the exile to Babylonia.

Jeremiah was a sensitive man who deeply loved his people, and who hated to have to pronounce judgment upon them. In many passages he spoke with deep emotion about the things he suffered because God had called him to be a prophet. The word of the Lord was like fire in his heart—he could not keep it back.

Some of the greatest words in the book point beyond Jeremiah's own troubled time to the day when there would be a new covenant, one that God's people would keep without a teacher to remind them, because it would be written on their hearts (31.31-34).

OUTLINE OF CONTENTS

---

1 This book is the account of what was said by Jeremiah son of Hilkiah, one of the priests of the town of Anathoth in the territory of Benjamin. ²The LORD spoke to Jeremiah in the thirteenth year that Josiah son of Amon was king of Judah, ³and he spoke to him again when Josiah's son Jehoiakim

1.2 2 K 22.3—23.27; 2 Ch 34.8—35.19   1.3 a 2 K 23.36—24.7; 2 Ch 36.5-8; b 2 K 24.18—25.21; 2 Ch 36.11-21 was king. After that, the LORD spoke to him many times, until the eleventh year of the reign of Zedekiah son of Josiah. In the fifth month of that year the people of Jerusalem were taken into exile.

The Call of Jeremiah

⁴The LORD said to me, ⁵"I chose you before I gave you life, and before you were born I selected you to be a prophet to the nations."

⁶I answered, "Sovereign LORD, I don't know how to speak; I am too young."

⁷But the LORD said to me, "Do not say that you are too young, but go to the people I send you to, and tell them everything I command you to say. ⁸Do not be afraid of them, for I will be with you to protect you. I, the LORD, have spoken!"

⁹Then the LORD reached out, touched my lips, and said to me, "Listen, I am giving you the words you must speak. ¹⁰Today I give you authority over nations and kingdoms to uproot and to pull down, to destroy and to overthrow, to build and to plant."

Two Visions

¹¹The LORD asked me, "Jeremiah, what do you see?"

I answered, "A branch of an almond tree."

¹²"You are right," the LORD said, "and I am watching^a to see that my words come true."

¹³Then the LORD spoke to me again. "What else do you see?" he asked.

I answered, "I see a pot boiling in the north, and it is about to tip over this way."

¹⁴He said to me, "Destruction will boil over from the north on all who live in this land, ¹⁵because I am calling all

the nations in the north to come. Their kings will set up their thrones at the gates of Jerusalem and around its walls

"I am giving you
the words you must speak." (1.9)

and also around the other cities of Judah. ¹⁶I will punish my people because they have sinned; they have abandoned me, have offered sacrifices to other gods, and have made idols and worshiped them. ¹⁷Get ready, Jeremiah; go and tell them everything I command you to say. Do not be afraid of them now, or I will make you even more afraid when you are with them. ¹⁸⁻¹⁹Listen, Jeremiah! Everyone in this land — the kings of Judah, the officials, the priests, and the people — will be against you. But today I am giving you the strength to resist them; you will be like a fortified city, an iron pillar, and a bronze wall. They will not defeat you, for I will be with you to protect you. I, the LORD, have spoken."

---

^{a} WATCHING: *This word in Hebrew sounds like the Hebrew for "almond."*

God's Care for Israel

2 The LORD told me ²to proclaim this message to everyone in Jerusalem.

"I remember how faithful you
were when you were
young,
how you loved me when we
were first married;
you followed me through the
desert,
through a land that had not
been planted.
³Israel, you belonged to me alone;
you were my sacred
possession.
I sent suffering and disaster
on everyone who hurt you.
I, the LORD, have spoken."

The Sin of Israel's Ancestors

⁴Listen to the LORD's message, you descendants of Jacob, you tribes of Israel. ⁵The LORD says:
"What accusation did your
ancestors bring
against me?
What made them turn away
from me?
They worshiped worthless idols
and became worthless
themselves.
⁶They did not care about me,
even though I rescued them
from Egypt
and led them through the
wilderness:
a land of deserts and sand
pits,
a dry and dangerous land
where no one lives
and no one will even travel.
⁷I brought them into a fertile
land,
to enjoy its harvests and its
other good things.
But instead they ruined my land;
they defiled the country I had
given them.

⁸The priests did not ask, 'Where
is the LORD?'
My own priests did not
know me.
The rulers rebelled against me;
the prophets spoke in the
name of Baal
and worshiped useless idols.

The LORD's Case against His People

⁹"And so I, the LORD, will state
my case against my
people again.
I will bring charges against their
descendants.
¹⁰Go west to the island of Cyprus,
and send someone eastward to
the land of Kedar.
You will see that nothing like
this has ever happened
before.
¹¹No other nation has ever
changed its gods,
even though they were not
real.
But my people have
exchanged me,
the God who has brought
them honor,
for gods that can do nothing
for them.
¹²And so I command the sky to
shake with horror,
to be amazed and astonished,
13   for my people have committed
two sins:
they have turned away from me,
the spring of fresh water,
and they have dug cisterns,
cracked cisterns that can hold
no water at all.

The Results of Israel's Unfaithfulness

¹⁴"Israel is not a slave;
he was not born into slavery.
Why then do his enemies
hunt him down?
¹⁵They have roared at him like
lions;

they have made his land a
desert,
and his towns lie in ruins,
completely abandoned.
¹⁶ Yes, the people of Memphis and
Tahpanhes
have cracked his skull.
¹⁷ Israel, you brought this on
yourself!
You deserted me, the LORD
your God,
while I was leading you along
the way.
¹⁸ What do you think you will gain
by going to Egypt
to drink water from the Nile?
What do you think you will gain
by going to Assyria
to drink water from the
Euphrates?
¹⁹ Your own evil will punish you,
and your turning from me will
condemn you.
You will learn how bitter and
wrong it is
to abandon me, the LORD
your God,
and no longer to remain
faithful to me.
I, the Sovereign LORD Almighty,
have spoken."

Israel Refuses to Worship the LORD

²⁰ The Sovereign LORD says,
"Israel, long ago you rejected my
authority;
you refused to obey me and
worship me.
On every high hill
and under every green tree
you worshiped fertility gods.
²¹ I planted you like a choice vine
from the very best seed.
But look what you have become!
You are like a rotten,
worthless vine.
²² Even if you washed with the
strongest soap,

I would still see the stain of
your guilt.
²³ How can you say you have not
defiled yourself,
that you have never
worshiped Baal?
Look how you sinned in the
valley;
see what you have done.
You are like a wild camel in
heat,
running around loose,
²⁴   rushing into the desert.*ᵇ*
When she is in heat, who can
control her?
No male that wants her has to
trouble himself;
she is always available in
mating season.
²⁵ Israel, don't wear your feet out,
or let your throat become dry
from chasing after other gods.
But you say, 'No! I can't turn
back.
I have loved foreign gods
and will go after them.' "

Israel Deserves to Be Punished

²⁶ The LORD says, "Just as a thief is
disgraced when caught, so all you people of Israel will be disgraced — your
kings and officials, your priests and
prophets. ²⁷ You will all be disgraced —
you that say that a tree is your father
and that a rock is your mother. This will
happen because you turned away from
me instead of turning to me. But when
you are in trouble, you ask me to come
and save you.
²⁸ "Where are the gods that you made
for yourselves? When you are in trouble, let them save you — if they can! Judah, you have as many gods as you have
cities. ²⁹ What is your complaint? Why
have you rebelled against me? ³⁰ I punished you, but it did no good; you would
not let me correct you. Like a raging
lion, you have murdered your prophets.

ᵇ Probable text rushing into the desert; *Hebrew* a wild donkey used to the desert.

31 People of Israel, listen to what I am saying. Have I been like a desert to you, like a dark and dangerous land? Why, then, do you say that you will do as you please, that you will never come back to me? 32 Does a young woman forget her jewelry, or a bride her wedding dress? But my people have forgotten me for more days than can be counted. 33 You certainly know how to chase after lovers. Even the worst of women can learn from you. 34 Your clothes are stained with the blood of the poor and innocent, not with the blood of burglars.

"But in spite of all this, 35 you say, 'I am innocent; surely the LORD is no longer angry with me.' But I, the LORD, will punish you because you deny that you have sinned. 36 You have cheapened yourself by turning to the gods of other nations. You will be disappointed by Egypt, just as you were by Assyria. 37 You will turn away from Egypt, hanging your head in shame. I, the LORD, have rejected those you trust; you will not gain anything from them."

Unfaithful Israel

3 The LORD says, "If a man divorces his wife, and she leaves him and becomes another man's wife, he cannot take her back again. This would completely defile the land. But, Israel, you have had many lovers, and now you want to return to me! 2 Look up at the hilltops. Is there any place where you have not acted like a prostitute? You waited for lovers along the roadside, as an Arab waits for victims in the desert. You have defiled the land with your prostitution. 3 That is why the rains were held back, and the spring showers did not come. You even look like a prostitute; you have no shame.

4 "And now you say to me, 'You are my father, and you have loved me ever since I was a child. 5 You won't always be angry; you won't be mad at me for-

Worshiping stones and trees (3.9)

ever.' Israel, that is what you said, but you did all the evil you could."

Israel and Judah Must Repent

6 When Josiah was king, the LORD said to me, "Have you seen what Israel, that unfaithful woman, has done? She has turned away from me, and on every high hill and under every green tree she has acted like a prostitute. 7 I thought that after she had done all this, she would surely return to me. But she did not return, and her unfaithful sister Judah saw it all. 8 Judah also saw that I divorced Israel and sent her away because she had turned from me and had become a prostitute. But Judah, Israel's unfaithful sister, was not afraid. She too became a prostitute 9 and was not at all ashamed. She defiled the land, and she committed adultery by worshiping stones and trees. 10 And after all this, Judah, Israel's unfaithful sister, only pretended to return to me; she was not sincere. I, the LORD, have spoken."

11 Then the LORD told me that, even though Israel had turned away from him, she had proved to be better than unfaithful Judah. 12 He told me to go and say to Israel, "Unfaithful Israel, come back to me. I am merciful and will not be angry; I will not be angry with you forever. 13 Only admit that you are guilty and that you have rebelled

3.6 2 K 22.1 – 23.30; 2 Ch 34.1 – 35.27

against the LORD, your God. Confess
that under every green tree you have
given your love to foreign gods and that
you have not obeyed my commands. I,
the LORD, have spoken.

14 "Unfaithful people, come back;
you belong to me. I will take one of you
from each town and two from each
clan, and I will bring you back to Mount
Zion. 15 I will give you rulers who obey
me, and they will rule you with wisdom
and understanding. 16 Then when you
have become numerous in that land,
people will no longer talk about my
Covenant Box. They will no longer
think about it or remember it; they will
not even need it, nor will they make another one. 17 When that time comes, Jerusalem will be called 'The Throne of
the LORD,' and all nations will gather
there to worship me. They will no
longer do what their stubborn and evil
hearts tell them. 18 Israel will join with
Judah, and together they will come
from exile in the country in the north
and will return to the land that I gave
your ancestors as a permanent possession."

The Idolatry of God's People

19 The LORD says,
    "Israel, I wanted to accept you as
        my child
        and give you a delightful land,
        the most beautiful land in all
            the world.
    I wanted you to call me father
        and never again turn away
            from me.
20 But like an unfaithful wife,
        you have not been faithful
            to me.
    I, the LORD, have spoken."

21 A noise is heard on the hilltops:

it is the people of Israel crying
        and pleading
    because they have lived sinful
        lives
    and have forgotten the LORD
        their God.
22 Return, all of you who have
        turned away from
        the LORD;
    he will heal you and make
        you faithful.

You say, "Yes, we are coming to the
LORD because he is our God. 23 We were
not helped at all by our pagan worship
on the hilltops. Help for Israel comes
only from the LORD our God. 24 But the
worship of Baal, the god of shame, has
made us lose flocks and herds, sons and
daughters — everything that our ancestors have worked for since ancient
times. 25 We should lie down in shame
and let our disgrace cover us. We and
our ancestors have always sinned
against the LORD our God; we have
never obeyed his commands."

A Call to Repentance

4 The LORD says, "People of Israel,
if you want to turn, then turn back
to me. If you are faithful to me and remove the idols I hate, 2 it will be right for

Turn back to me. (4.1)

you to swear by my name. Then*c* all
the nations will ask me to bless them,
and they will praise me."

3 The LORD says to the people of Judah and Jerusalem, "Plow up your

---

*c it will be right . . . name. Then; or and if you swear by my name and are truthful,
just, and righteous, then.*
4.3 Ho 10.12

The enemy is coming like clouds. (4.13)

unplowed fields; do not plant your seeds among thorns. ⁴ Keep your covenant with me, your LORD, and dedicate yourselves to me, you people of Judah and Jerusalem. If you don't, my anger will burn like fire because of the evil things you have done. It will burn, and there will be no one to put it out."

Judah Is Threatened with Invasion

⁵ Blow the trumpet throughout
    the land!
  Shout loud and clear!
Tell the people of Judah and
    Jerusalem
  to run to the fortified cities.
⁶ Point the way to Zion!
  Run for safety! Don't delay!
The LORD is bringing disaster
  and great destruction from
    the north.
⁷ Like a lion coming from its
    hiding place,
  a destroyer of nations has
    set out.
He is coming to destroy Judah.
The cities of Judah will be left
    in ruins,
  and no one will live in them.
⁸ So put on sackcloth, and weep
    and wail
  because the fierce anger of
    the LORD
  has not turned away from
    Judah.

⁹ The LORD said, "On that day kings and officials will lose their courage; priests will be shocked and prophets will be astonished."

¹⁰ Then I said, "Sovereign LORD, you have completely deceived the people of Jerusalem! You have said there would be peace, but a sword is at their throats."

¹¹ The time is coming when the people of Jerusalem will be told that a scorching wind is blowing in from the desert toward them. It will not be a gentle wind that only blows away the chaff — ¹² the wind that comes at the LORD's command will be much stronger than that! It is the LORD himself who is pronouncing judgment on his people.

Judah Is Surrounded by Enemies

¹³ Look, the enemy is coming like clouds. Their war chariots are like a whirlwind, and their horses are faster than eagles. We are lost! We are doomed!

¹⁴ Jerusalem, wash the evil from your heart, so that you may be saved. How long will you go on thinking sinful thoughts?

¹⁵ Messengers from the city of Dan and from the hills of Ephraim announce the bad news. ¹⁶ They have come to warn the nations and to tell Jerusalem that enemies are coming from a country far away. These enemies will shout against the cities of Judah ¹⁷ and will surround Jerusalem like men guarding a field, because her people have rebelled against the LORD. The LORD has spoken.

¹⁸ Judah, you have brought this on yourself by the way you have lived and by the things you have done. Your sin has caused this suffering; it has stabbed you through the heart.

Jeremiah's Sorrow for His People

¹⁹The pain! I can't bear the pain!
My heart! My heart is beating
　　wildly!
I can't keep quiet;
I hear the trumpets
　　and the shouts of battle.
²⁰One disaster follows another;
　　the whole country is left
　　　　in ruins.
Suddenly our tents are
　　destroyed;
　　their curtains are torn to
　　　　pieces.
²¹How long must I see the battle
　　raging
　　and hear the blasts of
　　　　trumpets?
²²The LORD says, "My people are
　　stupid;
　　they don't know me.
They are like foolish children;
　　they have no understanding.
They are experts at doing what
　　is evil,
　　but failures at doing what is
　　　　good."

Jeremiah's Vision of the Coming Destruction

²³I looked at the earth — it was a
　　barren waste;
　　at the sky — there was no
　　　　light.
²⁴I looked at the mountains — they
　　were shaking,
　　and the hills were rocking
　　　　back and forth.
²⁵I saw that there were no people;
　　even the birds had flown
　　　　away.
²⁶The fertile land had become a
　　desert;
　　its cities were in ruins
　　because of the LORD's fierce
　　　　anger.
(²⁷The LORD has said that the whole
earth will become a wasteland, but that
he will not completely destroy it.)
²⁸The earth will mourn;

the sky will grow dark.
The LORD has spoken
　　and will not change his mind.
He has made his decision
　　and will not turn back.
²⁹At the noise of the cavalry and
　　archers
　　everyone will run away.
Some will run to the forest;
　　others will climb up among
　　　　the rocks.
Every town will be left empty,
　　and no one will live in them
　　　　again.
³⁰Jerusalem, you are doomed!
　　Why do you dress in scarlet?
Why do you put on jewelry
　　and paint your eyes?
You are making yourself
　　beautiful for nothing!
　　Your lovers have rejected you
　　and want to kill you.
³¹I heard a cry, like a woman in
　　labor,
　　a scream like a woman
　　　　bearing her first child.
It was the cry of Jerusalem
　　gasping for breath,
　　stretching out her hand and
　　　　saying,
"I am doomed!
　　They are coming to kill me!"

The Sin of Jerusalem

5 People of Jerusalem, run
　　through your streets!
Look around! See for
　　yourselves!
Search the marketplaces!
Can you find one person
　　who does what is right
　　and tries to be faithful to God?
If you can, the LORD will forgive
　　Jerusalem.
²Even though you claim to
　　worship the LORD,
　　you do not mean what
　　　　you say.
³Surely the LORD looks for
　　faithfulness.

He struck you, but you paid no
   attention;
he crushed you, but you
   refused to learn.
You were stubborn and would
   not turn from your sins.
4 Then I thought, "These are only
   the poor and ignorant.
They behave foolishly;
   they don't know what their
     God requires,
   what the LORD wants them
     to do.
5 I will go to the people in power
   and talk with them.
Surely they know what their God
   requires,
   what the LORD wants them
     to do."
But all of them have rejected the
   LORD's authority
   and refuse to obey him.
6 That is why lions from the forest
   will kill them;
wolves from the desert will
   tear them to pieces,
and leopards will prowl
   through their towns.
If those people go out, they will
   be torn apart
because their sins are
   numerous
and time after time they have
   turned from God.
7 The LORD asked, "Why should I
   forgive the sins of my
   people?
They have abandoned me
   and have worshiped gods that
     are not real.
I fed my people until they were
   full,
but they committed adultery
   and spent their time with
     prostitutes.
8 They were like well-fed stallions
   wild with desire,
each lusting for his neighbor's
   wife.

9 Shouldn't I punish them for
   these things
   and take revenge on a nation
     such as this?
10 I will send enemies to cut down
   my people's vineyards,
but not to destroy them
   completely.
I will tell them to strip away the
   branches,
because those branches are
   not mine.
11 The people of Israel and Judah
   have betrayed me completely.
I, the LORD, have spoken."

The LORD Rejects Israel

12 The LORD's people have denied
him and have said, "He won't really do
anything.*d* We won't have hard times;
we won't have war or famine."
13-14 They have said that the prophets
are nothing but windbags and that they
have no message from the LORD. The
LORD God Almighty said to me, "Jeremiah, because these people have said
such things, I will make my words like
a fire in your mouth. The people will be
like wood, and the fire will burn
them up."

15 People of Israel, the LORD is bringing a nation from far away to attack you.
It is a strong and ancient nation, a nation whose language you do not know.
16 Their archers are mighty soldiers
who kill without mercy. 17 They will devour your crops and your food; they will
kill your sons and your daughters. They
will slaughter your flocks and your
herds and destroy your vines and fig
trees. The fortified cities in which you
trust will be destroyed by their army.
18 The LORD says, "Yet even in those
days I will not completely destroy my
people. 19 When they ask why I did all
these things, tell them, Jeremiah, that

---

d He won't . . . anything; *or* We don't want anything to do with him.

just as they turned away from me and served foreign gods in their own land, so they will serve strangers in a land that is not theirs."

God Warns His People

20 The LORD says, "Tell the descendants of Jacob, tell the people of Judah: 21 Pay attention, you foolish and stupid people, who have eyes, but cannot see, and have ears, but cannot hear. 22 I am the LORD; why don't you fear me? Why don't you tremble before me? I placed the sand as the boundary of the sea, a permanent boundary that it cannot cross. The sea may toss, but it cannot go beyond it; the waves may roar, but they cannot break through. 23 But you people! You are stubborn and rebellious; you have turned aside and left me. 24 You never thought to honor me, even though I send the autumn rains and the spring rains and give you the harvest season each year. 25 Instead, your sins have kept these good things from you.

26 "Evildoers live among my people; they lie in wait like those who lay nets to catch birds,*e* but they have set their traps to catch people. 27 Just as a hunter fills a cage with birds, they have filled their houses with loot. That is why they are powerful and rich, 28 why they are fat and well fed. There is no limit to their evil deeds. They do not give orphans their rights or show justice to the oppressed.

29 "But I, the LORD, will punish them for these things; I will take revenge on this nation. 30 A terrible and shocking thing has happened in the land: 31 prophets speak nothing but lies; priests rule as the prophets command, and my people offer no objections. But what will they do when it all comes to an end?"

Jerusalem Is Surrounded by Enemies

6 People of Benjamin, run for safety! Escape from Jerusalem! Sound the trumpet in Tekoa and build a signal fire in Beth Haccherem. Disaster and destruction are about to come from the north. 2 The city of Zion is beautiful, but it will be destroyed; 3 kings will camp there with their armies. They will pitch their tents around the city, and each of them will camp wherever they want. 4 They will say, "Prepare to attack Jerusalem! Get ready! We'll attack at noon!" But then they will say, "It's too late, the day is almost over, and the evening shadows are growing long. 5 We'll attack by night; we'll destroy the city's fortresses."

6 The LORD Almighty has ordered these kings to cut down trees and build mounds in order to besiege Jerusalem. He has said, "I will punish this city because it is full of oppression. 7 As a well keeps its water fresh, so Jerusalem keeps its evil fresh. I hear violence and destruction in the city; sickness and wounds are all I see. 8 People of Jerusalem, let these troubles be a warning to you, or else I will abandon you; I will turn your city into a desert, a place where no one lives."

Rebellious Israel

9 The LORD Almighty said to me, "Israel will be stripped clean like a vineyard from which every grape has been picked. So you must rescue everyone you can while there is still time."

10 I answered, "Who would listen to me if I spoke to them and warned them? They are stubborn and refuse to listen to your message; they laugh at what you tell me to say. 11 Your anger against them burns in me too, LORD, and I can't hold it in any longer."

Then the LORD said to me, "Pour out

---

e Probable text they . . . birds; *Hebrew unclear.*
5.21 Is 6.9, 10; Ez 12.2; Mk 8.18   **5.22** Job 38.8-11

my anger on the children in the streets and on the gatherings of the young people. Husbands and wives will be taken away, and even the very old will not be spared. 12 Their houses will be given to others, and so will their fields and their wives. I am going to punish the people of this land. 13 Everyone, great and small, tries to make money dishonestly; even prophets and priests cheat the people. 14 They act as if my people's wounds were only scratches. 'All is well,' they say, when all is not well. 15 Were they ashamed because they did these disgusting things? No, they were not at all ashamed; they don't even know how to blush. And so they will fall as others have fallen; when I punish them, that will be the end of them. I, the LORD, have spoken."

Israel Rejects God's Way

16 The LORD said to his people, "Stand at the crossroads and look. Ask for the ancient paths and where the best road is. Walk in it, and you will live in peace."

But they said, "No, we will not!" 17 Then the LORD appointed sentries to listen for the trumpet's warning. But they said, "We will not listen."

18 So the LORD said, "Listen, you nations, and learn what is going to happen to my people. 19 Listen, earth! As punishment for all their schemes I am bringing ruin on these people, because they have rejected my teaching and have not obeyed my words. 20 What do I care about the incense they bring me from Sheba, or the spices from a distant land? I will not accept their offerings or be pleased with their sacrifices. 21 And so I will make these people stumble and fall. Parents and children will die, and so will friends and neighbors."

Invasion from the North

22 The LORD says, "People are coming from a country in the north; a mighty nation far away is preparing for war. 23 They have taken up their bows and swords; they are cruel and merciless. They sound like the roaring sea, as they ride their horses. They are ready for battle against Jerusalem."

24 "We have heard the news," say the people of Jerusalem, "and our hands hang limp; we are seized by anguish

*"We have heard the news,
. . . and our hands hang limp." (6.24)*

and pain like a woman in labor. 25 We don't dare go to the countryside or walk on the roads, because our enemies are armed and terror is all around us."

26 The LORD says to his people, "Put on sackcloth and roll in ashes. Mourn with bitter tears as you would for an only child, because the one who comes to destroy you will suddenly attack. 27 Jeremiah, test my people, as you would test metal, and find out what they are like. 28 They are all stubborn rebels, hard as bronze and iron. They are all corrupt, going around and spreading gossip. 29 The furnace burns fiercely, but the waste metals do not melt and run off. It is useless to go on refining my people, because those who are evil are not taken away. 30 They will be called worthless dross, because I, the LORD, have rejected them."

6.14 Ez 13.10   **6.12-15** Jr 8.10-12

Jeremiah Preaches in the Temple

7 ¹⁻³ The Lord sent me to the gate of the Temple where the people of Judah went in to worship. He told me to stand there and announce what the Lord Almighty, the God of Israel, had to say to them: "Change the way you are living and the things you are doing, and I will let you go on living here. ⁴ Stop believing those deceitful words, 'We are safe! This is the Lord's Temple, this is the Lord's Temple, this is the Lord's Temple!'

⁵ "Change the way you are living and stop doing the things you are doing. Be fair in your treatment of one another. ⁶ Stop taking advantage of aliens, orphans, and widows. Stop killing innocent people in this land. Stop worshiping other gods, for that will destroy you. ⁷ If you change, I will let you go on living here in the land which I gave your ancestors as a permanent possession.

⁸ "Look, you put your trust in deceitful words. ⁹ You steal, murder, commit adultery, tell lies under oath, offer sacrifices to Baal, and worship gods that you had not known before. ¹⁰ You do these things I hate, and then you come and stand in my presence, in my own Temple, and say, 'We are safe!' ¹¹ Do you think that my Temple is a hiding place for robbers? I have seen what you are doing. ¹² Go to Shiloh,ᶠ the first place where I chose to be worshiped, and see what I did to it because of the sins of my people Israel. ¹³ You have committed all these sins, and even though I spoke to you over and over again, you refused to listen. You would not answer when I called you. ¹⁴ And so, what I did to Shiloh I will do to this Temple of mine, in which you trust. Here in this place that I gave to your ancestors and you, I will do the same thing that I did to Shiloh.

¹⁵ I will drive you out of my sight as I drove out your relatives, the people of Israel. I, the Lord, have spoken."

The People's Disobedience

¹⁶ The Lord said, "Jeremiah, do not pray for these people. Do not cry or pray on their behalf; do not plead with me, for I will not listen to you. ¹⁷ Don't you see what they are doing in the cities of Judah and in the streets of Jerusalem? ¹⁸ The children gather firewood, the men build fires, and the women mix dough to bake cakes for the goddess they call the Queen of Heaven. They also pour out offerings of wine to other gods, in order to hurt me. ¹⁹ But am I really the one they are hurting? No, they are hurting themselves and bringing shame on themselves. ²⁰ And so I, the Sovereign Lord, will pour out my fierce anger on this Temple. I will pour it out on people and animals alike, and even on the trees and the crops. My anger will be like a fire that no one can put out.

²¹ "My people, some sacrifices you burn completely on the altar, and some you are permitted to eat. But what I, the Lord, say is that you might as well eat them all. ²² I gave your ancestors no commands about burnt offerings or any other kinds of sacrifices when I brought them out of Egypt. ²³ But I did command them to obey me, so that I would be their God and they would be my people. And I told them to live the way I had commanded them, so that things would go well for them. ²⁴ But they did not obey or pay any attention. Instead, they did whatever their stubborn and evil hearts told them to do, and they became worse instead of better. ²⁵ From the day that your ancestors came out of Egypt until this very day I have kept on sending to you my servants, the

---

ᶠ SHILOH: *The city where the Covenant Box was kept in the time of Eli (see 1 S 1.3). The city was destroyed, probably by the Philistines.*

7.11 Mt 21.13; Mk 11.17; Lk 19.46   **7.12-14** Js 18.1; Ps 78.60; Jr 26.6   **7.18** Jr 44.17-19 prophets. 26 Yet no one listened or paid any attention. Instead, you became more stubborn and rebellious than your ancestors.

27 "So, Jeremiah, you will speak all these words to my people, but they will not listen to you; you will call them, but they will not answer. 28 You will tell them that their nation does not obey me, the LORD their God, or learn from their punishment. Faithfulness is dead. No longer is it even talked about.

Sinful Deeds in Hinnom Valley

29 "Mourn, people of Jerusalem;
cut off your hair and throw
it away.
Sing a funeral song on the
hilltops,
because I, the LORD, am
angry
and have rejected my people.

30 "The people of Judah have done an evil thing. They have placed their idols, which I hate, in my Temple and have defiled it. 31 In Hinnom Valley they have built an altar called Topheth, so that they can sacrifice their sons and daughters in the fire. I did not command them to do this — it did not even enter my mind. 32 And so, the time will come when it will no longer be called Topheth or Hinnom Valley, but Slaughter Valley. They will bury people there because there will be nowhere else to bury them. 33 The corpses will be food for the birds and wild animals, and there will be no one to scare them off. 34 The land will become a desert. In the cities of Judah and in the streets of Jerusalem I will put an end to the sounds of joy and gladness and to the happy sounds of wedding feasts.

8 "At that time the bones of the kings and of the officials of Judah, as well as the bones of the priests, of the prophets, and of the other people who lived in Jerusalem, will be taken out of their graves. 2 Instead of being gathered and buried, their bones will be like manure lying on the ground. They will be spread out before the sun, the moon, and the stars, which these people have loved and served, and which they have consulted and worshiped. 3 And the people of this evil nation who survive, who live in the places where I have scattered them, will prefer to die rather than to go on living. I, the LORD Almighty, have spoken."

Sin and Punishment

4 The LORD told me to say to his people, "When someone falls down, doesn't he get back up? If someone misses the road, doesn't he turn back? 5 Why then, my people, do you turn away from me without ever turning back? You cling to your idols and refuse to return to me. 6 I listened carefully, but you did not speak the truth. Not one of you has been sorry for your wickedness; not one of you has asked, 'What have I done wrong?' Each of you keep on going your own way, like a horse rushing into battle. 7 Even storks know when it is time to return; doves, swallows, and thrushes know when it is time to migrate. But, my people, you do not know the laws by which I rule you. 8 How can you say that you are wise and that you know my laws? Look, the laws have been changed by dishonest scribes. 9 Your wise men are put to shame; they are confused and trapped. They have rejected my words; what wisdom do they have now? 10 So I will give their fields to new owners and their wives to other men. Everyone, great and small, tries to make money dishonestly. Even prophets and priests cheat the people. 11 They act as if my people's wounds were only scratches. 'All is well,' they say, when all is not well. 12 My people, were you ashamed

7.31 a 2 K 23.10; Jr 32.35; b Lv 18.21   7.34 Jr 16.9; 25.10; Ba 2.23; Rev 18.23
8.11 Ez 13.10   8.10-12 Jr 6.12-15

Like a vine with no grapes (8.13)

because you did these disgusting things? No, you were not ashamed at all; you don't even know how to blush! And so you will fall as others have fallen; when I punish you, that will be the end of you. I, the LORD, have spoken.

13 "I wanted to gather my people, as a farmer gathers a harvest; but they are like a vine with no grapes, like a fig tree with no figs; even the leaves have withered. Therefore, I have allowed outsiders to take over the land."*g*

14 "Why are we sitting still?" God's people ask. "Come on, we will run to the fortified cities and die there. The LORD our God has condemned us to die; he has given us poison to drink, because we have sinned against him. 15 We hoped for peace and a time of healing, but it was no use; terror came instead. 16 Our enemies are already in the city of Dan; we hear the snorting of their horses. The whole land trembles when their horses neigh. Our enemies have come to destroy our land and everything in it, our city and all its people."

17 "Watch out!" the LORD says, "I am sending snakes among you, poisonous snakes that cannot be charmed, and they will bite you."

Jeremiah's Sorrow for His People

18 My sorrow cannot be healed;*h*
  I am sick at heart.
19 Listen! Throughout the land
   I hear my people crying out,
 "Is the LORD no longer in Zion?
   Is Zion's king no longer
      there?"
The LORD, their king, replies,
 "Why have you made me angry
      by worshiping your idols
   and by bowing down to your
      useless foreign gods?"
20 The people cry out,
 "The summer is gone, the
      harvest is over,
   but we have not been saved."

21 My heart has been crushed
   because my people are
      crushed;
  I mourn; I am completely
      dismayed.

I am sick at heart. (8.18)

22 Is there no medicine in Gilead? *i*
   Are there no doctors there?
  Why, then, have my people
      not been healed?

---

g Therefore . . . land; *Hebrew unclear.*   *h* Probable text My sorrow . . . healed; *Hebrew unclear.*   *i* GILEAD: *A region east of the Jordan, famous for plants that were used for medicinal purposes.*

9 I wish my head were a well of
water,
and my eyes a fountain of
tears,
so that I could cry day and night
for my people who have been
killed.
² I wish I had a place to stay in
the desert
where I could get away from
my people.
They are all unfaithful,
a mob of traitors.
³ They are always ready to tell lies;
dishonesty instead of truth
rules the land.

The LORD says,
"My people do one evil thing
after another
and do not acknowledge me
as their God."

⁴ Everyone must be on guard
against their friends,
and no one can trust their
relatives;
for all relatives are as deceitful
as Jacob,
and everyone slanders their
friends.
⁵⁻⁶ They all mislead their friends,
and no one tells the truth;
they have taught their tongues
to lie
and will not give up their
sinning.
They do one violent thing after
another,
and one deceitful act follows
another.

The LORD says that his people
reject him.
⁷ Because of this the LORD
Almighty says,
"I will refine my people like
metal
and put them to the test.
My people have done evil —
what else can I do with them?

⁸ Their tongues are like deadly
arrows;
they always tell lies.
Everyone speaks friendly words
to their neighbors,
but they are really setting a
trap for them.
⁹ Will I not punish them for these
things?
Will I not take revenge on a
nation like this?
I, the LORD, have spoken."

¹⁰ I said, "I will mourn for the
mountains
and weep for the pastures,
because they have dried up,
and no one travels through
them.
The sound of livestock is no
longer heard;
birds and wild animals have
fled and gone."

¹¹ The LORD says, "I will make
Jerusalem a pile of ruins,
a place where jackals live;
the cities of Judah will become a
desert,
a place where no one lives."

¹² I asked, "LORD, why is the land
devastated and dry as a desert, so that
no one travels through it? Who is wise
enough to understand this? To whom
have you explained it so that they can
tell others?"

¹³ The LORD answered, "This has
happened because my people have
abandoned the teaching that I gave
them. They have not obeyed me or done
what I told them. ¹⁴ Instead, they have
been stubborn and have worshiped the
idols of Baal as their ancestors taught
them to do. ¹⁵ So then, listen to what I,
the LORD Almighty, the God of Israel,
will do: I will give my people bitter
plants to eat and poison to drink. ¹⁶ I will
scatter them among nations that neither they nor their ancestors have
heard about, and I will send armies

against them until I have completely
destroyed them."

The People of Jerusalem
Cry Out for Help

¹⁷The LORD Almighty said,
"Think about what is happening!
Call for the mourners to come,
for the women who sing
funeral songs."

¹⁸The people said,
"Tell them to hurry and sing a
funeral song for us,
until our eyes fill with tears,
and our eyelids are wet from
crying."

¹⁹Listen to the sound of crying in
Zion:
"We are ruined!
We are completely disgraced!
We must leave our land;
our homes have been torn
down."

²⁰I said,
"Listen to the LORD, you women,
and pay attention to his
words.
Teach your daughters how to
mourn,
and your friends how to sing a
funeral song.
²¹Death has come in through our
windows
and entered our palaces;
it has cut down the children in
the streets
and the young men in the
marketplaces.
²²Dead bodies are scattered
everywhere,
like piles of manure on the
fields,

like grain cut and left behind
by the reapers,
grain that no one gathers.
This is what the LORD has told
me to say."

²³The LORD says,
"The wise should not boast of
their wisdom,
nor the strong of their
strength,
nor the rich of their wealth.
²⁴If any want to boast,
they should boast that they
know and understand me,
because my love is constant,
and I do what is just and
right.
These are the things that
please me.
I, the LORD, have spoken."

²⁵⁻²⁶The LORD says, "The time is
coming when I will punish the people
of Egypt, Judah, Edom, Ammon, Moab,
and the desert people, who have their
hair cut short.ʲ All these people are circumcised, but have not kept the covenant it symbolizes. None of these
people and none of the people of Israel
have kept my covenant."

Idolatry and True Worship

10 People of Israel, listen to the
message that the LORD has for
you. ²He says,
"Do not follow the ways of other
nations;
do not be disturbed by
unusual sights in the sky,
even though other nations are
terrified.
³The religion of these people is
worthless.
A tree is cut down in the forest;

ʲ HAIR CUT SHORT: *The desert people cut their hair short in honor of their god, a pagan
practice forbidden to the Israelites (see Lv 19.27).*
9.24 1 Co 1.31; 2 Co 10.17

it is carved by the tools of the
woodworker
4   and decorated with silver and
gold.
It is fastened down with nails
to keep it from falling over.
5 Such idols are like scarecrows in
a field of melons;
they cannot speak;
they have to be carried
because they cannot walk.
Do not be afraid of them:
they can cause you no harm,
and they can do you no good."

They cannot speak;
they have to be carried. (10.5)

6 LORD, there is no one like you;
you are mighty,
and your name is great and
powerful.
7 Who would not honor you, the
king of all nations?
You deserve to be honored.
There is no one like you
among all the wise men of the
nations
or among any of their kings.
8 All of them are stupid and
foolish.
What can they learn from
wooden idols?*k*
9 Their idols are covered with
silver from Spain

and with gold from Uphaz,
all the work of artists;
they are dressed in violet and
purple cloth
woven by skilled weavers.
10 But you, LORD, are the true God,
you are the living God
and the eternal king.
When you are angry, the world
trembles;
the nations cannot endure
your anger.

(11 You people must tell them that
the gods who did not make the earth
and the sky will be destroyed. They will
no longer exist anywhere on earth.)

A Hymn of Praise to God

12 The LORD made the earth by his
power;
by his wisdom he created the
world
and stretched out the
heavens.
13 At his command the waters
above the sky*l* roar;
he brings clouds from the
ends of the earth.
He makes lightning flash in
the rain
and sends the wind from his
storeroom.
14 At the sight of this, people feel
stupid and senseless;
those who make idols are
disillusioned,
because the gods they make
are false and lifeless.
15 They are worthless and should
be despised;
they will be destroyed when
the LORD comes to deal
with them.
16 The God of Jacob is not like
them;

k What can . . . idols?; *or* What their idols teach is worthless.   *l* WATERS ABOVE THE
SKY: *See Gn* 1.6-8.
10.7 Rev 15.4

he is the one who made
everything,
and he has chosen Israel to be
his very own people.
The LORD Almighty is his
name.

The Coming Exile

17 People of Jerusalem, you are under
siege! Gather up your belongings.
18 The LORD is going to throw you out of
this land; he is going to crush you until
not one of you is left. The LORD has
spoken.

19 The people of Jerusalem cried out,
"How badly we are hurt!
Our wounds will not heal.
And we thought this was
something we could
endure!
20 Our tents are ruined;
the ropes that held them have
broken.
Our children have all gone away;
there is no one left to put up
our tents again;
there is no one to hang their
curtains."

21 I answered, "Our leaders are
stupid;
they do not ask the LORD for
guidance.
This is why they have failed,
and our people have been
scattered.
22 Listen! News has come!
There is a great commotion in
a nation to the north;
its army will turn the cities of
Judah into a desert,
a place where jackals live."

23 LORD, I know that none of us are
in charge of our own
destiny;
none of us have control over
our own life.
24 Correct your people, LORD,
but do not be too hard on us

or punish us when you are
angry;
that would be the end of us.
25 Turn your anger on the nations
that do not worship you
and on the people who
reject you.
They have killed your people;
they have destroyed us
completely
and left our country in ruins.

Jeremiah and the Covenant

11 The LORD said to me, 2 "Listen
to the terms of the covenant.
Tell the people of Judah and of Jerusalem 3 that I, the LORD God of Israel,
have placed a curse on everyone who
does not obey the terms of this covenant. 4 It is the covenant I made with
their ancestors when I brought them
out of Egypt, the land that was like a
blazing furnace to them. I told them to
obey me and to do everything that I had
commanded. I told them that if they
obeyed, they would be my people and I
would be their God. 5 Then I would keep
the promise I made to their ancestors
that I would give them the rich and fertile land which they now have."

I said, "Yes, LORD."

6 Then the LORD said to me, "Go to
the cities of Judah and to the streets of
Jerusalem. Proclaim my message there
and tell the people to listen to the terms
of the covenant and to obey them.
7 When I brought their ancestors out of
Egypt, I solemnly warned them to obey
me, and I have kept on warning the
people until this day. 8 But they did not
listen or obey. Instead, everyone continued to be as stubborn and evil as
ever. I had commanded them to keep
the covenant, but they refused. So I
brought on them all the punishments
described in it."

9 Then the LORD said to me, "The
people of Judah and of Jerusalem are
plotting against me. 10 They have gone
back to the sins of their ancestors, who

refused to do what I said; they have worshiped other gods. Both Israel and Judah have broken the covenant that I made with their ancestors. ¹¹ So now I, the Lord, warn them that I am going to bring destruction on them, and they will not escape. And when they cry out to me for help, I will not listen to them. ¹² Then the people of Judah and of Jerusalem will go to the gods to whom they offer sacrifices and will cry out to them for help. But those gods will not be able to save them when this destruction comes. ¹³ The people of Judah have as many gods as they have cities, and the inhabitants of Jerusalem have set up as many altars for sacrifices to that disgusting god Baal as there are streets in the city. ¹⁴ Jeremiah, don't pray to me or plead with me on behalf of these people. When they are in trouble and call to me for help, I will not listen to them."

¹⁵ The Lord says, "The people I love are doing evil things. What right do they have to be in my Temple? Do they think they can prevent disaster by making promises*m* and by offering animal sacrifices? Will they then rejoice? ¹⁶ I once called them a leafy olive tree, full of beautiful fruit; but now, with a roar like thunder I will set its leaves on fire and break its branches.

I will set its leaves on fire. (11.16)

¹⁷ "I, the Lord Almighty, planted Israel and Judah; but now I threaten them with disaster. They have brought this on themselves because they have done wrong; they have made me angry by offering sacrifices to Baal."

A Plot against Jeremiah's Life

¹⁸ The Lord informed me of the plots that my enemies were making against me. ¹⁹ I was like a trusting lamb taken out to be killed, and I did not know that it was against me that they were planning evil things. They were saying, "Let's chop down the tree while it is still healthy;*n* let's kill him so that no one will remember him any more."

²⁰ Then I prayed, "Almighty Lord, you are a just judge; you test people's thoughts and feelings. I have placed my cause in your hands; so let me watch you take revenge on these people."

²¹ The people of Anathoth wanted me killed, and they told me that they would kill me if I kept on proclaiming the Lord's message. ²² So the Lord Almighty said, "I will punish them! Their young men will be killed in war; their children will die of starvation. ²³ I have set a time for bringing disaster on the people of Anathoth, and when that time comes, none of them will survive."

Jeremiah Questions the Lord

12 "Lord, if I argued my case with you,
you would prove to be right.
Yet I must question you about matters of justice.
Why are the wicked so prosperous?
Why do dishonest people succeed?
² You plant them, and they take root;

m One ancient translation promises; *Hebrew* many.   *n Probable text* while it is still
healthy; *Hebrew* with its bread.
11.20 Ws 1.6-9

they grow and bear fruit.
They always speak well of you,
    yet they do not really care
        about you.
³ But, LORD, you know me;
    you see what I do
    and how I love you.
Drag these evil people away like
        sheep to be butchered;
    guard them until it is time for
        them to be slaughtered.
⁴ How long will our land be dry,
    and the grass in every field be
        withered?
Animals and birds are dying
    because of the wickedness of
        our people,
    people who say, 'God doesn't
        see what we are doing.' "*

⁵ The LORD said,
"Jeremiah, if you get tired racing
        against people,
    how can you race against
        horses?
If you can't even stand up in
        open country,
    how will you manage in the
        jungle by the Jordan?
⁶ Even your relatives, members of
        your own family, have
        betrayed you;
    they join in the attacks
        against you.
Do not trust them, even though
        they speak friendly words."

The LORD's Sorrow because
of His People

⁷ The LORD says,
"I have abandoned Israel;
    I have rejected my chosen
        nation.
I have given the people I love
    into the power of their
        enemies.
⁸ My chosen people have turned
        against me;

like a lion in the forest
    they have roared at me,
    and so I hate them.
⁹ My chosen people are like a bird
    attacked from all sides by
        hawks.
Call the wild animals
    to come and join in the feast!
¹⁰ Many foreign rulers have
        destroyed my vineyard;
    they have trampled down my
        fields;
    they have turned my lovely
        land into a desert.
¹¹ They have made it a wasteland;
    it lies desolate before me.
The whole land has become a
        desert,
    and no one cares.
¹² Across all the desert highlands
    people have come to plunder.
I have sent war to destroy the
        entire land;
    no one can live in peace.
¹³ My people planted wheat, but
        gathered weeds;
    they have worked hard, but
        got nothing for it.
Because of my fierce anger
    their crops have failed."

The LORD's Promise to
Israel's Neighbors

¹⁴ The LORD says, "I have something
to say about Israel's neighbors who
have ruined the land I gave to my people Israel. I will take those wicked people away from their countries like an
uprooted plant, and I will rescue Judah
from them. ¹⁵ But after I have taken
them away, I will have mercy on them;
I will bring each nation back to its own
land and to its own country. ¹⁶ If with all
their hearts they will accept the religion
of my people and will swear, 'As the
LORD lives' — as they once taught my
people to swear by Baal — then they will
also be a part of my people and will

---

o Some ancient translations what we are doing; *Hebrew* our latter end.

prosper. [17] But if any nation will not obey, then I will completely uproot it and destroy it. I, the LORD, have spoken."

The Linen Shorts

13 The LORD told me to go and buy myself some linen shorts and to put them on; but he told me not to put them in water. [2] So I bought them and put them on. [3] Then the LORD spoke to me again and said, [4] "Go to the Euphrates River and hide the shorts in a hole in the rocks." [5] So I went and hid them near the Euphrates.

[6] Some time later the LORD told me to go back to the Euphrates and get the shorts. [7] So I went back, and when I found the place where I had hidden them, I saw that they were ruined and were no longer any good.

[8] Then the LORD spoke to me again. He said, [9] "This is how I will destroy the pride of Judah and the great pride of Jerusalem. [10] These evil people have refused to obey me. They have been as stubborn and wicked as ever, and have worshiped and served other gods. So then, they will become like these shorts that are no longer any good. [11] Just as shorts fit tightly around the waist, so I intended all the people of Israel and Judah to hold tightly to me. I did this so that they would be my people and would bring praise and honor to my name; but they would not obey me."

The Wine Jar

[12] The LORD God said to me, "Jeremiah, tell the people of Israel that every wine jar should be filled with wine. They will answer that they know every wine jar should be filled with wine. [13] Then tell them that I, the LORD, am going to fill the people in this land with wine until they are drunk: the kings, who are David's descendants, the priests, the prophets, and all the people

of Jerusalem. [14] Then I will smash them like jars against one another, old and young alike. No pity, compassion, or mercy will stop me from killing them."

Jeremiah Warns against Pride

[15] People of Israel, the LORD has
    spoken!
Be humble and listen to him.
[16] Honor the LORD, your God,
    before he brings darkness,
    and you stumble on the
        mountains;
before he turns into deep
        darkness
    the light you hoped for.
[17] If you will not listen,
    I will cry in secret because of
        your pride;
    I will cry bitterly, and my tears
        will flow
    because the LORD's people
        have been taken away as
        captives.

[18] The LORD said to me, "Tell the king and his mother to come down from their thrones, because their beautiful crowns have fallen from their heads. [p] [19] The towns of southern Judah are under siege; no one can get through to them. All the people of Judah have been taken away into exile."

[20] Jerusalem, look! Your enemies are coming down from the north! Where are the people entrusted to your care, your people you were so proud of? [21] What will you say when people you thought were your friends conquer you and rule over you? [q] You will be in pain like a woman giving birth. [22] If you ask why all this has happened to you — why your clothes have been torn off and you have been raped — it is because your sin is so terrible. [23] Can people change the color of their skin, or a leopard remove its spots? If they could, then you that do

---

[p] *Some ancient translations* from their heads; *Hebrew unclear.*   [q] *Probable text* What . . . over you; *Hebrew unclear.*

nothing but evil could learn to do what is right. 24 The LORD will scatter you like straw that is blown away by the desert wind. 25 He has said that this will be your fate. This is what he has decided to do with you, because you have forgotten him and have trusted in false gods. 26 The LORD himself will strip off your clothes and expose you to shame. 27 He has seen you do the things he hates. He has seen you go after pagan gods on the hills and in the fields, like a man lusting after his neighbor's wife or like a stallion after a mare. People of Jerusalem, you are doomed! When will you ever be pure?

The Terrible Drought

14 The LORD said to me concerning the drought,
2 "Judah is in mourning;
    its cities are dying,
its people lie on the ground in
    sorrow,
    and Jerusalem cries out for
        help.
3 The rich people send their
    servants for water;
they go to the cisterns,
    but find no water;
they come back with their
    jars empty.
Discouraged and confused,
    they hide their faces.
4 Because there is no rain
    and the ground is dried up,
the farmers are sick at heart;
    they hide their faces.
5 In the field the mother deer
    abandons her newborn fawn
    because there is no grass.
6 The wild donkeys stand on the
    hilltops
    and pant for breath like
        jackals;
their eyesight fails them
    because they have no food.
7 My people cry out to me,
    'Even though our sins
        accuse us,

They come back with their jars empty. (14.3)

help us, LORD, as you have
    promised.
We have turned away from you
    many times;
    we have sinned against you.
8 You are Israel's only hope;
    you are the one who saves us
        from disaster.
Why are you like a stranger in
    our land,
    like a traveler who stays for
        only one night?
9 Why are you like someone taken
    by surprise,
    like a soldier powerless to
        help?
Surely, LORD, you are with us!
    We are your people;
    do not abandon us.' "

10 The LORD says about these people, "They love to run away from me, and they will not control themselves. So I am not pleased with them. I will remember the wrongs they have done and punish them because of their sins."

11 The LORD said to me, "Do not ask me to help these people. 12 Even if they fast, I will not listen to their cry for help; and even if they offer me burnt offerings and grain offerings, I will not be pleased with them. Instead, I will kill

them in war and by starvation and disease."

[13] Then I said, "Sovereign LORD, you know that the prophets are telling the people that there will be no war or starvation, because you have promised, they say, that there will be only peace in our land."

[14] But the LORD replied, "The prophets are telling lies in my name; I did not send them, nor did I give them any orders or speak one word to them. The visions they talk about have not come from me; their predictions are worthless things that they have imagined. [15] I, the LORD, tell you what I am going to do to those prophets whom I did not send but who speak in my name and say war and starvation will not strike this land — I will kill them in war and by starvation. [16] The people to whom they have said these things will be killed in the same way. Their bodies will be thrown out into the streets of Jerusalem, and there will be no one to bury them. This will happen to all of them — including their wives, their sons, and their daughters. I will make them pay for their wickedness."

[17] The LORD commanded me to tell the people about my sorrow and to say:
"May my eyes flow with tears
day and night,
may I never stop weeping,
for my people are deeply
wounded
and are badly hurt.
[18] When I go out in the fields,
I see the bodies of men killed
in war;
when I go into the towns,
I see people starving to death.
Prophets and priests carry on
their work,
but they don't know what
they are doing."[r]

The People Plead with the LORD

[19] LORD, have you completely
rejected Judah?
Do you hate the people of
Zion?
Why have you hurt us so badly
that we cannot be healed?
We looked for peace, but nothing
good happened;
we hoped for healing, but
terror came instead.
[20] We have sinned against you,
LORD;
we confess our own sins
and the sins of our ancestors.
[21] Remember your promises and do
not despise us;
do not bring disgrace on
Jerusalem,
the place of your glorious
throne.
Do not break the covenant you
made with us.
[22] None of the idols of the nations
can send rain;
the sky by itself cannot make
showers fall.
We have put our hope in you,
O LORD our God,
because you are the one who
does these things.

Doom for the People of Judah

15 Then the LORD said to me, "Even if Moses and Samuel were standing here pleading with me, I would not show these people any mercy. Make them go away; make them get out of my sight. [2] When they ask you where they should go, tell them that I have said:
Some are doomed to die by
disease —
that's where they will go!
Others are doomed to die
in war —

---

[r] Prophets . . . doing; *or* Prophets and priests have been dragged away to a land they know nothing about.
15.1 a Ex 32.11-14; Nu 14.13-19; **b** 1 S 7.5-9   **15.2** Rev 13.10

that's where they will go!
Some are doomed to die of
    starvation —
    that's where they will go!
Others are doomed to be taken
    away as prisoners —
    that's where they will go!
³I, the LORD, have decided that four terrible things will happen to them: they will be killed in war; their bodies will be dragged off by dogs; birds will eat them, and wild animals will devour what is left over. ⁴I will make all the people of the world horrified at them because of what Hezekiah's son Manasseh did in Jerusalem when he was king of Judah."

⁵The LORD says,

"Who will pity you, people of
    Jerusalem,
    and who will grieve over you?
Who will stop long enough
    to ask how you are?
⁶You people have rejected me;
    you have turned your backs
        on me.
So I reached out and
        crushed you
    because I was tired of
        controlling my anger.ˢ
⁷In every town in the land
    I threw you to the wind like
        straw.
I destroyed you, my people,
    I killed your children
    because you did not stop your
        evil ways.
⁸There are more widows in your
        land
    than grains of sand by
        the sea.
I killed your young men in their
        prime
    and made their mothers
        suffer.
I suddenly struck them
    with anguish and terror.

⁹The mother who lost her seven
        children has fainted,
    gasping for breath.
Her daylight has turned to
        darkness;
    she is disgraced and sick at
        heart.
I will let your enemies kill
    those of you who are still
        alive.
I, the LORD, have spoken."

Jeremiah Complains to the LORD

¹⁰What an unhappy man I am! Why did my mother bring me into the world? I have to quarrel and argue with everyone in the land. I have not lent any money or borrowed any; yet everyone curses me. ¹¹LORD, may all their curses come true if I have not servedᵗ you well, if I have not pleaded with you on behalf of my enemies when they were in trouble and distress. (¹²No one can break iron, especially the iron from the north that is mixed with bronze.)

¹³The LORD said to me, "I will send enemies to carry away the wealth and treasures of my people, in order to punish them for the sins they have committed throughout the land. ¹⁴I will make them serve their enemies in a land they know nothing about, because my anger is like fire, and it will burn forever."

¹⁵Then I said, "LORD, you understand. Remember me and help me. Let me have revenge on those who persecute me. Do not be so patient with them that they succeed in killing me. Remember that it is for your sake that I am insulted. ¹⁶You spoke to me, and I listened to every word. I belong to you, LORD God Almighty, and so your words filled my heart with joy and happiness. ¹⁷I did not spend my time with other people, laughing and having a good time. In obedience to your orders I

ˢ you because . . . anger; or you; I was tired of feeling sorry for you. ᵗ *Probable text* LORD, . . . served; *Hebrew unclear.*
15.4 2 K 21.1-16; 2 Ch 33.1-9

stayed by myself and was filled with anger. [18] Why do I keep on suffering? Why are my wounds incurable? Why won't they heal? Do you intend to disappoint me like a stream that goes dry in the summer?"

[19] To this the LORD replied, "If you return, I will take you back, and you will be my servant again. If instead of talking nonsense you proclaim a worthwhile message, you will be my prophet again. The people will come back to you, and you will not need to go to them. [20] I will make you like a solid bronze wall as far as they are concerned. They will fight against you, but they will not defeat you. I will be with you to protect you and keep you safe. [21] I will rescue you from the power of wicked and violent people. I, the LORD, have spoken."

The LORD's Will for Jeremiah's Life

16 Again the LORD spoke to me and said, [2] "Do not marry or have children in a place like this. [3] I will tell you what is going to happen to the children who are born here and to their parents. [4] They will die of terrible diseases, and no one will mourn for them or bury them. Their bodies will lie like piles of manure on the ground. They will be killed in war or die of starvation, and their bodies will be food for the birds and the wild animals.

[5] "You must not enter a house where there is mourning. Do not grieve for anyone. I will no longer bless my people with peace or show them love and mercy. [6] The rich and the poor will die in this land, but no one will bury them or mourn for them. Not one of you will gash yourself or shave your head to show your grief. [7] No one will eat or drink with anyone to offer comfort when a loved one dies. No one will show sympathy, not even for someone who has lost a father or mother.

[8] "Do not enter a house where people are feasting. Do not sit down with them to eat and drink. [9] Listen to what I, the LORD Almighty, the God of Israel, have to say. I will silence the sounds of joy and gladness and the happy sounds of wedding feasts. The people here will live to see this happen.

[10] "When you tell them all this, they will ask you why I have decided to punish them so harshly. They will ask what crime they are guilty of and what sin they have committed against the LORD their God. [11] Then tell them that the LORD has said, 'Your ancestors turned away from me and worshiped and served other gods. They abandoned me and did not obey my teachings. [12] But you have done even worse than your ancestors. All of you are stubborn and evil, and you do not obey me. [13] So then, I will throw you out of this land into a land that neither you nor your ancestors have ever known. And there you will serve other gods day and night, and I will show you no mercy.'"

The Return from Exile

[14] The LORD says, "The time is coming when people will no longer swear by me as the living God who brought the people of Israel out of the land of Egypt. [15] Instead, they will swear by me as the living God who brought the people of Israel out of a northern land and out of all the other countries where I had scattered them. I will bring them back to their own country, to the land that I gave their ancestors. I, the LORD, have spoken."

The Coming Punishment

[16] The LORD says, "I am sending for many fishermen to come and catch these people. Then I will send for many hunters to hunt them down on every mountain and hill and in the caves among the rocks. [17] I see everything

they do. Nothing is hidden from me; their sins do not escape my sight. [18] I will make them pay double for their sin and wickedness, because they have defiled my land with idols that are as lifeless as corpses, and have filled it with their false gods."

Jeremiah's Prayer of Confidence in the LORD

[19] LORD, you are the one who protects me and gives me strength; you help me in times of trouble. Nations will come to you from the ends of the earth and say, "Our ancestors had nothing but false gods, nothing but useless idols. [20] Can people make their own gods? No, if they did, those would not really be gods."

[21] "So then," says the LORD, "once and for all I will make the nations know my power and my might; they will know that I am the LORD."

The Sin and Punishment of Judah

17 The LORD says, "People of Judah, your sin is written with an iron pen; it is engraved on your hearts with a diamond point and carved on the corners of your altars. [2] Your people worship at the altars and the symbols that have been set up for the goddess Asherah by every green tree and on the hilltops [3] and on the mountains in the open country. I will have your enemies take away your wealth and your treasures because of all the sins you have committed[u] throughout your land. [4] You will have to give up[v] the land I gave you, and I will make you serve your enemies in a land you know nothing about, because my anger is like a fire, and it will burn forever."

Various Sayings

[5] The LORD says,
"I will condemn those
  who turn away from me
and put their trust in human
    beings,
  in the strength of mortals.
[6] He is like a bush in the desert,
  which grows in the dry
    wasteland,
  on salty ground where
    nothing else grows.
Nothing good ever happens
  to him.

He is like a bush in the desert. (17.6)

[7] "But I will bless the person
  who puts his trust in me.
[8] He is like a tree growing near a
    stream
  and sending out roots to the
    water.
It is not afraid when hot weather
    comes,
  because its leaves stay green;

---

[u] *Probable text* because of all the sins you have committed; *Hebrew* your high places for sins.   [v] *Probable text* You ... give up; *Hebrew unclear.*
17.8 Ps 1.3

it has no worries when there is
no rain;
it keeps on bearing fruit.

9"Who can understand the human
heart?
There is nothing else so
deceitful;
it is too sick to be healed.
10I, the LORD, search the minds
and test the hearts of people.
I treat each of them according to
the way they live,
according to what they do."

11The person who gets money
dishonestly
is like a bird that hatches
eggs it didn't lay.
In the prime of life he will lose
his riches,
and in the end he is nothing
but a fool.

12Our Temple is like a glorious
throne,
standing on a high mountain
from the beginning.

13LORD, you are Israel's hope;
all who abandon you will be
put to shame.
They will disappear like names
written in the dust,w
because they have abandoned
you, the LORD,
the spring of fresh water.

Jeremiah Asks the LORD for Help

14LORD, heal me and I will be completely well; rescue me and I will be
perfectly safe. You are the one I praise!
15The people say to me, "Where are
those threats the LORD made against
us? Let him carry them out now!"
16But, LORD, I never urged you to
bring disaster on them;x I did not wish
a time of trouble for them. LORD, you
know this; you know what I have said.
17Do not be a terror to me; you are my
place of safety when trouble comes.
18Bring disgrace on those who persecute me, but spare me, LORD. Fill them
with terror, but do not terrify me. Bring
disaster on them and break them to
pieces.

On Observing the Sabbath

19The LORD said to me, "Jeremiah, go
and announce my message at the People's Gate, through which the kings of
Judah enter and leave the city; then go
to all the other gates of Jerusalem.
20Tell the kings and all the people of Judah and everyone who lives in Jerusalem and enters these gates, to listen to
what I say. 21Tell them that if they love
their lives, they must not carry any load
on the Sabbath; they must not carry
anything in through the gates of Jerusalem 22or carry anything out of their
houses on the Sabbath. They must not
work on the Sabbath; they must observe it as a sacred day, as I commanded their ancestors. 23Their ancestors did not listen to me or pay any
attention. Instead, they became stubborn; they would not obey me or learn
from me.
24"Tell these people that they must
obey all my commands. They must not
carry any load in through the gates of
this city on the Sabbath. They must observe the Sabbath as a sacred day and
must not do any work at all. 25Then
their kings and princes will enter the
gates of Jerusalem and have the same
royal power that David had. Together
with the people of Judah and of Jerusalem, they will ride in chariots and on
horses, and the city of Jerusalem will
always be filled with people. 26People

w disappear . . . dust; or go to the world of the dead.   x Probable text bring disaster
on them; Hebrew from being a shepherd after you.
17.10 a Rev 2.23; b Ps 62.12   17.21 Ne 13.15-22   17.22 Ex 20.8-10; Dt 5.12-14

will come from the towns of Judah and from the villages around Jerusalem; they will come from the territory of Benjamin, from the foothills, from the mountains, and from southern Judah. They will bring to my Temple burnt offerings and sacrifices, grain offerings and incense, as well as thank offerings. 27But they must obey me and observe the Sabbath as a sacred day. They must not carry any load through the gates of Jerusalem on that day, for if they do, I will set the gates of Jerusalem on fire. Fire will burn down the palaces of Jerusalem, and no one will be able to put it out."

Jeremiah at the Potter's House

18 The LORD said to me, 2"Go down to the potter's house, where I will give you my message." 3So I went there and saw the potter working at his wheel. 4Whenever a piece of pottery turned out imperfect, he would take the clay and make it into something else.

5Then the LORD said to me, 6"Don't I have the right to do with you people of Israel what the potter did with the clay? You are in my hands just like clay in the potter's hands. 7If at any time I say that I am going to uproot, break down, or destroy any nation or kingdom, 8but then that nation turns from its evil, I will not do what I said I would. 9On the other hand, if I say that I am going to plant or build up any nation or kingdom, 10but then that nation disobeys me and does evil, I will not do what I said I would. 11Now then, tell the people of Judah and of Jerusalem that I am making plans against them and getting ready to punish them. Tell them to stop living sinful lives — to change their ways and the things they are doing. 12They will answer, 'No, why should we? We will all be just as stubborn and evil as we want to be.'"

The People Reject the LORD

13The LORD says,
"Ask every nation if such a thing
  has ever happened before.
The people of Israel have
  done a terrible thing!
14Are Lebanon's rocky heights ever
  without snow?
Do its cool mountain streams
  ever run dry?
15Yet my people have
  forgotten me;
they burn incense to idols.
They have stumbled in the way
  they should go;
they no longer follow the old
  ways;
they walk on unmarked paths.
16They have made this land a
  thing of horror,
to be despised forever.
All who pass by will be shocked
  at what they see;
they will shake their heads in
  amazement.
17I will scatter my people before
  their enemies,
like dust blown by the east
  wind.
I will turn my back on them;
  I will not help them when the
  disaster comes."

A Plot against Jeremiah

18Then the people said, "Let's do something about Jeremiah! There will always be priests to instruct us, the wise to give us counsel, and prophets to proclaim God's message. Let's bring charges against him and stop listening to what he says."

19So I prayed, "LORD, hear what I am saying and listen to what my enemies are saying about me. 20Is evil the payment for good? Yet they have dug a pit for me to fall in. Remember how I came to you and spoke on their behalf, so that you would not deal with them in anger. 21But now, LORD, let their children starve to death; let them be killed in war. Let the women lose their husbands and children; let the men die of disease and the young men be killed in battle. ²² Send a mob to plunder their homes without warning; make them

"Lord, hear what I am saying." (18.19)

cry out in terror. They have dug a pit for me to fall in and have set traps to catch me. ²³ But, Lord, you know all their plots to kill me. Do not forgive their evil or pardon their sin. Throw them down in defeat and deal with them while you are angry."

The Broken Jar

19 The Lord told me to go and buy a clay jar. He also told me to take some of the elders of the people and some of the older priests, ² and to go through Potsherd Gate out to Hinnom Valley. There I was to proclaim the message that he would give me. ³ The Lord told me to say, "Kings of Judah and people of Jerusalem, listen to what I, the Lord Almighty, the God of Israel, have to say. I am going to bring such a disaster on this place that everyone who hears about it will be stunned. ⁴ I am going to do this because the people have abandoned me and defiled this place by

offering sacrifices here to other gods — gods that neither they nor their ancestors nor the kings of Judah have known anything about. They have filled this place with the blood of innocent people, ⁵ and they have built altars for Baal in order to burn their children in the fire as sacrifices. I never commanded them to do this; it never even entered my mind. ⁶ So then, the time will come when this place will no longer be called Topheth or Hinnom Valley. Instead, it will be known as Slaughter Valley. ⁷ In this place I will frustrate all the plans of the people of Judah and Jerusalem. I will let their enemies triumph over them and kill them in battle. I will give their corpses to the birds and the wild animals as food. ⁸ I will bring such terrible destruction on this city that everyone who passes by will be shocked and amazed. ⁹ The enemy will surround the city and try to kill its people. The siege will be so terrible that the people inside the city will eat one another and even their own children."

¹⁰ Then the Lord told me to break the jar in front of those who had gone with me ¹¹ and to tell them that the Lord Almighty had said, "I will break this people and this city, and it will be like this broken clay jar that cannot be put together again. People will bury their dead even in Topheth because there will be nowhere else to bury them. ¹² I promise that I will make this city and its inhabitants like Topheth. ¹³ The houses of Jerusalem, the houses of the kings of Judah, and indeed all the houses on whose roofs incense has been burned to the stars and where wine has been poured out as an offering to other gods — they will all be as unclean as Topheth."

¹⁴ Then I left Topheth, where the Lord had sent me to proclaim his message. I went and stood in the court of the Temple and told all the people

19.2 2 K 23.10; Jr 7.30-32; 32.34, 35   **19.5** Lv 18.21

¹⁵ that the Lᴏʀᴅ Almighty, the God of Israel, had said, "I am going to bring on this city and on every nearby town all the punishment that I said I would, because you are stubborn and will not listen to what I say."

The Lᴏʀᴅ told me to break the jar. (19.10)

Jeremiah's Conflict with Pashhur the Priest

20 When the priest Pashhur son of Immer, who was the chief officer of the Temple, heard me proclaim these things, ²he had me beaten and placed in chains near the upper Benjamin Gate in the Temple. ³The next morning, after Pashhur had released me from the chains, I said to him, "The Lᴏʀᴅ did not name you Pashhur. The name he has given you is 'Terror Everywhere.' ⁴The Lᴏʀᴅ himself has said, 'I am going to make you a terror to yourself and to your friends, and you will see them all killed by the swords of their enemies. I am going to put all the people of Judah under the power of the king of Babylonia; he will take some away as prisoners to his country and put others to death. ⁵I will also let their enemies plunder all the wealth of this city and seize all its possessions and property, even the treasures of the kings of Judah, and carry everything off to Babylonia. ⁶As for you, Pashhur, you and all your family will also be captured and taken off to Babylonia. There you will die and be buried,

along with all your friends to whom you have told so many lies.' "

Jeremiah Complains to the Lᴏʀᴅ

⁷Lᴏʀᴅ, you have deceived me,
    and I was deceived.
You are stronger than I am,
    and you have overpowered
        me.
Everyone makes fun of me;
    they laugh at me all day long.

⁸Whenever I speak, I have to
        cry out
    and shout, "Violence!
        Destruction!"
Lᴏʀᴅ, I am ridiculed and scorned
        all the time
    because I proclaim your
        message.
⁹But when I say, "I will forget the
        Lᴏʀᴅ
    and no longer speak in his
        name,"
then your message is like a fire
    burning deep within me.
I try my best to hold it in,
    but can no longer keep it
        back.
¹⁰I hear everybody whispering,
    "Terror is everywhere!
    So let's report him to the
        authorities!"
Even my close friends wait for
        my downfall.
"Perhaps he can be tricked,"
        they say;
    "then we can catch him and
        get revenge."
¹¹But you, Lᴏʀᴅ, are on my side,
        strong and mighty,
    and those who persecute me
        will fail.
They will be disgraced forever,
    because they cannot succeed.
Their disgrace will never be
        forgotten.
¹²But, Almighty Lᴏʀᴅ, you test
        people justly;

you know what is in their
hearts and minds.
So let me see you take revenge
on my enemies,
for I have placed my cause in
your hands.
13 Sing to the LORD!
Praise the LORD!
He rescues the oppressed from
the power of evil people.

14 Curse the day I was born!
Forget the day my mother gave
me birth!
15 Curse the one who made my
father glad
by bringing him the news,
"It's a boy! You have a son!"
16 May he be like those cities
that the LORD destroyed
without mercy.
May he hear cries of pain in the
morning
and the battle alarm at noon,
17   for not killing me before I
was born.
Then my mother's womb would
have been my grave.
18 Why was I born?
Was it only to have trouble
and sorrow,
to end my life in disgrace?

Jerusalem's Defeat Is Predicted

21 King Zedekiah of Judah sent to
me Pashhur son of Malchiah
and the priest Zephaniah son of Maaseiah with this request: 2 "Please speak to
the LORD for us, because King Nebuchadnezzar of Babylonia and his army
are besieging the city. Maybe the LORD
will perform one of his miracles for us
and force Nebuchadnezzar to retreat."
3 Then the LORD spoke to me, and I
told those who had been sent to me 4 to
tell Zedekiah that the LORD, the God of

Israel, had said, "Zedekiah, I am going
to defeat your army that is fighting
against the king of Babylonia and his
army. I will pile up your soldiers' weapons in the center of the city. 5 I will fight
against you with all my might, my anger, my wrath, and my fury. 6 I will kill
everyone living in this city; people and
animals alike will die of a terrible disease. 7 But as for you, your officials, and
the people who survive the war, the
famine, and the disease — I will let all of
you be captured by King Nebuchadnezzar and by your enemies, who want
to kill you. Nebuchadnezzar will put
you to death. He will not spare any of
you or show mercy or pity to any of you.
I, the LORD, have spoken."
8 Then the LORD told me to say to the
people, "Listen! I, the LORD, am giving
you a choice between the way that
leads to life and the way that leads to
death. 9 Anyone who stays in the city
will be killed in war or by starvation or
disease. But those who go out and surrender to the Babylonians, who are now
attacking the city, will not be killed;
they will at least escape with their life.
10 I have made up my mind not to spare
this city, but to destroy it. It will be
given over to the king of Babylonia, and
he will burn it to the ground. I, the
LORD, have spoken."

Judgment on the Royal House of Judah

11-12 The LORD told me to give this
message to the royal house of Judah,
the descendants of David: "Listen to
what I, the LORD, am saying. See that
justice is done every day. Protect the
person who is being cheated from the
one who is cheating him. If you don't,
the evil you are doing will make my anger burn like a fire that cannot be put
out. 13 You, Jerusalem, are sitting*y*

y You, Jerusalem, are sitting; *or* You are enthroned.
20.14-18 Job 3.1-19   **21.2** 2 K 25.1-11; 2 Ch 36.17-21

high above the valleys, like a rock rising above the plain. But I will fight against you. You say that no one can attack you or break through your defenses. [14] But I will punish you for what you have done. I will set your palace on fire, and the fire will burn down everything around it. I, the LORD, have spoken."

Jeremiah's Message to the Royal House of Judah

22 [1-2] The LORD told me to go to the palace of the king of Judah, the descendant of David, and there tell the king, his officials, and the people of Jerusalem to listen to what the LORD had said: [3] "I, the LORD, command you to do what is just and right. Protect the person who is being cheated from the one who is cheating him. Do not mistreat or oppress aliens, orphans, or widows; and do not kill innocent people in this holy place. [4] If you really do as I have commanded, then David's descendants will continue to be kings. And they, together with their officials and their people, will continue to pass through the gates of this palace in chariots and on horses. [5] But if you do not obey my commands, then I swear to you that this palace will fall into ruins. I, the LORD, have spoken."

[6] "To me, Judah's royal palace is as beautiful as the land of Gilead and as the Lebanon Mountains; but I will make it a desolate place where no one lives. [7] I am sending men to destroy it. They will all bring their axes, cut down its beautiful cedar pillars, and throw them into the fire.

[8] "Afterward many foreigners will pass by and ask one another why I, the LORD, have done such a thing to this great city. [9] Then they will answer that it is because you have abandoned your covenant with me, your God, and have worshiped and served other gods."

Jeremiah's Message concerning Joahaz

[10] People of Judah, do not weep for
King Josiah;
do not mourn his death.
But weep bitterly for Joahaz,
his son;
they are taking him away,
never to return,
never again to see the land
where he was born.

[11] The LORD says concerning Josiah's son Joahaz, who succeeded his father as king of Judah, "He has gone away from here, never to return. [12] He will die in the country where they have taken him, and he will never again see this land."

Jeremiah's Message concerning Jehoiakim

[13] Doomed is the one who builds
his house by injustice
and enlarges it by dishonesty;
who makes his people work for
nothing
and does not pay their wages.
[14] Doomed is the one who says,
"I will build myself a mansion
with spacious rooms upstairs."
So he puts windows in his
house,
panels it with cedar,
and paints it red.
[15] Does it make you a better king
if you build houses of cedar,
finer than those of others?
Your father enjoyed a full life.
He was always just and fair,
and he prospered in
everything he did.
[16] He gave the poor a fair trial,
and all went well with him.
That is what it means to know
the LORD.
[17] But you can only see your selfish
interests;
you kill the innocent

and violently oppress your
people.
The LORD has spoken.

18 So then, the LORD says about Josiah's son Jehoiakim, king of Judah,
"No one will mourn his death
or say,
'How terrible, my friend, how
terrible!'
No one will weep for him or cry,
'My lord! My king!'
19 With the funeral honors of a
donkey,
he will be dragged away
and thrown outside
Jerusalem's gates."

Jeremiah's Message about the Fate of Jerusalem

20 People of Jerusalem, go to
Lebanon and shout,
go to the land of Bashan
and cry;
call out from the mountains of
Moab,
because all your allies have
been defeated.
21 The LORD spoke to you when
you were prosperous,
but you refused to listen.
That is what you've done all your
life;
you never would obey the
LORD.
22 Your leaders will be blown away
by the wind,
your allies taken as prisoners
of war,
your city disgraced and put to
shame
because of all the evil you
have done.
23 You rest secure among the
cedars brought from
Lebanon;
but how pitiful you'll be when
pains strike you,

pains like those of a woman
in labor.

God's Judgment on Jehoiachin

24 The LORD said to King Jehoiachin,
son of King Jehoiakim of Judah, "As
surely as I am the living God, even if
you were the signet ring on my right
hand, I would pull you off 25 and give
you to people you are afraid of, people
who want to kill you. I will give you to
King Nebuchadnezzar of Babylonia
and his soldiers. 26 I am going to force
you and your mother into exile. You will
go to a country where neither of you
was born, and both of you will die there.
27 You will long to see this country
again, but you will never return."

28 I said, "Has King Jehoiachin become like a broken jar that is thrown
away and that no one wants? Is that
why he and his children have been
taken into exile to a land they know
nothing about?"
29 O land, land, land!
Listen to what the LORD has
said:
30 "This man is condemned to lose
his children,
to be a man who will never
succeed.
He will have no descendants
who will rule in Judah
as David's successors.
I, the LORD, have spoken."

Hope for the Future

23 How terrible will be the LORD's
judgment on those rulers who
destroy and scatter his people! 2 This is
what the LORD, the God of Israel, says
about the rulers who were supposed to
take care of his people: "You have not
taken care of my people; you have scattered them and driven them away. Now
I am going to punish you for the evil you
have done. 3 I will gather the rest of my
people from the countries where I have

22.18 2 K 23.36—24.6; 2 Ch 36.5-7   **22.24** 2 K 24.8-15; 2 Ch 36.9, 10 cattered them, and I will bring them back to their homeland. They will have many children and increase in number. I will appoint rulers to take care of them. My people will no longer be afraid or terrified, and I will not punish them again.[z] I, the LORD, have spoken."

5 The LORD says, "The time is coming when I will choose as king a righteous descendant of David. That king will rule wisely and do what is right and just throughout the land. 6 When he is king, the people of Judah will be safe, and the people of Israel will live in peace. He will be called 'The LORD Our Salvation.'

7 "The time is coming," says the LORD, "when people will no longer wear by me as the living God who brought the people of Israel out of the land of Egypt. 8 Instead, they will swear by me as the living God who brought the people of Israel out of a northern land and out of all the other countries where I had scattered them. Then they will live in their own land."

Jeremiah's Message about the Prophets

9 My heart is crushed,
   and I am trembling.
Because of the LORD,
   because of his holy words,
I am like a man who is drunk,
   someone who has had too
     much wine.
10 The land is full of people
     unfaithful to the LORD;
   they live wicked lives and
     misuse their power.
Because of the LORD's curse the
     land mourns
   and the pastures are dry.

11 The LORD says,
"The prophets and the priests
   are godless;

I have caught them doing evil
   in the Temple itself.
12 The paths they follow will be
     slippery and dark;
I will make them stumble
   and fall.
I am going to bring disaster on
     them;
the time of their punishment
   is coming.
I, the LORD, have spoken.
13 I have seen the sin of Samaria's
     prophets:
they have spoken in the name
     of Baal
and have led my people
   astray.
14 But I have seen the prophets in
     Jerusalem do even worse:
they commit adultery and
     tell lies;
they help people to do wrong,
   so that no one stops doing
     what is evil.
To me they are all as bad
   as the people of Sodom and
     Gomorrah.

15 "So then, this is what I, the LORD Almighty, say about the prophets of Jerusalem:
I will give them bitter plants
     to eat
   and poison to drink,
because they have spread
     ungodliness throughout
     the land."

16 The LORD Almighty said to the people of Jerusalem, "Do not listen to what the prophets say; they are filling you with false hopes. They tell you what they have imagined and not what I have said. 17 To the people who refuse to listen to what I have said, they keep saying that all will go well with them. And they tell everyone who is stubborn that disaster will never touch them."

18 I said, "None of these prophets has

I will not punish them again; *or* not one of them will be missing.
3.5, 6 Jr 33.14-16   **23.14** Gn 18.20; Ez 16.49

ever known the LORD's secret thoughts. None of them has ever heard or understood his message, or ever listened or paid attention to what he said. ¹⁹ His anger is a storm, a furious wind that will rage over the heads of the wicked, ²⁰ and it will not end until he has done everything he intends to do. In days to come his people will understand this clearly."

²¹ The LORD said, "I did not send these prophets, but even so they went. I did not give them any message, but still they spoke in my name. ²² If they had known my secret thoughts, then they could have proclaimed my message to my people and could have made them give up the evil lives they live and the wicked things they do.

²³ "I am a God who is everywhere and not in one place only. ²⁴ No one can hide where I cannot see them. Do you not know that I am everywhere in heaven and on earth? ²⁵ I know what those prophets have said who speak lies in my name and claim that I have given them my messages in their dreams. ²⁶ How much longer will those prophets mislead my people with the lies they have invented? ²⁷ They think that the dreams they tell will make my people forget me, just as their ancestors forgot me and turned to Baal. ²⁸ The prophet who has had a dream should say it is only a dream, but the prophet who has heard my message should proclaim that message faithfully. What good is straw compared with wheat? ²⁹ My message is like a fire and like a hammer that breaks rocks in pieces. ³⁰ I am against those prophets who take each other's words and proclaim them as my message. ³¹ I am also against those prophets who speak their own words and claim they came from me. ³² Listen to what I, the LORD, say! I am against the prophets who tell their dreams that are full of

lies. They tell these dreams and lead m[y] people astray with their lies and thei[r] boasting. I did not send them or orde[r] them to go, and they are of no help a[t] all to the people. I, the LORD, hav[e] spoken."

The LORD's Burden

³³ The LORD said to me, "Jeremiah[,] when one of my people or a prophet o[r] a priest asks you, 'What is the LORD'[s] message?' you are to say, 'You are [a] burden*ᵃ* to the LORD, and he is goin[g] to get rid of you.' ³⁴ If any of my peopl[e] or a prophet or a priest even uses th[e] words 'the LORD's burden,' I will punis[h] them and their families. ³⁵ Instead[,] each one of them should ask thei[r] friends and their relatives, 'What an[s]wer has the LORD given? What has th[e] LORD said?' ³⁶ So they must no longe[r] use the words 'the LORD's burden,' be[-]cause if any of them do, I will make m[y] message a real burden to them. Th[e] people have perverted the words o[f] their God, the living God, the LOR[D] Almighty. ³⁷ Jeremiah, ask the proph[-]ets, 'What answer did the LORD giv[e] you? What did the LORD say?' ³⁸ And i[f] they disobey my command and use th[e] words 'the LORD's burden,' then tel[l] them that ³⁹ I will certainly pick the[m] up*ᵇ* and throw them far away from m[e] both them and the city that I gave t[o] them and their ancestors. ⁴⁰ I will brin[g] on them everlasting shame and dis[-]grace that will never be forgotten."

Two Baskets of Figs

24 The LORD showed me two bas[-]kets of figs placed in front o[f] the Temple. (This was after King Neb[-]uchadnezzar of Babylonia had take[n] away Jehoiakim's son, King Jehoiachi[n] of Judah, as a prisoner from Jerusale[m] to Babylonia, together with the leader[s]

ᵃ The Hebrew word for message *and* burden *is the same.*   *ᵇ The Hebrew verb for* pick up *comes from the same root as the Hebrew word for* message *and* burden.

23.24 Ws 1.7; Si 16.17   **24.1** 2 K 24.12-16; 2 Ch 36.10

of Judah, the craftworkers, and the skilled workers.) [2] The first basket contained good figs, those that ripen early; the other one contained bad figs, too bad to eat. [3] Then the LORD said to me, "Jeremiah, what do you see?"

I answered, "Figs. The good ones are very good, and the bad ones are very bad, too bad to eat."

[4] So the LORD said to me, [5] "I, the LORD, the God of Israel, consider that the people who were taken away to Babylonia are like these good figs, and I will treat them with kindness. [6] I will watch over them and bring them back to this land. I will build them up and not tear them down; I will plant them and not pull them up. [7] I will give them the desire to know that I am the LORD. Then they will be my people, and I will be their God, because they will return to me with all their heart.

[8] "As for King Zedekiah of Judah, the politicians around him, and the rest of the people of Jerusalem who have stayed in this land or moved to Egypt — I, the LORD, will treat them all like these figs that are too bad to be eaten. [9] I will bring such a disaster on them that all the nations of the world will be terrified. People will make fun of them, make jokes about them, ridicule them, and use their name as a curse everywhere I scatter them. [10] I will bring war, starvation, and disease on them until there is not one of them left in the land that I gave to them and their ancestors."

The Enemy from the North

25 In the fourth year that Jehoiakim son of Josiah was king of Judah, I received a message from the LORD concerning all the people of Judah. (This was the first year that Nebuchadnezzar was king of Babylonia.) [2] I said to all the people of Judah and of Jerusalem, [3] "For twenty-three years,

from the thirteenth year that Josiah son of Amon was king of Judah until this very day, the LORD has spoken to me, and I have never failed to tell you what he said. But you have paid no attention. [4] You would not listen or pay attention, even though the LORD has continued to send you his servants the prophets. [5] They told you to turn from your wicked way of life and from the evil things you are doing, so that you could go on living in the land that the LORD gave you and your ancestors as a permanent possession. [6] They told you not to worship and serve other gods and not to make the LORD angry by worshiping the idols you had made. If you had obeyed the LORD, then he would not have punished you. [7] But the LORD himself says that you refused to listen to him. Instead, you made him angry with your idols and have brought his punishment on yourselves.

[8] "So then, because you would not listen to him, the LORD Almighty says, [9] 'I am going to send for all the peoples from the north and for my servant, King Nebuchadnezzar of Babylonia. I am going to bring them to fight against Judah and its inhabitants and against all the neighboring nations. I am going to destroy this nation and its neighbors and leave them in ruins forever, a terrible and shocking sight. I, the LORD, have spoken. [10] I will silence their shouts of joy and gladness and the happy sounds of wedding feasts. They will have no oil for their lamps, and there will be no more grain. [11] This whole land will be left in ruins and will be a shocking sight, and the neighboring nations will serve the king of Babylonia for seventy years. [12] After that I will punish Babylonia and its king for their sin. I will destroy that country and leave it in ruins forever. [13] I will punish Babylonia with all the disasters that I threatened to bring on the nations when I spoke

25.1 2 K 24.1; 2 Ch 36.5-7; Dn 1.1, 2　**25.10 a** Jr 7.34; 16.9; **b** Rev 18.22, 23　**25.11** 2 Ch 36.21; Jr 29.10; Dn 9.2

through Jeremiah — all the disasters recorded in this book. 14 I will pay the Babylonians back for what they have done, and many nations and great kings will make slaves of them.'"

God's Judgment on the Nations

15 The LORD, the God of Israel, said to me, "Here is a wine cup filled with my anger. Take it to all the nations to whom I send you, and make them drink from it. 16 When they drink from it, they will stagger and go out of their minds because of the war I am sending against them."

17 So I took the cup from the LORD's hand, gave it to all the nations to whom the LORD had sent me, and made them drink from it. 18 Jerusalem and all the towns of Judah, together with its kings and leaders, were made to drink from it, so that they would become a desert, a terrible and shocking sight, and so that people would use their name as a curse — as they still do.

19-26 Here is the list of all the others who had to drink from the cup:
the king of Egypt, his officials and leaders;
all the Egyptians and all the foreigners in Egypt;
all the kings of the land of Uz;
all the kings of the Philistine cities of Ashkelon, Gaza, Ekron, and what remains of Ashdod;
all the people of Edom, Moab, and Ammon;
all the kings of Tyre and Sidon;
all the kings of the Mediterranean lands;
the cities of Dedan, Tema, and Buz;
all the people who cut their hair short;
all the kings of Arabia;
all the kings of the desert tribes;
all the kings of Zimri, Elam, and Media;

all the kings of the north, far and near, one after another.

Every nation on the face of the earth had to drink from it. Last of all, the king of Babylonia will drink from it.

27 Then the LORD said to me, "Tell the people that I, the LORD Almighty, the God of Israel, am commanding them to drink until they are drunk and vomit, until they fall down and cannot get up, because of the war that I am sending against them. 28 And if they refuse to take the cup from your hand and drink from it, then tell them that the LORD Almighty has said that they will still have to drink from it. 29 I will begin my work of destruction in my own city. Do they think they will go unpunished? No, they will be punished, for I am going to send war on all the people on earth. I, the LORD Almighty, have spoken.

30 "You, Jeremiah, must proclaim everything I have said. You must tell these people,
'The LORD will roar from heaven and thunder from the heights of heaven.
He will roar against his people; he will shout like a man treading grapes.
Everyone on earth will hear him,
31 and the sound will echo to the ends of the earth.
The LORD has a case against the nations.
He will bring all people to trial and put the wicked to death.
The LORD has spoken.'"

32 The LORD Almighty says that disaster is coming on one nation after another, and a great storm is gathering at the far ends of the earth. 33 On that day the bodies of those whom the LORD has killed will lie scattered from one end of the earth to the other. No one will mourn for them, and they will not be taken away and buried. They will lie on the ground like piles of manure.

34 Cry, you leaders, you shepherds o

my people, cry out loud! Mourn and roll in the dust. The time has come for you to be slaughtered,[c] and you will be butchered like rams.[d] 35 There will be no way for you to escape. 36-37 You moan and cry out in distress because the LORD in his anger has destroyed your nation and left your peaceful country in ruins. 38 The LORD has abandoned his people[e] like a lion that leaves its cave. The horrors of war and the LORD's fierce anger have turned the country into a desert.

Jeremiah Is Brought to Trial

26 Soon after Jehoiakim son of Josiah became king of Judah, 2 the LORD said to me, "Stand in the court of the Temple and proclaim all I have commanded you to say to the people who come from the towns of Judah to worship there. Do not leave out anything. 3 Perhaps the people will listen and give up their evil ways. If they do, then I will change my mind about the destruction I plan to bring on them for all their wicked deeds."

4 The LORD told me to say to the people, "I, the LORD, have said that you must obey me by following the teaching that I gave you, 5 and by paying attention to the words of my servants, the prophets, whom I have kept on sending to you. You have never obeyed what they said. 6 If you continue to disobey, then I will do to this Temple what I did to Shiloh,[f] and all the nations of the world will use the name of this city as a curse."

7 The priests, the prophets, and all the people heard me saying these things in the Temple, 8 and as soon as I had finished all that the LORD had commanded me to speak, they grabbed me and shouted, "You ought to be killed for this! 9 Why have you said in the LORD's name that this Temple will become like Shiloh and that this city will be destroyed and no one will live in it?" Then the people crowded around me.

10 When the leaders of Judah heard what had happened, they hurried from the royal palace to the Temple and took their places at the New Gate. 11 Then the priests and the prophets said to the leaders and to the people, "This man deserves to be sentenced to death because he has spoken against our city. You heard him with your own ears."

12 Then I said, "The LORD sent me to proclaim everything that you heard me say against this Temple and against this city. 13 You must change the way you are living and the things you are doing, and must obey the LORD your God. If you do, he will change his mind about the destruction that he said he would bring on you. 14 As for me, I am in your power! Do with me whatever you think is fair and right. 15 But be sure of this: if you kill me, you and the people of this city will be guilty of killing an innocent man, because it is the LORD who sent me to give you this warning."

16 Then the leaders and the people said to the priests and the prophets, "This man spoke to us in the name of the LORD our God; he should not be put to death."

17 After that, some of the elders stood up and said to the people who had gathered, 18 "When Hezekiah was king of Judah, the prophet Micah of Moresheth told all the people that the LORD Almighty had said,

'Zion will be plowed like a field;
    Jerusalem will become a pile
        of ruins,
    and the Temple hill will
        become a forest.'

19 King Hezekiah and the people of

---

[c] Hebrew has an additional word, the meaning of which is unclear.   [d] One ancient translation rams; Hebrew vessels.   [e] The LORD ... people; or The LORD's people run away.   [f] SHILOH: See 7.12.

26.1 2 K 23.36—24.6; 2 Ch 36.5-7   **26.6** Js 18.1; Ps 78.60; Jr 7.12-14   **26.18** Mic 3.12

Judah did not put Micah to death. Instead, Hezekiah honored the LORD and tried to win his favor. And the LORD changed his mind about the disaster that he said he would bring on them. Now we are about to bring a terrible disaster on ourselves."

(20 There was another man, Uriah son of Shemaiah from Kiriath Jearim, who spoke in the name of the LORD against this city and nation just as Jeremiah did. 21 When King Jehoiakim and his soldiers and officials heard what Uriah had said, the king tried to have him killed. But Uriah heard about it; so he fled in terror and escaped to Egypt. 22 King Jehoiakim, however, sent Elnathan son of Achbor and some other men to Egypt to get Uriah. 23 They brought him back to King Jehoiakim, who had him killed and his body thrown into the public burial ground.)

24 But because I had the support of Ahikam son of Shaphan, I was not handed over to the people and killed.

Jeremiah Wears an Ox Yoke

27 Soon after Josiah's son Zedekiah became king of Judah, the LORD told me 2 to make myself a yoke out of leather straps and wooden crossbars and to put it on my neck. 3 Then the LORD told me to send a message*g* to the kings of Edom, Moab, Ammon, Tyre, and Sidon through their ambassadors who had come to Jerusalem to see King Zedekiah. 4 The LORD Almighty, the God of Israel, told me to command them to tell their kings that the LORD had said: 5 "By my great power and strength I created the world, human beings, and all the animals that live on the earth; and I give it to anyone I choose. 6 I am the one who has placed all these nations under the power of my servant, King Nebuchadnezzar of Babylonia, and I have made even the wild animals serve him. 7 All nations will serve him, and they will serve his son and his grandson until the time comes for his own nation to fall. Then his nation will serve powerful nations and great kings.

8 "But if any nation or kingdom will not submit to his rule, then I will punish that nation by war, starvation, and disease until I have let Nebuchadnezzar destroy it completely. 9 Do not listen to your prophets or to those who claim they can predict the future, either by dreams or by calling up the spirits of the dead or by magic. They all tell you not to submit to the king of Babylonia. 10 They are deceiving you and will cause you to be taken far away from your country. I will drive you out, and you will be destroyed. 11 But if any nation submits to the king of Babylonia and serves him, then I will let it stay on in its own land, to farm it and live there. I, the LORD, have spoken."

12 I said the same thing to King Zedekiah of Judah, "Submit to the king of Babylonia. Serve him and his people, and you will live. 13 Why should you and your people die in war or of starvation or disease? That is what the LORD has said will happen to any nation that does not submit to the king of Babylonia. 14 Do not listen to the prophets who tell you not to surrender to him. They are deceiving you. 15 The LORD himself has said that he did not send them and that they are lying to you in his name. And so he will drive you out, and you will be killed, you and the prophets who are telling you these lies."

16 Then I told the priests and the people that the LORD had said: "Do not listen to the prophets who say that the Temple treasures will soon be brought back from Babylonia. They are lying to you. 17 Don't listen to them! Submit to the king of Babylonia and you will live!

---

g Probable text a message; *Hebrew* them.

27.1 2 K 24.18-20; 2 Ch 36.11-13　**27.6** Ba 3.16, 17

Why should this city become a pile of ruins? 18 If they are really prophets and if they have my message, let them ask me, the LORD Almighty, not to allow the treasures that remain in the Temple and in the royal palace to be taken to Babylonia."

(19-20 When King Nebuchadnezzar took away to Babylonia the king of Judah, Jehoiachin son of Jehoiakim, and the leading men of Judah and Jerusalem, he left the columns, the bronze tank, the carts, and some of the other Temple treasures.) 21 "Listen to what I, the LORD Almighty, the God of Israel, say about the treasures that are left in the Temple and in the royal palace in Jerusalem: 22 They will be taken to Babylonia and will remain there until I turn my attention to them. Then I will bring them back and restore them to this place. I, the LORD, have spoken."

Jeremiah and the Prophet Hananiah

28 That same year,[h] in the fifth month of the fourth year that Zedekiah was king, Hananiah son of Azzur, a prophet from the town of Gibeon, spoke to me in the Temple. In the presence of the priests and of the people he told me 2 that the LORD Almighty, the God of Israel, had said: "I have broken the power of the king of Babylonia. 3 Within two years I will bring back to this place all the Temple treasures that King Nebuchadnezzar took to Babylonia. 4 I will also bring back the king of Judah, Jehoiachin son of Jehoiakim, along with all of the people of Judah who went into exile in Babylonia. Yes, I will break the power of the king of Babylonia. I, the LORD, have spoken."

5 Then in the presence of the priests and of all the people who were standing in the Temple, I said to Hananiah, 6 "Wonderful! I hope the LORD will do this! I certainly hope he will make your prophecy come true and will bring back from Babylonia all the Temple treasures and all the people who were taken away as prisoners. 7 But listen to what I say to you and to the people. 8 The prophets who spoke long ago, before my time and yours, predicted that war, starvation, and disease would come to many nations and powerful kingdoms. 9 But a prophet who predicts peace can only be recognized as a prophet whom the LORD has truly sent when that prophet's predictions come true."

10 Then Hananiah took the yoke off my neck, broke it in pieces, 11 and said in the presence of all the people, "The LORD has said that this is how he will break the yoke that King Nebuchadnezzar has put on the neck of all the nations; and he will do this within two years." Then I left.

12 Some time after this the LORD told me 13 to go and tell Hananiah: "The LORD has said that you may be able to break a wooden yoke, but he[i] will replace it with an iron yoke. 14 The LORD Almighty, the God of Israel, has said that he will put an iron yoke on all these nations and that they will serve King Nebuchadnezzar of Babylonia. The LORD has said that he will make even the wild animals serve Nebuchadnezzar."

15 Then I told Hananiah this, and added, "Listen, Hananiah! The LORD did not send you, and you are making these people believe a lie. 16 And so the LORD himself says that he is going to get rid of you. Before this year is over you will die because you have told the people to rebel against the LORD."

17 And Hananiah died in the seventh month of that same year.

One ancient translation That same year; *Hebrew* That same year at the beginning of his reign.   *i One ancient translation* he; *Hebrew* you.
28.1 2 K 24.18-20; 2 Ch 36.11-13

Jeremiah's Letter to the Jews in Babylonia

29 I wrote a letter to the priests, the prophets, the leaders of the people, and to all the others whom Nebuchadnezzar had taken away as prisoners from Jerusalem to Babylonia. ² I wrote it after King Jehoiachin, his mother, the palace officials, the leaders of Judah and of Jerusalem, the engravers, and the skilled workers had been taken into exile. ³ I gave the letter to Elasah son of Shaphan and to Gemariah son of Hilkiah, whom King Zedekiah of Judah was sending to King Nebuchadnezzar of Babylonia. It said:

⁴"The LORD Almighty, the God of Israel, says to all those people whom he allowed Nebuchadnezzar to take away as prisoners from Jerusalem to Babylonia: ⁵'Build houses and settle down. Plant gardens and eat what you grow in them. ⁶ Marry and have children. Then let your children get married, so that they also may have children. You must increase in numbers and not decrease. ⁷ Work for the good of the cities where I have made you go as prisoners. Pray to me on their behalf, because if they are prosperous, you will be prosperous too. ⁸ I, the LORD, the God of Israel, warn you not to let yourselves be deceived by the prophets who live among you or by any others who claim they can predict the future. Do not pay any attention to their ʲ dreams. ⁹ They are telling you lies in my name. I did not send them. I, the LORD Almighty, have spoken.'

¹⁰"The LORD says, 'When Babylonia's seventy years are over, I will show my concern for you and keep my promise to bring you back

home. ¹¹ I alone know the plans I have for you, plans to bring you prosperity and not disaster, plans to bring about the future you hope for.ᵏ ¹² Then you will call to me. You will come and pray to me, and I will answer you. ¹³ You will seek me, and you will find me because you will seek me with all your heart. ¹⁴ Yes, I say, you will find me, and I will restore you to your land. I will gather you from every country and from every place to which I have scattered you, and I will bring you back to the land from which I had sent you away into exile. I, the LORD, have spoken.'

¹⁵"You say that the LORD has given you prophets in Babylonia. ¹⁶ Listen to what the LORD says about the king who rules the kingdom that David ruled and about the people of this city, that is, your relatives who were not taken away as prisoners with you. ¹⁷ The LORD Almighty says, 'I am bringing war, starvation, and disease on them, and I will make them like figs that are too rotten to be eaten. ¹⁸ I will pursue them with war, starvation, and disease, and all the nations of the world will be horrified at what they see. Everywhere I scatter them, people will be shocked and terrified at what has happened to them. People will make fun of them and use their name as a curse. ¹⁹ This will happen to them because they did not obey the message that I kept on sending to them through my servants the prophets. They refused to listen. ²⁰ All of you whom I sent into exile in Babylonia, listen to what I, the LORD, say.'

²¹"The LORD Almighty, the God of Israel, has spoken about Ahab

ʲ *Probable text* their; *Hebrew* your.　　ᵏ the future you hope for; *or* a future full of hope.

29.1, 2 2 K 24.12-16; 2 Ch 36.10　**29.10** 2 Ch 36.21; Jr 25.11; Dn 9.2　**29.13** Dt 4.29; Ws 6.12, 13 son of Kolaiah and Zedekiah son of Maaseiah, who are telling you lies in his name. He has said that he will hand them over to the power of King Nebuchadnezzar of Babylonia, who will put them to death before your eyes. ²²When the people who were taken away as prisoners from Jerusalem to Babylonia want to bring a curse on someone, they will say, 'May the LORD treat you like Zedekiah and Ahab, whom the king of Babylonia roasted alive!' ²³This will be their fate because they are guilty of terrible sins—they have committed adultery and have told lies in the LORD's name. This was against the LORD's will; he knows what they have done, and he is a witness against them.[l] The LORD has spoken."

The Letter of Shemaiah

²⁴⁻²⁵The LORD Almighty, the God of Israel, gave me a message for Shemaiah of Nehelam, who had sent a letter in his own name to all the people of Jerusalem and to the priest Zephaniah son of Maaseiah and to all the other priests. In this letter Shemaiah wrote to Zephaniah:

²⁶"The LORD made you a priest in place of Jehoiada, and you are now the chief officer[m] in the Temple. It is your duty to see that every crazy person who pretends to be a prophet is placed in chains with an iron collar around the neck. ²⁷Why haven't you done this to Jeremiah of Anathoth, who has been speaking as a prophet to the people? ²⁸He must be stopped because he told the people in Babylonia that they would be prisoners there a long time and should build houses, settle down, plant gardens, and eat what they grow."

²⁹Zephaniah read the letter to me, ³⁰and then the LORD told me ³¹⁻³²to send to all the prisoners in Babylon this message about Shemaiah: "I, the LORD, will punish Shemaiah and all of his descendants. I did not send him, but he spoke to you as if he were a prophet, and he made you believe lies. He will have no descendants among you. He will not live to see the good things that I am going to do for my people, because he told them to rebel against me. I, the LORD, have spoken."

The LORD's Promises to His People

30 The LORD, the God of Israel, ²said to me, "Write down in a book everything that I have told you, ³because the time is coming when I will restore my people, Israel and Judah. I will bring them back to the land that I gave their ancestors, and they will take possession of it again. I, the LORD, have spoken."

⁴The LORD says to the people of Israel and Judah,

⁵"I heard a cry of terror,
a cry of fear and not of peace.
⁶Now stop and think!
Can a man give birth to a child?
Why then do I see every man
with his hands on
his stomach
like a woman in labor?
Why is everyone so pale?
⁷A terrible day is coming;
no other day can compare
with it—
a time of distress for my people,
but they will survive."

⁸The LORD Almighty says, "When that day comes, I will break the yoke that is around their neck and remove their chains, and they will no longer be

---

^l done, and he . . . them; or done; he saw them do it. ^m Some ancient translations officer; Hebrew officers.

the slaves of foreigners. ⁹Instead, they will serve me, the LORD their God, and a descendant of David, whom I will enthrone as king.

¹⁰"My people, do not be afraid;
    people of Israel, do not be
        terrified.
I will rescue you from that
        faraway land,
    from the land where you are
        prisoners.
You will come back home and
        live in peace;
    you will be secure, and no one
        will make you afraid.
¹¹I will come to you and save you.
I will destroy all the nations
    where I have scattered you,
    but I will not destroy you.
I will not let you go unpunished;
    but when I punish you, I will
        be fair.
I, the LORD, have spoken."

¹²The LORD says to his people,
"Your wounds are incurable,
    your injuries cannot be
        healed.
¹³There is no one to take care
        of you,
    no remedy for your sores,
    no hope of healing for you.
¹⁴All your lovers have
        forgotten you;
    they no longer care about you.
I have attacked you like an
        enemy;
    your punishment has been
        harsh
    because your sins are many
    and your wickedness is great.
¹⁵Complain no more about your
        injuries;
    there is no cure for you.
I punished you like this
    because your sins are many
    and your wickedness is great.
¹⁶But now, all who devour you will
        be devoured,

and all your enemies will be
    taken away as prisoners.
All who oppress you will be
        oppressed,
    and all who plunder you will
        be plundered.
¹⁷I will make you well again;
    I will heal your wounds,
    though your enemies say,
'Zion is an outcast;
    no one cares about her.'
I, the LORD, have spoken."

¹⁸The LORD says,
"I will restore my people to
        their land
    and have mercy on every
        family;
Jerusalem will be rebuilt,
    and its palace restored.
¹⁹The people who live there will
        sing praise;
    they will shout for joy.
By my blessing they will increase
        in numbers;
    my blessing will bring them
        honor.
²⁰I will restore the nation's ancient
        power
    and establish it firmly again;
    I will punish all who oppress
        them.
²¹⁻²²Their ruler will come from their
        own nation,
    their prince from their own
        people.
He will approach me when I
        invite him,
    for who would dare come
        uninvited?
They will be my people,
    and I will be their God.
I, the LORD, have spoken."

²³⁻²⁴The LORD's anger is a storm, a
furious wind that will rage over the
heads of the wicked. It will not end un
til he has done all that he intends to do

In days to come his people will understand this clearly.

Israel's Return Home

31 The LORD says, "The time is coming when I will be the God of all the tribes of Israel, and they will be my people. [2] In the desert I showed mercy to those people who had escaped death. When the people of Israel longed for rest, [3] I appeared to them[n] from far away. People of Israel, I have always loved you, so I continue to show you my constant love. [4] Once again I will rebuild you. Once again you will take up your tambourines and dance joyfully. [5] Once again you will plant vineyards on the hills of Samaria, and those who plant them will eat what the vineyards produce. [6] Yes, the time is coming when sentries will call out on the hills of Ephraim, 'Let's go up to Zion, to the LORD our God.'"

[7] The LORD says,
"Sing with joy for Israel,
    the greatest of the nations.
Sing your song of praise,
    'The LORD has saved his[o]
        people;
    he has rescued all who
        are left.'
[8] I will bring them from the north
    and gather them from the
        ends of the earth.
The blind and the lame will
        come with them,
    pregnant women and those
        about to give birth.
They will come back a great
    nation.
[9] My people will return weeping,
    praying as I lead them back.
I will guide them to streams of
    water,

on a smooth road where they
    will not stumble.
I am like a father to Israel,
    and Ephraim is my
        oldest son."

[10] The LORD says,
"Nations, listen to me
    and proclaim my words on the
        far-off shores.
I scattered my people, but I will
        gather them
    and guard them as a shepherd
        guards his flock.
[11] I have set Israel's people free
    and have saved them from a
        mighty nation.
[12] They will come and sing for joy
        on Mount Zion
    and be delighted with my
        gifts—
    gifts of grain and wine and
        olive oil,
    gifts of sheep and cattle.
They will be like a well-watered
        garden;
    they will have everything they
        need.
[13] Then the young women will
        dance and be happy,
    and men, young and old, will
        rejoice.
I will comfort them and turn
        their mourning into joy,
    their sorrow into gladness.
[14] I will fill the priests with the
        richest food
    and satisfy all the needs of
        my people.
I, the LORD, have spoken."

The LORD's Mercy on Israel

[15] The LORD says,
"A sound is heard in Ramah,

---

[n] *One ancient translation* them; *Hebrew* me.   [o] *Some ancient translations* The LORD
has saved his; *Hebrew* LORD, save your.
31.15 a Gn 35.16-19; **b** Mt 2.18

The young women will dance and be happy, and men, young and old, will rejoice. (31.13)

the sound of bitter weeping.
Rachel is crying for her children;
    they are gone,
    and she refuses to be
        comforted.
¹⁶ Stop your crying
    and wipe away your tears.
All that you have done for your
        children
    will not go unrewarded;
    they will return from the
        enemy's land.
¹⁷ There is hope for your future;
    your children will come back
        home.
I, the Lord, have spoken.

¹⁸ "I hear the people of Israel say
    in grief,
'Lord, we were like an untamed
        animal,
    but you taught us to obey.
Bring us back;
    we are ready to return to you,
    the Lord our God.

¹⁹ We turned away from you,
    but soon we wanted to return.
After you had punished us,
    we hung our heads in grief.
We were ashamed and disgraced
    because we sinned when we
        were young.'

²⁰ "Israel, you are my dearest child,
    the one I love best.
Whenever I mention your name,
    I think*p* of you with love.
My heart goes out to you;
    I will be merciful.
²¹ Set up signs and mark the road;
    find again the way by which
        you left.
Come back, people of Israel,
    come home to the towns
        you left.
²² How long will you hesitate,
    faithless people?
I have created something new
    and different,
    as different as a woman
        protecting a man."*q*

---

p I mention . . . I think; *or* I threaten to punish, I still think.   *q* as different . . . man;
Hebrew unclear.

The Future Prosperity of God's People

23 The LORD Almighty, the God of Israel, says, "When I restore the people to their land, they will once again say in the land of Judah and in its towns,

'May the LORD bless the sacred hill[r] of Jerusalem,
the holy place where he lives.'

24 People will live in Judah and in all its towns, and there will be farmers, and shepherds with their flocks. 25 I will refresh those who are weary and will satisfy with food everyone who is weak from hunger. 26 So then, people will say, 'I went to sleep and woke up refreshed.'

27 "I, the LORD, say that the time is coming when I will fill the land of Israel and Judah with people and animals. 28 And just as I took care to uproot, to pull down, to overthrow, to destroy, and to demolish them, so I will take care to plant them and to build them up. 29 When that time comes, people will no longer say,

'The parents ate the sour grapes,
But the children got the sour taste.'

30 Instead, those who eat sour grapes will have their own teeth set on edge; and everyone will die because of their own sin."

31 The LORD says, "The time is coming when I will make a new covenant with the people of Israel and with the people of Judah. 32 It will not be like the old covenant that I made with their ancestors when I took them by the hand and led them out of Egypt. Although I was like a husband to them, they did not keep that covenant. 33 The new covenant that I will make with the people of Israel will be this: I will put my law within them and write it on their hearts. I will be their God, and they will be my people. 34 None of them will have

to teach a neighbor to know the LORD, because all will know me, from the least to the greatest. I will forgive their sins and I will no longer remember their wrongs. I, the LORD, have spoken."

35 The LORD provides the sun for light by day,
the moon and the stars to shine at night.
He stirs up the sea and makes it roar;
his name is the LORD Almighty.
36 He promises that as long as the natural order lasts,
so long will Israel be a nation.
37 If one day the sky could be measured
and the foundations of the earth explored,
only then would he reject the people of Israel
because of all they have done.
The LORD has spoken.

38 "The time is coming," says the LORD, "when all of Jerusalem will be rebuilt as my city, from Hananel Tower west to the Corner Gate. 39 And the boundary line will continue from there on the west to the hill of Gareb and then around to Goah. 40 The entire valley, where the dead are buried and garbage is dumped, and all the fields above Kidron Brook as far as the Horse Gate to the east, will be sacred to me. The city will never again be torn down or destroyed."

Jeremiah Buys a Field

32 The LORD spoke to me in the tenth year that Zedekiah was king of Judah, which was also the eighteenth year of King Nebuchadnezzar of Babylonia. 2 At that time the army of the king of Babylonia was attacking

---

[r] SACRED HILL: *Mount Zion, the hill in Jerusalem which formed part of the Temple and palace area.*

31.29 Ez 18.2 31.31 Mt 26.28; Mk 14.24; Lk 22.20; 1 Co 11.25; 2 Co 3.6
31.31-34 He 8.8-12 31.33 He 10.16 31.34 He 10.17 32.1 2 K 25.1-7

Jerusalem, and I was locked up in the courtyard of the royal palace. ³King Zedekiah had imprisoned me there and had accused me of announcing that the LORD had said, "I am going to let the king of Babylonia capture this city, ⁴and King Zedekiah will not escape. He will be handed over to the king of Babylonia; he will see him face-to-face and will speak to him in person. ⁵Zedekiah will be taken to Babylonia, and he will remain there until I deal with him. Even if he fights the Babylonians, he will not be successful. I, the LORD, have spoken."

⁶The LORD told me ⁷that Hanamel, my uncle Shallum's son, would come to me with the request to buy his field at Anathoth in the territory of Benjamin, because I was his nearest relative and had the right to buy it for myself. ⁸Then, just as the LORD had said, Hanamel came to me there in the courtyard and asked me to buy the field. So I knew that the LORD had really spoken to me. ⁹I bought the field from Hanamel and weighed out the money to him; the price came to seventeen pieces of silver. ¹⁰I signed and sealed the deed, had it witnessed, and weighed out the money on scales. ¹¹Then I took both copies of the deed of purchase — the sealed copy containing the contract and its conditions, and the open copy — ¹²and gave them to Baruch, the son of Neriah and grandson of Mahseiah. I gave them to him in the presence of Hanamel and of the witnesses who had signed the deed of purchase and of the people who were sitting in the courtyard. ¹³Before them all I said to Baruch, ¹⁴"The LORD Almighty, the God of Israel, has ordered you to take these deeds, both the sealed deed of purchase and the open copy, and to place them in a clay jar, so that they may be preserved for years to come. ¹⁵The LORD Almighty, the God of Israel, has said

that houses, fields, and vineyards will again be bought in this land."

Jeremiah's Prayer

¹⁶After I had given the deed of purchase to Baruch, I prayed, ¹⁷"Sovereign LORD, you made the earth and the sky by your great power and might; nothing is too difficult for you. ¹⁸You have shown constant love to thousands, but you also punish people for the sins of their parents. You are a great and powerful God; you are the LORD Almighty. ¹⁹You make wise plans and do mighty things; you see everything that people do, and you reward them according to their actions. ²⁰Long ago you performed miracles and wonders in Egypt, and you have continued to perform them to this day, both in Israel and among all the other nations, so that you are now known everywhere. ²¹By means of miracles and wonders that terrified our enemies, you used your power and might to bring your people Israel out of Egypt. ²²You gave them this rich and fertile land, as you had promised their ancestors. ²³But when they came into this land and took possession of it, they did not obey your commands or live according to your teaching; they did nothing that you had ordered them to do. And so you brought all this destruction on them.

²⁴"The Babylonians have built siege mounds around the city to capture it, and they are attacking. War, starvation and disease will make the city fall into their hands. You can see that all you have said has come true. ²⁵Yet, Sovereign LORD, you are the one who ordered me to buy the field in the presence of witnesses, even though the city is about to be captured by the Babylonians."

²⁶Then the LORD said to me, ²⁷"I am the LORD, the God of all people. Nothing is too difficult for me. ²⁸I am going

to give this city over to King Nebuchadnezzar of Babylonia and his army; they
will capture it [29] and set it on fire. They
will burn it down, together with the
houses where people have made me angry by burning incense to Baal on the
rooftops and by pouring out wine offerings to other gods. [30] From the very beginning of their history the people of
Israel and the people of Judah have displeased me and made me angry by
what they have done. [31] The people of
this city have made me angry and furious from the day it was built. I have decided to destroy it [32] because of all the
evil that has been done by the people of
Judah and Jerusalem, together with
their kings and leaders, their priests
and prophets. [33] They turned their
backs on me; and though I kept on
teaching them, they would not listen
and learn. [34] They even placed their disgusting idols in the Temple built for my
worship, and they have defiled it.
[35] They have built altars to Baal in Hinnom Valley, to sacrifice their sons and
daughters to the god Molech. I did not
command them to do this, and it did not
even enter my mind that they would do
such a thing and make the people of Judah sin."

A Promise of Hope

[36] The LORD, the God of Israel, said to
me, "Jeremiah, the people are saying
that war, starvation, and disease will
make this city fall into the hands of the
king of Babylonia. Now listen to what
else I have to say. [37] I am going to gather
the people from all the countries where
I have scattered them in my anger and
fury, and I am going to bring them back
to this place and let them live here in
safety. [38] Then they will be my people,
and I will be their God. [39] I will give
them a single purpose in life: to honor
me for all time, for their own good and
the good of their descendants. [40] I will

make an eternal covenant with them. I
will never stop doing good things for
them, and I will make them fear me
with all their heart, so that they will
never turn away from me. [41] I will take
pleasure in doing good things for them,
and I will establish them permanently
in this land.

[42] "Just as I have brought this disaster on these people, so I am going to
give them all the good things that I
have promised. [43] The people are saying
that this land will be like a desert where
neither people nor animals live, and
that it will be given over to the Babylonians. But fields will once again be
bought in this land. [44] People will buy
them, and the deeds will be signed,
sealed, and witnessed. This will take
place in the territory of Benjamin, in
the villages around Jerusalem, in the
towns of Judah, and in the towns in the
hill country, in the foothills, and in
southern Judah. I will restore the people to their land. I, the LORD, have
spoken."

Another Promise of Hope

33 While I was still in prison in
the courtyard, the LORD's message came to me again. [2] The LORD,

The LORD's message came to me again. (33.1)

32.34 2 K 23.10; Jr 7.30, 31; 19.1-6   **32.35 a** 2 K 23.10; Jr 7.31; **b** Lv 18.21

who made the earth, who formed it and set it in place, spoke to me. He whose name is the LORD said, [3]"Call to me, and I will answer you; I will tell you wonderful and marvelous things that you know nothing about. [4]I, the LORD, the God of Israel, say that the houses of Jerusalem and the royal palace of Judah will be torn down as a result of the siege and the attack. [5]Some will fight against the Babylonians, who will fill the houses[s] with the corpses of those whom I am going to strike down in my anger and fury. I have turned away from this city because of the evil things that its people have done. [6]But I will heal this city and its people and restore them to health. I will show them abundant peace and security. [7]I will make Judah and Israel prosperous, and I will rebuild them as they were before. [8]I will purify them from the sins that they have committed against me, and I will forgive their sins and their rebellion. [9]Jerusalem will be a source of joy, honor, and pride to me; and every nation in the world will fear and tremble when they hear about the good things that I do for the people of Jerusalem and about the prosperity that I bring to the city."

[10]The LORD said, "People are saying that this place is like a desert, that it has no people or animals living in it. And they are right; the towns of Judah and the streets of Jerusalem are empty; no people or animals live there. But in these places you will hear again [11]the shouts of gladness and joy and the happy sounds of wedding feasts. You will hear people sing as they bring thank offerings to my Temple; they will say,

'Give thanks to the LORD
    Almighty,
  because he is good
    and his love is eternal.'

I will make this land as prosperous as it was before. I, the LORD, have spoken."

[12]The LORD Almighty said, "In this land that is like a desert and where no people or animals live, there will once again be pastures where shepherds can take their sheep. [13]In the towns in the hill country, in the foothills, and in southern Judah, in the territory of Benjamin, in the villages around Jerusalem, and in the towns of Judah, shepherds will once again count their sheep. I, the LORD, have spoken."

[14]The LORD said, "The time is coming when I will fulfill the promise that I made to the people of Israel and Judah. [15]At that time I will choose as king a righteous descendant of David. That king will do what is right and just throughout the land. [16]The people of Judah and of Jerusalem will be rescued and will live in safety. The city will be called 'The LORD Our Salvation.' [17]I, the LORD, promise that there will always be a descendant of David to be king of Israel [18]and that there will always be priests from the tribe of Levi to serve me and to offer burnt offerings, grain offerings, and sacrifices."

[19]The LORD said to me, [20]"I have made a covenant with the day and with the night, so that they always come at their proper times; and that covenant can never be broken. [21]In the same way I have made a covenant with my servant David that he would always have a descendant to be king, and I have made a covenant with the priests from the tribe of Levi that they would always serve me; and those covenants can never be broken. [22]I will increase the number of descendants of my servant David and the number of priests from the tribe of Levi, so that it will be as impossible to count them as it is to count the stars in the sky or the grains of sand on the seashore."

[s] *In verses 4 and 5* as a result . . . houses; *Hebrew unclear.*

33.11 1 Ch 16.34; 2 Ch 5.13; 7.3; Ezra 3.11; Ps 100.5; 106.1; 107.1; 118.1; 136.1
33.14-16 Jr 23.5, 6   **33.17** 2 S 7.12-16; 1 K 2.4; 1 Ch 17.11-14   **33.18** Nu 3.5-10

²³The LORD said to me, ²⁴"Have you noticed how people are saying that I have rejected Israel and Judah, the two families that I chose? And so they look with contempt on my people and no longer consider them a nation. ²⁵But I, the LORD, have a covenant with day and night, and I have made the laws that control earth and sky. ²⁶And just as surely as I have done this, so I will maintain my covenant with Jacob's descendants and with my servant David. I will choose one of David's descendants to rule over the descendants of Abraham, Isaac, and Jacob. I will be merciful to my people and make them prosperous again."

A Message for Zedekiah

34 The LORD spoke to me when King Nebuchadnezzar of Babylonia and his army, supported by troops from all the nations and races that were subject to him, were attacking Jerusalem and its nearby towns. The LORD, the God of Israel, told me to go and say to King Zedekiah of Judah, I, the LORD, will hand this city over to the king of Babylonia, and he will burn it down. ³You will not escape; you will be captured and handed over to him. You will see him face-to-face and talk to him in person; then you will go to Babylonia. ⁴Zedekiah, listen to what I say about you. You will not be killed in battle. ⁵You will die in peace, and as people burned incense when they buried your ancestors, who were kings before you, in the same way they will burn incense for you. They will mourn over you and say, 'Our king is dead!' I, the LORD, have spoken."

⁶Then I gave this message to King Zedekiah in Jerusalem ⁷while the army of the king of Babylonia was attacking the city. The army was also attacking Lachish and Azekah, the only other fortified cities left in Judah.

Deceitful Treatment of Slaves

⁸King Zedekiah and the people of Jerusalem had made an agreement to set free ⁹their Hebrew slaves, both male and female, so that no one would have an Israelite as a slave. ¹⁰All the people and their leaders agreed to free their slaves and never to enslave them again. They did set them free, ¹¹but later they changed their minds, took them back, and forced them to become slaves again.

¹²Then the LORD, ¹³the God of Israel, told me to say to the people: "I made a covenant with your ancestors when I rescued them from Egypt and set them free from slavery. I told them that ¹⁴every seven years they were to set free any Hebrew slave who had served them for six years. But your ancestors would not pay any attention to me or listen to what I said. ¹⁵Just a few days ago you changed your minds and did what pleased me. All of you agreed to set all Israelites free, and you made a covenant in my presence, in the Temple where I am worshiped. ¹⁶But then you changed your minds again and dishonored me. All of you took back the slaves whom you had set free as they desired, and you forced them into slavery again. ¹⁷So now, I, the LORD, say that you have disobeyed me; you have not given all Israelites their freedom. Very well, then, I will give you freedom: the freedom to die by war, disease, and starvation. I will make every nation in the world horrified at what I do to you. ¹⁸⁻¹⁹The officials of Judah and of Jerusalem, together with the palace officials, the priests, and all the leaders, made a covenant with me by walking between the two halves of a bull that they had cut in two. But they broke the covenant and did not keep its terms. So I will do to these people what they did to the bull. ²⁰I will hand them over to their enemies, who want to kill them, and their

^{34.1} 2 K 25.1-11; 2 Ch 36.17-21   **34.14** Ex 21.2; Dt 15.12

corpses will be eaten by birds and wild animals. [21] I will also hand over King Zedekiah of Judah and his officials to those who want to kill them. I will hand them over to the Babylonian army, which has stopped its attack against you. [22] I will give the order, and they will return to this city. They will attack it, capture it, and burn it down. I will make the towns of Judah like a desert where no one lives. I, the LORD, have spoken."

Jeremiah and the Rechabites

35 When Jehoiakim son of Josiah was king of Judah, the LORD said to me, [2] "Go to the members of the Rechabite clan and talk to them. Then bring them into one of the rooms in the Temple and offer them some wine." [3] So I took the entire Rechabite clan — Jaazaniah (the son of another Jeremiah, who was Habazziniah's son) and all his brothers and sons — [4] and brought them to the Temple. I took them into the room of the disciples of the prophet Hanan son of Igdaliah. This room was above the room of Maaseiah son of Shallum, an important official in the Temple, and near the rooms of the other officials. [5] Then I placed cups and bowls full of wine before the Rechabites, and I said to them, "Have some wine."

[6] But they answered, "We do not drink wine. Our ancestor Jonadab son of Rechab told us that neither we nor our descendants were ever to drink any wine. [7] He also told us not to build houses or farm the land and not to plant vineyards or buy them. He commanded us always to live in tents, so that we might remain in this land where we live like strangers. [8] We have obeyed all the instructions that Jonadab gave us. We ourselves never drink wine, and neither do our wives, our sons, or our daugh-

ters. [9-10] We do not build houses for homes — we live in tents — and we own no vineyards, fields, or grain. We have fully obeyed everything that our ancestor Jonadab commanded us. [11] But when King Nebuchadnezzar invaded the country, we decided to come to Jerusalem to get away from the Babylonian and Syrian armies. That is why we are living in Jerusalem."

[12-13] Then the LORD Almighty, the God of Israel, told me to go and say to the people of Judah and Jerusalem, "I the LORD, ask you why you refuse to listen to me and to obey my instructions [14] Jonadab's descendants have obeyed his command not to drink wine, and to this very day none of them drink any But I have kept on speaking to you, and you have not obeyed me. [15] I have continued to send you all my servants the prophets, and they have told you to give up your evil ways and to do what is right. They warned you not to worship and serve other gods, so that you could go on living in the land that I gave you and your ancestors. But you would not listen to me or pay any attention to me [16] Jonadab's descendants have obeyed the command that their ancestor gave them, but you people have not obeyed me. [17] So now, I, the LORD Almighty the God of Israel, will bring on you people of Judah and of Jerusalem all the destruction that I promised. I will do this because you would not listen when spoke to you, and you would not answer when I called you."

[18] Then I told the Rechabite clan that the LORD Almighty, the God of Israel had said, "You have obeyed the command that your ancestor Jonadab gave you; you have followed all his instructions, and you have done everything he commanded you. [19] So I, the LORD Almighty, the God of Israel, promise that Jonadab son of Rechab will always have a male descendant to serve me.

35.1 2 K 23.36 — 24.6; 2 Ch 36.5-7

Baruch wrote it all down
on a scroll.

Baruch read from the scroll.

Then the officials sent
Jehudi. (36.4,10,14)

Baruch Reads the Scroll
in the Temple

36 In the fourth year that Jehoia-kim son of Josiah was king of Judah, the LORD said to me, 2"Get a scroll and write on it everything that I have told you about Israel and Judah and all the nations. Write everything that I have told you from the time I first spoke to you, when Josiah was king, up to the present. 3 Perhaps when the people of Judah hear about all the destruction that I intend to bring on them, they will turn from their evil ways. Then I will forgive their wickedness and their sins."

4 So I called Baruch son of Neriah and dictated to him everything that the LORD had said to me. And Baruch wrote it all down on a scroll. 5 Then I gave Baruch the following instructions: "I am no longer allowed to go into the Temple. But I want you to go there the next time the people are fasting. You are to read the scroll aloud, so that they will hear everything that the LORD has said to me and that I have dictated to you. Do this where everyone can hear you, including the people of Judah who have come in from their towns. 7 Perhaps they will pray to the LORD and turn from their evil ways, because the LORD has threatened this people with his terrible anger and fury." 8 So Baruch read

the LORD's words in the Temple exactly as I had told him to do.

9 In the ninth month of the fifth year that Jehoiakim was king of Judah, the people fasted to gain the LORD's favor. The fast was kept by all who lived in Jerusalem and by all who came there from the towns of Judah. 10 Then, while all the people were listening, Baruch read from the scroll everything that I had said. He did this in the Temple, from the room of Gemariah son of Shaphan, the court secretary. His room was in the upper court near the entrance of the New Gate of the Temple.

The Scroll Is Read to the Officials

11 Micaiah, the son of Gemariah and grandson of Shaphan, heard Baruch read from the scroll what the LORD had said. 12 Then he went to the royal palace, to the room of the court secretary, where all the officials were in session. Elishama, the court secretary, Delaiah son of Shemaiah, Elnathan son of Achbor, Gemariah son of Shaphan, Zedekiah son of Hananiah, and all the other officials were there. 13 Micaiah told them everything that he had heard Baruch read to the people. 14 Then the officials sent Jehudi (the son of Nethaniah, grandson of Shelemiah, and great-grandson of Cushi) to tell Baruch to bring the scroll that he had read to the

36.1 2 K 24.1; 2 Ch 36.5-7; Dn 1.1, 2

"We must report this to the king."

As soon as Jehudi finished reading three or four columns the king cut them off . . . then I took another scroll. (36.16, 23, 32

people. Baruch brought them the scroll. 15"Sit down," they said, "and read the scroll to us." So Baruch did. 16After he had read it, they turned to one another in alarm and said to Baruch, "We must report this to the king." 17Then they asked him, "Tell us, now, how did you come to write all this? Did Jeremiah dictate it to you?"

18Baruch answered, "Jeremiah dictated every word of it to me, and I wrote it down in ink on this scroll."

19Then they told him, "You and Jeremiah must go and hide. Don't let anyone know where you are."

The King Burns the Scroll

20The officials put the scroll in the room of Elishama, the court secretary, and went to the king's court, where they reported everything to the king. 21Then the king sent Jehudi to get the scroll. He took it from the room of Elishama and read it to the king and all the officials who were standing around him. 22It was winter and the king was sitting in his winter palace in front of the fire. 23As soon as Jehudi finished reading three or four columns, the king cut them off with a small knife and threw them into the fire. He kept doing this until the entire scroll was burned up. 24But neither the king nor any of his officials who heard all this was afraid or showed any sign of sorrow. 25Although Elnathan, Delaiah, and Gemariah

begged the king not to burn the scroll he paid no attention to them. 26Then he ordered Prince Jerahmeel, together with Seraiah son of Azriel and Shele miah son of Abdeel, to arrest me and my secretary Baruch. But the LORD had hidden us.

Jeremiah Writes Another Scroll

27After King Jehoiakim had burned the scroll that I had dictated to Baruch the LORD told me 28to take another scroll and write on it everything that had been on the first one. 29The LORD told me to say to the king, "You have burned the scroll, and you have asked Jeremiah why he wrote that the king of Babylonia would come and destroy this land and kill its people and its animals 30So now, I, the LORD, say to you, King Jehoiakim, that no descendant of yours will ever rule over David's kingdom. Your corpse will be thrown out where it will be exposed to the sun during the day and to the frost at night. 31I will punish you, your descendants, and your officials because of the sins all of you commit. Neither you nor the people of Jerusalem and of Judah have paid any attention to my warnings, and so I will bring on all of you the disaster that I have threatened."

32Then I took another scroll and gave it to my secretary Baruch, and he wrote down everything that I dictated. He wrote everything that had been on the first scroll and similar messages that I dictated to him.

Zedekiah's Request to Jeremiah

37 King Nebuchadnezzar of Babylonia made Zedekiah son of Josiah king of Judah in the place of Jehoiachin son of Jehoiakim. 2 But neither Zedekiah nor his officials nor the people obeyed the message which the LORD had given me.

3 King Zedekiah sent Jehucal son of Shelemiah and the priest Zephaniah son of Maaseiah to ask me to pray to the LORD our God on behalf of our nation. 4 I had not yet been put in prison and was still moving about freely among the people. 5 The Babylonian army had been besieging Jerusalem, but when they heard that the Egyptian army had crossed the Egyptian border, they retreated.

6 Then the LORD, the God of Israel, told me 7 to say to Zedekiah, "The Egyptian army is on its way to help you, but it will return home. 8 Then the Babylonians will come back, attack the city, capture it, and burn it down. 9 I, the LORD, warn you not to deceive yourselves into thinking that the Babylonians will not come back, because they will. 10 Even if you defeat the whole Babylonian army, so that only wounded men are left, lying in their tents, they would still get up and burn this city to the ground."

Jeremiah Is Arrested and Imprisoned

11 The Babylonian army retreated from Jerusalem because the Egyptian army was approaching. 12 So I started to leave Jerusalem and go to the territory of Benjamin to take possession of my share of the family property. 13 But when I reached the Benjamin Gate, the officer in charge of the soldiers on duty there, a man by the name of Irijah, the son of Shelemiah and grandson of Han-

aniah, stopped me and said, "You are deserting to the Babylonians!"

14 I answered, "That's not so! I'm not deserting." But Irijah would not listen to me. Instead, he arrested me and took me to the officials. 15 They were furious with me and had me beaten and locked up in the house of Jonathan, the court secretary, whose house had been made into a prison. 16 I was put in an underground cell and kept there a long time.

17 Later on King Zedekiah sent for me, and there in the palace he asked me privately, "Is there any message from the LORD?"

"There is," I answered, and added, "You will be handed over to the king of Babylonia." 18 Then I asked, "What crime have I committed against you or your officials or this people, to make you put me in prison? 19 What happened to your prophets who told you that the king of Babylonia would not attack you or the country? 20 And now, Your Majesty, I beg you to listen to me and do what I ask. Please do not send me back to the prison in Jonathan's house. If you do, I will surely die there."

21 So King Zedekiah ordered me to be locked up in the palace courtyard. I stayed there, and each day I was given a loaf of bread from the bakeries until all the bread in the city was gone.

Jeremiah in a Dry Well

38 Shephatiah son of Mattan, Gedaliah son of Pashhur, Jehucal son of Shelemiah, and Pashhur son of Malchiah heard that I was telling the people that 2 the LORD had said, "Whoever stays on in the city will die in war or of starvation or disease. But those who go out and surrender to the Babylonians will not be killed; they will at least escape with their life." 3 I was also telling them that the LORD had said, "I am going to give the city to the Babylonian army, and they will capture it."

37.1 2 K 24.17; 2 Ch 36.10

⁴Then the officials went to the king and said, "This man must be put to death. By talking like this he is making the soldiers in the city lose their courage, and he is doing the same thing to everyone else left in the city. He is not trying to help the people; he only wants to hurt them."

⁵King Zedekiah answered, "Very well, then, do what you want to with him; I can't stop you." ⁶So they took me and let me down by ropes into Prince Malchiah's well, which was in the palace courtyard. There was no water in the well, only mud, and I sank down in it.

⁷However, Ebedmelech the Ethiopian,ᶠ a eunuch who worked in the royal palace, heard that they had put me in the well. At that time the king was holding court at the Benjamin Gate. ⁸So Ebedmelech went there and said to the king, ⁹"Your Majesty, what these men have done is wrong. They have put Jeremiah in the well, where he is sure to die of starvation, since there is no more food in the city." ¹⁰Then the king ordered Ebedmelech to take with him three men and to pull me out of the well before I died. ¹¹So Ebedmelech went with the men to the palace storeroom and got some worn-out clothing which he let down to me by ropes. ¹²He told me to put the rags under my arms, so that the ropes wouldn't hurt me. I did this, ¹³and they pulled me up out of the well. After that I was kept in the courtyard.

Zedekiah Asks Jeremiah's Advice

¹⁴On another occasion King Zedekiah had me brought to him at the third entrance to the Temple, and he said, "I am going to ask you a question, and I want you to tell me the whole truth."

And they pulled me up out of the well. (38.13)

¹⁵I answered, "If I tell you the truth, you will put me to death, and if I give you advice, you won't pay any attention."

¹⁶So King Zedekiah promised me in secret, "I swear by the living God, the God who gave us life, that I will not put you to death or hand you over to the men who want to kill you."

¹⁷Then I told Zedekiah that the LORD Almighty, the God of Israel, had said, "If you surrender to the king of Babylonia's officers, your life will be spared, and this city will not be burned down. Both you and your family will be spared. ¹⁸But if you do not surrender, then this city will be handed over to the Babylonians, who will burn it down, and you will not escape from them."

¹⁹But the king answered, "I am afraid of our own people who have deserted to the Babylonians. I may be handed over to them and tortured."

²⁰I said, "You will not be handed over

ᶠ *Hebrew* Cushite: *Cush is the ancient name of the extensive territory south of the First Cataract of the Nile River. This region was called Ethiopia in Graeco-Roman times, and included within its borders most of modern Sudan and some of present-day Ethiopia (Abyssinia).*

to them. I beg you to obey the LORD's message; then all will go well with you, and your life will be spared. ²¹But the LORD has shown me in a vision what will happen if you refuse to surrender. ²²In it I saw all the women left in Judah's royal palace being led out to the king of Babylonia's officers. Listen to what they were saying as they went:

'The king's best friends
    misled him,
  they overruled him.
And now that his feet have sunk
    in the mud,
  his friends have left him.' "

²³Then I added, "All your women and children will be taken out to the Babylonians, and you yourself will not escape from them. You will be taken prisoner by the king of Babylonia, and this city will be burned to the ground."

²⁴Zedekiah replied, "Don't let anyone know about this conversation, and your life will not be in danger. ²⁵If the officials hear that I have talked with you, they will come and ask you what we said. They will promise not to put you to death if you tell them everything. ²⁶Just tell them you were begging me not to send you back to prison to die there." ²⁷Then all the officials came and questioned me, and I told them exactly what the king had told me to say. There was nothing else they could do, because no one had overheard the conversation. ²⁸And I was kept in the palace courtyard until the day Jerusalem was captured.

The Fall of Jerusalem

39 In the tenth month of the ninth year that Zedekiah was king of Judah, King Nebuchadnezzar of Babylonia came with his whole army and attacked Jerusalem. ²On the ninth day of the fourth month of Zedekiah's elev-

enth year as king, the city walls were broken through.

(³When Jerusalem was captured,ᵘ all the high officials of the king of Babylonia came and took their places at the Middle Gate, including Nergal Sharezer, Samgar Nebo, Sarsechim, and another Nergal Sharezer.ᵛ)

⁴When King Zedekiah and all his soldiers saw what was happening, they tried to escape from the city during the night. They left by way of the royal garden, went through the gateway connecting the two walls, and escaped in the direction of the Jordan Valley. ⁵But the Babylonian army pursued them and captured Zedekiah in the plains near Jericho. Then they took him to King Nebuchadnezzar, who was in the city of Riblah in the territory of Hamath, and there Nebuchadnezzar passed sentence on him. ⁶At Riblah he put Zedekiah's sons to death while Zedekiah was looking on, and he also had the officials of Judah executed. ⁷After that, he had Zedekiah's eyes put out and had him placed in chains to be taken to Babylonia. ⁸Meanwhile, the Babylonians burned down the royal palace and the houses of the people and tore down the walls of Jerusalem. ⁹Finally Nebuzaradan, the commanding officer, took away as prisoners to Babylonia the people who were left in the city, together with those who had deserted to him. ¹⁰He left in the land of Judah some of the poorest people, who owned no property, and he gave them vineyards and fields.

Jeremiah's Release

¹¹But King Nebuchadnezzar commanded Nebuzaradan, the commanding officer, to give the following order: ¹²"Go and find Jeremiah and take good care of him. Do not harm him, but do

---

ᵘ When Jerusalem was captured; *these words are moved here from the end of chapter 38.* ᵛ *The names and titles of these men are unclear.*

38.28 Ez 33.21

for him whatever he wants." [13]So Nebuzaradan, together with the high officials Nebushazban and Nergal Sharezer and all the other officers of the king of Babylonia, [14]had me brought from the palace courtyard. They put me under the care of Gedaliah, the son of Ahikam and grandson of Shaphan, who was to see that I got home safely. And so I stayed there among the people.

Hope for Ebedmelech

[15]While I was still imprisoned in the palace courtyard, the LORD told me [16]to tell Ebedmelech the Ethiopian[w] that the LORD Almighty, the God of Israel, had said, "Just as I said I would, I am going to bring upon this city destruction and not prosperity. And when this happens, you will be there to see it. [17]But I, the LORD, will protect you, and you will not be handed over to the people you are afraid of. [18]I will keep you safe, and you will not be put to death. You will escape with your life because you have put your trust in me. I, the LORD, have spoken."

Jeremiah Stays with Gedaliah

40 The LORD spoke to me after Nebuzaradan, the commanding officer, had set me free at Ramah. I had been taken there in chains, along with all the other people from Jerusalem and Judah who were being taken away as prisoners to Babylonia.

[2]The commanding officer took me aside and said, "The LORD your God threatened this land with destruction, [3]and now he has done what he said he would. All this happened because your people sinned against the LORD and disobeyed him. [4]Now, I am taking the chains off your wrists and setting you free. If you want to go to Babylonia with me, you may do so, and I will take care of you. But if you don't want to go, you don't have to. You have the whole country to choose from, and you may go wherever you wish."

[5]When I did not answer,[x] Nebuzaradan said, "Go back to Gedaliah, the son of Ahikam and grandson of Shaphan, whom the king of Babylonia has made governor of the towns of Judah. You may stay with him and live among the people, or you may go anywhere you think you should." Then he gave me a present and some food to take with me, and let me go on my way. [6]I went to stay with Gedaliah in Mizpah and lived among the people who were left in the land.

Gedaliah, Governor of Judah
(2 Kings 25.22-24)

[7]Some of the Judean officers and soldiers had not surrendered. They heard that the king of Babylonia had made Gedaliah governor of the land and had placed him in charge of all those who had not been taken away to Babylonia—the poorest people in the land. [8]So Ishmael son of Nethaniah, Johanan son of Kareah, Seraiah son of Tanhumeth, the sons of Ephai from Netophah, and Jezaniah from Maacah went with their men to Gedaliah at Mizpah. [9]Gedaliah said to them, "I give you my word that there is no need for you to be afraid to surrender to the Babylonians. Settle in this land, serve the king of Babylonia, and all will go well with you. [10]I myself will stay in Mizpah and be your representative when the Babylonians come here. But you can gather and store up wine, fruit, and olive oil,

---

[w] Hebrew Cushite: *Cush is the ancient name of the extensive territory south of the First Cataract of the Nile River. This region was called Ethiopia in Graeco-Roman times, and included within its borders most of modern Sudan and some of present-day Ethiopia (Abyssinia).*   [x] When I did not answer; *or* Then, before he left.

40.7-9 2 K 25.22-24

and live in the villages you occupy." [11] Meanwhile, all the Israelites who were in Moab, Ammon, Edom, and other countries, heard that the king of Babylonia had allowed some Israelites to stay on in Judah and that he had made Gedaliah their governor. [12] So they left the places where they had been scattered, and returned to Judah. They came to Gedaliah at Mizpah, and there they gathered in large amounts of wine and fruit.

Gedaliah Is Murdered
(2 Kings 25.25, 26)

[13] After this, Johanan and the leaders of the soldiers who had not surrendered came to Gedaliah at Mizpah [14] and said to him, "Don't you know that King Baalis of Ammon has sent Ishmael to murder you?" But Gedaliah did not believe it. [15] Then Johanan said privately to him, "Let me go and kill Ishmael, and no one will know who did it. Why should he be allowed to murder you? That would cause all the Jews who have gathered around you to be scattered, and it would bring disaster on all the people who are left in Judah."

[16] But Gedaliah answered, "Don't do it! What you are saying about Ishmael is not true!"

41 In the seventh month of that year, Ishmael, the son of Nethaniah and grandson of Elishama, a member of the royal family and one of the king's chief officers, went to Mizpah with ten men to see Governor Gedaliah. While they were all eating a meal together, [2] Ishmael and the ten men with him pulled out their swords and killed Gedaliah. [3] Ishmael also killed all the Israelites who were with Gedaliah at Mizpah and the Babylonian soldiers who happened to be there.

[4] The next day, before anyone knew about Gedaliah's murder, [5] eighty men arrived from Shechem, Shiloh, and Samaria. They had shaved off their beards, torn their clothes, and gashed themselves. They were taking grain and incense to offer in the Temple. [6] So Ishmael went out from Mizpah to meet them, weeping as he went. When he came to them, he said, "Please come in to see Gedaliah." [7] As soon as they were inside the city, Ishmael and his men killed them and threw their bodies in a well.

[8] But there were ten men in the group who said to Ishmael, "Please don't kill us! We have wheat, barley, olive oil, and honey hidden in the fields." So he spared them. [9] The well into which Ishmael threw the bodies of the men he had killed was the large one[y] that King Asa had dug when he was being attacked by King Baasha of Israel. Ishmael filled the well with the bodies. [10] Then he made prisoners of the king's daughters and all the rest of the people in Mizpah, whom Nebuzaradan the commanding officer had placed under the care of Gedaliah. Ishmael took them prisoner and started off in the direction of the territory of Ammon.

[11] Johanan and all the army leaders with him heard of the crime that Ishmael had committed. [12] So they went after him with their men and overtook him near the large pool at Gibeon. [13] When Ishmael's prisoners saw Johanan and the leaders of the forces with him, they were glad, [14] and turned and ran to them. [15] But Ishmael and eight of his men got away from Johanan and escaped to the land of Ammon.

[16] Then Johanan and the leaders of the forces with him took charge of the people whom Ishmael had taken away as prisoners from Mizpah after murdering Gedaliah — soldiers, women, children, and eunuchs. [17-18] They were afraid of the Babylonians because Ishmael had murdered Gedaliah, whom

---

[y] *One ancient translation* was the large one; *Hebrew* by means of Gedaliah.

41.1-3 2 K 25.25

the king of Babylonia had made governor of the land. So they set out for Egypt, in order to get away from the Babylonians. On the way they stopped at Chimham near Bethlehem.

The People Ask Jeremiah to Pray for Them

42 Then all the army leaders, including Johanan son of Kareah and Azariah[z] son of Hoshaiah, came with people of every class [2] and said to me, "Please do what we ask you! Pray to the LORD our God for us. Pray for all of us who have survived. Once there were many of us; but now only a few of us are left, as you can see. [3] Pray that the LORD our God will show us the way we should go and what we should do."

[4] I answered, "Very well, then. I will pray to the LORD our God, just as you have asked, and whatever he says, I will tell you. I will not keep back anything from you."

[5] Then they said to me, "May the LORD be a true and faithful witness against us if we do not obey all the commands that the LORD our God gives you for us. [6] Whether it pleases us or not, we will obey the LORD our God, to whom we are asking you to pray. All will go well with us if we obey him."

The LORD's Answer to Jeremiah's Prayer

[7] Ten days later the LORD spoke to me; [8] so I called together Johanan, all the army leaders who were with him, and all the other people. [9] I said to them, "The LORD, the God of Israel, to whom you sent me with your request has said, [10] 'If you are willing to go on living in this land, then I will build you up and not tear you down; I will plant you and not pull you up. The destruction I brought on you has caused me great sorrow. [11] Stop being afraid of the king of Babylonia. I am with you, and I will rescue you from his power. [12] Because I am merciful, I will make him have mercy on you and let you go back home. I, the LORD, have spoken.'

[13-15] "But you people who are left in Judah must not disobey the LORD your God and refuse to live in this land. You must not say, 'No, we will go and live in Egypt, where we won't face war any more or hear the call to battle or go hungry.' If you say this, then the LORD Almighty, the God of Israel, says, 'If you are determined to go and live in Egypt, [16] then the war that you fear will overtake you, and the hunger you dread will follow you, and you will die there in Egypt. [17] All the people who are determined to go and live in Egypt will die either in war or of starvation or disease. Not one of them will survive, not one will escape the disaster that I am going to bring on them.'

[18] "The LORD, the God of Israel, says, 'Just as my anger and fury were poured out on the people of Jerusalem, so my fury will be poured out on you if you go to Egypt. You will be a horrifying sight; people will make fun of you and use your name as a curse. You will never see this place again.' "

[19] Then I continued, "The LORD has told you people who are left in Judah not to go to Egypt. And so I warn you now [20] that you are making a fatal mistake. You asked me to pray to the LORD our God for you, and you promised that you would do everything that he commands. [21] And now I have told you, but you are disobeying everything that the LORD our God sent me to tell you. [22] So then, remember this: you will die in war or of starvation or disease in the land where you want to go and live."

Jeremiah Is Taken to Egypt

43 I finished telling the people everything that the LORD their God had sent me to tell them. [2] Then

---

[z] *One ancient translation (see also 43.2)* Azariah; *Hebrew* Jezaniah.

They disobeyed the Lord's command and went into Egypt. (43.7)

Azariah son of Hoshaiah and Johanan son of Kareah and all the other arrogant men said to me, "You are lying. The Lord our God did not send you to tell us not to go and live in Egypt. ³Baruch son of Neriah has stirred you up against us, so that the Babylonians will gain power over us and can either kill us or take us away to Babylonia." ⁴So neither Johanan nor any of the army officers nor any of the people would obey the Lord's command to remain in the land of Judah. ⁵Then Johanan and all the army officers took everybody left in Judah away to Egypt, together with all the people who had returned from the nations where they had been scattered: ⁶the men, the women, the children, and the king's daughters. They took everyone whom Nebuzaradan the commanding officer had left under the care of Gedaliah, including Baruch and me. ⁷They disobeyed the Lord's command and went into Egypt as far as the city of Tahpanhes.

⁸There the Lord said to me, ⁹"Get some large stones and bury them in the mortar of the pavement*ᵃ* in front of the entrance to the government building here in the city, and let some of the Israelites see you do it. ¹⁰Then tell them that I, the Lord Almighty, the God of Israel, am going to bring my servant King Nebuchadnezzar of Babylonia to this place, and he*ᵇ* will put his throne over these stones that you*ᶜ* buried, and will spread the royal tent over them. ¹¹Nebuchadnezzar will come and de-feat Egypt. Those people who are doomed to die of disease will die of disease, those doomed to be taken away as prisoners will be taken away as prisoners, and those doomed to be killed in war will be killed in war. ¹²I will set fire to the temples of Egypt's gods, and the king of Babylonia will either burn their gods or carry them off. As shepherds pick their clothes clean of lice, so the king of Babylonia will pick the land of Egypt clean and then leave victorious. ¹³He will destroy the sacred stone monuments at Heliopolis in Egypt and will burn down the temples of the Egyptian gods."

The Lord's Message to the Israelites in Egypt

44 The Lord spoke to me concerning all the Israelites living in Egypt, in the cities of Migdol, Tahpanhes, and Memphis, and in the southern part of the country. ²The Lord Almighty, the God of Israel, said, "You yourselves have seen the destruction I brought on Jerusalem and all the other cities of Judah. Even now they are still in ruins, and no one lives in them ³because their people had done evil and had made me angry. They offered sacrifices to other gods and served gods that neither they nor you nor your ancestors ever worshiped. ⁴I kept sending you my servants the prophets, who told you not to do this terrible thing that I hate. ⁵But you would not listen or pay

ᵃ Probable text bury them . . . pavement; Hebrew unclear. ᵇ *Some ancient translations he; Hebrew I.* ᶜ *Some ancient translations you; Hebrew I.*
43.5-7 2 K 25.26

any attention. You would not give up your evil practice of sacrificing to other gods. 6 So I poured out my anger and fury on the towns of Judah and on the streets of Jerusalem, and I set them on fire. They were left in ruins and became a horrifying sight, as they are today.

7 "And so I, the LORD Almighty, the God of Israel, now ask why you are doing such an evil thing to yourselves. Do you want to bring destruction on men and women, children and babies, so that none of your people will be left? 8 Why do you make me angry by worshiping idols and by sacrificing to other gods here in Egypt, where you have come to live? Are you doing this just to destroy yourselves, so that every nation on earth will make fun of you and use your name as a curse? 9 Have you forgotten all the wicked things that have been done in the towns of Judah and in the streets of Jerusalem by your ancestors, by the kings of Judah and their wives, by you and your wives? 10 But to this day you have not humbled yourselves. You have not honored me or lived according to all the laws that I gave you and your ancestors.

11 "So then, I, the LORD Almighty, the God of Israel, will turn against you and destroy all Judah. 12 As for the people of Judah who are left and are determined to go and live in Egypt, I will see to it that all of them are destroyed. All of them, great and small, will die in Egypt, either in war or of starvation. They will be a horrifying sight; people will make fun of them and use their name as a curse. 13 I will punish those who live in Egypt, just as I punished Jerusalem — with war, starvation, and disease. 14 None of the people of Judah who are left and have come to Egypt to live will escape or survive. Not one of them will return to Judah, where they long to live once again. No one will return except a few refugees."

15 Then all the men who knew that their wives offered sacrifices to other gods, and all the women who were standing there, including the Israelites who lived in southern Egypt — a large crowd in all — said to me, 16 "We refuse to listen to what you have told us in the name of the LORD. 17 We will do everything that we said we would. We will offer sacrifices to our goddess, the Queen of Heaven, and we will pour out wine offerings to her, just as we and our ancestors, our king and our leaders, used to do in the towns of Judah and in the streets of Jerusalem. Then we had plenty of food, we were prosperous, and had no troubles. 18 But ever since we stopped sacrificing to the Queen of Heaven and stopped pouring out wine offerings to her, we have had nothing, and our people have died in war and of starvation."

19 And the women added, "When we baked cakes shaped like the Queen of Heaven, offered sacrifices to her, and poured out wine offerings to her, our husbands approved of what we were doing."

20 Then I said to all the men and the women who had answered me in this way, 21 "As for the sacrifices which you and your ancestors, your kings and your leaders, and the people of the land offered in the towns of Judah and in the streets of Jerusalem — do you think that the LORD did not know about them or that he forgot them? 22 This very day your land lies in ruins and no one lives in it. It has become a horrifying sight, and people use its name as a curse because the LORD could no longer endure your wicked and evil practices. 23 This present disaster has come on you because you offered sacrifices to other gods and sinned against the LORD by not obeying all his commands."

24-25 I told all the people, especially the women, what the LORD Almighty, the God of Israel, was saying to the people of Judah living in Egypt: "Both you and your wives have made solemn promises to the Queen of Heaven. You promised that you would offer sacrifices to her and pour out wine offerings to her, and you have kept your promises. Very well, then! Keep your promises! Carry out your vows! 26 But now listen to the vow that I, the LORD, have made in my mighty name to all you Israelites in Egypt: Never again will I let any of you use my name to make a vow by saying, 'I swear by the living Sovereign LORD!' 27 I will see to it that you will not prosper, but will be destroyed. All of you will die, either in war or of disease, until not one of you is left. 28 But a few of you will escape death and return from Egypt to Judah. Then the survivors will know whose words have come true, mine or theirs. 29 I, the LORD, will give you proof that I will punish you in this place and that my promise to bring destruction on you will come true. 30 I will hand over King Hophra of Egypt to his enemies who want to kill him, just as I handed over King Zedekiah of Judah to King Nebuchadnezzar of Babylonia, who was his enemy and wanted to kill him."

God's Promise to Baruch

45 In the fourth year that Jehoiakim son of Josiah was king of Judah, Baruch wrote down what I had dictated to him. Then I told him 2 that the LORD, the God of Israel, had said, "Baruch, 3 you are saying, 'I give up! The LORD has added sorrow to my troubles. I am worn out from groaning, and I can't find any rest!'

4 "But I, the LORD, am tearing down what I have built and pulling up what I have planted. I will do this to the entire earth. 5 Are you looking for special treatment for yourself? Don't do it. I am bringing disaster on all people, but you will at least escape with your life, wherever you go. I, the LORD, have spoken."

Egypt's Defeat at Carchemish

46 The LORD spoke to me about the nations, 2 beginning with Egypt. This is what he said about the army of King Neco of Egypt, which King Nebuchadnezzar of Babylonia defeated at Carchemish near the Euphrates River in the fourth year that Jehoiakim was king of Judah:

3 "The Egyptian officers shout,
    'Get your shields ready
        and march into battle!
4 Harness your horses and mount
        them!
Fall in line and put on your
        helmets!
    Sharpen your spears!
    Put on your armor!'

5 "But what do I see?" asks the
        LORD.
"They are turning back in terror.
Their soldiers are beaten back;
    overcome with fear, they run
        as fast as they can
    and do not look back.
6 Those who run fast cannot get
        away;
    the soldiers cannot escape.
In the north, by the Euphrates,
    they stumble and fall.
7 Who is this that rises like
        the Nile,
    like a river flooding its banks?
8 It is Egypt, rising like the Nile,
    like a river flooding its banks.
Egypt said, 'I will rise and cover
        the world;
    I will destroy cities and
        the people who live there.
9 Command the horses to go
    and the chariots to roll!
Send out the soldiers:

Command the horses to go. (46.9)

men from Ethiopia[d] and
    Libya, carrying shields,
and skilled archers from
    Lydia.' "

10 This is the day of the Sovereign
    LORD Almighty:
today he will take revenge;
today he will punish his
    enemies.
His sword will eat them until it
    is full,
and drink their blood until it
    is satisfied.
Today the Almighty sacrifices his
    victims
in the north, by the
    Euphrates.
11 People of Egypt, go to Gilead[e]
    and look for medicine!
All your medicine has proved
    useless;
nothing can heal you.
12 Nations have heard of your
    shame;
everyone has heard you cry.
One soldier trips over another,
and both of them fall to the
    ground.

The Coming of Nebuchadnezzar

13 When King Nebuchadnezzar of
Babylonia came to attack Egypt, the
LORD spoke to me. He said,
14 "Proclaim it in the towns of
    Egypt,

in Migdol, Memphis, and
    Tahpanhes:
'Get ready to defend yourselves;
all you have will be destroyed
    in war!
15 Why has your mighty god Apis
    fallen?
The LORD has struck him
    down!'
16 Your soldiers have stumbled and
    fallen;[f]
each one says to the other,
'Hurry! Let's go home to our
    people
and escape the enemy's
    sword!'

17 "Give the king of Egypt a new
    name —
'Noisy Braggart Who Missed
    His Chance.'
18 I, the LORD Almighty, am king.
I am the living God.
As Mount Tabor towers above
    the mountains
and Mount Carmel stands
    high above the sea,
so will be the strength of the one
    who attacks you.
19 Get ready to be taken prisoner,
    you people of Egypt!
Memphis will be made a desert,
a ruin where no one lives.
20 Egypt is like a splendid cow,
attacked by a stinging fly from
    the north.

[d] Hebrew *Cush*: *Cush is the ancient name of the extensive territory south of the First
Cataract of the Nile River. This region was called Ethiopia in Graeco-Roman times,
and included within its borders most of modern Sudan and some of present-day
Ethiopia (Abyssinia).*   [e] GILEAD: *See 8.22.*   [f] *Probable text* Your soldiers . . . fallen;
Hebrew unclear.
46.13 Jr 43.10-13

21 Even her hired soldiers
     are helpless as calves.
They did not stand and fight;
     all of them turned and ran.
The day of their doom had
         arrived,
     the time of their destruction.
22 Egypt runs away, hissing like
         a snake,
     as the enemy's army
         approaches.
They attack her with axes,
     like people cutting down trees
23   and destroying a thick forest.
Their soldiers are too many to
         count;
     they outnumber the locusts.
24 The people of Egypt are put to
         shame;
     they are conquered by the
         people of the north.
I, the LORD, have spoken."

25 The LORD Almighty, the God of Israel, says, "I am going to punish Amon,
the god of Thebes, together with Egypt
and its gods and kings. I am going to
take the king of Egypt and all who put
their trust in him, 26 and hand them
over to those who want to kill them, to
King Nebuchadnezzar of Babylonia
and his army. But later on, people will
live in Egypt again, as they did in times
past. I, the LORD, have spoken.

The LORD Will Save His People

27 "My people, do not be afraid,
     people of Israel, do not be
         terrified.
I will rescue you from that
     faraway land,
     from the land where you are
         prisoners.
You will come back home and
     live in peace;
     you will be secure, and no one
         will make you afraid.

28 I will come to you and save you.
I will destroy all the nations
     where I have scattered you,
     but I will not destroy you.
I will not let you go unpunished;
     but when I punish you, I will
         be fair.
I, the LORD, have spoken."

The LORD's Message about Philistia

47 Before the king of Egypt at-
tacked Gaza, the LORD spoke to
me about Philistia. 2 He said:
"Look! Waters are rising in the
         north
     and will rush like a river in
         flood.
They will cover the land and
     everything on it,
     cities and the people who live
         there.
People will call out for help;
     everyone on earth will cry
         bitterly.
3 They will hear the hoofbeats of
         horses,
     the clatter of chariots,
     the rumble of wheels.
Parents will not turn back for
     their children;
     their hands will hang limp at
         their sides.
4 The time has come to destroy
         Philistia,
     to cut off from Tyre and Sidon
     all the help that remains.
I, the LORD, will destroy the
         Philistines,
     all who came from the shores
         of Crete.
5 Great sorrow has come to the
     people of Gaza,
     and Ashkelon's people are
         silent.
How long will the rest of
     Philistia mourn?
6 You cry out, 'Sword of the LORD!

46.27, 28 Jr 30.10, 11   **47.1-7** Is 14.29-31; Ez 25.15-17; Jl 3.4-8; Am 1.6-8; Zep 2.4-7;
Zec 9.5-7

How long will you go on
  slashing?
Go back to your scabbard,
  stay there and rest!'
⁷But how can it rest,
  when I have given it work
    to do?
I have commanded it to attack
    Ashkelon
  and the people who live on
    the coast."

The Destruction of Moab

48 This is what the LORD
Almighty said about Moab:
"Pity the people of Nebo—
  their town is destroyed!
Kiriathaim is captured,
  its mighty fortress torn down,
  and its people put to shame;
² the splendor of Moab is gone.
The enemy have captured
    Heshbon
  and plot to destroy the nation
    of Moab.
The town of Madmen will be
    silenced;
  armies will march against it.
³The people of Horonaim cry out,
  'Violence! Destruction!'

⁴"Moab has been destroyed;
  listen to the children crying.
⁵Hear the sound of their sobs
  along the road up to Luhith,
  the cries of distress
  on the way down to
    Horonaim.
⁶'Quick, run for your lives!'
    they say.
  'Run like a wild desert
    donkey!'

⁷"Moab, you trusted in your
    strength and your wealth,
  but now even you will be
    conquered;

your god Chemosh will go into
    exile,
  along with his princes and
    priests.
⁸Not a town will escape the
    destruction;
  both valley and plain will be
    ruined.
I, the LORD, have spoken.
⁹Set up a tombstone for Moab;
  it will soon be destroyed.
Its towns will be left in ruins,
  and no one will live there
    again."

(¹⁰Curse those who do not do the
LORD's work with all their heart! Curse
those who do not slash and kill!)

The Cities of Moab Are Destroyed

¹¹The LORD said, "Moab has always
lived secure and has never been taken
into exile. Moab is like wine left to settle
undisturbed and never poured from jar
to jar. Its flavor has never been ruined,
and it tastes as good as ever.

¹²"So now, the time is coming when
I will send people to pour Moab out like
wine. They will empty its wine jars and
break them in pieces. ¹³Then the Moabites will be disillusioned with their
god Chemosh, just as the Israelites
were disillusioned with Bethel, a god in
whom they trusted.

¹⁴"Men of Moab, why do you claim
    to be heroes,
  brave soldiers tested in war?
¹⁵Moab and its cities are destroyed;
  its finest young men have
    been slaughtered.
I am the king, the LORD
    Almighty,
  and I have spoken.
¹⁶Moab's doom approaches;
  its ruin is coming soon.

¹⁷"Mourn for that nation, you that
    live nearby,
  all of you that know its fame.

48.1-47 Is 15.1 – 16.14; 25.10-12; Ez 25.8-11; Am 2.1-3; Zep 2.8-11

Say, 'Its powerful rule has been
  broken;
  its glory and might are no
  more.'
18 You that live in Dibon,
  come down from your place
    of honor
  and sit on the ground in the
    dust;
  Moab's destroyer is here
  and has left its forts in ruins.
19 You that live in Aroer,
  stand by the road and wait;
  ask those who are running
    away,
  find out from them what
    has happened.
20 'Moab has fallen,' they will
    answer,
  'weep for it; it is disgraced.
  Announce along the Arnon River
    that Moab is destroyed!'

21 "Judgment has come on the cities
of the plateau: on Holon, Jahzah,
Mephaath, 22 Dibon, Nebo, Beth Diblathaim, 23 Kiriathaim, Bethgamul, Beth-
meon, 24 Kerioth, and Bozrah. Judgment has come on all the cities of Moab,
far and near. 25 Moab's might has been
crushed; its power has been destroyed.
I, the LORD, have spoken."

Moab Will Be Humbled

26 The LORD said, "Make Moab
drunk, because it has rebelled against
me. Moab will roll in its own vomit, and
people will laugh. 27 Moab, remember
how you made fun of the people of Israel? You treated them as though they
had been caught with a gang of
robbers.

28 "You people who live in Moab,
leave your towns! Go and live on the
cliffs! Be like the dove that makes its
nest in the sides of a ravine. 29 Moab is
very proud! I have heard how proud, arrogant, and conceited the people are,

how much they think of themselves.
30 I, the LORD, know of their arrogance.
Their boasts amount to nothing, and
the things they do will not last. 31 And so
I will weep for everyone in Moab and for
the people of Kir Heres. 32 I will cry for
the people of Sibmah, even more than
for the people of Jazer. City of Sibmah,
you are like a vine whose branches
reach across the Dead Sea and go as far
as Jazer. But now your summer fruits
and your grapes have been destroyed.
33 Happiness and joy have been taken
away from the fertile land of Moab. I
have made the wine stop flowing from
the wine presses; there is no one to
make the wine and shout for joy.

34 "The people of Heshbon and Elealeh cry out,g and their cry can be heard
as far as Jahaz; it can be heard by the
people in Zoar, and it is heard as far as
Horonaim and Eglath Shelishiyah.
Even Nimrim Brook has dried up. 35 I
will stop the people of Moab from making burnt offerings at their places of
worship and from offering sacrifices to
their gods. I, the LORD, have spoken.

36 "So my heart mourns for Moab and
for the people of Kir Heres, like someone playing a funeral song on a flute,
because everything they owned is
gone. 37 All of them have shaved their
heads and cut off their beards. They
have all made gashes on their hands,
and everyone is wearing sackcloth.
38 On all the housetops of Moab and in
all its public squares there is nothing
but mourning, because I have broken
Moab like a jar that no one wants.
39 Moab has been shattered! Cry out!
Moab has been disgraced. It is in ruins,
and all the surrounding nations make
fun of it. I, the LORD, have spoken."

No Escape for Moab

40 The LORD has promised that a nation will swoop down on Moab like an
eagle with its outspread wings, 41 and

---

g *Probable text* Heshbon . . . cry out; *Hebrew unclear.*

the towns and fortresses will be captured. On that day Moab's soldiers will be as frightened as a woman in labor. ⁴² Moab will be destroyed and will no longer be a nation, because it rebelled against me. ⁴³ Terror, pits, and traps are waiting for the people of Moab. The LORD has spoken. ⁴⁴ Whoever tries to escape the terror will fall into the pits, and whoever climbs out of the pits will be caught in the traps, because the LORD has set the time for Moab's destruction. ⁴⁵ Helpless refugees try to find protection in Heshbon, the city that King Sihon once ruled, but it is in flames.^h Fire has burned up the frontiers and the mountain heights of the war-loving people of Moab. ⁴⁶ Pity the people of Moab! The people who worshiped Chemosh have been destroyed, and their sons and daughters have been taken away as prisoners.

⁴⁷ But in days to come the LORD will make Moab prosperous again. All of this is what the LORD has said will happen to Moab.

The LORD's Judgment on Ammon

49 This is what the LORD said about Ammon: "Where are the men of Israel? Is there no one to defend their land? Why have they let the people who worship Molech take the territory of the tribe of Gad and settle there? ² But the time is coming when I will make the people of the capital city of Rabbah hear the noise of battle, and it will be left in ruins and its villages burned to the ground. Then Israel will take its land back from those who took it from them. ³ People of Heshbon, cry out! Ai is destroyed! Women of Rabbah, go into mourning! Put on sackcloth and mourn. Run about in confusion. Your

god Molech will be taken into exile, together with his priests and princes. ⁴ Why do you unfaithful people boast? Your strength is failing. Why do you trust in your power and say that no one would dare attack you? ⁵ I will bring terror on you from every side. You will all run away. Each one will run for his life, and there will be no one to bring your troops together again.

⁶ "But later on I will make Ammon prosperous again. I, the LORD, have spoken."

The LORD's Judgment on Edom

⁷ This is what the LORD Almighty said about Edom: "Have the people of Edom lost their good judgment? Can their advisers no longer tell them what to do? Has all their wisdom disappeared? ⁸ People of Dedan, turn and run! Hide! I am going to destroy Esau's descendants because the time has come for me to punish them. ⁹ When people pick grapes, they leave a few on the vines, and when robbers come at night, they take only what they want. ¹⁰ But Iⁱ have stripped Esau's descendants completely and uncovered their hiding places, so that they can no longer hide. All the people of Edom are destroyed. Not one of them is left. ¹¹ Leave your orphans with me, and I will take care of them. Your widows can depend on me.

¹² "If even those who did not deserve to be punished had to drink from the cup of punishment, do you think that you will go unpunished? No, you must drink from the cup! ¹³ I myself have sworn that the city of Bozrah will become a horrifying sight and a desert; people will make fun of it and use its name as a curse. All the nearby villages

^h Heshbon, the city . . . flames; *or* the city of Heshbon, but it is in flames and the palace of King Sihon is burning.　　ⁱ they leave a few . . . they take only what they want. ¹⁰ But I; *or* they leave nothing . . . they take everything. ¹⁰ And so I.

49.1-6 Ez 21.28-32; 25.1-7; Am 1.13-15; Zep 2.8-11　　**49.7-22** Is 34.5-17; 63.1-6; Ez 25.12-14; 35.1-15; Am 1.11, 12; Ob 1-14; Ml 1.2-5　　**49.7** Ba 3.22, 23

Hide! (49.8)

will be in ruins forever. I, the Lᴏʀᴅ, have spoken."

¹⁴I said, "Edom, I have received a message from the Lᴏʀᴅ. He has sent a messenger to tell the nations to assemble their armies and to get ready to attack you. ¹⁵The Lᴏʀᴅ is going to make you weak, and no one will respect you. ¹⁶Your pride has deceived you. No one fears you as much as you think they do. You live on the rocky cliffs, high on top of the mountain; but even though you live as high up as an eagle, the Lᴏʀᴅ will bring you down. The Lᴏʀᴅ has spoken."

¹⁷The Lᴏʀᴅ said, "The destruction that will come on Edom will be so terrible that everyone who passes by will be shocked and terrified. ¹⁸The same thing will happen to Edom that happened to Sodom and Gomorrah, when they and the nearby towns were destroyed. No one will ever live there again. I, the Lᴏʀᴅ, have spoken. ¹⁹Like a lion coming out of the thick woods along the Jordan River up to the green pasture land, I will come and make the Edomites run away suddenly from their country. Then the leader I choose will rule the nation. Who can be compared to me? Who would dare challenge me? What ruler could oppose me? ²⁰So lis-

ten to the plan that I have made against the people of Edom, and to what I intend to do to the people of the city of Teman. Even their children will be dragged off, and everyone will be horrified. ²¹When Edom falls, there will be such a noise that the entire earth will shake, and the cries of alarm will be heard as far away as the Gulf of Aqaba. ²²The enemy will attack Bozrah like an eagle swooping down with outspread wings. On that day Edom's soldiers will be as frightened as a woman in labor."

The Lᴏʀᴅ's Judgment on Damascus

²³This is what the Lᴏʀᴅ said about Damascus: "The people in the cities of Hamath and Arpad are worried and troubled because they have heard bad news. Anxiety rolls over them like a sea, and they cannot rest. ²⁴The people of Damascus are weak and have fled in terror. They are in pain and misery like a woman in labor. ²⁵The famous city that used to be happyʲ is completely deserted. ²⁶On that day her young men will be killed in the city streets, and all her soldiers destroyed. ²⁷I will set the walls of Damascus on fire and will burn down King Benhadad's palaces. I, the Lᴏʀᴅ Almighty, have spoken."

ʲ Some ancient translations happy; Hebrew my happiness.
49.18 Gn 19.24, 25 **49.19** Ws 12.12 **49.23-27** Is 17.1-3; Am 1.3-5; Zec 9.1

Judgment on the Tribe of Kedar and the City of Hazor

28 This is what the LORD said about the tribe of Kedar and the districts controlled by Hazor, which were conquered by King Nebuchadnezzar of Babylonia: "Attack the people of Kedar and destroy that tribe of eastern people! **29** Seize their tents and their flocks, their tent curtains and everything in their tents. Take their camels and tell the people, 'Terror is all around you!'

30 "People of Hazor, I, the LORD, warn you to run far away and hide. King Nebuchadnezzar of Babylonia has plotted against you, and this is what he says, **31** 'Come on! We'll attack those people that feel safe and secure! Their city has no gates or locks and is completely unprotected.' **32** "Take their camels and all their livestock! I will scatter in every direction those people who cut their hair short, and I will bring disaster on them from every side. **33** Hazor will be made a desert forever, a place where only jackals live. No one will ever live there again. I, the LORD, have spoken."

The LORD's Judgment on Elam

34 Soon after Zedekiah became king of Judah, the LORD Almighty spoke to me about the country of Elam. **35** He said, "I will kill all the archers who have made Elam so powerful. **36** I will make winds blow against Elam from all directions, and I will scatter her people everywhere, until there is no country where her refugees have not gone. **37** I will make the people of Elam afraid of their enemies, who want to kill them. In my great anger I will destroy the people of Elam and send armies against them until I have wiped them out. **38** I will destroy their kings and leaders, and set up my throne there. **39** But later on I will make the people of Elam prosperous again. I, the LORD, have spoken."

Babylon's Capture

50 This is the message that the LORD gave me about the city of Babylon and its people:

2 "Tell the news to the nations!
　Proclaim it!
Give the signal and announce
　the news!
Do not keep it a secret!
Babylon has fallen!
　Her god Marduk has been
　shattered!
Babylon's idols are put to shame;
　her disgusting images are
　crushed!

3 "A nation from the north has come to attack Babylonia and will make it a desert. People and animals will run away, and no one will live there."

Israel's Return

4 The LORD says, "When that time comes, the people of both Israel and Judah will come weeping, looking for me, their God. **5** They will ask the way to Zion and then go in that direction. They will make an eternal covenant with me and never break it.

6 "My people are like sheep whose shepherds have let them get lost in the mountains. They have wandered like sheep from one mountain to another, and they have forgotten where their home is. **7** They are attacked by all who find them. Their enemies say, 'They sinned against the LORD, and so what we have done is not wrong. Their ancestors trusted in the LORD, and they themselves should have remained faithful to him.'

8 "People of Israel, run away from Babylonia! Leave the country! Be the first to leave! **9** I am going to stir up a group of strong nations in the north and make them attack Babylonia. They will line up in battle against the country and conquer it. They are skillful hunters, shooting arrows that never miss the mark. ¹⁰Babylonia will be looted, and those who loot it will take everything they want. I, the LORD, have spoken."

Babylon's Fall

¹¹The LORD says, "People of Babylonia, you plundered my nation. You are happy and glad, going about like a cow threshing grain or like a neighing horse, ¹²but your own great city will be humiliated and disgraced. Babylonia will be the least important nation of all; it will become a dry and waterless desert. ¹³Because of my anger no one will live in Babylon; it will be left in ruins, and all who pass by will be shocked and amazed.

¹⁴"Archers, line up for battle against Babylon and surround it. Shoot all your arrows at Babylon, because it has sinned against me, the LORD. ¹⁵Raise the war cry all around the city! Now Babylon has surrendered. Its walls have been broken through and torn down.ᵏ I am taking my revenge on the Babylonians. So take your revenge on them, and treat them as they have treated others. ¹⁶Do not let seeds be planted in that country nor let a harvest be gathered. Every foreigner living there will be afraid of the attacking army and will go back home."

Israel's Return

¹⁷The LORD says, "The people of Israel are like sheep, chased and scattered by lions. First, they were attacked by the emperor of Assyria, and then King Nebuchadnezzar of Babylonia gnawed on their bones. ¹⁸Because of this, I, the LORD Almighty, the God of Israel, will punish King Nebuchadnezzar and his country, just as I punished the emperor of Assyria. ¹⁹I will restore the people of Israel to their land. They will eat the food that grows on Mount Carmel and in the region of Bashan,

and they will eat all they want of the crops that grow in the territories of

Like sheep . . . scattered by lions (50.17)

Ephraim and Gilead. ²⁰When that time comes, no sin will be found in Israel and no wickedness in Judah, because I will forgive those people whose lives I have spared. I, the LORD, have spoken."

God's Judgment on Babylonia

²¹The LORD says, "Attack the people of Merathaim and of Pekod. Kill and destroy them.ˡ Do everything I command you. I, the LORD, have spoken. ²²The noise of battle is heard in the land, and there is great destruction. ²³Babylonia hammered the whole world to pieces, and now that hammer is shattered! All the nations are shocked at what has happened to that country. ²⁴Babylonia, you fought against me, and you have been caught in the trap I set for you, even though you did not know it. ²⁵I have opened the place where my weapons are stored, and in my anger I have taken them out, because I, the Sovereign LORD Almighty, have work to do in Babylonia. ²⁶Attack it from every side and break open the places where its grain is stored! Pile up the loot like piles of grain! Destroy the country! Leave nothing at all! ²⁷Kill all their soldiers! Slaughter them! The people of Babylonia are doomed! The time has come for them to be punished!"

(²⁸Refugees escape from Babylonia and come to Jerusalem, and they tell

---

ᵏ *Hebrew has an additional word, the meaning of which is unclear.*   ˡ *One ancient translation* them; *Hebrew* after them.

how the LORD our God took revenge for what the Babylonians had done to his Temple.)

²⁹"Tell the archers to attack Babylon. Send out everyone who knows how to use the bow and arrow. Surround the city and don't let anyone escape. Pay it back for all it has done, and treat it as it has treated others, because it acted with pride against me, the Holy One of Israel. ³⁰So its young men will be killed in the city streets, and all its soldiers will be destroyed on that day. I, the LORD, have spoken.

³¹"Babylonia, you are filled with pride, so I, the Sovereign LORD Almighty, am against you! The time has come for me to punish you. ³²Your proud nation will stumble and fall, and no one will help you up. I will set your cities on fire, and everything around will be destroyed."

³³The LORD Almighty says, "The people of Israel and of Judah are oppressed. All who captured them are guarding them closely and will not let them go. ³⁴But the one who will rescue them is strong—his name is the LORD Almighty. He himself will take up their cause and will bring peace to the earth, but trouble to the people of Babylonia."

³⁵The LORD says,
"Death to Babylonia!
    Death to its people,
    to its rulers, to its people
        of wisdom.
³⁶Death to its lying prophets—
    what fools they are!
    Death to its soldiers—
        how terrified they are!
³⁷Destroy its horses and chariots!
    Death to its hired soldiers—
        how weak they are!
    Destroy its treasures;
        plunder and loot.
³⁸Bring a drought on its land
    and dry up its rivers.

Babylonia is a land of terrifying
        idols
    that have made fools of the
        people.
³⁹"And so Babylon will be haunted by demons and evil spirits,ᵐ and by unclean birds. Never again will people live there, not for all time to come. ⁴⁰The same thing will happen to Babylon that happened to Sodom and Gomorrah, when I destroyed them and the nearby towns. No one will ever live there again. I, the LORD, have spoken.

⁴¹"People are coming from a
        country in the north,
    a mighty nation far away;
    many kings are preparing
        for war.
⁴²They have taken their bows and
        swords;
    they are cruel and merciless.
    They sound like the roaring sea,
        as they ride their horses.
    They are ready for battle against
        Babylonia.
⁴³The king of Babylonia hears the
        news,
    and his hands hang limp.
    He is seized by anguish,
        by pain like a woman in labor.

⁴⁴"Like a lion coming out of the thick woods along the Jordan up to the green pasture land, I, the LORD, will come and make the Babylonians run away suddenly from their city. Then the leader I choose will rule the nation. Who can be compared to me? Who would dare challenge me? What ruler could oppose me? ⁴⁵So listen to the plan that I have made against the city of Babylon and to what I intend to do to its people. Even their children will be dragged off, and everyone will be horrified. ⁴⁶When Babylon falls, there will be such a noise that the entire earth will shake, and the cries of alarm will be heard by the other nations."

ᵐ demons and evil spirits; *or* wildcats and jackals.
50.29 Rev 18.6   **50.39** Rev 18.2   **50.40** Gn 19.24, 25

Further Judgment on Babylonia

51 The LORD says, "I am bringing a destructive wind[n] against Babylonia and its people. ²I will send foreigners to destroy Babylonia like a wind that blows straw away. When that day of destruction comes, they will attack from every side and leave the land bare. ³Don't give its soldiers time to shoot their arrows or to put on their armor. Do not spare the young men! Destroy the whole army! ⁴They will be wounded and die in the streets of their cities. ⁵I, the LORD God Almighty, have not abandoned Israel and Judah, even though they have sinned against me, the Holy One of Israel. ⁶Run away from Babylonia! Run for your lives! Do not be killed because of Babylonia's sin. I am now taking my revenge and punishing it as it deserves. ⁷Babylonia was like a gold cup in my hand, making the whole world drunk. The nations drank its wine and went out of their minds. ⁸Babylonia has suddenly fallen and is destroyed! Mourn over it! Get medicine for its wounds, and maybe it can be healed. ⁹Foreigners living there said, 'We tried to help Babylonia, but it was too late. Let's leave now and go back

Run for your lives! (51.6)

home. God has punished Babylonia with all his might and has destroyed it completely.'"

¹⁰The LORD says, "My people shout, 'The LORD has shown that we are in the right. Let's go and tell the people in Jerusalem what the LORD our God has done.'"

¹¹The LORD has stirred up the kings of Media, because he intends to destroy Babylonia. That is how he will take revenge for the destruction of his Temple.

The attacking officers command, "Sharpen your arrows! Get your shields ready! ¹²Give the signal to attack Babylon's walls. Strengthen the guard! Post the sentries! Place troops in ambush!"

The LORD has done what he said he would do to the people of Babylonia. ¹³That country has many rivers and rich treasures, but its time is up, and its thread of life is cut. ¹⁴The LORD Almighty has sworn by his own life that

[n] destructive wind; *or* destroying spirit.
51.7 Rev 17.2-4; 18.3   **51.9** Rev 18.5
51.13 Rev 17.1

Give the signal to attack Babylon's walls. (51.12)

he will bring many men to attack Babylonia like a swarm of locusts, and they
will shout with victory.

A Hymn of Praise to God

¹⁵ The Lord made the earth by his
power;
by his wisdom he created the
world
and stretched out the
heavens.
¹⁶ At his command the waters
above the sky*ᵒ* roar;
he brings clouds from the
ends of the earth.
He makes lightning flash in
the rain
and sends the wind from his
storeroom.
¹⁷ At the sight of this, people feel
stupid and senseless;
those who make idols are
disillusioned
because the gods they make
are false and lifeless.
¹⁸ They are worthless and should
be despised;
they will be destroyed when
the Lord comes to deal
with them.
¹⁹ The God of Jacob is not like
them;
he is the one who made
everything,
and he has chosen Israel to
be his very own people.
The Lord Almighty is his
name.

The Lord's Hammer

²⁰ The Lord says,
"Babylonia, you are my hammer,
my weapon of war.
I used you to crush nations and
kingdoms,
²¹   to shatter horses and riders,
to shatter chariots and their
drivers,
²²   to kill men and women,
to slay old and young,
to kill boys and girls,
²³   to slaughter shepherds and
their flocks,
to slaughter farmers and their
plow horses,
to crush rulers and high
officials."

Babylonia's Punishment

²⁴ The Lord says, "You will see me
repay Babylonia and its people for all
the evil they did to Jerusalem. ²⁵ Babylonia, you are like a mountain that destroys the whole world, but I, the Lord,
am your enemy. I will take hold of
you, level you to the ground, and
leave you in ashes. ²⁶ None of the
stones from your ruins will ever be
used again for building. You will be
like a desert forever. I, the Lord,
have spoken.

²⁷ "Give the signal to attack! Blow the
trumpet so that the nations can hear!
Prepare the nations for war against
Babylonia! Tell the kingdoms of Ararat,
Minni, and Ashkenaz to attack. Appoint
an officer to lead the attack. Bring up
the horses like a swarm of locusts.
²⁸ Prepare the nations for war against
Babylonia. Send for the kings of Media,
their leaders and officials, and the armies of all the countries they control.
²⁹ The earth trembles and shakes because the Lord is carrying out his plan
to make Babylonia a desert, where no
one lives. ³⁰ The Babylonian soldiers
have stopped fighting and remain in
their forts. They have lost their courage
and have become helpless. The city
gates are broken down, and the houses
are on fire. ³¹ Messenger after messenger runs to tell the king of Babylonia
that his city has been broken into from
every side. ³² The enemy have captured
the river crossing and have set the for-

ᵒ WATERS ABOVE THE SKY: *See Gn 1.6-8.*

That country will become a pile of ruins where wild animals live. (51.37)

tresses on fire. The Babylonian soldiers have panicked. ³³ Soon the enemy will cut them down and trample them like grain on a threshing place. I, the LORD Almighty, the God of Israel, have spoken."

³⁴ The king of Babylonia cut
    Jerusalem up
    and ate it.
He emptied the city like a jar;
    like a monster he
        swallowed it.
He took what he wanted
    and threw the rest away.
³⁵ Let the people of Zion say,
    "May Babylonia be held
        responsible
    for the violence done to us!"
Let the people of Jerusalem say,
    "May Babylonia be held
        responsible
    for what we have suffered!"

The LORD Will Help Israel

³⁶ And so the LORD said to the people of Jerusalem, "I will take up your cause and will make your enemies pay for what they did to you. I will dry up the source of Babylonia's water and make its rivers go dry. ³⁷ That country will become a pile of ruins where wild animals live. It will be a horrible sight; no one will live there, and all who see it will be terrified. ³⁸ The Babylonians all roar like lions and growl like lion cubs. ³⁹ Are they greedy? I will prepare them a feast and make them drunk and happy. They will go to sleep and never wake up. ⁴⁰ I will take them to be slaughtered, like lambs, goats, and rams. I, the LORD, have spoken."

Babylon's Fate

⁴¹ The LORD says about Babylon: "The city that the whole world praised has been captured! What a horrifying sight Babylon has become to the nations! ⁴² The sea has rolled over Babylon and covered it with roaring waves. ⁴³ The towns have become a horrifying sight and are like a waterless desert, where no one lives or even travels. ⁴⁴ I will punish Bel, the god of Babylonia, and make him give up his stolen goods; the nations will not worship him any more.

"Babylon's walls have fallen. ⁴⁵ People of Israel, run away from there! Run for your life from my fierce anger. ⁴⁶ Do not lose courage or be afraid because of the rumors you hear. Every year a different rumor spreads — rumors of violence in the land and of one king fighting another. ⁴⁷ And so the time is coming when I will deal with Babylonia's idols. The whole country will be put to shame, and all its people will be killed. ⁴⁸ Everything on earth and in the sky will shout for joy when Babylonia falls to the people who come from the north to destroy it. ⁴⁹ Babylonia caused the death of people all over the world, and now Babylonia will fall because it caused the death of so many Israelites. I, the LORD, have spoken."

God's Message to the Israelites in Babylonia

⁵⁰ The LORD says to his people in Babylonia: "You have escaped death! Now go! Don't wait! Though you are far from home, think about me, your LORD, and remember Jerusalem. ⁵¹ You say, 'We've been disgraced and made ashamed; we feel completely helpless because foreigners have taken over the holy places in the Temple.' ⁵² So then, I say that the time is coming when I will deal with Babylon's idols, and the wounded will groan throughout the country. ⁵³ Even if Babylon could climb to the sky and build a strong fortress there, I would still send people to destroy it. I, the LORD, have spoken."

Further Destruction on Babylon

⁵⁴ The LORD says,
"Listen to the sound of crying in Babylon,
    of mourning for the destruction in the land.
⁵⁵ I am destroying Babylon
    and putting it to silence.
The armies rush in like roaring waves
    and attack with noisy shouts.
⁵⁶ They have come to destroy Babylon;
    its soldiers are captured,
    and their bows are broken.
I am a God who punishes evil,
    and I will treat Babylon as it deserves.

⁵⁷ I will make its rulers drunk —
    men of wisdom, leaders, and soldiers.
They will go to sleep and never wake up.
I, the king, have spoken;
    I am the LORD Almighty.
⁵⁸ The walls of mighty Babylon will be thrown to the ground,
    and its towering gates burned down.
The work of the nations is all for nothing;
    their efforts go up in flames.
I, the LORD Almighty, have spoken."

Jeremiah's Message Is Sent to Babylonia

⁵⁹ King Zedekiah's personal attendant was Seraiah, the son of Neriah and grandson of Mahseiah. In the fourth year that Zedekiah was king of Judah, Seraiah was going to Babylonia with him, and I gave him some instructions. ⁶⁰ I wrote in a book an account of all the destruction that would come on Babylonia, as well as all these other things about Babylonia. ⁶¹ I told Seraiah, "When you get to Babylon, be sure to read aloud to the people everything that is written here. ⁶² Then pray, 'LORD, you have said that you would destroy this place, so that there would be no living creatures in it, neither people nor animals, and it would be like a desert forever.' ⁶³ Seraiah, when you finish reading this book to the people, then tie it to a rock and throw it into the Euphrates River ⁶⁴ and say, 'This is what will happen to Babylonia — it will sink and never rise again because of the destruction that the LORD is going to bring on it.' "ᵖ

The words of Jeremiah end here.

ᵖ *One ancient translation* on it; *Hebrew* on it and they will become tired out.
51.49 Rev 18.24   **51.63, 64** Rev 18.21

The Fall of Jerusalem
(2 *Kings* 24.18 — 25.7)

52 Zedekiah was twenty-one years old when he became king of Judah, and he ruled in Jerusalem for

It will sink and never rise again. (51.64)

eleven years. His mother's name was Hamutal, the daughter of the Jeremiah who lived in the city of Libnah. ²King Zedekiah sinned against the LORD, just as King Jehoiakim had done. ³The LORD became so angry with the people of Jerusalem and Judah that he banished them from his sight.

Zedekiah rebelled against King Nebuchadnezzar of Babylonia, ⁴and so Nebuchadnezzar came with all his army and attacked Jerusalem on the tenth day of the tenth month of the ninth year of Zedekiah's reign. They set up camp outside the city, built siege walls around it, ⁵and kept it under siege until Zedekiah's eleventh year. ⁶On the ninth day of the fourth month of that same year, when the famine was so bad that the people had nothing left to eat, ⁷the city walls were broken through. Although the Babylonians were surrounding the city, all the soldiers escaped during the night. They left by way of the royal garden, went through the gateway connecting the two walls, and fled in the direction of the Jordan Valley. ⁸But the Babylonian army pursued King Zedekiah, captured him in the plains near Jericho, and all his soldiers deserted him. ⁹Zedekiah was taken to King Nebuchadnezzar, who was in the city of Riblah in the territory of Hamath, and there Nebuchadnezzar passed sentence on him. ¹⁰At Riblah he put Zedekiah's sons to death while Zedekiah was looking on and he also had the officials of Judah executed. ¹¹After that, he had Zedekiah's eyes put out and had him placed in chains and taken to Babylon. Zedekiah remained in prison in Babylon until the day he died.

The Destruction of the Temple
(2 *Kings* 25.8-17)

¹²On the tenth day of the fifth month of the nineteenth year of King Nebuchadnezzar of Babylonia, Nebuzaradan, adviser to the king and commander of his army, entered Jerusalem. ¹³He burned down the Temple, the palace, and the houses of all the important people in Jerusalem; ¹⁴and his soldiers tore down the city walls. ¹⁵Then Nebuzaradan took away to Babylonia⁹ the people who were left in the city, the remaining skilled workers, and those who had deserted to the Babylonians. ¹⁶But he left in Judah some of the poorest people, who owned

⁹ *Probable text* Babylonia; *Hebrew* Babylonia some of the poorest of the people.

52.4 Ez 24.2　**52.7** Ez 33.21　**52.11** Ez 12.13　**52.13** 1 K 9.8

So the people of Judah were carried away. (52.27)

no property, and he put them to work in the vineyards and fields.

17 The Babylonians broke in pieces the bronze columns and the carts that were in the Temple, together with the large bronze tank, and they took all the bronze to Babylon. 18 They also took away the shovels and the ash containers used in cleaning the altar, the tools used in tending the lamps, the bowls used for catching the blood from the sacrifices, the bowls used for burning incense, and all the other bronze articles used in the Temple service. 19 They took away everything that was made of gold or silver: the small bowls, the pans used for carrying live coals, the bowls for holding the blood from the sacrifices, the ash containers, the lampstands, the bowls used for incense, and the bowls used for pouring out wine offerings. 20 The bronze objects that King Solomon had made for the Temple — the two columns, the carts, the large tank, and the twelve bulls that supported it — were too heavy to weigh. 21-22 The two columns were identical: each one was 27 feet high and 18 feet around. They were hollow, and the metal was 3 inches thick. On top of each column was a bronze capital 7½ feet high, and all around it was a grillwork decorated with pomegranates, all of which was also made of bronze. 23 On the grillwork of each column there were a hundred pomegranates in all, and ninety-six of these were visible from the ground.

The People of Judah Are Taken to Babylonia
(2 Kings 25.18-21, 27-30)

24 In addition, Nebuzaradan, the commanding officer, took away as prisoners Seraiah the High Priest, Zephaniah the priest next in rank, and the three other important Temple officials. 25 From the city he took the officer who had been in command of the troops, seven of the king's personal advisers who were still in the city, the commander's assistant, who was in charge of military records, and sixty other important men. 26 Nebuzaradan took them to the king of Babylonia, who was in the city of Riblah 27 in the territory of Hamath. There the king had them beaten and put to death.

So the people of Judah were carried away from their land into exile. 28 This is the record of the people that Nebuchadnezzar took away as prisoners: in his seventh year as king he carried away 3,023; 29 in his eighteenth year, 832 from Jerusalem; 30 and in his twenty-third year, 745 — taken away by Nebuzaradan. In all, 4,600 people were taken away.

31 In the year that Evil-merodach became king of Babylonia, he showed kindness to King Jehoiachin of Judah by releasing him from prison. This happened on the twenty-fifth day of the twelfth month of the thirty-seventh year after Jehoiachin had been taken

away as a prisoner. ³²Evil-merodach treated him kindly and gave him a position of greater honor than he gave the other kings who were exiles with him in Babylonia. ³³So Jehoiachin was per-mitted to change from his prison clothes and to dine at the king's table for the rest of his life. ³⁴Each day for as long as he lived, he was given a regular allowance for his needs.

LAMENTATIONS

INTRODUCTION

The book of *Lamentations* is a collection of five poems lamenting the destruction of Jerusalem in 586 B.C., and its aftermath of ruin and exile. In spite of the mournful nature of most of the book, there is also the note of trust in God and hope for the future. These poems are used by the Jews in worship on the annual days of fasting and mourning which commemorate the national disaster of 586 B.C.

OUTLINE OF CONTENTS

The Sorrows of Jerusalem

1 How lonely lies Jerusalem, once
        so full of people!
    Once honored by the world,
        she is now like a widow;
    The noblest of cities has fallen
        into slavery.

² All night long she cries; tears
        run down her cheeks.
    Of all her former friends, not
        one is left to comfort her.
    Her allies have betrayed her
        and are all against
        her now.

³ Judah's people are helpless
        slaves, forced away
        from home.ᵃ
    They live in other lands, with
        no place to call
        their own —
    Surrounded by enemies, with
        no way to escape.

⁴ No one comes to the Temple
        now to worship on the
        holy days.
    The young women
        who sang there suffer,
        and the priests
        can only groan.

ᵃ *are helpless . . . home; or* fled from home, from the misery of slavery.
1.1 Ba 4.12

Like a widow . . . all night long she cries. (1.1-2)

The city gates stand empty,
and Zion is in agony.

⁵Her enemies succeeded; they
hold her in their power.
The LORD has made her
suffer for all her many
sins;
Her children have been
captured and taken away.

⁶The splendor of Jerusalem is a
thing of the past.
Her leaders are like deer that
are weak from hunger,
Whose strength is almost
gone as they flee from
the hunters.

⁷A lonely ruin now, Jerusalem
recalls her ancient
splendor.
When she fell to the enemy,
there was no one to
help her;
Her conquerors laughed at
her downfall.

⁸Her honor is gone; she is naked
and held in contempt.
She groans and hides her face
in shame.

Jerusalem made herself filthy
with terrible sin.

⁹Her uncleanness was easily seen,
but she showed no concern
for her fate.
Her downfall was terrible; no
one can comfort her.
Her enemies have won, and
she cries to the LORD
for mercy.

¹⁰The enemies robbed her of all
her treasures.
She saw them enter the
Temple itself,
Where the LORD had
forbidden Gentiles to go.

¹¹Her people groan as they look for
something to eat;
They exchange their treasures
for food to keep themselves
alive.
"Look at me, LORD," the city
cries; "see me in my
misery."

¹²"Look at me!" she cries to
everyone who passes by.ᵇ
"No one has ever had pain
like mine,
Pain that the LORD brought
on me in the time of
his anger.

¹³"He sent fire from above, a fire
that burned inside me.
He set a trap for me and
brought me to the ground.
Then he abandoned me and
left me in constant pain.

¹⁴"He took note of all my sins and
tied them all together;
He hung them around my
neck, and I grew weak
beneath the weight.

ᵇ Look . . . by; *or* May this not happen to you that pass by; *or* Does this mean nothing
to you that pass by?

The Lord gave me to my foes,
and I was helpless against
them.

15 "The Lord laughed at all my
strongest soldiers;
He sent an army to destroy
my young men.
He crushed my people like
grapes in a wine press.

16 "That is why my eyes are
overflowing with tears.
No one can comfort me; no
one can give me courage.
The enemy has conquered
me; my people have
nothing left.

17 "I stretch out my hands, but no
one will help me.
The LORD has called enemies
against me from every side;
They treat me like some filthy
thing.

18 "But the LORD is just, for I have
disobeyed him.
Listen to me, people
everywhere; look at me
in my pain.
My young men and women
have been taken away
captive.

19 "I called to my allies, but they
refused to help me.
The priests and the leaders
died in the city streets,
Looking for food to keep
themselves alive.

20 "Look, O LORD, at my agony, at
the anguish of my soul!
My heart is broken in sorrow
for my sins.

There is murder in the
streets; even indoors there
is death.

21 "Listen[c] to my groans; there is
no one to comfort me.
My enemies are glad that you
brought disaster on me.
Bring[d] the day you promised;
make my enemies suffer
as I do.

22 "Condemn them for all their
wickedness;
Punish them as you punished
me for my sins.
I groan in misery, and I am
sick at heart."

The Lord's Punishment of Jerusalem

2 The Lord in his anger has
covered Zion with
darkness.
Its heavenly splendor he has
turned into ruins.
On the day of his anger he
abandoned even his
Temple.

2 The Lord destroyed without
mercy every village
in Judah
And tore down the forts that
defended the land.
He brought disgrace on the
kingdom and its rulers.

3 In his fury he shattered the
strength of Israel;
He refused to help us when
the enemy came.
He raged against us like fire,
destroying everything.

4 He aimed his arrows at us like
an enemy;

---

c One ancient translation Listen; Hebrew They listened.   d One ancient translation
Bring; Hebrew You brought.

He killed all those who were
our joy and delight.
Here in Jerusalem we felt his
burning anger.

5 Like an enemy, the Lord has
destroyed Israel;
He has left her forts and
palaces in ruins.
He has brought on the people
of Judah unending sorrow.

6 He smashed to pieces the
Temple where we
worshiped him;
He has put an end to holy
days and Sabbaths.
King and priest alike have felt
the force of his anger.

7 The Lord rejected his altar and
deserted his holy Temple;
He allowed the enemy to tear
down its walls.
They shouted in victory where
once we had worshiped
in joy.

8 The LORD was determined that
the walls of Zion should
fall;
He measured them off to
make sure of total
destruction.
The towers and walls now lie
in ruins together.

9 The gates lie buried in rubble,
their bars smashed to
pieces.
The king and the noblemen
now are in exile.
The Law is no longer taught,
and the prophets have no
visions from the LORD.

10 Jerusalem's old men sit on the
ground in silence,
With dust on their heads and
sackcloth on their bodies.

Young women bow their
heads to the ground.

11 My eyes are worn out with
weeping; my soul is in
anguish.
I am exhausted with grief at
the destruction of my
people.
Children and babies are
fainting in the streets
of the city.

12 Hungry and thirsty, they cry to
their mothers;
They fall in the streets as
though they were
wounded,
And slowly die in their
mothers' arms.

13 O Jerusalem, beloved Jerusalem,
what can I say?
How can I comfort you? No
one has ever suffered
like this.
Your disaster is boundless as
the ocean; there is no
possible hope.

14 Your prophets had nothing to tell
you but lies;
Their preaching deceived you
by never exposing your sin.
They made you think you did
not need to repent.

15 People passing by the city look at
you in scorn.
They shake their heads and
laugh at Jerusalem's ruins:
"Is this that lovely city? Is this
the pride of the world?"

16 All your enemies mock you and
glare at you with hate.
They curl their lips and sneer,
"We have destroyed it!
This is the day we have
waited for!"

¹⁷The LORD has finally done what
 he threatened to do:
He has destroyed us without
 mercy, as he warned
 us long ago.
He gave our enemies victory,
 gave them joy at our
 downfall.

¹⁸O Jerusalem, let your very walls
 cry out to the Lord!^e
Let your tears flow like rivers
 night and day;
Wear yourself out with
 weeping and grief!

¹⁹All through the night get up
 again and again to cry
 out to the Lord;
Pour out your heart and beg
 him for mercy on your
 children—
Children starving to death on
 every street corner!

Get up again . . . to cry out to the Lord. (2.19)

²⁰Look, O LORD! Why are you
 punishing us like this?
Women are eating the bodies
 of the children they loved!
Priests and prophets are being
 killed in the Temple itself!

²¹Young and old alike lie dead in
 the streets,
Young men and women,
 killed by enemy swords.
You slaughtered them without
 mercy on the day of your
 anger.

²²You invited my enemies to hold a
 carnival of terror all
 around me,
And no one could escape on
 that day of your anger.
They murdered my children,
 whom I had raised and
 loved.

Punishment, Repentance, and Hope

3 I am one who knows what it is
 to be punished by God.
² He drove me deeper and
 deeper into darkness
³ And beat me again and again
 with merciless blows.

⁴He has left my flesh open and
 raw, and has broken
 my bones.
⁵ He has shut me in a prison of
 misery and anguish.
⁶ He has forced me to live in
 the stagnant darkness
 of death.

⁷He has bound me in chains; I
 am a prisoner with no
 hope of escape.
⁸ I cry aloud for help, but God
 refuses to listen;
⁹ I stagger as I walk; stone
 walls block me wherever
 I turn.

¹⁰He waited for me like a bear;
 he pounced on me
 like a lion.

^e *Probable text* O Jerusalem . . . Lord; *Hebrew* Their hearts cried out to the Lord, O wall
of Jerusalem.

11 He chased me off the road,
  tore me to pieces, and
  left me.
12 He drew his bow and made
  me the target for his
  arrows.

God refuses to listen. (3.8)

13 He shot his arrows deep into my
  body.
14 People laugh at me all day
  long; I am a joke to
  them all.
15 Bitter suffering is all he has
  given me for food and
  drink.

16 He rubbed my face in the ground
  and broke my teeth
  on rocks.
17 I have forgotten what health
  and peace and
  happiness are.
18 I do not have much longer to
  live; my hope in the LORD
  is gone.

19 The thought of my pain, my
  homelessness, is
  bitter poison.

20 I think of it constantly, and
  my spirit is depressed.
21 Yet hope returns when I
  remember this one thing:

22 The LORD's unfailing love and
  mercy still continue,
23 Fresh as the morning, as sure
  as the sunrise.
24 The LORD is all I have, and so
  in him I put my hope.

25 The LORD is good to everyone
  who trusts in him,
26 So it is best for us to wait in
  patience — to wait for him
  to save us —
27 And it is best to learn this
  patience in our youth.

28 When we suffer, we should sit
  alone in silent patience;
29 We should bow in submission,
  for there may still be hope.
30 Though beaten and insulted,
  we should accept it all.

31 The Lord is merciful and will not
  reject us forever.
32 He may bring us sorrow, but
  his love for us is sure
  and strong.
33 He takes no pleasure in
  causing us grief or pain.

34 The Lord knows when our spirits
  are crushed in prison;
35 He knows when we are
  denied the rights he
  gave us;
36 When justice is perverted in
  court, he knows.

37 The will of the Lord alone is
  always carried out.*f*
38 Good and evil alike take place
  at his command.

f The will . . . out; *or* No one can make anything happen unless the Lord is willing.

39 Why should we ever complain
    when we are punished
    for our sin?*g*

40 Let us examine our ways and
    turn back to the LORD.
41 Let us open our hearts to God
    in heaven and pray,
42 "We have sinned and rebelled,
    and you, O LORD, have
    not forgiven us.

43 "You pursued us and killed us;
    your mercy was hidden
    by your anger,
44 By a cloud of fury too thick
    for our prayers to get
    through.
45 You have made us the
    garbage dump of the world.

46 "We are insulted and mocked by
    all our enemies.
47 We have been through
    disaster and ruin; we live
    in danger and fear.
48 My eyes flow with rivers of
    tears at the destruction
    of my people.

49 "My tears will pour out in a
    ceaseless stream
50 Until the LORD looks down
    from heaven and sees us.
51 My heart is grieved when I
    see what has happened to
    the women of the city.

52 "I was trapped like a bird by
    enemies who had no cause
    to hate me.
53 They threw me alive into a pit
    and closed the opening
    with a stone.
54 Water began to close over me,
    and I thought death was
    near.

55 "From the bottom of the pit,
    O LORD, I cried out to you,
56 And when I begged you to
    listen to my cry, you heard.
57 You answered me and told me
    not to be afraid.

58 "You came to my rescue, Lord,
    and saved my life.
59 Judge in my favor; you know
    the wrongs done
    against me.
60 You know how my enemies
    hate me and how they
    plot against me.

61 "You have heard them insult me,
    O LORD; you know all
    their plots.
62 All day long they talk about
    me and make their plans.
63 From morning till night they
    make fun of me.

64 "Punish them for what they have
    done, O LORD;
65 Curse them and fill them with
    despair!
66 Hunt them down and wipe
    them off the earth!"

Jerusalem after Its Fall

4 Our glittering gold has grown
    dull;
    the stones of the Temple lie
    scattered in the streets.

2 Zion's young people were as
    precious to us as gold,
    but now they are treated like
    common clay pots.

3 Even a mother wolf will nurse
    her cubs,
    but my people are like
    ostriches, cruel to their
    young.

g Why should . . . sin?; *or* Why should we complain about being punished for sin, as long as we are still alive?

⁴They let their babies die of
hunger and thirst;
children are begging for food
that no one will give them.

⁵People who once ate the finest
foods die starving in
the streets;
those raised in luxury are
pawing through garbage
for food.

⁶My people have been punished
even more than the
inhabitants of Sodom,
which met a sudden downfall
at the hands of God.

⁷Our princes*ʰ* were undefiled and
pure as snow,
vigorous and strong, glowing
with health.

⁸Now they lie unknown in the
streets, their faces
blackened in death;
their skin, dry as wood, has
shriveled on their bones.

⁹Those who died in the war were
better off than those who
died later,
who starved slowly to death,
with no food to keep
them alive.

¹⁰The disaster that came to my
people brought horror;
loving mothers boiled their
own children for food.

¹¹The LORD turned loose the full
force of his fury;
he lit a fire in Zion that
burned it to the ground.

¹²No one anywhere, not even
rulers of foreign nations,

believed that any invader
could enter Jerusalem's
gates.

¹³But it happened, because her
prophets sinned and her
priests were guilty
of causing the death of
innocent people.

¹⁴Her leaders wandered through
the streets as though blind,
so stained with blood that no
one would touch them.

¹⁵"Get away!" people shouted.
"You're defiled! Don't
touch me!"
So they wandered from nation
to nation, welcomed by
no one.

¹⁶The LORD had no more concern
for them; he scattered
them himself.
He showed no regard for our
priests and leaders.

¹⁷For help that never came, we
looked until we could
look no longer.
We kept waiting for help from
a nation that had none to
give.

¹⁸The enemy was watching for us;
we could not even walk
in the streets.
Our days were over; the end
had come.

¹⁹Swifter than eagles swooping
from the sky, they chased
us down.
They tracked us down in the
hills; they took us by
surprise in the desert.

ʰ princes; *or* Nazirites.
4.6 Gn 19.24   **4.10** Dt 28.57; Ez 5.10

20 They captured the source of our
life, the king the LORD
had chosen,
the one we had trusted to
protect us from every
invader.

21 Laugh on, people of Edom and
Uz; be glad while you can.
Your disaster is coming too;
you too will stagger naked
in shame.

22 Zion has paid for her sin; the
LORD will not keep us
in exile any longer.
But Edom, the LORD will
punish you; he will expose
your guilty acts.

A Prayer for Mercy

5 Remember, O LORD, what has
happened to us.
Look at us, and see our
disgrace.

2 Our property is in the hands of
strangers;
foreigners are living in our
homes.

3 Our fathers have been killed by
the enemy,
and now our mothers are
widows.

4 We must pay for the water we
drink;
we must buy the wood we
need for fuel.

5 Driven hard like donkeys or
camels,
we are tired, but are allowed
no rest.

6 To get food enough to stay alive,
we went begging to Egypt
and Assyria.

7 Our ancestors sinned, but now
they are gone,
and we are suffering for their
sins.

8 Our rulers are no better than
slaves,
and no one can save us from
their power.

9 Murderers roam through the
countryside;
we risk our lives when we
look for food.

10 Hunger has made us burn with
fever
until our skin is as hot as an
oven.

11 Our wives have been raped on
Mount Zion itself;
in every Judean village our
daughters have been
forced to submit.

12 Our leaders have been taken and
hanged;
our elders are shown no
respect.

13 Our young men are forced to
grind grain like slaves;
boys go staggering under
heavy loads of wood.

14 The old people no longer sit at
the city gate,
and the young people no
longer make music.

15 Happiness has gone out of our
lives;
grief has taken the place of
our dances.

16 Nothing is left of all we were
proud of.
We sinned, and now we are
doomed.

¹⁷We are sick at our very hearts
and can hardly see through
our tears,

¹⁸because Mount Zion lies lonely
and deserted,
and wild jackals prowl
through its ruins.

¹⁹But you, O LORD, are king
forever
and will rule to the end of
time.

²⁰Why have you abandoned us so
long?
Will you ever remember us
again?

²¹Bring us back to you, LORD!
Bring us back!
Restore our ancient glory.

²²Or have you rejected us forever?
Is there no limit to your
anger?

The Book of
EZEKIEL

INTRODUCTION

The prophet Ezekiel lived in exile in Babylon during the period before and after the fall of Jerusalem in 586 B.C. His message was addressed both to the exiles in Babylonia and to the people of Jerusalem. *The Book of Ezekiel* has six principal parts: 1) God's call to Ezekiel to be a prophet. 2) Warnings to the people about God's judgment on them and about the coming fall and destruction of Jerusalem. 3) Messages from the Lord regarding his judgment upon the various nations that oppressed and misled his people. 4) Comfort for Israel after the fall of Jerusalem and the promise of a brighter future. 5) The prophecy against Gog. 6) Ezekiel's picture of a restored Temple and nation.

Ezekiel was a man of deep faith and great imagination. Many of his insights came in the form of visions, and many of his messages were expressed in vivid symbolic actions. Ezekiel emphasized the need for inner renewal of the heart and spirit, and the responsibility of each individual for his own sins. He also proclaimed his hope for the renewal of the life of the nation. As a priest, as well as prophet, he had special interest in the Temple and in the need for holiness.

OUTLINE OF CONTENTS

EZEKIEL'S FIRST VISION OF GOD
(1.1 – 7.27)

God's Throne

1 On the fifth day of the fourth month of the thirtieth year,[a] I, Ezekiel the priest, son of Buzi, was living with the Jewish exiles by the Chebar River in Babylonia. The sky opened, and I saw a vision of God. (² It was the fifth year since King Jehoiachin had been taken into exile.) ³ There in Babylonia beside the Chebar River, I heard the LORD speak to me, and I felt his power.

⁴ I looked up and saw a windstorm coming from the north. Lightning was flashing from a huge cloud, and the sky around it was glowing. Where the lightning was flashing, something shone like bronze. ⁵ At the center of the storm I saw what looked like four living

---

a **THIRTIETH YEAR:** *It is not known to what year this refers.*
1.1 Rev 19.11   **1.2** 2 K 24.10-16; 2 Ch 36.9, 10   **1.5** Rev 4.6

creatures in human form, [6] but each of them had four faces and four wings. [7] Their legs were straight, and they had hoofs like those of a bull. They shone like polished bronze. [8] In addition to their four faces and four wings, they each had four human hands, one under each wing. [9] Two wings of each creature were spread out so that the creatures formed a square, with their wing tips touching. When they moved, they moved as a group without turning their bodies.

[10] Each living creature had four different faces: a human face in front, a lion's face at the right, a bull's face at the left, and an eagle's face at the back. [11] Two wings[b] of each creature were raised so that they touched the tips of the wings of the creatures next to it, and their other two wings were folded against their bodies. [12] Each creature faced all four directions, and so the group could go wherever they wished, without having to turn.

[13] Among[c] the creatures there was something that looked like a blazing torch, constantly moving. The fire would blaze up and shoot out flashes of lightning. [14] The creatures themselves darted back and forth with the speed of lightning.

[15] As I was looking at the four creatures I saw four wheels touching the ground, one beside each of them.[d] [16] All four wheels were alike; each one shone like a precious stone, and each had another wheel intersecting it at right angles, [17] so that the wheels could move in any of the four directions. [18] The rims of the wheels were covered with eyes.[e] [19] Whenever the creatures moved, the wheels moved with them, and if the creatures rose up from the earth, so did the wheels. [20] The crea-

tures went wherever they wished, and the wheels did exactly what the creatures did, because the creatures controlled them. [21] So every time the creatures moved or stopped or rose in the air, the wheels did exactly the same.

[22] Above the heads of the creatures there was something that looked like a dome made of dazzling crystal. [23] There under the dome stood the creatures, each stretching out two wings toward the ones next to it and covering its body with the other two wings. [24] I heard the noise their wings made in flight; it sounded like the roar of the sea, like the noise of a huge army, like the voice of Almighty God. When they stopped flying, they folded their wings, [25] but there was still a sound coming from above the dome over their heads.

[26] Above the dome there was something that looked like a throne made of sapphire, and sitting on the throne was a figure that looked like a human being. [27] The figure seemed to be shining like bronze in the middle of a fire. It shone all over with a bright light [28] that had in it all the colors of the rainbow. This was the dazzling light which shows the presence of the LORD.

God Calls Ezekiel to Be a Prophet

When I saw this, I fell face downward on the ground. Then I heard a voice [1] saying, "Mortal man, stand up. I want to talk to you." [2] While the voice was speaking, God's spirit entered me and raised me to my feet, and I heard the voice continue, [3] "Mortal man, I am sending you to the people of Israel. They have rebelled and turned against me and are still rebels, just as their ancestors were. [4] They are stub-

---

[b] *Some ancient translations* Two wings; *Hebrew* Their faces, their wings.   [c] *Some ancient translations* Among; *Hebrew* And the likeness of.   [d] *Some ancient translations* them; *Hebrew* their faces.   [e] *Verse 18 in Hebrew is unclear.*

1.10 Ez 10.14; Rev 4.7   **1.13** Rev 4.5   **1.15-21** Ez 10.9-13   **1.18** Rev 4.8   **1.22** Rev 4.6   **1.24** Rev 1.4-15; 19.6   **1.26** Ez 10.1; Rev 4.2, 3   **1.27** Ez 8.2

born and do not respect me, so I am sending you to tell them what I, the Sovereign LORD, am saying to them. Whether those rebels listen to you or not, they will know that a prophet has been among them.

6 "But you, mortal man, must not be afraid of them or of anything they say. They will defy and despise you; it will be like living among scorpions. Still, don't be afraid of those rebels or of anything they say. 7 You will tell them whatever I tell you to say, whether they listen or not. Remember what rebels they are.

8 "Mortal man, listen to what I tell you. Don't be rebellious like them. Open your mouth and eat what I am going to give you." 9 I saw a hand reaching out toward me, and it was holding a

I saw a hand reaching out toward me. (2.9)

scroll. 10 The hand unrolled the scroll, and I saw that there was writing on both sides — cries of grief were written there, and wails and groans.

3 God said, "Mortal man, eat this scroll; then go and speak to the people of Israel."

2 So I opened my mouth, and he gave me the scroll to eat. 3 He said, "Mortal man, eat this scroll that I give you; fill your stomach with it." I ate it, and it tasted as sweet as honey.

4 Then God said, "Mortal man, go to the people of Israel and say to them whatever I tell you to say. 5 I am not sending you to a nation that speaks a difficult foreign language, but to the Israelites. 6 If I sent you to great nations that spoke difficult languages you didn't understand, they would listen to you. 7 But none of the people of Israel will be willing to listen; they will not even listen to me. All of them are stubborn and defiant. 8 Now I will make you as stubborn and as tough as they are. 9 I will make you as firm as a rock, as hard as a diamond; don't be afraid of those rebels."

10 God continued, "Mortal man, pay close attention and remember everything I tell you. 11 Then go to the people of your nation who are in exile and tell them what I, the Sovereign LORD, am saying to them, whether they pay attention to you or not."

12 Then God's spirit lifted me up, and I heard behind me the loud roar of a voice that said, "Praise the glory of the LORD in heaven above!" 13 I heard the wings of the creatures beating together in the air, and the noise of the wheels, as loud as an earthquake. 14 The power of the LORD came on me with great force, and as his spirit carried me off, I felt bitter and angry. 15 So I came to Tel Abib beside the Chebar River, where the exiles were living, and for seven days I stayed there, overcome by what I had seen and heard.

The LORD Appoints Ezekiel as a Lookout
(Ezekiel 33.1-9)

16 After the seven days had passed, the LORD spoke to me. 17 "Mortal man," he said, "I am making you a lookout for the nation of Israel. You will pass on to them the warnings I give you. 18 If I

2.9, 10 Rev 5.1   **3.1-3** Rev 10.9, 10

announce that someone evil is going to die but you do not warn him to change his ways so that he can save his life, he will die, still a sinner, but I will hold you responsible for his death. ¹⁹ If you do warn an evil man and he doesn't stop sinning, he will die, still a sinner, but your life will be spared.

²⁰ "If someone truly good starts doing evil and I put him in a dangerous situation, he will die if you do not warn him. He will die because of his sins — I will not remember the good he did — and I will hold you responsible for his death. ²¹ If you do warn a good man not to sin and he listens to you and doesn't sin, he will stay alive, and your life will also be spared."

But God's spirit entered me and raised me to my feet. (3.24)

Ezekiel Will Be Unable to Talk

²² I felt the powerful presence of the LORD and heard him say to me, "Get up and go out into the valley. I will talk to you there."

²³ So I went out into the valley, and there I saw the glory of the LORD, just as I had seen it beside the Chebar River. I fell face downward on the ground, ²⁴ but God's spirit entered me and raised me to my feet. The LORD said to me, "Go home and shut yourself up in the house. ²⁵ You will be tied with ropes, mortal man, and you will not be able to go out in public. ²⁶ I will paralyze your tongue so that you won't be able to warn these rebellious people. ²⁷ Then, when I speak to you again and give you back the power of speech, you will tell them what I, the Sovereign LORD, am saying. Some of them will listen, but some will ignore you, for they are a nation of rebels."

Ezekiel Acts Out the Siege of Jerusalem

4 God said, "Mortal man, get a brick, put it in front of you, and scratch lines on it to represent the city of Jerusalem. ² Then, to represent a siege, put trenches, earthworks, camps, and battering rams all around it. ³ Take an iron pan and set it up like a wall between you and the city. Face the city. It is under siege, and you are the one besieging it. This will be a sign to the nation of Israel.

⁴⁻⁵ "Then lie down on your left side, and I𝑓 will place on you the guilt of the nation of Israel. For 390 days you will stay there and suffer because of their guilt. I have sentenced you to one day for each year their punishment will last. ⁶ When you finish that, turn over on your right side and suffer for the guilt of Judah for forty days — one day for each year of their punishment.

⁷ "Fix your eyes on the siege of Jerusalem. Shake your fist at the city and prophesy against it. ⁸ I will tie you up so that you cannot turn from one side to the other until the siege is over.

⁹ "Now take some wheat, barley, beans, peas, millet, and spelt. Mix them all together and make bread. That is what you are to eat during the 390 days you are lying on your left side. ¹⁰ You will be allowed eight ounces of bread a day, and it will have to last until the

_____

𝑓 Probable text I; Hebrew you.

Shake your fist at the city and prophesy against it. (4.7)

next day. ¹¹ You will also have a limited amount of water to drink, two cups a day. ¹² You are to build a fire out of dried human excrement, bake bread on the fire, and eat it where everyone can see you."

¹³ The LORD said, "This represents the way the Israelites will have to eat food which the Law forbids,ᵍ when I scatter them to foreign countries."

¹⁴ But I replied, "No, Sovereign LORD! I have never defiled myself. From childhood on I have never eaten meat from any animal that died a natural death or was killed by wild animals. I have never eaten any food considered unclean."

¹⁵ So God said, "Very well. I will let you use cow dung instead, and you can bake your bread on that."

¹⁶ And he added, "Mortal man, I am going to cut off the supply of bread for Jerusalem. The people there will be distressed and anxious as they measure out the food they eat and the water they drink. ¹⁷ They will run out of bread and water; they will be in despair, and they will waste away because of their sins."

Ezekiel Cuts His Hair

5 The LORD said, "Mortal man, take a sharp sword and use it to shave off your beard and all your hair. Then weigh the hair on scales and divide it into three parts. ² Burn up a third of it in the city when the siege is over. Take another third and chop it up with your sword as you move around outside the city. Scatter the remaining third to the winds, and I will pursue it with my sword. ³ Keep back a few hairs and wrap them in the hem of your clothes. ⁴ Then take a few of them out again, throw them in the fire, and let them burn up. From them fire will spread to the whole nation of Israel."

⁵ The Sovereign LORD said, "Look at Jerusalem. I put her at the center of the world, with other countries all around her. ⁶ But Jerusalem rebelled against my commands and showed that she was more wicked than the other nations, more disobedient than the countries around her. Jerusalem rejected my commands and refused to keep my laws. ⁷ Now listen, Jerusalem, to what I, the Sovereign LORD, am saying. By not obeying my laws or keeping my commands, you have caused more trouble than the nations around you. You have followed the customs of other nations. ⁸ And so I, the Sovereign LORD, am telling you that I am your enemy. I will pass judgment on you where all the nations can see it. ⁹ Because of all the things you do that I hate, I will punish Jerusalem as I have never done before and will never do again. ¹⁰ As a result, parents in Jerusalem will eat their children, and children will eat their parents. I will punish you and scatter in every direction any who are left alive.

¹¹ "Therefore, as I am the living God — this is the word of the Sovereign LORD — because you defiled my Temple with all the evil, disgusting things you did, I will cut you down without mercy. ¹² A third of your people will die from sickness and hunger in the city; a third will be cut down by swords outside the city; and I will scatter the last third to the winds and pursue them with a sword.

ᵍ FOOD WHICH THE LAW FORBIDS: *The Law of Moses prohibited the eating of certain foods as being ritually unclean (see Lv 11).*
5.10 Lm 4.10

13"You will feel all the force of my anger and rage until I am satisfied. When all this happens, you will be convinced that I, the LORD, have spoken to you because I am outraged at your unfaithfulness. 14 Everyone from the nations around you who passes by will sneer at you and keep their distance.

15"When I am angry and furious with you and punish you, all the nations around you will be terrified. They will look at you with disgust and make fun of you. 16 I will cut off your supply of food and let you starve. You[h] will feel the pains of hunger like sharp arrows sent to destroy you. 17 I will send hunger and wild animals to kill your children, and will send sickness, violence, and war to kill you. I, the LORD, have spoken."

The LORD Condemns Idolatry

6 The LORD spoke to me. 2"Mortal man," he said, "look toward the mountains of Israel and give them my message. 3 Tell the mountains of Israel to hear the Sovereign LORD's word — to hear what I, the Sovereign LORD, am telling the mountains, the hills, the gorges, and the valleys: I will send a sword to destroy the places where people worship idols. 4 The altars will be torn down and the incense altars broken. All the people there will be killed in front of their idols. 5 I will scatter the corpses of the people of Israel; I will scatter their bones all around the altars. 6 All the cities of Israel will be destroyed, so that all their altars and their idols will be smashed to pieces, their incense altars will be shattered, and everything they made will disappear. 7 People will be killed everywhere, and those who survive will acknowledge that I am the LORD.

8"I will let some escape the slaughter and be scattered among the nations, 9 where they will live in exile. There they will remember me and know that I have punished them and disgraced them,[i] because their faithless hearts deserted me and they preferred idols to me. And they will be disgusted with themselves because of the evil and degrading things they have done. 10 They will know that I am the LORD and that my warnings were not empty threats."

11 The Sovereign LORD said, "Wring your hands! Stamp your feet! Cry in

h *Probable text* You; *Hebrew* They.   i *Some ancient translations* disgraced them; *Hebrew* I am disgraced.
5.17 Rev 6.8

Corpses will be scattered among the idols. (6.13)

sorrow because of all the evil, disgusting things the Israelites have done. They are going to die in war or of starvation or disease. 12 Those far away will get sick and die; those nearby will be killed in war; those who survive will starve to death. They will feel all the force of my anger. 13 Corpses will be scattered among the idols and around the altars, scattered on every high hill, on the top of every mountain, under every green tree and every large oak, in every place where they burned sacrifices to their idols. Then everyone will know that I am the LORD. 14 Yes, I will reach out and destroy their country. I will make it a wasteland from the southern desert to the city of Riblah in the north, not sparing any place where the Israelites live. Then everyone will know that I am the LORD."

The End Is Near for Israel

7 The LORD spoke to me. 2 "Mortal man," he said, "this is what I, the Sovereign LORD, am saying to the land of Israel: This is the end for the whole land!

3 "Israel, the end has come. You will feel my anger, because I am judging you for what you have done. I will pay you back for all your disgusting conduct. 4 I will not spare you or show you any mercy. I am going to punish you for the disgusting things you have done, so that you will know that I am the LORD."

5 This is what the Sovereign LORD is saying: "One disaster after another is coming on you. 6 It's all over. This is the end. You are finished. 7 The end is coming for you people who live in the land. The time is near when there will be no more celebrations at the mountain shrines, only confusion.*j*

8 "Very soon now you will feel all the force of my anger. I am judging you for what you have done, and I will pay you back for all your disgusting conduct. 9 I will not spare you or show you any mercy. I am going to punish you for the disgusting things you have done, so that you will know that I am the LORD and that I am the one who punishes you."

10 The day of disaster is coming. Violence is flourishing. Pride is at its height.*k* 11 Violence produces more wickedness. Nothing of theirs will remain, nothing of their wealth, their splendor, or their glory.

12 The time is coming. The day is near when buying and selling will have no more meaning, because God's punishment will fall on everyone alike. 13 No merchants will live long enough to get back what they have lost, because God's anger is on everyone. Those who are evil cannot survive.*l* 14 The trumpet blows, and everyone gets ready. But no one goes off to war, for God's anger will fall on everyone alike.

Punishment for Israel's Sins

15 There is fighting in the streets, and sickness and hunger in the houses. Anyone who is out in the country will die in the fighting, and anyone in the city will be a victim of sickness and hunger. 16 Some will escape to the mountains like doves frightened from

Some will escape to the mountains. (7.16)

---

j Probable text celebrations . . . confusion; *Hebrew unclear.* 　　*k Probable text* Pride is at its height; *Hebrew unclear.* 　　*l Verse 13 in Hebrew is unclear.*

the valleys. All of them will moan over their sins.[m] [17] Everyone's hands will be weak, and their knees will shake. [18] They will put on sackcloth and they will tremble all over. Their heads will be shaved, and they will all be disgraced. [19] They will throw their gold and silver away in the streets like garbage, because neither silver nor gold can save them when the LORD pours out his fury. They cannot use it to satisfy their desires or fill their stomachs. Gold and silver led them into sin. [20] Once they were proud of their beautiful jewels, but they used them to make disgusting idols. That is why the LORD has made their wealth repulsive to them.

[21] "I will let foreigners rob them," says the LORD, "and lawbreakers will take all their wealth and defile it. [22] I will not interfere when my treasured Temple is profaned, when robbers break into it and defile it.

[23] "Everything is in confusion[n] — the land is full of murders and the cities are full of violence. [24] I will bring the most evil nations here and let them have your homes. Your strongest men will lose their confidence when I let the nations profane the places where you worship. [25] Despair is coming. You will look for peace and never find it. [26] One disaster will follow another, and a steady stream of bad news will pour in. You will beg the prophets to reveal what they foresee. The priests will have nothing to teach the people, and the elders will have no advice to give. [27] The king will mourn, the prince will give up hope, and the people will shake with fear. I will punish you for all you have done, and will judge you in the same way as you have judged others. This will show you that I am the LORD."

EZEKIEL'S SECOND VISION OF GOD (8.1 — 10.22)

Idolatry in Jerusalem

8 On the fifth day of the sixth month of the sixth year of our exile, the leaders of the exiles from Judah were sitting in my house with me. Suddenly the power of the Sovereign LORD came on me. [2] I looked up and saw a vision of a fiery human form. From the waist down his body looked like fire, and from the waist up he was shining like polished bronze. [3] He reached out what seemed to be a hand and grabbed me by the hair. Then in this vision God's spirit lifted me high in the air and took me to Jerusalem. He took me to the inner entrance of the north gate of the Temple, where there was an idol that was an outrage to God.

[4] There I saw the dazzling light that shows the presence of Israel's God, just as I had seen it when I was by the Chebar River. [5] God said to me, "Mortal man, look toward the north." I looked, and there near the altar by the entrance of the gateway I saw the idol that was an outrage to God.

[6] God said to me, "Mortal man, do you see what is happening? Look at the disgusting things the people of Israel are doing here, driving me farther and farther away from my holy place. You will see even more disgraceful things than this."

[7] He took me to the entrance of the outer courtyard and showed me a hole in the wall. [8] He said, "Mortal man, break through the wall here." I broke through it and found a door. [9] He told me, "Go in and look at the evil, disgusting things they are doing there." [10] So I went in and looked. The walls were covered with drawings of snakes and other

---

[m] *Verse 16 in Hebrew is unclear.*   [n] *One ancient translation* Everything is in confusion; *Hebrew unclear.*

8.2 Ez 1.27   **8.4** Ez 1.28

unclean animals,*o* and of the other things which the Israelites were worshiping. ¹¹ Seventy Israelite leaders were there, including Jaazaniah son of Shaphan. Each one was holding an incense burner, and smoke was rising from the incense. ¹² God asked me, "Mortal man, do you see what the Israelite leaders are doing in secret? They are all worshiping in a room full of images. Their excuse is: 'The LORD doesn't see us! He has abandoned the country.'"

¹³ Then the LORD said to me, "You are going to see them do even more disgusting things than that." ¹⁴ So he took me to the north gate of the Temple and showed me women weeping over the death of the god Tammuz.*p*

¹⁵ He asked, "Mortal man, do you see that? You will see even more disgusting things." ¹⁶ So he took me to the inner courtyard of the Temple. There near the entrance of the sanctuary, between the altar and the porch, were about twenty-five men. They had turned their backs to the sanctuary and were bowing low toward the east, worshiping the rising sun.

¹⁷ The LORD said to me, "Mortal man, do you see that? These people of Judah are not satisfied with merely doing all the disgusting things you have seen here and with spreading violence throughout the country. No, they must come and do them right here in the Temple and make me even more angry. Look how they insult me in the most offensive way possible!*q* ¹⁸ They will feel all the force of my anger. I will not spare them or show them any mercy. They will shout prayers to me as loud as they can, but I will not listen to them."

Jerusalem Is Punished

9 Then I heard God shout, "Come here, you men who are going to punish the city. Bring your weapons with you." ² At once six men came from the outer north gate of the Temple, each one carrying a weapon. With them was a man dressed in linen clothes, carrying something to write with. They all came and stood by the bronze altar.

³ Then the dazzling light of the presence of the God of Israel rose up from the winged creatures*r* where it had been, and moved to the entrance of the Temple. The LORD called to the man dressed in linen, ⁴ "Go through the whole city of Jerusalem and put a mark on the forehead of everyone who is distressed and troubled because of all the disgusting things being done in the city."

⁵ And I heard God say to the other men, "Follow him through the city and kill. Spare no one; have mercy on no one. ⁶ Kill the old men, young men, young women, mothers, and children. But don't touch anyone who has the mark on his forehead. Start here at my Temple." So they began with the leaders who were standing there at the Temple.

⁷ God said to them, "Defile the Temple. Fill its courtyards with corpses. Get to work!" So they began to kill the people in the city.*s*

⁸ While the killing was going on, I was there alone. I threw myself face downward on the ground and shouted, "Sovereign LORD, are you so angry with Jerusalem that you are going to kill everyone left in Israel?"

---

o UNCLEAN ANIMALS: *The Law of Moses prohibited the eating of certain animals as being ritually unclean (see 4.13; Lv 11).*   *p* TAMMUZ: *A god who was thought to die when vegetation died and to come to life the next year. Women would mourn his ritual death.*   *q* IN THE MOST OFFENSIVE WAY POSSIBLE: *A reference to a pagan rite of putting a branch to the nose.*   *r* WINGED CREATURES: *See 1.5-12.*   *s* work!" So they ... city.; *or* work! Go on and start killing the people in the city!"

9.4 Rev 7.3; 9.4; 14.1

[9] God answered, "The people of Israel and Judah are guilty of terrible sins. They have committed murder all over the land and have filled Jerusalem with crime. They say that I, the LORD, have abandoned their country and that I don't see them. [10] But I will not have pity on them; I will do to them what they have done to others."

[11] Then the man wearing linen clothes returned and reported to the LORD, "I have carried out your orders."

The Glory of the LORD Leaves the Temple

10 I looked at the dome over the heads of the living creatures[t] and above them was something that seemed to be a throne made of sapphire. [2] God said to the man wearing linen clothes, "Go between the wheels under the creatures and fill your hands with burning coals. Then scatter the coals over the city."

I watched him go. [3] The creatures were standing to the south of the Temple when he went in, and a cloud filled the inner courtyard. [4] The dazzling light of the LORD's presence rose up from the creatures and moved to the entrance of the Temple. Then the cloud filled the Temple, and the courtyard was blazing with the light. [5] The noise made by the creatures' wings was heard even in the outer courtyard. It sounded like the voice of Almighty God.

[6] When the LORD commanded the man wearing linen clothes to take some fire from between the wheels that were under the creatures, the man went in and stood by one of the wheels. [7] One of the creatures reached his hand into the fire that was there among them, picked up some coals, and put them in the

hands of the man in linen. The man took the coals and left.

[8] I saw that each creature had what looked like a human hand under each of its wings. [9-10] I also saw that there were four wheels, all alike, one beside each creature. The wheels shone like precious stones, and each one had another wheel which intersected it at right angles. [11] When the creatures moved, they could go in any direction without turning. They all moved together in the direction they wanted to go, without having to turn around. [12] Their bodies, backs, hands, wings, and wheels were covered with eyes. [13] I heard a voice calling out, "Whirling wheels."

[14] Each creature had four faces. The first was the face of a bull, the second a human face, the third the face of a lion, and the fourth the face of an eagle. [15] (They were the same creatures that I had seen by the Chebar River.) When the creatures rose in the air [16] and moved, the wheels went with them. Whenever they spread their wings to fly, the wheels still went with them. [17] When the creatures stopped, the wheels stopped; and when the creatures flew, the wheels went with them, because the creatures controlled them.

[18] Then the dazzling light of the LORD's presence left the entrance of the Temple and moved to a place above the creatures. [19] They spread their wings and flew up from the earth while I was watching, and the wheels went with them. They paused at the east gate of the Temple, and the dazzling light was over them. [20] I recognized them as the same creatures which I had seen beneath the God of Israel at the Chebar River.

[21] Each of them had four faces, four wings, and what looked like a human hand under each wing. [22] Their faces

---

[t] LIVING CREATURES: *See 1.5-12.*

10.1 Ez 1.26; Rev 4.2   **10.2** Rev 8.5   **10.9-13** Ez 1.15-21   **10.12** Rev 4.8   **10.14** Ez 1.10; Rev 4.7

looked exactly like the faces[u] I had seen by the Chebar River. Each creature moved straight ahead.

Jerusalem Is Condemned

11 God's spirit lifted me up and took me to the east gate of the Temple. There near the gate I saw twenty-five men, including Jaazaniah son of Azzur and Pelatiah son of Benaiah, two leaders of the nation.

2 God said to me, "Mortal man, these men make evil plans and give bad advice in this city. 3 They say, 'We will soon be building houses again.[v] The city is like a cooking pot, and we are like the meat in it, but at least it protects us from the fire.' 4 Now then, denounce them, mortal man."

5 The spirit of the LORD took control of me, and the LORD told me to give the people this message: "People of Israel, I know what you are saying and what you are planning. 6 You have murdered so many people here in the city that the streets are full of corpses.

7 "So this is what I, the Sovereign LORD, am saying to you. This city is a cooking pot all right, but what is the meat? The corpses of those you have killed! You will not be here — I will throw you out of the city! 8 Are you afraid of swords? I will bring soldiers with swords to attack you. 9 I will take you out of the city and hand you over to foreigners. I have sentenced you to death, 10 and you will be killed in battle in your own country. Then everyone will know that I am the LORD. 11 This city will not protect you the way a pot protects the meat in it. I will punish you wherever you may be in the land of Israel. 12 You will know that I am the LORD and that while you were keeping the laws of the neighboring nations,

you were breaking *my* laws and disobeying *my* commands."

13 While I was prophesying, Pelatiah dropped dead. I threw myself face downward on the ground and shouted, "No, Sovereign LORD! Are you going to kill everyone left in Israel?"

God's Promise to the Exiles

14 The LORD spoke to me. 15 "Mortal man," he said, "the people who live in Jerusalem are talking about you and those of your nation who are in exile. They say, 'The exiles are too far away to worship the LORD. He has given us possession of the land.'

16 "Now tell your fellow exiles what I am saying. I am the one who sent them to live in far-off nations and scattered them in other countries. Yet, for the time being I will be present with them in the lands where they have gone.

17 "So tell them what I, the Sovereign LORD, am saying. I will gather them out of the countries where I scattered them, and will give the land of Israel back to them. 18 When they return, they are to get rid of all the filthy, disgusting idols they find. 19 I will give them a new heart and a new mind. I will take away their stubborn heart of stone and will give them an obedient heart. 20 Then they will keep my laws and faithfully obey all my commands. They will be my people, and I will be their God. 21 But I will punish the people who love to worship filthy, disgusting idols. I will punish them for what they have done." The Sovereign LORD has spoken.

God's Glory Leaves Jerusalem

22 The living creatures began to fly, and the wheels went with them. The dazzling light of the presence of the God of Israel was over them. 23 Then the

---

[u] *Probable text* the faces; *Hebrew* the faces and them.   [v] We will . . . again; *or* We won't be building houses any time soon.

11.19, 20 Ez 36.26-28   **11.22, 23** Ez 43.2-5

In the vision . . . (11.24)

dazzling light left the city and moved to the mountain east of it. ²⁴ In the vision the spirit of God lifted me up and brought me back to the exiles in Babylonia. Then the vision faded, ²⁵ and I told the exiles everything that the LORD had shown me.

The Prophet as a Refugee

12 The LORD spoke to me. ²"Mortal man," he said, "you are living among rebellious people. They have

eyes, but they see nothing; they have ears, but they hear nothing, because they are rebellious.

³"Now, mortal man, pack a bundle just as a refugee would and start out before nightfall. Let everyone see you leaving and going to another place. Maybe those rebels will notice you.ʷ ⁴While it is still daylight, pack your bundle for exile, so that they can see you, and then let them watch you leave in the evening as if you were going into exile. ⁵While they are watching, break

ʷ Maybe those . . . you; *or* Maybe they will then realize that they are rebels.
12.2 Is 6.9, 10; Jr 5.21; Mk 8.18

a hole through the wall of your house and take your pack out through it. ⁶Let them watch you putting your pack on your shoulder and going out into the dark with your eyes covered, so that you can't see where you are going. What you do will be a warning to the Israelites."

⁷I did what the LORD told me to do. That day I packed a bundle as a refugee would, and that evening as it was getting dark I dug a hole in the wall with my hands and went out. While everyone watched, I put the pack on my shoulder and left.

⁸The next morning the LORD spoke to me. ⁹"Mortal man," he said, "now that those Israelite rebels are asking you what you're doing, ¹⁰tell them what I, the Sovereign LORD, am saying to them. This message is for the prince ruling in Jerusalem and for all the people who live there. ¹¹Tell them that what you have done is a sign of what will happen to them — they will be refugees and captives. ¹²The prince who is ruling them will shoulder his pack in the dark and escape through a hole that they dig for him in the wall. He will cover his eyes and not see where he is going. ¹³But I will spread out my net and trap him in it. Then I will take him to the city of Babylon, where he will die without having seen it. ¹⁴I will scatter in every direction all the members of his court and his advisers and bodyguards, and people will search for them to kill them.

¹⁵"When I scatter them among the other nations and in foreign countries, they will know that I am the LORD. ¹⁶I will let a few of them survive the war, the famine, and the diseases, so that there among the nations they will realize how disgusting their actions have been and will acknowledge that I am the LORD."

The Sign of the Trembling Prophet

¹⁷The LORD spoke to me. ¹⁸"Mortal man," he said, "tremble when you eat, and shake with fear when you drink. ¹⁹Tell the whole nation that this is the message of the Sovereign LORD to the people of Jerusalem who are still living in their land: They will tremble when they eat and shake with fear when they drink. Their land will be stripped bare, because everyone who lives there is lawless. ²⁰Cities that are now full of people will be destroyed, and the country will be made a wilderness. Then they will know that I am the LORD."

A Popular Proverb and an Unpopular Message

²¹The LORD spoke to me. ²²"Mortal man," he said, "why do the people of Israel repeat this proverb: 'Time goes by, and predictions come to nothing'? ²³Now tell them what I, the Sovereign LORD, have to say about that. I will put an end to that proverb. It won't be repeated in Israel any more. Tell them instead: The time has come, and the predictions are coming true!

²⁴"Among the people of Israel there will be no more false visions or misleading prophecies. ²⁵I, the LORD, will speak to them, and what I say will be done. There will be no more delay. In your own lifetime, you rebels, I will do what I have warned you I would do. I have spoken," says the Sovereign LORD.

²⁶The LORD said to me, ²⁷"Mortal man, the Israelites think that your visions and prophecies are about the distant future. ²⁸So tell them that I, the Sovereign LORD, am saying: There will be no more delay. What I have said will be done. I, the Sovereign LORD, have spoken!"

12.13 2 K 25.7; Jr 52.11

Prophecy against False Male Prophets

13 The LORD spoke to me. [2]"Mortal man," he said, "denounce the prophets of Israel who make up their own prophecies. Tell them to listen to the word of the LORD."

[3]This is what the Sovereign LORD says: "These foolish prophets are doomed! They provide their own inspiration and invent their own visions. [4]People of Israel, your prophets are as useless as foxes living among the ruins of a city. [5]They don't guard the places where the walls have crumbled, nor do they rebuild the walls, and so Israel cannot be defended when war comes on the day of the LORD. [6]Their visions are false, and their predictions are lies. They claim that they are speaking my message, but I have not sent them. Yet they expect their words to come true! [7]I tell them: Those visions you see are false, and the predictions you make are lies. You say that they are my words, but I haven't spoken to you!"

[8]So the Sovereign LORD says to them, "Your words are false, and your visions are lies. I am against you. [9]I am about to punish you prophets who have false visions and make misleading predictions. You will not be there when my people gather to make decisions; your names will not be included in the list of the citizens of Israel; you will never return to your land. Then you will know that I am the Sovereign LORD.

[10]"The prophets mislead my people by saying that all is well. All is certainly not well! My people have put up a wall of loose stones, and then the prophets have come and covered it with whitewash. [11]Tell the prophets that their wall is going to fall down. I will send a pouring rain. Hailstones will fall on it, and a strong wind will blow against it. [12]The wall will collapse, and everyone will ask you what good the whitewash did."

[13]Now this is what the Sovereign LORD says: "In my anger I will send a strong wind, pouring rain, and hailstones to destroy the wall. [14]I intend to

I will send a strong wind, pouring rain, and hailstones to destroy the wall. (13.13)

break down the wall they whitewashed, to shatter it, and to leave the foundation stones bare. It will collapse and kill you all. Then everyone will know that I am the LORD.

[15]"The wall and those who covered it with whitewash will feel the force of my anger. Then I will tell you that the wall is gone and so are those who whitewashed it — [16]those prophets who assured Jerusalem that all was well, when all was not well!" The Sovereign LORD has spoken.

Prophecy against False Female Prophets

[17]The LORD said, "Now, mortal man, look at the women among your people who make up predictions. Denounce them [18]and tell them what the Sovereign LORD is saying to them:

"You women are doomed! You sew magic wristbands for everyone and make magic scarves for everyone to wear on their heads, so that they can have power over other people's lives. You want to possess the power of life and death over my people and to use it for your own benefit. [19]You dishonor me in front of my people in order to get a few handfuls of barley and a few pieces of bread. You kill people who don't deserve to die, and you keep people alive who don't deserve to live. So you tell lies to my people, and they believe you."

20 Now this is what the Sovereign LORD says: "I hate the wristbands that you use in your attempt to control life and death. I will rip them off your arms and set free the people that you were controlling. *x* **21** I will rip off your scarves and let my people escape from your power once and for all. Then you will know that I am the LORD.

22 "By your lies you discourage good people, whom I do not wish to hurt. You prevent evil people from giving up evil and saving their lives. **23** So now your false visions and misleading predictions are over. I am rescuing my people from your power, so that you will know that I am the LORD."

God Condemns Idolatry

14 Some of the leaders of the Israelites came to consult me about the LORD's will. **2** Then the LORD spoke to me. **3** "Mortal man," he said, "these men have given their hearts to idols and are letting idols lead them into sin. Do they think I will give them an answer? **4** "Now speak to them and tell them what I, the Sovereign LORD, am saying to them: Each of you Israelites who have given your heart to idols and let them lead you into sin and who then come to consult a prophet, will get an answer from me — the answer that your many idols deserve! **5** All those idols have turned the Israelites away from me, but by my answer I hope to win back their loyalty.

6 "Now then, tell the Israelites what I, the Sovereign LORD, am saying: Turn back and leave your disgusting idols.

7 "Whenever one of you Israelites or one of you foreigners who live in the Israelite community turn away from me and worship idols, and then go to consult a prophet, I, the LORD, will give you your answer! **8** I will oppose you. I will make an example of you. I will remove you from the community of my people, so that all of you will know that I am the LORD.

9 "If any prophets are deceived into giving a false answer, it is because I, the LORD, have deceived them. I will remove them from the people of Israel. **10** Both prophets and anyone who consults them will get the same punishment. **11** I will do this to keep the Israelites from deserting me and defiling themselves by their sins. They are to be my people, and I will be their God." The Sovereign LORD has spoken.

Noah, Danel, and Job

12 The LORD spoke to me. **13** "Mortal man," he said, "if a country sins and is unfaithful to me, I will reach out and destroy its supply of food. I will send a famine and kill people and animals alike. **14** Even if those three men, Noah, Danel,*y* and Job, were living there, their goodness would save only their own lives." The Sovereign LORD has spoken.

15 "Or I might send wild animals to kill the people, making the land so dangerous that no one could travel through it, **16** and even if those three men lived there — as surely as I, the Sovereign LORD, am the living God — they would not be able to save even their own children. They would save only their own lives, and the land would become a wilderness.

17 "Or I might bring war on that country and send destructive weapons to wipe out people and animals alike, **18** and even if those three men lived

---

x In verse 20 in Hebrew a word occurs twice, the meaning of which is unclear.
y Danel; or Daniel (see 28.3), an ancient hero, known for his righteous life.

there — as surely as I, the Sovereign LORD, am the living God — they would not be able to save even their children, but only their own lives.

19 "If I send an epidemic on that country and in my anger take many lives, killing people and animals, 20 even if Noah, Danel, and Job lived there — as surely as I, the Sovereign LORD, am the living God — they would not be able to save even their own children. Their goodness would save only their own lives."

21 This is what the Sovereign LORD is saying: "I will send my four worst punishments on Jerusalem — war, famine, wild animals, and disease — to destroy people and animals alike. 22 If some survive and save their children, look at them when they come to you. See how evil they are, and be convinced that the punishment I am bringing on Jerusalem is justified; 23 then you will know that there was good reason for everything I did." The Sovereign LORD has spoken.

A Parable about a Vine

15 The LORD spoke to me. 2 "Mortal man," he said, "how does a vine compare with a tree? What good is a branch of a grapevine compared with the trees of the forest? 3 Can you use it to make anything? Can you even make a peg out of it to hang things on? 4 It is only good for building a fire. And when the ends are burned up and the middle is charred, can you make anything out of it? 5 It was useless even before it was burned. Now that the fire has burned it and charred it, it is even more useless."

6 Now this is what the Sovereign LORD is saying: "Just as a vine is taken from the forest and burned, so I will take the people who live in Jerusalem

7 and will punish them. They have escaped one fire, but now fire will burn them up. When I punish them, you will know that I am the LORD. 8 They have

Can you make anything out of it? (15.4)

been unfaithful to me, and so I will make the country a wilderness." The Sovereign LORD has spoken.

Jerusalem the Unfaithful

16 The LORD spoke to me again. 2 "Mortal man," he said, "point out to Jerusalem what disgusting things she has done. 3 Tell Jerusalem what the Sovereign LORD is saying to her:

"You were born in the land of Canaan. Your father was an Amorite, and your mother was a Hittite.z 4 When you were born, no one cut your umbilical cord or washed youa or rubbed you with salt or wrapped you in cloths. 5 No one took enough pity on you to do any of these things for you. When you were born, no one loved you. You were thrown out in an open field.

6 "Then I passed by and saw you squirming in your own blood. You were covered with blood, but I wouldn't let you die. 7 I made you grow like a healthy plant. You grew strong and tall and became a young woman.b Your breasts were well-formed, and your hair had grown, but you were naked.

8 "As I passed by again, I saw that the time had come for you to fall in love. I

z AMORITE . . . HITTITE: *The Israelites regarded these people as immoral and idolatrous.* a *Hebrew has an additional word, the meaning of which is unclear.* b *Probable text* young woman; *Hebrew unclear.*
14.21 Rev 6.8

covered your naked body with my coat and promised to love you. Yes, I made a marriage covenant with you, and you became mine." This is what the Sovereign LORD says.

⁹"Then I took water and washed the blood off you. I rubbed olive oil on your skin. ¹⁰I dressed you in embroidered gowns and gave you shoes of the best leather, a linen headband, and a silk cloak. ¹¹I put jewels on you — bracelets and necklaces. ¹²I gave you a nose ring and earrings and a beautiful crown to wear. ¹³You had ornaments of gold and silver, and you always wore clothes of embroidered linen and silk. You ate bread made from the best flour, and had honey and olive oil to eat. Your beauty was dazzling, and you became a queen. ¹⁴You became famous in every nation for your perfect beauty, because I was the one who made you so lovely." This is what the Sovereign LORD says.

¹⁵"But you took advantage of your beauty and fame to sleep with everyone who came along.ᶜ ¹⁶You used some of your clothes to decorate your places of worship, and just like a prostitute,ᵈ you gave yourself to everyone. ¹⁷You took the silver and gold jewelry that I had given you, used it to make male images, and committed adultery with them. ¹⁸You took the embroidered clothes I gave you and put them on the images, and you offered to the images the olive oil and incense I had given you. ¹⁹I gave you food — the best flour, olive oil, and honey — but you offered it as a sacrifice to win the favor of idols." This is what the Sovereign LORD says.

²⁰"Then you took the sons and the daughters you had borne me and offered them as sacrifices to idols. Wasn't it bad enough to be unfaithful to me, ²¹without taking my children and sacrificing them to idols? ²²During your disgusting life as a prostitute you never once remembered your childhood — when you were naked, squirming in your own blood."

Jerusalem's Life as a Prostitute

²³The Sovereign LORD said, "You are doomed! Doomed! You did all that evil, and then ²⁴by the side of every road you built places to worship idols and practice prostitution. ²⁵You dragged your beauty through the mud. You offered yourself to everyone who came by, and you were more of a prostitute every day. ²⁶You let your lustful neighbors, the Egyptians, go to bed with you, and you used your prostitution to make me angry.

²⁷"Now I have raised my hand to punish you and to take away your share of my blessing. I have handed you over to the Philistines, who hate you and are disgusted with your immoral actions.

²⁸"Because you were not satisfied by the others, you went running after the Assyrians. You were their prostitute, but they didn't satisfy you either. ²⁹You were also a prostitute for the Babylonians, that nation of merchants, but they didn't satisfy you either."

³⁰Thisᵉ is what the Sovereign LORD is saying: "You have done all this like a shameless prostitute. ³¹On every street you built places to worship idols and practice prostitution. But you are not out for money like a common prostitute. ³²You are like a woman who commits adultery with strangers instead of loving her husband. ³³A prostitute is paid, but you gave presents to all your lovers and bribed them to come from everywhere to sleep with you. ³⁴You are a special kind of prostitute. No one forced you to become one. You didn't get paid; you paid them! Yes, you are different."

ᶜ Hebrew has two additional words, the meaning of which is unclear.   ᵈ Hebrew has four additional words, the meaning of which is unclear.   ᵉ Verse 30 in Hebrew begins with three words, the meaning of which is unclear.

God's Judgment on Jerusalem

35Now then, Jerusalem, you whore! Hear what the LORD is saying.

36This is what the Sovereign LORD says: "You stripped off your clothes, and like a prostitute, you gave yourself to your lovers and to all your disgusting idols, and you killed your children as sacrifices to idols. **37**Because of this I will bring all your former lovers together — the ones you liked and the ones you hated. I will bring them around you in a circle, and then I will strip off your clothes and let them see you naked. **38**I will condemn you for adultery and murder, and in my anger and fury I will punish you with death. **39**I will put you in their power, and they will tear down the places where you engage in prostitution and worship idols. They will take away your clothes and jewels and leave you completely naked.

40"They will stir up a crowd to stone you, and they will cut you to pieces with their swords. **41**They will burn your houses down and let crowds of women see your punishment. I will make you stop being a prostitute and make you stop giving gifts to your lovers. **42**Then my anger will be over, and I will be calm. I will not be angry or jealous any more. **43**You have forgotten how I treated you when you were young, and you have made me angry by all the things you did. That is why I have made you pay for them all. Why did you add sexual immorality to all the other disgusting things you did?" The Sovereign LORD has spoken.

Like Mother, Like Daughter

44The LORD said, "People will use this proverb about you, Jerusalem: 'Like mother, like daughter.' **45**You really are your mother's daughter. She detested her husband and her children. You are like your sisters, who hated their husbands and their children.

You and your sister cities had a Hittite mother and an Amorite*f* father.

46"Your older sister, with her villages, is Samaria, in the north. Your younger sister, with her villages, is Sodom, in the south. **47**Were you satisfied to follow in their footsteps and copy their disgusting actions? No, in only a little while you were acting worse than they were in everything you did.

48"As surely as I am the living God," the Sovereign LORD says, "your sister Sodom and her villages never did the evil that you and your villages have done. **49**She and her daughters were proud because they had plenty to eat and lived in peace and quiet, but they did not take care of the poor and the underprivileged. **50**They were proud and stubborn and did the things that I hate, so I destroyed them, as you well know.

51"Samaria did not sin half as much as you have. You have acted more disgustingly than she ever did. Your corruption makes your sisters look innocent by comparison. **52**And now you will have to endure your disgrace. Your sins are so much worse than those of your sisters that they look innocent beside you. Now blush and bear your shame, because you make your sisters look pure."

Sodom and Samaria Will Be Restored

53The LORD said to Jerusalem, "I will make them prosperous again — Sodom and her villages and Samaria and her villages. Yes, I will make you prosperous too. **54**You will be ashamed of yourself, and your disgrace will show your sisters how well-off they are. **55**They will become prosperous again, and you and your villages will also be restored. **56**Didn't you joke about Sodom in those days when you were proud **57**and before the evil you did had been exposed? Now you are just like her — a joke to the

f HITTITE . . . AMORITE: *See 16.3.*

Edomites, the Philistines, and your other neighbors who hate you. ⁵⁸You must suffer for the obscene, disgusting things you have done." The LORD has spoken.

A Covenant That Lasts Forever

⁵⁹The Sovereign LORD says, "I will treat you the way you deserve, because you ignored your promises and broke the covenant. ⁶⁰But I will honor the covenant I made with you when you were young, and I will make a covenant with you that will last forever. ⁶¹You will remember how you have acted, and be ashamed of it when you get your older sister and your younger sister back. I will let them be like daughters to you, even though this was not part of my covenant with you. ⁶²I will renew my covenant with you, and you will know that I am the LORD. ⁶³I will forgive all the wrongs you have done, but you will remember them and be too ashamed to open your mouth." The Sovereign LORD has spoken.

The Parable of the Eagles and the Vine

17 The LORD spoke to me. ²"Mortal man," he said, "tell the Israelites a parable ³to let them know what I, the Sovereign LORD, am saying to them: There was a giant eagle with beautiful feathers and huge wings, spread wide. He flew to the Lebanon Mountains and broke off the top of a cedar tree, ⁴which he carried to a land of commerce and placed in a city of merchants. ⁵Then he took a young plant from the land of Israel and planted it in a fertile field,*g* where there was always water to make it grow. ⁶The plant sprouted and became a low, wide-

spreading grapevine. The branches grew upward toward the eagle, and the roots grew deep. The vine was covered with branches and leaves.

He broke off the top of a cedar tree. (17.3)

⁷"There was another giant eagle with huge wings and thick plumage. And now the vine sent its roots toward him and turned its leaves toward him, in the hope that he would give it more water than there was in the garden where it was growing.*h* ⁸But the vine had already been planted in a fertile, well-watered field so that it could grow leaves and bear grapes and be a magnificent vine.

⁹"So I, the Sovereign LORD, ask: Will this vine live and grow? Won't the first eagle pull it up by its roots, pull off the grapes, and break off the branches and let them wither? It will not take much strength or a mighty nation to pull it up. ¹⁰Yes, it is planted, but will it live and grow? Won't it wither when the east wind strikes it? Won't it wither there where it is growing?"

The Parable Is Explained

¹¹The LORD said to me, ¹²"Ask these rebels if they know what the parable

---

g Hebrew has an additional word, the meaning of which is unclear. *h And now the vine . . . growing; or And now the vine turned away from the garden where it was growing and sent its roots toward him and turned its leaves toward him, in the hope that he would give it water.*

17.12-15 2 K 24.15-20; 2 Ch 36.10-13

It is planted, but will it live and grow? (17.10)

means. Tell them that the king of Babylonia came to Jerusalem and took the king and his officials back with him to Babylonia. 13 He took one of the king's family, made a treaty with him, and made him swear to be loyal. He took important men as hostages 14 to keep the nation from rising again and to make sure that the treaty would be kept. 15 But the king of Judah rebelled and sent agents to Egypt to get horses and a large army. Will he succeed? Can he get away with that? He cannot break the treaty and go unpunished!

16 "As surely as I am the living God," says the Sovereign LORD, "this king will die in Babylonia because he broke his oath and the treaty he had made with the king of Babylonia, who put him on the throne. 17 Even the powerful army of the king of Egypt will not be able to help him fight when the Babylonians build earthworks and dig trenches in order to kill many people. 18 He broke his oath and the treaty he had made. He did all these things, and now he will not escape."

19 The Sovereign LORD says, "As surely as I am the living God, I will punish him for breaking the treaty which he swore in my name to keep. 20 I will spread out a hunter's net and catch him in it. I will take him to Babylonia and punish him there, because he was unfaithful to me. 21 His best soldiers will be killed in battle, and the survivors will be scattered in every direction. Then you will know that I, the LORD, have spoken."

18.2 Jr 31.29

God's Promise of Hope

22 This is what the Sovereign LORD says:

"I will take the top of a tall cedar
  and break off a tender sprout;
I will plant it on a high
    mountain,
23   on Israel's highest mountain.
It will grow branches and bear
    seed
  and become a magnificent
    cedar.
Birds of every kind will live there
  and find shelter in its shade.
24 All the trees in the land will
    know
  that I am the LORD.
I cut down the tall trees
  and make small trees grow
    tall.
I wither up the green trees
  and make the dry trees
    become green.
I, the LORD, have spoken. I will do what
I have said I would do."

Individual Responsibility

18 The LORD spoke to me 2 and said, "What is this proverb people keep repeating in the land of Israel?

*I will spread out a hunter's net
and catch him in it. (17.20)*

Birds of every kind will live there. (17.23)

'The parents ate the sour grapes,
  But the children got the sour
    taste.'

³"As surely as I am the living God,"
says the Sovereign LORD, "you will not
repeat this proverb in Israel any more.
⁴The life of every person belongs to me,
the life of the parent as well as that of
the child. The person who sins is the
one who will die.

⁵"Suppose there is a truly good man,
righteous and honest. ⁶He doesn't worship the idols of the Israelites or eat the
sacrifices offered at forbidden shrines.
He doesn't seduce another man's wife
or have intercourse with a woman during her period. ⁷He doesn't cheat or rob
anyone. He returns what a borrower
gives him as security; he feeds the hungry and gives clothing to the naked.
⁸He doesn't lend money for profit. He
refuses to do evil and gives an honest
decision in any dispute. ⁹Such a man
obeys my commands and carefully
keeps my laws. He is righteous, and he
will live," says the Sovereign LORD.

¹⁰"Then suppose this man has a son
who robs and kills, who does any *i* of
these things ¹¹that the father never did.

He eats sacrifices offered at forbidden
shrines and seduces other men's wives.
¹²He cheats the poor, he robs, he keeps
what a borrower gives him as security.
He goes to pagan shrines, worships disgusting idols, ¹³and lends money for
profit. Will he live? No, he will not. He
has done all these disgusting things,
and so he will die. He will be to blame
for his own death.

¹⁴"Now suppose this second man has
a son. He sees all the sins his father
practiced, but does not follow his example. ¹⁵He doesn't worship the idols of
the Israelites or eat the sacrifices offered at forbidden shrines. He doesn't
seduce another man's wife ¹⁶or oppress
anyone or rob anyone. He returns what
a borrower gives him as security. He
feeds the hungry and gives clothing to
the naked. ¹⁷He refuses to do evil *j* and
doesn't lend money for profit. He keeps
my laws and obeys my commands. He
will not die because of his father's sins,
but he will certainly live. ¹⁸His father,
on the other hand, cheated and
robbed *k* and always did evil to everyone. And so he died because of the sins
he himself had committed.

¹⁹"But you ask, 'Why shouldn't the
son suffer because of his father's sins?'
The answer is that the son did what was
right and good. He kept my laws and
followed them carefully, and so he will
certainly live. ²⁰It is the one who sins
who will die. A son is not to suffer because of his father's sins, nor a father
because of the sins of his son. Good people will be rewarded for doing good, and
evil people will suffer for the evil they
do.

²¹"If someone evil stops sinning and
keeps my laws, if he does what is right
and good, he will not die; he will certainly live. ²²All his sins will be forgiven, and he will live, because he did

---

i Some ancient translations who does any; *Hebrew unclear.*   *j Some ancient*
translations (see also verse 8) to do evil; *Hebrew* from the poor.   *k Some ancient*
translations robbed; *Hebrew unclear.*
18.9 Lv 18.5   **18.20** Dt 24.16

what is right. ²³ Do you think I enjoy seeing evil people die?" asks the Sovereign LORD. "No, I would rather see them repent and live.

²⁴ "But if a righteous person stops doing good and starts doing all the evil, disgusting things that evil people do, will he go on living? No! None of the good he did will be remembered. He will die because of his unfaithfulness and his sins.

²⁵ "But you say, 'What the Lord does isn't right.' Listen to me, you Israelites. Do you think my way of doing things isn't right? It is your way that isn't right. ²⁶ When a righteous person stops doing good and starts doing evil and then dies, he dies because of the evil he has done. ²⁷ When someone evil stops sinning and does what is right and good, he saves his life. ²⁸ He realizes what he is doing and stops sinning, so

He realizes what he is doing and stops sinning. (18.28)

he will certainly not die, but go on living. ²⁹ And you Israelites say, 'What the Lord does isn't right.' You think my way isn't right, do you? It is your way that isn't right.

³⁰ "Now I, the Sovereign LORD, am telling you Israelites that I will judge each of you by what you have done. Turn away from all the evil you are doing, and don't let your sin destroy you. ³¹ Give up all the evil you have been do-

ing, and get yourselves new minds and hearts. Why do you Israelites want to die? ³² I do not want anyone to die," says the Sovereign LORD. "Turn away from your sins and live."

A Song of Sorrow

19 The LORD told me to sing this song of sorrow for two princes of Israel:

² What a lioness your mother was!
She raised her cubs among the
    fierce male lions.
³ She raised a cub and taught him
    to hunt;
  he learned to eat people.
⁴ The nations heard about him
    and trapped him in a pit.
  With hooks they dragged him off
    to Egypt.
⁵ She waited until she saw all
    hope was gone.
  Then she raised another of her
    cubs,
    and he grew into a fierce lion.
⁶ When he was full-grown,
  he prowled with the other
    lions.
  He too learned to hunt and eat
    people.
⁷ He wrecked forts,[l] he ruined
    towns.
  The people of the land were
    terrified
    every time he roared.
⁸ The nations gathered to
    fight him;
  people came from everywhere.
  They spread their hunting nets
    and caught him in their trap.
⁹ They put him in a cage
    and took him to the king of
    Babylonia.
  They kept him under guard,
    so that his roar would never
    be heard again
    on the hills of Israel.

---

[l] *One ancient translation* wrecked forts; *Hebrew unclear.*
18.32 Ws 1.13

¹⁰ Your mother was like a
    grapevine^m
    planted near a stream.
Because there was plenty of
    water,
    the vine was covered with
    leaves and fruit.
¹¹ Its branches were strong
    and grew to be royal scepters.
The vine grew tall enough to
    reach the clouds;
    everyone saw how leafy and
    tall it was.
¹² But angry hands pulled it up by
    the roots
    and threw it to the ground.
The east wind dried up its fruit.
Its branches were broken off;
    they dried up and were
    burned.
¹³ Now it is planted in the desert,
    in a dry and waterless land.
¹⁴ The stem of the vine caught fire;
    fire burned up its branches
    and fruit.
The branches will never again
    be strong,
    will never be royal scepters.
This is a song of sorrow; it has been
sung again and again.

The LORD's Will and Human Defiance

20 It was the tenth day of the fifth
month of the seventh year of
our exile. Some of the leaders of the Israelite community came to consult me
about the LORD's will, and they sat
down in front of me. ²Then the LORD
spoke to me. ³"Mortal man," he said,
"speak to these leaders and tell them
that the Sovereign LORD is saying: You
have come to ask my will, have you? As
surely as I am the living God, I will not
let you ask me anything. I, the
Sovereign LORD, have spoken.

⁴"Are you ready to pass sentence on
them, mortal man? Then do so. Remind
them of the disgusting things their ancestors did. ⁵Tell them what I am saying. When I chose Israel, I made them
a promise. I revealed myself to them in
Egypt and told them: I am the LORD
your God. ⁶It was then that I promised
to take them out of Egypt and lead them
to a land I had chosen for them, a rich
and fertile land, the finest land of all. ⁷I
told them to throw away the disgusting
idols they loved and not to make themselves unclean with the false gods of
Egypt, because I am the LORD their
God. ⁸But they defied me and refused to
listen. They did not throw away their
disgusting idols or give up the Egyptian
gods. I was ready to let them feel the
full force of my anger there in Egypt.
⁹But I did not, since that would have
brought dishonor to my name, for in the
presence of the people among whom
they were living I had announced to Israel that I was going to lead them out of
Egypt.

¹⁰"And so I led them out of Egypt into
the desert. ¹¹I gave them my commands and taught them my laws,
which bring life to anyone who obeys
them. ¹²I made the keeping of the Sabbath a sign of the agreement between
us, to remind them that I, the LORD,
make them holy. ¹³But even in the desert they defied me. They broke my
laws and rejected my commands,
which bring life to anyone who obeys
them. They completely profaned the
Sabbath. I was ready to let them feel the
force of my anger there in the desert
and to destroy them. ¹⁴But I did not,
since that would have brought dishonor
to my name among the nations which
had seen me lead Israel out of Egypt.
¹⁵So I made a vow in the desert that I
would not take them to the land I had
given them, a rich and fertile land, the
finest land of all. ¹⁶I made the vow because they had rejected my commands,
broken my laws, and profaned the

---

^m *Hebrew has an additional word, the meaning of which is unclear.*
20.5, 6 Ex 6.2-8   **20.11, 13** Lv 18.5   **20.12** Ex 31.13-17   **20.15** Nu 14.26-35

I gave them my commands. (20.11)

Sabbath — they preferred to worship their idols.

17 "But then I took pity on them. I decided not to kill them there in the desert. **18** Instead, I warned the young people among them: Do not keep the laws your ancestors made; do not follow their customs or defile yourselves with their idols. **19** I am the LORD your God. Obey my laws and my commands. **20** Make the Sabbath a holy day, so that it will be a sign of the covenant we made, and will remind you that I am the LORD your God.

21 "But that generation also defied me. They broke my laws and did not keep my commands, which bring life to anyone who obeys them. They profaned the Sabbath. I was ready to let them feel the force of my anger there in the desert and to kill them all. **22** But I

did not, since that would have brought dishonor to my name among the nations which had seen me bring Israel out of Egypt. **23** So I made another vow in the desert. I vowed that I would scatter them all over the world. **24** I did this because they had rejected my commands, broken my laws, profaned the Sabbath, and worshiped the same idols their ancestors had served.

25 "Then I gave them laws that are not good and commands that do not bring life. **26** I let them defile themselves with their own offerings, and I let them sacrifice their first-born sons. This was to punish them and show them that I am the LORD.

27 "Now then, mortal man, tell the Israelites what I, the Sovereign LORD, am saying to them. This is another way their ancestors insulted me by their unfaithfulness. **28** I brought them to the land I had promised to give them. When they saw the high hills and green trees, they offered sacrifices at all of them. They made me angry by the sacrifices they burned and by the wine they brought as offerings. **29** I asked them: What are these high places where you go? So they have been called 'High Places'[n] ever since. **30** Now tell the Israelites what I am saying: Why must you commit the same sins your ancestors did and go running after their idols? **31** Even today you offer the same gifts and defile yourselves with the same idols by sacrificing your children to them in the fire. And then you Israelites still come to ask what my will is! As surely as I, the Sovereign LORD, am the living God, I will not let you ask me anything. **32** You have made up your minds that you want to be like the other nations, like the people who live in other countries and worship trees and rocks. But that will never be.

[n] HIGH PLACES: *Pagan places of worship which the Hebrews were forbidden to use. The Hebrew word translated "High Places" sounds like the Hebrew for "where you go."*
20.23 Lv 26.33

God Punishes and Forgives

33 "As surely as I, the Sovereign LORD, am the living God, I warn you that in my anger I will rule over you with a strong hand, with all my power. 34 I will show you my power and my anger when I gather you together and bring you back from all the countries where you have been scattered. 35 I will bring you into the 'Desert of the Nations,' and there I will condemn you to your face. 36 I will now condemn you just as I condemned your ancestors in the Sinai Desert," says the Sovereign LORD.

37 "I will take firm control of you and make you obey my covenant. 38 I will take away from among you those who are rebellious and sinful. I will take them out of the lands where they are living now, but I will not let them return to the land of Israel. Then you will know that I am the LORD."

39 The Sovereign LORD says, "And now, all you Israelites, suit yourselves! Go on and serve your idols! But I warn you that after this you will have to obey me and stop dishonoring my holy name by offering gifts to your idols. 40 There in the land, on my holy mountain,ᵒ the high mountain of Israel, all you people of Israel will worship me. I will be pleased with you and will expect you to bring me your sacrifices, your best offerings, and your holy gifts. 41 After I bring you out of the countries where you have been scattered and gather you together, I will accept the sacrifices that you burn, and the nations will see that I am holy. 42 When I bring you back to Israel, the land that I promised I would give to your ancestors, then you will know that I am the LORD. 43 Then you will remember all the disgraceful things you did and how you defiled yourselves. You will be disgusted with yourselves because of all the evil things

you did. 44 When I act to protect my honor, you Israelites will know that I am the LORD, because I do not deal with you as your wicked, evil actions deserve." The Sovereign LORD has spoken.

Fire in the South

45 The LORD spoke to me. 46 "Mortal man," he said, "look toward the south. Speak against the south and prophesy against the forest of the south. 47 Tell the southern forest to hear what the Sovereign LORD is saying: Look! I am starting a fire, and it will burn up every tree in you, whether green or dry. Nothing will be able to put it out. It will spread from south to north, and everyone will feel the heat of the flames. 48 They will all see that I, the LORD, set it on fire and that no one can put it out."

49 But I protested, "Sovereign LORD, don't make me do it! Everyone is already complaining that I always speak in riddles."

The LORD's Sword

21 The LORD spoke to me. 2 "Mortal man," he said, "denounce Jerusalem. Denounce the places where people worship. Warn the land of Israel 3 that I, the LORD, am saying: I am your enemy. I will draw my sword and kill all of you, good and evil alike. 4 I will use my sword against everyone from south to north. 5 Everyone will know that I, the LORD, have drawn my sword and that I will not put it away.

6 "Mortal man, groan as if your heart is breaking with despair. Groan in sorrow where everyone can watch you. 7 When they ask you why you are groaning, tell them it is because of the news that is coming. When it comes, their hearts will be filled with fear, their hands will hang limp, their courage will fail, and their knees will tremble. The

---

ᵒ HOLY MOUNTAIN: *Mount Zion, the hill in Jerusalem which formed part of the Temple and palace area.*

time has come; it is here." The
Sovereign LORD has spoken.

⁸ The LORD said to me, ⁹ "Mortal man,
prophesy. Tell the people what I, the
Lord, am saying:

A sword, a sword is sharpened
    and polished.
¹⁰ It is sharpened to kill,
    polished to flash like
      lightning.
There can be no rejoicing,
    for my people have
      disregarded every warning
      and punishment.ᵖ
¹¹ The sword is being polished,
    to make it ready for use.
It is sharpened and polished,
    to be put in the hands of a
      killer.
¹² Howl in grief, mortal man;
    this sword is meant for my
      people
and for all the leaders of
    Israel.
They are going to be killed
    with all the rest of my people.
Beat your breast in despair!
¹³ I am testing my people,
    and if they refuse to repent,
    all these things will happen to
      them.�q

¹⁴ "Now, mortal man, prophesy. Clap
your hands, and the sword will strike
again and again. It is a sword that kills,
a sword that terrifiesʳ and slaughters.
¹⁵ It makes my people lose courage and
stumble. I am threatening their city
with a swordˢ that flashes like lightning and is ready to kill. ¹⁶ Cut to the
right and the left, you sharp sword! Cut
wherever you turn.ᵗ ¹⁷ I also will clap
my hands, and my anger will be over. I,
the LORD, have spoken."

The Sword of the King of Babylonia

¹⁸ The LORD spoke to me. ¹⁹ "Mortal
man," he said, "mark out two roads by
which the king of Babylonia can come
with his sword. Both of them are to start
in the same country. Put up a signpost
where the roads fork.ᵘ ²⁰ One will show
the king the way to the Ammonite city
of Rabbah, and the other the way to Judah, to the fortified city, Jerusalem.
²¹ The king of Babylonia stands by the
signpost at the fork of the road. To discover which way to go, he shakes the
arrows;ᵛ he consults his idols; he examines the liver of a sacrificed animal.
²² Now! His right hand holds the arrow
marked 'Jerusalem'! It tells him to go
and set up battering rams, to shout the
battle cry, to place battering rams
against the gates, to throw up earthworks, and to dig trenches. ²³ The people of Jerusalem won't believe this
because of the treaties they have made.
But this prediction is to remind them of
their sins and to warn them that they
will be captured. ²⁴ This then is what I,
the Sovereign LORD, am saying: Your
sins are exposed. Everyone knows how
guilty you are. You show your sins in
your every action. You stand condemned, and I will hand you over to
your enemies.

²⁵ "You wicked, unholy ruler of Israel, your day, the day of your final punishment, is coming. ²⁶ I, the Sovereign
LORD, have spoken. Take off your
crown and your turban. Nothing will be
the same again. Raise the poor to
power! Bring down those who are ruling! ²⁷ Ruin, ruin! Yes, I will make the
city a ruin. But this will not happen
until the one comes whom I have

chosen to punish the city. To him I will give it.

A Sword and the Ammonites

28 "Mortal man, prophesy. Announce what I, the Sovereign LORD, am saying to the Ammonites, who are insulting Israel. Say to them:

'A sword is ready to destroy;
It is polished to kill, to flash like lightning.

29 The visions that you see are false, and the predictions you make are lies. You are wicked and evil, and your day is coming, the day of your final punishment. The sword is going to fall on your necks.

30 'Put up the sword! I will judge you in the place where you were created, in the land where you were born. 31 You will feel my anger when I turn it loose on you like a blazing fire. And I will hand you over to brutal men, experts at destruction. 32 You will be destroyed by fire. Your blood will be shed in your own country, and no one will remember you any more.' " The LORD has spoken.

The Crimes of Jerusalem

22 The LORD spoke to me. 2 "Mortal man," he said, "are you ready to judge the city that is full of murderers? Make clear to her all the disgusting things she has done. 3 Tell the city what I, the Sovereign LORD, am saying: Because you have murdered so many of your own people and have defiled yourself by worshiping idols, your time is coming. 4 You are guilty of those murders and are defiled by the idols you made, and so your day is coming, your time is up! That is why I have let the nations make fun of you and all the countries sneer at you. 5 Countries nearby and countries far away sneer at

you because of your lawlessness. 6 All Israel's leaders trust in their own strength and commit murder. 7 None of you in the city honor your parents. You cheat foreigners and take advantage of widows and orphans. 8 You have no respect for the holy places, and you don't keep the Sabbath. 9 Some of your people tell lies about others in order to have them put to death. Some of them eat sacrifices offered to idols. Some are always satisfying their lusts. 10 Some of them sleep with their father's wife. Some force women to have intercourse with them during their period. 11 Some commit adultery, and others seduce their daughters-in-law or their half sisters. 12 Some of your people murder for pay. Some charge interest on the loans they make to other Israelites and get rich by taking advantage of them. They have forgotten me." The Sovereign LORD has spoken.

13 "I will bring my fist down on your robberies and murders. 14 Do you think you will have any courage left or have strength enough to lift your hand when I am finished with you? I, the LORD, have spoken, and I keep my word. 15 I will scatter your people to every country and nation and will put an end to your evil actions. 16 And so the other nations will dishonor you, but you will know that I am the LORD."

God's Refining Furnace

17 The LORD said to me, 18 "Mortal man, the Israelites are of no use to me. They are like waste metal — copper, tin, iron, and lead — left over after silver has been refined in a furnace. 19 So now I, the Sovereign LORD, am telling them that they are just as useless as that. I will bring them all together in Jerusalem 20 in the same way that the ore of silver, copper, iron, lead, and tin is put

---

21.28-32 Jr 49.1-6; Ez 25.1-7; Am 1.3-15; Zep 2.8-11   **22.7 a** Ex 20.12; Dt 5.16; **b** Ex 22.21, 22; Dt 24.17   **22.8** Lv 19.30; 26.2   **22.10, 11** Lv 18.7-20   **22.12** Ex 23.8; Dt 16.19; Ex 22.25; Lv 25.36, 37; Dt 23.19

in a refining furnace. My anger and rage will melt them the way fire melts ore. ²¹Yes, I will gather them in Jerusalem, build a fire under them, and melt them with my anger. ²²They will be melted in Jerusalem the way silver is melted in a furnace, and then they will know that they are feeling the anger of the LORD."

The Sins of Israel's Leaders

²³The LORD spoke to me again. ²⁴"Mortal man," he said, "tell the Israelites that their land is unholy, and so I am punishing it in my anger. ²⁵The leadersʷ are like lions roaring over the animals they have killed. They kill the people, take all the money and property they can get, and by their murders leave many widows. ²⁶The priests break my law and have no respect for what is holy. They make no distinction between what is holy and what is not. They do not teach the difference between clean and unclean things, and they ignore the Sabbath. As a result the people of Israel do not respect me. ²⁷The government officials are like wolves tearing apart the animals they have killed. They commit murder in order to get rich. ²⁸The prophets have hidden these sins like workers covering a wall with whitewash. They see false visions and make false predictions. They claim to speak the word of the Sovereign LORD, but I, the LORD, have not spoken to them. ²⁹The wealthy cheat and rob. They mistreat the poor and take advantage of foreigners. ³⁰I looked for someone who could build a wall, who could stand in the places where the walls have crumbled and defend the land when my anger is about to destroy it, but I could find no one. ³¹So I will turn my anger loose on them,

and like a fire I will destroy them for what they have done." The Sovereign LORD has spoken.

The Sinful Sisters

23 The LORD spoke to me. ²"Mortal man," he said, "there were once two sisters. ³When they were young, living in Egypt, they lost their virginity and became prostitutes. ⁴The older one was named Oholahˣ (she represents Samaria), and the younger one was named Oholibahʸ (she represents Jerusalem). I married both of them, and they bore me children. ⁵Although she was mine, Oholah continued to be a prostitute and was full of lust for her lovers from Assyria. ⁶They were soldiers in uniforms of purple, noblemen and high-ranking officers; all of them were handsome young cavalry officers. ⁷She was the whore for all the Assyrian officers, and her lust led her to defile herself by worshiping Assyrian idols. ⁸She continued what she had begun as a prostitute in Egypt, where she lost her virginity. From the time she was a young woman, men slept with her and treated her like a prostitute. ⁹So I handed her over to her Assyrian lovers whom she wanted so much. ¹⁰They stripped her naked, seized her sons and daughters, and then killed her with a sword. Women everywhere gossiped about her fate.

¹¹"Even though her sister Oholibah saw this, she was wilder and more of a prostitute than Oholah had ever been. ¹²She too was full of lust for the Assyrian noblemen and officers — soldiers in bright uniforms — and for the cavalry officers, all of those handsome young men. ¹³I saw that she was completely immoral, that the second sister was as bad as the first.

ʷ *One ancient translation* The leaders; *Hebrew* A conspiracy of her prophets.
ˣ OHOLAH: *This name in Hebrew means "her sanctuary."*   ʸ OHOLIBAH: *This name in Hebrew means "my sanctuary is in her."*
22.26 Lv 10.10

14-15"She sank deeper and deeper in her immorality. She was attracted by the images of high Babylonian officials carved into the wall and painted bright red, with sashes around their waists and fancy turbans on their heads. **16**As soon as she saw them, she was filled with lust and sent messengers to them in Babylonia. **17**The Babylonians came to have sex with her. They used her and defiled her so much that finally she became disgusted with them. **18**She exposed herself publicly and let everyone know she was a whore. I was as disgusted with her as I had been with her sister. **19**She became more of a prostitute than ever, acting the way she did as a young woman, when she was a prostitute in Egypt. **20**She was filled with lust for oversexed men who had all the lustfulness of donkeys or stallions." **21**Oholibah, you wanted to repeat the immorality you were guilty of as a young woman in Egypt, where men played with your breasts and you lost your virginity.)

God's Judgment on the Younger Sister

22"Now then, Oholibah, this is what I, the Sovereign LORD, am saying to you. You are tired of those lovers, but I will make them angry with you and bring them to surround you. **23**I will bring all the Babylonians and Chaldeans, men from Pekod, Shoa, and Koa, and all the Assyrians. I will gather all those handsome young noblemen and officers, all those important officials and high-ranking cavalry officers. **24**They will attack you from the north,[z] bringing a large army with chariots and supply wagons. Protected by shields and helmets, they will surround you. I will hand you over to them, and they will judge you by their own laws. **25**Because I am angry with you, I will let them deal with you in their anger. They will cut off your nose and your ears and kill your children. Yes, they will take your sons and daughters from you and burn them alive. **26**They will tear off your clothes and take your jewels. **27**I will put a stop to your lust and to the obscenities you have committed ever since you were in Egypt. You won't look at any more idols or think about Egypt any more."

28This is what the Sovereign LORD says: "I will hand you over to people you hate and are disgusted with. **29**And because they hate you, they will take away everything you have worked for and leave you stripped naked, exposed like a prostitute. Your lust and your prostitution **30**have brought this on you. You were a prostitute for the nations and defiled yourself with their idols. **31**You followed in your sister's footsteps, and so I will give you the same cup of punishment to drink."

32The Sovereign LORD says,
"You will drink from your
sister's cup;
it is large and deep.
Everyone will scorn and
mock you;
the cup is full.
33It will make you miserable
and drunk,
that cup of fear and ruin,
your sister Samaria's cup.
34You will drink and drain it dry,
and with its broken pieces
tear your breast.
I, the Sovereign LORD, have spoken."

35Now this is what the Sovereign LORD is saying: "Because you forgot me and turned your back on me, you will suffer for your lust and your prostitution."

God's Judgment on Both Sisters

36The LORD said to me, "Mortal man, are you ready to judge Oholah and Oholibah? Accuse them of the disgusting things they have done. **37**They have

---

z *One ancient translation* north; *Hebrew unclear.*

committed adultery and murder —
adultery with idols and murder of the
children they bore me. They sacrificed
my children to their idols. ³⁸ And that is
not all they did. They profaned my
Temple and broke the Sabbath, which
I had established. ³⁹ The very day that
they killed my children as sacrifices to
idols, they came to my Temple and profaned it!

⁴⁰ "Again and again they sent messengers to invite men to come from a
great distance, and the men came. The
two sisters would bathe and put on eye
shadow and jewelry. ⁴¹ They would sit
on a beautiful couch, and in front of
them they would have a table covered
with good things, including the incense
and the olive oil that I had given them.
⁴² The sound of a carefree crowd could
be heard, a group of men brought in
from the desert. They put bracelets on
the women's arms and beautiful
crowns on their heads. ⁴³ And I said to
myself that they were using as a prostitute a woman worn out by adultery.ᵃ
⁴⁴ They went back to these prostitutes
again and again. They went back to
Oholah and Oholibah, those immoral
women. ⁴⁵ Righteous men will condemn them on the charge of adultery
and murder, because they practice
adultery and their hands are stained
with blood."

⁴⁶ This is what the Sovereign Lord
says: "Bring a mob to terrorize them
and rob them. ⁴⁷ Let the mob stone
them and attack them with swords, kill
their children, and burn down their
houses. ⁴⁸ Throughout the land I will
put a stop to immorality, as a warning
to every woman not to commit adultery
as they did. ⁴⁹ And you two sisters — I
will punish you for your immorality and
your sin of worshiping idols. Then you
will know that I am the Sovereign
Lord."

The Corroded Cooking Pot

24 On the tenth day of the tenth
month of the ninth year of our
exile, the Lord spoke to me. ² "Mortal
man," he said, "write down today's date,
because this is the day that the king of
Babylonia is beginning the siege of Jerusalem. ³ Tell my rebellious people this
parable that I, the Sovereign Lord,
have for them:
Set the pot on the fire
and fill it up with water.

Set the pot on the fire. (24.3)

⁴ Put in the best pieces of meat —
the shoulders and the legs —
fill it with choice bony
pieces too.
⁵ Use the meat of the finest sheep;
pile the woodᵇ under the pot.
Let the water boil;
boil the bones and the meat."

⁶ This is what the Sovereign Lord
is saying: "The city of murderers is
doomed! It is like a corroded pot that is
never cleaned. Piece after piece of meat
is taken out, and not one is left. ⁷ There
was murder in the city, but the blood
was not spilled on the ground where
the dust could hide it; it was spilled on
a bare rock. ⁸ I have left the blood there
where it cannot be hidden, where it demands angry revenge."

⁹ This is what the Sovereign Lord is

ᵃ *Verses 42-43 in Hebrew are unclear.*   ᵇ *Probable text* wood; *Hebrew* bones.
24.2 2 K 25.1; Jr 52.4

saying: "The city of murderers is doomed! I myself will pile up the firewood. ¹⁰Bring more wood! Fan the flames! Cook the meat! Boil away the broth!ᶜ Burn up the bones! ¹¹Now set the empty bronze pot on the coals and let it get red-hot. Then the pot will be ritually pure again after the corrosion is burned off, ¹²although all that corrosion will not disappear in the flames.ᵈ ¹³Jerusalem, your immoral actions have defiled you. Although I tried to purify you, you remained defiled. You will not be pure again until you have felt the full force of my anger. ¹⁴I, the LORD, have spoken. The time has come for me to act. I will not ignore your sins or show pity or be merciful. You will be punished for what you have done." The Sovereign LORD has spoken.

The Death of the Prophet's Wife

¹⁵The LORD spoke to me. ¹⁶"Mortal man," he said, "with one blow I am going to take away the person you love most. You are not to complain or cry or shed any tears. ¹⁷Don't let your sobbing be heard. Do not go bareheaded or barefoot as a sign of mourning. Don't cover your face or eat the food that mourners eat."

¹⁸Early in the day I was talking with the people. That evening my wife died, and the next day I did as I had been told. ¹⁹The people asked me, "Why are you acting like this?"

²⁰So I said to them, "The LORD spoke to me and told me ²¹to give you Israelites this message: You are proud of the strength of the Temple. You like to look at it and to visit it, but the LORD is going to profane it. And the younger members of your families who are left in Jerusalem will be killed in war. ²²Then you will do what I have done. You will not cover your faces or eat the food that

mourners eat. ²³You will not go bareheaded or barefoot or mourn or cry. You will waste away because of your sins, and you will groan to one another. ²⁴Then I will be a sign to you; you will do everything I have done. The LORD says that when this happens, you will know that he is the Sovereign LORD."

²⁵The LORD said, "Now, mortal man, I will take away from them the strong Temple that was their pride and joy, which they liked to look at and to visit. And I will take away their sons and daughters. ²⁶On the day that I do this, some who escape the destruction will come and tell you about it. ²⁷That same day you will get back the power of speech which you had lost, and you will talk with them. In this way you will be a sign to the people, and they will know that I am the LORD."

Prophecy against Ammon

25 The LORD spoke to me. ²"Mortal man," he said, "denounce the country of Ammon. ³Tell them to listen to what I, the Sovereign LORD, am saying: You were delighted to see my Temple profaned, to see the land of Israel devastated, to see the people of Judah go into exile. ⁴Because you were glad, I will let the tribes from the eastern desert conquer you. They will set up their camps in your country and settle there. They will eat the fruit and drink the milk that should have been yours. ⁵I will turn the city of Rabbah into a place to keep camels, and the whole country of Ammon will become a place to keep sheep, so that you will know I am the LORD.

⁶"This is what the Sovereign LORD is saying: You clapped your hands and jumped for joy. You despised the land of Israel. ⁷Because you did, I will hand you over to other nations who will rob

---

ᶜ *Some ancient translations* Boil away the broth!; *Hebrew unclear.*   ᵈ *Verse 12 in Hebrew begins with two words, the meaning of which is unclear.*
25.1-7 Jr 49.1-6; Ez 21.28-32; Am 1.13-15; Zep 2.8-11

you and plunder you. I will destroy you so completely that you will not be a nation any more or have a country of your own. Then you will know that I am the LORD."

Prophecy against Moab

8 The Sovereign LORD said, "Because Moab[e] has said that Judah is like all the other nations, 9 I will let the cities that defend the border of Moab be attacked, including even the finest cities — Beth Jeshimoth, Baal Meon, and Kiriathaim. 10 I will let the tribes of the eastern desert conquer Moab, together with Ammon, so that Moab[f] will no longer be a nation. 11 I will punish Moab, and they will know that I am the LORD."

Prophecy against Edom

12 The Sovereign LORD said, "The people of Edom took cruel revenge on Judah, and that revenge has brought lasting guilt on Edom. 13 Now I announce that I will punish Edom and kill every person and animal there. I will make it a wasteland, from the city of Teman to the city of Dedan, and the people will be killed in battle. 14 My people Israel will take revenge on Edom for me, and they will make Edom feel my furious anger. Edom will know what it means to be the object of my revenge." The Sovereign LORD has spoken.

Prophecy against Philistia

15 The Sovereign LORD said, "The Philistines have taken cruel revenge on their agelong enemies and destroyed them in their hate. 16 And so I am announcing that I will attack the Philis-

tines and wipe them out. I will destroy everyone left living there on the Philistine Plain. 17 I will punish them severely and take full revenge on them. They will feel my anger. Then they will know that I am the LORD."

Prophecy against Tyre

26 On the first day of the ... month[g] of the eleventh year of our exile, the LORD spoke to me. 2 "Mortal man," he said, "this is what the people in the city of Tyre are cheering about. They shout, 'Jerusalem is shattered! Her commercial power is gone! She won't be our rival any more!'

3 "Now then, this is what I, the Sovereign LORD, am saying: I am your enemy, city of Tyre. I will bring many nations to attack you, and they will come like the waves of the sea. 4 They will destroy your city walls and tear down your towers. Then I will sweep away all the dust and leave only a bare rock. 5 Fishermen will dry their nets on it, there where it stands in the sea. I, the Sovereign LORD, have spoken. The nations will plunder Tyre, 6 and with their swords they will kill those who live in her towns on the mainland. Then Tyre will know that I am the LORD."

7 The Sovereign LORD says, "I am going to bring the greatest king of all — King Nebuchadnezzar of Babylonia — to attack Tyre. He will come from the north with a huge army, with horses and chariots and with cavalry. 8 Those who live in the towns on the mainland will be killed in the fighting. The enemy will dig trenches, build earthworks, and make a solid wall of shields against you. 9 They will pound in your walls with battering rams and

---

e Some ancient translations Moab; *Hebrew* Moab and Seir.   *f Probable text* Moab; *Hebrew* Ammon.   *g* month; *the Hebrew text does not specify the month.*
25.8-11 Is 15.1 — 16.14; 25.10-12; Jr 48.1-47; Am 2.1-3; Zep 2.8-11   **25.12-14** Is 34.5-17; 63.1-6; Jr 49.7-22; Ez 35.1-15; Am 1.11, 12; Ob 1-14; Ml 1.2-5   **25.15-17** Is 14.29-31; Jr 47.1-7; Jl 3.4-8; Am 1.6-8; Zep 2.4-7; Zec 9.5-7   **26.1 — 28.19** Is 23.1-18; Jl 3.4-8; Am 1.9, 10; Zec 9.1-4; Mt 11.21, 22; Lk 10.13, 14

tear down your towers with iron bars. [10] The clouds of dust raised by their horses will cover you. The noise of their horses pulling wagons and chariots will shake your walls as they pass through the gates of the ruined city. [11] Their cavalry will storm through your streets, killing your people with their swords. Your mighty pillars will be thrown to the ground. [12] Your enemies will help themselves to your wealth and merchandise. They will pull down your walls and shatter your luxurious houses. They will take the stones and wood and all the rubble, and dump them into the sea. [13] I will put an end to all your songs, and I will silence the music of your harps. [14] I will leave only a bare rock where fishermen can dry their nets. The city will never be rebuilt. I, the Sovereign LORD, have spoken."

[15] The Sovereign LORD has this to say to the city of Tyre: "When you are being conquered, the people who live along the coast will be terrified at the screams of those who are slaughtered. [16] All the kings of the seafaring nations will come down from their thrones. They will take off their robes and their embroidered clothes and sit trembling on the ground. They will be so terrified at your fate that they will not be able to stop trembling. [17] They will sing this funeral song for you:

The famous city is destroyed!
Her ships have been swept[h]
   from the seas.
The people of this city ruled the
   seas
And terrified all who lived on
   the coast.
[18] Now, on the day it has fallen,
The islands are trembling,
And their people are shocked at
   such destruction."

[19] The Sovereign LORD says: "I will make you as desolate as ruined cities where no one lives. I will cover you with the water of the ocean depths. [20] I will send you down to the world of the dead to join the people who lived in ancient times. I will make you stay in that underground world among eternal ruins, keeping company with the dead. As a result you will never again be inhabited and take your place[i] in the land of the living. [21] I will make you a terrifying example, and that will be the end of you. People may look for you, but you will never be found." The Sovereign LORD has spoken.

A Funeral Song for Tyre

27 The LORD said to me, [2] "Mortal man, sing a funeral song for Tyre, [3] that city which stands at the edge of the sea and does business with the people living on every seacoast. Tell her what the Sovereign LORD is saying:

"Tyre, you boasted of your
   perfect beauty.
[4] Your home is the sea.
Your builders made you like a
   beautiful ship;
[5] They used fir trees from Mount
   Hermon for timber
And a cedar from Lebanon for
   your mast.
[6] They took oak trees from Bashan
   to make oars;
They made your deck out of pine
   from Cyprus
And inlaid it with ivory.
[7] Your sails were made of linen,
Embroidered linen from Egypt,
Easily recognized from afar.
Your awnings were made of
   finest cloth,
Of purple from the island of
   Cyprus.
[8] Your oarsmen were from the
   cities of Sidon and Arvad.

---

[h] *Some ancient translations* swept; *Hebrew* inhabited.   [i] *One ancient translation* and take your place; *Hebrew unclear.*

26.13 Rev 18.22   **26.16-18** Rev 18.9, 10   **26.21** Rev 18.21

*That city which stands
at the edge of the sea (27.3)*

Your own skillful men were the
  sailors.
⁹The ship's carpenters
  Were well-trained men from
    Byblos.
  Sailors from every seagoing ship
  Did business in your shops.

¹⁰"Soldiers from Persia, Lydia, and
Libya served in your army. They hung
their shields and their helmets in your
barracks. They are the men who won
glory for you. ¹¹Soldiers from Arvad
guarded your walls, and troops from
Gamad guarded your towers. They
hung their shields on your walls. They
are the ones who made you beautiful.

¹²"You did business in Spain and
took silver, iron, tin, and lead in payment for your abundant goods. ¹³You
did business in Greece, Tubal, and Meshech and traded your goods for slaves
and for articles of bronze. ¹⁴You sold
your goods for workhorses, war-horses,
and mules from Beth Togarmah. ¹⁵The
people of Rhodes*ʲ* traded with you;
people of many coastal lands gave you
ivory and ebony in exchange for your
goods. ¹⁶The people of Syria bought
your merchandise and your many products. They gave emeralds, purple cloth,
embroidery, fine linen, coral, and rubies in payment for your wares. ¹⁷Ju-
dah and Israel paid for your goods with
wheat,*ᵏ* honey, olive oil, and spices.
¹⁸⁻¹⁹The people of Damascus bought
your merchandise and your products,
paying for them with wine from Helbon
and wool from Sahar.*ˡ* They traded
wrought iron and spices for your goods.
²⁰The people of Dedan traded saddle
blankets for your goods. ²¹The Arabians
and the rulers of the land of Kedar paid
for your merchandise with lambs,
sheep, and goats. ²²For your goods the
merchants of Sheba and Raamah
traded jewels, gold, and the finest
spices. ²³The cities of Haran, Canneh,
and Eden, the merchants of Sheba, the
cities of Asshur and Chilmad—they all
traded with you. ²⁴They sold you luxurious clothing, purple cloth, and embroidery, brightly colored carpets, and
well-made cords and ropes. ²⁵Your
merchandise was carried in fleets of the
largest cargo ships.

  "You were like a ship at sea
  Loaded with heavy cargo.
²⁶When your oarsmen brought you
    out to sea,

ʲ One ancient translation Rhodes; *Hebrew* Dedan.   *ᵏ Hebrew has two additional
words, the meaning of which is unclear.   ˡ Hebrew has three additional words, the
meaning of which is unclear.*
27.25-36 Rev 18.11-19

An east wind wrecked you far
    from land.
27 All your wealth of merchandise,
All the sailors in your crew,
Your ship's carpenters and your
    merchants,
Every soldier on board the
    ship —
All, all were lost at sea
When your ship was wrecked.
28 The shouts of the drowning
    sailors
    Echoed on the shore.

29 "Every ship is now deserted,
    And every sailor has gone ashore.
30 They all mourn bitterly for you,
    Throwing dust on their heads
        and rolling in ashes.
31 They shave their heads for you
And dress themselves in
    sackcloth.
Their hearts are bitter as they
    weep.
32 They chant a funeral song
    for you:
'Who can be compared to Tyre,
To Tyre now silent in the sea?
33 When your merchandise went
    overseas,
You filled the needs of every
    nation.
Kings were made rich
By the wealth of your goods.
34 Now you are wrecked in the sea;
You have sunk to the ocean
    depths.
Your goods and all who worked
    for you
Have vanished with you in
    the sea.'

35 "Everyone who lives along the
coast is shocked at your fate. Even their
kings are terrified, and fear is written
on their faces. 36 You are gone, gone forever, and merchants all over the world
are terrified, afraid that they will share
your fate."

Prophecy against the King of Tyre

28 The LORD spoke to me. 2 "Mortal man," he said, "tell the ruler
of Tyre what I, the Sovereign LORD, am
saying to him: Puffed up with pride,
you claim to be a god. You say that like
a god you sit on a throne, surrounded by
the seas. You may pretend to be a god,
but, no, you are mortal, not divine. 3 You
think you are wiser than Danel,[m] that
no secret can be kept from you. 4 Your
wisdom and skill made you rich with
treasures of gold and silver. 5 You made
clever business deals and kept on making profits. How proud you are of your
wealth!

6 "Now then, this is what I, the
Sovereign LORD, am saying: Because
you think you are as wise as a god, 7 I
will bring ruthless enemies to attack
you. They will destroy all the beautiful
things you have acquired by skill and
wisdom. 8 They will kill you and send
you to a watery grave. 9 When they
come to kill you, will you still claim that
you are a god? When you face your
murderers, you will be mortal and not
at all divine. 10 You will die like a dog
at the hand of godless foreigners. I,
the Sovereign LORD, have given the
command."

The Fall of the King of Tyre

11 The LORD spoke to me again.
12 "Mortal man," he said, "grieve for the
fate that is waiting for the king of Tyre.
Tell him what I, the Sovereign LORD,
am saying: You were once an example
of perfection. How wise and handsome
you were! 13 You lived in Eden, the garden of God, and wore gems of every
kind: rubies and diamonds; topaz,
beryl, carnelian, and jasper; sapphires,
emeralds, and garnets. You had ornaments of gold. They were made for
you[n] on the day you were created. 14 I
put a terrifying angel there to guard

---

m Danel; *or* Daniel *(see 14.14).*   *n Probable text* They were made for you; *Hebrew*
unclear.

you.*o* You lived on my holy mountain and walked among sparkling gems. [15]Your conduct was perfect from the day you were created until you began to do evil. [16]You were busy buying and selling, and this led you to violence and sin. So I forced you to leave my holy mountain, and the angel who guarded you drove you away from the sparkling gems. [17]You were proud of being handsome, and your fame made you act like a fool. Because of this I hurled you to the ground and left you as a warning to other kings. [18]You did such evil in buying and selling that your places of worship were corrupted. So I set fire to the city and burned it to the ground. All who look at you now see you reduced to ashes. [19]You are gone, gone forever, and all the nations that had come to know you are terrified, afraid that they will share your fate."

Prophecy against Sidon

[20]The LORD said to me, [21]"Mortal man, denounce the city of Sidon. [22]Tell the people there what I, the Sovereign LORD, say about them: I am your enemy, Sidon; people will praise me because of what I do to you. They will know that I am the LORD, when I show how holy I am by punishing those who live in you. [23]I will send diseases on you and make blood flow in your streets. You will be attacked from every side, and your people will be killed. Then you will know that I am the LORD."

Israel Will Be Blessed

[24]The LORD said, "None of the surrounding nations that treated Israel with scorn will ever again be like thorns and briers to hurt Israel. And they will know that I am the Sovereign LORD."

[25]The Sovereign LORD said, "I will bring back the people of Israel from the nations where I scattered them, and all the nations will know that I am holy. The people of Israel will live in their own land, the land that I gave to my servant Jacob. [26]They will live there in safety. They will build houses and plant vineyards. I will punish all their neighbors who treated them with scorn, and Israel will be secure. Then they will know that I am the LORD their God."

Prophecy against Egypt

29 On the twelfth day of the tenth month of the tenth year of our exile, the LORD spoke to me. [2]"Mortal man," he said, "denounce the king of Egypt. Tell him how he and all the land of Egypt will be punished. [3]Say that this is what the Sovereign LORD is telling the king of Egypt: I am your enemy, you monster crocodile, lying in the river. You say that the Nile is yours and that you made it.*p* [4]I am going to put a hook through your jaw and make the fish in your river stick fast to you. Then I will pull you up out of the Nile, with all the fish sticking to you. [5]I will throw you and all those fish into the desert. Your body will fall on the ground and be left unburied. I will give it to the birds and animals for food. [6]Then all the people of Egypt will know that I am the LORD."

The LORD says, "The Israelites relied on you Egyptians for support, but you were no better than a weak stick. [7]When they leaned on you, you broke, pierced their armpits, and made them wrench their backs.*q* [8]Now then, I, the Sovereign LORD, am telling you that I will have troops attack you with swords, and they will kill your people and your

---

o One ancient translation I put . . . you; *Hebrew unclear.* *p Some ancient translations* you made it; *Hebrew* you made yourself. *q One ancient translation* wrench their backs; *Hebrew* make their backs stand.

28.20-26 Jl 3.4-8; Zec 9.1, 2; Mt 11.21, 22; Lk 10.13, 14   **29.1—32.32** Is 19.1-25; Jr 46.2-26   **29.6** Is 36.6

I will pull you up out of the Nile. (29.4)

animals. ⁹Egypt will become an empty wasteland. Then you will know that I am the LORD.

"Because you said that the Nile is yours and you made it, ¹⁰I am your enemy and the enemy of your Nile. I will make all of Egypt an empty wasteland, from the city of Migdol in the north to the city of Aswan in the south, all the way to the Ethiopian ʳ border. ¹¹No human being or animal will walk through it. For forty years nothing will live there. ¹²I will make Egypt the most desolate country in the world. For forty years the cities of Egypt will lie in ruins, ruins worse than those of any other city. I will make the Egyptians refugees. They will flee to every country and live among other peoples."

¹³The Sovereign LORD says, "After forty years I will bring the Egyptians back from the nations where I have scattered them, ¹⁴and I will let them live in southern Egypt, their original home. There they will be a weak kingdom, ¹⁵the weakest kingdom of all, and they will never again rule other nations. I will make them so unimportant that they will not be able to bend any other nation to their will. ¹⁶Israel will never again depend on them for help. Egypt's fate will remind Israel how wrong it was to rely on them. Then Israel will know that I am the Sovereign LORD."

King Nebuchadnezzar Will Conquer Egypt

¹⁷On the first day of the first month of the twenty-seventh year of our exile, the LORD spoke to me. ¹⁸"Mortal man," he said, "King Nebuchadnezzar of Babylonia launched an attack on Tyre. He made his soldiers carry such heavy loads that their heads were rubbed bald and their shoulders were worn raw, but neither the king nor his army got anything for all their trouble. ¹⁹So now this is what I, the Sovereign LORD, am saying: I am giving the land of Egypt to King Nebuchadnezzar. He will loot and plunder it and carry off all the wealth of Egypt as his army's pay. ²⁰I am giving him Egypt in payment for his services, because his army was working for me. I, the Sovereign LORD, have spoken.

²¹"When that happens, I will make the people of Israel strong and let you, Ezekiel, speak out where everyone can hear you, so that they will know that I am the LORD."

ʳ *Hebrew* Cushite(Cush): *Cush is the ancient name of the extensive territory south of the First Cataract of the Nile River. This region was called Ethiopia in Graeco-Roman times, and included within its borders most of modern Sudan and some of present-day Ethiopia (Abyssinia).*

The LORD Will Punish Egypt

30 The LORD spoke to me again. 2 "Mortal man," he said, "prophesy and announce what I, the Sovereign LORD, am saying. You are to shout these words:

A day of terror is coming!
3 The day is near, the day when
    the LORD will act,
A day of clouds and trouble for
    the nations.
4 There will be war in Egypt
And great distress in Ethiopia.*
Many in Egypt will be killed;
The country will be plundered
And left in ruins.

5 "That war will also kill the soldiers hired from Ethiopia,* Libya, Lydia, Arabia, Kub, and even from among my own people."

6 The LORD says, "From Migdol in the north to Aswan in the south, all Egypt's defenders will be killed in battle. Egypt's proud army will be destroyed. I, the Sovereign LORD, have spoken. 7 The land will be the most desolate in the world, and its cities will be left totally in ruins. 8 When I set fire to Egypt and all her defenders are killed, then they will know that I am the LORD.

9 "When that day comes and Egypt is destroyed, I will send messengers in ships to arouse the unsuspecting people of Ethiopia,* and they will be terrified. That day is coming!"

10 The Sovereign LORD says, "I will use King Nebuchadnezzar of Babylonia to put an end to Egypt's wealth. 11 He and his ruthless army will come to devastate the land. They will attack Egypt with swords, and the land will be full of corpses. 12 I will dry up the Nile and put Egypt under the power of evil people. Foreigners will devastate the whole country. I, the LORD, have spoken."

13 The Sovereign LORD says, "I will destroy the idols and the false gods in Memphis. There will be no one to rule Egypt, and I will terrify all the people. 14 I will make southern Egypt desolate and set fire to the city of Zoan in the north. I will punish the capital city of Thebes. 15 I will let the city of Pelusium, Egypt's great fortress, feel my fury. I will destroy the wealth of Thebes. 16 I will set fire to Egypt, and Pelusium will be in agony. The walls of Thebes will be broken down, and the city will be flooded.* 17 The young men of the cities of Heliopolis and Bubastis will die in the war, and the other people will be taken prisoner. 18 Darkness will fall on Tahpanhes when I break the power of Egypt and put an end to the strength they were so proud of. A cloud will cover Egypt, and the people of all her cities will be taken prisoner. 19 When I punish Egypt in this way, they will know that I am the LORD."

The Broken Power of the King of Egypt

20 On the seventh day of the first month of the eleventh year of our exile, the LORD spoke to me. 21 "Mortal man," he said, "I have broken the arm of the king of Egypt. No one has bandaged it or put it in a sling so that it could heal and be strong enough to hold a sword again. 22 Now then, this is what I, the Sovereign LORD, say: I am the enemy of the king of Egypt. I am going to break both his arms—the good one and the one already broken—and the sword will fall from his hand. 23 I am going to scatter the Egyptians throughout the world. 24 Then I will make the arms of the king of Babylonia strong and put

---

r Hebrew Cushite(Cush): *Cush is the ancient name of the extensive territory south of the First Cataract of the Nile River. This region was called Ethiopia in Graeco-Roman times, and included within its borders most of modern Sudan and some of present-day Ethiopia (Abyssinia).*   *s One ancient translation* flooded; *Hebrew unclear.*

my sword in his hands. But I will break the arms of the king of Egypt, and he will groan and die in front of his enemy. 25 Yes, I will weaken him and strengthen the king of Babylonia. When I give him my sword and he points it toward Egypt, everyone will know that I am the LORD. 26 I will scatter the Egyptians throughout the world. Then they will know that I am the LORD."

Egypt Is Compared to a Cedar Tree

31 On the first day of the third month of the eleventh year of our exile, the LORD spoke to me. 2 "Mortal man," he said, "say to the king of Egypt and all his people:

How powerful you are!
    What can I compare you to?
3 You are like *t* a cedar in
        Lebanon,
    With beautiful, shady branches,
    A tree so tall it reaches the
        clouds. *u*
4 There was water to make it
        grow,
    And underground rivers to
        feed it.
    They watered the place where
        the tree was growing
    And sent streams to all the trees
        of the forest.
5 Because it was well-watered,
    It grew taller than other trees.
    Its branches grew thick and
        long.
6 Every kind of bird built nests in
        its branches;
    The wild animals bore their
        young in its shelter;
    The nations of the world rested
        in its shade.
7 How beautiful the tree was —
    So tall, with such long branches.

Its roots reached down to the
        deep-flowing streams.
8 No cedar in God's garden could
        compare with it.
    No fir tree ever had such
        branches,
    And no plane tree such limbs.
    No tree in God's own garden was
        so beautiful.
9 I made it beautiful, with
        spreading branches.
    It was the envy of every tree in
        Eden, the garden of God.

10 "Now then, I, the Sovereign LORD, will tell you what is going to happen to that tree that grew until it reached the clouds. *u* As it grew taller it grew proud; 11 so I have rejected it and will let a foreign ruler have it. He will give that tree what it deserves for its wickedness. 12 Ruthless foreigners will cut it down and leave it. Its branches and broken limbs will fall on every mountain and valley in the country. All the nations that have been living in its shade will go away. 13 The birds will come and perch on the fallen tree, and the wild animals will walk over its branches. 14 And so from now on, no tree, no matter how well-watered it is, will grow that tall again or push its top through the clouds *u* and reach such a height. All of them are doomed to die like mortals, doomed to join those who go down to the world of the dead."

15 This is what the Sovereign LORD says: "On the day when the tree goes to the world of the dead, I will make the underground waters cover it as a sign of mourning. I will hold back the rivers and not let the many streams flow out. Because the tree has died, I will bring darkness over the Lebanon Mountains and make all the trees of the forest wither. 16 When I send it down to the world of the dead, the noise of its

---

t Probable text You are like; *Hebrew* Assyria is. *Hebrew* thick branches.

31.8 Gn 2.9

u One ancient translation clouds;

No tree . . . will grow that tall again. (31.14)

downfall will shake the nations. All the trees of Eden and all the choice, well-watered trees of Lebanon who have gone to the world below will be pleased at its downfall. 17 They will go with it to the world of the dead to join those that have already fallen. And all who live under its shadow will be scattered among the nations.*v*

18 "The tree is the king of Egypt and all his people. Not even the trees in Eden were so tall and impressive. But now, like the trees of Eden, it will go down to the world of the dead and join the ungodly and those killed in battle. I have spoken," says the Sovereign LORD.

The King of Egypt Is Compared to a Crocodile

32 On the first day of the twelfth month of the twelfth year of our exile, the LORD spoke to me. 2 "Mortal man," he said, "give a solemn warning to the king of Egypt. Give him this message from me: You act like a lion among the nations, but you are more like a crocodile splashing through a river. You muddy the water with your feet and pollute the rivers. 3 When many nations gather, I will catch you in my net and let them drag the net ashore. 4 I will throw you out on the ground and bring all the birds and animals of the world to feed on you. 5 I will cover mountains and valleys with your rotting corpse. 6 I will pour out your

blood until it spreads over the mountains and fills the streams. 7 When I destroy you, I will cover the sky and blot out the stars. The sun will hide behind the clouds, and the moon will give no light. 8 I will put out all the lights of heaven and plunge your world into darkness. I, the Sovereign LORD, have spoken.

9 "Many nations will be troubled when I spread the news of your destruction through countries you never heard of. 10 What I do to you will shock many nations. When I swing my sword, kings will shudder with fright. On the day you fall, all of them will tremble in fear for their own lives."

11 The Sovereign LORD says to the king of Egypt, "You will face the sword of the king of Babylonia. 12 I will let soldiers from cruel nations draw their swords and kill all your people. All your people and everything else that you are proud of will be destroyed. 13 I will slaughter your cattle at every water hole. There will be no people or cattle to muddy the water any more. 14 I will let your waters settle and become clear and let your rivers run calm. I, the Sovereign LORD, have spoken. 15 When I make Egypt a desolate wasteland and destroy all who live there, they will know that I am the LORD. 16 This solemn warning will become a funeral song. The women of the nations will sing it to mourn for Egypt and all its

v Probable text And all . . . nations; *Hebrew unclear.*
32.7 Is 13.10; Mt 24.29; Mk 13.24, 25; Lk 21.25; Rev 6.12, 13; 8.12

people. I, the Sovereign LORD, have spoken."

The World of the Dead

[17] On the fifteenth day of the first month[w] of the twelfth year of our exile, the LORD spoke to me. [18] "Mortal man," he said, "mourn for all the many people of Egypt. Send them down with the other powerful nations to the world of the dead. [19] Say to them:

"Do you think you are more
     beautiful than anyone else?
You will go down to the world of
     the dead
     and lie there among the
       ungodly.

[20] "The people of Egypt will fall with those who are killed in battle. A sword is ready to kill them all.[x] [21] The greatest heroes and those who fought on the Egyptian side welcome the Egyptians to the world of the dead. They shout: 'The ungodly who were killed in battle have come down here, and here they lie!'

[22] "Assyria is there, with the graves of her soldiers all around. They were all killed in battle, [23] and their graves are in the deepest parts of the world of the dead. All her soldiers fell in battle, and their graves surround her tomb. Yet once they terrified the land of the living.

[24] "Elam is there, with the graves of her soldiers all around. They were all killed in battle, and they went down, uncircumcised, to the world of the dead. In life they spread terror, but now they lie dead and disgraced. [25] Elam lies down among those killed in battle, and the graves of her soldiers are all around her. They are all uncircumcised, all killed in battle. In life they spread terror, but now they lie dead and dis-

graced, sharing the fate of those killed in battle.

[26] "Meshech and Tubal are there, with the graves of their soldiers all around. They are all uncircumcised, all killed in battle. Yet once they terrified the living. [27] They were not given honorable burial like the heroes of ancient times,[y] who went fully armed to the world of the dead, their swords placed under their heads and their shields[z] over their bodies. These heroes were once powerful enough to terrify the living.

[28] "That is how the Egyptians will lie crushed among the uncircumcised who were killed in battle.

[29] "Edom is there with her kings and rulers. They were powerful soldiers, but now they lie in the world of the dead with the uncircumcised who were killed in battle.

[30] "All the princes of the north are there, and so are the Sidonians. Their power once spread terror, but now they go down in disgrace with those killed in battle and are laid to rest, uncircumcised. They share the disgrace of those who go down to the world of the dead.

[31] "The sight of all these who were killed in battle will be a comfort to the king of Egypt and his army," says the Sovereign LORD.

[32] "I caused the king of Egypt to terrorize the living, but he and all his army will be killed and laid to rest with all the uncircumcised who die in battle." The Sovereign LORD has spoken.

God Appoints Ezekiel as a Lookout
(Ezekiel 3.16-21)

33 The LORD spoke to me. [2] "Mortal man," he said, "tell your people what happens when I bring war to a land. The people of that country

---

[w] *One ancient translation* of the first month; *Hebrew does not have these words.*
[x] *Probable text* A sword . . . all; *Hebrew unclear.*
ancient times; *Hebrew* of the uncircumcised.
iniquities.
[y] *Some ancient translations of*
[z] *Probable text* shields; *Hebrew*

choose one of their number to be a lookout. ³When he sees the enemy approaching, he sounds the alarm to warn everyone. ⁴If someone hears it but pays no attention and the enemy comes and kills him, then he is to blame for his own death. ⁵His death is his own fault, because he paid no attention to the warning. If he had paid attention, he could have escaped. ⁶If, however, the lookout sees the enemy coming and does not sound the alarm, the enemy will come and kill those sinners, but I will hold the lookout responsible for their death.

⁷"Now, mortal man, I am making you a lookout for the nation of Israel. You must pass on to them the warnings I give you. ⁸If I announce that an evil person is going to die but you do not warn him to change his ways so that he can save his life, then he will die, still a sinner, and I will hold you responsible for his death. ⁹If you do warn an evil person and he doesn't stop sinning, he will die, still a sinner, but your life will be spared."

Individual Responsibility

¹⁰The LORD spoke to me. "Mortal man," he said, "repeat to the Israelites what they are saying: 'We are burdened with our sins and the wrongs we have done. We are wasting away. How can we live?' ¹¹Tell them that as surely as I, the Sovereign LORD, am the living God, I do not enjoy seeing sinners die. I would rather see them stop sinning and live. Israel, stop the evil you are doing. Why do you want to die?

¹²"Now, mortal man, tell the Israelites that when someone good sins, the good he has done will not save him. If an evil person stops doing evil, he won't be punished, and if a good man starts sinning, his life will not be spared. ¹³I may promise life to someone good, but if he starts thinking that his past good-

ness is enough and begins to sin, I will not remember any of the good he did. He will die because of his sins. ¹⁴I may warn someone evil that he is going to die, but if he stops sinning and does what is right and good — ¹⁵for example, if he returns the security he took for a loan or gives back what he stole — if he stops sinning and follows the laws that give life, he will not die, but live. ¹⁶I will forgive the sins he has committed, and he will live because he has done what is right and good.

¹⁷"And your people say that what I do isn't right! No, it's their way that isn't right. ¹⁸When someone righteous stops doing good and starts doing evil, he will die for it. ¹⁹When someone evil quits sinning and does what is right and good, he has saved his life. ²⁰But Israel, you say that what I do isn't right. I am going to judge you by what you do."

The News of Jerusalem's Fall

²¹On the fifth day of the tenth month of the twelfth year of our exile, someone who had escaped from Jerusalem came and told me that the city had fallen. ²²The evening before he came, I had felt the powerful presence of the LORD. When the man arrived the next morning, the LORD gave me back the power of speech.

The Sins of the People

²³The LORD spoke to me. ²⁴"Mortal man," he said, "the people who are living in the ruined cities of the land of Israel are saying: 'Abraham was only one man, and he was given the whole land. There are many of us, so now the land is ours.'

²⁵"Tell them what I, the Sovereign LORD, am saying: You eat meat with the blood still in it. You worship idols. You commit murder. What makes you think that the land belongs to you? ²⁶You rely on your swords. Your actions

are disgusting. Everyone commits adultery. What makes you think that the land is yours?

27 "Tell them that I, the Sovereign LORD, warn them that as surely as I am the living God, the people who live in the ruined cities will be killed. Those living in the country will be eaten by wild animals. Those hiding in the mountains and in caves will die of disease. 28 I will make the country a desolate wasteland, and the power they were so proud of will come to an end. The mountains of Israel will be so wild that no one will be able to travel through them. 29 When I punish the people for their sins and make the country a wasteland, then they will know that I am the LORD."

The Results of the Prophet's Message

30 The LORD said, "Mortal man, your people are talking about you when they meet by the city walls or in the doorways of their houses. They say to one another, 'Let's go and hear what word has come from the LORD now.' 31 So my people crowd in to hear what you have to say, but they don't do what you tell them to do. Loving words are on their lips, but they continue their greedy ways. 32 To them you are nothing more than an entertainer singing love songs or playing a harp. They listen to all your words and don't obey a single one of them. 33 But when all your words come true — and they will come true — then they will know that a prophet has been among them."

The Shepherds of Israel

34

The LORD spoke to me. 2 "Mortal man," he said, "denounce the rulers of Israel. Prophesy to them, and tell them what I, the Sovereign LORD, say to them: You are doomed, you shepherds of Israel! You take care of yourselves, but never tend the sheep.

They listen to all your words and don't obey a single one of them. (33.32)

3 You drink the milk, wear clothes made from the wool, and kill and eat the finest sheep. But you never tend the sheep. 4 You have not taken care of the weak ones, healed the ones that are sick, bandaged the ones that are hurt, brought back the ones that wandered off, or looked for the ones that were lost. Instead, you treated them cruelly. 5 Because the sheep had no shepherd, they were scattered, and wild animals killed and ate them. 6 So my sheep wandered over the high hills and the mountains. They were scattered over the face of the earth, and no one looked for them or tried to find them.

7 "Now, you shepherds, listen to what I, the LORD, am telling you. 8 As surely as I am the living God, you had better listen to me. My sheep have been attacked by wild animals that killed and ate them because there was no shepherd. My shepherds did not try to find the sheep. They were taking care of themselves and not the sheep. 9 So listen to me, you shepherds. 10 I, the Sovereign LORD, declare that I am your enemy. I will take my sheep away from you and never again let you be their shepherds; never again will I let you take care only of yourselves. I will

34.5 Nu 27.17; 1 K 22.17; Mt 9.36; Mk 6.34

Because the sheep had no shepherd (34.5)   *I myself will be the shepherd of my sheep. (34.15)*

rescue my sheep from you and not let you eat them.

The Good Shepherd

11"I, the Sovereign LORD, tell you that I myself will look for my sheep and take care of them **12** in the same way as shepherds take care of their sheep that were scattered and are brought together again. I will bring them back from all the places where they were scattered on that dark, disastrous day. **13** I will take them out of foreign countries, gather them together, and bring them back to their own land. I will lead them back to the mountains and the streams of Israel and will feed them in pleasant pastures. **14** I will let them graze in safety in the mountain meadows and the valleys and in all the green pastures of the land of Israel. **15** I myself will be the shepherd of my sheep, and I will find them a place to rest. I, the Sovereign LORD, have spoken.

16"I will look for those that are lost, bring back those that wander off, bandage those that are hurt, and heal those that are sick; but those that are fat and strong I will destroy, because I am a shepherd who does what is right.

17"Now then, my flock, I, the Sovereign LORD, tell you that I will judge each of you and separate the good from the bad, the sheep from the goats. **18** Some of you are not satisfied with eating the best grass; you even trample down what you don't eat! You drink the clear water and muddy what you don't drink! **19** My other sheep have to eat the grass you trample down and drink the water you muddy.

20"So now, I, the Sovereign LORD, tell you that I will judge between you strong sheep and the weak sheep. **21** You pushed the sick ones aside and butted them away from the flock. **22** But I will rescue my sheep and not let them be mistreated any more. I will judge each of my sheep and separate the good from the bad. **23** I will give them a king like my servant David to be their one shepherd, and he will take care of them. **24** I, the LORD, will be their God, and a king like my servant David will be their ruler. I have spoken. **25** I will make a covenant with them that guarantees their security. I will get rid of all the dangerous animals in the land, so that my sheep can live safely in the fields and sleep in the forests.

26 "I will bless them and let them live around my sacred hill.*a* There I will bless them with showers of rain when they need it. 27 The trees will bear fruit, the fields will produce crops, and everyone will live in safety on his own land. When I break my people's chains and set them free from those who made them slaves, then they will know that I am the LORD. 28 The heathen nations will not plunder them any more, and the wild animals will not kill and eat them. They will live in safety, and no one will terrify them. 29 I will give them fertile fields and put an end to hunger in the land. The other nations will not sneer at them any more. 30 Everyone will know that I protect Israel and that they are my people. I, the Sovereign LORD, have spoken.

31 "You, my sheep, the flock that I feed, are my people, and I am your God," says the Sovereign LORD.

God's Punishment of Edom

35 The LORD spoke to me. 2 "Mortal man," he said, "denounce the country of Edom. 3 Tell the people what I, the Sovereign LORD, am saying:
"I am your enemy, mountains
    of Edom!
I will make you a desolate
    wasteland.
4 I will leave your cities in ruins
    And your land desolate;
Then you will know that I am
    the LORD.

5 "You were Israel's constant enemy and let her people be slaughtered in the time of her disaster, the time of final punishment for her sins. 6 So then — as surely as I, the Sovereign LORD, am the living God — death is your fate, and you cannot escape it. You are guilty of*b*

murder, and murder will follow you. 7 I will make the hill country of Edom a wasteland and kill everyone who travels through it. 8 I will cover the mountains with corpses, and the bodies of those who are killed in battle will cover the hills and valleys. 9 I will make you desolate forever, and no one will live in your cities again. Then you will know that I am the LORD.

10 "You said that the two nations, Judah and Israel, together with their lands, belonged to you and that you would possess them, even though I, the LORD, was their God. 11 So then, as surely as I, the Sovereign LORD, am the living God, I will pay you back for your anger, your jealousy, and your hate toward my people. They will know that I am punishing you for what you did to them. 12 Then you will know that I, the LORD, heard you say with contempt that the mountains of Israel were desolate and that they were yours to devour. 13 I have heard the wild, boastful way you have talked against me."

14 The Sovereign LORD says, "I will make you so desolate that the whole world will rejoice at your downfall, 15 just as you rejoiced at the devastation of Israel, my own possession. The mountains of Seir, yes, all the land of Edom, will be desolate. Then everyone will know that I am the LORD."

God's Blessing on Israel

36 The LORD said, "Mortal man, speak to the mountains of Israel and tell them to listen to the message which I, 2 the Sovereign LORD, have for them: Israel's enemies gloated and said, 'Now those ancient hills are ours!'

3 "Prophesy, then, and announce what I, the Sovereign LORD, am saying. When the neighboring nations captured and plundered the mountains of

a SACRED HILL: *See* 20.40.   *b One ancient translation* are guilty of; *Hebrew* hate.
35.1-15 Is 34.5-17; 63.1-6; Jr 49.7-22; Ez 25.12-14; Am 1.11, 12; Ob 1-14; Ml 1.2-5

Israel, everyone made fun of Israel. [4] So now listen to what I, the Sovereign LORD, say to you mountains and hills, to you brooks and valleys, to you places that were left in ruins, and to you deserted cities which were plundered and mocked by all the surrounding nations.

[5] "I, the Sovereign LORD, have spoken out in the heat of my anger against the surrounding nations, and especially against Edom. With glee and contempt they captured my land and took possession of its pastures.

[6] "So prophesy to the land of Israel; tell the mountains, hills, brooks, and valleys what I, the Sovereign LORD, am saying in jealous anger because of the way the nations have insulted and humiliated them. [7] I, the Sovereign LORD, solemnly promise that the surrounding nations will be humiliated. [8] But on the mountains of Israel the trees will again grow leaves and bear fruit for you, my people Israel. You are going to come home soon. [9] I am on your side, and I will make sure that your land is plowed again and crops are planted on it. [10] I will make your population grow. You will live in the cities and rebuild everything that was left in ruins. [11] I will make people and cattle increase in number. There will be more of you than ever before, and you will have many children. I will let you live there as you used to live, and I will make you more prosperous than ever. Then you will know that I am the LORD. [12] I will bring you, my people Israel, back to live again in the land. It will be your own land, and it will never again let your children starve.

[13] "I, the Sovereign LORD, say: It is true that people say that the land eats people and that it robs the nation of its children. [14] But from now on it will no longer eat people and rob you of your children. I, the Sovereign LORD, have spoken. [15] The land will no longer have to listen to the nations making fun of it or see the peoples sneer at it. The land will no longer rob the nation of its children. I, the Sovereign LORD, have spoken."

Israel's New Life

[16] The LORD spoke to me. [17] "Mortal man," he said, "when the Israelites were living in their land, they defiled it by the way they lived and acted. I regarded their behavior as being as ritually unclean as a woman is during her monthly period.[c] [18] I let them feel the force of my anger because of the murders they had committed in the land and because of the idols by which they had defiled it. [19] I condemned them for the way they lived and acted, and I scattered them through foreign countries. [20] Wherever they went, they brought disgrace on my holy name, because people would say, 'These are the people of the LORD, but they had to leave his land.' [21] That made me concerned for my holy name, since the Israelites brought disgrace on it everywhere they went.

[22] "Now then, give the Israelites the message that I, the Sovereign LORD, have for them: What I am going to do is not for the sake of you Israelites, but for the sake of my holy name, which you have disgraced in every country where you have gone. [23] When I demonstrate to the nations the holiness of my great name — the name you disgraced among them — then they will know that I am the LORD. I, the Sovereign LORD, have spoken. I will use you to show the nations that I am holy. [24] I will take you from every nation and country and bring you back to your own land. [25] I will sprinkle clean water on you and make you clean from all your idols and everything else that has de-

---

[c] RITUALLY UNCLEAN ... PERIOD: *This is based on the view of ritual uncleanness described in the Law of Moses (see Lv 15.19).*

filed you. ²⁶ I will give you a new heart and a new mind. I will take away your stubborn heart of stone and give you an obedient heart. ²⁷ I will put my spirit in you and will see to it that you follow my laws and keep all the commands I have given you. ²⁸ Then you will live in the land I gave your ancestors. You will be my people, and I will be your God. ²⁹ I will save you from everything that defiles you. I will command the grain to be plentiful, so that you will not have any more famines. ³⁰ I will increase the yield of your fruit trees and your fields, so that there will be no more famines to disgrace you among the nations. ³¹ You will remember your evil conduct and the wrongs that you committed, and you will be disgusted with yourselves because of your sins and your iniquities. ³² Israel, I want you to know that I am not doing all this for your sake. I want you to feel the shame and disgrace of what you are doing. I, the Sovereign Lord, have spoken."

³³ The Sovereign Lord says, "When I make you clean from all your sins, I will let you live in your cities again and let you rebuild the ruins. ³⁴ Everyone who used to walk by your fields saw how overgrown and wild they were, but I will let you farm them again. ³⁵ Everyone will talk about how this land, which was once a wilderness, has become like the Garden of Eden, and how the cities which were torn down, looted, and left in ruins, are now inhabited and fortified. ³⁶ Then the neighboring nations that have survived will know that I, the Lord, rebuild ruined cities and replant waste fields. I, the Lord, have promised that I would do this — and I will."

³⁷ The Sovereign Lord says, "I will once again let the Israelites ask me for help, and I will let them increase in numbers like a flock of sheep. ³⁸ The cities that are now in ruins will then be as full of people as Jerusalem was once

full of the sheep which were offered as sacrifices at a festival. Then they will know that I am the Lord."

The Valley of Dry Bones

37 I felt the powerful presence of the Lord, and his spirit took me and set me down in a valley where the ground was covered with bones. ² He led me all around the valley, and I could see that there were very many

I could see that there were very many bones.
(37.2)

bones and that they were very dry. ³ He said to me, "Mortal man, can these bones come back to life?"

I replied, "Sovereign Lord, only you can answer that!"

⁴ He said, "Prophesy to the bones. Tell these dry bones to listen to the word of the Lord. ⁵ Tell them that I, the Sovereign Lord, am saying to them: I am going to put breath into you and bring you back to life. ⁶ I will give you sinews and muscles, and cover you with skin. I will put breath into you and bring you back to life. Then you will know that I am the Lord."

⁷ So I prophesied as I had been told. While I was speaking, I heard a rattling noise, and the bones began to join together. ⁸ While I watched, the bones were covered with sinews and muscles, and then with skin. But there was no breath in the bodies.

⁹ God said to me, "Mortal man, prophesy to the wind.ᵈ Tell the wind that the

---

ᵈ wind; *or* spirit. *The same Hebrew word may mean* wind, *or* spirit, *or* breath.
36.26-28 Ez 11.19, 20

Sovereign LORD commands it to come from every direction, to breathe into these dead bodies, and to bring them back to life."

¹⁰So I prophesied as I had been told. Breath entered the bodies, and they came to life and stood up. There were enough of them to form an army.

¹¹God said to me, "Mortal man, the people of Israel are like these bones. They say that they are dried up, without any hope and with no future. ¹²So prophesy to my people Israel and tell them that I, the Sovereign LORD, am going to open their graves. I am going to take them out and bring them back to the land of Israel. ¹³When I open the graves where my people are buried and bring them out, they will know that I am the LORD. ¹⁴I will put my breath in them, bring them back to life, and let them live in their own land. Then they will know that I am the LORD. I have promised that I would do this — and I will. I, the LORD, have spoken."

Judah and Israel in One Kingdom

¹⁵The LORD spoke to me again. ¹⁶"Mortal man," he said, "take a wooden stick and write on it the words, 'The kingdom of Judah.' Then take another stick and write on it the words, 'The kingdom of Israel.' ¹⁷Then hold the two sticks end to end in your hand so that they look like one stick. ¹⁸When your people ask you to tell them what this means, ¹⁹tell them that I, the Sovereign LORD, am going to take the stick representing Israel and put it with the one that represents Judah. Out of the two I will make one stick and hold it in my hand.

²⁰"Hold in your hand the two sticks and let the people see them. ²¹Then tell them that I, the Sovereign LORD, am going to take all my people out of the nations where they have gone, gather

them together, and bring them back to their own land. ²²I will unite them into one nation in the land, on the mountains of Israel. They will have one king to rule over them, and they will no longer be divided into two nations or split into two kingdoms. ²³They will not defile themselves with disgusting idols any more or corrupt themselves with sin. I will free them from all the ways in which they sin and betray me. I will purify them; they will be my people, and I will be their God. ²⁴A king like my servant David will be their king. They will all be united under one ruler and will obey my laws faithfully. ²⁵They will live on the land I gave to my servant Jacob, the land where their ancestors lived. They will live there forever, and so will their children and all their descendants. A king like my servant David will rule them forever. ²⁶I will make a covenant with them that guarantees their security forever. I will establish them and increase their population, and will see to it that my Temple stands forever in their land. ²⁷I will live there with them; I will be their God, and they will be my people. ²⁸When I place my Temple there to be among them forever, then the nations will know that I, the LORD, have chosen Israel to be my own people."

Gog as the Instrument of God

38 The LORD spoke to me. ²"Mortal man," he said, "denounce Gog, chief ruler of the nations of Meshech and Tubal in the land of Magog. Denounce him ³and tell him that I, the Sovereign LORD, am his enemy. ⁴I will turn him around, put hooks in his jaws, and drag him and all his troops away. His army, with its horses and uniformed riders, is enormous, and every soldier carries a shield and is armed with a sword. ⁵Troops from Persia,

Ethiopia,[e] and Libya are with him, and all have shields and helmets. [6] All the fighting men of the lands of Gomer and Beth Togarmah in the north are with him, and so are men from many other nations. [7] Tell him to get ready and have all his troops ready at his command. [8] After many years I will order him to invade a country where the people were brought back together from many nations and have lived without fear of war. He will invade the mountains of Israel, which were desolate and deserted so long, but where all the people now live in safety. [9] He and his army and the many nations with him will attack like a storm and cover the land like a cloud."

[10] This is what the Sovereign LORD says to Gog: "When that time comes, you will start thinking up an evil plan. [11] You will decide to invade a helpless country where the people live in peace and security in unwalled towns that have no defenses. [12] You will plunder and loot the people who live in cities that were once in ruins. They have been gathered from the nations, and now they have livestock and property and live at the crossroads of the world. [13] The people of Sheba and Dedan and the merchants from the towns of Spain will ask you, 'Have you assembled your army and attacked in order to loot and plunder? Do you intend to get silver and gold, livestock and property, and march off with all those spoils?' "

[14] So the Sovereign LORD sent me to tell Gog what he was saying to him: "Now while my people Israel live in security, you will set out[f] [15] to come from your place in the far north, leading a large, powerful army of soldiers from many nations, all of them on horseback. [16] You will attack my people Israel like a storm moving across the land. When

the time comes, I will send you to invade my land in order to show the nations who I am, to show my holiness by what I do through you. [17] You are the one I was talking about long ago, when I announced through my servants, the prophets of Israel, that in days to come I would bring someone to attack Israel." The Sovereign LORD has spoken.

God's Punishment of Gog

[18] The Sovereign LORD says, "On the day when Gog invades Israel, I will become furious. [19] I declare in the heat of my anger that on that day there will be a severe earthquake in the land of Israel. [20] Every fish and bird, every animal large and small, and every human being on the face of the earth will tremble for fear of me. Mountains will fall, cliffs will crumble, and every wall will collapse. [21] I will terrify Gog with all sorts of calamities.[g] I, the Sovereign LORD, have spoken. His men will turn their swords against one another. [22] I will punish him with disease and bloodshed. Torrents of rain and hail, together with fire and sulfur, will pour down on him and his army and on the many nations that are on his side. [23] In this way I will show all the nations that I am great and that I am holy. They will know then that I am the LORD."

The Defeat of Gog

39 The Sovereign LORD said, "Mortal man, denounce Gog, the chief ruler of the nations of Meshech and Tubal, and tell him that I am his enemy. [2] I will turn him in a new direction and lead him out of the far north until he comes to the mountains of Israel. [3] Then I will knock his bow out of his left hand and his arrows out of his

---

[e] *Hebrew* Cush: *Cush is the ancient name of the extensive territory south of the First Cataract of the Nile River. This region was called Ethiopia in Graeco-Roman times, and included within its borders most of modern Sudan and some of present-day Ethiopia (Abyssinia).*   [f] *One ancient translation* set out; *Hebrew* know.   [g] *One ancient translation* terrify . . . calamities; *Hebrew unclear.*

right hand. [4] Gog and his army and his allies will fall dead on the mountains of Israel, and I will let their bodies be food for all the birds and wild animals. [5] They will fall dead in the open field. I, the Sovereign LORD, have spoken. [6] I will start a fire in the land of Magog and along all the seacoasts where people live undisturbed, and everyone will know that I am the LORD. [7] I will make sure that my people Israel know my holy name, and I will not let my name be disgraced any more. Then the nations will know that I, the LORD, am the holy God of Israel."

[8] The Sovereign LORD said, "The day I spoke about is certain to come. [9] The people who live in the cities of Israel will go out and collect the abandoned weapons for firewood. They will build fires with the shields, bows, arrows, spears, and clubs, and have enough to last for seven years. [10] They will not have to gather firewood in the fields or cut down trees in the forest, because they will have the abandoned weapons to burn. They will loot and plunder those who looted and plundered them." The Sovereign LORD has spoken.

The Burial of Gog

[11] The LORD said, "When all this happens, I will give Gog a burial ground there in Israel, in Travelers' Valley, east of the Dead Sea.[h] Gog and all his army will be buried there, and the valley will be called 'The Valley of Gog's Army.' [12] It will take the Israelites seven months to bury all the corpses and make the land clean again. [13] Everyone in the land will help bury them, and they will be honored for this on the day of my victory. I, the Sovereign LORD, have spoken. [14] After the seven months are over, men will be chosen to travel through the land in order to find and bury those bodies [i] remaining on the ground, so that they can make the land clean. [15] As they go up and down the country, every time they find a human bone, they will put a marker beside it so that the gravediggers can come and bury it in the Valley of Gog's Army. [16] (There will be a town nearby named after the army.) And so the land will be made clean again."

[17] The Sovereign LORD said to me, "Mortal man, call all the birds and animals to come from all around to eat the sacrifice I am preparing for them. It will be a huge feast on the mountains of Israel, where they can eat meat and drink blood. [18] They are to eat the bodies of soldiers and drink the blood of the rulers of the earth, all of whom will be killed like rams or lambs or goats or fat bulls. [19] When I kill these people like sacrifices, the birds and animals are to eat all the fat they can hold and to drink blood until they are drunk. [20] At my table they will eat all they can hold of horses and their riders and of soldiers and fighting men. I, the Sovereign LORD, have spoken."

The Restoration of Israel

[21] The LORD said, "I will let the nations see my glory and show them how I use my power to carry out my just decisions. [22] The Israelites will know from then on that I am the LORD their God. [23] And the nations will know that the Israelites went into exile because of the sins which they committed against me. I turned away from them and let their enemies defeat them and kill them in battle. [24] I gave them what they deserved for their uncleanness and their wickedness, and I turned away from them."

[25] The Sovereign LORD said, "But now I will be merciful to Jacob's

---

[h] *Hebrew has four additional words, the meaning of which is unclear.*   [i] *Some ancient translations* those bodies; *Hebrew the* travelers.

39.17-20 Rev 19.17, 18

descendants, the people of Israel, and make them prosperous again. I will protect my holy name. 26 When they are once more living in safety in their own land, with no one to threaten them, they will be able to forget how they were disgraced for having betrayed me. 27 In order to show to the many nations that I am holy, I will bring my people back from all the countries where their enemies live. 28 Then my people will know that I am the LORD their God. They will know this, because I sent them into captivity and now gather them and bring them back to their own land, not leaving even one of them behind. 29 I will pour out my spirit on the people of Israel and never again turn away from them. I, the Sovereign LORD, have spoken."

A VISION OF THE FUTURE TEMPLE (40.1 — 48.35)

Ezekiel Is Taken to Jerusalem

40 It was the tenth day of the new year, which was the twenty-fifth year after we had been taken into exile and the fourteenth year after Jerusalem was captured. On that day I felt the powerful presence of the LORD, and he carried me away. 2 In a vision God took me to the land of Israel and put me on a high mountain. I saw in front of mej a group of buildings that looked like a city. 3 He took me closer, and I saw a man who shone like bronze. He was holding a linen tape measure and a measuring rod and was standing by a gateway. 4 He said to me, "Watch, mortal man. Listen carefully and pay close attention to everything I show you, because this is why you were brought here. You are

to tell the people of Israel everything you see."

The East Gate

5 What I saw was the Temple, and there was a wall around it. The man took his measuring rod, which was 10 feet long, and measured the wall. It was 10 feet high and 10 feet thick. 6 Then he went to the gateway that faced east. He went up the steps, and at the top he measured the entrance; it was 10 feet deep.k 7 Beyond it there was a passageway, which had three guardrooms on each side. Each of the rooms was square, 10 feet on each side, and the walls between them were 8 feet thick. Beyond the guardrooms there was a passageway 10 feet long that led to an entrance room which faced the Temple. 8-9 He measured this room and found it was 14 feet deep. It formed that end of the gateway which was nearest the Temple, and at its far end the walls were 4 feet thick. (10 These guardrooms on each side of the passageway were all the same size, and the walls between them were all of the same thickness.)

11 Next, the man measured the width of the passageway in the gateway. It was 22 feet altogether, and the space between the open gates was 16 feet. 12 In front of each of the guardrooms there was a low wall 20 inches high and 20 inches thick. (The rooms were 10 feet square.) 13 Then he measured the distance from the back walll of one room to the back walll of the room across the passageway from it, and it was 42 feet. 14 The room at the far end led out to a courtyard. He measured that room and found it was 34 feet wide.m 15 The total length of the gateway from the outside wall of the gate to the far side of the last room was 84 feet.

---

j One ancient translation in front of me; Hebrew in the south.   k One ancient translation deep; Hebrew deep, one entrance 10 feet deep.   l Probable text back wall; Hebrew roof.   m Verse 14 in Hebrew is unclear.

40.2 Rev 21.10   **40.3** Rev 11.1; 21.15   **40.5—42.20** 1 K 6.1-38; 2 Ch 3.1-9

16 There were small openings in the outside walls of all the rooms and also in the inner walls between the rooms. There were palm trees carved on the inner walls that faced the passageway.

The Outer Courtyard

17 The man took me through the gateway into the courtyard. There were thirty rooms built against the outer wall, and in front of them there was an area paved with stones, 18 which extended around the courtyard. This outer courtyard was at a lower level than the inner courtyard.

19 There was a gateway at a higher level that led to the inner courtyard. The man measured the distance between the two gateways, and it was 168 feet.[n]

The North Gate

20 Then the man measured the gateway on the north side that led into the outer courtyard. 21 The three guardrooms on each side of the passageway, the walls between them, and the entrance room all had the same measurements as those in the east gateway. The total length of the gateway was 84 feet and the width 42 feet. 22 The entrance room, the windows, and the carved palm trees were like those in the east gate. Here seven steps led up to the gate, and the entrance room was at the end facing the courtyard. 23 Across the courtyard from this north gateway was another gateway leading to the inner courtyard, just as there was on the east side. The man measured the distance between these two gateways, and it was 168 feet.

The South Gate

24 Next, the man took me to the south side, and there we saw another gateway. He measured its inner walls and its entrance room, and they were the same as the others. 25 There were windows in the rooms of this gateway just as in the others. The total length of the gateway was 84 feet and the width 42 feet. 26 Seven steps led up to it, and its entrance room was also at the end facing the courtyard. There were palm trees carved on the inner walls that faced the passageway. 27 Here, too, there was a gateway leading to the inner courtyard. The man measured the distance to this second gateway, and it was 168 feet.

The Inner Courtyard: The South Gate

28 The man took me through the south gateway into the inner courtyard. He measured the gateway, and it was the same size as the gateways in the outer wall. 29-30 Its guardrooms, its entrance room, and its inner walls were the same size as those in the other gateways. There were also windows in the rooms of this gateway. The total length was 84 feet and the width 42 feet. 31 Its entrance room faced the other courtyard, and palm trees were carved on the walls along the passageway. Eight steps led up to this gate.

The Inner Courtyard: The East Gate

32 The man took me through the east gateway into the inner courtyard. He measured the gateway, and it was the same size as the others. 33 Its guardrooms, its entrance room, and its inner walls measured the same as those in the other gateways. There were windows all around, and in the entrance room also. The total length was 84 feet and the width 42 feet. 34 The entrance room faced the outer courtyard. Palm trees were carved on the walls along the passageway. Eight steps led up to this gate.

[n] *Hebrew has two additional words, the meaning of which is unclear.*

The Inner Courtyard: The North Gate

35 Then the man took me to the north gateway. He measured it, and it was the same size as the others. 36 Like them, it also had guardrooms, decorated inner walls, an entrance room, and windows all around. Its total length was 84 feet and its width 42 feet. 37 The entrance room*o* faced the outer courtyard. Palm trees were carved on the walls along the passageway. Eight steps led up to this gate.

Buildings Near the North Gate

38 In the outer courtyard there was an annex attached to the inner gateway on the north side. It opened into the entrance room that faced the courtyard, and there they washed the carcasses of the animals to be burned whole as sacrifices. 39 In this entrance room there were four tables, two on each side of the room. It was on these tables that they killed the animals to be offered as sacrifices, either to be burned whole or to be sacrifices for sin or as repayment offerings. 40 Outside the room there were four similar tables, two on either side of the entrance of the north gate. 41 Altogether there were eight tables on which the animals to be sacrificed were killed: four inside the room and four out in the courtyard. 42 The four tables in the annex, used to prepare the offerings to be burned whole, were of cut stone. They were 20 inches high, and their tops were 30 inches square. All the equipment used in killing the sacrificial animals was kept on these tables. 43 Ledges 3 inches wide ran around the edge of the tables. All the meat to be offered in sacrifice was placed on the tables.*p*

44 Then he brought me into the inner court. There were two rooms opening on the inner court, one facing south beside the north gateway and the other facing north beside the south gateway.*q* 45 The man told me that the room which faced south was for the priests who served in the Temple, 46 and the room which faced north was for the priests who served at the altar. All the priests are descended from Zadok; they are the only members of the tribe of Levi who are permitted to go into the LORD's presence to serve him.

The Inner Courtyard and the Temple Building

47 The man measured the inner courtyard, and it was 168 feet square. The Temple was on the west side, and in front of it was an altar. 48 Then he took me into the entrance room of the Temple. He measured the entranceway: it was 9 feet deep and 24 feet wide,*r* with walls 5 feet thick on either side. 49 Steps led up to the entrance room, which was 34 feet wide and 20 feet deep.*s* There were two columns, one on each side of the entrance.

41 Next, the man took me into the central room, the Holy Place. He measured the passageway into it: it was 10 feet deep*t* 2 and 18 feet wide, with walls 8 feet thick on either side. He measured the room itself: it was 68 feet long and 34 feet wide.

3 Then he went to the innermost room. He measured the passageway into it: it was 3 feet deep and 10 feet wide, with walls on either side 12 feet thick.*u* 4 He measured the room itself,

---

o Some ancient translations entrance room; *Hebrew* inner wall.   *p Verse 43 in Hebrew is unclear.*   *q One ancient translation* Then . . . south gateway; *verse 44 in Hebrew is unclear.*   *r One ancient translation* and 24 feet wide; *Hebrew does not have these words.*   *s One ancient translation* 20 feet deep; *Hebrew* 18 feet deep.
t Hebrew has two additional words, the meaning of which is unclear.   *u One ancient translation* with walls on either side 12 feet thick; *Hebrew* and 12 feet thick.

and it was 34 feet square. This room was beyond the central room. Then he said to me, "This is the Most Holy Place."

The Rooms Built against the Temple Walls

⁵The man measured the thickness of the inner wall of the Temple building, and it was 10 feet. Against this wall, all around the Temple, was a series of small rooms 7 feet wide. ⁶These rooms were in three stories, with thirty rooms on each floor. The Temple's outer wall on each floor was thinner than on the floor below, so that the rooms could rest on the wall without being anchored into it. ⁷And so the Temple walls, when seen from the outside, seemed to have the same thickness all the way to the top. Against the Temple's outer wall, on the outside of the rooms, two wide stairways were built, so that it was possible to go from the lower story to the middle and the upper stories.ᵛ ⁸⁻¹¹The outside wall of these rooms was 8 feet thick; there was one door into the rooms on the north side of the Temple, and one into those on the south side. I saw that there was a terrace 8 feet wide around the Temple; it was 10 feet above the ground and it was level with the foundation of the rooms by the Temple walls. Between the terrace and the buildings used by the priests there was an open space 34 feet across, along the sides of the Temple.

The Building on the West

¹²At the far end of the open space on the west side of the Temple there was a building 150 feet long and 116 feet wide; its walls were 9 feet thick all around.

The Total Measurements of the Temple Building

¹³The man measured the outside of the Temple, and it was 168 feet long. And from the back of the Temple, across the open space to the far side of the building to the west, the distance was also 168 feet. ¹⁴The distance across the front of the Temple, including the open space on either side, was also 168 feet. ¹⁵He measured the length of the building to the west, including its galleries on both sides, and it was also 168 feet.

Details of the Temple Building

The entrance room of the Temple, the Holy Place, and the Most Holy Place ¹⁶were all paneled with wood from the floor to the windows. These windows could be covered.ʷ ¹⁷The inside walls of the Temple, up as high as above the doors, were completely covered with carvingsˣ ¹⁸of palm trees and winged creatures. Palm trees alternated with creatures, one following the other, all the way around the room. Each creature had two faces: ¹⁹a human face that was turned toward the palm tree on one side, and a lion's face that was turned toward the tree on the other side. It was like this all around the wall, ²⁰from the floor to above the doors. ²¹The doorposts of the Holy Place were square.

The Wooden Altar

In front of the entrance of the Most Holy Place there was something that looked like ²²a wooden altar. It was 5 feet high and 4 feet wide. Its corner posts, its base,ʸ and its sides were all made of wood. The man said to me, "This is the table which stands in the presence of the LORD."

ᵛ *Verse 7 in Hebrew is unclear.*   ʷ *Verse 16 in Hebrew is unclear.*   ˣ *Verse 17 in Hebrew is unclear.*   ʸ *Some ancient translations* base; *Hebrew* length.

The Doors

23 There was a door at the end of the passageway to the Holy Place and one also at the end of the passageway to the Most Holy Place. **24** They were double doors that swung open in the middle. **25** There were palm trees and winged creatures carved on the doors of the Holy Place, just as there were on the walls. And there was a wooden covering over the outside of the doorway of the entrance room. **26** At the sides of this room there were windows, and the walls were decorated with palm trees.[z]

Two Buildings Near the Temple

42 Then the man took me into the outer courtyard and led me to a building on the north side of the Temple, not far from the building at the west end of the Temple. **2** This building was 168 feet long and 84 feet wide. **3** On one side it faced the space 34 feet wide which was alongside the Temple, and on the other side it faced the pavement of the outer courtyard. It was built on three levels, each one set further back than the one below it. **4** Along the north side of this building was a passageway 16 feet wide and 168 feet long,[a] with entrances on that side. **5** The rooms at the upper level of the building were narrower than those at the middle and lower levels because they were set further back. **6** The rooms at all three levels were on terraces and were not supported by columns like the other buildings in the courtyard. **7-8** At the lower level the outer wall of the building was solid for 84 feet, half its length; and there were rooms in the remaining 84 feet. At the top level there were rooms in the entire length of the building. **9-10** Below these rooms at the east end of the building, where the wall of the courtyard began,[b] there was an entrance into the outer courtyard.

At the south[c] side of the Temple there was an identical building not far from the building at the west end of the Temple. **11** In front of the rooms there was a passageway just like the one on the north side. It had the same measurements, the same design, and the same kind of entrances. **12** There was a door under the rooms on the south side of the building, at the east end where the wall began.

13 The man said to me, "Both these buildings are holy. In them the priests who enter the LORD's presence eat the holiest offerings. Because the rooms are holy, the priests will place the holiest offerings there: the offerings of grain and the sacrifices offered for sin or as repayment offerings. **14** When priests have been in the Temple and want to go to the outer courtyard, they must leave in these rooms the holy clothing they wore while serving the LORD. They must put on other clothes before going out to the area where the people gather."

The Measurements of the Temple Area

15 When the man had finished measuring inside the Temple area, he took me out through the east gate and then measured the outside of the area. **16** He took the measuring rod and measured the east side, and it was 840 feet. **17-19** Then he measured the north side, the south side, and the west side; each side had the same length, 840 feet,[d] **20** so that the wall enclosed a square 840 feet on each side. The wall served to separate what was holy from what was not.

---

[z] *Hebrew has three additional words, the meaning of which is unclear.*   [a] *Some ancient translations* 168 feet long; *Hebrew* a way of 20 inches.   [b] *One ancient translation* where the wall of the courtyard began; *Hebrew* in the breadth of the wall of the courtyard.   [c] *One ancient translation* south; *Hebrew* east.   [d] *Verses 16-19 in Hebrew are unclear.*

The Lord Returns to the Temple

43 The man took me to the gate that faces east, ²and there I saw coming from the east the dazzling light of the presence of the God of Israel. God's voice sounded like the roar of the sea, and the earth shone with the dazzling light. ³This vision was like the one I had seen when God came to destroy Jerusalem, and the one I saw by the Chebar River. Then I threw myself face downward on the ground. ⁴The dazzling light passed through the east gate and went into the Temple.

⁵The Lord's spirit lifted me up and took me into the inner courtyard, where I saw that the Temple was filled with the glory of the Lord. ⁶The man stood beside me there, and I heard the Lord speak to me out of the Temple: ⁷"Mortal man, here is my throne. I will live here among the people of Israel and rule them forever. Neither the people of Israel nor their kings will ever again disgrace my holy name by worshiping other gods or by burying the corpses of^e their dead kings. ⁸The kings built the doorsills and doorposts of their palace right against the doorsills and doorposts of my Temple, so that there was only a wall between us. They disgraced my holy name by all the disgusting things they did, and so in my anger I destroyed them. ⁹Now they must stop worshiping other gods and remove the corpses of^f their kings. If they do, I will live among them forever."

¹⁰And the Lord continued, "Mortal man, tell the people of Israel about the Temple, and let them study its plan. Make them ashamed of their sinful actions. ¹¹Then if they are ashamed of what they have done, explain the plan of the Temple to them: its design, its entrances and exits, its shape, the arrangement of everything, and all its rules and regulations. Write all this down for them so that they can see how everything is arranged and can carry out all the rules. ¹²This is the law of the Temple: All the area surrounding it on the top of the mountain is sacred and holy."

The Altar

¹³These are the measurements of the altar, using the same unit of measure as in measuring the Temple. All around the base of the altar there was a gutter 20 inches deep and 20 inches wide, with a rim at the outside edge 10 inches high. ¹⁴The lowest section of the altar, from the top of the base, was 4 feet high. The next section was set back from the edge 20 inches all around, and was 7 feet high. The section after that was also set back from the edge 20 inches all around. ¹⁵This top section, on which the sacrifices were burned, was also 7 feet high. The projections on the four corners were higher than the rest of the top. ¹⁶The top of the altar was a square, 20 feet on each side. ¹⁷The middle section was also a square, 24 feet on each side, with a rim at the outside edge 10 inches high. (The gutter was 20 inches wide.) The steps going up the altar were on the east side.

The Consecration of the Altar

¹⁸The Sovereign Lord said to me, "Mortal man, listen to what I tell you. When the altar is built, you are to dedicate it by burning sacrifices on it and by sprinkling on it the blood of the animals that were sacrificed. ¹⁹Those priests belonging to the tribe of Levi who are descended from Zadok are the only ones who are to come into my presence to serve me. I, the Sovereign Lord, com-

---

^e by burying the corpses of; *or* by putting up monuments to.   ^f remove the corpses of; *or* remove the monuments to.

43.2 Ez 10.3, 4, 18, 19; 11.22, 23; Rev 1.15   **43.13-17** Ex 27.1, 2; 2 Ch 4.1
43.18-27 Ex 29.35-37; 1 Macc 4.52-56

nand this. You will give them a young
oull to offer as a sacrifice for sin. ²⁰You
are to take some of its blood and put it
on the projections on the top corners of
he altar, on the corners of the middle
ection of the altar, and all around its
dges. In this way you will purify the
altar and consecrate it. ²¹You are to
ake the bull that is offered as a sacrifice
for sin and burn it at the specified place
outside the Temple area. ²²The next
day you are to take a male goat without
any defects and offer it as a sacrifice for
sin. Purify the altar with its blood the
same way you did with the bull.
²³When you have finished doing that,
take a young bull and a young ram,
both of them without any defects, ²⁴and
bring them to me. The priests will
sprinkle salt on them and burn them as
an offering to me. ²⁵Each day for seven
days you are to offer a goat, a bull, and
a ram as sacrifices for sin. All of them
must be without any defects. ²⁶For
seven days the priests are to consecrate
the altar and make it ready for use.
²⁷When the week is over, the priests are
to begin offering on the altar the burnt
offerings and the fellowship offerings of
the people. Then I will be pleased with
all of you. I, the Sovereign LORD, have
spoken."

The Use of the East Gate

44 The man led me to the outer
gate at the east side of the
Temple area. The gate was closed, ²and
the LORD said to me, "This gate will stay
closed and will never be opened. No human being is allowed to use it, because
I, the LORD God of Israel, have entered
through it. It is to remain closed. ³The
ruling prince, however, may go there to
eat a holy meal in my presence. He is to
enter and leave the gateway through
the entrance room at the inner end."

Rules for Admission to the Temple

⁴Then the man took me through the
north gate to the front of the Temple. As
I looked, I saw that the Temple of the
LORD was filled with the dazzling light
of his presence. I threw myself face
downward on the ground, ⁵and the
LORD said to me, "Mortal man, pay attention to everything you see and hear.
I am going to tell you the rules and regulations for the Temple. Note carefully
which persons are allowed to go in and
out of the Temple, and which persons
are not allowed.

⁶"Tell those rebellious people of Is-
rael that I, the Sovereign LORD, will no
longer tolerate the disgusting things
that they have been doing. ⁷They have
profaned my Temple by letting uncircumcised foreigners, people who do not
obey me, enter the Temple when the fat
and the blood of the sacrifices are being
offered to me. So my people have broken my covenant by all the disgusting
things they have done. ⁸They have not
taken charge of the sacred rituals in my
Temple, but instead have put foreigners in charge.

⁹"I, the Sovereign LORD, declare that
no uncircumcised foreigner, no one
who disobeys me, will enter my Temple, not even a foreigner who lives
among the people of Israel."

The Levites Are Excluded from the Priesthood

¹⁰The LORD said to me, "I am punish-
ing those Levites who, together with
the rest of the people of Israel, deserted
me and worshiped idols. ¹¹They may
serve me in the Temple by taking
charge of the gates and by performing
the work of the Temple. They may kill
the animals which the people offer for
burnt offerings and for sacrifices, and
they are to be on duty to serve the people. ¹²But because they conducted the
worship of idols for the people of Israel
and in this way led the people into sin,
I, the Sovereign LORD, solemnly swear
that they must be punished. ¹³They are
not to serve me as priests or to go near
anything that is holy to me or to enter

the Most Holy Place. This is the punishment for the disgusting things they have done. [14] I am assigning to them the menial work that is to be done in the Temple."

The Priests

[15] The Sovereign LORD said, "Those priests belonging to the tribe of Levi who are descended from Zadok, however, continued to serve me faithfully in the Temple when the rest of the people of Israel turned away from me. So now they are the ones who are to serve me and come into my presence to offer me the fat and the blood of the sacrifices. [16] They alone will enter my Temple, serve at my altar, and conduct the Temple worship. [17] When they enter the gateway to the inner courtyard of the Temple, they are to put on linen clothing. They must not wear anything made of wool when they are on duty in the inner courtyard or in the Temple. [18] So that they won't perspire, they are to wear linen turbans and linen trousers, but no belt. [19] Before they go to the outer courtyard where the people are, they must first take off the clothes they wore on duty in the Temple and leave them in the holy rooms. They are to put on other clothing in order to keep their sacred clothing from harming the people.[g]

[20] "Priests must neither shave their heads nor let their hair grow long. They are to keep it a proper length. [21] Priests must not drink any wine before going into the inner courtyard. [22] No priest may marry a divorced woman; he is to marry only an Israelite virgin or the widow of another priest.

[23] "The priests are to teach my people the difference between what is holy and what is not, and between what is ritually clean and what is not. [24] When a legal dispute arises, the priests are to decide the case according to my laws. They are to keep the religious festivals according to my rules and regulations, and they are to keep the Sabbaths holy.

[25] "A priest is not to become ritually unclean by touching a corpse, unless it is one of his parents, one of his children, or a brother or an unmarried sister. [26] After he has become clean again, he must wait seven days [27] and then go into the inner courtyard of the Temple and offer a sacrifice for his purification, so that he can serve in the Temple again. I, the Sovereign LORD, have spoken.

[28] "The priests have the priesthood as their share of what I have given Israel to be handed down from one generation to another. They are not to hold property in Israel; I am all they need. [29] The grain offerings, the sin offerings, and the repayment offerings will be the priests' food, and they are to receive everything in Israel that is set apart for me. [30] The priests are to have the best of all the first harvest and of everything else that is offered to me. Each time the people bake bread, they are to give the priests the first loaf as an offering, and my blessing will rest on their homes. [31] The priests must not eat any bird or animal that dies a natural death or is killed by another animal."

The LORD's Portion of the Country

45 When the land is divided to give each tribe a share, one part is to be dedicated to the LORD. It is to be 10 miles long by 8 miles[h] wide. The entire area will be holy. [2] In this area there is to be a square plot of land

---

[g] HARMING THE PEOPLE: *It was believed that ordinary people would be harmed by touching something holy.*   [h] *One ancient translation* 8 miles; *Hebrew* 4 miles.

44.17, 18 Ex 28.39-43; Lv 16.4   **44.19** Lv 16.23   **44.20** Lv 21.5   **44.21** Lv 10.9
44.22 Lv 21.7, 13, 14   **44.23** Lv 10.10   **44.25** Lv 21.1-4   **44.28** Nu 18.20
44.29, 30 Nu 18.8-19   **44.31** Lv 22.8

for the Temple, 840 feet on each side, entirely surrounded by an open space 84 feet wide. ³Half of this area, a section 10 miles by 4 miles, is to be measured off; it will contain the Temple, the holiest place of all. ⁴It will be a holy part of the country, set aside for the priests who serve the LORD in his Temple. It will contain their houses and the section of land for the Temple. ⁵The other half of the area is to be set aside as the possession of the Levites, who do the work in the Temple. There will be towns there for them to live in.*ⁱ*

⁶Next to the holy area, another section, 10 miles long and 2 miles wide, is to be set aside for a city where any of the people of Israel may live.

Land for the Prince

⁷Land is also to be set aside for the ruling prince. From the west boundary of the holy area it will extend west to the Mediterranean Sea; and from the east boundary it will extend to the eastern border of the country, so that its length will be the same as the length of one of the areas allotted to the tribes of Israel. ⁸This area will be the share the ruling prince will have in the land of Israel, so that he will no longer oppress the people, but will let the rest of the country belong to the tribes of Israel.

Rules for the Prince

⁹The Sovereign LORD said, "You have sinned too long, you rulers of Israel! Stop your violence and oppression. Do what is right and just. You must never again drive my people off their land. I, the Sovereign LORD, am telling you this.

¹⁰"Everyone must use honest weights and measures:

¹¹"The *ephah* for dry measure is to be equal to the *bath* for liquid measure. The standard is the *homer*.*ʲ* The resulting measures are as follows:

1 *homer* = 10 *ephahs* = 10 *baths*

¹²"Your weights are to be as follows:

20 *gerahs* = 1 *shekel*ᵏ
60 *shekels* = 1 *mina*

¹³⁻¹⁵"This is the basis on which you are to make your offerings:

Wheat: 1/60th of your harvest
Barley: 1/60th of your harvest
Olive oil: 1/100th of the yield of
　　　your trees

(Measure it by the *bath*: 10 *baths* = 1 *homer* = 1 *kor*.)

Sheep: 1 sheep out of every 200
　　　from the meadows of Israel

"You are to bring grain offerings, animals to be burned whole, and animals for fellowship offerings, so that your sins will be forgiven. I, the Sovereign LORD, command it.

¹⁶"All the people of the land must take*ˡ* these offerings to the ruling prince of Israel. ¹⁷It will be his duty to provide the animals to be burned whole, the grain offerings, and the wine offerings for the whole nation of Israel at the New Moon Festivals, the Sabbaths, and the other festivals. He is to provide the sin offerings, the grain offerings, the offerings to be burned whole, and the fellowship offerings, to take away the sins of the people of Israel."

The Festivals
(Exodus 12.1-20; Leviticus 23.33-43)

¹⁸The Sovereign LORD said, "On the first day of the first month you are to

---

ⁱ One ancient translation towns there for them to live in; *Hebrew* twenty rooms.
ʲ HOMER: *A unit of dry or liquid measure, about 5 bushels or 175 quarts; so an ephah or a bath would be about 1/2 bushel or 17.5 quarts.*　ᵏ SHEKEL: *In Ezekiel's time this unit of weight was about 0.4 ounce or 11.4 grams.*　ˡ *Probable text* must take; *Hebrew unclear.*

45.10 Lv 19.36

sacrifice a bull without any defects and purify the Temple. ¹⁹The priest will take some of the blood of this sin offering and put it on the doorposts of the Temple, on the four corners of the altar, and on the posts of the gateways to the inner courtyard. ²⁰On the seventh day of the month you are to do the same thing on behalf of anyone who sins unintentionally or through ignorance. In this way you will keep the Temple holy.

²¹"On the fourteenth day of the first month you will begin the celebration of the Passover Festival. For seven days everyone will eat bread made without yeast. ²²On the first day of the festival the ruling prince must offer a bull as a sacrifice for his sins and for those of all the people. ²³On each of the seven days of the festival he is to sacrifice to the LORD seven bulls and seven rams without any defects and burn them whole. He is also to sacrifice a male goat each day as a sin offering. ²⁴For each bull and each ram that is sacrificed, there is to be an offering of half a bushel of grain and three quarts of olive oil.

²⁵"For the Festival of Shelters, which begins on the fifteenth day of the seventh month, the prince will offer on each of the seven days the same sacrifice for sin, the same offerings to be burned whole, and the same offerings of grain and olive oil."

The Prince and the Festivals

46 The Sovereign LORD says, "The east gateway to the inner courtyard must be kept closed during the six working days, but it is to be opened on the Sabbath and at the New Moon Festival. ²The ruling prince will go from the outer courtyard into the entrance room of the gateway and stand beside the posts of the gate while the priests burn his sacrifices whole and offer his fellowship offerings. There at the gate he must worship and then go

back out. The gate must not be shut until evening. ³Each Sabbath and each New Moon Festival all the people are also to bow down and worship the LORD in front of the gate. ⁴On the Sabbath the prince is to bring to the LORD, as sacrifices to be burned whole, six lambs and one ram, all without any defects. ⁵With each ram he is to bring an offering of half a bushel of grain, and with each lamb he is to bring whatever he wants to give. For each half-bushel of grain offering he is to bring three quarts of olive oil. ⁶At the New Moon Festival he will offer a young bull, six lambs, and a ram, all without any defects. ⁷With each bull and each ram the offering is to be half a bushel of grain, and with each lamb the offering is to be whatever the prince wants to give. Three quarts of olive oil are to be offered with each half-bushel of grain. ⁸The prince must leave the entrance room of the gateway and go out by the same way he went in.

⁹"When the people come to worship the LORD at any festival, those who enter by the north gate are to leave by the south gate after they have worshiped, and those who enter by the south gate are to leave by the north gate. No one may go out by the same way he entered, but must leave by the opposite gate. ¹⁰The prince is to come in when the people come, and leave when they leave. ¹¹On the feast days and at the festivals the grain offering will be half a bushel with each bull or ram, and whatever the worshiper wants to give with each lamb. Three quarts of olive oil are to be offered with each half-bushel of grain.

¹²"When the ruling prince wants to make a voluntary offering to the LORD, either an offering to be burned whole or a fellowship offering, the east gate to the inner courtyard will be opened for him. He is to make the offering in the same way he does on the Sabbath, and

45.21 Ex 12.1-20; Nu 28.16-25   **45.25** Lv 23.33-36; Nu 29.12-38

the gate is to be closed after he goes back out."

The Daily Offering

13 The LORD says, "Every morning a one-year-old lamb without any defects is to be burned whole as an offering to the LORD. This offering must be made every day. 14 Also an offering of five pounds of flour is to be made every morning, along with one quart of olive oil for mixing with the flour. The rules for this offering to the LORD are to be in force forever. 15 The lamb, the flour, and the olive oil are to be offered to the LORD every morning forever."

The Prince and the Land

16 The Sovereign LORD commands: 'If the ruling prince gives any of the land he owns to one of his sons as a present, it will belong to that son as a part of his family property. 17 But if the ruling prince gives any of his land to anyone who is in his service, it will become the prince's property again when the Year of Restoration[m] comes. It belongs to him, and only he and his sons can own it permanently. 18 The ruling prince must not take any of the people's property away from them. Any land he gives to his sons must be from the land that is assigned to him, so that he will not oppress any of my people by taking their land."

The Temple Kitchens

19 Then the man took me to the entrance of the rooms facing north near the gate on the south side of the inner courtyard. These are holy rooms for the priests. He pointed out a place on the west side of the rooms 20 and said, "This is the place where the priests are to boil the meat offered as sacrifices for sin or as repayment offerings, and to bake the offerings of flour, so that nothing holy is carried to the outer courtyard, where it might harm the people."[n]

21-22 Then he led me to the outer courtyard and showed me that in each of its four corners there was a smaller[o] courtyard, 68 feet long and 48 feet wide. 23 Each one had a stone wall around it, with fireplaces built against the wall. 24 The man told me, "These are the kitchens where the Temple servants are to boil the sacrifices the people offer."

The Stream Flowing from the Temple

47 The man led me back to the entrance of the Temple. Water was coming out from under the entrance and flowing east, the direction the Temple faced. It was flowing down from under the south part of the Temple past the south side of the altar. 2 The man then took me out of the Temple area by way of the north gate and led me around to the gate that faces east. A small stream of water was flowing out at the south side of the gate. 3 With his measuring rod the man measured 560 yards downstream to the east and told me to wade through the stream there. The water came only to my ankles. 4 Then he measured another 560 yards, and the water came up to my knees. Another 560 yards farther down, the water was up to my waist. 5 He measured 560 yards more, and there the stream was so deep I could not wade through it. It was too deep to cross

---

[m] YEAR OF RESTORATION: *Every fifty years, all Israelites were required to give freedom to any Israelites who had become slaves because of debts; they were also to give back to the original owner, or his heirs, any ancestral land that had been sold for debt (see Lv 25.8-55).*   [n] HARM THE PEOPLE: *See 44.19.*   [o] *One ancient translation* smaller; *Hebrew* enclosed.

46.17 Lv 25.10   **47.1** Zec 14.8; Jn 7.38; Rev 22.1

except by swimming. ⁶He said to me, "Mortal man, note all this carefully."

Then the man took me back to the riverbank, ⁷and when I got there, I saw that there were very many trees on each bank. ⁸He said to me, "This water flows through the land to the east and down into the Jordan Valley and to the Dead Sea. When it flows into the Dead Sea, it replaces the salt water of that sea with fresh water. ⁹Wherever the stream flows, there will be all kinds of animals and fish. The stream will make the water of the Dead Sea fresh, and wherever it flows, it will bring life. ¹⁰From the Springs of Engedi all the way to the Springs of Eneglaim, there will be fishermen on the shore of the sea, and they will spread out their nets there to dry. There will be as many different kinds of fish there as there are in the Mediterranean Sea. ¹¹But the water in the marshes and ponds along the shore will not be made fresh. They will remain there as a source of salt. ¹²On each bank of the stream all kinds of trees will grow to provide food. Their leaves will never wither, and they will never stop bearing fruit. They will have fresh fruit every month, because they are watered by the stream that flows from the Temple. The trees will provide food, and their leaves will be used for healing people."

The Boundaries of the Land

¹³The Sovereign LORD said, "These are the boundaries of the land that is to be divided among the twelve tribes, with the tribe of Joseph receiving two sections.ᵖ ¹⁴I solemnly promised your ancestors that I would give them possession of this land; now divide it equally among you.

¹⁵"The northern boundary runs eastward from the Mediterranean Sea to the city of Hethlon, to Hamath Pass, to the city of Zedad,�q ¹⁶to the cities of Berothah and Sibraim (they are located between the territory of the kingdom of Damascus and that of the kingdom of Hamath), and to the city of Ticon (located by the border of the district of Hauran). ¹⁷So the northern boundary runs from the Mediterranean eastward to Enon City, with the border regions of Damascus and Hamath to the north of it.

¹⁸"The eastern boundary runs south from a point between the territory of Damascus and that of Hauran, with the Jordan River forming the boundary between the land of Israel on the west and Gilead on the east, as far as Tamarʳ on the Dead Sea.

¹⁹"The southern boundary runs southwest from Tamar to the oasis of Kadesh Meribah and then northwest

ᵖ TWO SECTIONS: *The tribes of Manasseh and Ephraim, the sons of Joseph, were each given one section.* �q *One ancient translation* Hamath Pass, to the city of Zedad; *Hebrew* Zedad Pass to the city of Hamath. ʳ *Some ancient translations* Tamar; *Hebrew unclear.*

47.12 Rev 22.2

along the Egyptian border to the Mediterranean Sea.

20 "The western boundary is formed by the Mediterranean and runs north to a point west of Hamath Pass.

21 "Divide this land among your tribes; **22** it is to be your permanent possession. The foreigners who are living among you and who have had children born here are also to receive their share of the land when you divide it. They are to be treated like full Israelite citizens and are to draw lots for shares of the land along with the tribes of Israel. **23** All foreign residents will receive their share with the people of the tribe among whom they are living. I, the Sovereign LORD, have spoken."

The Division of the Land among the Tribes

48 **1-7** The northern boundary of the land runs eastward from the Mediterranean Sea to the city of Hethlon, to Hamath Pass, to Enon City, to the boundary between the kingdoms of Damascus and Hamath. Each tribe is to receive one section of land extending from the eastern boundary west to the Mediterranean Sea,ˢ in the following order from north to south:

Dan
Asher
Naphtali
Manasseh
Ephraim
Reuben
Judah

The Special Section in the Center of the Land

8 The next section of the land is to be set apart for special use. It is to be 10 miles wide from north to south, and the same length from east to west as the sections given to the tribes. The Temple will be located within this section.

9 In the center of this section, a special area 10 miles by 8 milesᵗ is to be dedicated to the LORD. **10** The priests are to have a portion of this holy area. From east to west their portion is to measure 10 miles, and from north to south, 4 miles. The Temple of the LORD is to be located in the middle of this area. **11** This holy area is to be for the priests who are descendants of Zadok. They served me faithfully and did not join the rest of the Israelites in doing wrong, as the other members of the tribe of Levi did. **12** So they are to have a special area next to the area belonging to the Levites, and it will be the holiest of all. **13** The Levites also are to have a special area, south of that of the priests. It too is to be 10 miles from east to west, by 4 miles from north to south. **14** The area dedicated to the LORD is the best part of all the land, and none of it may be sold or exchanged or transferred to anyone else. It is holy and belongs to the LORD.

15 The part of the special area that is left, 10 miles by 2 miles, is not holy, but is for the general use of the people. They may live there and use the land. The city is to be in the center of it, **16** and it will be a square, 2,520 yards on each side. **17** All around the city on each side there will be an open space 140 yards across. **18** The land that is left after the city has been built in the area immediately to the south of the holy area — 4 miles by 2 miles on the east and 4 miles by 2 miles on the west — is to be used as farmland by the people who live in the city. **19** Anyone who lives in the city, no matter which tribe he comes from, may farm that land.

20 And so the total area in the center of the section which was set apart will be a square measuring 10 miles on each side, and it will include the area occupied by the city.

21-22 To the east and to the west of this area which contains the Temple, the

---

ˢ *One ancient translation* extending . . . Sea; *Hebrew* having an eastern boundary and a western boundary.   ᵗ *Probable text (see 45.1)* 8 miles; *Hebrew* 4 miles.

priests' land, the Levites' land, and the city, the remaining land belongs to the ruling prince. It reaches east to the eastern boundary and west to the Mediterranean Sea, and is bounded on the north by the section belonging to Judah and on the south by the one belonging to Benjamin.

Land for the Other Tribes

23-27 South of this special section, each of the remaining tribes is to receive one section of land running from the eastern boundary west to the Mediterranean Sea, in the following order from north to south:

Benjamin
Simeon
Issachar
Zebulun
Gad

28 On the south side of the portion given to the tribe of Gad, the boundary runs southwest from Tamar to the oasis

48.30-34 Rev 21.12, 13

of Kadesh, and then northwest along the Egyptian border to the Mediterranean Sea.

29 The Sovereign LORD said, "That is the way the land is to be divided into sections for the tribes of Israel to possess."

The Gates of Jerusalem

30-34 There are twelve entrances to the city of Jerusalem. Each of the four walls measures 2,520 yards and has three gates in it, each named for one of the tribes. The gates in the north wall are named for Reuben, Judah, and Levi; those in the east wall, for Joseph, Benjamin, and Dan; those in the south wall, for Simeon, Issachar, and Zebulun; and those in the west wall are named for Gad, Asher, and Naphtali. 35 The total length of the wall on all four sides of the city is 10,080 yards. The name of the city from now on will be "The-LORD-Is-Here!"

The Book of
DANIEL

INTRODUCTION

The Book of Daniel was written during a time when the Jews were suffering greatly under the persecution and oppression of a pagan king. Using stories and accounts of visions, the writer encourages the people of his time with the hope that God will bring the tyrant down and restore sovereignty to God's people.

The book has two main parts: 1) Stories about Daniel and some of his fellow exiles, who through their faith in God and obedience to him triumph over their enemies. These stories are set in the time of the Babylonian and Persian Empires. 2) A series of visions seen by Daniel, which in the form of symbols present the successive rise and fall of several empires, beginning with Babylonia, and predict the downfall of the pagan oppressor and the victory of God's people.

OUTLINE OF CONTENTS

THE STORY OF DANIEL AND HIS FRIENDS (1.1 — 6.28)

The Young Men
at Nebuchadnezzar's Court

1 In the third year that Jehoiakim was king of Judah, King Nebuchadnezzar of Babylonia attacked Jerusalem and surrounded the city. ² The Lord let him capture King Jehoiakim and seize some of the Temple treasures. He took some prisoners back with him to the temple of his gods in Babylon, and put the captured treasures in the temple storerooms.

³ The king ordered Ashpenaz, his chief official, to select from among the Israelite exiles some young men of the royal family and of the noble families. ⁴ They had to be handsome, intelligent, well-trained, quick to learn, and free from physical defects, so that they would be qualified to serve in the royal court. Ashpenaz was to teach them to read and write the Babylonian language. ⁵ The king also gave orders that every day they were to be given the same food and wine as the members of the royal court. After three years of this training they were to appear before the king. ⁶ Among those chosen were Daniel, Hananiah, Mishael, and Azariah, all of whom were from the tribe of Judah.

1.1 2 K 24.1; 2 Ch 36.5-7   **1.2-4** 2 K 20.17, 18; 24.10-16; 2 Ch 36.10; Is 39.7, 8

7 The chief official gave them new names: Belteshazzar, Shadrach, Meshach, and Abednego.

8 Daniel made up his mind not to let himself become ritually unclean by eating the food and drinking the wine of the royal court, so he asked Ashpenaz to help him, 9 and God made Ashpenaz sympathetic to Daniel. 10 Ashpenaz, however, was afraid of the king, so he said to Daniel, "The king has decided what you are to eat and drink, and if you don't look as fit as the other young men, he may kill me."

11 So Daniel went to the guard whom Ashpenaz had placed in charge of him and his three friends. 12 "Test us for ten days," he said. "Give us vegetables to eat and water to drink. 13 Then compare us with the young men who are eating the food of the royal court, and base your decision on how we look."

14 He agreed to let them try it for ten days. 15 When the time was up, they looked healthier and stronger than all those who had been eating the royal food. 16 So from then on the guard let them continue to eat vegetables instead of what the king provided.

17 God gave the four young men knowledge and skill in literature and philosophy. In addition, he gave Daniel skill in interpreting visions and dreams.

18 At the end of the three years set by the king, Ashpenaz took all the young men to Nebuchadnezzar. 19 The king talked with them all, and Daniel, Hananiah, Mishael, and Azariah impressed him more than any of the others. So they became members of the king's court. 20 No matter what question the king asked or what problem he raised, these four knew ten times more than any fortuneteller or magician in his whole kingdom. 21 Daniel remained at the royal court until Cyrus, the emperor of Persia, conquered Babylonia.

Nebuchadnezzar's Dream

2 In the second year that Nebuchadnezzar was king, he had a dream. It worried him so much that he couldn't sleep, 2 so he sent for his fortunetellers, magicians, sorcerers, and wizards to come and explain the dream to him. When they came and stood before the king, 3 he said to them, "I'm worried about a dream I've had. I want to know what it means."

4 They answered the king in Aramaic,[a] "May Your Majesty live forever! Tell us your dream, and we will explain it to you."

5 The king said to them, "I have made up my mind that you must tell me the dream and then tell me what it means. If you can't, I'll have you torn limb from limb and make your houses a pile of ruins. 6 But if you can tell me both the dream and its meaning, I will reward you with gifts and great honor. Now then, tell me what the dream was and what it means."

7 They answered the king again, "If Your Majesty will only tell us what the dream was, we will explain it."

8 At that, the king exclaimed, "Just as I thought! You are trying to gain time because you see that I have made up my mind 9 to give all of you the same punishment if you don't tell me the dream. You have agreed among yourselves to go on telling me lies because you hope that in time things will change. Tell me what the dream was, and then I will know that you can also tell me what it means."

10 The advisers replied, "There is no one on the face of the earth who can tell Your Majesty what you want to know. No king, not even the greatest and most powerful, has ever made such a demand of his fortunetellers, magicians, and wizards. 11 What Your Majesty is asking for is so difficult that no one can

---

[a] *From here to the end of chapter 7, the language used is Aramaic, not Hebrew.*

HIGHLIGHTS FROM NEBUCHADNEZZAR'S DREAM INTERPRETED BY DANIEL
(Numbers refer to chapter and verse in Daniel)

do it for you except the gods, and they do not live among human beings."

¹²At that, the king flew into a rage and ordered the execution of all the royal advisers in Babylon. ¹³So the order was issued for all of them to be killed, including Daniel and his friends.

God Shows Daniel What the Dream Means

¹⁴Then Daniel went to Arioch, commander of the king's bodyguard, who had been ordered to carry out the execution. Choosing his words carefully, ¹⁵he asked Arioch why the king had issued such a harsh order. So Arioch told Daniel what had happened.

¹⁶Daniel went at once and obtained royal permission for more time, so that he could tell the king what the dream meant. ¹⁷Then Daniel went home and told his friends Hananiah, Mishael, and Azariah what had happened. ¹⁸He told them to pray to the God of heaven for mercy and to ask him to explain the mystery to them so that they would not be killed along with the other advisers in Babylon. ¹⁹Then that same night the mystery was revealed to Daniel in a vision, and he praised the God of heaven:

²⁰"God is wise and powerful!
Praise him forever and ever.
²¹ He controls the times and the
seasons;
he makes and unmakes kings;
it is he who gives wisdom and
understanding.
²² He reveals things that are deep
and secret;
he knows what is hidden in
darkness,
and he himself is surrounded
by light.
²³ I praise you and honor you, God
of my ancestors.
You have given me wisdom and
strength;
you have answered my prayer
and shown us what to tell the
king."

Daniel Tells the King the Dream and Explains It

²⁴So Daniel went to Arioch, whom the king had commanded to execute the royal advisers. He said to him, "Don't put them to death. Take me to the king, and I will tell him what his dream means."

²⁵At once Arioch took Daniel into King Nebuchadnezzar's presence and told the king, "I have found one of the Jewish exiles who can tell Your Majesty the meaning of your dream."

²⁶The king said to Daniel (who was also called Belteshazzar), "Can you tell me what I dreamed and what it means?"

²⁷Daniel replied, "Your Majesty, there is no wizard, magician, fortune-teller, or astrologer who can tell you that. ²⁸But there is a God in heaven, who reveals mysteries. He has informed Your Majesty what will happen in the future. Now I will tell you the dream, the vision you had while you were asleep.

²⁹"While Your Majesty was sleeping, you dreamed about the future; and God, who reveals mysteries, showed you what is going to happen. ³⁰Now, this mystery was revealed to me, not because I am wiser than anyone else, but so that Your Majesty may learn the meaning of your dream and understand the thoughts that have come to you.

³¹"Your Majesty, in your vision you saw standing before you a giant statue, bright and shining, and terrifying to look at. ³²Its head was made of the finest gold; its chest and arms were made of silver; its waist and hips of bronze, ³³its legs of iron, and its feet partly of iron and partly of clay. ³⁴While you were looking at it, a great stone broke loose from a cliff without anyone touching it, struck the iron and clay feet of the statue, and shattered them. ³⁵At once the iron, clay, bronze, silver, and gold crumbled and became like the dust on a threshing place in summer.

The wind carried it all away, leaving not a trace. But the stone grew to be a mountain that covered the whole earth. 36 "This was the dream. Now I will tell Your Majesty what it means. 37 Your Majesty, you are the greatest of all kings. The God of heaven has made you emperor and given you power, might, and honor. 38 He has made you ruler of all the inhabited earth and ruler over all the animals and birds. You are the head of gold. 39 After you there will be another empire, not as great as yours, and after that a third, an empire of bronze, which will rule the whole earth. 40 And then there will be a fourth empire, as strong as iron, which shatters and breaks everything. And just as iron shatters everything, it will shatter and crush all the earlier empires. 41 You also saw that the feet and the toes were partly clay and partly iron. This means that it will be a divided empire. It will have something of the strength of iron, because there was iron mixed with the clay. 42 The toes — partly iron and partly clay — mean that part of the empire will be strong and part of it weak. 43 You also saw that the iron was mixed with the clay. This means that the rulers of that empire will try to unite their families by intermarriage, but they will not be able to, any more than iron can mix with clay. 44 At the time of those rulers the God of heaven will establish a kingdom that will never end. It will never be conquered, but will completely destroy all those empires and then last forever. 45 You saw how a stone broke loose from a cliff without anyone touching it and how it struck the statue made of iron, bronze, clay, silver, and gold. The great God is telling Your Majesty what will happen in the future. I have told you exactly what you dreamed, and have given you its true meaning."

The King Rewards Daniel

46 Then King Nebuchadnezzar bowed to the ground and gave orders for sacrifices and offerings to be made to Daniel. 47 The king said, "Your God is the greatest of all gods, the Lord over kings, and the one who reveals mysteries. I know this because you have been able to explain this mystery." 48 Then he gave Daniel a high position, presented him with many splendid gifts, put him in charge of the province of Babylon, and made him the head of all the royal advisers. 49 At Daniel's request the king put Shadrach, Meshach, and Abednego in charge of the affairs of the province of Babylon; Daniel, however, remained at the royal court.

Nebuchadnezzar Commands Everyone to Worship a Gold Statue

3 King Nebuchadnezzar had a gold statue made, ninety feet high and nine feet wide, and he had it set up in the plain of Dura in the province of Babylon. 2 Then the king gave orders for all his officials to come together — the princes, governors, lieutenant governors, commissioners, treasurers, judges, magistrates, and all the other officials of the provinces. They were to attend the dedication of the statue which King Nebuchadnezzar had set up. 3 When all these officials gathered for the dedication and stood in front of the statue, 4 a herald announced in a loud voice, "People of all nations, races, and languages! 5 You will hear the sound of the trumpets, followed by the playing of oboes, lyres, zithers, and harps; and then all the other instruments will join in. As soon as the music starts, you are to bow down and worship the gold statue that King Nebuchadnezzar has set up. 6 Anyone who does not bow down and worship will immediately be thrown into a blazing furnace." 7 And so, as soon as they heard the sound of the instruments, the people of all the nations, races, and languages bowed down and worshiped the gold statue which King Nebuchadnezzar had set up.

Daniel's Three Friends Are Accused of Disobedience

⁸It was then that some Babylonians took the opportunity to denounce the Jews. ⁹They said to King Nebuchadnezzar, "May Your Majesty live forever! ¹⁰Your Majesty has issued an order that as soon as the music starts, everyone is to bow down and worship the gold statue, ¹¹and that anyone who does not bow down and worship it is to be thrown into a blazing furnace. ¹²There are some Jews whom you put in charge of the province of Babylon — Shadrach, Meshach, and Abednego — who are disobeying Your Majesty's orders. They do not worship your god or bow down to the statue you set up."

¹³At that, the king flew into a rage and ordered the three men to be brought before him. ¹⁴He said to them, "Shadrach, Meshach, and Abednego, is it true that you refuse to worship my god and to bow down to the gold statue I have set up? ¹⁵Now then, as soon as you hear the sound of the trumpets, oboes, lyres, zithers, harps, and all the other instruments, bow down and worship the statue. If you do not, you will immediately be thrown into a blazing furnace. Do you think there is any god who can save you?"

¹⁶Shadrach, Meshach, and Abednego answered, "Your Majesty, we will not try to defend ourselves. ¹⁷If the God whom we serve is able to save us from the blazing furnace and from your power, then he will.ᵇ ¹⁸But even if he doesn't, Your Majesty may be sure that we will not worship your god, and we will not bow down to the gold statue that you have set up."

Daniel's Three Friends Are Sentenced to Death

¹⁹Then Nebuchadnezzar lost his temper, and his face turned red with anger at Shadrach, Meshach, and Abednego. So he ordered the furnace to be heated seven times hotter than usual. ²⁰And he commanded the strongest men in his army to tie the three men up and throw them into the blazing furnace. ²¹So they tied them up, fully dressed — shirts, robes, caps and all — and threw them into the blazing furnace. ²²Now because the king had given strict orders for the furnace to be made extremely hot, the flames burned up the guards who took the men to the furnace. ²³Then Shadrach, Meshach, and Abednego, still tied up, fell into the heart of the blazing fire.

²⁴Suddenly Nebuchadnezzar leaped to his feet in amazement. He asked his officials, "Didn't we tie up three men and throw them into the blazing furnace?"

They answered, "Yes, we did, Your Majesty."

²⁵"Then why do I see four men walking around in the fire?" he asked. "They are not tied up, and they show no sign of being hurt — and the fourth one looks like an angel."ᶜ

The Three Men Are Released and Promoted

²⁶So Nebuchadnezzar went up to the door of the blazing furnace and called out, "Shadrach! Meshach! Abednego! Servants of the Supreme God! Come out!" And they came out at once. ²⁷All the princes, governors, lieutenant gov-

ᵇ If the God . . . will; or If it is true that we refuse to worship your god or bow down to the gold statue you set up, the God whom we serve is able to save us from the blazing furnace and from your power—and he will.   ᶜ angel; or a son of the gods; or a son of God.

The fourth one looks like an angel. (3.25)

ernors, and other officials of the king gathered to look at the three men, who had not been harmed by the fire. Their hair was not singed, their clothes were not burned, and there was no smell of smoke on them.

²⁸ The king said, "Praise the God of Shadrach, Meshach, and Abednego! He sent his angel and rescued these men who serve and trust him. They disobeyed my orders and risked their lives rather than bow down and worship any god except their own.

²⁹ "And now I command that if anyone of any nation, race, or language speaks disrespectfully of the God of Shadrach, Meshach, and Abednego, he is to be torn limb from limb, and his house is to be made a pile of ruins. There is no other god who can rescue like this."

³⁰ And the king promoted Shadrach, Meshach, and Abednego to higher positions in the province of Babylon.

Nebuchadnezzar's Second Dream

4 King Nebuchadnezzar sent the following message to the people of all nations, races, and languages in the world:

"Greetings! ² Listen to my account of the wonders and miracles which the Supreme God has shown me.

³ "How great are the wonders God
    shows us!
How powerful are the miracles
    he performs!
God is king forever; he will rule
    for all time.

⁴ "I was living comfortably in my palace, enjoying great prosperity. ⁵ But I had a frightening dream and saw terrifying visions while I was asleep. ⁶ I ordered all the royal advisers in Babylon to be brought to me so that they could tell me what the dream meant. ⁷ Then all the fortunetellers, magicians, wizards, and astrologers were brought in,

and I told them my dream, but they could not explain it to me. ⁸Then Daniel came in. (He is also called Belteshazzar, after the name of my god.) The spirit of the holy gods*ᵈ* is in him, so I told him what I had dreamed. I said to him: ⁹Belteshazzar, chief of the fortunetellers, I know that the spirit of the holy gods*ᵈ* is in you and that you understand all mysteries. This is*ᵉ* my dream. Tell me what it means.

¹⁰"While I was asleep, I had a vision of a huge tree in the middle of the earth. ¹¹It grew bigger and bigger until it reached the sky and could be seen by everyone in the world. ¹²Its leaves were beautiful, and it was loaded down with fruit — enough for the whole world to eat. Wild animals rested in its shade, birds built nests in its branches, and every kind of living being ate its fruit.

¹³"While I was thinking about the vision, I saw coming down from heaven an angel, alert and watchful. ¹⁴He proclaimed in a loud voice, 'Cut the tree down and chop off its branches; strip off its leaves and scatter its fruit. Drive the animals from under it and the birds out of its branches. ¹⁵But leave the stump in the ground with a band of iron and bronze around it. Leave it there in the field with the grass.

" 'Now let the dew fall on this man, and let him live with the animals and the plants. ¹⁶For seven years he will not have a human mind, but the mind of an animal. ¹⁷This is the decision of the alert and watchful angels. So then, let all people everywhere know that the Supreme God has power over human kingdoms and that he can give them to anyone he chooses — even to those who are least important.'

¹⁸"This is the dream I had," said King Nebuchadnezzar. "Now, Belteshazzar, tell me what it means. None of my royal advisers could tell me, but you can, because the spirit of the holy gods*ᶠ* is in you."

Daniel Explains the Dream

¹⁹At this, Daniel, who is also called Belteshazzar, was so alarmed that he could not say anything. The king said to him, "Belteshazzar, don't let the dream and its message alarm you."

Belteshazzar replied, "Your Majesty, I wish that the dream and its explanation applied to your enemies and not to you. ²⁰The tree, so tall that it reached the sky, could be seen by everyone in the world. ²¹Its leaves were beautiful, and it had enough fruit on it to feed the whole world. Wild animals rested under it, and birds made their nests in its branches.

²²"Your Majesty, you are the tree, tall and strong. You have grown so great that you reach the sky, and your power

So tall that it reached the sky (4.20)

ᵈ gods; *or* God.   *ᵉ Probable text* This is; *Aramaic* Visions of.   *ᶠ* gods; *or* God.

extends over the whole world. ²³ While Your Majesty was watching, an angel came down from heaven and said, 'Cut the tree down and destroy it, but leave the stump in the ground. Wrap a band of iron and bronze around it, and leave it there in the field with the grass. Let the dew fall on this man, and let him live there with the animals for seven years.'

Leave the stump in the ground. (4.23)

²⁴ "This, then, is what it means, Your Majesty, and this is what the Supreme God has declared will happen to you. ²⁵ You will be driven away from human society and will live with wild animals. For seven years you will eat grass like an ox and sleep in the open air, where the dew will fall on you. Then you will admit that the Supreme God controls all human kingdoms and that he can give them to anyone he chooses. ²⁶ The angel ordered the stump to be left in the ground. This means that you will become king again when you acknowledge that God rules all the world. ²⁷ So then, Your Majesty, follow my advice. Stop sinning, do what is right, and be merciful to the poor.ᵍ Then you will continue to be prosperous."

²⁸ All this did happen to King Nebuchadnezzar. ²⁹ Only twelve months later, while he was walking around on the roof of his royal palace in Babylon, ³⁰ he said, "Look how great Babylon is! I built it as my capital city to display my power and might, my glory and majesty."

³¹ Before the words were out of his mouth, a voice spoke from heaven, "King Nebuchadnezzar, listen to what I say! Your royal power is now taken away from you. ³² You will be driven away from human society, live with wild animals, and eat grass like an ox for seven years. Then you will acknowledge that the Supreme God has power over human kingdoms and that he can give them to anyone he chooses."

³³ The words came true immediately. Nebuchadnezzar was driven out of human society and ate grass like an ox. The dew fell on his body, and his hair grew as long as eagle feathers and his nails as long as bird claws.

Nebuchadnezzar Praises God

³⁴ "When the seven years had passed," said the king, "I looked up at the sky, and my sanity returned. I praised the Supreme God and gave honor and glory to the one who lives forever.

"He will rule forever,
  and his kingdom will last for
    all time.
³⁵ He looks on the people of the
    earth as nothing;
  angels in heaven and people
    on earth
  are under his control.
No one can oppose his will
  or question what he does.

³⁶ "When my sanity returned, my honor, my majesty, and the glory of my kingdom were given back to me. My officials and my noblemen welcomed me, and I was given back my royal power with even greater honor than before.

³⁷ "And now, I, Nebuchadnezzar, praise, honor, and glorify the King of Heaven. Everything he does is right and just, and he can humble anyone who acts proudly."

ᵍ Stop sinning . . . to the poor; *or* Make up for your sins by doing what is right and by being merciful to the poor.
4.27 Tb 12.9; Si 3.30   **4.34** Si 18.1

Belshazzar's Banquet

5 One night King Belshazzar invited a thousand noblemen to a great banquet, and they drank wine together. ² While they were drinking, Belshazzar gave orders to bring in the gold and silver cups and bowls which his father*ʰ* Nebuchadnezzar had carried off from the Temple in Jerusalem. The king sent for them so that he, his noblemen, his wives, and his concubines could drink out of them. ³ At once the gold cups and bowls were brought in, and they all drank wine out of them ⁴ and praised gods made of gold, silver, bronze, iron, wood, and stone.

⁵ Suddenly a human hand appeared and began writing on the plaster wall of the palace, where the light from the lamps was shining most brightly. And the king saw the hand as it was writing.

Suddenly a human hand appeared. (5.5)

⁶ He turned pale and was so frightened that his knees began to shake. ⁷ He shouted for someone to bring in the magicians, wizards, and astrologers. When they came in, the king said to them, "Anyone who can read this writing and tell me what it means will be dressed in robes of royal purple, wear a gold chain of honor around his neck, and be the third in power in the kingdom." ⁸ The royal advisers came forward, but none of them could read the writing or tell the king what it meant.

⁹ In his distress King Belshazzar grew even paler, and his noblemen had no idea what to do.

¹⁰ The queen mother heard the noise made by the king and his noblemen and entered the banquet hall. She said, "May Your Majesty live forever! Please do not be so disturbed and look so pale. ¹¹ There is a man in your kingdom who has the spirit of the holy gods*ⁱ* in him. When your father was king, this man showed good sense, knowledge, and wisdom like the wisdom of the gods. And King Nebuchadnezzar, your father,*ʲ* made him chief of the fortune-tellers, magicians, wizards, and astrologers. ¹² He has unusual ability and is wise and skillful in interpreting dreams, solving riddles, and explaining mysteries; so send for this man Daniel, whom the king named Belteshazzar, and he will tell you what all this means."

Daniel Explains the Writing

¹³ Daniel was brought at once into the king's presence, and the king said to him, "Are you Daniel, that Jewish exile whom my father the king brought here from Judah? ¹⁴ I have heard that the spirit of the holy gods*ᵏ* is in you and that you are skillful and have knowledge and wisdom. ¹⁵ The advisers and magicians were brought in to read this writing and tell me what it means, but they could not discover the meaning. ¹⁶ Now I have heard that you can find hidden meanings and explain mysteries. If you can read this writing and tell me what it means, you will be dressed in robes of royal purple, wear a gold chain of honor around your neck, and be the third in power in the kingdom."

¹⁷ Daniel replied, "Keep your gifts for yourself or give them to someone else. I will read for Your Majesty what has

ʰ There were several kings of Babylonia between Nebuchadnezzar and Belshazzar. Father may mean predecessor, or the name Nebuchadnezzar may be used for Nabonidus. ⁱ *gods; or God.* ʲ *your father (see 5.2).* ᵏ *gods; or God.*

been written and tell you what it means.

18 "The Supreme God made your father Nebuchadnezzar a great king and gave him dignity and majesty. 19 He was so great that people of all nations, races, and languages were afraid of him and trembled. If he wanted to kill someone, he did; if he wanted to keep someone alive, he did. He honored or disgraced anyone he wanted to. 20 But because he became proud, stubborn, and cruel, he was removed from his royal throne and lost his place of honor. 21 He was driven away from human society, and his mind became like that of an animal. He lived with wild donkeys, ate grass like an ox, and slept in the open air with nothing to protect him from the dew. Finally he admitted that the Supreme God controls all human kingdoms and can give them to anyone he chooses.

22 "But you, his son, have not humbled yourself, even though you knew all this. 23 You acted against the Lord of heaven and brought in the cups and bowls taken from his Temple. You, your noblemen, your wives, and your concubines drank wine out of them and praised gods made of gold, silver, bronze, iron, wood, and stone — gods that cannot see or hear and that do not know anything. But you did not honor the God who determines whether you live or die and who controls everything you do. 24 That is why God has sent the hand to write these words.

25 "This is what was written: 'Number, number, weight, divisions.' 26 And this is what it means: *number,* God has numbered the days of your kingdom and brought it to an end; 27 *weight,* you have been weighed on the scales and found to be too light; 28 *divisions,* your kingdom is divided up and given to the Medes and Persians."[l]

29 Immediately Belshazzar ordered his servants to dress Daniel in a robe of royal purple and to hang a gold chain of honor around his neck. And he made him the third in power in the kingdom. 30 That same night Belshazzar, the king of Babylonia, was killed; 31 and Darius the Mede, who was then sixty-two years old, seized the royal power.

Daniel in the Pit of Lions

6 Darius decided to appoint a hundred and twenty governors to hold office throughout his empire. 2 In addition, he chose Daniel and two others to supervise the governors and to look after the king's interests. 3 Daniel soon showed that he could do better work than the other supervisors or the governors. Because he was so outstanding, the king considered putting him in charge of the whole empire. 4 Then the other supervisors and the governors tried to find something wrong with the way Daniel administered the empire, but they couldn't, because Daniel was reliable and did not do anything wrong or dishonest. 5 They said to each other, "We are not going to find anything of which to accuse Daniel unless it is something in connection with his religion."

6 So they went to see the king and said, "King Darius, may Your Majesty live forever! 7 All of us who administer your empire — the supervisors, the governors, the lieutenant governors, and the other officials — have agreed that Your Majesty should issue an order and enforce it strictly. Give orders that for thirty days no one be permitted to request anything from any god or from any human being except from Your Majesty. Anyone who violates this order is to be thrown into a pit filled with lions. 8 So let Your Majesty issue this order and sign it, and it will be in force, a law of the Medes and Persians, which cannot be changed." 9 And so King Darius signed the order. 10 When Daniel

---

l PERSIANS: *In Aramaic the word for "Persians" sounds like the word for "division."*

learned that the order had been signed, he went home. In an upstairs room of his house there were windows that faced toward Jerusalem. There, just as he had always done, he knelt down at the open windows and prayed to God three times a day.

He knelt down at the open window. (6.10)

[11] When Daniel's enemies observed him praying to God, [12] all of them went together to the king to accuse Daniel. They said, "Your Majesty, you signed an order that for the next thirty days anyone who requested anything from any god or from any human being except you, would be thrown into a pit filled with lions."

The king replied, "Yes, that is a strict order, a law of the Medes and Persians, which cannot be changed."

[13] Then they said to the king, "Daniel, one of the exiles from Judah, does not respect Your Majesty or obey the order you issued. He prays regularly three times a day."

[14] When the king heard this, he was upset and did his best to find some way to rescue Daniel. He kept trying until sunset. [15] Then Daniel's enemies came back to the king and said to him, "Your Majesty knows that according to the laws of the Medes and Persians no order which the king issues can be changed."

[16] So the king gave orders for Daniel to be taken and thrown into the pit filled with lions. He said to Daniel, "May your God, whom you serve so loyally, rescue you." [17] A stone was put over the mouth of the pit, and the king placed his own royal seal and the seal of his noblemen on the stone, so that no one could rescue Daniel. [18] Then the king returned to the palace and spent a sleepless night, without food or any form of entertainment.

[19] At dawn the king got up and hurried to the pit. [20] When he got there, he called out anxiously, "Daniel, servant of the living God! Was the God you serve so loyally able to save you from the lions?"

[21] Daniel answered, "May Your Majesty live forever! [22] God sent his angel to shut the mouths of the lions so that they would not hurt me. He did this because he knew that I was innocent and because I have not wronged you, Your Majesty."

[23] The king was overjoyed and gave orders for Daniel to be pulled up out of the pit. So they pulled him up and saw that he had not been hurt at all, for he trusted God. [24] Then the king gave orders to arrest all those who had accused Daniel, and he had them thrown, together with their wives and children, into the pit filled with lions. Before they even reached the bottom of the pit, the lions pounced on them and broke all their bones.

[25] Then King Darius wrote to the people of all nations, races, and languages on earth:

"Greetings! [26] I command that throughout my empire everyone should fear and respect Daniel's God.

"He is a living God,
    and he will rule forever.
His kingdom will never be
    destroyed,
    and his power will never
      come to an end.

6.16 Bel 31-42   **6.22** Tb 4.17; 12.14, 15

He knew that I was innocent. (6.22)

²⁷ He saves and rescues;
   he performs wonders and
     miracles
   in heaven and on earth.
   He saved Daniel from being
     killed by the lions."
²⁸ Daniel prospered during the reign of Darius and the reign of Cyrus the Persian.

DANIEL DESCRIBES HIS VISIONS (7.1 – 12.13)

Daniel's Vision of the Four Beasts

7 In the first year that Belshazzar was king of Babylonia, I had a dream and saw a vision in the night. I wrote the dream down, and this is the record ²of what I saw that night:

Winds were blowing from all directions and lashing the surface of the ocean. ³Four huge beasts came up out of the ocean, each one different from the others. ⁴The first one looked like a lion, but had wings like an eagle. While I was watching, the wings were torn off. The beast was lifted up and made to stand up straight. And then a human mind was given to it.

⁵The second beast looked like a bear standing on its hind legs. It was holding three ribs between its teeth, and a voice said to it, "Go on, eat as much meat as you can!"

⁶While I was watching, another beast appeared. It looked like a leopard, but on its back there were four wings, like the wings of a bird, and it had four heads. It had a look of authority about it.

⁷As I was watching, a fourth beast appeared. It was powerful, horrible, terrifying. With its huge iron teeth it crushed its victims, and then it trampled on them. Unlike the other beasts, it had ten horns. ⁸While I was staring at the horns, I saw a little horn coming up among the others. It tore out three of the horns that were already there. This horn had human eyes and a mouth that was boasting proudly.

The Vision of the One Who Has Been Living Forever

⁹While I was looking, thrones were put in place. One who had been living forever sat down on one of the thrones. His clothes were white as snow, and his hair was like pure wool. His throne, mounted on fiery wheels, was blazing with fire, ¹⁰and a stream of fire was pouring out from it. There were many thousands of people there to serve him, and millions of people stood before him.

7.3 Rev 13.1; 17.8   **7.4-6** Rev 13.2   **7.7** Rev 12.3; 13.1   **7.8** Rev 13.5, 6   **7.9 a** Rev 20.4;
b Rev 1.14   **7.10 a** Rev 5.11; **b** Rev 20.12

The court began its session, and the books were opened.

11 While I was looking, I could still hear the little horn bragging and boasting. As I watched, the fourth beast was killed, and its body was thrown into the flames and destroyed. 12 The other beasts had their power taken away, but they were permitted to go on living for a limited time.

13 During this vision in the night, I saw what looked like a human being. He was approaching me, surrounded by clouds, and he went to the one who had been living forever and was presented to him. 14 He was given authority, honor, and royal power, so that the people of all nations, races, and languages would serve him. His authority would last forever, and his kingdom would never end.

The Visions Are Explained

15 The visions I saw alarmed me, and I was deeply disturbed.[m] 16 I went up to one of those standing there and asked him to explain it all. So he told me the meaning. 17 He said, "These four huge beasts are four empires which will arise on earth. 18 And the people of the Supreme God will receive royal power and keep it forever and ever."

19 Then I wanted to know more about the fourth beast, which was not like any of the others — the terrifying beast which crushed its victims with its bronze claws and iron teeth and then trampled on them. 20 And I wanted to know about the ten horns on its head and the horn that had come up afterward and had made three of the horns fall. It had eyes and a mouth and was boasting proudly. It was more terrifying than any of the others.

21 While I was looking, that horn made war on God's people and conquered them. 22 Then the one who had been living forever came and pronounced judgment in favor of[n] the people of the Supreme God. The time had arrived for God's people to receive royal power.

23 This is the explanation I was given: "The fourth beast is a fourth empire that will be on the earth and will be different from all other empires. It will crush the whole earth and trample it down. 24 The ten horns are ten kings who will rule that empire. Then another king will appear; he will be very different from the earlier ones and will overthrow three kings. 25 He will speak against the Supreme God and oppress God's people. He will try to change their religious laws and festivals, and God's people will be under his power for three and a half years. 26 Then the heavenly court will sit in judgment, take away his power, and destroy him completely. 27 The power and greatness of all the kingdoms on earth will be given to the people of the Supreme God. Their royal power will never end, and all rulers on earth will serve and obey them."

28 This is the end of the account. I was so frightened that I turned pale, and I kept everything to myself.

Daniel's Vision of a Ram and a Goat

8 In the third year that Belshazzar was king, I saw a second vision.[o] 2 In the vision I suddenly found myself in the walled city of Susa in the province of Elam. I was standing by the Ulai River, 3 and there beside the river I saw

---

[m] *Aramaic has two additional words, the meaning of which is unclear.*
[n] pronounced judgment in favor of; *or* gave the right to judge to.   [o] *Beginning at 8.1, the rest of this book is in Hebrew (see 2.4).*
7.13 Mt 24.30; 26.64; Mk 13.26; 14.62; Lk 21.27; Rev 1.7, 13; 14.14   **7.14** Rev 11.15
7.18 Rev 22.5   **7.21** Rev 13.7   **7.22** Rev 20.4   **7.24** Rev 17.12   **7.25** Rev 12.14; 13.5, 6
7.27 a Rev 20.4; **b** Rev 22.5

a ram that had two long horns, one of which was longer and newer than the other. [4] I watched the ram butting with his horns to the west, the north, and the south. No animal could stop him or escape his power. He did as he pleased and grew arrogant.

[5] While I was wondering what this meant, a goat came rushing out of the west, moving so fast that his feet didn't touch the ground. He had one prominent horn between his eyes. [6] He came toward the ram, which I had seen standing beside the river, and rushed at him with all his force. [7] I watched him attack the ram. He was so angry that he smashed into him and broke the two horns. The ram had no strength to resist. He was thrown to the ground and trampled on, and there was no one who could save him.

[8] The goat grew more and more arrogant, but at the height of his power his horn was broken. In its place four prominent horns came up, each pointing in a different direction. [9] Out of one of these four horns grew a little horn, whose power extended toward the south and the east and toward the Promised Land. [10] It grew strong enough to attack the army of heaven, the stars themselves, and it threw some of them to the ground and trampled on them. [11] It even defied the Prince of the heavenly army, stopped the daily sacrifices offered to him, and ruined the Temple. [12] People sinned there instead of offering the proper daily sacrifices,[p] and true religion was thrown to the ground. The horn was successful in everything it did.

[13] Then I heard one angel ask another, "How long will these things that were seen in the vision continue? How long will an awful sin replace the daily sacrifices? How long will the army of heaven and the Temple be trampled on?"

[14] I heard the other angel answer, "It will continue for 2,300 mornings and evenings, during which sacrifices will not be offered. Then the Temple will be restored."

The Angel Gabriel Explains the Vision

[15] I was trying to understand what the vision meant, when suddenly someone was standing in front of me. [16] I heard a voice call out over the Ulai River, "Gabriel, explain to him the meaning of what he saw." [17] Gabriel came and stood beside me, and I was so terrified that I fell to the ground.

He said to me, "Mortal man, understand the meaning. The vision has to do with the end of the world." [18] While he was talking, I fell to the ground unconscious. But he took hold of me, raised me to my feet, [19] and said, "I am showing you what the result of God's anger will be. The vision refers to the time of the end.

[20] "The ram you saw that had two horns represents the kingdoms of Media and Persia. [21] The goat represents the kingdom of Greece, and the prominent horn between his eyes is the first king. [22] The four horns that came up when the first horn was broken represent the four kingdoms into which that nation will be divided and which will not be as strong as the first kingdom.

[23] "When the end of those kingdoms is near and they have become so wicked that they must be punished, there will be a stubborn, vicious, and deceitful king. [24] He will grow strong—but not by his own power. He will cause terrible destruction and be successful in everything he does. He will bring destruction on powerful men and on God's own people. [25] Because he is cunning, he will succeed in his deceitful ways. He will be proud of himself and destroy many people without warning. He will

[p] People ... sacrifices; *Hebrew unclear.*
8.10 Rev 12.4   **8.16** Lk 1.19, 26

even defy the greatest King of all, but he will be destroyed without the use of any human power. 26 This vision about the evening and morning sacrifices which has been explained to you will come true. But keep it secret now, because it will be a long time before it does come true."

27 I was depressed and ill for several days. Then I got up and went back to the work that the king had assigned to me, but I was puzzled by the vision and could not understand it.

Daniel Prays for His People

9 Darius the Mede, who was the son of Xerxes, ruled over the kingdom of Babylonia. 2 In the first year of his reign I was studying the sacred books and thinking about the seventy years that Jerusalem would be in ruins, according to what the LORD had told the prophet Jeremiah. 3 And I prayed earnestly to the Lord God, pleading with him, fasting, wearing sackcloth, and sitting in ashes. 4 I prayed to the LORD my God and confessed the sins of my people.

I said, "Lord God, you are great, and we honor you. You are faithful to your covenant and show constant love to those who love you and do what you command.

5 "We have sinned, we have been evil, we have done wrong. We have rejected what you commanded us to do and have turned away from what you showed us was right. 6 We have not listened to your servants the prophets, who spoke in your name to our kings, our rulers, our ancestors, and our whole nation. 7 You, Lord, always do what is right, but we have always brought disgrace on ourselves. This is true of all of us who live in Judea and in Jerusalem and of all the Israelites whom you scat-

tered in countries near and far because they were unfaithful to you. 8 Our kings, our rulers, and our ancestors have acted shamefully and sinned against you, Lord. 9 You are merciful and forgiving, although we have rebelled against you. 10 We did not listen to you, O LORD our God, when you told us to live according to the laws which you gave us through your servants the prophets. 11 All Israel broke your laws and refused to listen to what you said. We sinned against you, and so you brought on us the curses that are written in the Law of Moses, your servant. 12 You did what you said you would do to us and our rulers. You punished Jerusalem more severely than any other city on earth, 13 giving us all the punishment described in the Law of Moses. But even now, O LORD our God, we have not tried to please you by turning from our sins or by following your truth. 14 You, O LORD our God, were prepared to punish us, and you did, because you always do what is right, and we did not listen to you.

15 "O Lord our God, you showed your power by bringing your people out of Egypt, and your power is still remembered. We have sinned; we have done wrong. 16 You have defended us in the past, so do not be angry with Jerusalem any longer. It is your city, your sacred hill.q All the people in the neighboring countries look down on Jerusalem and on your people because of our sins and the evil our ancestors did. 17 O God, hear my prayer and pleading. Restore your Temple, which has been destroyed; restore it so that everyone will know that you are God. 18 Listen to us, O God; look at us and see the trouble we are in and the suffering of the city that bears your name. We are praying to you because you are merciful, not because we have done right. 19 Lord, hear

q SACRED HILL: *Mount Zion (see Zion in Word List).*
9.2 Jr 25.11; 29.10   **9.7** Ba 1.15-17   **9.11** Ba 1.19-23   **9.15** Ba 2.11-13   **9.17** Ba 2.14
9.18 Ba 2.19

us. Lord, forgive us. Lord, listen to us, and act! In order that everyone will know that you are God, do not delay! This city and these people are yours."

"God, do not delay!" (9.19)

Gabriel Explains the Prophecy

20 I went on praying, confessing my sins and the sins of my people Israel and pleading with the LORD my God to restore his holy Temple. **21** While I was praying, Gabriel, whom I had seen in the earlier vision, came flying down to where I was. It was the time for the evening sacrifice to be offered. **22** He explained, "Daniel, I have come here to help you understand the prophecy. **23** When you began to plead with God, he answered you. He loves you, and so I have come to tell you the answer. Now pay attention while I explain the vision.

24 "Seven times seventy years is the length of time God has set for freeing your people and your holy city from sin and evil. Sin will be forgiven and eternal justice established, so that the vision and the prophecy will come true, and the holy Temple*r* will be rededicated. **25** Note this and understand it:

From the time the command is given to rebuild Jerusalem until God's chosen leader comes, seven times seven years will pass. Jerusalem will be rebuilt with streets and strong defenses, and will stand for seven times sixty-two years, but this will be a time of troubles. **26** And at the end of that time God's chosen leader will be killed unjustly.*s* The city and the Temple will be destroyed by the invading army of a powerful ruler. The end will come like a flood, bringing the war and destruction which God has prepared. **27** That ruler will have a firm agreement with many people for seven years, and when half this time is past, he will put an end to sacrifices and offerings. The Awful Horror*t* will be placed on the highest point of the Temple and will remain there until the one who put it there meets the end which God has prepared for him."

Daniel's Vision by the Tigris River

10 In the third year that Cyrus was emperor of Persia, a message was revealed to Daniel, who is also called Belteshazzar. The message was true but extremely hard to understand.*u* It was explained to him in a vision.

2 At that time I was mourning for three weeks. **3** I did not eat any rich food or any meat, drink any wine, or comb my hair until the three weeks were past.

4 On the twenty-fourth day of the first month of the year I was standing on the bank of the mighty Tigris River. **5** I looked up and saw someone who was wearing linen clothes and a belt of fine gold. **6** His body shone like a jewel. His face was as bright as a flash of

r Temple; *or* altar.   *s One ancient translation* unjustly; *Hebrew unclear.*   *t* THE
AWFUL HORROR: *A pagan image set up in the Jerusalem Temple by foreign conquerors*
(see 1 Macc 1.54-61).   *u* but extremely hard to understand; *or* and it was about a
great war.

9.21 Lk 1.19, 26   **9.27** Dn 11.31; 12.11; 1 Macc 1.44-50, 54; Mt 24.15; Mk 13.14
10.5, 6 Rev 1.13-15; 2.18; 19.12

lightning, and his eyes blazed like fire. His arms and legs shone like polished bronze, and his voice sounded like the roar of a great crowd.

7 I was the only one who saw the vision. Those who were with me did not see anything, but they were terrified and ran and hid. 8 I was left there alone, watching this amazing vision. I had no strength left, and my face was so changed that no one could have recognized me. 9 When I heard his voice, I fell to the ground unconscious and lay there face downward. 10 Then a hand took hold of me and raised me to my hands and knees; I was still trembling.

11 The angel said to me, "Daniel, God loves you. Stand up and listen carefully to what I am going to say. I have been sent to you." When he had said this, I stood up, still trembling.

12 Then he said, "Daniel, don't be afraid. God has heard your prayers ever since the first day you decided to humble yourself in order to gain understanding. I have come in answer to your prayer. 13 The angel prince of the kingdom of Persia opposed me for twenty-one days. Then Michael, one of the chief angels, came to help me, because I had been left there alone in Persia. 14 I have come to make you understand what will happen to your people in the future. This is a vision about the future."

15 When he said this, I stared at the ground, speechless. 16 Then the angel, who looked like a human being, reached out and touched my lips. I said to him, "Sir, this vision makes me so weak that I can't stop trembling. 17 I am like a slave standing before his master. How can I talk to you? I have no strength or breath left in me."

18 Once more he took hold of me, and I felt stronger. 19 He said, "God loves you, so don't let anything worry you or frighten you."

When he had said this, I felt even stronger and said, "Sir, tell me what you have to say. You have made me feel better."

20-21 He said, "Do you know why I came to you? It is to reveal to you what is written in the Book of Truth. Now I have to go back and fight the guardian angel of Persia. After that the guardian angel of Greece will appear. There is no one to help me except Michael, Israel's

11 guardian angel.v 1 He isw responsible for helping and defending me. 2 And what I am now going to tell you is true."

The Kingdoms of Egypt and Syria

The angel said, "Three more kings will rule over Persia, followed by a fourth, who will be richer than all the others. At the height of his power and wealth he will challenge the kingdom of Greece.

3 "Then a heroic king will appear. He will rule over a huge empire and do whatever he wants. 4 But at the height of his power his empire will break up and be divided into four parts. Kings not descended from him will rule in his place, but they will not have the power that he had.

5 "The king of Egypt will be strong. One of his generals, however, will be even stronger and rule a greater kingdom. 6 After a number of years the king of Egypt will make an alliance with the king of Syria and give him his daughter in marriage. But the alliance will not last, and she, her husband, her child,x and the servants who went with her will all be killed. 7 Soon afterward one of her relatives will become king. He will attack the army of the king of Syria, en-

v *Probable text* guardian angel; *Hebrew* guardian angel. And I, in the first year of Darius the Mede.   w *One ancient translation* He is; *Hebrew* I am.   x *Some ancient translations* her child; *Hebrew* her father.

10.13, 21 Rev 12.7

ter their fortress, and defeat them. 8 He will carry back to Egypt the images of their gods and the articles of gold and silver dedicated to those gods. After several years of peace 9 the king of Syria will invade Egypt, but he will be forced to retreat.

10 "The sons of the king of Syria will prepare for war and gather a large army. One of them will sweep on like a flood and attack an enemy fortress. 11 In his anger the king of Egypt will go to war against the king of Syria and capture his huge army. 12 He will be proud of his victory and of the many soldiers he has killed, but he will not continue to be victorious.

13 "The king of Syria will go back and gather a larger army than he had before. When the proper time comes, he will return with a large, well-equipped army. 14 Then many people will rebel against the king of Egypt. And some violent people from your nation, Daniel, will rebel because of a vision they have seen, but they will be defeated. 15 So the king of Syria will lay siege to a fortified city and capture it. The soldiers of Egypt will not continue to fight; even the best of them will not have enough strength. 16 The Syrian invader will do with them as he pleases, without opposition. He will stand in the Promised Land and have it completely in his power.

17 "The king of Syria will plan an expedition, using his whole army. Then, in order to destroy this enemy's kingdom, he will make an alliance with him and offer him his daughter*y* in marriage; but his plan will not succeed. 18 After that he will attack the nations by the sea and conquer many of them. But a foreign leader will defeat him and put an end to his arrogance; indeed he will turn the arrogance of Syria's king back on him.*z* 19 The king will return to the fortresses of his own land, but he

will be defeated, and that will be the end of him.

20 "He will be followed by another king, who will send an officer to oppress the people with taxes in order to increase the wealth of his kingdom. In a short time that king will be killed, but not publicly and not in battle."

The Evil King of Syria

21 The angel went on to explain: "The next king of Syria will be an evil man who has no right to be king, but he will come unexpectedly and seize power by trickery. 22 Anyone who opposes him, even God's High Priest, will be swept away and wiped out. 23 By making treaties, he will deceive other nations, and he will grow stronger and stronger, even though he rules only a small nation. 24 He will invade a wealthy province without warning and will do things that none of his ancestors ever did. Then he will divide among his followers the goods and property he has captured in war. He will make plans to attack fortresses, but his time will soon run out.

25 "He will boldly raise a large army to attack the king of Egypt, who will prepare to fight back with a huge and powerful army. But the king of Egypt will be deceived and will not be successful. 26 His closest advisers will ruin him. Many of his soldiers will be killed, and his army will be wiped out. 27 Then the two kings will sit down to eat at the same table, but their motives will be evil, and they will lie to each other. They will not get what they want, because the time for it has not yet come. 28 The king of Syria will return home with all the loot he has captured, determined to destroy the religion of God's people. He will do as he pleases and then return to his own land.

29 "Later on he will invade Egypt again, but this time things will turn out

---

y his daughter; *or* a young woman.   *z Probable text* his arrogance . . . on him; Hebrew *unclear*.

differently. ³⁰The Romans will come in ships and oppose him, and he will be frightened.

"Then he will turn back in a rage and try to destroy the religion of God's people. He will follow the advice of those who have abandoned that religion. ³¹Some of his soldiers will make the Temple ritually unclean. They will stop the daily sacrifices and set up The Awful Horror.ᵃ ³²By deceit the king will win the support of those who have already abandoned their religion, but those who follow God will fight back. ³³Wise leaders of the people will share their wisdom with many others. But for a while some of them will be killed in battle or be burned to death, and some will be robbed and made prisoners. ³⁴While the killing is going on, God's people will receive a little help, even though many who join them will do so for selfish reasons. ³⁵Some of those wise leaders will be killed, but as a result of this the people will be purified. This will continue until the end comes, the time that God has set.

³⁶"The king of Syria will do as he pleases. He will boast that he is greater than any god, superior even to the Supreme God. He will be able to do this until the time when God punishes him. God will do exactly what he has planned. ³⁷The king will ignore the god his ancestors served, and also the god that women love. In fact, he will ignore every god, because he will think he is greater than any of them. ³⁸Instead, he will honor the god who protects fortresses. He will offer gold, silver, jewels, and other rich gifts to a god his ancestors never worshiped. ³⁹To defend his fortresses, he will use people who worship a foreign god. He will give great honor to those who accept him as ruler, put them into high offices, and give them land as a reward.

⁴⁰"When the king of Syria's final hour has almost come, the king of Egypt will attack him, and the king of Syria will fight back with all his power, using chariots, horses, and many ships. He will invade many countries, like the waters of a flood. ⁴¹He will even invade the Promised Land and kill tens of thousands, but the countries of Edom, Moab, and what is left of Ammon will escape. ⁴²When he invades all those countries, even Egypt will not be spared. ⁴³He will take away Egypt's hidden treasures of gold and silver and its other prized possessions. He will conquer Libya and Ethiopia.ᵇ ⁴⁴Then news that comes from the east and the north will frighten him, and he will fight furiously, killing many people. ⁴⁵He will even set up his huge royal tents between the sea and the mountain on which the Temple stands. But he will die, with no one there to help him."

The Time of the End

12 The angel wearing linen clothes said, "At that time the great angel Michael, who guards your people, will appear. Then there will be a time of troubles, the worst since nations first came into existence. When that time comes, all the people of your nation whose names are written in God's book will be saved. ²Many of those who have already died will live again: some will enjoy eternal life, and some will suffer eternal disgrace. ³The

---

ᵃ THE AWFUL HORROR: See 9.27.   ᵇ Hebrew Cush: *Cush is the ancient name of the extensive territory south of the First Cataract of the Nile River. This region was called Ethiopia in Graeco-Roman times, and included within its borders most of modern Sudan and some of present-day Ethiopia (Abyssinia).*

11.30 2 Macc 5.11   **11.31** Dn 9.27; 12.11; Mt 24.15; Mk 13.14   **11.36 a** 2 Th 2.3, 4; **b** Rev 13.5, 6   **12.1 a** Rev 12.7; **b** Mt 24.21; Mk 13.19; Rev 7.14; 12.7   **12.2** Is 26.19; 2 Macc 7.9-11, 14; Mt 25.46; Jn 5.29   **12.3** 2 Esd 7.97

wise leaders will shine with all the brightness of the sky. And those who have taught many people to do what is right will shine like the stars forever."

⁴He said to me, "And now, Daniel, close the book and put a seal on it until the end of the world. Meanwhile, many people will waste their efforts trying to understand what is happening."

Daniel, close the book. (12.4)

⁵Then I saw two men standing by a river, one on each bank. ⁶One of them asked the angel who was standing further upstream, "How long will it be un-

til these amazing events come to an end?"

⁷The angel raised both hands toward the sky and made a solemn promise in the name of the Eternal God. I heard him say, "It will be three and a half years. When the persecution of God's people ends, all these things will have happened."

⁸I heard what he said, but I did not understand it. So I asked, "But, sir, how will it all end?"

⁹He answered, "You must go now, Daniel, because these words are to be kept secret and hidden until the end comes. ¹⁰Many people will be purified. Those who are wicked will not understand but will go on being wicked; only those who are wise will understand.

¹¹"From the time the daily sacrifices are stopped, that is, from the time of The Awful Horror,ᶜ 1,290 days will pass. ¹²Happy are those who remain faithful until 1,335 days are over!

¹³"And you, Daniel, be faithful to the end. Then you will die, but you will rise to receive your reward at the end of time."

ᶜ THE AWFUL HORROR: *See* 9.27.
12.4 Rev 22.10   **12.7 a** Rev 10.5; **b** Rev 12.14
Mt 24.15; Mk 13.14

12.10 Rev 22.11   **12.11** Dn 9.27; 11.31;

The Book of
HOSEA

INTRODUCTION

The prophet Hosea preached in the northern kingdom of Israel, after the prophet Amos, during the troubled times before the fall of Samaria in 721 B.C. He was especially concerned about the idolatry of the people and their faithlessness toward God. Hosea boldly pictured this faithlessness in terms of his own disastrous marriage to an unfaithful woman. Just as his wife Gomer turned out to be unfaithful to him, so God's people had deserted the Lord. For this, judgment would fall on Israel. Yet in the end God's constant love for his people would prevail, and he would win the nation back to himself and restore the relationship. This love is expressed in the moving words: "How can I give you up, Israel? How can I abandon you? . . . My heart will not let me do it! My love for you is too strong" (11.8).

OUTLINE OF CONTENTS

1 This is the message which the LORD gave Hosea son of Beeri during the time that Uzziah, Jotham, Ahaz, and Hezekiah were kings of Judah, and Jeroboam son of Jehoash was king of Israel.

Hosea's Wife and Children

2 When the LORD first spoke to Israel through Hosea, he said to Hosea, "Go and get married; your wife will be unfaithful, and your children will be just like her.[a] In the same way my people have left me and become unfaithful."

3 So Hosea married a woman named Gomer, the daughter of Diblaim. After the birth of their first child, a son, 4 the LORD said to Hosea, "Name him 'Jezreel,' because it will not be long before I punish the king of Israel for the murders that his ancestor Jehu committed at Jezreel.[b] I am going to put an end to Jehu's dynasty.[c] 5 And in Jezreel Valley I will at that time destroy Israel's military power."

6 Gomer had a second child — this time it was a daughter. The LORD said to Hosea, "Name her 'Unloved,' because I will no longer show love to the people of Israel or forgive them. 7 But to

---

a *get married; your wife . . . her; or* marry a prostitute, and have children by her who will be just as bad as she is.   b JEZREEL: *At this city Jehu assassinated the king of Israel and all the rest of the royal family, and became the first king of a new dynasty (see* 2 K 9–10). c Jehu's dynasty; *or* the kingdom of Israel.
1.1 a 2 K 15.1-7; 2 Ch 26.1-23; **b** 2 K 15.32-38; 2 Ch 27.1-8; **c** 2 K 16.1-20; 2 Ch 28.1-27; **d** 2 K 18.1 – 20.21; 2 Ch 29.1 – 32.33; **e** 2 K 14.23-29   **1.4** 2 K 10.11

the people of Judah I will show love. I, the LORD their God, will save them, but I will not do it by war — with swords or bows and arrows or with horses and horsemen."

⁸After Gomer had weaned her daughter, she became pregnant again and had another son. ⁹The LORD said to Hosea, "Name him 'Not-My-People,' because the people of Israel are not my people, and I am not their God."

Israel Is to Be Restored

¹⁰The people of Israel will become like the sand of the sea, more than can be counted or measured. Now God says to them, "You are not my people," but the day is coming when he will say to them, "You are the children of the living God!" ¹¹The people of Judah and the people of Israel will be reunited. They will choose for themselves a single leader, and once again they will grow and prosper in their land. Yes, the day of Jezreel*d* will be a great day!

2 ¹So call your fellow Israelites "God's People" and "Loved-by-the-Lord."

Unfaithful Gomer — Unfaithful Israel

²My children, plead with your mother — though she is no longer a wife to me, and I am no longer her husband. Plead with her to stop her adultery and prostitution. ³If she does not, I will strip her as naked as she was on the day she was born. I will make her like a dry and barren land, and she will die of thirst. ⁴⁻⁵I will not show mercy to her children; they are the children of a shameless prostitute.*e* She herself said, "I will go to my lovers — they give me food and water, wool and linen, olive oil and wine."

⁶So I am going to fence her in with thorn bushes and build a wall to block her way. ⁷She will run after her lovers but will not catch them. She will look for them but will not find them. Then she will say, "I am going back to my first husband — I was better off then than I am now."

⁸She would never acknowledge that I am the one who gave her the grain, the wine, the olive oil, and all the silver and gold that she used in the worship of Baal. ⁹So at harvest time I will take back my gifts of grain and wine, and will take away the wool and the linen I gave her for clothing. ¹⁰I will strip her naked in front of her lovers, and no one will be able to save her from my power. ¹¹I will put an end to all her festivities — her annual and monthly festivals and her Sabbath celebrations — all her religious meetings. ¹²I will destroy her grapevines and her fig trees, which she said her lovers gave her for serving them. I will turn her vineyards and orchards into a wilderness; wild animals will destroy them. ¹³I will punish her for the times that she forgot me, when she burned incense to Baal and put on her jewelry to go chasing after her lovers. The LORD has spoken.

The LORD's Love for His People

¹⁴So I am going to take her into the desert again; there I will win her back with words of love. ¹⁵I will give back to her the vineyards she had and make Trouble Valley a door of hope. She will respond to me there as she did when

---

d JEZREEL: *This name in Hebrew means "God sows" and suggests growth and prosperity.*   *e* the children of a shameless prostitute; *or* as shameless as their mother, a prostitute.

1.10 Ro 9.26   **2.15** Js 7.24-26

Let my people live in peace. (2.18)

she was young, when she came from Egypt. ¹⁶Then once again she will call me her husband—she will no longer call me her Baal.*f* ¹⁷I will never let her speak the name of Baal again.

¹⁸At that time I will make a covenant with all the wild animals and birds, so that they will not harm my people. I will also remove all weapons of war from the land, all swords and bows, and will let my people live in peace and safety.

¹⁹Israel, I will make you my wife;
 I will be true and faithful;
 I will show you constant love
  and mercy
 and make you mine forever.
²⁰I will keep my promise and make
  you mine,

and you will acknowledge me
  as LORD.
²¹⁻²²At that time I will answer the
  prayers of my people
  Israel.*g*
 I will make rain fall on the
  earth,
 and the earth will produce
  grain and grapes
  and olives.
²³I will establish my people in the
  land and make them
  prosper.
 I will show love to those who
  were called "Unloved,"
 and to those who were called
  "Not-My-People"
 I will say, "You are my
  people,"
 and they will answer, "You
  are our God."

f BAAL: *This title of the Canaanite god means "Lord"; another meaning of the word is* "husband." *g* ISRAEL: *The Hebrew text here refers to Israel as Jezreel (see 1.4, 11).*
2.23 Ro 9.25; 1 P 2.10

Hosea and the Unfaithful Woman

3 The LORD said to me, "Go again[h] and show your love for a woman who is committing adultery with a lover. You must love her just as I still love the people of Israel, even though they turn to other gods and like to take offerings of raisins to idols."[i]

2 So I paid fifteen pieces of silver and seven bushels of barley to buy her. 3 I told her that for a long time she would have to wait for me without being a prostitute or committing adultery; and during this time I would wait for her. 4 In just this way the people of Israel will have to live for a long time without kings or leaders, without sacrifices or sacred stone pillars, without idols or images to use for divination. 5 But the time will come when the people of Israel will once again turn to the LORD their God and to a descendant of David their king. Then they will fear the LORD and will receive his good gifts.

The LORD's Accusation against Israel

4 The LORD has an accusation to bring against the people who live in this land. Listen, Israel, to what he says: "There is no faithfulness or love in the land, and the people do not acknowledge me as God. 2 They make promises and break them; they lie, murder, steal, and commit adultery. Crimes increase, and there is one murder after another. 3 And so the land will dry up, and everything that lives on it will die. All the animals and birds, and even the fish, will die."

The LORD Accuses the Priests

4 The LORD says, "Let no one accuse the people or reprimand them — my complaint is against you priests.[j] 5 Night and day you blunder on, and the prophets do no better than you. I am going to destroy Israel, your mother. 6 My people are doomed because they do not acknowledge me. You priests have refused to acknowledge me and have rejected my teaching, and so I reject you and will not acknowledge your sons as my priests.

7 "The more of you priests there are, the more you sin against me, and so I will turn your honor into disgrace. 8 You grow rich from the sins of my people, and so you want them to sin more and more. 9 You will suffer the same punishment as the people! I will punish you and make you pay for the evil you do. 10 You will eat your share of the sacrifices, but still be hungry. You will worship the fertility gods, but still have no children, because you have turned away from me to follow other gods."

The LORD Condemns Pagan Worship

11 The LORD says, "Wine, both old and new, is robbing my people of their senses! 12 They ask for revelations from a piece of wood! A stick tells them what they want to know! They have left me. Like a woman who becomes a prostitute, they have given themselves to

They ask for revelations from a piece of wood! (4.12)

---

[h] The LORD . . . again; *or* The LORD spoke to me again. He said, "Go . . ."
[i] OFFERINGS OF RAISINS TO IDOLS: *Dried grapes were used in the worship of fertility gods, who were believed to give abundant harvests to their worshipers.* [j] *Probable text* my complaint is against you priests; *Hebrew* your people are like those with a complaint against the priests.

other gods. 13 At sacred places on the mountaintops they offer sacrifices, and on the hills they burn incense under tall, spreading trees, because the shade is so pleasant!

"As a result, your daughters serve as prostitutes, and your daughters-in-law commit adultery. 14 Yet I will not punish them for this, because you yourselves go off with temple prostitutes,*k* and together with them you offer pagan sacrifices. As the proverb says, 'A people without sense will be ruined.'

15 "Even though you people of Israel are unfaithful to me, may Judah not be guilty of the same thing. Don't worship at Gilgal or Bethaven,*l* or make promises there in the name of the living LORD. 16 The people of Israel are as stubborn as mules. How can I feed them like lambs in a meadow? 17 The people of Israel are under the spell of idols. Let them go their own way. 18 After drinking much wine, they delight in their prostitution, preferring disgrace to honor. 19 They will be carried away as by the wind, and they will be ashamed of their pagan sacrifices.*m, n*

5 "Listen to this, you priests! Pay attention, people of Israel! Listen, you that belong to the royal family! You are supposed to judge with justice — so judgment will fall on you! You have become a trap at Mizpah, a net spread on Mount Tabor, 2 a deep pit at Acacia City,*o* and I will punish all of you. 3 I know what Israel is like — she cannot hide from me. She has been unfaithful, and her people are unfit to worship me."

Hosea Warns against Idolatry

4 The evil that the people have done keeps them from returning to their God. Idolatry has a powerful hold on them, and they do not acknowledge the LORD. 5 The arrogance of the people of Israel cries out against them. Their sins make them stumble and fall, and the people of Judah fall with them. 6 They take their sheep and cattle to offer as sacrifices to the LORD, but it does them no good. They cannot find him, for he has left them. 7 They have been unfaithful to the LORD; their children do not belong to him. So now they and their lands will soon be destroyed.

War between Judah and Israel

8 Blow the war trumpets in Gibeah! Sound the alarm in Ramah! Raise the war cry at Bethaven!*p* Into battle, men of Benjamin! 9 The day of punishment is coming, and Israel will be ruined. People of Israel, this will surely happen!

10 The LORD says, "I am angry because the leaders of Judah have invaded Israel and stolen land from her. So I will pour out punishment on them like a flood. 11 Israel is suffering oppression; she has lost land that was rightfully hers, because she insisted on going for help to those who had none to give.*q* 12 I will bring destruction on Israel and ruin on the people of Judah.

13 "When Israel saw how sick she was and when Judah saw her own wounds, then Israel went to Assyria to ask the great emperor for help, but he could not cure them or heal their wounds. 14 I will attack the people of Israel and Judah

---

k TEMPLE PROSTITUTES: *These women were found in Canaanite temples, where fertility gods were worshiped. It was believed that intercourse with these prostitutes assured fertile fields and herds.* *l* BETHAVEN: *This name means "house of evil" or "house of idolatry" and in this passage refers to the city of Bethel, a name which means "house of God." See also 10.8.* *m* sacrifices; *some ancient translations* altars. *n* Verses 17-19 in Hebrew are unclear. *o* Probable text a deep pit at Acacia City; *Hebrew unclear.* *p* BETHAVEN: *This name means "house of evil" or "house of idolatry" and in this passage refers to the city of Bethel, a name which means "house of God." See also 10.8.* *q* Probable text those who had none to give; *Hebrew* command.

like a lion. I myself will tear them to pieces and then leave them. When I drag them off, no one will be able to save them.

15 "I will abandon my people until they have suffered enough for their sins and come looking for me. Perhaps in their suffering they will try to find me."

The People's Insincere Repentance

6 The people say, "Let's return to the LORD! He has hurt us, but he will be sure to heal us; he has wounded us, but he will bandage our wounds, won't he? 2 In two or three days he will revive us, and we will live in his presence. 3 Let us try to know the LORD. He will come to us as surely as the day dawns, as surely as the spring rains fall upon the earth."

4 But the LORD says, "Israel and Judah, what am I going to do with you? Your love for me disappears as quickly as morning mist; it is like dew, that vanishes early in the day. 5 That is why I have sent my prophets to you with my message of judgment and destruction. What I want from you is plain and clear: 6 I want your constant love, not your animal sacrifices. I would rather have my people know me than burn offerings to me.

7 "But as soon as they entered the land at Adam,r they broke the covenant I had made with them. 8 Gilead is a city full of evil people and murderers. 9 The priests are like a gang of robbers who wait in ambush for someone. Even on the road to the holy place at Shechem they commit murder. And they do all this evil deliberately! 10 I have seen a horrible thing in Israel: my people have defiled themselves by worshiping idols.

11 "And as for you, people of Judah, I

have set a time to punish you also for what you are doing.

7 "Whenever I want to heal my people Israel and make them prosperous again, all I can see is their wickedness and the evil they do. They cheat one another; they break into houses and steal; they rob people in the streets. 2 It never enters their heads that I will remember all this evil; but their sins surround them, and I cannot avoid seeing them."

Conspiracy in the Palace

3 The LORD says, "People deceive the king and his officers by their evil plots. 4 They are all treacherous and disloyal. Their hatred smolders like the fire in an oven, which is not stirred by the baker until the dough is ready to bake. 5 On the day of the king's celebration they made the king and his officials drunk and foolish with wine. 6 Yes, they burneds like an oven with their plotting. All night their anger smoldered, and in the morning it burst into flames.

7 "In the heat of their anger they murdered their rulers. Their kings have been assassinated one after another, but no one prays to me for help."

Israel and the Nations

8 The LORD says, "The people of Israel are like a half-baked loaf of bread. They rely on the nations around them 9 and do not realize that this reliance on foreigners has robbed them of their strength. Their days are numbered, but they don't even know it. 10 The arrogance of the people of Israel cries out against them. In spite of everything that has happened, they have not returned to me, the LORD their God. 11 Israel flits around like a silly pigeon; first her people call on Egypt for help, and then they run to Assyria! 12 But I will

---

r Probable text But . . . at Adam; Hebrew But like Adam.   s One ancient translation burned; Hebrew drew near.

6.6 Mt 9.13; 12.7

spread out a net and catch them like birds as they go by. I will punish them for the evil they have done.[t]

13"They are doomed! They have left me and rebelled against me. They will be destroyed. I wanted to save them, but their worship of me was false. 14They have not prayed to me sincerely, but instead they throw themselves down and wail as the heathen do. When they pray for grain and wine, they gash themselves like pagans. What rebels they are! 15Even though I was the one who brought them up and made them strong, they plotted against me. 16They keep on turning away from me to a god that is powerless.[u] They are as unreliable as a crooked bow. Because their leaders talk arrogantly, they will die a violent death, and the Egyptians will laugh."

The LORD Condemns Israel for Idol Worship

8 The LORD says, "Sound the alarm! Enemies are swooping down on my land like eagles! My people have broken the covenant I made with them and have rebelled against my teaching. 2Even though they call me their God and claim that they are my people and that they know me, 3they have rejected what is good. Because of this their enemies will pursue them.

4"My people chose kings, but they did it on their own. They appointed leaders, but without my approval. They took their silver and gold and made idols — for their own destruction. 5I hate the gold bull worshiped by the people of the city of Samaria. I am furious with them. How long will it be before they give up their idolatry? 6An Israelite craftsman made the idol, and it is not a god at all! The gold bull worshiped in Samaria will be smashed to pieces!

7When they sow the wind, they will reap a storm! A field of grain that doesn't ripen can never produce any bread. But even if it did, foreigners would eat it up. 8Israel has become like any other nation and is as useless as a broken pot. 9Stubborn as wild donkeys, the people of Israel go their own way. They have gone off to seek help from Assyria and have paid other nations to protect them. 10But now I am going to gather them together and punish them. Soon they will writhe in pain when the emperor of Assyria oppresses them.

11"The more altars the people of Israel build for removing sin, the more places they have for sinning! 12I write down countless teachings for the people, but they reject them as strange and foreign. 13They offer sacrifices to me and eat the meat of the sacrifices.[v] But I, the LORD, am not pleased with them, and now I will remember their sin and punish them for it; I will send them back to Egypt!

14"The people of Israel have built palaces, but they have forgotten their own Maker. The people of Judah have built fortified cities. But I will send fire that will burn down their palaces and their cities."

Hosea Announces Punishment for Israel

9 People of Israel, stop celebrating your festivals like pagans. You have turned away from your God and have been unfaithful to him. All over the land you have sold yourselves like prostitutes to the god Baal and have loved the grain you thought he paid you with! 2But soon you will not have enough grain and olive oil, and there will be no wine. 3The people of Israel will not remain in the LORD's land, but will have to go back to Egypt and will

---

[t] *Probable text* the evil they have done; *Hebrew* the report to their congregation.
[u] *Probable text* a god that is powerless; *Hebrew unclear.*   [v] They offer . . . the sacrifices; *Hebrew unclear.*

have to eat forbidden food^w in Assyria. ^{4}In those foreign lands they will not be able to make wine offerings to the LORD or bring their sacrifices to him. Their food will defile everyone who eats it, like food eaten at funerals. It will be used only to satisfy their hunger; none of it will be taken as an offering to the LORD's Temple. ^{5}And when the time comes for the appointed festivals in honor of the LORD, what will they do then? ^{6}When the disaster comes and the people are scattered, the Egyptians will gather them up — gather them for burial there at Memphis! Their treasures of silver and the places where their homes once stood will be overgrown with weeds and thorn bushes.

^{7}The time for punishment has come, the time when people will get what they deserve. When that happens, Israel will know it! "This prophet," you say, "is a fool. This inspired man is insane." You people hate me so much because your sin is so great. ^{8}God has sent me as a prophet to warn his people Israel. Yet wherever I go, you try to trap me like a bird. Even in God's Temple the people are the prophet's enemies. ^{9}They are hopelessly evil in what they do, just as they were at Gibeah.^{x} God will remember their sin and punish them for it.

Israel's Sin and Its Consequences

^{10}The LORD says, "When I first found Israel, it was like finding grapes growing in the desert. When I first saw your ancestors, it was like seeing the first ripe figs of the season. But when they came to Mount Peor, they began to worship Baal and soon became as disgusting as the gods they loved. ^{11}Israel's greatness will fly away like a bird, and there will be no more children born to them, no more women pregnant, no more children conceived. ^{12}But even if they did bring up children, I would take them away and not leave one alive. When I abandon these people, terrible things will happen to them."

^{13}LORD, I can see their children being hunted down^y and killed. ^{14}What shall I ask you to do to these people? Make their women barren! Make them unable to nurse their babies!

The LORD's Judgment on Israel

^{15}The LORD says, "All their evildoing began in Gilgal. It was there that I began to hate them. And because of the evil they have done, I will drive them out of my land. I will not love them any more; all their leaders have rebelled against me. ^{16}The people of Israel are like a plant whose roots have dried up and which bears no fruit. They will have no children, but even if they did, I would kill the children so dear to them."

The Prophet Speaks about Israel

^{17}The God I serve will reject his people, because they have not listened to him. They will become wanderers among the nations. **10** ^{1}The people of Israel were like a grapevine that was full of grapes. The more prosperous they were, the more altars they built. The more productive their land was, the more beautiful they made the sacred stone pillars they worship. ^{2}The people whose hearts are deceitful must now suffer for their sins. God will break down their altars and destroy their sacred pillars.

^{3}These people will soon be saying, "We have no king because we did not fear the LORD. But what could a king do

---

^{v} FORBIDDEN FOOD: *The Law of Moses prohibited the eating of certain foods as being ritually unclean (see Lv 11).* ^{x} GIBEAH: *At this city some Israelites of the tribe of Benjamin raped a Levite's concubine; this caused a civil war that almost wiped out the Benjaminites (see Jg 19–21).* ^{y} *Probable text* being hunted down; *Hebrew unclear.*

9.7 Lk 21.22   **9.9** Jg 19.1-30   **9.10** Nu 25.1-5

for us anyway?" ⁴They utter empty words and make false promises and useless treaties. Justice has become injustice, growing like poisonous weeds in a plowed field.

⁵The people who live in the city of Samaria will be afraid and will mourn the loss of the gold bull*z* at Bethaven.*a* They and the priests who serve the idol will weep over it. They will wail when it is stripped of its golden splendor. ⁶The idol will be carried off to Assyria as tribute to the great emperor. The people of Israel will be disgraced and put to shame because of the advice they followed. ⁷Their king will be carried off, like a chip of wood on water. ⁸The hilltop shrines of Aven,*a* where the people of Israel worship idols, will be destroyed. Thorns and weeds will grow up over their altars. The people will call out to the mountains, "Hide us!" and to the hills, "Cover us!"

Thorns and weeds will grow up over their altars. (10.8)

The LORD Pronounces Judgment on Israel

⁹The LORD says, "The people of Israel have not stopped sinning against me since the time of their sin at Gibeah.*b* So at Gibeah war will catch up with them. ¹⁰I will attack*c* this sinful people and punish them. Nations will join together against them, and they will be punished for their many sins.

¹¹"Israel was once like a well-trained young cow, ready and willing to thresh grain. But I decided to put a yoke*d* on her beautiful neck and to harness her for harder work. I made Judah pull the plow and Israel pull the harrow. ¹²I said, 'Plow new ground for yourselves, plant righteousness, and reap the blessings that your devotion to me will produce. It is time for you to turn to me, your LORD, and I will come and pour out blessings upon you.' ¹³But instead you planted evil and reaped its harvest. You have eaten the fruit produced by your lies.

"Because you trusted in your chariots*e* and in the large number of your soldiers, ¹⁴war will come to your people, and all your fortresses will be destroyed. It will be like the day when King Shalman destroyed the city of Betharbel in battle, and mothers and their children were crushed to death. ¹⁵That is what will happen to you, people of Bethel, because of the terrible evil that you have done. As soon as the battle begins, the king of Israel will die."

God's Love for His Rebellious People

11 The LORD says,
"When Israel was a child,
  I loved him
and called him out of Egypt
  as my son.*f*
²But the more I*g* called to him,

---

z Some ancient translations bull; *Hebrew* cows.   *a* BETHAVEN: *This name means "house of evil" or "house of idolatry" and in this passage refers to the city of Bethel, a name which means "house of God." In verse 8, Bethaven is called Aven. See also 4.15 and 5.8.*   *b* GIBEAH: *See 9.9.*   *c One ancient translation* I will attack; *Hebrew* In my desire.   *d Probable text* put a yoke; *Hebrew* spare.   *e One ancient translation* chariots; *Hebrew* way.   *f* him, and called him . . . son; *or* him; from the time he left Egypt I have called him my son.   *g One ancient translation* I; *Hebrew* they.
10.8 Lk 23.30; Rev 6.16   **10.9** Jg 19.1-30   **10.12** Jr 4.3   **11.1** Ex 4.22; Mt 2.15

the more he turned away
  from me.[h]
My people sacrificed to Baal;
  they burned incense to idols.
[3] Yet I was the one who taught
  Israel to walk.

I took my people up in my
  arms,[i]
  but they did not acknowledge
    that I took care of them.
[4] I drew them to me with affection
    and love.
  I picked them up and held
    them to my cheek;
  I bent down to them and fed
    them.[j]

[5] "They refuse to return to me, and so
they must return to Egypt, and Assyria
will rule them. [6] War will sweep
through their cities and break down the
city gates. It will destroy my people because they do what they themselves
think best. [7] They insist on turning
away from me. They will cry out because of the yoke that is on them, but
no one will lift it from them.[k]

[8] "How can I give you up, Israel?
  How can I abandon you?
  Could I ever destroy you as I did
    Admah,
  or treat you as I did Zeboiim?
My heart will not let me do it!
  My love for you is too strong.
[9] I will not punish you in my
    anger;
  I will not destroy Israel again.
For I am God and not a mere
    human being.
  I, the Holy One, am with you.
  I will not come to you in anger.

[10] "My people will follow me when I
roar like a lion at their enemies. They
will hurry to me from the west. [11] They
will come from Egypt, as swiftly as
birds, and from Assyria, like doves. I
will bring them to their homes again. I,
the LORD, have spoken."

Israel and Judah Are Condemned

[12] The LORD says, "The people of Israel have surrounded me with lies and
deceit, and the people of Judah are still
rebelling against me, the faithful and

12 holy God. [1] Everything that the
people of Israel do from morning to night is useless and destructive.
Treachery and acts of violence increase
among them. They make treaties with
Assyria and do business with Egypt."

[2] The LORD has an accusation to
bring against the people of Judah; he is
also going to punish Israel for the way
her people act. He will pay them back
for what they have done. [3] Their ancestor Jacob struggled with his twin
brother Esau while the two of them
were still in their mother's womb; when
Jacob grew up, he fought against
God — [4] he fought against an angel and
won. He wept and asked for a blessing.
And at Bethel God came to our ancestor
Jacob and spoke with him.[l] [5] This was
the LORD God Almighty — the LORD is
the name by which he is to be worshiped. [6] So now, descendants of Jacob,
trust in your God and return to him. Be
loyal and just, and wait patiently for
your God to act.

Further Words of Judgment

[7] The LORD says, "The people of Israel are as dishonest as the Canaanites;
they love to cheat their customers with
false scales. [8] 'We are rich,' they say.
'We've made a fortune. And no one can
accuse us of getting rich dishonestly.'
[9] But I, the LORD your God who led you
out of Egypt, I will make you live in

[h] *One ancient translation* me; *Hebrew* them.   [i] *One ancient translation* I . . . my
arms; *Hebrew* He . . . his arms.   [j] *Verse 4 in Hebrew is unclear.*   [k] *Verse 7 in
Hebrew is unclear.*   [l] *Some ancient translations* him; *Hebrew* us.
11.8 Dt 29.23   **12.3** Gn 25.26   **12.3, 4** Gn 32.24-26   **12.4** Gn 28.10-22   **12.9** Lv 23.42, 43

tents again, as you did when I came to you in the desert.

The altars there will become piles of stone. (12.11)

¹⁰"I spoke to the prophets and gave them many visions, and through the prophets I gave my people warnings. ¹¹Yet idols are worshiped in Gilead, and those who worship them will die. Bulls are sacrificed in Gilgal, and the altars there will become piles of stone in the open fields."

¹²Our ancestor Jacob had to flee to Mesopotamia, where, in order to get a wife, he worked for another man and took care of his sheep. ¹³The LORD sent a prophet to rescue the people of Israel from slavery in Egypt and to take care of them. ¹⁴The people of Israel have made the LORD bitterly angry; they deserve death for their crimes. Their Lord will punish them for the disgrace they have brought on him.

Final Judgment on Israel

13 In the past, when the tribe of Ephraim spoke, the other tribes of Israel were afraid; they looked up to Ephraim. But the people sinned by worshiping Baal, and for this they will die. ²They still keep on sinning by making metal images to worship — idols of silver, designed by human minds, made by human hands. And then they say, "Offer sacrifices to them!" How can anyone kiss those idols — idols in the shape of bulls!ᵐ

³And so these people will disappear like morning mist, like the dew that vanishes early in the day. They will be like chaff which the wind blows from the threshing place, like smoke from a chimney.

⁴The LORD says, "I am the LORD your God, who led you out of Egypt. You have no God but me. I alone am your savior. ⁵I took care of you in a dry, desert land. ⁶But when you entered the good land, you became full and satisfied, and then you grew proud and forgot me. ⁷So I will attack you like a lion. Like a leopard I will lie in wait along your path. ⁸I will attack you like a bear that has lost her cubs, and I will tear

How can anyone kiss those idols? (13.2)

ᵐ *Probable text* And then they ... bulls!; *Hebrew unclear*.
12.12 Gn 29.1-20 **12.13** Ex 12.50, 51 **13.5, 6** Dt 8.11-17

Like a leopard I will lie in wait. (13.7)

you open. Like a lion I will devour you on the spot, and will tear you to pieces like a wild animal.

9 "I will destroy you, people of Israel! Then who can help you?[n] 10 You asked for a king and for leaders, but how can they save the nation?[o] 11 In my anger I have given you kings, and in my fury I have taken them away.

12 "Israel's sin and guilt are on record, and the records are safely stored away. 13 Israel has a chance to live, but is too foolish to take it — like a child about to be born, who refuses to come out of the womb. 14 I will not save this people from the world of the dead or rescue them from the power of death. Bring on[p] your plagues, death! Bring on[p] your destruction, world of the dead! I will no longer have pity for this people. 15 Even though Israel flourishes like weeds,[q] I will send a hot east wind from the desert, and it will dry up their springs and wells. It will take away everything of value. 16 Samaria must be punished for rebelling against me. Her people will die in war; babies will be dashed to the ground, and pregnant women will be ripped open."

Hosea's Plea to Israel

14 Return to the LORD your God, people of Israel. Your sin has made you stumble and fall. 2 Return to the LORD, and let this prayer be your offering to him: "Forgive all our sins and accept our prayer, and we will praise you as we have promised. 3 Assyria can never save us, and war horses cannot protect us. We will never again say to our idols that they are our God. O LORD, you show mercy to those who have no one else to turn to."

The LORD Promises New Life for Israel

4 The LORD says,
"I will bring my people back
   to me.
I will love them with all my
   heart;
   no longer am I angry with
   them.
5 I will be to the people of Israel
   like rain in a dry land.
They will blossom like flowers;
   they will be firmly rooted
   like the trees of Lebanon.
6 They will be alive with new
   growth,
   and beautiful like olive trees.
They will be fragrant
   like the cedars of Lebanon.
7 Once again they will live under
   my protection.
They will grow crops of grain
   and be fruitful like a vineyard.
They will be as famous as the
   wine of Lebanon.

[n] *One ancient translation* who can help you?; *Hebrew* in me is your help.   [o] *Verse 10 in Hebrew is unclear.*   [p] *Some ancient translations* Bring on; *Hebrew* I will be.   [q] *Probable text* like weeds; *Hebrew* among brothers.

13.10 1 S 8.5, 6   **13.11 a** 1 S 10.17-24; **b** 1 S 15.26   **13.14** 1 Co 15.55

8 The people of Israel^r will have
   nothing more to do with idols;
I will answer their prayers
   and take care of them.
Like an evergreen tree I will
   shelter them;
I am the source of all their
   blessings."

Conclusion

9 May those who are wise understand what is written here, and may they take it to heart. The LORD's ways are right, and righteous people live by following them, but sinners stumble and fall because they ignore them.

^r *One ancient translation* The people of Israel; *Hebrew* Israel, I.

The Book of
JOEL

INTRODUCTION

Little is known about the prophet Joel, and it is not clear just when he lived. But it seems likely that the book comes from the fifth or fourth century B.C., during the time of the Persian Empire. Joel describes a terrible invasion of locusts and a devastating drought in Palestine. In these events he sees a sign of the coming day of the Lord, a time when the Lord will punish those who oppose his righteous will. The prophet conveys the Lord's call to the people to repent, and his promise of restoration and blessing for his people. Noteworthy is the promise that God will send his Spirit upon all the people, men and women, young and old alike.

OUTLINE OF CONTENTS

1 This is the LORD's message to Joel son of Pethuel.

The People Mourn the Destruction of the Crops

2 Pay attention, you older people;
   everyone in Judah, listen.
Has anything like this ever
   happened
   in your time or the time of
   your ancestors?

3 Tell your children about it;
   they will tell their children,
   who in turn will tell the next
   generation.

4 Swarm after swarm of locusts
   settled on the crops;
what one swarm left, the next
   swarm devoured.

5 Wake up and weep, you
   drunkards;
   cry, you wine-drinkers;

The ground mourns. (1.10)

the grapes for making new
wine have been destroyed.

6 An army of locusts has attacked
our land;
they are powerful and too
many to count;
their teeth are as sharp as
those of a lion.
7 They have destroyed our
grapevines
and chewed up our fig trees.
They have stripped off the bark,
till the branches are white.

8 Cry, you people, like a young
woman who mourns
the death
of the man she was going to
marry.
9 There is no grain or wine to offer
in the Temple;
the priests mourn because
they have no offerings
for the LORD.
10 The fields are bare;
the ground mourns
because the grain is
destroyed,
the grapes are dried up,

and the olive trees are
withered.
11 Grieve, you farmers;
cry, you that take care of the
vineyards,
because the wheat, the barley,
yes all the crops are
destroyed.
12 The grapevines and fig trees
have withered;
all the fruit trees have wilted
and died.
The joy of the people is gone.
13 Put on sackcloth and weep,
you priests who serve at the
altar!
Go into the Temple and mourn
all night!
There is no grain or wine to offer
your God.
14 Give orders for a fast;
call an assembly!
Gather the leaders
and all the people of Judah
into the Temple of the LORD
your God
and cry out to him!
15 The day of the LORD is near,
the day when the Almighty
brings destruction.
What terror that day will
bring!

.6 Rev 9.8   1.15 Is 13.6

16 We look on helpless as our crops
　　are destroyed.
　　There is no joy in the Temple
　　　of our God.
17 The seeds die in the dry earth.
　　There is no grain to be stored,
　　and so the empty granaries
　　　are in ruins.
18 The cattle are bellowing in
　　　distress
　　because there is no pasture
　　　for them;
　　the flocks of sheep also suffer.
19 I cry out to you, LORD,
　　because the pastures and
　　　trees are dried up,
　　as though a fire had burned
　　　them.
20 Even the wild animals cry out
　　　to you
　　because the streams have
　　　become dry.

The Locusts as a Warning of the Day of the LORD

2 Blow the trumpet; sound the
　　　alarm
　　on Zion, God's sacred hill.*
　Tremble, people of Judah!
　　The day of the LORD is
　　　coming soon.
2 It will be a dark and gloomy day,
　　a black and cloudy day.
　The great army of locusts
　　　advances
　　like darkness spreading over
　　　the mountains.
　There has never been anything
　　　like it,
　　and there never will be again.

3 Like fire they eat up the plants.
　In front of them the land is
　　like the Garden of Eden,
　　but behind them it is a barren
　　　desert.
　　Nothing escapes them.

4 They look like horses;
　　they run like war-horses.
5 As they leap on the tops of the
　　　mountains,
　　they rattle like chariots;
　　they crackle like dry grass
　　　on fire.
　They are lined up like a great
　　　army ready for battle.
6 As they approach, everyone is
　　　terrified;
　　every face turns pale.
7 They attack like warriors;
　　they climb the walls like
　　　soldiers.
　They all keep marching straight
　　　ahead
　　and do not change direction
8 　or get in each other's way.
　They swarm through defenses,
　　and nothing can stop them.
9 They rush against the city;
　　they run over the walls;
　　they climb up the houses
　　and go in through the
　　　windows like thieves.

10 The earth shakes as they
　　　advance;
　　the sky trembles.
　The sun and the moon grow
　　　dark,
　　and the stars no longer shine.
11 The LORD thunders commands
　　　to his army.
　The troops that obey him
　　are many and mighty.
　How terrible is the day of the
　　　LORD!
　　Who will survive it?

A Call to Repentance

12 "But even now," says the LORD,
　　"repent sincerely and return
　　　to me
　　with fasting and weeping and
　　　mourning.

---

a SACRED HILL: *Mount Zion (see Zion in Word List).*
2.4, 5 Rev 9.7-9　**2.10** Rev 8.12　**2.11** Rev 6.17

¹³Let your broken heart show your
  sorrow;
 tearing your clothes is not
  enough."

Come back to the LORD
  your God.
He is kind and full of mercy;
 he is patient and keeps his
  promise;
 he is always ready to forgive
  and not punish.

Let your broken heart show your sorrow. (2.13)

¹⁴Perhaps the LORD your God will
  change his mind
 and bless you with abundant
  crops.
Then you can offer him grain
  and wine.

¹⁵Blow the trumpet on Mount
  Zion;
 give orders for a fast and call
  an assembly!
¹⁶Gather the people together;
 prepare them for a sacred
  meeting;
 bring the old people;
 gather the children
 and the babies too.
 Even newly married couples
 must leave their homes and
  come.

¹⁷The priests, serving the LORD
  between the altar and the
  entrance of the Temple,
must weep and pray:
 "Have pity on your people,
  LORD.
Do not let other nations
 despise us and mock us
 by saying, 'Where is
  your God?' "

God Restores Fertility to the Land

¹⁸Then the LORD showed concern
  for his land;
 he had mercy on his people.
¹⁹He answered them:
 "Now I am going to give you
 grain and wine and olive oil,
 and you will be satisfied.
 Other nations will no longer
  despise you.
²⁰I will remove the locust army
  that came from the north
 and will drive some of them
  into the desert.
Their front ranks will be driven
  into the Dead Sea,
 their rear ranks into the
  Mediterranean.
 Their dead bodies will stink.
I will destroy them because of all
  they have done to you.

²¹"Fields, don't be afraid,
 but be joyful and glad
 because of all the LORD has
  done for you.
²²Animals, don't be afraid.
 The pastures are green;
 the trees bear their fruit,
 and there are plenty of figs
  and grapes.

²³"Be glad, people of Zion,
 rejoice at what the LORD your
  God has done for you.

2.17 1 Macc 7.36-38

He has given you the right
　　amount of autumn rain;[b]
he has poured down the
　　winter rain for you
and the spring rain as before.
24 The threshing places will be full
　　of grain;
the pits beside the presses will
　　overflow with wine and
　　olive oil.
25 I will give you back what you
　　lost
in the years when swarms of
　　locusts ate your crops.
It was I who sent this army
　　against you.
26 Now you will have plenty to eat,
　　and be satisfied.
You will praise the LORD
　　your God,
who has done wonderful
　　things for you.
My people will never be
　　despised again.
27 Then, Israel, you will know that
　　I am among you
and that I, the LORD, am
　　your God
and there is no other.
My people will never be
　　despised again.

The Day of the LORD

28 "Afterward I will pour out my
　　Spirit on everyone:
your sons and daughters will
　　proclaim my message;
your old people will have
　　dreams,
and your young people will
　　see visions.
29 At that time I will pour out my
　　Spirit
even on servants, both men
　　and women.

30 "I will give warnings of that day
　　in the sky and on the earth;
there will be bloodshed, fire,
　　and clouds of smoke.
31 The sun will be darkened,
　　and the moon will turn red
　　as blood
before the great and terrible
　　day of the LORD comes.
32 But all who ask the LORD for
　　help will be saved.
As the LORD has said,
　　'Some in Jerusalem will
　　escape;
those whom I choose will
　　survive.' "

God Will Judge the Nations

3 The LORD says,
"At that time I will restore
　　the prosperity of Judah and
　　Jerusalem.
2 I will gather all the nations
　　and bring them to the Valley
　　of Judgment.
There I will judge them
　　for all they have done to
　　my people.
They have scattered the
　　Israelites in foreign
　　countries
and divided Israel, my land.
3 They threw dice to decide
　　who would get the captives.
They sold boys and girls into
　　slavery
to pay for prostitutes and
　　wine.

4 "What are you trying to do to me,
Tyre, Sidon, and all of Philistia? Are you
trying to pay me back for something? If
you are, I will quickly pay me back!
5 You have taken my silver and gold and
carried my rich treasures into your tem-

---

[b] right amount of autumn rain; or autumn rain because he is just.
2.31 Mt 24.29; Mk 13.24, 25; Lk 21.25; Rev 6.12, 13　**2.28-32** Ac 2.17-21　**2.32** Ro 10.13
3.4-8 Is 23.1-18; Ez 26.1−28.26; Am 1.9, 10; Zec 9.1-4; Mt 11.21, 22; Lk 10.13, 14
3.4-8 Is 14.29-31; Jr 47.1-7; Ez 25.15-17; Am 1.6-8; Zep 2.4-7; Zec 9.5-7

ples. 6 You have taken the people of Judah and Jerusalem far from their own country and sold them to the Greeks. 7 Now I am going to bring them out of the places to which you have sold them. I will do to you what you have done to them. 8 I will let your sons and daughters be sold to the people of Judah; they will sell them to the far-off Sabeans. I, the LORD, have spoken.

9 "Make this announcement
      among the nations:
    'Prepare for war;
    call your warriors;
    gather all your soldiers and
      march!
10 Hammer the points of your plows
      into swords
    and your pruning knives into
      spears.
    Even the weak must fight.
11 Hurry[c] and come,
      all you surrounding nations,
    and gather in the valley.' "

    Send down, O LORD, your army
      to attack them!

12 "The nations must get ready
      and come to the Valley of
      Judgment.
    There I, the LORD, will sit
      to judge
      all the surrounding nations.
13 They are very wicked;
    cut them down like grain
      at harvest time;
    crush them as grapes are
      crushed
      in a full wine press
      until the wine runs over."

14 Thousands and thousands
      are in the Valley of Judgment.

    It is there that the day of the
      LORD
      will soon come.
15 The sun and the moon grow
      dark,
      and the stars no longer shine.

God Will Bless His People

16 The LORD roars from Mount
      Zion;
    his voice thunders from
      Jerusalem;
    earth and sky tremble.
    But he will defend his people.
17 "Then, Israel, you will know that
      I am the LORD your God.
    I live on Zion, my sacred hill.
    Jerusalem will be a sacred city;
    foreigners will never conquer
      it again.
18 At that time the mountains will
      be covered with vineyards,
    and cattle will be found on
      every hill;
    there will be plenty of water
      for all of Judah.
    A stream will flow from the
      Temple of the LORD,
    and it will water Acacia
      Valley.

19 "Egypt will become a desert,
      and Edom a ruined waste,
    because they attacked the land of
      Judah
    and killed its innocent people.
20-21 I will avenge[d] those who were
      killed;
    I will not spare the guilty.
    But Judah and Jerusalem will be
      inhabited forever,
    and I, the LORD, will live on
      Mount Zion."

---

[c] Probable text Hurry; Hebrew Help.   [d] Some ancient translations avenge; Hebrew declare innocent.

3.10 Is 2.4; Mic 4.3   **3.13 a** Rev 14.14-16; **b** Rev 14.19, 20; 19.15   **3.16** Am 1.2

The Book of
AMOS

INTRODUCTION

Amos was the first prophet in the Bible whose message was recorded at length. Although he came from a town in Judah, he preached to the people of the northern kingdom of Israel, about the middle of the eighth century B.C. It was a time of great prosperity, notable religious piety, and apparent security. But Amos saw that prosperity was limited to the wealthy, and that it fed on injustice and on oppression of the poor. Religious observance was insincere, and security more apparent than real. With passion and courage he preached that God would punish the nation. He called for justice to "flow like a stream," and said, "Perhaps the Lord will be merciful to the people of this nation who are still left alive" (5.15).

OUTLINE OF CONTENTS

---

1 These are the words of Amos, a shepherd from the town of Tekoa. Two years before the earthquake, when Uzziah was king of Judah and Jeroboam son of Jehoash was king of Israel, God revealed to Amos all these things about Israel.

² Amos said,

"The LORD roars from Mount
	Zion;
	his voice thunders from
		Jerusalem.
The pastures dry up,
	and the grass on Mount
		Carmel turns brown."

God's Judgment on Israel's Neighbors

Syria

³ The LORD says, "The people of Damascus have sinned again and again, and for this I will certainly punish them. They treated the people of Gilead with savage cruelty. ⁴ So I will send fire upon the palace built by King Hazael and I will burn down the fortresses of King Benhadad. ⁵ I will smash the city gates of Damascus and remove the inhabitants of Aven Valley and the ruler of Betheden. The people of Syria will be taken away as prisoners to the land of Kir."

Philistia

⁶ The LORD says, "The people of Gaza have sinned again and again, and for this I will certainly punish them. They carried off a whole nation and sold them as slaves to the people of Edom. ⁷ So I will send fire upon the city walls of Gaza and burn down its fortresses. ⁸ I

1.1 a 2 K 15.1-7; 2 Ch 26.1-23; **b** 2 K 14.23-29   **1.2** Jl 3.16   **1.3-5** Is 17.1-3; Jr 49.23-27;
Zec 9.1   **1.6-8** Is 14.29-31; Jr 47.1-7; Ez 25.15-17; Jl 3.4-8; Zep 2.4-7; Zec 9.5-7

I will send fire. (1.4—2.5)

will remove the rulers of the cities of Ashdod and Ashkelon. I will punish the city of Ekron, and all the Philistines who are left will die."

Tyre

⁹ The LORD says, "The people of Tyre have sinned again and again, and for this I will certainly punish them. They carried off a whole nation into exile in the land of Edom, and did not keep the treaty of friendship they had made. ¹⁰ So I will send fire upon the city walls of Tyre and burn down its fortresses."

Edom

¹¹ The LORD says, "The people of Edom have sinned again and again, and for this I will certainly punish them. They hunted down their relatives,ᵃ the Israelites, and showed them no mercy. Their anger had no limits, and they never let it die. ¹² So I will send fire upon the city of Teman and burn down the fortresses of Bozrah."

Ammon

¹³ The LORD says, "The people of Ammon have sinned again and again, and for this I will certainly punish them. In their wars for more territory they even ripped open pregnant women in Gilead. ¹⁴ So I will send fire upon the city walls of Rabbah and burn down its fortresses. Then there will be shouts on the day of battle, and the fighting will rage like a storm. ¹⁵ Their king and his officers will go into exile."

Moab

2 The LORD says, "The people of Moab have sinned again and again, and for this I will certainly punish them. They dishonored the bones of the king of Edom by burning them to ashes. ² I will send fire upon the land of Moab and burn down the fortresses of Kerioth. The people of Moab will die in the noise of battle while soldiers are shouting and trumpets are sounding. ³ I

ᵃ THEIR RELATIVES: *The Israelites were descended from Jacob, who was the brother of Esau, the ancestor of the Edomites.*

1.9, 10 Is 23.1-18; Ez 26.1—28.19; Jl 3.4-8; Zec 9.1-4; Mt 11.21, 22; Lk 10.13, 14
1.11, 12 Is 34.5-17; 63.1-6; Jr 49.7-22; Ez 25.12-14; 35.1-15; Ob 1-14; Ml 1.2-5
1.13-15 Jr 49.1-6; Ez 21.28-32; 25.1-7; Zep 2.8-11 **2.1-3** Is 15.1—16.14; 25.10-12; Jr 48.1-47; Ez 25.8-11; Zep 2.8-11

will kill the ruler of Moab and all the leaders of the land."

Judah

⁴The LORD says, "The people of Judah have sinned again and again, and for this I will certainly punish them. They have despised my teachings and have not kept my commands. They have been led astray by the same false gods that their ancestors served. ⁵So I will send fire upon Judah and burn down the fortresses of Jerusalem."

God's Judgment on Israel

⁶The LORD says, "The people of Israel have sinned again and again, and for this I will certainly punish them. They sell into slavery honest people who cannot pay their debts, the poor who cannot repay even the price of a pair of sandals. ⁷They trample*b* down the weak and helpless and push the poor out of the way. A man and his father have intercourse with the same slave woman, and so profane my holy name. ⁸At every place of worship people sleep on clothing that they have taken from the poor as security for debts. In the temple of their God they drink wine which they have taken from those who owe them money.

⁹"And yet, my people, it was for your sake that I totally destroyed the Amorites, who were as tall as cedar trees and as strong as oaks. ¹⁰I brought you out of Egypt, led you through the desert for forty years, and gave you the land of the Amorites to be your own. ¹¹I chose some of your sons to be prophets and some of your young men to be nazirites.*c* Isn't this true, people of Israel? I, the LORD, have spoken. ¹²But you

made the nazirites drink wine, and ordered the prophets not to speak my message. ¹³And now I will crush you to the ground, and you will groan like a cart loaded with grain. ¹⁴Not even fast runners will escape; strong men will lose their strength, and soldiers will not be able to save their own lives. ¹⁵Archers will not stand their ground, fast runners will not get away, and men on horses will not escape with their lives. ¹⁶On that day even the bravest soldiers will drop their weapons and run." The LORD has spoken.

3 People of Israel, listen to this message which the LORD has spoken about you, the entire nation that he brought out of Egypt: ²"Of all the nations on earth, you are the only one I have known and cared for. That is what makes your sins so terrible, and that is why I must punish you for them."

The Prophet's Task

³Do two people start traveling together without arranging to meet?

⁴Does a lion roar in the forest unless he has found a victim?

Does a young lion growl in his den unless he has caught something?

⁵Does a bird get caught in a trap if the trap has not been baited?

Does a trap spring unless something sets it off?

⁶Does the war trumpet sound in a city without making the people afraid?

Does disaster strike a city unless the LORD sends it?

⁷The Sovereign LORD never does anything without revealing his plan to his servants, the prophets.

⁸When a lion roars, who can keep from being afraid?

---

b trample; *Hebrew unclear.*   *c* NAZIRITES: *Israelites who showed their devotion to God by taking vows not to drink wine or beer or cut their hair or touch corpses (see Nu 6.1-8).*
2.9 Dt 3.8-11   **2.11** Nu 6.1-8

When the Sovereign LORD speaks, who can keep from proclaiming his message?

The Doom of Samaria

⁹Announce to those who live in the palaces of Egypt and Ashdod: "Gather together in the hills around Samaria and see the great disorder and the crimes being committed there."

¹⁰The LORD says, "These people fill their mansions with things taken by crime and violence. They don't even know how to be honest. ¹¹And so an enemy will surround their land, destroy their defenses, and plunder their mansions."

¹²The LORD says, "As a shepherd recovers only two legs or an ear of a sheep that a lion has eaten, so only a few will survive of Samaria's people, who now recline on luxurious couches.*d* ¹³Listen now, and warn the descendants of Jacob," says the Sovereign LORD Almighty. ¹⁴"On the day when I punish the people of Israel for their sins, I will destroy the altars of Bethel. The corners of every altar will be broken off and will fall to the ground. ¹⁵I will destroy winter houses and summer houses. The houses decorated with ivory will fall in ruins; every large house will be destroyed."

4 Listen to this, you women of Samaria, who grow fat like the well-fed cows of Bashan, who mistreat the weak, oppress the poor, and demand that your husbands keep you supplied with liquor! ²As the Sovereign LORD is holy, he has promised, "The days will come when they will drag you away with hooks; every one of you will be like a fish on a hook. ³You will be dragged to the nearest break in the wall and thrown out."*e*

Israel's Failure to Learn

⁴The Sovereign LORD says, "People of Israel, go to the holy place in Bethel and sin, if you must! Go to Gilgal and sin with all your might! Go ahead and bring animals to be sacrificed morning after morning, and bring your tithes every third day. ⁵Go on and offer your bread in thanksgiving to God, and brag about the extra offerings you bring! This is the kind of thing you love to do.

⁶"I was the one who brought famine to all your cities, yet you did not come back to me. ⁷I kept it from raining when your crops needed it most. I sent rain on one city, but not on another. Rain fell on one field, but another field dried up. ⁸Weak with thirst, the people of several cities went to a city where they hoped to find water, but there was not enough to drink. Still you did not come back to me.

⁹"I sent a scorching wind to dry up your crops. The locusts ate up all your gardens and vineyards, your fig trees and olive trees. Still you did not come back to me.

¹⁰"I sent a plague on you like the one I sent on Egypt. I killed your young men in battle and took your horses away. I filled your nostrils with the stink of dead bodies in your camps. Still you did not come back to me.

¹¹"I destroyed some of you as I destroyed Sodom and Gomorrah. Those of you who survived were like a burning stick saved from a fire. Still you did not come back to me," says the LORD. ¹²"So then, people of Israel, I am going to punish you. And because I am going to do this, get ready to face my judgment!"

¹³God is the one who made the mountains
and created the winds.

---

d luxurious couches; *Hebrew unclear.*   *e Hebrew has an additional word, the meaning of which is unclear.*

3.14 2 K 23.15   **4.6** Ws 12.2, 10   **4.11** Gn 19.24

Still you did not come back to me. (4.9)

He makes his thoughts known
　　to people;
　he changes day into night.
　He walks on the heights of
　　the earth.
This is his name: the LORD God
　　Almighty!

A Call to Repentance

5 Listen, people of Israel, to this funeral song which I sing over you:

2 Virgin Israel has fallen,
　Never to rise again!
　She lies abandoned on the
　　ground,
　And no one helps her up.

3 The Sovereign LORD says, "A city in
Israel sends out a thousand soldiers,
but only a hundred return; another city
sends out a hundred, but only ten come
back."

4 The LORD says to the people of Israel, "Come to me, and you will live.
5 Do not go to Beersheba to worship. Do
not try to find me at Bethel — Bethel
will come to nothing. Do not go to
Gilgal — her people are doomed to
exile."

6 Go to the LORD, and you will live. If
you do not go, he will sweep down like
fire on the people of Israel. The fire will
burn up the people of Bethel, and no
one will be able to put it out. 7 You are
doomed, you that twist justice and
cheat people out of their rights!

8 The LORD made the stars,
　　the Pleiades and Orion.
　He turns darkness into daylight
　　and day into night.
　He calls for the waters of the sea
　　and pours them out on
　　the earth.
　His name is the LORD.
9 He brings destruction on the
　　mighty and their
　　strongholds.

10 You people hate anyone who challenges injustice and speaks the whole
truth in court. 11 You have oppressed
the poor and robbed them of their grain.
And so you will not live in the fine stone
houses you build or drink wine from the
beautiful vineyards you plant. 12 I know
how terrible your sins are and how
many crimes you have committed. You
persecute good people, take bribes, and
prevent the poor from getting justice in
the courts. 13 And so, keeping quiet in
such evil times is the smart thing to do!

5.8 Job 9.9; 38.31

¹⁴Make it your aim to do what is right, not what is evil, so that you may live. Then the LORD God Almighty really will be with you, as you claim he is. ¹⁵Hate what is evil, love what is right, and see that justice prevails in the courts. Perhaps the LORD will be merciful to the people of this nation who are still left alive.

¹⁶And so the Sovereign LORD Almighty says, "There will be wailing and cries of sorrow in the city streets. Even farmers will be called to mourn the dead along with those who are paid to mourn. ¹⁷There will be wailing in all the vineyards. All this will take place because I am coming to punish you." The LORD has spoken.

¹⁸How terrible it will be for you who long for the day of the LORD! What good will that day do you? For you it will be a day of darkness and not of light. ¹⁹It will be like someone who runs from a lion and meets a bear! Or like someone who comes home and puts his hand on the wall — only to be bitten by a snake! ²⁰The day of the LORD will bring darkness and not light; it will be a day of gloom, without any brightness.

²¹The LORD says, "I hate your religious festivals; I cannot stand them! ²²When you bring me burnt offerings and grain offerings, I will not accept them; I will not accept the animals you have fattened to bring me as offerings. ²³Stop your noisy songs; I do not want to listen to your harps. ²⁴Instead, let justice flow like a stream, and righteousness like a river that never goes dry.

²⁵"People of Israel, I did not demand sacrifices and offerings during those forty years that I led you through the desert. ²⁶But now, because you have worshiped images of Sakkuth, your king god, and of Kaiwan, your star god, you will have to carry those images ²⁷when I take you into exile in a land beyond Damascus," says the LORD, whose name is Almighty God.

The Destruction of Israel

6 How terrible it will be for you that have such an easy life in Zion and for you that feel safe in Samaria — you great leaders of this great nation Israel, you to whom the people go for help! ²Go and look at the city of Calneh. Then go on to the great city of Hamath and on down to the Philistine city of Gath.

5.21, 22 Is 1.11-14　**5.25-27** Ac 7.42, 43

There will be wailing and cries of sorrow. (5.16)

Like someone who runs from a lion (5.19)

Were they any better than the kingdoms of Judah and Israel? Was their territory larger than yours? ³You refuse to admit that a day of disaster is coming, but what you do only brings that day closer. ⁴How terrible it will be for you that stretch out on your luxurious couches, feasting on veal and lamb! ⁵You like to compose songs, as David did, and play them on harps. ⁶You drink wine by the bowlful and use the finest perfumes, but you do not mourn over the ruin of Israel. ⁷So you will be the first to go into exile. Your feasts and banquets will come to an end.

⁸The Sovereign LORD Almighty has given this solemn warning: "I hate the pride of the people of Israel; I despise their luxurious mansions. I will give their capital city and everything in it to the enemy."

⁹If there are ten men left in a family, they will die. ¹⁰The dead man's relative, the one in charge of the funeral, will take the body out of the house. The relative will call to whoever is still left in the house, "Is anyone else there with you?"

The person will answer, "No!"

Then the relative will say, "Be quiet! We must be careful not even to mention the LORD's name."ᶠ

¹¹When the LORD gives the command, houses large and small will be smashed to pieces. ¹²Do horses gallop on rocks? Does anyone plow the sea with oxen? Yet you have turned justice into poison, and right into wrong.

¹³You brag about capturing the town of Lodebar.ᵍ You boast, "We were strong enough to take Karnaim."ʰ

¹⁴The LORD God Almighty himself says, "People of Israel, I am going to send a foreign army to occupy your country. It will oppress you from Hamath Pass in the north to the Brook of the Arabah in the south."

A Vision of Locusts

7 I had a vision from the Sovereign LORD. In it I saw him create a swarm of locusts just after the king's share of the hay had been cut and the grass was starting to grow again. ²In my vision I saw the locusts eat up every green thing in the land, and then I said, "Sovereign LORD, forgive your people! How can they survive? They are so small and weak!"

³The LORD changed his mind and said, "What you saw will not take place."

A Vision of Fire

⁴I had another vision from the Sovereign LORD. In it I saw him preparing to punish his people with fire. The fire burned up the great ocean under the earth and started to burn up the

---

ᶠ *Verse 10 in Hebrew is unclear.*   ᵍ LODEBAR: *This name sounds like the Hebrew for* "nothing."   ʰ KARNAIM: *The name of this small town means "horns," a symbol of strength.*

land. ⁵Then I said, "Stop, O Sovereign Lord! How can your people survive? They are so small and weak!"

⁶The Lord changed his mind again and said, "This will not take place either."

A Vision of a Plumb Line

⁷I had another vision from the Lord. In it I saw him standing beside a wall that had been built with the use of a plumb line, and there was a plumb line in his hand. ⁸He asked me, "Amos, what do you see?"

"A plumb line," I answered.

Then he said, "I am using it to show that my people are like a wall that is out of line. I will not change my mind again about punishing them. ⁹The places where Isaac's descendants worship will be destroyed. The holy places of Israel will be left in ruins. I will bring the dynasty of King Jeroboam to an end."

Amos and Amaziah

¹⁰Amaziah, the priest of Bethel, then sent a report to King Jeroboam of Israel: "Amos is plotting against you among the people. His speeches will destroy the country. ¹¹This is what he says: 'Jeroboam will die in battle, and the

"Stop, O Sovereign Lord!" (7.5)

people of Israel will be taken away from their land into exile.' "

¹²Amaziah then said to Amos, "That's enough, prophet! Go on back to Judah and do your preaching there. Let *them* pay you for it. ¹³Don't prophesy here at Bethel any more. This is the king's place of worship, the national temple."

¹⁴Amos answered, "I am not the kind of prophet who prophesies for pay. I am a herdsman, and I take care of fig trees. ¹⁵But the Lord took me from my work as a shepherd and ordered me to come and prophesy to his people Israel. ¹⁶So now listen to what the Lord says. You tell me to stop prophesying, to stop raving against the people of Israel. ¹⁷And so, Amaziah, the Lord says to you, 'Your wife will become a prostitute in the city, and your children will be killed in war. Your land will be divided up and

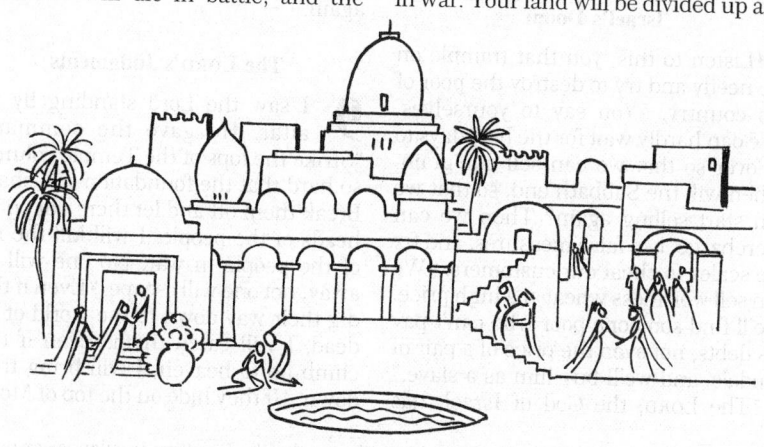

I hate the pride of the people of Israel. (6.8)

given to others, and you yourself will die in a heathen country. And the people of Israel will certainly be taken away from their own land into exile.' "

A Vision of a Basket of Fruit

8 I had another vision from the Sovereign LORD. In it I saw a basket of fruit. ²The LORD asked, "Amos, what do you see?"

"A basket of fruit," I answered.

The LORD said to me, "The end[i] has come for my people Israel. I will not

Amos, what do you see? (8.2)
"A basket of fruit."

change my mind again about punishing them. ³On that day the songs in the palace will become cries of mourning. There will be dead bodies everywhere. They will be cast out in silence."[j]

Israel's Doom

⁴Listen to this, you that trample on the needy and try to destroy the poor of the country. ⁵You say to yourselves, "We can hardly wait for the holy days to be over so that we can sell our grain. When will the Sabbath end, so that we can start selling again? Then we can overcharge, use false measures, and fix the scales to cheat our customers. ⁶We can sell worthless wheat at a high price. We'll find someone poor who can't pay his debts, not even the price of a pair of sandals, and we'll buy him as a slave."

⁷The LORD, the God of Israel, has

sworn, "I will never forget their evil deeds. ⁸And so the earth will quake, and everyone in the land will be in distress. The whole country will be shaken; it will rise and fall like the Nile River. ⁹The time is coming when I will make the sun go down at noon and the earth grow dark in daytime. I, the Sovereign LORD, have spoken. ¹⁰I will turn your festivals into funerals and change your glad songs into cries of grief. I will make you shave your heads and wear sackcloth, and you will be like parents mourning for their only child. That day will be bitter to the end.

¹¹"The time is coming when I will send famine on the land. People will be hungry, but not for bread; they will be thirsty, but not for water. They will hunger and thirst for a message from the LORD. I, the Sovereign LORD, have spoken. ¹²People will wander from the Dead Sea to the Mediterranean and then on around from the north to the east. They will look everywhere for a message from the LORD, but they will not find it. ¹³On that day even healthy young men and women will collapse from thirst. ¹⁴Those who swear by the idols of Samaria, who say, 'By the god of Dan' or 'By the god of Beersheba' — those people will fall and not rise again."

The LORD's Judgments

9 I saw the Lord standing by the altar. He gave the command: "Strike the tops of the Temple columns so hard that the foundation will shake. Break them off and let them fall on the heads of the people. I will kill the rest of the people in war. No one will get away; not one will escape. ²Even if they dig their way down to the world of the dead, I will catch them. Even if they climb up to heaven, I will bring them down. ³If they hide on the top of Mount

---

[i] END: *The Hebrew words for "end" and "fruit" sound alike.*   [j] out in silence; *or* out. Silence!

Carmel, I will search for them and catch them. If they hide from me at the bottom of the sea, I will command the sea monster[k] to bite them. [4] If they are taken away into captivity by their enemies, I will order them to be put to death. I am determined to destroy them, not to help them."

[5] The Sovereign Lord Almighty
    touches the earth,
    and it quakes;
    all who live there mourn.
The whole world rises and falls
    like the Nile River.
[6] The Lord builds his home in the
    heavens,
    and over the earth he puts the
    dome of the sky.
He calls for the waters of the sea
    and pours them out on the
    earth.
His name is the Lord!

[7] The Lord says, "People of Israel, I think as much of the people of Ethiopia[l] as I do of you. I brought the Philistines from Crete and the Syrians from Kir, just as I brought you from Egypt. [8] I, the Sovereign Lord, am watching this sinful kingdom of Israel, and I will destroy it from the face of the earth. But I will not destroy all the descendants of Jacob.

[9] "I will give the command and shake the people of Israel like grain in a sieve. I will shake them among the nations to remove all who are worthless. [10] The sinners among my people will be killed in war — all those who say, 'God will not let any harm come near us.' "

The Future Restoration of Israel

[11] The Lord says, "A day is coming when I will restore the kingdom of David, which is like a house fallen into ruins. I will repair its walls and restore it. I will rebuild it and make it as it was long ago. [12] And so the people of Israel will conquer what is left of the land of Edom and all the nations that were once mine," says the Lord, who will cause this to happen.

[13] "The days are coming," says the
    Lord,
    "when grain will grow faster
    than it can be harvested,
    and grapes will grow faster
    than the wine can
    be made.
The mountains will drip with
    sweet wine,
    and the hills will flow with it.
[14] I will bring my people back to
    their land.
They will rebuild their ruined
    cities and live there;
    they will plant vineyards and
    drink the wine;
    they will plant gardens and
    eat what they grow.
[15] I will plant my people on the
    land I gave them,
    and they will not be pulled up
    again."
The Lord your God has spoken.

---

[k] SEA MONSTER: *It was believed that the sea was inhabited by a great monster. This creature, like all others, was regarded as under God's control.*   [l] *Hebrew* Cush: *Cush is the ancient name of the extensive territory south of the First Cataract of the Nile River. This region was called Ethiopia in Graeco-Roman times, and included within its borders most of modern Sudan and some of present-day Ethiopia (Abyssinia).*
9.11, 12 Ac 15.16-18

The Book of
OBADIAH

INTRODUCTION

This short book comes from some undetermined time after the fall of Jerusalem in 586 B.C., when Edom, Judah's age-old enemy to the southeast, not only rejoiced over the fall of Jerusalem but took advantage of Judah's plight to loot the city and help the invader. Obadiah prophesied that Edom would be punished and defeated, along with other nations that were the enemies of Israel.

OUTLINE OF CONTENTS

---

¹This is the prophecy of Obadiah — what the Sovereign LORD said about the nation of Edom.

The LORD Will Punish Edom

The LORD has sent his
      messenger to the nations,
and we have heard his
      message:
"Get ready! Let us go to war
      against Edom!"
²The LORD says to Edom,
"I will make you weak;
      everyone will despise you.
³Your pride has deceived you.
Your capital is a fortress of solid
      rock;
      your home is high in the
      mountains,
and so you say to yourself,
      'Who can ever pull me down?'
⁴Even though you make your
      home
      as high as an eagle's nest,
      so that it seems to be among
      the stars,
yet I will pull you down.

⁵"When thieves come at night,
      they take only what they
      want.

Yet I will pull you down. (4)

When people gather grapes,
      they always leave a few.
But your enemies have wiped
      you out completely.
⁶Descendants of Esau, your
      treasures have been looted.
⁷Your allies have deceived you;
      they have driven you from
      your country.
People who were at peace with
      you have now
      conquered you.

1-14 Is 34.5-17; 63.1-6; Jr 49.7-22; Ez 25.12-14; 35.1-15; Am 1.11, 12; Ml 1.2-5

You should not have gloated. (12)

Those friends who ate with
   you have laid a trap
   for you;
   they say of you, 'Where is all
   that cleverness he had?'

8 "On the day I punish Edom,
   I will destroy their clever men
   and wipe out all their wisdom.
9 The fighting men of Teman will
   be terrified,
   and every soldier in Edom will
   be killed.

Reasons for Edom's Punishment

10 "Because you robbed and killed
   your relatives,[a] the
   descendants of Jacob,
   you will be destroyed and
   dishonored forever.
11 You stood aside on that day
   when enemies broke down
   their gates.
   You were as bad as those
   strangers
   who carried off Jerusalem's
   wealth

and divided it among
   themselves.
12 You should not have gloated
   over the misfortune of your
   relatives in Judah.
   You should not have been glad
   on the day of their ruin.
   You should not have laughed
   at them
   in their distress.
13 You should not have entered the
   city of my people
   to gloat over their suffering
   and to seize their riches
   on the day of their disaster.
14 You should not have stood at the
   crossroads
   to catch those trying to
   escape.
   You should not have handed
   them over to the enemy
   on the day of their distress.

God Will Judge the Nations

15 "The day is near when I, the
   LORD,
   will judge all nations.
   Edom, what you have done
   will be done to you.
   You will get back what you
   have given.
16 My people have drunk a bitter
   cup of punishment
   on my sacred hill.[b]

---

[a] YOUR RELATIVES: *The Israelites were descended from Jacob, who was the brother of Esau, the ancestor of the Edomites.*   [b] SACRED HILL: *Mount Zion (see Zion in Word List).*

But all the surrounding nations
will drink
a still more bitter cup of
punishment;
they will drink it all and
vanish away.

The Victory of Israel

17"But on Mount Zion some will
escape,
and it will be a sacred place.
The people of Jacob will possess
the land that is theirs by
right.
18 The people of Jacob and of
Joseph will be like fire;
they will destroy the people
of Esau
as fire burns stubble.
No descendant of Esau will
survive.
I, the LORD, have spoken.

19"People from southern Judah will
occupy Edom;
those from the western
foothills will capture
Philistia.
Israelites will possess the
territory of Ephraim and
Samaria;
the people of Benjamin will
take Gilead.
20 The army of exiles from northern
Israel
will return and conquer
Phoenicia as far north as
Zarephath.
The exiles from Jerusalem who
are in Sardis
will capture the towns of
southern Judah.
21 The victorious men of Jerusalem
will attack Edom and rule
over it.
And the LORD himself will be king."

The Book of
JONAH

INTRODUCTION

The Book of Jonah is unlike other prophetic books of the Bible in that it is a narrative, describing the adventures of a prophet who tried to disobey God's command. God told him to go to Nineveh, the capital of the great empire of Assyria, Israel's deadly enemy. But Jonah did not want to go there with God's message, because he was convinced that God would not carry out his threat to destroy the city. After a series of dramatic events, he reluctantly obeyed, and finally sulked when his message of doom did not come true.

The book portrays God's absolute sovereignty over his creation. But above all it portrays God as a God of love and mercy, who would rather forgive and save even the enemies of his people, than punish and destroy them.

OUTLINE OF CONTENTS

Jonah Disobeys the LORD

1 One day the LORD spoke to Jonah son of Amittai. ² He said, "Go to Nineveh, that great city, and speak out against it; I am aware of how wicked its people are." ³ Jonah, however, set out in the opposite direction in order to get away from the LORD. He went to Joppa, where he found a ship about to go to Spain. He paid his fare and went aboard with the crew to sail to Spain, where he would be away from the LORD.

⁴ But the LORD sent a strong wind on the sea, and the storm was so violent that the ship was in danger of breaking up. ⁵ The sailors were terrified and cried out for help, each one to his own god. Then, in order to lessen the danger,ᵃ they threw the cargoᵇ overboard.

Meanwhile, Jonah had gone below and was lying in the ship's hold, sound asleep.

⁶ The captain found him there and said to him, "What are you doing asleep? Get up and pray to your god for help. Maybe he will feel sorry for us and spare our lives."

⁷ The sailors said to each other, "Let's draw lots and find out who is to blame for getting us into this danger." They did so, and Jonah's name was drawn. ⁸ So they said to him, "Now, then, tell us! Who is to blame for this? What are you doing here? What country do you come from? What is your nationality?"

⁹ "I am a Hebrew," Jonah answered. "I worship the LORD, the God of heaven, who made land and sea." ¹⁰ Jonah went

---

ᵃ lessen the danger; *or* lighten the ship. ᵇ cargo; *or* equipment.
1.1 2 K 14.25

HIGHLIGHTS FROM THE LIFE OF JONAH (1, 2, 3, 4)

on to tell them that he was running away from the LORD.

The sailors were terrified, and said to him, "That was an awful thing to do!"[c] 11 The storm was getting worse all the time, so the sailors asked him, "What should we do to you to stop the storm?"

12 Jonah answered, "Throw me into the sea, and it will calm down. I know it is my fault that you are caught in this violent storm."

13 Instead, the sailors tried to get the ship to shore, rowing with all their might. But the storm was becoming worse and worse, and they got nowhere. 14 So they cried out to the LORD, "O LORD, we pray, don't punish us with death for taking this man's life! You, O LORD, are responsible for all this; it is your doing." 15 Then they picked Jonah up and threw him into the sea, and it calmed down at once. 16 This made the sailors so afraid of the LORD that they offered a sacrifice and promised to serve him.

17 At the LORD's command a large fish swallowed Jonah, and he was inside the fish for three days and three nights.

Jonah's Prayer

2 From deep inside the fish Jonah prayed to the LORD his God:
2 "In my distress, O LORD, I called to you,
    and you answered me.
From deep in the world of the dead
    I cried for help, and you heard me.
3 You threw me down into the depths,
    to the very bottom of the sea,
    where the waters were all around me,

and all your mighty waves
    rolled over me.
4 I thought I had been banished from your presence
    and would never see your holy Temple again.
5 The water came over me and choked me;
    the sea covered me completely,
    and seaweed wrapped around my head.
6 I went down to the very roots of the mountains,
    into the land whose gates lock shut forever.[d]
But you, O LORD my God,
    brought me back from the depths alive.
7 When I felt my life slipping away,
    then, O LORD, I prayed to you,
    and in your holy Temple you heard me.
8 Those who worship worthless idols
    have abandoned their loyalty to you.
9 But I will sing praises to you;
    I will offer you a sacrifice
    and do what I have promised.
    Salvation comes from the LORD!"
10 Then the LORD ordered the fish to spit Jonah up on the beach, and it did.

Jonah Obeys the LORD

3 Once again the LORD spoke to Jonah. 2 He said, "Go to Nineveh, that great city, and proclaim to the people the message I have given you." 3 So Jonah obeyed the LORD and went to Nineveh, a city so large that it took three days to walk through it. 4 Jonah started through the city, and after walking a whole day, he proclaimed, "In

---

[c] and said . . . to do!; *or* and asked him, "Why did you have to run away like that?"
[d] THE LAND WHOSE GATES LOCK SHUT FOREVER: *A reference to the world of the dead (see 2.2).*
1.17 Mt 12.40   **3.4, 5** Mt 12.41; Lk 11.32

forty days Nineveh will be destroyed!"

5 The people of Nineveh believed God's message. So they decided that everyone should fast, and all the people, from the greatest to the least, put on sackcloth to show that they had repented.

6 When the king of Nineveh heard about it, he got up from his throne, took off his robe, put on sackcloth, and sat down in ashes. 7 He sent out a proclamation to the people of Nineveh: "This is an order from the king and his officials: No one is to eat anything; all persons, cattle, and sheep are forbidden to eat or drink. 8 All persons and animals must wear sackcloth. Everyone must pray earnestly to God and must give up their wicked behavior and their evil actions. 9 Perhaps God will change his mind; perhaps he will stop being angry, and we will not die!"

10 God saw what they did; he saw that they had given up their wicked behavior. So he changed his mind and did not punish them as he had said he would.

Jonah's Anger and God's Mercy

4 Jonah was very unhappy about this and became angry. 2 So he prayed, "LORD, didn't I say before I left home that this is just what you would do? That's why I did my best to run away to Spain! I knew that you are a loving and merciful God, always patient, always kind, and always ready to change your mind and not punish. 3 Now then, LORD, let me die. I am better off dead than alive."

4 The LORD answered, "What right do you have to be angry?"

5 Jonah went out east of the city and sat down. He made a shelter for himself and sat in its shade, waiting to see what would happen to Nineveh. 6 Then the LORD God made a plant grow up over Jonah to give him some shade, so that he would be more comfortable. Jonah was extremely pleased with the plant. 7 But at dawn the next day, at God's command, a worm attacked the plant, and it died. 8 After the sun had risen, God sent a hot east wind, and Jonah was about to faint from the heat of the sun beating down on his head. So he wished he were dead.e "I am better off dead than alive," he said.

9 But God said to him, "What right do you have to be angry about the plant?"

Jonah replied, "I have every right to be angry — angry enough to die!"

10 The LORD said to him, "This plant grew up in one night and disappeared the next; you didn't do anything for it and you didn't make it grow — yet you feel sorry for it! 11 How much more, then, should I have pity on Nineveh, that great city. After all, it has more than 120,000 innocent children in it, as well as many animals!"

---

e wished he were dead; or prayed that he would die.
4.2 Ex 34.6   **4.3** 1 K 19.4

The Book of
MICAH

INTRODUCTION

The prophet Micah, a contemporary of Isaiah, was from a country town in Judah, the southern kingdom. He was convinced that Judah was about to face the same kind of national catastrophe that Amos had predicted for the northern kingdom, and for the same reason God would punish the hateful injustice of the people. Micah's message, however, contains more clear and notable signs of hope for the future.

Passages especially worth noting are the picture of universal peace under God (4.1-4); the prediction of a great king who would come from the family line of David and bring peace to the nation (5.2-5a); and, in a single verse (6.8), the summary of much that the prophets of Israel had to say: "What he requires of us is this: to do what is just, to show constant love, and to live in humble fellowship with our God."

OUTLINE OF CONTENTS

1 During the time that Jotham, Ahaz, and Hezekiah were kings of Judah, the LORD gave this message to Micah, who was from the town of Moresheth. The LORD revealed to Micah all these things about Samaria and Jerusalem.

A Lament for Samaria and Jerusalem

2 Hear this, all you nations;
   listen to this, all who live on
      earth!
The Sovereign LORD will testify
   against you.
   Listen! He speaks from his
      heavenly temple.
3 The LORD is coming from his
   holy place;

he will come down and walk
   on the tops of the
      mountains.
4 Then the mountains will melt
   under him
like wax in a fire;
   they will pour down into the
      valleys
   like water pouring down a
      hill.

5 All this will happen because the people of Israel have sinned and rebelled against God. Who is to blame for Israel's rebellion? Samaria, the capital city itself! Who is guilty of idolatry in Judah? Jerusalem itself! 6 So the LORD says, "I will make Samaria a pile of ruins in the open country, a place for planting grapevines. I will pour the rub-

ble of the city down into the valley, and will lay bare the city's foundations. ⁷All its precious idols will be smashed to pieces, everything given to its temple prostitutes will be destroyed by fire, and all its images will become a desolate heap. Samaria acquired these things for its fertility rites, and now her enemies will carry them off for temple prostitutes elsewhere."

⁸Then Micah said, "Because of this I will mourn and lament. To show my sorrow, I will walk around barefoot and naked. I will howl like a jackal and wail like an ostrich. ⁹Samaria's wounds cannot be healed, and Judah is about to suffer in the same way; destruction has reached the gates of Jerusalem itself, where my people live."

The Enemy Approaches Jerusalem

¹⁰Don't tell our enemies in Gath about our defeat; don't let them see you weeping. People of Beth Leaphrah,ᵃ show your despair by rolling in the dust! ¹¹You people of Shaphir, go into exile, naked and ashamed. Those who live in Zaanan do not dare to come out of their city. When you hear the people of Bethezel mourn, you will know that there is no refuge there. ¹²The people of Maroth anxiously wait for relief, because the Lord has brought disaster close to Jerusalem. ¹³You that live in Lachish, hitch the horses to the chariots. You imitated the sins of Israel and so caused Jerusalem to sin. ¹⁴And now, people of Judah, say good-bye to the town of Moresheth Gath. The kings of Israel will get no help from the town of Achzib.

¹⁵People of Mareshah, the Lord will hand you over to an enemy, who is going to capture your town. The leaders of Israel will go and hide in the cave at

Adullam. ¹⁶People of Judah, cut off your hair in mourning for the children you love. Make yourselves as bald as vultures, because your children will be taken away from you into exile.

The Fate of Those Who Oppress the Poor

2 How terrible it will be for those who lie awake and plan evil! When morning comes, as soon as they have the chance, they do the evil they planned. ²When they want fields, they seize them; when they want houses, they take them. No one's family or property is safe.

³And so the Lord says, "I am planning to bring disaster on you, and you will not be able to escape it. You are going to find yourselves in trouble, and then you will not walk so proudly any more. ⁴When that time comes, people will use the story about you as an example of disaster, and they will sing this song of despair about your experience:

We are completely ruined!
The Lord has taken our land
      away
And given it to those who took
      us captive."ᵇ

⁵So then, when the time comes for the land to be given back to the Lord's people, there will be no share for any of you.

⁶The people preach at me and say, "Don't preach at us. Don't preach about all that. God is not going to disgrace us. ⁷Do you think the people of Israel are under a curse?ᶜ Has the Lord lost his patience? Would he really do such things? Doesn't heᵈ speak kindly to those who do right?"

⁸The Lord replies, "You attack my

ᵃ BETH LEAPHRAH: *The prophet speaks of outlying towns (verses 10-14) which an enemy army approaching Jerusalem would attack.*   ᵇ *Probable text* those who took us captive; *Hebrew* rebels.   ᶜ *Probable text* under a curse; *Hebrew unclear.*   ᵈ *One ancient translation* Doesn't he; *Hebrew* Don't I.

"Don't preach at us." (2.6)

people[e] like enemies. Men return from battle, thinking they are safe at home, but there you are, waiting to steal the coats off their backs. ⁹You drive the women of my people out of the homes they love, and you have robbed their children of my blessings forever. ¹⁰Get up and go; there is no safety here any more. Your sins have doomed this place to destruction.

¹¹"These people want the kind of prophet who goes around full of lies and deceit and says, 'I prophesy that wine and liquor will flow for you.'

¹²"But I will gather you together, all you people of Israel that are left. I will bring you together like sheep returning to the fold. Like a pasture full of sheep, your land will once again be filled with many people."

¹³God will open the way for them and lead them out of exile. They will break out of the city gates and go free. Their king, the LORD himself, will lead them out.

Micah Denounces Israel's Leaders

3 Listen, you rulers of Israel! You are supposed to be concerned about justice, ²yet you hate what is good and you love what is evil. You skin my people alive and tear the flesh off their bones. ³You eat my people up.

You strip off their skin, break their bones, and chop them up like meat for the pot. ⁴The time is coming when you will cry out to the LORD, but he will not answer you. He will not listen to your prayers, for you have done evil.

⁵My people are deceived by prophets who promise peace to those who pay them, but threaten war for those who don't. To these prophets the LORD says, ⁶"Prophets, your day is almost over; the sun is going down on you. Because you mislead my people, you will have no more prophetic visions, and you will not be able to predict anything." ⁷Those who predict the future will be disgraced by their failure. They will all be humiliated because God does not answer them.

⁸But as for me, the LORD fills me with his spirit and power, and gives me a sense of justice and the courage to tell the people of Israel what their sins are. ⁹Listen to me, you rulers of Israel, you that hate justice and turn right into wrong. ¹⁰You are building God's city, Jerusalem, on a foundation of murder and injustice. ¹¹The city's rulers govern for bribes, the priests interpret the Law for pay, the prophets give their revelations for money — and they all claim that the LORD is with them. "No harm will come to us," they say. "The LORD is with us."

¹²And so, because of you, Zion will be plowed like a field, Jerusalem will become a pile of ruins, and the Temple hill will become a forest.

The LORD's Universal Reign of Peace
(Isaiah 2.2-4)

4 In days to come
the mountain where the
Temple stands
will be the highest one of all,
towering above all the hills.

---

[e] *Probable text* You attack my people; *Hebrew* Recently my people have attacked.
3.12 Jr 26.18

Many nations will come
    streaming to it,
² and their people will say,
    "Let us go up the hill of the
      LORD,*f*
    to the Temple of Israel's God.
He will teach us what he wants
    us to do;
we will walk in the paths he
    has chosen.

The prophets give their revelations for money.
(3.11)

For the LORD's teaching comes
    from Jerusalem;
    from Zion he speaks to his
      people."

³ He will settle disputes among the
    nations,
    among the great powers near
      and far.
They will hammer their swords
    into plows
    and their spears into pruning
      knives.
Nations will never again go
    to war,
    never prepare for battle again.
⁴ Everyone will live in peace
    among their own vineyards
    and fig trees,

and no one will make them
    afraid.
The LORD Almighty has
    promised this.

⁵ Each nation worships and obeys its
own god, but we will worship and obey
the LORD our God forever and ever.

Israel Will Return from Exile

⁶ "The time is coming," says the
LORD, "when I will gather together the
people I punished, those who have suffered in exile. ⁷ They are crippled and
far from home, but I will make a new
beginning with those who are left, and
they will become a great nation. I will
rule over them on Mount Zion from
that time on and forever."

⁸ And you, Jerusalem, where God,
like a shepherd from his lookout tower,
watches over his people, will once again
be the capital of the kingdom that was
yours. ⁹ Why do you cry out so loudly?
Why are you suffering like a woman in
labor? Is it because you have no king,
and your counselors are dead? ¹⁰ Twist
and groan,*g* people of Jerusalem, like a
woman giving birth, for now you will
have to leave the city and live in the
open country. You will have to go to
Babylon, but there the LORD will save
you from your enemies. ¹¹ Many nations
have gathered to attack you. They say,
"Jerusalem must be destroyed! We will
see this city in ruins!" ¹² But these nations do not know what is in the LORD's
mind. They do not realize that they
have been gathered together to be punished in the same way that grain is
brought in to be threshed.

¹³ The LORD says, "People of Jerusalem, go and punish your enemies! I will
make you as strong as a bull with iron
horns and bronze hoofs. You will crush
many nations, and the wealth they got

---

f HILL OF THE LORD: *Mount Zion (see Zion in Word List).*   *g Probable text* groan;
Hebrew bring forth.
4.3 Is 2.4; Jl 3.10   **4.4** Zec 3.10

by violence you will present to me, the Lord of the whole world."

5 People of Jerusalem, gather your forces![h] We are besieged! They are attacking the leader of Israel!

God Promises a Ruler from Bethlehem

2 The LORD says, "Bethlehem Ephrathah, you are one of the smallest towns in Judah, but out of you I will bring a ruler for Israel, whose family line goes back to ancient times."

3 So the LORD will abandon his people to their enemies until the woman who is to give birth has her son. Then those Israelites who are in exile will be reunited with their own people. 4 When he comes, he will rule his people with the strength that comes from the LORD and with the majesty of the LORD God himself. His people will live in safety because people all over the earth will acknowledge his greatness, 5 and he will bring peace.

Deliverance and Punishment

When the Assyrians invade our country and break through our defenses, we will send our strongest leaders to fight them. 6 By force of arms they will conquer Assyria, the land of Nimrod, and they [i] will save us from the Assyrians when they invade our territory.

7 The people of Israel who survive will be like refreshing dew sent by the LORD for many nations, like showers on growing plants. They will depend on God, not people. 8 Those who are left among the nations will be like a lion hunting for food in a forest or a pasture: it gets in among the sheep, pounces on them, and tears them to pieces — and there is no hope of rescue. 9 Israel will conquer her enemies and destroy them all.

10 The LORD says, "At that time I will take away your horses and destroy your chariots. 11 I will destroy the cities in your land and tear down all your defenses. 12 I will destroy the magic charms you use and leave you without any fortunetellers. 13 I will destroy your idols and sacred stone pillars; no longer will you worship the things that you yourselves have made. 14 I will pull down the images of the goddess Asherah in your land and destroy your cities. 15 And in my great anger I will take revenge on all nations that have not obeyed me."

The LORD's Case against Israel

6 Listen to the LORD's case against Israel.

Arise, O LORD, and present your case; let the mountains and the hills hear what you say.

2 You mountains, you everlasting foundations of the earth, listen to the LORD's case! The LORD has a case against his people. He is going to bring an accusation against Israel.

3 The LORD says, "My people, what have I done to you? How have I been a burden to you? Answer me. 4 I brought you out of Egypt; I rescued you from slavery; I sent Moses, Aaron, and Miriam to lead you. 5 My people, remember what King Balak of Moab planned to do to you and how Balaam son of Beor answered him. Remember the things that happened on the way from the camp at Acacia to Gilgal. Remember these things and you will realize what I did in order to save you."

What the LORD Requires

6 What shall I bring to the LORD, the God of heaven, when I come to worship him? Shall I bring the best calves to burn as offerings to him? 7 Will the LORD be pleased if I bring him thou-

---

[h] *Probable text* People . . . forces!; *Hebrew unclear.*   [i] *Probable text* they; *Hebrew* he.
5.2 Mt 2.6; Jn 7.42   **5.6** Gn 10.8-11   **6.4 a** Ex 12.50, 51; **b** Ex 4.10-16; **c** Ex 15.20
6.5 a Nu 22.2 – 24.25; **b** Js 3.1 – 4.19

sands of sheep or endless streams of olive oil? Shall I offer him my first-born child to pay for my sins? 8 No, the LORD has told us what is good. What he requires of us is this: to do what is just, to show constant love, and to live in humble fellowship with our God.

9 It is wise to fear the LORD. He calls to the city, "Listen, you people who assemble in the city!ʲ 10 In the houses of evil people are treasures which they got dishonestly. They use false measures, a thing that I hate.ᵏ 11 How can I forgive those who use false scales and weights?

How can I forgive those who use false scales and weights? (6.11)

12 Your rich people exploit the poor, and all of you are liars. 13 So I have already begunˡ your ruin and destruction because of your sins. 14 You will eat, but not be satisfied — in fact you will still be hungry. You will carry things off, but you will not be able to save them; anything you do save I will destroy in war. 15 You will sow grain, but not harvest the crop. You will press oil from olives, but never get to use it. You will make wine, but never drink it. 16 This will happen because you have followed the evil practices of King Omri and of his son, King Ahab. You have continued their policies, and so I will bring you to ruin, and everyone will despise you. Peopleᵐ everywhere will treat you with contempt."ⁿ

Israel's Moral Corruption

7 It's hopeless! I am like a hungry person who finds no fruit left on the trees and no grapes on the vines. All the grapes and all the tasty figs have been picked. 2 There is not an honest person left in the land, no one loyal to God. Everyone is waiting for a chance to commit murder. Everyone hunts down their own people. 3 They are all experts at doing evil. Officials and judges ask for bribes. The influential people tell them what they want, and so they scheme together.ᵒ 4 Even the best and most honest of them are as worthless as weeds.

The day has come when God will punish the people, as he warned them through their watchmen, the prophets. Now they are in confusion. 5 Don't believe your neighbor or trust your friend. Be careful what you say even to your husband or wife. 6 In these times sons treat their fathers like fools, daughters oppose their mothers, and young women quarrel with their mothers-in-law; your enemies are the members of your own family.

7 But I will watch for the LORD; I will wait confidently for God, who will save me. My God will hear me.

The LORD Brings Salvation

8 Our enemies have no reason to gloat over us. We have fallen, but we will rise again. We are in darkness now,

<hr />

ʲ *Probable text* who assemble in the city; *Hebrew* and who appointed it. Yet.   ᵏ *Verse 10 in Hebrew is unclear.*   ˡ *Some ancient translations* begun; *Hebrew* made sick.
ᵐ *One ancient translation* People; *Hebrew* My people.   ⁿ People . . . contempt; *or* As my people you will everywhere be treated with contempt.   ᵒ and so they scheme together; *Hebrew unclear.*
6.16 a 1 K 16.23-28; **b** 1 K 16.29-34; 21.25, 26   **7.6** Mt 10.35, 36; Lk 12.53

but the LORD will give us light. ⁹We have sinned against the LORD, so now we must endure his anger for a while. But in the end he will defend us and right the wrongs that have been done to us. He will bring us out to the light; we will live to see him save us. ¹⁰Then our enemies will see this and be disgraced—the same enemies who taunted us by asking, "Where is the LORD your God?" We will see them defeated, trampledᵖ down like mud in the streets.

¹¹People of Jerusalem, the time to rebuild the city walls is coming. At that time your territory will be enlarged. ¹²Your people will return to you from everywhere—from Assyria in the east, from Egypt in the south, from the region of the Euphrates River, from distant seas and far-off mountains. ¹³But the earth will become a desert because of the wickedness of those who live on it.

The LORD's Compassion on Israel

¹⁴Be a shepherd to your people, LORD, the people you have chosen. Although they live apart in the wilderness, there is fertile land around them.

Your people will return to you from everywhere.
(7.12)

Let them go and feed in the rich pastures of Bashan and Gilead, as they did long ago.

¹⁵Work miracles for us,�q LORD, as you did in the days when you brought us out of Egypt. ¹⁶The nations will see this and be frustrated in spite of all their strength. In dismay they will close their mouths and cover their ears. ¹⁷They will crawl in the dust like snakes; they will come from their fortresses, trembling and afraid. They will turn in fear to the LORD our God.

¹⁸There is no other god like you, O LORD; you forgive the sins of your people who have survived. You do not stay angry forever, but you take pleasure in showing us your constant love. ¹⁹You will be merciful to us once again. You will trample our sins underfoot and send them to the bottom of the sea! ²⁰You will show your faithfulness and constant love to your people, the descendants of Abraham and of Jacob, as you promised our ancestors long ago.

ᵖ We will see . . . trampled; *or* We will gloat over them as they lie trampled.
q *Probable text* Work miracles for us; *Hebrew* I will work miracles for him.

The Book of
NAHUM

INTRODUCTION

The Book of Nahum is a poem celebrating the fall of Nineveh, the capital city of Israel's ancient and oppressive enemy, the Assyrians. The fall of Nineveh, near the end of the seventh century B.C., is seen as the judgment of God upon a cruel and arrogant nation.

OUTLINE OF CONTENTS

1 This is a message about Nineveh, the account of a vision seen by Nahum, who was from Elkosh.

The Lord's Anger against Nineveh

² The Lord God tolerates no rivals;
  he punishes those who
    oppose him.
  In his anger he pays them
    back.
³ The Lord does not easily become
    angry,
  but he is powerful
  and never lets the guilty go
    unpunished.

Where the Lord walks, storms
    arise;
  the clouds are the dust raised
    by his feet!
⁴ He commands the sea, and it
    dries up!
  He makes the rivers go dry.
The fields of Bashan wither,
  Mount Carmel turns brown,
  and the flowers of Lebanon
    fade.

⁵ Mountains quake in the presence
    of the Lord;
  hills melt before him.
The earth shakes when the Lord
    appears;
  the world and all its people
    tremble.
⁶ When he is angry, who can
    survive?
Who can survive his terrible
    fury?
He pours out his flaming anger;
  rocks crumble to dust
    before him.

⁷ The Lord is good;
  he protects his people in times
    of trouble;
  he takes care of those who
    turn to him.
⁸ Like a great rushing flood he
  completely destroys his
    enemies;[a]
  he sends to their death those
    who oppose him.
⁹ What are you plotting against the
    Lord?
He will destroy you.

---

[a] *Some ancient translations* his enemies; *Hebrew* its place.
1.1—3.19 Is 10.5-34; 14.24-27; Zep 2.13-15

No one opposes him more
   than once.
¹⁰ Like tangled thorns and dry
      straw
   you drunkards will be
      burned up!

¹¹ From you, Nineveh, there came someone full of wicked schemes, who plotted against the LORD. ¹² This is what the LORD says to his people Israel: "Even though the Assyrians are strong and numerous, they will be destroyed and disappear. My people, I made you suffer, but I will not do it again. ¹³ I will now end Assyria's power over you and break the chains that bind you."

¹⁴ This is what the LORD has decreed about the Assyrians: "They will have no descendants to carry on their name. I will destroy the idols that are in the temples of their gods. I am preparing a grave for the Assyrians — they don't deserve to live!"

¹⁵ Look, a messenger is coming over the mountains with good news! He is on his way to announce the victory! People of Judah, celebrate your festivals and give God what you solemnly

Look, a messenger is coming! (1.15)

promised him. The wicked will never invade your land again. They have been totally destroyed!

The Fall of Nineveh

2 Nineveh, you are under attack!
   The power that will shatter you
      has come.
   Prepare the defenses!
   Guard the road!
   Prepare for battle!
(² The LORD is about to restore the glory of Israel, as it was before her enemies plundered her.)
³ The enemy soldiers carry red
      shields
   and wear uniforms of red.
   They are preparing to attack!
   Their chariots flash like fire!
   Their horses*ᵇ* prance!

⁴ Chariots dash wildly through the
      streets,
   rushing back and forth in the
      city squares.
   They flash like torches
   and dart about like lightning.
⁵ The officers are summoned;
   they stumble as they press
      forward.

   The attackers rush to the wall
   and set up the shield for the
      battering ram.
⁶ The gates by the river burst
      open;
   the palace is filled with terror.
⁷ The queen is taken captive;
   her servants moan like doves
   and beat their breasts in
      sorrow.
⁸ Like water from a broken dam
   the people rush from
      Nineveh!ᶜ
   "Stop! Stop!" the cry rings out —
   but no one turns back.

ᵇ Some ancient translations horses; *Hebrew* cypresses.   *ᶜ Probable text* Like water
... Nineveh; *Hebrew unclear.*
1.15 Is 52.7

⁹Plunder the silver!
    Plunder the gold!
    The city is full of treasure!

¹⁰Nineveh is destroyed, deserted,
        desolate!
    Hearts melt with fear;
    knees tremble, strength is
        gone;
    faces grow pale.

¹¹Where now is the city
    that was like a den of lions,
    the place where young lions
        were fed,
    where the lion and the lioness
        would go
    and their cubs would be safe?

¹²The lion killed his prey
    and tore it to pieces for his
        mate and her cubs;
    he filled his den with torn
        flesh.

¹³"I am your enemy!" says the LORD Almighty. "I will burn up your chariots. Your soldiers will be killed in war, and I will take away everything that you took from others. The demands of your envoys will no longer be heard."

3 Doomed is the lying, murderous
        city,
    full of wealth to be looted and
        plundered!

²Listen! The crack of the whip,
    the rattle of wheels,
    the gallop of horses,
    the jolting of chariots!

³Cavalry troops charge,
    swords flash, spears gleam!
Corpses are piled high,
    dead bodies without
        number —
    men stumble over them!

⁴Nineveh the whore is being
        punished.
Attractive and full of deadly
        charms,
    she enchanted nations and
        enslaved[d] them.

⁵The LORD Almighty says,
    "I will punish you, Nineveh!
    I will strip you naked
    and let the nations see you,
    see you in all your shame.

⁶I will treat you with contempt
    and cover you with filth.
    People will stare at you in
        horror.

⁷All who see you will shrink back.
    They will say, 'Nineveh lies in
        ruins!
    Who has any sympathy
        for her?
    Who will want to
        comfort her?' "

⁸Nineveh, are you any better than

---

d enslaved; *or* seduced.

Thebes, the capital of Egypt? She too had a river to protect her like a wall — the Nile was her defense. 9 She ruled Ethiopia*e* and Egypt, there was no limit to her power; Libya was her ally. 10 Yet the people of Thebes were carried off into exile. At every street corner their children were beaten to death. Their leading men were carried off in chains and divided among their captors.

11 Nineveh, you too will fall into a drunken stupor! You too will try to escape from your enemies. 12 All your fortresses will be like fig trees with ripe figs: shake the trees, and the fruit falls right into your mouth! 13 Your soldiers are helpless, and your country stands defenseless before your enemies. Fire will destroy the bars across your gates. 14 Draw water to prepare for a siege, and strengthen your fortresses! Trample the clay to make bricks, and get the brick molds ready! 15 No matter what you do, you will still be burned to death or killed in battle. You will be wiped out like crops eaten up by locusts.

You multiplied like locusts! 16 You produced more merchants than there are stars in the sky! But now they are gone, like locusts that spread their wings and fly away. 17 Your officials are like a swarm of locusts that stay in the walls on a cold day. But when the sun comes out, they fly away, and no one knows where they have gone!

18 Emperor of Assyria, your governors are dead, and your noblemen are asleep forever! Your people are scattered on the mountains, and there is no one to bring them home again. 19 There is no remedy for your injuries, and your wounds cannot be healed. All those who hear the news of your destruction clap their hands for joy. Did anyone escape your endless cruelty?

---

e Hebrew Cush: *Cush is the ancient name of the extensive territory south of the First Cataract of the Nile River. This region was called Ethiopia in Graeco-Roman times, and included within its borders most of modern Sudan and some of present-day Ethiopia (Abyssinia).*

The Book of
HABAKKUK

INTRODUCTION

The words of the prophet Habakkuk come from near the end of the seventh century B.C., at a time when the Babylonians were in power. He was deeply disturbed by the violence of these cruel people, and asked the Lord, "So why are you silent while they destroy people who are more righteous than they are?" (1.13). The Lord's answer was that he would take action in his own good time, and meanwhile "those who are righteous will live because they are faithful to God" (2.4).

The rest of the book is a prophecy of doom on the unrighteous, with a concluding psalm celebrating the greatness of God and expressing the undying faith of the poet.

OUTLINE OF CONTENTS

---

1 This is the message that the LORD revealed to the prophet Habakkuk.

Habakkuk Complains of Injustice

² O LORD, how long must I call for help before you listen, before you save us from violence? ³ Why do you make me see such trouble? How can you stand to look on such wrongdoing? Destruction and violence are all around me, and there is fighting and quarreling everywhere. ⁴ The law is weak and useless, and justice is never done. Evil people get the better of the righteous, and so justice is perverted.

The LORD's Reply

⁵ Then the LORD said to his people, "Keep watching the nations around you, and you will be astonished at what you see. I am going to do something that you will not believe when you hear about it. ⁶ I am bringing the Babylonians to power, those fierce, restless people. They are marching out across the world to conquer other lands. ⁷ They spread fear and terror, and in their pride they are a law to themselves.

⁸ "Their horses are faster than leopards, fiercer than hungry wolves. Their cavalry troops come riding from distant lands; their horses paw the ground. They come swooping down like eagles attacking their prey.

1.5 Ac 13.41   **1.6** 2 K 24.2

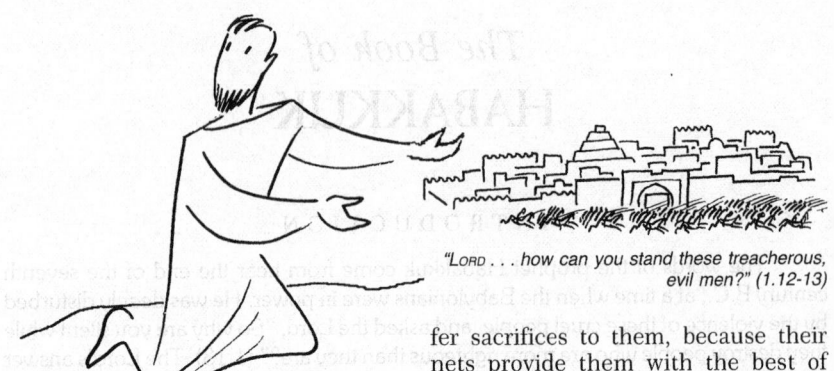

"Lord . . . how can you stand these treacherous, evil men?" (1.12-13)

⁹"Their armies advance in violent conquest, and everyone is terrified as they approach.ᵃ Their captives are as numerous as grains of sand. ¹⁰They treat kings with contempt and laugh at high officials. No fortress can stop them—they pile up earth against it and capture it. ¹¹Then they sweep on like the wind and are gone, these men whose power is their god."

Habakkuk Complains to the Lord Again

¹²Lord, from the very beginning you are God. You are my God, holy and eternal. Lord, my God and protector, you have chosen the Babylonians and made them strong so that they can punish us. ¹³But how can you stand these treacherous, evil men? Your eyes are too holy to look at evil, and you cannot stand the sight of people doing wrong. So why are you silent while they destroy people who are more righteous than they are?

¹⁴How can you treat people like fish or like a swarm of insects that have no ruler to direct them? ¹⁵The Babylonians catch people with hooks, as though they were fish. They drag them off in nets and shout for joy over their catch! ¹⁶They even worship their nets and offer sacrifices to them, because their nets provide them with the best of everything.

¹⁷Are they going to use their swords forever and keep on destroying nations without mercy?

The Lord's Answer to Habakkuk

2 I will climb my watchtower and wait to see what the Lord will tell me to say and what answer heᵇ will give to my complaint.

²The Lord gave me this answer: "Write down clearly on tablets what I reveal to you, so that it can be read at a glance. ³Put it in writing, because it is not yet time for it to come true. But the time is coming quickly, and what I show you will come true. It may seem slow in coming, but wait for it; it will certainly take place, and it will not be delayed. ⁴And this is the message: 'Those who are evil will not survive,ᶜ but those who are righteous will live because they are faithful to God.'"

Doom on the Unrighteous

⁵Wealth is deceitful. Greedy people are proud and restless—like death itself they are never satisfied. That is why they conquer nation after nation for themselves. ⁶The conquered people will taunt their conquerors and show their scorn for them. They will say, "You take what isn't yours, but you are

---

ᵃ *Probable text* and everyone . . . approach; *Hebrew unclear.*   ᵇ *One ancient translation* he; *Hebrew* I.   ᶜ *Probable text* will not survive; *Hebrew unclear.*
2.3 He 10.37   **2.4** Ro 1.17; Ga 3.11; He 10.38

doomed! How long will you go on getting rich by forcing your debtors to pay up?"

⁷But before you know it, you that have conquered others will be in debt yourselves and be forced to pay interest. Enemies will come and make you tremble. They will plunder you! ⁸You have plundered the people of many nations, but now those who have survived will plunder you because of the murders you have committed and because of your violence against the people of the world and its cities.ᵈ

⁹You are doomed! You have made your family rich with what you took by violence, and have tried to make your own home safe from harm and danger! ¹⁰But your schemes have brought shame on your family; by destroying many nations you have only brought ruin on yourself. ¹¹Even the stones of the walls cry out against you, and the rafters echo the cry.

¹²You are doomed! You founded a city on crime and built it up by murder. ¹³The nations you conquered wore themselves out in useless labor, and all they have built goes up in flames. The Lᴏʀᴅ Almighty has done this. ¹⁴But the earth will be as full of the knowledge of the Lᴏʀᴅ's glory as the seas are full of water.

¹⁵You are doomed! In your fury you humiliated and disgraced your neighbors; you made them stagger as though they were drunk. ¹⁶You in turn will be covered with shame instead of honor. You yourself will drink and stagger. The Lᴏʀᴅ will make you drink your own cup of punishment, and your honor will be turned to disgrace. ¹⁷You have cut down the forests of Lebanon; now you will be cut down. You killed its animals; now animals will terrify you. This will happen because of the murders you have committed and because

of your violence against the people of the world and its cities.ᵈ

¹⁸What's the use of an idol? It is only something that a human being has made, and it tells you nothing but lies. What good does it do for its maker to trust it — a god that can't even talk! ¹⁹You are doomed! You say to a piece of wood, "Wake up!" or to a block of stone, "Get up!" Can an idol reveal anything to you? It may be covered with silver and gold, but there is no life in it.

²⁰The Lᴏʀᴅ is in his holy Temple; let everyone on earth be silent in his presence.

A Prayer of Habakkuk

3 This is a prayer of the prophet Habakkuk:ᵉ

²O Lᴏʀᴅ, I have heard of what
　　you have done,
　　and I am filled with awe.
Now do again in our times
　　the great deeds you used
　　to do.
Be merciful, even when you are
　　angry.

³God is coming again from Edom;
　　the holy God is coming from
　　the hills of Paran.
His splendor covers the heavens,
　　and the earth is full of his
　　praise.
⁴He comes with the brightness
　　of lightning;
　　light flashes from his hand,
　　there where his power is
　　hidden.
⁵He sends disease before him
　　and commands death to
　　follow him.
⁶When he stops, the earth shakes;
　　at his glance the nations
　　tremble.

ᵈ the people ... cities; *or* the land, the city, and those who live in it.　　　ᵉ *Hebrew has an additional phrase, the meaning of which is unclear.*

2.13 Si 14.19　**2.14** Is 11.9

The eternal mountains are
        shattered;
    the everlasting hills sink
        down,
    the hills where he walked in
        ancient times.

7 I saw the people of Cushan
        afraid
    and the people of Midian
        tremble.
8 Was it the rivers that made you
        angry, Lord?
    Was it the sea that made you
        furious?
    You rode upon the clouds;
        the storm cloud was your
            chariot,
        as you brought victory to your
            people.
9 You got ready to use your bow,
    ready to shoot your arrows.*f*
    Your lightning split open the
        earth.
10 When the mountains saw you,
        they trembled;
    water poured down from
        the skies.
    The waters under the earth
        roared,
    and their waves rose high.
11 At the flash of your speeding
        arrows
    and the gleam of your shining
        spear,
    the sun and the moon stood
        still.
12 You marched across the earth
        in anger;
    in fury you trampled the
        nations.
13 You went out to save your
        people,
    to save your chosen king.

You struck down the leader of
        the wicked
    and completely destroyed his
        followers.*g*
14 Your arrows pierced the
        commander of his army
    when it came like a storm to
        scatter us,
    gloating like those who
        secretly oppress the poor.*h*
15 You trampled the sea with your
        horses,
    and the mighty waters
        foamed.

16 I hear all this, and I tremble;
    my lips quiver with fear.
    My body goes limp,
    and my feet stumble*i*
        beneath me.

    I will quietly wait for the time
        to come
    when God will punish those
        who attack us.

17 Even though the fig trees have
        no fruit
    and no grapes grow on the
        vines,
    even though the olive crop fails
    and the fields produce no
        grain,
    even though the sheep all die
    and the cattle stalls are
        empty,
18 I will still be joyful and glad,
    because the Lord God is my
        savior.
19 The Sovereign Lord gives me
        strength.
    He makes me sure-footed as
        a deer
    and keeps me safe on the
        mountains.

---

f Probable text ready to shoot your arrows; *Hebrew unclear.*   *g Probable text*
completely . . . followers; *Hebrew unclear.*   *h Verse 14 in Hebrew is unclear.*
i Probable text my feet stumble; *Hebrew* I am excited, because.
3.19 2 S 22.34; Ps 18.33

The Book of
ZEPHANIAH

INTRODUCTION

The prophet Zephaniah preached in the latter part of the seventh century B.C., probably in the decade before King Josiah's religious reforms of 621 B.C. The book contains the familiar prophetic themes: A day of doom and destruction is threatened, when Judah will be punished for her worship of other gods. The Lord will punish other nations also. Although Jerusalem is doomed, in time the city will be restored, with a humble and righteous people living there.

OUTLINE OF CONTENTS

1 This is the message that the LORD gave to Zephaniah during the time that Josiah son of Amon was king of Judah. (Zephaniah was descended from King Hezekiah through Amariah, Gedaliah, and Cushi.)

The Day of the LORD's Judgment

2 The LORD said, "I am going to destroy everything on earth, 3 all human beings and animals, birds and fish. I will bring about the downfall of[a] the wicked. I will destroy everyone, and no survivors will be left. I, the LORD, have spoken.

4 "I will punish the people of Jerusalem and of all Judah. I will destroy the last trace of the worship of Baal there, and no one will even remember the pagan priests who serve him. 5 I will destroy anyone who goes up on the roof and worships the sun, the moon, and the stars. I will also destroy those who worship me and swear loyalty to me, but then take oaths in the name of the god Molech. 6 I will destroy those who have turned back and no longer follow me, those who do not come to me or ask me to guide them."

7 The day is near when the LORD will sit in judgment; so be silent in his presence. The LORD is preparing to sacrifice his people and has invited enemies to plunder Judah. 8 "On that day of slaughter," says the LORD, "I will punish the officials, the king's sons, and all who practice foreign customs. 9 I will punish all who worship like pagans and who steal and kill in order to fill their master's house[b] with loot.

10 "On that day," says the LORD, "you will hear the sound of crying at the Fish Gate in Jerusalem. You will hear wailing in the newer part of the city and a great crashing sound in the hills.

---

[a] Probable text I will bring about the downfall of; Hebrew the stumbling blocks.
[b] their master's house; or the temple of their god.
1.1 2 K 22.1 — 23.30; 2 Ch 34.1 — 35.27

11 Wail and cry when you hear this, you that live in the lower part of the city, because all the merchants will be dead!

12 "At that time I will take a lamp and search Jerusalem. I will punish the people who are self-satisfied and confident, who say to themselves, 'The LORD never does anything, one way or the

The LORD never does anything, one way or the other. (1.12)

other.' 13 Their wealth will be looted and their houses destroyed. They will never live in the houses they are building or drink wine from the vineyards they are planting."

14 The great day of the LORD is near — very near and coming fast! That day will be bitter, for even[c] the bravest soldiers will cry out in despair! 15 It will be a day of fury, a day of trouble and distress, a day of ruin and destruction, a day of darkness and gloom, a black and cloudy day, 16 a day filled with the sound of war trumpets and the battle cry of soldiers attacking fortified cities and high towers.

17 The LORD says, "I will bring such disasters on the human race that everyone will grope about like someone blind. They have sinned against me, and now their blood will be poured out like water, and their dead bodies will lie rotting on the ground."

18 On the day when the LORD shows his fury, not even all their silver and gold will save them. The whole earth will be destroyed by the fire of his anger. He will put an end — a sudden end — to everyone who lives on earth.

A Plea for Repentance

2 Shameless nation, come to your senses 2 before you are driven away like chaff blown by the wind, before the burning anger of the LORD comes upon you, before the day when he shows his fury. 3 Turn to the LORD, all you humble people of the land, who obey his commands. Do what is right, and humble yourselves before the LORD. Perhaps you will escape punishment on the day when the LORD shows his anger.

The Doom of the Nations around Israel

4 No one will be left in the city of Gaza. Ashkelon will be deserted. The people of Ashdod will be driven out in half a day,[d] and the people of Ekron will be driven from their city. 5 You Philistines are doomed, you people who live along the coast. The LORD has passed sentence on you. He will destroy you, and not one of you will be left. 6 Your land by the sea will become open fields with shepherd's huts and sheep pens. 7 The people of Judah who survive will occupy your land. They will pasture their flocks there and sleep in the houses of Ashkelon. The LORD their

---

[c] *That day ... even; or* Listen! That terrible day is coming when even.   [d] *in half a day; or* by a surprise attack at noontime.

2.4-7 Is 14.29-31; Jr 47.1-7; Ez 25.15-17; Jl 3.4-8; Am 1.6-8; Zec 9.5-7

Owls will live among its ruins. (2.14)

God will be with them and make them prosper again.

[8] The LORD Almighty says, "I have heard the people of Moab and Ammon insulting and taunting my people, and boasting that they would seize their land. [9] As surely as I am the living LORD, the God of Israel, I swear that Moab and Ammon are going to be destroyed like Sodom and Gomorrah. They will become a place of salt pits and everlasting ruin, overgrown with weeds. Those of my people who survive will plunder them and take their land."

[10] That is how the people of Moab and Ammon will be punished for their pride and arrogance and for insulting the people of the LORD Almighty. [11] The LORD will terrify them. He will reduce the gods of the earth to nothing, and then every nation will worship him, each in its own land.

[12] The LORD will also put the people of Ethiopia[e] to death.

[13] The LORD will use his power to destroy Assyria. He will make the city of Nineveh a deserted ruin, a waterless desert. [14] It will be a place where flocks, herds, and animals of every kind will lie down. Owls will live among its ruins and hoot from the windows. Crows[f] will caw on the doorsteps. The cedar wood of her buildings will be stripped away. [15] That is what will happen to the city that is so proud of its own power and thinks it is safe. Its people think that their city is the greatest in the world. What a desolate place it will become, a place where wild animals will rest! Everyone who passes by will shrink back in horror.

Jerusalem's Sin and Redemption

3 Jerusalem is doomed, that corrupt, rebellious city that oppresses its own people. [2] It has not listened to the LORD or accepted his discipline. It has not put its trust in the LORD or asked for his help. [3] Its officials are like roaring lions; its judges are like hungry wolves, too greedy to leave a bone until morning. [4] The prophets are irresponsible and treacherous; the priests defile what is sacred, and twist the law of God to their own advantage. [5] But the LORD

[e] *Hebrew* Cush: *Cush is the ancient name of the extensive territory south of the First Cataract of the Nile River. This region was called Ethiopia in Graeco-Roman times, and included within its borders most of modern Sudan and some of present-day Ethiopia (Abyssinia).* [f] *Some ancient translations* Crows; *Hebrew* Desolation.

2.8-11 a Is 15.1—16.14; 25.10-12; Jr 48.1-47; Ez 25.8-11; Am 1.13-15; **b** Jr 49.1-6; Ez 21.28-32; 25.1-7; Am 1.13-15   **2.9** Gn 19.24   **2.12** Is 18.1-7   **2.13-15** Is 10.5-34; 14.24-27; Nh 1.1—3.19

is still in the city; he does what is right and never what is wrong. Every morning without fail, he brings justice to his people. And yet the unrighteous people there keep on doing wrong and are not ashamed.

6 The Lord says, "I have wiped out whole nations; I have destroyed their cities and left their walls and towers in ruins. The cities are deserted; the streets are empty — no one is left. **7** I thought that then my people would have reverence for me and accept my discipline, that they would never forget*g* the lesson I taught them. But soon they were behaving as badly as ever.

8 "Just wait," the Lord says. "Wait for the day when I rise to accuse the nations. I have made up my mind to gather nations and kingdoms in order to let them feel the force of my anger. The whole earth will be destroyed by the fire of my fury.

9 "Then I will change the people of the nations, and they will pray to me alone and not to other gods. They will all obey me. **10** Even from distant Ethiopia*h* my scattered people will bring offerings to me. **11** At that time you, my people, will no longer need to be ashamed that you rebelled against me. I will remove everyone who is proud and arrogant, and you will never again rebel against me on my sacred hill.*i* **12** I will leave there a humble and lowly people, who will come to me for help. **13** The people of Israel who survive will do no wrong to anyone, tell no lies, nor

try to deceive. They will be prosperous and secure, afraid of no one."

A Song of Joy

14 Sing and shout for joy, people
    of Israel!
  Rejoice with all your heart,
    Jerusalem!
15 The Lord has stopped your
    punishment;
  he has removed all your
    enemies.
  The Lord, the king of Israel, is
    with you;
  there is no reason now to be
    afraid.
16 The time is coming when they
    will say to Jerusalem,
  "Do not be afraid, city of Zion!
  Do not let your hands hang
    limp!
17 The Lord your God is with you;
  his power gives you victory.
  The Lord will take delight
    in you,
  and in his love he will give
    you new life.*j*
  He will sing and be joyful
    over you,
18   as joyful as people at a
    festival."
The Lord says,
  "I have ended the threat of doom
    and taken away your
    disgrace.*k*
19 The time is coming!
  I will punish your oppressors;
  I will rescue all the lame
    and bring the exiles home.
  I will turn their shame to honor,

---

g Some ancient translations they would never forget; *Hebrew* their dwelling would not be cut off.   *h Hebrew* Cush: *Cush is the ancient name of the extensive territory south of the First Cataract of the Nile River. This region was called Ethiopia in Graeco-Roman times, and included within its borders most of modern Sudan and some of present-day Ethiopia (Abyssinia).*   *i* SACRED HILL: *Mount Zion (see Zion in Word List).*   *j Some ancient translations* give you new life; *Hebrew* be silent.   *k Verse 18 in Hebrew is unclear.*
3.13 Rev 14.5

and all the world will praise
them.
20 The time is coming!
I will bring your scattered people
home;

I will make you famous
throughout the world
and make you prosperous
once again."
The LORD has spoken.

The Book of
HAGGAI

INTRODUCTION

The Book of Haggai is a collection of brief messages that came from the Lord through the prophet Haggai in 520 B.C. The people had returned from exile and had lived in Jerusalem for some years, but the Temple still lay in ruins. The messages urge the leaders of the people to rebuild the Temple, and the Lord promises prosperity and peace in the future for a renewed and purified people.

OUTLINE OF CONTENTS

The LORD's Command to Rebuild the Temple

1 During the second year that Darius was emperor of Persia, on the first day of the sixth month, the LORD spoke through the prophet Haggai. The message was for the governor of Judah, Zerubbabel son of Shealtiel, and for the High Priest, Joshua son of Jehozadak.

2 The LORD Almighty said to Haggai, "These people say that this is not the right time to rebuild the Temple." 3 The LORD then gave this message to the people through the prophet Haggai: 4 "My people, why should you be living in well-built houses while my Temple lies in ruins? 5 Don't you see what is happening to you? 6 You have planted much grain, but have harvested very

little. You have food to eat, but not enough to make you full. You have wine to drink, but not enough to get drunk on! You have clothing, but not enough to keep you warm. And workers cannot earn enough to live on. 7 Can't you see why this has happened? 8 Now go up into the hills, get lumber, and rebuild the Temple; then I will be pleased and will be worshiped as I should be.

9 "You hoped for large harvests, but they turned out to be small. And when you brought the harvest home, I blew it away.ᵃ Why did I do that? Because my Temple lies in ruins while every one of you is busy working on your own house. 10 That is why there is no rain and nothing can grow. 11 I have brought

ᵃ I blew it away; *or* I spoiled it.
1.1 Ezra 4.24—5.2; 6.14

Why should you be living in well-built houses while my Temple lies in ruins? (1.4)

drought on the land — on its hills, grain-fields, vineyards, and olive orchards — on every crop the ground produces, on people and animals, on everything you try to grow."

The People Obey the LORD's Command

¹²Then Zerubbabel and Joshua and all the people who had returned from the exile*b* in Babylonia, did what the LORD their God told them to do. They were afraid and obeyed the prophet Haggai, the LORD's messenger. ¹³Then Haggai gave the LORD's message to the people: "I will be with you — that is my promise." ¹⁴The LORD inspired everyone to work on the Temple: Zerubbabel, the governor of Judah; Joshua, the High Priest, and all the people who had returned from the exile.*b* They began working on the Temple of the LORD Almighty, their God, ¹⁵on the twenty-fourth day of the sixth month of the second year that Darius was emperor.

The Splendor of the New Temple

2 On the twenty-first day of the seventh month of that same year, the LORD spoke again through the prophet Haggai. ²He told Haggai to speak to Zerubbabel, the governor of Judah, to Joshua, the High Priest, and to the people, and to say to them, ³"Is there anyone among you who can still remember how splendid the Temple used to be? How does it look to you now? It must seem like nothing at all. ⁴But now don't be discouraged, any of you. Do the work, for I am with you. ⁵When you came out of Egypt, I promised that I would always be with you. I am still with you, so do not be afraid.

⁶"Before long I will shake heaven and earth, land and sea. ⁷I will overthrow all the nations, and their treasures will be brought here, and the Temple will be filled with wealth. ⁸All the silver and gold of the world is mine. ⁹The new Temple will be more splendid than the old one, and there I will

---

b who had returned from the exile; *or* who had not gone into exile.
2.3 Ezra 3.12 **2.5** Ex 29.45, 46 **2.6** He 12.26

give my people prosperity and peace." The LORD Almighty has spoken.

The Prophet Consults the Priests

¹⁰On the twenty-fourth day of the ninth month of the second year that Darius was emperor, the LORD Almighty spoke again to the prophet Haggai. ¹¹He said, "Ask the priests for a ruling on this question: ¹²Suppose someone takes a piece of consecrated meat from a sacrifice and carries it in a fold of his robe. If he then lets his robe touch any bread, cooked food, wine, olive oil, or any kind of food at all, will it make that food consecrated also?"

When the question was asked, the priests answered, "No."

¹³Then Haggai asked, "Suppose someone is defiled because he has touched a dead body. If he then touches any of these foods, will that make them defiled too?"

The priests answered, "Yes."

¹⁴Then Haggai said, "The LORD says that the same thing applies to the people of this nation and to everything they produce; and so everything they offer on the altar is defiled."

The LORD Promises His Blessing

¹⁵The LORD says, "Can't you see what has happened to you? Before you

started to rebuild the Temple, ¹⁶you would go to a pile of grain expecting to find twenty bushels, but there would be only ten. You would go to draw fifty gallons of wine from a vat, but find only twenty. ¹⁷I sent scorching winds and hail to ruin everything you tried to grow, but still you did not repent. ¹⁸Today is the twenty-fourth day of the ninth month, the day that the foundation of the Temple has been completed. See what is going to happen from now on. ¹⁹Although there is no grain left, and the grapevines, fig trees, pomegranates, and olive trees have not yet produced, yet from now on I will bless you."

The LORD's Promise to Zerubbabel

²⁰On that same day, the twenty-fourth of the month, the LORD gave Haggai a second message ²¹for Zerubbabel, the governor of Judah: "I am about to shake heaven and earth ²²and overthrow kingdoms and end their power. I will overturn chariots and their drivers; the horses will die, and their riders will kill one another. ²³On that day I will take you, Zerubbabel my servant, and I will appoint you to rule in my name. You are the one I have chosen." The LORD Almighty has spoken.

2.13 Nu 19.11-22

The Book of
ZECHARIAH

INTRODUCTION

The Book of Zechariah has two distinct parts: 1) *Chapters 1–8* Prophecies from the prophet Zechariah, dated at various times in the years from 520 to 518 B.C. These are largely in the form of visions, and deal with the restoration of Jerusalem, the rebuilding of the Temple, the purification of God's people, and the messianic age to come. 2) *Chapters 9–14* A collection of messages about the expected Messiah and the final judgment.

OUTLINE OF CONTENTS

The LORD Calls His People to Return to Him

1 In the eighth month of the second year that Darius was emperor of Persia, the LORD gave this message to the prophet Zechariah, the son of Berechiah and grandson of Iddo. ²The LORD Almighty told Zechariah to say to the people, "I, the LORD, was very angry with your ancestors, ³but now I say to you, 'Return to me, and I will return to you. ⁴Do not be like your ancestors. Long ago the prophets gave them my message, telling them not to live evil, sinful lives any longer. But they would not listen to me or obey me. ⁵Your ancestors and those prophets are no longer alive. ⁶Through my servants the prophets I gave your ancestors commands and warnings, but they disregarded them and suffered the consequences. Then they repented and acknowledged that I, the LORD Almighty, had punished them as they

deserved and as I had determined to do.'"

The Prophet's Vision of the Horses

⁷In the second year that Darius was emperor, on the twenty-fourth day of the eleventh month (the month of Shebat), the LORD gave me a message in a vision at night. ⁸I saw someone riding a red horse. He had stopped among some myrtle trees in a valley, and behind him were other horses — red, dappled, and white. ⁹I asked him, "Sir, what do these horses mean?"

He answered, "I will show you what they mean. ¹⁰The LORD sent them to go and inspect the earth."

¹¹They reported to the angel: "We have been all over the world and have found that the whole world lies helpless and subdued."

¹²Then the angel said, "Almighty LORD, you have been angry with Jerusalem and the cities of Judah for sev-

1.1 Ezra 4.24 — 5.1; 6.14   **1.8 a** Rev 6.4; **b** Rev 6.2

enty years now. How much longer will it be before you show them mercy?"

¹³The LORD answered the angel with comforting words, ¹⁴and the angel told me to proclaim what the LORD Almighty had said: "I have a deep love and concern for Jerusalem, my holy city, ¹⁵and I am very angry with the nations that enjoy quiet and peace. For while I was holding back my anger against my people, those nations made the sufferings of my people worse. ¹⁶So I have come back to Jerusalem to show mercy to the city. My Temple will be restored, and the city will be rebuilt."

¹⁷The angel also told me to proclaim: "The LORD Almighty says that his cities will be prosperous again and that he will once again help Jerusalem and claim the city as his own."

The Vision of the Horns

¹⁸In another vision I saw four ox horns. ¹⁹I asked the angel that had been speaking to me, "What do these horns mean?"

He answered, "They stand for the world powers that have scattered the people of Judah, Israel, and Jerusalem."

²⁰Then the LORD showed me four workers with hammers. ²¹I asked, "What have they come to do?"

He answered, "They have come to terrify and overthrow the nations that completely crushed the land of Judah and scattered its people."

The Vision of the Measuring Line

2 In another vision I saw a man with a measuring line in his hand. ²"Where are you going?" I asked.

"To measure Jerusalem," he answered, "to see how long and how wide it is."

³Then I saw the angel who had been speaking to me step forward, and an-

other angel came to meet him. ⁴The first one said to the other, "Run and tell that young man with the measuring line that there are going to be so many people and so much livestock in Jerusalem that it will be too big to have walls. ⁵The LORD has promised that he himself will be a wall of fire around the city to protect it and that he will live there in all his glory."

The Exiles Are Called to Come Home

⁶⁻⁷The LORD said to his people, "I scattered you in all directions. But now, you exiles, escape from Babylonia and return to Jerusalem. ⁸Anyone who strikes you strikes what is most precious to me."

So the LORD Almighty[a] sent me with this message for the nations that had plundered his people: ⁹"The LORD himself will fight against you, and you will be plundered by the people who were once your servants."

When this happens, everyone will know that the LORD Almighty sent me.

¹⁰The LORD said, "Sing for joy, people of Jerusalem! I am coming to live among you!"

¹¹At that time many nations will come to the LORD and become his people. He will live among you, and you will know that he has sent me to you. ¹²Once again Judah will be the special possession of the LORD in his sacred land, and Jerusalem will be the city he loves most of all.

¹³Be silent, everyone, in the presence of the LORD, for he is coming from his holy dwelling place.

The Prophet's Vision of the High Priest

3 In another vision the LORD showed me the High Priest Joshua standing before the angel of the

a Hebrew has two additional words, the meaning of which is unclear.
3.1 a Ezra 5.2; **b** Rev 12.10

LORD. And there beside Joshua stood Satan,[b] ready to bring an accusation against him. [2]The angel of the LORD[c] said to Satan, "May the LORD condemn you, Satan! May the LORD, who loves Jerusalem, condemn you. This man is like a stick snatched from the fire."

[3]Joshua was standing there, wearing filthy clothes. [4]The angel said to his heavenly attendants, "Take away the filthy clothes this man is wearing." Then he said to Joshua, "I have taken away your sin and will give you new clothes to wear."

[5]He commanded the attendants to put[d] a clean turban on Joshua's head. They did so, and then they put the new clothes on him while the angel of the LORD stood there.

[6]Then the angel told Joshua that [7]the LORD Almighty had said: "If you obey my laws and perform the duties I have assigned you, then you will continue to be in charge of my Temple and its courts, and I will hear your prayers, just as I hear the prayers of the angels who are in my presence. [8]Listen then, Joshua, you who are the High Priest; and listen, you fellow priests of his, you that are the sign of a good future: I will reveal my servant, who is called The Branch! [9]I am placing in front of Joshua a single stone with seven facets. I will engrave an inscription on it, and in a single day I will take away the sin of this land. [10]When that day comes, each of you will invite your neighbor to come and enjoy peace and security, surrounded by your vineyards and fig trees."

The Vision of the Lampstand

4 The angel who had been speaking to me came again and roused me as if I had been sleeping. [2]"What do you see?" he asked.

A single stone with seven facets (3.9)

"A lampstand made of gold," I answered. "At the top is a bowl for the oil. On the lampstand are seven lamps, each one with places for seven wicks. [3]There are two olive trees beside the lampstand, one on each side of it." [4]Then I asked the angel, "What do these things stand for, sir?"

[5]"Don't you know?" he asked me.

"No, I don't, sir," I replied.

[10b]The angel said to me, "The seven lamps are the seven eyes of the LORD, which see all over the earth."[e]

[11]Then I asked him, "What do the two olive trees on either side of the lampstand mean? [12]And what is the meaning of the two olive branches be-

[b] SATAN: *A supernatural being whose name indicates he was regarded as the opponent of human beings.*   [c] *One ancient translation* The angel of the LORD; *Hebrew* The LORD.   [d] *Some ancient translations* He commanded the attendants to put; *Hebrew* I said, "Let them put.   [e] *Verses 10b–14 are moved here from the end of the chapter in order to retain the natural sequence of the narrative.*

3.2 Jd 9   **3.8** Jr 23.5; 33.15; Zec 6.12   **3.10** Mic 4.4   **4.3** Rev 11.4   **4.6** Ezra 5.2   **4.10** Rev 5.6   **4.11** Rev 11.4

side the two gold pipes from which the olive oil pours?"

¹³He asked me, "Don't you know?"

"No, I don't, sir," I answered.

¹⁴Then he said, "These are the two men whom God has chosen and anointed to serve him, the Lord of the whole earth."

God's Promise to Zerubbabel

⁶The angel told me to give Zerubbabel this message from the LORD: "You will succeed, not by military might or by your own strength, but by my spirit. ⁷Obstacles as great as mountains will disappear before you. You will rebuild the Temple, and as you put the last stone in place, the people will shout, 'Beautiful, beautiful!' "

⁸Another message came to me from the LORD. ⁹He said, "Zerubbabel has laid the foundation of the Temple, and he will finish the building. When this happens, my people will know that it is I who sent you to them. ¹⁰ᵃThey are disappointed because so little progress is being made. But they will see Zerubbabel continuing to build the Temple, and they will be glad."

The Vision of the Flying Scroll

5 I looked again, and this time I saw a scroll flying through the air. ²The angel asked me what I saw. I answered, "A scroll flying through the air; it is thirty feet long and fifteen feet wide."

³Then he said to me, "On it is written the curse that is to go out over the whole land. On one side of the scroll it says that every thief will be removed from the land; and on the other side it says that everyone who tells lies under oath will also be taken away. ⁴The LORD Almighty says that he will send this curse out, and it will enter the house of every thief and the house of everyone

who tells lies under oath. It will remain in their houses and leave them in ruins."

The Vision of the Woman in the Basket

⁵The angel appeared again and said, "Look! Something else is coming!"

⁶"What is it?" I asked.

He replied, "It is a basket, and it stands for the sin𝒇 of the whole land."

⁷The basket had a lid made of lead. As I watched, the lid was raised, and there in the basket sat a woman!

There in the basket sat a woman! (5.7)

⁸The angel said, "This represents wickedness." Then he pushed her down into the basket and put the lid back down. ⁹I looked up and saw two women flying toward me with powerful wings like those of a stork. They picked up the basket and flew off with it.

¹⁰I asked the angel, "Where are they taking it?"

¹¹He answered, "To Babylonia, where they will build a temple for it. When the temple is finished, the basket will be placed there to be worshiped."

𝒇 *Some ancient translations* sin; *Hebrew* eye.

The Vision of the Four Chariots

6 I had another vision. This time I saw four chariots coming out from between two bronze mountains. ²The first chariot was pulled by red horses, the second by black horses, ³the third by white horses, and the fourth by dappled horses. ⁴Then I asked the angel, "Sir, what do these chariots mean?"

⁵He answered, "These are the four winds; they have just come from the presence of the Lord of all the earth."

⁶The chariot pulled by the black horses was going north to Babylonia, the white horses were going to the west, and the dappled horses were going to the country in the south. ⁷As the dappled horses came out, they were impatient to go and inspect the earth. The angel said, "Go and inspect the earth!"—and they did. ⁸Then the angel cried out to me, "The horses that went north to Babylonia have quieted the Lord's anger."

The Command to Crown Joshua

⁹The Lord gave me this message. ¹⁰He said, "Take the gifts given by the exiles Heldai, Tobijah, and Jedaiah, and go at once to the home of Josiah son of Zephaniah. All of them have returned from exile in Babylonia. ¹¹Make a crown out of the silver and gold they have given, and put it on the head of the High Priest, Joshua son of Jehozadak. ¹²Tell him that the Lord Almighty says, 'The man who is called The Branch will flourish where he is and rebuild the Lord's Temple. ¹³He is the one who will build it and receive the honor due a king, and he will rule his people. A priest will stand by his throne, and they will work together in peace and harmony.' ¹⁴The crown will be a memorial in the Lord's Temple in honor of Heldai,ᵍ Tobijah, Jedaiah, and Josiah."ʰ

¹⁵Men who live far away will come and help to rebuild the Temple of the Lord. And when it is rebuilt, you will know that the Lord Almighty sent me to you. This will all happen if you fully obey the commands of the Lord your God.

The Lord Condemns Insincere Fasting

7 In the fourth year that Darius was emperor, on the fourth day of the ninth month (the month of Kislev), the Lord gave me a message.

²The people of Bethel had sent Sharezer and Regemmelech and their men to the Temple of the Lord Almighty to pray for the Lord's blessing ³and to ask the priests and the prophets this question: "Should we continue to mourn because of the destruction of the Temple, by fasting in the fifth month as we have done for so many years now?"

⁴This is the message of the Lord that came to me. ⁵He said, "Tell the people of the land and the priests that when they fasted and mourned in the fifth and seventh months during these seventy years, it was not in honor of me. ⁶And when they ate and drank, it was for their own satisfaction."

⁷This is what the Lord said through the earlier prophets at the time when Jerusalem was prosperous and filled with people and when there were many people living not only in the towns around the city but also in the southern region and in the western foothills.

Disobedience, the Cause of Exile

⁸The Lord gave this message to Zechariah: ⁹"Long ago I gave these commands to my people: 'You must see that justice is done, and must show

---

ᵍ One ancient translation Heldai; Hebrew Helem. Hebrew Hen.   ʰ One ancient translation Josiah;

6.2 a Rev 6.4; **b** Rev 6.5   **6.3** Rev 6.2   **6.5** Rev 7.1   **6.12** Jr 23.5; 33.15; Zec 3.8

May you receive the same blessings that came to Judah and Israel! (8.13)

kindness and mercy to one another. ¹⁰Do not oppress widows, orphans, foreigners who live among you, or anyone else in need. And do not plan ways of harming one another.'

¹¹"But my people stubbornly refused to listen. They closed their minds ¹²and made their hearts as hard as rock. Because they would not listen to the teaching which I sent through the prophets who lived long ago, I became very angry. ¹³Because they did not listen when I spoke, I did not answer when they prayed. ¹⁴Like a storm I swept them away to live in foreign countries. This good land was left a desolate place, with no one living in it."

The Lord Promises to Restore Jerusalem

8 The Lord Almighty gave this message to Zechariah: ²"I have longed to help Jerusalem because of my deep love for her people, a love which has made me angry with her enemies. ³I will return to Jerusalem, my holy city, and live there. It will be known as the faithful city, and the hill of the Lord

Almightyⁱ will be called the sacred hill. ⁴Once again old men and women, so old that they use canes when they walk, will be sitting in the city squares. ⁵And the streets will again be full of boys and girls playing.

⁶"This may seem impossible to those of the nation who are now left, but it's not impossible for me. ⁷I will rescue my people from the lands where they have been taken, ⁸and will bring them back from east and west to live in Jerusalem. They will be my people, and I will be their God, ruling over them faithfully and justly.

⁹"Have courage! You are now hearing the same words the prophets spoke at the time the foundation was being laid for rebuilding my Temple. ¹⁰Before that time no one could afford to hire either men or animals, and no one was safe from enemies. I turned people against one another. ¹¹But now I am treating the survivors of this nation differently. ¹²They will plant their crops in peace. Their vines will bear grapes, the earth will produce crops, and there will be plenty of rain. I will give all these blessings to the people of my nation

8.1-8 An 1.9; 2.10; M 11.21, 23; L 10.13, 14; 9.9-11; 11.20-31; Jr 4.7; 17.2-3, 6; T] 2.17-18; R3 2.2, 2; J1 1.2.

ⁱ HILL OF THE LORD ALMIGHTY: *Mount Zion (see Zion in Word List).*

who survive. ¹³ People of Judah and Israel! In the past foreigners have cursed one another by saying, 'May the same disasters fall on you that fell on Judah and Israel!' But I will save you, and then those foreigners will say to one another, 'May you receive the same blessings that came to Judah and Israel!' So have courage and don't be afraid."

¹⁴ The LORD Almighty says, "When your ancestors made me angry, I planned disaster for them and did not change my mind, but carried out my plans. ¹⁵ But now I am planning to bless the people of Jerusalem and Judah. So don't be afraid. ¹⁶ These are the things you should do: Speak the truth to one another. In the courts give real justice — the kind that brings peace. ¹⁷ Do not plan ways of harming one another. Do not give false testimony under oath. I hate lying, injustice, and violence."

¹⁸ The LORD Almighty gave this message to Zechariah: ¹⁹ "The fasts held in the fourth, fifth, seventh, and tenth months will become festivals of joy and gladness for the people of Judah. You must love truth and peace."

²⁰ The LORD Almighty says, "The time is coming when people from many^j cities will come to Jerusalem. ²¹ Those from one city will say to those from another, 'We are going to worship the LORD Almighty and pray for his blessing. Come with us!' ²² Many^j peoples and powerful nations will come to Jerusalem to worship the LORD Almighty and to pray for his blessing. ²³ In those days ten foreigners will come to one Jew and say, 'We want to share in your destiny, because we have heard that God is with you.'"

Judgment on Neighboring Nations

9 This is the LORD's message:
He has decreed punishment for the land of Hadrach and for the city of Damascus. Not only the tribes of Israel but also the capital of Syria belong to the LORD. ² Hamath, which borders on Hadrach, also belongs to him, and so do the cities of Tyre and Sidon, with all their skill. ³ Tyre has built fortifications for herself and has piled up so much silver and gold that it is as common as dirt! ⁴ But the Lord will take away everything she has. He will throw her wealth into the sea, and the city will be burned to the ground.

⁵ The city of Ashkelon will see this and be afraid. The city of Gaza will see it and suffer great pain. So will Ekron, and her hopes will be shattered. Gaza will lose her king, and Ashkelon will be left deserted. ⁶ People of mixed race will live in Ashdod. The LORD says, "I will humble all these proud Philistines. ⁷ They will no longer eat meat with blood in it, or other forbidden food. All the survivors will become part of my people and be like a clan in the tribe of Judah. Ekron will become part of my people, as the Jebusites^k did. ⁸ I will guard my land and keep armies from passing through it. I will not allow tyrants to oppress my people any more. I have seen how my people have suffered."

The Future King

⁹ Rejoice, rejoice, people of Zion!
    Shout for joy, you people of
      Jerusalem!
   Look, your king is coming
      to you!
   He comes triumphant and
      victorious,

---

^{j} many; or great. ^{k} JEBUSITES: *The original inhabitants of Jerusalem, who became David's subjects after he captured the city.*
8.16 Eph 4.25   **9.1** Is 17.1-3; Jr 49.23-27; Am 1.3-5   **9.1-4** Is 23.1-18; Ez 26.1—28.26; Jl 3.4-8; Am 1.9, 10; Mt 11.21, 22; Lk 10.13, 14   **9.5-7** Is 14.29-31; Jr 47.1-7; Ez 25.15-17; Jl 3.4-8; Am 1.6-8; Zep 2.4-7   **9.9** Mt 21.5; Jn 12.15

but humble and riding on a
      donkey —
  on a colt, the foal of a donkey.

Look, your king is coming to you! (9.9)

¹⁰ The LORD says,
"I will remove the war chariots
      from Israel
  and take the horses from
      Jerusalem;
  the bows used in battle will be
      destroyed.
  Your king will make peace
      among the nations;
  he will rule from sea to sea,
  from the Euphrates River to
      the ends of the earth."

The Restoration of God's People

¹¹ The LORD says,
"Because of my covenant
      with you
  that was sealed by the blood
      of sacrifices,
  I will set your people free —
  free from the waterless pit of
      exile.
¹² Return, you exiles who now have
      hope;
  return to your place of safety.
  Now I tell you that I will repay
      you twice over
  with blessing for all you have
      suffered.

¹³ I will use Judah like a
      soldier's bow
  and Israel like the arrows.
  I will use the men of Zion like a
      sword,
  to fight the men of Greece."

¹⁴ The LORD will appear above his
      people;
  he will shoot his arrows like
      lightning.
  The Sovereign LORD will sound
      the trumpet;
  he will march in the storms
      from the south.
¹⁵ The LORD Almighty will protect
      his people,
  and they will destroy their
      enemies.
  They will shout in battle like
      drunk men
  and will shed the blood of
      their enemies;
  it will flow like the blood of a
      sacrifice
  poured on the altar from a
      bowl.ⁱ

¹⁶ When that day comes, the LORD
      will save his people,
  as a shepherd saves his flock
      from danger.
  They will shine in his land
  like the jewels of a crown.
¹⁷ How good and beautiful the land
      will be!
  The young people will grow
      strong on its grain and
      wine.

The LORD Promises Deliverance

10 Ask the LORD for rain in the
      spring of the year. It is the
LORD who sends rain clouds and
showers, making the fields green for
everyone. ² People consult idols and
fortunetellers, but the answers they get

ⁱ *Verse 15 in Hebrew is unclear.*
9.10 Ps 72.8   **9.11** Ex 24.8   **10.2** Mt 9.36; Mk 6.34

are lies and nonsense. Some interpret dreams, but only mislead you; the comfort they give is useless. So the people wander about like lost sheep. They are in trouble because they have no leader.

³The LORD says, "I am angry with those foreigners who rule my people, and I am going to punish them. The people of Judah are mine, and I, the LORD Almighty, will take care of them. They will be my powerful war-horses. ⁴From among them will come rulers, leaders, and commanders to govern my people.ᵐ ⁵The people of Judah will be victorious like soldiers who trample their enemies in the mud of the streets. They will fight because the LORD is with them, and they will defeat even the enemy cavalry.

> ⁶"I will make the people of Judah
> strong;
> I will rescue the people of
> Israel.
> I will have compassion on them
> and bring them all back
> home.
> They will be as though I had
> never rejected them.
> I am the LORD their God; I
> will answer their prayers.
> ⁷The people of Israel will be
> strong like soldiers,
> happy like those who have
> been drinking wine.
> Their descendants will remember
> this victory
> and be glad because of what
> the LORD has done.

> ⁸"I will call my people
> and gather them together.
> I will rescue them
> and make them as numerous
> as they used to be.

> ⁹Though I have scattered them
> among the nations,
> yet in far-off places they will
> remember me.
> They and their children will
> survive
> and return home together.
> ¹⁰From Egypt and Assyria I will
> bring them home
> and settle them in their own
> country.
> I will settle them in Gilead and
> Lebanon also;
> the whole land will be filled
> with people.
> ¹¹When they pass through their
> sea of trouble,
> I, the LORD, will strike the
> waves,
> and the depths of the Nile will
> go dry.
> Proud Assyria will be humbled,
> and mighty Egypt will lose
> her power.
> ¹²I will make my people strong;
> they will worship and
> obey me."

The LORD has spoken.

The Fall of the Tyrants

11 Open your doors, Lebanon,
> so that fire can burn down
> your cedar trees!ⁿ
> ²Weep and wail, cypress trees —
> the cedars have fallen;
> those glorious trees have been
> destroyed!
> Weep and wail, oaks of
> Bashan —
> the dense forest has been
> cut down!
> ³The rulers cry out in grief;
> their glory is gone!
> Listen to the roaring of the lions;

ᵐ *From among . . . people; or* All oppressors—rulers, leaders, and commanders—will depart together from Judah.   ⁿ CEDAR TREES: *Trees are used here as symbols of powerful nations or their kings.*
10.9, 10 Ba 2.20-32

their forest home along the
Jordan is destroyed!

The Two Shepherds

He has abandoned his flock. (11.17)

⁴The Lord my God said to me, "Act
the part of the shepherd⁰ of a flock of
sheep that are going to be butchered.
⁵Their owners kill them and go unpunished. They sell the meat and say,
'Praise the Lord! We are rich!' Even
their own shepherds have no pity on
them."

(⁶The Lord said, "I will no longer
pity anyone on earth. I myself will put
all the people in the power of their rulers. These rulers will devastate the
earth, and I will not save it from their
power.")

⁷Those who bought and sold the
sheep hired me, and I became the shepherd of the sheep that were going to be
butchered. I took two sticks: one I
called "Favor" and the other "Unity."
And I took care of the flock. ⁸I lost patience with three other shepherds, who
hated me, and I got rid of them all in a
single month. ⁹Then I said to the flock,
"I will not be your shepherd any longer.
Let those die who are to die. Let those
be destroyed who are to be destroyed.
Those who are left will destroy one another." ¹⁰Then I took the stick called
"Favor" and broke it, to cancel the covenant which the Lord had made with all
the nations. ¹¹So the covenant was canceled on that day. Those who bought
and sold the sheep were watching me,
and they knew that the Lord was
speaking through what I did. ¹²I said to
them, "If you are willing, give me my
wages. But if not, keep them." So they
paid me thirty pieces of silver as my
wages.

¹³The Lord said to me, "Put them in
the Temple treasury."ᵖ So I took the
thirty pieces of silver — the magnificent
sum they thought I was worth — and
put them in the Temple treasury.
¹⁴Then I broke the second stick, the
one called "Unity," and the unity of Judah and Israel was shattered.

¹⁵Then the Lord said to me, "Once
again act the part of a shepherd, this
time a worthless one. ¹⁶I have put a
shepherd in charge of my flock, but he
does not help the sheep that are threatened by destruction; nor does he look
for the lost, or heal those that are hurt,
or feed the healthy. Instead, he eats the
meat of the fattest sheep and tears off
their hoofs. ¹⁷That worthless shepherd
is doomed! He has abandoned his flock.

War will totally destroy his power. His arm will wither, and his right eye will go blind."

The Future Deliverance of Jerusalem

12 This is a message about Israel from the LORD, the LORD who spread out the skies, created the earth, and gave life to man. He says, ²"I will make Jerusalem like a cup of wine; the nations around her will drink and stagger like drunks. And when they besiege Jerusalem, the cities of the rest of Judah will also be besieged. ³But when that time comes, I will make Jerusalem like a heavy stone — any nation that tries to lift it will be hurt. All the nations of the world will join forces to attack her. ⁴At that time I will terrify all their horses and make all their riders go crazy. I will watch over the people of Judah, but I will make the horses of their enemies blind. ⁵Then the clans of Judah will say to themselves, 'The LORD God Almighty gives strength to his people who live in Jerusalem.'

⁶"At that time I will make the clans of Judah like a fire in a forest or in a field of ripe grain — they will destroy all the surrounding nations. The people of Jerusalem will remain safe in the city.

⁷"I, the LORD, will give victory to the armies of Judah first, so that the honor which the descendants of David and the people of Jerusalem will receive will be no greater than that of the rest of Judah. ⁸At that time the LORD will protect those who live in Jerusalem, and even the weakest among them will become as strong as David was. The descendants of David will lead them like the angel of the LORD, like God himself. ⁹At that time I will destroy every nation that tries to attack Jerusalem.

¹⁰"I will fill the descendants of David and the other people of Jerusalem with the spirit of mercy and the spirit of prayer. They will look at the one whom they stabbed to death, and they will mourn for him like those who mourn for an only child. They will mourn bitterly, like those who have lost their first-born son. ¹¹At that time the mourning in Jerusalem will be as great as the mourning for Hadad Rimmon*q* in the plain of Megiddo. ¹²⁻¹⁴Each family in the land will mourn by itself: the family descended from David, the family descended from Nathan, the family descended from Levi, the family descended from Shimei, and all the other families. Each family will mourn by itself, and the men of each family will mourn separately from the women.

13 "When that time comes," says the LORD Almighty, "a fountain will be opened to purify the descendants of David and the people of Jerusalem from their sin and idolatry. ²At that time I will remove the names of the idols from the land, and no one will remember them any more. I will get rid of anyone who claims to be a prophet and will take away the desire to worship idols. ³Then if anyone still insists on prophesying, his own father and mother will tell him that he must be put to death, because he claimed to speak the LORD's word, but spoke lies instead. When he prophesies, his own father and mother will stab him to death. ⁴When that time comes, no prophet will be proud of his visions or act like a prophet or wear a prophet's coarse garment in order to deceive people. ⁵Instead, he will say, 'I am not a prophet. I am a farmer — I have farmed the land all my life.' ⁶Then if someone asks him, 'What are those wounds on your chest?' he will answer, 'I got them at a friend's house.'"

---

q HADAD RIMMON: *Probably a name for Baal, the god of vegetation in Canaan and Syria. When the vegetation died each year, the worshipers thought that the god had died, and they mourned his death.*

12.10 Jn 19.37; Rev 1.7   **12.10-14** Mt 24.20; Rev 1.7

The Command to Kill God's Shepherd

7 The LORD Almighty says, "Wake up, sword, and attack the shepherd*r* who works for me! Kill him, and the sheep will be scattered. I will attack my people 8 and throughout the land two-thirds of the people will die. 9 And I will test the third that survives and will purify them as silver is purified by fire. I will test them as gold is tested. Then they will pray to me, and I will answer them. I will tell them that they are my people, and they will confess that I am their God."

Jerusalem and the Nations

14 The day when the LORD will sit in judgment is near. Then Jerusalem will be looted, and the loot will be divided up before your eyes. 2 The LORD will bring all the nations together to make war on Jerusalem. The city will be taken, the houses looted, and the women raped. Half of the people will go into exile, but the rest of them will not be taken away from the city. 3 Then the LORD will go out and fight against those nations, as he has fought in times past. 4 At that time he will stand on the Mount of Olives, to the east of Jerusalem. Then the Mount of Olives will be split in two from east to west by a large valley. Half of the mountain will move northward, and half of it southward. 5 You will escape through this valley that divides the mountain in two.*s* You will flee as your ancestors did when the earthquake struck in the time of King Uzziah of Judah. The LORD my God will come, bringing all the angels with him. 6 When that time comes, there will no longer be cold or frost,*t* 7 nor any darkness. There will always be daylight, even at nighttime. When this will happen is known only to the LORD.

8 When that day comes, fresh water will flow from Jerusalem, half of it to the Dead Sea and the other half to the Mediterranean. It will flow all year long, in the dry season as well as the wet. 9 Then the LORD will be king over all the earth; everyone will worship him as God and know him by the same name.

10 The whole region, from Geba in the north to Rimmon in the south, will be made level. Jerusalem will tower above the land around it; the city will reach from the Benjamin Gate to the Corner Gate, where there had been an earlier gate, and from the Tower of Hananel to the royal wine presses. 11 The people will live there in safety, no longer threatened by destruction.

12 The LORD will bring a terrible disease on all the nations that make war on Jerusalem. Their flesh will rot away while they are still alive; their eyes and their tongues will rot away.

13 At that time the LORD will make them so confused and afraid that everyone will seize the man next to him and attack him. 14 The men of Judah will fight to defend Jerusalem. They will take as loot the wealth of all the nations — gold, silver, and clothing in great abundance.

15 A terrible disease will also fall on the horses, the mules, the camels, and the donkeys — on all the animals in the camps of the enemy.

16 Then all of the survivors from the nations that have attacked Jerusalem will go there each year to worship the LORD Almighty as king and to celebrate the Festival of Shelters. 17 If any nation refuses to go and worship the LORD Almighty as king, then rain will not fall on their land. 18 If the Egyptians refuse to celebrate the Festival of Shelters,

---

r SHEPHERD: *See 11.4.*   *s Probable text* You will escape . . . in two; *Hebrew unclear.*
t Probable text cold or frost; *Hebrew unclear.*
13.7 Mt 26.31; Mk 14.27   **14.8** Ez 47.1; Jn 7.38; Rev 22.1   **14.11** Rev 22.3
14.16 Lv 23.39-43

then they will be struck by the same disease that the LORD will send on every nation that refuses to go. ¹⁹This will be the punishment that will fall on Egypt and on all the other nations if they do not celebrate the Festival of Shelters.

²⁰At that time even the harness bells of the horses will be inscribed with the words "Dedicated to the LORD." The cooking pots in the Temple will be as sacred as the bowls before the altar. ²¹Every cooking pot in Jerusalem and in all Judah will be set apart for use in the worship of the LORD Almighty. The people who offer sacrifices will use them for boiling the meat of the sacrifices. When that time comes, there will no longer be any merchant in the Temple of the LORD Almighty.

The Book of
MALACHI

INTRODUCTION

The Book of Malachi comes from some time in the fifth century B.C. after the Temple in Jerusalem was rebuilt. The prophet's main concern is to call priests and people to renew their faithfulness to their covenant with God. It is clear that there is laxity and corruption in the life and worship of God's people. Priests and people are cheating God by not giving him the offerings that are rightly due him, and by not living according to his teaching. But the Lord will come to judge and purify his people, sending ahead of him his messenger to prepare the way and to proclaim his covenant.

OUTLINE OF CONTENTS

1 This is the message that the LORD gave Malachi to tell the people of Israel.

The LORD's Love for Israel

²The LORD says to his people, "I have always loved you."

But they reply, "How have you shown your love for us?"

The LORD answers, "Esau and Jacob were brothers, but I have loved Jacob and his descendants, ³and have hated Esau and his descendants. I have devastated Esau's hill country and abandoned the land to jackals."

⁴If Esau's descendants, the Edom-

1.2, 3 Ro 9.13 **1.2-5** Is 34.5-17; 63.1-6; Jr 49.7-22; Ez 25.12-14; 35.1-15; Am 1.11, 12; Ob 1-14 tes, say, "Our towns have been destroyed, but we will rebuild them," then the LORD will reply, "Let them rebuild — I will tear them down again. People will call them 'The evil country' and 'The nation with whom the LORD is angry forever.' "

⁵ The people of Israel are going to see this with their own eyes, and they will say, "The LORD is mighty even outside the land of Israel!"

The LORD Reprimands the Priests

⁶ The LORD Almighty says to the priests, "Children honor their parents, and servants honor their masters. I am your father — why don't you honor me? I am your master — why don't you respect me? You despise me, and yet you ask, 'How have we despised you?' ⁷ This is how — by offering worthless food on my altar. Then you ask, 'How have we failed to respect you?' I will tell you — by showing contempt for my altar. ³ When you bring a blind or sick or lame animal to sacrifice to me, do you think there's nothing wrong with that? Try giving an animal like that to the governor! Would he be pleased with you or grant you any favors?"

⁹ Now, you priests, try asking God to be good to us. He will not answer your prayer, and it will be your fault. ¹⁰ The LORD Almighty says, "I wish one of you would close the Temple doors so as to prevent you from lighting useless fires on my altar. I am not pleased with you; I will not accept the offerings you bring me. ¹¹ People from one end of the world to the other honor me. Everywhere they burn incense to me and offer acceptable sacrifices. All of them honor me! ¹² But you dishonor me when you say that my altar is worthless and when you offer on it food that you despise. ¹³ You say, 'How tired we are of all this!' and

you turn up your nose at me. As your offering to me you bring a stolen animal or one that is lame or sick. Do you think I will accept that from you? ¹⁴ A curse on the cheater who sacrifices a worthless animal to me, when he has in his flock a good animal that he promised to give me! For I am a great king, and people of all nations fear me."

2 The LORD Almighty says to the priests, "This command is for you: ² You must honor me by what you do. If you will not listen to what I say, then I will bring a curse on you. I will put a curse on the things you receive for your support. In fact, I have already put a curse on them, because you do not take my command seriously. ³ I will punish your children and rub your faces in the dung of the animals you sacrifice — and you will be taken out to the dung heap. ⁴ Then you will know that I have given you this command, so that my covenant with the priests, the descendants of Levi, will not be broken.

⁵ "In my covenant I promised them life and well-being, and this is what I gave them, so that they might respect me. In those days they did respect and fear me. ⁶ They taught what was right, not what was wrong. They lived in harmony with me; they not only did what was right themselves, but they also helped many others to stop doing evil. ⁷ It is the duty of priests to teach the true knowledge of God. People should go to them to learn my will, because they are the messengers of the LORD Almighty.

⁸ "But now you priests have turned away from the right path. Your teaching has led many to do wrong. You have broken the covenant I made with you. ⁹ So I, in turn, will make the people of Israel despise you because you do not obey my will, and when you teach my people, you do not treat everyone alike."

The People's Unfaithfulness to God

¹⁰ Don't we all have the same father? Didn't the same God create us all? Then why do we break our promises to one another, and why do we despise the covenant that God made with our ancestors? ¹¹ The people of Judah have broken their promise to God and done a horrible thing in Jerusalem and all over the country. They have defiled the Temple which the LORD loves. Men have married women who worship foreign gods. ¹² May the LORD remove from the community of Israel those who did this, and never again let them participate in the offerings our nation brings to the LORD Almighty.ᵃ

¹³ This is another thing you do. You drown the LORD's altar with tears, weeping and wailing because he no longer accepts the offerings you bring him. ¹⁴ You ask why he no longer accepts them. It is because he knows you have broken your promise to the wife you married when you were young. She was your partner, and you have broken your promise to her, although you promised before God that you would be faithful to her. ¹⁵ Didn't God make you one body and spirit with her?ᵇ What was his purpose in this? It was that you should have children who are truly God's people. So make sure that none of you breaks his promise to his wife. ¹⁶ "I hate divorce," says the LORD God of Israel. "I hate it when one of you does such a cruel thing to his wife. Make sure that you do not break your promise to be faithful to your wife."

The Day of Judgment Is Near

¹⁷ You have tired the LORD out with your talk. But you ask, "How have we tired him?" By saying, "The LORD Almighty thinks all evildoers are good; in fact he likes them." Or by asking, "Where is the God who is supposed to be just?"

3 The LORD Almighty answers, "I will send my messenger to prepare the way for me. Then the Lord you are looking for will suddenly come to his Temple. The messenger you long to see will come and proclaim my covenant."

² But who will be able to endure the day when he comes? Who will be able to survive when he appears? He will be like strong soap, like a fire that refines metal. ³ He will come to judge like one who refines and purifies silver. As a metalworker refines silver and gold, so the LORD's messenger will purify the priests, so that they will bring to the LORD the right kind of offerings. ⁴ Then the offerings which the people of Judah and Jerusalem bring to the LORD will be pleasing to him, as they used to be in the past.

⁵ The LORD Almighty says, "I will appear among you to judge, and I will testify at once against those who practice magic, against adulterers, against those who give false testimony, those who cheat employees out of their wages, and those who take advantage of widows, orphans, and foreigners — against all who do not respect me.

The Payment of Tithes

⁶ "I am the LORD, and I do not change. And so you, the descendants of Jacob, are not yet completely lost. ⁷ You, like your ancestors before you, have turned away from my laws and have not

ᵃ One ancient translation May . . . Almighty; Hebrew unclear. God . . . her; Hebrew unclear.   ᵇ Probable text Didn't

3.1 Mt 11.10; Mk 1.2; Lk 1.76; 7.27   **3.2** Jl 2.11; Rev 6.17   **3.6** Si 48.10

I am the LORD, and I do not change. (3.6)

kept them. Turn back to me, and I will turn to you. But you ask, 'What must we do to turn back to you?' ⁸I ask you, is it right for a person to cheat God? Of course not, yet you are cheating me. 'How?' you ask. In the matter of tithes and offerings. ⁹A curse is on all of you because the whole nation is cheating me. ¹⁰Bring the full amount of your tithes to the Temple, so that there will be plenty of food there. Put me to the test and you will see that I will open the windows of heaven and pour out on you in abundance all kinds of good things. ¹¹I will not let insects destroy your crops, and your grapevines will be loaded with grapes. ¹²Then the people of all nations will call you happy, because your land will be a good place to live.

God's Promise of Mercy

¹³"You have said terrible things about me," says the LORD. "But you ask,

'What have we said about you?' ¹⁴You have said, 'It's useless to serve God. What's the use of doing what he says or of trying to show the LORD Almighty that we are sorry for what we have done? ¹⁵As we see it, proud people are the ones who are happy. Evil people not only prosper, but they test God's patience with their evil deeds and get away with it.' "

¹⁶Then the people who feared the LORD spoke to one another, and the LORD listened and heard what they said. In his presence, there was written down in a book a record of those who feared the LORD and respected him. ¹⁷"They will be my people," says the LORD Almighty. "On the day when I act, they will be my very own. I will be merciful to them as parents are merciful to the children who serve them. ¹⁸Once again my people will see the difference between what happens to the righteous and to the wicked, to the person who serves me and the one who does not."

The Day of the LORD Is Coming

4 The LORD Almighty says, "The day is coming when all proud and evil people will burn like straw. On that day they will burn up, and there will be nothing left of them. ²But for you who obey me, my saving power will rise on you like the sun and bring healing like the sun's rays. You will be as free and happy as calves let out of a stall. ³On the day when I act, you will overcome the wicked, and they will be like dust under your feet.

⁴"Remember the teachings of my servant Moses, the laws and commands

3.10 Lv 27.30; Nu 18.21-24; Dt 12.6; 14.22-29; Ne 13.12

which I gave him at Mount Sinai for all the people of Israel to obey.

5"But before the great and terrible day of the LORD comes, I will send you the prophet Elijah. 6 He will bring fathers and children together again; otherwise I would have to come and destroy your country."

4.5 Mt 11.14; 17.10-13; Mk 9.11-13; Lk 1.17; Jn 1.21

My saving power will rise on you like the sun. (4.2)

DEUTEROCANONICALS/ APOCRYPHA

Introduction

The following books, Tobit, Judith, Additions to Esther (Greek text), Wisdom of Solomon, Sirach, Baruch, Letter of Jeremiah, Additions to Daniel (Three Young Men, Susanna, Bel and the Dragon), 1 Maccabees, and 2 Maccabees, formed part of the Septuagint Greek text and were interspersed among other books of the Old Testament.

This Greek text was not only widely used by Jews but was known as well by numerous "God-fearing" Gentiles who were attracted to the high moral teachings of the Old Testament, even though they had not themselves become converts to Judaism. One can thus readily understand how and why early Christianity, as it spread among Greek-speaking Jews and Gentiles, employed this Greek text. In fact, the majority of Old Testament quotations in the New Testament are based on this translation.

Precisely when Jewish leadership officially adopted the traditional 39 books of the so-called "Hebrew Canon" is not known, nor is there agreement as to exactly what criteria were used in determining this canon. According to tradition the determination of the books of the Hebrew canon was made about A.D. 90, but there is evidence to believe that official and widespread agreement on this issue came somewhat later.

Among Christians it was apparently only in the fourth century that the issue of the canonicity of these books arose, a situation which is reflected in Jerome's placing these books in a separated section in his Vulgate translation of the Old Testament.

In 1546 at the Council of Trent the Roman Catholic Church officially declared these books to be sacred and canonical and to be accepted "with equal devotion and reverence."

At the time of the Reformation Martin Luther did not regard these books as Scripture but as "useful and good for reading." In his German translation of the Old Bible he followed the practice of Jerome in placing them at the end of the Old Testament with the superscription "Apocrypha." Protestants generally continued this practice in their translations of the Bible into such languages as Swedish, Norwegian, Danish, Slovenian, French, Spanish, and English (King James Version).

Among Christians who do not accept these books as Scripture there is, however, widespread agreement as to their importance in providing much valuable information on Jewish history, life, thought, worship, and religious practice during the centuries immediately prior to the time of Christ. Accordingly, they make possible a clearer understanding of the historical and cultural situation in which Jesus lived and taught.

Catholics speak of these books as "deuterocanonical," to indicate that their canonical status as Scripture was settled later than that of the protocanonical books. Protestants usually refer to these books as Apocrypha.

i

DEUTEROCANONICALS/
APOCRYPHA

Introduction

The following books: Tobit, Judith, Esther (the Greek text), Wisdom of Solomon, Sirach, Baruch, Letter of Jeremiah, Song of the Three Young Men, Susanna, Bel and the Dragon, 1 Maccabees, and 2 Maccabees, formed part of the Septuagint Greek text and were interspersed among other books of the Old Testament.

This Greek text was not only widely used by Jews but was known as well by numerous "God-fearing" Gentiles who were attracted to the high moral teachings of the Old Testament, even though they had not themselves become converts to Judaism. One can thus readily understand how and why early Christianity, as it spread among Greek-speaking Jews and Gentiles, employed this Greek text. In fact, the majority of Old Testament quotations in the New Testament are based on this translation.

Precisely when Jewish leadership officially adopted the traditional 39 books of the so-called "Hebrew Canon" is not known; nor is there agreement as to exactly what criteria were used in determining the canon. According to tradition the determination of the books of the Hebrew canon was made about A.D. 90, but there is evidence to believe that official and widespread agreement on this issue came somewhat later.

Among Christians it was apparently only in the fourth century that the issue of the canonicity of these books arose, a situation which is reflected in Jerome's placing these books in a separated section in his Vulgate translation of the Old Testament.

In 1546 at the Council of Trent the Roman Catholic Church officially declared these books to be sacred and canonical and to be accepted "with equal devotion and reverence."

At the time of the Reformation Martin Luther did not regard these books as Scripture but as "useful and good for reading." In his German translation of the Bible he followed the practice of Jerome in placing them at the end of the Old Testament with the superscription "Apocrypha." Protestants generally continued this practice in their translations of the Bible into such languages as Swedish, Norwegian, Danish, Slovenian, French, Spanish and English (King James Version).

Among Christians who do not accept these books as Scripture there is, however, widespread agreement as to their importance in providing much valuable information on Jewish history, life, thought, worship, and religious practice during the centuries immediately prior to the time of Christ. Accordingly, they make possible a clearer understanding of the historical and cultural situation in which Jesus lived and taught.

Catholics speak of these books as "deuterocanonical" to indicate that their canonical status as Scripture was settled later than that of the protocanonical books. Protestants usually refer to these books as Apocrypha.

The Book of
TOBIT

INTRODUCTION

The Book of Tobit, originally written in Hebrew or Aramaic, is a story which tells of miraculous help to God's faithful people and teaches Jewish piety and morality. The book offers a vivid picture of Jewish religion and culture in the period prior to the New Testament.

OUTLINE OF CONTENTS

---

1 I am Tobit and this is the story of my life. My father was Tobiel, my grandfather was Ananiel, and my great-grandfather was Aduel. Aduel's father was Gabael; his grandfather was Raphael; and his great-grandfather was Raguel, who belonged to the clan of Asiel, a part of the tribe of Naphtali. ²During the time that Shalmaneser was emperor of Assyria, I was taken captive in my hometown of Thisbe, located in northern Galilee, south of Kadesh in Naphtali, northwest of Hazor, and north of Phogor.

Tobit's Early Life

³All my life I have been honest and have tried to do what was right. I often gave money to help needy relatives and other Jews who had been deported with me to Nineveh, the capital of Assyria.

⁴When I was young, I lived in northern Israel. All the tribes in Israel were supposed to offer sacrifices in Jerusalem. It was the one city that God had chosen from among all the Israelite cities as the place where his holy and eternal home. But my entire tribe of Naphtali rejected the city of Jerusalem and the kings descended from David. ⁵Like everyone else in this tribe, my own family used to go to the city of Dan in the mountains of northern Galilee to offer sacrifices to the gold bull-calf which King Jeroboam of Israel had set up there.

1.2 2 K 17.3; 18.9   **1.5** 1 K 12.28, 29

Tobit's Faithfulness to His Religion

6 I was the only one in my family who regularly went to Jerusalem to celebrate the religious festivals, as the Law of Moses commands everyone to do. I would hurry off to Jerusalem with the first part of my harvest, the first-born of my animals, a tenth of my cattle, and the freshly clipped wool from my sheep. Then I would stand before the altar in the Temple, and give these offerings to the priests, the descendants of Aaron.

I would hurry off to Jerusalem with the first part of my harvest. (1.6)

7 I would give a tenth of my grain, wine, olive oil, pomegranates, figs, and other fruits to the Levites who served God in Jerusalem. Every year, except the seventh year when the land was at rest,[a] I would sell a second tenth of my possessions and spend the money in Jerusalem on the festival meal.

8 But every third year, I would give a third tithe[b] to widows and orphans and to foreigners living among my people, and we would eat the festival meal together. I did this in keeping with the Law of Moses, which Deborah, the mother of my grandfather Ananiel, had

taught me to obey. (I had been left an orphan when my father died.)

Tobit's Faithfulness in Exile

9 When I grew up, I married Anna, a member of my own tribe. We had a son and named him Tobias. **10** Later, I was taken captive and deported to Assyria, and that is how I came to live in Nineveh.

While we lived in Nineveh, all my relatives and the other Jews used to eat the same kind of food as the other people who lived there, **11** but I refused to do so. **12** Since I took seriously the commands of the Most High God, **13** he made Emperor Shalmaneser respect me, and I was placed in charge of purchasing all the emperor's supplies.

14 Before the emperor died, I made regular trips to the land of Media to buy things for him there. Once, when I was in the city of Rages in Media, I left some bags of money there with Gabael, Gabrias' brother, and asked him to keep them for me. There were more than 600 pounds of silver coins in those bags. **15** When Shalmaneser died, his son Sennacherib succeeded him as emperor. It soon became so dangerous to travel on the roads in Media that I could no longer go there.

Tobit Buries the Dead

16 While Shalmaneser was still emperor, I took good care of my own people whenever they were in need. **17** If they were hungry, I shared my food with them; if they needed clothes, I gave them some of my own. Whenever I saw that the dead body of one of my people had been thrown outside the city wall, I gave it a decent burial.

18 One day Sennacherib cursed God, the King of Heaven; God punished him, and Sennacherib had to retreat from

---

a THE LAND WAS AT REST: *See Lv 25.1-7.* money.

b a third tithe; *some manuscripts have the*

1.6 Dt 16.16   **1.17** Job 31.16-20

Judah. On his way back to Media he was so furious that he killed many Israelites. But I secretly removed the bodies and buried them; and when Sennacherib later searched for the bodies, he could not find them.

¹⁹ Then someone from Nineveh told the emperor that I was the one who had been burying his victims. As soon as I realized that the emperor knew all about me and that my life was in danger, I became frightened. So I ran away and hid. ²⁰ Everything I owned was seized and put in the royal treasury. My wife Anna and my son Tobias were all I had left.

Tobit's Nephew Rescues Him

²¹ About six weeks later, two of Sennacherib's sons assassinated him and then escaped to the mountains of Ararat. Another son, Esarhaddon, became emperor and put Ahikar, my brother Anael's son, in charge of all the financial affairs of the empire. ²² This was actually the second time Ahikar was appointed to this position, for when Sennacherib was emperor of Assyria, Ahikar had been wine steward, treasurer, and accountant, and had been in charge of the official seal. Since Ahikar was my nephew, he put in a good word for me with the emperor, and I was allowed to return to Nineveh.

A Family Celebration

2 When I returned home I was reunited with my wife Anna and my son Tobias. At the Harvest Festival, which is also called the Festival of Weeks, I sat down to a delicious meal. ² When I saw how much food there was on the table, I said to Tobias, "Son, go out and find one of our people who is living in poverty here in exile, someone who takes God's commands seriously. Bring him back with you, so that he can share this festival meal with us. I won't start eating until you come back."

A Murder in Nineveh

³ So Tobias went out to look for such a person. But he quickly returned, shouting, "Father! Father!"

"Yes, what is it?" I asked.

"One of our people has just been

You have already been hunted down once for burying the dead. (2.8)

murdered! Someone strangled him and threw his body into the marketplace."

⁴ I jumped up and left the table without even touching my food. I removed the body from the street and carried it to a little shed, where I left it until sunset, when I could bury it. ⁵ Then I returned home and washed, so as to purify myself. In deep sorrow I ate my dinner. ⁶ I was reminded of what the prophet Amos had said to the people of Bethel,

"Your festivals will be turned
     into funerals,
and your glad songs will
     become cries of grief."

I began to weep.

⁷ After sunset I went out, dug a grave, and buried the man. ⁸ My neighbors thought I was crazy. "Haven't you learned anything?" they asked. "You

"Take it straight back to its owners." (2.13)

have already been hunted down once for burying the dead, and you would have been killed if you had not run away. But here you are doing the same thing all over again."

Tobit Is Blinded

⁹That night I washed, so as to purify myself, and went out into my courtyard to sleep by the wall. It was a hot night, and I did not pull the cover up over my head. ¹⁰Sparrows were on the wall right above me, but I did not know it. Their warm droppings fell into my eyes, causing a white film to form on them. I went to one doctor after another, but the more they treated me with their medicines, the worse my eyes became, until finally I was completely blind.

For four years I could see nothing. My relatives were deeply concerned about my condition, and Ahikar supported me for two years before he went to the land of Elam.

A Family Quarrel

¹¹After Ahikar left, my wife Anna had to go to work, so she took up weaving, like many other women. ¹²The people she worked for would pay her when she delivered the cloth. One spring day, she cut a finished piece of cloth from the loom and took it to the people who had ordered it. They paid her the full price and also gave her a goat.

¹³When Anna came home with the goat, it began to bleat. I called out, "Where did that goat come from? You stole it, didn't you? Take it straight back to its owners. It's not right to eat stolen food!"

¹⁴"No!" she replied. "It was given to me as a gift in addition to what I got for the cloth." But I didn't believe her, and I blushed for shame for what she had done. I ordered her to return the goat to its owners, but she had the last word. "Now I see what you are really like!" she shouted. "Where is all that concern of yours for others? What about all those good deeds you used to do?"

Tobit's Prayer

3 I was so embarrassed and ashamed that I sighed and began to cry. Then, as I choked back my tears, I prayed:

²"You are righteous, O Lord!
 You are merciful[c] in all you do,
  faithful in all your ways.

---
[c] merciful; *some manuscripts add* and just.

You are the judge of this world. [d]

3-4 I beg you, treat me with
    kindness.
Do not punish me for my sins,
    not even for sins of which I
    am unaware.
My ancestors rebelled and
    disobeyed[e] your
    commands,
    but do not punish me for their
    sins.
You let our people be plundered,
    taken captive and killed.
You made an example of our
    people,
    an object of contempt and
    disgrace
    in all the nations where you
    scattered us.
5 You have often judged my
    ancestors for their sins
    and punished me for mine.
We were disloyal and rejected
    your commands,
    so our punishment has always
    been just.

6 "Now treat me as you please.
Take my life away and free me
    from this world;
    let my body return to the
    earth.
I would be better off dead.
I am tormented by insults I don't
    deserve,
    and weighed down with
    despair.
Lord, give the command—
    bring all my troubles to
    an end,
    take me to my eternal rest.
Don't reject my prayer.
I would rather die than live in
    misery
    and face such cruel insults."

Sarah's Troubles

7 That same day in the city of Ecbatana in Media, it happened that Sarah, the daughter of a man named Raguel, was insulted by one of her father's servant women. 8 Sarah had been married seven times, but the evil demon, Asmodeus, killed each husband before the marriage could be consummated. The servant woman said to Sarah, "You husband killer! Look at you! You've already had seven husbands, but not one of them lived long enough to give you a son.[f] 9 Why should you take it out on us? Why don't you go and join your dead husbands? I hope we never see a child of yours!"

10 Sarah was so depressed that she burst into tears and went upstairs determined to hang herself. But when she thought it over, she said to herself, "No, I won't do it! People would insult my father and say, 'You had only one child, a daughter whom you loved dearly, but she hanged herself because she felt so miserable.' Such grief would bring my gray-haired father to his grave, and I would be responsible. I won't kill myself; I'll just beg the Lord to let me die. Then I won't have to listen to those insults any longer!"

Sarah's Prayer

11 Then Sarah stood by the window, raised her arms in prayer, and said,

"God of mercy, worthy of our
    praise,
    may your name always be
    honored,
    may all your creation praise
    you forever.
12 "Lord, I look to you for help.
13 Speak the word and set me free
    from this life;

---

[d] You are the judge of this world; *some manuscripts have* You are always fair and just when you judge.   [e] My ancestors ... disobeyed; *some manuscripts have* I disobeyed.
[f] but ... son; *some manuscripts have* but it hasn't done you a bit of good.

Sarah's prayer (3.11)

then I will no longer have to
hear these insults.
14 You know, O Lord, that I'm still
a virgin;
I have never been defiled by
a man.
15 Never have I disgraced myself or
my father's name,
as long as we have lived in
this land of exile.
My father has no other child to
be his heir,
and there is no relative *g*
whom I can marry.
I have already lost seven
husbands,
so why should I live any
longer?
But if it is not your will to take
my life,
at least show mercy to me.
Don't let me hear those insults
again!"*h*

God Hears the Prayers of Tobit
and Sarah

16 As Tobit and Sarah were praying,
God in heaven heard their prayers
17 and sent his angel Raphael to help
them. He was sent to remove the white
film from Tobit's eyes, so that he could
see again, and to arrange a marriage between Sarah and Tobit's son Tobias,
who, as her cousin, had the right to
marry her. Raphael was also ordered to
expel the demon Asmodeus from
Sarah. At the very moment that Tobit
went back into his house from the
courtyard, Sarah, in her house in Ecbatana, was coming downstairs.

Tobit's Advice to Tobias

4 That same day, Tobit remembered the money that he had left
with Gabael at Rages in Media. 2 He
thought to himself, "Now that I have
asked God to let me die, I should call my
son Tobias and tell him about the
money."

3-4 So Tobit called Tobias and said to
him, "Son, when I die, give me a proper
burial. And after I'm gone, show respect to your mother. Take care of her
for the rest of her life, and when she
dies, bury her beside me. Remember,
she risked her life to bring you into
this world, so try to make her happy
and never do anything that would
worry her.

5 "Every day of your life, keep the
Lord our God in mind. Never sin deliberately or disobey any of his commands.
Always do what is right and never get
involved in anything evil. 6 Be honest,
and you will succeed in whatever
you do.

7 "Give generously to anyone who
faithfully obeys God.*i* If you are stingy

---

g RELATIVE: *In Israel it was customary to marry within one's own tribe.*   *h* at least
. . . again; *some manuscripts have* at least listen to my complaint.   *i The translation
of verses 7b-19b, accidentally omitted in the Greek manuscript that this translation
normally follows, is based on other Greek manuscripts.*
3.17 Nu 36.6-9; Tb 6.10-12   **4.7** Dt 15.7, 8; Pr 19.17; Si 3.30—4.6; 1 Jn 3.17

in giving to the poor, God will be stingy in giving to you. ⁸Give according to what you have. The more you have, the more you should give. Even if you have only a little, be sure to give something. ⁹This is as good as money saved. You will have your reward in a time of trouble. ¹⁰⁻¹¹Taking care of the poor is the kind of offering that pleases God in heaven. Do this, and you will be kept safe from the dark world of the dead.

¹²"Son, be on your guard against prostitutes. Above all, marry a woman of our tribe, because we are descendants of the prophets. Do not marry anyone who is not related to us. Remember that Noah, Abraham, Isaac and Jacob, our earliest ancestors, all married relatives. God blessed them with children, and so their descendants will inherit the land of Israel. ¹³Son, be loyal to your own relatives. Don't be too proud to marry one of them. Such pride leads to terrible frustration and ruin, just as laziness brings on severe poverty and causes starvation.

¹⁴"Pay your workers each day; never keep back their wages overnight. Honor God in this way, and he will reward you. Behave properly at all times. ¹⁵Never do to anyone else anything that you would not want someone to do to you.

"Do not drink so much wine that you get drunk, and do not let drinking become a habit.

¹⁶"Give food to the hungry and clothes to people in need. If you are prosperous, give generously, and do it gladly!

¹⁷"When one of God's faithful people has died, prepare food for the family,ʲ but never do this when someone evil dies.

¹⁸"Take the advice of sensible people, and never treat any useful advice lightly.

¹⁹"Take advantage of every opportunity to praise the Lord your God. Ask him to make you prosper in whatever you set out to do. He does not give his wisdom to the people of any other nation. He is the source of all good things, but he can also destroy you and bring you to certain death, if he wishes.

"Remember all my instructions. Don't forget them for one minute.

²⁰"Tobias, I want you to know that I once left a large sum of money with Gabrias' son, Gabael, at Rages in Media. ²¹We're poor now, but don't worry. If you obey God and avoid sin, he will be pleased with you and make you prosperous."

Travel Preparations

5 Then Tobias answered his father, "I'll do everything you told me. ²But how can I get the money back from Gabael? We have never even met each other. How can I prove to him who I am, so that he will trust me and give me the money? Besides that, I don't know how to get to Media."

³Tobit replied, "Gabael and I both signed a document. I then tore it in two, and we each took a half. I put his half with the money. That was twenty years ago! Now, go and find a reliable person to travel with you to Media and back, and we will pay him when you return. But you must get the money that I left with Gabael."

Tobias Meets Raphael

⁴Tobias then went out to look for someone who knew the way to Media and would travel with him. Almost as soon as he left the house, he found himself face-to-face with Raphael. Tobias did not know that Raphael was an angel of God, ⁵so he asked him where he was from.

"I am an Israelite," Raphael answered, "one of your distant relatives,

ʲ prepare . . . family; *or* put food on his grave.
4.15 Mt 7.12; Lk 6.31   **4.17** Dt 26.14   **4.21** 1 Ti 6.6-8   **5.4** He 13.2

and I have come here to Nineveh to find work."

"Do you know the way to Media?" Tobias asked.

⁶"Yes, I do," Raphael replied. "I have been there many times, and I know all the roads well. I used to stay with our relative Gabael, who lives there in the town of Rages.ᵏ It takes at least two days to travel there from Ecbatana, the capital city, because Rages is up in the mountains."

⁷Then Tobias said to Raphael, "Wait here for me, my friend, while I go in and tell my father. I would like for you to travel with me, and I will pay you for the journey."

⁸"All right," Raphael said, "I'll wait, but don't take too long."

⁹Tobias went in and told his father, "I have found an Israelite to travel with me."

"Call the man in," Tobit replied. "I would like to know what family and tribe he belongs to, and whether he is a reliable traveling companion for you."

Tobit Meets Raphael

So Tobias went out and called to Raphael, "My father would like to meet you." When Raphael came in, Tobit greeted him first.

Then Raphael returned the greeting, "I hope all is well with you."

But Tobit replied, "How can all be well with me? I'm blind and can't see a thing. It's like being dead and no longer able to see the light. I might as well be dead! I can hear people talking, but I can't see them."

"Cheer up!" Raphael said to him. "God is going to cure you soon, so don't worry!"

Tobit then said, "My son Tobias wants to go to Media. Can you go with him and show him the way? I will pay you, of course."

Raphael replied, "Certainly I can go with him. I have traveled there many times and I know all the roads in the mountains and on the plains."

¹⁰Tobit questioned him further, "Tell me, my friend, what family and tribe do you belong to?"

¹¹But Raphael asked, "Why do you need to know that?"

"Tell me the truth," said Tobit. "What is your name, and who are you?"

¹²Raphael replied, "My name is Azarias, and I am the son of the older Ananias, one of your relatives."

¹³Then Tobit said to him, "Welcome to our home! God bless you, my son. Please don't be offended because I wanted to know the truth about you and your family. As it turns out, you are from a good family and a relative at that! I knew Ananias and Nathan, the two sons of the older Shemaiah. They were always loyal to their religion. We used to travel together to Jerusalem and worship there. Your relatives are fine people, and you come from good stock. Have a safe journey."

¹⁴Tobit continued, "I will pay the normal daily wage plus expenses for both of you. ¹⁵Be a good companion to Tobias, and I will add a bonus to your wages."

¹⁶"I will go with him," Raphael said. "And don't worry; we will get there and back safely. The roads are not dangerous."

"God be with you!" Tobit replied. Then he called Tobias and said to him, "Son, get everything ready that you need for the journey, so that the two of you can be on your way. May God and his angel watch over you both and bring you back to me safe and sound."

Before leaving for Media, Tobias kissed his father and mother good-bye. Tobit said again, "Have a safe journey!"

¹⁷Then his mother began to cry. "How could you send my son away like

ᵏ Rages; *Greek* Ecbatana.
5.16 Gn 24.7, 40

this?" she complained. "He's our only means of support. Who will take care of us now? ¹⁸ Is that money so important to you that you are willing to risk your own son's life to get it back? ¹⁹ Why can't we be content to live on what the Lord has given us?"

²⁰ "Calm down," Tobit said to her. "He will get there and back safely, and with your own eyes you will see him return home safe and sound. ²¹ Now stop worrying about them, dear. A good angel will go with Tobias. He will have a successful journey and will come back in good health." At that, Anna calmed down and stopped crying.

Tobias Catches a Fish

6 So Tobias and the angel started out toward Media, taking Tobias' dog along with them. They walked on until sunset, then camped by the Tigris River. ² Tobias had gone down to wash his feet in the river, when suddenly a huge fish jumped up out of the water and tried to swallow one of his feet. Tobias let out a yell, ³ and the angel called to him, "Grab that fish! Don't let it get away."

Then Tobias grabbed the fish and dragged it up on the bank.

⁴ "Cut the fish open," the angel instructed, "and take out its gall bladder, heart, and liver. Keep these with you; they can be used for medicine, but throw away the guts."

⁵ Tobias did as the angel had told him. Then he cooked the fish, ate part of it, and salted the rest to take along with him.

The two continued on together until they were near Media. ⁶ Then Tobias asked, "Azarias, my friend, what diseases can be cured by this gall bladder, heart, and liver?"

⁷ The angel answered, "The heart and liver can be burned and used to chase away a demon or an evil spirit that is tormenting someone. The attacks will stop immediately, and the

person will never be troubled again. ⁸ You can use the gall bladder to treat someone whose eyes are covered with a white film. Just rub it on his eyes and

Grab that fish! (6.3)

blow on the film, and he will be able to see again."

On the Way to Ecbatana

⁹ When they had reached Media and were approaching the city of Ecbatana, ¹⁰ Raphael said, "Tobias, my friend."

"Yes, what is it?" Tobias asked.

Raphael continued, "Tonight we will stay at the home of your relative Raguel. He has only one child, a daughter named Sarah, ¹¹ and since you are her closest relative, you have the right to marry her. You also have the right to inherit all her father's property. ¹² She is sensible, brave, and very beautiful; and her father is a good man. Tonight I'll discuss the marriage proposal with her father, and he will consent to give her to you as your bride. Then, when we return home from the town of Rages, we will celebrate the marriage. Raguel cannot refuse to let you marry her, and he cannot let any other man have her. If he did, then according to the Law of Moses he would deserve the death penalty. He knows that you are the only man who has the right to marry his daughter and receive the inheritance, so follow my advice. Raguel and I will discuss the matter tonight and arrange your engagement to Sarah. When we get back from the city of Rages, we will take her home with us."

¹³Tobias then said to Raphael, "Azarias, my friend, I have already heard about Sarah's seven former husbands, and how each one dropped dead on his wedding night, even before he could get to bed. ¹⁴According to the story I heard, a demon killed them. He doesn't harm Sarah, but he kills every man who tries to get near her. I am afraid of this demon. I am an only child, and if I were to die, the sorrow would send my parents to their graves. They don't even have another son to bury them."

¹⁵The angel replied, "Have you already forgotten your father's instructions? He told you to marry a woman from your own tribe. So, listen carefully to what I say. Don't worry about the demon. Marry Sarah! I know that tonight Raguel will let Sarah marry you. ¹⁶When you go into the bedroom, take the fish's heart and liver with you and place them on the burning incense, ¹⁷so that the odor will spread throughout the room. When the demon smells it, he will leave and never come near Sarah again. But before you consummate the marriage, both of you must get up and pray for the Lord in heaven to be merciful to you and to protect you. Don't be afraid. Sarah was meant to be yours from the beginning of creation. You will rescue her from the demon, and she will go with you to your home. You and Sarah will have many children, whom you will love very much. So don't worry!"

Tobias listened very carefully to what Raphael had to say. He knew that Sarah was a relative on his father's side of the family. He began to fall in love with her and looked forward to marrying her.

7.6 Gn 33.4; 45.14; Lk 15.20

At Raguel's House

7 When Tobias and the angel Raphael had entered the city of Ecbatana, Tobias said, "Azarias, my friend, take me to see Raguel as quickly as you can." The angel brought him to Raguel's house, where they found him sitting at the entrance to his courtyard. Raphael and Tobias greeted him first; then he replied, "Come in, my friends. You are welcome in my home."

Raguel brought them into his house ²and said to his wife Edna, "Doesn't this young man look just like my cousin Tobit?"

³Edna asked them, "Where do you come from?"

"We are Israelites of the tribe of Naphtali," Tobias and Raphael answered, "but we are now living in exile in the city of Nineveh in Assyria."

⁴Edna said, "Do you know our cousin Tobit?"

"We certainly do know him," they answered.

"How is he?" she asked.

⁵"He is alive and well," they replied. Then Tobias added, "Tobit is my father." ⁶At that Raguel got up, and with tears of joy in his eyes he kissed Tobias. ⁷Then he said, "God bless you, my child. Your father is a good and noble man. What a terrible tragedy that such an honest and generous man should have lost his sight!" He threw his arms around Tobias' neck and wept on his shoulder. ⁸His wife Edna and his daughter Sarah also wept for Tobit.

Raguel gave Tobias and Raphael a warm welcome and had one of his rams slaughtered. After the guests had bathed and were about to sit down to eat, Tobias said to Raphael, "Azarias, my friend, when are you going to ask Raguel to let me marry Sarah?"

⁹But Raguel overheard the question and said to Tobias, ¹⁰"Eat and drink something first and enjoy yourself this

evening. You have the right to marry Sarah, and I cannot let anyone else marry her, because you are my closest relative. But I must tell you the truth, my son. ¹¹I have already given her to seven men, all of them relatives. Each one died on his wedding night, as soon as he entered the bedroom. But now, my son, have something to eat and drink. The Lord will take care of you both."

Tobias replied, "I won't eat or drink until you give me your word."

¹²Raguel agreed. "Certainly I will," he said. "I will give her to you just as the Law of Moses commands. God in heaven has arranged this marriage, so take her as your wife. From now on, you belong to each other. Sarah is yours today and forever. May the Lord of heaven keep both of you safe tonight. May he be merciful and kind to you."

The Marriage Ceremony

¹³Then Raguel called his daughter. When she came in, he took her by the hand and gave her to Tobias with his blessing, "Take her to be your wife according to the teachings in the Law of Moses. Take her safely with you to your father's house. May the God of heaven give you a happy life together."

¹⁴Raguel asked his wife to bring him a blank scroll so that he could write out the marriage contract. Edna brought him the scroll, and Raguel wrote out the agreement, saying that Sarah was given to Tobias according to the teachings in the Law of Moses. ¹⁵After the ceremony they began the meal.

¹⁶Raguel called his wife and said, "Get the spare room ready, my dear, and take Sarah there."

¹⁷Edna made up the bed as Raguel had told her. Then she took Sarah into the room with her, and Sarah began to cry.[l] But Edna wiped away her tears and said, ¹⁸"Don't worry, Sarah. I'm sure the Lord of heaven will make you happy this time and not sad. So cheer up, my dear." Then Edna left the room.

The Demon Is Expelled

8 When they had finished the meal, and it was time to go to bed, Sarah's parents led young Tobias to the bedroom. ²He remembered Raphael's instructions, so he took the fish's liver and heart out of the bag where he had been keeping them. Then he placed them on the burning incense. ³The smell drove the demon away from them, and he fled to Egypt.[m] Raphael chased after him and caught him there. At once he bound him hand and foot.

The Prayer of Tobias

⁴When Tobias and Sarah were alone behind closed doors, Tobias got up from the bed and said to his wife, "Get up, dear. Let's pray for the Lord to be merciful and to protect us." ⁵Sarah got up so that they could pray together and ask God for his protection. Then Tobias prayed:

"God of our ancestors, you are
    worthy of praise.
May your name be honored
    forever and ever
by all your creatures in
    heaven and on earth.
⁶You created Adam and gave him
    his wife Eve
to be his helper and support.
They became the parents of the
    whole human race.

---

[l] and Sarah began to cry; *some manuscripts have* and she began to cry.   [m] EGYPT: *Egypt was thought of as the most remote part of the world and the home of demons and evil spirits.*
8.3 Mt 12.43   **8.5** S of 3Y 3   **8.6** Gn 2.18

They went out to dig a grave. (8.9)

You said, 'It is not good for man
to live alone.
I will make a suitable helper
for him.'
[7] Lord, I have chosen Sarah
because it is right,
not because I lusted for her.
Please be merciful to us
and grant that we may grow
old together."
[8] Then they both said "Amen" [9] and
went to bed for the night.

Anxious Parents

Later that night, Raguel called his
servants, and together they went out to
dig a grave, [10] because Raguel thought,
"Tobias will probably die too, and people will laugh and make fun of us."
[11] When they finished digging the
grave, Raguel went back into the house
and said to his wife, [12] "Send one of the
servant women to find out if Tobias is
still alive. If he isn't, then we will bury
him before anyone finds out." [13] They
then sent a servant woman to take a
lamp and see if he was still alive. As she
opened the door, she could see that
both of them were sound asleep. [14] So
she went back and told Raguel and
Edna that Tobias was alive and unharmed. [15] Then Raguel[n] praised the
God of heaven:

Raguel's Prayer

"You are worthy of our praise,
O God.
May your people praise you
forever,
may they praise you with pure
hearts.
[16] I praise you because you have
made me glad;
you have been merciful to us,
and my worst fears did not
come true.
[17] You deserve our praise, O Lord;
you were merciful to this
young couple,
the only children of their
parents.
Now, grant them your mercy and
protection.
Let them live out their lives in
happiness and love."
[18] Then Raguel ordered his servants to
fill in the grave before dawn.

The Wedding Feast

[19] Raguel told his wife to bake
enough bread for a big feast. Then he
went out to the herd and brought back
two oxen and four rams, which he ordered his servants to slaughter in preparation for the wedding feast. [20] He
called for Tobias and vowed[o] that he

[n] Raguel; *some manuscripts have* they.
8.20 Gn 24.55

[o] vowed; *some manuscripts have* said.

would not let him leave for two weeks. "Stay, and we will eat and drink together," he said. "It will do my daughter good after her terrible suffering. [21] Then you may take half of what I own and go back to your parents safe and sound. You will inherit the other half when Edna and I die. Have no doubts about our love for you; from now on you are as much our son as Sarah is our daughter. You can be sure of that, my son."

The Journey to Rages

9 Then Tobias called Raphael and said to him, [2] "Azarias, take four of the servants with you, and two camels, and go to Gabael's house in the town of Rages. Give him the signed document, so that he will give you the money. Then bring him back with you for the wedding feast. [3-4] You know that my father is counting the days until I come home, and he will be very upset if I am even one day late. You know, too, how Raguel insists that I must stay, and I cannot disappoint him."

[5] So Raphael and the four servants went to Rages in Media, where they stayed at Gabael's house. Raphael gave him the signed document and told him that Tobit's son Tobias had recently married, and that Gabael was invited to the wedding feast. At once Gabael counted out the bags of money, which were still sealed, and they loaded them on the camels.[p] [6] Very early the next morning, they set out for the wedding feast. When Raphael and Gabael came to Raguel's house, they found Tobias at dinner. Tobias immediately got up and greeted Gabael. With tears in his eyes Gabael returned the greeting and added, "You are just like your honest and generous father. May the Lord in heaven bless you and your wife, your mother-in-law, and your father. Praise

God! He has let me live to see my cousin Tobias, who looks so much like his father."

Tobit and Anna Are Worried

10 Meanwhile, every day Tobit was keeping count of the time needed to travel to Rages and back. When the time was up and his son had not returned, Tobit said to his wife, [2] "What can be keeping him? Do you suppose Gabael has died? Maybe there is no one to give him the money." [3] Tobit was very worried.

[4] Then Anna said, "My son is dead. I'm sure of it." She began to weep and to mourn for Tobias, [5] "Oh, my son, the joy of my life, why did I ever let you leave home?"

[6] Tobit tried to comfort her. "Calm down, my dear," he said. "Don't worry. He will be all right. Something unexpected is probably keeping them there longer than we counted on. Besides, his companion is a reliable man and a relative at that. Don't let yourself get so upset over him, dear. I'm sure he is already on his way home."

[7] But she replied, "Be quiet and leave me alone! Don't try to fool me. My son is dead." Each day she would rush out of the house to the road which Tobias had taken and would watch for him until sunset. She would let no one comfort her,[q] and when she returned home she would weep and mourn for her son all night long, without sleeping.

Departure from Ecbatana

The two-week wedding feast which Raguel had promised to hold for his daughter Sarah came to an end. So Tobias went to him and asked, "Please let me go home now. I'm certain my parents have given up all hope of ever seeing me again. Please, Raguel, let me go home to my father. I have already told

---

p loaded them on the camels; *some manuscripts have* stacked them up.   *q* She would let no one comfort her; *some manuscripts have* She would not eat a bite.

Each day she would . . . watch for him until sunset. (10.7)

you the condition he was in when I left."

8 But Raguel answered, "Stay, my son. Stay here with me. I will send messengers to your father to tell him that you are all right."

9 But Tobias insisted, "No, I can't! Please let me go back to my father."

10 So Raguel gave Tobias his bride Sarah without further delay. He also gave Tobias half of everything he owned: slaves, cattle, sheep, donkeys, camels, clothes, money, and furniture. 11 Raguel embraced Tobias and sent them on their way with his blessing, "Good-bye, my son. Have a safe journey. May the Lord of heaven protect you and Sarah. And may I live to see your children." 12 Raguel then said to Sarah, "Go with your husband and live in his parents' house. From now on they are as much your parents as your own mother and I are. Let me hear only good things about you as long as I live." After saying good-bye he sent them on their way.

Then Edna said to Tobias, "Tobias my dear child, may the Lord bring you safely home. And may he let me live to see your children. The Lord is my witness; I am placing my daughter in your care. Never, at any time in your life, do

anything that would break her heart. Have a safe journey, Tobias. From now on, Sarah is your wife and I am your mother. May we all prosper as long as we live." Then Edna kissed them both and sent them safely on their way.

11 When Tobias left, he was as happy as could be. He praised the Lord of heaven and earth, the King of all the world, because his journey had been so successful, and he promised to honor Raguel and his wife as long as they lived.*r*

The Homecoming

As they came near the city of Kaserin, just outside Nineveh, 2 Raphael said, "Tobias, you know the condition your father was in when we left him. 3 We should go on ahead of your wife and get the house ready before everyone else arrives. 4 Be sure to bring the fish's gall bladder with you." So they went on ahead, and Tobias' dog ran along with*s* them.

5 Meanwhile, Anna sat looking down the road for her son. 6 Suddenly she saw him coming and she shouted out to Tobit, "Look! Our son is coming, and his friend is with him!"

7 Before they reached Tobit, Raphael said to Tobias, "Your father will be able

r successful, and . . . lived; *or* successful. And Raguel made Tobias promise to honor him and Edna as long as they lived.   *s* Tobias' dog . . . with; *some manuscripts have* the Lord accompanied.

to see again. [8] Just put the fish's gall bladder on his eyes like a plaster. The medicine will make the white film shrivel up so that you can peel it off, and your father will then regain his eyesight."

[9] Anna ran to her son, threw her arms around him, and exclaimed, "Now that I have seen you alive, my child, I can die in peace!" And she wept for joy.

Tobit's Cure

[10] Tobit got up and stumbled out through the entrance of the courtyard. [11] Tobias went up to him, holding the fish's gall bladder in his hand. He blew on his father's eyes and steadied him. "Don't worry now, father," he said. [12-13] Tobias then applied the gall, and beginning from the corners of Tobit's eyes, he peeled away the white film. [14] Tobit threw his arms around Tobias' neck and wept for joy. Then he exclaimed, "I can see you! My son, the light of my eyes!"

"Praise God. Praise him for his greatness.
Praise all his holy angels.
May he continue to bless us.
Praise all his angels forever.
[15] He brought this illness upon me,
but now I can see my son
Tobias!"

Then Tobias went happily into the house, praising God at the top of his voice. He told his father how successful he had been, that he had not only brought back the money, but had married Raguel's daughter Sarah, who was on her way and would soon arrive.

Sarah's Arrival

[16] Tobit was excited and praised God as he went out to meet his son's bride at the city gate. When the people of Nineveh saw him, they were amazed, because he was walking on his own, with no one leading him by the hand.

[17] Tobit praised God and told everyone how God in his mercy had restored his sight.

When Tobit met Sarah, he greeted her, "Welcome, daughter! Praise God for bringing you to us, my daughter. May God bless your father, as well as you and my son Tobias. Welcome to your new home. May you always be blessed with good health and happiness. Come in, daughter!"

It was a day of great joy for all the Jews of Nineveh. [18] Tobit's nephews Ahikar and Nadab came by to share Tobit's happiness with him.

The Angel Raphael

12 When the wedding feast was over, Tobit called his son Tobias and said to him, "Son, be sure to pay your traveling companion, and don't forget to give him a bonus."

[2] Tobias asked him, "Father, how much do you think I should pay him? I wouldn't mind giving him half of everything we brought back with us. [3] He brought me back home safe and sound; he went to get the money for me from Gabael; he rid my wife of a demon; and he cured your blindness. How much of a bonus should I give him?"

[4] Tobit answered, "Give him half of what he helped you bring back. He well deserves that."

[5] Tobias then called Raphael and said to him, "Here is half of what you helped me bring back. You have earned it; have a safe journey home."

[6] Then Raphael called the two men aside and said to them, "Praise God and tell everyone about the good things he has done for you, so that they too will honor him and sing his praises. Let everyone know what God has done. Never stop praising him.

[7] "It's a good idea to keep a king's secret, but what God does should be told

Tobit and Tobias were terrified. (12.16)

everywhere, so that he may be praised and honored.

"If you do good, no harm will come to you.

8"It is better to pray sincerely and to please God by helping the poor than to be rich and dishonest. It is better to give to the poor than to store up gold. 9Such generosity will save you from death and will wash away all your sins. Those who give to the poor will live full lives, 10but those who live a life of sin and wickedness are their own worst enemies.

11"I have already told you that a king's secret ought to be kept, but the things God does should be told to everyone. Now I will reveal to you the full truth and keep nothing back. 12Tobit, when you and Sarah prayed to the Lord, I was the one who brought your prayers into his glorious presence. I did the same thing each time you buried the dead. 13On the day you got up from the table without eating your meal in order to bury that corpse, God sent me to test you. 14But he also sent me to cure you and to rescue your daughter-in-law, Sarah, from her troubles. 15I am Raphael, one of the seven angels who stand in the glorious presence of the Lord, ready to serve him."

16Tobit and Tobias were terrified and fell to the ground, trembling with fear. 17But Raphael said to them, "Don't be afraid; everything is all right. Always remember to praise God. 18He wanted me to come and help you; I did not come on my own. So sing God's praises as long as you live. 19When you thought you saw me eating, I did not really eat anything; it only seemed so. 20While you are on this earth, you must praise the Lord God and give him thanks. Now I must go back to him who sent me. Write down everything that has happened to you."

21Then Raphael disappeared into the sky. Tobit and Tobias stood up, but they could no longer see him. 22They began to sing hymns of praise, giving thanks for all the mighty deeds God had done while his angel Raphael had been with them.

Tobit's Song of Praise

13 Then Tobit prayed:
"Praise the eternal God,
    praise the one who rules.
2He punishes us; then he shows
    us mercy.

12.8 Si 29.8-13   **12.9** Pr 11.4; Dn 4.27; Si 3.30   **12.12** Job 33.23, 24; Ac 10.4; Rev 8.3, 4
12.15 Zec 4.10; Lk 1.19; Rev 8.2

He sends us down to the
world of the dead,
then he brings us up from
the grave.
No one can escape his power.

3 "People of Israel, give thanks
among the nations,
where he sent you into exile;
4 even there he showed his
great power.
Let all who live hear your praise.
The Lord is our God and father
forever.

5 "Though he punished you for
your wickedness,
he will be merciful and bring
you home
from among the nations
where he scattered you.

6 "Turn to him with all your heart
and soul,
live in loyal obedience to him.
Then he will turn to you to
help you
and will no longer hide
himself.
Remember what God has done
for you,
and give thanks with all your
heart.
Praise the righteous Lord;
honor the eternal King.

"Although I live in exile in a
foreign land,
I will give thanks to the Lord
and will speak of his great
strength to a nation
of sinners.
'Turn away from your sins, and
do what pleases God!
Perhaps he will be gracious
and show you his mercy.'

7 "I praise my God and rejoice in
his greatness;
my whole being honors the
King of heaven.

8 "Let everyone tell of his
greatness
and sing his praises in
Jerusalem.

9 "Jerusalem, Holy City of our God,
he will punish you for the sins
of your people,
but he will be merciful to all
who do right.
10 So give thanks to the Lord, for
he is good.
Praise the eternal King. ^{t}
Your Temple will be rebuilt,
and your people will be happy
again.

"May the Lord make all your
exiles glad,
may he take care of your
suffering people
for as long as time shall last.

11 "Jerusalem, your light will shine
brightly for all the world,
and from far away many
nations will come to you.
Their people will come to honor
the Lord your God,
they will bring gifts for the
King of heaven.
In your streets many generations
will sing joyful praise,
your name will endure forever
as God's chosen city.
12 A curse will be on all who make
threats against you,
on all who destroy you and
tear down your walls,
on all who demolish your
towers and burn your
homes.

---

^{t} *Some manuscripts do not have verses 6b-10a* Although I live . . . Praise the eternal
King.
13.4 Is 63.16; Jr 3.4; Ws 14.3; Si 23.1, 4; Mt 6.9　　**13.9-18** Is 60.1-22; Rev 21.9—22.5

But all who honor you will be
blessed forever.

13 "Rejoice, Jerusalem, because of
your righteous people;
they will be gathered together
from exile
to praise the Lord of the ages.

14 "Happy are all who love you
and are pleased to see you
prosper.
Those who mourn over your
suffering now
will one day be happy;
your happiness will bring
them joy forever.

15 "I praise the Lord, the great
King;
16   Jerusalem will be rebuilt
and will be his home forever.

"Jerusalem, how happy I will be
when my descendants can see
your splendor
and give thanks to the King of
heaven.

"Your gates will be built with
sapphires and emeralds,
and all your walls with
precious stones.
Your towers will be made of gold,
and their fortifications of pure
gold.
17 Your streets will be paved with
rubies and precious jewels.
18 Joyful songs will ring out from
your gates,
and from all your houses
people will shout,
'Praise the Lord! Praise the
God of Israel!'

"Jerusalem, God will bless your
people,
and they will praise his holy
name forever."

With these words Tobit ended his
song of praise.

Tobit's Final Advice

14 1-2 Tobit was 62 years old when
he became blind, but after his
sight had been restored, he lived a very
full life. Once again he gave generously
to the poor, and he continued to praise
God and tell of his greatness. Tobit died
a peaceful death at the age of 112, and
was given an honorable burial in
Nineveh.

3 But just before Tobit died, he sent
for his son Tobias and told him, 4 "My
son, take your children and go at once
to Media. I believe that God's judgment
which his prophet Nahum announced
against Nineveh is about to take place.
Everything that God's prophets told Israel about Nineveh and Assyria will
happen. It will all come true, every
word of it, when the right time comes.
I am absolutely convinced that everything God has said is sure to come true.
God does not break his promises. It will
be safer for you in Media than in Assyria or Babylon.

"Those Jews who live in Israel will all
be scattered and taken from that good
land into exile. All Israel will become a
wasteland; Samaria and Jerusalem will
be abandoned cities. God's Temple will
be burned to the ground and will lie in
complete ruin for a while. 5 But God will
have mercy on his people again, and he
will bring them back to the land of Israel. They will rebuild the Temple, but
it will not be as splendid as the first
Temple, not until the proper time has
come. But when that time does come,
all the people of Israel will return from
exile, and they will rebuild the city of
Jerusalem in all its former splendor.
They will rebuild God's Temple in Jerusalem, just as Israel's prophets have
foretold.

6 "Then all the nations in the world

will come back to God. They will worship him as the only true God and give up the idols that led them into false worship. [7]The nations of the world will praise the everlasting God by doing what he demands.

"At that time God will save all the people of Israel who have been faithful to him. He will bring them together to Jerusalem, and let them take possession of the land of Abraham, and there they will live securely forever. All who love God with their heart and soul will rejoice, but all sinners and evil people will be wiped off the face of the earth. [8]"Now, my children, follow my instructions. Worship God sincerely and do what is pleasing to him. [9]Bring up your children to do what is right. Teach them that they must give to the poor and must always remember to praise God with all sincerity.

[10]"Tobias, my son, leave Nineveh now. Do not stay here. As soon as you bury your mother beside me, leave; do not stay another night within the city limits. It is a wicked city and full of immorality; the people here have no sense of shame. Remember what Nadab did to Ahikar his own uncle who had brought him up. He tried to kill Ahikar and forced him to go into hiding in a tomb. Ahikar came back into the light of day, but God sent Nadab down into everlasting darkness for what he had done. Ahikar escaped the deadly trap which Nadab had set for him, because Ahikar[u] had given generously to the poor. But Nadab fell into that fatal trap and it destroyed him. [11]So now, my children, you see what happens to those who show their concern for others, and how death awaits those who treat others unjustly. But now I am very weak."

Then they laid Tobit on his bed. He died and was given an honorable burial. [12]Later on, Tobit's wife died and was buried beside her husband. Then Tobias and his wife moved to Ecbatana in Media, where they lived with Raguel, Tobias' father-in-law. [13]Tobias took care of Edna and Raguel in their old age and showed them great respect. When at last they died, he buried them at Ecbatana. Tobias inherited Raguel's estate, as he had inherited the estate of his father Tobit.

[14]At the ripe old age of 117 Tobias died, [15]having lived long enough to hear about the destruction of Nineveh and to see King Cyaxares[v] of Media take the people away as captives. Tobias praised God for the way that he had punished the people of Nineveh and Assyria. As long as he lived he gave thanks for what God had done to Nineveh.

---

[u] Ahikar; *or* I.   [v] *Probable text* Cyaxares; *Greek unclear.*

The Book of
JUDITH

INTRODUCTION

The Book of Judith depicts a time when the Jewish nation was about to be crushed by an enemy army. Judith, the heroine of the story, is a deeply religious widow who observes all the requirements of the Law of Moses. She depends on God to help her complete the dramatic rescue of the nation by killing Holofernes.

OUTLINE OF CONTENTS

The War between Nebuchadnezzar and Arphaxad

1 While King Nebuchadnezzar was ruling over the Assyrians from his capital city of Nineveh, King Arphaxad ruled over the Medes from his capital city of Ecbatana. ² Around Ecbatana King Arphaxad built a wall 105 feet high and 75 feet thick of cut stones; each stone was 4 1/2 feet thick and 9 feet long. ³ At each gate he built a tower 150 feet high, with a foundation 90 feet thick. ⁴ Each gateway was 105 feet high and 60 feet wide — wide enough for his whole army to march through, with the infantry in formation.

⁵ In the twelfth year of his reign King Nebuchadnezzar went to war against King Arphaxad in the large plain around the city of Rages. ⁶ Many nations joined forces with King Arphaxad — all the people who lived in the mountains, those who lived along the Tigris, Euphrates, and Hydaspes rivers, as well as those who lived in the plain ruled by King Arioch of Elam. Many nations joined this Chelodite alliance.

⁷ Then King Nebuchadnezzar of Assyria sent a message to the Persians and to the people to the west, in the regions of Cilicia, Damascus, Lebanon, Antilebanon, to those along the coast, ⁸ and in the regions of Carmel, Gilead, northern Galilee, and Jezreel Valley. ⁹⁻¹⁰ The message also went to the people living in Samaria and the nearby towns, to those in the area west of the Jordan River as far as the cities of Jerusalem, Bethany, Chelous, and Kadesh, and to the district of Goshen. The message was also taken to the Egyptian cities of Tahpanhes, Rameses, Tanis, and Memphis, and the district up the Nile River to the Ethiopian[a] border. ¹¹ But everyone in this whole region ignored King Nebuchadnezzar's appeal and refused to take part in the war. They thought that he had no chance of win-

---

[a] *Greek* Ethiopian: *Ethiopia is the name given in Graeco-Roman times to the extensive territory south of the First Cataract of the Nile River. Cush was the ancient (Hebrew) name of this region which included within its borders most of modern Sudan and some of present-day Ethiopia (Abyssinia).*

ning the war, so they were not afraid of him and sent his messengers back disgraced and empty-handed.

¹²This made Nebuchadnezzar so furious that he vowed he would risk his entire kingdom to take revenge on all those people. He vowed that he would put to death the entire population of Cilicia, Damascus, Syria, Moab, Ammon, Judah, and Egypt — everyone from the Mediterranean Sea to the Persian Gulf.

This made Nebuchadnezzar so furious . . . (1.12)

¹³In the seventeenth year of his reign King Nebuchadnezzar led his army into battle against King Arphaxad. He defeated all of Arphaxad's forces, including his entire cavalry, and all his charioteers. ¹⁴Then Nebuchadnezzar occupied all the towns in the land of Media and advanced against the city of Ecbatana. He captured the city's towers, looted its markets, and made that beautiful city a ruin. ¹⁵He captured King Arphaxad in the mountains around Rages and killed him. After Ar-

phaxad's death, ¹⁶Nebuchadnezzar and his entire army returned to Nineveh with all the loot taken in battle. There they relaxed and feasted for four months.

The War against the Nations in the West

2 In the eighteenth year of Nebuchadnezzar's reign, on the twenty-second day of the first month of that year, he and his advisers decided to carry out his threat to take revenge on all those countries that had refused to help him. ²⁻³The king called his general staff and senior officers together and reported in detail how those countries had betrayed him. He and his officers agreed that everyone who had refused to help him in the war should be put to death. Then he described to them his plan of attack.

⁴At the close of the meeting, Nebuchadnezzar gave the following command to Holofernes, who was the general in command of his armies and second in command to the king: ⁵"I, Nebuchadnezzar, the great king and ruler of all the earth, command you to choose some experienced soldiers: 120,000 infantry and 12,000 cavalry. ⁶Then attack the lands to the west because they refused to respond to my appeal for help. ⁷Warn them that they must prepare their offerings of earth and water to show that they have surrendered unconditionally. I will make them feel the full force of my anger and completely destroy them. My armies will march over every foot of their land and plunder it as they go. ⁸I will fill the valleys with their dead bodies and will choke up every stream and river with so many corpses that they will all overflow. ⁹I will take captive all those who are left alive and carry them off to the ends of the earth.

¹⁰"But you, Holofernes, are ordered to go ahead of me and occupy all their territories in advance. If they surrender

Holofernes, commander in chief of the armies (2.4)

to you, hold them for me until I come to punish them. ¹¹But if they resist, do not spare them. Kill them and loot the entire region under your control. ¹²I have taken a solemn vow, and at the risk of my life and my royal power I am determined to do what I have vowed to do. ¹³Do not disobey me in any way. I am your king; remember that, and carry out without delay every order that I have given you."

The Campaign of Holofernes

¹⁴So Holofernes left the king and called together all the commanders, generals, and officers of the Assyrian army. ¹⁵Just as the king had ordered, he chose 120,000 of the best infantrymen and 12,000 of the best mounted archers ¹⁶and arranged them in battle formation. ¹⁷He also took along a very large number of camels, donkeys, and mules to carry the equipment, as well as many sheep, cattle, and goats for food. ¹⁸Every soldier received plenty of rations and a large payment of gold and silver from the royal treasury.

¹⁹Then Holofernes and his entire army set out, advancing ahead of King Nebuchadnezzar. The chariots, the cavalry, and the infantry marched out to overrun the entire western region.

²⁰Other troops went with them. There were so many that it was impossible to count them — they were like a swarm of locusts or like grains of sand in the desert.

²¹Three days after they had left the city of Nineveh, they reached the plains around Bectileth near the mountains north of Cilicia, where they set up camp. ²²From there Holofernes advanced into the hill country with his entire army, his infantry, cavalry, and chariots. ²³He totally destroyed the countries of Libya and Lydia, then plundered all the people of Rassis and the Ishmaelites who lived on the edge of the desert, south of the land of the Chelleans.

²⁴Then Holofernes crossed the Euphrates River and marched through the land of Mesopotamia, completely destroying all the walled towns along the Abron River as far as the sea. ²⁵He seized the territory of Cilicia, killing everyone who resisted him, and went as far as the southern borders of the land of Japheth, near Arabia. ²⁶He surrounded the Midianites, burned down their tents, and slaughtered their sheep.

²⁷Holofernes went down into the plains around Damascus during the

wheat harvest, burned all the fields, slaughtered the flocks and herds, looted the towns, devastated the entire countryside, and killed all the young men. ²⁸ Panic seized all the people who lived along the Mediterranean Sea, and they shook with fear. Everyone in the towns of Tyre, Sidon, Sur, Ocina, Jamnia, Ashdod, and Ashkelon was terrified.

The Peace Delegation to King Nebuchadnezzar

3 All these nations sent a peace delegation to King Nebuchadnezzar with this message: ²"We remain loyal to you, great King Nebuchadnezzar; we are ready to serve you and obey any command that you may wish to give us. ³ Our buildings, all our land, our wheat fields, our livestock, and our tents are at your disposal; use them in any way you wish. ⁴ Our people will be your slaves, and you may use our towns as you please."

⁵ After the peace delegation had brought this message, ⁶ Holofernes led Nebuchadnezzar's army down to the Mediterranean coast. He stationed guards in all the walled towns and selected certain local men in each of the towns as reserve troops. ⁷ The people in the towns and in the surrounding countryside welcomed Holofernes by wearing wreaths of flowers and dancing to the beat of drums. ⁸ But Holofernes destroyed all their places of worship[b] and cut down their sacred trees. He had been ordered to destroy all the gods of the land so that all the nations and tribes would worship only Nebuchadnezzar and pray to him as a god.

⁹ Then Holofernes passed through Jezreel Valley near Dothan, which faces the main ridge of the mountains of Judah, ¹⁰ and set up camp between Geba and Scythopolis. He stayed there for a month in order to get supplies for his army.

The Israelite Plan for Defense

4 The people of Judah heard what Holofernes, the commander of King Nebuchadnezzar's armies, had done to the other nations. They heard how he had looted and destroyed all their temples, ² and they were terrified of him and afraid of what he might do to Jerusalem and to the Temple of the Lord their God. ³ They had only recently returned home to Judah from exile and had just rededicated the Temple and its utensils and its altar after they had been defiled. ⁴ So they sent a warning to the whole region of Samaria and to the towns of Kona, Beth Horon, Belmain, Jericho, Choba, and Aesora, and to Salem Valley. ⁵ They immediately occupied the mountaintops, fortified the villages on the mountains, and stored up food in preparation for war. It was fortunate that they had recently harvested their fields.

⁶ The High Priest Joakim, who was in Jerusalem at that time, wrote to the people in the towns of Bethulia and Betomesthaim, which face Jezreel Valley near Dothan. ⁷ He ordered them to occupy the mountain passes which led into the land of Judah, where it would be easy to withstand an attack, since the approach was only wide enough for two people at a time to pass. ⁸ The Israelites carried out the orders given to them by the High Priest Joakim and the Council which met in Jerusalem.

Prayer before the War

⁹ The leaders of Israel prayed earnestly to God and fasted. ¹⁰ They put on

---

[b] *One ancient translation* places of worship; *Greek* territory.
3.8 Ex 34.13; 2 Ch 17.6   **4.10-12** Jon 3.7, 8; Es 4.1-3

They lay there in the Lord's presence. (4.11)

sackcloth — they and their wives, their children, their livestock, and every resident foreigner, every slave and hired laborer. 11-12 They also covered the altar with sackcloth. Then all the men, women, and children in Jerusalem lay face down on the ground in front of the Temple; they lay there in the Lord's presence, all in sackcloth, their heads covered with ashes. They joined together in earnest prayer to the God of Israel, begging him not to let their children be captured, their wives carried off, or their home towns destroyed. They pleaded with him not to give the Gentiles the satisfaction of destroying the Temple and dishonoring it. 13 The Lord heard their prayers and saw their distress. For many days the people of Judah and Jerusalem continued their fast in front of the Temple of the Lord Almighty. 14 The High Priest Joakim, the priests, and all the others who served in the Lord's Temple, wore sackcloth when they offered the daily burnt offering, the freewill offerings of the people, and the offerings made to fulfill a vow. 15 They put ashes on their turbans and cried out in prayer to the Lord, begging him to have mercy on the whole nation.

The War Council in the Camp of Holofernes

5 When Holofernes, the Assyrian general, heard that the Israelites had prepared for war, blocked the mountain passes, fortified the mountaintops, and set up roadblocks in the plains, 2 he boiled over with anger. He called together all the Moabite rulers, all the Ammonite generals, and all the governors of the region along the Mediterranean coast 3 and said to them, "You live in Canaan, so tell me about the people who live in these mountains. Which cities do they occupy? How large is their army? What is the source of their power and strength? Who is the king who leads their army? 4 Why have they alone, of all the people in the west, refused to come out and surrender to me?"

The Speech of Achior

5 Then Achior, the leader of all the Ammonites, answered Holofernes, "Sir, if you will please be so kind as to listen to me, I will tell you the truth about these people who live in the mountains near your camp. I will not lie to you.

4.13 Es 4.16 **4.14** Jl 2.17

⁶These people are the descendants of some Babylonians ⁷⁻⁸who abandoned the ways of their ancestors in order to worship the God of heaven. Finally, they were driven out of their land because they refused to worship their ancestors' gods. Then they fled to Mesopotamia, where they settled and lived for a long time.

⁹"Afterward, their god told them to leave Mesopotamia and go to the land of Canaan, where they settled and became very rich in gold, silver, and livestock. ¹⁰Later, when a famine struck all the land of Canaan, these Israelites, as they were later called, went down to Egypt and stayed there as long as there was enough food. While they were there, they became a large nation with so many people that they could not be counted. ¹¹So the king of Egypt turned against them. He took advantage of them and put them to work making bricks. He oppressed them and made them slaves. ¹²But they prayed to their god, and he sent disasters that left the Egyptians helpless. When the Egyptians drove them out of the country, ¹³their god dried up the Red Sea in front of them, ¹⁴and then led them along the way to Sinai and Kadesh Barnea.

"The Israelites drove out all the people who lived in the southern part of Canaan, ¹⁵occupied the land of the Amorites, wiped out the people of Heshbon, crossed the Jordan River, and took possession of the entire mountain region. ¹⁶They drove out the Canaanites, the Perizzites, the Jebusites, the Shechemites, and all the Girgashites. The Israelites have now lived in these mountains for a long time.

¹⁷"Their god hates wickedness, and as long as they did not sin against him, they prospered. ¹⁸But when they disobeyed him, they suffered heavy losses in many wars and were finally taken away as captives to a foreign country. The temple of their god was leveled and their cities were occupied by their enemies. ¹⁹But now that they have returned to their god, they have come back home from the countries where they had been scattered. They have again taken possession of the city of Jerusalem, where their temple is, and have resettled in the mountains that had remained uninhabited.

²⁰"Sir, if these people are now sinning against their god, even unknowingly, and if we can be sure that they are guilty of some offense, we can successfully attack them. ²¹But if they have not disobeyed the law of their god, then you should leave them alone, or he will defend them, and we will be disgraced before the whole world."

The Reaction of the Crowd

²²When Achior had finished his speech, all the people standing around the tent began to protest. Holofernes' own senior officers, as well as the Moabites and those from the Mediterranean coast, demanded that Achior be put to death.

²³"Why should we be afraid of these Israelites?" they asked. "They are weak; they can't put up a strong defense. ²⁴Let's go ahead! General Holofernes, your great army will slaughter them easily."

The Speech of Holofernes

6 When the noise of the crowd around the council had subsided, Holofernes spoke to Achior in front of the entire group, those from the Mediterranean coast, the Moabites, and the Ammonite mercenaries.ᶜ

ᶜ the Ammonite mercenaries; *some manuscripts do not have these words.*

5.9 Gn 11.31–12.5   **5.10** Gn 42.1-5; Ex 1.7   **5.11** Ex 1.8-14   **5.12** Ex 7.1–12.46
5.13 Ex 14.21, 22   **5.17** Dt 28.1-68

2"Achior,[d] who do you think you are, acting like a prophet? Who are you to tell us not to go to war against the Israelites because some god will defend them? Nebuchadnezzar is our god, and that's all that matters. He will send his army and wipe these Israelites off the face of the earth. Their god can't help them. 3 But we serve Nebuchadnezzar, and we will beat them as easily as if their whole army were one man. They will not be able to hold their ground against our cavalry; 4 it will overwhelm them. The mountains will be soaked with their blood, and the valleys will be filled with their corpses. After our attack, they will be completely wiped out; not a trace of them will be left. This is the command of Nebuchadnezzar, the lord of the whole earth, and he doesn't speak idle words. 5 Achior, you are nothing but an Ammonite mercenary, and you talk like a traitor. You will not see me again until I come and punish this race of runaway slaves. 6 And when I do, my soldiers will put you to death. You will be just another name on the casualty list.

7 "Now my men will take you into the mountains and leave you in one of the Israelite towns, 8 and you will die with the people there. 9 Why look so worried, Achior? Don't you think the town can stand against me? I will carry out all my threats; you can be sure of that!"

Achior Is Brought to Bethulia

10 Then Holofernes ordered his men, who were waiting in his tent, to seize Achior, take him to Bethulia, and hand him over to the Israelites. 11 So the men seized Achior and took him out of the camp into the valley. From there they led him into the mountains, as far as the spring which was below Bethulia. 12 When the men of that town saw them approaching, they picked up their weapons and ran to the top of the hill. Every man who used a sling as a weapon rained stones down on Holofernes' soldiers, and this stopped them from coming any farther up the mountain. 13 The Assyrians were forced to take cover along the mountainside, where they tied Achior up and left him lying at the foot of the mountain. Then they returned to Holofernes.

14 Later, when the Israelites came down from Bethulia, they untied Achior, brought him into the town, and took him before the town officials, 15 who at that time were Uzziah son of Micah, of the tribe of Simeon, Chabris son of Gothoniel, and Charmis son of Melchiel. 16 The officials called together the town elders, and all the women and the young men also ran to the assembly. Achior was brought before the people, and Uzziah began questioning him. 17 Achior told them what had been said at Holofernes' war council, what he himself had said to the Assyrian officers, and how Holofernes had boasted about what he would do to the Israelites. 18 When the people heard this, they fell on their knees and worshiped God. They prayed: 19 "O Lord God of heaven, look how our boastful enemies have humiliated your people! Have pity on us and help us." 20 Then they reassured Achior and praised him for what he had done. 21 After the assembly was over, Uzziah took Achior home with him, and gave a banquet there for the elders. All that night they prayed to the God of Israel for help.

The Siege of Bethulia

7 1-2 The next day Holofernes gathered his whole army together, as well as his allied forces. It was an immense army, consisting of 170,000 infantry and 12,000 cavalry, not counting the support troops who took care of the

---

[d] Achior; *some manuscripts add* you and your hired soldiers from Ephraim; *others add* you and your mercenaries from Ammon.

equipment. He ordered them to march on Bethulia, seize the mountain passes, and attack the Israelites. So they moved out ³and set up camp beside the spring in the valley near Bethulia. The camp was so wide that it spread out toward the town of Dothan as far as Balbaim, and so long that it stretched from Bethulia to Cyamon, which faces Jezreel Valley.

⁴When the Israelites saw the size of the army, they were terrified and said to one another, "Those soldiers are going to eat up everything in sight. There's not enough food in the mountains, valleys, and hills put together to feed an army like that." ⁵But in spite of their fear, all the Israelites took up their weapons, lighted signal fires on the towers, and remained on guard duty all night. ⁶The next day Holofernes led out his entire cavalry so that the Israelites in Bethulia could see them. ⁷He inspected the approaches to the town and the springs that supplied its water. He seized the springs and stationed guards there, before returning to camp.

⁸All the leaders of the Edomite and Moabite forces, along with the commanders of the troops from the Mediterranean coast, came to Holofernes and said, ⁹"Sir, if you listen to our advice, your troops will not suffer heavy losses. ¹⁰These Israelites do not rely on their weapons for defense but rather on the height of the mountains where they live, since the mountains are not easy to climb. ¹¹So then, General Holofernes, if you do not make a direct attack on them, your whole army will suffer no casualties. ¹²Stay in your camp and keep your soldiers in their quarters. Just command your men to blockade the springs at the foot of the mountains, ¹³because that's where the people of Bethulia come to draw their water. Then, when they are dying of thirst, they will surrender their town to you. Meanwhile, we and our men will go up

to the tops of the surrounding mountains, where we will set up camp and keep anyone from leaving the town. ¹⁴Everyone will starve to death — men, women, and children. Even before we attack, the streets will be littered with their corpses. ¹⁵In this way you can make them pay for their rebellion and for refusing to surrender peacefully to you."

¹⁶Holofernes and his entire staff were pleased with this suggestion, so he gave orders to put the plan into action. ¹⁷The Moabites and 5,000 Assyrians moved their camp into the valley to control the source of the town's water. ¹⁸The Edomites and the Ammonites went up into the mountains and set up their camp opposite the town of Dothan. They sent some of their men to the southeast in the direction of Acraba, near Chusi, which is beside the Mochmur River. The rest of the Assyrian army set up camp in the valley. Their camp was spread out over the whole countryside, because the number of tents and the amount of equipment needed for such a large army were immense.

¹⁹Then the Israelites cried out to the Lord their God for help. They had lost their courage, for with the enemy all around them there was no way to escape. ²⁰The entire Assyrian army — infantry, chariots, and cavalry — blockaded Bethulia for thirty-four days until the town ran out of water. ²¹All the reservoirs and cisterns went dry, so that the drinking water had to be rationed, and not a day passed when there was enough water to go around. ²²Children were becoming weak; everywhere throughout the town women and young people were collapsing. No one had any strength left.

²³All the people of the town — men, women, and children alike — gathered around Uzziah and the town officials

No one had any strength left. (7.22)

and shouted in protest, 24 "God will punish you for what you have done to us! You are to blame for what is happening, because you did not make peace with the Assyrians. 25 There is no one to help us now! God has put us in their power. We are exhausted and dying of thirst. 26 Call the Assyrians now and surrender to them, and let Holofernes and his army take the town and loot it. 27 We are better off as prisoners of war. They will make us slaves, but at least we will be alive, and we won't have to watch our wives and children dying before our eyes. 28 Heaven and earth are witnesses against you, and so is our God, the Lord of our ancestors, who is punishing us for their sins as well as ours. We can only hope and pray that he will not let these terrible things happen to us today."*e*

29 Everyone there began to weep loudly and to pray to the Lord their God. 30 Then Uzziah said to them, "Don't give up, my friends! Let's wait five more days to see if the Lord our God will be merciful to us. Surely he will not abandon us completely. 31 But if no help comes after five days, then I will do as you say." 32 So Uzziah dismissed the people. All the men returned to their guard posts on the walls and towers, while the women and children went back to their homes. The morale of the entire town was very low.

Judith, the Israelite Widow

8 At that time, Judith heard about Uzziah's decision. She was the daughter of Merari, the granddaughter of Ox and the great-granddaughter of Joseph. Joseph's ancestors were Oziel, Elkiah, Ananias, Gideon, Raphaim, Ahitub, Elijah, Hilkiah, Eliab, Nathanael, Salamiel, Sarasadai, and Israel. 2 Judith's husband Manasseh, who belonged to the same tribe and clan, had died during the barley harvest. 3 He had suffered a sunstroke while in the fields supervising the farm workers and later died in bed at home in Bethulia. He was buried in the family tomb in the field between Dothan and Balamon.

4 For three years and four months, Judith had lived as a widow. 5 In her grief she built a little shelter on the roof of her house and lived there, wearing sackcloth. 6 She fasted during that entire period except when fasting was forbidden: the day before the Sabbath and the Sabbath itself, the eve of the New Moon Festival and the Festival itself, and all the festivals and holidays observed by the people of Israel. 7 Judith was a very beautiful woman. Her husband had left her gold and silver, servants and slaves, livestock and fields. She continued to supervise the estate, 8 and no one ever said anything bad about Judith. She was a very religious woman.

e We can ... today; *some Greek manuscripts and ancient translations have* We demand that you surrender, as we have asked you to do today.
8.5 Jg 3.20; 2 K 4.10

Judith Meets with the Town Officials

9 Judith heard how the people were complaining bitterly against Uzziah, now that the water shortage had broken their morale. She learned that in answer to their complaints he had promised to surrender the town to the Assyrians after five days. **10** Judith sent a slave, the woman who managed her business affairs, to invite Uzziah,*f* Chabris, and Charmis, the town officials, to her home.

11 When the officials arrived, Judith said to them, "Please listen to me. You are the leaders of the people of Bethulia, but you were wrong to speak to the people as you did today. You should not have made a solemn promise before God that you would surrender the town to our enemies if the Lord did not come

Judith was a beautiful and attractive woman.
(8.7)

to our aid within a few days. **12** What right do you have to put God to the test as you have done today? Who are you to put yourselves in God's place in dealing with human affairs? **13** It is the Lord Almighty that you are putting to the

test! Will you never learn? **14** There is no way that you can understand what is in the depths of a human heart or find out what a person is thinking. Yet you dare to read God's mind and interpret his thoughts! How can you claim to understand God, the Creator? No, my friends, you must stop arousing the anger of the Lord our God! **15** If he decides not to come to our aid within five days, he still may rescue us at any time he chooses. Or he may let our enemies destroy us. **16** But you must not lay down conditions for the Lord our God! Do you think that he is like one of us? Do you think you can bargain with him or force him to make a decision? **17** No! Instead, we should ask God for his help and wait patiently for him to rescue us. If he wants to, he will answer our cry for help. **18** We do not worship gods made with human hands. Not one of our clans, tribes, towns, or cities has ever done that, even though our ancestors used to do so. **19** That is why God let their enemies kill them and take everything they had. It was a great defeat! **20** But since we worship no other God but the Lord, we can hope that he will not reject us or any of our people.

21 "If our town is taken by the enemy, the entire region of Judah will then fall, and our Temple in Jerusalem will be looted. And God will make us pay with our lives for allowing the Temple to be defiled. **22** He will hold us responsible for the slaughter and captivity of our people and for the destruction of the land we have inherited. We will be despised and mocked by the people in those nations to which we will be taken as slaves. **23** We are not going to win the favor of our enemies by surrendering to them now.*g* If we do surrender, the Lord our God will see that we are put to shame.

24 "No, my friends, we should set an

---

f Uzziah; *some Greek manuscripts do not have this word.*   *g* We are not . . . now; *or* No good will ever come out of our slavery.

8.12 Dt 6.16; Job 38.2   **8.14** Ro 11.33, 34; 1 Co 2.11

example for our own people. Not only their lives, but the fate of the Temple and the altar depend on us. 25 The Lord our God is putting us to the test, just as he tested our ancestors, and we should be thankful for that. 26 Remember how he put Abraham and Isaac to the test, and what happened to Jacob while he was working as a shepherd for his uncle Laban in Mesopotamia. 27 God is not testing our loyalty as severely as he did theirs. God is not sending this punishment on us as revenge, but as a warning to us who worship him."

28 Then Uzziah answered Judith, "Everything you have said makes good sense, and no one can argue with it. 29 This is not the first time you have shown wisdom. Ever since you were a child, all of us have recognized the soundness and maturity of your judgment. 30 But our people are dying of thirst. They forced us to say what we did and to make a solemn promise, which we cannot break. 31 So now, since you are a deeply religious woman, pray for our people; ask the Lord to send rain to fill our cisterns, so that we can get our strength back."

32 "All right," Judith replied, "I am going to do something which our Jewish people will never forget. 33 Tonight, the three of you must stand guard at the gate so that my slave woman and I can leave the town. And before the day comes on which you have promised to surrender, the Lord will use me to rescue the people of Israel. 34 But you must not ask me what I am going to do; I will explain it to you when it is all over."

35 Uzziah and the other officials said to her, "You have our blessing. May the Lord our God guide you as you take revenge on our enemies." Then they left Judith's rooftop shelter and returned to their posts.

Judith's Prayer

9 Then Judith put ashes on her head, opened her robe to reveal the sackcloth she was wearing under her clothes, and bowed down with her face to the floor. It was the time that the evening incense was being offered in the Temple in Jerusalem, and Judith prayed in a loud voice: 2 "O Lord, the God of my ancestor Simeon, remember how you armed Simeon with a sword to take revenge on those foreigners who seized Dinah, who was a virgin, tore off her clothes,[h] and defiled her; they stripped her naked and shamed her; they raped her and disgraced her, even though you had forbidden this. 3 That is why you let their leaders be killed — put to death on the same bed where they had raped the woman.[i] You destroyed them all, slaves, princes, and rulers on their thrones. 4 You let their wives be carried off, their daughters taken captive, and their possessions plundered by the Israelites, your chosen people, who were eager to do your will. Dinah's brothers were furious because of this disgrace to their family, so they called on you for help.

"O my God, listen to my prayer, the prayer of a widow. 5 Your hand guided all that happened then, and all that happened before and after. You have planned it all — what is happening now, and what is yet to be. Your plans have always been carried out. 6 Whatever you want to be done is as good as done. You know in advance all that you will do and what decisions you will make. 7 Now the Assyrians are stronger than ever; they take pride in their cavalry and their infantry. They rely on their weapons, but they do not know that you, O Lord, are a warrior who ends war. The Lord is your name. 8 In your anger, use your power to shatter their

---

[h] *Probable text* clothes; *Greek unclear.*
Greek unclear.
[i] *Probable text* put to death . . . woman;
8.26 Gn 22.1-18; 29.1 — 31.55　　**9.2** Gn 34.1-31

mighty army. They plan to defile your Temple, where you are worshiped, and to hack off the corners of your altar with their swords. ⁹ Look how proud and boastful they are! Pour out your fury upon them! I am only a widow, but give me the strength to carry out my plan. ¹⁰ Use my deceitful words to strike them all dead, master and slave alike. Let a woman's strength break their pride. ¹¹ Your power does not depend on the size and strength of an army. You are a God who cares for the humble and helps the oppressed. You give support and protection to people who are weak and helpless; you save those who have lost hope. ¹² Now hear my prayer, O God of my ancestor Simeon, the God in whom Israel trusts, ruler of heaven and earth, creator of the rivers and the seas, king of all creation. Hear my prayer and ¹³ let my deceitful words wound and kill those who have planned such cruelty against your covenant and your holy Temple, against Mount Zion and the land you have given your people. ¹⁴ Make your whole nation and every tribe recognize that you are God, almighty and all-powerful, and that you alone protect the people of Israel!"

Judith Goes to the Camp of Holofernes

10 When Judith had finished her prayer to the God of Israel, ² she stood up, called her slave woman, and went down into the house as she always did on Sabbaths and festival days. ³ She took off the sackcloth and her widow's clothes, took a bath, and put on rich perfumes. She brushed her hair, tied a ribbon around it, and dressed herself in the fine clothes she used to wear on joyful occasions when her husband Manasseh was still alive. ⁴ She put on sandals and all her finest jewelry: rings and earrings, and bracelets on her wrists and ankles. She made herself so beautiful that she was sure to attract

the attention of any man who saw her. ⁵ Judith gave her slave woman a leather bag of wine and a jar of oil to carry. She filled a bag with roasted barley, cakes of dried figs, and several loaves of bread baked according to Jewish food laws. She carefully wrapped all the food and dishes and gave them to her slave. ⁶ Then the two women left the house and went to the gates of Bethulia, where they found Uzziah and the town officials, Chabris and Charmis, standing guard. ⁷ When the men saw Judith after she had changed clothes and put on make-up, they were struck by her beauty and said to her, ⁸ "May the God of our ancestors bless you and make your plan successful, so that you may bring glory to Jerusalem and victory to Israel."

Judith prayed ⁹ and then said, "Order the gates to be opened for me. I am on my way to do what we were talking about." Then they ordered the young men to open the gates for her, ¹⁰ and Judith and her slave left the city. The men watched her as she went down the mountain into the valley, until she was out of sight.

¹¹ As the two women were walking through the valley, an Assyrian patrol met them. ¹² They arrested Judith and questioned her, "What is your nationality? Where did you come from, and where are you going?"

"I am a Hebrew," she answered, "but I am running away from the Israelites because God is going to let you destroy them. ¹³ I am on my way to see Holofernes, the general in command of your army, to give him some reliable information. I can show him how to advance into the mountains and take control of the entire region without a single casualty."

¹⁴ The men stared at her because she was so beautiful. They listened to her story and said, ¹⁵ "You have saved your life by coming down here to see our

9.13 Gk Est C.24, 25

They were greatly impressed by her beauty. (10.19)

general. Some of us will take you to his headquarters and present you to him. ¹⁶ Do not be afraid of him. Just tell him what you have told us, and he will treat you well." ¹⁷ They assigned a hundred men to escort Judith and her slave to the headquarters of Holofernes.

¹⁸ There was great commotion in the Assyrian camp as news of Judith's arrival spread from tent to tent. While she stood outside the tent of Holofernes waiting to be presented to him, many Assyrian soldiers came and stood around her. ¹⁹ They were greatly impressed by her beauty and wondered what kind of people the Israelites were. "Who can have contempt for people whose women are so beautiful?" they asked one another. "We had better kill all the men, or else these Jews will be able to charm the whole world."

²⁰ Then Holofernes' bodyguard and his personal servants came out and led Judith into the tent. ²¹ Holofernes was resting on his bed under a mosquito net woven of purple and gold thread and decorated with emeralds and other precious stones. ²² When the men told him that Judith had arrived, he came to the outer part of the tent. Silver lamps were carried ahead of him. ²³ When Judith came near him and his servants, they were all astonished at her beauty. She bowed down to the ground before Holofernes, but his servants helped her to her feet.

11 Holofernes said to Judith, "Don't worry; there's no need for you to be afraid. I have never hurt anyone who was willing to serve Nebuchadnezzar, king of the whole world. ² Even now, if your people up in the mountains had not insulted me, I would not have declared war on them. They have brought all this trouble on themselves. ³ But tell me, why have you left them and come to us? You will be safe here. No need to be afraid! We have spared your life tonight, and you are in no danger for the future. ⁴ No one here will harm you; everyone will treat you well, like all other servants of my master, Nebuchadnezzar."

⁵ Then Judith said to Holofernes, "Allow me to speak to you, my lord, and please listen to what I have to say. I will tell you the truth. ⁶ If you follow my advice, God will do something great with you, and my lord will not fail in his plan. ⁷ For I swear to you by the life and strength of Nebuchadnezzar, king of the whole world, who sent you to bring order to all the subjects of his kingdom, that not only have you made people

11.7 Jr 27.6; Dn 2.38

serve him, but because of you even the wild animals, the livestock, and the birds obey him. Because of you, Nebuchadnezzar and his entire kingdom will prosper.*j* ⁸We have heard how wise and clever you are. The whole world knows that you are the most competent, skilled, and accomplished general in the whole Assyrian Empire. ⁹Achior was rescued by the men of Bethulia, and has told us what he said at your war council. ¹⁰Please, sir, do not dismiss lightly what Achior told you, but take it seriously, because it is true. No one can harm or conquer our people unless they sin against their God.

¹¹"But you will not suffer any setbacks, nor will you fail to achieve your goal. When the Israelites sin and make their God angry, they will die. ¹²Their food supply has already run out, and the water shortage has become serious, so they have decided to kill their livestock and eat foods that God's Law clearly forbids them to eat. ¹³They have decided to eat the wheat set aside from the early harvest and the tithes of wine and oil, which are holy and are reserved for the priests who serve God in Jerusalem. The rest of us are forbidden even to touch this sacred food, ¹⁴but since the people in Jerusalem have already broken this law, the people of our town have sent messengers to the Council there requesting permission to do the same. ¹⁵On the day that they receive permission and actually eat the food, you will be able to destroy them. ¹⁶As soon as I learned about this, I ran away from my people. God has sent me to do something with you that will amaze everyone in the entire world who hears about it. ¹⁷Sir, I am a religious woman; I worship the God of heaven day and night. I will stay here in your camp, and each night I will go out into the valley to pray to God, and he will tell me when the Israelites have sinned. ¹⁸As soon as

I find out, I will come and tell you, and you can march out with your whole army. The Israelites will not be able to defend themselves against you. ¹⁹I will guide you through the central part of the land of Judah until we come to Jerusalem, where I will crown you king in the center of the city. You will scatter the people of Jerusalem like sheep without a shepherd. Not even a dog will dare to growl at you. God has revealed these things to me in advance and has sent me to report them to you."

²⁰Holofernes and his personal servants were pleased with what Judith had said, and they admired her wisdom. ²¹"She must be the wisest and most beautiful woman in the world," they commented one to another.

²²Then Holofernes said to her, "It's a good thing that God has sent you here to bring us victory and to destroy those who have insulted King Nebuchadnezzar. ²³Not only are you beautiful, but you know how to make a speech. If you do as you have promised, your God will be my God. You will live in King Nebuchadnezzar's palace and will be famous throughout the world."

Judith Remains Faithful to Her Religion

12 Holofernes commanded his men to take Judith to the table which was set with his silverware and to serve her some of his own special food and wine. ²But Judith refused. "I cannot eat your food," she said, "for I would be breaking the laws of my God. I will eat only what I have brought with me."

³"But what will you do when your food and wine are gone?" Holofernes asked. "Where will we get more food for you? There are no Israelites here in our camp."

⁴"Sir," Judith answered, "as surely as

j not only . . . prosper; *Greek unclear.*
11.13 Ex 23.19; Lv 27.30   **12.2** Dn 1.8; Gk Est C.28

"O Lord . . . help me with what I am about to do." (13.4)

you live, I have more than enough food to last until the Lord has used me to carry out his plan."

⁵ Then Holofernes' personal servants led Judith to a tent. She slept there until the time of the morning watch just before dawn, when she got up ⁶ and sent a message to Holofernes requesting permission to go out into the valley to pray. ⁷ Holofernes ordered his guards to let Judith leave the camp. So for three days Judith lived in the camp, and each night she would go out to the valley near Bethulia and bathe at the spring. ⁸ After she had bathed, she would pray to the Lord God to guide her in her plan to bring victory to Israel. ⁹ Then she would return to the camp ritually pure and remain in her tent until after the evening meal.

Holofernes' Banquet

¹⁰ On the fourth day of Judith's stay in the camp, Holofernes gave a banquet for his highest ranking officers, but he did not invite any of the officers who were on duty. ¹¹ He said to Bagoas, the eunuch who was in charge of his personal affairs, "Go and persuade the Hebrew woman, who is in your care, to come to my tent to eat and drink with us. ¹² It would be a shame to pass up an opportunity to make love to a woman like that. If I don't try to seduce her, she will laugh at me."

¹³ So Bagoas left Holofernes and went to Judith. "Lovely lady," he said, "the general invites you to his tent for some drinks. Come and enjoy yourself like the Assyrian women who serve in Nebuchadnezzar's palace. This is a great honor."

¹⁴ "I shall be glad to accept," Judith answered. "How could I refuse? I'll remember this happy night as long as I live."

¹⁵ So Judith got up and put on her prettiest clothes. Her slave woman went ahead of her and placed on the ground in front of Holofernes the lamb skins that Bagoas had given Judith to sit on when she ate. ¹⁶ Judith came into the tent and sat down there. Holofernes was aroused when he saw her and had an uncontrollable desire to make love to her. From the first day he had seen her, he had been waiting for a chance to seduce her. ¹⁷ "Join us for a drink and enjoy yourself," he said to her.

¹⁸ "I'll be glad to, sir," Judith replied; "this is the happiest day of my life." ¹⁹ But even then Judith ate and drank only what her slave had prepared. ²⁰ Holofernes was so charmed by her that he drank more wine than he had ever drunk at one time in his whole life.

13 Finally, when it got late, the guests excused themselves and left. Bagoas then closed up the tent from the outside and prevented Holofernes' servants from going in. So they all went to bed; everyone was very tired because the banquet had lasted so long. ²Judith was left alone in the tent with Holofernes who was lying drunk on his bed. ³Judith's slave woman was waiting outside the tent for Judith to go and pray, as she had done each night. Judith had also told Bagoas that she would be going out to pray as usual.

⁴All the guests and servants were now gone, and Judith and Holofernes were alone in the tent. Judith stood by Holofernes' bed and prayed silently, "O Lord, God Almighty, help me with what I am about to do for the glory of Jerusalem. ⁵Now is the time to rescue your chosen people and to help me carry out my plan to destroy the enemies who are threatening us." ⁶Judith went to the bedpost by Holofernes' head and took down his sword. ⁷She came closer, seized Holofernes by the hair of his head, and said, "O Lord, God of Israel, give me strength now." ⁸Then Judith raised the sword and struck him twice in the neck as hard as she could, chopping off his head. ⁹She rolled his body off the bed and took down the mosquito net from the bedposts. Then she came out and gave Holofernes' head to her slave, ¹⁰who put it in the food bag.

Judith and Her Slave Return to Bethulia

Then the two women left together, as they always did when they went to pray. After they had walked through the Assyrian camp, they crossed the valley and went up the mountainside until they came to the gates of Bethulia. ¹¹When they were a short distance away, Judith called out to the guards at the gate, "Open the gate! Open the gate! Our God is still with us. Today he has once again shown his strength in Israel and used his power against our enemies."

¹²When the men heard her voice, they hurried down to the gates and called for the town officials. ¹³Everyone, young and old, ran together to the gate. No one could believe that Judith had come back. They opened the gate for her and her slave and welcomed them. Then, when they had lit a fire to give some light and had gathered around the two women, ¹⁴Judith shouted, "Praise God, give him praise! Praise God, who has not held back his mercy from the people of Israel. Tonight he has used me to destroy our enemies." ¹⁵She then took the head out of the food bag and showed it to the people. "Here," she said, "is the head of Holofernes, the general of the Assyrian army, and here is the mosquito net from his bed, where he lay in a drunken stupor. The Lord used a woman to kill him. ¹⁶As the Lord lives, I swear that Holofernes never touched me, although my beauty deceived him and brought him to his ruin. I was not defiled or disgraced; the Lord took care of me through it all."

When the men heard her voice . . . (13.12)

¹⁷Everyone in the city was utterly amazed. They bowed down and worshiped God, praying together, "Our God, you are worthy of great praise. Today you have triumphed over the enemies of your people."

[18]Then Uzziah said, "Judith, my dear, the Most High God has blessed you more than any other woman on earth. How worthy of praise is the Lord God who created heaven and earth! He guided you as you cut off the head of our deadliest enemy. [19]Your trust in God will never be forgotten by those who tell of God's power. [20]May God give you everlasting honor for what you have done. May he reward you with blessings, because you remained faithful to him and did not hesitate to risk your own life to relieve the oppression of your people."

All the people replied, "Amen, amen!"

Judith's Plan

14 Then Judith said to them, "My friends, please follow my advice. In the morning, take this head and hang it on the town wall. [2]Appoint a leader for yourselves, and at sunrise have all your able-bodied men take their weapons and march out of the town with him, as if they were going down into the valley to attack the Assyrian outpost. [3]The Assyrian guards will grab their weapons and rush back to camp to wake up their officers. The officers will run to Holofernes' tent but will not find him, and the whole army will be terrified and retreat as you advance against them. [4]Then you and all the other Israelites will be able to follow them and kill them as they retreat. [5]But before you do any of this, send Achior the Ammonite to me. I want to see if he recognizes Holofernes, the man who spoke of Israel with contempt and sent Achior to us, thinking he would be killed along with the rest of us."

Achior's Conversion

[6]So they called Achior from Uzziah's house. But when he came and saw the head of Holofernes in the hands of one of the men, Achior fainted and fell to the floor. [7]When they had helped him up, Achior bowed at Judith's feet in respect. "May every family in the land of Judah praise you," he said, "and may every nation tremble with terror when they hear your name. [8]Please tell me how you managed to do this."

While all the people were gathered around, Judith told him everything that she had done from the day she left the town until that moment. [9]When she had finished her story, the people cheered so loudly that the whole town echoed with sounds of joy. [10]When Achior heard all that the God of Israel had done, he became a firm believer. He was circumcised and made a member of the Israelite community, as his descendants are to the present day.

Panic in Holofernes' Camp

[11]The next morning the Israelites hung the head of Holofernes on the wall of the town. All of them took up their weapons and went out in companies to the slopes in front of the town. [12]When the Assyrians saw what was happening, they sent word to their officers, and these reported the matter to their superiors. [13]These men then went to Holofernes' tent and said to Bagoas, "Wake up the general! Those worthless Israelites have dared to come down from the mountain to attack us; they are just asking to be destroyed."

[14]Bagoas went in and clapped his hands in front of the sleeping quarters of the tent, thinking that Holofernes was in bed with Judith. [15]When there was no answer, he drew the curtain aside and went in, and there he found the headless body sprawled over a footstool. [16]Bagoas let out a yell. He screamed, tore his clothes, and started groaning and weeping. [17]He went into the tent where Judith had stayed, but of course he did not find her. He rushed

out and shouted to the officers, [18]"They have tricked us! One Israelite woman has disgraced Nebuchadnezzar's whole kingdom. Look in there! Holofernes is lying dead on the ground and his head is gone!" [19]When the officers heard this, they tore their clothes in grief; and as the panic spread, wild cries and shouts were heard throughout the camp.

Israel's Victory

15 When the soldiers heard what had happened, they were horrified [2]and began to tremble with fear. They all scattered in different directions from the camp, making no effort to stay together as they tried to escape along the paths in the mountains and valleys. [3]The soldiers who had camped in the mountains around Bethulia also began to retreat. Then all the Israelite soldiers came charging down on them.

[4]Uzziah sent messengers to the towns of Betomesthaim, Bebai, Choba, and Kola, and throughout the land of Israel to tell everyone what had happened and to urge them to join in pursuing and destroying the enemy. [5]When they received the message, they all attacked the Assyrians and chased them as far as Choba, slaughtering them as they went. Even the people of Jerusalem and others living in the mountains joined the attack when the messengers told them what had happened in the Assyrian camp. The people of the regions of Gilead and Galilee blocked the path of the retreating Assyrians and inflicted heavy losses on them. They pursued them as far as the region around Damascus.

[6]The rest of the people in Bethulia went down to the Assyrian camp, plundered it and carried away enough loot to make themselves very rich. [7]When the Israelite soldiers returned from the slaughter, they helped themselves to what was left. There was so much of it that the people of the towns and villages in the hill country also shared in the loot.

Israel Celebrates the Victory

[8]The High Priest Joakim and the Council of Israel came from Jerusalem to see for themselves what great things the Lord had done for his people and to meet Judith and congratulate her. [9]When they arrived, they all praised her, "You are Jerusalem's crowning glory, the heroine of Israel, the pride

"You are . . . the heroine of Israel!" (15.9)

and joy of our people! [10]You have won this great victory for Israel by yourself. God, the Almighty, is pleased with what you have done. May he bless you as long as you live."

All the people responded, "Amen."

[11]It took the people thirty days to finish looting the camp of the Assyrians. Judith was given Holofernes' tent, all his silver, his bowls, his couches, and all his furniture. She took them and loaded as much as she could on her mule; then she brought her wagons and loaded them too. [12]All the Israelite women came to see her; they sang her praises and danced in her honor. On this joyful occasion Judith and the other women waved ivy-covered branches [13]and wore wreaths of olive leaves on their heads. Judith took her

place at the head of the procession to lead the women as they danced. All the men of Israel followed, wearing wreaths of flowers on their heads, carrying their weapons, and singing songs of praise.

Judith's Song of Praise

16 Then Judith sang a song of thanksgiving there with all Israel present, and the people joined in this song of praise. ²She sang,

"Praise my God and sing to him;
    praise the Lord with drums
        and cymbals;
    play a new song for him.
Praise him and call on him for
        help.
³The Lord is a warrior who
        ends war.
    He rescued me from my
        pursuers
    and brought me back to his
        people's camp.
⁴Down from the mountains of the
        north came the Assyrians,
    with their tens of thousands
        of soldiers.
    Their troops blocked the rivers in
        the valleys;
    their cavalry covered the
        mountains.
⁵They threatened to set fire to our
        country,
    slaughter our young men,
    dash our babies to the ground,
    take our children away as
        captives,
    and carry off all our young
        women.
⁶But the Lord Almighty tricked
        them;
    he used a woman to stop
        them.
⁷Their hero was not slain by
        young soldiers

or attacked and killed by
        mighty giants.
It was Judith, the daughter of
        Merari,
    who brought him down with
        her beauty.
⁸She gave victory to the oppressed
        people of Israel,
    when she took off her widow's
        clothes,
    and put on a linen dress to
        entice him.
She put on her rich perfumes
    and tied a ribbon around her
        hair.
⁹Her dainty sandal caught
        his eye;
    her beauty captured his heart.
Then the sword slashed through
        his neck.
¹⁰The Persians trembled at her
        daring;
    the Medes were amazed at
        her bravery.
¹¹Then our people shouted in
        victory.
    They had been weak and
        oppressed,
    but they forced the enemy to
        retreat in panic and fear.
¹²We are the descendants of
        slaves,
    but our enemies turned
        and ran;
    we killed them like runaway
        slaves.
    They were destroyed by the army
        of the Lord.

¹³"I will sing a new song to
        my God.
    O Lord, you are strong and
        glorious!
    You have never been
        defeated.
¹⁴Let all your creatures serve you.
    You gave the command,
    and all of them came into
        being;

16.13 Ps 144.9

you breathed on them,
and all of them were created.
No one can oppose your
    command.
15 The mountains and the seas
    tremble,
and rocks melt like wax when
    you come near.
But there is mercy for all who
    obey you.
16 The Lord is more pleased with
    those who obey him
than with all the choice meat
    on the altar,
or with all the most fragrant
    sacrifices.
17 The nations who rise up against
    my people are doomed.
The Lord Almighty will
    punish them on
    Judgment Day.
He will send fire and worms
    to devour their bodies,
and they will weep in pain
    forever."

Judith's Fame

18 When the people arrived in Jerusalem, they purified themselves and worshiped God. They presented their burnt offerings, freewill offerings, and gifts. 19 Judith dedicated to God all of Holofernes' property, which the people had given to her. And as a special offering in fulfillment of a vow, she presented to the Lord the mosquito net which she had taken from Holofernes' bed. 20 For three months the people continued to celebrate in front of the Temple in Jerusalem, and Judith stayed there with them.

21 When the celebrations had ended, everyone returned home, and Judith went back to Bethulia to live on her own estate. For the rest of her life she was famous throughout the land of Israel. 22 Many men wanted to marry her, but she never remarried after the death of her husband Manasseh. 23-24 Her fame continued to spread, and she lived in the house her husband had left her. Before she died, Judith divided her property among her husband's and her own close relatives and set her slave woman free. When she died in Bethulia at the age of 105, she was buried beside her husband, and the people of Israel mourned her death for seven days. 25 As long as Judith lived, and for many years after her death, no one dared to threaten the people of Israel.

16.16 1 S 15.22; Ps 51.16, 17; Ho 6.6

The Book of
ESTHER
(The Greek Version)

INTRODUCTION

The Book of Esther in Greek is a translation, adaptation, and expansion of *The Book of Esther* in Hebrew. The chain of events is much the same, but there are many variations in text, including different proper names and a strong religious tone. The six additions, shown as Chapters A–F in this translation, provide a different introduction and conclusion, introduce documents in an official style, and emphasize the religious elements by the addition of prayers and accounts of how they were answered.

OUTLINE OF CONTENTS

Mordecai's Strange Dream

A *a* 1-3 Mordecai, a Jew who belonged to the tribe of Benjamin, was taken into exile, along with King Jehoiachin of Judah, when King Nebuchadnezzar of Babylonia captured Jerusalem. Mordecai was the son of Jair, a descendant of Kish and Shimei. He now lived in the Persian city of Susa, where he was an important official in the royal court of Xerxes the great king.

During the second year of Xerxes' reign, on the first day of the month of Nisan, Mordecai had a dream. 4 He dreamed that there was great noise and confusion, loud thunder, and an earthquake, with terrible turmoil on the earth. 5 Then two huge dragons appeared, ready to fight each other. 6 They made a dreadful noise, and all the nations got ready to make war against God's nation of righteous people. 7 For the world it was a day of darkness and gloom, trouble and distress, destruction and ruin. 8 All of God's righteous people were troubled, in great fear of what was about to happen to them. They prepared for death, 9 but they cried out to God for help. In the dream their prayer was answered by a great river which came flowing out of a small spring. 10 The day dawned, the sun rose, and the humble people were made strong and destroyed their arrogant enemies.

11 Mordecai woke up from this dream in which he saw what God planned to do. He thought about it all day and tried to understand what it meant.

---

a Chapter A 1-17 corresponds to chapters 11.2–12.6 in a number of English translations.
A.1-3 2 K 24.10-16

Mordecai Saves the King's Life

¹²While Mordecai was resting in the courtyard of the palace, where two of the king's eunuchs, Gabatha and Tharra, were on guard, ¹³he overheard them plotting together. He listened carefully to what they were saying and learned that they were making plans to kill the king. So Mordecai went to King Xerxes and told him about the plot of the two eunuchs. ¹⁴The king had them questioned, and when they confessed, they were led away and executed.

¹⁵The king had an account of this written in the official records, and Mordecai also wrote an account of it. ¹⁶Then the king appointed Mordecai to a position at court and gave him many gifts as a reward for what he had done.

¹⁷But Haman son of Hammedatha, a Bougaean who was respected by the king, tried to cause trouble for Mordecai and his people the Jews, because Mordecai had been responsible for the death of the two eunuchs.

Queen Vashti Defies King Xerxes

1 ¹⁻²These things happened in the time of King Xerxes, who ruled 127 provinces, all the way from India to Ethiopia,ᵇ from his royal throne in Susa, Persia's capital city. ³In the third year of his reign, the king gave a banquet for all his advisers, the representatives of the other countries, the noblemen from Persia and Media, and the governors of the provinces. ⁴For six whole months he made a show of the riches of the imperial court with magnificent and expensive celebrations.

⁵After the feastᶜ the king gave a banquet for the people of other nations who were in the city. It lasted a week and was held in the palace courtyard, ⁶which was decorated with linen and cotton curtains, held by cords of purple linen attached to silver and gold blocks on marble and stone columns. Couches made of gold and silver had been placed in the courtyard, which was paved with green and white marble and mother-of-pearl. The couches were spread with a fine, thin fabric of many colors, with roses around the edges. ⁷There were gold and silver cups, and one of them, decorated with jewels worth more than a thousand tons of silver, had been set out for display. There was plenty of good wine from the king's own supply. ⁸There were no limits on the drinks. The king had given orders to the palace servants that they should provide him and his guests with as much as they wanted.

⁹Meanwhile, inside the royal palace Queen Vashti was giving a banquet for the women.

¹⁰On the seventh day of his banquet the king was feeling happy, so he called in the seven eunuchs who were his personal servants, Haman, Bazan, Tharra,

He overheard them plotting together. (A. v13)

ᵇ *Greek* Ethiopia: *Ethiopia is the name given in Graeco-Roman times to the extensive territory south of the First Cataract of the Nile River. Cush was the ancient (Hebrew) name of this region which included within its borders most of modern Sudan and some of present-day Ethiopia (Abyssinia).*   ᶜ feast; *some manuscripts have* wedding feast.

1.1, 2 Ezra 4.6

Boraze, Zatholta, Abataza, and Tharaba. [11] He ordered them to bring in the queen, so that he could place the royal crown on her head and show her off to the officials and all his guests, for she was a beautiful woman. [12] But Queen Vashti refused to obey and would not come with the servants. This embarrassed the king and made him furious.

[13] He told his advisers about Vashti's reply and asked them to give a legal opinion about what he should do. [14-15] Three of them, who were closest to the king and held the highest offices, came and told him what the law required and what should be done to Queen Vashti for disobeying the command he had given her through his servants. They were Arkesaeus, Sarsathaeus, and Malesear, officials of Persia and Media.

[16] Then the king told his officials and the governors of Media and Persia how the queen had defied him. So Muchaeus said to the king and everyone present: "Queen Vashti has insulted not only you but all of us as well. [17-18] As soon as our wives hear what the queen has done, they will be bold enough to defy their husbands and treat them with disrespect in the same way that Vashti has treated you. [19] If, then, it please Your Majesty, issue a royal proclamation that Vashti may never again appear before the king. Have it written into the laws of Media and Persia. Then give her place as queen to some better woman. There is no other way. [20] When your proclamation is made known all over this empire, then every woman will treat her husband with proper respect, whether he is rich or poor."

[21] The king and his officials liked this idea, and the king did as Muchaeus suggested. [22] To each of the royal provinces he sent a message in the language of that province, saying that

every husband must be respected in his own home.

Esther Becomes Queen

2 Later the king's anger cooled down. Although he no longer mentioned Vashti, he kept thinking about how he had condemned her. [2] So some of the king's advisers suggested, "Why don't you make a search to find some beautiful young women of good character? [3] You can appoint officials in every province of the empire and have them bring all these beautiful young virgins to your harem here in Susa. Put them in the care of Hegai, the eunuch who is in charge of your women, and let them be given cosmetics and whatever else they may need. [4] Then take the young woman you like best and make her queen in Vashti's place."

The king thought this was good advice, so he followed it.

[5] There in Susa lived a Jew named Mordecai son of Jair; he was from the tribe of Benjamin and was a descendant of Kish and Shimei. [6] He was among the captives whom King Nebuchadnezzar of Babylonia had taken into exile from Jerusalem. [7] Mordecai was the guardian of Esther, the daughter of his uncle Aminadab. She was a beautiful young woman, and after the death of her parents, Mordecai brought her up until she was grown. [d]

[8] When the king had issued his new proclamation, many young women were being brought to Susa, and Esther was among them. She too was put in the royal palace in the care of Hegai, who had charge of the harem. [9] Hegai liked Esther, and she won his favor. He lost no time in beginning her beauty treatment of massage and special diet. He assigned seven young women specially chosen from the royal palace to

[d] until she was grown; *or* and planned to marry her.
2.6 2 K 24.10-16; 2 Ch 36.10

serve her, and he treated her and her servants well.

10 Now, on the advice of Mordecai, Esther had kept secret the fact that she was Jewish. **11** Every day Mordecai would walk back and forth in front of the courtyard of the harem, watching to see what was going to happen to her. **12** The regular beauty treatment for the young women lasted a year: massages with oil of myrrh for six months and with beauty creams and cosmetics

The regular beauty treatment . . . lasted a year. (2.12)

for six more. **13** After that, each young woman was handed over to the person appointed to conduct her from the harem to the palace, and she was taken to the king. **14** She would go there in the evening, and the next morning she would be taken to another harem and put in the care of Hegai, the eunuch in charge. She would not go to the king again unless he asked for her by name.

15 The time came for Esther, the daughter of Aminadab the uncle of Mordecai, to go to the king. She had done everything that Hegai had advised, and she was admired by everyone who saw her. **16** So in Xerxes' seventh year as king, in the twelfth month, the month of Adar, she was brought to the king. **17** He fell in love with Esther, who pleased him more than any of the others, and he placed the queen's crown on her head. **18** Then the king gave a

week-long banquet for all his advisers and administrators to celebrate his marriage to Esther. He also granted a reduction of taxes for the whole empire.

Mordecai Saves the King's Life

19 Meanwhile Mordecai had been appointed to a high administrative position. **20** As for Esther, she had still not let it be known that she was Jewish. Mordecai had told her not to tell anyone, and she obeyed him in this, just as she had obeyed him when she was a little girl under his care. She continued to worship God and carry out God's commands, without abandoning her Jewish ways.

21 When the king promoted Mordecai to a higher position, the two palace eunuchs who were officers of the king's bodyguard became angry and plotted to assassinate the king. **22** Mordecai learned about it and told Queen Esther, who then told the king the details of the plot. **23** The king had the two men questioned, and both men were hanged. To honor Mordecai, the king ordered an account of this to be written down in the royal records, so that his valuable service would be remembered.

Haman Plots to Destroy the Jews

3 Some time later King Xerxes honored a man named Haman son of Hammedatha, a Bougaean, by promoting him to the position of prime minister. **2** The king ordered all the officials in his service to show their respect for Haman by bowing to him. They all did so, except Mordecai, who refused to bow to Haman. **3** The other officials in the royal service asked him why he was disobeying the king's command. **4** Day after day they urged him to give in, but he would not listen to them. "I am a Jew," he explained, "and I cannot bow to Haman." So they told Haman how Mordecai was defying the king's orders. **5** Haman was furious when he realized that Mordecai was not going to bow to him, **6** and so he made plans to kill every Jew in the whole Persian Empire.

⁷In the twelfth year of King Xerxes' reign, Haman ordered the lots to be cast to find out the right day and month to destroy the Jews, all in a single day. The fourteenth day of the month of Adar was the date chosen.

⁸So Haman told the king, "There is a certain race of people scattered among the nations all over your empire. They observe customs that are not like those of any other people. Moreover, they do not obey the laws of the empire, so it is not in your best interests to tolerate them. ⁹If it please Your Majesty, issue a decree that they are to be put to death. If you do this, I promise to put 375 tons of silver into the royal treasury."

¹⁰The king took off his ring, which was used to stamp official proclamations, and gave it to Haman to seal the decree that was to be written against the Jews. ¹¹The king told him, "Keep the money, and do whatever you want with that race of people."

¹²So on the thirteenth day of the first month, Haman called the king's secretaries and dictated a proclamation to be translated into every language in the empire and to be sent to all the rulers and governors. It was issued in the name of King Xerxes and sent to all the 127 provinces, which stretched from India to Ethiopia.ᵉ ¹³Runners took this proclamation to every province of the empire. It contained the instructions that on a single day in the twelfth month, the month of Adar, all Jews were to be killed and their belongings confiscated.ᶠ

Xerxes' Proclamation against the Jews

Bᵍ This is a copy of the decree:

"King Xerxes the Great sends the following decree to the governors of his 127 provinces, from India to Ethiopia,ʰ and to their subordinate officials:

²"After I became ruler of many nations and master of the whole world, I resolved that my subjects should always live at peace. I wanted this, not because of pride in my power but because I was always reasonable and governed my subjects with kindness. I determined to renew the peace that everyone longs for and to do what was necessary to create a civilized kingdom, safe for travel from one border to another.

³"I asked my advisers how to accomplish this goal, and Haman made a suggestion. He is distinguished among us as a man of great wisdom, and at all times he has demonstrated his concern for the welfare of the kingdom. Because of his unfailing loyalty, he has been raised to the second highest position in the empire. ⁴Recently Haman told us about a certain unruly people scattered among all the other peoples of the empire. He explained to us that these people have their own laws, are opposed to every other nation, and constantly ignore royal commands. As a result of their attitude, we are not able to establish the kind of unified government which we earnestly intend for the empire.

⁵"These people are hostile to our government and commit terrible crimes which threaten the security of the em-

---

ᵉ Greek Ethiopia: *Ethiopia is the name given in Graeco-Roman times to the extensive territory south of the First Cataract of the Nile River. Cush was the ancient (Hebrew) name of this region which included within its borders most of modern Sudan and some of present-day Ethiopia (Abyssinia).*   ᶠ *Chapter 3 continues after chapter B.*
ᵍ *Chapter B 1-7 corresponds to chapter 13.1-7 in a number of English translations.*
ʰ Greek Ethiopia: *Ethiopia is the name given in Graeco-Roman times to the extensive territory south of the First Cataract of the Nile River. Cush was the ancient (Hebrew) name of this region which included within its borders most of modern Sudan and some of present-day Ethiopia (Abyssinia).*

pire. They follow strange customs, obey their own laws, and stand alone in their constant opposition to all people. ⁶ In the light of these facts, we recommend the slaughter of the people referred to by Haman, our prime minister. All of them, including women and children, must be put to death; no one is to be spared. They are our enemies; we will show them no pity. This order is to be carried out this year on the fourteenth day of the twelfth month, the month of Adar. ⁷ These people, who have caused so much trouble for so long, will all die a violent death in a single day. From then on, our government will be secure and stable."

3 ¹⁴ The contents of the proclamation were made public in every province, and everyone was ordered to be prepared for that day.

¹⁵ The decree was also rapidly made public in the capital city of Susa. And while the king and Haman got drunk, the city of Susa was thrown into confusion.

Mordecai Asks for Esther's Help

4 When Mordecai learned of all that had been done, he tore his clothes in anguish. Then he dressed in sackcloth, covered his head with ashes, and ran through the city crying loudly, "An innocent nation is being destroyed!" ² When he came to the entrance of the palace, he stopped. He did not go in because no one in sackcloth and ashes was allowed inside. ³ Throughout all the provinces, wherever the king's proclamation was made known, there was loud mourning among the Jews. They wept, wailed, and put on sackcloth and ashes.

⁴ When Esther's servant women and eunuchs told her what Mordecai was doing, she was deeply disturbed. She sent Mordecai some clothes to put on

instead of the sackcloth, but he would not accept them. ⁵ Then she called Hathach, one of the palace eunuchs appointed as her servant, and told him to go to Mordecai and get the details of what was happening.ⁱ ⁷ Mordecai told him everything that had happened and how Haman had promised to put 375 tons of silver into the royal treasury if all the Jews were killed. ⁸ He gave Hathach a copy of the proclamation that had been issued in Susa, ordering the destruction of the Jews. Mordecai asked him to take it to Esther so that she might go and plead with the king and beg him to have mercy on her people. "Tell her," he said, "to remember the days when she was just an ordinary person being brought up under my care. Now, since Haman, the king's prime minister, has spoken against us and demands our death, she must pray to the Lord and then speak to the king about us. She must save us from death."

⁹ So Hathach did this, ¹⁰ and Esther gave him this message to take back to Mordecai: ¹¹ "If anyone, man or woman, goes to the inner courtyard and sees the king without being summoned, that person will be sentenced to death. Everyone in the empire knows that. Only if the king holds out his gold scepter to him can his life be spared. But it has been a month now since the king has sent for me."

¹² When Mordecai received Esther's message, ¹³ he sent her this warning: "Esther, don't imagine that you are safer than any of the other Jews in the empire. ¹⁴ If you keep quiet at a time like this, help will come to the Jews in some other way and they will be saved, but you will die and your father's family will come to an end. Yet, who knows? Maybe it was for a time like this that you were made queen!"

¹⁵ Esther sent Mordecai this reply:

ⁱ *Some manuscripts add verse 6:* Hathach went to Mordecai in the city square at the entrance to the palace.

¹⁶"Go and gather all the Jews in Susa together; hold a fast and pray for me. Don't eat or drink anything for three days and nights. My servant women and I will be doing the same. After that, I will go to the king, even though it is against the law. If I must die for doing it, I will die."

¹⁷Mordecai then left and did everything that Esther had told him to do.

Mordecai's Prayer

Cʲ Mordecai prayed to the Lord, calling to mind what the Lord had done in the past: ²"O Lord, you are the Lord and King of all creation, and everything obeys your commands. If you wish to save Israel, no one can stop you. ³You made heaven and earth and all the wonderful things on earth. ⁴You are the Lord of all, and there is no one who can stand against you. ⁵You know all things. You know, Lord, that when I refused to bow to that arrogant Haman, it was not because I was arrogant or trying to impress people. ⁶⁻⁷I simply did not want to honor any human being more than I honor God. I refuse to bow to anyone but you, my Lord; and this is not because of pride. If it would help to save Israel, I would be willing even to kiss the soles of his feet.

⁸⁻⁹"And now, O Lord, God and King, God of Abraham, spare your people; save us from our enemies. They are determined to destroy us; they are looking for a chance. Long ago you chose us to be your people and rescued us from the land of Egypt. Do not abandon us now. ¹⁰We are your chosen people, so listen to my prayer and be gracious to us. Turn our misfortune into joy so that we may live to sing your praises. Save us from death so that we can keep on praising you."

¹¹And all the people of Israel prayed loudly and earnestly because they were sure that they were going to die.

Esther's Prayer

¹²Queen Esther, in deep agony, turned to the Lord. ¹³She took off her splendid robes and put on garments of mourning and grief. Instead of her rich perfumes, she put ashes and dung on her head. She did all she could to destroy any dignity in her appearance. She let her tangled and uncombed hair hang down over her body that she had always taken such care to beautify. ¹⁴She prayed to the Lord God of Israel, "My Lord and King, only you are God. I am all alone, and I have no one to turn to but you. Help me! ¹⁵I am about to risk my life. ¹⁶O Lord, as long as I can remember, my family has told me how you chose Israel from all the nations and how in ancient times you singled out our ancestors to be your people forever. You have kept all your promises to them.

¹⁷"But we sinned against you. You handed us over to our enemies because

Esther's prayer (C. v12)

ʲ *Chapter C 1-30 corresponds to chapters 13.8—14.19 in a number of English translations.*

C.8, 9 Ex 3.6

In all her royal splendor (D. v2)

we worshiped their gods. ¹⁸We deserved your punishment, O Lord. ¹⁹But our enemies are no longer satisfied just to see us in slavery. They have made a solemn promise to their idols ²⁰not only to destroy the people who praise you, but to do away with your Law and to remove forever the glory of your house and altar. ²¹They want the whole world to praise worthless idols and stand in awe of mortal kings forever.

²²"Lord, these gods are nothing; do not surrender your power to them or give our enemies the chance to laugh at our downfall. Instead, turn their evil plans against them, and make an example of that man who first planned our destruction.

²³"Remember us, O Lord. Come to us in this time of trouble. Give me courage, King of all gods and Ruler over all earthly powers. ²⁴Give me the right words to say when I go in to face Xerxes, that savage lion. Change his heart so that he will turn against Haman, our enemy, and destroy him and his gang. ²⁵Come to our rescue, O Lord. Help me; I am all alone, and I have no one to turn to but you.

²⁶"You know everything, Lord. You know that I hate the honor I receive from these Gentiles. I detest the thought of having sex with any of these uncircumcised heathen. ²⁷But you know that I have no choice. I hate the crown I have to wear as queen on official occasions. I never wear it unless I have to; it's as disgusting as last month's rag. ²⁸I refuse to eat at Haman's table or honor the king by attending his parties, and I have never drunk any of the wine dedicated to his gods. ²⁹Since I came here, the only thing that has brought me joy is my worship of you, Lord God of Abraham.

³⁰"Almighty God, listen to the prayer of your people. Rescue us from these evildoers, and take away my fear."

Esther Goes to the King

D[k] Queen Esther prayed for three days. Then she took off the clothes she had been wearing and put on her splendid robes again. ²⁻³In all her royal splendor, she prayed again to her God and savior, who sees everything. Walking like a queen, she left her room accompanied by two servant women, one of them escorting her by

[k] *Chapter D 1-15 corresponds to chapter 15.1-16 in a number of English translations.*
C.24, 25 Jdt 9.13   **C.28** Dn 1.8; Jdt 12.2

the arm and [4] the other holding up the train of her robe. [5] Queen Esther's face was radiantly beautiful. She looked as cheerful as she was lovely, but in her heart she was terror-stricken. [6] She passed through all the doors and entered the throne room, where she stood before the king. He was seated on his royal throne, dressed in his glorious robes, which were covered with gold and precious jewels. It was an awe-inspiring sight. [7] His face glowed with splendor, but when he saw Esther, he stared at her with fierce anger. She grew weak and turned pale; she almost fainted and had to lean her head on her attendant's shoulder.

[8] But God changed the king's anger into tender concern. He quickly rose from his throne and took her in his arms until she was able to stand. He calmed her with comforting words. [9] "What is it, Esther?" he said to her. "I am your husband. There's no need to be afraid. [10] Our law applies only to ordinary people; you will not die. [11] Come here to me." [12] He lifted his gold scepter and touched her on the neck with it. Then he kissed her and said, "Tell me what you want."

[13] "When I looked at you, my lord, I thought I was seeing an angel of God," the queen answered, "and I was overcome by your awesome majesty. [14] You are so marvelous and your face is so full of kindness."

[15] But while she was speaking, she fainted again. [16] The king was concerned about her, and all his attendants tried to revive her.

Esther Invites the King and Haman to a Banquet

5 [l] [3] "What is it, Esther?" the king asked. "Tell me what you want, and you shall have it — even if it is half of my empire."

[4] Esther replied, "Today is a special day for me. If it please my lord, I would like you and Haman to be my guests tonight at a banquet I am preparing for you."

[5] The king then ordered Haman to come quickly, so that they could be Esther's guests. So the king and Haman went to Esther's banquet. [6] Over the wine the king again said to her, "Tell me what you want, Queen Esther."

[7] Esther replied, [8] "If my lord is kind enough to grant my request, I would like you and Haman to be my guests tomorrow at another banquet that I will prepare for you. It will be just like this one."

Haman Plots to Kill Mordecai

[9] When Haman left the king he was happy and in a good mood, until he saw Mordecai the Jew in the courtyard of the palace. That made him furious, [10] but he went on home. Then he invited his friends to his house and asked his wife Zeresh to join them. [11] He boasted to them about how rich he was and about the honor the king had paid him when he promoted him to high office and made him prime minister. [12] "What is more," Haman said, "Queen Esther gave a banquet for no one but the king and me, and we are invited back tomorrow. [13] But none of this means a thing to me as long as I see that Jew Mordecai sitting in the courtyard of the palace."

[14] Then his wife and all his friends suggested, "Why don't you have a gallows put up, seventy-five feet high? Tomorrow morning you can ask the king to have Mordecai hanged on it, and then you can go with the king to the banquet and enjoy yourself." Haman thought it was a good idea, so he had the gallows built.

---

[l] In Greek, chapter D replaces verses 1 and 2 in Hebrew.
5.3 Mk 6.23

. . . and Haman led him through the city. (6.11)

The King Honors Mordecai

6 That night the Lord kept the king from sleeping, so the king ordered his private secretary to bring the official records of the empire and read them to him. ² He read the account of how Mordecai had uncovered a plot to assassinate the king — the plot made by the two eunuchs who served as palace guards. ³ The king asked, "How have we honored and rewarded Mordecai for this?"

His servants answered, "You have done nothing for him."

⁴ Now just as the king was inquiring about Mordecai's good deed, Haman entered the courtyard. He had come to ask the king to have Mordecai hanged on the gallows that was now ready.

"Who is that in the courtyard?" the king asked.

⁵ The servants answered, "It is Haman; he is waiting to see you."

"Show him in," said the king.

⁶ So Haman came in, and the king said to him, "There is someone I wish very much to honor. What should I do for this man?"

Haman thought to himself, "Now who could the king want to honor so much? Me, of course."

⁷⁻⁸ So he answered the king, "Let the royal servants bring a fine linen robe for this man — one that you yourself wear.

And let them bring a horse that you yourself ride. ⁹ Then put that robe on the man you like so much and then have the nobleman lead him, mounted on the horse, through the city square. Have the nobleman announce as they go: 'See how the king rewards a man whom he wishes to honor!'"

¹⁰ Then the king said to Haman, "Fine! Do all that for Mordecai the Jew, who holds a high position in the palace; don't leave out a thing."

¹¹ So Haman got the robe and the horse, and he put the robe on Mordecai. Mordecai got on the horse, and Haman led him through the city square, announcing to the people as they went: "See how the king rewards a man whom he wishes to honor!"

¹² Mordecai then went back to the courtyard while Haman hurried home, covering his face in embarrassment. ¹³ He told his wife and all his friends everything that had happened to him. Then they all said to him, "You are beginning to lose power to Mordecai. He is a Jew, and you cannot overcome him. He will certainly defeat you, for the living God is with him!"

Haman Is Put to Death

¹⁴ While they were still talking, the palace eunuchs arrived to take Haman to Esther's banquet.

7 And so the king and Haman went to eat with Esther ²for a second time. Over the wine the king asked her again, "Now, Queen Esther, what do you want? Tell me and you shall have it. I'll even give you half the empire."

³Queen Esther answered, "If it please Your Majesty to grant my humble request, my wish is that I may live and that my people may live. ⁴My people and I have been sold into slavery; our possessions have been plundered, and now we are to be destroyed — all of us, including our children, will be slaves — and so far I have kept quiet. It isn't right that our enemy should be a member of the royal court."

⁵Then King Xerxes asked Esther, "Who dares to do such a thing?"

⁶Esther answered, "Our enemy is this evil man Haman!"

"Our enemy is this evil man Haman!" (7.6)

In terror Haman faced the king and queen. ⁷The king got up from the table and went outside to the palace gardens. Haman could see that he was in a dangerous situation, so he stayed behind to beg Queen Esther for his life. ⁸He had just thrown himself down on Esther's couch to beg for mercy, when the king came back into the room from the gardens. Seeing this, the king cried out, "Are you going to rape my wife here in my own palace?"

8.8 Dn 6.8

When Haman heard this, he turned away in despair. ⁹Then one of the eunuchs, whose name was Bougathan, said, "Haman has even gone so far as to build a gallows at his house so that he can hang Mordecai, who warned Your Majesty about the plot. And it's seventy-five feet high!"

"Hang Haman on it!" the king commanded.

¹⁰So Haman was hanged on the gallows that he had built for Mordecai. Then the king's anger cooled down.

The Jews Are Told to Fight Back

8 That same day King Xerxes gave Queen Esther all the property of Haman, the enemy of the Jews. Esther told the king that Mordecai was related to her, and Mordecai was invited to enter the king's presence. ²The king took off his ring with his seal on it (which he had taken back from Haman) and gave it to Mordecai. Esther put Mordecai in charge of Haman's property.

³Then Esther spoke to the king again, throwing herself at his feet. She begged him to do something to stop the evil plot that Haman had made against the Jews. ⁴The king held out the gold scepter to her, so she stood up ⁵and said, "If it please Your Majesty and if you care about me, please issue a proclamation to keep Haman's orders from being carried out — those orders he gave for the destruction of all the Jews in the empire. ⁶How can I endure it if this disaster comes on my people? How can I go on living if my whole nation is destroyed?"

⁷Then the king said to Esther, "I have hanged Haman for his plot against the Jews, and I have given you his property. If that is not enough, ⁸you may write to the Jews whatever you like; and you may write it in my name and stamp it with the royal seal, for a procla-

mation issued in the king's name and stamped with the royal seal cannot be revoked."

[9] On the twenty-third day of the first month, the month of Nisan, the king's secretaries were called and letters were written to the Jews and to the governors and administrators of all 127 provinces from India to Ethiopia.[m] The letters were written to each province in its own language. [10] They were written in the name of the king and stamped with the royal seal and they were delivered by runners.

[11] These letters explained that the king would allow the Jews in every city of the empire to live by their own laws and organize for self-defense. They were permitted to treat their opponents and enemies in any way they liked. [12] This decree was to take effect throughout the Persian Empire on the thirteenth day of Adar, the twelfth month.[n]

The King's Decree in Favor of the Jews

E[o] This is a copy of the decree: "Greetings from King Xerxes the Great to the governors of the 127 provinces, which extend from India to Ethiopia,[p] and to all those who are loyal to us.

[2] "Many people become increasingly arrogant when honors are given to them and favors are done for them. [3] They do not know what to do with so much good fortune, so they not only try to harm our subjects, but they even scheme against those who grant them favors. [4] They are never grateful for what people do for them, and they even think they can escape the judgment of God, who hates evil and sees everything. In their arrogance they listen to the flattery of ignorant, sinful people.

[5] "It often happens also that friends who have been entrusted with administrative responsibilities exert pressure on those in authority. They make their leaders their partners in killing people and bring about misfortunes that can never be remedied. [6] These friends, by their lies and deceitful ways, take advantage of the good will of their rulers.

[7] "You can see examples of this misuse of power not only in the stories that have been handed down to us from the past, but in the more recent outrageous things which have happened among you.

[8] "I intend to make sure that in the future my kingdom will remain untroubled and peaceful for all people. [9] This can be done by changing certain policies and by judging fairly each situation that comes to my attention.

[10] "Consider, for example, the case of Haman son of Hammedatha, a Macedonian. He is a foreigner with no Persian blood and with no trace of my generosity; but I welcomed him, [11] and he received the benefit of my concern and love for all people. He was, in fact, proclaimed 'Father' of the empire and received more honor than anyone else, except the king.

[12] "But his arrogance knew no limits, and he tried to murder me and take over the empire. [13] In his crafty and deceitful way, he asked that Mordecai be put to

---

[m] Greek Ethiopia: *Ethiopia is the name given in Graeco-Roman times to the extensive territory south of the First Cataract of the Nile River. Cush was the ancient (Hebrew) name of this region which included within its borders most of modern Sudan and some of present-day Ethiopia (Abyssinia).*   [n] Chapter 8 continues after chapter E.

[o] Chapter E 1-24 corresponds to chapter 16.1-24 in a number of English translations.

[p] Greek Ethiopia: *Ethiopia is the name given in Graeco-Roman times to the extensive territory south of the First Cataract of the Nile River. Cush was the ancient (Hebrew) name of this region which included within its borders most of modern Sudan and some of present-day Ethiopia (Abyssinia).*

death—Mordecai, who once saved my life and who has always supported me. He even asked for the death of Esther, our blameless queen, and in fact, the death of all the Jewish people. 14 His purpose was to leave us helpless and to allow the Macedonians to take over the Persian Empire. 15 Even though this wicked criminal plotted to wipe out the Jews, I find that they are not traitors at all but are governed by very just laws. 16 They worship the living God, the highest and greatest God, who has kept our empire in its excellent condition from the time of our ancestors until our own day.

17 "Therefore I advise you not to carry out the instructions issued in the letters sent out by Haman. 18 He is the person responsible for all of this, and he has been hanged, along with his entire family, at the gates of Susa. God, who governs all things, has given him the speedy punishment that he deserved.

19 "I order you to post copies of this decree in every public place. Permit the Jews to live by their own customs, 20 and give them support when they defend themselves against those who attack them on the day set for their destruction, the thirteenth day of Adar, the twelfth month. 21 God, who governs all things, has turned that day of destruction into a day of celebration for his chosen people.

22 "Include this day among your national holidays and celebrate it as a festival. 23 Now and in the future it will remind us and all our allies of the way God watches over our nation, and those who plot against us will be reminded of God's threat of destruction.

24 "Every province, every city, without exception, which does not obey these orders will feel my anger. It will be destroyed in battle and burned to the ground. No human being will ever go

there again, and even the birds and wild animals will avoid it forever.

8 q 13 "Post copies of this decree in plain view in every province, so that all the Jews can be ready to fight their enemies when that day comes."

Post copies of this decree in plain view in every province . . . Messengers on horses rode off at top speed. (8.13,14)

14 Messengers on horses rode off at top speed to carry out the orders of the king, and the decree was also made public in Susa.

15 Mordecai left the palace, wearing royal robes, a turban of fine purple linen, and a gold crown. When the people of Susa saw him, they cheered, 16 and the Jews were happy and joyful. 17 They held a joyful holiday with feasting and happiness in every city and province, wherever the king's proclamation was posted. In fact, many Gentiles were circumcised and became Jews, because they were now afraid of them.

q *Verses 1-12 precede chapter E.*

The Jews Destroy Their Enemies

9 On the thirteenth day of Adar, the day on which the royal proclamation was to take effect, ²it was the enemies of the Jews who were wiped out. People everywhere were afraid of the Jews, and no one could stand against them. ³In fact, the provincial governors, the administrators, and the royal scribes showed respect for the Jews, because they were all afraid of Mordecai. ⁴⁻⁵The royal decree had made his name known throughout the empire.

⁶In Susa, the capital city itself, the Jews killed five hundred people ⁷⁻¹⁰and looted their property. Among them were the ten sons of Haman son of Hammedatha, a Bougaean, the enemy of the Jews: Pharsannestain, Delphon, Phasga, Pharadatha, Barea, Sarbacha, Marmasima, Arouphaeus, Arsaeus, and Zabouthaeus.

¹¹That same day the number of people killed in Susa was reported to the king. ¹²He then said to Esther, "In Susa alone the Jews have killed five hundred people. What must they have done out in the provinces! Tell me what else you want, and you shall have it."

¹³Esther answered, "Let the Jews in Susa do again tomorrow what they were allowed to do today. And have the bodies of Haman's ten sons hung up." ¹⁴The king agreed and permitted the Jews to put the bodies of Haman's ten sons on public display. ¹⁵On the fourteenth day of Adar the Jews of Susa got together again and killed three hundred more people in the city. But they did no looting.

¹⁶The Jews in the provinces also organized and defended themselves. They rid themselves of their enemies by killing 15,000 people on the thirteenth day of Adar, but they did no looting. ¹⁷On the next day, the fourteenth, there was no more killing, and the Jews made it a joyful holiday of rest and feasting. ¹⁸The Jews of Susa, however, made the fifteenth a holiday, since they had slaughtered their enemies on the thirteenth and fourteenth and did not stop until the fifteenth. ¹⁹This is why Jews who live in small towns observe the fourteenth day of the month of Adar as a holiday, a time of giving gifts of food to one another, while the Jews in the large cities celebrate the holiday in the same way on the fifteenth.

The Festival of Purim

²⁰Mordecai had these events written down in a book and sent it to all the Jews, near and far, throughout the Persian Empire, ²¹telling them to observe the fourteenth and fifteenth days of Adar as holidays. ²²These were the days on which the Jews had rid themselves of their enemies. The Jews were to observe the whole month as a holiday, for this was a month that had been turned from a time of grief and despair into a time of joy and happiness. They were told to observe these days with feasts and parties, giving gifts of food to friends and to the poor. ²³So the Jews accepted all that Mordecai had written.

²⁴Mordecai had recorded how Haman son of Hammedatha, a Macedonian, had fought against the Jewish people, how he had made a decree and cast lots to determine the day he would destroy them, ²⁵and how he had gone to the king to request that Mordecai be hanged. But Haman suffered the same fate he had planned for the Jews — he and his sons were hanged from the gallows. ²⁶⁻²⁸Because of Mordecai's letter, because of all they had suffered, and because of all that had happened to them, the Jews accepted Mordecai's suggestion and made it a rule for themselves, their descendants, and anyone that might become a Jew, that these days should be properly observed as a memorial, generation after generation,

9.1 1 Macc 7.49; 2 Macc 15.36   **9.24-28** Es 3.7

in every city, province, and country. The Jews were to remember and observe these days of Purim for all time to come and never neglect them. (The holidays are called Purim because "purim" in their language is the word for "lots.")

29-30 Then Queen Esther, the daughter of Aminadab, along with Mordecai the Jew, wrote down what they had done, putting the queen's full authority behind the letter about Purim. **31** They both took responsibility for establishing the festival and made up their minds to observe it at all costs.*r* **32** Esther established the festival forever, and a written record was made of her official decree.

The Greatness of Xerxes and Mordecai

10 King Xerxes imposed taxes on the people of the coastal regions of his empire as well as on those of the interior. **2** His power and virtue, as well as the wealth and splendor of his empire, are recorded in the official records of the kings of Persia and Media. **3** Mordecai was second in rank only to King Xerxes himself. He was a great man in the empire and was honored by his fellow Jews. He was greatly loved, for he sought the welfare of his people.

Mordecai Remembers His Dream

F *s* Then Mordecai said, "God has caused all these things to happen! **2** And I am reminded of the dream I had about all of this. Every detail of the dream has come true: **3** the small spring that became a river, the dawn that turned into sunlight, and the abundance of water. The river is Esther, whom the king married and made his queen. **4** The two dragons represent Haman and me. **5** The nations are all those who have gathered together to destroy the Jews. **6** My nation is Israel, which cried out to God for help and was saved. The Lord saved his people! He rescued us from all these evils and performed great miracles and wonders that have never happened among other nations. **7** That is because God prepared one destiny for his own people and another for all other nations. **8** Then came the day and the hour when these two destinies were to be decided; the time had come for God to make a decision about the nations. **9** God remembered his chosen people and gave the verdict in their favor. **10** So each year for all time to come God's people will gather together in his presence on the fourteenth and fifteenth of the month of Adar, and celebrate with joy and happiness."

Postscript

During the fourth year of the reign of Ptolemy and Cleopatra, a man named Dositheus, who claimed to be a levitical priest, brought the preceding letter about the Purim festival. He was accompanied by his son Ptolemy, and they declared that the letter was genuine and that it had been translated by Lysimachus, son of Ptolemy, a member of a Jerusalem family.

---

r at all costs; *Greek unclear.*   *s Chapter F 1-10 corresponds to chapters 10.4—11.1 in a number of English translations.*

THE WISDOM OF SOLOMON

INTRODUCTION

This book was originally written in Greek by an unknown Jewish author. The book makes use of traditional Jewish material, as well as ideas borrowed from Greek philosophy, in order to teach that God rewards those who are faithful to him.

The Search for Justice

1 Love justice, you rulers of the world. Set your minds sincerely on the Lord, and look for him with all honesty. ²Those who do not try to test him will find him; he will show himself to those who trust him. ³Dishonest thoughts separate people from God, and if we are foolish enough to test him, his power will put us to shame. ⁴Wisdom will never be at home with anyone who is deceitful or a slave of sin. ⁵Everyone who is holy has learned to stay away from deceitful people. He will not stay around when foolish thoughts are being expressed; he will not feel comfortable when injustice is done.

God Is Aware of What We Say

⁶Wisdom is a spirit that is friendly to people, but she will not forgive anyone who speaks against God, for God knows our feelings and thoughts, and hears our every word. ⁷Since the Lord's spirit fills the entire world, and holds everything in it together, she knows every word that people say. ⁸No one who speaks wickedly will escape notice; sooner or later he will receive just punishment. ⁹The intentions of ungodly people will be closely examined; their words will be reported to the Lord, and then they will get the punishment that their wickedness deserves. ¹⁰God will tolerate no challenge, and since he hears everything, you cannot hide your complaining from him. ¹¹So be sure that you do not go around complaining — it does no good — and don't engage in bitter talk. The most secret things you say will have their consequences, and lying will destroy your soul.

God Did Not Create Death

¹²Do not bring on your own death by sinful actions. ¹³God did not invent death, and when living creatures die, it gives him no pleasure. ¹⁴He created everything so that it might continue to exist, and everything he created is wholesome and good. There is no

deadly poison in them. No, death does not rule this world, 15for God's justice does not die.

16 Ungodly people have brought death on themselves by the things they have said and done. They yearn for death as if it were a lover. They have gone into partnership with death, and it is just what they deserve.

Wicked Thinking

2 Wicked people are wrong when they say to themselves, "Our life is short and full of sorrow, and when its end comes, there is no escape. No one has ever been known to come back from the world of the dead. 2We were born by chance, and after life is over, we will be as if we had never been born at all. Our breath is no more than a puff of smoke; our mind is nothing more than a spark thrown off by the beating of our heart. 3When that spark dies, our body will crumble into ashes, and our breath will become part of the empty air. 4In time, no one will remember anything we ever did, and even our names will be forgotten. Our lives will pass away like the traces of clouds and vanish like fog in the heat of the sun. 5Our time on earth is like a passing shadow. There is no escape from the day of our death; it is fixed, and no one can postpone it."

6The wicked say, "Come on, then, let's enjoy the good things of life, and live in this world the way we did when we were young and free of care! 7Let's drink the most expensive wines and use the finest perfumes. Let's not miss a single flower in the springtime! 8Before the roses wither, let's pick them and wear them in our hair! 9Let's all join in and leave signs everywhere of our carefree revelry! Life owes us that much!

10"We'll oppress the poor, even if they are righteous. We'll show no re-

spect for widows or old people. 11We'll call ourselves right if we are strong enough to get what we want. No one ever got anywhere by being weak! 12Righteous people are nothing but a nuisance, so let's look for chances to get rid of them. They are against what we do; they accuse us of breaking the Law of Moses and violating the traditions of

Our lives will pass away like . . . clouds. (2.4)

our ancestors. 13They claim to know God, and they call themselves the Lord's children. 14We can't stand the sight of people like that; what they are contradicts our whole way of thinking. 15They are not like other people; they have strange ways. 16They think that our moral standards are so corrupt that everything we do should be avoided. They boast of having God for their Father, and believe that when all is said and done, only the righteous will be happy. 17But we'll see if that's true! Let's see what will happen when it's time for them to die! 18If the righteous really are God's children, God will save them from their enemies. 19So let's put

1.16 Pr 8.36; Is 28.15; Si 14.12　**2.6** Is 22.13; 1 Co 15.32

them to the test. We'll be cruel to them, and torment them; then we'll find out how calm and reasonable they are! We'll find out just how much they can stand! 20 We'll condemn them to a shameful death. After all, they say that God will protect them."

21 That is how evil people think, but they are wrong. They are blinded by their own wickedness. 22 They have never known God's secrets, never hoped for the rewards of a holy and blameless life. 23 When God created us, he did not intend for us to die; he made us like himself. 24 It was the Devil's jealousy that brought death into the world, and those who belong to the Devil are the ones who will die.

The Destiny of the Righteous

3 But righteous people are protected by God and will never suffer torment. 2 It is a foolish mistake to think that righteous people die and that their death is a terrible evil. 3 They leave us, but it is not a disaster. In fact, the righteous are at peace. 4 It might appear that they have suffered punishment, but they have the confident hope of immortality. 5-6 Their sufferings were minor compared with the blessings they will receive. God has tested them, like gold in a furnace, and found them worthy to be with him. He has accepted them, just as he accepts the sacrifices which his worshipers burn on the altar.

7 When God comes to reward the righteous, they will blaze out against the wicked like fire in dry straw. 8 They will rule over nations and peoples, and the Lord will be their king forever. 9 Those who have put their trust in God will come to understand the truth of his ways. Those who have been faithful will live with him in his love, for he is

kind and merciful to the ones whom he has chosen.*a*

The Destiny of the Wicked

10 The ungodly, however, will get the punishment their wicked thoughts deserve, because they rebelled against the Lord and ignored what was right.*b* 11 A man who has no use for wisdom or education has a miserable life in store for him. He has nothing to hope for. His labors are useless, and he will never accomplish anything worthwhile. 12 The woman he marries will turn out to be irresponsible, and his children will go wrong. 13 All his descendants will be under a curse.

The Importance of Virtue

On Judgment Day God will reward the woman who has never been able to have a child, provided she has not been guilty of adultery. Then she will be happy. 14 On that day, even the man who has been castrated will be rewarded with happiness, if he has kept the Law and has not stored up resentment against the Lord. Because he has been faithful, he will receive a special reward more precious than having children: a place in the Lord's heavenly Temple. 15 Honest deeds are like a tree that bears marvelous fruit. Wisdom is like a root that is alive and can always send up new shoots.

16 But children born of adultery or of a forbidden union will die an early death. 17 Yet even if they do live a long time, they will never amount to anything. They will not be respected in their old age, 18 and if they die young, they will have no hope or comfort on Judgment Day. 19 Children born of a forbidden union suffer a miserable fate.

---

a Some manuscripts add and he protects his own people *(see 4.15).* *b* what was right; *or* righteous people.

2.23 Gn 1.26, 27 **3.2** Ws 4.17 **3.5, 6** Ro 8.18; 2 Co 4.17

4 It is better to have virtue, even if it means having no children. Your virtue will be recognized by other people and by God, and you will be remembered for it forever. [2] Virtue provides an example for people to follow; when it is not there, they miss it. It has always been the finest prize a person can win, and it always will be so. It is the noblest of all the good qualities a person can have.

Wisdom is like a root that is alive and can always send up new shoots. (3.15)

[3] No matter how many children are born of a forbidden union, none of them will ever amount to anything. They are illegitimate; they can never lay a firm foundation for themselves, never take deep root. [4] Like trees with shallow roots, they put out leaves for a while, but they sway in the wind, and storms uproot them. [5] Their branches snap off before they mature; their fruit never ripens, and it is good for nothing. [6] On Judgment Day children born of a forbidden union will testify to the sin of their parents and act as witnesses against them.

[7] Righteous people, however, will find rest, even if they die young. [8] We honor old age, but not just because a person has lived a long time. [9] Wisdom and righteousness are signs of the maturity that should come with old age.

The Example of Enoch

[10] Once there was a man named Enoch who pleased God, and God loved him. While Enoch was still living among sinners, God took him away, [11] so that evil and falsehood could not corrupt his mind and soul. ([12] We all know that people can be so fascinated by evil that they cannot recognize what is good even when they are looking right at it. Innocent people can be so corrupted with desire that they can think of nothing but what they want.) [13] This man Enoch achieved in a few years' time a perfection that other people could never attain in a complete lifetime. [14] The Lord was pleased with Enoch's life and quickly took him out of this wicked world. People were aware of his departure but didn't understand. They never seemed to learn the lesson [15] that God is kind and merciful to his own people; he protects those whom he has chosen.

The Fate of the Wicked

[16] Even when righteous people are dead and gone, they put to shame the wicked people who live on after them. In their old age the wicked will be disgraced by young people who have already achieved perfection. [17] The wise may die young, but the wicked will never understand that this is the Lord's way of taking them off to safety. [18] They make light of a wise person's death, but the Lord will soon be laughing at them. When they die, they will not be given an honorable burial. Even the dead will hold them in scorn and disgust forever. [19] God will throw them to the ground and make them speechless. Like buildings shaken from their foundations, they will be reduced to piles of ruins. They will be in torment. People will soon forget all about them. [20] They will come in fear to the Judgment, where their sins will be counted; they will

This is the one we made fun of! (5.4)

stand condemned by their own lawless actions.

The Regrets of the Wicked

5 On that day someone righteous, full of confidence, will stand before those who oppressed him and made light of his labors. ² They will be amazed to see him safe and will tremble with terrible fear. ³ Then they will regret what they did, and groaning in anguish they will say to each other: ⁴ "This is the one we made fun of. We thought he was a joke. What fools we were! We thought he was crazy to live the way he did, and when he died, we didn't honor him. ⁵ And now here he is, one of God's own children, with a place of his own among God's people. ⁶ We were the ones who wandered off the right road. We never lived in the light of righteousness; we never caught the first glimmer of its light. ⁷ All our lives we wandered across unmarked deserts, instead of following the road which the Lord wanted us to travel. And this lawlessness led us to ruin. ⁸ We were so proud of ourselves — we bragged about how rich we were — and now, what good has it done us? ⁹ All those things are gone

now; they have disappeared like a shadow, like something you hear and then forget.

¹⁰ "A ship sails across the waves of the ocean, but when it is gone, it leaves no trace. You cannot tell it was ever there. ¹¹ A bird flies through the air, but leaves no sign that it has been there. It speeds along, riding through the thin air by the force of its wings, leaving behind no trace of its passing. ¹² An arrow splits the air when it is shot at a target, but at once the air closes up behind it, and no one can tell where it passed. ¹³ It is the same with us — we were born, and then we ceased to be. We left no sign of virtue behind us; we were destroyed by our wickedness."

¹⁴ What hope do wicked people have? Only the hope of straw blown about in the wind, the hope of ocean foam[c] that disappears in the storm, the hope of smoke in the breeze. Their hope lasts no longer than our memory of a guest who stays one day and leaves the next.

¹⁵ But the righteous live on forever. The Lord will reward them; the Most High will protect them. ¹⁶ He will give them royal splendor and a magnificent crown. He will shield them with his

[c] ocean foam; *some manuscripts have* frost.

powerful arm. [17] He will go out into battle determined to defeat his enemies, and use the creation itself as a weapon. [18] Righteousness will be his armor, genuine justice will be his helmet, [19] holiness will be his invincible shield. [20] He will sharpen his stern anger into a sword, and the forces of nature will join him in battle against those who are foolish enough to oppose him. [21] Bolts of lightning will strike right on target, as if the Lord had made a bow out of the clouds and was shooting arrows. [22] Hailstones will beat down on his enemies with terrible force. The oceans and rivers will come rushing over them in a devastating flood. [23] Great windstorms will blow them away like straw. Lawlessness will be the ruin of the whole world. Evil actions will cause governments to fall.

The Responsibility of Rulers

6 So then, you kings, you rulers the world over, listen to what I say, and learn from it. [2] You govern many lands and are proud that so many people are under your rule, [3] but this authority has been given to you by the Lord Most High. He will examine what you have done and what you plan to do. [4] You rule on behalf of God and his kingdom, and if you do not govern justly, if you do not uphold the law, if you do not live according to God's will, [5] you will suffer sudden and terrible punishment. Judgment is especially severe on those in power. [6] Common people may be mercifully forgiven for their wrongs, but those in power will face a severe judgment. [7] The Lord of all is not afraid of anyone, no matter how great they are. He himself made everyone, great and common alike, and he provides for all equally, [8] but he will judge the conduct of rulers more strictly. [9] It is for you, mighty kings, that I write these words, so that you may know how to act wisely and avoid mistakes. [10] These are holy matters, and if you treat them in a holy manner, you yourselves will be considered holy. If you have learned this lesson, you will be able to defend yourselves at the Judgment. [11] So then, make my teaching your treasure and joy, and you will be well instructed.

The Value of Wisdom

[12] Wisdom shines bright and never grows dim; those who love her and look for her can easily find her. [13] She is quick to make herself known to anyone who desires her. [14] Get up early in the morning to find her, and you will have no problem; you will find her sitting at your door. [15] To fasten your attention on Wisdom is to gain perfect understanding. If you look for her, you will soon find peace of mind, [16] because she will be looking for those who are worthy of her, and she will find you wherever you are. She is kind and will be with you in your every thought.

[17] Wisdom begins when you sincerely want to learn. To desire Wisdom is to love her; [18] to love her is to keep her laws; to keep her laws is to be certain of immortality; [19] immortality will bring you close to God. [20] This desire for Wisdom can prepare you to rule a kingdom. [21] So then, you that rule the nations, if you value your thrones and symbols of authority, honor Wisdom so that you may rule forever.

Solomon Wishes to Share His Wisdom

[22] I will tell you what Wisdom is, and how she came to be. I will not keep anything secret. I will trace her history from the beginning and make knowledge of her open to all. I will not ignore any part of the truth. [23] No jealous desire to guard my own knowledge will make me hold back anything. Wisdom has nothing in common with such an

5.17-23 Eph 6.11-17   **6.3** Ro 13.1

attitude. 24 No indeed — the more wise people there are, the safer the world will be. A sensible king can be depended on to give his people this kind of security. 25 So then, learn what I am about to teach you, and you will profit from it.

A King Is Like Everyone Else

7 1-2 Like every human being, I am mortal. I am a descendant of that first man, who was made from the soil. I was conceived from the sperm of a man, in the pleasure of intercourse. For nine months my flesh took shape in the blood of my mother's womb. 3 When I was born, I came into the world like anyone else. I began to breathe the same air we all breathe; and like everyone else, the first sound I made was a cry. 4 I was wrapped in cloths and cared for. 5 No king ever began life differently. 6 For all of us, there is one way into life, and there is one way out.

Solomon Declares His Love for Wisdom

7 Realizing that I was only human, I prayed and was given understanding. The spirit of Wisdom came to me. 8 I regarded her more highly than any throne or crown. Wealth was nothing compared to her. 9 Precious jewels could not equal her worth; beside Wisdom all the gold in the world is a handful of sand, and silver is nothing more than clay. 10 I valued her more than health and good looks. Hers is a brightness that never grows dim, and I preferred it to any other light.

11 When Wisdom came to me, all good things came with her. She brought me untold riches. 12 I was happy with them all, because Wisdom had brought them to me. I had not realized before that she was the source of all these things. 13 I was sincere in

learning from her, and now I am glad to share what I learned. 14 No one can ever exhaust the treasures of Wisdom. Use those treasures and you are God's friends; he approves of what you learn from her.

15 I pray to God that my thoughts may be worthy of what I have learned, and that I may speak according to his will. He is Wisdom's guide; he gives correction to those who are wise. 16 We are under his power and authority — we ourselves, our words, all our understanding and skills. 17 It is he who gave me true knowledge of the forces of nature: what the world is made of; how the elements behave; 18 how the calendar is determined by the movements of the sun, the changing seasons, 19 the constellations, and the cycles of years. 20 He has taught me about the nature of living creatures, the behavior of wild animals, the force of the winds, the reasoning powers of human beings, the different kinds of plants, and the use of their roots as medicine. 21 I learned things that were well known and things that had never been known before, 22 because Wisdom, who gave shape to everything that exists, was my teacher.

The Nature of Wisdom

The spirit of Wisdom is intelligent and holy. It is of one nature but reveals itself in many ways. It is not made of any material substance, and it moves about freely. It is clear, clean, and confident; it cannot be harmed.[d] It loves what is good. It is sharp and unconquerable, 23 kind, and a friend of humanity. It is dependable and sure, and has no worries. It has power over everything, and sees everything. It penetrates every spirit that is intelligent and pure, no matter how delicate its substance may be.

24 Wisdom moves more easily than

---

[d] cannot be harmed; or does no harm.

7.7 1 K 3.6-9; Ws 9.1-18

motion itself; she is so pure that she penetrates everything. 25 She is a breath of God's power — a pure and radiant stream of glory from the Almighty. Nothing that is defiled can ever steal its way into Wisdom. 26 She is a reflection of eternal light, a perfect mirror of God's activity and goodness. 27 Even though Wisdom acts alone, she can do anything. She makes everything new, although she herself never changes. From generation to generation she enters the souls of holy people, and makes them God's friends and prophets. 28 There is nothing that God loves more than people who are at home with Wisdom. 29 Wisdom is more beautiful than the sun and all the constellations. She is better than light itself, 30 because night always follows day, but evil never

8 overcomes Wisdom. 1 Her great power reaches into every part of the world, and she sets everything in useful order.

Solomon's Love for Wisdom

2 Wisdom has been my love. I courted her when I was young and wanted to make her my bride. I fell in love with her beauty. 3 She glorifies her noble origin by living with God, the Lord of all, who loves her. 4 She is familiar with God's mysteries and helps determine his course of action.

5 Is it good to have riches in this life? Nothing can make you richer than Wisdom, who makes everything function. 6 Is knowledge a useful thing to have? Nothing is better than Wisdom, who has given shape to everything that exists. 7 Do you love justice? All the virtues are the result of Wisdom's work: justice and courage, self-control and understanding. Life can offer us nothing more valuable than these. 8 Do you want to have wide experience? Wisdom knows the lessons of history and can anticipate the future. She knows how to interpret what people say and how to solve problems. She knows the miracles that God will perform, and how the movements of history will develop.

9 So I decided to take Wisdom home to live with me, because I knew that she would give me good advice and encourage me in times of trouble and grief. 10 I thought to myself, "Because of her I will be honored wherever people come together. The old men will respect me, even though I am young. 11 They will find that my opinions show deep insight, and those in power will admire me. 12 When I am silent, they will wait for me to speak, and when I speak, they will pay attention. Even when I speak at length, they will listen with concentration. 13 Because of Wisdom I will gain immortality; I will live forever in the memory of those who come after me. 14 I will hold power over nations and peoples; 15 dreaded tyrants will be seized with fear at the mention of my name. I will be famous, as a good king and as a brave soldier. 16 When I come home to Wisdom, I will find contentment because there is no conflict or pain in living with her, only happiness and joy."

17 And so I thought it over: to be wedded to Wisdom is to live forever, 18 to love her is to be perfectly happy, to do her work is to be rich beyond measure, to share her company is to have sound judgment, to converse with her is to be honored. Then I was determined to take Wisdom as my bride. 19 I had a pleasant personality even as a child. I had been fortunate enough to receive a good soul, or rather, I was given a sound body to live in because I was already good. 20 Still, I realized that I would never receive Wisdom unless God gave her to me — and knowing that only God could give her to me was itself a sign of understanding. So I prayed, begging the Lord with all my heart:

8.2 Si 15.2   **8.4** Pr 8.27-30

Solomon Prays for Wisdom

9 "God of my ancestors, merciful Lord, by your word you created everything. [2] By your Wisdom you made us humans to rule all creation, [3] to govern the world with holiness and righteousness, to administer justice with integrity. [4] Give me the Wisdom that sits beside your throne; give me a place among your children. [5] I am your slave, as was my mother before me. I am only human. I am not strong, and my life will be short. I have little understanding of the Law or of how to apply it. [6] Even if someone is perfect, he will be thought of as nothing without the Wisdom that comes from you. [7] You chose me over everyone else to be the king of your own people, to judge your sons and daughters. [8] You told me to build a temple on your sacred mountain, an altar in Jerusalem, the city you chose as your home. It is a copy of that temple in heaven, which you prepared at the beginning. [9] Wisdom is with you and knows your actions; she was present when you made the world. She knows what pleases you, what is right and in accordance with your commands. [10] Send her from the holy heavens, down from your glorious throne, so that she may work at my side, and I may learn what pleases you. [11] She knows and understands everything, and will guide me intelligently in what I do. Her glory will protect me. [12] Then I will judge your people fairly, and be worthy of my father's throne. My actions will be acceptable.

[13] "Who can ever learn the will of God? [14] Human reason is not adequate for the task, and our philosophies tend to mislead us, [15] because our mortal bodies weigh our souls down. The body is a temporary structure made of earth, a burden to the active mind. [16] All we can do is make guesses about things on earth; we must struggle to learn about things that are close to us. Who, then, can ever hope to understand heavenly things? [17] No one has ever learned your will, unless you first gave him Wisdom, and sent your holy spirit down to him. [18] In this way people on earth have been set on the right path, have learned what pleases you, and have been kept safe by Wisdom."

Wisdom Protected Adam

10 Wisdom protected the father of the world, the first man that was ever formed, when he alone had been created. She saved him from his own sinful act [2] and gave him the strength to master everything on earth.

Cain Abandoned Wisdom

[3] But there was an unrighteous man who abandoned Wisdom; he destroyed himself by killing his brother in a fit of anger.

Wisdom Protected Noah

[4] Because of that sin, the earth was flooded, but Wisdom saved it again. She guided a righteous man in his flimsy wooden boat.

Wisdom Helped Abraham

[5] Once when the nations were frustrated in their wicked plans, Wisdom recognized a righteous man and kept him innocent in God's sight. She gave him strength to obey God's command in spite of his love for his son.

Wisdom Rescued Lot

[6] Wisdom rescued a righteous man while ungodly people were dying. He escaped the flames that destroyed the Five Cities. [7] You can still see the evidence of their wickedness. The land

9.1-18 1 K 3.6-9; Ws 7.7   **10.1, 2** Gn 1.26-28   **10.3** Gn 4.8-13   **10.4** Gn 7.1–8.22
10.5 Gn 11.1-9; 12.1-3; 22.1-19   **10.6-9** Gn 19.1-29

Wisdom protects. (10)
(Numbers refer to verses of chapter 10)

there is barren and smoking. The plants bear fruit that never ripens, and a pillar of salt stands as a monument to one who did not believe. ⁸The people of those cities ignored Wisdom and could not tell right from wrong. Not only that, but the remains of their cities still remind us of the foolish way they lived, so that their failure can never be forgotten. ⁹But Wisdom rescued her servants from the danger.

Wisdom Protected Jacob

¹⁰A righteous man once had to escape from his brother's anger, and Wisdom guided him in the right way. She showed him God's kingdom and allowed him to know about holy things.ᵉ She made him prosperous and successful in his work. ¹¹When others were greedy for what he had, and wanted to take it away from him, Wisdom stood by him and made him rich. ¹²She protected him from his enemies who were waiting for a chance to attack him. She gave him victory in a hard fight, so that he might realize that nothing can make a person stronger than serving God.

Wisdom Rescued Joseph

¹³Once a righteous man was sold into slavery, but Wisdom did not abandon him. She kept him safe from sin. She went to prison with him ¹⁴and never left him until she had given him power over an empire and made him the ruler of people who had once oppressed him. She let it be known that a false accusation had been made against him, and she gave him eternal honor.

Wisdom Led the Israelites Out of Egypt

¹⁵Wisdom once rescued an innocent and holy people from a nation of oppressors. ¹⁶She entered the soul of one of God's servants andᶠ stood up to dreaded kings by performing miracles. ¹⁷She rewarded God's people for their hardships. She guided them along a miraculous journey. She gave them shade during the day and brilliant starlight at night. ¹⁸She led them through the deep waters of the Red Sea, ¹⁹but she drowned their enemies and washed their bodies up on the shore. ²⁰And so the righteous looted the ungodly. They sang hymns to your holy name, O Lord; together they praised you for defending them. ²¹Wisdom gave speech to those who could not speak; she even caused babies to speak clearly.

Wisdom Led the Israelites through the Desert

11 Wisdom brought success to the people of Israel through a holy prophet. ²They traveled across a desert where no one lived and camped in places where no human being had ever been. ³They stood up to their enemies and fought them off. ⁴When your people grew thirsty, they called to you, Lord, and you gave them water flowing out of solid rock. ⁵The disasters that punished the Egyptians saved your people when they were in trouble.

The Punishment of the Egyptians

⁶⁻⁸Because those enemies decreed that the babies of your people should be killed, you stirred up the sources of their everflowing river and made it foul with blood.

In the desert you let your people go thirsty, to give them a taste of how you had punished their enemies. And then, when they least expected it, you gave them plenty of water. ⁹When they were being tested, even though it was a

ᵉ holy things; *or* angels.   ᶠ and; *or* who.

10.10-12 Gn 27.43; 28.10-22; 32.24-30   **10.13, 14** Gn 37.12-36; 39.1-23; 41.37-44
10.15-21 Ex 1.1−15.21   **11.1-5** Ex 15.22−17.16

merciful discipline, they learned how wicked people were tortured when you judged them in anger. ¹⁰You tested your people, as parents test their children, to warn them. But you judged their enemies like a stern king and condemned them. ¹¹They suffered, whether they were near your people or far from them. ¹²Their sorrow was doubled; they groaned as they looked back on what had happened. ¹³When they learned that their punishment had been of benefit to your people, they realized that it was your work, Lord. ¹⁴The Egyptians had refused to have anything to do with that man who, long before as a baby, had been thrown out and exposed; but as things worked out, they came to be amazed at him. The righteous never suffered a thirst like theirs.

¹⁵Their wickedness misled them into silly ideas, so that they worshiped snakes and other disgusting animals, creatures without any powers of reason. Because of this, you punished them with millions of such animals, ¹⁶and taught them that punishment for sin takes the same form as the sin itself. ¹⁷Your almighty power, Lord, created the world out of material that had no form at all. You could easily have punished those people by sending an invasion of bears or savage lions. ¹⁸You could have created new and terrible animals, that could breathe fire or roar and send out clouds of smoke, or shoot out fearful sparks from their eyes. ¹⁹You could have made animals like these that would not have to attack those people to kill them, but could scare them to death just by looking at them. ²⁰But this was not necessary. You could have pursued them with your justice or struck them dead at the slightest hint of your power. But you have chosen to measure, count, and weigh everything you do.

11.15, 16 Ex 8.1-24; 10.12-15

God Is Powerful and Merciful

²¹You can show your great power any time you wish, and no one can

You could have created new and terrible animals. (11.18)

stand up against it. ²²In your sight the whole world is a grain of sand, barely heavy enough to tip a pair of scales, a drop of dew on the ground in the morning. ²³You are powerful enough to do anything, but you are merciful to everyone; you overlook our sins and give us time to repent. ²⁴You love everything that exists; you do not despise anything that you have made. If you had not liked it, you would not have made it in the first place. ²⁵How could anything last, if you did not want it to? How could it endure, if you had not created it? ²⁶You have allowed it all to exist, O Lord, because it is yours, and you love every **12** living thing. ¹Your immortal spirit is in every one of them, ²and so you gently correct those who sin against you. You remind them of what they are doing, and warn them about it, so that they may abandon their evil ways and put their trust in you, Lord.

The Sins of the Canaanites

3-4 You hated the people who lived in your holy land long ago, because they did horrible things: they practiced magic and conducted unholy worship; 5 they killed children without mercy and ate the flesh and blood of human beings. They were initiated into secret rituals*g* 6 in which parents murdered their own defenseless children. It was your will for our ancestors to destroy these people, 7 so that the land which you consider the most precious of all lands would be a suitable home for your people. 8 But even in this you showed mercy toward their enemies, since they were only human beings. You sent hornets ahead of your army, to destroy the enemy gradually. 9 You could have allowed the righteous to destroy those ungodly people in battle; you could have wiped them out immediately with wild animals or with one harsh command. 10 But instead, you carried out your sentence gradually, to give them a chance to repent, even though you knew that they came from evil stock, that they had been wicked since birth, and that they would never change their way of thinking. 11 Their whole nation was cursed from the start, and though you had not punished them for their sins, it was not because you were afraid of anyone.

God Is Sovereign

12 You created those wicked people, and no one can speak in their defense or condemn you for destroying them. No one can question what you have done or challenge your judgment. 13 All things are under your care, and there is no other god to whom you must justify your decisions. 14 No king or ruler on earth can accuse you of punishing those people unfairly. 15 You are righteous, and you rule everything right-

eously. You have never used your power to condemn a person who does not deserve to be punished. 16 Your strength is the source of justice. You can show mercy to everyone, because you are the Lord of all. 17 You show your strength when people doubt that your power is perfect, and you punish anyone who knows your power but dares to ignore it. 18 Even though you have absolute power, you are a merciful judge. You could take action against us whenever you like, but instead, you rule us with great patience.

19 By the things you have done you have taught your people that a person who is righteous must also be kind. You have given your people abundant hope by allowing them to repent of their sins. 20 You were very careful and patient in punishing your people's enemies; even when they deserved to die, you gave them every opportunity to give up their sinful ways. 21 But you judged your own people very strictly, even though you had made covenants with their ancestors and had solemnly promised to give them good things.

22 Yes, you punish us, but you punish our enemies ten thousand times more, so that when we judge others, we may remember your goodness, and when we are being judged, we may look for mercy.

The Punishment of the Egyptians

23 And so you tormented those who were foolish enough to live wickedly — you tormented them with the horrible things they worshiped. 24 They had wandered far away from the truth and worshiped the most disgusting and horrible animals. They were deceived as easily as little children. 25 And so you punished them for their stupidity, and your judgment made them look like fools. 26 It was a light punishment, but

g They were . . . rituals; *Greek unclear.*

12.3-7 Dt 12.31; 18.9-13   **12.8** Ex 23.28   **12.10** 2 Esd 9.11

those who pay no attention to such warnings deserve to feel the full weight of God's judgment. ²⁷When they were punished with those creatures they considered gods, they became bitterly disillusioned and recognized that the true God was the one they had always refused to acknowledge. That is why they suffered the final punishment.

The Foolishness of Nature Worship

13 Anyone who does not know God is simply foolish. Such people look at the good things around them and still fail to see the living God. They have studied the things he made, but they have not recognized the one who made them. ²Instead, they suppose that the gods who rule the world are fire or wind or storm or the circling stars or rushing water or the heavenly bodies. ³People were so delighted with the beauty of these things that they thought they must be gods, but they should have realized that these things have a master and that he is much greater than all of them, for he is the creator of beauty, and he created them. ⁴Since people are amazed at the power of these things, and how they behave, they ought to learn from them that their maker is far more powerful. ⁵When we realize how vast and beautiful the creation is, we are learning about the Creator at the same time.

⁶But maybe we are too harsh with these people. After all, they may have really wanted to find God, but couldn't. ⁷Surrounded by God's works, they keep on looking at them, until they are finally convinced that because the things they see are so beautiful, they must be gods. ⁸But still, these people really have no excuse. ⁹If they had enough intelligence to speculate about the nature of the universe, why did they never find the Lord of all things?

The Foolishness of Idolatry

¹⁰But the most miserable people of all are those who rest their hopes on lifeless things, who worship things that have been made by human hands — images of animals artistically made from gold and silver, or some useless stone carved by someone years ago. ¹¹A skilled woodworker may saw down some suitable tree, carefully strip off the bark, and then, with skillful craftsmanship, make from it an object that will serve some useful purpose. ¹²He will take the leftover pieces and use them as firewood to cook a meal that he can sit down to and enjoy. ¹³But among that scrap wood he may take one piece that isn't good for anything — maybe it's crooked and full of knots — and carefully carve it in his leisure time, using spare moments to shape it into the crude image of a person, ¹⁴or maybe of some worthless animal. He paints it all over with red, covering up every flaw in the work. ¹⁵Then he prepares a suitable place in the wall for it and fastens it in place with iron nails. ¹⁶He is careful to keep it from falling, because he knows it is only an idol and needs help; it cannot help itself. ¹⁷But he is not ashamed to pray to this lifeless thing about his marriage, his children, and his possessions. ¹⁸It is weak, but he prays to it for health. It is dead, but he prays to it for life. It has no experience, but he prays to it for help. It cannot walk, but he prays to it for a successful journey. ¹⁹Its hands have no power, but he asks it to help him — in business, in making money, and in his work.

Wooden Idols Compared with Noah's Wooden Boat

14 In the same way, a man getting ready to sail on the raging sea will call for help from a piece of wood that is not as strong as the ship he is

13.10 – 14.31 Is 44.9-20; Jr 10.1-16; Let Jr 8-73

about to board. ² Someone designed the ship out of a desire for profit, and a craftsman built it with skill. ³ But it is your care, O Father, that steers it; you give it a safe path through the waves of the sea. ⁴ People may go to sea even if they have no skill, because you can save them from any danger. ⁵ It is your will that the things you have made by your wisdom should be put to use. And so people can cross the sea in a boat and come safely to land, because they trust their lives to that small piece of wood.

. . . It is dead, but he prays to it for life. (13.18)

⁶ This was how it was in ancient times, when a proud race of giants was dying away. The hope of the world escaped on such a boat under your guidance and left the world a new generation to carry on the human race. ⁷ A blessing was on Noah's wooden boat that allowed righteousness to survive, ⁸ but a curse is on an idol made by human hands. A curse is also on the one who makes it, because he works on this perishable thing and then calls it a god. ⁹ Ungodly people and these ungodly things they make are equally hated by God, ¹⁰ who will punish both the things made and the people who made them. ¹¹ And so God's judgment will fall on pagan idols, because, even though they are made from something God created, they became horrible things that trap the souls of foolish people.

The Origins of Idolatry

¹² Sexual immorality began when idols were invented. They have corrupted human life ever since they were first made. ¹³ Idols have not always existed, nor will they exist forever. ¹⁴ It was human pride that brought them into the world, and that is why a quick end has been planned for them.

¹⁵ Once there was a father who was overwhelmed with grief at the untimely death of his child, so he made an image of that child who had been suddenly taken from him. He then honored a dead human being as a god, and handed on secret rituals and ceremonies to those who were under his authority. ¹⁶ As time went on, this ungodly custom became stronger. Finally it became law, and idols were being worshiped at the command of powerful rulers. ¹⁷ When people lived too far away to honor a ruler in his presence but were eager to pay honor to this absent king, they would imagine what he must look like, and would then make a likeness of him. ¹⁸ The ambitious artists who made these likenesses caused this worship to spread, even among people who did not know the king. ¹⁹ An artist might want to please some ruler, and so he would use his skill to make the likeness better looking than the actual person. ²⁰ Then people would be so attracted by the work of art, that the one whom they had earlier honored now became the object of their worship. ²¹ So all this became a deadly trap, because people who were grieving, or under royal authority, would take objects of stone or wood, and give them the honor reserved for the One God.

The Results of Idolatry

²² One thing led to another. It was not enough to be wrong about the knowledge of God. They lived in a state of evil warfare, but they were so ignorant that they called it peace. ²³ They murdered children in their initiation rituals,

You rule the universe with mercy. (15.1)

celebrated secret mysteries, and held wild ceremonial orgies with unnatural practices. ²⁴They no longer kept their lives or their marriages pure. A man might kill another by an act of treachery or cause him grief by committing adultery with his wife. ²⁵Everything was a complete riot of bloody murder, robbery, deceit, corruption, faithlessness, disorder, falsehood, ²⁶harassment of innocent people, ingratitude, moral decay, sexual perversion, broken marriages, adultery, and immorality. ²⁷The worship of idols, whose names should never be spoken, is the beginning and the end, the cause and the result of every evil. ²⁸People who worship them lose control of themselves in ecstasy, or pass off lies as prophecies, or live wickedly, or break their word without hesitation. ²⁹They tell lies under oath and expect no punishment, because the idols they put their trust in are lifeless. ³⁰But punishment will finally catch up with them, for two reasons: first, they were in error

about God when they worshiped idols, and second, they had so little regard for holiness that they made false statements to deceive people. ³¹When unrighteous people commit sin, they will be hunted down, not by the power of whatever thing they swear by, but by the punishment that sinners deserve.

The True God Gives Immortality

15 But you, our God, are kind and true and patient. You rule the universe with mercy. ²Even if we sin, we know your power and are still yours. But because we know that we belong to you, we will not sin. ³Knowing you is perfect righteousness. Recognizing your power is where immortality begins. ⁴We have not been misled by any evil product of human skill, by any useless object painted by some artist, or by any idol smeared with different colors. ⁵The sight of such things arouses the passions of foolish people and makes them desire a dead, lifeless image. ⁶Anyone who makes such a thing or desires it or worships it is in love with something evil, and gets what he deserves when he places his hopes in it.

The Foolishness of Worshiping Clay Idols

⁷A potter works the soft clay and carefully shapes each object for our use. Some things he makes are put to good use, and some are not, but he makes them all from the same clay, and shapes them in the same manner. The potter himself decides which objects shall be used for what purposes. ⁸He is a human being who was himself formed from earth only a short while earlier, and after a little while, when he must return the soul that was lent to him, he will go back to the same earth. He is a human being, but he wastes his labor shaping a useless god out of the same clay that he uses to make pots. ⁹His life will be short, and he will soon

have to die, but he is not concerned about that. He wants to compete with those who work in gold, silver, and bronze, and make things like they do. He takes great pride in the things he makes, but they are counterfeit. [10] His heart is made of ashes. His hope is cheaper than dirt. His life is not worth as much as his clay, [11] because he never came to know the God who shaped him, who breathed into him an active soul and a living spirit. [12] He thinks of human life as just a game, a market where he can make a profit. He believes that he must make money however he can, even by evil ways. [13] This man, who makes idols and fragile pots from the same clay, knows better than anyone else that he is sinning.

This man, who makes idols and fragile pots (15.13)

The Punishment of the Egyptians

[14] But the most foolish of all people, showing less sense than babies, were the enemies who oppressed your people, O Lord. [15] They thought that all their pagan idols were gods, even though idols cannot see with their eyes, cannot breathe through their nose, cannot hear with their ears, cannot feel with their fingers, and cannot walk on their legs. [16] Someone whose spirit is only borrowed made them. No one can ever make a god that is equal to a human being. [17] Every person will sooner or later die, but anything he makes with his wicked hands is dead from the start. He himself is better than what he worships. He at least is alive, but what he worships is not, and never has been. [18] Such people worship the most disgusting animals, including even the least intelligent ones. [19] Even as animals they are not attractive enough to make anyone want them. God himself passed them by when he put his approval and blessing on the rest of creation. [1] And so it was appropriate

16

that these people were punished by such creatures — tormented by swarms of them.

[2] But you, O Lord, did not punish your people in this way; instead, you showed them kindness. You sent them quails to eat, a rare, delicious food to satisfy their hunger. [3] You did all this so that the idolaters, when they were hungry, would be unable to eat because of the disgusting creatures sent to them. Your people, however, suffered hunger only a short while, and then they ate the finest food. [4] It was necessary for the oppressors to suffer relentless need, while your people saw how their enemies were being tormented.

[5] When terrible, fierce snakes attacked your people and were killing them with their poison, you did not remain angry long enough to destroy your people. [6] This trouble lasted for only a little while, as a warning. Then you gave them a healing symbol, the bronze snake, to remind them of what your Law requires. [7] If a person looked at that symbol, he was cured of the snakebite — not by what he saw, but by you, the savior of all mankind. [8] By doing this, you also convinced our enemies that you are the one who rescues people from every evil. [9] Our enemies died from the bites of locusts and flies; no way was found to cure them, because they deserved to be punished by such creatures. [10] But even poisonous snakes could not overcome your people,

16.2 Ex 16.11-13; Nu 11.31, 32   **16.5-7** Nu 21.6-9

because you had mercy, helped them, and cured them. ¹¹They were bitten so that they would remember your commands, but they were quickly rescued, in order to keep them from forgetting you completely and depriving themselves of your kindness. ¹²No medicine or ointment cured them. They were restored to health by your word, O Lord, the word which heals all humanity. ¹³You have power over life and death; you can bring a person to the brink of death and back again. ¹⁴A wicked person may kill someone, but cannot bring the dead person back to life or rescue a soul imprisoned in the world of the dead.

Disastrous Storms Hit Egypt

¹⁵No one can possibly escape from you. ¹⁶Look at those ungodly people: they refused to recognize you as God, so you punished them with your great power. They were overtaken by terrible storms of rain and hail and were completely destroyed by fire. ¹⁷The most amazing thing was that the fire burned all the more fiercely in the water, which usually puts fire out. All the forces of nature fight to defend those who are righteous. ¹⁸At one point the flames died down, so that they wouldn't destroy the creatures sent to punish the ungodly. Those people had to learn that they were being overtaken by your judgment. ¹⁹But at another point, when surrounded by water, the flames burned more fiercely than fire had ever burned before, and so destroyed the crops on the land where those unrighteous people lived.

The Israelites Receive Manna to Eat

²⁰But this disaster did not strike your people. Instead, you gave them the food of angels. From heaven you sent down bread that was ready to eat, and they did not have to prepare it. The food you gave delighted everyone, no matter what his taste. ²¹All this showed how lovingly you care for your children. That food satisfied the desire of everyone who ate it; it was changed to suit each person's taste. ²²It was food that under normal circumstances would vanish away like snow or ice, but now it did not melt even in the fire. This was meant to teach your people that the same fire that was destroying their enemies' crops during the heavy downpour of rain and hail ²³held back its power, so that your own righteous people might have food.

²⁴You created the universe; it is at your command. All creation uses its power to punish unrighteous people, but it becomes mild and kind to those who put their trust in you. ²⁵Creation assumed all kinds of forms to show how you provide generously for all who pray to you.[h] ²⁶This happened so that the people whom you loved, O Lord, might learn that they are not fed by what they can grow. It is your word that maintains those who put their trust in you. ²⁷The food that was not destroyed by the fire melted when the first ray of sunlight warmed it. ²⁸This was to teach us that we must get up before daybreak to give you thanks, and pray as the sun comes up. ²⁹But an ungrateful person's hope will melt away like frost, and drain away like water that is not being used.

Terror Strikes the Egyptians at Night

17 O Lord, your acts of judgment are marvelous and hard to explain; that is why people who had not been taught about them went astray. ²When lawless people imagined that they had your holy nation in their power, they were themselves imprisoned in a long night of darkness. They lay in their own houses, shut off from

[h] pray to you; *or* are in need.
16.20-29 Ex 16.1-36

your eternal care. ³They thought that their sins had been secret and unnoticed, shielded from view by a dark curtain of forgetfulness, but now they were horribly afraid, confused, and terrified by ghostly forms. ⁴Not even the dark corners where they lay could protect them from fear. They were surrounded by horrible noises; grim ghosts with gloomy faces appeared before their eyes. ⁵No fire had power to give them light, and the brilliant stars could do nothing to relieve that deathly darkness. ⁶There was only a dreadful fire, lit by no human hand, that shone on them, and in their terror they believed that the real world was even worse than the things they imagined. ⁷The illusions produced by their magic tricks were put to shame, and all the wisdom they had boasted of came to nothing. ⁸They had claimed they could drive away all the fears and illnesses of sick minds, but now they themselves were sick with silly, groundless fears. ⁹Even though nothing dangerous had actually happened, they were terrified by hissing snakes and animals advancing on them. ¹⁰And so they died, shaking with fear, afraid even to open their eyes, yet unable to keep them shut.

¹¹Wickedness is cowardly in itself and stands self-condemned.ⁱ Someone with a guilty conscience will always imagine things to be worse than they really are. ¹²Fear is nothing but the failure to use the help that reason gives. ¹³When you lack the confidence to rely on reason, you give in to the fears caused by ignorance.

¹⁴All night long those people slept the same restless sleep, even though the night held no power over them, since it came from the powerless depths of the world of the dead. ¹⁵They were chased by hideous forms and lay paralyzed as they surrendered themselves to the sudden, unexpected fear that came over them. ¹⁶People would suddenly collapse and lie locked in the chains of their own fear. ¹⁷Farmers, shepherds, and laborers out in the countryside were captured by the same inevitable fate and bound in the darkness by the same invisible chain. ¹⁸⁻¹⁹They were panic-stricken by the sighing of the wind or by the singing of birds in the trees or by the roar of rushing water or by the rumble of falling rock or by the sound of unseen creatures running about or by the savage roaring of wild animals or by the echoes from the mountains. ²⁰In the full light of day, the rest of the world went about its business undisturbed. ²¹Only those people were covered by this heavy night, a foretaste of the darkness of death that was waiting for them. They were a burden to themselves that was even heavier than the darkness.

Light Shines on the Israelites

18 Yet all the while a brilliant light was shining for your holy people. Their enemies heard their voices, but couldn't see them. They envied the good fortune of your people, who were not suffering. ²Those enemies could at least be thankful that the people they had wronged were not taking vengeance on them now, and so they begged them to leave.ʲ

³Then you guided your people as they traveled through a country they did not know. You guided them with a pillar of fire. It was like a sun that would not harm them on that glorious journey. ⁴But their enemies, who were not allowed to see the light, deserved to be prisoners in darkness, because they had made prisoners of your people. And it was through your people that the

eternal light of the Law was going to be given to the world.

The Death of the Egyptian First-Born

5 When your enemies were carrying out their resolve to kill the babies of your holy people, there was one child who was abandoned but later rescued. Then you punished your enemies by killing a great number of their own children. You drowned their whole army at one time in the rushing waters. 6 But our ancestors had been told in advance of what would happen that night, so that they would be cheered and encouraged by confident trust in your promises to them. 7 Your people knew that you would rescue the righteous nation and destroy their enemies. 8 With the same act you punished our enemies and did us the glorious honor of calling us to yourself.

9 During all this time devout people from this righteous nation were secretly offering sacrifices, giving their word to each other that they would keep God's law and share each other's blessings and dangers. Already they were chanting those ancient hymns of praise. 10 But their enemies' pitiful cries of grief echoed everywhere, as they mourned for their dead children. 11 Masters suffered the same punishment as their slaves; the king endured the same loss as the common people. 12 There were too many dead bodies to count. There were not enough people left to bury them all. In a single moment their dearest children died; all of them met death in the same way. 13 These people had paid no attention to any warning, but relied instead on their magical powers. But when their firstborn sons were killed, then they recognized that Israel was God's son.

14 The short night was half over, and all was quiet and peaceful, 15 when sud-denly your threats were carried out! An invincible word of judgment sped from your royal throne in heaven, straight down to that doomed land. It came like a soldier in fierce attack, 16 carrying out your firm command with a fearful weapon, standing with feet on the ground and head touching the sky, filling the land with death. 17 At that moment the people who were about to die had terrible nightmares and were seized by sudden fear. 18 All over the land they lay half-dead and let it be known why they were dying. 19 They knew why they were dying, because their horrible dreams had told them.

Aaron's Prayer Saves the Israelites from Death

20 Death also came to the righteous nation, for an epidemic struck many of them while they were in the desert, but your anger did not last long. 21 There was a certain blameless man who quickly took action to defend them. Acting as their priest, Aaron offered prayers and burned the incense used in asking forgiveness of sins. With prayers and incense as his weapons, he withstood your anger and ended the disaster. By doing this he proved that he was your servant. 22 He overcame the bitter difficulty,k but not by his own strength or by military force. Instead, he used prayer to stop the punishment, appealing to the promises you solemnly gave to our ancestors. 23 Dead bodies were already lying in piles, but he stepped in to hold your anger back and to keep it from harming those who were left alive. 24 He wore a long robe decorated with symbols of the universe. In honor of our ancestors he wore four rows of engraved stones on his chest, and your own majesty was represented by the ornament on his turban. 25 The Angel of Death was afraid of these things, and

---

k *Probable text* bitter difficulty; *Greek* crowd.
18.20-25 Nu 16.41-50

gave up. It was only a slight experience of your wrath, but it was enough.

The Suicidal Stupidity of the Egyptians

19 But the godless continued to feel your pitiless anger until the very end. You knew what they would do before they did it. ²You knew that even though they let your people go and made them leave quickly, they would change their minds and pursue them. ³⁻⁴While the Egyptians were still mourning at the graves of their dead, they forgot why all this had happened, and they foolishly decided that the people they had begged to leave were runaways. So they chased after them. They were led into this as part of the punishment they deserved, so that they would suffer the rest of the torments they were due to receive. ⁵They were to meet a strange death, while your people continued on their miraculous journey.

God Guides and Protects His People

⁶The whole nature of the universe was changed at your command so that your people would not be harmed. ⁷They saw the cloud over their camp and dry land where water had been. There was a grass-covered plain between the stormy waves of the Red Sea, making it easy for them to cross over. ⁸All your people, under your protection, saw this miracle and went across. ⁹They pranced about like horses let out to pasture; they skipped about like lambs and praised you, Lord, for saving them. ¹⁰They still remembered what life had been like when they were slaves—how the earth bred gnats instead of cattle, how the river produced huge numbers of frogs instead of fish. ¹¹⁻¹²Later, when they desperately wanted better food, quails came up from the sea to satisfy their hunger.

The quail was a bird they had never seen before.

The Punishment of the Egyptians

¹³But violent thunder gave warning of the punishment that was coming on those sinners. They suffered a well-deserved punishment for their great wickedness. No nation had ever hated strangers so bitterly. ¹⁴Other people had been known to refuse welcome to strangers who came to them, but these people made slaves of those who were their guests and who had shown them kindness. ¹⁵Every nation will be punished if it does not welcome foreigners, ¹⁶but these people, who had earlier welcomed the foreigners with happy celebrations and treated them as equals, later made them suffer cruelly. ¹⁷These people were also struck with blindness, like the men of Sodom who came to the door of that righteous man Lot. They found themselves in total darkness, as each one groped around to find his own door.

God's Miraculous Power

¹⁸On a harp each string keeps its own pitch, but each sound can be combined with others to make different melodies. That is how it was in those days, when the very elements entered into new combinations. Look at what happened! ¹⁹Land animals took to the water, and swimming creatures came up on the land. ²⁰Fire burned even in water, which could not put it out. ²¹And yet the flames could not burn the flesh of the perishable creatures walking in them and did not melt that heavenly food that would ordinarily have melted like frost.

²²Lord, you have made your people great—glorious in all respects. You have never neglected them. You have given them help, always, everywhere.

SIRACH
THE WISDOM OF JESUS, SON OF SIRACH
(Ecclesiasticus)

INTRODUCTION

The Wisdom of Jesus, Son of Sirach, also known as *Ecclesiasticus,* was written in Hebrew by a man named Joshua (or Jesus) and was later translated into Greek by his grandson. The book includes traditional Jewish wisdom material and makes a defense of Judaism by showing that God has given true wisdom to his people. Many subjects of a religious, moral, and practical nature are presented, sometimes at length and sometimes in short proverbial sayings.

OUTLINE OF CONTENTS

Foreword

The Law, the Prophets, and the later writers have left us a wealth of valuable teachings, and we should praise Israel for the instruction and wisdom they provide. But it is not enough that those who read them should gain understanding for themselves. Anyone who values learning should be able to help others by what he himself says and writes. That is why my grandfather Jesus devoted himself to reading the Law, the Prophets, and the other books of our ancestors. After he had mastered them, he was led to write a book of his own in order to share his wisdom and learning with others, so that anyone who shared his love for learning should have his book available as well, and be all the more able to live according to the Law.

Let me urge you, then, to read this book carefully and with an open mind. And please be patient in those places where, in spite of all my diligent efforts, I may not have translated some phrases very well. What was originally written in Hebrew does not always have exactly the same sense when it is translated into another language.[a] That is true not only of this book, but even of the Law itself, the Prophets, and the other books. The translations differ quite a bit from the original.

I came to Egypt in the thirty-eighth year of King Euergetes' reign and stayed for some time. While I was there, I had the opportunity for a good deal of study and felt the necessity of translating the following book. I wanted to use all my diligence and skill to complete it and make it available for all those living in foreign lands who wish to learn and who have the strength of character to live by the Law of Moses.

In Praise of Wisdom

1 All wisdom comes from the
Lord,
and Wisdom is with him
forever.
2 Who can count raindrops or the
sand along the shore?
Who can count the days of
eternity?
3 How high is the sky? How wide
is the earth?
How deep is the ocean? How
profound is Wisdom?
Can anyone find answers to
these questions?
4 Wisdom was created before
anything else;
understanding has always
existed.[b]
6 Has anyone ever been shown
where Wisdom originates?
Does anyone understand her
subtle cleverness?[c]
8 There is only one who is wise,

and we must stand in awe
before his throne.
9 The Lord himself created
Wisdom;
he saw her and recognized
her value,
and so he filled everything he
made with Wisdom.

Who can count raindrops? (1.2)

10 He gave some measure of
Wisdom to everyone,
but poured her out on those
who love him.

11 If you fear the Lord, honor and
pride will be yours;
you will be crowned with
happiness and joy.
12 To honor the Lord is a heartfelt
delight;
it will give you a long and
happy life,
13 and at the end of your days all
will go well for you.
God will bless you on the day
of your death.

---

[a] *The book of Sirach was written in Hebrew, but the writer of this foreword translated it into Greek.*   [b] *Some manuscripts add verse 5:* The source of Wisdom is the word of God on high; her ways are eternal commands.   [c] *Some manuscripts add verse 7:* To whom has the knowledge of Wisdom been revealed? Who has understood her great experience?

1.1 Pr 2.6   **1.9** Pr 8.22-31; Si 24.9

¹⁴To fear the Lord is the first step
to Wisdom.
Wisdom is given to the
faithful in their mothers'
wombs.
¹⁵She has lived with us from
ancient times,
and generations to come will
rely on her.
¹⁶To fear the Lord is Wisdom at
her fullest;
she satisfies us completely
with her gifts
¹⁷and fills our homes and our
barns
with all that our hearts can
desire.
¹⁸To fear the Lord is the flower of
Wisdom
that blossoms with peace and
good health.ᵈ
¹⁹She sends knowledge and
understanding like the
rain,
and increases the honor of
those who receive her.
²⁰To fear the Lord is the root of
Wisdom;
her branches are long life.ᵉ

Self-control

²²There is no excuse for unjustified
anger; it can bring about your downfall.
²³Wait and be patient, and later you will
be glad you did. ²⁴Keep quiet until the
right time to speak, and you will gain a
reputation for good sense.

Wisdom and Reverence for God

²⁵Wisdom has a treasury of wise sayings, but sinners have nothing but contempt for godliness. ²⁶If you want to be
wise, keep the Lord's commands, and
he will give you Wisdom in abundance.
²⁷Fearing the Lord is Wisdom and an
education in itself. He is pleased by loyalty and humility. ²⁸Be faithful in the
practice of your religion; when you worship the Lord, do it with all your heart.
²⁹Be careful about what you say, and
don't be a hypocrite. ³⁰Don't be arrogant; you may suffer a fall and be disgraced. The Lord will reveal your
secrets and humble you in front of
everyone in the synagogue, because
you did not come there with reverence
for the Lord, but with a heart full of
hypocrisy.

Faithfulness to God

2 My child, if you are going to serve
the Lord, be prepared for times
when you will be put to the test. ²Be
sincere and determined. Keep calm
when trouble comes. ³Stay with the
Lord; never abandon him, and you will
be prosperous at the end of your days.
⁴Accept whatever happens to you.
Even if you suffer humiliation, be patient. ⁵Gold is tested by fire, and human
character is tested in the furnace of humiliation. ⁶Trust the Lord, and he will
help you. Walk straight in his ways, and
put your hope in him.

⁷All you that fear the Lord, wait for
him to show you his mercy. Do not turn
away from him, or you will fall. ⁸All you
that fear the Lord, trust him, and you
will certainly be rewarded. ⁹All you that
fear the Lord, look forward to his blessings of mercy and eternal happiness.

¹⁰Think back to the ancient generations and consider this: has the Lord
ever disappointed anyone who put his
hope in him? Has the Lord ever abandoned anyone who held him in constant reverence? Has the Lord ever
ignored anyone who prayed to him?
¹¹The Lord is kind and merciful; he forgives our sins and keeps us safe in time

---

ᵈ *Some manuscripts add:* He saw her and recognized her value (*see 1.9*).   ᵉ *Some*
manuscripts add verse 21: Honoring the Lord takes sin away; where the fear of the
Lord is found, it turns away anger.
1.17 Ws 7.11   **1.20** Pr 3.16; 4.10   **2.5** Ws 3.5, 6; 1 P 1.7

of trouble. ¹²But those who lose their nerve are doomed — all those sinners who try to have it both ways! ¹³Doom is sure to come for those who lose their courage; they have no faith, and so they will have no protection. ¹⁴Doom is sure to come for those who lose their hope. What will they do when the Lord comes to judge them?

¹⁵Those who fear the Lord do not disobey his commands; those who love him will live as he wants them to live. ¹⁶Those who fear and love the Lord will try to please him and devote themselves to the Law. ¹⁷Those who fear the Lord are always ready to serve him. They humble themselves before him, and say, ¹⁸"We place our destiny in the hands of the Lord, not in human hands, because his mercy is as great as his majesty."

Duties to Parents

3 Children, listen to me; I am your father. Do what I tell you and you will be safe, ²for the Lord has given fathers authority over their children and given children the obligation to obey their mothers. ³If you respect your father, you can make up for your sins, ⁴and if you honor your mother, you are earning great wealth. ⁵If you respect your father, one day your own children will make you happy; the Lord will hear your prayers. ⁶If you obey the Lord by honoring your father and making your mother happy, you will live a long life. ⁷Obey your parents as if you were their slave. ⁸Honor your father in everything you do and say, so that you may receive his blessing. ⁹When parents give their blessing, they give strength to their children's homes, but when they curse their children, they destroy the very foundations.

¹⁰Never seek honor for yourself at your father's expense; it is not to your

Obey the Lord by . . . making your mother happy. (3.6)

credit if he is dishonored. ¹¹Your own honor comes from the respect that you show to your father. If children do not honor their mothers, it is their own disgrace. ¹²My child, take care of your father when he grows old; give him no cause for worry as long as he lives. ¹³Be sympathetic even if his mind fails him; don't look down on him just because you are strong and healthy. ¹⁴The Lord will not forget the kindness you show to your father; it will help you make up for your sins. ¹⁵When you are in trouble, the Lord will remember your kindness and will help you; your sins will melt away like frost in warm sunshine. ¹⁶Those who abandon their parents or give them cause for anger may as well be cursing the Lord; they are already under the Lord's curse.

Humility

¹⁷My child, be humble in everything you do, and people will appreciate it more than gifts.ᶠ ¹⁸The greater you become, the more humble you should be; then the Lord will be pleased with

ᶠ *Hebrew* people . . . gifts; *Greek* those whom the Lord approves will love you.

2.15, 16 Ws 6.18; Jn 14.15, 21, 23   **3.8** Ex 20.12   **3.18** Phil 2.3

you.⁹ 20 The Lord's power is great, and he is honored by those who are humble. 21 Don't try to understand things that are too hard for you, or investigate matters that are beyond your power to

The greater you become, the more humble you should be. (3.18)

know. 22 Concentrate on the Law, which has been given to you. You do not need to know about things which the Lord has not revealed, 23 so don't concern yourself with them. After all, what has been shown to you is beyond human power to understand. 24 Many people have been misled by their own opinions; their wrong ideas have warped their judgment.ʰ

26 Stubbornness will get you into trouble at the end. If you live dangerously, it will kill you. 27 A stubborn per-

son will be burdened down with troubles. Sinners go on adding one sin to another. 28 There is no cure for the troubles that arrogant people have; wickedness has taken deep root in them. 29 Intelligent people will learn from proverbs and parables. They listen well because they want to learn.

Giving to the Poor

30 Giving to the poor can make up for sin, just as water can put out a blazing fire. 31 Anyone who responds to others with acts of kindness is thinking of the future, because he will find help if he ever falls on hard times. 1 My child, don't prevent the poor from making a living, or keep them waiting in their need. 2 Never give a hungry person any cause for resentment or anger. 3 Don't add to the troubles of someone who is already desperate. If he is in need, don't put off giving to him. 4-5 Don't refuse to help a beggar who is in distress. Don't turn your back on a poor person or give him any reason to curse you. 6 If he becomes so bitter that he does curse you, his Creator will hear his prayer.

7 Make yourself popular in the synagogue. Bow your head to men of authority. 8 Listen to what the poor have to say, and answer them politely. 9 Protect people from those who want to wrong them, and be firm in your judgments. 10 Be like a father to orphans, and provide widows with the help their husbands can no longer give them. Then you will be like a child of the Most High, and he will love you more than your own mother does.

⁹ *Some Greek manuscripts add verse 19:* Many are exalted and esteemed, but God's secrets are revealed to the humble; *Hebrew:* God's mercy is great, and he reveals his secrets to those who are humble.   ʰ *Some Greek manuscripts add verse 25:* If you have no eyes, you cannot see; don't claim to have knowledge if you don't have it; *Hebrew has, after verse 27:* If you have no eyes, you cannot see; if you have no knowledge, you cannot have Wisdom.
3.22 Dt 29.29

Wisdom as a Teacher

11 Wisdom takes care of those who look for her; she raises them to greatness. **12** Loving her is loving life itself; rising early to look for her is pure joy. **13** Anyone who obtains Wisdom will be greatly honored. Wherever he goes, the Lord will bless him. **14** Wisdom's servants are the servants of the Holy One, and the Lord loves everyone who loves her. **15** Those who obey her will give sound judgments;*i* those who pay attention to her have true security. **16** Put your trust in Wisdom, and you will possess her and pass her on to your descendants. **17** At first, Wisdom will lead you along difficult paths. She will make you so afraid that you will think you cannot go on. The discipline she demands will be tormenting, and she will put you to the test with her requirements until she trusts you*j* completely. **18** Then she will come to you with no delay, reveal her secrets to you, and make you happy. **19** But if you go astray, she will abandon you and let you go to your own ruin.

Self-confidence

20 Take advantage of opportunities, but guard yourself against evil. Don't underrate yourself. **21** Humility deserves honor and respect, but a low opinion of yourself leads to sin. **22** Do not let others have their way at your expense; do not bring on your own ruin by giving up your rights. **23** Never hesitate to speak out when the occasion*k* calls for it. Don't hide your wisdom.*l* **24** Your wisdom and education can be known only by what you say. **25** Do not, however, go against the truth, and remember that you do not know everything. **26** Don't be ashamed to confess your sins; there's no point in trying to stop a river from flowing. **27** Don't allow yourself to be dominated by someone who is stupid or show partiality to influential people. **28** Stand up for what is right, even if it costs you your life; the Lord God will be fighting on your side.

29 Don't be quick to speak or lazy and negligent in your work. **30** Don't act like a lion at home or be suspicious of your servants. **31** Don't stick out your hand to get something if you're going to be tightfisted when the time comes to pay it back.

Don't Be Presumptuous

5 Don't rely on money to make you independent. **2** Don't think you have to have everything you want, and then spend your energy trying to get it. **3** Don't think that no one can exercise authority over you; if you do, the Lord is certain to punish you. **4** Don't think that you can sin and get away with it; the Lord does not mind waiting to punish you. **5** Don't be so certain of the Lord's forgiveness that you go on committing one sin after another. **6** Don't think that his mercy is so great that he will forgive your sins no matter how many they are. He does show mercy, but he also shows his furious anger with sinners. **7** Come back to the Lord quickly. Don't think that you can keep putting it off. His anger can come upon you suddenly, and you will die under his punishment. **8** Don't rely on dishonest wealth; it will do you no good on that day of disaster.

Sincerity and Self-control

9-10 Be certain about what you believe and consistent in what you say. Don't

---

i Hebrew give sound judgments; *Greek* judge nations.   *j* she trusts you; *or* you trust her.   *k Probable text* the occasion; *Greek* safety.   *l Hebrew* Don't hide your wisdom; *most Greek manuscripts do not have these words; other Greek manuscripts* Don't hide your wisdom for the sake of appearances.

4.31 Ac 20.35   **5.4** Ec 8.11

try to please everyone or agree with everything people say.*m* 11 Always be ready to listen, but take your time in answering. 12 Answer only if you know what to say, and if you don't know what

Answer only if you know what to say, and if you don't . . . keep quiet. (5.12)

to say, keep quiet. 13 Speaking can bring you either honor or disgrace; what you say can ruin you.

14 Don't get a reputation for being a gossip, and don't tell tales that will hurt people. Just as robbers will suffer disgrace, so liars will suffer severe condemnation. 15 Do nothing destructive,*n* whether it seems insignificant or not,

6 1 and do not be an enemy when you should be a friend. A bad reputation brings you the disgrace that lying sinners deserve. 2 Do not let your passions carry you away; this can tear your soul to pieces like a bull.*o* 3 You will be left like a dead tree without any leaves or fruit. 4 Evil desire will destroy you and make you a joke to your enemies.

Friendship

5 If you are polite and courteous, you will enjoy the friendship of many people. 6 Exchange greetings with many, but take advice from only one person out of a thousand. 7 When you make friends, don't be too quick to trust them; make sure that they have proved themselves. 8 Some people will be your friends only when it is convenient for them, but they won't stand by you in trouble. 9 Others will fall out with you over some argument, and then embarrass you by letting everyone know about it. 10-11 Others will sit at your table as long as things are going well; they will stick to you like your shadow and give orders to your servants, but they will not stand by you in trouble. 12 If your situation takes a turn for the worse, they will turn against you, and you won't be able to find them anywhere.

13 Stay away from your enemies and be on guard against your friends. 14 A loyal friend is like a safe shelter; find one, and you have found a treasure. 15 Nothing else is as valuable; there is no way of putting a price on it. 16 A loyal friend is like a medicine that keeps you in good health. Only those who fear the Lord can find such a friend. 17 A person who fears the Lord can make real friendships, because he will treat his friends as he does himself.*p*

Learn from Wisdom

18 My child, learn to value Wisdom while you are young, and you will still be able to find her when you grow old. 19 Work as hard to find Wisdom as a

m Hebrew everything people say; *Greek adds* That is what double-tongued sinners do.
n Hebrew Do nothing destructive; *Greek* Do not be ignorant in anything.   *o Verse 2 in both Greek and Hebrew is unclear.*   *p* because . . . himself; *or* because his friends will also fear the Lord.
6.19 Jas 5.7, 8

farmer works to plow and plant his fields; then you can expect a good harvest. You will have to work at it for a while, but you will soon be enjoying what you have earned. 20 Undisciplined people find Wisdom's demands too hard and don't have enough determination to meet them. 21 Her requirements are a burden heavier than they are willing to bear, and they quickly lay them aside. 22 "Discipline" means just that — discipline,*q* and not many people are able to discipline themselves.

23 My child, listen to me and take my advice. 24 Put Wisdom's chains around your feet and her yoke around your neck. 25 Carry her on your shoulder and don't be resentful of her bonds. 26 Follow Wisdom, and keep to her ways with all your heart. 27 Go looking for her, and she will reveal herself to you. Take hold of her and don't let go. 28 Then you will discover the peace of mind she offers, and she will become your joy. 29-30 The signs of slavery you wear will become signs of royal majesty. Her chains will be your protection, and you will wear her yoke like a magnificent robe. 31 You will wear Wisdom like a splendid crown.

32 My child, you can learn if you want to. You can be clever if you are determined to be. 33 If you are willing to listen, you will learn and become wise. 34 Go where the old people are; find someone who is wise, and stay with him. 35 Be ready to listen when religious people speak, and don't miss anything that shows insight. 36 If you find someone with understanding, get up early to call on him; wear out his doorstep with your visits.

37 Devote all your time to studying the Lord's commands and thinking about them. He will give you the insight and wisdom you are looking for.

Miscellaneous Advice

7 1-2 If you do no wrong, no wrong will ever come to you. 3 Do not plow the ground to plant seeds of injustice; you may reap a bigger harvest than you expect.

4 Don't ask the Lord for a place of honor or ask the king for an important position. 5 Don't try to convince the Lord that you are righteous or make a show of your wisdom before the king. 6 Don't set your heart on being a judge, unless you have the strength of character it takes to put an end to injustice. If you let yourself be influenced by someone in a position of power, your integrity will be damaged. 7 Don't commit any crime against the general public, and don't disgrace yourself among your townspeople.

8 Don't commit the same sin twice. The punishment you get the first time ought to be enough.

9 Don't think that God Most High is going to take into account how very generous you are and so accept any offering you decide to make.

10 Never get tired of praying, and never miss a chance to give to the poor.

11 Don't laugh at someone who has been humiliated. It is the Lord who humbles a person, but the Lord also raises him up again.

12 Don't think up lies to tell about your friends. 13 Don't tell lies at all. It never does any good.

14 In an official assembly, don't get up and talk a lot of nonsense. And don't repeat yourself when you pray.

15 Don't try to avoid farm work or other hard labor; the Most High has given us these jobs to do.

16 Don't join up with a crowd of sinners; remember that the Lord's punishment is sure to come.

q Hebrew "Discipline" . . . discipline; *Greek* "Wisdom" . . . wisdom.
6.37 Js 1.8; Ps 1.2

¹⁷ Be very humble, because the decay of death awaits us all. *r*

Relations with Others

¹⁸ Don't betray a friend for money. Don't betray a real friend for all the gold in the world.

¹⁹ Don't miss your chance to marry a wise and good woman. A gracious wife is worth more than gold.

²⁰ Don't mistreat servants who do their work well, or employees who do their best for you.

²¹ Show the same love to wise servants that you would show to yourself, *s* and let them have their freedom.

²² Take good care of any animals you own. If they make money for you, keep them.

²³ If you have sons, educate them. Teach them self-discipline while they are young.

Teach them self-discipline while they are young. (7.23)

²⁴ If you have daughters, keep them virtuous, and don't be too indulgent with them. ²⁵ When you give your daughter in marriage, you have finished a great task, but give her to a sensible man.

²⁶ If you have a good wife, do not divorce her, but do not trust yourself to someone you don't love.

²⁷ Honor your father with all your heart, and never forget how your mother suffered when you were born. ²⁸ Remember that you owe your life to them. How can you ever repay them for all they have done for you?

²⁹ Fear the Lord with all your heart, and have respect for his priests. ³⁰ Love your Creator with all your strength, and give his ministers your support. ³¹ Honor the Lord and respect the priests. Supply them with what you have been commanded to give: the first produce, the offering for sin, the shoulder of the sacrificial animal — all the required sacrifices and offerings.

³² Give your help to the poor, and the Lord will give you his perfect blessing. ³³ Be generous to every living soul, and be gracious to the memory of the dead. ³⁴ Show sympathy to those who have lost a loved one, and mourn with them. ³⁵ Do not hesitate to visit the sick. You will be loved for things like these. ³⁶ Whatever you do, remember that some day you must die. As long as you keep this in mind, you will never sin.

Using Common Sense

8 Do not challenge a person who has influence; you may fall into his power. ² Do not quarrel with someone rich; he may bribe people to turn against you. Gold has destroyed many people and corrupted kings. ³ Don't argue with someone who talks too much; you will just be adding fuel to his fire. ⁴ Don't make fun of someone who has bad manners; he may insult your ancestors. ⁵ Don't criticize someone if he is already turning away from sin. Remember that we are all guilty. ⁶ Never think less of someone because he is old;

r Hebrew the decay . . . all; *Greek* the punishment of the ungodly is fire and worms.
s Hebrew Show the same love . . . yourself; *Greek* Show love to a wise servant.
7.21 Ex 21.2; Dt 15.12-15   **7.27, 28** Ex 20.12

some of us are growing old, too. 7Don't be happy over the death of anyone; remember that all of us must die.

8Do not disregard what the wise have said. Study their proverbs; from them you can learn to be cultured and to serve great people. 9Pay attention to what old people say, for they learned from those who came before them. You can learn from them, and they can teach you how to have an answer ready when you need one.

10You should not provide a sinner with more opportunity to sin. You might get hurt yourself; it's as easy as getting burned while adding logs to a fire. 11You should not get up and walk out on someone who is insolent. He might twist your words and use them against you. 12You should not lend anything to someone more powerful than you. If you do, you might as well consider it lost. 13You should not guarantee anyone else's loan to an extent that you cannot afford. You must be prepared to pay any such guarantee. 14You should not bring a lawsuit against a judge. He will win because of his position. 15You should not travel with anyone who is reckless. It will cause you nothing but trouble. He will do any foolish thing he pleases, and you will die with him.

16You should not get into an argument with anyone who has a hot temper or go to some place where the two of you will be alone. Violence means nothing to such a person, and he will attack you when there is no one to help you. 17You should not ask a stupid person for advice. He will not be able to keep secret what you tell him. 18You should not do anything in front of a stranger that should be kept secret. There is no way of knowing what will happen if you do. 19You should not reveal your most private thoughts to anyone. If you do, you may as well throw away any chance of happiness. t

Advice about Women

9 Don't be jealous of the wife you love. You will only be teaching her how to do you harm. 2Do not surrender your dignity to any woman. 3Keep away from other men's wives u or they will trap you. 4Don't keep company with female musicians; they will trick you. 5Don't look too intently at a virgin, or you may find yourself forced to pay a bride price. 6Don't give yourself to prostitutes, or you may lose everything you own. 7So don't go looking about in the streets or wandering around in the rundown parts of town. 8When you see a good-looking woman, look the other way; don't let your mind dwell on the beauty of any woman who is not your wife. Many men have been led astray by a woman's beauty. It kindles passion

When you see a good-looking woman, look the other way. (9.8)

as if it were fire. 9Don't sit down to eat with another man's wife or join her for a drink. You may give in to the

---

t *Hebrew* If . . . happiness; *Greek* And don't let anyone do you a favor.   u *Hebrew* other men's wives; *Greek* immoral women.
9.1 Nu 5.12-15

temptation of her charms and be destroyed by your passion.

Friendships with Others

10 Never abandon old friends; you will never find a new one who can take their place. Friendship is like wine; it gets better as it grows older. [11] Don't be jealous of a sinner's success; you don't know what kind of disaster is in store for him. [12] Don't take pleasure in the things that make ungodly people happy; remember that they will be held guilty as long as they live. [13] If you keep away from someone who has the power to put you to death, you will not have to fear for your life; but if you must go near him, be very careful, or he may kill you. Be conscious that you are walking among hidden traps, that you are an easy target.

[14] Get to know the people around you as well as you can, and take advice only from those who are qualified to give it. [15] Engage in conversation with intelligent people, and let the Law of the Most High be the topic of your discussions. [16] Choose righteous people for your dinner companions. Your chief pride should be your fear of the Lord.

Rulers

[17] A skilled worker is admired for the things he makes, and a leader's wisdom is proved by his words. [18] Someone who speaks rashly and recklessly is feared and hated by everyone in town.

10 [1] A wise ruler will educate his people, and his government will be orderly. [2] All the officials and all the citizens will be like their ruler. [3] An uneducated king will ruin his people, but a government will grow strong if its rulers are wise. [4] The Lord sees to the government of the world and brings the right person to power at the right time. [5] The success of that person is in the Lord's hands. The Lord is the source of the honor given to any official.

Pride

[6] Don't be angry with someone for every little thing he does wrong. Don't do anything out of injured pride. [7] Arrogance and injustice are hated by both the Lord and people. [8] Injustice, arrogance, and wealth cause nations to fall from power, and others then rise to take their place. [9] We are only dust and ashes; what have we got to be proud of? Our body decays even while we are alive.[v] [10] A long illness puzzles the doctor.[w] Even a king may be alive today and dead tomorrow. [11] When a person dies, all he then possesses is worms, flies, and maggots.

[12] Pride has its beginning when a person abandons the Lord, his maker. [13] Pride is like a fountain pouring out sin, and whoever persists in it will be full of wickedness. That is why the Lord brought terrible punishments on some people and completely destroyed them. [14] The Lord has overthrown kings and put humbler people in their place. [15] The Lord has pulled up nations by the roots and established humbler ones in their place. [16] The Lord has overthrown empires and completely devastated their lands. [17] He destroyed some so completely that they are not even remembered any more. [18] The Creator never intended for human beings to be arrogant and violent.

People Who Should Be Honored

[19] Who deserves honor? The human race does, because people fear the Lord. Who does not deserve honor? The human race does not, because people break the Lord's commands. [20] A leader should be honored by those who follow

---

[v] Our body ... alive; *this sentence in both Greek and Hebrew is unclear.*
[w] A long ... doctor; *this sentence in both Greek and Hebrew is unclear.*
10.14 1 S 2.8; Lk 1.52

him, and the Lord honors those who fear him.ˣ

²²Rich people, famous people, and poor people all take pride in their fear of the Lord. ²³It is not right to refuse honor to a poor person who is intelligent, and it is not right to give honor to a sinner. ²⁴People of influence, rulers, and judges will be honored, but none of them is greater than a person who fears the Lord. ²⁵A slave who is wise will have free citizens serving him; and if they are sensible, they will not resent it.

Humility and Self-respect

²⁶When you do your work, don't make a show of your skill, and don't try to put on a show when you are in trouble. ²⁷It is better to work and have more than you need than to go around boasting but hungry.

²⁸My child, keep your self-respect, but remain modest. Value yourself at your true worth. ²⁹There is no excuse for a person to run himself down. No one respects a person who has no respect for himself. ³⁰Poor people can be honored for their good sense, and rich people can be honored for their wealth. ³¹If someone is honored while he is poor, think how much he will be honored if he becomes rich! If someone is despised while he is rich, think how much more he will be despised if he

11 becomes poor! ¹If a poor person is wise, he has good reason to be proud, and he will be thought of as someone great.

Appearances

²Do not compliment a person on his good looks. On the other hand, do not look down on someone who is unattractive. ³Compared to most flying things, a bee is very small, but the honey it

makes is the sweetest of foods. ⁴Don't make fun of someone who has fallen on hard times and is dressed in rags.ʸ The Lord does wonderful things that human beings never notice. ⁵Many are the kings who have ended their careers sitting on the ground, while their crowns were worn by those no one had heard of before. ⁶Many are the rulers who have suffered disgrace. Many are the famous people who have fallen into the power of others.

Be Cautious

⁷Before you start criticizing, get your facts straight and think the matter through. ⁸Don't interrupt while someone is speaking; hear what he has to say before you answer. ⁹Don't get into an argument over something that is none of your business. Don't take part in decisions that are being made by sinners.

¹⁰My child, don't get involved in too many things. If you try to do too much, you will suffer for it. You won't be able to finish your work, and you won't be able to get away from it either. ¹¹For instance, here is someone who never stops working like a slave, but gets further behind all the time. ¹²On the other hand, someone else may be very poor and not up to his task. He may be slow, and he may need help, but the Lord is pleased with him and pulls him out of his bad situation. ¹³When he is back on his feet again, everyone is astounded.

¹⁴Everything comes from the Lord: success and failure, poverty and wealth, life and death. ¹⁵Wisdom, understanding, knowledge of the Law, love, and the doing of good deeds — all these come from the Lord. ¹⁶Error and darkness have been with sinners from the beginning, and those who enjoy evil will have it with them into their old age. ¹⁷The Lord's gifts to religious people

---

ˣ *Some manuscripts add verse 21:* Success begins with fear of the Lord, but failure begins with stubbornness and arrogance.   ʸ *Hebrew* Don't . . . rags; *Greek* Don't take pride in fine clothes, and don't let compliments go to your head.

are gifts that endure. If he approves of you, you will always be successful. [18] Someone may grow rich by working hard and denying himself pleasure, but what does he get for it? [19] He says to himself, "Now I can finally sit back and enjoy what I have worked for." But he has no idea how long it will be before he must die and leave his wealth to others.

[20] Stand by your duty and stick to it; grow old at your work. [21] Don't be jealous of what sinners achieve; just stick to your own work, and trust the Lord. It is very easy for the Lord to make a poor person suddenly rich. [22] Devout people will receive the Lord's blessing as their reward, and that blessing can be given in a moment. [23] Don't be concerned about what you need, or what success the future holds for you. [24] On the other hand, don't think that you have everything you need or that nothing can go wrong for you in the future. [25] When things are going well, people don't think about hard times; and when things are going badly, they forget about prosperity. [26] The Lord can easily wait until the day of our death to reward or punish us. [27] At that time our deeds are open for all to see; all our happiness can be erased in that one moment of misery. [28] So then, don't think of anyone's life as happy until it is over, because all the evidence is not in until the person is dead. [z]

Be Careful in Choosing Friends

[29] Be careful about the kind of person you invite into your home, because clever people can fool you in many ways. [30] A proud person is a decoy to

But when you are successful, your enemies will act like friends. (12.9)

lure you into danger; like a spy, he will look for your weaknesses. [a] [31] He will make good appear evil and find fault with the noblest actions. [32] A single spark can set a pile of coals ablaze, and a sinner is just waiting for a chance to do violence. [33] Watch out for such people and their evil plans; they will ruin you permanently. [34] If you bring a stranger home with you, it will only cause trouble, even between you and your own family.

12 When you do a good deed, make sure you know who is benefiting from it; then what you do will not be wasted. [b] [2] You will be repaid for any kindness you show to a devout person. If he doesn't repay you, the Most High will. [3] No good ever comes to a person who gives comfort to the wicked; it is not a righteous act. [c] [4] Give to religious people, but don't help sinners. [5] Do good to humble people, but don't give anything to those who are not devout. Don't give them food, or they will use your kindness against you. Every good thing you do for such people will bring you twice as much trouble in return. [6] The Most High himself hates sinners, and he will punish them. [7] Give to good people, but do not help sinners.

[z] *Hebrew* all . . . dead; *Greek* a man will be known by his children.   [a] *Hebrew* look . . . weaknesses; *Greek* wait for your downfall.   [b] what you do . . . wasted; *or* you will be thanked for what you do.   [c] *Hebrew* gives . . . act; *Greek* makes evil a habit or refuses to give to the poor.

11.18, 19 Ps 49.10; Lk 12.16-21   **12.1** Mt 7.6

⁸When things are going well, it is hard to tell who your real friends are, but in hard times you can recognize your enemies; ⁹even your friends will leave you then. But when you are successful, your enemies will act like friends.ᵈ ¹⁰Never trust an enemy; his wickedness is as destructive as rust. ¹¹Watch out, and be on guard against him, even if he acts ever so humble. He is like a metal mirror that rusts away if you don't keep it polished. ¹²Seat an enemy at your right hand, and the next thing you know he'll be trying to get your own place of honor. Put him next to you, and he will overthrow you. Then you will realize the truth of my words, and be stung with regret when you remember them. ¹³Nobody feels sorry for snake charmers or wild animal tamers who get bitten, ¹⁴and nobody will feel sorry for you if you run around with sinners and get involved in their wrongdoing.

¹⁵An enemy will stay with you for a while, but not when trouble comes. ¹⁶He will speak fine words while he plots how to trap you. He will pretend to share your sorrows, but he will kill you if he gets a chance. ¹⁷If trouble comes your way, you will find him waiting, ready to trip you up while he pretends to help you. ¹⁸He will be a different person then, rubbing his hands, nodding his head, and spreading rumors about you.

13 If you touch tar, it will stick to you, and if you keep company with arrogant people, you will come to be just like them. ²Don't try to lift something too heavy for you, and don't keep company with people who are richer and more powerful than you. You cannot keep a clay pot next to an iron kettle; the pot will break if it hits the kettle. ³If a rich person wrongs someone, he can afford to add insult to

injury; but if a poor person is wronged, he is forced to apologize for himself. ⁴A rich person will use you as long as he can profit from it, but when you need him, he will leave you helpless. ⁵He will live with you as long as you have anything and will gladly drain you dry. ⁶If he needs you, he will trick you with his smiles and cheerful, kindly words. "Do you need anything?" he will ask. ⁷He will feed you until you are embarrassed. Finally, when he has drained you two or three times over, he will laugh at you. If you see him later, he will pretend he doesn't know you, and will pass you by.

He will feed you until you are embarrassed. (13.7)

⁸Be careful not to be misled; you can be enjoying yourself and suddenly find yourself humiliated. ⁹If you are invited to the home of someone influential, be reserved in your behavior. Then he will invite you more often. ¹⁰If you push yourself on him, he will put you in your place. On the other hand, if you keep your distance from him, he will forget about you. ¹¹Don't pretend to be his equal or trust everything he says. In spite of all of his long and polite conversation, he is testing you.

¹²If a person does not keep confidences, he is cruel; he will not hesitate to hurt you or have you put in jail. ¹³Keep your secrets to yourself and be

---

ᵈ *Hebrew* act like friends; *Greek* be sorry.

very careful, for you are always walking on dangerous ground.ᵉ

15 Every creature prefers its own kind, and people are no different. 16 Just as animals of the same species flock together, so people keep company with people like themselves. 17 A sinner has no more in common with a devout person than a wolf has with a lamb. 18 Rich people have no more in common with poor people than hyenas have with dogs. 19 The rich hunt down the poor just as lions hunt down wild donkeys in the open country. 20 Arrogant people have nothing but scorn for the humble, and the rich think of the poor in the same way. 21 When a rich person stumbles, his friends will steady him, but if a poor person falls, his friends will have nothing to do with him. 22 When someone rich makes a mistake, there are many people to cover up for him and explain away all the things he never should have said. But let someone poor make a mistake, and he gets nothing but criticism. Even if what he says makes good sense, nobody will listen. 23 When a rich person speaks, everyone is silent, and they praise him to the skies for what he says. But let a poor person speak, and everybody says, "Who is that?" They push him down if he so much as stumbles.

24 There is nothing wrong with being rich if you haven't sinned to get that way. But there is nothing sinful about being poor, either. Only the ungodly think so. 25 It's what is in your heart that makes the expression on your face happy or sad. 26 If you feel cheerful, you will look cheerful, although making up proverbs calls for some intense thought.

14 If a person never says anything carelessly, he is to be congratulated; he doesn't need to feel guilty. 2 If a person has a clear conscience and never gives up hope, he is certainly to be congratulated!

Responsible Use of Wealth

3 It isn't right for someone who is selfish to be rich. What use is money to a stingy person? 4 If you deny yourself in order to accumulate wealth, you are only accumulating it for someone else. Others will use your riches to live in luxury. 5 How can you be generous with others if you are stingy with yourself, if you are not willing to enjoy your own wealth? 6 No one is worse off than someone who is stingy with himself; it is a sin that brings its own punishment. 7 When such a person does something good, it is only by accident; his selfishness will sooner or later be evident. 8 A selfish person is evil; he turns his back on people's needs 9 and is never satisfied with what he has. Greedᶠ will shrivel up a person's soul. 10 Some people are too stingy to put bread on their own table.

11 My child, treat yourself as well as you can, and bring worthy offerings to the Lord. 12 Remember that death is coming for you some day, and you haven't been told when that will be. 13 Before that day comes, be kind to your friends; be as generous as you can. 14 Don't deny yourself a single day's happiness. If there is something you want to do and it is lawful, go ahead! 15 Some day all that you have worked for will be divided up and given to others. 16 So be generous; but also be willing to receive from others. Enjoy yourself, for you will not find any pleasures in the world of the dead. 17 The human body wears out like a piece of clothing. The ancient law decrees that we must die. 18 Human beings are like leaves on a

ᵉ Some manuscripts add verses 13b-14: When you hear this in your sleep, wake up! 14 As long as you live, love the Lord and call on him to rescue you. ᶠ Probable text Greed; Greek Wicked injustice.

spreading tree. New growth takes the place of the fallen leaves; while some of us die, others are being born. ¹⁹Everything made by human hands will decay and perish, along with the person who made it.

The Happiness of Having Wisdom

²⁰It is a happy person who is concerned with Wisdom and who uses good sense. ²¹Anyone who studies the ways of Wisdom will also learn her secrets. ²²Go after Wisdom like a hunter looking for game. ²³Look into her windows and listen at her doors. ²⁴Camp as close to her house as you can get, ²⁵and you will have a fine place to live. ²⁶⁻²⁷Build your home there, safe beneath her protecting branches, and shaded from the heat.ᵍ

15 If you fear the Lord, you will do this. Master his Law, and you will find Wisdom. ²She will come to welcome you, like a mother or a young bride. ³She will give you wisdom and knowledge like food and drink. ⁴Rely on her for support, and you will never know the disgrace of failure. ⁵She will make you more honored than all your neighbors; when you speak in the assembly, she will give you the right words. ⁶You will find happiness and genuine joy; your name will be remembered forever.

⁷But people who are foolish or sinful will never even catch sight of Wisdom. ⁸She will have nothing to do with conceited people; she never enters the mind of liars. ⁹It is not appropriate for a sinner to sing hymns of praise, because his worship is insincere. ¹⁰A hymn should be an expression of wisdom, inspired by the Lord himself.

Free Will

¹¹Don't blame the Lord for your sin; the Lord does not cause what he hates.ʰ ¹²Don't claim that he has misled you; he doesn't need the help of sinners to accomplish his purposes. ¹³The Lord hates evil in all its forms, and those who fear the Lord find nothing attractive in evil. ¹⁴When, in the beginning, the Lord created human beings, he left them free to do as they wished. ¹⁵If you want to, you can keep the Lord's commands. You can decide whether you will be loyal to him or not. ¹⁶He has placed fire and water before you; reach out and take whichever you want. ¹⁷You have a choice between life and death; you will get whichever you choose. ¹⁸The Lord's wisdom and power are great and he sees everything. ¹⁹He is aware of everything a person does, and he takes care of those who fear him. ²⁰He has never commanded anyone to be wicked or given anyone permission to sin.

God's Punishment of Sinners

16 A large family is nothing to be desired if the children are worthless. Godless children are nothing to be proud of. ²No matter how many children you have, don't look on them with pride unless they fear the Lord. ³Don't put much hope in their future or expect them to live a long time. One child who does the Lord's will is better than a thousand who do not.ⁱ It is better to go to your grave with no children at all than to have children who are godless.

⁴A city's population may grow because of the wisdom of one person, while a whole tribe of lawless people disappears. ⁵I have seen such things

---

ᵍ Hebrew Build . . . heat; Greek Let her protect your children. Live safe beneath her branches, shaded from the heat, surrounded by her glory.　　ʰ Hebrew the Lord does not cause what he hates; Greek do not do what the Lord hates.　　ⁱ Hebrew who does . . . do not; Greek is better than a thousand.

14.20-25 Pr 8.32-35　**15.11-20** Si 17.1-12

many times and have heard of even more striking examples. ⁶The Lord's flaming anger will break out against a small gathering of sinners or a disobedient nation. ⁷He did not forgive those ancient giants who rebelled against him, confident of their own strength. ⁸He detested the arrogance of the people among whom Lot lived, and he did not spare them. ⁹He showed no mercy on that nation which he doomed to destruction for its sins, ¹⁰nor on those 600,000 people on the march through the wilderness who gathered together in stubborn rebellion. ¹¹Even if there had been only one stubborn person, it would have been a miracle if he had escaped punishment. The Lord is merciful, but he can also become angry. He can be overwhelming in his forgiveness or in his anger. ¹²His punishment is as severe as his mercy is great. He judges people by what they have done. ¹³No sinner can escape with what he has stolen. The Lord will reward the patience of devout people. ¹⁴Every righteous person will be rewarded;ʲ everyone will get what he deserves.ᵏ

¹⁷Never say, "I will hide from the Lord. Nobody up there is going to give me a thought. How can I be noticed among so many people? The creation is so enormous, what am I worth? ¹⁸When the Lord comes, everything will tremble: the earth and the great waters beneath it, the sky and the heavens above it. ¹⁹The mountains will shake, and the foundations of the earth will shudder when he looks at them. ²⁰The Lord isn't going to give me a thought. Nobody cares what I do. ²¹If I

sin and am secretly disloyal, nobody will know it.ˡ ²²If I do what is right, nobody will tell the Lord about it. Who wants to wait for him, anyway? He is too slow in doing what he has said he would." ²³Only someone with very little sense, and foolishly misguided, would think things like that.

God's Wisdom in Creation

²⁴My child, listen and pay attention to me; you will gain knowledge if you do. ²⁵I will give you diligent and accurate instruction.

²⁶In the beginning the Lord did
his work of creation,ᵐ
and gave everything a place
of its own.
²⁷He arranged everything in an
eternal order
and decreed that it should be
that way forever.
Not one part of creation ever
grows hungry;
no part grows tired or stops
its work.
²⁸The parts do not crowd one
another,
and they never disobey his
word.
²⁹When the Lord had made all
this,
he looked at the earth and
filled it with good things.
³⁰He covered it with all kinds of
creatures
that must die and return to
the dust.

ʲ Hebrew Every . . . rewarded; Greek He makes room for every act of mercy. ᵏ Some manuscripts add verses 15-16: The Lord made the king of Egypt so stubborn that he would not acknowledge the Lord, in order that the world might know the Lord's works. ¹⁶He shows his mercy to all creation; he has divided his light from darkness with a plumb line. ˡ Hebrew ²⁰⁻²¹The Lord . . . know it; Greek ²⁰It is altogether too big for the human mind to handle. No one can understand his ways. ²¹Most of his works are just as invisible as the storm wind. ᵐ Hebrew In . . . creation; Greek In the judgment of the Lord his works are from the beginning.
16.7 Gn 6.4; Ws 14.6

17 Then the Lord formed
          human beings from
          the dust
    and sent each of them back to
        it again.
[2] He gave them only a limited time
        to live,
    but he gave them authority
        over everything on earth.
[3] He made them to be like himself,
    and gave them his[n] own
        strength.
[4] He made all other creatures
        afraid of them;
    he gave them authority over
        all the animals and birds.[o]
[6] He gave them their tongues,
        their eyes,
    their ears, their minds, and
        their consciences.
[7] He filled them with knowledge
        and understanding
    and showed them the
        difference between good
        and evil.
[8] He gave them his own insight
    to let them see the majesty of
        his creation.[p]
[10] They will praise his holy name
    and proclaim the greatness of
        all he does.
[11] He made knowledge available to
        them
    and gave them the Law as a
        source of life.
[12] He made an eternal covenant
        with them

and revealed his commands
    to them.
[13] They saw the splendor of his
        majesty
    and heard the glory of his
        voice.
[14] He warned them against
        unrighteousness
    and taught each person how
        to treat others.

God Is Judge

[15] The Lord is always aware of what
people do; there is no way to hide from
him.[q] [17] He gave each nation its own
ruler, but Israel is the Lord's own possession.[r] [19] The Lord is always watching what people do; everything they do
is as clear as day to him. [20] None of their
sins are hidden from him; he is aware
of them all.[s] [22] When we give to the
poor, the Lord considers it as precious
as a valuable ring. Human kindness is
as precious to him as life itself. [23] Later
he will judge the wicked and punish
them; they will get what they deserve.
[24] But the Lord will allow those who repent to return to him. He always gives
encouragement to those who are losing
hope.

A Call to Repentance

[25] Come to the Lord, and leave your
sin behind. Pray sincerely that he will
help you live a better life. [26] Return to
the Most High and turn away from sin.

---

[n] *Probable text* his; *Greek* their.   [o] *Some manuscripts add verse 5:* The Lord
gave them the five senses, but he also gave them a sixth—intelligence, and a
seventh—reason, which enables them to interpret what comes to them through the
senses.   [p] *Some manuscripts add verse 9:* and he allowed them to take pride forever
in his marvelous deeds.   [q] *Some manuscripts add verses 16-17a:* From childhood on
they tend to be evil; their heart is like stone, and they don't seem to be able to make it
more human. [17] He divided the nations of the whole earth.   [r] *Some manuscripts add
verse 18:* Israel is his first-born, whom he disciplines as he brings him up. He gives
him the light of his love and never neglects him.   [s] *Some manuscripts add verse 21:*
But the Lord is gracious and knows his creatures; so he has spared them rather than
abandon them.
17.1-3 Gn 1.26-28; 2.7   **17.7** Gn 2.17   **17.25, 26** Jr 3.12

Have an intense hatred for wickedness.
27 Those who are alive can give thanks
to the Lord, but can anyone in the world
of the dead sing praise to the Most
High? 28 A person who is alive and well
can sing the Lord's praises, but the
dead, who no longer exist, have no way
to give him thanks. 29 How great is the
Lord's merciful forgiveness of those
who turn to him! 30 But this is not the
nature of human beings;[t] not one of us
is immortal. 31 Nothing is brighter than
the sun, but even the sun's light fails
during an eclipse. How much easier it
is for human thoughts to be eclipsed by
evil! 32 The Lord can look out over all
the stars in the sky. Human beings?
They are dust and ashes.

The Greatness of God

18 The Lord, who lives forever,
created the whole universe,
2 and he alone is just.[u] 4 He has given
no one enough power to describe what
he has done, and no one can investigate
it completely. 5 Who can measure his
majestic power? Who can tell the whole
story of his merciful actions? 6 We cannot add to them; we cannot subtract
from them. There is no way to compre-
hend the marvelous things the Lord
has done. 7 When we come to the end of
that story, we have not even begun; we
are simply at a loss for words.

Human Beings Are Nothing

8 What are human beings? Of what
use are we? The good that we do — the
evil that we do — what does it all mean?
9 If we live a hundred years, we have
lived an unusually long time, 10 but

. . . a gift you resent giving. (18.18)

compared with all eternity, those years
are like a drop of water in the ocean, like
a single grain of sand. 11 That is why the
Lord is so patient with us, why he is so
free with his mercy. 12 He looks at us
and knows that we are doomed to die;
that is why he is so willing to forgive us.
13 We can show compassion to someone
we know, but the Lord shows compassion for all humanity. He corrects us;
he disciplines us; he teaches us. Like a
shepherd tending sheep, he brings us
back to himself. 14 He will have compassion on us if we accept his guidance
and are eager for him to show us where
we are wrong.

Kindness and Charity

15 My child, when you help someone,
don't reprimand him at the same time.
When you make a gift, don't say anything that hurts. 16 Your words count
for more than what you give. Even dew
gives some relief during a spell of hot
weather. 17 Yes, kind words are more
effective than the best of gifts, and
if you are really concerned, you will
give both. 18 It is stupid to be unkind

---

[t] But ... human beings; *or* People cannot have everything.   [u] *Some manuscripts add
verses 2b-3:* and there is no other besides him. 3 He guides the world with his hand,
and everything obeys him. He is the king of all things, and his power separates what is
holy from what is not.
17.27, 28 Ps 6.5; Is 38.18; Ba 2.17, 18

and insulting. No one's eyes are going to sparkle at a gift that you resent giving.

Self-examination

¹⁹Know what you are talking about before you speak, and give attention to your health before you get sick. ²⁰Examine your conscience before the Lord judges you; then when that time comes, he will forgive you. ²¹Humble yourself before you are punished with sickness. When you have sinned, show repentance. ²²If you make a promise to the Lord, keep it as soon as you can. Don't wait until you are about to die to set things straight. ²³But before you make such a promise, be prepared to keep it. Don't try to test the Lord's patience. ²⁴Think! Do you want him to be angry with you on the day you die? When you face his judgment, do you want him to turn his back on you? ²⁵When you have all you want, think what it is like to be hungry, what it is to be poor. ²⁶Things can change in a single day; the Lord can act very quickly. ²⁷If you are wise, you will be careful in everything you do. When sin is all around you, be especially careful that you do not become guilty. ²⁸Every intelligent person can recognize wisdom and will honor anyone who shows it. ²⁹If you appreciate wisdom when you hear it, you will become wise yourself, and your words will be a source of wisdom for others.

Self-control

³⁰Don't be controlled by your lust; keep your passions in check. ³¹If you allow yourself to satisfy your every desire, you will be a joke to your enemies. ³²Don't indulge in luxurious living; the expense of it will ruin you. ³³Don't make yourself a beggar by borrowing for expensive banquets when you don't

have enough money of your own. **19** ¹If you do, you_v will never get rich; if you don't pay attention to small matters, you will gradually ruin yourself. ²Wine and women make sensible men do foolish things. A man who goes to prostitutes gets more and more careless, ³and that carelessness will cost him his life. Worms will feed on his decaying body.

⁴It is silly to trust people too quickly. If you sin, you are hurting yourself. ⁵If wickedness makes you happy, you will be condemned.

Loose Talk

⁶Avoid idle talk, and you will avoid a lot of trouble. ⁷Never repeat what you hear, and you will have no regrets. ⁸Don't tell it to your friends or your enemies unless it would be sinful to keep it to yourself. ⁹Whoever hears you will take note of it, and sooner or later will hate you for it. ¹⁰Have you heard a rumor? Let it die with you. Be brave! It won't make you explode. ¹¹A foolish person trying to keep a secret suffers like a woman in labor. ¹²Any time he hears a secret, it's like an arrow stuck in his leg.

¹³If you hear that a friend has done something wrong, ask him about it. Maybe it isn't true. If it is true, he won't do it again. ¹⁴If you hear that a neighbor has said something he shouldn't, ask him about it. Maybe he didn't say it. If he did, he won't say it again. ¹⁵If you hear something bad about a friend, ask him about it. It might be a lie. Don't believe everything you hear. ¹⁶A person may say something carelessly and not really mean it. Everyone has sinned in this way at one time or another. ¹⁷If you hear something that makes you angry with your neighbor, ask him about it before you threaten him.

---

v Hebrew If you do, you; _Greek_ A worker who drinks too much.

Leave the matter to the Law of the Most High. *w*

Recognizing Real Wisdom

20 Fear the Lord and keep his Law; that is what Wisdom is all about. *x* 22 You may know everything there is to know about wickedness, but that does not make you wise. It is not sensible to follow the advice of sinners. 23 It is possible to use cleverness for wicked purposes, but some people act like fools because they don't know any better. 24 A devout person, even if he is not very intelligent, is better off than the cleverest of sinners. 25 It is possible to be marvelously clever and still be dishonest, or to get what you want by being absurdly polite.

26 Then there are those wicked people who go about looking very solemn and mournful, but who are only trying to deceive you. 27 They will turn their faces away and pretend not to hear you, but they'll take advantage of you when you least expect it. 28 If for some reason they are unable to sin now, they'll get around to it at the first opportunity. 29 You can know people by their appearance. The first time you look at them, you can tell if they have good sense. 30 Their character shows in the way they dress, the way they laugh, and the way they walk.

Knowing When to Talk

20 A person can be rebuked in the wrong way; it may be wiser to keep quiet than to speak. 2 But it is much better to rebuke the person than to keep your anger bottled up. 3 Admit when you are wrong, and you will avoid embarrassment. 4 Using force to get a

. . . and pretend not to hear you. (19.27)

point across is like a castrated man trying to rape a young woman. 5 Some people are thought to be wise because they don't talk much; others are disliked because they talk too much. 6 Some people keep quiet because they don't have anything to say; others keep quiet because they know the right time to speak. 7 A wise person will not speak until the right moment, but a bragging fool doesn't know when that time is. 8 No one can stand a person who talks too long and will not give others a chance to speak.

Sudden Changes of Fortune

9 Bad luck can sometimes lead to success, and a stroke of good luck can sometimes lead to loss.

---

w Some manuscripts add verses 17c-19: and don't be angry. 18 Fearing the Lord is the first step toward his accepting you; he will love you if you are wise. 19 Learn the Lord's commands. It is a discipline that gives life. Those who do what pleases him enjoy the fruit of the tree of immortality. *x Some manuscripts add verses 20b-21:* and what the knowledge of his omnipotence means. 21 If a servant refuses to obey his master, but later does obey, the master is still angry.

¹⁰Generosity will sometimes do you no good, but at other times it will repay you double.

¹¹Honor can be followed by disgrace, but there are people who have risen from obscurity to places of honor.

¹²Sometimes what seems like a real bargain can turn out to be a very expensive mistake.

¹³When a person with good judgment speaks, he wins friends. A stupid person, though, can shower compliments on everybody, and it won't help him a bit. ¹⁴If such a person gives you something, it won't do any good; it won't be as valuable as he thinks it is.ʸ ¹⁵He isn't generous with anything but criticism, which he will shout for all the world to hear. If he lends you something today, he'll want it back tomorrow. (Don't you hate people like that?) ¹⁶Then that fool will say, "Nobody likes me. Nobody appreciates what I do for them. They'll take what I give them, but then talk about me behind my back." ¹⁷And he's right—he's a constant joke to everyone.

No one can stand a person who talks too long. (20.8)

Inappropriate Talk

¹⁸A slip of the tongue is worse than a slip on the pavement; the wicked will go to ruin just as suddenly as a person slips and falls.

¹⁹An impolite person is like one of those off-color stories that ignorant people are always telling.

²⁰Nobody takes a proverb seriously when some fool quotes it at the wrong time.

²¹If a person is too poor to afford sin, he can rest without a guilty conscience.

²²You can lose all your self-respect by being reluctant to speak up in the presence of stupidity.

²³If you promise a friend something because you are too bashful to say no, you're needlessly making an enemy.

²⁴Lying is an ugly blot on a person's character, but ignorant people do it all the time. ²⁵A thief is better than a habitual liar, but both are headed for ruin. ²⁶A liar has no honor. He lives in constant disgrace.

Stewardship of Wisdom

²⁷Speak wisely, and you will get ahead in the world. Influential people appreciate good sense. ²⁸They will excuse your errors if they like you, so cultivate the soil and reap the harvest!

²⁹Gifts and bribes make even the wise blind to the truth, and prevent them from being honest in their criticism.

³⁰Wisdom that is not expressed is like a treasure that has been hidden— both are useless. ³¹But a person who covers up his foolishness is better than one who keeps his wisdom to himself.

Sin

21 My child, have you sinned? Don't do it again, and pray for forgiveness for what you have already done. ²Avoid sin as if it were a snake. If

---

ʸ it won't be . . . it is; *or* he only expects to be repaid.

you get too near, it will sink its teeth into your soul like a lion, and destroy you. ³Every lawless act leaves an incurable wound, like one left by a double-edged sword.

⁴If a person is insolent and arrogant, he may lose everything he has.

⁵When poor people pray, God hears them and quickly answers their prayers.

⁶If you refuse to accept correction, you are committing a sin; and if you fear the Lord, you will make a sincere change in your ways.

⁷Someone may be famous as a good speaker, but when he is wrong, a sensible person will detect it.

⁸Anyone who borrows money to build a house is just collecting stones for his own tomb.ᶻ

⁹A group of people who have no respect for the Law is like a pile of kindling; they will meet a fiery end. ¹⁰The road that sinners walk is smooth and paved, but it leads to the world of the dead.

Wisdom and Foolishness

¹¹Whoever wants to keep the Law must learn what the Law means. If you fear the Lord in every sense of the term, you will have wisdom. ¹²You have to be intelligent to learn anything; but there is such a thing as just pretending to be intelligent, which only makes people bitter. ¹³A wise person's knowledge is like a river that never runs dry, like an everflowing stream of good advice.

¹⁴A fool, on the other hand, has a mind like a jar with a hole in it; anything he learns is soon lost.

¹⁵When an educated person hears something that shows insight, it stimulates his mind and leads him on to other ideas. But when someone who is satisfied with ignorance hears it, he won't

like it, and will forget it as soon as he can. ¹⁶Listening to a foolish person talk is like traveling with a heavy load on your back, but it is a pleasure to hear what intelligent people have to say. ¹⁷The assembly will be eager to hear from an intelligent person and will take his opinion seriously.

¹⁸To an ignorant person, wisdom is as useless as a house gone to ruin. He has never even thought about the things he is so sure of. ¹⁹To a person without any sense, an education is like handcuffs, ²⁰⁻²¹but to a sensible person, it is like gold bracelets. An intelligent person will smile quietly while a fool roars with laughter. ²²⁻²³A stupid person will peep into someone's house through the door and then march right in, but someone with experience and good manners will have enough respect

A fool . . . has a mind like a jar with a hole in it. (21.14)

to wait outside. ²⁴Eavesdropping at doors is bad manners, and anyone with a sense of decency would be ashamed to do it.

²⁵Presumptuous people talk about things that are none of their business,ᵃ

ᶻ his own tomb; *some manuscripts have* the winter.　　ᵃ *Probable text*
Presumptuous . . . business; *Greek* The lips of strangers speak of these things.
21.5 Si 35.17-19

but the wise will consider the consequences of what they say. ²⁶Fools say whatever comes to mind; wise people think before they speak.

²⁷When a wicked person curses his enemy[b] he is cursing himself.

²⁸A gossip ruins his own character, and everyone in the neighborhood hates him.

Laziness and Foolishness

22 ¹⁻²Lazy people are no better than dung; they are repulsive, and no one wants to get near them.

³It is a disgrace to a father to have an undisciplined child, especially if it is a daughter. ⁴A sensible daughter will get a husband, but a shameless daughter brings her father grief. ⁵A girl with no sense of propriety will disgrace both her husband and her father; neither will have any respect for her.

⁶Lecturing your children can sometimes be as out of place as singing to people in mourning, but a whipping is a wise choice of discipline at any time.

⁷Trying to teach a fool is like gluing a broken pot back together, like waking someone out of a deep sleep. ⁸Explaining something to a fool is like explaining it to a sleepy person; when you have finished, he'll say, "What was that again?"[c]

¹¹We mourn for the dead because they have no access to light. We ought to mourn for fools, because they have no access to intelligence. In fact, we should go into deeper mourning for fools, because the life they lead is worse than death. The dead are at least at rest. ¹²For seven days we mourn the dead, but a foolish or ungodly person causes a lifetime of grief.

¹³Don't visit stupid people or spend a lot of time talking with them. Avoid them; then they can't contaminate you, and you can live in peace without being troubled or worn down by their foolishness. ¹⁴Such people are a heavier burden to bear than lead; and the only word that fits them is "fools." ¹⁵It is easier to carry a load of sand, salt, and iron than to put up with a stupid person.

¹⁶A wooden beam can be put into a building so firmly that an earthquake cannot shake it loose; a person can be trained to use reason and good sense so well that he keeps his head when a crisis comes. ¹⁷A mind that thinks things through intelligently is like a firm wall, finely decorated. ¹⁸Small stones on top of a wall[d] will not stay put when the wind blows, and a person whose stupid ideas have made him timid will not be able to stand up to frightening situations.

Friendship

¹⁹If you stick something in your eye, tears will flow; and if you hurt a person deeply, you will discover his true feelings. ²⁰If you throw rocks at birds, you will scare them away; and if you insult a friend, you will break up the friendship. ²¹⁻²²Even if you have a violent argument with a friend, and speak sharply, all is not lost. You can still make up with him. But any friend will leave you if you insult him, if you are arrogant, if you reveal his secrets, or if you turn on him unexpectedly.

²³Gain the confidence of your neighbor if he is poor; then you can share his happiness if he becomes successful. Stand by him when he is in trouble if you want to share with him when better times come his way.

---

[b] his enemy; or Satan.   [c] Some manuscripts add verses 9-10: Children who are brought up well do not show the humble origin of their parents. ¹⁰Children who are not brought up well, who are arrogant and conceited, are a stain on the noblest family.
[d] Small . . . wall; some manuscripts have A fence on top of a hill.
22.12 Gn 50.10; Jdt 16.24

24 Fumes and smoke appear before the flames do; insults come before violence.

25 I will never be afraid to protect a friend, and I will never turn a friend away if he needs me. 26 If I suffer because of him, everyone who learns of it will be on guard against him.

A Prayer for Help against Sin

27 I wish that a guard could be placed at my mouth, that my lips could be wisely sealed. It would keep me from making mistakes and prevent me from destroying myself with my own tongue!

23 O Lord, my Father and Master of my life, do not leave me at the mercy of my own words; don't let them cause my downfall. 2 I wish I could be whipped for my thoughts, so that Wisdom could discipline my mind. I would not want to be spared when I am wrong; I would not want a single sin to be overlooked! 3 Then I would not keep on sinning, making one mistake after another. I could not fall to my enemies and be humiliated by them.

4 O Lord, my Father, God of my life, keep me from being arrogant; 5 protect me from evil desires. 6 Keep me from being overcome by greed or lust; do not leave me at the mercy of these shameless passions.

Taking Oaths

7 My children, listen to what I have to say about proper speech; do as I teach you and you will never get trapped. 8 Sinners are caught by their own arrogant, insulting words.

9 Don't fall into the habit of taking oaths, and don't use God's holy name too freely. 10 A slave who is constantly beaten will never be free of bruises; someone who is always taking an oath by the Holy Name will never be free of sin. 11 Anyone who takes oaths all the time is sinful to the core, and punishment is never far away from his household. If he fails to fulfill his oath, he is guilty. If he ignores his oath, he is twice as guilty. If his oath was insincere in the first place, he cannot be pardoned and will have a house full of trouble.

Filthy Talk

12 There is one way of speaking that is like death itself—may no Israelite ever be guilty of it! Devout people do not wallow in such sin, and they will keep away from such behavior. 13 Don't fall into the habit of coarse, profane talk; it is sinful. 14 You might forget yourself while in the company of important people and make a fool of yourself with some foul word that comes to you naturally. Think how your parents would feel! You would curse the day you were born and wish you were dead! 15 If you fall into the habit of using offensive language, you will never break yourself of it as long as you live.

Sexual Sins

16 There are any number of ways to sin and bring down the Lord's anger, but sexual passion is a hot, blazing fire that cannot be put out at will; it can only burn itself out. A man who lives for nothing but sexual enjoyment will keep on until that fire destroys him. 17 To such a man all women are desirable, and he can never get enough as long as he lives.

18 The man who is unfaithful to his wife thinks to himself, "No one will ever know. It's dark in here, and no one sees me. I have nothing to worry about. As for the Most High, he won't even notice." 19 This man is only afraid of other people. He doesn't realize that the eyes of the Lord are 10,000 times brighter than the sun, that he sees everything

we do, even when we try to hide it. ²⁰He knew everything before he created the world, as well as after. ²¹That sinful man will be caught when he least expects it, and punished publicly.

²²The same is true of a woman who is unfaithful to her husband and presents him with a child by another man. ²³In the first place, she has broken the Law of the Most High. In the second place, she has wronged her husband. And in the third place, she has made a whore of herself by committing adultery and bearing the child of a man not her husband. ²⁴⁻²⁵The children will suffer for her sin. They will not be able to find a place in society or establish families. She herself will be brought before the assembly ²⁶and permanently disgraced. There will be a curse on her memory. After she is gone, ²⁷everyone will realize that nothing is better than fearing the Lord, nothing is sweeter than keeping his commands.

In Praise of Wisdom

24 Listen to Wisdom! She proudly sings her own praises among the Israelites, her own people, ²in the assembly of the Most High, in the presence of his power.ᵉ

³"I am the word spoken by the
　　Most High.
　I covered the earth like a
　　mist.
⁴I made my home in highest
　　heaven,
　my throne on a pillar of cloud.
⁵Alone I walked around the circle
　　of the sky
　and walked through the ocean
　　beneath the earth.

⁶I ruled overᶠ all the earth and
　　the ocean waves,
　over every nation, over every
　　people.
⁷I looked everywhere for a place
　　to settle,
　some part of the world to
　　make my home.
⁸Then my Creator, who created
　　the universe,
　told me where I was to live.
'Make your home in Israel,' he
　　said.
　'The descendants of Jacob will
　　be your people.'
⁹He created me in eternity, before
　　time began,
　and I will exist for all eternity
　　to come.
¹⁰I served him in the Sacred Tent
　and then made my home on
　　Mount Zion.
¹¹He settled me in the Beloved
　　City
　and gave me authority over
　　Jerusalem.
¹²I put down roots among an
　　honored people
　whom the Lord had chosen as
　　his own.
¹³I grew tall, like the cedars in
　　Lebanon,
　like the cypresses on Mount
　　Hermon,
¹⁴like the palm trees of Engedi,ᵍ
　like the roses of Jericho,
　like beautiful olive trees in the
　　fields,
　like plane trees growing by
　　the water.
¹⁵My breath was the spicy smell of
　　cinnamon,
　of sweet perfume and finest
　　myrrh,
　of stacte, onycha, and galbanum,

ᵉ power; *or* angels.　　ᶠruled over; *some manuscripts have* gained possession of.
ᵍ of Engedi; *some manuscripts have* on the seashore.
24.4 Ex 33.9, 10

the fragrant incense in the Sacred Tent.

16 Like an oak I spread out my branches,
    magnificent and graceful.
17 Like a grapevine I put out lovely shoots;
    my blossoms gave way to rich and glorious fruit.[h]
19 Come to me, all you that want me,
    and eat your fill of my fruit.
20 You will remember me as sweeter than honey,
    better than honey from the comb.
21 Eat me, and you will hunger for more;
    drink me, and you will thirst for more.
22 Obey me, and you will never have cause for embarrassment;
    do as I say, and you will be safe from sin."

Wisdom and the Law

23 Wisdom is the Law, the Law which Moses commanded us to keep, the covenant of God Most High, the inheritance of the synagogues of Israel.[i] 25 The Law overflows with Wisdom like the Pishon River, like the Tigris at fruit-picking time. 26 The Law brims over with understanding like the Euphrates, like the Jordan at harvest time. 27 It sparkles with teachings like the Nile,[j] like the Gihon at grape-picking time. 28 The first human being ever created never knew Wisdom completely, and the last person on earth will be no more successful. 29 The possibilities of Wisdom are vaster than the ocean; her resources are more profound than the deepest waters beneath the earth.

30 As for me, I thought of myself as an irrigation canal bringing water from a river into a garden. 31 I only intended to water my orchard and flower beds, but the canal soon became a river, and the river became a sea. 32 And so I present you with my learning; I hold it high, so that its light can be seen everywhere, like that of the rising sun. 33 Like an inspired prophet, I pour out my teachings, so that future generations can benefit from them. 34 Please realize that I have not done all this hard work for myself alone, but to help anyone who wants to be wise.

People Who Deserve Praise

25 There are three things in which I take special delight — things that are beautiful to the Lord and people alike:[k]
    brothers who get along with each other,
    neighbors who are friends,
        and a married couple who are happy together.
2 There are three kinds of people I cannot stand, whose behavior I find highly offensive:
    poor people who are arrogant,
    rich people who lie,
        and foolish old men who commit adultery.
3 Unless you learn what you can while you are young, you will never be wise when you reach old age. 4 Sound

---

[h] *Some manuscripts add verse 18:* I am the mother of beautiful love, of fear, knowledge, and holy hope. Since I am eternal, I am given to all my children, who are named by him.   [i] *Some manuscripts add verse 24:* Always be strong in the Lord; stay with him, so that he may make you strong. There is no God but the Lord Almighty, and no savior except him.   [j] *One ancient translation* It sparkles . . . Nile; *Greek* It makes teachings shine like light.   [k] *Some ancient translations* There are . . . alike; *Greek* I was made beautiful in three ways and I stood before the Lord and people in beauty.

judgment, good advice, and gray hair go together beautifully. ⁵Wisdom, understanding, and sound counsel are appropriate to the aged and the respected. ⁶Elderly people wear the crown of long experience, and they can boast of nothing finer than their fear of the Lord.

⁷I will tell you about ten kinds of people that I feel fortunate to know, especially fortunate in the case of the tenth:

someone who takes pride in his children,
someone who lives to see his enemies fall,
⁸a man fortunate enough to have an understanding wife,
a married couple who are well-matched,ˡ
a person who never speaks sinfully,
a person who doesn't have to work for someone less competent than himself,
⁹someone fortunate enough to have a real friend,ᵐ
a person that people are happy to listen to,
¹⁰and the really great one: someone who is wise.
But the greatest one of all is the person who fears the Lord.
¹¹Such a person has no equal, because the fear of the Lord is the most important thing in the world.ⁿ

Advice about Women

¹³No wound is as serious as wounded love. No troubles are as serious as the troubles that women cause. ¹⁴No sufferings are worse than the sufferings caused by people who hate you. No revenge is worse than revenge taken by an enemy. ¹⁵No poison is deadlier than the poison of a snake, and no anger is deadlier than the anger of a woman.ᵒ

¹⁶I would rather live in the same house with a lion or a dragon than with a bad wife. ¹⁷When a wife is in a bad mood, her expression changes until she looks like an angry bear. ¹⁸Her husband has to go and eat with the

Three things in which I take special delight . . .
(25.1)

ˡ *Hebrew and one ancient translation* a married couple . . . well-matched; *Greek does not have these words.*   ᵐ *Some ancient translations* real friend; *Greek* good sense.
ⁿ *Some manuscripts add verse 12:* Fearing the Lord is the first step toward loving him, and faith is the first step toward loyalty to him.   ᵒ *Some ancient translations* woman; *Greek* enemy.

neighbors, where he can't hold back his bitter sighs.

¹⁹ Compared with the troubles caused by a woman, any other trouble looks small. May such women suffer the fate of sinners!

²⁰ A quiet man living with a nagging wife is like an old man climbing up a sandy hill.

²¹ Never lose your head over a woman's beauty, and don't try to win a woman because she is wealthy.ᵖ ²² When a man is supported by his wife, there is sure to be anger, arrogance, and humiliation. ²³ A bad wife will make her husband gloomy and depressed, and break his heart. Show me a timid man who can never make up his mind, and I will show you a wife who doesn't make her husband happy. ²⁴ Sin began with a woman, and we must all die because of her. ²⁵ Don't let a bad wife have her way, any more than you would allow water to leak from your cistern. ²⁶ If she won't do as you tell her, divorce her.

26 The husband of a good wife is a fortunate man; he will live twice as long because of her. ² A fine wife is a joy to her husband, and he can live out his years in peace. ³ A good wife is among the precious blessings given to those who fear the Lord. ⁴ Whether such men are rich or poor, they will be happy and always look cheerful.

⁵ There are four things that scare me: vicious rumors spread around town, a gathering mob, false accusations — these are all worse than death. ⁶ But a woman jealous of another woman causes heartache and grief; her tongue lashes out at everyone.

⁷ A bad wife is like a yoke that doesn't fit. Trying to control her is like holding a scorpion. ⁸ A drunken woman is an infuriating sight; she can't conceal her shameless behavior. ⁹ You can tell an unfaithful wife by the bold and flirting look in her eyes.

¹⁰ If your daughter is determined to have her own way, keep a close watch on her. If you don't, she'll take advantage of any chance she gets. ¹¹ If she is too self-willed, be on guard, and don't be surprised if she disappoints you. ¹² She'll spread her legs anywhere for any man who wants her, just as a thirsty traveler will drink whatever water is available.

¹³ A gracious wife is her husband's delight; her abilities make him a stronger man.�q ¹⁴ A wife who doesn't

You can tell an unfaithful wife by . . . (26.9)

talk too much is a gift from the Lord. Such restraint is admirable beyond words. ¹⁵ A modest wife has endless charm; it is a quality too precious to measure. ¹⁶ The beauty of a good wife in her well-kept home is like the noonday sun shining in the Lord's sky. ¹⁷ Her beautiful face and attractive figure areʳ as lovely as the light from the sacred lampstand in the Temple, ¹⁸ and like its gold shaft set on its silver

---

ᵖ *Hebrew* because she is wealthy; *Greek does not have these words.*   q her abilities . . . man; *or* she knows how to keep him well-fed.   ʳ and attractive figure are; *or* as she grows older is.

base are her shapely legs and strong ankles.[s, t]

Sad Observations

28 There are two things that make me sad, and a third that makes me angry:
a soldier who has become poor,
intelligent people who are not respected,
and a righteous person who turns to evil.
The Lord will punish such a person with death!

29 A merchant can hardly avoid doing wrong; every salesman is guilty of sin.

27 **1** Many people have sinned while looking for a profit; if you want to be rich you have to keep blinders on your eyes. **2** It is hard to remove a peg that is stuck between two stones of a house, and it is just as hard to remove dishonesty from buying and selling. **3** Unless you are determined in your fear of the Lord, your house is going to come down on you.

Speech Reflects True Feelings

4 Your talk shows your faults; it is like a sieve that separates out the rubbish. **5** The way you think shows your character just as surely as a kiln shows any flaws in the pottery being fired. **6** You can tell how well a tree has been cared for by the fruit it bears, and you can tell

a person's feelings by the way he expresses himself. **7** Never praise anyone before you hear him talk; that is the real test.

Honesty

8 If you try to be honest, you can be, and it will improve your character as handsome clothing improves your appearance. **9** Birds come to roost with those of their own kind, and the habit of honesty comes to those who try to be honest. **10** Sin waits for those looking for a chance to sin, just as a lion waits for prey.

Foolish Talk

11 When devout people talk, what they say always makes sense, but foolish people are always contradicting themselves. **12** When you find yourself with stupid people, look for some excuse to leave, but when you are with serious-minded people, stay as long as you can.

13 The stories that foolish people tell are offensive, and they make jokes about the worst kinds of sin. **14** When such people curse, it is enough to make your hair stand on end, and when they start arguing among themselves, all you can do is to stop up your ears. **15** It is painful to listen to them insult each

---

[s] strong ankles; *some manuscripts have* firm breasts *or* determined heart.   [t] *Some manuscripts add verses 19-27:* My child, stay healthy while you are young, and don't give your strength to strangers. **20** Search the whole land for a fertile field, and plant it with your own seed, trusting your own good stock. **21** Then your children will survive and grow up confident of their good family. **22** A prostitute is like spit; a married woman who has affairs brings death to her lovers. **23** A lawless man will get a godless wife, as he deserves, but a man who honors the Lord will have a devout wife. **24** A shameless wife enjoys making a disgrace of herself, but a modest wife will act modestly even alone with her husband. **25** A self-willed woman is a bitch, but a woman with a sense of decency honors the Lord. **26** A wife who honors her husband will seem wise to everyone; but if she dishonors him by her overbearing attitude, everyone will know that she is ungodly. Fortunate is the husband of a good wife, because he will live twice as long. **27** A loud-mouthed, talkative woman is like a trumpet sounding the signal for attack, and any man who has such a wife will spend his life at war.
27.6 Mt 7.17; 12.33; Lk 6.44

All you can do is to stop up your ears. (27.14)

other, and such blustering can lead to violence.

Betraying Secrets

¹⁶ If you repeat secrets that have been told to you, you are destroying the confidence others have in you, and you will never have a close friend. ¹⁷ Respect your friends, and keep faith with them. If you do betray a friend's confidence, you may as well forget you have a friend. ¹⁸ You have killed that friendship just as surely as if you had taken a weapon and killed an enemy. ¹⁹ Your friend is gone. You can no more get him back than you can get a bird to come back to your hand once you let it go. ²⁰ Don't bother going after him. It's too late. He is gone, like a deer escaped from a trap. ²¹ Wounds can be bandaged and insults can be forgiven, but if you betray a confidence, it is hopeless.

Hypocrisy

²² When someone starts winking at you, he has something bad in mind, and nothing can stop him from going through with it. ²³ When he's with you, his talk is so nice! He compliments you on every word you say. But behind your back it's a different story; he will take what you have said and turn it against you. ²⁴ There is nothing in the world

that I hate as much as a person like that — and the Lord hates him too.

²⁵ Throw a stone straight up in the air and it will come down on your head. Strike a blow, and you yourself will be wounded. ²⁶ People who set traps fall into them themselves. ²⁷ People who hurt others will be hurt by their own actions and will have no idea why.

²⁸ Arrogant people insult others and make fun of them,ᵘ but someone is waiting like a lion for a chance to take revenge on them. ²⁹ Those who are happy to witness the downfall of devout people are going to fall into a trap and die a painful death.

Resentment

³⁰ Anger and a hot temper are horrible things, but sinners have both.

28 ¹ The Lord is taking note of your sins, and if you take vengeance on someone, the Lord will take vengeance on you. ² But if you forgive someone who has wronged you, your sins will be forgiven when you pray. ³ You cannot expect the Lord to pardon you while you are holding a grudge against someone else. ⁴ You yourself are a sinner, and if you won't forgive another person, you have no right to pray that the Lord will forgive your sins. ⁵ If you cannot get rid of your anger, you have no hope of forgiveness — you are only a human being. ⁶ Think about it! Some day you will die, and your body will decay. So give up hate and live by the Lord's commands, ⁷ the commands in the covenant of the Most High. Instead of getting upset over your neighbor's faults, overlook them.

Arguments

⁸ If you stay out of arguments, you will not sin so much, because a hot temper gets them started. ⁹ It is sinful to

---

ᵘ insult others . . . them; *or* will be insulted and mocked.
27.16-21 Pr 20.19; 25.9 **28.2** Mt 6.14; Mk 11.25

break up a friendship by creating hostility among people who get along well together. ¹⁰The more fuel, the hotter the fire. The more stubbornness, the hotter the argument. And the stronger or richer people are, the angrier they can afford to become. ¹¹An argument that blazes out suddenly can lead to violence. ¹²You can blow on a spark to make it glow, or you can spit on it to put it out. Either way, you do it with your mouth.

Vicious Talk

¹³Gossips and liars deserve to be cursed, because they have been the ruin of many people who were minding their own business. ¹⁴Many have had their lives ruined and have been driven from their homes because of people who meddled in their business. Such unwanted interference has resulted in the destruction of strong cities and the homes of respected people. ¹⁵Meddlers have caused faithful wives to be divorced, robbed of everything they had worked for. ¹⁶Anyone who pays attention to slander can never find peace of mind. ¹⁷A whip can raise a welt, but a vicious tongue can break bones. ¹⁸More people have died as a result of loose talk than were ever killed by swords. ¹⁹⁻²⁰Count yourself lucky if you have been spared the experience of having irresponsible talk directed against you — if you have never had that iron yoke around your neck or those heavy chains on your legs. ²¹Slander leads to a miserable death; but in fact, you'd be better off dead.

²²Devout people, however, cannot be overcome by slander; they cannot be burned by its flames. ²³Its victims are those who have abandoned the Lord; once the fire of slander has been lit among them, it cannot be put out. Slander will pounce on them like a lion and tear them to pieces like a leopard.

²⁴Don't you fence in your property? Don't you lock up your money? ²⁵Well, be just as careful with what you say. Weigh every word, and have a lock ready for your mouth. ²⁶Someone may be waiting for you to slip, and if you are not careful, you will stumble over your own words and fall down in front of him.

Loans and Repayment

29 Be kind enough to lend to your neighbor when he needs help. You are keeping the Lord's commands if you help him. ²If he needs something, lend it to him. And when you are in debt, pay it back as soon as you can. ³If you meet your obligations, you will always be able to borrow what you need. ⁴Many people treat a loan as something they found and can keep, causing embarrassment to those who helped them. ⁵Some people will speak politely, bow, and scrape until they get the loan they want, but when the time comes to pay it back, they'll put it off, say that it's inconvenient, and make a lot of worthless excuses. ⁶If the lender insists on being paid, he can count himself lucky to get back half. If he doesn't insist, the borrower has robbed him and made an unnecessary enemy. All the lender will get from him are curses, insults, and disrespect, but never any gratitude.

⁷Many people refuse to lend at all, not because they are stingy, but because[v] they don't want to be cheated if they can avoid it.

Generosity

⁸Nevertheless, be understanding with those who are poor. Don't keep

---

[v] not because … stingy, but because; *some manuscripts have* therefore, because of this wickedness.

28.13-26 Si 51.2-6; Jas 3.5-12   **29.1-7** Ex 22.25; Lv 25.35-38

Going from house to house is a miserable way to live. (29.24)

them waiting for your generosity. ⁹The Lord has commanded us to help the poor; don't refuse them the help they need. ¹⁰It is better to lose your money by helping a relative or a friend than to lose it by letting it rust away under a rock somewhere. ¹¹Use your wealth as the Most High has commanded; this will do you more good than keeping your money for yourself. ¹²Count among your treasures the fact that you give to the poor. It will save you from all kinds of trouble ¹³and will be a better defense against your enemies than the strongest shield or stoutest spear.

Guaranteeing Debts

¹⁴A good man is willing to guarantee his neighbor's debts. Only someone who has lost all sense of decency would refuse to do so. ¹⁵If someone does this favor for you, don't forget it; he has risked his good name for you. ¹⁶There are some ungrateful sinners who abandon those who stand behind them, and they cause them loss of property. ¹⁷Guaranteeing loans has ruined many

prosperous people and caused them unsettling storms of trouble. ¹⁸Influential people have lost their homes over it and have had to go wandering in foreign countries. ¹⁹A sinner who hopes to make a profit by guaranteeing a loan is going to find himself involved in lawsuits. ²⁰So help your neighbor as much as you can, but protect yourself against the dangers involved.

Home and Hospitality

²¹The necessities of life are water, food, clothing, and a home where you can have privacy. ²²It is better to be poor and live under your own crude roof than to enjoy lavish banquets in other people's homes. ²³Be happy with what you have, even if it isn't very much, and don't listen to anyone who would insult your home and family.ʷ ²⁴Going from house to house is a miserable way to live. Anywhere you go, you don't dare speak. ²⁵You welcome the guests and pour the drinks, and nobody thanks you. Instead, people humiliate you by saying things like: ²⁶"Stranger! Come

---

ʷ *don't listen . . . family; or* don't listen to insults from your family; *some manuscripts do not have these words; one ancient translation has* don't get a reputation for living off other people.

. . . so that he can be proud of him later. (30.1)

here and set the table! I want to eat what you've got there! Give it here! ²⁷Go away, stranger! I've got an important guest! My brother is coming to visit, and I need the room!"

²⁸Being denied hospitality or having a moneylender hound you — these are hard things for any sensitive person to endure.

Bringing up Children

30 A father who loves his son will whip him often, so that he can be proud of him later. ²If a son is disciplined, he will be of some use, and his father can boast of him to his friends. ³Anyone who gives good guidance to his son cannot only take pride in him among his friends, but he can make his enemies jealous. ⁴⁻⁵While the father is alive, the sight of his son makes him happy, and when he dies, he has no regrets. He is not really dead, because his son is like him. ⁶He has left someone to take vengeance on his enemies and to return the favors he owes his friends.

⁷But anyone who spoils his son will have to bandage his wounds.ˣ His heart will stop every time he hears a shout. ⁸An untamed horse is going to be stubborn, and an undisciplined son is no different. ⁹If you pamper your child and play with him, he will be a disappointment and a source of grief. ¹⁰Laugh with him now, and one day you will have to cry over him, grinding your teeth in regret. ¹¹Don't give him freedom while he is young, and don't overlook what he does wrong. ¹²Whip him while he is still a child, and make him respect your authority. If you don't, he will be stubborn and disobedient and cause you nothing but sorrow. ¹³So discipline your son and give him work to do, or else he will be an embarrassment to you.

Health

¹⁴It is better to be poor, but strong and healthy, than to be rich, but in poor health. ¹⁵A sound, healthy body and a cheerful attitudeʸ are more valuable than gold and jewels. ¹⁶Nothing can make you richer or give you greater happiness than those two things. ¹⁷It would be better to be dead, asleep forever, than to live in the misery of chronic illness. ¹⁸The finest food means nothing if you are too sick to eat it; it might as well be offered to an idol.ᶻ ¹⁹But there is no point in offering food to an idol; it can't eat it or smell it. It is just the same with someone whom the Lord has afflicted. ²⁰He looks at his food and sighs, like a castrated man hugging a young woman.

ˣ will have . . . wounds; *or* is going to be hurt. strong body.   ᶻ *Hebrew* offered to an idol; *Greek* placed on a grave.   ʸ *Hebrew* a cheerful attitude; *Greek* a

Cheerfulness and Sadness

²¹ Don't deliberately torture yourself by giving in to depression. ²² Happiness makes for a long life and makes it worth living. ²³ Enjoy yourself and be happy; don't worry all the time. Worry never did anybody any good, and it has destroyed many people. ²⁴ It will make you old before your time. Jealousy and anger will shorten your life. ²⁵ A cheerful person with a good attitude will have a good appetite and enjoy his food.

Problems Caused by Money

31 Worrying about money will make you lose weight and lose sleep. ² Worrying about business*a* will keep you from sleeping just as surely as a serious illness does.

³ Rich people work hard to make a lot of money; then they can sit back and live in luxury. ⁴ Poor people work hard and have nothing to show for it, and when they rest, they are still poor.

⁵ No one who loves money can be judged innocent; his efforts to get rich have led him into sin.*b* ⁶ Many people have been ruined because of money, brought face-to-face with disaster. ⁷ Money is a trap for those who are fascinated by it, a trap that every fool falls into.

⁸ A person who gets rich without sinfully chasing after money is fortunate. ⁹ Do you know anyone like that? If so, we will congratulate him for performing a miracle that no one else has ever been able to do. ¹⁰ If anyone has ever passed this test, he can well be proud. Has anyone ever known that he could get away with cheating someone, and not taken advantage of it? ¹¹ If so, he deserves his wealth, and everyone will praise him for his generosity.

Behavior at Dinner Parties

¹² When you sit down at a fancy banquet, don't let your mouth hang open,

Money is a trap for those who are fascinated by it. (31.7)

and don't say, "Look at all that food!" ¹³ It is impolite to have a greedy eye; remember that. Nothing in creation is greedier than the eye; that is why it sheds tears so often.*c* ¹⁴ Don't reach out for everything you see, and don't elbow people out of the way to get at the food. ¹⁵ Be considerate of the other people at the table and treat them the way you want to be treated. ¹⁶ When you get your food, eat it like a human being. Don't smack and slurp; nobody can stand that. ¹⁷ It's good manners to be the first to stop eating; stuffing yourself is offensive. ¹⁸ If there are many people present, don't try to be the first to be served. ¹⁹ A little bit is plenty for anyone with good manners. Besides, you won't be short of breath when you go to bed. ²⁰ People who eat too much get stomach aches and cannot sleep. If you don't overeat, you can get a good night's sleep and wake up early the next morning feeling fine. ²¹ But if you do get a

a Hebrew Worrying about business; *Greek* Sleepless worry. *b Hebrew* have . . . sin; *Greek* will destroy him. *c Hebrew* so often; *Greek* on every face.
30.21-25 Ec 11.9, 10

stomach ache from eating too much, go off and vomit[d] and you will feel better. [22] My child, if you listen to what I am saying and put it into practice, one of these days you will thank me for it. Be moderate[e] in everything you do, and you will never get sick.

[23] People appreciate a generous host, and he deserves their praise. [24] But everybody in town will complain about a host who is stingy with food, and their complaints are justified.

[25] Don't try to prove your manhood by how much you can drink. Wine has been the ruin of many. [26] An arrogant person's character shows through when he is in a drunken argument, in the same way that iron is tested when it is heated red-hot and then dipped in water. [27] Wine can put new life into you if you drink it in moderation. What would life be like without it? Wine was created to make us happy. [28] If you drink it in moderation and at the right time, it can lift your spirits and make you cheerful, [29] but if you drink when you are angry and upset, it leads to headaches, embarrassment, and disgrace.[f] [30] A drunken fool can lose his temper and hurt himself. His drinking makes him weak and an easy target for angry blows. [31] Never rebuke a person when you have both been drinking. Don't hurt his feelings while he is having a good time. It's not the time to criticize anyone, or to ask him to pay back a debt.

32 If you are chosen to preside at a banquet, don't put on airs. Just be like everyone else. Look after the guests before you sit down. [2] After you have performed your duties, you can sit down and enjoy yourself with the others. They will respect you for doing a good job.

[3] If you are older than most of the guests, you may talk; that is your right. But you should know what you are talking about and not interrupt the music. [4] If entertainment is being provided, don't keep up a steady conversation; it's the wrong time to show off your wit. [5] Music at a banquet where wine is served is like a ruby set in gold. [6] Good music and good wine — an emerald set in gold.

[7] If you are young, don't speak unless you have to, but never more than twice, and only if someone speaks to you first. [8] Come to the point and say it all in a few words. Show that you are well-informed, but stay quiet. [9] Don't treat important people as if you were their equal and don't make a nuisance of yourself by asking them a lot of questions.[g] [10] The reputation of a modest person goes before him, as lightning before thunder.

[11] Leave the party at the right time and never be the last to go. Don't linger at the door; just go straight home. [12] There you can enjoy yourself as you wish, but don't commit the sin of bragging. [13] And don't forget to thank your Creator for letting you enjoy so many good things.

Interpreting the Law

[14] If you fear the Lord, you will accept his correction. He will bless those who get up early in the morning to pray. [15] Study his Law, and you will master it, unless you are insincere about it, in which case you will fail. [16] If you fear the Lord, you will know what is right, and you will be famous for your fairness. [17] Sinners have no use for correction, and will interpret the Law to suit themselves.

[18] Sensible people will consider every

---

[d] go off and vomit; *some manuscripts have* get up in the middle of the meal.
[e] *Hebrew* moderate; *Greek* industrious.   [f] *Hebrew* when you are ... disgrace; *Greek* too much, it leads to bitterness, offense, and stumbling.   [g] *Hebrew* make ... questions; *Greek* keep talking when someone else is speaking.

opinion, but arrogant[h] people will let nothing stand in their way. [19] Never do anything without thinking it through, and once you have done something, don't look back and wish you had done something else. [20] Don't take a course of action that is dangerous, and don't make the same mistake twice.[i] [21] Don't be too sure of yourself, even when the way looks easy. [22] Always watch where you are going.[j] [23] Whatever you do be careful;[k] this is keeping the Lord's commands.

[24] Believing in the Law means keeping the Lord's commands.

If you trust the Lord, you cannot 33 lose. [1] No evil will ever come to a person who fears the Lord; however often danger comes, the Lord will come to the rescue. [2] A person who has no use for the Law doesn't have good sense, and anyone who is insincere about it is going to be tossed about like a boat in a storm. [3] If you are wise, you will believe in the Law; you will find it as reliable as the sacred lots.

[4] Prepare what you are going to say and people will listen to you. Use what you have learned before you start talking. [5] A foolish person's mind works like a cartwheel, going round and round in circles. [6] A sarcastic friend is like a wild horse that neighs no matter who tries to ride him.

People Are Not Alike

[7] Why are some days holier than others, even though the same sun rises on every day of the year? [8] It is because the Lord made them different by setting them apart as religious holidays and festivals. [9] He made some days holy and important, and made other days ordinary.

[10] Every human being was made from the earth, just as Adam was. [11] But the Lord, in his wisdom, made them all different and gave them different tasks. [12] He blessed some, making them honored and holy, keeping them near him. Others he cursed, humbling them and removing them from their positions. [13] Just as clay is in the potter's hands for him to shape as he pleases, so we are in the hands of our Creator for him to do with as he wishes.

[14] Good is the opposite of evil, life is the opposite of death, and sin is the opposite of devotion to the Lord. [15] Think about it: the Most High has made everything in pairs, each thing the opposite of something else.

[16] As for me, I have been the last to come on duty, as if going through vineyards to gather whatever the grape-pickers had left behind. But the Lord blessed me, and I did well,[l] like a grape-picker who has filled the wine press. [17] But I want you to know that I have not done all this work for myself alone, but for everyone who wants to learn. [18] Listen to me, all you great leaders! All you leaders of the assemblies, hear what I have to say!

Be Independent

[19] Never, as long as you live, give anyone power over you — whether son, wife, brother, or friend. Don't give your property to anyone; you might change your mind and have to ask for it back. [20] As long as you have breath in your body, don't let anyone lead your life for you. [21] It is better that your children be dependent on you than the other way around. [22] Keep control over all that you do; don't let anything stain your reputation. [23] Wait until the last moment of

---

[h] *Hebrew* arrogant; *Greek* foreign and arrogant.   [i] *Hebrew* make . . . twice; *Greek* stumble on stones.   [j] *Hebrew* watch . . . going; *Greek* look out for your children.
[k] *Hebrew* be careful; *Greek* have confidence in yourself.   [l] did well; *or* overtook the others.

33.3 Ex 28.30; Si 45.10

your life, when you are breathing your last, and then divide your property among your heirs.

Treatment of Slaves

24 A donkey should be given its fodder and its burden, and it should be beaten. A slave should be given food and work, and should be disciplined. 25 If you make your slave work, you can set your mind at ease. If you don't keep him busy, he will be looking for freedom. 26 You can use a harness and yoke to tame an animal, and a slave can be tortured in the stocks. 27 Keep him at work, and don't let him be idle; idleness can only teach him how to make trouble. 28 Work is what he needs. If he won't obey you, put him in chains.

29 But don't be too severe with anyone, and never be unfair. 30 If you have a slave, treat him as you would want to be treated; you bought him with your hard-earned money. 31 Treat him as a brother; you need him as you need yourself. If you mistreat him and he runs away, where are you going to look for him?

Dreams Mean Nothing

34 Foolish people are deceived by vain hopes, and dreams get them all excited. 2 A person who pays any attention at all to dreams is like someone who tries to catch shadows or chase the wind. 3 What you see in a dream is no more real than the reflection of your face in a mirror. 4 What is unreal can no more produce something real than what is dirty can produce something clean. 5 Dreams, divination, and omens are all nonsense. You see in them only what you want to see.m 6 Unless the Most High has sent you the dream, pay no attention to it. 7 Dreams have misled many people; they put

their faith in them, only to be disappointed. 8 The Law is complete without such falsehood. Wisdom, as spoken by the righteous, is also complete without it.

Travel

9 A well-traveledn person with wide experience knows many things and talks sense. 10 You can't know much if you haven't experienced much, but travel can make you more clever. 11 In my own travels I have seen many things and learned more than I can put into words. 12 I have been in danger of death many times, but I have always been able to escape by relying on past experience.

Fear the Lord

13 Those who fear the Lord will live, because they have put their trust in the one who can save them. 14 Fear the Lord, and you will have nothing else to fear. If your trust is in him, you will never act like a coward. 15 People who fear the Lord are fortunate, because they know where they can look for help. 16 The Lord watches over those who love him; he is their strong protection and firm support. He shelters them from the heat, shades them from the noonday sun, and keeps them from stumbling and falling. 17 He makes them cheerful and puts a sparkle in their eyes. He blesses them with life and health.

Offering Sacrifices

18 If you offer as a sacrifice an animal that you have obtained dishonestly, it is defective and unacceptable. 19 The Most High gets no pleasure from sacrifices made by ungodly people; no amount of sacrifices can make up for

---

m Probable text You see ... to see; Greek The mind has an imagination like a woman in labor.   n A well-traveled; some manuscripts have An educated.

34.1-8 Dt 13.1-5; 18.9-14

their sins. ²⁰Anyone who steals an animal from the poor to offer as a sacrifice is like someone who kills a boy before his father's eyes. ²¹Food means life itself to poor people, and taking it away

. . . taking it away from them is murder. (34.21)

from them is murder. ²²It is murder to deprive someone of his living or to cheat an employee of his wages.

²³When one person builds and somebody else tears down, has anything been accomplished but hard work? ²⁴When one person blesses and somebody else curses, which one is the Lord going to listen to? ²⁵If you touch a dead body and then purify yourself by washing, but then go and touch it again, what good did the washing do? ²⁶If you fast because of your sins, and then go out and commit the same sins over again, what have you gained by going without food? Who do you think is going to listen to your prayers?

35 Keeping the Law is worth many offerings; it is a fellowship offering in itself. ²Returning a kindness is like a grain offering; giving to the poor is like a thanksgiving offering. ³Keeping away from sin will please the Lord and make atonement for sin. ⁴But don't come to the Temple without an offering; ⁵the Law requires that you

bring one. ⁶When someone righteous offers a sacrifice and the fat drips down on the altar, a pleasant smell rises to the Most High. ⁷The Lord will accept the offerings made by a righteous person and will not forget them. ⁸Praise the Lord by making generous offerings to him; don't be stingy with the first of your crops. ⁹Be cheerful with every gift you make, and when you pay your tithes, do it gladly. ¹⁰Give to the Most High as he has given to you, just as generously as you can. ¹¹The Lord always repays and will do it many times over. ¹²But don't try to bribe him or rely on offerings that you have obtained dishonestly. He will not accept them.

God's Justice

The Lord is fair*ᵒ* and does not show partiality. ¹³He is not prejudiced against the poor; when someone prays who has been wronged, the Lord listens. ¹⁴When orphans and widows pour out their prayers, he does not ignore them. ¹⁵The tears running down a widow's cheek cry out in accusation against the one who has caused her distress.

¹⁶Serve the Lord willingly, and the Lord will accept you; your prayers will reach the skies. ¹⁷The prayer of a humble person goes past the clouds and keeps on going until it reaches the Lord Most High, where it stays until he answers by seeing that justice is done and that the guilty are punished.

¹⁸And the Lord will act quickly. He will show no patience with wicked people. He will take vengeance by crushing the heathen. He will completely wipe out the merciless and the arrogant, and will destroy the authority of the wicked. ¹⁹He will give each of us what our thoughts and actions deserve. Because of the Lord's mercy, his people will be happy when he has judged their

---

ᵒ Hebrew fair; *Greek* judge.
35.9 2 Co 9.7

case. ²⁰In times of trouble his mercy is as welcome as rain after a long drought.

A Prayer for Israel

36 O Lord God of the universe, look upon us and have mercy. ²Make every nation stand in fear of you. ³Take action against the foreign nations, and let them witness your power! ⁴You have used us to show them how holy you are; now use them to show us how great you are. ⁵Let them learn, as we have learned, that there is no God, O Lord, but you. ⁶Give new signs, perform new miracles; show us your glorious strength! ⁷⁻⁹Bring on that appointed time when everyone can talk about the great things you do. Pour out your furious, flaming anger, and let none of our enemies survive. Destroy those who have oppressed your people. ¹⁰Crush all those enemy rulers who think they are the only people in the world who matter! ¹¹Gather the tribes of Israel together again, and give them back their land as you gave it to them long ago. ¹²Lord, have mercy on Israel, the people who are known by your name, whom you called your first-born son. ¹³Take pity on Jerusalem, your holy city, where you chose to stay. ¹⁴Fill your Temple*p* on Mount Zion with your glory and with hymns of praise. ¹⁵Testify for your people, whom you created in the beginning; fulfill the prophecies that have been spoken in your name. ¹⁶Reward those who have put their faith in you, and vindicate your prophets. ¹⁷You have always been gracious to your people;*q* listen to your servants as we pray. Then everyone on earth will recognize that you are the Lord, the God of the ages.

Choosing a Wife

¹⁸Any kind of food can be eaten, but some foods are better than others. ¹⁹And just as the tongue can distinguish the flavors of different kinds of meat, so a sharp mind can detect lies. ²⁰A person with a warped mind causes trouble, but an experienced person knows how to pay it back.

²¹A woman has to take any man as a husband, but a man must choose his wife carefully. ²²A woman's beauty makes a man happy; there is no fairer sight for the human eye to see. ²³If the woman is kind and gentle in her speech, her husband is the most fortunate of men. ²⁴When a man marries, he gets the finest thing he will ever have — a wife to help and encourage him.

²⁵If property is not fenced in, thieves will wander in and help themselves. And if a man has no wife, he is a sighing wanderer; ²⁶people have no more trust in a homeless person who sleeps in a different place every night than they have in a wandering thief who goes from town to town.

False Friends

37 Anyone can claim to be your friend, but some people are friends in name only. ²The grief caused when a close friendship turns sour is as bad as death. ³This evil impulse we have! Why was it ever formed? How did

When a close friendship turns sour (37.2)

p Hebrew Temple; *Greek* people.   *q Hebrew* You have . . . people; *Greek* According to the blessing of Aaron on your people.

it manage to cover the earth with deceit? ⁴Some people will be your friend as long as things are going well, but they will turn against you when trouble comes. ⁵A real*ʳ* friend will help you against your enemies*ˢ* and protect you in the fight. ⁶Never forget such companions in battle;*ᵗ* share the results of your victory with them.

Caution in Taking Advice

⁷Anyone can give advice, but some people do so only in their own interest. ⁸Be careful when somebody offers you advice. Find out first what his interest in the matter is, because you can be sure that he is thinking primarily of himself. Why should he come out on top instead of you?*ᵘ* ⁹He will assure you that things look good, and then stand back to watch what happens to you.

¹⁰Don't ask advice of anyone who doesn't trust you, and don't give advice to anyone who is jealous of you.

¹¹Don't ask a woman for advice about a rival of hers,

a coward about war,
a merchant about a bargain,
a buyer about selling,
a stingy person about gratitude,
a cruel person about kindness,
a lazy person about work,
a casual worker about finishing
a job,
a lazy slave about a difficult task.

Pay no attention to any advice they may give.

¹²Instead, rely on someone who is religious and known to keep the Lord's commands, someone who is sympathetic with you, who will be sorry to see you fail. ¹³And trust your own judgment; no one's advice is more reliable. ¹⁴Sometimes your own intuition can tell you more than seven watchmen on a high tower. ¹⁵Above all, pray to the Most High that he will show you the right thing to do.

Wisdom and Confidence

¹⁶Planning and thought lie behind everything that is done. ¹⁷⁻¹⁸The mind concerns itself with four things: these are good and evil, life and death. They all begin in the mind,*ᵛ* but the tongue is their absolute ruler.

¹⁹Someone may have the ability to teach, but still not be of much use to himself. ²⁰He may be clever with words, but end up starving because people hate him. ²¹This may happen if he doesn't have good sense, if the Lord has not given him tact. ²²Someone may consider himself wise and let you know that he is certain about what he knows. ²³Anyone who really is wise will be the teacher of his people, and they can be certain that what he teaches is the truth. ²⁴Everyone will praise such a person and speak of him as fortunate. ²⁵A person's life has only a limited number of days, but the life of Israel cannot be measured in days at all. ²⁶The wise will win the confidence of others, and will be remembered forever.

Controlling the Appetite

²⁷My child, as you go through life, keep your appetite under control, and don't eat anything that you know is bad for you. ²⁸All food doesn't agree with everyone, and everyone doesn't like the same kinds of food. ²⁹Don't feel that you just have to have all sorts of fancy

---

ʳ Hebrew real; Greek does not have this word.   ˢ Hebrew against your enemies; Greek hoping to get a meal.   ᵗ Hebrew in battle; Greek in your soul.   ᵘ Hebrew Why . . . you?; Greek He may use his influence against you.   ᵛ Hebrew The mind . . . the mind; Greek There are four things that show the changes of the heart: good and evil, life and death.

food, and don't be a glutton over any food. ³⁰ If you eat too much, you'll get sick; if you do it all the time, you'll always have stomach trouble. ³¹ Gluttony has been the death of many people. Avoid it and live longer.

Sickness and Medicine

38 Give doctors the honor they deserve, for the Lord gave them their work to do.ʷ ² Their skill came from the Most High, and kings reward them for it. ³ Their knowledge gives them a position of importance, and powerful people hold them in high regard.

⁴ The Lord created medicines from the earth, and a sensible person will not hesitate to use them. ⁵ Didn't a tree once make bitter water fit to drink, so that the Lord's powerˣ might be known? ⁶ He gave medical knowledge to human beings, so that we would praise him for the miracles he performs. ⁷⁻⁸ The druggist mixes these medicines, and the doctor will use them to cure diseases and ease pain. There is no end to the activities of the Lord, who gives health to the people of the world.

⁹ My child, when you get sick, don't ignore it. Pray to the Lord, and he will make you well. ¹⁰ Confess all your sins and determine that in the future you will live a righteous life. ¹¹ Offer incense and a grain offering, as fine as you can afford.ʸ ¹² Then call the doctor—for the Lord created him—and keep him at your side; you need him. ¹³ There are times when you have to depend on his skill. ¹⁴ The doctor's prayer is that the Lord will make him able to ease his patients' pain and make them well again. ¹⁵ As for the person who sins against his Creator, he deserves to be sick.

Mourning for the Dead

¹⁶ My child, when someone dies, you should mourn. Weep and wail to show how deeply you feel the loss. Prepare the body in the proper way, and be present at the burial. ¹⁷ Weep bitterly and passionately; observe the proper period of mourning for the person. Mourn for a whole day or maybe two, to keep people from talking, but then pull yourself together and reconcile yourself to the loss. ¹⁸ Grief can undermine your health and even lead to your own death. ¹⁹ Grief lingers on after the death of a loved one, but it is not wise to let it lead you into poverty.

²⁰ Don't lose yourself in sorrow; drive it away.ᶻ Remember that we must all die sometime. ²¹ There is no way to bring the dead person back. All your sorrow does him no good, and it hurts you. Don't forget that. ²² You will die, just as he did. Today it was his turn; tomorrow it will be yours. ²³ When the dead have been laid to rest, let the memory of them fade. Once they are gone, take courage.

Scholarship and Other Occupations

²⁴ Scholars must have time to study if they are going to be wise; they must be relieved of other responsibilities. ²⁵ How can a farm hand gain knowledge, when his only ambition is to drive the oxen and make them work, when all he knows to talk about is livestock? ²⁶ He takes great pains to plow a straight furrow and will work far into the night to feed the animals.

²⁷ It is the same with the artist and the craftsman, who work night and day engraving precious stones, carefully working out new designs. They take great pains to produce a lifelike image,

---

ʷ *Hebrew* gave them their work to do; *Greek* created them.   ˣ the Lord's power; *or* its healing properties.   ʸ *Hebrew* as fine as you can afford; *Greek unclear.*   ᶻ drive it away; *or* put the memory of the person aside.
38.5 Ex 15.23-25   **38.16-23** Si 22.11, 12

All your sorrow does him no good. (38.21)

and will work far into the night to finish the work.

28 It is the same with the blacksmith at his anvil, planning what he will make from a piece of iron. The heat from the fire sears his skin as he sweats away at the forge. The clanging of the hammer deafens him[a] as he carefully watches the object he is working take shape. He takes great pains to complete his task, and will work far into the night to bring it to perfection.

29 It is the same with the potter, sitting at his wheel and turning it with his feet, always concentrating on his work, concerned with how many objects he can produce. **30** He works the clay with his feet until he can shape it with his hands; then he takes great pains to glaze it properly, and will work far into the night to clean out the kiln.

31 All of these people are skilled with their hands, each of them an expert at his own craft. **32** Without such people there could be no cities; no one would live or visit where these services were not available. **33** These people are not sought out to serve on the public councils, and they never attain positions of great importance. They do not serve as judges, and they do not understand legal matters. They have no education and are not known for their wisdom. You never hear them quoting proverbs. **34** But the work they do holds this world together. When they do their work, it is the same as offering prayer.[b]

39 But it is different with the person who devotes himself to studying the Law of the Most High. He examines the wisdom of all the ancient writers and concerns himself with the prophecies. **2** He memorizes the sayings of famous men and is a skilled interpreter of parables. **3** He studies the hidden meaning of proverbs and is able to

a Probable text deafens him; *Greek* renews his ears. *b* When . . . prayer; *or* When they pray, it is about their work.

discuss the obscure points of parables.
⁴Great people call on him for his services, and he is seen in the company of rulers. He travels to foreign lands in his efforts to learn about human good and evil. ⁵It is his practice to get up early and pray aloud to the Lord his Creator, asking the Most High to forgive his sins. ⁶Then, if the great Lord is willing, he will be filled with understanding. He will pour out a stream of wise sayings, and give thanks to the Lord in prayer. ⁷He will have knowledge to share and good advice to give, as well as insight into the Lord's secrets. ⁸He will demonstrate his learning in what he teaches,*c* and his pride will be in the Lord's Law and covenant. ⁹He will be widely praised for his wisdom, and it will never be lost, because people for generations to come will remember him. ¹⁰The Gentiles will talk about his wisdom, and he will be praised aloud in the assembly. ¹¹If he lives to old age, he will die famous, but if he is laid to rest before he is famous, he will be content.*d*

A Hymn in Praise of God

¹²Like the moon, I am full—full of more ideas to be discussed. ¹³Listen to me, you devout children of mine, and blossom like a rosebush on a stream bank. ¹⁴Bloom like a sweet-smelling lily, and send your fragrance into the air like incense. Sing the Lord's praises, and thank him for all that he has done. ¹⁵Proclaim his glory in grateful praise! To the music of the harp, sing this song:

¹⁶All that the Lord has done is
    very good;
  all that he commands is
    sooner or later done.

¹⁷No one should ask why things
    are as they are;
  these questions will be
    answered at the right time.
He commanded, and the water
    piled up high,
  great walls of water arose
    when he spoke.
¹⁸Whatever he commands is
    promptly done;
  there are no limits to his
    power to save.
¹⁹He sees all that every human
    being does;
  there is no way to hide from
    his sight.
²⁰He sees the whole of time, from
    beginning to end,
  and nothing takes him by
    surprise.*e*
²¹No one should ask why things
    are as they are;
  everything in creation has its
    purpose.

²²His blessings overflow like the
    Nile,
  enriching the world in a
    fertile flood.*f*
²³He turns fresh water into salt
    water,
  and he turns his anger on the
    nations.
²⁴For the devout, his ways are
    straight;
  for the wicked, they are laid
    with traps.
²⁵From the beginning he has made
    good things for the good
  and terrible things for sinners.
²⁶The basic needs of life are these:
    water, fire, iron, and salt,
  flour, honey, and milk,
  wine, clothing, and oil.
²⁷All these things are good for
    those who are devout,

---

c his learning . . . teaches; *or* the wisdom of what he has been taught.   *d* if he is . . . content; *Greek unclear.*   *e* takes him by surprise; *or* is too marvelous for him.   *f Hebrew* overflow . . . flood; *Greek* cover the dry land like a river and drench it like a flood.

but they turn into evils for
sinners.

28 There are winds that were
        created to bring
        punishment,
    fierce enough to move
        mountains.*g*
In times of judgment, they
        unleash their strength
    and calm the anger of their
        maker.

29-30 Vicious animals, scorpions, and
        snakes;
    the sword that destroys the
        wicked;
    fire, hail, famine, and disease;
        these have all been created as
        punishments.

31 They are all glad to obey the
        Lord's command
    and are ready to serve him
        here on earth.
    When their times of duty come,
        they never disobey.

(32 I was long convinced of this, so after
thinking it over I put*h* it in writing.)

33 Everything made by the Lord is
        good;
    he meets every need at the
        proper time.

34 No one can claim that some
        things are worse than
        others,
    for everything is good in its
        proper place.

35 Now then, sing praises with all
        your heart,
    and praise the name of the
        Lord!

The Misery of Human Life

40 Every person has been given a
great deal of work to do. A
heavy burden lies on all of us from the
day of our birth until the day we go back
to the earth, the mother of us all. 2 We
are confused and fearful, dreading the
day of our death — 3-4 all of us from the
king on his splendid throne wearing
royal robes and a crown, to the hum-
blest person dressed in burlap and living in poverty. 5 All through our lives we
meet anger, jealousy, and trouble.
Things disturb us; we live with furious
conflicts and with the fear of death.
Even when we go to bed, we think up
new troubles in our sleep. 6 We get little
rest, if any at all. When we sleep, it is
as if we were awake, disturbed by our
imaginations. If we dream that we are
running from an enemy, 7 just as we are
about to be caught,*i* we wake up and
are relieved to find there is nothing to
be afraid of.

8 Here is what all creatures, both human and animal, must face (but it is
seven times worse for sinners): 9 death,
violence, conflict, murder, disaster,
famine, sickness, epidemic. 10 All these
things were created because of the
wicked; they are the ones who have
caused destruction.*j* 11 Everything
that comes from the earth goes back to
the earth, just as all water flows into
the sea.

The Results of Evil

12 Nothing that comes from bribery
or injustice will last, but the effects of
loyalty will remain forever. 13 Wealth
that has been obtained dishonestly is
like a stream that runs full during a
thunderstorm, 14 tumbling rocks along
as it flows, but then suddenly goes
dry.*k* 15 The children of ungodly people
will not leave large families; they are
like plants trying to take root on rock,
16 like reeds along a river bank, withering*l* before any other plant. 17 Acts of

g Hebrew move mountains; *Greek* lash heavily.   *h* put; *or* left.   *i Probable text*
caught; *Greek* rescued.   *j Hebrew* have caused destruction; *Greek* caused the flood.
k Verses 13-14 are translated from Hebrew; verse 14 in Greek is unclear.   *l Hebrew*
withering; *Greek* pulled up.

kindness and charity are as lasting as eternity. *m*

The Joys of Human Life

18 Being independently wealthy or working for a living — both can make life pleasant, but it is better to find a treasure.

19 Your name can be preserved if you have children or if you establish a city, but finding Wisdom is a better way.

Owning livestock and orchards will make you famous, *n* but it is better to have a wife you love. *o*

20 Wine and music can make you happy, but a happy marriage *p* is even better.

21 Flutes and harps make fine music, but a pleasant voice is better than either.

22 Gracefulness and beauty please the eye, but not as much as new growth in the spring.

23 You can't go wrong with a good friend or neighbor, but an intelligent wife is *q* better than either.

24 Relatives and helpers are good to have in times of trouble, but it will be an even greater help if you have made a practice of giving to the poor.

25 Gold and silver provide security, but good advice is better.

26 Wealth and strength give confidence, but the fear of the Lord can give you even greater confidence. When you fear the Lord you need nothing more; it is all the support you need. **27** The fear of the Lord is like a rich garden of blessings; you could not want a more glorious shelter.

Begging

28 My child, don't live the life of a beggar; it is better to die than to beg. **29** If you have to depend on someone else for your food, you are not really living your own life. You pollute yourself by accepting food from another. Begging is torture to the soul of any sensitive person. *r* **30** A shameless person can make begging sound sweet, but something inside him burns.

Death

41 Death! The very thought of it is bitter to someone who is prosperous, living peacefully with his possessions, free of worries, and still able to enjoy his food.

2 Death! Its sentence is welcome to someone living in poverty, with failing health, very old, burdened with worries, blind, and without hope. *s*

3 Do not be afraid of death's decree. Remember that it came to those before you and will come to those after you. **4** The Lord has decreed it for every living creature. Who are you to object to what the Most High wishes? In the world of the dead no one will care whether you lived ten years, a hundred, or a thousand.

The Fate of the Wicked

5 The children of sinners, brought up in ungodly surroundings, turn out to be hateful people. **6** They will lose whatever they inherit, and their own descendants will live in permanent disgrace. **7** The children will put the blame for their disgrace on their ungodly parents.

---

m Hebrew Acts . . . eternity; *Greek* Kindness is a blessed garden, and charity lasts forever.   *n Hebrew* but finding Wisdom . . . famous; *Greek does not have these words.*   *o Hebrew* wife you love; *Greek* blameless wife.   *p Hebrew* a happy marriage; *Greek* the love of Wisdom.   *q Hebrew* an intelligent wife is; *Greek* a wife and a husband are.   *r Hebrew* Begging . . . person; *Greek* An intelligent and understanding person will avoid it.   *s Hebrew* blind, and without hope; *Greek* rebellious and without patience.

. . . when it is proper to be ashamed. (41.16)

8 You are doomed, you irreligious people who have abandoned the Law of the Most High God. **9** When you have children, disaster will strike them and you will be left with nothing but sorrow. There will be great joy whenever you stumble,[t] and even after your death you will be cursed. **10** What comes into being from nothing[u] will return to nothing;[u] so it will be with the godless, doomed to extinction.

11 A person's body amounts to nothing,[v] but a good reputation will last forever. **12** Protect your reputation; it will outlive you and last longer than a thousand treasures of gold. **13** A good life lasts only so long, but a good reputation will last forever.

A Sense of Decency

14 My children, do as I teach you and live at peace. Wisdom that is not expressed is like a treasure that has been hidden — both are useless. **15** A person who covers up his foolishness is better than one who keeps his wisdom to himself.

16 My children, listen and I will teach you the circumstances when it is proper to be ashamed.[w] Sometimes it is entirely out of place.

17 Before your parents, be ashamed of immoral behavior.

Before a ruler or an important person, be ashamed of a lie.

18 Before a judge, be ashamed of criminal behavior.

Before a public assembly, be ashamed of breaking the law.

Before a friend or partner, be ashamed of dishonesty.

19 Before your neighbors, be ashamed of theft.

Be ashamed of breaking a promise,[x]
   of leaning on the dinner table with your elbows,
   of stinginess when you are asked for something,

20   of not returning a greeting,
   of staring at a prostitute,

21   of turning down a relative's request,
   of depriving someone of what is rightly his,
   of staring at another man's wife,

22   of playing around with his slave woman (keep away from her bed!)
   of insulting your friends,

---

[t] *Hebrew* When you have . . . stumble; *Greek* You are born under a curse.   [u] *Hebrew* nothing; *Greek* earth.   [v] *Hebrew* A person's . . . nothing; *Greek* The death of a person's body is mourned.   [w] *Hebrew* My children . . . ashamed; *Greek* Show respect for what I say.   [x] *Hebrew* of breaking a promise; *Greek* of yourself before the truth of God.

of following up your gifts
  with criticism,
  23   of betraying secrets.
These are times when it is proper for
you to be ashamed, and people will respect you for it.

A Sense of Pride

42 On the other hand, it is possible to sin by giving in to other
people too much. Here are some things
you should not be ashamed of:
  ² the Law of the Most High and
    his covenant,
    judging even godless people
    fairly,
  ³ sharing expenses with a business
    partner or a traveling
    companion,
    sharing an inheritance,
  ⁴ using accurate weights and
    measures,
  ⁵ making a profit, whether great
    or small,
    bargaining with a merchant,
    disciplining your children often,
    beating a disloyal slave until the
    blood flows.
⁶ It is wise to lock things up if you
cannot trust your wife or if too many
people are around. ⁷ Keep an accurate
record of any deposits you make or of
anything you give or receive. ⁸ Don't
hesitate to correct someone who is acting foolishly or an old man who goes
around with prostitutes. All of this is
worthwhile advice, and if you follow it,
everyone will approve of your behavior.

Fathers and Daughters

⁹ Although he will not let his daughter know it, a father will lie awake at
night worrying about her. If she is
young, he worries that she might not
get married. If she is already married,
he worries about her happiness. ¹⁰ If
she is a virgin, he worries that she
might be seduced and become pregnant while living in his house. If she is
married, he worries that she might be
unfaithful, or that she might not be able
to have children.

¹¹ Keep a close watch over your
daughter if she is determined to have
her own way. If you don't, she may
make a fool of you in front of your enemies. You will be a constant joke to
everyone in town, a public disgrace.
Make sure that her room has no windows or any place where she can look
out to the entrance of the house. ʸ
¹² Don't let her show off her beauty in
front of men, or spend her time talking
with the women. ᶻ ¹³ Women hurt other
women just as moths damage clothing.

¹⁴ A man's wickedness is better than
a woman's goodness; women bring
shame and disgrace.

The Glory of God in Nature

¹⁵ Now I will remind you of the
    works of the Lord
    and describe the things I have
    seen.
  The words of the Lord brought
    his works into being,
    and the whole creation obeys
    his commands.
¹⁶ The light of the sun shines down
    on everything,
    and everything is filled with
    the Lord's glory.
¹⁷ Not even to his holy angels has
    the Lord given power
  to describe all his mighty
    deeds,
  even though he has given them
    power
  to stand unharmed in his
    glorious presence. ᵃ

ʸ *Hebrew* Make sure . . . house; *Greek does not have these words.*   ᶻ *Hebrew* Don't
let . . . women; *Greek unclear.*   ᵃ *Hebrew* even though . . . presence; *Greek* which
the Lord Almighty established so that everything may stand firm in his glory.
42.9-11 Si 7.24, 25; 26.10-12

18 He sees into the oceans and into
   the human heart,
   and he knows the secrets of
   both.
   The Most High knows
   everything that can be
   known
   and understands the signs of
   the ages.
19 He knows all that has ever been
   and all that ever will be;
   he uncovers the deepest of
   mysteries.
20 He takes notice of our every
   thought
   and hears our every word.
21 The orderly world shows the
   greatness of his wisdom;
   he is the same forever and
   ever.[b]
   Nothing can be added to him,
   and nothing taken away;
   he needs no one to give him
   advice.
22 All his works are beautiful,
   down to the smallest and
   faintest spark of light.[c]
23 All these things go on forever,
   and all of them have their
   purpose.
24 All things are in pairs, each the
   opposite of the other,
   but nothing the Lord made is
   incomplete.
25 Everything completes the
   goodness of something
   else.
   Could anyone ever see
   enough of this splendor?

43

How beautiful is the bright,
   clear sky above us!
   What a glorious sight it is!
2 The sun, when it appears,
   proclaims as it rises

how marvelous a thing it is,
   made by the Most High.
3 At noon it dries up the land;
   no one can stand its blazing
   heat.
4 The setting sun sets fire to the
   hilltops,
   like a metal furnace glowing
   from the heat.[d]
   It sends out fiery rays,
   blinding the eyes with its
   brightness.
5 The Lord, who made it, is great;
   it speeds on its way at his
   command.

6 There is also the moon, marking
   the passage of time,[e]
   an eternal sign of the
   changing seasons.
7 The moon determines the holy
   days.
   Its light grows full and then
   grows dim.
8 The "month" is named after the
   moon,
   marvelous to watch as it
   grows fuller each night,
   a signal light for the heavenly
   armies,
   shining out in the dome of
   the sky.

9 The shining stars make the night
   sky lovely,
   brilliant ornaments in the
   Lord's high heavens.
10 They stay in the places assigned
   to them by the Holy One
   and never relax their dutiful
   watch.
11 Look at the rainbow and praise
   its Creator!
   How magnificent, how
   radiant, its beauty!

---

[b] Hebrew he is . . . ever; Greek he is before eternity and is eternal.   [c] Hebrew down
to . . . spark of light; Greek unclear.   [d] Hebrew The setting . . . heat; Greek A man at
a furnace works with scorching heat, but the sun burns the hills three times as much.
[e] Hebrew marking . . . time; Greek unclear.

It spans the horizon in a circle of glory. (43.12)

12 Like a bow bent by the hands of
the Most High,
it spans the horizon in a circle
of glory.

13 He commands, and snow begins
to fall;
lightning strikes to carry out
his judgments.
14 The storerooms of the sky are
thrown open,
and the clouds roll out like
flying birds.
15 With his power he forms great
masses of clouds
and shatters the ice into
hailstones.
16-17 He speaks, and thunder twists
the earth in pain;
the mountains are shaken by
his strength.*f*

Whenever he wishes, the south
wind blows,
whirlwinds come, and
windstorms from the north.
He sends the snow fluttering
down like birds,
like locusts lighting on the
ground.
18 We marvel at its beautiful
whiteness,
and in fascination we watch it
fall.
19 He sprinkles frost over the
ground like salt,
and it freezes into thorny
flowers of ice.*g*
20 He sends the cold north wind
blowing
and the water hardens
into ice;
every lake and pond freezes over,
putting on a coat of icy armor.

f Hebrew by his strength; Greek when he appears.   *g Hebrew flowers of ice; Greek points.*

21 He scorches the wilderness hills
with drought,
and the grass turns brown
from its heat;
22 but a cloudy mist restores it all
to life
as the weather cools and dew
appears.

23 By his wisdom he calmed the
great oceans
and placed the islands there.
24 Sailors tell about the dangers of
the sea,
and we listen to their tales in
amazement.
25 In the sea are strange and
marvelous creatures:
huge monsters and all kinds
of living things.
26 Each of the Lord's messengers
succeeds at its task.
Everything is held together by
his word.

27 We could say much more and
never finish,
but it all means this: the Lord
is everything.
28 How can we find the power to
praise him?
He is greater than all his
creation.
29 The Lord is awesome in his
greatness;
his power is overwhelming.
30 Though you do your best to
praise him,
he is greater than you can
ever express.
Though you honor him tirelessly
and with all your strength,
you still cannot praise him
enough.
31 No one has seen him, no one
can describe him;

no one can praise him as he
deserves.
32 Mysteries greater than these are
still unknown;
we know only a fraction of
his works.
33 The Lord made the universe
and then gave wisdom to
devout people.

The Glory of God in History

44 So let us now give praise to
godly[h] men,
our ancestors of generations
past,
2 those whom the Lord honored
with great glory,
in whom his greatness has
been seen
from the beginning of time.
3 There were some who ruled
kingdoms,
and some who were known
for their strength.
Some were wise advisers,
and some spoke prophecies.
4 There were statesmen whose
policies governed the
people,
rulers who issued decrees,[i]
scholars who spoke wise
words,[j]
and those who used pointed
proverbs,[k]
5 poets, and composers of
music,
6 rich and powerful men living
peacefully at home.
7 All of these were famous in their
own times,
honored by the people of
their day.
8 Some of them left a reputation,
and people still praise them
today.

[h] *Hebrew godly; Greek famous.* [i] *Probable Hebrew text rulers who issued decrees;
Greek unclear.* [j] *Hebrew scholars ... words; Greek unclear.* [k] *Hebrew and
those ... proverbs; Greek does not have these words.*

IN PRAISE OF ANCESTORS (Chapters 44–50)

⁹There are others who are not
remembered,
as if they had never lived,
who died and were forgotten,
they, and their children after
them.

¹⁰But we will praise these
godly men,
whose righteous deeds have
never been forgotten.
¹¹Their reputations will be passed
on to their descendants,
and this will be their
inheritance.¹
¹²Their descendants continue to
keep the covenant
and always will, because of
what their ancestors did.
¹³Their family line will go on
forever,
and their fame will never
fade.
¹⁴Their bodies were laid to rest,
but their reputations will live
forever.
¹⁵Nations will tell about their
wisdom,
and God's people will praise
them.

Enoch

¹⁶Enoch pleased the Lord and was
taken up into heaven. He became an inspiration for repentance for all time to
come.

Noah

¹⁷Noah was a perfectly righteous
man. After destruction came, he gave
the human race a new start.ᵐ Because
of him there were people left on earth
when the flood was over. ¹⁸The Lord
made an eternal covenant with him,

promising that life would never again
be destroyed by a flood.

Abraham

¹⁹Abraham was the great ancestor of
many nations; his reputation was fault-
less.ⁿ ²⁰He kept the Law of the Most
High and made a covenant with him, a
covenant marked on his body. When he
was put to the test, he was found faithful. ²¹And so the Lord made him a solemn promise that his descendants
would be a blessing to the world; that
their number would be countless, like
the dust of the earth; that they would be
honored more than any other people on
earth; and that their land would extend
from sea to sea, from the Euphrates to
the ends of the earth.

Isaac and Jacob

²²⁻²³The Lord renewed that covenant
with Isaac, and then again with Jacob,
repeating the promise that Abraham's
descendants would be a blessing to the
whole human race. The Lord assured
Jacob that he would bless him; he gave
him the land that would be his, dividing
it into twelve parts, one for each of the
tribes.

Moses

45 From Jacob's descendants the
Lord raised up a godly man
who won the favor of everyone, loved by
God and people alike. This man was
Moses, whose very memory is a blessing. ²The Lord made him as glorious as
the angels and made his enemies fear
him. ³There in Egypt at his command
the disaster struck.ᵒ The Lord made
kings hold him in respect. The Lord
gave him his commands for his people

---

l Verse 11 in Greek is unclear.   *m Hebrew gave . . . start; Greek was taken in*
exchange for the human race.   *n Hebrew his reputation was faultless; Greek there*
was no one like him in reputation.   *ᵒ Hebrew struck; Greek stopped.*
44.16 Gn 5.24; He 11.5; Jd 14   **44.17, 18** Gn 6.9–9.17   **44.19-21** Gn 15.1–17.27;
22.1-18   **44.22, 23** Gn 17.19; 26.3-5; 27.28; 28.14   **45.1-5** Ex 6.28–11.10; 20.1-21

and showed him the dazzling light of his presence. [4]The Lord chose Moses out of the whole human race and consecrated him because of his loyalty and humility. [5]He let him hear his voice and led him into the dark cloud, where, face-to-face, he gave him the commandments, the Law that gives life and knowledge, so that Moses might teach the covenant regulations to the Israelites.

Aaron

[6]The Lord raised up Aaron, a holy man like his brother Moses, of the tribe of Levi. [7]He made an eternal covenant with him, giving him the privilege of serving as priest to the Lord's people. He honored him by clothing him with magnificent robes and fine ornaments, [8]perfect in their splendor. He granted him the symbols of authority: the linen shorts, the shirt, and the robe with the pomegranates around the hem. [9]Gold bells were also around its hem, so that when he walked, their ringing would be heard in the Temple, and the Lord would remember his people. [10]The Lord gave Aaron the sacred robe with the gold, blue, and purple embroidery; the breastpiece with the Urim and Thummim;[p] [11]the red yarn, spun by an expert; the precious stones with names engraved on them, mounted in a gold setting by a jeweler, placed on the breastpiece to remind the Lord of the twelve tribes of Israel. [12]He gave him the turban with the gold ornament engraved with the words "Dedicated to the Lord." It was expertly crafted, a beautiful work of art, and it was a high honor to wear it. [13]Before Aaron's time such beautiful things were never seen. No one but Aaron and his descendants ever wore them, or ever will. [14]The grain offering is to be presented twice a day and burned completely.

[15]Moses ordained Aaron to office by pouring the sacred anointing oil over his head. An eternal covenant was made with him and his descendants, that they would serve the Lord as his priests and bless the people in the Lord's name. [16]The Lord chose Aaron out of the whole human race to offer sacrifices, to burn fragrant incense to remind the Lord of his people, and to take away their sins. [17]He entrusted the commandments to Aaron's keeping and gave him the authority to make legal decisions and to teach Israel the Law.

[18]Once, while the people were in the wilderness, an angry group of jealous outsiders conspired against Moses. These were Dathan, Abiram, and Korah with their supporters. [19]The Lord saw what they were doing and became angry, so furious that he performed a miracle and destroyed them in a blazing fire. [20]Then he rewarded Aaron again, giving him a special honor: the right to the offerings of the first produce, so that the priests should have enough to eat. [21]Their food is the sacrifices offered to the Lord; the Lord gave this to Aaron and his descendants. [22]But Aaron, unlike the rest of the people, was to inherit no land, no special portion of his own. The Lord himself would be all he needed.

Phinehas

[23]Only Moses and Aaron were more famous for their intense devotion to the Lord than Phinehas son of Eleazar. He brought about forgiveness for Israel's sin by standing firm in brave determination when everyone else was in rebellion. [24]And so the Lord made a

---

[p] URIM AND THUMMIM: *Two objects used by the priest to determine God's will; it is not known precisely how they were used.*

45.6 Ex 4.14   **45.7-13** Ex 28.1-43   **45.15** Lv 8.1-36   **45.18, 19** Nu 16.1-35
45.22 Nu 18.20; Dt 12.12   **45.23-26** Nu 25.7-13

covenant with him, valid for all time to come, that he should be in charge of the sanctuary and of his people, that he and his descendants should hold the office of High Priest forever. ²⁵ Unlike the covenant made with David son of Jesse, from the tribe of Judah, where the kingship passed only from father to son, the priesthood was to pass from Aaron to all his descendants.

²⁶ Now praise the Lord, who is good, who has crowned you with glory!�q May he give you wisdom to judge his people fairly, so that their success and your authorityʳ may continue for all time to come.

Joshua

46 Joshuaˢ son of Nun was a great soldier and the next of the prophets after Moses. He lived up to the meaning of his name as the great deliverer of the Lord's chosen people. He defeated the enemies that attacked them, so that Israel could claim its land. ² How magnificent it was when he raised his arm and then led the attacks on the cities! ³ No one could stand up to him;ᵗ he was fighting a holy war for the Lord. ⁴ Remember how he held back the sun and made one day as long as two? ⁵ When his enemies were threatening him from every side, he prayed to the mighty Lord Most High, and his prayer was answered with a hailstorm of devastating force. ⁶ The Lord hurled the hail down on the enemyᵘ and destroyed them at the pass at Beth Horon, so that the nations would realize how strong Joshua was, since he was fighting as a devoted follower of the Lord.

Caleb

⁷ Joshua was loyal as long as Moses lived, both he and Caleb son of Jephunneh. They stood up to the whole community, made them stop their ungrateful complaining, and kept them from sinning. ⁸ Out of the 600,000 Israelites who marched through the wilderness, these two were the only ones spared and allowed to enter the rich and fertile land that was to be theirs. ⁹ The Lord made Caleb strong, and when he was an old man, he was still strong enough to go up into the hill country and capture it for himself and his descendants. ¹⁰ Then all of Israel could see how good it is to follow the Lord.

The Judges

¹¹ Then there were the judges, each of them famous in their own right, who never fell into idolatry and never abandoned the Lord. ¹² May their memory be honored! May these whom we honor spring from the grave to new life in their descendants!

Samuel

¹³ Samuel was loved by the Lord. As the Lord's prophet he established the kingdom and appointed rulers for the people. ¹⁴ He judged the nation in accordance with the Law of the Lord, and the Lord protected Israel. ¹⁵ Because Samuel was faithful, he was accepted as a true prophet. People trusted him as a seer because of his words. ¹⁶ When his enemies were threatening him from every side, he called upon the mighty Lord and offered him a young lamb as

---

q Hebrew Now praise . . . glory; Greek does not have these words.   ʳ Probable Hebrew text and your authority; Greek unclear.   ˢ JOSHUA: This name in Hebrew means "the Lord saves."   ᵗ Hebrew no one . . . to him; Greek No one before had ever been so brave.   ᵘ Probable text The Lord hurled . . . enemy; Greek unclear.
46.1-6 Js 1.1–11.23   **46.7-10** Nu 14.6-10; 11.21; Js 14.6-11   **46.11** Jg 1.1–16.31
46.13-20 1 S 3.19, 20; 7.9-11; 10.1; 12.3; 16.13; 28.18, 19

a sacrifice. ¹⁷ Then the Lord thundered from heaven with a mighty roar ¹⁸ and destroyed all the enemy^v rulers of Philistia. ¹⁹ When Samuel was about to die, he gave assurances before the Lord and the anointed king that he had never taken anyone's property, not even so much as a pair of shoes, and no one contradicted him. ²⁰ Even after he died, he prophesied to King Saul how he would die. Out of the grave he spoke as a prophet, to blot out his people's wickedness.

Nathan

47 After him came Nathan, who was a prophet at the time of David.

David

² As the choice fat portion of the fellowship offering is reserved for the Lord, so David was chosen from among the Israelites. ³ He played with lions and bears as if they were lambs or little goats. ⁴ When he was still a boy, he killed a giant to rescue his people. He put a stone in his sling, took aim, and put an end to Goliath's bragging. ⁵ He prayed to the Lord, the Most High, and was given the strength to kill that famous soldier, so that the nations would have respect for the power of his people. ⁶ The people honored him for killing his tens of thousands, and when he was crowned king, they praised him for being chosen by the Lord. ⁷ He wiped out all his enemies and permanently crushed the Philistines, so that they never again became a threat.

⁸ In everything David did, he gave thanks and praise to the Holy Lord, the Most High. He loved his Creator and sang praises to him with all his heart.

⁹ He put singers at the altar to provide beautiful music. ¹⁰ He set the times of the festivals throughout the year and made them splendid occasions; the Temple rang with the Lord's praises all day long. ¹¹ The Lord forgave David's sin and established his power forever. He made a covenant with him that he and his descendants would reign in splendor over Israel.

Solomon

¹² David prepared the way well for his son, a wise man, to rule after him. ¹³ There was no war while Solomon was king. God gave him peace on all his borders, so that he could build for the Lord a Temple which would stand forever. ¹⁴ How wise you were, Solomon, when you were young! Your knowledge was like the Nile^w in flood. ¹⁵ Your influence reached over all the world; your proverbs and riddles were known everywhere. ¹⁶ You were famous everywhere, and people loved you for bringing peace. ¹⁷ Nations around the world held you in admiration for your songs, proverbs, parables, and witty sayings. ¹⁸ You gathered silver and gold as if it were tin or lead, all in the name of the Lord God of Israel.

¹⁹ But your lust for women was your downfall. ²⁰ You stained your reputation and that of your descendants. They suffered punishment for that foolishness of yours, which caused them so much grief. ²¹ It divided the nation, and a rival kingdom arose in northern Israel. ²² But the Lord will always be merciful and keep all his promises.^x He will never destroy the descendants of David, whom he chose and who loved him. So for Israel's sake he allowed David's family to survive.

---

^v *Hebrew* enemy; *Greek* rulers of Tyre and.   ^w *Hebrew* the Nile; *Greek* a river.
^x *Hebrew* keep all his promises; *Greek* will not destroy what he made.

47.1 2 S 7.2, 3; 12.1   **47.2-11** 1 S 17.34—18.7; 2 S 5.7; 8.1; 12.13   **47.13-17** 1 K 4.21-32
47.18 1 K 10.21, 27   **47.19** 1 K 11.1   **47.21** 1 K 12.15-20   **47.22** 2 S 7.15

Rehoboam and Jeroboam

23 Solomon followed his ancestors in death and left one of his sons to rule after him. This was Rehoboam, a man of little intelligence and great foolishness,*y* whose policies caused a rebellion.

There was also the unspeakable*z* Jeroboam, who led northern Israel in sinful ways. **24** His people became so sinful that they were exiled from their land. **25** They tried all kinds of wickedness until the Lord took vengeance on them.

Elijah

48 Then there arose the fiery prophet Elijah, whose words blazed like a torch. **2** He brought a famine on the people, and many of them died because of his persistence. **3** Speaking in the name of the Lord, he kept the rain from coming, and on three occasions he called down fire. **4** Elijah, your miracles were marvelous! No one else can boast of such deeds! **5** In the name of the Most High, you brought a dead man back to life. **6** You brought a famous king down to sickness and death. **7** At Sinai you heard the Lord rebuke you and declare his determination to punish his enemies. **8** You anointed a king to be the instrument of that punishment, and a prophet to take your place. **9** You were taken up to heaven in a fiery whirlwind, a chariot drawn by fiery horses. **10** The scripture says that you are ready to appear at the designated time,*a* to cool God's anger before it breaks out in fury; that you "will bring parents and children together again,"

and restore the tribes of Israel. **11** Fortunate are those who live to see you come, as well as those who have already died in love, for we too shall live.*b*

Elisha

12 When Elijah was hidden by the whirlwind, Elisha was filled with his spirit. As long as he lived, he was not afraid of rulers, and they could not make him do as they wished. **13** Nothing was too hard for him. Even when he was dead, his body worked a miracle. **14** In life and in death he performed amazing miracles.

15 But in spite of all this, the people did not abandon their sinful ways until they were taken from their land as prisoners and scattered all over the world. This left the nation few in number, but those who remained were still ruled by the descendants of David. **16** Some of the people did what was pleasing to the Lord, but others committed sin after sin.

Hezekiah

17 Hezekiah prepared his city to resist a siege and provided it with a water supply. He had a tunnel built through solid rock with iron tools and had cisterns built to hold the water. **18** During his reign Sennacherib attacked the city and sent his chief official from Lachish. He challenged Jerusalem and boasted arrogantly. **19** The people lost their courage and shook with fear; they were in pain, like a woman in labor. **20** But they prayed to the merciful Lord, the Holy One in heaven, who quickly answered their prayers and sent Isaiah to save

y Hebrew great foolishness; *Greek* the people's fool.   *z Hebrew* the unspeakable (one); *Greek* Jeroboam son of Nebat.   *a Hebrew* you are . . . time; *Greek* unclear.
b Verse 11 in Greek is unclear.

47.23-25 1 K 11.43; 12.10-30; 2 K 17.6, 18   **48.1-11** 1 K 17.1-24; 18.38; 19.15, 16;
2 K 1.10-16; 2.11; Ml 4.5, 6   **48.12** 2 K 2.9,13   **48.13** 2 K 13.20, 21   **48.15** 2 K 18.11, 12
48.17 2 K 20.20   **48.18** 2 K 18.13-17   **48.20, 21** 2 K 19.15-20, 35

them. ²¹ The Lord struck the Assyrian camp; his angel wiped them out. ²² Yes, Hezekiah did what was pleasing to the Lord and firmly followed the example of his ancestor David. This was what was commanded by the great prophet Isaiah, whose visions were trusted. ²³ He made the sun move backward and lengthened the king's life. ²⁴ He comforted the mourners in Jerusalem. His powerful spirit looked into the future, ²⁵ and he predicted what was to happen before the end of time, hidden things that had not yet occurred.

Josiah

49 The memory of Josiah is as sweet as the fragrance of expertly blended incense, sweet as honey to the taste,ᶜ like music with wine at a banquet. ² He followed the correct policy of reforming the nation and removed the horrors of idolatry. ³ He was completely loyal to the Lord and strengthened true religion in those wicked times.

Jeremiah

⁴ All the kings, except David, Hezekiah, and Josiah, were terrible sinners, because they abandoned the Law of the Most High to the very end of the kingdom.ᵈ ⁵ They surrendered their power and honor to foreigners, ⁶ who set fire to the holy city and left its streets deserted, just as Jeremiah had predicted. ⁷ Jeremiah had been badly treated, even though he was chosen as a prophet before he was born, "to uproot and to pull

down, to destroy and to overthrow," but also "to build and to plant."

Ezekiel

⁸ It was Ezekiel who was shown the vision of the divine glory over the chariot and the living creatures. ⁹ He also referred to the prophet Job, who always did the right thing.ᵉ

The Twelve Prophets

¹⁰ May the bones of the twelve prophets rise to new life, because these men encouraged the people of Israel and saved them with confident hope.

Zerubbabel and Joshua

¹¹ How can we praise Zerubbabel? He was like a signet ring on the Lord's right hand, ¹² as was Joshua son of Jehozadak. They rebuilt the Lord's holy Temple, destined for eternal fame.

Nehemiah

¹³ The memory of Nehemiah is also great. He rebuilt the ruined walls of Jerusalem, installing the gates and bars. He rebuilt our homes.

The Patriarchs

¹⁴ No one else like Enoch has ever walked the face of the earth, for he was taken up from the earth. ¹⁵ No one else like Joseph has ever been born;ᶠ even his bones were honored.ᵍ ¹⁶ Shem, Seth, and Enoshʰ were highly

---

ᶜ *Hebrew* to the taste; *Greek* to everyone.   ᵈ *Hebrew* to the very end of the kingdom;
Greek and failed.   ᵉ *Probable Hebrew text* He also ... thing; *Greek unclear.*
ᶠ *Greek adds* the greatest of his brothers and the pride of his people; *Hebrew and one
ancient translation place these words in 50.1.*   ᵍ even ... honored; *or* the Lord
watched over his body.   ʰ *Hebrew* Shem, Seth, and Enosh; *Greek* Shem and Seth
among people.
48.23 2 K 20.10, 11   **49.1-3** 2 K 22.1; 22.11-13; 23.3, 25   **49.6, 7** Jr 1.4-10; 39.8
49.8, 9 Ez 1.3-15; 14.14-20   **49.11** Ezra 3.2; Hg 2.23   **49.12** Hg 1.1, 12   **49.13** Ne 6.15

honored, but Adam's glory was above that of any other living being.

Simon Son of Onias

50 The greatest of his brothers and the pride of his people[i] was the High Priest Simon son of Onias, who repaired the Temple [2]and laid the foundation for the high double wall and the fortifications of the Temple.[j] [3]The reservoir, as big as the bronze tank, was dug[k] while he was in office. [4]He made plans to protect his people from attack and fortified the city so that it could withstand a siege.

[5]How glorious he was when he came out of the Most Holy Place![l] [6]He was like the morning star shining through the clouds, like the full moon, [7]like the sun shining on the Temple of the Most High, like the rainbow gleaming in glory against the clouds, [8]like roses in springtime, like lilies beside a stream, like the cedars of Lebanon in summer, [9]like burning incense, like a cup made of hammered gold and decorated with all kinds of jewels, [10]like an olive tree loaded with fruit, like a cypress tree towering into the clouds.

[11]When Simon put on his magnificent robe and went up to the holy altar dressed in perfect splendor, he made the Temple courtyard a majestic sight. [12]When the priests handed him the portions of the sacrifice as he stood beside the altar with his assistants circling him like a wreath, he was like a young cedar of Lebanon surrounded by palm trees. [13]Those were the descendants of Aaron in their splendid garments, standing before the whole assembly of Israel, holding in their hands the offering made to the Lord. [14]When he had finished the service at the altar and had arranged the sacrifice to the Most High, the Almighty, [15]he reached for a cup and poured out sweet-smelling wine at the foot of the altar as an offering to the Most High, the universal King. [16]Then the priests shouted and blew their trumpets of hammered silver. They made a loud noise that the Most High would hear. [17]All the people immediately bowed down with their faces to the ground to worship their Lord, the Almighty, the Most High. [18]Then the choir began to sing his praises, and the beautiful music rang out. [19]The people kept praying to the merciful Lord Most High until the service of worship had come to a close. [20]Then Simon came down from the altar, raised his hands over the whole assembly of Israel, and reverently pronounced the blessing from the Lord, [21]while the people bowed a second time in worship to receive that blessing from the Most High.

A Benediction

[22]Now then, give praise to the God of the universe, who has done great things everywhere, who brings us up[m] from the time we are born, and deals with us mercifully. [23]May he give us happiness and allow us to have peace in Israel forever. [24]May he continue his mercy to us and rescue us in our time of need.

Three Hated Nations

[25]There are two nations that I detest, and a third that does not even deserve to be called a nation. [26]These are the Edomites,[n] the inhabitants of the Philistine cities, and the stupid Samaritans.

---

[i] The greatest ... people; *Hebrew and one ancient translation place the words at this point; Greek places them at 49.15.* [j] *Verse 2 in Greek is unclear.* [k] *Hebrew* dug; *Greek* reduced. [l] *Hebrew* Most Holy Place; *Greek* Most Holy Place among the people. [m] brings us up; *or* honors us. [n] *Hebrew* Edomites; *Greek* Samaritans.
50.20 Nu 6.24-27

The Wisdom of Jesus Son of Sirach

27 I, Jesus son of Sirach Eleazar *o* of Jerusalem, put all my wisdom into writing this book to provide instruction and knowledge for others. 28 May God bless everyone who gives attention to these teachings. Whoever takes them to heart will become wise. 29 Whoever lives by them will be strong enough for any occasion, because he will be walking in the light of the Lord.

A Song of Thanksgiving

51 I give you thanks, O Lord and King;
I praise you as my God and Savior.
I give you thanks,
2   for you have helped me and protected me.
You have rescued me from death,
from dangerous lies and slander.
3 You helped me when no one else would;
in your great mercy you saved me
from the many troubles I have known:
from the glaring hatred of my enemies,
who wanted to put an end to my life;
4 from suffocation in oppressive smoke
rising from fires that I did not light;
5 from death itself;
from vicious slander reported to the king.
6 I was once brought face-to-face with death;
7   enemies surrounded me everywhere.
I looked for someone to help me, but there was no one there.

8 But then, O Lord, I remembered how merciful you are
and what you had done in times past.
I remembered that you rescue those who rely on you,
that you save them from their enemies.
9 Then from here on earth I prayed to you
to rescue me from death.
10 I prayed, "O Lord, you are my father; *p*
do not abandon me to my troubles
when I am helpless against arrogant enemies.
11 I will always praise you and sing hymns of thanksgiving."
You answered my prayer,
12   and saved me from the threat of destruction.
And so I thank you and praise you.
O Lord, I praise you!

The Search for Wisdom

13 When I was still young, before I started out on my travels, I boldly prayed for Wisdom. 14 I went to the Temple and asked for her, and I will look for her as long as I live. 15 From my blossoming youth to my ripe old age she has been my delight. I have followed directly in her path ever since I was young. 16 I received Wisdom as soon as I began listening for her, and I have been rewarded with great knowledge. 17 I have always been a learner and am grateful to everyone who has been my teacher. 18 I was determined to live wisely and was devoted to the cause of goodness. I have no regrets. 19 I fought for Wisdom and was strict in my conduct. When I prayed, I sadly confessed how far short of Wisdom I fell. 20 But I

o Sirach Eleazar; *or* Sirach son of Eleazar. father of my Lord.

p Hebrew you are my father; *Greek*

was determined to have her, and I found her by keeping myself free from sin. I have grown in Wisdom since first I found her, and I will never be without her. 21 Because I was driven by the desire to find her, I have been richly rewarded. 22 The Lord gave me a gift for words, and I have used it in his praise.

23 Come to me, all you that need instruction, and learn in my school. 24 Why do you admit that you are ignorant and do nothing about it? 25 Here is what I say: It costs nothing to be wise. 26 Put on the yoke, and be willing to learn. The opportunity is always near. 27 See for yourselves! I have really not studied very hard, but I have found great contentment. 28 No matter how much it costs you to get Wisdom, it will be well worth it. 29 Be joyfully grateful for the Lord's mercy, and never be ashamed to praise him. 30 Do your duty at the proper time, and the Lord, at the time he thinks proper, will give you your reward.

The Book of
BARUCH

INTRODUCTION

The Book of Baruch is a collection of four distinct, short discourses, attributed to Baruch, the secretary of the prophet Jeremiah (Jeremiah 32.12; 36.4). These discourses, written at various times, probably in Hebrew originally, were later put together into a single document.

OUTLINE OF CONTENTS

Introduction

1 This book was written by Baruch son of Neraiah, grandson of Mahseiah, and a descendant of Zedekiah, Hasadiah, and Hilkiah. It was written in Babylon ²on the seventh day of the month*ᵃ* in the fifth year after the Babylonians captured Jerusalem and burned it down. ³⁻⁴Baruch read the book aloud to Jehoiachin son of Jehoiakim, king of Judah, and to all the people who lived in Babylon by the Sud River. Everyone came to hear it read — nobles, children of royal families, elders, in fact, all the people, no matter what their status.

⁵When the book was read, everyone cried, fasted, and prayed to the Lord. ⁶Then they all gave as much money as they could, ⁷and the collection was sent to Jerusalem to Jehoiakim the High Priest, son of Hilkiah and grandson of Shallum, and to the other priests and to all the people who were with him in Jerusalem.

⁸On the tenth day of the month of Sivan, Baruch took the sacred utensils which had been carried away from the Temple and returned them to Judah. These were the silver utensils which Zedekiah son of King Josiah of Judah had ordered made ⁹after King Nebuchadnezzar of Babylonia had deported Jehoiachin, the rulers, the skilled workers,*ᵇ* the nobles, and the common people and had taken them from Jerusalem to Babylon.

A Letter to Jerusalem

¹⁰The people wrote:

Please use the money we are sending you to buy animals for the burnt offerings and the sin offerings, to buy incense, and to provide the grain offerings. Offer them on the altar of the Lord our God, ¹¹and pray for King Nebuchadnezzar of Babylonia and his son Belshazzar, that they may live as long as the heavens last.

ᵃ THE MONTH: *The month is probably the fifth month of the Hebrew calendar (see 2 K 25.8; Jr 52.12).*   *ᵇ* skilled workers; *Greek* prisoners.
1.1 Jr 36.4   **1.3, 4** 2 K 24.8-17

Baruch read the book aloud. (1.3)

¹⁶ our kings, our rulers, our priests, our prophets, and our ancestors have been put to shame, ¹⁷ because we have sinned against the Lord our God ¹⁸ and have disobeyed him. We did not listen to him or live according to his commandments. ¹⁹ From the day the Lord brought our ancestors out of Egypt until the present day, we have continued to be unfaithful to him, and we have not hesitated to disobey him. ²⁰ Long ago, when the Lord led our ancestors out of Egypt, so that he could give us a rich and fertile land, he pronounced curses against us through his servant Moses. And today we are suffering because of those curses. ²¹ We refused to obey the word of the Lord our God which he spoke to us through the prophets. Instead, we all did as we pleased and went on our own evil way. We turned to other gods and did things the Lord hates.

2 "So the Lord carried out the threat he had made against us and against our judges, our kings, our rulers, and the people of Israel and Judah. ² Nowhere else on earth have such things happened as happened in Jerusalem when the Lord carried out the threats written in the Law of Moses. ³ Things were so bad that we even ate the flesh of our own sons and daughters. ⁴ The Lord scattered our people, handing us over to the control of all the nations around us, and they looked on us with reproach and horror. ⁵ We sinned against the Lord our God and refused to obey him. Therefore, our nation was conquered, instead of being victorious.

⁶ "The Lord our God is always righteous, but we and our ancestors are still burdened with our guilt. ⁷ Even though the Lord punished us as he had threatened, ⁸ we still did

¹² Then the Lord will strengthen us and be our guide. Nebuchadnezzar and his son Belshazzar will protect us, and we will be loyal to them as long as we live; then they will be pleased with us. ¹³ We ask you also to pray to the Lord God for us, because we have sinned against him, and he is still angry with us. ¹⁴ Please read this book that we are sending you and make your own confession of sin in the Temple on the first day of the Festival of Shelters and on other holy days of assembly.

A Confession of Sin

¹⁵ This is the confession you should make: "The Lord our God is righteous, but we are still covered with shame. All of us — the people of Judah, the people of Jerusalem,

not turn to him and pray that we would abandon our evil thoughts. ⁹⁻¹⁰We did not obey him or live by his just commands, so the Lord brought on us all the punishments he had kept ready for us.

The Prayer for Deliverance

¹¹"You, O Lord, are the God of Israel who brought your people out of Egypt with great power and with signs, miracles, and wonders. You showed your mighty strength and gained a glorious reputation, which is still recognized today. ¹²O Lord our God, we have sinned; we have been unfaithful; we have disobeyed all your commands. ¹³But do not be angry with us any longer. Here among the nations where you have scattered us, only a few of us are left. ¹⁴Listen to our prayer of petition, Lord, and rescue us for the sake of your own honor. Let those who have taken us into exile be pleased with us. ¹⁵Then the whole world will know that you are the Lord our God and that you have chosen the nation of Israel to be your own people.

¹⁶"O Lord, look down from heaven and see our misery. Listen to our prayer. ¹⁷Open your eyes and look upon us. Those in the world of the dead with no breath left in their bodies cannot offer praises to you or proclaim how just you are. ¹⁸Only the living, O Lord, can offer you praise and acknowledge your justice, even though they may be suffering greatly, bent and weak, hungry and with failing eyesight.

¹⁹"O Lord our God, we pray to you for mercy, but not because of any good things done by our ancestors and our kings. ²⁰You turned your anger and wrath against us, just as you had threatened to do when your servants the prophets spoke your word to

us and said, ²¹'Bend your backs and serve the king of Babylonia, and you can remain in the land that I gave to your ancestors. ²²But if you refuse to obey my command to serve him, ²³I will bring to an end every sound of joy and celebration in the towns of Judah and in Jerusalem. Even the happy sounds of wedding feasts will no longer be heard. The whole land will be desolate and uninhabited.'

²⁴"But we did not obey your command to serve the king of Babylonia, so you carried out the threat that you had made when you spoke through your servants the prophets, when you said that the bones of our kings and of our ancestors would be taken from their tombs and scattered. ²⁵And now here they lie exposed to the heat of the day and to the frost of the night. They died in torment from famine, war, and disease. ²⁶And because of the sin of the people of Israel and Judah, you have reduced your own Temple to ruins, even as it is today.

²⁷"But, Lord, you have been patient with us and have shown us great mercy, ²⁸as you promised through your servant Moses on the day you commanded him to write your Law in the presence of the Israelites. ²⁹'If you do not obey me,' you said, 'you will be reduced to a handful among the nations where I will scatter you. ³⁰I know that you will not obey me, because you are a stubborn people. But when you are taken into exile in another land, you will come to your senses. ³¹Then you will realize that I am the Lord your God, and I will give you a desire to know and a mind with which to understand. ³²There in the land of your exile you will praise me and remember me. ³³You will stop being so stubborn and wicked, for you will remember what happened to your

ancestors when they sinned against the Lord. ³⁴Then I will bring you back to the land that I solemnly promised to give to your ancestors, to Abraham, Isaac, and Jacob, and it will be yours again. I will increase your population, and you will never again be reduced to a small number. ³⁵I will make an everlasting covenant with you; I will be your God and you will be my people. I will never again remove you, the people of Israel, from the land that I gave you.'

3 "O Lord Almighty, God of Israel, from the depth of our troubled, weary souls we cry out to you. ²Hear us, O Lord, and have mercy on us, because we have sinned against you. ³You reign as king forever, but we die and are gone forever. ⁴O Lord Almighty, God of Israel, hear our prayer. We are no better off than the dead. Our ancestors sinned against you, the Lord their God. They refused to obey you, and we are suffering the consequences of their sin. ⁵Forget the sinful things that our ancestors did in the past; at a time like this, think only of your power and reputation, ⁶for you are the Lord our God, and we will praise you. ⁷You have made us fear you, so that we might pray to you. Here in exile we will praise you because we have turned away from the sins of our ancestors. ⁸You have scattered us among the nations, and you have made them despise and curse us. You are punishing us for the sins of our ancestors when they rebelled against you, the Lord our God."

In Praise of Wisdom

⁹Listen, Israel, to the commands that promise life; pay attention, and you will become wise. ¹⁰Why is it, Israel, that you find yourself in an enemy land? Why have you grown old in a foreign country? You are ritually unclean, like the dead; ¹¹you are already counted among the dead. But why? ¹²It is because you have left the source of Wisdom! ¹³If you had walked in God's ways, you would have lived in peace forever. ¹⁴Learn where understanding, strength, and insight are to be found. Then you will know where to find a long and full life, light to guide you, and peace.

¹⁵No one has ever found where Wisdom lives or has entered her treasure house, ¹⁶⁻¹⁷and those who have tried have vanished: the rulers of the nations, those who hunted wild animals and birds for sport, those who accumulated vast fortunes of silver and gold, which everyone trusts and will do anything to get, ¹⁸and those who worried and schemed to make money, but who left no trace of their work behind. ¹⁹They have all disappeared and gone down to the world of the dead. Others have come along to take their place. ²⁰A later generation was born and lived in the land, but they too did not discover the way to knowledge. They did not find the path to Wisdom or ever reach her. ²¹Their children also failed. ²²Wisdom was not found by the Canaanites. It has not been discovered by the Edomites ²³although they search after knowledge. The way to Wisdom has not been found by the merchants of Merran and Tema or by those who relate fables or by any others who seek understanding.

²⁴O Israel, how great is the universe in which God dwells! How vast is all that he possesses! ²⁵There is no end to it; there is no way to measure how wide or how high it is. ²⁶Here in early times the famous giants were born, a mighty race skilled in war. ²⁷But God did not choose them to be his people or show them the way of knowledge. ²⁸They

died out because they had neither understanding nor insight.

²⁹ No one has ever gone up into heaven to get Wisdom and bring her down out of the clouds. ³⁰ No one has sailed across the seas to find Wisdom or bought her with precious gold. ³¹ No one knows how to get to her or how to discover the path that leads to her.

³² The only one who knows Wisdom is God, and he knows all things. With his understanding he found her. He established the earth for all time and filled it with all kinds of animals. ³³ The light trembled and obeyed when he called. He sent it forth, and it appeared. ³⁴ He called the stars, and they promptly answered; they took their places and gladly shone to please the one who made them. ³⁵ He is our God, and there is none like him. ³⁶ He discovered the entire path leading to understanding and gave Wisdom to his servant Israel, whom he loved. ³⁷ From that time on, Wisdom appeared on earth and lived among us.

4 Wisdom is the book of God's commandments, the Law that will last forever. All who hold onto her will live, but those who abandon her will die. ² Turn to Wisdom, people of Israel, and take hold of her. Make your way toward the splendor of her light. ³ Do not surrender our glorious privileges to any other people. ⁴ How happy we are, people of Israel; we have the advantage of knowing what is pleasing to God!

Comfort for Jerusalem

⁵ Take courage, my people, you are the ones who keep Israel's name alive. ⁶ You were sold to Gentile nations, but not to be destroyed. Because you made God angry, he handed you over to your enemies. ⁷ When you offered sacrifices to demons instead of to God, you angered the one who made you. ⁸ You forgot the Eternal God, who had nourished you as a child, and so you brought grief to Jerusalem, who had been like a mother to you. ⁹ Jerusalem saw that God was punishing you because he was angry, and she said to all the neighboring cities, "Look at the great misery that God has brought on me. ¹⁰ I saw my sons and daughters taken into captivity, a captivity brought on them by the Eternal God. ¹¹ I brought up my children with great delight, but I cried and mourned when they were taken from me. ¹² Let no one take pleasure in my suffering now that I am a widow and so many of my children have been taken from me. They turned away from God's Law, and their sins have made me a deserted city. ¹³ They had no respect for his commandments and would not live by them; they refused to let him guide them in the way of righteousness.

¹⁴ "All you neighboring cities, come and consider how the Eternal God has sent my children into exile. ¹⁵ He brought against them a nation from far away, a shameless nation that speaks a foreign language and has no respect for the elderly and no pity for children. ¹⁶ These people carried off my beloved sons and took away my daughters, and I was left a widow, completely alone.

¹⁷ "My children in exile, I can do nothing to help you. ¹⁸ Only the one who brought this punishment upon you can rescue you from your enemies. ¹⁹ Go your own way, my children; live your own life! I am all alone. ²⁰ I have taken off the robes I wore during days of peace, and I have dressed myself like a person in mourning. I will cry out to the Eternal God for help as long as I live.

²¹ "Take courage, my children, and cry out to God for help. He will rescue you from oppression, from the power of your enemies. ²² I am confident that the

4.1 Si 24.23   **4.19** 2 Esd 2.2

I, the Eternal God, will send down fire on her. (4.35)

Eternal God will soon set you free. The Holy One, your eternal savior, will make me happy when he shows you mercy. ²³ I cried and wailed when you were taken away, but God will bring you back and will make me happy forever. ²⁴ Just as the neighboring cities watched as you were taken captive, so they will soon see the Eternal God coming in glorious splendor to rescue you. ²⁵ My children, endure God's punishment with patience. Your enemies have persecuted you, but you will soon see them destroyed and at your mercy. ²⁶ My children, I spoiled you with love, but you have had to follow rugged paths; you were carried off like sheep caught in an enemy raid.

²⁷ "Take courage, my children, and cry out to God for help. He punished you, but he will not forget you. ²⁸ Just as you were once determined to turn away from God, now turn back and serve him with ten times more determination. ²⁹ The one who brought these calamities upon you will rescue you and bring you everlasting joy."

Jerusalem Is Assured of Help

³⁰ Take courage, Jerusalem. God, who gave you your name, will now bring comfort to you. ³¹ Misery will come to those who mistreated you and then rejoiced when you fell. ³² Misery will come to those cities that made your children slaves. Misery will be the fate of Babylon, that city which swallowed up your children. ³³ Just as that city rejoiced when you fell and took delight in your ruin, so now she will mourn when she herself is deserted. ³⁴ I will turn her proud boastings into mourning and take away her large population in which she took pride. ³⁵ I, the Eternal God, will send down fire on her, and it will burn for many days. Her ruins will be haunted by demons for a long time to come.

³⁶ Look to the east, Jerusalem, and see the joy that God is bringing to you. ³⁷ Look, your children are coming home, the children that were taken from you. They have been gathered together from the east and from the west by the command of God, the Holy One. And now they are coming home, rejoicing in the glory of God.

5 Jerusalem, take off the clothes you have worn in your mourning and distress, and put on the eternal splendor of God's glory. ² Put around you the cloak of God's righteousness. Place on your head the crown of the glory of the Eternal God. ³ God will show your splendor to every nation on earth. ⁴ Forever he will say to you: "Your security comes from your righteousness, and your splendor from your devotion to me."[c]

⁵Get up, Jerusalem, stand on the mountaintop; see where God, the Holy One, is bringing your children together from the east and from the west. They are rejoicing that God has remembered them. ⁶Jerusalem, your children were led away by their enemies; they left you on foot, but God is bringing them back to you, carried in royal splendor. ⁷God has commanded that every high mountain and the everlasting hills shall be made low; he has commanded that the valleys shall be filled and the ground leveled, so that the people of Israel may come safely home in the glory of God. ⁸At the command of God, forests of fragrant trees will spring up to provide shade for the people of Israel. ⁹God will lead Israel home. They will return with great joy, guided by his mercy and righteousness, surrounded by the light of his glorious presence.

[c] Forever . . . devotion to me; *or* He will give you this name forever: "Peace from Righteousness and Glory from Godliness."

God will lead Israel home. . . . with great joy. (5.9)

The Letter of
JEREMIAH

INTRODUCTION

The Letter of Jeremiah is in the form of a letter, claiming to be written by the prophet Jeremiah to Jews who are about to be taken into exile. It consists primarily of a lengthy condemnation of idolatry.

OUTLINE OF CONTENTS

---

¹This is a copy of the letter sent by Jeremiah to the people of Jerusalem just before they were captured by the Babylonian king and taken to Babylon. It contains the message that God had commanded Jeremiah to give them.

The People Face a Long Captivity

²You have sinned against God. That is why you are about to be taken away as prisoners to Babylon by King Nebuchadnezzar. ³You will remain there in exile for many years, as long as seven generations; then God will lead you peacefully home from Babylon. ⁴There in Babylon you will see gods made of wood, silver, and gold — gods which people carry on their shoulders and which fill the heathen with fear. ⁵You must be careful never to imitate those Gentiles. Don't let their gods fill you with fear when you see them being carried in procession and being worshiped. ⁶Instead, say to yourselves, "It is you alone, Lord, that we must worship." ⁷God's angel will be there with you; he will take care of you.

The Helplessness of Idols

⁸Their idols are plated with silver and gold and have tongues that were carved by woodworkers. But they are not real gods, and they cannot speak. ⁹The people make gold crowns and put them on the heads of their gods, as if these idols were girls who love jewelry. ¹⁰Sometimes the priests steal the silver and gold from their gods and spend it on themselves; ¹¹they even give some of it to the temple prostitutes. People take these gods of wood, silver, and gold, and put clothes on them, as if they were human. ¹²But even though the gods are dressed in purple robes like kings, they still cannot keep themselves from being tarnished or protect themselves from termites. ¹³When dust from the temple settles on their faces, someone has to wipe it off for them. ¹⁴Like human judges they hold scepters in their hands, but they have no power to punish anyone who wrongs them. ¹⁵Sometimes they have daggers and axes in their hands, but they cannot protect themselves from being destroyed in war or from being carried off

by thieves. 16 All of this proves that they are not gods — do not worship them.

17 Those gods sitting in their temples are as useless as a broken bowl. Their eyes are filled with the dust that people kick up when they come in. 18 The priests fortify the temples with doors and bars and bolts, so that thieves cannot break in. The gods are locked up as securely as a prisoner about to be executed for a crime against the king. 19 The priests light lamps for the gods, far more than they need for their own use, but the idols can't see even one of them. 20 Their insides are eaten away by termites, just like the wooden beams of the temple, and their clothing is destroyed, but they don't even know it. 21 Their faces are blackened by the smoke in the temple. 22 Bats, swallows, and other birds perch on them, and even cats sit on them. 23 All of this proves that they are not gods — do not worship them.

24 These idols have been plated with gold to make them beautiful, but they do not shine unless someone polishes them. When they were being poured into molds, they felt nothing. 25 It makes no difference how high a price is paid for them; they are still unable to breathe. 26 See how useless they are! They can't walk on their own feet, but must be carried around. 27 Even those who take care of them are embarrassed when one of their gods falls to the ground and has to be picked up again. When someone stands one of them in a certain place, it cannot move, and if it is leaning over, it can never straighten itself up. Offering gifts to them is like giving gifts to a corpse. 28 Priests sell what is sacrificed to their gods and use the money on themselves. And the wives of the priests preserve the sacrifices with salt for later use, instead of sharing them with the poor and helpless. 29 Even women who are having their monthly period or women who have just given birth are allowed to touch the sacrifices. All of this proves

They . . . must be carried around. (1.26)

that they are not gods — do not worship them.

30 How can they ever be called gods, when women are allowed to make offerings to these things made of wood, silver, and gold? 31 The priests even sit in the temples when they are in mourning, with torn clothes and shaved, uncovered heads. 32 The priests roar and shout in the presence of their gods as if they were taking part in a funeral feast. 33 They take the clothing off their gods and give it to their wives and children. 34 It doesn't matter whether a person helps or harms these gods, since they cannot pay him back. They are not able to make anyone a king or to dethrone him, 35 and they cannot make a person wealthy or give him any money. If someone makes a vow to them but does not keep it, they will never make him pay. 36 They can never rescue a person from death, and they never help a weak person against one who is strong. 37 They cannot restore sight to the blind or save anyone in distress. 38 They cannot offer any mercy or give help to widows or orphans. 39 These things made of wood and covered with silver and gold are as powerless as stone taken from the mountains; and the people who

worship them will be put to shame.
⁴⁰How can anyone think that they are
gods or call them gods?

The Foolishness of Worshiping Idols

The Babylonians bring dishonor on
their own gods. ⁴¹When someone cannot speak, they take him to the temple
and ask Bel to give him the power of
speech, as if Bel could understand anything. ⁴²But even when the people realize that their gods cannot help, they are
stupid enough to go on worshiping
them. ⁴³Not only that, but women wrap
cords around themselves and sit alongside the road burning incense and offering themselves as prostitutes. When
one of them is taken off for sex, she returns to ridicule the woman next to her
who was not beautiful enough to be
chosen. ⁴⁴Everything about these idols
is false. How can anyone think that
they are gods or call them gods?

⁴⁵Woodworkers and goldsmiths
make these gods, so they can never be
anything other than what these people
want them to be. ⁴⁶Even their makers
do not live long lives, so how are they
able to create gods? ⁴⁷These people
leave nothing but deceit and disgrace
as an inheritance for future generations. ⁴⁸When wars and disturbances
come, the priests plan where they can
go into hiding with their gods. ⁴⁹These
idols are helpless in the face of wars and
disturbances. Why can't people realize
that these idols are not gods?

⁵⁰These idols are nothing more than
wood covered with silver and gold; one
day it will be clear that they are really
not gods at all. ⁵¹All nations and kings
will realize that idols are nothing more
than the work of human hands. They
do not have the power of a god, ⁵²and
anyone should know that they are not
really gods.

⁵³These gods can never make anyone a king or bring rain. ⁵⁴They can't

make decisions about their own affairs
or give justice to someone who has
been wronged; they can do absolutely
nothing. They are as useless as crows
flying around in the air. ⁵⁵When a temple catches on fire, the priests run away
to save themselves, while the gods
made of wood and covered with silver
and gold are left to burn like wooden
beams. ⁵⁶They can't fight kings or go to
war against enemies. How can anyone
believe that they are gods?

⁵⁷These gods of wood, covered with
silver and gold, cannot protect themselves from thieves and robbers ⁵⁸who
take off the silver and gold and the gods'
clothing and walk away with all of it.
The gods can do nothing to stop them.
⁵⁹Anything from a courageous king to a
useful piece of pottery is better than a
false god. Even a door is better than
a false god; a door at least protects the
things in the house. Even a wooden pillar in a palace is better than a false god.

⁶⁰God provided the sun, the moon,
and the stars to give light, and they
obey him. ⁶¹The same is true of lightning and wind. The lightning can be
seen far and wide, and the wind blows
everywhere. ⁶²When God commands
clouds to spread out over the whole
world, they obey. ⁶³When God sends
down fire from heaven to burn up
mountains and forests, it does what it is
told. Idols cannot do these things —
they can't even do a good imitation.
⁶⁴Why should they be called gods,
when they are not able to help us or
harm us in any way? ⁶⁵You know that
they are not gods — do not worship
them.

⁶⁶These gods have no power over
kings; they cannot pronounce curses
on them or grant them blessings.
⁶⁷They cannot produce for the nations
any signs in the sky; they cannot shine
like the sun or the moon. ⁶⁸Even wild
animals are better off than these idols;

41 Is 46.1

animals can at least run from danger to protect themselves. [69] So it is absolutely clear that they are not gods — do not worship them.

[70] These gods of theirs, made of wood and covered with silver and gold, are about as helpful as a scarecrow in a cucumber patch; they are no protection at all. [71] They do as much good as a thorn bush in a garden; instead of keeping birds away, they provide a perch for

them. These gods are like a dead body thrown out into the darkness. [72] The purple linen[a] robes they wear rot away, so we know that they are not gods. Finally they will be eaten by termites, and then no one anywhere will have any use for them.

[73] The righteous person has an advantage over others; he does not own any idols, and they can never make a fool of him.

---

[a] linen; *Greek* marble.

THE PRAYER OF AZARIAH AND THE SONG OF
THE THREE YOUNG MEN

INTRODUCTION

The Prayer of Azariah and the Song of the Three Young Men is one of the three major additions to *The Book of Daniel* in the Greek version. This insertion between 3.23 and 3.24 of *Daniel* gives the prayer of Azariah and the song of the three young men after King Nebuchadnezzar had them thrown into the blazing furnace.

OUTLINE OF CONTENTS

Prayer of Azariah   1-22
Description of the fiery furnace   23-27
The song of the three young men   28-68

The Prayer of Azariah

[1] The three young men, Hananiah, Mishael, and Azariah,[a] started walking around in the flames, singing hymns to God, and praising him as Lord. [2] Then Azariah stood still and

there in the fire he prayed aloud: [3] "O Lord, the God of our ancestors, we praise and adore you; may your name be honored forever. [4] You have treated us as we deserve. In everything you have done to us you are always honest, and when you bring us to judgment,

---

[a] HANANIAH, MISHAEL, AND AZARIAH: *These are the original names of Shadrach, Meshach, and Abednego (see Dn 1.6, 7).*
1 Dn 3.23

you are always fair. ⁵You did what was right when you brought disaster upon Jerusalem, the holy city of our ancestors. We deserved that judgment because of our sins. ⁶We disobeyed you, we turned our backs on you, and we are guilty of every sin. ⁷We did not do the things that you commanded us to do. If we had obeyed your laws, we would have prospered, ⁸but now we deserve the judgment and punishment that you have brought upon us. ⁹You have handed us over to lawless, hateful, and defiant enemies — to the most wicked king in the world. ¹⁰And now all of us who worship you are humiliated; we are too ashamed to open our mouths.

¹¹"Yet for the sake of your own honor, do not break your covenant with us and abandon us forever. ¹²Do not withhold your mercy from us. Keep your promises to Abraham, whom you loved, to Isaac, your servant, and to Jacob, the father of your holy people Israel. ¹³You promised to give them as many descendants as the stars in the sky or as the grains of sand along the seashore. ¹⁴But now, Lord, we are fewer in number than any other nation; wherever we are, we live in disgrace because of our sins. ¹⁵We are left without a king, without any prophets or leaders. There is no longer a Temple where we can go to offer you burnt offerings, sacrifices, gifts, or incense, no place where we can make offerings to you and find your mercy. ¹⁶But we come to you with repentant hearts and humble spirits, begging you to accept us just as if we had come with burnt offerings of rams and bulls and thousands of fat lambs. ¹⁷Accept our repentance as our sacrifice to you today, so that we may obey you with all our hearts. No one who trusts you will ever be disappointed. ¹⁸⁻¹⁹Now with all our hearts we promise to obey you, worship you, and come to you in prayer. Treat us with kindness

and mercy, and let us never be put to shame. ²⁰O Lord, rescue us with one of your miracles; bring honor to your name.

²¹"Bring disgrace and shame on all who harm us. Take away their might and power and crush their strength. ²²Let them know that you alone are Lord and God and that you rule in majesty over the whole world."

²³The king's servants who had thrown the three men into the furnace kept the fire hot by feeding it with oil, tar, flax, and brushwood. ²⁴The flames blazed up to a height of seventy-five feet ²⁵and even spread out and burned up the Babylonians standing near the furnace. ²⁶But an angel of the Lord came down into the fire where the three men were. He pushed aside the flames ²⁷so that it felt as if a cool breeze were blowing, and the fire did not touch the men at all or hurt them in any way.

The Song of the Three Young Men

²⁸There in the furnace the three young men again started singing together in praise of God:

²⁹"We praise you, O Lord, the God
    of our ancestors.
³⁰May your glorious, holy name
    be held in honor and
    reverence forever.
³¹May hymns be sung to your
    glory forever
    and may your holy presence
    be praised in that temple,
³²   where you sit on your
    heavenly throne above the
    winged creatures
    and look down to the world of
    the dead.
    May you be praised and
    honored forever.
³³May you be praised as you sit on
    your royal throne.

The three young men again started singing. (v.28)

May hymns be sung to your glory forever.
³⁴ May you be praised in the dome of the heavens.
May hymns be sung to your glory forever.

³⁵ "Praise the Lord, all creation;
sing his praise and honor him forever.
³⁶ Praise the Lord, skies above;
sing his praise and honor him forever.
³⁷ Praise the Lord, all angels of the Lord;
sing his praise and honor him forever.
³⁸ Praise the Lord, all waters above the sky;
sing his praise and honor him forever.
³⁹ Praise the Lord, all heavenly powers;
sing his praise and honor him forever.
⁴⁰ Praise the Lord, sun and moon;
sing his praise and honor him forever.
⁴¹ Praise the Lord, stars of heaven;
sing his praise and honor him forever.

⁴² Praise the Lord, rain and dew;
sing his praise and honor him forever.
⁴³ Praise the Lord, all winds;
sing his praise and honor him forever.
⁴⁴ Praise the Lord, fire and heat;
sing his praise and honor him forever.
⁴⁵ Praise the Lord, bitter cold and scorching heat;
sing his praise and honor him forever.
⁴⁶ Praise the Lord, dews and snows;
sing his praise and honor him forever.
⁴⁷ Praise the Lord, nights and days;
sing his praise and honor him forever.
⁴⁸ Praise the Lord, daylight and darkness;
sing his praise and honor him forever.
⁴⁹ Praise the Lord, ice and cold;
sing his praise and honor him forever.
⁵⁰ Praise the Lord, frost and snow;
sing his praise and honor him forever.
⁵¹ Praise the Lord, lightning and storm clouds;

sing his praise and honor him
forever.

52 "Let the earth praise the Lord;
sing his praise and honor him
forever.
53 Praise the Lord, mountains and
hills;
sing his praise and honor him
forever.
54 Praise the Lord, everything that
grows;
sing his praise and honor him
forever.
55 Praise the Lord, lakes and rivers;
sing his praise and honor him
forever.
56 Praise the Lord, springs of water;
sing his praise and honor him
forever.
57 Praise the Lord, whales and sea
creatures;
sing his praise and honor him
forever.
58 Praise the Lord, all birds;
sing his praise and honor him
forever.
59 Praise the Lord, all cattle and
wild animals;
sing his praise and honor him
forever.

60 "Praise the Lord, all people on
earth;
sing his praise and honor him
forever.
61 Praise the Lord, people of Israel;

sing his praise and honor him
forever.
62 Praise the Lord, priests of the
Lord;
sing his praise and honor him
forever.
63 Praise the Lord, servants of the
Lord;
sing his praise and honor him
forever.
64 Praise the Lord, all faithful
people;
sing his praise and honor him
forever.
65 Praise the Lord, all who are
humble and holy;
sing his praise and honor him
forever.
66 Praise the Lord, Hananiah,
Azariah, and Mishael;
sing his praise and honor him
forever.
He rescued us from the world of
the dead
and saved us from the power
of death.
He brought us out from the
burning furnace
and saved us from the fire.
67 Give thanks to the Lord, for he is
good
and his mercy lasts forever.
68 Praise the Lord, all who
worship him;
sing praise to the God of gods
and give him thanks,
for his mercy lasts forever."

The Book of
SUSANNA

INTRODUCTION

The Book of Susanna is a story that was added to *The Book of Daniel,* evidently when the latter was translated into Greek. The book tells how the beautiful and virtuous Susanna, falsely charged with adultery, is cleared by the wisdom and courage of Daniel.

OUTLINE OF CONTENTS

Susanna's Beauty Attracts Two Judges

¹In Babylon there lived a man named Joakim, ²who was married to Susanna, daughter of Hilkiah. Susanna was a beautiful woman and deeply religious. ³Her parents were devout Jews who had brought up their daughter to live according to the Law of Moses. ⁴Her husband Joakim was very wealthy. Lovely gardens surrounded his house, and the other Jews often gathered there for meetings, because they all thought so highly of him. ⁵⁻⁶Everyone who had a legal case to present would also go to Joakim's house, where two judges held court. These two leaders of the Jewish community had recently been appointed to office. They were the ones about whom the Lord said, "There is wickedness in Babylon; judges are failing to give guidance to the people."

⁷Every day at noon, when all the people left for lunch, Susanna used to take a walk in the gardens. ⁸The two judges were so attracted to her that they would wait around and watch for her. ⁹They became so obsessed with their desire for her that they lost interest both in prayer and in their responsibility as judges. ¹⁰They each wanted Susanna, but neither told the other how he felt, ¹¹for each was ashamed to admit his lust. ¹²So day after day they watched eagerly to catch sight of her.

¹³One day at noon they said to each other, "It's time for lunch; let's go home." ¹⁴So they both left and went their separate ways, but soon each one came back for a look at Susanna, and by accident they met each other. At first each tried to explain what he was doing there, but finally they both confessed their desire for Susanna. They decided to watch for a time when they might find her alone. ¹⁵⁻¹⁷So they kept waiting for the right opportunity.

The Judges Try to Seduce Susanna

One day Susanna went into the garden as usual with her two servant women. No one else was there, except the two judges, who had hidden themselves and were watching Susanna. It was very hot and she decided to take a bath. So she said to her servants, "Bring me some bath oil and some perfume, and lock the gates, so that I won't be

Each one came back for a look at Susanna. (v.14)

disturbed." ¹⁸ The servants locked the main gates and went out by the side door to get what Susanna had asked for. They did not notice the two men.

¹⁹ As soon as the servants had left, the two judges jumped out from their hiding place, ran to Susanna, ²⁰ and said to her, "The gates are locked and no one will see us. We are burning to have sex with you, so give us what we want. ²¹ If you don't, we will go to court and swear that we saw you send your servants away, so that you could be alone with a young man."

²² "There is no way out," Susanna moaned. "If I give in to you, I could be put to death for adultery. If I refuse, you will still have me trapped. ²³ But I would rather be your innocent victim than sin against the Lord." ²⁴ So she started screaming as loud as she could, and the two judges began shouting accusations, ²⁵ while one of them ran and unlocked the gates.

²⁶ As soon as the servants in the house heard all the noise, they ran into the gardens through the side door to find out what had happened to Susanna. ²⁷ The judges told their story, and the servants were shocked and

ashamed. Such a thing had never before been said about Susanna.

The Judges Testify against Susanna

²⁸ The next day, when the people assembled at Joakim's house, the two judges arrived, fully determined to carry out their wicked plan to have Susanna put to death. ²⁹ In front of all the people they said, "Send for Joakim's wife Susanna, the daughter of Hilkiah." When she was called, ³⁰ she came in with her parents, her children, and all her other relatives. ³¹ Susanna was so graceful and beautiful ³² that the two wicked men ordered her veil to be removed, so that they might enjoy looking at her. ³³ Her family and everyone else were in tears.

³⁴ Then the two judges stood up in front of the people, placed their hands on Susanna's head, and began making their accusations against her. ³⁵ She was crying, but she looked up to heaven because she trusted the Lord. ³⁶ The two men gave the following testimony: "We were walking in the gardens when this woman came in with her two servant women. She locked the main gates and asked the servants to leave. ³⁷ Then

a young man who had been hiding in the gardens came to her, and they lay down together. ³⁸We were in a corner of the gardens, and when we saw what was happening, we ran over ³⁹and caught them in the act. We tried to hold on to the man, but he was too strong for us. He ran and opened the gates and got away, ⁴⁰but we were able to hold the woman. We asked her who the man was, but she refused to tell us. We swear that our testimony is true." ⁴¹Because the two men were not only leaders in the community but also judges, the people believed their story and condemned Susanna to death.

Daniel Rescues Susanna

⁴²Then Susanna cried out in a loud voice, "Eternal God, nothing can be kept secret from you; you know everything before it happens. ⁴³Here I am about to die, but you know that I am innocent, that these men are lying. Why must I die?"

⁴⁴The Lord heard her prayer ⁴⁵and led a young man named Daniel to speak out, just as Susanna was being taken away to her death. ⁴⁶He shouted, "I refuse to be a party to her death!"

⁴⁷Everyone turned around to look at him and asked, "What are you talking about?"

⁴⁸Daniel stood up before them and said, "People of Israel, how foolish can you be? Are you going to condemn an Israelite woman to death on this kind of evidence? You haven't even tried to find out the truth. ⁴⁹Reopen the case. The testimony these men gave was a lie."

⁵⁰So all the people hurried back to where the trial had taken place, and the officials said to Daniel, "God has given you wisdom beyond your years, so come

and join us and explain to us what you mean."

⁵¹Daniel said to them, "Separate the two judges, and let me question them one at a time." ⁵²Then Daniel called the first judge and said, "You wicked old man, now you will have to answer for all the sins you have committed. ⁵³You have been giving unjust sentences. You have condemned the innocent and released the guilty, even though the Lord has said, 'Do not put an innocent person to death.' ⁵⁴Now if you really did see this couple making love, tell me, what tree were they under?"

"Under a small gum tree," he answered.

⁵⁵Daniel said, "All right! That lie will cost you your life. God's angel has already been given orders to chop^a you in two."

⁵⁶Then the first judge was led away and the second one was brought before Daniel. "You are more like a Canaanite than a Jew," Daniel said to him. "This woman's beauty has warped your judgment, and lust has corrupted your thinking. ⁵⁷You are used to having your way with the women of Israel because they have been afraid of you, but here is a Jewish woman, and she would not give in. ⁵⁸Now, tell me what tree you saw them under."

"Under a large oak tree," he answered.

⁵⁹Daniel said, "All right! That lie will cost you your life; God's angel is waiting with his sword in his hand, ready to cut^b you in two. Then we shall be rid of you both."

⁶⁰Then all the people shouted and praised God, who saves those who put their trust in him. ⁶¹They turned against the two judges because Daniel had proved that they had lied under oath. ⁶²The Law of Moses states that people who give false testimony shall

---

^a CHOP: *This word in Greek sounds like the Greek for "a small gum tree."*   ^b CUT: *This word in Greek sounds like the Greek for "a large oak tree."*

53 Ex 23.7   **62** Dt 19.16-21

receive the same punishment that the accused person would have received. And so the two judges were put to death, and the life of an innocent woman was saved. ⁶³Susanna's par-

ents, her husband, and all her relatives praised God because she had been proved innocent of the charges. ⁶⁴From that day on, Daniel was held in high regard.

BEL AND THE DRAGON

INTRODUCTION

Bel and the Dragon consists of two stories which were added to the Greek translation of *The Book of Daniel.* The first tells of Daniel's wisdom and courage in revealing the falseness of the idol Bel, and the second describes how he destroyed a dragon which was worshiped by the Babylonians.

OUTLINE OF CONTENTS

Daniel and the Priests of Bel

¹After the death of King Astyages, Cyrus of Persia took over his kingdom. ²Daniel was one of King Cyrus' closest companions, and the king thought more highly of Daniel than of any other of his advisers.

³The Babylonians had an idol named Bel. Each day the people had to provide Bel with an offering of twelve bushels of fine flour, forty sheep, and fifty gallons of wine. ⁴King Cyrus believed that Bel was a god, and each day he used to go and worship it. But Daniel worshiped his own God.

⁵One day the king asked Daniel, "Why don't you worship Bel?"

Daniel answered, "I do not worship idols made with human hands. I wor-

ship only the living God, who created heaven and earth and is the Lord of all human beings."

⁶"And don't you believe that our god Bel is really alive?" asked the king. "Haven't you seen how much he eats and drinks every day?"

⁷Daniel laughed and said, "Don't be fooled, Your Majesty. This god you call Bel is nothing more than clay covered with bronze; it has never eaten or drunk anything."

⁸⁻¹⁰At this the king became angry and called in all seventy of the priests of Bel. He said to them, "I warn you that you will be put to death, unless you can show me that it is Bel who is eating these offerings. If you prove to me that it is Bel, then I will have Daniel put to death for claiming that Bel is not a god."

3 Is 46.1; Jr 51.44

The king set out the food for Bel. (1.14)

Daniel agreed to this proposal.

11 Then they all went with the king into Bel's temple, where the priests said to the king, "Your Majesty, we will go out and let you place the food on the table and prepare the wine. When you leave, you may lock the door behind you and seal it with the royal seal. 12 In the morning when you return, if you find that Bel has not eaten everything, you can put us to death. But if he has, Daniel will die for making false accusations against us."

13 But the priests were not worried, because they had made a secret entrance underneath a table in the temple, so that they could go in every night and eat the offerings.

14 When the priests had left, the king set out the food for Bel. Then Daniel ordered his servants to bring some ashes and scatter them all over the floor of the temple. No one except the king saw them do this. After that they all went out, locked the door, sealed it with the royal seal, and left.

15 That night, as usual, the priests with their wives and children came into the temple by the secret entrance and ate all the food and drank all the wine.

16 Early the next morning, the king and Daniel went to the temple. 17 The king asked, "Have the seals been broken, Daniel?"

"No, Your Majesty, they have not been broken," he replied.

18 As soon as the door was opened, the king saw the empty table and shouted, "You are great, O Bel! You really are a god."

19 But Daniel began to laugh and said to the king, "Before you enter the temple, look at the floor and tell me whose footprints you see there."

20 "I see the footprints of men, women, and children," said the king, 21 and he became so angry that he had the priests and their families arrested and brought to him. They showed him the secret doors through which they had come in each night to eat the food placed on the table. 22 So the king had the priests put to death, and he gave Bel to Daniel, who destroyed the idol and tore down its temple.

He gave Bel to Daniel, who destroyed the idol. (1.22)

Daniel Kills the Dragon

23 There was also a huge dragon which the Babylonians worshiped. 24 One day the king said to Daniel, "You can't tell me that this god is not alive. So worship him!"

25 "I worship the Lord," replied Daniel. "He is the only living God. 26 And if Your Majesty will give me permission, I will kill this dragon of yours without using a sword or a club."

"You have my permission," answered the king.

²⁷So Daniel took some tar, some fat, and some hair and boiled them all together. He made cakes out of the mixture and fed them to the dragon. When the dragon ate them, it swelled up and burst open. "That's the kind of thing you Babylonians worship," said Daniel.

²⁸When the people of Babylon heard what had happened, they staged an angry demonstration against the king. "The king has become a Jew," they shouted. "First he destroyed Bel and slaughtered the priests, and now he has killed our dragon." ²⁹They went to the king and demanded that Daniel be handed over to them. "If you refuse," they warned the king, "we will put you and your family to death."

³⁰When the king saw that they meant what they said, he was forced to hand Daniel over to them. ³¹They threw him into a pit of lions, where they left him for six days. ³²There were seven lions in the pit, and normally they were fed two human bodies and two sheep each day. But they were given nothing to eat during these six days, in order to make sure that Daniel would be eaten.

Daniel Is Rescued from the Pit of Lions

³³At that time the prophet Habakkuk was in the land of Judah. He had cooked a stew and crumbled bread into it. He was carrying a bowl of it to the workers who were out in the fields harvesting grain, ³⁴when an angel of the Lord spoke to him, "Take the food you are carrying and give it to Daniel, who is in Babylon in a pit of lions."

³⁵Habakkuk answered, "Sir, I have never been to Babylon, and I don't know where the pit of lions is."

³⁶So the angel grabbed the prophet by the hair and took him to Babylon with the speed of the wind.ᵃ He set him down near the pit of lions. ³⁷Habakkuk called out, "Daniel! Daniel! God has sent you some food. Here, take it."

³⁸When Daniel heard Habakkuk, he prayed, "God, you did remember me; you never abandon those who love you." ³⁹Then he got up and ate the meal, and God's angel immediately took Habakkuk home.

⁴⁰Seven days after Daniel had been thrown to the lions, the king went to the pit to mourn for him. When he got there and looked in, there sat Daniel. ⁴¹The king shouted, "O Lord, the God of Daniel, how great you are. You alone are

The king shouted, "O Lord, the God of Daniel, how great you are." (1.41)

God." ⁴²So he pulled Daniel out of the pit and had those who had tried to kill Daniel thrown into it. And the lions ate them immediately, while the king watched.

ᵃ with the speed of the wind; *or* by the power of his spirit.
31, 32 Dn 6.16-24 **36** Ez 8.3

The First Book of the
MACCABEES

INTRODUCTION

The First Book of the Maccabees describes events in Jewish history from the time of Antiochus Epiphanes (175 B.C.) to the rise of John Hyrcanus (134 B.C.).

The historical interest of the book centers in the Hasmonean, or Maccabean, family, and it supports the view that they are divinely chosen to save Israel. The book also has a strong religious theme: God is at work in history and will give victory as a reward to those who are faithful to him.

OUTLINE OF CONTENTS

Alexander the Great

1 This history begins when Alexander the Great, son of Philip of Macedonia, marched from Macedonia and attacked Darius, king of Persia and Media. Alexander enlarged the Greek Empire by defeating Darius and seizing his throne. ²He fought many battles, captured fortified cities, and put the kings of the region to death. ³As he advanced to the ends of the earth, he plundered many nations; and when he had conquered the world, he became proud and arrogant. ⁴By building up a strong army, he dominated whole nations and their rulers, and forced everyone to pay him taxes.

⁵⁻⁷When Alexander had been emperor for twelve years, he fell ill and realized that he was about to die. He called together his generals, noblemen who had been brought up with him since his early childhood, and he divided his empire, giving a part to each of them. ⁸After his death, the generals took control, ⁹and each had himself crowned king of his own territory. The descendants of these kings ruled for many generations and brought a great deal of misery on the world.

Antiochus Epiphanes and the Renegade Jews
(2 Maccabees 4.7-17)

¹⁰The wicked ruler Antiochus Epiphanes, son of King Antiochus the Third of Syria, was a descendant of one of Alexander's generals. Antiochus Epiphanes had been a hostage in Rome before he became king of Syria in the year 137.ᵃ

¹¹At that time there appeared in the land of Israel a group of traitorous Jews who had no regard for the Law and who

---

ᵃ THE YEAR 137: *The dates in this book are counted from the beginning of the Syrian Kingdom in 312 B.C. The year 137 corresponds to 175 B.C.*
1.10 2 Macc 4.7

PALESTINE IN THE
TIME OF THE MACCABEES

Miles
0   40

Kms
0   40

Sidon

Damascus

MT. HERMON

S Y R I A

P H O E N I C I A

Tyre

MEDITERRANEAN

Kedesh

Hazor

Seleucia

SEA

Ptolemais

GALILEE

Baskama

Lake
Galilee

Karnaim

MT. CARMEL

Dor

Ephron

G I L E A D

Beth Shan

SAMARIA

Samaria

Jordan River

AMMON

Joppa

Lydda

Modein

Ephraim

Jamnia

Gezer

Beth
Horon

Berea

Mizpah

Jericho

Emmaus

Jerusalem

Azotus

Ekron

J U D E A

Bethbasi

Medeba

Ascalon

Marisa

Beth
Zechariah

Dead
Sea

Gaza

Bethzur

Hebron

P H I L I S T I A

I D U M E A

N A B A T E A

© United Bible Societies 1978

had a bad influence on many of our people. They said, "Let's come to terms with the Gentiles, for our refusal to associate with them has brought us nothing but trouble." 12 This proposal appealed to many people, 13 and some of them became so enthusiastic about it that they went to the king and received from him permission to follow Gentile customs. 14 They built in Jerusalem a stadium like those in the Greek cities. 15 They had surgery performed to hide their circumcision, abandoned the holy covenant, started associating with[b] Gentiles, and did all sorts of other evil things.

Antiochus Attacks Egypt

16 When Antiochus had firmly established himself as king, he decided to conquer Egypt and rule that country as well as Syria. 17 He invaded Egypt with a large fleet of ships and a powerful army, including chariots, elephants, and cavalry. 18 When the attack came, King Ptolemy of Egypt turned and fled, and many of his soldiers were killed. 19 Antiochus was able to capture the fortified cities of Egypt and plunder the whole land.

Antiochus Persecutes the Jews

20 In the year 143,[c] after the conquest of Egypt, Antiochus marched with a great army against the land of Israel and the city of Jerusalem. 21 In his arrogance, he entered the Temple and took away the gold altar, the lampstand with all its equipment, 22 the table for the bread offered to the Lord, the cups and bowls, the gold fire pans, the curtain, and the crowns. He also stripped all the gold from the front of the Temple 23 and carried off the silver and gold and everything else of value, including all the treasures that he could find stored there. 24 Then he took it all to his own country. He had also murdered many people and boasted arrogantly about it. 25 There was great mourning everywhere in the land of Israel.

26 Rulers and leaders groaned in
　　sorrow.
Young men and young women
　　grew weak.
The beauty of our women faded.
27 Every bridegroom sang a funeral
　　song,
　　and every bride sat mourning in
　　her room.

---

[b] started associating with; or married.
[c] THE YEAR 143: This corresponds to 169 B.C.
1.15 1 Co 7.18

Then he took it all to his own country. (1.24)

28 All our people were clothed with
shame,
and our land trembled for them.

29 Two years later Antiochus sent a
large army from Mysia[d] against the
towns of Judea. When the soldiers entered Jerusalem, 30 their commander
spoke to the people, offering them
terms of peace and completely deceiving them. Then he suddenly launched
a fierce attack on the city, dealing it a
major blow and killing many of the people. 31 He plundered the city, set it on
fire, and tore down its buildings and
walls. 32 He and his army took the
women and children as prisoners and
seized the cattle.

33 Then Antiochus and his forces
built high walls and strong towers in
the area north of the Temple, turning it
into a fort. 34 They brought in a group of
traitorous Jews and installed them
there. 35 They also brought in arms and
supplies and stored in the fort all the
loot that they had taken in Jerusalem.
This fort became a great threat to the
city.

36 The fort was a threat to the
Temple,
a constant, evil menace for
Israel.
37 Innocent people were murdered
around the altar;
the Holy Place was defiled by
murderers.
38 The people of Jerusalem fled
in fear,
and the city became a colony of
foreigners.
Jerusalem was foreign to its own
people,
who had been forced to abandon
the city.
39 Her Temple was as empty as a
wilderness;
her festivals were turned into
days of mourning,

her Sabbath joy into shame.
Her honor became an object of
ridicule.
40 Her shame was as great as her
former glory,
and her pride was turned into
deepest mourning.

41-43 Antiochus now issued a decree
that all nations in his empire should
abandon their own customs and become one people. All the Gentiles and
even many of the Israelites submitted
to this decree. They adopted the official
pagan religion, offered sacrifices to
idols, and no longer observed the
Sabbath.

44 The king also sent messengers
with a decree to Jerusalem and all the
towns of Judea, ordering the people to
follow customs that were foreign to the
country. 45 He ordered them not to offer
burnt offerings, grain offerings, or wine
offerings in the Temple, and commanded them to treat Sabbaths and festivals as ordinary work days. 46 They
were even ordered to defile the Temple
and the holy things in it.[e] 47 They were
commanded to build pagan altars, temples, and shrines, and to sacrifice pigs
and other unclean animals there.
48 They were forbidden to circumcise
their sons and were required to make
themselves ritually unclean in every
way they could, 49 so that they would
forget the Law which the Lord had
given through Moses and would disobey all its commands. 50 The penalty
for disobeying the king's decree was
death.

51 The king not only issued the same
decree throughout his whole empire,
but he also appointed officials to supervise the people and commanded each
town in Judea to offer pagan sacrifices.
52 Many of the Jews were ready to forsake the Law and to obey these officials. They defiled the land with their

---

[d] *Probable text* a large army from Mysia; *Greek* a tax collector with a large army.
[e] the holy things in it; *or* the priests.

evil, ⁵³ and their conduct forced all true Israelites to hide wherever they could.

⁵⁴ On the fifteenth day of the month of Kislev in the year 145,ᶠ King Antiochus set up "The Awful Horror" on the altar of the Temple, and pagan altars were built in the towns throughout Judea. ⁵⁵ Pagan sacrifices were offered in front of houses and in the streets. ⁵⁶ Any books of the Law which were found were torn up and burned, ⁵⁷ and anyone who was caught with a copy of the sacred books or who obeyed the Law was put to death by order of the king. ⁵⁸ Month after month these wicked people used their power against the Israelites caught in the towns.

⁵⁹ On the twenty-fifth of the month, these same evil people offered sacrifices on the pagan altar erected on top of the altar in the Temple. ⁶⁰ Mothers who had allowed their babies to be circumcised were put to death in accordance with the king's decree. ⁶¹ Their babies were hung around their necks, and their families and those who had circumcised them were put to death. ⁶² But many people in Israel firmly resisted the king's decree and refused to eat food that was ritually unclean. ⁶³ They preferred to die rather than break the holy covenant and eat unclean food — and many did die. ⁶⁴ In his anger God made Israel suffer terribly.

The Faithfulness of Mattathias

2 During that time, a priest of the Jehoiarib family named Mattathias, who was the son of John and the grandson of Simeon, moved from Jerusalem and settled in Modein. ² Mattathias had five sons: John (also called Gaddi), ³ Simon (also called Thassi), ⁴ Judas (also called Maccabeus), ⁵ Eleazar (also called Avaran), and Jonathan (also called Apphus).

⁶ When Mattathias saw all the sins

that were being committed in Judea and Jerusalem, ⁷ he said:

"Why was I born to see these
   terrible things,
   the ruin of my people and of
   the holy city?
Must I sit here helpless
   while the city is surrendered
   to enemies
   and the Temple falls into the
   hands of foreigners?
⁸ The Temple is like someone
   without honor.
⁹ Its splendid furnishings
   have been carried away as
   loot.
Our children have been killed in
   the streets,
   and our young men by the
   sword of the enemy.
¹⁰ Every nation in the world has
   occupied the city
   and robbed her of her
   possessions.
¹¹ All her ornaments have been
   stripped away;
   she is now a slave, no longer
   free.
¹² Look at our Temple, profaned by
   the Gentiles,
   emptied of all its splendor.
¹³ Why should we go on living?"

¹⁴ In their grief, Mattathias and his sons tore their clothes, put on sackcloth, and continued in deep mourning. ¹⁵ Then the king's officials, who were forcing the people to turn from God, came to the town of Modein to force the people there to offer pagan sacrifices. ¹⁶ Many of the Israelites came to meet them, including Mattathias and his sons. ¹⁷ The king's officials said to Mattathias, "You are a respected leader in this town, and you have the support of your sons and relatives. ¹⁸ Why not be the first one here to do what the king

ᶠ THE YEAR 145: *This corresponds to 167 B.C.*
1.54 Dn 9.27; 11.31; 12.11; 1 Macc 6.7; Mt 24.15; Mk 13.14   **1.60** 2 Macc 6.10

"We will not obey the king's decree." (2.22)

has commanded? All the Gentiles, the people of Judea, and all the people left in Jerusalem have already done so. If you do, you and your sons will be honored with the title of 'Friends of the King,' and you will be rewarded with silver and gold and many gifts."

¹⁹ Mattathias answered in a loud voice, "I don't care if every Gentile in this empire has obeyed the king and yielded to the command to abandon the religion of his ancestors. ²⁰ My children, my relatives, and I will continue to keep the covenant that God made with our ancestors. ²¹ With God's help we will never abandon his Law or disobey his commands. ²² We will not obey the king's decree, and we will not change our way of worship in the least."

²³ Just as he finished speaking, one of the men from Modein decided to obey the king's decree and stepped out in front of everyone to offer a pagan sacrifice on the altar that stood there. ²⁴ When Mattathias saw him, he became angry enough to do what had to be done. Shaking with rage, he ran forward and killed the man right there on the altar. ²⁵ He also killed the royal official who was forcing the people to sacrifice, and then he tore down the altar.

²⁶ In this way Mattathias showed his deep devotion for the Law, just as Phinehas had done when he killed Zimri son of Salu.

The Guerrilla Warfare of Mattathias

²⁷ Then Mattathias went through the town shouting, "Everyone who is faithful to God's covenant and obeys his Law, follow me!" ²⁸ With this, he and his sons fled to the mountains, leaving behind all they owned.

²⁹⁻³⁰ At that time also many of the Israelites who were seeking to be right with God through obedience to the Law went out to live in the wilderness, taking their children, their wives, and their livestock with them, because of the terrible oppression they were suffering. ³¹ The report soon reached the king's officials and the soldiers in the fort at Jerusalem that some men who had defied the king's command had gone into hiding in the wilderness. ³² A large force of soldiers pursued them, caught up with them, set up camp opposite them, and prepared to attack them on the Sabbath. ³³ "There is still time," they shouted out to the Jews. "Come out and

2.26 Nu 25.6-15   **2.32** 2 Macc 6.11

obey the king's command, and we will spare your lives."

34"We will not come out," they answered. "We will not obey the king's command, and we will not profane the Sabbath."

35The soldiers attacked them immediately, 36but the Jews did nothing to resist; they did not even throw stones or block the entrances to the caves where they were hiding. 37They said, "We will all die with a clear conscience. Let heaven and earth bear witness that you are slaughtering us unjustly." 38So the enemy attacked them on the Sabbath and killed the men, their wives, their children, and their livestock. A thousand people died.

39When Mattathias and his friends heard the news about this, they were greatly saddened 40and said to one another, "If all of us do as these other Jews have done and refuse to fight the Gentiles to defend our lives and our religion, we will soon be wiped off the face of the earth." 41On that day they decided that if anyone attacked them on the Sabbath, they would defend themselves, so that they would not all die as those Jews had died in the caves.

42Then Mattathias and his friends were joined by a group of devout and patriotic Jews, the strongest and bravest men in Israel, who had all volunteered to defend the Law. 43In addition, everyone who was fleeing from the persecution joined them and strengthened their forces. 44Now that they had an army, they gave vent to their anger by attacking the renegade Jews. Those who escaped were forced to flee to the Gentiles for safety. 45Mattathias and his friends went everywhere tearing down pagan altars 46and circumcising by force every uncircumcised boy they found within the borders of Israel. 47They were also successful in hunting down the arrogant Gentile officials.

48They rescued the Law of Moses from the Gentiles and their kings and broke the power of the wicked King Antiochus.

The Death of Mattathias

49When the time came for Mattathias to die, he said to his sons, "These are times of violence and distress. Arrogant people are in control and have made us an object of ridicule. 50But you, my sons, must be devoted to the Law and ready to die to defend God's covenant with our ancestors. 51Remember what our ancestors did and how much they accomplished in their day. Follow their example, and you will be rewarded with great glory and undying fame. 52Remember how Abraham put his trust in the Lord when he was tested and how the Lord was pleased with him and accepted him. 53Joseph, in his time of trouble, obeyed God's commands and became ruler over the land of Egypt. 54Phinehas, our ancestor, because of his burning devotion, was given the promise that his descendants would always be priests. 55Joshua was made a judge in Israel because he obeyed the command of Moses. 56Caleb brought back a good report to the community and was given a part of the land as a reward. 57David was made king and was given the promise that his descendants would always be kings because of his steadfast loyalty to God. 58Elijah, because of his great devotion to the Law, was taken up into heaven. 59Hananiah, Azariah, and Mishael were saved from the flames because they had faith. 60Daniel was a man of integrity, and the Lord rescued him from the mouth of the lions. 61Take each of these ancestors of ours as an example, and you will realize that no one who puts his trust in the Lord will ever lack strength. 62Don't be afraid of the

---

2.52 Gn 15.6; 22.15-18   **2.53** Gn 39.1—45.28   **2.55, 56** Nu 13.1—14.12   **2.57** 2 S 7.16
2.58 2 K 2.9-12   **2.59** Dn 3.8-30   **2.60** Dn 6.1-24; Bel 31-42

threats of a wicked man. Remember that he will die and all his splendor will end with worms feeding on his decaying body. ⁶³ Today he may be highly honored, but tomorrow he will disappear; his body will return to the earth and his scheming will come to an end. ⁶⁴ But you, my sons, be strong and courageous in defending the Law, because it is through the Law that you will earn great glory.

⁶⁵ "Your brother Simon is wise, so always listen to him as you would to me. ⁶⁶ Judas Maccabeus has been strong all his life; he will be your commander and will lead you in battle against the enemy. ⁶⁷ Call everyone who obeys God's Law to rally around you; then avenge the wrongs done to your people. ⁶⁸ Pay back the Gentiles for what they have done, and always obey the Law and its commands."

⁶⁹ Then Mattathias gave them his blessing and died. ⁷⁰ He was buried in the family tomb at Modein, and all the people of Israel went into deep mourning for him. This happened in the year 146.ᵍ

The Early Victories of Judas
(2 Maccabees 8.1-7)

3 Judas Maccabeus took the place of his father Mattathias. ² All his brothers and all the loyal followers of his father gave him their support, and they were happy to carry on Israel's war.

³ Judas brought greater glory to
    his people.
In his armor, he was like a giant.
He took up his weapons and
    went to war;
  with his own sword he
    defended his camp.
⁴ He was like a ferocious lion
    roaring as it attacks.

⁵ Judas hunted down those who
    broke the Law
  and set fire to all who
    oppressed his people.
⁶ In fear of him, lawless men
    huddled together in terror,
  not knowing which way to
    turn.
He advanced the cause of
    freedom by what he did.
⁷ He made life miserable for many
    kings,
  but brought joy to the people
    of Israel.
We will praise him forever for
    what he did.
⁸ He went through the towns of
    Judea
  and destroyed all the
    godless men.
He relieved Israel of its terrible
    suffering.ʰ
⁹ His fame spread to the ends of
    the earth,
  as he gathered together those
    who were threatened with
    death.

¹⁰ Then Apollonius assembled a Gentile army, including a large force from Samaria, to attack the people of Israel. ¹¹ When Judas learned of this, he marched out to battle, defeated the army, and killed Apollonius. Many Gentiles lost their lives, and the rest fled. ¹² When the spoils of war were collected, Judas took the sword of Apollonius and used it in battle until the day he died.

¹³ Seron, the general of the Syrian forces, learned that Judas had gathered together an army, consisting of a band of loyal men who were ready to fight under his command. ¹⁴ Seron said to himself, "I will make a reputation for myself throughout the empire by defeating Judas and his men, who have no respect for the king's command."

ᵍ THE YEAR 146: *This corresponds to 166 B.C.*   ʰ relieved Israel of its terrible suffering; *or* saved Israel from God's anger.

"It is the Lord's power that determines the outcome." (3.19)

15 Then he began a new campaign against Judas and was joined by a strong force of godless men who were eager to help him take vengeance on Israel. 16 When he approached the pass at Beth Horon, Judas went out to meet him with a small group of men. 17 When Judas' men saw the army coming against them, they asked, "How can our little group of men fight an army as big as that? Besides, we have not eaten all day, and we are tired!"

18 "It is not difficult," Judas answered, "for a small group to overpower a large one. It makes no difference to the Lord whether we are rescued by many people or by just a few. 19 Victory in battle does not depend on who has the largest army; it is the Lord's power that determines the outcome. 20 Our enemies are coming against us with great violence, intending to plunder our possessions and kill our wives and children. 21 But we are fighting for our lives and for our religion. 22 When we attack, the Lord will crush our enemies, so don't be afraid of them."

23 As soon as Judas had finished speaking, he and his men made a sudden attack against Seron and his army and crushed them. 24 They pursued them down the pass at Beth Horon to the plain and killed about 800 men. Those who escaped fled to Philistia. 25 After that, Gentiles everywhere began to be afraid of Judas and his brothers. 26 His fame reached the ears of King Antiochus, and people in every

nation talked about Judas and his victories.

The King Appoints Lysias as Governor

27 When Antiochus heard what had happened, he was furious. He ordered all the armies of his empire to assemble in one huge force. 28 From his treasury he paid a full year's wages to his soldiers and ordered them to be prepared for any emergency. 29 But then he found that the funds in his treasury were exhausted. Income from taxes had decreased because of the disorder and the troubles he had brought on the world by doing away with the laws which had been in force from the earliest times. 30 Antiochus had always given presents more lavishly than earlier kings, but now he was worried that he might not be able to continue this, or even to meet expenses — this had happened once or twice before. 31 He was very disturbed; but finally he decided to go to Persia, collect the taxes from the provinces there, and bring together a large sum of ready cash.

32 He appointed Lysias, an important man who had been granted the title "Relative of the King," as governor to take care of the king's affairs in the whole territory between the Euphrates River and the Egyptian border. 33 The king also made Lysias the guardian of his son Antiochus the Fifth until his own return. 34 He put Lysias in charge of all the elephants and of half his army, and then gave him detailed instructions

about what he wanted done, and in particular, what he wanted done with the inhabitants of Judea and Jerusalem. [35] Lysias was ordered to send an army against the Jews, especially the Jews in Jerusalem, to break their power and destroy them, so that no trace of them would remain. [36] He was ordered to take their land and give it to foreigners, who would settle the whole area. [37] Taking the other half of his army, the king set out from Antioch, his capital city, in the year 147.[i] He crossed the Euphrates River and marched through Mesopotamia.

The Victories of Judas
(2 Maccabees 8.8-29, 34-36)

[38] Lysias chose Nicanor, Gorgias, and Ptolemy son of Dorymenes as army commanders; all three were able men who bore the title "Friend of the King." [39] He put them in charge of 40,000 infantry and 7,000 cavalry and ordered them to invade the land of Judea and destroy it as the king had commanded. [40] These commanders set out with their entire force, and when they came to the plains near Emmaus, they made camp. [41] A force from Idumea[j] and Philistia joined them. The merchants of the region heard about the strength of the army, and they came to the camp with chains and a large amount of money, hoping to buy some Jewish slaves.

[42] Judas and his brothers saw that their situation was getting more and more difficult, with foreign armies camped within their own borders. They also learned that the king had commanded the complete destruction of the people. [43] So they determined to rebuild their ruined nation and fight for their country and the Temple. [44] Then the whole community came together to prepare for war and to pray for God's mercy.

[45] Jerusalem was as empty as a
    wilderness;
no citizens left or entered the
    city.
The holy Temple was profaned
    by foreigners,
and Gentiles camped in the
    city's fort;
so joy departed from the people
    of Israel,
and the sound of music was
    heard no more.

[46] Then Judas and his men assembled and marched to Mizpah, opposite Jerusalem, because the people of Israel had previously had a place of worship there. [47] In deep mourning, they fasted all that day, put on sackcloth, threw ashes on their heads, and tore their clothes. [48] The Gentiles would have consulted their idols in such a situation, but the Israelites unrolled the book of the Law to search for God's guidance. [49] They brought the priests' robes, the offerings of the first grain, and the tithes, and then they brought in some Nazirites who had completed their vows. [50] The whole community prayed, "Lord, what shall we do with these things? Where shall we take them, [51] now that your holy Temple has been trampled and profaned by Gentiles, and your priests mourn in disgrace? [52] The Gentiles have come to attack and destroy us. You know what they plan to do! [53] If you don't help us, how can we stand up against them?" [54] Then they blew trumpets and shouted loudly.

[55] After that, Judas divided his men into groups of ten, fifty, a hundred, and a thousand, placing officers in charge of each group. [56] Then, in obedience to the Law, he sent home everyone who had recently been married, built a house, or planted a vineyard, as well as anyone who was afraid. [57] Finally, the army marched out and took up positions south of Emmaus, [58] where Judas

---

[i] THE YEAR 147: *This corresponds to 165 B.C.*
3.56 Dt 20.5-8; Jg 7.3

[j] *Probable text* Idumea; *Greek* Syria.

said to them: "Prepare yourselves for battle and be courageous! Be ready early tomorrow morning to fight these Gentiles who have joined forces to attack us and destroy us and our Temple. ⁵⁹ It is better for us to die fighting than to stand idly by and watch the destruction of our nation and our Temple. ⁶⁰ But the Lord will do what he pleases."

4 Gorgias took 5,000 infantry and 1,000 of his most experienced cavalry and left camp by night, ² with men from the fort in Jerusalem as his guides. He had planned to make a surprise attack on the Jewish army, ³ but Judas learned of the plan and moved out with his men to attack the king's army at Emmaus ⁴ while Gorgias and his troops were still away from the camp. ⁵ When Gorgias and his army reached Judas' camp that night, they found no one there. They thought Judas and his men were trying to escape, so they started looking for them in the mountains.

⁶ At dawn Judas appeared in the plain with 3,000 men, not all of them as well armed as they would have liked. ⁷ They saw the huge Gentile army of experienced troops wearing armor and protected by cavalry. ⁸ But Judas said to his men, "Don't worry about the size of their army, and don't be frightened when they attack. ⁹ Remember how our ancestors were saved at the Red Sea when the king of Egypt was pursuing them with his army! ¹⁰ Now let us ask the Lord to have mercy on us. Let us pray that he will honor his covenant with our ancestors and crush this army when we attack today. ¹¹ Then all the Gentiles will know that Israel has a God who rescues and saves them."

¹² When the Gentiles saw Judas and his men preparing for battle, ¹³ they moved out of their camp to fight. Then Judas and his men sounded their trumpets ¹⁴ and attacked. The Gentiles broke ranks and fled to the plain, ¹⁵ but all the stragglers were killed. The Israelites pursued the enemy as far as Gezer, the plains of Idumea, and the towns of Azotus and Jamnia. Altogether they killed about 3,000 of the enemy.

¹⁶ When Judas and his army came back from the pursuit, ¹⁷⁻¹⁸ he said to his men, "Don't be greedy for loot. Gorgias and his army are nearby in the mountains, so there is still heavy fighting ahead of us. We must stand firm and fight. After that, you can safely take all the loot you want." ¹⁹ Judas was just finishing his speech when an enemy patrol on a scouting mission looked down from the mountains ²⁰ and saw that their army had been put to flight; they could tell from the smoke that their camp was burning. ²¹ When they saw all this, they were terrified, and when they also saw that Judas' army was in the plain ready for battle, ²² they all fled to Philistia. ²³ Then Judas returned to loot the enemy camp; he took large amounts of gold and silver, blue and purple cloth, and other rich plunder. ²⁴ When the Jews came back to their own camp, they sang a hymn: "The Lord is worthy of praise; his mercy endures forever." ²⁵ That day brought a great victory to the people of Israel.

Victory over Lysias
(2 Maccabees 11.1-12)

²⁶ The Gentile troops that escaped went to Lysias and reported all that had happened. ²⁷ When Lysias heard that his troops had lost the battle, he was shocked and disappointed that Israel had not been defeated as the king had commanded.

²⁸ In the following year Lysias gathered an army of 60,000 well-trained infantry and 5,000 cavalry, intending to conquer the Jews. ²⁹ They marched into Idumea and camped at Bethzur. Judas came to meet them with 10,000 men. ³⁰ When Judas saw how strong the

enemy's army was, he prayed, "We will praise you, Savior of Israel. You broke the attack of the giant by the hand of your servant David and you let Saul's son Jonathan and the young man who carried his weapons defeat the entire Philistine army. [31] Now in the same way let your people Israel defeat our enemy. Put them to shame, in spite of all their confidence in their infantry and cavalry. [32] Make them afraid; let their bold strength melt away; let them tremble at the prospect of defeat. [33] We love and worship you; so let us kill our enemies, that we may then sing your praises."

[34] The battle began, and in the hand-to-hand fighting about 5,000 of Lysias' men were killed. [35] When Lysias saw that his army was being defeated and when he saw the reckless courage of Judas and his men, who showed that they were ready to live or die with honor, he returned to Antioch. There he recruited some mercenaries and planned to return to Judea later with a much larger army.

The Purification of the Temple
(2 Maccabees 10.1-8)

[36] Judas and his brothers said, "Now that our enemies have been defeated, let's go to Jerusalem to purify the Temple and rededicate it." [37] So the whole army was assembled and went up to Mount Zion. [38] There they found the Temple abandoned, the altar profaned, the gates burned down, the courtyards grown up in a forest of weeds, and the priests' rooms torn down. [39] In their sorrow, they tore their clothes, cried loudly, threw ashes on their heads, [40] and fell face down on the ground. When the signal was given on the trumpets, everyone cried out to the Lord.

[41] Then Judas ordered some of his soldiers to attack the men in the fort, while he purified the Temple. [42] He chose some priests who were qualified and who were devoted to the Law. [43] They purified the Temple and took the stones that had been defiled and put them in an unclean place. [44] They discussed what should be done with the altar of burnt offerings, which had been desecrated [45] by the Gentiles, and decided to tear it down, so that it would not stand there as a monument to their shame. So they tore down the altar [46] and put the stones in a suitable place on the Temple hill, where they were to be kept until a prophet should appear and decide what to do with them. [47] Then they took uncut stones, as the Law of Moses required, and built a new altar like the old one. [48] They repaired the Temple, inside and out, and dedicated its courtyards. [49] They made new utensils for worship and brought the lampstand, the altar of incense, and the table for the bread into the Temple. [50] They burned incense on the altar and lit the lamps on the lampstand, and there was light in the Temple! [51] They placed the loaves of bread on the table, hung the curtains, and completed all the work.

[52-54] The twenty-fifth day of the ninth month, the month of Kislev, in the year 148[k] was the anniversary of the day the Gentiles had desecrated the altar. On that day a sacrifice was offered on the new altar in accordance with the Law of Moses. The new altar was dedicated and hymns were sung to the accompaniment of harps, lutes, and cymbals. [55] All the people bowed down with their faces to the ground and worshiped and praised the Lord for giving them victory.

[56] For eight days they celebrated the rededication of the altar. With great joy they brought burnt offerings and offered fellowship offerings and thank offerings. [57] They decorated the front of

---

[k] THE YEAR 148: *This corresponds to 164 B.C.*
4.47 Ex 20.25; Dt 27.5, 6   **4.52-54** 1 Macc 1.54

the Temple with gold crowns and shields, rebuilt the gates and the priests' rooms and put doors on them. ⁵⁸Now that the Jews had removed the shame which the Gentiles had brought, they held a great celebration. ⁵⁹Then Judas, his brothers, and the entire community of Israel decreed that the rededication of the altar should be celebrated with a festival of joy and gladness at the same time each year, beginning on the twenty-fifth of the month of Kislev and lasting for eight days.

⁶⁰Then they built high walls and strong towers around Mount Zion, so that the Gentiles could not come in and trample and defile it again. ⁶¹Judas placed a detachment of soldiers there to guard the Temple. He also fortified the town of Bethzur, so that the people of Israel would have a fortress facing Idumea.

Wars with Neighboring Nations
(2 Maccabees 10.14-33; 12.10-45)

5 When the neighboring nations heard that the Jews had built the altar and restored the Temple as it had been before, they were so furious ²that they made up their minds to destroy all the Jews who were living among them. So they began to murder and kill our people. ³The Idumeans were blockading the Israelites, so Judas went to war against them at Akrabattene, crushed them, and looted them. ⁴He also dealt with the people of Baean, who were a constant threat to the people of Israel, because they would lie in ambush waiting to trap Israelite travelers. ⁵He shut the Baeanites up in their forts, took a solemn oath that he would destroy them, and burned their forts with everyone in them. ⁶Then he marched against the land of Ammon, where he met a large and powerful army under the command of a man named Timothy. ⁷Judas

won many battles against them and finally defeated them. ⁸He captured Jazer and its surrounding villages and then returned to Judea.

⁹The Gentiles in Gilead assembled to attack and destroy the Israelites living in their territory. But the Israelites fled to the fortress of Dathema ¹⁰⁻¹¹and sent the following letter to Judas and his brothers: "The Gentiles around us are joining forces under Timothy. We have fled to this fortress for protection, and now they are getting ready to capture it and destroy us. ¹²Many of us have already been killed. Come rescue us! ¹³All the Jewish men in the region of Tob^l have been killed, their wives and their children have been taken captive, and their possessions have been carried off. A force of about 1,000 men has been destroyed there."

¹⁴This letter was still being read when other messengers, who had torn their clothes in sorrow, arrived with a report from Galilee. ¹⁵They said, "An army from Ptolemais, Tyre, Sidon, and all of Galilee has come together to destroy us."

¹⁶When Judas and the people heard all this, a great assembly was held to decide what should be done to help these countrymen, who were in such difficulty under enemy attack. ¹⁷Judas said to his brother Simon, "Choose some men and go rescue our fellow Jews in Galilee; our brother Jonathan and I will go to Gilead." ¹⁸Judas left the rest of his army to defend Judea and put the two leaders, Azariah and Joseph son of Zechariah, in charge of the people. ¹⁹He told them: "I am leaving you in command here, but don't go out and fight the Gentiles until we get back." ²⁰Then 3,000 men joined Simon for the march into Galilee, and 8,000 remained with Judas for the march into Gilead.

²¹Simon went into Galilee and fought many battles with the Gentiles. He defeated them ²²and pursued them

^l in the region of Tob; *or* who were fighting with Tobias.

Judas and his men saw a vast army attacking the fortress. (5.30)

all the way to the city of Ptolemais, killing about 3,000 of them, and taking the loot. 23 Then he took the Jews who were in Galilee and Arbatta, with their wives, their children, and all they owned, and brought them back to Judea with him. There was great rejoicing.

24 During this time, Judas Maccabeus and his brother Jonathan had crossed the Jordan River and had marched for three days through the desert. 25 They met some friendly Nabateans who told them all that had happened to the Jews in Gilead. 26 They reported that many Jews were imprisoned in the fortified cities of Bozrah, Bosor, Alema, Chaspho, Maked, and Karnaim, 27 while others were imprisoned in the smaller towns of Gilead. They also reported that the enemy was drawn up to make an attack the next day on the Jewish fortresses, hoping to destroy all the Jews in a single day.

28 So Judas and his army suddenly turned and attacked Bozrah by the desert road, captured the town, and killed every man in it. They looted the town and set it on fire. 29 They left there and marched all night to the fortress at Dathema. 30 At dawn Judas and his men saw a vast army attacking the fortress; they were bringing up ladders, siege platforms, and battering rams in an effort to capture it. 31 When Judas heard the noise, the shouts, and the

sound of trumpets coming from the city, he realized that the battle had begun, 32 so he said to his men, "Fight today for our fellow Jews!"

33 He ordered his men to march in three columns and attack the enemy from the rear. As they moved forward, they blew trumpets and shouted prayers. 34 When the army under Timothy's command saw that it was Judas Maccabeus, the soldiers turned and fled. Judas crushed them and killed about 8,000 men that day.

35 Then Judas turned aside to attack the town of Alema; *m* he captured it and killed all the men in it. He looted the town and set fire to it. 36 From there he went on and captured Chaspho, Maked, Bosor, and the other towns of Gilead.

37 After this, Timothy gathered another army and camped opposite Raphon, on the other side of a river. 38 Judas sent some men to spy on the camp, and they reported back to him that all the Gentiles in the region had joined Timothy and had formed a large army. 39 Timothy had also hired Arab mercenaries to help him, and these were camped on the other side of the river ready to attack Judas. So Judas went out to meet them in battle.

40 As Judas and his army came closer to the water, Timothy said to his officers, "If he keeps on coming and crosses

---

m ALEMA: *The name of the town is not certain.*

the river, we won't be able to turn back his attack, and he will defeat us. ⁴¹But if he is afraid and stops on the other side of the river, we will cross over to attack and defeat him." ⁴²When Judas reached the bank of the river, he gave orders to his officers to let no one stop but to push everyone forward into battle. ⁴³Judas was the first to cross the river against the enemy, and all his men followed him. The Gentiles broke ranks before them, threw away their arms, and fled to the pagan temple at Karnaim. ⁴⁴But Judas and his men took the city and burned down the temple with all who were in it. With Karnaim overthrown, the Gentiles could no longer offer any resistance to Judas.

⁴⁵Then Judas gathered together all the Jews in Gilead to take them back to Judea with him. It was a large group of all kinds of people, together with their wives and children and all that they owned. ⁴⁶They went as far as Ephron, a large, well-fortified town. It was impossible to go around it on either side, and the road passed directly through the town. ⁴⁷But the people there would not let them pass and blocked the town gates with stones. ⁴⁸Then Judas sent a friendly message to them: "Let us pass through your territory to return home. No one will harm you; we will just pass through." But they still refused to open the gates.

⁴⁹So Judas told everyone in the group, except the fighting men, to camp where they were. ⁵⁰The fighting men were ordered to take up their positions and attack the town. They fought all day and all night, until they had taken it. ⁵¹Judas had all the men of Ephron put to death, plundered the town, and leveled it. Then he and his army marched through the town over the dead bodies. ⁵²They crossed the Jordan into the wide plain opposite Beth Shan. ⁵³Throughout the whole march Judas kept gathering up the stragglers and encouraging the people until they reached the land of Judea. ⁵⁴With thanksgiving and rejoicing, they went up to Mount Zion and sacrificed burnt offerings because they had returned safely without a single loss.

⁵⁵While Judas and Jonathan were in Gilead and their brother Simon was attacking Ptolemais in Galilee, ⁵⁶Joseph and Azariah, the commanders of the army in Judea, heard about their brave deeds and victories. ⁵⁷They said to one another, "Let's go to war with the Gentiles around us and win some fame for ourselves." ⁵⁸So they and their men attacked Jamnia. ⁵⁹Gorgias and his men went out of the town to meet them in battle. ⁶⁰They defeated Joseph and Azariah and pursued them as far as the borders of Judea. At least 2,000 Israelite men were killed that day. ⁶¹This great defeat came about because the Jewish commanders wanted to be heroes and refused to obey Judas and his brothers. ⁶²Besides, they did not belong to the family of the Maccabees, whom God had chosen to bring freedom to the people of Israel.

⁶³But Judas Maccabeus and his brothers won great respect among all the Israelites and all the Gentiles. When people heard of their fame, ⁶⁴large crowds gathered to praise them.

⁶⁵Then Judas and his brothers went to war against the Edomites to the south. He attacked Hebron and its surrounding towns, destroyed its fortifications, and burned down the towers around it. ⁶⁶Then he marched into the land of the Philistines and passed through Marisa.ⁿ ⁶⁷That day a number of priests were killed in battle because they wanted to be heroes and foolishly went out to fight. ⁶⁸Judas turned aside to Azotus in Philistia. He pulled down the altars, burned the images of their gods, plundered their towns, and then returned to Judea.

ⁿ *Some ancient translations* Marisa; *Greek* Samaria.

The Death of Antiochus the Fourth
(2 Maccabees 1.11-17; 9.1-29; 10.9-11)

6 As King Antiochus the Fourth was passing through Mesopotamia, he heard of a city in Persia, named Elymais, which was famous for its riches in silver and gold. ² The temple was very rich, containing gold shields, armor, and weapons left there by Alexander, son of King Philip of Macedonia, who was the first to rule the Greek Empire. ³ Antiochus came and tried to take the city and loot it, but he didn't succeed, because the citizens had learned what he was planning to do, ⁴ and they drew up their troops to resist him. In great frustration he withdrew to return to Babylonia.

⁵ In Persia a messenger reached him with the news that the armies he had sent into Judea had been defeated. ⁶ Lysias and his strong army had been forced to flee from the Jews, who were now reinforced by the additional weapons, supplies, and loot they had taken from the defeated armies. ⁷ The Jews had pulled down the thing they called "The Awful Horror" that Antiochus had built on the altar in Jerusalem. They had also surrounded the Temple with high walls, as it had been before, and had taken and fortified the town of Bethzur, one of the king's own towns.

⁸ When the king heard this report, he was so dumbfounded and terribly shaken that he went to bed in a fit of deep depression because things had not turned out as he had hoped. ⁹ He remained ill for a long time, as waves of despair swept over him, until he finally realized that he was going to die. ¹⁰ He called together all those to whom he had given the title "Friends of the King" and said to them, "I cannot sleep, and my heart is broken with grief and worry. ¹¹ At first I asked myself why these great waves of trouble were

The king . . . went to bed in a fit of deep depression. (6.8)

sweeping over me, since I have been kind and well-liked during my reign. ¹² But then I remembered the wrongs I did in Jerusalem when I took all the silver and gold objects from the Temple and tried without any good reason to destroy the inhabitants of Judea. ¹³ I know this is why all these terrible things have happened to me and I am about to die in deep despair here in this foreign land."

¹⁴ Then he called Philip, one of his most trusted advisers, and put him in charge of his whole empire. ¹⁵ He gave him his crown, robe, and official ring, and authorized him to educate his son Antiochus the Fifth and bring him up to be king. ¹⁶ King Antiochus died there in the year 149.ᵒ

¹⁷ When Lysias learned that the king had died, he made the young Antiochus king in place of his father. He had brought up Antiochus from childhood and now gave him the name Eupator.

The Campaign of Antiochus the Fifth and Lysias
(2 Maccabees 13.1-26; 11.22-26)

¹⁸ Meanwhile, the enemies in the fort at Jerusalem had been blockading the people of Israel in the area around the Temple, constantly causing them trouble and giving support to the Gentiles.

ᵒ THE YEAR 149: *This corresponds to 163 B.C.*
6.7 1 Macc 1.54

19 So Judas decided to get rid of them and called all the people together to besiege the fort. 20 The people assembled and laid siege to the fort in the year 150.ᵖ They built siege platforms and battering rams.

21 But some of the men under siege escaped, and together with some of the renegade Jews, they went to the king and said, 22 "How long are you going to wait before you take revenge for what was done to our countrymen? 23 We were willing to serve your father, follow his orders, and obey his decrees. 24 But what good did it do us? Now our own countrymen have become our enemies.�q In fact, they have killed as many of us as they could find and have stolen our possessions. 25 But we are not the only ones they have harmed; they have attacked all their neighbors. 26 And now they have laid siege to the fort in Jerusalem and are planning to take it. They have also fortified the Temple and Bethzur. 27 Unless you act immediately, they will do even more, and you will not be able to stop them."

28 When the king heard this, he was furious. He brought together all the army commanders, the cavalry officers, and his most trusted advisers. 29 He also hired mercenary soldiers from other countries and from the Greek islands. 30 His forces numbered 100,000 infantry, 20,000 cavalry, and 32 elephants trained for war. 31 The king and his army passed through Idumea and laid siege to Bethzur, where they fought for a long time. They built battering rams and siege platforms, but the defenders fought bravely and came out of the town and burned down the platforms.

32 Then Judas withdrew his troops from the fort in Jerusalem and set up his camp at Beth Zechariah, blocking the advance of the king's army. 33 Early the next morning, the king rapidly moved his army along the road to Beth Zechariah, where his troops took up battle positions and blew trumpets. 34 They got the elephants ready for battle by showing them grape juice and mulberry juice. 35 The huge animals were distributed among the infantry units. A thousand men, protected by chain armor and bronze helmets, were stationed with each elephant. Each animal was also accompanied by a special force of 500 cavalry, 36 which always remained with the elephant. 37 A strong, protected wooden platform was securely fastened by a special harness to the back of each elephant. Threeʳ soldiers rode on each animal, in addition to the elephant driver. 38 Lysias placed the rest of the cavalry on the two flanks of the army where they could be protected by the infantry while harassing the enemy. 39 The sunlight, reflected off the bronze and gold shields, shone on the mountains and flashed like burning torches. 40 Part of the king's army was spread out over the higher ground of the mountain slopes and part over the lower land, but they all moved forward steadily and in good order. 41 All the people were terrified when they heard the noise made by the clashing of weapons and the marching of that great and powerful army.

42 Judas and his army advanced into battle, and immediately killed 600 of the king's army. 43 When Eleazar Avaran saw that one of the elephants was larger than the others and that it was covered with royal armor, he thought that the king was riding on it. 44 Eleazar sacrificed his life to save his people and to gain eternal fame. 45 He ran boldly toward the elephant, which was in the middle of a battalion of infantry. He rushed forward killing men to the right and left, so that the enemy soldiers fell back before him on both sides. 46 He slipped in under the elephant and stabbed it to death, and it fell on him

---

ᵖ THE YEAR 150: *This corresponds to 162 B.C.* and besieged the fort.   ʳ *Probable text* Three; *Greek* Thirty *or* Thirty-two.   �q enemies; *some manuscripts add* and killed him. [47] But when the Jews realized how strong the royal army was and how determined it was to fight, they retreated.

[48] The king and his army advanced to fight the Jews at Jerusalem and laid siege to the whole of Judea and Jerusalem. [49] He made peace with the Jews of Bethzur, who then left the town. There had not been enough food in the town for them to withstand the siege because it was the sabbatical year, when no crops were planted. [50] The king occupied Bethzur and stationed a body of troops there to guard it. [51] Then he surrounded the Temple and besieged it for a long time. He set up siege platforms, battering rams, catapults for throwing fire and stones, and other weapons to throw spears and rocks. [52] The defenders also made war machines to oppose those of the enemy, and so the battle went on for a long time. [53] But there was no food left in the Temple storage bins because it was the sabbatical year, and the people who had fled from the Gentiles and taken refuge in Judea had eaten all the food that had been stored there. [54] The shortage of food had been so severe that many people had scattered to their homes, and only a few men were left in the Temple.

[55] Meanwhile, Philip, who had been appointed by King Antiochus before his death to educate his son to be king, [56] returned from Persia and Media. He had come back with the royal army and planned to take control of the government. When Lysias heard this news, [57] he made rapid preparations to depart. He said to the young king, to his officers, and to his men, "We are growing weaker each day; we are short of provisions, and this place we are besieging is strong. Besides, there are pressing government affairs which need our attention. [58] So now let's arrange a truce and make a peace treaty with the Jews and their whole nation. [59] We will allow

them to follow their own laws and customs as they did before. All this trouble started when we provoked them by abolishing their laws and customs."

[60] This recommendation was well received by the king and the officers, so Lysias proposed peace terms to the Jews, and they accepted them. [61] When the king and his officers solemnly agreed to abide by these terms, the Jews came out of their fortress. [62] But when the king entered the Temple area on Mount Zion and saw the strong fortifications, he broke his word and ordered the walls surrounding the Temple to be torn down. [63] Then he hurriedly left and returned to Antioch, where he found Philip in control of the city. The king attacked the city and took it by force.

The High Priest Alcimus and the Campaign of Nicanor
(2 Maccabees 14.1-36; 15.1-36)

7 In the year 151,[s] Demetrius son of Seleucus left Rome and with a few men landed at a town on the Mediterranean coast, where he proclaimed himself king. [2] As he was making his way to the royal palace of his ancestors, the soldiers arrested Antiochus the Fifth and Lysias, planning to take them to Demetrius. [3] When Demetrius heard about it, he said, "I don't want to see them." [4] So the soldiers killed them, and Demetrius took the throne.

[5] Then all the godless traitorous Jews led by Alcimus, who wanted to be High Priest, went to Demetrius. [6] They brought accusations against the other Jews and said, "Judas and his brothers have killed everybody who supported you, and they have driven us out of our country. [7] We advise you to send someone whom you can trust to go and inspect all the damage done to our property and the king's territory and to

[s] THE YEAR 151: *This corresponds to 161 B.C.*

punish Judas, his brothers, and all who support them."

⁸ King Demetrius chose one of his advisers, a man by the name of Bacchides, who was the governor of Greater Syria. He was an important man in the empire and loyal to the king. ⁹ He was sent along with the godless Alcimus, whom the king had appointed High Priest; Alcimus had orders to take revenge on the Jews. ¹⁰ They left Antioch and arrived in Judea with a large army. Bacchides tried to trick Judas and his brothers by sending to them messengers with offers of peace. ¹¹ But when Judas and his brothers saw what a large army they had brought, they did not believe what the messengers said.

¹² A group of teachers of the Law came to Alcimus and Bacchides, asking for justice. ¹³ These devout and patriotic men were the first of the Jews to try to make peace with Alcimus and Bacchides. ¹⁴ They trusted Alcimus, who was a priest descended from Aaron, and they thought he would not cause them any harm. ¹⁵ Alcimus assured them of his peaceful intentions and solemnly promised that no harm would come to them or their friends. ¹⁶ But as soon as they began to trust him, he arrested 60 of them and put them all to death on the same day. As the scripture says,

¹⁷ "The blood of your faithful people
    was poured out,
  their bodies were scattered
      around Jerusalem,
  and there was no one left to bury
      the dead."

¹⁸ When this happened, all the people were afraid of Alcimus and Bacchides, and they said, "They don't know what truth or justice means. They gave their solemn word and then broke it!" ¹⁹ Bacchides left Jerusalem and set up his headquarters at Beth Zaith. He ordered the arrest of some of the faithful Jews and even many of the renegades who had willingly joined him; he had them

killed and thrown into a deep pit. ²⁰ Bacchides put the country under the control of Alcimus, left troops there to help him, and returned to the king.

²¹ Alcimus then began his struggle to establish himself as High Priest. ²² Every troublemaker in the country joined him. They gained control of the land of Judea and caused great difficulties for the Jews. ²³ Judas saw that the trouble Alcimus and his men had caused was even worse than the damage done by the Gentiles. ²⁴ So he went around the whole country of Judea taking revenge on all the men who had willingly joined Alcimus and preventing them from leaving the towns and going into the country. ²⁵ When Alcimus saw that Judas and his men were growing more powerful and when he realized that he would not be able to stand against them, he returned to the king and accused them of great crimes.

²⁶ Then the king sent Nicanor, one of his most honored officers, who hated the Jews, with orders to exterminate them. ²⁷ Nicanor came to Jerusalem with a big army. He tried to trick Judas and his brothers by sending peace offers. He said, ²⁸ "There need not be any quarrel between you and me. I will come to you with a small escort for a friendly private conversation." ²⁹ When he came to Judas, they exchanged polite greetings, but Judas' enemies were ready to kidnap him. ³⁰ When Judas learned that Nicanor's visit was part of a plot against him, he was afraid and decided not to meet him again. ³¹ Nicanor realized that his plan had been discovered, so he left Jerusalem to meet Judas in battle near Capharsalama. ³² About 500 of Nicanor's men were killed, and the rest of the army escaped to the fort in Jerusalem.

³³ Some time later Nicanor went to Mount Zion. Some of the priests left the Temple and, along with some of the leaders of the people, went to welcome

him with words of peace and to show him the burnt offering that was being sacrificed on behalf of the king. 34 But he ridiculed them and made them ceremonially unclean by spitting on them. He spoke proudly 35 and angrily threatened them with an oath, "Unless Judas and his army are surrendered to me immediately, I will burn this Temple down as soon as I return after my victory." And he left in a rage.

36 The priests went into the courtyard and stood facing the altar and the Temple. They started weeping and prayed, 37 "Lord, you chose this Temple to bear your name and to be a place of prayer and intercession for your people. 38 Now, take vengeance on this man and his army; let them die in battle. Remember how they spoke evil of you, and let none of them survive."

39 Nicanor left Jerusalem and set up his headquarters at Beth Horon, where the Syrian army joined him. 40 Meanwhile, Judas set up camp at Adasa with 3,000 men. There Judas prayed, 41 "Lord, the Scriptures tell us that when a king sent messengers to insult you, your angel went out and killed 185,000 of his soldiers. 42 Now, in the same way, crush this army before us today and let everyone know that Nicanor is being punished because he insulted your holy Temple. Punish him as his wickedness deserves."

43 The armies met in battle on the thirteenth day of the month of Adar, and Nicanor's army was defeated. Nicanor himself was the first to be killed in the battle, 44 and when his soldiers saw that he was dead, they threw down their weapons and fled. 45 The Jews pursued them all day long from Adasa to Gezer. As they followed, they kept sounding the call to battle on the trumpets, 46 and from all the surrounding villages of Judea people came out and attacked the fleeing enemy from the sides. This forced them back toward the

Jews who were chasing them, and all of the enemy were killed in the fight. Not one of them survived.

47 The Jews took the loot and then cut off Nicanor's head and his right arm, which he had extended so arrogantly. They brought his head and his arm to be put on display outside Jerusalem. 48 There was great rejoicing among the Jews. They set that day aside as a special day of celebration, 49 and decreed that the thirteenth day of Adar should be observed as an annual day of celebration. 50 There was peace in the land of Judea for a little while.

The Treaty with the Romans

8 Judas had heard about the Romans and their reputation as a military power. He knew that they welcomed all those who joined them as allies and that those who came to them could be sure of the friendship of Rome. 2 People had told him about the wars the Romans had fought and their heroic acts among the Gauls, whom they had conquered and forced to pay taxes. 3 He had been told what they had done in Spain when they captured the silver mines and the gold mines there. 4 By careful planning and persistence, they had conquered the whole country, even though it was far from Rome. They had overcome the kings from distant lands who had fought against them; they had defeated them so badly that the survivors had to pay annual taxes. 5 They had fought and conquered Philip and Perseus, kings of Macedonia, and all who had joined them against Rome. 6 They had even defeated Antiochus the Great, king of Syria, who had attacked them with 120 elephants, cavalry, chariots, and a powerful army. 7 They took him alive and forced him and his successors to pay heavy taxes, to give hostages, and to surrender 8 India, Media, Lydia, and some of their best lands. They took these and gave them to King Eumenes.[t]

⁹When the Greeks made plans to attack and destroy them, ¹⁰the Romans learned of the plans and sent a general to fight against them. The Romans killed many of the Greeks, took their wives and children captive, plundered their possessions, occupied their land, tore down their fortresses, and made them slaves, as they are today. ¹¹They also destroyed or made slaves of other kingdoms, the islands, and everyone who had ever fought against them. ¹²But they maintained their friendship with their allies and those who relied on them for protection. They conquered kings near and far, and everyone who heard of their reputation was afraid of them. ¹³They helped some men to become kings, while they deposed others; they had become a world power. ¹⁴In spite of all this, no Roman ever tried to advance his own position by wearing a crown or putting on royal robes. ¹⁵They created a senate, and each day 320 senators came together to deliberate about the affairs of the people and their well-being. ¹⁶Each year they entrusted to one man the responsibility of governing them and controlling their whole territory. Everyone obeyed this one man, and there was no envy or jealousy among them.

¹⁷Judas chose Eupolemus, the son of John and grandson of Accos, and Jason son of Eleazar and sent them to Rome to make a treaty of friendship and alliance with the Romans. ¹⁸He did this to eliminate Syrian oppression, since the Jews clearly saw that they were being reduced to slavery. ¹⁹After a long and difficult journey, Eupolemus and Jason reached Rome and entered the Senate. They addressed the assembly in these terms: ²⁰"Judas Maccabeus, his brothers, and the Jewish people have sent us here to make a mutual defense treaty with you, so that we may be officially recorded as your friends and allies."

²¹The Romans accepted the proposal, ²²and what follows is a copy of the letter which was engraved on bronze tablets and sent to Jerusalem to remain there as a record of the treaty:

²³"May things go well forever for the Romans and for the Jewish nation on land and sea! May they never have enemies, and may they never go to war! ²⁴But if war is declared first against Rome or any of her allies anywhere, ²⁵the Jewish nation will come to her aid with wholehearted support, as the situation may require. ²⁶And to those at war with her, the Jews shall not give or supply food, arms, money, or ships, as was agreed in Rome. The Jews must carry out their obligations without receiving anything in return.

²⁷"In the same way, if war is declared first against the Jewish nation, the Romans will come to their aid with hearty support, as the situation may require. ²⁸And to their enemies there shall not be given or supplied food, arms, money, or ships, as was agreed in Rome. The Romans must carry out their obligations without deception.

²⁹"These are the terms of the treaty that the Romans have made with the Jewish people. ³⁰But if, in the future, both parties shall agree to add or remove anything, they shall act on their decision, and whatever they add or remove shall be valid.

³¹"Furthermore, concerning the wrongs which King Demetrius is doing against the Jews, we have written him as follows, 'Why have you treated our friends and allies, the Jews, so harshly? ³²If they complain to us about you one more time, we will support their cause and go to war against you on land and sea.'"

---

[t] KING EUMENES: *This is King Eumenes II, king of Pergamum from 197–158 B.C.*
8.17 2 Macc 4.11   **8.22** 1 Macc 14.18

The Death of Judas

9 When Demetrius heard that Nicanor and his army had been annihilated, he again sent Bacchides and Alcimus to the land of Judea, this time with the Syrian wing of the army. [2]They moved along Gilgal Road, laid siege to Mesaloth in Arbela, captured it, and killed many people. [3]In the first month of the year 152,[u] they set up camp opposite Jerusalem. [4]From there they marched to Berea with 20,000 infantry and 2,000 cavalry.

[5]Judas had camped at Elasa, with 3,000 experienced soldiers. [6]But when they saw the enormous size of the enemy army, they were terrified. So many men deserted that only 800 Jewish soldiers were left. [7]When Judas saw that his army was dwindling away and that the battle was about to begin, he was worried because there was not enough time to bring his army together. [8]He was discouraged, but he said to those who were still with him, "Let's prepare for the attack; maybe we can still defeat them."

[9]His men tried to talk him out of it. "We are not strong enough," they said. "Let's retreat now and save our lives. Then we can return with reinforcements and fight the enemy. We don't have enough men now."

[10]Judas replied, "Never let it be said that I ran from a battle. If our time has come, let's die bravely for our fellow Jews and not leave any stain on our honor."

[11]The Syrian army came out of the camp and took up battle positions against the Jews. The cavalry was divided into two parts. The shock troops were in the front lines, but the archers and those who used slings went ahead of the main formation. [12]Bacchides took his position on the right. The infantry advanced, protected on both sides by the cavalry, and the war trumpets were blown. The soldiers of Judas also sounded their trumpets. [13]The ground shook from the noise when the two armies met, and they fought from morning until evening.

[14]When Judas saw that Bacchides and the main force of the Syrian army was on the right, all his bravest men joined him, [15]and they crushed the Syrians' right wing. They pursued them as far as the foothills.[v] [16]But when the Syrians on the left wing saw that their right wing had been crushed, they turned to attack Judas and his men from the rear. [17]The fighting became very fierce, and many on both sides were killed. [18]Finally Judas himself was killed. Then all his men fled. [19]Jonathan and Simon took their brother's body and buried it in the family tomb at Modein, [20]and there at the tomb they wept for him. All Israel mourned for him in great sorrow for many days. They said, [21]"It can't be! The mighty hero and savior of Israel has been killed!"

[22]The other deeds of Judas, his battles, his courageous deeds, and his great accomplishments, were too many to write down.

Jonathan Succeeds Judas

[23]After the death of Judas, the lawless traitors began to reappear everywhere in Judea, and all the wicked people returned. [24]Also at that time there was a severe famine, and the whole country went over to the side of the renegades. [25]Bacchides deliberately appointed some renegade Jews as rulers over the country. [26]These men hunted down the friends of Judas and brought them all before Bacchides, and he subjected them to torture and humiliation. [27]It was a time of great trouble for Israel, worse than anything

[u] THE YEAR 152: *This corresponds to 160 B.C.* Mount Azotus.

[v] *Probable text* the foothills; *Greek* Mount Azotus.

They kept watch and saw a noisy crowd loaded down with baggage. (9.39)

that had happened to them since the time prophets ceased to appear among them.

²⁸ Then all the friends of Judas came together and said to Jonathan, ²⁹ "Since your brother Judas died, there has been no one like him to lead us against our enemies, against Bacchides and those of our own nation who oppose us. ³⁰ So today we choose you to succeed him as our ruler and commander to carry on our war." ³¹ Jonathan accepted the leadership that day and took the place of his brother Judas.

The Campaigns of Jonathan

³² When Bacchides learned of this, he made up his mind to kill Jonathan. ³³ But when this news reached Jonathan, he fled, with his brother Simon and their men, to the wilderness of Tekoa and set up camp at the pool of Asphar. (³⁴ Bacchides learned about this on the Sabbath and crossed the Jordan with his whole army.ʷ) ³⁵ Jonathan sent his brother John, who was responsible for the soldiers' families, to ask the Nabateans, with whom he was on friendly terms, for permission to store with them the large amount of baggage they had. ³⁶ But the Jambrites of Medeba attacked John, took him captive, and carried off all the baggage. ³⁷ Some time later Jonathan and his brother Si-

mon learned that the Jambrites were about to celebrate an important wedding and that there would be a bridal procession from the town of Nadabath. The bride was the daughter of one of the great princes of Canaan. ³⁸ Jonathan and Simon had wanted revenge for the death of their brother John, so they and their men went up on one of the mountains and hid. ³⁹ They kept watch and saw a noisy crowd loaded down with baggage. The bridegroom, his friends, and his relatives were on their way to meet the bride's party. They were heavily armed and were playing musical instruments and drums. ⁴⁰ The Jews attacked from their ambush and killed many of them; the rest escaped into the mountains, while the Jews carried off all their possessions. ⁴¹ So the wedding was turned into a time of mourning and their joyful music into funeral songs. ⁴² Jonathan and Simon had taken full revenge for the death of their brother, and they returned to the marshes along the Jordan.

⁴³ Bacchides heard about this and arrived on the Sabbath at the banks of the Jordan with a large army. ⁴⁴ Jonathan said to his men, "Now we must fight for our lives. We are in a worse situation than we have ever been in before. ⁴⁵ The enemy is in front of us, the river is behind us, and marshes and thickets are on both sides of us; there is no way

ʷ *Verse 34 is probably misplaced and belongs with verse 43.*

out. ⁴⁶So pray now for the Lord to save us from our enemies."

⁴⁷The battle began and Jonathan and his men were just about to kill Bacchides, when he escaped to the rear of the army. ⁴⁸So Jonathan and his men jumped into the Jordan and swam to the other side to escape, and the Syrian army did not cross the river to follow them. ⁴⁹That day Bacchides lost about 1,000 men.

⁵⁰After Bacchides returned to Jerusalem, the Syrians built fortifications with high walls and barred gates for a number of towns in Judea: Emmaus, Beth Horon, Bethel, Timnath, Pirathon, Tephon, and the fortress in Jericho. ⁵¹In all of these he placed troops to harass the Jews. ⁵²He also strengthened the fortifications of the towns of Bethzur and Gezer and of the fort in Jerusalem. He placed army units in them and stored up supplies there. ⁵³Then he took the sons of the leading men of the country as hostages and imprisoned them in the fort.

⁵⁴In the second month of the year 153,ˣ the High Priest Alcimus ordered that the wall of the inner court of the Temple be torn down. This would have destroyed what the prophets had accomplished; but just as the work began, ⁵⁵he had a stroke, and work was stopped. Paralyzed and unable to open his mouth, he could not speak or even make a will for his family. ⁵⁶He died in great torment. ⁵⁷When Bacchides learned that Alcimus was dead, he returned to King Demetrius, and the land of Judea had peace for two years.

⁵⁸Then all the renegades got together and said, "Look, Jonathan and his men are living in peace and security. If we bring Bacchides here now, he can capture them all in a single night." ⁵⁹They went to discuss the matter with Bacchides, ⁶⁰and he set out with a large army. He sent secret letters to all his allies in Judea, asking them to seize Jonathan and his men. But they were not able to do so because the plot was discovered. ⁶¹Jonathan and his men captured 50 of the traitorous leaders who had been involved in the plot and put them to death. ⁶²Then Jonathan, Simon, and their forces withdrew to Bethbasi in the wilderness. They rebuilt the fallen fortifications and strengthened the town's defenses. ⁶³When Bacchides learned about all this, he got his whole army together and alerted his supporters in Judea. ⁶⁴He attacked Bethbasi from all sides and built siege platforms. After the battle had gone on for a long time, ⁶⁵Jonathan slipped out into the country with a small body of men and left his brother Simon in charge of the town. ⁶⁶Jonathan defeated Odomera and his people, and then attacked and destroyed the Phasirite camp. Once defeated, they joined Jonathan and advanced with him in his attack against Bacchides. ⁶⁷At the same time, Simon and his men rushed from the town and burned the siege platforms. ⁶⁸In the battle Bacchides was pressed so hard that all his plans came to nothing, and he was defeated. ⁶⁹He was so furious with the traitorous Jews who had urged him to come to Judea that he put many of them to death.

Then Bacchides decided to return to his own country, ⁷⁰but when Jonathan learned of this, he sent ambassadors to Bacchides to arrange for peace terms and the return of Jewish prisoners. ⁷¹Bacchides agreed to do as Jonathan asked and gave him his solemn promise that he would let him live in peace the rest of his life. ⁷²Bacchides handed over the prisoners and returned to his own country. Never again did he come into Jewish territory. ⁷³War came to an end in Israel. Jonathan settled in Michmash and began to govern the people and to eliminate the renegade Jews from Israel.

ˣ THE YEAR 153: *This corresponds to 159 B.C.*

Alexander Epiphanes Makes Jonathan High Priest

10 In the year 160,[y] Alexander Epiphanes,[z] son of Antiochus the Fourth, landed at Ptolemais and captured it. The people welcomed him as their king. [2] When King Demetrius heard of it, he gathered a large army and went out to meet him in battle. [3] At that time Demetrius sent Jonathan a friendly letter full of flattery, [4] in the hope of winning Jonathan over to his side and making peace with the Jews before Alexander made a treaty with them against him. [5] Demetrius thought that Jonathan would certainly remember all the wrongs he had done to him, his brothers, and the entire Jewish nation. [6] And so Demetrius made Jonathan his ally and gave him authority to raise an army and equip it. He also ordered that the hostages held in the fort at Jerusalem should be handed over to Jonathan. [7] So Jonathan went to Jerusalem and read the letter to all the people and to the men in the fort. [8] These men were terrified when they learned that the king had given Jonathan authority to raise an army. [9] They handed the hostages over to him, and he returned them to their parents.

[10] Jonathan set up headquarters in Jerusalem and began to rebuild and restore the city. [11] He ordered the builders to use squared stones for the city walls and for the protecting wall around Mount Zion. This was done. [12] The foreigners deserted the fortresses that Bacchides had built; [13] each man left his post and returned to his own country. [14] But some of the Jews who had abandoned the Law of Moses and its commands were still left in Bethzur, which served as their last place of refuge.

[15] King Alexander learned of the promises Demetrius had made to Jonathan and he also learned about Jonathan himself, about the battles he had fought, his courageous deeds, and the troubles he and his brothers had endured. [16] He was certain that he would never find another man like Jonathan and so decided to make him his friend and ally. [17] He wrote Jonathan a letter:

[18] "King Alexander to his friend Jonathan, greetings.

[19] I have heard that you are a brave man who has earned the right to be a friend of the king. [20] I have this day appointed you as High Priest of your nation and conferred upon you the title of 'Friend of the King.' You are to be our ally and give us your support." He also sent him a royal robe and a gold crown. [21] Jonathan put on the robes of the High Priest in the seventh month of the year 160[a] at the Festival of Shelters. He raised an army and stored up a large supply of weapons.

Jonathan Supports Alexander Epiphanes

[22] When Demetrius heard this, he was distressed and said, [23] "How did we manage to let Alexander get ahead of us? He has strengthened his position by making an alliance with the Jews. [24] I also will write them a friendly letter offering high positions and gifts, so that they will support me."

[25] He wrote:

"King Demetrius to the nation of the Jews, greetings. [26] We are delighted to learn that you have kept your obligations under our treaty, remained loyal to us, and have not gone over to the side of our enemies. [27] Now if you continue to remain loyal to us, we will reward you well. [28] We will grant you exemptions from many taxes and allow you other

---

privileges. ²⁹I hereby grant all the Jewish people release and exemption from payment of regular taxes, salt taxes, and other special taxes. ³⁰Furthermore, from this day I release you from your obligation to pay me one third of the grain harvest and one half of the fruit harvest. From now on I will not demand these payments from Judea or from the three districts that have been added to Judea from Samaria and Galilee. ³¹Jerusalem and its surrounding territory is to be recognized as a holy city and to be exempt from the payment of all taxes. ³²I also give up my authority over the fort in Jerusalem and place it under the High Priest, who may station there anyone he wishes to guard it. ³³I freely grant release to all Jews who are prisoners of war anywhere in my kingdom. All of them will be exempt from taxes, even on their cattle.*b* ³⁴No taxes shall be collected from any Jew anywhere in my kingdom on Sabbaths, New Moon Festivals, and other holy days. Furthermore, no taxes shall be collected three days before or after the major holy days. ³⁵No one has the right on any of these days to demand payment or to trouble you in any way.

³⁶"Jews may be enlisted in the royal army up to a total of 30,000 men, and they will receive the same pay as other royal troops. ³⁷Some of them may be stationed in the great royal fortresses, and others assigned to responsible positions in the government. They shall have Jews as their leaders and officers, and they shall be allowed to follow their own laws and customs, just as the king has permitted for the people of Judea.

³⁸"The three districts added to Judea from the territory of Samaria will be completely incorporated into Judea and placed under the authority of the High Priest alone. ³⁹I give to the Temple in Jerusalem for its operating expenses the revenues from the city of Ptolemais and the lands belonging to it. ⁴⁰I also promise to make an annual gift of 15,000 silver coins from appropriate accounts within the royal treasury. ⁴¹The total accumulated state subsidy, which we have failed to pay in recent years, shall be paid, and the payments continued from now on for the work of the Temple. ⁴²In addition to this, we will no longer require the 5,000 silver coins annually from the Temple income. This money belongs to the priests serving in the Temple. ⁴³Whoever owes a debt to the king or any other debt and takes refuge in the Temple in Jerusalem or in any area that belongs to it may not be arrested nor may his property anywhere in my kingdom be confiscated. ⁴⁴The expenses for rebuilding and renovating the Temple shall be provided from the royal treasury. ⁴⁵Likewise, the expenses for rebuilding the walls of Jerusalem and its surrounding fortifications, as well as the walls of designated towns in Judea, shall be provided from the royal treasury."

⁴⁶When Jonathan and the people heard the proposals made by King Demetrius, they refused to believe them or accept them, because they remembered how harshly he had treated them and what terrible troubles he had caused them. ⁴⁷They preferred to give their allegiance to Alexander because he had been the first to open peace negotiations, and they remained his allies as long as he lived.

⁴⁸King Alexander raised a large army and took up battle positions facing Demetrius. ⁴⁹But when the armies of the

---

b This sentence in Greek is unclear.
10.30 1 Macc 11.34

Ptolemy and his daughter Cleopatra left Egypt. (10.57)

two kings met in battle, the army of Alexander^c turned and ran. Demetrius^d pursued them and won the battle. ⁵⁰Alexander^e fought bitterly until sundown, but Demetrius was killed that day.

⁵¹Then Alexander sent ambassadors to King Ptolemy the Sixth of Egypt with this message:

⁵²"I have returned to my kingdom and taken my seat on the throne of my ancestors. I have taken over the government, and I am now in control of the country. ⁵³I made war on Demetrius, defeated him and his army, and I have taken over his kingdom. ⁵⁴Now I am ready to make an alliance. Give me your daughter in marriage, and I will give both of you such gifts as you deserve."

⁵⁵King Ptolemy replied, "It was a great day when you returned to your country and took the throne of your ancestors. ⁵⁶I agree to your proposals, but first meet me at Ptolemais. We can get acquainted there, and I will give you my daughter in marriage."

⁵⁷So in the year 162^f Ptolemy and his daughter Cleopatra^g left Egypt and arrived at Ptolemais. ⁵⁸King Alexander met them, and Ptolemy gave him his daughter in marriage. The wedding was celebrated there in Ptolemais with royal splendor.

⁵⁹King Alexander wrote asking Jonathan to come to meet him. ⁶⁰So Jonathan, in a show of splendor, went to Ptolemais and met the two kings. He presented them with gifts of silver and gold, and he also gave many gifts to the high officials who had accompanied them. Everyone was favorably impressed with him. ⁶¹At the same time some traitorous Jews who wanted to make trouble for Jonathan made accusations against him, but King Alexander paid no attention to them. ⁶²He gave orders that Jonathan should be given royal robes to wear, ⁶³and he honored him by letting him sit at his side. Alexander told his officers to take Jonathan into the center of the city and to announce that no one was to bring charges against him for any reason and

^c Alexander; *some manuscripts have* Demetrius.   ^d Demetrius; *some manuscripts have* Alexander.   ^e Alexander; *some manuscripts have* Demetrius.   ^f THE YEAR 162: *This corresponds to 150 B.C.*   ^g CLEOPATRA: *This was Cleopatra Thea, also known as Cleopatra the Third, and not to be confused with Cleopatra the Seventh (69–30 B.C.), who was involved in the history of Caesar and Mark Antony.*

no one was to cause him any kind of trouble. ⁶⁴When his accusers saw the honors given to him, heard the announcement, and saw him clothed in royal robes, they all fled. ⁶⁵The king further honored Jonathan by enrolling him in the First Order of the "Friends of the King" and by making him general and governor of his province. ⁶⁶Jonathan returned to Jerusalem pleased and successful.

Jonathan's Victory over Apollonius

⁶⁷In the year 165 ʰ Demetrius the Second, the son of Demetrius the First, left Crete and arrived in Syria, the land of his ancestors. ⁶⁸When King Alexander heard about this, he was worried and returned to Antioch, the capital of Syria. ⁶⁹Demetrius reappointed Apollonius governor of Greater Syria. Apollonius raised a large army, set up camp near Jamnia, and sent the following message to Jonathan the High Priest: ⁷⁰"Because of you I am being ridiculed, but why do you, there in your mountains, continue this rebellion when no one supports you? ⁷¹If you really have any confidence in your army, come down here on the plain and fight, where we can test each other's strength. Study the situation, and you will find that I have the support of the forces from the cities. ⁷²You will learn who I am and who our allies are, and you will discover that you have no chance of standing against us. Your predecessors have already been beaten twice on their own ground; ⁷³so how do you expect to defeat my cavalry and the kind of army I have here on the plain? Down here there is not so much as a pebble to hide behind and no way to escape."

⁷⁴When Jonathan received this message from Apollonius, he became angry. He took 10,000 elite troops from Jerusalem; his brother Simon also brought troops, and their two forces ⁷⁵set up camp outside of Joppa. The men of the city refused to let them in because there was a detachment of Apollonius' troops there, but Jonathan attacked, ⁷⁶and the men in the city became so frightened that they opened the gates, allowing Jonathan to capture Joppa. ⁷⁷When Apollonius heard what had happened, he took 3,000 cavalry and a large army of infantry and pretended to retreat south toward Azotus. However, relying upon the strength of his cavalry, he marched into the plain with his main force, ⁷⁸⁻⁷⁹positioning 1,000 cavalry where they could attack Jonathan's forces from the rear. Jonathan continued his pursuit as far as Azotus, where the two armies met in battle. ⁸⁰Not until then did Jonathan realize that he was caught in an ambush. His army was surrounded, and enemy arrows rained down on them from morning until evening. ⁸¹But Jonathan's men stood firm, as he had ordered, and the attacking cavalry grew tired. ⁸²Then, when the cavalry was exhausted, Simon appeared on the scene with his forces and attacked and overwhelmed the enemy infantry, who broke ranks and fled. ⁸³The cavalry, which by now was scattered all over the battlefield, fled to Azotus, where they took refuge in the temple of Dagon, their god. ⁸⁴But Jonathan set fire to the city and to the temple of Dagon, burning to death all those who had taken refuge there. Then he set fire to the surrounding towns and looted them. ⁸⁵That day about 8,000 were either killed in the battle or burned to death. ⁸⁶Jonathan left and set up camp at Ascalon, where the people of the city came out to welcome him with great honors. ⁸⁷Jonathan and his men returned to Jerusalem with large quantities of loot.

⁸⁸When King Alexander heard what

ʰ THE YEAR 165: *This corresponds to 147 B.C.*

Jonathan had done, he gave him even greater honors. ⁸⁹He sent him a gold shoulder buckle, which is given only to those honored with the title "Relative of the King." He also gave him the city of Ekron and its surrounding territory.

The Fall of Alexander Epiphanes

11 King Ptolemy the Sixth of Egypt assembled an army of soldiers more numerous than the grains of sand along the seashore, and he also gathered a great fleet of ships. He intended to trap Alexander, take his kingdom, and add it to his own, ²so he went to Syria with promises of peace, and the citizens opened their gates to him and welcomed him. King Alexander had ordered them to do this because Ptolemy was his father-in-law. ³But as Ptolemy moved north, he stationed a detachment of troops in each town. ⁴When he reached Azotus, the people there showed him the burned ruins of the temple of Dagon and all the destruction in the city and the surrounding towns. There were corpses everywhere. The bodies of the men Jonathan had burned to death during the battle were now stacked up along Ptolemy's route. ⁵The people told him what Jonathan had done, hoping that he would hold him responsible, but Ptolemy said nothing. ⁶Jonathan, with all the proper ceremony, went to Joppa to meet him. They exchanged greetings and spent the night there. ⁷Jonathan accompanied him as far as the Eleutherus River before returning to Jerusalem. ⁸In this way King Ptolemy, in his plot against Alexander, took control of the towns along the coast as far north as Seleucia-by-the-sea.

⁹From there King Ptolemy sent this message to King Demetrius: "Let's make a treaty. My daughter is now Alexander's wife, but I will take her back and give her to you and let you rule over your father's kingdom. ¹⁰I regret that I ever gave her to Alexander, because he has tried to kill me." ¹¹Ptolemy made this accusation against Alexander because he wanted to take over his kingdom. ¹²So he took his daughter away from Alexander and gave her to Demetrius; he broke off all relations with Alexander, and they became open enemies. ¹³Then Ptolemy entered Antioch and assumed the crown of Syria; so he wore both the crown of Egypt and the crown of Syria.

¹⁴King Alexander was in Cilicia at the time because the people of that region were in a state of rebellion. ¹⁵But when he heard what Ptolemy had done, he moved to attack him. Ptolemy met him with a large force and won a decisive victory. ¹⁶While Ptolemy reached the peak of his power, Alexander fled to Arabia to find protection, ¹⁷but an Arab named Zabdiel cut off his head and sent it to Ptolemy. ¹⁸Two days later Ptolemy himself died, and the troops he had left in the fortresses were then killed by the local citizens. ¹⁹So in the year 167ⁱ Demetrius the Second became king.

Jonathan Wins the Favor of Demetrius the Second

²⁰About that time Jonathan gathered the men of Judea to attack the fort in Jerusalem. They built many siege platforms to use in the attack. ²¹But some traitorous Jews who hated their own nation went to King Demetrius the Second and told him that Jonathan was laying siege to the fort in Jerusalem. ²²When Demetrius heard this, he was furious and immediately moved his headquarters to Ptolemais. He wrote to Jonathan and ordered him to lift the siege and to meet him for a conference in Ptolemais without a moment's delay.

²³When Jonathan got the message, he gave orders for the siege to continue,

---

ⁱ THE YEAR 167: *This corresponds to 145 B.C.*

and then chose some Jewish leaders and some priests to go with him. At the risk of his life, ²⁴he went to the king in Ptolemais, taking along robes, silver and gold, and many other gifts. He made a good impression on the king. ²⁵Although some lawless traitors of his own nation had made accusations against Jonathan, ²⁶the king still treated him just as his predecessors had done. He honored him in the presence of all his advisers, ²⁷and confirmed him as High Priest, restoring all his former honors and appointing him to the highest rank among the "Friends of the King."

²⁸Jonathan asked the king to release the territory of Judea and the three regions of Samaria*ʲ* from the payment of taxes, promising that if Demetrius would do that, he would pay him a lump sum of 22,000 pounds of silver. ²⁹The king agreed and wrote a letter to Jonathan to confirm all this:

³⁰"King Demetrius to King Jonathan and to the Jewish nation, greetings.

³¹"For your information I am sending a copy of the letter I have written to the Honorable Lasthenes about you:

³²"'King Demetrius to the Honorable Lasthenes, greetings. ³³I have decided to grant the Jewish nation certain benefits because they are our loyal allies and keep their treaty obligations. ³⁴I confirm their rights to the land of Judea and the three regions of Ephraim, Lydda, and Arimathea, which are hereby annexed to Judea from Samaria with all the lands belonging to them. This will be of benefit to everyone who goes to Jerusalem to offer sacrifice, since payments of the annual tax on produce and fruit from these lands will no longer be made to the king, but to the Temple. ³⁵And I also grant them relief from the payment of revenues now due me from tithes, tolls, salt taxes, and special taxes. ³⁶None of the provisions mentioned in this letter shall ever be canceled in the future.

³⁷"'You are required to see that a complete copy of this decree is made and given to Jonathan, to be posted in a prominent place on the Temple hill.'"

Jonathan Helps Demetrius the Second

³⁸When King Demetrius saw that the land was peaceful under his rule and there was no further resistance, he disbanded his whole army and sent everyone home, except the soldiers he had hired from the Greek islands. This made all the soldiers who had served under his predecessors hate him because they had lost their source of income. ³⁹One of Alexander's former supporters, Trypho, saw that all the soldiers were complaining about Demetrius, so he went to Imalkue, the Arab who was responsible for bringing up Alexander's young son Antiochus. ⁴⁰Trypho stayed there for a long time and kept urging Imalkue to hand the boy over to him, so that he could make him king in place of his father. He also told Imalkue about the decrees of Demetrius and how the soldiers hated him.

⁴¹Jonathan sent a message to King Demetrius asking him to remove his troops from the fort in Jerusalem and from the fortresses in Judea, since they kept harassing the Jews. ⁴²Demetrius replied: "I will do what you request, and when the opportunity presents itself, I will bestow upon you and your nation the highest honors. ⁴³But now you can help me by sending soldiers to fight for me, because all of my troops have revolted."

⁴⁴So Jonathan sent 3,000 trained sol-

ʲ Probable text three regions of Samaria; *Greek* three regions and Samaria.
11.34 1 Macc 10.30

diers to Antioch. The king was delighted when they arrived, ⁴⁵because a mob of 120,000 had gathered in the city determined to kill him. ⁴⁶But he escaped to the palace while the mob took control of the streets and began to riot. ⁴⁷Then the king called on the Jewish soldiers for help, and they all rushed to his aid. They went through the whole city and killed at least 100,000 people. ⁴⁸They saved the king's life, but they plundered and burned the city. ⁴⁹When the people saw that the Jews had complete control of the city, they lost courage and appealed to the king, requesting ⁵⁰him to arrange a truce and stop the Jewish attack. ⁵¹The rebels threw down their arms and surrendered. The king and everyone in his kingdom now had great respect for the Jews, who returned to Jerusalem with a great deal of loot. ⁵²Demetrius was firmly established as king, and the country was at peace under his rule, ⁵³but he broke all his promises and turned against Jonathan. He did not reward him for his loyal service, but instead continued to harass him.

Jonathan Supports Antiochus the Sixth

⁵⁴Some time later, Trypho returned with the young boy Antiochus and crowned him king. ⁵⁵All the soldiers that Demetrius had dismissed then came to the support of the young king. They defeated Demetrius, and he fled. ⁵⁶Trypho captured the elephants and took control of Antioch. ⁵⁷The young King Antiochus wrote to Jonathan and confirmed him as High Priest and as ruler over the four regions and gave him the title "Friend of the King." ⁵⁸He sent him a set of gold tableware and authorized him to drink from gold cups, to wear a royal robe, and to wear the gold shoulder buckle awarded to "Relatives of the King." ⁵⁹He also appointed Jonathan's brother Simon as governor of the territory from the Phoenician coast to the Egyptian border.

⁶⁰Jonathan then marched with his army through the towns of Greater Syria, and all the Syrian forces joined him as allies. He went to Ascalon, where the people welcomed him with great honors. ⁶¹Then he went to Gaza, but the people there barred their gates against him. So he laid siege to the city and burned and looted the surrounding area. ⁶²The people of Gaza then asked for peace, and Jonathan arranged a truce. He took the sons of the leaders and sent them to Jerusalem as hostages. After that he marched on as far as Damascus.

⁶³Jonathan learned that the officers of Demetrius had come to Kedesh in Galilee with a large army, intending to keep him from carrying out his plan. ⁶⁴So he left his brother Simon in Judea and set out to meet them in battle. ⁶⁵Then Simon laid siege to Bethzur and fought against it for a long time. ⁶⁶The people asked for peace terms, and Simon agreed. He then took over the town, drove the people out, and stationed a detachment of troops there.

⁶⁷Jonathan and his army set up camp by Lake Galilee. Early the next morning he marched his troops to the plain of Hazor, ⁶⁸where the main force of the foreign army was advancing to meet him. Unknown to Jonathan, they had left a detachment of troops in ambush in the mountains, ⁶⁹and when the men in ambush came out and attacked, ⁷⁰Jonathan's entire army turned and ran. No one was left, except two officers, Mattathias son of Absalom and Judas son of Chalphi. ⁷¹Jonathan was humiliated, so he tore his clothes, threw dust on his head, and prayed. ⁷²Then he turned back to the battle, crushed the enemy, and put them to flight. ⁷³When his own fleeing soldiers saw this, they turned back and joined him in pursuit. They chased the enemy all the way back to their camp at Kedesh and then took over the camp. ⁷⁴At least 3,000 enemy soldiers were killed

that day. Jonathan then returned to Jerusalem.

Alliances with Rome and Sparta

12 When Jonathan saw that things were working out to his advantage, he chose ambassadors and sent them to Rome to confirm and renew friendship with the Romans. ²He also sent letters with a similar message to Sparta and other places. ³The ambassadors went to Rome, where they were admitted to the Senate chamber, and reported that the High Priest Jonathan and the Jewish nation had sent them to renew the earlier ties of friendship and alliance with Rome. ⁴The Romans provided them with letters to the authorities in each country through which they would pass, guaranteeing them safe conduct in their return to the land of Judea.

⁵Here is a copy of the letter Jonathan wrote to the Spartans:

⁶"Jonathan the High Priest, the national council of leaders, the priests, and the rest of the people of Judea, to our brothers in Sparta, greetings. ⁷At an earlier time, your King Arius sent a letter to our High Priest Onias, stating that our two nations are related, as the attached copy shows. ⁸Onias received your ambassador with full honors and acknowledged receipt of your letter, which declared our alliance and friendship. ⁹And now, although we are not in need of such alliances, since we find our source of strength in the holy books we possess, ¹⁰we have written to renew our ties of brotherhood and friendship with you. We do not wish to become total strangers, and it has now been many years since your last communication. ¹¹Throughout the years we have taken every opportunity, on our festival days and other suitable days, to remember you when we have offered our sacrifices and made our prayers, as it is fitting and proper for brothers to do. ¹²We also are pleased that fame has come to you. ¹³But we have had one series of troubles after another and have had to fight many wars, because we have been under constant attack by surrounding nations. ¹⁴During this time of war, we did not wish to trouble you or our other allies and friends, ¹⁵since we do have the help of the Lord, who has defeated our enemies and rescued us from them. ¹⁶So we have chosen Numenius son of Antiochus together with Antipater son of Jason and sent them as ambassadors to Rome to renew our ties of friendship and alliance with the Romans. ¹⁷We have also ordered them to go to you with our greetings and deliver this letter about the renewal of our ties of brotherhood. ¹⁸And now we request an answer to this letter.

¹⁹"The following is a copy of the earlier letter:

²⁰" 'King Arius of Sparta to Onias the High Priest, greetings. ²¹We have found a document about the Spartans and the Jews indicating that we are related and that both of our nations are descended from Abraham. ²²Now that we have discovered this, please send us a report about your situation. ²³In reply, we will send you a letter indicating that we are willing to share our possessions, including cattle and property, if you will do the same. We have given orders to our ambassadors to give you a full report about these matters.' "

Campaigns of Jonathan and Simon

²⁴Jonathan learned that the officers of Demetrius had returned to attack him with an even larger army than before. ²⁵Jonathan did not want to give them an opportunity to penetrate his own territory, so he left Jerusalem and went to meet them in the region of Ha-

math. 26 Jonathan sent spies into the enemy camp, who reported to him that the enemy forces were making plans to attack the Jews by night. 27 At sunset Jonathan ordered all his soldiers to be on the alert and to have their weapons ready for a surprise attack any time during the night. He also stationed guards all around the camp. 28 When the enemy soldiers learned that Jonathan and his men were ready for battle, they were panic-stricken and fled, leaving

They were panic-stricken and fled, leaving their campfires burning. (12.28)

their campfires burning. 29 Jonathan and his men saw the campfires but did not realize what had happened until the next morning. 30 Jonathan then set out after them, but he could not overtake them because they had already crossed the Eleutherus River. 31 Then Jonathan turned aside and attacked a tribe of Arabs called Zabadeans. He defeated them and plundered their possessions. 32 Then he broke camp and went to Damascus, inspecting the entire area along the way.

33 Meanwhile, Simon had also set out on a campaign and had advanced as far as Ascalon and the neighboring fortresses. Then he turned aside to Joppa 34 and stationed a detachment of soldiers there because he had heard that the people were planning to hand over the fortress of Joppa to the soldiers of Demetrius.

35 When Jonathan returned, he called the council of the leaders together and made plans with them to build fortresses in Judea, 36 to increase the height of the walls of Jerusalem, and to build a high wall to separate the fort from the city. This would isolate the fort, making it impossible for the enemy to buy or sell anything. 37 The people worked together to strengthen the city's defenses because a part of the east wall along the Kidron Valley had collapsed and the Chaphenatha section was in need of repair. 38 Simon also rebuilt the town of Adida in the foothills. He fortified it and constructed barred gates for it.

Trypho Captures Jonathan

39 Then Trypho plotted a rebellion against King Antiochus so that he could make himself king of Syria. 40 He was afraid, however, that Jonathan would not agree to this and would go to war against him to prevent it. So Trypho got his army ready and went to Beth Shan in the hope of capturing Jonathan and putting him to death. 41 But Jonathan also came to Beth Shan with 40,000 well-trained soldiers. 42 When Trypho saw how large an army Jonathan had brought with him, he was afraid to take action. 43 So he received Jonathan with all honors, presented him to all his advisers, gave him gifts, and ordered his advisers and soldiers to obey Jonathan as they would him. 44 He asked Jonathan, "Why have you put these soldiers to so much trouble when we are not at war? 45 Why don't you send them home? Choose a few men to stay with you, and then accompany me to Ptolemais. I will hand the city over to you, as well as the rest of the fortresses, the troops, and all the officials. Then I will turn around and leave. In fact, that's why I am here." 46 Jonathan believed

him, and following his advice, sent his soldiers back to Judea. [47] He took 3,000 men with him, but left 2,000 of them in Galilee, while only 1,000 accompanied him the rest of the way. [48] But when Jonathan entered Ptolemais, the people of the city locked the gates, arrested him, and killed everyone who had come with him.

[49] Trypho sent infantry and cavalry units to Galilee and Jezreel Valley to kill the rest of Jonathan's soldiers. [50] The Jewish troops thought that Jonathan had been captured and killed, along with all those who had accompanied him, so they encouraged one another and marched out in battle formation. [51] When the approaching enemy forces saw that the Jews were ready to fight for their lives, they turned back. [52] Then the Jewish soldiers returned to Judea safely, but terribly afraid. The whole nation was in deep mourning, assuming that Jonathan and all his men had been killed. [53] All the surrounding nations now tried to destroy them. They thought that the Jews had no leaders or allies and that the time was ripe to annihilate them and put an end to their history.

Simon Leads the Jews

13 Simon learned that Trypho had assembled a large army and that he had plans to invade Judea and devastate it. [2] He realized that this news had brought panic and fear to the people, so he went to Jerusalem, called the people together, [3] and tried to encourage them by saying, "You know how much my father's family, my brothers, and I have done for the sake of the Law of Moses and the Temple. You also know about the wars we have fought and the troubles we have had. [4] All my brothers have been killed fighting for our Law, our Temple, and our nation, and I am the only one left. [5] But never let it be said that I tried to save my own life in a time of danger; I do not con-

sider myself better than my brothers. [6] Not in the least! It is true that in their hatred all the Gentile nations have gathered together to destroy us, but I will fight to defend my nation, the Temple, and your loved ones."

[7] These words immediately revived the morale of the people, [8] and they answered with a loud shout, "You are now our leader in place of your brothers Judas and Jonathan. [9] Fight our wars, and we will do whatever you ask." [10] So Simon gathered together all the soldiers and hurried to complete the walls of Jerusalem and to strengthen all its defenses. [11] He sent Jonathan son of Absalom to Joppa with a large army. This Jonathan drove out the people who were there and occupied the town.

[12] Trypho left Ptolemais with a large army to invade Judea, taking Simon's brother Jonathan along with him as a prisoner. [13] Simon set up camp at Adida at the edge of the plain. [14] When Trypho learned that Simon had succeeded his brother Jonathan and that he was ready to meet him in battle, he sent this message to him: [15] "I am holding your brother Jonathan under arrest because while he was in office he did not pay his debts to the royal treasury. [16] However, I will release him if you will pay me 6,000 pounds of silver and send two of his sons as hostages to guarantee that he will not revolt against us when he is released."

[17] Although Simon knew that they were deceiving him, he sent for the money and the two sons because he did not want to arouse the hostility of the Jews. [18] He was afraid that they might later say that Jonathan was put to death because Simon would not send the money and the boys. [19] So he did as Trypho had demanded, but Trypho broke his promise and did not release Jonathan.

[20] Then Trypho made his move to invade the land and destroy it, circling around by the road to Adora. But Simon and his army moved along facing him

wherever he went. 21 The enemy soldiers in the fort in Jerusalem kept sending messengers to Trypho urging him to come to them quickly by way of the desert and to send them supplies. 22 Trypho got all his cavalry ready for the invasion, but that night there was a heavy snowstorm, and he was not able to move up into the hills. So he withdrew and went into Gilead. 23 When he was near Baskama, he had Jonathan put to death and his body buried there. 24 Then Trypho turned and went back to his own country.

25 Simon had the body of his brother Jonathan brought to Modein, to be buried in the town of their ancestors. 26 Everyone in Israel was in deep sorrow at the loss of Jonathan, and they mourned for him a long time. 27 Over the tomb of his father and his brothers Simon built a high monument that could be seen from a great distance. It was covered front and back with polished stone. 28 He constructed seven pyramids side by side for his father, his mother, and his four brothers. 29 For the pyramids he created a setting of tall columns on which there were carvings. Some of these carvings were of suits of armor and some were of ships. It was a monument to their victories, which travelers from overseas could visit. k 30 The tomb which he built in Modein is still there today.

31 Meanwhile, Trypho assassinated the young king, Antiochus the Sixth, 32 and took over his kingdom in Syria. He brought that country great troubles.

33 Simon rebuilt the fortresses of Judea with high towers, strong walls, and barred gates; then he placed stores of supplies there. 34 He sent ambassadors to King Demetrius the Second to ask for tax relief for the land, since Trypho was doing nothing but robbing them. 35 King Demetrius sent the following letter in reply:

36 "King Demetrius to the High Priest Simon, the friend of kings, to the Jewish nation, and to their leaders, greetings. 37 I have received the gold crown and the gold palm branch which you sent, and I am prepared to make a peace treaty with you and to instruct our tax officials to grant you exemptions. 38 Our previous agreements with you are confirmed, and the fortresses which you have built are to remain yours. 39 I grant you pardon for treaty violations committed up to the present date, and I release you from payment of the special tax still due and any other taxes that have been collected up to this time in Jerusalem. 40 All Jews who are qualified may enroll in the royal service. Let us have peace."

41 So in the year 170 l the yoke of the Gentile oppressors was removed from the Jews. 42 People began to date their documents and contracts with these words: "In the first year of Simon, the great High Priest, commander and leader of the Jews."

43 At that time Simon laid siege to Gezer and surrounded it with his army. He built a movable siege platform, brought it up to the town wall, attacked one of the towers, and captured it. 44 The men who had been on the siege platform then moved rapidly into the town, and this created great confusion. 45 The men of the town, their wives, and their children tore their clothes in distress and climbed up on the top of the town wall. They pleaded loudly with Simon for a truce. 46 "Have mercy on us," they begged. "Don't punish us as we deserve!"

47 So Simon came to terms with them and ended the fighting. He made the people leave the town; then he purified the houses in which there had been idols. When that was done, he and his men entered the town singing hymns

---

k Verses 28-29 in Greek are unclear.   l THE YEAR 170: This corresponds to 142 B.C.
13.43 2 Macc 10.32-38

and songs of praise. [48] He eliminated everything that would make the town ritually unclean and settled it with people who would obey every command contained in the Law of Moses. He strengthened the defenses of the town and built himself a palace there.

[49] Those in the fort in Jerusalem were now prevented from leaving to buy or sell anything. They were suffering from severe hunger and many of them had died of starvation. [50] Finally they appealed to Simon for a truce. He agreed, removed them from the fort, and purified it. [51] On the twenty-third day of the second month, in the year 171,[m] there was a great celebration in the city because this terrible threat to the security of Israel had come to an end. Simon and his men entered the fort singing hymns of praise and thanksgiving, while carrying palm branches and playing harps, cymbals, and lyres. [52] Simon issued a decree that the day should be joyfully

Simon and his men entered the fort. (13.51)

celebrated every year. He strengthened the defenses of the Temple hill on the side facing the fort, and he and his men made their headquarters there. [53] Simon's son John was now a grown man, so Simon made him commander of the whole army, and John set up headquarters at Gezer.

In Praise of Simon

14 In the year 172[n] King Demetrius the Second gathered his army and went to Media to seek additional help for his war against Trypho. [2] When King Arsaces the Sixth of Persia and Media heard that Demetrius had entered his territory, he sent one of his commanders with some troops to capture Demetrius alive. [3] They attacked and defeated the army of Demetrius, took him captive, and brought him back to King Arsaces, who threw him in prison.

[4] The land of Judea was at peace as long as Simon lived. During his entire reign, he used his position of power and influence to do what was good for his people, and they were always pleased with him as their ruler. [5] He added to his reputation when he captured the port of Joppa and opened up the route to the Greek islands. [6] He not only enlarged the territory of his nation and gained control of the whole country, [7] but he brought back many prisoners of war and captured Gezer, Bethzur, and the fort in Jerusalem. He purified the fort, and there was no one to oppose him.

[8] The Jews farmed their land in peace; the land produced its crops and the trees bore fruit. [9] The young men showed off their splendid military uniforms, while the old men sat around the city squares and talked about the great things that had happened. [10] Simon supplied the cities with food and pro-

---

[m] THE YEAR 171: *This corresponds to 141 B.C.*   [n] THE YEAR 172: *This corresponds to 140 B.C.*

vided them with weapons of defense. His fame spread everywhere. ¹¹He brought peace to the country, and Israel's joy knew no bounds. ¹²Everyone lived in peace among his own grapevines and fig trees, and no one made them afraid. ¹³In those days all the enemy kings had been defeated, and there was no one left in the land to fight the Jews. ¹⁴Simon provided help for all the poor among his people, and guided by the Law of Moses, he eliminated all wicked and lawless men. ¹⁵He provided the Temple with splendid furnishings and added a large number of utensils for use in worship.

¹⁶When the news that Jonathan had died reached Rome and Sparta, it brought great sorrow. ¹⁷But when the Spartans heard that Simon had succeeded his brother as High Priest and that he was in control of the country and its towns, ¹⁸they engraved on bronze tablets a renewal of the treaty of friendship which they had made with his brothers Judas and Jonathan and sent the tablets to him. ¹⁹These were read to the assembly in Jerusalem. ²⁰What follows is a copy of the letter sent by the Spartans:

"The people of Sparta and their rulers to Simon the High Priest, to the leaders and the priests of the Jews, and to all our Jewish brothers, greetings. ²¹The delegation that you sent to our people has told us how respected and renowned you are. Their visit has been a source of joy for us, ²²and a report of their visit has been written down in our public records, as follows: 'Numenius son of Antiochus and Antipater son of Jason, honored representatives of the Jews, appeared before us to renew their treaty of friendship. ²³The assembly of the people was pleased to receive these men with all honors and to place a copy of their report in the public archives, so that the people of Sparta may have it on record. A copy of this document has been made for the High Priest Simon.'"

²⁴Later, Simon sent Numenius to Rome with the gift of a large gold shield weighing half a ton, to confirm the Jews' alliance with the Romans.

²⁵When the people of Israel heard about all this, they asked themselves, "How can we express our thanks to Simon and his sons? ²⁶He, his brothers, and his father's whole family have been towers of strength for our nation. They have fought off our enemies and set the nation free."

So they recorded this on bronze tablets and set them up on columns on Mount Zion. ²⁷The inscription read as follows:

"On the eighteenth day of the month of Elul in the year 172,ⁿ that is, in the third year of Simon, the High Priest,ᵒ ²⁸at a great assembly of priests, people, officials, and national leaders the following facts were made known to us: ²⁹Often when wars broke out in the country, Simon son of Mattathias, a priest of the Jehoiarib family, and his brothers risked their lives in protecting our nation, our Temple, and our Law against our enemies. They have brought great glory to our nation. ³⁰Jonathan united our people and became the High Priest before he died. ³¹The enemies of the Jews plotted to invade the land and defile the Temple. ³²Then Simon assumed command and fought for his country. He spent a large amount of his own money to provide weapons and wages for his nation's armed forces. ³³He fortified the towns of Judea, and especially Bethzur on the border, where enemy weapons had

ⁿ THE YEAR 172: *This corresponds to 140 B.C. meaning of which is unclear.*
14.18 1 Macc 8.22

ᵒ *Greek has an additional word, the*

previously been stored. He stationed a detachment of soldiers there. ³⁴ He fortified the seaport of Joppa and the city of Gezer on the border of Azotus, which was previously occupied by enemy soldiers. He settled Jews there and provided the towns with everything that the people needed.ᵖ ³⁵ When the people saw Simon's patriotism and how he wanted to bring glory to his nation, they made him their leader and High Priest. They did this because of all that he had accomplished through his loyalty and because he had brought about justice and had tried in every way to bring glory to his nation.

³⁶ "Under his leadership the Gentiles were driven out of the land. Enemy soldiers were forced out of the area north of the Temple, where they had built the fort, from which the soldiers used to go out and defile the holy Temple. ³⁷ Simon settled Jews in the fort, strengthened it for the security of the country and the city of Jerusalem, and increased the height of the city walls. ³⁸ As a result, King Demetrius confirmed him as High Priest, ³⁹ gave him the title of "Friend of the King," and treated him with great honor. ⁴⁰ Demetrius did this because he had heard that the Romans were calling the Jews their friends, allies, and brothers and that they had received Simon's delegation with full honors.

⁴¹ "Therefore,�q the Jews and their priests are happy to have Simon and his descendants as their leaders and High Priests, until a true prophet appears. ⁴² Simon shall govern their country, have charge of the Temple, and shall be their military commander. He shall be in charge of military supplies, fortifications, and public works. ⁴³ The people must obey him in everything. All govern-

ment contracts shall be drawn up in his name. He shall have the right to wear royal robes with the gold shoulder buckle.

⁴⁴ "No one, priest or people, shall have the legal right to annul any of these decisions, to alter or change any of Simon's orders, to convene any assembly in the country without his permission, or to wear royal robes with the gold shoulder buckle. ⁴⁵ Anyone who disobeys or disregards these regulations shall be subject to punishment.

⁴⁶ "The people gave their unanimous approval to grant Simon the right to act in accordance with these regulations. ⁴⁷ Simon consented and agreed to be supreme leader: High Priest, commander of the armies, and governor of the Jews and the priests."

⁴⁸ It was decided that this declaration should be engraved on bronze tablets and set up in a prominent place within the Temple area ⁴⁹ and that copies should be placed in the Temple treasury, where Simon and his sons would have access to them.

Antiochus the Seventh Asks for Simon's Support

15 From the Greek islands Antiochus son of King Demetrius wrote the following letter to Simon the High Priest and governor of the Jews and to the whole nation:

² "King Antiochus to Simon, the High Priest and governor, and to the Jewish nation, greetings. ³ As you know, the kingdom of my ancestors has been seized by traitors. I have decided to reclaim it and restore its former greatness. I have raised a large army of mercenary troops and have fitted out warships. ⁴ I plan to invade the land and to attack those

---

ᵖ that the people needed; *or* that was needed to keep them in repair.   q Therefore; *some manuscripts have* and that.

who have destroyed many of the towns and ruined the country.

⁵"Now therefore, I confirm all exemptions from taxes and payments granted you by former kings. ⁶I authorize you to mint your own coins as legal currency in your own country. ⁷Jerusalem and the Temple shall be free of taxation. All the weapons that you have manufactured and the defenses you have built and now occupy shall remain yours. ⁸In addition, all debts now owed to the royal treasury, or which may in the future fall due, are permanently canceled. ⁹As soon as I have regained control of my kingdom, I will confer upon you, your nation, and the Temple such great honors that the glory of your country will be evident to the whole world."

¹⁰In the year 174ʳ Antiochus invaded the land of his ancestors. Most of the soldiers came over to his side, so that there were very few left with Trypho. ¹¹Trypho, pursued by Antiochus, fled to the coastal city of Dor, ¹²realizing that he was in a desperate situation, now that all his troops had deserted him. ¹³Then Antiochus laid siege to Dor with 120,000 well-trained soldiers and 8,000 cavalry. ¹⁴With his ships joining the attack, he completely surrounded the town and brought such pressure on it that no one was able to enter or leave.

Rome Supports the Jews

¹⁵Meanwhile, Numenius and those with him arrived in Jerusalem from Rome with the following letter addressed to various kings and countries:

¹⁶"From Lucius, consul of the Romans, to King Ptolemy, greetings. ¹⁷A delegation from our friends and allies the Jews has come to us to renew the earlier treaty of friendship and alliance. They were sent by the High Priest Simon and the Jewish people, ¹⁸and they have brought as a gift a gold shield weighing half a ton. ¹⁹So we have decided to write to various kings and countries urging them not to harm the Jews, their towns, or their country in any way. They must not make war against the Jews or give support to those who attack them. ²⁰We have decided to accept the shield and grant them protection. ²¹Therefore if any traitors escape from Judea and seek refuge in your land, hand them over to Simon the High Priest, so that he may punish them according to Jewish law."

²²Lucius wrote the same letter to King Demetrius, to Attalus, Ariarathes, and Arsaces, ²³and to all the following countries: Sampsames, Sparta, Delos, Myndos, Sicyon, Caria, Samos, Pamphylia, Lycia, Halicarnassus, Rhodes, Phaselis, Cos, Side, Aradus, Gortyna, Cnidus, Cyprus, and Cyrene. ²⁴A copy of the letter was also sent to Simon the High Priest.

Antiochus the Seventh Breaks with Simon

²⁵King Antiochus laid siege to Dor for a second time, keeping it under constant attack. He built siege platforms, and his blockade kept Trypho and his men from going in or out. ²⁶Simon sent 2,000 well-trained soldiers to help Antiochus, as well as silver and gold and a great deal of equipment. ²⁷But Antiochus refused to accept them, canceled all the previous agreements that he had made with Simon, and became his enemy. ²⁸Then Antiochus sent his trusted official Athenobius to negotiate with Simon. He told Simon, "You are occupying Joppa, Gezer, and the fort in Jerusalem, cities that belong to my kingdom. ²⁹You have devastated those

---

ʳ THE YEAR 174: *This corresponds to 138 B.C.*
15.15 1 Macc 12.16

regions and brought great trouble to the country. You have seized control of many places in my kingdom. 30 Now you must hand back these cities that you have captured, and you must give me the tax money that you have taken from places that you occupied outside the territory of Judea. 31 If you are unwilling to do this, then you must pay me 30,000 pounds of silver, and 30,000 additional pounds of silver to compensate me for damages and for lost taxes. If you refuse to do either of these, we will go to war against you."

32 When Athenobius came to Jerusalem and saw the splendor of Simon's court, the gold and silver tableware in his banquet hall, and the rest of the display of great wealth, he was amazed. He delivered the king's message to Simon, 33 and Simon answered, "We have never taken land away from other nations or confiscated anything that belonged to other people. On the contrary, we have simply taken back property that we inherited from our ancestors, land that had been unjustly taken away from us by our enemies at one time or another. 34 We are now only making use of this opportunity to recover our ancestral heritage. 35 As for Joppa and Gezer, which you claim, we will give you 6,000 pounds of silver, in spite of the fact that the people of those cities have done great harm to our nation."

Athenobius made no reply, 36 but he returned to the king in a rage. When he told the king what Simon had said, and reported on the splendor of Simon's court and all that he had seen, the king became violently angry.

John's Victory over Cendebeus

37 In the meantime, Trypho had boarded a ship and escaped to the town of Orthosia. 38 King Antiochus appointed Cendebeus as commander of the coastal area, provided him with infantry and cavalry, 39 and gave him orders to move against Judea. He also ordered him to rebuild the town of Kedron and fortify its gates, so that he could fight against the Jewish people. The king himself continued to pursue Trypho.

40 Cendebeus then came to Jamnia and began to harass the Jews by invading Judea, capturing people, and murdering them. 41 He rebuilt Kedron and stationed some cavalry and infantry units there, so that they could make attacks and patrol the roads of Judea, as the king had ordered.

16 Simon's son John left Gezer and went to report to his father what Cendebeus had done. 2 Simon said to John and Judas, his two oldest sons, "All my father's family, my brothers, and I have fought Israel's battles all our lives, and many times we have been successful in saving Israel. 3 I am old now, but you, thanks to God, are in the prime of life. You must take my place and that of my brother in fighting for our nation. And may God himself be with you."

4 Then John raised an Israelite army of 20,000 trained soldiers and cavalry and marched out against Cendebeus. They spent the night in Modein, 5 and then early the next morning they moved into the plain. There a large army of infantry and cavalry moved to meet them, but there was a river between the two armies. 6 John and his army took up battle positions facing the enemy, but when John saw that his soldiers were afraid to cross the river, he crossed ahead of them, and his men saw him and followed. 7 John divided his army and placed his cavalry in the middle of the infantry, because there was a large number of enemy cavalry. 8 The trumpets sounded the attack, and Cendebeus and his army were defeated, and many of them were killed. The rest ran back to their fortress at Kedron. 9 Judas was wounded in the battle, but his brother John continued to pursue the enemy as far as Kedron, which Cendebeus had rebuilt. 10 The

escaping soldiers fled to the towers in the fields at Azotus, and John set fire to the city. On that day, 2,000 enemy soldiers were killed, and John returned safely to Judea.

The Murder of Simon and Two of His Sons

11 Simon the High Priest had appointed Ptolemy son of Abubus commander for the Plain of Jericho. Ptolemy was very rich, 12 because he was Simon's son-in-law. 13 But he became too ambitious and wanted to take over the country. So he devised a plan to assassinate Simon and his sons. 14 Simon, together with his sons Mattathias and Judas, was visiting the towns in the area, in order to take care of their needs. They arrived in Jericho in the month of Shebat, the eleventh month, in the year 177.*s* 15 Ptolemy, still plotting to murder Simon and his two sons, received them in a small fortress called Dok, which he had built. He gave a great banquet for them, but he had men hidden within the fortress. 16 When Simon and his sons were drunk, Ptolemy and his men came out of hiding and with

swords in hand rushed into the banquet hall, where they killed Simon, his two sons, and some of the servants. 17 With this horrible act of treachery, Ptolemy returned evil for good.

18 Then Ptolemy wrote a report of what he had done and sent it to the king. In the letter he requested that troops be sent to help him and that the country and the cities be turned over to him. 19 He wrote a letter to the army officers inviting them to join him and promising them silver, gold, and gifts. Then he sent some of his men to Gezer to kill John, 20 and others to take control of Jerusalem and the Temple hill. 21 But someone ran to Gezer ahead of Ptolemy's men and reported to John that his father and his brothers had been killed and that Ptolemy was sending his soldiers to kill him. 22 John was horrified at this news, but, because he had been warned in advance, he was able to capture and put to death the men who had been sent to kill him.

23 Now the rest of what John did from the time he succeeded his father: his wars, his deeds of courage, his rebuilding of walls, and his other accomplishments, 24 are all written in the chronicles of his reign as High Priest.

---

s THE YEAR 177: *This corresponds to 134 B.C.*

The Second Book of the
MACCABEES

INTRODUCTION

The Second Book of the Maccabees is a condensation of a five-volume history by Jason of Cyrene. The book reports events in Jewish history from the time of the High Priest, Onias the Third (about 180 B.C.), to the death of Nicanor (161 B.C.), and parallels in part the events described in the early chapters of *1 Maccabees*. There is a strong emphasis on loyalty to the law and on God's reward to martyrs who die for their faith.

OUTLINE OF CONTENTS

A Letter to the Jews in Egypt

1 "From the Jews of Jerusalem and Judea to those in Egypt, warm greetings.

² "May God be good to you and keep the covenant he made with Abraham, Isaac, and Jacob, his faithful servants. ³ May he fill each of you with the desire to worship him and to do his will eagerly with all your heart and soul. ⁴ May he enable you to understand his Law and his commands. May he give you peace, ⁵ answer your prayers, forgive your sins, and never abandon you in times of trouble. ⁶ Here in Judah we are now praying for you.

⁷ "In the year 169,ᵃ when Demetrius the Second was king of Syria, we wrote to tell you about the persecution and the hard times that came upon us in the years after Jason revolted against authority in the Holy Land. ⁸ Jason and his men set fire to the Temple gates and

slaughtered innocent people. Then we prayed to the Lord and he answered our prayers. So we sacrificed animals, gave offerings of grain, lit the lamps in the Temple, and set out the sacred loaves. ⁹ This is why we urge you to celebrate in the month of Kislev a festival similar to the Festival of Shelters. Written in the year 188."ᵇ

A LETTER TO ARISTOBULUS

The Death of King Antiochus

¹⁰ "From the Jews of Jerusalem and Judea, the Jewish Senate, and Judas, to Aristobulus, a descendant of priests and the teacher of King Ptolemy, and to the Jews in Egypt, greetings and good health.

¹¹ "We thank God because he saved us from great danger. We were like men ready to fight against a king, ¹² but God drove the enemy from our holy

---

ᵃ THE YEAR 169: *This corresponds to 143 B.C.*

ᵇ THE YEAR 188: *This corresponds to 124 B.C.*

Everyone looked on in amazement. (1.22)

city. [13] When King Antiochus arrived in Persia, his army seemed impossible to defeat, but they were cut to pieces in the temple of the goddess Nanea by an act of treachery on the part of her priests. [14] King Antiochus had gone to the temple with some of his most trusted advisers, so that he might marry the goddess and then take away most of the temple treasures as a wedding gift. [15] After the priests had laid out the treasure, he and a few of his men went into the temple to collect it. But the priests closed the doors behind him [16] and stoned him and his men from trap doors hidden in the ceiling. Then they cut up the bodies and threw the heads to the people outside. [17] Praise God for punishing those evil men! Praise him for everything!

Fire Consumes Nehemiah's Sacrifice

[18] "On the twenty-fifth day of the month of Kislev we will celebrate the Festival of Rededication just as we celebrate the Festival of Shelters. We thought it important to remind you of this, so that you too may celebrate this festival. In this way you will remember how fire appeared when Nehemiah offered sacrifices after he had rebuilt the Temple and the altar. [19] At the time when our ancestors were being taken to exile in Persia, a few devout priests took some fire from the altar and secretly hid it in the bottom of a dry cistern. They hid the fire so well that no one ever discovered it. [20] Years later, when it pleased God, the Persian emperor sent Nehemiah back to Jerusalem, and Nehemiah told the descendants of those priests to find the fire. They reported to us that they had found no fire but only some oily liquid. Nehemiah then told them to scoop some up and bring it to him. [21] When everything for the sacrifice had been placed on the altar, he told the priests to pour the liquid over both the wood and the sacrifice. [22] After this was done and some time had passed, the sun appeared from behind the clouds, and suddenly everything on the altar burst into flames. Everyone looked on in amazement. [23] Then, while the fire was consuming the sacrifice, Jonathan the High Priest led the people in prayer, and Nehemiah and all the people responded.

Nehemiah's Prayer

[24] "Nehemiah's prayer went something like this: 'Lord God, Creator of all

1.13-16 1 Macc 6.1-4; 2 Macc 9.1-10

things, you are awesome and strong, yet merciful and just. You alone are king. No one but you is kind; [25] no one but you is gracious and just. You are almighty and eternal, forever ready to rescue Israel from trouble. You chose our ancestors to be your own special people. [26] Accept this sacrifice which we offer on behalf of all Israel; protect your chosen people and make us holy. [27] Free those who are slaves in foreign lands and gather together our scattered people. Have mercy on our people, who are mistreated and despised, so that all other nations will know that you are our God. [28] Punish the brutal and arrogant people who have oppressed us, [29] and then establish your people in your holy land, as Moses said you would.'

The Persian Emperor Hears about the Fire

[30] "Then the priests sang hymns. [31] After the sacrifices had been consumed, Nehemiah gave orders for the rest of the liquid to be poured over some large stones. [32] Immediately a fire blazed up, but it was extinguished by a flame from the fire on the altar.

[33] "News of what had happened spread everywhere. The Persian emperor heard that a liquid had been found in the place where the priests had hidden the altar fire, just before they were taken into exile. He also heard that Nehemiah and his friends had used this liquid to burn the sacrifice on the altar. [34] When the emperor investigated the matter and found out that this was true, he had the area fenced off and made into a shrine. [35] It became a substantial source of income for him, and he used the money for gifts to anyone who was in his good favor. [36] Nehemiah and his friends called the liquid *nephthar*, which means 'purification,' but most people call it 'naphtha.'

Jeremiah Hides the Tent of the Lord's Presence

2 "We know from the records that Jeremiah the prophet instructed the people who were being taken into exile to hide some of the fire from the altar, as we have just mentioned. [2] We also know that he taught them God's Law and warned them not to be deceived by the ornamented gold and silver idols which they would see in the land of their exile. [3] And then he urged them never to abandon the Law.

[4] "These same records also tell us that Jeremiah, acting under divine guidance, commanded the Tent of the Lord's Presence and the Covenant Box to follow him to the mountain where Moses had looked down on the land which God had promised our people. [5] When Jeremiah got to the mountain, he found a huge cave and there he hid the Tent of the Lord's Presence, the Covenant Box, and the altar of incense. Then he sealed up the entrance.

[6] "Some of Jeremiah's friends tried to follow him and mark the way, but they could not find the cave. [7] When Jeremiah learned what they had done, he reprimanded them, saying, 'No one must know about this place until God gathers his people together again and shows them mercy. [8] At that time he will reveal where these things are hidden, and the dazzling light of his presence will be seen in the cloud, as it was in the time of Moses and on the occasion when Solomon prayed that the Temple might be dedicated in holy splendor.'

How Solomon Celebrated the Festival

[9] "We are also told how the wise King Solomon offered a sacrifice of dedication at the completion of the Temple, [10] and that when he prayed, fire came down from heaven and consumed the sacrifices, just as it had done earlier

2.8 Ex 16.10; 24.16; 1 K 8.10, 11

. . . but they could not find the cave. (2.6)

when Moses prayed. ¹¹Moses had explained that the sin offering was consumed by fire because it was not eaten. ¹²Solomon celebrated the festival for eight days.

Nehemiah's Library

¹³"These same facts are found in the royal records and in the memoirs of Nehemiah, who established a library and collected the writings of David, letters of the kings concerning offerings, and books about the kings and prophets. ¹⁴Judas also collected the books that had been scattered because of the war, and we still have them. ¹⁵If you ever need any of these books, let us know, and we will send them.

An Invitation to Celebrate the Festival

¹⁶"Since we are about to celebrate the Festival of Rededication, we are

writing to you, advising you to celebrate it as well. ¹⁷God has saved all his people and has restored to all of us our holy land, the kingship, the priesthood, and the Temple services, ¹⁸just as he promised in his Law. He has rescued us from terrible evils and has purified the Temple, and we are confident that in his mercy he will soon gather us to his holy Temple from every nation under the sun."

Author's Preface

¹⁹Jason of Cyrene has recorded in five volumes the story of Judas Maccabeus and his brothers, the purification of the great Temple, and the dedication of its altar. ²⁰He has described the battles with Antiochus Epiphanes and with his son Eupator, ²¹and he has told of the heavenly visions that appeared to those who fought bravely and enthusiastically to defend Judaism. Our forces

were few in number, but they plundered the entire country and routed the heathen forces. [22] They recaptured the Temple famous throughout the world, liberated Jerusalem, and restored the laws that were in danger of being abolished. They were able to do all these things because the Lord was merciful and kind to them.

[23] I will now try to summarize in a single book the five volumes written by Jason. [24] The number of details and the bulk of material can be overwhelming for anyone who wants to read an account of the events. [25] But I have attempted to simplify it for all readers; those who read for sheer pleasure will find enjoyment and those who want to memorize the facts will not find it difficult. [26] Writing such a summary is a difficult task, demanding hard work and sleepless nights. [27] It is as difficult as preparing a banquet that people of different tastes will enjoy. But I am happy to undergo this hardship in order to please my readers. [28] I will leave the matter of details to the original author and attempt to give only a summary of the events. [29] I am not the builder of a new house who is concerned with every detail of the structure, but simply a painter whose only concern is to make the house look attractive. [30] The historian must master his subject, examine every detail, and then explain it carefully, [31] but whoever is merely writing a summary should be permitted to give a brief account without going into a detailed discussion. [32] So then, without any further comment, I will begin my story. It would be foolish to write such a long introduction that the story itself would have to be cut short.

The Argument between Onias and Simon

3 When Onias[c] was High Priest in Jerusalem, the holy city enjoyed peace and prosperity, and its laws were strictly obeyed, because he was devout and hated evil. [2] The kings of Syria and Egypt honored the Temple and presented it with expensive gifts, [3] and King Seleucus,[d] ruler of all Asia, even used to pay the costs of the Temple sacrifices from the revenues he collected.

[4] But a man by the name of Simon, of the tribe of Bilgah,[e] the chief administrative official of the Temple, lost an argument he had with Onias over the regulations governing the city market. [5] At this time Apollonius son of Thraseus was the governor of Greater Syria. Simon went to him [6] and said that there was so much money in the Temple treasury that it could not be counted, and since the money was not needed for sacrifices, it might as well be placed under the king's control.

Heliodorus Is Sent to Jerusalem

[7] When Apollonius met with the king, he told him about the money, and the king ordered Heliodorus, his chief minister, to get it for him. [8] Heliodorus set out at once on his mission, but he claimed that he was only making a tour of inspection of the cities of Greater Syria. [9] After he had arrived in Jerusalem and had been warmly received by the High Priest, he explained the real reason for his visit and asked if what he had been told was true. [10-11] The High Priest then stated that Simon, that devil of a man, had not been telling the truth. There was indeed some money in the Temple treasury, but part of it was set aside for widows and orphans and part of it belonged to Hyrcanus son of To-

---

[c] ONIAS: *This is Onias the Third, son of Simon the Second (see 4.4-6; Si 50.1-21).*
[d] SELEUCUS: *This is Seleucus the Fourth, known as Philopator, son of Antiochus the Third, 187–175 B.C.*   [e] *Some ancient translations* Bilgah *(see Ne 12.5,18); Greek* Benjamin.

bias, a very important man. He also pointed out that the total amount was only 30,000 pounds of silver and 15,000 pounds of gold. 12 He added that it was absolutely impossible that anyone should be permitted to take the money of those people who had placed their trust in the sanctity and safety of this world-famous Temple.

Heliodorus Plans to Enter the Temple

13 But Heliodorus insisted that the money should be taken for the royal treasury, as the king had ordered. 14 So he set a day and went into the Temple to supervise the counting of the money. This caused an uproar throughout the entire city. 15 Priests, wearing their priestly robes, threw themselves face downward before the altar and begged God to keep the money safe, since he had given the laws designed to protect the money that people deposited in the Temple. 16 It was heartbreaking to see the High Priest. His face turned pale, revealing the agony of his soul, 17 and his body was trembling with fear, reflecting the pain in his heart. 18 People ran from their houses to join together in prayer that the Temple might not be defiled. 19 Women, wearing nothing but skirts of sackcloth, crowded the streets. Young girls whose parents had never allowed them to be seen in public ran to the gates or to the walls of the city, or just stared out of their windows. 20 But wherever they went, they lifted their hands to God in prayer. 21 What a pitiful sight it was to see the High Priest in such great agony and frustration and to see everyone in the city confused and lying face down on the ground.

The Lord Protects His Temple

22 While everyone was begging the Lord Almighty to protect the money that had been entrusted to his care, 23 Heliodorus went on with his plan. 24 But at the very moment that he and

It was heartbreaking to see the High Priest. (3.16)

his bodyguards arrived at the treasury, the Lord of all supernatural powers caused such a vision to appear that everyone who had dared to enter with Heliodorus was panic-stricken and weak with fear at this display of the Lord's power. 25 In the vision they saw a horse and a rider. The horse had a richly decorated bridle, and its rider, dressed in gold armor, was frightening. Suddenly the horse rushed at Heliodorus, then reared up and struck at him with its hoofs. 26 Heliodorus also saw two unusually strong and handsome young men, wearing very fine clothes. They stood on either side of him and beat him unmercifully. 27 He immediately fell to the ground unconscious, and his men put him on a stretcher 28 and carried him out. Only a moment earlier this man had entered the treasury with a large group of men, including all his bodyguards, but now he was being carried away helpless. So they all*f* openly acknowledged the mighty power of God.

Onias Prays for Heliodorus' Recovery

²⁹Heliodorus lay there unable to speak and without hope of recovery from this demonstration of God's power. ³⁰But the Jews praised Almighty God because he had miraculously protected his Temple and had brought great happiness where only minutes before there had been fear and confusion. ³¹Some of Heliodorus' friends quickly asked Onias the High Priest to pray that the Most High would spare the life of this man who was at the point of death. ³²So the High Priest offered a sacrifice in the hope that God would save Heliodorus, for he did not want the king to think that the Jews had done this to the man he had sent. ³³While Onias was offering the sacrifice, the two young men, wearing the same clothes as before, again appeared to Heliodorus and said, "Be grateful to the High Priest; the Lord has spared your life because of him. ³⁴Remember that it was the Lord of heaven who punished you. Now go and tell everyone of his great power." When they had said this, they disappeared.

Heliodorus Praises God

³⁵So Heliodorus offered a sacrifice to the Lord and made many promises, because the Lord had spared his life. Then he said good-bye to Onias and returned with his army to the king. ³⁶There he told everyone what the Lord, the most powerful of all gods, had done.

³⁷When the king asked Heliodorus who would be the best man to send on the next mission to Jerusalem, Heliodorus replied, ³⁸"If you have an enemy or

know of someone plotting against your government, send him. He will come back badly beaten, if he comes back at all, for some strange power from God is at work there. ³⁹The God of heaven watches over the Temple; he strikes down and destroys anyone who comes to harm it." ⁴⁰That is the story of how the Temple treasury was protected from Heliodorus.

Simon Accuses Onias

4 But Simon (mentioned earlier as the one who informed Apollonius about the money and brought trouble on the nation) also lied about Onias, claiming that he was responsible for the attack on Heliodorus and for the difficulties that followed. ²He dared to accuse Onias of plotting against the government—Onias who not only had made donations to Jerusalem and had protected the Temple, but who was eager to see that all our laws were obeyed. ³⁻⁴Apollonius son of Menestheus, the governor of Greater Syria, encouraged Simon in every evil thing he did, and Simon's opposition finally grew so strong that one of his trusted followers committed several murders. Onias realized how dangerous the situation had become, ⁵so he went to the king, not for the purpose of making accusations against his own people, but for the common good of all Jews, both in their private and public lives. ⁶He realized that without the king's cooperation there was no hope for peace, and Simon would keep on with his foolishness.

Jason Introduces Greek Customs

⁷Later, when King Seleucus died and Antiochus (known as Epiphanes) became king, Jason the brother of Onias became High Priest by corrupt

---

f they all; *some manuscripts have* he.
4.7 1 Macc 1.10

means. [8] He went to see [g] the king and offered him 27,000 pounds of silver with 6,000 more pounds to be paid later. [9] Jason also offered him an additional 11,250 pounds of silver for the authority to establish a stadium where young men could train and to enroll the people of Jerusalem as citizens of Antioch. [h]

[10] The king gave his approval, and just as soon as Jason took over the office of High Priest, he made the people of Jerusalem change to the Greek way of life. [11] He began by abolishing the favors that John had secured for the Jews from previous Syrian kings. (John was the father of the Eupolemus who later went to Rome to make an alliance and to establish ties of friendship.) Jason also did away with our Jewish customs and introduced new customs that were contrary to our Law. [12] With great enthusiasm he built a stadium near the Temple hill and led our finest young men to adopt the Greek custom of participating in athletic events. [13] Because of the unrivaled wickedness of Jason, that ungodly and illegitimate High Priest, the craze for the Greek way of life and for foreign customs reached such a point [14] that even the priests lost all interest in their sacred duties. They lost interest in the Temple services and neglected the sacrifices. Just as soon as the signal was given, they would rush off to take part in the games that were forbidden by our Law. [15] They did not care about anything their ancestors had valued; they prized only Greek honors. [16] And this turned out to be the source of all their troubles, for the very people whose ways they admired and whose customs they tried to imitate became their enemies and oppressed them. [17] It is a serious thing to disregard God's Law, as you will see from the following events.

Jerusalem under Syrian Influence

[18] Once when the king was present for the athletic games that were held every five [i] years in the city of Tyre, [19] that worthless Jason sent some men there from Jerusalem, who were also enrolled as citizens of Antioch, to take 22,500 pounds of silver to pay for a sacrifice to the god Hercules. But even these men did not think it was fitting to use such a large sum of money for a sacrifice, and [20] so the money originally intended as a sacrifice to Hercules was used for the construction of warships.

[21] When Apollonius son of Menestheus was sent to Egypt to attend the crowning of Philometor as king, Antiochus learned that Philometor was opposed to his policies. Antiochus became concerned about the security of his own kingdom, so he went to Joppa and then on to Jerusalem. [22] There he was welcomed with great splendor by Jason and the people of the city who went out to greet him, shouting and carrying torches. From Jerusalem Antiochus led his army to Phoenicia.

Menelaus Becomes High Priest

[23] Three years later, Jason sent Menelaus (brother of the Simon [j] mentioned earlier) to take some money to the king and to get his decision on several important matters. [24] But when he stood before the king, Menelaus impressed him with his show of authority and offered 22,500 pounds of silver more than Jason had offered for his appointment to the office of High Priest. [25] As a result Menelaus returned to Jerusalem with papers from the king, confirming him as High Priest. But he possessed no other qualifications; he had the temper of a cruel tyrant and could be as fierce as a wild animal. [26] So Jason, who had cheated his own

---

[g] went to see; *or* wrote to.   [h] the people . . . Antioch; *or* the men of Jerusalem as supporters of King Antiochus.   [i] five; *or* four.   [j] SIMON: *See 3.4.*

4.11 1 Macc 8.17

brother out of the office of High Priest, was now forced to flee to the land of Ammon. [27]Menelaus continued to be High Priest, but he never paid any of the money he had promised the king. [28]However, Sostratus, the captain of the fort in Jerusalem, kept demanding the money, since it was his responsibility to collect it. So finally, the two men were summoned to appear before the king concerning the matter. [29]Menelaus left his brother Lysimachus as acting High Priest, while Sostratus left the fort under the command of Crates, the commander of the mercenary troops from Cyprus.

The Murder of Onias

[30]Meanwhile, there was a revolt in the Cilician cities of Tarsus and Mallus, because the king had given those cities to Antiochis, his mistress. [31]So the king left Andronicus, one of his high officials, in command, while he hurried off to Cilicia to restore order. [32]Menelaus took advantage of this opportunity and presented Andronicus with some of the gold objects he had removed from the Temple in Jerusalem. He had already sold some of them to the city of Tyre and to other nearby cities. [33]When Onias heard about this, he fled for safety to a temple at Daphne near the city of Antioch and openly accused Menelaus. [34]Then Menelaus secretly persuaded Andronicus to kill Onias. So Andronicus went to Onias and deceived him with a friendly greeting and with promises of safety. Although Onias was suspicious, Andronicus finally lured him away from the safety of the temple and immediately murdered him in cold blood.

Andronicus Is Punished

[35]The Jews and Gentiles were very angry because Onias had been murdered. [36]So when the king returned

from the territory of Cilicia, the Jews of Antioch went to him and protested against this senseless killing. Many Gentiles felt the same way about the crime. [37]King Antiochus was deeply grieved and was so filled with sorrow that he was moved to tears when he recalled the wisdom and self-control that Onias had shown throughout his life. [38]Antiochus became so angry that he tore off Andronicus' royal robe, stripped him naked, and marched him around the city to the very spot where Onias had been murdered. Then Antiochus had this bloodthirsty murderer put to death. This was how the Lord gave him the punishment he deserved.

Lysimachus Is Killed

[39]Meanwhile, with the support of his brother Menelaus, Lysimachus had on numerous occasions robbed the Jerusalem Temple and had taken many of its gold objects. When word of this spread around, crowds began to gather in protest against Lysimachus. [40]Finally, the crowds were becoming dangerous and were beginning to get out of control, so Lysimachus sent 3,000 armed men to attack them. They were led by Auranus, a man as stupid as he was old. [41]When the Jews in the Temple courtyard realized what was happening, they picked up rocks, pieces of wood, or simply handfuls of ashes from the altar and threw them at Lysimachus and his men in the confusion. [42]They killed a few of Lysimachus' men, wounded many of them, and all the rest ran for their lives. Lysimachus himself, that temple robber, was killed near the Temple treasury.

Menelaus Is Brought to Trial

[43]Because of this incident Menelaus was brought to trial. [44]When the king came to the city of Tyre, the Jewish authorities in Jerusalem sent three men

Attacking and counterattacking (5.3)

to bring charges against Menelaus. 45 When Menelaus saw that he was losing the case, he offered Ptolemy son of Dorymenes a large bribe to persuade the king to decide in his favor. 46 Ptolemy then asked the king to go outside the courtroom with him, as though to get some fresh air, and there he persuaded him to change his mind 47 and declare Menelaus innocent of the charges against him. So Menelaus was set free, although he had caused the trouble; but the three men, whom even the cruel Scythians would have declared innocent, were sentenced to death. 48 The three men had spoken in defense of Jerusalem, its people,[k] and the sacred objects stolen from the Temple, but they were quickly and unjustly executed. 49 Some of the people of Tyre, however, showed their disgust with this crime and their respect for these men by giving them a splendid funeral. 50 Menelaus stayed on in his position because of the greed of those in power. He grew more evil every day and became the worst enemy of his own people.

Visions of a Battle

5 About this time Antiochus the Fourth made a second attack against Egypt. 2 For nearly forty days people all over Jerusalem saw visions of cavalry troops in gold armor charging across the sky. The riders were armed with spears and their swords were drawn. 3 They were lined up in battle against one another, attacking and counterattacking. Shields were clashing, there was a rain of spears, and arrows flew through the air. All the different kinds of armor and the gold bridles on the horses flashed in the sunlight. 4 Everyone in the city prayed that these visions might be a good sign.

Jason Attacks Jerusalem

5 When a false report began to spread that Antiochus had died, Jason took more than a thousand men and suddenly attacked Jerusalem. They drove back those stationed on the city walls and finally captured the city. Menelaus fled for safety to the fort, near the Temple hill, 6 while Jason and his men went on slaughtering their fellow Jews without mercy. Jason did not realize that success against one's own people is the worst kind of failure. He even considered his success a victory over enemies, rather than a defeat of his own people. 7 But Jason did not take over the government. Instead he was forced to flee once again to the territory of the Ammonites, and in the end his evil plot brought him nothing but shame and

[k] its people; *some manuscripts also have* the surrounding villages.

disgrace, ⁸ and he died in misery. Aretas, the ruler of the Arabs, imprisoned him; he was looked upon as a criminal and despised because he had betrayed his own people; everyone was hunting for him, and he had to run from town to town. He fled to Egypt for safety, ⁹ then to Greece, hoping to find refuge among the Spartans, who were related to the Jews. Finally, this man, who had forced so many others to flee from their own country, died as a fugitive in a foreign land. ¹⁰ Jason had killed many people and left their bodies unburied, but now his own death was unmourned. He was not given a funeral or even buried with his ancestors.

Antiochus Attacks Jerusalem
(1 Maccabees 1.20-63)

¹¹ When the news of what had happened in Jerusalem reached Antiochus, he thought the whole country of Judea was in revolt, and he became as furious as a wild animal. So he left Egypt and took Jerusalem by storm, ¹² giving his men orders to cut down without mercy everyone they met and to slaughter anyone they found hiding in the houses. ¹³ They murdered everyone — men and women, boys and girls; even babies were butchered. ¹⁴ Three days later Jerusalem had lost 80,000 people: 40,000 killed in the attack and at least that many taken away to be sold as slaves.

¹⁵ But Antiochus was still not satisfied. He even dared to enter the holiest Temple in all the world, guided by Menelaus, who had become a traitor both to his religion and to his people. ¹⁶ With his filthy and unholy hands, Antiochus swept away the sacred objects of worship and the gifts which other kings had given to increase the glory and honor of the Temple. ¹⁷ He was so thrilled with his conquest that he did not realize that the Lord had let his holy Temple be defiled because the sin of the people of Jerusalem had made him

angry for a while. ¹⁸ If the people of Jerusalem had not been involved in so many sins, Antiochus would have been punished immediately and prevented from taking such a foolish action. He would have suffered the same fate as Heliodorus, who was sent by King Seleucus to inspect the treasury. ¹⁹ But the Lord did not choose his people for the sake of his Temple; he established his Temple for the sake of his people. ²⁰ So the Temple shared in the people's suffering but also later shared in their prosperity. The Lord abandoned it when he became angry, but restored it when his anger had cooled down.

Another Attack against Jerusalem

²¹ Antiochus took 135,000 pounds of silver from the Temple and hurried off to Antioch. Such was his arrogance that he felt he could make ships sail across dry land or troops march across the sea. ²² He appointed governors to cause trouble for the people. In Jerusalem he placed Philip, a man from Phrygia who was more evil than Antiochus himself. ²³ At Mount Gerizim he placed Andronicus. In addition to these, there was Menelaus, who mistreated his fellow Jews far worse than the governors did. Antiochus hated the Jews so much ²⁴ that he sent an army of 22,000 mercenary troops from Mysia to Jerusalem under the command of a man named Apollonius, with orders to kill every man in the city and to sell the women and boys as slaves. ²⁵ Apollonius arrived in Jerusalem, pretending to be on a peace mission. Then on a Sabbath, when all the Jews were observing the day of rest, he led his troops, who were fully armed, in a parade outside the city. ²⁶ Suddenly he commanded his men to kill everyone who had come out to see them. They rushed into the city and murdered a great many people.

²⁷ But Judas Maccabeus and about nine others escaped into the barren mountains, where they lived like wild

animals. In order not to defile themselves, they ate only plants which they found growing there.

The Jews Are Persecuted Because of Their Faith

6 Not long after that, the king sent an elderly Athenian[l] to force the Jews to abandon their religion and the customs of their ancestors. [2]He was also to defile their Temple by dedicating it to the Olympian god Zeus.[m] The temple on Mount Gerizim was to be officially named "Temple of Zeus the God of Hospitality," as the people who lived there had requested.

[3]The oppression was harsh and almost intolerable. [4]Gentiles filled the Temple with drinking parties and all sorts of immorality. They even had intercourse with prostitutes there. Forbidden objects were brought into the Temple, [5]and the altar was covered with detestable sacrifices prohibited by our Law. [6]It was impossible to observe the Sabbath, to celebrate any of the traditional festivals, or even so much as to admit to being a Jew. [7]Each month when the king's birthday was celebrated, the Jews were compelled by brute force to eat the intestines of sacrificial animals. Then, during the festival in honor of the wine god Dionysus, they were required to wear ivy wreaths on their heads and march in procession. [8]On the advice of Ptolemy,[n] the neighboring Greek cities were also instructed to require Jews to eat the sacrifices; [9]they were told to put to death every Jew who refused to adopt the Greek way of life. It was easy to see that hard times were ahead. [10]For example, two women were arrested for having their babies circumcised. They were paraded around the city with their babies hung from their breasts; then they were thrown down from the city wall. [11]On another occasion, Philip was told that some Jews had gathered in a nearby cave to observe the Sabbath in secret. Philip attacked and burned them all alive. They had such respect for the Sabbath that they would not fight to defend themselves.

The Lord Punishes and Shows Mercy

[12]I beg you not to become discouraged as you read about the terrible things that happened. Consider that this was the Lord's way of punishing his people, not of destroying them. [13]In fact, it is a sign of kindness to punish a person immediately for his sins, rather than to wait a long time. [14]The Lord does not treat us as he does other nations: he waits patiently until they have become deeply involved in sin before he punishes them, [15]but he punishes us before we have sinned too much. [16]So the Lord is always merciful to us, his own people. Although he punishes us with disasters, he never abandons us. [17]I have made these few observations by way of reminder. We will now get on with the story.

Eleazar Dies for His Faith

[18]There was an elderly and highly respected teacher of the Law by the name of Eleazar, whose mouth was being forced open to make him eat pork. [19-20]But he preferred an honorable death rather than a life of disgrace. So he spit out the meat and went willingly

---

[l] elderly Athenian; *or* an elder of Athens, *or* Athenaios the elder, *or* Geron an Athenian; *some manuscripts have* an elderly Antiochean; *or* an elder of Antioch.   [m] ZEUS: *The supreme god of the Greeks; Mount Olympus was thought to be his home.*   [n] Ptolemy (*see 4.45*); *some manuscripts have* the people of Ptolemais.
6.10 1 Macc 1.60, 61   **6.11** 1 Macc 2.32-38   **6.18** Lv 11.7, 8; He 11.35

His courageous death was remembered as a glorious example. (6.31)

to the place of torture, showing how people should have courage to refuse unclean food, even if it costs them their lives. 21-22 Those in charge of the sacrifice had been friends of Eleazar for a long time, and because of this friendship they told him privately to bring meat that was lawful for him to eat. He need only pretend to eat the pork, they said, and in this way he would not be put to death.

23 But Eleazar made a decision worthy of his gray hair and advanced age. All his life he had lived in perfect obedience to God's holy laws, so he replied, "Kill me, here and now. 24 Such deception is not worthy of a man of my years. Many young people would think that I had denied my faith after I was ninety years old. 25 If I pretended to eat this meat, just to live a little while longer, it would bring shame and disgrace on me and lead many young people astray. 26 For the present I might be able to es-

cape what you could do to me, but whether I live or die, I cannot escape Almighty God. 27 If I die bravely now, it will show that I deserved my long life. 28 It will also set a good example of the way young people should be willing and glad to die for our sacred and respected laws."

As soon as he said these things, he went*o* off to be tortured, 29 and the very people who had treated him kindly a few minutes before, now turned against him, because they thought he had spoken like a madman. 30 When they had beaten him almost to the point of death, he groaned and said, "The Lord possesses all holy knowledge. He knows I could have escaped these terrible sufferings and death, yet he also knows that I gladly suffer these things, because I fear him."

31 So Eleazar died. But his courageous death was remembered as a glorious example, not only by young people, but by the entire nation as well.

o went; *some manuscripts have* was dragged.

A Mother and Her Sons Die for Their Faith

7 On another occasion a Jewish mother and her seven sons were arrested. The king was having them beaten to force them to eat pork. ²Then one of the young men said, "What do you hope to gain by doing this? We would rather die than abandon the traditions of our ancestors."

³This made the king so furious that he gave orders for huge pans and kettles to be heated red hot, ⁴and it was done immediately. Then he told his men to cut off the tongue of the one who had spoken and to scalp him and chop off his hands and feet, while his mother and six brothers looked on. ⁵After the young man had been reduced to a helpless mass of breathing flesh, the king gave orders for him to be carried over and thrown into one of the pans. As a cloud of smoke streamed up from the pan, the brothers and their mother encouraged one another to die bravely, saying, ⁶"The Lord God is looking on and understands our suffering. Moses made this clear when he wrote a song condemning those who had abandoned the Lord. He said, 'The Lord will have mercy on those who serve him.'"

⁷After the first brother had died in this way, the soldiers started amusing themselves with the second one by tearing the hair and skin from his head. Then they asked him, "Now will you eat this pork, or do you want us to chop off your hands and feet one by one?"

⁸He replied in his native language, "I will never eat it!" So the soldiers tortured him, just as they had the first one, ⁹but with his dying breath he cried out to the king, "You butcher! You may kill us, but the King of the universe will raise us from the dead and give us eternal life, because we have obeyed his laws."

¹⁰The soldiers began entertaining themselves with the third brother. When he was ordered to stick out his tongue, he quickly did so. Then he bravely held out his hands ¹¹and courageously said, "God gave these to me. But his laws mean more to me than my hands, and I know God will give them back to me again." ¹²The king and those with him were amazed at his courage and at his willingness to suffer.

¹³After he had died, the soldiers tortured the fourth one in the same cruel way, ¹⁴but his final words were, "I am glad to die at your hands, because we have the assurance that God will raise us from death. But there will be no resurrection to life for you, Antiochus!"

¹⁵When the soldiers took the fifth boy and began torturing him, ¹⁶he looked the king squarely in the eye and said, "You have the power to do whatever you want with us, even though you also are mortal. But do not think that God has abandoned our people. ¹⁷Just wait. God will use his great power to torture you and your descendants."

¹⁸Then the soldiers took the sixth boy, and just before he died he said, "Make no mistake. We are suffering what we deserve, because we have sinned against our God. That's why all these terrible things are happening to us. ¹⁹But don't think for a minute that you will avoid being punished for fighting against God."

²⁰The mother was the most amazing one of them all, and she deserves a special place in our memory. Although she saw her seven sons die in a single day, she endured it with great courage because she trusted in the Lord. ²¹She combined womanly emotion with manly courage and spoke words of encouragement to each of her sons in their native language. ²²"I do not know how your life began in my womb," she would say, "I was not the one who gave you life and breath and put together each part of your body. ²³It was God

"King Antiochus . . . I refuse to obey your orders." (7.30)

who did it, God who created the universe, the human race, and all that exists. He is merciful and he will give you back life and breath again, because you love his laws more than you love yourself."

24 Antiochus was sure that the mother was making fun of him, so he did his best to convince her youngest son to abandon the traditions of his ancestors. He promised not only to make the boy rich and famous, but to place him in a position of authority and to give him the title "Friend of the King." 25 But the boy paid no attention to him, so Antiochus tried to persuade the boy's mother to talk him into saving his life, 26 and after much persuasion she agreed to do so. 27 Leaning over her son, she fooled the cruel tyrant by saying in her native language, "My son, have pity on me. Remember that I carried you in my womb for nine months and nursed you for three years. I have taken care of you and looked after all your needs up to the present day. 28 So I urge you, my child, to look at the sky and the earth. Consider everything you see there, and realize that God made it all from nothing, just as he made the human race. 29 Don't be afraid of this butcher. Give up your life willingly and prove yourself worthy of your brothers, so that by God's mercy I may receive you back with them at the resurrection."

30 Before she could finish speaking, the boy said, "King Antiochus, what are you waiting for? I refuse to obey your orders. I only obey the commands in the Law which Moses gave to our ancestors. 31 You have thought up all kinds of cruel things to do to our people, but you won't escape the punishment that God has in store for you. 32-33 It is true that our living Lord is angry with us and is making us suffer because of our sins, in order to correct and discipline us. But this will last only a short while, for we are still his servants, and he will forgive us. 34 But you are the cruelest and most disgusting thing that ever lived. So don't fool yourself with illusions of greatness while you punish God's people. 35 There is no way for you to escape punishment at the hands of the almighty and all-seeing God. 36 My brothers suffered briefly because of our faithfulness to God's covenant, but now they have entered eternal life.p But you will fall under God's judgment and be punished as you deserve for your arrogance. 37 I now give up my body and my

p briefly . . . life; *or* briefly, but now they have entered eternal life because of our covenant with God.

life for the laws of our ancestors, just as my brothers did. But I also beg God to show mercy to his people quickly and to torture you until you are forced to acknowledge that he alone is God. ³⁸May my brothers and I be the last to suffer the anger of Almighty God, which he has justly brought upon our entire nation."

³⁹These words of ridicule made Antiochus so furious that he had the boy tortured even more cruelly than his brothers. ⁴⁰And so the boy died, with absolute trust in the Lord, never unfaithful for a minute.

⁴¹Last of all, the mother was put to death.

⁴²But I have said enough about the Jews being tortured and being forced to eat the intestines of sacrificial animals.

Judas Maccabeus Revolts
(1 Maccabees 3.1-26)

8 Judas Maccabeus and his friends went secretly from village to village until they had gathered a force of about 6,000 Jewish men who had remained faithful to their religion. ²They begged the Lord to help his people, now trampled under foot by all nations, to take pity on the Temple, now defiled by pagans, ³and to have mercy on Jerusalem, now destroyed and almost leveled to the ground. ⁴They also asked the Lord to show his hatred of evil by taking revenge on those who were murdering his people, mercilessly slaughtering innocent children, and saying evil things against the Lord.

⁵When Judas had finally organized his forces, the Gentiles were unable to stand against him, because the Lord's anger against Israel had now turned to mercy. ⁶⁻⁷Judas would make sudden attacks on towns and villages and burn them. He captured strategic positions and routed many enemy troops, finding that he was most successful at night. People everywhere spoke of his bravery.

Ptolemy Sends Nicanor to Attack Judas
(1 Maccabees 3.38-41)

⁸When Philip, governor of Jerusalem, realized that Judas was gaining ground little by little and that his victories were becoming more and more frequent, he wrote a letter to Ptolemy, governor of Greater Syria, requesting his help in defending the royal interests. ⁹Ptolemy immediately appointed Nicanor son of Patroclus, who was also in the closest circle of the King's Friends, and sent him with more than 20,000 troops of various nationalities to wipe out the entire Jewish race. Ptolemy also appointed Gorgias, a general of wide military experience, to go with him. ¹⁰King Antiochus owed the Romans 150,000 pounds of silver; Nicanor planned to pay off the debt by selling Jewish prisoners of war as slaves.

¹¹So he at once sent word to the towns along the coast, informing them that he would be selling Jews for less than a pound of silver each. But he did not know of the judgment that Almighty God had in store for him.

Judas Learns of Nicanor's Plans
(1 Maccabees 3.42-54)

¹²Judas learned that Nicanor was advancing with his army toward Judea, so he informed his men. ¹³Some were cowardly and did not believe in the justice of God, and they ran away as fast as they could. ¹⁴But others sold all their remaining possessions so that the Lord would consider them worthy to be saved from the godless Nicanor, who had sold them as slaves even before the battle had taken place. ¹⁵They prayed that if God was not willing to do this for their sake alone, he might be willing to rescue them because of the covenants he had made with their ancestors, and because he, the great and wonderful God, had called them to be his people. ¹⁶Judas brought together all 6,000 of

his men and encouraged them not to be frightened or to flee in panic at the sight of the large number of Gentile troops who were marching against them without cause. Instead they should fight bravely, [17] never forgetting the crimes the Gentiles had committed against the Temple and how they had made Jerusalem suffer terribly and had done away with Jewish traditions. [18] "They rely on their weapons and their daring," Judas said, "but we trust in Almighty God, who is able to destroy not only these troops, but, if necessary, the entire world, with a mere nod of his head."

[19] Then Judas went on to remind them of the ways God had helped their ancestors: during the time of Sennacherib 185,000 of the enemy had been destroyed; [20] and once in Babylonia 8,000 Jews came to the aid of 4,000 Macedonians, defeating 120,000 Galatians and taking a great deal of loot, all because of God's help.

Judas Defeats Nicanor
(1 Maccabees 3.55 — 4.27)

[21] Judas' words encouraged his men and made them willing to die for their religion and their country. He then divided his army into four divisions [22] of about 1,500 men each, with himself and his brothers Simon, Joseph, and Jonathan each in charge of a division. [23] After ordering Eleazar to read aloud[q] from the holy book, he gave his men the battle cry: "God will help us," and personally led the attack against Nicanor.

[24] Almighty God fought on their side, and they killed more than 9,000 of the enemy. They wounded many others and put the entire enemy army to flight. [25] They seized the money from the people who had come to buy them as slaves. Then they pursued the enemy a long way, until they had to return, [26] because it was almost time for the Sab-

bath to begin. [27] When they had collected the enemy's weapons and looted the dead, they celebrated the Sabbath, praising the Lord and giving thanks to him, because he had brought them safely to that day and had given them the first sign of his mercy. [28] When the Sabbath was over, they gave some of the loot to the victims of persecution and to the widows and orphans; then they divided the rest among their own families. [29] Afterward they joined together in prayer to the merciful Lord, asking him to look favorably upon his servants.

Judas Defeats Timothy and Bacchides

[30] The Jews later fought against the forces of Timothy and Bacchides and killed more than 20,000 of them. They captured some very high fortresses and took a lot of loot, which they divided equally among themselves and the widows, orphans, old men, and the victims of persecution. [31] They carefully collected all the enemy's weapons and stored them in strategic places, but the rest of the loot was taken to Jerusalem. [32] They executed the commanding officer of Timothy's forces, a godless man who had caused the Jews much suffering. [33] While celebrating their victory in the city of their ancestors, they burned alive those men who had set fire to the Temple gates. The dead included Callisthenes, who had hidden in a small house; and so he received the punishment he deserved for his evil deeds.

[34] In this way, the evil Nicanor, who had brought a thousand merchants to buy the Jews, [35] was defeated with the help of the Lord by the very people he despised so much. He threw off his splendid uniform and fled all alone like a runaway slave, until he reached Antioch. He had succeeded only in destroying his entire army. [36] This man, who

---

[q] *Probable text* After . . . aloud; *Greek unclear.*
8.23 1 Macc 3.48

had tried to pay a debt to Rome by selling the people of Jerusalem, showed that the Jews could not be defeated. God was their mighty Defender, because they obeyed the laws he had given them.

The Lord Punishes Antiochus
(1 Maccabees 6.1-7; 2 Maccabees 1.11-17)

9 About this time Antiochus was retreating in disorder from Persia, ² where he had entered the city of Persepolis and had attempted to rob a temple and take control of the city. The people took up arms and attacked Antiochus, forcing his army to retreat in disgrace. ³ When he reached Ecbatana, he was told what had happened to the forces of Nicanor and Timothy. ⁴ He became furious and decided to make the Jews pay for the defeat he had suffered. So he ordered his chariot driver not to stop until they reached Jerusalem. With great arrogance he said, "I will turn Jerusalem into a graveyard full of Jews."

But he did not know that he was heading straight for God's judgment. ⁵ In fact, as soon as he had said these words, the all-seeing Lord, the God of Israel, struck him down with an invisible but fatal blow. He was seized with sharp intestinal pains for which there was no relief — ⁶ a fitting punishment for the man who had tortured others in so many terrible ways! ⁷ But this in no way caused him to give up his pride. Instead he became more arrogant than ever, and breathing out fiery threats against the Jews, he gave orders to drive even faster. As a result he fell out of his chariot with such a thud that it made every bone in his body ache. ⁸ His arrogant pride made him think he had the superhuman strength to make ocean waves obey him and to weigh high mountains on a pair of scales. But suddenly he fell flat on the ground and had to be carried off on a stretcher, a clear sign to everyone of God's power.

⁹ Even the eyes of this godless man were crawling with worms and he lived in terrible pain and agony. The stink was so bad that his entire army was sickened, ¹⁰ and no one was able to come close enough to carry him around. Yet only a short while before, he thought he could take hold of the stars.

No one was able to come close enough. (9.10)

Antiochus Makes a Promise to God
(1 Maccabees 6.8-17)

¹¹ Antiochus was deeply depressed and suffered constant pain because of the punishment that God had brought on him, so he finally came to his senses and gave up his arrogant pride. ¹² Then, when he could no longer endure his own stink, he said, "It is right that all mortals should be subject to God and not think that they are his equal." ¹³ The time of the Lord's mercy had come to an end for Antiochus, but this worthless man made the Lord a promise: ¹⁴ "I once intended to level Jerusalem to the ground and make that holy city a graveyard full of Jews," he said, "but now I declare it a free city. ¹⁵ I had planned to throw out the dead bodies of the Jews and their children for the wild animals and the birds to eat, for I did not consider them worth burying. But now I intend to grant them the same privileges as the citizens of Athens enjoy. ¹⁶ I once looted the Temple and took its sacred utensils, but I will fill it with splendid

gifts and with better utensils than before, and I will pay the cost of the sacrifices from my own resources. [17] Besides all this, I will become a Jew myself and go wherever people live, telling them of God's power."

Antiochus' Letter to the Jews

[18] Antiochus was in despair and could find no relief from his pain, because God was punishing him as he deserved, so he wrote the following letter to the Jews:

[19] "King Antiochus to the Jews, my most distinguished subjects. Warm greetings and best wishes for your health and prosperity.

[20] "I hope that you and your families are in good health and that all goes well with you. My hope is in God, [21] and I remember with a deep sense of joy the respect and kindness that you have shown me.

"On my way home from Persia I fell violently ill, and so I thought it best to begin making plans for the general welfare of the people. [22] I have not given up hopes of getting well; in fact I am fully confident that I will recover. [23] But I recall that my father used to appoint a successor whenever he went on a military campaign east of the Euphrates. [24] He did this so that if something unexpected happened, or if some bad news came back, then his subjects would not be afraid, for they knew who had been left in command. [25] Also, I know how the rulers along the frontiers of my kingdom are constantly on the lookout for any opportunity that may come along. That is why I have appointed my son Antiochus to succeed me as king. I have frequently entrusted him to your care and recommended him to you when I went on my regular visits to the provinces east of the Euphrates. (He is receiving a copy of the letter which follows.) [26] Now I strongly urge each of you to keep in mind the good things that I have done for you, both individually and as a nation, and to continue in your good will toward me and my son. [27] I am confident that he will treat you with fairness and kindness, just as I have always done."

[28] And so, this murderer, who had cursed God, suffered the same terrible agonies he had brought on others, and then died a miserable death in the mountains of a foreign land. [29] One of his close friends, Philip, took his body home; but, because he was afraid of Antiochus' son, he went on to King Ptolemy Philometor of Egypt.

The Rededication of the Temple
(1 Maccabees 4.36-61)

10 Judas Maccabeus and his followers, under the leadership of the Lord, recaptured the Temple and the city of Jerusalem. [2] They tore down the altars which foreigners had set up in the marketplace and destroyed the other places of worship that had been built. [3] They purified the Temple and built a new altar. Then, with new fire started by striking flint, they offered sacrifice for the first time in two years, burned incense, lighted the lamps, and set out the sacred loaves. [4] After they had done all this, they lay face down on the ground and prayed that the Lord would never again let such disasters strike them. They begged him to be merciful when he punished them for future sins and not hand them over any more to barbaric, pagan Gentiles. [5] They rededicated the Temple on the twenty-fifth day of the month of Kislev, the same day of the same month on which the Temple had been desecrated by the Gentiles. [6] The happy celebration lasted eight days, like the Festival of Shelters, and the people remembered how only a short time before, they had spent the Festival of Shelters wandering like wild animals in the mountains and living in caves. [7]But now, carrying green palm branches and sticks decorated with ivy, they paraded around, singing grateful praises to him who had brought about the purification of his own Temple. [8]Everyone agreed that the entire Jewish nation should celebrate this festival each year.

Ptolemy Macron Commits Suicide

[9]The days of Antiochus Epiphanes had come to an end. [10]Now we will tell about Antiochus Eupator, the son of this godless man, and give a summary of the evil effects of his wars. [11]When he became king he appointed a man by the name of Lysias to be in charge of the affairs of state and to be chief governor of Greater Syria, [12]replacing Ptolemy Macron, who had been the first governor to treat the Jews fairly. Macron had established peaceful relations with them in an attempt to make up for the wrongs they had suffered. [13]As a result the King's Friends went to Eupator and accused Macron of treachery, because he had abandoned the island of Cyprus, which King Philometor of Egypt had placed under his command, and had gone over to Antiochus Epiphanes. In fact, everyone called Macron a traitor. No longer able to maintain the respect that his office demanded, he committed suicide by taking poison.

Judas Maccabeus Defeats the Idumeans
(1 Maccabees 5.1-8)

[14]When Gorgias became governor of Idumea, he kept a force of mercenaries and attacked the Jews at every opportunity. [15]Not only this, but the Idumeans themselves controlled certain strategic fortresses and were constantly harassing the Jews. They welcomed those who fled from Jerusalem and did every-

thing they could to keep the country in a perpetual state of war. [16]So Judas Maccabeus and his men, after offering prayers for God's help, rushed out and made a vigorous attack against the Idumean fortresses. [17]They beat back those who were defending the walls and captured the fortresses, killing everyone they found, a total of about 20,000 people.

[18]About 9,000 of the enemy, however, managed to take refuge in two easily defended forts, with everything they needed to withstand a siege. [19]Judas had to go on to some other places in the country, where he was more urgently needed, but he left behind Simon and Joseph, together with Zacchaeus and his men. This force was large enough to continue the siege, [20]but some of Simon's men were greedy, and when they were offered 140 pounds of silver, they let some of the enemy escape from the forts. [21]When Judas heard what had happened, he called together the leaders of his troops and accused those men of selling their brothers by setting their enemies free to fight against them. [22]Then he executed the traitors and immediately captured the two forts. [23]Judas was always successful in battle, and in his assault on those two forts he killed more than 20,000 men.

Judas Defeats Timothy

[24]Timothy, who had been defeated by the Jews once before, had gathered a large number of cavalry from Asia and a tremendous force of mercenary troops and was now advancing to take Judea by armed attack. [25]But as the enemy forces were approaching, Judas and his men prayed to God. They put on sackcloth, threw dirt on their heads, [26]and lay face downward on the steps of the altar, begging God to help them by

fighting against their enemies, as he had promised in his Law.

27 When they had finished praying, they took up their weapons, went out a good distance from Jerusalem, and stopped for the night not far from the enemy. 28 At daybreak the two armies joined in battle. The Jewish forces depended upon both their bravery and their trust in the Lord for victory, while the enemy relied only on their ability to fight fiercely. 29 When the fighting was at its worst, the enemy saw five handsome men riding on horses with gold bridles and leading the Jewish forces. 30 These five men surrounded Judas, protecting him with their own armor and showering the enemy with arrows and thunderbolts. The enemy forces then became so confused and bewildered that they broke ranks, and the Jews cut them to pieces, 31 slaughtering 20,500 infantry and 600 cavalry.

32 Timothy himself escaped to the strongly defended fort of Gezer, where his brother Chaereas was in command. 33 Judas and his men besieged the fort for four days with great enthusiasm, 34 but those inside trusted to the security of their positions and shouted all sorts of terrible insults against the Jews and their God. 35 At dawn on the fifth day, twenty of Judas' men, burning with anger at these insults, bravely climbed the wall and with savage fury chopped down everyone they met. 36 At the same time, others climbed the walls on the other side of the fort and set the towers on fire. Many of the enemy were burned to death as the flames spread. A third force broke down the gates and let in the rest of Judas' men to capture the city. 37 Timothy had hidden in a cistern, but they killed him, as well as his brother Chaereas and Apollophanes.

38 When it was over, the Jews celebrated by singing hymns and songs of thanksgiving to the Lord, who had shown them great kindness and had given them victory.

Judas Maccabeus Defeats Lysias
(1 Maccabees 4.26-35)

11 Not long after Timothy was defeated, Lysias, the King's guardian and relative, and head of the

Twenty of Judas' men . . . bravely climbed the wall. (10.35)

government, heard what had happened. He became angry 2 and led 80,000 infantry and all his cavalry against the Jews with the intention of turning Jerusalem into a Greek city. 3 The Temple would be taxed, as were all Gentile places of worship, and the office of High Priest would be up for sale each year. 4 Lysias was so pleased with his tens of thousands of infantry, his thousands of cavalry, and his eighty elephants that he failed to take into account the power of God. 5 He invaded Judea and attacked the fort of Bethzur, about twenty miles south of Jerusalem.

6 When Judas and his men heard that Lysias was laying siege to their forts, they and all the people cried and wept, begging the Lord to send a good angel

to save them. ⁷Judas was the first to take up his weapons, and he urged the others to join him in risking their lives to help the other Jews. So with great eagerness they all set out together. ⁸But they had not gone far from Jerusalem, when suddenly they noticed they were being led by a horseman dressed in white and carrying gold weapons. ⁹Immediately all of them together thanked God for his mercy; he had made them brave enough to attack not only men, but even the most savage animals or even walls of iron. ¹⁰So they marched in battle formation, and with them went the one whom the Lord in his mercy had sent to fight on their side. ¹¹Then they charged into the enemy like lions, killing 11,000 infantry and 1,600 cavalry, and forcing the rest to run for their lives. ¹²Most of those who ran were wounded and had lost their weapons, and Lysias himself managed to escape only because he ran away like a coward.

Lysias Makes Peace with the Jews
(1 Maccabees 6.56-61)

¹³Lysias was no fool. As he thought about the defeat he had suffered, he realized it was because the mighty God had fought for the Jews, making it impossible for them to be defeated. So he sent a message to the Jews, ¹⁴trying to persuade them to agree to a just settlement and promising to do all he could to make the king friendly toward them.ʳ ¹⁵Judas Maccabeus considered what would be best for the people, and so he agreed to all the proposals Lysias had made, since the king had granted every written request that Judas had presented to Lysias.ˢ

The Letter of Lysias to the Jews

¹⁶Here is a copy of the letter which Lysias wrote to the Jews:

"Lysias to the Jewish people, greetings. ¹⁷Your representatives John and Absalom have delivered to me the official document you sent with them, and they have asked me to agree to what is contained in it. ¹⁸I have informed the king of the matters that needed to be brought to his attention, and he has agreed to do whatever is possible. ¹⁹If you continue to be loyal to the government, I will do everything I can in the future to benefit your nation. ²⁰I have instructed your representatives and mine to meet with you to discuss the details of these matters. ²¹May all go well with you. Dated the twenty-fourth day of the month of Dioscorinthius in the year 148."ᵗ

The King's Letter to Lysias

²²Here is a copy of the King's letter:
"King Antiochus to the honorable Lysias, greetings. ²³Now that my father has gone to be with the gods, I want the subjects of my kingdom to conduct their own affairs without interference. ²⁴I understand that the Jews do not wish to adopt the Greek way of life, as my father had intended, but prefer their own way of life and have requested that they be allowed to live according to their own customs. ²⁵Since I desire that they live undisturbed like the other nations in my empire, I hereby decree that their Temple be restored to them and that they be allowed to live according to the customs of their ancestors. ²⁶Please inform them of this decision and assure them of my friendship, so that they may conduct their own affairs in peace, without anything to worry about."
²⁷Here is a copy of the king's letter to the Jewish people:

ʳ to do . . . them; *Greek unclear.* ˢ since . . . Lysias; *or* and the king granted every written request that Judas presented to Lysias. ᵗ THE YEAR 148: *This corresponds to 164 B.C.*

"King Antiochus to the Jewish leaders and all the Jews, greetings. 28 I hope that all is going well for you. I am in good health. 29 Menelaus has informed me of your desire to return home and attend to your own affairs. 30 So then, those of you who return home by the thirtieth of the month of Xanthicus may rest assured that you have nothing to fear. 31 You may continue to observe your food laws and other laws, as you used to do, and no Jew will be punished for any crime done in ignorance. 32 I am sending Menelaus to set your minds at ease. 33 May all go well with you. Dated the fifteenth day of the month of Xanthicus in the year 148."*t*

The Letter of the Romans to the Jews

34 The Romans also sent the Jews the following letter:

"Quintus Memmius and Titus Manius, representatives of the Romans, to the Jews, greetings. 35 We are in complete agreement with all that has been granted to you by the honorable Lysias. 36 We are now on our way to Antioch, so please examine carefully those matters that Lysias referred to the king. Then send a reply to us immediately so that we can represent your best interests before him. Do this as soon as you can, 37 without delay, so that we may know what you have decided. 38 May all go well with you. Dated the fifteenth day of the month of Xanthicus in the year 148."

The Jews of Joppa Are Murdered

12 When the peace agreement between the Jews and the Syrians was completed, Lysias returned to the king, and the Jews went back to their farming. 2 But some of the local governors, Timothy and Apollonius son of Gennaeus, as well as Hieronymus and Demophon, would not let them live in peace; and neither would Nicanor, the commander of the mercenaries from Cyprus.

3 About this time, the people of Joppa did a cruel thing to the Jews of their city. They pretended to be friendly to the Jews and invited them and their families to go sailing with them on ships they had provided. 4 Since all the people of the town had decided to do this, the Jews suspected nothing and accepted the invitation out of a feeling of good will. But when they were out at sea, the people of Joppa drowned all two hundred of them.

The people of Joppa drowned all two hundred of them. (12.4)

5 As soon as Judas heard of this inhuman thing that had been done to those Jews, he informed his men. 6 After they had prayed to God, the just judge, they attacked the murderers. Under cover of darkness they set fire to the harbor, burning all the ships, and killing everyone they found hiding there. 7 The gates of the city were locked, so Judas withdrew; but he was determined to return at some other time and wipe out everyone living there.

8 Judas heard that the people of Jamnia had plans to kill the Jews of their city also. 9 So he attacked Jamnia at

---

t THE YEAR 148: *This corresponds to 164 B.C.*

He sent the women and the children on ahead with the baggage. (12.21)

night, setting fire to its harbor and the ships there. The flames could be seen as far as Jerusalem, thirty miles away.

Judas' Victories in the Region of Gilead
(1 Maccabees 5.9-54)

10 When Judas and his men were about a mile away from Jamnia on their way to meet Timothy in battle, they were attacked by more than 5,000 Arabs, supported by 500 cavalry. **11** It was a hard fight, but with the help of God they defeated these desert tribesmen, who then asked to be on friendly terms with the Jews, promising to give them some livestock and offering to help them in other ways as well. **12** Judas thought their friendship might prove useful in many ways, so he agreed to make peace with them; after that the Arabs returned to their tents.

13 Judas also attacked the heavily fortified walled city of Caspin. The people who lived there were a mixed population of Gentiles **14** who relied on the strength of their walls and felt confident that they had enough food stored up to last through a siege. So they made fun of Judas and his men, shouting out insults against them and profanities against their God. **15** But the Jews prayed to the Almighty Lord of the universe, who had torn down the walls of Jericho in the days of Joshua without using battering rams or siege weapons. Then they made a fierce attack against the wall **16** and because it was God's will, they captured the city. The Jews slaughtered so many people that a nearby lake, which was about a quarter of a mile wide, seemed to be overflowing with blood.

Judas Defeats Timothy's Army
(1 Maccabees 5.37-44)

17 From the city of Caspin, Judas and his men marched about 95 miles, until they came to the Jewish settlement of Charax, near the city of Tob. **18** But they did not find Timothy there, because he had already left the region. He had been able to do nothing there except leave behind a strong garrison in one place. **19** Two of Judas' generals, Dositheus and Sosipater, attacked the garrison and killed all 10,000 men stationed there. **20** Then Judas divided his army into several divisions, placing Dositheus and Sosipater each in command of a division, and hurried after Timothy, who had a force of 120,000 infantry and 2,500 cavalry. **21** When Timothy found out that Judas was coming after him, he sent the women and the children on ahead with the baggage to the city of

Karnaim, which was almost impossible to besiege or even to reach, because of the narrow passes that led up to it. 22 But at the moment that Judas' first division came into sight, the enemy forces were thrown into panic by a vision sent by God, who sees everything. In terror they began to run wildly about and many of them were wounded by the swords of their own men. 23 So Judas and his men pursued them as hard as they could, killing at least 30,000 of the enemy. 24 Timothy himself was captured by the troops of Dositheus and Sosipater. But he was very shrewd and managed to convince them that many of their relatives were his prisoners and would be put to death if anything happened to him. 25 Finally, after he had promised to send their relatives home safely, they let him go free.

Judas Wins Other Victories
(1 Maccabees 5.45-54)

26 Next, Judas attacked the city of Karnaim and the temple of the goddess Atargatis there, killing 25,000 people 27 and completely destroying both the city and the temple. Then he attacked the fortified city of Ephron where Lysias and[u] people of all nationalities were living. Strong young men took up their positions in front of the walls and fought bravely, while inside the city were stored large quantities of military supplies and weapons. 28 But the Jews prayed for help to the Lord, who crushes the power of his enemies. So they captured the city and killed about 25,000 people. 29 From there they hurried on to the city of Beth Shan, seventy-five miles north of Jerusalem. 30 The Jews there told Judas how kindly the people of the city had treated them, especially during hard times. 31 So Judas and his men thanked the people

and urged them to show the same good will toward the Jews in the future. Then they left for Jerusalem, where they arrived shortly before the Harvest Festival.

Judas Defeats Gorgias

32 After Pentecost (as the Harvest Festival is called in Greek) Judas and his men quickly marched out against Gorgias, the governor of Idumea, 33 who met them with 3,000 infantry and 400 cavalry. 34 In the battle that followed, a few Jews were killed. 35 Then a Jew from the city of Tob,[v] a powerful cavalry soldier by the name of Dositheus, grabbed Gorgias by his cloak and started dragging him away by brute force, intending to take the worthless man alive. But suddenly one from the Thracian cavalry rushed at Dositheus and chopped off his arm, allowing Gorgias to escape to the city of Marisa. 36 By now the Jewish men under the command of Esdrias had been fighting for a long time and were exhausted. So Judas prayed that the Lord would show that he was on their side and in command of their troops. 37 Then, while Judas sang a hymn in his native language as a battle cry, the Jews made a surprise attack against Gorgias and his men and put them to flight.

Prayers for Those Killed in Battle

38 After the battle Judas led his men to the town of Adullam. It was the day before the Sabbath, so they purified themselves according to Jewish custom and then observed the holy day. 39 By the following day it was urgent that they gather up the bodies of the men who had been killed in battle and bury them in their family tombs. 40 But on each of the dead, hidden under their clothes, they found small images of the

---

[u] *Lysias and; some manuscripts do not have these words.*   [v] *a Jew from the city of Tob; some manuscripts have one of Bacenor's men.*

12.32 Ex 23.16   **12.40** Dt 7.25

gods worshiped in Jamnia, which the Law forbids Jews to wear. Everyone then knew why these men had been killed. [41] So they praised the ways of the Lord, the just judge, who reveals what is hidden, [42] and they begged him that this sin might be completely blotted out. Then, Judas, that great man, urged the people to keep away from sin, because they had seen for themselves what had happened to those men who had sinned. [43] He also took up a collection from all his men, totaling about four pounds of silver, and sent it to Jerusalem to provide for a sin offering. Judas did this noble thing because he believed in the resurrection of the dead. [44] If he had not believed that the dead would be raised, it would have been foolish and useless to pray for them. [45] In his firm and devout conviction that all of God's faithful people would receive a wonderful reward, Judas made provision for a sin offering to set free from their sin those who had died.

Menelaus Is Put to Death

13 In the year 149 [w] Judas Maccabeus and his followers found out that Antiochus Eupator was marching against Judea with a large army [2] and that Lysias, the young king's guardian and the head of his government, was with him. They [x] had a force of Greek troops consisting of 110,000 infantry, 5,300 cavalry, 22 elephants, and 300 chariots with sharp blades attached to their wheels.

[3] Menelaus, trying to take advantage of the situation, went over to their side and urged them on, not because he was concerned for the country, but because he hoped to be confirmed as High Priest. [4] But God, the King of kings, made Antiochus furious with Menelaus. Lysias proved to Antiochus that this criminal had been the source of all his troubles, so Antiochus ordered him

to be taken to the city of Berea and put to death in the way that it was done there. [5] In that city there is a tower about 75 feet high. It is filled with ashes, and all around the inside of the tower is a platform sloping down into the ashes. [6] People accused of crimes against the gods or of any other serious crime are taken there and thrown down to their death. [7] Menelaus was put to death in that way, without even having the privilege of a burial, [8] and that was just what he deserved. He had often profaned the sacred ashes of the altar fire in the Temple, and now he met his death in ashes.

A Battle Near the City of Modein

[9] King Antiochus arrogantly continued his barbaric invasion of Judah, intending to deal with the Jews more harshly than his father had ever done. [10] When Judas learned of this, he told the people to pray to the Lord day and night, because they were in danger of losing their Law, their country, and their holy Temple. As never before, they needed his help and protection [11] to keep their newly restored country from falling into the hands of godless Gentiles. [12] For three days the people did nothing but lie face down on the ground, fasting and crying, begging the merciful Lord for his help. Then Judas spoke words of encouragement to the people, urging them to get ready for action.

[13] Afterward, Judas met privately with the Jewish leaders and decided to march out with God's help to battle against the king, rather than to wait for Antiochus to invade Judea and besiege Jerusalem. [14] Then, leaving the outcome of the battle to the Creator of the world, Judas encouraged his men to fight bravely and to be willing to die for their laws, the Temple, Jerusalem, their country, and their whole way of

---

[w] THE YEAR 149: *This corresponds to 163 B.C.*　　　[x] They; *Greek unclear.*

life. They set up camp near the city of Modein. 15 Judas gave his men the battle cry, "Victory comes from God," and that night, with a picked force of his bravest young men, he attacked the area near the king's tent and killed as many as 2,000 men. They also stabbed to death*y* the lead elephant and its keeper. 16 Everyone in camp was terrified and in panic when Judas and his men finally left victoriously 17 just before dawn. The help and protection of the Lord had made all this possible.

Antiochus the Fifth Makes a Treaty with the Jews
(1 Maccabees 6.48-63)

18 This taste of Jewish daring was enough to convince King Antiochus that he had to find some better way of capturing the Jewish positions. 19 He attacked the strong Jewish fort of Bethzur, but was repeatedly beaten back and finally defeated. 20 Judas sent supplies to the men who were defending the fort, 21 but a Jewish soldier by the name of Rhodocus gave some secret information to the enemy. He was found out, however, caught, and put to death. 22 The king made a second attempt to come to terms with the people of Bethzur, and when he had reached an agreement with them, he withdrew his forces. Then he went to attack Judas, but again he was defeated. 23 Meanwhile, Philip had been left at Antioch in charge of the government, but King Antiochus learned that he had revolted. The king did not know what to do, so he initiated peace talks with the Jews, agreed to their terms, and promised to be just in his treatment of them. To put the treaty into effect, he offered a sacrifice, gave a generous gift to show his respect for the Temple, 24 and graciously received Judas Maccabeus.

After that, the king appointed Hegemonides to be governor of the territory between the cities of Ptolemais and Gerar, 25 and then he himself went on to Ptolemais. The people there were angry because of the treaty he had made with the Jews — so angry, in fact, that they wanted the treaty canceled. 26 But Lysias made a public speech, defending the treaty as well as he could. After he had calmed the people down and convinced them that he was right, he returned to Antioch.

In this way King Antiochus' invasion was turned into a retreat.

Alcimus Speaks against Judas
(1 Maccabees 7.1-21)

14 Three years later, Judas and his men learned that Demetrius son of Seleucus had sailed into the port of Tripolis with a powerful army and a fleet. 2 It was reported that he had killed King Antiochus and his guardian Lysias and had taken over the country.

3 There was a man by the name of Alcimus, who had formerly been High Priest but who had gladly adopted the Greek way of life during the revolt. Realizing that he could never again be High Priest and fearful of what the Jews might do to him, 4 he went to see King Demetrius in the year 151.*z* On this occasion he presented the king with a gold crown and a palm branch, together with some olive branches traditionally presented to the Temple, but he said nothing about his plans. 5 Later, however, he got the chance to put his foolish plans into effect when Demetrius summoned him to a meeting of his advisers and asked him what the Jews were intending to do.

Alcimus said, 6 "The followers of Judas Maccabeus think of themselves as

y Probable text stabbed to death; *Greek unclear.*   *z* THE YEAR 151: *This corresponds to 161 B.C.*

devout and patriotic; they love war and are constantly inciting the people to rebellion and will never leave the nation in peace. 7 It is their fault that I no

He went to see King Demetrius. (14.4)

longer hold the glorious position of High Priest, to which I am entitled by birth. And so I have come here, 8 primarily out of a genuine concern for your interests as king, but also out of consideration for my own people, for the foolish policies of Judas and his followers have brought terrible suffering on our entire nation. 9 When Your Majesty has examined all the details of these matters, please act in your usual kind and generous manner to relieve the oppression of our nation and its people. 10 As long as Judas is alive, it will be impossible for our nation to enjoy peace."

Demetrius Sends Nicanor to Attack Judas

11 As soon as Alcimus had finished his speech, the other advisers quickly seized this opportunity to arouse Demetrius' anger against Judas, because they also hated him. 12 So King Demetrius immediately appointed Nicanor, who was the commander of his elephant forces, to be governor of Judea, and sent him there 13 with orders to kill Judas, scatter his followers, and make Alcimus High Priest of the greatest Temple in all the world. 14 All the foreigners in Judea, who had fled from Judas' attacks, now rushed to join forces with Nicanor, because they thought that any defeat or trouble that came to the Jews would be to their own advantage.

15 The Jews heard that Nicanor was attacking and that the foreigners in their country were giving him their support. So they threw dirt on themselves and prayed to their God, who had chosen their nation as his possession forever and had never failed to help them in time of need. 16 Then Judas, their leader, gave the orders, and they immediately marched out to engage the enemy in battle near the village of Adasa.^a 17 Judas' brother Simon was fighting Nicanor but was gradually losing the battle because of an unexpected move on the part of the enemy. 18 However, when Nicanor heard how bravely and courageously Judas and his men were fighting for their country, he decided not to settle the matter in battle. 19 Instead, he sent Posidonius, Theodotus, and Mattathias to make a treaty with the Jews.

20 After the terms of the treaty had been worked out in detail, Nicanor informed his troops, and they unanimously agreed. 21 Then a day was set on which the leaders would meet in

---

^a *Probable text* Adasa; *Greek* Dessau.
14.15-25 1 Macc 7.27, 28

private. Ceremonial chairs were brought out from each camp and set up. ²²Judas had taken the precaution of placing battle-ready troops in strategic places, in case of sudden treachery on the part of the enemy. But the two leaders had a friendly meeting. ²³Nicanor stayed on in Jerusalem for some time after that. He did not mistreat the Jews in any way, and even sent away the people who had come over to his side. ²⁴The two men became the best of friends, and Judas was Nicanor's constant companion. ²⁵Nicanor urged him to marry and start a family. So Judas did this and settled down to a peaceful life.

Nicanor Turns against Judas

²⁶When Alcimus noticed how well Nicanor and Judas were getting along, he obtained a copy of the treaty and went to see King Demetrius. He told the king that Nicanor was disloyal to the government, because he had appointed the traitor Judas to be his successor. ²⁷These false accusations infuriated the king, and in his anger he wrote to Nicanor, informing him that he was dissatisfied with the treaty and ordering him to arrest Judas Maccabeus and send him to Antioch at once. ²⁸When this message reached Nicanor, he was hurt and didn't know what to do, because he did not like having to break an agreement with a man who had kept his part of the bargain. ²⁹Yet it was impossible for him to ignore the king's command, so he began looking for a way to trap Judas. ³⁰Judas, however, noticed that Nicanor was becoming hostile and rude toward him, and he knew that this was a bad sign. So he gathered a large number of his followers and went into hiding.

³¹When Nicanor realized that Judas had outsmarted him, he went to the great and holy Temple at the time when the priests were offering sacrifice and ordered them to surrender Judas to him. ³²But the priests declared under oath that they had no idea where Judas was hiding. ³³Then Nicanor raised his right arm in the direction of the Temple and made a solemn threat: "If you do not hand Judas over to me as a prisoner, I will level God's Temple to the ground, demolish this altar, and on this spot build a glorious temple to Dionysus." ³⁴Then he left, and immediately the priests lifted their arms toward heaven and prayed to God, the faithful Defender of our nation: ³⁵"Lord, you are in need of nothing, yet it has pleased you to place your Temple here and to live among us. ³⁶You alone are holy, and your Temple has only recently been purified, so now protect its holiness forever."

Razis Dies for His Country

³⁷One of the leaders in Jerusalem, a man by the name of Razis, was denounced to Nicanor. It was said that he had helped his people in many ways and was so highly respected by them that he was known as "the Father of the Jews." ³⁸During the early days of the revolution he had risked his life for Judaism and had been brought to trial because of his loyalty. ³⁹Wanting to show clearly how much he disliked the Jews, Nicanor sent more than 500 soldiers to arrest Razis, ⁴⁰because he thought his arrest would be a crippling blow to the Jews. ⁴¹The soldiers were about to capture the tower where Razis had gone. They were forcing open the gates to the courtyard, and the order had been given to set the door on fire. Razis realized there was no escape, so he tried to commit suicide with his sword, ⁴²preferring to die with honor rather than suffer humiliation at the hands of evil men.

⁴³Under the pressure of the moment, Razis misjudged the thrust of the

14.31 1 Macc 7.29, 30

sword, and it did not kill him. So, while the soldiers were swarming into the room, he rushed to the wall and jumped off like a brave hero into the crowd below. ⁴⁴The crowd quickly moved back, and he fell in the space they left. ⁴⁵Still alive, and burning with courage, he got up, and with blood gushing from his wounds, he ran through the crowd and finally climbed a steep rock. ⁴⁶Now completely drained of blood, he tore out his intestines with both hands and threw them at the crowd, and as he did so, he prayed for the Lord of life and breath to give them back to him. That was how he died.

Nicanor's Cruel Plan

15 Nicanor learned that Judas and his men were in the region of Samaria, and so he decided to attack them on a Sabbath, when he could do so without any danger to himself. ²The Jews who were forced to accompany his army begged him not to do such a cruel and savage thing, but to respect the day that the all-seeing God had honored and made the most holy of all days. ³Then Nicanor, the lowest creature on earth, asked if there was some sovereign ruler in heaven who had commanded them to honor the Sabbath. ⁴And the Jews replied, "Yes; the living Lord, who rules in heaven, commanded us to honor the Sabbath."

⁵But Nicanor answered, "I am the ruler on earth, and I order you to take up your weapons and to do what the king commands." However, he did not succeed in carrying out his cruel plan.

Judas Prepares His Troops for Battle

⁶In his arrogance Nicanor had boasted that he would set up a monument in honor of his victory over Judas. ⁷But Judas was fully confident that the Lord would help him, ⁸so he urged his men not to be afraid of the enemy. He encouraged them to remember how the Almighty had helped them in times past and to rest assured that he would give them victory this time also. ⁹He renewed their hope by reading to them from the Law and the Prophets and by reminding them of the battles they had already won. ¹⁰When his men were ready for battle, he gave them their orders and at the same time pointed out how the Gentiles could not be trusted, because they never kept their treaties. ¹¹He armed all his men, not by encouraging them to trust in shields and spears, but by inspiring them with courageous words. He also lifted their morale by telling them about his dream, a kind of vision that they could trust in.

¹²He told them that he had seen a vision of Onias, the former High Priest, that great and wonderful man of humble and gentle disposition, who was an outstanding orator and who had been taught from childhood how to live a virtuous life. With outstretched arms Onias was praying for the entire Jewish nation. ¹³Judas then saw an impressive white-haired man of great dignity and authority. ¹⁴Onias said: "This is God's prophet Jeremiah, who loves the Jewish people and offers many prayers for us and for Jerusalem, the holy city."

¹⁵Then Jeremiah stretched out his right hand and gave Judas a gold sword, saying as he did so, ¹⁶"This holy sword is a gift from God. Take it and destroy your enemies."

¹⁷The eloquent words that Judas spoke encouraged everyone to be brave, and inspired boys to fight like men. Their city, their religion, and their Temple were in danger. So the Jews made up their minds not to waste any time, but to make a daring attack against the enemy and bravely decide their fate in hand-to-hand combat. ¹⁸They were not so concerned about their own families and relatives as they were about their sacred Temple. ¹⁹And the people who had to stay in Jerusalem were deeply concerned about how a battle on open ground would turn out.

The Defeat and Death of Nicanor

20 Everyone was waiting to see who would win the battle. The enemy troops

"This holy sword is a gift from God." (15.16)

were already moving forward, with their cavalry on each side of them, and their elephants placed in strategic positions. **21** Judas Maccabeus looked at the huge enemy force, the variety of their weapons, and their fierce elephants. Then he raised his hands toward heaven and prayed to the Lord, who works miracles, because he knew that the Lord gives victory to those who deserve it, not to those who have a strong army. **22** Judas said: "Lord, when Hezekiah was king of Judah, you sent your angel, who killed 185,000 of King Sennacherib's men. **23** Now once again, Lord of heaven, send your good angel to make our enemies shake and tremble with fear. **24** With your great power, destroy these people who have slandered you and have come out to attack your chosen people." So Judas ended his prayer.

25 Nicanor and his army moved forward to the sound of trumpets and battle songs, **26** but Judas and his men went into battle calling on God for help.

27 So by fighting with their hands and praying to God in their hearts, the Jews killed more than 35,000 of the enemy. How grateful they were for the help they had received from God! **28** When the battle was over and they were going home celebrating their victory, they noticed Nicanor in full armor lying dead on the battlefield. **29** Then with loud shouts they praised the Lord in their native language.

30 Judas Maccabeus, who had always fought with all his body and soul for his own people, never losing the patriotism of his youth, ordered his men to cut off Nicanor's head and right arm and to take them to Jerusalem. **31** When they arrived in the city, he called together all the people, stationed the priests before the altar, and sent for the men in the fort. **32** He showed them the head of the evil Nicanor and the arm which that wicked man had arrogantly stretched out against the sacred Temple of the Almighty God. **33** Then he cut out the tongue of that godless man, promising to feed it bit by bit to the birds and to hang up his head opposite the Temple, as evidence of what his foolishness did for him. **34** Everyone there looked up to heaven and praised the Lord, who had revealed his power and had kept his Temple from being defiled. **35** Judas hung Nicanor's head from the wall of the fort, as a clear proof to everyone of the Lord's help. **36** By unanimous vote it was decided that this day would never be forgotten, but would be celebrated each year on the eve of Mordecai's Day,^b which is the thirteenth day of the twelfth month, called Adar in Aramaic.

Concluding Words

37 That is how things turned out for Nicanor. The city of Jerusalem remained in the possession of the Jewish

^b MORDECAI'S DAY: *The Festival of Purim (see Es 9.17-22).*
15.22 2 K 19.35   **15.25-35** 1 Macc 7.43-50   **15.36** 1 Macc 7.49

people from that time on, so I will end my story here. [38] If it is well written and to the point, I am pleased; if it is poorly written and uninteresting, I have still done my best. [39] We know it is un-healthy to drink wine or water alone, whereas wine mixed with water makes a delightfully tasty drink. So also a good story skillfully written gives pleasure to those who read it. With this I conclude.

SOME ADDITIONAL BOOKS

SOME ADDITIONAL BOOKS

Introduction

The following books: 1 Esdras, 2 Esdras, and the Prayer of Manasseh, are included by many Protestants in the Apocrypha. However, they are not accepted as canonical by Roman Catholics. 1 Esdras and the Prayer of Manasseh constituted a part of the Septuagint Greek text of the Old Testament used by Christians during the early centuries of Christianity. The book of 2 Esdras may not have been in its final form until toward the end of the second century A.D.

The First Book of
ESDRAS

INTRODUCTION

The First Book of Esdras parallels the account given in *2 Chronicles 35–36, Ezra,* and *Nehemiah 6–8,* although there are omissions, additions, and variations in both order and detail. The most distinctive new material is the debate before the emperor in chapters 3 and 4.

Josiah Celebrates the Passover
(*2 Kings 23.21-23; 2 Chronicles 35.1-9*)

1 King Josiah celebrated the Passover at Jerusalem in honor of the Lord; on the fourteenth day of the first month they killed the animals for the festival. ² Josiah assigned the priests, dressed in their priestly robes, to serve in the Temple according to the daily order. ³ He also instructed the Levites, the Temple servants, to purify themselves for the Lord's service, so that they could put the sacred Covenant Box of the Lord in the Temple that King Solomon, the son of David, had built. ⁴ Josiah said to them, "You must no longer carry it from place to place, but you are to serve the Lord your God and minister to his people Israel. Get ready by family and clan to carry out your duties ⁵ according to the directions given by King David and the splendid way that they were carried out by his son King Solomon. Take your places in the Temple in proper order according to your family divisions as Levites serving the Lord for the people of Israel. ⁶ Kill the Passover lambs and goats and prepare the sacrifices for your people. Then celebrate the Passover according to the instructions that the Lord gave to Moses."

⁷ Josiah gave to the people who were present 30,000 young sheep and goats and 3,000 calves. These were a gift from the royal estates to carry out the promise he had made to the people, the priests, and the Levites. ⁸ The officials in charge of the Temple — Hilkiah, Zechariah, and Jehiel — also gave the priests 2,600 sheep and 300 calves for the sacrifices during the festival. ⁹ And the army commanders — Conaniah, Shemaiah and his brother Nethanel, Hashabiah, Ochiel, and Joram — contributed 5,000 sheep and 700 calves for the Levites to offer as sacrifices.

¹⁰-¹¹ Here is what happened. The priests and the Levites, dressed in the proper manner and carrying the unleavened bread, came that morning to present the offerings to the Lord

The priests and the Levites . . . carrying the unleavened bread (1.10)

according to the instructions in the Law of Moses. They took their positions in front of the people in the order of tribal and family divisions. ¹²The Levites roasted the Passover sacrifices and then boiled them in pots and kettles, making a pleasant smell. ¹³Then they distributed the meat to all the people. After that was done, they took meat for themselves and for the priests, the descendants of Aaron, ¹⁴because the priests were kept busy until night burning the fat of the sacrifices. ¹⁵⁻¹⁶The guards at the Temple gates and the Temple singers of the Levite clan of Asaph (with Asaph, Zechariah, and Eddinus, who were representatives of the king) remained at the places assigned to them by King David's instructions. They did not need to leave their posts, because the other Levites prepared the Passover for them.

¹⁷⁻¹⁸So, as King Josiah had commanded, everything that related to the sacrifices offered to the Lord was done that day; the Passover Festival was celebrated, and the sacrifices were offered on the altar. ¹⁹All the people of Israel who were present at that time kept the Passover and observed the Festival of Unleavened Bread for seven days. ²⁰Since the days of the prophet Samuel, the Passover had never been celebrated so well. ²¹⁻²²None of the former kings of Israel had ever celebrated a Passover like this one celebrated by King Josiah in Jerusalem in the eighteenth year of his reign; it was celebrated by the priests, the Levites, and all the people of Judah and Israel.

The End of Josiah's Reign
(*2 Kings* 23.28-30; *2 Chronicles* 35.20-27)

²³The Lord was pleased with everything Josiah did, for he was a very reli-

1.12 Ex 12.8, 9   **1.19** Ex 12.1-20

gious man. [24] But the ancient records also tell the story of those who sinned and rebelled against the Lord during Josiah's reign. They sinned more than any other nation or kingdom and did things that offended the Lord so much that his judgment fell on the people of Israel.

[25] After Josiah had done all these things, the king of Egypt led an army to fight at Carchemish on the Euphrates River. Josiah tried to stop him, [26] but the king of Egypt sent Josiah this message: "The war I am fighting does not concern you, King of Judah. [27] The Lord God did not send me to fight you; my battle is on the Euphrates River. The Lord is with me, and he is urging me on; so withdraw your troops and don't oppose the Lord." [28] But Josiah did not go back to his chariot and withdraw. He refused to listen to what the Lord had said through the prophet Jeremiah and decided to fight. [29] He went into battle on the plain of Megiddo, and the Egyptian commanders attacked him.

[30] King Josiah ordered his servants, "Take me off the battlefield; I'm badly hurt." So they took him out of the line of battle immediately, [31] and he got into a second chariot and was taken back to Jerusalem. There he died and was buried in the royal tomb. [32] All the people of Judah mourned his death.

The prophet Jeremiah composed a lament for King Josiah. It has become a custom in Israel for the leaders and their wives to sing this song when they mourn for him. [33] These things are recorded in *The History of the Kings of Judah.* Everything that Josiah did, how he gained his fame and his understanding of the Law, what he did earlier and what is told here, is all recorded in *The History of the Kings of Israel and Judah.*

King Joahaz of Judah
(2 Kings 23.30-35; 2 Chronicles 36.1-4)

[34] The people of Judah chose Josiah's son Joahaz[a] and made him king. Joahaz was twenty-three years old, [35] and he ruled Judah and Jerusalem for three months. Then the king of Egypt deposed him [36] and made the nation pay 7,500 pounds of silver and 75 pounds of gold as tribute. [37] The king of Egypt appointed Joahaz's brother Jehoiakim king of Judah and Jerusalem. [38] Jehoiakim put the leading men of the nation in prison, then had his brother Zarius arrested and brought back from Egypt.

King Jehoiakim of Judah
(2 Kings 23.36 — 24.7; 2 Chronicles 36.5-8)

[39] Jehoiakim was twenty-five years old when he became king of Judah and Jerusalem. He sinned against the Lord. [40] King Nebuchadnezzar of Babylonia invaded Judah, captured Jehoiakim, and took him to Babylonia in bronze chains. [41] Nebuchadnezzar also carried off some of the sacred utensils from the Temple and put them in his own temple in Babylon. [42] The stories about Jehoiakim, his depravity, and the godless way he lived are recorded in *The Chronicles of the Kings.*

King Jehoiachin of Judah
(2 Kings 24.8-17; 2 Chronicles 36.9, 10)

[43] Jehoiachin was eighteen years old when he succeeded his father Jehoiakim as king, [44] and he ruled in Jerusalem for three months and ten days. He too sinned against the Lord. [45] A year later King Nebuchadnezzar had Jehoiachin taken to Babylonia as a prisoner; Nebuchadnezzar also carried off sacred utensils from the Temple. [46] Then he

---

a Joahaz; *some manuscripts have* Jeconiah.

1.37 Jr 22.11, 12   **1.39** Jr 22.18, 19; 26.1   **1.40** Dn 1.1, 2   **1.45** Jr 22.24-30; 24.1; 29.1, 2; Ez 17.12

made Zedekiah king of Judah and Jerusalem.

King Zedekiah of Judah
(2 Kings 24.18-20; 2 Chronicles 36.11, 12; Jeremiah 52.1-3a)

Zedekiah was then twenty-one years old, and he ruled for eleven years. ⁴⁷He sinned against the Lord and refused to listen to the prophet Jeremiah, who spoke the word of the Lord.

The Fall of Jerusalem
(2 Kings 25.1-21; 2 Chronicles 36.13-21; Jeremiah 52.3b-11)

⁴⁸Although King Nebuchadnezzar had forced Zedekiah to swear in the Lord's name that he would be loyal to him, Zedekiah broke his oath and rebelled against him. He stubbornly refused to obey the commands of the Lord, the God of Israel. ⁴⁹In addition, the leaders of the people and even the chief priests did more godless and lawless things than all the corrupt heathen; they defiled the Temple of the Lord, which he had made holy. ⁵⁰The God of their ancestors had continued to send prophets to call them back from their sins, because he wanted to spare them and the Temple. ⁵¹But when the Lord spoke through his prophets, the people made fun of them and laughed. ⁵²At last the Lord became so angry with his people and their depraved ways that he ordered the kings of Babylonia to attack them. ⁵³The Babylonians killed the young men of Judah all around the Temple and did not spare anyone, young or old, man or woman. The Lord handed them all over to their enemies. ⁵⁴The Babylonians carried off all the sacred utensils from the Temple, the

treasure chests,*ᵇ* and the wealth of the king; they took everything away to Babylon, leaving nothing behind. ⁵⁵They burned down the Temple, broke down the city wall, set fire to its towers, ⁵⁶and completely destroyed all its beauty. Nebuchadnezzar forced all the survivors to be led away to Babylon, ⁵⁷where they served him and his descendants as slaves until the rise of the Persian Empire. And so what the Lord had foretold through the prophet Jeremiah was fulfilled: ⁵⁸"The land will lie desolate for seventy years to make up for the Sabbath rest*ᶜ* that has not been observed."

Cyrus Commands the Jews to Return
(2 Chronicles 36.22, 23; Ezra 1.1-11)

2 In the first year that Cyrus of Persia was emperor,*ᵈ* the Lord made come true what he had said through the prophet Jeremiah. ²He prompted Cyrus to issue the following command and send it out in writing to be read aloud everywhere in his empire:

³"This is the command of Cyrus, emperor of Persia. The Lord of Israel, the Lord Most High, has appointed me ruler over the whole world ⁴and has given me the responsibility of building a Temple for him in Jerusalem in Judah. ⁵May the Lord be with those of you who are his people. You are to go to Jerusalem and rebuild the Temple of the Lord of Israel, the Lord who lives in Jerusalem. ⁶If any of his people in exile need help to return, their neighbors must give them this help, providing them with silver and gold ⁷and other gifts, with horses and pack animals, as well as anything else offered for the Temple

---

ᵇ treasure chests; *some manuscripts have* the equipment of the Covenant Box.
ᶜ SABBATH REST: *A reference to the requirement of the Law that every seventh year the land was not to be farmed (see Lv 25.1-7).* *ᵈ* EMPEROR: *King Cyrus of Persia occupied the city of Babylon in 539 B.C. and began to reign as the emperor of Babylonia.*
1.48 Ez 17.15 **1.58** Jr 25.11; 29.10 **2.3** Is 44.28

They took everything away to Babylon. (1.54)

of the Lord in Jerusalem in fulfillment of a vow."

⁸ Then the heads of the clans of the tribes of Judah and Benjamin, the priests and the Levites, and everyone else whose heart the Lord had moved, got ready to go and rebuild the Lord's Temple in Jerusalem. ⁹ Their neighbors helped them with everything, giving them silver, gold, horses, and pack animals. Many of their neighbors were also led to give a large number of other things, in fulfillment of vows.

¹⁰ Emperor Cyrus gave them back the sacred utensils that King Nebuchadnezzar had taken from Jerusalem and had put in the temple of his idols. ¹¹ He brought them out and handed them over to Mithredath, chief of the royal treasury, ¹² who delivered them to Sheshbazzar, the governor of Judah. ¹³ Here is the inventory of the utensils:

gold bowls for offerings 1,000

silver bowls for offerings	1,000
silver fire pans	29
small gold bowls	30
small silver bowls	2,410
other utensils	1,000

¹⁴ In all there were 5,469 gold and silver bowls and other utensils, ¹⁵ and Sheshbazzar took these with him when he and the other exiles went from Babylon to Jerusalem.

Opposition to Rebuilding Jerusalem
(Ezra 4.7-24)

¹⁶ In the reign of Emperor Artaxerxes of Persia, Bishlam, Mithredath, Tabeel, Rehum, Beltethmus, Shimshai the secretary of the province, and their associates who lived in Samaria and elsewhere wrote the following letter in protest against the Jews who were living in Judah and Jerusalem:

17 "To Your Majesty Emperor Artaxerxes from your servants, the official correspondent Rehum, the secretary Shimshai, the other members of the council, and the judges of Greater Syria and Phoenicia.

18 "We want Your Majesty to know that the Jews who came here from your other territories have settled in Jerusalem and are rebuilding that evil and rebellious city. They are restoring the marketplaces, repairing the walls, and laying the foundations for a Temple. 19 If this city is rebuilt and its walls are completed, the people will stop paying taxes and will even rebel against royal authority. 20 Since work on the Temple has already begun, we consider it appropriate not to overlook such an important matter 21 but to bring it to the attention of Your Majesty. Then, if it seems proper to you, a search may be made in the records your ancestors kept. 22 You will find information about these matters in the historical records, and you will discover that this city has always been rebellious and given trouble to other cities and kings. 23 The Jews have used it from ancient times as a base for rebellions and wars. That is why the city was destroyed. 24 We therefore declare to you that if this city is rebuilt and its walls are restored, Your Majesty will no longer be able to enter Greater Syria and Phoenicia."

25 The emperor sent the following answer to the official correspondent Rehum, Beltethmus, the secretary Shimshai, and their associates who lived in Samaria, Syria, and Phoenicia:

26 "After reading the letter which you sent me, I gave orders for an investigation to be made, and it has indeed been found that from ancient times Jerusalem has revolted against royal authority, 27 and its people have been involved in insurrections and wars. Powerful and cruel kings have reigned there and have ruled over Greater Syria and Phoenicia, from which they collected taxes. 28 Therefore I am now issuing orders that those men be prevented from rebuilding the city and that necessary steps be taken to insure that these orders will not be disobeyed, 29 so that this trouble spot will no longer be a threat to the royal interests."

30 As soon as this letter from Emperor Artaxerxes was read, Rehum, Shimshai the secretary, and their associates hurried to Jerusalem with a force of cavalry and a large number of armed troops and began interfering with the rebuilding of the Temple. The work had to stop, and no more was done until the second year of the reign of Emperor Darius of Persia.

They stopped the builders. (2.30)

The Debate of the Bodyguards before the Emperor

3 The Emperor Darius gave a great banquet for all those under him, all the members of his family and staff, all the leading officials of Persia and Media, 2 all his chief officers, administrators, and the governors of the 127 provinces stretching from India to Ethi-

opia.*e* ³When everyone had enough to eat and drink, they left, and Darius went to bed. He fell asleep but soon awoke.

A Contest Is Proposed

⁴Then the three young men who served Emperor Darius as his personal bodyguard said to one another, ⁵"Let each one of us name the one thing that he considers the strongest thing in the world. The emperor will decide who has given the wisest answer to this question and will give magnificent gifts and prizes to the winner. ⁶He will wear royal robes, drink from a gold cup, and sleep in a gold bed. He will have a chariot with gold-studded bridles, wear a fine linen turban, and have a gold necklace. ⁷Because of his wisdom he will be an adviser to the emperor and will be given the title "Relative of the Emperor."

⁸Then each of them wrote down the best answer he could think of, sealed it, and put it under the emperor's pillow. They said to one another, ⁹"When the emperor wakes up, the statements will be given to him. He and the three leading officials of Persia will decide who gave the wisest answer. The winner will be given the prize on the basis of what he has written." ¹⁰The first wrote, "There is nothing stronger than wine." ¹¹The second wrote, "There is nothing stronger than the emperor." ¹²And the third wrote, "There is nothing stronger than a woman, but truth can conquer anything."

¹³When the emperor woke up, the written statements were given to him, and he read them. ¹⁴Then he sent messengers and called together all the leading officials of Persia and Media, including the chief officers, adminis-

trators, governors, and commissioners. ¹⁵He took his seat in the council chamber and had the three statements read aloud. ¹⁶"Bring in the three young men," he said, "and let them explain their answers." So when they were brought in, ¹⁷they were asked to explain what they had written.

The Speech about Wine

The bodyguard who had written about the strength of wine spoke first: ¹⁸"Gentlemen," he began, "wine is clearly the strongest thing in the world. It confuses the mind of everyone who drinks it. ¹⁹It has exactly the same effect on everyone: king or orphan, slave or free, rich or poor. ²⁰It makes every thought happy and carefree, and makes one forget every sorrow and responsibility. ²¹It makes everyone feel rich, ignore the power of kings and officials, and talk as if he owned the whole world. ²²When men drink wine, they forget who their friends and neighbors are, and then they are soon drawing their swords to fight them. ²³Then, when they sober up, they don't remember what they have done. ²⁴Gentlemen," he concluded, "if wine makes men act in this way, it certainly must be the strongest thing in the world."

The Speech about the Emperor

4 The bodyguard who had written about the strength of the emperor spoke next. ²"Gentlemen," he began, "nothing in the world is stronger than men, since they rule over land and sea and, in fact, over everything in the world. ³But the emperor is the strongest of them all; he is their lord and master, and men obey him, no matter what he commands. ⁴If he tells them to make war on one another, they do it. If he

---

e Greek Ethiopia: *Ethiopia is the name given in Graeco-Roman times to the extensive territory south of the First Cataract of the Nile River. Cush was the ancient (Hebrew) name of this region which included within its borders most of modern Sudan and some of present-day Ethiopia (Abyssinia).*

sends them out against his enemies, they go, even if they have to break down mountains, walls, or towers. 5 They may kill or be killed, but they never disobey the emperor's orders. If they are victorious, they bring him all their loot and everything else they have taken in battle. 6 Farmers do not go out to war, but even they bring to the emperor a part of everything that they harvest, and they compel one another to pay taxes to the emperor. 7 Although the emperor is only one man, if he orders people to kill, they kill; if he orders them to set prisoners free, they do it; 8 if he orders them to attack, they do; if he orders destruction, they destroy; if he orders them to build, they build; 9 if he orders crops to be destroyed or fields to be planted, it is done. 10 Everybody, soldier or civilian, obeys the emperor. And when he sits down to eat or drink and then falls asleep, 11 his servants stand guard around him, without being able to go and take care of their own affairs, for they never disobey him. 12 Gentlemen," he concluded, "since people obey the emperor like this, certainly nothing in the world is stronger than he is."

The Speech about Women

13 The bodyguard who had written about women and the truth—it was Zerubbabel—spoke last. 14 "Gentlemen," he began, "the emperor is certainly powerful, men are numerous, and wine is strong, but who rules and controls them all? It is women! 15 Women gave birth to the emperor and all the men who rule over land and sea. 16 Women brought them into the world. Women brought up the men who planted the vineyards from which wine comes. 17 Women make the clothes that men wear; women bring honor to men; in fact, without women, men couldn't live.

18 "Men may accumulate silver or gold or other beautiful things, but if they see a woman with a pretty face or a good figure, 19 they will leave it all to gape and stare, and they will desire her more than their wealth. 20 A man will leave his own father, who brought him up, and leave his own country to get married. 21 He will forget his father, his mother, and his country to spend the rest of his life with his wife. 22 So you must recognize that women are your masters. Don't you work and sweat and then take all that you have earned and give it to your wives? 23 A man will take his sword and go out to attack, rob and steal, and sail the seas and rivers. 24 He may have to face lions or travel in the dark, but when he has robbed, stolen, and plundered, he will bring the loot home to the woman he loves.

25 "A man loves his wife more than his parents. 26 Some men are driven out of their minds on account of a woman, and others become slaves for the sake of a woman. 27 Others have been put to death, have ruined their lives, or have committed crimes because of a woman. 28 So now do you believe me?

"The emperor's power is certainly great—no nation has the courage to attack him. 29 But once I saw him with Apame, his concubine, the daughter of the famous Bartacus. While sitting at the emperor's right, 30 she took his crown off his head, put it on her own, and then slapped his face with her left hand. 31 All the emperor did was look at her with his mouth open. Whenever she smiles at him, he smiles back; and when she gets angry with him, he flatters her and teases her until she is in a good mood again. 32 Gentlemen, if women can do all that, surely there can be nothing stronger in the world." 33 The emperor and his officials just looked at one another.

The Speech about Truth

Then Zerubbabel began to speak about truth. 34 "Yes, gentlemen," he said, "women are very strong. But think of how big the earth is, how high the sky is; think how fast the sun moves, as it rapidly circles the whole sky in a single day. ³⁵ If the sun can do this, it is certainly great. But truth is greater and stronger than all of these things. ³⁶ Everyone on earth honors truth; heaven praises it; all creation trembles in awe before it.

"There is not the slightest injustice in truth.ᶠ ³⁷ You will find injustice in wine, the emperor, women, all human beings, in all they do, and in everything else. There is no truth in them; they are unjust and they will perish. ³⁸ But truth endures and is always strong; it will continue to live and reign forever. ³⁹ Truth shows no partiality or favoritism; it does what is right, rather than what is unjust or evil. Everyone approves what truth does; ⁴⁰ its decisions are always fair. Truth is strong, royal, powerful, and majestic forever. Let all things praise the God of truth!"

The Response

⁴¹ When Zerubbabel had finished speaking, all the people shouted, "Truth is great—there is nothing stronger!"

⁴² Then the emperor said to him, "You may ask anything you want, even more than what was agreed, and I will give it to you. You will be my adviser, and you will be granted the title 'Relative of the Emperor.'"

⁴³ Zerubbabel replied, "Your Majesty, permit me to remind you of the solemn vow you took on the day you became emperor. You promised to rebuild Jerusalem ⁴⁴ and to send back all the treasures that had been taken from the city. Remember that when Cyrus made a vow to destroy Babylon, he set these things aside and solemnly promised to send them back to Jerusalem. ⁴⁵ You also promised to rebuild the Temple, which the Edomites burned down

when the Babylonians devastated the land of Judah. ⁴⁶ So, Your Majesty, because you are a man of generosity, I beg you to fulfill the solemn promise you made to the King of heaven."

⁴⁷ Then Emperor Darius stood up, kissed Zerubbabel, and wrote letters for him to all the treasurers, governors, and administrators in the provinces, ordering them to provide safe conduct for

The Emperor Darius stood up and kissed Zerubbabel. (4.47)

him and all those going with him to rebuild Jerusalem. ⁴⁸ He also wrote letters to all the governors in Greater Syria and Phoenicia, with special instructions to those in Lebanon, to transport cedar logs to Jerusalem and help Zerubbabel rebuild the city.

⁴⁹ The emperor also provided letters for all the Jews who wished to return to Jerusalem. These letters guaranteed their freedom and ordered all governors, treasurers, and other administrators not to interfere with them in any way. ⁵⁰ All the land that they acquired was to be exempt from taxation, and the Edomites were to surrender the villages they had taken from the Jews. ⁵¹ Each year 1,500 pounds of silver

ᶠ in truth; *some manuscripts have* with God.
4.45 Ob 10-14

would be given for the construction of the Temple until it was finished. ⁵² In addition, 750 pounds of silver would be given each year to provide for the seventeen burnt offerings to be offered in the Temple each day. ⁵³ All the Jews who left Babylonia to build the city of Jerusalem would be granted their freedom, together with their children and the priests.

⁵⁴ The emperor's orders gave specific instructions, as follows: the priests must be supported, their robes for the Temple service must be provided, ⁵⁵ the Levites must be supported until the Temple and Jerusalem are completely rebuilt, ⁵⁶ and land and wages must be provided for all the guards of the city. ⁵⁷ He also reaffirmed Cyrus' instructions that all the small utensils and Temple treasures that Cyrus had set aside should be returned to Jerusalem.

⁵⁸ Then the young man Zerubbabel left the council chamber, turned toward Jerusalem, looked up to heaven, and praised the King of heaven: ⁵⁹ "Lord, all praise belongs to you; you are the source of all victory and wisdom, ⁶⁰ and I thank you, O Lord of our ancestors, for giving wisdom to me, your servant."

⁶¹ Zerubbabel took the emperor's letters and went to Babylon, where he told the other Jews everything that had happened. ⁶² They praised the God of their ancestors because he had made it possible for them ⁶³ to go and rebuild Jerusalem and the Temple which bears his name. For seven days they held a joyful celebration, accompanied by music.

The List of Those Who Returned from Exile
(Ezra 2.1-70; Nehemiah 7.4-73)

5 After this, the heads of clans were chosen, tribe by tribe, to go to Jerusalem with their wives, children,

slaves, and animals. ² Emperor Darius sent a thousand cavalry troops to escort them safely back to Jerusalem. ³ He sent them off to the music of drums and flutes, while all the rest of the Jewish people danced for joy.

⁴ These are the names, by tribes, clans, and families, of the men who returned: ⁵ Among the priests, descendants of Phinehas son of Aaron, was Joshua, son of Jozadak and grandson of Seraiah. He was accompanied by Zerubbabel,^g who was the son of Shealtiel of the family of David, of the line of Perez, of the tribe of Judah. ⁶ He was the one who had spoken the wise words before Emperor Darius of Persia. They left Babylon in the second year of his reign in Nisan, the first month.

⁷ These are the Jewish men who returned from exile. Their families had been living in Babylonia since King Nebuchadnezzar had taken them there as prisoners. ⁸ They returned to Jerusalem and the rest of Judah, each to his own hometown. Their leaders were Zerubbabel, Joshua, Nehemiah, Seraiah, Resaiah, Eneneus, Mordecai, Beelsarus, Aspharasus, Reeliah, Rehum, and Baanah.

^{9-17a} The following is a list of the clans of Israel, with the number of those from each clan who returned with their leaders from exile:

Parosh	2,172
Shephatiah	472
Arah	756
Pahath Moab (descendants of Jeshua and Joab)	2,812
Elam	1,254
Zattu	945
Chorbe	705
Bani	648
Bebai	623
Azgad	1,322
Adonikam	667
Bigvai	2,066

---

^g *Probable text* He was accompanied by Zerubbabel; *Greek* and Joakim son of Zerubbabel.

Adin	454
Ater (also called Hezekiah)	92
Kilan and Azetas	67
Azaru	432
Annias	101
Arom	—
Bezai	323
Arsiphurith	112
Baiterus	3,005

17b-23 People whose ancestors had lived in the following towns also returned:

Bethlehem	123
Netophah	55
Anathoth	158
Beth Azmaveth	42
Kiriath Jearim	25
Chephirah and Beeroth	743
the towns of the Chadiasans and the Ammidians	422
Ramah and Geba	621
Michmash	122
Bethel	52
Magbish	156
The other Elam and Ono	725
Jericho	345
Senaah	3,330

24-25 The following is the list of the priestly clans that returned from exile:

Jedaiah (descendants of Jeshua and Anasib)	972
Immer	1,052
Pashhur	1,247
Harim	1,017

26-28 Clans of Levites who returned from exile:

Jeshua, Kadmiel, Bannas, and Sudias	74
Temple musicians (descendants of Asaph)	128
Temple guards (descendants of Shallum, Ater, Talmon, Akkub, Hatita, and Shobai)	139

29-32 Clans of Temple workmen who returned from exile:

Esau, Hasupha, Tabbaoth, Keros, Siaha, Padon, Lebanah, Hagabah, Akkub, Uthai, Ketab, Hagab, Shamlai, Hanan, Cathua, Geddur, Jairus, Daisan, Noeba, Chaseba, Gazera, Uzza, Phinoe, Asara, Besai, Asnah, Meunim, Nephisim, Akub, Hakupha, Asur, Pharakim, Bazluth, Mehida, Cutha, Charea, Barkos, Sisera, Temah, Neziah, Hatipha

33-34 Clans of Solomon's servants who returned from exile:

Hassophereth, Peruda, Jaalah, Lozon, Giddel, Shephatiah, Agia, Phochereth Hazzebaim, Sarothie, Masiah, Gas, Addus, Subas, Apherra, Barodis, Shaphat, Adlon

35 The total number of descendants of the Temple workmen and of Solomon's servants who returned from exile was 372.

36-37 There were 652 belonging to the clans of Delaiah (descendants of Tobiah) and Nekoda who returned from the towns of Tel Melah and Tel Harsha, with their leaders Cherub, Addan, and Immer; but these could not prove that they were descendants of Israelites.

38-39 The following clans, who claimed to be priestly clans, could find no record to prove their ancestry: Habaiah, Hakkoz, Jaddus (the ancestor of the clan of Jaddus had married Agia, one of the daughters of Barzillai, and had taken the name of his father-in-law's clan). Since they were unable to prove who their ancestors were, they were not allowed to function as priests. **40** Nehemiah the governor [h] told them that they could not eat the food offered to God until there was a High Priest

---

[h] *Probable meaning* the governor; *Greek* and Attharias.
5.40 Nu 27.21

who could use the Revelation and Truth.[i]

41-43 The total number of Israelites (twelve years old or older, not counting servants) 42,360

Male and female servants	7,337
Male and female musicians	245
Camels	435
Horses	7,036
Mules	245
Donkeys	5,525

44 When the exiles arrived at the place of God's Temple in Jerusalem, some of the leaders of the clans took a vow to rebuild the Temple on its old site, to the best of their ability. 45 They promised to contribute for the rebuilding and the service of the Temple 1,000 pounds of gold, 5,000 pounds of silver, and 100 robes for priests.

46 The priests, the Levites, and some of the people settled in or near Jerusalem; the musicians and the Temple guards settled in nearby towns; and the rest of the Israelites settled in the towns where their ancestors had lived.

Worship Begins Again
(Ezra 3.1-6)

47 By the seventh month the people of Israel were all settled in their towns. Then they all assembled in the open square in front of the first gate on the east side of the Temple area. 48 Joshua son of Jehozadak, his fellow priests, and Zerubbabel son of Shealtiel, together with his relatives, prepared the altar of the God of Israel, 49 so that they could burn sacrifices on it according to the instructions written in the Law of Moses, the man of God. 50 Some of the local people, even though they were stronger

than the Jews and opposed to them, joined them[j] in rebuilding the altar where it had stood before. Then the Jews began once again to burn the regular morning and evening sacrifices on the altar. 51 They celebrated the Festival of Shelters, according to the regulations, each day offering the sacrifices required for that day. 52 They also offered the normal daily sacrifices, as well as those required for the Sabbath, the New Moon Festival, and the other regular assemblies for worship. 53 Although the people had not yet rebuilt God's Temple, everyone who had made a vow to God began to offer sacrifices on the first day of the seventh month.

The Rebuilding of the Temple Begins
(Ezra 3.7-13)

54 The people gave money to pay the stonemasons and the carpenters; they gave food, drink, 55 and carts to be sent to the cities of Tyre and Sidon in exchange for cedar logs from Lebanon, which were to be floated to the harbor at Joppa. All of this was done according to the orders given by Emperor Cyrus of Persia.

56-57 So in the second month of the year after they came back to the site of the Temple in Jerusalem, they started the work and began laying the foundation. Zerubbabel, Joshua, and the rest of the Jewish people, the priests, and the Levites — in fact, all the exiles who had come back to Jerusalem, joined in the work. 58 The Levites twenty years of age or older were put in charge of rebuilding the Temple for the Lord. The Levite Jeshua and his sons and relatives, his brother Kadmiel, the sons of Jeshua Emadabun, the sons of Joda son of Iliadun, and all their sons and relatives — in fact, all the Levites joined

[i] REVELATION AND TRUTH: *This is the Greek translation of Urim and Thummim, two objects used by the priest to determine God's will; it is not known precisely how they were used.* [j] *Some of . . . joined them; Greek unclear.*

5.46 1 Ch 9.2; Ne 11.3 **5.52** Nu 28.11—29.39

All the people blew trumpets and shouted. (5.62)

together to take charge of the rebuilding of the Temple.

While the workers were building the Temple of the Lord, [59] the priests in their robes took their places with trumpets and other musical instruments in their hands, and the Levites of the clan of Asaph stood there with cymbals. [60] They praised the Lord and gave thanks to him according to the instructions handed down from the time of King David. [61] They sang psalms praising the Lord, repeating the refrain: "The goodness of the Lord and his glorious presence are with all Israel forever." [62] All the people blew trumpets and shouted with all their might, praising the Lord because the Temple was being rebuilt. [63] Some of the older priests, Levites, and heads of clans had seen the first Temple, and when they came and saw the building of this Temple, they cried and wailed. [64] Others who were there blew trumpets and shouted for joy. [65] The crowd blew the trumpets so loud that the blast could be heard far away, but no one nearby could hear the blast of the trumpets because the sound made by those who were crying and wailing was so loud.

Opposition to the Rebuilding of the Temple
(Ezra 4.1-5)

[66] The enemies of the tribes of Judah and Benjamin heard the sound of the trumpets and came to see what it meant. [67] When they learned that those who had returned from exile were rebuilding the Temple of the Lord, the God of Israel, [68] they went to Zerubbabel, Joshua, and the heads of the clans and said, "Let us join you in building the Temple. [69] We worship the same Lord you worship and we have been offering sacrifices to him ever since Emperor Esarhaddon [k] of Assyria sent us here to live."

[70] Zerubbabel, Joshua, and the heads of the clans told them, "We don't need your help in building the Temple for the Lord our God. [71] We will build it ourselves, just as Emperor Cyrus of Persia commanded us."

[72] Then the people who had been living in the land began to harass [l] the Jews; they cut off their supplies and kept them from building. [73] These people plotted, agitated, and rioted so much that they prevented the Temple from being completed during the reign

[k] ESARHADDON: *Greek* Asbasareth.   [l] *Probable text* harass; *Greek unclear.*
5.59, 60 1 Ch 25.1   **5.61** 1 Ch 16.34; 2 Ch 5.11-14; Ps 100.5; 106.1; 118.1; 136.1; Jr 33.11   **5.67, 68** 2 K 17.24-41

of Emperor Cyrus. The work was halted until Darius became emperor, two years later.

Work on the Temple Begins Again
(Ezra 5.1-17)

6 In the second year of the reign of Emperor Darius, the two prophets, Haggai and Zechariah son of Iddo, began to speak in the name of the Lord God of Israel to the Jews who lived in Judah and Jerusalem. ²When Zerubbabel son of Shealtiel and Joshua son of Jehozadak heard their messages, they began to rebuild the Temple in Jerusalem, and the two prophets helped them.

³Almost at once Governor Sisinnes of Greater Syria and Phoenicia, with Shethar Bozenai and the other officials, came to Jerusalem and demanded: ⁴"Who gave you orders to build this Temple and complete this roof and everything else? Who is doing this work?" ⁵But the Lord was with the people who had returned from exile and was watching over the Jewish leaders, ⁶and they were allowed to continue building until Emperor Darius could be informed and his reply received. ⁷Here is the report that the Persian officials sent to the emperor:

⁸"To Emperor Darius, greetings.

"Your Majesty should know that we went to Judah and to Jerusalem and there we found the leaders of the Jews who have returned from exile ⁹building a large new Temple for the Lord with expensive, shaped stone blocks and with wooden beams set in the walls. ¹⁰The work is being done rapidly and is moving ahead steadily; yet they are taking great care and doing their work beautifully.

¹¹"We then asked the leaders of the people to tell us who had given them orders to rebuild the Temple and lay the foundations for the buildings. ¹²We also asked them who their leaders were and demanded a list of their names, so that we could inform you.

¹³"They answered, 'We are servants of the Lord who created heaven and earth. ¹⁴This Temple was built and equipped many years ago by a very powerful king of Israel. ¹⁵But because our ancestors sinned against Israel's Lord in heaven and made him angry, he let them be conquered by King Nebuchadnezzar of Babylonia, a king of the Chaldean dynasty. ¹⁶The Temple was demolished and burned, and the people were taken into exile in Babylonia. ¹⁷Then, in the first year of his reign as emperor of Babylonia, Cyrus issued orders for the Temple to be rebuilt. ¹⁸He gave back the sacred gold and silver utensils which Nebuchadnezzar had taken from the Temple in Jerusalem and had placed in his own temple in Babylon. Emperor Cyrus turned these utensils over to Zerubbabel and the governor, Sheshbazzar. ¹⁹The Emperor told Sheshbazzar to take them and return them to the Temple in Jerusalem, and to rebuild the Temple where it had stood before. ²⁰So Sheshbazzar came and laid its foundation, and construction has continued from then until the present, but the Temple is still not finished.'

²¹"Now, if it please Your Majesty, have a search made in the royal records in Babylon ²²to find whether or not the building of this Temple in Jerusalem had the approval of Emperor Cyrus, and then, if it please Your Majesty, inform us what your will is in this matter."

6.1 Zec 1.1   **6.2** Hg 1.12; Zec 4.6-9   **6.15, 16** 2 K 25.8-12; 2 Ch 36.17-20; Jr 52.12-15
6.17 Ezra 1.2-11; 1 Esd 2.3-15

Emperor Cyrus' Order
Is Rediscovered
(Ezra 6.1-5)

²³ So Emperor Darius ordered a search to be made in the royal records that were kept in Babylon. It was, however, in the fortress of Ecbatana in the province of Media that a scroll was found, containing the following record: ²⁴ "In the first year of his reign Emperor Cyrus ordered the rebuilding of the Temple in Jerusalem, where sacrifices are continually offered. ²⁵ The Temple is to be 90 feet high and 90 feet wide. The walls must be built with one layer of new local wood on top of each three layers of shaped stone. All expenses are to be paid by the royal treasury. ²⁶ Also the gold and silver utensils which King Nebuchadnezzar brought to Babylon from the Temple in Jerusalem are to be returned to their proper place in the Jerusalem Temple."

Emperor Darius Orders the
Work to Continue
(Ezra 6.6-12)

²⁷ Then Emperor Darius gave strict orders to Sisinnes, governor of Greater Syria and Phoenicia, Shethar Bozenai, the other officials, and the local officials to stay away from Jerusalem and let Zerubbabel, the servant of the Lord and governor of Judah, and the other Jewish leaders rebuild the Temple of the Lord where it stood before. ²⁸ "And I also command," he continued, "that it be completely rebuilt and that, until it is finished, every effort be made to help the Jews who have returned from exile. ²⁹ From the taxes received in Greater Syria and Phoenicia a contribution shall be made on a regular basis to these men, payable to Governor Zerubbabel, for bulls, sheep, and lambs to be used in their sacrifices to the Lord. ³⁰ In the same way, each year and without

further question, wheat, salt, wine, and olive oil are to be supplied, according to the daily needs indicated by the priests. ³¹ This must be done so that they can make wine offerings to God Most High for me and my children and pray for his blessing on our lives." ³² He also gave these orders: "If anyone disobeys the commands as written above or fails to carry them out, he is to be hanged on a wooden beam taken from his own house, and his property is to be turned over to the emperor. ³³ May the Lord who is worshiped at Jerusalem destroy any king or nation that tries to stop the work or damage the Temple there. ³⁴ I, Emperor Darius, issue the command that these orders be carried out in every detail."

The Temple Is Dedicated
(Ezra 6.13-18)

7 Then Governor Sisinnes, Shethar Bozenai, and the other officials did exactly as the emperor had commanded ² and gave careful supervision to the work on the Temple, helping the Jewish leaders and Temple officials. ³ The workers made good progress with the building of the Temple, encouraged by the prophets Haggai and Zechariah. ⁴ The Jews completed the building according to the command of the Lord, the God of Israel, and with the permission of Cyrus, Darius, and Artaxerxes, emperors of Persia. ⁵ The Temple was completed on the twenty-third day of the month of Adar in the sixth year of the reign of Emperor Darius. ⁶ Then the people of Israel — the priests, the Levites, and all the others who had returned from exile and joined them — carried out all the commands in the Law of Moses. ⁷ For the dedication they offered 100 bulls, 200 sheep, and 400 lambs as sacrifices, ⁸ and 12 goats as offerings for sin, one goat for the leader of each tribe of Israel. ⁹ The

priests in their robes and the Levites took their positions, family by family, for the Temple services of the Lord, the God of Israel, according to the instructions contained in the book of Moses. The Temple guards stood at each gate.

The Passover
(Ezra 6.19-22)

¹⁰ The people of Israel who had returned from exile celebrated the Passover on the fourteenth day of the first month of the following year. The priests and Levites had purified themselves at the same time. ¹¹ Not all the Jews who had returned purified themselves at that time, but the Levites did.ᵐ ¹² The Levites killed the animals for the Passover sacrifices for all the people who had returned, for the priests, and for themselves. ¹³ The sacrifices were eaten by all the Israelites who had returned from exile; they worshiped the Lord and rejected the pagan ways of the other people who were living in the land. ¹⁴ For seven days they celebrated the Festival of Unleavened Bread. They rejoiced in the presence of the Lord, ¹⁵ the God of Israel, because he had made the plans of the emperor of Assyriaⁿ favorable to them and had supported them in their work.

Ezra Arrives in Jerusalem
(Ezra 7.1-10)

8 Many years later, when Artaxerxes was emperor of Persia, a man named Ezra came from Babylon. He traced his ancestry back to Aaron, the High Priest, as follows: Ezra was the son of Seraiah, son of Azariah, son of Hilkiah, son of Shallum, ² son of Zadok, son of Ahitub, son of Amariah,

When Artaxerxes was emperor (8.1)

son of Azariah, son of Bukki, son of Abishua, son of Phinehas, son of Eleazar, son of Aaron.

³⁻⁴ Ezra was a scholar with a thorough knowledge of the Law, which the God of Israel had given to Moses. The emperor had a high regard for him and approved all the requests he made. Ezra set out from Babylonia ⁵ for Jerusalem with a group of Israelites which included priests, Levites, Temple musicians, Temple guards, and workmen. ⁶ They left Babylonia on the first day of the first month in the seventh year of the reign of Artaxerxes. God gave them a safe journey, and they arrived in Jerusalem on the first day of the fifth month. ⁷ Ezra had a thorough knowledge of the Law of the Lord and ne-

---

ᵐ *Verse 11 in Greek is unclear.*   ⁿ EMPEROR OF ASSYRIA: *Apparently a reference to the Persian emperor who then also ruled the territory once occupied by Assyria, Israel's ancient enemy.*

7.10 Ex 12.1-20

glected none of its details. As a result he could teach all its laws and regulations to all the people of Israel.

The Document That Emperor Artaxerxes Gave to Ezra
(Ezra 7.11-26)

8 The following is a copy of the decree that Emperor Artaxerxes gave to Ezra, the priest and scholar of the Law of the Lord:

9 "From Emperor Artaxerxes to the priest Ezra, scholar of the Law of the Lord, greetings.

10 "In my generosity I have decided to decree that throughout my empire any of the Jews who so desire, including priests and Levites, may go with you to Jerusalem. **11** I and the seven counselors who have the title 'Friends of the Emperor' have decided that all who wish to do so may go with you. **12** Let them investigate the conditions in Jerusalem and Judah to see how well the Law of the Lord is being obeyed. **13** Let them also take with them to Jerusalem the gifts which I and my counselors have vowed to give to the Lord of Israel, including all the silver and gold belonging to the Lord which may be found in Babylonia, **14** and all that is given by the people of Israel for the Temple of their Lord. The silver and gold are to be collected to buy bulls, rams, lambs, and everything else that is necessary, **15** so that sacrifices may be offered on the altar of the Lord in Jerusalem.

16 "You may use the silver and gold for whatever you and the rest of your people desire, in accordance with the will of your God. **17-18** You may obtain from the royal treasury the sacred vessels of the Lord that are being entrusted to you for use in the Temple of your God in Jerusalem, as well as anything else you may need for the Temple service.

19 "I command all the treasury officials in Greater Syria and Phoenicia to provide promptly for Ezra, the priest and scholar of the Law of God Most High, everything he asks for, **20** up to a limit of 7,500 pounds of silver, 500 bushels of wheat, 550 gallons of wine, and as much salt as may be needed. **21** You must be careful to do everything that the Law requires in order to honor God Most High and so make sure that he is never angry with me or with those who reign after me. **22** You are forbidden to collect any taxes from the priests, Levites, musicians, guards, workmen, or anyone else connected with this Temple. No one has the right to impose any burden on them.

23 "You, Ezra, using the wisdom that comes from God, shall appoint administrators and judges to govern all the people in Greater Syria and Phoenicia who live by the Law of your God. You must teach that Law to anyone who does not know it. **24** If anyone disobeys the laws of your God or the laws of the empire, he is to be punished promptly: by death, by fine, by exile, or by some other punishment."

Ezra Praises God
(Ezra 7.27, 28)

25 Ezra said, "Praise the Lord, the Lord alone! He has made the emperor willing to restore the glory of the Temple of the Lord in Jerusalem. **26** By God's grace, I have won the respect of the emperor, his counselors, all his Friends, and all his powerful officials. **27** The Lord my God has given me courage, and I have been able to persuade many men to return with me."

The People Who Returned from Exile
(Ezra 8.1-14)

28 This is the list of the leaders of the clans and families who had been in exile in Babylonia and returned with Ezra to Jerusalem when Artaxerxes was emperor:

29-40 Gershom, of the clan of Phinehas

Gamael, of the clan of Ithamar

Hattush son of Shecaniah, of the clan of David

Zechariah, of the clan of Parosh, with 150 men of his clan (there were records of their family line)

Eliehoenai son of Zechariah, of the clan of Pahath Moab, with 200 men

Shecaniah son of Jehaziel, of the clan of Zattu, with 300 men

Ebed son of Jonathan, of the clan of Adin, with 250 men

Jeshaiah son of Gotholiah, of the clan of Elam, with 70 men

Zeraiah son of Michael, of the clan of Shephatiah, with 70 men

Obadiah son of Jehiel, of the clan of Joab, with 212 men

Shelomith son of Josiphiah, of the clan of Bani, with 160 men

Zechariah son of Bebai, of the clan of Bebai, with 28 men

Johanan son of Hakkatan, of the clan of Azgad, with 110 men

Eliphelet, Jeuel, and Shemaiah, of the clan of Adonikam, with 70 men (they returned at a later date)

Uthai son of Istalcurus, of the clan of Bigvai, with 70 men

Ezra Finds Priests and Levites for the Temple
(Ezra 8.15-20)

41 I assembled the entire group at Theras River, and we camped there for three days. I inspected them 42 and found that there were no priests or Levites in the group, 43-44 so I sent a message to ten of the leaders who were

competent men: Eliezer, Iduel, Maasmas, Elnathan, Shemaiah, Jarib, Nathan, Elnathan, Zechariah, and Meshullam. 45 I told them to go to Iddo, the chief official at the treasury, 46 and ask him, his associates, and the treasury officials to send us priests to serve in the Temple of our Lord. 47 With God's help, they sent us some able men: Sherebiah, a Levite from the clan of Mahli, with eighteen of his sons and relatives, 48 and Hashabiah, Annunus, and his brother Jeshaiah of the clan of Hananiah, with twenty of their sons. 49 There were also 220 Temple workmen whose ancestors had been designated by King David and his officials to assist the Levites. They were all listed in the register by name.

Ezra Leads the People in Fasting and Prayer
(Ezra 8.21-23)

50 There by Theras River I made a vow that the young men should fast in the presence of our Lord and ask him for a safe journey for us, our children, and our animals. 51 I would have been ashamed to ask the emperor for infantry and cavalry to accompany us and protect us from our enemies, 52 because I had told him that our Lord by his strength blesses and protects those who trust him. 53 So once again we prayed for our Lord to protect us, and he answered our prayers.

The Gifts for the Temple
(Ezra 8.24-30)

54 From among the leading priests I chose Sherebiah, Hashabiah, and ten others. 55 Then I weighed out the silver, the gold, and the sacred utensils which the emperor, his advisers and officials, and the people of Israel had given to be used in the Temple, and I gave it to the priests. 56-57 This is what I gave them:

silver	25 tons
silver utensils	7,500 pounds
gold	7,500 pounds

gold bowls   20
fine bronze bowls
  that looked like
  gold   12

58 I said to the priests, "You are sacred to the Lord, the Lord of our ancestors, and so are the utensils and the silver and gold brought to him in fulfillment of a vow. **59** Guard them carefully until you reach the Temple. There in the priests' rooms, turn them over to the leaders of the priests and the Levites and to the leaders of the people of Israel in Jerusalem." **60** So the priests and the Levites took charge of the silver, the gold, and the utensils for Jerusalem and brought them to the Temple.

The Return to Jerusalem
(Ezra 8.31-36)

61 It was on the twelfth day of the first month that we left Theras River, and with the Lord's presence and protection we reached Jerusalem. He protected us from all our enemies on our journey, and we arrived safely. **62** After we had been there three days, we went to the Temple, weighed the silver and gold and turned it all over to Meremoth the priest, son of Uriah. **63** With him were Eleazar son of Phinehas and two Levites, Jozabad son of Jeshua and Moeth son of Sabannus. **64** Everything was counted and weighed, and a complete record was made at the same time.

65 All those who had returned from exile then offered sacrifices to the Lord, the God of Israel. They offered 12 bulls for all Israel, 96 rams, **66** and 72 lambs; they also offered 12 goats as a fellowship offering. They sacrificed all these animals to the Lord. **67** Then they took the decree the emperor had given them and gave it to the governors and officials of Greater Syria and Phoenicia, who then honored the Jewish people and the Temple of the Lord.

Ezra Learns of Intermarriages with Non-Jews
(Ezra 9.1-15)

68 After all this had been done, some of the leaders of the people of Israel came and told me that **69** the people, the leaders, the priests, and the Levites had not kept themselves separate from the people in the neighboring countries of Edom, Moab, and Egypt, or from the Canaanites, Hittites, Perizzites, and Jebusites. They were doing the same disgusting things which those people did. **70** God's holy people had become contaminated because Jewish men were marrying foreign women. Even the leaders and the officials had taken part in this breaking of the Law from the very beginning. **71** As soon as I heard this, I tore my clothes and my sacred robe in despair. I also tore my hair and my beard, and sat down crushed with anxiety and grief. **72** I sat there grieving about this sin until it was time for the evening sacrifice to be offered, when people began to gather around me — all those who were disturbed by what the Lord of Israel had said.

73 Then I got up from where I had been fasting, and still wearing my torn clothes, I knelt in prayer and stretched out my hands to the Lord. **74** I said, "O Lord, I am ashamed and confused

"O Lord, I am ashamed and confused in your presence." (8.74)

in your presence. 75 Our sins tower over our heads; they reach as high as the heavens. 76 This has been true from the days of our ancestors until now; we, your people, have sinned greatly. 77 Because of our sins and the sins of our ancestors, we and our relatives, our kings, and our priests have fallen into the hands of foreign kings, and we have been slaughtered, robbed, and carried away as prisoners. We have been totally disgraced, as we still are today. 78 Now, Lord, for a short time you have shown us great mercy. You have allowed just a few of us to survive in order to carry on the name Israel here in your holy Temple. 79 You have let the light of our nation shine again, after feeding us and taking care of us during the time of our slavery. 80 Even when we were slaves you did not abandon us; you made the emperors of Persia favor us, so that they gave us food, 81 restored the glory of your Temple, rebuilt the city of Jerusalem out of its ruins, and gave us a place of security here in Judah and Jerusalem.

82 "But now, Lord, what can we say, after you have done all this for us? We have again disobeyed the commands that you gave us through your servants, the prophets. They told us that 83 the land we were to occupy was an impure land because the heathen people who lived in it filled it with their disgusting deeds. 84 They told us that we should never intermarry with those people 85 and never seek peaceful relations with them if we wanted to be strong and enjoy the land and pass it on to our descendants forever. 86 Even after everything that has happened to us in punishment for our sins, we know that you, Lord, have punished us less than we deserve 87 and have allowed us to survive. But we have rebelled again, broken your Law, and intermarried with these wicked people. 88 Yet you were not angry enough to destroy us

completely and leave none of us alive, with no descendants and without our name. 89 Lord of Israel, you are faithful; you have allowed us to survive. 90 We confess our guilt to you; we have no right to come into your presence."

The Plan for Ending Mixed Marriages
(Ezra 10.1-17)

91 While Ezra was bowing in prayer in front of the Temple, weeping and confessing these sins, a large group of people from Jerusalem — men, women, and children — gathered around him, all of them weeping bitterly. 92 Then Shecaniah son of Jehiel, one of the Israelites, said to Ezra, "We have sinned against the Lord by marrying foreign women, but even so, there is still hope for Israel. 93 Now we must make a solemn promise to the Lord that we will send all these foreign women and their children away. 94 We will do what you and the others who obey the Law of the Lord advise us to do. 95 It is your responsibility to act. We are behind you, so go ahead and get it done."

96 So Ezra began by making the leaders of the priests, of the Levites, and of the rest of the people take an oath that they would divorce their foreign wives.

9 Then Ezra went from the court of the Temple into the living quarters of Jehohanan son of Eliashib 2 and spent the night there grieving over the people's terrible violation of the Law. He did not eat or drink anything.

3 A message was sent throughout Jerusalem and Judah, calling all those who had returned from exile to meet in Jerusalem, 4 by order of the leaders of the people. If anyone failed to come within two or three days, his cattle would be confiscated, and he would lose his right to be a member of the community.

5 Within the three days, on the twentieth day of the ninth month, all the

8.84, 85 Ex 34.11-16; Dt 7.1-5

men of the tribes of Judah and Benjamin came to Jerusalem 6 and assembled in the Temple square. Everyone was shivering from the cold because it was wintertime.

7 Then Ezra stood up and spoke to them, "You have broken the Law and brought guilt on Israel by marrying foreign women. 8 Now then, tell the truth and confess your sins to the Lord, the God of our ancestors, 9 and do what he requires. Separate yourselves from the foreigners living in our land and get rid of your foreign wives."

10 The people shouted in reply, "We will do whatever you say." 11 But they added, "The crowd is too big, and it's wintertime. We can't stand here in the open like this. This isn't something that can be settled in one or two days, since so many of us are involved in this sin. 12 Let our officials stay in Jerusalem and take charge of the matter. Then let anyone who has a foreign wife come at an appointed time, 13 together with the leaders and the judges of his city. In this way God's anger over this situation will be turned away." 14 Jonathan son of Asahel and Jahzeiah son of Tikvah assumed responsibility for the plan; and Meshullam, Levi, and Shabbethai served with them as judges.

15 The returned exiles carried out the investigation in full. 16 Ezra the priest appointed men from among the heads of the clans and recorded their names. On the first day of the tenth month they began their investigation. 17 And within the next three months they investigated all the cases of men with foreign wives.

The Men Who Had Foreign Wives
(Ezra 10.18-44)

18 The following is a list of the men who had foreign wives:

Priests, listed by clans:

19 Clan of Joshua and his brothers, sons of Jozadak: Maaseiah, Eliezar, Ja-

rib, and Jodan. 20 They promised to divorce their wives, and they offered rams as a sacrifice for their sins.

21 Clan of Immer: Hanani, Zebadiah, Manes, Shemaiah, Jehiel, and Azariah

22 Clan of Pashhur: Elioenai, Maaseiah, Ishmael, Nathanael, Okidelus, and Elasah

23 *Levites:*

Jozabad, Shimei, Kelaiah (also called Kelita), Pethahiah, Judah, and Jonah

24 *Musicians:*

Eliashib and Bacchurus

25 *Temple guards:*

Shallum and Telem

26 *Others:*

Clan of Parosh: Ramiah, Izziah, Malchijah, Milelos, Eleazar, Asebiah, Benaiah

27 Clan of Elam: Mattaniah, Zechariah, Jezriel, Abdi, Jeremoth, and Elijah

28 Clan of Zattu: Elioenai, Eliashib, Othoniah, Jeremoth, Zabad, and Zerdaiah

29 Clan of Bebai: Jehohanan, Hananiah, Zabbai, and Emathis

30 Clan of Bani: Meshullam, Malluch, Adaiah, Jashub, Sheal, and Jeremoth

31 Clan of Addi: Naathus, Moossias, Laccunus, Naidus, Bescaspasmys, Sesthel, Belnuus, and Manasseas

32 Clan of Annan: Elionas, Asiah, Melchiah, Sabbaiah, and Simon Chosamaeus

33 Clan of Hashum: Mattenai, Mattattah, Zabad, Eliphelet, Manasseh, and Shimei

34 Clan of Bani: Jeremai, Maadai, Amram, Joel, Mamdai, Bedeiah, Vaniah, Carabasion, Eliashib, Machnadebai, Eliasis, Binnui, Elialis, Shimei, Shelemiah, and Nathaniah

Clan of Ezora: Shashai, Azarel, Azael, Shemaiah, Amariah, and Joseph

35 Clan of Nebo: Mattithiah, Zabad, Iddo, Joel, and Benaiah

All the people . . . had gathered to hear it. (9.40)

36 All these men had foreign wives. They divorced them and sent them and their children away.

Ezra Reads the Law to the People
(Nehemiah 7.73 – 8.12)

37 The priests, the Levites, and many of the ordinary people of Israel settled in Jerusalem and its vicinity. By the seventh month the other Israelites were all settled in their towns. On the first day of that month **38** they all assembled in Jerusalem in the square just inside the east gate of the Temple. **39** They asked Ezra, the High Priest and scholar of the Law which the Lord had given Israel through Moses, to bring the book of the Law. **40** So Ezra brought it to the place where all the people — men, women, and all the priests — had gathered to hear it. **41** There in the square by the gate he read the Law to them from dawn until noon, and they all listened attentively.

9.37 1 Ch 9.2; Ne 11.3

42 Ezra was standing on a wooden platform that had been built for the occasion. **43** The following men stood at his right: Mattathiah, Shema, Ananiah, Azariah, Uriah, Hezekiah, and Baalsamos; **44** and the following stood at his left: Pedaiah, Mishael, Malchijah, Lothasubus, Nabariah, and Zechariah.

45 Ezra took his seat on the platform in a prominent place where everyone could see him. As soon as he took the book of the Law **46** and opened it, all the people stood up. Ezra said, "Praise the Lord, God Most High, God Almighty, Ruler of all."

47 All the people raised their arms in the air and answered, "Amen!" They knelt down in worship, with their faces to the ground.

48 The following Levites taught the Law of the Lord to the people: Jeshua, Anniuth, Sherebiah, Jamin, Akkub, Shabbethai, Hodiah, Maiannas, Kelita, Azariah, Jozabad, Hanan, and

Peliah. They read the Law to the people and explained what was read.

⁴⁹⁻⁵⁰ When the people heard what the Law required, they were so moved that they began to weep. The governor*ᵒ* said to Ezra, the priest and scholar of the Law, and to all the Levites who were teaching the people, "This day is holy to the Lord; ⁵¹ go home and have a feast. Share your food and wine with those who don't have any. ⁵² Today is

holy to the Lord, so don't be sad. He will restore your former glory."

⁵³ The Levites gave the command to all the people: "This day is holy; do not be sad." ⁵⁴ So all the people went home and joyfully ate and drank and shared what they had with those who had nothing. They celebrated ⁵⁵ because they understood what had been read to them.

Then they assembled. . . .*ᵖ*

ᵒ Probable meaning The governor; *Greek* Attharates. *must have continued (see Ne 8.13).*

ᵖ Originally the Greek text

The Second Book of ESDRAS

INTRODUCTION

The Second Book of Esdras is primarily an apocalypse (or series of visions and revelations) that was written by an unknown Jewish author in Hebrew or Aramaic. This was translated into Greek, and an introduction and appendix of Christian origin were added. The original and the Greek translation have disappeared, and the text is now preserved primarily in Latin. The main part of the work reports seven revelations that were given to Shealtiel (identified with Ezra) and answers questions about the problem of evil, suffering, persecution, the end of the world, judgment, and the new world.

OUTLINE OF CONTENTS

1 This is the second book of the prophet Ezra. He was the son of Seraiah, the grandson of Azariah, and a descendant of Hilkiah, Shallum, Zadok, Ahitub, 2 Ahijah, Phinehas, Eli, Amariah, Azariah, Meraioth, Arna, Uzzi, Borith, Abishua, Phinehas, Eleazar, 3 and Aaron, of the tribe of Levi.

The Rejection of Israel

When I, Ezra, was a captive in Media during the reign of Artaxerxes, king of Persia, 4 the Lord said to me, 5 "Go and remind my people and their children of the sins they have committed against me, and let them tell their grandchildren. 6 My people have sinned even more than their ancestors, for they have forgotten me and offered sacrifices to foreign gods. 7 I rescued them from Egypt, where they were slaves, but they have done things that made me angry and have refused to listen to my warnings.

8 "Ezra, tear your hair in grief and call down on these people all the disasters they deserve. They are rebellious and refuse to obey my Law. 9 How much longer can I tolerate these people for whom I have done so much? 10 For their sake I overthrew many kings and crushed the king of Egypt together with his officials and all his army. 11 I destroyed all the nations that opposed them, and in the east I scattered the people of the provinces of Tyre and Sidon and killed all the enemies of Israel.

12 "Ezra, tell them that the Lord says: 13 I brought you across the Red Sea and made safe roads for you where there were none. I made Moses your leader and gave you Aaron as your priest. 14 I provided you with light from a pillar of fire and performed great miracles among you, but you have forgotten me. I, the Lord, have spoken.

15 "The Lord Almighty says: I sent you quails as a sign of my care for you. I provided you with camps where you could be safe, but all you did there was complain. 16 Even when I destroyed your enemies, you did not appreciate what I had done. You have never done anything but complain. 17 Have you forgotten the blessings I gave you? There in the desert when you were hungry and thirsty you cried out to me: 18 'Why have you brought us out to this desert to kill us? Being slaves to the Egyptians was better than coming here to die.' 19 I was moved by your bitter groans and gave you manna, the bread of angels. 20 When you were thirsty, I split the rock and all the water you needed flowed out. To protect you from the heat, I provided you with shade trees. 21 I divided fertile lands among you and drove out the Canaanites, the Perizzites, and the Philistines who opposed your advance. What more could I have done for you?

22 "The Lord Almighty says: There in the desert by the river of bitter water when you were thirsty and cursed me, 23 in spite of your insults I did not send fire upon you. Instead, I made the water fit to drink by throwing wood into the river. 24 People of Israel, what can I do with you? People of Judah, you refuse to obey me. So I will turn to other nations and make them my people. They will keep my laws. 25 Because you have abandoned me, I will abandon you. You will beg me for mercy, but I will show you none. 26 When you pray to me, I will not hear you. You never hesitate to commit murder; your hands are stained with the blood of those you have killed. 27 It is not me that you have betrayed; you have betrayed yourselves.

Israel Is to Be Replaced

28 "The Lord Almighty says: I have pleaded with you as a father pleads with

---

1.1-3 Ezra 7.1-5; 1 Esd 8.1, 2   **1.5** Is 58.1   **1.10** Ex 14.28   **1.13** Ex 14.29   **1.14** Ex 13.21
1.15 Ex 16.13   **1.17, 18** Nu 14.3   **1.20** Nu 20.11; Ws 11.4   **1.22, 23** Ex 15.22-25

his sons, as a mother pleads with her daughters, or as a nursemaid pleads with her small children. 29 I begged you to be my people so that I could be your God, to be my children so that I could be your father. 30 I gathered you together as a hen gathers her chicks under her wings. But now what can I do with you? I will banish you from my sight; 31 and even when you offer sacrifices to me, I will turn away from you. Your religious festivals, your New Moon celebrations, or your circumcision ceremonies mean nothing to me. 32 I sent to you my servants, the prophets, but you killed them and mutilated their corpses. I will make you pay for murdering them.

33 "The Lord Almighty says: Your Temple is abandoned. I will scatter you like straw blown away by the wind. 34 Your children will have no descendants because they rejected my commandments and did what I hated, just as you did. 35 I will give your home to a people that is about to appear. They will believe me, even though they have not yet heard of me. They will do what I command, even though I never performed any miracles for them. 36 They have not seen the prophets, but they will live by their ancient teachings. 37 I give my solemn promise that I will bless those people, and their little children will laugh and shout for joy. Those people have never seen me, but deep within them they will believe my words.

38 "Now, Father Ezra, look with pride at the people you see coming from the east. 39 Look at the leaders I have given them: Abraham, Isaac, Jacob, Hosea, Amos, Micah, Joel, Obadiah, Jonah, 40 Nahum, Habakkuk, Zephaniah, Haggai, Zechariah, and Malachi (who is also called the Lord's messenger).

2 "The Lord says: I led my people out of slavery in Egypt; I gave them commandments through my servants, the prophets, but they refused to listen and ignored my teachings. 2 Jerusalem, the mother who brought them into the world, says to them, 'Go your own way, my children; I am now a widow left completely alone. 3 I took great delight in bringing you up, but you sinned against the Lord God and did what I knew was wrong, so I mourned in deep grief when I lost you. 4 What can I do for you, now that I am a widow and left completely alone? Go, my children, and ask the Lord for mercy.'

5 "Father Ezra, I call on you to testify against these people as their mother has done, because they have refused to keep my covenant. 6 Now bring confusion on them and ruin on their mother, so that they will have no descendants. 7 They will be scattered among the nations, and no one on earth will remember them any longer, for they have despised my covenant.

8 "How terrible will be your punishment, Assyria. You have let wicked people hide within your borders. Remember, sinful nation, what I did to Sodom and Gomorrah. 9 Their land now lies covered with lumps of tar and heaps of ashes. That is what I do to people who do not obey me.

10 "The Lord says to Ezra: Announce to my new people that I will give them the kingdom of Jerusalem, which I had planned to give to Israel. 11 I will take the dazzling light of my presence away from Israel and will give to my new people the eternal Temple that I had prepared for Israel. 12 The tree of life will fill the air around them with its fragrance. They will never have to work; they will never grow tired. 13 Ask, and you will receive. Pray that the number of the days you have to wait will be reduced. Even

---

1.30 Mt 23.37; Lk 13.34　**1.35, 36** Ro 10.14-20　**2.2** Is 54.1; Ga 4.26, 27; Ba 4.19
2.8 Gn 19.24　**2.12** Rev 2.7; 22.2, 14　**2.13** Mt 7.7, 8; 25.34

now the kingdom has been prepared for you, so stay alert. [14] Call heaven and earth to witness that I, the living God, have abolished evil and created good.

[15] "Mother Jerusalem, take your children in your arms. Guide their steps in safe paths; raise them with the same delight that a dove has in raising her young. I, the Lord, have chosen you. [16] I will raise your dead from their graves because I recognize them as my people. [17] Jerusalem, mother of these people, do not be afraid; I, the Lord, have chosen you.

[18] "I will send my servants Isaiah and Jeremiah to help you. At their request I have consecrated and prepared for you twelve trees, heavy with different kinds of fruit, [19] twelve fountains flowing with milk and honey, and seven high mountains covered with roses and lilies. I will make your children very happy there. [20] Now, Jerusalem, come to the defense of widows, take the side of the fatherless, give to the poor, protect orphans, give clothing to those who have none, [21] take care of those who are broken and weak, do not make fun of those who are crippled, protect the disabled, and help the blind to catch a vision of my dazzling splendor. [22] Keep both the old and the young safe within your walls. [23] Whenever you find a dead body, bury it and mark the grave, and I will give you a place of honor when I raise the dead.

[24] "Be calm, my people; your time to rest will come. [25] Take care of your children like a faithful nursemaid and guide their steps in safe paths, [26] so that none of them will be lost. When the time comes, I will hold you responsible for them. [27] Don't worry; when the day of trouble and distress comes, others will cry and mourn, but you will be happy and rich. [28] The other nations will be jealous of you, but they will not be able to harm you.

[29] "I will protect you with my power and save your children from hell. [30] Be happy, Jerusalem, you and your children, because I, the Lord, will rescue you. [31] Remember your children who are asleep in their graves; I, the Lord Almighty, am merciful, and I will bring them out from the place where they lie hidden in the earth. [32] Until I come, hold your children close and tell them about my grace and mercy, which are like a spring that never runs dry."

Ezra on Mount Sinai

[33] I, Ezra, was on Mount Sinai when the Lord ordered me to go to the people of Israel. But when I went to them, they rejected me and refused to listen to what the Lord commanded. [34] That is why I am speaking to you Gentiles. You are ready to listen and understand: "Wait for your shepherd who is coming very soon, at the end of the age, to give you eternal rest. [35] Be ready to receive the blessings of the kingdom, for eternal light will shine on you forever. [36] Flee from the darkness of this present age and accept the joyful splendor prepared for you. I testify publicly for my savior. [37] The Lord has appointed him, so accept him and be happy. Give thanks to God, who has called you into his heavenly kingdom. [38] Stand up and see the number of those who have received the Lord's mark and who share in his banquet. [39] They have left the darkness of this age and have received shining white robes from the Lord. [40] So now, Jerusalem, welcome these people who have kept the Law of the Lord, and this will complete the list of those whom God has assigned to you. [41] The children you longed for have returned; their number is now complete. So pray that the Lord's kingdom may come and that your people, whom God chose before he created the world, may become holy."

2.18 Rev 22.2   2.23 Tb 1.17-19   2.26 Jn 17.12

Ezra on Mount Zion

42 I, Ezra, saw an enormous crowd on Mount Zion, too many people to count. They were all singing and praising the Lord. **43** Standing in the middle of this crowd was a very tall young man, taller than any of the others. He was placing a crown on the head of each person, but he towered above them all. I was spellbound by the sight, **44** and I asked the angel, "Who are these people, sir?"

45 He replied, "These are people who have taken off their mortal robes and have put on immortal ones. They have confessed their faith in God, and now they are being given crowns and palm branches as symbols of their victory."

46 Then I asked the angel, "Who is the young man who is putting the crowns on their heads and giving them the palms?"

47 "He is the Son of God," the angel replied, "and all these people confessed their faith in him while they lived on earth." Then I began to praise those who had stood for the Lord so bravely. **48** And the angel said to me, "Go and tell my people what you have seen, the many marvelous wonders of the Lord."

THE FIRST VISION

Ezra's Prayer of Complaint

3 Thirty years after the fall of Jerusalem, I, Shealtiel (also known as Ezra), was in Babylon. I was lying on my bed, troubled and disturbed, **2** as I thought about the ruins of Jerusalem and the prosperity of those who lived in Babylon. **3** I was deeply disturbed and began to express my fears to God Most High. **4** "O Lord and Master," I said, "you, and you alone, spoke the word at the beginning of creation and formed the world. At your command the dust **5** produced the lifeless body of Adam.

Then with your hands you shaped it, you breathed into it the breath of life, and he began to live. **6** You brought him into the Garden of Eden, which you yourself had planted before the earth was made. **7** You gave him just one commandment, but he disobeyed it, and you immediately made him and his descendants subject to death.

"From Adam were born more nations, tribes, clans, and families than can be counted. **8** All the nations did whatever they wished; they sinned against you and rejected your commands. But you did nothing to stop them. **9** Then again, after a while, you brought on the flood and destroyed the world's population. **10** They all suffered the same fate: as death had come to Adam, so now death came to a whole generation in the flood. **11** But you spared one man, Noah, with his family and all his righteous descendants.

12 "The number of people living on earth began to increase, and the number of families, tribes, and nations grew. They too fell into sin and were worse than the generations before them. **13** But then you chose Abraham. **14** You loved him, and to him alone in the dead of night, you secretly disclosed how the world would end. **15** You made an everlasting covenant with him and promised him that you would never abandon his descendants. You gave him Isaac, and to Isaac you gave Jacob and Esau. **16** You chose Jacob, and his descendants became a great nation, but you rejected Esau.

17 "You rescued the descendants of Jacob from Egypt and led them to Mount Sinai. **18** There you bent down the skies, shook*a* the earth, moved the world, made the waters beneath the earth tremble, and brought disorder to the universe. **19** The dazzling light of your presence passed through the four

---

a Some ancient translations shook; *Latin* steadied.

2.42 Rev 7.9   **3.1** Ezra 3.2; 5.2; Ne 12.1   **3.7** Ws 1.13, 14; 2.23, 24   **3.8** Gn 6.12
3.9 Gn 6.9 – 8.22

gates of fire, earthquake, wind, and frost, in order to give the Law and its commandments to Jacob's descendants, the people of Israel. 20 Yet you did not remove their evil impulse, but let your Law guide their lives. 21 The first man, Adam, weighed down with an evil impulse, sinned and was defeated, and the same was true of all of his descendants. 22 So the disease became permanent, and although the Law was in the hearts of the people, so also was the root of evil! That is why what was good passed away, while what was evil continued.

23 "Many years later you sent your servant David 24 and told him to build a city which would bear your name and in which sacrifices would be offered to you. 25 This was done for many years, but then the inhabitants of the city disobeyed you 26 and sinned just like Adam and all his descendants, because they had the same evil impulse. 27 So you handed over your own city to your enemies.

28 "I said to myself, 'Perhaps Babylon has been allowed to conquer Jerusalem because the people who live there are better than we are.' 29 But when I got to Babylon, I saw more sins than I could count, and now for thirty years I have seen many sinners here. So I was perplexed 30 when I saw how you tolerate sinners and do not punish them, how you protect your enemies and yet destroy your own people. 31 You haven't given the faintest hint as to how these ways of yours can be changed. Surely Babylon is no better than Jerusalem. 32 No other nation, except Israel, has ever known you or accepted your covenants. 33 But Israel was never rewarded, and never profited from its labor. I have traveled widely in the other nations, and I have seen how prosperous they are, although they don't keep your com-

mands. 34 Now then, Lord, if you would just weigh our sins on the scales against those of the rest of the world, it would be perfectly clear that their sins are heavier. 35 There has never been a time when the people of the world did not sin against you; but has any other nation kept your commands as well as Israel has? 36 You may find individuals who have, but you won't find a nation that has done so."

The Human Mind Cannot Understand God's Ways

4 The angel Uriel, who had been sent to me, replied, 2 "You can't even understand what happens in this world. Do you think you can understand the ways of God Most High?"

3 "Yes, sir, I do!" I answered.

The angel continued, "I have been sent to ask you to solve three riddles about what happens in this world. 4 If you can explain even one of them to me, I will answer your questions about God's ways and teach you why the human race has an evil impulse."

5 "I agree, sir," I said.

Then he said to me, "Good! How do you weigh out a pound of fire? How do you measure a bushel*b* of wind? How do you bring back a day that has passed?"

6 I answered, "Why do you ask me such questions? No human being could answer them."

7 Then he said, "What if I had asked you how many dwelling places there are at the bottom of the sea? How many rivers flow into the waters beneath the earth? How many rivers are there above the dome of the sky? Where are the exits from the world of the dead? Where are the entrances to*c* Paradise? 8 If I had asked you these questions, you might have answered, 'I have never

---

b Some ancient translations bushel; *Latin* blast.   *c Some ancient translations* exits from . . . entrances to; *Latin* exits from.

3.20 Si 15.14

gone down into the waters beneath the earth, and I have not yet entered the world of the dead. I have never gone up to heaven.' ⁹But all I have asked you about is fire, wind, and the day that has just passed — things that you have experienced. Yet you have given me no answer. ¹⁰You can't even understand things that you have been familiar with since you were a child. ¹¹How then can your little mind understand the ways of God Most High? Can someone already worn down by this corrupt world understand the ways of the incorruptible God?"

Weigh out a pound of fire . . . measure a bushel of wind. (4.5)

When I heard this, I fell face downward on the ground[d] ¹²and said to him, "It would have been better if we had never been born than to have to live in a world of sin and suffering without understanding why things happen as they do."

¹³The angel Uriel answered, "I once went into the woods and heard the trees plotting together. ¹⁴They were saying, 'Let's go to war against the sea and push it back, so that we may have more room.' ¹⁵But the waves of the sea also plotted together and said, 'Let's con-

quer the woods and extend our territory.' ¹⁶But all the plotting of the trees was useless because fire came and destroyed them. ¹⁷And the plotting of the sea was just as useless because the sand stood firm and blocked its advance. ¹⁸Now, if you were the judge and had to decide between them, which would you pronounce right?"

¹⁹I replied, "They were both wrong, because trees belong on the land, and waves belong in the sea."

²⁰"You have given the right answer," he said. "So why can't you see the answer to your own problems? ²¹For just as trees have their place on land, and waves have their place in the sea, so the people of this world can understand only what goes on in this world, and only heavenly beings can understand what goes on in heaven."

The End of the Age

²²"Please tell me, sir," I asked, "why then was I given the ability to understand anything? ²³I am not interested in asking questions about what goes on in the heavens; I am only concerned about things that go on around us. Why has God allowed Israel to be disgraced by foreign nations? Why has he let the nation he loves be handed over to the power of godless nations? Why do the Law and the covenant that were given to our ancestors mean nothing any more? ²⁴Why do we die as quickly as insects? Why is our life shorter than a breath? Why does God think us unworthy of his mercy? ²⁵Why doesn't God do something to help his own people? These are the questions that I want to ask."

²⁶Uriel answered, "If you live long enough, you will be surprised at what you will see, because this age is rapidly passing away. ²⁷This age is so full of misery and imperfection that it cannot

---

[d] *Verse 11 in Latin is unclear.*
4.21 Is 55.8, 9; Jn 3.31; 1 Co 2.14

hold all the blessings that God has promised the righteous in the time to come. 28 The evil about which you have asked me has already been planted, but the time for its harvesting has not yet arrived. 29 This evil must be harvested, and this world where it was planted must be removed, before the new age where the good is to be planted can appear. 30 At the beginning of time one grain of evil seed was sown in the heart of Adam. See how much wickedness it has already produced! Think of how much more it will produce before it is cut down and threshed out at Judgment Day. 31 You can see for yourself what a big crop this one evil seed has produced. 32 How terrible will be the harvest on Judgment Day when these countless heads of grain are threshed out!"

33 Then I asked, "How long do we have to wait before this happens? Why are our lives so short and so full of misery?"

34 Uriel answered, "Don't be in a greater hurry than God Most High! You are thinking only of yourself, but God has to be concerned about everybody.*e* 35 Your questions are the same ones asked by the souls of the righteous dead in the places where God is keeping them waiting: 'How long must we wait here? When will the day of judgment come, when we will get our reward?' 36 The archangel Jeremiel answers them, 'It will happen as soon as the complete number of those who have suffered as you have are here. For God has weighed this age, 37 measured the years, and numbered the days. Nothing will be changed until time has run its predetermined course.'"

38 "But, sir," I replied, "all of us here on earth are such wicked sinners. 39 Is it possible that because of our sin the righteous dead are having to wait for their reward?"

40 His answer was, "Can a pregnant woman keep her child from being born after her nine months are up?"

41 "No, sir, she cannot," I answered.

And he continued, "In the world of the dead, the place where God has stored the souls is like a womb. 42 It is as eager to return the souls entrusted to it from the beginning of the world as a woman is to end her labor pains. 43 When that happens, you will have the answer to all your questions."

44 "Please, sir," I asked, "if you think I am able to understand it, can you 45 tell me one more thing? Is the time that is still to come longer than the past that has already gone by? 46 I know how long the past has been, but I don't know the future."

47 "Come here and stand at my right," he commanded, "and I will show you a vision and explain its meaning." 48 So I stood by him and looked, and I saw a blazing fire pass by in front of me, and when it was gone, I saw that smoke was still there. 49 Then a rain cloud passed by in front of me, bringing a heavy downpour of rain; and when the downpour was over, there was still a light rain. 50 "Think about this," said Uriel. "Just as the downpour was greater than the light rain that followed it and the fire was greater than the smoke left behind, in the same way the time that has passed is much longer than the time to come. The time that is left is like the light rain and the smoke."

The Signs of the End

51 "Please tell me," I asked, "do you think I will live until that time? If not, who will be alive when it happens?"

52 He answered, "I can tell you some of the signs of the end, if that is what

---

e Verse 34 in Latin is unclear.

4.30 2 Esd 3.20   **4.36** 2 Esd 2.41; Rev 6.11
4.51 — 5.19 Mt 24.4-31; Mk 13.5-27;
Lk 21.8-28

Wickedness will increase. (5.2)

you are asking about; but I am not here to tell you how long you will live, and in any case, I don't know.

5 "But these are the signs: The time will come when all people on earth will be in the grip of great confusion.*f* The way of truth will be hidden, and no faith will be left in the land. ²Wickedness will increase until it has become worse than you have ever known it to be. ³The country that you now see ruling the world will lie in ruins, with no inhabitant or traveler there. ⁴After that,*g* if God Most High lets you live long enough, you will see that country in confusion. The sun will suddenly start shining at night, and the moon in the daytime. ⁵Blood will drip from trees; stones will speak; nations will be in confusion; the movement of the stars will be changed. ⁶A king unwanted by anyone will begin to rule, and the birds will fly away. ⁷Fish will be washed up on the shores of the Dead Sea. The voice of one whom many do not know will be heard at night; everyone will hear it. ⁸The earth will break open*h* in many places and begin spouting out flames. Wild animals will leave the fields and forests. At their monthly periods women will bear monsters. ⁹Fresh

water will become salty. Friends everywhere will attack one another. Then understanding will disappear, and reason will go into hiding, ¹⁰and they will not be found even though many may look for them. Everywhere on earth wickedness and violence will increase. ¹¹One country will ask a neighboring country if justice or anyone who does right has come that way, but the answer will always be 'No.' ¹²At that time people will hope for much, but will get nothing; they will work hard, but will never succeed at anything. ¹³These are the signs of the end that I am permitted to show you. But if you begin to pray again and continue to weep and fast for seven more days, you will hear even greater things."

¹⁴Then I woke up, and I was trembling violently. I was so disturbed that I was about to faint, ¹⁵but the angel that had come to talk with me took hold of me, strengthened me, and set me on my feet.

¹⁶The next night, Phaltiel, who was a leader of the people, came to me and asked, "Where have you been? And why do you look so sad? ¹⁷Don't you know that the people of Israel in the land of their exile have been put in your

---

f Some ancient translations confusion; *Latin unclear.*   *g* After that; *Latin unclear.*
h One ancient translation The earth will break open; *Latin* Chaos will appear.
5.2 Mt 24.12   **5.5** Hb 2.11

care? ¹⁸So get up and eat. Do not abandon us like a shepherd leaving his flock to the attacks of savage wolves."

¹⁹"Leave me alone," I answered, "do not come near me for the next seven days. Then come back." So he left.

THE SECOND VISION

Ezra's Prayer and Uriel's Answer

²⁰Then, crying and mourning, I fasted seven days, as the angel Uriel had commanded me to do. ²¹At the end of the seven days, I was again deeply troubled, ²²but I recovered my ability to think, and again I began to speak with God Most High. ²³"Lord and Master," I said, "from all the forests and plants on earth you have chosen this one vine. ²⁴From all the countries of the world, you have chosen this one small land. From all the flowers in the world, you have chosen this one lily. ²⁵From all the water in the deep oceans, you have filled up this one river. From all the cities that have ever been built, you have set apart this one city, Jerusalem, as your own. ²⁶From all the birds that were created, you chose this one dove. From all the animals that were made, you chose this one lamb. ²⁷From all the nations of the world, you chose this one nation to be your own, and you gave its people your Law, which is honored by people everywhere.

²⁸"And now, Lord, since all of this is true, why have you dishonoredⁱ this one people more than all others by handing them over to many nations? Why have you scattered your own people, ²⁹who believed in your covenants? Why have you let them be trampled by people who rejected your promises? ³⁰If you are so angry with your own people, you yourself ought to punish them."

³¹When I had finished speaking, the angel who had come to me on a previous night was sent to me again. ³²He said, "Listen carefully to me, and I will teach you more."

³³"Please go on, sir," I said.

So he continued, "Are you worried about the people of Israel? Do you think you love them more than God, who made them?"

³⁴"No, sir," I replied. "I spoke as I did because I was so confused and upset. I am always troubled whenever I try to think about the ways of God Most High or to understand even a small part of what he does."

³⁵"You cannot understand!" he answered.

And I asked, "Why not, sir? In that case, why was I born? Why didn't I die before I was born? Then I wouldn't have seen the sufferings and troubles of the people of Israel."

³⁶The angel said to me, "I will answer you if you can do the following things: Tell me how many people are yet to be born; collect scattered raindrops for me; make dead flowers bloom again; ³⁷open the rooms where the winds are locked up and make them blow for me; show me the picture of a sound. If you can do these things, I will answer your questions about the sufferings of the people of Israel."

³⁸I answered, "Lord and master, no one can do these things, except God, who is not confined to this world. ³⁹How can I give you any kind of answer? What do I know?"

⁴⁰He continued, "You could not do even one of the things that I asked you to do. How can you expect to understand God's judgments or why God has promised his love to his people?"

Descending Generations

⁴¹Then I said, "But, Lord God, your concern is with the people who will be

_____

ⁱ *Some ancient translations* dishonored; *Latin* prepared.
5.35 Job 3.11

alive at the end of the world. What will happen to those who live before that time? What about us? What about those who came before us, and those who will live after us?"

⁴²He answered me, "The final judgment can be compared to a circle, and just as a circle has no beginning or end, so those who come early will not be too early, and those who come late will not be too late."

The final judgment can be compared to a circle. (5.42)

⁴³I replied, "But couldn't you have created all human beings, those of the past, the present, and the future, so that they would all live at the same time? In that way, you could have had your final judgment sooner."

⁴⁴He answered, "The creation cannot move faster than the Creator. And besides, the world wouldn't have been able to hold all the people if everyone had been created at the same time."

⁴⁵"Why, then," I asked, "did you just now tell me that one day you would bring back to life at the same time every creature that ever lived? If the world can hold them all then, it can hold them now."

⁴⁶He answered, "That would be like asking a woman who has given birth to ten children why she didn't have them all at once, instead of one at a time."

⁴⁷"That would be impossible," I answered. "She can't have them all at once."

⁴⁸"In the same way," he continued, "I have made the world like a womb so that it produces human beings at regular intervals. ⁴⁹The rule that neither a young child nor an old woman can give birth to a baby also applies to the world that I have created."

⁵⁰Then I said, "Since you have brought up the subject, may I ask if the world you have been talking about is still young or is it approaching old age?"

⁵¹He replied, "You can learn the answer from any woman who has given birth to several children. ⁵²Ask her why her younger children do not grow as tall as her older children. ⁵³She will tell you that those born while she was young and healthy are much stronger than those born when she was getting old and becoming weak. ⁵⁴You will notice that you are smaller than people of earlier generations; ⁵⁵those who come later will be smaller still. This shows you that creation is already getting old and losing the strength of her youth."

God Will Bring the End of the World

⁵⁶"If you please, Lord," I asked, "will you show me the one through whom you will bring judgment on your creation?"

6 He said to me, "I made this decision before I created the world: before the gates of the world were standing; before the winds were brought together to blow, ²or the lightning flashed, or the thunder rolled; before the foundations of Paradise were laid, ³or the beautiful flowers appeared; before the powers that move the stars were established, or the armies of angels assembled; ⁴before the air was

5.52 Gn 6.4; Nu 13.33

piled up high, or the divisions of the heavens given their names; before I chose Mount Zion as my footstool; ⁵before the present age was planned, or the scheming of its sinners was rejected, or my seal was placed on those who obeyed the Law and laid up a treasure of faithfulness. ⁶Even then, I decided that since I, and I alone, had created the world, I, and I alone, would bring it to an end."

⁷Then I asked, "How long a period of time will divide the ages? When will the first age end and the next age begin?"

⁸He answered, "The interval will be no longer than that between Abraham and Abraham.ʲ He was the grandfather of both Jacob and Esau, and when they were born, Jacob was holding Esau's heel. ⁹Esau represents the end of this age, and Jacob represents the beginning of the new age. ¹⁰So, if Jacob's hand is the beginning and Esau's heel is the end,ᵏ do not try to find a space in between."

The Signs of the End

¹¹"Lord and Master," I said, "please hear my request. ¹²On that earlier night you showed me some of the signs of the end; now please show me the rest."

¹³"Stand up," he said, "and you will hear a very loud voice. ¹⁴If the place where you are standing is violently shaken ¹⁵while the voice is speaking, don't be afraid. The message will be about the end of the world, and the foundations of the world will understand ¹⁶that the voice is speaking about them. They will tremble and quake because they know that they will undergo a change when the end comes."

¹⁷When he said this, I stood up and listened. I heard a voice that sounded like a roaring river. ¹⁸It said, "The time is near when I will come to judge the people living on the earth. ¹⁹I will punish those who have hurt others with their injustice. Jerusalem's humiliation will come to an end, ²⁰and this age which is about to pass away will have the final seal put on it. Then I will give the following signs: the books will be opened across the sky for all to see.

Like a giant scroll spread across the sky (6.20)

²¹Children only a year old will speak. Pregnant women will give birth after only three or four months, and their premature babies will live and run about. ²²Planted fields will suddenly become bare, and full barns will suddenly become empty. ²³Then the trumpet will sound, and sudden terror will grip the heart of everyone when they hear it. ²⁴Friends will fight like ene-

---

ʲ Abraham; *some manuscripts have* Isaac. *Latin unclear.*

ᵏ *Some ancient translations* So . . . end;

6.17 Rev 1.15; 14.2; 19.6   **6.20** Dn 7.10; 12.1; Ml 3.16; Rev 20.12   **6.23** 1 Co 15.51, 52; 1 Th 4.16

mies, and the earth and its people will be terrified. Rivers will stop flowing and stand still for three hours.

25 "Those who survive all these things that I have predicted will be rescued when I bring to an end this world that I created. 26 They will see those who never died but were taken up alive into heaven. The hearts and minds of people on earth will be changed. 27 Evil will be destroyed and deceit eliminated. 28 Faith will grow strong, corruption will be overcome, and truth, which has not produced fruit for so long, will make itself felt again."

29 While the voice was speaking, the ground beneath me began to rock back and forth. *l* 30 Then the angel said to me, "These are the things that I have come to show you tonight. *m* 31 Now if you will pray and fast for seven more days, I will come back and tell you even greater things, *n* 32 because God Most High has heard your prayer; the Mighty God has seen the pure and righteous life that you have lived since your youth. 33 That is why he has sent me to show you all these things and to tell you not to be afraid but to trust him. 34 Do not be so quick to raise useless questions in the present age; then you will not be so quick to do so in the final age."

THE THIRD VISION

Why God's People Suffer

35 After that, I mourned and fasted for seven more days, as I had done before, and so I completed the three weeks of fasting that I had been commanded to observe. 36 On the eighth night I was again deeply troubled, and I began to speak to God Most High. 37 I was very tense and my heart was uneasy, 38 but I said, "O Lord, at the beginning of creation you spoke the word. On the first day you commanded, 'Let the universe be made,' and your word carried out that command. 39 At that time the spirit was moving, darkness and silence were everywhere, and no human voice was yet heard. *o* 40 Then you commanded that a ray of light shine out of the room where it was stored, so that your works could be seen. 41 On the second day you created the angel of the sky and commanded him to separate the water, so that part of it would move up above the dome of the sky and part remain below. 42 On the third day you commanded the water that covered the earth to come together in one place and cover one-seventh of the earth's surface. Then you dried out the rest of the earth's surface to make dry land, so that it might be cultivated and planted and used in your service. 43 Your word went out and completed the work immediately. 44 In an instant all kinds of fruits and vegetables appeared, enough kinds to satisfy every taste. There were flowers of indescribable fragrances and of the most magnificent colors. These things were made on the third day. 45 On the fourth day the bright-shining sun, the light of the moon, and the arrangement of the stars were created by your command. 46 You commanded them to serve the human race, which would soon be created. 47 On the fifth day you commanded the part of the earth covered by water to produce birds and fish; and it was done. 48 At your command, the still and lifeless water brought forth living creatures, so that the nations might proclaim your wonderful works. 49 Then you singled out two of the living creatures; you named one of them

---

l Some ancient translations the ground ... forth; *Latin unclear.* *m One ancient translation* tonight; *Latin unclear.* *n Some ancient translations* things; *Latin adds* in the daytime. *o Some ancient translations* yet heard; *Latin adds* from you.

6.26 Gn 5.24; 2 K 2.11, 12; Si 44.16; Ml 4.5, 6 **6.38** Ps 33.6; He 11.3; 2 P 3.5
6.49-52 Job 7.12; Ps 74.12-15

Behemoth and the other Leviathan.
50 You separated them from each other
because the sea wasn't big enough to
hold them both. 51 You let Behemoth
live on a part of the land that you dried
up on the third day of creation; it is a
land of a thousand mountains. 52 You
let Leviathan live in the sea. You kept
them both alive, so that your chosen
people may feast on them at the time
you choose. 53 On the sixth day you
commanded the earth to produce the
animals, domestic and wild, large and
small. 54 More important than all of
these, you created Adam and put him
in charge of everything that you had
made. And all of us, the people you have
chosen, are descended from him.

55 "O Lord, I have told you all this because you said that you created this
first world for the sake of your people.
56 You said that, in spite of their great
numbers, all the other nations which
descended from Adam are nothing,
worth no more than a drop of water, no
more than spit. 57 But now, Lord, those
nations that are considered as nothing
are ruling over us and destroying us.
58 We are your people, and you have
called us your first-born, your only
child, your witness, your loved one, but
we have been handed over to the power
of these other nations. 59 If this world
was really created for the sake of your
people, why don't we have possession of
it? How much longer must we wait?"

7 When I had finished speaking,
the same angel that had been sent
to me on the earlier nights appeared
again. 2 He said, "Stand up, Ezra, and
listen to what I have come to tell you."

3 "Go ahead, sir," I said.

He continued, "Picture in your mind
a broad,ᵖ immense sea spreading over
a vast area, 4 but with an entrance no
wider than a river. 5 No one who wishes
to enter that sea, whether to visit it or
control it, can reach its broad expanse

of water without passing through the
narrow entrance. 6 Or take another example: Picture a city built on a plain.
The city is full of all kinds of good
things, 7 but the entrance to it is narrow
and steep, with fire on one side and
deep water on the other. 8 The one path
between the fire and the water is so narrow that only one person at a time may
walk on it. 9 If anyone inherits this city,
he cannot take possession of his inheritance without passing through this
dangerous entrance."

10 "That is right, sir," I said.

"That is how it is with the people of
Israel," he added. 11 "I made this world
for their sake, but when Adam broke
my commands, the world came under
my judgment. 12 Then the entrances
into this world were made narrow and
difficult to travel. They were rough,
dangerous, and few in number. 13 But
the entrances to the great world to
come are wide and safe and lead to immortality. 14 Everyone who lives must
walk the narrow and meaningless ways
of this world in order to receive the
blessings stored up in the world to
come. 15 So, Ezra, why are you upset
and disturbed by the thought thatᵠ you
are mortal and must die? 16 Why don't
you think about the age to come, rather
than the present age?"

17 I answered, "Lord and master, in
your Law you said that the righteous
would receive all these blessings, but
that the wicked would perish. 18 The
righteous then can endure all the difficulties of this narrow way because they
look forward to the broad and open life
of the future, but the wicked must pass
through the narrow way without any
hope of seeing the broad open life."

19 The angel replied, "Do you think
you are a better judge than God? Do
you think you are wiser than God Most
High? 20 It is better to let many people
of the present age perish than to allow

ᵖ Some ancient translations broad; Latin deep.   ᵠ by the thought that; or since.
7.11 Ro 5.18-20   7.15, 16 2 Co 4.18

them to neglect the Law that God has given them. 21 God has given clear commandments to everyone coming into this world, telling them what they should do to obtain life and to avoid punishment. 22 But the wicked would not listen and refused to obey him. In their foolishness 23 they have made their own wicked and deceitful plans. They denied the existence of God Most High and refused to follow his ways. 24 They have rejected his Law, refused to accept his promises, disobeyed his decrees, and failed to do what he commanded. 25 That's the reason, Ezra, that there is emptiness for the empty and fullness for the full.

The Messianic Kingdom and the Final Judgment

26 "The time is coming when these signs will take place. The invisible city will appear,*r* and the land that is now hidden will be seen. 27 Everyone who survives the calamities I have predicted will also see the wonderful things I will do. 28 My son the Messiah*s* will be revealed, together with those who come with him. He will bring four hundred years of happiness to all these survivors. 29 At the end of that time, my son the Messiah and all human beings will die. 30 Then the world will return to its original silence, and for seven days it will be like it was at the beginning. No one will be left alive. 31 After seven days this corrupt age will pass out of existence and a new age will be awakened. 32 The ground will give up the dead who sleep there in silence, and the souls of the dead will be released from the places where they have been kept. 33 God Most High will appear on his judgment seat. Mercy and patience will vanish completely 34 and be replaced by judgment. Truth and faithfulness will once again stand firm. 35 The good and bad that people have done will be fully revealed, and reward and punishment will follow immediately.*t* 36 The pit of torment, the fires of hell, will appear, and opposite them the Paradise of joy and rest.

37 "Then God Most High will say to the nations that have been raised from the dead, 'Look! I am the one whom you have denied and refused to serve; it is my commands that you have rejected. 38 Look around you; there is joy and peace in one direction, fire and torment in the other.' That's what he will say to them on Judgment Day.

39 "On Judgment Day there will be no sun, moon, or stars; 40 no cloud, thunder, or lightning; no wind, water, or air; no darkness, evening, or morning; 41 no summer, spring, or winter; no heat, frost, or cold; no hail, rain, or dew; 42 no noon, night, or dawn; no daylight, brightness, or light. The only light will be the dazzling brightness of God Most High, making it possible for everyone to see. 43 The judgment will last seven years. 44 That's the arrangement I have made for Judgment Day, but I have revealed these things only to you."

Only a Few Will Be Saved

45 Then I said, "Lord, I repeat what I said earlier: How fortunate are the people who can live now and obey your commands! 46 But what about those for whom I have been praying? There is no one in the present generation who has not sinned, no one who has not broken your covenant. 47 Now I understand

r Some ancient translations The invisible city will appear; *Latin* The bride will appear and the appearing city.   *s Some ancient translations* the Messiah; *Latin* Jesus.
t Verses 36-105 are not found in the King James Version, but they have been restored from ancient sources.
7.32 Dn 12.2   **7.36** Lk 16.23, 24; Rev 9.2

that the world to come will bring joy to only a few, but torment to many. ⁴⁸ The evil impulse within us has grown and it has led us away from God's ways, brought us to ruin, put us on the way to death and destruction, and taken us far from life. It has destroyed not only a few, but almost everyone who was ever created."

⁴⁹ "Listen to me," the angel said, "and I will teach you further and correct your thinking. ⁵⁰ Because only a few will be saved, God created two worlds, instead of only one. ⁵¹ As you say, only a few people are righteous, but there are large numbers of wicked people. But listen: ⁵² If you had only a few precious stones, would you add lumps of lead and clay to them in order to have more?"^u

⁵³ "Surely no one would do that, sir," I answered.

⁵⁴ "Take another illustration," he continued. "The earth itself will give you an answer if you humbly ask it ⁵⁵ whether it produces more gold, silver, copper, iron, lead, or clay. ⁵⁶ There is more silver than gold, more copper than silver, more iron than copper, more lead than iron, and more clay than lead. ⁵⁷ So judge for yourself which are more desirable and valuable, common things or rare things."

⁵⁸ I answered, "Lord and master, the common things are cheap; it is the rare things that are valuable."

⁵⁹ "All right," he replied, "so draw the logical conclusion: the person who has what is scarce has more reason to be pleased than the person who has what is plentiful. ⁶⁰ It's the same with the judgment^v that I have promised: I will be pleased with the few who will be saved, because they are the ones who now praise and honor me and make my name known. ⁶¹ I will not be sad about the large number of people who will be lost, because even now they last no longer than a vapor; they disappear like fire and smoke; they catch fire, blaze up, and quickly go out."

⁶² Then I said to the earth, "Look at what you have done! When you gave birth to the rest of creation you gave birth to reason. ⁶³ It would have been better if you had never been created. Then we humans would never have had the power of reasoning! ⁶⁴ But as it is now, our reason grows up with us and then torments us, because we realize that we are going to die! ⁶⁵ Compared to us who must bear this sorrow, the dumb animals must be happy. ⁶⁶ They are much better off than we are. They do not have to look forward to the judgment; they are not aware of any torment or salvation that is promised to them after death. ⁶⁷ What good is it to us that we are going to be given life in the future if it is to be a life of terrible torment? ⁶⁸ Everyone who is born is caught in the web of sin, is full of wickedness and burdened with guilt. ⁶⁹ I think it would be better if after death we did not have to face judgment."

⁷⁰ The angel replied, "When God Most High was creating the world, as well as Adam and his descendants, the first thing he did was to get everything ready for the judgment. ⁷¹ So you ought to learn from your own words. You said that your reason grows up with you, ⁷² and that's the point. The people of this world used their reason and sinned; they received God's commands but did not keep them; they accepted the Law and then disobeyed it. And that's why they will suffer torment. ⁷³ What excuse can they offer at the judgment? How can they answer at the last day? ⁷⁴ God Most High has been very patient with the people of this world for a long time, but it has not been for their sake. He has done it for the sake of the age to come."

---

^u *One ancient translation* would you . . . more; *Latin unclear.*   ^v *Some ancient translations* judgment; *Latin* creation.

The Soul after Death

⁷⁵Then I said, "Sir, may I ask you, please, to explain to me what happens when we die, when each of us must give back our soul? Will we be kept at rest until the time when you begin to make your new creation, or will our torment begin immediately?"

⁷⁶"I will answer that question also," he replied, "but do not include yourself among those who will be tormented because they have no use for religion. ⁷⁷After all, you have a treasure of good works stored up with God Most High, which will not be shown to you until the last days. ⁷⁸But to answer your question about death: When God Most High has pronounced the final decree that a person shall die, the soul leaves the body to return to the one who gave it. Immediately it praises the glory of God Most High. ⁷⁹Let me explain first about people who had no use for the ways of God Most High and hated those who worshiped him. ⁸⁰There is no place where their souls can go for rest; they must wander around forever in torment, grief, and sorrow. Their torment will progress in seven stages. ⁸¹First, they ignore the Law of God Most High. ⁸²Second, they can no longer make a sincere repentance and obtain life. ⁸³Third, they see the reward stored up for those who put their faith in the covenants of God Most High. ⁸⁴Fourth, they think about the torment that has been stored up for them in the last days. ⁸⁵Fifth, they see angels guarding the homes of other souls in complete silence. ⁸⁶Sixth, they recognize that they must soon be tormented.ʷ ⁸⁷Seventh, and worst of all, when they see the glory of God Most High, they are sick with remorse and shame. They cringe in fear, because while they were living they sinned against him. And now they are about to come before him to be judged on the last day.

⁸⁸"Now let me explain about those who followed the ways of God Most High and what will happen when the time comes for them to leave their mortal bodies. ⁸⁹While they lived on earth, through constant difficulty and danger, they served God Most High and carefully kept the Law given by the Lawgiver. ⁹⁰This is what they will receive: ⁹¹They will rejoice when they see the great glory of God. He will receive them, and they will enter their rest in seven stages of joy. ⁹²The first joy is to have struggled hard and won the victory over the evil impulse which was formed in them, but which did not succeed in leading them from life into death. ⁹³The second is to see the endless wandering of the souls of the wicked and the punishment that is waiting for them. ⁹⁴The third is to know what a good report their Maker has given about them, that during their lifetime they kept the Law that was entrusted to them. ⁹⁵The fourth is to appreciate the rest that they are to enjoy in the places where they have been brought together, guarded by angels, in complete silence, and with the glory that is waiting for them at the last day. ⁹⁶The fifth is to rejoice that they have now escaped the corrupt world and that they will receive the future life as their possession. They can see both the narrow, troubledˣ world from which they have been freed and the spacious world they will receive and enjoy forever. ⁹⁷The sixth is to be shown how their faces will shine like the sun and how they are to be like the light of the stars that never die. ⁹⁸The seventh joy, and best of all, is when they rush to meet God face-to-face, with perfect trust and happiness, without any fear or shame. They served him during their lifetime and now they will receive from him

---

ʷ *Verse 86 in Latin is unclear.*   ˣ *Some ancient translations* troubled; *Latin unclear.*
7.97 Dn 12.3; Mt 13.43   **7.98** Mt 5.8; He 12.14; 1 Jn 3.2; Rev 22.4

their reward in glory. [99] These rewards that I have been telling you about are those that have been prepared for the souls of the righteous. I described to you earlier the torment that the rebellious will suffer."

[100] Then I asked, "When the souls of the righteous are separated from their bodies, will they be given time to see what you have told me about?"

[101] "They will be free for seven days," he answered, "and during that time they will be able to see the things I have told you about. After that they will be brought together with the other souls in their homes."

The Finality of Judgment and the Salvation of the Few

[102] Then I said, "Sir, please tell me whether the righteous will be able to ask God Most High to show mercy on the unrighteous on Judgment Day.

. . . they rush to meet God face-to-face. (7.98)

[103] Will fathers be able to pray for their children, children for parents, brothers for brothers, relatives for those near to them, and friends[y] for those dear to them?"

[104] "I will be happy to tell you," he replied. "Judgment Day is final[z] and sets the final seal on truth for all to see. You know that in this age a father cannot send his son to be sick[a] for him or sleep or eat or be healed for him. An owner cannot send his slave to do these things for him, nor can a person send his best friend. [105] In the same way, on that day, no one will be able to pray for another person. Each person will receive the punishment or reward for his own sinfulness or righteousness."[b]

[106] "If that is so," I answered, "how can we explain what we find in the Scriptures? Abraham prayed for the people of Sodom, and Moses for our ancestors who sinned in the desert. [107] Later, Joshua prayed for the people of Israel in the time of Achan, [108] and Samuel prayed for them in the days of Saul.[c] David prayed at the time of the epidemic, and Solomon prayed for those who were going to worship in the Temple. [109] Elijah prayed that the people might have rain and for a dead person to come back to life. [110] Hezekiah prayed for the people during the time of Sennacherib. And there are many other examples. [111] If righteous people prayed for the unrighteous during such times when corruption increased and injustice multiplied, why won't the same thing happen at the Judgment Day?"

[112] "The present age is not the end of everything," the angel answered. "Even in this age, the glorious presence of God is not[d] always seen. That is why

[y] Some ancient translations friends; Latin the confident.   [z] One ancient translation final; Latin bold.   [a] Some ancient translations be sick; Latin understand.
[b] Verses 106-140 are the equivalent of verses 36-70 in the King James Version.
[c] Some ancient translations in the days of Saul; Latin does not have these words.
[d] Some ancient translations is not; Latin is.

7.106 Gn 18.23; Ex 32.11 **7.107** Js 7.6, 7 **7.108** 1 S 7.9; 2 S 24.17; 1 K 8.22, 23, 30
7.109 1 K 18.42, 45; 17.20, 21 **7.110** 2 K 19.15-19

the strong have prayed for the weak during this age. [113]But the Judgment Day will be the end of the present age and the beginning of the future age. Then all corruption will end, [114]self-indulgence and disloyalty will be eliminated. Righteousness and truth will reach their full maturity. [115]So on Judgment Day, no one will be able to have mercy on those who have been condemned, and no one will be able to harm those who have been acquitted."

[116]I answered, "I made this point before, and I will make it again. It would have been better if the earth had never produced Adam, or when it had done so, if it had made him so that he could not sin. [117]What good is it for any of us to have life in the present age, when it is full of misery and when all we can look forward to after death is punishment? [118]O Adam, what have you done? Your sin was not only your own downfall; it was also the downfall of all of us who are your descendants. [119]What good is it to us that we have the promise of immortal life, when we have committed sins that condemn us to death? [120]What good is the hope of eternity, when we find ourselves in such a completely hopeless situation? [121]What good is it that safe and secure homes have been prepared for us in the future world, when we have lived such wicked lives? [122]What good is the promise that the glorious presence of God Most High will protect those who have lived pure lives, when our own lives have been so full of sin? [123]What good is it that Paradise is shown to us, that its imperishable fruit can heal us and provide all we need? We can never go there [124]because we have lived unacceptable lives.[e] [125]What good is it that the faces of those who practice self-control will shine more brightly than the stars,

when our own faces will be blacker than the night? [126]Never in our whole lives, when we sinned, did we think about what we would have to suffer after death."

[127]The angel replied, "Here is the meaning of the conflict that every person on earth must endure: [128]If he is defeated, he must suffer the things you have just told me about, but if he is victorious, he will receive the rewards that I have just mentioned. [129]That is why Moses long ago urged the people to choose life so that they might live. [130]But they did not believe him or the prophets who came after him, and they did not believe me when I spoke to them. [131]So the sadness over their destruction is nothing compared to the great joy over the salvation of those who believe."

[132]I answered, "Sir, I know that God Most High is spoken of as merciful because he shows mercy to those who have not yet entered this world. [133]He is called compassionate because he shows compassion to those who repent and obey his Law. [134]He is thought of as patient because he is patient with his own creatures who have sinned. [135]He is known as generous because he prefers to give rather than to demand. [136]And he is known as very forgiving because he continues to forgive sinners of the past, present, and future. [137]If he did not continue to forgive, there would be no life for this world or the people in it. [138]He is spoken of as pardoning because, if it were not for his goodness in pardoning sinners, not one person in ten thousand would gain life. [139]He is called judge because he pardons and blots out the many sins of those who were created by his word. [140]If he did not, only a handful of the whole human race would be left."[f]

---

[e] *Probable text* unacceptable lives; *Latin* in unacceptable places.   [f] *Verses 106-140 are the equivalent of verses 36-70 in the King James Version.*
7.123 Ez 47.12; Rev 22.2   **7.129** Dt 30.19

8 The angel replied, "God Most High made this world for many people, but the future world for only a few. ²Ezra, let me give you an illustration. If you ask the earth, it will tell you that it produces a large amount of clay for pots but only a small amount of gold dust. And that's the way it is with the

A large amount of clay . . . but only a small amount of gold dust (8.2)

present world: ³many have been created, but only a few will be saved."

Ezra Prays for His People

⁴I said to myself, "I must search for wisdom and try to understand. ⁵I was brought into this world without my consent,ᵍ and I will leave it against my will. God has given me only a few short years as my span of life."

⁶Then I prayed, "O Lord above, permit me, your humble servant, to offer this prayer: Plant a seed within us, and let it grow until it produces new hearts and minds, so that sinful humanity may have life. ⁷For you alone are God, and you created all of us, as the scripture says. ⁸You give life and provide arms and legs to the body formed in the

womb, where it is kept safe in the elements of fire and water. The body which you form is carried in the womb for nine months, ⁹and you alone provide safety for the protecting womb and the protected body. Then when the womb delivers what was created in it, ¹⁰your command produces milk from the breasts of the human body. ¹¹The infant you created is fed in this way for a while, and then you continue to provide your mercy. ¹²You raise the person on your righteousness, teach him your Law, and discipline him with your wisdom. ¹³You are his Creator and, as you wish, you can take away his life or allow him to live. ¹⁴But if you are so ready to destroy a person that was so carefully created at your command, why was he created in the first place?

¹⁵"Now, Lord, I must say this: You may know what is best in regard to the rest of the human race, but I mourn for your own people — ¹⁶I am disturbed and grieved for your own nation Israel, the descendants of Jacob. ¹⁷So I want to pray for them and for myself, because I can see how all of us who live on this earth have failed, ¹⁸and I know that judgment will soon come upon us. ¹⁹So please hear me and listen to my prayer."

The prayer that Ezra prayed before he was taken up into heaven begins here. He prayed, ²⁰"O Lord, you live forever, and the highest heavens are yours. ²¹Your throne is more wonderful than anything we can imagine; your glory surpasses our understanding; the heavenly army of angels stands trembling before you. ²²They are ready to turn themselves into wind or fire at your command. Your word is everlastingly true. ²³Your mighty commands accomplish fearful things. With one look, you dry up the deep oceans, and you can melt the mountains with your anger. Your truth lasts forever.ʰ

ᵍ *One ancient translation* without my consent; *Latin* to obey.   ʰ *Some ancient translations* lasts forever; *Latin* testifies.
8.3 Mt 22.14   **8.22** Ps 104.4; He 1.7

24 O Lord, you created me, and I am your servant, so listen to my prayer. 25 As long as I have life and understanding, I cannot keep silent.

26 "Do not take account of the sins of your people; rather, consider those who have served you faithfully. 27 Pay no attention to godless people and what they do, but take into account those who have kept your covenant in spite of all their sufferings. 28 Do not think about those who have lived wicked lives, but remember those who have gladly confessed you as God. 29 Do not destroy your people because of those who have lived like animals, but be mindful of those who have taught your Law in such a wonderful way. 30 Do not be angry with those you consider worse than animals, but show your love to those who have always trusted in your glorious presence.

31 "It is true that we and our ancestors have lived our lives in ways that bring death, but it is because of us who are sinners that you are called merciful. 32 You will surely be called merciful if you choose to take pity on us — we are sinners without any righteous deeds to our credit. 33 Those who are righteous will receive their reward on the basis of the many good works that they have stored up with you.

34 "What are human beings that you should be angry with them? What is this mortal race that you should be so bitter against it? 35 To speak the truth, no person was ever born who did not sin; there is no one living who is not guilty. 36 Therefore, Lord, your righteousness and goodness will certainly be made known when you show your mercy to those who have no treasure of good deeds."

37 The Lord answered me, "Part of what you have said is correct, and things will happen as you have indicated. 38 You can be sure that I will give no thought to those who have sinned or to their creation, death, judgment, or destruction. 39 Instead, I will find my joy in the creation of the righteous, their earthly journey, their salvation, and their final reward. 40 Things will happen just as I have said. 41 The farmer plants many seeds and puts out many plants, but not all of them take root or come up at the right time. That's the way it is with this world. Not everyone who has been placed in this world will be saved."

42 Then I said, "Please let me speak. 43 The farmer's seed may not come up because you did not send rain at the right time, or it may be ruined by too much rain. 44 But people are different. You formed them with your own hands; you created them to be like you; and you made everything for their benefit. How can you compare them to a farmer's seed? 45 It's impossible, O Lord[i] above! Spare the people who are your own. Have pity on them. Show your mercy to the people you have created."

46 He answered, "The present is for those who live now, and the future for those who are to come. 47 You are certainly not able to love what I have created more than I do. Never again consider yourself among the unrighteous, as you have done so often. 48 Yet I am very pleased 49 that you have shown proper humility and not boasted by thinking of yourself as righteous. 50 The people of this world who have lived their lives in pride and arrogance will suffer many things in the last days. 51 But, Ezra, you should be thinking about the glory that is waiting for you and those like you. 52 For all of you, Paradise has been opened, the tree of life has been planted, the world to come has been made ready, all your needs have been provided, the heavenly city has been built, full rest from your labors

---

i Some ancient translations O Lord; *Latin does not have these words.*

8.52 1 P 1.4

has been offered, goodness and wisdom have been perfected. [53] The source of evil has been sealed off, so that it cannot reach you; all sickness has been removed, death[j] has been taken away, hell is gone, and corruption has disappeared. [54] All suffering has been taken away, and the treasure of immortality is at last revealed.

[55] "So don't ask any more questions about the large number of people who are lost. [56] For when they had the opportunity to choose, they despised God Most High, had contempt for his Law, and refused to follow his ways. [57] In addition, they mistreated the righteous servants of God. [58] They even said to themselves that there was no God, although they knew that they must die. [59] So the joys I have described are waiting for you, while thirst and torment are in store for them. But God Most High did not want anyone to perish. [60] He created everyone and prepared life for everyone, but those he created dishonored the name of their Creator and were ungrateful to the one who offered them life. [61] That is why the day on which I will judge them is near. [62] I have made this known to you and a few others like you, but not to everyone."

The Signs of the End

I answered, [63] "Sir, you have shown me many signs which you will perform in the last days, but you have not told me how I can know when this will happen."

9 He answered, "Consider all these things very carefully. When you see that some of the signs I have told you about have appeared, [2] you will know that the time has come when God Most High will bring judgment on the world he has created. [3] There will be earthquakes, national rebellions, international intrigues, unstable leaders, and confused rulers. When you see these things happening, [4] you will know that they are what God Most High has spoken about since the beginning of creation. [5] The beginning and the end[k] of everything that happens in this world are clear. [6] The same is true in the world above:[l] wonders and miracles show the beginning of events, and mighty signs show when they end.

[7] "Some people will escape destruction and be saved by their good works or by their faith. All of them [8] will survive the dangers I have described and will enjoy the salvation provided in the land that I have set apart from eternity as my own. [9] Then those who have ignored my ways and held them in contempt will be surprised when they find themselves in continual torment. [10] This will include all those who ignored me while they were alive, even though they accepted the blessings I gave them. [11] It will include all those who scorned my Law during the time they were free to do so and all those who refused to repent when they still had the chance. [12] The torment they will have to suffer after death will force them to recognize the truth. [13] Therefore, Ezra, you should stop asking questions about how the wicked will be punished. Instead, be concerned about how and when the righteous will be saved. The world was created for them and belongs to them."

[14] I said, [15] "I must repeat what I said before. The lost far outnumber those who are saved — [16] it is like a wave compared with a drop of water."

[17] He answered, "The seed to be planted depends on the soil; the color of the flower depends on the kind of flower; the quality of a product depends

---

[j] *Some ancient translations* death; *Latin does not have this word.*   [k] *One ancient translation* The beginning and the end; *Latin unclear.*   [l] *The same . . . above; Latin unclear.*

8.59 Lk 16.24   **9.11** Ws 12.10, 20; He 12.17

on the skill of the worker; and the size of the harvest depends on how hard the farmer has worked. 18 Before I created this world or the people who would live in it, no one opposed me, because no one existed. 19 When I had created the world, I supplied it with an abundance of food and a Law of profound wisdom, but the people I created lived corrupt lives. 20 I looked at my world and saw that it was ruined. I saw that my earth was in danger of being destroyed by the wicked plans of the people who had come into it. 21 When I saw this, I found it very difficult to spare them, but I saved a few for myself, one grape out of a bunch and one tree out of a great forest. *m* 22 So let them perish — all those people who were born only to be lost. But let my chosen people be kept safe — those for whom I worked so hard to bring to perfection.

23 "And now, Ezra, you must wait seven more days, but do not fast this time. 24 Go to a field of wild flowers where no one has ever lived and eat nothing but the flowers — do not eat any meat or drink any wine. 25 Pray the whole time to God Most High. Then I will come and talk with you again."

THE FOURTH VISION

The Law Remains

26 I obeyed the angel's command and went to a field called Ardat. I sat there among the flowers and ate the wild plants, and that was enough food for me. 27 After seven days I was lying on the grass, and once again my thoughts began to trouble me. 28 Then I began to speak and said to God Most High, 29 "O Lord, you revealed yourself to our ancestors when they were traveling through the trackless, barren desert after they had left Egypt. You said to them, 30 'Listen to me, people of Israel.

31 I am giving you my Law. It will be like a seed planted among you that produces fruit, and it will be your crowning glory forever.' 32 Our ancestors received the Law, but they disobeyed its commands. Yet the fruit of the Law was not destroyed — it could not be destroyed because it was yours. 33 Those who had received the Law were destroyed because they did not guard the good seed that was sown in them. 34-35 The usual thing is that the container remains after its contents have been destroyed, for example, seed in the ground, a ship on the sea, or food in a bowl. But this is not the case with us sinners. 36 The Law was placed in our hearts, and we are the ones who will be destroyed because we have sinned. 37 The Law will not be destroyed; it will remain in all its glory."

The Vision of the Weeping Woman

38 While I was saying these things to myself, I looked around and saw a woman on my right. She was weeping and wailing, terribly upset; her clothes were torn, and there were ashes on her head. 39 I immediately put my own troubles out of my mind, turned to the woman, 40 and asked, "Why are you crying? Why are you so upset?"

41 "Please, sir," she answered, "leave me alone and let me go on crying and mourning; I am bitter and depressed."

42 "Tell me what's wrong," I said.

43 She answered, "Sir, I was married for thirty years, but I was never able to have a child. 44 During those thirty years I prayed every day and every hour, day and night, to God Most High for a child. 45 After thirty years God answered my prayer; he saw my suffering, took away my distress, and gave me a son. What great joy this brought to my husband and me and to all our neighbors! We sang the praises of the Almighty. 46 I brought our son up with

---

m Some ancient translations a great forest; *Latin* great tribes.
9.29 Ex 19.9; 24.10; Dt 4.12

She was weeping and wailing. (9.38)

the greatest care, ⁴⁷and when he was grown, I chose a wife for him and prepared for the wedding.

10 "On the wedding night when my son entered the bedroom, he dropped dead. ²So we put out all the wedding lamps, and all my neighbors came to comfort me. I remained in control of myself until the evening of the second day, ³when they all left. That night I got up and came out to this field, as you see. ⁴I have decided never to return to that town. I am going to stay here in constant mourning, neither eating nor drinking anything until I die."

⁵When she told me this, I put aside my own thoughts and spoke sharply to her: ⁶"You are the most foolish woman I ever met. Don't you see what our people are suffering? Don't you know all that has happened to us? ⁷Jerusalem, the mother of us all, is overcome with grief and shame. You ought to be mourning for her ⁸and sharing the grief and sorrow of all of us. But you are mourning for that one son of yours. ⁹Ask the earth; let her tell you that she is the one who ought to be mourning for the vast multitudes of people that she has brought to birth. ¹⁰All of us who are living came originally from her, and there are more to come. Almost all of us go straight to destruction—the vast multitude of earth's children are lost. ¹¹So who has more right to mourn, you for your one son, or the earth, which has lost so many? ¹²⁻¹³I know what you are thinking; you think that your sorrow is worse than the earth's. You think that it is only natural for earth's multitudes to live and then die, but you have lost your own flesh and blood which you brought to birth with such trouble and pain. But let me tell you ¹⁴that from the time God created the earth she has suffered as much in producing human beings for God as you did in childbirth. ¹⁵So keep your tears to yourself, and be brave about what has happened to you. ¹⁶If you will accept God's decision as just, you will get your son back at the right time, and you will receive the praise due a mother. ¹⁷Go back to the city and to your husband."

¹⁸"No," she answered, "I will never go back; I am going to stay here and die."

¹⁹⁻²⁰"Don't do that," I continued. "Consider the misfortunes and sorrows of Jerusalem, and you won't feel so sorry for yourself. ²¹You can see that our place of worship is in ruins, our altar has been torn down, our Temple has been destroyed, ²²our musical instruments lie quiet, our hymns have been silenced, our joy has ended, the light of the sacred lamp has been put out, our Covenant Box has been carried off, our sacred utensils have been desecrated, the name of our God has been profaned, our leaders have been dishonored, our priests have been burned to death, our Levites have been taken captive, our

virgins have been raped, our wives have been violated, our devout men have been carried off, our children have been abandoned, our young people have been made slaves, and our strong soldiers have been made helpless. 23 Worst of all, Jerusalem, once marked as God's own city, has lost its glory and has been handed over to our enemies. 24 So put aside all your sorrow and grief. May God Most High, the Almighty, be merciful to you and give you peace. May he give you rest from your troubles."

25 While I was speaking to the woman, her face suddenly began to shine with a light that flashed like lightning. I was afraid to stand near her and wondered what all this meant. 26 Suddenly she let out a loud and terrifying cry that shook the earth. 27 When I looked up, I could no longer see the woman, but there was a city built*n* on huge foundations. I was afraid and shouted, 28 "Where is the angel Uriel, who came to me earlier? It is his fault that I am so confused. My prayer is useless, and I have nothing to hope for but death."

Uriel's Interpretation of the Vision

29 I was still speaking when the angel Uriel appeared again. He saw me 30 lying there unconscious like a corpse, so he took hold of my right hand, gave me strength, and stood me on my feet. Then he asked, 31 "What's the matter? Why are you so disturbed and confused?"

32 I answered, "You abandoned me completely! I did as you told me and came out to this field, but I cannot explain what I am seeing."

33 "Stand up straight," he answered, "and I will explain it to you."

34 "Sir," I answered, "please explain it

to me. I will die in my frustration if you leave me, 35 for I cannot understand what I have seen and heard. 36 Or is my mind playing tricks on me, and is this just a bad dream? 37 I beg you, sir, tell me what this vision means."

38 The angel said, "Now listen closely, and I will explain the meaning of these things that you fear. God Most High has revealed many secrets to you 39 because he has seen that you have lived a righteous life and have always grieved and mourned for your people and for Jerusalem. 40 This is what the vision means: A woman appeared to you a little while ago, 41 and when you saw that she was mourning, you tried to console her. 42-43 The woman told you about the death of her son. Then she vanished from your sight, and a whole city*o* appeared. This is the meaning: 44 The woman you saw is Jerusalem, which you now see as a completed city. 45 When she told you that for thirty years she had had no children, it meant that for three thousand*p* years no offerings had yet been made there. 46 Then Solomon built the city, and sacrifices began to be offered there. At that time the childless woman gave birth to her son. 47 When she told you that she took great care in bringing the son up, that referred to the period when Jerusalem was inhabited. 48 When she told you of the death of her son on his wedding day, that meant the destruction of Jerusalem. 49 So in the vision you saw how she mourned for her son, and you tried to console her for what had happened — this is what was to be revealed to you. 50 When God Most High saw that you were grieving for the woman with all your heart and soul, he showed you all her glory and majestic beauty. 51 That is why I told you to go and stay in the field where no one had

---

n Some ancient translations built; *Latin* being built.   *o Some ancient translations* whole city; *Latin* city being built.   *p Some ancient translations* three thousand; *Latin* three.

10.27 He 11.10; Rev 21.9-27

ever lived, [52] for I knew that God Most High was going to show you these things. [53] I told you to go to the field where no foundation had ever been built, [54] because nothing built by human hands could stand in the place where the city of God Most High was about to be revealed.

[55] "So don't be afraid. Go into the city and look at its beautiful and majestic buildings. See as much as you can. [56] After that, you will hear as much as you can. [57] You are more fortunate than most people, and only a few have the reputation with God Most High that you have. [58] Remain here until tomorrow night, [59] and he will show you in dreams and visions what he plans to do for those who will be living on the earth in the last days." So I slept there that night and the next, as I had been told.

THE FIFTH VISION

The Vision of an Eagle

11 The second night I had a dream. I saw an eagle coming up out of the sea. It had twelve wings

I saw an eagle coming up out of the sea. (11.1)

and three heads. [2] As I looked, it spread out its wings over the whole world. Winds blew on it from every direction, and clouds[q] gathered over it. [3] Then

from its wings I saw rival wings begin to grow, but they were small and insignificant. [4] All three heads of the eagle were asleep, even the middle one, which was larger than the others. [5] While I was watching, the eagle flew up in the air and became ruler of the whole earth and all its people. [6] I saw how everything on earth was brought under the eagle's control — no one on earth was able to oppose it. [7] Then I saw the eagle stand up on its claws and say to its wings, [8] "Not all of you are to wake up at the same time; you must sleep where you are and wake up when your turn comes, [9] and the heads must wake up last." [10] I looked again and saw that the voice was not coming from any of the eagle's heads but from the middle of its body. [11] I counted its rival wings, and there were eight of them.

[12] I saw one of the wings on the right side rise up and govern the whole world. [13] After its rule came to an end, it vanished so completely that it left no trace. Then the next wing rose up and governed for a long time. [14] When its rule was coming to an end and it was about to vanish like the first wing, [15] a voice said to it, [16] "Listen, you have ruled the world for a long time, and I want you to hear this message before you disappear: [17] No one after you will rule as long as you did — not even half as long." [18] The third wing rose up and governed as the earlier ones had done; then it also vanished. [19] The same thing happened to all the other wings: one after the other they rose to power and then vanished.

[20] I kept looking, and after a while the other small wings on the right side rose up to seize power. Some of them governed briefly and quickly disappeared, [21] while others rose up but were never able to govern. [22] Then I noticed that the twelve large wings and two of the small wings had disappeared. [23] Noth-

---

[q] *Some ancient translations* clouds; *Latin does not have this word.*
11.1 Dn 7.3, 4; Rev 13.1

ing was left on the eagle's body except the three sleeping heads and the six small wings. 24 I kept watching, and suddenly two of the six small wings left the others and moved under the head on the right side, while the other four remained where they were. 25 Then I saw that these four small wings were plotting to rise up and seize power. 26 One of them rose up, but it quickly disappeared. 27 The second one also rose up, but it disappeared even more quickly than the first. 28 I saw that the two remaining small wings were also plotting to seize control for themselves. 29 While they were making their plans, one of the sleeping heads suddenly awoke. It was the one in the middle, the one that was larger than the other two. 30 Then I saw that it was joined by the other heads, 31 and when it turned to eat up the two little wings that were planning to seize power, the other two heads helped it. 32 This head gained power over the whole world, established an oppressive rule over people everywhere, and exercised more power over the world than any of the other wings had done before. 33 Then, as I watched, the middle head disappeared just as suddenly as the wings had done. 34 Two heads were left, and they also gained power over the earth and its people; 35 but while I was still watching, the head on the right ate up the head on the left.

36 Then I heard a voice which said, "Ezra, look straight ahead and think about what you see."

37 I looked and saw what appeared to be an angry lion come roaring out of the forest. I heard it speak in human language to the eagle and say, 38 "Listen, Eagle, to what I have to say to you; it is the message of God Most High: 39 You are the only one left of the four animals that I appointed to govern my world and to bring the ages of this world to an end. 40 You are the fourth animal and you have conquered all the animals that

came before you. As long as you have been in this world, you have ruled it through terror, oppression, and deceit, 41 with a total disregard for truth. 42 You have viciously attacked harmless people who were living in peace; you have hated those who spoke the truth, and you have loved liars. You have destroyed the homes of those who were prosperous and have torn down the walls of those who did you no harm. 43 God Most High knows how proud and arrogant you are. The Almighty One 44 has looked back over the world he established. The end has come; the final age is over. 45 So, Eagle, the time has come for you to vanish, along with your big, terrible wings, your small, wicked wings, your evil heads, your awful claws, and your whole worthless body. 46 The entire world will be set free from your violence and renewed as it sets its hope on the judgment and mercy of God, who created it."

12 While the lion was speaking in this way to the eagle, I looked 2 and saw that the last head of the eagle was gone. Then the two small wings that had moved over to that head rose up to govern, but their rule was short and full of trouble. 3 They disappeared before my eyes, and the whole body of the eagle burst into flames, and the world was terrified.

The Interpretation of the Vision

I was so disturbed and so afraid that I woke up. I said, 4 "I have brought this on myself, because I have tried to study the ways of God Most High. 5 I am mentally exhausted and completely worn out. The terrible fears I have experienced this night have taken my last bit of strength. 6 All I can do now is pray to God Most High to give me strength until the end." 7 Then I prayed, "Master and Lord, if it is true that you consider me more righteous than many others and if you hear my prayers, then I beg you, ⁸give me strength. Show me, O Lord, the full meaning of this terrifying vision, and set my mind at ease. ⁹After all, you did consider me worthy to be shown the end of this age."

¹⁰God's angel said to me, "Here is the interpretation of the vision you saw. ¹¹The eagle you saw coming up out of the sea represents the fourth kingdom in the vision that your brother Daniel saw. ¹²But he was not given the same interpretation of it that I am giving you. ¹³The time is coming when an empire will be established on earth that is more terrible than any before it. ¹⁴Twelve kings will rule over it, one after the other. ¹⁵The second king will rule longer than any of the others. ¹⁶That is the meaning of the twelve wings that you saw.

¹⁷"You heard the voice speaking from the middle of the eagle's body, instead of from its heads. ¹⁸That means that after the rule of the second king, a great struggle for power will take place, and the empire will be in danger of breaking up. But that will not happen, and the empire will regain its earlier power.

¹⁹"You saw the eight small wings growing out of the eagle's big wings. That means ²⁰that eight kings will rise up in the empire, but their rule will be brief and unimportant. ²¹Two of them will appear briefly near the middle of the period, four of them will not appear until near the end, and two will be left until the very end.

²²"You saw the three heads that were asleep. That means ²³that in the last days of the empire, God Most High will raise up three kings; they ʳ will restore much of the empire and rule over the world ²⁴and its people with more harshness than any before them. The reason they are called the eagle's heads ²⁵is that these three kings will bring to a

head and complete the godless work of the eagle. ²⁶You saw the largest head disappear. This means that one of the kings will die in his bed, in great agony. ²⁷The other two will die in battle. ²⁸One of them will kill the other; then he also will be killed in battle at the end of time.

²⁹"You saw the two small wings moving under the head on the right side. ³⁰That means that God Most High has kept them until the end, but their rule was short and full of trouble, as you saw.

³¹"You saw the angry lion come roaring out of the forest, and you heard it speak to the eagle and rebuke it for the evil that it had done and for all that it had said. ³²The lion represents the Messiah, whom God Most High has held back until the end. He will be a descendant of David and will come and speak ˢ to the rulers. He will rebuke them for their wickedness, their sinfulness, and their contempt for God's ways. ³³While they are still living, he will bring them to judgment, condemn them for their sin, and destroy them. ³⁴But he will have mercy on the rest of my people, those who are left in my land; he will set them free and make them happy until the end comes, the Judgment Day about which I told you at the beginning.

³⁵"That is the dream you had, and that is its interpretation. ³⁶But you are the only one that God Most High has considered worthy to reveal this secret to. ³⁷So write in a book everything you saw, and put it in a safe hiding place. ³⁸Then teach these secrets to those who are wise among your people, those who will be able to understand them and keep them secret. ³⁹But you must stay here seven more days, so that God Most High may reveal to you whatever he wishes." Then the angel left me.

ʳ Some ancient translations they; Latin he. speak; Latin does not have these words.
12.11 Dn 7.7   **12.32** Dn 7.13, 14

ˢ Some ancient translations He will . . .

"What wrong have we done to you?" (12.41)

The People Come to Ezra

⁴⁰When the seven days had passed and all the people heard that I had not yet returned to the city, all of them, rich and poor, came and asked me, ⁴¹"What wrong have we done to you? How have we mistreated you? Why have you abandoned us and settled down in this place? ⁴²You are the only one of all our prophets who is left. You are like the last bunch of grapes in a vineyard, like a lantern in a dark place, like a safe harbor for a ship in a storm. ⁴³Haven't we suffered enough already? ⁴⁴If you abandon us, it would have been better if we had died like the others in the fire that destroyed Jerusalem. ⁴⁵We are no better than those who died." Then they all started crying loudly.

I answered, ⁴⁶"Be brave, Israel, put away your sorrow. ⁴⁷God Most High will keep you in mind; the Almighty One has not forgotten you in all your troubles. ⁴⁸And I haven't left you or abandoned you. I came here to pray for Jerusalem in her time of trouble and to ask mercy for her and for your Temple, now in disgrace. ⁴⁹Please return to your homes, all of you. I will come back to you in a few days." ⁵⁰So they left me and went back to the city.

THE SIXTH VISION

The Vision

⁵¹I stayed in the field for seven days, as the angel had commanded me. I ate nothing but wild flowers; I was a vegetarian in those days.

13 The seven days passed, and the following night I had a dream. ²In my dream I saw a wind coming up out of the sea and stirring up great waves. ³As I watched, the wind brought with it out of the sea what looked like a man,*ᵗ* and he was flying*ᵘ* on the clouds. When he turned his face, everything he looked at began to tremble, ⁴and when he spoke, everyone who heard his voice melted like wax in a fire.

⁵I looked again and saw a crowd too large to count. They were people gathered together from all parts of the world to fight against the man who had come up out of the sea. ⁶Then I watched the man carve out a high mountain and fly up on it. ⁷I tried to see the place or the region from which the mountain was carved, but I couldn't. ⁸Then I saw that all the people who had come together to make war against him were terrified, but they still prepared to fight him. ⁹When the man saw the great crowd

---

ᵗ Some ancient translations the wind . . . man; *Latin does not have these words.*
ᵘ Some ancient translations flying; *Latin growing strong.*
13.3 Dn 7.13; 2 Esd 13.32   **13.6** Dn 2.45

The wind brought with it out of the sea what looked like a man. (13.3)

advancing to attack him, he did not take up any weapons. [10] The only thing I saw was what looked like a stream of fire coming out of his mouth. He sent a flaming wind from his lips and a storm of sparks from his tongue. The stream of fire, the flaming wind, and the great storm combined [11] and swept down on the crowd that was coming to attack him, and burned them all up. In a single moment, that crowd too large to count vanished, and there was nothing left but powdery ashes and the smell of smoke. I was shocked when I saw what had happened.

[12] Then I saw the man come down from the mountain and call another large crowd to come to him — this was a peace-loving crowd. [13] All sorts of people came: some were happy, some were sad, some had their hands and feet tied, and some brought others as a gift to the Lord.

The Interpretation of the Vision

I was so frightened that I woke up. I prayed to God Most High and said, [14] "Lord, you have been showing me all these marvelous things. You have considered me worthy and have heard my prayers. [15] Now please show me the meaning of this dream also. [16] I have been thinking how terrible it will be for

the people who will be living in those days, but how much worse for those who do not survive. [17] They will be in great sorrow [18] because they will not enjoy any of the pleasures reserved for the last days. [19] But how terrible also for those who do survive; they will have to face great dangers and many troubles, as these dreams have shown. [20] Nevertheless, it is better to pass through these dangers and reach the end than to disappear like a cloud from this world and never see what takes place in the last days."

He answered, [21] "I will explain to you the meaning of the vision and answer the questions you have asked. [22] You have raised questions about those who will survive until the end. The answer is that [23] the one who brings the dangers in those days will also protect from danger the people who have stored up good works and faithfulness with God the Almighty One. [24] You may be certain that those who survive are far more fortunate than those who die.

[25] "This is the meaning of the vision. The man you saw coming up out of the sea [26] represents the one whom God Most High has kept ready for many ages. He will free the world he created and establish the new order for those who survive. [27] You saw the wind, fire,

and storm going out of the man's mouth, 28 and you saw that without the use of a spear or any other weapon he destroyed the great crowd that was advancing to attack him. This means that 29 the time is near when God Most High will begin to free the people on earth. 30 At that time everyone will be close to panic. 31 They will begin to make war against one another, city against city, region against region, nation against nation, and kingdom against kingdom. 32 When that happens, the signs I told you about earlier will take place, and then I will reveal my son, whom you saw as a man coming out of the sea. 33 When they hear his voice, all the nations will leave their own territory, forget their wars with one another, 34 and come together in one great crowd too large to count, as you saw in your dream. The nations will unite with the single purpose of making war on my son. 35 He will take his stand on the top of Mount Zion, 36 and the new Jerusalem will be seen by everyone. It will be completed and fully built, just as in your dream you saw the mountain carved out, but not by human hands. 37 Then my son will condemn the assembled nations for their godlessness. That is what the storm meant. 38 He will confront them with the wicked plans they have made and also with the torments they must endure. That is what the flames meant. Then he will easily destroy them by means of *v* the Law. That is what the fire meant.

39 "You saw him gather another great crowd of peace-loving people. 40 These are the ten tribes of Israel who were taken away into captivity in the time of King Hoshea. King Shalmaneser of Assyria captured them and deported them to a foreign land east of the Euphrates River. 41 But the ten tribes decided not to stay in that land among the many Gentiles, so they moved farther east to a country where no human beings had ever lived before. 42 There they hoped to keep their laws, which they had failed to keep in their own country. 43 When they had to make the difficult passage across the Euphrates, 44 God Most High performed miracles for them and blocked the channels of the river until they had crossed over. 45 Their long journey through that region, which is named Arzareth, took a year and a half, 46 and they have lived there ever since. Now in these last days they are coming back home, 47 and once again God Most High will block the channels of the river, so that they may cross over. That is the meaning of the great crowd of peace-loving people you saw. 48 But they will also have with them all of your own people who are left and who are found within the borders of my holy land. 49 When the time comes for my son to destroy the crowd that has gathered from every nation, he will protect his people who are left 50 and perform many great miracles for them."

51 Then I said, "Lord and Master, please tell me why the man came up out of the sea."

52 He answered, "No one can explore the bottom of the sea to find out what is there. In the same way, no human being can see my son or those who come with him until the day that has been fixed. 53 That is the meaning of your dream. You alone have been given this information, 54 because you have given up your own interests to devote yourself to mine and to the study of my Law. 55 You have dedicated your life to wisdom, and understanding has been like a mother to you. 56 That is why God Most High has rewarded you by showing you these things. After three days, I will come back and tell you about other profound wonders."

---

v One ancient translation by means of; *Latin* and.
13.31 Mt 24.7   **13.36** 2 Esd 7.26; Rev 21.2, 9   **13.40** 2 K 17.1-6

THE SEVENTH VISION

The Voice from the Bush

⁵⁷I went for a walk in the field, worshiping and praising God Most High for the miracles he performs in his own good time. ⁵⁸For he controls the ages and what happens in them. I remained there for three days.

14 On the third day, while I was sitting under an oak tree, ²suddenly a voice came out of a bush near me and called, "Ezra! Ezra!"

I stood up and answered, "Here I am, Lord."

A voice came out of a bush near me. (14.2)

³The voice continued, "I revealed myself from a bush and spoke to Moses when my people were slaves in Egypt. ⁴I sent him to lead them out of Egypt, and I brought them to Mount Sinai. I kept Moses with me there on the mountain for a long time, ⁵while I told him the secrets about the ages and the end of time. I told him ⁶what to make public and what to keep secret. ⁷Now I command you ⁸to memorize the signs, visions, and interpretations that I have given you. ⁹You will be taken out of this

world into the heavenly world where you and others like you will live with my son until the end of time. ¹⁰The world is no longer young; it is rapidly approaching old age. ¹¹The whole history of the world is divided into twelve periods, and the tenth period has already arrived ¹²and it is half over; only two and a half parts remain. ¹³So set your house in order, warn your people, comfort those who are humble, and teach those who are wise.ʷ Then say goodbye to this mortal life. ¹⁴Put earthly cares away from you, throw down your human burdens, and lay aside your weak human nature. ¹⁵Put all your anxieties aside, and get ready to leave this world quickly. ¹⁶You have seen many evil things already, but far worse things are about to happen. ¹⁷As the world grows older and weaker, the evils that will come upon its people will multiply. ¹⁸Truth will depart and falsehood will draw ever nearer. The eagle you saw in your vision is just about to arrive."

Ezra Reproduces the Sacred Writings

¹⁹I replied, "Let me speakˣ in your presence, Lord. ²⁰I am ready to depart, as you have commanded, and I will warn the present generation; but who will warn the people who have not yet been born? This world is a dark place, and its people have no light. ²¹Your Law has been destroyed by fire, so no one can know what you have done in the past or what you are planning to do in the future. ²²Please send your holy spirit to me, so that I can write down everything that has been done in this world from the beginning, everything that was written in your Law. Then in these last days, people will be able to find the right way and obtain life if they want to."

ʷ *Some ancient translations* teach . . . wise; *Latin does not have these words.*
ˣ *Some ancient translations* Let me speak; *Latin does not have these words.*
14.2 Ex 3.4

They took turns writing down what I said. (14.42)

²³ He answered, "Go and call the people together and tell them not to look for you for forty days. ²⁴ Prepare a large number of writing tablets, and take with you these five men who can write fast: Seraiah, Dabriah, Shelemiah, Ethan, and Asiel. ²⁵ Then come here, and I will light the lamp of understanding in your heart, and it will not go out until you have finished what you are supposed to write. ²⁶ When you have finished your work, you will make some of it public, and you will give the rest to some wise people, who will keep it secret. Tomorrow at this time you will begin to write."

²⁷ I did as I was commanded and called all the people together. I said, ²⁸ "Listen to what I have to say, people of Israel. ²⁹ At first our ancestors lived as foreigners in Egypt, but then they were set free ³⁰ and received from God the life-giving Law. But they did not keep it, and when your turn came, you did not keep it either. ³¹ God gave you the holy land as your own possession, but you were as sinful as your ancestors and did not follow the ways that God Most High had commanded. ³² God is a just judge, so after a while he took away

what he had given you. ³³ Now you are in exile here, but you are closer to Jerusalem than some of your own people. ʸ ³⁴ But if you will discipline your thoughts and be willing to learn, you will be kept safe in this life and will be granted mercy after death, ³⁵ for Judgment Day comes after death. We will be brought back to life, and the righteous people will be made known, while what the godless have done will be exposed. ³⁶ But now for forty days, no one is to come near me or try to find me."

³⁷ As I had been commanded, I took the five men, and we went to the field and stayed there. ³⁸ On the next day I suddenly heard a voice saying, "Ezra, open your mouth and drink what I am giving you." ³⁹ So I opened my mouth, and I was handed a cup full of a fiery-colored liquid, ⁴⁰ which I took and drank. When I had drunk it, my mind overflowed with understanding, and wisdom increased within me as my memory became perfect. ⁴¹ I began to speak and went on talking without stopping. ⁴² God Most High also gave wisdom to the five men with me, and they took turns writing down what I

ʸ but . . . own people; *Latin unclear.*

said. They used an alphabet[z] that they had not known before, and worked for forty days, writing in the daytime and eating at night. ⁴³I spoke all day long, and I was not silent even at night. ⁴⁴During the forty days, ninety-four[a] books were written.

⁴⁵At the end of the forty days, God Most High said to me, "You are now to make public the first twenty-four[b] books[c] that you wrote, so that everyone, whether they are worthy or not, may read them. ⁴⁶But the last seventy books that you wrote are to be held back and to be given only to those who are wise among your people, ⁴⁷because these books contain a flood of understanding, a fountain of wisdom, and a river of knowledge." ⁴⁸Then I did as I was told.

ADDITIONAL PROPHECIES

The Coming Disasters

15 The Lord says, "Proclaim to my people the prophetic messages that I will give you, ²and then have them written down, because they are true and will be fulfilled. ³Do not be afraid of those who plot against you or be disturbed by their unbelief. ⁴All unbelievers will die because of their unbelief."

⁵The Lord says, "I am going to bring terrible disasters on the whole world — war and famine, death and destruction, ⁶because wickedness has spread everywhere, and evil has reached its limit."

⁷"Therefore," the Lord says, ⁸"I will no longer remain silent about the wickedness of these godless people; I will no longer tolerate it. They have murdered innocent people, and the blood they have spilled cries out to me for revenge;

the souls of the righteous are constantly pleading for vengeance. ⁹Let there be no doubt," says the Lord, "I will hear the plea of all the innocent people who have been murdered and I will take vengeance for what has been done to them.

¹⁰"My people are being led to the slaughter like a flock of sheep. They will no longer have to live in Egypt; ¹¹I will use all my strength and power to bring them out of that land. I will bring disasters upon the Egyptians, as I did earlier, and I will destroy their country. ¹²The whole land will be in mourning; it will be shaken to its foundations when I, the Lord, strike it and pound on it. ¹³The farmers will mourn because their seed will fail to sprout, and their trees will be destroyed by blight, hail, and terrible storms.

¹⁴"The world and the people in it are doomed. ¹⁵The war that will bring their destruction is very near. Nations will arm themselves and fight against other nations. ¹⁶There will be great political turmoil, with one group trying to overpower another and gain control, while ignoring the legitimate government. ¹⁷There will no longer be free access to the cities, ¹⁸because the struggle for power will bring destruction, terror, and total confusion wherever people live. ¹⁹Driven by famine and terrible suffering, people will assault their neighbors and mercilessly plunder their possessions."

²⁰God says, "I am calling together all the kings of the earth to come from north, south, east, and west to turn back and restore what they have taken. ²¹I will pay them back with the same harsh treatment they have always given to my chosen people." The Lord says, ²²"I will use my power, and there

---

[z] *Some ancient translations* an alphabet; *Latin unclear.*   [a] *Some ancient translations* ninety-four; *Latin unclear.*   [b] *Some ancient translations* twenty-four; *Latin does not have this word.*   [c] TWENTY-FOUR BOOKS: *The Hebrew Bible contains twenty-four books, corresponding to the thirty-nine books of the Christian Old Testament.*

will be no mercy for sinners; I will put to death all who have murdered innocent people. 23 My anger has become so fierce that fire has blazed out to burn up the foundations of the earth and to burn up sinners like straw. 24 Sinners who do not keep my commands are doomed," says the Lord. 25 "I will have no mercy on them! Out of my sight, you rebels! Do not defile my holy Temple."

A Terrifying Vision

26 God is aware of all those who sin against him, and he will hand them over to death and destruction. 27 Terrible disasters have already come upon the world, and there is no escape. You have sinned against God, and he will not rescue you.

28 Then in the east you will suddenly see a fearsome sight. 29 Arab armies with many chariots will advance like dragons. As soon as they start out, the sound of their hissing will spread across the world and bring fear and trembling to everyone who hears it. 30 The Carmonians will come out of the forest in a fierce rage like wild boars advancing in full strength to attack the dragons. With their tusks they will tear up a large part of Assyria, 31 but the dragons will unite their forces, regain their former strength, and win the victory. They will turn and pursue the wild boars, 32 who will be thrown into panic, beaten into silence, and forced to turn and run. 33 The wild boars will be ambushed in Assyria, and one of them will be killed. This will bring fear and panic to their army and indecision to their kings.

34 Then suddenly clouds — terrible, angry storm clouds — will cover the sky from one end to the other. 35 They will collide head-on and release their violence upon the earth. The blood of war will be as deep as a horse's belly 36 or someone's thigh or a camel's knee. 37 Everywhere on earth people will tremble in fear at the horrible sight. 38 Then great storm clouds will move in from the north and the south, and others from the west. 39 But the winds from the east will prevail and push back those angry storm clouds that were about to bring destruction.d 40-41 Huge, powerful, angry storm clouds will arise and ruin the whole world and its people. A terrible storm of fire, hail, and flashing swords will come sweeping down on those who have power and authority.e Every river will overflow into the fields, and the floods 42 will demolish cities, walls, mountains, hills, forests, and crops. 43-44 This destruction will press on until it reaches Babylon and engulfs it in a raging storm of ruin. The dust and the smoke will form a great cloud reaching to the sky, and all the neighboring cities will mourn for Babylon. 45 Anyone who survives will become a slave to those who destroyed the city.

Asia Is Doomed

46-47 You, Asia, are to be pitied. You are doomed! You have enjoyed the splendor and glory of Babylon. You have imitated her and dressed up your daughters to look like prostitutes to please and gratify your lovers, who have always lusted for you. 48 Because you have imitated that vile prostitute in everything she has done or planned, God has this to say: 49 "I will send disasters upon you. I will make you a widow and send poverty, famine, war, and epidemics to destroy your homes and bring ruin and death. 50 The power of which you boast will wither like a flower when the burning heat is sent upon you. 51 You will be a wretched, weak woman so bruised, beaten, and wounded that

---

d Verse 39 in Latin is unclear.   e those who have power and authority; or every hill and mountain.

15.46-48 Rev 14.8; 17.4, 5

you will no longer attract your wealthy lovers. ⁵²I would not punish you so severely," says the Lord, ⁵³"if you had not murdered my chosen people. But you took great delight in striking them, and when you were drunk, you boasted about killing them.

⁵⁴"Paint your face! ⁵⁵You will be paid for your work as a prostitute; you will get what you have earned. ⁵⁶I will pay you back," says the Lord, "for what you have done to my chosen people. I will bring disaster on you. ⁵⁷You will be put to death, and your children will starve. Your cities will be torn down, and the people out in the country will be killed. ⁵⁸Those in the mountains will starve; their hunger and thirst will drive them to eat their own flesh and drink their own blood. ⁵⁹You will be more miserable than anyone has ever been, but there will be still more punishment to come. ⁶⁰The army that destroyed Babylon will march back through your country and devastate your peaceful city; they will destroy your beautiful country and leave most of it in ruins. ⁶¹Your country will be destroyed like straw in a fire. ⁶²They will burn up all your forests and orchards. All over your land, your cities and mountains will be covered with ruins. ⁶³Your splendor will vanish; your children will be carried off as prisoners; your possessions will be plundered."

16 Babylonia, Asia, Egypt, and Syria, you are doomed! ²Put on your clothes of mourning, your sackcloth and goat's hair. Cry and wail for your children because the time for your destruction is near. ³I am sending war on you, and no one can stop it. ⁴I am sending fire on you, and no one can put it out. ⁵I am sending disasters on you, and no one can stop them from coming. ⁶Can anyone stop a hungry lion in the forest or put out a fire that is burning in straw ⁷or turn back an arrow shot by a strong archer? ⁸When the Lord God sends disaster, no one can hold it back. ⁹No one can escape the blazing anger

of the Lord. ¹⁰When he sends lightning, no one can keep from trembling; and when it thunders, everyone is afraid. ¹¹When the Lord makes his threats, no one can keep from falling to the ground in his presence. ¹²The foundations of the earth tremble. There is violent churning in the deepest part of the sea. Even the creatures in the sea are in turmoil when the Lord makes his glorious power felt. ¹³He is like a mighty archer whose strong right arm bends the bow. His arrows are sharp and never miss their mark once they are shot out toward any part of the earth. ¹⁴He has already sent out his disasters toward the earth, and they will not miss their target. ¹⁵The fire has been lit, and it cannot be put out until it burns up the foundations of the earth. ¹⁶The disasters are on their way toward the earth, and like an arrow shot by a strong archer, they cannot be turned back.

¹⁷I'm doomed! I'm doomed! Who will rescue me in those days? ¹⁸Troubles will come, and many people will groan. Famine will come, and many will die. Wars will come, and the world powers will tremble. Disasters will come, and everyone will be terrified. What will people do when these disasters come?

Troubles will come, and many people will groan. (16.18)

¹⁹Famine, epidemics, troubles, and suffering are sent to punish and correct people. ²⁰But in spite of all this, they will not turn away from their sins; they soon forget their punishment. ²¹The time is coming when food will be so cheap that people will think a time of peace and plenty has arrived. But then disasters will spring up everywhere — wars, famine, and great confusion. ²²Many people on earth will starve to death, and those who escape starvation will be killed in war. ²³Their corpses will be thrown out like garbage, and there will be no one left to comfort the living. The earth will be deserted and its cities demolished. ²⁴There will be no one left to plow the land or plant it. ²⁵Trees will bear their fruit, but there will be no one left to pick it. ²⁶Grapes will ripen, but there will be no one left to make wine. There will be desolation everywhere, ²⁷and a person will long to see the face of another human being or even to hear another person's voice. ²⁸Only ten will be left out of a whole city, and in the countryside, only two, who have hidden in the forest or in caves. ²⁹When an olive grove is harvested, three or four olives may be left on each tree. ³⁰When grapes in a vineyard are picked, a few bunches may be left even by those who look carefully. ³¹That is how it will be in those days. Three or four will be missed by the soldiers who search through the houses to kill everyone. ³²The land will be left empty; the fields will be overgrown with briers; the roads and paths will be covered with weeds and thorns because there will be no sheep to graze along them. ³³Young women will be in mourning because there is no one to marry them; wives will be in mourning because they have lost their husbands; daughters will be in mourning because there is no one to help them. ³⁴All the young men will be killed in the war, and all the married men will die in the famine.

God's People Must Prepare for the End

³⁵Now listen to my message, you people who serve the Lord. ³⁶It is the Lord's message, so receive it and believe what he says. ³⁷The disasters are approaching rapidly, and they will not be delayed. ³⁸A woman in the ninth month of pregnancy may suffer labor pains for several hours, but when the time comes for the baby to be born, there is no longer any delay. ³⁹In the same way, the disasters that are coming on the earth will not be delayed, and the world will groan when it is caught in its labor pains.

⁴⁰Listen to my message, my people, and get ready for the battle. When the disasters come, you must live as people whose home is not in this world. ⁴¹⁻⁴²Merchants must not expect to make a profit from what they sell; they must be ready to run for their lives. Their customers must expect to lose whatever they buy. Whoever builds a house should not plan to live in it. ⁴³Farmers should not expect to harvest their crops or pick their grapes. ⁴⁴Those who marry must not expect to have children, and those who don't marry must live as if they had been widowed. ⁴⁵Anything that is done will be useless. ⁴⁶Foreigners will harvest the crops, seize the wealth, tear down the houses, and carry off the children as slaves. Anyone who has children will be bringing them up to be slaves or to die of starvation. ⁴⁷Anyone who makes money will do so only to see it violently taken away. The more possessions people gather, the more they spend on their cities and houses, the more attention they give to their personal appearance, ⁴⁸the more angry the Lord will become with them because of their sin. This is what the Lord says. ⁴⁹Just as a respectable woman despises a prostitute, ⁵⁰so righteousness despises sinfulness, no matter how attractive it may look. Righteousness will expose every sin in

the world and condemn it face-to-face when her Defender comes. ⁵¹So do not imitate sinfulness or what it does, ⁵²for in a very short time sinfulness will be swept out of the world and righteousness will rule among us.

⁵³Sinners must not deny their sins. Those who say that they have not sinned against God and his majesty are only bringing fiery shame upon themselves. ⁵⁴The Lord certainly knows everything that people do; he knows their plans and innermost thoughts. ⁵⁵When the Lord said, "Let the world be created," it was done! When he said, "Let the sky be created," that was done too. ⁵⁶He set the stars in place by his command, and he knows how many of them there are. ⁵⁷He knows what is in the deepest part of the sea and the treasures that are there. He has measured the sea and everything that is in it. ⁵⁸By his word he confined the sea to its place and put the land on top of the water. ⁵⁹The Lord stretched out the sky and fixed it firmly over the water like a dome. ⁶⁰He put springs of water in the desert and lakes in the high mountains, so that water could flow down in the rivers and water the land. ⁶¹The Lord created human beings and gave each one of them a heart. He gave them life, breath, and understanding, ⁶²which is the spirit of God the Almighty, who created everything and who knows all secrets and sees into all hidden places. ⁶³My people, the Lord knows everything you plan and the secret thoughts of your heart. Sinners who try to hide their sins are doomed. ⁶⁴The Lord will carefully examine everything you have done and bring you to judgment. ⁶⁵On that day you will be thrown into utter

confusion; all your sins will be publicly exposed and the wicked things you have done will witness against you. ⁶⁶What will you do then? How will you hide your sins from God and his angels? ⁶⁷God is your judge, so fear him! Abandon your sins, put away the evil you have done, and never sin again. Then God will save you from all these disasters.

⁶⁸A vast mob of people is ready now to descend on you and devour you like flames. They will drag some of you off and force you to eat pagan sacrifices. ⁶⁹If you give in to them, they will ridicule you, mock you, and humiliate you. ⁷⁰In many places near the cities ᶠ there will be violent persecution against those who fear the Lord. ⁷¹The attackers will act like wild people; they will plunder and destroy without pity all those who still fear the Lord. ⁷²They will turn them out of their homes and take away all their possessions. ⁷³This will be the time of testing for my chosen people, and they will prove to be as pure as refined gold.

⁷⁴But listen to what the Lord says: "My chosen people, the time of terrible suffering is near, but I will rescue you. ⁷⁵Don't be afraid or have any doubts; I am your God and I will lead you. ⁷⁶If you keep my laws and commands," says the Lord, "you must not let your sins weigh you down or control you. ⁷⁷Those who are chained by their sins, overwhelmed by the evil they have done, are doomed. They will be like a field overgrown with brush, with the path across it so choked with thorns that no one can get through. ⁷⁸It is abandoned and doomed to be destroyed by fire."

ᶠ In ... cities; *Latin unclear.*
16.73 Zec 13.9; 1 P 1.7

THE PRAYER OF MANASSEH

INTRODUCTION

The Prayer of Manasseh is a beautiful short prayer of repentance. It is presented as a prayer by Manasseh, the wicked king of Judah, referred to in *2 Chronicles 33.12,18,19.*

1 Lord Almighty, God of our
ancestors,
God of Abraham, Isaac,
and Jacob,
God of their righteous
descendants,
2 you created the universe
and all the splendor that
fills it.
3 The sea obeys your command
and never overflows its
bounds.
The power of your wonderful,
glorious name
keeps the ocean depths in
their place.
4 When you show your power,
all creation trembles.
5 Your glorious splendor is
overwhelming,
and your anger is more than
sinners can endure.
6 But the mercy you promise is
also greater
than we can understand or
measure.
7 For you are the Lord Most High;
you are patient and show
mercy and compassion.
You make our punishment easier
to bear
when we suffer for our sins.

O Lord, in your great goodness
and mercy
you promise forgiveness and
salvation
to those who repent of their
sin against you. *a*
8 You, Lord, are the God of
righteous people.
Repentance was not necessary
for Abraham, Isaac, and
Jacob,
for they did not sin
against you.
But for sinners like me
you have made repentance
possible.
9 I have committed more sins
than there are grains of sand
along the seashore.
They are so many, Lord, they
are so many.
I have done so much that is
wrong
that I am not worthy to turn
my face toward heaven.
10 I am crushed beneath the weight
of my sin; *b*
I am bowed down by its heavy
iron chain.
I can find no relief,
for I have made you angry.

---

a O Lord ... against you; *some manuscripts do not have these words.*   *b crushed
... my sin; Greek unclear.*
1 2 Ch 33.11-13, 18, 19   **9** 2 K 21.1-18

I have set up idols
everywhere;
I have done what you hate.

11 But now I bow in deep humility,
praying for your mercy.

12 I have sinned, Lord, I have
sinned;
I confess the wicked things
I have done.

13 I beg you, Lord, I earnestly pray:
forgive me, forgive me.
Do not destroy me because of
my sins;
do not stay angry with me
forever

or store up punishment for me.
Do not condemn me to the world
of the dead,
for you, O Lord, forgive those
who repent.

14 Show me all your mercy and
kindness and save me,
even though I do not
deserve it.

15 Then I will go on praising you as
long as I live.
All the heavenly powers sing
your praises,
and your glory endures
forever. Amen.

NEW TESTAMENT

PALESTINE IN THE TIME OF JESUS

Miles
0   40

Kms
0   40

MEDITERRANEAN

SEA

PHOENICIA

LEBANON MTS.

SYRIA

Abila
ABILENE

Damascus

MT. HERMON

Sidon

Zarephath

Tyre

Caesarea Philippi

GALILEE

Ptolemais

Chorazin
Capernaum
Magadan

Bethsaida

Lake
Galilee

Cana   Tiberias

MT. CARMEL

Nazareth
MT. TABOR

Nain

Gadara

TEN TOWNS

Caesarea

Salim
Aenon

SAMARIA

Samaria

MT. EBAL

MT. GERIZIM Sychar

Gerasa

Jordan River

P E R E A

Joppa

Arimathea?

Ephraim

Jericho

Azotus

Emmaus
Jerusalem Bethany
Qumran

Ascalon

JUDEA

Bethlehem

Gaza

Hebron

Dead

Sea

IDUMEA

N A B A T E A

© United Bible Societies, 1976

The Gospel according to
MATTHEW

INTRODUCTION

The Gospel according to Matthew tells the good news that Jesus is the promised Savior, the one through whom God fulfilled the promises he made to his people in the Old Testament. This good news is not only for the Jewish people, among whom Jesus was born and lived, but for the whole world.

Matthew is carefully arranged. It begins with the birth of Jesus, describes his baptism and temptation, and then takes up his ministry of preaching, teaching, and healing in Galilee. After this the Gospel records Jesus' journey from Galilee to Jerusalem and the events of Jesus' last week, culminating in his crucifixion and resurrection.

This Gospel presents Jesus as the great Teacher, who has the authority to interpret the Law of God, and who teaches about the Kingdom of God. Much of his teaching is gathered by subject matter into five collections: (1) the Sermon on the Mount, which concerns the character, duties, privileges, and destiny of the citizens of the Kingdom of heaven (chapters 5–7); (2) instructions to the twelve disciples for their mission (chapter 10); (3) parables about the Kingdom of heaven (chapter 13); (4) teaching on the meaning of discipleship (chapter 18); and (5) teaching about the end of the present age and the coming of the Kingdom of God (chapters 24–25).

OUTLINE OF CONTENTS

The Ancestors of Jesus Christ
(Luke 3.23-38)

1 This is the list of the ancestors of Jesus Christ, a descendant of David, who was a descendant of Abraham. ²⁻⁶ᵃ From Abraham to King David, the following ancestors are listed: Abraham, Isaac, Jacob, Judah and his brothers; then Perez and Zerah (their mother was Tamar), Hezron, Ram, Amminadab, Nahshon, Salmon, Boaz (his mother was Rahab), Obed (his mother was Ruth), Jesse, and King David.

⁶ᵇ⁻¹¹ From David to the time when the people of Israel were taken into exile in Babylon, the following ancestors are listed: David, Solomon (his mother was

1.11 2 K 24.14, 15; 2 Ch 36.10; Jr 27.20

the woman who had been Uriah's wife), Rehoboam, Abijah, Asa, Jehoshaphat, Jehoram, Uzziah, Jotham, Ahaz, Hezekiah, Manasseh, Amon, Josiah, and Jehoiachin and his brothers.

12-16 From the time after the exile in Babylon to the birth of Jesus, the following ancestors are listed: Jehoiachin, Shealtiel, Zerubbabel, Abiud, Eliakim, Azor, Zadok, Achim, Eliud, Eleazar, Matthan, Jacob, and Joseph, who married Mary, the mother of Jesus, who was called the Messiah.

17 So then, there were fourteen generations from Abraham to David, and fourteen from David to the exile in Babylon, and fourteen from then to the birth of the Messiah.

The Birth of Jesus Christ
(Luke 2.1-7)

18 This was how the birth of Jesus Christ took place. His mother Mary was engaged to Joseph, but before they were married, she found out that she was going to have a baby by the Holy Spirit. 19 Joseph was a man who always did what was right, but he did not want to disgrace Mary publicly; so he made plans to break the engagement privately. 20 While he was thinking about this, an angel of the Lord appeared to him in a dream and said, "Joseph, descendant of David, do not be afraid to take Mary to be your wife. For it is by the Holy Spirit that she has conceived. 21 She will have a son, and you will name him Jesus — because he will save his people from their sins."

22 Now all this happened in order to make come true what the Lord had said through the prophet, 23 "A virgin will become pregnant and have a son, and he will be called Immanuel" (which means, "God is with us").

24 So when Joseph woke up, he married Mary, as the angel of the Lord had told him to. 25 But he had no sexual rela-tions with her before she gave birth to her son. And Joseph named him Jesus.

Visitors from the East

2 Jesus was born in the town of Bethlehem in Judea, during the time when Herod was king. Soon afterward, some men who studied the stars came from the East to Jerusalem 2 and asked, "Where is the baby born to be the king of the Jews? We saw his star when it came up in the east, and we have come to worship him."

3 When King Herod heard about this, he was very upset, and so was everyone else in Jerusalem. 4 He called together all the chief priests and the teachers of the Law and asked them, "Where will the Messiah be born?"

5 "In the town of Bethlehem in Judea," they answered. "For this is what the prophet wrote:

6 'Bethlehem in the land of Judah,
    you are by no means the least
        of the leading cities of
            Judah;
    for from you will come a leader
        who will guide my people
            Israel.'"

7 So Herod called the visitors from the East to a secret meeting and found out from them the exact time the star had appeared. 8 Then he sent them to Bethlehem with these instructions: "Go and make a careful search for the child; and when you find him, let me know, so that I too may go and worship him."

9-10 And so they left, and on their way they saw the same star they had seen in the East. When they saw it, how happy they were, what joy was theirs! It went ahead of them until it stopped over the place where the child was. 11 They went into the house, and when they saw the child with his mother Mary, they knelt down and worshiped him. They brought out their gifts of gold, frankin-

---

1.18 Lk 1.27   **1.21** Si 46.1; Lk 1.31   **1.23** Is 7.14 (LXX)   **1.25** Lk 2.21   **2.6** Mic 5.2

The star . . . went ahead of them. (2.9-10)

cense, and myrrh, and presented them to him.

¹²Then they returned to their country by another road, since God had warned them in a dream not to go back to Herod.

The Escape to Egypt

¹³After they had left, an angel of the Lord appeared in a dream to Joseph and said, "Herod will be looking for the child in order to kill him. So get up, take the child and his mother and escape to Egypt, and stay there until I tell you to leave."

¹⁴Joseph got up, took the child and his mother, and left during the night for Egypt, ¹⁵where he stayed until Herod died. This was done to make come true what the Lord had said through the prophet, "I called my Son out of Egypt."

The Killing of the Children

¹⁶When Herod realized that the visitors from the East had tricked him, he was furious. He gave orders to kill all the boys in Bethlehem and its neighborhood who were two years old and younger — this was done in accordance with what he had learned from the visitors about the time when the star had appeared.

¹⁷In this way what the prophet Jeremiah had said came true:
¹⁸"A sound is heard in Ramah,
 the sound of bitter weeping.
 Rachel is crying for her children;
  she refuses to be comforted,
  for they are dead."

The Return from Egypt

¹⁹After Herod died, an angel of the Lord appeared in a dream to Joseph in Egypt ²⁰and said, "Get up, take the child and his mother, and go back to the land of Israel, because those who tried to kill the child are dead." ²¹So Joseph got up, took the child and his mother, and went back to Israel.

²²But when Joseph heard that Archelaus had succeeded his father Herod as king of Judea, he was afraid to go there. He was given more instructions in a dream, so he went to the province of Galilee ²³and made his home in a town named Nazareth. And so what the prophets had said came true: "He will be called a Nazarene."

The Preaching of John the Baptist
(Mark 1.1-8; Luke 3.1-18; John 1.19-28)

3 At that time John the Baptist came to the desert of Judea and started preaching. ²"Turn away from your sins," he said, "because the Kingdom of heaven is near!" ³John was the man the prophet Isaiah was talking about when he said,
  "Someone is shouting in the
   desert,
  'Prepare a road for the Lord;
   make a straight path for him
   to travel!'"
⁴John's clothes were made of camel's hair; he wore a leather belt around his waist, and his food was locusts and wild honey. ⁵People came to him from Jerusalem, from the whole province of Judea, and from all over the country near

---

2.15 Ho 11.1   **2.18** Jr 31.15   **2.23** Mk 1.24; Lk 2.39; Jn 1.45   **3.2** Mt 4.17; Mk 1.15
3.3 Is 40.3 (LXX)   **3.4** 2 K 1.8

the Jordan River. ⁶They confessed their sins, and he baptized them in the Jordan.

⁷When John saw many Pharisees and Sadducees coming to him to be baptized, he said to them, "You snakes — who told you that you could escape from the punishment God is about to send? ⁸Do those things that will show that you have turned from your sins. ⁹And don't think you can escape punishment by saying that Abraham is your ancestor. I tell you that God can take these rocks and make descendants for Abraham! ¹⁰The ax is ready to cut down the trees at the roots; every tree that does not bear good fruit will be cut down and thrown in the fire. ¹¹I baptize you with water to show that you have repented, but the one who will come after me will baptize you with the Holy Spirit and fire. He is much greater than I am; and I am not good enough even to carry his sandals. ¹²He has his winnowing shovel with him to thresh out all the grain. He will gather his wheat into his barn, but he will burn the chaff in a fire that never goes out."

The Baptism of Jesus
(Mark 1.9-11; Luke 3.21, 22)

¹³At that time Jesus arrived from Galilee and came to John at the Jordan to be baptized by him. ¹⁴But John tried to make him change his mind. "I ought to be baptized by you," John said, "and yet you have come to me!"

¹⁵But Jesus answered him, "Let it be so for now. For in this way we shall do all that God requires." So John agreed.

¹⁶As soon as Jesus was baptized, he came up out of the water. Then heaven was opened to him, and he saw the Spirit of God coming down like a dove and lighting on him. ¹⁷Then a voice said from heaven, "This is my own dear Son, with whom I am pleased."

The Temptation of Jesus
(Mark 1.12, 13; Luke 4.1-13)

4 Then the Spirit led Jesus into the desert to be tempted by the Devil. ²After spending forty days and nights without food, Jesus was hungry. ³Then the Devil came to him and said, "If you are God's Son, order these stones to turn into bread."

"Order these stones to turn into bread!" (4.3)

⁴But Jesus answered, "The scripture says, 'Human beings cannot live on bread alone, but need every word that God speaks.'"

⁵Then the Devil took Jesus to Jerusalem, the Holy City, set him on the highest point of the Temple, ⁶and said to him, "If you are God's Son, throw yourself down, for the scripture says,

'God will give orders to his
    angels about you;
they will hold you up with
    their hands,
so that not even your feet will
    be hurt on the stones.'"

⁷Jesus answered, "But the scripture also says, 'Do not put the Lord your God to the test.'"

3.7 Mt 12.34; 23.33   **3.9** Jn 8.33   **3.10** Mt 7.19   **3.12** Ws 5.14, 23   **3.17** Gn 22.2; Ps 2.7; Is 42.1; Mt 12.18; 17.5; Mk 1.11; Lk 9.35   **4.1** He 2.18; 4.15   **4.4** Dt 8.3   **4.6** Ps 91.11, 12   **4.7** Dt 6.16

⁸Then the Devil took Jesus to a very high mountain and showed him all the kingdoms of the world in all their greatness. ⁹"All this I will give you," the Devil said, "if you kneel down and worship me."

¹⁰Then Jesus answered, "Go away, Satan! The scripture says, 'Worship the Lord your God and serve only him!'"

¹¹Then the Devil left Jesus; and angels came and helped him.

Jesus Begins His Work in Galilee
(Mark 1.14, 15; Luke 4.14, 15)

¹²When Jesus heard that John had been put in prison, he went away to Galilee. ¹³He did not stay in Nazareth, but went to live in Capernaum, a town by Lake Galilee, in the territory of Zebulun and Naphtali. ¹⁴This was done to make come true what the prophet Isaiah had said,

¹⁵"Land of Zebulun and land of Naphtali,
  on the road to the sea, on the other side of the Jordan,
  Galilee, land of the Gentiles!
¹⁶The people who live in darkness will see a great light.
  On those who live in the dark land of death
    the light will shine."

¹⁷From that time Jesus began to preach his message: "Turn away from your sins, because the Kingdom of heaven is near!"

Jesus Calls Four Fishermen
(Mark 1.16-20; Luke 5.1-11)

¹⁸As Jesus walked along the shore of Lake Galilee, he saw two brothers who were fishermen, Simon (called Peter) and his brother Andrew, catching fish in the lake with a net. ¹⁹Jesus said to them, "Come with me, and I will teach you to catch people." ²⁰At once they left their nets and went with him.

²¹He went on and saw two other brothers, James and John, the sons of Zebedee. They were in their boat with their father Zebedee, getting their nets ready. Jesus called them, ²²and at once they left the boat and their father, and went with him.

Jesus Teaches, Preaches, and Heals
(Luke 6.17-19)

²³Jesus went all over Galilee, teaching in the synagogues, preaching the Good News about the Kingdom, and healing people who had all kinds of disease and sickness. ²⁴The news about him spread through the whole country of Syria, so that people brought to him all those who were sick, suffering from all kinds of diseases and disorders: people with demons, and epileptics, and paralytics — and Jesus healed them all. ²⁵Large crowds followed him from Galilee and the Ten Towns, from Jerusalem, Judea, and the land on the other side of the Jordan.

The Sermon on the Mount

5 Jesus saw the crowds and went up a hill, where he sat down. His disciples gathered around him, ²and he began to teach them:

True Happiness
(Luke 6.20-23)

³"Happy are those who know they are spiritually poor;
  the Kingdom of heaven belongs to them!
⁴"Happy are those who mourn;
  God will comfort them!
⁵"Happy are those who are humble;
  they will receive what God has promised!

4.10 Dt 6.13   4.12 Mt 14.3; Mk 6.17; Lk 3.19, 20   4.13 Jn 2.12   4.15, 16 Is 9.1, 2
4.17 Mt 3.2   4.23 Mt 9.35; Mk 1.39   5.4 Is 61.2   5.5 Ps 37.11

6"Happy are those whose greatest
desire is to do what
God requires;
God will satisfy them fully!
7"Happy are those who are
merciful to others;
God will be merciful to them!
8"Happy are the pure in heart;
they will see God!
9"Happy are those who work for
peace;
God will call them his
children!
10"Happy are those who are
persecuted because they
do what God requires;
the Kingdom of heaven
belongs to them!
11"Happy are you when people insult
you and persecute you and tell all kinds
of evil lies against you because you are
my followers. 12Be happy and glad, for
a great reward is kept for you in heaven.
This is how the prophets who lived before you were persecuted.

Salt and Light
(Mark 9.50; Luke 14.34, 35)

13"You are like salt for the whole
human race. But if salt loses its saltiness, there is no way to make it salty
again. It has become worthless, so it is
thrown out and people trample on it.
14"You are like light for the whole
world. A city built on a hill cannot be
hid. 15No one lights a lamp and puts it
under a bowl; instead it is put on the
lampstand, where it gives light for
everyone in the house. 16In the same
way your light must shine before people, so that they will see the good things
you do and praise your Father in
heaven.

Teaching about the Law

17"Do not think that I have come to
do away with the Law of Moses and the
teachings of the prophets. I have not
come to do away with them, but to
make their teachings come true. 18Re-
member that as long as heaven and
earth last, not the least point nor the
smallest detail of the Law will be done
away with—not until the end of all
things.ᵃ 19So then, whoever disobeys
even the least important of the commandments and teaches others to do
the same, will be least in the Kingdom
of heaven. On the other hand, whoever
obeys the Law and teaches others to do
the same, will be great in the Kingdom
of heaven. 20I tell you, then, that you
will be able to enter the Kingdom of
heaven only if you are more faithful
than the teachers of the Law and the
Pharisees in doing what God requires.

Teaching about Anger

21"You have heard that people were
told in the past, 'Do not commit murder; anyone who does will be brought to
trial.' 22But now I tell you: if you are an-
gryᵇ with your brother you will be
brought to trial, if you call your brother
'You good-for-nothing!' you will be
brought before the Council, and if
you call your brother a worthless fool
you will be in danger of going to the fire
of hell. 23So if you are about to offer
your gift to God at the altar and there
you remember that your brother has
something against you, 24leave your
gift there in front of the altar, go at once
and make peace with your brother,
and then come back and offer your
gift to God.
25"If someone brings a lawsuit
against you and takes you to court, set-

ᵃ the end of all things; *or* all its teachings come true.   ᵇ if you are angry; *some manuscripts have* if without cause you are angry.

5.6 Is 55.1, 2; Si 24.21   **5.8** Ps 24.3, 4; 2 Esd 7.98   **5.10** 1 P 3.14   **5.11** 1 P 4.14
5.12 2 Ch 36.16; Si 2.8; Ac 7.52   **5.13** Mk 9.50; Lk 14.34, 35   **5.14** Jn 8.12; 9.5
5.15 Mk 4.21; Lk 8.16; 11.33   **5.16** 1 P 2.12   **5.18** Lk 16.17   **5.21** Ex 20.13; Dt 5.17

tle the dispute while there is time, before you get to court. Once you are there, you will be turned over to the judge, who will hand you over to the police, and you will be put in jail. 26 There you will stay, I tell you, until you pay the last penny of your fine.

Teaching about Adultery

27 "You have heard that it was said, 'Do not commit adultery.' 28 But now I tell you: anyone who looks at a woman and wants to possess her is guilty of committing adultery with her in his heart. 29 So if your right eye causes you to sin, take it out and throw it away! It is much better for you to lose a part of your body than to have your whole body thrown into hell. 30 If your right hand causes you to sin, cut it off and throw it away! It is much better for you to lose one of your limbs than to have your whole body go off to hell.

Teaching about Divorce
(Matthew 19.9; Mark 10.11, 12; Luke 16.18)

31 "It was also said, 'Anyone who divorces his wife must give her a written notice of divorce.' 32 But now I tell you: if a man divorces his wife for any cause other than her unfaithfulness, then he is guilty of making her commit adultery if she marries again; and the man who marries her commits adultery also.

Teaching about Vows

33 "You have also heard that people were told in the past, 'Do not break your promise, but do what you have vowed to the Lord to do.' 34 But now I tell you: do not use any vow when you make a promise. Do not swear by heaven, for it is God's throne; 35 nor by earth, for it is

the resting place for his feet; nor by Jerusalem, for it is the city of the great King. 36 Do not even swear by your head, because you cannot make a single hair white or black. 37 Just say 'Yes' or 'No' — anything else you say comes from the Evil One.

Teaching about Revenge
(Luke 6.29, 30)

38 "You have heard that it was said, 'An eye for an eye, and a tooth for a tooth.' 39 But now I tell you: do not take revenge on someone who wrongs you. If anyone slaps you on the right cheek, let him slap your left cheek too. 40 And if someone takes you to court to sue you for your shirt, let him have your coat as well. 41 And if one of the occupation troops forces you to carry his pack one mile, carry it two miles. 42 When someone asks you for something, give it to him; when someone wants to borrow something, lend it to him.

Love for Enemies
(Luke 6.27, 28, 32-36)

43 "You have heard that it was said, 'Love your friends, hate your enemies.' 44 But now I tell you: love your enemies and pray for those who persecute you, 45 so that you may become the children of your Father in heaven. For he makes his sun to shine on bad and good people alike, and gives rain to those who do good and to those who do evil. 46 Why should God reward you if you love only the people who love you? Even the tax collectors do that! 47 And if you speak only to your friends, have you done anything out of the ordinary? Even the pagans do that! 48 You must be perfect — just as your Father in heaven is perfect.

5.27 Ex 20.14; Dt 5.18   **5.29** Mt 18.9; Mk 9.47   **5.30** Mt 18.8; Mk 9.43   **5.31** Dt 24.1-4; Mt 19.7; Mk 10.4   **5.32** Mt 19.9; Mk 10.11, 12; Lk 16.18; 1 Co 7.10, 11   **5.33 a** Lv 19.12; **b** Nu 30.2; Dt 23.21   **5.34 a** Jas 5.12; **b** Is 66.1; Mt 23.22   **5.35 a** Is 66.1; **b** Ps 48.2 **5.38** Ex 21.24; Lv 24.20; Dt 19.21   **5.43** Si 12.4-7   **5.45** Si 4.10   **5.48** Lv 19.2; Dt 18.13

Teaching about Charity

6 "Make certain you do not perform your religious duties in public so that people will see what you do. If you do these things publicly, you will not have any reward from your Father in heaven.

2 "So when you give something to a needy person, do not make a big show of it, as the hypocrites do in the houses of worship and on the streets. They do it so that people will praise them. I assure you, they have already been paid

Do not make a big show of it. (6.2)

in full. 3 But when you help a needy person, do it in such a way that even your closest friend will not know about it. 4 Then it will be a private matter. And your Father, who sees what you do in private, will reward you.

Teaching about Prayer
(Luke 11.2-4)

5 "When you pray, do not be like the hypocrites! They love to stand up and pray in the houses of worship and on the street corners, so that everyone will see them. I assure you, they have al-

ready been paid in full. 6 But when you pray, go to your room, close the door, and pray to your Father, who is unseen. And your Father, who sees what you do in private, will reward you.

7 "When you pray, do not use a lot of meaningless words, as the pagans do, who think that their gods will hear them because their prayers are long. 8 Do not be like them. Your Father already knows what you need before you ask him. 9 This, then, is how you should pray:

'Our Father in heaven:
    May your holy name be
        honored;
10   may your Kingdom come;
    may your will be done on
        earth as it is in
        heaven.
11   Give us today the food we
        need.*c*
12   Forgive us the wrongs we
        have done,
        as we forgive the wrongs
            that others have done
            to us.
13   Do not bring us to hard
        testing,
        but keep us safe from the
            Evil One.'*d*

14 "If you forgive others the wrongs they have done to you, your Father in heaven will also forgive you. 15 But if you do not forgive others, then your Father will not forgive the wrongs you have done.

Teaching about Fasting

16 "And when you fast, do not put on a sad face as the hypocrites do. They neglect their appearance so that everyone will see that they are fasting. I assure you, they have already been paid in full. 17 When you go without food,

c we need; or for today, or for tomorrow.   *d Some manuscripts add For yours is the kingdom, and the power, and the glory forever. Amen.*

6.1 Mt 23.5   **6.5** Lk 18.10-14   **6.7** Si 7.14   **6.14, 15** Mk 11.25, 26   **6.14** Si 28.1-5   **6.17** Jdt 10.3

wash your face and comb your hair, [18] so that others cannot know that you are fasting — only your Father, who is unseen, will know. And your Father, who sees what you do in private, will reward you.

Riches in Heaven
(Luke 12.33, 34)

[19] "Do not store up riches for yourselves here on earth, where moths and rust destroy, and robbers break in and steal. [20] Instead, store up riches for yourselves in heaven, where moths and rust cannot destroy, and robbers cannot break in and steal. [21] For your heart will always be where your riches are.

The Light of the Body
(Luke 11.34-36)

[22] "The eyes are like a lamp for the body. If your eyes are sound, your whole body will be full of light; [23] but if your eyes are no good, your body will be in darkness. So if the light in you is darkness, how terribly dark it will be!

God and Possessions
(Luke 16.13; 12.22-31)

[24] "You cannot be a slave of two masters; you will hate one and love the other; you will be loyal to one and despise the other. You cannot serve both God and money.

[25] "This is why I tell you: do not be worried about the food and drink you need in order to stay alive, or about clothes for your body. After all, isn't life worth more than food? And isn't the body worth more than clothes? [26] Look at the birds: they do not plant seeds, gather a harvest and put it in barns; yet your Father in heaven takes care of them! Aren't you worth much more

than birds? [27] Can any of you live a bit longer [e] by worrying about it?

[28] "And why worry about clothes? Look how the wild flowers grow: they do not work or make clothes for themselves. [29] But I tell you that not even King Solomon with all his wealth had clothes as beautiful as one of these flowers. [30] It is God who clothes the wild grass — grass that is here today and gone tomorrow, burned up in the oven. Won't he be all the more sure to clothe you? What little faith you have!

Aren't you worth much more than birds? (6.26)

[31] "So do not start worrying: 'Where will my food come from? or my drink? or my clothes?' [32] (These are the things the pagans are always concerned about.) Your Father in heaven knows that you need all these things. [33] Instead, be concerned above everything else with the Kingdom of God and with what he requires of you, and he will provide you with all these other things. [34] So do not worry about tomorrow; it will have enough worries of its own. There is no need to add to the troubles each day brings.

Judging Others
(Luke 6.37, 38, 41, 42)

7 "Do not judge others, so that God will not judge you, [2] for God will judge you in the same way you judge others, and he will apply to you the

---

[e] live a bit longer; *or* grow a bit taller.

6.19 Jas 5.2, 3   **6.20** Si 29.11   **6.29** 1 K 10.4-7; 2 Ch 9.3-6   **7.2** Mk 4.24

same rules you apply to others. ³Why, then, do you look at the speck in your brother's eye and pay no attention to the log in your own eye? ⁴How dare you say to your brother, 'Please, let me take that speck out of your eye,' when you have a log in your own eye? ⁵You hypocrite! First take the log out of your own eye, and then you will be able to see clearly to take the speck out of your brother's eye.

⁶"Do not give what is holy to dogs — they will only turn and attack you. Do not throw your pearls in front of pigs — they will only trample them underfoot.

Ask, Seek, Knock
(Luke 11.9-13)

⁷"Ask, and you will receive; seek, and you will find; knock, and the door will be opened to you. ⁸For everyone who asks will receive, and anyone who seeks will find, and the door will be opened to those who knock. ⁹Would any of you who are fathers give your son a stone when he asks for bread? ¹⁰Or would you give him a snake when he asks for a fish? ¹¹As bad as you are, you know how to give good things to your children. How much more, then, will your Father in heaven give good things to those who ask him!

¹²"Do for others what you want them to do for you: this is the meaning of the Law of Moses and of the teachings of the prophets.

The Narrow Gate
(Luke 13.24)

¹³"Go in through the narrow gate, because the gate to hell is wide and the road that leads to it is easy, and there are many who travel it. ¹⁴But the gate to life is narrow and the way that leads to it is hard, and there are few people who find it.

A Tree and Its Fruit
(Luke 6.43, 44)

¹⁵"Be on your guard against false prophets; they come to you looking like sheep on the outside, but on the inside they are really like wild wolves. ¹⁶You will know them by what they do. Thorn bushes do not bear grapes, and briers do not bear figs. ¹⁷A healthy tree bears good fruit, but a poor tree bears bad fruit. ¹⁸A healthy tree cannot bear bad fruit, and a poor tree cannot bear good fruit. ¹⁹And any tree that does not bear good fruit is cut down and thrown in the fire. ²⁰So then, you will know the false prophets by what they do.

I Never Knew You
(Luke 13.25-27)

²¹"Not everyone who calls me 'Lord, Lord' will enter the Kingdom of heaven, but only those who do what my Father in heaven wants them to do. ²²When the Judgment Day comes, many will say to me, 'Lord, Lord! In your name we spoke God's message, by your name we drove out many demons and performed many miracles!' ²³Then I will say to them, 'I never knew you. Get away from me, you wicked people!'

The Two House Builders
(Luke 6.47-49)

²⁴"So then, anyone who hears these words of mine and obeys them is like a wise man who built his house on rock. ²⁵The rain poured down, the rivers flooded over, and the wind blew hard against that house. But it did not fall, because it was built on rock.

²⁶"But anyone who hears these words of mine and does not obey them is like a foolish man who built his house on sand. ²⁷The rain poured down, the rivers flooded over, the wind blew hard

7.7, 8 2 Esd 2.13   **7.12** Tb 4.15; Lk 6.31   **7.13, 14** Si 15.17   **7.16** Si 27.6   **7.19** Mt 3.10; Lk 3.9   **7.20** Mt 12.33   **7.23** Ps 6.8

against that house, and it fell. And what a terrible fall that was!"

The Authority of Jesus

28When Jesus finished saying these things, the crowd was amazed at the way he taught. **29**He wasn't like the teachers of the Law; instead, he taught with authority.

Jesus Heals a Man
(Mark 1.40-45; Luke 5.12-16)

8 When Jesus came down from the hill, large crowds followed him. **2**Then a man suffering from a dreaded skin disease came to him, knelt down before him, and said, "Sir, if you want to, you can make me clean."*f*

3Jesus reached out and touched him. "I do want to," he answered. "Be clean!" At once the man was healed of his disease. **4**Then Jesus said to him, "Listen! Don't tell anyone, but go straight to the priest and let him examine you; then in order to prove to everyone that you are cured, offer the sacrifice that Moses ordered."

Jesus Heals a Roman Officer's Servant
(Luke 7.1-10)

5When Jesus entered Capernaum, a Roman officer met him and begged for help: **6**"Sir, my servant is sick in bed at home, unable to move and suffering terribly."

7"I will go and make him well," Jesus said.

8"Oh no, sir," answered the officer. "I do not deserve to have you come into my house. Just give the order, and my servant will get well. **9**I, too, am a man under the authority of superior officers, and I have soldiers under me. I order this one, 'Go!' and he goes; and I order that one, 'Come!' and he comes; and I

order my slave, 'Do this!' and he does it."

10When Jesus heard this, he was surprised and said to the people following him, "I tell you, I have never found anyone in Israel with faith like this. **11**I assure you that many will come from the east and the west and sit down with Abraham, Isaac, and Jacob at the feast in the Kingdom of heaven. **12**But those who should be in the Kingdom will be thrown out into the darkness, where they will cry and gnash their teeth." **13**Then Jesus said to the officer, "Go home, and what you believe will be done for you."

And the officer's servant was healed that very moment.

Jesus Heals Many People
(Mark 1.29-34; Luke 4.38-41)

14Jesus went to Peter's home, and there he saw Peter's mother-in-law sick in bed with a fever. **15**He touched her hand; the fever left her, and she got up and began to wait on him.

16When evening came, people brought to Jesus many who had demons in them. Jesus drove out the evil spirits with a word and healed all who were sick. **17**He did this to make come true what the prophet Isaiah had said, "He himself took our sickness and carried away our diseases."

The Would-Be Followers of Jesus
(Luke 9.57-62)

18When Jesus noticed the crowd around him, he ordered his disciples to go to the other side of the lake. **19**A teacher of the Law came to him. "Teacher," he said, "I am ready to go with you wherever you go."

20Jesus answered him, "Foxes have holes, and birds have nests, but the Son

---

f MAKE ME CLEAN: *This disease was considered to make a person ritually unclean.*
7.28, 29 Mk 1.22; Lk 4.32   **8.4** Lv 14.1-32   **8.9** Ba 3.33-35   **8.11** Lk 13.29
8.12 Mt 22.13; 25.30; Lk 13.28   **8.17** Is 53.4

of Man has no place to lie down and rest."

21 Another man, who was a disciple, said, "Sir, first let me go back and bury my father."

22 "Follow me," Jesus answered, "and let the dead bury their own dead."

Jesus Calms a Storm
(Mark 4.35-41; Luke 8.22-25)

23 Jesus got into a boat, and his disciples went with him. 24 Suddenly a fierce storm hit the lake, and the boat was in danger of sinking. But Jesus was asleep. 25 The disciples went to him and woke him up. "Save us, Lord!" they said. "We are about to die!"

26 "Why are you so frightened?" Jesus answered. "What little faith you have!" Then he got up and ordered the winds and the waves to stop, and there was a great calm.

27 Everyone was amazed. "What kind of man is this?" they said. "Even the winds and the waves obey him!"

Jesus Heals Two Men with Demons
(Mark 5.1-20; Luke 8.26-39)

28 When Jesus came to the territory of Gadara on the other side of the lake, he was met by two men who came out of the burial caves there. These men had demons in them and were so fierce that no one dared travel on that road. 29 At once they screamed, "What do you want with us, you Son of God? Have you come to punish us before the right time?"

30 Not far away there was a large herd of pigs feeding. 31 So the demons begged Jesus, "If you are going to drive us out, send us into that herd of pigs."

32 "Go," Jesus told them; so they left and went off into the pigs. The whole herd rushed down the side of the cliff into the lake and was drowned.

33 The men who had been taking care of the pigs ran away and went into the town, where they told the whole story and what had happened to the men with the demons. 34 So everyone from the town went out to meet Jesus; and when they saw him, they begged him to leave their territory.

Jesus Heals a Paralyzed Man
(Mark 2.1-12; Luke 5.17-26)

9 Jesus got into the boat and went back across the lake to his own town, g 2 where some people brought to him a paralyzed man, lying on a bed. When Jesus saw how much faith they had, he said to the paralyzed man, "Courage, my son! Your sins are forgiven."

3 Then some teachers of the Law said to themselves, "This man is speaking blasphemy!"

4 Jesus perceived what they were thinking, and so he said, "Why are you thinking such evil things? 5 Is it easier to say, 'Your sins are forgiven,' or to say, 'Get up and walk'? 6 I will prove to you, then, that the Son of Man has authority on earth to forgive sins." So he said to the paralyzed man, "Get up, pick up your bed, and go home!"

7 The man got up and went home. 8 When the people saw it, they were afraid, and praised God for giving such authority to people.

Jesus Calls Matthew
(Mark 2.13-17; Luke 5.27-32)

9 Jesus left that place, and as he walked along, he saw a tax collector, named Matthew, sitting in his office. He said to him, "Follow me."

Matthew got up and followed him.

10 While Jesus was having a meal in Matthew's house, h many tax collectors and other outcasts came and joined

---

g HIS OWN TOWN: *Capernaum (see 4.13).* Jesus') house.

h in Matthew's house; *or in his (that is,*

8.21 Tb 4.3, 4   **9.10, 11** Lk 15.1, 2

Jesus and his disciples at the table. [11]Some Pharisees saw this and asked his disciples, "Why does your teacher eat with such people?"

[12]Jesus heard them and answered, "People who are well do not need a doctor, but only those who are sick. [13]Go and find out what is meant by the scripture that says: 'It is kindness that I want, not animal sacrifices.' I have not come to call respectable people, but outcasts."

The Question about Fasting
(Mark 2.18-22; Luke 5.33-39)

[14]Then the followers of John the Baptist came to Jesus, asking, "Why is it that we and the Pharisees fast often, but your disciples don't fast at all?"

[15]Jesus answered, "Do you expect the guests at a wedding party to be sad as long as the bridegroom is with them? Of course not! But the day will come when the bridegroom will be taken away from them, and then they will fast.

[16]"No one patches up an old coat with a piece of new cloth, for the new patch will shrink and make an even bigger hole in the coat. [17]Nor does anyone pour new wine into used wineskins, for the skins will burst, the wine will pour out, and the skins will be ruined. Instead, new wine is poured into fresh wineskins, and both will keep in good condition."

The Official's Daughter and the Woman Who Touched Jesus' Cloak
(Mark 5.21-43; Luke 8.40-56)

[18]While Jesus was saying this, a Jewish official came to him, knelt down before him, and said, "My daughter has just died; but come and place your hands on her, and she will live."

[19]So Jesus got up and followed him, and his disciples went along with him.

[20]A woman who had suffered from severe bleeding for twelve years came up behind Jesus and touched the edge of his cloak. [21]She said to herself, "If only I touch his cloak, I will get well."

"If only I touch his cloak . . ." (9.21)

[22]Jesus turned around and saw her, and said, "Courage, my daughter! Your faith has made you well." At that very moment the woman became well.

[23]Then Jesus went into the official's house. When he saw the musicians for the funeral and the people all stirred up, [24]he said, "Get out, everybody! The little girl is not dead — she is only sleeping!" Then they all started making fun of him. [25]But as soon as the people had been put out, Jesus went into the girl's room and took hold of her hand, and she got up. [26]The news about this spread all over that part of the country.

Jesus Heals Two Blind Men

[27]Jesus left that place, and as he walked along, two blind men started following him. "Have mercy on us, Son of David!" they shouted.

[28]When Jesus had gone indoors, the two blind men came to him, and he asked them, "Do you believe that I can heal you?"

"Yes, sir!" they answered.

[29]Then Jesus touched their eyes and

9.13 a Mt 12.7; b Ho 6.6

said, "Let it happen, then, just as you believe!" — 30 and their sight was restored. Jesus spoke sternly to them, "Don't tell this to anyone!"

31 But they left and spread the news about Jesus all over that part of the country.

Jesus Heals a Man Who Could Not Speak

32 As the men were leaving, some people brought to Jesus a man who could not talk because he had a demon. 33 But as soon as the demon was driven out, the man started talking, and everyone was amazed. "We have never seen anything like this in Israel!" they exclaimed.

34 But the Pharisees said, "It is the chief of the demons who gives Jesus the power to drive out demons."

Jesus Has Pity for the People

35 Jesus went around visiting all the towns and villages. He taught in the synagogues, preached the Good News about the Kingdom, and healed people with every kind of disease and sickness. 36 As he saw the crowds, his heart was filled with pity for them, because they were worried and helpless, like sheep without a shepherd. 37 So he said to his disciples, "The harvest is large, but there are few workers to gather it in. 38 Pray to the owner of the harvest that he will send out workers to gather in his harvest."

The Twelve Apostles
(Mark 3.13-19; Luke 6.12-16)

10 Jesus called his twelve disciples together and gave them authority to drive out evil spirits and to heal every disease and every sickness.

2 These are the names of the twelve apostles: first, Simon (called Peter) and his brother Andrew; James and his brother John, the sons of Zebedee; 3 Philip and Bartholomew; Thomas and Matthew, the tax collector; James son of Alphaeus, and Thaddaeus; 4 Simon the Patriot, and Judas Iscariot, who betrayed Jesus.

The Mission of the Twelve
(Mark 6.7-13; Luke 9.1-6)

5 These twelve men were sent out by Jesus with the following instructions: "Do not go to any Gentile territory or any Samaritan towns. 6 Instead, you are to go to the lost sheep of the people of Israel. 7 Go and preach, 'The Kingdom of heaven is near!' 8 Heal the sick, bring the dead back to life, heal those who suffer from dreaded skin diseases, and drive out demons. You have received without paying, so give without being paid. 9 Do not carry any gold, silver, or copper money in your pockets; 10 do not carry a beggar's bag for the trip or an extra shirt or shoes or a walking stick. Workers should be given what they need.

11 "When you come to a town or village, go in and look for someone who is willing to welcome you, and stay with him until you leave that place. 12 When you go into a house, say, 'Peace be with you.' 13 If the people in that house welcome you, let your greeting of peace remain; but if they do not welcome you, then take back your greeting. 14 And if some home or town will not welcome you or listen to you, then leave that place and shake the dust off your feet. 15 I assure you that on the Judgment Day God will show more mercy to the people of Sodom and Gomorrah than to the people of that town!

9.34 Mt 10.25; 12.24; Mk 3.22; Lk 11.15   9.35 Mt 4.23; Mk 1.39; Lk 4.44
9.36 Nu 27.17; 1 K 22.17; 2 Ch 18.16; Ez 34.5; Mk 6.34   9.37, 38 Lk 10.2
10.10 1 Co 9.14; 1 Ti 5.18   10.14 Ac 13.51   10.15 a Mt 11.24; b Gn 19.24-28
10.7-15 Lk 10.4-12

Coming Persecutions
(Mark 13.9-13; Luke 21.12-17)

¹⁶"Listen! I am sending you out just like sheep to a pack of wolves. You must be as cautious as snakes and as gentle as doves. ¹⁷Watch out, for there will be those who will arrest you and take you to court, and they will whip you in the synagogues. ¹⁸For my sake you will be brought to trial before rulers and kings, to tell the Good News to them and to the Gentiles. ¹⁹When they bring you to trial, do not worry about what you are going to say or how you will say it; when the time comes, you will be given what you will say. ²⁰For the words you will speak will not be yours; they will come from the Spirit of your Father speaking through you.

²¹"People will hand over their own brothers to be put to death, and fathers will do the same to their children; children will turn against their parents and have them put to death. ²²Everyone will hate you because of me. But whoever holds out to the end will be saved. ²³When they persecute you in one town, run away to another one. I assure you that you will not finish your work in all the towns of Israel before the Son of Man comes.

²⁴"No pupil is greater than his teacher; no slave is greater than his master. ²⁵So a pupil should be satisfied to become like his teacher, and a slave like his master. If the head of the family is called Beelzebul, the members of the family will be called even worse names!

Whom to Fear
(Luke 12.2-7)

²⁶"So do not be afraid of people. Whatever is now covered up will be uncovered, and every secret will be made known. ²⁷What I am telling you in the dark you must repeat in broad daylight, and what you have heard in private you must announce from the housetops. ²⁸Do not be afraid of those who kill the body but cannot kill the soul; rather be afraid of God, who can destroy both body and soul in hell. ²⁹For only a penny you can buy two sparrows, yet not one sparrow falls to the ground without your Father's consent. ³⁰As for you, even the hairs of your head have all been counted. ³¹So do not be afraid; you are worth much more than many sparrows!

Confessing and Rejecting Christ
(Luke 12.8, 9)

³²"Those who declare publicly that they belong to me, I will do the same for them before my Father in heaven. ³³But those who reject me publicly, I will reject before my Father in heaven.

Not Peace, but a Sword
(Luke 12.51-53; 14.26, 27)

³⁴"Do not think that I have come to bring peace to the world. No, I did not come to bring peace, but a sword. ³⁵I came to set sons against their fathers, daughters against their mothers, daughters-in-law against their mothers-in-law; ³⁶your worst enemies will be the members of your own family.

³⁷"Those who love their father or mother more than me are not fit to be my disciples; those who love their son or daughter more than me are not fit to be my disciples. ³⁸Those who do not take up their cross and follow in my steps are not fit to be my disciples. ³⁹Those who try to gain their own life

---

10.16 Lk 10.3   **10.17-20** Mk 13.9-11; Lk 12.11, 12; 21.12-15   **10.21** Mk 13.12; Lk 21.16
10.22 a Mt 24.9; Mk 13.13; Lk 21.17; **b** Mt 24.13; Mk 13.13   **10.24 a** Lk 6.40; **b** Jn 13.16;
15.20   **10.25** Mt 9.34; 12.24; Mk 3.22; Lk 11.15   **10.26** Mk 4.22; Lk 8.17
10.33 2 Ti 2.12   **10.35, 36** Mic 7.6   **10.38** Mt 16.24; Mk 8.34; Lk 9.23   **10.39** Mt 16.25;
Mk 8.35; Lk 9.24; 17.33; Jn 12.25

will lose it; but those who lose their life for my sake will gain it.

Rewards
(Mark 9.41)

40 "Whoever welcomes you welcomes me; and whoever welcomes me welcomes the one who sent me. 41 Whoever welcomes God's messenger because he is God's messenger, will share in his reward. And whoever welcomes a good man because he is good, will share in his reward. 42 You can be sure that whoever gives even a drink of cold water to one of the least of these my followers because he is my follower, will certainly receive a reward."

The Messengers from John the Baptist
(Luke 7.18-35)

11 When Jesus finished giving these instructions to his twelve disciples, he left that place and went off to teach and preach in the towns near there.

2 When John the Baptist heard in prison about the things that Christ was doing, he sent some of his disciples to him. 3 "Tell us," they asked Jesus, "are you the one John said was going to come, or should we expect someone else?"

4 Jesus answered, "Go back and tell John what you are hearing and seeing: 5 the blind can see, the lame can walk, those who suffer from dreaded skin diseases are made clean,^{i} the deaf hear, the dead are brought back to life, and the Good News is preached to the poor. 6 How happy are those who have no doubts about me!"

7 While John's disciples were leaving, Jesus spoke about him to the crowds: "When you went out to John in the desert, what did you expect to see? A blade of grass bending in the wind? 8 What did you go out to see? A man dressed up in fancy clothes? People who dress like that live in palaces! 9 Tell me, what did you go out to see? A prophet? Yes indeed, but you saw much more than a prophet. 10 For John is the one of whom the scripture says: 'God said, I will send my messenger ahead of you to open the way for you.' 11 I assure you that John the Baptist is greater than anyone who has ever lived. But the one who is least in the Kingdom of heaven is greater than John. 12 From the time John preached his message until this very day the Kingdom of heaven has suffered violent attacks,^{j} and violent men try to seize it. 13 Until the time of John all the prophets and the Law of Moses spoke about the Kingdom; 14 and if you are willing to believe their message, John is Elijah, whose coming was predicted. 15 Listen, then, if you have ears!

16 "Now, to what can I compare the people of this day? They are like children sitting in the marketplace. One group shouts to the other, 17 'We played wedding music for you, but you wouldn't dance! We sang funeral songs, but you wouldn't cry!' 18 When John came, he fasted and drank no wine, and everyone said, 'He has a demon in him!' 19 When the Son of Man came, he ate and drank, and everyone said, 'Look at this man! He is a glutton and wine drinker, a friend of tax collectors and other outcasts!' God's wisdom, however, is shown to be true by its results."

The Unbelieving Towns
(Luke 10.13-15)

20 The people in the towns where Jesus had performed most of his mira-

---

^{i} MADE CLEAN: *See 8.2.* ^{j} has suffered violent attacks; *or* has been coming violently.
10.40 a Lk 10.16; Jn 13.20; **b** Mk 9.37; Lk 9.48   **11.5 a** Is 35.5, 6; **b** Is 61.1   **11.10** Ml 3.1
11.12, 13 Lk 16.16   **11.14** Ml 4.5; Mt 17.10-13; Mk 9.11-13

cles did not turn from their sins, so he reproached those towns. 21 "How terrible it will be for you, Chorazin! How terrible for you too, Bethsaida! If the miracles which were performed in you had been performed in Tyre and Sidon, the people there would have long ago put on sackcloth and sprinkled ashes on themselves, to show that they had turned from their sins! 22 I assure you that on the Judgment Day God will show more mercy to the people of Tyre and Sidon than to you! 23 And as for you, Capernaum! Did you want to lift yourself up to heaven? You will be thrown down to hell! If the miracles which were performed in you had been performed in Sodom, it would still be in existence today! 24 You can be sure that on the Judgment Day God will show more mercy to Sodom than to you!"

Come to Me and Rest
(Luke 10.21, 22)

25 At that time Jesus said, "Father, Lord of heaven and earth! I thank you because you have shown to the unlearned what you have hidden from the wise and learned. 26 Yes, Father, this was how you were pleased to have it happen.

27 "My Father has given me all things. No one knows the Son except the Father, and no one knows the Father except the Son and those to whom the Son chooses to reveal him.

28 "Come to me, all of you who are tired from carrying heavy loads, and I will give you rest. 29 Take my yoke and put it on you, and learn from me, because I am gentle and humble in spirit; and you will find rest. 30 For the yoke I will give you is easy, and the load I will put on you is light."

Come to me, all of you who are tired. (11.28)

The Question about the Sabbath
(Mark 2.23-28; Luke 6.1-5)

12 Not long afterward Jesus was walking through some wheat fields on a Sabbath. His disciples were hungry, so they began to pick heads of wheat and eat the grain. 2 When the Pharisees saw this, they said to Jesus, "Look, it is against our Law for your disciples to do this on the Sabbath!"

3 Jesus answered, "Have you never read what David did that time when he and his men were hungry? 4 He went into the house of God, and he and his men ate the bread offered to God, even though it was against the Law for them to eat it — only the priests were allowed to eat that bread. 5 Or have you not read in the Law of Moses that every Sabbath the priests in the Temple actually break the Sabbath law, yet they are not guilty? 6 I tell you that there is something here greater than the Temple. 7 The scripture says, 'It is kindness that I want, not animal sacrifices.' If you really knew what this means, you would not condemn people who are not guilty; 8 for the Son of Man is Lord of the Sabbath."

The Man with a Paralyzed Hand
(Mark 3.1-6; Luke 6.6-11)

9 Jesus left that place and went to a synagogue, 10 where there was a man

---

11.21 Is 23.1-18; Ez 26.1–28.26; Jl 3.4-8; Am 1.9, 10; Zec 9.2-4   **11.23 a** Is 14.13-15; **b** Gn 19.24-28   **11.24** Mt 10.15; Lk 10.12   **11.27 a** Jn 3.35; **b** Jn 1.18; 10.15 **11.28-30** Si 6.24-30; 24.19; 51.23-26   **11.29** Jr 6.16   **12.1** Dt 23.25   **12.3, 4** 1 S 21.1-6 **12.4** Lv 24.9   **12.5** Nu 28.9, 10   **12.7 a** Mt 9.13; **b** Ho 6.6

who had a paralyzed hand. Some people were there who wanted to accuse Jesus of doing wrong, so they asked him, "Is it against our Law to heal on the Sabbath?"

11 Jesus answered, "What if one of you has a sheep and it falls into a deep hole on the Sabbath? Will you not take hold of it and lift it out? 12 And a human being is worth much more than a sheep! So then, our Law does allow us to help someone on the Sabbath." 13 Then he said to the man with the paralyzed hand, "Stretch out your hand."

He stretched it out, and it became well again, just like the other one. 14 Then the Pharisees left and made plans to kill Jesus.

God's Chosen Servant

15 When Jesus heard about the plot against him, he went away from that place; and large crowds followed him. He healed all the sick 16 and gave them orders not to tell others about him. 17 He did this so as to make come true what God had said through the prophet Isaiah:

18 "Here is my servant, whom I
    have chosen,
  the one I love, and with
    whom I am pleased.
I will send my Spirit upon him,
  and he will announce my
    judgment to the nations.
19 He will not argue or shout,
  or make loud speeches in
    the streets.
20 He will not break off a bent reed,
  nor put out a flickering lamp.
He will persist until he causes
  justice to triumph,
21   and on him all peoples will
    put their hope."

Jesus and Beelzebul
(*Mark 3.20-30; Luke 11.14-23*)

22 Then some people brought to Jesus a man who was blind and could not talk because he had a demon. Jesus healed the man, so that he was able to talk and see. 23 The crowds were all amazed at what Jesus had done. "Could he be the Son of David?" they asked.

24 When the Pharisees heard this, they replied, "He drives out demons only because their ruler Beelzebul gives him power to do so."

25 Jesus knew what they were thinking, and so he said to them, "Any country that divides itself into groups which fight each other will not last very long. And any town or family that divides itself into groups which fight each other will fall apart. 26 So if one group is fighting another in Satan's kingdom, this means that it is already divided into groups and will soon fall apart! 27 You say that I drive out demons because Beelzebul gives me the power to do so. Well, then, who gives your followers the power to drive them out? What your own followers do proves that you are wrong! 28 No, it is not Beelzebul, but God's Spirit, who gives me the power to drive out demons, which proves that the Kingdom of God has already come upon you.

29 "No one can break into a strong man's house and take away his belongings unless he first ties up the strong man; then he can plunder his house.

30 "Anyone who is not for me is really against me; anyone who does not help me gather is really scattering. 31 For this reason I tell you: people can be forgiven any sin and any evil thing they say; k but whoever says evil things against the Holy Spirit will not be forgiven. 32 Anyone who says something

---

k evil thing they say; *or* evil thing they say against God.

12.11 Lk 14.5   **12.18-21** Is 42.1-4 (LXX)   **12.24** Mt 9.34; 10.25   **12.29** Tb 8.3
12.30 Mk 9.40   **12.32** Lk 12.10

against the Son of Man can be forgiven; but whoever says something against the Holy Spirit will not be forgiven — now or ever.

A Tree and Its Fruit
(Luke 6.43-45)

33"To have good fruit you must have a healthy tree; if you have a poor tree, you will have bad fruit. A tree is known by the kind of fruit it bears. 34 You snakes — how can you say good things when you are evil? For the mouth speaks what the heart is full of. 35 A good person brings good things out of a treasure of good things; a bad person brings bad things out of a treasure of bad things.

36"You can be sure that on the Judgment Day you will have to give account of every useless word you have ever spoken. 37 Your words will be used to judge you — to declare you either innocent or guilty."

The Demand for a Miracle
(Mark 8.11, 12; Luke 11.29-32)

38Then some teachers of the Law and some Pharisees spoke up. "Teacher," they said, "we want to see you perform a miracle."

39"How evil and godless are the people of this day!" Jesus exclaimed. "You ask me for a miracle? No! The only miracle you will be given is the miracle of the prophet Jonah. 40 In the same way that Jonah spent three days and nights in the big fish, so will the Son of Man spend three days and nights in the depths of the earth. 41 On the Judgment Day the people of Nineveh will stand up and accuse you, because they turned

from their sins when they heard Jonah preach; and I tell you that there is something here greater than Jonah! 42 On the Judgment Day the Queen of Sheba will stand up and accuse you, because she traveled all the way from her country to listen to King Solomon's wise teaching; and I assure you that there is something here greater than Solomon!

The Return of the Evil Spirit
(Luke 11.24-26)

43"When an evil spirit goes out of a person, it travels over dry country looking for a place to rest. If it can't find one, 44 it says to itself, 'I will go back to my house.' So it goes back and finds the house empty, clean, and all fixed up. 45 Then it goes out and brings along seven other spirits even worse than itself, and they come and live there. So when it is all over, that person is in worse shape than at the beginning. This is what will happen to the evil people of this day."

Jesus' Mother and Brothers
(Mark 3.31-35; Luke 8.19-21)

46Jesus was still talking to the people when his mother and brothers arrived. They stood outside, asking to speak with him. 47 So one of the people there said to him, "Look, your mother and brothers are standing outside, and they want to speak with you."[l]

48Jesus answered, "Who is my mother? Who are my brothers?" 49 Then he pointed to his disciples and said, "Look! Here are my mother and my brothers! 50 Whoever does what my Father in heaven wants is my brother, my sister, and my mother."

---

[l] *Some manuscripts do not have verse 47.*

12.33 Si 27.6; Mt 7.20; Lk 6.44   **12.34 a** Mt 3.7; 23.33; Lk 3.7; **b** Mt 15.18; Lk 6.45
12.38 Mt 16.1; Mk 8.11; Lk 11.16   **12.39** Mt 16.4; Mk 8.12   **12.40** Jon 1.17
12.41 Jon 3.5   **12.42** 1 K 10.1-10; 2 Ch 9.1-12

The Parable of the Sower
(Mark 4.1-9; Luke 8.4-8)

13 That same day Jesus left the house and went to the lakeside, where he sat down to teach. ²The crowd that gathered around him was so large that he got into a boat and sat in it, while the crowd stood on the shore. ³He used parables to tell them many things.

"Once there was a man who went out to sow grain. ⁴As he scattered the seed in the field, some of it fell along the path, and the birds came and ate it up. ⁵Some of it fell on rocky ground, where there was little soil. The seeds soon sprouted, because the soil wasn't deep. ⁶But when the sun came up, it burned the young plants; and because the roots had not grown deep enough, the plants soon dried up. ⁷Some of the seed fell among thorn bushes, which grew up and choked the plants. ⁸But some seeds fell in good soil, and the plants bore grain: some had one hundred grains, others sixty, and others thirty."

⁹And Jesus concluded, "Listen, then, if you have ears!"

The Purpose of the Parables
(Mark 4.10-12; Luke 8.9, 10)

¹⁰Then the disciples came to Jesus and asked him, "Why do you use parables when you talk to the people?"

¹¹Jesus answered, "The knowledge about the secrets of the Kingdom of heaven has been given to you, but not to them. ¹²For the person who has something will be given more, so that he will have more than enough; but the person who has nothing will have taken away from him even the little he has. ¹³The reason I use parables in talking to them is that they look, but do not see, and they listen, but do not hear or understand. ¹⁴So the prophecy of Isaiah applies to them:

'This people will listen and listen, but not understand; they will look and look, but not see, ¹⁵because their minds are dull, and they have stopped up their ears and have closed their eyes. Otherwise, their eyes would see, their ears would hear, their minds would understand, and they would turn to me, says God, and I would heal them.'

¹⁶"As for you, how fortunate you are! Your eyes see and your ears hear. ¹⁷I assure you that many prophets and many of God's people wanted very much to see what you see, but they could not, and to hear what you hear, but they did not.

Jesus Explains the Parable of the Sower
(Mark 4.13-20; Luke 8.11-15)

¹⁸"Listen, then, and learn what the parable of the sower means. ¹⁹Those who hear the message about the Kingdom but do not understand it are like the seeds that fell along the path. The Evil One comes and snatches away what was sown in them. ²⁰The seeds that fell on rocky ground stand for those who receive the message gladly as soon as they hear it. ²¹But it does not sink deep into them, and they don't last long. So when trouble or persecution comes because of the message, they give up at once. ²²The seeds that fell among thorn bushes stand for those who hear the message; but the worries about this life and the love for riches choke the message, and they don't bear fruit. ²³And the seeds sown in the good soil stand for those who hear the message and understand it: they bear fruit,

---

13.2 Lk 5.1-3   **13.12** Mt 25.29; Mk 4.25; Lk 8.18; 19.26   **13.14, 15** Is 6.9, 10 (LXX)
13.16, 17 Lk 10.23, 24

some as much as one hundred, others sixty, and others thirty."

The Parable of the Weeds

²⁴ Jesus told them another parable: "The Kingdom of heaven is like this. A man sowed good seed in his field. ²⁵ One night, when everyone was asleep, an enemy came and sowed weeds among the wheat and went away. ²⁶ When the plants grew and the heads of grain began to form, then the weeds showed up. ²⁷ The man's servants came to him and said, 'Sir, it was good seed you sowed in your field; where did the weeds come from?' ²⁸ 'It was some enemy who did this,' he answered. 'Do you want us to go and pull up the weeds?' they asked him. ²⁹ 'No,' he answered, 'because as you gather the weeds you might pull up some of the wheat along with them. ³⁰ Let the wheat and the weeds both grow together until harvest. Then I will tell the harvest workers to pull up the weeds first, tie them in bundles and burn them, and then to gather in the wheat and put it in my barn.'"

The Parable of the Mustard Seed
(Mark 4.30-32; Luke 13.18, 19)

³¹ Jesus told them another parable: "The Kingdom of heaven is like this. A man takes a mustard seed and sows it in his field. ³² It is the smallest of all seeds, but when it grows up, it is the biggest of all plants. It becomes a tree, so that birds come and make their nests in its branches."

The Parable of the Yeast
(Luke 13.20, 21)

³³ Jesus told them still another parable: "The Kingdom of heaven is like this. A woman takes some yeast and mixes it with a bushel of flour until the whole batch of dough rises."

Jesus' Use of Parables
(Mark 4.33, 34)

³⁴ Jesus used parables to tell all these things to the crowds; he would not say a thing to them without using a parable. ³⁵ He did this to make come true what the prophet had said,

"I will use parables when I
    speak to them;
I will tell them things
    unknown since the
    creation of the world."

Jesus Explains the Parable
of the Weeds

³⁶ When Jesus had left the crowd and gone indoors, his disciples came to him and said, "Tell us what the parable about the weeds in the field means."

³⁷ Jesus answered, "The man who sowed the good seed is the Son of Man; ³⁸ the field is the world; the good seed is the people who belong to the Kingdom; the weeds are the people who belong to the Evil One; ³⁹ and the enemy who sowed the weeds is the Devil. The harvest is the end of the age, and the harvest workers are angels. ⁴⁰ Just as the weeds are gathered up and burned in the fire, so the same thing will happen at the end of the age: ⁴¹ the Son of Man will send out his angels to gather up out of his Kingdom all those who cause people to sin and all others who do evil things, ⁴² and they will throw them into the fiery furnace, where they will cry and gnash their teeth. ⁴³ Then God's people will shine like the sun in their Father's Kingdom. Listen, then, if you have ears!

The Parable of the Hidden Treasure

⁴⁴ "The Kingdom of heaven is like this. A man happens to find a treasure hidden in a field. He covers it up again,

13.35 Ps 78.2   **13.43** 2 Esd 7.97

and is so happy that he goes and sells everything he has, and then goes back and buys that field.

The Parable of the Pearl

45 "Also, the Kingdom of heaven is like this. A man is looking for fine pearls, 46 and when he finds one that is unusually fine, he goes and sells everything he has, and buys that pearl.

The Parable of the Net

47 "Also, the Kingdom of heaven is like this. Some fishermen throw their net out in the lake and catch all kinds of fish. 48 When the net is full, they pull it to shore and sit down to divide the fish: the good ones go into the buckets, the worthless ones are thrown away. 49 It will be like this at the end of the age: the angels will go out and gather up the evil people from among the good 50 and will throw them into the fiery furnace, where they will cry and gnash their teeth.

New Truths and Old

51 "Do you understand these things?" Jesus asked them.

"Yes," they answered.

52 So he replied, "This means, then, that every teacher of the Law who becomes a disciple in the Kingdom of heaven is like a homeowner who takes new and old things out of his storage room."

Jesus Is Rejected at Nazareth
(Mark 6.1-6; Luke 4.16-30)

53 When Jesus finished telling these parables, he left that place 54 and went back to his hometown. He taught in the synagogue, and those who heard him were amazed. "Where did he get such wisdom?" they asked. "And what about

his miracles? 55 Isn't he the carpenter's son? Isn't Mary his mother, and aren't James, Joseph, Simon, and Judas his brothers? 56 Aren't all his sisters living here? Where did he get all this?" 57 And so they rejected him.

Jesus said to them, "A prophet is respected everywhere except in his hometown and by his own family." 58 Because they did not have faith, he did not perform many miracles there.

The Death of John the Baptist
(Mark 6.14-29; Luke 9.7-9)

14 At that time Herod, the ruler of Galilee, heard about Jesus. 2 "He is really John the Baptist, who has come back to life," he told his officials. "That is why he has this power to perform miracles."

3 For Herod had earlier ordered John's arrest, and he had him tied up and put in prison. He had done this because of Herodias, his brother Philip's wife. 4 For some time John the Baptist had told Herod, "It isn't right for you to be married to Herodias!" 5 Herod wanted to kill him, but he was afraid of the Jewish people, because they considered John to be a prophet.

6 On Herod's birthday the daughter of Herodias danced in front of the whole group. Herod was so pleased 7 that he promised her, "I swear that I will give you anything you ask for!"

8 At her mother's suggestion she asked him, "Give me here and now the head of John the Baptist on a plate!"

9 The king was sad, but because of the promise he had made in front of all his guests he gave orders that her wish be granted. 10 So he had John beheaded in prison. 11 The head was brought in on a plate and given to the girl, who took it to her mother. 12 John's disciples came, carried away his body, and buried it; then they went and told Jesus.

13.57 Jn 4.44   **14.3, 4** Lk 3.19, 20   **14.4** Lv 18.16; 20.21

Jesus Feeds Five Thousand
(Mark 6.30-44; Luke 9.10-17;
John 6.1-14)

¹³When Jesus heard the news about John, he left there in a boat and went to a lonely place by himself. The people heard about it, and so they left their towns and followed him by land. ¹⁴Jesus got out of the boat, and when he saw the large crowd, his heart was filled with pity for them, and he healed their sick.

¹⁵That evening his disciples came to him and said, "It is already very late, and this is a lonely place. Send the people away and let them go to the villages to buy food for themselves."

¹⁶"They don't have to leave," answered Jesus. "You yourselves give them something to eat!"

¹⁷"All we have here are five loaves and two fish," they replied.

¹⁸"Then bring them here to me," Jesus said. ¹⁹He ordered the people to sit down on the grass; then he took the five loaves and the two fish, looked up to heaven, and gave thanks to God. He broke the loaves and gave them to the disciples, and the disciples gave them to the people. ²⁰Everyone ate and had enough. Then the disciples took up twelve baskets full of what was left over. ²¹The number of men who ate was about five thousand, not counting the women and children.

Jesus Walks on the Water
(Mark 6.45-52; John 6.15-21)

²²Then Jesus made the disciples get into the boat and go on ahead to the other side of the lake, while he sent the people away. ²³After sending the people away, he went up a hill by himself to pray. When evening came, Jesus was there alone; ²⁴and by this time the boat was far out in the lake, tossed about by the waves, because the wind was blowing against it.

²⁵Between three and six o'clock in the morning Jesus came to the disci-

ples, walking on the water. ²⁶When they saw him walking on the water, they were terrified. "It's a ghost!" they said, and screamed with fear.

²⁷Jesus spoke to them at once. "Courage!" he said. "It is I. Don't be afraid!"

²⁸Then Peter spoke up. "Lord, if it is really you, order me to come out on the water to you."

²⁹"Come!" answered Jesus. So Peter got out of the boat and started walking on the water to Jesus. ³⁰But when he noticed the strong wind, he was afraid and started to sink down in the water. "Save me, Lord!" he cried.

³¹At once Jesus reached out and grabbed hold of him and said, "What little faith you have! Why did you doubt?"

³²They both got into the boat, and the wind died down. ³³Then the disciples in the boat worshiped Jesus. "Truly you are the Son of God!" they exclaimed.

Jesus Heals the Sick in Gennesaret
(Mark 6.53-56)

³⁴They crossed the lake and came to land at Gennesaret, ³⁵where the people recognized Jesus. So they sent for the sick people in all the surrounding country and brought them to Jesus. ³⁶They begged him to let the sick at least touch the edge of his cloak; and all who touched it were made well.

The Teaching of the Ancestors
(Mark 7.1-13)

15 Then some Pharisees and teachers of the Law came from Jerusalem to Jesus and asked him, ²"Why is it that your disciples disobey the teaching handed down by our ancestors? They don't wash their hands in the proper way before they eat!"

³Jesus answered, "And why do you disobey God's command and follow

your own teaching? [4] For God said, 'Respect your father and your mother,' and 'If you curse your father or your mother, you are to be put to death.' [5] But you teach that if people have something they could use to help their father or mother, but say, 'This belongs to God,' [6] they do not need to honor their father.[m] In this way you disregard God's command, in order to follow your own teaching. [7] You hypocrites! How right Isaiah was when he prophesied about you:

[8] 'These people, says God, honor
    me with their words,
but their heart is really far
    away from me.
[9] It is no use for them to
    worship me,
because they teach human
    rules as though they
    were my laws!'"

The Things That Make a
Person Unclean
(Mark 7.14-23)

[10] Then Jesus called the crowd to him and said to them, "Listen and understand! [11] It is not what goes into your mouth that makes you ritually unclean; rather, what comes out of it makes you unclean."

[12] Then the disciples came to him and said, "Do you know that the Pharisees had their feelings hurt by what you said?"

[13] "Every plant which my Father in heaven did not plant will be pulled up," answered Jesus. [14] "Don't worry about them! They are blind leaders of the blind; and when one blind man leads another, both fall into a ditch."

[15] Peter spoke up, "Explain this saying to us."

[16] Jesus said to them, "You are still no more intelligent than the others.

[17] Don't you understand? Anything that goes into your mouth goes into your stomach and then on out of your body. [18] But the things that come out of the mouth come from the heart, and these are the things that make you ritually unclean. [19] For from your heart come the evil ideas which lead you to kill, commit adultery, and do other immoral things; to rob, lie, and slander others. [20] These are the things that make you unclean. But to eat without washing your hands as they say you should — this doesn't make you unclean."

A Woman's Faith
(Mark 7.24-30)

[21] Jesus left that place and went off to the territory near the cities of Tyre and Sidon. [22] A Canaanite woman who lived

They are blind leaders of the blind. (15.14)

in that region came to him. "Son of David!" she cried out. "Have mercy on me, sir! My daughter has a demon and is in a terrible condition."

[23] But Jesus did not say a word to her. His disciples came to him and begged him, "Send her away! She is following us and making all this noise!"

---

[m] their father; *some manuscripts have* their father or mother.

15.4 a Ex 20.12; Dt 5.16; **b** Ex 21.17; Lv 20.9   **15.8, 9** Is 29.13 (LXX)   **15.14** Lk 6.39
15.18 Mt 12.34

24 Then Jesus replied, "I have been sent only to the lost sheep of the people of Israel."

25 At this the woman came and fell at his feet. "Help me, sir!" she said.

26 Jesus answered, "It isn't right to take the children's food and throw it to the dogs."

27 "That's true, sir," she answered, "but even the dogs eat the leftovers that fall from their masters' table."

28 So Jesus answered her, "You are a woman of great faith! What you want will be done for you." And at that very moment her daughter was healed.

Jesus Heals Many People

29 Jesus left there and went along by Lake Galilee. He climbed a hill and sat down. 30 Large crowds came to him, bringing with them the lame, the blind, the crippled, the dumb, and many other sick people, whom they placed at Jesus' feet; and he healed them. 31 The people were amazed as they saw the dumb speaking, the crippled made whole, the lame walking, and the blind seeing; and they praised the God of Israel.

Jesus Feeds Four Thousand
(Mark 8.1-10)

32 Jesus called his disciples to him and said, "I feel sorry for these people, because they have been with me for three days and now have nothing to eat. I don't want to send them away without feeding them, for they might faint on their way home."

33 The disciples asked him, "Where will we find enough food in this desert to feed this crowd?"

34 "How much bread do you have?" Jesus asked.

"Seven loaves," they answered, "and a few small fish."

35 So Jesus ordered the crowd to sit down on the ground. 36 Then he took the seven loaves and the fish, gave thanks to God, broke them, and gave them to the disciples; and the disciples gave them to the people. 37 They all ate and had enough. Then the disciples took up seven baskets full of pieces left over. 38 The number of men who ate was four thousand, not counting the women and children.

39 Then Jesus sent the people away, got into a boat, and went to the territory of Magadan.

The Demand for a Miracle
(Mark 8.11-13; Luke 12.54-56)

16 Some Pharisees and Sadducees who came to Jesus wanted to trap him, so they asked him to perform a miracle for them, to show that God approved of him. 2 But Jesus answered, "When the sun is setting, you say, 'We are going to have fine weather, because the sky is red.' 3 And early in the morning you say, 'It is going to rain, because the sky is red and dark.' You can predict the weather by looking at the sky, but you cannot interpret the signs concerning these times![n] 4 How evil and godless are the people of this day! You ask me for a miracle? No! The only miracle you will be given is the miracle of Jonah."

So he left them and went away.

The Yeast of the Pharisees and Sadducees
(Mark 8.14-21)

5 When the disciples crossed over to the other side of the lake, they forgot to take any bread. 6 Jesus said to them, "Take care; be on your guard against the yeast of the Pharisees and Sadducees."

7 They started discussing among themselves, "He says this because we didn't bring any bread."

8 Jesus knew what they were saying,

---

n Some manuscripts do not have the words of Jesus in verses 2-3.
16.1 Mt 12.38; Lk 11.16   **16.4** Mt 12.39; Lk 11.29   **16.6** Lk 12.1

so he asked them, "Why are you discussing among yourselves about not having any bread? What little faith you have! 9 Don't you understand yet? Don't you remember when I broke the five loaves for the five-thousand men? How many baskets did you fill? 10 And what about the seven loaves for the four thousand men? How many baskets did you fill? 11 How is it that you don't understand that I was not talking to you about bread? Guard yourselves from the yeast of the Pharisees and Sadducees!"

12 Then the disciples understood that he was not warning them to guard themselves from the yeast used in bread but from the teaching of the Pharisees and Sadducees.

Peter's Declaration about Jesus
(Mark 8.27-30; Luke 9.18-21)

13 Jesus went to the territory near the town of Caesarea Philippi, where he asked his disciples, "Who do people say the Son of Man is?"

14 "Some say John the Baptist," they answered. "Others say Elijah, while others say Jeremiah or some other prophet."

15 "What about you?" he asked them. "Who do you say I am?"

16 Simon Peter answered, "You are the Messiah, the Son of the living God."

17 "Good for you, Simon son of John!" answered Jesus. "For this truth did not come to you from any human being, but it was given to you directly by my Father in heaven. 18 And so I tell you, Peter: you are a rock, and on this rock foundation I will build my church, and not even death will ever be able to overcome it. 19 I will give you the keys of the Kingdom of heaven; what you prohibit on earth will be prohibited in heaven,

and what you permit on earth will be permitted in heaven."

20 Then Jesus ordered his disciples not to tell anyone that he was the Messiah.

Jesus Speaks about His Suffering and Death
(Mark 8.31 — 9.1; Luke 9.22-27)

21 From that time on Jesus began to say plainly to his disciples, "I must go to Jerusalem and suffer much from the elders, the chief priests, and the teachers of the Law. I will be put to death, but three days later I will be raised to life."

22 Peter took him aside and began to rebuke him. "God forbid it, Lord!" he said. "That must never happen to you!"

23 Jesus turned around and said to Peter, "Get away from me, Satan! You are an obstacle in my way, because these thoughts of yours don't come from God, but from human nature."

24 Then Jesus said to his disciples, "If any of you want to come with me, you must forget yourself, carry your cross, and follow me. 25 For if you want to save your own life, you will lose it; but if you lose your life for my sake, you will find it. 26 Will you gain anything if you win the whole world but lose your life? Of course not! There is nothing you can give to regain your life. 27 For the Son of Man is about to come in the glory of his Father with his angels, and then he will reward each one according to his deeds. 28 I assure you that there are some here who will not die until they have seen the Son of Man come as King."

The Transfiguration
(Mark 9.2-13; Luke 9.28-36)

17 Six days later Jesus took with him Peter and the brothers James and John and led them up

16.9 Mt 14.17-21 **16.10** Mt 15.34-38 **16.14** Mt 14.1, 2; Mk 6.14, 15; Lk 9.7, 8
16.16 Jn 6.68, 69 **16.19** Mt 18.18; Jn 20.23 **16.24** Mt 10.38; Lk 14.27 **16.25** Mt 10.39;
Lk 17.33; Jn 12.25 **16.27 a** Mt 25.31; **b** Ps 62.12; Ro 2.6

a high mountain where they were alone. [2]As they looked on, a change came over Jesus: his face was shining like the sun, and his clothes were dazzling white. [3]Then the three disciples saw Moses and Elijah talking with Jesus. [4]So Peter spoke up and said to Jesus, "Lord, how good it is that we are here! If you wish, I will make three tents here, one for you, one for Moses, and one for Elijah."

[5]While he was talking, a shining cloud came over them, and a voice from the cloud said, "This is my own dear Son, with whom I am pleased — listen to him!"

[6]When the disciples heard the voice, they were so terrified that they threw themselves face downward on the ground. [7]Jesus came to them and touched them. "Get up," he said. "Don't be afraid!" [8]So they looked up and saw no one there but Jesus.

[9]As they came down the mountain, Jesus ordered them, "Don't tell anyone about this vision you have seen until the Son of Man has been raised from death."

[10]Then the disciples asked Jesus, "Why do the teachers of the Law say that Elijah has to come first?"

[11]"Elijah is indeed coming first," answered Jesus, "and he will get everything ready. [12]But I tell you that Elijah has already come and people did not recognize him, but treated him just as they pleased. In the same way they will also mistreat the Son of Man."

[13]Then the disciples understood that he was talking to them about John the Baptist.

Jesus Heals a Boy with a Demon
(Mark 9.14-29; Luke 9.37-43a)

[14]When they returned to the crowd, a man came to Jesus, knelt before him, [15]and said, "Sir, have mercy on my son! He is an epileptic and has such terrible attacks that he often falls in the fire or into water. [16]I brought him to your disciples, but they could not heal him."

[17]Jesus answered, "How unbelieving and wrong you people are! How long must I stay with you? How long do I have to put up with you? Bring the boy here to me!" [18]Jesus gave a command to the demon, and it went out of the boy, and at that very moment he was healed.

[19]Then the disciples came to Jesus in private and asked him, "Why couldn't we drive the demon out?"

[20]"It was because you do not have enough faith," answered Jesus. "I assure you that if you have faith as big as a mustard seed, you can say to this hill, 'Go from here to there!' and it will go. You could do anything!"[o]

Jesus Speaks Again about His Death
(Mark 9.30-32; Luke 9.43b-45)

[22]When the disciples all came together in Galilee, Jesus said to them, "The Son of Man is about to be handed over to those [23]who will kill him; but three days later he will be raised to life."

The disciples became very sad.

Payment of the Temple Tax

[24]When Jesus and his disciples came to Capernaum, the collectors of the Temple tax came to Peter and asked, "Does your teacher pay the Temple tax?"

[25]"Of course," Peter answered.

---

o Some manuscripts add verse 21: But only prayer and fasting can drive this kind out; nothing else can *(see Mk 9.29).*

17.5 a Gn 22.2; Ps 2.7; Is 42.1; Mt 3.17; 12.18; Mk 1.11; Lk 3.22; **b** Dt 18.15
17.1-5 2 P 1.17, 18　**17.10** Ml 4.5　**17.11** Si 48.10　**17.12** Mt 11.14　**17.20** Mt 21.21;
Mk 11.23; 1 Co 13.2　**17.24** Ex 30.13; 38.26

When Peter went into the house, Jesus spoke up first, "Simon, what is your opinion? Who pays duties or taxes to the kings of this world? The citizens of the country or the foreigners?"

²⁶"The foreigners," answered Peter.

"Well, then," replied Jesus, "that means that the citizens don't have to pay. ²⁷But we don't want to offend these people. So go to the lake and drop in a line. Pull up the first fish you hook, and in its mouth you will find a coin worth enough for my Temple tax and yours. Take it and pay them our taxes."

Who Is the Greatest?
(Mark 9.33-37; Luke 9.46-48)

18 At that time the disciples came to Jesus, asking, "Who is the greatest in the Kingdom of heaven?"

²So Jesus called a child to come and stand in front of them, ³and said, "I assure you that unless you change and

"Unless you change and become like children . . ." (18.3)

become like children, you will never enter the Kingdom of heaven. ⁴The greatest in the Kingdom of heaven is the one who humbles himself and becomes like

this child. ⁵And whoever welcomes in my name one such child as this, welcomes me.

Temptations to Sin
(Mark 9.42-48; Luke 17.1, 2)

⁶"If anyone should cause one of these little ones to lose his faith in me, it would be better for that person to have a large millstone tied around his neck and be drowned in the deep sea. ⁷How terrible for the world that there are things that make people lose their faith! Such things will always happen — but how terrible for the one who causes them!

⁸"If your hand or your foot makes you lose your faith, cut it off and throw it away! It is better for you to enter life without a hand or a foot than to keep both hands and both feet and be thrown into the eternal fire. ⁹And if your eye makes you lose your faith, take it out and throw it away! It is better for you to enter life with only one eye than to keep both eyes and be thrown into the fire of hell.

The Parable of the Lost Sheep
(Luke 15.3-7)

¹⁰"See that you don't despise any of these little ones. Their angels in heaven, I tell you, are always in the presence of my Father in heaven.ᵖ

¹²"What do you think a man does who has one hundred sheep and one of them gets lost? He will leave the other ninety-nine grazing on the hillside and go and look for the lost sheep. ¹³When he finds it, I tell you, he feels far happier over this one sheep than over the ninety-nine that did not get lost. ¹⁴In just the same way yourᵍ Father in heaven does not want any of these little ones to be lost.

ᵖ *Some manuscripts add verse 11:* For the Son of Man came to save the lost (*see Lk 19.10*).　　ᵍ *your; some manuscripts have* my.

18.1 Lk 22.24　**18.3** Mk 10.15; Lk 18.17　**18.8** Mt 5.30　**18.9** Mt 5.29　**18.10** Tb 12.15
18.11 Lk 19.10

He will . . . go and look for the lost sheep.
(18.12)

When Someone Sins

15"If your brother sins against you,*r* go to him and show him his fault. But do it privately, just between yourselves. If he listens to you, you have won your brother back. 16But if he will not listen to you, take one or two other persons with you, so that 'every accusation may be upheld by the testimony of two or more witnesses,' as the scripture says. 17And if he will not listen to them, then tell the whole thing to the church. Finally, if he will not listen to the church, treat him as though he were a pagan or a tax collector.

Prohibiting and Permitting

18"And so I tell all of you: what you prohibit on earth will be prohibited in heaven, and what you permit on earth will be permitted in heaven.

19"And I tell you more: whenever two of you on earth agree about anything you pray for, it will be done for you by my Father in heaven. 20For where two or three come together in my name, I am there with them."

The Parable of the Unforgiving Servant

21Then Peter came to Jesus and asked, "Lord, if my brother keeps on sinning against me, how many times do I have to forgive him? Seven times?"

22"No, not seven times," answered Jesus, "but seventy times seven,*s* 23because the Kingdom of heaven is like this. Once there was a king who decided to check on his servants' accounts. 24He had just begun to do so when one of them was brought in who owed him millions of dollars. 25The servant did not have enough to pay his debt, so the king ordered him to be sold as a slave, with his wife and his children and all that he had, in order to pay the debt. 26The servant fell on his knees before the king. 'Be patient with me,' he begged, 'and I will pay you everything!' 27The king felt sorry for him, so he forgave him the debt and let him go.

28"Then the man went out and met one of his fellow servants who owed him a few dollars. He grabbed him and started choking him. 'Pay back what you owe me!' he said. 29His fellow servant fell down and begged him, 'Be patient with me, and I will pay you back!' 30But he refused; instead, he had him thrown into jail until he should pay the debt. 31When the other servants saw what had happened, they were very upset and went to the king and told him everything. 32So he called the servant in. 'You worthless slave!' he said. 'I forgave you the whole amount you owed me, just because you asked me to. 33You should have had mercy on your fellow servant, just as I had mercy on

r Some manuscripts do not have against you. seventy-seven times.　　*s* seventy times seven; *or*

18.15 Lk 17.3　**18.16** Dt 19.15　**18.18** Mt 16.19; Jn 20.23　**18.21, 22** Lk 17.3, 4
18.22 Gn 4.24

you.' [34] The king was very angry, and he sent the servant to jail to be punished until he should pay back the whole amount."

[35] And Jesus concluded, "That is how my Father in heaven will treat every one of you unless you forgive your brother from your heart."

Jesus Teaches about Divorce
(Mark 10.1-12)

19 When Jesus finished saying these things, he left Galilee and went to the territory of Judea on the other side of the Jordan River. [2] Large crowds followed him, and he healed them there.

[3] Some Pharisees came to him and tried to trap him by asking, "Does our Law allow a man to divorce his wife for whatever reason he wishes?"

[4] Jesus answered, "Haven't you read the scripture that says that in the beginning the Creator made people male and female? [5] And God said, 'For this reason a man will leave his father and mother and unite with his wife, and the two will become one.' [6] So they are no longer two, but one. No human being must separate, then, what God has joined together."

[7] The Pharisees asked him, "Why, then, did Moses give the law for a man to hand his wife a divorce notice and send her away?"

[8] Jesus answered, "Moses gave you permission to divorce your wives because you are so hard to teach. But it was not like that at the time of creation. [9] I tell you, then, that any man who divorces his wife for any cause other than her unfaithfulness, commits adultery if he marries some other woman."

[10] His disciples said to him, "If this is how it is between a man and his wife, it is better not to marry."

[11] Jesus answered, "This teaching does not apply to everyone, but only to those to whom God has given it. [12] For there are different reasons why men cannot marry: some, because they were born that way; others, because men made them that way; and others do not marry for the sake of the Kingdom of heaven. Let him who can accept this teaching do so."

Jesus Blesses Little Children
(Mark 10.13-16; Luke 18.15-17)

[13] Some people brought children to Jesus for him to place his hands on them and to pray for them, but the disciples scolded the people. [14] Jesus said, "Let the children come to me and do not stop them, because the Kingdom of heaven belongs to such as these."

[15] He placed his hands on them and then went away.

The Rich Young Man
(Mark 10.17-31; Luke 18.18-30)

[16] Once a man came to Jesus. "Teacher," he asked, "what good thing must I do to receive eternal life?"

[17] "Why do you ask me concerning what is good?" answered Jesus. "There is only One who is good. Keep the commandments if you want to enter life."

[18] "What commandments?" he asked.

Jesus answered, "Do not commit murder; do not commit adultery; do not steal; do not accuse anyone falsely; [19] respect your father and your mother; and love your neighbor as you love yourself."

[20] "I have obeyed all these commandments," the young man replied. "What else do I need to do?"

[21] Jesus said to him, "If you want to be perfect, go and sell all you have and give the money to the poor, and you will

---

19.4 Gn 1.27; 5.2   **19.5** Gn 2.24   **19.7** Dt 24.1-4; Mt 5.31   **19.9** Mt 5.32; 1 Co 7.10, 11
19.18 a Ex 20.13; Dt 5.17; **b** Ex 20.14; Dt 5.18; **c** Ex 20.15; Dt 5.19; **d** Ex 20.16; Dt 5.20
19.19 a Ex 20.12; Dt 5.16; **b** Lv 19.18

have riches in heaven; then come and follow me."

22 When the young man heard this, he went away sad, because he was very rich.

23 Jesus then said to his disciples, "I assure you: it will be very hard for rich people to enter the Kingdom of heaven. **24** I repeat: it is much harder for a rich person to enter the Kingdom of God than for a camel to go through the eye of a needle."

25 When the disciples heard this, they were completely amazed. "Who, then, can be saved?" they asked.

26 Jesus looked straight at them and answered, "This is impossible for human beings, but for God everything is possible."

27 Then Peter spoke up. "Look," he said, "we have left everything and followed you. What will we have?"

28 Jesus said to them, "You can be sure that when the Son of Man sits on his glorious throne in the New Age, then you twelve followers of mine will also sit on thrones, to rule the twelve tribes of Israel. **29** And everyone who has left houses or brothers or sisters or father or mother or children or fields for my sake, will receive a hundred times more and will be given eternal life. **30** But many who now are first will be last, and many who now are last will be first.

The Workers in the Vineyard

20 "The Kingdom of heaven is like this. Once there was a man who went out early in the morning to hire some men to work in his vineyard. **2** He agreed to pay them the regular wage, a silver coin a day, and sent them to work in his vineyard. **3** He went out again to the marketplace at nine o'clock and saw some men standing there doing nothing, **4** so he told them, 'You also

go and work in the vineyard, and I will pay you a fair wage.' **5** So they went. Then at twelve o'clock and again at three o'clock he did the same thing. **6** It was nearly five o'clock when he went to the marketplace and saw some other men still standing there. 'Why are you wasting the whole day here doing nothing?' he asked them. **7** 'No one hired us,' they answered. 'Well, then, you go and work in the vineyard,' he told them.

8 "When evening came, the owner told his foreman, 'Call the workers and pay them their wages, starting with those who were hired last and ending with those who were hired first.' **9** The men who had begun to work at five o'clock were paid a silver coin each. **10** So when the men who were the first to be hired came to be paid, they thought they would get more; but they too were given a silver coin each. **11** They took their money and started grumbling against the employer. **12** 'These men who were hired last worked only one hour,' they said, 'while we put up with a whole day's work in the hot sun — yet you paid them the same as you paid us!' **13** 'Listen, friend,' the owner answered one of them, 'I have not cheated you. After all, you agreed to do a day's work for one silver coin. **14** Now take your pay and go home. I want to give this man who was hired last as much as I gave you. **15** Don't I have the right to do as I wish with my own money? Or are you jealous because I am generous?' "

16 And Jesus concluded, "So those who are last will be first, and those who are first will be last."

Jesus Speaks a Third Time about His Death
(Mark 10.32-34; Luke 18.31-34)

17 As Jesus was going up to Jerusalem, he took the twelve disciples aside

19.28 a Mt 25.31; **b** Lk 22.30　**19.30** Mt 20.16; Lk 13.30　**20.8** Lv 19.13; Dt 24.15
20.16 Mt 19.30; Mk 10.31; Lk 13.30

and spoke to them privately, as they walked along. [18]"Listen," he told them, "we are going up to Jerusalem, where the Son of Man will be handed over to the chief priests and the teachers of the Law. They will condemn him to death [19]and then hand him over to the Gentiles, who will make fun of him, whip him, and crucify him; but three days later he will be raised to life."

A Mother's Request
(Mark 10.35-45)

[20]Then the wife of Zebedee came to Jesus with her two sons, bowed before him, and asked him for a favor.

[21]"What do you want?" Jesus asked her.

She answered, "Promise me that these two sons of mine will sit at your right and your left when you are King."

[22]"You don't know what you are asking for," Jesus answered the sons. "Can you drink the cup of suffering that I am about to drink?"

"We can," they answered.

[23]"You will indeed drink from my cup," Jesus told them, "but I do not have the right to choose who will sit at my right and my left. These places belong to those for whom my Father has prepared them."

[24]When the other ten disciples heard about this, they became angry with the two brothers. [25]So Jesus called them all together and said, "You know that the rulers of the heathen have power over them, and the leaders have complete authority. [26]This, however, is not the way it shall be among you. If one of you wants to be great, you must be the servant of the rest; [27]and if one of you wants to be first, you must be the slave of the others — [28]like the Son of Man, who did not come to be served, but to serve and to give his life to redeem many people."

Jesus Heals Two Blind Men
(Mark 10.46-52; Luke 18.35-43)

[29]As Jesus and his disciples were leaving Jericho, a large crowd was following. [30]Two blind men who were sitting by the road heard that Jesus was passing by, so they began to shout, "Son of David! Have mercy on us, sir!"

[31]The crowd scolded them and told them to be quiet. But they shouted even more loudly, "Son of David! Have mercy on us, sir!"

[32]Jesus stopped and called them. "What do you want me to do for you?" he asked them.

[33]"Sir," they answered, "we want you to give us our sight!"

[34]Jesus had pity on them and touched their eyes; at once they were able to see, and they followed him.

The Triumphant Entry into Jerusalem
(Mark 11.1-11; Luke 19.28-40; John 12.12-19)

21 As Jesus and his disciples approached Jerusalem, they came to Bethphage at the Mount of Olives. There Jesus sent two of the disciples on ahead [2]with these instructions: "Go to the village there ahead of you, and at once you will find a donkey tied up with her colt beside her. Untie them and bring them to me. [3]And if anyone says anything, tell him, 'The Master[t] needs them'; and then he will let them go at once."

[4]This happened in order to make come true what the prophet had said:
[5]"Tell the city of Zion,
    Look, your king is coming
        to you!
    He is humble and rides on a
        donkey
    and on a colt, the foal of a
        donkey."

[6]So the disciples went and did what Jesus had told them to do: [7]they

[t] The Master; or Their owner.
20.25, 26 Lk 22.25, 26   **20.26, 27** Mt 23.11; Mk 9.35; Lk 22.26   **21.5** Zec 9.9

brought the donkey and the colt, threw their cloaks over them, and Jesus got on. ⁸A large crowd of people spread their cloaks on the road while others cut branches from the trees and spread them on the road. ⁹The crowds walking in front of Jesus and those walking behind began to shout, "Praise to David's Son! God bless him who comes in the name of the Lord! Praise be to God!"

"God bless him who comes in the name of the Lord!" (21.9)

¹⁰When Jesus entered Jerusalem, the whole city was thrown into an uproar. "Who is he?" the people asked.

¹¹"This is the prophet Jesus, from Nazareth in Galilee," the crowds answered.

Jesus Goes to the Temple
(Mark 11.15-19; Luke 19.45-48; John 2.13-22)

¹²Jesus went into the Temple and drove out all those who were buying and selling there. He overturned the tables of the moneychangers and the stools of those who sold pigeons, ¹³and said to them, "It is written in the Scriptures that God said, 'My Temple will be called a house of prayer.' But you are making it a hideout for thieves!"

¹⁴The blind and the crippled came to him in the Temple, and he healed them. ¹⁵The chief priests and the teachers of the Law became angry when they saw the wonderful things he was doing and the children shouting in the Temple, "Praise to David's Son!" ¹⁶So they asked Jesus, "Do you hear what they are saying?"

"Indeed I do," answered Jesus. "Haven't you ever read this scripture? 'You have trained children and babies to offer perfect praise.'"

¹⁷Jesus left them and went out of the city to Bethany, where he spent the night.

Jesus Curses the Fig Tree
(Mark 11.12-14, 20-24)

¹⁸On his way back to the city early next morning, Jesus was hungry. ¹⁹He saw a fig tree by the side of the road and went to it, but found nothing on it except leaves. So he said to the tree, "You will never again bear fruit!" At once the fig tree dried up.

²⁰The disciples saw this and were astounded. "How did the fig tree dry up so quickly?" they asked.

²¹Jesus answered, "I assure you that if you believe and do not doubt, you will be able to do what I have done to this fig

21.9 Ps 118.25, 26　**21.13** Is 56.7; Jr 7.11　**21.16** Ps 8.2 (LXX)　**21.21** Mt 17.20; 1 Co 13.2

tree. And not only this, but you will even be able to say to this hill, 'Get up and throw yourself in the sea,' and it will. 22 If you believe, you will receive whatever you ask for in prayer."

The Question about Jesus' Authority
(Mark 11.27-33; Luke 20.1-8)

23 Jesus came back to the Temple; and as he taught, the chief priests and the elders came to him and asked, "What right do you have to do these things? Who gave you such right?"

24 Jesus answered them, "I will ask you just one question, and if you give me an answer, I will tell you what right I have to do these things. 25 Where did John's right to baptize come from: was it from God or from human beings?"

They started to argue among themselves, "What shall we say? If we answer, 'From God,' he will say to us, 'Why, then, did you not believe John?' 26 But if we say, 'From human beings,' we are afraid of what the people might do, because they are all convinced that John was a prophet." 27 So they answered Jesus, "We don't know."

And he said to them, "Neither will I tell you, then, by what right I do these things.

The Parable of the Two Sons

28 "Now, what do you think? There was once a man who had two sons. He went to the older one and said, 'Son, go and work in the vineyard today.' 29 'I don't want to,' he answered, but later he changed his mind and went. 30 Then the father went to the other son and said the same thing. 'Yes, sir,' he answered, but he did not go. 31 Which one of the two did what his father wanted?"

"The older one," they answered.

So Jesus said to them, "I tell you: the tax collectors and the prostitutes are going into the Kingdom of God ahead of you. 32 For John the Baptist came to you

showing you the right path to take, and you would not believe him; but the tax collectors and the prostitutes believed him. Even when you saw this, you did not later change your minds and believe him.

The Parable of the Tenants in the Vineyard
(Mark 12.1-12; Luke 20.9-19)

33 "Listen to another parable," Jesus said. "There was once a landowner who planted a vineyard, put a fence around it, dug a hole for the wine press, and built a watchtower. Then he rented the vineyard to tenants and left home on a trip. 34 When the time came to gather the grapes, he sent his slaves to the tenants to receive his share of the harvest. 35 The tenants grabbed his slaves, beat one, killed another, and stoned another. 36 Again the man sent other slaves, more than the first time, and the tenants treated them the same way. 37 Last of all he sent his son to them. 'Surely they will respect my son,' he said. 38 But when the tenants saw the son, they said to themselves, 'This is the owner's son. Come on, let's kill him, and we will get his property!' 39 So they grabbed him, threw him out of the vineyard, and killed him.

40 "Now, when the owner of the vineyard comes, what will he do to those tenants?" Jesus asked.

41 "He will certainly kill those evil men," they answered, "and rent the vineyard out to other tenants, who will give him his share of the harvest at the right time."

42 Jesus said to them, "Haven't you ever read what the Scriptures say?

'The stone which the builders
    rejected as worthless
turned out to be the most
    important of all.
This was done by the Lord;
    what a wonderful sight it is!'

21.32 Lk 3.12; 7.29, 30   21.33 Is 5.1, 2   21.42 Ps 118.22, 23

43"And so I tell you," added Jesus, "the Kingdom of God will be taken away from you and given to a people who will produce the proper fruits."[u]

45The chief priests and the Pharisees heard Jesus' parables and knew that he was talking about them, **46**so they tried to arrest him. But they were afraid of the crowds, who considered Jesus to be a prophet.

The Parable of the Wedding Feast
(Luke 14.15-24)

22 Jesus again used parables in talking to the people. **2**"The Kingdom of heaven is like this. Once there was a king who prepared a wedding feast for his son. **3**He sent his servants to tell the invited guests to come to the feast, but they did not want to come. **4**So he sent other servants with this message for the guests: 'My feast is ready now; my steers and prize calves have been butchered, and everything is ready. Come to the wedding feast!' **5**But the invited guests paid no attention and went about their business: one went to his farm, another to his store, **6**while others grabbed the servants, beat them, and killed them. **7**The king was very angry; so he sent his soldiers, who killed those murderers and burned down their city. **8**Then he called his servants and said to them, 'My wedding feast is ready, but the people I invited did not deserve it. **9**Now go to the main streets and invite to the feast as many people as you find.' **10**So the servants went out into the streets and gathered all the people they could find, good and bad alike; and the wedding hall was filled with people.

11"The king went in to look at the guests and saw a man who was not wearing wedding clothes. **12**'Friend, how did you get in here without wed-

ding clothes?' the king asked him. But the man said nothing. **13**Then the king told the servants, 'Tie him up hand and foot, and throw him outside in the dark. There he will cry and gnash his teeth.' "

14And Jesus concluded, "Many are invited, but few are chosen."

The Question about Paying Taxes
(Mark 12.13-17; Luke 20.20-26)

15The Pharisees went off and made a plan to trap Jesus with questions. **16**Then they sent to him some of their disciples and some members of Herod's party. "Teacher," they said, "we know that you tell the truth. You teach the truth about God's will for people, without worrying about what others think, because you pay no attention to anyone's status. **17**Tell us, then, what do you think? Is it against our Law to pay taxes to the Roman Emperor, or not?"

18Jesus, however, was aware of their evil plan, and so he said, "You hypocrites! Why are you trying to trap me? **19**Show me the coin for paying the tax!"

They brought him the coin, **20**and he asked them, "Whose face and name are these?"

21"The Emperor's," they answered.

So Jesus said to them, "Well, then, pay to the Emperor what belongs to the Emperor, and pay to God what belongs to God."

22When they heard this, they were amazed; and they left him and went away.

The Question about Rising from Death
(Mark 12.18-27; Luke 20.27-40)

23That same day some Sadducees came to Jesus and claimed that people will not rise from death. **24**"Teacher," they said, "Moses said that if a man who has no children dies, his brother must marry the widow so that they can have

---

[u] *Some manuscripts add verse 44:* Whoever falls on this stone will be cut to pieces; and if the stone falls on someone, it will crush him to dust *(see Lk 20.18).*
22.13 Mt 8.12; 25.30; Lk 13.28   **22.14** 2 Esd 8.3   **22.23** Ac 23.8   **22.24** Dt 25.5

children who will be considered the dead man's children. 25 Now, there were seven brothers who used to live here. The oldest got married and died without having children, so he left his widow to his brother. 26 The same thing happened to the second brother, to the third, and finally to all seven. 27 Last of all, the woman died. 28 Now, on the day when the dead rise to life, whose wife will she be? All of them had married her."

29 Jesus answered them, "How wrong you are! It is because you don't know the Scriptures or God's power. 30 For when the dead rise to life, they will be like the angels in heaven and will not marry. 31 Now, as for the dead rising to life: haven't you ever read what God has told you? He said, 32 'I am the God of Abraham, the God of Isaac, and the God of Jacob.' He is the God of the living, not of the dead."

33 When the crowds heard this, they were amazed at his teaching.

The Great Commandment
(Mark 12.28-34; Luke 10.25-28)

34 When the Pharisees heard that Jesus had silenced the Sadducees, they came together, 35 and one of them, a teacher of the Law, tried to trap him with a question. 36 "Teacher," he asked, "which is the greatest commandment in the Law?"

37 Jesus answered, " 'Love the Lord your God with all your heart, with all your soul, and with all your mind.' 38 This is the greatest and the most important commandment. 39 The second most important commandment is like it: 'Love your neighbor as you love yourself.' 40 The whole Law of Moses and the teachings of the prophets depend on these two commandments."

The Question about the Messiah
(Mark 12.35-37; Luke 20.41-44)

41 When some Pharisees gathered together, Jesus asked them, 42 "What do you think about the Messiah? Whose descendant is he?"

"He is David's descendant," they answered.

43 "Why, then," Jesus asked, "did the Spirit inspire David to call him 'Lord'? David said,

44 'The Lord said to my Lord:
    Sit here at my right side
    until I put your enemies
        under your feet.'

45 If, then, David called him 'Lord,' how can the Messiah be David's descendant?"

46 No one was able to give Jesus any answer, and from that day on no one dared to ask him any more questions.

Jesus Warns against the Teachers of the Law and the Pharisees
(Mark 12.38, 39; Luke 11.43, 46; 20.45, 46)

23 Then Jesus spoke to the crowds and to his disciples. 2 "The teachers of the Law and the Pharisees are the authorized interpreters of Moses' Law. 3 So you must obey and follow everything they tell you to do; do not, however, imitate their actions, because they don't practice what they preach. 4 They tie onto people's backs loads that are heavy and hard to carry, yet they aren't willing even to lift a finger to help them carry those loads. 5 They do everything so that people will see them. Look at the straps with scripture verses on them which they wear on their foreheads and arms, and notice how large they are! Notice also how long are the tassels on their cloaks!ᵛ 6 They love the best places at feasts and

---

ᵛ TASSELS ON THEIR CLOAKS: *These tassels were worn as a sign of devotion to God (see Nu 15.37-41).*

22.30 Ws 5.5   **22.32** Ex 3.6   **22.37** Dt 6.5   **22.39** Lv 19.18   **22.35-40** Lk 10.25-28
22.44 Ps 110.1   **23.5 a** Mt 6.1; **b** Dt 6.8; **c** Nu 15.38

They aren't willing even to lift a finger to help them. (23.4)

the reserved seats in the synagogues; [7] they love to be greeted with respect in the marketplaces and to have people call them 'Teacher.' [8] You must not be called 'Teacher,' because you are all equal and have only one Teacher. [9] And you must not call anyone here on earth 'Father,' because you have only the one Father in heaven. [10] Nor should you be called 'Leader,' because your one and only leader is the Messiah. [11] The greatest one among you must be your servant. [12] Whoever makes himself great will be humbled, and whoever humbles himself will be made great.

Jesus Condemns Their Hypocrisy
(Mark 12.40; Luke 11.39-42, 44, 52; 20.47)

[13] "How terrible for you, teachers of the Law and Pharisees! You hypocrites! You lock the door to the Kingdom of heaven in people's faces, but you yourselves don't go in, nor do you allow in those who are trying to enter! [w]

[15] "How terrible for you, teachers of the Law and Pharisees! You hypocrites! You sail the seas and cross whole countries to win one convert; and when you succeed, you make him twice as deserving of going to hell as you yourselves are!

[16] "How terrible for you, blind guides! You teach, 'If someone swears by the Temple, he isn't bound by his vow; but if he swears by the gold in the Temple, he is bound.' [17] Blind fools! Which is more important, the gold or the Temple which makes the gold holy? [18] You also teach, 'If someone swears by the altar, he isn't bound by his vow; but if he swears by the gift on the altar, he is bound.' [19] How blind you are! Which is the more important, the gift or the altar which makes the gift holy? [20] So then, when a person swears by the altar, he is swearing by it and by all the gifts on it; [21] and when he swears by the Temple, he is swearing by it and by God, who lives there; [22] and when someone swears by heaven, he is swearing by God's throne and by him who sits on it.

[23] "How terrible for you, teachers of the Law and Pharisees! You hypocrites! You give to God one tenth even of the seasoning herbs, such as mint, dill, and cumin, but you neglect to obey the really important teachings of the Law, such as justice and mercy and honesty. These you should practice, without neglecting the others. [24] Blind guides! You strain a fly out of your drink, but swallow a camel!

[25] "How terrible for you, teachers of the Law and Pharisees! You hypocrites!

[w] *Some manuscripts add verse 14:* How terrible for you, teachers of the Law and Pharisees! You hypocrites! You take advantage of widows and rob them of their homes, and then make a show of saying long prayers! Because of this your punishment will be all the worse! (*see Mk 12.40*).

23.11 Mt 20.26, 27; Mk 9.35; 10.43, 44; Lk 22.26   **23.12** Lk 14.11; 18.14   **23.22** Is 66.1; Mt 5.34   **23.23** Lv 27.30

You clean the outside of your cup and plate, while the inside is full of what you have gotten by violence and selfishness. 26 Blind Pharisee! Clean what is inside the cup first, and then the outside will be clean too!

27 "How terrible for you, teachers of the Law and Pharisees! You hypocrites! You are like whitewashed tombs, which look fine on the outside but are full of bones and decaying corpses on the inside. 28 In the same way, on the outside you appear good to everybody, but inside you are full of hypocrisy and sins.

Jesus Predicts Their Punishment
(Luke 11.47-51)

29 "How terrible for you, teachers of the Law and Pharisees! You hypocrites! You make fine tombs for the prophets and decorate the monuments of those who lived good lives; 30 and you claim that if you had lived during the time of your ancestors, you would not have done what they did and killed the prophets. 31 So you actually admit that you are the descendants of those who murdered the prophets! 32 Go on, then, and finish up what your ancestors started! 33 You snakes and children of snakes! How do you expect to escape from being condemned to hell? 34 And so I tell you that I will send you prophets and wise men and teachers; you will kill some of them, crucify others, and whip others in the synagogues and chase them from town to town. 35 As a result, the punishment for the murder of all innocent people will fall on you, from the murder of innocent Abel to the murder of Zechariah son of Berechiah, whom you murdered between the Temple and the altar. 36 I tell you indeed: the punishment for all these murders will fall on the people of this day!

Jesus' Love for Jerusalem
(Luke 13.34, 35)

37 "Jerusalem, Jerusalem! You kill the prophets and stone the messengers God has sent you! How many times I wanted to put my arms around all your people, just as a hen gathers her chicks under her wings, but you would not let me! 38 And so your Temple will be abandoned and empty. 39 From now on, I tell you, you will never see me again until you say, 'God bless him who comes in the name of the Lord.'"

Jesus Speaks of the Destruction of the Temple
(Mark 13.1, 2; Luke 21.5, 6)

24 Jesus left and was going away from the Temple when his disciples came to him to call his attention to its buildings. 2 "Yes," he said, "you may well look at all these. I tell you this: not a single stone here will be left in its place; every one of them will be thrown down."

Troubles and Persecutions
(Mark 13.3-13; Luke 21.7-19)

3 As Jesus sat on the Mount of Olives, the disciples came to him in private. "Tell us when all this will be," they asked, "and what will happen to show that it is the time for your coming and the end of the age."

4 Jesus answered, "Watch out, and do not let anyone fool you. 5 Many men, claiming to speak for me, will come and say, 'I am the Messiah!' and they will fool many people. 6 You are going to hear the noise of battles close by and the news of battles far away; but do not be troubled. Such things must happen, but they do not mean that the end has come. 7 Countries will fight each other; kingdoms will attack one another. There will be famines and earthquakes

---

23.27 Ac 23.3   **23.33** Mt 3.7; 12.34; Lk 3.7   **23.35 a** Gn 4.8; **b** 2 Ch 24.20, 21
23.38 Jr 22.5   **23.39** Ps 118.26   **24.3** 2 Esd 4.51—5.19   **24.7** 2 Esd 13.31

everywhere. 8 All these things are like the first pains of childbirth.

9 "Then you will be arrested and handed over to be punished and be put to death. Everyone will hate you because of me. 10 Many will give up their faith at that time; they will betray one another and hate one another. 11 Then many false prophets will appear and fool many people. 12 Such will be the spread of evil that many people's love will grow cold. 13 But whoever holds out to the end will be saved. 14 And this Good News about the Kingdom will be preached through all the world for a witness to all people; and then the end will come.

The Awful Horror
(Mark 13.14-23; Luke 21.20-24)

15 "You will see 'The Awful Horror' of which the prophet Daniel spoke. It will be standing in the holy place." (Note to the reader: understand what this means!) 16 "Then those who are in Judea must run away to the hills. 17 Someone who is on the roof of a house must not take the time to go down and get any belongings from the house. 18 Someone who is in the field must not go back to get a cloak. 19 How terrible it will be in those days for women who are pregnant and for mothers with little babies! 20 Pray to God that you will not have to run away during the winter or on a Sabbath! 21 For the trouble at that time will be far more terrible than any there has ever been, from the beginning of the world to this very day. Nor will there ever be anything like it again. 22 But God has already reduced the number of days; had he not done so, nobody would survive. For the sake of his chosen people, however, God will reduce the days.

23 "Then, if anyone says to you, 'Look, here is the Messiah!' or 'There he is!' — do not believe it. 24 For false Messiahs and false prophets will appear; they will perform great miracles and wonders in order to deceive even God's chosen people, if possible. 25 Listen! I have told you this ahead of time.

26 "Or, if people should tell you, 'Look, he is out in the desert!' — don't go there; or if they say, 'Look, he is hiding here!' — don't believe it. 27 For the Son of Man will come like the lightning which flashes across the whole sky from the east to the west.

28 "Wherever there is a dead body, the vultures will gather.

The Coming of the Son of Man
(Mark 13.24-27; Luke 21.25-28)

29 "Soon after the trouble of those days, the sun will grow dark, the moon will no longer shine, the stars will fall from heaven, and the powers in space will be driven from their courses. 30 Then the sign of the Son of Man will appear in the sky; and all the peoples of earth will weep as they see the Son of Man coming on the clouds of heaven with power and great glory. 31 The great trumpet will sound, and he will send out his angels to the four corners of the earth, and they will gather his chosen people from one end of the world to the other.

The Lesson of the Fig Tree
(Mark 13.28-31; Luke 21.29-33)

32 "Let the fig tree teach you a lesson. When its branches become green and tender and it starts putting out leaves, you know that summer is near. 33 In the same way, when you see all these things, you will know that the time is

---

24.9 Mt 10.22　**24.13** Mt 10.22　**24.15** Dn 9.27; 11.31; 12.11; 1 Macc 1.54; 6.7
24.17, 18 Lk 17.31　**24.21** Dn 12.1; Rev 7.14　**24.26, 27** Lk 17.23, 24　**24.28** Lk 17.37
24.29 a Is 13.10; Jl 2.10, 31; 3.15; Rev 6.12; **b** Is 13.10; Ez 32.7; Jl 2.10; 3.15; **c** Is 34.4;
Rev 6.13　**24.30** Dn 7.13; Zec 12.10-14; Rev 1.7

near, ready to begin.* 34 Remember that all these things will happen before the people now living have all died. 35 Heaven and earth will pass away, but my words will never pass away.

No One Knows the Day and Hour
(Mark 13.32-37; Luke 17.26-30, 34-36)

36 "No one knows, however, when that day and hour will come — neither the angels in heaven nor the Son; *y* the Father alone knows. 37 The coming of the Son of Man will be like what happened in the time of Noah. 38 In the days before the flood people ate and drank, men and women married, up to the very day Noah went into the boat; 39 yet they did not realize what was happening until the flood came and swept them all away. That is how it will be when the Son of Man comes. 40 At that time two men will be working in a field: one will be taken away, the other will be left behind. 41 Two women will be at a mill grinding meal: one will be taken away, the other will be left behind. 42 Watch out, then, because you do not know what day your Lord will come. 43 If the owner of a house knew the time when the thief would come, you can be sure that he would stay awake and not let the thief break into his house. 44 So then, you also must always be ready, because the Son of Man will come at an hour when you are not expecting him.

The Faithful or the Unfaithful Servant
(Luke 12.41-48)

45 "Who, then, is a faithful and wise servant? It is the one that his master has placed in charge of the other servants to give them their food at the proper time. 46 How happy that servant is if his master finds him doing this when he comes home! 47 Indeed, I tell you, the master will put that servant in charge of all his property. 48 But if he is a bad servant, he will tell himself that his master will not come back for a long time, 49 and he will begin to beat his fellow servants and to eat and drink with drunkards. 50 Then that servant's master will come back one day when the servant does not expect him and at a time he does not know. 51 The master will cut him in pieces *z* and make him share the fate of the hypocrites. There he will cry and gnash his teeth.

The Parable of the Ten Young Women

25 "At that time the Kingdom of heaven will be like this. Once there were ten young women who took their oil lamps and went out to meet the bridegroom. 2 Five of them were foolish, and the other five were wise. 3 The foolish ones took their lamps but did not take any extra oil with them, 4 while the wise ones took containers full of oil for their lamps. 5 The bridegroom was late in coming, so they began to nod and fall asleep.

6 "It was already midnight when the cry rang out, 'Here is the bridegroom! Come and meet him!' 7 The ten young women woke up and trimmed their lamps. 8 Then the foolish ones said to the wise ones, 'Let us have some of your oil, because our lamps are going out.' 9 'No, indeed,' the wise ones answered, 'there is not enough for you and for us. Go to the store and buy some for yourselves.' 10 So the foolish ones went off to buy some oil; and while they were gone, the bridegroom arrived. The five who were ready went in with him to the wedding feast, and the door was closed.

11 "Later the others arrived. 'Sir, sir! Let us in!' they cried out. 12 'Certainly

---

x the time is near, ready to begin; *or* he is near, ready to come.   *y Some manuscripts do not have* nor the Son.   *z* cut him in pieces; *or* throw him out.

24.37 Gn 6.5-8   **24.39** Gn 7.6-24   **24.43, 44** Lk 12.39, 40   **25.1** Lk 12.35
25.11, 12 Lk 13.25

not! I don't know you,' the bridegroom answered."

¹³And Jesus concluded, "Watch out, then, because you do not know the day or the hour.

The Parable of the Three Servants
(Luke 19.11-27)

¹⁴"At that time the Kingdom of heaven will be like this. Once there was a man who was about to leave home on a trip; he called his servants and put them in charge of his property. ¹⁵He gave to each one according to his ability: to one he gave five thousand gold coins, to another he gave two thousand, and to another he gave one thousand. Then he left on his trip. ¹⁶The servant who had received five thousand coins went at once and invested his money and earned another five thousand. ¹⁷In the same way the servant who had received two thousand coins earned another two thousand. ¹⁸But the servant who had received one thousand coins went off, dug a hole in the ground, and hid his master's money.

¹⁹"After a long time the master of those servants came back and settled accounts with them. ²⁰The servant who had received five thousand coins came in and handed over the other five thousand. 'You gave me five thousand coins, sir,' he said. 'Look! Here are another five thousand that I have earned.' ²¹'Well done, you good and faithful servant!' said his master. 'You have been faithful in managing small amounts, so I will put you in charge of large amounts. Come on in and share my happiness!' ²²Then the servant who had been given two thousand coins came in and said, 'You gave me two thousand coins, sir. Look! Here are another two thousand that I have earned.' ²³'Well done, you good and faithful servant!' said his master. 'You have

been faithful in managing small amounts, so I will put you in charge of large amounts. Come on in and share my happiness!' ²⁴Then the servant who had received one thousand coins came in and said, 'Sir, I know you are a hard man; you reap harvests where you did not plant, and you gather crops where you did not scatter seed. ²⁵I was afraid, so I went off and hid your money in the ground. Look! Here is what belongs to you.' ²⁶'You bad and lazy servant!' his master said. 'You knew, did you, that I reap harvests where I did not plant, and gather crops where I did not scatter seed? ²⁷Well, then, you should have deposited my money in the bank, and I would have received it all back with interest when I returned. ²⁸Now, take the money away from him and give it to the one who has ten thousand coins. ²⁹For to every person who has something, even more will be given, and he will have more than enough; but the person who has nothing, even the little that he has will be taken away from him. ³⁰As for this useless servant—throw him outside in the darkness; there he will cry and gnash his teeth.'

The Final Judgment

³¹"When the Son of Man comes as King and all the angels with him, he will sit on his royal throne, ³²and the people of all the nations will be gathered before him. Then he will divide them into two groups, just as a shepherd separates the sheep from the goats. ³³He will put the righteous people at his right and the others at his left. ³⁴Then the King will say to the people on his right, 'Come, you that are blessed by my Father! Come and possess the kingdom which has been prepared for you ever since the creation of the world. ³⁵I was hungry and you fed

25.14-30 Lk 19.11-27   **25.29** Mt 13.12; Mk 4.25; Lk 8.18   **25.30** Mt 8.12; 22.13; Lk 13.28
25.31 a Mt 16.27; **b** Mt 19.28   **25.35, 36** Si 7.32-36

me, thirsty and you gave me a drink; I was a stranger and you received me in your homes, 36 naked and you clothed me; I was sick and you took care of me, in prison and you visited me.' 37 The righteous will then answer him, 'When, Lord, did we ever see you hungry and feed you, or thirsty and give you a drink? 38 When did we ever see you a stranger and welcome you in our homes, or naked and clothe you? 39 When did we ever see you sick or in prison, and visit you?' 40 The King will reply, 'I tell you, whenever you did this for one of the least important of these followers of mine, you did it for me!'

41 "Then he will say to those on his left, 'Away from me, you that are under God's curse! Away to the eternal fire which has been prepared for the Devil and his angels! 42 I was hungry but you would not feed me, thirsty but you would not give me a drink; 43 I was a stranger but you would not welcome me in your homes, naked but you would not clothe me; I was sick and in prison but you would not take care of me.' 44 Then they will answer him, 'When, Lord, did we ever see you hungry or thirsty or a stranger or naked or sick or in prison, and we would not help you?' 45 The King will reply, 'I tell you, whenever you refused to help one of these least important ones, you refused to help me.' 46 These, then, will be sent off to eternal punishment, but the righteous will go to eternal life."

The Plot against Jesus
(Mark 14.1, 2; Luke 22.1, 2; John 11.45-53)

26 When Jesus had finished teaching all these things, he said to his disciples, 2 "In two days, as you know, it will be the Passover Festi-

val, and the Son of Man will be handed over to be crucified."

3 Then the chief priests and the elders met together in the palace of Caiaphas, the High Priest, 4 and made plans to arrest Jesus secretly and put him to death. 5 "We must not do it during the festival," they said, "or the people will riot."

Jesus Is Anointed at Bethany
(Mark 14.3-9; John 12.1-8)

6 Jesus was in Bethany at the house of Simon, a man who had suffered from a dreaded skin disease. 7 While Jesus was eating, a woman came to him with an alabaster jar filled with an expensive perfume, which she poured on his head. 8 The disciples saw this and became angry. "Why all this waste?" they asked. 9 "This perfume could have been sold for a large amount and the money given to the poor!"

10 Jesus knew what they were saying, and so he said to them, "Why are you bothering this woman? It is a fine and beautiful thing that she has done for me. 11 You will always have poor people with you, but you will not always have me. 12 What she did was to pour this perfume on my body to get me ready for burial. 13 Now, I assure you that wherever this gospel is preached all over the world, what she has done will be told in memory of her."

Judas Agrees to Betray Jesus
(Mark 14.10, 11; Luke 22.3-6)

14 Then one of the twelve disciples — the one named Judas Iscariot — went to the chief priests 15 and asked, "What will you give me if I betray Jesus to you?" They counted out thirty silver coins and gave them to him. 16 From then on Judas was looking for a good chance to hand Jesus over to them.

25.46 Dn 12.2   **26.2** Ex 12.1-27   **26.7** Lk 7.37, 38   **26.11** Dt 15.11   **26.15** Zec 11.12

Thirty silver coins (26.15)

Jesus Eats the Passover Meal with His Disciples
(Mark 14.12-21; Luke 22.7-13, 21-23; John 13.21-30)

¹⁷On the first day of the Festival of Unleavened Bread the disciples came to Jesus and asked him, "Where do you want us to get the Passover meal ready for you?"

¹⁸"Go to a certain man in the city," he said to them, "and tell him: 'The Teacher says, My hour has come; my disciples and I will celebrate the Passover at your house.'"

¹⁹The disciples did as Jesus had told them and prepared the Passover meal.

²⁰When it was evening, Jesus and the twelve disciples sat down to eat. ²¹During the meal Jesus said, "I tell you, one of you will betray me."

²²The disciples were very upset and began to ask him, one after the other, "Surely, Lord, you don't mean me?"

²³Jesus answered, "One who dips his bread in the dish with me will betray me. ²⁴The Son of Man will die as the Scriptures say he will, but how terrible for that man who will betray the Son of Man! It would have been better for that man if he had never been born!"

²⁵Judas, the traitor, spoke up. "Surely, Teacher, you don't mean me?" he asked.

Jesus answered, "So you say."

The Lord's Supper
(Mark 14.22-26; Luke 22.14-20; 1 Corinthians 11.23-25)

²⁶While they were eating, Jesus took a piece of bread, gave a prayer of thanks, broke it, and gave it to his disciples. "Take and eat it," he said; "this is my body."

²⁷Then he took a cup, gave thanks to God, and gave it to them. "Drink it, all of you," he said; ²⁸"this is my blood, which seals God's covenant, my blood poured out for many for the forgiveness of sins. ²⁹I tell you, I will never again drink this wine until the day I drink the new wine with you in my Father's Kingdom."

³⁰Then they sang a hymn and went out to the Mount of Olives.

Jesus Predicts Peter's Denial
(Mark 14.27-31; Luke 22.31-34; John 13.36-38)

³¹Then Jesus said to them, "This very night all of you will run away and leave me, for the scripture says, 'God will kill the shepherd, and the sheep of the flock will be scattered.' ³²But after I am raised to life, I will go to Galilee ahead of you."

³³Peter spoke up and said to Jesus, "I will never leave you, even though all the rest do!"

³⁴Jesus said to Peter, "I tell you that before the rooster crows tonight, you will say three times that you do not know me."

³⁵Peter answered, "I will never say that, even if I have to die with you!"

And all the other disciples said the same thing.

Jesus Prays in Gethsemane
(Mark 14.32-42; Luke 22.39-46)

³⁶Then Jesus went with his disciples to a place called Gethsemane, and he

26.23 Ps 41.9 **26.28 a** Ex 24.8; **b** Jr 31.31-34 **26.31** Zec 13.7 **26.32** Mt 28.16

"Take this cup of suffering from me!" (26.39)

said to them, "Sit here while I go over there and pray." 37 He took with him Peter and the two sons of Zebedee. Grief and anguish came over him, 38 and he said to them, "The sorrow in my heart is so great that it almost crushes me. Stay here and keep watch with me."

39 He went a little farther on, threw himself face downward on the ground, and prayed, "My Father, if it is possible, take this cup of suffering from me! Yet not what I want, but what you want."

40 Then he returned to the three disciples and found them asleep; and he said to Peter, "How is it that you three were not able to keep watch with me for even one hour? 41 Keep watch and pray that you will not fall into temptation. The spirit is willing, but the flesh is weak."

42 Once more Jesus went away and prayed, "My Father, if this cup of suf-

They could not keep their eyes open. (26.43)

fering cannot be taken away unless I drink it, your will be done." 43 He returned once more and found the disciples asleep; they could not keep their eyes open.

44 Again Jesus left them, went away, and prayed the third time, saying the same words. 45 Then he returned to the disciples and said, "Are you still sleeping and resting? Look! The hour has come for the Son of Man to be handed over to the power of sinners. 46 Get up, let us go. Look, here is the man who is betraying me!"

The Arrest of Jesus
(Mark 14.43-50; Luke 22.47-53; John 18.3-12)

47 Jesus was still speaking when Judas, one of the twelve disciples, arrived. With him was a large crowd armed with swords and clubs and sent by the chief priests and the elders. 48 The traitor had given the crowd a signal: "The man I kiss is the one you want. Arrest him!"

49 Judas went straight to Jesus and said, "Peace be with you, Teacher," and kissed him.

50 Jesus answered, "Be quick about it, friend!"*a*

Then they came up, arrested Jesus, and held him tight. 51 One of those who were with Jesus drew his sword and

a Be quick about it, friend!; *or* Why are you here, friend?

struck at the High Priest's slave, cutting off his ear. ⁵²"Put your sword back in its place," Jesus said to him. "All who take the sword will die by the sword. ⁵³Don't you know that I could call on my Father for help, and at once he would send me more than twelve armies of angels? ⁵⁴But in that case, how could the Scriptures come true which say that this is what must happen?"

⁵⁵Then Jesus spoke to the crowd, "Did you have to come with swords and clubs to capture me, as though I were an outlaw? Every day I sat down and taught in the Temple, and you did not arrest me. ⁵⁶But all this has happened in order to make come true what the prophets wrote in the Scriptures."

Then all the disciples left him and ran away.

Jesus before the Council
(Mark 14.53-65; Luke 22.54, 55, 63-71;
John 18.13, 14, 19-24)

⁵⁷Those who had arrested Jesus took him to the house of Caiaphas, the High Priest, where the teachers of the Law and the elders had gathered together. ⁵⁸Peter followed from a distance, as far as the courtyard of the High Priest's house. He went into the courtyard and sat down with the guards to see how it would all come out. ⁵⁹The chief priests and the whole Council tried to find some false evidence against Jesus to put him to death; ⁶⁰but they could not find any, even though many people came forward and told lies about him. Finally two men stepped up ⁶¹and said, "This man said, 'I am able to tear down God's Temple and three days later build it back up.'"

⁶²The High Priest stood up and said to Jesus, "Have you no answer to give to this accusation against you?" ⁶³But Jesus kept quiet. Again the High Priest spoke to him, "In the name of the living God I now put you under oath: tell us

if you are the Messiah, the Son of God."

⁶⁴Jesus answered him, "So you say. But I tell all of you: from this time on you will see the Son of Man sitting at the right side of the Almighty and coming on the clouds of heaven!"

⁶⁵At this the High Priest tore his clothes and said, "Blasphemy! We don't need any more witnesses! You have just heard his blasphemy! ⁶⁶What do you think?"

They answered, "He is guilty and must die."

⁶⁷Then they spat in his face and beat him; and those who slapped him ⁶⁸said, "Prophesy for us, Messiah! Guess who hit you!"

Peter Denies Jesus
(Mark 14.66-72; Luke 22.56-62;
John 18.15-18, 25-27)

⁶⁹Peter was sitting outside in the courtyard when one of the High Priest's servant women came to him and said, "You, too, were with Jesus of Galilee."

⁷⁰But he denied it in front of them all. "I don't know what you are talking about," he answered, ⁷¹and went on out to the entrance of the courtyard. Another servant woman saw him and said to the men there, "He was with Jesus of Nazareth."

⁷²Again Peter denied it and answered, "I swear that I don't know that man!"

⁷³After a little while the men standing there came to Peter. "Of course you are one of them," they said. "After all, the way you speak gives you away!"

⁷⁴Then Peter said, "I swear that I am telling the truth! May God punish me if I am not! I do not know that man!"

Just then a rooster crowed, ⁷⁵and Peter remembered what Jesus had told him: "Before the rooster crows, you will say three times that you do not know me." He went out and wept bitterly.

26.55 Lk 19.47; 21.37   **26.61** Jn 2.19   **26.64** Dn 7.13   **26.65, 66** Lv 24.16   **26.67** Is 50.6

Jesus Is Taken to Pilate
(Mark 15.1; Luke 23.1, 2; John 18.28-32)

27 Early in the morning all the chief priests and the elders made their plans against Jesus to put him to death. ²They put him in chains, led him off, and handed him over to Pilate, the Roman governor.

The Death of Judas
(Acts 1.18, 19)

³When Judas, the traitor, learned that Jesus had been condemned, he repented and took back the thirty silver coins to the chief priests and the elders. ⁴"I have sinned by betraying an innocent man to death!" he said.

"What do we care about that?" they answered. "That is your business!"

⁵Judas threw the coins down in the Temple and left; then he went off and hanged himself.

⁶The chief priests picked up the coins and said, "This is blood money, and it is against our Law to put it in the Temple treasury." ⁷After reaching an agreement about it, they used the money to buy Potter's Field, as a cemetery for foreigners. ⁸That is why that field is called "Field of Blood" to this very day.

⁹Then what the prophet Jeremiah had said came true: "They took the thirty silver coins, the amount the people of Israel had agreed to pay for him, ¹⁰and used the money to buy the potter's field, as the Lord had commanded me."

Pilate Questions Jesus
(Mark 15.2-5; Luke 23.3-5; John 18.33-38)

¹¹Jesus stood before the Roman governor, who questioned him. "Are you the king of the Jews?" he asked.

"So you say," answered Jesus. ¹²But he said nothing in response to the accusations of the chief priests and elders. ¹³So Pilate said to him, "Don't you hear all these things they accuse you of?"

¹⁴But Jesus refused to answer a single word, with the result that the Governor was greatly surprised.

Jesus Is Sentenced to Death
(Mark 15.6-15; Luke 23.13-25; John 18.39 – 19.16)

¹⁵At every Passover Festival the Roman governor was in the habit of setting free any one prisoner the crowd asked for. ¹⁶At that time there was a well-known prisoner named Jesus Barabbas. ¹⁷So when the crowd gathered, Pilate asked them, "Which one do you want me to set free for you? Jesus Barabbas or Jesus called the Messiah?" ¹⁸He knew very well that the Jewish authorities had handed Jesus over to him because they were jealous.

¹⁹While Pilate was sitting in the judgment hall, his wife sent him a message: "Have nothing to do with that innocent man, because in a dream last night I suffered much on account of him."

²⁰The chief priests and the elders persuaded the crowd to ask Pilate to set Barabbas free and have Jesus put to death. ²¹But Pilate asked the crowd, "Which one of these two do you want me to set free for you?"

"Barabbas!" they answered.

²²"What, then, shall I do with Jesus called the Messiah?" Pilate asked them.

"Crucify him!" they all answered.

²³But Pilate asked, "What crime has he committed?"

Then they started shouting at the top of their voices: "Crucify him!"

²⁴When Pilate saw that it was no use to go on, but that a riot might break out, he took some water, washed his hands in front of the crowd, and said, "I am not

27.3-8 Ac 1.18, 19   **27.9, 10** Zec 11.12, 13   **27.24** Dt 21.6-9

responsible for the death of this man! This is your doing!"

25 The whole crowd answered, "Let the responsibility for his death fall on us and on our children!"

26 Then Pilate set Barabbas free for them; and after he had Jesus whipped, he handed him over to be crucified.

The Soldiers Make Fun of Jesus
(Mark 15.16-20; John 19.2, 3)

27 Then Pilate's soldiers took Jesus into the governor's palace, and the whole company gathered around him. 28 They stripped off his clothes and put a scarlet robe on him. 29 Then they made a crown out of thorny branches and placed it on his head, and put a stick in his right hand; then they knelt before him and made fun of him. "Long live the King of the Jews!" they said. 30 They spat on him, and took the stick and hit him over the head. 31 When they had finished making fun of him, they took the robe off and put his own clothes back on him. Then they led him out to crucify him.

Jesus Is Crucified
(Mark 15.21-32; Luke 23.26-43;
John 19.17-27)

32 As they were going out, they met a man from Cyrene named Simon, and the soldiers forced him to carry Jesus' cross. 33 They came to a place called Golgotha, which means, "The Place of the Skull." 34 There they offered Jesus wine mixed with a bitter substance; but after tasting it, he would not drink it.

35 They crucified him and then divided his clothes among them by throwing dice. 36 After that they sat there and watched him. 37 Above his head they put the written notice of the accusation against him: "This is Jesus, the King of the Jews." 38 Then they crucified two bandits with Jesus, one on his right and the other on his left.

39 People passing by shook their heads and hurled insults at Jesus: 40 "You were going to tear down the Temple and build it back up in three days! Save yourself if you are God's Son! Come on down from the cross!"

41 In the same way the chief priests and the teachers of the Law and the elders made fun of him: 42 "He saved others, but he cannot save himself! Isn't he the king of Israel? If he will come down off the cross now, we will believe in him! 43 He trusts in God and claims to be God's Son. Well, then, let us see if God wants to save him now!"

44 Even the bandits who had been crucified with him insulted him in the same way.

The Death of Jesus
(Mark 15.33-41; Luke 23.44-49;
John 19.28-30)

45 At noon the whole country was covered with darkness, which lasted for three hours. 46 At about three o'clock Jesus cried out with a loud shout, *"Eli, Eli, lema sabachthani?"* which means, "My God, my God, why did you abandon me?"

47 Some of the people standing there heard him and said, "He is calling for Elijah!" 48 One of them ran up at once, took a sponge, soaked it in cheap wine, put it on the end of a stick, and tried to make him drink it.

49 But the others said, "Wait, let us see if Elijah is coming to save him!"

50 Jesus again gave a loud cry and breathed his last.

51 Then the curtain hanging in the Temple was torn in two from top to

27.34 Ps 69.21   **27.35** Ps 22.18   **27.39** Ps 22.7; 109.25; Si 12.17, 18; 13.7
27.40 Mt 26.61; Jn 2.19   **27.43** Ps 22.8; Ws 2.18-20   **27.46** Ps 22.1   **27.48** Ps 69.21
27.51 Ex 26.31-33

bottom. The earth shook, the rocks split apart, [52] the graves broke open, and many of God's people who had died were raised to life. [53] They left the graves, and after Jesus rose from death, they went into the Holy City, where many people saw them.

[54] When the army officer and the soldiers with him who were watching Jesus saw the earthquake and everything else that happened, they were terrified and said, "He really was the Son of God!"

[55] There were many women there, looking on from a distance, who had followed Jesus from Galilee and helped him. [56] Among them were Mary Magdalene, Mary the mother of James and Joseph, and the wife of Zebedee.

The Burial of Jesus
(Mark 15.42-47; Luke 23.50-56; John 19.38-42)

[57] When it was evening, a rich man from Arimathea arrived; his name was Joseph, and he also was a disciple of Jesus. [58] He went into the presence of Pilate and asked for the body of Jesus. Pilate gave orders for the body to be given to Joseph. [59] So Joseph took it, wrapped it in a new linen sheet, [60] and placed it in his own tomb, which he had just recently dug out of solid rock. Then he rolled a large stone across the entrance to the tomb and went away. [61] Mary Magdalene and the other Mary were sitting there, facing the tomb.

The Guard at the Tomb

[62] The next day, which was a Sabbath, the chief priests and the Pharisees met with Pilate [63] and said, "Sir, we remember that while that liar was still alive he said, 'I will be raised to life three days later.' [64] Give orders, then,

for his tomb to be carefully guarded until the third day, so that his disciples will not be able to go and steal the body, and then tell the people that he was raised from death. This last lie would be even worse than the first one."

[65] "Take a guard," Pilate told them; "go and make the tomb as secure as you can."

[66] So they left and made the tomb secure by putting a seal on the stone and leaving the guard on watch.

The Resurrection
(Mark 16.1-10; Luke 24.1-12; John 20.1-10)

28 After the Sabbath, as Sunday morning was dawning, Mary Magdalene and the other Mary went to look at the tomb. [2] Suddenly there was a violent earthquake; an angel of the Lord came down from heaven, rolled the stone away, and sat on it. [3] His appearance was like lightning, and his clothes were white as snow. [4] The guards were so afraid that they trembled and became like dead men.

[5] The angel spoke to the women. "You must not be afraid," he said. "I know you are looking for Jesus, who was crucified. [6] He is not here; he has been raised, just as he said. Come here and see the place where he was lying. [7] Go quickly now, and tell his disciples, 'He has been raised from death, and now he is going to Galilee ahead of you; there you will see him!' Remember what I have told you."

[8] So they left the tomb in a hurry, afraid and yet filled with joy, and ran to tell his disciples.

[9] Suddenly Jesus met them and said, "Peace be with you." They came up to him, took hold of his feet, and worshiped him. [10] "Do not be afraid," Jesus said to them. "Go and tell my brothers

27.55, 56 Lk 8.2, 3   **27.63** Mt 16.21; 17.23; 20.19; Mk 8.31; 9.31; 10.33, 34; Lk 9.22; 18.31-33

to go to Galilee, and there they will see me."

The Report of the Guard

11 While the women went on their way, some of the soldiers guarding the tomb went back to the city and told the chief priests everything that had happened. 12 The chief priests met with the elders and made their plan; they gave a large sum of money to the soldiers 13 and said, "You are to say that his disciples came during the night and stole his body while you were asleep. 14 And if the Governor should hear of this, we will convince him that you are innocent, and you will have nothing to worry about."

15 The guards took the money and did what they were told to do. And so that is the report spread around by the Jews to this very day.

Jesus Appears to His Disciples
(Mark 16.14-18; Luke 24.36-49; John 20.19-23; Acts 1.6-8)

16 The eleven disciples went to the hill in Galilee where Jesus had told them to go. 17 When they saw him, they worshiped him, even though some of them doubted. 18 Jesus drew near and said to them, "I have been given all authority in heaven and on earth. 19 Go, then, to all peoples everywhere and make them my disciples: baptize them in the name of the Father, the Son, and the Holy Spirit, 20 and teach them to obey everything I have commanded you. And I will be with you always, to the end of the age."

28.16 Mt 26.32; Mk 14.28   **28.19** Ac 1.8

The Gospel according to
MARK

INTRODUCTION

The Gospel according to Mark begins with the statement that it is "the Good News about Jesus Christ, the Son of God." Jesus is pictured as a man of action and authority. His authority is seen in his teaching, in his power over demons, and in forgiving people's sins. Jesus speaks of himself as the Son of Man, who came to give his life to set people free from sin.

Mark presents the story of Jesus in a straightforward, vigorous way, with emphasis on what Jesus did, rather than on his words and teachings. After a brief prologue about John the Baptist and the baptism and temptation of Jesus, the writer immediately takes up Jesus' ministry of healing and teaching. As time goes on, the followers of Jesus come to understand him better, but Jesus' opponents become more hostile. The closing chapters report the events of Jesus' last week of earthly life, especially his crucifixion and resurrection.

The two endings to the Gospel, which are enclosed in brackets, are generally regarded as written by someone other than the author of *Mark*.

OUTLINE OF CONTENTS

The Preaching of John the Baptist
(Matthew 3.1-12; Luke 3.1-18; John 1.19-28)

1 This is the Good News about Jesus Christ, the Son of God.[a] ²It began as the prophet Isaiah had written:

"God said, 'I will send my
     messenger ahead of you
     to open the way for you.'
³Someone is shouting in the
     desert,
'Get the road ready for the
     Lord;
make a straight path for him
     to travel!' "

⁴So John appeared in the desert, baptizing and preaching.[b] "Turn away from your sins and be baptized," he told the people, "and God will forgive your

---

[a] *Some manuscripts do not have* the Son of God.   [b] John appeared in the desert, baptizing and preaching; *some manuscripts have* John the Baptist appeared in the desert, preaching.

1.2 Ml 3.1   **1.3** Is 40.3 (LXX)

At once they left their nets. (1.18)

sins." ⁵ Many people from the province of Judea and the city of Jerusalem went out to hear John. They confessed their sins, and he baptized them in the Jordan River.

⁶ John wore clothes made of camel's hair, with a leather belt around his waist, and his food was locusts and wild honey. ⁷ He announced to the people, "The man who will come after me is much greater than I am. I am not good enough even to bend down and untie his sandals. ⁸ I baptize you with water, but he will baptize you with the Holy Spirit."

The Baptism and Temptation of Jesus
(Matthew 3.13 — 4.11; Luke 3.21, 22; 4.1-13)

⁹ Not long afterward Jesus came from Nazareth in the province of Galilee, and was baptized by John in the Jordan. ¹⁰ As soon as Jesus came up out of the water, he saw heaven opening and the Spirit coming down on him like a dove. ¹¹ And a voice came from heaven, "You are my own dear Son. I am pleased with you."

¹² At once the Spirit made him go into the desert, ¹³ where he stayed forty days, being tempted by Satan. Wild ani-

mals were there also, but angels came and helped him.

Jesus Calls Four Fishermen
(Matthew 4.12-22; Luke 4.14, 15; 5.1-11)

¹⁴ After John had been put in prison, Jesus went to Galilee and preached the Good News from God. ¹⁵ "The right time has come," he said, "and the Kingdom of God is near! Turn away from your sins and believe the Good News!"

¹⁶ As Jesus walked along the shore of Lake Galilee, he saw two fishermen, Simon and his brother Andrew, catching fish with a net. ¹⁷ Jesus said to them, "Come with me, and I will teach you to catch people." ¹⁸ At once they left their nets and went with him.

¹⁹ He went a little farther on and saw two other brothers, James and John, the sons of Zebedee. They were in their boat getting their nets ready. ²⁰ As soon as Jesus saw them, he called them; they left their father Zebedee in the boat with the hired men and went with Jesus.

A Man with an Evil Spirit
(Luke 4.31-37)

²¹ Jesus and his disciples came to the town of Capernaum, and on the next Sabbath Jesus went to the synagogue

---

1.6 2 K 1.8   **1.11** Gn 22.2; Ps 2.7; Is 42.1; Mt 3.17; 12.18; Mk 9.7; Lk 3.22   **1.15** Mt 3.2

and began to teach. ²²The people who heard him were amazed at the way he taught, for he wasn't like the teachers of the Law; instead, he taught with authority.

²³Just then a man with an evil spirit came into the synagogue and screamed, ²⁴"What do you want with us, Jesus of Nazareth? Are you here to destroy us? I know who you are — you are God's holy messenger!"

²⁵Jesus ordered the spirit, "Be quiet, and come out of the man!"

²⁶The evil spirit shook the man hard, gave a loud scream, and came out of him. ²⁷The people were all so amazed that they started saying to one another, "What is this? Is it some kind of new teaching? This man has authority to give orders to the evil spirits, and they obey him!"

²⁸And so the news about Jesus spread quickly everywhere in the province of Galilee.

Jesus Heals Many People
(Matthew 8.14-17; Luke 4.38-41)

²⁹Jesus and his disciples, including James and John, left the synagogue and went straight to the home of Simon and Andrew. ³⁰Simon's mother-in-law was sick in bed with a fever, and as soon as Jesus arrived, he was told about her. ³¹He went to her, took her by the hand, and helped her up. The fever left her, and she began to wait on them.

³²After the sun had set and evening had come, people brought to Jesus all the sick and those who had demons. ³³All the people of the town gathered in front of the house. ³⁴Jesus healed many who were sick with all kinds of diseases and drove out many demons. He would not let the demons say anything, because they knew who he was.

Took her by the hand, and . . . the fever left her. (1.31)

Jesus Preaches in Galilee
(Luke 4.42-44)

³⁵Very early the next morning, long before daylight, Jesus got up and left the house. He went out of town to a lonely place, where he prayed. ³⁶But Simon and his companions went out searching for him, ³⁷and when they found him, they said, "Everyone is looking for you."

³⁸But Jesus answered, "We must go on to the other villages around here. I have to preach in them also, because that is why I came."

³⁹So he traveled all over Galilee, preaching in the synagogues and driving out demons.

Jesus Heals a Man
(Matthew 8.1-4; Luke 5.12-16)

⁴⁰A man suffering from a dreaded skin disease came to Jesus, knelt down, and begged him for help. "If you want to," he said, "you can make me clean."ᶜ

⁴¹Jesus was filled with pity,ᵈ and reached out and touched him. "I do want to," he answered. "Be clean!" ⁴²At once the disease left the man, and he was clean. ⁴³Then Jesus spoke sternly to him and sent him away at once, ⁴⁴after saying to him, "Listen, don't tell anyone about this. But go straight to

ᶜ MAKE ME CLEAN: *This disease was considered to make a person ritually unclean.*
ᵈ pity; *some manuscripts have* anger.

1.22 Mt 7.28, 29   **1.39** Mt 4.23; 9.35   **1.44** Lv 14.1-32 the priest and let him examine you; then in order to prove to everyone that you are cured, offer the sacrifice that Moses ordered."

45 But the man went away and began to spread the news everywhere. Indeed, he talked so much that Jesus could not go into a town publicly. Instead, he stayed out in lonely places, and people came to him from everywhere.

Jesus Heals a Paralyzed Man
(Matthew 9.1-8; Luke 5.17-26)

2 A few days later Jesus went back to Capernaum, and the news spread that he was at home. 2 So many people came together that there was no room left, not even out in front of the door. Jesus was preaching the message to them 3 when four men arrived, carrying a paralyzed man to Jesus. 4 Because of the crowd, however, they could not get the man to him. So they made a hole in the roof right above the place where Jesus was. When they had made an opening, they let the man down, lying on his mat. 5 Seeing how much faith they had, Jesus said to the paralyzed man, "My son, your sins are forgiven."

6 Some teachers of the Law who were sitting there thought to themselves, 7 "How does he dare talk like this? This is blasphemy! God is the only one who can forgive sins!"

8 At once Jesus knew what they were thinking, so he said to them, "Why do you think such things? 9 Is it easier to say to this paralyzed man, 'Your sins are forgiven,' or to say, 'Get up, pick up your mat, and walk'? 10 I will prove to you, then, that the Son of Man has authority on earth to forgive sins." So he said to the paralyzed man, 11 "I tell you, get up, pick up your mat, and go home!"

12 While they all watched, the man got up, picked up his mat, and hurried away. They were all completely amazed

and praised God, saying, "We have never seen anything like this!"

Jesus Calls Levi
(Matthew 9.9-13; Luke 5.27-32)

13 Jesus went back again to the shore of Lake Galilee. A crowd came to him, and he started teaching them. 14 As he walked along, he saw a tax collector, Levi son of Alphaeus, sitting in his office. Jesus said to him, "Follow me." Levi got up and followed him.

15 Later on Jesus was having a meal in Levi's house.*e* A large number of tax collectors and other outcasts was following Jesus, and many of them joined him and his disciples at the table. 16 Some teachers of the Law, who were Pharisees, saw that Jesus was eating with these outcasts and tax collectors, so they asked his disciples, "Why does he eat with such people?"

17 Jesus heard them and answered, "People who are well do not need a doctor, but only those who are sick. I have not come to call respectable people, but outcasts."

The Question about Fasting
(Matthew 9.14-17; Luke 5.33-39)

18 On one occasion the followers of John the Baptist and the Pharisees were fasting. Some people came to Jesus and asked him, "Why is it that the disciples of John the Baptist and the disciples of the Pharisees fast, but yours do not?"

19 Jesus answered, "Do you expect the guests at a wedding party to go without food? Of course not! As long as the bridegroom is with them, they will not do that. 20 But the day will come when the bridegroom will be taken away from them, and then they will fast.

21 "No one uses a piece of new cloth to patch up an old coat, because the new patch will shrink and tear off some

e in Levi's house; *or* in his *(that is,* Jesus') house.

of the old cloth, making an even bigger hole. 22 Nor does anyone pour new wine into used wineskins, because the wine will burst the skins, and both the wine and the skins will be ruined. Instead, new wine must be poured into fresh wineskins."

The Question about the Sabbath
(Matthew 12.1-8; Luke 6.1-5)

23 Jesus was walking through some wheat fields on a Sabbath. As his disciples walked along with him, they began to pick the heads of wheat. 24 So the Pharisees said to Jesus, "Look, it is against our Law for your disciples to do that on the Sabbath!"

25 Jesus answered, "Have you never read what David did that time when he needed something to eat? He and his men were hungry, 26 so he went into the house of God and ate the bread offered to God. This happened when Abiathar was the High Priest. According to our Law only the priests may eat this bread — but David ate it and even gave it to his men."

27 And Jesus concluded, "The Sabbath was made for the good of human beings; they were not made for the Sabbath. 28 So the Son of Man is Lord even of the Sabbath."

The Man with a Paralyzed Hand
(Matthew 12.9-14; Luke 6.6-11)

3 Then Jesus went back to the synagogue, where there was a man who had a paralyzed hand. 2 Some people were there who wanted to accuse Jesus of doing wrong; so they watched him closely to see whether he would cure the man on the Sabbath. 3 Jesus said to the man, "Come up here to the front." 4 Then he asked the people, "What does our Law allow us to do on the Sabbath? To help or to harm? To save someone's life or to destroy it?"

But they did not say a thing. 5 Jesus was angry as he looked around at them, but at the same time he felt sorry for them, because they were so stubborn and wrong. Then he said to the man, "Stretch out your hand." He stretched it out, and it became well again. 6 So the Pharisees left the synagogue and met at once with some members of Herod's party, and they made plans to kill Jesus.

A Crowd by the Lake

7 Jesus and his disciples went away to Lake Galilee, and a large crowd followed him. They had come from Galilee, from Judea, 8 from Jerusalem, from the territory of Idumea, from the territory on the east side of the Jordan, and from the region around the cities of Tyre and Sidon. All these people came to Jesus because they had heard of the things he was doing. 9 The crowd was so large that Jesus told his disciples to get a boat ready for him, so that the people would not crush him. 10 He had healed many people, and all the sick kept pushing their way to him in order to touch him. 11 And whenever the people who had evil spirits in them saw him, they would fall down before him and scream, "You are the Son of God!"

12 Jesus sternly ordered the evil spirits not to tell anyone who he was.

Jesus Chooses the Twelve Apostles
(Matthew 10.1-4; Luke 6.12-16)

13 Then Jesus went up a hill and called to himself the men he wanted. They came to him, 14 and he chose twelve, whom he named apostles. "I have chosen you to be with me," he told them. "I will also send you out to preach, 15 and you will have authority to drive out demons."

16 These are the twelve he chose: Simon (Jesus gave him the name Peter); 17 James and his brother John, the sons of Zebedee (Jesus gave them the name Boanerges, which means "Men of

---

2.23 Dt 23.25 **2.26** Lv 24.9 **2.25, 26** 1 S 21.1-6 **3.9, 10** Mk 4.1; Lk 5.1-3

The crowd was so large . . . (3.9)

Thunder"); ¹⁸ Andrew, Philip, Bartholomew, Matthew, Thomas, James son of Alphaeus, Thaddaeus, Simon the Patriot, ¹⁹ and Judas Iscariot, who betrayed Jesus.

Jesus and Beelzebul
(Matthew 12.22-32; Luke 11.14-23; 12.10)

²⁰ Then Jesus went home. Again such a large crowd gathered that Jesus and his disciples had no time to eat. ²¹ When his family heard about it, they set out to take charge of him, because people were saying, "He's gone mad!"

²² Some teachers of the Law who had come from Jerusalem were saying, "He has Beelzebul in him! It is the chief of the demons who gives him the power to drive them out."

²³ So Jesus called them to him and spoke to them in parables: "How can Satan drive out Satan? ²⁴ If a country divides itself into groups which fight each other, that country will fall apart. ²⁵ If a family divides itself into groups which fight each other, that family will fall apart. ²⁶ So if Satan's kingdom divides into groups, it cannot last, but will fall apart and come to an end.

²⁷ "No one can break into a strong man's house and take away his belongings unless he first ties up the strong man; then he can plunder his house. ²⁸ "I assure you that people can be forgiven all their sins and all the evil things they may say. ᶠ ²⁹ But whoever says evil things against the Holy Spirit will never be forgiven, because he has committed an eternal sin." (³⁰ Jesus said this because some people were saying, "He has an evil spirit in him.")

Jesus' Mother and Brothers
(Matthew 12.46-50; Luke 8.19-21)

³¹ Then Jesus' mother and brothers arrived. They stood outside the house and sent in a message, asking for him. ³² A crowd was sitting around Jesus, and they said to him, "Look, your mother and your brothers and sisters are outside, and they want you."

³³ Jesus answered, "Who is my mother? Who are my brothers?" ³⁴ He looked at the people sitting around him and said, "Look! Here are my mother and my brothers! ³⁵ Whoever does what God wants is my brother, my sister, my mother."

ᶠ evil things they may say; or evil things they may say against God.
3.22 Mt 9.34; 10.25   **3.29** Lk 12.10

The Parable of the Sower
(Matthew 13.1-9; Luke 8.4-8)

4 Again Jesus began to teach beside Lake Galilee. The crowd that gathered around him was so large that he got into a boat and sat in it. The boat was out in the water, and the crowd stood on the shore at the water's edge. ²He used parables to teach them many things, saying to them:

³"Listen! Once there was a man who went out to sow grain. ⁴As he scattered the seed in the field, some of it fell along the path, and the birds came and ate it up. ⁵Some of it fell on rocky ground, where there was little soil. The seeds soon sprouted, because the soil wasn't deep. ⁶Then, when the sun came up, it burned the young plants; and because the roots had not grown deep enough, the plants soon dried up. ⁷Some of the seed fell among thorn bushes, which grew up and choked the plants, and they didn't bear grain. ⁸But some seeds fell in good soil, and the plants sprouted, grew, and bore grain: some had thirty grains, others sixty, and others one hundred."

⁹And Jesus concluded, "Listen, then, if you have ears!"

The Purpose of the Parables
(Matthew 13.10-17; Luke 8.9, 10)

¹⁰When Jesus was alone, some of those who had heard him came to him with the twelve disciples and asked him to explain the parables. ¹¹"You have been given the secret of the Kingdom of God," Jesus answered. "But the others, who are on the outside, hear all things by means of parables, ¹²so that,

'They may look and look,
    yet not see;
they may listen and listen,
    yet not understand.

For if they did, they would turn to God,
    and he would forgive them.'"

Jesus Explains the Parable of the Sower
(Matthew 13.18-23; Luke 8.11-15)

¹³Then Jesus asked them, "Don't you understand this parable? How, then, will you ever understand any parable? ¹⁴The sower sows God's message. ¹⁵Some people are like the seeds that fall along the path; as soon as they hear the message, Satan comes and takes it away. ¹⁶Other people are like the seeds that fall on rocky ground. As soon as they hear the message, they receive it gladly. ¹⁷But it does not sink deep into them, and they don't last long. So when trouble or persecution comes because of the message, they give up at once. ¹⁸Other people are like the seeds sown among the thorn bushes. These are the ones who hear the message, ¹⁹but the worries about this life, the love for riches, and all other kinds of desires crowd in and choke the message, and they don't bear fruit. ²⁰But other people are like seeds sown in good soil. They hear the message, accept it, and bear fruit: some thirty, some sixty, and some one hundred."

A Lamp under a Bowl
(Luke 8.16-18)

²¹Jesus continued, "Does anyone ever bring in a lamp and put it under a bowl or under the bed? Isn't it put on the lampstand? ²²Whatever is hidden away will be brought out into the open, and whatever is covered up will be uncovered. ²³Listen, then, if you have ears!"

²⁴He also said to them, "Pay attention to what you hear! The same rules you use to judge others will be used by God to judge you — but with even greater se-

4.1 Lk 5.1-3   **4.12** Is 6.9, 10 (LXX)   **4.21** Mt 5.15; Lk 11.33   **4.22** Mt 10.26; Lk 12.2
4.24 Mt 7.2; Lk 6.38

Waves began to spill over into the boat (4.37) . . . and there was a great calm. (4.39)

verity. ²⁵Those who have something will be given more, and those who have nothing will have taken away from them even the little they have."

The Parable of the Growing Seed

²⁶Jesus went on to say, "The Kingdom of God is like this. A man scatters seed in his field. ²⁷He sleeps at night, is up and about during the day, and all the while the seeds are sprouting and growing. Yet he does not know how it happens. ²⁸The soil itself makes the plants grow and bear fruit; first the tender stalk appears, then the head, and finally the head full of grain. ²⁹When the grain is ripe, the man starts cutting it with his sickle, because harvest time has come.

The Parable of the Mustard Seed
(Matthew 13.31, 32, 34; Luke 13.18, 19)

³⁰"What shall we say the Kingdom of God is like?" asked Jesus. "What para-

ble shall we use to explain it? ³¹It is like this. A man takes a mustard seed, the smallest seed in the world, and plants it in the ground. ³²After a while it grows up and becomes the biggest of all plants. It puts out such large branches that the birds come and make their nests in its shade."

³³Jesus preached his message to the people, using many other parables like these; he told them as much as they could understand. ³⁴He would not speak to them without using parables, but when he was alone with his disciples, he would explain everything to them.

Jesus Calms a Storm
(Matthew 8.23-27; Luke 8.22-25)

³⁵On the evening of that same day Jesus said to his disciples, "Let us go across to the other side of the lake." ³⁶So they left the crowd; the disciples

4.25 Mt 13.12; 25.29; Lk 19.26   **4.29** Jl 3.13

got into the boat in which Jesus was already sitting, and they took him with them. Other boats were there too. 37 Suddenly a strong wind blew up, and the waves began to spill over into the boat, so that it was about to fill with water. 38 Jesus was in the back of the boat, sleeping with his head on a pillow. The disciples woke him up and said, "Teacher, don't you care that we are about to die?"

39 Jesus stood up and commanded the wind, "Be quiet!" and he said to the waves, "Be still!" The wind died down, and there was a great calm. 40 Then Jesus said to his disciples, "Why are you frightened? Do you still have no faith?"

41 But they were terribly afraid and began to say to one another, "Who is this man? Even the wind and the waves obey him!"

Jesus Heals a Man with Evil Spirits
(Matthew 8.28-34; Luke 8.26-39)

5 Jesus and his disciples arrived on the other side of Lake Galilee, in the territory of Gerasa. 2 As soon as Jesus got out of the boat, he was met by a man who came out of the burial caves there. This man had an evil spirit in him 3 and lived among the tombs. Nobody could keep him tied with chains any more; 4 many times his feet and his hands had been tied, but every time he broke the chains and smashed the irons on his feet. He was too strong for anyone to control him. 5 Day and night he wandered among the tombs and through the hills, screaming and cutting himself with stones.

6 He was some distance away when he saw Jesus; so he ran, fell on his knees before him, 7 and screamed in a loud voice, "Jesus, Son of the Most High God! What do you want with me? For God's sake, I beg you, don't punish me!" (8 He said this because Jesus was saying, "Evil spirit, come out of this man!")

9 So Jesus asked him, "What is your name!"

The man answered, "My name is 'Mob' — there are so many of us!" 10 And he kept begging Jesus not to send the evil spirits out of that region.

11 There was a large herd of pigs near by, feeding on a hillside. 12 So the spirits begged Jesus, "Send us to the pigs, and let us go into them." 13 He let them go, and the evil spirits went out of the man and entered the pigs. The whole herd — about two thousand pigs in all — rushed down the side of the cliff into the lake and was drowned.

14 The men who had been taking care of the pigs ran away and spread the news in the town and among the farms. People went out to see what had happened, 15 and when they came to Jesus, they saw the man who used to have the mob of demons in him. He was sitting there, clothed and in his right mind; and they were all afraid. 16 Those who had seen it told the people what had happened to the man with the demons, and about the pigs.

17 So they asked Jesus to leave their territory.

18 As Jesus was getting into the boat, the man who had had the demons begged him, "Let me go with you!"

19 But Jesus would not let him. Instead, he told him, "Go back home to your family and tell them how much the Lord has done for you and how kind he has been to you."

20 So the man left and went all through the Ten Towns, telling what Jesus had done for him. And all who heard it were amazed.

Jairus' Daughter and the Woman Who Touched Jesus' Cloak
(Matthew 9.18-26; Luke 8.40-56)

21 Jesus went back across to the other side of the lake. There at the lakeside a large crowd gathered around him.

²²Jairus, an official of the local synagogue, arrived, and when he saw Jesus, he threw himself down at his feet ²³and begged him earnestly, "My little daughter is very sick. Please come and place your hands on her, so that she will get well and live!"

²⁴Then Jesus started off with him. So many people were going along with Jesus that they were crowding him from every side.

²⁵There was a woman who had suffered terribly from severe bleeding for twelve years, ²⁶even though she had been treated by many doctors. She had spent all her money, but instead of getting better she got worse all the time. ²⁷She had heard about Jesus, so she came in the crowd behind him, ²⁸saying to herself, "If I just touch his clothes, I will get well."

²⁹She touched his cloak, and her bleeding stopped at once; and she had the feeling inside herself that she was healed of her trouble. ³⁰At once Jesus knew that power had gone out of him, so he turned around in the crowd and asked, "Who touched my clothes?"

³¹His disciples answered, "You see how the people are crowding you; why do you ask who touched you?"

³²But Jesus kept looking around to see who had done it. ³³The woman realized what had happened to her, so she came, trembling with fear, knelt at his feet, and told him the whole truth. ³⁴Jesus said to her, "My daughter, your faith has made you well. Go in peace, and be healed of your trouble."

³⁵While Jesus was saying this, some messengers came from Jairus' house and told him, "Your daughter has died. Why bother the Teacher any longer?"

³⁶Jesus paid no attention to *g* what they said, but told him, "Don't be afraid, only believe." ³⁷Then he did not let anyone else go on with him except Peter and James and his brother John.

³⁸They arrived at Jairus' house, where Jesus saw the confusion and heard all the loud crying and wailing. ³⁹He went in and said to them, "Why all this confusion? Why are you crying? The child is not dead — she is only sleeping!"

⁴⁰They started making fun of him, so he put them all out, took the child's father and mother and his three disciples, and went into the room where the child was lying. ⁴¹He took her by the hand and said to her, *"Talitha, koum,"* which means, "Little girl, I tell you to get up!"

⁴²She got up at once and started walking around. (She was twelve years old.) When this happened, they were completely amazed. ⁴³But Jesus gave them strict orders not to tell anyone, and he said, "Give her something to eat."

Jesus Is Rejected at Nazareth
(Matthew 13.53-58; Luke 4.16-30)

6 Jesus left that place and went back to his hometown, followed by his disciples. ²On the Sabbath he began to teach in the synagogue. Many people were there; and when they heard him, they were all amazed. "Where did he get all this?" they asked. "What wisdom is this that has been given him? How does he perform miracles? ³Isn't he the carpenter, the son of Mary, and the brother of James, Joseph, Judas, and Simon? Aren't his sisters living here?" And so they rejected him.

⁴Jesus said to them, "Prophets are respected everywhere except in their own hometown and by their relatives and their family."

⁵He was not able to perform any miracles there, except that he placed his hands on a few sick people and healed them. ⁶He was greatly surprised, because the people did not have faith.

---

g paid no attention to; *or* overheard.
5.26 Tb 2.10   **6.4** Jn 4.44

Jesus Sends Out the Twelve Disciples
(Matthew 10.5-15; Luke 9.1-6)

Then Jesus went to the villages around there, teaching the people. [7] He called the twelve disciples together and sent them out two by two. He gave them authority over the evil spirits [8] and ordered them, "Don't take anything with you on the trip except a walking stick — no bread, no beggar's bag, no money in your pockets. [9] Wear sandals, but don't carry an extra shirt." [10] He also told them, "Wherever you are welcomed, stay in the same house until you leave that place. [11] If you come to a town where people do not welcome you or will not listen to you, leave it and shake the dust off your feet. That will be a warning to them!"

[12] So they went out and preached that people should turn away from their sins. [13] They drove out many demons, and rubbed olive oil on many sick people and healed them.

The Death of John the Baptist
(Matthew 14.1-12; Luke 9.7-9)

[14] Now King Herod[h] heard about all this, because Jesus' reputation had spread everywhere. Some people were saying, "John the Baptist has come back to life! That is why he has this power to perform miracles."

[15] Others, however, said, "He is Elijah."

Others said, "He is a prophet, like one of the prophets of long ago."

[16] When Herod heard it, he said, "He is John the Baptist! I had his head cut off, but he has come back to life!" [17] Herod himself had ordered John's arrest, and he had him tied up and put in prison. Herod did this because of Herodias, whom he had married, even though she was the wife of his brother Philip. [18] John the Baptist kept telling Herod, "It isn't right for you to marry your brother's wife!"

[19] So Herodias held a grudge against John and wanted to kill him, but she could not because of Herod. [20] Herod was afraid of John because he knew that John was a good and holy man, and so he kept him safe. He liked to listen to him, even though he became greatly disturbed every time he heard him.

[21] Finally Herodias got her chance. It was on Herod's birthday, when he gave a feast for all the top government officials, the military chiefs, and the leading citizens of Galilee. [22] The daughter of Herodias[i] came in and danced, and pleased Herod and his guests. So the king said to the girl, "What would you like to have? I will give you anything you want." [23] With many vows he said to her, "I swear that I will give you anything you ask for, even as much as half my kingdom!"

[24] So the girl went out and asked her mother, "What shall I ask for?"

"The head of John the Baptist," she answered.

[25] The girl hurried back at once to the king and demanded, "I want you to give me here and now the head of John the Baptist on a plate!"

[26] This made the king very sad, but he could not refuse her because of the vows he had made in front of all his guests. [27] So he sent off a guard at once with orders to bring John's head. The guard left, went to the prison, and cut John's head off; [28] then he brought it on a plate and gave it to the girl, who gave it to her mother. [29] When John's disciples heard about this, they came and got his body, and buried it.

---

[h] KING HEROD: *Herod Antipas, ruler of Galilee.* [i] The daughter of Herodias; *some manuscripts have* His daughter Herodias.

6.11 Ac 13.51 **6.8-11** Lk 10.4-11 **6.13** Jas 5.14 **6.14, 15** Mt 16.14; Mk 8.28; Lk 9.19 **6.17, 18** Lk 3.19, 20

Jesus Feeds Five Thousand
(Matthew 14.13-21; Luke 9.10-17;
John 6.1-14)

30 The apostles returned and met with Jesus, and told him all they had done and taught. **31** There were so many people coming and going that Jesus and his disciples didn't even have time to eat. So he said to them, "Let us go off by ourselves to some place where we will be alone and you can rest a while." **32** So they started out in a boat by themselves to a lonely place.

33 Many people, however, saw them leave and knew at once who they were; so they went from all the towns and ran ahead by land and arrived at the place ahead of Jesus and his disciples. **34** When Jesus got out of the boat, he saw this large crowd, and his heart was filled with pity for them, because they were like sheep without a shepherd. So he began to teach them many things. **35** When it was getting late, his disciples came to him and said, "It is already very late, and this is a lonely place. **36** Send the people away, and let them go to the nearby farms and villages in order to buy themselves something to eat."

37 "You yourselves give them something to eat," Jesus answered.

They asked, "Do you want us to go and spend two hundred silver coins *j* on bread in order to feed them?"

38 So Jesus asked them, "How much bread do you have? Go and see."

When they found out, they told him, "Five loaves and also two fish."

39 Jesus then told his disciples to make all the people divide into groups and sit down on the green grass. **40** So the people sat down in rows, in groups of a hundred and groups of fifty. **41** Then Jesus took the five loaves and the two fish, looked up to heaven, and gave thanks to God. He broke the loaves and gave them to his disciples to distribute to the people. He also divided the two fish among them all. **42** Everyone ate and had enough. **43** Then the disciples took up twelve baskets full of what was left of the bread and the fish. **44** The number of men who were fed was five thousand.

Jesus Walks on the Water
(Matthew 14.22-33; John 6.15-21)

45 At once Jesus made his disciples get into the boat and go ahead of him to Bethsaida, on the other side of the lake, while he sent the crowd away. **46** After saying good-bye to the people, he went away to a hill to pray. **47** When evening came, the boat was in the middle of the lake, while Jesus was alone on land. **48** He saw that his disciples were straining at the oars, because they were rowing against the wind; so sometime between three and six o'clock in the morning, he came to them, walking on the water. He was going to pass them by, *k* **49** but they saw him walking on the water. "It's a ghost!" they thought, and

"It's a ghost!" (6.49)

screamed. **50** They were all terrified when they saw him.

Jesus spoke to them at once, "Courage!" he said. "It is I. Don't be afraid!" **51** Then he got into the boat with them, and the wind died down. The disciples were completely amazed, **52** because

---

j SILVER COINS: *A silver coin was the daily wage of a rural worker (see Mt 20.2).*
k pass them by; *or* join them.
6.34 Nu 27.17; 1 K 22.17; 2 Ch 18.16; Ez 34.5; Mt 9.36

they had not understood the real meaning of the feeding of the five thousand; their minds could not grasp it.

Jesus Heals the Sick in Gennesaret
(Matthew 14.34-36)

53 They crossed the lake and came to land at Gennesaret, where they tied up the boat. 54 As they left the boat, people recognized Jesus at once. 55 So they ran throughout the whole region; and wherever they heard he was, they brought to him the sick lying on their mats. 56 And everywhere Jesus went, to villages, towns, or farms, people would take their sick to the marketplaces and beg him to let the sick at least touch the edge of his cloak. And all who touched it were made well.

The Teaching of the Ancestors
(Matthew 15.1-9)

7 Some Pharisees and teachers of the Law who had come from Jerusalem gathered around Jesus. 2 They noticed that some of his disciples were eating their food with hands that were ritually unclean—that is, they had not washed them in the way the Pharisees said people should.

(3 For the Pharisees, as well as the rest of the Jews, follow the teaching they received from their ancestors: they do not eat unless they wash their hands in the proper way; 4 nor do they eat anything that comes from the market unless they wash it first.*l* And they follow many other rules which they have received, such as the proper way to wash cups, pots, copper bowls, and beds.*m*)

5 So the Pharisees and the teachers of the Law asked Jesus, "Why is it that your disciples do not follow the teaching handed down by our ancestors, but instead eat with ritually unclean hands?"

6 Jesus answered them, "How right Isaiah was when he prophesied about you! You are hypocrites, just as he wrote:

'These people, says God, honor
    me with their words,
but their heart is really far
    away from me.
7 It is no use for them to
    worship me,
because they teach human
    rules
as though they were my laws!'

8 "You put aside God's command and obey human teachings."

9 And Jesus continued, "You have a clever way of rejecting God's law in order to uphold your own teaching. 10 For Moses commanded, 'Respect your father and your mother,' and, 'If you curse your father or your mother, you are to be put to death.' 11 But you teach that if people have something they could use to help their father or mother, but say, 'This is Corban' (which means, it belongs to God), 12 they are excused from helping their father or mother. 13 In this way the teaching you pass on to others cancels out the word of God. And there are many other things like this that you do."

The Things That Make a Person Unclean
(Matthew 15.10-20)

14 Then Jesus called the crowd to him once more and said to them, "Listen to me, all of you, and understand. 15 There is nothing that goes into you from the outside which can make you ritually unclean. Rather, it is what comes out of you that makes you unclean."*n*

---

l anything that comes from the market unless they wash it first; *or* anything after they come from the market unless they wash themselves first.   *m Some manuscripts do not have* and beds.   *n Some manuscripts add verse 16:* Listen, then, if you have ears! *(see 4.23).*

7.6, 7 Is 29.13 (LXX)   **7.10 a** Ex 20.12; Dt 5.16; **b** Ex 21.17; Lv 20.9

17 When he left the crowd and went into the house, his disciples asked him to explain this saying. **18** "You are no more intelligent than the others," Jesus said to them. "Don't you understand? Nothing that goes into you from the outside can really make you unclean, **19** because it does not go into your heart but into your stomach and then goes on out of the body." (In saying this, Jesus declared that all foods are fit to be eaten.)

20 And he went on to say, "It is what comes out of you that makes you unclean. **21** For from the inside, from your heart, come the evil ideas which lead you to do immoral things, to rob, kill, **22** commit adultery, be greedy, and do all sorts of evil things; deceit, indecency, jealousy, slander, pride, and folly — **23** all these evil things come from inside you and make you unclean."

A Woman's Faith
(Matthew 15.21-28)

24 Then Jesus left and went away to the territory near the city of Tyre. He went into a house and did not want anyone to know he was there, but he could not stay hidden. **25** A woman, whose daughter had an evil spirit in her, heard about Jesus and came to him at once and fell at his feet. **26** The woman was a Gentile, born in the region of Phoenicia in Syria. She begged Jesus to drive the demon out of her daughter. **27** But Jesus answered, "Let us first feed the children. It isn't right to take the children's food and throw it to the dogs."

28 "Sir," she answered, "even the dogs under the table eat the children's leftovers!"

29 So Jesus said to her, "Because of that answer, go back home, where you will find that the demon has gone out of your daughter!"

30 She went home and found her child lying on the bed; the demon had indeed gone out of her.

Jesus Heals a Deaf-Mute

31 Jesus then left the neighborhood of Tyre and went on through Sidon to Lake Galilee, going by way of the territory of the Ten Towns. **32** Some people brought him a man who was deaf and could hardly speak, and they begged Jesus to place his hands on him. **33** So Jesus took him off alone, away from the crowd, put his fingers in the man's ears, spat, and touched the man's tongue. **34** Then Jesus looked up to heaven, gave a deep groan, and said to the man, *"Ephphatha,"* which means, "Open up!"

35 At once the man was able to hear, his speech impediment was removed, and he began to talk without any trouble. **36** Then Jesus ordered the people not to speak of it to anyone; but the more he ordered them not to, the more they told it. **37** And all who heard were completely amazed. "How well he does everything!" they exclaimed. "He even causes the deaf to hear and the dumb to speak!"

Jesus Feeds Four Thousand People
(Matthew 15.32-39)

8 Not long afterward another large crowd came together. When the people had nothing left to eat, Jesus called the disciples to him and said, **2** "I feel sorry for these people, because they have been with me for three days and now have nothing to eat. **3** If I send them home without feeding them, they will faint as they go, because some of them have come a long way."

4 His disciples asked him, "Where in this desert can anyone find enough food to feed all these people?"

5 "How much bread do you have?" Jesus asked.

"Seven loaves," they answered.

6 He ordered the crowd to sit down on the ground. Then he took the seven loaves, gave thanks to God, broke them, and gave them to his disciples to distribute to the crowd; and the disciples did so. 7They also had a few small fish. Jesus gave thanks for these and told the disciples to distribute them too. 8-9Everybody ate and had enough— there were about four thousand people. Then the disciples took up seven baskets full of pieces left over. Jesus sent the people away 10and at once got into a boat with his disciples and went to the district of Dalmanutha.

The Pharisees Ask for a Miracle
(Matthew 16.1-4)

11Some Pharisees came to Jesus and started to argue with him. They wanted to trap him, so they asked him to perform a miracle to show that God approved of him. 12But Jesus gave a deep groan and said, "Why do the people of this day ask for a miracle? No, I tell you! No such proof will be given to these people!"

13He left them, got back into the boat, and started across to the other side of the lake.

The Yeast of the Pharisees and of Herod
(Matthew 16.5-12)

14The disciples had forgotten to bring enough bread and had only one loaf with them in the boat. 15"Take care," Jesus warned them, "and be on your guard against the yeast of the Pharisees and the yeast of Herod."

16They started discussing among themselves: "He says this because we don't have any bread."

17Jesus knew what they were saying, so he asked them, "Why are you discussing about not having any bread? Don't you know or understand yet? Are your minds so dull? 18You have eyes— can't you see? You have ears—can't you hear? Don't you remember 19when

I broke the five loaves for the five thousand people? How many baskets full of leftover pieces did you take up?"

"Twelve," they answered.

20"And when I broke the seven loaves for the four thousand people," asked Jesus, "how many baskets full of leftover pieces did you take up?"

"Seven," they answered.

21"And you still don't understand?" he asked them.

Jesus Heals a Blind Man at Bethsaida

22They came to Bethsaida, where some people brought a blind man to Jesus and begged him to touch him. 23Jesus took the blind man by the hand and led him out of the village. After spitting on the man's eyes, Jesus placed his hands on him and asked him, "Can you see anything?"

24The man looked up and said, "Yes, I can see people, but they look like trees walking around."

25Jesus again placed his hands on the man's eyes. This time the man looked intently, his eyesight returned, and he saw everything clearly. 26Jesus then sent him home with the order, "Don't go back into the village."

Peter's Declaration about Jesus
(Matthew 16.13-20; Luke 9.18-21)

27Then Jesus and his disciples went away to the villages near Caesarea Philippi. On the way he asked them, "Tell me, who do people say I am?"

28"Some say that you are John the Baptist," they answered; "others say that you are Elijah, while others say that you are one of the prophets."

29"What about you?" he asked them. "Who do you say I am?"

Peter answered, "You are the Messiah."

8.11 Mt 12.38; Lk 11.16 **8.12** Mt 12.39; Lk 11.29 **8.15** Lk 12.1 **8.18** Jr 5.21; Ez 12.2; Mk 4.12 **8.28** Mk 6.14, 15; Lk 9.7, 8 **8.29** Jn 6.68, 69

. . . you must forget yourself, carry your cross, and follow me. (8.34)

³⁰ Then Jesus ordered them, "Do not tell anyone about me."

Jesus Speaks about His Suffering and Death
(Matthew 16.21-28; Luke 9.22-27)

³¹ Then Jesus began to teach his disciples: "The Son of Man must suffer much and be rejected by the elders, the chief priests, and the teachers of the Law. He will be put to death, but three days later he will rise to life." ³² He made this very clear to them. So Peter took him aside and began to rebuke him. ³³ But Jesus turned around, looked at his disciples, and rebuked Peter. "Get away from me, Satan," he said. "Your thoughts don't come from God but from human nature!"

³⁴ Then Jesus called the crowd and his disciples to him. "If any of you want to come with me," he told them, "you must forget yourself, carry your cross, and follow me. ³⁵ For if you want to save your own life, you will lose it; but if you lose your life for me and for the gospel, you will save it. ³⁶ Do you gain anything if you win the whole world but lose your life? Of course not! ³⁷ There is nothing you can give to regain your life. ³⁸ If you are ashamed of me and of my teaching in this godless and wicked day, then the Son of Man will be ashamed of you when he comes in the glory of his Father with the holy angels."

9 And he went on to say, "I tell you, there are some here who will not die until they have seen the Kingdom of God come with power."

The Transfiguration
(Matthew 17.1-13; Luke 9.28-36)

² Six days later Jesus took with him Peter, James, and John, and led them up a high mountain, where they were alone. As they looked on, a change came over Jesus, ³ and his clothes became shining white — whiter than anyone in the world could wash them. ⁴ Then the three disciples saw Elijah and Moses talking with Jesus. ⁵ Peter spoke up and said to Jesus, "Teacher, how good it is that we are here! We will make three tents, one for you, one for Moses, and one for Elijah." ⁶ He and the others were so frightened that he did not know what to say.

⁷ Then a cloud appeared and covered them with its shadow, and a voice came from the cloud, "This is my own dear Son — listen to him!" ⁸ They took a quick look around but did not see anyone else; only Jesus was with them.

⁹ As they came down the mountain, Jesus ordered them, "Don't tell anyone what you have seen, until the Son of Man has risen from death."

¹⁰ They obeyed his order, but among themselves they started discussing the matter, "What does this 'rising from

8.34 Mt 10.38; Lk 14.27   **8.35** Mt 10.39; Lk 17.33; Jn 12.25   **9.2-7** 2 P 1.17, 18
9.7 Mt 3.17; Mk 1.11; Lk 3.22

death' mean?" ¹¹ And they asked Jesus, "Why do the teachers of the Law say that Elijah has to come first?"

¹² His answer was, "Elijah is indeed coming first in order to get everything ready. Yet why do the Scriptures say that the Son of Man will suffer much and be rejected? ¹³ I tell you, however, that Elijah has already come and that people treated him just as they pleased, as the Scriptures say about him."

Jesus Heals a Boy with an Evil Spirit
(Matthew 17.14-21; Luke 9.37-43a)

¹⁴ When they joined the rest of the disciples, they saw a large crowd around them and some teachers of the Law arguing with them. ¹⁵ When the people saw Jesus, they were greatly surprised, and ran to him and greeted him. ¹⁶ Jesus asked his disciples, "What are you arguing with them about?"

¹⁷ A man in the crowd answered, "Teacher, I brought my son to you, because he has an evil spirit in him and cannot talk. ¹⁸ Whenever the spirit attacks him, it throws him to the ground, and he foams at the mouth, grits his teeth, and becomes stiff all over. I asked your disciples to drive the spirit out, but they could not."

¹⁹ Jesus said to them, "How unbelieving you people are! How long must I stay with you? How long do I have to put up with you? Bring the boy to me!" ²⁰ They brought him to Jesus.

As soon as the spirit saw Jesus, it threw the boy into a fit, so that he fell on the ground and rolled around, foaming at the mouth. ²¹ "How long has he been like this?" Jesus asked the father.

"Ever since he was a child," he replied. ²² "Many times the evil spirit has tried to kill him by throwing him in the fire and into water. Have pity on us and help us, if you possibly can!"

²³ "Yes," said Jesus, "if you yourself can! Everything is possible for the person who has faith."

²⁴ The father at once cried out, "I do have faith, but not enough. Help me have more!"

²⁵ Jesus noticed that the crowd was closing in on them, so he gave a command to the evil spirit. "Deaf and dumb spirit," he said, "I order you to come out of the boy and never go into him again!"

²⁶ The spirit screamed, threw the boy into a bad fit, and came out. The boy looked like a corpse, and everyone said, "He is dead!" ²⁷ But Jesus took the boy by the hand and helped him rise, and he stood up.

²⁸ After Jesus had gone indoors, his disciples asked him privately, "Why couldn't we drive the spirit out?"

²⁹ "Only prayer can drive this kind out," answered Jesus; "nothing else can."

Jesus Speaks Again about His Death
(Matthew 17.22, 23; Luke 9.43b-45)

³⁰ Jesus and his disciples left that place and went on through Galilee. Jesus did not want anyone to know where he was, ³¹ because he was teaching his disciples: "The Son of Man will be handed over to those who will kill him. Three days later, however, he will rise to life."

³² But they did not understand what this teaching meant, and they were afraid to ask him.

Who Is the Greatest?
(Matthew 18.1-5; Luke 9.46-48)

³³ They came to Capernaum, and after going indoors Jesus asked his disciples, "What were you arguing about on the road?"

³⁴ But they would not answer him, because on the road they had been arguing among themselves about who was the greatest. ³⁵ Jesus sat down,

9.11 Ml 4.5; Mt 11.14   **9.12** Si 48.10   **9.34** Lk 22.24   **9.35** Mt 20.26, 27; 23.11; Mk 10.43, 44; Lk 22.26

called the twelve disciples, and said to them, "Whoever wants to be first must place himself last of all and be the servant of all." 36 Then he took a child and had him stand in front of them. He put his arms around him and said to them, 37 "Whoever welcomes in my name one of these children, welcomes me; and whoever welcomes me, welcomes not only me but also the one who sent me."

Whoever Is Not against Us Is for Us
(Luke 9.49, 50)

38 John said to him, "Teacher, we saw a man who was driving out demons in your name, and we told him to stop, because he doesn't belong to our group."

39 "Do not try to stop him," Jesus told them, "because no one who performs a miracle in my name will be able soon afterward to say evil things about me. 40 For whoever is not against us is for us. 41 I assure you that anyone who gives you a drink of water because you belong to me will certainly receive a reward.

Temptations to Sin
(Matthew 18.6-9; Luke 17.1, 2)

42 "If anyone should cause one of these little ones to lose faith in me, it would be better for that person to have a large millstone tied around the neck and be thrown into the sea. 43 So if your hand makes you lose your faith, cut it off! It is better for you to enter life without a hand than to keep both hands and go off to hell, to the fire that never goes out.*o* 45 And if your foot makes you lose your faith, cut it off! It is better for you to enter life without a foot than to keep both feet and be thrown into hell.*p*

47 And if your eye makes you lose your faith, take it out! It is better for you to enter the Kingdom of God with only one eye than to keep both eyes and be thrown into hell. 48 There 'the worms that eat them never die, and the fire that burns them is never put out.'

49 "Everyone will be purified by fire as a sacrifice is purified by salt.

50 "Salt is good; but if it loses its saltiness, how can you make it salty again?

"Have the salt of friendship among yourselves, and live in peace with one another."

Jesus Teaches about Divorce
(Matthew 19.1-12; Luke 16.18)

10 Then Jesus left that place, went to the province of Judea, and crossed the Jordan River. Crowds came flocking to him again, and he taught them, as he always did.

2 Some Pharisees came to him and tried to trap him. "Tell us," they asked, "does our Law allow a man to divorce his wife?"

3 Jesus answered with a question, "What law did Moses give you?"

4 Their answer was, "Moses gave permission for a man to write a divorce notice and send his wife away."

5 Jesus said to them, "Moses wrote this law for you because you are so hard to teach. 6 But in the beginning, at the time of creation, 'God made them male and female,' as the scripture says. 7 'And for this reason a man will leave his father and mother and unite with his wife,*q* 8 and the two will become one.' So they are no longer two, but one. 9 No human being must separate, then, what God has joined together."

o Some manuscripts add verse 44: There 'the worms that eat them never die, and the fire that burns them is never put out' *(see verse 48).*   *p* Some manuscripts add verse 46: There 'the worms that eat them never die, and the fire that burns them is never put out' *(see verse 48).*   *q* Some manuscripts do not have and unite with his wife.

9.37 Mt 10.40; Lk 10.16; Jn 13.20   **9.40** Mt 12.30; Lk 11.23   **9.41** Mt 10.42   **9.43** Mt 5.30   **9.47** Mt 5.29   **9.48** Is 66.24   **9.50** Mt 5.13; Lk 14.34, 35   **10.4** Dt 24.1-4; Mt 5.31   **10.6** Gn 1.27; 5.2   **10.7, 8** Gn 2.24

10 When they went back into the house, the disciples asked Jesus about this matter. 11 He said to them, "A man who divorces his wife and marries another woman commits adultery against his wife. 12 In the same way, a woman who divorces her husband and marries another man commits adultery."

Jesus Blesses Little Children
(Matthew 19.13-15; Luke 18.15-17)

13 Some people brought children to Jesus for him to place his hands on them, but the disciples scolded the people. 14 When Jesus noticed this, he was angry and said to his disciples, "Let the children come to me, and do not stop them, because the Kingdom of God belongs to such as these. 15 I assure you that whoever does not receive the Kingdom of God like a child will never enter it." 16 Then he took the children in his arms, placed his hands on each of them, and blessed them.

The Rich Man
(Matthew 19.16-30; Luke 18.18-30)

17 As Jesus was starting on his way again, a man ran up, knelt before him, and asked him, "Good Teacher, what must I do to receive eternal life?"

18 "Why do you call me good?" Jesus asked him. "No one is good except God alone. 19 You know the commandments: 'Do not commit murder; do not commit adultery; do not steal; do not accuse anyone falsely; do not cheat; respect your father and your mother.'"

20 "Teacher," the man said, "ever since I was young, I have obeyed all these commandments."

21 Jesus looked straight at him with love and said, "You need only one thing. Go and sell all you have and give the money to the poor, and you will have riches in heaven; then come and follow me." 22 When the man heard this, gloom spread over his face, and he went away sad, because he was very rich.

23 Jesus looked around at his disciples and said to them, "How hard it will be for rich people to enter the Kingdom of God!"

24 The disciples were shocked at these words, but Jesus went on to say, "My children, how hard it is to enter the Kingdom of God! 25 It is much harder for a rich person to enter the Kingdom of God than for a camel to go through the eye of a needle."

26 At this the disciples were completely amazed and asked one another, "Who, then, can be saved?"

27 Jesus looked straight at them and answered, "This is impossible for human beings but not for God; everything is possible for God."

28 Then Peter spoke up, "Look, we have left everything and followed you."

29 "Yes," Jesus said to them, "and I tell you that those who leave home or brothers or sisters or mother or father or children or fields for me and for the gospel, 30 will receive much more in this present age. They will receive a hundred times more houses, brothers, sisters, mothers, children, and fields — and persecutions as well; and in the age to come they will receive eternal life. 31 But many who are now first will be last, and many who are now last will be first."

Jesus Speaks a Third Time about His Death
(Matthew 20.17-19; Luke 18.31-34)

32 Jesus and his disciples were now on the road going up to Jerusalem. Jesus was going ahead of the disciples, who were filled with alarm; the people who followed behind were afraid. Once again Jesus took the twelve disciples

---

10.11, 12 Mt 5.32; 1 Co 7.10, 11 **10.15** Mt 18.3 **10.19 a** Ex 20.13; Dt 5.17; **b** Ex 20.14; Dt 5.18; **c** Ex 20.15; Dt 5.19; **d** Ex 20.16; Dt 5.20; **e** Ex 20.12; Dt 5.16 **10.31** Mt 20.16; Lk 13.30

aside and spoke of the things that were going to happen to him. ³³"Listen," he told them, "we are going up to Jerusalem where the Son of Man will be handed over to the chief priests and the teachers of the Law. They will condemn him to death and then hand him over to the Gentiles, ³⁴who will make fun of him, spit on him, whip him, and kill him; but three days later he will rise to life."

The Request of James and John
(Matthew 20.20-28)

³⁵Then James and John, the sons of Zebedee, came to Jesus. "Teacher," they said, "there is something we want you to do for us."

³⁶"What is it?" Jesus asked them.

³⁷They answered, "When you sit on your throne in your glorious Kingdom, we want you to let us sit with you, one at your right and one at your left."

³⁸Jesus said to them, "You don't know what you are asking for. Can you drink the cup of suffering that I must drink? Can you be baptized in the way I must be baptized?"

³⁹"We can," they answered.

Jesus said to them, "You will indeed drink the cup I must drink and be baptized in the way I must be baptized. ⁴⁰But I do not have the right to choose who will sit at my right and my left. It is God who will give these places to those for whom he has prepared them."

⁴¹When the other ten disciples heard about it, they became angry with James and John. ⁴²So Jesus called them all together to him and said, "You know that those who are considered rulers of the heathen have power over them, and the leaders have complete authority. ⁴³This, however, is not the way it is among you. If one of you wants to be great, you must be the servant of the rest; ⁴⁴and if one of you wants to be first, you must be the slave of all. ⁴⁵For

even the Son of Man did not come to be served; he came to serve and to give his life to redeem many people."

Jesus Heals Blind Bartimaeus
(Matthew 20.29-34; Luke 18.35-43)

⁴⁶They came to Jericho, and as Jesus was leaving with his disciples and a large crowd, a blind beggar named Bartimaeus son of Timaeus was sitting by the road. ⁴⁷When he heard that it was Jesus of Nazareth, he began to shout, "Jesus! Son of David! Have mercy on me!"

⁴⁸Many of the people scolded him and told him to be quiet. But he shouted even more loudly, "Son of David, have mercy on me!"

⁴⁹Jesus stopped and said, "Call him."

So they called the blind man. "Cheer up!" they said. "Get up, he is calling you."

⁵⁰So he threw off his cloak, jumped up, and came to Jesus.

⁵¹"What do you want me to do for you?" Jesus asked him.

"Teacher," the blind man answered, "I want to see again."

⁵²"Go," Jesus told him, "your faith has made you well."

At once he was able to see and followed Jesus on the road.

The Triumphant Entry into Jerusalem
(Matthew 21.1-11; Luke 19.28-40; John 12.12-19)

11 As they approached Jerusalem, near the towns of Bethphage and Bethany, they came to the Mount of Olives. Jesus sent two of his disciples on ahead ²with these instructions: "Go to the village there ahead of you. As soon as you get there, you will find a colt tied up that has never been ridden. Untie it and bring it here. ³And if someone asks you why you are doing that,

10.38 Lk 12.50   **10.42, 43** Lk 22.25, 26   **10.43, 44** Mt 23.11; Mk 9.35; Lk 22.26

say that the Master[r] needs it and will send it back at once."

[4] So they went and found a colt out in the street, tied to the door of a house. As they were untying it, [5] some of the bystanders asked them, "What are you doing, untying that colt?"

[6] They answered just as Jesus had told them, and the crowd let them go. [7] They brought the colt to Jesus, threw their cloaks over the animal, and Jesus got on. [8] Many people spread their cloaks on the road, while others cut branches in the field and spread them on the road. [9] The people who were in front and those who followed behind began to shout, "Praise God! God bless him who comes in the name of the Lord! [10] God bless the coming kingdom of King David, our father! Praise be to God!"

[11] Jesus entered Jerusalem, went into the Temple, and looked around at everything. But since it was already late in the day, he went out to Bethany with the twelve disciples.

Jesus Curses the Fig Tree
(Matthew 21.18, 19)

[12] The next day, as they were coming back from Bethany, Jesus was hungry. [13] He saw in the distance a fig tree covered with leaves, so he went to see if he could find any figs on it. But when he came to it, he found only leaves, because it was not the right time for figs. [14] Jesus said to the fig tree, "No one shall ever eat figs from you again!"

And his disciples heard him.

Jesus Goes to the Temple
(Matthew 21.12-17; Luke 19.45-48; John 2.13-22)

[15] When they arrived in Jerusalem, Jesus went to the Temple and began to drive out all those who were buying and selling. He overturned the tables of the moneychangers and the stools of those who sold pigeons, [16] and he would not let anyone carry anything through the Temple courtyards. [17] He then taught the people: "It is written in the Scriptures that God said, 'My Temple will be called a house of prayer for the people of all nations.' But you have turned it into a hideout for thieves!"

[18] The chief priests and the teachers of the Law heard of this, so they began looking for some way to kill Jesus. They were afraid of him, because the whole crowd was amazed at his teaching.

[19] When evening came, Jesus and his disciples left the city.

The Lesson from the Fig Tree
(Matthew 21.20-22)

[20] Early next morning, as they walked along the road, they saw the fig tree. It was dead all the way down to its roots. [21] Peter remembered what had happened and said to Jesus, "Look, Teacher, the fig tree you cursed has died!"

[22] Jesus answered them, "Have faith in God. [23] I assure you that whoever tells this hill to get up and throw itself in the sea and does not doubt in his heart, but believes that what he says will happen, it will be done for him. [24] For this reason I tell you: When you pray and ask for something, believe that you have received it, and you will be given whatever you ask for. [25] And when you stand and pray, forgive anything you may have against anyone, so that your Father in heaven will forgive the wrongs you have done."[s]

[r] the Master; *or* its owner.   [s] *Some manuscripts add verse 26:* If you do not forgive others, your Father in heaven will not forgive the wrongs you have done (*see Mt 6.15).*
11.9 Ps 118.25, 26   **11.17 a** Is 56.7; **b** Jr 7.11   **11.23** Mt 17.20; 1 Co 13.2
11.25, 26 Mt 6.14, 15

The Question about Jesus' Authority
(Matthew 21.23-27; Luke 20.1-8)

27 They arrived once again in Jerusalem. As Jesus was walking in the Temple, the chief priests, the teachers of the Law, and the elders came to him 28 and asked him, "What right do you have to do these things? Who gave you such right?"

29 Jesus answered them, "I will ask you just one question, and if you give me an answer, I will tell you what right I have to do these things. 30 Tell me, where did John's right to baptize come from: was it from God or from human beings?"

31 They started to argue among themselves: "What shall we say? If we answer, 'From God,' he will say, 'Why, then, did you not believe John?' 32 But if we say, 'From human beings . . .' " (They were afraid of the people, because everyone was convinced that John had been a prophet.) 33 So their answer to Jesus was, "We don't know."

Jesus said to them, "Neither will I tell you, then, by what right I do these things."

The Parable of the Tenants in the Vineyard
(Matthew 21.33-46; Luke 20.9-19)

12 Then Jesus spoke to them in parables: "Once there was a man who planted a vineyard, put a fence around it, dug a hole for the wine press, and built a watchtower. Then he rented the vineyard to tenants and left home on a trip. 2 When the time came to gather the grapes, he sent a slave to the tenants to receive from them his share of the harvest. 3 The tenants grabbed the slave, beat him, and sent him back without a thing. 4 Then the owner sent another slave; the tenants beat him over the head and treated him shamefully. 5 The owner sent another

slave, and they killed him; and they treated many others the same way, beating some and killing others. 6 The only one left to send was the man's own dear son. Last of all, then, he sent his son to the tenants. 'I am sure they will respect my son,' he said. 7 But those tenants said to one another, 'This is the owner's son. Come on, let's kill him, and his property will be ours!' 8 So they grabbed the son and killed him and threw his body out of the vineyard.

9 "What, then, will the owner of the vineyard do?" asked Jesus. "He will come and kill those tenants and turn the vineyard over to others. 10 Surely you have read this scripture?

'The stone which the builders
    rejected as worthless
turned out to be the most
    important of all.
11 This was done by the Lord;
    what a wonderful sight it is!' "

12 The Jewish leaders tried to arrest Jesus, because they knew that he had told this parable against them. But they were afraid of the crowd, so they left him and went away.

The Question about Paying Taxes
(Matthew 22.15-22; Luke 20.20-26)

13 Some Pharisees and some members of Herod's party were sent to Jesus to trap him with questions. 14 They came to him and said, "Teacher, we know that you tell the truth, without worrying about what people think. You pay no attention to anyone's status, but teach the truth about God's will for people. Tell us, is it against our Law to pay taxes to the Roman Emperor? Should we pay them or not?"

15 But Jesus saw through their trick and answered, "Why are you trying to trap me? Bring a silver coin, and let me see it."

16 They brought him one, and he

12.1 Is 5.1, 2   **12.10, 11** Ps 118.22, 23

asked, "Whose face and name are these?"

"The Emperor's," they answered.

[17] So Jesus said, "Well, then, pay to the Emperor what belongs to the Emperor, and pay to God what belongs to God."

And they were amazed at Jesus.

The Question about Rising from Death
(Matthew 22.23-33; Luke 20.27-40)

[18] Then some Sadducees, who say that people will not rise from death, came to Jesus and said, [19]"Teacher, Moses wrote this law for us: 'If a man dies and leaves a wife but no children, that man's brother must marry the widow so that they can have children who will be considered the dead man's children.' [20] Once there were seven brothers; the oldest got married and died without having children. [21] Then the second one married the woman, and he also died without having children. The same thing happened to the third brother, [22] and then to the rest: all seven brothers married the woman and died without having children. Last of all, the woman died. [23] Now, when all the dead rise to life on the day of resurrection, whose wife will she be? All seven of them had married her."

[24] Jesus answered them, "How wrong you are! And do you know why? It is because you don't know the Scriptures or God's power. [25] For when the dead rise to life, they will be like the angels in heaven and will not marry. [26] Now, as for the dead being raised: haven't you ever read in the Book of Moses the passage about the burning bush? There it is written that God said to Moses, 'I am the God of Abraham, the God of Isaac, and the God of Jacob.' [27] He is the God of the living, not of the dead. You are completely wrong!"

The Great Commandment
(Matthew 22.34-40; Luke 10.25-28)

[28] A teacher of the Law was there who heard the discussion. He saw that Jesus had given the Sadducees a good answer, so he came to him with a question: "Which commandment is the most important of all?"

[29] Jesus replied, "The most important one is this: 'Listen, Israel! The Lord our God is the only Lord.[t] [30] Love the Lord your God with all your heart, with all your soul, with all your mind, and with all your strength.' [31] The second most important commandment is this: 'Love your neighbor as you love yourself.' There is no other commandment more important than these two."

[32] The teacher of the Law said to Jesus, "Well done, Teacher! It is true, as you say, that only the Lord is God and that there is no other god but he. [33] And you must love God with all your heart and with all your mind and with all your strength; and you must love your neighbor as you love yourself. It is more important to obey these two commandments than to offer on the altar animals and other sacrifices to God."

[34] Jesus noticed how wise his answer was, and so he told him, "You are not far from the Kingdom of God."

After this nobody dared to ask Jesus any more questions.

The Question about the Messiah
(Matthew 22.41-46; Luke 20.41-44)

[35] As Jesus was teaching in the Temple, he asked the question, "How can the teachers of the Law say that the Messiah will be the descendant of David? [36] The Holy Spirit inspired David to say:

'The Lord said to my Lord:
    Sit here at my right side

---

[t] The Lord our God is the only Lord; *or* The Lord is our God, the Lord alone.

12.18 Ac 23.8   **12.19** Dt 25.5   **12.26** Ex 3.6   **12.29, 30** Dt 6.4, 5   **12.31** Lv 19.18
12.32 Dt 4.35   **12.33** Ho 6.6   **12.28-34** Lk 10.25-28   **12.36** Ps 110.1

until I put your enemies
under your feet.'
37 David himself called him 'Lord'; so
how can the Messiah be David's
descendant?"

Jesus Warns against the Teachers of the Law
(Matthew 23.1-36; Luke 20.45-47)

A large crowd was listening to Jesus
gladly. 38 As he taught them, he said,
"Watch out for the teachers of the Law,
who like to walk around in their long
robes and be greeted with respect in the
marketplace, 39 who choose the reserved seats in the synagogues and the
best places at feasts. 40 They take advantage of widows and rob them of
their homes, and then make a show of
saying long prayers. Their punishment
will be all the worse!"

The Widow's Offering
(Luke 21.1-4)

41 As Jesus sat near the Temple treasury, he watched the people as they
dropped in their money. Many rich men
dropped in a lot of money; 42 then a poor
widow came along and dropped in two
little copper coins, worth about a
penny. 43 He called his disciples together and said to them, "I tell you that
this poor widow put more in the offering box than all the others. 44 For the
others put in what they had to spare of
their riches; but she, poor as she is, put
in all she had — she gave all she had to
live on."

Jesus Speaks of the Destruction of the Temple
(Matthew 24.1, 2; Luke 21.5, 6)

13 As Jesus was leaving the Temple, one of his disciples said,
"Look, Teacher! What wonderful
stones and buildings!"
2 Jesus answered, "You see these

great buildings? Not a single stone here
will be left in its place; every one of
them will be thrown down."

Troubles and Persecutions
(Matthew 24.3-14; Luke 21.7-19)

3 Jesus was sitting on the Mount of
Olives, across from the Temple, when
Peter, James, John, and Andrew came
to him in private. 4 "Tell us when this
will be," they said, "and tell us what will
happen to show that the time has come
for all these things to take place."
5 Jesus said to them, "Watch out, and
don't let anyone fool you. 6 Many men,
claiming to speak for me, will come and
say, 'I am he!' and they will fool many
people. 7 And don't be troubled when
you hear the noise of battles close by
and news of battles far away. Such
things must happen, but they do not
mean that the end has come. 8 Countries will fight each other; kingdoms
will attack one another. There will be
earthquakes everywhere, and there will
be famines. These things are like the
first pains of childbirth.
9 "You yourselves must watch out.
You will be arrested and taken to court.
You will be beaten in the synagogues;
you will stand before rulers and kings
for my sake to tell them the Good News.
10 But before the end comes, the gospel
must be preached to all peoples. 11 And
when you are arrested and taken to
court, do not worry ahead of time about
what you are going to say; when the
time comes, say whatever is then given
to you. For the words you speak will not
be yours; they will come from the Holy
Spirit. 12 Men will hand over their own
brothers to be put to death, and fathers
will do the same to their children. Children will turn against their parents and
have them put to death. 13 Everyone
will hate you because of me. But whoever holds out to the end will be saved.

13.4 2 Esd 4.51—5.19   13.9-11 Mt 10.17-20; Lk 12.11, 12   13.13 Mt 10.22

The Awful Horror
(Matthew 24.15-28; Luke 21.20-24)

14"You will see 'The Awful Horror' standing in the place where he should not be." (Note to the reader: understand what this means!) "Then those who are in Judea must run away to the hills. 15 Someone who is on the roof of a house must not lose time by going down into the house to get anything to take along. 16 Someone who is in the field must not go back to the house for a cloak. 17 How terrible it will be in those days for women who are pregnant and for mothers with little babies! 18 Pray to God that these things will not happen in the winter! 19 For the trouble of those days will be far worse than any the world has ever known from the very beginning when God created the world until the present time. Nor will there ever be anything like it again. 20 But the Lord has reduced the number of those days; if he had not, nobody would survive. For the sake of his chosen people, however, he has reduced those days.

21"Then, if anyone says to you, 'Look, here is the Messiah!' or, 'Look, there he is!' — do not believe it. 22 For false Messiahs and false prophets will appear. They will perform miracles and wonders in order to deceive even God's chosen people, if possible. 23 Be on your guard! I have told you everything ahead of time.

The Coming of the Son of Man
(Matthew 24.29-31; Luke 21.25-28)

24"In the days after that time of trouble the sun will grow dark, the moon will no longer shine, 25 the stars will fall from heaven, and the powers in space will be driven from their courses. 26 Then the Son of Man will appear, coming in the clouds with great power and glory. 27 He will send the angels out to the four corners of the earth to gather God's chosen people from one end of the world to the other.

The Lesson of the Fig Tree
(Matthew 24.32-35; Luke 21.29-33)

28"Let the fig tree teach you a lesson. When its branches become green and tender and it starts putting out leaves, you know that summer is near. 29 In the same way, when you see these things happening, you will know that the time is near, ready to begin.*u* 30 Remember that all these things will happen before the people now living have all died. 31 Heaven and earth will pass away, but my words will never pass away.

No One Knows the Day or Hour
(Matthew 24.36-44)

32"No one knows, however, when that day or hour will come — neither the angels in heaven, nor the Son; only the Father knows. 33 Be on watch, be alert, for you do not know when the time will come. 34 It will be like a man who goes away from home on a trip and leaves his servants in charge, after giving to each one his own work to do and after telling the doorkeeper to keep watch. 35 Watch, then, because you do not know when the master of the house is coming — it might be in the evening or at midnight or before dawn or at sunrise. 36 If he comes suddenly, he must not find you asleep. 37 What I say to you, then, I say to all: Watch!"

---

u the time is near, ready to begin; *or* he is near, ready to come.

13.14 Dn 9.27; 11.31; 12.11; 1 Macc 1.54; 6.7 **13.15, 16** Lk 17.31 **13.19** Dn 12.1; Rev 7.14 **13.24 a** Is 13.10; Jl 2.10, 31; 3.15; Rev 6.12; **b** Is 13.10; Ez 32.7 **13.25 a** Is 34.4; Rev 6.13; **b** Jl 2.10 **13.26** Dn 7.13; Rev 1.7 **13.32** Mt 24.36 **13.34** Lk 12.36-38

The Plot against Jesus
(Matthew 26.1-5; Luke 22.1, 2;
John 11.45-53)

14 It was now two days before the Festival of Passover and Unleavened Bread. The chief priests and the teachers of the Law were looking for a way to arrest Jesus secretly and put him to death. ²"We must not do it during the festival," they said, "or the people might riot."

Jesus Is Anointed at Bethany
(Matthew 26.6-13; John 12.1-8)

³Jesus was in Bethany at the house of Simon, a man who had suffered from a dreaded skin disease. While Jesus was eating, a woman came in with an alabaster jar full of a very expensive perfume made of pure nard. She broke the jar and poured the perfume on Jesus' head. ⁴Some of the people there became angry and said to one another, "What was the use of wasting the perfume? ⁵It could have been sold for more than three hundred silver coins*ᵛ* and the money given to the poor!" And they criticized her harshly.

⁶But Jesus said, "Leave her alone! Why are you bothering her? She has done a fine and beautiful thing for me. ⁷You will always have poor people with you, and any time you want to, you can help them. But you will not always have me. ⁸She did what she could; she poured perfume on my body to prepare it ahead of time for burial. ⁹Now, I assure you that wherever the gospel is preached all over the world, what she has done will be told in memory of her."

Judas Agrees to Betray Jesus
(Matthew 26.14-16; Luke 22.3-6)

¹⁰Then Judas Iscariot, one of the twelve disciples, went off to the chief priests in order to betray Jesus to them. ¹¹They were pleased to hear what he had to say, and promised to give him money. So Judas started looking for a good chance to hand Jesus over to them.

Jesus Eats the Passover Meal with His Disciples
(Matthew 26.17-25; Luke 22.7-14, 21-23; John 13.21-30)

¹²On the first day of the Festival of Unleavened Bread, the day the lambs for the Passover meal were killed, Jesus' disciples asked him, "Where do you want us to go and get the Passover meal ready for you?"

¹³Then Jesus sent two of them with these instructions: "Go into the city, and a man carrying a jar of water will meet you. Follow him ¹⁴to the house he enters, and say to the owner of the house: 'The Teacher says, Where is the room where my disciples and I will eat the Passover meal?' ¹⁵Then he will show you a large upstairs room, fixed up and furnished, where you will get everything ready for us."

¹⁶The disciples left, went to the city, and found everything just as Jesus had told them; and they prepared the Passover meal.

¹⁷When it was evening, Jesus came with the twelve disciples. ¹⁸While they were at the table eating, Jesus said, "I tell you that one of you will betray me — one who is eating with me."

¹⁹The disciples were upset and began to ask him, one after the other, "Surely you don't mean me, do you?"

²⁰Jesus answered, "It will be one of you twelve, one who dips his bread in the dish with me. ²¹The Son of Man will die as the Scriptures say he will; but how terrible for that man who will betray the Son of Man! It would have been

---

ᵛ SILVER COINS: *See 6.37.*

14.1 Ex 12.1-27   **14.3** Lk 7.37, 38   **14.7** Dt 15.11   **14.18** Ps 41.9

better for that man if he had never been born!"

The Lord's Supper
(Matthew 26.26-30; Luke 22.14-20;
1 Corinthians 11.23-25)

22 While they were eating, Jesus took a piece of bread, gave a prayer of thanks, broke it, and gave it to his disciples. "Take it," he said, "this is my body."

"This is my body." (14.22)

23 Then he took a cup, gave thanks to God, and handed it to them; and they all drank from it. 24 Jesus said, "This is my blood which is poured out for many, my blood which seals God's covenant. 25 I tell you, I will never again drink this wine until the day I drink the new wine in the Kingdom of God."

26 Then they sang a hymn and went out to the Mount of Olives.

Jesus Predicts Peter's Denial
(Matthew 26.31-35; Luke 22.31-34;
John 13.36-38)

27 Jesus said to them, "All of you will run away and leave me, for the scripture says, 'God will kill the shepherd, and the sheep will all be scattered.' 28 But after I am raised to life, I will go to Galilee ahead of you."

29 Peter answered, "I will never leave you, even though all the rest do!"

30 Jesus said to Peter, "I tell you that before the rooster crows two times to-

night, you will say three times that you do not know me."

31 Peter answered even more strongly, "I will never say that, even if I have to die with you!"

And all the other disciples said the same thing.

Jesus Prays in Gethsemane
(Matthew 26.36-46; Luke 22.39-46)

32 They came to a place called Gethsemane, and Jesus said to his disciples, "Sit here while I pray." 33 He took Peter, James, and John with him. Distress and anguish came over him, 34 and he said to them, "The sorrow in my heart is so great that it almost crushes me. Stay here and keep watch."

35 He went a little farther on, threw himself on the ground, and prayed that, if possible, he might not have to go through that time of suffering. 36 "Father," he prayed, "my Father! All things are possible for you. Take this cup of suffering away from me. Yet not what I want, but what you want."

37 Then he returned and found the three disciples asleep. He said to Peter, "Simon, are you asleep? Weren't you able to stay awake for even one hour?" 38 And he said to them, "Keep watch, and pray that you will not fall into temptation. The spirit is willing, but the flesh is weak."

39 He went away once more and prayed, saying the same words. 40 Then he came back to the disciples and found them asleep; they could not keep their eyes open. And they did not know what to say to him.

41 When he came back the third time, he said to them, "Are you still sleeping and resting? Enough! The hour has come! Look, the Son of Man is now being handed over to the power of sinners. 42 Get up, let us go. Look, here is the man who is betraying me!"

14.24 a Ex 24.8; **b** Jr 31.31-34   **14.27** Zec 13.7   **14.28** Mt 28.16

The Arrest of Jesus
(Matthew 26.47-56; Luke 22.47-53; John 18.3-12)

⁴³ Jesus was still speaking when Judas, one of the twelve disciples, arrived. With him was a crowd armed with swords and clubs and sent by the chief priests, the teachers of the Law, and the elders. ⁴⁴ The traitor had given the crowd a signal: "The man I kiss is the one you want. Arrest him and take him away under guard."

⁴⁵ As soon as Judas arrived, he went up to Jesus and said, "Teacher!" and kissed him. ⁴⁶ So they arrested Jesus

So they arrested Jesus and held him tight. (14.46)

and held him tight. ⁴⁷ But one of those standing there drew his sword and struck at the High Priest's slave, cutting off his ear. ⁴⁸ Then Jesus spoke up and said to them, "Did you have to come with swords and clubs to capture me, as though I were an outlaw? ⁴⁹ Day after day I was with you teaching in the Temple, and you did not arrest me. But the Scriptures must come true."

⁵⁰ Then all the disciples left him and ran away.

⁵¹ A certain young man, dressed only in a linen cloth, was following Jesus. They tried to arrest him, ⁵² but he ran away naked, leaving the cloth behind.

Jesus before the Council
(Matthew 26.57-68; Luke 22.54, 55, 63-71; John 18.13, 14, 19-24)

⁵³ Then Jesus was taken to the High Priest's house, where all the chief priests, the elders, and the teachers of the Law were gathering. ⁵⁴ Peter followed from a distance and went into the courtyard of the High Priest's house. There he sat down with the guards, keeping himself warm by the fire. ⁵⁵ The chief priests and the whole Council tried to find some evidence against Jesus in order to put him to death, but they could not find any. ⁵⁶ Many witnesses told lies against Jesus, but their stories did not agree.

⁵⁷ Then some men stood up and told this lie against Jesus: ⁵⁸ "We heard him say, 'I will tear down this Temple which men have made, and after three days I will build one that is not made by men.'" ⁵⁹ Not even they, however, could make their stories agree.

⁶⁰ The High Priest stood up in front of them all and questioned Jesus, "Have you no answer to the accusation they bring against you?"

⁶¹ But Jesus kept quiet and would not say a word. Again the High Priest questioned him, "Are you the Messiah, the Son of the Blessed God?"

⁶² "I am," answered Jesus, "and you will all see the Son of Man seated at the right side of the Almighty and coming with the clouds of heaven!"

⁶³ The High Priest tore his robes and said, "We don't need any more witnesses! ⁶⁴ You heard his blasphemy. What is your decision?"

They all voted against him: he was guilty and should be put to death.

⁶⁵ Some of them began to spit on Jesus, and they blindfolded him and hit him. "Guess who hit you!" they said. And the guards took him and slapped him.

14.49 Lk 19.47; 21.37 **14.58** Jn 2.19 **14.62** Dn 7.13 **14.64** Lv 24.16

Peter Denies Jesus
(Matthew 26.69-75; Luke 22.56-62; John 18.15-18, 25-27)

⁶⁶Peter was still down in the courtyard when one of the High Priest's servant women came by. ⁶⁷When she saw Peter warming himself, she looked straight at him and said, "You, too, were with Jesus of Nazareth."

⁶⁸But he denied it. "I don't know . . . I don't understand what you are talking about," he answered, and went out into the passageway. Just then a rooster crowed.ʷ

⁶⁹The servant woman saw him there and began to repeat to the bystanders, "He is one of them!" ⁷⁰But Peter denied it again.

A little while later the bystanders accused Peter again, "You can't deny that you are one of them, because you, too, are from Galilee."

⁷¹Then Peter said, "I swear that I am telling the truth! May God punish me if I am not! I do not know the man you are talking about!"

⁷²Just then a rooster crowed a second time, and Peter remembered how Jesus had said to him, "Before the rooster crows two times, you will say three times that you do not know me." And he broke down and cried.

Jesus before Pilate
(Matthew 27.1, 2, 11-14; Luke 23.1-5; John 18.28-38)

15 Early in the morning the chief priests met hurriedly with the elders, the teachers of the Law, and the whole Council, and made their plans. They put Jesus in chains, led him away, and handed him over to Pilate. ²Pilate questioned him, "Are you the king of the Jews?"

Jesus answered, "So you say."

³The chief priests were accusing Jesus of many things, ⁴so Pilate questioned him again, "Aren't you going to answer? Listen to all their accusations!"

⁵Again Jesus refused to say a word, and Pilate was amazed.

Jesus Is Sentenced to Death
(Matthew 27.15-26; Luke 23.13-25; John 18.39 – 19.16)

⁶At every Passover Festival Pilate was in the habit of setting free any one prisoner the people asked for. ⁷At that time a man named Barabbas was in prison with the rebels who had committed murder in the riot. ⁸When the crowd gathered and began to ask Pilate for the usual favor, ⁹he asked them, "Do you want me to set free for you the king of the Jews?" ¹⁰He knew very well that the chief priests had handed Jesus over to him because they were jealous.

¹¹But the chief priests stirred up the crowd to ask, instead, that Pilate set Barabbas free for them. ¹²Pilate spoke again to the crowd, "What, then, do you want me to do with the one you call the king of the Jews?"

¹³They shouted back, "Crucify him!"

¹⁴"But what crime has he committed?" Pilate asked.

They shouted all the louder, "Crucify him!"

¹⁵Pilate wanted to please the crowd, so he set Barabbas free for them. Then he had Jesus whipped and handed him over to be crucified.

The Soldiers Make Fun of Jesus
(Matthew 27.27-31; John 19.2, 3)

¹⁶The soldiers took Jesus inside to the courtyard of the governor's palace and called together the rest of the company. ¹⁷They put a purple robe on Jesus, made a crown out of thorny

---

ʷ *Some manuscripts do not have* Just then a rooster crowed.

branches, and put it on his head. ¹⁸ Then they began to salute him: "Long live the King of the Jews!" ¹⁹ They beat him over the head with a stick, spat on him, fell on their knees, and bowed down to him. ²⁰ When they had finished making fun of him, they took off the purple robe and put his own clothes back on him. Then they led him out to crucify him.

Jesus Is Crucified
(Matthew 27.32-44; Luke 23.26-43; John 19.17-27)

²¹ On the way they met a man named Simon, who was coming into the city from the country, and the soldiers forced him to carry Jesus' cross. (Simon was from Cyrene and was the father of Alexander and Rufus.) ²² They took Jesus to a place called Golgotha, which means "The Place of the Skull." ²³ There they tried to give him wine mixed with a drug called myrrh, but

Jesus would not drink it. ²⁴ Then they crucified him and divided his clothes among themselves, throwing dice to

Throwing dice (15.24)

see who would get which piece of clothing. ²⁵ It was nine o'clock in the morning when they crucified him. ²⁶ The notice of the accusation against him said: "The King of the Jews." ²⁷ They also crucified two bandits with Jesus, one on his right and the other on his left.ˣ

²⁹ People passing by shook their heads and hurled insults at Jesus: "Aha! You were going to tear down the Temple and build it back up in three days! ³⁰ Now come down from the cross and save yourself!"

³¹ In the same way the chief priests and the teachers of the Law made fun of Jesus, saying to one another, "He saved others, but he cannot save himself! ³² Let us see the Messiah, the king of Israel, come down from the cross now, and we will believe in him!"

And the two who were crucified with Jesus insulted him also.

The Death of Jesus
(Matthew 27.45-56; Luke 23.44-49; John 19.28-30)

³³ At noon the whole country was covered with darkness, which lasted for three hours. ³⁴ At three o'clock Jesus cried out with a loud shout, *"Eloi, Eloi, lema sabachthani?"* which means, "My God, my God, why did you abandon me?"

³⁵ Some of the people there heard him and said, "Listen, he is calling for Elijah!" ³⁶ One of them ran up with a sponge, soaked it in cheap wine, and put it on the end of a stick. Then he held it up to Jesus' lips and said, "Wait! Let us see if Elijah is coming to bring him down from the cross!"

ˣ *Some manuscripts add verse 28:* In this way the scripture came true which says, "He shared the fate of criminals" *(see Lk 22.37).*

15.21 Ro 16.13   **15.24** Ps 22.18   **15.28** Is 53.12   **15.29 a** Ps 22.7; 109.25; **b** Mk 14.58; Jn 2.19   **15.34** Ps 22.1   **15.36** Ps 69.21

37 With a loud cry Jesus died.

38 The curtain hanging in the Temple was torn in two, from top to bottom. **39** The army officer who was standing there in front of the cross saw how Jesus had died.*y* "This man was really the Son of God!" he said.

40 Some women were there, looking on from a distance. Among them were Mary Magdalene, Mary the mother of the younger James and of Joseph, and Salome. **41** They had followed Jesus while he was in Galilee and had helped him. Many other women who had come to Jerusalem with him were there also.

The Burial of Jesus
(Matthew 27.57-61; Luke 23.50-56; John 19.38-42)

42-43 It was toward evening when Joseph of Arimathea arrived. He was a respected member of the Council, who was waiting for the coming of the Kingdom of God. It was Preparation day (that is, the day before the Sabbath), so Joseph went boldly into the presence of Pilate and asked him for the body of Jesus. **44** Pilate was surprised to hear that Jesus was already dead. He called the army officer and asked him if Jesus had been dead a long time. **45** After hearing the officer's report, Pilate told Joseph he could have the body. **46** Joseph bought a linen sheet, took the body down, wrapped it in the sheet, and placed it in a tomb which had been dug out of solid rock. Then he rolled a large stone across the entrance to the tomb. **47** Mary Magdalene and Mary the mother of Joseph were watching and saw where the body of Jesus was placed.

The Resurrection
(Matthew 28.1-8; Luke 24.1-12; John 20.1-10)

16 After the Sabbath was over, Mary Magdalene, Mary the mother of James, and Salome bought spices to go and anoint the body of Jesus. **2** Very early on Sunday morning, at sunrise, they went to the tomb. **3-4** On the way they said to one another, "Who will roll away the stone for us from the entrance to the tomb?" (It was a very large stone.) Then they looked up and saw that the stone had already been rolled back. **5** So they entered the tomb, where they saw a young man sitting at the right, wearing a white robe — and they were alarmed.

6 "Don't be alarmed," he said. "I know you are looking for Jesus of Nazareth, who was crucified. He is not here — he has been raised! Look, here is the place where he was placed. **7** Now go and give this message to his disciples, including Peter: 'He is going to Galilee ahead of you; there you will see him, just as he told you.'"

8 So they went out and ran from the tomb, distressed and terrified. They said nothing to anyone, because they were afraid.

So they went out and ran. (16.8)

---

y had died; *some manuscripts have* had cried out and died.
15.38 Ex 26.31-33   **15.40, 41** Lk 8.2, 3   **16.7** Mt 26.32; Mk 14.28

The disciples went and preached everywhere. (16.20)

AN OLD ENDING TO THE GOSPEL [z]

Jesus Appears to Mary Magdalene
(Matthew 28.9, 10; John 20.11-18)

[9 After Jesus rose from death early on Sunday, he appeared first to Mary Magdalene, from whom he had driven out seven demons. 10 She went and told his companions. They were mourning and crying; 11 and when they heard her say that Jesus was alive and that she had seen him, they did not believe her.

Jesus Appears to Two Followers
(Luke 24.13-35)

12 After this, Jesus appeared in a different manner to two of them while they were on their way to the country. 13 They returned and told the others, but these would not believe it.

Jesus Appears to the Eleven
(Matthew 28.16-20; Luke 24.36-49; John 20.19-23; Acts 1.6-8)

14 Last of all, Jesus appeared to the eleven disciples as they were eating. He scolded them, because they did not have faith and because they were too stubborn to believe those who had seen him alive. 15 He said to them, "Go throughout the whole world and preach the gospel to all people. 16 Whoever believes and is baptized will be saved; whoever does not believe will be condemned. 17 Believers will be given the

---

z *Some manuscripts and ancient translations do not have this ending to the Gospel (verses 9-20).*

16.15 Ac 1.8

power to perform miracles: they will drive out demons in my name; they will speak in strange tongues; [18] if they pick up snakes or drink any poison, they will not be harmed; they will place their hands on sick people, and these will get well."

Jesus Is Taken Up to Heaven
(Luke 24.50-53; Acts 1.9-11)

[19] After the Lord Jesus had talked with them, he was taken up to heaven and sat at the right side of God. [20] The disciples went and preached everywhere, and the Lord worked with them and proved that their preaching was true by the miracles that were performed.]

ANOTHER OLD ENDING [a]

[[9] The women went to Peter and his friends and gave them a brief account of all they had been told. [10] After this, Jesus himself sent out through his disciples from the east to the west the sacred and everliving message of eternal salvation.]

[a] *Some manuscripts and ancient translations have this shorter ending to the Gospel in addition to the longer ending (verses 9-20).*
16.19 Ac 1.9-11

The Gospel according to
LUKE

INTRODUCTION

The Gospel according to Luke presents Jesus as both the promised Savior of Israel and as the Savior of all people. Luke records that Jesus was called by the Spirit of the Lord to "bring good news to the poor," and this Gospel is filled with a concern for people with all kinds of need. The note of joy is also prominent in Luke, especially in the opening chapters that announce the coming of Jesus, and again at the conclusion, when Jesus ascends to heaven. The story of the growth and spread of the Christian faith after the ascension of Jesus is told by the same writer in the book of *Acts*.

Parts 2 and 6 (see the outline below) contain much material that is found only in this Gospel, such as the stories about the song of the angels and the shepherds' visit at the birth of Jesus, Jesus in the Temple as a boy, and the parables of the Good Samaritan and the Lost Son. Throughout the Gospel great emphasis is placed on prayer, the Holy Spirit, the role of women in the ministry of Jesus, and God's forgiveness of sins.

OUTLINE OF CONTENTS

Introduction

1 Dear Theophilus:
Many people have done their best to write a report of the things that have taken place among us. ²They wrote what we have been told by those who saw these things from the beginning and who proclaimed the message. ³And so, Your Excellency, because I have carefully studied all these matters from their beginning, I thought it would be good to write an orderly account for you. ⁴I do this so that you will know the full truth about everything which you have been taught.

The Birth of John the Baptist Is Announced

⁵During the time when Herod was king of Judea,ᵃ there was a priest

---

ᵃ JUDEA: *The term here refers to the whole land of Palestine.*
1.5 1 Ch 24.10

named Zechariah, who belonged to the priestly order of Abijah. His wife's name was Elizabeth; she also belonged to a priestly family. 6 They both lived good lives in God's sight and obeyed fully all the Lord's laws and commands. 7 They had no children because Elizabeth could not have any, and she and Zechariah were both very old.

8 One day Zechariah was doing his work as a priest in the Temple, taking his turn in the daily service. 9 According to the custom followed by the priests, he was chosen by lot to burn incense on the altar. So he went into the Temple of the Lord, 10 while the crowd of people outside prayed during the hour when the incense was burned. 11 An angel of the Lord appeared to him, standing at the right side of the altar where the incense was burned. 12 When Zechariah saw him, he was alarmed and felt afraid. 13 But the angel said to him, "Don't be afraid, Zechariah! God has heard your prayer, and your wife Elizabeth will bear you a son. You are to name him John. 14 How glad and happy you will be, and how happy many others will be when he is born! 15 John will be great in the Lord's sight. He must not drink any wine or strong drink. From his very birth he will be filled with the Holy Spirit, 16 and he will bring back many of the people of Israel to the Lord their God. 17 He will go ahead of the Lord, strong and mighty like the prophet Elijah. He will bring fathers and children together again; he will turn disobedient people back to the way of thinking of the righteous; he will get the Lord's people ready for him."

18 Zechariah said to the angel, "How shall I know if this is so? I am an old man, and my wife is old also."

19 "I am Gabriel," the angel answered. "I stand in the presence of God, who sent me to speak to you and tell you this good news. 20 But you have not believed my message, which will come true at the right time. Because you have not believed, you will be unable to speak; you will remain silent until the day my promise to you comes true."

21 In the meantime the people were waiting for Zechariah and wondering why he was spending such a long time in the Temple. 22 When he came out, he could not speak to them, and so they knew that he had seen a vision in the Temple. Unable to say a word, he made signs to them with his hands.

23 When his period of service in the Temple was over, Zechariah went back home. 24 Some time later his wife Elizabeth became pregnant and did not leave the house for five months. 25 "Now at last the Lord has helped me," she said. "He has taken away my public disgrace!"

The Birth of Jesus Is Announced

26 In the sixth month of Elizabeth's pregnancy God sent the angel Gabriel to a town in Galilee named Nazareth. 27 He had a message for a young woman promised in marriage to a man named Joseph, who was a descendant of King David. Her name was Mary. 28 The angel came to her and said, "Peace be with you! The Lord is with you and has greatly blessed you!"

29 Mary was deeply troubled by the angel's message, and she wondered what his words meant. 30 The angel said to her, "Don't be afraid, Mary; God has been gracious to you. 31 You will become pregnant and give birth to a son, and you will name him Jesus. 32 He will be great and will be called the Son of the Most High God. The Lord God will make him a king, as his ancestor David was, 33 and he will be the king of the

1.15 Nu 6.3   1.17 Ml 4.5, 6; Si 48.10, 11   1.19 Dn 8.16; 9.21; Tb 12.15   1.27 Mt 1.18
1.31 Mt 1.21   1.32, 33 2 S 7.12, 13, 16; Is 9.7

descendants of Jacob forever; his kingdom will never end!"

34 Mary said to the angel, "I am a virgin. How, then, can this be?"

35 The angel answered, "The Holy Spirit will come on you, and God's power will rest upon you. For this reason the holy child will be called the Son of God. 36 Remember your relative Elizabeth. It is said that she cannot have children, but she herself is now six months pregnant, even though she is very old. 37 For there is nothing that God cannot do."

38 "I am the Lord's servant," said Mary; "may it happen to me as you have said." And the angel left her.

Mary Visits Elizabeth

39 Soon afterward Mary got ready and hurried off to a town in the hill country of Judea. 40 She went into Zechariah's house and greeted Elizabeth. 41 When Elizabeth heard Mary's greeting, the baby moved within her. Elizabeth was filled with the Holy Spirit 42 and said in a loud voice, "You are the most blessed of all women, and blessed is the child you will bear! 43 Why should this great thing happen to me, that my Lord's mother comes to visit me? 44 For as soon as I heard your greeting, the baby within me jumped with gladness. 45 How happy you are to believe that the Lord's message to you will come true!"

Mary's Song of Praise

46 Mary said,
"My heart praises the Lord;
47   my soul is glad because of
        God my Savior,
48   for he has remembered me,
        his lowly servant!
From now on all people will call
        me happy,

49   because of the great things
        the Mighty God has
        done for me.
His name is holy;
50   from one generation to
        another
        he shows mercy to those who
        honor him.
51 He has stretched out his
        mighty arm
        and scattered the proud with
        all their plans.
52 He has brought down mighty
        kings from their thrones,
        and lifted up the lowly.
53 He has filled the hungry with
        good things,
        and sent the rich away with
        empty hands.
54 He has kept the promise he
        made to our ancestors,
        and has come to the help of
        his servant Israel.
55 He has remembered to show
        mercy to Abraham
        and to all his descendants
        forever!"

56 Mary stayed about three months with Elizabeth and then went back home.

The Birth of John the Baptist

57 The time came for Elizabeth to have her baby, and she gave birth to a son. 58 Her neighbors and relatives heard how wonderfully good the Lord had been to her, and they all rejoiced with her.

59 When the baby was a week old, they came to circumcise him, and they were going to name him Zechariah, after his father. 60 But his mother said, "No! His name is to be John."

61 They said to her, "But you don't have any relative with that name!"

1.37 Gn 18.14   **1.42** Jdt 13.18   **1.48** 1 S 1.11   **1.52** Job 5.11; 12.19; Si 10.14
1.55 Gn 17.7   **1.46-55** 1 S 2.1-10   **1.59** Lv 12.3

62 Then they made signs to his father, asking him what name he would like the boy to have.

63 Zechariah asked for a writing pad and wrote, "His name is John." How surprised they all were! 64 At that moment Zechariah was able to speak again, and he started praising God. 65 The neighbors were all filled with fear, and the news about these things spread through all the hill country of Judea. 66 Everyone who heard of it thought about it and asked, "What is this child going to be?" For it was plain that the Lord's power was upon him.

Zechariah's Prophecy

67 John's father Zechariah was filled with the Holy Spirit, and he spoke God's message:

68 "Let us praise the Lord, the God of Israel!
He has come to the help of his people and has set them free.
69 He has provided for us a mighty Savior,
a descendant of his servant David.
70 He promised through his holy prophets long ago
71   that he would save us from our enemies,
from the power of all those who hate us.
72 He said he would show mercy to our ancestors
and remember his sacred covenant.
73-74 With a solemn oath to our ancestor Abraham
he promised to rescue us from our enemies
and allow us to serve him without fear,
75 so that we might be holy and righteous before him
all the days of our life.
76 "You, my child, will be called a prophet of the Most High God.
You will go ahead of the Lord to prepare his road for him,
77 to tell his people that they will be saved
by having their sins forgiven.
78 Our God is merciful and tender.
He will cause the bright dawn of salvation to rise on us
79   and to shine from heaven on all those who live in the dark shadow of death,
to guide our steps into the path of peace."

80 The child grew and developed in body and spirit. He lived in the desert until the day when he appeared publicly to the people of Israel.

The Birth of Jesus
(Matthew 1.18-25)

2 At that time Emperor Augustus ordered a census to be taken throughout the Roman Empire. 2 When this first census took place, Quirinius was the governor of Syria. 3 Everyone, then, went to register himself, each to his own hometown.

4 Joseph went from the town of Nazareth in Galilee to the town of Bethlehem in Judea, the birthplace of King David. Joseph went there because he was a descendant of David. 5 He went to register with Mary, who was promised in marriage to him. She was pregnant, 6 and while they were in Bethlehem, the time came for her to have her baby. 7 She gave birth to her first son, wrapped him in cloths and laid him in a manger — there was no room for them to stay in the inn.

The Shepherds and the Angels

8 There were some shepherds in that part of the country who were spending the night in the fields, taking care of

1.76 Ml 3.1   **1.79** Is 9.2

their flocks. ⁹An angel of the Lord appeared to them, and the glory of the Lord shone over them. They were terribly afraid, ¹⁰but the angel said to them, "Don't be afraid! I am here with good news for you, which will bring great joy to all the people. ¹¹This very day in David's town your Savior was born — Christ the Lord! ¹²And this is what will prove it to you: you will find a baby wrapped in cloths and lying in a manger."

¹³Suddenly a great army of heaven's angels appeared with the angel, singing praises to God:

¹⁴"Glory to God in the highest
heaven,
and peace on earth to those
with whom he is pleased!"

¹⁵When the angels went away from them back into heaven, the shepherds said to one another, "Let's go to Bethlehem and see this thing that has happened, which the Lord has told us."

¹⁶So they hurried off and found Mary and Joseph and saw the baby lying in the manger. ¹⁷When the shepherds saw him, they told them what the angel had said about the child. ¹⁸All who heard it were amazed at what the shepherds said. ¹⁹Mary remembered all these things and thought deeply about them. ²⁰The shepherds went back, singing praises to God for all they had heard and seen; it had been just as the angel had told them.

Jesus Is Named

²¹A week later, when the time came for the baby to be circumcised, he was named Jesus, the name which the angel had given him before he had been conceived.

Jesus Is Presented in the Temple

²²The time came for Joseph and Mary to perform the ceremony of purifi-

Mary remembered all these things. (2.19)

cation, as the Law of Moses commanded. So they took the child to Jerusalem to present him to the Lord, ²³as it is written in the law of the Lord: "Every first-born male is to be dedicated to the Lord." ²⁴They also went to offer a sacrifice of a pair of doves or two young pigeons, as required by the law of the Lord.

²⁵At that time there was a man named Simeon living in Jerusalem. He was a good, God-fearing man and was waiting for Israel to be saved. The Holy Spirit was with him ²⁶and had assured him that he would not die before he had seen the Lord's promised Messiah. ²⁷Led by the Spirit, Simeon went into the Temple. When the parents brought the child Jesus into the Temple to do for him what the Law required, ²⁸Simeon took the child in his arms and gave thanks to God:

²⁹"Now, Lord, you have kept your
promise,
and you may let your servant
go in peace.
³⁰With my own eyes I have seen
your salvation,
³¹ which you have prepared in
the presence of all peoples:
³²A light to reveal your will to the
Gentiles

2.9 Tb 5.4   **2.21 a** Lv 12.3; **b** Lk 1.31   **2.23** Ex 13.2, 12   **2.22-24** Lv 12.6-8   **2.32** Is 42.6;
49.6; 52.10

and bring glory to your people Israel."

33 The child's father and mother were amazed at the things Simeon said about him. 34 Simeon blessed them and said to Mary, his mother, "This child is chosen by God for the destruction and the salvation of many in Israel. He will be a sign from God which many people will speak against 35 and so reveal their secret thoughts. And sorrow, like a sharp sword, will break your own heart."

36-37 There was a very old prophet, a widow named Anna, daughter of Phanuel of the tribe of Asher. She had been married for only seven years and was now eighty-four years old.*b* She never left the Temple; day and night she worshiped God, fasting and praying. 38 That very same hour she arrived and gave thanks to God and spoke about the child to all who were waiting for God to set Jerusalem free.

The Return to Nazareth

39 When Joseph and Mary had finished doing all that was required by the Law of the Lord, they returned to their hometown of Nazareth in Galilee. 40 The child grew and became strong; he was full of wisdom, and God's blessings were upon him.

The Boy Jesus in the Temple

41 Every year the parents of Jesus went to Jerusalem for the Passover Festival. 42 When Jesus was twelve years old, they went to the festival as usual. 43 When the festival was over, they started back home, but the boy Jesus stayed in Jerusalem. His parents did not know this; 44 they thought that he was with the group, so they traveled a whole day and then started looking for him among their relatives and friends. 45 They did not find him, so they went back to Jerusalem looking for him.

46 On the third day they found him in the Temple, sitting with the Jewish teachers, listening to them and asking questions. 47 All who heard him were amazed at his intelligent answers.

. . . sitting with the Jewish teachers (2.46)

48 His parents were astonished when they saw him, and his mother said to him, "Son, why have you done this to us? Your father and I have been terribly worried trying to find you."

49 He answered them, "Why did you have to look for me? Didn't you know that I had to be in my Father's house?" 50 But they did not understand his answer.

51 So Jesus went back with them to Nazareth, where he was obedient to them. His mother treasured all these things in her heart. 52 Jesus grew both in body and in wisdom, gaining favor with God and people.

The Preaching of John the Baptist
(Matthew 3.1-12; Mark 1.1-8; John 1.19-28)

3 It was the fifteenth year of the rule of Emperor Tiberius; Pontius Pilate was governor of Judea, Herod was ruler of Galilee, and his brother Philip was ruler of the territory of Iturea and Trachonitis; Lysanias was ruler of Abilene, 2 and Annas and Caiaphas were High Priests. At that time the word of God came to John son of Zechariah in the desert. 3 So John went throughout

---

b was now eighty-four years old; *or* had been a widow eighty-four years.
2.36, 37 Jdt 8.4, 5   **2.39** Mt 2.23   **2.41** Ex 12.1-27; Dt 16.1-8   **2.52** 1 S 2.26; Pr 3.4

the whole territory of the Jordan River, preaching, "Turn away from your sins and be baptized, and God will forgive your sins." ⁴As it is written in the book of the prophet Isaiah:

"Someone is shouting in the
    desert:
'Get the road ready for the
    Lord;
make a straight path for him
    to travel!
⁵Every valley must be filled up,
    every hill and mountain
    leveled off.
The winding roads must be
    made straight,
    and the rough paths made
    smooth.
⁶The whole human race will see
    God's salvation!' "

⁷Crowds of people came out to John to be baptized by him. "You snakes!" he said to them. "Who told you that you could escape from the punishment God is about to send? ⁸Do those things that will show that you have turned from your sins. And don't start saying among yourselves that Abraham is your ancestor. I tell you that God can take these rocks and make descendants for Abraham! ⁹The ax is ready to cut down the trees at the roots; every tree that does not bear good fruit will be cut down and thrown in the fire."

¹⁰The people asked him, "What are we to do, then?"

¹¹He answered, "Whoever has two shirts must give one to the man who has none, and whoever has food must share it."

¹²Some tax collectors came to be baptized, and they asked him, "Teacher, what are we to do?"

¹³"Don't collect more than is legal," he told them.

¹⁴Some soldiers also asked him, "What about us? What are we to do?"

He said to them, "Don't take money from anyone by force or accuse anyone falsely. Be content with your pay."

¹⁵People's hopes began to rise, and they began to wonder whether John perhaps might be the Messiah. ¹⁶So John said to all of them, "I baptize you with water, but someone is coming who is much greater than I am. I am not good enough even to untie his sandals. He will baptize you with the Holy Spirit and fire. ¹⁷He has his winnowing shovel with him, to thresh out all the grain and gather the wheat into his barn; but he will burn the chaff in a fire that never goes out."

¹⁸In many different ways John preached the Good News to the people and urged them to change their ways. ¹⁹But John reprimanded Governor Herod, because he had married Herodias, his brother's wife, and had done many other evil things. ²⁰Then Herod did an even worse thing by putting John in prison.

The Baptism of Jesus
(Matthew 3.13-17; Mark 1.9-11)

²¹After all the people had been baptized, Jesus also was baptized. While he was praying, heaven was opened, ²²and the Holy Spirit came down upon him in bodily form like a dove. And a voice came from heaven, "You are my own dear Son. I am pleased with you."

The Ancestors of Jesus
(Matthew 1.1-17)

²³When Jesus began his work, he was about thirty years old. He was the son, so people thought, of Joseph, who was the son of Heli, ²⁴the son of Matthat, the son of Levi, the son of Melchi, the son of Jannai, the son of Joseph, ²⁵the son of Mattathias, the son of Amos, the son of Nahum, the son of

3.4-6 Is 40.3-5 (LXX)   **3.7** Mt 12.34; 23.33   **3.8** Jn 8.33   **3.9** Mt 7.19   **3.12** Lk 7.29
3.19, 20 Mt 14.3, 4; Mk 6.17, 18   **3.22** Gn 22.2; Ps 2.7; Is 42.1; Mt 3.17; Mk 1.11;
Lk 9.35

Esli, the son of Naggai, [26] the son of Maath, the son of Mattathias, the son of Semein, the son of Josech, the son of Joda, [27] the son of Joanan, the son of Rhesa, the son of Zerubbabel, the son of Shealtiel, the son of Neri, [28] the son of Melchi, the son of Addi, the son of Cosam, the son of Elmadam, the son of Er, [29] the son of Joshua, the son of Eliezer, the son of Jorim, the son of Matthat, the son of Levi, [30] the son of Simeon, the son of Judah, the son of Joseph, the son of Jonam, the son of Eliakim, [31] the son of Melea, the son of Menna, the son of Mattatha, the son of Nathan, the son of David, [32] the son of Jesse, the son of Obed, the son of Boaz, the son of Salmon, the son of Nahshon, [33] the son of Amminadab, the son of Admin, the son of Arni, the son of Hezron, the son of Perez, the son of Judah, [34] the son of Jacob, the son of Isaac, the son of Abraham, the son of Terah, the son of Nahor, [35] the son of Serug, the son of Reu, the son of Peleg, the son of Eber, the son of Shelah, [36] the son of Cainan, the son of Arphaxad, the son of Shem, the son of Noah, the son of Lamech, [37] the son of Methuselah, the son of Enoch, the son of Jared, the son of Mahalaleel, the son of Kenan, [38] the son of Enosh, the son of Seth, the son of Adam, the son of God.

The Temptation of Jesus
(Matthew 4.1-11; Mark 1.12, 13)

4 Jesus returned from the Jordan full of the Holy Spirit and was led by the Spirit into the desert, [2] where he was tempted by the Devil for forty days. In all that time he ate nothing, so that he was hungry when it was over.

[3] The Devil said to him, "If you are God's Son, order this stone to turn into bread."

[4] But Jesus answered, "The scripture says, 'Human beings cannot live on bread alone.' "

[5] Then the Devil took him up and showed him in a second all the kingdoms of the world. [6] "I will give you all this power and all this wealth," the Devil told him. "It has all been handed over to me, and I can give it to anyone I choose. [7] All this will be yours, then, if you worship me."

[8] Jesus answered, "The scripture says, 'Worship the Lord your God and serve only him!' "

[9] Then the Devil took him to Jerusalem and set him on the highest point of the Temple, and said to him, "If you are God's Son, throw yourself down from here. [10] For the scripture says, 'God will order his angels to take good care of you.' [11] It also says, 'They will hold you up with their hands so that not even your feet will be hurt on the stones.' "

[12] But Jesus answered, "The scripture says, 'Do not put the Lord your God to the test.' "

[13] When the Devil finished tempting Jesus in every way, he left him for a while.

Jesus Begins His Work in Galilee
(Matthew 4.12-17; Mark 1.14, 15)

[14] Then Jesus returned to Galilee, and the power of the Holy Spirit was with him. The news about him spread throughout all that territory. [15] He taught in the synagogues and was praised by everyone.

Jesus Is Rejected at Nazareth
(Matthew 13.53-58; Mark 6.1-6)

[16] Then Jesus went to Nazareth, where he had been brought up, and on the Sabbath he went as usual to the synagogue. He stood up to read the Scriptures [17] and was handed the book of the prophet Isaiah. He unrolled the scroll and found the place where it is written,

[18] "The Spirit of the Lord is
    upon me,

4.4 Dt 8.3   **4.8** Dt 6.13   **4.10, 11** Ps 91.11, 12   **4.12** Dt 6.16   **4.18, 19** Is 61.1, 2 (LXX)

because he has chosen me to
bring good news to
the poor.
He has sent me to proclaim
liberty to the captives
and recovery of sight to the
blind,
to set free the oppressed
19   and announce that the time
has come
when the Lord will save his
people."

²⁰Jesus rolled up the scroll, gave it back to the attendant, and sat down. All the people in the synagogue had their eyes fixed on him, ²¹as he said to them, "This passage of scripture has come true today, as you heard it being read."

²²They were all well impressed with him and marveled at the eloquent words that he spoke. They said, "Isn't he the son of Joseph?"

²³He said to them, "I am sure that you will quote this proverb to me, 'Doctor, heal yourself.' You will also tell me to do here in my hometown the same things you heard were done in Capernaum. ²⁴I tell you this," Jesus added, "prophets are never welcomed in their hometown. ²⁵Listen to me: it is true that there were many widows in Israel during the time of Elijah, when there was no rain for three and a half years and a severe famine spread throughout the whole land. ²⁶Yet Elijah was not sent to anyone in Israel, but only to a widow living in Zarephath in the territory of Sidon. ²⁷And there were many people suffering from a dreaded skin disease who lived in Israel during the time of the prophet Elisha; yet not one of them was healed, but only Naaman the Syrian."

²⁸When the people in the synagogue heard this, they were filled with anger. ²⁹They rose up, dragged Jesus out of town, and took him to the top of the hill on which their town was built. They meant to throw him over the cliff, ³⁰but he walked through the middle of the crowd and went his way.

A Man with an Evil Spirit
(Mark 1.21-28)

³¹Then Jesus went to Capernaum, a town in Galilee, where he taught the people on the Sabbath. ³²They were all amazed at the way he taught, because he spoke with authority. ³³In the synagogue was a man who had the spirit of an evil demon in him; he screamed out in a loud voice, ³⁴"Ah! What do you want with us, Jesus of Nazareth? Are you here to destroy us? I know who you are: you are God's holy messenger!"

³⁵Jesus ordered the spirit, "Be quiet and come out of the man!" The demon threw the man down in front of them and went out of him without doing him any harm.

³⁶The people were all amazed and said to one another, "What kind of words are these? With authority and power this man gives orders to the evil spirits, and they come out!" ³⁷And the report about Jesus spread everywhere in that region.

Jesus Heals Many People
(Matthew 8.14-17; Mark 1.29-34)

³⁸Jesus left the synagogue and went to Simon's home. Simon's mother-in-law was sick with a high fever, and they spoke to Jesus about her. ³⁹He went and stood at her bedside and ordered the fever to leave her. The fever left her, and she got up at once and began to wait on them.

⁴⁰After sunset all who had friends who were sick with various diseases brought them to Jesus; he placed his hands on every one of them and healed them all. ⁴¹Demons also went out from many people, screaming, "You are the Son of God!"

Jesus gave the demons an order and

4.24 Jn 4.44   **4.25** 1 K 17.1   **4.26** 1 K 17.8-16   **4.27** 2 K 5.1-14   **4.32** Mt 7.28, 29 would not let them speak, because they knew he was the Messiah.

Jesus Preaches in the Synagogues
(Mark 1.35-39)

⁴²At daybreak Jesus left the town and went off to a lonely place. The people started looking for him, and when they found him, they tried to keep him from leaving. ⁴³But he said to them, "I must preach the Good News about the Kingdom of God in other towns also, because that is what God sent me to do."

⁴⁴So he preached in the synagogues throughout the country.

Jesus Calls the First Disciples
(Matthew 4.18-22; Mark 1.16-20)

5 One day Jesus was standing on the shore of Lake Gennesaret while the people pushed their way up to him to listen to the word of God. ²He saw two boats pulled up on the beach; the fishermen had left them and were washing the nets. ³Jesus got into one of the boats — it belonged to Simon — and asked him to push off a little from the shore. Jesus sat in the boat and taught the crowd.

⁴When he finished speaking, he said to Simon, "Push the boat out further to the deep water, and you and your partners let down your nets for a catch."

⁵"Master," Simon answered, "we worked hard all night long and caught nothing. But if you say so, I will let down the nets." ⁶They let them down and caught such a large number of fish that the nets were about to break. ⁷So they motioned to their partners in the other boat to come and help them. They came and filled both boats so full of fish that the boats were about to sink. ⁸When Simon Peter saw what had happened, he fell on his knees before Jesus and said, "Go away from me, Lord! I am a sinful man!"

They . . . caught such a large number of fish. (5.6)

⁹He and the others with him were all amazed at the large number of fish they had caught. ¹⁰The same was true of Simon's partners, James and John, the sons of Zebedee. Jesus said to Simon, "Don't be afraid; from now on you will be catching people."

¹¹They pulled the boats up on the beach, left everything, and followed Jesus.

Jesus Heals a Man
(Matthew 8.1-4; Mark 1.40-45)

¹²Once Jesus was in a town where there was a man who was suffering from a dreaded skin disease. When he saw Jesus, he threw himself down and begged him, "Sir, if you want to, you can make me clean!"ᶜ

¹³Jesus reached out and touched him. "I do want to," he answered. "Be clean!" At once the disease left the man. ¹⁴Jesus ordered him, "Don't tell anyone, but go straight to the priest and let him examine you; then to prove to everyone that you are cured, offer the sacrifice as Moses ordered."

¹⁵But the news about Jesus spread all the more widely, and crowds of people came to hear him and be healed

ᶜ MAKE ME CLEAN: *This disease was considered to make a person ritually unclean.*
5.1-3 Mt 13.1, 2; Mk 3.9, 10; 4.1   **5.5** Jn 21.3   **5.6** Jn 21.6   **5.14** Lv 14.1-32

from their diseases. 16But he would go away to lonely places, where he prayed.

Jesus Heals a Paralyzed Man
(Matthew 9.1-8; Mark 2.1-12)

17One day when Jesus was teaching, some Pharisees and teachers of the Law were sitting there who had come from every town in Galilee and Judea and from Jerusalem. The power of the Lord was present for Jesus to heal the sick. 18Some men came carrying a paralyzed man on a bed, and they tried to carry him into the house and put him in front of Jesus. 19Because of the crowd, however, they could find no way to take him in. So they carried him up on the roof, made an opening in the tiles, and let him down on his bed into the middle

They . . . let him down on his bed into the middle of the group. (5.19)

of the group in front of Jesus. 20When Jesus saw how much faith they had, he said to the man, "Your sins are forgiven, my friend."

21The teachers of the Law and the Pharisees began to say to themselves, "Who is this man who speaks such blasphemy! God is the only one who can forgive sins!"

22Jesus knew their thoughts and said

to them, "Why do you think such things? 23Is it easier to say, 'Your sins are forgiven you,' or to say, 'Get up and walk'? 24I will prove to you, then, that the Son of Man has authority on earth to forgive sins." So he said to the paralyzed man, "I tell you, get up, pick up your bed, and go home!"

25At once the man got up in front of them all, took the bed he had been lying on, and went home, praising God. 26They were all completely amazed! Full of fear, they praised God, saying, "What marvelous things we have seen today!"

Jesus Calls Levi
(Matthew 9.9-13; Mark 2.13-17)

27After this, Jesus went out and saw a tax collector named Levi, sitting in his office. Jesus said to him, "Follow me." 28Levi got up, left everything, and followed him.

29Then Levi had a big feast in his house for Jesus, and among the guests was a large number of tax collectors and other people. 30Some Pharisees and some teachers of the Law who belonged to their group complained to Jesus' disciples. "Why do you eat and drink with tax collectors and other outcasts?" they asked.

31Jesus answered them, "People who are well do not need a doctor, but only those who are sick. 32I have not come to call respectable people to repent, but outcasts."

The Question about Fasting
(Matthew 9.14-17; Mark 2.18-22)

33Some people said to Jesus, "The disciples of John fast frequently and offer prayers, and the disciples of the Pharisees do the same; but your disciples eat and drink."

34Jesus answered, "Do you think you can make the guests at a wedding party go without food as long as the bride-

5.30 Lk 15.1, 2

groom is with them? Of course not! ³⁵ But the day will come when the bridegroom will be taken away from them, and then they will fast."

³⁶ Jesus also told them this parable: "You don't tear a piece off a new coat to patch up an old coat. If you do, you will have torn the new coat, and the piece of new cloth will not match the old. ³⁷ Nor do you pour new wine into used wineskins, because the new wine will burst the skins, the wine will pour out, and the skins will be ruined. ³⁸ Instead, new wine must be poured into fresh wineskins! ³⁹ And you don't want new wine after drinking old wine. 'The old is better,' you say."

The Question about the Sabbath
(Matthew 12.1-8; Mark 2.23-28)

6 Jesus was walking through some wheat fields on a Sabbath. His disciples began to pick the heads of wheat, rub them in their hands, and eat the grain. ² Some Pharisees asked, "Why are you doing what our Law says you cannot do on the Sabbath?"

³ Jesus answered them, "Haven't you read what David did when he and his men were hungry? ⁴ He went into the house of God, took the bread offered to God, ate it, and gave it also to his men. Yet it is against our Law for anyone except the priests to eat that bread."

⁵ And Jesus concluded, "The Son of Man is Lord of the Sabbath."

The Man with a Paralyzed Hand
(Matthew 12.9-14; Mark 3.1-6)

⁶ On another Sabbath Jesus went into a synagogue and taught. A man was there whose right hand was paralyzed. ⁷ Some teachers of the Law and some Pharisees wanted a reason to accuse Jesus of doing wrong, so they watched him closely to see if he would heal on the Sabbath. ⁸ But Jesus knew

their thoughts and said to the man, "Stand up and come here to the front." The man got up and stood there. ⁹ Then Jesus said to them, "I ask you: What does our Law allow us to do on the Sabbath? To help or to harm? To save someone's life or destroy it?" ¹⁰ He looked around at them all; then he said[d] to the man, "Stretch out your hand." He did so, and his hand became well again.

¹¹ They were filled with rage and began to discuss among themselves what they could do to Jesus.

Jesus Chooses the Twelve Apostles
(Matthew 10.1-4; Mark 3.13-19)

¹² At that time Jesus went up a hill to pray and spent the whole night there praying to God. ¹³ When day came, he called his disciples to him and chose twelve of them, whom he named apostles: ¹⁴ Simon (whom he named Peter) and his brother Andrew; James and John, Philip and Bartholomew, ¹⁵ Matthew and Thomas, James son of Alphaeus, and Simon (who was called the Patriot), ¹⁶ Judas son of James, and Judas Iscariot, who became the traitor.

Jesus Teaches and Heals
(Matthew 4.23-25)

¹⁷ When Jesus had come down from the hill with the apostles, he stood on a level place with a large number of his disciples. A large crowd of people was there from all over Judea and from Jerusalem and from the coast cities of Tyre and Sidon; ¹⁸ they had come to hear him and to be healed of their diseases. Those who were troubled by evil spirits also came and were healed. ¹⁹ All the people tried to touch him, for power was going out from him and healing them all.

---

[d] said; *some manuscripts have* said angrily.
6.1 Dt 23.25   **6.4** Lv 24.9   **6.3, 4** 1 S 21.1-6

Happiness and Sorrow
(Matthew 5.1-12)

20 Jesus looked at his disciples and said,

"Happy are you poor;
 the Kingdom of God is yours!
21 "Happy are you who are
 hungry now;
 you will be filled!
"Happy are you who weep now;
 you will laugh!
22 "Happy are you when people hate you, reject you, insult you, and say that you are evil, all because of the Son of Man! **23** Be glad when that happens and dance for joy, because a great reward is kept for you in heaven. For their ancestors did the very same things to the prophets.

24 "But how terrible for you who
 are rich now;
 you have had your easy life!
25 "How terrible for you who are
 full now;
 you will go hungry!
"How terrible for you who
 laugh now;
 you will mourn and weep!
26 "How terrible when all people speak well of you; their ancestors said the very same things about the false prophets.

Love for Enemies
(Matthew 5.38-48; 7.12a)

27 "But I tell you who hear me: Love your enemies, do good to those who hate you, **28** bless those who curse you, and pray for those who mistreat you. **29** If anyone hits you on one cheek, let him hit the other one too; if someone takes your coat, let him have your shirt as well. **30** Give to everyone who asks you for something, and when someone takes what is yours, do not ask for it back. **31** Do for others just what you want them to do for you.

32 "If you love only the people who love you, why should you receive a blessing? Even sinners love those who love them! **33** And if you do good only to those who do good to you, why should you receive a blessing? Even sinners do that! **34** And if you lend only to those from whom you hope to get it back, why should you receive a blessing? Even sinners lend to sinners, to get back the same amount! **35** No! Love your enemies and do good to them; lend and expect nothing back. You will then have a great reward, and you will be children of the Most High God. For he is good to the ungrateful and the wicked. **36** Be merciful just as your Father is merciful.

Judging Others
(Matthew 7.1-5)

37 "Do not judge others, and God will not judge you; do not condemn others, and God will not condemn you; forgive others, and God will forgive you. **38** Give to others, and God will give to you. Indeed, you will receive a full measure, a generous helping, poured into your hands — all that you can hold. The measure you use for others is the one that God will use for you."

39 And Jesus told them this parable: "One blind man cannot lead another one; if he does, both will fall into a ditch. **40** No pupils are greater than their teacher; but all pupils, when they have completed their training, will be like their teacher.

41 "Why do you look at the speck in your brother's eye, but pay no attention to the log in your own eye? **42** How can you say to your brother, 'Please, brother, let me take that speck out of your eye,' yet cannot even see the log in your own eye? You hypocrite! First take the log out of your own eye, and then you will be able to see clearly to take the speck out of your brother's eye.

6.22 1 P 4.14   **6.23** 2 Ch 36.16; Ac 7.52   **6.31** Tb 4.15; Mt 7.12   **6.35** Si 4.10, 11
6.39 Mt 15.14   **6.40** Mt 10.24, 25; Jn 13.16; 15.20

A Tree and Its Fruit
(Matthew 7.16-20; 12.33-35)

43 "A healthy tree does not bear bad fruit, nor does a poor tree bear good fruit. **44** Every tree is known by the fruit it bears; you do not pick figs from thorn bushes or gather grapes from bramble bushes. **45** A good person brings good out of the treasure of good things in his heart; a bad person brings bad out of his treasure of bad things. For the mouth speaks what the heart is full of.

The Two House Builders
(Matthew 7.24-27)

46 "Why do you call me, 'Lord, Lord,' and yet don't do what I tell you? **47** Anyone who comes to me and listens to my words and obeys them — I will show you what he is like. **48** He is like a man who, in building his house, dug deep and laid the foundation on rock. The river flooded over and hit that house but could not shake it, because it was well built. **49** But anyone who hears my words and does not obey them is like a man who built his house without laying a foundation; when the flood hit that house it fell at once — and what a terrible crash that was!"

Jesus Heals a Roman Officer's Servant
(Matthew 8.5-13)

7 When Jesus had finished saying all these things to the people, he went to Capernaum. **2** A Roman officer there had a servant who was very dear to him; the man was sick and about to die. **3** When the officer heard about Jesus, he sent some Jewish elders to ask him to come and heal his servant. **4** They came to Jesus and begged him earnestly, "This man really deserves your help. **5** He loves our people and he himself built a synagogue for us." **6** So Jesus went with them. He was not far from the house when the officer sent friends to tell him, "Sir, don't trouble yourself. I do not deserve to have you come into my house, **7** neither do I consider myself worthy to come to you in person. Just give the order, and my servant will get well. **8** I, too, am a man placed under the authority of superior officers, and I have soldiers under me. I order this one, 'Go!' and he goes; I order that one, 'Come!' and he comes; and I order my slave, 'Do this!' and he does it."

9 Jesus was surprised when he heard this; he turned around and said to the crowd following him, "I tell you, I have never found faith like this, not even in Israel!"

10 The messengers went back to the officer's house and found his servant well.

Jesus Raises a Widow's Son

11 Soon afterward[e] Jesus went to a town named Nain, accompanied by his disciples and a large crowd. **12** Just as he arrived at the gate of the town, a funeral procession was coming out. The dead man was the only son of a woman who was a widow, and a large crowd from the town was with her. **13** When the Lord saw her, his heart was filled with pity for her, and he said to her, "Don't cry." **14** Then he walked over and touched the coffin, and the men carrying it stopped. Jesus said, "Young man! Get up, I tell you!" **15** The dead man sat up and began to talk, and Jesus gave him back to his mother.

16 They all were filled with fear and praised God. "A great prophet has appeared among us!" they said; "God has come to save his people!"

17 This news about Jesus went out through all the country and the surrounding territory.

---

e Soon afterward; *some manuscripts have* The next day.
6.44 Mt 12.33   **6.45** Mt 12.34

The Messengers from John the Baptist
(Matthew 11.2-19)

[18] When John's disciples told him about all these things, he called two of them [19] and sent them to the Lord to ask him, "Are you the one John said was going to come, or should we expect someone else?"

[20] When they came to Jesus, they said, "John the Baptist sent us to ask if you are the one he said was going to come, or should we expect someone else?"

[21] At that very time Jesus healed many people from their sicknesses, diseases, and evil spirits, and gave sight to many blind people. [22] He answered John's messengers, "Go back and tell John what you have seen and heard: the blind can see, the lame can walk, those who suffer from dreaded skin diseases are made clean,*f* the deaf can hear, the dead are raised to life, and the Good News is preached to the poor. [23] How happy are those who have no doubts about me!"

[24] After John's messengers had left, Jesus began to speak about him to the crowds: "When you went out to John in the desert, what did you expect to see? A blade of grass bending in the wind? [25] What did you go out to see? A man dressed up in fancy clothes? People who dress like that and live in luxury are found in palaces! [26] Tell me, what did you go out to see? A prophet? Yes indeed, but you saw much more than a prophet. [27] For John is the one of whom the scripture says: 'God said, I will send my messenger ahead of you to open the way for you.' [28] I tell you," Jesus added, "John is greater than anyone who has ever lived. But the one who is least in the Kingdom of God is greater than John."

[29] All the people heard him; they and especially the tax collectors were the ones who had obeyed God's righteous demands and had been baptized by John. [30] But the Pharisees and the teachers of the Law rejected God's purpose for themselves and refused to be baptized by John.

[31] Jesus continued, "Now to what can I compare the people of this day? What are they like? [32] They are like children sitting in the marketplace. One group shouts to the other, 'We played wedding music for you, but you wouldn't dance! We sang funeral songs, but you wouldn't cry!' [33] John the Baptist came, and he fasted and drank no wine, and you said, 'He has a demon in him!' [34] The Son of Man came, and he ate and drank, and you said, 'Look at this man! He is a glutton and wine drinker, a friend of tax collectors and other outcasts!' [35] God's wisdom, however, is shown to be true by all who accept it."

Jesus at the Home of Simon the Pharisee

[36] A Pharisee invited Jesus to have dinner with him, and Jesus went to his house and sat down to eat. [37] In that town was a woman who lived a sinful life. She heard that Jesus was eating in the Pharisee's house, so she brought an alabaster jar full of perfume [38] and stood behind Jesus, by his feet, crying and wetting his feet with her tears. Then she dried his feet with her hair, kissed them, and poured the perfume on them. [39] When the Pharisee saw this, he said to himself, "If this man really were a prophet, he would know who this woman is who is touching him; he would know what kind of sinful life she lives!"

[40] Jesus spoke up and said to him, "Simon, I have something to tell you."

"Yes, Teacher," he said, "tell me."

f MADE CLEAN: *See 5.12.*

7.22 a Is 35.5, 6; **b** Is 61.1   **7.27** Ml 3.1   **7.29, 30** Mt 21.32; Lk 3.12   **7.37, 38** Mt 26.7; Mk 14.3; Jn 12.3

41"There were two men who owed money to a moneylender," Jesus began. "One owed him five hundred silver coins, and the other owed him fifty. **42**Neither of them could pay him back, so he canceled the debts of both. Which one, then, will love him more?"

43"I suppose," answered Simon, "that it would be the one who was forgiven more."

"You are right," said Jesus. **44**Then he turned to the woman and said to Simon, "Do you see this woman? I came into your home, and you gave me no water for my feet, but she has washed my feet with her tears and dried them with her hair. **45**You did not welcome me with a kiss, but she has not stopped kissing my feet since I came. **46**You provided no olive oil for my head, but she has covered my feet with perfume. **47**I tell you, then, the great love she has shown proves that her many sins have been forgiven. But whoever has been forgiven little shows only a little love."

48Then Jesus said to the woman, "Your sins are forgiven."

49The others sitting at the table began to say to themselves, "Who is this, who even forgives sins?"

50But Jesus said to the woman, "Your faith has saved you; go in peace."

Women Who Accompanied Jesus

8 Some time later Jesus traveled through towns and villages, preaching the Good News about the Kingdom of God. The twelve disciples went with him, **2**and so did some women who had been healed of evil spirits and diseases: Mary (who was called Magdalene), from whom seven demons had been driven out; **3**Joanna, whose husband Chuza was an officer in Herod's court; and Susanna, and many other women who used their own resources to help Jesus and his disciples.

The Parable of the Sower
(Matthew 13.1-9; Mark 4.1-9)

4People kept coming to Jesus from one town after another; and when a great crowd gathered, Jesus told this parable:

5"Once there was a man who went out to sow grain. As he scattered the seed in the field, some of it fell along the path, where it was stepped on, and the birds ate it up. **6**Some of it fell on rocky ground, and when the plants sprouted, they dried up because the soil had no moisture. **7**Some of the seed fell among thorn bushes, which grew up with the plants and choked them. **8**And some seeds fell in good soil; the plants grew and bore grain, one hundred grains each."

And Jesus concluded, "Listen, then, if you have ears!"

The Purpose of the Parables
(Matthew 13.10-17; Mark 4.10-12)

9His disciples asked Jesus what this parable meant, **10**and he answered, "The knowledge of the secrets of the Kingdom of God has been given to you, but to the rest it comes by means of parables, so that they may look but not see, and listen but not understand.

Jesus Explains the Parable
of the Sower
(Matthew 13.18-23; Mark 4.13-20)

11"This is what the parable means: the seed is the word of God. **12**The seeds that fell along the path stand for those who hear; but the Devil comes and takes the message away from their hearts in order to keep them from believing and being saved. **13**The seeds that fell on rocky ground stand for those who hear the message and receive it gladly. But it does not sink deep into

8.2, 3 Mt 27.55, 56; Mk 15.40, 41; Lk 23.49   **8.10** Is 6.9 (LXX)

them; they believe only for a while but when the time of testing comes, they fall away. [14] The seeds that fell among thorn bushes stand for those who hear; but the worries and riches and pleasures of this life crowd in and choke them, and their fruit never ripens. [15] The seeds that fell in good soil stand for those who hear the message and retain it in a good and obedient heart, and they persist until they bear fruit.

A Lamp under a Bowl
(Mark 4.21-25)

[16] "No one lights a lamp and covers it with a bowl or puts it under a bed. Instead, it is put on the lampstand, so that people will see the light as they come in.

[17] "Whatever is hidden away will be brought out into the open, and whatever is covered up will be found and brought to light.

[18] "Be careful, then, how you listen; because those who have something will be given more, but whoever has nothing will have taken away from them even the little they think they have."

Jesus' Mother and Brothers
(Matthew 12.46-50; Mark 3.31-35)

[19] Jesus' mother and brothers came to him, but were unable to join him because of the crowd. [20] Someone said to Jesus, "Your mother and brothers are standing outside and want to see you."

[21] Jesus said to them all, "My mother and brothers are those who hear the word of God and obey it."

Jesus Calms a Storm
(Matthew 8.23-27; Mark 4.35-41)

[22] One day Jesus got into a boat with his disciples and said to them, "Let us go across to the other side of the lake." So they started out. [23] As they were sailing, Jesus fell asleep. Suddenly a strong wind blew down on the lake, and the boat began to fill with water, so that they were all in great danger. [24] The disciples went to Jesus and woke him up, saying, "Master, Master! We are about to die!"

Jesus got up and gave an order to the wind and to the stormy water; they quieted down, and there was a great calm. [25] Then he said to the disciples, "Where is your faith?"

But they were amazed and afraid, and said to one another, "Who is this man? He gives orders to the winds and waves, and they obey him!"

Jesus Heals a Man with Demons
(Matthew 8.28-34; Mark 5.1-20)

[26] Jesus and his disciples sailed on over to the territory of Gerasa,[g] which is across the lake from Galilee. [27] As Jesus stepped ashore, he was met by a man from the town who had demons in him. For a long time this man had gone without clothes and would not stay at home, but spent his time in the burial caves. [28] When he saw Jesus, he gave a loud cry, threw himself down at his feet, and shouted, "Jesus, Son of the Most High God! What do you want with me? I beg you, don't punish me!" [29] He said this because Jesus had ordered the evil spirit to go out of him. Many times it had seized him, and even though he was kept a prisoner, his hands and feet tied with chains, he would break the chains and be driven by the demon out into the desert.

[30] Jesus asked him, "What is your name?"

"My name is 'Mob,' " he answered — because many demons had gone into

---

[g] Gerasa; *some manuscripts have* Gadara *(see Mt 8.28); others have* Gergesa.
8.16 Mt 5.15; Lk 11.33 **8.17** Mt 10.26; Lk 12.2 **8.18** Mt 25.29; Lk 19.26

him. [31] The demons begged Jesus not to send them into the abyss.[h]

[32] There was a large herd of pigs near by, feeding on a hillside. So the demons begged Jesus to let them go into the pigs, and he let them. [33] They went out of the man and into the pigs. The whole herd rushed down the side of the cliff into the lake and was drowned.

[34] The men who had been taking care of the pigs saw what happened, so they ran off and spread the news in the town and among the farms. [35] People went out to see what had happened, and when they came to Jesus, they found the man from whom the demons had gone out sitting at the feet of Jesus, clothed and in his right mind; and they were all afraid. [36] Those who had seen it told the people how the man had been cured. [37] Then all the people from that territory asked Jesus to go away, because they were terribly afraid. So Jesus got into the boat and left. [38] The man from whom the demons had gone out begged Jesus, "Let me go with you."

But Jesus sent him away, saying, [39] "Go back home and tell what God has done for you."

The man went through the town, telling what Jesus had done for him.

Jairus' Daughter and the Woman Who Touched Jesus' Cloak
(*Matthew 9.18-26; Mark 5.21-43*)

[40] When Jesus returned to the other side of the lake, the people welcomed him, because they had all been waiting for him. [41] Then a man named Jairus arrived; he was an official in the local synagogue. He threw himself down at Jesus' feet and begged him to go to his home, [42] because his only daughter, who was twelve years old, was dying.

As Jesus went along, the people were crowding him from every side. [43] Among them was a woman who had suffered from severe bleeding for twelve years; she had spent all she had on doctors,[i] but no one had been able to cure her. [44] She came up in the crowd behind Jesus and touched the edge of his cloak, and her bleeding stopped at once. [45] Jesus asked, "Who touched me?"

Everyone denied it, and Peter said, "Master, the people are all around you and crowding in on you."

[46] But Jesus said, "Someone touched me, for I knew it when power went out of me." [47] The woman saw that she had been found out, so she came trembling and threw herself at Jesus' feet. There in front of everybody, she told him why she had touched him and how she had been healed at once. [48] Jesus said to her, "My daughter, your faith has made you well. Go in peace."

[49] While Jesus was saying this, a messenger came from the official's house. "Your daughter has died," he told Jairus; "don't bother the Teacher any longer."

[50] But Jesus heard it and said to Jairus, "Don't be afraid; only believe, and she will be well."

[51] When he arrived at the house, he would not let anyone go in with him except Peter, John, and James, and the child's father and mother. [52] Everyone there was crying and mourning for the child. Jesus said, "Don't cry; the child is not dead—she is only sleeping!"

[53] They all made fun of him, because they knew that she was dead. [54] But Jesus took her by the hand and called out, "Get up, child!" [55] Her life returned, and she got up at once, and Jesus ordered them to give her something to

---

[h] ABYSS: *It was thought that the demons were to be imprisoned in the depths of the earth until their final punishment.*   [i] *Some manuscripts do not have* she had spent all she had on doctors.

eat. [56] Her parents were astounded, but Jesus commanded them not to tell anyone what had happened.

Jesus Sends Out the Twelve Disciples
(Matthew 10.5-15; Mark 6.7-13)

9 Jesus called the twelve disciples together and gave them power and authority to drive out all demons and to cure diseases. [2] Then he sent them out to preach the Kingdom of God and to heal the sick, [3] after saying to them, "Take nothing with you for the trip: no walking stick, no beggar's bag, no food, no money, not even an extra shirt. [4] Wherever you are welcomed, stay in the same house until you leave that town; [5] wherever people don't welcome you, leave that town and shake the dust off your feet as a warning to them."

[6] The disciples left and traveled through all the villages, preaching the Good News and healing people everywhere.

Herod's Confusion
(Matthew 14.1-12; Mark 6.14-29)

[7] When Herod, the ruler of Galilee, heard about all the things that were happening, he was very confused, because some people were saying that John the Baptist had come back to life. [8] Others were saying that Elijah had appeared, and still others that one of the prophets of long ago had come back to life. [9] Herod said, "I had John's head cut off; but who is this man I hear these things about?" And he kept trying to see Jesus.

Jesus Feeds Five Thousand
(Matthew 14.13-21; Mark 6.30-44; John 6.1-14)

[10] The apostles came back and told Jesus everything they had done. He took them with him, and they went off by themselves to a town named Bethsaida. [11] When the crowds heard about it, they followed him. He welcomed them, spoke to them about the Kingdom of God, and healed those who needed it.

[12] When the sun was beginning to set, the twelve disciples came to him and said, "Send the people away so that they can go to the villages and farms around here and find food and lodging, because this is a lonely place."

[13] But Jesus said to them, "You yourselves give them something to eat."

They answered, "All we have are five loaves and two fish. Do you want us to go and buy food for this whole crowd?" [14] (There were about five thousand men there.)

Jesus said to his disciples, "Make the people sit down in groups of about fifty each."

[15] After the disciples had done so, [16] Jesus took the five loaves and two fish, looked up to heaven, thanked God for them, broke them, and gave them to the disciples to distribute to the people. [17] They all ate and had enough, and the disciples took up twelve baskets of what was left over.

Peter's Declaration about Jesus
(Matthew 16.13-19; Mark 8.27-29)

[18] One day when Jesus was praying alone, the disciples came to him. "Who do the crowds say I am?" he asked them.

[19] "Some say that you are John the Baptist," they answered. "Others say that you are Elijah, while others say that one of the prophets of long ago has come back to life."

[20] "What about you?" he asked them. "Who do you say I am?"

Peter answered, "You are God's Messiah."

9.5 Ac 13.51   **9.3-5** Lk 10.4-11   **9.7, 8** Mt 16.14; Mk 8.28; Lk 9.19   **9.19** Mt 14.1, 2; Mk 6.14, 15; Lk 9.7, 8   **9.20** Jn 6.68, 69

They all ate and had enough. (9.17)

Jesus Speaks about His Suffering and Death
(Matthew 16.20-28; Mark 8.30 — 9.1)

21 Then Jesus gave them strict orders not to tell this to anyone. **22** He also told them, "The Son of Man must suffer much and be rejected by the elders, the chief priests, and the teachers of the Law. He will be put to death, but three days later he will be raised to life."

23 And he said to them all, "If you want to come with me, you must forget yourself, take up your cross every day, and follow me. **24** For if you want to save your own life, you will lose it, but if you lose your life for my sake, you will save it. **25** Will you gain anything if you win the whole world but are yourself lost or defeated? Of course not! **26** If you are ashamed of me and of my teaching, then the Son of Man will be ashamed of you when he comes in his glory and in the glory of the Father and of the holy angels. **27** I assure you that there are some here who will not die until they have seen the Kingdom of God."

The Transfiguration
(Matthew 17.1-8; Mark 9.2-8)

28 About a week after he had said these things, Jesus took Peter, John, and James with him and went up a hill to pray. **29** While he was praying, his face changed its appearance, and his clothes became dazzling white. **30** Suddenly two men were there talking with him. They were Moses and Elijah, **31** who appeared in heavenly glory and talked with Jesus about the way in which he would soon fulfill God's purpose by dying in Jerusalem. **32** Peter and his companions were sound asleep, but they woke up and saw Jesus' glory and the two men who were standing with him. **33** As the men were leaving Jesus, Peter said to him, "Master, how good it is that we are here! We will make three tents, one for you, one for Moses, and one for Elijah." (He did not really know what he was saying.)

34 While he was still speaking, a cloud appeared and covered them with its shadow; and the disciples were

9.23 Mt 10.38; Lk 14.27 **9.24** Mt 10.39; Lk 17.33; Jn 12.25

afraid as the cloud came over them. [35] A voice said from the cloud, "This is my Son, whom I have chosen — listen to him!"

[36] When the voice stopped, there was Jesus all alone. The disciples kept quiet about all this and told no one at that time anything they had seen.

Jesus Heals a Boy with an Evil Spirit
(Matthew 17.14-18; Mark 9.14-27)

[37] The next day Jesus and the three disciples went down from the hill, and a large crowd met Jesus. [38] A man shouted from the crowd, "Teacher! I beg you, look at my son — my only son! [39] A spirit attacks him with a sudden shout and throws him into a fit, so that he foams at the mouth; it keeps on hurting him and will hardly let him go! [40] I begged your disciples to drive it out, but they couldn't."

[41] Jesus answered, "How unbelieving and wrong you people are! How long must I stay with you? How long do I have to put up with you?" Then he said to the man, "Bring your son here."

[42] As the boy was coming, the demon knocked him to the ground and threw him into a fit. Jesus gave a command to the evil spirit, healed the boy, and gave him back to his father. [43] All the people were amazed at the mighty power of God.

Jesus Speaks Again about His Death
(Matthew 17.22, 23; Mark 9.30-32)

The people were still marveling at everything Jesus was doing, when he said to his disciples, [44] "Don't forget what I am about to tell you! The Son of Man is going to be handed over to the power of human beings." [45] But the disciples did not know what this meant. It had been hidden from them so that

they could not understand it, and they were afraid to ask him about the matter.

Who Is the Greatest?
(Matthew 18.1-5; Mark 9.33-37)

[46] An argument broke out among the disciples as to which one of them was the greatest. [47] Jesus knew what they were thinking, so he took a child, stood him by his side, [48] and said to them, "Whoever welcomes this child in my name, welcomes me; and whoever welcomes me, also welcomes the one who sent me. For the one who is least among you all is the greatest."

Whoever Is Not against You Is for You
(Mark 9.38-40)

[49] John spoke up, "Master, we saw a man driving out demons in your name, and we told him to stop, because he doesn't belong to our group."

[50] "Do not try to stop him," Jesus said to him and to the other disciples, "because whoever is not against you is for you."

A Samaritan Village Refuses to Receive Jesus

[51] As the time drew near when Jesus would be taken up to heaven, he made up his mind and set out on his way to Jerusalem. [52] He sent messengers ahead of him, who went into a village in Samaria to get everything ready for him. [53] But the people there would not receive him, because it was clear that he was on his way to Jerusalem. [54] When the disciples James and John saw this, they said, "Lord, do you want us to call fire down from heaven to destroy them?"[j]

---

[j] *Some manuscripts add* as Elijah did.

9.35 Is 42.1; Mt 3.17; 12.18; Mk 1.11; Lk 3.22   **9.28-35** 2 P 1.17, 18   **9.46** Lk 22.24
9.48 Mt 10.40; Lk 10.16; Jn 13.20   **9.54** 2 K 1.9-16

⁵⁵Jesus turned and rebuked them.ᵏ ⁵⁶Then Jesus and his disciples went on to another village.

The Would-Be Followers of Jesus
(Matthew 8.19-22)

⁵⁷As they went on their way, a man said to Jesus, "I will follow you wherever you go."

⁵⁸Jesus said to him, "Foxes have holes, and birds have nests, but the Son of Man has no place to lie down and rest."

⁵⁹He said to another man, "Follow me."

But that man said, "Sir, first let me go back and bury my father."

⁶⁰Jesus answered, "Let the dead bury their own dead. You go and proclaim the Kingdom of God."

⁶¹Someone else said, "I will follow you, sir; but first let me go and say good-bye to my family."

⁶²Jesus said to him, "Anyone who starts to plow and then keeps looking back is of no use for the Kingdom of God."

Jesus Sends Out the Seventy-Two

10 After this the Lord chose another seventy-twoˡ men and sent them out two by two, to go ahead of him to every town and place where he himself was about to go. ²He said to them, "There is a large harvest, but few workers to gather it in. Pray to the owner of the harvest that he will send out workers to gather in his harvest. ³Go! I am sending you like lambs among wolves. ⁴Don't take a purse or a beggar's bag or shoes; don't stop to greet anyone on the road. ⁵Whenever you go into a house, first say, 'Peace be with this house.' ⁶If someone who is peace-loving lives there, let your greeting of peace remain on that person; if not, take back your greeting of peace. ⁷Stay in that same house, eating and drinking whatever they offer you, for workers should be given their pay. Don't move around from one house to another. ⁸Whenever you go into a town and are made welcome, eat what is set before you, ⁹heal the sick in that town, and say to the people there, 'The Kingdom of God has come near you.' ¹⁰But whenever you go into a town and are not welcomed, go out in the streets and say, ¹¹'Even the dust from your town that sticks to our feet we wipe off against you. But remember that the Kingdom of God has come near you!' ¹²I assure you that on the Judgment Day God will show more mercy to Sodom than to that town!

The Unbelieving Towns
(Matthew 11.20-24)

¹³"How terrible it will be for you, Chorazin! How terrible for you too, Bethsaida! If the miracles which were performed in you had been performed in Tyre and Sidon, the people there would have long ago sat down, put on sackcloth, and sprinkled ashes on themselves, to show that they had turned from their sins! ¹⁴God will show more mercy on the Judgment Day to Tyre and Sidon than to you. ¹⁵And as for you, Capernaum! Did you want to

---

ᵏ *Some manuscripts add* and said, "You don't know what kind of a Spirit you belong to; for the Son of Man did not come to destroy human lives, but to save them."
ˡ seventy-two; *some manuscripts have* seventy.
9.61 1 K 19.20   **10.2** Mt 9.37, 38   **10.3** Mt 10.16   **10.7** 1 Co 9.14; 1 Ti 5.18
10.10, 11 Ac 13.51   **10.4-11** Mt 10.7-14; Mk 6.8-11; Lk 9.3-5   **10.12 a** Gn 19.24-28;
Mt 11.24; **b** Mt 10.15   **10.13** Is 23.1-18; Ez 26.1—28.26; Jl 3.4-8; Am 1.9, 10; Zec 9.2-4
10.15 Is 14.13-15

lift yourself up to heaven? You will be thrown down to hell!"

16 Jesus said to his disciples, "Whoever listens to you listens to me; whoever rejects you rejects me; and whoever rejects me rejects the one who sent me."

The Return of the Seventy-Two

17 The seventy-two[m] men came back in great joy. "Lord," they said, "even the demons obeyed us when we gave them a command in your name!"

18 Jesus answered them, "I saw Satan fall like lightning from heaven. 19 Listen! I have given you authority, so that you can walk on snakes and scorpions and overcome all the power of the Enemy, and nothing will hurt you. 20 But don't be glad because the evil spirits obey you; rather be glad because your names are written in heaven."

Jesus Rejoices
(Matthew 11.25-27; 13.16, 17)

21 At that time Jesus was filled with joy by the Holy Spirit[n] and said, "Father, Lord of heaven and earth! I thank you because you have shown to the unlearned what you have hidden from the wise and learned. Yes, Father, this was how you were pleased to have it happen.

22 "My Father has given me all things. No one knows who the Son is except the Father, and no one knows who the Father is except the Son and those to whom the Son chooses to reveal him."

23 Then Jesus turned to the disciples and said to them privately, "How fortunate you are to see the things you see!

24 I tell you that many prophets and kings wanted to see what you see, but they could not, and to hear what you hear, but they did not."

The Parable of the Good Samaritan

25 A teacher of the Law came up and tried to trap Jesus. "Teacher," he asked, "what must I do to receive eternal life?"

26 Jesus answered him, "What do the Scriptures say? How do you interpret them?"

27 The man answered, " 'Love the Lord your God with all your heart, with all your soul, with all your strength, and with all your mind'; and 'Love your neighbor as you love yourself.' "

28 "You are right," Jesus replied; "do this and you will live."

29 But the teacher of the Law wanted to justify himself, so he asked Jesus, "Who is my neighbor?"

30 Jesus answered, "There was once a man who was going down from Jerusalem to Jericho when robbers attacked him, stripped him, and beat him up, leaving him half dead. 31 It so happened that a priest was going down that road;

His heart was filled with pity. (10.33)

---

[m] seventy-two; *some manuscripts have* seventy *(see verse 1).*   [n] by the Holy Spirit; *some manuscripts have* by the Spirit; *others have* in his spirit.

10.16 Mt 10.40; Mk 9.37; Lk 9.48; Jn 13.20   **10.19** Ps 91.13   **10.22 a** Jn 3.35; **b** Jn 10.15   **10.25-28** Mt 22.35-40; Mk 12.28-34   **10.27 a** Dt 6.5; **b** Lv 19.18   **10.28** Lv 18.5

but when he saw the man, he walked on by on the other side. 32 In the same way a Levite also came there, went over and looked at the man, and then walked on by on the other side. 33 But a Samaritan who was traveling that way came upon the man, and when he saw him, his heart was filled with pity. 34 He went over to him, poured oil and wine on his wounds and bandaged them; then he put the man on his own animal and took him to an inn, where he took care of him. 35 The next day he took out two silver coins and gave them to the innkeeper. 'Take care of him,' he told the innkeeper, 'and when I come back this way, I will pay you whatever else you spend on him.' "

36 And Jesus concluded, "In your opinion, which one of these three acted like a neighbor toward the man attacked by the robbers?"

37 The teacher of the Law answered, "The one who was kind to him."

Jesus replied, "You go, then, and do the same."

Jesus Visits Martha and Mary

38 As Jesus and his disciples went on their way, he came to a village where a woman named Martha welcomed him in her home. 39 She had a sister named Mary, who sat down at the feet of the Lord and listened to his teaching. 40 Martha was upset over all the work she had to do, so she came and said, "Lord, don't you care that my sister has left me to do all the work by myself? Tell her to come and help me!"

41 The Lord answered her, "Martha, Martha! You are worried and troubled over so many things, 42 but just one is needed. Mary has chosen the right thing, and it will not be taken away from her."

Jesus' Teaching on Prayer
(Matthew 6.9-13; 7.7-11)

11 One day Jesus was praying in a certain place. When he had finished, one of his disciples said to him, "Lord, teach us to pray, just as John taught his disciples."

2 Jesus said to them, "When you pray, say this:
    'Father:
        May your holy name be honored;
        may your Kingdom come.
3   Give us day by day the food we need.*o*
4   Forgive us our sins,
            for we forgive everyone who does us wrong.
        And do not bring us to hard testing.' "

5 And Jesus said to his disciples, "Suppose one of you should go to a friend's house at midnight and say, 'Friend, let me borrow three loaves of bread. 6 A friend of mine who is on a trip has just come to my house, and I don't have any food for him!' 7 And suppose your friend should answer from inside, 'Don't bother me! The door is already locked, and my children and I are in bed. I can't get up and give you anything.' 8 Well, what then? I tell you that even if he will not get up and give you the bread because you are his friend, yet he will get up and give you everything you need because you are not ashamed to keep on asking. 9 And so I say to you: Ask, and you will receive; seek, and you will find; knock, and the door will be opened to you. 10 For those who ask will receive, and those who seek will find, and the door will be opened to anyone who knocks. 11 Would any of you who are fathers give your son a snake when he asks for fish?

---

o the food we need; *or* food for the next day.
10.33, 34 2 Ch 28.15   **10.38, 39** Jn 11.1

¹²Or would you give him a scorpion when he asks for an egg? ¹³As bad as you are, you know how to give good things to your children. How much more, then, will the Father in heaven give the Holy Spirit to those who ask him!"

Jesus and Beelzebul
(Matthew 12.22-30; Mark 3.20-27)

¹⁴Jesus was driving out a demon that could not talk; and when the demon went out, the man began to talk. The crowds were amazed, ¹⁵but some of the people said, "It is Beelzebul, the chief of the demons, who gives him the power to drive them out."

¹⁶Others wanted to trap Jesus, so they asked him to perform a miracle to show that God approved of him. ¹⁷But Jesus knew what they were thinking, so he said to them, "Any country that divides itself into groups which fight each other will not last very long; a family divided against itself falls apart. ¹⁸So if Satan's kingdom has groups fighting each other, how can it last? You say that I drive out demons because Beelzebul gives me the power to do so. ¹⁹If this is how I drive them out, how do your followers drive them out? Your own followers prove that you are wrong! ²⁰No, it is rather by means of God's power that I drive out demons, and this proves that the Kingdom of God has already come to you.

²¹"When a strong man, with all his weapons ready, guards his own house, all his belongings are safe. ²²But when a stronger man attacks him and defeats him, he carries away all the weapons the owner was depending on and divides up what he stole.

²³"Anyone who is not for me is really against me; anyone who does not help me gather is really scattering.

The Return of the Evil Spirit
(Matthew 12.43-45)

²⁴"When an evil spirit goes out of a person, it travels over dry country looking for a place to rest. If it can't find one, it says to itself, 'I will go back to my house.' ²⁵So it goes back and finds the house clean and all fixed up. ²⁶Then it goes out and brings seven other spirits even worse than itself, and they come and live there. So when it is all over, that person is in worse shape than at the beginning."

True Happiness

²⁷When Jesus had said this, a woman spoke up from the crowd and said to him, "How happy is the woman who bore you and nursed you!"

²⁸But Jesus answered, "Rather, how happy are those who hear the word of God and obey it!"

The Demand for a Miracle
(Matthew 12.38-42)

²⁹As the people crowded around Jesus, he went on to say, "How evil are the people of this day! They ask for a miracle, but none will be given them except the miracle of Jonah. ³⁰In the same way that the prophet Jonah was a sign for the people of Nineveh, so the Son of Man will be a sign for the people of this day. ³¹On the Judgment Day the Queen of Sheba will stand up and accuse the people of today, because she traveled all the way from her country to listen to King Solomon's wise teaching; and there is something here, I tell you, greater than Solomon. ³²On the Judgment Day the people of Nineveh will stand up and accuse you, because they turned from their sins when they heard Jonah preach; and I assure you that there is something here greater than Jonah!

11.15 Mt 9.34; 10.25   **11.16** Mt 12.38; 16.1; Mk 8.11   **11.23** Mk 9.40   **11.29** Mt 16.4; Mk 8.12   **11.30** Jon 3.4   **11.31** 1 K 10.1-10; 2 Ch 9.1-12   **11.32** Jon 3.5

The Light of the Body
(Matthew 5.15; 6.22, 23)

33"No one lights a lamp and then hides it or puts it under a bowl;*p* instead, it is put on the lampstand, so that people may see the light as they come in. 34Your eyes are like a lamp for the body. When your eyes are sound, your whole body is full of light; but when your eyes are no good, your whole body will be in darkness. 35Make certain, then, that the light in you is not darkness. 36If your whole body is full of light, with no part of it in darkness, it will be bright all over, as when a lamp shines on you with its brightness."

Jesus Accuses the Pharisees and the Teachers of the Law
(Matthew 23.1-36; Mark 12.38-40)

37When Jesus finished speaking, a Pharisee invited him to eat with him; so he went in and sat down to eat. 38The Pharisee was surprised when he noticed that Jesus had not washed before eating. 39So the Lord said to him, "Now then, you Pharisees clean the outside of your cup and plate, but inside you are full of violence and evil. 40Fools! Did not God, who made the outside, also make the inside? 41But give what is in your cups and plates to the poor, and everything will be ritually clean for you.

42"How terrible for you Pharisees! You give to God one tenth of the seasoning herbs, such as mint and rue and all the other herbs, but you neglect justice and love for God. These you should practice, without neglecting the others.

43"How terrible for you Pharisees! You love the reserved seats in the synagogues and to be greeted with respect in the marketplaces. 44How terrible for you! You are like unmarked graves which people walk on without knowing it."

45One of the teachers of the Law said to him, "Teacher, when you say this, you insult us too!"

46Jesus answered, "How terrible also for you teachers of the Law! You put onto people's backs loads which are hard to carry, but you yourselves will not stretch out a finger to help them carry those loads. 47How terrible for you! You make fine tombs for the prophets — the very prophets your ancestors murdered. 48You yourselves admit, then, that you approve of what your ancestors did; they murdered the prophets, and you build their tombs. 49For this reason the Wisdom of God said, 'I will send them prophets and messengers; they will kill some of them and persecute others.' 50So the people of this time will be punished for the murder of all the prophets killed since the creation of the world, 51from the murder of Abel to the murder of Zechariah, who was killed between the altar and the Holy Place. Yes, I tell you, the people of this time will be punished for them all!

52"How terrible for you teachers of the Law! You have kept the key that opens the door to the house of knowledge; you yourselves will not go in, and you stop those who are trying to go in!"

53When Jesus left that place, the teachers of the Law and the Pharisees began to criticize him bitterly and ask him questions about many things, 54trying to lay traps for him and catch him saying something wrong.

A Warning against Hypocrisy
(Matthew 10.26, 27)

12 As thousands of people crowded together, so that they were stepping on each other, Jesus said

---

p Some manuscripts do not have or puts it under a bowl.
11.33 Mt 5.15; Mk 4.21; Lk 8.16 **11.42** Lv 27.30 **11.51 a** Gn 4.8; **b** 2 Ch 24.20, 21
12.1 Mt 16.6; Mk 8.15

first to his disciples, "Be on guard against the yeast of the Pharisees — I mean their hypocrisy. ²Whatever is covered up will be uncovered, and every secret will be made known. ³So then, whatever you have said in the dark will be heard in broad daylight, and whatever you have whispered in private in a closed room will be shouted from the housetops.

Whom to Fear
(Matthew 10.28-31)

⁴"I tell you, my friends, do not be afraid of those who kill the body but cannot afterward do anything worse. ⁵I will show you whom to fear: fear God, who, after killing, has the authority to throw into hell. Believe me, he is the one you must fear!

⁶"Aren't five sparrows sold for two pennies? Yet not one sparrow is forgotten by God. ⁷Even the hairs of your head have all been counted. So do not be afraid; you are worth much more than many sparrows!

Confessing and Rejecting Christ
(Matthew 10.32, 33; 12.32; 10.19, 20)

⁸"I assure you that those who declare publicly that they belong to me, the Son of Man will do the same for them before the angels of God. ⁹But those who reject me publicly, the Son of Man will also reject them before the angels of God.

¹⁰"Whoever says a word against the Son of Man can be forgiven; but whoever says evil things against the Holy Spirit will not be forgiven.

¹¹"When they bring you to be tried in the synagogues or before governors or rulers, do not be worried about how you will defend yourself or what you will say. ¹²For the Holy Spirit will teach you at that time what you should say."

The Parable of the Rich Fool

¹³A man in the crowd said to Jesus, "Teacher, tell my brother to divide with me the property our father left us."

¹⁴Jesus answered him, "Friend, who gave me the right to judge or to divide the property between you two?" ¹⁵And he went on to say to them all, "Watch out and guard yourselves from every kind of greed; because your true life is not made up of the things you own, no matter how rich you may be."

¹⁶Then Jesus told them this parable: "There was once a rich man who had land which bore good crops. ¹⁷He began to think to himself, 'I don't have a place to keep all my crops. What can I do? ¹⁸This is what I will do,' he told himself; 'I will tear down my barns and build bigger ones, where I will store the grain and all my other goods. ¹⁹Then I will say to myself, Lucky man! You have all the good things you need for many years. Take life easy, eat, drink, and enjoy yourself!' ²⁰But God said to him, 'You fool! This very night you will have to give up your life; then who will get all these things you have kept for yourself?'"

²¹And Jesus concluded, "This is how it is with those who pile up riches for themselves but are not rich in God's sight."

Trust in God
(Matthew 6.25-34)

²²Then Jesus said to the disciples, "And so I tell you not to worry about the food you need to stay alive or about the clothes you need for your body. ²³Life is much more important than food, and the body much more important than clothes. ²⁴Look at the crows: they don't plant seeds or gather a harvest; they don't have storage rooms or barns; God feeds them! You are worth so much more than birds! ²⁵Can any of you live

12.2 Mk 4.22; Lk 8.17　**12.10** Mt 12.32; Mk 3.29　**12.11, 12** Mt 10.19, 20; Mk 13.11; Lk 21.14, 15　**12.19** Si 11.19

a bit longer *q* by worrying about it? 26 If you can't manage even such a small thing, why worry about the other things? 27 Look how the wild flowers grow: they don't work or make clothes for themselves. But I tell you that not even King Solomon with all his wealth had clothes as beautiful as one of these flowers. 28 It is God who clothes the wild grass — grass that is here today and gone tomorrow, burned up in the oven. Won't he be all the more sure to clothe you? What little faith you have!

So I tell you not to worry. (12.22)

29 "So don't be all upset, always concerned about what you will eat and drink. 30 (For the pagans of this world are always concerned about all these things.) Your Father knows that you need these things. 31 Instead, be concerned with his Kingdom, and he will provide you with these things.

Riches in Heaven
(Matthew 6.19-21)

32 "Do not be afraid, little flock, for your Father is pleased to give you the Kingdom. 33 Sell all your belongings and give the money to the poor. Provide for yourselves purses that don't wear out, and save your riches in heaven, where they will never decrease, because no thief can get to them, and no moth can destroy them. 34 For your heart will always be where your riches are.

Watchful Servants

35 "Be ready for whatever comes, dressed for action and with your lamps lit, 36 like servants who are waiting for their master to come back from a wedding feast. When he comes and knocks, they will open the door for him at once. 37 How happy are those servants whose master finds them awake and ready when he returns! I tell you, he will take off his coat, have them sit down, and will wait on them. 38 How happy they are if he finds them ready, even if he should come at midnight or even later! 39 And you can be sure that if the owner of a house knew the time when the thief would come, he would not let the thief break into his house. 40 And you, too, must be ready, because the Son of Man will come at an hour when you are not expecting him."

The Faithful or the Unfaithful Servant
(Matthew 24.45-51)

41 Peter said, "Lord, does this parable apply to us, or do you mean it for everyone?"

42 The Lord answered, "Who, then, is the faithful and wise servant? He is the one that his master will put in charge, to run the household and give the other servants their share of the food at the proper time. 43 How happy that servant is if his master finds him doing this when he comes home! 44 Indeed, I tell you, the master will put that servant in charge of all his property. 45 But if that servant says to himself that his master is taking a long time to come back and if he begins to beat the other servants, both the men and the women, and eats and drinks and gets drunk, 46 then the master will come back one day when the servant does not expect him and at a time he does not know. The master

---

q live a bit longer; *or* grow a bit taller.

12.27 1 K 10.4-7; 2 Ch 9.3-6 **12.35** Mt 25.1-13 **12.36** Mk 13.34-36
12.39, 40 Mt 24.43, 44

will cut him in pieces[r] and make him share the fate of the disobedient.

[47] "The servant who knows what his master wants him to do, but does not get himself ready and do it, will be punished with a heavy whipping. [48] But the servant who does not know what his master wants, and yet does something for which he deserves a whipping, will be punished with a light whipping. Much is required from the person to whom much is given; much more is required from the person to whom much more is given.

Jesus the Cause of Division
(Matthew 10.34-36)

[49] "I came to set the earth on fire, and how I wish it were already kindled! [50] I have a baptism to receive, and how distressed I am until it is over! [51] Do you suppose that I came to bring peace to the world? No, not peace, but division. [52] From now on a family of five will be divided, three against two and two against three. [53] Fathers will be against their sons, and sons against their fathers; mothers will be against their daughters, and daughters against their mothers; mothers-in-law will be against their daughters-in-law, and daughters-in-law against their mothers-in-law."

Understanding the Time
(Matthew 16.2, 3)

[54] Jesus said also to the people, "When you see a cloud coming up in the west, at once you say that it is going to rain — and it does. [55] And when you feel the south wind blowing, you say that it is going to get hot — and it does. [56] Hypocrites! You can look at the earth and the sky and predict the weather; why, then, don't you know the meaning of this present time?

Settle with Your Opponent
(Matthew 5.25, 26)

[57] "Why do you not judge for yourselves the right thing to do? [58] If someone brings a lawsuit against you and takes you to court, do your best to settle the dispute before you get to court. If you don't, you will be dragged before the judge, who will hand you over to the police, and you will be put in jail. [59] There you will stay, I tell you, until you pay the last penny of your fine."

Turn from Your Sins or Die

13 At that time some people were there who told Jesus about the Galileans whom Pilate had killed while they were offering sacrifices to God. [2] Jesus answered them, "Because those Galileans were killed in that way, do you think it proves that they were worse sinners than all other Galileans? [3] No indeed! And I tell you that if you do not turn from your sins, you will all die as they did. [4] What about those eighteen people in Siloam who were killed when the tower fell on them? Do you suppose this proves that they were worse than all the other people living in Jerusalem? [5] No indeed! And I tell you that if you do not turn from your sins, you will all die as they did."

The Parable of the Unfruitful Fig Tree

[6] Then Jesus told them this parable: "There was once a man who had a fig tree growing in his vineyard. He went looking for figs on it but found none. [7] So he said to his gardener, 'Look, for three years I have been coming here looking for figs on this fig tree, and I haven't found any. Cut it down! Why should it go on using up the soil?' [8] But the gardener answered, 'Leave it alone, sir, just one more year; I will dig around it and put in some fertilizer. [9] Then if

---

[r] cut him in pieces; *or* throw him out.
12.50 Mk 10.38   **12.53** Mic 7.6

the tree bears figs next year, so much the better; if not, then you can have it cut down.'"

Jesus Heals a Crippled Woman on the Sabbath

¹⁰One Sabbath Jesus was teaching in a synagogue. ¹¹A woman there had an evil spirit that had kept her sick for eighteen years; she was bent over and could not straighten up at all. ¹²When Jesus saw her, he called out to her, "Woman, you are free from your sickness!" ¹³He placed his hands on her, and at once she straightened herself up and praised God.

¹⁴The official of the synagogue was angry that Jesus had healed on the Sabbath, so he spoke up and said to the people, "There are six days in which we should work; so come during those days and be healed, but not on the Sabbath!"

¹⁵The Lord answered him, "You hypocrites! Any one of you would untie your ox or your donkey from the stall and take it out to give it water on the Sabbath. ¹⁶Now here is this descendant of Abraham whom Satan has kept in bonds for eighteen years; should she not be released on the Sabbath?" ¹⁷His answer made his enemies ashamed of themselves, while the people rejoiced over all the wonderful things that he did.

The Parable of the Mustard Seed
(Matthew 13.31, 32; Mark 4.30-32)

¹⁸Jesus asked, "What is the Kingdom of God like? What shall I compare it with? ¹⁹It is like this. A man takes a mustard seed and plants it in his field. The plant grows and becomes a tree, and the birds make their nests in its branches."

The Parable of the Yeast
(Matthew 13.33)

²⁰Again Jesus asked, "What shall I compare the Kingdom of God with? ²¹It is like this. A woman takes some yeast and mixes it with a bushel of flour until the whole batch of dough rises."

The Narrow Door
(Matthew 7.13, 14, 21-23)

²²Jesus went through towns and villages, teaching the people and making his way toward Jerusalem. ²³Someone asked him, "Sir, will just a few people be saved?"

Jesus answered them, ²⁴"Do your best to go in through the narrow door; because many people will surely try to go in but will not be able. ²⁵The master of the house will get up and close the door; then when you stand outside and begin to knock on the door and say, 'Open the door for us, sir!' he will answer you, 'I don't know where you come from!' ²⁶Then you will answer, 'We ate and drank with you; you taught in our town!' ²⁷But he will say again, 'I don't know where you come from. Get away from me, all you wicked people!' ²⁸How you will cry and gnash your teeth when you see Abraham, Isaac, and Jacob, and all the prophets in the Kingdom of God, while you are thrown out! ²⁹People will come from the east and the west, from the north and the south, and sit down at the feast in the Kingdom of God. ³⁰Then those who are now last will be first, and those who are now first will be last."

Jesus' Love for Jerusalem
(Matthew 23.37-39)

³¹At that same time some Pharisees came to Jesus and said to him, "You must get out of here and go somewhere else, because Herod wants to kill you."

13.14 Ex 20.9, 10; Dt 5.13, 14   **13.27** Ps 6.8   **13.28** Mt 22.13; 25.30
13.28, 29 Mt 8.11, 12   **13.30** Mt 19.30; 20.16; Mk 10.31

32 Jesus answered them, "Go and tell that fox: 'I am driving out demons and performing cures today and tomorrow, and on the third day I shall finish my work.' 33 Yet I must be on my way today, tomorrow, and the next day; it is not right for a prophet to be killed anywhere except in Jerusalem.

34 "Jerusalem, Jerusalem! You kill the prophets, you stone the messengers God has sent you! How many times I wanted to put my arms around all your people, just as a hen gathers her chicks under her wings, but you would not let me! 35 And so your Temple will be abandoned. I assure you that you will not see me until the time comes when you say, 'God bless him who comes in the name of the Lord.'"

Jesus Heals a Sick Man

14 One Sabbath Jesus went to eat a meal at the home of one of the leading Pharisees; and people were watching Jesus closely. 2 A man whose legs and arms were swollen came to Jesus, 3 and Jesus spoke up and asked the teachers of the Law and the Pharisees, "Does our Law allow healing on the Sabbath or not?"

4 But they would not say a thing. Jesus took the man, healed him, and sent him away. 5 Then he said to them, "If any one of you had a child or an ox that happened to fall in a well on a Sabbath, would you not pull it out at once on the Sabbath itself?"

6 But they were not able to answer him about this.

Humility and Hospitality

7 Jesus noticed how some of the guests were choosing the best places, so he told this parable to all of them: 8 "When someone invites you to a wedding feast, do not sit down in the best place. It could happen that someone

more important than you has been invited, 9 and your host, who invited both of you, would have to come and say to you, 'Let him have this place.' Then you would be embarrassed and have to sit in the lowest place. 10 Instead, when you are invited, go and sit in the lowest place, so that your host will come to you and say, 'Come on up, my friend, to a better place.' This will bring you honor in the presence of all the other guests. 11 For those who make themselves great will be humbled, and those who humble themselves will be made great."

12 Then Jesus said to his host, "When you give a lunch or a dinner, do not invite your friends or your brothers or your relatives or your rich neighbors — for they will invite you back, and in this way you will be paid for what you did. 13 When you give a feast, invite the poor, the crippled, the lame, and the blind; 14 and you will be blessed, because they are not able to pay you back. God will repay you on the day the good people rise from death."

The Parable of the Great Feast
(Matthew 22.1-10)

15 When one of the guests sitting at the table heard this, he said to Jesus, "How happy are those who will sit down at the feast in the Kingdom of God!"

16 Jesus said to him, "There was once a man who was giving a great feast to which he invited many people. 17 When it was time for the feast, he sent his servant to tell his guests, 'Come, everything is ready!' 18 But they all began, one after another, to make excuses. The first one told the servant, 'I have bought a field and must go and look at it; please accept my apologies.' 19 Another one said, 'I have bought five pairs of oxen and am on my way to try them out; please accept my apologies.' 20 Another one said, 'I have just gotten

13.34 2 Esd 1.30   **13.35** Ps 118.26   **14.5** Mt 12.11   **14.8-10** Pr 25.6, 7   **14.11** Mt 23.12; Lk 18.14

married, and for that reason I cannot come.' ²¹ The servant went back and told all this to his master. The master was furious and said to his servant, 'Hurry out to the streets and alleys of the town, and bring back the poor, the crippled, the blind, and the lame.' ²² Soon the servant said, 'Your order has been carried out, sir, but there is room for more.' ²³ So the master said to the servant, 'Go out to the country roads and lanes and make people come in, so that my house will be full. ²⁴ I tell you all that none of those who were invited will taste my dinner!' "

The Cost of Being a Disciple
(Matthew 10.37, 38)

²⁵ Once when large crowds of people were going along with Jesus, he turned and said to them, ²⁶ "Those who come to me cannot be my disciples unless they love me more than they love father and mother, wife and children, brothers and sisters, and themselves as well. ²⁷ Those who do not carry their own cross and come after me cannot be my disciples. ²⁸ If one of you is planning to build a tower, you sit down first and figure out what it will cost, to see if you have enough money to finish the job. ²⁹ If you don't, you will not be able to finish the tower after laying the foundation; and all who see what happened will make fun of you. ³⁰ 'You began to build but can't finish the job!' they will say. ³¹ If a king goes out with ten thousand men to fight another king who comes against him with twenty thousand men, he will sit down first and decide if he is strong enough to face that other king. ³² If he isn't, he will send messengers to meet the other king to ask for terms of peace while he is still a long way off. ³³ In the same way," concluded Jesus, "none of you can be my disciple unless you give up everything you have.

Worthless Salt
(Matthew 5.13; Mark 9.50)

³⁴ "Salt is good, but if it loses its saltiness, there is no way to make it salty again. ³⁵ It is no good for the soil or for the manure pile; it is thrown away. Listen, then, if you have ears!"

The Lost Sheep
(Matthew 18.12-14)

15 One day when many tax collectors and other outcasts came to listen to Jesus, ² the Pharisees and the teachers of the Law started grumbling, "This man welcomes outcasts and even eats with them!" ³ So Jesus told them this parable:
⁴ "Suppose one of you has a hundred sheep and loses one of them — what do you do? You leave the other ninety-nine sheep in the pasture and go looking for the one that got lost until you find it. ⁵ When you find it, you are so happy that you put it on your shoulders ⁶ and carry it back home. Then you call your friends and neighbors together and say to them, 'I am so happy I found my lost sheep. Let us celebrate!' ⁷ In the same way, I tell you, there will be more joy in heaven over one sinner who repents than over ninety-nine respectable people who do not need to repent.

The Lost Coin

⁸ "Or suppose a woman who has ten silver coins loses one of them — what does she do? She lights a lamp, sweeps her house, and looks carefully everywhere until she finds it. ⁹ When she finds it, she calls her friends and neighbors together, and says to them, 'I am so happy I found the coin I lost. Let us celebrate!' ¹⁰ In the same way, I tell you, the angels of God rejoice over one sinner who repents."

14.26 Mt 10.37   **14.27** Mt 10.38; 16.24; Mk 8.34; Lk 9.23   **15.1, 2** Lk 5.29, 30

The Lost Son

[11] Jesus went on to say, "There was once a man who had two sons. [12] The younger one said to him, 'Father, give me my share of the property now.' So the man divided his property between his two sons. [13] After a few days the younger son sold his part of the property and left home with the money. He went to a country far away, where he wasted his money in reckless living. [14] He spent everything he had. Then a severe famine spread over that country, and he was left without a thing. [15] So he went to work for one of the citizens of that country, who sent him out to his farm to take care of the pigs. [16] He wished he could fill himself with the bean pods the pigs ate, but no one gave him anything to eat. [17] At last he came to his senses and said, 'All my father's hired workers have more than they can

"Here I am about to starve!" (15.17)

eat, and here I am about to starve! [18] I will get up and go to my father and say, "Father, I have sinned against God and against you. [19] I am no longer fit to be called your son; treat me as one of your hired workers."' [20] So he got up and started back to his father.

"He was still a long way from home when his father saw him; his heart was filled with pity, and he ran, threw his arms around his son, and kissed him. [21] 'Father,' the son said, 'I have sinned against God and against you. I am no longer fit to be called your son.' [22] But the father called to his servants. 'Hurry!' he said. 'Bring the best robe and put it on him. Put a ring on his finger and shoes on his feet. [23] Then go and get the prize calf and kill it, and let us celebrate with a feast! [24] For this son

of mine was dead, but now he is alive; he was lost, but now he has been found.' And so the feasting began.

[25] "In the meantime the older son was out in the field. On his way back, when he came close to the house, he heard the music and dancing. [26] So he called one of the servants and asked him, 'What's going on?' [27] 'Your brother has come back home,' the servant answered, 'and your father has killed the prize calf, because he got him back safe and sound.' [28] The older brother was so angry that he would not go into the house; so his father came out and begged him to come in. [29] But he spoke back to his father, 'Look, all these years I have worked for you like a slave, and I have never disobeyed your orders. What have you given me? Not even a goat for me to have a feast with my friends! [30] But this son of yours wasted all your property on prostitutes, and when he comes back home, you kill the prize calf for him!' [31] 'My son,' the father answered, 'you are always here with me, and everything I have is yours. [32] But we had to celebrate and be happy, because your brother was dead, but now he is alive; he was lost, but now he has been found.'"

The Shrewd Manager

16 Jesus said to his disciples, "There was once a rich man who had a servant who managed his property. The rich man was told that the manager was wasting his master's money, [2] so he called him in and said, 'What is this I hear about you? Turn in a complete account of your handling of my property, because you cannot be my manager any longer.' [3] The servant said to himself, 'My master is going to dismiss me from my job. What shall I do? I am not strong enough to dig ditches, and I am ashamed to beg. [4] Now I know what I will do! Then when my job is gone, I shall have friends who will welcome me in their homes.' [5] So he called in all the people who were in debt to his master. He asked the first one, 'How much do you owe my master?' 6'One hundred barrels of olive oil,' he answered. 'Here is your account,' the manager told him; 'sit down and write fifty.' 7Then he asked another one, 'And you — how much do you owe?' 'A thousand bushels of wheat,' he answered. 'Here is your account,' the manager told him; 'write eight hundred.' 8As a result the master of this dishonest manager praised him for doing such a shrewd thing; because the people of this world are much more shrewd in handling their affairs than the people who belong to the light."

9And Jesus went on to say, "And so I tell you: make friends for yourselves with worldly wealth, so that when it gives out, you will be welcomed in the eternal home. 10Whoever is faithful in small matters will be faithful in large ones; whoever is dishonest in small matters will be dishonest in large ones. 11If, then, you have not been faithful in handling worldly wealth, how can you be trusted with true wealth? 12And if you have not been faithful with what belongs to someone else, who will give you what belongs to you?

13"No servant can be the slave of two masters; such a slave will hate one and love the other or will be loyal to one and despise the other. You cannot serve both God and money."

Some Sayings of Jesus
(Matthew 11.12, 13; 5.31, 32;
Mark 10.11, 12)

14When the Pharisees heard all this, they made fun of Jesus, because they loved money. 15Jesus said to them, "You are the ones who make yourselves look right in other people's sight, but

God knows your hearts. For the things that are considered of great value by people are worth nothing in God's sight.

16"The Law of Moses and the writings of the prophets were in effect up to the time of John the Baptist; since then the Good News about the Kingdom of God is being told, and everyone forces their way in. 17But it is easier for heaven and earth to disappear than for the smallest detail of the Law to be done away with.

18"Any man who divorces his wife and marries another woman commits adultery; and the man who marries a divorced woman commits adultery.

The Rich Man and Lazarus

19"There was once a rich man who dressed in the most expensive clothes and lived in great luxury every day. 20There was also a poor man named Lazarus, covered with sores, who used to be brought to the rich man's door, 21hoping to eat the bits of food that fell from the rich man's table. Even the dogs would come and lick his sores. 22The poor man died and was carried by the angels to sit beside Abraham at the feast in heaven. The rich man died and was buried, 23and in Hades,s where he was in great pain, he looked up and saw Abraham, far away, with Lazarus at his side. 24So he called out, 'Father Abraham! Take pity on me, and send Lazarus to dip his finger in some water and cool off my tongue, because I am in great pain in this fire!' 25But Abraham said, 'Remember, my son, that in your lifetime you were given all the good things, while Lazarus got all the bad things. But now he is enjoying himself here, while you are in pain. 26Besides all that, there is a deep pit lying between us, so that those who want to

---

s HADES: *The world of the dead.*
16.9 Tb 4.9-11   **16.13** Mt 6.24   **16.16** Mt 11.12, 13   **16.17** Mt 5.18   **16.18** Mt 5.32;
1 Co 7.10, 11   **16.23, 24** 2 Esd 7.36; 8.59

cross over from here to you cannot do so, nor can anyone cross over to us from where you are.' 27 The rich man said, 'Then I beg you, father Abraham, send Lazarus to my father's house, 28 where I have five brothers. Let him go and warn them so that they, at least, will not come to this place of pain.' 29 Abraham said, 'Your brothers have Moses and the prophets to warn them; your brothers should listen to what they say.' 30 The rich man answered, 'That is not enough, father Abraham! But if someone were to rise from death and go to them, then they would turn from their sins.' 31 But Abraham said, 'If they will not listen to Moses and the prophets, they will not be convinced even if someone were to rise from death.'"

Sin
(Matthew 18.6, 7, 21, 22; Mark 9.42)

17 Jesus said to his disciples, "Things that make people fall into sin are bound to happen, but how terrible for the one who makes them happen! 2 It would be better for him if a large millstone were tied around his neck and he were thrown into the sea than for him to cause one of these little ones to sin. 3 So watch what you do!

"If your brother sins, rebuke him, and if he repents, forgive him. 4 If he sins against you seven times in one day, and each time he comes to you saying, 'I repent,' you must forgive him."

Faith

5 The apostles said to the Lord, "Make our faith greater."

6 The Lord answered, "If you had faith as big as a mustard seed, you could say to this mulberry tree, 'Pull yourself up by the roots and plant yourself in the sea!' and it would obey you.

A Servant's Duty

7 "Suppose one of you has a servant who is plowing or looking after the sheep. When he comes in from the field, do you tell him to hurry along and eat his meal? 8 Of course not! Instead, you say to him, 'Get my supper ready, then put on your apron and wait on me while I eat and drink; after that you may have your meal.' 9 The servant does not deserve thanks for obeying orders, does he? 10 It is the same with you; when you have done all you have been told to do, say, 'We are ordinary servants; we have only done our duty.'"

Jesus Heals Ten Men

11 As Jesus made his way to Jerusalem, he went along the border between Samaria and Galilee. 12 He was going into a village when he was met by ten men suffering from a dreaded skin disease. They stood at a distance 13 and shouted, "Jesus! Master! Have pity on us!"

14 Jesus saw them and said to them, "Go and let the priests examine you."

On the way they were made clean.*t*
15 When one of them saw that he was healed, he came back, praising God in a loud voice. 16 He threw himself to the ground at Jesus' feet and thanked him. The man was a Samaritan. 17 Jesus spoke up, "There were ten who were healed; where are the other nine? 18 Why is this foreigner the only one who came back to give thanks to God?" 19 And Jesus said to him, "Get up and go; your faith has made you well."

The Coming of the Kingdom
(Matthew 24.23-28, 37-41)

20 Some Pharisees asked Jesus when the Kingdom of God would come. His answer was, "The Kingdom of God does not come in such a way as to be seen.

t MADE CLEAN: *See 5.12.*

17.3 Mt 18.15   **17.14** Lv 14.1-32

"Where are the other nine?" (17.17)

²¹ No one will say, 'Look, here it is!' or, 'There it is!'; because the Kingdom of God is within you."ᵘ

²² Then he said to the disciples, "The time will come when you will wish you could see one of the days of the Son of Man, but you will not see it. ²³ There will be those who will say to you, 'Look, over there!' or, 'Look, over here!' But don't go out looking for it. ²⁴ As the lightning flashes across the sky and lights it up from one side to the other, so will the Son of Man be in his day. ²⁵ But first he must suffer much and be rejected by the people of this day. ²⁶ As it was in the time of Noah so shall it be in the days of the Son of Man. ²⁷ Everybody kept on eating and drinking, and men and women married, up to the very day Noah went into the boat and the flood came and killed them all. ²⁸ It will be as it was in the time of Lot. Everybody kept on eating and drinking, buying and selling, planting and building. ²⁹ On the day Lot left Sodom, fire and sulfur rained down from heaven and killed them all. ³⁰ That is how it will be on the day the Son of Man is revealed.

³¹ "On that day someone who is on the roof of a house must not go down into the house to get any belongings; in the same way anyone who is out in the field must not go back to the house. ³² Remember Lot's wife! ³³ Those who try to save their own life will lose it; those who lose their life will save it. ³⁴ On that night, I tell you, there will be two people sleeping in the same bed: one will be taken away, the other will be left behind. ³⁵ Two women will be grinding meal together: one will be taken away, the other will be left behind."ᵛ

³⁷ The disciples asked him, "Where, Lord?"

Jesus answered, "Wherever there is a dead body, the vultures will gather."

The Parable of the Widow and the Judge

18 Then Jesus told his disciples a parable to teach them that they should always pray and never become discouraged. ² "In a certain town there was a judge who neither feared God nor respected people. ³ And there was a widow in that same town who kept coming to him and pleading for her rights, saying, 'Help me against my opponent!' ⁴ For a long time the judge refused to act, but at last he said to himself, 'Even though I don't fear God or respect people, ⁵ yet because of all the trouble this widow is giving me, I will see to it that she gets her rights. If I

ᵘ within you; *or* among you, *or* will suddenly appear among you.   ᵛ *Some manuscripts add verse 36:* Two men will be working in a field: one will be taken away, the other will be left behind (*see* Mt 24.40).
17.26 Gn 6.5-8   **17.27** Gn 7.6-24   **17.28, 29** Gn 18.20–19.25   **17.31** Mt 24.17, 18; Mk 13.15, 16   **17.32** Gn 19.26   **17.33** Mt 10.39; 16.25; Mk 8.35; Lk 9.24; Jn 12.25

don't, she will keep on coming and finally wear me out!' "

⁶And the Lord continued, "Listen to what that corrupt judge said. ⁷Now, will God not judge in favor of his own people who cry to him day and night for help? Will he be slow to help them? ⁸I tell you, he will judge in their favor and do it quickly. But will the Son of Man find faith on earth when he comes?"

The Parable of the Pharisee and the Tax Collector

⁹Jesus also told this parable to people who were sure of their own goodness and despised everybody else. ¹⁰"Once there were two men who went up to the Temple to pray: one was a Pharisee, the other a tax collector. ¹¹The Pharisee stood apart by himself and prayed,ʷ 'I thank you, God, that I am not greedy, dishonest, or an adulterer, like everybody else. I thank you that I am not like that tax collector over there. ¹²I fast two days a week, and I give you one tenth of all my income.' ¹³But the tax collector stood at a distance and would not even raise his face to heaven, but beat on his breast and said, 'God, have pity on me, a sinner!' ¹⁴I tell you," said Jesus, "the tax collector, and not the Pharisee, was in the right with God when he went home. For those who make themselves great will be humbled, and those who humble themselves will be made great."

Jesus Blesses Little Children
(Matthew 19.13-15; Mark 10.13-16)

¹⁵Some people brought their babies to Jesus for him to place his hands on them. The disciples saw them and scolded them for doing so, ¹⁶but Jesus called the children to him and said, "Let

the children come to me and do not stop them, because the Kingdom of God belongs to such as these. ¹⁷Remember this! Whoever does not receive the Kingdom of God like a child will never enter it."

The Rich Man
(Matthew 19.16-30; Mark 10.17-31)

¹⁸A Jewish leader asked Jesus, "Good Teacher, what must I do to receive eternal life?"

¹⁹"Why do you call me good?" Jesus asked him. "No one is good except God alone. ²⁰You know the commandments: 'Do not commit adultery; do not commit murder; do not steal; do not accuse anyone falsely; respect your father and your mother.' "

²¹The man replied, "Ever since I was young, I have obeyed all these commandments."

²²When Jesus heard this, he said to him, "There is still one more thing you need to do. Sell all you have and give the money to the poor, and you will have riches in heaven; then come and follow me." ²³But when the man heard this, he became very sad, because he was very rich.

²⁴Jesus saw that he was sad and said, "How hard it is for rich people to enter the Kingdom of God! ²⁵It is much harder for a rich person to enter the Kingdom of God than for a camel to go through the eye of a needle."

²⁶The people who heard him asked, "Who, then, can be saved?"

²⁷Jesus answered, "What is humanly impossible is possible for God."

²⁸Then Peter said, "Look! We have left our homes to follow you."

²⁹"Yes," Jesus said to them, "and I assure you that anyone who leaves home

---

ʷ stood apart by himself and prayed; *some manuscripts have* stood up and prayed to himself.

18.7 Si 35.19   **18.13** Man 8   **18.14** Mt 23.12; Lk 14.11   **18.20 a** Ex 20.14; Dt 5.18; **b** Ex 20.13; Dt 5.17; **c** Ex 20.15; Dt 5.19; **d** Ex 20.16; Dt 5.20; **e** Ex 20.12; Dt 5.16

or wife or brothers or parents or children for the sake of the Kingdom of God 30 will receive much more in this present age and eternal life in the age to come."

Jesus Speaks a Third Time about His Death
(Matthew 20.17-19; Mark 10.32-34)

31 Jesus took the twelve disciples aside and said to them, "Listen! We are going to Jerusalem where everything the prophets wrote about the Son of Man will come true. 32 He will be handed over to the Gentiles, who will make fun of him, insult him, and spit on him. 33 They will whip him and kill him, but three days later he will rise to life."

34 But the disciples did not understand any of these things; the meaning of the words was hidden from them, and they did not know what Jesus was talking about.

Jesus Heals a Blind Beggar
(Matthew 20.29-34; Mark 10.46-52)

35 As Jesus was coming near Jericho, there was a blind man sitting by the road, begging. 36 When he heard the crowd passing by, he asked, "What is this?"

37 "Jesus of Nazareth is passing by," they told him.

38 He cried out, "Jesus! Son of David! Have mercy on me!"

39 The people in front scolded him and told him to be quiet. But he shouted even more loudly, "Son of David! Have mercy on me!"

40 So Jesus stopped and ordered the blind man to be brought to him. When he came near, Jesus asked him, 41 "What do you want me to do for you?"

"Sir," he answered, "I want to see again."

42 Jesus said to him, "Then see! Your faith has made you well."

43 At once he was able to see, and he followed Jesus, giving thanks to God. When the crowd saw it, they all praised God.

Jesus and Zacchaeus

19 Jesus went on into Jericho and was passing through. 2 There was a chief tax collector there named Zacchaeus, who was rich. 3 He was trying to see who Jesus was, but he was a little man and could not see Jesus because of the crowd. 4 So he ran ahead of

He was a little man. (19.3)

the crowd and climbed a sycamore tree to see Jesus, who was going to pass that way. 5 When Jesus came to that place, he looked up and said to Zacchaeus, "Hurry down, Zacchaeus, because I must stay in your house today."

6 Zacchaeus hurried down and welcomed him with great joy. 7 All the people who saw it started grumbling, "This man has gone as a guest to the home of a sinner!"

8 Zacchaeus stood up and said to the Lord, "Listen, sir! I will give half my belongings to the poor, and if I have cheated anyone, I will pay back four times as much."

9 Jesus said to him, "Salvation has come to this house today, for this man,

also, is a descendant of Abraham. 10 The Son of Man came to seek and to save the lost."

The Parable of the Gold Coins
(Matthew 25.14-30)

11 While the people were listening to this, Jesus continued and told them a parable. He was now almost at Jerusalem, and they supposed that the Kingdom of God was just about to appear. 12 So he said, "There was once a man of high rank who was going to a country far away to be made king, after which he planned to come back home. 13 Before he left, he called his ten servants and gave them each a gold coin and told them, 'See what you can earn with this while I am gone.' 14 Now, his own people hated him, and so they sent messengers after him to say, 'We don't want this man to be our king.'

15 "The man was made king and came back. At once he ordered his servants to appear before him, in order to find out how much they had earned. 16 The first one came and said, 'Sir, I have earned ten gold coins with the one you gave me.' 17 'Well done,' he said; 'you are a good servant! Since you were faithful in small matters, I will put you in charge of ten cities.' 18 The second servant came and said, 'Sir, I have earned five gold coins with the one you gave me.' 19 To this one he said, 'You will be in charge of five cities.' 20 Another servant came and said, 'Sir, here is your gold coin; I kept it hidden in a handkerchief. 21 I was afraid of you, because you are a hard man. You take what is not yours and reap what you did not plant.' 22 He said to him, 'You bad servant! I will use your own words to condemn you! You know that I am a hard man, taking what is not mine and reaping what I have not planted.

23 Well, then, why didn't you put my money in the bank? Then I would have received it back with interest when I returned.' 24 Then he said to those who were standing there, 'Take the gold coin away from him and give it to the servant who has ten coins.' 25 But they said to him, 'Sir, he already has ten coins!' 26 'I tell you,' he replied, 'that to those who have something, even more will be given; but those who have nothing, even the little that they have will be taken away from them. 27 Now, as for those enemies of mine who did not want me to be their king, bring them here and kill them in my presence!' "

The Triumphant Approach to Jerusalem
(Matthew 21.1-11; Mark 11.1-11; John 12.12-19)

28 After Jesus said this, he went on in front of them toward Jerusalem. 29 As he came near Bethphage and Bethany at the Mount of Olives, he sent two disciples ahead 30 with these instructions: "Go to the village there ahead of you; as you go in, you will find a colt tied up that has never been ridden. Untie it and bring it here. 31 If someone asks you why you are untying it, tell him that the Master[x] needs it."

32 They went on their way and found everything just as Jesus had told them. 33 As they were untying the colt, its owners said to them, "Why are you untying it?"

34 "The Master needs it," they answered, 35 and they took the colt to Jesus. Then they threw their cloaks over the animal and helped Jesus get on. 36 As he rode on, people spread their cloaks on the road.

37 When he came near Jerusalem, at the place where the road went down

---

[x] the Master; or its owner.
19.10 Mt 18.11   **19.26** Mt 13.12; Mk 4.25; Lk 8.18   **19.11-27** Mt 25.14-30

the Mount of Olives, the large crowd of his disciples began to thank God and praise him in loud voices for all the great things that they had seen: ³⁸"God bless the king who comes in the name of the Lord! Peace in heaven and glory to God!"

³⁹Then some of the Pharisees in the crowd spoke to Jesus. "Teacher," they said, "command your disciples to be quiet!"

⁴⁰Jesus answered, "I tell you that if they keep quiet, the stones themselves will start shouting."

Jesus Weeps over Jerusalem

⁴¹He came closer to the city, and when he saw it, he wept over it, ⁴²saying, "If you only knew today what is needed for peace! But now you cannot see it! ⁴³The time will come when your enemies will surround you with barricades, blockade you, and close in on you from every side. ⁴⁴They will completely destroy you and the people within your walls; not a single stone will they leave in its place, because you did not recognize the time when God came to save you!"

Jesus Goes to the Temple
(Matthew 21.12-17; Mark 11.15-19; John 2.13-22)

⁴⁵Then Jesus went into the Temple and began to drive out the merchants, ⁴⁶saying to them, "It is written in the Scriptures that God said, 'My Temple will be a house of prayer.' But you have turned it into a hideout for thieves!"

⁴⁷Every day Jesus taught in the Temple. The chief priests, the teachers of the Law, and the leaders of the people wanted to kill him, ⁴⁸but they could not find a way to do it, because all the people kept listening to him, not wanting to miss a single word.

The Question about Jesus' Authority
(Matthew 21.23-27; Mark 11.27-33)

20 One day when Jesus was in the Temple teaching the people and preaching the Good News, the chief priests and the teachers of the Law, together with the elders, came ²and said to him, "Tell us, what right do you have to do these things? Who gave you such right?"

³Jesus answered them, "Now let me ask you a question. Tell me, ⁴did John's right to baptize come from God or from human beings?"

⁵They started to argue among themselves, "What shall we say? If we say, 'From God,' he will say, 'Why, then, did you not believe John?' ⁶But if we say, 'From human beings,' this whole crowd here will stone us, because they are convinced that John was a prophet." ⁷So they answered, "We don't know where it came from."

⁸And Jesus said to them, "Neither will I tell you, then, by what right I do these things."

The Parable of the Tenants in the Vineyard
(Matthew 21.33-46; Mark 12.1-12)

⁹Then Jesus told the people this parable: "There was once a man who planted a vineyard, rented it out to tenants, and then left home for a long time. ¹⁰When the time came to gather the grapes, he sent a slave to the tenants to receive from them his share of the harvest. But the tenants beat the slave and sent him back without a thing. ¹¹So he sent another slave; but the tenants beat him also, treated him shamefully, and sent him back without a thing. ¹²Then he sent a third slave; the tenants wounded him, too, and threw him out. ¹³Then the owner of the vineyard said, 'What shall I do? I will send my own

19.38 Ps 118.26   **19.46** Is 56.7; Jr 7.11   **19.47** Lk 21.37   **20.9** Is 5.1

dear son; surely they will respect him!'
¹⁴ But when the tenants saw him, they
said to one another, 'This is the owner's
son. Let's kill him, and his property will
be ours!' ¹⁵ So they threw him out of the
vineyard and killed him.

"What, then, will the owner of the
vineyard do to the tenants?" Jesus
asked. ¹⁶ "He will come and kill those
men, and turn the vineyard over to
other tenants."

When the people heard this, they
said, "Surely not!"

¹⁷ Jesus looked at them and asked,
"What, then, does this scripture mean?

'The stone which the builders
        rejected as worthless
    turned out to be the most
        important of all.'

¹⁸ Everyone who falls on that stone will
be cut to pieces; and if that stone falls
on someone, that person will be
crushed to dust."

The Question about Paying Taxes
(Matthew 22.15-22; Mark 12.13-17)

¹⁹ The teachers of the Law and the
chief priests tried to arrest Jesus on the
spot, because they knew that he had
told this parable against them; but they
were afraid of the people. ²⁰ So they
looked for an opportunity. They bribed
some men to pretend they were sincere,
and they sent them to trap Jesus with
questions, so that they could hand him
over to the authority and power of the
Roman Governor. ²¹ These spies said to
Jesus, "Teacher, we know that what
you say and teach is right. We know
that you pay no attention to anyone's
status, but teach the truth about God's
will for people. ²² Tell us, is it against
our Law for us to pay taxes to the Roman Emperor, or not?"

²³ But Jesus saw through their trick
and said to them, ²⁴ "Show me a silver

coin. Whose face and name are these
on it?"

"The Emperor's," they answered.

²⁵ So Jesus said, "Well, then, pay to
the Emperor what belongs to the Emperor, and pay to God what belongs
to God."

²⁶ There before the people they could
not catch him in a thing, so they kept
quiet, amazed at his answer.

The Question about Rising from Death
(Matthew 22.23-33; Mark 12.18-27)

²⁷ Then some Sadducees, who say
that people will not rise from death,
came to Jesus and said, ²⁸ "Teacher,
Moses wrote this law for us: 'If a man
dies and leaves a wife but no children,
that man's brother must marry the
widow so that they can have children
who will be considered the dead man's
children.' ²⁹ Once there were seven
brothers; the oldest got married and
died without having children. ³⁰ Then
the second one married the woman,
³¹ and then the third. The same thing
happened to all seven — they died without having children. ³² Last of all, the
woman died. ³³ Now, on the day when
the dead rise to life, whose wife will she
be? All seven of them had married her."

³⁴ Jesus answered them, "The men
and women of this age marry, ³⁵ but the
men and women who are worthy to rise
from death and live in the age to come
will not then marry. ³⁶ They will be like
angels and cannot die. They are the
children of God, because they have
risen from death. ³⁷ And Moses clearly
proves that the dead are raised to life. In
the passage about the burning bush he
speaks of the Lord as 'the God of Abraham, the God of Isaac, and the God of
Jacob.' ³⁸ He is the God of the living, not
of the dead, for to him all are alive."

³⁹ Some of the teachers of the Law
spoke up, "A good answer, Teacher!"

20.17 Ps 118.22   **20.27** Ac 23.8   **20.28** Dt 25.5   **20.37** Ex 3.6

⁴⁰For they did not dare ask him any more questions.

The Question about the Messiah
(Matthew 22.41-46; Mark 12.35-37)

⁴¹Jesus asked them, "How can it be said that the Messiah will be the descendant of David? ⁴²For David himself says in the book of Psalms,

'The Lord said to my Lord:
Sit here at my right side
⁴³   until I put your enemies as a
footstool under your feet.'

⁴⁴David called him 'Lord'; how, then, can the Messiah be David's descendant?"

Jesus Warns against the Teachers of the Law
(Matthew 23.1-36; Mark 12.38-40)

⁴⁵As all the people listened to him, Jesus said to his disciples, ⁴⁶"Be on your guard against the teachers of the Law, who like to walk around in their long robes and love to be greeted with respect in the marketplace; who choose the reserved seats in the synagogues and the best places at feasts; ⁴⁷who take advantage of widows and rob them of their homes, and then make a show of saying long prayers! Their punishment will be all the worse!"

The Widow's Offering
(Mark 12.41-44)

21 Jesus looked around and saw rich people dropping their gifts in the Temple treasury, ²and he also saw a very poor widow dropping in two little copper coins. ³He said, "I tell you that this poor widow put in more than all the others. ⁴For the others offered their gifts from what they had to spare of their riches; but she, poor as she is, gave all she had to live on."

Jesus Speaks of the Destruction of the Temple
(Matthew 24.1, 2; Mark 13.1, 2)

⁵Some of the disciples were talking about the Temple, how beautiful it looked with its fine stones and the gifts offered to God. Jesus said, ⁶"All this you see — the time will come when not a single stone here will be left in its place; every one will be thrown down."

Troubles and Persecutions
(Matthew 24.3-14; Mark 13.3-13)

⁷"Teacher," they asked, "when will this be? And what will happen in order to show that the time has come for it to take place?"

⁸Jesus said, "Watch out; don't be fooled. Many men, claiming to speak for me, will come and say, 'I am he!' and, 'The time has come!' But don't follow them. ⁹Don't be afraid when you hear of wars and revolutions; such things must happen first, but they do not mean that the end is near."

¹⁰He went on to say, "Countries will fight each other; kingdoms will attack one another. ¹¹There will be terrible earthquakes, famines, and plagues everywhere; there will be strange and terrifying things coming from the sky. ¹²Before all these things take place, however, you will be arrested and persecuted; you will be handed over to be tried in synagogues and be put in prison; you will be brought before kings and rulers for my sake. ¹³This will be your chance to tell the Good News. ¹⁴Make up your minds ahead of time not to worry about how you will defend yourselves, ¹⁵because I will give you such words and wisdom that none of your enemies will be able to refute or contradict what you say. ¹⁶You will be handed over by your parents, your brothers, your relatives, and your

friends; and some of you will be put to death. 17 Everyone will hate you because of me. 18 But not a single hair from your heads will be lost. 19 Stand firm, and you will save yourselves.

Jesus Speaks of the Destruction of Jerusalem
(Matthew 24.15-21; Mark 13.14-19)

20 "When you see Jerusalem surrounded by armies, then you will know that it will soon be destroyed. 21 Then those who are in Judea must run away to the hills; those who are in the city must leave, and those who are out in the country must not go into the city. 22 For those will be 'The Days of Punishment,' to make come true all that the Scriptures say. 23 How terrible it will be in those days for women who are pregnant and for mothers with little babies! Terrible distress will come upon this land, and God's punishment will fall on this people. 24 Some will be killed by the sword, and others will be taken as prisoners to all countries; and the heathen will trample over Jerusalem until their time is up.

The Coming of the Son of Man
(Matthew 24.29-31; Mark 13.24-27)

25 "There will be strange things happening to the sun, the moon, and the stars. On earth whole countries will be in despair, afraid of the roar of the sea and the raging tides. 26 People will faint from fear as they wait for what is coming over the whole earth, for the powers in space will be driven from their courses. 27 Then the Son of Man will appear, coming in a cloud with great power and glory. 28 When these things begin to happen, stand up and raise your heads, because your salvation is near."

The Lesson of the Fig Tree
(Matthew 24.32-35; Mark 13.28-31)

29 Then Jesus told them this parable: "Think of the fig tree and all the other trees. 30 When you see their leaves beginning to appear, you know that summer is near. 31 In the same way, when you see these things happening, you will know that the Kingdom of God is about to come.

32 "Remember that all these things will take place before the people now living have all died. 33 Heaven and earth will pass away, but my words will never pass away.

The Need to Watch

34 "Be careful not to let yourselves become occupied with too much feasting and drinking and with the worries of this life, or that Day may suddenly catch you 35 like a trap. For it will come upon all people everywhere on earth. 36 Be on watch and pray always that you will have the strength to go safely through all those things that will happen and to stand before the Son of Man."

37 Jesus spent those days teaching in the Temple, and when evening came, he would go out and spend the night on the Mount of Olives. 38 Early each morning all the people went to the Temple to listen to him.

The Plot against Jesus
(Matthew 26.1-5; Mark 14.1, 2; John 11.45-53)

22 The time was near for the Festival of Unleavened Bread, which is called the Passover. 2 The chief priests and the teachers of the Law were afraid of the people, and so they were trying to find a way of putting Jesus to death secretly.

21.22 Ho 9.7   **21.25** Is 13.10; Ez 32.7; Jl 2.31; Rev 6.12, 13   **21.27** Dn 7.13; Rev 1.7
21.37 Lk 19.47   **22.1** Ex 12.1-27

Judas Agrees to Betray Jesus
(Matthew 26.14-16; Mark 14.10, 11)

³Then Satan entered into Judas, called Iscariot, who was one of the twelve disciples. ⁴So Judas went off and spoke with the chief priests and the officers of the Temple guard about how he could betray Jesus to them. ⁵They were pleased and offered to pay him money. ⁶Judas agreed to it and started looking for a good chance to hand Jesus over to them without the people knowing about it.

Jesus Prepares to Eat the Passover Meal
(Matthew 26.17-25; Mark 14.12-21; John 13.21-30)

⁷The day came during the Festival of Unleavened Bread when the lambs for the Passover meal were to be killed. ⁸Jesus sent Peter and John with these instructions: "Go and get the Passover meal ready for us to eat."

⁹"Where do you want us to get it ready?" they asked him.

¹⁰He answered, "As you go into the city, a man carrying a jar of water will meet you. Follow him into the house that he enters, ¹¹and say to the owner of the house: 'The Teacher says to you, Where is the room where my disciples and I will eat the Passover meal?' ¹²He will show you a large furnished room upstairs, where you will get everything ready."

¹³They went off and found everything just as Jesus had told them, and they prepared the Passover meal.

The Lord's Supper
(Matthew 26.26-30; Mark 14.22-26; 1 Corinthians 11.23-25)

¹⁴When the hour came, Jesus took his place at the table with the apostles.

¹⁵He said to them, "I have wanted so much to eat this Passover meal with you before I suffer! ¹⁶For I tell you, I will never eat it until it is given its full meaning in the Kingdom of God."

¹⁷Then Jesus took a cup, gave thanks to God, and said, "Take this and share it among yourselves. ¹⁸I tell you that from now on I will not drink this wine until the Kingdom of God comes."

¹⁹Then he took a piece of bread, gave thanks to God, broke it, and gave it to them, saying, "This is my body, which is given for you. Do this in memory of me." ²⁰In the same way, he gave them the cup after the supper, saying, "This cup is God's new covenant sealed with my blood, which is poured out for you.ʸ

²¹"But, look! The one who betrays me is here at the table with me! ²²The Son of Man will die as God has decided, but how terrible for that man who betrays him!"

²³Then they began to ask among themselves which one of them it could be who was going to do this.

The Argument about Greatness

²⁴An argument broke out among the disciples as to which one of them should be thought of as the greatest. ²⁵Jesus said to them, "The kings of the pagans have power over their people, and the rulers claim the title 'Friends of the People.' ²⁶But this is not the way it is with you; rather, the greatest one among you must be like the youngest, and the leader must be like the servant. ²⁷Who is greater, the one who sits down to eat or the one who serves? The one who sits down, of course. But I am among you as one who serves.

ʸ *Some manuscripts do not have the words of Jesus after* This is my body *in verse 19, and all of verse 20.*

22.20 Jr 31.31-34   **22.21** Ps 41.9   **22.24** Mt 18.1; Mk 9.34; Lk 9.46   **22.26** Mt 23.11; Mk 9.35   **22.25, 26** Mt 20.25-27; Mk 10.42-44   **22.27** Jn 13.12-15

²⁸"You have stayed with me all through my trials; ²⁹and just as my Father has given me the right to rule, so I will give you the same right. ³⁰You will eat and drink at my table in my Kingdom, and you will sit on thrones to rule over the twelve tribes of Israel.

Jesus Predicts Peter's Denial
(Matthew 26.31-35; Mark 14.27-31;
John 13.36-38)

³¹"Simon, Simon! Listen! Satan has received permission to test all of you, to separate the good from the bad, as a farmer separates the wheat from the chaff. ³²But I have prayed for you, Simon, that your faith will not fail. And when you turn back to me, you must strengthen your brothers."

³³Peter answered, "Lord, I am ready to go to prison with you and to die with you!"

³⁴"I tell you, Peter," Jesus said, "the rooster will not crow tonight until you have said three times that you do not know me."

Purse, Bag, and Sword

³⁵Then Jesus asked his disciples, "When I sent you out that time without purse, bag, or shoes, did you lack anything?"

"Not a thing," they answered.

³⁶"But now," Jesus said, "whoever has a purse or a bag must take it; and whoever does not have a sword must sell his coat and buy one. ³⁷For I tell you that the scripture which says, 'He shared the fate of criminals,' must come true about me, because what was written about me is coming true."

³⁸The disciples said, "Look! Here are two swords, Lord!"

"That is enough!"^z he replied.

Jesus Prays on the Mount of Olives
(Matthew 26.36-46; Mark 14.32-42)

³⁹Jesus left the city and went, as he usually did, to the Mount of Olives; and the disciples went with him. ⁴⁰When he arrived at the place, he said to them, "Pray that you will not fall into temptation."

⁴¹Then he went off from them about the distance of a stone's throw and knelt down and prayed. ⁴²"Father," he said, "if you will, take this cup of suffering away from me. Not my will, however, but your will be done." ⁴³An angel from heaven appeared to him and strengthened him. ⁴⁴In great anguish he prayed even more fervently; his sweat was like drops of blood falling to the ground.^a

⁴⁵Rising from his prayer, he went back to the disciples and found them asleep, worn out by their grief. ⁴⁶He said to them, "Why are you sleeping? Get up and pray that you will not fall into temptation."

The Arrest of Jesus
(Matthew 26.47-56; Mark 14.43-50;
John 18.3-11)

⁴⁷Jesus was still speaking when a crowd arrived, led by Judas, one of the twelve disciples. He came up to Jesus to kiss him. ⁴⁸But Jesus said, "Judas, is it with a kiss that you betray the Son of Man?"

⁴⁹When the disciples who were with Jesus saw what was going to happen, they asked, "Shall we use our swords, Lord?" ⁵⁰And one of them struck the High Priest's slave and cut off his right ear.

⁵¹But Jesus said, "Enough of this!" He touched the man's ear and healed him.

⁵²Then Jesus said to the chief priests and the officers of the Temple guard and the elders who had come there to

---

^z That is enough; *or* Enough of this.   ^a *Some manuscripts do not have verses 43-44.*
22.30 Mt 19.28   **22.35** Mt 10.9, 10; Mk 6.8, 9; Lk 9.3; 10.4   **22.37** Is 53.12

get him, "Did you have to come with swords and clubs, as though I were an outlaw? 53 I was with you in the Temple every day, and you did not try to arrest me. But this is your hour to act, when the power of darkness rules."

Peter Denies Jesus
(Matthew 26.57, 58, 69-75; Mark 14.53, 54, 66-72; John 18.12-18, 25-27)

54 They arrested Jesus and took him away into the house of the High Priest; and Peter followed at a distance. 55 A fire had been lit in the center of the courtyard, and Peter joined those who were sitting around it. 56 When one of the servant women saw him sitting there at the fire, she looked straight at him and said, "This man too was with Jesus!"

57 But Peter denied it, "Woman, I don't even know him!"

"Woman, I don't even know him!" (22.57)

58 After a little while a man noticed Peter and said, "You are one of them, too!"

But Peter answered, "Man, I am not!"

59 And about an hour later another man insisted strongly, "There isn't any doubt that this man was with Jesus, because he also is a Galilean!"

60 But Peter answered, "Man, I don't know what you are talking about!"

At once, while he was still speaking, a rooster crowed. 61 The Lord turned

around and looked straight at Peter, and Peter remembered that the Lord had said to him, "Before the rooster crows tonight, you will say three times that you do not know me." 62 Peter went out and wept bitterly.

Jesus Is Mocked and Beaten
(Matthew 26.67, 68; Mark 14.65)

63 The men who were guarding Jesus made fun of him and beat him. 64 They blindfolded him and asked him, "Who hit you? Guess!" 65 And they said many other insulting things to him.

Jesus before the Council
(Matthew 26.59-66; Mark 14.55-64; John 18.19-24)

66 When day came, the elders, the chief priests, and the teachers of the Law met together, and Jesus was brought before the Council. 67 "Tell us," they said, "are you the Messiah?"

He answered, "If I tell you, you will not believe me; 68 and if I ask you a question, you will not answer. 69 But from now on the Son of Man will be seated at the right side of Almighty God."

70 They all said, "Are you, then, the Son of God?"

He answered them, "You say that I am."

71 And they said, "We don't need any witnesses! We ourselves have heard what he said!"

Jesus before Pilate
(Matthew 27.1, 2, 11-14; Mark 15.1-5; John 18.28-38)

23 The whole group rose up and took Jesus before Pilate, 2 where they began to accuse him: "We caught this man misleading our people, telling them not to pay taxes to the Emperor and claiming that he himself is the Messiah, a king."

22.53 Lk 19.47; 21.37

³Pilate asked him, "Are you the king of the Jews?"

"So you say," answered Jesus.

⁴Then Pilate said to the chief priests and the crowds, "I find no reason to condemn this man."

⁵But they insisted even more strongly, "With his teaching he is starting a riot among the people all through Judea. He began in Galilee and now has come here."

Jesus before Herod

⁶When Pilate heard this, he asked, "Is this man a Galilean?" ⁷When he learned that Jesus was from the region ruled by Herod, he sent him to Herod, who was also in Jerusalem at that time. ⁸Herod was very pleased when he saw Jesus, because he had heard about him and had been wanting to see him for a long time. He was hoping to see Jesus perform some miracle. ⁹So Herod asked Jesus many questions, but Jesus made no answer. ¹⁰The chief priests and the teachers of the Law stepped forward and made strong accusations against Jesus. ¹¹Herod and his soldiers made fun of Jesus and treated him with contempt; then they put a fine robe on him and sent him back to Pilate. ¹²On that very day Herod and Pilate became friends; before this they had been enemies.

Jesus Is Sentenced to Death
(Matthew 27.15-26; Mark 15.6-15; John 18.39 — 19.16)

¹³Pilate called together the chief priests, the leaders, and the people, ¹⁴and said to them, "You brought this man to me and said that he was misleading the people. Now, I have examined him here in your presence, and I have not found him guilty of any of the crimes you accuse him of. ¹⁵Nor did Herod find him guilty, for he sent him back to us. There is nothing this man has done to deserve death. ¹⁶So I will have him whipped and let him go."ᵇ

¹⁸The whole crowd cried out, "Kill him! Set Barabbas free for us!" (¹⁹Barabbas had been put in prison for a riot that had taken place in the city, and for murder.)

²⁰Pilate wanted to set Jesus free, so he appealed to the crowd again. ²¹But they shouted back, "Crucify him! Crucify him!"

²²Pilate said to them the third time, "But what crime has he committed? I cannot find anything he has done to deserve death! I will have him whipped and set him free."

²³But they kept on shouting at the top of their voices that Jesus should be crucified, and finally their shouting succeeded. ²⁴So Pilate passed the sentence on Jesus that they were asking for. ²⁵He set free the man they wanted, the one who had been put in prison for riot and murder, and he handed Jesus over for them to do as they wished.

Jesus Is Crucified
(Matthew 27.32-44; Mark 15.21-32; John 19.17-27)

²⁶The soldiers led Jesus away, and as they were going, they met a man from Cyrene named Simon who was coming into the city from the country. They seized him, put the cross on him, and made him carry it behind Jesus.

²⁷A large crowd of people followed him; among them were some women who were weeping and wailing for him. ²⁸Jesus turned to them and said, "Women of Jerusalem! Don't cry for me, but for yourselves and your children. ²⁹For the days are coming when people will say, 'How lucky are the women who never had children, who never bore babies, who never nursed

---

ᵇ *Some manuscripts add verse 17:* At every Passover Festival Pilate had to set free one prisoner for them (*see Mk 15.6*).

them!' ³⁰That will be the time when people will say to the mountains, 'Fall on us!' and to the hills, 'Hide us!' ³¹For if such things as these are done when the wood is green, what will happen when it is dry?"

They . . . put the cross on him, and made him carry it. (23.26)

³²Two other men, both of them criminals, were also led out to be put to death with Jesus. ³³When they came to the place called "The Skull," they crucified Jesus there, and the two criminals, one on his right and the other on his left. ³⁴Jesus said, "Forgive them, Father! They don't know what they are doing."ᶜ

They divided his clothes among themselves by throwing dice. ³⁵The people stood there watching while the Jewish leaders made fun of him: "He saved others; let him save himself if he is the Messiah whom God has chosen!"

³⁶The soldiers also made fun of him: they came up to him and offered him cheap wine, ³⁷and said, "Save yourself if you are the king of the Jews!"

³⁸Above him were written these words: "This is the King of the Jews."

³⁹One of the criminals hanging there hurled insults at him: "Aren't you the Messiah? Save yourself and us!"

⁴⁰The other one, however, rebuked him, saying, "Don't you fear God? You received the same sentence he did. ⁴¹Ours, however, is only right, because we are getting what we deserve for what we did; but he has done no wrong." ⁴²And he said to Jesus, "Remember me, Jesus, when you come as King!"

⁴³Jesus said to him, "I promise you that today you will be in Paradise with me."

The Death of Jesus
(Matthew 27.45-56; Mark 15.33-41; John 19.28-30)

⁴⁴⁻⁴⁵It was about twelve o'clock when the sun stopped shining and darkness covered the whole country until three o'clock; and the curtain hanging in the Temple was torn in two. ⁴⁶Jesus cried out in a loud voice, "Father! In your hands I place my spirit!" He said this and died.

"Father! In your hands I place my spirit!" (23.46)

⁴⁷The army officer saw what had happened, and he praised God, saying, "Certainly he was a good man!"

⁴⁸When the people who had gathered there to watch the spectacle saw what happened, they all went back home, beating their breasts in sorrow. ⁴⁹All those who knew Jesus personally,

ᶜ *Some manuscripts do not have* Jesus said, "Forgive them, Father! They don't know what they are doing."

23.30 Ho 10.8; Rev 6.16   **23.34** Ps 22.18   **23.35** Ps 22.7   **23.36** Ps 69.21
23.45 Ex 26.31-33   **23.46** Ps 31.5   **23.49** Lk 8.2, 3

including the women who had followed him from Galilee, stood at a distance to watch.

The Burial of Jesus
(Matthew 27.57-61; Mark 15.42-47; John 19.38-42)

50-51 There was a man named Joseph from Arimathea, a town in Judea. He was a good and honorable man, who was waiting for the coming of the Kingdom of God. Although he was a member of the Council, he had not agreed with their decision and action. 52 He went into the presence of Pilate and asked for the body of Jesus. 53 Then he took the body down, wrapped it in a linen sheet, and placed it in a tomb which had been dug out of solid rock and which had never been used. 54 It was Friday, and the Sabbath was about to begin.

55 The women who had followed Jesus from Galilee went with Joseph and saw the tomb and how Jesus' body was placed in it. 56 Then they went back home and prepared the spices and perfumes for the body.

On the Sabbath they rested, as the Law commanded.

The Resurrection
(Matthew 28.1-10; Mark 16.1-8; John 20.1-10)

24 Very early on Sunday morning the women went to the tomb, carrying the spices they had prepared. 2 They found the stone rolled away from the entrance to the tomb, 3 so they went in; but they did not find the body of the Lord Jesus. 4 They stood there puzzled about this, when suddenly two men in bright shining clothes stood by them. 5 Full of fear, the women bowed down to the ground, as the men said to them, "Why are you looking among the dead

for one who is alive? 6 He is not here; he has been raised. Remember what he said to you while he was in Galilee:

"He is not here; he has been raised." (24.6)

7 'The Son of Man must be handed over to sinners, be crucified, and three days later rise to life.' "

8 Then the women remembered his words, 9 returned from the tomb, and told all these things to the eleven disciples and all the rest. 10 The women were Mary Magdalene, Joanna, and Mary the mother of James; they and the other women with them told these things to the apostles. 11 But the apostles thought that what the women said was nonsense, and they did not believe them. 12 But Peter got up and ran to the tomb; he bent down and saw the grave cloths but nothing else. Then he went back home amazed at what had happened.*d*

The Walk to Emmaus
(Mark 16.12, 13)

13 On that same day two of Jesus' followers were going to a village named Emmaus, about seven miles from Jerusalem, 14 and they were talking to each other about all the things that had happened. 15 As they talked and discussed, Jesus himself drew near and walked

---

d Some manuscripts do not have verse 12.

23.56 Ex 20.10; Dt 5.14   **24.6, 7** Mt 16.21; 17.22, 23; 20.18, 19; Mk 8.31; 9.31; 10.33, 34; Lk 9.22; 18.31-33 along with them; ¹⁶they saw him, but somehow did not recognize him. ¹⁷Jesus said to them, "What are you talking about to each other, as you walk along?"

They stood still, with sad faces. ¹⁸One of them, named Cleopas, asked him, "Are you the only visitor in Jerusalem who doesn't know the things that have been happening there these last few days?"

¹⁹"What things?" he asked.

"The things that happened to Jesus of Nazareth," they answered. "This man was a prophet and was considered by God and by all the people to be powerful in everything he said and did. ²⁰Our chief priests and rulers handed him over to be sentenced to death, and he was crucified. ²¹And we had hoped that he would be the one who was going to set Israel free! Besides all that, this is now the third day since it happened. ²²Some of the women of our group surprised us; they went at dawn to the tomb, ²³but could not find his body. They came back saying they had seen a vision of angels who told them that he is alive. ²⁴Some of our group went to the tomb and found it exactly as the women had said, but they did not see him."

²⁵Then Jesus said to them, "How foolish you are, how slow you are to believe everything the prophets said! ²⁶Was it not necessary for the Messiah to suffer these things and then to enter his glory?" ²⁷And Jesus explained to them what was said about himself in all the Scriptures, beginning with the books of Moses and the writings of all the prophets.

²⁸As they came near the village to which they were going, Jesus acted as if he were going farther; ²⁹but they held him back, saying, "Stay with us; the day is almost over and it is getting dark." So he went in to stay with them. ³⁰He sat down to eat with them, took

the bread, and said the blessing; then he broke the bread and gave it to them. ³¹Then their eyes were opened and they recognized him, but he disappeared from their sight. ³²They said to each other, "Wasn't it like a fire burning in us when he talked to us on the road and explained the Scriptures to us?"

³³They got up at once and went back to Jerusalem, where they found the eleven disciples gathered together with the others ³⁴and saying, "The Lord is risen indeed! He has appeared to Simon!"

³⁵The two then explained to them what had happened on the road, and how they had recognized the Lord when he broke the bread.

Jesus Appears to His Disciples
(Matthew 28.16-20; Mark 16.14-18;
John 20.19-23; Acts 1.6-8)

³⁶While the two were telling them this, suddenly the Lord himself stood among them and said to them, "Peace be with you."*e*

³⁷They were terrified, thinking that they were seeing a ghost. ³⁸But he said to them, "Why are you alarmed? Why are these doubts coming up in your minds? ³⁹Look at my hands and my feet, and see that it is I myself. Feel me, and you will know, for a ghost doesn't have flesh and bones, as you can see I have."

⁴⁰He said this and showed them his hands and his feet.*f* ⁴¹They still could not believe, they were so full of joy and wonder; so he asked them, "Do you have anything here to eat?" ⁴²They gave him a piece of cooked fish, ⁴³which he took and ate in their presence.

⁴⁴Then he said to them, "These are the very things I told you about while I was still with you: everything written

e Some manuscripts do not have and said to them, "Peace be with you."   *f Some manuscripts do not have verse 40.*

As he was blessing them . . . (24.51)

about me in the Law of Moses, the writings of the prophets, and the Psalms had to come true."

⁴⁵ Then he opened their minds to understand the Scriptures, ⁴⁶ and said to them, "This is what is written: the Messiah must suffer and must rise from death three days later, ⁴⁷ and in his name the message about repentance and the forgiveness of sins must be preached to all nations, beginning in Jerusalem. ⁴⁸ You are witnesses of these things. ⁴⁹ And I myself will send upon you what my Father has promised. But you must wait in the city until

the power from above comes down upon you."

Jesus Is Taken Up to Heaven
(Mark 16.19, 20; Acts 1.9-11)

⁵⁰ Then he led them out of the city as far as Bethany, where he raised his hands and blessed them. ⁵¹ As he was blessing them, he departed from them and was taken up into heaven.*g* ⁵² They worshiped him and went back into Jerusalem, filled with great joy, ⁵³ and spent all their time in the Temple giving thanks to God.

g Some manuscripts do not have and was taken up into heaven.

24.49 Ac 1.4 **24.50, 51** Ac 1.9-11 **24.51** Si 50.20

The Gospel according to
JOHN

INTRODUCTION

The Gospel according to John presents Jesus as the eternal Word of God, who "became a human being and lived among us." As the book itself says, this Gospel was written so that its readers might believe that Jesus is the promised Savior, the Son of God, and that through their faith in him they may have life (20.31).

After an introduction that identifies the eternal Word of God with Jesus, the first part of the Gospel presents various miracles which show that Jesus is the promised Savior, the Son of God. These are followed by discourses that explain what is revealed by the miracles. This part of the book tells how some people believed in Jesus and became his followers, while others opposed him and refused to believe. Chapters 13–17 record at length the close fellowship of Jesus with his disciples on the night of his arrest, and his words of preparation and encouragement to them on the eve of his crucifixion. The closing chapters tell of Jesus' arrest and trial, his crucifixion and resurrection, and his appearances to his disciples after the resurrection.

The story of the woman caught in adultery (8.1-11) is placed in brackets because many manuscripts and early translations omit it, while others include it in other places.

John emphasizes the gift of eternal life through Christ, a gift which begins now and which comes to those who respond to Jesus as the way, the truth, and the life. A striking feature of *John* is the symbolic use of common things from everyday life to point to spiritual realities, such as water, bread, light, the shepherd and his sheep, and the grapevine and its fruit.

OUTLINE OF CONTENTS

The Word of Life

1 In the beginning the Word already existed; the Word was with God, and the Word was God. ²From the very beginning the Word was with God. ³Through him God made all things; not one thing in all creation was made without him. ⁴The Word was the source of life,ᵃ and this life brought light to people. ⁵The light shines in the

---

ᵃ The Word was the source of life; *or* What was made had life in union with the Word.

darkness, and the darkness has never put it out.

⁶God sent his messenger, a man named John, ⁷who came to tell people about the light, so that all should hear the message and believe. ⁸He himself was not the light; he came to tell about the light. ⁹This was the real light — the light that comes into the world and shines on all people.

¹⁰The Word was in the world, and though God made the world through him, yet the world did not recognize him. ¹¹He came to his own country, but his own people did not receive him. ¹²Some, however, did receive him and believed in him; so he gave them the right to become God's children. ¹³They did not become God's children by natural means, that is, by being born as the children of a human father; God himself was their Father.

¹⁴The Word became a human being and, full of grace and truth, lived among us. We saw his glory, the glory which he received as the Father's only Son.

¹⁵John spoke about him. He cried out, "This is the one I was talking about when I said, 'He comes after me, but he is greater than I am, because he existed before I was born.'"

¹⁶Out of the fullness of his grace he has blessed us all, giving us one blessing after another. ¹⁷God gave the Law through Moses, but grace and truth came through Jesus Christ. ¹⁸No one has ever seen God. The only Son, who is the same as God and is at the Father's side, he has made him known.

John the Baptist's Message
(Matthew 3.1-12; Mark 1.1-8;
Luke 3.1-18)

¹⁹The Jewish authorities in Jerusalem sent some priests and Levites to John to ask him, "Who are you?"

²⁰John did not refuse to answer, but spoke out openly and clearly, saying: "I am not the Messiah."

²¹"Who are you, then?" they asked. "Are you Elijah?"

"No, I am not," John answered.

"Are you the Prophet?"ᵇ they asked.

"No," he replied.

²²"Then tell us who you are," they said. "We have to take an answer back to those who sent us. What do you say about yourself?"

²³John answered by quoting the prophet Isaiah:

"I am 'the voice of someone
    shouting in the desert:
Make a straight path for the
    Lord to travel!'"

²⁴The messengers, who had been sent by the Pharisees, ²⁵thenᶜ asked John, "If you are not the Messiah nor Elijah nor the Prophet, why do you baptize?"

²⁶John answered, "I baptize with water, but among you stands the one you do not know. ²⁷He is coming after me, but I am not good enough even to untie his sandals."

²⁸All this happened in Bethany on the east side of the Jordan River, where John was baptizing.

The Lamb of God

²⁹The next day John saw Jesus coming to him, and said, "There is the Lamb of God, who takes away the sin of the world! ³⁰This is the one I was talking about when I said, 'A man is coming

---

ᵇ THE PROPHET: *The one who was expected to appear and announce the coming of the Messiah.*   ᶜ The messengers, who had been sent by the Pharisees, then; *or* Those who had been sent were Pharisees; they.

1.6 Mt 3.1; Mk 1.4; Lk 3.1, 2   **1.21 a** Ml 4.5; **b** Dt 18.15, 18; Si 48.10, 11
1.23 Is 40.3 (LXX)

after me, but he is greater than I am, because he existed before I was born.' 31 I did not know who he would be, but I came baptizing with water in order to make him known to the people of Israel."

32 And John gave this testimony: "I saw the Spirit come down like a dove

I saw the Spirit come down like a dove. (1.32)

from heaven and stay on him. 33 I still did not know that he was the one, but God, who sent me to baptize with water, had said to me, 'You will see the Spirit come down and stay on a man; he is the one who baptizes with the Holy Spirit.' 34 I have seen it," said John, "and I tell you that he is the Son of God."

The First Disciples of Jesus

35 The next day John was standing there again with two of his disciples, 36 when he saw Jesus walking by. "There is the Lamb of God!" he said.

37 The two disciples heard him say this and went with Jesus. 38 Jesus turned, saw them following him, and asked, "What are you looking for?"

They answered, "Where do you live, Rabbi?" (This word means "Teacher.")

39 "Come and see," he answered. (It was then about four o'clock in the afternoon.) So they went with him and saw where he lived, and spent the rest of that day with him.

40 One of them was Andrew, Simon Peter's brother. 41 At once he found his brother Simon and told him, "We have found the Messiah." (This word means "Christ.") 42 Then he took Simon to Jesus.

Jesus looked at him and said, "Your name is Simon son of John, but you will be called Cephas." (This is the same as Peter and means "a rock.")

Jesus Calls Philip and Nathanael

43 The next day Jesus decided to go to Galilee. He found Philip and said to him, "Come with me!" (44 Philip was from Bethsaida, the town where Andrew and Peter lived.) 45 Philip found Nathanael and told him, "We have found the one whom Moses wrote about in the book of the Law and whom the prophets also wrote about. He is Jesus son of Joseph, from Nazareth."

46 "Can anything good come from Nazareth?" Nathanael asked.

"Come and see," answered Philip.

47 When Jesus saw Nathanael coming to him, he said about him, "Here is a real Israelite; there is nothing false in him!"

48 Nathanael asked him, "How do you know me?"

Jesus answered, "I saw you when you were under the fig tree before Philip called you."

49 "Teacher," answered Nathanael, "you are the Son of God! You are the King of Israel!"

50 Jesus said, "Do you believe just because I told you I saw you when you were under the fig tree? You will see much greater things than this!" 51 And he said to them, "I am telling you the truth: you will see heaven open and

1.51 Gn 28.12

God's angels going up and coming down on the Son of Man."

The Wedding in Cana

2 Two days later there was a wedding in the town of Cana in Galilee. Jesus' mother was there, ²and Jesus and his disciples had also been invited to the wedding. ³When the wine had given out, Jesus' mother said to him, "They are out of wine."

⁴"You must not tell me what to do," Jesus replied. "My time has not yet come."

⁵Jesus' mother then told the servants, "Do whatever he tells you."

⁶The Jews have rules about ritual washing, and for this purpose six stone water jars were there, each one large enough to hold between twenty and thirty gallons. ⁷Jesus said to the servants, "Fill these jars with water." They

"Fill these jars with water." (2.7)

filled them to the brim, ⁸and then he told them, "Now draw some water out and take it to the man in charge of the feast." They took him the water, ⁹which now had turned into wine, and he tasted it. He did not know where this wine had come from (but, of course, the servants who had drawn out the water

knew); so he called the bridegroom ¹⁰and said to him, "Everyone else serves the best wine first, and after the guests have drunk a lot, he serves the ordinary wine. But you have kept the best wine until now!"

¹¹Jesus performed this first miracle in Cana in Galilee; there he revealed his glory, and his disciples believed in him.

¹²After this, Jesus and his mother, brothers, and disciples went to Capernaum and stayed there a few days.

Jesus Goes to the Temple
(Matthew 21.12, 13; Mark 11.15-17; Luke 19.45, 46)

¹³It was almost time for the Passover Festival, so Jesus went to Jerusalem. ¹⁴There in the Temple he found people selling cattle, sheep, and pigeons, and also the moneychangers sitting at their tables. ¹⁵So he made a whip from cords and drove all the animals out of the Temple, both the sheep and the cattle; he overturned the tables of the moneychangers and scattered their coins; ¹⁶and he ordered those who sold the pigeons, "Take them out of here! Stop making my Father's house a marketplace!" ¹⁷His disciples remembered that the scripture says, "My devotion to your house, O God, burns in me like a fire."

¹⁸The Jewish authorities came back at him with a question, "What miracle can you perform to show us that you have the right to do this?"

¹⁹Jesus answered, "Tear down this Temple, and in three days I will build it again."

²⁰"Are you going to build it again in three days?" they asked him. "It has taken forty-six years to build this Temple!"

²¹But the temple Jesus was speaking about was his body. ²²So when he was raised from death, his disciples remembered that he had said this, and they

2.12 Mt 4.13　　**2.13** Ex 12.1-27　　**2.17** Ps 69.9　　**2.19** Mt 26.61; 27.40; Mk 14.58; 15.29

believed the scripture and what Jesus had said.

Jesus' Knowledge of Human Nature

²³ While Jesus was in Jerusalem during the Passover Festival, many believed in him as they saw the miracles he performed. ²⁴ But Jesus did not trust himself to them, because he knew them all. ²⁵ There was no need for anyone to tell him about them, because he himself knew what was in their hearts.

Jesus and Nicodemus

3 There was a Jewish leader named Nicodemus, who belonged to the party of the Pharisees. ² One night he went to Jesus and said to him, "Rabbi, we know that you are a teacher sent by God. No one could perform the miracles you are doing unless God were with him."

³ Jesus answered, "I am telling you the truth: no one can see the Kingdom of God without being born again."^d

⁴ "How can a grown man be born again?" Nicodemus asked. "He certainly cannot enter his mother's womb and be born a second time!"

⁵ "I am telling you the truth," replied Jesus, "that no one can enter the Kingdom of God without being born of water and the Spirit. ⁶ A person is born physically of human parents, but is born spiritually of the Spirit. ⁷ Do not be surprised because I tell you that you must all be born again.^d ⁸ The wind blows wherever it wishes; you hear the sound it makes, but you do not know where it comes from or where it is going. It is like that with everyone who is born of the Spirit."

⁹ "How can this be?" asked Nicodemus.

¹⁰ Jesus answered, "You are a great teacher in Israel, and you don't know this? ¹¹ I am telling you the truth: we speak of what we know and report what we have seen, yet none of you is willing to accept our message. ¹² You do not believe me when I tell you about the things of this world; how will you ever believe me, then, when I tell you about the things of heaven? ¹³ And no one has ever gone up to heaven except the Son of Man, who came down from heaven."^e

¹⁴ As Moses lifted up the bronze snake on a pole in the desert, in the same way the Son of Man must be lifted up, ¹⁵ so that everyone who believes in him may have eternal life. ¹⁶ For God loved the world so much that he gave his only Son, so that everyone who believes in him may not die but have eternal life. ¹⁷ For God did not send his Son into the world to be its judge, but to be its savior.

¹⁸ Those who believe in the Son are not judged; but those who do not believe have already been judged, because they have not believed in God's only Son. ¹⁹ This is how the judgment works: the light has come into the world, but people love the darkness rather than the light, because their deeds are evil. ²⁰ Those who do evil things hate the light and will not come to the light, because they do not want their evil deeds to be shown up. ²¹ But those who do what is true come to the light in order that the light may show that what they did was in obedience to God.

Jesus and John

²² After this, Jesus and his disciples went to the province of Judea, where he spent some time with them and baptized. ²³ John also was baptizing in Ae-

---

^d again; *or* from above.   ^e *The quotation may continue through verse 21.*
3.12 Ws 9.16, 17   **3.13** Ba 3.29   **3.14** Nu 21.9; Ws 16.5-7

non, not far from Salim, because there was plenty of water in that place. People were going to him, and he was baptizing them. (24 This was before John had been put in prison.)

25 Some of John's disciples began arguing with a Jew*f* about the matter of ritual washing. 26 So they went to John and told him, "Teacher, you remember the man who was with you on the east side of the Jordan, the one you spoke about? Well, he is baptizing now, and everyone is going to him!"

27 John answered, "No one can have anything unless God gives it. 28 You yourselves are my witnesses that I said, 'I am not the Messiah, but I have been sent ahead of him.' 29 The bridegroom is the one to whom the bride belongs; but the bridegroom's friend, who stands by and listens, is glad when he hears the bridegroom's voice. This is how my own happiness is made complete. 30 He must become more important while I become less important."

He Who Comes from Heaven

31 He who comes from above is greater than all. He who is from the earth belongs to the earth and speaks about earthly matters, but he who comes from heaven is above all. 32 He tells what he has seen and heard, yet no one accepts his message. 33 But whoever accepts his message confirms by this that God is truthful. 34 The one whom God has sent speaks God's words, because God gives him the fullness of his Spirit. 35 The Father loves his Son and has put everything in his power. 36 Whoever believes in the Son has eternal life; whoever disobeys the Son will not have life, but will remain under God's punishment.

Jesus and the Samaritan Woman

4 The Pharisees heard that Jesus was winning and baptizing more disciples than John. (2 Actually, Jesus himself did not baptize anyone; only his disciples did.) 3 So when Jesus heard what was being said, he left Judea and went back to Galilee; 4 on his way there he had to go through Samaria.

5 In Samaria he came to a town named Sychar, which was not far from the field that Jacob had given to his son Joseph. 6 Jacob's well was there, and Jesus, tired out by the trip, sat down by the well. It was about noon.

7 A Samaritan woman came to draw some water, and Jesus said to her, "Give

"Give me a drink of water." (4.7)

me a drink of water." (8 His disciples had gone into town to buy food.)

9 The woman answered, "You are a Jew, and I am a Samaritan — so how can you ask me for a drink?" (Jews will not use the same cups and bowls that Samaritans use.)*g*

10 Jesus answered, "If you only knew what God gives and who it is that is asking you for a drink, you would ask him, and he would give you life-giving water."

11 "Sir," the woman said, "you don't have a bucket, and the well is deep.

---

f a Jew; *some manuscripts have* some Jews. bowls that Samaritans use; *or* Jews will have nothing to do with Samaritans.

g Jews will not use the same cups and

3.24 Mt 14.3; Mk 6.17; Lk 3.19, 20   **3.28** Jn 1.20   **3.35** Mt 11.27; Lk 10.22
4.5 Gn 33.19; Js 24.32   **4.9** Ezra 4.1-5; Ne 4.1, 2

Where would you get that life-giving water? 12 It was our ancestor Jacob who gave us this well; he and his children and his flocks all drank from it. You don't claim to be greater than Jacob, do you?"

13 Jesus answered, "Those who drink this water will get thirsty again, 14 but those who drink the water that I will give them will never be thirsty again. The water that I will give them will become in them a spring which will provide them with life-giving water and give them eternal life."

15 "Sir," the woman said, "give me that water! Then I will never be thirsty again, nor will I have to come here to draw water."

16 "Go and call your husband," Jesus told her, "and come back."

17 "I don't have a husband," she answered.

Jesus replied, "You are right when you say you don't have a husband. 18 You have been married to five men, and the man you live with now is not really your husband. You have told me the truth."

19 "I see you are a prophet, sir," the woman said. 20 "My Samaritan ancestors worshiped God on this mountain, but you Jews say that Jerusalem is the place where we should worship God."

21 Jesus said to her, "Believe me, woman, the time will come when people will not worship the Father either on this mountain or in Jerusalem. 22 You Samaritans do not really know whom you worship; but we Jews know whom we worship, because it is from the Jews that salvation comes. 23 But the time is coming and is already here, when by the power of God's Spirit people will worship the Father as he really is, offering him the true worship that he wants. 24 God is Spirit, and only by the power of his Spirit can people worship him as he really is."

25 The woman said to him, "I know that the Messiah will come, and when he comes, he will tell us everything."

26 Jesus answered, "I am he, I who am talking with you."

27 At that moment Jesus' disciples returned, and they were greatly surprised to find him talking with a woman. But none of them said to her, "What do you want?" or asked him, "Why are you talking with her?"

28 Then the woman left her water jar, went back to the town, and said to the people there, 29 "Come and see the man who told me everything I have ever done. Could he be the Messiah?" 30 So they left the town and went to Jesus.

31 In the meantime the disciples were begging Jesus, "Teacher, have something to eat!"

32 But he answered, "I have food to eat that you know nothing about."

33 So the disciples started asking among themselves, "Could somebody have brought him food?"

34 "My food," Jesus said to them, "is to obey the will of the one who sent me and to finish the work he gave me to do. 35 You have a saying, 'Four more months and then the harvest.' But I tell you, take a good look at the fields; the crops are now ripe and ready to be harvested! 36 The one who reaps the harvest is being paid and gathers the crops for eternal life; so the one who plants and the one who reaps will be glad together. 37 For the saying is true, 'Someone plants, someone else reaps.' 38 I have sent you to reap a harvest in a field where you did not work; others worked there, and you profit from their work."

39 Many of the Samaritans in that town believed in Jesus because the woman had said, "He told me everything I have ever done." 40 So when the Samaritans came to him, they begged him to stay with them, and Jesus stayed there two days.

41 Many more believed because of his message, 42 and they told the woman, "We believe now, not because of what you said, but because we ourselves

have heard him, and we know that he really is the Savior of the world."

Jesus Heals an Official's Son

⁴³After spending two days there, Jesus left and went to Galilee. ⁴⁴For he himself had said, "Prophets are not respected in their own country." ⁴⁵When he arrived in Galilee, the people there welcomed him, because they had gone to the Passover Festival in Jerusalem and had seen everything that he had done during the festival.

⁴⁶Then Jesus went back to Cana in Galilee, where he had turned the water into wine. A government official was there whose son was sick in Capernaum. ⁴⁷When he heard that Jesus had come from Judea to Galilee, he went to him and asked him to go to Capernaum and heal his son, who was about to die. ⁴⁸Jesus said to him, "None of you will ever believe unless you see miracles and wonders."

⁴⁹"Sir," replied the official, "come with me before my child dies."

⁵⁰Jesus said to him, "Go; your son will live!"

The man believed Jesus' words and went. ⁵¹On his way home his servants met him with the news, "Your boy is going to live!"

⁵²He asked them what time it was when his son got better, and they answered, "It was one o'clock yesterday afternoon when the fever left him." ⁵³Then the father remembered that it was at that very hour when Jesus had told him, "Your son will live." So he and all his family believed.

⁵⁴This was the second miracle that Jesus performed after coming from Judea to Galilee.

The Healing at the Pool

5 After this, Jesus went to Jerusalem for a religious festival. ²Near the Sheep Gate in Jerusalem there is a pool ʰ with five porches; in Hebrew it is called Bethzatha.ⁱ ³A large crowd of sick people were lying on the porches — the blind, the lame, and the paralyzed.ʲ ⁵A man was there who had been sick for thirty-eight years. ⁶Jesus saw him lying there, and he knew that the man had been sick for such a long time; so he asked him, "Do you want to get well?"

⁷The sick man answered, "Sir, I don't have anyone here to put me in the pool when the water is stirred up; while I am trying to get in, somebody else gets there first."

⁸Jesus said to him, "Get up, pick up your mat, and walk." ⁹Immediately the man got well; he picked up his mat and started walking.

The day this happened was a Sabbath, ¹⁰so the Jewish authorities told the man who had been healed, "This is a Sabbath, and it is against our Law for you to carry your mat."

¹¹He answered, "The man who made me well told me to pick up my mat and walk."

¹²They asked him, "Who is the man who told you to do this?"

¹³But the man who had been healed did not know who Jesus was, for there was a crowd in that place, and Jesus had slipped away.

¹⁴Afterward, Jesus found him in the Temple and said, "Listen, you are well now; so stop sinning or something worse may happen to you."

¹⁵Then the man left and told the Jewish authorities that it was Jesus

---

ʰ Near the Sheep Gate . . . a pool; *or* Near the Sheep Pool . . . a place.   ⁱ Bethzatha; *some manuscripts have* Bethesda.   ʲ *Some manuscripts add verses 3b-4:* They were waiting for the water to move, ⁴because every now and then an angel of the Lord went down into the pool and stirred up the water. The first sick person to go into the pool after the water was stirred up was healed from whatever disease he had.
4.44 Mt 13.57; Mk 6.4; Lk 4.24   **4.45** Jn 2.23   **4.46** Jn 2.1-11   **5.10** Ne 13.19; Jr 17.21

who had healed him. ¹⁶ So they began to persecute Jesus, because he had done this healing on a Sabbath. ¹⁷ Jesus answered them, "My Father is always working, and I too must work."

¹⁸ This saying made the Jewish authorities all the more determined to kill him; not only had he broken the Sabbath law, but he had said that God was his own Father and in this way had made himself equal with God.

The Authority of the Son

¹⁹ So Jesus answered them, "I tell you the truth: the Son can do nothing on his own; he does only what he sees his Father doing. What the Father does, the Son also does. ²⁰ For the Father loves the Son and shows him all that he himself is doing. He will show him even greater things to do than this, and you will all be amazed. ²¹ Just as the Father raises the dead and gives them life, in the same way the Son gives life to those he wants to. ²² Nor does the Father himself judge anyone. He has given his Son the full right to judge, ²³ so that all will honor the Son in the same way as they honor the Father. Whoever does not honor the Son does not honor the Father who sent him.

²⁴ "I am telling you the truth: those who hear my words and believe in him who sent me have eternal life. They will not be judged, but have already passed from death to life. ²⁵ I am telling you the truth: the time is coming — the time has already come — when the dead will hear the voice of the Son of God, and those who hear it will come to life. ²⁶ Just as the Father is himself the source of life, in the same way he has made his Son to be the source of life. ²⁷ And he has given the Son the right to judge, because he is the Son of Man. ²⁸ Do not be surprised at this; the time is coming when all the dead will hear

his voice ²⁹ and come out of their graves: those who have done good will rise and live, and those who have done evil will rise and be condemned.

Witnesses to Jesus

³⁰ "I can do nothing on my own authority; I judge only as God tells me, so my judgment is right, because I am not trying to do what I want, but only what he who sent me wants.

³¹ "If I testify on my own behalf, what I say is not to be accepted as real proof. ³² But there is someone else who testifies on my behalf, and I know that what he says about me is true. ³³ John is the one to whom you sent your messengers, and he spoke on behalf of the truth. ³⁴ It is not that I must have a human witness; I say this only in order that you may be saved. ³⁵ John was like a lamp, burning and shining, and you were willing for a while to enjoy his light. ³⁶ But I have a witness on my behalf which is even greater than the witness that John gave: what I do, that is, the deeds my Father gave me to do, these speak on my behalf and show that the Father has sent me. ³⁷ And the Father, who sent me, also testifies on my behalf. You have never heard his voice or seen his face, ³⁸ and you do not keep his message in your hearts, for you do not believe in the one whom he sent. ³⁹ You study the Scriptures, because you think that in them you will find eternal life. And these very Scriptures speak about me! ⁴⁰ Yet you are not willing to come to me in order to have life.

⁴¹ "I am not looking for human praise. ⁴² But I know what kind of people you are, and I know that you have no love for God in your hearts. ⁴³ I have come with my Father's authority, but you have not received me; when, however, someone comes with his own authority,

5.18 Ws 2.16   **5.29** Dn 12.2   **5.33** Jn 1.19-27; 3.27-30   **5.35** Si 48.1   **5.37** Mt 3.17;
Mk 1.11; Lk 3.22   **5.39** Ba 4.1

you will receive him. ⁴⁴You like to receive praise from one another, but you do not try to win praise from the one who alone is God; how, then, can you believe me? ⁴⁵Do not think, however, that I am the one who will accuse you to my Father. Moses, in whom you have put your hope, is the very one who will accuse you. ⁴⁶If you had really believed Moses, you would have believed me, because he wrote about me. ⁴⁷But since you do not believe what he wrote, how can you believe what I say?"

Jesus Feeds Five Thousand
(Matthew 14.13-21; Mark 6.30-44; Luke 9.10-17)

6 After this, Jesus went across Lake Galilee (or, Lake Tiberias, as it is also called). ²A large crowd followed him, because they had seen his miracles of healing the sick. ³Jesus went up a hill and sat down with his disciples. ⁴The time for the Passover Festival was near. ⁵Jesus looked around and saw that a large crowd was coming to him, so he asked Philip, "Where can we buy enough food to feed all these people?" (⁶He said this to test Philip; actually he already knew what he would do.)

⁷Philip answered, "For everyone to have even a little, it would take more than two hundred silver coins ᵏ to buy enough bread."

⁸Another one of his disciples, Andrew, who was Simon Peter's brother, said, ⁹"There is a boy here who has five loaves of barley bread and two fish. But they will certainly not be enough for all these people."

¹⁰"Make the people sit down," Jesus told them. (There was a lot of grass there.) So all the people sat down; there were about five thousand men. ¹¹Jesus took the bread, gave thanks to God, and distributed it to the people who were sitting there. He did the same with the

fish, and they all had as much as they wanted. ¹²When they were all full, he said to his disciples, "Gather the pieces left over; let us not waste a bit." ¹³So they gathered them all and filled twelve baskets with the pieces left over from the five barley loaves which the people had eaten.

¹⁴Seeing this miracle that Jesus had performed, the people there said, "Surely this is the Prophetˡ who was to come into the world!" ¹⁵Jesus knew that they were about to come and seize him in order to make him king by force; so he went off again to the hills by himself.

Jesus Walks on the Water
(Matthew 14.22-33; Mark 6.45-52)

¹⁶When evening came, Jesus' disciples went down to the lake, ¹⁷got into a boat, and went back across the lake toward Capernaum. Night came on, and Jesus still had not come to them. ¹⁸By then a strong wind was blowing and stirring up the water. ¹⁹The disciples had rowed about three or four miles when they saw Jesus walking on the water, coming near the boat, and they were terrified. ²⁰"Don't be afraid," Jesus told them, "it is I!" ²¹Then they willingly took him into the boat, and immediately the boat reached land at the place they were heading for.

The People Seek Jesus

²²Next day the crowd which had stayed on the other side of the lake realized that there had been only one boat there. They knew that Jesus had not gone in it with his disciples, but that they had left without him. ²³Other boats, which were from Tiberias, came to shore near the place where the crowd had eaten the bread after the Lord had given thanks. ²⁴When the crowd saw that Jesus was not there, nor his

---

ᵏ SILVER COINS: *A silver coin was the daily wage of a rural worker (see Mt 20.2).*
ˡ THE PROPHET: *See 1.21.*

disciples, they got into those boats and went to Capernaum, looking for him.

Jesus the Bread of Life

²⁵When the people found Jesus on the other side of the lake, they said to him, "Teacher, when did you get here?"

²⁶Jesus answered, "I am telling you the truth: you are looking for me because you ate the bread and had all you wanted, not because you understood my miracles. ²⁷Do not work for food that spoils; instead, work for the food that lasts for eternal life. This is the food which the Son of Man will give you, because God, the Father, has put his mark of approval on him."

²⁸So they asked him, "What can we do in order to do what God wants us to do?"

²⁹Jesus answered, "What God wants you to do is to believe in the one he sent."

³⁰They replied, "What miracle will you perform so that we may see it and believe you? What will you do? ³¹Our ancestors ate manna in the desert, just as the scripture says, 'He gave them bread from heaven to eat.' "

³²"I am telling you the truth," Jesus said. "What Moses gave you was not^m the bread from heaven; it is my Father who gives you the real bread from heaven. ³³For the bread that God gives is he who comes down from heaven and gives life to the world."

³⁴"Sir," they asked him, "give us this bread always."

³⁵"I am the bread of life," Jesus told them. "Those who come to me will never be hungry; those who believe in me will never be thirsty. ³⁶Now, I told you that you have seen me but will not believe. ³⁷Everyone whom my Father gives me will come to me. I will never turn away anyone who comes to me, ³⁸because I have come down from heaven to do not my own will but the will of him who sent me. ³⁹And it is the will of him who sent me that I should not lose any of all those he has given me, but that I should raise them all to life on the last day. ⁴⁰For what my Father wants is that all who see the Son and believe in him should have eternal life. And I will raise them to life on the last day."

⁴¹The people started grumbling about him, because he said, "I am the bread that came down from heaven." ⁴²So they said, "This man is Jesus son of Joseph, isn't he? We know his father and mother. How, then, does he now say he came down from heaven?"

⁴³Jesus answered, "Stop grumbling among yourselves. ⁴⁴People cannot come to me unless the Father who sent me draws them to me; and I will raise them to life on the last day. ⁴⁵The prophets wrote, 'Everyone will be taught by God.' Anyone who hears the Father and learns from him comes to me. ⁴⁶This does not mean that anyone has seen the Father; he who is from God is the only one who has seen the Father. ⁴⁷I am telling you the truth: he who believes has eternal life. ⁴⁸I am the bread of life. ⁴⁹Your ancestors ate manna in the desert, but they died. ⁵⁰But the bread that comes down from heaven is of such a kind that whoever eats it will not die. ⁵¹I am the living bread that came down from heaven. If you eat this bread, you will live forever. The bread that I will give you is my flesh, which I give so that the world may live."

⁵²This started an angry argument among them. "How can this man give us his flesh to eat?" they asked.

⁵³Jesus said to them, "I am telling you the truth: if you do not eat the flesh of the Son of Man and drink his blood, you will not have life in yourselves. ⁵⁴Those who eat my flesh and drink my

---

^m What Moses gave you was not; *or* It was not Moses who gave you.
6.27 Si 24.19-22   **6.31** Ex 16.4, 15; Ps 78.24; Ws 16.20, 21   **6.45** Is 54.13

blood have eternal life, and I will raise them to life on the last day. 55 For my flesh is the real food; my blood is the real drink. 56 Those who eat my flesh and drink my blood live in me, and I live in them. 57 The living Father sent me, and because of him I live also. In the same way whoever eats me will live because of me. 58 This, then, is the bread that came down from heaven; it is not like the bread that your ancestors ate, but then later died. Those who eat this bread will live forever."

59 Jesus said this as he taught in the synagogue in Capernaum.

The Words of Eternal Life

60 Many of his followers heard this and said, "This teaching is too hard. Who can listen to it?"

61 Without being told, Jesus knew that they were grumbling about this, so he said to them, "Does this make you want to give up? 62 Suppose, then, that you should see the Son of Man go back up to the place where he was before? 63 What gives life is God's Spirit; human power is of no use at all. The words I have spoken to you bring God's lifegiving Spirit. 64 Yet some of you do not believe." (Jesus knew from the very beginning who were the ones that would not believe and which one would betray him.) 65 And he added, "This is the very reason I told you that no people can come to me unless the Father makes it possible for them to do so."

66 Because of this, many of Jesus' followers turned back and would not go with him any more. 67 So he asked the twelve disciples, "And you — would you also like to leave?"

68 Simon Peter answered him, "Lord, to whom would we go? You have the words that give eternal life. 69 And now we believe and know that you are the Holy One who has come from God."

70 Jesus replied, "I chose the twelve of you, didn't I? Yet one of you is a devil!" 71 He was talking about Judas, the son of Simon Iscariot. For Judas, even though he was one of the twelve disciples, was going to betray him.

Jesus and His Brothers

7 After this, Jesus traveled in Galilee; he did not want to travel in Judea, because the Jewish authorities there were wanting to kill him. 2 The time for the Festival of Shelters was near, 3 so Jesus' brothers said to him, "Leave this place and go to Judea, so that your followers will see the things that you are doing. 4 People don't hide what they are doing if they want to be well known. Since you are doing these things, let the whole world know about you!" (5 Not even his brothers believed in him.)

6 Jesus said to them, "The right time for me has not yet come. Any time is right for you. 7 The world cannot hate you, but it hates me, because I keep telling it that its ways are bad. 8 You go on to the festival. I am not going n to this festival, because the right time has not come for me." 9 He said this and then stayed on in Galilee.

Jesus at the Festival of Shelters

10 After his brothers had gone to the festival, Jesus also went; however, he did not go openly, but secretly. 11 The Jewish authorities were looking for him at the festival. "Where is he?" they asked.

12 There was much whispering about him in the crowd. "He is a good man," some people said. "No," others said, "he fools the people." 13 But no one talked about him openly, because they were afraid of the Jewish authorities.

14 The festival was nearly half over when Jesus went to the Temple and

n I am not going; *some manuscripts have* I am not yet going.
6.63 Ws 9.13-18   **6.68, 69** Mt 16.16; Mk 8.29; Lk 9.20   **7.2** Lv 23.34; Dt 16.13

began teaching. 15 The Jewish authorities were greatly surprised and said,
"How does this man know so much
when he has never been to school?"

16 Jesus answered, "What I teach is
not my own teaching, but it comes from
God, who sent me. 17 Whoever is willing
to do what God wants will know
whether what I teach comes from God
or whether I speak on my own authority. 18 Those who speak on their own authority are trying to gain glory for
themselves. But he who wants glory for
the one who sent him is honest, and
there is nothing false in him. 19 Moses
gave you the Law, didn't he? But not
one of you obeys the Law. Why are you
trying to kill me?"

20 "You have a demon in you!" the
crowd answered. "Who is trying to
kill you?"

21 Jesus answered, "I performed one
miracle, and you were all surprised.
22 Moses ordered you to circumcise your
sons (although it was not Moses but
your ancestors who started it), and so
you circumcise a boy on the Sabbath.
23 If a boy is circumcised on the Sabbath
so that Moses' Law is not broken, why
are you angry with me because I made
a man completely well on the Sabbath?
24 Stop judging by external standards,
and judge by true standards."

Is He the Messiah?

25 Some of the people of Jerusalem
said, "Isn't this the man the authorities
are trying to kill? 26 Look! He is talking
in public, and they say nothing against
him! Can it be that they really know
that he is the Messiah? 27 But when
the Messiah comes, no one will know
where he is from. And we all know
where this man comes from."

28 As Jesus taught in the Temple, he
said in a loud voice, "Do you really know
me and know where I am from? I have
not come on my own authority. He who
sent me, however, is truthful. You do
not know him, 29 but I know him, because I come from him and he sent
me."

30 Then they tried to seize him, but
no one laid a hand on him, because his
hour had not yet come. 31 But many in
the crowd believed in him and said,
"When the Messiah comes, will he
perform more miracles than this
man has?"

Guards Are Sent to Arrest Jesus

32 The Pharisees heard the crowd
whispering these things about Jesus, so
they and the chief priests sent some
guards to arrest him. 33 Jesus said, "I
shall be with you a little while longer,
and then I shall go away to him who
sent me. 34 You will look for me, but you
will not find me, because you cannot go
where I will be."

35 The Jewish authorities said among
themselves, "Where is he about to go so
that we shall not find him? Will he go
to the Greek cities where our people
live, and teach the Greeks? 36 He says
that we will look for him but will not
find him, and that we cannot go where
he will be. What does he mean?"

Streams of Life-Giving Water

37 On the last and most important day
of the festival Jesus stood up and said in
a loud voice, "Whoever is thirsty should
come to me, and 38 whoever believes in
me should drink. As the scripture says,
'Streams of life-giving water will pour
out from his side.' "o 39 Jesus said this
about the Spirit, which those who believed in him were going to receive. At

o *Jesus' words in verses 37-38 may be translated:* "Whoever is thirsty should come to
me and drink. 38 As the scripture says, 'Streams of life-giving water will pour out from
within anyone who believes in me.' "

7.22 a Lv 12.3; **b** Gn 17.10 **7.23** Jn 5.9 **7.37** Lv 23.36 **7.38** Ez 47.1; Zec 14.8

that time the Spirit had not yet been given, because Jesus had not been raised to glory.

Division among the People

40 Some of the people in the crowd heard him say this and said, "This man is really the Prophet!"*p*

41 Others said, "He is the Messiah!"

But others said, "The Messiah will not come from Galilee! **42** The scripture says that the Messiah will be a descendant of King David and will be born in Bethlehem, the town where David lived." **43** So there was a division in the crowd because of Jesus. **44** Some wanted to seize him, but no one laid a hand on him.

The Unbelief of the Jewish Authorities

45 When the guards went back, the chief priests and Pharisees asked them, "Why did you not bring him?"

46 The guards answered, "Nobody has ever talked the way this man does!"

47 "Did he fool you, too?" the Pharisees asked them. **48** "Have you ever known one of the authorities or one Pharisee to believe in him? **49** This crowd does not know the Law of Moses, so they are under God's curse!"

50 One of the Pharisees there was Nicodemus, the man who had gone to see Jesus before. He said to the others, **51** "According to our Law we cannot condemn people before hearing them and finding out what they have done."

52 "Well," they answered, "are you also from Galilee? Study the Scriptures and you will learn that no prophet ever comes *q* from Galilee."

The Woman Caught in Adultery

8 [Then everyone went home, but Jesus went to the Mount of Olives. **2** Early the next morning he went back to the Temple. All the people gathered around him, and he sat down and began to teach them. **3** The teachers of the Law and the Pharisees brought in a woman who had been caught committing adultery, and they made her stand before them all. **4** "Teacher," they said to Jesus, "this woman was caught in the very act of committing adultery. **5** In our Law Moses commanded that such a woman must be stoned to death. Now, what do you say?" **6** They said this to trap Jesus, so that they could accuse him. But he bent over and wrote on the ground with his finger. **7** As they stood there asking him questions, he straightened up and said to them, "Whichever one of you has committed no sin may throw the first stone at her." **8** Then he bent over again and wrote on the ground. **9** When they heard this, they all left, one by one, the older ones first. Jesus was left alone, with the woman still standing there. **10** He straightened up and said to her, "Where are they? Is there no one left to condemn you?"

11 "No one, sir," she answered.

"Well, then," Jesus said, "I do not condemn you either. Go, but do not sin again."]*r*

Jesus the Light of the World

12 Jesus spoke to the Pharisees again. "I am the light of the world," he said. "Whoever follows me will have the light of life and will never walk in darkness."

13 The Pharisees said to him, "Now

---

p THE PROPHET: *See 1.21.*   *q* no prophet ever comes; *one manuscript has* the Prophet will not come.   *r* *Many manuscripts and early translations do not have this passage (8.1-11); others have it after Jn 21.24; others have it after Lk 21.38; one manuscript has it after Jn 7.36.*

7.42 2 S 7.12; Mic 5.2   **7.50** Jn 3.1, 2   **8.5** Lv 20.10; Dt 22.22-24   **8.7** Su 34
8.12 Ws 7.26; Mt 5.14; Jn 9.5   **8.13** Jn 5.31

you are testifying on your own behalf; what you say proves nothing."

¹⁴"No," Jesus answered, "even though I do testify on my own behalf, what I say is true, because I know where I came from and where I am going. You do not know where I came from or where I am going. ¹⁵You make judgments in a purely human way; I pass judgment on no one. ¹⁶But if I were to do so, my judgment would be true, because I am not alone in this; the Father who sent me is with me. ¹⁷It is written in your Law that when two witnesses agree, what they say is true. ¹⁸I testify on my own behalf, and the Father who sent me also testifies on my behalf."

¹⁹"Where is your father?" they asked him.

"You know neither me nor my Father," Jesus answered. "If you knew me, you would know my Father also."

²⁰Jesus said all this as he taught in the Temple, in the room where the offering boxes were placed. And no one arrested him, because his hour had not come.

You Cannot Go Where I Am Going

²¹Again Jesus said to them, "I will go away; you will look for me, but you will die in your sins. You cannot go where I am going."

²²So the Jewish authorities said, "He says that we cannot go where he is going. Does this mean that he will kill himself?"

²³Jesus answered, "You belong to this world here below, but I come from above. You are from this world, but I am not from this world. ²⁴That is why I told you that you will die in your sins. And you will die in your sins if you do not believe that 'I Am Who I Am'."

²⁵"Who are you?" they asked him.

Jesus answered, "What I have told you from the very beginning.ˢ ²⁶I have much to say about you, much to condemn you for. The one who sent me, however, is truthful, and I tell the world only what I have heard from him."

²⁷They did not understand that Jesus was talking to them about the Father. ²⁸So he said to them, "When you lift up the Son of Man, you will know that 'I Am Who I Am'; then you will know that I do nothing on my own authority, but I say only what the Father has instructed me to say. ²⁹And he who sent me is with me; he has not left me alone, because I always do what pleases him."

³⁰Many who heard Jesus say these things believed in him.

The Truth Will Set You Free

³¹So Jesus said to those who believed in him, "If you obey my teaching, you are really my disciples; ³²you will know the truth, and the truth will set you free."

³³"We are the descendants of Abraham," they answered, "and we have never been anybody's slaves. What do you mean, then, by saying, 'You will be free'?"

³⁴Jesus said to them, "I am telling you the truth: everyone who sins is a slave of sin. ³⁵A slave does not belong to a family permanently, but a son belongs there forever. ³⁶If the Son sets you free, then you will be really free. ³⁷I know you are Abraham's descendants. Yet you are trying to kill me, because you will not accept my teaching. ³⁸I talk about what my Father has shown me, but you do what your father has told you."

³⁹They answered him, "Our father is Abraham."

"If you really were Abraham's children," Jesus replied, "you would doᵗ

ˢ What I have told you from the very beginning; *or* Why should I speak to you at all?

ᵗ If you really were . . . you would do; *some manuscripts have* If you are . . . do.

8.17 Dt 19.15   **8.32** 1 Esd 4.38   **8.33** Mt 3.9; Lk 3.8

the same things that he did. ⁴⁰All I have ever done is to tell you the truth I heard from God, yet you are trying to kill me. Abraham did nothing like this! ⁴¹You are doing what your father did."

"God himself is the only Father we have," they answered, "and we are his true children."

⁴²Jesus said to them, "If God really were your Father, you would love me, because I came from God and now I am here. I did not come on my own authority, but he sent me. ⁴³Why do you not understand what I say? It is because you cannot bear to listen to my message. ⁴⁴You are the children of your father, the Devil, and you want to follow your father's desires. From the very beginning he was a murderer and has never been on the side of truth, because there is no truth in him. When he tells a lie, he is only doing what is natural to him, because he is a liar and the father of all lies. ⁴⁵But I tell the truth, and that is why you do not believe me. ⁴⁶Which one of you can prove that I am guilty of sin? If I tell the truth, then why do you not believe me? ⁴⁷He who comes from God listens to God's words. You, however, are not from God, and that is why you will not listen."

Jesus and Abraham

⁴⁸They asked Jesus, "Were we not right in saying that you are a Samaritan and have a demon in you?"

⁴⁹"I have no demon," Jesus answered. "I honor my Father, but you dishonor me. ⁵⁰I am not seeking honor for myself. But there is one who is seeking it and who judges in my favor. ⁵¹I am telling you the truth: whoever obeys my teaching will never die."

⁵²They said to him, "Now we know for sure that you have a demon! Abraham died, and the prophets died, yet you say that whoever obeys your teach-

ing will never die. ⁵³Our father Abraham died; you do not claim to be greater than Abraham, do you? And the prophets also died. Who do you think you are?"

⁵⁴Jesus answered, "If I were to honor myself, that honor would be worth nothing. The one who honors me is my Father—the very one you say is your God. ⁵⁵You have never known him, but I know him. If I were to say that I do not know him, I would be a liar like you. But I do know him, and I obey his word. ⁵⁶Your father Abraham rejoiced that he was to see the time of my coming; he saw it and was glad."

⁵⁷They said to him, "You are not even fifty years old—and you have seen Abraham?"ᵘ

⁵⁸"I am telling you the truth," Jesus replied. "Before Abraham was born, 'I Am'."

⁵⁹Then they picked up stones to throw at him, but Jesus hid himself and left the Temple.

Jesus Heals a Man Born Blind

9 As Jesus was walking along, he saw a man who had been born blind. ²His disciples asked him, "Teacher, whose sin caused him to be born blind? Was it his own or his parents' sin?"

³Jesus answered, "His blindness has nothing to do with his sins or his parents' sins. He is blind so that God's power might be seen at work in him. ⁴As long as it is day, we must do the work of him who sent me; night is coming when no one can work. ⁵While I am in the world, I am the light for the world."

⁶After he said this, Jesus spat on the ground and made some mud with the spittle; he rubbed the mud on the man's eyes ⁷and told him, "Go and wash your face in the Pool of Siloam."

ᵘ you have seen Abraham?; *some manuscripts have* has Abraham seen you?
8.44 Ws 1.13; 2.24　**9.5** Mt 5.14; Jn 8.12

(This name means "Sent.") So the man went, washed his face, and came back seeing.

8 His neighbors, then, and the people who had seen him begging before this, asked, "Isn't this the man who used to sit and beg?"

9 Some said, "He is the one," but others said, "No he isn't; he just looks like him."

So the man himself said, "I am the man."

10 "How is it that you can now see?" they asked him.

11 He answered, "The man called Jesus made some mud, rubbed it on my eyes, and told me to go to Siloam and wash my face. So I went, and as soon as I washed, I could see."

12 "Where is he?" they asked.

"I don't know," he answered.

The Pharisees Investigate the Healing

13 Then they took to the Pharisees the man who had been blind. 14 The day that Jesus made the mud and cured him of his blindness was a Sabbath. 15 The Pharisees, then, asked the man again how he had received his sight. He told them, "He put some mud on my eyes; I washed my face, and now I can see."

16 Some of the Pharisees said, "The man who did this cannot be from God, for he does not obey the Sabbath law."

Others, however, said, "How could a man who is a sinner perform such miracles as these?" And there was a division among them.

17 So the Pharisees asked the man once more, "You say he cured you of your blindness — well, what do you say about him?"

"He is a prophet," the man answered.

18 The Jewish authorities, however, were not willing to believe that he had been blind and could now see, until they called his parents 19 and asked them, "Is this your son? You say that he

was born blind; how is it, then, that he can now see?"

20 His parents answered, "We know that he is our son, and we know that he was born blind. 21 But we do not know how it is that he is now able to see, nor do we know who cured him of his blindness. Ask him; he is old enough, and he can answer for himself!" 22 His parents said this because they were afraid of the Jewish authorities, who had already agreed that anyone who said he believed that Jesus was the Messiah would be expelled from the synagogue. 23 That is why his parents said, "He is old enough; ask him!"

24 A second time they called back the man who had been born blind, and said to him, "Promise before God that you will tell the truth! We know that this man who cured you is a sinner."

25 "I do not know if he is a sinner or not," the man replied. "One thing I do know: I was blind, and now I see."

26 "What did he do to you?" they asked. "How did he cure you of your blindness?"

27 "I have already told you," he answered, "and you would not listen. Why do you want to hear it again? Maybe you, too, would like to be his disciples?"

28 They insulted him and said, "You are that fellow's disciple; but we are Moses' disciples. 29 We know that God spoke to Moses; as for that fellow, however, we do not even know where he comes from!"

30 The man answered, "What a strange thing that is! You do not know where he comes from, but he cured me of my blindness! 31 We know that God does not listen to sinners; he does listen to people who respect him and do what he wants them to do. 32 Since the beginning of the world nobody has ever heard of anyone giving sight to a person born blind. 33 Unless this man came from God, he would not be able to do a thing."

34 They answered, "You were born and brought up in sin — and you are try-

ing to teach us?" And they expelled him from the synagogue.

Spiritual Blindness

35 When Jesus heard what had happened, he found the man and asked him, "Do you believe in the Son of Man?"

36 The man answered, "Tell me who he is, sir, so that I can believe in him!"

37 Jesus said to him, "You have already seen him, and he is the one who is talking with you now."

38 "I believe, Lord!" the man said, and knelt down before Jesus.

39 Jesus said, "I came to this world to judge, so that the blind should see and those who see should become blind."

40 Some Pharisees who were there with him heard him say this and asked him, "Surely you don't mean that we are blind, too?"

41 Jesus answered, "If you were blind, then you would not be guilty; but since you claim that you can see, this means that you are still guilty."

The Parable of the Shepherd

10 Jesus said, "I am telling you the truth: the man who does not enter the sheep pen by the gate, but climbs in some other way, is a thief and a robber. **2** The man who goes in through the gate is the shepherd of the sheep. **3** The gatekeeper opens the gate for him; the sheep hear his voice as he calls his own sheep by name, and he leads them out. **4** When he has brought them out, he goes ahead of them, and the sheep follow him, because they know his voice. **5** They will not follow someone else; instead, they will run away from such a person, because they do not know his voice."

6 Jesus told them this parable, but they did not understand what he meant.

Jesus the Good Shepherd

7 So Jesus said again, "I am telling you the truth: I am the gate for the sheep. **8** All others who came before me are thieves and robbers, but the sheep did not listen to them. **9** I am the gate. Those who come in by me will be saved; they will come in and go out and find pasture. **10** The thief comes only in order to steal, kill, and destroy. I have come in order that you might have life — life in all its fullness.

11 "I am the good shepherd, who is willing to die for the sheep. **12** When the hired man, who is not a shepherd and does not own the sheep, sees a wolf coming, he leaves the sheep and runs away; so the wolf snatches the sheep and scatters them. **13** The hired man runs away because he is only a hired man and does not care about the sheep. **14-15** I am the good shepherd. As the Father knows me and I know the Father, in the same way I know my sheep and they know me. And I am willing to die for them. **16** There are other sheep which belong to me that are not in this sheep pen. I must bring them, too; they will listen to my voice, and they will become[v] one flock with one shepherd.

17 "The Father loves me because I am willing to give up my life, in order that I may receive it back again. **18** No one takes my life away from me. I give it up of my own free will. I have the right to give it up, and I have the right to take it back. This is what my Father has commanded me to do."

19 Again there was a division among the people because of these words. **20** Many of them were saying, "He has a demon! He is crazy! Why do you listen to him?"

21 But others were saying, "A man with a demon could not talk like this!

---

v they will become; *some manuscripts have* there will be.
10.11 Si 18.13   **10.15** Mt 11.27; Lk 10.22

How could a demon give sight to blind people?"

Jesus Is Rejected

22 It was winter, and the Festival of the Dedication of the Temple was being celebrated in Jerusalem. 23 Jesus was walking in Solomon's Porch in the Temple, 24 when the people gathered around him and asked, "How long are you going to keep us in suspense? Tell us the plain truth: are you the Messiah?"

25 Jesus answered, "I have already told you, but you would not believe me. The deeds I do by my Father's authority speak on my behalf; 26 but you will not believe, for you are not my sheep. 27 My sheep listen to my voice; I know them, and they follow me. 28 I give them eternal life, and they shall never die. No one can snatch them away from me. 29 What my Father has given me is greater*w* than everything, and no one can snatch them away from the Father's care. 30 The Father and I are one."

31 Then the people again picked up stones to throw at him. 32 Jesus said to them, "I have done many good deeds in your presence which the Father gave me to do; for which one of these do you want to stone me?"

33 They answered, "We do not want to stone you because of any good deeds, but because of your blasphemy! You are only a man, but you are trying to make yourself God!"

34 Jesus answered, "It is written in your own Law that God said, 'You are gods.' 35 We know that what the scripture says is true forever; and God called those people gods, the people to whom his message was given. 36 As for me, the Father chose me and sent me into the world. How, then, can you say that I blaspheme because I said that I am the Son of God? 37 Do not believe me, then, if I am not doing the things my Father wants me to do. 38 But if I do them, even though you do not believe me, you should at least believe my deeds, in order that you may know once and for all that the Father is in me and that I am in the Father."

39 Once more they tried to seize Jesus, but he slipped out of their hands.

40 Jesus then went back again across the Jordan River to the place where John had been baptizing, and he stayed there. 41 Many people came to him. "John performed no miracles," they said, "but everything he said about this man was true." 42 And many people there believed in him.

The Death of Lazarus

11 A man named Lazarus, who lived in Bethany, became sick. Bethany was the town where Mary and her sister Martha lived. (2 This Mary was the one who poured the perfume on the Lord's feet and wiped them with her hair; it was her brother Lazarus who was sick.) 3 The sisters sent Jesus a message: "Lord, your dear friend is sick."

4 When Jesus heard it, he said, "The final result of this sickness will not be the death of Lazarus; this has happened in order to bring glory to God, and it will be the means by which the Son of God will receive glory."

5 Jesus loved Martha and her sister and Lazarus. 6 Yet when he received the news that Lazarus was sick, he stayed where he was for two more days. 7 Then he said to the disciples, "Let us go back to Judea."

8 "Teacher," the disciples answered,

---

w What my Father has given me is greater; *some manuscripts have* My Father, who gave them to me, is greater.

10.22 1 Macc 4.36, 52-59; 2 Macc 1.18; 10.5   **10.29** Ws 3.1   **10.33** Lv 24.16
10.34 Ps 82.6   **10.40** Jn 1.28   **11.1** Lk 10.38, 39   **11.2** Jn 12.3

"just a short time ago the people there wanted to stone you; and are you planning to go back?"

9 Jesus said, "A day has twelve hours, doesn't it? So those who walk in broad daylight do not stumble, for they see the light of this world. **10** But if they walk during the night they stumble, because they have no light." **11** Jesus said this and then added, "Our friend Lazarus has fallen asleep, but I will go and wake him up."

12 The disciples answered, "If he is asleep, Lord, he will get well."

13 Jesus meant that Lazarus had died, but they thought he meant natural sleep. **14** So Jesus told them plainly, "Lazarus is dead, **15** but for your sake I am glad that I was not with him, so that you will believe. Let us go to him."

16 Thomas (called the Twin) said to his fellow disciples, "Let us all go along with the Teacher, so that we may die with him!"

Jesus the Resurrection and the Life

17 When Jesus arrived, he found that Lazarus had been buried four days before. **18** Bethany was less than two miles from Jerusalem, **19** and many Judeans had come to see Martha and Mary to comfort them about their brother's death.

20 When Martha heard that Jesus was coming, she went out to meet him, but Mary stayed in the house. **21** Martha said to Jesus, "If you had been here, Lord, my brother would not have died! **22** But I know that even now God will give you whatever you ask him for."

23 "Your brother will rise to life," Jesus told her.

24 "I know," she replied, "that he will rise to life on the last day."

25 Jesus said to her, "I am the resurrection and the life. Those who believe in me will live, even though they die;

26 and those who live and believe in me will never die. Do you believe this?"

27 "Yes, Lord!" she answered. "I do believe that you are the Messiah, the Son of God, who was to come into the world."

Jesus Weeps

28 After Martha said this, she went back and called her sister Mary privately. "The Teacher is here," she told her, "and is asking for you." **29** When Mary heard this, she got up and hurried out to meet him. (**30** Jesus had not yet arrived in the village, but was still in the place where Martha had met him.) **31** The people who were in the house with Mary comforting her followed her when they saw her get up and hurry out. They thought that she was going to the grave to weep there.

32 Mary arrived where Jesus was, and as soon as she saw him, she fell at his feet. "Lord," she said, "if you had been here, my brother would not have died!"

33 Jesus saw her weeping, and he saw how the people with her were weeping also; his heart was touched, and he was deeply moved. **34** "Where have you buried him?" he asked them.

"Come and see, Lord," they answered.

35 Jesus wept. **36** "See how much he loved him!" the people said.

37 But some of them said, "He gave sight to the blind man, didn't he? Could he not have kept Lazarus from dying?"

Lazarus Is Brought to Life

38 Deeply moved once more, Jesus went to the tomb, which was a cave with a stone placed at the entrance. **39** "Take the stone away!" Jesus ordered.

Martha, the dead man's sister, answered, "There will be a bad smell, Lord. He has been buried four days!"

40 Jesus said to her, "Didn't I tell you that you would see God's glory if you

11.24 2 Macc 7.22, 23; 12.44

believed?" [41] They took the stone away. Jesus looked up and said, "I thank you, Father, that you listen to me. [42] I know that you always listen to me, but I say this for the sake of the people here, so that they will believe that you sent me." [43] After he had said this, he called out in

"Lazarus, come out!" (11.43)

a loud voice, "Lazarus, come out!" [44] He came out, his hands and feet wrapped in grave cloths, and with a cloth around his face. "Untie him," Jesus told them, "and let him go."

The Plot against Jesus
(Matthew 26.1-5; Mark 14.1, 2; Luke 22.1, 2)

[45] Many of the people who had come to visit Mary saw what Jesus did, and they believed in him. [46] But some of them returned to the Pharisees and told them what Jesus had done. [47] So the Pharisees and the chief priests met with the Council and said, "What shall we do? Look at all the miracles this man is performing! [48] If we let him go on in this way, everyone will believe in him, and the Roman authorities will take action and destroy our Temple and our nation!"

[49] One of them, named Caiaphas, who was High Priest that year, said, "What fools you are! [50] Don't you realize that it is better for you to have one man die for the people, instead of having the whole nation destroyed?" [51] Actually, he

did not say this of his own accord; rather, as he was High Priest that year, he was prophesying that Jesus was going to die for the Jewish people, [52] and not only for them, but also to bring together into one body all the scattered people of God.

[53] From that day on the Jewish authorities made plans to kill Jesus. [54] So Jesus did not travel openly in Judea, but left and went to a place near the desert, to a town named Ephraim, where he stayed with the disciples.

[55] The time for the Passover Festival was near, and many people went up from the country to Jerusalem to perform the ritual of purification before the festival. [56] They were looking for Jesus, and as they gathered in the Temple, they asked one another, "What do you think? Surely he will not come to the festival, will he?" [57] The chief priests and the Pharisees had given orders that if anyone knew where Jesus was, he must report it, so that they could arrest him.

Jesus Is Anointed at Bethany
(Matthew 26.6-13; Mark 14.3-9)

12 Six days before the Passover, Jesus went to Bethany, the home of Lazarus, the man he had raised from death. [2] They prepared a dinner for him there, which Martha helped serve; Lazarus was one of those who were sitting at the table with Jesus. [3] Then Mary took a whole pint of a very expensive perfume made of pure nard, poured it on Jesus' feet, and wiped them with her hair. The sweet smell of the perfume filled the whole house. [4] One of Jesus' disciples, Judas Iscariot — the one who was going to betray him — said, [5] "Why wasn't this perfume sold for three hundred silver coins[x] and the money given to the poor?" [6] He said this, not because he

[x] SILVER COINS: *See* 6.7.
12.3 Lk 7.37, 38

cared about the poor, but because he was a thief. He carried the money bag and would help himself from it.

[7] But Jesus said, "Leave her alone! Let her keep what she has for the day of my burial. [8] You will always have poor people with you, but you will not always have me."

The Plot against Lazarus

[9] A large number of people heard that Jesus was in Bethany, so they went there, not only because of Jesus but also to see Lazarus, whom Jesus had raised from death. [10] So the chief priests made plans to kill Lazarus too, [11] because on his account many Jews were rejecting them and believing in Jesus.

The Triumphant Entry into Jerusalem
(Matthew 21.1-11; Mark 11.1-11; Luke 19.28-40)

[12] The next day the large crowd that had come to the Passover Festival heard that Jesus was coming to Jerusalem. [13] So they took branches of palm trees and went out to meet him, shouting, "Praise God! God bless him who comes in the name of the Lord! God bless the King of Israel!"

[14] Jesus found a donkey and rode on it, just as the scripture says,

[15] "Do not be afraid, city of Zion!
Here comes your king,
    riding on a young donkey."

[16] His disciples did not understand this at the time; but when Jesus had been raised to glory, they remembered that the scripture said this about him and that they had done this for him. [17] The people who had been with Jesus when he called Lazarus out of the grave and raised him from death had reported what had happened. [18] That was why the crowd met him — because they heard that he had performed this miracle. [19] The Pharisees then said to one another, "You see, we are not succeeding at all! Look, the whole world is following him!"

Some Greeks Seek Jesus

[20] Some Greeks were among those who had gone to Jerusalem to worship during the festival. [21] They went to Philip (he was from Bethsaida in Galilee) and said, "Sir, we want to see Jesus."

[22] Philip went and told Andrew, and the two of them went and told Jesus. [23] Jesus answered them, "The hour has now come for the Son of Man to receive great glory. [24] I am telling you the truth: a grain of wheat remains no more than a single grain unless it is dropped into the ground and dies. If it does die, then it produces many grains. [25] Those who love their own life will lose it; those who hate their own life in this world will keep it for life eternal. [26] Whoever wants to serve me must follow me, so that my servant will be with me where I am. And my Father will honor anyone who serves me.

Jesus Speaks about His Death

[27] "Now my heart is troubled — and what shall I say? Shall I say, 'Father, do not let this hour come upon me'? But that is why I came — so that I might go through this hour of suffering. [28] Father, bring glory to your name!"

Then a voice spoke from heaven, "I have brought glory to it, and I will do so again."

[29] The crowd standing there heard the voice, and some of them said it was thunder, while others said, "An angel spoke to him!"

[30] But Jesus said to them, "It was not for my sake that this voice spoke, but for yours. [31] Now is the time for this world to be judged; now the ruler of this world will be overthrown. [32] When I am

12.8 Dt 15.11   **12.13** Ps 118.25, 26; 1 Macc 13.51   **12.15** Zec 9.9   **12.25** Mt 10.39;
16.25; Mk 8.35; Lk 9.24; 17.33

lifted up from the earth, I will draw everyone to me." (³³In saying this he indicated the kind of death he was going to suffer.)

³⁴The crowd answered, "Our Law tells us that the Messiah will live forever. How, then, can you say that the Son of Man must be lifted up? Who is this Son of Man?"

³⁵Jesus answered, "The light will be among you a little longer. Continue on your way while you have the light, so that the darkness will not come upon you; for the one who walks in the dark does not know where he is going. ³⁶Believe in the light, then, while you have it, so that you will be the people of the light."

The Unbelief of the People

After Jesus said this, he went off and hid himself from them. ³⁷Even though he had performed all these miracles in their presence, they did not believe in him, ³⁸so that what the prophet Isaiah had said might come true:

"Lord, who believed the message we told?
To whom did the Lord reveal his power?"

³⁹And so they were not able to believe, because Isaiah also said,

⁴⁰"God has blinded their eyes
and closed their minds,
so that their eyes would not see,
and their minds would not understand,
and they would not turn to me, says God,
for me to heal them."

⁴¹Isaiah said this because he saw Jesus' glory and spoke about him.

⁴²Even then, many Jewish authorities believed in Jesus; but because of the Pharisees they did not talk about it openly, so as not to be expelled from the synagogue. ⁴³They loved human approval rather than the approval of God.

Judgment by Jesus' Words

⁴⁴Jesus said in a loud voice, "Whoever believes in me believes not only in me but also in him who sent me. ⁴⁵Whoever sees me sees also him who sent me. ⁴⁶I have come into the world as light, so that everyone who believes in me should not remain in the darkness. ⁴⁷If people hear my message and do not obey it, I will not judge them. I came, not to judge the world, but to save it. ⁴⁸Those who reject me and do not accept my message have one who will judge them. The words I have spoken will be their judge on the last day! ⁴⁹This is true, because I have not spoken on my own authority, but the Father who sent me has commanded me what I must say and speak. ⁵⁰And I know that his command brings eternal life. What I say, then, is what the Father has told me to say."

Jesus Washes His Disciples' Feet

13 It was now the day before the Passover Festival. Jesus knew that the hour had come for him to leave this world and go to the Father. He had always loved those in the world who were his own, and he loved them to the very end.

²Jesus and his disciples were at supper. The Devil had already put into the heart of Judas, the son of Simon Iscariot, the thought of betraying Jesus.ʸ ³Jesus knew that the Father had given him complete power; he knew that he had come from God and was going to God. ⁴So he rose from the table, took off his outer garment, and tied a towel around his waist. ⁵Then he poured some water into a washbasin and began to wash the disciples' feet and dry them

---

ʸ *The Devil . . . betraying Jesus; or* The Devil had already decided that Judas, the son of Simon Iscariot, would betray Jesus.
12.34 Ps 110.4; Is 9.7; Ez 37.25; Dn 7.14   **12.38** Is 53.1 (LXX)   **12.40** Is 6.10 (LXX)

The disciples looked at one another. (13.22)

with the towel around his waist. 6 He came to Simon Peter, who said to him, "Are you going to wash my feet, Lord?"

7 Jesus answered him, "You do not understand now what I am doing, but you will understand later."

8 Peter declared, "Never at any time will you wash my feet!"

"If I do not wash your feet," Jesus answered, "you will no longer be my disciple."

9 Simon Peter answered, "Lord, do not wash only my feet, then! Wash my hands and head, too!"

10 Jesus said, "Those who have taken a bath are completely clean and do not have to wash themselves, except for their feet. z All of you are clean — all except one." (11 Jesus already knew who was going to betray him; that is why he said, "All of you, except one, are clean.")

12 After Jesus had washed their feet, he put his outer garment back on and returned to his place at the table. "Do you understand what I have just done to you?" he asked. 13 "You call me Teacher and Lord, and it is right that you do so, because that is what I am. 14 I, your Lord and Teacher, have just washed your feet. You, then, should wash one another's feet. 15 I have set an example for you, so that you will do just what I have done for you. 16 I am telling you the truth: no slaves are greater than their master, and no messengers are greater than the one who sent them. 17 Now that you know this truth, how happy you will be if you put it into practice!

18 "I am not talking about all of you; I know those I have chosen. But the scripture must come true that says, 'The man who shared my food turned against me.' 19 I tell you this now before it happens, so that when it does happen, you will believe that 'I Am Who I Am.' 20 I am telling you the truth: whoever receives anyone I send receives me also; and whoever receives me receives him who sent me."

Jesus Predicts His Betrayal
(Matthew 26.20-25; Mark 14.17-21; Luke 22.21-23)

21 After Jesus had said this, he was deeply troubled and declared openly, "I am telling you the truth: one of you is going to betray me."

22 The disciples looked at one another, completely puzzled about whom he meant. 23 One of the disciples, the one whom Jesus loved, was sitting next to Jesus. 24 Simon Peter motioned to him and said, "Ask him whom he is talking about."

25 So that disciple moved closer to Jesus' side and asked, "Who is it, Lord?"

26 Jesus answered, "I will dip some bread in the sauce and give it to him; he is the man." So he took a piece of bread, dipped it, and gave it to Judas, the son of Simon Iscariot. 27 As soon as Judas took the bread, Satan entered into him. Jesus said to him, "Hurry and do what you must!" 28 None of the others at the table understood why Jesus said this to him. 29 Since Judas was in charge of the

z *Some manuscripts do not have* except for their feet.
13.12-15 Lk 22.27 **13.16** Mt 10.24; Lk 6.40; Jn 15.20 **13.18** Ps 41.9 **13.20** Mt 10.40; Mk 9.37; Lk 9.48; 10.16

money bag, some of the disciples thought that Jesus had told him to go and buy what they needed for the festival, or to give something to the poor.

30 Judas accepted the bread and went out at once. It was night.

The New Commandment

31 After Judas had left, Jesus said, "Now the Son of Man's glory is revealed; now God's glory is revealed through him. 32 And if God's glory is revealed through him, then God will reveal the glory of the Son of Man in himself, and he will do so at once. 33 My children, I shall not be with you very much longer. You will look for me; but I tell you now what I told the Jewish authorities, 'You cannot go where I am going.' 34 And now I give you a new commandment: love one another. As I have loved you, so you must love one another. 35 If you have love for one another, then everyone will know that you are my disciples."

Jesus Predicts Peter's Denial
(Matthew 26.31-35; Mark 14.27-31; Luke 22.31-34)

36 "Where are you going, Lord?" Simon Peter asked him.

"You cannot follow me now where I am going," answered Jesus; "but later you will follow me."

37 "Lord, why can't I follow you now?" asked Peter. "I am ready to die for you!"

38 Jesus answered, "Are you really ready to die for me? I am telling you the truth: before the rooster crows you will say three times that you do not know me.

Jesus the Way to the Father

14 "Do not be worried and upset," Jesus told them. "Believe*a* in God and believe also in me. 2 There are many rooms in my Father's house, and I am going to prepare a place for you. I would not tell you this if it were not so.*b* 3 And after I go and prepare a place for you, I will come back and take you to myself, so that you will be where I am. 4 You know the way that leads to the place where I am going."

5 Thomas said to him, "Lord, we do not know where you are going; so how can we know the way to get there?"

6 Jesus answered him, "I am the way, the truth, and the life; no one goes to the Father except by me. 7 Now that you have known me," he said to them, "you will know*c* my Father also, and from now on you do know him and you have seen him."

8 Philip said to him, "Lord, show us the Father; that is all we need."

9 Jesus answered, "For a long time I have been with you all; yet you do not know me, Philip? Whoever has seen me has seen the Father. Why, then, do you say, 'Show us the Father'? 10 Do you not believe, Philip, that I am in the Father and the Father is in me? The words that I have spoken to you," Jesus said to his disciples, "do not come from me. The Father, who remains in me, does his own work. 11 Believe me when I say that I am in the Father and the Father is in me. If not, believe because of the things I do. 12 I am telling you the truth: those who believe in me will do what I do — yes, they will do even greater things, because I am going to the Father. 13 And I will do whatever you ask for in my name, so that the Father's glory will be shown through the Son. 14 If you

---

a Believe; *or* You believe.   *b* There are . . . were not so; *or* There are many rooms in my Father's house; if it were not so, would I tell you that I am going to prepare a place for you?   *c* Now that you have known me . . . you will know; *some manuscripts have* If you had known me . . . you would know.

13.33 Jn 7.34   **13.34** Jn 15.12, 17; 1 Jn 3.23; 2 Jn 5   **14.6** Ba 3.13, 14 ask me[d] for anything in my name, I will do it.

The Promise of the Holy Spirit

15 "If you love me, you will obey my commandments. **16** I will ask the Father, and he will give you another Helper, who will stay with you forever. **17** He is the Spirit, who reveals the truth about God. The world cannot receive him, because it cannot see him or know him. But you know him, because he remains with you and is[e] in you.

18 "When I go, you will not be left all alone; I will come back to you. **19** In a little while the world will see me no more, but you will see me; and because I live, you also will live. **20** When that day comes, you will know that I am in my Father and that you are in me, just as I am in you.

21 "Those who accept my commandments and obey them are the ones who love me. My Father will love those who love me; I too will love them and reveal myself to them."

22 Judas (not Judas Iscariot) said, "Lord, how can it be that you will reveal yourself to us and not to the world?"

23 Jesus answered him, "Those who love me will obey my teaching. My Father will love them, and my Father and I will come to them and live with them. **24** Those who do not love me do not obey my teaching. And the teaching you have heard is not mine, but comes from the Father, who sent me.

25 "I have told you this while I am still with you. **26** The Helper, the Holy Spirit, whom the Father will send in my name, will teach you everything and make you remember all that I have told you.

27 "Peace is what I leave with you; it is my own peace that I give you. I do not give it as the world does. Do not be worried and upset; do not be afraid. **28** You heard me say to you, 'I am leaving, but

I will come back to you.' If you loved me, you would be glad that I am going to the Father; for he is greater than I. **29** I have told you this now before it all happens, so that when it does happen, you will believe. **30** I cannot talk with you much longer, because the ruler of this world is coming. He has no power over me, **31** but the world must know that I love the Father; that is why I do everything as he commands me.

"Come, let us go from this place.

Jesus the Real Vine

15 "I am the real vine, and my Father is the gardener. **2** He breaks off every branch in me that does not bear fruit, and he prunes every branch that does bear fruit, so that it will be clean and bear more fruit. **3** You have been made clean already by the teaching I have given you. **4** Remain united to me, and I will remain united to you. A branch cannot bear fruit by itself; it can do so only if it remains in the vine. In the same way you cannot bear fruit unless you remain in me.

5 "I am the vine, and you are the branches. Those who remain in me, and I in them, will bear much fruit; for you can do nothing without me. **6** Those who do not remain in me are thrown out like a branch and dry up; such branches are gathered up and thrown into the fire, where they are burned. **7** If you remain in me and my words remain in you, then you will ask for anything you wish, and you shall have it. **8** My Father's glory is shown by your bearing much fruit; and in this way you become my disciples. **9** I love you just as the Father loves me; remain in my love. **10** If you obey my commands, you will remain in my love, just as I have obeyed my Father's commands and remain in his love.

11 "I have told you this so that my joy

---

[d] *Some manuscripts do not have* me.   [e] *is; some manuscripts have* will be.
14.15 Ws 6.18   **14.21** Ws 6.12, 18; Si 4.14

may be in you and that your joy may be complete. 12 My commandment is this: love one another, just as I love you. 13 The greatest love you can have for your friends is to give your life for them. 14 And you are my friends if you do what I command you. 15 I do not call you servants any longer, because servants do not know what their master is doing. Instead, I call you friends, because I have told you everything I heard from my Father. 16 You did not choose me; I chose you and appointed you to go and bear much fruit, the kind of fruit that endures. And so the Father will give you whatever you ask of him in my name. 17 This, then, is what I command you: love one another.

The World's Hatred

18 "If the world hates you, just remember that it has hated me first. 19 If you belonged to the world, then the world would love you as its own. But I chose you from this world, and you do not belong to it; that is why the world hates you. 20 Remember what I told you: 'Slaves are not greater than their master.' If people persecuted me, they will persecute you too; if they obeyed my teaching, they will obey yours too. 21 But they will do all this to you because you are mine; for they do not know the one who sent me. 22 They would not have been guilty of sin if I had not come and spoken to them; as it is, they no longer have any excuse for their sin. 23 Whoever hates me hates my Father also. 24 They would not have been guilty of sin if I had not done among them the things that no one else ever did; as it is, they have seen what I did, and they hate both me and my Father. 25 This, however, was bound to happen so that what is written in their Law may come true: 'They hated me for no reason at all.'

26 "The Helper will come — the Spirit, who reveals the truth about God and who comes from the Father. I will send him to you from the Father, and he will speak about me. 27 And you, too, will speak about me, because you have been with me from the very beginning.

16 "I have told you this, so that you will not give up your faith. 2 You will be expelled from the synagogues, and the time will come when those who kill you will think that by doing this they are serving God. 3 People will do these things to you because they have not known either the Father or me. 4 But I have told you this, so that when the time comes for them to do these things, you will remember what I told you.

The Work of the Holy Spirit

"I did not tell you these things at the beginning, for I was with you. 5 But now I am going to him who sent me, yet none of you asks me where I am going. 6 And now that I have told you, your hearts are full of sadness. 7 But I am telling you the truth: it is better for you that I go away, because if I do not go, the Helper will not come to you. But if I do go away, then I will send him to you. 8 And when he comes, he will prove to the people of the world that they are wrong about sin and about what is right and about God's judgment. 9 They are wrong about sin, because they do not believe in me; 10 they are wrong about what is right, because I am going to the Father and you will not see me any more; 11 and they are wrong about judgment, because the ruler of this world has already been judged.

12 "I have much more to tell you, but now it would be too much for you to bear. 13 When, however, the Spirit comes, who reveals the truth about

15.12 Jn 13.34; 15.17; 1 Jn 3.23; 2 Jn 5   **15.20** Mt 10.24; Lk 6.40; Jn 13.16
15.25 Ps 35.19; 69.4   **16.13** Ws 9.11

God, he will lead you into all the truth. He will not speak on his own authority, but he will speak of what he hears and will tell you of things to come. 14 He will give me glory, because he will take what I say and tell it to you. 15 All that my Father has is mine; that is why I said that the Spirit will take what I give him and tell it to you.

Sadness and Gladness

16 "In a little while you will not see me any more, and then a little while later you will see me."

17 Some of his disciples asked among themselves, "What does this mean? He tells us that in a little while we will not see him, and then a little while later we will see him; and he also says, 'It is because I am going to the Father.' 18 What does this 'a little while' mean? We don't know what he is talking about!"

19 Jesus knew that they wanted to question him, so he said to them, "I said, 'In a little while you will not see me, and then a little while later you will see me.' Is this what you are asking about among yourselves? 20 I am telling you the truth: you will cry and weep, but the world will be glad; you will be sad, but your sadness will turn into gladness. 21 When a woman is about to give birth, she is sad because her hour of suffering has come; but when the baby is born, she forgets her suffering, because she is happy that a baby has been born into the world. 22 That is how it is with you: now you are sad, but I will see you again, and your hearts will be filled with gladness, the kind of gladness that no one can take away from you.

23 "When that day comes, you will not ask me for anything. I am telling you the truth: the Father will give you whatever you ask of him in my name.ƒ
24 Until now you have not asked for any-

thing in my name; ask and you will receive, so that your happiness may be complete.

Victory over the World

25 "I have used figures of speech to tell you these things. But the time will come when I will not use figures of speech, but will speak to you plainly about the Father. 26 When that day comes, you will ask him in my name; and I do not say that I will ask him on your behalf, 27 for the Father himself loves you. He loves you because you love me and have believed that I came from God. 28 I did come from the Father, and I came into the world; and now I am leaving the world and going to the Father."

29 Then his disciples said to him, "Now you are speaking plainly, without using figures of speech. 30 We know now that you know everything; you do not need to have someone ask you questions. This makes us believe that you came from God."

31 Jesus answered them, "Do you believe now? 32 The time is coming, and is already here, when all of you will be scattered, each of you to your own home, and I will be left all alone. But I am not really alone, because the Father is with me. 33 I have told you this so that you will have peace by being united to me. The world will make you suffer. But be brave! I have defeated the world!"

Jesus Prays for His Disciples

17 After Jesus finished saying this, he looked up to heaven and said, "Father, the hour has come. Give glory to your Son, so that the Son may give glory to you. 2 For you gave him authority over all people, so that he might give eternal life to all those you

---

ƒ the Father will give you whatever you ask of him in my name; *some manuscripts have* if you ask the Father for anything, he will give it to you in my name.

"Father, the hour has come." (17.1)

I came from you, and they believe that you sent me.

9 "I pray for them. I do not pray for the world but for those you gave me, for they belong to you. 10 All I have is yours, and all you have is mine; and my glory is shown through them. 11 And now I am coming to you; I am no longer in the world, but they are in the world. Holy Father! Keep them safe by the power of your name, the name you gave me,*g* so that they may be one just as you and I are one. 12 While I was with them, I kept them safe by the power of your name, the name you gave me.*h* I protected them, and not one of them was lost, except the man who was bound to be lost — so that the scripture might come true. 13 And now I am coming to you, and I say these things in the world so that they might have my joy in their hearts in all its fullness. 14 I gave them your message, and the world hated them, because they do not belong to the world, just as I do not belong to the world. 15 I do not ask you to take them out of the world, but I do ask you to keep them safe from the Evil One. 16 Just as I do not belong to the world, they do not belong to the world. 17 Dedicate them to yourself by means of the truth; your word is truth. 18 I sent them into the world, just as you sent me into the world. 19 And for their sake I dedicate myself to you, in order that they, too, may be truly dedicated to you.

20 "I pray not only for them, but also for those who believe in me because of their message. 21 I pray that they may all be one. Father! May they be in us, just as you are in me and I am in you. May they be one, so that the world will believe that you sent me. 22 I gave them the same glory you gave me, so that

gave him. 3 And eternal life means to know you, the only true God, and to know Jesus Christ, whom you sent. 4 I have shown your glory on earth; I have finished the work you gave me to do. 5 Father! Give me glory in your presence now, the same glory I had with you before the world was made.

6 "I have made you known to those you gave me out of the world. They belonged to you, and you gave them to me. They have obeyed your word, 7 and now they know that everything you gave me comes from you. 8 I gave them the message that you gave me, and they received it; they know that it is true that

g Keep them safe by the power of your name, the name you gave me; *some manuscripts have* By the power of your name keep safe those you have given me.
h I kept them safe by the power of your name, the name you gave me; *some manuscripts have* By the power of your name I kept safe those you have given me.
17.3 Ws 15.3   **17.12** Ps 41.9; 2 Esd 2.26; Jn 13.18

they may be one, just as you and I are one: 23 I in them and you in me, so that they may be completely one, in order that the world may know that you sent me and that you love them as you love me.

24 "Father! You have given them to me, and I want them to be with me where I am, so that they may see my glory, the glory you gave me; for you loved me before the world was made. 25 Righteous Father! The world does not know you, but I know you, and these know that you sent me. 26 I made you known to them, and I will continue to do so, in order that the love you have for me may be in them, and so that I also may be in them."

The Arrest of Jesus
(Matthew 26.47-56; Mark 14.43-50; Luke 22.47-53)

18 After Jesus had said this prayer, he left with his disciples and went across Kidron Brook. There was a garden in that place, and Jesus and his disciples went in. 2 Judas, the traitor, knew where it was, because many times Jesus had met there with his disciples. 3 So Judas went to the garden, taking with him a group of Roman soldiers, and some Temple guards sent by the chief priests and the Pharisees; they were armed and carried lanterns and torches. 4 Jesus knew everything that was going to happen to him, so he stepped forward and asked them, "Who is it you are looking for?"

5 "Jesus of Nazareth," they answered.

"I am he," he said.

Judas, the traitor, was standing there with them. 6 When Jesus said to them, "I am he," they moved back and fell to the ground. 7 Again Jesus asked them, "Who is it you are looking for?"

"Jesus of Nazareth," they said.

8 "I have already told you that I am he," Jesus said. "If, then, you are looking for me, let these others go." (9 He said this so that what he had said might come true: "Father, I have not lost even one of those you gave me.")

10 Simon Peter, who had a sword, drew it and struck the High Priest's slave, cutting off his right ear. The name of the slave was Malchus. 11 Jesus said to Peter, "Put your sword back in its place! Do you think that I will not drink the cup of suffering which my Father has given me?"

Jesus before Annas

12 Then the Roman soldiers with their commanding officer and the Jewish guards arrested Jesus, tied him up, 13 and took him first to Annas. He was the father-in-law of Caiaphas, who was High Priest that year. 14 It was Caiaphas who had advised the Jewish authorities that it was better that one man should die for all the people.

Peter Denies Jesus
(Matthew 26.69, 70; Mark 14.66-68; Luke 22.55-57)

15 Simon Peter and another disciple followed Jesus. That other disciple was well known to the High Priest, so he went with Jesus into the courtyard of the High Priest's house, 16 while Peter stayed outside by the gate. Then the other disciple went back out, spoke to the girl at the gate, and brought Peter inside. 17 The girl at the gate said to Peter, "Aren't you also one of the disciples of that man?"

"No, I am not," answered Peter.

18 It was cold, so the servants and guards had built a charcoal fire and were standing around it, warming themselves. So Peter went over and stood with them, warming himself.

18.11 Mt 26.39; Mk 14.36; Lk 22.42   **18.14** Jn 11.49, 50

The High Priest Questions Jesus
(Matthew 26.59-66; Mark 14.55-64; Luke 22.66-71)

19 The High Priest questioned Jesus about his disciples and about his teaching. **20** Jesus answered, "I have always spoken publicly to everyone; all my teaching was done in the synagogues and in the Temple, where all the people come together. I have never said anything in secret. **21** Why, then, do you question me? Question the people who heard me. Ask them what I told them — they know what I said."

22 When Jesus said this, one of the guards there slapped him and said, "How dare you talk like that to the High Priest!"

23 Jesus answered him, "If I have said anything wrong, tell everyone here what it was. But if I am right in what I have said, why do you hit me?"

24 Then Annas sent him, still tied up, to Caiaphas the High Priest.

Peter Denies Jesus Again
(Matthew 26.71-75; Mark 14.69-72; Luke 22.58-62)

25 Peter was still standing there keeping himself warm. So the others said to him, "Aren't you also one of the disciples of that man?"

But Peter denied it. "No, I am not," he said.

26 One of the High Priest's slaves, a relative of the man whose ear Peter had cut off, spoke up. "Didn't I see you with him in the garden?" he asked.

27 Again Peter said "No" — and at once a rooster crowed.

Jesus before Pilate
(Matthew 27.1, 2, 11-14; Mark 15.1-5; Luke 23.1-5)

28 Early in the morning Jesus was taken from Caiaphas' house to the governor's palace. The Jewish authorities did not go inside the palace, for they wanted to keep themselves ritually clean, in order to be able to eat the Passover meal. **29** So Pilate went outside to them and asked, "What do you accuse this man of?"

30 Their answer was, "We would not have brought him to you if he had not committed a crime."

31 Pilate said to them, "Then you yourselves take him and try him according to your own law."

They replied, "We are not allowed to put anyone to death." (**32** This happened in order to make come true what Jesus had said when he indicated the kind of death he would die.)

33 Pilate went back into the palace and called Jesus. "Are you the king of the Jews?" he asked him.

34 Jesus answered, "Does this question come from you or have others told you about me?"

35 Pilate replied, "Do you think I am a Jew? It was your own people and the chief priests who handed you over to me. What have you done?"

36 Jesus said, "My kingdom does not belong to this world; if my kingdom belonged to this world, my followers would fight to keep me from being handed over to the Jewish authorities. No, my kingdom does not belong here!"

37 So Pilate asked him, "Are you a king, then?"

Jesus answered, "You say that I am a king. I was born and came into the world for this one purpose, to speak about the truth. Whoever belongs to the truth listens to me."

38 "And what is truth?" Pilate asked.

Jesus Is Sentenced to Death
(Matthew 27.15-31; Mark 15.6-20; Luke 23.13-25)

Then Pilate went back outside to the people and said to them, "I cannot find

18.32 Jn 3.14; 12.32

"And what is truth?" (18.38)

any reason to condemn him. ³⁹ But according to the custom you have, I always set free a prisoner for you during the Passover. Do you want me to set free for you the king of the Jews?"

⁴⁰ They answered him with a shout, "No, not him! We want Barabbas!" (Barabbas was a bandit.)

"No, not him! We want Barabbas!" (18.40)

19 Then Pilate took Jesus and had him whipped. ² The soldiers made a crown out of thorny branches and put it on his head; then they put a purple robe on him ³ and came to him and said, "Long live the King of the Jews!" And they went up and slapped him.

⁴ Pilate went back out once more and said to the crowd, "Look, I will bring him out here to you to let you see that I cannot find any reason to condemn

him." ⁵ So Jesus came out, wearing the crown of thorns and the purple robe. Pilate said to them, "Look! Here is the man!"

⁶ When the chief priests and the Temple guards saw him, they shouted, "Crucify him! Crucify him!"

Pilate said to them, "You take him, then, and crucify him. I find no reason to condemn him."

⁷ The crowd answered back, "We have a law that says he ought to die, because he claimed to be the Son of God."

⁸ When Pilate heard this, he was even more afraid. ⁹ He went back into the palace and asked Jesus, "Where do you come from?"

But Jesus did not answer. ¹⁰ Pilate said to him, "You will not speak to me? Remember, I have the authority to set you free and also to have you crucified."

¹¹ Jesus answered, "You have authority over me only because it was given to you by God. So the man who handed me over to you is guilty of a worse sin."

¹² When Pilate heard this, he tried to find a way to set Jesus free. But the crowd shouted back, "If you set him free, that means that you are not the Emperor's friend! Anyone who claims to be a king is a rebel against the Emperor!"

¹³ When Pilate heard these words, he took Jesus outside and sat down on the judge's seat in the place called "The Stone Pavement." (In Hebrew the name is "Gabbatha.") ¹⁴ It was then almost noon of the day before the Passover. Pilate said to the people, "Here is your king!"

¹⁵ They shouted back, "Kill him! Kill him! Crucify him!"

Pilate asked them, "Do you want me to crucify your king?"

The chief priests answered, "The only king we have is the Emperor!"

¹⁶ Then Pilate handed Jesus over to them to be crucified.

19.11 Ws 6.3

Jesus Is Crucified
(Matthew 27.32-44; Mark 15.21-32;
Luke 23.26-43)

So they took charge of Jesus. ¹⁷He went out, carrying his cross, and came to "The Place of the Skull," as it is called. (In Hebrew it is called "Golgotha.") ¹⁸There they crucified him; and

He went out, carrying his cross. (19.17)

they also crucified two other men, one on each side, with Jesus between them. ¹⁹Pilate wrote a notice and had it put on the cross. "Jesus of Nazareth, the King of the Jews," is what he wrote. ²⁰Many people read it, because the place where Jesus was crucified was not far from the city. The notice was written in Hebrew, Latin, and Greek. ²¹The chief priests said to Pilate, "Do not write 'The King of the Jews,' but rather, 'This man said, I am the King of the Jews.'"

²²Pilate answered, "What I have written stays written."

²³After the soldiers had crucified Jesus, they took his clothes and divided them into four parts, one part for each soldier. They also took the robe, which was made of one piece of woven cloth without any seams in it. ²⁴The soldiers said to one another, "Let's not tear it; let's throw dice to see who will get it." This happened in order to make the scripture come true:

"They divided my clothes among
    themselves
    and gambled for my robe."
And this is what the soldiers did.

²⁵Standing close to Jesus' cross were his mother, his mother's sister, Mary the wife of Clopas, and Mary Magdalene. ²⁶Jesus saw his mother and the disciple he loved standing there; so he said to his mother, "He is your son."

²⁷Then he said to the disciple, "She is your mother." From that time the disciple took her to live in his home.

The Death of Jesus
(Matthew 27.45-56; Mark 15.33-41;
Luke 23.44-49)

²⁸Jesus knew that by now everything had been completed; and in order to make the scripture come true, he said, "I am thirsty."

²⁹A bowl was there, full of cheap wine; so a sponge was soaked in the wine, put on a stalk of hyssop, and lifted up to his lips. ³⁰Jesus drank the wine and said, "It is finished!"

Then he bowed his head and gave up his spirit.

Jesus' Side Is Pierced

³¹Then the Jewish authorities asked Pilate to allow them to break the legs of the men who had been crucified, and to take the bodies down from the crosses. They requested this because it was Friday, and they did not want the bodies to stay on the crosses on the Sabbath, since the coming Sabbath was especially holy. ³²So the soldiers went and broke the legs of the first man and then of the other man who had been crucified with Jesus. ³³But when they came to Jesus, they saw that he was already dead, so they did not break his legs. ³⁴One of the soldiers, however, plunged his spear into Jesus' side, and at once blood and water poured out. (³⁵The one who saw this happen has spoken of it,

19.24 Ps 22.18   **19.28** Ps 69.21; 22.15

so that you also may believe.*i* What he said is true, and he knows that he speaks the truth.) 36 This was done to make the scripture come true: "Not one of his bones will be broken." 37 And there is another scripture that says, "People will look at him whom they pierced."

The Burial of Jesus
(Matthew 27.57-61; Mark 15.42-47; Luke 23.50-56)

38 After this, Joseph, who was from the town of Arimathea, asked Pilate if he could take Jesus' body. (Joseph was a follower of Jesus, but in secret, because he was afraid of the Jewish authorities.) Pilate told him he could have the body, so Joseph went and took it away. 39 Nicodemus, who at first had gone to see Jesus at night, went with Joseph, taking with him about one hundred pounds of spices, a mixture of myrrh and aloes. 40 The two men took Jesus' body and wrapped it in linen cloths with the spices according to the Jewish custom of preparing a body for

The two men took Jesus' body. (19.40)

burial. 41 There was a garden in the place where Jesus had been put to death, and in it there was a new tomb where no one had ever been buried.

42 Since it was the day before the Sabbath and because the tomb was close by, they placed Jesus' body there.

The Empty Tomb
(Matthew 28.1-8; Mark 16.1-8; Luke 24.1-12)

20 Early on Sunday morning, while it was still dark, Mary Magdalene went to the tomb and saw that the stone had been taken away from the entrance. 2 She went running to Simon Peter and the other disciple, whom Jesus loved, and told them, "They have taken the Lord from the tomb, and we don't know where they have put him!"

3 Then Peter and the other disciple went to the tomb. 4 The two of them were running, but the other disciple ran faster than Peter and reached the tomb first. 5 He bent over and saw the linen cloths, but he did not go in. 6 Behind him came Simon Peter, and he went straight into the tomb. He saw the linen cloths lying there 7 and the cloth which had been around Jesus' head. It was not lying with the linen cloths but was rolled up by itself. 8 Then the other disciple, who had reached the tomb first, also went in; he saw and believed. (9 They still did not understand the scripture which said that he must rise from death.) 10 Then the disciples went back home.

Jesus Appears to Mary Magdalene
(Matthew 28.9, 10; Mark 16.9-11)

11 Mary stood crying outside the tomb. While she was still crying, she bent over and looked in the tomb 12 and saw two angels there dressed in white, sitting where the body of Jesus had been, one at the head and the other at

i believe; *some manuscripts have* continue to believe.
19.36 Ex 12.46; Nu 9.12; Ps 34.20   **19.37** Zec 12.10; Rev 1.7   **19.39** Jn 3.1, 2

the feet. ¹³"Woman, why are you crying?" they asked her.

She answered, "They have taken my Lord away, and I do not know where they have put him!"

¹⁴Then she turned around and saw Jesus standing there; but she did not know that it was Jesus. ¹⁵"Woman, why are you crying?" Jesus asked her. "Who is it that you are looking for?"

She thought he was the gardener, so she said to him, "If you took him away, sir, tell me where you have put him, and I will go and get him."

¹⁶Jesus said to her, "Mary!"

She turned toward him and said in Hebrew, "Rabboni!" (This means "Teacher.")

¹⁷"Do not hold on to me," Jesus told her, "because I have not yet gone back up to the Father. But go to my brothers and tell them that I am returning to him who is my Father and their Father, my God and their God."

¹⁸So Mary Magdalene went and told the disciples that she had seen the Lord and related to them what he had told her.

Jesus Appears to His Disciples
(Matthew 28.16-20; Mark 16.14-18; Luke 24.36-49)

¹⁹It was late that Sunday evening, and the disciples were gathered together behind locked doors, because they were afraid of the Jewish authorities. Then Jesus came and stood among them. "Peace be with you," he said. ²⁰After saying this, he showed them his hands and his side. The disciples were filled with joy at seeing the Lord. ²¹Jesus said to them again, "Peace be with you. As the Father sent me, so I send you." ²²Then he breathed on them and said, "Receive the Holy Spirit. ²³If you forgive people's sins, they are forgiven; if you do not forgive them, they are not forgiven."

Jesus and Thomas

²⁴One of the twelve disciples, Thomas (called the Twin), was not with them when Jesus came. ²⁵So the other disciples told him, "We have seen the Lord!"

Thomas said to them, "Unless I see the scars of the nails in his hands and put my finger on those scars and my hand in his side, I will not believe."

²⁶A week later the disciples were together again indoors, and Thomas was with them. The doors were locked, but Jesus came and stood among them and said, "Peace be with you." ²⁷Then he said to Thomas, "Put your finger here, and look at my hands; then reach out your hand and put it in my side. Stop your doubting, and believe!"

"Look at my hands. . . . Stop your doubting, and believe!" (20.27)

²⁸Thomas answered him, "My Lord and my God!"

²⁹Jesus said to him, "Do you believe because you see me? How happy are those who believe without seeing me!"

The Purpose of This Book

³⁰In his disciples' presence Jesus performed many other miracles which are not written down in this book. ³¹But these have been written in order that you may believe *i* that Jesus is the

---

i believe; *some manuscripts have* continue to believe.
20.23 Mt 16.19; 18.18

Messiah, the Son of God, and that through your faith in him you may have life.

Jesus Appears to Seven Disciples

21 After this, Jesus appeared once more to his disciples at Lake Tiberias. This is how it happened. ² Simon Peter, Thomas (called the Twin), Nathanael (the one from Cana in Galilee), the sons of Zebedee, and two other disciples of Jesus were all together. ³ Simon Peter said to the others, "I am going fishing."

"We will come with you," they told him. So they went out in a boat, but all that night they did not catch a thing. ⁴ As the sun was rising, Jesus stood at the water's edge, but the disciples did not know that it was Jesus. ⁵ Then he asked them, "Young men, haven't you caught anything?"

"Not a thing," they answered.

⁶ He said to them, "Throw your net out on the right side of the boat, and you will catch some." So they threw the net out and could not pull it back in, because they had caught so many fish.

⁷ The disciple whom Jesus loved said to Peter, "It is the Lord!" When Peter heard that it was the Lord, he wrapped his outer garment around him (for he had taken his clothes off) and jumped into the water. ⁸ The other disciples came to shore in the boat, pulling the net full of fish. They were not very far from land, about a hundred yards away. ⁹ When they stepped ashore, they saw a charcoal fire there with fish on it and some bread. ¹⁰ Then Jesus said to them, "Bring some of the fish you have just caught."

¹¹ Simon Peter went aboard and dragged the net ashore full of big fish, a hundred and fifty-three in all; even though there were so many, still the net did not tear. ¹² Jesus said to them, "Come and eat." None of the disciples

Simon Peter . . . dragged the net ashore. (21.11)

dared ask him, "Who are you?" because they knew it was the Lord. ¹³ So Jesus went over, took the bread, and gave it to them; he did the same with the fish.

¹⁴ This, then, was the third time Jesus appeared to the disciples after he was raised from death.

Jesus and Peter

¹⁵ After they had eaten, Jesus said to Simon Peter, "Simon son of John, do you love me more than these others do?"

"Yes, Lord," he answered, "you know that I love you."

Jesus said to him, "Take care of my lambs." ¹⁶ A second time Jesus said to him, "Simon son of John, do you love me?"

"Yes, Lord," he answered, "you know that I love you."

Jesus said to him, "Take care of my sheep." ¹⁷ A third time Jesus said, "Simon son of John, do you love me?"

Peter became sad because Jesus asked him the third time, "Do you love me?" and so he said to him, "Lord, you know everything; you know that I love you!"

Jesus said to him, "Take care of my

sheep. [18] I am telling you the truth: when you were young, you used to get ready and go anywhere you wanted to; but when you are old, you will stretch out your hands and someone else will tie you up and take you where you don't want to go." [19] (In saying this, Jesus was indicating the way in which Peter would die and bring glory to God.) Then Jesus said to him, "Follow me!"

Jesus and the Other Disciple

[20] Peter turned around and saw behind him that other disciple, whom Jesus loved — the one who had leaned close to Jesus at the meal and had asked, "Lord, who is going to betray you?" [21] When Peter saw him, he asked Jesus, "Lord, what about this man?"

21.20 Jn 13.25

[22] Jesus answered him, "If I want him to live until I come, what is that to you? Follow me!"

[23] So a report spread among the followers of Jesus that this disciple would not die. But Jesus did not say he would not die; he said, "If I want him to live until I come, what is that to you?"

[24] He is the disciple who spoke of these things, the one who also wrote them down; and we know that what he said is true.

Conclusion

[25] Now, there are many other things that Jesus did. If they were all written down one by one, I suppose that the whole world could not hold the books that would be written.

THE ACTS
of the Apostles

INTRODUCTION

The Acts of the Apostles is a continuation of *The Gospel according to Luke.* Its chief purpose is to tell how Jesus' early followers, led by the Holy Spirit, spread the Good News about him "in Jerusalem, in all of Judea and Samaria, and to the ends of the earth" (1.8). It is the story of the Christian movement as it began among the Jewish people and went on to become a faith for the whole world. The writer was also concerned to reassure his readers that the Christians were not a subversive political threat to the Roman Empire, and that the Christian faith was the fulfillment of the Jewish religion.

Acts may be divided into three principal parts, reflecting the ever widening area in which the Good News about Jesus was proclaimed and the church established: (1) the beginning of the Christian movement in Jerusalem following the ascension of Jesus; (2) expansion into other parts of Palestine; and (3) further expansion, into the Mediterranean world as far as Rome.

An important feature of *Acts* is the activity of the Holy Spirit, who comes with power upon the believers in Jerusalem on the day of Pentecost and continues to guide and strengthen the church and its leaders throughout the events reported in the book. The early Christian message is summarized in a number of sermons, and the events recorded in *Acts* show the power of this message in the lives of the believers and in the fellowship of the church.

OUTLINE OF CONTENTS

1

Dear Theophilus:
In my first book I wrote about all the things that Jesus did and taught from the time he began his work [2] until the day he was taken up to heaven. Before he was taken up, he gave instructions by the power of the Holy Spirit to the men he had chosen as his apostles. [3] For forty days after his death he appeared to them many times in ways that proved beyond doubt that he was alive. They saw him, and he talked with them about the Kingdom of God. [4] And when they came together,[a] he gave them this order: "Do not leave Jerusalem, but wait for the gift I told you about, the gift my Father promised. [5] John baptized with water, but in a few days you will be baptized with the Holy Spirit."

Jesus Is Taken Up to Heaven

[6] When the apostles met together with Jesus, they asked him, "Lord, will you at this time give the Kingdom back to Israel?"

[7] Jesus said to them, "The times and occasions are set by my Father's own authority, and it is not for you to know when they will be. [8] But when the Holy Spirit comes upon you, you will be filled with power, and you will be witnesses for me in Jerusalem, in all of Judea and Samaria, and to the ends of the earth." [9] After saying this, he was taken up to heaven as they watched him, and a cloud hid him from their sight.

[10] They still had their eyes fixed on the sky as he went away, when two men dressed in white suddenly stood beside them [11] and said, "Galileans, why are you standing there looking up at the sky? This Jesus, who was taken from you into heaven, will come back in the same way that you saw him go to heaven."

Judas' Successor

[12] Then the apostles went back to Jerusalem from the Mount of Olives, which is about half a mile away from the city. [13] They entered the city and went up to the room where they were staying: Peter, John, James and Andrew, Philip and Thomas, Bartholomew and Matthew, James son of Alphaeus, Simon the Patriot, and Judas son of James. [14] They gathered frequently to pray as a group, together with the women and with Mary the mother of Jesus and with his brothers.

[15] A few days later there was a meeting of the believers, about a hundred and twenty in all, and Peter stood up to speak. [16] "My friends," he said, "the scripture had to come true in which the Holy Spirit, speaking through David, made a prediction about Judas, who was the guide for those who arrested Jesus. [17] Judas was a member of our group, for he had been chosen to have a part in our work."

([18] With the money that Judas got for his evil act he bought a field, where he fell to his death; he burst open and all his insides spilled out. [19] All the people living in Jerusalem heard about it, and so in their own language they call that field Akeldama, which means "Field of Blood.")

[20] "For it is written in the book of Psalms,

'May his house become empty;
     may no one live in it.'
It is also written,
'May someone else take his place
        of service.'

---

[a] when they came together; *or* while he was staying with them, *or* while he was eating with them.

1.1 Lk 1.1-4   **1.4** Lk 24.49   **1.5** Mt 3.11; Mk 1.8; Lk 3.16; Jn 1.33   **1.8** Mt 28.19; Mk 16.15; Lk 24.47, 48   **1.9** Mk 16.19; Lk 24.50, 51   **1.13** Mt 10.2-4; Mk 3.16-19; Lk 6.14-16   **1.18, 19** Mt 27.3-8   **1.20 a** Ps 69.25; **b** Ps 109.8

21-22"So then, someone must join us as a witness to the resurrection of the Lord Jesus. He must be one of the men who were in our group during the whole time that the Lord Jesus traveled about with us, beginning from the time John preached his message of baptism[b] until the day Jesus was taken up from us to heaven."

23 So they proposed two men: Joseph, who was called Barsabbas (also known as Justus), and Matthias. **24** Then they prayed, "Lord, you know the thoughts of everyone, so show us which of these two you have chosen **25** to serve as an apostle in the place of Judas, who left to go to the place where he belongs." **26** Then they drew lots to choose between the two men, and the one chosen was Matthias, who was added to the group of eleven apostles.

The Coming of the Holy Spirit

2 When the day of Pentecost came, all the believers were gathered together in one place. **2** Suddenly there was a noise from the sky which sounded like a strong wind blowing, and it filled the whole house where they were sitting. **3** Then they saw what looked like tongues of fire which spread out and touched each person there. **4** They were all filled with the Holy Spirit and began to talk in other languages, as the Spirit enabled them to speak.

5 There were Jews living in Jerusalem, religious people who had come from every country in the world. **6** When they heard this noise, a large crowd gathered. They were all excited, because all of them heard the believers talking in their own languages. **7** In amazement and wonder they exclaimed, "These people who are talking like this are Galileans! **8** How is it, then,

that all of us hear them speaking in our own native languages? **9** We are from Parthia, Media, and Elam; from Mesopotamia, Judea, and Cappadocia; from Pontus and Asia, **10** from Phrygia and Pamphylia, from Egypt and the regions of Libya near Cyrene. Some of us are from Rome, **11** both Jews and Gentiles converted to Judaism, and some of us are from Crete and Arabia — yet all of us hear them speaking in our own languages about the great things that God has done!" **12** Amazed and confused, they kept asking each other, "What does this mean?"

13 But others made fun of the believers, saying, "These people are drunk!"

Peter's Message

14 Then Peter stood up with the other eleven apostles and in a loud voice began to speak to the crowd: "Fellow Jews and all of you who live in Jerusalem, listen to me and let me tell you what this

"Fellow Jews . . . listen to me!" (2.14)

means. **15** These people are not drunk, as you suppose; it is only nine o'clock in the morning. **16** Instead, this is what the prophet Joel spoke about:

17 'This is what I will do in the last days, God says:

---

[b] John preached his message of baptism; or John baptized him.

1.22 a Mt 3.16; Mk 1.9; Lk 3.21; **b** Mk 16.19; Lk 24.51   **2.1** Lv 23.15-21; Dt 16.9-11
2.17-21 Jl 2.28-32 (LXX)

I will pour out my Spirit on
everyone.
Your sons and daughters will
proclaim my message;
your young men will see
visions,
and your old men will have
dreams.
18 Yes, even on my servants, both
men and women,
I will pour out my Spirit in
those days,
and they will proclaim my
message.
19 I will perform miracles in the
sky above
and wonders on the earth
below.
There will be blood, fire, and
thick smoke;
20   the sun will be darkened,
and the moon will turn red
as blood,
before the great and glorious
Day of the Lord comes.
21 And then, whoever calls out to
the Lord for help will
be saved.'

22 "Listen to these words, fellow Israelites! Jesus of Nazareth was a man
whose divine authority was clearly
proven to you by all the miracles and
wonders which God performed through
him. You yourselves know this, for it
happened here among you. 23 In accordance with his own plan God had already decided that Jesus would be
handed over to you; and you killed him
by letting sinful men crucify him. 24 But
God raised him from death, setting him
free from its power, because it was impossible that death should hold him
prisoner. 25 For David said about him,
'I saw the Lord before me at all
times;
he is near me, and I will not
be troubled.
26 And so I am filled with gladness,

and my words are full of joy.
And I, mortal though I am,
will rest assured in hope,
27 because you will not abandon me
in the world of the dead;
you will not allow your
faithful servant to rot in
the grave.
28 You have shown me the paths
that lead to life,
and your presence will fill me
with joy.'

29 "My friends, I must speak to you
plainly about our famous ancestor King
David. He died and was buried, and his
grave is here with us to this very day.
30 He was a prophet, and he knew what
God had promised him: God had made
a vow that he would make one of David's descendants a king, just as David
was. 31 David saw what God was going
to do in the future, and so he spoke
about the resurrection of the Messiah
when he said,
'He was not abandoned in the
world of the dead;
his body did not rot in the
grave.'
32 God has raised this very Jesus from
death, and we are all witnesses to this
fact. 33 He has been raised to the right
side of God, his Father, and has received from him the Holy Spirit, as he
had promised. What you now see and
hear is his gift that he has poured out
on us. 34 For it was not David who went
up into heaven; rather he said,
'The Lord said to my Lord:
Sit here at my right side
35 until I put your enemies as a
footstool under your feet.'
36 "All the people of Israel, then, are
to know for sure that this Jesus, whom
you crucified, is the one that God has
made Lord and Messiah!"
37 When the people heard this, they
were deeply troubled and said to Peter

2.23 Mt 27.35; Mk 15.24; Lk 23.33; Jn 19.18   **2.24** Mt 28.5, 6; Mk 16.6; Lk 24.5
2.25-28 Ps 16.8-11 (LXX)   **2.30** Ps 132.11; 2 S 7.12, 13   **2.34, 35** Ps 110.1

and the other apostles, "What shall we do, brothers?"

³⁸ Peter said to them, "Each one of you must turn away from your sins and be baptized in the name of Jesus Christ, so that your sins will be forgiven; and you will receive God's gift, the Holy Spirit. ³⁹ For God's promise was made to you and your children, and to all who are far away — all whom the Lord our God calls to himself."

⁴⁰ Peter made his appeal to them and with many other words he urged them, saying, "Save yourselves from the punishment coming on this wicked people!" ⁴¹ Many of them believed his message and were baptized, and about three thousand people were added to the group that day. ⁴² They spent their time in learning from the apostles, taking part in the fellowship, and sharing in the fellowship meals and the prayers.

Life among the Believers

⁴³ Many miracles and wonders were being done through the apostles, and everyone was filled with awe. ⁴⁴ All the believers continued together in close fellowship and shared their belongings with one another. ⁴⁵ They would sell their property and possessions, and distribute the money among all, according to what each one needed. ⁴⁶ Day after day they met as a group in the Temple, and they had their meals together in their homes, eating with glad and humble hearts, ⁴⁷ praising God, and enjoying the good will of all the people. And every day the Lord added to their group those who were being saved.

A Lame Beggar Is Healed

3 One day Peter and John went to the Temple at three o'clock in the afternoon, the hour for prayer. ² There at the Beautiful Gate, as it was called, was a man who had been lame all his life. Every day he was carried to the

gate to beg for money from the people who were going into the Temple. ³ When he saw Peter and John going in, he begged them to give him something. ⁴ They looked straight at him, and Peter said, "Look at us!" ⁵ So he looked at them, expecting to get something from them. ⁶ But Peter said to him, "I have no money at all, but I give you what I have: in the name of Jesus Christ of Nazareth

"... I give you what I have." (3.6)

I order you to get up and walk!" ⁷ Then he took him by his right hand and helped him up. At once the man's feet and ankles became strong; ⁸ he jumped up, stood on his feet, and started walking around. Then he went into the Temple with them, walking and jumping and praising God. ⁹ The people there saw him walking and praising God, ¹⁰ and when they recognized him as the beggar who had sat at the Beautiful Gate, they were all surprised and amazed at what had happened to him.

Peter's Message in the Temple

¹¹ As the man held on to Peter and John in Solomon's Porch, as it was called, the people were amazed and ran to them. ¹² When Peter saw the people, he said to them, "Fellow Israelites, why are you surprised at this, and why do you stare at us? Do you think that it was by means of our own power or godliness that we made this man walk? ¹³ The

God of Abraham, Isaac, and Jacob, the God of our ancestors, has given divine glory to his Servant Jesus. But you handed him over to the authorities, and you rejected him in Pilate's presence, even after Pilate had decided to set him free. 14 He was holy and good, but you rejected him, and instead you asked Pilate to do you the favor of turning loose a murderer. 15 You killed the one who leads to life, but God raised him from death — and we are witnesses to this. 16 It was the power of his name that gave strength to this lame man. What you see and know was done by faith in his name; it was faith in Jesus that has made him well, as you can all see.

17 "And now, my friends, I know that what you and your leaders did to Jesus was due to your ignorance. 18 God announced long ago through all the prophets that his Messiah had to suffer; and he made it come true in this way. 19 Repent, then, and turn to God, so that he will forgive your sins. If you do, 20 times of spiritual strength will come from the Lord, and he will send Jesus, who is the Messiah he has already chosen for you. 21 He must remain in heaven until the time comes for all things to be made new, as God announced through his holy prophets of long ago. 22 For Moses said, 'The Lord your God will send you a prophet, just as he sent me,c and he will be one of your own people. You are to obey everything that he tells you to do. 23 Anyone who does not obey that prophet shall be separated from God's people and destroyed.' 24 And all the prophets who had a message, including Samuel and those who came after him, also announced what has been happening these days. 25 The promises of God through his prophets are for you, and you share in the covenant which God made with your ancestors. As he said to

Abraham, 'Through your descendants I will bless all the people on earth.' 26 And so God chose his Servant and sent him to you first, to bless you by making every one of you turn away from your wicked ways.''

Peter and John before the Council

4 Peter and John were still speaking to the people when some priests,d the officer in charge of the Temple guards, and some Sadducees arrived. 2 They were annoyed because the two apostles were teaching the people that Jesus had risen from death, which proved that the dead will rise to life. 3 So they arrested them and put them in jail until the next day, since it was already late. 4 But many who heard the message believed; and the number grew to about five thousand.

5 The next day the Jewish leaders, the elders, and the teachers of the Law gathered in Jerusalem. 6 They met with the High Priest Annas and with Caiaphas, John, Alexander, and the others who belonged to the High Priest's family. 7 They made the apostles stand before them and asked them, "How did you do this? What power do you have or whose name did you use?"

8 Peter, full of the Holy Spirit, answered them, "Leaders of the people and elders: 9 if we are being questioned today about the good deed done to the lame man and how he was healed, 10 then you should all know, and all the people of Israel should know, that this man stands here before you completely well through the power of the name of Jesus Christ of Nazareth — whom you crucified and whom God raised from death. 11 Jesus is the one of whom the scripture says,

'The stone that you the builders despised

---

c just as he sent me; or like me.   d priests; some manuscripts have chief priests.
3.14 Mt 27.15-23; Mk 15.6-14; Lk 23.13-23; Jn 19.12-15   **3.22** Dt 18.15, 18 (LXX)
3.23 Dt 18.19   **3.25** Gn 22.18   **4.11** Ps 118.22

turned out to be the most important of all.' [12] Salvation is to be found through him alone; in all the world there is no one else whom God has given who can save us."

[13] The members of the Council were amazed to see how bold Peter and John were and to learn that they were ordinary men of no education. They realized then that they had been companions of Jesus. [14] But there was nothing that they could say, because they saw the man who had been healed standing there with Peter and John. [15] So they told them to leave the Council room, and then they started discussing among themselves. [16] "What shall we do with these men?" they asked. "Everyone in Jerusalem knows that this extraordinary miracle has been performed by them, and we cannot deny it. [17] But to keep this matter from spreading any further among the people, let us warn these men never again to speak to anyone in the name of Jesus."

[18] So they called them back in and told them that under no condition were they to speak or to teach in the name of Jesus. [19] But Peter and John answered them, "You yourselves judge which is right in God's sight — to obey you or to obey God. [20] For we cannot stop speaking of what we ourselves have seen and heard." [21] So the Council warned them even more strongly and then set them free. They saw that it was impossible to punish them, because the people were all praising God for what had happened. [22] The man on whom this miracle of healing had been performed was over forty years old.

The Believers Pray for Boldness

[23] As soon as Peter and John were set free, they returned to their group and told them what the chief priests and the elders had said. [24] When the believers heard it, they all joined together in prayer to God: "Master and Creator of heaven, earth, and sea, and all that is in them! [25] By means of the Holy Spirit you spoke through our ancestor David, your servant, when he said,

'Why were the Gentiles furious; why did people make their useless plots?
[26] The kings of the earth prepared themselves,
and the rulers met together against the Lord and his Messiah.'

[27] For indeed Herod and Pontius Pilate met together in this city with the Gentiles and the people of Israel against Jesus, your holy Servant, whom you made Messiah. [28] They gathered to do everything that you by your power and will had already decided would happen. [29] And now, Lord, take notice of the threats they have made, and allow us, your servants, to speak your message with all boldness. [30] Reach out your hand to heal, and grant that wonders and miracles may be performed through the name of your holy Servant Jesus."

[31] When they finished praying, the place where they were meeting was shaken. They were all filled with the Holy Spirit and began to proclaim God's message with boldness.

The Believers Share Their Possessions

[32] The group of believers was one in mind and heart. None of them said that any of their belongings were their own, but they all shared with one another everything they had. [33] With great power the apostles gave witness to the resurrection of the Lord Jesus, and God poured rich blessings on them all. [34] There was no one in the group who was in need. Those who owned fields or

4.24 Ex 20.11; Ne 9.6; Ps 146.6   **4.25, 26** Ps 2.1, 2 (LXX)   **4.27 a** Lk 23.7-11; **b** Mt 27.1, 2; Mk 15.1; Lk 23.1; Jn 18.28, 29   **4.32** Ac 2.44, 45

houses would sell them, bring the money received from the sale, ³⁵ and turn it over to the apostles; and the money was distributed according to the needs of the people.

³⁶ And so it was that Joseph, a Levite born in Cyprus, whom the apostles called Barnabas (which means "One who Encourages"), ³⁷ sold a field he owned, brought the money, and turned it over to the apostles.

Ananias and Sapphira

5 But there was a man named Ananias, who with his wife Sapphira sold some property that belonged to them. ² But with his wife's agreement he kept part of the money for himself and turned the rest over to the apostles. ³ Peter said to him, "Ananias, why did you let Satan take control of you and make you lie to the Holy Spirit by keeping part of the money you received for the property? ⁴ Before you sold the property, it belonged to you; and after you sold it, the money was yours. Why, then, did you decide to do such a thing? You have not lied to people — you have lied to God!" ⁵ As soon as Ananias heard this, he fell down dead; and all who heard about it were terrified. ⁶ The young men came in, wrapped up his body, carried him out, and buried him.

⁷ About three hours later his wife, not knowing what had happened, came in. ⁸ Peter asked her, "Tell me, was this the full amount you and your husband received for your property?"

"Yes," she answered, "the full amount."

⁹ So Peter said to her, "Why did you and your husband decide to put the Lord's Spirit to the test? The men who buried your husband are at the door right now, and they will carry you out too!" ¹⁰ At once she fell down at his feet and died. The young men came in and saw that she was dead, so they carried

her out and buried her beside her husband. ¹¹ The whole church and all the others who heard of this were terrified.

Miracles and Wonders

¹² Many miracles and wonders were being performed among the people by the apostles. All the believers met together in Solomon's Porch. ¹³ Nobody outside the group dared join them, even though the people spoke highly of them. ¹⁴ But more and more people were added to the group — a crowd of men and women who believed in the Lord. ¹⁵ As a result of what the apostles were doing, sick people were carried out into the streets and placed on beds and mats so that at least Peter's shadow might fall on some of them as he passed

. . . at least Peter's shadow might fall on some of them. (5.15)

by. ¹⁶ And crowds of people came in from the towns around Jerusalem, bringing those who were sick or who had evil spirits in them; and they were all healed.

The Apostles Are Persecuted

¹⁷ Then the High Priest and all his companions, members of the local

party of the Sadducees, became extremely jealous of the apostles; so they decided to take action. [18] They arrested the apostles and put them in the public jail. [19] But that night an angel of the Lord opened the prison gates, led the apostles out, and said to them, [20] "Go and stand in the Temple, and tell the people all about this new life." [21] The apostles obeyed, and at dawn they entered the Temple and started teaching.

The High Priest and his companions called together all the Jewish elders for a full meeting of the Council; then they sent orders to the prison to have the apostles brought before them. [22] But when the officials arrived, they did not find the apostles in prison, so they returned to the Council and reported, [23] "When we arrived at the jail, we found it locked up tight and all the guards on watch at the gates; but when we opened the gates, we found no one inside!" [24] When the chief priests and the officer in charge of the Temple guards heard this, they wondered what had happened to the apostles. [25] Then a man came in and said to them, "Listen! The men you put in prison are in the Temple teaching the people!" [26] So the officer went off with his men and brought the apostles back. They did not use force, however, because they were afraid that the people might stone them.

[27] They brought the apostles in, made them stand before the Council, and the High Priest questioned them. [28] "We gave you strict orders not to teach in the name of this man," he said; "but see what you have done! You have spread your teaching all over Jerusalem, and you want to make us responsible for his death!"

[29] Peter and the other apostles answered, "We must obey God, not men. [30] The God of our ancestors raised Jesus from death, after you had killed him by nailing him to a cross. [31] God raised him to his right side as Leader and Savior, to give the people of Israel the opportunity to repent and have their sins forgiven. [32] We are witnesses to these things — we and the Holy Spirit, who is God's gift to those who obey him."

[33] When the members of the Council heard this, they were so furious that they wanted to have the apostles put to death. [34] But one of them, a Pharisee named Gamaliel, who was a teacher of the Law and was highly respected by all the people, stood up in the Council. He ordered the apostles to be taken out for a while, [35] and then he said to the Council, "Fellow Israelites, be careful what you do to these men. [36] You remember that Theudas appeared some time ago, claiming to be somebody great, and about four hundred men joined him. But he was killed, all his followers were scattered, and his movement died out. [37] After that, Judas the Galilean appeared during the time of the census; he drew a crowd after him, but he also was killed, and all his followers were scattered. [38] And so in this case, I tell you, do not take any action against these men. Leave them alone! If what they have planned and done is of human origin, it will disappear, [39] but if it comes from God, you cannot possibly defeat them. You could find yourselves fighting against God!"

The Council followed Gamaliel's advice. [40] They called the apostles in, had them whipped, and ordered them never again to speak in the name of Jesus; and then they set them free. [41] As the apostles left the Council, they were happy, because God had considered them worthy to suffer disgrace for the sake of Jesus. [42] And every day in the Temple and in people's homes they continued to teach and preach the Good News about Jesus the Messiah.

5.28 Mt 27.25 **5.39** 2 Macc 7.19

The Seven Helpers

6 Some time later, as the number of disciples kept growing, there was a quarrel between the Greek-speaking Jews and the native Jews. The Greek-speaking Jews claimed that their widows were being neglected in the daily distribution of funds. ²So the twelve apostles called the whole group of believers together and said, "It is not right for us to neglect the preaching of God's word in order to handle finances. ³So then, friends, choose seven men among you who are known to be full of the Holy Spirit and wisdom, and we will put them in charge of this matter. ⁴We ourselves, then, will give our full time to prayer and the work of preaching."

⁵The whole group was pleased with the apostles' proposal, so they chose Stephen, a man full of faith and the Holy Spirit, and Philip, Prochorus, Nicanor, Timon, Parmenas, and Nicolaus, a Gentile from Antioch who had earlier been converted to Judaism. ⁶The group presented them to the apostles, who prayed and placed their hands on them.

⁷And so the word of God continued to spread. The number of disciples in Jerusalem grew larger and larger, and a great number of priests accepted the faith.

The Arrest of Stephen

⁸Stephen, a man richly blessed by God and full of power, performed great miracles and wonders among the people. ⁹But he was opposed by some men who were members of the synagogue of the Freedmen*e* (as it was called), which had Jews from Cyrene and Alexandria. They and other Jews from the provinces of Cilicia and Asia started arguing with Stephen. ¹⁰But the Spirit gave Stephen such wisdom that when he spoke, they could not refute him. ¹¹So they bribed some men to say, "We heard him speaking against Moses and against God!" ¹²In this way they stirred up the people, the elders, and the teachers of the Law. They seized Stephen and took him before the Council. ¹³Then they brought in some men to tell lies about him. "This man," they said, "is always talking against our sacred Temple and the Law of Moses. ¹⁴We heard him say that this Jesus of Nazareth will tear down the Temple and change all the customs which have come down to us from Moses!" ¹⁵All those sitting in the Council fixed their eyes on Stephen and saw that his face looked like the face of an angel.

Stephen's Speech

7 The High Priest asked Stephen, "Is this true?"

²Stephen answered, "Brothers and fathers, listen to me! Before our ancestor Abraham had gone to live in Haran, the God of glory appeared to him in Mesopotamia ³and said to him, 'Leave your family and country and go to the land that I will show you.' ⁴And so he left his country and went to live in Haran. After Abraham's father died, God made him move to this land where you now live. ⁵God did not then give Abraham any part of it as his own, not even a square foot of ground, but God promised to give it to him, and that it would belong to him and to his descendants. At the time God made this promise, Abraham had no children. ⁶This is what God said to him: 'Your descendants will live in a foreign country, where they will be slaves and will be badly treated for four hundred years. ⁷But I will pass judgment on the people

e FREEDMEN: *These were Jews who had been slaves, but had bought or been given their freedom.*

7.2, 3 Gn 12.1   **7.4 a** Gn 11.31; **b** Gn 12.4   **7.5** Gn 12.7; 13.15; 15.18; 17.8
7.6, 7 Gn 15.13, 14   **7.7** Ex 3.12

that they will serve, and afterward your descendants will come out of that country and will worship me in this place.' ⁸Then God gave to Abraham the ceremony of circumcision as a sign of the covenant. So Abraham circumcised Isaac a week after he was born; Isaac circumcised his son Jacob, and Jacob circumcised his twelve sons, the famous ancestors of our race.

⁹"Jacob's sons became jealous of their brother Joseph and sold him to be a slave in Egypt. But God was with him ¹⁰and brought him safely through all his troubles. When Joseph appeared before the king of Egypt, God gave him a pleasing manner and wisdom, and the king made Joseph governor over the country and the royal household. ¹¹Then there was a famine all over Egypt and Canaan, which caused much suffering. Our ancestors could not find any food, ¹²and when Jacob heard that there was grain in Egypt, he sent his sons, our ancestors, on their first visit there. ¹³On the second visit Joseph made himself known to his brothers, and the king of Egypt came to know about Joseph's family. ¹⁴So Joseph sent a message to his father Jacob, telling him and the whole family, seventy-five people in all, to come to Egypt. ¹⁵Then Jacob went to Egypt, where he and his sons died. ¹⁶Their bodies were taken to Shechem, where they were buried in the grave which Abraham had bought from the clan of Hamor for a sum of money.

¹⁷"When the time drew near for God to keep the promise he had made to Abraham, the number of our people in Egypt had grown much larger. ¹⁸At last a king who did not know about Joseph began to rule in Egypt. ¹⁹He tricked our ancestors and was cruel to them, forcing them to put their babies out of their homes, so that they would die. ²⁰It was at this time that Moses was born, a very beautiful child. He was cared for at home for three months, ²¹and when he was put out of his home, the king's daughter adopted him and brought him up as her own son. ²²He was taught all the wisdom of the Egyptians and became a great man in words and deeds.

²³"When Moses was forty years old, he decided to find out how his fellow Israelites were being treated. ²⁴He saw one of them being mistreated by an Egyptian, so he went to his help and took revenge on the Egyptian by killing him. (²⁵He thought that his own people would understand that God was going to use him to set them free, but they did not understand.) ²⁶The next day he saw two Israelites fighting, and he tried to make peace between them. 'Listen, men,' he said, 'you are fellow Israelites; why are you fighting like this?' ²⁷But the one who was mistreating the other pushed Moses aside. 'Who made you ruler and judge over us?' he asked. ²⁸'Do you want to kill me, just as you killed that Egyptian yesterday?' ²⁹When Moses heard this, he fled from Egypt and went to live in the land of Midian. There he had two sons.

³⁰"After forty years had passed, an angel appeared to Moses in the flames of a burning bush in the desert near Mount Sinai. ³¹Moses was amazed by what he saw, and went near the bush to get a better look. But he heard the Lord's voice: ³²'I am the God of your ancestors, the God of Abraham, Isaac, and Jacob.' Moses trembled with fear and dared not look. ³³The Lord said to him, 'Take your sandals off, for the place

7.8 a Gn 17.10-14; **b** Gn 21.2-4; **c** Gn 25.26; **d** Gn 29.31 – 35.18   **7.9 a** Gn 37.11;
b Gn 37.28; **c** Gn 39.2, 21   **7.10** Gn 41.39-41   **7.11** Gn 42.1, 2   **7.13 a** Gn 45.1;
b Gn 45.16   **7.14 a** Gn 45.9, 10, 17, 18; **b** Gn 46.27 (LXX)   **7.15 a** Gn 46.1-7; **b** Gn 49.33
7.16 Gn 23.3-16; 33.19; 50.7-13; Js 24.32   **7.17, 18** Ex 1.7, 8   **7.19 a** Ex 1.10, 11;
b Ex 1.22   **7.20** Ex 2.2   **7.21** Ex 2.3-10   **7.23-29** Ex 2.11-15   **7.29** Ex 18.3, 4
7.30-34 Ex 3.1-10

where you are standing is holy ground. ³⁴ I have seen the cruel suffering of my people in Egypt. I have heard their groans, and I have come down to set them free. Come now; I will send you to Egypt.'

³⁵ "Moses is the one who was rejected by the people of Israel. 'Who made you ruler and judge over us?' they asked. He is the one whom God sent to rule the people and set them free with the help of the angel who appeared to him in the burning bush. ³⁶ He led the people out of Egypt, performing miracles and wonders in Egypt and at the Red Sea and for forty years in the desert. ³⁷ Moses is the one who said to the people of Israel, 'God will send you a prophet, just as he sent me,*f* and he will be one of your own people.' ³⁸ He is the one who was with the people of Israel assembled in the desert; he was there with our ancestors and with the angel who spoke to him on Mount Sinai, and he received God's living messages to pass on to us.

³⁹ "But our ancestors refused to obey him; they pushed him aside and wished that they could go back to Egypt. ⁴⁰ So they said to Aaron, 'Make us some gods who will lead us. We do not know what has happened to that man Moses, who brought us out of Egypt.' ⁴¹ It was then that they made an idol in the shape of a bull, offered sacrifice to it, and had a feast in honor of what they themselves had made. ⁴² So God turned away from them and gave them over to worship the stars of heaven, as it is written in the book of the prophets:

'People of Israel! It was not
    to me
that you slaughtered and
    sacrificed animals

for forty years in the desert.
⁴³ It was the tent of the god
    Molech that you carried,
and the image of Rephan,
    your star god;
they were idols that you had
    made to worship.
And so I will send you into exile
    beyond Babylon.'

⁴⁴ "Our ancestors had the Tent of God's presence with them in the desert. It had been made as God had told Moses to make it, according to the pattern that Moses had been shown. ⁴⁵ Later on, our ancestors who received the tent from their fathers carried it with them when they went with Joshua and took over the land from the nations that God drove out as they advanced. And it stayed there until the time of David. ⁴⁶ He won God's favor and asked God to allow him to provide a dwelling place for the God of Jacob.*g* ⁴⁷ But it was Solomon who built him a house.

⁴⁸ "But the Most High God does not live in houses built by human hands; as the prophet says,

⁴⁹ 'Heaven is my throne, says the
    Lord,
and the earth is my footstool.
What kind of house would you
    build for me?
Where is the place for me to
    live in?
⁵⁰ Did not I myself make all these
    things?'

⁵¹ "How stubborn you are!" Stephen went on to say. "How heathen your hearts, how deaf you are to God's message! You are just like your ancestors: you too have always resisted the Holy Spirit! ⁵² Was there any prophet that

---

f just as he sent me; *or* like me.　　*g* the God of Jacob; *some manuscripts have* the people of Israel.

7.35 Ex 2.14　**7.36 a** Ex 7.3; **b** Ex 14.21; **c** Nu 14.33　**7.37** Dt 18.15, 18
7.38 Ex 19.1 – 20.17; Dt 5.1-33　**7.40** Ex 32.1　**7.41** Ex 32.2-6
7.42, 43 Am 5.25-27 (LXX)　**7.44** Ex 25.9, 40　**7.45** Js 3.14-17　**7.46** 2 S 7.1-16;
1 Ch 17.1-14　**7.47** 1 K 6.1-38; 2 Ch 3.1-17　**7.49, 50** Is 66.1, 2　**7.51** Is 63.10

your ancestors did not persecute? They killed God's messengers, who long ago announced the coming of his righteous Servant. And now you have betrayed and murdered him. ⁵³ You are the ones who received God's law, that was handed down by angels — yet you have not obeyed it!"

The Stoning of Stephen

⁵⁴ As the members of the Council listened to Stephen, they became furious and ground their teeth at him in anger. ⁵⁵ But Stephen, full of the Holy Spirit, looked up to heaven and saw God's glory and Jesus standing at the right side of God. ⁵⁶ "Look!" he said. "I see heaven opened and the Son of Man standing at the right side of God!"

⁵⁷ With a loud cry the Council members covered their ears with their hands. Then they all rushed at him at once, ⁵⁸ threw him out of the city, and stoned him. The witnesses left their cloaks in the care of a young man named Saul. ⁵⁹ They kept on stoning Stephen as he called out to the Lord, "Lord Jesus, receive my spirit!" ⁶⁰ He knelt down and cried out in a loud voice, "Lord! Do not remember this sin against them!" He said this and died.

8 And Saul approved of his murder.

Saul Persecutes the Church

That very day the church in Jerusalem began to suffer cruel persecution. All the believers, except the apostles, were scattered throughout the provinces of Judea and Samaria. ² Some devout men buried Stephen, mourning for him with loud cries.

³ But Saul tried to destroy the church; going from house to house, he dragged out the believers, both men and women, and threw them into jail.

The Gospel Is Preached in Samaria

⁴ The believers who were scattered went everywhere, preaching the message. ⁵ Philip went to the principal city*ʰ*

Saul approved of his murder. (8.1)

in Samaria and preached the Messiah to the people there. ⁶ The crowds paid close attention to what Philip said, as they listened to him and saw the miracles that he performed. ⁷ Evil spirits came out from many people with a loud cry, and many paralyzed and lame people were healed. ⁸ So there was great joy in that city.

⁹ A man named Simon lived there, who for some time had astounded the Samaritans with his magic. He claimed that he was someone great, ¹⁰ and everyone in the city, from all classes of society, paid close attention to him. "He is that power of God known as 'The Great Power,'" they said. ¹¹ They paid this attention to him because for such a long time he had astonished them with his magic. ¹² But when they believed Philip's message about the good news of the Kingdom of God and about Jesus Christ, they were baptized, both men and women. ¹³ Simon himself also believed; and after being baptized, he stayed close to Philip and was astounded when he saw the great wonders and miracles that were being performed.

ʰ the principal city; *some manuscripts have* a city.
8.3 Ac 22.4, 5; 26.9-11

PALESTINE AND SYRIA

¹⁴The apostles in Jerusalem heard that the people of Samaria had received the word of God, so they sent Peter and John to them. ¹⁵When they arrived, they prayed for the believers that they might receive the Holy Spirit. ¹⁶For the Holy Spirit had not yet come down on any of them; they had only been baptized in the name of the Lord Jesus. ¹⁷Then Peter and John placed their hands on them, and they received the Holy Spirit.

¹⁸Simon saw that the Spirit had been given to the believers when the apostles placed their hands on them. So he offered money to Peter and John, ¹⁹and said, "Give this power to me too, so that anyone I place my hands on will receive the Holy Spirit."

²⁰But Peter answered him, "May you

and your money go to hell, for thinking that you can buy God's gift with money! ²¹You have no part or share in our work, because your heart is not right in God's sight. ²²Repent, then, of this evil plan of yours, and pray to the Lord that he will forgive you for thinking such a thing as this. ²³For I see that you are full of bitter envy and are a prisoner of sin."

²⁴Simon said to Peter and John, "Please pray to the Lord for me, so that none of these things you spoke of will happen to me."

²⁵After they had given their testimony and proclaimed the Lord's message, Peter and John went back to Jerusalem. On their way they preached the Good News in many villages of Samaria.

Philip and the Ethiopian Official

²⁶ An angel of the Lord said to Philip, "Get ready and go south[i] to the road that goes from Jerusalem to Gaza." (This road is not used nowadays.)[j] ²⁷⁻²⁸ So Philip got ready and went. Now an Ethiopian eunuch, who was an important official in charge of the treasury of the queen of Ethiopia, was on his way home. He had been to Jerusalem to worship God and was going back home in his carriage. As he rode along, he was reading from the book of the prophet Isaiah. ²⁹ The Holy Spirit said to Philip, "Go over to that carriage and stay close to it." ³⁰ Philip ran over and heard him reading from the book of the prophet Isaiah. He asked him, "Do you understand what you are reading?"

³¹ The official replied, "How can I understand unless someone explains it to me?" And he invited Philip to climb up and sit in the carriage with him. ³² The passage of scripture which he was reading was this:

> "He was like a sheep that is
>   taken to be slaughtered,
> like a lamb that makes no
>   sound when its wool
>   is cut off.
> He did not say a word.
> ³³ He was humiliated, and justice
>   was denied him.
> No one will be able to tell
>   about his descendants,
> because his life on earth has
>   come to an end."

³⁴ The official asked Philip, "Tell me, of whom is the prophet saying this? Of himself or of someone else?" ³⁵ Then Philip began to speak; starting from this passage of scripture, he told him the Good News about Jesus. ³⁶ As they traveled down the road, they came to a place where there was some water, and the official said, "Here is some water. What is to keep me from being baptized?"[k]

³⁸ The official ordered the carriage to stop, and both Philip and the official went down into the water, and Philip baptized him. ³⁹ When they came up out of the water, the Spirit of the Lord took Philip away. The official did not see him again, but continued on his way, full of joy. ⁴⁰ Philip found himself in Azotus; he went on to Caesarea, and on the way he preached the Good News in every town.

The Conversion of Saul
(Acts 22.6-16; 26.12-18)

9 In the meantime Saul kept up his violent threats of murder against the followers of the Lord. He went to the High Priest ² and asked for letters of introduction to the synagogues in Damascus, so that if he should find there any followers of the Way of the Lord, he would be able to arrest them, both men and women, and bring them back to Jerusalem.

³ As Saul was coming near the city of Damascus, suddenly a light from the sky flashed around him. ⁴ He fell to the ground and heard a voice saying to him, "Saul, Saul! Why do you persecute me?"

⁵ "Who are you, Lord?" he asked.

"I am Jesus, whom you persecute," the voice said. ⁶ "But get up and go into the city, where you will be told what you must do."

⁷ The men who were traveling with Saul had stopped, not saying a word; they heard the voice but could not see anyone. ⁸ Saul got up from the ground and opened his eyes, but could not see

---

i south; *or* at midday.   *j* This road is not used nowadays; *or* This is the desert road.
k *Some manuscripts add verse 37:* Philip said to him, "You may be baptized if you believe with all your heart." "I do," he answered; "I believe that Jesus Christ is the Son of God."
8.32, 33 Is 53.7, 8 (LXX)

"Who are you, Lord?" (9.5)

a thing. So they took him by the hand and led him into Damascus. ⁹For three days he was not able to see, and during that time he did not eat or drink anything.

¹⁰There was a believer in Damascus named Ananias. He had a vision, in which the Lord said to him, "Ananias!"

"Here I am, Lord," he answered.

¹¹The Lord said to him, "Get ready and go to Straight Street, and at the house of Judas ask for a man from Tarsus named Saul. He is praying, ¹²and in a vision he has seen a man named Ananias come in and place his hands on him so that he might see again."

¹³Ananias answered, "Lord, many people have told me about this man and about all the terrible things he has done to your people in Jerusalem. ¹⁴And he has come to Damascus with authority from the chief priests to arrest all who worship you."

¹⁵The Lord said to him, "Go, because I have chosen him to serve me, to make my name known to Gentiles and kings and to the people of Israel. ¹⁶And I myself will show him all that he must suffer for my sake."

¹⁷So Ananias went, entered the house where Saul was, and placed his hands on him. "Brother Saul," he said,

"the Lord has sent me — Jesus himself, who appeared to you on the road as you were coming here. He sent me so that you might see again and be filled with the Holy Spirit." ¹⁸At once something like fish scales fell from Saul's eyes, and he was able to see again. He stood up and was baptized; ¹⁹and after he had eaten, his strength came back.

Saul Preaches in Damascus

Saul stayed for a few days with the believers in Damascus. ²⁰He went straight to the synagogues and began to preach that Jesus was the Son of God.

²¹All who heard him were amazed and asked, "Isn't he the one who in Jerusalem was killing those who worship that man Jesus? And didn't he come here for the very purpose of arresting those people and taking them back to the chief priests?"

²²But Saul's preaching became even more powerful, and his proofs that Jesus was the Messiah were so convincing that the Jews who lived in Damascus could not answer him.

²³After many days had gone by, the Jews met together and made plans to kill Saul, ²⁴but he was told of their plan. Day and night they watched the city gates in order to kill him. ²⁵But one night Saul's followers took him and let him down through an opening in the wall, lowering him in a basket.

Saul in Jerusalem

²⁶Saul went to Jerusalem and tried to join the disciples. But they would not believe that he was a disciple, and they were all afraid of him. ²⁷Then Barnabas came to his help and took him to the apostles. He explained to them how Saul had seen the Lord on the road and that the Lord had spoken to him. He also told them how boldly Saul had preached in the name of Jesus in Damascus. ²⁸And so Saul stayed with

9.18 Tb 11.13-15 **9.23-25** 2 Co 11.32, 33

them and went all over Jerusalem, preaching boldly in the name of the Lord. 29 He also talked and disputed with the Greek-speaking Jews, but they tried to kill him. 30 When the believers found out about this, they took Saul to Caesarea and sent him away to Tarsus.

31 And so it was that the church throughout Judea, Galilee, and Samaria had a time of peace. Through the help of the Holy Spirit it was strengthened and grew in numbers, as it lived in reverence for the Lord.

Peter in Lydda and Joppa

32 Peter traveled everywhere, and on one occasion he went to visit God's people who lived in Lydda. 33 There he met a man named Aeneas, who was paralyzed and had not been able to get out of bed for eight years. 34 "Aeneas," Peter said to him, "Jesus Christ makes you well. Get up and make your bed." At once Aeneas got up. 35 All the people living in Lydda and Sharon saw him, and they turned to the Lord.

36 In Joppa there was a woman named Tabitha, who was a believer. (Her name in Greek is Dorcas, meaning "a deer.") She spent all her time doing good and helping the poor. 37 At that time she got sick and died. Her body was washed and laid in a room upstairs. 38 Joppa was not very far from Lydda, and when the believers in Joppa heard that Peter was in Lydda, they sent two men to him with the message, "Please hurry and come to us." 39 So Peter got ready and went with them. When he arrived, he was taken to the room upstairs, where all the widows crowded around him, crying and showing him all the shirts and coats that Dorcas had made while she was alive. 40 Peter put them all out of the room, and knelt down and prayed; then he turned to the body and said, "Tabitha, get up!" She opened her eyes, and when she saw Pe-

ter, she sat up. 41 Peter reached over and helped her get up. Then he called all the believers, including the widows, and presented her alive to them. 42 The news about this spread all over Joppa, and many people believed in the Lord. 43 Peter stayed on in Joppa for many days with a tanner of leather named Simon.

Peter and Cornelius

10 There was a man in Caesarea named Cornelius, who was a captain in the Roman army regiment called "The Italian Regiment." 2 He was a religious man; he and his whole family worshiped God. He also did much to help the Jewish poor people and was constantly praying to God. 3 It was about three o'clock one afternoon when he had a vision, in which he clearly saw an angel of God come in and say to him, "Cornelius!"

4 He stared at the angel in fear and said, "What is it, sir?"

The angel answered, "God is pleased with your prayers and works of charity, and is ready to answer you. 5 And now send some men to Joppa for a certain man whose full name is Simon Peter. 6 He is a guest in the home of a tanner of leather named Simon, who lives by the sea." 7 Then the angel went away, and Cornelius called two of his house servants and a soldier, a religious man who was one of his personal attendants. 8 He told them what had happened and sent them off to Joppa.

9 The next day, as they were on their way and coming near Joppa, Peter went up on the roof of the house about noon in order to pray. 10 He became hungry and wanted something to eat; while the food was being prepared, he had a vision. 11 He saw heaven opened and something coming down that looked like a large sheet being lowered by its four corners to the earth. 12 In it were all

10.9 Jdt 8.5

kinds of animals, reptiles, and wild birds. 13 A voice said to him, "Get up, Peter; kill and eat!"

14 But Peter said, "Certainly not, Lord! I have never eaten anything ritually unclean or defiled."

15 The voice spoke to him again, "Do not consider anything unclean that God has declared clean." 16 This happened three times, and then the thing was taken back up into heaven.

17 While Peter was wondering about the meaning of this vision, the men sent by Cornelius had learned where Simon's house was, and they were now standing in front of the gate. 18 They called out and asked, "Is there a guest here by the name of Simon Peter?"

19 Peter was still trying to understand what the vision meant, when the Spirit said, "Listen! Three*l* men are here looking for you. 20 So get ready and go down, and do not hesitate to go with them, for I have sent them." 21 So Peter went down and said to the men, "I am the man you are looking for. Why have you come?"

22 "Captain Cornelius sent us," they answered. "He is a good man who worships God and is highly respected by all the Jewish people. An angel of God told him to invite you to his house, so that he could hear what you have to say." 23 Peter invited the men in and had them spend the night there.

The next day he got ready and went with them; and some of the believers from Joppa went along with him. 24 The following day he arrived in Caesarea, where Cornelius was waiting for him, together with relatives and close friends that he had invited. 25 As Peter was about to go in, Cornelius met him, fell at his feet, and bowed down before him. 26 But Peter made him rise. "Stand up," he said, "I myself am only a man." 27 Peter kept on talking to Cornelius as

he went into the house, where he found many people gathered. 28 He said to them, "You yourselves know very well that a Jew is not allowed by his religion to visit or associate with Gentiles. But God has shown me that I must not consider any person ritually unclean or defiled. 29 And so when you sent for me, I came without any objection. I ask you, then, why did you send for me?"

30 Cornelius said, "It was about this time three days ago that I was praying*m* in my house at three o'clock in the afternoon. Suddenly a man dressed in shining clothes stood in front of me 31 and said: 'Cornelius! God has heard your prayer and has taken notice of your works of charity. 32 Send someone to Joppa for a man whose full name is Simon Peter. He is a guest in the home of Simon the tanner of leather, who lives by the sea.' 33 And so I sent for you at once, and you have been good enough to come. Now we are all here in the presence of God, waiting to hear anything that the Lord has instructed you to say."

Peter's Speech

34 Peter began to speak: "I now realize that it is true that God treats everyone on the same basis. 35 Those who fear him and do what is right are acceptable to him, no matter what race they belong to. 36 You know the message he sent to the people of Israel, proclaiming the Good News of peace through Jesus Christ, who is Lord of all. 37 You know of the great event that took place throughout the land of Israel, beginning in Galilee after John preached his message of baptism. 38 You know about Jesus of Nazareth and how God poured out on him the Holy Spirit and power. He went everywhere, doing good and healing all who were under

l Three; *some manuscripts have* Some; *one manuscript has* Two.   *m* praying; *some manuscripts have* fasting and praying.
10.34 Dt 10.17

the power of the Devil, for God was with him. 39 We are witnesses of everything that he did in the land of Israel and in Jerusalem. Then they put him to death by nailing him to a cross. 40 But God raised him from death three days later and caused him to appear, 41 not to everyone, but only to the witnesses that God had already chosen, that is, to us who ate and drank with him after he rose from death. 42 And he commanded us to preach the gospel to the people and to testify that he is the one whom God has appointed judge of the living and the dead. 43 All the prophets spoke about him, saying that all who believe in him will have their sins forgiven through the power of his name."

The Gentiles Receive the Holy Spirit

44 While Peter was still speaking, the Holy Spirit came down on all those who were listening to his message. 45 The Jewish believers who had come from Joppa with Peter were amazed that God had poured out his gift of the Holy Spirit on the Gentiles also. 46 For they heard them speaking in strange tongues and praising God's greatness. Peter spoke up: 47 "These people have received the Holy Spirit, just as we also did. Can anyone, then, stop them from being baptized with water?" 48 So he ordered them to be baptized in the name of Jesus Christ. Then they asked him to stay with them for a few days.

Peter's Report to the Church at Jerusalem

11 The apostles and the other believers throughout Judea heard that the Gentiles also had received the word of God. 2 When Peter went to Jerusalem, those who were in favor of circumcising Gentiles criticized him, saying, 3 "You were a guest in the home of uncircumcised Gentiles, and you even ate with them!" 4 So Peter gave them a complete account of what had happened from the very beginning:

5 "While I was praying in the city of Joppa, I had a vision. I saw something coming down that looked like a large sheet being lowered by its four corners from heaven, and it stopped next to me. 6 I looked closely inside and saw domesticated and wild animals, reptiles, and wild birds. 7 Then I heard a voice saying to me, 'Get up, Peter; kill and eat!' 8 But I said, 'Certainly not, Lord! No ritually unclean or defiled food has ever entered my mouth.' 9 The voice spoke again from heaven, 'Do not consider anything unclean that God has declared clean.' 10 This happened three times, and finally the whole thing was drawn back up into heaven. 11 At that very moment three men who had been sent to me from Caesarea arrived at the house where I was[n] staying. 12 The Spirit told me to go with them without hesitation. These six fellow believers from Joppa accompanied me to Caesarea, and we all went into the house of Cornelius. 13 He told us how he had seen an angel standing in his house, who said to him, 'Send someone to Joppa for a man whose full name is Simon Peter. 14 He will speak words to you by which you and all your family will be saved.' 15 And when I began to speak, the Holy Spirit came down on them just as on us at the beginning. 16 Then I remembered what the Lord had said: 'John baptized with water, but you will be baptized with the Holy Spirit.' 17 It is clear that God gave those Gentiles the same gift that he gave us when we believed in the Lord Jesus Christ; who was I, then, to try to stop God!"

18 When they heard this, they stopped their criticism and praised God, saying, "Then God has given to the

---

n I was; *some manuscripts have* we were.
11.16 Ac 1.5

Gentiles also the opportunity to repent and live!"

The Church at Antioch

¹⁹ Some of the believers who were scattered by the persecution which took place when Stephen was killed went as far as Phoenicia, Cyprus, and Antioch, telling the message to Jews only. ²⁰ But other believers, who were from Cyprus and Cyrene, went to Antioch and proclaimed the message to Gentiles *o* also, telling them the Good News about the Lord Jesus. ²¹ The Lord's power was with them, and a great number of people believed and turned to the Lord.

²² The news about this reached the church in Jerusalem, so they sent Barnabas to Antioch. ²³ When he arrived and saw how God had blessed the people, he was glad and urged them all to be faithful and true to the Lord with all their hearts. ²⁴ Barnabas was a good man, full of the Holy Spirit and faith, and many people were brought to the Lord.

²⁵ Then Barnabas went to Tarsus to look for Saul. ²⁶ When he found him, he took him to Antioch, and for a whole year the two met with the people of the church and taught a large group. It was at Antioch that the believers were first called Christians.

²⁷ About that time some prophets went from Jerusalem to Antioch. ²⁸ One of them, named Agabus, stood up and by the power of the Spirit predicted that a severe famine was about to come over all the earth. (It came when Claudius was emperor.) ²⁹ The disciples decided that they each would send as much as they could to help their fellow believers who lived in Judea. ³⁰ They did this, then, and sent the money to the church elders by Barnabas and Saul.

More Persecution

12 About this time King Herod *p* began to persecute some members of the church. ² He had James, the brother of John, put to death by the sword. ³ When he saw that this pleased the Jews, he went ahead and had Peter arrested. (This happened during the time of the Festival of Unleavened Bread.) ⁴ After his arrest Peter was put in jail, where he was handed over to be guarded by four groups of four soldiers each. Herod planned to put him on trial in public after Passover. ⁵ So Peter was kept in jail, but the people of the church were praying earnestly to God for him.

Peter Is Set Free from Prison

⁶ The night before Herod was going to bring him out to the people, Peter was sleeping between two guards. He was tied with two chains, and there were guards on duty at the prison gate. ⁷ Suddenly an angel of the Lord stood there, and a light shone in the cell. The angel shook Peter by the shoulder, woke him up, and said, "Hurry! Get up!" At once the chains fell off Peter's hands. ⁸ Then the angel said, "Tighten your belt and put on your sandals." Peter did so, and the angel said, "Put your cloak around you and come with me." ⁹ Peter followed him out of the prison, not knowing, however, if what the angel was doing was real; he thought he was seeing a vision. ¹⁰ They passed by the first guard station and then the second, and came at last to the iron gate that opens into the city. The gate opened for them by itself, and they went out. They walked down a street, and suddenly the angel left Peter.

¹¹ Then Peter realized what had happened to him, and said, "Now I know that it is really true! The Lord sent his angel to rescue me from Herod's power

o Gentiles; *some manuscripts have* Greek-speaking Jews *or* Greek-speaking people.
p KING HEROD: *Herod Agrippa I, ruler of all Palestine.*
11.19 Ac 8.1-4   **11.28** Ac 21.10   **12.4** Ex 12.1-27

and from everything the Jewish people expected to happen."

¹²Aware of his situation, he went to the home of Mary, the mother of John Mark, where many people had gathered and were praying. ¹³Peter knocked at the outside door, and a servant named Rhoda came to answer it. ¹⁴She recognized Peter's voice and was so happy that she ran back in without opening the door, and announced that Peter was standing outside. ¹⁵"You are crazy!" they told her. But she insisted that it was true. So they answered, "It is his angel."

¹⁶Meanwhile Peter kept on knocking. At last they opened the door, and when they saw him, they were amazed. ¹⁷He motioned with his hand for them to be quiet, and he explained to them how the Lord had brought him out of prison. "Tell this to James and the rest of the believers," he said; then he left and went somewhere else.

¹⁸When morning came, there was a tremendous confusion among the guards — what had happened to Peter? ¹⁹Herod gave orders to search for him, but they could not find him. So he had the guards questioned and ordered them put to death.

After this, Herod left Judea and spent some time in Caesarea.

The Death of Herod

²⁰Herod was very angry with the people of Tyre and Sidon, so they went in a group to see him. First they convinced Blastus, the man in charge of the palace, that he should help them. Then they went to Herod and asked him for peace, because their country got its food supplies from the king's country.

²¹On a chosen day Herod put on his royal robes, sat on his throne, and made a speech to the people. ²²"It isn't a man speaking, but a god!" they shouted. ²³At once the angel of the Lord struck Herod down, because he did not give honor to God. He was eaten by worms and died.

²⁴Meanwhile the word of God continued to spread and grow.

²⁵Barnabas and Saul finished their mission and returned from*q* Jerusalem, taking John Mark with them.

Barnabas and Saul Are Chosen and Sent

13 In the church at Antioch there were some prophets and teachers: Barnabas, Simeon (called the Black), Lucius (from Cyrene), Manaen (who had been brought up with Governor Herod*r*), and Saul. ²While they were serving the Lord and fasting, the Holy Spirit said to them, "Set apart for me Barnabas and Saul, to do the work to which I have called them."

³They fasted and prayed, placed their hands on them, and sent them off.

In Cyprus

⁴Having been sent by the Holy Spirit, Barnabas and Saul went to Seleucia and sailed from there to the island of Cyprus. ⁵When they arrived at Salamis, they preached the word of God in the synagogues. They had John Mark with them to help in the work.

⁶They went all the way across the island to Paphos, where they met a certain magician named Bar-Jesus, a Jew who claimed to be a prophet. ⁷He was a friend of the governor of the island, Sergius Paulus, who was an intelligent man. The governor called Barnabas and Saul before him because he wanted to hear the word of God. ⁸But they were opposed by the magician Elymas (that

q from; some manuscripts have to.   *r* HEROD: *Herod Antipas, ruler of Galilee (see Lk 3.1).*
12.20-23 2 Macc 9.5-28

is his name in Greek), who tried to turn the governor away from the faith. [9] Then Saul — also known as Paul — was filled with the Holy Spirit; he looked straight at the magician [10] and said, "You son of the Devil! You are the enemy of everything that is good. You are full of all kinds of evil tricks, and you always keep trying to turn the Lord's truths into lies! [11] The Lord's hand will come down on you now; you will be blind and will not see the light of day for a time."

At once Elymas felt a dark mist cover his eyes, and he walked around trying to find someone to lead him by the hand. [12] When the governor saw what had happened, he believed; for he was greatly amazed at the teaching about the Lord.

In Antioch in Pisidia

[13] Paul and his companions sailed from Paphos and came to Perga, a city in Pamphylia, where John Mark left them and went back to Jerusalem. [14] They went on from Perga and arrived in Antioch in Pisidia, and on the Sabbath they went into the synagogue and sat down. [15] After the reading from the Law of Moses and from the writings of the prophets, the officials of the synagogue sent them a message: "Friends, we want you to speak to the people if you have a message of encouragement for them." [16] Paul stood up, motioned with his hand, and began to speak:

"Fellow Israelites and all Gentiles here who worship God: hear me! [17] The God of the people of Israel chose our ancestors and made the people a great nation during the time they lived as foreigners in Egypt. God brought them out of Egypt by his great power, [18] and for forty years he endured[s] them in the desert. [19] He destroyed seven nations in the land of Canaan and made his people the owners of the land. [20] All of this took about 450 years.

"After this[t] he gave them judges until the time of the prophet Samuel. [21] And when they asked for a king, God gave them Saul son of Kish from the tribe of Benjamin, to be their king for forty years. [22] After removing him, God made David their king. This is what God said about him: 'I have found that David son of Jesse is the kind of man I like, a man who will do all I want him to do.' [23] It was Jesus, a descendant of David, whom God made the Savior of the people of Israel, as he had promised. [24] Before Jesus began his work, John preached to all the people of Israel that they should turn from their sins and be baptized. [25] And as John was about to finish his mission, he said to the people, 'Who do you think I am? I am not the one you are waiting for. But listen! He is coming after me, and I am not good enough to take his sandals off his feet.'

[26] "My fellow Israelites, descendants of Abraham, and all Gentiles here who worship God: it is to us that this message of salvation has been sent! [27] For the people who live in Jerusalem and their leaders did not know that he is the Savior, nor did they understand the words of the prophets that are read every Sabbath. Yet they made the prophets' words come true by condemning Jesus. [28] And even though they could find no reason to pass the death sentence on him, they asked Pi-

---

[s] he endured; *some manuscripts have* he took care of.   [t] All of this took about 450 years. After this; *or* Some 450 years later.

13.17 a Ex 1.7; **b** Ex 12.51   **13.18** Nu 14.34; Dt 1.31   **13.19 a** Dt 7.1; **b** Js 14.1   **13.20 a** Jg 2.16; **b** 1 S 3.20   **13.21 a** 1 S 8.5; **b** 1 S 10.21   **13.22 a** 1 S 13.14; **b** 1 S 16.12; Ps 89.20   **13.24** Mk 1.4; Lk 3.3   **13.25 a** Jn 1.20; **b** Mt 3.11; Mk 1.7; Lk 3.16; Jn 1.27   **13.28** Mt 27.22, 23; Mk 15.13, 14; Lk 23.21-23; Jn 19.15

late to have him put to death. 29 And after they had done everything that the Scriptures say about him, they took him down from the cross and placed him in a tomb. 30 But God raised him from death, 31 and for many days he appeared to those who had traveled with him from Galilee to Jerusalem. They are now witnesses for him to the people of Israel. 32-33 And we are here to bring the Good News to you: what God promised our ancestors he would do, he has now done for us, who are their descendants, by raising Jesus to life. As it is written in the second Psalm,

'You are my Son;
        today I have become your
            Father.'

34 And this is what God said about raising him from death, never to rot away in the grave:

'I will give you the sacred and
        sure blessings
    that I promised to David.'

35 As indeed he says in another passage,

'You will not allow your faithful
        servant to rot in the grave.'

36 For David served God's purposes in his own time, and then he died, was buried with his ancestors, and his body rotted in the grave. 37 But this did not happen to the one whom God raised from death. 38-39 All of you, my fellow Israelites, are to know for sure that it is through Jesus that the message about forgiveness of sins is preached to you; you are to know that everyone who believes in him is set free from all the sins from which the Law of Moses could not set you free. 40 Take care, then, so that what the prophets said may not happen to you: u

41 'Look, you scoffers! Be
        astonished and die!
    For what I am doing today

is something that you will
    not believe,
    even when someone explains
        it to you!' "

42 As Paul and Barnabas were leaving the synagogue, the people invited them to come back the next Sabbath and tell them more about these things. 43 After the people had left the meeting, Paul and Barnabas were followed by many Jews and by many Gentiles who had been converted to Judaism. The apostles spoke to them and encouraged them to keep on living in the grace of God.

44 The next Sabbath nearly everyone in the town came to hear the word of the Lord. 45 When the Jews saw the crowds, they were filled with jealousy; they disputed what Paul was saying and insulted him. 46 But Paul and Barnabas spoke out even more boldly: "It was necessary that the word of God should be spoken first to you. But since you reject it and do not consider yourselves worthy of eternal life, we will leave you and go to the Gentiles. 47 For this is the commandment that the Lord has given us:

'I have made you a light for the
        Gentiles,
    so that all the world may be
        saved.' "

48 When the Gentiles heard this, they were glad and praised the Lord's message; and those who had been chosen for eternal life became believers.

49 The word of the Lord spread everywhere in that region. 50 But the Jews stirred up the leading men of the city and the Gentile women of high social standing who worshiped God. They started a persecution against Paul and Barnabas and threw them out of their region. 51 The apostles shook the dust off their feet in protest against them

---

u *Some manuscripts do not have* to you.

13.29 Mt 27.57-61; Mk 15.42-47; Lk 23.50-56; Jn 19.38-42   **13.31** Ac 1.3   **13.33** Ps 2.7
13.34 Is 55.3 (LXX)   **13.35** Ps 16.10   **13.41** Hb 1.5 (LXX)   **13.47** Is 42.6; 49.6
13.51 Mt 10.14; Mk 6.11; Lk 9.5; 10.11

and went on to Iconium. 52 The believers in Antioch were full of joy and the Holy Spirit.

In Iconium

14 The same thing happened in Iconium: Paul and Barnabas went to the synagogue and spoke in such a way that a great number of Jews and Gentiles became believers. 2 But the Jews who would not believe stirred up the Gentiles and turned them against the believers. 3 The apostles stayed there for a long time, speaking boldly about the Lord, who proved that their message about his grace was true by giving them the power to perform miracles and wonders. 4 The people of the city were divided: some were for the Jews, others for the apostles.

5 Then some Gentiles and Jews, together with their leaders, decided to mistreat the apostles and stone them. 6 When the apostles learned about it, they fled to the cities of Lystra and Derbe in Lycaonia and to the surrounding territory. 7 There they preached the Good News.

In Lystra and Derbe

8 In Lystra there was a crippled man who had been lame from birth and had never been able to walk. 9 He sat there and listened to Paul's words. Paul saw that he believed and could be healed, so he looked straight at him 10 and said in a loud voice, "Stand up straight on your feet!" The man jumped up and started walking around. 11 When the crowds saw what Paul had done, they started shouting in their own Lycaonian language, "The gods have become like men and have come down to us!" 12 They gave Barnabas the name Zeus, and Paul the name Hermes, because he was the chief speaker. 13 The priest of the god Zeus, whose temple stood just outside the town, brought bulls and flowers to the gate, for he and the crowds wanted to offer sacrifice to the apostles.

14 When Barnabas and Paul heard what they were about to do, they tore their clothes and ran into the middle of the crowd, shouting, 15 "Why are you doing this? We ourselves are only human beings like you! We are here to announce the Good News, to turn you away from these worthless things to the living God, who made heaven, earth, sea, and all that is in them. 16 In the past he allowed all people to go their own way. 17 But he has always given evidence of his existence by the good things he does: he gives you rain from heaven and crops at the right times; he gives you food and fills your hearts with happiness." 18 Even with these words the apostles could hardly keep the crowd from offering a sacrifice to them.

19 Some Jews came from Antioch in Pisidia and from Iconium; they won the crowds over to their side, stoned Paul and dragged him out of the town, thinking that he was dead. 20 But when the believers gathered around him, he got up and went back into the town. The next day he and Barnabas went to Derbe.

The Return to Antioch in Syria

21 Paul and Barnabas preached the Good News in Derbe and won many disciples. Then they went back to Lystra, to Iconium, and on to Antioch in Pisidia. 22 They strengthened the believers and encouraged them to remain true to the faith. "We must pass through many troubles to enter the Kingdom of God," they taught. 23 In each church they appointed elders, and with prayers and fasting they commended them to the Lord, in whom they had put their trust.

24 After going through the territory of Pisidia, they came to Pamphylia.

14.15 Ex 20.11; Ps 146.6

PAUL'S 1st AND 2nd JOURNEYS
- - - - - - - First Journey
———— Second Journey

© United Bible Societies 1978

²⁵ There they preached the message in Perga and then went to Attalia, ²⁶ and from there they sailed back to Antioch, the place where they had been commended to the care of God's grace for the work they had now completed.

²⁷ When they arrived in Antioch, they gathered the people of the church together and told them about all that God had done with them and how he had opened the way for the Gentiles to believe. ²⁸ And they stayed a long time there with the believers.

The Meeting at Jerusalem

15 Some men came from Judea to Antioch and started teaching the believers, "You cannot be saved unless you are circumcised as the Law of Moses requires." ² Paul and Barnabas got into a fierce argument with them about this, so it was decided that Paul and Barnabas and some of the others in Antioch should go to Jerusalem and see the apostles and elders about this matter.

³ They were sent on their way by the church; and as they went through

Phoenicia and Samaria, they reported how the Gentiles had turned to God; this news brought great joy to all the believers. ⁴ When they arrived in Jerusalem, they were welcomed by the church, the apostles, and the elders, to whom they told all that God had done through them. ⁵ But some of the believers who belonged to the party of the Pharisees stood up and said, "The Gentiles must be circumcised and told to obey the Law of Moses."

⁶ The apostles and the elders met together to consider this question. ⁷ After a long debate Peter stood up and said, "My friends, you know that a long time ago God chose me from among you to preach the Good News to the Gentiles, so that they could hear and believe. ⁸ And God, who knows the thoughts of everyone, showed his approval of the Gentiles by giving the Holy Spirit to them, just as he had to us. ⁹ He made no difference between us and them; he forgave their sins because they believed. ¹⁰ So then, why do you now want to put God to the test by laying a load on the backs of the believers which neither our ancestors nor we ourselves were

15.1 Lv 12.3   **15.7** Ac 10.1-43   **15.8** Ac 10.44; Ac 2.4

able to carry? 11 No! We believe and are saved by the grace of the Lord Jesus, just as they are."

12 The whole group was silent as they heard Barnabas and Paul report all the miracles and wonders that God had performed through them among the Gentiles. 13 When they had finished speaking, James spoke up: "Listen to me, my friends! 14 Simon has just explained how God first showed his care for the Gentiles by taking from among them a people to belong to him. 15 The words of the prophets agree completely with this. As the scripture says,

16 'After this I will return, says the Lord,
        and restore the kingdom of David.
    I will rebuild its ruins
        and make it strong again.
17 And so all the rest of the human race will come to me,
        all the Gentiles whom I have called to be my own.
18 So says the Lord, who made this known long ago.'

19 "It is my opinion," James went on, "that we should not trouble the Gentiles who are turning to God. 20 Instead, we should write a letter telling them not to eat any food that is ritually unclean because it has been offered to idols; to keep themselves from sexual immorality; and not to eat any animal that has been strangled, or any blood. 21 For the Law of Moses has been read for a very long time in the synagogues every Sabbath, and his words are preached in every town."

The Letter to the Gentile Believers

22 Then the apostles and the elders, together with the whole church, decided to choose some men from the group and send them to Antioch with Paul and Barnabas. They chose two men who were highly respected by the believers, Judas, called Barsabbas, and Silas, 23 and they sent the following letter by them:

"We, the apostles and the elders, your brothers, send greetings to all our brothers of Gentile birth who live in Antioch, Syria, and Cilicia. 24 We have heard that some who went from our group have troubled and upset you by what they said; they had not, however, received any instruction from us. 25 And so we have met together and have all agreed to choose some messengers and send them to you. They will go with our dear friends Barnabas and Paul, 26 who have risked their lives in the service of our Lord Jesus Christ. 27 We send you, then, Judas and Silas, who will tell you in person the same things we are writing. 28 The Holy Spirit and we have agreed not to put any other burden on you besides these necessary rules: 29 eat no food that has been offered to idols; eat no blood; eat no animal that has been strangled; and keep yourselves from sexual immorality. You will do well if you take care not to do these things. With our best wishes."

30 The messengers were sent off and went to Antioch, where they gathered the whole group of believers and gave them the letter. 31 When the people read it, they were filled with joy by the message of encouragement. 32 Judas and Silas, who were themselves prophets, spoke a long time with them, giving them courage and strength. 33 After spending some time there, they were sent off in peace by the believers and went back to those who had sent them.ᵛ

35 Paul and Barnabas spent some time in Antioch, and together with many others they taught and preached the word of the Lord.

ᵛ *Some manuscripts add verse 34:* But Silas decided to stay there.
15.16-18 Am 9.11, 12 (LXX) **15.20 a** Ex 34.15-17; **b** Lv 18.6-23; **c** Lv 17.10-16

Paul and Barnabas Separate

36 Some time later Paul said to Barnabas, "Let us go back and visit the believers in every town where we preached the word of the Lord, and let us find out how they are getting along." **37** Barnabas wanted to take John Mark with them, **38** but Paul did not think it was right to take him, because he had not stayed with them to the end of their mission, but had turned back and left them in Pamphylia. **39** There was a sharp argument, and they separated: Barnabas took Mark and sailed off for Cyprus, **40** while Paul chose Silas and left, commended by the believers to the care of the Lord's grace. **41** He went through Syria and Cilicia, strengthening the churches.

Timothy Goes with Paul and Silas

16 Paul traveled on to Derbe and Lystra, where a Christian named Timothy lived. His mother, who was also a Christian, was Jewish, but his father was a Greek. **2** All the believers in Lystra and Iconium spoke well of Timothy. **3** Paul wanted to take Timothy along with him, so he circumcised him. He did so because all the Jews who lived in those places knew that Timothy's father was Greek. **4** As they went through the towns, they delivered to the believers the rules decided upon by the apostles and elders in Jerusalem, and they told them to obey those rules. **5** So the churches were made stronger in the faith and grew in numbers every day.

In Troas: Paul's Vision

6 They traveled through the region of Phrygia and Galatia because the Holy Spirit did not let them preach the message in the province of Asia. **7** When they reached the border of Mysia, they tried to go into the province of Bithynia, but the Spirit of Jesus did not allow them. **8** So they traveled right on through[w] Mysia and went to Troas. **9** That night Paul had a vision in which he saw a Macedonian standing and begging him, "Come over to Macedonia and help us!" **10** As soon as Paul had this vision, we got ready to leave for Macedonia, because we decided that God had called us to preach the Good News to the people there.

In Philippi: the Conversion of Lydia

11 We left by ship from Troas and sailed straight across to Samothrace, and the next day to Neapolis. **12** From there we went inland to Philippi, a city of the first district of Macedonia;[x] it is also a Roman colony. We spent several days there. **13** On the Sabbath we went out of the city to the riverside, where we thought there would be a place where Jews gathered for prayer. We sat down and talked to the women who gathered there. **14** One of those who heard us was Lydia from Thyatira, who was a dealer in purple cloth. She was a woman who worshiped God, and the Lord opened her mind to pay attention to what Paul was saying. **15** After she and the people of her house had been baptized, she invited us, "Come and stay in my house if you have decided that I am a true believer in the Lord." And she persuaded us to go.

In Prison at Philippi

16 One day as we were going to the place of prayer, we were met by a young servant woman who had an evil spirit that enabled her to predict the future. She earned a lot of money for her

---

[w] *traveled right on through; or passed by.*

[x] *a city of the first district of Macedonia;* some manuscripts have *a leading city of the district of Macedonia, or a leading city of that district in Macedonia.*

15.38 Ac 13.13

owners by telling fortunes. 17 She followed Paul and us, shouting, "These men are servants of the Most High God! They announce to you how you can be saved!" 18 She did this for many days, until Paul became so upset that he turned around and said to the spirit, "In the name of Jesus Christ I order you to come out of her!" The spirit went out of her that very moment. 19 When her owners realized that their chance of making money was gone, they seized Paul and Silas and dragged them to the authorities in the public square. 20 They brought them before the Roman officials and said, "These men are Jews, and they are causing trouble in our city. 21 They are teaching customs that are against our law; we are Roman citizens, and we cannot accept these customs or practice them." 22 And the crowd joined in the attack against Paul and Silas.

Then the officials tore the clothes off Paul and Silas and ordered them to be whipped. 23 After a severe beating, they were thrown into jail, and the jailer was ordered to lock them up tight. 24 Upon receiving this order, the jailer threw them into the inner cell and fastened their feet between heavy blocks of wood.

25 About midnight Paul and Silas were praying and singing hymns to God, and the other prisoners were listening to them. 26 Suddenly there was a violent earthquake, which shook the prison to its foundations. At once all the doors opened, and the chains fell off all the prisoners. 27 The jailer woke up, and when he saw the prison doors open, he thought that the prisoners had escaped; so he pulled out his sword and was about to kill himself. 28 But Paul shouted at the top of his voice, "Don't harm yourself! We are all here!"

29 The jailer called for a light, rushed in, and fell trembling at the feet of Paul and Silas. 30 Then he led them out and asked, "Sirs, what must I do to be saved?"

31 They answered, "Believe in the Lord Jesus, and you will be saved — you and your family." 32 Then they preached the word of the Lord to him and to all the others in the house. 33 At that very hour of the night the jailer took them and washed their wounds; and he and all his family were baptized at once. 34 Then he took Paul and Silas up into his house and gave them some food to eat. He and his family were filled with joy, because they now believed in God.

35 The next morning the Roman authorities sent police officers with the order, "Let those men go."

36 So the jailer told Paul, "The officials have sent an order for you and Silas to be released. You may leave, then, and go in peace."

37 But Paul said to the police officers, "We were not found guilty of any crime, yet they whipped us in public — and we are Roman citizens! Then they threw us in prison. And now they want to send us away secretly? Not at all! The Roman officials themselves must come here and let us out."

38 The police officers reported these words to the Roman officials; and when they heard that Paul and Silas were Roman citizens, they were afraid. 39 So

"Sirs, what must I do to be saved?" (16.30)

they went and apologized to them; then they led them out of the prison and asked them to leave the city. [40] Paul and Silas left the prison and went to Lydia's house. There they met the believers, spoke words of encouragement to them, and left.

In Thessalonica

17 Paul and Silas traveled on through Amphipolis and Apollonia and came to Thessalonica, where there was a synagogue. [2] According to his usual habit Paul went to the synagogue. There during three Sabbaths he held discussions with the people, quoting [3] and explaining the Scriptures, and proving from them that the Messiah had to suffer and rise from death. "This Jesus whom I announce to you," Paul said, "is the Messiah." [4] Some of them were convinced and joined Paul and Silas; so did many of the leading women and a large group of Greeks who worshiped God.

[5] But some Jews were jealous and gathered worthless loafers from the streets and formed a mob. They set the whole city in an uproar and attacked the home of a man named Jason, in an attempt to find Paul and Silas and bring them out to the people. [6] But when they did not find them, they dragged Jason and some other believers before the city authorities and shouted, "These men have caused trouble everywhere! Now they have come to our city, [7] and Jason has kept them in his house. They are all breaking the laws of the Emperor, saying that there is another king, whose name is Jesus." [8] With these words they threw the crowd and the city authorities in an uproar. [9] The authorities made Jason and the others pay the required amount of money to be released, and then let them go.

In Berea

[10] As soon as night came, the believers sent Paul and Silas to Berea. When they arrived, they went to the synagogue. [11] The people there were more open-minded than the people in Thessalonica. They listened to the message with great eagerness, and every day they studied the Scriptures to see if what Paul said was really true. [12] Many of them believed; and many Greek women of high social standing and many Greek men also believed. [13] But when the Jews in Thessalonica heard that Paul had preached the word of God in Berea also, they came there and started exciting and stirring up the mobs. [14] At once the believers sent Paul away to the coast; but both Silas and Timothy stayed in Berea. [15] The men who were taking Paul went with him as far as Athens and then returned to Berea with instructions from Paul that Silas and Timothy should join him as soon as possible.

In Athens

[16] While Paul was waiting in Athens for Silas and Timothy, he was greatly upset when he noticed how full of idols the city was. [17] So he held discussions in the synagogue with the Jews and with the Gentiles who worshiped God, and also in the public square every day with the people who happened to come by. [18] Certain Epicurean and Stoic teachers also debated with him. Some of them asked, "What is this ignorant show-off trying to say?"

Others answered, "He seems to be talking about foreign gods." They said this because Paul was preaching about Jesus and the resurrection.*y* [19] So they took Paul, brought him before the city council, the Areopagus, and said, "We would like to know what this new teaching is that you are talking about.

---

y JESUS AND THE RESURRECTION: *In Greek, the feminine noun "resurrection" could be understood to be the name of a goddess.*

20 Some of the things we hear you say sound strange to us, and we would like to know what they mean." (21 For all the citizens of Athens and the foreigners who lived there liked to spend all their time telling and hearing the latest new thing.)

22 Paul stood up in front of the city council and said, "I see that in every way you Athenians are very religious. 23 For as I walked through your city and looked at the places where you worship, I found an altar on which is written, 'To an Unknown God.' That which you worship, then, even though you do not know it, is what I now proclaim to you. 24 God, who made the world and everything in it, is Lord of heaven and earth and does not live in temples made by human hands. 25 Nor does he need anything that we can supply by working for him, since it is he himself who gives life and breath and everything else to everyone. 26 From one human being he created all races of people and made them live throughout the whole earth. He himself fixed beforehand the exact times and the limits of the places where they would live. 27 He did this so that they would look for him, and perhaps find him as they felt around for him. Yet God is actually not far from any one of us; 28 as someone has said,

'In him we live and move and
    exist.'

It is as some of your poets have said,

'We too are his children.'

29 Since we are God's children, we should not suppose that his nature is anything like an image of gold or silver or stone, shaped by human art and skill. 30 God has overlooked the times when people did not know him, but now he commands all of them everywhere to turn away from their evil ways. 31 For he has fixed a day in which he will judge the whole world with justice by means of a man he has chosen. He has given

proof of this to everyone by raising that man from death!"

32 When they heard Paul speak about a raising from death, some of them made fun of him, but others said, "We want to hear you speak about this again." 33 And so Paul left the meeting. 34 Some men joined him and believed, among whom was Dionysius, a member of the council; there was also a woman named Damaris, and some other people.

In Corinth

18 After this, Paul left Athens and went on to Corinth. 2 There he met a Jew named Aquila, born in Pontus, who had recently come from Italy with his wife Priscilla, for Emperor Claudius had ordered all the Jews to leave Rome. Paul went to see them, 3 and stayed and worked with them, because he earned his living by making tents, just as they did. 4 He held discussions in the synagogue every Sabbath, trying to convince both Jews and Greeks.

5 When Silas and Timothy arrived from Macedonia, Paul gave his whole time to preaching the message, testifying to the Jews that Jesus is the Messiah. 6 When they opposed him and said evil things about him, he protested by shaking the dust from his clothes and saying to them, "If you are lost, you yourselves must take the blame for it! I am not responsible. From now on I will go to the Gentiles." 7 So he left them and went to live in the house of a Gentile named Titius Justus, who worshiped God; his house was next to the synagogue. 8 Crispus, who was the leader of the synagogue, believed in the Lord, together with all his family; and many other people in Corinth heard the message, believed, and were baptized.

9 One night Paul had a vision in

17.23 Ws 13.1   **17.24, 25** 1 K 8.27; Is 42.5; Ac 7.48   **17.25** 2 Macc 14.35
17.26 2 Macc 7.23   **17.27** Ws 13.6-9

which the Lord said to him, "Do not be afraid, but keep on speaking and do not give up, [10] for I am with you. No one will be able to harm you, for many in this city are my people." [11] So Paul stayed there for a year and a half, teaching the people the word of God.

[12] When Gallio was made the Roman governor of Achaia, Jews there got together, seized Paul, and took him into court. [13] "This man," they said, "is trying to persuade people to worship God in a way that is against the law!"

[14] Paul was about to speak when Gallio said to the Jews, "If this were a matter of some evil crime or wrong that has been committed, it would be reasonable for me to be patient with you Jews. [15] But since it is an argument about words and names and your own law, you yourselves must settle it. I will not be the judge of such things!" [16] And he drove them out of the court. [17] They all grabbed Sosthenes, the leader of the synagogue, and beat him in front of the court. But that did not bother Gallio a bit.

The Return to Antioch

[18] Paul stayed on with the believers in Corinth for many days, then left them and sailed off with Priscilla and Aquila for Syria. Before sailing from Cenchreae he had his head shaved because of a vow he had taken.[z] [19] They arrived in Ephesus, where Paul left Priscilla and Aquila. He went into the synagogue and held discussions with the Jews. [20] The people asked him to stay longer, but he would not consent. [21] Instead, he told them as he left, "If it is the will of God, I will come back to you." And so he sailed from Ephesus.

[22] When he arrived at Caesarea, he went to Jerusalem and greeted the church, and then went to Antioch.

[23] After spending some time there, he left and went through the region of Galatia and Phrygia, strengthening all the believers.

Apollos in Ephesus and Corinth

[24] At that time a Jew named Apollos, who had been born in Alexandria, came to Ephesus. He was an eloquent speaker and had a thorough knowledge of the Scriptures. [25] He had been instructed in the Way of the Lord, and with great enthusiasm he proclaimed and taught correctly the facts about Jesus. However, he knew only the baptism of John. [26] He began to speak boldly in the synagogue. When Priscilla and Aquila heard him, they took him home with them and explained to him more correctly the Way of God. [27] Apollos then decided to go to Achaia, so the believers in Ephesus helped him by writing to the believers in Achaia, urging them to welcome him. When he arrived, he was a great help to those who through God's grace had become believers. [28] For with his strong arguments he defeated the Jews in public debates by proving from the Scriptures that Jesus is the Messiah.

Paul in Ephesus

19 While Apollos was in Corinth, Paul traveled through the interior of the province and arrived in Ephesus. There he found some disciples [2] and asked them, "Did you receive the Holy Spirit when you became believers?"

"We have not even heard that there is a Holy Spirit," they answered.

[3] "Well, then, what kind of baptism did you receive?" Paul asked.

"The baptism of John," they answered.

[4] Paul said, "The baptism of John was

---

[z] A VOW HE HAD TAKEN: *This refers to the Jewish custom of shaving the head as a sign that a vow has been kept.*

18.18 Nu 6.18   **19.4** Mt 3.11; Mk 1.4, 7, 8; Lk 3.4, 16; Jn 1.26, 27 for those who turned from their sins; and he told the people of Israel to believe in the one who was coming after him — that is, in Jesus."

5 When they heard this, they were baptized in the name of the Lord Jesus. 6 Paul placed his hands on them, and the Holy Spirit came upon them; they spoke in strange tongues and also proclaimed God's message. 7 They were about twelve men in all.

8 Paul went into the synagogue and for three months spoke boldly with the people, holding discussions with them and trying to convince them about the Kingdom of God. 9 But some of them were stubborn and would not believe, and before the whole group they said evil things about the Way of the Lord. So Paul left them and took the believers with him, and every day[a] he held discussions in the lecture hall of Tyrannus. 10 This went on for two years, so that all the people who lived in the province of Asia, both Jews and Gentiles, heard the word of the Lord.

The Sons of Sceva

11 God was performing unusual miracles through Paul. 12 Even handkerchiefs and aprons he had used were taken to the sick, and their diseases were driven away, and the evil spirits would go out of them. 13 Some Jews who traveled around and drove out evil spirits also tried to use the name of the Lord Jesus to do this. They said to the evil spirits, "I command you in the name of Jesus, whom Paul preaches." 14 Seven brothers, who were the sons of a Jewish High Priest named Sceva, were doing this.

15 But the evil spirit said to them, "I know Jesus, and I know about Paul; but you — who are you?"

16 The man who had the evil spirit in him attacked them with such violence that he overpowered them all. They ran away from his house, wounded and with their clothes torn off. 17 All the Jews and Gentiles who lived in Ephesus heard about this; they were all filled with fear, and the name of the Lord Jesus was given greater honor. 18 Many of the believers came, publicly admitting and revealing what they had done. 19 Many of those who had practiced magic brought their books together and burned them in public. They added up the price of the books, and the total came to fifty thousand silver coins.[b] 20 In this powerful way the word of the Lord[c] kept spreading and growing stronger.

The Riot in Ephesus

21 After these things had happened, Paul made up his mind[d] to travel through Macedonia and Achaia and go on to Jerusalem. "After I go there," he said, "I must also see Rome." 22 So he sent Timothy and Erastus, two of his helpers, to Macedonia, while he spent more time in the province of Asia.

23 It was at this time that there was serious trouble in Ephesus because of the Way of the Lord. 24 A certain silversmith named Demetrius made silver models of the temple of the goddess Artemis, and his business brought a great deal of profit to the workers. 25 So he called them all together with others whose work was like theirs and said to them, "Men, you know that our prosperity comes from this work. 26 Now, you can see and hear for yourselves what this fellow Paul is doing. He says that hand-made gods are not gods at all, and he has succeeded in convincing

---

[a] Some manuscripts add from 11:00 a.m. until 4:00 p.m.
coin was the daily wage of a rural worker (see Mt 20.2).
so, by the power of the Lord, the message.
by the Spirit, decided.

[b] SILVER COINS: A silver
[c] In this ... Lord; or And
[d] Paul made up his mind; or Paul, led

PAUL'S THIRD JOURNEY

many people, both here in Ephesus and in nearly the whole province of Asia. ²⁷ There is the danger, then, that this business of ours will get a bad name. Not only that, but there is also the danger that the temple of the great goddess Artemis will come to mean nothing and that her greatness will be destroyed — the goddess worshiped by everyone in Asia and in all the world!"

²⁸ As the crowd heard these words, they became furious and started shouting, "Great is Artemis of Ephesus!" ²⁹ The uproar spread throughout the whole city. The mob grabbed Gaius and Aristarchus, two Macedonians who were traveling with Paul, and rushed with them to the theater. ³⁰ Paul himself wanted to go before the crowd, but the believers would not let him. ³¹ Some of the provincial authorities, who were his friends, also sent him a message begging him not to show himself in the theater. ³² Meanwhile the whole meeting was in an uproar: some people were shouting one thing, others were shouting something else, because most of them did not even know why they had come together. ³³ Some of the people concluded that Alexander was responsible, since the Jews made him go up to the front. Then Alexander motioned with his hand for the people to be silent, and he tried to make a speech of defense. ³⁴ But when they recognized that he was a Jew, they all shouted together the same thing for two hours: "Great is Artemis of Ephesus!"

³⁵ At last the city clerk was able to calm the crowd. "Fellow Ephesians!" he said. "Everyone knows that the city of Ephesus is the keeper of the temple of the great Artemis and of the sacred stone that fell down from heaven. ³⁶ Nobody can deny these things. So then, you must calm down and not do anything reckless. ³⁷ You have brought these men here even though they have not robbed temples or said evil things about our goddess. ³⁸ If Demetrius and his workers have an accusation against anyone, we have the authorities and the regular days for court; charges can be made there. ³⁹ But if there is something more that you want, it will have to be settled in a legal meeting of citizens. ⁴⁰ For after what has happened today, there is the danger that we will be accused of a riot. There is no excuse for all this uproar, and we would not be able to give a good reason for it." ⁴¹ After saying this, he dismissed the meeting.

To Macedonia and Achaia

20 After the uproar died down, Paul called together the believers and with words of encouragement said good-bye to them. Then he left and went on to Macedonia. ² He went through those regions and encouraged the people with many messages. Then he came to Achaia, ³ where he stayed three months. He was getting ready to go to Syria when he discovered that there were Jews plotting against him; so he decided to go back through Macedonia. ⁴ Sopater son of Pyrrhus, from Berea, went with him; so did Aristarchus and Secundus, from Thessalonica; Gaius, from Derbe; Tychicus and Trophimus, from the province of Asia; and Timothy. ⁵ They went ahead and waited for us in Troas. ⁶ We sailed from Philippi after the Festival of Unleavened Bread, and five days later we joined them in Troas, where we spent a week.

Paul's Last Visit to Troas

⁷ On Saturday*ᵉ* evening we gathered together for the fellowship meal. Paul spoke to the people and kept on speaking until midnight, since he was going to leave the next day. ⁸ Many lamps were burning in the upstairs room where we were meeting. ⁹ A young man named Eutychus was sitting in the window, and as Paul kept on talking, Eutychus got sleepier and sleepier, until he finally went sound asleep and fell from the third story to the ground. When they picked him up, he was dead. ¹⁰ But Paul went down and threw himself on him and hugged him. "Don't worry," he said, "he is still alive!" ¹¹ Then he went back upstairs, broke bread, and ate. After talking with them for a long time, even until sunrise, Paul left. ¹² They took the young man home alive and were greatly comforted.

ᵉ Saturday; or Sunday.
20.24 2 Ti 4.7

From Troas to Miletus

¹³ We went on ahead to the ship and sailed off to Assos, where we were going to take Paul aboard. He had told us to do this, because he was going there by land. ¹⁴ When he met us in Assos, we took him aboard and went on to Mitylene. ¹⁵ We sailed from there and arrived off Chios the next day. A day later we came to Samos, and the following day we reached Miletus. ¹⁶ Paul had decided to sail on by Ephesus, so as not to lose any time in the province of Asia. He was in a hurry to arrive in Jerusalem by the day of Pentecost, if at all possible.

Paul's Farewell Speech to the Elders of Ephesus

¹⁷ From Miletus Paul sent a message to Ephesus, asking the elders of the church to meet him. ¹⁸ When they arrived, he said to them, "You know how I spent the whole time I was with you, from the first day I arrived in the province of Asia. ¹⁹ With all humility and many tears I did my work as the Lord's servant during the hard times that came to me because of the plots of some Jews. ²⁰ You know that I did not hold back anything that would be of help to you as I preached and taught in public and in your homes. ²¹ To Jews and Gentiles alike I gave solemn warning that they should turn from their sins to God and believe in our Lord Jesus. ²² And now, in obedience to the Holy Spirit I am going to Jerusalem, not knowing what will happen to me there. ²³ I only know that in every city the Holy Spirit has warned me that prison and troubles wait for me. ²⁴ But I reckon my own life to be worth nothing to me; I only want to complete my mission and finish the work that the Lord Jesus gave me to do,

which is to declare the Good News about the grace of God.

²⁵"I have gone about among all of you, preaching the Kingdom of God. And now I know that none of you will ever see me again. ²⁶So I solemnly declare to you this very day: if any of you should be lost, I am not responsible. ²⁷For I have not held back from announcing to you the whole purpose of God. ²⁸So keep watch over yourselves and over all the flock which the Holy Spirit has placed in your care. Be shepherds of the church of God,*f* which he made his own through the blood of his Son.*g* ²⁹I know that after I leave, fierce wolves will come among you, and they will not spare the flock. ³⁰The time will come when some men from your own group will tell lies to lead the believers away after them. ³¹Watch, then, and remember that with many tears, day and night, I taught every one of you for three years.

³²"And now I commend you to the care of God and to the message of his grace, which is able to build you up and give you the blessings God has for all his people. ³³I have not wanted anyone's silver or gold or clothing. ³⁴You yourselves know that I have worked with these hands of mine to provide everything that my companions and I have needed. ³⁵I have shown you in all things that by working hard in this way we must help the weak, remembering the words that the Lord Jesus himself said, 'There is more happiness in giving than in receiving.'"

³⁶When Paul finished, he knelt down with them and prayed. ³⁷They were all crying as they hugged him and kissed him good-bye. ³⁸They were especially sad because he had said that they would never see him again. And so they went with him to the ship.

Paul Goes to Jerusalem

21 We said good-bye to them and left. After sailing straight across, we came to Cos; the next day we reached Rhodes, and from there we went on to Patara. ²There we found a ship that was going to Phoenicia, so we went aboard and sailed away. ³We came to where we could see Cyprus, and then sailed south of it on to Syria. We went ashore at Tyre, where the ship was going to unload its cargo. ⁴There we found some believers and stayed with them a week. By the power of the Spirit they told Paul not to go to Jerusalem. ⁵But when our time with them was over, we left and went on our way. All of them, together with their wives and children, went with us out of the city to the beach, where we all knelt and prayed. ⁶Then we said good-bye to one another, and we went on board the ship while they went back home.

⁷We continued our voyage, sailing from Tyre to Ptolemais, where we greeted the believers and stayed with them for a day. ⁸On the following day we left and arrived in Caesarea. There we stayed at the house of Philip the evangelist, one of the seven men who had been chosen as helpers in Jerusalem. ⁹He had four unmarried daughters who proclaimed God's message. ¹⁰We had been there for several days when a prophet named Agabus arrived from Judea. ¹¹He came to us, took Paul's belt, tied up his own feet and hands with it, and said, "This is what the Holy Spirit says: The owner of this belt will be tied up in this way by the Jews in Jerusalem, and they will hand him over to the Gentiles."

¹²When we heard this, we and the others there begged Paul not to go to Jerusalem. ¹³But he answered, "What are you doing, crying like this and

---

f God; *some manuscripts have* the Lord.   *g* through the blood of his Son; *or* through the sacrificial death of his Son; *or* through his own blood.
21.8 Ac 6.5; 8.5   **21.10** Ac 11.28

breaking my heart? I am ready not only to be tied up in Jerusalem but even to die there for the sake of the Lord Jesus."

14 We could not convince him, so we gave up and said, "May the Lord's will be done."

15 After spending some time there, we got our things ready and left for Jerusalem. 16 Some of the disciples from Caesarea also went with us and took us to the house of the man we were going to stay with[h] — Mnason, from Cyprus, who had been a believer since the early days.

Paul Visits James

17 When we arrived in Jerusalem, the believers welcomed us warmly. 18 The next day Paul went with us to see James; and all the church elders were present. 19 Paul greeted them and gave a complete report of everything that God had done among the Gentiles through his work. 20 After hearing him, they all praised God. Then they said, "Brother Paul, you can see how many thousands of Jews have become believers, and how devoted they all are to the Law. 21 They have been told that you have been teaching all the Jews who live in Gentile countries to abandon the Law of Moses, telling them not to circumcise their children or follow Jewish customs. 22 They are sure to hear that you have arrived. What should be done, then? 23 This is what we want you to do. There are four men here who have taken a vow. 24 Go along with them and join them in the ceremony of purification and pay their expenses; then they will be able to shave their heads.[i] In this way everyone will know that there is no truth in any of the things that they have been told about you, but that you yourself live in ac-

cordance with the Law of Moses. 25 But as for the Gentiles who have become believers, we have sent them a letter telling them we decided that they must not eat any food that has been offered to idols, or any blood, or any animal that has been strangled, and that they must keep themselves from sexual immorality."

26 So Paul took the men and the next day performed the ceremony of purification with them. Then he went into the Temple and gave notice of how many days it would be until the end of the period of purification, when a sacrifice would be offered for each one of them.

Paul Is Arrested in the Temple

27 But just when the seven days were about to come to an end, some Jews from the province of Asia saw Paul in the Temple. They stirred up the whole crowd and grabbed Paul. 28 "People of Israel!" they shouted. "Help! This is the man who goes everywhere teaching everyone against the people of Israel, the Law of Moses, and this Temple. And now he has even brought some Gentiles into the Temple and defiled this holy place!" (29 They said this because they had seen Trophimus from Ephesus with Paul in the city, and they thought that Paul had taken him into the Temple.)

30 Confusion spread through the whole city, and the people all ran together, grabbed Paul, and dragged him out of the Temple. At once the Temple doors were closed. 31 The mob was trying to kill Paul, when a report was sent up to the commander of the Roman troops that all of Jerusalem was rioting. 32 At once the commander took some officers and soldiers and rushed down to

---

[h] and took us to the house of the man we were going to stay with; or bringing with them the man at whose house we were going to stay.   [i] SHAVE THEIR HEADS: See 18.18.

21.23, 24 Nu 6.13-21   **21.25** Ac 15.29   **21.29** Ac 20.4

the crowd. When the people saw him with the soldiers, they stopped beating Paul. 33 The commander went over to Paul, arrested him, and ordered him to be bound with two chains. Then he asked, "Who is this man, and what has he done?" 34 Some in the crowd shouted one thing, others something else. There was such confusion that the commander could not find out exactly what had happened, so he ordered his men to take Paul up into the fort. 35 They got as far as the steps with him, and then the soldiers had to carry him because the mob was so wild. 36 They were all coming after him and screaming, "Kill him!"

Paul Defends Himself

37 As the soldiers were about to take Paul into the fort, he spoke to the commander: "May I say something to you?"

"You speak Greek, do you?" the commander asked. 38 "Then you are not that Egyptian fellow who some time ago started a revolution and led four thousand armed terrorists out into the desert?"

39 Paul answered, "I am a Jew, born in Tarsus in Cilicia, a citizen of an important city. Please let me speak to the people."

40 The commander gave him permission, so Paul stood on the steps and motioned with his hand for the people to be silent. When they were quiet, Paul spoke to them in Hebrew:

22 "My fellow Jews, listen to me as I make my defense before you!" 2 When they heard him speaking to them in Hebrew, they became even quieter; and Paul went on:

3 "I am a Jew, born in Tarsus in Cilicia, but brought up here in Jerusalem as a student of Gamaliel. I received strict instruction in the Law of our ancestors and was just as dedicated to God as are all of you who are here today.

4 I persecuted to the death the people who followed this Way. I arrested men and women and threw them into prison. 5 The High Priest and the whole Council can prove that I am telling the truth. I received from them letters written to fellow Jews in Damascus, so I went there to arrest these people and bring them back in chains to Jerusalem to be punished.

Paul Tells of His Conversion
(Acts 9.1-19; 26.12-18)

6 "As I was traveling and coming near Damascus, about midday a bright light from the sky flashed suddenly around me. 7 I fell to the ground and heard a voice saying to me, 'Saul, Saul! Why do you persecute me?' 8 'Who are you, Lord?' I asked. 'I am Jesus of Nazareth, whom you persecute,' he said to me. 9 The men with me saw the light, but did not hear the voice of the one who was speaking to me. 10 I asked, 'What shall I do, Lord?' and the Lord said to me, 'Get up and go into Damascus, and there you will be told everything that God has determined for you to do.' 11 I was blind because of the bright light, and so my companions took me by the hand and led me into Damascus.

12 "In that city was a man named Ananias, a religious man who obeyed our Law and was highly respected by all the Jews living there. 13 He came to me, stood by me, and said, 'Brother Saul, see again!' At that very moment I saw again and looked at him. 14 He said, 'The God of our ancestors has chosen you to know his will, to see his righteous Servant, and to hear him speaking with his own voice. 15 For you will be a witness for him to tell everyone what you have seen and heard. 16 And now, why wait any longer? Get up and be baptized and have your sins washed away by praying to him.'

22.3 Ac 5.34-39   **22.4, 5** Ac 8.3; 26.9-11

Paul's Call to Preach to the Gentiles

17 "I went back to Jerusalem, and while I was praying in the Temple, I had a vision, 18 in which I saw the Lord, as he said to me, 'Hurry and leave Jerusalem quickly, because the people here will not accept your witness about me.' 19 'Lord,' I answered, 'they know very well that I went to the synagogues and arrested and beat those who believe in you. 20 And when your witness Stephen was put to death, I myself was there, approving of his murder and taking care of the cloaks of his murderers.' 21 'Go,' the Lord said to me, 'for I will send you far away to the Gentiles.' "

22 The people listened to Paul until he said this; but then they started shouting at the top of their voices, "Away with him! Kill him! He's not fit to live!" 23 They were screaming, waving their clothes, and throwing dust up in the air. 24 The Roman commander ordered his men to take Paul into the fort, and he told them to whip him in order to find out why the Jews were screaming like this against him. 25 But when they had tied him up to be whipped, Paul said to the officer standing there, "Is it lawful for you to whip a Roman citizen who hasn't even been tried for any crime?"

26 When the officer heard this, he went to the commander and asked him, "What are you doing? That man is a Roman citizen!"

27 So the commander went to Paul and asked him, "Tell me, are you a Roman citizen?"

"Yes," answered Paul.

28 The commander said, "I became one by paying a large amount of money."

"But I am one by birth," Paul answered.

29 At once the men who were going to question Paul drew back from him; and

the commander was frightened when he realized that Paul was a Roman citizen and that he had put him in chains.

Paul before the Council

30 The commander wanted to find out for sure what the Jews were accusing Paul of; so the next day he had Paul's chains taken off and ordered the chief priests and the whole Council to meet. Then he took Paul and made him stand before them.

23 Paul looked straight at the Council and said, "My fellow Israelites! My conscience is perfectly clear about the way in which I have lived before God to this very day." 2 The High Priest Ananias ordered those who were standing close to Paul to strike him on the mouth. 3 Paul said to him, "God will certainly strike you — you whitewashed wall! You sit there to judge me according to the Law, yet you break the Law by ordering them to strike me!"

4 The men close to Paul said to him, "You are insulting God's High Priest!"

5 Paul answered, "My fellow Israelites, I did not know that he was the High Priest. The scripture says, 'You must not speak evil of the ruler of your people.' "

6 When Paul saw that some of the group were Sadducees and the others were Pharisees, he called out in the Council, "Fellow Israelites! I am a Pharisee, the son of Pharisees. I am on trial here because of the hope I have that the dead will rise to life!"

7 As soon as he said this, the Pharisees and Sadducees started to quarrel, and the group was divided. (8 For the Sadducees say that people will not rise from death and that there are no angels or spirits; but the Pharisees believe in all three.) 9 The shouting became louder, and some of the teachers of the

22.20 Ac 7.58   **23.3** Mt 23.27, 28   **23.5** Ex 22.28   **23.6** Ac 26.5; Phil 3.5   **23.8** Mt 22.23; Mk 12.18; Lk 20.27

Law who belonged to the party of the Pharisees stood up and protested strongly: "We cannot find a thing wrong with this man! Perhaps a spirit or an angel really did speak to him!"

¹⁰The argument became so violent that the commander was afraid that Paul would be torn to pieces. So he ordered his soldiers to go down into the group, get Paul away from them, and take him into the fort.

¹¹That night the Lord stood by Paul and said, "Don't be afraid! You have given your witness for me here in Jerusalem, and you must also do the same in Rome."

The Plot against Paul's Life

¹²The next morning some Jews met together and made a plan. They took a vow that they would not eat or drink anything until they had killed Paul. ¹³There were more than forty who planned this together. ¹⁴Then they went to the chief priests and elders and said, "We have taken a solemn vow together not to eat a thing until we have killed Paul. ¹⁵Now then, you and the Council send word to the Roman commander to bring Paul down to you, pretending that you want to get more accurate information about him. But we will be ready to kill him before he ever gets here."

¹⁶But the son of Paul's sister heard about the plot; so he went to the fort and told Paul. ¹⁷Then Paul called one of the officers and said to him, "Take this young man to the commander; he has something to tell him." ¹⁸The officer took him, led him to the commander, and said, "The prisoner Paul called me and asked me to bring this young man to you, because he has something to say to you."

¹⁹The commander took him by the hand, led him off by himself, and asked him, "What do you have to tell me?"

²⁰He said, "The Jewish authorities have agreed to ask you tomorrow to take Paul down to the Council, pretending that the Council wants to get more accurate information about him. ²¹But don't listen to them, because there are more than forty men who will be hiding and waiting for him. They have taken a vow not to eat or drink until they have killed him. They are now ready to do it and are waiting for your decision."

²²The commander said, "Don't tell anyone that you have reported this to me." And he sent the young man away.

Paul Is Sent to Governor Felix

²³Then the commander called two of his officers and said, "Get two hundred soldiers ready to go to Caesarea, together with seventy horsemen and two hundred spearmen, and be ready to leave by nine o'clock tonight. ²⁴Provide some horses for Paul to ride and get him safely through to Governor Felix." ²⁵Then the commander wrote a letter that went like this:

²⁶"Claudius Lysias to His Excellency, Governor Felix: Greetings. ²⁷The Jews seized this man and were about to kill him. I learned that he is a Roman citizen, so I went with my soldiers and rescued him. ²⁸I wanted to know what they were accusing him of, so I took him down to their Council. ²⁹I found out that he had not done a thing for which he deserved to die or be put in prison; the accusation against him had to do with questions about their own law. ³⁰And when I was informed that there was a plot against him, at once I decided to send him to you. I have told his accusers to make their charges against him before you."

³¹The soldiers carried out their orders. They got Paul and took him that night as far as Antipatris. ³²The next day the foot soldiers returned to the fort and left the horsemen to go on with him. ³³They took him to Caesarea, delivered the letter to the governor, and turned Paul over to him. ³⁴The

governor read the letter and asked Paul what province he was from. When he found out that he was from Cilicia, [35] he said, "I will hear you when your accusers arrive." Then he gave orders for Paul to be kept under guard in the governor's headquarters.

The Case Against Paul

24 Five days later the High Priest Ananias went to Caesarea with some elders and a lawyer named Tertullus. They appeared before Governor Felix and made their charges against Paul. [2] Then Paul was called in, and Tertullus began to make his accusation, as follows:

"Your Excellency! Your wise leadership has brought us a long period of peace, and many necessary reforms are being made for the good of our country. [3] We welcome this everywhere and at all times, and we are deeply grateful to you. [4] I do not want to take up too much of your time, however, so I beg you to be kind and listen to our brief account. [5] We found this man to be a dangerous nuisance; he starts riots among Jews all over the world and is a leader of the party of the Nazarenes. [6] He also tried to defile the Temple, and we arrested him.[j] [8] If you question this man, you yourself will be able to learn from him all the things that we are accusing him of." [9] The Jews joined in the accusation and said that all this was true.

Paul's Defense before Felix

[10] The governor then motioned to Paul to speak, and Paul said,

"I know that you have been a judge over this nation for many years, and so I am happy to defend myself before you. [11] As you can find out for yourself, it was no more than twelve days ago that I went to Jerusalem to worship. [12] The Jews did not find me arguing with anyone in the Temple, nor did they find me stirring up the people, either in the synagogues or anywhere else in the city. [13] Nor can they give you proof of the accusations they now bring against me. [14] I do admit this to you: I worship the God of our ancestors by following that Way which they say is false. But I also believe in everything written in the Law of Moses and the books of the prophets. [15] I have the same hope in God that these themselves have, namely, that all people, both the good and the bad, will rise from death. [16] And so I do my best always to have a clear conscience before God and people.

[17] "After being away from Jerusalem for several years, I went there to take some money to my own people and to offer sacrifices. [18] It was while I was doing this that they found me in the Temple after I had completed the ceremony of purification. There was no crowd with me and no disorder. [19] But some Jews from the province of Asia were there; they themselves ought to come before you and make their accusations if they have anything against me. [20] Or let these who are here tell what crime they found me guilty of when I stood before the Council — [21] except for the one thing I called out when I stood before them: 'I am being tried by you today for believing that the dead will rise to life.' "

[22] Then Felix, who was well informed about the Way, brought the hearing to a close. "When the commander Lysias arrives," he told them, "I will decide your case." [23] He ordered the officer in charge of Paul to keep him under guard, but to give him some freedom and allow his friends to provide for his needs.

---

[j] *Some manuscripts add verses 6b-8a:* We planned to judge him according to our own law, [7] but the commander Lysias came, and with great violence took him from us. [8] Then Lysias gave orders that his accusers should come before you.

24.17, 18 Ac 21.17-28   **24.21** Ac 23.6

Paul before Felix and Drusilla

²⁴ After some days Felix came with his wife Drusilla, who was Jewish. He sent for Paul and listened to him as he talked about faith in Christ Jesus. ²⁵ But as Paul went on discussing about goodness, self-control, and the coming Day of Judgment, Felix was afraid and said, "You may leave now. I will call you again when I get the chance." ²⁶ At the same time he was hoping that Paul would give him some money; and for this reason he would call for him often and talk with him.

²⁷ After two years had passed, Porcius Festus succeeded Felix as governor. Felix wanted to gain favor with the Jews so he left Paul in prison.

Paul Appeals to the Emperor

25 Three days after Festus arrived in the province, he went from Caesarea to Jerusalem, ² where the chief priests and the Jewish leaders brought their charges against Paul. They begged Festus ³ to do them the favor of having Paul come to Jerusalem, for they had made a plot to kill him on the way. ⁴ Festus answered, "Paul is being kept a prisoner in Caesarea, and I myself will be going back there soon. ⁵ Let your leaders go to Caesarea with me and accuse the man if he has done anything wrong."

⁶ Festus spent another eight or ten days with them and then went to Caesarea. On the next day he sat down in the judgment court and ordered Paul to be brought in. ⁷ When Paul arrived, the Jews who had come from Jerusalem stood around him and started making many serious charges against him, which they were not able to prove. ⁸ But Paul defended himself: "I have done nothing wrong against the Law of the Jews or against the Temple or against the Roman Emperor."

⁹ But Festus wanted to gain favor with the Jews, so he asked Paul, "Would you be willing to go to Jerusa-lem and be tried on these charges before me there?"

¹⁰ Paul said, "I am standing before the Emperor's own judgment court, where I should be tried. I have done no wrong to the Jews, as you yourself well know. ¹¹ If I have broken the law and done something for which I deserve the death penalty, I do not ask to escape it. But if there is no truth in the charges they bring against me, no one can hand me over to them. I appeal to the Emperor."

¹² Then Festus, after conferring with his advisers, answered, "You have appealed to the Emperor, so to the Emperor you will go."

Paul before Agrippa and Bernice

¹³ Some time later King Agrippa and Bernice came to Caesarea to pay a visit of welcome to Festus. ¹⁴ After they had been there several days, Festus explained Paul's situation to the king: "There is a man here who was left a prisoner by Felix; ¹⁵ and when I went to Jerusalem, the Jewish chief priests and elders brought charges against him and asked me to condemn him. ¹⁶ But I told them that we Romans are not in the habit of handing over any who are accused of a crime before they have met their accusers face-to-face and have had the chance of defending themselves against the accusation. ¹⁷ When they came here, then, I lost no time, but on the very next day I sat in the judgment court and ordered the man to be brought in. ¹⁸ His opponents stood up, but they did not accuse him of any of the evil crimes that I thought they would. ¹⁹ All they had were some arguments with him about their own religion and about a man named Jesus, who has died; but Paul claims that he is alive. ²⁰ I was undecided about how I could get information on these matters, so I asked Paul if he would be willing to go to Jerusalem and be tried there on these charges. ²¹ But Paul appealed; he

asked to be kept under guard and to let the Emperor decide his case. So I gave orders for him to be kept under guard until I could send him to the Emperor."

²²Agrippa said to Festus, "I would like to hear this man myself."

"You will hear him tomorrow," Festus answered.

²³The next day Agrippa and Bernice came with great pomp and ceremony and entered the audience hall with the military chiefs and the leading men of the city. Festus gave the order, and Paul was brought in. ²⁴Festus said, "King Agrippa and all who are here with us: You see this man against whom all the Jewish people, both here and in Jerusalem, have brought complaints to me. They scream that he should not live any longer. ²⁵But I could not find that he had done anything for which he deserved the death sentence. And since he himself made an appeal to the Emperor, I have decided to send him. ²⁶But I have nothing definite about him to write to the Emperor. So I have brought him here before you — and especially before you, King Agrippa! — so that, after investigating his case, I may have something to write. ²⁷For it seems unreasonable to me to send a prisoner without clearly indicating the charges against him."

Paul Defends Himself before Agrippa

26 Agrippa said to Paul, "You have permission to speak on your own behalf." Paul stretched out his hand and defended himself as follows:

²"King Agrippa! I consider myself fortunate that today I am to defend myself before you from all the things these Jews accuse me of, ³particularly since you know so well all the Jewish customs and disputes. I ask you, then, to listen to me with patience.

⁴"All the Jews know how I have lived ever since I was young. They know how I have spent my whole life, at first in my own country and then in Jerusalem. ⁵They have always known, if they are willing to testify, that from the very first I have lived as a member of the strictest party of our religion, the Pharisees. ⁶And now I stand here to be tried because of the hope I have in the promise that God made to our ancestors — ⁷the very thing that the twelve tribes of our people hope to receive, as they worship God day and night. And it is because of this hope, Your Majesty, that I am being accused by these Jews! ⁸Why do you who are here find it impossible to believe that God raises the dead?

⁹"I myself thought that I should do everything I could against the cause of Jesus of Nazareth. ¹⁰That is what I did in Jerusalem. I received authority from the chief priests and put many of God's people in prison; and when they were sentenced to death, I also voted against them. ¹¹Many times I had them punished in the synagogues and tried to make them deny their faith. I was so furious with them that I even went to foreign cities to persecute them.

Paul Tells of His Conversion
(Acts 9.1-19; 22.6-16)

¹²"It was for this purpose that I went to Damascus with authority and orders from the chief priests. ¹³It was on the road at midday, Your Majesty, that I saw a light much brighter than the sun, coming from the sky and shining around me and the men traveling with me. ¹⁴All of us fell to the ground, and I heard a voice say to me in Hebrew, 'Saul, Saul! Why are you persecuting me? You are hurting yourself by hitting back, like an ox kicking against its owner's stick.' ¹⁵'Who are you, Lord?' I asked. And the Lord answered, 'I am Jesus, whom you persecute. ¹⁶But get up and stand on your feet. I have appeared to you to appoint you as my serv-

26.5 Ac 23.6; Phil 3.5   **26.8** 2 Macc 7.9   **26.9-11** Ac 8.3; 22.4, 5 ant. You are to tell others what you have seen of me[k] today and what I will show you in the future. [17]I will rescue you from the people of Israel and from the Gentiles to whom I will send you. [18]You are to open their eyes and turn them from the darkness to the light and from the power of Satan to God, so that through their faith in me they will have their sins forgiven and receive their place among God's chosen people.'

Paul Tells of His Work

[19]"And so, King Agrippa, I did not disobey the vision I had from heaven. [20]First in Damascus and in Jerusalem and then in the whole country of Israel and among the Gentiles, I preached that they must repent of their sins and turn to God and do the things that would show they had repented. [21]It was for this reason that these Jews seized me while I was in the Temple, and they tried to kill me. [22]But to this very day I have been helped by God, and so I stand here giving my witness to all, to small and great alike. What I say is the very same thing which the prophets and Moses said was going to happen: [23]that the Messiah must suffer and be the first one to rise from death, to announce the light of salvation to the Jews and to the Gentiles."

[24]As Paul defended himself in this way, Festus shouted at him, "You are mad, Paul! Your great learning is driving you mad!"

[25]Paul answered, "I am not mad, Your Excellency! I am speaking the sober truth. [26]King Agrippa! I can speak to you with all boldness, because you know about these things. I am sure that you have taken notice of every one of them, for this thing has not happened hidden away in a corner. [27]King Agrippa, do you believe the prophets? I know that you do!"

[28]Agrippa said to Paul, "In this short time do you think you will make me a Christian?"

[29]"Whether a short time or a long time," Paul answered, "my prayer to God is that you and all the rest of you who are listening to me today might become what I am — except, of course, for these chains!"

[30]Then the king, the governor, Bernice, and all the others got up, [31]and after leaving they said to each other, "This man has not done anything for which he should die or be put in prison." [32]And Agrippa said to Festus, "This man could have been released if he had not appealed to the Emperor."

Paul Sails for Rome

27 When it was decided that we should sail to Italy, they handed Paul and some other prisoners over to Julius, an officer in the Roman army regiment called "The Emperor's Regiment." [2]We went aboard a ship from Adramyttium, which was ready to leave for the seaports of the province of Asia, and we sailed away. Aristarchus, a Macedonian from Thessalonica, was with us. [3]The next day we arrived at Sidon. Julius was kind to Paul and allowed him to go and see his friends, to be given what he needed. [4]We went on from there, and because the winds were blowing against us, we sailed on the sheltered side of the island of Cyprus. [5]We crossed over the sea off Cilicia and Pamphylia and came to Myra in Lycia. [6]There the officer found a ship from Alexandria that was going to sail for Italy, so he put us aboard.

[7]We sailed slowly for several days and with great difficulty finally arrived off the town of Cnidus. The wind would not let us go any farther in that direction, so we sailed down the sheltered side of the island of Crete, passing by

---

[k] *Some manuscripts do not have* of me.
26.20 Ac 9.20, 28, 29   **26.23** a 1 Co 15.20; b Is 42.6; 49.6

The ship hit a sandbank. (27.41)

Cape Salmone. 8 We kept close to the coast and with great difficulty came to a place called Safe Harbors, not far from the town of Lasea.

9 We spent a long time there, until it became dangerous to continue the voyage, for by now the Day of Atonement[l] was already past. So Paul gave them this advice: 10 "Men, I see that our voyage from here on will be dangerous; there will be great damage to the cargo and to the ship, and loss of life as well." 11 But the army officer was convinced by what the captain and the owner of the ship said, and not by what Paul said. 12 The harbor was not a good one to spend the winter in; so almost everyone was in favor of putting out to sea and trying to reach Phoenix, if possible, in order to spend the winter there. Phoenix is a harbor in Crete that faces southwest and northwest.[m]

The Storm at Sea

13 A soft wind from the south began to blow, and the men thought that they could carry out their plan, so they pulled up the anchor and sailed as close as possible along the coast of Crete.

14 But soon a very strong wind — the one called "Northeaster" — blew down from the island. 15 It hit the ship, and since it was impossible to keep the ship headed into the wind, we gave up trying and let it be carried along by the wind. 16 We got some shelter when we passed to the south of the little island of Cauda. There, with some difficulty we managed to make the ship's boat secure. 17 They pulled it aboard and then fastened some ropes tight around the ship. They were afraid that they might run into the sandbanks off the coast of Libya, so they lowered the sail and let the ship be carried by the wind. 18 The violent storm continued, so on the next day they began to throw some of the ship's cargo overboard, 19 and on the following day they threw part of the ship's equipment overboard. 20 For many days we could not see the sun or the stars, and the wind kept on blowing very hard. We finally gave up all hope of being saved.

21 After everyone had gone a long time without food, Paul stood before them and said, "You should have listened to me and not have sailed from

---

[l] DAY OF ATONEMENT: *This was celebrated toward the end of September or beginning of October, at which time bad weather made sailing dangerous.* [m] southwest and northwest; *or* northeast and southeast.

Crete; then we would have avoided all this damage and loss. [22]But now I beg you, take courage! Not one of you will lose your life; only the ship will be lost. [23]For last night an angel of the God to whom I belong and whom I worship came to me [24]and said, 'Don't be afraid, Paul! You must stand before the Emperor. And God in his goodness to you has spared the lives of all those who are sailing with you.' [25]So take courage, men! For I trust in God that it will be just as I was told. [26]But we will be driven ashore on some island."

[27]It was the fourteenth night, and we were being driven in the Mediterranean by the storm. About midnight the sailors suspected that we were getting close to land. [28]So they dropped a line with a weight tied to it and found that the water was one hundred and twenty feet deep; a little later they did the same and found that it was ninety feet deep. [29]They were afraid that the ship would go on the rocks, so they lowered four anchors from the back of the ship and prayed for daylight. [30]Then the sailors tried to escape from the ship; they lowered the boat into the water and pretended that they were going to put out some anchors from the front of the ship. [31]But Paul said to the army officer and soldiers, "If the sailors don't stay on board, you have no hope of being saved." [32]So the soldiers cut the ropes that held the boat and let it go.

[33]Just before dawn, Paul begged them all to eat some food: "You have been waiting for fourteen days now, and all this time you have not eaten a thing. [34]I beg you, then, eat some food; you need it in order to survive. Not even a hair of your heads will be lost." [35]After saying this, Paul took some bread, gave thanks to God before them all, broke it, and began to eat. [36]They took courage, and every one of them also ate some food. [37]There was a total of 276[n] of us on board. [38]After everyone had eaten

enough, they lightened the ship by throwing all the wheat into the sea.

The Shipwreck

[39]When day came, the sailors did not recognize the coast, but they noticed a bay with a beach and decided that, if possible, they would run the ship aground there. [40]So they cut off the anchors and let them sink in the sea, and at the same time they untied the ropes that held the steering oars. Then they raised the sail at the front of the ship so that the wind would blow the ship forward, and we headed for shore. [41]But the ship hit a sandbank and went aground; the front part of the ship got stuck and could not move, while the back part was being broken to pieces by the violence of the waves.

[42]The soldiers made a plan to kill all the prisoners, in order to keep them from swimming ashore and escaping. [43]But the army officer wanted to save Paul, so he stopped them from doing this. Instead, he ordered everyone who could swim to jump overboard first and swim ashore; [44]the rest were to follow, holding on to the planks or to some broken pieces of the ship. And this was how we all got safely ashore.

In Malta

28 When we were safely ashore, we learned that the island was called Malta. [2]The natives there were very friendly to us. It had started to rain and was cold, so they built a fire and made us all welcome. [3]Paul gathered up a bundle of sticks and was putting them on the fire when a snake came out on account of the heat and fastened itself to his hand. [4]The natives saw the snake hanging on Paul's hand and said to one another, "This man must be a murderer, but Fate will not let him live, even though he escaped from the sea." [5]But Paul shook the snake off into the

[n] 276; *some manuscripts have* 275; *others have* about 76.

PAUL'S JOURNEY
TO ROME
© United Bible Societies 1978

fire without being harmed at all. [6] They were waiting for him to swell up or suddenly fall down dead. But after waiting for a long time and not seeing anything unusual happening to him, they changed their minds and said, "He is a god!"

[7] Not far from that place were some fields that belonged to Publius, the chief of the island. He welcomed us kindly and for three days we were his guests. [8] Publius' father was in bed, sick with fever and dysentery. Paul went into his room, prayed, placed his hands on him, and healed him. [9] When this happened, all the other sick people on the island came and were healed. [10] They gave us many gifts, and when we sailed, they put on board what we needed for the voyage.

From Malta to Rome

[11] After three months we sailed away on a ship from Alexandria, called "The Twin Gods," which had spent the winter in the island. [12] We arrived in the city of Syracuse and stayed there for three days. [13] From there we sailed on

and arrived in the city of Rhegium. The next day a wind began to blow from the south, and in two days we came to the town of Puteoli. [14] We found some believers there who asked us to stay with them a week. And so we came to Rome. [15] The believers in Rome heard about us and came as far as the towns of Market of Appius and Three Inns to meet us. When Paul saw them, he thanked God and was greatly encouraged.

In Rome

[16] When we arrived in Rome, Paul was allowed to live by himself with a soldier guarding him.

[17] After three days Paul called the local Jewish leaders to a meeting. When they had gathered, he said to them, "My fellow Israelites, even though I did nothing against our people or the customs that we received from our ancestors, I was made a prisoner in Jerusalem and handed over to the Romans. [18] After questioning me, the Romans wanted to release me, because they found that I had done nothing for which I deserved to die. [19] But when the

Jews opposed this, I was forced to appeal to the Emperor, even though I had no accusation to make against my own people. 20 That is why I asked to see you and talk with you. As a matter of fact, I am bound in chains like this for the sake of him for whom the people of Israel hope."

21 They said to him, "We have not received any letters from Judea about you, nor have any of our people come from there with any news or anything bad to say about you. 22 But we would like to hear your ideas, because we know that everywhere people speak against this party to which you belong."

23 So they set a date with Paul, and a large number of them came that day to the place where Paul was staying. From morning till night he explained to them his message about the Kingdom of God, and he tried to convince them about Jesus by quoting from the Law of Moses and the writings of the prophets. 24 Some of them were convinced by his words, but others would not believe. 25 So they left, disagreeing among themselves, after Paul had said this one thing: "How well the Holy Spirit spoke

through the prophet Isaiah to your ancestors! 26 For he said,

'Go and say to this people:
You will listen and listen, but
     not understand;
you will look and look, but
     not see,
27 because this people's minds are
     dull,
and they have stopped up
     their ears
and closed their eyes.
Otherwise, their eyes would see,
     their ears would hear,
     their minds would
     understand,
and they would turn to me,
     says God,
and I would heal them.' "

28 And Paul concluded: "You are to know, then, that God's message of salvation has been sent to the Gentiles. They will listen!"o

30 For two years Paul lived in a place he rented for himself, and there he welcomed all who came to see him. 31 He preached about the Kingdom of God and taught about the Lord Jesus Christ, speaking with all boldness and freedom.

o *Some manuscripts add verse 29:* After Paul said this, the Jews left, arguing violently among themselves.
28.26, 27 Is 6.9, 10 (LXX)

Paul's Letter to the
ROMANS

INTRODUCTION

Paul's Letter to the Romans was written to prepare the way for a visit Paul planned to make to the church at Rome. His plan was to work among the Christians there for a while and then, with their support, to go on to Spain. He wrote to explain his understanding of the Christian faith and its practical implications for the lives of Christians. The book contains Paul's most complete statement of his message.

After greeting the people of the church at Rome and telling them of his prayers for them, Paul states the theme of the letter: "The gospel reveals how God puts people right with himself: it is through faith from beginning to end" (1.17).

Paul then develops this theme. All people, both Jews and Gentiles, need to be put right with God, for all alike are under the power of sin. People are put right with God through faith in Jesus Christ. Next Paul describes the new life in union with Christ that results from this new relation with God. The believer has peace with God and is set free by God's Spirit from the power of sin and death. In chapters 5–8 Paul also discusses the purpose of the Law of God and the power of God's Spirit in the believer's life. Then the apostle wrestles with the question of how Jews and Gentiles fit into the plan of God for all people. He concludes that the Jewish rejection of Jesus is part of God's plan for bringing all people within the reach of God's grace in Jesus Christ, and he believes that the Jews will not always reject Jesus. Finally Paul writes about how the Christian life should be lived, especially about the way of love in relations with others. He takes up such themes as service to God, the duty of Christians to the state and to one another, and questions of conscience. He ends the letter with personal messages and with words of praise to God.

OUTLINE OF CONTENTS

---

1 From Paul, a servant of Christ Jesus and an apostle chosen and called by God to preach his Good News.

² The Good News was promised long ago by God through his prophets, as written in the Holy Scriptures. ³ It is about his Son, our Lord Jesus Christ: as to his humanity, he was born a descendant of David; ⁴ as to his divine holiness, he was shown with great power to be the Son of God by being raised from death. ⁵ Through him God

gave me the privilege of being an apostle for the sake of Christ, in order to lead people of all nations to believe and obey. [6] This also includes you who are in Rome, whom God has called to belong to Jesus Christ.

[7] And so I write to all of you in Rome whom God loves and has called to be his own people:

May God our Father and the Lord Jesus Christ give you grace and peace.

Prayer of Thanksgiving

[8] First, I thank my God through Jesus Christ for all of you, because the whole world is hearing about your faith. [9] God is my witness that what I say is true — the God whom I serve with all my heart by preaching the Good News about his Son. God knows that I remember you [10] every time I pray. I ask that God in his good will may at last make it possible for me to visit you now. [11] For I want very much to see you, in order to share a spiritual blessing with you to make you strong. [12] What I mean is that both you and I will be helped at the same time, you by my faith and I by yours.

[13] You must remember, my friends, that many times I have planned to visit you, but something has always kept me from doing so. I want to win converts among you also, as I have among other Gentiles. [14] For I have an obligation to all peoples, to the civilized and to the savage, to the educated and to the ignorant. [15] So then, I am eager to preach the Good News to you also who live in Rome.

The Power of the Gospel

[16] I have complete confidence in the gospel; it is God's power to save all who believe, first the Jews and also the Gentiles. [17] For the gospel reveals how God

puts people right with himself: it is through faith from beginning to end. As the scripture says, "The person who is put right with God through faith shall live."[a]

Human Guilt

[18] God's anger is revealed from heaven against all the sin and evil of the people whose evil ways prevent the truth from being known. [19] God punishes them, because what can be known about God is plain to them, for God himself made it plain. [20] Ever since God created the world, his invisible qualities, both his eternal power and his divine nature, have been clearly seen; they are perceived in the things that God has made. So those people have no excuse at all! [21] They know God, but they do not give him the honor that belongs to him, nor do they thank him. Instead, their thoughts have become complete nonsense, and their empty

Their thoughts have become complete nonsense. (1.21)

minds are filled with darkness. [22] They say they are wise, but they are fools; [23] instead of worshiping the immortal God, they worship images made to look

[a] put right with God through faith shall live; *or* put right with God shall live through faith.

1.13 Ac 19.21   **1.16** Mk 8.38   **1.17** Hb 2.4   **1.20** Ws 13.1-9; Si 17.8   **1.21** Eph 4.17, 18
1.23 Dt 4.16-18; Ws 11.15; 12.24; 13.10-19

like mortals or birds or animals or reptiles.

24 And so God has given those people over to do the filthy things their hearts desire, and they do shameful things with each other. 25 They exchange the truth about God for a lie; they worship and serve what God has created instead of the Creator himself, who is to be praised forever! Amen.

26 Because they do this, God has given them over to shameful passions. Even the women pervert the natural use of their sex by unnatural acts. 27 In the same way the men give up natural sexual relations with women and burn with passion for each other. Men do shameful things with each other, and as a result they bring upon themselves the punishment they deserve for their wrongdoing.

28 Because those people refuse to keep in mind the true knowledge about God, he has given them over to corrupted minds, so that they do the things that they should not do. 29 They are filled with all kinds of wickedness, evil, greed, and vice; they are full of jealousy, murder, fighting, deceit, and malice. They gossip 30 and speak evil of one another; they are hateful to God, insolent,[b] proud, and boastful; they think of more ways to do evil; they disobey their parents; 31 they have no conscience; they do not keep their promises, and they show no kindness or pity for others. 32 They know that God's law says that people who live in this way deserve death. Yet, not only do they continue to do these very things, but they even approve of others who do them.

God's Judgment

2 Do you, my friend, pass judgment on others? You have no excuse at all, whoever you are. For when you judge others and then do the same things which they do, you condemn yourself. 2 We know that God is right when he judges the people who do such things as these. 3 But you, my friend, do those very things for which you pass judgment on others! Do you think you will escape God's judgment? 4 Or perhaps you despise his great kindness, tolerance, and patience. Surely you know that God is kind, because he is trying to lead you to repent. 5 But you have a hard and stubborn heart, and so you are making your own punishment even greater on the Day when God's anger and righteous judgments will be revealed. 6 For God will reward each of us according to what we have done. 7 Some people keep on doing good, and seek glory, honor, and immortal life; to them God will give eternal life. 8 Other people are selfish and reject what is right, in order to follow what is wrong; on them God will pour out his anger and fury. 9 There will be suffering and pain for all those who do what is evil, for the Jews first and also for the Gentiles. 10 But God will give glory, honor, and peace to all who do what is good, to the Jews first and also to the Gentiles. 11 For God judges everyone by the same standard.

12 The Gentiles do not have the Law of Moses; they sin and are lost apart from the Law. The Jews have the Law; they sin and are judged by the Law. 13 For it is not by hearing the Law that people are put right with God, but by doing what the Law commands. 14 The Gentiles do not have the Law; but whenever they do by instinct what the Law commands, they are their own law, even though they do not have the Law. 15 Their conduct shows that what the Law commands is written in their hearts. Their consciences also show that this is true, since their thoughts sometimes accuse them and sometimes defend them. 16 And so, according

---

b are hateful to God, insolent; or hate God, and are insolent.

2.1 Mt 7.1; Lk 6.37   **2.4** Ws 11.23   **2.6** Ps 62.12; Pr 24.12   **2.11** Dt 10.17

to the Good News I preach, this is how it will be on that Day when God through Jesus Christ will judge the secret thoughts of all.

The Jews and the Law

17 What about you? You call yourself a Jew; you depend on the Law and boast about God; 18 you know what God wants you to do, and you have learned from the Law to choose what is right; 19 you are sure that you are a guide for the blind, a light for those who are in darkness, 20 an instructor for the foolish, and a teacher for the ignorant. You are certain that in the Law you have the full content of knowledge and of truth. 21 You teach others — why don't you teach yourself? You preach, "Do not steal" — but do you yourself steal? 22 You say, "Do not commit adultery" — but do you commit adultery? You detest idols — but do you rob temples? 23 You boast about having God's law — but do you bring shame on God by breaking his law? 24 The scripture says, "Because of you Jews, the Gentiles speak evil of God."

25 If you obey the Law, your circumcision is of value; but if you disobey the Law, you might as well never have been circumcised. 26 If the Gentile, who is not circumcised, obeys the commands of the Law, will not God regard him as though he were circumcised? 27 And so you Jews will be condemned by the Gentiles because you break the Law, even though you have it written down and are circumcised; but they obey the Law, even though they are not physically circumcised. 28 After all, who is a real Jew, truly circumcised? It is not the man who is a Jew on the outside, whose circumcision is a physical thing. 29 Rather, the real Jew is the person

who is a Jew on the inside, that is, whose heart has been circumcised, and this is the work of God's Spirit, not of the written Law. Such a person receives praise from God, not from human beings.

3 Do the Jews then have any advantage over the Gentiles? Or is there any value in being circumcised? 2 Much, indeed, in every way! In the first place, God trusted his message to the Jews. 3 But what if some of them were not faithful? Does this mean that God will not be faithful? 4 Certainly not! God must be true, even though all human beings are liars. As the scripture says,

"You must be shown to be right
     when you speak;
   you must win your case when
     you are being tried."

5 But what if our doing wrong serves to show up more clearly God's doing right? Can we say that God does wrong when he punishes us? (This would be the natural question to ask.) 6 By no means! If God is not just, how can he judge the world?

7 But what if my untruth serves God's glory by making his truth stand out more clearly? Why should I still be condemned as a sinner? 8 Why not say, then, "Let us do evil so that good may come"? Some people, indeed, have insulted me by accusing me of saying this very thing! They will be condemned, as they should be.

No One Is Righteous

9 Well then, are we Jews in any better condition than the Gentiles? Not at all! c I have already shown that Jews and Gentiles alike are all under the power of sin. 10 As the Scriptures say:

c any better condition than the Gentiles? Not at all!; or any worse condition than the Gentiles? Not altogether.

2.24 Is 52.5 (LXX)   **2.29** Dt 30.6   **3.4** Ps 51.4 (LXX)   **3.10-12** Ps 14.1-3 (LXX); Ps 53.1-3 (LXX)

"There is no one who is
righteous,
11   no one who is wise
or who worships God.
12 All have turned away from God;
they have all gone wrong;
no one does what is right,
not even one.
13 Their words are full of deadly
deceit;
wicked lies roll off their
tongues,
and dangerous threats, like
snake's poison, from their
lips;
14   their speech is filled with
bitter curses.
15 They are quick to hurt and kill;
16   they leave ruin and
destruction wherever
they go.
17 They have not known the path
of peace,
18   nor have they learned
reverence for God."

19 Now we know that everything in
the Law applies to those who live under
the Law, in order to stop all human excuses and bring the whole world under
God's judgment. 20 For no one is put
right in God's sight by doing what the
Law requires; what the Law does is to
make us know that we have sinned.

How We Are Put Right with God

21 But now God's way of putting people right with himself has been revealed. It has nothing to do with law,
even though the Law of Moses and the
prophets gave their witness to it. 22 God
puts people right through their faith in
Jesus Christ. God does this to all who
believe in Christ, because there is no
difference at all: 23 everyone has sinned
and is far away from God's saving presence. 24 But by the free gift of God's
grace all are put right with him through
Christ Jesus, who sets them free.
25-26 God offered him, so that by his
blood[d] he should become the means by
which people's sins are forgiven
through their faith in him. God did this
in order to demonstrate that he is righteous. In the past he was patient and
overlooked people's sins; but in the
present time he deals with their sins, in
order to demonstrate his righteousness.
In this way God shows that he himself
is righteous and that he puts right
everyone who believes in Jesus.

27 What, then, can we boast about?
Nothing! And what is the reason for
this? Is it that we obey the Law? No,
but that we believe. 28 For we conclude
that a person is put right with God only
through faith, and not by doing what
the Law commands. 29 Or is God the
God of the Jews only? Is he not the God
of the Gentiles also? Of course he is.
30 God is one, and he will put the Jews
right with himself on the basis of their
faith, and will put the Gentiles right
through their faith. 31 Does this mean
that by this faith we do away with the
Law? No, not at all; instead, we uphold
the Law.

The Example of Abraham

4 What shall we say, then, of Abraham, the father of our race? What
was his experience? 2 If he was put
right with God by the things he did, he
would have something to boast about —
but not in God's sight. 3 The scripture
says, "Abraham believed God, and because of his faith God accepted him as
righteous." 4 A person who works is paid
wages, but they are not regarded as a
gift; they are something that has been

---

[d] by his blood; *or* by his sacrificial death.
3.13 a Ps 5.9 (LXX); **b** Ps 140.3   **3.14** Ps 10.7 (LXX)   **3.15-17** Is 59.7, 8   **3.18** Ps 36.1
3.20 Ps 143.2; Ga 2.16   **3.22** Ga 2.16   **3.30** Dt 6.4; Ga 3.20   **4.3** Gn 15.6; Ga 3.6

earned. ⁵But those who depend on faith, not on deeds, and who believe in the God who declares the guilty to be innocent, it is this faith that God takes into account in order to put them right with himself. ⁶This is what David meant when he spoke of the happiness of the person whom God accepts as righteous, apart from anything that person does:

⁷"Happy are those whose wrongs
    are forgiven,
  whose sins are pardoned!
⁸Happy is the person whose sins
    the Lord will not keep
    account of!"

⁹Does this happiness that David spoke of belong only to those who are circumcised? No indeed! It belongs also to those who are not circumcised. For we have quoted the scripture, "Abraham believed God, and because of his faith God accepted him as righteous." ¹⁰When did this take place? Was it before or after Abraham was circumcised? It was before, not after. ¹¹He was circumcised later, and his circumcision was a sign to show that because of his faith God had accepted him as righteous before he had been circumcised. And so Abraham is the spiritual father of all who believe in God and are accepted as righteous by him, even though they are not circumcised. ¹²He is also the father of those who are circumcised, that is, of those who, in addition to being circumcised, also live the same life of faith that our father Abraham lived before he was circumcised.

God's Promise Is Received through Faith

¹³When God promised Abraham and his descendants that the world would belong to him, he did so, not because

Abraham obeyed the Law, but because he believed and was accepted as righteous by God. ¹⁴For if what God promises is to be given to those who obey the Law, then faith means nothing and God's promise is worthless. ¹⁵The Law brings down God's anger; but where there is no law, there is no disobeying of the law.

¹⁶And so the promise was based on faith, in order that the promise should be guaranteed as God's free gift to all of Abraham's descendants — not just to those who obey the Law, but also to those who believe as Abraham did. For Abraham is the spiritual father of us all; ¹⁷as the scripture says, "I have made you father of many nations." So the promise is good in the sight of God, in whom Abraham believed — the God who brings the dead to life and whose command brings into being what did not exist. ¹⁸Abraham believed and hoped, even when there was no reason for hoping, and so became "the father of many nations." Just as the scripture says, "Your descendants will be as many as the stars." ¹⁹He was then almost one hundred years old; but his faith did not weaken when he thought of his body, which was already practically dead, or of the fact that Sarah could not have children. ²⁰His faith did not leave him, and he did not doubt God's promise; his faith filled him with power, and he gave praise to God. ²¹He was absolutely sure that God would be able to do what he had promised. ²²That is why Abraham, through faith, "was accepted as righteous by God." ²³The words "he was accepted as righteous" were not written for him alone. ²⁴They were written also for us who are to be accepted as righteous, who believe in him who raised Jesus our Lord from death. ²⁵Because of our sins he was given over to die, and he

4.7, 8 Ps 32.1, 2   **4.11** Gn 17.10   **4.13** Gn 17.4-6; 22.17, 18; Ga 3.29   **4.14** Ga 3.18
4.16 Ga 3.7   **4.17** Gn 17.5   **4.18** Gn 15.5   **4.19** Gn 17.17   **4.25** Is 53.4, 5

was raised to life in order to put us right with God.

Right with God

5 Now that we have been put right with God through faith, we have[e] peace with God through our Lord Jesus Christ. [2] He has brought us by faith into this experience of God's grace, in which we now live. And so we boast[f] of the hope we have of sharing God's glory! [3] We also boast[g] of our troubles, because we know that trouble produces endurance, [4] endurance brings God's approval, and his approval creates hope. [5] This hope does not disappoint us, for God has poured out his love into our hearts by means of the Holy Spirit, who is God's gift to us.

[6] For when we were still helpless, Christ died for the wicked at the time that God chose. [7] It is a difficult thing for someone to die for a righteous person. It may even be that someone might dare to die for a good person. [8] But God has shown us how much he loves us — it was while we were still sinners that Christ died for us! [9] By his blood[h] we are now put right with God; how much more, then, will we be saved by him from God's anger! [10] We were God's enemies, but he made us his friends through the death of his Son. Now that we are God's friends, how much more will we be saved by Christ's life! [11] But that is not all; we rejoice because of what God has done through our Lord Jesus Christ, who has now made us God's friends.

Adam and Christ

[12] Sin came into the world through one man, and his sin brought death with it. As a result, death has spread to the whole human race because everyone has sinned. [13] There was sin in the world before the Law was given; but where there is no law, no account is kept of sins. [14] But from the time of Adam to the time of Moses, death ruled over all human beings, even over those who did not sin in the same way that Adam did when he disobeyed God's command.

Adam was a figure of the one who was to come. [15] But the two are not the same, because God's free gift is not like Adam's sin. It is true that many people died because of the sin of that one man. But God's grace is much greater, and so is his free gift to so many people through the grace of the one man, Jesus Christ. [16] And there is a difference between God's gift and the sin of one man. After the one sin, came the judgment of "Guilty"; but after so many sins, comes the undeserved gift of "Not guilty!" [17] It is true that through the sin of one man death began to rule because of that one man. But how much greater is the result of what was done by the one man, Jesus Christ! All who receive God's abundant grace and are freely put right with him will rule in life through Christ.

[18] So then, as the one sin condemned all people, in the same way the one righteous act sets all people free and gives them life. [19] And just as all people were made sinners as the result of the disobedience of one man, in the same way they will all be put right with God as the result of the obedience of the one man.

[20] Law was introduced in order to increase wrongdoing; but where sin increased, God's grace increased much more. [21] So then, just as sin ruled by means of death, so also God's grace rules by means of righteousness, lead-

---

[e] we have; *some manuscripts have* let us have.   [f] we boast; *or* let us boast.   [g] We also boast; *or* Let us also boast.   [h] By his blood; *or* By his sacrificial death.

5.12 Gn 3.6; Ws 2.24   **5.18** 2 Esd 7.11

So that we should no longer be the slaves of sin. (6.6)

ing us to eternal life through Jesus Christ our Lord.

Dead to Sin but Alive in Union with Christ

6 What shall we say, then? Should we continue to live in sin so that God's grace will increase? ² Certainly not! We have died to sin — how then can we go on living in it? ³ For surely you know that when we were baptized into union with Christ Jesus, we were baptized into union with his death. ⁴ By our baptism, then, we were buried with him and shared his death, in order that, just as Christ was raised from death by the glorious power of the Father, so also we might live a new life.

⁵ For since we have become one with him in dying as he did, in the same way we shall be one with him by being raised to life as he was. ⁶ And we know that our old being has been put to death with Christ on his cross, in order that the power of the sinful self might be destroyed, so that we should no longer be the slaves of sin. ⁷ For when we die, we are set free from the power of sin. ⁸ Since we have died with Christ, we believe that we will also live with him. ⁹ For we know that Christ has been raised from death and will never die again — death will no longer rule over him. ¹⁰ And so, because he died, sin has no power over him; and now he lives his life in fellowship with God. ¹¹ In the same way you are to think of yourselves as dead, so far as sin is concerned, but living in fellowship with God through Christ Jesus.

¹² Sin must no longer rule in your mortal bodies, so that you obey the desires of your natural self. ¹³ Nor must you surrender any part of yourselves to sin to be used for wicked purposes. Instead, give yourselves to God, as those who have been brought from death to life, and surrender your whole being to him to be used for righteous purposes. ¹⁴ Sin must not be your master; for you do not live under law but under God's grace.

Slaves of Righteousness

15 What, then? Shall we sin, because we are not under law but under God's grace? By no means! 16 Surely you know that when you surrender yourselves as slaves to obey someone, you are in fact the slaves of the master you obey—either of sin, which results in death, or of obedience, which results in being put right with God. 17 But thanks be to God! For though at one time you were slaves to sin, you have obeyed with all your heart the truths found in the teaching you received. 18 You were set free from sin and became the slaves of righteousness. 19 (I use everyday language because of the weakness of your natural selves.) At one time you surrendered yourselves entirely as slaves to impurity and wickedness for wicked purposes. In the same way you must now surrender yourselves entirely as slaves of righteousness for holy purposes.

20 When you were the slaves of sin, you were free from righteousness. 21 What did you gain from doing the things that you are now ashamed of? The result of those things is death! 22 But now you have been set free from sin and are the slaves of God. Your gain is a life fully dedicated to him, and the result is eternal life. 23 For sin pays its wage—death; but God's free gift is eternal life in union with Christ Jesus our Lord.

An Illustration from Marriage

7 Certainly you will understand what I am about to say, my friends, because all of you know about law. The law rules over people only as long as they live. 2 A married woman, for example, is bound by the law to her husband as long as he lives; but if he dies, then she is free from the law that bound her to him. 3 So then, if she lives with another man while her husband is alive, she will be called an adulteress; but if her husband dies, she is legally a free woman and does not commit adultery if she marries another man. 4 That is how it is with you, my friends. As far as the Law is concerned, you also have died because you are part of the body of Christ; and now you belong to him who was raised from death in order that we might be useful in the service of God. 5 For when we lived according to our human nature, the sinful desires stirred up by the Law were at work in our bodies, and all we did ended in death. 6 Now, however, we are free from the Law, because we died to that which once held us prisoners. No longer do we serve in the old way of a written law, but in the new way of the Spirit.

Law and Sin

7 Shall we say, then, that the Law itself is sinful? Of course not! But it was the Law that made me know what sin is. If the Law had not said, "Do not desire what belongs to someone else," I would not have known such a desire. 8 But by means of that commandment sin found its chance to stir up all kinds of selfish desires in me. Apart from law, sin is a dead thing. 9 I myself was once alive apart from law; but when the commandment came, sin sprang to life, 10 and I died. And the commandment which was meant to bring life, in my case brought death. 11 Sin found its chance, and by means of the commandment it deceived me and killed me.

12 So then, the Law itself is holy, and the commandment is holy, right, and good. 13 But does this mean that what is good caused my death? By no means! It was sin that did it; by using what is good, sin brought death to me, in order that its true nature as sin might be revealed. And so, by means of the commandment sin is shown to be even more terribly sinful.

7.7 Ex 20.17; Dt 5.21   7.11 Gn 3.13

The Conflict in Us

14 We know that the Law is spiritual; but I am a mortal, sold as a slave to sin. **15** I do not understand what I do; for I don't do what I would like to do, but instead I do what I hate. **16** Since what I do is what I don't want to do, this shows that I agree that the Law is right. **17** So I am not really the one who does this thing; rather it is the sin that lives in me. **18** I know that good does not live in me — that is, in my human nature. For even though the desire to do good is in me, I am not able to do it. **19** I don't do the good I want to do; instead, I do the evil that I do not want to do. **20** If I do what I don't want to do, this means that I am no longer the one who does it; instead, it is the sin that lives in me.

21 So I find that this law is at work: when I want to do what is good, what is evil is the only choice I have. **22** My inner being delights in the law of God. **23** But I see a different law at work in my body — a law that fights against the law which my mind approves of. It makes me a prisoner to the law of sin which is at work in my body. **24** What an unhappy man I am! Who will rescue me from this body that is taking me to death? **25** Thanks be to God, who does this through our Lord Jesus Christ!

This, then, is my condition: on my own I can serve God's law only with my mind, while my human nature serves the law of sin.

Life in the Spirit

8 There is no condemnation now for those who live in union with Christ Jesus. **2** For the law of the Spirit, which brings us life in union with Christ Jesus, has set me *i* free from the law of sin and death. **3** What the Law could not do, because human nature was weak, God did. He condemned sin in human nature by sending his own Son, who came with a nature like our sinful nature, to do away with sin. **4** God did this so that the righteous demands of the Law might be fully satisfied in us who live according to the Spirit, and not according to human nature. **5** Those who live as their human nature tells them to, have their minds controlled by what human nature wants. Those who live as the Spirit tells them to, have their minds controlled by what the Spirit wants. **6** To be controlled by human nature results in death; to be controlled by the Spirit results in life and peace. **7** And so people become enemies of God when they are controlled by their human nature; for they do not obey God's law, and in fact they cannot obey it. **8** Those who obey their human nature cannot please God.

9 But you do not live as your human nature tells you to; instead, you live as the Spirit tells you to — if, in fact, God's Spirit lives in you. Whoever does not have the Spirit of Christ does not belong to him. **10** But if Christ lives in you, the Spirit is life for you *j* because you have been put right with God, even though your bodies are going to die because of sin. **11** If the Spirit of God, who raised Jesus from death, lives in you, then he who raised Christ from death will also give life to your mortal bodies by the presence of his Spirit in you.

12 So then, my friends, we have an obligation, but it is not to live as our human nature wants us to. **13** For if you live according to your human nature, you are going to die; but if by the Spirit you put to death your sinful actions, you will live. **14** Those who are led by God's Spirit are God's children. **15** For the Spirit that God has given you does not make you slaves and cause you to be afraid; instead, the Spirit makes you God's children, and by the Spirit's

---

i me; *some manuscripts have* you; *others have* us.   *j* the Spirit is life for you; *or* your spirit is alive.

7.15 Ga 5.17   **8.11** 1 Co 3.16   **8.15-17** Ga 4.5-7   **8.15** Mk 14.36; Ga 4.6

power we cry out to God, "Father! my Father!" 16God's Spirit joins himself to our spirits to declare that we are God's children. 17Since we are his children, we will possess the blessings he keeps for his people, and we will also possess with Christ what God has kept for him; for if we share Christ's suffering, we will also share his glory.

The Future Glory

18I consider that what we suffer at this present time cannot be compared at all with the glory that is going to be revealed to us. 19All of creation waits with eager longing for God to reveal his children. 20For creation was condemned to lose its purpose, not of its own will, but because God willed it to be so. Yet there was the hope 21that creation itself would one day be set free from its slavery to decay and would share the glorious freedom of the children of God. 22For we know that up to the present time all of creation groans with pain, like the pain of childbirth. 23But it is not just creation alone which groans; we who have the Spirit as the first of God's gifts also groan within ourselves as we wait for God to make us his children and^k set our whole being free. 24For it was by hope that we were saved; but if we see what we hope for, then it is not really hope. For who of us hopes for something we see? 25But if we hope for what we do not see, we wait for it with patience.

26In the same way the Spirit also comes to help us, weak as we are. For we do not know how we ought to pray; the Spirit himself pleads with God for us in groans that words cannot express. 27And God, who sees into our hearts, knows what the thought of the Spirit is; because the Spirit pleads with God on behalf of his people and in accordance with his will.

28We know that in all things God works for good with those who love him,^{l} those whom he has called according to his purpose. 29Those whom God had already chosen he also set apart to become like his Son, so that the Son would be the first among many believers. 30And so those whom God set apart, he called; and those he called, he put right with himself, and he shared his glory with them.

God's Love in Christ Jesus

31In view of all this, what can we say? If God is for us, who can be against us? 32Certainly not God, who did not even keep back his own Son, but offered him for us all! He gave us his Son — will he not also freely give us all things? 33Who will accuse God's chosen people? God himself declares them not guilty! 34Who, then, will condemn them? Not Christ Jesus, who died, or rather, who was raised to life and is at the right side of God, pleading with him for us! 35Who, then, can separate us from the love of Christ? Can trouble do it, or hardship or persecution or hunger or poverty or danger or death? 36As the scripture says,

"For your sake we are in danger
    of death at all times;
  we are treated like sheep that
        are going to be
        slaughtered."

37No, in all these things we have complete victory through him who loved us! 38For I am certain that nothing can separate us from his love: neither death nor life, neither angels nor other heavenly rulers or powers, neither the present nor the future, 39neither the world above nor the world below —

---

^{k} *Some manuscripts do not have* make us his children and. ^{l} in all things God works for good with those who love him; *some manuscripts have* all things work for good for those who love God.

8.18 Ws 3.5, 6   **8.20** Gn 3.17-19   **8.23** 2 Co 5.2-4   **8.36** Ps 44.22

there is nothing in all creation that will ever be able to separate us from the love of God which is ours through Christ Jesus our Lord.

God and His People

9 I am speaking the truth; I belong to Christ and I do not lie. My conscience, ruled by the Holy Spirit, also assures me that I am not lying [2]when I say how great is my sorrow, how endless the pain in my heart [3]for my people, my own flesh and blood! For their sake I could wish that I myself were under God's curse and separated from Christ. [4]They are God's people; he made them his children and revealed his glory to them; he made his covenants[m] with them and gave them the Law; they have the true worship; they have received God's promises; [5]they are descended from the famous Hebrew ancestors; and Christ, as a human being, belongs to their race. May God, who rules over all, be praised forever![n] Amen.

[6]I am not saying that the promise of God has failed; for not all the people of Israel are the people of God. [7]Nor are all of Abraham's descendants the children of God. God said to Abraham, "It is through Isaac that you will have the descendants I promised you." [8]This means that the children born in the usual way[o] are not the children of God; instead, the children born as a result of God's promise are regarded as the true descendants. [9]For God's promise was made in these words: "At the right time[p] I will come back, and Sarah will have a son."

[10]And this is not all. For Rebecca's two sons had the same father, our ancestor Isaac. [11-12]But in order that the choice of one son might be completely the result of God's own purpose, God said to her, "The older will serve the younger." He said this before they were born, before they had done anything either good or bad; so God's choice was based on his call, and not on anything they had done. [13]As the scripture says, "I loved Jacob, but I hated Esau."

[14]Shall we say, then, that God is unjust? Not at all. [15]For he said to Moses, "I will have mercy on anyone I wish; I will take pity on anyone I wish." [16]So then, everything depends, not on what we humans want or do, but only on God's mercy. [17]For the scripture says to the king of Egypt, "I made you king in order to use you to show my power and to spread my fame over the whole world." [18]So then, God has mercy on anyone he wishes, and he makes stubborn anyone he wishes.

God's Anger and Mercy

[19]But one of you will say to me, "If this is so, how can God find fault with anyone? Who can resist God's will?" [20]But who are you, my friend, to talk back to God? A clay pot does not ask the man who made it, "Why did you make me like this?" [21]After all, the man who makes the pots has the right to use the clay as he wishes, and to make two pots from the same lump of clay, one for special occasions and the other for ordinary use.

[22]And the same is true of what God

---

[m] covenants; *some manuscripts have* covenant.   [n] May God, who rules over all, be praised forever!; *or* And may he, who is God ruling over all, be praised forever!
[o] CHILDREN BORN IN THE USUAL WAY: *This refers to the descendants Abraham had through Ishmael, his son by Hagar (see Ga 4.22-23).*   [p] At the right time; *or* At this time next year.

9.4 Ex 4.22   **9.7** Gn 21.12   **9.9** Gn 18.10   **9.12** Gn 25.23   **9.13** Ml 1.2, 3   **9.15** Ex 33.19
9.17 Ex 9.16 (LXX)   **9.20** Is 29.16; 45.9; Ws 12.12   **9.21** Ws 15.7; Si 33.13
9.22 Ws 12.20, 21

has done. He wanted to show his anger and to make his power known. But he was very patient in enduring those who were the objects of his anger, who were doomed to destruction. 23 And he also wanted to reveal his abundant glory, which was poured out on us who are the objects of his mercy, those of us whom he has prepared to receive his glory. 24 For we are the people he called, not only from among the Jews but also from among the Gentiles. 25 This is what he says in the book of Hosea:

"The people who were not mine
    I will call 'My People.'
The nation that I did not love
    I will call 'My Beloved.'
26 And in the very place where they
    were told, 'You are not
    my people,'
there they will be called the
    children of the living God."

27 And Isaiah exclaims about Israel: "Even if the people of Israel are as many as the grains of sand by the sea, yet only a few of them will be saved; 28 for the Lord will quickly settle his full account with the world." 29 It is as Isaiah had said before, "If the Lord Almighty had not left us some descendants, we would have become like Sodom, we would have been like Gomorrah."

Israel and the Gospel

30 So we say that the Gentiles, who were not trying to put themselves right with God, were put right with him through faith; 31 while God's people, who were seeking a law that would put them right with God, did not find it. 32 And why not? Because they did not depend on faith but on what they did. And so they stumbled over the "stumbling stone" 33 that the scripture speaks of:

"Look, I place in Zion a stone
    that will make people
    stumble,
    a rock that will make them
    fall.
But whoever believes in him will
    not be disappointed."

10 My friends, how I wish with all my heart that my own people might be saved! How I pray to God for them! 2 I can assure you that they are deeply devoted to God; but their devotion is not based on true knowledge. 3 They have not known the way in which God puts people right with himself, and instead, they have tried to set up their own way; and so they did not submit themselves to God's way of putting people right. 4 For Christ has brought the Law to an end, so that everyone who believes is put right with God.

Salvation Is for All

5 Moses wrote this about being put right with God by obeying the Law: "Whoever obeys the commands of the Law will live." 6 But what the scripture says about being put right with God through faith is this: "You are not to ask yourself, Who will go up into heaven?" (that is, to bring Christ down). 7 "Nor are you to ask, Who will go down into the world below?" (that is, to bring Christ up from death). 8 What it says is this: "God's message is near you, on your lips and in your heart" — that is, the message of faith that we preach. 9 If you confess that Jesus is Lord and believe that God raised him from death, you will be saved. 10 For it is by our faith that we are put right with God; it is by our confession that we are saved. 11 The scripture says, "Whoever believes in him will not be disappointed." 12 This

---

9.25 Ho 2.23   **9.26** Ho 1.10   **9.27, 28** Is 10.22, 23 (LXX)   **9.29** Is 1.9 (LXX)
9.33 Is 28.16 (LXX)   **10.5** Lv 18.5   **10.6-8** Dt 30.12-14   **10.11** Is 28.16 (LXX)

includes everyone, because there is no difference between Jews and Gentiles; God is the same Lord of all and richly blesses all who call to him. [13] As the scripture says, "Everyone who calls out to the Lord for help will be saved."

[14] But how can they call to him for help if they have not believed? And how can they believe if they have not heard the message? And how can they hear if the message is not proclaimed? [15] And how can the message be proclaimed if the messengers are not sent out? As the scripture says, "How wonderful is the coming of messengers who bring good news!" [16] But not all have accepted the Good News. Isaiah himself said, "Lord, who believed our message?" [17] So then, faith comes from hearing the message, and the message comes through preaching Christ.

[18] But I ask: Is it true that they did not hear the message? Of course they did — for as the scripture says:

"The sound of their voice went
     out to all the world;
   their words reached the ends
     of the earth."

[19] Again I ask: Did the people of Israel not understand? Moses himself is the first one to answer:

"I will use a so-called nation
   to make my people jealous;
 and by means of a nation of fools
   I will make my people angry."

[20] And Isaiah is even bolder when he says,

"I was found by those who were
     not looking for me;
   I appeared to those who were
     not asking for me."

[21] But concerning Israel he says, "All day long I held out my hands to welcome a disobedient and rebellious people."

God's Mercy on Israel

11 I ask, then: Did God reject his own people? Certainly not! I myself am an Israelite, a descendant of Abraham, a member of the tribe of Benjamin. [2] God has not rejected his people, whom he chose from the beginning. You know what the scripture says in the passage where Elijah pleads with God against Israel: [3] "Lord, they have killed your prophets and torn down your altars; I am the only one left, and they are trying to kill me." [4] What answer did God give him? "I have kept for myself seven thousand men who have not worshiped the false god Baal." [5] It is the same way now: there is a small number left of those whom God has chosen because of his grace. [6] His choice is based on his grace, not on what they have done. For if God's choice were based on what people do, then his grace would not be real grace.

[7] What then? The people of Israel did not find what they were looking for. It was only the small group that God chose who found it; the rest grew deaf to God's call. [8] As the scripture says, "God made their minds and hearts dull; to this very day they cannot see or hear." [9] And David says,

"May they be caught and trapped
     at their feasts;
   may they fall, may they be
     punished!
[10] May their eyes be blinded so that
     they cannot see;
   and make them bend under
     their troubles at all times."

[11] I ask, then: When the Jews stumbled, did they fall to their ruin? By no means! Because they sinned, salvation has come to the Gentiles, to make the Jews jealous of them. [12] The sin of the Jews brought rich blessings to the world, and their spiritual poverty

---

10.13 Jl 2.32   **10.15** Is 52.7   **10.16** Is 53.1 (LXX)   **10.18** Ps 19.4 (LXX)   **10.19** Dt 32.21
10.20 Is 65.1 (LXX)   **10.21** Is 65.2 (LXX)   **11.1** Phil 3.5   **11.3** 1 K 19.10, 14
11.4 1 K 19.18   **11.8** Dt 29.4; Is 29.10   **11.9, 10** Ps 69.22, 23 (LXX)

brought rich blessings to the Gentiles. Then, how much greater the blessings will be when the complete number of Jews is included!

The Salvation of the Gentiles

13 I am speaking now to you Gentiles: As long as I am an apostle to the Gentiles, I will take pride in my work. 14 Perhaps I can make the people of my own race jealous, and so be able to save some of them. 15 For when they were rejected, all other people were changed from God's enemies into his friends. What will it be, then, when they are accepted? It will be life for the dead!

16 If the first piece of bread is given to God, then the whole loaf is his also; and if the roots of a tree are offered to God, the branches are his also. 17 Some of the branches of the cultivated olive tree have been broken off, and a branch of a wild olive tree has been joined to it. You Gentiles are like that wild olive tree, and now you share the strong spiritual life of the Jews. 18 So then, you must not despise those who were broken off like branches. How can you be proud? You are just a branch; you don't support the roots — the roots support you.

19 But you will say, "Yes, but the branches were broken off to make room for me." 20 That is true. They were broken off because they did not believe, while you remain in place because you do believe. But do not be proud of it; instead, be afraid. 21 God did not spare the Jews, who are like natural branches; do you think he will spare you? 22 Here we see how kind and how severe God is. He is severe toward those who have fallen, but kind to you — if you continue in his kindness. But if you do not, you too will be broken off. 23 And if the Jews abandon their unbelief, they will be put back in the place where they were; for God

is able to do that. 24 You Gentiles are like the branch of a wild olive tree that is broken off and then, contrary to nature, is joined to a cultivated olive tree. The Jews are like this cultivated tree; and it will be much easier for God to join these broken-off branches to their own tree again.

God's Mercy on All

25 There is a secret truth, my friends, which I want you to know, for it will keep you from thinking how wise you are. It is that the stubbornness of the people of Israel is not permanent, but will last only until the complete number of Gentiles comes to God. 26 And this is how all Israel will be saved. As the scripture says,

"The Savior will come from Zion
    and remove all wickedness
        from the descendants
            of Jacob.
27 I will make this covenant with
            them
        when I take away their sins."

28 Because they reject the Good News, the Jews are God's enemies for the sake of you Gentiles. But because of God's choice, they are his friends because of their ancestors. 29 For God does not change his mind about whom he chooses and blesses. 30 As for you Gentiles, you disobeyed God in the past; but now you have received God's mercy because the Jews were disobedient. 31 In the same way, because of the mercy that you have received, the Jews now disobey God, in order that they also may now *q* receive God's mercy. 32 For God has made all people prisoners of disobedience, so that he might show mercy to them all.

Praise to God

33 How great are God's riches! How deep are his wisdom and knowledge!

---

q Some manuscripts do not have now.

11.26 Is 59.20, 21 (LXX)   **11.27** Is 27.9 (LXX)   **11.33** Is 55.8; Ws 17.1

Who can explain his decisions? Who can understand his ways? ³⁴As the scripture says,

"Who knows the mind of the
    Lord?
Who is able to give him
    advice?
³⁵Who has ever given him
    anything,
    so that he had to pay it back?"
³⁶For all things were created by him, and all things exist through him and for him. To God be the glory forever! Amen.

Life in God's Service

12 So then, my friends, because of God's great mercy to us I appeal to you: Offer yourselves as a living sacrifice to God, dedicated to his service and pleasing to him. This is the true worship that you should offer. ²Do not conform yourselves to the standards of this world, but let God transform you inwardly by a complete change of your mind. Then you will be able to know the will of God — what is good and is pleasing to him and is perfect.

³And because of God's gracious gift to me I say to every one of you: Do not think of yourself more highly than you should. Instead, be modest in your thinking, and judge yourself according to the amount of faith that God has given you. ⁴We have many parts in the one body, and all these parts have different functions. ⁵In the same way, though we are many, we are one body in union with Christ, and we are all joined to each other as different parts of one body. ⁶So we are to use our different gifts in accordance with the grace that God has given us. If our gift is to

speak God's message, we should do it according to the faith that we have; ⁷if it is to serve, we should serve; if it is to teach, we should teach; ⁸if it is to encourage others, we should do so. Whoever shares with others should do it generously; whoever has authority should work hard; whoever shows kindness to others should do it cheerfully.

⁹Love must be completely sincere. Hate what is evil, hold on to what is good. ¹⁰Love one another warmly as Christians, and be eager to show respect for one another. ¹¹Work hard and do not be lazy. Serve the Lord with a heart full of devotion. ¹²Let your hope keep you joyful, be patient in your troubles, and pray at all times. ¹³Share your belongings with your needy fellow Christians, and open your homes to strangers.

¹⁴Ask God to bless those who persecute you — yes, ask him to bless, not to curse. ¹⁵Be happy with those who are happy, weep with those who weep. ¹⁶Have the same concern for everyone. Do not be proud, but accept humble duties.ʳ Do not think of yourselves as wise.

¹⁷If someone has done you wrong, do not repay him with a wrong. Try to do what everyone considers to be good. ¹⁸Do everything possible on your part to live in peace with everybody. ¹⁹Never take revenge, my friends, but instead let God's anger do it. For the scripture says, "I will take revenge, I will pay back, says the Lord." ²⁰Instead, as the scripture says: "If your enemies are hungry, feed them; if they are thirsty, give them a drink; for by doing this you will make them burn with shame." ²¹Do not let evil defeat you; instead, conquer evil with good.

ʳ accept humble duties; *or* make friends with humble people.

11.34 Is 40.13 (LXX)   **11.35** Job 41.11   **11.36** 1 Co 8.6   **12.4, 5** 1 Co 12.12
12.6-8 1 Co 12.4-11   **12.14** Mt 5.44; Lk 6.28   **12.15** Si 7.34   **12.16** Pr 3.7
12.19 Dt 32.35   **12.20** Pr 25.21, 22 (LXX)

Duties toward State Authorities

13 Everyone must obey state authorities, because no authority exists without God's permission, and the existing authorities have been put there by God. ² Whoever opposes the existing authority opposes what God has ordered; and anyone who does so will bring judgment on himself. ³ For rulers are not to be feared by those who do good, but by those who do evil. Would you like to be unafraid of those in authority? Then do what is good, and they will praise you, ⁴ because they are God's servants working for your own good. But if you do evil, then be afraid of them, because their power to punish is real. They are God's servants and carry out God's punishment on those who do evil. ⁵ For this reason you must obey the authorities — not just because of God's punishment, but also as a matter of conscience.

⁶ That is also why you pay taxes, because the authorities are working for God when they fulfill their duties. ⁷ Pay, then, what you owe them; pay them your personal and property taxes, and show respect and honor for them all.

Duties toward One Another

⁸ Be under obligation to no one — the only obligation you have is to love one another. Whoever does this has obeyed the Law. ⁹ The commandments, "Do not commit adultery; do not commit murder; do not steal; do not desire what belongs to someone else" — all these, and any others besides, are summed up in the one command, "Love your neighbor as you love yourself." ¹⁰ If you love others, you will never do them wrong; to love, then, is to obey the whole Law.

¹¹ You must do this, because you know that the time has come for you to wake up from your sleep. For the mo-ment when we will be saved is closer now than it was when we first believed. ¹² The night is nearly over, day is almost here. Let us stop doing the things that belong to the dark, and let us take up weapons for fighting in the light. ¹³ Let us conduct ourselves properly, as people who live in the light of day — no orgies or drunkenness, no immorality or indecency, no fighting or jealousy. ¹⁴ But take up the weapons of the Lord Jesus Christ, and stop paying attention to your sinful nature and satisfying its desires.

Do Not Judge Others

14 Welcome those who are weak in faith, but do not argue with them about their personal opinions. ² Some people's faith allows them to eat anything, but the person who is weak in the faith eats only vegetables. ³ The person who will eat anything is not to despise the one who doesn't; while the one who eats only vegetables is not to pass judgment on the one who will eat anything; for God has accepted that person. ⁴ Who are you to judge the servants of someone else? It is their own Master who will decide whether they succeed or fail. And they will succeed, because the Lord is able to make them succeed.

⁵ Some people think that a certain day is more important than other days, while others think that all days are the same. We each should firmly make up our own minds. ⁶ Those who think highly of a certain day do so in honor of the Lord; those who will eat anything do so in honor of the Lord, because they give thanks to God for the food. Those who refuse to eat certain things do so in honor of the Lord, and they give thanks to God. ⁷ We do not live for ourselves only, and we do not die for ourselves

13.1 Ws 6.3   **13.6, 7** Mt 22.21; Mk 12.17; Lk 20.25   **13.9 a** Ex 20.14; Dt 5.18; **b** Ex 20.13; Dt 5.17; **c** Ex 20.15; Dt 5.19; **d** Ex 20.17; Dt 5.21; **e** Lv 19.18 **14.1-6** Col 2.16

only. 8 If we live, it is for the Lord that we live, and if we die, it is for the Lord that we die. So whether we live or die, we belong to the Lord. 9 For Christ died and rose to life in order to be the Lord of the living and of the dead. 10 You then, who eat only vegetables — why do you pass judgment on others? And you who eat anything — why do you despise other believers? All of us will stand before God to be judged by him. 11 For the scripture says,

"As surely as I am the living
    God, says the Lord,
everyone will kneel before me,
and everyone will confess that
    I am God."

12 Every one of us, then, will have to give an account to God.

Do Not Make Others Fall

13 So then, let us stop judging one another. Instead, you should decide never to do anything that would make others stumble or fall into sin. 14 My union with the Lord Jesus makes me certain that no food is of itself ritually unclean; but if you believe that some food is unclean, then it becomes unclean for you. 15 If you hurt others because of something you eat, then you are no longer acting from love. Do not let the food that you eat ruin the person for whom Christ died! 16 Do not let what you regard as good get a bad name. 17 For God's Kingdom is not a matter of eating and drinking, but of the righteousness, peace, and joy which the Holy Spirit gives. 18 And when you serve Christ in this way, you please God and are approved by others.

19 So then, we must always aim*s* at those things that bring peace and that help strengthen one another. 20 Do not, because of food, destroy what God has done. All foods may be eaten, but it is

wrong to eat anything that will cause someone else to fall into sin. 21 The right thing to do is to keep from eating meat, drinking wine, or doing anything else that will make other believers fall. 22 Keep what you believe about this matter, then, between yourself and God. Happy are those who do not feel guilty when they do something they judge is right! 23 But if they have doubts about what they eat, God condemns them when they eat it, because their action is not based on faith. And anything that is not based on faith is sin.

Please Others, Not Yourselves

15 We who are strong in the faith ought to help the weak to carry their burdens. We should not please ourselves. 2 Instead, we should all please other believers for their own good, in order to build them up in the faith. 3 For Christ did not please himself. Instead, as the scripture says, "The insults which are hurled at you have fallen on me." 4 Everything written in the Scriptures was written to teach us, in order that we might have hope through the patience and encouragement which the Scriptures give us. 5 And may God, the source of patience and encouragement, enable you to have the same point of view among yourselves by following the example of Christ Jesus, 6 so that all of you together may praise with one voice the God and Father of our Lord Jesus Christ.

The Gospel to the Gentiles

7 Accept one another, then, for the glory of God, as Christ has accepted you. 8 For I tell you that Christ's life of service was on behalf of the Jews, to show that God is faithful, to make his promises to their ancestors come true, 9 and to enable even the Gentiles to

s we must always aim; *some manuscripts have* we always aim.

14.10 2 Co 5.10   **14.11** Is 45.23 (LXX)   **15.3** Ps 69.9   **15.4** 1 Macc 12.9; 2 Macc 15.9
15.9 2 S 22.50; Ps 18.49

praise God for his mercy. As the scripture says,

"And so I will praise you among
the Gentiles;
I will sing praises to you."

10 Again it says,

"Rejoice, Gentiles, with God's
people!"

11 And again,

"Praise the Lord, all Gentiles;
praise him, all peoples!"

12 And again, Isaiah says,

"A descendant of Jesse will
appear;
he will come to rule the
Gentiles,
and they will put their hope
in him."

13 May God, the source of hope, fill you with all joy and peace by means of your faith in him, so that your hope will continue to grow by the power of the Holy Spirit.

Paul's Reason for Writing So Boldly

14 My friends: I myself feel sure that you are full of goodness, that you have all knowledge, and that you are able to teach one another. 15 But in this letter I have been quite bold about certain subjects of which I have reminded you. I have been bold because of the privilege God has given me 16 of being a servant of Christ Jesus to work for the Gentiles. I serve like a priest in preaching the Good News from God, in order that the Gentiles may be an offering acceptable to God, dedicated to him by the Holy Spirit. 17 In union with Christ Jesus, then, I can be proud of my service for God. 18 I will be bold and speak only about what Christ has done through me to lead the Gentiles to obey God. He has done this by means of words and deeds, 19 by the power of miracles and wonders, and by the power of the Spirit of God. And so, in traveling all the way from Jerusalem to Illyricum, I have proclaimed fully the Good News about Christ. 20 My ambition has always been to proclaim the Good News in places where Christ has not been heard of, so as not to build on a foundation laid by someone else. 21 As the scripture says,

"Those who were not told about
him will see,
and those who have not heard
will understand."

Paul's Plan to Visit Rome

22 And so I have been prevented many times from coming to you. 23 But now that I have finished my work in these regions and since I have been wanting for so many years to come to see you, 24 I hope to do so now. I would like to see you on my way to Spain, and be helped by you to go there, after I have enjoyed visiting you for a while. 25 Right now, however, I am going to Jerusalem in the service of God's people there. 26 For the churches in Macedonia and Achaia have freely decided to give an offering to help the poor among God's people in Jerusalem. 27 That decision was their own; but, as a matter of fact, they have an obligation to help them. Since the Jews shared their spiritual blessings with the Gentiles, the Gentiles ought to use their material blessings to help the Jews. 28 When I have finished this task and have turned over to them all the money that has been raised for them, I shall leave for Spain and visit you on my way there. 29 When I come to you, I know that I shall come with a full measure of the blessing of Christ.

30 I urge you, friends, by our Lord Jesus Christ and by the love that the

15.10 Dt 32.43   15.11 Ps 117.1   15.12 Is 11.10 (LXX)   15.21 Is 52.15 (LXX)
15.22 Ro 1.13   15.25, 26 1 Co 16.1-4   15.27 1 Co 9.11

Spirit gives: join me in praying fervently to God for me. [31] Pray that I may be kept safe from the unbelievers in Judea and that my service in Jerusalem may be acceptable to God's people there. [32] And so I will come to you full of joy, if it is God's will, and enjoy a refreshing visit with you. [33] May God, our source of peace, be with all of you. Amen.

Personal Greetings

16 I recommend to you our sister Phoebe, who serves the church at Cenchreae. [2] Receive her in the Lord's name, as God's people should, and give her any help she may need from you; for she herself has been a good friend to many people and also to me.

[3] I send greetings to Priscilla and Aquila, my fellow workers in the service of Christ Jesus; [4] they risked their lives for me. I am grateful to them — not only I, but all the Gentile churches as well. [5] Greetings also to the church that meets in their house.

Greetings to my dear friend Epaenetus, who was the first in the province of Asia to believe in Christ. [6] Greetings to Mary, who has worked so hard for you. [7] Greetings also to Andronicus and Junia,[t] fellow Jews who were in prison with me; they are well known among the apostles, and they became Christians before I did.

[8] My greetings to Ampliatus, my dear friend in the fellowship of the Lord. [9] Greetings also to Urbanus, our fellow worker in Christ's service, and to Stachys, my dear friend. [10] Greetings to Apelles, whose loyalty to Christ has been proved. Greetings to those who belong to the family of Aristobulus. [11] Greetings to Herodion, a fellow Jew,

and to the Christians in the family of Narcissus.

[12] My greetings to Tryphaena and Tryphosa, who work in the Lord's service, and to my dear friend Persis, who has done so much work for the Lord. [13] I send greetings to Rufus, that outstanding worker in the Lord's service, and to his mother, who has always treated me like a son. [14] My greetings to Asyncritus, Phlegon, Hermes, Patrobas, Hermas, and all the other Christians with them. [15] Greetings to Philologus and Julia, to Nereus and his sister, to Olympas and to all of God's people who are with them.

[16] Greet one another with the kiss of peace. All the churches of Christ send you their greetings.

Greet one another with the kiss of peace. (16.16)

Final Instructions

[17] I urge you, my friends: watch out for those who cause divisions and upset people's faith and go against the teaching which you have received. Keep away from them! [18] For those who do such things are not serving Christ our Lord, but their own appetites. By their fine words and flattering speech they deceive innocent people. [19] Everyone has heard of your loyalty to the gospel,

---

[t] Junia; *or* Junias; *some manuscripts have* Julia.
16.3 Ac 18.2   **16.13** Mk 15.21

and for this reason I am happy about you. I want you to be wise about what is good, but innocent in what is evil. [20] And God, our source of peace, will soon crush Satan under your feet.

The grace of our Lord Jesus be with you. [u]

[21] Timothy, my fellow worker, sends you his greetings; and so do Lucius, Jason, and Sosipater, fellow Jews.

[22] I, Tertius, the writer of this letter, send you Christian greetings.

[23] My host Gaius, in whose house the church meets, sends you his greetings; Erastus, the city treasurer, and our brother Quartus send you their greetings. [v]

Concluding Prayer of Praise

[25] Let us give glory to God! He is able to make you stand firm in your faith, according to the Good News I preach about Jesus Christ and according to the revelation of the secret truth which was hidden for long ages in the past. [26] Now, however, that truth has been brought out into the open through the writings of the prophets; and by the command of the eternal God it is made known to all nations, so that all may believe and obey.

[27] To the only God, who alone is all-wise, be glory through Jesus Christ forever! Amen. [w]

---

[u] *Some manuscripts omit this sentence.*   [v] *Some manuscripts add verse 24: The* grace of our Lord Jesus Christ be with you all. Amen; *others add this after verse 27.* [w] *Some manuscripts have verses 25-27 here and after 14.23; others have them only after 14.23; one has them after 15.33.*

16.21 Ac 16.1   **16.23 a** Ac 19.29; 1 Co 1.14; **b** 2 Ti 4.20

Paul's First Letter to the
CORINTHIANS

INTRODUCTION

Paul's First Letter to the Corinthians was written to deal with problems of Christian life and faith that had arisen in the church which Paul had established at Corinth. At that time Corinth was a great cosmopolitan Greek city, the capital of the Roman province of Achaia. It was noted for its thriving commerce, proud culture, widespread immorality, and variety of religions.

The apostle's chief concerns are with problems such as divisions and immorality in the church, and with questions about sex and marriage, matters of conscience, church order, gifts of the Holy Spirit, and the resurrection. With deep insight he shows how the Good News speaks to these questions.

Chapter 13, which presents love as the best of God's gifts to his people, is probably the most widely known passage in the book.

OUTLINE OF CONTENTS

1

From Paul, who was called by the will of God to be an apostle of Christ Jesus, and from our brother Sosthenes —

² To the church of God which is in Corinth, to all who are called to be God's holy people, who belong to him in union with Christ Jesus, together with all people everywhere who worship our Lord Jesus Christ, their Lord and ours:

³ May God our Father and the Lord Jesus Christ give you grace and peace.

Blessings in Christ

⁴ I always give thanks to my God for you because of the grace he has given you through Christ Jesus. ⁵ For in union with Christ you have become rich in all things, including all speech and all knowledge. ⁶ The message about Christ has become so firmly established in you ⁷ that you have not failed to receive a single blessing, as you wait for our Lord Jesus Christ to be revealed. ⁸ He will also keep you firm to the end, so that you will be faultless on the Day of our Lord Jesus Christ. ⁹ God

1.2 Ac 18.1

is to be trusted, the God who called you to have fellowship with his Son Jesus Christ, our Lord.

Divisions in the Church

10 By the authority of our Lord Jesus Christ I appeal to all of you, my friends, to agree in what you say, so that there will be no divisions among you. Be completely united, with only one thought and one purpose. **11** For some people from Chloe's family have told me quite plainly, my friends, that there are quarrels among you. **12** Let me put it this way: each one of you says something different. One says, "I follow Paul"; another, "I follow Apollos"; another, "I follow Peter"; and another, "I follow Christ." **13** Christ has been divided[a] into groups! Was it Paul who died on the cross for you? Were you baptized as Paul's disciples?

14 I thank God that I did not baptize any of you except Crispus and Gaius. **15** No one can say, then, that you were baptized as my disciples. (**16** Oh yes, I also baptized Stephanas and his family; but I can't remember whether I baptized anyone else.) **17** Christ did not send me to baptize. He sent me to tell the Good News, and to tell it without using the language of human wisdom, in order to make sure that Christ's death on the cross is not robbed of its power.

Christ the Power and the Wisdom of God

18 For the message about Christ's death on the cross is nonsense to those who are being lost; but for us who are being saved it is God's power. **19** The scripture says,

"I will destroy the wisdom of
the wise

and set aside the
understanding of
the scholars."

20 So then, where does that leave the wise? or the scholars? or the skillful debaters of this world? God has shown that this world's wisdom is foolishness!

21 For God in his wisdom made it impossible for people to know him by means of their own wisdom. Instead, by means of the so-called "foolish" message we preach, God decided to save those who believe. **22** Jews want miracles for proof, and Greeks look for wisdom. **23** As for us, we proclaim the crucified Christ, a message that is offensive to the Jews and nonsense to the Gentiles; **24** but for those whom God has called, both Jews and Gentiles, this message is Christ, who is the power of God and the wisdom of God. **25** For what seems to be God's foolishness is wiser than human wisdom, and what seems to be God's weakness is stronger than human strength.

26 Now remember what you were, my friends, when God called you. From the human point of view few of you were wise or powerful or of high social standing. **27** God purposely chose what the world considers nonsense in order to shame the wise, and he chose what the world considers weak in order to shame the powerful. **28** He chose what the world looks down on and despises and thinks is nothing, in order to destroy what the world thinks is important. **29** This means that no one can boast in God's presence. **30** But God has brought you into union with Christ Jesus, and God has made Christ to be our wisdom. By him we are put right with God; we become God's holy people and are set free. **31** So then, as the scripture says, "Whoever wants to boast must boast of what the Lord has done."

---

a Christ has been divided; *some manuscripts have* Christ cannot be divided.

1.12 Ac 18.24   **1.14 a** Ac 18.8; **b** Ac 19.29; Ro 16.23   **1.16** 1 Co 16.15
1.19 Is 29.14 (LXX)   **1.20 a** Job 12.17; Is 19.12; 33.18; **b** Is 44.25   **1.21** Ws 13.1-9
1.31 Jr 9.24

The Message about the Crucified Christ

2 When I came to you, my friends, to preach God's secret truth,[b] I did not use big words and great learning. [2] For while I was with you, I made up my mind to forget everything except Jesus Christ and especially his death on the cross. [3] So when I came to you, I was weak and trembled all over with fear, [4] and my teaching and message were not delivered with skillful words of human wisdom, but with convincing proof of the power of God's Spirit. [5] Your faith, then, does not rest on human wisdom but on God's power.

God's Wisdom

[6] Yet I do proclaim a message of wisdom to those who are spiritually mature. But it is not the wisdom that belongs to this world or to the powers that rule this world — powers that are losing their power. [7] The wisdom I proclaim is God's secret wisdom, which is hidden from human beings, but which he had already chosen for our glory even before the world was made. [8] None of the rulers of this world knew this wisdom. If they had known it, they would not have crucified the Lord of glory. [9] However, as the scripture says,

"What no one ever saw or heard,
 what no one ever thought
  could happen,
is the very thing God prepared
  for those who love him."

[10] But[c] it was to us that God made known his secret by means of his Spirit. The Spirit searches everything, even the hidden depths of God's purposes. [11] It is only our own spirit within us that knows all about us; in the same way, only God's Spirit knows all about God.

[12] We have not received this world's spirit; instead, we have received the Spirit sent by God, so that we may know all that God has given us.

[13] So then, we do not speak in words taught by human wisdom, but in words taught by the Spirit, as we explain spiritual truths to those who have the Spirit.[d] [14] Whoever does not have the Spirit cannot receive the gifts that come from God's Spirit. Such a person really does not understand them, and they seem to be nonsense, because their value can be judged only on a spiritual basis. [15] Whoever has the Spirit, however, is able to judge the value of everything, but no one is able to judge him.
[16] As the scripture says,

"Who knows the mind of the
  Lord?
Who is able to give him
  advice?"

We, however, have the mind of Christ.

Servants of God

3 As a matter of fact, my friends, I could not talk to you as I talk to people who have the Spirit; I had to talk to you as though you belonged to this world, as children in the Christian faith. [2] I had to feed you milk, not solid food, because you were not ready for it. And even now you are not ready for it, [3] because you still live as the people of this world live. When there is jealousy among you and you quarrel with one another, doesn't this prove that you belong to this world, living by its standards? [4] When one of you says, "I follow Paul," and another, "I follow Apollos" — aren't you acting like worldly people?

[5] After all, who is Apollos? And who is Paul? We are simply God's servants, by whom you were led to believe. Each

---

b God's secret truth; some manuscripts have the testimony about God.   *c But; some manuscripts have* For.   *d to those who have the Spirit; or* with words given by the Spirit.

2.3 Ac 18.9   **2.8** Ba 3.14-17   **2.9** Is 64.4; Si 1.9, 10   **2.16** Is 40.13 (LXX)
3.2 He 5.12, 13   **3.4** 1 Co 1.12

one of us does the work which the Lord gave him to do: ⁶I planted the seed, Apollos watered the plant, but it was God who made the plant grow. ⁷The one who plants and the one who waters really do not matter. It is God who matters, because he makes the plant grow. ⁸There is no difference between the one who plants and the one who waters; God will reward each one according to the work each has done. ⁹For we are partners working together for God, and you are God's field.

It was God who made the plant grow. (3.6)

You are also God's building. ¹⁰Using the gift that God gave me, I did the work of an expert builder and laid the foundation, and someone else is building on it. But each of you must be careful how you build. ¹¹For God has already placed Jesus Christ as the one and only foundation, and no other foundation can be laid. ¹²Some will use gold or silver or precious stones in building on the foundation; others will use wood or grass or straw. ¹³And the quality of each person's work will be seen when the Day of Christ exposes it. For on that Day fire will reveal everyone's work; the fire will test it and show its real quality. ¹⁴If what was built on the foundation sur-

vives the fire, the builder will receive a reward. ¹⁵But if your work is burnt up, then you will lose it; but you yourself will be saved, as if you had escaped through the fire.

¹⁶Surely you know that you are God's temple and that God's Spirit lives in you! ¹⁷God will destroy anyone who destroys God's temple. For God's temple is holy, and you yourselves are his temple.

¹⁸You should not fool yourself. If any of you think that you are wise by this world's standards, you should become a fool, in order to be really wise. ¹⁹For what this world considers to be wisdom is nonsense in God's sight. As the scripture says, "God traps the wise in their cleverness"; ²⁰and another scripture says, "The Lord knows that the thoughts of the wise are worthless." ²¹No one, then, should boast about what human beings can do. Actually everything belongs to you: ²²Paul, Apollos, and Peter; this world, life and death, the present and the future—all these are yours, ²³and you belong to Christ, and Christ belongs to God.

Apostles of Christ

4 You should think of us as Christ's servants, who have been put in charge of God's secret truths. ²The one thing required of such servants is that they be faithful to their master. ³Now, I am not at all concerned about being judged by you or by any human standard; I don't even pass judgment on myself. ⁴My conscience is clear, but that does not prove that I am really innocent. The Lord is the one who passes judgment on me. ⁵So you should not pass judgment on anyone before the right time comes. Final judgment must wait until the Lord comes; he will bring to light the dark secrets and expose the hidden purposes of people's minds. And

3.6 a Ac 18.4-11; **b** Ac 18.24-28   **3.16** 1 Co 6.19; 2 Co 6.16   **3.19** Job 5.13   **3.20** Ps 94.11
4.4 Ws 17.11

then all will receive from God the praise they deserve.

6 For your sake, my friends, I have applied all this to Apollos and me, using the two of us as an example, so that you may learn what the saying means, "Observe the proper rules." None of you should be proud of one person and despise another. 7 Who made you superior to others? Didn't God give you everything you have? Well, then, how can you boast, as if what you have were not a gift?

8 Do you already have everything you need? Are you already rich? Have you become kings, even though we are not? Well, I wish you really were kings, so that we could be kings together with you. 9 For it seems to me that God has given the very last place to us apostles, like people condemned to die in public as a spectacle for the whole world of angels and of human beings. 10 For Christ's sake we are fools; but you are wise in union with Christ! We are weak, but you are strong! We are despised, but you are honored! 11 To this very moment we go hungry and thirsty; we are clothed in rags; we are beaten; we wander from place to place; 12 we wear ourselves out with hard work. When we are cursed, we bless; when we are persecuted, we endure; 13 when we are insulted, we answer back with kind words. We are no more than this world's garbage; we are the scum of the earth to this very moment!

14 I write this to you, not because I want to make you feel ashamed, but to instruct you as my own dear children. 15 For even if you have ten thousand guardians in your Christian life, you have only one father. For in your life in union with Christ Jesus I have become your father by bringing the Good News to you. 16 I beg you, then, to follow my example. 17 For this purpose I am sending to you Timothy, who is my own dear and faithful son in the Christian life.

He will remind you of the principles which I follow in the new life in union with Christ Jesus and which I teach in all the churches everywhere.

18 Some of you have become proud because you have thought that I would not be coming to visit you. 19 If the Lord is willing, however, I will come to you soon, and then I will find out for myself the power which these proud people have, and not just what they say. 20 For the Kingdom of God is not a matter of words but of power. 21 Which do you prefer? Shall I come to you with a whip, or in a spirit of love and gentleness?

Immorality in the Church

5 Now, it is actually being said that there is sexual immorality among you so terrible that not even the heathen would be guilty of it. I am told that a man is sleeping with his stepmother! 2 How, then, can you be proud? On the contrary, you should be filled with sadness, and the man who has done such a thing should be expelled from your fellowship. 3-4 And even though I am far away from you in body, still I am there with you in spirit; and as though I were there with you, I have in the name of our Lord Jesus already passed judgment on the man who has done this terrible thing. As you meet together, and I meet with you in my spirit, by the power of our Lord Jesus present with us, 5 you are to hand this man over to Satan for his body to be destroyed, so that his spirit may be saved in the Day of the Lord.

6 It is not right for you to be proud! You know the saying, "A little bit of yeast makes the whole batch of dough rise." 7 You must remove the old yeast of sin so that you will be entirely pure. Then you will be like a new batch of dough without any yeast, as indeed I know you actually are. For our Passover Festival is ready, now that Christ, our

4.12 Ac 18.3   **4.16** 1 Co 11.1; Phil 3.17   **5.1** Dt 22.30   **5.6** Ga 5.9   **5.7** Ex 12.5

Passover lamb, has been sacrificed. [8] Let us celebrate our Passover, then, not with bread having the old yeast of sin and wickedness, but with the bread that has no yeast, the bread of purity and truth.

[9] In the letter that I wrote you I told you not to associate with immoral people. [10] Now I did not mean pagans who are immoral or greedy or are thieves, or who worship idols. To avoid them you would have to get out of the world completely. [11] What I meant was that you should not associate with a person who calls himself a believer but is immoral or greedy or worships idols or is a slanderer or a drunkard or a thief. Don't even sit down to eat with such a person. [12-13] After all, it is none of my business to judge outsiders. God will judge them. But should you not judge the members of your own fellowship? As the scripture says, "Remove the evil person from your group."

Lawsuits against Fellow Christians

6 If any of you have a dispute with another Christian, how dare you go before heathen judges instead of letting God's people settle the matter? [2] Don't you know that God's people will judge the world? Well, then, if you are to judge the world, aren't you capable of judging small matters? [3] Do you not know that we shall judge the angels? How much more, then, the things of this life! [4] If such matters come up, are you going to take them to be settled by people who have no standing in the church? [5] Shame on you! Surely there is at least one wise person in your fellowship who can settle a dispute between fellow Christians. [6] Instead, one Christian goes to court against another and lets unbelievers judge the case! [7] The very fact that you have legal disputes among yourselves shows that you have failed completely. Would it

not be better for you to be wronged? Would it not be better for you to be robbed? [8] Instead, you yourselves wrong one another and rob one another, even other believers! [9] Surely you know that the wicked will not possess God's Kingdom. Do not fool yourselves; people who are immoral or who worship idols or are adulterers or homosexual perverts [10] or who steal or are greedy or are drunkards or who slander others or are thieves — none of these will possess God's Kingdom. [11] Some of you were like that. But you have been purified from sin; you have been dedicated to God; you have been put right with God by the Lord Jesus Christ and by the Spirit of our God.

Use Your Bodies for God's Glory

[12] Someone will say, "I am allowed to do anything." Yes; but not everything is good for you. I could say that I am allowed to do anything, but I am not going to let anything make me its slave. [13] Someone else will say, "Food is for the stomach, and the stomach is for food." Yes; but God will put an end to both. The body is not to be used for sexual immorality, but to serve the Lord; and the Lord provides for the body. [14] God raised the Lord from death, and he will also raise us by his power.

[15] You know that your bodies are parts of the body of Christ. Shall I take a part of Christ's body and make it part of the body of a prostitute? Impossible! [16] Or perhaps you don't know that the man who joins his body to a prostitute becomes physically one with her? The scripture says quite plainly, "The two will become one body." [17] But he who joins himself to the Lord becomes spiritually one with him.

[18] Avoid immorality. Any other sin a man commits does not affect his body; but the man who is guilty of sexual immorality sins against his own body.

5.8 Ex 13.7; Dt 16.3   **5.13** Dt 13.5; 17.7 (LXX)   **6.12** 1 Co 10.23   **6.16** Gn 2.24

¹⁹ Don't you know that your body is the temple of the Holy Spirit, who lives in you and who was given to you by God? You do not belong to yourselves but to God; ²⁰ he bought you for a price. So use your bodies for God's glory.

Questions about Marriage

7 Now, to deal with the matters you wrote about.

A man does well not to marry.ᵉ ² But because there is so much immorality, every man should have his own wife, and every woman should have her own husband. ³ A man should fulfill his duty as a husband, and a woman should fulfill her duty as a wife, and each should satisfy the other's needs. ⁴ A wife is not the master of her own body, but her husband is; in the same way a husband is not the master of his own body, but his wife is. ⁵ Do not deny yourselves to each other, unless you first agree to do so for a while in order to spend your time in prayer; but then resume normal marital relations. In this way you will be kept from giving in to Satan's temptation because of your lack of self-control.

⁶ I tell you this not as an order, but simply as a permission. ⁷ Actually I would prefer that all of you were as I am; but each one has a special gift from God, one person this gift, another one that gift.

⁸ Now, to the unmarried and to the widows I say that it would be better for you to continue to live alone as I do. ⁹ But if you cannot restrain your desires, go ahead and marry — it is better to marry than to burn with passion.

¹⁰ For married people I have a command which is not my own but the Lord's: a wife must not leave her husband; ¹¹ but if she does, she must re-main single or else be reconciled to her husband; and a husband must not di-vorce his wife.

¹² To the others I say (I, myself, not the Lord): if a Christian man has a wife who is an unbeliever and she agrees to go on living with him, he must not di-vorce her. ¹³ And if a Christian woman is married to a man who is an unbe-liever and he agrees to go on living with her, she must not divorce him. ¹⁴ For the unbelieving husband is made ac-ceptable to God by being united to his wife, and the unbelieving wife is made acceptable to God by being united to her Christian husband. If this were not so, their children would be like pagan children; but as it is, they are accepta-ble to God. ¹⁵ However, if the one who is not a believer wishes to leave the Christian partner, let it be so. In such cases the Christian partner, whether husband or wife, is free to act. God has called you to live in peace. ¹⁶ How can you be sure, Christian wife, that you will not saveᶠ your husband? Or how can you be sure, Christian husband, that you will not saveᶠ your wife?

Live As God Called You

¹⁷ Each of you should go on living ac-cording to the Lord's gift to you, and as you were when God called you. This is the rule I teach in all the churches. ¹⁸ If a circumcised man has accepted God's call, he should not try to remove the marks of circumcision; if an uncircum-cised man has accepted God's call, he should not get circumcised. ¹⁹ For whether or not a man is circumcised means nothing; what matters is to obey God's commandments. ²⁰ Each of you should remain as you were when you accepted God's call. ²¹ Were you a slave

---

ᵉ A man does well not to marry; or You say that a man does well not to marry.
ᶠ How can you be sure . . . that you will not save; or How do you know . . . that you will save.

6.19 1 Co 3.16; 2 Co 6.16   **7.10, 11** Mt 5.32; 19.9; Mk 10.11, 12; Lk 16.18
7.18 1 Macc 1.15

when God called you? Well, never mind; but if you have a chance to become free, use it.*g* ²²For a slave who has been called by the Lord is the Lord's free person; in the same way a free person who has been called by Christ is his slave. ²³God bought you for a price; so do not become slaves of people. ²⁴My friends, each of you should remain in fellowship with God in the same condition that you were when you were called.

Questions about the Unmarried and the Widows

²⁵Now, concerning what you wrote about unmarried people: I do not have a command from the Lord, but I give my opinion as one who by the Lord's mercy is worthy of trust.

²⁶Considering the present distress, I think it is better for a man to stay as he is. ²⁷Do you have a wife? Then don't try to get rid of her. Are you unmarried? Then don't look for a wife. ²⁸But if you do marry, you haven't committed a sin; and if an unmarried woman marries, she hasn't committed a sin. But I would rather spare you the everyday troubles that married people will have.

²⁹What I mean, my friends, is this: there is not much time left, and from now on married people should live as though they were not married; ³⁰those who weep, as though they were not sad; those who laugh, as though they were not happy; those who buy, as though they did not own what they bought; ³¹those who deal in material goods, as though they were not fully oc-

cupied with them. For this world, as it is now, will not last much longer.

³²I would like you to be free from worry. An unmarried man concerns himself with the Lord's work, because he is trying to please the Lord. ³³But a married man concerns himself with worldly matters, because he wants to please his wife; ³⁴and so he is pulled in two directions. An unmarried woman or a virgin concerns herself with the Lord's work, because she wants to be dedicated both in body and spirit; but a married woman concerns herself with worldly matters, because she wants to please her husband.

³⁵I am saying this because I want to help you. I am not trying to put restrictions on you. Instead, I want you to do what is right and proper, and to give yourselves completely to the Lord's service without any reservation.

³⁶In the case of an engaged couple who have decided not to marry: if the man feels that he is not acting properly toward the young woman and if his passions are too strong and he feels that they ought to marry, then they should get married, as he wants to.*h* There is no sin in this. ³⁷But if a man, without being forced to do so, has firmly made up his mind not to marry,*i* and if he has his will under complete control and has already decided in his own mind what to do—then he does well not to marry the young woman.*j* ³⁸So the man who marries*k* does well, but the one who doesn't marry*l* does even better.

³⁹A married woman is not free as long as her husband lives; but if her husband dies, then she is free to be

---

g but if you have a chance to become free, use it; *or* but even if you have a chance to become free, choose rather to make the best of your condition as a slave.   *h* an engaged couple . . . as he wants to; *or* a man and his unmarried daughter: if he feels that he is not acting properly toward her, and if she is at the right age to marry, then he should do as he wishes and let her get married.   *i* not to marry; *or* not to let his daughter get married.   *j* marry the young woman; *or* let her get married.
k marries; *or* lets his daughter get married.   *l* doesn't marry; *or* doesn't let her get married.

married to any man she wishes, but only if he is a Christian. ⁴⁰She will be happier, however, if she stays as she is. That is my opinion, and I think that I too have God's Spirit.

The Question about Food Offered to Idols

8 Now, concerning what you wrote about food offered to idols. It is true, of course, that "all of us have knowledge," as they say. Such knowledge, however, puffs a person up with pride; but love builds up. ²Those who think they know something really don't know as they ought to know. ³But the person who loves God is known by him.

⁴So then, about eating the food offered to idols: we know that an idol stands for something that does not really exist; we know that there is only the one God. ⁵Even if there are so-called "gods," whether in heaven or on earth, and even though there are many of these "gods" and "lords," ⁶yet there is for us only one God, the Father, who is the Creator of all things and for whom we live; and there is only one Lord, Jesus Christ, through whom all things were created and through whom we live.

⁷But not everyone knows this truth. Some people have been so used to idols that to this day when they eat such food they still think of it as food that belongs to an idol; their conscience is weak, and they feel they are defiled by the food. ⁸Food, however, will not improve our relation with God; we shall not lose anything if we do not eat, nor shall we gain anything if we do eat.

⁹Be careful, however, not to let your freedom of action make those who are weak in the faith fall into sin. ¹⁰Suppose a person whose conscience is weak in this matter sees you, who have so-called "knowledge," eating in the temple of an idol; will not this encourage him to eat food offered to idols? ¹¹And so this weak person, your brother for whom Christ died, will perish because of your "knowledge"! ¹²And in this way you will be sinning against Christ by sinning against other Christians and wounding their weak conscience. ¹³So then, if food makes a believer sin, I will never eat meat again, so as not to make a believer fall into sin.

Rights and Duties of an Apostle

9 Am I not a free man? Am I not an apostle? Haven't I seen Jesus our Lord? And aren't you the result of my work for the Lord? ²Even if others do not accept me as an apostle, surely you do! Because of your life in union with the Lord you yourselves are proof of the fact that I am an apostle.

³When people criticize me, this is how I defend myself: ⁴Don't I have the right to be given food and drink for my work? ⁵Don't I have the right to follow the example of the other apostles and the Lord's brothers and Peter, by taking a Christian wife with me on my trips? ⁶Or are Barnabas and I the only ones who have to work for our living? ⁷What soldiers ever have to pay their own expenses in the army? What farmers do not eat the grapes from their own vineyard? What shepherds do not use the milk from their own sheep?

⁸I don't have to limit myself to these everyday examples, because the Law says the same thing. ⁹We read in the Law of Moses, "Do not muzzle an ox when you are using it to thresh grain." Now, is God concerned about oxen? ¹⁰Didn't he really mean us when he said that? Of course that was written for us. Anyone who plows and anyone who reaps should do their work in the hope of getting a share of the crop. ¹¹We have sown spiritual seed among you. Is it too much if we reap material

9.9 Dt 25.4; 1 Ti 5.18   **9.11** Ro 15.27

benefits from you? ¹²If others have the right to expect this from you, don't we have an even greater right?

But we haven't made use of this right. Instead, we have endured everything in order not to put any obstacle in the way of the Good News about Christ. ¹³Surely you know that the men who work in the Temple get their food from the Temple and that those who offer the sacrifices on the altar get a share of the sacrifices. ¹⁴In the same way, the Lord has ordered that those who preach the gospel should get their living from it.

¹⁵But I haven't made use of any of these rights, nor am I writing this now in order to claim such rights for myself. I would rather die first! Nobody is going to turn my rightful boast into empty words! ¹⁶I have no right to boast just because I preach the gospel. After all, I am under orders to do so. And how terrible it would be for me if I did not preach the gospel! ¹⁷If I did my work as a matter of free choice, then I could expect to be paid; but I do it as a matter of duty, because God has entrusted me with this task. ¹⁸What pay do I get, then? It is the privilege of preaching the Good News without charging for it, without claiming my rights in my work for the gospel.

¹⁹I am a free man, nobody's slave; but I make myself everybody's slave in order to win as many people as possible. ²⁰While working with the Jews, I live like a Jew in order to win them; and even though I myself am not subject to the Law of Moses, I live as though I were when working with those who are, in order to win them. ²¹In the same way, when working with Gentiles, I live like a Gentile, outside the Jewish Law, in order to win Gentiles. This does not mean that I don't obey God's law; I am really under Christ's law. ²²Among the weak in faith I become weak like one of

them, in order to win them. So I become all things to all people, that I may save some of them by whatever means are possible.

²³All this I do for the gospel's sake, in order to share in its blessings. ²⁴Surely you know that many runners take part in a race, but only one of them wins the prize. Run, then, in such a way as to win the prize. ²⁵Every athlete in training submits to strict discipline, in order to be crowned with a wreath that will not last; but we do it for one that will last forever. ²⁶That is why I run straight for the finish line; that is why I am like a boxer who does not waste his punches. ²⁷I harden my body with blows and bring it under complete control, to keep myself from being disqualified after having called others to the contest.

Only one of them wins the prize. (9.24)

Warnings against Idols

10 I want you to remember, my friends, what happened to our ancestors who followed Moses. They were all under the protection of the cloud, and all passed safely through the Red Sea. ²In the cloud and in the sea they were all baptized as followers of Moses. ³All ate the same spiritual bread ⁴and drank the same spiritual drink. They drank from the spiritual rock that went with them; and that rock was

9.13 Dt 18.1   **9.14** Mt 10.10; Lk 10.7   **9.25** Ws 4.2; 5.16   **10.1 a** Ex 13.21, 22;
b Ex 14.22-29   **10.3** Ex 16.35   **10.4** Ex 17.6; Nu 20.11

Christ himself. [5] But even then God was not pleased with most of them, and so their dead bodies were scattered over the desert.

[6] Now, all of this is an example for us, to warn us not to desire evil things, as they did, [7] nor to worship idols, as some of them did. As the scripture says, "The people sat down to a feast which turned into an orgy of drinking and sex." [8] We must not be guilty of sexual immorality, as some of them were — and in one day twenty-three thousand of them fell dead. [9] We must not put the Lord[m] to the test, as some of them did — and they were killed by snakes. [10] We must not complain, as some of them did — and they were destroyed by the Angel of Death.

[11] All these things happened to them as examples for others, and they were written down as a warning for us. For we live at a time when the end is about to come.

[12] If you think you are standing firm you had better be careful that you do not fall. [13] Every test that you have experienced is the kind that normally comes to people. But God keeps his promise, and he will not allow you to be tested beyond your power to remain firm; at the time you are put to the test, he will give you the strength to endure it, and so provide you with a way out.

[14] So then, my dear friends, keep away from the worship of idols. [15] I speak to you as sensible people; judge for yourselves what I say. [16] The cup we use in the Lord's Supper and for which we give thanks to God: when we drink from it, we are sharing in the blood of Christ. And the bread we break: when we eat it, we are sharing in the body of Christ. [17] Because there is the one loaf

We all share the same loaf. (10.17)

of bread, all of us, though many, are one body, for we all share the same loaf.

[18] Consider the people of Israel; those who eat what is offered in sacrifice share in the altar's service to God. [19] Do I imply, then, that an idol or the food offered to it really amounts to anything? [20] No! What I am saying is that what is sacrificed on pagan altars is offered to demons, not to God. And I do not want you to be partners with demons. [21] You cannot drink from the Lord's cup and also from the cup of demons; you cannot eat at the Lord's table and also at the table of demons. [22] Or do we want to make the Lord jealous? Do we think that we are stronger than he?

[23] "We are allowed to do anything," so they say. That is true, but not everything is good. "We are allowed to do anything" — but not everything is helpful. [24] None of you should be looking out for your own interests, but for the interests of others.

[25] You are free to eat anything sold in the meat market, without asking any questions because of your conscience. [26] For, as the scripture says, "The earth and everything in it belong to the Lord."

[27] If an unbeliever invites you to a meal and you decide to go, eat what is

---

[m] the Lord; *some manuscripts have* Christ.

10.5 Nu 14.29, 30   10.6 Nu 11.4   10.7 Ex 32.6   10.8 Nu 25.1-18   10.9 Nu 21.5, 6
10.10 Nu 16.41-49   10.13 Jdt 8.25-27; Si 15.11-20   10.16 Mt 26.26-28; Mk 14.22-24;
Lk 22.19, 20   10.18 Lv 7.6   10.20 Dt 32.17 (LXX)   10.22 Dt 32.21   10.23 1 Co 6.12
10.26 Ps 24.1

set before you, without asking any questions because of your conscience. 28 But if someone tells you, "This food was offered to idols," then do not eat that food, for the sake of the one who told you and for conscience' sake — 29 that is, not your own conscience, but the other person's conscience.

"Well, then," someone asks, "why should my freedom to act be limited by another person's conscience? 30 If I thank God for my food, why should anyone criticize me about food for which I give thanks?"

31 Well, whatever you do, whether you eat or drink, do it all for God's glory. 32 Live in such a way as to cause no trouble either to Jews or Gentiles or to the church of God. 33 Just do as I do; I try to please everyone in all that I do, not thinking of my own good, but of the good of all, so that they might be saved.

11 Imitate me, then, just as I imitate Christ.

Covering the Head in Worship

2 I praise you because you always remember me and follow the teachings that I have handed on to you. 3 But I want you to understand that Christ is supreme over every man, the husband is supreme over his wife, and God is supreme over Christ. 4 So a man who prays or proclaims God's message in public worship with his head covered disgraces Christ. 5 And any woman who prays or proclaims God's message in public worship with nothing on her head disgraces her husband; there is no difference between her and a woman whose head has been shaved. 6 If the woman does not cover her head, she might as well cut her hair. And since it is a shameful thing for a woman to shave her head or cut her hair, she should cover her head. 7 A man has no need to cover his head, because he reflects the image and glory of God. But

woman reflects the glory of man; 8 for man was not created from woman, but woman from man. 9 Nor was man created for woman's sake, but woman was created for man's sake. 10 On account of the angels, then, a woman should have a covering over her head to show that she is under her husband's authority. 11 In our life in the Lord, however, woman is not independent of man, nor is man independent of woman. 12 For as woman was made from man, in the same way man is born of woman; and it is God who brings everything into existence.

13 Judge for yourselves whether it is proper for a woman to pray to God in public worship with nothing on her head. 14 Why, nature itself teaches you that long hair on a man is a disgrace, 15 but on a woman it is a thing of beauty. Her long hair has been given her to serve as a covering. 16 But if anyone wants to argue about it, all I have to say is that neither we nor the churches of God have any other custom in worship.

The Lord's Supper
(Matthew 26.26-29; Mark 14.22-25;
Luke 22.14-20)

17 In the following instructions, however, I do not praise you, because your meetings for worship actually do more harm than good. 18 In the first place, I have been told that there are opposing groups in your meetings; and this I believe is partly true. (19 No doubt there must be divisions among you so that the ones who are in the right may be clearly seen.) 20 When you meet together as a group, it is not the Lord's Supper that you eat. 21 For as you eat, you each go ahead with your own meal, so that some are hungry while others get drunk. 22 Don't you have your own homes in which to eat and drink? Or would you rather despise the church of God and put to shame the people who

---

11.1 1 Co 4.16; Phil 3.17   **11.7** Gn 1.26, 27   **11.8, 9** Gn 2.18-23

are in need? What do you expect me to say to you about this? Shall I praise you? Of course I don't!

²³For I received from the Lord the teaching that I passed on to you: that the Lord Jesus, on the night he was betrayed, took a piece of bread, ²⁴gave thanks to God, broke it, and said, "This is my body, which is for you. Do this in memory of me." ²⁵In the same way, after the supper he took the cup and said, "This cup is God's new covenant, sealed with my blood. Whenever you drink it, do so in memory of me."

²⁶This means that every time you eat this bread and drink from this cup you proclaim the Lord's death until he comes. ²⁷It follows that if one of you eats the Lord's bread or drinks from his cup in a way that dishonors him, you are guilty of sin against the Lord's body and blood. ²⁸So then, you should each examine yourself first, and then eat the bread and drink from the cup. ²⁹For if you do not recognize the meaning of the Lord's body when you eat the bread and drink from the cup, you bring judgment on yourself as you eat and drink. ³⁰That is why many of you are sick and weak, and several have died. ³¹If we would examine ourselves first, we would not come under God's judgment. ³²But we are judged and punished by the Lord, so that we shall not be condemned together with the world.

³³So then, my friends, when you gather together to eat the Lord's Supper, wait for one another. ³⁴And if any of you are hungry, you should eat at home, so that you will not come under God's judgment as you meet together. As for the other matters, I will settle them when I come.

Gifts from the Holy Spirit

12 Now, concerning what you wrote about the gifts from the Holy Spirit.

I want you to know the truth about them, my friends. ²You know that while you were still heathen, you were led astray in many ways to the worship of lifeless idols. ³I want you to know that no one who is led by God's Spirit can say "A curse on Jesus!" and no one can confess "Jesus is Lord," without being guided by the Holy Spirit.

⁴There are different kinds of spiritual gifts, but the same Spirit gives them. ⁵There are different ways of serving, but the same Lord is served. ⁶There are different abilities to perform service, but the same God gives ability to all for their particular service. ⁷The Spirit's presence is shown in some way in each person for the good of all. ⁸The Spirit gives one person a message full of wisdom, while to another person the same Spirit gives a message full of knowledge. ⁹One and the same Spirit gives faith to one person, while to another person he gives the power to heal. ¹⁰The Spirit gives one person the power to work miracles; to another, the gift of speaking God's message; and to yet another, the ability to tell the difference between gifts that come from the Spirit and those that do not. To one person he gives the ability to speak in strange tongues, and to another he gives the ability to explain what is said. ¹¹But it is one and the same Spirit who does all this; as he wishes, he gives a different gift to each person.

One Body with Many Parts

¹²Christ is like a single body, which has many parts; it is still one body, even though it is made up of different parts. ¹³In the same way, all of us, whether Jews or Gentiles, whether slaves or free, have been baptized into the one body by the same Spirit, and we have all been given the one Spirit to drink.

¹⁴For the body itself is not made up of only one part, but of many parts. ¹⁵If

11.25 a Ex 24.8; Jr 31.31-34; **b** Ex 24.6-8   **12.4-11** Ro 12.6-8   **12.12** Ro 12.4, 5

the foot were to say, "Because I am not a hand, I don't belong to the body," that would not keep it from being a part of the body. [16] And if the ear were to say, "Because I am not an eye, I don't belong to the body," that would not keep it from being a part of the body. [17] If the whole body were just an eye, how could it hear? And if it were only an ear, how could it smell? [18] As it is, however, God put every different part in the body just as he wanted it to be. [19] There would not be a body if it were all only one part! [20] As it is, there are many parts but one body.

[21] So then, the eye cannot say to the hand, "I don't need you!" Nor can the head say to the feet, "Well, I don't need you!" [22] On the contrary, we cannot do without the parts of the body that seem to be weaker; [23] and those parts that we think aren't worth very much are the ones which we treat with greater care; while the parts of the body which don't look very nice are treated with special modesty, [24] which the more beautiful parts do not need. God himself has put the body together in such a way as to give greater honor to those parts that need it. [25] And so there is no division in the body, but all its different parts have the same concern for one another. [26] If one part of the body suffers, all the other parts suffer with it; if one part is praised, all the other parts share its happiness.

[27] All of you are Christ's body, and each one is a part of it. [28] In the church God has put all in place: in the first place apostles, in the second place prophets, and in the third place teachers; then those who perform miracles, followed by those who are given the power to heal or to help others or to direct them or to speak in strange tongues. [29] They are not all apostles or prophets or teachers. Not everyone has the power to work miracles [30] or to heal diseases or to speak in strange tongues or to explain what is said. [31] Set your hearts, then, on the more important gifts.

Best of all, however, is the following way.

Love

13 I may be able to speak the languages of human beings and even of angels, but if I have no love, my speech is no more than a noisy gong or a clanging bell. [2] I may have the gift of inspired preaching; I may have all knowledge and understand all secrets; I may have all the faith needed to move mountains — but if I have no love, I am nothing. [3] I may give away everything I have, and even give up my body to be burned[n] — but if I have no love, this does me no good.

[4] Love is patient and kind; it is not jealous or conceited or proud; [5] love is not ill-mannered or selfish or irritable; love does not keep a record of wrongs; [6] love is not happy with evil, but is happy with the truth. [7] Love never gives up; and its faith, hope, and patience never fail.

[8] Love is eternal. There are inspired messages, but they are temporary; there are gifts of speaking in strange tongues, but they will cease; there is knowledge, but it will pass. [9] For our gifts of knowledge and of inspired messages are only partial; [10] but when what is perfect comes, then what is partial will disappear.

[11] When I was a child, my speech, feelings, and thinking were all those of a child; now that I am an adult, I have no more use for childish ways. [12] What we see now is like a dim image in a mirror; then we shall see face-to-face. What I know now is only partial; then it will be complete — as complete as God's knowledge of me.

[n] to be burned; *some manuscripts have* in order to boast.
12.28 Eph 4.11   **13.2** Mt 17.20; 21.21; Mk 11.23

What we see now is like a dim image in a mirror. (13.12)

Then we shall see face-to-face. (13.12)

13 Meanwhile these three remain: faith, hope, and love; and the greatest of these is love.

More about Gifts from the Spirit

14 It is love, then, that you should strive for. Set your hearts on spiritual gifts, especially the gift of proclaiming God's message. 2 Those who speak in strange tongues do not speak to others but to God, because no one understands them. They are speaking secret truths by the power of the Spirit. 3 But those who proclaim God's message speak to people and give them help, encouragement, and comfort. 4 Those who speak in strange tongues help only themselves, but those who proclaim God's message help the whole church.

5 I would like for all of you to speak in strange tongues; but I would rather that you had the gift of proclaiming God's message. For the person who proclaims God's message is of greater value than the one who speaks in strange tongues — unless there is someone present who can explain what is said, so that the whole church may be helped. 6 So when I come to you, my friends, what use will I be to you if I speak in strange tongues? Not a bit, unless I bring you some revelation from God or some knowledge or some inspired message or some teaching.

7 Take such lifeless musical instruments as the flute or the harp — how will anyone know the tune that is being played unless the notes are sounded distinctly? 8 And if the one who plays the bugle does not sound a clear call, who will prepare for battle? 9 In the same way, how will anyone understand what you are talking about if your message given in strange tongues is not clear? Your words will vanish in the air! 10 There are many different languages in the world, yet none of them is without meaning. 11 But if I do not know the language being spoken, those who use it will be foreigners to me and I will be a foreigner to them. 12 Since you are eager to have the gifts of the Spirit, you must try above everything else to make greater use of those which help to build up the church.

13 The person who speaks in strange tongues, then, must pray for the gift to explain what is said. 14 For if I pray in this way, my spirit prays indeed, but my mind has no part in it. 15 What should I do, then? I will pray with my spirit, but I will pray also with my mind; I will sing

with my spirit, but I will sing also with my mind. 16 When you give thanks to God in spirit only, how can ordinary people taking part in the meeting say "Amen" to your prayer of thanksgiving? They have no way of knowing what you are saying. 17 Even if your prayer of thanks to God is quite good, other people are not helped at all.

18 I thank God that I speak in strange tongues much more than any of you. 19 But in church worship I would rather speak five words that can be understood, in order to teach others, than speak thousands of words in strange tongues.

20 Do not be like children in your thinking, my friends; be children so far as evil is concerned, but be grown up in your thinking. 21 In the Scriptures it is written,

"By means of people speaking
strange languages
I will speak to my people, says
the Lord.
I will speak through lips of
foreigners,
but even then my people will
not listen to me."

22 So then, the gift of speaking in strange tongues is proof for unbelievers, not for believers, while the gift of proclaiming God's message is proof for believers, not for unbelievers.

23 If, then, the whole church meets together and everyone starts speaking in strange tongues — and if some ordinary people or unbelievers come in, won't they say that you are all crazy? 24 But if everyone is proclaiming God's message when some unbelievers or ordinary people come in, they will be convinced of their sin by what they hear. They will be judged by all they hear, 25 their secret thoughts will be brought into the open, and they will bow down and worship God, confessing, "Truly God is here among you!"

Order in the Church

26 This is what I mean, my friends. When you meet for worship, one person has a hymn, another a teaching, another a revelation from God, another a message in strange tongues, and still another the explanation of what is said. Everything must be of help to the church. 27 If someone is going to speak in strange tongues, two or three at the most should speak, one after the other, and someone else must explain what is being said. 28 But if no one is there who can explain, then the one who speaks in strange tongues must be quiet and speak only to himself and to God. 29 Two or three who are given God's message should speak, while the others are to judge what they say. 30 But if someone sitting in the meeting receives a message from God, the one who is speaking should stop. 31 All of you may proclaim God's message, one by one, so that everyone will learn and be encouraged. 32 The gift of proclaiming God's message should be under the speaker's control, 33 because God does not want us to be in disorder but in harmony and peace.

As in all the churches of God's people, 34 the women should keep quiet in the meetings. They are not allowed to speak; as the Jewish Law says, they must not be in charge. 35 If they want to find out about something, they should ask their husbands at home. It is a disgraceful thing for a woman to speak in a church meeting.

36 Or could it be that the word of God came from you? Or are you the only ones to whom it came? 37 If anyone supposes he is God's messenger or has a spiritual gift, he must realize that what I am writing to you is the Lord's command. 38 But if he does not pay attention to this, pay no attention to him.

39 So then, my friends, set your heart

14.21 Is 28.11, 12

on proclaiming God's message, but do not forbid the speaking in strange tongues. 40 Everything must be done in a proper and orderly way.

The Resurrection of Christ

15 And now I want to remind you, my friends, of the Good News which I preached to you, which you received, and on which your faith stands firm. 2 That is the gospel, the message that I preached to you. You are saved by the gospel if you hold firmly to it — unless it was for nothing that you believed.

3 I passed on to you what I received, which is of the greatest importance: that Christ died for our sins, as written in the Scriptures; 4 that he was buried and that he was raised to life three days later, as written in the Scriptures; 5 that he appeared to Peter and then to all twelve apostles. 6 Then he appeared to more than five hundred of his followers at once, most of whom are still alive, although some have died. 7 Then he appeared to James, and afterward to all the apostles.

8 Last of all he appeared also to me — even though I am like someone whose birth was abnormal.*o* 9 For I am the least of all the apostles — I do not even deserve to be called an apostle, because I persecuted God's church. 10 But by God's grace I am what I am, and the grace that he gave me was not without effect. On the contrary, I have worked harder than any of the other apostles, although it was not really my own doing, but God's grace working with me. 11 So then, whether it came from me or from them, this is what we all preach, and this is what you believe.

Those who sleep in death will also be raised. (15.20)

Our Resurrection

12 Now, since our message is that Christ has been raised from death, how can some of you say that the dead will not be raised to life? 13 If that is true, it means that Christ was not raised; 14 and if Christ has not been raised from death, then we have nothing to preach and you have nothing to believe. 15 More than that, we are shown to be lying about God, because we said that he raised Christ from death — but if it is true that the dead are not raised to life, then he did not raise Christ. 16 For if the dead are not raised, neither has Christ been raised. 17 And if Christ has not been raised, then your faith is a delusion and you are still lost in your sins. 18 It would also mean that the believers in Christ who have died are lost. 19 If our hope in Christ is good for this life only and no more,*p* then we deserve more pity than anyone else in all the world.

20 But the truth is that Christ has

---

o whose birth was abnormal; *or* who was born at the wrong time.   *p* If our hope in Christ is good for this life only and no more; *or* If all we have in this life is our hope in Christ.

15.3 Is 53.5-12   **15.4** Ps 16.8-10; Mt 12.40; Ac 2.24-32   **15.5 a** Lk 24.34; **b** Mt 28.16, 17; Mk 16.14; Lk 24.36; Jn 20.19   **15.8** Ac 9.3-6   **15.9** Ac 8.3

been raised from death, as the guarantee that those who sleep in death will also be raised. ²¹ For just as death came by means of a man, in the same way the rising from death comes by means of a man. ²² For just as all people die because of their union with Adam, in the same way all will be raised to life because of their union with Christ. ²³ But each one will be raised in proper order: Christ, first of all; then, at the time of his coming, those who belong to him. ²⁴ Then the end will come; Christ will overcome all spiritual rulers, authorities, and powers, and will hand over the Kingdom to God the Father. ²⁵ For Christ must rule until God defeats all enemies and puts them under his feet. ²⁶ The last enemy to be defeated will be death. ²⁷ For the scripture says, "God put *all* things under his feet." It is clear, of course, that the words "all things" do not include God himself, who puts all things under Christ. ²⁸ But when all things have been placed under Christ's rule, then he himself, the Son, will place himself under God, who placed all things under him; and God will rule completely over all.

²⁹ Now, what about those people who are baptized for the dead? What do they hope to accomplish? If it is true, as some claim, that the dead are not raised to life, why are those people being baptized for the dead? ³⁰ And as for us — why would we run the risk of danger every hour? ³¹ My friends, I face death every day! The pride I have in you, in our life in union with Christ Jesus our Lord, makes me declare this. ³² If I have, as it were, fought "wild beasts" here in Ephesus simply from human motives, what have I gained? But if the dead are not raised to life, then, as the saying goes, "Let us eat and drink, for tomorrow we will die."

³³ Do not be fooled. "Bad companions ruin good character." ³⁴ Come back to your right senses and stop your sinful ways. I declare to your shame that some of you do not know God.

The Resurrection Body

³⁵ Someone will ask, "How can the dead be raised to life? What kind of body will they have?" ³⁶ You fool! When you plant a seed in the ground, it does not sprout to life unless it dies. ³⁷ And what you plant is a bare seed, perhaps a grain of wheat or some other grain, not the full-bodied plant that will later grow up. ³⁸ God provides that seed with the body he wishes; he gives each seed its own proper body.

³⁹ And the flesh of living beings is not all the same kind of flesh; human beings have one kind of flesh, animals another, birds another, and fish another.

⁴⁰ And there are heavenly bodies and earthly bodies; the beauty that belongs to heavenly bodies is different from the beauty that belongs to earthly bodies. ⁴¹ The sun has its own beauty, the moon another beauty, and the stars a different beauty; and even among stars there are different kinds of beauty.

⁴² This is how it will be when the dead are raised to life. When the body is buried, it is mortal; when raised, it will be immortal. ⁴³ When buried, it is ugly and weak; when raised, it will be beautiful and strong. ⁴⁴ When buried, it is a physical body; when raised, it will be a spiritual body. There is, of course, a physical body, so there has to be a spiritual body. ⁴⁵ For the scripture says, "The first man, Adam, was created a living being"; but the last Adam is the life-giving Spirit. ⁴⁶ It is not the spiritual that comes first, but the physical, and then the spiritual. ⁴⁷ The first Adam, made of earth, came from the earth; the second Adam came from heaven. ⁴⁸ Those who belong to the earth are like the one who was made of earth; those who are of heaven are like the one

15.25 Ps 110.1   **15.27** Ps 8.6   **15.29** 2 Macc 12.44   **15.32** Is 22.13   **15.45** Gn 2.7

who came from heaven. [49] Just as we wear the likeness of the man made of earth, so we will wear [q] the likeness of the Man from heaven.

[50] What I mean, friends, is that what is made of flesh and blood cannot share in God's Kingdom, and what is mortal cannot possess immortality.

[51-52] Listen to this secret truth: we shall not all die, but when the last trumpet sounds, we shall all be changed in an instant, as quickly as the blinking of an eye. For when the trumpet sounds, the dead will be raised, never to die again, and we shall all be changed. [53] For what is mortal must be changed into what is immortal; what will die must be changed into what cannot die. [54] So when this takes place, and the mortal has been changed into the immortal, then the scripture will come true: "Death is destroyed; victory is complete!"

[55] "Where, Death, is your victory?
Where, Death, is your power to
    hurt?"

[56] Death gets its power to hurt from sin, and sin gets its power from the Law. [57] But thanks be to God who gives us the victory through our Lord Jesus Christ!

[58] So then, my dear friends, stand firm and steady. Keep busy always in your work for the Lord, since you know that nothing you do in the Lord's service is ever useless.

The Offering for Needy Believers

16 Now, concerning what you wrote about the money to be raised to help God's people in Judea. You must do what I told the churches in Galatia to do. [2] Every Sunday each of you must put aside some money, in proportion to what you have earned, and save it up, so that there will be no need to collect money when I come. [3] After I come, I shall give letters of introduction to those you have approved, and send them to take your gift to Jerusalem. [4] If it seems worthwhile for me to go, then they can go along with me.

Paul's Plans

[5] I shall come to you after I have gone through Macedonia — for I have to go through Macedonia. [6] I shall probably spend some time with you, perhaps the whole winter, and then you can help me to continue my trip, wherever it is I shall go next. [7] I want to see you more than just briefly in passing; I hope to spend quite a long time with you, if the Lord allows.

[8] I will stay here in Ephesus until the day of Pentecost. [9] There is a real opportunity here for great and worthwhile work, even though there are many opponents.

[10] If Timothy comes your way, be sure to make him feel welcome among you, because he is working for the Lord, just as I am. [11] No one should look down on him, but you must help him continue his trip in peace, so that he will come back to me; for I am expecting him back with the believers.

[12] Now, about brother Apollos. I have often encouraged him to visit you with the other believers, but he is not completely convinced [r] that he should go at this time. When he gets the chance, however, he will go.

Final Words

[13] Be alert, stand firm in the faith, be brave, be strong. [14] Do all your work in love.

[15] You know about Stephanas and his

---

[q] we will wear; *some manuscripts have* let us wear.   [r] he is not completely convinced; *or* it is not at all God's will.

15.51, 52 2 Esd 6.23; 1 Th 4.15-17   **15.54** Is 25.8   **15.55** Ho 13.14 (LXX)
16.1 Ro 15.25, 26   **16.5** Ac 19.21   **16.8** Lv 23.15-21; Dt 16.9-11   **16.8, 9** Ac 19.8-10
16.10 1 Co 4.17   **16.15** 1 Co 1.16

family; they are the first Christian converts in Achaia and have given themselves to the service of God's people. I beg you, my friends, [16] to follow the leadership of such people as these, and of anyone else who works and serves with them.

[17] I am happy about the coming of Stephanas, Fortunatus, and Achaicus; they have made up for your absence [18] and have cheered me up, just as they cheered you up. Such men as these deserve notice.

[19] The churches in the province of Asia send you their greetings; Aquila

16.19 Ac 18.2

and Priscilla and the church that meets in their house send warm Christian greetings. [20] All the believers here send greetings.

Greet one another with the kiss of peace.

[21] With my own hand I write this: *Greetings from Paul.*

[22] Whoever does not love the Lord — a curse on him!

Marana tha — Our Lord, come!

[23] The grace of the Lord Jesus be with you.

[24] My love be with you all in Christ Jesus.

Paul's Second Letter to the
CORINTHIANS

INTRODUCTION

Paul's Second Letter to the Corinthians was written during a difficult period in his relation with the church at Corinth. Some members of the church had evidently made strong attacks against Paul, but he shows his deep longing for reconciliation and expresses his great joy when this is brought about.

In the first part of the letter Paul discusses his relationship with the church at Corinth, explaining why he had responded with severity to insult and opposition in the church and expressing his joy that this severity had resulted in repentance and reconciliation. Then he appeals to the church for a generous offering to help the needy Christians in Judea. In the final chapters Paul defends his apostleship against a few people at Corinth who had set themselves up as true apostles, while accusing Paul of being a false one.

OUTLINE OF CONTENTS

The offering for the Christians in Judea   8.1 — 9.15
Paul's defense of his authority as an apostle   10.1 — 13.10
Conclusion   13.11-13

---

1 From Paul, an apostle of Christ Jesus by God's will, and from our brother Timothy —
To the church of God in Corinth, and to all God's people throughout Achaia:
[2] May God our Father and the Lord Jesus Christ give you grace and peace.

Paul Gives Thanks to God

[3] Let us give thanks to the God and Father of our Lord Jesus Christ, the merciful Father, the God from whom all help comes! [4] He helps us in all our troubles, so that we are able to help others who have all kinds of troubles, using the same help that we ourselves

Help others who have all kinds of troubles. (1.4)

have received from God. [5] Just as we have a share in Christ's many sufferings, so also through Christ we share in God's great help. [6] If we suffer, it is for your help and salvation; if we are helped, then you too are helped and given the strength to endure with patience the same sufferings that we also endure. [7] So our hope in you is never shaken; we know that just as you share

in our sufferings, you also share in the help we receive.

[8] We want to remind you, friends, of the trouble we had in the province of Asia. The burdens laid upon us were so great and so heavy that we gave up all hope of staying alive. [9] We felt that the death sentence had been passed on us. But this happened so that we should rely, not on ourselves, but only on God, who raises the dead. [10] From such terrible dangers of death[a] he saved us, and will save us; and we have placed our hope in him that he will save us again, [11] as you help us by means of your prayers for us. So it will be that the many prayers for us will be answered, and God will bless us; and many will raise their voices to him in thanksgiving for us.

The Change in Paul's Plans

[12] We are proud that our conscience assures us that our lives in this world, and especially our relations with you, have been ruled by God-given frankness[b] and sincerity, by the power of God's grace and not by human wisdom. [13-14] We write to you only what you can read and understand. But even though you now understand us only in part, I hope that you will come to understand us completely, so that in the Day of our Lord Jesus you can be as proud of us as we shall be of you.

[15] I was so sure of all this that I made plans at first to visit you, in order that you might be blessed twice. [16] For I

---

a terrible dangers of death; *some manuscripts have* terrible death.   *b* frankness; *some manuscripts have* holiness.

1.1 Ac 18.1   **1.8** 1 Co 15.32   **1.16** Ac 19.21

planned to visit you on my way to Macedonia and again on my way back, in order to get help from you for my trip to Judea. [17] In planning this, did I appear fickle? When I make my plans, do I make them from selfish motives, ready to say "Yes, yes" and "No, no" at the same time? [18] As surely as God speaks the truth, my promise to you was not a "Yes" and a "No." [19] For Jesus Christ, the Son of God, who was preached among you by Silas, Timothy, and myself, is not one who is "Yes" and "No." On the contrary, he is God's "Yes"; [20] for it is he who is the "Yes" to all of God's promises. This is why through Jesus Christ our "Amen" is said to the glory of God. [21] It is God himself who makes us, together with you, sure of our life in union with Christ; it is God himself who has set us apart, [22] who has placed his mark of ownership upon us, and who has given us the Holy Spirit in our hearts as the guarantee of all that he has in store for us.

[23] I call God as my witness — he knows my heart! It was in order to spare you that I decided not to go to Corinth. [24] We are not trying to dictate to you what you must believe; we know that you stand firm in the faith. Instead, we are working with you for your own happiness.

2 So I made up my mind not to come to you again to make you sad. [2] For if I were to make you sad, who would be left to cheer me up? Only the very persons I had made sad. [3] That is why I wrote that letter to you — I did not want to come to you and be made sad by the very people who should make me glad. For I am convinced that when I am happy, then all of you are happy too. [4] I wrote you with a greatly troubled and distressed heart and with many tears; my purpose was not to make you sad, but to make you realize how much I love you all.

Forgiveness for the Offender

[5] Now, if anyone has made somebody sad, he has not done it to me but to all of you — in part, at least. (I say this because I do not want to be too hard on him.) [6] It is enough that this person has been punished in this way by most of you. [7] Now, however, you should forgive him and encourage him, in order to keep him from becoming so sad as to give up completely. [8] And so I beg you to let him know that you really do love him. [9] I wrote you that letter because I wanted to find out how well you had stood the test and whether you are always ready to obey my instructions. [10] When you forgive people for what they have done, I forgive them too. For when I forgive — if, indeed, I need to forgive anything — I do it in Christ's presence because of you, [11] in order to keep Satan from getting the upper hand over us; for we know what his plans are.

Paul's Anxiety in Troas

[12] When I arrived in Troas to preach the Good News about Christ, I found that the Lord had opened the way for the work there. [13] But I was deeply worried, because I could not find our brother Titus. So I said good-bye to the people there and went on to Macedonia.

Victory through Christ

[14] But thanks be to God! For in union with Christ we are always led by God as prisoners in Christ's victory procession. God uses us to make the knowledge about Christ spread everywhere like a sweet fragrance. [15] For we are like a sweet-smelling incense offered by Christ to God, which spreads among those who are being saved and those who are being lost. [16] For those who are being lost, it is a deadly stench that kills; but for those who are being saved,

it is a fragrance that brings life. Who, then, is capable for such a task? [17]We are not like so many others, who handle God's message as if it were cheap merchandise; but because God has sent us, we speak with sincerity in his presence, as servants of Christ.

Servants of the New Covenant

3 Does this sound as if we were again boasting about ourselves? Could it be that, like some other people, we need letters of recommendation to you or from you? [2]You yourselves are the letter we have, written on our hearts for everyone to know and read. [3]It is clear that Christ himself wrote this letter and sent it by us. It is written, not with ink but with the Spirit of the living God, and not on stone tablets but on human hearts.

[4]We say this because we have confidence in God through Christ. [5]There is nothing in us that allows us to claim that we are capable of doing this work. The capacity we have comes from God; [6]it is he who made us capable of serving the new covenant, which consists not of a written law but of the Spirit. The written law brings death, but the Spirit gives life.

[7]The Law was carved in letters on stone tablets, and God's glory appeared when it was given. Even though the brightness on Moses' face was fading, it was so strong that the people of Israel could not keep their eyes fixed on him. If the Law, which brings death when it is in force, came with such glory, [8]how much greater is the glory that belongs to the activity of the Spirit! [9]The system which brings condemnation was glorious; how much more glorious is the activity which brings salvation! [10]We may say that because of the far brighter

glory now the glory that was so bright in the past is gone. [11]For if there was glory in that which lasted for a while, how much more glory is there in that which lasts forever!

[12]Because we have this hope, we are very bold. [13]We are not like Moses, who had to put a veil over his face so that the people of Israel would not see the brightness fade and disappear. [14]Their minds, indeed, were closed; and to this very day their minds are covered with the same veil as they read the books of the old covenant. The veil is removed only when a person is joined to Christ. [15]Even today, whenever they read the Law of Moses, the veil still covers their minds. [16]But it can be removed, as the scripture says about Moses: "His veil was removed when he turned to the Lord."[c] [17]Now, "the Lord" in this passage is the Spirit; and where the Spirit of the Lord is present, there is freedom. [18]All of us, then, reflect the glory of the Lord with uncovered faces; and that same glory, coming from the Lord, who is the Spirit, transforms us into his likeness in an ever greater degree of glory.

Spiritual Treasure in Clay Pots

4 God in his mercy has given us this work to do, and so we do not become discouraged. [2]We put aside all secret and shameful deeds; we do not act with deceit, nor do we falsify the word of God. In the full light of truth we live in God's sight and try to commend ourselves to everyone's good conscience. [3]For if the gospel we preach is hidden, it is hidden only from those who are being lost. [4]They do not believe, because their minds have been kept in the dark by the evil god of this world. He keeps them from seeing the light shining on them, the light that comes from the

---

c Verse 16 may be translated: But the veil is removed whenever someone turns to the Lord.

3.3 a Ex 24.12; **b** Jr 31.33; Ez 11.19; 36.26   **3.6** Jr 31.31   **3.7** Ex 34.29   **3.13** Ex 34.33
3.16 Ex 34.34

Good News about the glory of Christ, who is the exact likeness of God. [5] For it is not ourselves that we preach; we preach Jesus Christ as Lord, and ourselves as your servants for Jesus' sake. [6] The God who said, "Out of darkness the light shall shine!" is the same God who made his light shine in our hearts, to bring us the knowledge of God's glory shining in the face of Christ.

[7] Yet we who have this spiritual treasure are like common clay pots, in order to show that the supreme power belongs to God, not to us. [8] We are often troubled, but not crushed; sometimes in doubt, but never in despair; [9] there are many enemies, but we are never without a friend; and though badly hurt at times, we are not destroyed. [10] At all times we carry in our mortal bodies the death of Jesus, so that his life also may be seen in our bodies. [11] Throughout our lives we are always in danger of death for Jesus' sake, in order that his life may be seen in this mortal body of ours. [12] This means that death is at work in us, but life is at work in you.

[13] The scripture says, "I spoke because I believed." In the same spirit of faith we also speak because we believe. [14] We know that God, who raised the Lord Jesus to life, will also raise us up with Jesus and take us, together with you, into his presence. [15] All this is for your sake; and as God's grace reaches more and more people, they will offer to the glory of God more prayers of thanksgiving.

Living by Faith

[16] For this reason we never become discouraged. Even though our physical being is gradually decaying, yet our spiritual being is renewed day after day. [17] And this small and temporary trouble we suffer will bring us a tremendous and eternal glory, much greater than the trouble. [18] For we fix our attention, not on things that are seen, but on things that are unseen. What can be seen lasts only for a time, but what cannot be seen lasts forever.

5 For we know that when this tent we live in — our body here on earth — is torn down, God will have a house in heaven for us to live in, a home he himself has made, which will last forever. [2] And now we sigh, so great is our desire that our home which comes from heaven should be put on over us; [3] by being clothed with it we shall not be without a body. [4] While we live in this earthly tent, we groan with a feeling of oppression; it is not that we want to get rid of our earthly body, but that we want to have the heavenly one put on over us, so that what is mortal will be transformed by life. [5] God is the one who has prepared us for this change, and he gave us his Spirit as the guarantee of all that he has in store for us.

[6] So we are always full of courage. We know that as long as we are at home in the body we are away from the Lord's home. [7] For our life is a matter of faith, not of sight. [8] We are full of courage and would much prefer to leave our home in the body and be at home with the Lord. [9] More than anything else, however, we want to please him, whether in our home here or there. [10] For all of us must appear before Christ, to be judged by him. We will each receive what we deserve, according to everything we have done, good or bad, in our bodily life.

Friendship with God through Christ

[11] We know what it means to fear the Lord, and so we try to persuade others. God knows us completely, and I hope that in your hearts you know me as well. [12] We are not trying again to recommend ourselves to you; rather, we are trying to give you a good reason to be proud of us, so that you will be able to answer those who boast about peo-

4.6 Gn 1.3　**4.13** Ps 116.10 (LXX)　**5.1** Ws 9.15　**5.10** Ro 14.10

ple's appearance and not about their character. [13] Are we really insane? It is for God's sake. Or are we sane? Then it is for your sake. [14] We are ruled by the love of Christ, now that we recognize that one man died for everyone, which means that they all share in his death. [15] He died for all, so that those who live should no longer live for themselves, but only for him who died and was raised to life for their sake.

[16] No longer, then, do we judge anyone by human standards. Even if at one time we judged Christ according to human standards, we no longer do so. [17] Anyone who is joined to Christ is a new being; the old is gone, the new has come. [18] All this is done by God, who through Christ changed us from enemies into his friends and gave us the task of making others his friends also. [19] Our message is that God was making all human beings his friends through Christ.[d] God did not keep an account of their sins, and he has given us the message which tells how he makes them his friends.

[20] Here we are, then, speaking for Christ, as though God himself were making his appeal through us. We plead on Christ's behalf: let God change you from enemies into his friends! [21] Christ was without sin, but for our sake God made him share our sin in order that in union with him we might share the righteousness of God.

6 In our work together with God, then, we beg you who have received God's grace not to let it be wasted. [2] Hear what God says:

"When the time came for me to
   show you favor,
   I heard you;
when the day arrived for me to
   save you,
   I helped you."

Listen! This is the hour to receive God's favor; today is the day to be saved!

[3] We do not want anyone to find fault with our work, so we try not to put obstacles in anyone's way. [4] Instead, in everything we do we show that we are God's servants by patiently enduring troubles, hardships, and difficulties. [5] We have been beaten, jailed, and mobbed; we have been overworked and have gone without sleep or food. [6] By our purity, knowledge, patience, and kindness we have shown ourselves to be God's servants — by the Holy Spirit, by our true love, [7] by our message of truth, and by the power of God. We have righteousness as our weapon, both to attack and to defend ourselves. [8] We are honored and disgraced; we are insulted and praised. We are treated as liars, yet we speak the truth; [9] as unknown, yet we are known by all; as though we were dead, but, as you see, we live on. Although punished, we are not killed; [10] although saddened, we are always glad; we seem poor, but we make many people rich; we seem to have nothing, yet we really possess everything.

[11] Dear friends in Corinth! We have spoken frankly to you; we have opened our hearts wide. [12] It is not we who have closed our hearts to you; it is you who have closed your hearts to us. [13] I speak now as though you were my children: show us the same feelings that we have for you. Open your hearts wide!

Warning against Pagan Influences

[14] Do not try to work together as equals with unbelievers, for it cannot be done. How can right and wrong be partners? How can light and darkness live together? [15] How can Christ and the Devil agree? What does a believer have in common with an unbeliever?

---

[d] God was making all human beings his friends through Christ; *or* God was in Christ making all human beings his friends.

6.2 Is 49.8   **6.5** Ac 16.23

16 How can God's temple come to terms with pagan idols? For we are the temple of the living God! As God himself has said,

"I will make my home with my
            people
        and live among them;
I will be their God,
        and they shall be my people."
17 And so the Lord says,
"You must leave them
        and separate yourselves from
            them.
Have nothing to do with what is
        unclean,
        and I will accept you.
18 I will be your father,
        and you shall be my sons and
            daughters,
        says the Lord Almighty."

7 All these promises are made to us, my dear friends. So then, let us purify ourselves from everything that makes body or soul unclean, and let us be completely holy by living in awe of God.

Paul's Joy

2 Make room for us in your hearts. We have wronged no one; we have ruined no one, nor tried to take advantage of anyone. 3 I do not say this to condemn you; for, as I have said before, you are so dear to us that we are always together, whether we live or die. 4 I am so sure of you; I take such pride in you! In all our troubles I am still full of courage; I am running over with joy.

5 Even after we arrived in Macedonia, we did not have any rest. There were troubles everywhere, quarrels with others, fears in our hearts. 6 But God, who encourages the downhearted, encouraged us with the coming of Titus. 7 It was not only his coming that cheered us, but also his report of

how you encouraged him. He told us how much you want to see me, how sorry you are, how ready you are to defend me; and so I am even happier now.

8 For even if that letter of mine made you sad, I am not sorry I wrote it. I could have been sorry when I saw that it made you sad for a while. 9 But now I am happy — not because I made you sad, but because your sadness made you change your ways. That sadness was used by God, and so we caused you no harm. 10 For the sadness that is used by God brings a change of heart that leads to salvation — and there is no regret in that! But sadness that is merely human causes death. 11 See what God did with this sadness of yours: how earnest it has made you, how eager to prove your innocence! Such indignation, such alarm, such feelings, such devotion, such readiness to punish wrongdoing! You have shown yourselves to be without fault in the whole matter.

12 So, even though I wrote that letter, it was not because of the one who did wrong or the one who was wronged. Instead, I wrote it to make plain to you, in God's sight, how deep your devotion to us really is. 13 That is why we were encouraged.

Not only were we encouraged; how happy Titus made us with his happiness over the way in which all of you helped to cheer him up! 14 I did boast of you to him, and you have not disappointed me. We have always spoken the truth to you, and in the same way the boast we made to Titus has proved true. 15 And so his love for you grows stronger, as he remembers how all of you were ready to obey his instructions, how you welcomed him with fear and trembling. 16 How happy I am that I can depend on you completely!

6.16 a 1 Co 3.16; 6.19; b Lv 26.12; Ez 37.27 Is 43.6; Jr 31.9 7.5 2 Co 2.13   6.17 Is 52.11   6.18 2 S 7.14; 1 Ch 17.13;

Christian Giving

8 Our friends, we want you to know what God's grace has accomplished in the churches in Macedonia. [2] They have been severely tested by the troubles they went through; but their joy was so great that they were extremely generous in their giving, even though they are very poor. [3] I can assure you that they gave as much as they could, and even more than they could. Of their own free will [4] they begged us and pleaded for the privilege of having a part in helping God's people in Judea. [5] It was more than we could have hoped for! First they gave themselves to the Lord; and then, by God's will they gave themselves to us as well. [6] So we urged Titus, who began this work, to continue it and help you complete this special service of love. [7] You are so rich in all you have: in faith, speech, and knowledge, in your eagerness to help and in your love for us.[e] And so we want you to be generous also in this service of love.

[8] I am not laying down any rules. But by showing how eager others are to help, I am trying to find out how real your own love is. [9] You know the grace of our Lord Jesus Christ; rich as he was, he made himself poor for your sake, in order to make you rich by means of his poverty.

[10] My opinion is that it is better for you to finish now what you began last year. You were the first, not only to act, but also to be willing to act. [11] On with it, then, and finish the job! Be as eager to finish it as you were to plan it, and do it with what you now have. [12] If you are eager to give, God will accept your gift on the basis of what you have to give, not on what you don't have.

[13-14] I am not trying to relieve others by putting a burden on you; but since you have plenty at this time, it is only fair that you should help those who are in need. Then, when you are in need and they have plenty, they will help you. In this way both are treated equally. [15] As the scripture says, "The one who gathered much did not have too much, and the one who gathered little did not have too little."

Titus and His Companions

[16] How we thank God for making Titus as eager as we are to help you! [17] Not only did he welcome our request; he was so eager to help that of his own free will he decided to go to you. [18] With him we are sending the brother who is highly respected in all the churches for his work in preaching the gospel. [19] And besides that, he has been chosen and appointed by the churches to travel with us as we carry out this service of love for the sake of the Lord's glory and in order to show that we want to help.

[20] We are being careful not to stir up any complaints about the way we handle this generous gift. [21] Our purpose is to do what is right, not only in the sight of the Lord, but also in the sight of others.

[22] So we are sending our brother with them; we have tested him many times and found him always very eager to help. And now that he has so much confidence in you, he is all the more eager to help. [23] As for Titus, he is my partner and works with me to help you; as for the other brothers who are going with him, they represent the churches and bring glory to Christ. [24] Show your love to them, so that all the churches will be sure of it and know that we are right in boasting about you.

Help for Needy Believers

9 There is really no need for me to write you about the help being sent to God's people in Judea. [2] I know

---

[e] *your love for us; some manuscripts have* our love for you.
8.1-4 Ro 15.26   **8.15** Ex 16.18   **8.21** Pr 3.4 (LXX)

that you are willing to help, and I have boasted of you to the people in Macedonia. "The believers in Achaia," I said, "have been ready to help since last year." Your eagerness has stirred up most of them. ³Now I am sending these believers, so that our boasting about you in this matter may not turn out to be empty words. But, just as I said, you will be ready with your help. ⁴However, if the people from Macedonia should come with me and find out that you are not ready, how ashamed we would be — not to speak of your shame — for feeling so sure of you! ⁵So I thought it was necessary to urge these believers to go to you ahead of me and get ready in advance the gift you promised to make. Then it will be ready when I arrive, and it will show that you give because you want to, not because you have to.

⁶Remember that the person who plants few seeds will have a small crop; the one who plants many seeds will have a large crop. ⁷You should each give, then, as you have decided, not with regret or out of a sense of duty; for God loves the one who gives gladly. ⁸And God is able to give you more than you need, so that you will always have all you need for yourselves and more than enough for every good cause. ⁹As the scripture says,

"He gives generously to the needy;
his kindness lasts forever."

¹⁰And God, who supplies seed for the sower and bread to eat, will also supply you with all the seed you need and will make it grow and produce a rich harvest from your generosity. ¹¹He will always make you rich enough to be generous at all times, so that many will thank God for your gifts which they receive from us. ¹²For this service you perform not only meets the needs of God's people, but also produces an outpouring of gratitude to God. ¹³And because of the proof which this service of

yours brings, many will give glory to God for your loyalty to the gospel of Christ, which you profess, and for your generosity in sharing with them and everyone else. ¹⁴And so with deep affection they will pray for you because of the extraordinary grace God has shown you. ¹⁵Let us thank God for his priceless gift!

Paul Defends His Ministry

10 I, Paul, make a personal appeal to you — I who am said to be meek and mild when I am with you, but harsh with you when I am away. By the gentleness and kindness of Christ ²I beg you not to force me to be harsh when I come; for I am sure I can deal harshly with those who say that we act from worldly motives. ³It is true that we live in the world, but we do not fight from worldly motives. ⁴The weapons we use in our fight are not the world's weapons but God's powerful weapons, which we use to destroy strongholds. We destroy false arguments; ⁵we pull down every proud obstacle that is raised against the knowledge of God; we take every thought captive and make it obey Christ. ⁶And after you have proved your complete loyalty, we will be ready to punish any act of disloyalty.

⁷You are looking at the outward appearance of things. Are there some there who reckon themselves to belong to Christ? Well, let them think again about themselves, because we belong to Christ just as much as they do. ⁸For I am not ashamed, even if I have boasted somewhat too much about the authority that the Lord has given us — authority to build you up, not to tear you down. ⁹I do not want it to appear that I am trying to frighten you with my letters. ¹⁰Someone will say, "Paul's letters are severe and strong, but when he is with us in person, he is weak, and his words are nothing!" ¹¹Such a person

must understand that there is no difference between what we write in our letters when we are away and what we will do when we are there with you.

¹²Of course we would not dare classify ourselves or compare ourselves with those who rate themselves so highly. How stupid they are! They make up their own standards to measure themselves by, and they judge themselves by their own standards! ¹³As for us, however, our boasting will not go beyond certain limits; it will stay within the limits of the work which God has set for us, and this includes our work among you. ¹⁴And since you are within those limits, we were not going beyond them when we came to you, bringing the Good News about Christ. ¹⁵So we do not boast about the work that others have done beyond the limits God set for us. Instead, we hope that your faith may grow and that we may be able to do a much greater work among you, always within the limits that God has set.

Preach the Good News in other countries beyond you. (10.16)

¹⁶Then we can preach the Good News in other countries beyond you and shall not have to boast about work already done in someone else's field.

¹⁷But as the scripture says, "Whoever wants to boast must boast about what the Lord has done." ¹⁸For it is when the Lord thinks well of us that we are really approved, and not when we think well of ourselves.

Paul and the False Apostles

11 I wish you would tolerate me, even when I am a bit foolish. Please do! ²I am jealous for you, just as God is; you are like a pure virgin whom I have promised in marriage to one man only, Christ himself. ³I am afraid that your minds will be corrupted and that you will abandon your full and pure devotion to Christ — in the same way that Eve was deceived by the snake's clever lies. ⁴For you gladly tolerate anyone who comes to you and preaches a different Jesus, not the one we preached; and you accept a spirit and a gospel completely different from the Spirit and the gospel you received from us!

⁵I do not think that I am the least bit inferior to those very special so-called "apostles" of yours! ⁶Perhaps I am an amateur in speaking, but certainly not in knowledge; we have made this clear to you at all times and in all conditions.

⁷I did not charge you a thing when I preached the Good News of God to you; I humbled myself in order to make you important. Was that wrong of me? ⁸While I was working among you, I was paid by other churches. I was robbing them, so to speak, in order to help you. ⁹And during the time I was with you I did not bother you for help when I needed money; the believers who came from Macedonia brought me everything I needed. As in the past, so in the future: I will never be a burden to you! ¹⁰By Christ's truth in me, I promise that this boast of mine will not be silenced anywhere in all of Achaia. ¹¹Do I say this because I don't love you? God knows I love you!

¹²I will go on doing what I am doing now, in order to keep those other

10.17 Jr 9.24   **11.3** Gn 3.1-5, 13   **11.9** Phil 4.15-18

"apostles" from having any reason for boasting and saying that they work in the same way that we do. [13] Those men are not true apostles — they are false apostles, who lie about their work and disguise themselves to look like real apostles of Christ. [14] Well, no wonder! Even Satan can disguise himself to look like an angel of light! [15] So it is no great thing if his servants disguise themselves to look like servants of righteousness. In the end they will get exactly what their actions deserve.

Paul's Sufferings as an Apostle

[16] I repeat: no one should think that I am a fool. But if you do, at least accept me as a fool, just so I will have a little to boast of. [17] Of course what I am saying now is not what the Lord would have me say; in this matter of boasting I am really talking like a fool. [18] But since there are so many who boast for merely human reasons, I will do the same. [19] You yourselves are so wise, and so you gladly tolerate fools! [20] You tolerate anyone who orders you around or takes advantage of you or traps you or looks down on you or slaps you in the face. [21] I am ashamed to admit that we were too timid to do those things!

But if anyone dares to boast about something — I am talking like a fool — I will be just as daring. [22] Are they Hebrews? So am I. Are they Israelites? So am I. Are they Abraham's descendants? So am I. [23] Are they Christ's servants? I sound like a madman — but I am a better servant than they are! I have worked much harder, I have been in prison more times, I have been whipped much more, and I have been near death more often. [24] Five times I was given the thirty-nine lashes by the Jews; [25] three times I was whipped by the Romans; and once I was stoned. I have been in three shipwrecks, and once I spent

twenty-four hours in the water. [26] In my many travels I have been in danger from floods and from robbers, in danger from my own people and from Gentiles; there have been dangers in the cities, dangers in the wilds, dangers on the high seas, and dangers from false friends. [27] There has been work and toil; often I have gone without sleep; I have been hungry and thirsty; I have often been without enough food, shelter, or clothing. [28] And not to mention other things, every day I am under the pressure of my concern for all the churches. [29] When someone is weak, then I feel weak too; when someone is led into sin, I am filled with distress.

[30] If I must boast, I will boast about things that show how weak I am. [31] The God and Father of the Lord Jesus — blessed be his name forever! — knows that I am not lying. [32] When I was in Damascus, the governor under King Aretas placed guards at the city gates to arrest me. [33] But I was let down in a basket through an opening in the wall and escaped from him.

Paul's Visions and Revelations

12 I have to boast, even though it doesn't do any good. But I will now talk about visions and revelations given me by the Lord. [2] I know a certain Christian man who fourteen years ago was snatched up to the highest heaven (I do not know whether this actually happened or whether he had a vision — only God knows). [3-4] I repeat, I know that this man was snatched to Paradise (again, I do not know whether this actually happened or whether it was a vision — only God knows), and there he heard things which cannot be put into words, things that human lips may not speak. [5] So I will boast about this man — but I will not boast about myself, except the things that show how weak I am.

11.23 Ac 16.23   **11.24** Dt 25.3   **11.25 a** Ac 16.22; **b** Ac 14.19   **11.26 a** Ac 9.23; **b** Ac 14.5
11.32, 33 Ac 9.23-25

6 If I wanted to boast, I would not be a fool, because I would be telling the truth. But I will not boast, because I do not want any of you to have a higher opinion of me than you have as a result of what you have seen me do and heard me say.

7 But to keep me from being puffed up with pride because of the many wonderful things I saw, I was given a painful physical ailment, which acts as Satan's messenger to beat me and keep me from being proud. 8 Three times I prayed to the Lord about this and asked him to take it away. 9 But his answer was: "My grace is all you need, for my power is greatest when you are weak." I am most happy, then, to be proud of my weaknesses, in order to feel the protection of Christ's power over me. 10 I am content with weaknesses, insults, hardships, persecutions, and difficulties for Christ's sake. For when I am weak, then I am strong.

Paul's Concern for the Corinthians

11 I am acting like a fool — but you have made me do it. You are the ones who ought to show your approval of me. For even if I am nothing, I am in no way inferior to those very special "apostles" of yours. 12 The many miracles and wonders that prove that I am an apostle were performed among you with much patience. 13 How were you treated any worse than the other churches, except that I did not bother you for financial help? Please forgive me for being so unfair!

14 This is now the third time that I am ready to come to visit you — and I will not make any demands on you. It is you I want, not your money. After all, children should not have to provide for their parents, but parents should provide for their children. 15 I will be glad to spend all I have, and myself as well, in order to help you. Will you love me less because I love you so much?

16 You will agree, then, that I was not a burden to you. But someone will say that I was tricky, and trapped you with lies. 17 How? Did I take advantage of you through any of the messengers I sent? 18 I begged Titus to go, and I sent the other believer with him. Would you say that Titus took advantage of you? Do not he and I act from the very same motives and behave in the same way?

19 Perhaps you think that all along we have been trying to defend ourselves before you. No! We speak as Christ would have us speak in the presence of God, and everything we do, dear friends, is done to help you. 20 I am afraid that when I get there I will find you different from what I would like you to be and you will find me different from what you would like me to be. I am afraid that I will find quarreling and jealousy, hot tempers and selfishness, insults and gossip, pride and disorder. 21 I am afraid that the next time I come my God will humiliate me in your presence, and I shall weep over many who sinned in the past and have not repented of the immoral things they have done — their lust and their sexual sins.

Final Warnings and Greetings

13 This is now the third time that I am coming to visit you. "Any accusation must be upheld by the evidence of two or more witnesses" — as the scripture says. 2 I want to tell those of you who have sinned in the past, and all the others; I said it before during my second visit to you, but I will say it again now that I am away: the next time I come nobody will escape punishment. 3 You will have all the proof you want that Christ speaks through me. When he deals with you, he is not weak; instead, he shows his power among you.

13.1 Dt 17.6; 19.15

⁴For even though it was in weakness that he was.put to death on the cross, it is by God's power that he lives. In union with him we also are weak; but in our relations with you we shall share God's power in his life.

⁵Put yourselves to the test and judge yourselves, to find out whether you are living in faith. Surely you know that Christ Jesus is in you? — unless you have completely failed. ⁶I trust you will know that we are not failures. ⁷We pray to God that you will do no wrong — not in order to show that we are a success, but so that you may do what is right, even though we may seem to be failures. ⁸For we cannot do a thing against the truth, but only for it. ⁹We are glad when we are weak but you are strong.

And so we also pray that you will become perfect. ¹⁰That is why I write this while I am away from you; it is so that when I arrive I will not have to deal harshly with you in using the authority that the Lord has given me — authority to build you up, not to tear you down.

¹¹And now, my friends, good-bye! Strive for perfection; listen to my appeals; agree with one another; live in peace. And the God of love and peace will be with you.

¹²Greet one another with the kiss of peace.

All of God's people send you their greetings.

¹³The grace of the Lord Jesus Christ, the love of God, and the fellowship of the Holy Spirit be with you all.

Paul's Letter to the
GALATIANS

INTRODUCTION

As the good news about Jesus began to be preached and welcomed among people who were not Jews, the question arose as to whether a person must obey the Law of Moses in order to be a true Christian. Paul had argued that this was not necessary—that in fact, the only sound basis for life in Christ was faith, by which all are put right with God. But among the churches of Galatia, a Roman province in Asia Minor, there had come people who opposed Paul and claimed that one must also observe the Law of Moses in order to be right with God.

Paul's Letter to the Galatians was written in order to bring back to true faith and practice those people who were being misled by this false teaching. Paul begins by defending his right to be called an apostle of Jesus Christ. He insists that his call to be an apostle came from God, not from any human authority, and that his mission was especially to the non-Jews. Then he develops the argument that it is by faith alone that people are put right with God. In the concluding chapters Paul shows that Christian conduct flows naturally from the love that results from faith in Christ.

OUTLINE OF CONTENTS

1 From Paul, whose call to be an apostle did not come from human beings or by human means, but from Jesus Christ and God the Father, who raised him from death. ²All the believers who are here join me in sending greetings to the churches of Galatia:

³May God our Father and the Lord Jesus Christ give you grace and peace.

⁴In order to set us free from this present evil age, Christ gave himself for our sins, in obedience to the will of our God and Father. ⁵To God be the glory forever and ever! Amen.

The One Gospel

⁶I am surprised at you! In no time at all you are deserting the one who called you by the grace of Christ,ᵃ and are accepting another gospel. ⁷Actually, there is no "other gospel," but I say this because there are some people who are upsetting you and trying to change the gospel of Christ. ⁸But even if we or an angel from heaven should preach to you a gospel that is different from the one we preached to you, may he be condemned to hell! ⁹We have said it before, and now I say it again: if anyone

---

ᵃ by the grace of Christ; *some manuscripts have* by his grace.

preaches to you a gospel that is different from the one you accepted, may he be condemned to hell!

10 Does this sound as if I am trying to win human approval? No indeed! What I want is God's approval! Am I trying to be popular with people? If I were still trying to do so, I would not be a servant of Christ.

How Paul Became an Apostle

11 Let me tell you, my friends, that the gospel I preach is not of human origin. 12 I did not receive it from any human being, nor did anyone teach it to me. It was Jesus Christ himself who revealed it to me.

13 You have been told how I used to live when I was devoted to the Jewish religion, how I persecuted without mercy the church of God and did my best to destroy it. 14 I was ahead of most other Jews of my age in my practice of the Jewish religion, and was much more devoted to the traditions of our ancestors.

15 But God in his grace chose me even before I was born, and called me to serve him. And when he decided 16 to reveal his Son to me, so that I might preach the Good News about him to the Gentiles, I did not go to anyone for advice, 17 nor did I go to Jerusalem to see those who were apostles before me. Instead, I went at once to Arabia, and then I returned to Damascus. 18 It was three years later that I went to Jerusalem to obtain information from Peter, and I stayed with him for two weeks. 19 I did not see any other apostle except James,[b] the Lord's brother.

20 What I write is true. God knows that I am not lying!

21 Afterward I went to places in Syria and Cilicia. 22 At that time the members of the churches in Judea did not know me personally. 23 They knew only what others were saying: "The man who used to persecute us is now preaching the faith that he once tried to destroy!" 24 And so they praised God because of me.

Paul and the Other Apostles

2 Fourteen years later I went back to Jerusalem with Barnabas, taking Titus along with me. 2 I went because God revealed to me that I should go. In a private meeting with the leaders I explained the gospel message that I preach to the Gentiles. I did not want my work in the past or in the present to be a failure. 3 My companion Titus, even though he is Greek, was not forced to be circumcised, 4 although some wanted it done. Pretending to be believers, these men slipped into our group as spies, in order to find out about the freedom we have through our union with Christ Jesus. They wanted to make slaves of us, 5 but in order to keep the truth of the gospel safe for you, we did not give in to them for a minute.

6 But those who seemed to be the leaders — I say this because it makes no difference to me what they were; God does not judge by outward appearances — those leaders, I say, made no new suggestions to me. 7 On the contrary, they saw that God had given me the task of preaching the gospel to the Gentiles, just as he had given Peter the task of preaching the gospel to the Jews. 8 For by God's power I was made an apostle to the Gentiles, just as Peter was made an apostle to the Jews. 9 James, Peter, and John, who seemed to be the leaders, recognized that God had given me this special task; so they shook hands with Barnabas and me, as

---

[b] any other apostle except James; or any other apostle; the only other person I saw was James.

1.13 Ac 8.3; 22.4, 5; 26.9-11   1.14 Ac 22.3   1.15, 16 Ac 9.3-6; 22.6-10; 26.13-18
1.18 Ac 9.26-30   2.1 Ac 11.30; 15.2   2.6 Dt 10.17

a sign that we were all partners. We agreed that Barnabas and I would work among the Gentiles and they among the Jews. [10] All they asked was that we should remember the needy in their group, which is the very thing I have[c] been eager to do.

Paul Rebukes Peter at Antioch

[11] But when Peter came to Antioch, I opposed him in public, because he was clearly wrong. [12] Before some men who had been sent by James arrived there, Peter had been eating with the Gentile believers. But after these men arrived, he drew back and would not eat with the Gentiles, because he was afraid of those who were in favor of circumcising them. [13] The other Jewish believers also started acting like cowards along with Peter; and even Barnabas was swept along by their cowardly action. [14] When I saw that they were not walking a straight path in line with the truth of the gospel, I said to Peter in front of them all, "You are a Jew, yet you have been living like a Gentile, not like a Jew. How, then, can you try to force Gentiles to live like Jews?"

Jews and Gentiles Are Saved by Faith

[15] Indeed, we are Jews by birth and not "Gentile sinners," as they are called. [16] Yet we know that a person is put right with God only through faith in Jesus Christ, never by doing what the Law requires. We, too, have believed in Christ Jesus in order to be put right with God through our faith in Christ, and not by doing what the Law requires. For no one is put right with God by doing what the Law requires. [17] If, then, as we try to be put right with God by our union with Christ, we are found to be sinners, as much as the Gentiles are — does this mean that Christ is serving the cause of sin? By no means! [18] If I start to rebuild

the system of Law that I tore down, then I show myself to be someone who breaks the Law. [19] So far as the Law is concerned, however, I am dead — killed by the Law itself — in order that I might live for God. I have been put to death with Christ on his cross, [20] so that it is no longer I who live, but it is Christ who lives in me. This life that I live now, I live by faith in the Son of God, who loved me and gave his life for me. [21] I refuse to reject the grace of God. But if a person is put right with God through the Law, it means that Christ died for nothing!

Law or Faith

3 You foolish Galatians! Who put a spell on you? Before your very eyes you had a clear description of the death of Jesus Christ on the cross! [2] Tell me this one thing: did you receive God's Spirit by doing what the Law requires or by hearing the gospel and believing it? [3] How can you be so foolish! You began by God's Spirit; do you now want to finish by your own power? [4] Did all your experience mean nothing at all? Surely it meant something! [5] Does God give you the Spirit and work miracles among you because you do what the Law requires or because you hear the gospel and believe it?

[6] Consider the experience of Abraham; as the scripture says, "He believed God, and because of his faith God accepted him as righteous." [7] You should realize, then, that the real descendants of Abraham are the people who have faith. [8] The scripture predicted that God would put the Gentiles right with himself through faith. And so the scripture announced the Good News to Abraham: "Through you God will bless all people." [9] Abraham believed and was blessed; so all who believe are blessed as he was.

---

c have; *or* had.
2.16 a Ps 143.2; Ro 3.20; **b** Ro 3.22　**3.6** Gn 15.6; Ro 4.3　**3.7** Ro 4.16　**3.8** Gn 12.3

¹⁰Those who depend on obeying the Law live under a curse. For the scripture says, "Whoever does not always obey everything that is written in the book of the Law is under God's curse!" ¹¹Now, it is clear that no one is put right with God by means of the Law, because the scripture says, "Only the person who is put right with God through faith shall live."*d* ¹²But the Law has nothing to do with faith. Instead, as the scripture says, "Whoever *does* everything the Law requires will live."

¹³But by becoming a curse for us Christ has redeemed us from the curse that the Law brings; for the scripture says, "Anyone who is hanged on a tree is under God's curse." ¹⁴Christ did this in order that the blessing which God promised to Abraham might be given to the Gentiles by means of Christ Jesus, so that through faith we might receive the Spirit promised by God.

The Law and the Promise

¹⁵My friends, I am going to use an everyday example: when two people agree on a matter and sign an agreement, no one can break it or add anything to it. ¹⁶Now, God made his promises to Abraham and to his descendant. The scripture does not use the plural "descendants," meaning many people, but the singular "descendant," meaning one person only, namely, Christ. ¹⁷What I mean is that God made a covenant with Abraham and promised to keep it. The Law, which was given four hundred and thirty years later, cannot break that covenant and cancel God's promise. ¹⁸For if God's gift depends on the Law, then it no longer depends on his promise. However, it was because of his promise that God gave that gift to Abraham.

¹⁹What, then, was the purpose of the Law? It was added in order to show what wrongdoing is, and it was meant to last until the coming of Abraham's descendant, to whom the promise was made. The Law was handed down by angels, with a man acting as a go-between. ²⁰But a go-between is not needed when only one person is involved; and God is one.*e*

The Purpose of the Law

²¹Does this mean that the Law is against God's promises? No, not at all! For if human beings had received a law that could bring life, then everyone could be put right with God by obeying it. ²²But the scripture says that the whole world is under the power of sin; and so the gift which is promised on the basis of faith in Jesus Christ is given to those who believe.

You are all one in union with Christ Jesus. (3.28)

d put right with God through faith shall live; *or* put right with God shall live through faith.   *e* and God is one; *or* and God acts alone.

3.10 Dt 27.26 (LXX)   **3.11** Hb 2.4   **3.12** Lv 18.5   **3.13** Dt 21.23   **3.17** Ex 12.40
3.18 Ro 4.14

²³But before the time for faith came, the Law kept us all locked up as prisoners until this coming faith should be revealed. ²⁴And so the Law was in charge of us until Christ came, in order that we might then be put right with God through faith. ²⁵Now that the time for faith is here, the Law is no longer in charge of us.

²⁶It is through faith that all of you are God's children in union with Christ Jesus. ²⁷You were baptized into union with Christ, and now you are clothed, so to speak, with the life of Christ himself. ²⁸So there is no difference between Jews and Gentiles, between slaves and free people, between men and women; you are all one in union with Christ Jesus. ²⁹If you belong to Christ, then you are the descendants of Abraham and will receive what God has promised.

4 But now to continue — the son who will receive his father's property is treated just like a slave while he is young, even though he really owns everything. ²While he is young, there are men who take care of him and manage his affairs until the time set by his father. ³In the same way, we too were slaves of the ruling spirits of the universe before we reached spiritual maturity. ⁴But when the right time finally came, God sent his own Son. He came as the son of a human mother and lived under the Jewish Law, ⁵to redeem those who were under the Law, so that we might become God's children.

⁶To show that you are ƒ his children, God sent the Spirit of his Son into our hearts, the Spirit who cries out, "Father, my Father." ⁷So then, you are no longer a slave but a child. And since you are his child, God will give you all that he has for his children.

You are no longer a slave. (4.7)

Paul's Concern for the Galatians

⁸In the past you did not know God, and so you were slaves of beings who are not gods. ⁹But now that you know God — or, I should say, now that God knows you — how is it that you want to turn back to those weak and pitiful ruling spirits? Why do you want to become their slaves all over again? ¹⁰You pay special attention to certain days, months, seasons, and years. ¹¹I am worried about you! Can it be that all my work for you has been for nothing?

¹²I beg you, my friends, be like me. After all, I am like you. You have not done me any wrong. ¹³You remember why I preached the gospel to you the first time; it was because I was sick. ¹⁴But even though my physical condition was a great trial to you, you did not despise or reject me. Instead, you received me as you would an angel from heaven; you received me as you would Christ Jesus. ¹⁵You were so happy! What has happened? I myself can say that you would have taken out your own eyes, if you could, and given them to me. ¹⁶Have I now become your enemy by telling you the truth?

¹⁷Those other people show a deep

ƒ To show that you are; or Because you are.

3.29 Ro 4.13   **4.5-7** Ro 8.15-17   **4.6** 2 Esd 10.7

interest in you, but their intentions are not good. All they want is to separate you from me, so that you will have the same interest in them as they have in you. [18] Now, it is good to have such a deep interest if the purpose is good — this is true always, and not merely when I am with you. [19] My dear children! Once again, just like a mother in childbirth, I feel the same kind of pain for you until Christ's nature is formed in you. [20] How I wish I were with you now, so that I could take a different attitude toward you. I am so worried about you!

The Example of Hagar and Sarah

[21] Let me ask those of you who want to be subject to the Law: do you not hear what the Law says? [22] It says that Abraham had two sons, one by a slave woman, the other by a free woman. [23] His son by the slave woman was born in the usual way, but his son by the free woman was born as a result of God's promise. [24] These things can be understood as a figure: the two women represent two covenants. The one whose children are born in slavery is Hagar, and she represents the covenant made at Mount Sinai. [25] Hagar, who stands for Mount Sinai in Arabia, is *g* a figure of the present city of Jerusalem, in slavery with all its people. [26] But the heavenly Jerusalem is free, and she is our mother. [27] For the scripture says,

> "Be happy, you childless woman!
> Shout and cry with joy, you
>   who never felt the pains
>   of childbirth!
> For the woman who was
>   deserted will have more
>   children
> than the woman whose
>   husband never left her."

[28] Now, you, my friends, are God's children as a result of his promise, just as Isaac was. [29] At that time the son who was born in the usual way persecuted the one who was born because of God's Spirit; and it is the same now. [30] But what does the scripture say? It says, "Send the slave woman and her son away; for the son of the slave woman will not have a part of the father's property along with the son of the free woman." [31] So then, my friends, we are not the children of a slave woman but of a free woman.

Preserve Your Freedom

5 Freedom is what we have — Christ has set us free! Stand, then, as free people, and do not allow yourselves to become slaves again.

[2] Listen! I, Paul, tell you that if you allow yourselves to be circumcised, it means that Christ is of no use to you at all. [3] Once more I warn any man who allows himself to be circumcised that he is obliged to obey the whole Law. [4] Those of you who try to be put right with God by obeying the Law have cut yourselves off from Christ. You are outside God's grace. [5] As for us, our hope is that God will put us right with him; and this is what we wait for by the power of God's Spirit working through our faith. [6] For when we are in union with Christ Jesus, neither circumcision nor the lack of it makes any difference at all; what matters is faith that works through love.

[7] You were doing so well! Who made you stop obeying the truth? How did he persuade you? [8] It was not done by God, who calls you. [9] "It takes only a little yeast to make the whole batch of dough rise," as they say. [10] But I still feel confident about you. Our life in union with

---

g Hagar . . . is; *some manuscripts have* Sinai is a mountain in Arabia, and it is.
4.22 a Gn 16.15; **b** Gn 21.2   **4.26** 2 Esd 2.2; 10.7   **4.27** Is 54.1   **4.29** Gn 21.9
4.30 Gn 21.10   **5.9** 1 Co 5.6

Help carry one another's burdens. (6.2)

the Lord makes me confident that you will not take a different view and that whoever is upsetting you will be punished by God.

¹¹ But as for me, my friends, if I continue to preach that circumcision is necessary, why am I still being persecuted? If that were true, then my preaching about the cross of Christ would cause no trouble. ¹² I wish that the people who are upsetting you would go all the way; let them go on and castrate themselves!

¹³ As for you, my friends, you were called to be free. But do not let this freedom become an excuse for letting your physical desires control you. Instead, let love make you serve one another. ¹⁴ For the whole Law is summed up in one commandment: "Love your neighbor as you love yourself." ¹⁵ But if you act like wild animals, hurting and harming each other, then watch out, or you will completely destroy one another.

The Spirit and Human Nature

¹⁶ What I say is this: let the Spirit direct your lives, and you will not satisfy the desires of the human nature. ¹⁷ For what our human nature wants is opposed to what the Spirit wants, and what the Spirit wants is opposed to what our human nature wants. These

two are enemies, and this means that you cannot do what you want to do. ¹⁸ If the Spirit leads you, then you are not subject to the Law.

¹⁹ What human nature does is quite plain. It shows itself in immoral, filthy, and indecent actions; ²⁰ in worship of idols and witchcraft. People become enemies and they fight; they become jealous, angry, and ambitious. They separate into parties and groups; ²¹ they are envious, get drunk, have orgies, and do other things like these. I warn you now as I have before: those who do these things will not possess the Kingdom of God.

²² But the Spirit produces love, joy, peace, patience, kindness, goodness, faithfulness, ²³ humility, and self-control. There is no law against such things as these. ²⁴ And those who belong to Christ Jesus have put to death their human nature with all its passions and desires. ²⁵ The Spirit has given us life; he must also control our lives. ²⁶ We must not be proud or irritate one another or be jealous of one another.

Bear One Another's Burdens

6 My friends, if someone is caught in any kind of wrongdoing, those of you who are spiritual should set him right; but you must do it in a gentle way. And keep an eye on yourselves, so

5.14 Lv 19.18   **5.17** Ro 7.15-23

that you will not be tempted, too. ²Help carry one another's burdens, and in this way you will obey*h* the law of Christ. ³If you think you are something when you really are nothing, you are only deceiving yourself. ⁴You should each judge your own conduct. If it is good, then you can be proud of what you yourself have done, without having to compare it with what someone else has done. ⁵For each of you have to carry your own load.

⁶If you are being taught the Christian message, you should share all the good things you have with your teacher.

⁷Do not deceive yourselves; no one makes a fool of God. You will reap exactly what you plant. ⁸If you plant in the field of your natural desires, from it you will gather the harvest of death; if you plant in the field of the Spirit, from the Spirit you will gather the harvest of eternal life. ⁹So let us not become tired of doing good; for if we do not give up, the time will come when we will reap the harvest. ¹⁰So then, as often as we have the chance, we should do good to everyone, and especially to those who belong to our family in the faith.

h you will obey; *some manuscripts have* obey.

Final Warning and Greeting

¹¹See what big letters I make as I write to you now with my own hand! ¹²The people who are trying to force you to be circumcised are the ones who want to show off and boast about external matters. They do it, however, only so that they may not be persecuted for the cross of Christ. ¹³Even those who practice circumcision do not obey the Law; they want you to be circumcised so that they can boast that you submitted to this physical ceremony. ¹⁴As for me, however, I will boast only about the cross of our Lord Jesus Christ; for by means of his cross the world is dead to me, and I am dead to the world. ¹⁵It does not matter at all whether or not one is circumcised; what does matter is being a new creature. ¹⁶As for those who follow this rule in their lives, may peace and mercy be with them — with them and with all of God's people!

¹⁷To conclude: let no one give me any more trouble, because the scars I have on my body show that I am the slave of Jesus.

¹⁸May the grace of our Lord Jesus Christ be with you all, my friends. Amen.

Paul's Letter to the
EPHESIANS

INTRODUCTION

Paul's Letter to the Ephesians is concerned first of all with "God's plan . . . to bring all creation together, everything in heaven and on earth, with Christ as head" (1.10). It is also an appeal to God's people to live out the meaning of this great plan for the unity of the whole human race through oneness with Jesus Christ.

In the first part of *Ephesians* the writer develops the theme of unity by speaking of the way in which God the Father has chosen his people, how they are forgiven and set free from their sins through Jesus Christ the Son, and how God's great promise is guaranteed by the Holy Spirit. In the second part he appeals to the readers to live in such a way that their oneness in Christ may become real in their life together.

Several figures of speech are used to show the oneness of God's people in union with Christ: the church is like a body, with Christ as the head; or like a building, with Christ as the cornerstone; or like a wife, with Christ as the husband. This letter rises to great heights of expression as the writer is moved by the thought of God's grace in Christ. Everything is seen in the light of Christ's love, sacrifice, forgiveness, grace, and purity.

OUTLINE OF CONTENTS

---

1 From Paul, who by God's will is an apostle of Christ Jesus —

To God's people in Ephesus,[a] who are faithful in their life in union with Christ Jesus:

2 May God our Father and the Lord Jesus Christ give you grace and peace.

Spiritual Blessings in Christ

3 Let us give thanks to the God and Father of our Lord Jesus Christ! For in our union with Christ he has blessed us by giving us every spiritual blessing in the heavenly world. 4 Even before the world was made, God had already chosen us to be his through our union with Christ, so that we would be holy and without fault before him.

Because of his love 5 God[b] had already decided that through Jesus Christ he would make us his children — this was his pleasure and purpose. 6 Let us praise God for his glorious grace, for the free gift he gave us in his dear Son! 7 For by the blood of

---

[a] *Some manuscripts do not have* in Ephesus. *or* before him, and to live in love. God.

[b] before him. Because of his love God;

1.1 Ac 18.19-21; 19.1   **1.7** Col 1.14

Let us . . . praise God's glory. (1.12)

Christ[c] we are set free, that is, our sins are forgiven. How great is the grace of God, ⁸ which he gave to us in such large measure!

In all his wisdom and insight ⁹ God did what he had purposed, and made known to us the secret plan he had already decided to complete by means of Christ. ¹⁰ This plan, which God will complete when the time is right, is to bring all creation together, everything in heaven and on earth, with Christ as head.

¹¹ All things are done according to God's plan and decision; and God chose us to be his own people in union with Christ because of his own purpose, based on what he had decided from the

[c] by the blood of Christ; *or* by the sacrificial death of Christ.

very beginning. [12] Let us, then, who were the first to hope in Christ, praise God's glory!

[13] And you also became God's people when you heard the true message, the Good News that brought you salvation. You believed in Christ, and God put his stamp of ownership on you by giving you the Holy Spirit he had promised. [14] The Spirit is the guarantee that we shall receive what God has promised his people, and this assures us that God will give complete freedom to those who are his. Let us praise his glory!

Paul's Prayer

[15] For this reason, ever since I heard of your faith in the Lord Jesus and your love for all of God's people, [16] I have not stopped giving thanks to God for you. I remember you in my prayers [17] and ask the God of our Lord Jesus Christ, the glorious Father, to give you the Spirit, who will make you wise and reveal God to you, so that you will know him. [18] I ask that your minds may be opened to see his light, so that you will know what is the hope to which he has called you, how rich are the wonderful blessings he promises his people, [19] and how very great is his power at work in us who believe. This power working in us is the same as the mighty strength [20] which he used when he raised Christ from death and seated him at his right side in the heavenly world. [21] Christ rules there above all heavenly rulers, authorities, powers, and lords; he has a title superior to all titles of authority in this world and in the next. [22] God put all things under Christ's feet and gave him to the church as supreme Lord over all things. [23] The church is Christ's body, the completion of him who himself completes all things everywhere.[d]

From Death to Life

2 In the past you were spiritually dead because of your disobedience and sins. [2] At that time you followed the world's evil way; you obeyed the ruler of the spiritual powers in space, the spirit who now controls the people who disobey God. [3] Actually all of us were like them and lived according to our natural desires, doing whatever suited the wishes of our own bodies and minds. In our natural condition we, like everyone else, were destined to suffer God's anger.

[4] But God's mercy is so abundant, and his love for us is so great, [5] that while we were spiritually dead in our disobedience he brought us to life with Christ. It is by God's grace that you have been saved. [6] In our union with Christ Jesus he raised us up with him to rule with him in the heavenly world. [7] He did this to demonstrate for all time to come the extraordinary greatness of his grace in the love he showed us in Christ Jesus. [8-9] For it is by God's grace that you have been saved through faith. It is not the result of your own efforts, but God's gift, so that no one can boast about it. [10] God has made us what we are, and in our union with Christ Jesus he has created us for a life of good deeds, which he has already prepared for us to do.

One in Christ

[11] You Gentiles by birth — called "the uncircumcised" by the Jews, who call themselves the circumcised (which refers to what men do to their bodies) — remember what you were in the past. [12] At that time you were apart from Christ. You were foreigners and did not belong to God's chosen people. You had no part in the covenants, which were based on God's promises to his people,

---

[d] who himself completes all things everywhere; *or* who is himself completely filled with God's fullness.

1.20 Ps 110.1   **1.22** Ps 8.6   **1.22, 23** Col 1.18   **2.1-5** Col 2.13

and you lived in this world without hope and without God. ¹³But now, in union with Christ Jesus you, who used to be far away, have been brought near by the blood of Christ.ᵉ ¹⁴For Christ himself has brought us peace by making Jews and Gentiles one people. With his own body he broke down the wall that separated them and kept them enemies. ¹⁵He abolished the Jewish Law with its commandments and rules, in order to create out of the two races one new people in union with himself, in this way making peace. ¹⁶By his death on the cross Christ destroyed their enmity; by means of the cross he united both races into one body and brought them back to God. ¹⁷So Christ came and preached the Good News of peace to all — to you Gentiles, who were far away from God, and to the Jews, who were near to him. ¹⁸It is through Christ that all of us, Jews and Gentiles, are able to come in the one Spirit into the presence of the Father.

¹⁹So then, you Gentiles are not foreigners or strangers any longer; you are now citizens together with God's people and members of the family of God. ²⁰You, too, are built upon the foundation laid by the apostles and prophets,ᶠ the cornerstone being Christ Jesus himself. ²¹He is the one who holds the whole building together and makes it grow into a sacred temple dedicated to the Lord. ²²In union with him you too are being built together with all the others into a place where God lives through his Spirit.

Paul's Work for the Gentiles

3 For this reason I, Paul, the prisoner of Christ Jesus for the sake of you Gentiles, pray to God. ²Surely you have heard that God in his grace has given me this work to do for your good.

³God revealed his secret plan and made it known to me. (I have written briefly about this, ⁴and if you will read what I have written, you can learn about my understanding of the secret of Christ.) ⁵In past times human beings were not told this secret, but God has revealed it now by the Spirit to his holy apostles and prophets. ⁶The secret is that by means of the gospel the Gentiles have a part with the Jews in God's blessings; they are members of the same body and share in the promise that God made through Christ Jesus.

⁷I was made a servant of the gospel by God's special gift, which he gave me through the working of his power. ⁸I am less than the least of all God's people; yet God gave me this privilege of taking to the Gentiles the Good News about the infinite riches of Christ, ⁹and of making all people see how God's secret plan is to be put into effect. God, who is the Creator of all things, kept his secret hidden through all the past ages, ¹⁰in order that at the present time, by means of the church, the angelic rulers and powers in the heavenly world might learn of his wisdom in all its different forms. ¹¹God did this according to his eternal purpose, which he achieved through Christ Jesus our Lord. ¹²In union with Christ and through our faith in him we have the boldness to go into God's presence with all confidence. ¹³I beg you, then, not to be discouraged because I am suffering for you; it is all for your benefit.

The Love of Christ

¹⁴For this reason I fall on my knees before the Father, ¹⁵from whom every family in heaven and on earth receives its true name. ¹⁶I ask God from the wealth of his glory to give you power through his Spirit to be strong in your

---

ᵉ *by the blood of Christ; or by the sacrificial death of Christ.*   ᶠ *the foundation laid by the apostles and prophets; or the foundation, that is, the apostles and prophets.*
2.15 Col 2.14   **2.16** Col 1.20   **2.17** Is 57.19   **3.4-6** Col 1.26, 27

inner selves, [17] and I pray that Christ will make his home in your hearts through faith. I pray that you may have your roots and foundation in love, [18] so that you, together with all God's people, may have the power to understand how broad and long, how high and deep, is Christ's love. [19] Yes, may you come to know his love — although it can never be fully known — and so be completely filled with the very nature of God.

[20] To him who by means of his power working in us is able to do so much more than we can ever ask for, or even think of: [21] to God be the glory in the church and in Christ Jesus for all time, forever and ever! Amen.

The Unity of the Body

4 I urge you, then — I who am a prisoner because I serve the Lord: live a life that measures up to the standard God set when he called you. [2] Be always humble, gentle, and patient. Show your love by being tolerant with one another. [3] Do your best to preserve the unity which the Spirit gives by means of the peace that binds you together. [4] There is one body and one Spirit, just as there is one hope to which God has called you. [5] There is one Lord, one faith, one baptism; [6] there is one God and Father of all people, who is Lord of all, works through all, and is in all.

[7] Each one of us has received a special gift in proportion to what Christ has given. [8] As the scripture says,

"When he went up to the very
    heights,
he took many captives
    with him;
he gave gifts to people."

[9] Now, what does "he went up" mean? It means that first he came down to the lowest depths of the earth.[g] [10] So the one who came down is the same one

who went up, above and beyond the heavens, to fill the whole universe with his presence. [11] It was he who "gave gifts to people"; he appointed some to be apostles, others to be prophets, others to be evangelists, others to be pastors and teachers. [12] He did this to prepare all God's people for the work of Christian service, in order to build up the body of Christ. [13] And so we shall all come together to that oneness in our faith and in our knowledge of the Son of God; we shall become mature people, reaching to the very height of Christ's full stature. [14] Then we shall no longer be children, carried by the waves and blown about by every shifting wind of the teaching of deceitful people, who lead others into error by the tricks they invent. [15] Instead, by speaking the truth in a spirit of love, we must grow up in every way to Christ, who is the head. [16] Under his control all the different parts of the body fit together, and the whole body is held together by every joint with which it is provided. So when each separate part works as it should, the whole body grows and builds itself up through love.

The New Life in Christ

[17] In the Lord's name, then, I warn you: do not continue to live like the heathen, whose thoughts are worthless [18] and whose minds are in the dark. They have no part in the life that God gives, for they are completely ignorant and stubborn. [19] They have lost all feeling of shame; they give themselves over to vice and do all sorts of indecent things without restraint.

[20] That was not what you learned about Christ! [21] You certainly heard about him, and as his followers you were taught the truth that is in Jesus. [22] So get rid of your old self, which made you live as you used to — the old self

[g] the lowest depths of the earth; *or* the lower depths, the earth itself.

3.18 Si 1.3   **4.2** Col 3.12, 13   **4.8** Ps 68.18   **4.16** Col 2.19   **4.22** Col 3.9

that was being destroyed by its deceitful desires. ²³ Your hearts and minds must be made completely new, ²⁴ and you must put on the new self, which is created in God's likeness and reveals itself in the true life that is upright and holy.

²⁵ No more lying, then! Each of you must tell the truth to the other believer, because we are all members together in the body of Christ. ²⁶ If you become angry, do not let your anger lead you into sin, and do not stay angry all day.

Do not let your anger lead you into sin. (4.26)

²⁷ Don't give the Devil a chance. ²⁸ If you used to rob, you must stop robbing and start working, in order to earn an honest living for yourself and to be able to help the poor. ²⁹ Do not use harmful words, but only helpful words, the kind that build up and provide what is needed, so that what you say will do good to those who hear you. ³⁰ And do not make God's Holy Spirit sad; for the Spirit is God's mark of ownership on you, a guarantee that the Day will come when God will set you free. ³¹ Get rid of all bitterness, passion, and anger. No more shouting or insults, no more hateful feelings of any sort. ³² Instead, be kind and tender-hearted to one an-

other, and forgive one another, as God has forgiven you through Christ.

Living in the Light

5 Since you are God's dear children, you must try to be like him. ² Your life must be controlled by love, just as Christ loved us and gave his life for us as a sweet-smelling offering and sacrifice that pleases God.

³ Since you are God's people, it is not right that any matters of sexual immorality or indecency or greed should even be mentioned among you. ⁴ Nor is it fitting for you to use language which is obscene, profane, or vulgar. Rather you should give thanks to God. ⁵ You may be sure that no one who is immoral, indecent, or greedy (for greed is a form of idolatry) will ever receive a share in the Kingdom of Christ and of God.

⁶ Do not let anyone deceive you with foolish words; it is because of these very things that God's anger will come upon those who do not obey him. ⁷ So have nothing at all to do with such people. ⁸ You yourselves used to be in the darkness, but since you have become the Lord's people, you are in the light. So you must live like people who belong to the light, ⁹ for it is the light ʰ that brings a rich harvest of every kind of goodness, righteousness, and truth. ¹⁰ Try to learn what pleases the Lord. ¹¹ Have nothing to do with the worthless things that people do, things that belong to the darkness. Instead, bring them out to the light. (¹² It is really too shameful even to talk about the things they do in secret.) ¹³ And when all things are brought out to the light, then their true nature is clearly revealed; ¹⁴ for anything that is clearly revealed becomes light.ⁱ That is why it is said,

"Wake up, sleeper,

ʰ the light; *some manuscripts have* the Spirit.   ⁱ anything that is clearly revealed becomes light; *or it is light that clearly reveals everything.*

4.24 a Col 3.10; **b** Gn 1.26; Ws 9.3   **4.25** Zec 8.16   **4.26** Ps 4.4 (LXX)   **4.32** Col 3.13
5.2 Ex 29.18; Ps 40.6

and rise from death,
and Christ will shine on you."

15 So be careful how you live. Don't live like ignorant people, but like wise people. 16 Make good use of every opportunity you have, because these are evil days. 17 Don't be fools, then, but try to find out what the Lord wants you to do.

18 Do not get drunk with wine, which will only ruin you; instead, be filled with the Spirit. 19 Speak to one another with the words of psalms, hymns, and sacred songs; sing hymns and psalms to the Lord with praise in your hearts. 20 In the name of our Lord Jesus Christ, always give thanks for everything to God the Father.

Wives and Husbands

21 Submit yourselves to one another because of your reverence for Christ. 22 Wives, submit yourselves to your husbands as to the Lord. 23 For a husband has authority over his wife just as Christ has authority over the church; and Christ is himself the Savior of the church, his body. 24 And so wives must submit themselves completely to their husbands just as the church submits itself to Christ.

25 Husbands, love your wives just as Christ loved the church and gave his life for it. 26 He did this to dedicate the church to God by his word, after making it clean by washing it in water, 27 in order to present the church to himself in all its beauty — pure and faultless, without spot or wrinkle or any other imperfection. 28 Men ought to love their wives just as they love their own bodies. A man who loves his wife loves himself. (29 None of us ever hate our own bodies. Instead, we feed them, and take care of them, just as Christ does the church;

30 for we are members of his body.) 31 As the scripture says, "For this reason a man will leave his father and mother and unite with his wife, and the two will become one." 32 There is a deep secret truth revealed in this scripture, which I understand as applying to Christ and the church. 33 But it also applies to you: every husband must love his wife as himself, and every wife must respect her husband.

Children and Parents

6 Children, it is your Christian duty to[j] obey your parents, for this is the right thing to do. 2 "Respect your father and mother" is the first commandment that has a promise added: 3 "so that all may go well with you, and you may live a long time in the land."

4 Parents, do not treat your children in such a way as to make them angry. Instead, raise them with Christian discipline and instruction.

Slaves and Masters

5 Slaves, obey your human masters with fear and trembling; and do it with a sincere heart, as though you were serving Christ. 6 Do this not only when they are watching you, because you want to gain their approval; but with all your heart do what God wants, as slaves of Christ. 7 Do your work as slaves cheerfully, as though you served the Lord, and not merely human beings. 8 Remember that the Lord will reward each of us, whether slave or free, for the good work we do.

9 Masters, behave in the same way toward your slaves and stop using threats. Remember that you and your slaves belong to the same Master in heaven, who judges everyone by the same standard.

---

j Some manuscripts do not have it is your Christian duty to.

5.16 Col 4.5　**5.19, 20** Col 3.16, 17　**5.22** Col 3.18; 1 P 3.1　**5.25** Col 3.19; 1 P 3.7
5.31 Gn 2.24　**6.1** Col 3.20　**6.2, 3** Ex 20.12; Dt 5.16　**6.4** Col 3.21　**6.5-8** Col 3.22-25
6.9 a Col 4.1; **b** Dt 10.17; Col 3.25

The Whole Armor of God

[10] Finally, build up your strength in union with the Lord and by means of his mighty power. [11] Put on all the armor that God gives you, so that you will be able to stand up against the Devil's evil tricks. [12] For we are not fighting against human beings but against the wicked spiritual forces in the heavenly world, the rulers, authorities, and cosmic powers of this dark age. [13] So put on God's armor now! Then when the evil day comes, you will be able to resist the enemy's attacks; and after fighting to the end, you will still hold your ground.

[14] So stand ready, with truth as a belt tight around your waist, with righteousness as your breastplate, [15] and as your shoes the readiness to announce the Good News of peace. [16] At all times carry faith as a shield; for with it you will be able to put out all the burning arrows shot by the Evil One. [17] And accept salvation as a helmet, and the word of God as the sword which the Spirit gives you. [18] Do all this in prayer, asking for God's help. Pray on every occasion, as the Spirit leads. For this reason keep alert and never give up; pray always for all God's people. [19] And pray also for me, that God will give me a message when I am ready to speak, so that I may speak boldly and make known the gospel's secret. [20] For the sake of this gospel I am an ambassador, though now I am in prison. Pray that I may be bold in speaking about the gospel as I should.

Final Greetings

[21] Tychicus, our dear brother and faithful servant in the Lord's work, will give you all the news about me, so that you may know how I am getting along. [22] That is why I am sending him to you — to tell you how all of us are getting along and to encourage you.

[23] May God the Father and the Lord Jesus Christ give to all Christians peace and love with faith. [24] May God's grace be with all those who love our Lord Jesus Christ with undying love.

6.11 Ws 5.17 **6.14-17** Ws 5.18-23 **6.14 a** Is 11.5; **b** Is 59.17 **6.15** Is 52.7 **6.17** Is 59.17
6.21 Ac 20.4; 2 Ti 4.12 **6.21, 22** Col 4.7, 8

Paul's Letter to the
PHILIPPIANS

INTRODUCTION

Paul's Letter to the Philippians was written to the first church that Paul established on European soil, in the Roman province of Macedonia. It was written while the apostle was in prison, and at a time when he was troubled by the opposition of other Christian workers toward himself and was distressed by false teaching in the church at Philippi. Yet this letter breathes a joy and confidence that can be explained only by Paul's deep faith in Jesus Christ.

The immediate reason for writing the letter was to thank the Philippian Christians for the gift which they had sent to help him in his time of need. He uses this opportunity to reassure them, so that they may have courage and confidence in spite of all his troubles and their own as well. He pleads with them to have the humble attitude of Jesus, rather than to be controlled by selfish ambition and pride. He reminds them that their life in union with Christ is a gift of God's grace which they have received through faith, not through obedience to the ceremonies of the Jewish Law. He writes of the joy and peace that God gives to those who live in union with Christ.

This letter is marked by its emphasis on joy, confidence, unity, and perseverance in the Christian faith and life. It also reveals the deep affection Paul had for the church at Philippi.

OUTLINE OF CONTENTS

1 From Paul and Timothy, servants of Christ Jesus —

To all God's people in Philippi who are in union with Christ Jesus, including the church leaders and helpers:

2 May God our Father and the Lord Jesus Christ give you grace and peace.

Paul's Prayer for His Readers

3 I thank my God for you every time I think of you; 4 and every time I pray for you all, I pray with joy 5 because of the way in which you have helped me in the work of the gospel from the very first day until now. 6 And so I am sure that God, who began this good work in you, will carry it on until it is finished

1.1 Ac 16.12

on the Day of Christ Jesus. [7] You are always in my heart! And so it is only right for me to feel as I do about you. For you have all shared with me in this privilege that God has given me, both now that I am in prison and also while I was free to defend the gospel and establish it firmly. [8] God is my witness that I tell the truth when I say that my deep feeling for you all comes from the heart of Christ Jesus himself.

[9] I pray that your love will keep on growing more and more, together with true knowledge and perfect judgment, [10] so that you will be able to choose what is best. Then you will be free from all impurity and blame on the Day of Christ. [11] Your lives will be filled with the truly good qualities which only Jesus Christ can produce, for the glory and praise of God.

To Live Is Christ

[12] I want you to know, my friends, that the things that have happened to me have really helped the progress of the gospel. [13] As a result, the whole palace guard and all the others here know that I am in prison because I am a servant of Christ. [14] And my being in prison has given most of the believers more confidence in the Lord, so that they grow bolder all the time to preach the message[a] fearlessly.

[15] Of course some of them preach Christ because they are jealous and quarrelsome, but others from genuine good will. [16] These do so from love, because they know that God has given me the work of defending the gospel. [17] The others do not proclaim Christ sincerely, but from a spirit of selfish ambition; they think that they will make more trouble for me while I am in prison.

[18] It does not matter! I am happy about it — just so Christ is preached in every way possible, whether from

wrong or right motives. And I will continue to be happy, [19] because I know that by means of your prayers and the help which comes from the Spirit of Jesus Christ I shall be set free. [20] My deep desire and hope is that I shall never fail in my duty, but that at all times, and especially right now, I shall be full of courage, so that with my whole being I shall bring honor to Christ, whether I live or die. [21] For what is life? To me, it is Christ. Death, then, will bring more. [22] But if by continuing to live I can do more worthwhile work, then I am not sure which I should choose. [23] I am pulled in two directions. I want very much to leave this life and be with Christ, which is a far better thing; [24] but for your sake it is much more important that I remain alive. [25] I am sure of this, and so I know that I will stay. I will stay on with you all, to add to your progress and joy in the faith, [26] so that when I am with you again, you will have even more reason to be proud of me in your life in union with Christ Jesus.

[27] Now, the important thing is that your way of life should be as the gospel of Christ requires, so that, whether or not I am able to go and see you, I will hear that you are standing firm with one common purpose and that with only one desire you are fighting together for the faith of the gospel. [28] Don't be afraid of your enemies; always be courageous, and this will prove to them that they will lose and that you will win, because it is God who gives you the victory. [29] For you have been given the privilege of serving Christ, not only by believing in him, but also by suffering for him. [30] Now you can take part with me in the battle. It is the same battle you saw me fighting in the past, and as you hear, the one I am fighting still.

---

[a] the message; *some manuscripts have* God's message.

1.13 Ac 28.30   **1.30** Ac 16.19-40

Christ's Humility and Greatness

2 Your life in Christ makes you strong, and his love comforts you. You have fellowship with the Spirit,[b] and you have kindness and compassion for one another. [2] I urge you, then, to make me completely happy by having the same thoughts, sharing the same love, and being one in soul and mind. [3] Don't do anything from selfish ambition or from a cheap desire to boast, but be humble toward one another, always considering others better than yourselves. [4] And look out for one another's interests, not just for your own. [5] The attitude you should have is the one that Christ Jesus had:

> [6] He always had the nature of God,
> but he did not think that by
> force he should try to
> remain[c] equal with God.
> [7] Instead of this, of his own free
> will he gave up all he had,
> and took the nature of a
> servant.
> He became like a human being
> and appeared in human
> likeness.
> [8] He was humble and walked the
> path of obedience all the
> way to death —
> his death on the cross.
> [9] For this reason God raised him to
> the highest place above
> and gave him the name that
> is greater than any other
> name.
> [10] And so, in honor of the name of
> Jesus
> all beings in heaven, on earth,
> and in the world below[d]
> will fall on their knees,
> [11] and all will openly proclaim that
> Jesus Christ is Lord,
> to the glory of God the Father.

Shining as Lights in the World

[12] So then, dear friends, as you always obeyed me when I was with you, it is even more important that you obey me now while I am away from you. Keep on working with fear and trembling to complete your salvation, [13] because God is always at work in you to make you willing and able to obey his own purpose.

[14] Do everything without complaining or arguing, [15] so that you may be innocent and pure as God's perfect children, who live in a world of corrupt and sinful people. You must shine among them like stars lighting up the sky, [16] as you offer them the message of life. If you do so, I shall have reason to be proud of you on the Day of Christ, because it will show that all my effort and work have not been wasted.

[17] Perhaps my life's blood is to be poured out like an offering on the sacrifice that your faith offers to God. If that is so, I am glad and share my joy with you all. [18] In the same way, you too must be glad and share your joy with me.

Timothy and Epaphroditus

[19] If it is the Lord's will, I hope that I will be able to send Timothy to you soon, so that I may be encouraged by news about you. [20] He is the only one who shares my feelings and who really cares about you. [21] Everyone else is concerned only with their own affairs, not with the cause of Jesus Christ. [22] And you yourselves know how he has proved his worth, how he and I, like a son and his father, have worked together for the sake of the gospel. [23] So I hope to send him to you as soon as I know how things are going to turn out

---

[b] You have fellowship with the Spirit; *or* The Spirit has brought you into fellowship with one another. [c] remain; *or* become. [d] WORLD BELOW: *It was thought that the dead continued to exist in a dark world under the ground.*
2.10, 11 Is 45.23 (LXX) **2.15** Dt 32.5

for me. [24] And I trust in the Lord that I myself will be able to come to you soon.

[25] I have thought it necessary to send to you our brother Epaphroditus, who has worked and fought by my side and who has served as your messenger in helping me. [26] He is anxious to see you all and is very upset because you had heard that he was sick. [27] Indeed he was sick and almost died. But God had pity on him, and not only on him but on me, too, and spared me an even greater sorrow. [28] I am all the more eager, then, to send him to you, so that you will be glad again when you see him, and my own sorrow will disappear. [29] Receive him, then, with joy, as a believer in the Lord. Show respect to all such people as he,

Receive him . . . as a believer. (2.29)

[30] because he risked his life and nearly died for the sake of the work of Christ, in order to give me the help that you yourselves could not give.

The True Righteousness

3 In conclusion, my friends, be joyful in your union with the Lord. I don't mind repeating what I have written before, and you will be safer if I do so. [2] Watch out for those who do evil things, those dogs, those who insist on cutting the body. [3] It is we, not they, who have received the true circumcision, for we worship God by means of his Spirit and rejoice in our life in union with Christ Jesus. We do not put any trust in external ceremonies. [4] I could, of course, put my trust in such things. If any of you think you can trust in external ceremonies, I have even more reason to feel that way. [5] I was circumcised when I was a week old. I am an Israelite by birth, of the tribe of Benjamin, a pure-blooded Hebrew. As far as keeping the Jewish Law is concerned, I was a Pharisee, [6] and I was so zealous that I persecuted the church. As far as a person can be righteous by obeying the commands of the Law, I was without fault. [7] But all those things that I might count as profit I now reckon as loss for Christ's sake. [8] Not only those things; I reckon everything as complete loss for the sake of what is so much more valuable, the knowledge of Christ Jesus my Lord. For his sake I have thrown everything away; I consider it all as mere garbage, so that I may gain Christ [9] and be completely united with him. I no longer have a righteousness of my own, the kind that is gained by obeying the Law. I now have the righteousness that is given through faith in Christ, the righteousness that comes from God and is based on faith. [10] All I want is to know Christ and to experience the power of his resurrection, to share in his sufferings and become like him in his death, [11] in the hope that I myself will be raised from death to life.

Running toward the Goal

[12] I do not claim that I have already succeeded or have already become perfect. I keep striving to win the prize for which Christ Jesus has already won me to himself. [13] Of course, my friends, I really do not[e] think that I have already won it; the one thing I do, however, is

---

[e] not; *some manuscripts have* not yet.

3.5 a Ro 11.1; **b** Ac 23.6; 26.5   **3.6** Ac 8.3; 22.4; 26.9-11 to forget what is behind me and do my best to reach what is ahead. ¹⁴So I run straight toward the goal in order to win the prize, which is God's call through Christ Jesus to the life above.

I run straight toward the goal. (3.14)

¹⁵All of us who are spiritually mature should have this same attitude. But if some of you have a different attitude, God will make this clear to you. ¹⁶However that may be, let us go forward according to the same rules we have followed until now.

¹⁷Keep on imitating me, my friends. Pay attention to those who follow the right example that we have set for you. ¹⁸I have told you this many times before, and now I repeat it with tears: there are many whose lives make them enemies of Christ's death on the cross. ¹⁹They are going to end up in hell, because their god is their bodily desires. They are proud of what they should be ashamed of, and they think only of things that belong to this world. ²⁰We, however, are citizens of heaven, and we eagerly wait for our Savior, the Lord Jesus Christ, to come from heaven. ²¹He will change our weak mortal bodies and make them like his own glorious body, using that power by which he is able to bring all things under his rule.

Instructions

4 So then, my friends, how dear you are to me and how I miss you! How happy you make me, and how proud I am of you! — this, dear friends, is how you should stand firm in your life in the Lord.

²Euodia and Syntyche, please, I beg you, try to agree as sisters in the Lord. ³And you too, my faithful partner, I want you to help these women; for they have worked hard with me to spread the gospel, together with Clement and all my other fellow workers, whose names are in God's book of the living.

⁴May you always be joyful in your union with the Lord. I say it again: rejoice!

⁵Show a gentle attitude toward everyone. The Lord is coming soon. ⁶Don't worry about anything, but in all your prayers ask God for what you need, always asking him with a thankful heart. ⁷And God's peace, which is far beyond human understanding, will keep your hearts and minds safe in union with Christ Jesus.

⁸In conclusion, my friends, fill your minds with those things that are good and that deserve praise: things that are true, noble, right, pure, lovely, and honorable. ⁹Put into practice what you learned and received from me, both from my words and from my actions. And the God who gives us peace will be with you.

Thanks for the Gift

¹⁰In my life in union with the Lord it is a great joy to me that after so long a time you once more had the chance of showing that you care for me. I don't mean that you had stopped caring for me — you just had no chance to show it. ¹¹And I am not saying this because I feel neglected, for I have learned to be satisfied with what I have. ¹²I know what it is to be in need and what it is to

3.17 1 Co 4.16; 11.1

have more than enough. I have learned this secret, so that anywhere, at any time, I am content, whether I am full or hungry, whether I have too much or too little. [13] I have the strength to face all conditions by the power that Christ gives me.

[14] But it was very good of you to help me in my troubles. [15] You Philippians know very well that when I left Macedonia in the early days of preaching the Good News, you were the only church to help me; you were the only ones who shared my profits and losses. [16] More than once when I needed help in Thessalonica, you sent it to me. [17] It is not that I just want to receive gifts; rather, I want to see profit added to your account. [18] Here, then, is my receipt for everything you have given me — and it

has been more than enough! I have all I need now that Epaphroditus has brought me all your gifts. They are like a sweet-smelling offering to God, a sacrifice which is acceptable and pleasing to him. [19] And with all his abundant wealth through Christ Jesus, my God will supply all your needs. [20] To our God and Father be the glory forever and ever! Amen.

Final Greetings

[21] Greetings to each one of God's people who belong to Christ Jesus. The believers here with me send you their greetings. [22] All God's people here send greetings, especially those who belong to the Emperor's palace.

[23] May the grace of the Lord Jesus Christ be with you all.

4.16 Ac 17.1   **4.15, 16** 2 Co 11.9   **4.18** Ex 29.18

Paul's Letter to the
COLOSSIANS

INTRODUCTION

Paul's Letter to the Colossians was written to the church at Colossae, a town in Asia Minor east of Ephesus. This church had not been established by Paul, but was in an area for which Paul felt responsible, as he sent out workers from Ephesus, the capital of the Roman province of Asia. Paul had learned that there were false teachers in the church at Colossae who insisted that in order to know God and have full salvation one must worship certain "spiritual rulers and authorities." In addition, these teachers said, one must submit to special rites such as circumcision and must observe strict rules about foods and other matters.

Paul writes to oppose these teachings with the true Christian message. The heart of his reply is that Jesus Christ is able to give full salvation and that these other beliefs and practices actually lead away from him. Through Christ, God created the world and through him he is bringing it back to himself. Only in union with Christ is there hope of salvation for the world. Paul then spells out the implications of this great teaching for the lives of believers.

It is noteworthy that Tychicus, who took this letter to Colossae for Paul, was accompanied by Onesimus, the slave on whose behalf Paul wrote *Philemon*.

OUTLINE OF CONTENTS

---

1 From Paul, who by God's will is an apostle of Christ Jesus, and from our brother Timothy—

² To God's people in Colossae, who are our faithful friends in union with Christ:

May God our Father give you grace and peace.

Prayer of Thanksgiving

³ We always give thanks to God, the Father of our Lord Jesus Christ, when we pray for you. ⁴ For we have heard of your faith in Christ Jesus and of your love for all God's people. ⁵ When the true message, the Good News, first came to you, you heard about the hope it offers. So your faith and love are based on what you hope for, which is kept safe for you in heaven. ⁶ The gospel keeps bringing blessings and is spreading throughout the world, just as it has among you ever since the day you first heard about the grace of God and came to know it as it really is. ⁷ You learned of God's grace from Epaphras, our dear

fellow servant, who is Christ's faithful worker on our *a* behalf. [8] He has told us of the love that the Spirit has given you.

[9] For this reason we have always prayed for you, ever since we heard about you. We ask God to fill you with the knowledge of his will, with all the wisdom and understanding that his Spirit gives. [10] Then you will be able to live as the Lord wants and will always do what pleases him. Your lives will produce all kinds of good deeds, and you will grow in your knowledge of God. [11-12] May you be made strong with all the strength which comes from his glorious power, so that you may be able to endure everything with patience. And with joy give thanks to *b* the Father, who has made you fit to have your share of what God has reserved for his people in the kingdom of light. [13] He rescued us from the power of darkness and brought us safe into the kingdom of his dear Son, [14] by whom we are set free, that is, our sins are forgiven.

The Person and Work of Christ

[15] Christ is the visible likeness of the invisible God. He is the first-born Son, superior to all created things. [16] For through him God created everything in heaven and on earth, the seen and the unseen things, including spiritual powers, lords, rulers, and authorities. God created the whole universe through him and for him. [17] Christ existed before all things, and in union with him all things have their proper place. [18] He is the head of his body, the church; he is the source of the body's life. He is the first-born Son, who was raised from death, in order that he alone might have the first place in all things. [19] For it was by God's own decision that the

Son has in himself the full nature of God. [20] Through the Son, then, God decided to bring the whole universe back to himself. God made peace through his Son's blood *c* on the cross and so brought back to himself all things, both on earth and in heaven.

[21] At one time you were far away from God and were his enemies because of the evil things you did and thought. [22] But now, by means of the physical death of his Son, God has made you his friends, in order to bring you, holy, pure, and faultless, into his presence. [23] You must, of course, continue faithful on a firm and sure foundation, and must not allow yourselves to be shaken from the hope you gained when you heard the gospel. It is of this gospel that I, Paul, became a servant — this gospel which has been preached to everybody in the world.

Paul's Work as a Servant of the Church

[24] And now I am happy about my sufferings for you, for by means of my physical sufferings I am helping to complete what still remains of Christ's sufferings on behalf of his body, the church. [25] And I have been made a servant of the church by God, who gave me this task to perform for your good. It is the task of fully proclaiming his message, [26] which is the secret he hid through all past ages from all human beings but has now revealed to his people. [27] God's plan is to make known his secret to his people, this rich and glorious secret which he has for all peoples. And the secret is that Christ is in you, which means that you will share in the glory of God. [28] So we preach Christ to everyone. With all possible wisdom we

---

a our; *some manuscripts have* your.   *b* with patience. And with joy give thanks to; *or* with patience and joy. And give thanks to.   *c* his Son's blood; *or* his Son's sacrificial death.

1.14 Eph 1.7   **1.15** Ws 7.26   **1.18** Eph 1.22, 23   **1.20** Eph 2.16

warn and teach them in order to bring each one into God's presence as a mature individual in union with Christ. [29]To get this done I toil and struggle, using the mighty strength which Christ supplies and which is at work in me.

2 Let me tell you how hard I have worked for you and for the people in Laodicea and for all others who do not know me personally. [2]I do this in order that they may be filled with courage and may be drawn together in love, and so have the full wealth of assurance which true understanding brings. In this way they will know God's secret, which is Christ himself.[d] [3]He is the key that opens all the hidden treasures of God's wisdom and knowledge.

[4]I tell you, then, do not let anyone deceive you with false arguments, no matter how good they seem to be. [5]For even though I am absent in body, yet I am with you in spirit, and I am glad as I see the resolute firmness with which you stand together in your faith in Christ.

Fullness of Life in Christ

[6]Since you have accepted Christ Jesus as Lord, live in union with him. [7]Keep your roots deep in him, build your lives on him, and become stronger in your faith, as you were taught. And be filled with thanksgiving.

[8]See to it, then, that no one enslaves you by means of the worthless deceit of human wisdom, which comes from the teachings handed down by human beings and from the ruling spirits of the universe, and not from Christ. [9]For the full content of divine nature lives in Christ, in his humanity, [10]and you have been given full life in union with him.

He is supreme over every spiritual ruler and authority.

[11]In union with Christ you were circumcised, not with the circumcision that is made by human beings, but with the circumcision made by Christ, which consists of being freed from the power of this sinful self. [12]For when you were baptized, you were buried with Christ, and in baptism you were also raised with Christ through your faith in the active power of God, who raised him from death. [13]You were at one time spiritually dead because of your sins and because you were Gentiles without the Law. But God has now brought you to life with Christ. God forgave us all our sins; [14]he canceled the unfavorable record of our debts with its binding rules and did away with it completely by nailing it to the cross. [15]And on that cross Christ freed himself from the power of the spiritual rulers and authorities;[e] he made a public spectacle of them by leading them as captives in his victory procession.

[16]So let no one make rules about what you eat or drink or about holy days or the New Moon Festival or the Sabbath. [17]All such things are only a shadow of things in the future; the reality is Christ. [18]Do not allow yourselves to be condemned by anyone who claims to be superior because of special visions and who insists on false humility and the worship of angels. For no reason at all, such people are all puffed up by their human way of thinking [19]and have stopped holding on to Christ, who is the head of the body. Under Christ's control the whole body is nourished and held together by its joints and ligaments, and it grows as God wants it to grow.

---

d God's secret, which is Christ himself; *some manuscripts have* God's secret; *others have* the secret of God the Father of Christ; *others have* the secret of the God and Father, and of Christ.   *e* Christ freed himself from the power of the spiritual rulers and authorities; *or* Christ stripped the spiritual rulers and authorities of their power.

2.12 Ro 6.4   **2.13** Eph 2.1-5   **2.14** Eph 2.15   **2.16** Ro 14.1-6   **2.19** Eph 4.16

Dying and Living with Christ

20 You have died with Christ and are set free from the ruling spirits of the universe. Why, then, do you live as though you belonged to this world? Why do you obey such rules as **21** "Don't handle this," "Don't taste that," "Don't touch the other"? **22** All these refer to things which become useless once they are used; they are only human rules and teachings. **23** Of course such rules appear to be based on wisdom in their forced worship of angels, and false humility, and severe treatment of the body; but they have no real value in controlling physical passions.

3 You have been raised to life with Christ, so set your hearts on the things that are in heaven, where Christ sits on his throne at the right side of God. **2** Keep your minds fixed on things there, not on things here on earth. **3** For you have died, and your life is hidden with Christ in God. **4** Your real life is Christ and when he appears, then you too will appear with him and share his glory!

The Old Life and the New

5 You must put to death, then, the earthly desires at work in you, such as sexual immorality, indecency, lust, evil passions, and greed (for greed is a form of idolatry). **6** Because of such things God's anger will come upon those who do not obey him.*f* **7** At one time you yourselves used to live according to such desires, when your life was dominated by them.

8 But now you must get rid of all these things: anger, passion, and hateful feelings. No insults or obscene talk must ever come from your lips. **9** Do not lie to one another, for you have put off the old self with its habits **10** and have

put on the new self. This is the new being which God, its Creator, is constantly renewing in his own image, in order to bring you to a full knowledge of himself. **11** As a result, there is no longer any distinction between Gentiles and Jews, circumcised and uncircumcised, barbarians, savages, slaves, and free, but Christ is all, Christ is in all.

12 You are the people of God; he loved you and chose you for his own. So then, you must clothe yourselves with compassion, kindness, humility, gentleness, and patience. **13** Be tolerant with one another and forgive one another whenever any of you has a complaint against someone else. You must forgive one another just as the Lord has forgiven you. **14** And to all these qualities add love, which binds all things together in perfect unity. **15** The peace that Christ gives is to guide you in the decisions you make; for it is to this peace that God has called you together in the one body. And be thankful. **16** Christ's message in all its richness must live in your hearts. Teach and instruct one another with all wisdom. Sing psalms, hymns, and sacred songs; sing to God with thanksgiving in your hearts. **17** Everything you do or say, then, should be done in the name of the Lord Jesus, as you give thanks through him to God the Father.

Personal Relations in the New Life

18 Wives, submit yourselves to your husbands, for that is what you should do as Christians.

19 Husbands, love your wives and do not be harsh with them.

20 Children, it is your Christian duty to obey your parents always, for that is what pleases God.

21 Parents, do not irritate your chil-

---

f Some manuscripts do not have upon those who do not obey him.

3.1 Ps 110.1   **3.9** Eph 4.22   **3.10 a** Eph 4.24; **b** Gn 1.26   **3.12, 13** Eph 4.2   **3.13** Eph 4.32
3.16, 17 Eph 5.19, 20   **3.18** Eph 5.22; 1 P 3.1   **3.19** Eph 5.25; 1 P 3.7   **3.20** Eph 6.1
3.21 Eph 6.4

dren, or they will become discouraged.

²²Slaves, obey your human masters in all things, not only when they are watching you because you want to gain their approval; but do it with a sincere heart because of your reverence for the Lord. ²³Whatever you do, work at it with all your heart, as though you were working for the Lord and not for people. ²⁴Remember that the Lord will give you as a reward what he has kept for his people. For Christ is the real Master you serve. ²⁵And all wrongdoers will be repaid for the wrong things they do, because God judges everyone by the same standard.

4 Masters, be fair and just in the way you treat your slaves. Remember that you too have a Master in heaven.

Instructions

²Be persistent in prayer, and keep alert as you pray, giving thanks to God. ³At the same time pray also for us, so that God will give us a good opportunity to preach his message about the secret of Christ. For that is why I am now in prison. ⁴Pray, then, that I may speak, as I should, in such a way as to make it clear.

⁵Be wise in the way you act toward those who are not believers, making good use of every opportunity you have. ⁶Your speech should always be pleasant and interesting, and you should know how to give the right answer to everyone.

Final Greetings

⁷Our dear friend Tychicus, who is a faithful worker and fellow servant in the Lord's work, will give you all the news about me. ⁸That is why I am sending him to you, in order to cheer you up by telling you how all of us are getting along. ⁹With him goes Onesimus, that dear and faithful friend, who belongs to your group. They will tell you everything that is happening here.

¹⁰Aristarchus, who is in prison with me, sends you greetings, and so does Mark, the cousin of Barnabas. (You have already received instructions to welcome Mark if he comes your way.) ¹¹Joshua, also called Justus, sends greetings too. These three are the only Jewish believers who work with me for the Kingdom of God, and they have been a great help to me.

¹²Greetings from Epaphras, another member of your group and a servant of Christ Jesus. He always prays fervently for you, asking God to make you stand firm, as mature and fully convinced Christians, in complete obedience to God's will. ¹³I can personally testify to his hard work for you and for the people in Laodicea and Hierapolis. ¹⁴Luke, our dear doctor, and Demas send you their greetings.

¹⁵Give our best wishes to the believers in Laodicea and to Nympha and the church that meets in her house.^g ¹⁶After you read this letter, make sure that it is read also in the church at Laodicea. At the same time, you are to read the letter that the believers in Laodicea will send you. ¹⁷And tell Archippus, "Be sure to finish the task you were given in the Lord's service."

¹⁸With my own hand I write this: *Greetings from Paul.* Do not forget my chains!

May God's grace be with you.

---

g Nympha . . . her house; *some manuscripts have* Nymphas . . . his house.

3.22-25 Eph 6.5-8   **3.25** Dt 10.17; Eph 6.9   **4.1** Eph 6.9   **4.5** Eph 5.16   **4.6** Ws 8.12
4.7 Ac 20.4; 2 Ti 4.12   **4.7, 8** Eph 6.21, 22   **4.9** Phm 10-12   **4.10 a** Ac 19.29; 27.2;
Phm 24; **b** Ac 12.12, 25; 13.13; 15.37-39   **4.12** Col 1.7; Phm 23   **4.14 a** 2 Ti 4.11;
Phm 24; **b** 2 Ti 4.10; Phm 24   **4.17** Phm 2

Paul's First Letter to the
THESSALONIANS

INTRODUCTION

Thessalonica was the capital city of the Roman province of Macedonia. Paul established a church there after he left Philippi. Soon, however, there was opposition from Jews who were jealous of Paul's success in preaching the Christian message among the non-Jews who had become interested in Judaism. Paul was forced to leave Thessalonica and go on to Berea. Later on, after he reached Corinth, Paul received a personal report from his companion and fellow worker Timothy about the situation in the church at Thessalonica.

Paul's First Letter to the Thessalonians was then written to encourage and reassure the Christians there. He gives thanks for the news about their faith and love; he reminds them of the kind of life he had lived while he was with them, and then answers questions that had arisen in the church about the return of Christ: Could a believer who died before Christ's return still share in the eternal life that his return will bring? And when will Christ come again? Paul takes this occasion to tell them to go on working quietly while waiting in hope for Christ's return.

OUTLINE OF CONTENTS

---

1 From Paul, Silas, and Timothy —
To the people of the church in Thessalonica, who belong to God the Father and the Lord Jesus Christ:
May grace and peace be yours.

The Life and Faith of the Thessalonians

2 We always thank God for you all and always mention you in our prayers. 3 For we remember before our God and Father how you put your faith into practice, how your love made you work so hard, and how your hope in our Lord Jesus Christ is firm. 4 Our friends, we know that God loves you and has chosen you to be his own. 5 For we brought the Good News to you, not with words only, but also with power and the Holy Spirit, and with complete conviction of its truth. You know how we lived when we were with you; it was for your own good. 6 You imitated us and the Lord; and even though you suffered much, you received the message with the joy that comes from the Holy Spirit. 7 So

1.1 Ac 17.1   1.6 Ac 17.5-9

you became an example to all believers in Macedonia and Achaia. [8] For not only did the message about the Lord go out from you throughout Macedonia and Achaia, but the news about your faith in God has gone everywhere. There is nothing, then, that we need to say. [9] All those people speak about how you received us when we visited you, and how you turned away from idols to God, to serve the true and living God [10] and to wait for his Son to come from heaven — his Son Jesus, whom he raised from death and who rescues us from God's anger that is coming.

Paul's Work in Thessalonica

2 Our friends, you yourselves know that our visit to you was not a failure. [2] You know how we had already been mistreated and insulted in Philippi before we came to you in Thessalonica. And even though there was much opposition, our God gave us courage to tell you the Good News that comes from him. [3] Our appeal to you is not based on error or impure motives, nor do we try to trick anyone. [4] Instead, we always speak as God wants us to, because he has judged us worthy to be entrusted with the Good News. We do not try to please people, but to please God, who tests our motives. [5] You know very well that we did not come to you with flattering talk, nor did we use words to cover up greed — God is our witness! [6] We did not try to get praise from anyone, either from you or from others, [7] even though as apostles of Christ we could have made demands on you. But we were gentle when we were with you, like a mother[a] taking care of her children. [8] Because of our love for you we were ready to share with you not only the Good News from God but even

our own lives. You were so dear to us! [9] Surely you remember, our friends, how we worked and toiled! We worked day and night so that we would not be any trouble to you as we preached to you the Good News from God.

[10] You are our witnesses, and so is God, that our conduct toward you who believe was pure, right, and without fault. [11] You know that we treated each one of you just as parents treat their own children. [12] We encouraged you, we comforted you, and we kept urging you to live the kind of life that pleases God, who calls you to share in his own Kingdom and glory.

[13] And there is another reason why we always give thanks to God. When we brought you God's message, you heard it and accepted it, not as a message from human beings but as God's message, which indeed it is. For God is at work in you who believe. [14] Our friends, the same things happened to you that happened to the churches of God in Judea, to the people there who belong to Christ Jesus. You suffered the same persecutions from your own people that they suffered from the Jews, [15] who killed the Lord Jesus and the prophets, and persecuted us. How displeasing they are to God! How hostile they are to everyone! [16] They even tried to stop us from preaching to the Gentiles the message that would bring them salvation. In this way they have brought to completion all the sins they have always committed. And now God's anger has at last come down on them!

Paul's Desire to Visit Them Again

[17] As for us, friends, when we were separated from you for a little while — not in our thoughts, of course, but only in body — how we missed you and how

---

[a] we were gentle when we were with you, like a mother; *some manuscripts have* we were like children when we were with you; we were like a mother.

2.2 a Ac 16.19-24; **b** Ac 17.1-9   **2.14** Ac 17.5   **2.15** Ac 9.23, 29; 13.45, 50; 14.2, 5, 19; 17.5, 13; 18.12

hard we tried to see you again! ¹⁸ We wanted to return to you. I myself tried to go back more than once, but Satan would not let us. ¹⁹ After all, it is you — you, no less than others! — who are our hope, our joy, and our reason for boasting of our victory in the presence of our Lord Jesus when he comes. ²⁰ Indeed, you are our pride and our joy!

3 Finally, we could not bear it any longer. So we decided to stay on alone in Athens ² while we sent Timothy, our brother who works with us for God in preaching the Good News about Christ. We sent him to strengthen you and help your faith, ³ so that none of you should turn back because of these persecutions. You yourselves know that such persecutions are part of God's will for us. ⁴ For while we were still with you, we told you ahead of time that we were going to be persecuted; and as you well know, that is exactly what happened. ⁵ That is why I had to send Timothy. I could not bear it any longer, so I sent him to find out about your faith. Surely it could not be that the Devil had tempted you and all our work had been for nothing!

⁶ Now Timothy has come back, and he has brought us the welcome news about your faith and love. He has told us that you always think well of us and that you want to see us just as much as we want to see you. ⁷ So, in all our trouble and suffering we have been encouraged about you, friends. It was your faith that encouraged us, ⁸ because now we really live if you stand firm in your life in union with the Lord. ⁹ Now we can give thanks to our God for you. We thank him for the joy we have in his presence because of you. ¹⁰ Day and night we ask him with all our heart to let us see you personally and supply what is needed in your faith.

¹¹ May our God and Father himself

and our Lord Jesus prepare the way for us to come to you! ¹² May the Lord make your love for one another and for all people grow more and more and become as great as our love for you. ¹³ In this way he will strengthen you, and you will be perfect and holy in the presence of our God and Father when our Lord Jesus comes with all who belong to him.[b]

A Life That Pleases God

4 Finally, our friends, you learned from us how you should live in order to please God. This is, of course, the way you have been living. And now we beg and urge you in the name of the Lord Jesus to do even more. ² For you know the instructions we gave you by the authority of the Lord Jesus. ³ God wants you to be holy and completely free from sexual immorality. ⁴ Each of you should know how to live with your wife[c] in a holy and honorable way, ⁵ not with a lustful desire, like the heathen who do not know God. ⁶ In this matter, then, none of you should do wrong to other Christians or take advantage of them. We have told you this before, and we strongly warned you that the Lord will punish those who do that. ⁷ God did not call us to live in immorality, but in holiness. ⁸ So then, whoever rejects this teaching is not rejecting a human being, but God, who gives you his Holy Spirit.

⁹ There is no need to write you about love for each other. You yourselves have been taught by God how you should love one another. ¹⁰ And you have, in fact, behaved like this toward all the believers in all of Macedonia. So we beg you, our friends, to do even more. ¹¹ Make it your aim to live a quiet life, to mind your own business, and to earn your own living, just as we told

---

b all who belong to him; *or* all his angels. body.

3.1 Ac 17.15   **3.6** Ac 18.5

c live with your wife; *or* control your

you before. [12] In this way you will win the respect of those who are not believers, and you will not have to depend on anyone for what you need.

The Lord's Coming

[13] Our friends, we want you to know the truth about those who have died, so that you will not be sad, as are those who have no hope. [14] We believe that Jesus died and rose again, and so we believe that God will take back with Jesus those who have died believing in him.

[15] What we are teaching you now is the Lord's teaching: we who are alive on the day the Lord comes will not go ahead of those who have died. [16] There will be the shout of command, the archangel's voice, the sound of God's trumpet, and the Lord himself will come down from heaven. Those who have died believing in Christ will rise to life first; [17] then we who are living at that time will be gathered up along with them in the clouds to meet the Lord in the air. And so we will always be with the Lord. [18] So then, encourage one another with these words.

Be Ready for the Lord's Coming

5 There is no need to write you, friends, about the times and occasions when these things will happen. [2] For you yourselves know very well that the Day of the Lord will come as a thief comes at night. [3] When people say, "Everything is quiet and safe," then suddenly destruction will hit them! It will come as suddenly as the pains that come upon a woman in labor, and people will not escape. [4] But you, friends, are not in the darkness, and the Day should not take you by surprise like a thief. [5] All of you are people who belong to the light, who belong to the day. We

do not belong to the night or to the darkness. [6] So then, we should not be sleeping like the others; we should be awake and sober. [7] It is at night when people sleep; it is at night when they get drunk. [8] But we belong to the day, and we should be sober. We must wear faith and love as a breastplate, and our hope of salvation as a helmet. [9] God did not choose us to suffer his anger, but to possess salvation through our Lord Jesus Christ, [10] who died for us in order that we might live together with him, whether we are alive or dead when he comes. [11] And so encourage one another and help one another, just as you are now doing.

Final Instructions and Greetings

[12] We beg you, our friends, to pay proper respect to those who work among you, who guide and instruct you in the Christian life. [13] Treat them with the greatest respect and love because of the work they do. Be at peace among yourselves.

[14] We urge you, our friends, to warn the idle, encourage the timid, help the weak, be patient with everyone. [15] See that no one pays back wrong for wrong, but at all times make it your aim to do good to one another and to all people.

[16] Be joyful always, [17] pray at all times, [18] be thankful in all circumstances. This is what God wants from you in your life in union with Christ Jesus.

[19] Do not restrain the Holy Spirit; [20] do not despise inspired messages. [21] Put all things to the test: keep what is good [22] and avoid every kind of evil.

[23] May the God who gives us peace make you holy in every way and keep your whole being — spirit, soul, and body — free from every fault at the coming of our Lord Jesus Christ. [24] He who calls you will do it, because he is faithful.

4.15-17 1 Co 15.51, 52   **4.15** Si 48.11   **4.16** 2 Esd 6.23   **5.2** Mt 24.43; Lk 12.39; 2 P 3.10
5.8 Is 59.17; Eph 6.13-17

25 Pray also for us, friends.
26 Greet all the believers with the kiss of peace.
27 I urge you by the authority of the Lord to read this letter to all the believers.
28 The grace of our Lord Jesus Christ be with you.

Paul's Second Letter to the
THESSALONIANS

INTRODUCTION

Confusion over the expected return of Christ continued to cause disturbances in the church at Thessalonica. *Paul's Second Letter to the Thessalonians* deals with the belief that the day of the Lord's coming had already arrived. Paul corrects this idea, pointing out that before Christ returns, evil and wickedness will reach a climax under the leadership of a mysterious figure called "the Wicked One," who would be opposed to Christ.

The apostle emphasizes the need for his readers to remain steady in their faith in spite of trouble and suffering, to work for a living as did Paul and his fellow workers, and to persevere in doing good.

OUTLINE OF CONTENTS

1 From Paul, Silas, and Timothy — To the people of the church in Thessalonica, who belong to God our Father and the Lord Jesus Christ:
2 May God our Father and the Lord Jesus Christ give you grace and peace.

The Judgment at Christ's Coming

3 Our friends, we must thank God at all times for you. It is right for us to do so, because your faith is growing so much and the love each of you has for the others is becoming greater. 4 That is why we ourselves boast about you in the churches of God. We boast about the way you continue to endure and believe through all the persecutions and sufferings you are experiencing.

5 All of this proves that God's judgment is just and as a result you will become worthy of his Kingdom, for which you are suffering. 6 God will do what is

right: he will bring suffering on those who make you suffer, [7]and he will give relief to you who suffer and to us as well. He will do this when the Lord Jesus appears from heaven with his mighty angels, [8]with a flaming fire, to punish those who reject God and who do not obey the Good News about our Lord Jesus. [9]They will suffer the punishment of eternal destruction, separated from the presence of the Lord and from his glorious might, [10]when he comes on that Day to receive glory from all his people and honor from all who believe. You too will be among them, because you have believed the message that we told you. [11]That is why we always pray for you. We ask our God to make you worthy of the life he has called you to live. May he fulfill by his power all your desire for goodness and complete your work of faith. [12]In this way the name of our Lord Jesus will receive glory from you, and you from him, by the grace of our God and of the Lord[a] Jesus Christ.

The Wicked One

2 Concerning the coming of our Lord Jesus Christ and our being gathered together to be with him: I beg you, my friends, [2]not to be so easily confused in your thinking or upset by the claim that the Day of the Lord has come. Perhaps it is thought that we said this while prophesying or preaching, or that we wrote it in a letter. [3]Do not let anyone deceive you in any way. For the Day will not come until the final Rebellion takes place and the Wicked One appears, who is destined to hell. [4]He will oppose every so-called god or object of worship and will put himself above them all. He will even go in and sit down in God's Temple and claim to be God.

[5]Don't you remember? I told you all this while I was with you. [6]Yet there is something that keeps this from happening now, and you know what it is. At the proper time, then, the Wicked One will appear. [7]The Mysterious Wickedness is already at work, but what is going to happen will not happen until the one who holds it back is taken out of the way. [8]Then the Wicked One will be revealed, but when the Lord Jesus comes, he will kill him with the breath from his mouth and destroy him with his dazzling presence. [9]The Wicked One will come with the power of Satan and perform all kinds of false miracles and wonders, [10]and use every kind of wicked deceit on those who will perish. They will perish because they did not welcome and love the truth so as to be saved. [11]And so God sends the power of error to work in them so that they believe what is false. [12]The result is that all who have not believed the truth, but have taken pleasure in sin, will be condemned.

You Are Chosen for Salvation

[13]We must thank God at all times for you, friends, you whom the Lord loves. For God chose you as the first[b] to be saved by the Spirit's power to make you his holy people and by your faith in the truth. [14]God called you to this through the Good News we preached to you; he called you to possess your share of the glory of our Lord Jesus Christ. [15]So then, our friends, stand firm and hold on to those truths which we taught you, both in our preaching and in our letter.

[16]May our Lord Jesus Christ himself and God our Father, who loved us and in his grace gave us unfailing courage and a firm hope, [17]encourage you and strengthen you to always do and say what is good.

---

[a] our God and of the Lord; *or* our God and Lord.　　[b] as the first; *some manuscripts have* from the beginning.

1.9 Is 2.10　**2.1** 1 Th 4.15-17　**2.4** Dn 11.36; Ez 28.2　**2.8** Is 11.4　**2.9** Mt 24.24

Pray for Us

3 Finally, our friends, pray for us that the Lord's message may continue to spread rapidly and be received with honor, just as it was among you. [2] Pray also that God will rescue us from wicked and evil people; for not everyone believes the message.

[3] But the Lord is faithful, and he will strengthen you and keep you safe from the Evil One. [4] And the Lord gives us confidence in you, and we are sure that you are doing and will continue to do what we tell you.

[5] May the Lord lead you into a greater understanding of God's love and the endurance that is given by Christ.

The Obligation to Work

[6] Our friends, we command you in the name of our Lord Jesus Christ to keep away from all believers who are living a lazy life and who do not follow the instructions that we gave them. [7] You yourselves know very well that you should do just what we did. We were not lazy when we were with you. [8] We did not accept anyone's support without paying for it. Instead, we worked and toiled; we kept working day and night so as not to be an expense to any of you. [9] We did this, not because we do not have the right to demand our support; we did it to be an example for you to follow. [10] While we were with you, we used to tell you, "Whoever refuses to work is not allowed to eat."

[11] We say this because we hear that there are some people among you who live lazy lives and who do nothing except meddle in other people's business. [12] In the name of the Lord Jesus Christ we command these people and warn them to lead orderly lives and work to earn their own living.

[13] But you, friends, must not become tired of doing good. [14] It may be that some there will not obey the message we send you in this letter. If so, take note of them and have nothing to do with them, so that they will be ashamed. [15] But do not treat them as enemies; instead, warn them as believers.

Do not treat them as enemies. (3.15)

Final Words

[16] May the Lord himself, who is our source of peace, give you peace at all times and in every way. The Lord be with you all.

[17] With my own hand I write this: *Greetings from Paul.* This is the way I sign every letter; this is how I write.

[18] May the grace of our Lord Jesus Christ be with you all.

Paul's First Letter to
TIMOTHY

INTRODUCTION

Timothy, a young Christian from Asia Minor, was the son of a Jewish mother and a Greek father. He became a companion and assistant to Paul in his missionary work. *Paul's First Letter to Timothy* deals with three main concerns.

The letter is first of all a warning against false teaching in the church. This teaching, a mixture of Jewish and non-Jewish ideas, was based on the belief that the physical world is evil and that one can attain salvation only by special secret knowledge and by practices such as avoiding certain foods and not marrying. The letter also contains instructions about church administration and worship, with a description of the kind of character that church leaders and helpers should have. Finally, Timothy is advised how to be a good servant of Jesus Christ and about the responsibilities that he has toward various groups of believers.

OUTLINE OF CONTENTS

---

1 From Paul, an apostle of Christ Jesus by order of God our Savior and Christ Jesus our hope —

² To Timothy, my true son in the faith:

May God the Father and Christ Jesus our Lord give you grace, mercy, and peace.

Warnings against False Teaching

³ I want you to stay in Ephesus, just as I urged you when I was on my way to Macedonia. Some people there are teaching false doctrines, and you must order them to stop. ⁴ Tell them to give up those legends and those long lists of ancestors, which only produce arguments; they do not serve God's plan, which is known by faith. ⁵ The purpose of this order is to arouse the love that comes from a pure heart, a clear conscience, and a genuine faith. ⁶ Some people have turned away from these and have lost their way in foolish discussions. ⁷ They want to be teachers of God's law, but they do not understand their own words or the matters about which they speak with so much confidence.

⁸ We know that the Law is good if it is used as it should be used. ⁹ It must be remembered, of course, that laws are made, not for good people, but for lawbreakers and criminals, for the godless and sinful, for those who are not religious or spiritual, for those who kill their fathers or mothers, for murderers, ¹⁰ for the immoral, for sexual perverts,

for kidnappers, for those who lie and give false testimony or who do anything else contrary to sound doctrine. [11] That teaching is found in the gospel that was entrusted to me to announce, the Good News from the glorious and blessed God.

Gratitude for God's Mercy

[12] I give thanks to Christ Jesus our Lord, who has given me strength for my work. I thank him for considering me worthy and appointing me to serve him, [13] even though in the past I spoke evil of him and persecuted and insulted him. But God was merciful to me because I did not yet have faith and so did not know what I was doing. [14] And our Lord poured out his abundant grace on me and gave me the faith and love which are ours in union with Christ Jesus. [15] This is a true saying, to be completely accepted and believed: Christ Jesus came into the world to save sinners. I am the worst of them, [16] but God was merciful to me in order that Christ Jesus might show his full patience in dealing with me, the worst of sinners, as an example for all those who would later believe in him and receive eternal life. [17] To the eternal King, immortal and invisible, the only God — to him be honor and glory forever and ever! Amen.

[18] Timothy, my child, I entrust to you this command, which is in accordance with the words of prophecy spoken in the past about you. Use those words as weapons in order to fight well, [19] and keep your faith and a clear conscience. Some people have not listened to their conscience and have made a ruin of their faith. [20] Among them are Hymenaeus and Alexander, whom I have punished by handing them over to the power of Satan; this will teach them to stop their blasphemy.

Church Worship

2 First of all, then, I urge that petitions, prayers, requests, and thanksgivings be offered to God for all

Christ Jesus came into the world to save sinners. (1.15)

people; [2] for kings and all others who are in authority, that we may live a quiet and peaceful life with all reverence toward God and with proper conduct. [3] This is good and it pleases God our Savior, [4] who wants everyone to be saved and to come to know the truth. [5] For there is one God, and there is one who brings God and human beings together, the man Christ Jesus, [6] who gave himself to redeem the whole human race. That was the proof at the right time that God wants everyone to be saved, [7] and that is why I was sent as an apostle and teacher of the Gentiles, to proclaim the message of faith and

1.13 Ac 8.3; 9.4, 5   **2.7** 2 Ti 1.11

truth. I am not lying; I am telling the truth!

8 In every church service I want the men to pray, men who are dedicated to God and can lift up their hands in prayer without anger or argument. 9 I also want the women to be modest and sensible about their clothes and to dress properly; not with fancy hair styles or with gold ornaments or pearls or expensive dresses, 10 but with good deeds, as is proper for women who claim to be religious. 11 Women should learn in silence and all humility. 12 I do not allow them to teach or to have authority over men; they must keep quiet. 13 For Adam was created first, and then Eve. 14 And it was not Adam who was deceived; it was the woman who was deceived and broke God's law. 15 But a woman will be saved through having children,*a* if she perseveres*b* in faith and love and holiness, with modesty.

Leaders in the Church

3 This is a true saying: If a man is eager to be a church leader, he desires an excellent work. 2 A church leader must be without fault; he must have only one wife,*c* be sober, self-controlled, and orderly; he must welcome strangers in his home; he must be able to teach; 3 he must not be a drunkard or a violent man, but gentle and peaceful; he must not love money; 4 he must be able to manage his own family well and make his children obey him with all respect. 5 For if a man does not know how to manage his own family, how can he take care of the church of God? 6 He must be mature in the faith, so that he will not swell up with pride and be condemned, as the Devil was. 7 He should be a man who is re-

spected by the people outside the church, so that he will not be disgraced and fall into the Devil's trap.

Helpers in the Church

8 Church helpers must also have a good character and be sincere; they must not drink too much wine or be greedy for money; 9 they should hold to the revealed truth of the faith with a clear conscience. 10 They should be tested first, and then, if they pass the test, they are to serve. 11 Their wives*d* also must be of good character and must not gossip; they must be sober and honest in everything. 12 A church helper must have only one wife,*e* and be able to manage his children and family well. 13 Those helpers who do their work well win for themselves a good standing and are able to speak boldly about their faith in Christ Jesus.

The Great Secret

14 As I write this letter to you, I hope to come and see you soon. 15 But if I delay, this letter will let you know how we should conduct ourselves in God's household, which is the church of the living God, the pillar and support of the truth. 16 No one can deny how great is the secret of our religion:

He appeared in human form,
was shown to be right by
the Spirit,*f*
and was seen by angels.
He was preached among the
nations,
was believed in throughout
the world,
and was taken up to
heaven.

---

a will be saved through having children; *or* will be kept safe through childbirth.　*b* if she perseveres; *or* if they persevere.　*c* have only one wife; *or* be married only once.　*d* Their wives; *or* Women helpers.　*e* have only one wife; *or* be married only once.　*f* was shown to be right by the Spirit; *or* and, in spiritual form, was shown to be right.
2.9 1 P 3.3　**2.13 a** Gn 2.7; **b** Gn 2.21, 22　**2.14** Gn 3.1-6　**3.2-7** Titus 1.6-9

False Teachers

4 The Spirit says clearly that some people will abandon the faith in later times; they will obey lying spirits and follow the teachings of demons. ²Such teachings are spread by deceitful liars, whose consciences are dead, as if burnt with a hot iron. ³Such people teach that it is wrong to marry and to eat certain foods. But God created those foods to be eaten, after a prayer of thanks, by those who are believers and have come to know the truth. ⁴Everything that God has created is good; nothing is to be rejected, but everything is to be received with a prayer of thanks, ⁵because the word of God and the prayer make it acceptable to God.

A Good Servant of Christ Jesus

⁶If you give these instructions to the believers, you will be a good servant of Christ Jesus, as you feed yourself spiritually on the words of faith and of the true teaching which you have followed. ⁷But keep away from those godless legends, which are not worth telling. Keep yourself in training for a godly life. ⁸Physical exercise has some value, but spiritual exercise is valuable in every way, because it promises life both for the present and for the future. ⁹This is a true saying, to be completely accepted and believed. ¹⁰We struggle*g* and work hard, because we have placed our hope in the living God, who is the Savior of all and especially of those who believe.

¹¹Give them these instructions and these teachings. ¹²Do not let anyone look down on you because you are young, but be an example for the believers in your speech, your conduct, your love, faith, and purity. ¹³Until I come, give your time and effort to the public reading of the Scriptures and to preaching and teaching. ¹⁴Do not ne-glect the spiritual gift that is in you, which was given to you when the prophets spoke and the elders laid their hands on you. ¹⁵Practice these things and devote yourself to them, in order that your progress may be seen by all. ¹⁶Watch yourself and watch your teaching. Keep on doing these things, because if you do, you will save both yourself and those who hear you.

Responsibilities toward Believers

5 Do not rebuke an older man, but appeal to him as if he were your father. Treat the younger men as your brothers, ²the older women as mothers, and the younger women as sisters, with all purity.

³Show respect for widows who really are all alone. ⁴But if a widow has children or grandchildren, they should learn first to carry out their religious duties toward their own family and in this way repay their parents and grandparents, because that is what pleases God. ⁵A widow who is all alone, with no one to take care of her, has placed her hope in God and continues to pray and ask him for his help night and day. ⁶But a widow who gives herself to pleasure has already died, even though she lives. ⁷Give them these instructions, so that no one will find fault with them. ⁸But if any do not take care of their relatives, especially the members of their own family, they have denied the faith and are worse than an unbeliever.

⁹Do not add any widow to the list of widows unless she is over sixty years of age. In addition, she must have been married only once*h* ¹⁰and have a reputation for good deeds: a woman who brought up her children well, received strangers in her home, performed humble duties for other Christians, helped

g struggle; *some manuscripts have* are reviled.   *h* married only once; *or* faithful to
her husband.
5.5 Jdt 8.4-6

people in trouble, and devoted herself to doing good.

11 But do not include younger widows in the list; because when their desires make them want to marry, they turn away from Christ, 12 and so become guilty of breaking their earlier promise to him. 13 They also learn to waste their time in going around from house to house; but even worse, they learn to be gossips and busybodies, talking of things they should not. 14 So I would prefer that the younger widows get married, have children, and take care of their homes, so as to give our enemies no chance of speaking evil of us. 15 For some widows have already turned away to follow Satan. 16 But if any Christian woman has widows in her family, she must take care of them and not put the burden on the church, so that it may take care of the widows who are all alone.

17 The elders who do good work as leaders should be considered worthy of receiving double pay, especially those who work hard at preaching and teaching. 18 For the scripture says, "Do not muzzle an ox when you are using it to thresh grain" and "Workers should be given their pay." 19 Do not listen to an accusation against an elder unless it is brought by two or more witnesses. 20 Rebuke publicly all those who commit sins, so that the rest may be afraid.

21 In the presence of God and of Christ Jesus and of the holy angels I solemnly call upon you to obey these instructions without showing any prejudice or favor to anyone in anything you do. 22 Be in no hurry to lay hands on people to dedicate them to the Lord's service. Take no part in the sins of others; keep yourself pure.

23 Do not drink water only, but take a little wine to help your digestion, since you are sick so often.

24 The sins of some people are plain to see, and their sins go ahead of them to judgment; but the sins of others are seen only later. 25 In the same way good deeds are plainly seen, and even those that are not so plain cannot be hidden.

6 Those who are slaves must consider their masters worthy of all respect, so that no one will speak evil of the name of God and of our teaching. 2 Slaves belonging to Christian masters must not despise them, for they are believers too. Instead, they are to serve them even better, because those who benefit from their work are believers whom they love.

False Teaching and True Riches

You must teach and preach these things. 3 Whoever teaches a different doctrine and does not agree with the true words of our Lord Jesus Christ and with the teaching of our religion 4 is swollen with pride and knows nothing. He has an unhealthy desire to argue and quarrel about words, and this brings on jealousy, disputes, insults, evil suspicions, 5 and constant arguments from people whose minds do not function and who no longer have the truth. They think that religion is a way to become rich.

6 Well, religion does make us very rich, if we are satisfied with what we have. 7 What did we bring into the world? Nothing! What can we take out of the world? Nothing! 8 So then, if we have food and clothes, that should be enough for us. 9 But those who want to get rich fall into temptation and are caught in the trap of many foolish and harmful desires, which pull them down to ruin and destruction. 10 For the love of money is a source of all kinds of evil. Some have been so eager to have it that they have wandered away from the faith and have broken their hearts with many sorrows.

5.18 a Dt 25.4; **b** Mt 10.10; Lk 10.7   **5.19** Dt 17.6; 19.15

Personal Instructions

11 But you, man of God, avoid all these things. Strive for righteousness, godliness, faith, love, endurance, and gentleness. **12** Run your best in the race of faith, and win eternal life for yourself; for it was to this life that God called you when you firmly professed your faith before many witnesses. **13** Before God, who gives life to all things, and before Christ Jesus, who firmly professed his faith before Pontius Pilate, I command you **14** to obey your orders and keep them faithfully until the Day when our Lord Jesus Christ will appear. **15** His appearing will be brought about at the right time by God, the blessed and only Ruler, the King of kings and the Lord of lords. **16** He alone is immortal; he lives in the light that no one can approach. No one has ever seen him; no one can ever see him.

6.13 Jn 18.37

To him be honor and eternal power! Amen.

17 Command those who are rich in the things of this life not to be proud, but to place their hope, not in such an uncertain thing as riches, but in God, who generously gives us everything for our enjoyment. **18** Command them to do good, to be rich in good works, to be generous and ready to share with others. **19** In this way they will store up for themselves a treasure which will be a solid foundation for the future. And then they will be able to win the life which is true life.

20 Timothy, keep safe what has been entrusted to your care. Avoid the profane talk and foolish arguments of what some people wrongly call "Knowledge." **21** For some have claimed to possess it, and as a result they have lost the way of faith.

God's grace be with you all.

Paul's Second Letter to
TIMOTHY

INTRODUCTION

Paul's Second Letter to Timothy consists largely of personal advice to Timothy, as a younger colleague and assistant. The main theme is endurance. Timothy is advised and encouraged to keep on witnessing faithfully to Jesus Christ, to hold to the true teaching of the Good News and the Old Testament, and to do his duty as teacher and evangelist, all in the face of suffering and opposition.

Timothy is especially warned about the dangers of becoming involved in "foolish and ignorant arguments" that do no good, but only ruin the people who listen to them.

In all this, Timothy is reminded of the example of the writer's own life and purpose — his faith, patience, love, endurance, and suffering in persecution.

OUTLINE OF CONTENTS

1 From Paul, an apostle of Christ Jesus by God's will, sent to proclaim the promised life which we have in union with Christ Jesus —

² To Timothy, my dear son:

May God the Father and Christ Jesus our Lord give you grace, mercy, and peace.

Thanksgiving and Encouragement

³ I give thanks to God, whom I serve with a clear conscience, as my ancestors did. I thank him as I remember you always in my prayers night and day. ⁴ I remember your tears, and I want to see you very much, so that I may be filled with joy. ⁵ I remember the sincere faith you have, the kind of faith that your grandmother Lois and your mother Eunice also had. I am sure that you have it also. ⁶ For this reason I remind you to keep alive the gift that God gave you when I laid my hands on you. ⁷ For the Spirit that God has given us does not make us timid; instead, his Spirit fills us with power, love, and self-control.

⁸ Do not be ashamed, then, of witnessing for our Lord; neither be ashamed of me, a prisoner for Christ's sake. Instead, take your part in suffering for the Good News, as God gives you the strength for it. ⁹ He saved us and called us to be his own people, not because of what we have done, but because of his own purpose and grace. He gave us this grace by means of Christ Jesus before the beginning of time,

¹⁰but now it has been revealed to us through the coming of our Savior, Christ Jesus. He has ended the power of death and through the gospel has revealed immortal life.

¹¹God has appointed me as an apostle and teacher to proclaim the Good News, ¹²and it is for this reason that I suffer these things. But I am still full of confidence, because I know whom I have trusted, and I am sure that he is able to keep safe until that Day what he has entrusted to me.ᵃ ¹³Hold firmly to the true words that I taught you, as the example for you to follow, and remain in the faith and love that are ours in union with Christ Jesus. ¹⁴Through the power of the Holy Spirit, who lives in us, keep the good things that have been entrusted to you.

¹⁵You know that everyone in the province of Asia, including Phygelus and Hermogenes, has deserted me. ¹⁶May the Lord show mercy to the family of Onesiphorus, because he cheered me up many times. He was not ashamed that I am in prison, ¹⁷but as soon as he arrived in Rome, he started looking for me until he found me. ¹⁸May the Lord grant him his mercy on that Day! And you know very well how much he did for me in Ephesus.

A Loyal Soldier of Christ Jesus

2 As for you, my son, be strong through the grace that is ours in union with Christ Jesus. ²Take the teachings that you heard me proclaim in the presence of many witnesses, and entrust them to reliable people, who will be able to teach others also.

³Take your part in suffering, as a loyal soldier of Christ Jesus. ⁴A soldier on active duty wants to please his commanding officer and so does not get mixed up in the affairs of civilian life. ⁵An athlete who runs in a race cannot win the prize unless he obeys the rules. ⁶The farmer who has done the hard work should have the first share of the harvest. ⁷Think about what I am saying, because the Lord will enable you to understand it all.

⁸Remember Jesus Christ, who was raised from death, who was a descendant of David, as is taught in the Good News I preach. ⁹Because I preach the Good News, I suffer and I am even chained like a criminal. But the word of God is not in chains, ¹⁰and so I endure everything for the sake of God's chosen people, in order that they too may obtain the salvation that comes through Christ Jesus and brings eternal glory. ¹¹This is a true saying:

"If we have died with him,
      we shall also live with him.
¹²If we continue to endure,
      we shall also rule with him.
If we deny him,
      he also will deny us.
¹³If we are not faithful,
      he remains faithful,
      because he cannot be false
      to himself."

An Approved Worker

¹⁴Remind your people of this, and give them a solemn warning in God's presence not to fight over words. It does no good, but only ruins the people who listen. ¹⁵Do your best to win full approval in God's sight, as a worker who is not ashamed of his work, one who correctly teaches the message of God's truth. ¹⁶Keep away from profane and foolish discussions, which only drive people farther away from God. ¹⁷Such teaching is like an open sore that eats away the flesh. Two men who have taught such things are Hymenaeus and Philetus. ¹⁸They have left the way of truth and are upsetting the faith of some believers by saying that our resur-

---

ᵃ what he has entrusted to me; *or* what I have entrusted to him.
1.11 1 Ti 2.7   **2.12** Mt 10.33; Lk 12.9

rection has already taken place. [19]But the solid foundation that God has laid cannot be shaken; and on it are written these words: "The Lord knows those who are his" and "Those who say that they belong to the Lord must turn away from wrongdoing."

[20]In a large house there are dishes and bowls of all kinds: some are made of silver and gold, others of wood and clay; some are for special occasions, others for ordinary use. [21]Those who make themselves clean from all those evil things, will be used for special purposes, because they are dedicated and useful to their Master, ready to be used for every good deed. [22]Avoid the passions of youth, and strive for righteousness, faith, love, and peace, together with those who with a pure heart call out to the Lord for help. [23]But keep away from foolish and ignorant arguments; you know that they end up in quarrels. [24]As the Lord's servant, you must not quarrel. You must be kind toward all, a good and patient teacher, [25]who is gentle as you correct your opponents, for it may be that God will give them the opportunity to repent and come to know the truth. [26]And then they will come to their senses and escape from the trap of the Devil, who had caught them and made them obey his will.

The Last Days

3 Remember that there will be difficult times in the last days. [2]People will be selfish, greedy, boastful, and conceited; they will be insulting, disobedient to their parents, ungrateful, and irreligious; [3]they will be unkind, merciless, slanderers, violent, and fierce; they will hate the good; [4]they will be treacherous, reckless, and swollen with pride; they will love pleasure

rather than God; [5]they will hold to the outward form of our religion, but reject its real power. Keep away from such people. [6]Some of them go into people's houses and gain control over weak women who are burdened by the guilt of their sins and driven by all kinds of desires, [7]women who are always trying to learn but who can never come to know the truth. [8]As Jannes and Jambres were opposed to Moses, so also these people are opposed to the truth — people whose minds do not function and who are failures in the faith. [9]But they will not get very far, because everyone will see how stupid they are. That is just what happened to Jannes and Jambres.

Last Instructions

[10]But you have followed my teaching, my conduct, and my purpose in life; you have observed my faith, my patience, my love, my endurance, [11]my persecutions, and my sufferings. You know all that happened to me in Antioch, Iconium, and Lystra, the terrible persecutions I endured! But the Lord rescued me from them all. [12]Everyone who wants to live a godly life in union with Christ Jesus will be persecuted; [13]and evil persons and impostors will keep on going from bad to worse, deceiving others and being deceived themselves. [14]But as for you, continue in the truths that you were taught and firmly believe. You know who your teachers were, [15]and you remember that ever since you were a child, you have known the Holy Scriptures, which are able to give you the wisdom that leads to salvation through faith in Christ Jesus. [16]All Scripture is inspired by God and is useful[b] for teaching the truth, rebuking error, correcting faults, and giving instruction for right living,

---

[b] All Scripture is inspired by God and is useful; *or* Every scripture inspired by God is also useful.

2.19 Nu 16.5   **3.8** Ex 7.11   **3.11 a** Ac 13.14-52; **b** Ac 14.1-7; **c** Ac 14.8-20

[17] so that the person who serves God may be fully qualified and equipped to do every kind of good deed.

4 In the presence of God and of Christ Jesus, who will judge the living and the dead, and because he is coming to rule as King, I solemnly urge you [2] to preach the message, to insist upon proclaiming it (whether the time is right or not), to convince, reproach, and encourage, as you teach with all patience. [3] The time will come when people will not listen to sound doctrine, but will follow their own desires and will collect for themselves more and more teachers who will tell them what they are itching to hear. [4] They will turn away from listening to the truth and give their attention to legends. [5] But you must keep control of yourself in all circumstances; endure suffering, do the work of a preacher of the Good News, and perform your whole duty as a servant of God.

[6] As for me, the hour has come for me to be sacrificed; the time is here for me to leave this life. [7] I have done my best in the race, I have run the full distance, and I have kept the faith.[c] [8] And now there is waiting for me the victory prize of being put right with God, which the Lord, the righteous Judge, will give me on that Day — and not only to me, but to all those who wait with love for him to appear.

Personal Words

[9] Do your best to come to me soon. [10] Demas fell in love with this present world and has deserted me, going off to Thessalonica. Crescens went to Galatia, and Titus to Dalmatia. [11] Only Luke is with me. Get Mark and bring him

with you, because he can help me in the work. [12] I sent Tychicus to Ephesus. [13] When you come, bring my coat that I left in Troas with Carpus; bring the books too, and especially the ones made of parchment.

The victory prize . . . (4.8)

[14] Alexander the metalworker did me great harm; the Lord will reward him according to what he has done. [15] Be on your guard against him yourself, because he was violently opposed to our message.

[16] No one stood by me the first time I defended myself; all deserted me. May God not count it against them! [17] But the Lord stayed with me and gave me strength, so that I was able to proclaim the full message for all the Gentiles to hear; and I was rescued from being sentenced to death. [18] And the Lord will rescue me from all evil and take me safely into his heavenly Kingdom. To him be the glory forever and ever! Amen.

Final Greetings

[19] I send greetings to Priscilla and Aquila and to the family of Onesiphorus. [20] Erastus stayed in Corinth, and I left

[c] kept the faith; *or* been true to my promise.
4.10 a Col 4.14; Phm 24; **b** 2 Co 8.23; Ga 2.3; Titus 1.4   **4.11 a** Col 4.14; Phm 24; **b** Ac 12.12, 25; 13.13; 15.37-39; Col 4.10; Phm 24   **4.12** Ac 20.4; Eph 6.21, 22; Col 4.7, 8   **4.13** Ac 20.6   **4.14 a** 1 Ti 1.20; **b** Ps 62.12; Ro 2.6   **4.19 a** Ac 18.2; **b** 2 Ti 1.16, 17   **4.20 a** Ac 19.22; Ro 16.23; **b** Ac 20.4; 21.29

Trophimus in Miletus, because he was sick. ²¹ Do your best to come before winter.

Eubulus, Pudens, Linus, and Clau-dia send their greetings, and so do all the other Christians.

²² The Lord be with your spirit.

God's grace be with you all.

Paul's Letter to
TITUS

INTRODUCTION

Titus was a Gentile convert to Christianity who became a fellow worker and assistant to Paul in his missionary work. *Paul's Letter to Titus* is addressed to his young helper in Crete, who had been left there to supervise the work of the church. The letter expresses three main concerns.

First, Titus is reminded of the kind of character that church leaders should have, especially in view of the bad character of many Cretans. Next, Titus is advised how to teach the various groups in the church, the older men, the older women (who are, in turn, to teach the younger women), the young men, and the slaves. Finally, the writer gives Titus advice regarding Christian conduct, especially the need to be peaceful and friendly, and to avoid hatred, argument, and division in the church.

OUTLINE OF CONTENTS

Introduction   1.1-4
Church officers   1.5-16
Duties of various groups in the church   2.1-15
Exhortations and warning   3.1-11
Conclusion   3.12-15

1 From Paul, a servant of God and an apostle of Jesus Christ.

I was chosen and sent to help the faith of God's chosen people and to lead them to the truth taught by our religion, ² which is based on the hope for eternal life. God, who does not lie, promised us this life before the beginning of time, ³ and at the right time he revealed it in his message. This was en-trusted to me, and I proclaim it by order of God our Savior.

⁴ I write to Titus, my true son in the faith that we have in common.

May God the Father and Christ Jesus our Savior give you grace and peace.

Titus' Work in Crete

⁵ I left you in Crete, so that you could put in order the things that still needed

1.4 2 Co 8.23; Ga 2.3; 2 Ti 4.10

doing and appoint church elders in every town. Remember my instructions: [6] an elder must be without fault; he must have only one wife,[a] and his children must be believers and not have the reputation of being wild or disobedient. [7] For since a church leader is in charge of God's work, he should be without fault. He must not be arrogant or quick-tempered, or a drunkard or violent or greedy for money. [8] He must be hospitable and love what is good. He must be self-controlled, upright, holy, and disciplined. [9] He must hold firmly to the message which can be trusted and which agrees with the doctrine. In this way he will be able to encourage others with the true teaching and also to show the error of those who are opposed to it.

[10] For there are many, especially the converts from Judaism, who rebel and deceive others with their nonsense. [11] It is necessary to stop their talk, because they are upsetting whole families by teaching what they should not, and all for the shameful purpose of making money. [12-13] It was a Cretan himself, one of their own prophets, who spoke the truth when he said, "Cretans are always liars, wicked beasts, and lazy gluttons." For this reason you must rebuke them sharply, so that they may have a healthy faith [14] and no longer hold on to Jewish legends and to human commandments which come from people who have rejected the truth. [15] Everything is pure to those who are themselves pure; but nothing is pure to those who are defiled and unbelieving, for their minds and consciences have been defiled. [16] They claim that they know God, but their actions deny it. They are hateful and disobedient, not fit to do anything good.

Sound Doctrine

2 But you must teach what agrees with sound doctrine. [2] Instruct the older men to be sober, sensible, and self-controlled; to be sound in their faith, love, and endurance. [3] In the same way instruct the older women to behave as women should who live a holy life. They must not be slanderers or slaves to wine. They must teach what is good, [4] in order to train the younger women to love their husbands and children, [5] to be self-controlled and pure, and to be good housewives who submit themselves to their husbands, so that no one will speak evil of the message that comes from God.

[6] In the same way urge the young men to be self-controlled. [7] In all things you yourself must be an example of good behavior. Be sincere and serious in your teaching. [8] Use sound words that cannot be criticized, so that your enemies may be put to shame by not having anything bad to say about us.

[9] Slaves are to submit themselves to their masters and please them in all things. They must not talk back to them [10] or steal from them. Instead, they must show that they are always good and faithful, so as to bring credit to the teaching about God our Savior in all they do.

[11] For God has revealed his grace for the salvation of all people. [12] That grace instructs us to give up ungodly living and worldly passions, and to live self-controlled, upright, and godly lives in this world, [13] as we wait for the blessed Day we hope for, when the glory of our great God and Savior Jesus Christ[b] will appear. [14] He gave himself for us, to rescue us from all wickedness and to make us a pure people who belong to him alone and are eager to do good.

[15] Teach these things and use your

---

[a] have only one wife; *or* be married only once.   [b] our great God and Savior Jesus Christ; *or* the great God and our Savior Jesus Christ.
1.6-9 1 Ti 3.2-7   **2.14 a** Ps 130.8; **b** Ex 19.5; Dt 4.20; 7.6; 14.2; 1 P 2.9

full authority as you encourage and rebuke your hearers. Let none of them look down on you.

Christian Conduct

3 Remind your people to submit to rulers and authorities, to obey them, and to be ready to do good in every way. ² Tell them not to speak evil of anyone, but to be peaceful and friendly, and always to show a gentle attitude toward everyone. ³ For we ourselves were once foolish, disobedient, and wrong. We were slaves to passions and pleasures of all kinds. We spent our lives in malice and envy; others hated us and we hated them. ⁴ But when the kindness and love of God our Savior was revealed, ⁵ he saved us. It was not because of any good deeds that we ourselves had done, but because of his own mercy that he saved us, through the Holy Spirit, who gives us new birth and new life by washing us. ⁶ God poured out the Holy Spirit abundantly on us through Jesus Christ our Savior, ⁷ so that by his grace we might be put right with God and come into possession of the eternal life we hope for. ⁸ This is a true saying.

I want you to give special emphasis to these matters, so that those who believe in God may be concerned with giving their time to doing good deeds, which are good and useful for everyone. ⁹ But avoid stupid arguments, long lists of ancestors, quarrels, and fights about the Law. They are useless and worthless. ¹⁰ Give at least two warnings to those who cause divisions, and then have nothing more to do with them. ¹¹ You know that such people are corrupt, and their sins prove that they are wrong.

Final Instructions

¹² When I send Artemas or Tychicus to you, do your best to come to me in Nicopolis, because I have decided to spend the winter there. ¹³ Do your best to help Zenas the lawyer and Apollos to get started on their travels, and see to it that they have everything they need. ¹⁴ Our people must learn to spend their time doing good, in order to provide for real needs; they should not live useless lives.

¹⁵ All who are with me send you greetings. Give our greetings to our friends in the faith.

God's grace be with you all.

3.12 Ac 20.4; Eph 6.21, 22; Col 4.7, 8; 2 Ti 4.12   **3.13** Ac 18.24; 1 Co 16.12

Paul's Letter to
PHILEMON

INTRODUCTION

Philemon was a prominent Christian, probably a member of the church at Colossae and the owner of a slave named Onesimus. This slave had run away from his master, and then somehow he had come in contact with Paul, who was then in prison. Through Paul, Onesimus became a Christian. *Paul's Letter to Philemon* is an appeal to Philemon to be reconciled to his slave, whom Paul is sending back to him, and to welcome him not only as a forgiven slave but as a Christian brother.

OUTLINE OF CONTENTS

---

[1] From Paul, a prisoner for the sake of Christ Jesus, and from our brother Timothy —

To our friend and fellow worker Philemon, [2] and the church that meets in your house, and our sister Apphia, and our fellow soldier Archippus:

[3] May God our Father and the Lord Jesus Christ give you grace and peace.

Philemon's Love and Faith

[4] Brother Philemon, every time I pray, I mention you and give thanks to my God. [5] For I hear of your love for all of God's people and the faith you have in the Lord Jesus. [6] My prayer is that our fellowship with you as believers will bring about a deeper understanding of every blessing which we have in our life in union with Christ. [7] Your love, dear brother, has brought me great joy and much encouragement! You have cheered the hearts of all of God's people.

A Request for Onesimus

[8] For this reason I could be bold enough, as your brother in Christ, to order you to do what should be done. [9] But because I love you, I make a request instead. I do this even though I am Paul, the ambassador of Christ Jesus, and at present also a prisoner for his sake.[a] [10] So I make a request to you on behalf of Onesimus, who is my own son in Christ; for while in prison I have become his spiritual father. [11] At one time he was of no use to you, but now he is useful[b] both to you and to me.

[12] I am sending him back to you now, and with him goes my heart. [13] I would like to keep him here with me, while I

---

[a] the ambassador of Christ Jesus, and at present also a prisoner for his sake; *or* an old man, and at present a prisoner for the sake of Christ Jesus.   [b] *The Greek name Onesimus means "useful."*
2 Col 4.17   **10** Col 4.9

am in prison for the gospel's sake, so that he could help me in your place. ¹⁴ However, I do not want to force you to help me; rather, I would like for you to do it of your own free will. So I will not do anything unless you agree.

¹⁵ It may be that Onesimus was away from you for a short time so that you might have him back for all time. ¹⁶ And now he is not just a slave, but much more than a slave: he is a dear brother in Christ. How much he means to me! And how much more he will mean to

Welcome him back. (17)

you, both as a slave and as a brother in the Lord!

¹⁷ So, if you think of me as your partner, welcome him back just as you would welcome me. ¹⁸ If he has done you any wrong or owes you anything, charge it to my account. ¹⁹ Here, I will write this with my own hand: *I, Paul, will pay you back.* (I should not have to remind you, of course, that you owe your very self to me.) ²⁰ So, my brother, please do me this favor for the Lord's sake; as a brother in Christ, cheer me up!

²¹ I am sure, as I write this, that you will do what I ask — in fact I know that you will do even more. ²² At the same time, get a room ready for me, because I hope that God will answer the prayers of all of you and give me back to you.

Final Greetings

²³ Epaphras, who is in prison with me for the sake of Christ Jesus, sends you his greetings, ²⁴ and so do my co-workers Mark, Aristarchus, Demas, and Luke.

²⁵ May the grace of the Lord Jesus Christ be with you all.

23 Col 1.7; 4.12   **24 a** Ac 12.12, 25; 13.13; 15.37-39; Col 4.10; **b** Ac 19.29; 27.2; Col 4.10; **c** Col 4.14; 2 Ti 4.10; **d** Col 4.14; 2 Ti 4.11

The Letter to the
HEBREWS

INTRODUCTION

The Letter to the Hebrews was written to a group of Christians who, faced with increasing opposition, were in danger of abandoning the Christian faith. The writer encourages them in their faith primarily by showing that Jesus Christ is the true and final revelation of God. In doing this he emphasizes three truths: (1) Jesus is the eternal Son of God, who learned true obedience to the Father through the suffering that he endured. As the Son of God, Jesus is superior to the prophets of the Old Testament, to the angels, and to Moses himself. (2) Jesus has been declared by God to be an eternal priest, superior to the priests of the Old Testament. (3) Through Jesus the believer is saved from sin, fear, and death; and Jesus, as High Priest, provides the true salvation, which was only foreshadowed by the rituals and animal sacrifices of the Hebrew religion.

By citing the example of the faith of some famous persons in Israel's history (chapter 11), the writer appeals to his readers to remain faithful, and in chapter 12 he urges his readers to continue faithful to the end, with eyes fixed on Jesus, and to endure whatever suffering and persecution may come to them. The book closes with words of advice and warning.

OUTLINE OF CONTENTS

God's Word through His Son

1 In the past God spoke to our ancestors many times and in many ways through the prophets, ²but in these last days he has spoken to us through his Son. He is the one through whom God created the universe, the one whom God has chosen to possess all things at the end. ³He reflects the brightness of God's glory and is the exact likeness of God's own being, sustaining the universe with his powerful word. After achieving forgiveness for

1.2 Ws 7.22   **1.3** Ws 7.25, 26; 8.1

the sins of all human beings, he sat down in heaven at the right side of God, the Supreme Power.

The Greatness of God's Son

4 The Son was made greater than the angels, just as the name that God gave him is greater than theirs. 5 For God never said to any of his angels,

"You are my Son;
    today I have become your
        Father."

Nor did God say about any angel,

"I will be his Father,
    and he will be my Son."

6 But when God was about to send his first-born Son into the world, he said,

"All of God's angels must
    worship him."

7 But about the angels God said,

"God makes his angels winds,
    and his servants flames
        of fire."

8 About the Son, however, God said:

"Your kingdom, O God, will last*a*
    forever and ever!
You rule over your*b* people
    with justice.
9 You love what is right and hate
    what is wrong.
That is why God, your God, has
    chosen you
and has given you the joy of
    an honor far greater
than he gave to your
    companions."

10 He also said,

"You, Lord, in the beginning
    created the earth,
and with your own hands you
    made the heavens.
11 They will disappear, but you will
    remain;

they will all wear out like
    clothes.
12 You will fold them up like a coat,
    and they will be changed like
        clothes.
But you are always the same,
    and your life never ends."

13 God never said to any of his angels:

"Sit here at my right side
until I put your enemies
    as a footstool under your feet."

14 What are the angels, then? They are spirits who serve God and are sent by him to help those who are to receive salvation.

The Great Salvation

2 That is why we must hold on all the more firmly to the truths we have heard, so that we will not be carried away. 2 The message given to our ancestors by the angels was shown to be true, and those who did not follow it or obey it received the punishment they deserved. 3 How, then, shall we escape if we pay no attention to such a great salvation? The Lord himself first announced this salvation, and those who heard him proved to us that it is true. 4 At the same time God added his witness to theirs by performing all kinds of miracles and wonders and by distributing the gifts of the Holy Spirit according to his will.

The One Who Leads Us to Salvation

5 God has not placed the angels as rulers over the new world to come — the world of which we speak. 6 Instead, as it is said somewhere in the Scriptures:

"What are human beings, O God,
    that you should think
        of them;

---

a Your kingdom, O God, will last; *or* God is your kingdom.   *b* your; *some manuscripts have* his.

1.5 a Ps 2.7; b 2 S 7.14; 1 Ch 17.13   1.6 Dt 32.43 (LXX)   1.7 Ps 104.4 (LXX)
1.8, 9 Ps 45.6, 7   1.10-12 Ps 102.25-27 (LXX)   1.13 Ps 110.1   1.14 Tb 12.14, 15
2.6-8 Ps 8.4-6

mere human beings, that you
should care for them?
7 You made them for a little while
lower than the angels;
you crowned them with glory
and honor,*c*
8   and made them rulers over all
things."
It says that God made them "rulers over
all things"; this clearly includes everything. We do not, however, see human
beings ruling over all things now. 9 But
we do see Jesus, who for a little while
was made lower than the angels, so that
through God's grace he should die for
everyone. We see him now crowned
with glory and honor because of the
death he suffered. 10 It was only right
that God, who creates and preserves all
things, should make Jesus perfect
through suffering, in order to bring
many children to share his glory. For
Jesus is the one who leads them to
salvation.
11 He purifies people from their sins,
and both he and those who are made
pure all have the same Father. That is
why Jesus is not ashamed to call them
his family. 12 He says to God,
"I will tell my people what you
have done;
I will praise you in their
meeting."
13 He also says, "I will put my trust in
God." And he also says, "Here I am with
the children that God has given me."
14 Since the children, as he calls
them, are people of flesh and blood,
Jesus himself became like them and
shared their human nature. He did this
so that through his death he might destroy the Devil, who has the power over
death, 15 and in this way set free those
who were slaves all their lives because
of their fear of death. 16 For it is clear
that it is not the angels that he helps.
Instead, he helps the descendants of
Abraham. 17 This means that he had to
become like his people in every way, in
order to be their faithful and merciful
High Priest in his service to God, so that
the people's sins would be forgiven.
18 And now he can help those who are
tempted, because he himself was
tempted and suffered.

Jesus Is Greater than Moses

3 My Christian friends, who also
have been called by God! Think of
Jesus, whom God sent to be the High
Priest of the faith we profess. 2 He was
faithful to God, who chose him to do
this work, just as Moses was faithful in
his work in God's house. 3 A man who
builds a house receives more honor
than the house itself. In the same way
Jesus is worthy of much greater honor
than Moses. 4 Every house, of course, is
built by someone — and God is the one
who has built all things. 5 Moses was
faithful in God's house as a servant,
and he spoke of the things that God
would say in the future. 6 But Christ is
faithful as the Son in charge of God's
house. We are his house if we keep up
our courage and our confidence in
what we hope for.

A Rest for God's People

7 So then, as the Holy Spirit says,
"If you hear God's voice today,
8   do not be stubborn, as your
ancestors were when they
rebelled against God,
as they were that day in the
desert when they put him
to the test.
9 There they put me to the test
and tried me, says God,
although they had seen what
I did for forty years.
10 And so I was angry with those
people and said,

---

c Many manuscripts add: You made them rulers over everything you made *(see Ps 8.6).*
2.12 Ps 22.22   **2.13 a** Is 8.17 (LXX); **b** Is 8.18   **2.16** Is 41.8, 9   **3.2** Nu 12.7
3.7-11 Ps 95.7-11 (LXX)

'They are always disloyal
and refuse to obey my
commands.'
11 I was angry and made a solemn
promise:
'They will never enter the
land where I would have
given them rest!' "

12 My friends, be careful that none of you have a heart so evil and unbelieving that you will turn away from the living God. 13 Instead, in order that none of you be deceived by sin and become stubborn, you must help one another every day, as long as the word "Today" in the scripture applies to us. 14 For we are all partners with Christ if we hold firmly to the end the confidence we had at the beginning.

15 This is what the scripture says:
"If you hear God's voice today,
do not be stubborn, as your
ancestors were
when they rebelled
against God."

16 Who were the people who heard God's voice and rebelled against him? All those who were led out of Egypt by Moses. 17 With whom was God angry for forty years? With the people who sinned, who fell down dead in the desert. 18 When God made his solemn promise, "They will never enter the land where I would have given them rest" — of whom was he speaking? Of those who rebelled. 19 We see, then, that they were not able to enter the land, because they did not believe.

4 Now, God has offered us the promise that we may receive that rest he spoke about. Let us take care, then, that none of you will be found to have failed to receive that promised rest. 2 For we have heard the Good News, just as they did. They heard the message, but it did them no good, because when they heard it, they did not accept it with faith. 3 We who believe, then, do receive that rest which God promised. It is just as he said,

"I was angry and made a solemn
promise:
'They will never enter the
land where I would have
given them rest!' "

He said this even though his work had been finished from the time he created the world. 4 For somewhere in the Scriptures this is said about the seventh day: "God rested on the seventh day from all his work." 5 This same matter is spoken of again: "They will never enter that land where I would have given them rest." 6 Those who first heard the Good News did not receive that rest, because they did not believe. There are, then, others who are allowed to receive it. 7 This is shown by the fact that God sets another day, which is called "Today." Many years later he spoke of it through David in the scripture already quoted:

"If you hear God's voice today,
do not be stubborn."

8 If Joshua had given the people the rest that God had promised, God would not have spoken later about another day. 9 As it is, however, there still remains for God's people a rest like God's resting on the seventh day. 10 For those who receive that rest which God promised will rest from their own work, just as God rested from his. 11 Let us, then, do our best to receive that rest, so that no one of us will fail as they did because of their lack of faith.

12 The word of God is alive and active, sharper than any double-edged sword. It cuts all the way through, to where soul and spirit meet, to where joints and marrow come together. It judges the desires and thoughts of the heart. 13 There is nothing that can be hid from God; everything in all creation is exposed and lies open before his eyes.

3.15 Ps 95.7, 8 (LXX)   **3.16-18** Nu 14.1-35   **4.3** Ps 95.11   **4.4** Gn 2.2   **4.5** Ps 95.11
4.7 Ps 95.7, 8 (LXX)   **4.8** Dt 31.7; Js 22.4   **4.10** Gn 2.2   **4.13** Ws 1.6

And it is to him that we must all give an account of ourselves.

Jesus the Great High Priest

[14] Let us, then, hold firmly to the faith we profess. For we have a great High Priest who has gone into the very presence of God — Jesus, the Son of God. [15] Our High Priest is not one who cannot feel sympathy for our weaknesses. On the contrary, we have a High Priest who was tempted in every way that we are, but did not sin. [16] Let us have confidence, then, and approach God's throne, where there is grace. There we will receive mercy and find grace to help us just when we need it.

5 Every high priest is chosen from his fellow-men and appointed to serve God on their behalf, to offer sacrifices and offerings for sins. [2] Since he himself is weak in many ways, he is able to be gentle with those who are ignorant and make mistakes. [3] And because he is himself weak, he must offer sacrifices not only for the sins of the people but also for his own sins. [4] No one chooses for himself the honor of being a high priest. It is only by God's call that a man is made a high priest — just as Aaron was.

[5] In the same way, Christ did not take upon himself the honor of being a high priest. Instead, God said to him,

"You are my Son;
today I have become your
Father."

[6] He also said in another place,

"You will be a priest forever,
in the priestly order of
Melchizedek."[d]

[7] In his life on earth Jesus made his prayers and requests with loud cries and tears to God, who could save him

from death. Because he was humble and devoted, God heard him. [8] But even though he was God's Son, he learned through his sufferings to be obedient. [9] When he was made perfect, he became the source of eternal salvation for all those who obey him, [10] and God declared him to be high priest, in the priestly order of Melchizedek.[d]

Warning against Abandoning the Faith

[11] There is much we have to say about this matter, but it is hard to explain to you, because you are so slow to understand. [12] There has been enough time for you to be teachers — yet you still need someone to teach you the first lessons of God's message. Instead of eating solid food, you still have to drink milk. [13] Anyone who has to drink milk is still a child, without any experience in the matter of right and wrong. [14] Solid food, on the other hand, is for adults, who through practice are able to distinguish between good and evil.

6 Let us go forward, then, to mature teaching and leave behind us the first lessons of the Christian message. We should not lay again the foundation of turning away from useless works and believing in God; [2] of the teaching about baptisms[e] and the laying on of hands; of the resurrection of the dead and the eternal judgment. [3] Let us go forward! And this is what we will do, if God allows.

[4] For how can those who abandon their faith be brought back to repent again? They were once in God's light; they tasted heaven's gift and received their share of the Holy Spirit; [5] they knew from experience that God's word is good, and they had felt the powers of the coming age. [6] And then they abandoned their faith! It is impossible to

---

[d] in the priestly order of Melchizedek; *or* like Melchizedek; *or* in the line of succession to Melchizedek.   [e] baptisms; *or* purification ceremonies.

5.3 Lv 9.7   **5.4** Ex 28.1   **5.5** Ps 2.7   **5.6** Ps 110.4   **5.7** Mt 26.36-46; Mk 14.32-42; Lk 22.39-46   **5.12, 13** 1 Co 3.2

bring them back to repent again, because they are again crucifying the Son of God and exposing him to public shame.

⁷God blesses the soil which drinks in the rain that often falls on it and which grows plants that are useful to those for whom it is cultivated. ⁸But if it grows thorns and weeds, it is worth nothing; it is in danger of being cursed by God and will be destroyed by fire.

⁹But even if we speak like this, dear friends, we feel sure about you. We know that you have the better blessings that belong to your salvation. ¹⁰God is not unfair. He will not forget the work you did or the love you showed for him in the help you gave and are still giving to other Christians. ¹¹Our great desire is that each of you keep up your eagerness to the end, so that the things you hope for will come true. ¹²We do not want you to become lazy, but to be like those who believe and are patient, and so receive what God has promised.

God's Sure Promise

¹³When God made his promise to Abraham, he made a vow to do what he had promised. Since there was no one greater than himself, he used his own name when he made his vow. ¹⁴He said, "I promise you that I will bless you and give you many descendants." ¹⁵Abraham was patient, and so he received what God had promised. ¹⁶When we make a vow, we use the name of someone greater than ourselves, and the vow settles all arguments. ¹⁷To those who were to receive what he promised, God wanted to make it very clear that he would never change his purpose; so he added his vow to the promise. ¹⁸There are these two things, then, that cannot change and about which God cannot lie. So we

who have found safety with him are greatly encouraged to hold firmly to the hope placed before us. ¹⁹We have this hope as an anchor for our lives. It is safe and sure, and goes through the curtain of the heavenly temple into the inner sanctuary. ²⁰On our behalf Jesus has gone in there before us and has become a high priest forever, in the priestly order of Melchizedek.ʲ

The Priest Melchizedek

7 This Melchizedek was king of Salem and a priest of the Most High God. As Abraham was coming back from the battle in which he defeated the four kings, Melchizedek met him and blessed him, ²and Abraham gave him one tenth of all he had taken. (The first meaning of Melchizedek's name is "King of Righteousness"; and because he was king of Salem, his name also means "King of Peace.") ³There is no record of Melchizedek's father or mother or of any of his ancestors; no record of his birth or of his death. He is like the Son of God; he remains a priest forever.

⁴You see, then, how great he was. Abraham, our famous ancestor, gave him one tenth of all he got in the battle. ⁵And those descendants of Levi who are priests are commanded by the Law to collect one tenth from the people of Israel, that is, from their own people, even though they are also descendants of Abraham. ⁶Melchizedek was not descended from Levi, but he collected one tenth from Abraham and blessed him, the man who received God's promises. ⁷There is no doubt that the one who blesses is greater than the one who is blessed. ⁸In the case of the priests the tenth is collected by men who die; but as for Melchizedek the tenth was collected by one who lives, as the scripture

ʲ in the priestly order of Melchizedek (see 5.6).

6.8 Gn 3.17, 18   **6.14** Gn 22.16, 17   **6.19** Lv 16.2   **6.20** Ps 110.4   **7.1, 2** Gn 14.17-20
7.5 Nu 18.21

says. [9] And, so to speak, when Abraham paid the tenth, Levi (whose descendants collect the tenth) also paid it. [10] For Levi had not yet been born, but was, so to speak, in the body of his ancestor Abraham when Melchizedek met him.

[11] It was on the basis of the levitical priesthood that the Law was given to the people of Israel. Now, if the work of the levitical priests had been perfect, there would have been no need for a different kind of priest to appear, one who is in the priestly order of Melchizedek,[f] not of Aaron. [12] For when the priesthood is changed, there also has to be a change in the law. [13] And our Lord, of whom these things are said, belonged to a different tribe, and no member of his tribe ever served as a priest. [14] It is well known that he was born a member of the tribe of Judah; and Moses did not mention this tribe when he spoke of priests.

Another Priest, like Melchizedek

[15] The matter becomes even plainer; a different priest has appeared, who is like Melchizedek. [16] He was made a priest, not by human rules and regulations, but through the power of a life which has no end. [17] For the scripture says, "You will be a priest forever, in the priestly order of Melchizedek."[f] [18] The old rule, then, is set aside, because it was weak and useless. [19] For the Law of Moses could not make anything perfect. And now a better hope has been provided through which we come near to God.

[20] In addition, there is also God's vow. There was no such vow when the others were made priests. [21] But Jesus became a priest by means of a vow when God said to him,

"The Lord has made a solemn
promise
and will not take it back:

'You will be a priest forever.' "

[22] This difference, then, also makes Jesus the guarantee of a better covenant.

[23] There is another difference: there were many of those other priests, because they died and could not continue their work. [24] But Jesus lives on forever, and his work as priest does not pass on to someone else. [25] And so he is able, now and always, to save those who come to God through him, because he lives forever to plead with God for them.

[26] Jesus, then, is the High Priest that meets our needs. He is holy; he has no fault or sin in him; he has been set apart from sinners and raised above the heavens. [27] He is not like other high priests; he does not need to offer sacrifices every day for his own sins first and then for the sins of the people. He offered one sacrifice, once and for all, when he offered himself. [28] The Law of Moses appoints men who are imperfect to be high priests; but God's promise made with the vow, which came later than the Law, appoints the Son, who has been made perfect forever.

Jesus Our High Priest

8 The whole point of what we are saying is that we have such a High Priest, who sits at the right of the throne of the Divine Majesty in heaven. [2] He serves as high priest in the Most Holy Place, that is, in the real tent which was put up by the Lord, not by human hands.

[3] Every high priest is appointed to present offerings and animal sacrifices to God, and so our High Priest must also have something to offer. [4] If he were on earth, he would not be a priest at all, since there are priests who offer the gifts required by the Jewish Law. [5] The work they do as priests is really only a copy and a shadow of what is in heaven.

---

[f] in the priestly order of Melchizedek (see 5.6).
7.17 Ps 110.4   **7.21** Ps 110.4   **7.27** Lv 9.7   **8.1** Ps 110.1   **8.5** Ex 25.40

It is the same as it was with Moses. When he was about to build the Sacred Tent, God told him, "Be sure to make everything according to the pattern you were shown on the mountain." 6But now, Jesus has been given priestly work which is superior to theirs, just as the covenant which he arranged between God and his people is a better one, because it is based on promises of better things.

7If there had been nothing wrong with the first covenant, there would have been no need for a second one. 8But God finds fault with his people when he says,

"The days are coming, says the Lord,
    when I will draw up a new
        covenant with the people
        of Israel and with the
        people of Judah.
9It will not be like the covenant
    that I made with their
    ancestors
on the day I took them by the
    hand and led them out of
    Egypt.
They were not faithful to the
    covenant I made with
    them,
and so I paid no attention to
    them.
10Now, this is the covenant that I
    will make with the people
    of Israel
in the days to come, says the
    Lord:
I will put my laws in their minds
    and write them on their
    hearts.
I will be their God,
    and they will be my people.
11None of them will have to teach
    their friends
or tell their neighbors,
    'Know the Lord.'

For they will all know me,
    from the least to the greatest.
12I will forgive their sins
    and will no longer remember
        their wrongs."
13By speaking of a new covenant, God has made the first one old; and anything that becomes old and worn out will soon disappear.

Earthly and Heavenly Worship

9 The first covenant had rules for worship and a place made for worship as well. 2A tent was put up, the outer one, which was called the Holy Place. In it were the lampstand and the table with the bread offered to God. 3Behind the second curtain was the tent called the Most Holy Place. 4In it were the gold altar for the burning of incense and the Covenant Box all covered with gold and containing the gold jar with the manna in it, Aaron's stick that had sprouted leaves, and the two stone tablets with the commandments written on them. 5Above the Box were the winged creatures representing God's presence, with their wings spread over the place where sins were forgiven. But now is not the time to explain everything in detail.

6This is how those things have been arranged. The priests go into the outer tent every day to perform their duties, 7but only the high priest goes into the inner tent, and he does so only once a year. He takes with him blood which he offers to God on behalf of himself and for the sins which the people have committed without knowing they were sinning. 8The Holy Spirit clearly teaches from all these arrangements that the way into the Most Holy Place has not yet been opened as long as the outer tent still stands. 9This is a symbol which points to the present time. It

---

8.8-12 Jr 31.31-34 (LXX)   **9.2 a** Ex 26.1-30; **b** Ex 25.31-40; **c** Ex 25.23-30
9.3 Ex 26.31-33   **9.4 a** Ex 30.1-6; **b** Ex 25.10-16; **c** Ex 16.33; **d** Nu 17.8-10; **e** Ex 25.16;
Dt 10.3-5   **9.5** Ex 25.18-22   **9.6** Nu 18.2-6   **9.7** Lv 16.2-34

means that the offerings and animal sacrifices presented to God cannot make the worshiper's heart perfect, [10]since they have to do only with food, drink, and various purification ceremonies. These are all outward rules, which apply only until the time when God will establish the new order.

[11]But Christ has already come as the High Priest of the good things that are already here.[g] The tent in which he serves is greater and more perfect; it is not a tent made by human hands, that is, it is not a part of this created world. [12]When Christ went through the tent and entered once and for all into the Most Holy Place, he did not take the blood of goats and bulls to offer as a sacrifice; rather, he took his own blood and obtained eternal salvation for us. [13]The blood of goats and bulls and the ashes of a burnt calf are sprinkled on the people who are ritually unclean, and this purifies them by taking away their ritual impurity. [14]Since this is true, how much more is accomplished by the blood of Christ! Through the eternal Spirit he offered himself as a perfect sacrifice to God. His blood will purify our consciences from useless rituals, so that we may serve the living God.

[15]For this reason Christ is the one who arranges a new covenant, so that those who have been called by God may receive the eternal blessings that God has promised. This can be done because there has been a death which sets people free from the wrongs they did while the first covenant was in effect.

[16]In the case of a will it is necessary to prove that the person who made it has died, [17]for a will means nothing while the person who made it is alive; it goes into effect only after his death. [18]That is why even the first covenant[h]

went into effect only with the use of blood. [19]First, Moses proclaimed to the people all the commandments as set forth in the Law. Then he took the blood of bulls and goats, mixed it with water, and sprinkled it on the book of the Law and all the people, using a sprig of hyssop and some red wool. [20]He said, "This is the blood which seals the covenant that God has commanded you to obey." [21]In the same way Moses also sprinkled the blood on the Sacred Tent and over all the things used in worship. [22]Indeed, according to the Law almost everything is purified by blood, and sins are forgiven only if blood is poured out.

Christ's Sacrifice Takes Away Sins

[23]Those things, which are copies of the heavenly originals, had to be purified in that way. But the heavenly things themselves require much better sacrifices. [24]For Christ did not go into a Holy Place made by human hands, which was a copy of the real one. He went into heaven itself, where he now appears on our behalf in the presence of God. [25]The Jewish high priest goes into the Most Holy Place every year with the blood of an animal. But Christ did not go in to offer himself many times, [26]for then he would have had to suffer many times ever since the creation of the world. Instead, now when all ages of time are nearing the end, he has appeared once and for all, to remove sin through the sacrifice of himself. [27]Everyone must die once, and after that be judged by God. [28]In the same manner Christ also was offered in sacrifice once to take away the sins of many. He will appear a second time, not to deal with sin, but to save those who are waiting for him.

[g] already here; *some manuscripts have* coming.   [h] COVENANT: *In Greek the same word means "will" and "covenant."*

9.13 a Lv 16.15, 16; b Nu 19.9, 17-19   **9.19, 20** Ex 24.6-8   **9.21** Lv 8.15   **9.22** Lv 17.11   **9.28** Is 53.12

10

The Jewish Law is not a full and faithful model of the real things; it is only a faint outline of the good things to come. The same sacrifices are offered forever, year after year. How can the Law, then, by means of these sacrifices make perfect the people who come to God? ² If the people worshiping God had really been purified from their sins, they would not feel guilty of sin any more, and all sacrifices would stop. ³ As it is, however, the sacrifices serve year after year to remind people of their sins. ⁴ For the blood of bulls and goats can never take away sins.

⁵ For this reason, when Christ was about to come into the world, he said to God:

"You do not want sacrifices and
        offerings,
    but you have prepared a body
        for me.
    ⁶ You are not pleased with animals
        burned whole on the altar
    or with sacrifices to take away
        sins.
    ⁷ Then I said, 'Here I am,
    to do your will, O God,
        just as it is written of me in
        the book of the Law.' "

⁸ First he said, "You neither want nor are you pleased with sacrifices and offerings or with animals burned on the altar and the sacrifices to take away sins." He said this even though all these sacrifices are offered according to the Law. ⁹ Then he said, "Here I am, O God, to do your will." So God does away with all the old sacrifices and puts the sacrifice of Christ in their place. ¹⁰ Because Jesus Christ did what God wanted him to do, we are all purified from sin by the offering that he made of his own body once and for all.

¹¹ Every Jewish priest performs his services every day and offers the same sacrifices many times; but these sacrifices can never take away sins. ¹² Christ, however, offered one sacrifice for sins, an offering that is effective forever, and then he sat down at the right side of God. ¹³ There he now waits until God puts his enemies as a footstool under his feet. ¹⁴ With one sacrifice, then, he has made perfect forever those who are purified from sin.

¹⁵ And the Holy Spirit also gives us his witness. First he says,

¹⁶ "This is the covenant that I will
        make with them
    in the days to come, says the
        Lord:
    I will put my laws in their hearts
    and write them on their
        minds."

¹⁷ And then he says, "I will not remember their sins and evil deeds any longer." ¹⁸ So when these have been forgiven, an offering to take away sins is no longer needed.

Let Us Come Near to God

¹⁹ We have, then, my friends, complete freedom to go into the Most Holy Place by means of the death of Jesus. ²⁰ He opened for us a new way, a living way, through the curtain—that is, through his own body. ²¹ We have a great priest in charge of the house of God. ²² So let us come near to God with a sincere heart and a sure faith, with hearts that have been purified from a guilty conscience and with bodies washed with clean water. ²³ Let us hold on firmly to the hope we profess, because we can trust God to keep his promise. ²⁴ Let us be concerned for one another, to help one another to show love and to do good. ²⁵ Let us not give up the habit of meeting together, as some are doing. Instead, let us encourage

10.5-7 Ps 40.6-8 (LXX)   **10.11** Ex 29.38   **10.12, 13** Ps 110.1   **10.16** Jr 31.33
10.17 Jr 31.34   **10.22** Lv 8.30; Ez 36.25

Let us not give up the habit of meeting together. (10.25)

one another all the more, since you see that the Day of the Lord is coming nearer.

26 For there is no longer any sacrifice that will take away sins if we purposely go on sinning after the truth has been made known to us. 27 Instead, all that is left is to wait in fear for the coming Judgment and the fierce fire which will destroy those who oppose God! 28 Anyone who disobeys the Law of Moses is put to death without any mercy when judged guilty from the evidence of two or more witnesses. 29 What, then, of those who despise the Son of God? who treat as a cheap thing the blood of God's covenant which purified them from sin? who insult the Spirit of grace? Just think how much worse is the punishment they will deserve! 30 For we know who said, "I will take revenge, I will repay"; and who also said, "The Lord will judge his people." 31 It is a terrifying thing to fall into the hands of the living God!

32 Remember how it was with you in the past. In those days, after God's light had shone on you, you suffered many things, yet were not defeated by the struggle. 33 You were at times publicly insulted and mistreated, and at other times you were ready to join those who were being treated in this way. 34 You shared the sufferings of prisoners, and when all your belongings were seized, you endured your loss gladly, because you knew that you still possessed something much better, which would last forever. 35 Do not lose your courage, then, because it brings with it a great reward. 36 You need to be patient, in order to do the will of God and receive what he promises. 37 For, as the scripture says,

"Just a little while longer,
  and he who is coming will
    come;
  he will not delay.
38 My righteous people, however,
    will believe and live;
  but if any of them turns back,
  I will not be pleased
    with them."

39 We are not people who turn back and are lost. Instead, we have faith and are saved.

10.27 Is 26.11 (LXX) 10.28 Dt 17.6; 19.15 10.29 Ex 24.8 10.30 a Dt 32.35; b Dt 32.36
10.37, 38 Hb 2.3, 4 (LXX)

Faith

11 To have faith is to be sure of the things we hope for, to be certain of the things we cannot see. [2] It was by their faith that people of ancient times won God's approval.

[3] It is by faith that we understand that the universe was created by God's word, so that what can be seen was made out of what cannot be seen.

[4] It was faith that made Abel offer to God a better sacrifice than Cain's. Through his faith he won God's approval as a righteous man, because God himself approved of his gifts. By means of his faith Abel still speaks, even though he is dead.

[5] It was faith that kept Enoch from dying. Instead, he was taken up to God, and nobody could find him, because God had taken him up. The scripture says that before Enoch was taken up, he had pleased God. [6] No one can please God without faith, for whoever comes to God must have faith that God exists and rewards those who seek him.

[7] It was faith that made Noah hear God's warnings about things in the future that he could not see. He obeyed God and built a boat in which he and his family were saved. As a result, the world was condemned, and Noah received from God the righteousness that comes by faith.

[8] It was faith that made Abraham obey when God called him to go out to a country which God had promised to give him. He left his own country without knowing where he was going. [9] By faith he lived as a foreigner in the country that God had promised him. He lived in tents, as did Isaac and Jacob, who received the same promise from God. [10] For Abraham was waiting for the city which God has designed and built, the city with permanent foundations.

[11] It was faith that made Abraham able to become a father, even though he was too old and Sarah herself could not have children. He [i] trusted God to keep his promise. [12] Though Abraham was practically dead, from this one man came as many descendants as there are stars in the sky, as many as the numberless grains of sand on the seashore.

[13] It was in faith that all these persons died. They did not receive the things God had promised, but from a long way off they saw them and welcomed them, and admitted openly that they were foreigners and refugees on earth. [14] Those who say such things make it clear that they are looking for a country of their own. [15] They did not keep thinking about the country they had left; if they had, they would have had the chance to return. [16] Instead, it was a better country they longed for, the heavenly country. And so God is not ashamed for them to call him their God, because he has prepared a city for them.

[17] It was faith that made Abraham offer his son Isaac as a sacrifice when God put Abraham to the test. Abraham was the one to whom God had made the promise, yet he was ready to offer his only son as a sacrifice. [18] God had said to him, "It is through Isaac that you will have the descendants I promised." [19] Abraham reckoned that God was able to raise Isaac from death — and, so to speak, Abraham did receive Isaac back from death.

[20] It was faith that made Isaac promise blessings for the future to Jacob and Esau.

---

[i] It was faith . . . children. He; *some manuscripts have* It was faith that made Sarah herself able to conceive, even though she was too old to have children. She.

11.2 Si 44.10−50.21; 1 Macc 2.51-64   **11.3** Gn 1.1; Ps 33.6, 9; Jn 1.3   **11.4** Gn 4.3-10
11.5 Gn 5.21-24 (LXX) ; Si 44.16   **11.7** Gn 6.13-22   **11.8** Gn 12.1-5   **11.9** Gn 35.27
11.11 Gn 18.11-14; 21.2   **11.12** Gn 15.5; 22.17; 32.12   **11.13** Gn 23.4; 1 Ch 29.15;
Ps 39.12   **11.17** Gn 22.1-14   **11.18** Gn 21.12   **11.20** Gn 27.27-29, 39, 40

21 It was faith that made Jacob bless each of the sons of Joseph just before he died. He leaned on the top of his walking stick and worshiped God.

22 It was faith that made Joseph, when he was about to die, speak of the departure of the Israelites from Egypt, and leave instructions about what should be done with his body.

23 It was faith that made the parents of Moses hide him for three months after he was born. They saw that he was a beautiful child, and they were not afraid to disobey the king's order.

24 It was faith that made Moses, when he had grown up, refuse to be called the son of the king's daughter. 25 He preferred to suffer with God's people rather than to enjoy sin for a little while. 26 He reckoned that to suffer scorn for the Messiah was worth far more than all the treasures of Egypt, for he kept his eyes on the future reward.

27 It was faith that made Moses leave Egypt without being afraid of the king's anger. As though he saw the invisible God, he refused to turn back. 28 It was faith that made him establish the Passover and order the blood to be sprinkled on the doors, so that the Angel of Death would not kill the first-born sons of the Israelites.

29 It was faith that made the Israelites able to cross the Red Sea as if on dry land; when the Egyptians tried to do it, the water swallowed them up.

30 It was faith that made the walls of Jericho fall down after the Israelites had marched around them for seven days. 31 It was faith that kept the prostitute Rahab from being killed with those who disobeyed God, for she gave the Israelite spies a friendly welcome.

32 Should I go on? There isn't enough time for me to speak of Gideon, Barak, Samson, Jephthah, David, Samuel, and the prophets. 33 Through faith they fought whole countries and won. They did what was right and received what God had promised. They shut the mouths of lions, 34 put out fierce fires, escaped being killed by the sword. They were weak, but became strong; they were mighty in battle and defeated the armies of foreigners. 35 Through faith women received their dead relatives raised back to life.

Others, refusing to accept freedom, died under torture in order to be raised to a better life. 36 Some were mocked and whipped, and others were put in chains and taken off to prison. 37 They were stoned, they were sawed in two, they were killed by the sword. They went around clothed in skins of sheep or goats — poor, persecuted, and mistreated. 38 The world was not good enough for them! They wandered like refugees in the deserts and hills, living in caves and holes in the ground.

39 What a record all of these have won by their faith! Yet they did not receive what God had promised, 40 because God had decided on an even better plan for us. His purpose was that only in company with us would they be made perfect.

God Our Father

12 As for us, we have this large crowd of witnesses around us. So then, let us rid ourselves of everything that gets in the way, and of the sin which holds on to us so tightly, and let us run with determination the race that lies before us. 2 Let us keep our eyes fixed on Jesus, on whom our faith de-

11.21 a Gn 48.1-20; **b** Gn 47.31 (LXX)   **11.22** Gn 50.24, 25; Ex 13.19   **11.23 a** Ex 2.2;
b Ex 1.22   **11.24** Ex 2.10-12   **11.28** Ex 12.21-30   **11.29** Ex 14.21-31   **11.30** Js 6.12-21
11.31 a Js 6.22-25; **b** Js 2.1-21   **11.32 a** Jg 6.11—8.32; **b** Jg 4.6—5.31; **c** Jg 13.2—16.31;
d Jg 11.1—12.7; **e** 1 S 16.1—1 K 2.11; **f** 1 S 1.1—25.1   **11.33** Dn 6.1-27   **11.34** Dn 3.1-30
11.35 1 K 17.17-24; 2 K 4.25-37; 2 Macc 6.18—7.42   **11.36** 1 K 22.26, 27;
2 Ch 18.25, 26; Jr 20.2; 37.15; 38.6   **11.37** 2 Ch 24.21

pends from beginning to end. He did not give up because of the cross! On the contrary, because of the joy that was waiting for him, he thought nothing of the disgrace of dying on the cross, and he is now seated at the right side of God's throne.

³Think of what he went through; how he put up with so much hatred from sinners! So do not let yourselves become discouraged and give up. ⁴For in your struggle against sin you have not yet had to resist to the point of being killed. ⁵Have you forgotten the encouraging words which God speaks to you as his children?

"My child, pay attention when
    the Lord corrects you,
and do not be discouraged
    when he rebukes you.
⁶Because the Lord corrects
    everyone he loves,
and punishes everyone he
    accepts as a child."

⁷Endure what you suffer as being a father's punishment; your suffering shows that God is treating you as his children. Was there ever a child who was not punished by his father? ⁸If you are not punished, as all his children are, it means you are not real children, but bastards. ⁹In the case of our human fathers, they punished us and we respected them. How much more, then, should we submit to our spiritual Father and live! ¹⁰Our human fathers punished us for a short time, as it seemed right to them; but God does it for our own good, so that we may share his holiness. ¹¹When we are punished, it seems to us at the time something to make us sad, not glad. Later, however, those who have been disciplined by such punishment reap the peaceful reward of a righteous life.

Instructions and Warnings

¹²Lift up your tired hands, then, and strengthen your trembling knees! ¹³Keep walking on straight paths, so that the lame foot may not be disabled, but instead be healed.

¹⁴Try to be at peace with everyone, and try to live a holy life, because no one will see the Lord without it. ¹⁵Guard against turning back from the grace of God. Let no one become like a bitter plant that grows up and causes many troubles with its poison. ¹⁶Let no one become immoral or unspiritual like Esau, who for a single meal sold his rights as the older son. ¹⁷Afterward, you know, he wanted to receive his father's blessing; but he was turned back, because he could not find any way to change what he had done, even though in tears he looked for it.ʲ

¹⁸You have not come, as the people of Israel came, to what you can feel, to Mount Sinai with its blazing fire, the darkness and the gloom, the storm, ¹⁹the blast of a trumpet, and the sound of a voice. When the people heard the voice, they begged not to hear another word, ²⁰because they could not bear the order which said, "If even an animal touches the mountain, it must be stoned to death." ²¹The sight was so terrifying that Moses said, "I am trembling and afraid!"

²²Instead, you have come to Mount Zion and to the city of the living God, the heavenly Jerusalem, with its thousands of angels. ²³You have come to the joyful gathering of God's first-born, whose names are written in heaven. You have come to God, who is the judge of all people, and to the spirits of good people made perfect. ²⁴You have come to Jesus, who arranged the new covenant, and to the sprinkled blood that

ʲ he looked for it; *or* he tried to get the blessing.
12.5, 6 Job 5.17; Pr 3.11, 12 (LXX)   **12.12** Is 35.3 (LXX)   **12.13** Pr 4.26 (LXX)
12.15 Dt 29.18 (LXX)   **12.16** Gn 25.29-34   **12.17** Gn 27.30-40   **12.18, 19** Ex 19.16-22;
20.18-21; Dt 4.11, 12; 5.22-27   **12.20** Ex 19.12, 13   **12.21** Dt 9.19   **12.24** Gn 4.10

*For this reason
Jesus also died outside the city. (13.12)*

promises much better things than does the blood of Abel.

25 Be careful, then, and do not refuse to hear him who speaks. Those who refused to hear the one who gave the divine message on earth did not escape. How much less shall we escape, then, if we turn away from the one who speaks from heaven! 26 His voice shook the earth at that time, but now he has promised, "I will once more shake not only the earth but heaven as well." 27 The words "once more" plainly show that the created things will be shaken and removed, so that the things that cannot be shaken will remain.

28 Let us be thankful, then, because we receive a kingdom that cannot be shaken. Let us be grateful and worship God in a way that will please him, with reverence and awe; 29 because our God is indeed a destroying fire.

How to Please God

13 Keep on loving one another as Christians. 2 Remember to welcome strangers in your homes. There were some who did that and welcomed angels without knowing it. 3 Remember those who are in prison, as though you were in prison with them. Remember those who are suffering, as though you were suffering as they are.

4 Marriage is to be honored by all, and husbands and wives must be faithful to each other. God will judge those who are immoral and those who commit adultery.

5 Keep your lives free from the love of money, and be satisfied with what you have. For God has said, "I will never leave you; I will never abandon you." 6 Let us be bold, then, and say,

"The Lord is my helper,
    I will not be afraid.
What can anyone do to me?"

7 Remember your former leaders, who spoke God's message to you. Think back on how they lived and died, and imitate their faith. 8 Jesus Christ is the same yesterday, today, and forever. 9 Do not let all kinds of strange teachings lead you from the right way. It is good to receive inner strength from God's grace, and not by obeying rules about foods; those who obey these rules have not been helped by them.

10 The priests who serve in the Jewish place of worship have no right to eat any of the sacrifice on our altar. 11 The Jewish high priest brings the blood of the animals into the Most Holy Place to offer it as a sacrifice for sins; but the bodies of the animals are burned outside the camp. 12 For this reason Jesus also died outside the city, in order to purify the people from sin with his own

12.25 Ex 20.22   **12.26** Hg 2.6 (LXX)   **12.29** Dt 4.24   **13.2** Gn 18.1-8; 19.1-3; Tb 5.4, 5
13.4 Ws 3.13   **13.5** Dt 31.6, 8; Js 1.5   **13.6** Ps 118.6 (LXX)   **13.11** Lv 16.27

blood. ¹³ Let us, then, go to him outside the camp and share his shame. ¹⁴ For there is no permanent city for us here on earth; we are looking for the city which is to come. ¹⁵ Let us, then, always offer praise to God as our sacrifice through Jesus, which is the offering presented by lips that confess him as Lord. ¹⁶ Do not forget to do good and to help one another, because these are the sacrifices that please God.

¹⁷ Obey your leaders and follow their orders. They watch over your souls without resting, since they must give to God an account of their service. If you obey them, they will do their work gladly; if not, they will do it with sadness, and that would be of no help to you.

¹⁸ Keep on praying for us. We are sure we have a clear conscience, because we want to do the right thing at all times. ¹⁹ And I beg you even more earnestly to pray that God will send me back to you soon.

ᵏ his blood; *or* his sacrificial death.

Closing Prayer

²⁰⁻²¹ God has raised from death our Lord Jesus, who is the Great Shepherd of the sheep as the result of his blood,ᵏ by which the eternal covenant is sealed. May the God of peace provide you with every good thing you need in order to do his will, and may he, through Jesus Christ, do in us what pleases him. And to Christ be the glory forever and ever! Amen.

Final Words

²² I beg you, my friends, to listen patiently to this message of encouragement; for this letter I have written you is not very long. ²³ I want you to know that our brother Timothy has been let out of prison. If he comes soon enough, I will have him with me when I see you.

²⁴ Give our greetings to all your leaders and to all God's people. The believers from Italy send you their greetings. ²⁵ May God's grace be with you all.

The Letter from

JAMES

INTRODUCTION

The Letter from James is a collection of practical instructions, written to "all God's people scattered over the whole world." The writer uses many vivid figures of speech to present instructions regarding practical wisdom and guidance for Christian attitudes and conduct. From the Christian perspective he deals with a variety of topics such as riches and poverty, temptation, good conduct, prejudice, faith and actions, the use of the tongue, wisdom, quarreling, pride and humility, judging others, boasting, patience, and prayer.

The letter emphasizes the importance of actions along with faith, in the practice of the Christian religion.

OUTLINE OF CONTENTS

---

1 From James, a servant of God and of the Lord Jesus Christ:

Greetings to all God's people scattered over the whole world.

Faith and Wisdom

2 My friends, consider yourselves fortunate when all kinds of trials come your way, 3 for you know that when your faith succeeds in facing such trials, the result is the ability to endure. 4 Make sure that your endurance carries you all the way without failing, so that you may be perfect and complete, lacking nothing. 5 But if any of you lack wisdom, you should pray to God, who will give it to you; because God gives generously and graciously to all. 6 But when you pray, you must believe and not doubt at all. Whoever doubts is like a wave in the sea that is driven and blown about by the wind. 7-8 If you are like that, unable to make up your mind and undecided in all you do, you must not think that you will receive anything from the Lord.

1.1 Mt 13.55; Mk 6.3; Ac 15.13; Ga 1.19   **1.2** Ws 3.5, 6   **1.5** Ws 8.20; Si 51.13, 14

Poverty and Riches

9 Those Christians who are poor must be glad when God lifts them up, 10 and the rich Christians must be glad when God brings them down. For the rich will pass away like the flower of a wild plant. 11 The sun rises with its blazing heat and burns the plant; its flower falls off, and its beauty is destroyed. In the same way the rich will be destroyed while they go about their business.

Testing and Tempting

12 Happy are those who remain faithful under trials, because when they succeed in passing such a test, they will receive as their reward the life which God has promised to those who love him. 13 If we are tempted by such trials, we must not say, "This temptation comes from God." For God cannot be tempted by evil, and he himself tempts no one. 14 But we are tempted when we are drawn away and trapped by our own evil desires. 15 Then our evil desires conceive and give birth to sin; and sin, when it is full-grown, gives birth to death.

16 Do not be deceived, my dear friends! 17 Every good gift and every perfect present comes from heaven; it comes down from God, the Creator of the heavenly lights, who does not change or cause darkness by turning. 18 By his own will he brought us into being through the word of truth, so that we should have first place among all his creatures.

Hearing and Doing

19 Remember this, my dear friends! Everyone must be quick to listen, but slow to speak and slow to become angry. 20 Human anger does not achieve God's righteous purpose. 21 So get rid of every filthy habit and all wicked conduct. Submit to God and accept the word that he plants in your hearts, which is able to save you.

22 Do not deceive yourselves by just listening to his word; instead, put it into practice. 23 If you listen to the word, but do not put it into practice you are like people who look in a mirror and see themselves as they are. 24 They take a good look at themselves and then go away and at once forget what they look like. 25 But if you look closely into the perfect law that sets people free, and keep on paying attention to it and do not simply listen and then forget it, but put it into practice — you will be blessed by God in what you do.

26 Do any of you think you are religious? If you do not control your tongue, your religion is worthless and you deceive yourself. 27 What God the Father considers to be pure and genuine religion is this: to take care of orphans and widows in their suffering and to keep oneself from being corrupted by the world.

Warning against Prejudice

2 My friends, as believers in our Lord Jesus Christ, the Lord of glory, you must never treat people in different ways according to their outward appearance. 2 Suppose a rich man wearing a gold ring and fine clothes comes to your meeting, and a poor man in ragged clothes also comes. 3 If you show more respect to the well-dressed man and say to him, "Have this best seat here," but say to the poor man, "Stand over there, or sit here on the floor by my feet," 4 then you are guilty of creating distinctions among yourselves and of making judgments based on evil motives.

5 Listen, my dear friends! God chose the poor people of this world to be rich in faith and to possess the kingdom which he promised to those who love him. 6 But you dishonor the poor! Who

1.10, 11 Is 40.6, 7 (LXX)   **1.13** Si 15.11-20   **1.19** Si 5.11

are the ones who oppress you and drag you before the judges? The rich! ⁷They are the ones who speak evil of that good name which has been given to you.

⁸You will be doing the right thing if you obey the law of the Kingdom, which is found in the scripture, "Love your neighbor as you love yourself." ⁹But if you treat people according to their outward appearance, you are guilty of sin, and the Law condemns you as a lawbreaker. ¹⁰Whoever breaks one commandment is guilty of breaking them all. ¹¹For the same one who said, "Do not commit adultery," also said, "Do not commit murder." Even if you do not commit adultery, you have become a lawbreaker if you commit murder. ¹²Speak and act as people who will be judged by the law that sets us free. ¹³For God will not show mercy when he judges the person who has not been merciful; but mercy triumphs over judgment.

Faith and Actions

¹⁴My friends, what good is it for one of you to say that you have faith if your actions do not prove it? Can that faith save you? ¹⁵Suppose there are brothers or sisters who need clothes and don't have enough to eat. ¹⁶What good is there in your saying to them, "God bless you! Keep warm and eat well!" — if you don't give them the necessities of life? ¹⁷So it is with faith: if it is alone and includes no actions, then it is dead.

¹⁸But someone will say, "One person has faith, another has actions." My answer is, "Show me how anyone can have faith without actions. I will show you my faith by my actions." ¹⁹Do you believe that there is only one God? Good! The demons also believe — and

tremble with fear. ²⁰You fool! Do you want to be shown that faith without actions is useless?ᵃ ²¹How was our ancestor Abraham put right with God? It was through his actions, when he offered his son Isaac on the altar. ²²Can't you see? His faith and his actions worked together; his faith was made perfect through his actions. ²³And the scripture came true that said, "Abraham believed God, and because of his faith God accepted him as righteous." And so Abraham was called God's friend. ²⁴You see, then, that it is by our actions that we are put right with God, and not by our faith alone.

²⁵It was the same with the prostitute Rahab. She was put right with God through her actions, by welcoming the Israelite spies and helping them to escape by a different road.

²⁶So then, as the body without the spirit is dead, also faith without actions is dead.

The Tongue

3 My friends, not many of you should become teachers. As you know, we teachers will be judged with greater strictness than others. ²All of us often make mistakes. But if a person never makes a mistake in what he says, he is perfect and is also able to control his whole being. ³We put a bit into the mouth of a horse to make it obey us, and we are able to make it go where we want. ⁴Or think of a ship: big as it is and driven by such strong winds, it can be steered by a very small rudder, and it goes wherever the pilot wants it to go. ⁵So it is with the tongue: small as it is, it can boast about great things.

Just think how large a forest can be set on fire by a tiny flame! ⁶And the

---

ᵃ useless; *some manuscripts have* dead.

2.8 Lv 19.18   **2.11 a** Ex 20.14; Dt 5.18; **b** Ex 20.13; Dt 5.17   **2.21** Gn 22.1-14; Si 44.19-21; 1 Macc 2.52   **2.23 a** Gn 15.6; **b** 2 Ch 20.7; Is 41.8   **2.25** Js 2.1-21
3.2 Si 5.9-15; 14.1; 28.13-26   **3.6** Si 5.13; 28.22

tongue is like a fire. It is a world of wrong, occupying its place in our bodies and spreading evil through our whole being. It sets on fire the entire course of our existence with the fire that comes to it from hell itself. [7]We humans are able to tame and have tamed all other creatures — wild animals and birds, reptiles and fish. [8]But no one has ever been able to tame the tongue. It is evil and uncontrollable, full of deadly poison. [9]We use it to give thanks to our Lord and Father and also to curse other people, who are created in the likeness of God. [10]Words of thanksgiving and cursing pour out from the same mouth. My friends, this should not happen! [11]No spring of water pours out sweet water and bitter water from the same opening. [12]A fig tree, my friends, cannot bear olives; a grapevine cannot bear figs, nor can a salty spring produce sweet water.

The Wisdom from Above

[13]Are there any of you who are wise and understanding? You are to prove it by your good life, by your good deeds performed with humility and wisdom. [14]But if in your heart you are jealous, bitter, and selfish, don't sin against the truth by boasting of your wisdom. [15]Such wisdom does not come down from heaven; it belongs to the world, it is unspiritual and demonic. [16]Where there is jealousy and selfishness, there is also disorder and every kind of evil. [17]But the wisdom from above is pure first of all; it is also peaceful, gentle, and friendly; it is full of compassion and produces a harvest of good deeds; it is free from prejudice and hypocrisy. [18]And goodness is the harvest that is produced from the seeds the peacemakers plant in peace.

Friendship with the World

4 Where do all the fights and quarrels among you come from? They come from your desires for pleasure, which are constantly fighting within you. [2]You want things, but you cannot have them, so you are ready to kill; you strongly desire things, but you cannot get them, so you quarrel and fight. You do not have what you want because you do not ask God for it. [3]And when you ask, you do not receive it, because your motives are bad; you ask for things to use for your own pleasures. [4]Unfaithful people! Don't you know that to be the world's friend means to be God's enemy? If you want to be the world's friend, you make yourself God's enemy. [5]Don't think that there is no truth in the scripture that says, "The spirit that God placed in us is filled with fierce desires."[b] [6]But the grace that God gives is even stronger. As the scripture says, "God resists the proud, but gives grace to the humble."

[7]So then, submit yourselves to God. Resist the Devil, and he will run away from you. [8]Come near to God, and he will come near to you. Wash your hands, you sinners! Purify your hearts, you hypocrites! [9]Be sorrowful, cry, and weep; change your laughter into crying, your joy into gloom! [10]Humble yourselves before the Lord, and he will lift you up.

Warning against Judging One Another

[11]Do not criticize one another, my friends. If you criticize or judge another Christian, you criticize and judge the Law. If you judge the Law, then you are no longer one who obeys the Law, but one who judges it. [12]God is the only lawgiver and judge. He alone can save and destroy. Who do you think you are, to judge someone else?

---

[b] The spirit . . . fierce desires; or God yearns jealously over the spirit that he placed in us.
3.9 Gn 1.26   **3.13** Si 19.20-30   **4.6** Pr 3.34 (LXX)

Warning against Boasting

13 Now listen to me, you that say, "Today or tomorrow we will travel to a certain city, where we will stay a year and go into business and make a lot of money." 14 You don't even know what your life tomorrow will be! You are like a puff of smoke, which appears for a moment and then disappears. 15 What you should say is this: "If the Lord is willing, we will live and do this or that." 16 But now you are proud, and you boast; all such boasting is wrong.

17 So then, if we do not do the good we know we should do, we are guilty of sin.

Warning to the Rich

5 And now, you rich people, listen to me! Weep and wail over the miseries that are coming upon you! 2 Your riches have rotted away, and your clothes have been eaten by moths. 3 Your gold and silver are covered with rust, and this rust will be a witness against you and will eat up your flesh like fire. You have piled up riches in these last days. 4 You have not paid any wages to those who work in your fields. Listen to their complaints! The cries of those who gather in your crops have reached the ears of God, the Lord Almighty. 5 Your life here on earth has been full of luxury and pleasure. You have made yourselves fat for the day of slaughter. 6 You have condemned and murdered innocent people, and they do not resist you.*c*

Patience and Prayer

7 Be patient, then, my friends, until the Lord comes. See how patient farmers are as they wait for their land to produce precious crops. They wait patiently for the autumn and spring rains. 8 You also must be patient. Keep your hopes high, for the day of the Lord's coming is near.

9 Do not complain against one another, my friends, so that God will not judge you. The Judge is near, ready to appear. 10 My friends, remember the prophets who spoke in the name of the Lord. Take them as examples of patient endurance under suffering. 11 We call them happy because they endured. You have heard of Job's patience, and you know how the Lord provided for him in the end. For the Lord is full of mercy and compassion.

12 Above all, my friends, do not use an oath when you make a promise. Do not swear by heaven or by earth or by anything else. Say only "Yes" when you mean yes, and "No" when you mean no, and then you will not come under God's judgment.

13 Are any among you in trouble? They should pray. Are any among you happy? They should sing praises. 14 Are any among you sick? They should send for the church elders, who will pray for them and rub olive oil on them in the name of the Lord. 15 This prayer made in faith will heal the sick; the Lord will restore them to health, and the sins they have commit-

This prayer made in faith will heal the sick. (5.15)

c people, and they do not resist you; *or* people. Will God not resist you?
4.13, 14 Pr 27.1   **4.13** Ws 2.4; 5.9-13   **5.2, 3** Mt 6.19   **5.3** Si 29.10-12   **5.4** Dt 24.14, 15
5.6 Ws 2.10-20   **5.11 a** Job 1.21, 22; 2.10; **b** Ps 103.8   **5.12** Mt 5.34-37   **5.14** Mk 6.13

ted will be forgiven. 16 So then, confess your sins to one another and pray for one another, so that you will be healed. The prayer of a good person has a powerful effect. 17 Elijah was the same kind of person as we are. He prayed earnestly that there would be no rain, and no rain fell on the land for three and a half years. 18 Once again he prayed, and

the sky poured out its rain and the earth produced its crops.

19 My friends, if any of you wander away from the truth and another one brings you back again, 20 remember this: whoever turns a sinner back from the wrong way will save that sinner's soul[d] from death and bring about the forgiveness of many sins.

---

[d] that sinner's soul; *or* his own soul.

5.16 Si 4.26　**5.17** 1 K 17.1; 18.1; Si 48.2, 3　**5.18** 1 K 18.42-45　**5.20** Pr 10.12; Tb 12.9;
1 P 4.8

The First Letter from PETER

INTRODUCTION

The First Letter from Peter was addressed to Christians, here called "God's chosen people," who were scattered throughout the northern part of Asia Minor. The main purpose of the letter is to encourage the readers, who were facing persecution and suffering for their faith. The writer does this by reminding his readers of the Good News about Jesus Christ, whose death, resurrection, and promised coming gave them hope. In the light of this they are to accept and endure their suffering, confident that it is a test of the genuineness of their faith and that they will be rewarded on "the Day when Jesus Christ is revealed."

Along with his encouragement in time of trouble, the writer also urges his readers to live as people who belong to Christ.

OUTLINE OF CONTENTS

1 From Peter, apostle of Jesus Christ—

To God's chosen people who live as refugees scattered throughout the provinces of Pontus, Galatia, Cappadocia, Asia, and Bithynia. ²You were chosen according to the purpose of God the Father and were made a holy people by his Spirit, to obey Jesus Christ and be purified by his blood.

May grace and peace be yours in full measure.

A Living Hope

³Let us give thanks to the God and Father of our Lord Jesus Christ! Because of his great mercy he gave us new life by raising Jesus Christ from death. This fills us with a living hope, ⁴and so we look forward to possessing the rich blessings that God keeps for his people. He keeps them for you in heaven, where they cannot decay or spoil or fade away. ⁵They are for you, who through faith are kept safe by God's power for the salvation which is ready to be revealed at the end of time.

⁶Be glad about this, even though it may now be necessary for you to be sad for a while because of the many kinds of trials you suffer. ⁷Their purpose is to prove that your faith is genuine. Even gold, which can be destroyed, is tested by fire; and so your faith, which is much more precious than gold, must also be tested, so that it may endure. Then you will receive praise and glory and honor on the Day when Jesus Christ is revealed. ⁸You love him, although you have not seen him, and you believe in him, although you do not now see him. So you rejoice with a great and glorious joy which words cannot express, ⁹because you are receiving the salvation of your souls, which is the purpose of your faith in him.

¹⁰It was concerning this salvation that the prophets made careful search and investigation, and they prophesied about this gift which God would give you. ¹¹They tried to find out when the time would be and how it would come.ᵃ This was the time to which Christ's Spirit in them was pointing, in predicting the sufferings that Christ would have to endure and the glory that would follow. ¹²God revealed to these prophets that their work was not for their own benefit, but for yours, as they spoke about those things which you have now heard from the messengers who announced the Good News by the power of the Holy Spirit sent from heaven. These are things which even the angels would like to understand.

A Call to Holy Living

¹³So then, have your minds ready for action. Keep alert and set your hope completely on the blessing which will be given you when Jesus Christ is revealed. ¹⁴Be obedient to God, and do not allow your lives to be shaped by those desires you had when you were still ignorant. ¹⁵Instead, be holy in all that you do, just as God who called you is holy. ¹⁶The scripture says, "Be holy because I am holy."

¹⁷You call him Father, when you pray to God, who judges all people by the same standard, according to what each one has done; so then, spend the rest of your lives here on earth in reverence for him. ¹⁸For you know what was paid to set you free from the worthless manner of life handed down by your ancestors. It was not something that can be destroyed, such as silver or gold; ¹⁹it was the costly sacrifice of Christ, who was like a lamb without defect or flaw. ²⁰He had been chosen by God before the creation of the world and was re-

---

ᵃ when the time would be and how it would come; *or* who the person would be and when he would come.

1.4 2 Esd 8.52   **1.7** 2 Esd 16.73   **1.16** Lv 11.44, 45; 19.2

vealed in these last days for your sake.
21 Through him you believe in God, who
raised him from death and gave him
glory; and so your faith and hope are
fixed on God.

22 Now that by your obedience to the
truth you have purified yourselves and
have come to have a sincere love for
other believers, love one another earnestly with all your heart. *b* 23 For
through the living and eternal word of
God you have been born again as the
children of a parent who is immortal,
not mortal. 24 As the scripture says,

"All human beings are like grass,
    and all their glory is like wild
        flowers.
The grass withers, and the
    flowers fall,
25   but the word of the Lord
        remains forever."

This word is the Good News that was
proclaimed to you.

The Living Stone and the Holy Nation

2 Rid yourselves, then, of all evil; no
more lying or hypocrisy or jealousy or insulting language. 2 Be like
newborn babies, always thirsty for the
pure spiritual milk, so that by drinking
it you may grow up and be saved. 3 As
the scripture says, "You have found out
for yourselves how kind the Lord is."

4 Come to the Lord, the living stone
rejected by people as worthless but chosen by God as valuable. 5 Come as living
stones, and let yourselves be used in
building the spiritual temple, where
you will serve as holy priests to offer
spiritual and acceptable sacrifices to
God through Jesus Christ. 6 For the
scripture says,

"I chose a valuable stone,
    which I am placing as the
        cornerstone in Zion;

and whoever believes in him
    will never be disappointed."

7 This stone is of great value for you that
believe; but for those who do not
believe:

"The stone which the builders
    rejected as worthless
turned out to be the most
    important of all."

8 And another scripture says,

"This is the stone that will make
    people stumble,
    the rock that will make them
        fall."

They stumbled because they did not believe in the word; such was God's will
for them.

9 But you are the chosen race, the
King's priests, the holy nation, God's
own people, chosen to proclaim the
wonderful acts of God, who called you
out of darkness into his own marvelous
light. 10 At one time you were not God's
people, but now you are his people; at
one time you did not know God's mercy,
but now you have received his mercy.

Slaves of God

11 I appeal to you, my friends, as
strangers and refugees in this world!
Do not give in to bodily passions, which
are always at war against the soul.
12 Your conduct among the heathen
should be so good that when they accuse you of being evildoers, they will
have to recognize your good deeds and
so praise God on the Day of his coming.

13 For the sake of the Lord submit
yourselves to every human authority: to
the Emperor, who is the supreme authority, 14 and to the governors, who
have been appointed by him to punish
the evildoers and to praise those who do
good. 15 For God wants you to silence
the ignorant talk of foolish people by

---

b with all your heart; *some manuscripts have* with a pure heart.
1.24, 25 Is 40.6-8 (LXX)   **2.3** Ps 34.8   **2.6** Is 28.16 (LXX)   **2.7** Ps 118.22   **2.8** Is 8.14, 15
2.9 a Ex 19.5, 6; Is 43.20 (LXX); **b** Ex 19.5; Dt 4.20; 7.6; 14.2; Titus 2.14; **c** Is 43.21;
d Is 9.2   **2.10** Ho 2.23

the good things you do. [16] Live as free people; do not, however, use your freedom to cover up any evil, but live as God's slaves. [17] Respect everyone, love other believers, honor God, and respect the Emperor.

The Example of Christ's Suffering

[18] You servants must submit yourselves to your masters and show them complete respect, not only to those who are kind and considerate, but also to those who are harsh. [19] God will bless you for this, if you endure the pain of undeserved suffering because you are conscious of his will. [20] For what credit is there if you endure the beatings you deserve for having done wrong? But if you endure suffering even when you have done right, God will bless you for it. [21] It was to this that God called you, for Christ himself suffered for you and left you an example, so that you would follow in his steps. [22] He committed no sin, and no one ever heard a lie come from his lips. [23] When he was insulted, he did not answer back with an insult; when he suffered, he did not threaten, but placed his hopes in God, the righteous Judge. [24] Christ himself carried our sins in his body to the cross, so that we might die to sin and live for righteousness. It is by his wounds that you have been healed. [25] You were like sheep that had lost their way, but now you have been brought back to follow the Shepherd and Keeper of your souls.

Wives and Husbands

3 In the same way you wives must submit yourselves to your husbands, so that if any of them do not believe God's word, your conduct will win them over to believe. It will not be necessary for you to say a word, [2] because they will see how pure and reverent your conduct is. [3] You should not use outward aids to make yourselves beautiful, such as the way you fix your hair, or the jewelry you put on, or the dresses you wear. [4] Instead, your beauty should consist of your true inner self, the ageless beauty of a gentle and quiet spirit, which is of the greatest value in God's sight. [5] For the devout women of the past who placed their hope in God used to make themselves beautiful by submitting themselves to their husbands. [6] Sarah was like that; she obeyed Abraham and called him her master. You are now her daughters if you do good and are not afraid of anything.

[7] In the same way you husbands must live with your wives with the proper understanding that they are more delicate than you. Treat them with respect, because they also will receive, together with you, God's gift of life. Do this so that nothing will interfere with your prayers.

Suffering for Doing Right

[8] To conclude: you must all have the same attitude and the same feelings; love one another, and be kind and humble with one another. [9] Do not pay back evil with evil or cursing with cursing; instead, pay back with a blessing, because a blessing is what God promised to give you when he called you. [10] As the scripture says,

"If you want to enjoy life
　and wish to see good times,
you must keep from speaking
　evil
　and stop telling lies.
[11] You must turn away from evil
　and do good;
you must strive for peace with
　all your heart.
[12] For the Lord watches over the
　righteous
　and listens to their prayers;

2.22 Is 53.9   **2.23** Is 53.7   **2.24, 25** Is 53.5, 6 (LXX)   **3.1** Eph 5.22; Col 3.18   **3.3** 1 Ti 2.9
3.6 Gn 18.12   **3.7** Eph 5.25; Col 3.19   **3.10-12** Ps 34.12-16 (LXX)

but he opposes those who do evil."

13 Who will harm you if you are eager to do what is good? 14 But even if you should suffer for doing what is right, how happy you are! Do not be afraid of anyone, and do not worry. 15 But have reverence for Christ in your hearts, and honor him as Lord. Be ready at all times to answer anyone who asks you to explain the hope you have in you, 16 but do it with gentleness and respect. Keep your conscience clear, so that when you are insulted, those who speak evil of your good conduct as followers of Christ will become ashamed of what they say. 17 For it is better to suffer for doing good, if this should be God's will, than for doing evil. 18 For Christ died[c] for sins once and for all, a good man on behalf of sinners, in order to lead you to God. He was put to death physically, but made alive spiritually, 19 and in his spiritual existence he went and preached to the imprisoned spirits. 20 These were the spirits of those who had not obeyed God when he waited patiently during the days that Noah was building his boat. The few people in the boat — eight in all — were saved by the water, 21 which was a symbol pointing to baptism, which now saves you. It is not the washing off of bodily dirt, but the promise made to God from a good conscience. It saves you through the resurrection of Jesus Christ, 22 who has gone to heaven and is at the right side of God, ruling over all angels and heavenly authorities and powers.

Changed Lives

4 Since Christ suffered physically, you too must strengthen yourselves with the same way of thinking that he had; because whoever suffers physically is no longer involved with sin. 2 From now on, then, you must live the rest of your earthly lives controlled by God's will and not by human desires. 3 You have spent enough time in the past doing what the heathen like to do. Your lives were spent in indecency, lust, drunkenness, orgies, drinking parties, and the disgusting worship of idols. 4 And now the heathen are surprised when you do not join them in the same wild and reckless living, and so they insult you. 5 But they will have to give an account of themselves to God, who is ready to judge the living and the dead. 6 That is why the Good News was preached also to the dead, to those who had been judged in their physical existence as everyone is judged; it was preached to them so that in their spiritual existence they may live as God lives.

Good Managers of God's Gifts

7 The end of all things is near. You must be self-controlled and alert, to be able to pray. 8 Above everything, love one another earnestly, because love covers over many sins. 9 Open your homes to each other without complaining. 10 Each one, as a good manager of God's different gifts, must use for the good of others the special gift he has received from God. 11 Those who preach must preach God's messages; those who serve must serve with the strength that God gives them, so that in all things praise may be given to God through Jesus Christ, to whom belong glory and power forever and ever. Amen.

Suffering as a Christian

12 My dear friends, do not be surprised at the painful test you are suffering, as though something unusual were happening to you. 13 Rather be glad that you are sharing Christ's sufferings, so that you may be full of joy when his glory is revealed. 14 Happy are

---

[c] died; *many manuscripts have* suffered.

3.14 Mt 5.10   **3.14, 15** Is 8.12, 13   **3.20** Gn 6.1 – 7.24   **4.8** Pr 10.12; Tb 12.9

you if you are insulted because you are Christ's followers; this means that the glorious Spirit, the Spirit of God, is resting on you. [15] If you suffer, it must not be because you are a murderer or a thief or a criminal or a meddler in other people's affairs. [16] However, if you suffer because you are a Christian, don't be ashamed of it, but thank God that you bear Christ's name.

[17] The time has come for judgment to begin, and God's own people are the first to be judged. If it starts with us, how will it end with those who do not believe the Good News from God? [18] As the scripture says,

"It is difficult for good people to
    be saved;
what, then, will become of
    godless sinners?"

[19] So then, those who suffer because it is God's will for them, should by their good actions trust themselves completely to their Creator, who always keeps his promise.

The Flock of God

5 I, who am an elder myself, appeal to the church elders among you. I am a witness of Christ's sufferings, and I will share in the glory that will be revealed. I appeal to you [2] to be shepherds of the flock that God gave you and to take care of it willingly, as God wants you to, and not unwillingly. Do your work, not for mere pay, but from a real desire to serve. [3] Do not try to rule over those who have been put in your care, but be examples to the flock. [4] And when the Chief Shepherd appears, you will receive the glorious crown which will never lose its brightness.

[5] In the same way you younger people must submit yourselves to your elders. And all of you must put on the apron of humility, to serve one another; for the scripture says, "God resists the proud, but shows favor to the humble." [6] Humble yourselves, then, under God's mighty hand, so that he will lift you up in his own good time. [7] Leave all your worries with him, because he cares for you.

[8] Be alert, be on watch! Your enemy, the Devil, roams around like a roaring lion, looking for someone to devour. [9] Be firm in your faith and resist him, because you know that other believers in all the world are going through the same kind of sufferings. [10] But after you have suffered for a little while, the God of all grace, who calls you to share his eternal glory in union with Christ, will himself perfect you and give you firmness, strength, and a sure foundation. [11] To him be the power forever! Amen.

Final Greetings

[12] I write you this brief letter with the help of Silas, whom I regard as a faithful Christian. I want to encourage you and give my testimony that this is the true grace of God. Stand firm in it.

[13] Your sister church in Babylon,[d] also chosen by God, sends you greetings, and so does my son Mark. [14] Greet one another with the kiss of Christian love.

May peace be with all of you who belong to Christ.

---

[d] BABYLON: *As in the book of Revelation, this probably refers to Rome.*
4.18 Pr 11.31 (LXX)   **5.2** Jn 21.15-17   **5.5** Pr 3.34 (LXX)   **5.6** Mt 23.12; Lk 14.11; 18.14
5.7 Si 2.1-18   **5.12** Ac 15.22, 40   **5.13** Ac 12.12, 25; 13.13; 15.37-39; Col 4.10; Phm 24

The Second Letter from
PETER

INTRODUCTION

The Second Letter from Peter is addressed to a wide circle of early Christians. Its main concern is to combat the work of false teachers and the immorality which results from such teaching. The answer to these problems is found in holding to the true knowledge of God and of the Lord Jesus Christ, knowledge which has been conveyed by persons who themselves have seen Jesus and have heard him teach. The writer is especially concerned with the teaching of those who claim that Christ will not return again. He says that the apparent delay in Christ's return is due to the fact that God "does not want anyone to be destroyed, but wants all to turn away from their sins."

OUTLINE OF CONTENTS

---

1 From Simon Peter, a servant and apostle of Jesus Christ —

To those who through the righteousness of our God and Savior Jesus Christ have been given a faith as precious as ours:

² May grace and peace be yours in full measure through your knowledge of God and of Jesus our Lord.

God's Call and Choice

³ God's divine power has given us everything we need to live a truly religious life through our knowledge of the one who called us to share in his own*a* glory and goodness. ⁴ In this way he has given us the very great and precious gifts he promised, so that by means of these gifts you may escape from the destructive lust that is in the world, and may come to share the divine nature. ⁵ For this very reason do your best to add goodness to your faith; to your goodness add knowledge; ⁶ to your knowledge add self-control; to your self-control add endurance; to your endurance add godliness; ⁷ to your godliness add Christian affection; and to your Christian affection add love. ⁸ These are the qualities you need, and if you have them in abundance, they will make you active and effective in your knowledge of our Lord Jesus Christ. ⁹ But if you do not have them, you are so shortsighted that you cannot see and have forgotten that you have been purified from your past sins.

¹⁰ So then, my friends, try even harder to make God's call and his choice of you a permanent experience; if you do so, you will never abandon

---

a to share in his own; *some manuscripts have* through his.

To make God's call . . . a permanent experience (1.10)

from the Supreme Glory, saying, "This is my own dear Son, with whom I am pleased!" ¹⁸ We ourselves heard this voice coming from heaven, when we were with him on the holy mountain.

¹⁹ So we are even more confident of the message proclaimed by the prophets. You will do well to pay attention to it, because it is like a lamp shining in a dark place until the Day dawns and the light of the morning star shines in your hearts. ²⁰ Above all else, however, remember that none of us can explain by ourselves a prophecy in the Scriptures. ²¹ For no prophetic message ever came just from the human will, but people were under the control of the Holy Spirit as they spoke the message that came from God.

your faith.ᵇ ¹¹ In this way you will be given the full right to enter the eternal Kingdom of our Lord and Savior Jesus Christ.

¹² And so I will always remind you of these matters, even though you already know them and are firmly grounded in the truth you have received. ¹³ I think it only right for me to stir up your memory of these matters as long as I am still alive. ¹⁴ I know that I shall soon put off this mortal body, as our Lord Jesus Christ plainly told me. ¹⁵ I will do my best, then, to provide a way for you to remember these matters at all times after my death.

Eyewitnesses of Christ's Glory

¹⁶ We have not depended on made-up stories in making known to you the mighty coming of our Lord Jesus Christ. With our own eyes we saw his greatness. ¹⁷ We were there when he was given honor and glory by God the Father, when the voice came to him

False Teachers

2 False prophets appeared in the past among the people, and in the same way false teachers will appear among you. They will bring in destructive, untrue doctrines, and will deny the Master who redeemed them, and so they will bring upon themselves sudden destruction. ² Even so, many will follow their immoral ways; and because of what they do, others will speak evil of the Way of truth. ³ In their greed these false teachers will make a profit out of telling you made-up stories. For a long time now their Judge has been ready, and their Destroyer has been wide awake!

⁴ God did not spare the angels who sinned, but threw them into hell, where they are kept chained in darkness,ᶜ waiting for the Day of Judgment. ⁵ God did not spare the ancient world, but brought the flood on the world of godless people; the only ones he saved were Noah, who preached righteousness, and seven other people. ⁶ God con-

---

ᵇ abandon your faith; *or* fall into sin.   ᶜ chained in darkness; *some manuscripts have* in dark pits.

1.17, 18 Mt 17.1-5; Mk 9.2-7; Lk 9.28-35   **2.5** Gn 6.1 — 7.24; Ws 10.4   **2.6** Gn 19.24

demned the cities of Sodom and Gomorrah, destroying them with fire, and made them an example of what will happen to the godless. [7] He rescued Lot, a good man, who was distressed by the immoral conduct of lawless people. [8] That good man lived among them, and day after day he suffered agony as he saw and heard their evil actions. [9] And so the Lord knows how to rescue godly people from their trials and how to keep the wicked under punishment for the Day of Judgment, [10] especially those who follow their filthy bodily lusts and despise God's authority.

These false teachers are bold and arrogant, and show no respect for the glorious beings above; instead, they insult them. [11] Even the angels, who are so much stronger and mightier than these false teachers, do not accuse them with insults in the presence of the Lord. [12] But these people act by instinct, like wild animals born to be captured and killed; they attack with insults anything they do not understand. They will be destroyed like wild animals, [13] and they will be paid with suffering for the suffering they have caused. Pleasure for them is to do anything in broad daylight that will satisfy their bodily appetites; they are a shame and a disgrace as they join you in your meals, all the while enjoying their deceitful ways! [14] They want to look for nothing but the chance to commit adultery; their appetite for sin is never satisfied. They lead weak people into a trap. Their hearts are trained to be greedy. They are under God's curse! [15] They have left the straight path and have lost their way; they have followed the path taken by Balaam son of Beor, who loved the money he would get for doing wrong [16] and was rebuked for his sin. His donkey spoke with a human voice and stopped the prophet's insane action.

[17] These people are like dried-up springs, like clouds blown along by a storm; God has reserved a place for them in the deepest darkness. [18] They make proud and stupid statements, and use immoral bodily lusts to trap those who are just beginning to escape from among people who live in error. [19] They promise them freedom while they themselves are slaves of destructive habits — for we are slaves of anything that has conquered us. [20] If people have escaped from the corrupting forces of the world through their knowledge of our Lord and Savior Jesus Christ, and then are again caught and conquered by them, such people are in worse condition at the end than they were at the beginning. [21] It would have been much better for them never to have known the way of righteousness than to know it and then turn away from the sacred command that was given them. [22] What happened to them shows that the proverbs are true: "A dog goes back to what it has vomited" and "A pig that has been washed goes back to roll in the mud."

The Promise of the Lord's Coming

3 My dear friends, this is now the second letter I have written you. In both letters I have tried to arouse pure thoughts in your minds by reminding you of these things. [2] I want you to remember the words that were spoken long ago by the holy prophets, and the command from the Lord and Savior which was given you by your apostles. [3] First of all, you must understand that in the last days some people will appear whose lives are controlled by their own lusts. They will make fun of you [4] and will ask, "He promised to come, didn't he? Where is he? Our ancestors have already died, but everything is still the same as it was since the creation of the world!" [5] They purposely ignore the fact that long ago God gave a command, and the heavens and earth were created. The earth was formed out of water and by water, [6] and it was also by water, the water of the flood, that the old world was destroyed. [7] But the heavens and the earth that now exist are being preserved by the same command of God, in order to be destroyed by fire. They are being kept for the day when godless people will be judged and destroyed.

[8] But do not forget one thing, my dear friends! There is no difference in the Lord's sight between one day and a thousand years; to him the two are the same. [9] The Lord is not slow to do what he has promised, as some think. Instead, he is patient with you, because he does not want anyone to be destroyed, but wants all to turn away from their sins.

[10] But the Day of the Lord will come like a thief. On that Day the heavens will disappear with a shrill noise, the heavenly bodies will burn up and be destroyed, and the earth with everything in it will vanish. [d] [11] Since all these things will be destroyed in this way, what kind of people should you be? Your lives should be holy and dedicated to God, [12] as you wait for the Day of God and do your best to make it come

soon — the Day when the heavens will burn up and be destroyed, and the heavenly bodies will be melted by the heat. [13] But we wait for what God has promised: new heavens and a new earth, where righteousness will be at home.

[14] And so, my friends, as you wait for that Day, do your best to be pure and faultless in God's sight and to be at peace with him. [15] Look on our Lord's patience as the opportunity he is giving you to be saved, just as our dear friend Paul wrote to you, using the wisdom that God gave him. [16] This is what he says in all his letters when he writes on the subject. There are some difficult things in his letters which ignorant and unstable people explain falsely, as they do with other passages of the Scriptures. So they bring on their own destruction.

[17] But you, my friends, already know this. Be on your guard, then, so that you will not be led away by the errors of lawless people and fall from your safe position. [18] But continue to grow in the grace and knowledge of our Lord and Savior Jesus Christ. To him be the glory, now and forever! Amen.

[d] vanish; *some manuscripts have* be found; *others have* be burned up; *one has* be found destroyed.

3.6 Gn 7.11   **3.8** Ps 90.4   **3.10** Mt 24.43; Lk 12.39; 1 Th 5.2; Rev 16.15   **3.13** Is 65.17; 66.22; Rev 21.1

The First Letter of
JOHN

INTRODUCTION

The First Letter of John has two main purposes: to encourage its readers to live in fellowship with God and with his Son, Jesus Christ, and to warn them against following false teaching that would destroy this fellowship. This teaching was based on the belief that evil results from contact with the physical world, and so Jesus, the Son of God, could not really have been a human being. Those teachers claimed that to be saved was to be set free from concern with life in this world; and they also taught that salvation had nothing to do with matters of morality or of love for others.

In opposition to this teaching the writer clearly states that Jesus Christ was a real human being, and he emphasizes that all who believe in Jesus and love God must also love one another.

OUTLINE OF CONTENTS

The Word of Life

1 We write to you about the Word of life, which has existed from the very beginning. We have heard it, and we have seen it with our eyes; yes, we have seen it, and our hands have touched it. ² When this life became visible, we saw it; so we speak of it and tell you about the eternal life which was with the Father and was made known to us. ³ What we have seen and heard we announce to you also, so that you will join with us in the fellowship that we have with the Father and with his Son Jesus Christ. ⁴ We write this in order that our *a* joy may be complete.

God Is Light

⁵ Now the message that we have heard from his Son and announce is this: God is light, and there is no darkness at all in him. ⁶ If, then, we say that we have fellowship with him, yet at the same time live in the darkness, we are lying both in our words and in our actions. ⁷ But if we live in the light — just as he is in the light — then we have fellowship with one another, and the blood of Jesus, his Son, purifies us from every sin.

⁸ If we say that we have no sin, we deceive ourselves, and there is no truth in us. ⁹ But if we confess our sins to

---

a our; *some manuscripts have* your.
1.1 Jn 1.1   **1.2** Jn 1.14

God, he will keep his promise and do what is right: he will forgive us our sins and purify us from all our wrongdoing. ¹⁰If we say that we have not sinned, we make a liar out of God, and his word is not in us.

Christ Our Helper

2 I am writing this to you, my children, so that you will not sin; but if anyone does sin, we have someone who pleads with the Father on our behalf—Jesus Christ, the righteous one. ²And Christ himself is the means by which our sins are forgiven, and not our sins only, but also the sins of everyone.

³If we obey God's commands, then we are sure that we know him. ⁴If we say that we know him, but do not obey his commands, we are liars and there is no truth in us. ⁵But if we obey his word, we are the ones whose love for God has really been made perfect. This is how we can be sure that we are in union with God: ⁶if we say that we remain in union with God, we should live just as Jesus Christ did.

The New Command

⁷My dear friends, this command I am writing you is not new; it is the old command, the one you have had from the very beginning. The old command is the message you have already heard. ⁸However, the command I now write you is new, because its truth is seen in Christ and also in you. For the darkness is passing away, and the real light is already shining.

⁹If we say that we are in the light, yet hate others, we are in the darkness to this very hour. ¹⁰If we love others, we live in the light, and so there is nothing in us that will cause someone else[b] to

sin. ¹¹But if we hate others, we are in the darkness; we walk in it and do not know where we are going, because the darkness has made us blind.

If we love others . . . if we hate others. (2.10,11)

¹²I write to you, my children, because your sins are forgiven for the sake of Christ. ¹³I write to you, fathers, because you know him who has existed from the beginning. I write to you, young people, because you have defeated the Evil One.

¹⁴I write to you, my children, because you know the Father. I write to you, fathers, because you know him who has existed from the beginning. I write to you, young people, because you are strong; the word of God lives in you, and you have defeated the Evil One.

¹⁵Do not love the world or anything that belongs to the world. If you love the world, you do not love the Father. ¹⁶Everything that belongs to the world—what the sinful self desires, what people see and want, and everything in this world that people are so proud of—none of this comes from the Father; it all comes from the world. ¹⁷The world and everything in it that people desire is passing away; but those who do the will of God live forever.

---

b someone else; or us.
2.7 Jn 13.34

The Enemy of Christ

18 My children, the end is near! You were told that the Enemy of Christ would come; and now many enemies of Christ have already appeared, and so we know that the end is near. **19** These people really did not belong to our fellowship, and that is why they left us; if they had belonged to our fellowship, they would have stayed with us. But they left so that it might be clear that none of them really belonged to us.

20 But you have had the Holy Spirit poured out on you by Christ, and so all of you know the truth. **21** I write you, then, not because you do not know the truth; instead, it is because you do know it, and you also know that no lie ever comes from the truth.

22 Who, then, is the liar? It is those who say that Jesus is not the Messiah. Such people are the Enemy of Christ — they reject both the Father and the Son. **23** For those who reject the Son reject also the Father; those who accept the Son have the Father also.

24 Be sure, then, to keep in your hearts the message you heard from the beginning. If you keep that message, then you will always live in union with the Son and the Father. **25** And this is what Christ himself promised to give us — eternal life.

26 I am writing this to you about those who are trying to deceive you. **27** But as for you, Christ has poured out his Spirit on you. As long as his Spirit remains in you, you do not need anyone to teach you. For his Spirit teaches you about everything, and what he teaches is true, not false. Obey the Spirit's teaching, then, and remain in union with Christ.

28 Yes, my children, remain in union with him, so that when he appears we may be full of courage and need not hide in shame from him on the Day he comes. **29** You know that Christ is righteous; you should know, then, that everyone who does what is right is God's child.

Children of God

3 See how much the Father has loved us! His love is so great that we are called God's children — and so, in fact, we are. This is why the world does not know us: it has not known God. **2** My dear friends, we are now God's children, but it is not yet clear what we shall become. But we know that when Christ appears, we shall be like him, because we shall see him as he really is. **3** Everyone who has this hope in Christ keeps himself pure, just as Christ is pure.

4 Whoever sins is guilty of breaking God's law, because sin is a breaking of the law. **5** You know that Christ appeared in order to take away sins,[c] and that there is no sin in him. **6** So everyone who lives in union with Christ does not continue to sin; but whoever continues to sin has never seen him or known him.

7 Let no one deceive you, my children! Whoever does what is right is righteous, just as Christ is righteous. **8** Whoever continues to sin belongs to the Devil, because the Devil has sinned from the very beginning. The Son of God appeared for this very reason, to destroy what the Devil had done.

9 Those who are children of God do not continue to sin, for God's very nature is in them; and because God is their Father, they cannot continue to sin. **10** Here is the clear difference between God's children and the Devil's children: those who do not do what is right or do not love others are not God's children.

---

[c] sins; *some manuscripts have* our sins.
3.1 Jn 1.12   **3.5** Jn 1.29

Love One Another

[11] The message you heard from the very beginning is this: we must love one another. [12] We must not be like Cain; he belonged to the Evil One and murdered his own brother Abel. Why did Cain murder him? Because the things he himself did were wrong, and the things his brother did were right. [13] So do not be surprised, my friends, if the people of the world hate you. [14] We know that we have left death and come over into life; we know it because we love others. Those who do not love are still under the power of death. [15] Those who hate others are murderers, and you know that murderers do not have eternal life in them. [16] This is how we know what love is: Christ gave his life for us. We too, then, ought to give our lives for others! [17] If we are rich and see others in need, yet close our hearts against them, how can we claim that we love God? [18] My children, our love should not be just words and talk; it must be true love, which shows itself in action.

Courage before God

[19] This, then, is how we will know that we belong to the truth; this is how we will be confident in God's presence. [20] If our conscience condemns us, we know that God is greater than our conscience and that he knows everything. [21] And so, my dear friends, if our conscience does not condemn us, we have courage in God's presence. [22] We receive from him whatever we ask, because we obey his commands and do what pleases him. [23] What he commands is that we believe in his Son Jesus Christ and love one another, just as Christ commanded us. [24] Those who obey God's commands live in union with God and God lives in union with them. And because of the Spirit that

God has given us we know that God lives in union with us.

The True Spirit and the False Spirit

4 My dear friends, do not believe all who claim to have the Spirit, but test them to find out if the spirit they have comes from God. For many false prophets have gone out everywhere. [2] This is how you will be able to know whether it is God's Spirit: anyone who acknowledges that Jesus Christ came as a human being has the Spirit who comes from God. [3] But anyone who denies this about Jesus does not have the Spirit from God. The spirit that he has is from the Enemy of Christ; you heard that it would come, and now it is here in the world already.

[4] But you belong to God, my children, and have defeated the false prophets, because the Spirit who is in you is more powerful than the spirit in those who belong to the world. [5] Those false prophets speak about matters of the world, and the world listens to them because they belong to the world. [6] But we belong to God. Whoever knows God listens to us; whoever does not belong to God does not listen to us. This, then, is how we can tell the difference between the Spirit of truth and the spirit of error.

God Is Love

[7] Dear friends, let us love one another, because love comes from God. Whoever loves is a child of God and knows God. [8] Whoever does not love does not know God, for God is love. [9] And God showed his love for us by sending his only Son into the world, so that we might have life through him. [10] This is what love is: it is not that we have loved God, but that he loved us and sent his Son to be the means by which our sins are forgiven.

[11] Dear friends, if this is how God loved us, then we should love one an-

other. ¹²No one has ever seen God, but if we love one another, God lives in union with us, and his love is made perfect in us.

¹³We are sure that we live in union with God and that he lives in union with us, because he has given us his Spirit. ¹⁴And we have seen and tell others that the Father sent his Son to be the Savior of the world. ¹⁵If we declare that Jesus is the Son of God, we live in union with God and God lives in union with us. ¹⁶And we ourselves know and believe the love which God has for us.

God is love, and those who live in love live in union with God and God lives in union with them. ¹⁷Love is made perfect in us in order that we may have courage on the Judgment Day; and we will have it because our life in this world is the same as Christ's. ¹⁸There is no fear in love; perfect love drives out all fear. So then, love has not been made perfect in anyone who is afraid, because fear has to do with punishment.

¹⁹We love because God first loved us. ²⁰If we say we love God, but hate others, we are liars. For we cannot love God, whom we have not seen, if we do not love others, whom we have seen.

Perfect love drives out all fear. (4.18)

Whoever believes that Jesus is the Messiah is a child of God. (5.1)

²¹The command that Christ has given us is this: whoever loves God must love others also.

Our Victory over the World

5 Whoever believes that Jesus is the Messiah is a child of God; and whoever loves a father loves his child also. ²This is how we know that we love God's children: it is by loving God and obeying his commands. ³For our love for God means that we obey his commands. And his commands are not too hard for us, ⁴because every child of God is able to defeat the world. And we win the victory over the world by means of our faith. ⁵Who can defeat the world? Only the person who believes that Jesus is the Son of God.

The Witness about Jesus Christ

⁶Jesus Christ is the one who came with the water of his baptism and the blood of his death. He came not only with the water, but with both the water and the blood. And the Spirit himself testifies that this is true, because the Spirit is truth. ⁷There are three witnesses: ⁸the Spirit, the water, and the blood; and all three give the same testimony. ⁹We believe human testimony; but God's testimony is much stronger, and he has given this testimony about his Son. ¹⁰So those who believe in the Son of God have this testimony in their

own heart; but those who do not believe God, have made a liar of him, because they have not believed what God has said about his Son. ¹¹ The testimony is this: God has given us eternal life, and this life has its source in his Son. ¹² Whoever has the Son has this life; whoever does not have the Son of God does not have life.

Eternal Life

¹³ I am writing this to you so that you may know that you have eternal life — you that believe in the Son of God. ¹⁴ We have courage in God's presence, because we are sure that he hears us if we ask him for anything that is according to his will. ¹⁵ He hears us whenever we ask him; and since we know this is true, we know also that he gives us what we ask from him.

¹⁶ If you see a believer commit a sin

5.11 Jn 3.36

that does not lead to death, you should pray to God, who will give that person life. This applies to those whose sins do not lead to death. But there is sin which leads to death, and I do not say that you should pray to God about that. ¹⁷ All wrongdoing is sin, but there is sin which does not lead to death.

¹⁸ We know that no children of God keep on sinning, for the Son of God keeps them safe, and the Evil One cannot harm them.

¹⁹ We know that we belong to God even though the whole world is under the rule of the Evil One.

²⁰ We know that the Son of God has come and has given us understanding, so that we know the true God. We live in union with the true God — in union with his Son Jesus Christ. This is the true God, and this is eternal life.

²¹ My children, keep yourselves safe from false gods!

The Second Letter of
JOHN

INTRODUCTION

The Second Letter of John was written by "the Elder" to "the dear Lady and to her children," probably meaning a local church and its members. The brief message is an appeal to love one another and a warning against false teachers and their teachings.

OUTLINE OF CONTENTS

---

¹ From the Elder —

To the dear Lady and to her children,ᵃ whom I truly love. And I am not the only one, but all who know the truth love you, ² because the truth remains in us and will be with us forever.

³ May God the Father and Jesus Christ, the Father's Son, give us grace, mercy, and peace; may they be ours in truth and love.

Truth and Love

⁴ How happy I was to find that some of your children live in the truth, just as the Father commanded us. ⁵ And so I ask you, dear Lady: let us all love one another. This is no new command I am writing you; it is the command which we have had from the beginning. ⁶ This love I speak of means that we must live in obedience to God's commands. The command, as you have all heard from the beginning, is that you must all live in love.

⁷ Many deceivers have gone out over the world, people who do not acknowledge that Jesus Christ came as a human being. Such a person is a deceiver and the Enemy of Christ. ⁸ Be on your guard, then, so that you will not lose what weᵇ have worked for, but will receive your reward in full.

⁹ Anyone who does not stay with the teaching of Christ, but goes beyond it, does not have God. Whoever does stay with the teaching has both the Father and the Son. ¹⁰ So then, if some come to you who do not bring this teaching, do not welcome them in your homes; do not even say, "Peace be with you." ¹¹ For anyone who wishes them peace becomes their partner in the evil things they do.

Final Words

¹² I have so much to tell you, but I would rather not do it with paper and ink; instead, I hope to visit you and talk

---

ᵃ LADY AND . . . HER CHILDREN: *This probably refers to a church and its members (also in verses 4, 5).*   ᵇ we; *some manuscripts have* you.

5 Jn 13.34; 15.12, 17

with you personally, so that we shall be completely happy.

send you their greetings.

*CHILDREN OF YOUR DEAR SISTER: *This probably refers to the members of the church to which the writer belonged.*

The Third Letter of
JOHN

INTRODUCTION

The Third Letter of John was written by "the Elder" to a church leader named Gaius. The writer praises Gaius because of his help to other Christians, and warns against a man named Diotrephes.

OUTLINE OF CONTENTS

¹From the Elder—

To my dear Gaius, whom I truly love.

²My dear friend, I pray that everything may go well with you and that you may be in good health — as I know you are well in spirit. ³I was so happy when some Christians arrived and told me how faithful you are to the truth — just as you always live in the truth. ⁴Nothing makes me happier than to hear that my children live in the truth.

Gaius Is Praised

⁵My dear friend, you are so faithful in the work you do for other Christians, even when they are strangers. ⁶They have spoken to the church here about your love. Please help them to continue their trip in a way that will please God. ⁷For they set out on their trip in the service of Christ without accepting any help from unbelievers. ⁸We Christians, then, must help these people, so that we may share in their work for the truth.

Diotrephes and Demetrius

⁹I wrote a short letter to the church; but Diotrephes, who likes to be their leader, will not pay any attention to what I say. ¹⁰When I come, then, I will bring up everything he has done: the terrible things he says about us and the

1 Ac 19.29; Ro 16.23; 1 Co 1.14

lies he tells! But that is not enough for him; he will not receive the Christians when they come, and even stops those who want to receive them and tries to drive them out of the church!

11 My dear friend, do not imitate what is bad, but imitate what is good. Whoever does good belongs to God; whoever does what is bad has not seen God.

12 Everyone speaks well of Demetrius; truth itself speaks well of him.

And we add our testimony, and you know that what we say is true.

Final Greetings

13 I have so much to tell you, but I do not want to do it with pen and ink. 14 I hope to see you soon, and then we will talk personally.

15 Peace be with you.

All your friends send greetings. Greet all our friends personally.

The Letter from
JUDE

INTRODUCTION

The Letter from Jude was written to warn against false teachers who claimed to be believers. In this brief letter, which is similar in content to *2 Peter,* the writer encourages his readers "to fight on for the faith which once and for all God has given to his people."

OUTLINE OF CONTENTS

1 From Jude, servant of Jesus Christ, and brother of James —

To those who have been called by God, who live in the love of God the Father and the protection of Jesus Christ:

2 May mercy, peace, and love be yours in full measure.

False Teachers

3 My dear friends, I was doing my best to write to you about the salvation we share in common, when I felt the need of writing at once to encourage you to fight on for the faith which once and for all God has given to his people. 4 For some godless people have slipped

1 Mt 13.55; Mk 6.3

in unnoticed among us, persons who distort the message about the grace of our God in order to excuse their immoral ways, and who reject Jesus Christ, our only Master and Lord. Long ago the Scriptures predicted the condemnation they have received.

5 For even though you know all this, I want to remind you of how the Lord[a] once rescued the people of Israel from Egypt, but afterward destroyed those who did not believe. 6 Remember the angels who did not stay within the limits of their proper authority, but abandoned their own dwelling place: they are bound with eternal chains in the darkness below, where God is keeping them for that great Day on which they will be condemned. 7 Remember Sodom and Gomorrah, and the nearby towns, whose people acted as those angels did and indulged in sexual immorality and perversion: they suffer the punishment of eternal fire as a plain warning to all.

8 In the same way also, these people have visions which make them sin against their own bodies; they despise God's authority and insult the glorious beings above. 9 Not even the chief angel Michael did this. In his quarrel with the Devil, when they argued about who would have the body of Moses, Michael did not dare condemn the Devil with insulting words, but said, "The Lord rebuke you!" 10 But these people attack with insults anything they do not understand; and those things that they know by instinct, like wild animals, are the very things that destroy them. 11 How terrible for them! They have followed the way that Cain took. For the sake of money they have given themselves over to the error that Balaam committed. They have rebelled as Korah rebelled, and like him they are destroyed. 12 With their shameless carousing they are like dirty spots in your fellowship meals. They take care only of themselves. They are like clouds carried along by the wind, but bringing no rain. They are like trees that bear no fruit, even in autumn, trees that have been pulled up by the roots and are completely dead. 13 They are like wild waves of the sea, with their shameful deeds showing up like foam. They are like wandering stars, for whom God has reserved a place forever in the deepest darkness.

14 It was Enoch, the seventh[b] direct descendant from Adam, who long ago prophesied this about them: "The Lord will come with many thousands of his holy angels 15 to bring judgment on all, to condemn them all for the godless deeds they have performed and for all the terrible words that godless sinners have spoken against him!"

16 These people are always grumbling and blaming others; they follow their own evil desires; they brag about themselves and flatter others in order to get their own way.

Warnings and Instructions

17 But remember, my friends, what you were told in the past by the apostles of our Lord Jesus Christ. 18 They said to you, "When the last days come, people will appear who will make fun of you, people who follow their own godless desires." 19 These are the people who cause divisions, who are controlled by their natural desires, who do not have the Spirit. 20 But you, my friends, keep on building yourselves up on your most sacred faith. Pray in the power of the Holy Spirit, 21 and keep yourselves in

---

[a] the Lord; *some manuscripts have* Jesus, *which in Greek is the same as* Joshua.
[b] SEVENTH: *This numbering includes both the first and the last in the series of seven names from Adam to Enoch.*

5 a Ex 12.51; **b** Nu 14.29, 30   7 Gn 19.1-24   9 a Dn 10.13, 21; 12.1; Rev 12.7; **b** Dt 34.6; **c** Zec 3.2   11 a Gn 4.3-8; **b** Nu 22.1-35; **c** Nu 16.1-35   14 Gn 5.18, 21-24   18 2 P 3.3

the love of God, as you wait for our Lord Jesus Christ in his mercy to give you eternal life.

22 Show mercy toward those who have doubts; 23 save others by snatching them out of the fire; and to others show mercy mixed with fear, but hate their very clothes, stained by their sinful lusts.

Prayer of Praise

24 To him who is able to keep you from falling and to bring you faultless and joyful before his glorious presence — 25 to the only God our Savior, through Jesus Christ our Lord, be glory, majesty, might, and authority, from all ages past, and now, and forever and ever! Amen.

THE REVELATION
to John

INTRODUCTION

The Revelation to John was written at a time when Christians were being persecuted because of their faith in Jesus Christ as Lord. The writer's main concern is to give his readers hope and encouragement, and to urge them to remain faithful during times of suffering and persecution.

For the most part the book consists of several series of revelations and visions presented in symbolic language that would have been understood by Christians of that day, but would have remained a mystery to all others. As with the themes of a symphony, the themes of this book are repeated again and again in different ways through the various series of visions. Although there are differences of opinion regarding the details of interpretation of the book, the central theme is clear: through Christ the Lord, God will finally and totally defeat all of his enemies, including Satan, and will reward his faithful people with the blessings of a new heaven and a new earth when this victory is complete.

OUTLINE OF CONTENTS

---

1 This book is the record of the events that Jesus Christ revealed. God gave him this revelation in order to show to his servants what must happen very soon. Christ made these things known to his servant John by sending his angel to him, ² and John has told all that he has seen. This is his report concerning the message from God and the truth revealed by Jesus Christ. ³ Happy is the one who reads this book, and happy are those who listen to the words of this prophetic message and obey what is written in this book! For the time is near when all these things will happen.

Greetings to the Seven Churches

⁴From John to the seven churches in the province of Asia:

Grace and peace be yours from God, who is, who was, and who is to come, and from the seven spirits in front of his throne, ⁵and from Jesus Christ, the faithful witness, the first to be raised from death and who is also the ruler of the kings of the world.

He loves us, and by his sacrificial death he has freed us from our sins ⁶and made us a kingdom of priests to serve his God and Father. To Jesus Christ be the glory and power forever and ever! Amen.

⁷Look, he is coming on the clouds! Everyone will see him, including those who pierced him. All peoples on earth will mourn over him. So shall it be!

⁸"I am the first and the last," says the Lord God Almighty, who is, who was, and who is to come.

A Vision of Christ

⁹I am John, your brother, and as a follower of Jesus I am your partner in patiently enduring the suffering that comes to those who belong to his Kingdom. I was put on the island of Patmos because I had proclaimed God's word and the truth that Jesus revealed. ¹⁰On the Lord's day the Spirit took control of me, and I heard a loud voice, that sounded like a trumpet, speaking behind me. ¹¹It said, "Write down what you see, and send the book to the churches in these seven cities: Ephesus, Smyrna, Pergamum, Thyatira, Sardis, Philadelphia, and Laodicea."

¹²I turned around to see who was talking to me, and I saw seven gold lampstands, ¹³and among them there was what looked like a human being, wearing a robe that reached to his feet, and a gold band around his chest. ¹⁴His hair was white as wool, or as snow, and his eyes blazed like fire; ¹⁵his feet shone like brass that has been refined and polished, and his voice sounded like a roaring waterfall. ¹⁶He held seven stars in his right hand, and a sharp two-edged sword came out of his mouth. His face was as bright as the midday sun. ¹⁷When I saw him, I fell down at his feet like a dead man. He placed his right hand on me and said, "Don't be afraid! I am the first and the last. ¹⁸I am the living one! I was dead, but now I am alive forever and ever. I have authority over death and the world of the dead. ¹⁹Write, then, the things you see, both the things that are now and the things that will happen afterward. ²⁰Here is the secret meaning of the seven stars that you see in my right hand, and of the seven gold lampstands: the seven stars are the angels of the seven churches, and the seven lampstands are the seven churches.

The Message to Ephesus

2 "To the angel of the church in Ephesus write:

"This is the message from the one who holds the seven stars in his right hand and who walks among the seven gold lampstands. ²I know what you have done; I know how hard you have worked and how patient you have been. I know that you cannot tolerate evil people and that you have tested those who say they are apostles but are not, and have found out that they are liars. ³You are patient, you have suffered for my sake, and you have not given up. ⁴But this is what I have against you: you do not love me now as you did at

---

1.4 a Ex 3.14; **b** Rev 4.5　**1.5 a** Is 55.4; **b** Ps 89.27　**1.6** Ex 19.6; Rev 5.10　**1.7 a** Dn 7.13; Mt 24.30; Mk 13.26; Lk 21.27; 1 Th 4.17; **b** Zec 12.10; Jn 19.34, 37; **c** Zec 12.10; Mt 24.30　**1.8 a** Rev 22.13; **b** Ex 3.14　**1.13 a** Dn 7.13; **b** Dn 10.5　**1.14** Dn 7.9　**1.14, 15** Dn 10.6　**1.15** Ez 1.24; 43.2; 2 Esd 6.17　**1.17** Is 44.6; 48.12; 2 Esd 10.30; Rev 2.8; 22.13

first. [5] Think how far you have fallen! Turn from your sins and do what you did at first. If you don't turn from your sins, I will come to you and take your lampstand from its place. [6] But this is what you have in your favor: you hate what the Nicolaitans do, as much as I do.

[7] "If you have ears, then, listen to what the Spirit says to the churches!

"To those who win the victory I will give the right to eat the fruit of the tree of life that grows in the Garden of God.

The Message to Smyrna

[8] "To the angel of the church in Smyrna write:

"This is the message from the one who is the first and the last, who died and lived again. [9] I know your troubles; I know that you are poor — but really you are rich! I know the evil things said against you by those who claim to be Jews but are not; they are a group that belongs to Satan! [10] Don't be afraid of anything you are about to suffer. Listen! The Devil will put you to the test by having some of you thrown into prison, and your troubles will last ten days. Be faithful to me, even if it means death, and I will give you life as your prize of victory.

[11] "If you have ears, then, listen to what the Spirit says to the churches!

"Those who win the victory will not be hurt by the second death.

The Message to Pergamum

[12] "To the angel of the church in Pergamum write:

"This is the message from the one who has the sharp two-edged sword. [13] I know where you live, there where Satan has his throne. You are true to me,

and you did not abandon your faith in me even during the time when Antipas, my faithful witness, was killed there where Satan lives. [14] But there are a few things I have against you: there are some among you who follow the teaching of Balaam, who taught Balak how to lead the people of Israel into sin by persuading them to eat food that had been offered to idols and to practice sexual immorality. [15] In the same way you have people among you who follow the teaching of the Nicolaitans. [16] Now turn from your sins! If you don't, I will come to you soon and fight against those people with the sword that comes out of my mouth.

[17] "If you have ears, then, listen to what the Spirit says to the churches!

"To those who win the victory I will give some of the hidden manna. I will also give each of them a white stone on which is written a new name that no one knows except the one who receives it.

The Message to Thyatira

[18] "To the angel of the church in Thyatira write:

"This is the message from the Son of God, whose eyes blaze like fire, whose feet shine like polished brass. [19] I know what you do. I know your love, your faithfulness, your service, and your patience. I know that you are doing more now than you did at first. [20] But this is what I have against you: you tolerate that woman Jezebel, who calls herself a messenger of God. By her teaching she misleads my servants into practicing sexual immorality and eating food that has been offered to idols. [21] I have given her time to repent of her sins, but she does not want to turn from her immorality. [22] And so I will throw her on a bed

2.7 a Gn 2.9; 2 Esd 2.12; Rev 22.2; **b** Ez 28.13; 31.8 (LXX)   **2.8** Is 44.6; 48.12; Rev 1.17; 22.13   **2.11** Rev 20.14; 21.8   **2.14 a** Nu 22.5, 7; 31.16; Dt 23.4; **b** Nu 25.1-3
2.17 a Ex 16.14, 15; 16.33, 34; Jn 6.48-50; **b** Is 62.2; 65.15   **2.20** 1 K 16.31; 2 K 9.22, 30

where she and those who committed adultery with her will suffer terribly. I will do this now unless they repent of the wicked things they did with her. ²³I will also kill her followers, and then all the churches will know that I am the one who knows everyone's thoughts and wishes. I will repay each of you according to what you have done.

²⁴"But the rest of you in Thyatira have not followed this evil teaching; you have not learned what the others call 'the deep secrets of Satan.' I say to you that I will not put any other burden on you. ²⁵But until I come, you must hold firmly to what you have. ²⁶⁻²⁸To those who win the victory, who continue to the end to do what I want, I will give the same authority that I received from my Father: I will give them authority over the nations, to rule them with an iron rod and to break them to pieces like clay pots. I will also give them the morning star.

²⁹"If you have ears, then, listen to what the Spirit says to the churches!

The Message to Sardis

3 "To the angel of the church in Sardis write:

"This is the message from the one who has the seven spirits of God and the seven stars. I know what you are doing; I know that you have the reputation of being alive, even though you are dead! ²So wake up, and strengthen what you still have before it dies completely. For I find that what you have done is not yet perfect in the sight of my God. ³Remember, then, what you were taught and what you heard; obey it and turn from your sins. If you do not wake up, I will come upon you like a thief, and you will not even know the time when I will come. ⁴But a few of you

there in Sardis have kept your clothes clean. You will walk with me, clothed in white, because you are worthy to do so. ⁵Those who win the victory will be clothed like this in white, and I will not remove their names from the book of the living. In the presence of my Father and of his angels I will declare openly that they belong to me.

⁶"If you have ears, then, listen to what the Spirit says to the churches!

The Message to Philadelphia

⁷"To the angel of the church in Philadelphia write:

"This is the message from the one who is holy and true. He has the key that belonged to David, and when he opens a door, no one can close it, and when he closes it, no one can open it. ⁸I know what you do; I know that you have a little power; you have followed my teaching and have been faithful to me. I have opened a door in front of you, which no one can close. ⁹Listen! As for that group that belongs to Satan, those liars who claim that they are Jews but are not, I will make them come and bow down at your feet. They will all know that I love you. ¹⁰Because you have kept my command to endure, I will also keep you safe from the time of trouble which is coming upon the world to test all the people on earth. ¹¹I am coming soon. Keep safe what you have, so that no one will rob you of your victory prize. ¹²I will make those who are victorious pillars in the temple of my God, and they will never leave it. I will write on them the name of my God and the name of the city of my God, the new Jerusalem, which will come down out of heaven from my God. I will also write on them my new name.

¹³"If you have ears, then, listen to what the Spirit says to the churches!

2.23 a Ps 7.9; Jr 17.10; **b** Ps 62.12   **2.26, 27** Ps 2.8, 9 (LXX)   **3.3** Mt 24.43, 44;
Lk 12.39, 40; Rev 16.15   **3.5 a** Ex 32.32, 33; Ps 69.28; Rev 20.12; **b** Mt 10.32; Lk 12.8
3.7 Is 22.22; Job 12.14   **3.9 a** Is 49.23; 60.14; **b** Is 43.4   **3.12 a** Rev 21.2; **b** Is 62.2; 65.15

The Message to Laodicea

14"To the angel of the church in Laodicea write:

"This is the message from the Amen, the faithful and true witness, who is the origin[a] of all that God has created. 15 I know what you have done; I know that you are neither cold nor hot. How I wish you were either one or the other! 16 But because you are lukewarm, neither hot nor cold, I am going to spit you out of my mouth! 17 You say, 'I am rich and well off; I have all I need.' But you do not know how miserable and pitiful you are! You are poor, naked, and blind. 18 I advise you, then, to buy gold from me, pure gold, in order to be rich. Buy also white clothing to dress yourself and cover up your shameful nakedness. Buy also some ointment to put on your eyes, so that you may see. 19 I rebuke and punish all whom I love. Be in earnest, then, and turn from your sins. 20 Listen! I stand at the door and knock; if any hear my voice and open the door, I will come into their house and eat with them, and they will eat with me. 21 To those who win the victory I will give the right to sit beside me on my throne, just as I have been victorious and now sit by my Father on his throne.

22 "If you have ears, then, listen to what the Spirit says to the churches!"

Worship in Heaven

4 At this point I had another vision and saw an open door in heaven. And the voice that sounded like a trumpet, which I had heard speaking to me before, said, "Come up here, and I will show you what must happen after this." 2 At once the Spirit took control of me. There in heaven was a throne with someone sitting on it. 3 His face gleamed like such precious stones as jasper and carnelian, and all around the throne there was a rainbow the color of an emerald. 4 In a circle around the

I stand at the door and knock. (3.20)

throne were twenty-four other thrones, on which were seated twenty-four elders dressed in white and wearing crowns of gold. 5 From the throne came flashes of lightning, rumblings, and peals of thunder. In front of the throne seven lighted torches were burning, which are the seven spirits of God. 6 Also in front of the throne there was what looked like a sea of glass, clear as crystal.

Surrounding the throne on each of its sides, were four living creatures covered with eyes in front and behind. 7 The first one looked like a lion; the second looked like a bull; the third had a face like a human face; and the fourth looked like an eagle in flight. 8 Each one of the four living creatures had six wings, and they were covered with eyes, inside and out. Day and night they never stop singing:

"Holy, holy, holy, is the Lord
    God Almighty,

---

a origin; or ruler.

3.14 Pr 8.22   **3.19** Pr 3.12; He 12.6   **4.2, 3** Ez 1.26-28; 10.1   **4.5 a** Ex 19.16; Tb 12.15; Rev 8.5; 11.19; 16.18; **b** Ez 1.13; **c** Rev 1.4; Zec 4.2   **4.6** Ez 1.22   **4.6, 7** Ez 1.5-10; 10.14   **4.8 a** Ez 1.18; 10.12; **b** Is 6.2, 3

who was, who is, and who
is to come."

9 The four living creatures sing songs
of glory and honor and thanks to the
one who sits on the throne, who lives
forever and ever. When they do so,
10 the twenty-four elders fall down before the one who sits on the throne, and
worship him who lives forever and ever.
They throw their crowns down in front
of the throne and say,

11 "Our Lord and God! You are
worthy
to receive glory, honor, and
power.
For you created all things,
and by your will they were
given existence and life."

The Scroll and the Lamb

5 I saw a scroll in the right hand of
the one who sits on the throne; it
was covered with writing on both sides
and was sealed with seven seals. 2 And
I saw a mighty angel, who announced
in a loud voice, "Who is worthy to break
the seals and open the scroll?" 3 But
there was no one in heaven or on earth
or in the world below *b* who could open
the scroll and look inside it. 4 I cried bitterly because no one could be found
who was worthy to open the scroll or
look inside it. 5 Then one of the elders
said to me, "Don't cry. Look! The Lion
from Judah's tribe, the great descendant of David, has won the victory, and
he can break the seven seals and open
the scroll."

6 Then I saw a Lamb standing in the
center of the throne, surrounded by the
four living creatures and the elders.
The Lamb appeared to have been
killed. It had seven horns and seven
eyes, which are the seven spirits of God
that have been sent through the whole
earth. 7 The Lamb went and took the

scroll from the right hand of the one
who sits on the throne. 8 As he did so,
the four living creatures and the
twenty-four elders fell down before the
Lamb. Each had a harp and gold bowls
filled with incense, which are the
prayers of God's people. 9 They sang a
new song:

"You are worthy to take the scroll
and to break open its seals.
For you were killed, and by your
sacrificial death you
bought for God
people from every tribe,
language, nation, and race.
10 You have made them a kingdom
of priests to serve our God,
and they shall rule on earth."

11 Again I looked, and I heard angels,
thousands and millions of them! They
stood around the throne, the four living
creatures, and the elders, 12 and sang in
a loud voice:

"The Lamb who was killed is
worthy
to receive power, wealth,
wisdom, and strength,
honor, glory, and praise!"

13 And I heard every creature in heaven,
on earth, in the world below, and in the
sea — all living beings in the universe —
and they were singing:

"To him who sits on the throne
and to the Lamb,
be praise and honor, glory
and might,
forever and ever!"

14 The four living creatures answered,
"Amen!" And the elders fell down and
worshiped.

The Seals

6 Then I saw the Lamb break open
the first of the seven seals, and I
heard one of the four living creatures
say in a voice that sounded like

---

b WORLD BELOW: *The world of the dead (see 1.18).*
5.1 Ez 2.9, 10; Is 29.11   **5.5 a** Gn 49.9; **b** Is 11.1, 10   **5.6 a** Is 53.7; **b** Zec 4.10
5.8 Ps 141.2   **5.9** Ps 33.3; 98.1; Is 42.10   **5.10** Ex 19.6; Rev 1.6   **5.11** Dn 7.10

thunder, "Come!" ²I looked, and there was a white horse. Its rider held a bow, and he was given a crown. He rode out as a conqueror to conquer.

³Then the Lamb broke open the second seal; and I heard the second living creature say, "Come!" ⁴Another horse came out, a red one. Its rider was given the power to bring war on the earth, so that people should kill each other. He was given a large sword.

⁵Then the Lamb broke open the third seal; and I heard the third living creature say, "Come!" I looked, and there was a black horse. Its rider held a pair of scales in his hand. ⁶I heard what sounded like a voice coming from among the four living creatures, which said, "A quart of wheat for a day's wages, and three quarts of barley for a day's wages. But do not damage the olive trees and the vineyards!"

⁷Then the Lamb broke open the fourth seal; and I heard the fourth living creature say, "Come!" ⁸I looked, and there was a pale-colored horse. Its rider was named Death, and Hades[c] followed close behind. They were given authority over one fourth of the earth, to kill by means of war, famine, disease, and wild animals.

⁹Then the Lamb broke open the fifth seal. I saw underneath the altar the souls of those who had been killed because they had proclaimed God's word and had been faithful in their witnessing. ¹⁰They shouted in a loud voice, "Almighty Lord, holy and true! How long will it be until you judge the people on earth and punish them for killing us?" ¹¹Each of them was given a white robe, and they were told to rest a little while longer, until the complete number of other servants and believers were killed, as they had been.

¹²And I saw the Lamb break open the sixth seal. There was a violent earthquake, and the sun became black like coarse black cloth, and the moon turned completely red like blood. ¹³The stars fell down to the earth, like unripe figs falling from the tree when a strong wind shakes it. ¹⁴The sky disappeared like a scroll being rolled up, and every mountain and island was moved from its place. ¹⁵Then the kings of the earth, the rulers and the military chiefs, the rich and the powerful, and all other people, slave and free, hid themselves in caves and under rocks on the mountains. ¹⁶They called out to the mountains and to the rocks, "Fall on us and hide us from the eyes of the one who sits on the throne and from the anger of the Lamb! ¹⁷The terrible day of their anger is here, and who can stand up against it?"

The 144,000 People of Israel

7 After this I saw four angels standing at the four corners of the earth, holding back the four winds so that no wind should blow on the earth or the sea or against any tree. ²And I saw another angel coming up from the east with the seal of the living God. He called out in a loud voice to the four angels to whom God had given the power to damage the earth and the sea. ³The angel said, "Do not harm the earth, the sea, or the trees, until we mark the servants of our God with a seal on their foreheads." ⁴And I was told that the number of those who were marked with God's seal on their foreheads was 144,000. They were from the twelve tribes of Israel, ⁵⁻⁸twelve thousand from each tribe: Judah, Reuben, Gad, Asher,

---

[c] HADES: *The world of the dead (see 1.18).*

6.2 Zec 1.8; 6.3, 6   **6.4** Zec 1.8; 6.2   **6.5** Zec 6.2, 6   **6.8** Ez 14.21   **6.11** 2 Esd 4.36
6.12 a Rev 11.13; 16.18; **b** Is 13.10; Jl 2.10, 31; 3.15; Mt 24.29; Mk 13.24, 25; Lk 21.25
6.13, 14 Is 34.4   **6.14** Rev 16.20   **6.15** Is 2.19, 21   **6.16** Ho 10.8; Lk 23.30   **6.17** Jl 2.11;
Ml 3.2   **7.1** Jr 49.36; Dn 7.2; Zec 6.5   **7.3** Ez 9.4, 6

Naphtali, Manasseh, Simeon, Levi, Issachar, Zebulun, Joseph, and Benjamin.

The Enormous Crowd

⁹After this I looked, and there was an enormous crowd — no one could count all the people! They were from every race, tribe, nation, and language, and they stood in front of the throne and of the Lamb, dressed in white robes and holding palm branches in their hands. ¹⁰They called out in a loud voice: "Salvation comes from our God, who sits on the throne, and from the Lamb!" ¹¹All the angels stood around the throne, the elders, and the four living creatures. Then they threw themselves face downward in front of the throne and worshiped God, ¹²saying, "Amen! Praise, glory, wisdom, thanksgiving, honor, power, and might belong to our God forever and ever! Amen!"

¹³One of the elders asked me, "Who are these people dressed in white robes, and where do they come from?"

¹⁴"I don't know, sir. You do," I answered.

He said to me, "These are the people who have come safely through the terrible persecution. They have washed their robes and made them white with the blood of the Lamb. ¹⁵That is why they stand before God's throne and serve him day and night in his temple. He who sits on the throne will protect them with his presence. ¹⁶Never again will they hunger or thirst; neither sun nor any scorching heat will burn them, ¹⁷because the Lamb, who is in the center of the throne, will be their shepherd, and he will guide them to springs of life-giving water. And God will wipe away every tear from their eyes."

The Seventh Seal

8 When the Lamb broke open the seventh seal, there was silence in heaven for about half an hour. ²Then I saw the seven angels who stand before God, and they were given seven trumpets.

³Another angel, who had a gold incense container, came and stood at the altar. He was given a lot of incense to add to the prayers of all God's people and to offer it on the gold altar that stands before the throne. ⁴The smoke of the burning incense went up with the prayers of God's people from the hands of the angel standing before God. ⁵Then the angel took the incense container, filled it with fire from the altar, and threw it on the earth. There were rumblings and peals of thunder, flashes of lightning, and an earthquake.

The Trumpets

⁶Then the seven angels with the seven trumpets prepared to blow them.

⁷The first angel blew his trumpet. Hail and fire, mixed with blood, came pouring down on the earth. A third of the earth was burned up, a third of the trees, and every blade of green grass.

⁸Then the second angel blew his trumpet. Something that looked like a huge mountain on fire was thrown into the sea. A third of the sea was turned into blood, ⁹a third of the living creatures in the sea died, and a third of the ships were destroyed.

¹⁰Then the third angel blew his trumpet. A large star, burning like a torch, dropped from the sky and fell on a third of the rivers and on the springs of water. ¹¹(The name of the star is "Bitterness.") A third of the water turned bitter, and many people died from

7.9 2 Esd 2.42   **7.14** Dn 12.1; Mt 24.21; Mk 13.19   **7.16** Is 49.10;   **7.17** a Ps 23.1; Ez 34.23; **b** Ps 23.2; Is 49.10; **c** Is 25.8   **8.3 a** Am 9.1; **b** Ex 30.1, 3   **8.5 a** Lv 16.12; Ez 10.2; **b** Ex 19.16; Rev 11.19; 16.18   **8.6, 7** Ws 11.5 – 12.2   **8.7** Ex 9.23-25; Ez 38.22 **8.10** Is 14.12   **8.11** Jr 9.15

drinking the water, because it had turned bitter.

¹²Then the fourth angel blew his trumpet. A third of the sun was struck, and a third of the moon, and a third of the stars, so that their light lost a third of its brightness; there was no light during a third of the day and a third of the night also.

¹³Then I looked, and I heard an eagle that was flying high in the air say in a loud voice, "O horror! horror! How horrible it will be for all who live on earth when the sound comes from the trumpets that the other three angels must blow!"

9 Then the fifth angel blew his trumpet. I saw a star which had fallen down to the earth, and it was given the key to the abyss.*ᵈ* ²The star opened the abyss, and smoke poured out of it, like the smoke from a large furnace; the sunlight and the air were darkened by the smoke from the abyss. ³Locusts came down out of the smoke upon the earth, and they were given the same kind of power that scorpions have. ⁴They were told not to harm the grass or the trees or any other plant; they could harm only the people who did not have the mark of God's seal on their foreheads. ⁵The locusts were not allowed to kill these people, but only to torture them for five months. The pain caused by the torture is like the pain caused by a scorpion's sting. ⁶During those five months they will seek death, but will not find it; they will want to die, but death will flee from them.

⁷The locusts looked like horses ready for battle; on their heads they had what seemed to be crowns of gold, and their faces were like human faces. ⁸Their hair was like women's hair, their teeth were like lions' teeth. ⁹Their chests

were covered with what looked like iron breastplates, and the sound made by their wings was like the noise of many horse-drawn chariots rushing into battle. ¹⁰They have tails and stings like those of a scorpion, and it is with their tails that they have the power to hurt people for five months. ¹¹They have a king ruling over them, who is the angel in charge of the abyss. His name in Hebrew is Abaddon; in Greek the name is Apollyon (meaning "The Destroyer").

¹²The first horror is over; after this there are still two more horrors to come.

¹³Then the sixth angel blew his trumpet. I heard a voice coming from the four corners of the gold altar standing before God. ¹⁴The voice said to the sixth angel, "Release the four angels who are bound at the great Euphrates River!" ¹⁵The four angels were released; for this very hour of this very day of this very month and year they had been kept ready to kill a third of all the human race. ¹⁶I was told the number of the mounted troops: it was two hundred million. ¹⁷And in my vision I saw the horses and their riders: they had breastplates red as fire, blue as sapphire, and yellow as sulfur. The horses' heads were like lions' heads, and from their mouths came out fire, smoke, and sulfur. ¹⁸A third of the human race was killed by those three plagues: the fire, the smoke, and the sulfur coming out of the horses' mouths. ¹⁹For the power of the horses is in their mouths and also in their tails. Their tails are like snakes with heads, and they use them to hurt people.

²⁰The rest of the human race, all those who had not been killed by these plagues, did not turn away from what they themselves had made. They did not stop worshiping demons, nor the

---

ᵈ ABYSS: *The place in the depths of the earth where the demons were imprisoned until their final punishment.*

8.12 Is 13.10; Ez 32.7; Jl 2.10, 31; 3.15   **9.2** Gn 19.28; 2 Esd 7.36   **9.3** Ex 10.12-15; Ws 16.9   **9.4** Ez 9.4   **9.6** Job 3.21; Jr 8.3   **9.7** Jl 2.4   **9.8** Jl 1.6   **9.9** Jl 2.5   **9.13** Ex 30.1-3   **9.17** Ws 11.17, 18   **9.20** Ps 115.4-7; 135.15-17; Dn 5.23

idols of gold, silver, bronze, stone, and wood, which cannot see, hear, or walk. [21] Nor did they repent of their murders, their magic, their sexual immorality, or their stealing.

The Angel and the Little Scroll

10 Then I saw another mighty angel coming down out of heaven. He was wrapped in a cloud and had a rainbow around his head; his face was like the sun, and his legs were like columns of fire. [2] He had a small scroll open in his hand. He put his right foot on the sea and his left foot on the land, [3] and called out in a loud voice that sounded like the roar of lions. After he had called out, the seven thunders answered with a roar. [4] As soon as they spoke, I was about to write. But I heard a voice speak from heaven, "Keep secret what the seven thunders have said; do not write it down!"

[5] Then the angel that I saw standing on the sea and on the land raised his right hand to heaven [6] and took a vow in the name of God, who lives forever and ever, who created heaven, earth, and the sea, and everything in them. The angel said, "There will be no more delay! [7] But when the seventh angel blows his trumpet, then God will accomplish his secret plan, as he announced to his servants, the prophets."

[8] Then the voice that I had heard speaking from heaven spoke to me again, saying, "Go and take the open scroll which is in the hand of the angel standing on the sea and on the land."

[9] I went to the angel and asked him to give me the little scroll. He said to me, "Take it and eat it; it will turn sour in your stomach, but in your mouth it will be sweet as honey."

[10] I took the little scroll from his hand and ate it, and it tasted sweet as honey in my mouth. But after I swallowed it, it turned sour in my stomach. [11] Then I was told, "Once again you must proclaim God's message about many nations, races, languages, and kings."

The Two Witnesses

11 I was then given a stick that looked like a measuring-rod, and was told, "Go and measure the temple of God and the altar, and count those who are worshiping in the temple. [2] But do not measure the outer courts, because they have been given to the heathen, who will trample on the Holy City for forty-two months. [3] I will send my two witnesses dressed in sackcloth, and they will proclaim God's message during those 1,260 days."

[4] The two witnesses are the two olive trees and the two lamps that stand before the Lord of the earth. [5] If anyone tries to harm them, fire comes out of their mouths and destroys their enemies; and in this way whoever tries to harm them will be killed. [6] They have authority to shut up the sky so that there will be no rain during the time they proclaim God's message. They have authority also over the springs of water, to turn them into blood; they have authority also to strike the earth with every kind of plague as often as they wish.

[7] When they finish proclaiming their message, the beast that comes up out of the abyss will fight against them. He will defeat them and kill them, [8] and their bodies will lie in the street of the great city, where their Lord was crucified. The symbolic name of that city is Sodom, or Egypt. [9] People from all nations, tribes, languages, and races will look at their bodies for three and a half days and will not allow them to be buried. [10] The people of the earth will be

---

10.5-7 Ex 20.11; Dt 32.40; Dn 12.7; Am 3.7   **10.8-10** Ez 2.8—3.3   **11.1** Ez 40.3; Zec 2.1, 2   **11.2** Lk 21.24   **11.4** Zec 4.3, 11-14   **11.6 a** 1 K 17.1; **b** Ex 7.17-19; **c** 1 S 4.8   **11.7 a** Dn 7.7; Rev 13.5-7; 17.8; **b** Dn 7.21   **11.8** Is 1.9, 10

happy because of the death of these two. They will celebrate and send presents to each other, because those two prophets brought much suffering upon the whole human race. [11] After three and a half days a life-giving breath came from God and entered them, and they stood up; and all who saw them were terrified. [12] Then the two prophets heard a loud voice say to them from heaven, "Come up here!" As their enemies watched, they went up into heaven in a cloud. [13] At that very moment there was a violent earthquake; a tenth of the city was destroyed, and seven thousand people were killed. The rest of the people were terrified and praised the greatness of the God of heaven.

[14] The second horror is over, but the third horror will come soon!

The Seventh Trumpet

[15] Then the seventh angel blew his trumpet, and there were loud voices in heaven, saying, "The power to rule over the world belongs now to our Lord and his Messiah, and he will rule forever and ever!" [16] Then the twenty-four elders who sit on their thrones in front of God threw themselves face downward and worshiped God, [17] saying:

"Lord God Almighty, the one
    who is and who was!
We thank you that you have
    taken your great power
    and have begun to rule!
[18] The heathen were filled with
    rage,
because the time for your
    anger has come,
    the time for the dead to be
    judged.
The time has come to reward
    your servants, the prophets,

and all your people, all who
    have reverence for you,
    great and small alike.
The time has come to destroy
    those who destroy the
    earth!"

[19] God's temple in heaven was opened, and the Covenant Box was seen there. Then there were flashes of lightning, rumblings and peals of thunder, an earthquake, and heavy hail.

The Woman and the Dragon

12 Then a great and mysterious sight appeared in the sky. There was a woman, whose dress was the sun and who had the moon under her feet and a crown of twelve stars on her head. [2] She was soon to give birth, and the pains and suffering of childbirth made her cry out.

[3] Another mysterious sight appeared in the sky. There was a huge red dragon with seven heads and ten horns and a crown on each of his heads. [4] With his tail he dragged a third of the stars out of the sky and threw them down to the earth. He stood in front of the woman, in order to eat her child as soon as it was born. [5] Then she gave birth to a son, who will rule over all nations with an iron rod. But the child was snatched away and taken to God and his throne. [6] The woman fled to the desert, to a place God had prepared for her, where she will be taken care of for 1,260 days.

[7] Then war broke out in heaven. Michael and his angels fought against the dragon, who fought back with his angels; [8] but the dragon was defeated, and he and his angels were not allowed to stay in heaven any longer. [9] The huge

11.11 Ez 37.10   **11.12** 2 K 2.11   **11.13** Rev 6.12; 16.18   **11.15** Ex 15.18; Dn 2.44; 7.14, 27   **11.18 a** Ps 2.5; 110.5; **b** Ps 115.13   **11.19** 2 Macc 2.4-8; **a** Rev 8.5; 16.18; **b** Rev 16.21   **12.3** Dn 7.7   **12.4** Dn 8.10   **12.5 a** Is 66.7; **b** Ps 2.9   **12.7** Dn 10.13, 21; 12.1; Jd 9   **12.9 a** Gn 3.1; **b** Lk 10.18

dragon was thrown out — that ancient serpent, named the Devil, or Satan, that deceived the whole world. He was thrown down to earth, and all his angels with him.

10 Then I heard a loud voice in heaven saying, "Now God's salvation has come! Now God has shown his power as King! Now his Messiah has shown his authority! For the one who stood before our God and accused believers day and night has been thrown out of heaven. 11 They won the victory over him by the blood of the Lamb and by the truth which they proclaimed; and they were willing to give up their lives and die. 12 And so be glad, you heavens, and all you that live there! But how terrible for the earth and the sea! For the Devil has come down to you, and he is filled with rage, because he knows that he has only a little time left."

13 When the dragon realized that he had been thrown down to the earth, he began to pursue the woman who had given birth to the boy. 14 She was given the two wings of a large eagle in order to fly to her place in the desert, where she will be taken care of for three and a half years, safe from the dragon's attack. 15 And then from his mouth the dragon poured out a flood of water after the woman, so that it would carry her away. 16 But the earth helped the woman; it opened its mouth and swallowed the water that had come from the dragon's mouth. 17 The dragon was furious with the woman and went off to fight against the rest of her descendants, all those who obey God's commandments and are faithful to the truth revealed by Jesus. 18 And the dragon stood*e* on the seashore.

The Two Beasts

13 Then I saw a beast coming up out of the sea. It had ten horns and seven heads; on each of its horns there was a crown, and on each of its heads there was a name that was insulting to God. 2 The beast looked like a leopard, with feet like a bear's feet and a mouth like a lion's mouth. The dragon gave the beast his own power, his throne, and his vast authority. 3 One of the heads of the beast seemed to have been fatally wounded, but the wound had healed. The whole earth was amazed and followed the beast. 4 Everyone worshiped the dragon because he had given his authority to the beast. They worshiped the beast also, saying, "Who is like the beast? Who can fight against it?"

5 The beast was allowed to make proud claims which were insulting to God, and it was permitted to have authority for forty-two months. 6 It began to curse God, his name, the place where he lives, and all those who live in heaven. 7 It was allowed to fight against God's people and to defeat them, and it was given authority over every tribe, nation, language, and race. 8 All people living on earth will worship it, except those whose names were written before the creation of the world in the book of the living which belongs to the Lamb that was killed.

9 "Listen, then, if you have ears! 10 Whoever is meant to be captured will surely be captured; whoever is meant to be killed by the sword will surely be killed by the sword. This calls for endurance and faith on the part of God's people."

11 Then I saw another beast, which came up out of the earth. It had two

---

e And the dragon stood; *some manuscripts have* And I stood, *connecting this verse with what follows.*

12.10 Job 1.9-11; Zec 3.1   **12.14** Dn 7.25; 12.7   **13.1** 2 Esd 11.1; **a** Dn 7.3; **b** Rev 17.3, 7-12   **13.2** Dn 7.4-6   **13.5, 6** Dn 7.8, 25; 11.36   **13.7** Dn 7.21   **13.8** Ps 69.28   **13.10** Jr 15.2; 43.11

horns like a lamb's horns, and it spoke like a dragon. [12] It used the vast authority of the first beast in its presence. It forced the earth and all who live on it to worship the first beast, whose wound had healed. [13] This second beast performed great miracles; it made fire come down out of heaven to earth in the sight of everyone. [14] And it deceived all the people living on earth by means of the miracles which it was allowed to perform in the presence of the first beast. The beast told them to build an image in honor of the beast that had been wounded by the sword and yet lived. [15] The second beast was allowed to breathe life into the image of the first beast, so that the image could talk and put to death all those who would not worship it. [16] The beast forced all the people, small and great, rich and poor, slave and free, to have a mark placed on their right hands or on their foreheads. [17] No one could buy or sell without this mark, that is, the beast's name or the number that stands for the name.

[18] This calls for wisdom. Whoever is intelligent can figure out the meaning of the number of the beast, because the number stands for the name of someone. Its number is 666.

The Lamb and His People

14 Then I looked, and there was the Lamb standing on Mount Zion; with him were 144,000 people who have his name and his Father's name written on their foreheads. [2] And I heard a voice from heaven that sounded like a roaring waterfall, like a loud peal of thunder. It sounded like the music made by musicians playing their harps. [3] The 144,000 people stood before the throne, the four living creatures, and the elders; they were singing a new song, which only they could learn. Of the whole human race they are the only ones who have been redeemed. [4] They are the men who have kept themselves pure by not having sexual relations with women; they are virgins. They follow the Lamb wherever he goes. They have been redeemed from the rest of the human race and are the first ones to be offered to God and to the Lamb. [5] They have never been known to tell lies; they are faultless.

The Three Angels

[6] Then I saw another angel flying high in the air, with an eternal message of Good News to announce to the peoples of the earth, to every race, tribe, language, and nation. [7] He said in a loud voice, "Honor God and praise his greatness! For the time has come for him to judge all people. Worship him who made heaven, earth, sea, and the springs of water!"

[8] A second angel followed the first one, saying, "She has fallen! Great Babylon has fallen! She made all peoples drink her wine — the strong wine of her immoral lust!"

[9] A third angel followed the first two, saying in a loud voice, "Those who worship the beast and its image and receive the mark on their forehead or on their hand [10] will themselves drink God's wine, the wine of his fury, which he has poured at full strength into the cup of his anger! All who do this will be tormented in fire and sulfur before the holy angels and the Lamb. [11] The smoke of the fire that torments them goes up forever and ever. There is no relief day or night for those who worship the beast and its image, for anyone who has the mark of its name."

[12] This calls for endurance on the part of God's people, those who obey God's commandments and are faithful to Jesus.

[13] Then I heard a voice from heaven

14.1 Ez 9.4; Rev 7.3   **14.2** 2 Esd 6.17   **14.5** Zep 3.13   **14.8** Is 21.9; Jr 51.8; Rev 18.2
14.10 a Is 51.17; **b** Gn 19.24; Ez 38.22   **14.11** Is 34.10

saying, "Write this: Happy are those who from now on die in the service of the Lord!"

"Yes indeed!" answers the Spirit. "They will enjoy rest from their hard work, because the results of their service go with them."

The Harvest of the Earth

¹⁴Then I looked, and there was a white cloud, and sitting on the cloud was what looked like a human being, with a crown of gold on his head and a sharp sickle in his hand. ¹⁵Then another angel came out from the temple and cried out in a loud voice to the one who was sitting on the cloud, "Use your sickle and reap the harvest, because the time has come; the earth is ripe for the harvest!" ¹⁶Then the one who sat on the cloud swung his sickle on the earth, and the earth's harvest was reaped.

¹⁷Then I saw another angel come out of the temple in heaven, and he also had a sharp sickle. ¹⁸Then another angel, who is in charge of the fire, came from the altar. He shouted in a loud voice to the angel who had the sharp sickle, "Use your sickle, and cut the grapes from the vineyard of the earth, because the grapes are ripe!" ¹⁹So the angel swung his sickle on the earth, cut the grapes from the vine, and threw them into the wine press of God's furious anger. ²⁰The grapes were squeezed out in the wine press outside the city, and blood came out of the wine press in a flood two hundred miles long and about five feet deep.

The Angels with the Last Plagues

15 Then I saw in the sky another mysterious sight, great and amazing. There were seven angels with

seven plagues, which are the last ones, because they are the final expression of God's anger.

²Then I saw what looked like a sea of glass mixed with fire. I also saw those who had won the victory over the beast and its image and over the one whose name is represented by a number. They were standing by the sea of glass, holding harps that God had given them ³and singing the song of Moses, the servant of God, and the song of the Lamb:

"Lord God Almighty,
    how great and wonderful
        are your deeds!
King of the nations,ᶠ
    how right and true are your
        ways!
⁴Who will not stand in awe of
        you, Lord?
Who will refuse to declare
        your greatness?
You alone are holy.
All the nations will come
    and worship you,
        because your just actions
            are seen by all."

⁵After this I saw the temple in heaven open, with the Sacred Tent in it. ⁶The seven angels who had the seven plagues came out of the temple, dressed in clean shining linen and with gold bands tied around their chests. ⁷Then one of the four living creatures gave the seven angels seven gold bowls full of the anger of God, who lives forever and ever. ⁸The temple was filled with smoke from the glory and power of God, and no one could go into the temple until the seven plagues brought by the seven angels had come to an end.

ᶠ nations; *some manuscripts have* ages.

14.14 Dn 7.13   **14.15** Jl 3.13   **14.20** Is 63.3; Lm 1.15; Rev 19.15   **15.3** Ex 15.1
15.4 a Jr 10.7; **b** Ps 86.9   **15.5** Ex 38.21   **15.8** Ex 40.34; 1 K 8.10, 11; 2 Ch 5.13, 14;
Is 6.4

The Bowls of God's Anger

16 Then I heard a loud voice speaking from the temple to the seven angels: "Go and pour out the seven bowls of God's anger on the earth!"

² The first angel went and poured out his bowl on the earth. Terrible and painful sores appeared on those who had the mark of the beast and on those who had worshiped its image.

³ Then the second angel poured out his bowl on the sea. The water became like the blood of a dead person, and every living creature in the sea died.

⁴ Then the third angel poured out his bowl on the rivers and the springs of water, and they turned into blood. ⁵ I heard the angel in charge of the waters say, "The judgments you have made are just, O Holy One, you who are and who were! ⁶ They poured out the blood of God's people and of the prophets, and so you have given them blood to drink. They are getting what they deserve!" ⁷ Then I heard a voice from the altar saying, "Lord God Almighty! True and just indeed are your judgments!"

⁸ Then the fourth angel poured out his bowl on the sun, and it was allowed to burn people with its fiery heat. ⁹ They were burned by the fierce heat, and they cursed the name of God, who has authority over these plagues. But they would not turn from their sins and praise his greatness.

¹⁰ Then the fifth angel poured out his bowl on the throne of the beast. Darkness fell over the beast's kingdom, and people bit their tongues because of their pain, ¹¹ and they cursed the God of heaven for their pains and sores. But they did not turn from their evil ways.

¹² Then the sixth angel poured out his bowl on the great Euphrates River. The river dried up, to provide a way for the kings who come from the east. ¹³ Then I saw three unclean spirits that looked like frogs. They were coming out of the mouth of the dragon, the mouth of the beast, and the mouth of the false prophet. ¹⁴ They are the spirits of demons that perform miracles. These three spirits go out to all the kings of the world, to bring them together for the battle on the great Day of Almighty God.

¹⁵ "Listen! I am coming like a thief! Happy is he who stays awake and guards his clothes, so that he will not walk around naked and be ashamed in public!"

¹⁶ Then the spirits brought the kings together in the place that in Hebrew is called Armageddon.

¹⁷ Then the seventh angel poured out his bowl in the air. A loud voice came from the throne in the temple, saying, "It is done!" ¹⁸ There were flashes of lightning, rumblings and peals of thunder, and a terrible earthquake. There has never been such an earthquake since the creation of human beings; this was the worst earthquake of all! ¹⁹ The great city was split into three parts, and the cities of all countries were destroyed. God remembered great Babylon and made her drink the wine from his cup—the wine of his furious anger. ²⁰ All the islands disappeared, all the mountains vanished. ²¹ Huge hailstones, each weighing as much as a hundred pounds, fell from the sky on people, who cursed God on account of the plague of hail, because it was such a terrible plague.

The Famous Prostitute

17 Then one of the seven angels who had the seven bowls came to me and said, "Come, and I will show you how the famous prostitute is to be

16.2 Ex 9.10   16.4 Ex 7.17-21; Ps 78.44   16.10 Ex 10.21   16.12 Is 11.15
16.15 Mt 24.43, 44; Lk 12.39, 40; Rev 3.3   16.16 2 K 23.29; Zec 12.11   16.18 Rev 8.5;
11.13, 19   16.19 Is 51.17   16.20 Rev 6.14   16.21 Ex 9.23; Rev 11.19   17.1 Jr 51.13

punished, that great city that is built near many rivers. ² The kings of the earth practiced sexual immorality with her, and the people of the world became drunk from drinking the wine of her immorality."

³ The Spirit took control of me, and the angel carried me to a desert. There I saw a woman sitting on a red beast that had names insulting to God written all over it; the beast had seven heads and ten horns. ⁴ The woman was dressed in purple and scarlet, and covered with gold ornaments, precious stones, and pearls. In her hand she held a gold cup full of obscene and filthy things, the result of her immorality. ⁵ On her forehead was written a name that has a secret meaning: "Great Babylon, the mother of all prostitutes and perverts in the world." ⁶ And I saw that the woman was drunk with the blood of God's people and the blood of those who were killed because they had been loyal to Jesus.

When I saw her, I was completely amazed. ⁷ "Why are you amazed?" the angel asked me. "I will tell you the secret meaning of the woman and of the beast that carries her, the beast with seven heads and ten horns. ⁸ That beast was once alive, but lives no longer; it is about to come up from the abyss and will go off to be destroyed. The people living on earth whose names have not been written before the creation of the world in the book of the living, will all be amazed as they look at the beast. It was once alive; now it no longer lives, but it will reappear.

⁹ "This calls for wisdom and understanding. The seven heads are seven hills, on which the woman sits. They are also seven kings: ¹⁰ five of them have fallen, one still rules, and the other one has not yet come; when he comes, he must rule only a little while.

¹¹ And the beast that was once alive, but lives no longer, is itself an eighth king who is one of the seven and is going off to be destroyed.

¹² "The ten horns you saw are ten kings who have not yet begun to rule, but who will be given authority to rule as kings for one hour with the beast. ¹³ These ten all have the same purpose, and they give their power and authority to the beast. ¹⁴ They will fight against the Lamb; but the Lamb, together with his called, chosen, and faithful followers, will defeat them, because he is Lord of lords and King of kings."

¹⁵ The angel also said to me, "The waters you saw, on which the prostitute sits, are nations, peoples, races, and languages. ¹⁶ The ten horns you saw and the beast will hate the prostitute; they will take away everything she has and leave her naked; they will eat her flesh and destroy her with fire. ¹⁷ For God has placed in their hearts the will to carry out his purpose by acting together and giving to the beast their power to rule until God's words come true.

¹⁸ "The woman you saw is the great city that rules over the kings of the earth."

The Fall of Babylon

18 After this I saw another angel coming down out of heaven. He had great authority, and his splendor brightened the whole earth. ² He cried out in a loud voice: "She has fallen! Great Babylon has fallen! She is now haunted by demons and unclean spirits; all kinds of filthy and hateful birds live in her. ³ For all the nations have drunk her wine — the strong wine of her immoral lust. The kings of the earth practiced sexual immorality with her, and the merchants of the world

---

17.2 Is 23.17; Jr 51.7   **17.3** Rev 13.1   **17.4** Jr 51.7   **17.8 a** Dn 7.7; Rev 11.7; **b** Ps 69.28
17.12 Dn 7.24   **18.2 a** Is 21.9; Jr 51.8; Rev 14.8; **b** Is 13.21; Jr 50.39   **18.3** Is 23.17;
Jr 51.7

This great and mighty city Babylon! (18.10)

grew rich from her unrestrained lust."

⁴Then I heard another voice from heaven, saying,

"Come out, my people! Come
out from her!
You must not take part in
her sins;
you must not share in her
punishment!
⁵For her sins are piled up as
high as heaven,
and God remembers her
wicked ways.
⁶Treat her exactly as she has
treated you;
pay her back double for all
she has done.
Fill her cup with a drink twice
as strong
as the drink she prepared
for you.
⁷Give her as much suffering and
grief
as the glory and luxury she
gave herself.
For she keeps telling herself:
'Here I sit, a queen!
I am no widow,

I will never know grief!'
⁸Because of this, in one day she
will be struck with
plagues—
disease, grief, and famine.
And she will be burned with fire,
because the Lord God, who
judges her, is mighty."

⁹The kings of the earth who took part in her immorality and lust will cry and weep over the city when they see the smoke from the flames that consume her. ¹⁰They stand a long way off, because they are afraid of sharing in her suffering. They say, "How terrible! How awful! This great and mighty city Babylon! In just one hour you have been punished!"

¹¹The merchants of the earth also cry and mourn for her, because no one buys their goods any longer; ¹²no one buys their gold, silver, precious stones, and pearls; their goods of linen, purple cloth, silk, and scarlet cloth; all kinds of rare woods and all kinds of objects made of ivory and of expensive wood, of bronze, iron, and marble; ¹³and cinnamon, spice, incense, myrrh, and frank-

18.4 Is 48.20; Jr 50.8; 51.6, 45   **18.5** Gn 18.20, 21; Jr 51.9   **18.6** Ps 137.8; Jr 50.29
18.7, 8 Is 47.7-9   **18.9, 10** Ez 26.16, 17   **18.11** Ez 27.31, 36   **18.12, 13** Ez 27.12, 13, 22

incense; wine and oil, flour and wheat, cattle and sheep, horses and carriages, slaves, and even human lives. ¹⁴The merchants say to her, "All the good things you longed to own have disappeared, and all your wealth and glamor are gone, and you will never find them again!" ¹⁵The merchants, who became rich from doing business in that city, will stand a long way off, because they are afraid of sharing in her suffering. They will cry and mourn, ¹⁶and say, "How terrible! How awful for the great city! She used to dress herself in linen, purple, and scarlet, and cover herself with gold ornaments, precious stones, and pearls! ¹⁷And in one hour she has lost all this wealth!"

All the ships' captains and passengers, the sailors and all others who earn their living on the sea, stood a long way off, ¹⁸and cried out as they saw the smoke from the flames that consumed her: "There never has been another city like this great city!" ¹⁹They threw dust on their heads, they cried and mourned, saying, "How terrible! How awful for the great city! She is the city where all who have ships sailing the seas became rich on her wealth! And in one hour she has lost everything!"

²⁰Be glad, heaven, because of her destruction! Be glad, God's people and the apostles and prophets! For God has condemned her for what she did to you!

²¹Then a mighty angel picked up a stone the size of a large millstone and threw it into the sea, saying, "This is how the great city Babylon will be violently thrown down and will never be seen again. ²²The music of harps and of human voices, of players of the flute and the trumpet, will never be heard in you again! No workman in any trade will ever be found in you again; and the

sound of the millstone will be heard no more! ²³Never again will the light of a lamp be seen in you; no more will the voices of brides and grooms be heard in you. Your merchants were the most powerful in all the world, and with your false magic you deceived all the peoples of the world!"

²⁴Babylon was punished because the blood of prophets and of God's people was found in the city; yes, the blood of all those who have been killed on earth.

19 After this I heard what sounded like the roar of a large crowd of people in heaven, saying, "Praise God! Salvation, glory, and power belong to our God! ²True and just are his judgments! He has condemned the prostitute who was corrupting the earth with her immorality. God has punished her because she killed his servants." ³Again they shouted, "Praise God! The smoke from the flames that consume the great city goes up forever and ever!" ⁴The twenty-four elders and the four living creatures fell down and worshiped God, who was seated on the throne. They said, "Amen! Praise God!"

The Wedding Feast of the Lamb

⁵Then there came from the throne the sound of a voice, saying, "Praise our God, all his servants and all people, both great and small, who have reverence for him!" ⁶Then I heard what sounded like a crowd, like the sound of a roaring waterfall, like loud peals of thunder. I heard them say, "Praise God! For the Lord, our Almighty God, is King! ⁷Let us rejoice and be glad; let us praise his greatness! For the time has come for the wedding of the Lamb, and his bride has prepared herself for it. ⁸She has been given clean shining

18.15 Ez 27.31, 36   18.17 Is 23.14; Ez 27.26-30   18.18 Ez 27.32   18.19 Ez 27.30-34
18.20 Dt 32.43; Jr 51.48   18.21 a Jr 51.63, 64; b Ez 26.21   18.22 Ez 26.13; Is 24.8
18.22, 23 Jr 7.34; 25.10   18.24 Jr 51.49   19.2 Dt 32.43; 2 K 9.7   19.3 Is 34.10
19.5 Ps 115.13   19.6 2 Esd 6.17; a Ez 1.24; b Ps 93.1; 97.1; 99.1

linen to wear." (The linen is the good deeds of God's people.)

⁹Then the angel said to me, "Write this: Happy are those who have been invited to the wedding feast of the Lamb." And the angel added, "These are the true words of God."

¹⁰I fell down at his feet to worship him, but he said to me, "Don't do it! I am a servant together with you and with other believers, all those who hold to the truth that Jesus revealed. Worship God!"

For the truth that Jesus revealed is what inspires the prophets.

The Rider on the White Horse

¹¹Then I saw heaven open, and there was a white horse. Its rider is called Faithful and True; it is with justice that he judges and fights his battles. ¹²His eyes were like a flame of fire, and he wore many crowns on his head. He had a name written on him, but no one except himself knows what it is. ¹³The robe he wore was covered with blood. His name is "The Word of God." ¹⁴The armies of heaven followed him, riding on white horses and dressed in clean white linen. ¹⁵Out of his mouth came a sharp sword, with which he will defeat the nations. He will rule over them with a rod of iron, and he will trample out the wine in the wine press of the furious anger of the Almighty God. ¹⁶On his robe and on his thigh was written the name: "King of kings and Lord of lords."

¹⁷Then I saw an angel standing on the sun. He shouted in a loud voice to all the birds flying in midair: "Come and gather together for God's great feast! ¹⁸Come and eat the flesh of kings, generals, and soldiers, the flesh of horses and their riders, the flesh of all people, slave and free, great and small!"

¹⁹Then I saw the beast and the kings of the earth and their armies gathered to fight against the one who was riding the horse and against his army. ²⁰The beast was taken prisoner, together with the false prophet who had performed miracles in his presence. (It was by those miracles that he had deceived those who had the mark of the beast and those who had worshiped the image of the beast.) The beast and the false prophet were both thrown alive into the lake of fire that burns with sulfur. ²¹Their armies were killed by the sword that comes out of the mouth of the one who was riding the horse; and all the birds ate all they could of their flesh.

The Thousand Years

20 Then I saw an angel coming down from heaven, holding in his hand the key of the abyss and a heavy chain. ²He seized the dragon, that ancient serpent — that is, the Devil, or Satan — and chained him up for a thousand years. ³The angel threw him into the abyss, locked it, and sealed it, so that he could not deceive the nations any more until the thousand years were over. After that he must be set loose for a little while.

⁴Then I saw thrones, and those who sat on them were given the power to judge. I also saw the souls of those who had been executed because they had proclaimed the truth that Jesus revealed and the word of God. They had not worshiped the beast or its image, nor had they received the mark of the beast on their foreheads or their hands. They came to life and ruled as kings with Christ for a thousand years. ⁵(The rest of the dead did not come to life until the thousand years were over.) This is the first raising of the dead. ⁶Happy and

19.9 Mt 22.2, 3   19.11 a Ez 1.1; b Ps 96.13; Is 11.4   19.12 Dn 10.6   19.13 Ws 18.14-18
19.15 a Ps 2.9; b Is 63.3; Jl 3.13; Rev 14.20   19.17, 18 Ez 39.17-20   19.20 Rev 13.1-18
20.2 Gn 3.1   20.4 Dn 7.9, 22

greatly blessed are those who are included in this first raising of the dead. The second death has no power over them; they shall be priests of God and of Christ, and they will rule with him for a thousand years.

The Defeat of Satan

7 After the thousand years are over, Satan will be set loose from his prison, 8 and he will go out to deceive the nations scattered over the whole world, that is, Gog and Magog. Satan will bring them all together for battle, as many as the grains of sand on the seashore. 9 They spread out over the earth and surrounded the camp of God's people and the city that he loves. But fire came down from heaven and destroyed them. 10 Then the Devil, who deceived them, was thrown into the lake of fire and sulfur, where the beast and the false prophet had already been thrown; and they will be tormented day and night forever and ever.

The Final Judgment

11 Then I saw a great white throne and the one who sits on it. Earth and heaven fled from his presence and were seen no more. 12 And I saw the dead, great and small alike, standing before the throne. Books were opened, and then another book was opened, the book of the living. The dead were judged according to what they had done, as recorded in the books. 13 Then the sea gave up its dead. Death and the world of the dead also gave up the dead they held. And all were judged according to what they had done. 14 Then death and the world of the dead were thrown into the lake of fire. (This lake of fire is the second death.) 15 Those who did not have their name written in the book of the living were thrown into the lake of fire.

The New Heaven and the New Earth

21 Then I saw a new heaven and a new earth. The first heaven and the first earth disappeared, and the sea vanished. 2 And I saw the Holy City, the new Jerusalem, coming down out of heaven from God, prepared and ready, like a bride dressed to meet her husband. 3 I heard a loud voice speaking from the throne: "Now God's home is with people! He will live with them, and they shall be his people. God himself will be with them, and he will be their God. 4 He will wipe away all tears from their eyes. There will be no more death, no more grief or crying or pain. The old things have disappeared."

5 Then the one who sits on the throne said, "And now I make all things new!" He also said to me, "Write this, because these words are true and can be trusted." 6 And he said, "It is done! I am the first and the last, the beginning and the end. To anyone who is thirsty I will give the right to drink from the spring of the water of life without paying for it. 7 Those who win the victory will receive this from me: I will be their God, and they will be my children. 8 But cowards, traitors, perverts, murderers, the immoral, those who practice magic, those who worship idols, and all liars — the place for them is the lake burning with fire and sulfur, which is the second death."

The New Jerusalem

9 One of the seven angels who had the seven bowls full of the seven last plagues came to me and said, "Come, and I will show you the Bride, the wife of the Lamb." 10 The Spirit took control

---

20.8 a Ez 7.2; b Ez 38.2, 9, 15   20.11, 12 Dn 7.9, 10   20.12 2 Esd 6.20   21.1 Is 65.17; 66.22; 2 P 3.13   21.2 2 Esd 13.36; a Is 52.1; b Rev 3.12; c Is 61.10   21.3 Ez 37.27; Lv 26.11, 12   21.4 a Is 25.8; b Is 35.10; 65.19   21.6 Is 55.1   21.7 2 S 7.14; Ps 89.26, 27   21.10 Ez 40.2; 2 Esd 10.27

of me, and the angel carried me to the top of a very high mountain. He showed me Jerusalem, the Holy City, coming down out of heaven from God [11] and shining with the glory of God. The city shone like a precious stone, like a jasper, clear as crystal. [12] It had a great, high wall with twelve gates and with twelve angels in charge of the gates. On the gates were written the names of the twelve tribes of the people of Israel. [13] There were three gates on each side: three on the east, three on the south, three on the north, and three on the west. [14] The city's wall was built on twelve foundation stones, on which were written the names of the twelve apostles of the Lamb. [15] The angel who spoke to me had a gold measuring stick to measure the city, its gates, and its wall. [16] The city was perfectly square, as wide as it was long. The angel measured the city with his measuring stick: it was fifteen hundred miles long and was as wide and as high as it was long. [17] The angel also measured the wall, and it was 216 feet high,[g] according to the standard unit of measure which he was using.[h] [18] The wall was made of jasper, and the city itself was made of pure gold, as clear as glass. [19] The foundation stones of the city wall were adorned with all kinds of precious stones. The first foundation stone was jasper, the second sapphire, the third agate, the fourth emerald, [20] the fifth onyx, the sixth carnelian, the seventh yellow quartz, the eighth beryl, the ninth topaz, the tenth chalcedony, the eleventh turquoise, the twelfth amethyst. [21] The twelve gates were twelve pearls; each gate was made from a single pearl. The street of the city was of pure gold, transparent as glass.

[22] I did not see a temple in the city, because its temple is the Lord God Almighty and the Lamb. [23] The city has no need of the sun or the moon to shine on it, because the glory of God shines on it, and the Lamb is its lamp. [24] The peoples of the world will walk by its light, and the kings of the earth will bring their wealth into it. [25] The gates of the city will stand open all day; they will never be closed, because there will be no night there. [26] The greatness and the wealth of the nations will be brought into the city. [27] But nothing that is impure will enter the city, nor anyone who does shameful things or tells lies. Only those whose names are written in the Lamb's book of the living will enter the city.

22 The angel also showed me the river of the water of life, sparkling like crystal, and coming from the throne of God and of the Lamb [2] and flowing down the middle of the city's street. On each side of the river was the tree of life, which bears fruit twelve times a year, once each month; and its leaves are for the healing of the nations. [3] Nothing that is under God's curse will be found in the city.

The throne of God and of the Lamb will be in the city, and his servants will worship him. [4] They will see his face, and his name will be written on their foreheads. [5] There shall be no more night, and they will not need lamps or sunlight, because the Lord God will be their light, and they will rule as kings forever and ever.

The Coming of Jesus

[6] Then the angel said to me, "These words are true and can be trusted. And

---

[g] high; *or thick.*   [h] *In verses 16 and 17 the Greek text speaks of "12,000 furlongs" and "144 cubits" which may have symbolic significance.*
21.12, 13 Ez 48.30-35   **21.15** Ez 40.3   **21.18-21** Is 54.11, 12   **21.18** Tb 13.16, 17
21.23 Is 60.19, 20   **21.24** Is 60.3   **21.25, 26** Is 60.11   **21.27** Is 52.1; Ez 44.9
22.1 Ez 47.1; Zec 14.8   **22.2** Gn 2.9; 2 Esd 2.12; 7.123   **22.3** Zec 14.11 (cp. Gn 3.17)
22.4 2 Esd 7.98   **22.5 a** Is 60.19; **b** Dn 7.18

the Lord God, who gives his Spirit to the prophets, has sent his angel to show his servants what must happen very soon."

⁷"Listen!" says Jesus. "I am coming soon! Happy are those who obey the prophetic words in this book!"

⁸I, John, have heard and seen all these things. And when I finished hearing and seeing them, I fell down at the feet of the angel who had shown me these things, and I was about to worship him. ⁹But he said to me, "Don't do it! I am a servant together with you and with your brothers the prophets and of all those who obey the words in this book. Worship God!" ¹⁰And he said to me, "Do not keep the prophetic words of this book a secret, because the time is near when all this will happen. ¹¹Whoever is evil must go on doing evil, and whoever is filthy must go on being filthy; whoever is good must go on doing good, and whoever is holy must go on being holy."

¹²"Listen!" says Jesus. "I am coming soon! I will bring my rewards with me, to give to each one according to what he has done. ¹³I am the first and the last, the beginning and the end."

¹⁴Happy are those who wash their robes clean and so have the right to eat the fruit from the tree of life and to go through the gates into the city. ¹⁵But outside the city are the perverts and those who practice magic, the immoral and the murderers, those who worship idols and those who are liars both in words and deeds.

¹⁶"I, Jesus, have sent my angel to announce these things to you in the churches. I am descended from the family of David; I am the bright morning star."

¹⁷The Spirit and the Bride say, "Come!"

Everyone who hears this must also say, "Come!"

Come, whoever is thirsty; accept the water of life as a gift, whoever wants it.

Conclusion

¹⁸I, John, solemnly warn everyone who hears the prophetic words of this book: if any add anything to them, God will add to their punishment the plagues described in this book. ¹⁹And if any take anything away from the prophetic words of this book, God will take away from them their share of the fruit of the tree of life and of the Holy City, which are described in this book.

²⁰He who gives his testimony to all this says, "Yes indeed! I am coming soon!"

So be it. Come, Lord Jesus!

²¹May the grace of the Lord Jesus be with everyone. *i*

---

i everyone; *some manuscripts have* God's people; *others have* all of God's people.
22.11 Dn 12.10   **22.12 a** Is 40.10; 62.11; **b** Ps 28.4; Is 40.10; Jr 17.10   **22.13 a** Rev 1.8; **b** Is 44.6; 48.12; Rev 1.17; 2.8   **22.14** Gn 2.9; 3.22   **22.16** Is 11.1, 10   **22.17** Is 55.1 **22.18, 19** Dt 4.2; 12.32

APPENDICES

WORD LIST

PASSAGES FROM THE SEPTUAGINT

CHRONOLOGY OF THE BIBLE

MAPS-MAP INDEX

SUBJECT INDEX

LECTIONARY GUIDE

WORD LIST

This Word List identifies many objects or cultural features whose meaning may not be known to all readers.

Abib The first month of the Hebrew calendar, corresponding to the period from about mid-March to about mid-April. This month is also called Nisan.

Abyss The place in the depths of the earth where the demons were imprisoned until their final punishment.

Acacia A flowering tree, a type of mimosa, with hard and durable wood.

Adar The twelfth month of the Hebrew calendar, corresponding to the period from about mid-February to about mid-March.

Agate A semiprecious stone of various colors, but usually white and brown.

Alabaster A soft stone of usually light creamy color, from which vases and jars were made.

Aloes A sweet-smelling substance, derived from a plant. It was used medicinally and as a perfume.

Amen A Hebrew word which means "it is so" or "may it be so." It can also be translated "certainly," "truly," or "surely." In Revelation 3.14 it is used as a title for Christ.

Amethyst A semiprecious stone, usually purple or violet in color.

Anoint To pour or rub olive oil on someone in order to honor him or to appoint him to some special work. The Israelite kings were anointed as a sign of their taking office, and so the king could be called "the anointed one." In a figurative sense, "The Anointed One" is the title of the one whom God chose and appointed as Savior and Lord.

Apostle Principally one of the group of twelve men whom Jesus chose to be his special followers and helpers. It is also used in the New Testament to re-

fer to Paul and other Christian workers. The word may have the sense of "messenger."

Areopagus A hill in Athens where the city council used to meet. For this reason the council itself was called Areopagus, even after it no longer met on the hill.

Artemis The Greek name of an ancient goddess of fertility, worshiped especially in Asia Minor.

Asherah A goddess of fertility worshiped by the Canaanites; her male counterpart was Baal. After the Hebrews invaded Canaan, many of them began worshiping these two gods.

Astarte A goddess of fertility and war who was widely worshiped in the ancient Near East.

Atonement, Day of The most important of Israel's holy days, when the High Priest would offer sacrifice for the sins of the people of Israel (Leviticus 16). It was held on the 10th day of the seventh month of the Hebrew calendar (around October 1). The Jewish name for this day is Yom Kippur.

Baal The god of fertility worshiped by the Canaanites; his female counterpart was Asherah. After the Hebrews invaded Canaan, many of them began worshiping these two gods.

Baal-of-the-Covenant A name by which the god Baal was known by the people of Shechem.

Balsam A tree from which sweet-smelling resin was obtained; the resin was used for perfume and medicine.

Barley A cultivated grain similar to wheat, grown as a food crop.

Beelzebul A New Testament name given to the Devil as the chief of the evil spirits.

Beryl A semiprecious stone, usually green or bluish green in color.

Breastplate Part of a soldier's armor, made of leather or metal; it covered the chest and sometimes the back as a protection against arrows and the blows of a sword.

Bul The eighth month of the Hebrew calender, corresponding to the period from about mid-October to about mid-November.

Burnt offering A type of sacrifice in which all the parts of the animal were completely burned on the altar; in other sacrifices only certain parts of the animal were burned.

Calamus A sweet-smelling reed-like plant.

Capital The top part of a column supporting a roof.

Carnelian A semiprecious stone, usually red in color.

Cassia A spice made from the bark of a tree; it closely resembles cinnamon.

Chalcedony A semiprecious stone, usually milky or gray in color.

Christ Originally a title, the Greek equivalent of the Hebrew word "Messiah." It means "the anointed one." Jesus was called the Christ because he was the one whom God chose and sent as Savior and Lord.

Circumcise To cut off the foreskin of the penis. As a sign of God's covenant with his people Israelite boys were circumcised eight days after they were born (Genesis 17.9-14).

Concubine A servant woman who, although not a wife, had sexual relations with her master. She had important legal rights, and her master was referred to as her husband.

Coral A brightly colored stony substance found in the sea; it was used as jewelry.

Council The supreme religious court of the Jews, composed of seventy leaders of the Jewish people and presided over by the High Priest.

Covenant An agreement, either between persons or between God and a person or a people. God made a covenant with Noah (Genesis 9.8-17) and with Abraham (Genesis 17.1-8), but in the Old Testament the term usually refers to the covenant made between God and the people of Israel at the time of Moses (Exodus 24.4-8).

Covenant Box The wooden chest covered with gold, in which were kept the two stone tablets on which were written the Ten Commandments. It has traditionally been called the Ark of the Covenant.

Cumin A small plant whose seeds are ground up and used for seasoning foods.

Cush The term "Cush" in the Old Testament Hebrew text normally designates the territory extending south from the First Cataract of the Nile River at Aswan. It was known in Graeco-Roman times as Ethiopia (Gk., *Aithiopia*), and later as Nubia. This extensive region included within its borders most of modern Sudan and some of present-day Ethiopia (Abyssinia). In Genesis 10, the Table of Nations, verses 8-12 are included under the genealogy of Egyptian Cush, yet all the peoples named are in Mesopotamia. Apparently the Hebrew designation for the Babylonian Kassites was "Cush" as well, thus resulting in the mixing of the two regions. Genesis 2.13 may be another reference to Babylonian Cush.

Cymbals A pair of thin pieces of metal held in the hands and struck together rhythmically in music.

David's City In the Old Testament the reference is generally to that part of the city of Jerusalem which was captured from the Jebusites by King David. In the New Testament the reference is to the town of Bethlehem, David's boyhood home, where Jesus was born.

Dedication, Festival of The Jewish festival, lasting eight days, which celebrated the restoration and rededication in 165 B.C. of the Temple altar by the Jewish patriot Judas Maccabeus. The festival began on the 25th day of the month Kislev (around December 10). The Jewish name for this festival is Hanukkah.

Defile To make ritually unclean or impure. Certain foods and practices were prohibited by the Law of Moses because they were thought to make a person ritually or ceremonially unclean. Such a person could not take part in the public worship until he had performed certain rituals which would remove the defilement.

Demon An evil spirit with the power to harm people; it was regarded as a messenger and servant of the Devil.

Dill A small garden plant whose stems, leaves, and seeds are used for seasoning food.

Dipper: Big Dipper and **Little Dipper** Two groups of stars which in the Northern Hemisphere are visible in the northern sky. The star at the end of the "handle" of the Little Dipper is Polaris, the North Star.

Disciple A person who follows and learns from someone else. In the New Testament the word is used of the followers of John the Baptist and especially of the followers of Jesus, particularly the twelve apostles.

Divination The attempt to discover a message from God or the gods by examining such things as marked stones or the liver of a sacrificed animal.

Dragon A legendary beast, thought to be like a huge lizard. It is also called a serpent and appears as a figure of the Devil (Revelation 12.3–13.4; 20.2, 3).

Elders In the Old Testament this is a name given to certain respected leaders of a tribe, nation, or city. In the New Testament three different groups are called elders: (1) in the Gospels the elders are influential Jewish religious leaders, some of whom were members of the supreme Council; (2) in Acts 11–21 and the Letters the elders are Christian church officers who had general responsibility for the work of the church; (3) in Revelation the twenty-four elders are part of God's court in heaven, perhaps as representatives of God's people.

Elul The sixth month of the Hebrew calendar, corresponding to the period from about mid-August to about mid-September.

Ephod The Hebrew term traditionally transliterated as "ephod" is of uncertain meaning in a number of contexts. Generally it refers to some type of priestly garment which was worn over the shoulder by the High Priest and with which the Urim and Thummim were associated. In certain contexts, however, the Hebrew term refers to an object of worship, and in some other passages, it evidently refers to an object used to foretell future events.

Epicureans Those who followed the teaching of Epicurus (died 270 B.C.), a Greek philosopher who taught that happiness is the highest good in life.

Epileptic A person who suffers from a nervous disease causing convulsions and fainting.

Ethanim The seventh month of the Hebrew calendar, corresponding to the period from about mid-September to about mid-October; it was later called Tishri.

Ethiopia See "Cush."

Eunuch A man who has been made physically incapable of having normal sexual relations. Eunuchs were often important officials in the courts of ancient kings, and the term may have come to be used of such officials in general, regardless of their sexual condition.

Fast To go without food for a while as a religious duty.

Feldspar A colorful, rather hard rock, often glassy in appearance.

Fellowship offerings A type of sacrifice offered to insure a right relationship with God. Only a portion of the animal was burned on the altar; the rest was eaten by the worshipers or the priests.

Flax A small cultivated plant; the fibers of its stem are spun into thread used in making linen cloth.

Frankincense A valuable incense, made from the sap of a certain tree. This incense was probably imported from Arabia.

Garnet A semiprecious stone, usually red in color.

Gazelle A kind of antelope, known for its beauty and gracefulness.

Gentile A person who is not a Jew.

Hades The Greek name used in the New Testament to refer to the world of the dead.

Harrow A farm implement used to break up the ground and level it after plowing.

Harvest Festival The Israelite festival celebrating the wheat harvest, held in the latter part of May, fifty days after Passover. The Jewish name for this festival is Shavuoth (the Feast of Weeks). It has also been called Pentecost.

Hermes The name of a Greek god who served as messenger of the gods.

Herod's party A political party in New Testament times composed of Jews who favored being ruled by one of the descendants of Herod the Great rather than by the Roman governor.

High Priest The priest who occupied the highest office in the Jewish priestly system and was president of the supreme Council of the Jews. Once a year (on the Day of Atonement) he would enter the Most Holy Place in the Temple and offer sacrifice for himself and for the sins of the people of Israel.

Hyssop A small bushy plant, used in religious ceremonies to sprinkle liquids.

Incense Material which is burned in order to produce a pleasant smell. The Israelites used it in their worship.

Jackal A small wild animal resembling a fox.

Jasper A semiprecious stone of various colors. The jasper mentioned in the Bible was probably green, or else clear.

Javelin A short, light spear used by soldiers in ancient times.

Kislev The ninth month of the Hebrew calendar, corresponding to the period from about mid-November to about mid-December.

Law The name which the Jews applied to the first five books of the Old Testament, also called "The Books of Moses." Sometimes, however, the name is applied in a more general way to the entire Old Testament.

Leviathan A legendary animal associated with water, in some passages identified by some scholars as the crocodile. In a figurative sense it may represent the chaos that existed before God created the world (Isaiah 27.1; Psalm 74.14).

Levite (1) A member of the tribe of Levi; (2) a man who assisted the priest in the performance of religious duties.

Levitical priest A Hebrew priest descended from the tribe of Levi. All priests were supposed to be members of the tribe of Levi, but in later times not all members of the tribe of Levi were priests.

Living creatures (also referred to as "winged creatures" and traditionally called "cherubim") symbols of God's majesty and associated with his presence. For a description of such creatures see Exodus 25.18-20; Ezekiel 1.5-13; 10; Revelation 4.6-9.

LORD in this translation represents the Hebrew name Yahweh (traditionally represented by Jehovah), corresponding either to the occurrence of the name itself or to a pronoun standing for the name.

Lyre A kind of harp.

Mandrake A small plant; it was believed that eating its root or fruit would make a woman more easily able to have children.

Manna A food eaten by the Israelites during their travels in the wilderness. It was white and flaky and looked like small seeds (Exodus 16.14-21; Numbers 11.7-9).

Medium A person who believes that he or she can communicate with the dead.

Messiah A Hebrew title (meaning "the anointed one") given to the promised Savior, whose coming was foretold by the Hebrew prophets; the corresponding Greek term "the Christ" has the same meaning.

Mildew A fungus that appears on various objects, especially in damp weather.

Millet A cultivated grain that was grown as a food crop.

Molech One of the gods of the ancient people of Canaan.

Most Holy Place The innermost room of the Tent of the LORD's presence or the Temple. The Covenant Box was kept there. Only the High Priest could enter the Most Holy Place, and he did so only once a year, on the Day of Atonement.

Mustard A large plant which grows from a very small seed. The seeds were ground into powder and used as spice on food.

Myrrh A sweet-smelling resin that was highly prized. It served as a medicine (Mark 15.23) and was used by the Jews in preparing bodies for burial (John 19.39).

Myrtle A kind of evergreen shrub or tree.

Nard An expensive perfume made from a plant.

Nazarene Someone from the town of Nazareth. The name was used as a title for Jesus and also as a name for the early Christians (Acts 24.5).

Nazirite A person who took a special vow of self-dedication. Such a person was not to drink beer or wine, cut his hair, or touch a dead body (Numbers 6.1-21). The vow could be taken for a certain period of time, but some persons were dedicated to God as Nazirites from their birth.

New Moon Festival A religious observance held by the Israelites on the day of each new moon.

New Year Festival The Jewish name for this festival is "Rosh Hashanah."

Nisan The first month of the Hebrew calendar, corresponding to the period from about mid-March to about mid-April. The month is also called Abib.

Onyx A semiprecious stone of various colors.

Orion A group of prominent stars visible during winter evenings.

Outcasts In the Gospels this name, which in many translations appears as "sinners," refers to those Jews who had been excluded from synagogue worship because they violated rules about foods that should not be eaten and about associating with people who were not Jews. Such outcasts were despised by many of their fellow Jews, and Jesus was criticized for associating with them (Mark 2.15-17; Luke 7.34; 15.1, 2).

Parable A story which teaches spiritual truth; it was often used by Jesus.

Paradise A name for heaven (Luke 23.43; 2 Corinthians 12.3).

Paralytic A person who suffers from a disease that prevents movement of part or all of the body.

Passover The Israelite festival, on the 14th day of the month Nisan (around April 1), which celebrated the deliverance of the ancient Hebrews from their captivity in Egypt. The Angel of Death killed the first-born in the Egyptian homes but passed over the Hebrew homes (Exodus 12.23-27). The Jewish name for this festival is Pesach.

Pentecost, Day of The Greek name for the Israelite festival of wheat harvest (see Harvest Festival). The name Pentecost (meaning "fiftieth") comes from the fact that the feast was held fifty days after Passover.

Pervert One who commits unnatural sexual acts.

Pharisees A Jewish religious party during the time of Jesus. They were strict in obeying the Law of Moses and other regulations which had been added to it through the centuries.

Pistachio nut A small greenish nut.

Pleiades A small group of stars visible during winter evenings.

Pomegranate A reddish fruit about the size of a large apple; it has a hard rind and is full of tasty seeds.

Preparation, Day of The sixth day of the week (Friday), on which the Jews made the required preparation to observe the Sabbath (Saturday).

Prophet A person who proclaims a message from God. The term usually refers to certain men in the Old Testament, but the New Testament speaks of prophets in the early church. John the Baptist is also called a prophet.

Purim The Jewish religious holiday held on the 14th day of the month Adar (around March 1), celebrating the deliverance of the Jews from Haman by Esther and Mordecai. The story is told in the book of Esther.

Quartz A semiprecious stone of various colors, but usually clear.

Rabbi A Hebrew word which means "my teacher."

Red Sea Evidently referred originally to (1) a series of lakes and marshes between the head of the Gulf of Suez and the Mediterranean, the region generally regarded as the site of the events described in Exodus 13, and

was also used to designate (2) the Gulf of Suez, (3) the Gulf of Aqaba.

Rephan The name of an ancient god that was worshiped as the ruler of the planet Saturn.

Resin A fragrant, gummy substance produced from the sap of certain trees and shrubs.

Restoration, Year of The year, coming every fifty years, when the ancient Israelites returned to the original owner any property they were holding, freed their Israelite slaves, and did not cultivate their fields.

Sabbath The seventh day of the Jewish week (from sundown on Friday to sundown on Saturday), a holy day on which no work was permitted.

Sackcloth A coarse cloth made of goats' hair, which was worn as a sign of mourning or distress.

Sadducees A small Jewish religious party in New Testament times, composed largely of priests. They based their beliefs primarily on the first five books of the Old Testament and differed in several matters of belief and practice from the larger party of the Pharisees.

Samaritan A name used to refer to a native of Samaria, the region between Judea and Galilee. Because of differences in politics, race, customs, and religion (including especially the central place of worship), there was much bad feeling between the Jews and the Samaritans.

Sanctuary A building dedicated to the worship of God. Sometimes the word refers to the central place of worship and not to the whole building.

Sapphire A very valuable stone, usually blue in color.

Scepter A short rod held by kings to symbolize their authority.

Scorpion A small creature which has eight legs and a long tail with a poisonous sting. It can inflict a very painful, and sometimes fatal, wound.

Scribe A person whose business it was to write documents for others or to copy written material. Some scribes were employed by ancient kings to prepare official documents, and some of them became important officials.

Scriptures In the New Testament the word refers to the collected body of Hebrew sacred writings, known to Christians as the Old Testament. Various names are used: the Law (or the Law of Moses) and the prophets (Matthew 5.17; 7.12; Luke 2.22; 24.44; Acts 13.15; 28.23); the Holy Scriptures (Romans 1.2; 2 Timothy 3.15); the old covenant (2 Corinthians 3.14). The singular "scripture" refers to a single passage of the Old Testament.

Serpent A name given to the dragon, which appears in the New Testament as a figure of the Devil (Revelation 12.3-17; 20.2, 3).

Seventh year The year, coming every seventh year, when the ancient Israelites did not cultivate their fields and when debts were canceled.

Shebat The eleventh month of the Hebrew calendar, corresponding to the period from about mid-January to about mid-February.

Shelters, Festival of A joyous festival celebrated by the Israelites in the fall after the completion of the harvest. In order to help them remember the years when their ancestors wandered through the wilderness, the Israelites constructed rough shelters to live in during the festival. The Jewish name for this festival is Sukkoth. It has been traditionally called the Feast of Tabernacles or the Feast of Booths.

Sickle A tool consisting of a curved metal blade and a wooden handle, used for cutting wheat and other crops.

Sivan The third month of the Hebrew calendar, corresponding to the period from about mid-May to about mid-June.

Snuffer The Hebrew word translated "snuffer" apparently identifies an implement used to trim the oil lamps used in the Tent of the LORD's presence or the Temple.

Sorcerer A person who works magic for evil purposes.

Stoics Those who followed the teachings of the Greek philosopher Zeno (died 265 B.C.), who taught that happiness is to be found in being free from pleasure and pain.

Sulfur In the Bible this refers to a sulfur compound which burns with great heat and produces an unpleasant smell.

Synagogue A place where Jews met every Sabbath day for their public worship. It probably also served as a center for Jewish social life and a school for Jewish children.

Tambourine A small drum with pieces of metal in the rim, held in the hand and shaken. In biblical times it was generally used by women.

Tassel A group of threads or cords, fastened together at one end and loose at the other. The Israelites were commanded to wear these on their clothes (Numbers 15.37-41).

Teachers of the Law Men who in New Testament times taught and interpreted the teachings of the Old Testament, especially the first five books.

Tebeth The tenth month of the Hebrew calendar, corresponding to the period from about mid-December to about mid-January.

Tenant A man who grows crops on land owned by someone else, and turns over a part of the harvest to the owner to pay for the use of his land.

Tent of the LORD's presence The large tent described in detail in Exodus 26, where the Israelites worshiped God until Solomon built the Temple. It has traditionally been called the Tabernacle or Tent of meeting.

Tithe A tenth part of a person's produce or income, given for religious purposes.

Topaz A semiprecious stone, usually yellow in color.

Turban A head covering worn by men, made by cloth wrapped around the head.

Turquoise A semiprecious stone, blue or bluish green in color.

Unleavened Bread, Festival of The Israelite festival, lasting seven days after Passover; it also celebrated the deliverance of the ancient Hebrews from Egypt. The name came from the practice of not using leaven (yeast) in making bread during that week (Exodus 12.14-20). It was held from the 15th to the 22nd day of the month Nisan (around the first week of April).

Urim and Thummim Two small objects used by Israelite priests to determine God's will.

Vow A strong declaration or promise, usually made while calling upon God to punish the speaker if the statement should prove to be not true or if the promise were not kept.

Winged creatures (also referred to as "living creatures" and traditionally called "cherubim") symbols of God's majesty and associated with his presence. For a description of such creatures see Exodus 25.18-20; Ezekiel 1.5-13; 10; Revelation 4.6-9.

Winnowing shovel A tool like a shovel or a large fork, used to separate the wheat from the chaff.

Wreath Flowers or leaves arranged in a circle, to be placed on a person's head. In ancient times a wreath of leaves was the prize given to winners in athletic contests.

Yeast A substance, also called leaven, which is added to dough made from the flour of wheat or barley to make it rise before being baked into bread.

Yoke A heavy bar of wood fitted over the necks of two oxen to make it possible for them to pull a plow or a cart. The word is used figuratively to describe the moral lessons that a teacher passes on to his pupils.

Zeus The name of the supreme god of the Greeks.

Zion Originally a designation for "David's City," the Jebusite stronghold captured by King David's forces. The term "Zion" was later extended in meaning to refer to the hill on which the Temple stood.

Ziv The second month of the Hebrew calendar, corresponding to the period from about mid-April to about mid-May.

NEW TESTAMENT PASSAGES
QUOTED OR PARAPHRASED FROM THE SEPTUAGINT

The writers of the New Testament generally quoted or paraphrased the ancient Greek translation of the Old Testament, commonly known as the Septuagint Version (LXX), made some two hundred years before the time of Christ. In a number of instances this version differs significantly in meaning from the Masoretic Hebrew text, and as a special help to the reader such occurrences of LXX quotations, paraphrases, or evident allusions are listed here. The following translations of the LXX passages reflect in general the wording of *Today's English Version* of the New Testament. When, however, a LXX quotation occurs several times in the New Testament, the TEV wording of the translation may vary because of evident differences in meaning or emphasis reflected in the different contexts. Chapter and verse numbers are those of the English Bible.

Matthew 1.23 (Isaiah 7.14) A virgin will become pregnant and have a son.

Matthew 3.3 (Isaiah 40.3) Someone is shouting in the desert, "Prepare a road for the Lord; make a straight path for our God to travel!"

Matthew 12.21 (Isaiah 42.4) And on him all people will put their hope.

Matthew 13.14, 15 (Isaiah 6.9, 10) This people will listen and listen, but not understand; they will look and look, but not see, because their minds are dull, and they have stopped up their ears, and have closed their eyes. Otherwise, their eyes would see, their ears would hear, their minds would understand, and they would turn to me, says God, and I would heal them.

Matthew 15.8, 9 (Isaiah 29.13) These people, says God, . . . honor me with their words, but their heart is really far away from me. It is no use for them to worship me, because they teach man-made rules and laws.

Matthew 21.16 (Psalm 8.2) You have trained children and babies to offer perfect praise.

Mark 1.3 (Isaiah 40.3) Someone is shouting in the desert, "Get the road ready for the Lord; make a straight path for our God to travel!"

Mark 4.12 (Isaiah 6.9, 10) This people will listen and listen, but not understand; they will look and look, but not see . . .; for if they did . . ., they would turn to me, says God, and I would heal them.

Mark 7.6, 7 (Isaiah 29.13) These people, says God, . . . honor me with their words, but their heart is really far away from me. It is no use for them to worship me, because they teach man-made rules and laws.

Luke 3.4-6 (Isaiah 40.3-5) Someone is shouting in the desert: "Get the road ready for the Lord, make a straight path for our God to travel! Every valley must be filled up, every hill and mountain leveled off. All the winding roads must be made straight, and the rough paths made smooth. . . . All people will see God's salvation!"

Luke 4.18 (Isaiah 61.1) The Spirit of the Lord is upon me, because he has chosen me to bring good news to the poor. He has sent me . . . to proclaim liberty to the captives and recovery of sight to the blind.

Luke 8.10 (Isaiah 6.9) You will listen and listen, but not understand; you will look and look, but not see.

John 1.23 (Isaiah 40.3) The voice of someone shouting in the desert: . . .

"Make a straight path for our God to travel!"

John 12.38 (Isaiah 53.1) Lord, who believed the message we told?

John 12.40 (Isaiah 6.10) This people's minds are dull, and they have stopped up their ears and have closed their eyes. Otherwise, their eyes would see, and their ears would hear, their minds would understand, and they would turn to me, says God, for me to heal them.

Acts 2.19, 20 (Joel 2.30, 31) There will be blood, fire, and thick smoke; the sun will be darkened, and the moon will turn red as blood, before the great and glorious Day of the Lord comes.

Acts 2.25-28 (Psalm 16.8-11) I saw the Lord before me at all times. He is near me, and I will not be troubled. And so I am filled with gladness, and my words are full of joy. And I, mortal though I am, will rest assured in hope, because you will not abandon me in the world of the dead; you will not allow your faithful servant to rot in the grave. You have shown me the paths that lead to life, and your presence will fill me with joy.

Acts 3.22 (Deuteronomy 18.15) You are to obey him in all things.

Acts 4.25, 26 (Psalm 2.1, 2) Why were the Gentiles furious; why did people make their useless plots? The kings of the earth prepared themselves, and the rulers met together.

Acts 7.14 (Genesis 46.27) Seventy-five people.

Acts 7.42, 43 (Amos 5.25-27) People of Israel! It was not to me that you slaughtered and sacrificed animals for forty years in the desert. It was the tent of the god Molech that you carried, and the image of Rephan, your star god; they were idols that you had made for yourselves. And so I will send you into exile beyond Damascus.

Acts 8.33 (Isaiah 53.8) He was humiliated, and justice was denied him. No one will be able to tell about his descendants, because his life on earth has come to an end.

Acts 13.34 (Isaiah 55.3) I will make an everlasting covenant with you, the sacred and sure blessings I promised to David.

Acts 13.41 (Habakkuk 1.5) Look, you scoffers! Be much astonished and die!

Acts 15.16, 17 (Amos 9.11, 12) In that day, says the Lord, I will restore the kingdom of David. I will rebuild its ruins, and make it strong again. . . . . And so all the rest of the human race will come to me, all the Gentiles whom I have called to be my own.

Acts 28.26, 27 (Isaiah 6.9, 10) Go and say to this people: You will listen and listen, but not understand; you will look and look, but not see, because this people's minds are dull, and they have stopped up their ears and closed their eyes. Otherwise, their eyes would see, their ears would hear, their minds would understand, and they would turn to me, says God, and I would heal them.

Romans 2.24 (Isaiah 52.5) Because of you Jews, the Gentiles continually speak evil of God.

Romans 3.4 (Psalm 51.4) You must be shown to be right when you speak; you must win your case when you are being tried.

Romans 3.12 (Psalms 14.3; 53.3) All have turned away from God; they have all gone wrong.

Romans 3.13 (Psalm 5.9) Wicked lies roll off their tongues.

Romans 3.14 (Psalm 10.7) Their speech is filled with bitter curses and guile.

Romans 9.17 (Exodus 9.16) To use you to show my power.

Romans 9.27, 28 (Isaiah 10.22, 23) Even if the people of Israel are as many as the grains of sand by the sea, yet only a few of them will be saved; for God will quickly and justly settle his full account with all the world.

Romans 9.29 (Isaiah 1.9) If the Lord Almighty had not left us some descendants.

Romans 9.33 (Isaiah 28.16) Whoever believes in him will not be disappointed.

Romans 10.11 (Isaiah 28.16) Whoever believes in him will not be disappointed.

Romans 10.16 (Isaiah 53.1) Lord, who believed our message?

Romans 10.18 (Psalm 19.4) The sound of their voice went out to all the world; their words reached the ends of the earth.

Romans 10.20 (Isaiah 65.1) I appeared to those who were not looking for me, I was found by those who were not asking for me.

Romans 10.21 (Isaiah 65.2) All day long I held out my hands to welcome a disobedient and rebellious people.

Romans 11.9, 10 (Psalm 69.22, 23) May they fall, may they be punished! . . . Make them bend under their troubles at all times.

Romans 11.26, 27 (Isaiah 59.20, 21) The Savior will come for the sake of Zion, and remove all wickedness from the descendants of Jacob. I will make this covenant with them, (Isaiah 27.9) when I take away their sins.

Romans 11.34 (Isaiah 40.13) Who knows the mind of the Lord?

Romans 12.20 (Proverbs 25.21, 22) If your enemies are hungry, feed them; if they are thirsty, give them a drink; for by doing this you will make them burn with shame.

Romans 14.11 (Isaiah 45.23) Everyone will kneel before me, and everyone will confess that I am God.

Romans 15.12 (Isaiah 11.10) On that day a descendant of Jesse will appear; he will come to rule the Gentiles, and they will put their hope in him.

Romans 15.21 (Isaiah 52.15) Those who were not told about him will see, and those who have not heard will understand.

1 Corinthians 1.19 (Isaiah 29.14) I will destroy the wisdom of the wise, and hide the understanding of the scholars.

1 Corinthians 2.16 (Isaiah 40.13) Who knows the mind of the Lord?

1 Corinthians 5.13 (Deuteronomy 17.7) Remove the evil man from your group.

1 Corinthians 10.20 (Deuteronomy 32.17) What is sacrificed on pagan altars is offered to demons, not to God.

1 Corinthians 15.55 (Hosea 13.14) Where, Death, is your punishment? Where, Hades, is your power to hurt?

2 Corinthians 4.13 (Psalm 116.10) I spoke because I believed.

2 Corinthians 8.21 (Proverbs 3.4) Make it your purpose to do what is right, not only in the sight of the Lord, but also in the sight of man.

Galatians 3.10 (Deuteronomy 27.26) Whoever does not always obey everything that is written in this Law is under God's curse.

Ephesians 4.26 (Psalm 4.4) If you become angry, do not let your anger lead you into sin.

Philippians 2.11 (Isaiah 45.23) And all will openly proclaim God.

Hebrews 1.6 (Deuteronomy 32.43) All of God's sons must worship him.

Hebrews 1.7 (Psalm 104.4) God makes his angels winds, and his servants a flaming fire.

Hebrews 1.10-12 (Psalm 102.25-27) You, Lord, in the beginning created the earth. . . . You will fold them up like a coat, and they will be changed.

Hebrews 2.7 (Psalm 8.5) You made him for a little while lower than the angels.

Hebrews 3.7-9 (Psalm 95.7-9) If you hear God's voice today, do not be stubborn as your ancestors were when they rebelled against God, as they were that day in the desert when they put him to the test. There they put me to the test and tried me, says God, although they saw what I did.

Hebrews 3.15 (Psalm 95.7, 8) If you hear God's voice today, do not be stubborn as your ancestors were when they rebelled against God.

Hebrews 4.7 (Psalm 95.7, 8) If you hear God's voice today, do not be stubborn.

Hebrews 8.9 (Jeremiah 31.32) They were not faithful to the covenant I made with them, and so I paid no attention to them.

Hebrews 10.5 (Psalm 40.6) You do not want sacrifices and offerings, but you have prepared a body for me.

Hebrews 10.27 (Isaiah 26.11) The fierceness . . . and now fire will destroy those who oppose God.

Hebrews 10.38b (Habakkuk 2.4a) If he turns back, I will not be pleased with him.

Hebrews 11.5 (Genesis 5.24) Enoch pleased God, and nobody could find him, because God had taken him up.

Hebrews 11.21 (Genesis 47.31) He leaned on the top of his walking stick and worshiped God.

Hebrews 12.5, 6 (Proverbs 3.11, 12) Son, pay attention when the Lord corrects you, and do not be discouraged when he rebukes you. Because the Lord corrects everyone he loves, and punishes everyone he accepts as a son.

Hebrews 12.13 (Proverbs 4.26) Keep walking on straight paths.

Hebrews 12.15 (Deuteronomy 29.18) A bitter plant that grows up.

Hebrews 12.26 (Haggai 2.6) I will once more shake heaven and earth.

Hebrews 13.6 (Psalm 118.6) The Lord is my helper; I will not fear what anyone may do to me.

James 1.10, 11 (Isaiah 40.6, 7) Like the flower of a wild plant. . . . Its flower falls off.

James 4.6 (Proverbs 3.34) The Lord resists the proud, but gives grace to the humble.

1 Peter 1.24 (Isaiah 40.6, 7) All human beings are like grass, and all their glory is like wild flowers. The grass withers, and the flowers fall.

1 Peter 2.6 (Isaiah 28.16) I chose a valuable and costly stone, which I am placing as the cornerstone in the foundations of Zion, and whoever believes in him will never be disappointed.

1 Peter 2.9 (Isaiah 43.20) The chosen race, (Exodus 19.5, 6) the King's priests, the holy nation, (Isaiah 43.21) my own people, chosen to proclaim my wonderful acts.

1 Peter 3.10 (Psalm 34.12) Whoever wishes life and wants to see good times.

1 Peter 4.18 (Proverbs 11.31) It is difficult for good people to be saved; what, then, will become of godless sinners?

1 Peter 5.5 (Proverbs 3.34) The Lord resists the proud, but shows favor to the humble.

Revelation 2.7 (Ezekiel 28.13; 31.8, 9) The Garden of God.

Revelation 2.27 (Psalm 2.9) You will rule them with an iron rod.

CHRONOLOGY OF THE BIBLE

PREHISTORY

THE BEGINNINGS: EVENTS IN PREHISTORY

Creation

Adam and Eve in the Garden

Cain and Abel

Noah and the Flood

The Tower of Babylon

2000 B.C.

THE ANCESTORS OF THE ISRAELITES

Abraham comes to Palestine. c. 1900

Isaac is born to Abraham.

Jacob is born to Isaac.

1800 B.C.

Jacob has twelve sons, who become the ancestors of the twelve tribes of Israel. The most prominent of these sons is Joseph, who becomes adviser to the King of Egypt.

THE ISRAELITES IN EGYPT

The descendants of Jacob are enslaved in Egypt. c. 1700 — c. 1290

1600 B.C.

1250 B.C.

Moses leads the Israelites out of Egypt. c. 1290

The Israelites wander in the wilderness. During this time Moses receives the Law on Mount Sinai. c. 1290 — c. 1250

THE CONQUEST AND SETTLEMENT OF CANAAN

Joshua leads the first stage of the invasion of Canaan. c. 1250

Israel remains a loose confederation of tribes, and leadership is exercised by heroic figures known as the Judges.

THE UNITED ISRAELITE KINGDOM

Reign of Saul   c. 1030 — c. 1010

1000 B.C.

Reign of David   c. 1010 — c. 970

Reign of Solomon c. 970 — 931

*A circa date is only an approximation. Generally speaking, the earlier the time, the less precise is the dating. From the time of the death of Solomon in 931 B.C. to the Edict of Cyrus in 538 B.C., the dates given are fairly accurate, but even in this epoch a possible error of a year or two must be allowed for.

CHRONOLOGY OF THE BIBLE

DATE

THE TWO ISRAELITE KINGDOMS

950 B.C.

JUDAH (Southern Kingdom)

Kings

Rehoboam 931-913

Abijah 913-911

900 B.C.

Asa 911-870

Jehoshaphat 870-848

Prophets

Elijah

850 B.C.

Jehoram 848-841
Ahaziah 841
Queen Athaliah
841-835

Elisha

Joash 835-796

800 B.C.

Amaziah 796-781

Uzziah 781-740

Jonah

Amos

750 B.C.

Jotham 740-736

Ahaz 736-716

Hosea

Micah   Isaiah

Hezekiah 716-687

ISRAEL (Northern Kingdom)

Kings

Jeroboam 931-910

Nadab 910-909

Baasha 909-886

Elah 886-885
Zimri 7 days in 885
Omri 885-874

Ahab 874-853

Ahaziah 853-852
Joram 852-841
Jehu 841-814

Jehoahaz 814-798

Jehoash 798-783

Jeroboam II 783-743

Zechariah 6 mo. in 743
Shallum 1 mo. in 743
Menahem 743-738
Pekahiah 738-737
Pekah 737-732
Hoshea 732-723
Fall of Samaria 722

700 B.C.

THE LAST YEARS OF THE KINGDOM OF JUDAH

Manasseh 687-642

650 B.C.

Amon 642-640

Josiah 640-609

Joahaz 3 mo. in 609

Jehoiakim 609-598

Prophets

Zephaniah

Nahum

Jeremiah

Habakkuk?

600 B.C.

Jehoiachin 3 mo. in 598

Zedekiah 598-587

Ezekiel

Fall of Jerusalem July 587 or 586

CHRONOLOGY OF THE BIBLE

550 B.C.

THE EXILE AND THE RESTORATION

The Jews taken into exile in Babylonia after the fall of Jerusalem

Persian rule begins. 539

Prophets

Edict of Cyrus allows Jews to return. 538

Haggai   Zechariah

Foundations of New Temple laid. 520

Obadiah   Daniel

Restoration of the walls of Jerusalem
  445-443

Malachi

Joel?

400 B.C.

THE TIME BETWEEN THE TESTAMENTS

Alexander the Great establishes Greek rule in Palestine. 333

Palestine is ruled by the Ptolemies, descendants of one of
  Alexander's generals, who had been given the position of
  ruler over Egypt. 323 to 198

200 B.C.

Palestine is ruled by the Seleucids, descendants of one of
  Alexander's generals, who had acquired the rule of
  Syria. 198 to 166

Jewish revolt under Judas Maccabeus reestablishes Jewish
  independence. Palestine is ruled by Judas' family and
  descendants, the Hasmoneans. 166 to 63

The Roman general Pompey takes Jerusalem 63 B.C.
  Palestine is ruled by puppet kings appointed by Rome. One of
  these is Herod the Great, who rules from 37 B.C. to 4 B.C.

THE TIME OF THE NEW TESTAMENT

A.D. 1

Birth of Jesus*

Ministry of John the Baptist; baptism of Jesus and
  beginning of his public ministry

Death and resurrection of Jesus

A.D. 30

Conversion of Paul (Saul of Tarsus) *c.* A.D. 37

Ministry of Paul *c.* A.D. 41 to A.D. 65

Final imprisonment of Paul *c.* A.D. 65

*The present era was calculated to begin with the birth of Jesus Christ, that is, in A.D. 1
(A.D. standing for *Anno Domini* 'in the year of the Lord'). However, the original calcula-
tion was later found to be wrong by a few years, so that the birth of Christ took place
perhaps about 6 B.C.

EGYPT AND SINAI

© United Bible Societies, 1976

DIVISION OF CANAAN

Miles 0 — 40
Kms 0 — 40

MEDITERRANEAN

SEA

SIDONIANS
LEBANON MTS.
HITTITES
ARAMEANS

Sidon
Damascus
MT. HERMON

DAN
Dan (Laish)

Tyre

ASHER

NAPHTALI

Hazor

MANASSEH (EAST)

Lake Galilee
Ashtaroth

MT. CARMEL

ZEBULUN
MT. TABOR
Endor

Dor
Megiddo
Shunem
ISSACHAR
Jezreel
MT. GILBOA

Ramoth

Jordan River

MANASSEH (WEST)

Jabesh

Shechem

GAD

AMMONITES

Joppa
Shiloh

EPHRAIM
Bethel
Gilgal
Ai
BENJAMIN
Gibeah
Jericho
Jerusalem

Rabbah

DAN

Bethpeor

Ashdod
Libnah

Ashkelon
Bethlehem

REUBEN

Gath?
Lachish
Hebron
Dead

Gaza

JUDAH
Engedi
Sea

Gath?

PHILISTINES

MOABITES

Beersheba
Hormah

SIMEON

The Negev

EDOMITES

© United Bible Societies, 1976

Kadesh

SIDONIANS
LEBANON MTS.
Gebal

BETHREHOB

SYRIA
Damascus

Sidon

MT. HERMON

Tyre

Abel • Dan

Hazor • MAACAH

Bashan

Cabul • GESHUR • Ashtaroth

MT. CARMEL

Dor • Megiddo
Jezreel

Edrei

Taanach •
MT. GILBOA

Jabesh

Ramoth

Shechem

Zarethan

Jabbok

Jazer

Gathrimmon

Joppa

Beth
Horon

Bethel

Rabbah

AMMONITES

Gezer
Jericho

Ashdod • Ekron
Jerusalem

Heshbon

Ashkelon

Medeba

Gaza • Gath?

PHILISTINES

Hebron

Dibon

Aroer

Debir

Dead
Sea

Gerar • Ziklag?

Beersheba

MOABITES

Kir Heres

Tamar

AMALEKITES

Bozrah

Kadesh Barnea

EDOMITES

Sela

The

Desert

The

Negev

UNITED ISRAELITE
KINGDOM

| 0 | Miles | 60 |

| 0 | Kms | 60 |

© United Bible Societies, 1976

Eziongeber

GULF OF
AQABA

MEDITERRANEAN SEA

Jordan R.

JERUSALEM IN OLD TESTAMENT TIMES

Wall of Zion (Jebusite)
Solomon's Expansion
Later Monarchic Wall
Post-exilic Wall

Hananel Tower

Altar
Temple

NEW CITY

Palace

Post-exilic Tombs

UPPER CITY

Manasseh's Wall?

Solomon's Wall

Nehemiah's Wall

Gate

City of David

Ophel

Gihon Spring

To Mount of Olives

Hezekiah's Tunnel

Central Valley

Kidron Valley

Lower Pool

Old Pool

Siloam

Steps

Royal Garden

Hinnom Valley

Enrogel Spring

© United Bible Societies, 1976

THE KINGDOMS OF
ISRAEL AND JUDAH

Miles 0 — 40
Kms 0 — 40

MEDITERRANEAN
SEA

Sidon
Zarephath
Tyre

PHOENICIA

LEBANON MTS.

Damascus

MT. HERMON
SYRIA

Dan
Kedesh
Hazor

GALILEE

BASHAN
Lake
Galilee

MT. CARMEL

Megiddo
Shunem
Jezreel
Ramoth

ISRAEL

Samaria
Shechem

GILEAD

AMMON

Joppa
Shiloh

Bethel
Gilgal
Geba
Jericho

Ekron
Ashdod
Libnah
Ashkelon
Jerusalem
Bethlehem

PHILISTIA
Gath?
Lachish
Hebron
Gaza
JUDAH
Dead
Sea
Gath?

Beersheba

MOAB

EDOM

© United Bible Societies 1978

Jordan River

PALESTINE IN THE TIME OF THE MACCABEES

PALESTINE IN THE TIME OF JESUS

Miles 0 — 40

Kms 0 — 40

MEDITERRANEAN

SEA

Sidon

Zarephath

SYRIA

Abila

ABILENE

Damascus

LEBANON MTS.

MT. HERMON

Tyre

PHOENICIA

Caesarea Philippi

Ptolemais

GALILEE

Chorazin

Capernaum

Bethsaida

Magadan

Lake

Galilee

Cana

Tiberias

MT. CARMEL

Nazareth

Nain

MT.
TABOR

Gadara

Caesarea

TEN TOWNS

Salim

SAMARIA

Aenon

Samaria

Gerasa

MT. EBAL

MT. GERIZIM

Sychar

Joppa

Arimathea?

Jordan River

PEREA

Ephraim

Jericho

Emmaus

Bethany

Azotus

Jerusalem

Qumran

Ascalon

JUDEA

Bethlehem

Gaza

Hebron

Dead

Sea

IDUMEA

NABATEA

© United Bible Societies, 1976

Antioch
Iconium
PISIDIA
Lystra
Derbe
CILICIA
Tarsus
PAMPHYLIA
Attalia
Perga
LYCIA
Patara
Myra
Seleucia
Antioch
SYRIA
Euphrates R.

CYPRUS
Salamis

Paphos

MEDITERRANEAN

SEA

PALESTINE AND SYRIA

Sidon
Tyre
Damascus
PHOENICIA
Ptolemais
Caesarea
Samaria
Joppa
Lydda
Azotus
Jerusalem
Gaza
JUDEA

Alexandria

Miles 0 200

Kms 0 200

PAUL'S THIRD JOURNEY

© United Bible Societies 1978

Philippi • Neapolis
Thessalonica
Berea
MACEDONIA
ACHAIA
Corinth
Athens
CHIOS
Mitylene
Assos
Troas
MYSIA
GALATIA
PHRYGIA
Antioch
ASIA
Ephesus
Iconium
CAPPADOCIA
Colossae
Derbe
CILICIA
Tarsus
Antioch
Miletus
SAMOS
COS
Patara
RHODES
CYPRUS
SYRIA
CRETE
MEDITERRANEAN
SEA
Tyre
Ptolemais
Caesarea
JUDEA
Jerusalem

Miles
0   300
Kms
0   300

PAUL'S JOURNEY TO ROME

© United Bible Societies 1978

MAP INDEX

Except for the last four, the maps are also located in various parts of the text, as follows:

SUBJECT INDEX

BARABBAS, Mt 27.16-26 **1468**; Mk 15.7-15 **1500**; Lk 23.18 **1551**; Jn 18.40 **1587**

BAR-JESUS, Ac 13.6 **1613**

BARNABAS, Ac 4.36 **1600**; 11.22-26,30 **1612**; 12.25 **1613**; 13.1−15.41 **1613**; 1 Co 9.6 **1669**; Ga 2.1,9,13 **1694**; Col 4.10 **1719**

BARTHOLOMEW, Mt 10.3 **1436**; Mk 3.18 **1477**; Lk 6.14 **1516**; Ac 1.13 **1594**

BARTIMAEUS, Mk 10.46 **1491**

BATHSHEBA, 2 S 11.3−12.24 **368**; 1 K 1.15-21 **393**

BEATITUDES, Mt 5.3-12 **1427**; Lk 6.20-23 **1517**

BEELZEBUL, Mt 10.25 **1437**; 12.24,27 **1440**; Mk 3.22 **1477**; Lk 11.15,18,19 **1529**; see DEVIL, SATAN

BEL, Is 46.1 **857**; Jr 50.2 **952**; Let Jer 40 **1276**; Bel 3-22 **1284**

BELSHAZZAR, Dn 5.1-9,30 **1044**; 7.1 **1047**; 8.1 **1048**

"BENEDICTUS," Lk 1.67-79 **1508**

BEREA, Ac 17.10,13 **1621**; 20.4 **1626**

BERNICE, Ac 25.13,23 **1633**; 26.30 **1635**

BETHANY

(a) near Jerusalem, Mt 21.17 **1455**; 26.6 **1464**; Jn 11.1,18 **1574**; 12.1 **1576**

(b) near the Jordan River, Jn 1.28 **1557**

BETHEL, Gn 12.8 **14**; 28.10-19 **34**; Js 16.2 **266**; 18.13,22 **269**; Jg 1.22-26 **278**; 20.1,18,27 **304**; 1 S 7.16 **323**; 1 K 13.1-32 **415**; 2 K 2.23-24 **434**; Jr 48.13 **948**; Am 3.14 **1077**; 7.10-17 **1081**; Ho 4.15 **1060**; 1 Macc 9.50 **1310**

BETHLEHEM, Gn 35.19 **45**; Ru 1.19 **309**; 1 S 16.4 **335**; 2 S 23.14-16 **389**; Mic 5.2 **1096**; Mt 2.1,5-8,16 **1424**; Lk 2.4,15 **1508**

BETHPHAGE, Mt 21.1 **1454**; Mk 11.1 **1491**; Lk 19.29 **1543**

BETHSAIDA, Mt 11.21 **1439**; Mk 6.45 **1483**; 8.22 **1486**; Lk 9.10 **1523**; Jn 1.44 **1558**

BETHULIA, Jdt 4.6 **1153**; 6.10-14 **1156**; 7.6−8.36 **1157**; 13.10−15.7 **1165**

BISHOPS, see CHURCH MINISTERS

BLOOD

(a) of animals, Gn 9.4 **10**; Ex 12.7,13 **79**; 24.8 **98**; Lv 16.18,19 **137**; 17.11 **139**; 1 S 14.31-34 **332**; Ac 15.29 **1618**; He 9.12,13,18-22,25 **1750**; 11.28 **1754**

(b) of men, Gn 4.10-11 **6**; 37.22 **48**; 1 Ch 28.3 **503**; Mt 23.30,35 **1460**; Rev 16.6 **1798**; 17.6 **1799**; 18.24 **1801**

(c) of Christ, Mt 26.28 **1465**; Mk 14.24 **1498**; Lk 22.20 **1548**; Jn 6.53-56 **1566**; 19.34 **1588**; 1 Co 10.16 **1671**; 11.25,27 **1673**; Eph 1.7 **1701**; Col 1.20 **1716**; He 9.12,14 **1750**; 10.29 **1752**; 12.24 **1755**; 13.12,20 **1756**; 1 P 1.2,19 **1764**; 1 Jn 1.7 **1773**; 5.6,8 **1777**; Rev 7.14 **1791**; 12.11 **1795**; 19.13 **1802**

BOAZ, Ru 2.3-14 **309**; 3.6-13 **311**; 4.1-22 **312**; Mt 1.5 **1423**

BREAD

(a) material, Ex 12.14-20 **79**; 13.3-10 **81**; 23.14-15 **97**; Js 9.3-15 **256**; Ez 4.9-13 **974**; Mt 4.3,4 **1426**; 15.26,33 **1447**; 16.5-12 **1447**; Mk 6.8,37 **1482**; Lk 7.33 **1519**; 24.30,35 **1554**; Jn 6.7 **1565**; 21.9-13 **1591**

(b) figurative, Jn 6.32-59 **1566**

(c) offered to God, Ex 25.30 **99**; 1 S 21.1-6 **343**; 1 K 7.48 **405**; Mt 12.4 **1439**; Mk 2.26 **1476**; Lk 6.4 **1516**; He 9.2 **1749**

(d) Lord's Supper, Mt 26.26 **1465**; Mk 14.22 **1498**; Lk 22.19 **1548**; Ac 2.46 **1597**; 1 Co 11.23-28 **1673**

BURIAL

(a) Jesus, Mt 27.59-60 **1470**; Mk 14.8 **1497**; 15.46 **1502**; Lk 23.53-56 **1553**; Jn 12.7 **1577**; 19.38-42 **1589**

(b) other, Gn 23.19 **26**; 50.13 **64**; Dt 34.6 **246**; 2 S 21.14 **385**; Tb 1.17-18 **1132**; 2.4 **1133**; Mt 14.12 **1444**; Ac 2.19 **1596**; 5.6,10 **1600**; 8.2 **1605**

(c) figurative, Ps 16.10 **648**; Ho 13.14 **1067**; Ro 6.4 **1647**; Col 2.12 **1717**

CAESAR

(a) title of Roman emperor, Mt 22.17-21 **1457**; Mk 12.14-17 **1493**; Lk 20.22-25 **1545**

(b) Augustus, Lk 2.1 **1508**

(c) Tiberius, Lk 3.1 **1510**; Jn 19.12,15 **1587**

(d) Claudius, Ac 11.28 **1612**; 18.2 **1622**

(e) Nero, Ac 25.8-12,21 **1633**; Phil 4.22 **1714**; 1 P 2.13,17 **1765**

CAESAREA

(a) seaport, Ac 8.40 **1607**; 9.30 **1609**; 10.1,24 **1609**; 11.11 **1611**; 12.19 **1613**; 21.8,16 **1627**; 23.23,33 **1631**; 25.1,4,6,13 **1633**

(b) Philippi, Mt 16.13 **1448**; Mk 8.27 **1486**

CAIAPHAS, Mt 26.3,57-66 **1464**; Lk 3.2 **1510**; Jn 11.49 **1576**; 18.13,14,24,28 **1585**; Ac 4.6 **1598**

CAIN, Gn 4.1-24 **5**; He 11.4 **1753**; 1 Jn 3.12 **1776**; Jd 11 **1782**

CANA, Jn 2.1-11 **1559**; 4.46 **1563**

CANAAN, name for Palestine, Gn 12.5 **13**; 47.4 **59**; Ex 6.4 **72**; Nu 13.2 **169**; Dt 32.49 **243**; Js 24.3 **275**; Jg 4.2,23 **281**; Ps 105.11 **718**

CAPERNAUM, Mt 4.13 **1427**; 8.5 **1433**; 11.23 **1439**; 17.24 **1449**; Mk 1.21 **1473**; 9.33 **1488**; Jn 2.12 **1559**; 6.17,24,59 **1565**

CARMEL, mountain in Palestine, 1 K 18.17-46 **422**; 2 K 2.25 **434**; 4.25 **437**; Jr 46.18 **946**; Am 9.3 **1082**

CHIEF PRIEST, Lv 21.10-15 **143**; 2 Ch 26.19-20 **533**; Ezra 7.1-6 **555**; Jr 52.24 **960**; Mt 2.4 **1424**; 21.15 **1455**; 27.1,3,6 **1468**; Mk 8.31 **1487**; 15.1,3,10,11 **1500**; Lk 9.22 **1524**; 20.1,19 **1544**; Jn 7.32 **1568**; 19.6,15,21 **1587**; Ac 4.23 **1599**; 5.24 **1601**; 9.14,21 **1608**; 25.2,15 **1633**; see HIGH PRIEST

CHURCH(ES), Mt 16.18 **1448**; 18.17 **1451**; Ac 2.47 **1597**; 9.31 **1609**; 20.28 **1627**; Ro 16.1,5,23 **1659**; 1 Co 1.2 **1661**; 12.28 **1674**; 14.4-5,12,23-40 **1675**; Eph 1.22 **1703**; 5.23-32 **1707**; 1 P 2.4-10 **1765**; Rev 1.6,11 **1785**; 2.1–3.22 **1785**

CHURCH MINISTERS

(a) *general,* 1 Co 12.28-30 **1674**; Eph 4.11 **1705**

(b) *bishops, overseers,* Ac 20.28 **1627**; Phil 1.1 **1709**; 1 Ti 3.1-7 **1729**; Titus 1.7-9

(c) *elders,* Ac 11.30 **1612**; 14.23 **1616**; 15.2,4,6,22 **1617**; 20.17 **1626**; 1 Ti 4.14 **1730**; 5.17-20 **1731**; Titus 1.5-6 **1737**; Jas 5.14 **1762**; 1 P 5.1 **1768**; 2 Jn 1 **1779**; 3 Jn 1 **1780**

(d) *church helper(s),* Phil 1.1 **1709**; 1 Ti 3.8-13 **1729**

CILICIA, 1 K 10.28 **411**; Ac 6.9 **1602**; 15.23,41 **1618**; 22.3 **1629**; Ga 1.21 **1694**

CIRCUMCISE, -CISION

(a) *literal,* Gn 17.10-27 **17**; 34.14-17,24 **43**; Ex 4.24-26 **70**; 12.43-48 **80**; Js 5.2-9 **251**; 1 Macc 1.15,60-61 **1289**; 2.46 **1293**; 2 Macc 6.10 **1339**; Lk 1.59 **1507**; 2.21 **1509**; Jn 7.22-23 **1568**; Ac 7.8 **1603**; 15.1,5 **1617**; 16.3 **1619**; Ro 2.25-29 **1643**; 3.1 **1643**; 4.9-12 **1645**; 1 Co 7.18-19 **1667**; Ga 2.3 **1694**; 5.2 **1698**; 6.12,13,15 **1700**; Phil 3.5 **1712**

(b) *figurative,* Phil 3.3 **1712**; Col 2.11 **1717**

CLEOPAS, Lk 24.18 **1554**

COMING

(a) *of the Lord,* Is 26.21 **831**; 66.18 **882**; Mic 1.2-5 **1092**; Zec 14.5 **1125**; Ml 3.1,2 **1128**

(b) *of Christ, Lord, son of man, second coming,* Mt 16.27-28 **1448**; 24.3,26-44 **1460**; 25.31-46 **1463**; Mk 13.24-37 **1496**; Lk 12.39-40 **1532**; 17.22-30 **1540**; 21.25-28 **1547**; Jn 14.2-4,18-24 **1580**; Ac 1.11 **1594**; Phil 3.20-21 **1713**; 1 Th 2.19 **1722**; 4.15–5.11 **1723**; 2 Th 1.7-10 **1725**; 2.1-15 **1725**; He 9.27-28 **1750**; 2 P 3.3-13 **1771**; 1 Jn 2.28 **1775**; 3.2 **1775**; Rev 22.7,12,17,20 **1805**

COMMAND, -MENTS

(a) *Mosaic,* Ex 20.2-17 **92**; Dt 4—28 **206**; 5.6-21 **208**; Js 22.5 **273**; 2 Macc 13.10 **1353**; Si 24.23-27 **1232**; Ws 18.4 **1203**; Ba 4.1 **1271**; Mt 5.21, 27,31,33,38,43 **1428**; 19.7,17 **1452**; Mk 1.44 **1474**; 12.28-34 **1494**; Jn 8.5 **1569**; Ro 7.7-13 **1648**; 13.8-10 **1656**; Jas 2.8 **1760**; see LAW

(b) *Christ's,* Mt 5.22,28,32,34-37,39-42,44-45,48 **1428**; Jn 12.49-50 **1578**; 13.34 **1580**; 15.10-14,17 **1581**; 1 Jn 2.7-8 **1774**; 3.21-24 **1776**; 2 Jn 5,6 **1779**

CONSCIENCE, Ws 17.11 **1203**; Ro 2.15 **1642**; 9.1 **1651**; 13.5 **1656**; 1 Co 8.7-13 **1669**; 10.25-30 **1671**; Titus 1.15 **1738**; 1 P 3.16,21 **1767**

CORINTH, Ac 18.1-17 **1622**; 19.1 **1623**; 1 Co **1660**; 2 Co **1680**

CORNELIUS, Ac 10.1-48 **1609**

CORNERSTONE, Is 28.16 **833**; Eph 2.20 **1704**; 1 P 2.6-7 **1765**

COVENANT, with Noah, Gn 6.18 **8**; 9.9 **10**; with Abraham, Isaac, and Jacob, Gn 15.18 **16**; 17.2 **17**; Ex 2.24 **68**; 6.4-5 **72**; with Phinehas, Nu 25.12-13 **188**; with David, 2 Ch 21.7 **527**; with Israel (or, Old) Ex 19.3-8 **91**; 24.7,8 **98**; 34.10,27 **110**; Dt 4.23 **207**; 7.9-11 **211**; 1 Ch 16.14-18 **490**; Ac 3.25 **1598**; 7.8 **1603**; 2 Co 3.14 **1683**; Ga 3.17 **1696**; Eph 2.12 **1703**; He 9.1,4,15,18,20 **1749**; New, Jr 31.31-34 **929**; Mt 26.28 **1465**; Mk 14.24 **1498**; Lk 22.20 **1548**; 1 Co 11.25 **1673**; 2 Co 3.6 **1683**; He 7.22 **1748**; 8.6-13 **1749**; 9.15 **1750**; 10.16,29 **1751**; 12.24 **1755**; 13.20 **1757**

COVET, ·OUSNESS, Ex 20.17 **93**; Dt
5.21 **209**; Js 7.21 **254**; Lk 12.15 **1531**;
Ro 1.29 **1642**; 7.7-10 **1648**; Eph 5.3,5
1706; Col 3.5 **1718**; Jas 4.2 **1761**

CREATE, ·TION, universe, Gn 1.1—2.4 **1**;
2 Macc 7.28 **1342**; Ws 11.17,24-25
1196; Jn 1.3 **1556**; Col 1.16 **1716**;
He 1.2 **1742**; 11.3 **1753**; Rev 10.6
1793; stars, Is 40.26 **846**; man, Gn
1.26-30 **3**; 2.4-25 **3**; new heart, Ps
51.10 **677**; new nature, Eph 4.24 **1706**

CRETE, ·ANS, Dt 2.23 **204**; Jr 47.4 **947**;
Am 9.7 **1083**; Ac 27.7-21 **1635**; Titus
1.5,12 **1737**

CROSS
(a) *Christ*, Mt 27.32,40,42 **1469**; 1 Co
1.17-18 **1662**; Ga 5.11 **1699**; 6.12,14
1700; Eph 2.16 **1704**; Col 1.20 **1716**;
2.14 **1717**; He 12.2 **1754**
(b) *disciples*, Mt 10.38 **1437**; 16.24 **1448**;
Mk 8.34 **1487**; Lk 9.23 **1524**; 14.27
1536

CROWN
(a) *literal*, 2 S 1.10 **356**; 12.30 **371**; Ps
89.39 **707**; 1 Macc 4.57 **1298**; 10.20
1311; Mt 27.29 **1469**; Mk 15.17
1500; Jn 19.2,5 **1587**
(b) *figurative*, Ps 8.4-5 **643**; Pr 4.9 **755**;
16.31 **767**; Si 1.11 **1207**; 6.31 **1213**;
Phil 4.1 **1713**; 2 Ti 2.5 **1734**; He 2.7,9
1744; 1 P 5.4 **1768**; Rev 2.10 **1786**;
6.2 **1790**; 14.14 **1797**

CYPRUS, Is 23.1,12 **827**; Jr 2.10 **886**; Ez
27.6 **1003**; Ac 4.36 **1600**; 13.4-12
1613; 15.39 **1619**

CYRENE, Mt 27.32 **1469**; Mk 15.21
1501; Lk 23.26 **1551**; Ac 2.10 **1595**;
11.20 **1612**

CYRUS, Ezra 1.1-11 **548**; Is 44.28 **855**;
45.1-14 **855**; Dn 1.21 **1037**; 6.28
1047; 10.1 **1051**; Bel 1 **1284**

DAMASCUS, Gn 14.15 **15**; 2 S 8.5-6
365; 2 K 5.12 **438**; 8.7,9 **442**; 14.28
452; 16.5-12 **454**; Is 7.1—8.6 **812**; Jdt
1.12 **1151**; 2.27 **1152**; 15.5 **1167**;
1 Macc 11.62 **1317**; 12.32 **1319**; Ac
9.2-25,27 **1607**; 22.5-16 **1629**;
26.12-20 **1634**; 2 Co 11.32 **1690**; Ga
1.17 **1694**

DARIUS
(a) *I, king of Persia*, Ezra 4.5 **552**; 5.5-7
553; 6.1-15 **554**; Ne 12.22 **579**; Hg
1.1 **1111**; Zec 1.1 **1114**
(b) *III, king of Persia*, 1 Macc 1.1 **1287**
(c) *the Mede*, Dn 5.31 **1045**; 6.1,6-
9,25-28 **1045**; 9.1 **1050**

DARKNESS
(a) *literal*, Gn 1.2 **1**; 15.12 **16**; Ex 10.21
78; Ps 139.12 **745**; Ws 17.1—18.4
1202; Mt 27.45 **1469**; Mk 15.33
1501; He 12.18 **1755**
(b) *spiritual*, Is 5.20 **811**; Mt 4.16 **1427**;
Lk 22.53 **1550**; Jn 1.5 **1556**; 3.19
1560; 12.35,46 **1578**; 2 Co 4.6 **1684**;
Eph 5.8,11 **1706**; 1 Jn 1.5-6 **1773**;
2.8-11 **1774**

DAVID, anointed by Samuel, 1 S 16.1-13
334; played the harp for Saul,
16.14-23 **335**; killed Goliath, 17 **336**;
won Jonathan's friendship, 18.1-4 **339**;
incurred Saul's jealousy, 18.5-9 **339**;
married Michal, 18.20-29 **340**; fled
from Saul, 19—22 **340**; fought against
the Philistines, 23 **345**; spared Saul at
Engedi, 24 **346**; David and Abigail, 25
348; spared Saul at Ziph, 26 **350**;
lived among the Philistines, 27.1—28.2
351; 29 **352**; defeated the Amalekites,
30 **353**; made king over Judah, 2 S
2.1-7 **357**; made king over Israel,
5.1-16 **361**; brought ark to Jerusalem,
6 **362**; God's covenant with, 7 **363**;
extended his kingdom, 8 **364**; and
Bathsheba, 11.1—12.25 **368**; fled Absalom's revolt, 15—16 **374**; returned
to Jerusalem, 19 **381**; last words,
23.2-7 **388**; numbered Israel and Judah, 24 **390**; charged Solomon, 1 K
2.1-9 **394**; died, 2.10-12 **395**; *see also*
1 K 2.45 **397**; 12.19,20 **414**; 1 Ch
11—29 **483**; Jr 21.12 **914**; 33.15,17
932; Si 45.25 **1260**; 47.2-11 **1261**;
48.15 **1262**; Mt 1.1,6,17 **1423**;
22.41-45 **1458**; Lk 2.11 **1509**; Ac 1.16
1594; 2.25,29,34 **1596**; 7.45 **1604**;
13.22,34,36 **1614**; Ro 1.3 **1640**; 4.6
1645; 2 Ti 2.8 **1734**; Rev 3.7 **1787**;
5.5 **1789**; 22.16 **1805**

DAY OF JUDGMENT *see* JUDGE (c)
DEACONS *see* CHURCH MINISTERS
DEATH
(a) *physical*, Gn 2.17 **3**; 3.19 **5**; 4.8-16 **6**;
Dt 30.19 **239**; Ru 1.17 **309**; Job 3.21
596; Ps 89.48 **708**; 116.15 **729**; Pr
7.27 **758**; Ec 9.1-6,10 **791**; 12.5-7
794; Si 10.11 **1216**; 14.17 **1220**;
25.24 **1234**; Ws 2.24 **1187**; 4.7-19
1188; Jn 11.11-44 **1575**; 1 Co 15.20-
28,54-56 **1677**; 1 Th 4.13-16 **1723**;
Rev 6.8 **1790**
(b) *figurative*, Ro 6.1-11 **1647**; 7.4-6,9-
13,24 **1648**; Jas 1.15 **1759**; 5.10
1762; 1 Jn 3.14 **1776**; 5.16,17 **1778**;
Rev 20.6,14 **1802**

EZRA, Ezra 7—10 **555**; Ne 8 **571**;
12.26,36 **579**

FAITH
  (a) *general,* Is 7.9 **813**; 28.16 **833**; Mt 9.2
  1434; 17.20 **1449**; 21.21-22 **1455**; Lk
  17.6 **1539**; Ro 1.16-17 **1641**; 3.27-31
  1644; 5.1 **1646**; 2 Co 5.7 **1684**; Ga
  3.2,6-14,22-26 **1695**; He 11.1 **1753**;
  Jas 1.6 **1758**; 2.14-26 **1760**
  (b) *in God,* Gn 15.6 **16**; Ps 78.22 **698**;
  2 Macc 7.40 **1343**; Si 2.6-13 **1208**;
  11.21 **1218**; Ws 12.2 **1196**; 16.26
  1202; Mk 11.22-24 **1492**; Jn 12.44-45
  1578; 14.1 **1580**; Ro 4.1-25 **1644**;
  Ga 3.6 **1695**; He 11.1-40 **1753**; Jas
  2.23 **1760**
  (c) *in Christ,* Mt 8.13 **1433**; 9.28-29
  1435; Mk 2.5 **1475**; 5.34,36 **1481**;
  9.23-24 **1488**; Jn 1.7,12,50 **1557**;
  3.15-16,18-19,36 **1560**; 6.29,35,40
  1566; 9.35-38 **1573**; 11.15,25-27
  1575; 20.29,31 **1590**; Ac 3.16 **1598**;
  16.31 **1620**; Ro 3.22-26 **1644**;
  10.6-17 **1652**; Ga 2.16,20 **1695**; 1 Jn
  3.23 **1776**; 5.1,5,10,13 **1777**

FALSE
  (a) *gods,* 2 K 17.15 **455**; Ps 40.4 **668**; Jr
  10.11 **900**; 14.22 **906**; Ws 13.1—14.31
  1198; 15.7-19 **1200**; Bel 3-30 **1284**;
  see IDOL
  (b) *prophet(s),* Dt 13.1-5 **219**; 18.20-22
  224; 1 K 22.5-25 **429**; Jr 23.16-32
  917; 28.15,16 **923**; Ez 13.17,19 **984**;
  Mic 3.11 **1094**; Mt 7.15 **1432**;
  24.11,24 **1461**; Mk 13.22 **1496**; Ac
  13.6 **1613**; 2 P 2.1 **1770**; 1 Jn 4.1
  1776; Rev 2.20 **1786**; 19.20 **1802**;
  20.10 **1803**
  (c) *Messiahs,* Mt 24.24 **1461**; Mk 13.22
  1496

FAST, -ING
  (a) *general,* 2 S 12.23 **371**; 2 Ch 20.3
  525; Ezra 8.21 **558**; Ne 9.1 **573**; Es
  4.3,16 **587**; Jr 14.12 **905**; Jl 2.12-15
  1070; Zec 7.1-7 **1118**; Jdt 4.13 **1154**;
  8.6 **1158**; 1 Macc 3.47 **1296**; 2 Macc
  13.12 **1353**; Si 34.26 **1244**; Ba 1.5
  1267; Mk 2.18 **1475**; Lk 2.37 **1510**;
  18.12 **1541**
  (b) *day of Atonement,* Lv 16 **136**;
  23.26-32 **146**
  (c) *Jesus' teaching,* Mt 6.16-18 **1430**;
  9.14-15 **1435**; Mk 2.18-20 **1475**; Lk
  5.33-35 **1515**

  (d) *Christian,* Ac 13.2-3 **1613**; 14.23
  1616

FATHER, title of God, Ps 89.26 **707**; Is
  63.16 **880**; Ml 1.6 **1127**; Tb 13.4
  1147; Si 23.1,4 **1230**; 51.10 **1265**;
  Ws 14.3 **1199**; Mt 5.48 **1429**; 6.8-9,32
  1430; 7.21 **1432**; 11.25-27 **1439**; Mk
  14.36 **1498**; Lk 2.49 **1510**; 12.30,32
  1532; 23.34,46 **1552**; Jn 1.18 **1557**;
  5.17-27,36-45 **1564**; 10.29-38 **1574**;
  14.6-11 **1580**; 17.1-26 **1583**; Ro 8.15
  1649; Ga 4.6 **1697**; He 12.5-9 **1755**;
  1 Jn 3.1-2 **1775**

FELIX, Ac 23.24,26 **1631**; 24.2-27 **1632**

FESTIVAL(S)
  (a) *Passover,* Ex 12.18-19,27,43-48 **79**;
  13.3-10 **81**; Dt 16.1-8 **222**; Js 5.10
  252; 2 K 23.21-23 **465**; 2 Ch 35.1-19
  545; Ezra 6.19-20 **555**; Mt
  26.2,5,17-19 **1464**; 27.15 **1468**; Mk
  14.1-2,12-16 **1497**; 15.6 **1500**; Lk
  2.41-43 **1510**; 22.1,8-13 **1547**; Jn
  2.13,23 **1559**; 6.4 **1565**; 11.55-56
  1576; 12.1,12,20 **1576**; 13.1,29
  1578; 19.14 **1587**; Ac 12.4 **1612**;
  1 Co 5.7 **1665**; He 11.28 **1754**
  (b) *unleavened bread,* Ex 12.15-20 **79**;
  13.6-7 **81**; 2 Ch 35.17 **545**; Ezra 6.22
  555; Mt 26.17 **1465**; Mk 14.1,12
  1497; Lk 22.1,7 **1547**; Ac 12.3 **1612**;
  20.6 **1626**
  (c) *Pentecost* (or *weeks,* or *day of firstfruits*),
  Ex 23.16 **97**; 34.22 **110**; Lv 23.15-21
  145; Dt 16.9-12 **222**; 2 Ch 8.13 **514**;
  Tb 2.1 **1133**; 2 Macc 12.31 **1352**; Ac
  2.1 **1595**; 20.16 **1626**; 1 Co 16.8
  1679
  (d) *tabernacles, booths, ingathering,* Lv
  23.34,42 **146**; Dt 16.13-16 **222**; 2 Ch
  9.12-13 **515**; Zec 14.16-19 **1125**; Jn
  7.2-14,37 **1567**
  (e) *new moon,* Nu 10.10 **165**; 28.11-14
  191; 1 S 20.5 **341**; Am 8.5 **1082**; Jdt
  8.6 **1158**; 1 Macc 10.34 **1312**; Col
  2.16 **1717**
  (f) *others,* trumpets, Nu 29.1 **192**; Purim,
  Es 9.21-32 **591**; Gk Est 9.24-28 **1183**;
  2 Macc 15.36 **1358**; dedication of temple, 1 Macc 4.59 **1299**; 2 Macc 10.1-8
  1346; Jn 10.22 **1574**
  (g) *unspecified,* Lm 2.6-7 **964**; Ho 9.5
  1063; Jn 5.1 **1563**; Col 2.16 **1717**

FESTUS, Ac 24.27 **1633**; 25.1—26.32
  1633

FORGIVE, -NESS
  (a) *general,* Ex 29.36 **104**; 32.30-32
  108; Lv 4.20-35 **121**; Dt 21.8 **227**;

1459; Mk 9.43,45,47 **1489**; Lk 10.15
1526; 12.5 **1531**; Ro 10.7 **1652**; Jas
3.6 **1760**; 2 P 2.4 **1770**; Rev 9.1-2,11
1792; 11.7 **1793**; 20.1-3 **1802**

HEROD
(a) *the Great, king of Judea,* Mt 2.1-22
1424; Lk 1.5 **1505**
(b) *Antipas, tetrarch of Galilee,* Mt 14.1-10
1444; Mk 6.14-27 **1482**; 8.15 **1486**;
Lk 3.1,19 **1510**; 9.7,9 **1523**; 13.31
1534; 23.6-12,15 **1551**; Ac 4.27
1599; 13.1 **1613**
(c) *Agrippa I, see* AGRIPPA (a)
(d) *Agrippa II, see* AGRIPPA (b)

HERODIAS, Mt 14.3,6 **1444**; Mk
6.17,19,22 **1482**; Lk 3.19 **1511**

**HEZEKIAH, son of Ahaz and king of
Judah,** 2 K 18—20 **456**; 2 Ch 29—32
535; Is 36—39 **840**; 2 Macc 15.22
1358; Si 48.17-23 **1262**; Mt 1.9,10
1423

HIGH PRIEST
(a) *Jewish,* Nu 35.25,28,32 **199**; 2 K
22.4,8 **462**; Ne 3.1,20 **564**; Zec 3.1,8
1115; 1 Macc 10.20 **1311**; 2 Macc
3.16-17 **1333**; 4.7-13 **1334**; Si
50.1-21 **1264**; Mt 26.3,51,57-66
1464; Mk 14.47,53-64,66 **1499**; Lk
22.50 **1549**; Jn 11.49-51 **1576**;
18.13,15,19-24,26 **1585**; Ac 4.6 **1598**;
5.17,21,27 **1600**; 7.1 **1602**; 19.14
1624; 24.1 **1632**; He 8.3 **1748**;
9.7,25 **1749**; 13.11 **1756**; *see* CHIEF
PRIEST
(b) *Christ,* He 2.17 **1744**; 3.1 **1744**;
4.14,15 **1746**; 5.1-6,10 **1746**; 6.20
1747; 7.15—8.6 **1748**

HITTITE, Gn 15.20 **16**; 23.3-20 **25**; Ex
23.28 **97**; 2 S 11.3-24 **368**; 1 K 10.29
411; 11.1 **411**

HOLOFERNES, Jdt 2.4—7.18 **1151**;
10.13—14.18 **1161**

HOLY SPIRIT
(a) *in life and teaching of Jesus,* Mt 1.18,20
1424; 3.11,16 **1426**; 4.1 **1426**;
12.18,28,31,32 **1440**; Mk 1.8 **1473**;
Lk 1.35 **1507**; 4.14,18 **1512**; 10.21
1527; Jn 1.33 **1558**; 3.5,6,8,34 **1560**;
14.17,26 **1581**; 15.26 **1582**; 16.13
1582; 20.22 **1590**; Ac 1.2,5,8 **1594**
(b) *in early Church,* Ac 2.1-4,17,18,33,38
1595; 5.3,9,32 **1600**; 8.15-19,29,39
1606; 9.17,31 **1608**; 10.19,38,44-47
1610; 11.12,15-17,24,28 **1611**;
13.2,4,9,52 **1613**; 19.1-7 **1623**
(c) *in letters of Paul,* Ro 8 **1649**; 1 Co
12.1-13 **1673**; Ga 5 **1698**

HUSBAND
(a) *literal,* Gn 3.6,16 **4**; Nu 5.13,20,27
160; Ru 1.3-12 **308**; Es 1.17,20 **584**;
Pr 12.4 **762**; 31.11 **782**; Tb 7.12
1141; 8.6 **1141**; 1 Co 7.2-4,10-
16,34,39 **1667**; Eph 5.22-28,33 **1707**;
Col 3.18-19 **1718**; 1 P 3.1,5,7 **1766**
(b) *figurative,* Is 54.5 **869**; Ho 2.2,7,16
1057; 2 Co 11.2 **1689**; Ga 4.27 **1698**

ICONIUM, Ac 13.51—14.6 **1615**;
14.19,21 **1616**; 16.2 **1619**; 2 Ti 3.11
1735

IDOL, Lv 19.4 **140**; Dt 29.17 **238**; 1 K
15.12 **418**; 2 K 17.12,15 **455**; 2 Ch
33.7,15 **542**; Ps 96.5 **712**; 115.4-8
728; 135.15-18 **742**; Is 40.18-20
846; 41.7(fn) **847**; 44.9-20 **854**;
46.1-7 **857**; Jr 10.3-5 **899**; Ez 36.25
1016; Ho 4.17 **1060**; Let Jer 4-73
1274; Bel 3-22 **1284**; Ac 7.41 **1604**;
17.16 **1621**; 1 Co 8.1,4,7,10 **1669**;
2 Co 6.16 **1686**; 1 Th 1.9 **1721**;
1 Jn 5.21 **1778**; Rev 2.14,20 **1786**;
see FALSE (a)

IMMANUEL, Is 7.14 **813**; 8.8 **814**; Mt
1.23 **1424**

ISAAC, Gn 18.1-15 **18**; 21.1-7 **23**; 22.1-19
24; 24 **26**; 25.19-26 **29**; 27.1-40 **32**;
35.27-29 **45**; Si 44.22-23 **1258**; Mt 1.2
1423; 8.11 **1433**; Ac 7.8 **1603**; Ro
9.7,10 **1651**; Ga 4.28 **1698**; He
11.9,17-18,20 **1753**; Jas 2.21 **1760**

ISAIAH, 2 K 19—20 **458**; Is 1.1 **805**; 6
812; 7.3 **812**; 8.3 **813**; 37—39 **841**;
Si 48.22-25 **1263**; Mt 3.3 **1425**; 4.14
1427; 8.17 **1433**; 12.17 **1440**; 13.14
1442; 15.7 **1446**; Mk 1.2 **1472**; Lk
3.4 **1511**; 4.17 **1512**; Jn 1.23 **1557**;
12.38-41 **1578**; Ac 8.28,30 **1607**;
28.25 **1639**; Ro 9.27-29 **1652**;
10.16,20-21 **1653**; 15.12 **1658**

ISHMAEL, Gn 16.3,15 **17**; 17.25-26 **18**;
21.8-21 **23**; 25.9,12-17 **29**; 28.9 **34**

ISRAEL
(a) *name given to Jacob,* Gn 32.22-32 **41**
(b) *descendants of Jacob,* Gn 34.7 **43**; Ex
32.4 **107**; Dt 4.1 **206**
(c) *other uses of term:* name for the ten
tribes of the northern kingdom, 1 S
11.8 **328**; 17.52 **338**; name for united
monarchy, 1 K 11.42 **413**; name for
the northern kingdom, 1 K 12.16,20
414; 15.25-31 **419**; Ho 1.1 **1056**;
name for returning exiles, Ezra 9.1
558; Ne 9.2 **573**

1465; Mk 14.32-42 **1498**; Lk 22.39-46 **1549**; arrest, trial, crucifixion, death, and burial, Mt 26.47−27.66 **1466**; Mk 14.43−15.47 **1499**; Lk 22.47−23.56 **1549**; Jn 18.1−19.42 **1585**

(g) *resurrection, appearances, ascension*, Mt 28.1-20 **1470**; Mk 16.1-20 **1502**; Lk 24.1-53 **1553**; Jn 20.1−21.25 **1589**; Ac 1.1-11 **1594**; 1 Co 15.4-8 **1677**; *see* RESURRECTION (b)

JEZEBEL
(a) *wife of Ahab, king of Israel*, 1 K 16.31 **420**; 19.1-2 **424**; 21.1-25 **428**; 2 K 9.7-10,30-37 **444**
(b) *name given to women who lured Christians to fornication and idolatry*, Rev 2.20-23 **1786**

JOAB, 2 S 2.12-32 **357**; 3.22-30 **359**; 11.6-21 **368**; 14.28-33 **374**; 18.10-16 **380**; 20.7-23 **384**; 1 K 2.28-34 **396**

JOHN
(a) *the Baptist*, Mt 3.1-15 **1425**; 11.2-19 **1438**; 14.2-12 **1444**; 21.25-32 **1456**; Mk 1.4-11 **1472**; 6.14-29 **1482**; 11.29-33 **1493**; Lk 1.13-25,57-80 **1506**; 3.2-20 **1510**; 7.18-33 **1519**; 11.1 **1528**; Jn 1.6-36 **1557**; 3.23-30 **1560**
(b) *son of Zebedee*, Mt 4.21 **1427**; Mk 1.29 **1474**; 5.37 **1481**; 9.2,38 **1487**; 10.35,41 **1491**; 13.3 **1495**; Lk 9.49,54 **1525**; 22.8 **1548**; Ac 3.1-11 **1597**; 4.13-21 **1599**; 8.14-17 **1606**; Ga 2.9 **1694**
(c) *author of Revelation*, Rev 1.1,4,9 **1784**; 22.8 **1805**
(d) *father of Simon Peter*, Jn 1.42 **1558**; 21.15-17 **1591**
(e) *Mark*, Ac 12.12,25 **1613**; 13.5,13 **1613**; 15.37,39 **1619**; Col 4.10 **1719**; 2 Ti 4.11 **1736**; Phm 24 **1741**; 1 P 5.13 **1768**
(f) *of family of high priest Annas*, Ac 4.6 **1598**

JONAH, 2 K 14.25 **451**; Jon **1086**; Mt 12.39-41 **1441**; 16.4 **1447**; Lk 11.29-32 **1529**

JONATHAN
(a) *son of Saul*, 1 S 13.2-4 **329**; 14.1-15,36-46 **330**; 18.1-5 **339**; 20 **341**; 31.2 **354**; 2 S 1.11-27 **356**
(b) *son of Matthias*, 1 Macc 2.1-5 **1291**; 9.23−12.53 **1308**

JOPPA, Js 19.46 **270**; 2 Ch 2.16 **508**; Ezra 3.7 **551**; Jon 1.3 **1089**; 1 Macc 10.75 **1314**; 2 Macc 4.21 **1335**; Ac

9.36-43 **1609**; 10.5-8,23,32 **1609**; 11.5,13 **1611**

JORDAN, Gn 13.10-11 **14**; 32.10 **41**; Dt 4.22 **207**; Js 1.2 **247**; 3.17 **250**; 2 S 19.15 **382**; 2 K 2.7 **433**; 5.10 **438**; 6.4 **439**; Jr 12.5 **903**; Jdt 1.9 **1150**; 1 Macc 5.24 **1300**; 9.43-48 **1309**; Mt 3.5-6,13 **1425**; Mk 1.5,9 **1473**; 10.1 **1489**; Lk 3.3 **1510**; Jn 1.28 **1557**; 10.40 **1574**

JOSEPH
(a) *son of Jacob*, Gn 30.22-24 **37**; 37.5−50.26 **47**; Js 24.32 **276**; Ps 105.17-22 **719**; Si 49.15 **1263**; Jn 4.5 **1561**; Ac 7.9-14 **1603**
(b) *husband of Mary*, Mt 1.16-25 **1424**; 2.13-15,19-23 **1425**; Lk 1.27 **1506**; 2.4,16 **1508**; 4.22 **1513**; Jn 1.45 **1558**; 6.42 **1566**
(c) *brother of Jesus*, Mt 13.55 **1444**; Mk 6.3 (called Joses) **1481**
(d) *brother of James, "the younger,"* Mt 27.56 **1470**; Mk 15.40,47 (called Joses) **1502**
(e) *of Arimathea*, Mt 27.57-60 **1470**; Mk 15.42-46 **1502**; Lk 23.50-53 **1553**; Jn 19.38-42 **1589**
(f) *Barsabbas*, Ac 1.23 **1595**
(g) *Barnabas*, Ac 4.36 **1600**

JOSHUA, Ex 17.8-13 **89**; 24.13 **98**; 33.11 **109**; Nu 13.1-16 **169**; 14.6-9 **170**; 27.18-23 **190**; Dt 31.23 **240**; Js **246**; Si 46.1-8 **1260**; Ac 7.45 **1604**; He 4.8 **1745**

JOSIAH, king of Judah, 2 K 21.24−23.30 **462**; 2 Ch 33.25−35.27 **543**; Si 49.1-7 **1263**

JUDAH
(a) *son of Jacob and tribe of his descendants*, Gn 29.35 **36**; 37.26-28 **48**; 38 **49**; 44.14-34 **57**; 49.8-12 **62**; Dt 33.7 **244**; He 7.14 **1748**
(b) *name for the southern kingdom*, 1 K 14.21 **417**; 15.1,9 **418**; Is 1.1 **805**; Ho 1.1 **1056**

JUDAS
(a) *Iscariot*, Mt 10.4 **1436**; 26.14,25,47 **1464**; 27.3 **1468**; Mk 3.19 **1477**; 14.10,43 **1497**; Lk 22.3,47-48 **1548**; Jn 6.71 **1567**; 12.4 **1576**; 13.2,26,29 **1578**; 18.2-3,5 **1585**; Ac 1.16,25 **1594**
(b) *brother of Jesus*, Mt 13.55 **1444**; Mk 6.3 **1481**
(c) *apostle*, Jn 14.22 **1581**
(d) *the Galilean*, Ac 5.37 **1601**
(e) *of Damascus*, Ac 9.11 **1608**

LOVE
> (a) *God*, Ex 20.6 **93**; 34.6 **110**; Dt 5.10 **209**; 7.8 **211**; Ps 25.6-7,10 **655**; 103.17 **716**; Is 54.8,10 **869**; Ho 11.1-4 **1064**; Si 2.18 **1209**; 18.13 **1224**; Ws 11.24 **1196**; Jn 3.16 **1560**; 14.23 **1581**; 16.27 **1583**; Ro 5.5,8 **1646**; 8.39 **1650**; Eph 1.5 **1701**; 2.4 **1703**; 1 Jn 3.1 **1775**; 4.7-12 **1776**
>
> (b) *Christ*, Jn 11.3,5 **1574**; 13.1,34 **1578**; 14.31 **1581**; 15.9-10,12 **1581**; Ro 8.35,37 **1650**; 2 Co 5.14 **1685**; Ga 2.20 **1695**; Eph 3.19 **1705**; 5.2 **1706**; Rev 1.5 **1785**

LUKE, Col 4.14 **1719**; 2 Ti 4.11 **1736**; Phm 24 **1741**

LYDIA, Ac 16.14,40 **1619**

LYSTRA, Ac 14.6,8,21 **1616**; 16.1-2 **1619**; 2 Ti 3.11 **1735**

MACEDONIA, 1 Macc 1.1 **1287**; 2 Macc 8.20 **1344**; Ac 16.9-10,12 **1619**; 19.21-22 **1624**; 20.1,3 **1626**; Ro 15.26 **1658**; 2 Co 2.13 **1682**; 7.5 **1686**; 8.1 **1687**; Phil 4.15 **1714**; 1 Th 1.7-8 **1720**; 1 Ti 1.3 **1727**

"MAGNIFICAT," Lk 1.46-55 **1507**

MANNA, Ex 16.1-4,12-15,22-35 **87**; Nu 11.7-9 **166**; Js 5.12 **252**; Ne 9.20 **574**; Ws 16.20-29 **1202**; Jn 6.31,49 **1566**; He 9.4 **1749**; Rev 2.17 **1786**

MARK *see* JOHN (e)

MARTHA, Lk 10.38-41 **1528**; Jn 11.1-40 **1574**; 12.2 **1576**

MARTYRS (*seven brothers*), 2 Macc 7 **1341**

MARY
> (a) *mother of Jesus*, Mt 1.16,18,20 **1424**; 2.11 **1424**; 13.55 **1444**; Mk 6.3 **1481**; Lk 1.27,30,34,38,39,41,46,56 **1506**; 2.5,16,19,34 **1508**; Jn 2.1-5,12 **1559**; 19.25-27 **1588**; Ac 1.14 **1594**
>
> (b) *Magdalene*, Mt 27.56,61 **1470**; 28.1 **1470**; Mk 15.40,47 **1502**; 16.1,9 **1502**; Lk 8.2 **1520**; 24.10 **1553**; Jn 19.25 **1588**; 20.1-18 **1589**
>
> (c) *mother of James and Joseph*, Mt 27.56,61 **1470**; 28.1 **1470**; Mk 15.40,47 **1502**; 16.1 **1502**; Lk 24.10 **1553**; Jn 19.25 **1588**
>
> (d) *of Bethany*, Lk 10.39,42 **1528**; Jn 11.1-2,19,20,28,31-32,45 **1574**; 12.3 **1576**
>
> (e) *mother of John Mark*, Ac 12.12 **1613**

MATTHEW, Mt 9.9 **1434**; Mk 3.18 **1477**; Lk 6.15 **1516**; *see* LEVI (b)

MATTHIAS, Ac 1.23,26 **1595**

MELCHIZEDEK, Gn 14.18-20 **15**; Ps 110.4 **726**; He 5.6,10 **1746**; 6.20 **1747**; 7.1-11,15,17 **1747**

MERCY, -IFUL
> (a) *God*, Ex 33.19 **109**; 34.6-7 **110**; Dt 4.31 **207**; Ps 25.16 **656**; 51.1 **676**; 103.8 **716**; Dn 9.9 **1050**; Ho 11.8 **1065**; Jon 4.2 **1091**; Tb 8.4-7 **1141**; Jdt 7.30 **1158**; 13.14 **1165**; Si 2.11 **1208**; Ws 11.23,26 **1196**; 12.22 **1197**; 15.1 **1200**; Lk 1.50,54,58,72,78 **1507**; 6.36 **1517**; Ro 9.15-16,18,23 **1651**; 11.30-32 **1654**; Eph 2.4 **1703**; 1 Ti 1.2,13,16 **1727**; Titus 3.5 **1739**; 1 P 1.3 **1764**; 2.10 **1765**
>
> (b) *Christ*, Mt 9.27 **1435**; 15.22 **1446**; 17.15 **1449**; 20.30-31 **1454**; He 2.17 **1744**; Jd 21 **1782**

MICHAEL, Dn 10.13,21 **1052**; 12.1 **1054**; Jd 9 **1782**; Rev 12.7 **1794**

MIDIAN, -ITE
> (a) *son of Abraham by Keturah*, Gn 25. 1-6 **29**
>
> (b) *people of Midian, and region occupied by them*, Gn 36.31-39 **46**; 37.28,36 **48**; Ex 3.1 **68**; Nu 22.4,7 **182**; 25 **188**; 31 **194**; Jg 6−8 **284**; Is 9.4 **815**; 60.6 **875**; Ac 7.29 **1603**

MIRACLES
> (a) *of Jesus: general*: Mt 4.23-24 **1427**; 8.16 **1433**; 9.35 **1436**; 12.15 **1440**; 14.14,35-36 **1445**; 15.30-31 **1447**; 19.2 **1452**; 21.14 **1455**; Mk 1.32-34,39 **1474**; 3.9-12 **1476**; 6.5,53-56 **1481**; Lk 4.40-41 **1513**; 5.15 **1514**; 6.18-19 **1516**; 7.21 **1519**; 9.11 **1523**; Jn 2.23 **1560**; 3.2 **1560**; 6.2 **1565**; 12.37 **1578**; 20.30 **1590**; Ac 10.38 **1610**; *driving out demons*: blind and dumb, Mt 12.22 **1440**; daughter of Canaanite woman, Mt 15.21-28 **1446**; Mk 7.24-30 **1485**; dumb man, Mt 9.32-33 **1436**; Lk 11.14 **1529**; epileptic boy, Mt 17.14-20 **1449**; Mk 9.14-21 **1488**; Lk 9.37-43 **1525**; Gadarene men, Mt 8.28-34 **1434**; Mk 5.1-20 **1480**; Lk 8.26-39 **1521**; man in Capernaum, Mk 1.23-28 **1474**; Lk 4.33-37 **1513**; Mary Magdalene, Mk 16.9 **1503**; Lk 8.2 **1520**; woman in synagogue, Lk 13.10-17 **1534**; *other cures*: blind Bartimaeus, Mt 20.29-34 **1454**; Mk 10.46-52 **1491**; Lk 18.35-43 **1542**; blind man at Bethsaida, Mk 8.22-26 **1486**; two blind men, Mt 9.27-31 **1435**; deaf mute, Mk 7.31-37

1485; leper, Mt 8.1-4 **1433**; Mk 1.40-45 **1474**; Lk 5.12-16 **1514**; ten lepers, Lk 17.11-19 **1539**; man born blind, Jn 9.1-7 **1571**; man with dropsy, Lk 14.1-6 **1535**; man with withered hand, Mt 12.9-14 **1439**; Mk 3.1-6 **1476**; Lk 6.6-11 **1516**; paralytic in Capernaum, Mt 9.1-8 **1434**; Mk 2.1-12 **1475**; Lk 5.17-26 **1515**; paralytic in Jerusalem, Jn 5.1-9 **1563**; Peter's mother-in-law, Mt 8.14-15 **1433**; Mk 1.29-31 **1474**; Lk 4.38-39 **1513**; servant of army officer, Mt 8.5-13 **1433**; Lk 7.1-10 **1518**; slave of high priest, Lk 22.50-51 **1549**; son of official, Jn 4.46-54 **1563**; woman with flow of blood, Mt 9.20-22 **1435**; Mk 5.25-34 **1481**; Lk 8.43-48 **1522**; *raising of dead*: daughter of Jairus, Mt 9.18-26 **1435**; Mk 5.21-43 **1480**; Lk 8.40-56 **1522**; son of widow of Nain, Lk 7.11-17 **1518**; Lazarus, Jn 11.1-44 **1574**; *other miracles*: coin in fish's mouth, Mt 17.24-27 **1449**; cursing of fig tree, Mt 21.19 **1455**; Mk 11.14,20 **1492**; feeding five thousand, Mt 14.13-21 **1445**; Mk 6.30-44 **1483**; Lk 9.10-17 **1523**; Jn 6.1-14 **1565**; feeding four thousand, Mt 15.32-39 **1447**; Mk 8.1-10 **1485**; great catch of fish, Lk 5.4-10 **1514**; another catch of fish, Jn 21.6-11 **1591**; stilling the storm, Mt 8.23-27 **1434**; Mk 4.35-41 **1479**; Lk 8.22-25 **1521**; walking on the water, Mt 14.22-33 **1445**; Mk 6.45-52 **1483**; Jn 6.16-21 **1565**; water changed to wine, Jn 2.1-11 **1559**

(b) *miracles of others*: *in OT*: of Moses, Ex 4.3-7 **70**; 7.10–10.28 **73**; 14.21-28 **83**; 15.25 **87**; 17.6 **89**; Nu 16.32 **174**; 20.11 **179**; 21.8-9 **181**; of Joshua, Js 3 **249**; 6 **252**; 10.12-14 **258**; of Samuel, 1 S 12.18 **329**; of Elijah, 1 K 17.1,14,22 **421**; 18.38,41-45 **423**; 2 K 1.10 **432**; 2.8 **433**; of Elisha, 2 K 2.14,21,24 **433**; 3.16-20 **435**; 4.4-7,35,41,43-44 **436**; 5.10,14,27 **438**; 6.6,18 **440**; 13.21 **450**; of Isaiah, 2 K 20.7,11 **460**; of Daniel, Dn 6.22 **1046**; *in NT*: of apostles, Mt 10.1,8 **1436**; Mk 6.7,13 **1482**; Lk 9.2,6 **1523**; Ac 5.12,16 **1600**; of the seventy, Lk 10.9,17 **1526**; of Peter, Ac 3.6-8 **1597**; 9.34,40-41 **1609**; of Philip, Ac 8.6,7,13 **1605**; of Paul, Ac 13.11 **1614**; 14.9,10 **1616**; 16.18 **1620**; 19.11-12 **1624**; 2 Co 12.12 **1691**

MOAB, -ITE, Gn 19.37 **22**; Ex 15.15 **86**; Nu 21.11-15,26-30 **181**; 22.1-36 **182**; 25.1 **188**; Dt 1.5 **202**; 34.1-8 **246**; Jg 3.12-30 **280**; Ru 1.1-6,22 **308**; 2 K 3.4-26 **434**; Is 15.1-9 **821**; 16.2-14 **822**; Jr 48.1-47 **948**; Jdt 5.2 **1154**

MOSES

(a) *person*, born, Ex 2.1-4 **67**; adopted by Pharaoh's daughter, 2.5-10 **67**; trained at Egyptian court, Ac 7.22 **1603**; killed Egyptian, Ex 2.11-12 **67**; fled to Midian, 2.15-20 **68**; married Zipporah, 2.21-22 **68**; called by God, 3.1–4.17 **68**; returned to Egypt, 4.18-31 **70**; interceded with Pharaoh, 5–11 **71**; crossed the Red Sea, 14 **83**; sang for victory, 15.1-18 **86**; appointed rulers, 18.13-26 **90**; met with God on Sinai, 19.3-13 **91**; 24–31 **98**; enraged by Israel's idolatry, 32 **107**; talked with the Lord, 33–34 **108**; built tabernacle, 35–40 **111**; numbered the people, Nu 1 **154**; vindicated before Aaron and Miriam, 12 **168**; sent twelve spies to Canaan, 13.1-20 **169**; consecrated Joshua as his successor, 27.18-23 **190**; Dt 31.23 **240**; recounted Israel's history, 1–3 **201**; exhorted Israel to obedience, 4.1-40 **206**; song of Moses, 32.1-43 **241**; viewed Canaan, 3.23-27 **206**; 32.48-52 **243**; 34.1-4 **246**; blessed the tribes, 33 **244**; death and burial in Moab, 34.5-7 **246**; *see also* Js 1.5 **247**; Ps 77.20 **696**; 103.7 **716**; Mic 6.4 **1096**; Si 45.1-5 **1258**; Mt 8.4 **1433**; 17.3-4 **1449**; 19.7-8 **1452**; Lk 16.29,31 **1539**; 20.37 **1545**; Jn 3.14 **1560**; 5.45-46 **1565**; 9.28-29 **1572**; Ac 3.22 **1598**; 6.11,14 **1602**; 7.20-44 **1603**; 15.1,21 **1617**; Ro 9.15 **1651**; 10.5,19 **1652**; 2 Co 3.7,13 **1683**; He 3.2-5,16 **1744**; 11.23-24 **1754**; Jd 9 **1782**; Rev 15.3 **1797**

(b) *law of, book of,* Js 8.31-32 **256**; 23.6 **274**; 1 K 2.3 **395**; 2 K 23.25 **465**; Ezra 3.2 **551**; Ne 8.1 **571**; Mk 12.26 **1494**; Lk 2.22 **1509**; 24.44 **1554**; Jn 1.17,45 **1557**; Ac 13.39 **1615**; 15.5 **1617**; 28.23 **1639**; 2 Co 3.15 **1683**; *see* LAW

MOUNT OF OLIVES, 2 S 15.30 **376**; Zec 14.4 **1125**; Mt 21.1 **1454**; 24.3 **1460**; 26.30 **1465**; Mk 11.1 **1491**; 13.3 **1495**; 14.26 **1498**; Lk 19.29,37 **1543**; 21.37 **1547**; 22.39 **1549**; Jn 8.1 **1569**; Ac 1.12 **1594**

PHARISEE(S), Mt 3.7 **1426**; 9.11,14,34 **1435**; 12.2,14,24,38 **1439**; 15.1,12 **1445**; 16.1,6,11-12 **1447**; 19.3 **1452**; 22.15 **1457**; 23.2,13-15,23,25-29 **1458**; 27.62 **1470**; Lk 7.36-50 **1519**; 16.14 **1538**; 18.10-11 **1541**; Jn 1.24 **1557**; 3.1 **1560**; 7.32,45-48 **1568**; Ac 15.5 **1617**; 23.6-9 **1630**; 26.5 **1634**

PHILADELPHIA, Rev 3.7 **1787**

PHILIP

(a) *tetrarch*, Lk 3.1 **1510**

(b) *first husband of Herodias*, Mt 14.3 **1444**; Mk 6.17 **1482**

(c) *apostle*, Mt 10.3 **1436**; Jn 1.43-48 **1558**; 6.5-7 **1565**; 12.21-22 **1577**; 14.8-9 **1580**

(d) *deacon and evangelist*, Ac 6.5 **1602**; 8.5-40 **1605**; 21.8 **1627**

PHILIPPI, Ac 16.12 **1619**; 20.6 **1626**; Phil 1.1 **1709**; 1 Th 2.2 **1721**

PHILISTINES, Gn 10.14 **12**; 21.32-34 **24**; Jg 3.3,31 **280**; 10.6-8,11 **292**; 13.1,5 **295**; 14.1-4 **296**; 15−16 **297**; 1 S 4−6 **319**; 13.1−14.31 **329**; 17.19-51 **337**; Jr 47.1-7 **947**; Ez 25.15-17 **1002**; Am 1.6-8 **1074**; 9.7 **1083**; Zec 9.5-7 **1120**

PILATE, Mt 27 **1468**; Mk 15 **1500**; Lk 3.1 **1510**; 13.1 **1533**; 23 **1550**; Jn 18.28−19.42 **1586**; Ac 3.13 **1597**; 4.27 **1599**; 13.28 **1614**; 1 Ti 6.13 **1732**

PRAYER(S)

(a) *in OT*, Gn 20.7,17 **23**; 25.21 **29**; 1 S 1.10-17,26-27 **315**; 2 S 7.18-27 **364**; 1 K 8.22-54 **406**; 18.36-37 **423**; 1 Ch 29.10-19 **504**; 2 Ch 6.13−7.1 **511**; Ne 1.5-11 **562**; 9.6-37 **573**; Job 42.8-9 **638**; Ps 4.1 **641**; 65.2 **685**; Pr 15.8-29 **765**; Is 1.15 **805**; 38.5 **843**; 56.7 **871**; Jr 14.7-9,11 **905**; Dn 9.3-28 **1050**; *see also* Tb 3.16 **1136**; 12.8,12 **1146**; Jdt 4.9-15 **1153**; 9 **1160**; Gk Est 4.17−17g **1176**; 1 Macc 5.33 **1300**; 7.37 **1306**; 12.11 **1318**; Si 7.10,14 **1213**; 39.5 **1249**; S of 3 Y 2-22 **1277**; Su 42-43 **1283**

(b) *teaching of Jesus*, Mt 5.44 **1429**; 6.5-15 **1430**; Lk 11.1-13 **1528**; 18.1-8 **1540**

(c) *in life of Jesus*, Mt 14.19,23 **1445**; 26.36-44 **1465**; Mk 1.35 **1474**; 6.46 **1483**; 14.32-39 **1498**; Lk 3.21 **1511**; 5.16 **1515**; 6.12 **1516**; 9.18,29 **1523**; 11.1 **1528**; 22.32,41-45 **1549**; Jn 17.1-26 **1583**; He 5.7 **1746**

(d) *teaching in the Epistles*, Ro 8.26 **1650**;

1 Co 14.13-15 **1675**; Eph 6.18 **1708**; Phil 4.6 **1713**; Col 4.2 **1719**; 1 Th 5.17 **1723**; 1 Ti 2.1,8 **1728**; Jas 5.13-18 **1762**; 1 Jn 5.16 **1778**; Jd 20 **1782**

PRISCILLA, Ac 18.2,18,26 **1622**; Ro 16.3 **1659**; 1 Co 16.19 **1680**; 2 Ti 4.19 **1736**

PROPHET(S), -ESS

(a) *of OT*, Gn 20.7 **23**; Nu 11.29 **167**; 12.6 **168**; Dt 13.1-3,5 **219**; 18.15,18-22 **224**; 34.10-12 **246**; 1 S 9.9 **324**; 10.5-6,10-13 **326**; 28.6,15 **351**; Jr 1.5 **885**; 14.14-16 **906**; 23.9,11-31 **917**; 27.9-10,14-18 **922**; Ez 13.2-10,16 **984**; Zec 7.3 **1118**; 13.3-6 **1124**; *references in NT*, Mt 1.22 **1424**; 2.5,15,17,23 **1424**; 4.14 **1427**; 11.13 **1438**; 23.29-31,37 **1460**; Lk 13.34 **1535**; Ac 2.16,30 **1595**; 3.18,21,24,25 **1598**; 8.28,30,34 **1607**; Ro 1.2 **1640**; He 1.1 **1742**; 1 P 1.10 **1764**

(b) *of NT*: Anna, Lk 2.36 **1510**; John the Baptist, Mt 11.9 **1438**; 14.5 **1444**; 21.26 **1456**; Mk 11.32 **1493**; Lk 1.76 **1508**; 7.26 **1519**; 20.6 **1544**; Jesus, Mt 13.57 **1444**; 21.11,46 **1455**; Mk 6.15 **1482**; Lk 7.16,39 **1518**; 13.33 **1535**; 24.19 **1554**; Jn 4.19,44 **1562**; 9.17 **1572**; "the prophet," Jn 1.21,25 **1557**; 6.14 **1565**; 7.40 **1569**; Ac 3.22-23 **1598**; Christian, Ac 11.27-28 **1612**; 13.1 **1613**; 15.32 **1618**; 1 Co 12.28-29 **1674**; Eph 4.11 **1705**; Rev 18.20,24 **1801**; 22.9 **1805**; the two witnesses, Rev 11.3-12 **1793**

(c) *false, see* FALSE

QUIRINIUS (Cyrenius, AV), Lk 2.2 **1508**

RACHEL, Gn 29.6-31 **35**; 30.1-8 **36**; 31.4-5,14-16,19,32-35 **38**; 33 **42**; 35.16-20 **45**; Jr 31.15 **927**; Mt 2.18 **1425**

RAHAB, Js 2.1-21 **248**; 6.22-25 **253**; Mt 1.5 **1423**; He 11.31 **1754**; Jas 2.25 **1760**

REBECCA, Gn 22.23 **25**; 24.15-67 **27**; 25.21-28 **29**; 27.1−28.5 **32**; Ro 9.10 **1651**

RESURRECTION

(a) *in OT*, 1 K 17.22 **421**; 2 K 4.35 **437**; 13.21 **450**; Is 26.19 **831**; Dn 12.2 **1054**

(b) *in NT*: interpretation of Jesus' resurrection, Ac 2.24,31-32 **1596**; 5.30

Ac 15.23,41 **1618**; 18.18 **1623**; 20.3 **1626**; 21.3 **1627**

TABERNACLE, Israelite center of worship before Temple was built, Ex 25.8-9 **99**; 26—27 **100**; 35.21—36.38 **112**; 40 **117**; Nu 1.50-53 **155**; 10.15-23 **165**; Js 22.29 **274**; 1 Ch 6.32,48 **477**; 21.28-30 **496**; *see* TENT

TABITHA, Ac 9.36,40 **1609**

TARSUS, Ac 9.30 **1609**; 11.25 **1612**; 21.39 **1629**; 22.3 **1629**

TAX

(a) *general,* Ex 30.11-16 **105**; Nu 31.25-41 **194**; 2 Ch 24.6-11 **530**; Ne 5.4 **568**; 1 Macc 3.31 **1295**; 10.29-35,41-42 **1312**; 11.28-35 **1316**; Mt 17.24 **1449**; 22.17,19 **1457**; Mk 12.14 **1493**; Ro 13.6-7 **1656**

(b) *collector(s),* Mt 9.10-11 **1434**; 11.19 **1438**; 21.31-32 **1456**; Mk 2.15-16 **1475**; Lk 3.12 **1511**; 5.27,29-30 **1515**; 7.29,34 **1519**; 15.1 **1536**; 18.10-14 **1541**; 19.2-10 **1542**

TEMPLE

(a) *Solomon's,* 1 K 5.2-18 **400**; 6—8 **400**; 2 K 18.15-16 **457**; 24.13 **466**; 25.13-17 **467**; 1 Ch 28.10 **503**; 2 Ch 2.2—7.2 **507**; Si 47.13 **1261**

(b) *Zerubbabel's,* Ezra 3.6-11 **551**; 5.11-17 **554**; 6.5-22 **554**; Hg 1.14-15 **1112**; Zec 4.7,9 **1116**; Tb 14.5 **1148**; 1 Macc 4.36-59 **1298**; 2 Macc 10.1-8 **1346**

(c) *Herod's,* Mt 4.5 **1426**; 21.12-17,23 **1455**; 24.1 **1460**; 26.55,61 **1467**; 27.5,40,51 **1468**; Mk 11.15,27 **1492**; 13.1 **1495**; 15.38 **1502**; Lk 1.9,21-22 **1506**; 2.27,46 **1509**; 19.45,47 **1544**; 20.1 **1544**; 21.1,5 **1546**; 24.53 **1555**; Jn 2.14-17 **1559**; 7.14,28 **1567**; 8.20 **1570**; 10.32 **1574**; Ac 2.46 **1597**; 3.1-3,8,10 **1597**; 5.20,21,25 **1601**; 21.26-30 **1628**

(d) *figurative,* Jn 2.18-22 **1559**; 1 Co 3.16-17 **1664**; 2 Co 6.16 **1686**; Eph 2.21 **1704**

(e) *in the vision of Ezekiel,* Ez 40—46 **1021**

TENT

(a) *the tabernacle,* Ex 25.8-9 **99**; 26—27 **100**; 29.4,10-11 **103**; 31.6-7 **106**; 33.7-11 **108**; 35.21—36.38 **112**; 40.22-35 **117**; Lv 4.4-7 **121**; Nu 1.50-53 **155**; 10.11-21 **165**; Js 22.29

274; 1 S 2.22 **317**; 2 S 7.2 **363**; 1 Ch 6.32,48 **477**; 21.28-30 **496**; Ac 7.44 **1604**; He 9.1-10,21 **1749**; *see* TABERNACLE

(b) *figurative,* He 8.2 **1748**; 9.11 **1750**; Rev 15.5 **1797**

TERTULLUS, Ac 24.1-2 **1632**

THADDAEUS, Mt 10.3 **1436**; Mk 3.18 **1477**

THESSALONICA, -NS, Ac 17.1,11,13 **1621**; Phil 4.16 **1714**; 1 Th 1.1 **1720**; 2 Th 1.1 **1724**

THOMAS, Mt 10.3 **1436**; Mk 3.18 **1477**; Lk 6.15 **1516**; Jn 11.16 **1575**; 14.5 **1580**; 20.24-28 **1590**; 21.2 **1591**; Ac 1.13 **1594**

THOUSAND YEARS, Ps 90.4 **708**; 2 P 3.8 **1772**; Rev 20.1-7 **1802**

THUMMIM, *see* URIM AND THUMMIM

THYATIRA, Ac 16.14 **1619**; Rev 2.18,24 **1786**

TIBERIAS,

(a) *city of,* Jn 6.23 **1565**

(b) *lake, see* GALILEE (a)

TIBERIUS *see* CAESAR (c)

TIGLATH PILESER, TIGLATH PILNESER, PUL, 2 K 15.19(*fn*),29 **453**; 16.7-10 **454**; 1 Ch 5.6,26 **475**; 2 Ch 28.20-21 **535**

TIMOTHY, Ac 16.1,3 **1619**; 17.14,15 **1621**; 18.5 **1622**; 19.22 **1624**; 20.4 **1626**; Ro 16.21 **1660**; 1 Co 4.17 **1665**; 16.10 **1679**; 2 Co 1.1,19 **1681**; Phil 1.1 **1709**; 2.19,22 **1711**; Col 1.1 **1715**; 1 Th 1.1 **1720**; 3.2,6 **1722**; 2 Th 1.1 **1724**; 1 Ti 1.2,18 **1727**; 6.20 **1732**; 2 Ti 1.2 **1733**; Phm 1 **1740**; He 13.23 **1757**

TITUS, 2 Co 2.13 **1682**; 7.6,13,14 **1686**; 8.6,16,23 **1687**; 12.18 **1691**; Ga 2.1,3 **1694**; 2 Ti 4.10 **1736**; Titus 1.4 **1737**

TONGUES (speaking in tongues), Ac 2.3,4,11 **1595**; 10.46 **1611**; 19.6 **1624**; 1 Co 12.10,28,30 **1673**; 13.1,8 **1674**; 14.2-40 **1675**

TROAS, Ac 16.8,11 **1619**; 20.5-6 **1626**; 2 Co 2.12 **1682**; 2 Ti 4.13 **1736**

TYCHICUS, Ac 20.4 **1626**; Eph 6.21 **1708**; Col 4.7 **1719**; 2 Ti 4.12 **1736**; Titus 3.12 **1739**

TYRE, 2 S 5.11 **361**; 1 K 5.1 **400**; 7.13-14 **404**; Is 23.1-18 **827**; Ez 26.1—28.19 **1002**; Am 1.9-10 **1075**; Jdt 2.28 **1153**; 1 Macc 5.15 **1299**; 2 Macc 4.18 **1335**; Mt 11.21-22 **1439**; 15.21 **1446**; Mk 7.24,31 **1485**; Lk 6.17 **1516**; 10.13-14 **1526**; Ac 12.20 **1613**; 21.3,7 **1627**

UNLEAVENED BREAD *see* FESTIVAL(S)
URIM AND THUMMIM, Ex 28.28-30
   102; Lv 8.8 **126**; Nu 27.21 **191**; Dt
   33.8-10 **244**; 1 S 14.41 **332**; 18.6
   339; Ezra 2.63 **550**; Ne 7.65 **571**

VINE, Gn 40.9-10 **51**; Jg 9.8-13 **290**; 1 K
   4.25 **399**; Ps 80.8-9 **701**; Ez 17.6-10
   989; 19.10-14 **993**; Jn 15.1,4,5 **1581**;
   Rev 14.18 **1797**
VINEYARD, Gn 9.20 **11**; 1 K 21.2-16
   428; Is 5.1-7 **809**; Am 9.14 **1083**; Mt
   20.1-16 **1453**; 21.28-32,33-43 **1456**;
   Mk 12.1-12 **1493**; Lk 20.9-18 **1544**
VIRGIN, -ITY, Ex 22.16-17 **96**; Jg
   11.37-38 **294**; Es 2.2-4 **584**; Mt 1.23
   1424; Lk 1.27 **1506**; 2 Co 11.2 **1689**

WIDOW, Ex 22.22-24 **96**; Dt 10.18 **215**;
   Ru 1.3 **308**; 1 K 17.9,10,20 **421**; Lm
   1.1 **961**; Jdt 8.1-8 **1158**; Mk
   12.40,42-44 **1495**; Lk 7.12 **1518**;
   18.3-5 **1540**; 21.2-3 **1546**; Ac 6.1
   1602; 9.39,41 **1609**; 1 Co 7.8 **1667**;
   1 Ti 5.3-16 **1730**
WIFE
   (a) *literal,* Gn 2.24 **4**; Ex 20.17 **93**; Dt
      5.21 **209**; 22.13-22 **228**; Ezra 10.2-4
      559; Pr 6.29 **757**; 18.22 **769**; 19.14
      770; Ml 2.13-16 **1128**; Tb 10.12
      1144; Si 26.1-4 **1234**; 1 Co 7.2-4,10-
      16,27,33,39 **1667**; Eph 5.22-33 **1707**;
      Col 3.18-19 **1718**; 1 P 3.1-7 **1766**
   (b) *figurative,* Is 54.6 **869**; Rev 19.7
      1801; 21.9 **1803**; 22.17 **1805**
WINE
   (a) *literal,* Gn 9.21-24 **11**; Nu 6.2-4 **161**;
      Jg 9.13 **290**; 13.4,7,13-14 **295**; 1 S
      1.14-15 **315**; Ps 104.15 **717**; Pr 20.1
      770; 23.29-35 **774**; 31.4-7 **782**; Jr
      35.2-8 **934**; Dn 1.8 **1037**; Si 19.2
      1225; 31.25-31 **1241**; Mt 9.17 **1435**;
      Mk 2.22 **1476**; 15.23 **1501**; Lk 1.15
      1506; 5.37-39 **1516**; Jn 2.3-10 **1559**;
      Ro 14.21 **1657**; Eph 5.18 **1707**; 1 Ti
      3.8 **1729**; 5.23 **1731**
   (b) *figurative,* Is 55.1 **870**; Jr 25.15-29
      920; Rev 6.6 **1790**; 14.8,10 **1796**;
      17.2 **1799**; 18.3 **1799**
WINGED CREATURES, Gn 3.24 **5**; Ex
   25.18-20 **99**; Nu 7.89 **163**; 1 S 4.4
   319; 1 K 6.23-28 **403**; 8.6-7 **406**; Ps
   18.10 **649**; 80.1 **700**; Is 37.16 **842**; Ez

10.1-22 **980**; 41.18 **1024**; He 9.5
   1749
WORLD OF THE DEAD (Sheol), Gn
   37.35 **49**; Nu 16.30-33 **174**; Ps 9.17
   644; 139.8 **744**; Is 14.9-15 **820**; Lk
   16.23 **1538**; Rev 1.18 **1785**; 20.14
   1803
WRATH, of God, Ex 32.11-14 **107**; Nu
   16.43-46 **175**; 25.10-11 **188**; 2 K
   22.11-17 **463**; Job 4.9 **597**; Ps 6.1
   642; 30.5 **658**; 85.3-5 **704**; Is
   51.17-22 **866**; 60.10 **876**; Mic 5.15
   1096; Zep 1.15,18 **1108**; 2 Macc 5.20
   1338; 8.5 **1343**; Si 5.6-7 **1211**; 16.11
   1222; Ws 5.20 **1190**; 11.9 **1195**; 16.5
   1201; Ba 1.13 **1268**; Mt 3.7 **1426**; Lk
   3.7 **1511**; 21.23 **1547**; Jn 3.36 **1561**;
   Ro 1.18 **1641**; 2.5-8 **1642**; 5.9 **1646**;
   9.22 **1651**; 13.4-5 **1656**; Eph 2.3
   1703; 5.6 **1706**; Col 3.6 **1718**; 1 Th
   2.16 **1721**; Rev 6.17 **1790**; 14.10,19
   1796; 15.1,7 **1797**

XERXES, Ezra 4.6 **552**; Es 1−10 **583**

YES, Mt 5.37 **1429**; 2 Co 1.17-20 **1682**
YOKE, Jr 27.1,2 **922**; 28.10-14 **923**; Mt
   11.29-30 **1439**

ZACCHAEUS, Lk 19.1-10 **1542**
ZEBEDEE, Mt 4.21 **1427**; 20.20 **1454**;
   27.56 **1470**; Mk 1.19-20 **1473**; 10.35
   1491; Lk 5.10 **1514**; Jn 21.2 **1591**
ZECHARIAH
   (a) *prophet,* Ezra 5.1 **553**; 6.14 **555**; Zec
      1.1 **1114**; 7.1 **1118**
   (b) *priest, father of John the Baptist,* Lk
      1.5-67 **1505**
ZERUBBABEL, Ezra 2.2 **549**; 3.2-8 **551**;
   5.2 **553**; Hg 1.1−2.23 **1111**; Zec
   4.1-10 **1116**; Si 49.11-12 **1263**
ZION
   (a) *hill on which city of Jerusalem stood,*
      2 S 5.7 **361**; 1 Ch 11.5 **484**
   (b) *Mt. Moriah on which Temple stood,* Is
      8.18 **814**; Jl 3.17 **1073**
   (c) *term for Jerusalem in entirety,* Ps 48
      674; 97.8 **713**; Mt 21.5 **1454**; Jn
      12.15 **1577**; Ro 9.33 **1652**; 11.26
      1654
   (d) *heavenly Jerusalem,* He 12.22 **1755**;
      Rev 14.1 **1796**

SHARING GOD'S WORD WITH THE WORLD

This Bible represents a legacy of translating God's Word into the language of the people – into languages that will bring the Scriptures to life in the hearts of readers and hearers. The American Bible Society works with scholars from many countries to faithfully translate the Scriptures into languages and formats that speak clearly to both mind and heart. We encourage people everywhere to engage with the inspired Word of God – to embody its message and to experience a relationship with God through its reading.

To this end the American Bible Society, a not-for-profit Christian organization, offers programs to churches, other Bible-centered organizations, and individuals that connect people with God's living Word, and support the work of more than 100 other Bible Societies worldwide. Since our founding in 1816, people have generously supported the American Bible Society in its global mission to translate, publish, and provide Scriptures that are easily understood and affordable.

In many areas of the world, and even within the United States, the cost of a Bible often represents a hardship for many who thirst for God's Word. Thanks to the faithful support of many individuals, churches, and ministry partners, the American Bible Society continues to respond to the Scripture needs of the underserved and under engaged through effective programs and ministry partnerships.

We invite you to participate with us as we share God's Word with the world. To find how, please contact us at:

American Bible Society
1865 Broadway
New York, New York 10023-7505
1-888-227-8262
www.americanbible.org